A Guide to *Psychology: Concepts and Applications*, Second Edition

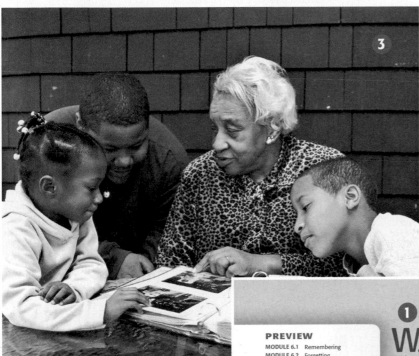

6

Memory

Chapter-Opening Features

① **Chapter Opener** follows the Preview and provides an interesting vignette or overview that introduces the reader to the topics covered in the chapter.

② **"Did You Know That..."** consists of a chapter-opening bulleted list of questions meant to stimulate student thinking and preview many of the issues to be discussed in the chapter modules. At the end of each question, a page reference is given to allow students to follow up on areas of interest.

③ **Art Program** Both the text's illustrations and photos were carefully conceived, researched, and created with the goal of presenting a clear, concise, diverse, and pedagogically sound art program.

PREVIEW

② **DID YOU KNOW THAT . . .**

- A man was able to memorize lists of hundreds of meaningless syllables and recite them again fifteen years later? (p. 217)
- Some research subjects did better on a memory test when they were submerged in water? (p. 219)
- The World Wide Web was modeled on the way the human brain works? (p. 226)
- You may be a skilled typist but not be able to name the keys in each row of the keyboard from memory? (p. 227)
- It may seem that memories of traumatic events like 9/11 are seared in our brains as exact records of these experiences, but evidence shows they are not any more accurate than ordinary memories? (p. 230)
- People can be misled into believing they saw a yield sign at an accident scene when they actually saw a stop sign? (p. 231)
- Fewer than half of the people tested in a research study could pick out the correct drawing of a penny? (p. 239)
- If your hippocampus were removed, each new experience would come and go without any permanent trace left in your brain that the event ever happened? (p. 245)

①

We are a nation that loves competitions. We watch or engage in competitions of all kinds, from sporting contests and tractor-pulls to the perennial game shows and award ceremonies on TV. But memory competitions? These are one of the newest entries in the competitive field. In the U.S. and world memory championships, experts compete in various challenges, such as recalling long lists of words or random numbers, or matching names to the faces of people they've seen in photographs. Some recent champions have demonstrated amazing feats of memory. The U.S. record holder in 1997 succeeded in memorizing in a mere 34.03 seconds each card (suit and number) in the order in which it appeared in a shuffled deck of fifty-two cards ("Instant Recall," 2000). But none of the feats of the recent champions can hold a candle to those of a Russian known only by his first initial, S., who had perhaps the most prodigious memory ever studied. He could repeat seventy randomly selected numbers in the precise order in which he had just heard them (Luria, 1968). Even more amazingly, he could memorize lists of hundreds of meaningless syllables and recite them not only immediately after studying them, but also when tested again some fifteen years later. He memorized long mathematical formulas that were utterly meaningless to him except as an enormously long string of numbers and symbols. After but a single reading, he could recite stanza after stanza of Dante's *Divine Comedy* in Italian, even though he could not speak the language (Rupp, 1998).

Imagine what it would be like to have such an extraordinary memory—to be able to remember everything you read word for word or to recall lists of facts you learned years ago. Yet if S.'s life story is any indication, it may be just as well you don't possess such a prodigious memory. S. didn't have an easy time of it. His mind was so crammed with meaningless details that he couldn't see the forest for the trees. He had difficulty distinguishing between the trivial and the significant (Turkington, 1996). He even had difficulty holding conversations, since individual words opened a floodgate of associations that distracted him from what the other person was saying. He was also unable to shift gears when new information conflicted with fixed images he held in memory. For example, he had difficulty recognizing people who had changed small details of their appearance, such as by getting a haircut or wearing a new suit. Unfortunately, S.'s life didn't end well. He spent the last years of his life confined to a mental hospital.

Most of us will probably never possess the memory of someone like S., nor would we even want to. Yet learning how our memory works and what we can do to improve it can help us meet many of life's challenges, from performing better in school or on the job to remembering to water the plants before leaving the house.

Our study of memory begins with a discussion of the underlying processes that make memory possible. We then consider the loss of information that results from forgetting and the role of the brain in creating and storing memories. We end with some practical suggestions for improving your memory. ■

217

Module Features

4 Survey Questions introduce each module and help students test their recall of the major concepts in the module. These study questions are repeated in the Module Review to reinforce learning and aid the study process.

5 Key Concepts are numbered concepts extracted from the text and placed in the margins next to key discussions within the modules. These concepts are interspersed throughout the text to help students identify and recall the major concepts covered in each module.

6 Integrated Media Resources The Online Study Center icons throughout the chapter highlight media resources available on the student website. These resources support key concepts in the text and include tutorials, animations, and weblinks.

7 Pioneer Boxes provide a glimpse into the lives of key researchers who helped shape the field of psychology.

8 Key Terms appear boldfaced within the text proper and in the margin alongside the introduction of each key term discussion. At the end of each chapter, a list of key terms is provided with page references for easy location by the reader.

MODULE 7.3
Intelligence

4
- What is intelligence, and how is it measured?
- What constitutes a good intelligence test?
- What are some examples of the misuse of intelligence tests?
- What are some of the major theories of intelligence?
- Is intelligence determined by heredity or environment?

Perhaps no subject in psychology has sparked as much controversy as intelligence. Psychologists have long argued about how to define it, how to measure it, what factors govern it, whether different racial and ethnic groups have more or less of it, and if so, what accounts for these differences. These debates are still very much at the forefront of contemporary psychology.

What Is Intelligence?

Just what is **intelligence**? Is it the ability to acquire knowledge from books or formal schooling? Or might it be "street smarts"—practical intelligence of the kind we see in people who survive by their wits rather than by knowledge acquired in school? Is it the ability to solve problems? Or is it the ability to adapt to the demands of the environment? Psychologists believe intelligence may be all these things and more. Though definitions of intelligence vary, a central belief of each is that intelligence is the ability to adapt to the environment. Perhaps the most widely used definition of intelligence is the one offered by psychologist David Wechsler (1975): "Intelligence is the global capacity of the individual to act purposefully, to think rationally, and to deal effectively with the environment."

Some theorists believe there are many different forms of intelligence, perhaps even multiple intelligences. Before we explore theories of intelligence, let us consider the history and nature of intelligence testing in modern times and also discuss the extremes of intelligence.

5 CONCEPT 7.20
Though theorists define intelligence in different ways, one widely used definition holds that intelligence is the capacity to act purposefully, think rationally, and deal effectively with the environment.

6 Online Study Center
Improve Your Grade
Tutorials: Test Your Intelligence

How Is Intelligence Measured?

The earliest attempts at measuring intelligence in the modern age were undertaken by Sir Francis Galton (1822–1911), an Englishman of many talents. Galton, a cousin of naturalist Charles Darwin, was a successful inventor, geographer, meteorologist, and mathematician (Hunt, 1993). He also was an amateur psycholo-

---

7 THE PIONEERS   The View from the Train

Max Wertheimer

As train passengers often do, Max Wertheimer stared out at the passing landscape. What he observed outside his window would forever alter his life and launch a new movement in psychology (Hunt, 1993). What captured his attention was the illusion that objects in the distance—telegraph poles, houses, and hilltops—appeared to be moving along with the train, even though they were obviously standing still.

Countless other people had observed the same phenomenon of apparent movement but had paid little if any attention to it. Apparent movement is best known as the basis of motion pictures. In 1890, Thomas Edison had shown that he could create the appearance of moving pictures by stringing together still photographs on a strip of film and then illuminating them in quick succession on a screen. Whereas Edison was content to produce apparent movement without attempting to explain it, Wertheimer was intrigued to find out why the phenomenon occurred. He had the idea that the illusion was not a trick of the eye but reflected higher-level processes in the brain that created the perception of movement. He promptly canceled his vacation and began experimental studies of the phenomenon. The experiments that he conducted with two assistants, Wolfgang Köhler (1887–1967) and Kurt Koffka (1886–1943), led to discoveries about the nature of perception—the processes by which we organize our sense impressions and form meaningful representations of the world around us.

CONCEPT 1.7
Freud held that our behavior is largely determined by unconscious forces and motives that lie beyond the reach of ordinary awareness.

ceived of the unconscious as the repository of primitive sexual and aggressive drives or instincts and of the wishes, impulses, and urges that arise from those drives or instincts. He believed that the motives underlying our behavior involve sexual and aggressive impulses that lie in the murky depths of the unconscious, hidden away from our ordinary awareness of ourselves. In other words, we may do or say things without understanding the true motives that prompted these behaviors.

Freud also believed that early childhood experiences play a determining role in shaping our personalities and behavior, including abnormal behaviors like excessive fears or phobias. He held that abnormal behavior patterns are rooted in unconscious conflicts originating in childhood. These conflicts involve a dynamic struggle within the unconscious mind between unacceptable sexual or aggressive impulses striving for expression and opposing mental forces seeking to keep this threatening material out of conscious awareness. Thus, Freud's view of psychology, and that of his followers, is often called the **psychodynamic perspective**.

Unlike Wundt, James, and Watson, Freud was a therapist, and his main aim was to help people overcome psychological problems. He developed a form of psychotherapy or "talk therapy" that he called **psychoanalysis** (discussed in Chapter 14). Psychoanalysis is a type of mental detective work. It incorporates methods, such as analysis of dreams and of "slips of the tongue," that Freud believed could be used to gain insight into the nature of the underlying motives and conflicts of which his patients were unaware. Freud maintained that once these unconscious conflicts were brought into the light of conscious awareness, they could be successfully resolved, or "worked through," during the course of therapy.

Contemporary Perspectives in Psychology

What do we find when we look over the landscape of psychology today? For one thing, we find a discipline that owes a great debt to its founders but that is constantly reinventing itself to meet new challenges. Not all schools of thought

8 psychodynamic perspective   The view that behavior is influenced by the struggle between unconscious sexual or aggressive impulses and opposing forces that try to keep this threatening material out of consciousness.
psychoanalysis   Freud's method of psychotherapy; it focuses on uncovering and working through the unconscious conflicts he believed were at the root of psychological problems.

Emphasis on Application and Critical Thinking

9 **"Try This Out"** features "hands-on" activities or exercises in which students can apply their knowledge of psychological concepts discussed in the chapter.

10 **Application Module** Each chapter ends with a short applied module aimed at helping students see how psychological principles are used to deal with real-world problems and issues, and provides tips on how to apply this knowledge in their own lives.

11 **"Reality Check"** boxes encourage students to examine common beliefs and misconceptions in the light of evidence. Each box consists of three parts: the Claim, the Evidence, and the Take-Away Message.

CONCEPT 7.31
Evidence indicates that genetic and environmental factors interact in complex ways in shaping intelligence.

REALITY CHECK

THE CLAIM IQ is determined at birth.

THE EVIDENCE Evidence supports roles for both heredity and environment in determining intelligence or IQ. Environmental factors, such as an intellectually stimulating home environment, a healthy diet, and formal enrichment programs like Head Start, can foster intellectual development and help children achieve higher IQ scores than they might otherwise.

THE TAKE-AWAY MESSAGE Intelligence, as measured by IQ, is not fixed at birth but is determined by an interplay of genetic and environmental influences.

Yet heredity doesn't tell the whole story. Refer again to Figure 7.18. Notice that the correlation for the IQ scores of MZ twins raised together is greater than the correlation for the IQ scores of MZ twins raised apart. Since MZ twins share the same genes, the difference in these correlations is evidence that the environment also plays a role in determining IQ. Environmental influences also contribute to intellectual development. A home environment that emphasizes verbal interaction, reading, and exploration can foster children's intellectual development.

Taken together, the evidence makes a compelling case that both genetic and environmental factors interact in complex ways in determining intelligence (Dickens & Flynn, 2001; Garlick, 2003). We also have learned that heredity helps shape intelligence throughout the life span, not just during early development (e.g., McGue & Christensen, 2001). Studies of twins in their eighties show similarities in intelligence virtually identical to those among adolescent twins (McClearn et al., 1997).

But just how much of intelligence is explained by genetics and how much by the environment? The **heritability** of a trait is the degree to which genetic factors explain the variability within the population on the trait (Benson, 2004b; Merikangas & Risch, 2003). A heritability estimate of 50 percent for intelligence—at least intelligence as measured by IQ tests—would mean that genetics accounts for 50 percent of the differences (variability) among people in IQ scores; the environment or other unspecified factors would account for the rest.

Heritability estimates of intelligence vary, typically ranging from about 50 to 75 percent (Gottesman, 1997; Scarr, Weinberg, & Waldman, 1993). However, although genetics may account for 50 to 75 percent of variability of IQ scores in the population, we cannot conclude that 50 to 75 percent of a given person's IQ results from genetic factors and the rest from environmental or other influences. Heritability estimates apply to differences among people in the population in general, not to the role that genetics plays in any given individual. Complicating the picture further is recent evidence that heredity plays a larger and stronger role in determining differences in IQ among children from more affluent families than among those from poorer families (Turkheimer et al., 2003).

12 **"Exploring Psychology"** sections help students to delve deeper into contemporary issues and controversies in psychology, learn more about emerging research, and relate the text material to their own lives.

heritability The degree to which heredity accounts for variations on a given trait within a population.

EXPLORING PSYCHOLOGY
Racial/Ethnic Differences in IQ

Controversy continues to swirl concerning the meaning of racial/ethnic differences in IQ scores. Evidence shows that, on average, White Americans of European descent (Euro-Americans) score higher on IQ tests than African Americans—about 15 points higher (Fagan & Holland, 2002). This gap in IQ scores exists even when differences in income levels are taken into account (Cowley, 1994). African American students also tend to lag behind Euro-American students in scores on reading

13 **Thinking Critically About Psychology** provides an end-of-chapter opportunity for students to sharpen their analytical skills by answering a critical-thinking question or questions. Sample answers/solutions are provided in an appendix.

13 Thinking Critically About Psychology

Based on your reading of this chapter, answer the following questions. Then, to evaluate your progress in developing critical thinking skills, compare your answers to the sample answers found in Appendix A.

The case of Phineas Gage is one of the best-known case studies in the annals of psychology. In 1848, as you already know, Gage suffered an accident in which a metal rod pierced his cheek and brain and penetrated the top of his head. Yet not only did he survive this horrific accident, but he also managed to pick himself up and speak to workers who came to his aid. Though he survived his injuries, his personality changed—so much so that people would remark, "Gage is no longer Gage."

1. Why do you think Gage's injury affected his personality but not the basic life functions that the brain controls, such as breathing and heart rate?

2. How might the nature of the injury that Gage sustained explain why this once polite and courteous man became aggressive and unruly?

Student Review Features

 Concept Charts summarize and review major concepts and visually make relational connections for students.

 Module Reviews test knowledge through "Q & A" recitation of answers to survey questions and through the use of self-scoring quizzes. Answers are provided at the end of the chapter.

 "Tying it Together" appears at the end of each chapter, helping students see how the modules are integrated within the chapter structure as a whole.

CONCEPT CHART 3.3 Hearing

Source of sensory information	Sound waves
Receptor organs	The ears. The outer ear funnels sound waves through the eardrum to the middle ear, where they are amplified by three tiny bones and transmitted through the oval window to the inner ear.
Receptor cells	Hair cells on the basilar membrane within the cochlea of the inner ear
Pitch perception	Three theories contribute to our understanding of pitch perception. Frequency theory appears to account for pitch perception of low-frequency sounds below 1,000 cycles per second. Place theory alone seems to account for pitch perception of high-frequency sounds above 4,000 cycles per second. The volley principle appears to explain pitch perception of moderate-frequency sounds in the range of approximately 1,000 to 4,000 cycles per second.

MODULE 3.3 REVIEW
Hearing: The Music of Sound

RECITE IT

How does the ear enable us to hear sound?

- Sound waves enter the outer ear and are funneled to the eardrum, causing it to vibrate. This mechanical energy is conveyed to tiny bones in the middle ear—the hammer, anvil, and stirrup—and then through the oval window to the cochlea in the inner ear.
- The organ of Corti in the cochlea is lined with hair cells that bend in response to the vibrations, triggering neural impulses that are fed through the auditory nerve to the auditory cortex in the temporal lobes of the brain, which leads to the experience of hearing.

What determines our perception of pitch?

- Perception of pitch is likely determined by a combination of the place on the basilar membrane of greatest vibration (place theory), the frequency of neural impulses (frequency theory), and the sequencing of firing of groups of neurons along the basilar membrane (volley principle).

What are the main types and causes of deafness?

- The main types of deafness are conduction deafness, usually caused by damage to the middle ear, and nerve deafness, usually caused by damage to the hair cells of the inner ear or to the auditory nerve.

RECALL IT

1. Which characteristics of sound waves give rise to the perception of loudness and pitch?

2. According to the frequency theory of pitch perception, our ability to detect differences in pitch is due to
   a. the rate of vibration of the basilar membrane.
   b. the location along the basilar membrane where the greatest vibration occurs.
   c. the alternation between areas of greater and lesser vibration of the basilar membrane.
   d. the rate of vibration of the oval window.

3. Match these parts of the ear with the descriptions that follow: (a) eardrum; (b) ossicles; (c) cochlea; (d) basilar membrane; (e) organ of Corti; (f) hair cells.
   i. a membrane that separates the outer ear from the middle ear
   ii. sensory receptors for hearing
   iii. a gelatinous structure attached to the basilar membrane and lined with sensory receptors
   iv. the membrane in the cochlea that moves in response to sound vibrations
   v. three small bones in the middle ear that conduct sound vibrations
   vi. a snail-shaped bony tube in the inner ear in which fluid moves in response to the vibrations of the oval window

THINK ABOUT IT

- What characteristics of sound waves give rise to the perception of loudness and pitch?

- What steps are you taking to protect your hearing from the damaging effects of noise? Are you doing enough?

TYING IT TOGETHER

Sensation and perception are processes that enable us to sense and make sense of the world around us. The early psychologists laid out a number of basic concepts of sensation, including the absolute threshold, the difference threshold, and Weber's law (Module 3.1). Each of our sensory systems transforms sources of stimulation into information the brain can use to produce sensations. With vision, light energy is transformed into sensations of visual images (Module 3.2). With hearing, vibrations caused by sound waves impact on structures in the inner ear, where they are converted into auditory messages that the brain uses to create sensations of sound (Module 3.3). Through our other senses—the chemical, skin, and body senses—we are able to experience sensations of odor, taste, touch, pressure, warmth and cold, pain, and body position and movement (Module 3.4).

Perception is the process by which we take sensory information and organize it in ways that allow us to form meaningful impressions of the world around us. Some areas of perception remain steeped in controversy, especially claims about subliminal perception and extrasensory perception (Module 3.5). Psychologists and other professionals apply their knowledge of sensation and perception in helping people cope more effectively with chronic pain (Module 3.6).

PSYCHOLOGY
CONCEPTS AND APPLICATIONS
SECOND EDITION WITH STUDENT STUDY GUIDE

Jeffrey S. Nevid
St. John's University

Study Guide by

Patricia S. Laser
Bucks County Community College

Revised by

Rachelle Lipshultz
Ann Arundel Community College

HOUGHTON MIFFLIN COMPANY
Boston   New York

PSYCHOLOGY: CONCEPTS AND APPLICATIONS, SECOND EDITION
by Jeffrey S. Nevid
Copyright © 2007 by Houghton Mifflin Company. All rights reserved.

Publisher: Charles Hartford
Sponsoring Editor: Jane Potter
Development Editor: Laura Hildebrand
Senior Project Editor: Carol Newman
Editorial Assistant: Deborah Berkman
Senior Art and Design Coordinator: Jill Haber
Senior Photo Editor: Jennifer Meyer Dare
Composition Buyer: Chuck Dutton
Designer: Henry Rachlin
Manufacturing Coordinator: Karen Banks Fawcett
Marketing Manager: Laura McGinn
Marketing Associate: Erin Lane

STUDY GUIDE, PSYCHOLOGY: CONCEPTS AND APPLICATIONS, SECOND EDITION
by Patricia S. Laser and Rachelle Lipshultz
Copyright © 2007 by Houghton Mifflin Company. All rights reserved.

Vice President, Publisher: Charles Hartford
Sponsoring Editor: Jane Potter
Assistant Editor: Liz Hogan
Editorial Assistant: Deborah Berkman
Digital Ancillary Producer: Sean McGann
Marketing Manager: Laura McGinn
Marketing Associate: Erin Lane

Custom Publishing Editor: Dan Luciano
Custom Publishing Production Manager: Tina Kozik
Project Coordinator: Georgia Young

Cover Image: © Getty Images

This book contains select works from existing Houghton Mifflin Company resources and was produced by Houghton Mifflin Custom Publishing for collegiate use. As such, those adopting and/or contributing to this work are responsible for editorial content, accuracy, continuity and completeness.

Printed in the United States of America.

ISBN-13: 978-0-618-73478-8
ISBN-10: 0-618-73478-3
N-06047

3 4 5 6 7 8 9 – AB – 08 07 06

 Houghton Mifflin
Custom Publishing

222 Berkeley Street • Boston, MA 02116

Address all correspondence and order information to the above address.

Brief Contents

Contents

7   Thinking, Language, and Intelligence   252

8   Motivation and Emotion   294

Features

The Pioneers

Concept Charts

Try This Out

Application Modules

Exploring Psychology

Preface

Welcome to the Second Edition of *Psychology: Concepts and Applications*. As instructors, we are challenged every day in the classroom to help our students succeed in today's learning environment. I approached the task of writing this text with that fundamental challenge in mind. I drew upon my experience in the classroom and research evidence from the science of psychology to build a learning-centric pedagogical framework. We have learned a great deal about the processes of learning and memory that we can bring to the classroom and incorporate in our textbooks. I also believe that empirical research on textbook pedagogy can lead to innovative ways of transforming the modern textbook into a more effective learning tool.

Research-Based Text Development

In our research laboratory, we conducted studies on two key pedagogical features embodied in this text, **modularization** and **concept signaling**.[1] The results of these studies gave me confidence that combining a modular approach with the pedagogical tool of concept signaling would help students better organize their study efforts and master key concepts in the field. This text is literally the product of the research program we undertook in our laboratory and honed through field-testing in classrooms around the country.

A textbook is more than its pedagogy, of course. Each author has a distinctive voice and style of writing. Throughout my writings, I have endeavored to speak directly to students and to make the material accessible to students at all levels. Psychology is a vibrant, dynamic discipline, and I have tried to approach the writing of this text with the same enthusiasm that psychologists bring to their research, teaching, and professional work every day.

---

[1] Nevid, J. S., & Carmony, T. M. (2002). Traditional versus modular format in presenting textual material in introductory psychology. *Teaching of Psychology, 29,* 237–238.

Nevid, J. S., & Lampmann, J. L. (2001, April). *Do pedagogical aids in textbooks enhance learning?* Paper presented at the 15th Annual Conference on Undergraduate Teaching of Psychology, Ellenville, NY.

Nevid, J. S. (2003, September). *Helping students get the point: Concept signaling as a pedagogical aid.* Paper presented at the conference, Taking Off: Best Practices in Teaching Introductory Psychology, Atlanta, GA.

Nevid, J. S., & Lampmann, J. L. (2003). Effects on content acquisition of signaling key concepts in text material. *Teaching of Psychology, 30,* 227–229.

Nevid, J. S. (2004, January). *Graphing psychology: The effective use of graphs and figures in teaching introductory psychology.* Invited address presented at the 26th Annual National Institute on the Teaching of Psychology, St. Petersburg, FL.

Nevid, J. S. (2004, February). *Evidence-based pedagogy: Using research to find new ways to help students learn.* Invited address presented at the 11th Midwest Institute for Students and Teachers of Psychology (MISTOP), Glen Ellyn, IL.

A Unique Pedagogy: The Concept-Based Module

If you thumb through the pages of this text, you'll see that it is organized in a series of individualized study units called *modules*. Each module is a cohesive study unit organized around a set of key concepts in a particular area of study. The text also incorporates a unique signaling tool called *concept signaling,* a method of extracting and signaling or "calling out" key concepts in the margins of the text.

Signaling is an effective tool for helping people encode important information. Textbooks traditionally have used a form of signaling in which key terms are boldfaced and defined in the margins of the text. This form of signaling helps students learn the technical vocabulary in the field. As an instructor, I want my students to learn key terms, but I recognize it is even more important for them to learn and retain the key concepts that comprise the basic units of knowledge in the field. This text uses signaling as a pedagogical aid to help students encode and retain both key terms and key concepts.

Why a Modular Approach?

The primary advantage of a modular format is that it breaks down complex chapters into smaller instructional units called modules. Many of our students juggle jobs, families, and careers. Tight for time, they need to balance studying with other life responsibilities. The modular approach helps busy students organize their study efforts by allowing them to focus on one module at a time rather than trying to tackle a whole chapter at once.

The majority of the student participants in our research program preferred a modular format over the traditional textbook format (57.3 percent versus 38.5 percent, with 4.2 percent expressing no preference) (Nevid & Carmony, 2002). In addition, we discovered that students who preferred a modular format performed significantly better on quizzes when material was presented in this manner rather than in the traditional narrative format. It stands to reason that if students prefer a particular approach, they will become more engaged in reading texts written in that format—an outcome that may translate into improved performance.

Learning Benefits of Concept Signaling

In a later study (Nevid & Lampman, 2003), we explored whether signaling key concepts by means of extracting and highlighting them in the margins of the text would enhance learning of this material. Though some students easily extract key concepts from text material, many others struggle to recognize the key points the author tries to convey. As instructors, we may only become aware of these struggles at examination time. Many students are able to cull facts or figures from text material, but have difficulty extracting the broader concepts that comprise the basic building blocks of knowledge in the field.

To examine the learning effects of signaling concepts, we had students read the same text passage under one of two conditions—one that highlighted key concepts in the margins and another that did not. We used a randomized, counterbalanced design to control for order effects and tested our research participants on a multiple-choice quiz shortly after a 20-minute study period. Our results showed that signaling key concepts significantly improved test performance overall as well as on the subset of items directly testing knowledge of key concepts. **Students who read the text material with concept signaling averaged 83 percent correct on items assessing key concepts, as compared to an average of 76.5 percent among students who read the same material without concept signaling.**

Concept signaling is a tool that can help students encode and retain key concepts. We did not expect, nor did we find, that concept signaling would improve student performance on quiz items assessing the surrounding material in the text that was not signaled. Our results only reinforce what instructors have known for years—that students should not use pedagogical aids (whether they be chapter summaries, running glossaries, study breaks, interim quizzes, or cued concepts) as substitutes for reading the text in its entirety. Students should be advised to use signaled concepts as an aid to help them gauge their knowledge of these important points, not as a substitute for reading the whole chapter.

We also polled student participants on which format they preferred—the one with signaled concepts or the one without. More than three out of four students preferred the signaling format and found it easier to understand and more clearly presented than the non-signaled format. (These findings were interesting in light of the fact that the material was exactly the same in both formats; the only difference was the signaling of key concepts).

Building Upon the Core

The defining features of the text that make it a learning-centric and student-friendly text are carried into the new edition. Users who are familiar with the text will recognize that the pedagogical platform of concept-based modules remains very much at the core of the text. The engaging writing style and use of many personal examples and vignettes helps make the text material accessible to students from varied backgrounds. The built-in pedagogical tools, such as keyed and numbered concepts, running glossary, Concept Charts, and the SQ3R+ study method help students master complex material. The Pioneers feature provides behind-the-scene glimpses into the personal lives of leading contributors to the field.

What's New in this Edition?
New Features

This edition includes several new features designed to stimulate critical thinking, engage interest, help students recognize relational connections between concepts, and review text material.

NEW . . . Reality Check This new critical thinking feature helps students examine common beliefs and misconceptions in the light of evidence. Each of these capsulized features (there's one per chapter) consists of three parts: the Claim, the Evidence, and the Take-Away Message. Examples include the following:

- Humans only use 10 percent of our brains (Ch. 2)
- ESP exists (Ch. 3)
- Skinner raised his daughter in a Skinner box. (Ch. 5)
- Girls are not good at math. (Ch. 11)
- Mental disorders affect relatively few people. (Ch. 13)

NEW . . . Exploring Psychology This new feature focuses on specific aspects of psychology. In these sections, I explore contemporary issues and controversies in psychology, highlight emerging research, and personalize the material by relating it to significant life concerns, such as suicide (Ch. 13) and the risks posed by unsafe sexual behaviors (Ch. 11). Here is a sampling:

- Anatomy of a Research Study: The Shooter Bias (Ch. 1)
- Driving While Distracted: Risks of Divided Consciousness (Ch. 4)
- Are Recovered Memories Credible? (Ch. 6)
- Does Day Care Affect Attachment? (Ch. 9)
- Cohabitation: Trial Marriage or Marriage Alternative? (Ch. 10)
- Making It in America: The Challenge of Acculturative Stress (Ch. 15)

NEW . . . Concept Maps for Psychology This unique print supplement helps students form linkages among key concepts. Concept maps are visual learning tools that are widely used in many fields, including education and computer science. These visual-spatial diagrams help students make relational connections between concepts.

NEW . . . Module Reviews The structure and content of these reviews have been changed to better help students gauge their knowledge of the text material. One important difference in this new edition is that review sections are placed at the end of each module, rather than compiled at the end of the chapter. This change allows each module to be a fully self-contained study unit. Each module review consists of three parts:

- **Recite It:** Here students have the opportunity to recite their answers to the survey questions that introduced the module. This question-and-answer format encourages active learning and adopts the SQ3R model to encourage recitation of answers to survey questions. Students not only can recite their answers to the questions, but they can then compare their answers to sample answers presented in the text.

- **Recall It:** Students test their knowledge by answering a variety of questions, including fill-in, multiple choice, short answer, and matching questions.

- **Think About It:** These thought-provoking questions encourage students to think critically about information contained in the module.

Expanded and Updated Coverage

Expanded Coverage of Neuroscience Neuroscientists are making important contributions to our understanding of the relationships between brain and behavior. A full listing of neuroscience content in the text is found in a tabbing guide available on the **Online Teaching Center**. Here are some examples:

- Use of brain scans in personality and memory research ("Looking Under the Hood," Ch. 2)

- Research using fMRI to investigate why it is impossible to tickle yourself (Ch. 2)

- Brain structures involved in controlling sleep-wake cycles (Ch. 4)

- Brain imaging study of hypnosis (Ch. 4)

- Brain-imaging study of response to alcohol words (Ch. 4)

- Role of SWS sleep, as well as REM sleep, in consolidating daily experiences into long-term memories (Ch. 6)

- Brain mechanisms involved in regulating appetite (Ch. 8)

- Research linking reduced utilization of serotonin in the brain to suicidal behavior (Ch. 13)

- New research on brain abnormalities in people with OCD, schizophrenia, and bipolar disorder (Ch. 13)

Expanded Coverage of Positive Psychology Positive psychology is an emerging movement within psychology that has been growing in momentum during the past few years. This edition features expanded coverage of positive psychology, including a new section on research on personal happiness (Ch. 8). For a full listing of positive psychology coverage, including such topics as love, optimism, and happiness, see the accompanying tabbing guide available on the **Online Teaching Center**.

Updated Research Throughout Importantly, the text has been thoroughly updated from start to finish. The field of psychology stands still for no author! New research developments are reported daily in our professional journals and circulated widely in the popular media. As you thumb through the pages of this edition, you will find more than 1,000 new citations of research findings and theoretical developments appearing in the scientific literature since the last edition. Here is but a small sampling of new research included in the Second Edition:

- Anatomy of a research study—the Shooter Bias study (Ch. 1)

- New research on the effectiveness of meditation in helping to relieve chronic pain (Ch. 3)

- New research on the risks posed by distracted driving (Ch. 4)

- New research showing the role of parental modeling in learning styles of dealing with conflicts in intimate relationships (Ch. 5)

- New research on induction of false memories, including the "Bugs Bunny" memory study (Ch. 6)

- New research on the "Flynn Effect" in developing countries (Ch. 7)

- New research on the role of body dissatisfaction and peer pressure in predicting bulimic behavior in young women (Ch 8)

- New section on the growing interest in happiness research (Ch. 8)

- New research on relationships between TV viewing and attentional difficulties in children (Ch. 9)

- New research on relationship between new marriage and happiness (Ch. 10)

- New research showing that men express greater confidence in using computers than do women of equal quantitative skills (Ch. 11)

- New research examining personalities of mountain climbers attempting to scale Mt. Everest (Ch. 12)

- New research on the effectiveness of virtual reality therapy (Ch. 14)

- New research showing that newlyweds whose bodies pumped out more stress hormones during the first year of marriage were more likely to get divorced within ten years than were newlyweds with a lower stress response (Ch. 15)

- New research showing that people with baby-faced features are more likely to elicit help than people with more mature facial features (Ch. 16)

Figure 1
The Four E's of Effective Learning (EL)

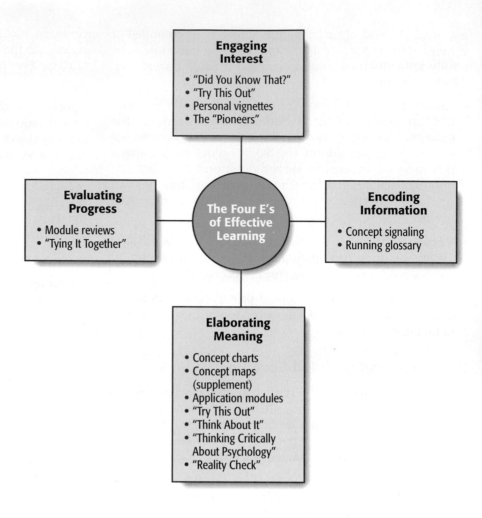

New Pioneers Boxes   Two additional Pioneers boxes are included in this edition: Tim Berners-Lee, the inventor of the World Wide Web who is profiled in Chapter 6 ("Weaving the Web"); and Stanley Milgram, who is profiled in Chapter 16 ("The Man Who Shocked the World").

A Complete Learning System Based on the Four E's of Effective Learning

The text provides a broad perspective on psychology that covers the history, methods of research, major theories, and research findings of the discipline, as well as applications of knowledge gained from contemporary research to the problems and challenges we face in today's world. But a text needs to be more than a compendium of information. It needs to be an effective learning tool.

The features of the text form a complete learning system that is grounded in research on memory, learning, and textbook pedagogy. The pedagogy incorporates four key elements of *effective learning* that I call the "**Four E's** (see Figure 1):

- Engaging Interest
- Encoding Information
- Elaborating Meaning
- Evaluating Progress

Engaging Interest

Learning begins with focused attention. A textbook can be an effective learning tool only if it succeeds in engaging and retaining the student's interest. Without focused attention, information is not likely to be encoded or retained.

This text is designed not only to generate interest but also to involve students directly in the material they read. Personal vignettes are used to draw the reader into the material and illustrate how the concepts discussed in the chapter relate to personal experiences. In addition, two distinctive pedagogical features are designed to further involve the student in the material.

"Did You Know That..."   These chapter-opening questions whet students' appetite for the material presented in the chapter and encourage them to read further. Some questions debunk common myths and misconceptions; others highlight interesting historical features or bring recent research developments into focus. Accompanying page numbers are provided for easy cross-referencing to the chapter sections in which the information is discussed. A small sample follows:

Did You Know That . . .

- The mechanism that makes motion pictures possible lies in the viewer, not the projector? (Ch. 3)

- Practicing smiling can lift your mood? (Ch. 8)

- The "Big Five" is not the name of a new NCAA basketball conference but the label used to describe the leading trait theory of personality today? (Ch. 12)

- Gestalt therapists have their clients talk to an empty chair? (Ch. 14)

- Waitresses who write helpful messages on the backs of customer's checks tend to get larger tips? (Ch. 16)

"Try This Out" These "hands-on" exercises encourage students to apply psychological concepts to their own experiences. Whether the topic involves using the principle of scaffolding to help a child acquire a particular skill, or performing a personal experiment on lucid dreaming, students can work through problems, generate solutions, and test out concepts and principles. They can participate in *active learning* by directly applying the text concepts to real-life situations, rather than simply reading about them.

"Try This Out" activities also offer suggestions for *service learning* through participation in research and volunteer experiences, while the self-scoring questionnaires in this feature allow students to evaluate their behavior and attitudes about specific issues.

Encoding Information

What image appears on the back of a $10 bill? Though we may have handled countless numbers of $10 bills in our lifetime, many of us are stumped when it comes to identifying the image on the back. (The answer is the U.S. Treasury). The more important question is why this question leaves so many people stumped. As discussed in the text (Ch. 6) with the related example of the image on the back of a nickel, information must first be encoded in order to be retained. We tend to encode only enough information as we need to know. Since we don't need to know the images on the backs of coins or paper bills in order to use this currency, this information may never have been encoded in memory in the first place.

Learning and retaining key concepts in text material also requires that information is first encoded. The pedagogical technique of signaling or cueing can help people encode important information. Textbook authors have long used forms of signaling, such as headings and highlighted key terms. This text features two types of signaling, the *running glossary* and *concept signaling*.

Running Glossary Key terms are highlighted in the text and defined in the margins. Students need not interrupt their

reading to thumb through a glossary at the end of the text whenever they encounter an unfamiliar term. A full glossary is presented at the end of the text as well.

Concept Signaling Concept signaling is designed to help students encode and retain key concepts and involves extracting key concepts and highlighting them in the margins of the text. More than **500 key concepts** appear in the margins of the text, numbered consecutively throughout each chapter for easy reference and are correlated to questions in the test bank. Here is but a small sample:

Concept 2.7
An action potential is generated according to the all-or-none principle—it is produced only if the level of excitation is sufficient.

Concept 9.16
A more securely attached infant is likely to be better adjusted in childhood and adolescence than a less securely attached infant.

Concept 16.8
The self-serving bias is widespread in Western cultures but virtually absent in some Eastern cultures.

Elaborating Meaning

Though information must first be encoded to be learned, new learning needs to be strengthened to help ensure long-term retention. We can help strengthen newly learned information by rote memorization, such as by mental rehearsal of definitions of key terms. But deeper processing and more enduring learning requires **elaborative rehearsal** in which we reflect on the meaning of the material and relate it our life experiences. This text provides several pedagogical features designed to foster both deeper processing and elaborative rehearsal.

Concept Charts Each module contains a Concept Chart that summarizes and reviews the key concepts in tabular form. Concept Charts reinforce knowledge of major concepts and help students make connections among concepts.

Application Modules The final module in each chapter is an application module. These modules illustrate how psychologists apply the knowledge they have gained from their research studies to real-life problems. Students will also see how they can apply the knowledge they gain from reading the chapter to their own lives. See the Features section on page xviii for a chapter-by-chapter listing of the application modules in the text.

"Try This Out"   These exercises not only engage students' interest, but also encourage them to apply the concepts they learn to their own experiences.

Critical Thinking Features   The critical thinking features included in this edition ("Think About It," "Thinking Critically About Psychology," and "Reality Check") encourage deeper processing by encouraging reflection and critical evaluation of commonly held beliefs, assumptions, and claims in the light of scientific evidence.

Strengthening Learning Through Repeated Rehearsal   Concepts are presented in several forms to reinforce learning—through discussion in the text, in Concept Charts, in marginal inserts, and in schematic diagrams in the text. The use of different contexts for presenting information strengthens new learning.

Evaluating Progress

The text contains built-in study aids to help students review material and evaluate their progress. These tools can help students prepare for exams and gauge whether they are integrating important concepts. Module Reviews test knowledge through "Q & A" recitation of answers to survey questions and through the use of self-scoring quizzes. "Tying It Together" sections appear at the end of each chapter to help students review how the modules are integrated within the chapter structure as a whole.

Additional Features of the Text
Targeting Critical Thinking Skills

Throughout the text, students are encouraged to challenge preconceived assumptions about human behavior and to think critically about claims made in the media in the light of scientific evidence. In addition to the "Think About It" and "Reality Check" critical thinking features, students are presented with critical thinking questions at the end of each chapter in the "Thinking Critically About Psychology" section. Students can sharpen their critical thinking skills by answering challenging questions that require them to analyze problems and evaluate claims in light of the information presented in the chapter. They may then compare their own answers to the critical thinking questions to sample responses provided in the appendix.

Targeting Technology as a Tool for Learning

The learning environment of today is much different from the one I experienced when I sat in my first undergraduate class in psychology. One important change has been the increased availability of computerized resources. The text is supported by enhanced multimedia resources: Online Teaching and Study Centers, and Eduspace.

Targeting Study Skills

The *survey, question, read, recite, review* (SQ3R) study method is a widely used technique for enhancing learning and encouraging students to adopt a more active role in the learning process. This text uses an SQ3R+ study method that incorporates the traditional elements of SQ3R along with an additional feature called "Think About It," which poses questions at the end of each module that help foster critical thinking skills.

- **Survey and Question**   Survey methods are incorporated within both the chapter structure and the modular structure. Each chapter opens with a preview section showing the contents and organization of the chapter (including a numbered list of modules presented in the chapter), and the material covered in the modules is described in the introductory section preceding the first module. In addition, survey questions begin each module to highlight important learning objectives and encourage students to use questions as advance organizers for studying.

- **Read**   The writing style has been carefully developed for reading level, content, and style. Students are often addressed directly to engage them in the material and encourage them to examine how the information may relate to their own personal experiences.

- **Recite and Review**   Each module ends with a review section that contains a "Recite It" feature that encourages students to recite answers to the survey questions that introduced the module and a "Recall It" feature that has students test their knowledge by completing a brief quiz comprising a variety of types of questions (e.g., multiple-choice, fill-in, matching, short answers). Concept Charts in each module provide further opportunities for students to review the knowledge they have acquired.

- **Think About It**   The text goes beyond review and recitation by posing thought-provoking questions in each module review. This feature encourages critical thinking and reflection on how text material relates to one's personal experiences.

Integrating Diversity

A primary objective of this text is to raise students' awareness of the importance of issues relating to diversity. Discussion of cultural and gender issues is therefore integrated within the main body of the text rather than relegated to boxed features.

For a reference guide to the integrated coverage of gender and sociocultural issues in the text, see the complete listings available at the **Online Teaching Center**.

Ancillaries

Even the most comprehensive text is incomplete without ancillaries. The ones accompanying *Psychology: Concepts and Applications,* Second Edition, help make it a complete teaching and learning package.

Teacher Ancillaries

Online Instructor's Resource Manual The *Online Instructor's Resource Manual* contains a variety of resources to aid instructors in preparing and presenting text material in a manner that meets their personal preferences and course needs. It begins with a comprehensive preface, which covers preparation, pitfalls, planning, execution, resources, and best practices for both new and seasoned instructors. Each chapter provides a preview, goals, lecture suggestions and activity planner to help organize classes. These assets can be accessed through the *Online Teaching Center* or the *HM ClassPrep CD-ROM.*

Test Bank The *Test Bank* contains over 2,500 items specifically developed for *Psychology: Concepts and Applications,* Second Edition. Multiple-choice questions and essay questions with answers are written both at the chapter and the modular level to provide flexibility to the instructor. All questions are labeled by type (factual, conceptual, applied), learning objective, module reference number, and page reference for easier use in creating exams. **New to this edition, each question is given the concept number that matches the marginal concept in the text to which it corresponds.** The test bank is available on the *HMClassPrep CD-ROM with HM Testing.*

HM ClassPrep CD-ROM with HM Testing *HM ClassPrep CD-ROM with HM Testing* is a CD-ROM that collects in one place, materials that instructors might want to have available electronically. It contains PowerPoint® slides of lecture outlines and art from the textbook, as well as the *Instructor's Resource Manual,* and the computerized test bank (HM Testing). HM Testing offers delivery of test questions in an easy-to-use format and contains 2,500 multiple-choice and essay questions with answers. All questions are labeled by type (factual, conceptual, applied), learning objective, module reference number, page reference, and concept. Additionally, the test bank questions are written both at the chapter level and the module level, to provide instructors with flexible options for customizing their exams.

PowerPoint® Presentations PowerPoint® presentations consist of an extensive set of slides providing lecture sequences that include tables, figures, and charts from the main text.

The slides are available on the *Online Teaching Center* as well as on the *HMClassPrep* CD-ROM.

Classroom Response System (CRS) Classroom Response System (CRS) content, available on the *Online Teaching Center* and on the *HM ClassPrep* CD-ROM, allows instructors to perform "on-the-spot" assessments, deliver quick quizzes, gauge students' understanding of a particular question or concept, and take their class roster easily. Students receive immediate feedback on how well they understand concepts covered in the text, and where they need to improve. Answer slides provide the correct answer and explanation of why the answer is correct. Houghton Mifflin content is compatible with the GTCO Personal Response System and the eInstruction Classroom Perfromance System.

HM ClassPresent CD-ROM The *HM ClassPresent CD-ROM* includes over forty newly developed animations spanning twenty-two topic areas. These animations can be inserted into PowerPoint® presentations and projected during a lecture, to illustrate difficult concepts from the text.

Online Teaching Center http://college.hmco.com/pic/nevid2e *Online Teaching Center* http://college.hmco.com/pic/nevid2e is a comprehensive gallery of online resources, including the complete Instructor's Resource Manual and Media Integration Guide, downloadable PDFs of the overhead transparencies, PowerPoint® lecture outlines, CRS content, and selected art from the textbook.

Eduspace *Eduspace* is a powerful course management system that enables instructors to create all or part of their courses online using the widely recognized tools of Blackboard™ and text-specific content from Nevid, *Psychology: Concepts and Applications,* Second Edition. Instructors and students have access to automatically graded online homework quizzes, *Psych in Film* video clips with quizzes, and tutorials with accompanying pedagogy.

Blackboard/Web CT Cartridges Blackboard/Web CT Cartridges allow instructors to utilize, customize, and administer many of the instructor resources, such as chapter outlines, an activity planner, PowerPoint® slides, handouts, and a wealth of testing material developed specifically for this edition.

Houghton Mifflin Psych in Film® DVD or VHS Houghton Mifflin Psych in Film® DVD or VHS is available to adopters. This supplement contains thirty-five clips from Universal Studios films illustrating key concepts in psychology. Clips from films such as *Schindler's List* and *Snow Falling on Cedars,* are combined with commentary and discussion questions to help bring psychology alive for students and demonstrate its relevance to contemporary life and culture. Teaching tips are also included.

Student Ancillaries

NEW . . . *Concept Maps for Psychology* Offered for the first time in introductory psychology, *Concept Maps for Psychology* are visual-spatial diagrams that show relational connections among concepts. Concept Maps are visual learning tools that help students recognize linkages among concepts discussed in the chapter. They do not require students to learn any additional material. To make these maps an even more effective learning tool, they are accompanied by thought questions that encourage deeper processing by making the material more personally meaningful. In addition, each map is correlated with a set of multiple-choice questions in the *Eduspace* homework quizzes, which help students assess their knowledge of this material.

Study Guide The Study Guide focuses on providing students with resources aimed at improving study skills and comprehension of the text material. For each chapter, this guide provides a one-page detailed outline, a list of objectives, chapter overview, key terms and concepts, and self-testing exercises and activities. In addition, students are provided an integrated set of media resources to further improve and expand their understanding of the main concepts of the course.

Online Study Center http://college.hmco.com/pic/nevid2e
Online Study Center http://college.hmco.com/pic/nevid2e is a comprehensive gallery of online resources available to students using *Psychology: Concepts and Applications,* Second Edition. Organized by category and chapter topic, these resources include ACE practice tests, tutorials, Critical Thinking Activities, Concept Charts, and a variety of web links. A passkey is required to access high-value content on the student site. If a passkey is not packaged with this text, please go to http://college.hmco.com/pic/nevid2e to obtain one.

Eduspace Eduspace is a customizable, powerful, and interactive platform that allows students to access a variety of online resources that help them study and complete assignments. Students have access to automatically graded online homework quizzes, *Psych in Film* video clips with quizzes, and tutorials with accompanying pedagogy.

Acknowledgments

First, I am indebted to the thousands of psychologists and other scientists whose work has informed the writing of both this edition and the first edition of the text. Thanks to their efforts, the field of psychology has had an enormous impact in broadening our understanding of ourselves and enhancing the quality of our lives. On a more personal level, I owe a debt of gratitude to the many colleagues and publishing professionals who helped shape this manuscript into its present form. Let me begin by thanking the professional colleagues who reviewed the manuscript and helped me refine it through several stages of development:

Patricia Abbott, D'Youville College
Denise M. Arehart, University of Colorado, Denver
James E. Arruda, Mercer University
David R. Barkmeier, Northeastern University
Howard Berthold, Lycoming College
Kathleen Bey, Palm Beach Community College
Cheryl Bluestone, Queensborough Community College/CUNY
Reba M. Bowman, Tennessee Temple University
John W. Bouseman, Hillsborough Community College
Deborah S. Briihl, Valdosta State University
Charles Brodie, Georgia Perimeter College
John P. Broida, University of Southern Maine
Winfield Brown, Florence Darlington Technical College
Lawrence R. Burns, Grand Valley State University
Adam Butler, University of Northern Iowa
Bernard J. Carducci, Indiana University Southeast
Elaine Cassel, Marymount University, Lord Fairfax Community College
Hank Cetula, Adrian College
Matthew G. Chin, University of Central Florida
Sharon Church, Highland Community College
Saundra K. Ciccarelli, Gulf Coast Community College
Russell D. Clark, University of North Texas
Wanda Clark, South Plains College
Susan Clayton, The College of Wooster
Sandra Cole, New Hampshire Community Technical College
Larry J. Cology, Owens Community College
Robert S. Coombs, Southern Adventist University
Mary Webber Coplen, Hutchinson Community College
Richard S. Coyle, California State University, Chico
George J. Demakis, Elmhurst College
Robin DesJardin, John Tyler Community College
Victor Duarte, North Idaho College
Mary H. Dudley, Howard College
Vera Dunwoody, Chaffey College
Gianna Durso-Finley, New England Institute of Technology
Steven I. Dworkin, University of North Carolina, Wilmington
Rebecca F. Eaton, The University of Alabama, Huntsville
Tami Eggleston, McKendree College
Julie Felender, Fullerton College
Oney D. Fitzpatrick, Lamar University
William F. Ford, Bucks County Community College
Lenore Frigo, College of Southern Idaho
Grace Galliano, Kennesaw State University
David Griese, State University of New York, Farmingdale
Dr. Jackie Griswold, Holyoke Community College

Frank Hager, Allegany College of Maryland

Lynn Haller, Morehead State University

Debra Hope, University of Nebraska, Lincoln

Senqi Hu, Humboldt State University

Amanda M. Maynard, State University of New York at New Paltz

Les Parrott, Seattle Pacific University

Janet R. Pascal, DeVry Institute of Technology, Kansas City

Christine M. Paynard, University of Detroit Mercy

Lillian M. Range, University of Southern Mississippi

Darren R. Ritzer, George Mason University

John Sanford, Laramie County Community College

H. R. Schiffman, Rutgers University

Pennie S. Seibert, Boise State University

Benjamin Wallace, Cleveland State University

Nancy White, Coastal Carolina Community College

David Yells, Utah Valley State College

Arthur D. VanDeventer, Thomas Nelson Community College

Jeanette Youngblood, Arkansas State University, Newport

Michael J. Zeller, Minnesota State University

Otto Zinser, East Tennessee State University

Second, I would like to thank the countless instructors and students who participated in our extensive market research conducted in the early stages of the text's development—including the instructors and students at Valencia Community College and the University of Central Florida, who provided us with great insight into their introductory psychology courses; the instructors who participated in the teleconference sessions and raised many important issues that impacted the day-to-day challenges of this course; and the 700-plus respondents who participated in our national survey on introductory psychology and this text. The overwhelming response we received from these professionals proved to be a rich resource throughout the development of the text. Many thanks also to the supplements team who helped produce wonderful teaching tools and study tools to accompany the text: Tami Eggleston, McKendree College and Gabie E. Smith, Elon University (*Instructor's Manual*); Rachelle Lipschultz, Anne Arundel Community College (*Study Guide*); Christine M. Vanchella, South Georgia College (*Test Bank*); Billa Reiss, St. John's University (*CRS*); David Strohmetz, Monmouth University (PowerPoint® slides); and Lora Harpster, Salt Lake Community College (Ace quizzes).

Third, I would like a special thanks to Dr. Celia Reaves of Monroe Community College for her helpful suggestions of cartoons that convey psychological concepts in a medium that is both informative and entertaining.

Finally, but certainly not the least of all, I am grateful to the people at Houghton Mifflin who made this book possible, especially Jane Potter, senior sponsoring editor, who began as the marketing manager for the text and then moved to the editorial side; Rita Lombard and Laura Hildebrand, two of the finest developmental editors an author could ever find; senior project editor Carol Newman, who brought the project together and continues to oversee its production, including reining me in whenever necessary; marketing manager Laura McGinn, who uncannily has a sense of how to best serve instructor's needs, and marketing associate, Erin Lane. Many thanks to the supplements team who produced both the print and electronic ancillaries: Lynn Baldridge, discipline product manager; Liz Hogan, editorial associate; Deborah Berkman, editorial assistant; Sean McGann, digital ancillary producer; Jaime Smith, media developer; Walter Holland, production assistant; and Audra Bayette, sr. project manager. I am indebted to photo editor Ann Schroeder, who found even the most difficult-to-find photographs, Susan Zorn, copyeditor, and the many other talented and committed professionals at Houghton Mifflin. I thank you all.

Jeff Nevid
New York, New York
askauthor@hotmail.com or *jnevid@hotmail.com*

A Message to Students

How to Use This Textbook

You are about to embark on a journey through the field of psychology. As with any journey, it is helpful to have markers or road signs to help you navigate your course. This text provides a number of convenient markers to help you know where you've been and where you're headed. Take a moment to familiarize yourself with the terrain you're going to encounter in your journey. It centers on the unique organizational framework represented in this text—the concept-based modular format.

Why a concept-based modular approach? There are three key reasons:

1. **To help you organize your study activities.** The modular approach breaks down large chapters into smaller units of instruction. Rather than try to digest an entire chapter at once, you can chew on one module at a time.

2. **To help you master the material.** Each module is a self-contained unit of instruction. At the end of each module you'll find a module review section designed to help you review the material in the module and test your knowledge before moving ahead.

3. **To help you learn key concepts that form the foundations of knowledge in each area of study.** As you make your way through each module, you will be learning a set of basic concepts and how they relate to the theoretical and research foundations of the field of psychology.

How to Use the SQ3R+ Study Method

This text includes a built-in study system called the SQ3R+ study method, a system designed to help students develop more effective study habits that expands upon the SQ3R method developed by psychologist Francis P. Robinson. SQ3R is an acronym that stands for five key features: *survey, question, read, recite,* and *review.* This text adds an additional section—"Think About It." Here's how you can best use the method to master the material:

1. **Survey** Preview each chapter before reading it. Scan the outline and the introductory section to get a sense of how the chapter is organized and what general topics are covered. Familiarizing yourself with the contents of a chapter before reading it can activate related information that you already hold in memory, thereby assisting you in acquiring and retaining new information.

2. **Question** This text incorporates survey questions at the start of each module that highlight key issues addressed in the module. Jot down these questions in a notebook or computer file so that you can answer them as you read along. You may also find it helpful to generate additional questions. Developing good questioning skills allows you to become a more active learner, which can enhance your ability to understand and retain information.

3. **Read** Read the material in the module in order to answer the survey questions and learn additional information.

4. **Recite** When you reach the end of the module, you'll see a Module Review. The review is intended to help you gauge your progress. The Module Review consists of three sections: *Recite It, Recall It,* and *Think About It.* The *Recite It* section contains the survey questions that began the module, with sample answers provided. Try reciting the answers to each question to yourself before looking at the sample answers. Then compare your answers with the sample answers provided. Hearing yourself speak the answers may further enhance your retention and later retrieval of the information you have read. That's why it is important for you to recite the answers first before looking at the sample answers provided in the text.

5. **Review** Establish a study schedule for reviewing the material on a regular basis. Test yourself each time you reread the material to further boost long-term retention. Use the *Recall It* section in the Module Review as a means of testing yourself. You may also go online and take self-scoring, ACE practice tests on the companion website.

6. **Think About It** The "Think About It" section in the Module Review poses thought-provoking questions that encourage you to apply your critical thinking skills and to reflect on how the material relates to your own experiences.

I hope you enjoy your journey through psychology. It began for me in my freshman year in college and has continued for me with a sense of wonder and joy ever since.

Please email your comments, questions, or suggestions to me at either *askauthor@hotmail.com* or *jnevid@hotmail.com.*

Jeff Nevid
New York, NY

About the Author

Dr. Jeffrey Nevid is Professor of Psychology at St. John's University in New York. He received his doctorate from the State University of New York at Albany and completed a post-doctoral fellowship in evaluation research at Northwestern University.

Dr. Nevid has conducted research in many areas of psychology, including health psychology, clinical and community psychology, social psychology, gender and human sexuality, adolescent development, and textbook pedagogy. His research publications have appeared in such journals as *Health Psychology, Journal of Consulting and Clinical Psychology, Journal of Community Psychology, Journal of Youth and Adolescence, Behavior Therapy, Psychology and Marketing, Professional Psychology, Teaching of Psychology, Sex Roles,* and *Journal of Social Psychology,* among others. Dr. Nevid also served as Editorial Consultant for the journals *Health Psychology* and *Psychology and Marketing* and as Associate Editor for *Journal of Consulting and Clinical Psychology.* He is actively involved in conducting further research on advances in textbook pedagogy.

Dr. Nevid has coauthored several other college texts, including *Abnormal Psychology in a Changing World,* published by Prentice Hall, *Human Sexuality in a World of Diversity,* published by Allyn and Bacon, and *Psychology and the Challenges of Life: Adjustment in the New Millennium,* published by John Wiley & Sons. He also authored several books on AIDS and sexually transmitted diseases published by Allyn and Bacon, including *A Student's Guide to AIDS and Other Sexually Transmitted Diseases* and *Choices: Sex in the Age of AIDS.* He lives in New York with his wife Judy and his children Michael and Daniella.

Psychology
Concepts and Applications

1

Introduction to Psychology and Methods of Research

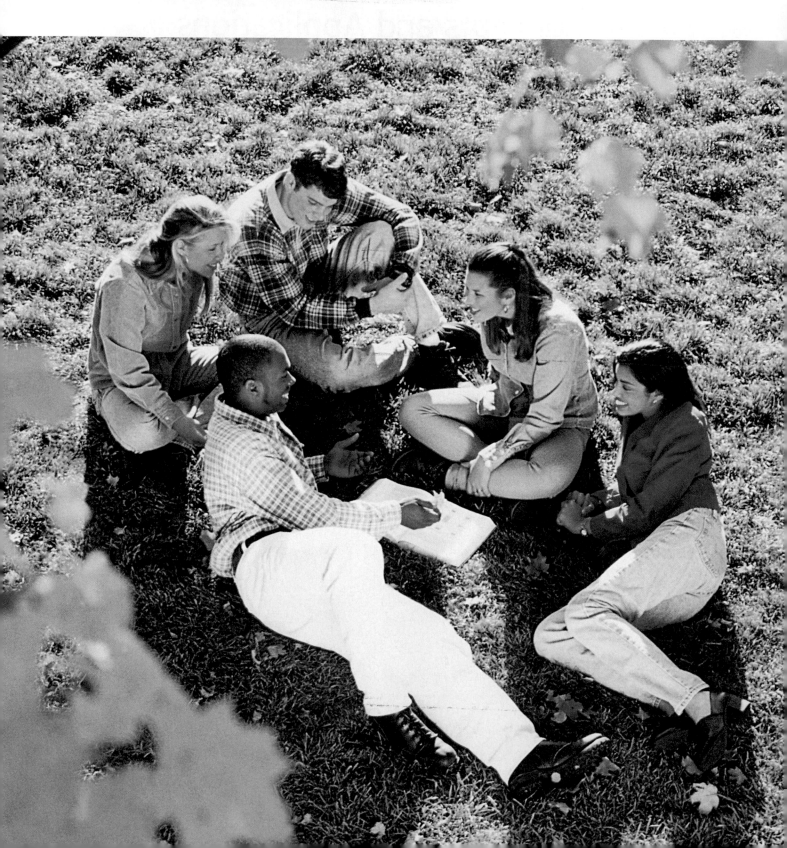

DID YOU KNOW THAT . . .

- One of the founders of modern psychology was such a poor student he was actually left back a grade in school? (p. 6)
- A movement that once dominated psychology believed that psychologists should turn away from the study of the mind? (p. 7)
- A major school of psychology was inspired by the view from a train? (p. 9)
- In comparison with their parents, young people today are twice as likely to classify themselves as multiracial? (p. 14)
- When it comes to hitting a baseball, your expectations about the type of pitch the pitcher will throw can get in the way of your hitting? (p. 22)
- A student successfully completed all Ph.D. requirements at Johns Hopkins University but was refused a doctorate because she was a woman? (p. 22)
- Placebo effects tend to be stronger for measures that rely on subjective ratings, such as feelings of pain, than on objective measures, such as blood pressure? (p. 33)
- You can obtain listings and abstracts of articles from major psychology journals by using your home computer (and most are free of charge)? (p. 42)

Let me introduce you to the field of psychology, the science of behavior and mental processes. This is probably not your first exposure to many of the topics we will study. Your earliest encounter with the subject matter of psychology most likely began many years ago. Perhaps it came as you first wondered about why people do what they do or how their personalities differ. Perhaps you wondered why your third-grade classmate just couldn't seem to sit still and often disrupted the class. Or perhaps you wondered about the meaning of those nightly meanderings of the mind we call dreams. Maybe you wondered mostly about yourself, about who you are and why you do the things you do. Perhaps one of the reasons you are taking this course is to learn more about yourself.

You may find answers to many questions you have about the behavior of humans and nonhuman animals in this introductory course in psychology. But you may not find all the answers you are seeking. There is still so much we do not understand, so much that remains to be explored. This text, like the field of psychology itself, is really about the process of exploration—the quest for knowledge about behavior and mental processes.

Psychology is a scientific discipline, but what makes it scientific? One answer is that it values evidence over opinion and tradition—even honored tradition or the opinions of respected scholars and thinkers. Psychologists don't dismiss opinion, tradition, or even folklore. Yet as scientists, they require that opinions, assumptions, beliefs, and theories, whether about love, dreams, or other aspects of the human experience, be tested and scrutinized in the light of the available evidence. Psychologists seek answers to the questions they and others have posed about human nature by using scientific methods of study and investigation. Like other scientists, they are professional skeptics. They have confidence only in those theories that can be tied to observable evidence. As in all branches of science, investigators within the field of psychology gather evidence to test their theories, beliefs, and assumptions.

Before we go further with our exploration of psychology, let us define what we mean by the term *psychology*. Though many definitions of psychology have been proposed, the one most widely used today defines psychology as the science of behavior and mental processes. But what do these terms mean—*behavior and mental processes*? Broadly speaking, anything an organism does is a form of behavior. Sitting in a chair is a form of behavior. Reading and studying are forms of behavior, as is watching TV. Making yourself a sandwich is a form of behavior, as is talking on the telephone, smiling at someone, dancing, or simply raising your arm. Even thinking and dreaming are forms of behavior—things you do—even if no one else can directly observe what you are thinking or dreaming.

Mental processes are private experiences that constitute our inner life as individuals. These private experiences include thoughts, feelings, dreams and daydreams, sensations, perceptions, and beliefs that others cannot directly observe or experience. Among the challenges psychologists face is finding ways of making such inner experiences available to scientific study.

Before we begin exploring how psychologists study behavior and mental processes, let us take the story of psychology back to its origins to see how it developed as a scientific discipline and where it stands today. ■

MODULE 1.1

Foundations of Modern Psychology

- What is psychology?
- What are the origins of psychology?
- What were the major early schools of psychology?
- What are the major contemporary perspectives in psychology?

CONCEPT 1.1
Psychology is the scientific discipline that studies behavior and mental processes.

CONCEPT 1.2
Although psychology is a relatively young science, interest in understanding the nature of mind and behavior can be traced back to ancient times.

Online Study Center

Improve Your Grade
Tutorials: Psychology vs. Common Sense

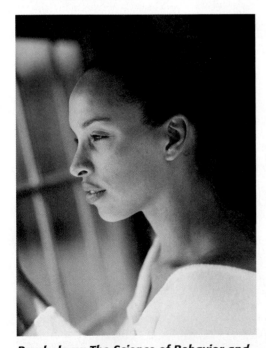

Psychology: The Science of Behavior and Mental Processes Psychologists study what we do and what we think, feel, dream, sense, and perceive. They use scientific methods to guide their investigations of behavior and mental processes.

This first module sets the stage for our study of psychology. It describes the development of psychology as a scientific discipline. How did psychology develop? What were the important influences that shaped its development as a scientific discipline? Here we address those questions by recounting a brief history of psychology. Let us begin by noting that although psychology is still a young science, its origins can be traced back to ancient times.

Origins of Psychology

The story of psychology has no clear beginning. We cannot mark its birth on any calendar. We can speculate that the story very likely began when early humans developed the capacity to reflect on human nature. Perhaps they were curious, as many of us are today, about what makes people tick. But what they may have thought or said about the nature of human beings remains unknown, as no record exists of their musings.

The word **psychology** is derived from two Greek roots, *psyche,* meaning "mind," and *logos,* meaning "study" or "knowledge." So it is fitting that we turn to the philosophers of the classical period of ancient Greece, around 500 to 300 B.C. The ancient Greek philosophers who had the most profound influence on psychological thought were Socrates (ca. 469–399 B.C.), Plato (ca. 428–348 B.C.), and Aristotle (ca. 384–332 B.C.).

We know of Socrates through the writings of his most eminent pupil, Plato. Socrates, whose famous credo was "know thyself," emphasized the importance of self-examination and personal reflection. He believed the unexamined life is not worth living. His theme of self-exploration remains one of the most enduring in modern psychology. Plato had also learned from Socrates that we should not rely on our senses to acquire knowledge about the world, since the world that is given to us by our senses is an imperfect copy of reality. The notion that our senses are not to be trusted as windows to the truth resonates with modern psychologists who study how our senses can deceive us in the form of visual illusions (see Chapter 3). Like Socrates before him, Plato believed that to acquire true knowledge we should rely on thought and reason, not on information that comes to us through our imperfect senses.

Aristotle, Plato's most famous student, thought differently. He was trained as a naturalist, so it is not surprising he came to believe that knowledge could be acquired by the senses through careful observation. Aristotle held that the pursuit of knowledge should be based on experience with the world around us, not on pure thought or reasoning. Aristotelian thinking came to influence the development of the modern sciences, as can be seen in the emphasis those sciences place on experimentation and careful observation as pathways to knowledge.

While most ancient Greeks believed that the gods interfered in people's daily lives, Aristotle maintained that people should believe in what they can see and touch. He was one of the first to write about natural causes of human behavior rather than appealing to divine or supernatural explanations. Aristotle even explained the ways in which one thought leads to another; his ideas on the *association* of thoughts are still found in contemporary views of learning and thinking. Aristo-

1860	• Gustav Fechner publishes *Elements of Psychophysics*
1875	• William James gives first psychology lecture at Harvard
1878	• G. Stanley Hall receives first Ph.D. in psychology in the U.S.
1879	• Wilhelm Wundt establishes first psychology laboratory
1883	• First American psychology laboratory established at Johns Hopkins University by G. Stanley Hall
1887	• G. Stanley Hall initiates the *American Journal of Psychology*
1889	• James Mark Baldwin establishes first Canadian psychology laboratory at University of Toronto
1890	• James writes first psychology text, *Principles of Psychology*
1892	• American Psychological Association (APA) formed; G. Stanley Hall first president
1894	• Margaret Floy Washburn is first woman to receive a Ph.D. in psychology
1895	• Sigmund Freud publishes first work on psychology
1896	• Lightner Witmer establishes the first psychology clinic in the U.S.
1900	• Freud publishes *The Interpretation of Dreams*
1905	• Two Frenchmen, Alfred Binet and Théodore Simon, announce development of the first intelligence test, which they describe as "a measuring scale of intelligence" • Mary Whiton Calkins becomes first female president of APA
1908	• Ivan Pavlov's work on conditioning first appears in an American scientific journal
1910	• Max Wertheimer and colleagues begin research on Gestalt psychology
1913	• Watson publishes the behaviorist manifesto, *Psychology as the Behaviorist Views It*
1920	• Francis Sumner is first African American to receive a Ph.D. in psychology in the U.S. • Henry Alston is first African American to publish his research findings in a major psychology journal in the U.S.

Figure 1.1   Psychology, the Early Days: A Timeline

psychology   The science of behavior and mental processes.

psychophysics   The study of the relationships between features of physical stimuli, such as their intensity, and the sensations we experience in response to them.

introspection   Inward focusing on mental experiences, such as sensations or feelings.

tle also said that people and lower animals are primarily motivated to seek pleasure and avoid pain. This view has become a mainstay of modern theories of motivation.

Even as we consider the contributions of the ancient Greek philosophers, we shouldn't forget that other systems of thought about human nature were taking root elsewhere around the same time—in Africa, the Middle East, and the Far East, where the philosopher and essayist Confucius (ca. 551–479 B.C.) was to become the most influential and respected thinker in Chinese history. Confucius believed that people have an inborn capacity to do good and that evil is the product of a bad environment or a lack of education, not an evil nature. As we'll see, the belief that environmental influences play a key role in determining behavior finds expression in modern schools of thought in psychology. Confucius also believed that people should be governed by moral principles (rather than profit motives) and that they should cultivate their minds to the utmost. Contemporary psychologists have also turned their attention to issues of moral reasoning and moral development, as we'll see in Chapter 10.

Psychology remained largely an interest of philosophers, theologians, and writers for several thousand years. It did not begin to emerge as a scientific discipline until the late nineteenth century. One of the first scientists to study psychological processes was the German physiologist Gustav Theodor Fechner (1801–1887). Fechner studied **psychophysics**, the ways in which the intensity and other physical characteristics of stimuli, such as light and sound, give rise to our psychological experience of them (their brightness, loudness, and so on). In 1860, Fechner published his findings in his book *Elements of Psychophysics*. In the 1850s, another German physiologist, Hermann von Helmholtz (1821–1894), developed a theory of how people perceive color. We'll return to the contributions of Fechner and von Helmholtz when we consider processes of sensation and perception in Chapter 3.

The founding of psychology as an independent science is usually credited to a German scientist, Wilhelm Wundt (1832–1920) (see the Pioneers box on page 6). The credit is given to Wundt (pronounced *Voont*) because he established the first scientific laboratory dedicated to the study of psychology (E. Taylor, 2000). With the founding of Wundt's laboratory in Leipzig, Germany, in 1879, psychology made the transition from philosophy to science (Benjamin, 2000).

Like any scientific discipline, the field of psychology is an unfolding story of exploration and discovery. In this text, you will encounter many of the explorers and discoverers who have shaped the continuing story of psychology. The bridge from ancient thought to the present starts with Wundt; there we encounter his disciple Edward Titchener and structuralism, the school with which both men were associated. (See Figure 1.1 for a timeline of the early days of psychology.)

Wilhelm Wundt, Edward Titchener, and Structuralism   Wilhelm Wundt was interested in studying people's mental experiences. He used a method called **introspection**, or careful self-examination and reporting of one's conscious experience—what one is perceiving, feeling, thinking, or sensing at each particular moment in time. For example, he would expose people to a visual or auditory stimulus, a light or a sound, and ask them to report their conscious reactions to the stimulus (what it sounded like, how long it lasted, how it felt).

THE PIONEERS | The Boy Who Daydreamed Too Much

Wilhelm Wundt

It is curious that the founder of psychology as an independent science was Wilhelm Wundt, a man whose early life experiences gave no inkling that he would go on to establish a new science. A poor student as a boy, Wundt was even required to repeat a grade. The problem for young Wilhelm was that he daydreamed too much. He would drift off during class, a practice that continued even during his university days. He would often be found sitting with an open book in his hand, staring off into space rather than reading his assigned text (a practice this author hopes you

don't emulate too closely when you open your psychology text).

While in his twenties, Wundt suffered a serious illness from which it seemed he would not recover. Yet he did not despair. Instead, he used the experience as an opportunity to probe deeply into his mind so he could analyze the experience of dying. But Wundt survived. He went on to graduate from medical school and from there to launch a successful research career as a physiologist. Later, he would apply his scientific training to his true passion, the understanding of conscious experience. In establishing the first psychology laboratory, the man who had once been left back in school because he was so absorbed in his own thoughts became the first scientist of the mind.

CONCEPT 1.3
Structuralism was an early school of psychology that attempted to understand how the mind is structured by breaking down mental experiences into their smallest components.

In his laboratory, Wundt and his students conducted rather simple experiments. The purpose was to develop a model of conscious experience by breaking it down into its component parts—sensations, perceptions, and feelings—and then to determine how these elements are evoked by such stimuli as lights, sounds, and colors and how they are related to each other. For example, people would be asked to listen to a metronome running at different rates of speed and to report their conscious reactions. A rapid beat might be experienced as exciting, a slower one as relaxing.

Edward Titchener (1867–1927), an Englishman who was a disciple of Wundt, brought Wundt's teachings and methods of introspection to the United States and other English-speaking countries. The school of psychology identified with Wundt and Titchener became known as **structuralism**, an approach that attempted to define the structure of the mind by breaking down mental experiences into their component parts.

The first American to work in Wundt's experimental laboratory was the psychologist G. Stanley Hall (1844–1924) (Johnson, 2000). In 1892, Hall founded the American Psychological Association (APA), now the largest organization of psychologists in the United States, and he served as its first president (Pate, 2000). Nine years earlier, in 1883, he had established the first psychology laboratory in the United States, which was housed at Johns Hopkins University (Benjamin, 2000). Although Hall played a pivotal role in the early days of psychology in the United States, the psychologist generally recognized as the founder of American psychology was the Harvard psychologist William James.

CONCEPT 1.4
William James, the founder of functionalism, believed that psychology should focus on how our behavior and mental processes help us adapt to the demands we face in the world.

William James and Functionalism   William James (1842–1910) was trained as a medical doctor but made important contributions to both psychology and philosophy (Pate, 2000). Although he used introspection, he shifted the focus to the *functions* of behavior. Unlike the structuralists, he did not believe that conscious experience could be parceled into discrete elements. Rather, he believed that mental experience is best understood in terms of the functions or purposes it serves.

James founded **functionalism**, the school of psychology that focused on how behavior helps individuals adapt to the demands placed on them in the environ-

Basketball-Playing Raccoon   When particular behaviors are reinforced, even a raccoon can be taught to shoot a basketball.

ment. Whereas structuralists were concerned with mental structures, functionalists were concerned with the functions of mental processes (Willingham, 2001). Functionalists examined the roles or functions that underlie our mental processes—*why* we do *what* we do. James believed that we develop habits, such as the characteristic ways in which we use a fork or a spoon, because they enable us to perform more effectively in meeting the demands of daily life.

James was influenced by Charles Darwin's theory of evolution. Darwin (1809–1882) believed that all life forms, including humans, had evolved from earlier life forms by adapting over time to the demands of their natural environments. He believed that evolution could be explained by **natural selection**, the process by which members of a species that are best adapted to the environment are the ones most likely to survive and pass along their traits to succeeding generations. In effect, nature selects them to survive and multiply. Over time, species will come to be dominated by members that possess adaptive traits, such as the ability to obtain food and avoid predators (Gaulin & McBurney, 2001). When environmental conditions change, as may occur during long periods of drought or with major shifts in temperature or climate, the species that survive will be those that possess traits that enable them to adjust to these changes. Other species not so well equipped will die out.

James extended Darwin's theory of evolution to psychology by advancing the idea that the most adaptive behaviors in an individual are the ones most likely to grow stronger and become habitual, while less useful or adaptive behaviors will likely disappear. So adaptive behaviors are more likely to endure, at least most of the time. But psychologists today are also interested in why some people engage in behavior that is *mal*adaptive, such as smoking or gambling, despite the harmful effects of such behavior.

James was also concerned with the **stream of consciousness**, the continuous current of thoughts that seem to flow endlessly through our awareness or consciousness like a river or stream. We will return to James's contributions to our understanding of conscious experience in Chapter 4.

John Watson and Behaviorism   In the early 1900s, a new force in psychology gathered momentum. It was called **behaviorism**, and its credo was that psychology should limit itself to the study of overt behavior that observers could record and measure. The founder of behaviorism was the American psychologist John Broadus Watson (1878–1958). Watson reasoned that since you can never observe another person's mental processes, psychology would never advance as a science unless it eliminated mentalistic concepts like mind, consciousness, thinking, and feeling. He rejected introspection as a method of scientific inquiry and proposed that psychology should become a science of behavior, not mental processes (Rilling, 2000; Tweney & Budzynski, 2000; Willingham, 2001). In this respect, he shared with the ancient Greek philosopher Aristotle the belief that science should rely on observable events. Watson appealed to his fellow psychologists, as scientists, to focus on what they could observe—responses, reflexes, and other observable behaviors.

Watson believed that the environment molds the behavior of humans and other animals. He even boasted that if he were given control over the lives of infants, he could determine the kinds of adults they would become:

> *Give me a dozen healthy infants, well-formed, and my own specified world to bring them up in and I'll guarantee to take any one at random and train him to become any type of specialist I might suggest—doctor, lawyer, merchant-chief and, yes, even beggar-man and thief, regardless of his talents, penchants, tendencies, abilities, vocations, and the race of his ancestors. (Watson, 1924, p. 82)*

CONCEPT 1.5

Behaviorism was based on the belief that psychology would only advance as a science if it turned away from the study of mental processes and limited itself to the study of observable behaviors that could be recorded and measured.

structuralism   The school of psychology that attempts to understand the structure of the mind by breaking it down into its component parts.

functionalism   The school of psychology that focuses on the adaptive functions of behavior.

natural selection   The evolutionary process by which individuals of a species that are best adapted to their environments are the ones most likely to survive and pass along their traits to succeeding generations.

stream of consciousness   The continuous flow of conscious thoughts.

behaviorism   The school of psychology that holds that psychology should limit itself to the study of overt, observable behavior.

No one, of course, took up Watson's challenge, so we never will know how "a dozen healthy infants" would have fared under his direction. Psychologists today, however, believe that human development is much more complex than Watson thought. Few would believe that Watson could have succeeded in meeting the challenge he posed.

By the 1920s, behaviorism had become the main school of psychology in the United States, and it remained the dominant force in American psychology for several generations. Its popularity owed a great deal to the work of the Harvard University psychologist B. F. Skinner (1904–1990). Skinner studied how behavior is shaped by rewards and punishments, the environmental consequences that follow specific responses. He showed that he could train animals to perform simple behaviors by rewarding particular responses. Thus, for example, a rat could learn to press a bar and a pigeon to peck a button if they were rewarded for these responses by receiving pellets of food. He also showed how more complex behaviors could be learned and maintained by manipulation of rewards, which he called *reinforcers*. In some of his more colorful demonstrations of the use of reinforcement, he trained a pigeon to play a tune on a toy piano and a pair of pigeons to play a type of Ping-Pong in which the birds rolled a ball back and forth between them. These methods could even be used to teach a raccoon to shoot a basketball, although the three-point shot is probably beyond its range.

Although Skinner studied mainly pigeons and rats, he believed that the same principles of learning he observed in laboratory animals could be applied to humans as well. He argued that human behavior is as much a product of environmental consequences as is the behavior of other animals. Everything we do, from saying "excuse me" when we sneeze, to attending class, to making a sandwich, represents responses learned through reinforcement, even though we cannot expect to recall the many reinforcement occasions involved in acquiring and maintaining these behaviors.

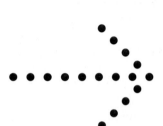

Figure 1.2   What Is This?

💡 **CONCEPT 1.6**
Gestalt psychology was based on a core principle that the brain organizes our perceptions of the world such that we perceive organized patterns or wholes, not individual bits and pieces of sense experiences added together.

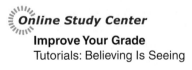

Online Study Center

Improve Your Grade
Tutorials: Believing Is Seeing

Gestalt psychology   The school of psychology that holds that the brain structures our perceptions of the world in terms of meaningful patterns or wholes.

gestalt   A German word meaning "unitary form" or "pattern."

unconscious   In Freudian theory, the part of the mind that lies outside the range of ordinary awareness and that contains primitive drives or instincts and unacceptable urges, wishes, or ideas.

Max Wertheimer and Gestalt Psychology   In 1910, at about the time Watson was appealing to psychologists to abandon the study of the mind, another young psychologist, Max Wertheimer (1880–1943), was traveling by train through central Germany on his way to a vacation in the Rhineland (see the Pioneers box on page 9). What he saw from the train would lead him to found a new movement in psychology. Called **Gestalt psychology**, it is the school of psychology that studies the ways in which the brain organizes and structures our perceptions of the world.

The Gestalt psychologists rejected the structuralist belief that mental experience could be understood by breaking it down into its component parts. The German word **gestalt** can be roughly translated as "unitary form" or "pattern." The Gestaltists believed that the brain organizes how we see the world so that we perceive unified or organized wholes, not individual bits and pieces of sense experiences added together. The well-known Gestalt maxim that the "whole is greater than the sum of the parts" expresses this core belief. You perceive the dots in Figure 1.2 not as a formless array of individual dots, but as representing an arrow. When you see a large number of black objects flying overhead, you instantly recognize them as a flock of birds flying in formation. In other words, your brain interprets what your eyes see as organized patterns or wholes. Although Gestalt psychology extended into other areas of psychology, especially learning, it is best known for its contributions to perception, as we shall see in Chapter 3.

Sigmund Freud and Psychoanalysis   Around the time that behaviorism and Gestalt psychology were establishing a foothold in organized psychology, a very different model of psychology was emerging. It was based on the writings of an Austrian physician named Sigmund Freud (1856–1939). Freud's psychology focused not only on the mind but also on a region of the mind that lay beyond the reach of ordinary consciousness—a region he called the **unconscious**. Freud con-

THE PIONEERS | The View from the Train

Max Wertheimer

As train passengers often do, Max Wertheimer stared out at the passing landscape. What he observed outside his window would forever alter his life and launch a new movement in psychology (Hunt, 1993). What captured his attention was the illusion that objects in the distance—telegraph poles, houses, and hilltops—appeared to be moving along with the train, even though they were obviously standing still.

Countless other people had observed the same phenomenon of apparent movement but had paid little if any attention to it. Apparent movement is best known as the basis of motion pictures. In 1890, Thomas Edison had shown that he could create the appearance of moving pictures by stringing together still photographs on a strip of film and then illuminating them in quick succession on a screen. Whereas Edison was content to produce apparent movement without attempting to explain it, Wertheimer was intrigued to find out why the phenomenon occurred. He had the idea that the illusion was not a trick of the eye but reflected higher-level processes in the brain that created the perception of movement. He promptly canceled his vacation and began experimental studies of the phenomenon. The experiments that he conducted with two assistants, Wolfgang Köhler (1887–1967) and Kurt Koffka (1886–1943), led to discoveries about the nature of perception—the processes by which we organize our sense impressions and form meaningful representations of the world around us.

CONCEPT 1.7
Freud held that our behavior is largely determined by unconscious forces and motives that lie beyond the reach of ordinary awareness.

ceived of the unconscious as the repository of primitive sexual and aggressive drives or instincts and of the wishes, impulses, and urges that arise from those drives or instincts. He believed that the motives underlying our behavior involve sexual and aggressive impulses that lie in the murky depths of the unconscious, hidden away from our ordinary awareness of ourselves. In other words, we may do or say things without understanding the true motives that prompted these behaviors.

Freud also believed that early childhood experiences play a determining role in shaping our personalities and behavior, including abnormal behaviors like excessive fears or phobias. He held that abnormal behavior patterns are rooted in unconscious conflicts originating in childhood. These conflicts involve a dynamic struggle within the unconscious mind between unacceptable sexual or aggressive impulses striving for expression and opposing mental forces seeking to keep this threatening material out of conscious awareness. Thus, Freud's view of psychology, and that of his followers, is often called the **psychodynamic perspective**.

Unlike Wundt, James, and Watson, Freud was a therapist, and his main aim was to help people overcome psychological problems. He developed a form of psychotherapy or "talk therapy" that he called **psychoanalysis** (discussed in Chapter 14). Psychoanalysis is a type of mental detective work. It incorporates methods, such as analysis of dreams and of "slips of the tongue," that Freud believed could be used to gain insight into the nature of the underlying motives and conflicts of which his patients were unaware. Freud maintained that once these unconscious conflicts were brought into the light of conscious awareness, they could be successfully resolved, or "worked through," during the course of therapy.

psychodynamic perspective The view that behavior is influenced by the struggle between unconscious sexual or aggressive impulses and opposing forces that try to keep this threatening material out of consciousness.

psychoanalysis Freud's method of psychotherapy; it focuses on uncovering and working through the unconscious conflicts he believed were at the root of psychological problems.

Contemporary Perspectives in Psychology

What do we find when we look over the landscape of psychology today? For one thing, we find a discipline that owes a great debt to its founders but that is constantly reinventing itself to meet new challenges. Not all schools of thought

CONCEPT 1.8

Although some early schools of psychology have essentially disappeared, contemporary perspectives in the field, including the behavioral, psychodynamic, humanistic, physiological, cognitive, and sociocultural perspectives, continue to evolve and to shape our understandings of behavior.

CONCEPT 1.9

Many psychologists today subscribe to a broadly based learning perspective, called social-cognitive theory, that emphasizes environmental and cognitive influences on behavior.

CONCEPT 1.10

The psychodynamic perspective focuses on the role of unconscious motivation (inner wishes and impulses of which we are unaware) and the importance of childhood experiences in shaping personality.

behavioral perspective An approach to the study of psychology that focuses on the role of learning in explaining observable behavior.

social-cognitive theory A contemporary learning-based model that emphasizes the roles played by both cognitive factors and environmental or situational factors in determining behavior.

behavior therapy A form of therapy that involves the systematic application of the principles of learning.

humanistic psychology The school of psychology that holds that free will and conscious choice are essential aspects of the human experience.

have survived the test of time. Structuralism, for one, has essentially disappeared from the landscape; others maintain small groups of devoted followers who remain true to the original precepts. But by and large, the early schools of psychology—functionalism, behaviorism, Gestalt psychology, psychoanalysis—have continued to evolve or have been consolidated within broader perspectives. Today, the landscape of psychology can be divided into six major perspectives: the behavioral, psychodynamic, humanistic, physiological, cognitive, and sociocultural.

The Behavioral Perspective The linchpin of the **behavioral perspective**, which focuses on observable behavior and the important role of learning in behavior, is, of course, behaviorism. However, many psychologists believe that traditional behaviorism is too simplistic or limited to explain complex human behavior. Though traditional behaviorism continues to influence modern psychology, it is no longer the dominant force it was during its heyday in the early to mid-1900s (Evans, 1999b).

Many psychologists today adopt a broader, learning-based perspective called **social-cognitive theory** (formerly called *social-learning theory*). This perspective originated in the 1960s with a group of learning theorists who broke away from traditional behaviorism (see Chapter 12). They believed that behavior is shaped not only by environmental factors, such as rewards and punishments, but also by *cognitive* factors, such as the value placed on different objects or goals (e.g., getting good grades) and expectancies about the outcomes of behavior ("If I do X, then Y will follow"). Social-cognitive theorists challenged their fellow psychologists to find ways to study these mental processes rather than casting them aside as unscientific, as traditional behaviorists would. Traditional behaviorists may not deny that thinking occurs, but they do believe that mental processes lie outside the range of scientific study.

The behavioral perspective led to the development of a major school of therapy, **behavior therapy**. Behavior therapy involves the systematic application of learning principles that are grounded in the behaviorist tradition of Watson and Skinner. Whereas the psychoanalyst is concerned with the workings of the unconscious mind, the behavior therapist helps people acquire more adaptive behaviors to overcome psychological problems like fears and social inhibitions. Today, many behavior therapists subscribe to a broader therapeutic approach, called *cognitive-behavioral therapy,* which incorporates techniques for changing maladaptive thoughts as well as overt behaviors (Dobson & Dozois, 2001) (see Chapter 14).

The Psychodynamic Perspective The psychodynamic perspective remains a vibrant force in psychology. Like other contemporary perspectives in psychology, it continues to evolve. As we'll see in Chapter 12, "neo-Freudians" (psychodynamic theorists who have followed in the Freudian tradition) tend to place less emphasis on basic drives like sex and aggression than Freud did and more emphasis on processes of self-awareness, self-direction, and conscious choice.

Psychodynamic theory has had an influence that extends well beyond the field of psychology. Its focus on our inner lives—our fantasies, wishes, dreams, and hidden motives—has had a profound impact on popular literature, art, and culture. Beliefs that psychological problems may be rooted in childhood and that people may not be consciously aware of their deeper motives and wishes continue to be widely endorsed, even by people not formally schooled in Freudian psychology.

The Humanistic Perspective: A "Third Force" in Psychology In the 1950s, another force began to achieve prominence in psychology. Known as **humanistic psychology**, it was a response to the two forces that dominated psychology at that time (i.e., behaviorism and Freudian psychology), and for that reason, it became known as a "third force" in psychology. Humanistic psychologists, includ-

CONCEPT 1.11
Humanistic psychologists emphasize personal freedom and responsibility for our behavior and the value of self-awareness and acceptance of our true selves.

CONCEPT 1.12
The physiological perspective examines relationships between biological processes and behavior.

CONCEPT 1.13
Evolutionary psychology subscribes to the view that our behavior is influenced by inherited predispositions or tendencies that may have increased the likelihood of survival for ancestral humans.

humanistic perspective An approach to the study of psychology that applies the principles of humanistic psychology.

physiological perspective An approach to the study of psychology that focuses on the relationships between biological processes and behavior.

evolutionary psychology A branch of psychology that focuses on the role of evolutionary processes in shaping behavior.

ing the Americans Abraham Maslow (1908–1970) and Carl Rogers (1902–1987), rejected the deterministic views of behaviorism and psychodynamic psychology—beliefs that human behavior is determined by the environment (in the case of behaviorism) or by the interplay of unconscious forces and motives lying outside the person's awareness (in the case of Freudian psychology). Humanistic psychologists believe that free will and conscious choice are essential aspects of the human experience.

Psychologists who adopt a **humanistic perspective** believe that psychology should focus on conscious experiences, even if those experiences are subjective and cannot be directly observed and scientifically measured. Humanistic psychologists view each of us as individuals who possess distinctive clusters of traits and abilities and unique frames of reference or perspectives on life. They emphasize the value of self-awareness and of becoming an authentic person by being true to oneself. They also stress the creative potentials of individuals and their ability to make choices that give their lives meaning and purpose.

The Physiological Perspective The **physiological perspective** examines relationships between biological processes and behavior. It is not identified with any one contributor, but rather with many psychologists and neuroscientists who focus on the biological bases of behavior and mental processes.

Sitting atop your shoulders is a wondrous mass of tissue—your brain—that governs virtually everything you do. The brain is the center of an incredibly complex living computer, the nervous system, that allows you to sense the world around you, to think and feel, to move through space, to regulate heartbeat and other bodily functions, and to coordinate what you see and hear with what you do. Your nervous system also allows you to visualize the world you see and worlds that never were.

Physiological psychologists conduct a wide range of studies that explore the biological bases of behavior and mental processes, including the roles of heredity, hormones, and the nervous system. As we'll see in Chapter 6, some of these investigators study the functioning of the nerve cells that enable us to learn and to remember what we've learned. Some examine how particular brain structures control our sleep-wake cycles (see Chapter 4) and regulate our motivational and emotional states (see Chapter 8). Others study the role of biological factors in abnormal behavior (see Chapter 13). Unraveling the biological bases of psychological or mental disorders like schizophrenia and depression remains a daunting challenge, but investigators have made important strides in this direction.

Heredity clearly plays a key role in our physical development. Heredity is why we grow arms rather than wings; it determines the color of our skin and eyes and our vulnerability to many diseases. Heredity also plays a role in many psychological traits and attributes that we shall touch upon in this text, from intelligence (see Chapter 7) to personality (see Chapter 12) to abnormal behavior (Chapter 13).

Evolutionary psychology is a movement within modern psychology that takes the physiological perspective and applies principles derived from Darwin's theory of evolution to the broad range of psychology. Evolutionary psychologists believe that through the process of natural selection, heredity shapes not only physical traits but also behavioral characteristics or traits (Durrant & Ellis, 2003). Evolutionary psychologists examine a wide range of behaviors in different species that they believe are influenced by evolutionary processes, including aggression, mating behavior, and altruistic behavior (i.e., self-sacrifice of the individual to help perpetuate the group) (Gaulin & McBurney, 2001; Richards, 2002; Thornhill & Palmer, 2000). They suspect that many aspects of human behavior also have evolutionary roots (Bjorklund, 2003; de Waal, 2002; Kenrick, Li, & Butner, 2003; McAndrew & Milenkovic, 2002).

Evolutionary psychologists do not argue that human behavior is simply the product of genetic programming. Rather, they hold that certain behavioral

Might There Be an Evolutionary Basis to Human Aggression? Evolutionary psychologists believe behavioral tendencies that had survival value to ancestral humans, such as aggressiveness, may have been passed down the genetic highway to modern humans. Even our penchant for aggressive sports might reflect these genetic undercurrents.

 CONCEPT 1.14

The cognitive perspective focuses on understanding the mental processes by which people gain knowledge about themselves and the world around them.

 CONCEPT 1.15

The sociocultural perspective places behavior within a broad social context by examining the influences of ethnicity, gender, lifestyles, socioeconomic status, and culture.

cognitive perspective An approach to the study of psychology that focuses on the processes by which we acquire knowledge.

sociocultural perspective An approach to the study of psychology that emphasizes the role of social and cultural influences on behavior.

tendencies or *predispositions* that may have helped ancestral humans survive could have been passed along genetically to successive generations, all the way down the genetic highway to us. These tendencies may increase the likelihood of certain behaviors, such as aggressive behaviors. But whether these predispositions lead to actual behavior (whether a person becomes aggressive or not) also depends on environmental factors, such as family and cultural influences.

The Cognitive Perspective Like Wilhelm Wundt, cognitive psychologists study people's mental processes in an effort to understand how people gain knowledge about themselves and the world around them (Basic Behavioral Science Task Force, 1996b). The word *cognitive* comes from the Latin word *cognitio,* meaning "knowledge." Psychologists who adopt the **cognitive perspective** study the mental processes by which we acquire knowledge—how we learn, form concepts, solve problems, make decisions, and use language. Some cognitive psychologists apply principles of computer information processing (i.e., the methods by which computers process information to solve problems) to explain how humans process, store, retrieve, and manipulate information.

Cognitive psychologists make no apology for studying mental experience; they believe the methods they use to study cognitions are well grounded in the scientific tradition. After all, no one has ever observed subatomic particles like protons and neutrons, but that hasn't prevented physicists from conducting scientific studies that attempt to investigate their properties. Chapter 7 examines the intriguing research findings reported by cognitive psychologists.

The Sociocultural Perspective Psychologists who adopt a **sociocultural perspective** examine how behavior and attitudes are shaped by the social and cultural influences to which people are exposed. These psychologists focus on the influences of ethnicity, gender, lifestyle, income level, and culture on behavior and mental processes. They have brought issues relating to diversity to the forefront of psychological research and thinking. Diversity in psychology is not limited to differences in ethnicity. It also relates to differences in age, gender, sexual orientation, and disability status (see Bingham et al., 2002; Garnets, 2002; Olkin, 2002; Reid, 2002). Nearly one in five adult Americans (19 percent) under the age of 65 have a disability (Farberman, 2003).

Consider the types of questions that psychologists adopting the sociocultural perspective might pose: Does susceptibility to visual illusions vary across cultures?

Who We Are   Our society is becoming increasingly ethnically diverse, to such an extent that the traditional majority group in the United States, Whites of European background, will become the minority at some point this century.

Are there gender differences in basic abilities in math or verbal skills? How does culture influence concepts of the self? Are there ethnic differences in drug-use patterns, and if so, how might we account for them? Are there ethnic differences in intelligence, and if so, what do we make of them? What role does acculturation play in the psychological adjustment of immigrant groups? We return to these questions in later chapters of this text.

The Increasing Diversity of Contemporary Society   The importance of taking sociocultural factors into account in explaining human behavior is underscored by the increasing diversity of our society (Clay, 2005; Yali & Revenson, 2004). Ethnic minorities presently constitute about 31 percent of the U.S. population (see Figure 1.3). But by the middle of the century the percentage of ethnic minorities in the United States is expected to rise to nearly 50 percent. In Canada, non-Whites accounted for about 13 percent of the population in 2001, up from about 9 percent in 1991 ("Statistics Canada," 2003).

We prefer using the term *ethnic minority* instead of *race* because a biologically based concept of race does not seem to square with findings from modern genetics (Smedley & Smedley, 2005). In other words, genetic tests fail to reveal distinct genetic groupings that correspond to traditional racial classifications (Bonham, Warshauer-Baker, & Collins, 2005). Many scholars, though certainly not all, believe that race is a social construct, not a biological construct, in effect a convenient way for classifying individuals according to their ethnic or ancestral backgrounds (Anderson & Nickerson, 2005; Sternberg, Grigorenko, & Kidd, 2005). In this text, we use terms like *ethnicity, culture,* and *ethnic identity* when referring to traditional "racial" distinctions. We also recognize that ethnic or cultural groups often differ in their values, customs, and traditions (Helms, Jernigan, & Mascher, 2005). Consequently, it is important to consider differences of ethnicity and culture in attempting to understand human diversity.

Hispanic Americans (Latinos/Latinas) and African Americans constitute the nation's largest ethnic minority groups, each accounting for about 13 percent of the population (again, see Figure 1.3). Asian Americans/Pacific Islanders account for about 4 percent of the U.S. population, whereas Native Americans constitute about 1 percent. Hispanic Americans and Asian Americans are the two fastest-growing population groups in the United States: they increased by more than 60 percent and 48 percent, respectively, during the 1990s ("Asian Americans and

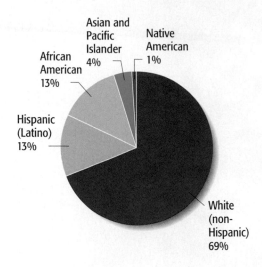

Figure 1.3 Composition of U.S. Population

Source: U.S. Census Bureau, 2005.
Note: Percentages are rounded off and based on the most recent estimates.

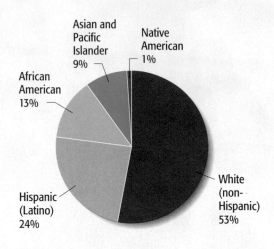

Figure 1.4 Projected U.S. Population in the Year 2050

Source: U.S. Census Bureau, 2005.
Note: Percentages are rounded off.

Census 2000 Results," 2003; Schmitt, 2001a, 2001b). Asian Americans are also the most diverse U.S. population group, encompassing people of Chinese, Filipino, Indian, Korean, Cambodian, Vietnamese, Japanese, and other Asian backgrounds (Mays, 2003).

Now contrast Figure 1.3 with Figure 1.4, which shows the expected changes in the ethnic composition of the U.S. population by the year 2050. You can see that European Americans (Whites), who in 1950 constituted 90 percent of the population (El Nasser, 2004), will constitute only about half of the U.S. population a century later.

Traditional "racial" identities are also becoming blurred by the increasing numbers of people who identify themselves in nontraditional categories. Nearly half (42 percent) of Hispanics (Latinos/Latinas) in the U.S. census in 2000 endorsed the "other" category rather than one of the traditional "racial" identities (White, Black, Asian, American Indian or Alaskan native, or Pacific Islander/Hawaiian) (Navarro, 2000). Many Hispanics identify themselves as *moreno, trigueno,* or *indio*—terms that indicate ancestry and variations in skin tones.

Blurring traditional boundaries further are the increased proportions of people in the United States and Canada who consider themselves biracial, multiracial, or multiethnic. People with multiracial backgrounds, such as golfer Tiger Woods, baseball player Derek Jeter, and singer Mariah Carey, are not easily classified on the basis of traditional "racial" distinctions. According to the U.S. census of 2000, nearly 7 million Americans described themselves as multiracial (Schmitt, 2001b, 2001c). In comparison with their parents, young people today are twice as likely to consider themselves multiracial (C. Takahashi, 2001). This increasing diversity reflects the fact that the number of marriages between people of different ethnic groups has been roughly doubling in each decade (Kristof, 2002).

Psychologists recognize that research samples need to be broadly representative of the populations to which they wish to generalize their findings. Much of the past research in psychology focused almost exclusively on White, middle-class, male college students. But we should not assume that findings based on such narrowly defined groups of individuals necessarily generalize to other groups who have different life experiences.

Mariah Carey, Tiger Woods, and Derek Jeter Traditional racial distinctions do not easily apply to many people of multiracial backgrounds.

Summary of Contemporary Perspectives Each major perspective in contemporary psychology focuses on different aspects of behavior or psychological functioning. No one perspective is necessarily right and the others wrong; rather, each has something unique to offer to our understanding of human behavior. Moreover, none offers a complete view. Given the complexity of human behavior and experience, it is not surprising that psychology has spawned multiple pathways for approaching its subject matter. It is also not surprising that many psychologists today identify with an eclectic approach to understanding human behavior—one that draws on theories and principles representing different perspectives. We should recognize, too, that contemporary psychology is not divided as neatly into different schools of thought as it seemed to be in its early days. There is considerable room for overlap among the different perspectives.

In addition to the six major perspectives that dot the landscape of contemporary psychology, a growing movement within psychology, called **positive psychology**, is directed toward the study of the positive aspects of human experience, such as love, happiness, spirituality, and altruism (Kogan, 2001; Seligman, 2003; Seligman & Csikszentmihalyi, 2000, 2001). Much of psychology is directed toward understanding human weaknesses and deficits, which include troubling emotional states, effects of traumatic stress, and problem behaviors such as violence and drug addiction. Founded by psychologist Martin Seligman, positive psychology balances the scales by focusing on our virtues and strengths, not our flaws. Throughout the text we will discuss many areas of interest in positive psychology, including love, helping behavior, optimism, successful aging, happiness, self-esteem, self-actualization, and creativity.

In Concept Chart 1.1, the first of many such charts in the text, you'll find examples of the kinds of general questions that psychologists from each of the major contemporary perspectives might ask, as well as the kinds of questions they might pose to learn more about specific topics. These topics are introduced here to help you distinguish between the various perspectives in contemporary psychology. They will be discussed further in later chapters.

CONCEPT 1.16

Positive psychology is a growing movement within psychology that encourages greater exploration of human strengths and assets, such as the capacity to love and be loved, optimism, spirituality, and positive emotions.

positive psychology A contemporary movement within psychology that emphasizes the study of human virtues and assets, rather than weaknesses and deficits.

CONCEPT CHART 1.1 Contemporary Perspectives in Psychology: How They Differ

Perspective	General Questions	Questions About Specific Topics		
		Aggression	**Depression**	**Obesity**
Behavioral	How do early learning experiences shape our behavior as adults?	How is aggressive behavior learned? How is it rewarded or reinforced? Does exposure to violence in the media or among one's peers play a role?	How is depression related to changes in reinforcement patterns? What social skills are needed to establish and maintain social relationships that could serve as sources of reinforcement?	How might unhealthy eating habits lead to obesity? How might we change those habits?
Psychodynamic	How do unresolved conflicts from childhood affect adult behavior? How can people be helped to cope with these conflicts?	How is aggression related to unconscious impulses? Against whom are these impulses really directed?	How might depression be related to unresolved loss? Might it represent anger turned inward?	Might obesity relate to childhood conflicts revolving around unresolved needs for love and support? Might food have become a substitute for love?
Humanistic	How do people pursue goals that give their lives a sense of meaning and purpose?	Might violence be related to frustration arising when people are blocked from pursuing their goals? How might we turn this around to prevent violence?	Might depression be related to a lack of self-esteem or a threat to one's self-image? Might it stem from a sense of purposelessness or lack of meaning in life?	What sets the stage for obesity? Does food have a special meaning for obese people? How can we help them to find other sources of satisfaction?
Physiological	How do biological structures and processes make behavior possible? What roles do nature (heredity) and nurture (environment) play in such areas as intelligence, language development, and aggression?	What brain mechanisms control aggressive behavior? Might brain abnormalities explain violent behavior in some people?	How are changes in brain chemistry related to depression? What genetic links might there be?	Is obesity inherited? What genes are involved? How would knowledge of a genetic basis of obesity lead to new approaches to treatment or prevention?
Cognitive	How do people solve problems, make decisions, and develop language?	What thoughts trigger aggressive responses? What beliefs do aggressive people hold that might increase their potential for violence?	What types of thinking patterns are related to depression? How might they be changed to help people overcome depression or prevent it from occurring?	How does obesity affect a person's self-concept? What thoughts lead to eating binges? How might they be changed?
Sociocultural	How do concepts of self differ across cultures? How do social and cultural influences shape behavior?	What social conditions give rise to drug use and aggressive behavior? Does our society condone or even reward certain forms of violence, such as sexual aggression against women or spousal abuse?	Is depression linked to social stresses, such as poverty or unemployment? Why is depression more common among certain groups of people, especially women? Does it have to do with their expected social roles?	Are some groups at greater risk of obesity than others? Do cultural differences in dietary patterns and customs play a role?

MODULE 1.1 REVIEW

Foundations of Modern Psychology

RECITE IT

What is psychology?

- Psychology is the science of behavior and mental processes.

What are the origins of psychology?

- Though systematic attempts to explain human behavior can be traced to philosophers in ancient times, psychology emerged as a scientific discipline in the nineteenth century with Wundt's founding of the first psychological laboratory in Leipzig, Germany, in 1879.

What were the major early schools of psychology?

- Structuralism is the earliest school of psychology. It was identified with Wilhelm Wundt and Edward Titchener, and it attempted to break down mental experiences into their component parts—sensations, perceptions, and feelings.

- Functionalism is the school of psychology founded by William James. It attempts to explain our behavior in terms of the functions it serves in helping us adapt to the environment.

- Behaviorism is the school of psychology begun by James Watson. It holds that psychology should limit itself to observable phenomena—namely, behavior.

- Gestalt psychology is the school of psychology founded by Max Wertheimer. It is grounded in the belief that the brain structures our perceptions of the world in terms of organized patterns or wholes.

- Psychoanalysis, the school of thought originated by Sigmund Freud, emphasizes the role of unconscious motives and conflicts in determining human behavior.

What are the major contemporary perspectives in psychology?

- The behavioral perspective focuses on observable behavior and the influences of learning processes in behavior.

- The psychodynamic perspective represents the model of psychology developed by Freud and his followers. It holds that our behavior and personalities are shaped by unconscious motives and conflicts that lie outside the range of ordinary awareness.

- The humanistic perspective reflects the views of humanistic psychologists such as Carl Rogers and Abraham Maslow, who emphasized the importance of subjective conscious experience and personal freedom and responsibility.

- The physiological perspective examines the ways in which behavior and mental experience are influenced by biological processes such as heredity, hormones, and the workings of the brain and other parts of the nervous system.

- The cognitive perspective focuses on mental processes that allow us to gain knowledge about ourselves and the world.

- The sociocultural perspective examines how our behavior and attitudes are shaped by social and cultural influences.

RECALL IT

1. Socrates, known to us through the writings of his student Plato, was an ancient Greek philosopher who had a profound effect on early psychological thinking. For what credo is he best remembered today?

2. The scientist generally credited with the founding of psychology as an independent science was _____.

3. The early school of psychology called _____ was concerned with investigating the structure of the mind.

4. The school of psychology that believes psychology should be limited to the study of observable behavior is called _____.

5. Gestalt psychology focuses on: (a) the organization of the mind; (b) the ways in which the brain organizes and structures our perceptions of the world; (c) the functions of behavior; (d) the role of self-actualization in motivating behavior.

6. Which psychological perspective originated with Sigmund Freud?

7. Humanistic psychologists rejected the notions that unconscious processes or environmental influences determine our behavior. Rather, they emphasized the importance of conscious _____ in understanding behavior.

Answers to Recall It questions are placed at the end of the chapter.

THINK ABOUT IT

- Suppose you attempted to explain behavior in terms of how people's habits help them adapt to the environmental demands they face. What early school of psychology would you be adopting in your approach?

- Suppose you wanted to understand behavior in terms of underlying forces within the personality that influence behavior even though the person may not be aware of them. What early school of psychology would this approach represent?

- Humanistic psychologists emphasize the importance of finding a purpose or meaning in life. What are your purposes in life? How can you make your own life more meaningful?

MODULE 1.2
Psychologists: Who They Are and What They Do

- What are the two general types of research that psychologists conduct?
- What are the various specialties in psychology?
- What changes have occurred in the ethnic and gender characteristics of psychologists over time?

Online Study Center

Improve Your Grade
Tutorial: Specialty Areas of Psychology

CONCEPT 1.17
The field of psychology consists of a large and ever-growing number of specialty areas.

basic research   Research focused on acquiring knowledge even if such knowledge has no direct practical application.

applied research   Research that attempts to find solutions to specific problems.

experimental psychologists Psychologists who apply experimental methods to the study of behavior.

comparative psychologists   Psychologists who study behavorial similarities and differences among animal species.

physiological psychologists Psychologists who focus on the biological underpinnings of behavior.

When you think of a psychologist, do you form a mental image of someone working in a hospital or clinic who treats people with psychological problems? This image describes one particular type of psychologist—a clinical psychologist. But there are many other types. Psychology is a diverse profession because of the large number of areas in the field and because of the many different roles psychologists perform. Some psychologists teach and conduct research. Others provide psychological services to individuals or to organizations, such as schools or businesses. Psychologists are usually identified with one particular specialty or subfield within psychology—for example, experimental, clinical, developmental, educational, or social psychology.

Some psychologists conduct **basic research**—research that seeks to expand our understanding of psychological phenomena even if such knowledge does not lead directly to any practical benefits. These psychologists typically work for universities or government agencies. Other psychologists conduct **applied research**—research intended to find solutions to specific problems. For example, a psychologist might apply research on learning and memory to studying methods of enhancing the educational experiences of children with mental retardation. Still other psychologists work in applied areas of psychology in which they provide services to people or organizations. These include clinical, counseling, school, and industrial/organizational psychologists. Many of these applied psychologists also conduct research in the areas in which they practice. In this module, we take a closer look at the various types of psychologists.

Specialty Areas of Psychology

All psychologists study behavior and mental processes, but they pursue this knowledge in different ways, in different settings, and from different perspectives. Most of them earn doctoral degrees in their area of specialization. The Ph.D. is the most common doctoral degree and is awarded after the completion of required graduate coursework and a dissertation, which involves an original research project. Some psychologists seeking practice careers may earn a Doctor of Psychology degree (Psy.D.), a doctoral degree that is focused more on practitioner skills than on research skills. Others may pursue graduate programs in schools of education and be awarded a doctorate in education (Ed.D.). In some speciality areas, such as school psychology and industrial/organizational (I/O) psychology, the Master's degree is recognized as the entry-level degree for professional work in the field. The following sections provide a run-down of some of the major specialty areas within the field of psychology, as well as some emerging ones.

Major Specialty Areas   Concept Chart 1.2 provides an overview of the major specialties in psychology discussed in this section. Figure 1.5 shows the percentages of psychologists working in major specialty areas, and Figure 1.6 summarizes where psychologists work.

Experimental psychologists apply experimental methods to the study of behavior and mental processes. They study such processes as learning, sensation and perception, and cognition. Some experimental psychologists, called **comparative**

CONCEPT CHART 1.2   Specialty Areas of Psychology

Types of Psychologists	Nature of Specialty	Typical Questions Studied
Experimental psychologists	Conduct research on learning, cognition, sensation and perception, biological bases of behavior, and animal behavior	How do various states of arousal affect learning? What brain centers are responsible for memory?
Clinical psychologists	Evaluate and treat people with psychological problems and disorders, such as depression and schizophrenia	How can we diagnose anxiety? Is depression treated more effectively with psychotherapy or drug therapy?
Counseling psychologists	Help people with adjustment problems	What kind of occupation would this student find fulfilling? Why does this person find it difficult to make friends?
School psychologists	Work in school systems to help children with academic problems or special needs	Would this child profit from special education, or would he or she be better off in a regular classroom?
Educational psychologists	Construct standardized psychological and educational tests (such as the SAT); improve course planning and instructional methods	Is this test a valid predictor of success in college? How can we teach algebra more efficiently?
Developmental psychologists	Study physical, cognitive, social, and personality development across the life span	At what age do children begin to walk or speak? What types of crises do people face in middle or later adulthood?
Personality psychologists	Study the psychological characteristics that make each of us unique	What is the structure of personality? How do we measure personality?
Social psychologists	Study the nature and causes of people's thoughts, feelings, and behavior in social situations	What are the origins of prejudice? Why do people do things as members of groups that they would not do as individuals?
Environmental psychologists	Study the ways in which people's behavior and mental processes influence, and are influenced by, their physical environments	What are the effects of city life on people? How does overcrowding affect people's health and behavior?
Industrial/Organizational psychologists	Study the relationships between people and their work environments	How can we find out who would perform well in this position? How can we make hiring and promotion fairer? How can we enhance employees' motivation?
Health psychologists	Study the relationships between psychological factors and the prevention and treatment of physical illness	How can we help people avoid risky sexual behaviors? How can we help people quit smoking and start to exercise?
Consumer psychologists	Study relationships between psychological factors and consumers' preferences and purchasing behavior	Why do people select particular brands? What types of people prefer a particular type of product?

psychologists, seek to understand animal behavior for its own sake and possibly for what it might teach us about human behavior (Dewsbury, 2000). Others, called **physiological psychologists** (also called *biological psychologists*), study the biological bases of behavior.

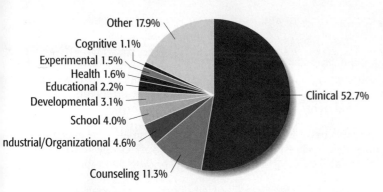

Figure 1.5   **Psychologists' Areas of Specialization**
Clinical psychologists make up the largest group of psychologists, followed by counseling psychologists and industrial/organizational psychologists.

Source: American Psychological Association, 2004.

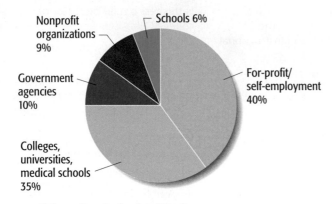

Figure 1.6   **Where Psychologists Work**
The largest group of psychologists work in settings providing psychological services. Many work at colleges and universities as teachers, researchers, administrators, or supervisors of psychologists in training. Some also work in schools or government agencies.

Source: American Psychological Association, 2003a.

clinical psychologists   Psychologists who use psychological techniques to evaluate and treat individuals with mental or psychological disorders.

psychiatrists   Medical doctors who specialize in the diagnosis and treatment of mental or psychological disorders.

counseling psychologists   Psychologists who help people clarify their goals, make life decisions, and overcome problems they face in their lives.

school psychologists   Psychologists who evaluate and assist children with learning problems or other special needs.

educational psychologists   Psychologists who study issues relating to the measurement of intelligence and the processes involved in educational or academic achievement.

Clinical psychologists evaluate and treat people with psychological disorders, such as depression and anxiety disorders. They may use psychotherapy to help people overcome psychological problems or cope better with the stresses they face in their lives. These psychologists may administer psychological tests to better understand people's problems or to evaluate their intellectual abilities or personalities. Many conduct research in the field or train future psychologists. Many others work in hospitals, clinics, or private practice or university settings. As Figure 1.5 shows, clinical psychologists represent the largest group of psychologists.

The professional roles of clinical psychologists in evaluating and treating psychological disorders often overlap with those of **psychiatrists**, medical doctors who complete residency training in the medical specialty of psychiatry. Unlike psychiatrists, however, psychologists cannot prescribe drugs. But even these lines may be blurring, since small numbers of psychologists have been trained in a specialized program to prescribe drugs to treat psychological disorders (Dittmann, 2003c; Foxhall, 2000b, 2000c).

Counseling psychologists help people who have adjustment problems that are not usually as severe as the kinds of problems treated by clinical psychologists. If you did not know what course of study to follow in college, or if you were having a difficult time adjusting to college, you might talk to a counseling psychologist about it. In addition to helping people with academic decisions, counseling psychologists may help with vocational decisions or marital problems. They use counseling methods to help people clarify their goals and to find ways of surmounting the obstacles they face. Many work in college counseling centers or community-based counseling or mental health centers.

School psychologists work in school systems, where they help children with academic, emotional, and behavioral problems and evaluate students for placement in special education programs (Quinn & McDougal, 1998). They are also team players who work collaboratively with teachers and other professionals in providing a broad range of services for children (DeAngelis, 2000).

Educational psychologists develop tests that measure intellectual ability or academic potential, help gear training approaches to students' learning styles, and create ways of helping students reach their maximum academic potential. Many conduct research; among the issues they study are the nature of intelligence, how teachers can enhance the learning process, and why some children are more highly motivated than others to do well in school (Webster & Beveridge, 1997).

Developmental psychologists study people's physical, cognitive, social, and personality development throughout the life span. *Child psychologists* are developmental psychologists who limit their focus to child development.

Personality psychologists seek to understand the nature of personality—the cluster of psychological characteristics and behaviors that distinguishes us as unique individuals and leads us to act consistently over time. In particular, they study how personality is structured and how it develops and changes (Derlega, Winstead, & Jones, 1999).

Social psychologists study how group or social influences affect behavior and attitudes. While personality psychologists look within the individual's psychological make-up to explain behavior, social psychologists focus on how groups affect individuals and, in some cases, how individuals affect groups.

Environmental psychologists study relationships between the physical environment and behavior. They are concerned with the ways in which people's behaviors and mental processes influence, and are influenced by, their physical environments. They examine such issues as the effects of outdoor temperature on aggression; the psychological impact of environmental factors like noise, air pollution, housing design, and overcrowding; and links between exposure to lead and IQ scores in children (e.g., Canfield et al., 2003).

Industrial/organizational (I/O) psychologists study people at work. They are concerned with such issues as job satisfaction, personnel selection and training, leadership qualities, the effects of organizational structure on productivity and work performance, and challenges posed by changes in the workplace. They may use psychological tests to determine the fit between applicants' abilities and interests and the jobs available within an organization or corporation. Some I/O psychologists engage in *human factors research,* which examines ways of making instrumentation and systems (e.g., airplane gauges and computer systems) more efficient and easier to use.

Health psychologists study how such psychological factors as stress, lifestyle, and attitude affect physical health. They apply this knowledge in developing disease prevention programs and interventions to improve the quality of life of patients with chronic diseases, such as heart disease, cancer, and HIV/AIDS (Schneiderman et al., 2001).

Consumer psychologists are interested in understanding consumer behavior—why people purchase particular products and particular brands. They examine consumers' attitudes toward different products and toward different ways of advertising or packaging products, even the type of music played in stores to put people in a good mood to entice them to buy (DeAngelis, 2004b; Khamsi, 2004). In one research example, consumer psychologists showed that people who buy minivans tended to be more "other-oriented"—more involved with family, friends, and community—than people who purchased SUVs. By contrast, SUV buyers tended to be more pleasure seeking and "self-oriented" (Bradsher, 2000).

Emerging Specialty Areas   When G. Stanley Hall founded the American Psychological Association (APA) in 1892, it had 31 charter members (Benjamin, 1997); today, the membership exceeds 150,000. It's no wonder that psychology's interests and specialties cover so wide a range, including such emerging specialty areas as neuropsychology, geropsychology, forensic psychology, and sport psychology.

Neuropsychologists study relationships between the brain and behavior. While some neuropsychologists limit their activities to research, *clinical neuropsychologists* use specialized tests to evaluate the cognitive effects of brain injuries and strokes. These tests can help them pinpoint the particular areas of the brain affected by

developmental psychologists Psychologists who focus on processes involving physical, cognitive, social, and personality development.

personality psychologists Psychologists who study the psychological characteristics and behaviors that distinguish us as individuals and lead us to act consistently over time.

social psychologists Psychologists who study group or social influences on behavior and attitudes.

environmental psychologists Psychologists who study relationships between the physical environment and behavior.

industrial/organizational (I/O) psychologists Psychologists who study people's behavior at work.

health psychologists Psychologists who focus on the relationship between psychological factors and physical health.

consumer psychologists Psychologists who study why people purchase particular products and brands.

neuropsychologists Psychologists who study relationships between the brain and behavior.

Neuropsychologists at Work Neuropsychologists use specialized psychological tests to study the effects of brain injuries and stroke on cognitive processes. The test shown here requires individuals to fit shapes into the appropriate cut-outs while they are blindfolded.

injury or disease. Clinical neuropsychologists may also work with rehabilitation specialists in designing programs to help people who have suffered various forms of brain damage regain as much of their functioning as possible.

Geropsychologists are interested in the psychological processes associated with aging. They may work with geriatric patients to help them cope with the stresses of later life, including retirement, loss of loved ones, and declining physical health.

Forensic psychologists work within the legal system (Otto & Heilbrun, 2002). They may perform psychological evaluations in child custody cases, testify about the competence of defendants to stand trial, develop psychological profiles of criminal types, give expert testimony in court on psychological issues, or assist attorneys in selecting potential jury members.

Sport psychologists apply psychology to sports and athletic competition (Meyers et al., 2001; Singer, 2003). Some sport psychologists use psychological techniques to help athletes improve their performance (Jaffe, 2004; Van Raalte & Brewer, 2002). These techniques include relaxation training, mental imagery, positive self-talk, and mental tips (Hacker, 2002; Hays, 2002). Sport psychologists also help athletes handle competitive pressures and balance travel, family, and life demands. Others develop rating scales to measure various aspects of sports performance, including jump-shooting in basketball and qualities associated with better performance in football by players in different positions (Libkuman, Love, & Donn, 1998; Lindeman et al., 2000).

Psychologist Rob Gray's (2002) research confirmed what pitchers have known since the earliest days of baseball, that you can fool a hitter by mixing up the speed of pitches. In analyzing the swings of six male college-level baseball players, Gray found larger errors in the timing of their swings when a fastball was thrown after three consecutive slow pitches than when it was thrown after three consecutive fast pitches. In other words, the batter's expectations got in the way of their hitting. Gray's findings underscore the importance of cognitive factors in athletic performance. According to baseball great Ted Williams, whom many people consider the greatest hitter ever, "Proper thinking is 50 percent of effective hitting" (cited in Williams & Underwood, 1970, p. 30).

Professional Psychology: Becoming More Diverse

The early psychologists shared more than just a yearning to understand behavior: almost all of them were White males of European background. The ranks of women in the early days of psychology were slim, and the ranks of ethnic minorities even slimmer. Back then, women and minority group members faced many barriers in pursuing careers in psychology, as they did in numerous other professions. The earliest woman pioneer in psychology was Christine Ladd-Franklin (1847–1930). She completed all the requirements for a Ph.D. at Johns Hopkins University in 1882, but the university refused to award her the degree because at that time it did not issue doctoral degrees to women. Nonetheless, she went on to pursue a distinguished research career in psychology, during which she developed a new theory of color vision. She finally received her Ph.D. in 1926 (Furumoto, 1992).

Another woman pioneer was Mary Whiton Calkins (1863–1930). A brilliant student of William James, Calkins completed all her Ph.D. requirements at Harvard, but Harvard denied her a doctorate; like Johns Hopkins, it did not grant doctoral degrees to women. She was offered the doctorate through Radcliffe College, a women's academy affiliated with Harvard, which she refused. Not easily deterred, she went on to have a distinguished career in psychology—teaching and conducting important research on learning and short-term memory (Evans, 1999c). In 1905, she became the first female president of the APA.

Margaret Floy Washburn (1871–1939) encountered similar discrimination when she pursued studies in psychology at Columbia University. In 1894, having

CONCEPT 1.18
Women and minority members faced difficult obstacles in pursuing careers in psychology in the early days of the profession.

geropsychologists   Psychologists who focus on psychological processes involved in aging.

forensic psychologists   Psychologists involved in the application of psychology to the legal system.

sport psychologists   Psychologists who apply psychology to understanding and improving athletic performance.

Mary Whilton Calkins

Margaret Floy Washburn

Gilbert Haven Jones

found a more receptive environment at Cornell University, she became the first woman in the United States to earn a Ph.D. in psychology (Evans, 1999c). She wrote an influential book, *The Animal Mind,* and in 1921 became the second female president of the APA.

In 1909, Gilbert Haven Jones (1883–1966), an African American, received a doctorate in psychology from a university in Germany. It wasn't until 1920, however, at Clark University in Worcester, Massachusetts, that Francis Sumner (1895–1954) became the first African American to receive a doctorate in psychology in the United States. Sumner went on to a distinguished career in teaching and research. He helped establish the psychology department at Howard University and served as its chairperson until his death in 1954 (Evans, 1999d).

In 1920, the same year Sumner earned his doctorate, J. Henry Alston became the first African American to publish his research findings (on the perception of warmth and cold) in a major U.S. psychology journal.

THE PIONEERS
Inherently Unequal

Kenneth and Mamie Clark

Kenneth Clark, an African American social psychologist, was born in 1914 and grew up in the community of Harlem in New York City. He attended Howard University in Washington, D.C., where he met his wife, Mamie Phipps-Clark (1917–1983). They both went on to earn doctorates in psychology from Columbia University. The research they conducted together demonstrated the negative effects of school segregation on the self-concept of African American children. They argued that African American children come to believe they must be inferior because they were prevented from attending school with White children. In a classic study in 1939, the Clarks found that African American preschool children preferred playing with a white doll rather than a black one and attributed more positive characteristics to the white doll (Clark & Clark, 1939). Kenneth Clark's writings on the personality development of African American children were cited by the U.S. Supreme Court in its landmark 1954 decision, *Brown* v. *Board of Education of Topeka, Kansas,* which held that separate schools were inherently unequal (Dingfelder, 2004a; Keppel, 2002; Tomes, 2004).

In 1946, Mamie Phipps-Clark established the Northside Center for Child Development in Harlem, a center providing psychological services to children from the community. Kenneth Clark taught at the City University of New York from 1942 until his retirement in 1975 and was the first African American to be appointed to a permanent professorship there. He wrote extensively on the psychological effects of prejudice in such books as *Prejudice and Your Child* (1955), *Dark Ghetto* (1965), and *A Possible Reality* (1972). In 1971, he became the first African American psychologist to serve as APA president. Clark died in 2005 at the age of ninety.

Figure 1.7   Ethnicities of Doctorate Recipients in Psychology
Though the percentages of minority-group members in the field of psychology have increased over the years, White Americans of European background still constitute the great majority of new doctorate recipients in the field.

Source: National Science Foundation, 2004.

Figure 1.8   Women Ph.D. Recipients in Psychology
Women now represent about two-thirds of new Ph.D.s in psychology, as compared to about one-third in 1976.

Source: American Psychological Association, 2003b.

CONCEPT 1.19
Though the field of psychology has become more diverse, people of color are still underrepresented in professional psychology.

CONCEPT 1.20
The profession of psychology has undergone a major gender shift in recent years.

It took another fifty years (until 1971) before the first—and, to this date, the only—African American psychologist, Kenneth Clark (1914–2005), was elected president of the APA (see the Pioneers box). In 1999, Richard Suinn became the first Asian American psychologist to be elected president of the APA.

In recent years, as increasing numbers of ethnic minorities have entered the field of psychology, the professional ranks of psychologists have become more diverse. Figure 1.7 shows the ethnic make-up of new doctorate recipients in psychology. Despite the increased diversity, ethnic minorities are still underrepresented in the profession (Evans, 1999d). For example, there is but one Native American psychologist for every 30,000 Native Americans (Rabasca, 2000a).

A different picture emerges when we examine gender shifts in professional psychology. Women constitute an ever-increasing proportion of degree recipients in psychology. They now account for about two-thirds of the undergraduate degrees and doctorates in the field (Kohout, 2001; Kyle, 2000) (see Figure 1.8). This gender shift mirrors the increased representation of women in occupations traditionally dominated by men, including medicine and law. However, the gender shift is occurring at a faster rate in psychology than in other professions.

MODULE 1.2 REVIEW

Psychologists: Who They Are and What They Do

RECITE IT

What are the two general types of research that psychologists conduct?

- Some conduct basic research that focuses on expanding our understanding and knowledge, whereas others conduct applied research that focuses on finding answers or solutions to particular problems.

What are the various specialties in psychology?

- These include major subfields such as clinical and counseling psychology, school psychology, and experimental psychology, as well as emerging specialty areas such as geropsychology, forensic psychology, and sport psychology.

What changes have occurred in the ethnic and gender characteristics of psychologists over time?

- Though psychology is now a more diverse discipline, African Americans and other minority groups remain underrepresented in the professional ranks of psychologists.

- Unlike in the early days of the profession, when women were actively excluded from pursuing professional careers, they now constitute the lion's share of new psychologists.

RECALL IT

1. _____ research focuses on expanding our understanding and knowledge, whereas _____ research focuses on finding answers or solutions to particular problems.

2. Match the following types of psychologists with the type of work they do: (a) counseling psychologists; (b) developmental psychologists; (c) environmental psychologists; (d) consumer psychologists.
   i. study changes in behaviors and attitudes throughout the life cycle
   ii. study effects of outdoor temperature on aggression
   iii. study psychological characteristics of people who buy particular products
   iv. help students adjust to college life

3. Psychologists who study relationships between the brain and behavior are called _____.

4. The first African American to receive a doctorate in psychology in the United States was _____.
   (a) Mary Whiton Calkins
   (b) Francis Sumner
   (c) Gilbert Haven Jones
   (d) Kenneth Clark

Answers to Recall It questions are placed at the end of the chapter.

THINK ABOUT IT

- If you were uncertain about what career to pursue and wanted help sorting through the vocational choices best suited to you, what type of psychologist would you consult?

- Or suppose you read in a newspaper about a psychologist who was studying how people's behavior changes when they become part of an unorganized mob. What type of psychologist would this person likely be?

MODULE 1.3
Research Methods in Psychology

- **What are the major objectives of science?**
- **What is the scientific method, and what are its four general steps?**
- **What are the major research methods psychologists use?**
- **What general ethical guidelines must psychologists follow in their research?**
- **What is an example of a specific ethical guideline?**

 CONCEPT 1.21
To understand behavior, you must first describe it as accurately and clearly as possible.

Psychologists are trained to be skeptical of claims and arguments that are not grounded in evidence. They are especially skeptical of public opinion and folklore. What distinguishes psychology from other inquiries into human nature, including philosophy, theology, and poetry, is the use of scientific methods to gain knowledge. Psychologists adopt an **empirical approach**; that is, they base their beliefs on evidence gathered from experiments and careful observation.

The Objectives of Science: To Describe, Explain, Predict, and Control

The major objectives of science are to describe, explain, predict, and control events. As scientists dedicated to understanding behavior and mental processes and to using that understanding for human betterment, psychologists share these goals.

Description   Clear and accurate description is a cornerstone of science. Psychologists use methods of careful observation to make unbiased and accurate descriptions. Consider the following vignette, which is based on an actual classroom experience:

empirical approach   A method of developing knowledge based on evaluating evidence gathered from experiments and careful observation.

Imagine you are a student in an experimental psychology class. On the first day of class your professor, a distinguished woman of about fifty, walks in, carrying a small wire-mesh cage containing a white rat. She smiles, removes the rat from the cage, and places the rat on the desk. She then asks the class to describe the rat's behavior.

As a serious student, you attend closely. The animal moves to the edge of the desk, pauses, peers over the edge, and seems to jiggle its whiskers at the floor below. It maneuvers along the edge of the desk, tracking the perimeter. Now and then it pauses and vibrates its whiskers downward in the direction of the floor. The professor picks up the rat and returns it to the cage. She asks the class to describe the animal's behavior.

A student responds, "The rat seems to be looking for a way to escape."

Another student: "It is reconnoitering its environment, examining it." Reconnoitering? you think. That student has seen too many war movies.

The professor writes each response on the blackboard. Another student raises her hand. "The rat is making a visual search of the environment," she says. "Maybe it's looking for food."

The professor prompts other students for their descriptions.

"It's looking around," says one.

"Trying to escape," says another.

Your turn arrives. Trying to be scientific, you say, "We can't say what its motivation might be. All we know is that it's scanning its environment."

"How so?" the professor asks.

"Visually," you reply, confidently.

The professor writes the response and then turns to the class, shaking her head. "Each of you observed the rat," she said, "but none of you described its behavior. Each of you made certain inferences—that the rat was 'looking for a way down' or 'scanning its environment,' or 'looking for food,' and the like. These are not unreasonable inferences, but they are inferences, not descriptions. They also happen to be wrong. You see, the rat is blind. It's been blind since birth. It couldn't possibly be looking around, at least not in a visual sense."

(From Nevid, Rathus, & Greene, 2003, pp. 17–18)

As you can see from this vignette, scientific description depends on careful observation. Psychologists are trained to distinguish between observations and **inferences**—conclusions drawn from observations. Inferences play an important role in science; they enable us to jump from the particular to the general, from what we observe about an individual's behavior to the more general category of behavior that it might represent. Yet we need to distinguish between describing what we observe and making inferences based on those observations. Consider the question "Have you ever observed abnormal behavior?" The answer, scientifically speaking, is no. You can only observe behavior. Labeling behavior as abnormal (or normal) is an inference, not an observation.

How, then, might you accurately and objectively describe the rat's behavior? You might give a detailed accounting of the animal's movements, such as exactly how far it moves in each direction, how long it pauses before turning, how it moves its head from side to side, and so on. Careful observation and description of behavior provide data for developing theories that can help us better understand the phenomena we study and perhaps also predict future occurrences.

Explanation   If we were to limit ourselves to description, we would be left with a buzzing confusion of unconnected observations. Psychologists, like other scientists, construct theories to help them understand the phenomena they study. **Theories** are explanations that organize observations into meaningful patterns and that account for relationships among observed events in terms of underlying mecha-

inferences   Conclusions drawn from observations.

theories   Formulations that account for relationships among observed events or experimental findings in ways that make them more understandable and predictable.

nisms. Social-cognitive theory, for instance, attempts to explain behavior in terms of the influence of situational factors, such as rewards and punishments, and of cognitive factors, such as values and expectancies.

Theories are judged by how useful they are in accounting for a given set of observations or experimental findings. Scientists recognize that even the best of theories are but crude approximations of ultimate truth. They understand that alternative theories with even better explanations of the evidence derived from careful observation may come along later.

A combination of theories, rather than any one theory, may best account for a given set of facts. For example, as you'll discover in Chapter 3, the best available explanation of color vision combines elements of two competing theories.

Prediction   Scientists draw on their theoretical understanding of events to make predictions about future occurrences.

Theories help make events more understandable. They also help us in making predictions about future occurrences and in suggesting ways of controlling them. Based on social-cognitive theory, for example, we might expect young people who have positive expectancies about alcohol or drug use—who believe these substances will make them more popular or have other desired outcomes—will be more likely to use them. By changing expectancies—by helping young people see the negative outcomes associated with alcohol or drug use—we may help them avoid using them.

A theory linking stress and depression might lead us to predict that stressful experiences, such as marital conflict or prolonged unemployment, would increase the risk of depression. If evidence supports this link (and it does; see Chapter 13), we might be able to prevent depression by providing counseling to people in times of stress.

Certainly not all scientific predictions about future events are borne out by the evidence. But even when contrary findings occur, they are useful to scientists in helping them reformulate or refine their theories, which may then enable them to make more accurate predictions.

Control   The fourth objective of science is control of events. The science of physics enabled people to harness nuclear power and to create the electronic superhighway, the Internet. Biological and medical sciences have enabled society to control many infectious diseases through vaccination programs and other public health initiatives, even to the extent of eradicating some historic scourges, such as smallpox.

Psychologists do not seek to control people or manipulate them to do their bidding. Rather, they find methods of using psychological knowledge to help people gain greater mastery and control over their own lives. Psychotherapy, for one, has helped people gain better control over negative emotional states, such as anxiety and depression; improve their relationships with others; and develop their unique potentials. Nonetheless, myths and misconceptions about psychology abound; Table 1.1 provides a sampling.

Psychologists seek yet another kind of control—control over the variables they study. **Variables** are factors that vary in an experiment, such as the dosage level of an experimental drug. In a study of memory, to see what factors affect recall, psychologists might control such variables as length of exposure to a list of words to be later recalled or number of repetitions of the word list.

As we'll see later in this chapter, psychologists subscribe to a code of ethics that respects the dignity and welfare of their clients and those who participate in their research studies. This code recognizes that people have a basic right to make their own decisions and to exercise choices, including the choice of whether to participate in psychological research.

CONCEPT 1.22
Psychologists seek to explain events by developing theories that lead to predictions that can be tested through research and careful observation.

CONCEPT 1.23
Control has two meanings in psychological research: control of the variables under study and using knowledge gained from research to help people attain better control over their lives.

variables   Factors or measures that vary within an experiment or among individuals.

TABLE 1.1 Common Misconceptions About Psychology

Myth	Fact
Psychologists can read people's minds.	No, psychologists cannot read people's minds. As one prominent psychologist put it, "If you want to know what people are thinking, ask them. They just might tell you."
Psychology is not a true science.	Psychology is indeed a true science because it is grounded in the scientific method.
Psychologists manipulate people like puppets.	Psychologists help people change their behavior and achieve their goals. They do not manipulate or control people.
There can be only one true psychological theory; all the others must be false.	No one theory accounts for all forms of behavior. Theories are more or less useful to the degree they account for the available evidence and lead to accurate predictions of future behavior. Some theories account for some types of behavior better than others, but many have value in accounting for some forms of behavior.
Psychotherapy is useless.	A large body of evidence shows that psychotherapy is indeed effective (see Chapter 14).
People cannot change—they are what they are.	Evidence shows that people can indeed change their behavior and their ways of relating to others.

CONCEPT 1.24

Scientists use the scientific method to test out predictions derived from theory, observation, experience, or commonly held beliefs.

CONCEPT 1.25

Scientists frame their research questions in the form of hypotheses, or specific predictions about the outcomes they expect to find.

scientific method A method of inquiry involving careful observation and use of experimental methods.

hypothesis A precise prediction about the outcomes of an experiment.

statistics The branch of mathematics involving the tabulation, analysis, and interpretation of numerical data.

statistical significance A term representing that a finding is unlikely to have been due to chance or random fluctuations.

replication The attempt to duplicate findings.

case study method An in-depth study of one or more individuals.

The Scientific Method: How We Know What We Know

Like other scientific disciplines, psychology uses the scientific method in its pursuit of knowledge. The **scientific method** is a framework for acquiring knowledge based on careful observation and the use of experimental methods. It can be conceptualized in terms of four general steps that scientists use to test their ideas and to expand and refine their knowledge: (1) developing a research question, (2) framing the research question in the form of a hypothesis, (3) gathering evidence to test the hypothesis, and (4) drawing conclusions about the hypothesis. Figure 1.9 illustrates these steps.

1. *Developing a research question.* Psychologists generate research questions from many sources, including theory, careful observation, previous experience, and commonly held beliefs. For example, a researcher might be interested in the question "Does exposure to stress increase risk of the common cold?"

2. *Framing the research question in the form of a hypothesis.* An investigator reframes the research question in the form of a **hypothesis**—a precise prediction that can be tested through research. Hypotheses are often drawn from theory. For example, a researcher might theorize that stress weakens the immune system, the body's defense system against disease, leaving us more vulnerable to various kinds of illness, including the common cold. Based on this theoretical model, the investigator might frame the research question in the form of a testable hypothesis: "People who encounter high levels of stress in their lives are more likely to develop a common cold after exposure to cold viruses than are people with lower levels of stress."

Investigators may also develop hypotheses based on common beliefs or assumptions about behavior. Consider the commonly held belief that "opposites attract." An opposing belief is that people are attracted to those similar to themselves—that "birds of a feather flock together." A specific hypothesis drawn from the latter belief might be phrased as follows: "Most people choose romantic partners who are similar in educational level."

3. *Gathering evidence to test the hypothesis.* The investigator develops a research design or strategy for gathering evidence to provide a scientific test of the hypothesis. The type of research method used depends on the nature of the problem.

Developing a Research Question	Forming a Hypothesis	Gathering Evidence	Drawing Conclusions
Drawing on theory, observations, experiences, or common beliefs to formulate a researchable question	Reframing the question so that it becomes a specific prediction that can be tested through research	Testing the hypothesis	Using statistical methods of analysis to determine whether the data support the hypothesis

Figure 1.9   General Steps in the Scientific Method

CONCEPT 1.26

Psychologists evaluate the results of scientific studies by using statistical tests to determine if relationships between variables or differences between groups are unlikely to be due to chance.

Testing a Hypothesis   Psychologists frame testable hypotheses that guide their research. For example, a psychologist might hypothesize that romantic partners with similar interests and attitudes are more likely to remain together than are couples with dissimilar interests and attitudes. Preferences for the same clothing styles may have no bearing on the longevity of the relationship, however.

CONCEPT 1.27

Psychologists use a variety of research methods to learn about behavior and mental processes, including the case study, survey, naturalistic observation, correlational, and experimental methods.

In the stress and common cold example, the investigator might classify people into high-stress and low-stress groups and then expose them (with their permission, of course) to cold viruses to see if the high-stress group is more likely to develop a common cold. Researchers who have used this methodology (Cohen et al., 1998) found that people under high levels of chronic stress associated with prolonged unemployment or persistent family conflict were more likely to develop a cold after viral exposure than were people in the low-stress comparison group.

4. *Drawing conclusions about the hypothesis.* Investigators draw conclusions about their hypotheses based on the evidence their research has produced. To test their hypotheses, they turn to **statistics**, the branch of mathematics involving methods of tabulating and analyzing numerical data. Investigators use statistical methods to determine whether relationships between variables (e.g., stress and vulnerability to the common cold) or differences between groups (e.g., an experimental group that receives a treatment versus a control group that does not) are statistically significant.

Statistical significance refers to a finding that is unlikely to have been due to chance or random fluctuations. Researchers use tests of significance to determine whether a finding meets a particular threshold of statistical significance, such as a likelihood of less than 5 percent that the finding could have been due to chance. The statistical methods that psychologists and other scientists use are discussed in the statistics appendix at the end of this book. When research findings do not support the study's hypotheses, scientists may adjust the theories from which the hypotheses were derived. Research findings may suggest new avenues of research and changes to psychological theories.

Replication is another important factor in drawing conclusions. **Replication** is the attempt to duplicate findings reported by others to determine whether they will occur again under the same experimental conditions. Scientists have more confidence in findings that can be reliably replicated by others.

Research Methods: How We Learn What We Know

The scientific method is a framework psychologists use to take their ideas for a test ride. Now let's consider the particular methods they use to acquire knowledge about behavior and mental processes: the case study, the survey, naturalistic observation, the correlational method, and the experimental method.

The Case Study Method   The **case study method** is a painstaking, in-depth study of one or more individuals. The psychologist draws information from interviews, observation, or written records. Sigmund Freud, for example, based much of his theory of personality and abnormal behavior on data from intensive observation and study of the patients he treated in his clinical practice. The Swiss scientist Jean Piaget (1896–1980) developed a theory of cognitive development by closely observing and interviewing a small number of children. Many of the early findings on brain function came from studies of brain-injured patients that matched the

CONCEPT 1.28
Case studies can provide a wealth of information and suggest testable hypotheses, but they lack the controls found in scientific experiments.

CONCEPT 1.29
Through survey research, psychologists can gather information about the attitudes and behaviors of large numbers of people, but the information they obtain may be subject to memory gaps and biases.

survey method A research method that uses structured interviews or questionnaires to gather information about groups of people.

structured interview An interview in which a set of specific questions is asked in a particular order.

questionnaire A written set of questions or statements to which people reply by marking their responses on an answer form.

population All the individuals or organisms that constitute particular groups.

samples Subsets of a population.

random sampling A method of sampling in which each individual in the population has an equal chance of being selected.

social desirability bias The tendency to respond to questions in a socially desirable manner.

volunteer bias The type of bias that arises when people who volunteer to participate in a survey or research study have characteristics that make them unrepresentative of the population from which they were drawn.

naturalistic observation method A method of research based on careful observation of behavior in natural settings.

types of injuries they sustained with particular deficits in memory functioning and motor skills.

Problems with case studies can arise when investigators rely on people's memories of their past experiences, such as childhood experiences. These memories may not be trustworthy because of gaps or distortions in memory. As discussed in Chapter 6, researchers find that memory often plays tricks on people, leading them to false or distorted recollections of events. People may also withhold important information out of embarrassment or shame. To present a more favorable impression, some may even purposefully deceive the researcher. Interviewers themselves may perhaps unintentionally lead people to distort their reports or recollections in ways that reflect the interviewers' own biases or expectations. In other words, interviewers may hear only what they expect or want to hear and observers may see only what they want or expect to see. In sum, though case studies can provide a treasure-trove of information and lead to testable hypotheses, they lack the rigorous controls of scientific experiments.

The Survey Method The **survey method** gathers information from target groups of people through the use of structured interviews or questionnaires. A **structured interview** is an interview that follows a preset series of questions in a particular order. A **questionnaire** is a written set of questions or statements to which people can reply by marking responses on an answer form.

Psychologists and other researchers conduct survey research to learn about the characteristics, beliefs, attitudes, and behaviors of certain populations. In survey research, a **population** represents the total group of people who are the subjects of interest. For example, a population might consist of all persons eighteen years of age or older in the United States, or perhaps all high school seniors. Generally speaking, it is impractical to study an entire population; an exception would be a very small population that could be studied in its entirety, such as the population of students living in a particular dormitory. In virtually all cases, however, surveys are conducted on **samples**, or segments, of populations.

To draw conclusions about a population based on the results of a sample, the sample must be representative of the target population. Representative samples allow researchers to *generalize,* or transfer, their results from a sample to the population it represents. To create representative samples, researchers use **random sampling**, a technique whereby individuals are selected at random from a given population for participation in a sample. This often entails the use of a computer program that randomly selects names of individuals or households within a given population. Political polls reported in the media typically use random samples of likely voters to predict outcomes of elections.

Like case studies, surveys may be limited by gaps in people's memories. Participants may also give answers that they believe are socially desirable rather than reflective of what they truly feel or believe. This response style results from what is called a **social desirability bias**. For example, many people exaggerate how frequently they attend church (Espenshade, 1993). Social desirability may be especially strong in situations where people have a considerable stake in what others think of them (McGovern & Nevid, 1986). Another form of bias in survey research is **volunteer bias**. This arises when people who volunteer to participate in surveys or other research studies are not representative of the population from which they are drawn.

The Naturalistic Observation Method The **naturalistic observation method** takes the laboratory "into the field" to directly observe the behavior of humans or other animal species in their natural habitats or environments. The people or other animals serving as research participants may behave more "naturally" in their natural environments than they would in the artificial confines of the experimental laboratory. Psychologists have observed children at home with their

Naturalistic Observation The famed naturalist Jane Goodall used naturalistic observation (also called a field study) to study the behavior of chimpanzees in Africa.

CONCEPT 1.30
With the naturalistic observation method, researchers in the field can examine behavior as it unfolds, but they run the risk of influencing the behavior they are observing.

Online Study Center

Improve Your Grade
Tutorial: Connect the Dots

CONCEPT 1.31
With the correlational method, we can examine how variables are related to each other but cannot determine cause-and-effect relationships.

correlational method A research method that examines relationships between variables.

correlation coefficient A statistical measure of association between variables that can vary from −1.00 to +1.00.

parents to learn more about parent-child interactions and in schoolyards and classrooms to see how children relate to each other. Because people may act differently when they know they are being observed, the observers try to avoid interfering with the behaviors they are observing. To further minimize this potential bias, the observers may spend time allowing the people they are observing to get accustomed to them so that they begin acting more naturally before any actual measurement takes place. Observers may also position themselves so that the individuals they are observing cannot see them.

Problems with this method may arise if observers introduce their own biases. For example, if observers have a preconceived idea about how a parent's interaction with a child affects the child's behavior, they may tend to see what they expect to see. To guard against this, pairs of observers may be used to check for consistency between observers. Experimenters may also make random spot checks to see that observers are recording their measurements accurately.

Animals in laboratory or zoolike environments may act differently than they do in their natural habitats. To learn more about chimp behavior, naturalist Jane Goodall lived for many years among chimpanzees in their natural environment. Gradually she came to be accepted by the chimps. Her observations disputed the long-held belief that only humans use tools. For example, she watched as chimps used a stick as a tool, inserting it into a termite mound to remove termites, which they then ate. Not only did chimpanzees use tools, but they also showed other humanlike behavior, such as kissing when greeting one another.

Though the method of naturalistic observation may lack the controls available in controlled experiments, it can provide important insights into behavior as it occurs under natural conditions.

The Correlational Method Psychologists use the **correlational method** to examine relationships between variables they do not directly manipulate or control. In Chapter 15, we will read about findings that show a correlation, or link, between optimism and outcomes following coronary bypass surgery. That is, patients who hold more optimistic attitudes tend to encounter fewer serious complications following this form of heart surgery than do less optimistic patients. In Chapter 9, we will find that maternal smoking during pregnancy is correlated with an increased risk of sudden infant death syndrome (SIDS) in babies.

A **correlation coefficient** is a statistical measure of association between two variables. Correlation coefficients can vary from −1.00 to +1.00. Coefficients with a positive sign reflect a positive correlation, in which higher values in one variable are associated with higher values in the other variable (e.g., the higher the level of

Are Your Brains in Your Feet? Though shoe size and vocabulary size are correlated in children, we should not infer that the size of a child's foot determines his or her vocabulary.

stress, the greater the likelihood of depression). A negative correlation, which is denoted by a negative sign, means the reverse: higher values in one variable are associated with lower values in the other. For example, level of education is negatively correlated with violent crime. The higher the correlation coefficient (the closer it is to -1.00 or $+1.00$), the stronger the relationship is.

Correlations are useful because they allow us to predict one variable on the basis of the other. A perfect correlation of $+1.00$ or -1.00 allows us to predict with certainty. Let's say we discovered a perfect correlation between certain genetic characteristics and the likelihood of developing a particular disease. Knowing that you possessed those genetic characteristics would allow us to know with certainty whether you will develop the disease. However, virtually all relationships, especially those of interest to psychologists, are less than perfect (varying between 0.00 and either $+1$ or -1). For example, while intelligence is correlated with academic achievement, not everyone with a high score on intelligence tests succeeds in school. A zero correlation means that there is no relationship between the two variables, that one variable is useless in predicting the other.

You may have heard the expression "correlation is not causation." *The fact that two variables are correlated, even highly correlated, doesn't mean that one causes the other.* For example, shoe size in children correlates strongly with vocabulary. While you may argue that some people seem to have more smarts in their little toes than others have in their whole brains, I don't think you'd argue that a growing foot causes vocabulary to expand. Rather, shoe size and vocabulary are correlated because older children tend to have larger feet and a larger vocabulary than younger children. Likewise, we cannot conclude that a correlation between optimism and postsurgical outcomes, or between maternal smoking and SIDS, means that these variables are causally related. It is possible that optimistic patients have other resources available, such as greater social support, which improves their odds of recovery. Mothers who smoke during pregnancy may engage in other behaviors that put their infants at risk of SIDS.

Though the correlational method is limited in terms of specifying underlying causes, it has several benefits:

- *It offers clues to underlying causes.* Though correlational relationships cannot determine cause-and-effect relationships, they may point to possible causal factors that can be followed up in experimental research. For example, evidence of a correlation between smoking and lung cancer led to experimental studies with animals that showed that exposure to cigarette smoke induced the formation of cancerous lesions in the lungs.

- *It can identify groups of people at high risk for physical or behavioral problems.* Knowing that a relationship exists between the positive expectancies of adolescents toward alcohol use and the later development of problem drinking may direct us toward developing alcoholism prevention efforts that focus on changing attitudes of youngsters before drinking problems arise.

- *It increases understanding of relationships between variables or events.* Such an understanding is one of the major objectives of science. From time to time in this text, we explore such relationships. For example, in Chapter 11 we look at the relationships between gender and mathematical and verbal abilities, and in Chapters 13 and 15 we explore whether stress is related not only to psychological disorders but also to physical illness.

CONCEPT 1.32
With the experimental method, researchers can explore cause-and-effect relationships by directly manipulating causal (independent) variables and observing their effects on measured (dependent) variables under controlled conditions.

experimental method A method of scientific investigation involving the manipulation of independent variables and observation or measurement of their effects on dependent variables under controlled conditions.

independent variables Factors that are manipulated in an experiment.

dependent variables The effects or outcomes of an experiment that are believed to be dependent on the values of the independent variables.

control groups Groups of research participants in an experimental study who do not receive the experimental treatment or intervention.

random assignment A method of randomly assigning research participants to experimental or control groups.

placebo An inert substance or experimental condition that resembles the active treatment.

placebo effects Positive outcomes of an experiment resulting from a participant's expectations about the effects of treatment rather than from the experimental treatment itself.

single-blind studies In drug research, studies in which research participants are kept uninformed about whether they are receiving the experimental drug or a placebo.

double-blind studies In drug research, studies in which both participants and experimenters are kept uninformed about which participants receive the active drug and which receive the placebo.

The Experimental Method With the **experimental method**, investigators directly explore cause-and-effect relationships by manipulating certain variables, called **independent variables**, and observing their effects on certain *measured* variables, called **dependent variables**. The dependent variables are so called because they are thought to depend on the independent, or manipulated, variable. Experimenters attempt to hold constant all other factors or conditions to ensure that the independent variable alone is the cause of the observed changes in the dependent variables.

Consider an experiment that examined whether the popularity of women's names affects judgments of their physical attractiveness. The experimenter paired women's photographs with either a currently popular name, such as Jessica, Jennifer, or Christine, or a traditional name that had fallen out of favor, such as Harriet, Gertrude, or Ethel (Garwood et al., 1980). You may not be surprised that the women who were assigned popular names were rated as more attractive than the women who were given out-of-fashion names. The experimenter controlled the *independent variable* (type of name) by randomly assigning popular or old-fashioned names to women's photographs and measured the effects of the independent variable on the *dependent variable* (ratings of attractiveness).

Experimenters typically use **control groups** to ensure that the effects of an independent variable are not due to other factors, such as the passage of time. For example, in a study examining the effects of alcohol intake on aggressive behavior, the experimental group would receive a dose of alcohol but the control group would not. The investigator would then observe whether the group given alcohol showed more aggressive behavior in a laboratory task than the control group.

In well-designed studies, experimenters use **random assignment** to place participants randomly in experimental groups or control groups. Random assignment balances experimental and control groups in terms of the background and personality characteristics of the people who constitute the groups. This method of assignment gives us confidence that differences between groups in how they perform on dependent measures are due to the independent variable or variables and not to the characteristics of the people making up the groups (Ioannidis et al., 2001). However, random assignment is not always feasible or ethically responsible. For example, ethical experimenters would never randomly assign children to be exposed to abuse or neglect to see what effects these experiences might have on their development. They rely on correlational methods to examine these relationships, even though such methods may not necessarily determine cause and effect.

Experimenters may wish to keep research participants and themselves in the dark concerning which groups receive which treatments. In drug studies, research participants are typically assigned to receive either an active drug or a **placebo**, an inert pill, or "sugar pill," made to resemble the active drug (Charney et al., 2002; Kaptchuk, Eisenberg, & Komaroff, 2002a, 2002b). The purpose is to control for **placebo effects**—positive outcomes that reflect a person's hopeful expectancies rather than the chemical properties of the drug itself (Kirsch, 2004). If you took an antibiotic drug that would have no effect on your condition for twenty-four hours, but you didn't know that and began feeling better an hour after taking it, you may have been experiencing a placebo effect. Placebos tend to have stronger effects on subjective feelings of distress or pain than on medical conditions that can be objectively measured, such as blood pressure (Bailar, 2001; Hrobjartsson & Gotzsche, 2001).

In drug studies, experimenters attempt to control for expectancy effects by preventing research participants from knowing whether they are receiving the active drug or a placebo. In **single-blind studies**, only the research participants are kept in the dark. In **double-blind studies**, both the research participants and the experimenters (prescribing physicians and other researchers) are "blinded" (kept uninformed) with respect to which participants are receiving the active drug.

TRY THIS OUT
Getting Involved

You can learn about psychological research first-hand by volunteering as a research subject or a research assistant. Most psychology departments provide opportunities for students to participate in faculty research as participants, research assistants, or both. Ask your instructor or department chairperson about how you can participate in the department's research activities. Serving as a research assistant will provide you with a front-row view of cutting-edge developments in the field and with opportunities to obtain valuable research experience, which you may need when applying for jobs or admission to graduate school.

CONCEPT 1.33
Psychologists engaged in research must follow ethical guidelines that are designed to protect the welfare of research participants.

ethics review committees Committees that evaluate whether proposed studies meet ethical guidelines.

informed consent Agreement to participate in a study following disclosure of information about the purposes and nature of the study and its potential risks and benefits.

Keeping the experimenters "blind" helps prevent their own expectancies from affecting the results.

Unfortunately, the "blinds" in many double-blind studies are more like venetian blinds with the slats slightly open; that is, patients and doctors are often able to guess at greater than chance levels of accuracy whether a placebo or an active drug is being used (Kirsch et al., 2002; Kirsch, Scoboria, & Moore, 2002; Mooney, White, & Hatsukami, 2004). Active drugs often have telltale side effects that give their presence away. Though they may not be perfect, well-constructed double-blind, randomized studies are an important means of evaluating the effectiveness of new medications (Leber, 2000; Leon, 2000).

Concept Chart 1.3 summarizes the research methods we have discussed. You can gain more direct experience with the research process by becoming involved in research yourself, as discussed in the nearby Try This Out box.

Ethical Principles in Psychological Research

Psychologists subscribe to a code of ethics that respects the dignity and welfare of their clients and those who participate in their research studies. This code recognizes that people have a basic right to make their own decisions and to exercise choices, including the choice of whether to participate in psychological research. Ethical guidelines also prohibit psychologists from using methods that would harm research participants or clients (American Psychological Association, 2002).

People who participate in experiments may be harmed not only by physical interventions, such as experimental drugs that have adverse effects, but also by psychological interventions, such as being goaded into aggressive behavior that leads to feelings of guilt or shame. Invasions of privacy are another concern.

Today, nearly all institutions in which biomedical and behavioral research is conducted, such as hospitals, colleges, and research foundations, have **ethics review committees**. These committees, which are usually composed of professionals and laypersons, must put their stamp of approval on all research proposals before the research can be carried out at their institutions. The committees review the proposals to see if they comply with ethical guidelines and advise the researchers concerning the potential harm of their proposed methods. In cases where individuals may experience harm or discomfort, the committees must weigh the potential benefits of the research against the potential harm. If the committees believe that the proposed research might be unacceptably harmful, they withhold approval.

One of the foremost ethical requirements is that investigators obtain **informed consent** from research participants before they begin participating in the study. This means that participants must be given enough information about the study's methods and purposes to make an "informed" decision about whether they wish to participate. Participants must also be free to withdraw from the study at any time.

Many studies of historic importance in psychology, including the famous Milgram studies on obedience to authority (see Chapter 16), have required that research participants be deceived as to the true purposes of the study. The APA's *Ethical Principles of Psychologists and Code of Conduct* (American Psychological Association, 2002) specifies the conditions that psychologists must meet to use deceptive practices in research. These conditions include a determination that the research is justified by its scientific, educational, or practical value; that no non-deceptive alternative research strategy is possible; that research participants are not misled about any research that can reasonably be expected to result in physical harm or severe emotional distress; and that participants receive an explanation of the deception at the earliest time that it is feasible to give it.

Psychologists must also maintain the *confidentiality* of the records of research participants and of the clients they treat. That is, they must respect people's right

CONCEPT CHART 1.3   How Psychologists Do Research

What Researchers Do	Comments	Approaches to Research Questions About Love
In the **case study method,** the researcher interviews or observes an individual (or small group of individuals) or examines historical records of the lives of particular individuals.	The accuracy of case studies may be jeopardized by gaps or errors in people's memories or by their efforts to make a favorable impression on the researcher.	A psychologist interested in the reasons people choose their mates might conduct in-depth interviews with several married persons.
In the **survey method,** the researcher uses questionnaires or interviews to obtain information about a particular group of people.	Psychologists may use surveys to explore the attitudes of thousands of people about such topics as abortion, premarital sex, or leisure pursuits. Results of surveys may be compromised by volunteer bias and other problems.	Psychologists might survey thousands of individuals about the characteristics of the people they have chosen as mates.
In the **naturalistic observation method,** the researcher observes behavior in the field—that is, where it occurs naturally.	Psychologists attempt not to interfere with the behaviors they are observing. They may spend considerable time allowing their research participants to become accustomed to them before they begin their observations.	Psychologists might observe from a distance how lovers walk together and how they look at each other.
In the **correlational method,** the researcher uses statistical methods to reveal and describe positive and negative relationships (correlations) between variables.	This method may suggest the presence of cause and effect, but it does not demonstrate it. The degree to which variables are statistically associated is expressed as a correlation coefficient, which varies from -1.00 to $+1.00$.	Psychologists might study relationships between feelings of love, self-esteem, and sexual satisfaction.
In the **experimental method,** the psychologist manipulates one or more independent variables (makes changes in the participants' environments) and observes their effects on one or more dependent (measured) variables. Experiments are conducted to establish cause-and-effect relationships between independent and dependent variables.	Participants in experimental groups receive an experimental treatment; those in control groups do not. All other conditions are held constant to ensure that the independent variable alone is the cause of the observed effects. Random assignment to groups helps ensure that groups do not differ in characteristics that might affect the outcome.	Psychologists might expose dating partners to an experimental treatment in which they share an arousing experience, such as watching an emotionally powerful movie, and then measure the treatment's effects on the partners' feelings toward each other. (The control group would be exposed to a neutral movie.)

Online Study Center

Resources
Weblinks: Ethical Guidelines in Animal Research

to privacy by keeping their records secure and by not disclosing their identities or the information they provide to others. There are times, however, when societal laws require that psychologists disclose confidential information acquired through the course of research or clinical practice, as when a participant or a client in therapy threatens to do physical harm to someone else.

Ethical guidelines also extend to the use of animals in psychological research. The design of research projects often precludes the use of human participants, and in such cases, the researchers use animals as research subjects.. For example, to determine which behaviors are instinctive and which are not, scientists have reared birds and fish in isolation from other members of their species; such research could not be conducted with humans because of the harmful effects of separating infants from their families. Scientists routinely test experimental drugs on animals to determine harmful effects before human trials are begun. Scientists who study the brain may destroy parts of the brains of laboratory animals, such as rats and monkeys, to learn how these parts of the brain are connected with behavior. (In Chapter 8, you will see how destruction of different parts of the brain causes laboratory animals to either overeat or stop eating completely.)

Issues concerning the ethical treatment of animals in research studies have risen to the fore in recent years. On one side of the debate are those who argue that significant advances in medicine and psychology could not have occurred without such research (Fowler, 1992). Yet recent polls find that most psychologists believe it is unethical to kill animals or expose them to pain, regardless of the potential benefits of the research to humans (Plous, 1996). According to APA ethical guidelines, animals may not be harmed or subjected to stress unless there is no alternative way to conduct the research and the goals of the research are justified by their intended scientific, educational, or practical value (APA, 2002). Researchers must also obtain approval from their ethics review committees to ensure that ethical practices are followed.

EXPLORING PSYCHOLOGY
Anatomy of a Research Study: The Shooter Bias

Do you consider yourself prejudiced? Perhaps not, but the results of a recent study may lead you to consider whether your behavior, like those of the college students in this study, may be influenced by stereotypes you might consciously reject. Stereotypes are discussed further in Chapter 16, but here let us note that they are generalized beliefs that all members of particular groups or categories, such as people of a particular gender or ethnicity, share certain common characteristics.

In this study, social psychologists simulated the type of situation faced by police officers who must make split-second decisions about whether to use their weapons in ambiguous situations—situations in which someone facing them may be holding a gun or merely an object resembling a gun (Correll et al., 2002). The scenario modeled a real-life tragedy in 1999 in which New York City police officers searching for a rape suspect fired upon and killed an unarmed 22-year-old West African immigrant, Amadou Diallo. The police officers observed the man reaching into his pocket and believed he was reaching for a gun. The "gun" turned out to be his wallet.

In a series of experiments, investigators used a specialized videogame designed to simulate the situation in which a police officer is confronted with an ambiguous but potentially dangerous figure and must decide whether to shoot or not to shoot. The question was, Would the ethnicity or race of a target figure make a difference in the decision to shoot? Here we go under the hood and examine the workings of the first of these studies.

Study Hypothesis (What They Predicted Would Occur) A hypothesis is a predicted outcome, but it is far from a wild guess. Hypotheses are informed by a careful review of theory and prior research. Based on earlier theories of stereotyping, the investigators hypothesized that ethnicity would be a determining factor in the decision to shoot or not shoot a target (Table 1.2 gives the experimental conditions in the study).

The Police Officer's Dilemma Police officers may need to make split-second decisions about whether to use their weapons in ambiguous situations in which they confront someone who is pointing an object at them that looks like a gun but might actually be an object that merely resembles a gun. Psychological research may help us understand whether the decision to shoot or not shoot under these circumstances may be influenced by underlying racial biases.

Procedure (What They Did and How They Did It) Upon arriving at the laboratory, the participants were met by a male experimenter who briefly described the study as an investigation of perceptual vigilance, the ability to monitor and respond quickly to a variety of stimuli. Detailed instructions were then given for completing the experimental task, which involved playing a particular videogame. The participants were also informed that monetary prizes of $30, $20, and $10 would be given to the people receiving the highest score and the next two highest scores, respectively, and that five additional prizes would be distributed randomly to those scoring in the top 30 percent. The purpose of the prizes was to motivate participants to perform their best.

TABLE 1.2   Experimental Design in Police Officer's Dilemma Study

		Ethnicity of Target	
		African American	White
Object	Gun	African American target with a gun	White target with a gun
	No Gun	African American target with no gun	White target with no gun

Participants were told that when an armed target appeared on a screen, they should act as though they were in imminent danger and shoot the target as quickly as possible. But they were not to shoot at unarmed targets. To "shoot" a target, they needed to press a button labeled "shoot." They were to press another button labeled "don't shoot" if the target was unarmed. They had to make the decision to shoot or not shoot as quickly as possible once the target appeared. Targets were shown for a brief duration that varied randomly from 500 to 1,000 milliseconds. The targets were presented in a slide-show fashion against the different backgrounds. From the perspective of the participants, the target seemed to simply appear on the background.

Participants were instructed to use separate hands for each button and to rest their hands on a center console between trials. They received a designated number of points for correctly shooting an armed target and lost points for incorrectly shooting an unarmed target or failing to shoot an armed target. Participants received 10 points for a "hit" (correctly shooting an armed target) and 5 points for a "nonshoot" (not shooting an unarmed target). The highest penalty (loss of 40 points) was given for failing to protect themselves in a potential life-or-death situation by not shooting an armed target. Making the mistake of shooting an innocent suspect (unarmed target) was assessed 20 points. Failing to respond within the designated time interval resulted in a timed-out penalty of 10 points.

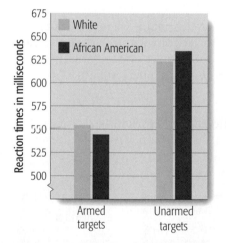

Figure 1.10   Reaction Times in Police Officer's Dilemma Study
Response times were shorter for armed targets when the target was African American than when the target was White. The reverse was the case when the target was unarmed. Do you think your responses would be affected by the ethnicity of the target?

Source: Adapted from Correll et al., 2002.

Results and Discussion (What They Found and What It Means)   Statistical analyses were performed on two dependent measures, *reaction time* (time interval from presentation of stimulus target to response) and *error rate* (proportion of errors in relation to total number of trials). Errors were defined as failures to shoot an armed target and shooting an unarmed target.

The most important finding was that reaction times depended on a combination of object type (target armed versus unarmed) and ethnicity of target (African American versus White). Participants fired more quickly when an armed target was African American than when an armed target was White. Participants also responded more quickly in deciding *not to shoot* an unarmed target when the target was White than when the target was African American (see Figure 1.10). Pause over these findings and consider how you might explain them.

The error rate was quite low, about 4 percent overall. The results on accuracy were not strong enough to lead to any firm conclusions. So the investigators conducted a second study to replicate and extend the results of the first study. They made the decision task more difficult by shortening the amount of time they gave the participants to respond. In the second experiment, the investigators found that participants were more likely to mistakenly shoot an unarmed African American figure than an unarmed White figure.

Taken together, these results support the existence of a "shooter bias"—that is, a tendency to respond more quickly to shoot an armed African American target than an armed White target and to err more often by shooting an unarmed African American than an unarmed White. Errors of omission (failing to shoot an armed assailant) and commission (shooting an innocent person) can have tragic results for a police officer in the first case and for an innocent civilian in the second.

None of the participants in these first two studies were African American. But a "shooter bias" was also found in a diverse sample in a subsequent study that included African American participants. The investigators believe that the constant barrage of images in the popular media depicting African Americans in violent roles reinforces the cultural stereotype of African Americans as violent. Once the

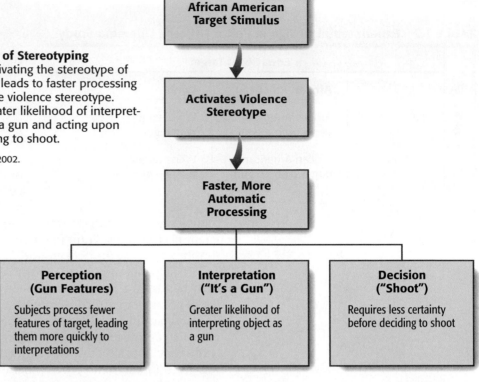

Figure 1.11
Fateful Decisions: The Role of Stereotyping
This model suggests that activating the stereotype of African Americans as violent leads to faster processing of stimuli associated with the violence stereotype. Consequently, there is a greater likelihood of interpreting an ambiguous object as a gun and acting upon that interpretation by deciding to shoot.

Source: Adapted from Correll et al., 2002.

violence stereotype is activated, it leads to a greater likelihood of interpreting an object as a gun when it is in the hands of an African American (see Figure 1.11).

Does a "shooter bias" exist among trained police officers? We don't yet know, but future research may give us the answer. If a bias does exist, might specialized police training programs help reduce or eliminate it? Again, we must await future research. As the investigators concluded, social-psychological theory and research may prove invaluable in the effort to identify, understand, and eventually control processes that bias decisions to shoot (and possibly kill) a person because of his or her ethnicity (Correll et al., 2002).

Citing References Psychologists use a particular style for citing references that was developed by the American Psychological Association. Here is the reference style for journal articles, using the Correll et al. study as an example:

Bibliographic information

Before moving on, you may wish to review Concept Chart 1.3, which summarizes the research methods we have discussed.

MODULE 1.3 REVIEW

Research Methods in Psychology

RECITE IT

What are the major objectives of science?

- The major objectives are description, explanation, prediction, and control of events or variables.

What is the scientific method, and what are its four general steps?

- The scientific method is a set of guiding principles that directs the scientific process.

- The scientific method comprises four general steps that guide research: (1) developing a research question, (2) formulating a hypothesis, (3) gathering evidence, and (4) drawing conclusions.

What are the major research methods psychologists use?

- These include the case study method, the survey method, the naturalistic observation method, the correlational method, and the experimental method.

What general ethical guidelines must psychologists follow in their research?

- Psychologists are committed to following ethical guidelines that promote the dignity of the individual, human welfare, and scientific integrity.

- Psychologists are precluded from using methods that harm research participants or clients and must receive approval of their research protocols from ethics review committees before undertaking research with humans or animals.

What is an example of a specific ethical guideline?

- One of the specific ethical provisions in research with humans is confidentiality, which requires that investigators keep the records and identities of research participants private and secure.

RECALL IT

1. A conclusion drawn from observations is called a(n) _____.

2. Psychologists adopt a scientific approach to studying behavior and mental processes, which comprises four principal objectives: description, _____, prediction, and control of events.

3. A distinct advantage of the naturalistic _____ method, when used correctly, is that it provides a view of behavior that occurs in natural settings.

4. Which research method is best suited to providing evidence of cause-and-effect relationships?

5. Ethical guidelines in psychological research are designed to protect research participants from physical or psychological _____.

Answers to Recall It questions are placed at the end of the chapter.

THINK ABOUT IT

- Perhaps you won't be surprised by research findings that adolescents with tattoos are more likely to engage in riskier behavior than their nontattooed peers (Roberts & Ryan, 2002). Tattooed youth are more likely to smoke cigarettes, engage in binge drinking, use marijuana, and join gangs. But does tattooing cause these risky behaviors? Or can you think of other explanations for the links between tattooing and high-risk behavior?

- Can you think of other examples in which two variables are correlated but not causally related?

- Suppose you were interested in studying the relationship between alcohol use and grades among college students. Assume you couldn't control whether students used alcohol or how much they used. What then would be the value of this type of research? Would you be able to conclude that alcohol use affects grades? Why or why not?

APPLICATION MODULE 1.4
Becoming a Critical Thinker

CONCEPT 1.34
Critical thinking involves adopting a skeptical, questioning attitude toward commonly held beliefs and assumptions and weighing arguments in terms of the available evidence.

Critical thinking involves adopting a questioning attitude, in which we weigh evidence carefully and thoughtfully analyze the claims and arguments of others. It is a way of evaluating information by maintaining a skeptical attitude toward what you hear and read, even what you read in the pages of this text.

Critical thinking requires a willingness to challenge conventional wisdom and common knowledge that many of us take for granted. When you think critically, you maintain an open mind and suspend belief until you can obtain and evaluate evidence that either supports or refutes a particular claim or statement. You find *reasons* to support your beliefs, rather than relying on impressions or "gut feelings." In this text, you'll be able to hone your critical thinking skills by answering the questions posed in the "Thinking Critically About Psychology" sections, which appear at the end of every chapter.

Features of Critical Thinking

Critical thinkers maintain a healthy skepticism. They question assumptions and claims made by others and demand to see the evidence upon which conclusions are based. Here are some suggestions for thinking critically about psychology (adapted from Nevid, Rathus, & Rubinstein, 1998):

1. *Question everything.* Critical thinkers do not blindly accept the validity of claims made by others, even claims made by authority figures, such as political or religious leaders, scientists, or even textbook authors. They keep an open mind and weigh the evidence upon which claims are made.

2. *Clarify what you mean.* Whether a claim is true or false may depend on how we define the terms we use. Consider the claim "Stress is bad for you." If we define stress only in terms of the pressures and hassles of daily life, then perhaps there is some truth to that claim. But if we define stress more broadly to include any events that impose a pressure on us to adjust, even positive events like the birth of a child or a promotion at work, then certain kinds of stress may actually be desirable (see Chapter 15). Perhaps we even need a certain amount of stress to be active and alert.

3. *Avoid oversimplifying.* Consider the claim "Alcoholism is inherited." In Chapter 4, we review evidence indicating that genetic factors may contribute to alcoholism. But the origins of alcoholism, as well as the origins of many other psychological and physical disorders, are more complex. Genetics alone does not tell the whole story. Many disorders involve the interplay of biological, psychological, and environmental factors, the nature of which we are only beginning to unravel.

4. *Avoid overgeneralizing.* People from China and Japan and other East Asian cultures tend to be more reserved about disclosing information about themselves to strangers than are Americans or Europeans (see Chapter 16). Yet this doesn't mean that every person from these East Asian cultures is more withholding or that every American or European is more disclosing.

5. *Don't confuse correlation with causation.* As you'll see in Chapter 10, girls who show earlier signs of puberty than their peers (e.g., early breast development) tend to have lower self-esteem, a more negative body image, and more emotional problems. But do physical changes associated with early puberty cause these negative psychological consequences, or might other factors be involved in explaining these links, such as how people react to these changes?

critical thinking The adoption of a skeptical, questioning attitude and careful scrutiny of claims or arguments.

6. *Consider the assumptions upon which claims are based.* Consider the claim that homosexuality is a psychological disorder. The claim rests in part on underlying assumptions about the nature of psychological disorders. What is a psychological disorder? What criteria are used to determine whether someone has a psychological disorder? Do gays, lesbians, or people with a bisexual sexual orientation meet these criteria? Is there evidence to support these assertions? In Chapter 13, you will see that mental health professionals no longer classify homosexuality as a psychological disorder.

7. *Examine sources of claims.* In their publications, scientists cite the sources on which they base their claims. (See this book's reference list, which cites the sources used in its preparation.) When examining source citations, note such features as publication dates (to determine whether the sources are outdated or current) and the journals or other periodicals in which the sources may have appeared (to see whether they are well-respected scientific journals or questionable sources). Source citations allow readers to check the original sources for themselves to see if the information provided is accurate.

8. *Question the evidence upon which claims are based.* Are claims based on sound scientific evidence or on anecdotes and personal testimonials that cannot be independently verified? In Chapter 6, we consider the controversy over so-called recovered memories—memories of childhood sexual abuse that suddenly reappear during adulthood, usually during the course of psychotherapy or hypnosis. Are such memories accurate? Or might they be tales spun of imaginary thread?

9. *Consider alternative ways of explaining claims.* Do you believe in the existence of extrasensory perception (ESP)? Some people claim to have extrasensory skills that enable them, simply by using their minds, to read other people's minds, to transmit their thoughts to others, or to move objects or change their shapes. Are such claims believable? Or might more mundane explanations account for these strange phenomena, such as coincidence, deliberate fabrication, or sleight-of-hand? In Chapter 3, we consider the case of a psychic who claims to have relied on her extrasensory ability in finding a missing person. Was it ESP? Or might there be other explanations?

Online Study Center

Resources

Weblinks: PsychPORT—Psychology News and Information

Thinking Critically About Online Information

Critical Thinking Adopt a skeptical attitude when using the Internet. Check out the credibility of the source of the material and be wary of information provided by companies or marketers seeking to promote or sell particular products or services.

One of the beauties of the Internet is that any user can post information that others can access. Yet this freedom carries with it the risk that posted information may be inaccurate (Eysenbach et al., 2003). Investigators have found that online health information is often inaccurate or misleading and difficult for many people to understand (Benotsch, Kalichman, & Weinhardt, 2004; Berland et al., 2001). Yet the Internet can be an effective vehicle for distributing information that may not be accessible through other sources, such as information young people can use to prevent sexually transmitted diseases (Keller & Brown, 2002). Investigators have also found that women with breast cancer benefit psychologically from seeking health-related information on the Internet (Fogel, 2003).

Critical thinkers don't suspend their skeptical attitude when they go online. They check out the credentials of the source by asking questions like these: Who is posting the material? Is the source a well-respected institution? Or is it an individual or group of individuals with no apparent credentials and perhaps with an axe to grind?

The most trustworthy online information comes from well-known scientific sources, such as leading scientific journals, government agencies like the National Institutes of Health, and major professional organizations, like the American Psychological Association and the American Psychological Society. One reason articles in scientific journals are so trustworthy is that they undergo a process of peer review in which independent scientists carefully scrutinize them before they are accepted for publication. Many leading scientific organizations provide links to abstracts (brief descriptions) of recent works. Much of this information is available without charge.

Sad to say, many people never question the information that comes to them on the printed page or on their computer screens. But as a critical thinker, you can evaluate assertions and claims for yourself. The critical thinking sections found at the end of each chapter will give you an opportunity to sharpen your critical thinking skills.

Another caution about Internet use is advised for students who are concerned about their grades. Recent evidence from a survey of college students showed that students who were heavier recreational users of the Internet were more likely than lighter users to report that their Internet use had hurt their academic performance (Kubey, Lavin, & Barrows, 2001). The link between heavy Internet use and poorer academic performance was much stronger for Internet use involving chat rooms and MUDs (a form of fantasy game playing called Multiple User Dungeons) than for email or newsgroups.

TYING IT TOGETHER

We began our study by focusing on the foundations of psychology as an organized field of study (Module 1.1). The early psychologists were all experimentalists, but as psychology matured as a profession it embraced a wider range of specialties. Today, it is a diverse discipline because of these many specialties and because of the diverse roles psychologists perform as researchers, teachers, and clinicians. Over time, it has also become more representative of the gender and ethnic diversity of the larger society (Module 1.2). At its core, psychology is a scientific discipline, and psychologists apply scientific methods in studying behavior and mental processes (Module 1.3). Psychologists are trained to be critical thinkers who are skeptical of claims and arguments not grounded in evidence. We, too, can learn to think critically by maintaining a skeptical, questioning attitude and examining claims in light of the evidence (Module 1.4).

Thinking Critically About Psychology

Here is the first critical thinking exercise you will encounter in this text. Based on your reading of the chapter, answer the following questions. Then, to evaluate your progress in developing critical thinking skills, compare your answers with the sample answers in Appendix A.

An experimenter claims that listening to a professor's lectures while you sleep can help improve your grades. The experimenter based this conclusion on the following data:

The experimenter invited students in a large introductory psychology class to participate in a study in which they would be given audiotapes of the professor's lectures and asked to play them back while they slept. Each of the thirty-six students who agreed to participate received a specially equipped audiotape player. Secured in the machine with tamper-proof sealing tape were recordings of each lecture given in the two weeks before the final examination. The tape player automatically played the tape two hours after the students went to bed. At other times, the play button was deactivated so that the students could not play the tape.

After the final examination, the experimenter compared the grades of the participating students with those of a group of students selected from the same class who had not participated in the study. The results showed that participating students achieved higher test grades.

1. **Do you believe the experimenter's claims are justified? Why or why not?**

2. **What other factors might account for the observed differences in test scores between the two groups?**

3. **How might you design the study differently to strengthen the experimenter's conclusion?**

Key Terms

psychology *(p. 4)*
psychophysics *(p. 5)*
introspection *(p. 5)*
structuralism *(p. 6)*
functionalism *(p. 6)*
natural selection *(p. 7)*
stream of consciousness *(p. 7)*
behaviorism *(p. 7)*
Gestalt psychology *(p. 8)*
gestalt *(p. 8)*
unconscious *(p. 8)*
psychodynamic perspective *(p. 9)*
psychoanalysis *(p. 9)*
behavioral perspective *(p. 10)*
social-cognitive theory *(p. 10)*
behavior therapy *(p. 10)*
humanistic psychology *(p. 10)*
humanistic perspective *(p. 11)*
physiological perspective *(p. 11)*
evolutionary psychology *(p. 11)*
cognitive perspective *(p. 12)*
sociocultural perspective *(p. 12)*
positive psychology *(p. 15)*
basic research *(p. 18)*
applied research *(p. 18)*
experimental psychologists *(p. 18)*
comparative psychologists *(p. 18)*

physiological psychologists *(p. 19)*
clinical psychologists *(p. 20)*
psychiatrists *(p. 20)*
counseling psychologists *(p. 20)*
school psychologists *(p. 20)*
educational psychologists *(p. 20)*
developmental psychologists *(p. 20)*
personality psychologists *(p. 20)*
social psychologists *(p. 20)*
environmental psychologists *(p. 21)*
industrial/organizational (I/O)
  psychologists *(p. 21)*
health psychologists *(p. 21)*
consumer psychologists *(p. 21)*
neuropsychologists *(p. 21)*
geropsychologists *(p. 22)*
forensic psychologists *(p. 22)*
sport psychologists *(p. 22)*
empirical approach *(p. 25)*
inferences *(p. 26)*
theories *(p. 26)*
variables *(p. 27)*
scientific method *(p. 28)*
hypothesis *(p. 28)*
statistics *(p. 29)*
statistical significance *(p. 29)*
replication *(p. 29)*

case study method *(p. 29)*
survey method *(p. 30)*
structured interview *(p. 30)*
questionnaire *(p. 30)*
population *(p. 30)*
samples *(p. 30)*
random sampling *(p. 30)*
social desirability bias *(p. 30)*
volunteer bias *(p. 30)*
naturalistic observation method *(p. 30)*
correlational method *(p. 31)*
correlation coefficient *(p. 31)*
experimental method *(p. 33)*
independent variables *(p. 33)*
dependent variables *(p. 33)*
control groups *(p. 33)*
random assignment *(p. 33)*
placebo *(p. 33)*
placebo effects *(p. 33)*
single-blind studies *(p. 33)*
double-blind studies *(p. 33)*
ethics review committees *(p. 34)*
informed consent *(p. 34)*
critical thinking *(p. 40)*

ANSWERS TO RECALL IT QUESTIONS

Module 1.1: 1. Know thyself; 2. Wilhelm Wundt; 3. structuralism; 4. behaviorism; 5. b; 6. psychodynamic perspective; 7. choice.

Module 1.2: 1. Basic, applied; 2. (a) iv, (b) i, (c) ii, (d) iii; 3. neuropsychologists; 4. b.

Module 1.3: 1. inference; 2. explanation; 3. observation; 4. experimental; 5. harm.

Biological Foundations of Behavior

DID YOU KNOW THAT . . .

- The messages carried by nerve cells need to be ferried by chemical messengers across a tiny gap that separates one nerve cell from another? (p. 50)

- Our bodies produce natural painkillers that are chemically similar to morphine and other narcotic drugs? (p. 52)

- Thanks to a weblike network of cells in the brain, we can sleep undisturbed by the sound of a truck rumbling by, but be awakened in a flash by the sound of a child's faint cry? (p. 61)

- Fetuses not only suck their thumbs in the womb, but 95 percent of them suck their right thumbs? (p. 73)

- The likelihood of your hair swirling in a clockwise or counterclockwise direction is related to your handedness? (p. 73)

- Though a man survived an accident in which a thick metal rod was driven right through his skull, his personality changed so much that people thought he no longer was himself? (pp. 74–75)

- Both men's and women's bodies produce the male sex hormone testosterone? (p. 81)

- Scientists have deciphered the entire human genetic code and posted it on the Internet? (p. 83)

I n *The Man Who Mistook His Wife for a Hat,* neurologist Oliver Sacks (1985) recounts the case of a Dr. P, a distinguished music teacher who had lost the ability to recognize objects by sight. Not only was he unable to recognize the faces of his students; he also sometimes perceived faces in objects when none existed. He would pat the fire hydrants and parking meters, believing them to be young children. As Dr. P was preparing to leave Sack's office one day after a physical examination, he looked about for his hat, and then

reached out his hand, and took hold of his wife's head, tried to lift it off, to put it on. He had apparently mistaken his wife for a hat! His wife looked as if she was used to such things. (Sacks, 1985, p. 10)

Dr. P's odd behavior may seem amusing in some respects, but his deficits in visual perception were caused by a large tumor in the part of the brain responsible for processing visual information. Perhaps the most remarkable aspect of Dr. P's case was his extraordinary ability to manage many tasks of daily life despite his nearly complete lack of visual perception. He was able to shower, dress himself, and eat meals by using music to coordinate his actions. He would sing various songs to himself to organize his efforts—eating songs and dressing songs, and so on. But when the music stopped, he would lose the ability to make sense of the world. If his dressing song was interrupted, for instance, he would lose his train of thought and be unable to recognize the clothes his wife had laid out for him or even to recognize his own body.

Dr. P's case reveals just how dependent we are on the brain. But it reveals something more: the remarkable capacity of the human brain to adapt to challenges imposed by physical illness or disability. The human brain can be regarded as the most remarkable feat of engineering ever achieved. Weighing a mere three pounds on the average, it is a living supercomputer of far more elegant design than any machine today's Silicon Valley wizards could hope to create. Yes, computers can crank out in a matter of milliseconds a stream of computations that would take teams of the most gifted humans years or even decades to accomplish. But even the most advanced computers lack the capacity for the basic insights and creativity that the human brain can achieve. What computer has written noteworthy music or a decent poem? What computer is aware of itself or aware that it even exists? Such wonders remain the stuff of science fiction.

To perform its many functions, the brain needs to communicate with the senses and other parts of the body. It does so through an information highway that took millions of years to construct. This complex network, of which the brain is a part, is called the *nervous system*.

In this chapter, we take an inward journey of discovery to explore the biological bases of our behavior, thinking processes, and moods. We begin the journey by studying the structure and workings of the fundamental unit of the nervous system: the nerve cell, or *neuron*. We then examine the workings of the two major divisions of the nervous system, the *central nervous system* (the brain and spinal cord) and the *peripheral nervous system,* the part that connects the central nervous system to other parts of the body. Finally, we consider how our behavior is influenced by the endocrine system and heredity. ■

MODULE 2.1

Neurons: The Body's Wiring

- **What is a neuron?**
- **What are the parts of a neuron?**
- **What are the types of neurons and types of cells found in the nervous system?**
- **How is a neural impulse generated and transmitted from one neuron to another?**
- **What roles do neurotransmitters play in psychological functioning?**

Neurons do wondrous things, such as informing your **brain** when light strikes your eye and carrying messages from the brain that command your muscles to raise your arms and your heart to pump blood. They also enable you to think, plan, even to dream. They enable you to read this page and to wonder what will be in the next paragraph.

In this module, we first look at the structure of an individual neuron and then observe how neurons communicate with one another to transmit information within the nervous system.

The Structure of the Neuron

CONCEPT 2.1

Neurons are the basic building blocks of the nervous system—the body's wiring through which messages are transmitted within the nervous system.

Neurons, the basic building blocks of the nervous system, are body cells that are specialized for transmitting information or messages in the form of electrical impulses. Each neuron is a single cell consisting of a cell body (or *soma*), an axon, and dendrites. Figure 2.1 illustrates these structures; Concept Chart 2.1 summarizes their functions. The **soma** is the main body of the cell. It houses the cell nucleus, which contains the cell's genetic material, and it carries out the *metabolic,* or life-sustaining, functions of the cell. Each neuron also has an **axon**, a long cable that projects trunklike from the soma and conducts outgoing messages to other neurons.

Figure 2.1   The Neuron
A neuron, or nerve cell, consists of a cell body, or soma, which houses the cell nucleus; an axon, which carries the neural message; and dendrites, which receive messages from adjacent neurons. Terminal buttons are swellings at the end of the axon from which neurotransmitter molecules are released to ferry the message to other neurons. The axons of many neurons are covered with a type of insulating layer, called a myelin sheath, that speeds transmission of neural impulses.

Dendrite

Direction of neural impulse

Axon

Cell nucleus

Cell body

Axon   Myelin sheath

Node of Ranvier

Axon terminal buttons

CONCEPT CHART 2.1   Parts of the Neuron

Part	Description	Functions
Soma	Cell body containing the nucleus	Performs metabolic, or life-sustaining, functions of the cell
Axon	Long cable projecting from the soma	Carries neural impulses to the terminal buttons
Terminal Buttons	Swellings at ends of axons	Release chemicals, called neurotransmitters, that carry neural messages to adjacent neurons
Dendrites	Fibers that project from the soma	Receive messages from neighboring neurons

CONCEPT 2.2

The nervous system has three types of neurons: sensory neurons, motor neurons, and interneurons.

neurons Nerve cells.

brain The mass of nerve tissue encased in the skull that controls virtually everything we are and everything we do.

soma The cell body of a neuron; contains the nucleus of the cell and carries out the cell's metabolic functions.

axon The tubelike part of a neuron that carries messages away from the cell body toward other neurons.

terminal buttons Swellings at the tips of axons from which neurotransmitters are dispatched into the synapse.

neurotransmitters Chemical messengers that transport nerve impulses from one nerve cell to another.

synapse The small fluid-filled gap between neurons through which neurotransmitters carry neural impulses.

dendrites Treelike structures projecting from the soma that receive neural messages from neighboring neurons.

sensory neurons Neurons that transmit information from sensory organs, muscles, and inner organs to the spinal cord and brain.

motor neurons Neurons that convey nerve impulses from the central nervous system to muscles and glands.

glands Body organs or structures that produce secretions.

hormones Secretions from endocrine glands that help regulate bodily processes.

interneurons Nerve cells in the central nervous system that connect neurons to neurons; in the brain, they are involved in processing information.

nerve A bundle of axons from different neurons that transmit nerve impulses.

The axons of the neurons in your brain may be only a few thousandths of an inch long. Other axons, such as those that run from your spinal cord to your toes, are several feet long. Axons may branch off like the stems of plants, fanning out in different directions. At the ends of these branches are knoblike swellings called **terminal buttons**. It is here that chemicals called **neurotransmitters** are stored and released. Neurons don't actually touch each other. Rather, the neurotransmitters they manufacture ferry outgoing messages to neighboring neurons across the **synapse**, a tiny gap that separates one neuron from another.

Dendrites are rootlike structures that project from the soma. Dendrites have receptor sites, or docking stations, that enable them to receive neurotransmitters released by neighboring neurons. Through its dendrites, each neuron may receive messages from thousands of other neurons (Kennedy, 2000).

The nervous system has three types of neurons: sensory neurons, motor neurons, and interneurons. These different types play specialized roles in the nervous system.

Sensory neurons (also called *afferent neurons*) transmit information about the outside world to the spinal cord and brain. This information first registers on your sensory organs. So when someone touches your hand, sensory receptors within the skin transmit the message through sensory neurons to the spinal cord and brain, where the information is processed, resulting in the feeling of touch. Sensory neurons also carry information from your muscles and inner organs to your spinal cord and brain.

Motor neurons (also called *efferent neurons*) convey messages from the brain and spinal cord to the muscles that control the movements of your body. They also convey messages to your **glands**, causing them to release **hormones**, chemical substances that help regulate bodily processes.

Interneurons (also called *associative neurons*) are the most common type of neuron in the nervous system. They connect neurons to neurons. In the spinal cord, they connect sensory neurons to motor neurons. In the brain, they form complex assemblages of interconnected nerve cells that process information from sensory organs and that control higher mental functions, such as planning and thinking.

A neuron is not the same thing as a nerve. A **nerve** is a bundle of axons from different neurons. The cell body of the neuron, or soma, is not part of the nerve. An individual nerve, such as the optic nerve, which transmits messages from the eyes to the brain, consists of more than a million axons. Although individual axons are microscopic, a nerve may be visible to the naked eye.

CONCEPT 2.3

The nervous system has two types of cells, neurons and glial cells.

CONCEPT 2.4

Many axons are covered with a protective coating, called a myelin sheath, that speeds the transmission of neural impulses.

CONCEPT 2.5

The nervous system is a massive communication network that connects billions of neurons throughout your body.

CONCEPT 2.6

A neuron fires when a stimulus triggers electrochemical changes along its cell membrane that lead to a chain reaction within the cell.

glial cells   Small but numerous cells in the nervous system that support neurons and that form the myelin sheath found on many axons.

myelin sheath   A layer of protective insulation that covers the axons of certain neurons and helps speed transmission of nerve impulses.

nodes of Ranvier   Gaps in the myelin sheath that create noninsulated areas along the axon.

multiple sclerosis (MS)   A disease of the central nervous system in which the myelin sheath that insulates axons is damaged or destroyed.

ions   Electrically charged chemical particles.

resting potential   The electrical potential across the cell membrane of a neuron in its resting state.

Neurons are not the only cells found in the nervous system. Scientists today believe that neurons only account for about 50 percent of brain volume (Gottesman & Hanson, 2005). Most of the remaining cells in the brain consist of smaller cells called **glial cells**. These cells act as a kind of glue to help hold neurons together. The word *glial* is derived from the Greek word for "glue." Glial cells also have other functions. They support the nervous system by nourishing neurons, removing their waste products, and assisting them in communicating with one another (Helmuth, 2001). Recently, scientists discovered that glial cells in the spinal cord also serve to amplify pain signals (Watkins & Maier, 2003).

Glial cells serve yet another important function: they form the **myelin sheath**, a fatty layer of cells that, like the insulation that wraps around electrical wires, acts as a protective shield on many axons. The insulation provided by the myelin sheath helps speed transmission of neural impulses, thus allowing muscles to move more efficiently and smoothly.

As shown in Figure 2.1, myelinated axons resemble a string of sausages that are pinched in at "the waist" at various points, creating gaps called **nodes of Ranvier**. The neural impulse appears to jump from node to node as it speeds down the axon. Because myelin sheaths are white, the parts of the nervous system that contain myelinated axons are referred to as "white matter."

Multiple sclerosis (MS) is a chronic and often crippling disease of the central nervous system that results in the eventual destruction of the myelin sheath on nerve cells (Vastag, 2001). Some 350,000 Americans suffer from MS, which typically strikes its victims when they are between the ages of twenty and forty (Cowan & Kandel, 2001; Jacobs, Munschauer, & Pullicino, 2000). The loss of myelin slows the transmission of nerve impulses. This leads to a range of symptoms; in the most severe cases, the person loses the ability to speak, walk, write, or even breathe.

How Neurons Communicate

The human brain is densely packed with more than 100 billion neurons, perhaps as many as a trillion or more (Johnson, 1994). From the time we are born, as we begin learning about the world around us, our brains become an increasingly complex network of some 100 trillion connections between neurons (Blakeslee, 2003). These complex assemblages of cells form intricate circuits in the brain that allow us to interpret the world around us and respond to external stimuli, as well as to organize our behavior, think, feel, and use language.

Neurons accomplish these tasks by sending messages to one another. Let us break down the process into smaller steps to see how it works.

Both inside and outside the neuron are electrically charged atoms and molecules called **ions**. Like the poles of a battery, ions have either a positive (+) or negative (−) charge. The movements of ions across the cell wall, or *cell membrane*, cause electrochemical changes in the cell that generate an electrical signal to travel down the cell's axon in the form of a neural impulse. The most important ions in this process are two types of positively charged ions, *sodium* ions and *potassium* ions. The movement of ions through the cell membrane is controlled by a series of gates, or tiny doors, that open to allow ions to enter the cell and close to shut them out.

When a neuron is at rest (not being stimulated), the gates that control the passage of sodium ions are closed. A greater concentration of positively charged sodium ions remains outside the cell, causing the cell to have a slightly negative charge, called a **resting potential**, relative to the surrounding fluid. The resting potential of a neuron is about −70 millivolts (mV) (a millivolt is one-thousandth of a volt). Like a charged battery sitting on a shelf, a neuron in the resting state holds a store of potential energy that can be used to generate ("fire") a neural impulse in response to stimulation. It awaits a source of stimulation that will temporarily reverse the electrical charges within the cell, causing it to fire.

Figure 2.2   An Action Potential

When a neuron in a resting state is stimulated, sodium gates in the cell membrane open, allowing positively charged sodium ions to rush into the cell. When stimulation is sufficiently strong, the cell suddenly shifts from a negative to a positive charge. The sudden reversal of charge is an action potential, an electrical charge that shoots down the axon, momentarily reversing the charge as it goes along the cell membrane. Once the action potential passes, sodium gates close, preventing further inflows of positively charged sodium ions, and the cell pumps out positively charged ions, mostly potassium ions. This restores the cell's negatively charged resting state, allowing it to fire again in response to stimulation.

CONCEPT 2.7

An action potential is generated according to the all-or-none principle—it is produced only if the level of excitation is sufficient.

depolarization   A positive shift in the electrical charge in the neuron's resting potential, making it less negatively charged.

action potential   An abrupt change from a negative to a positive charge of a nerve cell, also called a neural impulse.

all-or-none principle   The principle by which neurons will fire only when a change in the level of excitation occurs that is sufficient to produce an action potential.

refractory period   A temporary state in which a neuron is unable to fire in response to continued stimulation.

When the cell is stimulated, usually by neurotransmitters released from adjoining neurons, sodium gates at the base of the axon open. Positively charged sodium ions from the surrounding fluid then rush in, causing the area inside the cell membrane at the point of excitation to become less negatively charged. This process is called **depolarization**. When stimulation is sufficiently strong, as when enough of a neurotransmitter is present, depolarization quickly spreads along the axon. When this wave of depolarization reaches a critical threshold, the neuron abruptly shifts from a negative charge to a positive charge of about +40 mV. The sudden reversal of electrical charge is called an **action potential**, or *neural impulse*. The action potential shoots down the entire length of the axon as a wave of changing electrical charges. We refer to this action as the "firing" of a neuron, or as a *spike* (see Figure 2.2).

Once an action potential reaches the end of an axon, it causes the release of neurotransmitters from the terminal buttons that carry the neural message to the next neuron. Action potentials are generated according to the **all-or-none principle**. A neuron will fire completely (generate an action potential) if sufficient stimulation is available, or it will not fire; there is no halfway point. Different axons generate action potentials of different speeds, depending on such characteristics as their thickness (generally the thicker the axon, the faster the speed) and whether or not they are covered with a myelin sheath (which speeds transmission). Speeds of action potentials range from between two miles an hour to a few hundred miles an hour. Even the most rapid neural impulses are much slower than a speeding bullet, which travels at the rate of several hundred miles a minute. Neural impulses reach their destinations in small fractions of seconds—fast enough to pull your hand in an instant from a burning surface, but perhaps not fast enough to avoid a burn.

For about one-thousandth of a second (one millisecond) after firing, a neuron busies itself preparing to fire again. Sodium gates along the cell membrane close, preventing further inflows of positively charged sodium ions into the cell. The cell pumps out positively charged ions, mostly potassium ions, and as it rids itself of these positive ions, the neuron's negatively charged resting potential is restored. Then, in a slower process, the cell restores the electrochemical balance by pumping out sodium ions and drawing in some potassium ions, making it possible for another action potential to occur. But during the time these changes are occurring, called a **refractory period**, the neuron, like a gun being reloaded, is temporarily incapable of firing. But *temporarily* truly means *temporarily,* for a neuron can "reload" hundreds of times per second.

Neurotransmitters: The Nervous System's Chemical Messengers

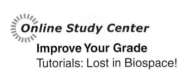

CONCEPT 2.8

When the neural impulse reaches the axon's terminal buttons, it triggers the release of chemicals that either increase or decrease the likelihood that neighboring cells will fire.

Neurons don't actually touch. As you read about earlier, they are separated by a tiny fluid-filled gap called a synapse, which measures less than a millionth of an inch across. Neural impulses cannot jump even this tiniest of gaps. They must be ferried across the synapse by chemical agents or messengers called neurotransmitters. When a neuron fires, tiny vesicles (or sacs) in the axon's terminal buttons release molecules of neurotransmitters, which then move out into the synaptic gap, like a flotilla of ships casting off into the sea (see Figure 2.3). Neurotransmitters carry messages that control activities ranging from contraction of muscles to move our bodies, to stimulation of glands to release hormones, to the psychological states of thinking and emotion.

Each specific type of neurotransmitter has a particular chemical structure, or three-dimensional shape. It fits into only one kind of **receptor site**, like a key fitting into a lock. When neurotransmitters dock at receptor sites, they lock into place, causing chemical changes in the receiving (or *postsynaptic*) neuron. These changes have either an *excitatory effect* or an *inhibitory effect*. Excitatory effects make an action potential more likely to occur. Inhibitory effects put the brakes on an action potential, making it less likely to occur. Some neurotransmitters have excitatory effects, others inhibitory effects, and still others have both excitatory and inhibitory effects. The nervous system depends on a balance between excitation and inhibition, or the turning on and turning off of neurons, in order to function smoothly and efficiently (Chih, Engelman, & Scheiffele, 2005).

Figure 2.3   How Neurons Communicate
Neural impulses are carried by neurotransmitters released by the terminal buttons of the transmitting neuron. These chemical messengers travel across the tiny synapse and are taken up by receptor sites on the dendrites of the receiving neuron. Neurotransmitter molecules that do not dock at receptor sites are decomposed in the synaptic gap or are reabsorbed by the transmitting neuron.

Online Study Center

Improve Your Grade
Tutorials: Lost in Biospace!

receptor site   A site on the receiving neuron in which neurotransmitters dock.

Several processes normally prevent excitatory neurotransmitters from continuing to stimulate a receiving cell. One process, called **reuptake**, is nature's own version of recycling. Through reuptake, neurotransmitters not taken up by the receiving cell are reabsorbed by their vesicles to be used again. In another process, **enzymes** in the synapse break down neurotransmitters, which are then eliminated from the body in the urine. In yet another process, terminal buttons release **neuromodulators**, chemicals that either increase or decrease the sensitivity of the receiving neuron to neurotransmitters.

Normal psychological functioning depends on the smooth transmission of messages between neurons in the brain. Your ability to think clearly, move your arms and legs at will, feel pain or emotions like joy, fear, or anger—everything you do, feel, or think—depends on neurotransmitters. When the body produces too little or too much neurotransmitter, problems may occur. Sometimes receptor sites allow too many neurotransmitter molecules to dock, or they do not accept neurotransmitters properly. Excesses or deficits of particular neurotransmitters in the brain, or irregularities in how they function, are associated with many disorders. For example, irregularities in neurotransmitter functioning are linked to eating disorders (see Chapter 8) and to depression and schizophrenia (see Chapter 13).

Drugs or chemicals that block the actions of neurotransmitters by occupying their receptor sites are called **antagonists**. By locking into these receptor sites, antagonists prevent transmission of the messages carried by the neurotransmitter (Gründer, Carlsson, & Wong, 2003). Consider *dopamine*, a neurotransmitter involved in controlling muscle contractions and in learning, memory, and emotional processing. It is of special interest to psychologists because irregularities in the utilization of dopamine in the brain may help explain the development of **schizophrenia**, a severe mental disorder affecting between 2 and 3 million people in the United States (McGuire, 2000). People with schizophrenia may experience **hallucinations** (the phenomenon of "hearing voices" or seeing things that are not there) and **delusions**—fixed, false ideas, such as believing that aliens have taken over their bodies. *Antipsychotic drugs* are antagonists that block receptor sites for dopamine (Gründer, Carlsson, & Wong, 2003). They help control hallucinations and delusional thinking in many schizophrenia patients (see Chapter 14).

Parkinson's disease is a degenerative brain disease that leads to a progressive loss of motor function, or physical movement (Carroll, 2004). Parkinson's sufferers experience tremors (shakiness), muscle rigidity and stiffness, and difficulty walking and controlling the movements of their fingers and hands. These symptoms result from the loss of dopamine-producing cells in an area of the brain

CONCEPT 2.9
Irregularities in neurotransmitter functioning are implicated in many psychological disorders, including eating disorders, depression, and schizophrenia.

reuptake   The process by which neurotransmitters are reabsorbed by the transmitting neuron.

enzymes   Organic substances that produce certain chemical changes in other organic substances through a catalytic action.

neuromodulators   Chemicals released in the nervous system that influence the sensitivity of the receiving neuron to neurotransmitters.

antagonists   Drugs that block the actions of neurotransmitters by occupying the receptor sites in which the neurotransmitters dock.

schizophrenia   A severe and chronic psychological disorder characterized by disturbances in thinking, perception, emotions, and behavior.

hallucinations   Perceptions experienced in the absence of external stimuli.

delusions   Fixed but patently false beliefs, such as believing that one is being hounded by demons.

Parkinson's disease   A progressive brain disease involving destruction of dopamine-producing brain cells and characterized by muscle tremors, shakiness, rigidity, and difficulty in walking and controlling fine body movements.

Michael J. Fox
Michael J. Fox quit his starring role in a hit TV show to focus his efforts on fighting Parkinson's disease, the degenerative brain disease from which he was suffering.

involved in regulating body movement. According to one expert, "Dopamine is like the oil in the engine of a car. . . . If the oil is there, the car runs smoothly. If not, it seizes up" (cited in Carroll, 2004, p. F5).   Parkinson's affects an estimated 1.5 million Americans, including former heavyweight boxing champion Muhammad Ali and actor Michael J. Fox ("NSAID Use," 2003). Genetic factors play a key role in determining susceptibility to the disease (Bonifati et al., 2003; Nussbaum & Ellis, 2003).

In contrast to antagonists, which compete with neurotransmitters at the same receptor sites, other drugs, called **agonists**, enhance the activity of neurotransmitters. Agonists work by either increasing the availability or effectiveness of neurotransmitters or by binding to their receptor sites and mimicking their actions. The mild **stimulant** caffeine, for example, increases the availability of a neurotransmitter called *glutamate,* an excitatory neurotransmitter that helps keep the central nervous system aroused (Goff & Coyle, 2001).

Stronger stimulants, such as **amphetamines** and cocaine, are agonists that increase the availability of dopamine in the brain by blocking its reuptake by the transmitting neuron. Since dopamine is a key neurotransmitter in neural pathways in the brain that regulate states of pleasure, increased availability of dopamine in these pathways may account for the pleasurable "high" these drugs produce (Friedman, 2002; Kauer, 2003; Leyton et al., 2002). (We'll return to this topic in Chapter 4.).

Alcohol and antianxiety drugs like Valium act as agonists by increasing the sensitivity of receptor sites to the inhibitory neurotransmitter *gamma-aminobutyric acid* (GABA). GABA regulates nervous activity by preventing neurons from overly exciting their neighbors. Thus, drugs that boost GABA's effects have a calming or relaxing effect. Reduced levels of GABA in the brain may play a role in emotional disorders in which anxiety is a core feature, such as panic disorder (Goddard et al., 2001).

The neurotransmitter *norepinephrine* (also called *noradrenaline*) is a chemical cousin of the hormone *epinephrine* (also called *adrenaline*). Norepinephrine does double duty as a neurotransmitter and a hormone (see Module 2.6). Another neurotransmitter, *serotonin,* functions mostly as an inhibitory neurotransmitter in regulating emotional responses, feelings of satiation after eating, and sleep.

Drugs that help relieve depression, called **antidepressants**, are agonists that increase the levels or activity of norepinephrine and serotonin in the brain. The widely used antidepressant *fluoxetine* (brand name Prozac) increases the availability of serotonin by interfering with the reuptake of the chemical by the transmitting neuron (discussed further in Chapter 14).

Did you know that the brain naturally produces neurotransmitters that are chemical cousins to narcotic drugs like morphine and heroin? In a classic research study, Candace Pert and Solomon Snyder (1973) traced morphine in the brain of an animal to see where it would be taken up. Once they found the receptor sites (locks) for the drug, they searched out the keys that would fit into them. The chemicals they discovered are inhibitory neurotransmitters called **endorphins** (short for *endogenous morphine,* morphine that "develops from within"). (Narcotics and other psychoactive drugs are discussed further in Chapter 4.)

Endorphins are the body's natural painkillers (Watkins & Maier, 2003). They are similar in chemical structure to narcotic drugs. Like morphine, heroin, and other narcotics, they deaden pain by fitting into receptor sites for chemicals that carry pain messages to the brain, thereby locking out pain messages. They also produce feelings of well-being and pleasure and may contribute to the "runner's high" experienced by many long-distance runners. Morphine and heroin are agonists, since they mimic the effects of naturally occurring endorphins on the body.

agonists Drugs that either increase the availability or effectiveness of neurotransmitters or mimic their actions.

stimulant A drug that activates the central nervous system, such as cocaine or nicotine.

amphetamines A class of synthetically derived stimulant drugs, such as methamphetamine or "speed."

antidepressants Drugs that combat depression by affecting the levels or activity of neurotransmitters in the brain.

endorphins Natural chemicals released in the brain that have pain-killing and pleasure-inducing effects.

MODULE 2.1 REVIEW

Neurons: The Body's Wiring

RECITE IT

What is a neuron?

- A neuron is a nerve cell, the basic building block of the nervous system through which information in the form of neural impulses is transmitted.

What are the parts of a neuron?

- Like other cells, neurons have a cell body, or soma, that houses the cell nucleus and carries out the metabolic work of the cell. Each neuron also has an axon, a long cable that conducts outgoing messages (neural impulses) to other neurons, as well as dendrites, which are fibers that receive neural messages from other neurons. Terminal buttons are swellings at the ends of the axon that release neurotransmitters, which are chemical messengers that carry the message to adjacent neurons.

What are the types of neurons and types of cells found in the nervous system?

- The nervous system has three types of neurons: sensory neurons, which carry information from sensory organs and internal bodily organs and tissues to the spinal cord and brain; motor neurons, which carry messages from the central nervous system to the muscles and inner organs; and interneurons, which connect neurons with each other.

- The nervous system has two types of cells: neurons, the nerve cells that conduct neural impulses, and glial cells, which support and nourish neurons. Glial cells also form the myelin sheath that covers some axons and that speeds transmission of neural impulses.

How is a neural impulse generated and transmitted from one neuron to another?

- Neural impulses are electrochemical events. When a neuron is stimulated beyond a threshold level, there is a rapid shift in its polarity from a negative to a positive charge. This reversal of charge, called an action potential or neural impulse, is generated along the length of the axon to the terminal buttons.

- When a neural impulse reaches the terminal buttons, it triggers the release of neurotransmitters, the chemical messengers that carry the message across the synapse to neighboring neurons. Neurotransmitters can have either excitatory or inhibitory effects on the neurons at which they dock.

What roles do neurotransmitters play in psychological functioning?

- Neurotransmitters are involved in many aspects of psychological functioning, including thinking and emotional response. Irregularities in the functioning of particular neurotransmitters are implicated in various disorders, including schizophrenia and depression.

RECALL IT

1. The part of the neuron that houses the cell nucleus is the _____.

2. The nervous system has three types of neurons: _____ neurons, which transmit sensory information to the spinal cord; _____ neurons, which transmit commands to muscles that control body movements and to glands, causing them to release hormones; and _____, which connect neurons to neurons.

3. Which of the following is *not* correct?
   a. A myelin sheath helps speed transmission of neural impulses.
   b. The myelin sheath is formed by glial cells.
   c. Myelin sheaths are white.
   d. Myelin covers all parts of a neuron except the axon.

4. When a neuron is at rest,
   a. a greater concentration of sodium ions remains outside the nerve cell.
   b. the cell has a slightly positive charge (relative to surrounding fluid).
   c. the state is known as an action potential.
   d. it is in a state of depolarization.

5. The terminal buttons at the end of the axon release _____ that carry the signal across the synapse and dock at receptor sites on the receiving neuron.

THINK ABOUT IT

- Why is a neuron in a resting state like a battery sitting on a shelf?

- What is an action potential? How is it generated? What happens when it reaches the end of an axon?

- A scientist develops a drug that blocks the actions of cocaine by locking into the same receptor sites as cocaine. So long as a person is taking the drug, cocaine will no longer produce a high. Would this drug be an antagonist or an agonist to cocaine? Why?

The Nervous System: Your Body's Information Superhighway

- How is the nervous system organized?
- What are spinal reflexes?
- What is the autonomic nervous system?
- What is the relationship between the sympathetic and parasympathetic divisions of the autonomic nervous system?

CONCEPT 2.10

The nervous system has two major parts: the central nervous system, which consists of the brain and spinal cord, and the peripheral nervous system, which consists of the nerves that connect the central nervous system to sensory organs, muscles, and glands.

Inside your body is an information superhighway that conducts information in the form of neural impulses. This superhighway, the **nervous system**, is an intricate network of neurons that are organized in a complex communication network. The nervous system is divided into two major parts, the *central nervous system* and the *peripheral nervous system* (see Figure 2.4).

The Central Nervous System: Your Body's Master Control Unit

The **central nervous system** consists of the brain and spinal cord. You can compare these two components to the central processing unit of a computer: together they constitute a master control system that regulates everything in your body, from the rate at which your heart beats, to the movements of your eyes as you scan these words, to your higher mental processes, such as thinking and reasoning. The central nervous system also enables you to sense the world around you and make sense of the sensations you experience (see Chapter 3).

The crowning glory of your central nervous system is your brain, that wondrous organ that regulates life processes and that enables you to think, plan, and create. Fortunately, this tender mass of tissue is cushioned in a hard, bony shell called the skull.

As you'll see in Module 2.3, one way of studying the brain is by exploring its three major parts: the hindbrain, or lower brain; the midbrain; and the forebrain, the highest region where thoughts and your sense of self "live." This module will consider the other major part of the central nervous system, the spinal cord, which is the brain's link to the peripheral nervous system.

Central Nervous System { Brain
Spinal cord

Peripheral Nervous System

Figure 2.4 Parts of the Nervous System
The nervous system has two major divisions, the central nervous system (brain and spinal cord) and the peripheral nervous system, which connects the central nervous system with sensory organs, muscles, and glands.

The Spinal Cord The **spinal cord**, a column of nerves nearly as thick as your thumb, is literally an extension of the brain. It begins at the base of your brain and runs down the center of your back, ending just below the waist. This cord is a neural pathway that transmits information between the brain and the peripheral nervous system. It receives incoming information from your sense organs and other

(a) The Knee-Jerk Reflex

(b) The Withdrawal Reflex

Figure 2.5 Anatomy of a Spinal Reflex
Tapping the knee *(a)* sends a signal through a sensory neuron to the spinal cord, where the information is transmitted directly to a motor neuron, which in turn signals muscles in the thigh to contract, causing the leg to kick forward. Touching a hot stove *(b)* sends a signal through a sensory neuron to the spinal cord, where it is relayed through an interneuron to a motor neuron, which signals muscles in the hand to contract, causing the hand to withdraw from the hot object.

CONCEPT 2.11

The spinal cord is an information highway that conducts information between the brain and the peripheral nervous system.

nervous system The network of nerve cells for communicating and processing information from within and outside the body.

central nervous system The part of the nervous system that consists of the brain and spinal cord.

spinal cord The column of nerves that transmits information between the brain and the peripheral nervous system.

spine The protective bony column that houses the spinal cord.

reflex An automatic, unlearned response to particular stimuli.

spinal reflex A reflex controlled at the level of the spinal cord that may involve as few as two neurons.

peripheral body parts and carries outgoing commands from your brain to muscles, glands, and organs throughout your body.

The spinal cord is encased in a protective bony column called the **spine** (also called the *spinal column*) that runs down the middle of the back. Despite this protection, it can suffer injury. In severe spinal cord injuries, signals cannot be transmitted between the brain and the peripheral organs, which can result in paralysis and an inability to breathe on one's own.

The spinal cord is not simply a conduit for the neural transmission of signals between the brain and the peripheral nervous system. It also controls some *spinal reflexes* that let you respond as quickly as possible to particular types of stimuli. A **reflex** is an automatic, unlearned reaction to a stimulus; a **spinal reflex** is a reflex controlled at the level of the spinal cord: in other words, a reflex that bypasses the brain. An example of a spinal reflex is the jerk your knee gives when a doctor who's examining you taps it lightly with a hammer. Some spinal reflexes, including the knee-jerk response, involve just two neurons, one sensory neuron and one motor neuron (see Figure 2.5). In other cases, such as the reflexive withdrawal of the hand upon touching a hot object, a third neuron in the spinal cord, an interneuron, transmits information from the incoming sensory neuron to the outgoing motor neuron.

Spinal reflexes allow us to respond almost instantly and with great efficiency to particular stimuli. The knee-jerk reflex takes a mere fifty milliseconds from the time the knee is tapped until the time the leg jerks forward (as compared with the hundreds of milliseconds it takes to voluntarily flex your leg). To appreciate the value of spinal reflexes, recall the times you've pulled your hand away from a hot stove or blinked when a gust of wind sent particles of debris hurtling toward your eyeballs. By saving the many milliseconds it would take to send a message to your brain, have it interpreted, and have a command sent back along the spinal highway to motor neurons, spinal reflexes can spell the difference between a minor injury and a serious one.

The Peripheral Nervous System: Your Body's Link to the Outside World

The central nervous system depends on a constant flow of information from the internal organs and sensory receptors, as well as on its ability to convey information to the muscles and glands that it regulates. These functions are performed by the **peripheral nervous system** (PNS), the part of the nervous system that connects your central nervous system with other parts of your body. Concept Chart 2.2 shows the organization of the nervous system.

Without the peripheral nervous system, your brain would be like a computer chip disconnected from the computer hardware, a marvelous feat of engineering but unable to function. Without information transmitted from your sensory organs—your eyes, ears, tongue, nose, and skin—you would be unable to perceive the world. Without commands sent to your muscles, you would be unable to act upon the world. The PNS is divided into two parts, the *somatic nervous system* and the *autonomic nervous system*.

The Somatic Nervous System   The **somatic nervous system** transmits messages between your central nervous system and your sensory organs and muscles. It not only enables you to perceive the world, but it also ensures that your muscles will

CONCEPT 2.12

The somatic nervous system is the part of the peripheral nervous system that controls voluntary movements of muscles and relays information between the central nervous system and sensory organs.

CONCEPT CHART 2.2   Organization of the Nervous System

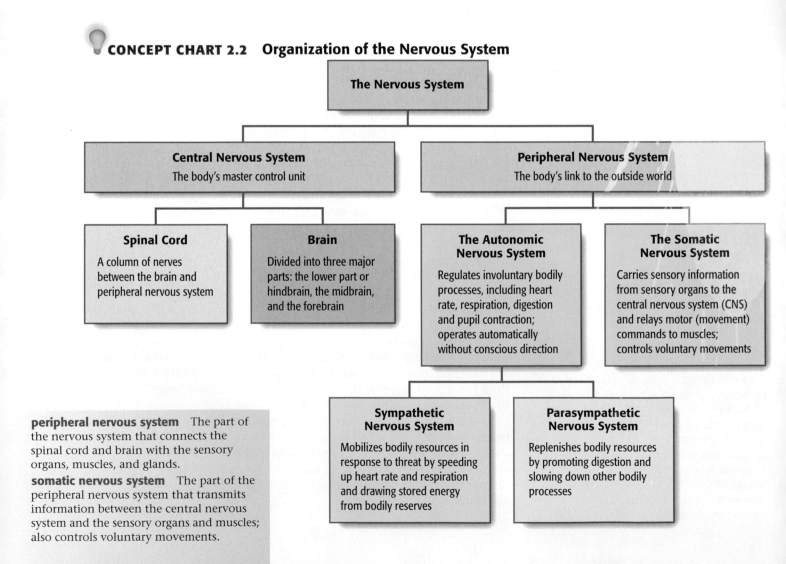

peripheral nervous system   The part of the nervous system that connects the spinal cord and brain with the sensory organs, muscles, and glands.

somatic nervous system   The part of the peripheral nervous system that transmits information between the central nervous system and the sensory organs and muscles; also controls voluntary movements.

contract in response to an intentional command or a stimulus that triggers a reflex action. And, finally, it regulates subtle movements that maintain posture and balance.

The somatic nervous system is composed of sensory and motor neurons. As noted in Module 2.1, sensory neurons send messages from the sensory organs to the spinal cord and brain. In this way, information about stimuli that impinge upon our senses (light, sound, odors, taste, pressure on our skin, and so on) is transmitted to the central nervous system. The brain then interprets these messages, allowing you to perceive a beautiful sunset or a threatening animal, distinguish a whisper from the rustling of the wind, determine whether you are sitting in a reclining or upright position, and experience sensations of warmth, cold, and pain.

The central nervous system processes the information it receives and sends messages back through motor neurons that control movements such as walking and running, pulling your arm back reflexively upon touching a hot object, raising and lowering your arms at will, and the tiny, almost imperceptible, movements that regulate your balance and posture.

CONCEPT 2.13

Like an automatic pilot, the autonomic nervous system, a division of the peripheral nervous system, automatically controls such involuntary bodily processes as heartbeat, respiration, and digestion.

CONCEPT 2.14

The autonomic nervous system is divided into two branches that have largely opposite effects: the sympathetic nervous system, the body's alarm system that heightens states of arousal, and the parasympathetic nervous system, which tones down bodily arousal and helps replenish bodily resources.

The Autonomic Nervous System   The **autonomic nervous system (ANS)** is the part of the peripheral nervous system that controls such internal bodily processes as heartbeat, respiration, digestion, and dilation of the pupils. The ANS does these tasks automatically, regulating these vital bodily processes without your having to think about them. (*Autonomic* means "automatic.") You can, however, exercise some voluntary control over some of these functions, as by intentionally breathing more rapidly or slowly.

The ANS is itself composed of two divisions, or branches, that have largely opposite effects, the *sympathetic nervous system* and the *parasympathetic nervous system*. Figure 2.6 compares these two branches. The **sympathetic nervous system** speeds up bodily processes and draws energy from stored reserves. It accelerates your heart rate and breathing rate and provides more fuel or energy for the body to use by releasing sugar (glucose) from the liver. This extra energy allows the body to meet increased physical demands during vigorous physical activity or times of stress. Activation of the sympathetic nervous system is often accompanied by strong emotions, such as anxiety, fear, or anger. That is why we sense our hearts beating faster when we are anxious or angered.

The **parasympathetic nervous system** fosters bodily processes, such as digestion, that replenish stores of energy. Digestion provides the body with fuel by converting food into glucose (blood sugar), which cells use as a source of energy. The parasympathetic nervous system also helps conserve energy by slowing down other bodily processes. The sympathetic nervous system speeds up your heart; the parasympathetic slows it down. The sympathetic nervous system turns off (inhibits) digestive activity; the parasympathetic turns it on. The parasympathetic system is in command whenever you are relaxing or digesting a meal.

autonomic nervous system   The part of the peripheral nervous system that automatically regulates involuntary bodily processes, such as breathing, heart rate, and digestion.

sympathetic nervous system   The branch of the autonomic nervous system that accelerates bodily processes and releases the stores of energy needed to meet increased physical demands.

parasympathetic nervous system   The branch of the autonomic nervous system that regulates bodily processes, such as digestion, that replenish stores of energy.

Figure 2.6 Opposing Effects of Sympathetic and Parasympathetic Nervous Systems
The sympathetic and parasympathetic nervous systems have generally opposite effects. For example, the sympathetic system accelerates heart rate and breathing, whereas the parasympathetic system slows down these bodily responses and helps restore spent bodily resources by stimulating digestive processes.

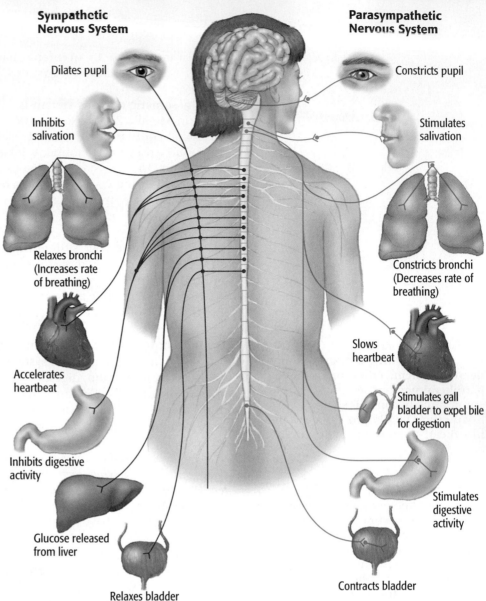

Sympathetic Nervous System

Dilates pupil

Inhibits salivation

Relaxes bronchi (Increases rate of breathing)

Accelerates heartbeat

Inhibits digestive activity

Glucose released from liver

Relaxes bladder

Parasympathetic Nervous System

Constricts pupil

Stimulates salivation

Constricts bronchi (Decreases rate of breathing)

Slows heartbeat

Stimulates gall bladder to expel bile for digestion

Stimulates digestive activity

Contracts bladder

MODULE 2.2 REVIEW

The Nervous System: Your Body's Information Superhighway

RECITE IT

How is the nervous system organized?

• The major divisions of the nervous system are the central nervous system, which consists of the brain and spinal cord, and the peripheral nervous system, which connects the central nervous system to the rest of the body.

What are spinal reflexes?

• Spinal reflexes are automatic, unlearned responses that are controlled at the level of the spinal cord. They may involve as few as two neurons.

How is the peripheral nervous system organized?

• The peripheral nervous system is divided into the somatic nervous system and autonomic nervous system. The autonomic nervous system is further divided into the sympathetic and parasympathetic branches.

What is the autonomic nervous system?

• The autonomic nervous system is the part of the peripheral nervous system that automatically regulates such internal bodily processes as heartbeat, respiration, digestion, and pupil dilation.

What is the relationship between the sympathetic and parasympathetic divisions of the autonomic nervous system?

• These two divisions have largely opposite effects. The sympathetic nervous system speeds up bodily processes that expend energy, while the parasympathetic system slows down some bodily processes and fosters others, such as digestion, that replenish stores of energy.

RECALL IT

1. The two major divisions in the human nervous system are the _____ nervous system and the _____ nervous system.

2. Spinal _____ are automatic, unlearned responses that are controlled at the level of the spinal cord.

3. The peripheral nervous system is divided into the _____ nervous system, which conveys information between the central nervous system and sensory organs and muscles, and the _____ nervous system, which automatically controls internal bodily processes.

4. The parasympathetic nervous system
   a. slows down some bodily processes, which helps conserve stores of energy.
   b. is part of the central nervous system.
   c. is responsible for the "fight-or-flight" response.
   d. draws energy from bodily reserves to meet stressful demands on the body.

THINK ABOUT IT

• As you're running to catch a bus, your breathing quickens, and your heart starts pounding. Which part of your peripheral nervous system kicks into gear at such a time?

• Were there any times in your life when a spinal reflex prevented serious injury?

MODULE 2.3

The Brain: Your Crowning Glory

■ **How is the brain organized, and what are the functions of its various parts?**

■ **How is the cerebral cortex organized?**

■ **What are the major functions associated with the four lobes of the cerebral cortex?**

 CONCEPT 2.15

The brain is divided into three major parts: the hindbrain, the midbrain, and the forebrain.

That wondrous organ, the human brain, consists of billions of nerve cells linked together through synaptic connections into very complex networks (Saffran & Schwartz, 2003). Let us take a tour of the brain, beginning with the lowest level, the *hindbrain*—the part of the brain where the spinal cord enters the skull and widens. We then work our way upward, first to the *midbrain*, which lies above the hindbrain, and then to the *forebrain*, which lies in the highest part of the brain. Concept Chart 2.3 shows these major brain structures.

The Hindbrain

hindbrain   The lowest and, in evolutionary terms, oldest part of the brain; includes the medulla, pons, and cerebellum.

medulla   A structure in the hindbrain involved in regulating basic life functions, such as heartbeat and respiration.

pons   A structure in the hindbrain involved with sleep and wakefulness.

brainstem   The "stalk" in the lower part of the brain that connects the spinal cord to higher regions of the brain.

The lowest part of the brain, the **hindbrain**, is also the oldest part in evolutionary terms. The hindbrain includes the *medulla, pons,* and *cerebellum*. These structures control such basic life-support functions as breathing and heart rate.

The **medulla** and **pons** contain sensory neurons that transmit information from the spinal cord to the forebrain. The medulla is the section of the hindbrain that lies closest to the spinal cord. It forms the marrow, or core, of the **brainstem**, the "stem" or "stalk" that connects the spinal cord to the higher regions of the brain (see Figure 2.7). (*Medulla* is a Latin word meaning "marrow.") The medulla controls such vital bodily processes as heart rate and breathing, and such reflexes as swallowing, coughing, and sneezing. The pons lies directly above the medulla.

CONCEPT CHART 2.3 Major Structures of the Human Brain

Forebrain

Cerebral Cortex
Higher mental functions including thinking, language, learning, memory, emotions, and control of voluntary movement

Corpus Callosum
Bundle of nerve fibers that connect the two cerebral hemispheres

Thalamus
Relay station for sorting and integrating sensory input; regulation of sleep-wake cycles

Limbic System
Emotional processing, motivated behavior, and learning and memory functioning; consists of amygdala, hippocampus, parts of the hypothalamus and thalamus, and nearby structures

Basal Ganglia
Regulation of movement and coordination

Midbrain

Reticular Formation
Regulation of attentional processes and states of alertness and arousal

Spinal cord

Hindbrain

Pons
Conveying sensory information from the spinal cord to the forebrain; regulation of states of wakefulness and sleep

Cerebellum
Regulation of balance and coordination

Medulla
Conveying sensory information from the spinal cord to the forebrain; control of basic bodily processes including heart rate and breathing and certain reflexes

 CONCEPT 2.16
The hindbrain, the lowest part of the brain, contains structures that control basic bodily functions, such as breathing and heart rate.

 CONCEPT 2.17
The midbrain contains nerve pathways for relaying messages between the hindbrain and the forebrain, as well as structures that control some automatic movements.

cerebellum A structure in the hindbrain involved in controlling coordination and balance.
midbrain The part of the brain that lies on top of the hindbrain and below the forebrain.

It contains nerve fibers that conduct information from the spinal cord and lower parts of the brain through the midbrain to the forebrain. It also helps regulate states of wakefulness and sleep.

Located behind the pons, the **cerebellum** is involved in controlling balance and coordination. Injury to the cerebellum can lead not only to problems with balance and coordination, but also to difficulties in initiating voluntary movements, such as lifting an arm or a leg.

As we continue our brief tour of the brain, we come to the midbrain, the part of the brain that serves as a major relay station for information passing between the lower brain and the forebrain.

The Midbrain

The **midbrain**, which lies above the hindbrain, contains nerve pathways that connect the hindbrain with the forebrain. Structures in the midbrain perform important roles, including control of automatic movements of the eye muscles, which allows you to keep your eyes focused on an object as your head changes position in relation to the object. Parts of the midbrain make up the brainstem (see Figure 2.7).

Figure 2.7   The Brainstem
The brainstem reaches from the top of the spinal cord up through the midbrain to the forebrain. It connects the spinal cord to the higher regions of the brain.

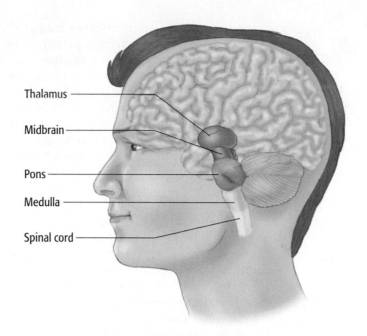

Thalamus

Midbrain

Pons

Medulla

Spinal cord

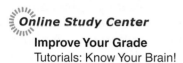
Online Study Center

Improve Your Grade
Tutorials: Know Your Brain!

The **reticular formation** (also called the *reticular activating system,* or *RAS*) is a weblike network of neurons that rises from the hindbrain and passes through the midbrain to the thalamus in the forebrain. The reticular formation plays a key role in regulating states of attention, alertness, and arousal. It screens visual and auditory information, filtering out irrelevant information while allowing important information to reach the higher processing centers of the brain, even when we are asleep. Thanks to the reticular formation, we can screen out familiar sounds that might disturb our sleep, such as the sound of a nearby fan or air conditioner, but be awakened by sounds that may require our immediate attention, such as a fire alarm or a child's faint cry. Depressants, such as alcohol, dampen the activity of the reticular formation, leading to drowsiness and diminished alertness.

CONCEPT 2.18
The largest part of the brain, the forebrain, controls higher mental functions, such as thinking, problem solving, use of language, planning, and memory.

reticular formation   A weblike formation of neurons involved in regulating states of attention, alertness, and arousal.
forebrain   The largest and uppermost part of the brain; contains the thalamus, hypothalamus, limbic system, basal ganglia, and cerebral cortex.
thalamus   A structure in the forebrain that serves as a relay station for sensory information and that plays a key role in regulating states of wakefulness and sleep.
basal ganglia   An assemblage of neurons lying in the forebrain that is important in controlling movement and coordination.
hypothalamus   A small, pea-sized structure in the forebrain that helps regulate many vital bodily functions, including body temperature and reproduction, as well as emotional states, aggression, and response to stress.

The Forebrain

The **forebrain**, located toward the top and front of the brain, is the largest part of the brain. The major structures in the forebrain are the *thalamus,* the *hypothalamus,* the *limbic system,* and the *cerebral cortex.*

The **thalamus** is a relay station near the middle of the brain. It consists of a pair of egg-shaped structures that route information from sense receptors for touch, vision, hearing, and taste (but not smell) to the processing centers of the brain located in the cerebral cortex. The thalamus first sorts through sensory information, sending information about vision to one area, information about hearing to another, and so on. From these relay stations in the thalamus, the information is then transmitted to the appropriate parts of the cerebral cortex for processing. The thalamus helps regulate states of sleep and wakefulness (Balkin et al., 2002). It also receives input from the **basal ganglia**, a cluster of nerve cells in the forebrain involved in regulating coordination and voluntary movement, such as walking.

Just beneath the thalamus is the **hypothalamus** (*hypo* meaning "under"), a pea-sized structure weighing a mere four grams. Despite its small size, the hypothalamus helps regulate many vital bodily functions, such as hunger and thirst, fluid concentrations, body temperature, and reproductive processes, as well as emotional states, aggressive behavior, and response to stress. As you will see in Module 2.6, the hypothalamus is part of the endocrine system, and it triggers the release of hormones throughout the body. Electrical stimulation of particular parts of the hypothalamus in other mammals, such as rats, can generate, or "switch on," stereotypical behavior patterns that range from eating to attacking rivals, courting behaviors, mounting attempts, and caring for the young.

The **limbic system** is a group of interconnected structures that includes the *amygdala, hippocampus,* parts of the *thalamus* and *hypothalamus,* and other nearby interconnected structures (see Concept Chart 2.3). The limbic system is much more evolved in mammals than in lower animals. It plays an important role in memory and emotional processing.

Referring again to Concept Chart 2.3, we find within the limbic system the **amygdala**, a set of two almond-shaped structures (*amygdala* is derived from the Greek root for "almond"). The amygdala helps regulate states of emotional arousal, especially states of aggression, rage, and fear that are evoked by unpleasant or aversive stimuli (see Chapter 8) (Hamann et al., 2003; LeDoux, 2000).

The **hippocampus** resembles a "sea horse," from which it derives its name. Located just behind the amygdala, it plays an important role in the formation of memories (see Chapter 6).

Our journey through the brain now brings us to the uppermost part of the forebrain, the cerebral cortex. Because it is responsible for our ability to think, use language, calculate, organize, and create, we devote the entire next section to a discussion of the cerebral cortex.

The Cerebral Cortex: The Brain's Thinking, Calculating, Organizing, and Creative Center

The **cerebral cortex** forms the thin, outer layer of the largest part of the forebrain, which is called the **cerebrum**. The cerebrum consists of two large masses, the right and left **cerebral hemispheres**. The cerebral cortex covers the cerebrum like a cap and derives its name from the Latin words for brain (*cerebrum*) and bark (*cortex*). A thick bundle of nerve fibers, called the **corpus callosum** (Latin for "thick body" or "hard body") connects the cerebral hemispheres and forms a pathway by which the hemispheres share information and communicate with each other. Structures in the brain that lie beneath the cerebral cortex are called *subcortical* structures (*sub,* meaning "below," the cortex).

Though a mere one-eighth of an inch thick, no thicker than a napkin, the cerebral cortex accounts for more than 80 percent of the brain's total mass. The cortex consists of unmyelinated neurons and so is called gray matter because of its grayish appearance. It owes its wrinkled or convoluted appearance to contours created by ridges and valleys. These contours enable its large surface area to be packed tightly within the confines of the skull (see Concept Chart 2.3). Its massive size in relation to the other parts of the brain reflects the amount of the brain devoted to higher mental functions such as thinking, language use, and problem solving. Only in humans does the cortex account for so great a portion of the brain (see Figure 2.8). The cortex also controls voluntary movement, states of motivation and emotional arousal, and processing of sensory information.

CONCEPT 2.19
The limbic system plays an important role in the regulation of memory and emotions.

CONCEPT 2.20
The cerebrum is divided into two hemispheres and is covered by a thin, outer layer, the cerebral cortex, that is responsible for higher mental functions.

CONCEPT 2.21
The corpus callosum is a bundle of nerve fibers that connects the two hemispheres of the brain, allowing them to share information.

CONCEPT 2.22
Each cerebral hemisphere has four main parts, or lobes: the occipital, parietal, frontal, and temporal lobes.

Figure 2.8 The Size of the Cerebral Cortex in Humans and Other Animals
The cerebral cortex accounts for a much greater portion of the brain in humans than in other animals.

Frog   Rat   Cat   Chimpanzee   Human

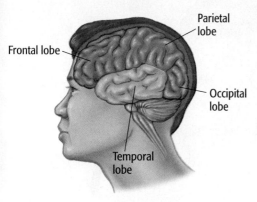

Figure 2.9   Lobes of the Cerebral Cortex
The cerebral cortex is divided into four parts, or lobes: the occipital, parietal, frontal, and temporal lobes.

TABLE 2.1   The Lobes of the Cerebral Cortex

Structure	Functions
Occipital lobes	Process visual information, giving rise to sensations of vision
Parietal lobes	Process information relating to sensations of touch, pressure, temperature (hot and cold), pain, and body movement
Frontal lobes	Control motor responses and higher mental functions, such as thinking, planning, problem solving, decision making, and accessing and acting on stored memories
Temporal lobes	Process auditory information, giving rise to sensations of sound

Each hemisphere of the cerebral cortex is divided into four parts, or *lobes,* as shown in Figure 2.9. So, for example, when we speak of the left frontal lobe, we mean the frontal lobe contained in the left hemisphere, not the frontal lobe contained in the right hemisphere. The functions of the lobes are summarized in Table 2.1. Generally speaking, each of the cerebral hemispheres controls feeling and movement on the opposite side of the body.

The **occipital lobes**, located in the back of the head, process visual information. We experience vision when a source of light stimulates receptors in the eyes and causes neurons in the occipital lobes to fire (discussed further in Chapter 3). Perhaps you have had the experience of "seeing stars" after being struck on this region of the head.

The **parietal lobes** are located on the sides of the brain, directly above and in front of the occipital lobes. At the front of the parietal lobes lies a strip of nerve cells called the **somatosensory cortex**, which processes sensory information received from receptors in the skin giving rise to our experience of touch, pressure, temperature (hotness or coldness), and pain. Like your eyes and ears, your skin is a sensory organ that provides information about the world. The somatosensory cortex also receives information from receptors in your muscles and joints to keep you aware of the position of the parts of your body as you move about.

Figure 2.10 illustrates how specific parts of the somatosensory cortex correspond to sensory information (touch, pressure, pain, and temperature) received from specific parts of the body. For example, electrical stimulation of particular parts of the somatosensory cortex can make it seem as though your shoulder or your leg were experiencing touch or pressure.

The strange-looking "figure" shown in Figure 2.11 is not some creature from the latest *Star Wars* installment. Sensory information from some parts of the body is transmitted to larger areas of the somatosensory cortex than is sensory information from other parts. This is because the brain devotes more of its capabilities to parts of the body that require greater sensitivity or control, such as the hands. Nor are the parts of the body represented in the somatosensory cortex in a way that directly corresponds to where they lie in the body. For example, sensory input from the genitals projects to an area that lies beneath the part receiving input from the toes, and the area that responds to stimulation of the tongue does not lie within the area that responds to stimulation of the lips (see Figure 2.10). No one can say why this is so, but each of us knows the precise areas of our body that are touched. We know, for instance, when it is our lips that are touched and not our tongue, and vice versa.

The **frontal lobes** are located in the front part of the brain, just behind the forehead. Scientists call the frontal lobes the "executive center" of the brain, because they believe they contain your "you": the part that accesses your memories, mulls things over, has self-awareness, and decides that the red plaid shirt is just

limbic system   A formation of structures in the forebrain that includes the hippocampus, amygdala, and parts of the thalamus and hypothalamus; is involved in memory and emotional processing.

amygdala   A set of almond-shaped structures in the limbic system believed to play an important role in aggression, rage, and fear.

hippocampus   A structure in the limbic system involved in memory formation.

cerebral cortex   The wrinkled, outer layer of gray matter that covers the cerebral hemispheres; controls higher mental functions, such as thought and language.

cerebrum   The largest mass of the forebrain, consisting of two cerebral hemispheres.

cerebral hemispheres   The right and left masses of the cerebrum, which are joined by the corpus callosum.

corpus callosum   The thick bundle of nerve fibers that connects the two cerebral hemispheres.

occipital lobes   The parts of the cerebral cortex, located at the back of both cerebral hemispheres, that process visual stimuli.

parietal lobes   The parts of the cerebral cortex, located on the side of each cerebral hemisphere, that process bodily sensations.

somatosensory cortex   The part of the parietal lobe that processes information about touch and pressure on the skin, as well as the position of the parts of our bodies as we move about.

frontal lobes   The parts of the cerebral cortex, located at the front of the cerebral hemispheres, that are considered the "executive center" of the brain because of their role in higher mental functions.

Figure 2.10   Somatosensory Cortex and Motor Cortex
Here we see how various parts of the body are mapped in the somatosensory cortex and the motor cortex. The mapping structure of the two cortexes is nearly a mirror image. But notice how body parts are not mapped onto these cortexes in relation to where they actually lie in the body. The size of the projections of the parts of the body in each cortex corresponds to the degree of sensitivity or need for control of these parts.

Somatosensory Cortex

Motor Cortex

Figure 2.11   A Creature from *Star Wars*?
Actually, this is an artist's rendering of how we would appear if the size of our body parts were in proportion to the areas of the somatosensory cortex that process sensory information from these parts. Because much more cortex is devoted to the fingers and hands than to elbows or thighs, we can discern much finer differences in sensations of touch with our fingertips.

motor cortex   A region of the frontal lobes involved in regulating body movement.

temporal lobes   The parts of the cerebral cortex lying beneath and somewhat behind the frontal lobes that are involved in processing auditory stimuli.

association areas   Parts of the cerebral cortex that piece together sensory information to form meaningful perceptions of the world and perform higher mental functions.

"too retro." Like the central processing unit of a computer, parts of the frontal lobes retrieve memories from storage, place them in active memory, manipulate them, and make decisions based on them. For example, your frontal lobes pull sensory memories about visual cues, sounds, odors, and even tastes from storage, so that the second time you see that oblong-shaped red pepper sitting innocently in your bowl of Kung Pao chicken, you'll remember not to bite into it. Your frontal lobes also allow you to solve problems, make decisions, plan actions, weigh evidence, and carry out coordinated actions.

Recent evidence further indicates that the frontal lobes are involved in processing emotional states, such as happiness and sadness (Davidson et al., 2000, 2002). In addition, they enable you to suppress tendencies to act on impulse, such as when you restrain yourself from telling your boss or professor what you really think of him or her.

The frontal lobes contain the **motor cortex**, which is located just across the border that separates them from the parietal lobes (see Figures 2.9 and 2.10). The motor cortex controls voluntary movements of specific parts of the body. For example, some neurons in the motor cortex control movements of the hands. When an electrode is used to stimulate a certain part of the motor cortex (a painless procedure sometimes used during brain surgery), muscles on the other side of the body contract. Depending on the electrode placement, the patient may lift a finger or tense a muscle in the leg. The representation of the body on the motor cortex is similar to that mapped out on the somatosensory cortex, as you can see in Figure 2.10.

The **temporal lobes** lie beneath and somewhat behind the frontal lobes, directly above the ears. The temporal lobes receive and process sensory information from the ears, producing the experience of hearing (discussed in Chapter 3).

The great majority of cortex consists of **association areas**, which are found in each lobe. These areas are more highly developed in humans than in other organisms. They are responsible for performing higher mental functions, such as piecing together sensory input to form meaningful perceptions of the world, thinking, learning, producing and understanding speech, solving math problems, planning activities, creating masterworks of architecture, and perhaps even composing the next hit song.

We cannot identify the precise locations where higher mental functions occur. Association areas are linked within intricate networks of neurons connecting many parts of the brain, the architecture of which we are only beginning to discern.

Online Study Center

Resources
Weblinks: The Brain Center;
The Whole Brain Atlas

CONCEPT 2.23
Most of the cerebral cortex consists of association areas that are responsible for higher mental functions.

MODULE 2.3 REVIEW

The Brain: Your Crowning Glory

RECITE IT

How is the brain organized, and what are the functions of its various parts?

- The brain has three major sections. The hindbrain, which houses the medulla, pons, and cerebellum, is involved in controlling basic bodily functions. The midbrain houses nerve bundles that relay messages between the hindbrain and the forebrain; it also houses structures that help regulate automatic movement and the weblike reticular formation that is involved in regulating attention, alertness, and arousal as well as filtering out irrelevant sensory information. The forebrain is the largest part of the brain; its major structures are the thalamus, the hypothalamus, the limbic system, and the cerebral cortex.

- The thalamus relays sensory information to the cerebral cortex and helps regulate states of sleep and wakefulness.

- The hypothalamus plays a key role in controlling many vital bodily processes.

- The limbic system, which includes the amygdala, hippocampus, and parts of the thalamus and hypothalamus, is involved in memory and emotional processing.

- The cerebral cortex is responsible for processing sensory information, for higher mental functions such as thought, problem solving, and language, and for controlling voluntary movement, among other functions.

How is the cerebral cortex organized?

- Each hemisphere of the cerebral cortex has four lobes: the frontal, parietal, temporal, and occipital lobes. The corpus callosum is a nerve bundle that connects the two hemispheres.

What are the major functions associated with the four lobes of the cerebral cortex?

- The occipital lobes are primarily involved with vision; the parietal lobes, with somatosensory processing; the temporal lobes, with hearing; and the frontal lobes, with motor control and higher mental functions, including retrieving and acting upon stored memories, solving problems, making decisions, and carrying out coordinated actions.

RECALL IT

1. In an evolutionary sense, the "oldest" part of the brain is the _____.

2. Match the following parts of the brain with the functions they control: (a) medulla; (b) cerebellum; (c) thalamus; (d) cerebral cortex.
   i.   balance and coordination
   ii. thinking and organizing
   iii. relay of sensory information to the cerebral cortex
   iv. heart rate and breathing

3. Which of the following is *not* correct? The cerebral cortex
   a. is the part of the brain most directly responsible for reasoning, language, and problem solving.
   b. is divided into four lobes.
   c. forms the outer layer of the cerebral hemispheres.
   d. accounts for a much smaller percentage of brain mass in humans than in other animals.

4. Most of the cerebral cortex consists of _____ areas that are responsible for integrating sensory information and performing higher mental functions.

THINK ABOUT IT

• Why does the text refer to your brain as your "crowning glory"?

• A person suffers a serious fall and sustains severe damage to the back of the head. What sensory processes are most likely to be affected by the injury?

MODULE 2.4

Methods of Studying the Brain

■ What recording and imaging techniques are used to study brain functioning?
■ What experimental methods do scientists use to study brain functioning?

CONCEPT 2.24

Modern technology provides ways of studying the structure and function of the brain without the need for invasive techniques.

EEG (electroencephalograph) A device that records electrical activity in the brain.

CT (computed tomography) scan A computer-enhanced imaging technique in which an X-ray beam is passed through the body at different angles to generate a three-dimensional image of bodily structures (also called a *CAT* scan, short for *computed axial tomography*).

PET (positron emission tomography) scan An imaging technique in which a radioactive sugar tracer is injected into the bloodstream and used to measure levels of activity of various parts of the brain.

MRI (magnetic resonance imaging) A technique that uses a magnetic field to create a computerized image of internal bodily structures.

Scientists use various methods of studying brain structures and their functioning. One method is to observe the effects of diseases or injuries on the brain. As a result of this type of observation, scientists have known for nearly two centuries that damage to the left side of the brain is connected with loss of sensation or movement on the right side of the body, and vice versa. Thus, we recognize that the brain's motor control mechanisms must cross over from each cerebral hemisphere to the other side of the body.

Over the years, scientists have also used invasive experimental methods to study the brain at work, including surgical procedures. Today, thanks to advanced technology, they have other, less invasive recording and imaging methods at their disposal. Concept Chart 2.4 summarizes both types of methods.

Recording and Imaging Techniques

Today, we have available a range of techniques that allow us literally to peer into the working brain and other parts of the body without surgery. These techniques are used to diagnose brain diseases and survey brain damage, as well as to help us learn more about brain functioning. Neuroscientists can probe the brain while the subject is awake and alert.

The **EEG (electroencephalograph)** is an instrument that records electrical activity in the brain (see Figure 2.12). Electrodes are attached to the scalp to measure the electrical currents, or *brain waves*, that are conducted between them. The EEG

💡 CONCEPT CHART 2.4   Methods of Studying the Brain

Recording and Imaging Techniques	Description
EEG (electroencephalograph)	A device that uses electrodes attached to the skull to record brain wave activity
CT (computed tomography) scan	A computer-enhanced X-ray technique that can provide images of the internal structures of the brain
PET (positron emission tomography) scan	A method that can provide a computer-generated image of the brain, formed by tracing the amounts of glucose used in different parts of the brain during different types of activity
MRI (magnetic resonance imaging)	A method of producing computerized images of the brain and other body parts by measuring the signals they emit when placed in a strong magnetic field

Experimental Techniques	Description
Lesioning	Destruction of brain tissue in order to observe the effects on behavior
Electrical recording	Placement of electrodes in brain tissue to record changes in electrical activity in response to particular stimuli
Electrical stimulation	The use of a mild electric current to observe the effects of stimulating various parts of the brain

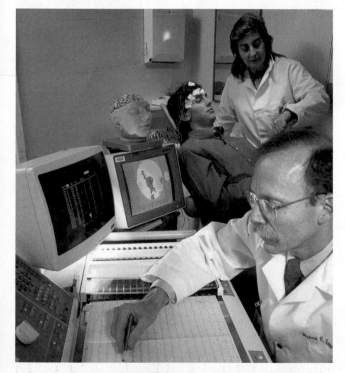

Figure 2.12   The Electroencephalograph (EEG) The EEG is a device that records electrical activity in the brain in the form of brain wave patterns. It is used to study the brains of people with physical or psychological disorders and to explore brain wave patterns during stages of sleep.

is used to study electrical activity in the brains of people with physical or psychological disorders and to explore brain wave patterns during stages of sleep.

The **CT (computed tomography) scan** (also called a *CAT* scan) is an imaging technique in which a computer measures the reflection of a narrow X-ray beam from various angles as it passes through the brain or other bodily structures; it thus produces a three-dimensional image of the inside of the body (see Figure 2.13). The CT scan can reveal brain abnormalities associated with blood clots, tumors, and brain injuries (Haydel et al., 2000). It is also used to explore structural abnormalities that may be present in the brains of people with schizophrenia or other severe psychological disorders.

Whereas the CT scan reveals information about the shape and size of structures in the brain, the **PET (positron emission tomography) scan** provides a computerized image of the brain and other organs at work. The subject receives an injection of a radioactive isotope that acts as a tracer in the bloodstream. How the tracer is metabolized (converted by cells into energy) in the brain reveals the parts of the brain that are more active than others. More active areas metabolize more of the tracer than less active ones (see Figure 2.14). The PET scan can reveal which parts of the brain are most active when we are reading and writing, daydreaming, listening to music, or experiencing emotions ("Brain Scans," 2000; Damasio et al., 2000). From these patterns, we can determine which parts of the brain are involved in particular functions.

MRI (magnetic resonance imaging) provides a detailed image of the brain or other body parts. To produce a brain image, a technician places the person's head within a doughnut-shaped device that emits a strong magnetic field, aligning the atoms that spin in the brain. The basic idea, according to the MRI's inventor, is to stuff a human being into a large magnet (Weed, 2003). A burst of radio waves

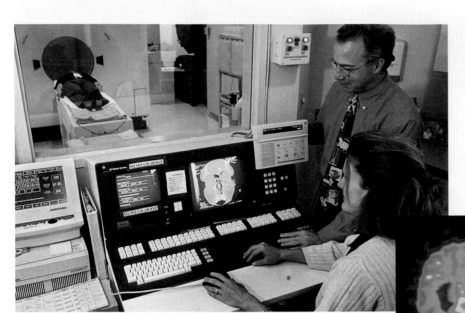

Figure 2.13 CT Scan
The CT scan provides a three-dimensional X-ray image of bodily structures. It can reveal structural abnormalities in the brain that may be associated with blood clots, tumors, brain injuries, or psychological disorders, such as schizophrenia.

Figure 2.14 PET Scan
The PET scan measures the metabolic activity of the brain. More active regions are highlighted in yellow and red, whereas less active regions are shown in blues and greens. Here we see PET scan images of the brain of an alcoholic patient during withdrawal. By comparing relative levels of brain activity following 10 days (top row) and 30 days (bottom row) of withdrawal, we can observe that the brain becomes more active with greater length of time without alcohol.

REALITY CHECK

THE CLAIM We use only 10 percent of our brains.

THE EVIDENCE This long-standing myth has become so ingrained in popular culture that many people just assume it must be true. Not only do we lack any scientific support for this belief, but the claim actually contradicts what we know about the human brain (Beyerstein, 1999). For example, brain-imaging studies show no large areas of the brain that remain inactive most of the time. Even during sleep, there are no completely inactive areas.

THE TAKE-AWAY MESSAGE Although we might not fully utilize our brains to our utmost creative potential, there is no basis to the belief that large parts of the brain, let alone 90 percent, lie unused.

directed at the person disrupts the atoms, which release signals as they become realigned. A computer then integrates the signals into an image of the brain.

A newer MRI technique, called *functional MRI (fMRI),* takes snapshots of the brain in action (see Figure 2.15). Whereas traditional MRI is limited to mapping brain structures, functional MRI is used to study both the function and the structure of the human brain.

Investigators use functional MRI to identify parts of the brain that are engaged when we perform particular tasks, such as seeing, hearing, remembering, using language, cooperating with others, and experiencing emotions, even romantic feelings of love (Berthoz et al., 2002; Ingram & Siegle, 2001; Rilling et al., 2002). Though the PET scan can also map brain functions, fMRI is less invasive in that it does not require injections of radioactive isotopes. fMRI is also used to examine brain abnormalities in people with psychological disorders such as autism (Allen & Courchesne, 2003) and schizophrenia (Barch et al., 2002).

Functional MRI may well have helped clear up a long-standing scientific mystery: why it is impossible to tickle yourself (Provine, 2004). Using this method, British researchers peered into the brains of people as they tickled themselves and as they were being tickled by a mechanical device (Begley, 2000c).The part of the brain that processes touch, the somatosensory cortex, showed more activity when people were being tickled than when they tickled themselves. When we tickle ourselves, the sensation we experience is expected and so it doesn't come as a surprise. The cerebellum, the brain structure involved in coordinating complex movements

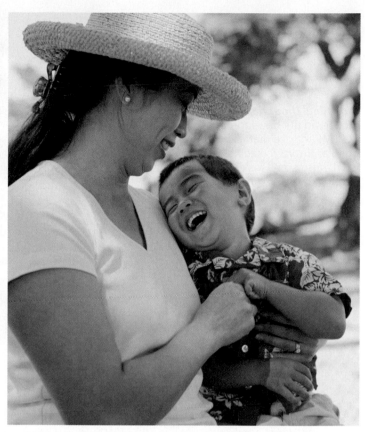

Figure 2.15 Functional Magnetic Resonance Imaging (fMRI)
Like the PET scan, the fMRI allows us to peer into the working brain. Here we see images of the brain when a person thinks about performing certain gestures (top), such as using a hammer or writing with a pen, and when actually performing these acts (bottom). The left hemisphere is depicted on the right side of the image, while the right hemisphere is shown on the left. Areas in red are associated with greater levels of brain activity.

A Ticklish Question   Why is it that you can't tickle yourself? Researchers using a brain-imaging technique believe they have the answer.

💡 **CONCEPT 2.25**
Experimental methods used to study brain functioning include lesioning, electrical recording, and electrical stimulation.

lesioning   In studies of brain functioning, the intentional destruction of brain tissue in order to observe the effects on behavior.

electrical recording   As a method of investigating brain functioning, a process of recording the electrical changes that occur in a specific neuron or groups of neurons in the brain in relation to particular activities or behaviors.

including tickling, sends a signal that blocks the "tickling message" from getting through to the somatosensory cortex. However, being tickled by someone else involves an unexpected sensation that the brain treats as a potential threat requiring attention, and so no blocking of the tickling message occurs. The brain mechanisms that enable us to distinguish between expected sensations, like self-tickling, and unexpected sensations, like being tickled by others, may have developed in early human history as a means of detecting the touch of a predator.

Experimental Methods

Scientists sometimes use invasive methods to investigate brain functioning. In one such method, called **lesioning**, the investigator destroys parts of the brain in experimental animals and then observes the effects. For example, destroying one part of a rhesus monkey's limbic system causes the animal to fly into a rage at the slightest provocation. But destroy another part of this system, and the monkey shows a placid response to all manner of provocation. Destroy one part of a rat's hypothalamus, and it gorges itself on food until it becomes extremely obese; destroy another part, and it stops eating. These experiments point to the parts of the brain involved in these and other forms of behavior.

Other experimental techniques for studying brain function include *electrical recording* and *electrical stimulation*. In **electrical recording**, electrodes are implanted into particular neurons, groups of neurons, or nerves in particular parts of the brain. These provide a record of electrical changes in response to particular stimuli. Some experimental techniques are so refined that investigators can record

Watching Thoughts   Dr. Keith Thulborn is a pioneer in the development of a powerful new MRI device that allows us to see the brain as it thinks (see Module 2.8). Images from these scans may help in the diagnosis and treatment of brain disorders.

electrical activity from a single brain cell. Using these methods, scientists discovered how individual neurons in the visual cortex respond to particular types of visual stimuli (see Chapter 3).

electrical stimulation   As a method of investigating brain functioning, a process of electrically stimulating particular parts of the brain to observe the effects on behavior.

With the technique of **electrical stimulation**, investigators pass a mild electric current through particular parts of the brain and observe the effects. In this way, they can learn which parts of the brain are involved in controlling which behaviors. For example, we mentioned earlier how stimulation of parts of the hypothalamus in rats and other animals switches on stereotypical behavior patterns.

MODULE 2.4 REVIEW

Methods of Studying the Brain

RECITE IT

What recording and imaging techniques are used to study brain functioning?

• These techniques include the EEG, CT scan, PET scan, and MRI.

What experimental methods do scientists use to study brain functioning?

• Lesioning is a method of destroying certain parts of the brains of laboratory animals in order to observe the effects.

• Electrical recording involves implanting electrodes in the brain to record changes in brain activity associated with certain activities or behaviors.

• Electrical stimulation entails passing a mild electric current through parts of the brain so that the effects on these parts can be observed.

RECALL IT

1. Which of the following is a computer-enhanced imaging technique that uses X-ray beams to study structural abnormalities of the brain?
   a. fMRI   c. CT scan
   b. PET scan   d. MRI

2. Functional MRI (fMRI)
   a. is used to study both brain structure and brain functioning.
   b. involves an invasive technique known as lesioning.
   c. is a controversial procedure with ethical implications.
   d. is based on a sophisticated type of X-ray technique.

3. In the experimental technique for brain study called lesioning,
   a. parts of the brain of living organisms are destroyed.
   b. electrodes are surgically implanted in the brain.
   c. parts of the brain are electrically stimulated to observe the effects on behavior.
   d. connections between the brain and spinal cord are severed.

THINK ABOUT IT

• What brain-imaging techniques do scientists use to study the functioning of the brain? to study the structures of the brain?

• What is your opinion about using animals in experimental brain research? What safeguards do you think should be observed in this kind of research?

MODULE 2.5

The Divided Brain: Specialization of Function

- What are the major differences between the left and right hemispheres?
- What determines handedness?
- What are the major causes of brain damage, and what effects do they have on psychological functioning?
- What can we learn about brain lateralization from studies of "split-brain" patients?

If you stub your left toe, cells in your right parietal lobe will "light up," producing sensations of pain. Conversely, a blow to your right toe will register in your left parietal lobe. This is because the sensory cortex in each hemisphere is connected to sensory receptors on the opposite sides of the body. Likewise, the motor cortex in your right frontal lobe controls the movements of the left side of your body, and vice versa. Thus, if we were to stimulate your left motor cortex in a certain spot, the fingers on your right hand would involuntarily contract. As we see next, evidence indicates that the right and left hemispheres are also specialized for certain types of functions.

The Brain at Work: Lateralization and Integration

CONCEPT 2.26

In most people, the left hemisphere is specialized for the use of language and logical analysis, while the right hemisphere is specialized for spatial processing and other nonverbal tasks.

The term **lateralization** refers to the division of functions between the right and left hemispheres (see Concept Chart 2.5) (Hoff, 2003; Peretz & Zatorre, 2005). Generally speaking, the left hemisphere in most people appears to be dominant for language abilities: speaking, reading, and writing. The left hemisphere also appears to be dominant for tasks requiring logical analysis, problem solving, and mathematical computations.

CONCEPT CHART 2.5   Lateralization of Brain Functions

Areas of Left-Hemisphere Dominance	Areas of Right-Hemisphere Dominance
Verbal functions (for right-handers and most left-handers), including spoken and written use of language, as well as logical analysis, problem solving, and mathematical computation	Nonverbal functions, including understanding spatial relationships (e.g., in jigsaw puzzles or maps), recognizing faces and interpreting gestures, perceiving musical pitches, and recognizing and expressing emotions

Language dominance is associated with handedness. For about 95 percent of right-handed people and even for about 70 percent of left-handed people, the left hemisphere is dominant for language functions (Damasio & Damasio, 1992; Pinker, 1994; Springer & Deutsch, 1993). For about 15 percent of left-handed people, the right hemisphere is dominant for language functions. The other 15 percent of left-handers show patterns of mixed dominance.

The right hemisphere in most people appears dominant for nonverbal processing, such as understanding spatial relationships (e.g., piecing together puzzles, arranging blocks to match designs, reading maps), recognizing faces, interpreting people's gestures and facial expressions, processing the pitch of musical sounds, and perceiving and expressing emotions.

Despite differences in functionality of the two hemispheres, people are not either "left-brained" or "right-brained" (Benson, 2003a; Gazzaniga, 1995). The functions of the hemispheres largely overlap, and messages rapidly zip back and

lateralization The specialization of the right and left cerebral hemispheres for particular functions.

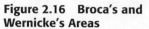

Figure 2.16   Broca's and Wernicke's Areas
Broca's area is an egg-shaped part of the frontal lobe that plays a key role in the production of speech. Wernicke's area, which is located in the temporal lobe, enables us to understand written or spoken language.

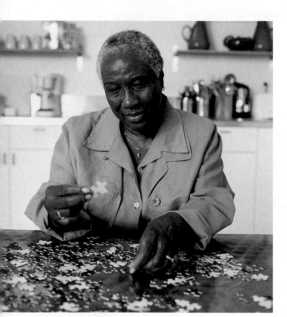

Lateralization of Brain Function   The right hemisphere is dominant for spatial tasks, such as solving jigsaw puzzles, whereas the left hemisphere is dominant for verbal tasks, such as speaking, reading, and writing.

forth across the corpus callosum, the bundle of nerve fibers that connects the hemispheres. Even though one hemisphere or the other may be dominant for a particular task, both hemispheres share the work in performing most tasks.

The French surgeon Paul Broca (1824–1880) was one of the pioneers in the discovery of the language areas of the brain. His most important discovery involved a male patient, fifty-one years old, who was admitted to the ward suffering from gangrene in his leg. The patient was also nearly unable to speak. He understood clearly what he heard, but his verbal utterances were limited primarily to one meaningless sound (*tan*).

The patient died a few days after being admitted. While conducting an autopsy, Broca found that an egg-shaped part of the left frontal lobe of the patient's brain had degenerated. The surgeon concluded that this area of the brain, now known as **Broca's area** in his honor, is essential to the production of speech (see Figure 2.16).

Broca's area is one of the brain's two vital language areas. The other, which is in the left temporal lobe, is **Wernicke's area** (see Figure 2.16), named after the German researcher Karl Wernicke (1848–1905). Wernicke's area is responsible for our ability to understand language in written or spoken form. Wernicke's and Broca's areas are connected by nerve fibers, so that there is an ongoing interaction between understanding language and being able to produce it or express it. Significant damage to Broca's area or Wernicke's area, or to the nerve connections between them, can lead to different forms of **aphasia**, the loss or impairment of the ability to understand or express language.

Handedness: Why Are People Not More Even-Handed?

CONCEPT 2.27
Scientists suspect that handedness is strongly influenced by genetics.

Broca's area   An area of the left frontal lobe involved in speech.
Wernicke's area   An area of the left temporal lobe involved in processing written and spoken language.
aphasia   Loss or impairment of the ability to understand or express language.

Though we may not be "right-brained" or "left-brained," most of us are primarily either right-handed or left-handed. Handedness runs in families (see Table 2.2), which points to the role of either heredity or family influences in its development. We don't yet know what causes handedness, but many scientists believe that genetic factors play an important role (Corballis, 2001; Jones & Martin, 2001). However, handedness differs in about one in five sets of identical twins (one twin may be right-handed, the other left-handed). Identical twins have identical genes, so if handedness were purely genetic in origin, we would not observe this difference. Thus, factors other than genetics must also contribute to handedness (Rosenbaum, 2000).

Already a Rightie? The proportions of fetuses sucking their right or left thumbs parallel those of right-handed and left-handed people in the population, suggesting that handedness preferences may begin to develop before birth.

TABLE 2.2   Parents' Handedness and Child's Odds of Being Left-Handed

Parents Who Are Left-Handed	Child's Odds
Neither parent	1 in 50
One parent	1 in 6
Both parents	1 in 2

Source: Springer and Deutsch, 1993.

Social factors that may influence handedness include family pressures on children to use their right hand for writing. Prenatal hormones may also play a role, as evidence links left-handedness to high levels of male sex hormones during prenatal development (Coren, 1992). This may explain why twice as many males as females turn out to be left-handed. Hormonal influences also depend on genetic factors, so the picture becomes yet more complex. Evidence does indicate that handedness preferences begin to develop before birth. In an ultrasound-based study of more than two hundred fetuses, researchers found that more than 95 percent of them sucked their right thumbs, while fewer than 5 percent sucked their left thumbs (Hepper, Shahidullah, & White, 1990). These percentages correspond closely to the distribution of right-handers and left-handers in the population.

Whatever the origins of handedness may be, forcibly imposing right-handedness on children may cause them to become secretive about using their left hands (e.g., by switching to the left hand when they are not being observed) and to develop emotional problems.

Brain Plasticity

CONCEPT 2.28
The brain is capable of reorganizing itself to a certain extent to adapt to new functions, sometimes even when half of it is surgically removed.

In some cases of epilepsy and other neurological disorders, damage to one of the cerebral hemispheres is so severe that it must be surgically removed. Remarkably, most patients who undergo this radical procedure are able to function normally, at least when the operation is performed before the age of thirteen. Until that age, the functions of the left and right hemispheres appear to be quite flexible, or "plastic." When children under thirteen have the left (language-dominant) hemisphere removed, the right hemisphere is able to reorganize itself and adapt to new demands by developing language functions (Zuger, 1997). This is an amazing example of adaptability, perhaps even more amazing than the ability of a lizard to regenerate a lost limb.

TRY THIS OUT

Which Way Does Your Hair Swirl?

Are you looking for something to do while waiting out long delays at airports? Why not follow the lead of National Cancer Institute investigator Amar Klar and examine the swirls on people's heads? While observing people at airports and shopping malls, Klar noticed an interesting pattern in the swirl directions of the hair on their heads (Klar, 2003; Pearson, 2003). More than 95 percent of right-handers had hair that swirled clockwise, whereas left-handers and people who were ambidextrous were equally likely to have swirls in either direction. Perhaps the same genes are involved in controlling both hair swirls and handedness.

TRY THIS OUT

Learning Through Volunteering

To learn first-hand about the effects of stroke and brain injuries, consider spending a few hours a week volunteering at a local rehabilitation center or clinic. Volunteers may assist occupational therapists, physical therapists, rehabilitation counselors, and other professionals. Or they may be asked to spend time with patients in the role of a companion or attentive listener. The work can be personally rewarding and give you the opportunity to see whether you might be well suited for a career in rehabilitation.

Stroke   Most strokes occur when a clot blocks the flow of blood in an artery serving the brain, resulting in damage or death to brain cells. In this photo of a stroke victim's brain, the area of dead tissue appears as the dark blue area on the right.

Also rather amazing is that the visual cortex can switch gears when it is not needed for processing visual information. For example, the visual cortex in a person with blindness may reorganize itself to process sensory information from touch receptors in the fingertips, enabling the person to read Braille (L.G. Cohen et al., 1997).

The ability of the brain to adapt and reorganize itself following trauma or surgical alteration is called **plasticity**. When one part of the brain is damaged by injury or disease, another part of the brain may take over its functions to a certain extent. Seeking to capitalize on the brain's ability to heal itself, physicians are now stimulating healthy neurons in the brains of stroke victims, hoping that these neurons will take over the functions that stroke-damaged neurons are no longer able to serve (Carmichael, 2004a). In the most common form of **stroke**, a clot blocks an artery that supplies blood to the brain, depriving brain cells of life-sustaining oxygen and causing damage or death to the affected brain tissue (Adler, 2004). The result can be paralysis, loss of speech, and even death. Each year, some 500,000 Americans suffer a stroke, and some 150,000 die as a result (see the nearby Try This Out feature).

As with patients who undergo surgical removal of one of their cerebral hemispheres, plasticity is greatest among young children whose brains are not fully lateralized. How the brain accomplishes these feats of reorganization, whether in building new circuitry or altering existing circuitry, remains uncertain. Yet, as in the case of many brain injuries and strokes, there are limits to how well the brain can compensate for damage to brain tissue.

CONCEPT 2.29

Brain damage can result in subtle or profound consequences in physical and psychological functioning.

plasticity   The ability of the brain to adapt itself after trauma or surgical alteration.

stroke   The sudden loss of consciousness and resulting paralysis, loss of sensation, and other disability or death resulting from blockage of blood to a part of the brain or from bleeding in the brain.

Brain Damage and Psychological Functioning

Many people have made remarkable recoveries from brain damage resulting from stroke or head trauma, perhaps none more remarkable than the recovery of Phineas Gage, a nineteenth-century railroad worker whose case astounded the medical practitioners of his time. One day in 1848, Gage, a 25-year-old construction foreman, was packing blasting powder for a dynamite charge and accidentally set it off. The blast shot an inch-thick metal rod through his cheek and brain and out through the top of his head (Ratiu & Talos, 2004). Gage fell to the ground, but to the astonishment of his co-workers, he soon stood up, dusted himself off, and spoke to them. He was helped home, where his wounds were bandaged.

Figure 2.17   Yet He Survived
This illustration of the path of the metal rod through Phineas Gage's skull shows just how remarkable it was that he survived.

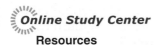

Online Study Center

Resources
Weblinks: Phineas Gage
Information Page

prefrontal cortex The area of the frontal lobe that lies in front of the motor cortex and that is involved in higher mental functions, including thinking, planning, impulse control, and weighing the consequences of behavior.

laceration A type of brain trauma in which a foreign object, such as a bullet or a piece of shrapnel, pierces the skull and injures the brain.

concussion A jarring of the brain caused by a blow to the head.

Gage's wounds healed within two months, and he was able to function despite the massive head injury he had suffered. However, changes in his personality soon began to occur, suggesting more subtle forms of brain damage. The formerly polite, conscientious worker became an irresponsible drifter (Jennings, 1999). He also started brawling and drinking heavily. Those who knew him before the accident said, "Gage is no longer Gage."

Gage's skull is now on display at Harvard University. The trajectory of the metal rod is obvious (see Figure 2.17). With near-surgical precision, it apparently missed the parts of the brain controlling language and movement but damaged the **prefrontal cortex**, the area of the frontal lobe that lies in front of the motor cortex.

The prefrontal cortex is the part of the brain that weighs the consequences of our actions, makes plans for the future, solves problems, makes decisions, and constrains impulsive behavior. Scientists suspect that it is where the seat of intelligence is located (Duncan et al., 2000). Contemporary research with patients who have suffered damage to the prefrontal cortex also points to the important role that this part of the brain plays in making moral judgments or decisions (e.g., S. W. Anderson et al., 1999). Scientists think there may be a kind of "morality circuit" in the prefrontal cortex, which if damaged can impair the person's ability to adhere to moral and social codes.

Head Trauma In a head trauma, the brain is injured by a blow to, or jarring of, the head or by the piercing of the skull by a foreign object. The injury Gage suffered is called a **laceration**, a form of head trauma that occurs when a foreign object (a metal rod in Gage's case) penetrates the skull and damages the brain. The effects of a laceration can range from mild impairment to immediate death, depending on the location and extent of the injury. Damage to the frontal lobes can also lead to a range of psychological effects, including changes of mood and personality, as was the case for Phineas Gage.

Another form of head trauma is a **concussion**, an injury to the brain resulting from a blow to the head that may result in momentary loss of consciousness. A mild concussion suffered on the football field is not likely to have lasting consequences. But a severe concussion or repeated concussions can lead to permanent brain damage, which may include memory and attention deficits, emotional instability, and slurred speech (see the nearby Try This Out).

TRY THIS OUT

Raising Your Awareness About Disability

Volunteering at a rehabilitation center can help raise your awareness about the needs of people with disabilities. There are also things you can do on your own to become more aware of the challenges posed by sensory and motor disabilities. Here are some suggestions offered by Professors Stephen Wurst and Karen Wolford of SUNY Oswego: (1) to simulate a hand (motor) disability, splinter two fingers together on your dominant hand and go about your daily routine (excepting any activities, like driving, where it might pose a risk); (2) to simulate the challenge posed by mutism, try not talking for a specified period of time; and (3) to simulate an auditory disability, use ear plugs such as those found at your local pharmacy (being careful to avoid any activities in which lack of hearing might pose a risk). These exercises are merely simulations, but they can give you a glimpse into the kinds of challenges that people with disabilities face in their daily lives.

Research on Split-Brain Patients: Does the Left Hand Know What the Right Hand Is Doing?

Imagine that one side of your cerebral cortex could not communicate with the other side because the neural fiber that connects the two, the corpus callosum, was cut. You'd literally have a brain that was split in two parts. In the 1960s, neurosurgeons began treating some severe cases of **epilepsy** with a surgical procedure that split the brain in two by severing the corpus callosum.

Epilepsy is a neurological disorder characterized by seizures marked by sudden, violent neural discharges of electrical activity in the brain. In many cases, these discharges resemble a neural Ping-Pong match: the electrical discharges begin in one cerebral hemisphere and thunder into the other. As they bounce back and forth, they create a kind of wild electrical storm in the brain. Fortunately, most people with epilepsy are able to avoid or control seizures with medication. But for some, surgery is needed to prevent the electrical activity in one hemisphere from crossing into the other. Patients undergoing this surgery are known as **split-brain patients**.

Split-brain patients retain their intellectual abilities and their distinctive personalities, which is all the more remarkable given that the surgery prevents their two cerebral hemispheres from communicating. The two hemispheres do appear to be of two minds about certain things (Gazzaniga, 1999). We might sometimes joke that it seems as if our left hand doesn't know what our right hand is doing. But for split-brain patients, the joke strikes closer to home, as was illustrated in landmark research conducted by Nobel Prize winner Roger Sperry and his colleague Michael Gazzaniga.

In a typical experiment, these researchers placed a familiar object, such as a key, in the left hands of split-brain patients (Gazzaniga, 1992). When blindfolded, the patients could not name the object they were holding, but they were able to use the key to open a lock. The question is, *why?*

Recall that the somatosensory cortex in the right hemisphere processes sensory information from the left side of the body (the touch of a key placed in the left hand, for instance). Since the right hemisphere shares this information with the left hemisphere, speech centers in the left hemisphere can respond by naming the object that is felt by the left hand. Consequently, people whose brains function normally ordinarily have no trouble naming a familiar object placed in their left hands even if they can't see it.

Now consider the case of split-brain patients. For them, the right hemisphere cannot transmit information to the speech centers in the left hemisphere, so it is impossible for the patient to name an object held in the left hand. The right hemisphere literally cannot "say" what the left hand is holding (Gazzaniga, 1995). Yet despite the lack of ability to name the object, the right hemisphere recognizes the object by touch and can demonstrate how it is used through the use of hand movements.

In perception studies with split-brain patients, researchers briefly flash pictures of objects on a screen and then ask the patients to identify them by naming them or by selecting them from among a group of objects hidden behind the screen (see Figure 2.18). The experimenters vary whether the stimuli are projected to the left or the right visual cortex. If you look straight ahead and project a vertical line dividing your field of view into a right half and a left half, the area to the left of the line represents your left visual field. Information presented to the left visual field crosses over and is processed by the visual cortex in the right hemisphere. Conversely, information presented to the right of your field of view (to the right visual field) is projected to the visual cortex in the left hemisphere. (The visual cortex for each hemisphere is located in the occipital lobe.) For people with an intact corpus

---

CONCEPT 2.30
The results of split-brain operations show that, under some conditions, the right hand literally doesn't know what the left hand is doing.

---

epilepsy A neurological disorder characterized by seizures marked by sudden, violent discharges of electrical activity in the brain.

split-brain patients Persons whose corpus callosum has been surgically severed.

Figure 2.18   Split-Brain Study
The right part of this figure shows that information from the right half of the
visual field is transmitted to the occipital cortex in the left hemisphere;
conversely, information from the left half of the visual field goes to the right
occipital cortex for processing. In split-brain patients, information received by
one hemisphere cannot be transferred to the other.

In a typical study with split-brain patients, investigators present a visual
stimulus to each hemisphere individually. When an object, such as a pencil,
is flashed in the right visual field *(a)*, the visual information is transmitted to
the patient's left hemisphere. Since the left hemisphere controls language,
the patient can correctly name the object. But when visual information is
presented in the left visual field and transmitted to the nonverbal right
hemisphere *(b)*, the patient is unable to name it. However, the patient is
able to pick out the object by touch from a group of hidden objects when
using the left hand *(c)*, since the tactile information from the left hand projects
to the right hemisphere, which has already "seen" the object.

callosum, information is quickly exchanged between the hemispheres, but in split-
brain patients, one hemisphere cannot communicate with the other.

Now, let's say an image is flashed to the right visual field of a split-brain patient. The left hemisphere processes the information and the patient is able to
name the object ("I saw a pencil"). This is not surprising when you consider that
the left hemisphere in most people controls speech. But what happens when the
picture of the object is flashed on the left side of the screen, which projects information to the right hemisphere, the one without language function? In this case,

the patient cannot say what, if anything, is seen. The patient is likely to report, "I saw nothing." However, because the right hemisphere can recognize objects by touch, the patient is able to use the left hand to select the correct object from among those hidden behind the screen.

Findings from studies of split-brain patients help us understand the importance of the left hemisphere in speech and language production. Perhaps more revealing is the observation that split-brain patients appear to be quite normal in their outward behavior (Sperry, 1982). Apparently their brains are able to adopt new strategies for processing information and solving problems that do not rely on communication between the hemispheres. Once again, this speaks to the remarkable ability of the human brain to adapt to new demands.

MODULE 2.5 REVIEW

The Divided Brain: Specialization of Function

RECITE IT

What are the major differences between the left and right hemispheres?

- In most people, the left hemisphere appears to play a larger role in verbal tasks, including the use of language and logic, while the right hemisphere is specialized for tasks involving nonverbal processing, such as understanding spatial relationships, recognizing faces, and appreciating music and art.

What determines handedness?

- Genetic factors appear to be a strong determinant of handedness, although hormonal factors and social and cultural influences may also play a role.

What are the major causes of brain damage, and what effects do they have on psychological functioning?

- The major causes of brain damage are laceration, concussion, and stroke. The psychological effects of brain trauma can be profound impairments in speech, vision, memory, reasoning, motor skills, and personality.

What can we learn about brain lateralization from studies of "split-brain" patients?

- Studies of split-brain patients, whose left and right cerebral hemispheres are surgically disconnected, can help us better understand the specialized functions of each cerebral hemisphere.

RECALL IT

1. Whereas for most people the _____ hemisphere appears to be dominant for language functions, the _____ hemisphere appears to be dominant for nonverbal functions.

2. The part of the brain directly involved in speech production is called _____ area, and the area primarily responsible for the ability to understand written or spoken language is called _____ area.

3. Which of the following is *not* true?
   a. Handedness runs in families.
   b. Handedness is determined entirely by genetic factors.
   c. Researchers have found that the great majority of fetuses suck their right thumbs.
   d. Imposing right-handedness on left-handed children can lead to emotional problems.

THINK ABOUT IT

- Why is it incorrect to say that someone is either right-brained or left-brained?

- What are the risks of trying to impose right-handedness on left-handed children?

MODULE 2.6

The Endocrine System: The Body's Other Communication System

- What are the major endocrine glands?
- What roles do hormones play in behavior?

The nervous system is not the only means by which parts of the body communicate with each other. The *endocrine system* is also a communication system, although it is vastly slower than the nervous system. The messages it sends are conveyed through blood vessels rather than a network of nerves. The messengers it uses are hormones, which, as you may recall from Module 2.1, are chemical substances that help regulate bodily processes. Here we explore the endocrine system and the role that it plays in behavior.

Endocrine Glands: The Body's Pumping Stations

CONCEPT 2.31
Endocrine glands distributed throughout the body help coordinate many bodily functions.

The **endocrine system** is composed of glands located in various parts of the body that release secretions, called hormones, directly into the bloodstream. Figure 2.19 shows the location of many of the major endocrine glands in the body. Concept Chart 2.6 summarizes the functions of the hormones they release.

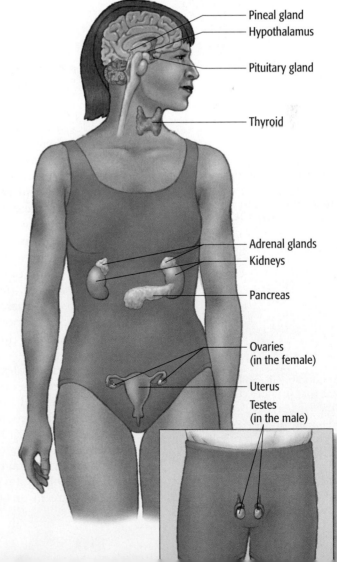

Figure 2.19   Major Glands of the Endocrine System
The endocrine system consists of glands that release secretions, called hormones, directly into the bloodstream.

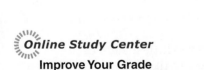
Online Study Center
  Improve Your Grade
  Tutorials: The Endocrine System

endocrine system   The body's system of glands that release their secretions, called hormones, directly into the bloodstream.

CONCEPT CHART 2.6   The Endocrine System

Gland/Hormone	Function
Pituitary gland	
Growth hormone	Stimulates growth, especially of bones
ACTH	Stimulates adrenal cortex to secrete cortical steroids
Oxytocin	Stimulates uterine contractions during childbirth and release of milk following childbirth
Hypothalamus	
Releasing factors	Stimulate the pituitary gland to release other hormones, including growth hormone
Pineal gland	
Melatonin	Helps regulate sleep-wake cycles
Pancreas	
Insulin	Facilitates entry of blood glucose (sugar) into cells; involved in regulation of blood sugar levels
Thyroid gland	
Thyroid hormones	Involved in regulating metabolic rate, growth, and maturation
Adrenal glands	
Cortical steroids	Help body cope with stress; promote muscle development; stimulate the liver to release stores of sugar
Epinephrine (adrenaline) and Norepinephrine (noradrenaline)	Speed up bodily processes, such as heart rate and breathing rate
Ovaries	
Estrogen	Fosters female sexual maturation; helps regulate menstrual cycle
Progesterone	Helps maintain pregnancy; helps regulate menstrual cycle
Testes	
Testosterone	Promotes sperm production; fosters male sexual differentiation during prenatal development; promotes sexual maturation in pubertal males

CONCEPT 2.32

Hormones are released by endocrine glands directly into your bloodstream, and from there they travel to specific receptor sites on target organs and issues.

pancreas An endocrine gland located near the stomach that produces the hormone insulin.

diabetes A metabolic disease involving the insufficient production of insulin or failure to efficiently use the insulin that is produced.

homeostasis The tendency of systems to maintain a steady, internally balanced state.

The endocrine system regulates important bodily processes, such as growth, reproduction, and metabolism. To do so, it relies on hormones to communicate its messages to organs and other bodily tissues. (The word *hormone* is derived from Greek roots that mean "to stimulate" or "to excite.")

Like neurotransmitters, hormones lock into receptor sites on target cells to trigger changes in these cells. For example, *insulin,* a hormone produced by the **pancreas**, regulates the concentration of glucose (sugar) in the blood. Like a key fitting into a lock, insulin opens glucose receptors on cells, allowing sugar to pass from the bloodstream into the cells where it is used as fuel. Unlike neurotransmitters, which are found only in the nervous system, hormones travel through the bloodstream system to their destinations.

In people with **diabetes**, the pancreas produces too little insulin or none at all, or cells in the body cannot efficiently utilize the insulin that is available. Thus, too much glucose circulates in the blood. It is eventually excreted in the urine, while cells remain starved for nourishment. Lacking glucose, cells begin burning fat and even muscle as fuel. Unless diabetes is controlled, excess glucose in the blood can damage sensitive body organs and lead to serious complications, such as blindness, heart disease, and kidney failure. In some cases, nerve damage or poor circulation in the lower extremities necessitates amputation.

One of the important functions of the endocrine system is helping to maintain an internally balanced state, or **homeostasis**, in the body. When the level of sugar in the blood exceeds a certain threshold, or set point—as may happen when you eat a meal rich in carbohydrates (sugars and starches)—the pancreas releases more insulin into the bloodstream. Insulin stimulates cells throughout the body to draw more

CONCEPT 2.33
In concert with the nervous system, the endocrine system helps the body maintain a state of equilibrium, or homeostasis.

 CONCEPT 2.34
The pituitary gland is often called the "master gland" because it helps regulate so many other endocrine glands.

pituitary gland An endocrine gland in the brain that produces various hormones involved in growth, regulation of the menstrual cycle, and childbirth.

pineal gland A small endocrine gland in the brain that produces the hormone melatonin, which is involved in regulating sleep-wake cycles.

adrenal glands A pair of endocrine glands located just above the kidneys that produce various stress-related hormones.

thyroid gland An endocrine gland in the neck that secretes hormones involved in regulating metabolic functions and physical growth.

gonads Sex glands (testes in men and ovaries in women) that produce sex hormones and germ cells (sperm in the male and egg cells in the female).

ovaries The female gonads, which secrete the female sex hormones estrogen and progesterone and produce mature egg cells.

testes The male gonads, which produce sperm and secrete the male sex hormone testosterone.

germ cells Sperm and egg cells from which new life develops.

glucose from the blood, which decreases the level of glucose in the body. As this level declines to its set point, the pancreas reduces the amount of insulin it secretes.

The two most important endocrine glands in the body, the hypothalamus and the **pituitary gland**, are located in the brain. The pituitary is often referred to as the "master gland" because it affects so many bodily processes. But even the so-called master gland operates under the control of another "master": the hypothalamus.

The hypothalamus secretes hormones known as *releasing factors* that cause the nearby pituitary gland to release other hormones. For example, the hypothalamus releases *growth-hormone releasing factor (hGRF)*, which stimulates the pituitary to release *growth hormone (GH)*, which in turn promotes physical growth. Other pituitary hormones cause other glands, such as the testes in men and ovaries in women, to release their own hormones. The process is akin to a series of falling dominoes.

In addition to the hypothalamus and pituitary, the brain houses another endocrine gland, the **pineal gland**, which releases *melatonin*, a hormone that helps regulate sleep-wake cycles (see Chapter 4). The **adrenal glands** are a pair of glands that lie above the kidneys. They have an outer layer, called the *adrenal cortex,* and a core, called the *adrenal medulla.* The pituitary hormone *ACTH* stimulates the adrenal cortex to secrete hormones called *cortical steroids,* which promote muscle development and stimulate the liver to release stores of sugar in times of stress. More energy thus becomes available in response to stressful situations, such as emergencies in which the organism faces the imminent threat of a predator attack. Other stress hormones, *epinephrine* and *norepinephrine,* are released by the adrenal medulla. They help prepare the body to deal with stress by speeding up bodily processes, such as heart rate and respiration rate.

As noted earlier in the chapter, some chemicals, like norepinephrine, do double duty: they function both as neurotransmitters in the nervous system and as hormones in the bloodstream. In the brain, norepinephrine—and to a lesser degree, epinephrine—function as neurotransmitters. Norepinephrine plays an important role in the nervous system in regulating mood, alertness, and appetite.

The **thyroid gland**, which is located at the base of the neck, produces hormones, including *thyroxin,* that control the rate of body metabolism, the speed at which the body turns food into energy. The **gonads** are the sex glands: **ovaries** in women and **testes** in men. The gonads produce the **germ cells**: egg cells in women and sperm in men. The ovaries also produce the female sex hormones *estrogen* and *progesterone,* which help regulate the menstrual cycle. Progesterone also stimulates growth of the female reproductive organs and helps the uterus maintain pregnancy.

The testes produce the male sex hormone, *testosterone,* which leads to the development of male sex organs in male fetuses. Following puberty in males, release of testosterone by the testes fosters growth of the male genitals, development of a beard, and deepening of the voice.

Though the nervous system and endocrine system are separate systems, they are closely intertwined. The brain regulates the activity of the endocrine system so that the body responds not as separate systems, but as an integrated whole. It does this through the autonomic nervous system. In times of stress, for example, the sympathetic nervous system transmits commands from the brain to the adrenal medulla, which then releases the stress hormones epinephrine and norepinephrine to help prepare the body to deal with stress (discussed further in Chapter 15).

Hormones and Behavior

Though human behavior is more strongly influenced by learning and experience than by hormones, hormones do play a role. For example, higher levels of the male sex hormone testosterone are linked to greater physical aggressiveness in both men and women (Pope, Kouri, & Hudson, 2000; Sullivan, 2000; Zuckerman, 2003). (Testosterone is produced in both men's and women's bodies, but in lesser amounts in women.) Ingestion of anabolic steroids (synthetic testosterone),

CONCEPT 2.35
Hormones are linked to a wide range of behaviors and mood states.

CONCEPT 2.36
Hormonal factors may be involved in explaining PMS, a syndrome affecting about three out of four women.

premenstrual syndrome (PMS) A cluster of physical and psychological symptoms occurring in the few days preceding the menstrual flow.

which some people use to build up muscle mass, is also linked to increased aggressive and belligerent behavior. On the other hand, deficiencies of testosterone can lead to loss of sexual desire in both men and women.

Excesses and deficiencies in hormone levels are associated with many physical and psychological disorders For example, excesses of thyroid hormones are associated with states of anxiety and irritability, whereas deficiencies can lead to sluggishness and weight gain and can impair intellectual development in children.

During the menstrual cycle, levels of estrogen and progesterone shift dramatically. Most women, about three out of four, experience some form of **premenstrual syndrome (PMS)**, a constellation of physical and psychological symptoms in the days leading up to menstruation each month. These symptoms may include anxiety, depression, irritability, weight gain resulting from fluid retention, and abdominal discomfort. The cause or causes of PMS are unclear, but mounting evidence suggests that hormones play a role. We lack solid evidence to support the belief that hormonal imbalances—too much or too little circulating estrogen or progesterone—are causally responsible for PMS (Chrisler & Johnston-Robledo, 2002). It may turn out that differences in sensitivity to these hormones, not to their levels per se, predisposes some women to PMS (Rubinow & Schmidt, 1995). It is also conceivable that estrogen affects mood by influencing serotonin activity in the brain (Rubinow, Schmidt, & Roca, 1998). Other factors—such as how women cope with menstrual symptoms, what their cultures teach them about menstruation, and their general mood states—may also influence the likelihood of a woman's experiencing PMS.

MODULE 2.6 REVIEW

The Endocrine System: The Body's Other Communication System

RECITE IT

What are the major endocrine glands?

- The major endocrine glands are the pituitary gland, hypothalamus, pineal gland, pancreas, adrenal glands, thyroid gland, and gonads (testes in males and ovaries in females).

What roles do hormones play in behavior?

- The male sex hormone testosterone is linked to aggressiveness and sexual desire.

- Excesses of thyroxin can cause anxiety and irritability, whereas having too little of the hormone can lead to sluggishness and weight gain and slow intellectual development in children.

- Female sex hormones appear to play a role in the development of PMS, although the precise role remains to be determined.

RECALL IT

1. Although it is vastly slower than the nervous system, the _____ system is another communication system in the human body.

2. The endocrine system consists of a network of that directly release their secretions, called _____, into the bloodstream.

3. What term is used to describe an internally balanced state in the body?

4. The gland known as the "master gland" because of its role in many bodily processes is the _____ gland.

5. In diabetes,
   a. the body either produces insufficient insulin or is unable to utilize the insulin it produces.
   b. the pineal gland fails to release sufficient melatonin.
   c. the adrenal cortex fails to release sufficient cortical steroids.
   d. the somatic nervous system does not adequately direct endocrine functions.

THINK ABOUT IT

- Do you believe your behavior is influenced by your hormones? Why or why not?

- Why does the text refer to the endocrine system as the body's other communication system?

MODULE 2.7

Genes and Behavior: A Case of Nature *and* Nurture

- What roles do genetic factors play in human behavior?
- What are the methods used to study genetic influences on behavior?

Within every living organism is a set of inherited instructions that determines whether it will have lungs or gills, a penis or a vagina, blue eyes or green. This set of instructions, called a **genotype**, constitutes a master plan for building and maintaining a living organism. The genetic instructions are encoded in the organism's **genes**, the basic units of heredity that are passed along from parent to offspring.

Genes are composed of the complex, double-stranded spiraling molecule called **deoxyribonucleic acid (DNA)** (Gaulin & McBurney, 2001), and they are linked together on long strands called **chromosomes** that reside in the cell nucleus. Scientists believe there may some 30,000 genes in the human genome, the genetic blueprint that contains the precise chemical sequence that constitutes human DNA. They are not completely sure about this number, however; it may turn out to be higher or lower (Wade, 2003b).

Each cell in the body contains the full complement of human genes, except for germ cells (egg cells and sperm cells). These carry half of the person's genetic code. Children inherit half of their chromosomes and the genes they carry from their mothers and half from their fathers. During conception, the twenty-three chromosomes in the mother's egg cell unite with the twenty-three chromosomes in the father's sperm cell, forming the normal human complement of forty-six chromosomes arranged in twenty-three pairs. With the exception of identical twins, no two people share the same genetic code.

Having recently succeeded in cracking the human genetic code or *genome,* scientists are now able to read the entire genetic script of a human being. The human genome has even been placed on the Internet to enable scientists to study it (Baltimore, 2000). Through continuing research on our genetic code, scientists seek to understand how genes work and to identify specific genes involved in physical and mental disorders (Gottesman & Hanson, 2005; Plomin et al., 2003; Tecott, 2003). They hope the human genome will yield new insights into the genetic origins of different diseases and spur development of gene-based therapies that will block the actions of harmful genes and harness the actions of useful ones (Plomin & McGuffin, 2003; Sapolsky, 2003).

Genetic factors clearly determine physical characteristics like eye color and hair color, but what about their role in behavior? Is our behavior a product of our genes, our environment, or both?

Genetic Influences on Behavior

Genes influence many patterns of behavior in other species (Plomin et al., 2003). Some dogs are bold or placid in temperament; others are yappy. They all share enough genes to make them dogs and not cats, but they may differ greatly from one another in their behavior and physical traits. People have selectively bred animals to enhance specific behavior patterns as well as physical traits. But what about human behavior?

Evidence shows that heredity influences many human traits and characteristics, including intelligence, shyness, aggressiveness, and sociability, as well as special aptitudes in music and art, and even preferences for different types of occupations (Bouchard, 2004; Ellis & Bonin, 2003; Plomin & Crabbe, 2000; Schwartz et al.,

CONCEPT 2.37
The view held by most scientists today is that both heredity and environment interact in complex ways in shaping our personalities and intellectual abilities.

Online Study Center

Improve Your Grade
Tutorials: Genetic Contributions to Behavior

genotype   An organism's genetic code.

genes   Basic units of heredity that contain the individual's genetic code.

deoxyribonucleic acid (DNA)   The basic chemical material in chromosomes that carries the individual's genetic code.

chromosomes   Rodlike structures in the cell nucleus that house the individual's genes.

2003). Genes also appear to contribute to our tendencies to have a happy or sad disposition (Lykken, 1999) and even to our propensity to marry (Johnson et al., 2004). Heredity also plays an important role in many psychological disorders, including anxiety disorders, substance abuse, mood disorders, and schizophrenia (Merikangas & Risch, 2003; Plomin & McGuffin, 2003; Waterworth, Bassett, & Brzustowicz, 2002).

The genotype, or genetic code, is a kind of recipe for determining the features or traits of an organism. But whether the genotype becomes expressed in the organism's observable traits, or **phenotype**, depends on a complex interaction of genes and the environment (Crabbe, 2002). Psychological traits, such as shyness, intelligence, or a predisposition to schizophrenia or alcoholism, appear to be **polygenic traits**, which means that they are influenced by multiple genes interacting with the environment in complex ways. In other words, no one gene accounts for complex psychological traits (Uhl & Grow, 2004). Most psychologists believe that psychological traits are influenced by the combination of nature (genetics) and nurture (environment and culture), not simply one or the other (Plomin et al., 2003; Snibbe, 2004).

Thus, genes do not dictate what our lives or our personalities will become (Maxson, 2003). Rather, genetic factors can create a *predisposition* or *likelihood* (not a certainty) that particular behaviors, abilities, personality traits, or psychological disorders will emerge. Other factors, such as family relationships, stress, and learning experiences, play a large role in determining *how*, or even *if*, genetic factors become expressed in observable behaviors or psychological traits (Ridley, 2003; Sapolsky, 2000).

Landmark research by psychologist David Reiss and his colleagues showed that the degree to which genetic influences on the personality trait of shyness become expressed in childrens' overt behavior depends on the interactions they have with their parents and other important people in their lives (Reiss et al., 2000). Overprotective parents may accentuate an underlying genetic tendency toward shyness, whereas those who encourage more outgoing behavior may help a shy child overcome it. But how can we separate the effects of environment from those of genetics? We next consider several methods scientists use to untangle these effects.

Kinship Studies: Untangling the Roles of Heredity and Environment

Scientists rely on several methods to examine genetic contributions to behavior, including familial association studies, twin studies, and adoptee studies. Concept Chart 2.7 provides a summary of these three basic types of kinship studies.

Familial Association Studies   The more closely related people are, the more genes they have in common. Each parent shares 50 percent of his or her genes with his or her children, as do siblings with each other. More distant relatives, such as uncles, aunts, and cousins, have fewer genes in common, but they still have a greater percentage of common genes than do unrelated people (see Figure 2.20). Therefore, if genes help determine a given trait or disorder, we would expect more closely related people to be more likely to share the trait or disorder in question (Gottesman & Gould, 2003).

Familial association studies have been used to study family linkages in schizophrenia (see Figure 2.21). Consistent with a role for genetics in the development of this disorder, we find a greater risk of the disorder among closer blood relatives of schizophrenia patients than among more distant relatives. The risk among blood relatives rises from 2 percent among first cousins and uncles and aunts to 48 percent among identical twins. Note, however, the following limitation. The closer

phenotype   The observable physical and behavioral characteristics of an organism, representing the influences of the genotype and environment.

polygenic traits   Traits that are influenced by multiple genes interacting in complex ways.

familial association studies   Studies that examine the degree to which disorders or characteristics are shared among family members.

CONCEPT CHART 2.7   Types of Kinship Studies

Type of Study	Method of Analysis	Evaluation
Familial association study	Analysis of shared traits or disorders among family members in relation to their degree of kinship	Provides supportive evidence of genetic contribution to behavior when concordance is greater among more closely related family members than among more distantly related ones; limited because the closer their blood relationship, the more likely people are to share similar environments
Twin study	Analysis of differences in the rates of overlap (concordance) for a given trait or disorder between identical and fraternal twins	Provides strong evidence of the role of genetic factors in behavior when concordance rates are greater among identical twins than among fraternal twins; may be biased by greater environmental similarity between identical twins than fraternal twins
Adoptee study	Analysis of similarity in traits or prevalences of psychological or physical disorders between adoptees and their biological and adoptive parents, or between identical twins reared apart and those reared together	The clearest way of separating the roles of heredity and environment, but may overlook common environmental factors in reared-apart twins early in life

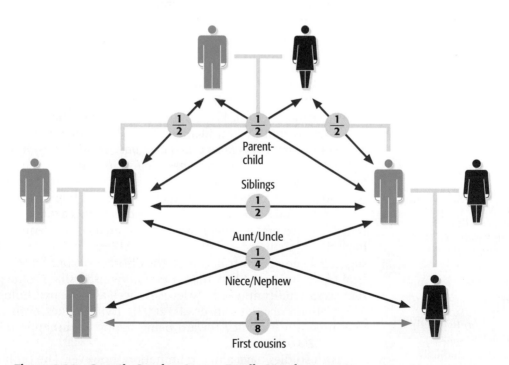

Figure 2.20   Genetic Overlap Among Family Members
As you can see in this family tree, the more closely related people are, the more genes they have in common. The fractions represent the proportion of genetic overlap. For example, siblings have one-half of their genes in common, while uncles or aunts share one-quarter of their genes with their nephews and nieces.

Figure 2.21
Familial Risk in Schizophrenia
The risk of developing schizophrenia generally increases with the closeness of the family relationship with someone who has the disorder. We also need to look at other sources of evidence, such as data from twin studies and adoption studies, to help disentangle the effects of nature and nurture.

Source: Adapted from Gottesman, McGuffin, and Farmer, 1987.

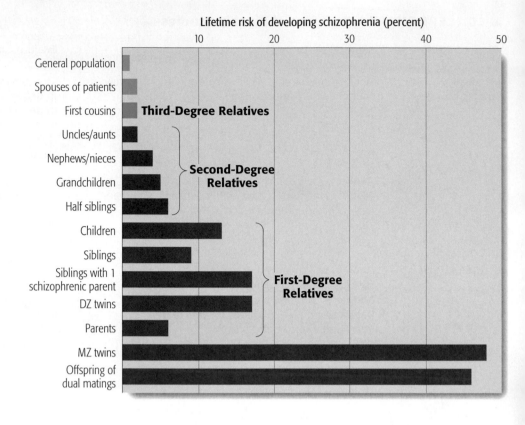

their blood relationship, the more likely people are to share common environments. Thus, researchers look to other types of studies, such as twin studies and adoptee studies, to help disentangle the relative contributions of heredity and environment.

Twin Studies   In the case of **identical twins** (also called *monozygotic*, or *MZ*, twins), a fertilized egg cell, or **zygote**, splits into two cells, and each one develops into a separate person. Because their genetic code had been carried in the single cell before it split in two, identical twins have the same genetic make-up. In the case of **fraternal twins** (also called *dizygotic*, or *DZ*, twins), the mother releases two egg cells in the same month. They are fertilized by different sperm cells, and each fertilized egg cell then develops into a separate person. Fraternal twins thus share only 50 percent of their genetic make-up, as do other brothers and sisters.

In **twin studies**, researchers compare **concordance rates**, or percentages of shared traits or disorders. A higher rate of concordance (percentage of time both twins have the same disorder or trait) among MZ twins than among DZ twins strongly suggests a genetic contribution to the disorder or trait. Researchers find that identical twins are more likely than fraternal twins to share some psychological traits, such as sociability and activity levels, as well as some psychological disorders, such as schizophrenia (Plomin et al., 2003). Twin studies even suggest that people may inherit a tendency toward being happy or unhappy (Lykken & Csikszentmihalyi, 2001).

Twin studies have a major limitation, however. The problem is that identical twins may be treated more alike than fraternal twins. Thus, environmental factors, not genes, may account for their higher rates of concordance. For example, identical twins may be encouraged to dress alike, take the same courses, even play the same musical instrument. Investigators believe that, despite this limitation, twin studies provide useful information on genetic contributions to personality and intellectual development (Winerman, 2004a).

identical twins   Twins who developed from the same zygote and so have identical genes (also called *monozygotic*, or *MZ*, twins).

zygote   A fertilized egg cell.

fraternal twins   Twins who developed from separate zygotes and so have 50 percent of their genes in common (also called *dizygotic*, or *DZ*, twins).

twin studies   Studies that examine the degree to which concordance rates between co-twins for particular disorders or characteristics vary in relation to whether the twins are identical or fraternal.

concordance rates   In twin studies, the percentages of cases in which both members of twin pairs share the same trait or disorder.

adoptee studies   Studies that examine whether adoptees are more similar to their biological or adoptive parents with respect to their psychological traits or the disorders they develop.

Adoptee Studies   The clearest way to separate the roles of environment and heredity is to conduct **adoptee studies**, which compare adopted children with both their adoptive parents and biological parents (Merikangas & Risch, 2003). If they tend to be more like their adoptive parents in their psychological traits or the disorders they develop, we can argue that environment plays the more dominant role. If they tend to be more like their biological parents, we may assume that heredity has a greater influence.

When identical twins are separated at an early age and reared apart in separate adoptive families, we can attribute any differences between them to environmental factors since their genetic make-up is the same. This natural experiment—separating identical twins at an early age—does not happen often, but when it does, it provides a special opportunity to examine the role of nature and nurture. One such study found little difference in the degree of similarity between identical twins reared apart as compared with those reared together across a range of personality traits (Tellegen et al., 1988).

These findings suggest that heredity plays an important role in personality development. Yet studies of twins reared apart may overlook common environmental factors. Since twins are rarely adopted at birth, they may have shared a common environment during infancy. Many continue to meet periodically throughout their lives. Thus, twins reared apart may have opportunities to be influenced by others in their shared environments or to influence each other, quite apart from their genetic overlap.

All in all, despite the weaknesses of methods used to separate the roles of heredity and environment, a wealth of findings using different methodologies underscores the important role of genetics in shaping personality and intellectual development. The influence genes have on our psychological development does not mean that genetics is destiny. Genetic factors provide a *range* for the expression of various traits, while environmental factors help determine how *or if* these traits are expressed.

MODULE 2.7 REVIEW

Genes and Behavior:
A Case of Nature *and* Nurture

RECITE IT

What roles do genetic factors play in human behavior?

• Genetic factors interact in complex ways with environmental influences in determining many types of personality traits as well as intellectual development.

What are the methods used to study genetic influences on behavior?

• Three types of kinship studies are used to study the role of genetics in human behavior: familial association studies, twin studies, and adoptee studies.

RECALL IT

1. _____are the basic units of heredity that carry the organism's genotype, or genetic make-up.

2. Polygenic traits are
   a. traits that are influenced by multiple genes.
   b. traits that are influenced by polygenic genes.
   c. traits that are determined by genetic defects.
   d. traits that are fully determined by combinations of genes.

3. What are the basic types of studies used to examine the influence of genetics on behavior?

4. Dizygotic (fraternal) twins result when
   a. a zygote is formed and then splits into two cells.
   b. two egg cells are fertilized by different sperm.
   c. two different sperm fertilize the same egg cell, which then divides in half.
   d. two zygotes are formed from the fertilization of the same egg cell.

THINK ABOUT IT

- What aspects of your personality, if any, do you believe were influenced by your genetic inheritance?

- What methods do researchers use to disentangle the influences of heredity and environment on behavior? What are the limitations of these methods?

APPLICATION MODULE 2.8

Looking Under the Hood: Scanning the Human Brain

Advances in cognitive neuroscience made possible by sophisticated brain-imaging techniques are broadening our understanding of how the brain works. Here we consider some of the cutting-edge applications of brain scanning that allow us to peer into the working brain.

Memory and Cognitive Research

Using advanced scanning techniques, investigators recently reported identifying and recording activities in specific brain circuits of laboratory animals that correspond to particular experiences in the animals' lives (Bartho et al., 2004; Csicsvari et al., 2003). Research along these lines is still in its infancy, but it is conceivable that we may one day be able to identify memory circuits in the human brain that hold the repository of our life experiences. In another application, investigators at the University of Illinois at Chicago used a high-resolution MRI scanner to "watch" a person's thoughts. They were able to create images of discrete patterns of neural activity in a person's brain on a thought-by-thought basis (Thulborn, 2003).

Personality Research

Brain scans may be useful in revealing underlying personality traits. Recently, test subjects were shown a mix of positive and negative images, such as those in Figure 2.22, while researchers tracked the neural activity in their brains using a high-tech imaging technique. The results showed differences in brain activity between people with different personality features or traits. In response to these positive and negative images, the brains of people who had personality traits of extraversion (were sociable, outgoing, and people-oriented) showed different patterns of activity than those who had traits of neuroticism (were anxious and worrisome) As the lead investigator, psychologist Turhan Canli put it, "If I know what the conditions are under which I see [a certain] activation pattern, I can make a good prediction as to what this person's personality traits are" (quoted in Pepper, 2005).

Online Study Center

Improve Your Grade
Tutorials: Methods of Studying the Living Brain

The Test
Subjects are shown mixed "positive" and "negative" images, like the images shown below. Meanwhile, brain scans track the differences in the patterns of activity among their brains' neurons.

1. The Extrovert
"Positive" images stimulate these areas in people who are more social and show positive emotions.

2. The Neurotic
"Negative" images provoke these responses among people prone to anxiety and negative emotions.

Figure 2.22
Scanning Personalities
The brains of people with different personality traits (extroversion vs. neuroticism) show different patterns of activity in response to positive and negative images. Research along these lines may help us learn more about relationships between brain functioning and personality types.

Source: Adapted from *Newsweek,* Feb. 21, 2005, p. E26.

Personnel Selection

Brain scans may also come into use in employment screenings. In addition to filling out traditional background and interest inventories, employers may begin peering inside the head of a job applicant (Pepper, 2005). Psychologist Turhan Canli has begun testing how differences in brain activation patterns in response to positive and negative images may reveal which individuals might be better suited for particular tasks.

Diagnosing Psychological Disorders

Brain scans might also be used to diagnose psychological or psychiatric disorders. Teams of experimenters are actively engaged in research exploring the use of brain scans in detecting signs of abnormal behavior patterns such as bipolar disorder, schizophrenia, and attention-deficit hyperactivity disorder (ADHD). Investigators hope to uncover signs of psychological disorders through scanning techniques, in much the same way that scanning techniques are presently used to reveal tumors and other physical disorders (Raeburn, 2005). These techniques are presently limited to experimental use, but one day, perhaps one day soon, they may become as common as chest X-rays or even dental X-rays.

TYING IT TOGETHER

In this chapter, we explored the biological underpinnings of behavior. Our ability to sense and make sense of the world around us, to coordinate our movements, and to think, learn, remember, and solve problems is dependent on the functioning of our nervous system. The basic units of the nervous system are neurons, nerve cells that transmit information and work together in complex assemblages in the brain to process information (Module 2.1). The nervous system consists of two major branches, the central nervous system, consisting of the brain and spinal cord, and the peripheral nervous system, which connects the central nervous system to the body's sensory organs, muscles, and glands. The spinal cord links the brain and the peripheral nervous system. The peripheral nervous system comprises the somatic nervous system (which allows us to perceive the outside world and to move our bodies) and the autonomic nervous system, which controls automatic bodily processes such as heart rate and digestion. The autonomic nervous system is further divided into the sympathetic nervous system, which speeds up bodily processes and draws energy from stored reserves, and the parasympathetic nervous system, which slows down bodily processes to conserve energy and helps replenish bodily stores of energy (Module 2.2).

The brain comprises three major parts: the hindbrain, the midbrain, and the forebrain. The largest mass of the forebrain is comprised of two hemispheres that are covered by the cerebral cortex, which is responsible for thinking, language, and other higher mental functions. Each hemisphere is divided into four lobes that each have particular functions: the occipital, parietal, frontal, and temporal (Module 2.3). Investigators explore the workings of the brain, the centerpiece of the central nervous system, by using brain-imaging techniques and experimental methods (Module 2.4). Based on studies of brain functioning, it appears that the left hemisphere of the brain is dominant for language and logical functions, whereas the right hemisphere of the brain appears to be dominant for nonverbal functions, such as understanding spatial relationships (Module 2.5).

The nervous system is not the only communication system in the body. The endocrine system consists of glands that release hormones that travel through the bloodstream to distant parts of the body. Hormones lock into receptor sites on specific target cells, triggering changes in these cells that are needed to regulate and coordinate important bodily processes. Hormones may also influence our behavior and moods (Module 2.6). Another biological influence on our behavior is heredity. Most psychologists believe that both genetic and environmental factors influence our behavior in varying degrees (Module 2.7).

Through the use of advanced brain-scanning techniques, investigators are peering into the working brain to learn more about memory, cognition, personality, abnormal behavior, and even the suitability of particular applicants for particular jobs (Module 2.8).

Thinking Critically About Psychology

Based on your reading of this chapter, answer the following questions. Then, to evaluate your progress in developing critical thinking skills, compare your answers to the sample answers found in Appendix A.

The case of Phineas Gage is one of the best-known case studies in the annals of psychology. In 1848, as you already know, Gage suffered an accident in which a metal rod pierced his cheek and brain and penetrated the top of his head. Yet not only did he survive this horrific accident, but he also managed to pick himself up and speak to workers who came to his aid. Though he survived his injuries, his personality changed—so much so that people would remark, "Gage is no longer Gage."

1. **Why do you think Gage's injury affected his personality but not the basic life functions that the brain controls, such as breathing and heart rate?**

2. **How might the nature of the injury that Gage sustained explain why this once polite and courteous man became aggressive and unruly?**

Key Terms

neurons (p. 46)
brain (p. 46)
soma (p. 46)
axon (p. 46)
terminal buttons (p. 47)
neurotransmitters (p. 47)
synapse (p. 47)
dendrites (p. 47)
sensory neurons (p. 47)
motor neurons (p. 47)
glands (p. 47)
hormones (p. 47)
interneurons (p. 47)
nerve (p. 47)
glial cells (p. 48)
myelin sheath (p. 48)
nodes of Ranvier (p. 48)
multiple sclerosis (MS) (p. 48)
ions (p. 48)
resting potential (p. 48)
depolarization (p. 49)
action potential (p. 49)
all-or-none principle (p. 49)
refractory period (p. 49)
receptor site (p. 50)
reuptake (p. 51)
enzymes (p. 51)
neuromodulators (p. 51)
antagonists (p. 51)
schizophrenia (p. 51)
hallucinations (p. 51)
delusions (p. 51)
Parkinson's disease (p. 51)
agonists (p. 52)
stimulant (p. 52)
amphetamines (p. 52)
antidepressants (p. 52)
endorphins (p. 52)
nervous system (p. 54)
central nervous system (p. 54)

spinal cord (p. 54)
spine (p. 55)
reflex (p. 55)
spinal reflex (p. 55)
peripheral nervous system (p. 56)
somatic nervous system (p. 56)
autonomic nervous system (p. 57)
sympathetic nervous system (p. 57)
parasympathetic nervous system (p. 57)
hindbrain (p. 59)
medulla (p. 59)
pons (p. 59)
brainstem (p. 59)
cerebellum (p. 60)
midbrain (p. 60)
reticular formation (p. 61)
forebrain (p. 61)
thalamus (p. 61)
basal ganglia (p. 61)
hypothalamus (p. 61)
limbic system (p. 62)
amygdala (p. 62)
hippocampus (p. 62)
cerebral cortex (p. 62)
cerebrum (p. 62)
cerebral hemispheres (p. 62)
corpus callosum (p. 62)
occipital lobes (p. 63)
parietal lobes (p. 63)
somatosensory cortex (p. 63)
frontal lobes (p. 63)
motor cortex (p. 65)
temporal lobes (p. 65)
association areas (p. 65)
EEG (electroencephalograph) (p. 66)
CT (computed tomography) scan (p. 67)
PET (positron emission tomography) scan (p. 67)
MRI (magnetic resonance imaging) (p. 67)

lesioning (p. 69)
electrical recording (p. 69)
electrical stimulation (p. 70)
lateralization (p. 71)
Broca's area (p. 72)
Wernicke's area (p. 72)
aphasia (p. 72)
plasticity (p. 74)
stroke (p. 74)
prefrontal cortex (p. 75)
laceration (p. 75)
concussion (p. 75)
epilepsy (p. 76)
split-brain patients (p. 76)
endocrine system (p. 79)
pancreas (p. 80)
diabetes (p. 80)
homeostasis (p. 80)
pituitary gland (p. 81)
pineal gland (p. 81)
adrenal glands (p. 81)
thyroid gland (p. 81)
gonads (p. 81)
ovaries (p. 81)
testes (p. 81)
germ cells (p. 81)
premenstrual syndrome (PMS) (p. 82)
genotype (p. 83)
genes (p. 83)
deoxyribonucleic acid (DNA) (p. 83)
chromosomes (p. 83)
phenotype (p. 84)
polygenic traits (p. 84)
familial association studies (p. 84)
identical twins (p. 86)
zygote (p. 86)
fraternal twins (p. 86)
twin studies (p. 86)
concordance rates (p. 86)
adoptee studies (p. 87)

ANSWERS TO RECALL IT QUESTIONS
Module 2.1: 1. soma; 2. sensory, motor, interneurons; 3. d; 4. a; 5. neurotransmitters.
Module 2.2: 1. central, peripheral; 2. reflexes; 3. somatic, autonomic; 4. a.
Module 2.3: 1. hindbrain; 2. (a) iv, (b) i, (c) iii, (d) ii; 3. d; 4. association.
Module 2.4: 1. c; 2. a; 3. a.
Module 2.5: 1. left, right; 2. Broca's, Wernicke's; 3. b.
Module 2.6: 1. endocrine; 2. glands, hormones; 3. homeostasis; 4. pituitary; 5. a.
Module 2.7: 1. genes; 2. a; 3. familial association studies, twin studies, and adoptee studies; 4. b.

Sensation and Perception

DID YOU KNOW THAT . . .

■ Our sense of smell may not be as keen as that of dogs, but humans can detect the presence of even one drop of perfume dispersed through a small house? (p. 94)

■ You are likely to be able to detect a change in the pitch of a person's voice when it varies by as little as one-third of 1 percent, but it takes about a 10 percent change in the volume of your neighbor's stereo before you notice any difference in loudness? (p. 95)

■ Roy G. Biv is one of the most famous names learned by psychology students, but he is not a real person? (p. 98)

■ The hair cells in the inner ear that serve as sense receptors for hearing don't actually contain tiny hairs? (p. 107)

■ Listening to music on an iPod or similar device at too high a volume can permanently damage your hearing? (p. 109)

■ Salmon use the sense of smell to sniff out the streams of their birth when they return to spawn? (p. 112)

■ Cats are insensitive to the taste of sweets? (p. 113)

■ Some people are born with a distaste for broccoli? (p. 113)

■ Newborn babies prefer the sounds of their mothers' voices to the voices of other women? (p. 119)

■ The mechanism that makes motion pictures possible lies in the viewer, not the projector? (p. 127)

One day, my infant daughter Daniella turned into a giant. Or so it seemed. I was making a video recording of her fledgling attempts to crawl. All was going well until she noticed the camera. She then started crawling toward this funny man holding the camera—me. As she approached, her image in the viewfinder grew larger and larger, eventually so large that she blotted out all other objects in my view. The image of my daughter that was cast upon my eyes was of a large and ever-growing giant! But I didn't panic. Despite the information my eyes were transmitting to my brain, I understood my daughter was not morphing into a giant. Fortunately, we tend to perceive objects to be their actual size despite changes in the size of the image they project on our eyes as they grow nearer. Yet the sensation of seeing your infant grow to be a giant before your eyes can be an unsettling experience, especially when the "giant" then attempts to mouth the camera.

We are continually bombarded with stimuli from the outside world that impinge on our sensory organs. The world is a medley of lights and sounds that strike our eyes and ears, and of chemical substances that waft past our noses or land on our tongues as we consume food or drink liquids. In this chapter, you will see how your sense organs respond to external stimuli and transform these stimuli into sensory signals your brain uses to produce *sensations* of vision, hearing, touch, smell, and taste. You will learn how your brain assembles bits and pieces of sensory information into meaningful impressions of the world that are called *perceptions*. You will also learn how your brain senses changes in the position of your body, so you can move about without stumbling or losing your balance. Our sensory systems operate at blinding speeds, but the real marvel is how the brain processes all the information it receives from the body's sensory organs, making it possible for us not only to sense the world around us, but also to make sense of it. As the example of my "giant" daughter illustrates, sensation and perception are different processes. What we perceive may not correspond to what our eyes observe.

The study of sensation and perception is critical to psychology because our investigation of behavior and mental processes begins with input from the world around us and the way the senses and brain interpret that information. Let us proceed, first, to explore how our sensory systems operate. Then we will explore how the brain assembles the sensory information it receives to form perceptions that help us make sense of the colors, sounds, fragrances, and tastes that form the rich tapestry of sensory experience. ■

MODULE 3.1

Sensing Our World: Basic Concepts of Sensation

- What is sensation?
- What is the difference between absolute thresholds and difference thresholds?
- What factors contribute to signal detection?
- What is sensory adaptation?

CONCEPT 3.1
Sensation is the process by which physical stimuli that impinge on our sensory organs are converted into neural impulses that the brain uses to create our experiences of vision, touch, hearing, taste, smell, and so on.

CONCEPT 3.2
Sensory receptors convert sources of sensory stimuli, such as light and sound, into neural impulses the brain can use to create sensations.

CONCEPT 3.3
Psychophysics is the study of relationships between the features of physical stimuli, such as the intensity of lights and sounds, and the sensations we experience in response to these stimuli.

CONCEPT 3.4
Our sensory systems vary in the amounts of stimulation needed to detect the presence of a stimulus and the differences among stimuli.

sensation The process by which we receive, transform, and process stimuli from the outside world to create sensory experiences of vision, touch, hearing, taste, smell, and so on.

sensory receptors Specialized cells that detect sensory stimuli and convert them into neural impulses.

psychophysics The study of the relationships between features of physical stimuli, such as their intensity, and the sensations we experience in response to them.

absolute threshold The smallest amount of a given stimulus a person can sense.

difference threshold The minimal difference in the magnitude of energy needed for people to detect a difference between two stimuli.

Sensation is the process by which we receive stimuli that impinge on our sensory organs and transform them into neural impulses, or signals, that the brain uses to create experiences of vision, hearing, taste, smell, touch, and so on.

Each of our sense organs contains specialized cells, called **sensory receptors**, that detect stimuli from the outside world, such as light, sound, and odors. They are found throughout the body in such organs as the eyes, ears, nose, and mouth, as well as in less obvious locations, such as the joints and muscles of the body and the entirety of the skin. In this module, we examine how sensory receptors respond to external stimuli and how they convert these stimuli into messages the brain uses to create sensations.

Our venture into sensation leads us back to **psychophysics**, the study of how physical sources of stimulation—light, sound, odors, and so on—relate to our experience of these stimuli in the form of sensations. Psychophysics began with the work of the nineteenth-century German scientist Gustav Theodor Fechner. Though Wilhelm Wundt is credited with establishing the first psychological laboratory in 1879, some historians believe that the publication of Fechner's *Elements of Psychophysics* in 1860 signaled the beginning of the scientific approach to psychology.

We begin our study of sensation by examining the common characteristics that relate to the functioning of our sensory systems: thresholds, signal detection, and sensory adaptation.

Absolute and Difference Thresholds: Is Something There? Is Something *Else* There?

Our sensory receptors are remarkably sensitive to certain types of stimuli. On a clear, dark night we can detect a flickering candle thirty miles away. We can also detect about one drop of perfume spread through a small house. The **absolute threshold** is the smallest amount of a stimulus that a person can reliably detect. Table 3.1 lists absolute thresholds for the senses of vision, hearing, taste, smell, and touch.

People differ in their absolute thresholds. Some are more sensitive than others to certain kinds of sensory stimulation, such as sounds or odors. Fechner sought to determine the absolute thresholds for various senses by presenting people with stimuli of different magnitudes, such as brighter and duller lights, and then asking them whether they could see them. According to this method, the absolute threshold is defined as the minimal level of stimulus energy that people can detect 50 percent of the time. Stimuli detected less than 50 percent of the time are considered below the absolute threshold. Stimuli that can be detected more often are above the threshold.

The nineteenth-century German scientist Ernst Weber (1795–1878) (pronounced Vay-ber) studied the smallest differences between stimuli that people were able to perceive. The minimal difference between two stimuli that people can reliably detect is the **difference threshold**, or *just-noticeable difference (jnd)*. Just-noticeable differences apply to each of our senses.

TABLE 3.1   Absolute Thresholds for Various Senses

Sense	Stimulus	Receptors	Threshold
Vision	Light energy	Rods and cones in the eyes	The flame from a single candle flickering about thirty miles away on a dark, clear night
Hearing	Sound waves	Hair cells in the inner ear	The ticking of a watch placed about twenty feet away from a listener in a quiet room
Taste	Chemical substances that contact the tongue	Taste buds on the tongue	About one teaspoon of sugar dissolved in two gallons of water
Smell	Chemical substances that enter the nose	Receptor cells in the upper nostrils	About one drop of perfume dispersed in a small house
Touch	Movement of, or pressure on, the skin	Nerve endings in the skin	The wing of a bee falling on the cheek from about one centimeter away

Source: Adapted from Galanter, 1962.

TABLE 3.2
Examples of Weber's Constants

Sensation	Weber's Constant (Approximate)
Saltiness of food	1/5
Pressure on skin	1/7
Loudness of sounds	1/10
Odor	1/20
Heaviness of weights	1/50
Brightness of lights	1/60
Pitch of sounds	1/333

CONCEPT 3.5

Our ability to detect a stimulus depends not only on the physical properties of the stimulus, but also on background characteristics as well as our own psychological and physiological characteristics.

Weber's law   The principle that the amount of change in a stimulus needed to detect a difference is given by a constant ratio or fraction, called a constant, of the original stimulus.

signal-detection theory   The belief that the detection of a stimulus depends on factors such as the intensity of the stimulus, the level of background stimulation, and the biological and psychological characteristics of the perceiver.

How do difference thresholds apply to the range of stimuli we perceive with our senses? Weber summarized his findings in what is now known as **Weber's law**. According to this law, the amount you must change a stimulus to detect a difference is given by a constant fraction or proportion (called a *constant*) of the original stimulus. For example, Weber's constant for noticing a difference in weights is about 1/50 (or 2 percent). This means that if you were lifting a 50-pound weight, you would probably not notice a difference unless the weight were increased or reduced by about 2 percent (or 1 pound). But if you were lifting a 200-pound weight, the weight would have to be increased by about 4 pounds (2 percent) for you to notice the difference. Though the absolute weight needed to detect a difference is about quadruple as you increase the initial weight from 50 pounds to 200, the fraction remains the same (1/50).

Weber found that the difference threshold differed for each of the senses. People are noticeably more sensitive to changes in the pitch of a sound than to changes in volume. They perceive the difference if you raise or lower the pitch of your voice by as little as one-third of 1 percent (1/333). Yet they will not sense any decrease in the loudness of a stereo amplifier until you reduce the sound by about 10 percent. Also, the louder the stereo is blasting, the more you'll need to reduce the volume in absolute terms before people notice a difference. Table 3.2 lists Weber's constants for various senses.

Weber's constants for these stimuli have practical meanings. First, if you are going to sing, you had better be right on pitch (hit the note precisely), or people are going to groan. But you might be able to raise the volume on your stereo a little without the next-door neighbor noticing the difference. Then, too, your neighbor may not notice it if you lower the stereo by a notch.

Signal Detection: More Than a Matter of Energy

Scientists who study psychophysics describe sounds, flashes of light, and other stimuli as *signals*. According to **signal-detection theory**, the threshold for detecting a signal depends not only on the properties of the stimulus itself, such as its intensity—the loudness of a sound, for example—but also on the level of background stimulation, or noise, and, importantly, on the biological and psycho-

CONCEPT CHART 3.1   Basic Concepts in Sensation

Sensation	The transformation of stimuli that impinge on our sense organs into neural signals the brain processes to create sensory experiences of vision, touch, sound, taste, smell, and so on
Absolute threshold	The smallest amount of a stimulus that a person can reliably detect
Difference threshold	The minimal difference between two stimuli that people can reliably detect; also called *just-noticeable difference*
Weber's law	The law stating that the amount of change in a stimulus needed to detect a difference can be expressed as a constant ratio or fraction of the original stimulus
Signal-detection theory	The belief that the ability to detect a signal varies with the characteristics of the perceiver, the background, and the stimulus itself
Sensory adaptation	The process by which sensory systems adapt to constant stimuli by becoming less sensitive to them

 CONCEPT 3.6

According to signal-detection theory, the ability to detect a stimulus depends not only on the properties of the stimulus, but also on the level of background stimulation and the biological and psychological characteristics of the perceiver.

logical characteristics of the perceiver. The sensitivity or degree of sharpness of an individual's sensory systems (e.g., the acuity of your eyesight or hearing) partially determines whether a signal is detected. The organism's physical condition also plays a role. For instance, your sense of smell is duller when you have a cold and your nose is stuffed. Levels of fatigue or alertness also contribute to signal detection.

Psychological factors, including attention levels and states of motivation like hunger, also play important roles in signal detection. As you are walking down a darkened street by yourself late at night, you may be especially attentive to even the slightest sounds because they may signal danger. You may fail to notice the same sounds as you walk along the same street in broad daylight. If you haven't eaten for a while, you may be more likely to notice aromas of food wafting from a nearby kitchen than if you had just consumed a hearty meal.

Sensory Adaptation: Turning the Volume Down

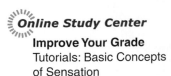 **CONCEPT 3.7**

Through the process of sensory adaptation, our sensory systems deal with repeated exposure to the same stimuli by becoming less sensitive to them.

Through the process of **sensory adaptation**, sensory systems become *less* sensitive to constant or unchanging stimuli. When you are wearing a new wristwatch or ring, you may at first be aware of the sensation of pressure on your skin, but after a while you no longer notice it. We may be thankful for sensory adaptation when, after a few minutes of exposure, the water in a crisp mountain lake seems warmer and the odors in a locker room become less noticeable. However, sensory adaptation may not occur when we are repeatedly exposed to certain strong stimuli, such as the loud wail of a car alarm. In such cases, our sensory systems show no change in sensitivity to the stimulus. Concept Chart 3.1 reviews the basic concepts in sensation.

Online Study Center

Improve Your Grade
Tutorials: Basic Concepts of Sensation

sensory adaptation   The process by which sensory receptors adapt to constant stimuli by becoming less sensitive to them.

MODULE 3.1 REVIEW

Sensing Our World: Basic Concepts of Sensation

RECITE IT

What is sensation?

- Sensation is the process of taking information from the world, transforming it into neural impulses, and transmitting these signals to the brain, where they are processed to produce experiences of vision, hearing, smell, taste, touch, and so on.

What is the difference between absolute thresholds and difference thresholds?

- An absolute threshold is the smallest amount of a stimulus that a person can sense. A difference threshold, or just-noticeable difference (jnd), is the minimal difference in magnitude of energy needed for people to detect a difference between two stimuli.

What factors contribute to signal detection?

- Factors affecting signal detection include the intensity of the stimulus; the level of background stimulation, or noise; the biological characteristics of the perceiver, such as the sharpness of the person's sensory system and levels of fatigue or alertness; and psychological factors, such as attention levels and states of motivation.

What is sensory adaptation?

- Sensory adaptation is the process by which sensory systems become less sensitive to unchanging stimuli.

RECALL IT

1. Specialized cells in the sense organs, which are geared to detect stimuli in the external environment, are called
   a. feature detectors.
   b. threshold detectors.
   c. sensory receptors.
   d. signal detectors.

2. The smallest amount of stimulation that a person can reliably detect is called a(n)
   a. minimal sensory field.
   b. absolute threshold.
   c. just-noticeable difference.
   d. vector of constants.

3. The amount, expressed as a ratio, that we need to increase the strength of a stimulus to be able to detect a difference is called _____ constant.

4. Jill notices the humming sound made by an air conditioner when she first enters the room, but within a few minutes she is no longer aware of the sound. What sensory process does this illustrate?

THINK ABOUT IT

- You've probably noticed that when you draw a bath it seems hotter at first than it does a minute or two later. Based on your reading of the text, explain this phenomenon.

- Let's say you're using a recipe that calls for fifteen grams of salt. According to Weber's constant for saltiness, which is 1/5, how much more salt must you add to make the recipe noticeably saltier?

MODULE 3.2

Vision: Seeing the Light

- How do the eyes process light?
- What are feature detectors, and what role do they play in visual processing?
- What are the two major theories of color vision?
- What are the two major forms of color blindness?

CONCEPT 3.8
Vision is the process by which light energy is converted into neural impulses that the brain interprets to produce the experience of sight.

Vision is the process by which light energy is converted into signals (neural impulses) that the brain interprets to produce the experience of sight. Our sense of vision allows us to receive visual information from a mere few inches away, as when we read from a book held close to our eyes, to many billions of miles away, as when we observe twinkling stars on a clear night. To understand vision, we first need to consider the source of physical energy that gives rise to vision: light.

Figure 3.1 The Electromagnetic Spectrum
Visible light occupies only a small portion of the range of electromagnetic radiation that is called the electromagnetic spectrum.

Radio and television   Microwave   Infrared   Ultraviolet   X-rays   Cosmic rays   Gamma rays

10^{14} 10^{13} 10^{12} 10^{11} 10^{10} 10^{9} 10^{8} 10^{7} 10^{6} 10^{5} 10^{4} 10^{3} 10^{2} 10^{1} 1 10^{-1} 10^{-2} 10^{-3} 10^{-4} 10^{-5}

Wavelength (in nanometers)

Light: The Energy of Vision

Light is physical energy in the form of electromagnetic radiation (electrically charged particles). X-rays, ultraviolet waves, and radio waves are other forms of electromagnetic energy. Visible light is the portion of the spectrum of electromagnetic radiation that gives rise to our sense of vision. As you can see in Figure 3.1, the visible spectrum occupies only a small portion of the full spectrum of electromagnetic radiation. It consists of the wavelengths from approximately 300 to 750 nanometers (a nanometer is one-billionth of a meter).

Different wavelengths within the visible spectrum give rise to the experience of different colors (see Figure 3.2). Violet has the shortest wavelength (about 400-billionths of a meter long), and red has the longest (about 700-billionths of a meter). Psychology students are often told that they can remember the order of the colors of the spectrum by thinking of the name Roy G. Biv (standing for red, orange, yellow, green, blue, indigo, and violet).

> **CONCEPT 3.9**
> Light, a form of physical energy, is the stimulus to which receptors in the eyes respond, giving rise to our sense of vision.

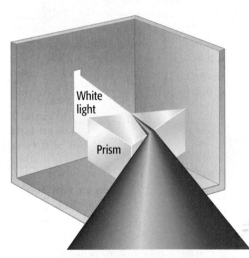

White light

Prism

Figure 3.2 The Color Spectrum
A prism separates white light into the various hues that make up the part of the electromagnetic spectrum that is visible to humans.

> **CONCEPT 3.10**
> Light enters the eye through the cornea and then passes through the pupil and then through the lens, which focuses it on the retina, where it comes into contact with photoreceptor cells, the rods and cones, that convert light energy into neural signals that are transmitted to the brain.

The Eye: The Visionary Sensory Organ

The eye is the organ with receptor cells that respond to light. Light enters the eye through the **cornea**, a transparent covering on the eye's surface (see Figure 3.3). A muscle called the **iris** contracts or expands to determine the amount of light that enters. The iris is colored, most often brown or blue, and gives the eye its color. The **pupil** of the eye is the black opening inside the iris. The iris increases or decreases the size of the pupil reflexively to adjust to the amount of light entering the eye. The brighter the light, the smaller the iris makes the pupil. Under darkened conditions, the iris opens to allow more light to enter the pupil so that we can see more clearly. Because these are reflex actions, they happen automatically (you don't have to think about them).

The light enters the eye through the cornea and then passes through the pupil and **lens**. Through a process called **accommodation**, the lens changes its shape to adjust for the distance of the object, which helps focus the visual image on a thin sheet of neural tissue in the inner surface of the eye called the **retina** (Pasternak, Bisley, & Calkins, 2003). Like the film in a camera, the retina receives the image as light strikes it. But the retina is much more sophisticated than photographic film. It contains two kinds of **photoreceptors**, specialized receptor cells that are sensitive to light.

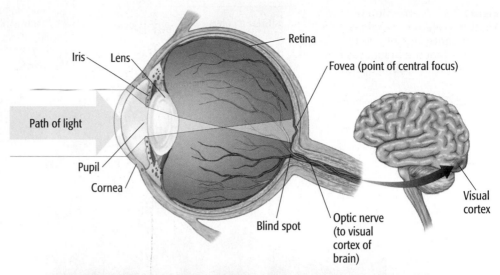

Figure 3.3   Parts of the Eye
Light enters the eye through the cornea. The iris adjusts reflexively to control the size of the pupil. The lens focuses the light on the retina, especially on the fovea, the point of central focus that gives rise to clearest vision.

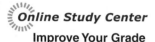

Online Study Center

Improve Your Grade
Tutorials: Conversion of Light into Neural Impulses

CONCEPT 3.11

Rods, which are more sensitive to light than cones are, are responsible for peripheral vision and vision in dim light, whereas cones allow us to detect colors and to discern fine details of objects under bright illumination.

cornea   A transparent covering on the eye's surface through which light enters.

iris   The pigmented, circular muscle in the eye that regulates the size of the pupil to adjust to changes in the level of illumination.

pupil   The black opening inside the iris that allows light to enter the eye.

lens   The structure in the eye that focuses light rays on the retina.

accommodation   The process by which the lens changes its shape to focus images more clearly on the retina.

retina   The light-sensitive layer of the inner surface of the eye that contains photoreceptor cells.

photoreceptors   Light-sensitive cells (rods and cones) in the eye upon which light registers.

rods   Photoreceptors that are sensitive only to the intensity of light (light and dark).

cones   Photoreceptors that are sensitive to color.

bipolar cells   A layer of interconnecting cells in the eye that connect photoreceptors to ganglion cells.

Figure 3.4   Rods and Cones
This close-up image of a portion of the retina shows cones (large reddish conelike objects on the left side of the photograph) and rods (more numerous rodlike objects).

When light hits the retina, it comes into contact with these photoreceptors. Because of their shapes, they are called **rods** and **cones** (see Figure 3.4). The normal eye has about 120 million rods and 6 million cones. The rods and cones convert the physical energy of light into neural signals that the brain processes to create visual sensations.

Have you ever noticed that when lighting is dim, you tend to make out the shapes of objects but not their colors? That's because cones are responsible for color vision but are less sensitive to light than rods are. Rods allow us to detect objects in low light. They are sensitive only to the intensity or brightness of light, not colors. They are also responsible for *peripheral vision*—the ability to detect objects, especially moving objects, at the edges (sides, as well as the top and bottom) of our visual field. Cones allow us to discern not only colors but also fine details of objects in bright light. Some animals, including certain birds, have only cones in their eyes (Gaulin & McBurney, 2001). They can see only during daylight hours when the cones are activated. Because they become totally blind at night, they must return to their roosts as evening approaches.

The neural signals produced by the rods and cones pass back through a layer of interconnecting cells called **bipolar cells** and then through a layer of neurons

**Figure 3.5   Conversion of
Light into Neural Impulses**
Light is converted into neural
impulses that the brain uses to
produce the sensation of vision.

1. Light enters eye,
triggering changes
in photoreceptor cells
(rods and cones)

2. Neural impulse
travels back through
bipolar cells and
then ganglion cells

Light

Light

Light

Back of eye

Retina
Area of
detail

Optic
nerve

3. Axon from each
ganglion cell
becomes one fiber
in optic nerve

Rod
Cone
Optic nerve

Ganglion
cells

Bipolar
cells

4. Neural impulse
travels to brain

Online Study Center

Improve Your Grade
Tutorials: What's So Complicated
About Seeing?

CONCEPT 3.12
**Objects are seen most clearly when their
images are focused on the fovea, a part
of the retina that contains only cones.**

ganglion cells   Nerve cells in the back of
the eye that transmit neural impulses in
response to light stimulation, the axons of
which make up the optic nerve.

optic nerve   The nerve that carries neural
impulses generated by light stimulation
from the eye to the brain.

blind spot   The area in the retina where
the optic nerve leaves the eye and that
contains no photoreceptor cells.

fovea   The area near the center of the
retina that contains only cones and that is
the center of focus for clearest vision.

called **ganglion cells** (see Figure 3.5). The axon projecting from each ganglion cell
makes up one nerve fiber in the **optic nerve**. The optic nerve, which consists of a
million or so ganglion axons, transmits visual information to the brain. In the
brain, this information is routed to the thalamus, a major relay station, and from
there to the visual cortex. The visual cortex lies in the occipital lobes, the part of
the cerebral cortex that processes visual information and produces the experience
of vision.

The part of the retina where the optic nerve leaves the eye is known as the
blind spot (see Figure 3.6). Because it contains no photoreceptors (rods or cones),
we do not see images that form on the blind spot. By contrast, the **fovea** is the part
of the retina that corresponds to the center of our gaze and that gives rise to our
sharpest vision (see Figure 3.3). It contains only cones (Pasternak et al., 2003).
Focusing our eyes on an object brings its image to bear directly on the fovea (see
Try This Out on page 101).

Farther away from the fovea, the proportion of cones decreases while the proportion of rods increases. Rods show the opposite pattern: they are few and far between close to the fovea and more densely packed farther away from the fovea.
The far ends of the retina contain only rods.

Visual acuity, or sharpness of vision, is the ability to discern visual details.
Many of us have impaired visual acuity. People who need to be unusually close to
objects to discern their details are *nearsighted*. People who need to be unusually far
away from objects to see them clearly are *farsighted*. Nearsightedness and farsightedness result from abnormalities in the shape of the eye. Nearsightedness can occur
when the eyeball is too long or the cornea is too curved. In either case, distant
objects are focused in front of the retina. Farsightedness can occur when the eyeball is too short so that light from nearby objects is focused behind the retina. People with nearsightedness or farsightedness can correct their vision by wearing
eyeglasses or contact lenses.

Figure 3.6   Blind Spot
Because there are no receptor cells in the blind spot—no rods or cones—images formed on the blind spot cannot be seen. You can demonstrate this for yourself by closing your left eye and, while focusing on the dot, slowly move the book farther away to about a distance of a foot. You'll notice there is a point at which the stack of money disappears. We are not typically aware of our blind spots because our eyes are constantly moving and because they work together to compensate for any loss of vision when an image falls on the blind spot.

Feature Detectors: Getting Down to Basics

In 1981, David Hubel and Torsten Wiesel received a Nobel Prize for unraveling a small piece of the puzzle of how we transform sensory information into rich visual experiences of the world around us. They discovered that the visual cortex contains nerve cells that respond only when an animal (in their studies, a cat) is shown a line with a particular orientation—horizontal, vertical, or diagonal (Hubel, 1988; Hubel & Wiesel, 1979). Some of these nerve cells respond only to lines that form right angles; others, to dots of light that move from right to left across the visual field; and yet others, to dots of light that move from left to right. Hubel and Wiesel made their discoveries by implanting a tiny electrode in individual cells in the cat's visual cortex. They then flashed different visual stimuli on a screen within the cat's field of vision and observed which cells fired in response to which types of stimuli. Neurons that respond to specific features of the visual stimulus are called **feature detectors**.

Yet we do not see a world composed of scattered bits and pieces of sensory data, of lines, angles, and moving points of light. Somehow the visual cortex compiles information from various cells, combining them to form meaningful patterns. How do we go from recognizing specific features of a stimulus—its individual angles, lines, and edges—to discerning a meaningful pattern, such as letters, numbers, words, or the human face? Scientists believe that complex assemblages of neurons in the brain work together to analyze relationships among specific features of objects. Hubel and Wiesel opened a door to understanding the beginning steps in this process at the level of the individual feature detector. Yet we are still a long way from understanding how the brain transforms sensory stimulation into the rich visual world we experience.

Color Vision: Sensing a Colorful World

To be able to perceive different colors, color receptors in the retina of the eye must transmit different messages to the brain when visible lights having different wavelengths stimulate them. How are these messages transmitted? Two nineteenth-century German scientists, Hermann von Helmholtz (1821–1894) and Ewald Hering (1834–1918), proposed different answers to this question.

Helmholtz contributed to many fields of science, but he is perhaps best known to psychologists for his work on color vision. He was impressed by the earlier work on color vision by the English scientist Thomas Young (1773–1829) (Martindale, 2001). Young had reversed the process by which a prism breaks light

---

CONCEPT 3.13
The brain's visual cortex contains cells so specialized that they fire only when they detect precise angles, lines, or points of light.

TRY THIS OUT
Reading Sideways
Hold a book or magazine to the side and try reading it. Why do you suppose the words are blurry, if you can make them out at all?

Online Study Center
Improve Your Grade
Tutorials: Monochromotopia

feature detectors   Specialized neurons in the visual cortex that respond only to particular features of visual stimuli, such as horizontal or vertical lines.

Figure 3.7 Primary Colors
The three primary colors of light—red, green, and blue-violet—combine to form white. Thomas Young showed that you could create any color of light by mixing these component colors and varying their brightnesses. For example, a combination of red and green light creates yellow.

down into component colors. He shone overlapping lights of red, green, and blue-violet onto a screen and found that he could create light of any color in the spectrum by varying the brightness of the lights (see Figure 3.7). Where all three lights overlapped, there was white light—the color of sunlight.

Building on Young's work, Helmholtz proposed what is now known as the Young-Helmholtz theory, or **trichromatic theory** (from Greek roots meaning "three" and "color"). Helmholtz believed that Young's experimental results showed that the eyes have three types of color receptors—red, green, and blue-violet. We now call these color receptors cones. These three types of cones have differing sensitivities to different wavelengths of light. Blue-violet cones are most sensitive to short wavelengths; green cones, to middle wavelengths; and red cones, to long wavelengths. According to the trichromatic theory, the response pattern of these three types of cones allows us to see different colors. So when green cones are most strongly activated, we see green. But when a combination of different types of cones is activated, we see other colors, just as mixing paint of different colors produces yet other colors. For example, when red and green receptors are stimulated at the same time, we see yellow.

Hering developed a different theory of color vision based on his work with *afterimages*. An **afterimage** is what you see if you gaze at a visual stimulus for a while and then look at a neutral surface, such as a sheet of white paper.

The flag in Figure 3.8 has all the shapes in the American flag, but the colors are off. Instead of being red, white, and blue, this flag is green, black, and yellow. Now, although you may not particularly wish to defend this oddly colored flag, gaze at it for a minute. (Give yourself a full minute.) Then shift your gaze to a white sheet of paper. You are likely to see a more familiar flag; this is because red is the afterimage of green, white is the afterimage of black, and blue is the afterimage of yellow.

Hering's work with afterimages led to him to develop the **opponent-process theory** of color vision. Opponent-process theory, like trichromatic theory, suggests that the eyes have three types of color receptors. According to this theory, however, each type of receptor consists of a pair of opposing receptors. Rather than there being separate receptors for red, green, and blue-violet, some receptors are sensitive to red or green; others, to blue or yellow; and others, to black or white. The black-white receptors detect brightness or shades of gray; the red-green and blue-yellow pairs detect differences in colors.

Figure 3.8 Afterimages
The colors in the American flag shown here can be set right by performing a simple experiment. Stare at the dot in the center of the flag for about sixty seconds. Then quickly shift your gaze to a white wall or white sheet of paper. You will see the more familiar colors of the American flag as afterimages.

Hering believed that color vision arises from pairs of opposing processes. According to his theory, red-green receptors do not simultaneously transmit messages for red and green. Rather, they transmit messages for either one or the other. When the red cone is activated, the green one is blocked, or inhibited, and so we see red. Yet prolonged transmission of any one message, such as red or green, disturbs the balance of neural activity, making it more difficult to inhibit the opposing color receptor. Thus, according to Hering's theory, if you stare at the green, black, and yellow flag in Figure 3.8 for a minute or so, you will disturb the balance of neural activity, producing an *opponent process*. The afterimage of red, white, and blue you experience represents the eye's attempt to reestablish a balance between the two opposing receptors.

Which model of color vision has it right—the trichromatic model or the opponent-process model? Contemporary research shows that both theories are right to a certain extent (Hergenhahn, 1997; Hubel, 1988). The trichromatic theory is correct at the receptor level, since the photochemistry of cones responds in the way described by trichromatic theory—some are sensitive to red light; others, to green light; and still others, to blue-violet light. But Hering's opponent-process theory is correct in terms of the behavior of cells that lie between the cones and the occipital lobe of the cerebral cortex, including bipolar and ganglion cells. These cells operate in an opponent-process fashion. Some are turned on by red light but are prevented (inhibited) from firing by green light. Others are turned on by green light but are inhibited by red light. Most authorities today believe that color vision includes elements of both trichromatic and opponent-process theories.

Trichromats are people with normal color vision who can discern all the colors of the visible spectrum—red, green, and blue-violet—as well as colors formed by various combinations of these hues.

About one out of every forty thousand people is completely color-blind. Such people are referred to as **monochromats** because they see only in black and white, as in an old movie or TV show. Because of a genetic defect, they have only one type of cone, so their brains cannot discern differences in the wavelengths of light that normally give rise to color. They can detect only brightness, so the world appears in shades of gray.

Much more common are **dichromats**—people who lack one of the three types of cones, making it difficult to distinguish between certain types of colors. The most common form is red-green color blindness, a genetic defect that makes it difficult to discriminate reds from greens. About 8 percent of men have red-green color blindness, as compared with fewer than 1 percent of women. Much less common is blue-yellow color blindness, in which the person has difficulty distinguishing blues from yellows. Figure 3.9 shows a plate from a test used to assess color blindness.

CONCEPT 3.14
The major theories of color, trichromatic theory and opponent-process theory, may each partially account for color vision.

CONCEPT 3.15
The most common form of color blindness is red-green color blindness, in which people cannot tell reds from greens.

trichromatic theory A theory of color vision that posits that the ability to see different colors depends on the relative activity of three types of color receptors in the eye (red, green, and blue-violet).

afterimage The visual image of a stimulus that remains after the stimulus is removed.

opponent-process theory A theory of color vision that holds that the experience of color results from opposing processes involving two sets of color receptors, red-green receptors and blue-yellow receptors, and that another set of opposing receptors, black-white, is responsible for detecting differences in brightness.

trichromats People with normal color vision who can discern all the colors of the visual spectrum.

monochromats People who have no color vision and can see only in black and white.

dichromats People who can see some colors but not others.

Figure 3.9 Color Blindness
What do you see? People with normal color vision will see the triangle in this array of dots. People with red-green color blindness will not perceive it.

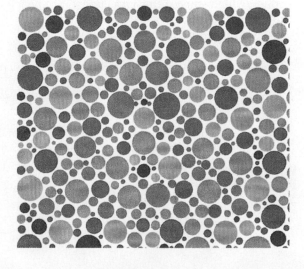

CONCEPT CHART 3.2   Vision

Source of sensory information	Visible light
Receptor organs	The eyes. Light enters through the cornea and pupil and is focused on the retina.
Receptor cells	The retina has two kinds of photoreceptors. Rods are sensitive to the intensity of light, which is the basis of our sense of light and dark. Cones are sensitive to differences in the wavelengths of light, which is the basis of color vision. Visual information is transmitted to the brain by means of the optic nerve.
Color vision	Two major theories of color vision have been proposed, the trichromatic theory and the opponent-process theory. Each theory appears to account for some aspects of color vision.

People with red-green color blindness might put on one green sock and one red sock, as long as they were similar in brightness. But they would not confuse green with blue. Red-green color blindness appears to be a sex-linked genetic defect that is carried on the X sex chromosome (Neitz & Neitz, 1995). As noted, more males than females are affected by this condition. Because males have only one X chromosome, whereas females have two, a defect on one X chromosome is more likely to be expressed in males than in females. Concept Chart 3.2 provides an overview of vision.

MODULE 3.2 REVIEW

Vision: Seeing the Light

RECITE IT

How do the eyes process light?

- Light enters the eye through the cornea and passes through the pupil and then the lens, which focuses the image on the retina.

- The light then stimulates photoreceptor cells, rods or cones, which convert the light energy into neural impulses that are carried first through bipolar cells and then to ganglion cells that terminate in the optic nerve.

- When we focus on an object, we bring its image to bear on the fovea, the cone-rich part of the retina in which we have our sharpest vision.

- Cones allow us to see colors but are less sensitive to light than rods are.

- Rods allow us to see objects in black and white in dim light; they are also responsible for peripheral vision.

What are feature detectors, and what role do they play in visual processing?

- Feature detectors are specialized cells in the visual cortex that respond only to specific features of visual stimuli, such as horizontal or vertical lines.

What are the two major theories of color vision?

- The trichromatic theory, or Young-Helmholtz theory, proposes that there are three kinds of color receptors (red, green, and blue-violet) and that all the colors in the spectrum can be generated by the simultaneous stimulation of a combination of these color receptors.

- The opponent-process theory developed by Ewald Hering proposes that there are three pairs of receptors (red-green, blue-yellow, black-white) and that opposing processes within each pair determine our experience of color.

What are the two major forms of color blindness?

- The two major forms of color blindness are complete color blindness (lack of any ability to discern colors) and partial color blindness (red-green or blue-yellow color blindness).

RECALL IT

1. The photoreceptors in the retina that are responsible for peripheral vision and vision in dim light are called _____; those responsible for color vision and for discerning fine details in bright light are called _____.

2. Rods are most heavily concentrated around the fovea. True or false?

3. Match the following parts of the eye with their respective functions: (a) iris; (b) pupil; (c) lens; (d) retina; (e) fovea; (f) blind spot.
   i. the part of the eye that focuses the visual image on the retina
   ii. inner surface of the eye in which the photo-receptors are found
   iii. the part of the retina from which the optic nerve leaves the eye
   iv. muscle controlling the size of the pupil
   v. area on the retina responsible for clearest vision
   vi. opening through which light enters the eye

THINK ABOUT IT

• Explain the phenomenon of afterimages by drawing upon Hering's opponent-process theory of color vision.

• Are you color blind? Do you know anyone who is? What type of color blindness do you (they) have? How has it affected your life, if at all? Have you (they) learned skills to compensate for color blindness?

MODULE 3.3

Hearing: The Music of Sound

■ How does the ear enable us to hear sound?

■ What determines our perception of pitch?

■ What are the main types and causes of deafness?

CONCEPT 3.16

Sound vibrations are the stimuli transformed by receptors in the ears into signals the brain uses to let you experience the sounds of the world around you.

The chattering of birds, the voices of children playing in the yard, the stirring melodies of Tchaikovsky—we sense all these sounds by means of hearing, or **audition**. We hear by sensing sound waves, which result from changes in the pressure of air or water. When sound waves impinge upon the ear, they cause parts of the ear to vibrate. These vibrations are then converted into electrical signals that are sent to the brain.

Sound: Sensing Waves of Vibrations

Like visible light, sound is a form of energy that travels in waves. Yet while light can travel through the empty reaches of outer space, sound exists only in a medium, such as air, liquids, gases, or even solids (which is why you may hear your neighbor's stereo through a solid wall). A vibrating object causes molecules of air (or other substances, such as water) to vibrate. For example, your voice is produced when your vocal cords vibrate. The resulting vibrations spread outward from the source in the form of sound waves that are characterized by such physical properties as *amplitude* (the height of the wave, which is a measure of the amount of energy in the sound wave) and *frequency* (the number of complete waves, or cycles, per second) (see Figure 3.10).

The amplitude of sound waves determines their perceived loudness and is measured in *decibels* (dB). For each ten-decibel increase, loudness of the sound increases tenfold. Thus, a sound of twenty decibels is actually ten times, not two times, louder than a sound of ten decibels.

audition   The sense of hearing.

Figure 3.10 Sound Waves
Sound waves vary in such physical properties as amplitude, or height of the wave, and frequency, or number of complete cycles per second. Differences in amplitude give rise to perceptions of loudness, whereas differences in frequency lead to perceptions of pitch.

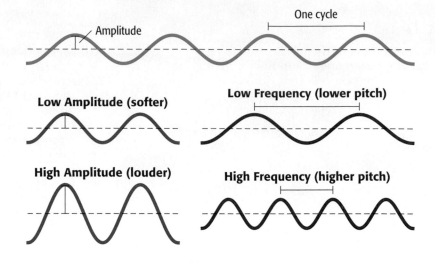

pitch The highness or lowness of a sound that corresponds to the frequency of the sound wave.

eardrum A sheet of connective tissue separating the outer ear from the middle ear that vibrates in response to auditory stimuli and transmits sound waves to the middle ear.

ossicles Three tiny bones in the middle ear (the hammer, anvil, and stirrup) that vibrate in response to vibrations of the eardrum.

oval window The membrane-covered opening that separates the middle ear from the inner ear.

cochlea The snail-shaped organ in the inner ear that contains sensory receptors for hearing.

basilar membrane The membrane in the cochlea that is attached to the organ of Corti.

organ of Corti A gelatinous structure in the cochlea containing the hair cells that serve as auditory receptors.

hair cells The auditory receptors that transform vibrations caused by sound waves into neural impulses that are then transmitted to the brain via the auditory nerve.

auditory nerve The nerve that carries neural impulses from the ear to the brain, which gives rise to the experience of hearing.

Light travels at 186,000 miles per second, which means that it takes about one and one-third seconds for a beam of light from the moon to reach the earth (a distance of about 240,000 miles). Sound is a slowpoke by comparison. Sound travels through air at only about 1,130 feet per second (or 770 miles per *hour*). Therefore, it may take about five seconds for the thunder from lightning a mile away to reach your ears. But most of the sounds that matter to us—the voice of a teacher or a lover, the screeches and whines of cars and buses, and the sounds of music—are so close that they seem to reach us in no time at all.

Although sound travels more slowly than light, the vibrations that give rise to sound still occur many times a second. The frequency with which they occur per second provides information that the brain uses to produce perceptions of **pitch**, or how high or low a sound seems. The human ear senses sound waves that vary in frequency from about 20 to perhaps 20,000 cycles per second. Sound waves that are higher in frequency are perceived as being higher in pitch. Women's voices are usually higher than men's because their vocal cords tend to be shorter and thus vibrate more rapidly (at a greater frequency). The shorter strings on a harp (or in a piano) produce higher notes than the longer strings because they vibrate more rapidly.

The Ear: A Sound Machine

The ear is structured to capture sound waves, reverberate with them, and convert them into messages that are relayed to the brain in the form of neural impulses (see Figure 3.11). The outer ear funnels sound waves to the **eardrum**, a tight membrane that vibrates in response to them. The vibrations are then transmitted through three tiny bones in the middle ear called the **ossicles** (literally "little bones"). The first of these to vibrate, the "hammer" (*malleus*), is connected to the eardrum. It strikes the "anvil" (*incus*), which in turn strikes the "stirrup" (*stapes*), causing it to vibrate. The vibration is transmitted from the stirrup to the **oval window**, a membrane to which the stirrup is attached. The oval window connects the middle ear to a snail- or coiled-shaped, fluid-filled tubular structure in the inner ear, called the **cochlea** (*cochlea* is the Greek word for "snail") (Hackett & Kaas, 2003).

When we hear a sound, physical movements in the inner ear become transformed into electrical signals that the brain can interpret (Ashmore, 2004). Here's how it works: Vibrations of the oval window cause waves of motion in fluid within the cochlea in the inner ear. The motion of this fluid causes a structure within the cochlea, the **basilar membrane**, to vibrate.

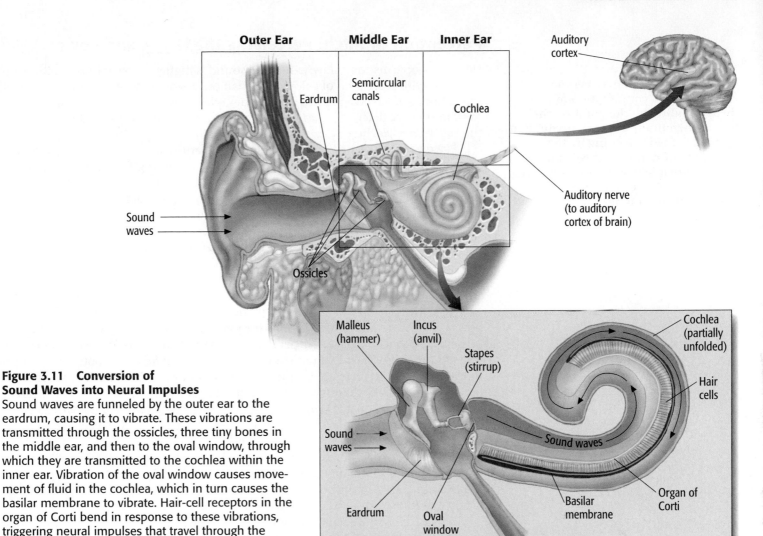

Figure 3.11 Conversion of Sound Waves into Neural Impulses
Sound waves are funneled by the outer ear to the eardrum, causing it to vibrate. These vibrations are transmitted through the ossicles, three tiny bones in the middle ear, and then to the oval window, through which they are transmitted to the cochlea within the inner ear. Vibration of the oval window causes movement of fluid in the cochlea, which in turn causes the basilar membrane to vibrate. Hair-cell receptors in the organ of Corti bend in response to these vibrations, triggering neural impulses that travel through the auditory nerve to the brain.

CONCEPT 3.17

Sound waves cause parts of the ear to vibrate; this mechanical vibration in turn affects sensory receptors in the inner ear, called hair cells, triggering auditory messages to be sent to the brain.

The basilar membrane is attached to a gelatinous structure called the **organ of Corti**, which is lined with 15,000 or so **hair cells** that serve as auditory receptors. These hair cells are not real hairs, but cells with 100 or so hairlike projections sticking out from their surfaces (Kros, 2005). The movement of the basilar membrane as it vibrates causes these hair cells to bend, which in turn triggers a neural message that is transmitted to the brain by way of the **auditory nerve**. The message is received by the auditory cortex, located in the temporal lobes of the cerebral cortex. The auditory cortex then processes the message, producing our experience of sound.

Your brain determines where a sound is coming from by comparing the sounds you receive in your two ears. Unless sounds originate from sources equally distant from both ears—for example, exactly in front of or above you—they reach one ear before the other. Although you might not be able to say exactly how much sooner you hear a sound in one ear than in the other, your brain can detect a difference as small as 1/10,000th of a second. It uses such information to help locate the source of a sound. More distant sounds tend to be softer, just as more distant objects look smaller, which provides yet another cue for locating sounds.

Perception of Pitch: Perceiving the Highs and Lows

How do people distinguish whether one sound is higher or lower in pitch than another? As with perception of color, more than one theory is needed to help us understand how we perceive pitch. Two theories, *place theory* and *frequency theory*, help explain how we detect high and low pitches, and a combination of the two, called the *volley principle*, helps explain how we detect mid-range pitches.

Place theory, originally developed by Hermann von Helmholtz, suggests that people perceive a sound to have a certain pitch according to the place along the basilar membrane that vibrates the most when sound waves of particular frequencies strike the ear. It is as though neurons line up along the basilar membrane like so many keys on a piano, standing ready to respond by producing sounds of different pitch when they are "struck" (Azar, 1996a).

Georg von Békésy (1957) won a Nobel Prize for showing that high-frequency sounds cause the greatest vibration of hair cells close to the oval window, whereas those with lower frequencies cause the greatest vibration farther down the basilar membrane. Hair cells at the point of maximal vibration, like the crest of a wave, excite particular neurons that inform the brain about their location. The brain uses this information to code sounds for pitch. However, low-frequency sounds—those below about 4,000 cycles per second—cannot be coded for location because they do not cause the membrane to vibrate the most at any one spot. Yet we know that people can detect sounds with frequencies as low as 20 cycles per second.

Enter **frequency theory**, which may account for how we perceive the pitch of sounds of about 20 to 1,000 cycles per second. According to frequency theory, the basilar membrane vibrates at the same frequency as the sound wave itself. In other words, a sound wave with a frequency of 200 cycles per second would cause the basilar membrane to vibrate at that rate and generate a corresponding number of neural impulses to the brain. In this case, there would be 200 neural impulses to the brain per second. But frequency theory also has its limitations. Most importantly, neurons cannot fire more frequently than about 1,000 times per second.

What, then, do we make of sounds with frequencies between 1,000 and 4,000 cycles per second? We bridge that gap by means of the **volley principle**. In one of nature's many surprises, it seems that groups of neurons along the basilar membrane fire in volleys, or alternating succession (as when one group of soldiers stands and fires while an alternate group kneels and reloads). By firing in rotation, groups of neurons combine their frequencies of firing to fill the gap.

In sum, frequency theory best explains pitch perception for low-frequency sounds, whereas place theory best explains pitch of high-frequency sounds. A combination of frequency and place theory, called the volley principle, suggests how we perceive the pitch of mid-range sounds.

place theory   The belief that pitch depends on the place along the basilar membrane that vibrates the most in response to a particular auditory stimulus.

frequency theory   The belief that pitch depends on the frequency of vibration of the basilar membrane and the volley of neural impulses transmitted to the brain via the auditory nerve.

volley principle   The principle that relates the experience of pitch to the alternating firing of groups of neurons along the basilar membrane.

Are You Protecting Your Hearing?

Nearly thirty million Americans have hearing problems, and as many as two million are deaf. There are many causes of hearing loss and deafness, including birth defects, disease, advanced age, and injury—especially the kind of injury caused by exposure to loud noise. Repeated or prolonged exposure to noise at a level of 85 decibels or higher can damage hearing, as can even brief exposure to sounds of 120 decibels or louder. Figure 3.12 shows the decibel levels of many familiar sounds. The clamor at most bars and clubs reaches 110 to 120 decibels, and even headphones can register 100 decibels or more (O'Connor, 2005). Many aging rock musicians, DJ's, and frequent concertgoers are now suffering from hearing loss.

Noise effects are not limited to urban dwellers. Even in our pristine national parks, helicopter noise is a major impediment to enjoying the experience and even appreciating the beauty of the landscape (Mace et al., 2000; Mace, Bell & Loomis, 1999).

Figure 3.12 Sounds and Decibels
Permanent hearing loss may occur from prolonged exposure to sound over 85 decibels (dB). Exposure to 120 decibels or higher creates an immediate danger to hearing. Most people can detect faint sounds at a decibel level just above 0 dB.

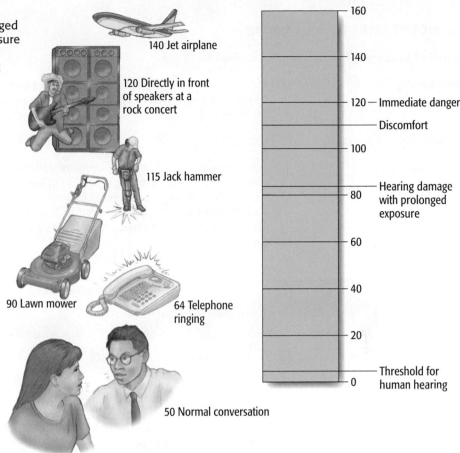

140 Jet airplane

120 Directly in front of speakers at a rock concert

115 Jack hammer

90 Lawn mower

64 Telephone ringing

50 Normal conversation

160
140
120 — Immediate danger
Discomfort
100
80 — Hearing damage with prolonged exposure
60
40
20
0 — Threshold for human hearing

There are two main types of deafness: conduction deafness and nerve deafness.

Conduction deafness is usually caused by damage to the middle ear. The eardrum may be punctured, or the three bones that amplify sound waves and conduct them to the inner ear may lose the ability to vibrate properly. People who experience conduction deafness may benefit from hearing aids that amplify sound waves.

Nerve deafness is usually caused by damage to the hair cells of the inner ear or to the auditory nerve. Exposure to loud sounds, disease, and aging can cause nerve deafness. The "ringing sensation" that can follow exposure to loud noises may indicate damage to hair cells. Cochlear implants, or "artificial ears," are sometimes successful in transmitting sounds past damaged hair cells to the auditory nerve. They work by converting sounds into electrical impulses. But these implants cannot correct for damage to the auditory nerve itself. If the auditory nerve does not function, even sounds that cause the hair cells on the basilar membrane to dance frantically will not be sensed in the auditory cortex of the brain.

Hearing loss in later life is not inevitable. It is largely due to years of abuse from loud music and noise. Here are some suggestions for avoiding exposure to excessive noise and helping to prevent noise-induced hearing loss later in life:

• When you can't avoid excessive noise, as in worksites, wear hearing protectors or earplugs.

• Turn down the volume when listening to music, especially music piped through headphones or earphones. Avoid attending ear-splitting concerts.

• If you live in a particularly noisy area, organize your neighbors to pressure government officials to seek remedies.

Before moving on, you may wish to review the basic concepts in hearing that are outlined in Concept Chart 3.3.

conduction deafness A form of deafness, usually involving damage to the middle ear, in which there is a loss of conduction of sound vibrations through the ear.

nerve deafness Deafness associated with nerve damage, usually involving damage to the hair cells or the auditory nerve itself.

CONCEPT CHART 3.3   Hearing

Source of sensory information	Sound waves
Receptor organs	The ears. The outer ear funnels sound waves through the eardrum to the middle ear, where they are amplified by three tiny bones and transmitted through the oval window to the inner ear.
Receptor cells	Hair cells on the basilar membrane within the cochlea of the inner ear
Pitch perception	Three theories contribute to our understanding of pitch perception. Frequency theory appears to account for pitch perception of low-frequency sounds below 1,000 cycles per second. Place theory alone seems to account for pitch perception of high-frequency sounds above 4,000 cycles per second. The volley principle appears to explain pitch perception of moderate-frequency sounds in the range of approximately 1,000 to 4,000 cycles per second.

MODULE 3.3 REVIEW

Hearing: The Music of Sound

RECITE IT

How does the ear enable us to hear sound?

- Sound waves enter the outer ear and are funneled to the eardrum, causing it to vibrate. This mechanical energy is conveyed to tiny bones in the middle ear—the hammer, anvil, and stirrup—and then through the oval window to the cochlea in the inner ear.

- The organ of Corti in the cochlea is lined with hair cells that bend in response to the vibrations, triggering neural impulses that are fed through the auditory nerve to the auditory cortex in the temporal lobes of the brain, which leads to the experience of hearing.

What determines our perception of pitch?

- Perception of pitch is likely determined by a combination of the place on the basilar membrane of greatest vibration (place theory), the frequency of neural impulses (frequency theory), and the sequencing of firing of groups of neurons along the basilar membrane (volley principle).

What are the main types and causes of deafness?

- The main types of deafness are conduction deafness, usually caused by damage to the middle ear, and nerve deafness, usually caused by damage to the hair cells of the inner ear or to the auditory nerve.

RECALL IT

1. Which characteristics of sound waves give rise to the perception of loudness and pitch?

2. According to the frequency theory of pitch perception, our ability to detect differences in pitch is due to
   a. the rate of vibration of the basilar membrane.
   b. the location along the basilar membrane where the greatest vibration occurs.
   c. the alternation between areas of greater and lesser vibration of the basilar membrane.
   d. the rate of vibration of the oval window.

3. Match these parts of the ear with the descriptions that follow: (a) eardrum; (b) ossicles; (c) cochlea; (d) basilar membrane; (e) organ of Corti; (f) hair cells.
   i. a membrane that separates the outer ear from the middle ear
   ii. sensory receptors for hearing
   iii. a gelatinous structure attached to the basilar membrane and lined with sensory receptors
   iv. the membrane in the cochlea that moves in response to sound vibrations
   v. three small bones in the middle ear that conduct sound vibrations
   vi. a snail-shaped bony tube in the inner ear in which fluid moves in response to the vibrations of the oval window

THINK ABOUT IT

- What characteristics of sound waves give rise to the perception of loudness and pitch?

- What steps are you taking to protect your hearing from the damaging effects of noise? Are you doing enough?

MODULE 3.4

Our Other Senses: Chemical, Skin, and Body Senses

- How do we sense odors and tastes?
- What are the skin senses?
- What are the kinesthetic and vestibular senses?

We usually think of five senses—sight, hearing, smell, taste, and touch. Yet there are actually more. Here we take a look at the chemical, skin, and body senses. These are the sensory systems that allow us to smell, taste, and touch and that keep us informed about the position and movement of our bodies.

The nose and tongue are like human chemistry laboratories. Smell and taste are chemical senses because they are based on the chemical analysis of molecules of substances that waft past the nose or that land on the tongue. The chemical senses allow us to perform chemistry on the fly.

Olfaction: What Your Nose Knows

Many chemical substances found in the air, such as carbon monoxide, have no odor. Though they enter our noses as we breathe them in, they do not stimulate **olfaction**, our sense of smell. They are odorless because odor receptors in the nose do not detect their chemical structures. Stimulation of the sense of smell depends on the shape of the molecules of chemical substances.

Though our olfactory system may not be as sensitive as that of dogs or cats, it is nonetheless exquisitely sensitive, allowing us to discern some ten thousand different substances on the basis of the shape of their molecules. In 2004, two scientists were awarded the Nobel Prize for medicine based on their discovery of the family of genes that give rise to the 1,000 or so different types of odor receptors in the nasal passageway ("Americans Axel, Buck Win Nobel," 2004). All told, we have some five million odor receptors of different types.

When molecules of different substances waft into the nose, they fit into particular odor receptors as keys fit into locks, triggering olfactory messages to be carried to the brain along the **olfactory nerve** (DiLorenzo & Youngentob, 2003) (see Figure 3.13). The smell of a freshly baked bread or brewed coffee activates an array

CONCEPT 3.20

The sense of smell depends on receptors in the nose that detect thousands of chemical substances and transmit information about them to the brain.

Figure 3.13   Olfaction
Receptor cells high in the nose respond to the molecular shapes of chemical substances, triggering nerve impulses that travel through the olfactory nerve to the olfactory bulb in the brain. This process gives rise to sensations of specific odors.

Olfactory bulb

Olfactory nerve

Receptor cells in olfactory membrane

Nasal passage

olfaction   The sense of smell.
olfactory nerve   The nerve that carries impulses from olfactory receptors in the nose to the brain.

A Sexy Scent? Scientists find that exposure to male sweat induces hormonal and mood changes in women. Whether bodily secretions or scents induce sexual attraction in people remains a question that scientists (as well as fragrance companies) continue to explore.

CONCEPT 3.21
Pheromones are chemical substances that play various roles in animal behavior, but their functions in human behavior remain unclear.

olfactory bulb The area in the front of the brain above the nostrils that receives sensory input from olfactory receptors in the nose.

pheromones Chemical substances that are emitted by many species and that have various functions, including sexual attraction.

of these odor receptors. This olfactory information is then processed by the brain, giving rise to odors corresponding to these particular chemical stimuli. The intensity of the odor appears to be a function of the number of olfactory receptors that are stimulated simultaneously.

Smell is the only sense in which sensory information does not go through the thalamus on its way to the cerebral cortex. Instead, olfactory information travels through the olfactory nerve directly to the **olfactory bulb**, a structure in the front of the brain above the nostrils. This information is then routed to the olfactory cortex in the temporal lobe and to several structures in the limbic system, which, as noted in Chapter 2, has important roles in emotion and memory. The connections between the olfactory system and the limbic system may account for the close relationship between odors and emotional memories. A whiff of chocolate pudding simmering on the stove or of someone's perfume may bring back strong feelings associated with childhood experiences or a particular person.

Olfaction plays a key role in perceiving flavors of foods. Actually, much of what we think we are tasting is actually what we are smelling (DiLorenzo & Youngentob, 2003). Without the sense of smell, the flavor of a steak might not be all that different from that of cardboard. An apple might taste the same as a raw potato. In laboratory studies, people were unable to identify tastes of coffee and chocolate when their sense of smell was blocked (DiLorenzo & Youngentob, 2003). A declining sense of smell in later life may be the major reason many older people complain that food doesn't taste as good as it once did.

Our sensory organs were shaped over the course of millions of years of adaptation to the environment. Olfaction, among our other senses, is critical to our survival. It helps us avoid rotten and potentially harmful foods long before we put our tongue to them. In various animal species, olfaction serves other functions as well. Fur seals and many other animal species recognize their own young from the pack on the basis of smell. Salmon roam the seven seas but sniff out the streams of their birth at spawning time on the basis of a few molecules of water emitted by those streams.

Many species emit chemical substances called **pheromones** that play important roles in numerous behaviors, including attracting mates, marking territory, establishing dominance hierarchies, controlling aggression, and organizing food-gathering efforts (DiLorenzo & Youngentob, 2003; Gaulin & McBurney, 2001; Rodriguez et al., 2000). Pheromones are found in bodily secretions, such as urine or vaginal secretions, and are detected by other members of the species through the sense of smell or taste.

We know that pheromones contribute to sexual attraction in various species of both animals and insects. But do they serve a similar purpose in humans?

TRY THIS OUT
The Smell of Taste

Ever notice that food tastes bland when your nose is stuffed? To demonstrate how olfaction affects your sense of taste, try eating a meal while holding your nostrils closed. What effect does it have on your ability to taste your food? on your enjoyment of the meal?

Although most mammals have specialized organs in the nose that they use to detect pheromones, claims that humans possess such an organ remain controversial. Presently, it is not clear what role, if any, pheromones play in human sexual behavior (Doty, 2001; Jacob et al., 2002).

Suffice it to say that what the nose knows remains an open question. Yet recent evidence suggests that the nose may indeed "know" more than we had believed. For example, evidence shows that substances present in the underarm secretions of young women can increase the women's sexual attractiveness to men (McCoy & Pitino, 2002). Moreover, scientists recently discovered that male sweat relaxes women (Pilcher, 2003). Researchers applied male perspiration (disguised by fragrance) to the lips of women volunteers for a period of six hours (Preti et al., 2003). The women were led to believe they were testing other chemical compounds, such as fragrances and alcohol. Exposure to these dabs of male perspiration affected levels of a female reproductive hormone and induced feelings of relaxation. However, none of the women exposed to the male perspiration reported feeling sexually aroused.

Taste: The Flavorful Sense

Taste, like our other senses, plays an important role in adaptation and survival. We rely on both taste and smell to discriminate between healthy, nutritious food and spoiled or rotten food. (The sense organs are not perfect, however; some poisonous substances are undetectable by smell or taste.)

There are thousands of different kinds of food and thousands of different flavors. Yet there are only four basic tastes: sweet, sour, salty, and bitter. The *flavor* of a food results from combinations of these taste qualities, the aroma of the food, its texture, and its temperature.

Tastes are sensed by receptors called **taste cells**. These are nerve cells located within pores or openings on the tongue called **taste buds**. Most taste buds are found near the edges and back of the tongue. Yet people without tongues can also sense taste because additional taste receptors are located on the roof of the mouth, inside the cheeks, and in the throat. Some taste receptors are more sensitive to a specific taste quality; others respond to several tastes. Despite these sensitivities, appropriate stimulation of virtually any part of the tongue that contains taste receptors can produce any of the primary tastes (Shiffman, 2000). Taste receptors differ from other neurons in that they regenerate very quickly—within a week to ten days. This is a good thing because people kill them off regularly by eating very hot food, such as pizza that is just out of the oven.

Why do some people like their food spicy, while others like it plain? Differences in cultural background certainly play a part in taste preferences. Babies may even be exposed to such cultural preferences in flavors when breast-feeding (Azar, 1998b). If a mother consumes garlic or vanilla, for example, the nursing baby will spend more time savoring these flavors by keeping the milk longer in its mouth.

Genetic factors play a significant role in determining taste sensitivities and preferences (Bartoshuk & Beauchamp, 1994; J. E. Brody, 2001a; Collins, 2005). Some people inherit a greater sensitivity to sweetness than others, and some inherit a sensitivity to bitter tastes. Cats are completely insensitive to sweets because they lack sweet taste receptors (DiLorenzo & Youngentob, 2003). But pigs do have a "sweet tooth" because they have these receptors. It might be accurate to say that while humans may eat like pigs, pigs may also eat like humans.

About one in four people (more women than men) are born with a very dense network of taste buds that makes them overly sensitive to certain tastes (Goode, 2001a). These people are called "supertasters." Supertasters may recoil at the sharp or bitter tastes of many fruits and vegetables, including broccoli, or find sugary foods sickeningly sweet. Researchers find both gender and ethnic or racial differences in taste sensitivity. For example, Asian women are most likely to be super-

CONCEPT 3.22
Like the sense of smell, the sense of taste depends on receptors that detect chemical substances and transmit information about them to the brain.

taste cells   Nerve cells that are sensitive to tastes.
taste buds   Pores or openings on the tongue containing taste cells.

CONCEPT CHART 3.4 Chemical, Skin, and Body Senses

Chemical Senses	**Olfaction**	Source of sensory information	Molecules of the substance being sensed
		Receptor organ	The nose
		Receptor cells	Receptors in each nostril that can sense about 10,000 different substances on the basis of their molecular shapes
	Taste	Source of sensory information	Molecules of the substance being sensed
		Receptor organs	Mainly taste buds on the tongue, although there are additional receptors elsewhere in the mouth and throat
		Receptor cells	Taste receptors that are sensitive to one or more of four basic tastes: sweet, sour, salty, and bitter
Skin Senses	**Skin Senses**	Source of sensory information	Touch, pressure, warmth, cold, and pain
		Receptor organ	The skin (pain can also originate in many other parts of the body)
		Receptor cells	Receptors that code for touch, pressure, warmth, cold, and pain
Body Senses	**Kinesthesis**	Source of sensory information	Movement and relative position of body parts
		Receptor cells	Receptors located mainly in joints, ligaments, and muscles
	Vestibular Sense	Source of sensory information	Motion of the body and orientation in space
		Receptor organs	Semicircular canals and vestibular sacs in the inner ear
		Receptor cells	Hair-cell receptors that respond to the movement of fluid in the semicircular canals and to shifts in the position of crystals in vestibular sacs

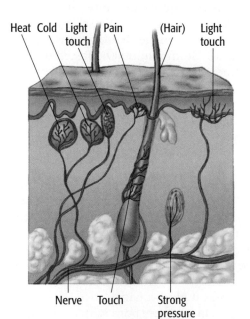

Heat Cold Light touch Pain (Hair) Light touch

Nerve Touch Strong pressure

Figure 3.14 Your Largest Sensory Organ—Your Skin
The skin contains receptors that are sensitive to touch, pressure, warm and cold temperatures, and pain.

tasters, while White men are much less likely to belong to this group (Carpenter, 2000d). Recently, scientists discovered what we might term a tasty gene: a gene that allows one to taste a particular bitter-flavored chemical (Kim et al., 2003). The gene controls the shape of the specific receptor on the tongue that responds to this chemical.

These genetic traits help determine dietary choices. For example, some people who load their meat with salt may be nearly taste-blind to salt, another genetic trait. Others are extremely sensitive to salt, pepper, and other spices. Concept Chart 3.4 reviews the chemical senses—olfaction and taste.

The Skin Senses: Your Largest Sensory Organ

You may not think of your skin as a sensory organ. But it is actually the body's largest sensory organ. It contains receptors for the body's **skin senses** that code for sensations of touch, pressure, warmth, cold, and pain. Some skin receptors respond to just one type of stimulation, such as pressure or warmth. Others respond to more than one type of stimulation.

Nearly one-half million receptors for touch and pressure are distributed throughout the body. They transmit sensory information to the spinal cord, which relays it to the *somatosensory cortex,* the part of the cerebral cortex that processes information from our skin receptors and makes us aware of how and where we have been touched. Many touch receptors are located near the surface of the skin (see Figure 3.14). They fire when the skin is lightly touched—for example, caressed,

CONCEPT 3.23

Sensory receptors in the skin are sensitive to touch, pressure, temperature, and pain, and they transmit information about these stimuli to your brain.

Blocking Pain Applying an ice pack to an injured area may reduce pain. Based on your reading of the text, how would you explain this phenomenon?

CONCEPT 3.24

The gate-control theory of pain proposes that the spinal cord contains a gating mechanism that controls the transmission of pain messages to the brain.

skin senses The senses of touch, pressure, warmth, cold, and pain that involve stimulation of sensory receptors in the skin.

gate-control theory of pain The belief that a neural gate in the spinal cord opens to allow pain messages to reach the brain and closes to shut them out.

stroked, or patted. Other receptors at deeper levels beneath the skin fire in response to pressure.

Receptors for temperature are also found just beneath the skin. Scientists generally agree that specific receptors exist for warmth and cold. In one of nature's more interesting surprises, sensations of hotness are produced by simultaneous stimulation of receptors for warmth and cold. If you were to clutch coiled pipes with warm and cold water circulating through them, you might feel as though your hand were being burned. Then, if the pipes were uncoiled, you would find that neither one by itself could give rise to sensations of hotness.

Reflect for a moment about what it might mean if you did not experience pain. At first thought, not sensing pain might seem to be a good thing. After all, why go through life with headaches, toothaches, and backaches if you do not have to do so? Yet a life without pain could be a short one.

Pain is a sign that something is wrong. Without the experience of pain, you might not notice splinters, paper cuts, burns, and the many sources of injury, irritation, and infection that can ultimately threaten life if not attended to promptly. Sip a cup of coffee that is too hot and receptors on your tongue send signals to your brain that cause you to wince and stop drinking to prevent further damage (Kalb, 2003b). Pain is usually adaptive—that is, by alerting us to damage to bodily tissues, it increases our chances of survival (Watkins & Maier, 2003). Pain is a signal that something is wrong, which leads us to search for and do something about the source of the pain.

Pain receptors are located not just in the skin, but also in other parts of the body, including muscles, joints, ligaments, and the pulp of the teeth—the source of tooth pain. We can feel pain in most parts of the body. Pain can be particularly acute where nerve endings are densely packed, as in the fingers and face. Sadly, some people are born without any pain receptors (Kalb, 2003b). Their bodies have no way of signaling danger, so most struggle as best they can to deal with assorted cuts, burns, and bruises. Sadly, most die young from injuries they sustain or from infections that take root in sites that suffer repetitive injuries.

People use many homespun remedies to control pain, such as rubbing or scratching a painful area or applying an ice pack. Why do these methods sometimes help? One possible answer lies in a theory developed by psychologist Ronald Melzack and biologist Patrick Wall (1965, 1983). According to their **gate-control theory of pain**, a gating mechanism in the spinal cord opens and closes to let pain messages through to the brain or to shut them out. The "gate" is not an actual physical structure in the spinal cord, but rather a pattern of nervous system activity that results in either blocking pain signals or letting them through.

Using this theory, we can say that rubbing or applying cold or warmth creates a bottleneck at the "gate" that may block out pain signals. It does this because the nerve fibers that carry sensory signals for warmth, cold, and touch are thicker and faster than those carrying signals associated with dull or throbbing pain (Coderre, Mogil, & Bushnell, 2003). Thus an ice pack reduces pain not only by curbing inflammation and swelling, which contribute to pain, but also by temporarily blocking out the signals for pain. However, the first sharp pangs of pain you experience when you stub your toe or cut your finger are carried by large nerve pathways and apparently cannot be blocked out. This is a good thing, as it ensures that pain messages register quickly in the brain, alerting you instantly to the part of your body that has been injured.

The brain also plays a critical role in controlling pain because it signals the release of *endorphins*. As you may recall from Chapter 2, endorphins are neurotransmitters that are similar in chemical composition to narcotic drugs, such as heroin, that have painkilling effects. They lock into receptor sites in the spinal cord that transmit pain messages, thereby closing the "pain gate" and preventing pain messages from reaching the brain. Yet endorphins are not effective in blocking all sources of pain.

Acupuncture Used for centuries by Chinese physicians, the benefits of acupuncture are still being debated by Western scientists.

CONCEPT 3.25
Sensory receptors in your joints, ligaments, and muscles transmit information that the brain uses to keep you aware of the position and movement of parts of your body.

CONCEPT 3.26
Sensory organs within your inner ears respond to gravitational forces and provide the brain with the sensory information it needs to maintain your balance and to know the position of your body in space.

acupuncture An ancient Chinese practice of inserting and rotating thin needles in various parts of the body in order to release natural healing energy.

kinesthesis The sense that keeps us informed about movement of the parts of the body and their position in relation to each other.

vestibular sense The sense that keeps us informed about balance and the position of our body in space.

semicircular canals Three curved, tube-like canals in the inner ear that are involved in sensing changes in the direction and movement of the head.

vestibular sacs Organs in the inner ear that connect the semicircular canals.

The release of endorphins may explain the benefits of a traditional Chinese medical practice called **acupuncture**. Thin needles are inserted at "acupuncture points" on the body and rotated by the acupuncturist. According to traditional Chinese beliefs, manipulation of the needles releases the body's natural healing energy. Though Western medicine has scoffed at the notion of acupuncture releasing a natural healing energy, acupuncture can provide relief from some forms of chronic pain, including chronic headaches (Vickers et al., 2004). However, some scientists believe that any pain relief that acupuncture might provide is due to a placebo effect (Johnson, 1993). For a summary of the skin senses, see Concept Chart 3.4.

The Kinesthetic and Vestibular Senses: Of Grace and Balance

Kinesthesis is the body sense that keeps you informed about the movement of various parts of your body and their positions in relation to one another, even when your eyes are shut or you are in the dark. These sources of information are transmitted to the brain from receptors in the joints, ligaments, and muscles. It is kinesthesis that allows you to ride a bicycle without watching the movements of your legs. Kinesthesis also allows you to perfect the motions of swinging a bat, typing without looking at a keyboard, and washing the back of your neck. You may occasionally watch what you are doing, but most of the time your movements are based on feedback from your joints, ligaments, and muscles. All these tasks are accomplished automatically, without your thinking about them.

The **vestibular sense** is the sensory system that monitors the position of your body in space and helps you maintain your balance. It also allows you to know when the train or car in which you are riding is speeding up, slowing down, coming to a stop, or reversing direction. When the position of your head changes—rotates, tilts, or moves forward, backward, or sideways—movement of fluid within the **semicircular canals** in your inner ear, and shifts in the position of crystals in the **vestibular sacs** that connect the canals, stimulate hair-cell receptors (see Figure 3.15). These receptors then transmit messages to the brain that are interpreted as information about the position and movement of the head in relation to the external world (Lackner & DiZio, 2005; Sage et al., 2005).

If you spin around and around and come to an abrupt stop, you are likely to feel dizzy. The reason is that fluid in your ears' semicircular canals keeps swirling about for a while after you stop, making it seem as if the world is still spinning. We may experience *motion sickness* when our vestibular and visual senses receive conflicting information about movement, as when we are riding in a car headed in one direction while observing a moving train headed in the other direction. For a summary of the kinesthetic and vestibular senses, see Concept Chart 3.4.

Kinesthesis Our kinesthetic sense allows us to fine-tune the movements of our body.

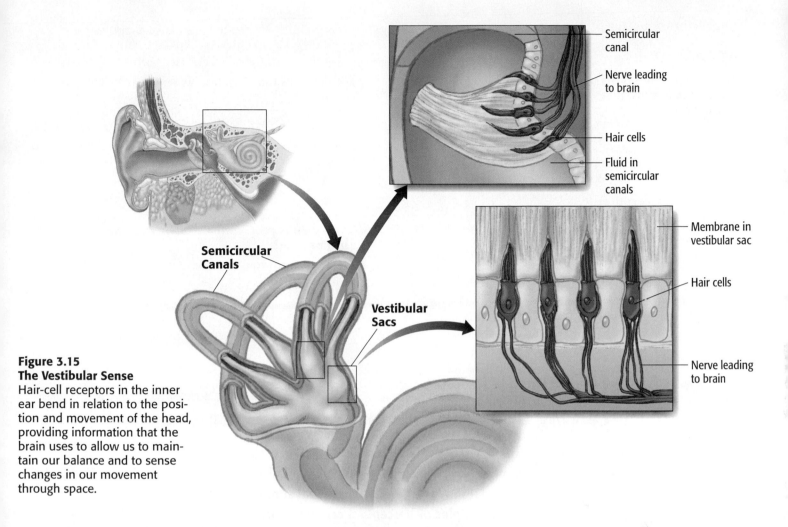

Semicircular canal

Nerve leading to brain

Hair cells

Fluid in semicircular canals

Membrane in vestibular sac

Hair cells

Nerve leading to brain

Semicircular Canals

Vestibular Sacs

Figure 3.15
The Vestibular Sense
Hair-cell receptors in the inner ear bend in relation to the position and movement of the head, providing information that the brain uses to allow us to maintain our balance and to sense changes in our movement through space.

MODULE 3.4 REVIEW

Our Other Senses: Chemical, Skin, and Body Senses

RECITE IT

How do we sense odors and tastes?

- Olfaction, or sense of smell, depends on receptors in the nostrils that are capable of sensing different chemical substances on the basis of their molecular shapes. This information is transmitted to the brain for processing, giving rise to the sensation of odor.

- The sense of taste involves stimulation of taste receptors located in taste buds, mostly on the tongue. Some taste receptors are more sensitive to one basic type of taste (sweet, sour, salty, bitter) while others respond to several tastes.

What are the skin senses?

- The skin senses enable us to detect touch, pressure, temperature, and pain. Different receptors in the skin respond to these stimuli and transmit the information to the brain for processing.

- The gate theory of pain holds that there is a gating mechanism in the spinal cord that opens to allow pain messages through to the brain to signal that something is wrong and closes to shut them off.

What are the kinesthetic and vestibular senses?

- The kinesthetic sense enables you to sense the movement of various parts of your body and their positions in relation to one another. Receptors in the joints, ligaments, and muscles transmit information about body movement and position to the brain for processing.

- The vestibular sense is the sensory system that enables you to detect your body's position and maintain your balance. As the position of your head changes, messages are transmitted to the brain, which interprets them as information about the position of your body in space.

RECALL IT

1. Olfactory receptors in the nose recognize different chemical substances on the basis of their
   a. aromas.
   b. molecular shapes.
   c. density.
   d. vibrations.

2. The tongue contains specialized _____ that are sensitive to different tastes.

3. Chemicals that function as sexual attractants are called _____.

4. What kinds of sensory receptors are found in the skin?

5. John is learning to swing a golf club. He relies on his _____ sense to know how far back he is swinging the club.

THINK ABOUT IT

- Selling cars is no longer simply a matter of performance, value, styling, and safety. Now aroma has entered the picture, as General Motor has begun imbuing all new Cadillacs with a sweet scent they call *Nuance* (Hakim, 2003). Do you think people will be led by their noses when buying their next car?

- Do you believe you are led around by your nose? How is your behavior affected by aromas?

MODULE 3.5

Perceiving Our World: Principles of Perception

- **What is perception?**
- **How is perception influenced by attention and perceptual set?**
- **What are the two general modes of processing visual stimuli?**
- **What are the Gestalt principles of perceptual organization?**
- **What is perceptual constancy, and what cues do we use to perceive depth and movement?**
- **What are visual illusions?**
- **Does subliminal perception exist?**
- **Does evidence support the existence of ESP?**

 CONCEPT 3.27

Through the process of perception, the brain pieces together sensory information to form meaningful impressions of the world.

Figure 3.16   Perception vs. Reality?
Which of the circles in the middle of these two groupings is larger?

Perception is the process by which the brain interprets sensory information, turning it into meaningful representations of the external world. Through perception, the brain attempts to make sense of the mass of sensory stimuli that impinge on our sensory organs. Were it not for perception, the world would seem like a continually changing hodgepodge of disconnected sensations—a buzzing confusion of lights, sounds, and other sensory impressions. The brain brings order to the mix of sensations we experience, organizing them into coherent pictures of the world around us. Perception is an active process in which the brain pieces together bits and pieces of sensory information to form meaningful impressions of the world. Consider what you see on this page: when the dots of black ink register on your retina, your brain transforms these images into meaningful symbols you perceive as letters. To paraphrase Shakespeare, sensation without perception would be "full of sound and fury but signifying nothing."

Our perceptions help us make sense of the world, but they may not accurately reflect external reality. Look at the central circles in the left and right configurations in Figure 3.16. Which of these two circles is larger? If you were to measure the diameter of each central circle with a ruler, you would find that they are exactly the same size. Yet you may perceive the central circle at the right to be larger than the one at the left. This is because the circle on the right is presented within an array of smaller circles, and your brain takes into account the context in which these shapes appear.

In this module, we explore basic concepts of perception, paying particular attention to visual perception—the area of perception that has captured the most research attention.

Attention: Did You Notice That?

CONCEPT 3.28
Many factors affect our attention to particular stimuli, including motivation and repeated exposure.

Attention is the first step in perception. Through **selective attention**, you limit your attention to certain stimuli while filtering out other stimuli. Selective attention prevents you from being flooded with extraneous information. It allows you to focus on the words you are reading but not perceive the sound of a car passing outside the window or the feeling of your toes touching the inside of your shoes. We tend to pay selective attention to sensory signals that are most meaningful or important to us. For example, a parent in a deep sleep may perceive the faint cry of an infant in the next room but be undisturbed by the wail of a siren from an ambulance passing just outside the house.

Motivational states, such as hunger and thirst, play important roles in attention. When we are hungry, we are more likely than when we've just eaten to pay attention to odors wafting out of a restaurant. We also are more likely to notice billboards on the side of the road advertising nearby restaurants. I recall one professor who had the habit of dropping the words *midterm exam* into his lectures when he felt the class was nodding off. That seemed to motivate his students to pay closer attention.

Online Study Center
Resources
Weblinks: Online Visual
Perception Experiments

Repeated exposure may also increase attention to particular stimuli. Prenatal auditory exposure may explain why three-day-old infants prefer the sounds of their mother's voice—as measured by head turning—to the voices of other women (Freeman, Spence, & Oliphant, 1993).

On the other hand, exposure to a constant stimulus can lead us to become *habituated,* or accustomed, to it. When you first turn on an air conditioner or fan, you may notice the constant humming sound it makes. But after a time, you no longer respond to it , even though the sound continues to impinge on the sensory receptors in your ears. Your brain has adapted to the constant stimulus by essentially tuning it out. **Habituation** makes sense from an evolutionary perspective, since constant stimuli are less likely than changing stimuli to require an adaptive response.

Perceptual Set: Seeing What You Expect to See

CONCEPT 3.29
Our interpretations of stimuli depend in part on what we expect to happen in particular situations.

Perceptual set is the tendency for our perceptions to be influenced by expectations or preconceptions. Do you see the number 13 or the letter B in Figure 3.17? In a classic study, Jerome Bruner and A. Leigh Minturn (1955) showed this figure to research participants after they had seen either a series of numbers or a series of letters. Among those who had viewed the number series, 83 percent said the stimulus was the number 13. Of those who had seen the letter series, 93 percent said the stimulus was a B. Similarly, devoted fans of science fiction might be more likely than others to perceive flickering lights in the night sky as a UFO. Figure 3.18 shows another example of a perceptual set.

perception The process by which the brain integrates, organizes, and interprets sensory impressions to create representations of the world.

selective attention The process by which we attend to meaningful stimuli and filter out irrelevant or extraneous stimuli.

habituation Reduction in the strength of a response to a constant or repeated stimulus.

perceptual set The tendency for perceptions to be influenced by one's expectations or preconceptions.

Figure 3.17
What Do You See Here, the Letter B or the Number 13?
Your answer may depend on your perceptual set.

13

(a)

(b)

(c)

Figure 3.18   A Duck or a Rabbit?
The figure in *a* appears to be a duck when you see it after viewing the figure in *c*. But if you first observed the figure in *b*, then the figure in *a* appears to be a rabbit.

 CONCEPT 3.30
The brain forms meaningful visual patterns using two different modes of processing visual stimuli, bottom-up processing and top-down processing.

CONCEPT 3.31
Gestalt psychologists described how the brain constructs meaning from sensations by organizing them into recognizable patterns.

Figure 3.19   Do You Know These Men?
At first glance, you may have thought you recognized President George W. Bush and Vice President Dick Cheney. Actually, the photo of Cheney was doctored by combining the facial features of Bush with Cheney's hairline. We tend to recognize faces on the basis of their large-scale features rather than by piecing together smaller details.

Modes of Visual Processing: Bottom-Up vs. Top-Down

As noted earlier, Hubel and Wiesel's (1979) work on feature detectors showed that specialized receptors in the visual cortex respond only to specific visual features, such as straight lines, angles, or moving points of light. Two general modes of visual processing, *bottom-up processing* and *top-down processing,* help account for how the brain transforms such bits and pieces of visual stimuli into meaningful patterns.

In **bottom-up processing**, the brain assembles specific features of shapes, such as angles and lines, to form patterns that we can compare with stored images we have seen before. For example, the brain combines individual lines and angles to form a pattern we recognize as the number "4." Bottom-up processing may also be used to combine the individual elements of letters and words into recognizable patterns. But how is it that we can read handwriting in which the same letter is never formed twice in exactly the same way? In this style of processing, called **top-down processing**, we recognize patterns as meaningful wholes without first piecing together their component parts (Ansorge & Heumann, 2003). Top-down processing is based on acquired experience and knowledge with patterns, but it is not perfect. Perhaps you've had the experience of thinking you recognized someone approaching you from a distance, only to find out you were mistaken as you got a closer look at the person. You made the mistake because of the tendency to perceive faces on the basis of their whole patterns rather than by building them up feature by feature (see Figure 3.19). Let's now take a look at how we organize our visual perceptions.

Gestalt Principles of Perceptual Organization

You'll recall from Chapter 1 that Max Wertheimer, while aboard a moving train, observed the apparent movement of stationary objects in the distance and that this perception led him to establish the school of psychology known as Gestalt psychology.

Now let's return to Figure 3.16 on page 118. Each of the central circles in the figure is perceived as part of a whole—in this case, as part of a grouping of seven circles. The central circle on the left clearly appears to be smaller than the surrounding circles. The central circle on the right clearly appears larger than the circles that surround it. Even though the central circles are the same size, their context creates the perception that the central circle on the right is larger. But that is because we *perceive* the circles within their contexts, or wholes—not because we are able to *sense* a difference in size with our eyes.

Max Wertheimer and other early Gestalt psychologists studied how the human brain assembles bits of sensory stimulation into meaningful wholes. On the basis of their findings, they formulated **laws of perceptual organization**. Here we consider laws of figure-ground perception and laws of grouping.

Figure and Ground   Look around as you are walking down the street. What do you see? Are there people milling about? Are there clouds in the sky? Gestalt psychologists have shown that people, clouds, and other objects are perceived in terms of *figure,* and the background against which the figures are perceived (the street, for the people; the sky, for the clouds) serves as the *ground.* Figures have shapes, but ground does not (Baylis & Cale, 2001). We recognize and attend to figures, not backgrounds (Vecera, Vogel, & Woodman, 2002). We perceive objects as figures when they have shapes or other characteristics, such as distinctive coloring, against the backdrop of the ground in which they appear (Adelson, 2002).

Sometimes, however, when we perceive an outline, it may be unclear what constitutes the figure and what constitutes the ground. Does Figure 3.20 show a vase, or does it show two profiles? Which is the figure, and which is the ground? Outline alone does not tell the tale, because the same outline describes a vase and human profiles.

Let's now consider Figure 3.21, an ambiguous figure that can be perceived in different ways depending on how you organize your perceptions. Take a minute to focus on it before reading further.

Did you see an old woman or a young one? Are you able to switch back and forth? (Hints: The old woman is facing forward and downward, while the young woman is facing diagonally away. The old woman's nose is the young woman's chin, and her left eye is her counterpart's left ear.) Whether you see an old woman or a young woman depends on how you organize your perceptual experience—which parts you take to be the figure and which parts you take to be the ground. Figure 3.22 provides an example in which figure and ground are less ambiguous.

Gestalt Laws of Grouping   People tend to perceive sensory stimuli in terms of their contexts, grouping bits and pieces of sensory information into unitary forms or wholes. Gestalt psychologists described several principles of grouping, including *proximity, similarity, continuity, closure,* and *connectedness.*

Figure 3.23*a* illustrates **proximity,** or nearness. Most observers would perceive the figure as consisting of three sets of parallel lines rather than six separate lines, although six lines are sensed. That is, we use the relative closeness of the lines as a perceptual cue for organizing them into a group.

How would you describe Figure 3.23*b*? Do you perceive nine separate geometric shapes or two columns of X's and one column of ●'s? If you describe it in terms of X's and ●'s, you are using the principle of **similarity**—that is, grouping figures that are similar to one another (in this case, geometric figures that resemble each other). If you see four bare-chested young men at a football game who've painted

Figure 3.20   Reversible Figure
Whether you see two profiles facing each other in this picture or a vase depends on your perception of figure and ground. See if you can shift back and forth between perceiving the profiles and the vase by switching the parts you take to be figure and those you take to be ground.

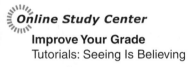
Online Study Center
Improve Your Grade
Tutorials: Seeing Is Believing

bottom-up processing   A mode of perceptual processing by which the brain recognizes meaningful patterns by piecing together bits and pieces of sensory information.

top-down processing   A mode of perceptual processing by which the brain identifies patterns as meaningful wholes rather than as piecemeal constructions.

laws of perceptual organization   The principles identified by Gestalt psychologists that describe the ways in which the brain groups bits of sensory stimulation into meaningful wholes or patterns.

proximity   The principle that objects that are near each other will be perceived as belonging to a common set.

similarity   The principle that objects that are similar will be perceived as belonging to the same group.

Figure 3.21   Ambiguous Figure
Do you see an old woman or a young one? If you have trouble switching between the two, look at Figure 3.22, in which figure and ground are less ambiguous.

Figure 3.22 Old/Young Woman
The figure on the right shows the downward-looking "old woman" more clearly as figure than as ground, while the one on the left highlights the figural aspects of the "young woman" looking away from the perceiver. Now look back at Figure 3.21 and see if you can't switch back between the two impressions.

(a) Proximity **(b) Similarity** **(c) Continuity** **(d) Closure** **(e) Connectedness**

Figure 3.23 Gestalt Laws of Grouping
Gestalt psychologists recognized that people group objects according to certain organizational principles. Here we see examples of five such principles: proximity, similarity, continuity, closure, and connectedness.

TRY THIS OUT

Your Neighborhood Gestalt

Take a walk through your neighborhood or local area. Look around you. How many examples of the Gestalt laws of perceptual organization can you identify?

CONCEPT 3.32
We tend to perceive objects as having a constant size, shape, color, and brightness even when the image they cast on our retinas changes.

their bodies in the colors of the home team, you are likely to perceive them as a group distinct from other fans.

Figure 3.23c represents another way we group stimuli, by **continuity**, which is the tendency to perceive a series of stimuli as a unified form when the stimuli appear to represent a continuous pattern. Here we perceive two intersecting continuous lines, one curved and one straight, rather than four separate lines.

Now, check Figure 3.23d. You sense a number of short lines, but do you perceive a meaningless array of lines or a broken triangle? If you perceive the triangle, your perception draws on the principle of **closure**—grouping disconnected pieces of information into a meaningful whole. You perceive a complete form even when there are gaps in the form. This illustrates the principle for which Gestalt psychologists are best known—that the whole is more than the sum of the parts.

Figure 3.23e gives an example of **connectedness**—the tendency to perceive objects as belonging together when they are positioned together or are moving together. Thus, you perceive three sets of connected triangles rather than six triangles with three interspersing lines. Perhaps you have noticed this tendency while watching two people walk down a street next to each other and being surprised when they suddenly walk off in different directions without saying goodbye. In such circumstances, we tend to perceive the people as belonging together because they are moving together (Sekuler & Bennett, 2001). To test some of these principles, see the nearby Try This Out.

Perceptual Constancy

Another way in which we organize perceptions is through **perceptual constancy**—the tendency to perceive the size, shape, color, and brightness of an object as remaining the same even when the image it casts on the retina changes. We could

Figure 3.24 Shape Constancy
Perception of an object's shape remains the same even when the image it casts on the retina changes with the angle of view. You perceive three rectangular doors, despite the fact that the image each projects on the retina is different.

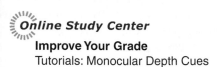
continuity The principle that a series of stimuli will be perceived as representing a unified form.

closure The perceptual principle that people tend to piece together disconnected bits of information to perceive whole forms.

connectedness The principle that objects positioned together or moving together will be perceived as belonging to the same group.

perceptual constancy The tendency to perceive the size, shape, color, and brightness of an object as remaining the same even when the image it casts on the retina changes.

shape constancy The tendency to perceive an object as having the same shape despite differences in the images it casts on the retina as the viewer's perspective changes.

size constancy The tendency to perceive an object as having the same size despite changes in the images it casts on the retina as the viewing distance changes.

color constancy The tendency to perceive an object as having the same color despite changes in lighting conditions.

brightness constancy The tendency to perceive objects as retaining their brightness even when they are viewed in dim light.

not adjust to our world very well without perceptual constancy. The world is constantly shifting before our eyes as we look at objects from different distances and perspectives. Just turning our heads changes the geometry of an object projected on the retina. Yet we don't perceive objects as changing before our eyes. We perceive them as constant—a good thing, since they are indeed constant. For example, the ability to perceive that a tiger is a tiger and not a pussycat regardless of the distance from which the animal is viewed could be a life-saving mechanism.

The tendency to perceive an object as being the same shape even when the object is viewed from different perspectives is **shape constancy**. If you observe a round bowl on a table from different angles, the image it casts on your retina changes shape. Nonetheless, you perceive the bowl as round. In other words, its shape remains constant despite the change in your angle of view. Similarly, you perceive a door as having an unchanging shape despite differences in the image it casts upon your retina depending on whether it is open or closed (see Figure 3.24). Moreover, as you approach the bowl at eye level, its size—in terms of the size of the retinal image—grows. As you move farther away from it, the size of its retinal image decreases. Yet you continue to perceive the bowl as being the same size, just as I knew my daughter did not suddenly become a giant as she approached the camera. The tendency to perceive an object as being the same size despite changes in the size of the retinal image it casts is **size constancy**.

Experience teaches people about distance and perspective. We learn that an object seen at a distance will look smaller than when it is close and that an object seen from different perspectives will appear to have different shapes.

People also perceive objects as retaining their color even when lighting conditions change. This tendency is called **color constancy**. For example, if your car is red, you perceive it to be red even though it may look grayish as evening falls. The tendency for the perceived brightness or lightness of an object to remain relatively constant despite changes in illumination is called **brightness constancy** or *lightness constancy* (Wilcox & Duke, 2003). For example, a piece of white chalk placed in the shade on a sunny day reflects less light than does a black hockey puck placed directly in sunlight. Yet we perceive the chalk to be brighter than the hockey puck.

Cues to Depth Perception

How do we know that some objects are closer than others? The answer is that we normally use both binocular and monocular cues for judging distance or depth.

CONCEPT 3.33
Our perception of depth depends on both monocular and binocular cues for judging distance.

Figure 3.25
Binocular Cues for Depth
When we rely on binocular cues for judging the depth of a nearby object, our eyes must converge on the object, which can give us that cross-eyed look.

binocular cues Cues for depth that involve both eyes, such as retinal disparity and convergence.
retinal disparity A binocular cue for distance based on the slight differences in the visual impressions formed in both eyes.
convergence A binocular cue for distance based on the degree of tension required to focus two eyes on the same object.
monocular cues Cues for depth that can be perceived by each eye alone, such as relative size and interposition.

Binocular Cues for Depth For **binocular cues**, we depend on both eyes. Because our eyes are a few inches apart, each eye receives slightly different images of the world. The brain interprets the difference in the two retinal images—the **retinal disparity** between them—as cues to the relative distances of objects. The closer the object, the greater the retinal disparity.

You can readily see how retinal disparity works by holding a finger an inch in front of your nose. First close your left eye and look at the finger only with your right eye. The finger looks as if it is off to the left. Then close your right eye and look at the finger with your left eye. The finger seems off to the right. The finger appears to move from side to side as you open and close each eye. The distance between the two apparent fingers corresponds to the retinal disparity between the two images that form on your retina. Now hold a finger straight ahead at arm's length away from your eyes. Again close one eye and focus on the finger. Then close that eye and open the other. The finger may still seem to "move," but there will be less distance between the two "fingers" because retinal disparity is smaller at greater distances.

Now let's try an experiment to illustrate the binocular cue of **convergence**, which depends on the muscular tension produced by turning both eyes inward to form a single image. Hold a finger once more at arm's length. Keeping both eyes open, concentrate on the finger so that you perceive only one finger. Now bring it slowly closer to your eyes, maintaining the single image. As you do, you will feel tension in your eye muscles. This is because your eyes are *converging,* or looking inward, to maintain the single image, as shown in Figure 3.25. The closer the object—in this case, the finger—the greater the tension. Your brain uses the tension as a cue for depth perception.

Monocular Cues for Depth **Monocular cues** depend on one eye only. When people drive, they use a combination of binocular and monocular cues to judge the distance of other cars and of the surrounding scenery. Although there are advantages to using binocular cues, most people can get by driving with monocular cues, if they need to do so. Monocular cues include relative size, interposition, relative clarity, texture gradient, linear perspective, and shadowing.

- *Relative Size.* When two objects are believed to be the same size, the one that appears larger is perceived to be closer (see Figure 3.26a).

- *Interposition.* When objects block or otherwise obscure our view of other objects, we perceive the obscured object as farther away. Notice that in Figure 3.26b we perceive the horses in front to be closer than the ones that are partially blocked.

- *Relative Clarity.* Smog, dust, smoke, and water droplets in the atmosphere create a "haze" that makes distant objects appear more blurry than nearer objects (see Figure 3.26c). You may have noticed how much closer faraway mountains appear on a really clear day.

- *Texture Gradient.* The relative coarseness or smoothness of an object is used as a cue for distance. Closer objects appear to have a coarser or more detailed texture than more distant objects. Thus, the texture of flowers that are farther away is smoother than the texture of those that are closer (Figure 3.26d).

- *Linear Perspective.* Linear perspective is the perception of parallel lines converging as they recede into the distance. As we look straight ahead, objects and the distances between them appear smaller the farther away they are from us. Thus, the road ahead of the driver, which consists of parallel lines, appears to grow narrower as it recedes into the distance (Figure 3.26e). It may even seem to end in a point.

- *Shadowing.* Patterns of light and dark, or shadowing, create the appearance of three-dimensional objects or curving surfaces. Shadowing can make an object

Figure 3.26 Monocular Cues for Depth
We use many different monocular cues to judge depth, including:

(a) Relative size

(b) Interposition

(c) Relative clarity

(d) Texture gradient

(e) Linear perspective

(f) Shadowing

appear to be concave or convex. Notice how the dents that appear in Figure 3.26f look like bumps when the image is turned upside down. We perceive objects that are lighter on top and darker on the bottom to be bumps, whereas the opposite is the case for dents (Gaulin & McBurney, 2001).

Motion Perception

CONCEPT 3.34
We use two basic cues in perceiving movement: the path of the image as it crosses the retina and the changing size of the object.

We use various cues to perceive motion. One is the actual movement of an object across our field of vision as the image it projects moves from point to point on the retina. The brain interprets the swath that the image paints across the retina as a sign of movement (Derrington, 2004). Another cue is the changing size of an object. Objects appear larger when they are closer. When you are driving and you see the cars ahead suddenly looming much larger, you perceive that you are moving faster than they are—so fast you may need to slam on the brakes to avoid a collision. When cars ahead grow smaller, they appear to be moving faster than you are.

Visual Illusions: Do Your Eyes Deceive You?

CONCEPT 3.35
Visual illusions are misperceptions of visual stimuli in which it seems that our eyes are playing tricks on us.

Our eyes sometimes seem to play tricks on us in the form of **visual illusions**. Figure 3.27 shows two well-known visual illusions: the *Müller-Lyer illusion (a)* and the *Ponzo illusion (b)*. In both cases, what you think you see isn't exactly what you get when you pull out a ruler. Although the center lines in *(a)* are actually the same length, as are the center lines in *(c)* and *(d)*, the line on the right in *(a)* seems longer, as does the center line in *(d)* compared to the one in *(c)*. The figure with the inward wings creates the impression of an outward corner of a room that appears

visual illusions Misperceptions of visual stimuli.

Figure 3.27   Müller-Lyer Illusion and Ponzo Illusion
Visual illusions involve misperceptions in which our eyes seem to be playing tricks on us.

| (a) Müller-Lyer Illusion | (b) Ponzo Illusion | (c) | (d) |

to be closer *(c)*. The figure with the outward wings suggests the inner corner of a room *(d)*, which makes the center line seem farther away.

Although no one explanation may fully account for the Müller-Lyer illusion, a partial explanation may involve how the brain interprets size and distance cues. As you'll recall from the discussion of size constancy, people tend to perceive an object as remaining the same size even as the image it projects on the retina changes in relation to distance from the observer. But when two objects of the same size appear to be at different distances from the observer, the one that is judged to be farther away is perceived to be larger. In the Müller-Lyer illusion, the figure with the outward wings suggests the inner corner of a room, which makes the center line seem farther away. The figure with the inward wings creates the impression of an outward corner of a room that appears to be closer to the observer. Since both center lines actually create the same-size image on the retina, the brain interprets the one that appears to be farther away as being longer.

Now consider the Ponzo illusion (also called the railroad illusion). Which of the two horizontal lines in Figure 3.27*b* looks longer? Why do you think people generally perceive the line at the top to be longer? Converging lines may create an impression of linear perspective, leading us to perceive the upper line as farther away. As with the Müller-Lyer illusion, since lines of equal length cast the same-size image on the retina, the one perceived as farther away is judged to be longer.

Figure 3.28   Impossible Figure
Notice how the figure makes sense if you look at certain of its features, but not when you take all its features into account.

Another type of illusion involves *impossible figures,* such as the one in Figure 3.28. Impossible figures fool the brain into creating the impression of a whole figure when the figure is viewed from certain perspectives. An impossible figure appears to make sense when you look at parts of it, but not when you try to take into account the characteristics of the whole figure.

The well-known *moon illusion* has baffled people for ages (see Figure 3.29). When a full moon appears near the horizon, it may seem enormous compared with its "normal" size—that is, its apparent size when it is high in the evening sky. Actually, the image the moon casts on the retina is the same size whether it sits high in the sky or just over the horizon. We don't have an entirely satisfactory explanation of this illusion. One leading theory, the *relative-size hypothesis*, relates the phenomenon to the amount of space surrounding the perceived object. When the moon is at the horizon, it appears larger by comparison with objects far off in the distance, such as tall trees and mountains. When the moon is high in the sky, there is nothing to compare it with except the vast featureless wastes of space, and this comparison makes it seem smaller.

You can test out the moon illusion for yourself by looking at the full moon on the horizon. Then, to remove any distance cues, look again at the moon through a rolled-up magazine. You'll find that the moon appears to shrink in size. One

stroboscopic movement   A type of apparent movement based on the rapid succession of still images, as in motion pictures.

Figure 3.29   Moon Illusion
The moon illusion refers to the perception that the moon is larger when at the horizon than when it is high in the sky.

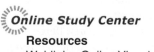
problem with the relative-size hypothesis is that it doesn't account for all situations in which the phenomenon is observed, including a planetarium in which the moon is depicted in the absence of intervening landscape cues (Suzuki, 1991).

We have discussed how we perceive actual movement, but there are also interesting examples of *apparent movement,* such as **stroboscopic movement** (see Figure 3.30). Stroboscopic movement puts the motion in motion pictures. We perceive the rapid progression of illuminated still images to be a seamless "motion picture." The film itself contains a series of still images projected at more than twenty pictures, or "frames," per second. Each frame differs somewhat from the one shown before. This is nothing but a quick slide show; the "movie" mechanism lies within us—the viewers.

Before reading further, you may wish to review Concept Chart 3.5, which shows the relationships among the concepts we use to explain how people form perceptions of the world.

Cultural Differences in Perceiving Visual Illusions

Suppose you lived in a culture in which structures with corners and angles were uncommon. Would you be as likely to experience the Müller-Lyer illusion as someone raised in, say, Cleveland or Dallas? To find out, Darhl Pedersen and John Wheeler (1983) tested two groups of Navajo Indians on the Müller-Lyer illusion.

Figure 3.30   Stroboscopic Movement
The perception of movement in "moving pictures" is a feature of the viewer, not the projector.

CONCEPT 3.36

The susceptibility to visual illusions is influenced by cultural factors, such as the types of structures to which people in a particular culture are accustomed.

One group lived in rectangular houses that provided daily exposure to angles and corners. Another group lived in traditional rounded huts with fewer of these cues. Those living in the rounded huts were less likely to be deceived by the Müller-Lyer illusion, suggesting that prior experience plays a role in determining susceptibility to the illusion. Other studies have produced similar results. For example, the illusion was observed less frequently among the Zulu people of southern Africa, who also live in rounded structures (Segall, 1994).

The **carpentered-world hypothesis** was put forth to account for cultural differences in susceptibility to the Müller-Lyer illusion (Segall, Campbell, & Herskovits, 1966). A carpentered world is one, like our own, that is dominated by structures (buildings, rooms, and furniture) in which straight lines meet at right angles. People living in noncarpentered worlds, which consist largely of rounded structures, are less prone to the illusion because of their limited experience with angular structures. Cultural experience, rather than race, seems the determinant. Zulus who move to cities where they become accustomed to seeing angular structures are more likely to be fooled by the illusion (Segall, Campbell, & Herskovits, 1963).

Studies with the Ponzo (railroad) illusion also show cultural differences. The illusion is less prominent among the people of Guam, an island with a hilly terrain and no long, uninterrupted highways or railroads (Leibowitz, 1971).

The lesson here goes beyond cultural differences in visual illusions. Perception is influenced not only by our sensory systems, but also by our experience of living in a particular culture. People from different cultures may perceive the physical world differently. Consider a classic example offered by the anthropologist Colin Turnbull (1961). Turnbull took Kenge, an African pygmy guide, on his first trip outside the dense forest into the open plain. When Kenge saw buffalo several miles away on the plain, he took them to be insects. When he got closer to the animals and recognized them as buffalo, he was aghast at how the animals had been able to grow so quickly. Why would Kenge mistake a buffalo for an insect? In Kenge's culture, people lived in remote villages in a dense forest. He had never before had an unobstructed view of objects at a great distance. He lacked the experience needed to acquire size constancy for distant objects—to learn that objects retain their size even as the image they project on our eyes grows smaller.

Next we focus on two controversies in perception that have sparked a continuing debate within both the scientific community and the society at large.

carpentered-world hypothesis
An attempt to explain the Müller-Lyer illusion in terms of the cultural experience of living in a carpentered, right-angled world like our own.

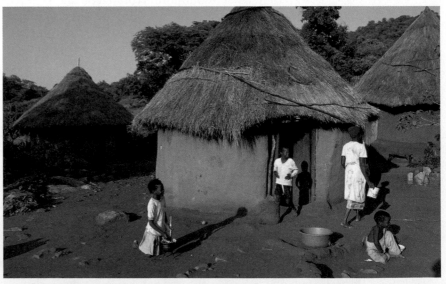

Carpentered-World Hypothesis According to the carpentered-world hypothesis, people living in cultures in which right-angled structures are rare are less prone to the Müller-Lyer illusion.

CONCEPT CHART 3.5   Overview of Perception

Basic Concepts	**Selective attention**	We tend to pay attention to the types of sensory information that are important to us. Such factors as motivational states and repeated exposure influence whether we attend to particular stimuli.
Modes of Perceptual Processing	**Perceptual set**	Our expectations or preconceptions may lead us to interpret stimuli in ways that conform to those expectations or preconceptions.
	Habituation	The process of adapting to a constant or repeated stimulus by becoming less responsive to it.
	Perceptual constancy	The tendency to perceive objects as unchanging in size, shape, color, and brightness despite changes in perspective, distance, or lighting conditions.
	Bottom-up processing	The process by which the brain forms perceptions by piecing together bits and pieces of sensory data to form meaningful patterns
	Top-down processing	The process by which the brain forms perceptions by recognizing whole patterns without first piecing together their component parts
Gestalt Principles of Perceptual Organization	**Figure-ground**	The tendency to perceive the visual environment in terms of figures (objects) that stand out from the surrounding background, or ground
	Principles of Grouping — **Proximity**	The tendency to perceive objects as belonging together when they are close to one another
	Similarity	The tendency to group objects that have similar characteristics
	Continuity	The tendency to perceive a series of stimuli as a unified form when they appear to represent a continuous pattern
	Closure	The tendency to group disconnected pieces of information into a meaningful whole
	Connectedness	The tendency to perceive objects as belonging together when they are positioned together or are moving together
Cues for Depth Perception	*Binocular Cues* — **Retinal disparity**	The disparity in the images of objects projected onto the retina, which the brain uses as a cue to the distance of the objects. Nearby objects produce greater retinal disparity.
	Convergence	Turning the eyes inward to focus on a nearby object, which creates muscular tension that the brain uses as a cue for depth perception. The closer the object, the more the eyes must converge to maintain the single image.
	Monocular Cues — **Relative size**	An object that appears larger than another object believed to be of the same size is judged to be closer.
	Interposition	Objects that are obscured by other objects are perceived as being farther away.
	Relative clarity	Nearby objects are clearer than more distant objects.
	Texture gradient	The details of nearby objects appear to have a coarser texture than those of distant objects.
	Linear perspective	Objects and the spaces between them look smaller as they become more distant. Thus, parallel lines appear to converge as they recede into the distance.
	Shadowing	Shadows can create the appearance of curving surfaces or three dimensions, giving the impression of depth.
Controversies in Perception	**Subliminal perception**	Perception of stimuli presented below the threshold of conscious awareness
	Extrasensory perception (ESP)	Perception occurring without the benefit of the known senses

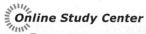

Online Study Center

Resources
Weblinks: Subliminal Research

CONCEPT 3.37

Though we sometimes perceive things we are not conscious of perceiving, there is no evidence that our attitudes or behavior are influenced by subliminal cues.

CONCEPT 3.38

Claims of ESP remain just that—claims that have not met the rigorous tests of scientific inquiry.

subliminal perception Perception of stimuli that are presented below the threshold of conscious awareness.

extrasensory perception (ESP) Perception that occurs without benefit of the known senses.

parapsychology The study of paranormal phenomena.

telepathy Communication of thoughts from one mind to another that occurs without using the known senses.

clairvoyance The ability to perceive objects and events without using the known senses.

precognition The ability to foretell the future.

psychokinesis The ability to move objects by mental effort alone.

Ganzfeld procedure A method of studying telepathy in which a sender attempts to mentally transmit information to a receiver who is in a sensory-restricted environment in another room.

EXPLORING PSYCHOLOGY
Controversies in Perception:
Subliminal Perception and Extrasensory Perception

In 1957, a newspaper reported that popcorn sales at a local movie theater had soared after the message EAT POPCORN was flashed across the screen at speeds too fast to register in moviegoers' conscious awareness. Though the report turned out to be a hoax (Pratkanis, 1992), it sparked a continuing controversy over whether **subliminal perception**—perception of stimuli flashed so quickly that they do not register in conscious awareness—could affect attitudes and behavior. Jumping on the subliminal bandwagon, marketers began claiming that subliminal messages embedded in audiotapes could help people boost memory power, lose weight, and even stop smoking. But is there evidence to support these beliefs?

An even more controversial topic is **extrasensory perception (ESP)**—perception that occurs without benefit of the known senses. Is it possible to read people's minds or to know the contents of a letter in a sealed envelope? Here we consider these controversies in light of scientific evidence.

Subliminal Perception: Did You See Something Flash By? A recent national poll found that two-thirds of Americans believe that subliminal perception exists (Onion, 2000). But does scientific evidence support this belief? The answer, researchers report, is *yes,* but it is a qualified *yes.* The effects of subliminal perception appear to be subtle and to depend on very precise experimental conditions (Greenwald & Draine, 1997).

We know from laboratory studies that, under strict experimental conditions, people can detect stimuli presented below the threshold of awareness (Dijksterhuis & Smith, 2002; Greenwald et al., 2003; Hull et al., 2002). Sheila Murphy and Robert Zajonc (1993) flashed either a smiling face or a frowning face to research participants at speeds too fast for them to perceive consciously. Yet those who were flashed the smiling face later reacted more favorably to a set of Chinese characters than those who had been flashed the frowning face. Apparently, some features of the subliminally presented stimulus had been perceived, even though participants could not report what they had seen. However, no convincing evidence exists that subliminal messages in ads or audiotapes influence our behavior or attitudes, lead us to purchase certain products, or help us become more successful in life (Druckman & Bjork, 1991; K. H. Smith & Rogers, 1994).

Extrasensory Perception: Is It for Real? A man claims to be able to bend spoons with his mind. A woman claims to be able to find the bodies of crime victims aided by nothing more than a piece of clothing worn by the victim. Another woman claims to be able to foretell future events. The study of such *paranormal phenomena*—events that cannot be explained by known physical, psychological, or biological mechanisms—is called **parapsychology**. The major focus of paranormal psychology is *extrasensory perception,* the so-called "sixth sense" by which people claim they can perceive objects or events without using the known senses. The forms of paranormal phenomena most commonly identified with ESP are *telepathy, clairvoyance, precognition,* and *psychokinesis.*

Telepathy refers to the purported ability to project one's thoughts into other people's minds or to read what is in their minds—to perceive their thoughts or feelings without using the known senses. **Clairvoyance** is the perception of events that are not available to the senses. The clairvoyant may claim to know what someone across town is doing at that precise moment or to identify the contents of a sealed envelope. **Precognition** is the ability to foretell the future. **Psychokinesis** (formerly called *telekinesis*) is the ability to move objects without touching them. Strictly speaking, psychokinesis is not a form of ESP since it does not involve perception, but for the sake of convenience it is often classified as such.

REALITY CHECK

THE CLAIM ESP exists.

THE EVIDENCE Psychics and fortune-tellers make their livings based on people's beliefs that ESP and other paranormal phenomena are real. However, despite decades of research, we lack any compelling scientific evidence that ESP exists. Though an absence of evidence is not sufficient to prove that something doesn't exist, the burden of proof falls on those making such claims of extraordinary phenomena.

THE TAKE-AWAY MESSAGE
No convincing scientific exists supporting the existence of ESP and other paranormal phenomena.

Beliefs in ESP are widespread. A recent study showed that believers in paranormal phenomena tended to view a demonstration of psychic abilities as an example of the paranormal, even when they were informed beforehand that the effect was simply a magic trick (Hergovich, 2004). Evidence also shows that virtually all college students believe in some aspect of ESP, especially telepathy (Beins, 2002). But a study of college students at a mid-sized university in Arizona showed stronger beliefs in the paranormal among first-year college students than among seniors (Fitzpatrick & Shook, 1994). Perhaps greater exposure to college courses instills a more critical attitude toward these beliefs.

Critical thinkers maintain an appropriate skepticism about claims of paranormal phenomena that seem to defy the laws of nature. Many claims of ESP have proven to be hoaxes, whereas others may be explained as random or chance occurrences.

Perhaps the strongest evidence to date for the existence of ESP comes from studies that have used the **Ganzfeld procedure**, which involves placing a "sender" and a "receiver" in separate, soundproof rooms. Ping-Pong balls are taped to the receiver's eyes, while white noise (static) is played into the receiver's ears through headphones. This setup reduces external stimuli to a minimum, which presumably would allow weak extrasensory signals to come through more clearly. The sender then concentrates on a randomly selected visual image (a picture of a particular object) selected from an array of four images. After half an hour, the receiver selects the image he or she believes the sender had been focusing on. By chance alone, the receiver should be right 25 percent of the time. Some researchers report a small but significant increase over chance, a finding that may indicate an ESP effect (D. J. Bem & Honorton, 1994). However, other investigators question the validity of these findings (Milton & Wiseman, 2001).

What should we make of all this? Despite many years of scientific study, we lack any reliable, replicable findings of ESP that have withstood scientific scrutiny. As critical thinkers, we need to maintain a skeptical attitude and insist that claims of extrasensory abilities be reliably demonstrated under tightly controlled conditions before we are willing to accept them.

MODULE 3.5 REVIEW

Perceiving Our World: Principles of Perception

RECITE IT

What is perception?
- Perception is the process by which sensory experiences are organized into meaningful representations or impressions of the world.

How is perception influenced by attention and perceptual set?
- Through the process of selective attention we focus on the most meaningful stimuli impinging upon us at any one time.
- Attention is influenced by such factors as motivational states and repeated exposure.
- The tendency for perceptions to be influenced by expectations and preconceptions is known as a perceptual set.

What are the two general modes of processing visual stimuli?
- The two general modes of visual processing are bottom-up processing, which involves piecing together specific features of visual stimuli to form meaningful patterns, and top-down processing, which involves recognizing patterns as meaningful wholes without first piecing together their component parts.

What are the Gestalt principles of perceptual organization?
- The Gestalt principles of perceptual organization include laws of figure-ground perception and laws of grouping (proximity, similarity, continuity, closure, and connectedness).

What is perceptual constancy, and what cues do we use to perceive depth and movement?
- Perceptual constancy is the tendency to perceive an object to be of the same shape, size, color, and brightness even when the images it casts on the retina change in response to changes in viewing perspective, distance, and lighting.
- Binocular cues include retinal disparity and convergence. Monocular cues include relative size, interposition, relative clarity, texture gradient, linear perspective, and shadowing.

- The movement of an object across our field of vision stimulates an array of points on the retina, which the brain interprets as movement. The changing size of the object is another cue for movement.

What are visual illusions?

- Visual illusions are misperceptions of visual stimuli in which our eyes seem to play tricks on us. Examples include the Müller-Lyer illusion, the Ponzo illusion, and the moon illusion.
- The brain may be fooled into perceiving apparent movement, as in the case of stroboscopic motion.

RECALL IT

1. The process by which the brain turns sensations into meaningful impressions of the external world is called _____.

2. The ability to focus on the words you are reading and to tune out irrelevant stimuli is called _____ attention.

3. The term used to describe the tendency for our expectations and preconceived notions to influence how we perceive events is _____.

4. What Gestalt principle describes the tendency to perceive objects as belonging together when they are positioned together or moving together?

THINK ABOUT IT

- Drawing upon your understanding of Gestalt principles of perceptual organization, explain how perceptions differ from photographic images.

Does subliminal perception exist?

- Some limited forms of subliminal perception exist, but there is no evidence that exposure to subliminally presented messages in everyday life affects attitudes or behavior.

Does evidence support the existence of ESP?

- There is no hard evidence acceptable to a majority of scientists that proves the existence of such forms of ESP as telepathy, clairvoyance, precognition, and psychokinesis.

5. Which of the following is *not* a monocular cue for depth?
   a. convergence   c. interposition
   b. relative clarity   d. shadowing

6. Subliminal perception involves
   a. acquiring knowledge or insight without using the known senses.
   b. perceiving information presented below the level of conscious awareness.
   c. perceiving stimuli in an underwater environment.
   d. sensory systems that can transmit all of a stimulus's features.

- Have you ever had any unusual experiences that you believe involved ESP? Think critically. What alternative explanations might account for these experiences?

APPLICATION MODULE 3.6
The Psychology of Pain Management

CONCEPT 3.39

People who suffer chronic pain may gain better control over their symptoms by using distraction, creating logjams at the "pain gate," doing something enjoyable, changing their thoughts and attitudes, obtaining accurate information, and practicing meditation and biofeedback.

The brain is a marvel of engineering. By allowing us to experience the first pangs of pain, it alerts us to danger. Without such a warning, we might not pull our hand away from a hot object in time to prevent burns (Kalb, 2003b). Then, by releasing endorphins, the brain gradually shuts the gate on pain.

But pain can turn bad. Millions of people suffer from chronic pain that persists despite the absence of any current tissue damage (Springen, 2003; Watkins & Maier, 2003). New technologies and approaches to managing chronic pain are being introduced to clinical practice each year. Although pain has a biological basis, researchers have found that psychological factors may influence the severity of pain and how well patients are able to cope with it. In this module, we focus on the role of psychological factors in pain management. However, before attempting to treat pain yourself, consult a health professional to determine the source of the pain and an appropriate course of treatment.

Distraction

Online Study Center

Improve Your Grade
Tutorials: Pain—Where Does
It Come From?

We've learned from experimental studies that people report lower levels of pain when they focus their attention away from the pain (Coderre et al., 2003). Chronic pain sufferers may thus be better able to cope with pain when they distract themselves, such as by exercising or becoming immersed in a good book or video. Children with cancer have learned to reduce the unpleasant side effects of chemotherapy by playing videogames (Redd, 1995). While receiving intravenous injections of nausea-inducing cancer drugs, the children focus on combating monsters on the video screen. Similarly, when faced with a painful medical or dental procedure, you can help keep your mind off your pain by focusing on a pleasing picture on the wall or some other stimulus or by letting your mind become absorbed in a pleasant fantasy.

Creating a Bottleneck at the "Gate"

As noted earlier, the gate-control theory of pain holds that other sensory stimuli may temporarily block pain messages from passing through a neural gate in the spinal cord. You can attempt to create a traffic jam at the gate by lightly rubbing an irritated area. Interestingly, applying both heat and cold may help because each sends messages through the spinal cord that compete for attention. Cold packs have the additional advantage of reducing inflammation.

Doing Something Enjoyable

Investigators find that priming positive emotions helps reduce pain intensity, whereas priming negative emotions actually increases it (Meagher, Arnau, & Rhudy, 2001). Negative emotions may increase attention to aversive stimuli, which in turn might magnify their effects. By engaging in pleasant activities (seeing a good movie), you may succeed in both distracting yourself and priming positive emotions.

Changing Thoughts and Attitudes

How people interpret their pain can affect how much pain they feel and how well they cope with it (Nuland, 2003). Researchers find that pain patients who have pessimistic thoughts ("I can no longer do anything. . . . It isn't fair I have to live this way") report more severe pain and distress during flare-ups than those who maintain more positive thoughts (Gil et al., 1990). Negative thoughts can lead to perceptions of lack of control, which in turn can produce feelings of helplessness and hopelessness. Psychologists help pain sufferers examine their thoughts and replace negative or pessimistic self-evaluations with rational alternatives like "Don't give in to hopelessness. Focus on what you need to do to cope with this pain." Changing thoughts and attitudes may not eliminate pain, but it can help people cope more effectively with their pain symptoms (Blanchard & Diamond, 1996).

Biofeedback Training Through biofeedback training, people can learn to alter some internal bodily processes, such as heart rate, blood pressure, muscle tension, body temperature, and certain types of brain wave patterns.

Coping With Pain What are the various coping skills that people can use to manage pain?

meditation A process of focused attention that induces a relaxed, contemplative state.

biofeedback training (BFT) A method of learning to control certain bodily responses by using information transmitted by physiological monitoring equipment.

electromyographic (EMG) biofeedback A form of biofeedback training that involves feedback about changes in the level of muscle tension in the forehead or elsewhere in the body.

thermal biofeedback A form of biofeedback training that involves feedback about changes in temperature and blood flow in selected parts of the body; used in the treatment of migraine headaches.

migraine headache A prolonged, intense headache brought on by changes in blood flow in the brain's blood vessels.

Obtaining Accurate Information

One of the most effective psychological methods for managing pain is obtaining factual and thorough information about the source of the pain and the available treatments. Many people try to avoid thinking about pain and its implications. Obtaining information helps people take an active role in controlling pain.

Meditation and Biofeedback

Evidence supports the effectiveness of meditation in helping to relieve chronic pain (Baer, 2003; Oz, 2003; Roemer & Orsillo, 2003). **Meditation** typically involves a process of focused attention that induces a relaxed, contemplative state. There are many different forms of meditation, but most of them involve narrowing attention by repeating a word, thought, or phrase or by maintaining a steady focus on one object, such as a burning candle or the design on a vase (see Chapter 4).

Biofeedback training (BFT) can be used to help relieve headache pain. Psychologists have found that providing people with feedback about their internal bodily functions ("biofeedback") can help them gain greater awareness and some degree of voluntary control over physiological processes. In BFT, individuals are attached to monitoring equipment that provides them with a continual stream of information about their internal physiological functioning. A rising tone may indicate increasing heart rate or muscle tension, while a lower tone indicates changes in the opposite direction. People use biofeedback signals as cues to help them learn strategies to modify their heart rates, blood pressure, muscle tension, body temperature, brain wave patterns, and other physiological processes.

In one form of BFT, **electromyographic (EMG) biofeedback**, electrodes placed on the forehead or elsewhere on the body monitor muscle tension. A tone is used to indicate increases or decreases in muscle tension. By learning to lower the tone, people develop the ability to relax their forehead muscles, which can reduce the pain of tension headaches (Holroyd, 2002).

In another form of BFT, **thermal biofeedback**, devices that measure temperature are attached to the body, generally around a finger. A tone is used to indicate changes in temperature. The temperature in the fingers rises as blood flow to the extremities increases, leading to changes in blood flow throughout the body, including the brain. Some people learn they can raise the temperature in their fingers simply by imagining a finger growing warmer. This form of biofeedback training is useful in treating **migraine headaches**, the intense, throbbing headaches associated with changes in blood flow in the brain (Durham, 2004).

In Chapter 4 we discuss another psychological technique used in controlling pain—hypnosis (Coderre et al., 2003).

TYING IT TOGETHER

Sensation and perception are processes that enable us to sense and make sense of the world around us. The early psychologists laid out a number of basic concepts of sensation, including the absolute threshold, the difference threshold, and Weber's law (Module 3.1). Each of our sensory systems transforms sources of stimulation into information the brain can use to produce sensations. With vision, light energy is transformed into sensations of visual images (Module 3.2). With hearing, vibrations caused by sound waves impact on structures in the inner ear, where they are converted into auditory messages that the brain uses to create sensations of sound (Module 3.3). Through our other senses—the chemi-

cal, skin, and body senses—we are able to experience sensations of odor, taste, touch, pressure, warmth and cold, pain, and body position and movement (Module 3.4).

Perception is the process by which we take sensory information and organize it in ways that allow us to form meaningful impressions of the world around us. Some areas of perception remain steeped in controversy, especially claims about subliminal perception and extrasensory perception (Module 3.5). Psychologists and other professionals apply their knowledge of sensation and perception in helping people cope more effectively with chronic pain (Module 3.6).

Thinking Critically About Psychology

Based on your reading of this chapter, answer the following questions. Then, to evaluate your progress in developing critical thinking skills, compare your answers to the sample answers found in Appendix A.

A few years ago, a police department asked a woman who claimed to have psychic abilities to help them locate an elderly man who had disappeared in a wooded area outside of town. Despite an extended search of the area, the police had been unable to locate the man. Working only from a photograph of the man and a map of the area, the woman circled an area of the map where she felt the man might be found. The police were amazed to discover the man's body in the area she had indicated. He had died of natural causes, and his body had been hidden by a dense thicket of bushes.

Critical thinkers adopt a skeptical attitude toward claims of ESP. They evaluate the evidence and consider more plausible alternative explanations. Consider these questions:

1. **Do you believe this case demonstrates the existence of ESP? Why or why not?**

2. **What, if any, additional information would you need to help you evaluate the woman's claims or to generate alternative explanations?**

Key Terms

sensation (p. 94)
sensory receptors (p. 94)
psychophysics (p. 94)
absolute threshold (p. 94)
difference threshold (p. 94)
Weber's law (p. 95)
signal-detection theory (p. 95)
sensory adaptation (p. 96)
cornea (p. 98)
iris (p. 98)
pupil (p. 98)
lens (p. 98)
accommodation (p. 98)
retina (p. 98)
photoreceptors (p. 98)
rods (p. 99)
cones (p. 99)
bipolar cells (p. 99)
ganglion cells (p. 100)
optic nerve (p. 100)
blind spot (p. 100)
fovea (p. 100)
feature detectors (p. 101)
trichromatic theory (p. 102)
afterimage (p. 102)
opponent-process theory (p. 102)
trichromats (p. 103)
monochromats (p. 103)
dichromats (p. 103)
audition (p. 105)
pitch (p. 106)
eardrum (p. 106)

ossicles (p. 106)
oval window (p. 106)
cochlea (p. 106)
basilar membrane (p. 106)
organ of Corti (p. 107)
hair cells (p. 107)
auditory nerve (p. 107)
place theory (p. 108)
frequency theory (p. 108)
volley principle (p. 108)
conduction deafness (p. 109)
nerve deafness (p. 109)
olfaction (p. 111)
olfactory nerve (p. 111)
olfactory bulb (p. 112)
pheromones (p. 112)
taste cells (p. 113)
taste buds (p. 113)
skin senses (p. 114)
gate-control theory of pain (p. 115)
acupuncture (p. 116)
kinesthesis (p. 116)
vestibular sense (p. 116)
semicircular canals (p. 116)
vestibular sacs (p. 116)
perception (p. 118)
selective attention (p. 119)
habituation (p. 119)
perceptual set (p. 119)
bottom-up processing (p. 120)
top-down processing (p. 120)
laws of perceptual organization (p. 120)

proximity (p. 121)
similarity (p. 121)
continuity (p. 122)
closure (p. 122)
connectedness (p. 122)
perceptual constancy (p. 122)
shape constancy (p. 123)
size constancy (p. 123)
color constancy (p. 123)
brightness constancy (p. 123)
binocular cues (p. 124)
retinal disparity (p. 124)
convergence (p. 124)
monocular cues (p. 124)
visual illusions (p. 125)
stroboscopic movement (p. 127)
carpentered-world hypothesis (p. 128)
subliminal perception (p. 130)
extrasensory perception (ESP) (p. 130)
parapsychology (p. 130)
telepathy (p. 130)
clairvoyance (p. 130)
precognition (p. 130)
psychokinesis (p. 130)
Ganzfeld procedure (p. 131)
meditation (p. 134)
biofeedback training (BFT) (p. 134)
electromyographic (EMG) biofeedback (p. 134)
thermal biofeedback (p. 134)
migraine headache (p. 134)

ANSWERS TO RECALL IT QUESTIONS

Module 3.1: 1. c; 2. b; 3. Weber's; 4. sensory adaptation.

Module 3.2: 1. rods, cones; 2. false; 3. (a) iv, (b) vi, (c) i, (d) ii, (e) v, (f) iii.

Module 3.3: 1. amplitude and frequency; 2. a; 3. (a) i, (b) v, (c) vi, (d) iv, (e) iii, (f) ii.

Module 3.4: 1. b; 2. taste cells; 3. pheromones; 4. touch, pressure, warmth, cold, and pain; 5. kinesthetic.

Module 3.5: 1. perception; 2. selective; 3. perceptual set; 4. connectedness; 5. a; 6. b.

4

Consciousness

DID YOU KNOW THAT . . .

- Directing all your attention on performing routine mechanical tasks can be counterproductive? (p. 139)

- Dividing your attention between driving and using a car phone is about as dangerous as driving with a blood alcohol concentration at the legal limit? (p. 141)

- Body temperature does not remain at a steady 98.6 degrees Fahrenheit throughout the day? (p. 143)

- One of the smartest things you can do to make sure that what you learn today is remembered tomorrow is to make getting a good night's sleep part of your study plan? (p. 146)

- Dreams don't occur in a flash but unfold in near real time, typically running from about 5 to 45 minutes. (p. 149)

- Coca-Cola once contained cocaine? (p. 165)

- You may be hooked on a drug you have with breakfast every morning? (p. 167)

- It can be dangerous—indeed deadly—to let a person who blacks out from drinking too much "sleep it off"? (pp. 175–176)

Think about what you are doing right now. Are you fully absorbed in reading this page? Or is your attention divided between two or more tasks? While you are reading, are you also listening to music or musing about your plans for the weekend?

We live in a multitasking world today in which we keep one eye on one thing and another eye (or ear) on another. The word *multitasking* entered the popular vocabulary with the introduction of computer systems that allowed users to perform two or more tasks at the same time, such as word processing and emailing. With advances in technology, multitasking has spilled into our daily lives. We make lists on our palmtop organizers or PDAs while attending lectures, talk on cell phones while shopping, and send emails or IM our buddies while listening to the latest hit song we just downloaded.

People today say they are multitasking more than ever before. For example, most of the people surveyed in a recent poll (54 percent) said that they read email while talking on the phone (Shellenbarger, 2003b).

Computers are becoming ever more sophisticated and capable of handling multiple tasks without a hitch, but what about the human brain? How well equipped are we to divide our attention between two or more tasks at once?

Though multitasking may be a timesaver, scientific findings back up the common perception that it is difficult to do two things well at the same time (Oberauer & Kliegl, 2004). Doing two things at once can be dangerous in some situations, such as when talking on a car phone while driving (Logan, 2003). The effort needed to perform multiple tasks at the same time can overload our mental resources and make us less efficient (Rubinstein, Meyer, & Evans, 2001). The effort needed to perform multiple tasks at the same time can overload our mental resources, making us less efficient in performing some tasks, especially complex tasks, such as balancing our checkbook, while speaking on the phone (Rubinstein, Meyer, & Evans, 2001). As we'll see, doing two things at once can even be dangerous, such as when talking on a car phone while driving. But we'll also see that paying too close attention to routine mechanical tasks may be counterproductive.

The very fact that we are capable of multitasking means that we can divide our consciousness, or state of mental awareness, between different activities. We can focus part of our awareness on one task while engaging another part on something else.

In this chapter we set out on an inward exploration of human consciousness. After examining different states of consciousness, we consider various ways in which people have sought to alter their ordinary consciousness, such as by practicing meditation, undergoing hypnosis, or using mind-altering drugs. We consider the psychological and physiological effects of these drugs and the risks they pose.

Psychologist have long been interested in studying consciouness. But the problem of applying scientific methods to studying something as subjective as a person's consciousness prompted many early psychologists, especially the behaviorists, to abandon the effort. Though behaviorism dominated scientific psychology from the 1920s through the 1950s, especially in the United States, the development of the cognitive and humanistic movements helped bring the study of conscious experience back within mainstream psychology. ■

MODULE 4.1

States of Consciousness

■ **What are states of consciousness? What are some examples?**

Multitasking
Are you a multitasker?

CONCEPT 4.1
States of consciousness range from alert wakefulness to deep sleep.

CONCEPT 4.2
The selectivity of consciousness allows us to direct our attention to meaningful stimuli, events, or experiences while filtering out other stimuli.

consciousness   A state of awareness of ourselves and of the world around us.

states of consciousness   Levels of consciousness ranging from alert wakefulness to unconsciousness during deep sleep.

focused awareness   A state of heightened alertness in which one is fully absorbed in the task at hand.

William James is widely regarded as the father of American psychology. As noted in the Pioneers box, he was such an early figure in the field that he had no formal schooling in psychology when he began teaching it himself in 1875. James was interested in the nature of **consciousness**, which he described as a stream of thoughts. To James, consciousness was not a fixed state or a collection of "chopped bits" of disconnected thoughts and experiences. Rather, it was a continuous process of thinking in which one thought flows into another, like water flowing continuously down a river (James 1890/1970). Psychologists today generally define consciousness as a state of awareness of ourselves and of the world around us. Yet like James, psychologists recognize that consciousness comprises a continual flow of mental experiences. In other words, your consciousness consists of whatever you happen to be aware of at each particular moment in time—your thoughts, feelings, sensations, and perceptions of the outside world.

Our **states of consciousness** shift during the course of a day from periods of alert wakefulness to those of drifting consciousness and unconsciousness, as during sleep. In this module, we describe these states of consciousness, beginning with the levels of awareness you are likely to experience during the course of a day: focused awareness, drifting consciousness, and divided consciousness.

Focused Awareness

Consciousness is *selective:* we have the ability to direct our attention to certain objects, events, or experiences while filtering out extraneous stimuli. The selectivity of consciousness enables us to achieve a heightened state of alert wakefulness called **focused awareness**. In a state of focused awareness, we are wide awake, fully alert, and completely engrossed in the task at hand. We pay little if any heed to distracting external stimuli (traffic noises, rumbling air conditioners) or even disturbing internal stimuli (hunger pangs, nagging aches and pains). Focused awareness is needed when performing tasks requiring fixed attention, such as learning to play a new song on the piano or mastering a challenging math problem.

TRY THIS OUT

Savoring Your Food

How does mental focusing affect your experience of eating a meal? Try this out: Focus your attention completely on your next meal. Avoid talking, watching TV, or reading while eating. Notice the shape, color, and texture of the food. Take a deep whiff of the aroma of the food before chewing. Then slowly chew each morsel, savoring the distinctive flavor of each bite. Mix different foods together in your mouth to appreciate their distinctive flavors and how they blend together in a mélange of taste. What differences do you notice between this experience and your usual dining experience?

| **The Student Becomes the Professor**

William James

William James, the brother of the famous novelist Henry James, had trained to be a medical doctor. Though he received a medical degree, he never practiced medicine. Instead he pursued an academic career, teaching biology, philosophy, and later psychology at Harvard University. As a young Harvard professor, he gave his first course in psychology in 1875, even though he had never had a psychology course or any instruction in the field. In fact, the first psychology lecture he ever attended was the one he gave himself (Hothersall, 1995). Since psychology did not yet exist as a discipline, his lack of preparation is not surprising. At the time there were also no psychology textbooks. It would be another fifteen years, in fact, before the first textbook on psychology would appear. It was written by James and was entitled *The Principles of Psychology* (James, 1890/1970).

 CONCEPT 4.3
States of drifting consciousness are associated with mental meanderings called daydreams.

Drifting Consciousness

It is difficult to maintain a state of focused awareness for an extended period of time. Before long, your mind may start drifting from thought to thought. This state of **drifting consciousness** may lead to **daydreaming**, a form of consciousness during a waking state in which your mind wanders to dreamy thoughts or fantasies. You may be studying for an exam when before long you begin daydreaming about the upcoming school break or perhaps what you intend to buy at the grocery store that night. We are particularly prone to daydreams when we are bored or engaged in unstructured activities, such as waiting for a bus. These mental wanderings may bring us to a realm of fantasy in which we take brief trips in our imaginations. However, most daydreams involve mundane tasks of everyday life. Despite the popular belief, relatively few have sexual themes (Klinger, 1987).

Divided Consciousness

CONCEPT 4.4
Our ability to divide consciousness allows us to perform more than one activity at a time.

Learning a new skill typically requires focused awareness. When learning to drive, for example, you need to pay close attention to how far to turn the wheel when steering into a curve, how much pressure to apply to the brakes when stopping, and so on. But after a time, driving may become so routine that you experience a state of divided consciousness and divide your attention between driving and other thoughts, such as trying to remember the words of a song or fantasizing about a vacation.

We typically perform well-honed tasks best, like typing or working a clutch on a car, when we don't concentrate too closely on how we are performing the task. To paraphrase the famed pianist, Vladimir Horowitz, the worst thing that can happen to skilled pianists during a performance is that they begin thinking about what their fingers are doing. In a recent study, investigators found that expert soccer players dribbled better through a slalom course when they were distracted than when they paid close attention to the side of the foot that had last made contact with the ball (Beilock et al., 2002). However, when they used their nondominant foot, they once again had to pay close attention, as did novice soccer players.

States of **divided consciousness** occur when we simultaneously perform two different activities, each of which demands some level of attention. Typically, one of these activities is a mechanical task, such as driving or doing the dishes. When

drifting consciousness A state of awareness characterized by drifting thoughts or mental imagery.

daydreaming A form of consciousness during a waking state in which one's mind wanders to dreamy thoughts or fantasies.

divided consciousness A state of awareness characterized by divided attention to two or more tasks or activities performed at the same time.

Divided Consciousness The ability to divide consciousness allows us to multitask. But the combination of driving and using a car phone or cell phone is associated with an increased risk of motor vehicle accidents.

performing these tasks, part of our mind seems to be on "automatic pilot" while the other part is free to think about other things. Still, consciousness can abruptly shift back to a state of focused awareness under certain circumstances. When driving in a blinding rainstorm, for example, you need to focus your full awareness on your driving. Even on a sunny day, it can be dangerous to divide your attention between driving and other demanding tasks, such as talking on a cell phone (see Exploring Psychology).

Unconsciousness

Sleeping and dreaming are states of **unconsciousness** in which we are relatively unaware of our external surroundings. Yet we may still be responsive to certain types of stimuli that are personally meaningful or relevant. As noted in Chapter 3, people may sleep soundly through the wail of a passing ambulance but be awakened instantly by their child's soft cry. The lowest levels of consciousness are states of deep unconsciousness resulting from head trauma, surgical anesthesia, or coma. A person in a coma may have no awareness of the outside world for months or even years.

In everyday speech, we use the term *unconscious* to refer to a lack of awareness. Freudian theorists, however, use the term to refer to a part of the mind that functions outside of conscious awareness. Freud's theory of the unconscious mind is discussed further in Chapter 12.

States of awareness that differ from one's usual waking state are called **altered states of consciousness**. Altered states of consciousness may occur during our waking states when we daydream, when we meditate or undergo hypnosis, or when we use mind-altering drugs like alcohol and marijuana. Repetitive physical activity, such as long-distance running or lap swimming, also may induce an altered state of consciousness—one in which the outside world seems to fade out of awareness. In some altered states, the person may experience changes in the sense of time (time may seem to stand still or speed up) and in sensory experiences (colors may seem more vibrant or, as in some drug-induced states, the person may hear voices or see visions). In Modules 4.2 to 4.4, we explore the range of human consciousness, from states of sleep and wakefulness to altered states of consciousness. Concept Chart 4.1 offers an overview of the states of consciousness.

CONCEPT 4.5
At the lower end of the continuum of awareness are states of sleeping and dreaming.

CONCEPT 4.6
Altered states of consciousness may be induced in different ways, such as by practicing meditation or undergoing hypnosis, or by using mind-altering drugs.

unconsciousness In ordinary use, a term referring to lack of awareness of one's surroundings or to loss of consciousness.

altered states of consciousness States of awareness that differ from one's usual waking state.

CONCEPT CHART 4.1   States of Consciousness

State of Consciousness	Level of Alertness/Attention	Examples or Features
Focused awareness	High; fully awake and alert	Learning a new skill; watching an engrossing movie
Drifting consciousness	Variable or shifting	Daydreaming, or letting one's thoughts wander
Divided consciousness	Medium; attention split between two activities	Thinking of other things while exercising or driving a car
Sleeping and dreaming	Low	States of unconsciousness in which the person is generally unaware of external surroundings but may respond to certain stimuli
Deep unconsciousness	Nil	Complete loss of consciousness with little or no awareness of the outside world; may be caused by a blow to the head, surgical anesthesia, or coma
Altered states of consciousness	Variable	Changes in consciousness associated with hypnosis, meditation, and drug use

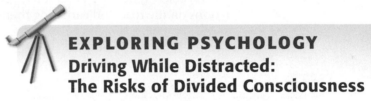

EXPLORING PSYCHOLOGY
Driving While Distracted: The Risks of Divided Consciousness

With the introduction of car phones and cell phones, states of divided attention on the road have raised new safety concerns. According to one study, drivers are four times more likely to have an automobile accident when they are talking on a car phone than when they are not (Redelmeier & Tibshirani, 1997). Driving while using a phone appears to be about as dangerous as driving with a blood alcohol concentration at the legal limit. The increased risk is associated most strongly with loss of concentration, not fiddling with the phone itself; whether the phone is hand-held or hands free, driving performance is impaired (Drucker, 2004; Nagourney, 2003).

The hazards of dividing one's attention while driving are not limited to phone use (see Table 4.1) (Hafner & George, 2005; Recarte & Nunes, 2003). Fussing with

TABLE 4.1   Driving While Distracted

A Canadian survey asked drivers whether they had engaged in the behaviors below while driving and whether they had observed other drivers engaging in the same behaviors.

Behaviors	Yourself %	Another Driver %
Drinking beverages (e.g., coffee, soft drinks)	65	74
Eating	53	66
Using a cell phone	35	79
Arguing with passengers	27	41
Disciplining children	18	33
Reading	8	26
Putting on make-up, shaving, or combing hair	8	43
Using PDAs, laptops, or other high-tech devices	5	21

Source: Adapted from *2003 Nerves of Steel* survey, commissioned by The Steel Alliance and the Canada Safety Council: http://www.safety-council.org/info/traffic/distract.html.

a child in the back seat, carrying on a complex or heated conversation with a passenger, putting on make-up, eating or drinking, and picking out a playlist on an iPod are also distracting, even dangerously so. According to a study by an automotive insurance group, the three most dangerous foods to eat while driving are (1) coffee, (2) hot soup, and (3) tacos (Strillacci, 2003). Soups, coffee, and other beverages find ways of spilling out of the cup, but any form of eating while driving can be dangerous.

People don't realize just how distracted they are, says Peter Kissinger, president of AAA's Foundation for Traffic Safety ("Driver Study," 2003). He notes that "talking to a passenger seems quite safe, but even something that simple takes away from the road." On the other hand, the results of a recent driving simulation study showed that listening to a radio at a moderate volume did not impair driving performance (Strayer & Johnston, 2001). Listening to a radio may not engage our attention resources as fully as carrying on a conversation with a passenger or talking on a cell phone.

According to the National Highway Traffic Safety Administration, distraction accounts for an estimated 25 percent of all police-reported motor vehicle crashes (Strillacci, 2003). A study by the California Highway Patrol revealed that cell phone use was the most frequent cause of inattention accidents; second was fiddling with the car's stereo system ("New Studies," 2003). Becoming aware of these many distractions on the road and curtailing them may help save a life, possibly your own.

MODULE 4.1 REVIEW

States of Consciousness

RECITE IT

What are states of consciousness? What are some examples?

- States of consciousness are different levels of awareness that occur during the course of the day, ranging from alert wakefulness to states of unconsciousness during sleep.

- Altered states of consciousness are states of awareness during wakefulness that differ from a person's usual waking state, such as when one undergoes hypnosis, takes a mind-altering drug, or runs a marathon.

RECALL IT

1. The nineteenth-century psychologist William James likened consciousness to
   a. water flowing continuously down a river.
   b. a drifting cloud.
   c. a swirling ocean.
   d. a state of tranquility.

2. The _____ of consciousness allows us to focus on meaningful stimuli, events, and experiences.

3. The state of awareness in which we are completely alert and engrossed in a task is known as _____ awareness.

4. Meditation, hypnosis, and the use of mind-altering drugs are among the ways people seek to experience _____ states of consciousness.

THINK ABOUT IT

- William James likened consciousness to water flowing continuously down a river. Can you think of other metaphors for representing consciousness?

MODULE 4.2
Sleeping and Dreaming

- How are our sleep-wake cycles regulated?
- What are the stages of sleep, and what functions does sleep serve?
- Why do we dream?
- What are sleep disorders?

We spend about a third of our lives sleeping. During sleep, we enter our own private theater of the mind—a realm of dreams in which the mind weaves tales ranging from the mundane and ordinary to the fantastic and bizarre. The laws of the physical world don't apply when we dream. Objects change shape, one person may be transformed into another, and scenes move abruptly without regard to the physical limits of time and place. Though we've learned much about sleeping and dreaming, many mysteries remain. We lack a consensus about such basic questions as "Why do we sleep?" and "Why do we dream?" In this module, we venture into the mysterious domain of sleep and dreams. We begin by examining the bodily mechanisms responsible for our sleep-wake cycles.

Sleep and Wakefulness: A Circadian Rhythm

Many bodily processes—sleep-wake cycles, as well as body temperature, hormonal secretions, blood pressure, and heart rate—fluctuate daily in a pattern called a **circadian rhythm**. The word *circadian* is derived from the Latin roots *circa* ("about") and *dies* ("day"). Circadian (daily) rhythms are found in virtually all species, including organisms as varied as humans, bees, and even plants and trees (Foster & Kreitzman, 2004; A. Underwood, 2004). These rhythms are synchronized with the 24-hour cycle of day and night. In humans, the sleep-wake cycle operates on a circadian rhythm that is close to 24 hours in length (Lavie, 2001). Human body temperature is not maintained at a steady 98.6 degrees Fahrenheit throughout the day. It follows a circadian rhythm in which it falls a few degrees during the middle of the night, rises in early morning, and then peaks by mid-day.

The circadian rhythm is controlled by a kind of body clock inside the brain. A small area of the hypothalamus, the *suprachiasmatic nucleus* (SCN), is a circadian center that regulates sleeping and wakefulness on roughly a 24-hour cycle (Refinetti, 2000; Yamaguchi et al., 2003). When light enters the eye, its energy is transformed into neural impulses that travel to the SCN (Berson, Dunn, & Takao, 2002; He et al., 2002). The SCN in turn regulates the pineal gland, which, as noted in Chapter 2, is a gland in the brain that releases the hormone melatonin (Barinaga, 2002). Melatonin helps synchronize the body's sleep-wake cycle by making us feel sleepy. Exposure to darkness during evening hours increases the production of melatonin. During exposure to bright light, melatonin production falls off, which helps us maintain wakefulness during daylight hours. (This might also explain why we often feel sleepy on cloudy days.)

Frequent time shifts can play havoc with the body's circadian rhythms. If you've ever traveled by plane across several time zones, you've probably experienced jet lag. **Jet lag** occurs when a change in local time conflicts with your internal body clock, making it difficult to fall asleep earlier than usual or to stay awake later than usual, depending on whether you've lost time by traveling east or gained time by traveling west. Jet lag is associated not only with disruption of sleep-wake cycles, but also with irritability, fatigue, and difficulty in concentrating.

For occasional travelers, jet lag may be only a mild annoyance. But shift workers who pull duty at night, when their body temperatures are normally low, must

CONCEPT 4.7
A clocklike mechanism in the hypothalamus is responsible for regulating our sleep-wake cycles.

CONCEPT 4.8
Your internal body clock does not adjust easily to time shifts associated with changes in time zones or shift work.

circadian rhythm   The pattern of fluctuations in bodily processes that occur regularly each day.

jet lag   A disruption of sleep-wake cycles caused by the shifts in time zones that accompany long-distance air travel.

often fight to stay awake (R. Sullivan, 1998). Night-shift workers in sensitive positions, such as air traffic controllers, firefighters, and nuclear power workers, tend to be less alert, sleepier, more fatigued, and less able to perform their jobs than day-shift workers in similar positions (G. Costa, 1996; Luna, French, & Mindtcha, 1997). Exposure to bright light for a few minutes at the start of a night shift may help reset circadian rhythms, since light exposure has been associated with better job performance and improved sleep patterns in shift workers (Kamei et al., 1994).

The Stages of Sleep

The electroencephalograph (EEG) is one of several devices researchers use to determine how our bodies respond when we sleep. The EEG tracks brain waves, which vary in intensity or amplitude (height of the wave) and speed or frequency (wave cycles per second). When you are awake and alert, your brain wave pattern is dominated by fast, low-amplitude *beta waves*. As you close your eyes and relax in bed, you enter a state of relaxed wakefulness. In this state, your brain wave pattern is dominated by slower, rhythmic cycles called *alpha waves*. When you slip into sleep, the EEG shows that you progress through several distinct stages characterized by different brain wave patterns (see Figure 4.1).

Stages 1 to 4: From Light to Deep Sleep   When you enter Stage 1 sleep, brain waves become small and irregular with varying frequencies. You can be easily awakened during this stage and may not even realize that you had been sleeping. Stage 2 sleep begins about two minutes after Stage 1 sleep and is characterized by bursts of brain wave activity that are represented by spindle-shaped waves called

CONCEPT 4.9
During sleep, your body cycles through four stages, followed by a period of REM sleep, in which most dreaming occurs.

Figure 4.1   Brain Wave Patterns During Wakefulness and Sleep
Here we see the characteristic brain wave patterns associated with each stage of sleep. *(a)* Ordinary wakefulness: fast, low-amplitude beta waves; *(b)* relaxed wakefulness: rhythmic alpha waves; *(c)* Stage 1 sleep: small, irregular brain waves with varying frequencies; *(d)* Stage 2 sleep: sleep spindles; *(e)* Stage 3 and Stage 4 sleep: large, slow, delta waves; *(f)* REM sleep: rapid, active pattern similar to that in ordinary wakefulness.

Online Study Center
Improve Your Grade
Tutorials: Sleeping in Stages

(a) Ordinary Wakefulness
Fast, low-amplitude beta waves

(b) Relaxed Wakefulness
Rhythmic alpha waves

(c) Stage 1 Sleep
Small, irregular brain waves

(d) Stage 2 Sleep
Appearance of spindle-shaped waves called sleep spindles
Sleep spindle

(e) Stage 3/ Stage 4 Sleep
Appearance of large, slow delta waves
Delta activity

(f) REM Sleep
Similar to ordinary wakefulness

Figure 4.2   REM Sleep Through the Night
Notice how periods of REM sleep become longer as sleep progresses through the night.

sleep spindles. You spend more than half your sleep time in Stage 2 sleep. This is a deeper stage of sleep, but you can still be readily awakened. Stages 3 and 4 of sleep, called *delta sleep* or *slow-wave sleep (SWS)*, are characterized by the appearance of large, slow brain waves called *delta waves.* This is the period of deep sleep during which it is becomes difficult to arouse you. The distinction between Stage 3 and Stage 4 is based on the proportion of delta waves. In Stage 3, delta waves constitute 50 percent or fewer of brain wave patterns; in Stage 4, they constitute more than 50 percent.

REM Sleep: The Stuff of Which Dreams Are Made

Rapid-eye-movement (REM) sleep is the stage of sleep in which one's eyes dart about under closed eyelids. After Stage 4 sleep, by about fifty to eighty minutes after falling asleep, the sleeper briefly recycles through Stages 3 and 2 and from there enters REM sleep.

REM is the stage of sleep most closely associated with dreaming (Latta & Van Cauter, 2003; Stickgold et al., 2001). Dreams also occur during Stages 1 to 4, collectively called non-REM (NREM) sleep, but they are generally briefer, less frequent, and more thoughtlike than those experienced during REM sleep.

The brain becomes more active during REM sleep, which is why it is sometimes called *active* sleep. Brain wave patterns during REM sleep are similar to those during states of alert wakefulness. REM sleep is also called *paradoxical sleep.* What makes it paradoxical is that despite a high level of brain activity, muscle activity is blocked to the point that the person is practically paralyzed. This is indeed fortunate, as it prevents injuries that might occur if the dreamer were suddenly to bolt from bed and try to enact a dream.

Sleep cycles generally repeat about every ninety minutes. The average person has about four or five sleep cycles during a night's sleep. It may take about an hour to reach Stage 4 sleep in the first cycle and then another 30 or 40 minutes to reach REM. As the night goes on, the amount of time spent in REM sleep increases (Latta & Van Cauter, 2003) (see Figure 4.2). Moreover, Stage 4 sleep disappears during the course of the night, which means that we progress faster to REM sleep as the night wears on. Concept Chart 4.2 summarizes the different states of wakefulness and stages of sleep.

Why Do We Sleep?

Humans and nearly all other animals sleep, although the average length of sleep varies across species (see Figure 4.3). The near universality of sleep suggests that it serves a basic survival function. One line of speculation is that sleep is protective: it keeps the organism out of harm's way. A sleeping animal may be less conspicuous to predators roaming about at night and less likely to suffer dangerous falls or accidents that could arise from moving about in the dark (Gaulin & McBurney, 2001).

Sleep also helps conserve energy, as animals use less bodily energy when they are sleeping than when they are moving about during the waking state. But perhaps the major function of sleep is restorative in nature. Sleep may help the brain recover from daily wear-and-tear and replenish proteins the body uses during wakefulness. The view that sleep is restorative is consistent with feeling rested and mentally alert after a good night's sleep.

Evidence also suggests that sleep helps us consolidate newly learned information into lasting memories (Gais & Born, 2004; Huber et al., 2004; Stickgold et al.,

CONCEPT 4.10

Three major functions of sleep have been proposed: a protective function, an energy-conservation function, and a restorative function.

rapid-eye-movement (REM) sleep
The stage of sleep that involves rapid eye movements and that is most closely associated with periods of dreaming.

CONCEPT CHART 4.2 Wakefulness and Sleep

State of Wakefulness/ Stage of Sleep	Characteristic Brain Wave Pattern	Key Features
Alert wakefulness	Fast, low-amplitude beta waves	State of focused attention or active thought
Relaxed wakefulness	Slower, rhythmic alpha waves	State of resting quietly with eyes closed
Stage 1 sleep	Small, irregular brain waves with varying frequencies	Light sleep from which the person can be easily awakened
Stage 2 sleep	Sleep spindles	Deeper sleep, but the sleeper is still readily awakened
Stage 3 sleep	Large, slow delta waves	Deep sleep (called delta sleep or slow-wave sleep) from which it is difficult to arouse the sleeper
Stage 4 sleep	Dominance of delta waves	Deepest level of sleep
REM sleep	Rapid, active pattern, similar to that in alert wakefulness	Sleep in which the brain becomes more active but muscle activity is blocked (also called active sleep or paradoxical sleep); stage associated with dreaming

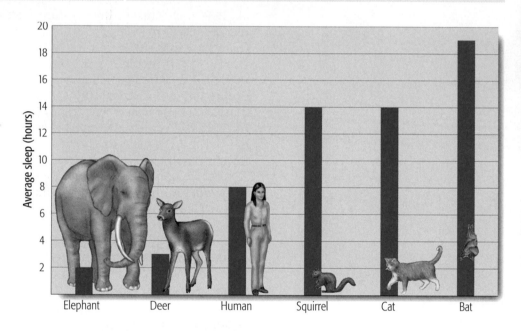

Figure 4.3 Average Length of Sleep Among Different Mammals
The average amount of sleep varies across animal species.

2001). Thus, if you want to retain new learning (including what you study in your textbooks), make sure that getting a good night's sleep is part of your study plan.

We also have evidence that sleep bolsters the body's ability to defend itself against disease-causing agents (Winerman, 2004). Not surprisingly, you may find yourself more susceptible to the common cold and other ailments when you've gone without your necessary quota of sleep.

Dreams and Dreaming

Why do we dream? The short answer is that no one really knows. In all likelihood dreams have multiple functions. One possible function of REM sleep is consolidating fresh memories into lasting memories (Huber et al., 2004; Ribeiro & Nicolelis, 2004). However, some evidence suggests that slow-wave sleep (SWS) may play a more direct role in memory consolidation than REM sleep (Gais & Born, 2004).

CONCEPT 4.11
Though we all dream while asleep, the question of why we dream remains unanswered.

Figure 4.4   Activation-Synthesis Hypothesis
According to the activation-synthesis hypothesis, dreams arise when the cerebral cortex attempts to make sense of random electrical discharges emanating from the brainstem during REM sleep.

2. Cerebral cortex creates meaning from these random signals, weaving dream stories that integrate personal memories and stored information

Example: Electrical signals generated from neurons in the brainstem that control balance and posture are synthesized by the cortex in a dream of the person riding on a roller-coaster

1. Neurons in the brainstem spontaneously generate random discharges of electrical activity

Online Study Center
Improve Your Grade
Tutorials: The Activation-Synthesis Hypothesis

Ernest Hartmann, a leading dream investigator, believes that dreams help us sort through possible solutions to everyday problems and concerns (cited in Talan, 1998). Another prominent view of dreaming, called the **activation-synthesis hypothesis** (Hobson, 2002; Hobson & McCarley, 1977), holds that dreams represent an attempt by the cerebral cortex to make sense of the random discharges of electrical activity that occur during REM sleep. The electrical activity arises from the brainstem, the part of the brain responsible for such basic functions as breathing and heart rate (see Figure 4.4). According to this hypothesis, the cerebral cortex creates a story line based on the individual's store of knowledge and memories to explain these random signals and the emotions and sensory experiences they generate.

Parts of the brain involved in emotions, memory, and visual processing are activated during REM sleep, while other parts, including parts of the cerebral cortex that are involved in logical thought, show decreased activity during REM sleep. This pattern of neural activity suggests why dreams may lack the orderliness or logic of ordinary conscious thought—why they may form from bits and pieces of emotionally charged memories and vivid imagery that unfold in a chaotic sequence of events.

Even if dreams emanate from a hodgepodge of electrical discharges from the deep recesses of the brain, they may be filled with personal meaning because they are based on individual memories and associations. But what, if anything, do they mean?

activation-synthesis hypothesis   The proposition that dreams represent the brain's attempt to make sense of the random discharges of electrical activity that occur during REM sleep.

Why Do We Dream? Although speculations about dreams abound, their meaning remains a mystery.

Sigmund Freud (1900) had an answer to this question that continues to fascinate and challenge us. He believed that dreams represent a form of *wish fulfillment*. According to Freud, dreams contain symbols that represent the sleeper's underlying wishes, usually of a sexual or aggressive nature. Freud called dreams the "royal road" to the unconscious, but he believed you needed a kind of psychological roadmap to interpret them because the dream symbols mask their true meanings. Freud distinguished between two types of dream content:

1. *Manifest content.* The manifest content refers to events that occur in the dream. You might dream, for example, of driving fast and getting a speeding ticket from a police officer.

2. *Latent content.* This is the true, underlying meaning of the dream, disguised in the form of dream symbols. The disguise conceals the dream's real meaning, thereby helping preserve sleep by preventing emotionally threatening material from waking you up. Driving fast might symbolize an unacceptable sexual wish. The police officer, a symbol of male authority, might represent your father punishing you for having the sexual wish.

In Freud's view, phallic objects like trees, skyscrapers, snakes, and guns are symbols of male genitalia, and enclosed objects like boxes, closets, and ovens are symbols of female genitalia. But Freud believed we shouldn't rush to judgment when interpreting dream symbols—that sometimes "a cigar is just a cigar." He also recognized that the same dream events might have different meanings for different people, so individual analysis is necessary to ferret out their meanings (Lear, 2000; Pesant & Zadra, 2004).

Dream interpretation makes for an interesting exercise, but how do we know that our interpretations are accurate? Unfortunately, although the meaning of dreams has been studied and debated for more than a century since Freud's initial work, we still lack any objective means of verifying the accuracy of dream interpretations. Nor is there evidence that dreams serve the function of preserving sleep, as Freud alleged (Fisher & Greenberg, 1978). Nevertheless, we should credit Freud with raising our awareness that dreams may have a psychological meaning and may express emotional issues (Squier & Domhoff, 1998).

TRY THIS OUT
Dream a Little Dream for Me

Can you determine what you dream about? To find out, try this experiment:

1. Before retiring for the night, select a topic to dream about—for example, meeting a famous person or playing your favorite sport—and put a pen and pad within handy reach of your bed.

2. For ten or fifteen minutes before retiring, mentally rehearse the dream by fantasizing about the topic.

3. Upon retiring, say to yourself, "I think I'll dream some more about this."

4. As you grow sleepier, return to the fantasy, but don't resist letting your mind wander off.

5. When you awake, whether in the middle of the night or the next morning, lie still while you recollect what you dreamed about and then immediately reach for your pen and pad and write down the dream content.

6. Evaluate your results. Were you able to program your dream in advance?

TABLE 4.2   Questions and Answers About Dreams

Do dreams foretell the future?	People who believe they have had prophetic dreams may point to one or two "hits" (correspondences between dream events and real-life events). But they overlook the many times when they dreamed about an event that did not occur. No credible scientific evidence supports the belief that dreams foretell the future. Any correspondence between a dream event and the same event in real life may be explained as mere coincidence.
Do we dream in color?	We cannot give a definitive answer, since we must rely on dream reports (people recalling their dreams upon awakening) rather than direct dream experience. But in laboratory-based sleep studies, people report that they dream in color.
Do animals dream?	Nonhuman animals cannot tell us whether they dream, so the question is moot. We know from laboratory studies that nonhuman mammals show the same brain activation patterns as humans when they sleep. Consequently, it is reasonable to assume that other animals have perceptual, emotional, and memory experiences when they sleep. Perhaps these experiences constitute a kind of wordless dream state.
Do dreams occur in a flash?	Actually, dreams events unfold in near real time. Dreams typically last from about 5 to 45 minutes.
Do blind people dream?	People who have been blind since birth do dream, but they do not have visual images in their dreams. Their dreams may involve sensations other than visual images, such as tactile, auditory, and bodily sensations. People who lose their sight after about the age of 7 do retain the capacity to have visual images when they dream, at least for some twenty or thirty years after losing their vision.
If you dream about falling from a high place, will you die if you fail to wake up in time?	Certainly not. Many people have dreams of falling and hitting the ground or even of dying, but they don't actually fall or die.

Source: Hobson, 2002; Kerr & Homhoff, 2004; NewScientist.com, among other sources.

Whatever the underlying meaning of dreams may be, some people report **lucid dreams**—dreams in which they are aware that they are dreaming (Patrick & Durndell, 2004). Lucid dreams seem to occur almost exclusively during REM sleep (LaBerge, 2003). Some lucid dreamers claim they can determine beforehand what they will dream about or can consciously direct the action of a dream as it unfolds. However, we have little evidence to support such claims. Moreover, relatively few people report experiencing lucid dreams on a regular basis.

On the other hand, psychologists find that either thinking about something shortly before sleep or trying not to think about something increases the likelihood of dreaming about it (A. O'Connor, 2004b; Wegner, Wenzlaff, & Kozak, 2004). So trying to keep something out of the mind can have the unintended consequence of making it more likely to pop up in dreams. All the mental energy expended in suppressing a thought may actually tag the thought as something meaningful that the mind incorporates in the nightly mental musings we call dreams. Table 4.2 examines some common questions people often ask about dreams.

Online Study Center
Improve Your Grade
Tutorials: How Are You Sleeping?

Sleep Disorders:
When Normal Sleep Eludes Us

CONCEPT 4.12
Sleep disorders are disturbances of sleep that prevent a person from getting a good night's sleep and remaining awake or alert during the day.

Sleep disorders—disturbances of sleep that interfere with getting a good night's sleep and remaining alert during the day—affect about 70 million people in the United States (R. Sullivan, 1998). Sleep disorders are sometimes evaluated in specialized sleep centers, where troubled sleepers can be wired to physiological monitoring equipment as they sleep to determine the particular type of sleep disorder they may have.

lucid dreams   Dreams in which the dreamer is aware that he or she is dreaming.

An estimated 9 to 12 percent of adults suffer from chronic **insomnia**, the most commonly occurring sleep disorder (Espie, 2002). People with insomnia have difficulty falling asleep, remaining asleep, or returning to sleep after night-time awakenings (Pallesen et al., 2001). Insomnia prevents people from achieving restorative sleep, the type of sleep that leaves them feeling refreshed and alert in the morning.

Insomnia is caused by many factors, including substance abuse, physical illness, and psychological disorders like depression (Morin, 2000). If the underlying problem is resolved, chances are that sleep patterns will return to normal. Worrying can also interfere with sleep, as it is accompanied by increased body arousal. Thus, bringing daily worries and concerns to bed can lead to insomnia or poor-quality sleep (Thomsen et al., 2003),. People who have trouble falling asleep may also begin worrying about not getting enough sleep, which can bump up their arousal level even more. They may find that the harder they try to fall asleep, the more difficult it becomes. The lesson here is that sleep is a natural function that cannot be forced.

Narcolepsy is characterized by sudden, unexplained "sleep attacks" during daytime hours. People with narcolepsy may be engaged in conversation one moment and fall fast asleep in the next. Narcolepsy is associated with **cataplexy**, a sudden loss of muscle tone or control that can result in the person suddenly collapsing to the floor (Krahn & Gonzalez-Arriaza, 2004; Siegel, 2004).

Sleep attacks can be very dangerous. Household accidents due to falls are common. Even more disturbing are reports that the majority of people with narcolepsy have episodes in which they suddenly fall asleep while driving (Aldrich, 1992). Narcolepsy may be caused by a loss of brain cells in an area of the hypothalamus responsible for producing a sleep-regulating chemical (Mignot & Thorsby, 2001). Currently available treatments for narcolepsy include daytime naps and use of stimulant drugs (amphetamines) to help maintain wakefulness.

People with **sleep apnea** may literally stop breathing momentarily as many as five hundred times during a night's sleep (the word *apnea* means "without breath"). The cause is a structural defect, such as an overly thick palate or enlarged tonsils that partially or fully block the flow of air through the upper airways. People with sleep apnea usually awaken the next morning with no memory of these episodes. However, their fitful sleep patterns deprive them of solid sleep so that they are sleepy during the day and have difficulty functioning at their best. For reasons that aren't clear, people with sleep apnea have an increased risk of hypertension (high blood pressure), a major risk factor in cardiovascular disease (Nieto et al., 2000). They also snore very loudly (described as "industrial strength" snoring) because of their narrowed airways. Experts estimate that as many as 18 million Americans suffer from sleep apnea (D. Smith, 2001b). It is more common in men, especially middle-aged men, and among obese people. Sleep apnea may be treated with mechanical appliances, such as a nose mask that exerts pressure to keep the upper airway passages open during sleep, or with surgery that opens narrowed airways.

People with **nightmare disorder** have frequent, disturbing nightmares. Children are especially prone to nightmare disorder. Nightmares are storylike dreams that contain threats to the dreamer's life or safety. The action of the nightmare may be vivid and intense, such as falling through space or fleeing from attackers or giant insects. Nightmares typically take place during REM sleep. People are usually more susceptible to nightmares when they are under emotional stress, have high fevers, or are suffering from sleep deprivation.

People with **sleep terror disorder** have frequent "night terrors," which are more intense than ordinary nightmares. Unlike nightmares, which occur mainly during REM sleep, night terrors occur during deep sleep. The disorder primarily affects children, and it affects boys more often than girls. Night terrors begin with a loud panicky scream. The child may sit up in bed, appear dazed and frightened,

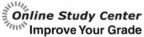
Online Study Center
Improve Your Grade
Tutorials: Identifying Sleep Disorders

insomnia Difficulty falling asleep, remaining asleep, or returning to sleep after nighttime awakenings.

narcolepsy A disorder characterized by sudden unexplained "sleep attacks" during the day.

cataplexy Sudden, involuntary loss of muscular tone or control.

sleep apnea Temporary cessation of breathing during sleep.

nightmare disorder A sleep disorder involving a pattern of frequent, disturbing nightmares.

sleep terror disorder A sleep disorder involving repeated episodes of intense fear during sleep, causing the person to awake abruptly in a terrified state.

sleepwalking disorder A sleep disorder characterized by repeated episodes of sleepwalking.

and be able to remember only fragmentary dream images, rather than the detailed dream stories that typically are remembered after nightmares. Most children outgrow the problem by adolescence.

Sleepwalking disorder is another sleep disorder that occurs more often in children than in adults. Occasional sleepwalking is common in children. But as many as 5 percent of children have a sleepwalking disorder in which sleepwalking episodes become persistent. During these episodes, the person remains soundly asleep while walking about with eyes open and perhaps an expressionless look on his or her face. Though sleepwalkers generally avoid knocking into things, accidents do occur. The following morning, the sleepwalker usually remembers nothing of the nighttime wanderings. Sleepwalking typically occurs during deep, dreamless sleep. Despite the belief to the contrary, there is no harm in awakening a sleepwalker. Sleeptalking is sometimes associated with sleep disorders such as sleepwalking and obstructive sleep apnea syndrome, but in most cases it is not linked to mental health problems (Hublin et al., 1998).

Sleep disorders are often treated with sleep medications that help induce sleep. However, these drugs can lead to physiological dependence and should be used for only a brief period of time, a few weeks at most (Pollack, 2004b). Psychologists have obtained good results in treating insomnia using cognitive-behavioral approaches that help people develop more adaptive sleep habits, including techniques such as those described in Module 4.5 of this chapter (Espie, 2002; Pollack, 2004a; Rybarczyk et al., 2002). Sleep experts believe that cognitive-behavioral techniques are just as effective as sleep medication in treating insomnia in the short term and more effective over the long term (Smith, 2001b).

Sleep Deprivation: Getting By on Less, but at What Cost?

CONCEPT 4.13
Though people vary in how much sleep they need, most people require seven to nine hours of sleep to feel refreshed and to perform at their best.

People vary in their need for sleep. Most require between seven and nine hours of sleep to feel fully refreshed and to function at their best (Kelley, 1997). Yet more than 60 percent of Americans report sleeping fewer than seven hours a night (Winerman, 2004c), and one person out of four says that sleep problems impair his or her ability to function during the day (National Sleep Foundation, 2005).

Though some people may need only 5 or 6 hours of sleep, many of these "short sleepers" are actually sleep-deprived and don't realize it. College students report averaging only 6 to 6.9 hours sleep a night, which may help explain the grogginess many students experience during the day (Markel, 2003). In addition, only about 15 percent of high school students report sleeping the recommended 8.5 hours they need (Kantrowitz & Springen, 2003). One of the reasons for not getting enough sleep is that we tend to go bed late. A recent survey found that more than a third of adults (34 percent) report going to bed after midnight (see Figure 4.5).

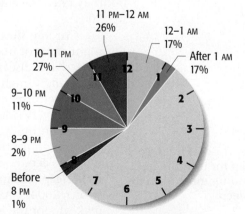

Figure 4.5   When America Goes to Bed
Living in a "24/7" world in which we can watch movies and news all night long or even order a pizza at 2 A.M. has taken its toll on America's sleep habits. One reason that many Americans don't get enough sleep is that they are going to bed too late.

Source: Adapted from *Sleepless in America,* a survey conducted by the ACNielsen Company, April 2005, retrieved from http://us.acnielsen.com/news/20050404.shtml.

Note: Percentages do not sum to 100% due to rounding.

Figure 4.6   Changes in Sleep Patterns in Childhood
During early childhood, the proportion of REM sleep declines, while the proportion of non-REM sleep increases.

Sleep Deprived   Sleep deprivation does not just leave you feeling groggy; it also slows your reaction times and impairs your concentration, memory, and problem-solving ability.

💡 **CONCEPT 4.14**
When people are deprived of REM sleep, they tend to make up for it in the next sleep period by spending more of their sleep time in REM sleep.

Sleep patterns change during the life cycle. Newborn infants sleep for about two-thirds of the day (see Figure 4.6). Infants spend about one-half of their sleep time in REM sleep, while adults spend about one-fifth. Children spend more time in REM sleep than adults, but as they mature, the proportion of REM sleep declines, while periods of NREM sleep and wakefulness increase. During adulthood, the amounts of total sleep declines, as does the amounts of REM sleep and deep sleep (Blackman, 2000; Van-Cauter, Leproult, & Plat, 2000). By the time we reach our sixties or seventies, we may require only six hours of sleep per night.

Temporary periods of sleep deprivation are not associated with ill effects to our health. If you miss a few hours of sleep, you may feel a little groggy the next day but will probably muddle through. Even so, sleep deprivation tends to slow reaction times; impair concentration, memory, and problem-solving ability; make it more difficult to retain newly acquired information; and impair performance on academic tasks, including math tasks (Bowman, 2000; Carpenter, 2000c; Harrison & Horne, 2000; Stickgold, LaTanya, & Hobson, 2000). Sleep deprivation is also among the most common causes of motor vehicle accidents. Such accidents are most likely to occur in the early morning hours when drivers are typically at their sleepiest.

Don't be alarmed if you miss a few hours of sleep; rather, attempt to restore your normal sleep pattern the following night. But chronic sleep deprivation is a serious concern because it puts a damper on our psychological well-being or happiness. Women in a recent study who reported sleeping poorly rated their daily experiences at the same (low) level of enjoyment as the typical person rates commuting. Those who slept well rated their daily experiences about as highly as they rated the enjoyment of watching TV (Kahneman et al., 2004; "New Method," 2004).

Chronic sleep deprivation, which occurs commonly among people working night shifts or frequently changing shifts, is associated with increased risks of cardiovascular disease and other medical problems (Latta & Van Cauter, 2003). Nor surprisingly, night work is also associated with increased risks of accidents and impaired performance. Nor should we be surprised that when extended work shifts among overworked medical interns are eliminated, the frequency of attentional failures during work shifts declines (Lockley et al., 2004).

It's not just the total amount of sleep that affects our functioning, but also the type of sleep. From laboratory studies in which volunteers have been deprived of REM sleep, we know that loss of REM sleep impairs learning ability and memory (Greer, 2004c). After REM deprivation, people experience a "rebound effect": they make up for the loss by spending more of their next sleep period in REM sleep.

MODULE 4.2 REVIEW

Sleeping and Dreaming

RECITE IT

How are our sleep-wake cycles regulated?

- The suprachiasmatic nucleus (SCN), a clocklike mechanism in the hypothalamus, regulates our sleep-wake cycles according to a circadian rhythm that approximates the 24-hour day.

What are the stages of sleep, and what functions does sleep serve?

- In addition to REM sleep, there are four non-REM stages of sleep (Stages 1 through 4); in these stages, sleep becomes increasingly deeper. The brain is relatively active during REM sleep, which is when most dreaming occurs.

- Though no one knows for sure, sleep experts suspect that sleep may serve several functions, including a protective function, an energy-conservation function, and a restorative function.

RECALL IT

1. Many bodily processes, including body temperature, heart rate, and sleep-wake cycles, fluctuate daily in a pattern called a _____ rhythm.

2. Deep sleep, which is characterized by delta brain wave patterns, occurs during Stages _____ and _____ of sleep.

3. Sleep may help the body replenish resources expended during wakefulness. What is this function of sleep called?

Why do we dream?

- Again, no one can say for sure, but theories include the belief that dreams are needed to consolidate memories and experiences that occur during the day into long-term memory, Hartmann's view that dreams help people work out their everyday problems, the activation-synthesis hypothesis, and Freud's view that dreaming helps preserve sleep by disguising potentially threatening wishes or impulses in the form of dream symbols.

What are sleep disorders?

- Sleep disorders are disturbances in the amount or quality of sleep. They include insomnia, narcolepsy, sleep apnea, nightmare disorder, sleep terror disorder, and sleepwalking. The most common sleep disorder is insomnia.

4. Match each of the sleep disorders listed with the appropriate description below: i. narcolepsy; ii. sleep terror disorder; iii. sleep apnea; iv. nightmare disorder;

   a. frequent, frightening dreams that usually occur during REM sleep, temporary cessation of breathing during sleep
   b. intense nightmares that occur during deep sleep and primarily affect children
   c. sudden, unexplained "sleep attacks" during the day
   d. temporary cessation of breathing during sleep

THINK ABOUT IT

- Have you experienced jet lag? How did it affect you? What might you do differently in the future to cope with it? One suggestion is to gradually alter your body clock by adjusting the time you go to bed by an hour a day for several days before your trip. If you will be away for only a brief time, you might be better off to follow your body clock as much as possible during the trip.

- Many college students disrupt their normal sleep-wake cycles by staying up to all hours of the night and then napping during the day to catch up on missed sleep. They may feel as though they are continually suffering from jet lag. What would you suggest to help someone get his or her sleep cycle back on track?

- How would you rate your sleep habits? What specific changes can you make to improve them? (For some suggestions on developing healthier sleep habits, see Module 4.5.)

- Apply each of the major theories of dreaming—Hartmann's belief that dreams allow us to sort through potential solutions to everyday problems and concerns, Freud's wish-fulfillment theory, and the activation-synthesis hypothesis—to a particular dream or dreams you are able to recall. Which of these theories do you believe best account for your dream or dreams?

MODULE 4.3

Altering Consciousness Through Meditation and Hypnosis

- What is meditation?
- What is hypnosis?
- What are the major theories of hypnosis?

We venture now from considering states of ordinary wakefulness and sleep to considering states of altered consciousness. People use many methods to alter their states of conscious awareness. Some turn to drugs; others turn to such practices as meditation and hypnosis. You might not think of meditation and hypnosis as having much in common, but both involve rituals that focus on narrowing attention or concentration to achieve an altered state of consciousness.

Meditation: Achieving a Peaceful State by Focusing Your Attention

CONCEPT 4.15
Meditation involves practices that induce an altered state of consciousness through techniques of focused attention.

People from many different cultures practice meditation, which, as you may recall from Chapter 3, is a process of focused attention that induces a relaxed, contemplative state. To remove all other thoughts from consciousness, practitioners of meditation narrow their attention to a single object or thought. The particular meditative technique used varies among cultures. In ancient Egypt, practitioners stared at an oil-burning lamp, a custom that inspired the tale of Aladdin's lamp. Yogis focus on the design of a vase or other graphic symbol. Other practitioners focus on a burning candle.

In **transcendental meditation (TM)**, practitioners narrow their attention by repeating a particular phrase or sound (such as *om*), which is known as a **mantra**. In **mindfulness meditation**, people focus on the thoughts and physical sensations they experience on a moment-to-moment basis (Baer, 2003; Hayes & Wilson, 2003). The underlying principle is to be focused in the moment, becoming fully aware of mental experiences without evaluating or judging those experiences as they unfold.

Meditation Meditation can induce a relaxed but alert state.

transcendental meditation (TM) A form of meditation in which practitioners focus their attention by repeating a particular mantra.

mantra A sound or phrase chanted repeatedly during transcendental meditation.

mindfulness meditation A form of meditation in which one adopts a state of nonjudgmental attention to the unfolding of experience on a moment-to-moment basis.

Mindfulness meditation is based on Buddhist meditation practices (Kabat-Zinn, 2003). The Dalai Lama, the Buddhist spiritual leader, describes mindfulness as "a state of alertness in which the mind does not get caught up in thoughts or sensations, but lets them come and go, much like watching a river flow by" (Gyatso, 2003, p. A29). Mindfulness meditation has caught the interest of Western researchers who see potential in using the technique to treat a variety of physical and mental health problems (Baer, 2003; Brown & Ryan, 2003; Grossman et al., 2004; Logsdon-Conradsen, 2002).

Some practitioners of meditation believe it does more than just relax the body and mind, that it can expand consciousness to help them achieve a state of pure awareness or inner peace. Perhaps meditation achieves these effects by helping people tune out the outside world, thus allowing them more opportunity for inward focus. Yet many people practice meditation not to expand consciousness, but to find relief from the stress of everyday life. Evidence shows that regular practice of meditation can lower blood pressure and help relieve the effects of stress on the body (e.g., Barnes, Treiber, & Johnson, 2004). Meditation is also useful in the treatment of psychological and physical disorders, such as alcohol and substance abuse disorders, anxiety disorders, and chronic pain (e.g., Alexander, Robinson, & Rainforth, 1995; Oz, 2003).

Online Study Center
Improve Your Grade
Tutorials: Hypnosis Myths

Hypnosis: "You Are Now Getting Sleepier"

CONCEPT 4.16
Hypnosis is not sleep, but a relaxed state of focused attention in which a person may become more responsive to suggestions.

Hypnosis is derived from the Greek word *hypnos,* meaning "sleep." People who undergo hypnosis may feel sleepier, but they are not asleep. Though you may find many different definitions of the term, **hypnosis** is most commonly defined as an altered state of consciousness characterized by focused attention, deep relaxation, and heightened susceptibility to suggestion. Techniques for inducing hypnosis vary, but they usually include a narrowing of attention to the hypnotist's voice. During a hypnotic induction, the hypnotist may ask the person to focus on an object, such as a swinging watch, and listen only to the sound of his or her voice. The hypnotist may also suggest that the person's eyelids are getting heavier and heavier and that the person is becoming sleepy.

Once the person becomes deeply relaxed, the hypnotist begins giving the person hypnotic suggestions that may lead to unusual experiences. These experiences include **hypnotic age regression** (reliving past events, usually from childhood) and **hypnotic analgesia** (loss of feeling or responsiveness to pain in certain parts of the body). Other hypnotic experiences include distortions of reality: seeing,

Hypnosis The first clinical use of hypnosis occurred more than two hundred years ago. Today, the use of hypnosis ranges from treating those with chronic pain to helping people stop smoking.

hypnosis An altered state of consciousness characterized by focused attention, deep relaxation, and heightened susceptibility to suggestion.

hypnotic age regression A hypnotically induced experience that involves reexperiencing past events in one's life.

hypnotic analgesia A loss of feeling or responsiveness to pain in certain parts of the body during hypnosis.

hearing, or feeling something that is not present in reality (a *positive* hallucination), or not perceiving something, such as a pen or a chair, that truly does exist (a *negative* hallucination). Another kind of hypnotic experience in response to hypnotic suggestions is **posthypnotic amnesia**, an inability to recall what happened during hypnosis. About one in four college students shows posthypnotic amnesia in response to suggestions (J. F. Kirsch et al., 1995; J. F. Kirsch & Lynn, 1998). Yet another type of hypnotic experience is **posthypnotic suggestion**, in which the hypnotist plants the idea that, after coming out of the hypnotic state, people will respond in particular ways (such as touching their ears or scratching their heads) when they hear a cue word—for example, *elephant*. A person may respond in the suggested way but deny any awareness of having performed the behavior.

Theories of Hypnosis

Despite more than one hundred years of scientific study, there is still no consensus about what hypnosis is or even how it should be defined (Vaitl et al., 2005). One view of hypnosis is that it is a trance state, an altered state of awareness characterized by heightened *suggestibility*. Suggestibility is the readiness with which one complies with suggestions offered by others, including a hypnotist. Some psychologists reject the view that hypnosis is a trance state, or even that it constitutes an altered state of consciousness. An alternative view proposes that hypnosis is best understood in terms of the social demands of the hypnotic situation (I. Kirsch, 1994). This view, generally called the *role-playing model*, proposes that hypnosis is a social interaction that exists between a hypnotist and a person assuming the role of a "good" hypnotic subject—one who faithfully follows the hypnotist's directions. This doesn't mean that hypnotic subjects are necessarily faking their responses, any more than you are faking when you perform the role of a good student, as when you raise your hand before speaking in class. In support of the role-playing model, investigators find that people who supposedly are hypnotically regressed to childhood do not accurately display childlike behavior; instead, they act like adults playing the role of children (McGreal & Evans, 1994; Nash, 1987). On the other hand, a recent brain-imaging study showed that patterns of brain activity in subjects who were hypnotized differed from those in subjects who were *acting* as if they were hypnotized (Kosslyn et al., 2000). More research in this area is needed, but there appears to be something more to hypnosis than just role playing (Bryant & Mallard, 2002).

One leading theorist who believed that hypnosis is a special state of consciousness was psychologist Ernest Hilgard. According to Hilgard's (1977, 1994) **neodissociation theory**, hypnosis involves a splitting off or dissociation of a part of consciousness. It is this dissociated part that follows the hypnotist's suggestions. Another part, called the **hidden observer**, remains detached from the hypnotic experience but continues to monitor everything that happens. In hypnotic pain relief, for example, subjects may be able to split off, or dissociate, the part of consciousness that is aware of the pain (the hidden observer) from another part that is not.

Hilgard demonstrated the hidden-observer phenomenon with a *cold pressor test* (Hilgard, Morgan, & Macdonald, 1975). In this test, subjects had one of their hands submerged in ice water, while their other hand was free to press a key to indicate if "any part of them" felt pain. Subjects were asked every few seconds to verbally report the level of pain on a rating scale. Hypnotized subjects given the suggestion that they would not feel pain reported that they felt little pain, but their key-pressing responses indicated that a "part of them" (the hidden observer) was aware of the pain (see Figure 4.7). Critics of neodissociation theory claim that even the hidden observer may be a product of suggestion rather than a special state of divided consciousness (J. F. Kirsch & Lynn, 1998).

Responsiveness to hypnotic suggestions may have more to do with the efforts

CONCEPT 4.17
Two theoretical models that have guided recent research on hypnosis are the role-playing model and neodissociation theory.

REALITY CHECK

THE CLAIM A hypnotist can make you do things you wouldn't ordinarily do.

THE EVIDENCE The belief that hypnotists have special powers that give them control over a hypnotized subject may be part of the mystique of hypnosis, but it is not consistent with scientific views of hypnosis. During hypnosis, people remain aware of what they are doing and why they are doing it. They can refuse at any time to comply with a request that makes them uncomfortable.

THE TAKE-AWAY MESSAGE People cannot be hypnotized involuntarily or made to do things during hypnosis that are against their will.

posthypnotic amnesia An inability to recall what happened during hypnosis.

posthypnotic suggestion A hypnotist's suggestion that the subject will respond in a particular way following hypnosis.

neodissociation theory A theory of hypnosis based on the belief that hypnosis represents a state of dissociated (divided) consciousness.

hidden observer Hilgard's term for a part of consciousness that remains detached from the hypnotic experience but aware of everything that happens during it.

Figure 4.7   Perception of Pain During Hypnosis
Ernest Hilgard believed that the difference between hypnotized subjects' verbal reports of the intensity of pain and their automatic key-pressing responses during the cold pressor test indicates the presence of a "hidden observer" that closely monitors the level of pain.

and skills of the hypnotic subject than with those of the hypnotist (I. Kirsch & Lynn, 1995). In effect, all forms of hypnosis may involve self-hypnosis, or willingness of the hypnotic subject to become absorbed in the hypnotic experience by vividly imagining the alternate realities suggested by the hypnotist. For example, in hypnotic age regression, people do not actually relive childhood incidents or experiences; they merely imagine that they are again children (T. X. Barber, 1999).

Though most people can be hypnotized to some extent, some are more hypnotizable, or susceptible to suggestions, than others. Typical characteristics of highly hypnotizable people include a well-developed fantasy life, a vivid sense of imagination, a tendency to be forgetful, and a positive attitude toward hypnosis (T. X. Barber, 1999; Barrett, 1996). These traits help them think along with the hypnotist—to imagine whatever the hypnotist suggests, perhaps so vividly that it seems real to them.

Hypnosis has a legitimate therapeutic role in treating a wide range of problems, from anxiety to pain to the challenges of losing weight and quitting smoking (Keefe, Abernethy, & Campbell, 2005; Patterson, 2004). Hypnosis may even give the body's immune system a boost in times of stress (Kiecolt-Glaser et al., 2001; Patterson & Jensen, 2003). Although hypnosis appears to have therapeutic benefits, it should be used only as an adjunct to treatment, not as a substitute for conventional treatments. For a summary of altering consciousness through meditation and hypnosis, see Concept Chart 4.3.

CONCEPT 4.18
The effectiveness of hypnosis may have more to do with the psychological characteristics of the hypnotized subject than the skills of the hypnotist.

CONCEPT CHART 4.3   Altering Consciousness Through Meditation and Hypnosis

Technique	Method of Induction	Key Points
Meditation	Narrowing attention to a single object, word, or thought or performing a repetitive ritual	Meditation relaxes the body and mind, helps combat stress, and can help people cope with pain. Some people believe it leads to a state of inner peace or spiritual enlightenment, but others practice it for its stress- and pain-relieving effects.
Hypnosis	Narrowing attention to the hypnotist's voice or repetitive stimulus	Debate about the nature of hypnosis continues. Role-playing theory and neodissociation theory have emerged as the major contemporary theories of hypnosis. All forms of hypnosis may actually involve self-hypnosis.

MODULE 4.3 REVIEW

Altering Consciousness Through Meditation and Hypnosis

RECITE IT

What is meditation?

• Meditation is an altered state of consciousness induced by narrowing attention to a single object, word, or thought or performing a repetitive ritual.

• Meditation produces a relaxed state that may have therapeutic benefits in relieving stress and pain.

What is hypnosis?

• Although there is no consensus about the nature of hypnosis, it has traditionally been defined as an altered

state of consciousness characterized by focused attention, deep relaxation, and heightened susceptibility to suggestion. Hypnosis is increasingly being used within mainstream psychology and medicine.

What are the major theories of hypnosis?

• The two major contemporary views of hypnosis are the role-playing model, which proposes that hypnosis is a form of social role playing, and neodissociation theory, which holds that hypnosis is a state of divided consciousness.

RECALL IT

1. The type of meditation in which practitioners focus their attention by repeating a mantra is called _____.

2. The loss of feeling or responsiveness to pain as a result of hypnotic suggestion is called _____.

3. The concept of a "hidden observer" is a key feature of which theory of hypnosis?

THINK ABOUT IT

• Have you ever practiced meditation? How did it affect your state of consciousness?

• Were you ever hypnotized? If so, what was the experience like? Whether or not you've experienced hypnosis, has reading this module changed any of your views about hypnosis? If so, how?

• Do you believe the concept of the "hidden observer" is an example of a special state of consciousness? Why or why not?

MODULE 4.4

Altering Consciousness Through Drugs

■ **When does drug use cross the line from use to abuse and dependence?**

■ **What are the different types of psychoactive drugs, and what effects do they have?**

■ **What factors contribute to alcohol and drug-abuse problems?**

■ **What treatment alternatives are available to help people with drug problems?**

 CONCEPT 4.19

Psychoactive substances—depressants, stimulants, and hallucinogens—are drugs that alter the user's mental state.

psychoactive drugs Chemical substances that affect a person's mental or emotional state.

Most people who want to change their states of waking consciousness don't turn to meditation or hypnosis. They are more likely to pop a pill, drink an alcoholic beverage, or smoke a joint.

Psychoactive drugs are chemical substances that act on the brain to affect emotional or mental states. They affect mood, thought processes, perceptions, and behavior. People use psychoactive drugs for many reasons: to change their level of alertness (stimulants to perk them up; depressants to relax them and make them drowsy so they can fall asleep), to alter their mental states by getting "high" or induce feelings of intense pleasure (a euphoric "rush"), to blunt awareness of the stresses and strains of daily life, or to seek some type of inner truth.

Some psychoactive drugs, including heroin, cocaine, and marijuana, are illegal or *illicit*. Others, such as alcohol and nicotine (found in tobacco), are legally available, but restrictions are placed on their use or sale. Another legal psychoactive drug, caffeine, is so widely used that many people don't realize they are ingesting a psychoactive drug when they drink a caffeinated beverage or eat a chocolate bar (which contains caffeine).

According to a 2003 survey, nearly one in four students in grades six through twelve reports using illicit drugs, with marijuana being the most used of these drugs ("Teen Drug Use," 2003). More than half of today's high school seniors also report having used illicit drugs at some point in their lives—and, again, marijuana is the illegal substance most commonly cited (M. Miller, 2000). Although only about one in fifty high school seniors has used heroin, about one in ten has used cocaine, and one in four has used marijuana (Irwin, Burg, & Cart, 2002). But the use of illicit drugs is dwarfed by the use of two legally available substances, alcohol and tobacco (see Figure 4.8). Alcoholic beverages contain the depressant drug alcohol, and tobacco products, such as cigarettes, contain the stimulant drug nicotine.

In this module, we examine drugs that alter consciousness or levels of alertness. We consider their effects, the risks they pose to health, the factors that may lead people to use and abuse them, and ways of helping people with substance abuse problems. We begin by defining the terms that professionals use to characterize problems associated with the misuse of drugs.

Figure 4.8   Rates of Drug Use in the United States
Nearly half of U.S. adults have used an illicit drug at some point in their lives. About one in twelve is a current user—that is, reporting use of an illicit drug in the past month. However, two psychoactive substances that adults can use legally—alcohol and tobacco—are much more widely used than any illicit drug.

Source: Substance Abuse and Mental Health Services Administration (SAMSHA), 2004.

When Does Use Become Abuse? Many people use alcohol socially, but when does use cross over into abuse? According to mental health professionals, drug use becomes drug abuse when it leads to damaging or dangerous consequences.

Drug Abuse: When Drug Use Causes Harm

💡 **CONCEPT 4.20**
Drug use crosses the line to abuse when it becomes maladaptive and either causes or contributes to personal, occupational, or health-related problems.

Drug use becomes *drug abuse* when repeated use causes or aggravates personal, occupational, or health-related problems (American Psychiatric Association, 2000). **Drug abuse** is maladaptive or dangerous use of a chemical substance. If drug use impairs a person's health or ability to function at home, in school, or on the job, or if it becomes associated with dangerous behavior such as drinking and driving, the person has crossed the line from use to abuse. If you repeatedly miss school or work because you are drunk or "sleeping it off," you are abusing alcohol. You may not admit you have a drug problem, but you do. People who abuse more than one drug at a time are called **polyabusers**.

Drug Dependence: When the Drug Takes Control

Drug abuse often leads to **drug dependence**, a severe drug-related problem characterized by impaired control over the use of a drug. People who become dependent on a drug feel compelled to use the drug or powerless to stop using it, even when they know the drug use is ruining their lives.

Drug dependence is usually, but not always, associated with *physiological dependence* (also called *chemical dependence*). In **physiological dependence**, a person's body chemistry changes as the result of repeated use of a drug so that the body comes to depend on having a steady supply of the drug. When physiologically dependent people abruptly stop their drug use, they may experience a cluster of unpleasant and sometimes dangerous symptoms called a **withdrawal syndrome** (also called an *abstinence syndrome*). Another frequent sign of physiological dependence is **tolerance**, the need to increase the amount of a drug so that it has the same effect.

Professionals use the terms *drug abuse* and *drug dependence* to describe the different types of substance-use disorders. Laypeople more often use the term *drug addiction*, but it has different meanings to different people. Here, let us define **drug addiction** (also called *chemical addiction*) as a pattern of drug dependence accompanied by physiological dependence. By this definition, we consider people to be addicted when they feel powerless to control their use of the drug *and* have developed signs of physiological dependence—typically a withdrawal syndrome

Bear in mind that people may become *psychologically* dependent on a drug without becoming physiologically dependent on it. **Psychological dependence** is a pattern of compulsive or habitual use of a drug that serves a psychological need,

---

drug abuse Maladaptive or dangerous use of a chemical substance.

polyabusers People who abuse more than one drug at a time.

drug dependence A severe drug-related problem characterized by impaired control over the use of the drug.

physiological dependence A state of physical dependence on a drug caused by repeated usage that changes body chemistry.

withdrawal syndrome A cluster of symptoms associated with abrupt withdrawal from a drug.

tolerance A form of physical habituation to a drug in which increased amounts are needed to achieve the same effect.

drug addiction Drug dependence accompanied by signs of physiological dependence, such as the development of a withdrawal syndrome.

psychological dependence A pattern of compulsive or habitual use of a drug to satisfy a psychological need.

CONCEPT 4.21

People who are psychologically dependent on drugs use them habitually or compulsively to cope with stress or to relieve negative feelings.

CONCEPT 4.22

Depressants are addictive drugs that can be deadly when used in high doses or when mixed with other drugs.

CONCEPT 4.23

Alcohol is the most widely used and abused depressant.

Online Study Center
Improve Your Grade
Tutorials: Test Your Alcohol Knowledge

such as lessening anxiety or escaping from stress. People who are unhappy or depressed may come to depend on alcohol or other drugs to blunt negative feelings or to cope with personal problems or conflicts with others (Holahan et al., 2004).

Now let us turn to the major classes of psychoactive drugs: depressants, stimulants, and hallucinogens.

Depressants

Depressants are drugs that reduce central nervous system activity, which in turn depresses (slows down) such bodily processes as heart rate and respiration rate. The major types of depressants are alcohol, barbiturates and tranquilizers, and opioids. Psychologically, depressants induce feelings of relaxation and provide relief from states of anxiety and tension. Some depressants also produce a "rush" of pleasure. In high doses, depressants can kill by arresting vital bodily functions, such as breathing. Depressants are highly addictive and can be dangerous, even lethal, in overdose or when mixed with other drugs. The deaths of famed entertainers Marilyn Monroe and Judy Garland were blamed on the deadly mix of barbiturates and alcohol.

Alcohol: The Most Widely Used and Abused Depressant   *Alcohol* is an **intoxicant**, a chemical substance that produces a state of drunkenness. The more a person drinks, the stronger the intoxicating effects become. Table 4.3 summarizes the behavioral effects of drinking. Impairment of driving skills begins with even the first drink. With heavier doses, the depressant effects of the drug on the central nervous system can induce a state of stupor, unconsciousness, and even death.

Women typically become intoxicated at lower doses of alcohol than men do. One reason is that women usually weigh less than men, and the less people weigh, the less alcohol it usually takes to produce intoxication. But another reason is that women have less of an enzyme that breaks down alcohol in the stomach than men do and thus more pure alcohol reaches their bloodstreams. The rule of thumb is that a single drink for a woman is equal in its effects to two drinks for a man (Springen & Kantrowitz, 2004). Yet women's greater sensitivity to alcohol can

depressants   Drugs, such as alcohol and barbiturates, that dampen central nervous system activity.

intoxicant   A chemical substance that induces a state of drunkenness.

TABLE 4.3   Behavioral Effects of Blood Alcohol Concentrations

Blood Alcohol Concentration (BAC)	Behavioral Effects
0.05 %	Lowered alertness; usually a "high" feeling; release of inhibitions; impaired judgment
0.10	Slowed reaction times; impaired motor function; less caution
0.15	Large, consistent decreases in reaction time
0.20	Marked depression in sensory and motor capability; decidedly intoxicated
0.25	Severe motor disturbance; staggering; sensory perceptions greatly impaired
0.30	Stuporous but conscious; no comprehension of the external world
0.35	Condition equivalent to surgical anesthesia; minimal level at which death occurs
0.40	Death in about 50 percent of cases

Source: Ray & Ksir, 1990.

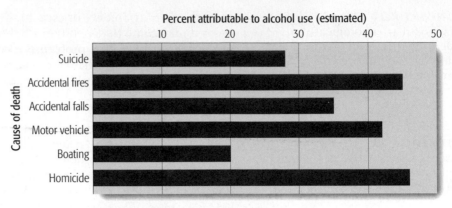

Figure 4.9   Alcohol Use and Causes of Death
Alcohol use is involved in a large percentage of homicides, suicides, and deaths due to motor vehicle accidents and other types of mishaps.

Source: National Institute on Alcohol Abuse and Alcoholism, 1996.

CONCEPT 4.24
Alcohol has various psychological effects: it clouds judgment; impairs attention, concentration, and the ability to weigh the consequences of behavior; and reduces inhibitions and thus leads to aggressive or impulsive behavior.

work in their favor in that it may serve as a biological constraint on excessive drinking.

Alcohol directly affects the brain, clouding judgment and impairing concentration and attention, as well as the ability to weigh the consequences of behavior (MacDonald et al., 2000). Thus, people may do or say things when they are drinking that they might not otherwise. They may also take unnecessary risks without considering the consequences of their actions, which can have tragic results, such as in the case of driving while intoxicated or having unsafe sex.

Alcohol also has a *disinhibiting* (inhibition-releasing) effect, which may lead to aggressive or impulsive behavior (Curtin et al., 2001). Not everyone who drinks becomes aggressive or acts foolishly or recklessly, of course. Individual differences play a large role. Yet alcohol use is associated with many forms of aggression, from rape and spousal abuse to other violent crimes, such as robbery, assault, and homicide (J. J. Collins & Messerschmidt, 1993; S. E. Martin, 1992). We examine the relationships between alcohol and violent behavior in Chapter 16.

Alcohol accounts for more than 100,000 deaths per year in the United States. Most of these deaths are the result of alcohol-related diseases and accidents, particularly motor vehicle accidents (Hingson et al., 2000; Kalb, 2001a; O'Donnell, 2003). One reason that drinking and driving is dangerous is that alcohol can impair depth perception, making it difficult to judge distances between cars (Nawrot, Nordenstrom, & Olson, 2004).

Alcohol-related accidents are the leading cause of death among young people in the 17- to 24-year age range (Ham & Hope, 2003). All told, alcohol claims the lives of about 1,400 college students each year, with most of these deaths resulting from alcohol-related motor vehicle accidents (Sink, 2004). Alcohol is also linked to about 25 percent of suicides and about 45 percent of homicides in the United States (see Figure 4.9).

Alcoholism   Most people who drink alcohol do so in moderation. However, about one in ten adult Americans—approximately 14 million people—suffers from **alcoholism** (alcohol dependence), a form of chemical dependence in which people become physically dependent on alcohol and unable to control their use of the drug (Leary, 1996; Miller & Brown, 1997). Relatively few people who suffer from alcoholism, perhaps only 5 percent, fit the stereotype of the "skid-row bum." Most have families and work for a living. They are the kinds of people you're likely

CONCEPT 4.25
Only a small percentage of people with alcoholism fit the stereotype of the "skid-row" bum.

alcoholism   A chemical addiction characterized by impaired control over the use of alcohol and physiological dependence on it.

Which of These People Suffers from Alcoholism?   The fact is that any one of these people might suffer from alcoholism. People struggling with alcoholism may be your neighbors, friends, or loved ones.

to meet in your daily life: neighbors, coworkers, friends, and even family members. Yet alcoholism is an equal-opportunity destroyer, leading to devastating health problems, motor vehicle accidents, and ruined careers and marriages. Alcoholism typically develops in early adulthood, usually between the ages of 20 and 40, although it may develop in teenagers and even in younger children.

Alcohol abuse involving regular, heavy consumption of alcohol can damage nearly every major organ and body system. Heavy drinking often has its most damaging effects on the liver, the organ that primarily metabolizes (breaks down) alcohol. *Cirrhosis of the liver,* an irreversible scarring of liver tissue typically caused by alcohol abuse, accounts for some 26,000 deaths annually in the United States.

Ironically, despite the health risks associated with heavy drinking, recent research links moderate use of alcohol (one to two drinks per day) to a lower risk of heart attacks and strokes and to a lower death rate overall (e.g., Carmichael, 2003a; Mukamal et al., 2003). This research is correlational, so we cannot yet draw conclusions about the beneficial effects of alcohol on our health. But scientists suspect that moderate use of alcohol may increase high-density lipoproteins (HDLs), the "good" cholesterol that helps remove blockages from arteries (I. J. Goldberg et al., 2001; Wood, Vinson, & Sher, 2001).

CONCEPT 4.26
Barbiturates and tranquilizers are depressants that help calm the nervous system, but they are addictive and potentially dangerous in high doses, especially when mixed with other drugs, such as alcohol.

Barbiturates and Tranquilizers   *Barbiturates* are calming or sedating drugs that have several legitimate medical uses. They are used to regulate high blood pressure, to block pain during surgery, and to control epileptic seizures. Yet they are also highly addictive and used illicitly as street drugs to induce states of euphoria and relaxation. Among the more widely used barbiturates are amobarbital, pentobarbital, phenobarbital, and secobarbital. Methaqualone (brand names, Quaalude and Sopor; street names, "ludes" and "sopors") is a sedating drug with effects similar to those of barbiturates, and with similar risks.

Barbiturates can induce drowsiness and slurred speech and impair motor skills and judgment. Overdoses can lead to convulsions, coma, and death. The mixture of barbiturates or methaqualone with alcohol can be especially dangerous and potentially lethal. People who are physiologically dependent on barbiturates or methaqualone should withdraw under careful medical supervision, since abrupt withdrawal can cause convulsions and even death.

Tranquilizers are a class of depressants widely used to treat anxiety and insomnia. Though they are less toxic than barbiturates, they can be dangerous in high doses, especially if combined with alcohol or other drugs. They also carry a risk of addiction, so they should not be used for extended periods of time. The most widely used tranquilizers include Valium, Xanax, and Halcion, which are members of the *benzodiazepine* family of drugs. Benzodiazepines act by boosting the availability of the neurotransmitter GABA in the brain (see Chapter 2). GABA, an inhibitory neurotransmitter, reduces excess nervous system activity.

Opioids *Opioids* (also called *opiates*) are **narcotics**, addictive drugs that have pain-relieving and sleep-inducing properties. They include morphine, heroin, and codeine, naturally occurring drugs derived from the poppy plant. Synthetic opioids, including Demerol, Percodan, and Darvon, are manufactured in a laboratory to have effects similar to those of the natural opioids. Opioids produce a "rush" of pleasurable excitement and dampen awareness of personal problems, which are two main reasons for their popularity as illicit street drugs.

Opioids have legitimate medical uses as painkillers. They are routinely used to deaden postsurgical pain and for some other pain conditions. Because of their high potential for addiction, their medical use is strictly regulated. However, they are sometimes obtained and used illegally, as in the case of *OxyContin,* a prescription painkiller widely misused as a street drug (Adler, 2003; Belluck, 2003).

Opioids are similar in chemical structure to endorphins and lock into the same receptor sites in the brain. You'll recall from Chapter 2 that endorphins are neurotransmitters that block pain signals and regulate states of pleasure. Opioids mimic the actions of endorphins, our own "natural opioids," thereby stimulating brain centers that produce pleasurable sensations.

Heroin, the most widely abused opioid, induces a euphoric rush that lasts perhaps five to fifteen minutes. The rush is so intense and pleasurable that users liken it to the pleasure of orgasm. After the rush fades, a second phase sets in that is characterized by a relaxed, drowsy state. Worries and concerns seem to evaporate, which is why heroin often appeals to people seeking a psychological escape from their problems. This mellow state soon fades, too, leading the habitual user to seek another "fix" to return to the drugged state. Tolerance develops, and users begin needing higher doses, which can lead to dangerous overdoses. The life of the heroin addict is usually organized around efforts to obtain and use the drug. Many turn to crime or prostitution to support their habit. Users who become addicted to heroin may undergo a severe withdrawal syndrome, which fortunately is not life-threatening.

Stimulants

A **stimulant** is a drug that heightens the activity of the central nervous system. Examples of stimulants include amphetamines, cocaine, MDMA ("Ecstasy"), nicotine, and caffeine. Stimulants can produce both physiological and psychological dependence. Some, like amphetamines and cocaine, can induce a pleasurable "high."

Amphetamines Like the synthetic opioids, *amphetamines* are not found in nature; they are chemicals manufactured in a laboratory. They activate the sympathetic branch of the autonomic nervous system, causing heart rate, breathing rate, and blood pressure to rise. At low doses, they boost mental alertness and concentration, reduce fatigue, and lessen the need for sleep. At high doses, they can induce an intense, pleasurable rush.

Amphetamines act on the brain by boosting levels of the neurotransmitters norepinephrine and dopamine (Leyton et al., 2002). The increased supply of these chemicals induces neurons to keep firing, which helps maintain high levels of arousal and alertness. Amphetamines produce pleasurable feelings by directly stimulating the reward pathways in the brain.

CONCEPT 4.27
Opioids, such as morphine and heroin, are depressants that induce a euphoric high.

CONCEPT 4.28
Stimulants increase activity in the central nervous system, heightening states of alertness and in some cases producing a pleasurable "high" feeling.

narcotics Addictive drugs that have pain-relieving and sleep-inducing properties.
stimulant A drug that activates the central nervous system, such as cocaine or nicotine.

The most widely used amphetamines are amphetamine sulfate (brand name, Benzedrine; street name, "bennies"), methamphetamine (Methedrine, or "speed"), and dextroamphetamine (Dexedrine, or "dexies"). They can be used in pill form, smoked in a relatively pure form of methamphetamine called "ice" or "crystal meth," or injected in the form of liquid methamphetamine.

More than a million Americans use amphetamines in one form or another, nearly three times as many as use heroin (Bonné, 2001). Overdoses, which often occur as users develop tolerance to the drug and keep increasing the amount they consume, can have dangerous, even fatal, consequences. In high doses, amphetamines can cause extreme restlessness, loss of appetite, tremors, and cardiovascular irregularities that may result in coma or death. High doses can also induce *amphetamine psychosis,* a psychotic reaction characterized by hallucinations and delusions that resembles acute episodes of schizophrenia. Brain-imaging studies show that methamphetamine abuse can damage the brain, causing deficits in learning, memory, and other functions (Thompson et al., 2004; Toomey et al., 2003).

CONCEPT 4.29

Cocaine is a highly addictive stimulant that induces a euphoric high by directly stimulating reward pathways in the brain.

Cocaine   *Cocaine* is a natural stimulant derived from the leaves of the coca plant. Cocaine can be administered in several ways. It can be sniffed in powder form, smoked in a hardened form called *crack,* injected in liquid form, or ingested as a tea brewed from coca leaves. You may be surprised to learn that when Coca-Cola was introduced in 1886, it contained cocaine and was soon being marketed as "the ideal brain tonic." (Cocaine was removed from Coca-Cola in the early twentieth century, but the beverage is still flavored with a nonpsychoactive extract from the coca plant.)

Like amphetamines, cocaine increases brain levels of the neurotransmitters norepinephrine and dopamine (Friedman, 2002). This helps maintain high levels of bodily arousal and mental alertness. Also like amphetamines, cocaine directly stimulates reward pathways in the brain, inducing feelings of extreme pleasure or euphoria. Though amphetamines and cocaine have similar effects, the high induced by cocaine is typically shorter-lived, especially in the form of crack. Smoking crack delivers the drug almost instantaneously to the brain, producing an immediate, intense high. But the high fades within five or ten minutes, leaving the user craving more. Many cocaine abusers go on binges lasting perhaps twelve to thirty-six hours. They will then abstain for several days until cravings for the drug once again prompt another binge.

Over time, regular use of cocaine damages brain circuits that produce feelings of pleasure ("Cocaine Impairs," 2003). This helps explain why cocaine abusers often become depressed when they stop using the drug. Regular use of cocaine can also damage the heart and circulatory system and other body organs. High doses can have life-threatening or fatal consequences, including irregular heart rhythms, heart stoppage, strokes caused by spasms of blood vessels in the brain, and respiratory arrest (cessation of breathing) (A. Goldstein, 1994).

Prolonged use may also lead to psychological problems, such as anxiety, irritability, and depression. At high doses, cocaine can induce a type of psychosis, called *cocaine psychosis,* that is characterized by hallucinations and delusions of persecution (unfounded beliefs that one is being pursued by others or by mysterious forces).

Cocaine is highly addictive and can lead to a withdrawal syndrome involving intense cravings for the drug, feelings of depression, and an inability to experience pleasure in the activities of everyday life. People addicted to cocaine will often return to using the drug to gain relief from these unpleasant withdrawal symptoms. Tolerance also develops quickly, yet another sign of the physically addicting properties of cocaine. Users may also become psychologically dependent on the drug, using it compulsively to deal with life stress.

"Ecstasy" The drug Ecstasy has become increasingly popular among young people, especially among those who frequent late-night dance clubs. Use of the drug can impair learning ability and memory functioning, and high doses can be lethal.

MDMA ("Ecstasy")

MDMA (3,4-methylenedioxymethamphetamine), better known as *Ecstasy,* is an amphetamine-like drug synthesized in underground laboratories. MDMA produces mild euphoric and hallucinogenic effects. It is especially popular among high school and college students and is widely available in many late-night dance clubs in U.S. cities (Strote & Wechsler, 2002). Though the number of new users has begun to decline, more than 10 million Americans have used the drug at least once (SAMHSA, 2005).

MDMA use can lead to undesirable psychological effects, such as depression, anxiety, insomnia, and even states of paranoia or psychotic symptoms. Heavy use of the drug is associated with cognitive deficits, including problems with memory functioning, learning ability, and attention (Buchert et al., 2004; Eisner, 2005). The drug has physical effects as well, such as increased heart rate and blood pressure, a tense or chattering jaw, and feelings of body warmth and/or chills. High doses can lead to loss of consciousness, seizures, and even death in severe cases (SAMHSA, 2005). Perceptions do not always square with reality, however, as many teens see no risk in experimenting with MDMA ("Teens See Little Risk," 2003).

CONCEPT 4.30

Nicotine, a stimulant, is an addictive substance found in tobacco.

Nicotine

Nicotine is a mild but highly addictive stimulant drug. It is found naturally in tobacco, and users typically administer the drug by smoking, snorting, or chewing tobacco. Physiological dependence can begin within the first few weeks of cigarette smoking. Nicotine use can also lead to psychological dependence, as we see in people who smoke habitually as a means of coping with the stress of everyday life.

As a stimulant, nicotine speeds up the heart rate, dampens appetite, and produces a mild rush or psychological kick. It increases states of arousal, alertness, and concentration. But it may also have "paradoxical" effects, such as inducing feelings of relaxation or mental calmness. In fact, since nicotine causes the release of endorphins in the brain, it can produce states of pleasure and reduce pain.

You certainly are aware by now that smoking is dangerous. But just how dangerous is it? Let's look at the evidence:

- Smoking is the major preventable cause of death in the United States and elsewhere in the world, accounting annually for more than 400,000 deaths in this country and about 4 million deaths worldwide (Brundtland, 2000; Mokdad, Marks, & Stroup, 2004; Schneiderman, 2004).

- According to the U.S. Surgeon General, smokers die an average thirteen to fourteen years earlier than nonsmokers ("Surgeon General Warns," 2004).

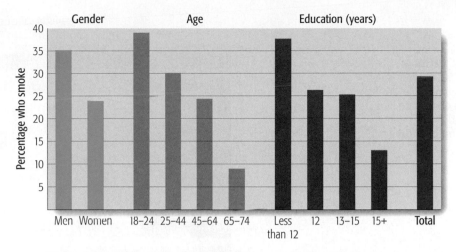

Figure 4.10   Who Smokes?
Older people and people with fifteen or more years of education are less likely to smoke than are younger people and those with fewer years of education.

Source: U.S. Department of Health and Human Services, 2001.

CONCEPT 4.31
Caffeine, a mild stimulant found in coffee, tea, cola drinks, chocolate, and other substances, is the most widely used psychoactive drug.

Becoming a Statistic   Smoking is the major preventable cause of death in the United States and elsewhere in the world, accounting annually for more than 400,000 deaths in this country and about 4 million deaths worldwide.

• Cigarette smoking is responsible for nearly one in three cancer deaths in the United States, most of them due to lung cancer. It may surprise you to learn that more women die from lung cancer than from breast cancer (Springen, 2004). Lung cancer is now the leading cancer killer of both men and women.

• Smoking is a major contributor to cardiovascular disease (heart and artery disease), the biggest killer of all, and to other serious health problems, including emphysema, cancers of the cervix, kidney, pancreas and stomach, and even cataracts ("Surgeon General Warns," 2004).

Smoking is more prevalent among men than women, among younger adults, and among less-educated people (see Figure 4.10, also Droomers, Schrijvers, & Mackenbach, 2002; Shields et al., 2005). Overall, more than 25 percent of Americans age 12 and above smoke cigarettes (NIDA Notes, 2004), a rate that has hardly budged in recent years. About one in eight (12 percent) high school students currently smokes. Tobacco use often begins in adolescence and is difficult to eliminate once a pattern of regular use is established.

Caffeine   *Caffeine,* a mild stimulant found in coffee, tea, cola drinks, chocolate, and other substances (see Figure 4.11), is our most widely used psychoactive drug. Americans consume perhaps 500 million or more cups of coffee a day, or more than two cups for every adult. Regular use of caffeine leads to physiological dependence. If your daily routine includes one or more cups of coffee or caffeinated tea and you feel on edge or have headaches when you go without your daily supply of caffeine, chances are you're physiologically dependent, or "hooked," on caffeine. Drinking just a cup or two of coffee or tea or even a few cans of caffeinated soft drinks each day can lead to physiological dependence. And it's not just coffee

Milligrams of caffeine

Source	Milligrams
Drip coffee (8 fl oz)	~235
Instant coffee (8 fl oz)	~165
Decaf coffee (8 fl oz)	~5
Hot tea (8 fl oz)	~50
Instant iced tea (8 fl oz)	~35
Cola (12 fl oz)	~50
Milk chocolate (1 oz)	~10
Excedrin	~130
No Doz tablets	~200

Figure 4.11
Sources of Caffeine
Caffeine is found not only in coffee, tea, and cola drinks, but also in chocolate, No Doz tablets, and even the common pain reliever Excedrin.

or tea that can give you a caffeine jolt. For example, cola drinks and other popular drinks such as Red Bull, Mountain Dew, and Dr Pepper contain hefty doses of caffeine (Lowrey, 2004).

The good news is that most caffeine users are able to control their use of the drug despite being physiologically dependent on it. In other words, they may limit themselves to one or two cups of coffee a day without feeling uncontrollable urges to increase their usage. Fortunately, too, caffeine is not known to be associated with health risks when used in moderation. However, caffeine use may increase the risk of miscarriage during pregnancy (Cnattingius et al., 2000). Caffeine can help increase wakefulness and mental alertness, but it can also have negative effects, such as jitteriness or nervousness, especially at higher dosages (from 200 to 600 milligrams).

Hallucinogens

CONCEPT 4.32
Hallucinogens alter or distort sensory perceptions and produce feelings of relaxation in some people but paranoid or panicky feelings in others.

Hallucinogens are drugs that alter sensory perceptions, producing distortions or hallucinations in visual, auditory, or other sensory forms. They are also called *psychedelics,* a word that literally means "mind-revealing." Hallucinogens may induce feelings of relaxation and calmness in some users but cause feelings of paranoia or panic in others. Though they are not known to produce physiological dependence, they can lead to psychological dependence when users come to depend on them for help in coping with problems or stressful life experi-

Our Most Widely Used Drug Caffeine is the most widely used psychoactive drug. Most regular users can control their use of the drug despite being physiologically dependent on it.

LSD Trip The hallucinogen LSD can produce vivid perceptual distortions and outright hallucinations. Some users experience "bad trips," which are characterized by panicky feelings and even psychotic states.

ences. Hallucinogens include LSD, mescaline, psilocybin, PCP, and marijuana. Of these, the two most widely used are LSD and marijuana.

LSD   *LSD* (lysergic acid diethylamide; street name, "acid") produces vivid hallucinations and other sensory distortions. The experience of using the drug is called a "trip," and it may last as long as twelve hours. More than a half million Americans reported using LSD in 2003 (NIDA Notes, 2004).

LSD has various effects on the body, including pupil dilation and increases in heart rate, blood pressure, and body temperature. It may also produce sweating, tremors, loss of appetite, and sleeplessness. The psychological effects on the user are variable and unpredictable. Users often report distortions of time and space. Higher doses are likely to produce more vivid displays of colors and outright hallucinations. The psychological effects depend not only on the amount used, but also on the user's personality, expectancies about the drug, and the context in which it used. Some users experience "bad trips," in which they suffer intense anxiety or panic or have psychotic reactions, such as delusions of persecution. Others have flashbacks, which involve a sudden reexperiencing of some of the perceptual distortions of an LSD trip. Flashbacks may occur without warning in the weeks, months, or years following the use of LSD.

Mescaline, Psilocybin, and PCP   For centuries, Native Americans have used the hallucinogens *mescaline* (derived from the cactus plant) and *psilocybin* (derived from certain mushrooms) for religious purposes. *PCP* (phencyclidine), or "angel dust," is a synthetic drug that produces **delirium**, a state of mental confusion characterized by excitement, disorientation, and difficulty in focusing attention. PCP can produce distortions in the sense of time and space, feelings of unreality, and vivid, sometimes frightening, hallucinations. It may lead to feelings of paranoia and blind rage and prompt bizarre or violent behavior. High doses can lead to coma and death.

Marijuana   *Marijuana* ("pot," "weed," "grass," "reefer," "dope") is derived from the cannabis plant. The psychoactive chemical in marijuana is THC (delta-9-tetrahydrocannabinol). The leaves of the plant are ground up and may be smoked in a pipe or rolled into "joints." The most potent form of the drug, called hashish ("hash"), is derived from the resin of the plant, which contains the highest concentration of THC. Though marijuana and hashish are usually smoked, some users ingest the drug by eating parts of the plant or foods into which the cannabis leaves have been baked.

Marijuana is generally classified as a hallucinogen because it alters perceptions and can produce hallucinations, especially in high doses or when used by susceptible individuals. At lower doses, users may feel relaxed and mildly euphoric. It may seem as if time is passing more slowly. Bodily sensations may seem more pronounced, which can create anxiety or even panicky feelings in some users (e.g., a pronounced sense of the heartbeat may cause some users to fear they are having a heart attack). High doses can cause nausea and vomiting, feelings of disorientation, panic attacks, and even paranoia (Johns, 2001).

Marijuana is the most widely used illicit drug in the United States and throughout the Western world (NIDA Notes, 2004). More than 40 percent of U.S. adults have used marijuana at least once in their lives (Iversen, 2000). About 6 percent of adult Americans are current users (NIDA Notes, 2004).

The issue of whether marijuana is physiologically addictive remains unresolved. However, recent evidence points to a definable withdrawal syndrome in

CONCEPT 4.33
Marijuana induces feelings of relaxation and mild euphoria at low doses, but it can produce hallucinations in high doses or when used by susceptible individuals.

hallucinogens   Drugs that alter sensory experiences and produce hallucinations.
delirium   A mental state characterized by confusion, disorientation, difficulty in focusing attention, and excitable behavior.

long-term heavy users of the drug who stop using it abruptly (Budney et al., 2004). It is certainly the case that marijuana use can lead to psychological dependence if people come to rely on it to deal with stress or personal difficulties.

Marijuana use is also linked to increased risk of later use of harder drugs such as heroin and cocaine (Kandel, 2003). Whether it plays a direct role in the progression to harder drugs remains an open question. In any event, programs that aim at preventing or stopping marijuana use appear to prevent progression to the use of harder drugs (Kandel, 2002).

Marijuana use also has some adverse physiological effects. It increases heart rate and possibly blood pressure, and therefore can put people with cardiovascular problems at risk (A. Goldstein, 1994). Because marijuana distorts perceptions and can impair motor performance and coordination, marijuana and driving are an especially dangerous combination. In addition, because THC affects parts of the brain involved in learning and memory, long-term use may lead to problems in these areas (Solowij et al., 2002; Verhovek, 2000). Finally, use of marijuana and hashish introduces cancer-causing agents into the body, increasing the risk of cancer (Iversen, 2000). Though marijuana use is also associated with greater risk of developing psychological problems, such as depression and anxiety, researchers can't yet say whether it actually causes these problems (Patton et al., 2002; Rey & Tennant, 2002).

In Concept Chart 4.4, you'll find a listing of the major types of psychoactive drugs in terms of their potential for psychological and physiological dependence, major psychological effects, and major risks.

Understanding Drug Abuse

To better understand the problems of drug use and abuse, we need to consider social, biological, and psychological factors (e.g., Ham & Hope, 2005; Kahler et al., 2003).

Sociocultural Influences   The pleasurable effects of drugs, peer pressure, and exposure to family members who smoke or use alcohol or other drugs are important influences in leading young people to begin experimenting with these substances (Read et al., 2003). Although people may begin to use drugs to "fit in" or appear "cool" in the eyes of peers, they generally continue using drugs because of the pleasurable effects of the drugs themselves.

Some young people who feel alienated from mainstream culture come to identify with subcultures in which drug use is sanctioned or encouraged, such as the gang subculture. Unemployment is another social factor linked to drug abuse. Young adults who are out of work are more than twice as likely as their employed peers to turn to drugs (USDHHS, 1991b). The relationship appears to be two-sided: drug abuse may increase the likelihood of unemployment, while unemployment may increase the likelihood of drug abuse.

Use of alcohol and other drugs is strongly affected by cultural norms. Cultural beliefs and customs may either encourage or discourage drinking. Some ethnic groups—Jews, Greeks, Italians, and Asians, for example—have low rates of alcoholism, largely because of tight social controls imposed on excessive and underage drinking. Traditional Hispanic cultures place severe restrictions on women's use of alcohol, especially on heavy drinking. Not surprisingly, highly acculturated Hispanic American women who have been exposed to the loose constraints on female drinking in mainstream U.S. society are much more likely to drink heavily than are relatively unacculturated Hispanic American women (Caetano, 1987). In traditional Islamic cultures, alcohol is prohibited altogether.

Ethnic and racial groups also differ in their reported use of illicit drugs. Figure 4.12 shows the reported rates of cocaine and marijuana use by African Americans and (non-Hispanic) White Americans. The data are drawn from an ongoing survey

CONCEPT 4.34
Drug abuse and dependence are complex problems arising from an interplay of social, biological, and psychological factors.

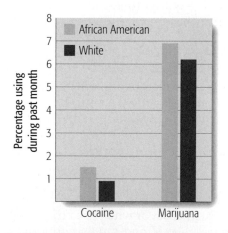

Figure 4.12   Ethnicity and Drug Use
This figure shows the percentages of African Americans and White Americans who report using cocaine and marijuana during the past month. The data are from an ongoing federally sponsored study of drug-use patterns in the United States. But can we infer from these data that use of these illicit drugs is a problem associated with minority-group status?

Source: Substance Abuse and Mental Health Services Administration (SAMSHA), 2004

CONCEPT CHART 4.4   Major Types of Psychoactive Drugs

	Drug	Potential for Psychological/ Physiological Dependence	Major Psychological Effects	Major Risks
Hallucinogens	Alcohol	Yes/Yes	Induces relaxation, mild euphoria, and intoxication; relieves anxiety; reduces mental alertness and inhibitions; impairs concentration, judgment, coordination, and balance	With heavy use, can cause liver disorders and other physical problems; in overdose, can cause coma or death
	Barbiturates and tranquilizers	Yes/Yes	Reduces mental alertness; induces relaxation and calm; may produce pleasurable rush (barbiturates)	High addictive potential; dangerous in overdose and when mixed with alcohol and other drugs
	Opioids	Yes/Yes	Induces relaxation and a euphoric rush; may temporarily blot out awareness of personal problems	High addictive potential; in overdose, may cause sudden death
Stimulants	Amphetamines	Yes/Yes	Boosts mental alertness; reduces need for sleep; induces pleasurable rush; causes loss of appetite	In high doses, can induce psychotic symptoms and cardiovascular irregularities that may lead to coma or death
	Cocaine	Yes/Yes	Effects similar to those of amphetamines but shorter-lived	High addictive potential; risk of sudden death from overdose; in high doses, can have psychotic effects; risk of nasal defects from "snorting"
	MDMA ("Ecstasy")	Yes/Yes	Mild euphoria and hallucinogenic effects	High doses can be lethal; may lead to depression or other psychological effects; may impair learning, attention, and memory
	Nicotine	Yes/Yes	Increases mental alertness; produces mild rush but paradoxically may have relaxing and calming effects	Strong addictive potential; implicated in various cancers, cardiovascular disease, and other physical disorders
	Caffeine	Yes/Yes	Increases mental alertness and wakefulness	In high doses, can cause jitteriness and sleeplessness; may increase risk of miscarriage during pregnancy
Depressants	LSD	Yes/No	Produces hallucinations and other sensory distortions	Intense anxiety, panic, or psychotic reactions associated with "bad trips"; flashbacks
	Marijuana	Yes/No	Induces relaxation and mild euphoria; can produce hallucinations	In high doses, can cause nausea, vomiting, disorientation, panic, and paranoia; possible health risks from regular use

of American households. Later in the chapter we will ask you to think critically about these data. Do they in fact demonstrate that race or ethnicity is responsible for these differences?

Biological Influences   With prolonged use of a drug, the body comes to depend on a steady supply of it and the person becomes physiologically dependent on the drug. As people become chemically dependent, they may continue using drugs primarily to avoid unpleasant withdrawal symptoms and cravings that occur when they stop using them.

Peer Pressure Social pressure from friends is an important influence on alcohol and drug use among young people.

Self-Medication? Many problem drinkers use alcohol in an attempt to wash away their problems or troubling emotions.

We have strong evidence of genetic factors at work in drug dependence, including alcoholism, heroin addiction, and even nicotine (smoking) addiction (Dodd et al., 2004; Feng et al., 2004; Wall, Carr, & Ehlers, 2003; Xu et al., 2004). For one thing, we know that alcoholism tends to run in families (Chassin, Flora, & King, 2004). But more direct evidence of a genetic contribution comes from findings that identical twins are more likely to share the disorder than are fraternal twins (Alterman et al., 2003;Liu et al., 2004). Scientists believe that multiple genes (not any one gene alone) act together with environmental factors to increase the likelihood of developing substance abuse problems (Crabbe, 2002; Dick & Foroud, 2003;Kendler et al., 2003). Some people may have a genetic tendency that makes the effects of certain drugs especially rewarding or stimulating.

Another genetic factor, at least for alcoholism, may be inheritance of a greater tolerance for the drug's negative effects (the nausea and so on), which may make it more difficult to learn when to say *no more*. People who inherit a greater sensitivity to the negative effects of alcohol—those whose bodies more readily "put the brakes" on excess drinking—may be less likely to develop problems with alcohol abuse or dependence (Pihl, Peterson, & Finn, 1990; Pollock, 1992). Thus, ironically, having a greater ability to hold one's liquor may put one at greater risk of developing problems with alcohol.

We also need to consider the role of neurotransmitters in drug abuse. Drugs such as cocaine, alcohol, heroin, amphetamines, and marijuana have pleasurable or euphoric effects because they increase levels of the neurotransmitter dopamine in the brain, a chemical that activates the brain's reward or pleasure circuits (Adler, 2003; Kauer, 2003; Saal et al., 2003). Investigators in one recent study examined differences in brain activity in response to alcohol-related words in two groups of women, an alcohol-dependent group and a group of light social drinkers (Tapert et al., 2004). The investigators showed sets of alcohol-related words (*keg, binge*) and neutral words (*fig, shave*) on a screen while the women's brains were being scanned. The results showed that women suffering from alcoholism (alcohol dependence) had greater activation in parts of the brain (the left frontal lobes and the limbic system) that are associated with the positive, reward value of alcohol use (see Figure 4.13). If the brain's reward circuitry becomes activated by alcohol-related cues, even by the mere mention of alcohol-related words, people struggling with alcoholism may be more prone to experience cravings and relapse in response to such cues.

Chronic use of drugs alters the delicate biochemistry of the brain's natural dopamine system, making it more difficult for the person to reap pleasure from the normal activities of everyday life, such as enjoying a good meal or attending a

Figure 4.13   Your Brain in Response to Alcohol Words
Investigators used functional magnetic resonance imaging (fMRI) to study brain activity in response to alcohol cue words in two groups of women, an alcohol-dependent group and a group of light social drinkers. The brains of alcohol-dependent women showed greater activity in parts of the limbic system and frontal lobes of the left hemisphere (indicated by yellow/orange colors). These parts of the brain are involved in reward pathways that are activated by consumption of alcohol and other drugs. Thus, mere exposure to words associated with alcohol can have similar effects on the brain as the drug itself, at least in women suffering from alcohol dependence.

Source: Tapert et al., 2004.

concert ("Cocaine Impairs," 2003). The chronic drug user comes to depend on drugs to produce feelings of pleasure or to erase negative feelings, such as anxiety or depression. Without drugs, life may no longer seem worth living.

Endorphins too are affected by drug abuse. Opioids lock into the same receptor sites as endorphins. Therefore, when the brain becomes accustomed to having opioids available, it suppresses production of endorphins. The person dependent on opioids comes to rely on them to perform the pain-relieving and pleasure-inducing functions normally served by endorphins.

Psychological Influences   Psychological factors, such as feelings of hopelessness, the need to seek sensation, and the desire to escape troubling emotions, are major contributors to the development of drug use and dependence. Young people from troubled backgrounds may turn to drugs out of a sense of futility and despair. People with a high need for sensation—those who become easily bored with the ordinary activities that fill most people's days—may come to rely on drugs to provide the stimulation they seek. Other people use alcohol or other drugs as a form of self-medication to relieve anxiety or emotional pain, or to temporarily escape from their problems or conflicts with others (Delfino, Jamner, & Whalen, 2001; Ozegovic, Bikos, & Szymanski, 2001).

Cognitive factors, such as favorable attitudes toward drugs and positive expectancies about their effects, also play important roles in determining whether young people use and abuse alcohol and other drugs (Fischer et al., 2004; Morawska & Oei, 2005; Wiers & Kummeling, 2004). In one research study, the strongest factor determining whether adolescents began using alcohol was a positive expectancy that alcohol would make them more socially outgoing (G. T. Smith et al., 1995). In another study, fifth and seventh graders with more positive impressions of smokers (perceiving them as "cool," "independent," or "good looking") were more likely to start smoking by the time they entered the ninth grade than were peers who had more negative impressions (Dinh et al., 1995). Yet times may be changing. In a recent study of adolescents in a Midwestern community, more negative attitudes toward smoking were found than was the case a generation ago in the same community (Chassin et al., 2003).

Media advertising, such as beer commercials, can create positive associations with alcohol use. Evidence shows that college students give more positive ratings, and are better able to recall, alcohol advertisements than virtually any other product category tested (Zinser, Freeman, & Ginnings, 1999). The success of drug prevention efforts may depend on our ability to change the images young people have of drug use even before they light up their first cigarette or take their first drink.

Drug Treatment

The most effective drug-treatment programs use a variety of approaches in dealing with the wide range of problems faced by people with drug-abuse problems (Litt et al., 2003). People with chemical dependencies may first need to undergo **detoxification**, a process in which their bodies are cleared of addictive drugs. To ensure that medical monitoring is available, detoxification usually requires a hospital stay. Follow-up services, including mental health services, can assist people in remaining free of drugs by helping them address the serious psychological problems that often occur together with substance abuse or dependence, especially mood disorders and anxiety disorders (Grant et al., 2004).

Therapeutic drugs may be used in combination with psychological counseling to combat addiction (Kiefer et al., 2003). Methadone, a synthetic opioid, is one such drug; when used in normal doses, it does not produce the rush or stuporous state associated with heroin, but it does curb withdrawal symptoms from heroin (Belluck, 2003). It can help heroin abusers gain employment and get their lives back on track. In addition, participation in a self-help program, such as the twelve-step program of Alcoholics Anonymous (AA), can motivate individuals to rebuild their lives free of drugs, especially when people commit themselves to abstinence goals and stick with the program more consistently (Moos & Moos, 2004; McCrady & Epstein, 2004). Though many treatment resources are available, unfortunately a great many people with alcohol and drug problems do not get the help they need. A recent study of more than 1,000 people with diagnosed substance-abuse disorders in the Canadian province of Ontario underscored the problem: only one in three ever received any form of substance-abuse treatment (Cunningham & Breslin, 2004).

EXPLORING PSYCHOLOGY
Binge Drinking: A Dangerous College Pastime

About two out of three college students drink alcohol at least once monthly, although most of them are under the legal drinking age (see Table 4.4). Drinking has become so ingrained in college life that it is virtually as much a part of the college experience as attending a dance or basketball game. Drinking among college students tends to be limited to weekends and is greater at the start of the semester when academic requirements are minimal than at the end during exam time (Del Boca et al., 2004).

Binge drinking on campus has become a prime concern among parents and school officials, and for good reason. Overall, about two out of five college students engage in binge drinking (Ham & Hope, 2003). *Binge drinking* is usually defined as having five or more drinks (for men) or four or more drinks (for women) on one occasion. A recent study of 236 university students showed that on "heavy" drinking nights, students averaged nearly ten drinks and achieved blood

---

CONCEPT 4.35

Effective drug treatment requires a multifaceted approach to helping people free themselves of chemical dependence and develop more adaptive ways of coping with their problems.

Online Study Center
Resources

Weblinks: Alcoholics Anonymous; Getting Help with Dependency

CONCEPT 4.36

Binge drinking is linked to increased risks of alcohol dependence, alcohol overdoses, unsafe or unplanned sex, and driving while impaired, among other problems.

detoxification A process of clearing drugs or toxins from the body.

Death by Alcohol Samantha Spady, a 19-year-old Colorado State University sophomore, died from alcohol poisoning after an evening of heavy drinking with her friends. At the time of her death, she had a blood alcohol concentration over five times the legal limit for driving.

TABLE 4.4   Alcohol Use Among College Students

Level of Alcohol Use	Percentage
Some time in their lifetime	86.6
Within the past year	83.2
Within the past 30 days	67.4
Daily within the past 30 days	3.6
Five or more drinks in a row during the last 2 weeks	39.3

Source: Johnston, O'Malley, & Bachman, 2001.

alcohol concentrations (BACs) of .25 (Alexander & Bowen, 2004). See Table 4.3 for the behavioral effects of a BAC of .25.

Drinking at a young age and engaging in binge drinking are strong predictors of later alcoholism (Chassin et al., 2002). Young people who start drinking before the age of fifteen are five times more likely than their peers to develop alcohol dependence (Kluger, 2001). Binge drinkers also face additional risks. For example, they are fourteen times more likely than other adults to drive while impaired (Naimi et al., 2003).

College students who binge-drink are also three times more likely than their peers to engage in unsafe or unplanned sexual activities, which increases their risks of both unwanted pregnancies and sexually transmitted diseases (Cooper, 1992; Kruger & Jerrells, 1992). The slogan from a recent public health campaign bears repeating: "First you get drunk. Then you get stupid. Then you get AIDS." A recent study of students from a southwestern university lends support to this message by showing that the greater the frequency and amount of alcohol consumed, the greater the likelihood of engaging in risky sexual behavior (Fierros-Gonzalez & Brown, 2002).   Excessive drinking has long been associated with social functions in fraternities and sororities. Though many fraternal organizations encourage their members to behave responsibly, evidence links drinking behavior to membership in these groups (Montgomery & Haemmerlie, 1993; Ozegovic et al., 2001). Many Greek organizations now ban alcohol beverages, including beer (Denizel-Lewis, 2005). But problem drinking on campus extends beyond fraternal organizations. A recent study shows that attendance at college was associated with an increased likelihood of occasional bouts of heavy drinking among women (Slutske et al., 2004). Pause for a moment and consider what it might be about the college experience that contributes to problem drinking.

Now consider some of the more immediate dangers of heavy drinking. Binge drinking and related drinking games (beer chugging or downing a series of shots) place drinkers at risk of coma or death from overdoses of alcohol (Zernike, 2005). Choking on one's own vomit is a frequent cause of alcohol-induced deaths. Heavy drinking can cause people to vomit reflexively, but the drug's depressant effects on the central nervous system interfere with the normal vomiting response. As a result, vomit accumulates in the air passages, sometimes causing asphyxiation and death. Many students who play drinking games don't stop until they become too drunk or too sick to continue (Johnson, 2002). Participation in drinking games is also strongly related to risks of being either a victim or perpetrator of sexual aggression (Johnson, Wendel, & Hamilton, 1998).

Prompt medical attention is needed if a person overdoses on alcohol. But how can you tell if a person has drunk too much? Table 4.5 lists some signs of alcohol overdose. If a person is unresponsive or unconscious, you may be tempted to walk away and let the person "sleep it off." You may think you have no right to interfere, and you may doubt that the person is in danger. However, an unconscious

TABLE 4.5   Signs of Alcohol Overdose

- Failure to respond when talked to or shouted at
- Failure to respond to being pinched, shaken, or poked
- Inability to stand unaided
- Failure to wake up
- Purplish or clammy skin
- Rapid pulse rate, irregular heart rhythm, low blood pressure, or difficulty breathing

person is definitely in danger and should not be left alone. Don't simply assume that he or she will "sleep it off." Stay with the person until you or someone else can obtain medical attention. Most important, call a physician or local emergency number immediately and ask for advice. If you were in the place of a person who showed signs of overdosing on alcohol, wouldn't you want someone to intervene to save your life?

MODULE 4.4 REVIEW

Altering Consciousness Through Drugs

RECITE IT

When does drug use cross the line from use to abuse and dependence?

- Drug use becomes drug abuse when it involves the maladaptive or dangerous use of a drug (use that causes or aggravates personal, occupational, or physical problems).

- Drug abuse frequently leads to drug dependence, a state of impaired control over the use of a drug. It is often accompanied by signs of physiological dependence.

- Physiological dependence means that the person's body has come to depend on having a steady supply of the drug. When psychologically dependent, people rely on a drug as a way of coping with anxiety, stress, and other negative feelings.

What are the different types of psychoactive drugs, and what effects do they have?

- Depressants, such as alcohol, barbiturates, tranquilizers, and opioids, are addictive drugs that reduce the activity of the central nervous system. Among other effects, they reduce states of bodily arousal, relieve anxiety and tension, and, in the case of barbiturates and opioids, produce a pleasurable or euphoric rush.

- Stimulants, which include amphetamines, cocaine, MDMA ("Ecstasy"), nicotine, and caffeine, heighten the activity of the nervous system. Stimulants may induce feelings of euphoria, but they also can lead to physiological dependence. Cocaine directly stimulates reward pathways in the brain, producing states of euphoria, but it is a highly addictive and dangerous drug. MDMA is a chemical knock

off of amphetamines that can have serious psychological and physical consequences. Nicotine, a mild stimulant, is the addictive substance found in tobacco. Though regular use of caffeine may lead to psychological dependence, most users can maintain control over their consumption of it.

- Hallucinogens are drugs that alter sensory perceptions and produce hallucinations. They include LSD, mescaline, psilocybin, PCP, and marijuana. PCP ("angel dust") is a synthetic drug that produces delirium, a state of confusion and disorientation that may be accompanied by hallucinations and violent behavior. Marijuana, the most widely used illicit drug, has a range of effects depending on dosage level.

What factors contribute to alcohol and drug-abuse problems?

- In addition to the reinforcing effects of the drugs themselves, social, biological, and psychological factors contribute to drug abuse. Among the contributing social factors are peer pressure and exposure to family members and friends who use drugs. Biological factors include high tolerance for negative drug effects. Psychological factors include feelings of hopelessness and the desire to escape troubling emotions.

What treatment alternatives are available to help people with drug problems?

- Approaches to treating people with drug problems include detoxification programs, professional counseling, the use of therapeutic drugs, and self-help programs such as Alcoholics Anonymous.

RECALL IT

1. Chemical substances that alter mental states are called _____ drugs.

2. When repeated use of a drug alters a person's body chemistry so that the body comes to rely on having a steady supply of the drug, the condition is called
   a. drug abuse.
   b. drug misuse.
   c. psychological dependence.
   d. physiological dependence.

3. Alcohol and heroin belong to which class of drugs?

4. What is the most widely used and abused depressant?

5. _____ are drugs that are widely used in treating anxiety and insomnia but that can become addictive when used for extended periods of time.

6. Hallucinogens are drugs that alter sensory perceptions and produce hallucinations. Which of the following is *not* a hallucinogen?
   a. cocaine
   b. marijuana
   c. LSD
   d. psilocybin

THINK ABOUT IT

- What roles do positive and negative reinforcement play in problems of drug abuse and dependence?

- Should marijuana be legalized? Why or why not?

APPLICATION MODULE 4.5
Getting Your Zs

Many people have difficulty falling asleep or getting enough sleep to feel refreshed upon awakening. Since insomnia may result from an underlying medical or psychological disorder, it is best to have the condition evaluated by a health professional. In many cases, however, insomnia reflects unhealthy sleep habits. Fortunately, people can change such habits by becoming better aware of behavioral patterns and making adaptive changes in behavior (Edinger et al., 2001; Quesnel et al., 2003). Here are some suggestions for developing healthier sleep habits (Nevid et al., 1998):

- *Adopt a regular sleep schedule.* Help get your internal body clock in sync by retiring and awakening at about the same times every day. You may cut yourself some slack on weekends, but be aware that sleeping late in the morning can throw off your body clock.

- *Don't try to force sleep.* Sleep is a natural process that cannot be forced. If you are wide-eyed and full of energy, allow your body and mind to wind down before going to bed.

- *Establish a regular bedtime routine.* Adopt a regular routine before going to bed. You may find that reading, watching TV, or practicing a relaxation or meditation technique helps prepare you for sleep.

- *Establish the proper cues for sleeping.* Make your bed a cue for sleeping by limiting as much as possible other activities in bed, such as eating, reading, watching TV, or talking on the telephone.

CONCEPT 4.37
Developing healthy sleep habits can help people overcome insomnia not caused by underlying physical or psychological problems.

Making Your Bed a Cue for Sleeping
If you have a problem with insomnia, you might find it helpful to make your bed a stronger cue for sleep by limiting other activities in bed, such as eating, reading, watching TV, or talking on the phone.

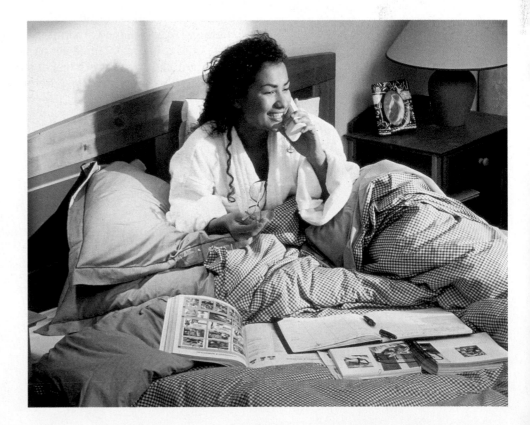

- *Avoid tossing and turning.* If you can't fall asleep within twenty minutes, don't continue tossing and turning. Get out of bed, move to another room, and achieve a state of relaxation by reading, listening to calming music, or meditating. When you are feeling relaxed, return to bed. Repeat this process as necessary until you are able to fall asleep.

- *Avoid daytime naps if you miss sleep.* Many people try to make up for nighttime sleeplessness by napping during the day. Napping can throw off your natural body clock, making it more difficult to fall asleep the following night.

- *Don't take your problems to bed.* Retiring to bed should be conducive to sleeping, not to mulling over your problems or organizing your daily schedule. Tell yourself you'll think about tomorrow, tomorrow. Or, before you go to bed, write reminder notes to yourself about the things you need to do the following day.

- *Use mental imagery.* Picturing relaxing scenes in your mind—for example, imagining yourself basking in the sun on a tropical beach or walking through a pristine forest—can help you slip from ordinary consciousness into the realm of sleep.

- *Adopt a regular exercise program.* Vigorous exercise can help relieve the stresses of daily life and prepare the body for restful sleep. But avoid exercising for several hours before sleep, since exercise increases states of bodily arousal.

- *Limit your intake of caffeine, especially in the afternoon or evening.* The caffeine in coffee, tea, and other substances can increase states of bodily arousal for up to ten hours. Also avoid smoking, not only because of its harmful effects on your health but also because tobacco contains nicotine, a mild stimulant.

- *Practice rational "self-talk."* Disturbing thoughts you silently mumble to yourself under your breath can lead to anxiety and worry that may keep you up well into the night. Replace such anxious "self-talk" with coping thoughts. For example, instead of thinking, "I must get to sleep or I'll be a wreck tomorrow," substitute a thought like "I might not feel as sharp as usual but I'm not going to fall apart. I've gotten by with little sleep before and can do so again." Don't fall into the trap of blowing things out of proportion.

TYING IT TOGETHER

Our state of consciousness, or level of awareness, shifts during the course of a day from periods of focused awareness through states of drifting and divided consciousness to states of unconsciousness experienced during sleeping and dreaming (Module 4.1). When we sleep, we experience a state of unconsciousness in which we are generally unaware of our external surroundings but can respond to certain kinds of stimuli (Module 4.2). Some people seek to achieve altered states of consciousness through meditation or hypnosis (Module 4.3) or by using mind-altering drugs (Module 4.4). By applying our knowledge of sleep-wake cycles and adopting healthy sleep habits to keep our body clocks in sync, we can help ensure that we receive the restful sleep we need (Module 4.5).

Thinking Critically About Psychology

Based on your reading of this chapter, answer the following questions. Then, to evaluate your progress in developing critical thinking skills, compare your answers to the sample answers found in Appendix A.

Do statistics lie? While statistics may not actually lie, they can certainly mislead if we don't apply critical thinking skills when interpreting them. Recall Figure 4.12 from page 170, which showed racial/ethnic differences in reported use of cocaine and marijuana. These survey results showed that African Americans were more likely to report using these drugs within the past month than were (non-Hispanic) White Americans. Now apply your critical thinking skills to answer the following questions:

1. **Does this evidence demonstrate that ethnicity accounts for differences in rates of drug use? Why or why not?**

2. **What other explanations might account for these findings?**

Key Terms

consciousness *(p. 138)*
states of consciousness *(p. 138)*
focused awareness *(p. 138)*
drifting consciousness *(p. 139)*
daydreaming *(p. 139)*
divided consciousness *(p. 139)*
unconsciousness *(p. 140)*
altered states of consciousness *(p. 140)*
circadian rhythm *(p. 143)*
jet lag *(p. 143)*
rapid-eye-movement (REM) sleep *(p. 145)*
activation-synthesis hypothesis *(p. 147)*
lucid dreams *(p. 149)*
insomnia *(p. 150)*
narcolepsy *(p. 150)*
cataplexy *(p. 150)*
sleep apnea *(p. 150)*

nightmare disorder *(p. 150)*
sleep terror disorder *(p. 150)*
sleepwalking disorder *(p. 151)*
transcendental meditation (TM) *(p. 154)*
mantra *(p. 154)*
mindfulness meditation *(p. 154)*
hypnosis *(p. 155)*
hypnotic age regression *(p. 155)*
hypnotic analgesia *(p. 155)*
posthypnotic amnesia *(p. 156)*
posthypnotic suggestion *(p. 156)*
neodissociation theory *(p. 156)*
hidden observer *(p. 156)*
psychoactive drugs *(p. 158)*
drug abuse *(p. 160)*
polyabusers *(p. 160)*
drug dependence *(p. 160)*

physiological dependence *(p. 160)*
withdrawal syndrome *(p. 160)*
tolerance *(p. 160)*
drug addiction *(p. 160)*
psychological dependence *(p. 160)*
depressants *(p. 161)*
intoxicant *(p. 161)*
alcoholism *(p. 162)*
narcotics *(p. 164)*
stimulants *(p. 164)*
hallucinogens *(p. 168)*
delirium *(p. 169)*
detoxification *(p. 174)*

ANSWERS TO RECALL IT QUESTIONS

Module 4.1: 1. a; 2. selectivity; 3. focused; 4. altered.
Module 4.2: 1. circadian; 2. 3, 4; 3. restorative; 4. i. c, ii. b, iii. d, iv. a.
Module 4.3: 1. transcendental meditation; 2. hypnotic analgesia; 3. neodissociation theory.
Module 4.4: 1. psychoactive; 2. d; 3. depressants; 4. alcohol; 5. tranquilizers; 6. a.

Learning

DID YOU KNOW THAT . . .

- Feelings of déjà-vu may be a type of conditioned response? (p. 185)

- Phobias may be acquired through the same principles of classical conditioning that Pavlov discovered from his studies of digestion in dogs? (p. 189)

- Salivating to the sound of a tone may not be harmful, but salivating at the sight of a Scotch bottle may well be dangerous to people battling alcoholism? (p. 190)

- Principles of classical conditioning were put into practice on a ranch to prevent coyotes from killing sheep? (pp. 190–191)

- Pigeons show forms of superstitious behavior that psychologists believe are learned in much the same way as humans learn superstitious behavior? (p. 196)

- We can apply the principles of learning to explain how slot machines become "one-armed bandits"? (p. 201)

- Scheduling tests on specific days may inadvertently reinforce cramming just before exams and slacking off afterward? (p. 202)

- Many people develop fears of various creatures even though they have had no direct negative experiences with them? (p. 211)

I hate eggs. It's not just the taste of eggs I can't stand. The smell, the feel, the very sight of eggs is enough to make me sick. Watching other people eat eggs can make me nauseous. It's not that I'm allergic to eggs. I like all kinds of baked goods that are made with eggs. I'm fine with eggs as long as they are cooked into other foods so they are no longer recognizable as, well, eggs. But eggs themselves, especially runny eggs, fill me with disgust.

I wasn't born with disgust for eggs. Nor did I always dislike eggs. My parents tell me I was actually quite fond of eggs as a young child. But somewhere along the line, I acquired an aversion to eggs. Chances are I had an unpleasant experience with eggs. No, I don't think I was chased around a barn by a clutch of crazed chickens. Most likely, I had an experience in which eggs made me sick. Or perhaps I was forced to eat eggs when I wasn't feeling well. In any event, I have no memory of it. All I know is that I hate eggs and have hated them for as long as I can recall.

I have described my aversion to eggs to introduce you to the topic of learning. Some responses, such as pulling your hand away from a hot stove, are reflexive. We don't learn reflexes; we are biologically equipped to perform them automatically. Other behaviors develop naturally as the result of maturation. As a child's muscles mature, the child becomes capable of lifting heavier weights or throwing a ball a longer distance. But other responses, such as my aversion to eggs, are acquired through *experience*. Psychologists generally define *learning* as a relatively permanent change in behavior that results from experience. It is through experience that we learn about the world and develop new skills, such as riding a bicycle or cooking a soufflé. Acquired taste preferences or aversions, including my aversion to eggs, are also learned behaviors. Note the use of the term *relatively permanent* in the definition of learning. Psychologists believe that for learning to occur, changes in behavior must be enduring. But change need not be permanent. It is possible to unlearn behavior. For example, you would need to unlearn the behavior of driving on the right side of the road if you wanted to drive in a country where people drive on the left side of the road.

Psychologists recognize that learning is adaptive; it enables organisms to adapt their behavior to the demands of the environment. Through learning, organisms acquire behaviors that increase their chances of survival. Even taste aversions can be adaptive. They prevent animals, including humans, from eating foods that have sickened or poisoned them in the past. But not all learned responses are adaptive. My own aversion to eggs limits the range of foods I might enjoy. By and large, however, learning helps prepare organisms to meet the demands that their environments impose on them.

Psychologists study many forms of learning, including three major types that are the focus of this chapter: classical conditioning, operant conditioning, and cognitive learning. ■

MODULE 5.1

Classical Conditioning: Learning Through Association

- What is learning?
- What is classical conditioning?
- What roles do extinction, spontaneous recovery, stimulus generalization, discrimination, and higher-order conditioning play in classical conditioning?
- What stimulus characteristics strengthen conditioned responses?
- What is the cognitive perspective on classical conditioning?
- What are some examples of classical conditioning in daily life?

CONCEPT 5.1
Pavlov's discovery that dogs would salivate to particular sounds in his laboratory led him to discover a process of learning called classical conditioning, which involves learning by association.

Do your muscles tighten at the sound of a dentist's drill? Do you suddenly begin to salivate when you drive by your favorite bakery? You weren't born with these responses—you learned them. But how does **learning** occur?

We begin with the work of Ivan Pavlov (1849–1936), a Russian scientist who discovered the form of learning called **classical conditioning**. Although Pavlov's discovery is among the most important in psychology, it actually occurred quite by accident. As described in the nearby Pioneers box, Pavlov was studying the digestive system in dogs when he noticed that the animals began salivating to sounds in his laboratory that had become associated with feeding.

You can think of classical conditioning as *learning by association*. If you associate the sound of a dentist's drill with pain because of past experiences, the stimulus of that sound will probably cause you to respond with the muscle tension that is a natural reflex to pain. If you associate a certain bakery with a particularly tasty treat, you may find yourself salivating as you drive or walk by the bakery. Classically conditioned responses are learned by experiences in which one stimulus is paired with another that elicits these naturally occurring reactions. Although classical conditioning is a relatively simple form of learning, it plays an important role in our lives—as you will see in this module.

Principles of Classical Conditioning

Pavlov performed many experiments in classical conditioning. In a typical experiment, he harnessed dogs in an apparatus similar to the one shown in Figure 5.1. When food is placed on a dog's tongue, the dog naturally salivates. This reflexive

Figure 5.1 Apparatus Similar to One Used in Pavlov's Experiments on Conditioning
In Pavlov's studies, a research assistant positioned behind a mirror sounded a tone as food was placed on the dog's tongue. After several pairings of the tone and food, the dog acquired a conditioned response of salivation. The amount of saliva dripping through a tube to a collection vial was taken as the measure of the strength of the conditioned response.

learning A relatively permanent change in behavior acquired through experience.
classical conditioning The process of learning by which a previously neutral stimulus comes to elicit an identical or similar response to one originally elicited by another stimulus as the result of the pairing of the two stimuli.

Recording cylinder to measure amount of saliva

Collection tube for saliva

THE PIONEERS | An Accidental Discovery

Ivan Pavlov

The Russian physiologist Ivan Pavlov won a Nobel Prize for his experimental work on digestive processes (Dewsbury, 1997; Windholz, 1997). Yet he is best known to us today for an accidental discovery he made in the course of his research on digestion in dogs. He took the occasion of his Nobel Prize address to inform the scientific community of an unusual phenomenon he had observed in his laboratory.

Pavlov had surgically inserted a small pouch in the stomachs of dogs to collect gastric juices, which he then examined to see how the stomach reacts when animals eat. But the dogs' stomachs did not react as Pavlov expected. Even before the dogs started eating, their stomachs secreted gastric juices and their salivary glands secreted saliva. Apparently, these responses occurred when the laboratory assistant wheeled in the metal food carts or when the dogs heard the carts banging against each other. Did the dogs "know" they were about to be fed? Did their thoughts trigger a gastric response?

Pavlov, a hard-nosed physiologist, had no regard for such mentalistic notions. He believed the response was a physiological reflex—an involuntary, automatic response to a particular stimulus. He argued that the reflex was triggered in the brain by stimuli associated with feeding. He called this phenomenon a "conditional reflex." We now call it a "conditioned response" (*conditioned* meaning "acquired" or "learned"). Pavlov spent the rest of his career studying this form of learning, which is now known as *classical conditioning*.

behavior is called an **unconditioned response (UR)** (*unconditioned* means "unlearned"). A stimulus that elicits an unconditioned response—in this case, the dog's food—is called an **unconditioned stimulus (US)**.

Figure 5.2 outlines the steps involved in a Pavlovian experiment. As you can see in Figure 5.2b, the introduction of a **neutral stimulus (NS)**, such as a tone or buzzer, does not naturally elicit a response of salivation. It may produce other responses, however. A dog's ears may turn up in response to a sound, but the dog doesn't naturally salivate when it hears a tone or buzzer. However, through repeated pairings of the neutral stimulus and the unconditioned stimulus (Figure

Figure 5.2   Diagramming Classical Conditioning
In classical conditioning, a neutral stimulus (the tone) is paired with an unconditioned stimulus (food) that normally elicits an unconditioned response (salivation). With repeated pairings, the neutral stimulus becomes a conditioned stimulus that elicits the conditioned response of salivation.

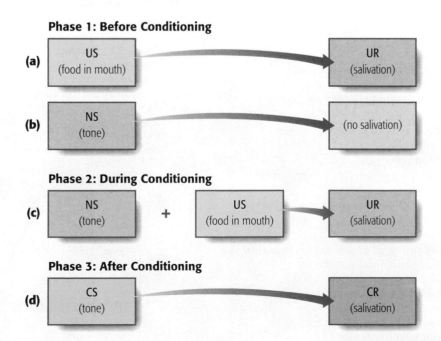

Phase 1: Before Conditioning

(a) US (food in mouth) → UR (salivation)

(b) NS (tone) → (no salivation)

Phase 2: During Conditioning

(c) NS (tone) + US (food in mouth) → UR (salivation)

Phase 3: After Conditioning

(d) CS (tone) → CR (salivation)

unconditioned response (UR)   An unlearned response to a stimulus.
unconditioned stimulus (US)   A stimulus that elicits an unlearned response.
neutral stimulus (NS)   A stimulus that before conditioning does not produce a particular response.

5.2*c*), the dog acquires a *learned* response: salivation in response to the tone or buzzer alone (Figure 5.2*d*). Salivation to the sound of a tone or buzzer alone is called a **conditioned response (CR)**. A previously neutral stimulus becomes a **conditioned stimulus (CS)** when it is repeatedly paired with an unconditioned stimulus and begins to elicit the conditioned response. In addition to showing that salivation (CR) could be made to occur in response to a stimulus that did not naturally elicit the response, Pavlov observed that the strength of the conditioned response (the amount of salivation) increased with the number of pairings of the CS and US.

We next examine other characteristics of classical conditioning: extinction and spontaneous recovery, stimulus generalization, discrimination, higher-order conditioning, and stimulus characteristics that strengthen conditioned responses.

 CONCEPT 5.2

Through the process of extinction, conditioned responses gradually weaken and eventually disappear as the result of the repeated presentation of the conditioned stimulus in the absence of the unconditioned stimulus.

 CONCEPT 5.3

Extinguished responses are not forgotten but may return spontaneously in the future if the conditioned stimulus is presented again.

CONCEPT 5.4

Stimulus generalization has survival value by enabling organisms to generalize their learned responses to new stimuli that are similar to an original threatening stimulus.

Extinction and Spontaneous Recovery Pavlov noticed that the conditioned response of salivation to the sound of a tone would gradually weaken and eventually disappear when he repeatedly presented the tone in the absence of the US (food). This process is called **extinction** (see Figure 5.3). The extinguished response is not forgotten or lost to memory. It may return spontaneously at a later time when the animal is again exposed to the conditioned stimulus. This phenomenon is called **spontaneous recovery**. However, the recovered response will once again extinguish if the CS continues to occur in the absence of the US.

Pavlov discovered that when the CS and US are paired again after extinction has occurred, the response is likely to be learned more quickly than in the original conditioning. In many cases, the animal needs only one or two pairings. The process of relearning a conditioned response after extinction is called **reconditioning**.

Stimulus Generalization and Stimulus Discrimination Pavlov found that once animals were trained to salivate to a particular stimulus, such as a tone, they would also salivate, but less strongly, to related stimuli that varied along some continuum, such as pitch. A tone with a higher or lower pitch, for example, would elicit some degree of salivation. The tendency of stimuli that are similar to the conditioned stimulus to elicit a conditioned response is called **stimulus generalization**. Generally speaking, the greater the difference between the original stimulus and the related stimulus, the weaker the conditioned response is. Were it not for stimulus generalization, the animal would need to be conditioned to respond to each stimulus no matter how slightly it varied from the original conditioned stimulus.

conditioned response (CR) An acquired or learned response to a conditioned stimulus.

conditioned stimulus (CS) A previously neutral stimulus that comes to elicit a conditioned response after it has been paired with an unconditioned stimulus.

extinction The gradual weakening and eventual disappearance of a conditioned response.

spontaneous recovery The spontaneous return of a conditioned response following extinction.

reconditioning The process of relearning a conditioned response following extinction.

stimulus generalization The tendency for stimuli that are similar to the conditioned stimulus to elicit a conditioned response.

Figure 5.3 Strength of a Conditioned Response
With repeated pairings of the conditioned stimulus (CS) and unconditioned stimulus (US), the conditioned response (CR) increases in strength. When the CS is repeatedly presented alone, the CR gradually weakens and eventually is extinguished. After a period of time has elapsed, however, spontaneous recovery of the response may occur. But when the CS is again presented in the absence of the US, extinction reoccurs.

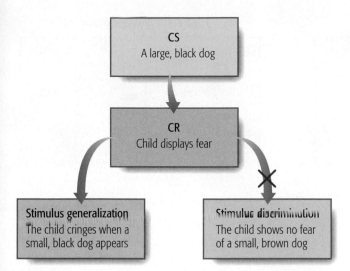

Figure 5.4   Stimulus Generalization and Discrimination
In stimulus generalization, a conditioned response generalizes to stimuli that are similar to the original conditioned stimulus. In stimulus discrimination, the organism learns to differentiate its responses to related stimuli.

 CONCEPT 5.5
By learning to differentiate among related stimuli, we are able to fine-tune our responses to the environment.

Stimulus generalization has survival value. It allows us to respond to a range of stimuli that are similar to an original threatening stimulus. Perhaps you were menaced or bitten by a large dog when you were young. Because of stimulus generalization, you may find yourself tensing up whenever you see a large dog approaching. Not all large dogs are dangerous, of course, but stimulus generalization helps prepare us just in case.

Have you ever walked into a room and suddenly felt uncomfortable or anxious for no apparent reason? Your emotional reaction may be a conditioned response to generalized stimuli in the environment that are similar to cues associated with unpleasant experiences in the past. Perhaps, too, you may have experienced déjà-vu—a feeling of having been in a place before when you've never actually been there. Stimulus generalization provides one explanation of such experiences. The feeling of familiarity in novel situations may involve a process of conditioning in which responses are evoked by generalized stimuli in these new environments that resemble conditioned stimuli encountered before. A fleeting odor, the way light bounces off a ceiling, even the color of walls—all are cues that may evoke conditioned responses acquired in other settings.

Stimulus discrimination, the ability to differentiate among related stimuli, represents the opposite side of the coin to stimulus generalization. This ability allows us to fine-tune our responses to the environment. Suppose, for example, that an animal in a laboratory study receives a mild shock shortly after exposure to a CS (a tone) (Domjan, 2005). After a few pairings of the tone and shock, the animal shows signs of fear (cowering, urinating) to the tone alone. The tone is the CS, the shock is the US, and the pairing of the two leads to the acquisition of a CR of fear to the tone alone. Now, let's say the pairings of the tone and the shock continue but are interspersed with a tone of a higher pitch that is not accompanied by a shock. What happens next is that the animal learns to discriminate between the two stimuli, responding with fear to the original tone but remaining calm when the higher-pitched tone is sounded.

Stimulus discrimination in daily life allows us to differentiate between threatening and nonthreatening stimuli. For example, through repeated uneventful encounters with certain breeds of dogs, we may learn to respond with fear to a large dog of an unfamiliar breed but not to the friendly Labrador that lives next door. Figure 5.4 illustrates the processes of stimulus generalization and stimulus discrimination.

Higher-Order Conditioning   In **higher-order conditioning**, a new stimulus becomes a conditioned stimulus when it is paired with an established conditioned stimulus that already elicits the conditioned response (see Figure 5.5). What is learned is the association between two conditioned stimuli, or a CS-CS connection. Consider, for example, a couple that has favorite song that was previously associated with positive feelings they had towards one another when they first met or fell in love. The song becomes a conditioned stimulus (CS) that elicits these positive feelings (the CR). Other cues associated with the song, such as the jingle associated with the radio station that regularly played the song or even the name of the singer, may become conditioned stimuli that elicit a similar response. Concept Chart 5.1 presents an overview of the major concepts in classical conditioning.

Stimulus Characteristics That Strengthen Conditioned Responses   Psychologists have identified several key factors relating to the timing and intensity of stimuli that serve to strengthen conditioned responses:

stimulus discrimination   The tendency to differentiate among stimuli so that stimuli that are related to the original conditioned stimulus, but not identical to it, fail to elicit a conditioned response.
higher-order conditioning   The process by which a new stimulus comes to elicit a conditioned response as a result of its being paired with a conditioned stimulus that already elicits the conditioned response.

Figure 5.5
Higher-Order Conditioning
In higher-order conditioning, a previously neutral stimulus becomes a conditioned stimulus when it is paired with an already established conditioned stimulus.

Original Conditioning

Higher-Order Conditioning

 CONCEPT 5.6

The strength of a classically conditioned response depends on the frequency of pairings and the timing of the stimuli, as well as the intensity of the US.

Online Study Center
Improve Your Grade
Tutorials: Understanding Classical Conditioning

1. *Frequency of pairings.* Generally, the more often the CS is paired with the US, the stronger and more reliable the conditioned response will be. In some cases, however, even a single pairing can produce a strong conditioned response. An airline passenger who experiences a sudden free-fall during a flight may develop an immediate and enduring fear of flying.

2. *Timing.* The strongest conditioned responses occur when the CS is presented first and remains present throughout the administration of the US. Weaker conditioned responses develop when the CS is presented first but is withdrawn before the US is introduced. Other timing sequences, such as the simultaneous presentation of the CS and US, produce even weaker conditioned responses, if any at all.

3. *Intensity of US.* A stronger US will typically lead to faster conditioning than a weaker one. For example, a puff of air (US) may be delivered shortly after a conditioned stimulus (e.g., a tone or light) is presented. The air puff produces a reflexive eye-blinking response (UR). After a few pairings, a conditioned eye-blink (CR) occurs in response to the CS (tone or light) alone. A stronger air puff will lead to faster conditioning than a weaker one.

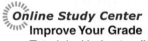 **CONCEPT CHART 5.1   Key Concepts in Classical Conditioning**

Concept	Description	Example: Fear of Dentistry
Classical conditioning	A form of learning in which a response identical or similar to one originally elicited by an unconditioned stimulus (US) is made in response to a conditioned stimulus (CS) based on the pairing of the two stimuli	Pairing pain during dental visits with cues (stimuli) in the dentist's office leads to the development of a fear response to the environmental cues alone.
Extinction	Gradual weakening and eventual disappearance of the conditioned response (CR) when the CS is repeatedly presented without the US	The use of anesthetics and painless dental techniques leads to the gradual reduction and elimination of fear of dentistry.
Spontaneous recovery	Spontaneous return of the CR sometime after extinction occurs	Fear of dentistry returns spontaneously a few months or years after extinction
Stimulus generalization	CR evoked by stimuli that are similar to the original CS	Person experiences fear when visiting the office of a new dentist.
Stimulus discrimination	CR not evoked by stimuli that are related but not identical to the CS	Person experiences fear in response to the sight of a dentist's drill but not to equipment used for cleaning teeth.
Higher-order conditioning	CR evoked by a new stimulus that is paired with a CS that already elicits the response	Person cringes upon hearing the dentist's name.

CONCEPT 5.7

In Rescorla's view, classical conditioning involves a cognitive process by which organisms learn to anticipate events based on cues or signals that reliably predict the events.

A Cognitive Perspective on Classical Conditioning

Psychologist Robert Rescorla (1967, 1988) challenged the conventional behaviorist view that classical conditioning is explained simply by the repeated pairings of a previously neutral stimulus and an unconditioned stimulus. He argued that conditioning depends on the informational value that the conditioned stimulus acquires in *predicting* the occurrence of the unconditioned stimulus. Consider a study in which Rescorla exposed laboratory rats to a series of electric shocks (US) that were preceded by a tone (CS) either on *all* occasions or on *most*, but not all, occasions. The rats whose shocks were always preceded by the tone learned a conditioned response of fear to the tone alone, whereas the rats whose shocks were usually, but not always, preceded by the tone did not. Rescorla argued that classical conditioning depends on more than the simple pairing of stimuli; it requires that the CS come to reliably predict the occurrence of the US.

Rescorla adopted a cognitive perspective in explaining classical conditioning. To Rescorla, humans and other animals actively seek information that helps them predict the occurrence of important events in their environment. Pavlov's conditioned stimuli were cues that his laboratory dogs used to predict that food was coming. One stimulus (the bell or tone) provided important information about the occurrence of another (food) (Holland & Ball, 2003).

Rescorla's model has important survival implications. Dogs and other animals may be more likely to survive if they learn to respond with salivation to cues that food is present, since salivation helps them prepare to swallow food. Animals are also more likely to survive if they learn a fear response (heightened bodily arousal) to cues that signal the presence of threatening stimuli. Consider an animal that hears a sound or gets a whiff of an odor (a CS) previously associated with the presence of a particular predator (a US). By responding quickly with heightened arousal to such a stimulus, the animal is better prepared to take defensive action if the predator appears. Thus, classical conditioning serves as a kind of built-in early warning system.

Rescorla's model also explains why you are likely to develop a fear of dentistry more quickly if you experience pain during each dental visit than if you have pain only every now and then. In other words, the more reliably the CS (dental cues) signals the occurrence of the US (pain), the stronger the conditioned response is likely to be.

Examples of Classical Conditioning

Pavlov's studies might merit only a footnote in the history of psychology if classical conditioning were limited to the salivary responses of dogs. But Pavlovian conditioning played an important role in psychology, especially in the development of behaviorism. John B. Watson, the founder of behaviorism, believed that Pavlov's principles of conditioning could explain emotional responses in humans. In 1919, Watson set out with Rosalie Rayner, a student who was later to become his wife, to prove that a fear response could be acquired through classical conditioning. (As noted in the Pioneers box on page 189, Watson left his mark not only on psychology, but also on the world of advertising.) After taking a look at Watson and Rayner's experiment, we consider other examples of conditioning in humans.

Classical Conditioning of Fear Responses   As their subject, Watson and Rayner selected an 11-month-old boy whom they called Albert B., but who is better known in the annals of psychology as "Little Albert" (Watson & Rayner, 1920). Albert had previously shown no fear of a white rat that was placed near him and had even reached out to stroke the animal (see Figure 5.6). In the experimental procedure, the rat was placed close to Albert, and as he reached for it, the experimenters

CONCEPT 5.8

Classical conditioning helps explain the development of conditioned emotional reactions, such as conditioned fear responses.

Figure 5.6 The Conditioning of "Little Albert"

Before Conditioning	During Conditioning	After Conditioning	Stimulus Generalization
Child shows no fear of white rat	White rat (CS) is paired with loud sound (US) that naturally evokes fear response	Child shows fear (CR) of white rat alone (CS)	Child shows fear reaction (CR) to related stimuli

John Watson and Rosalie Rayner with Little Albert

banged a steel bar with a hammer just behind his head, creating a loud sound. Watson believed that loud sounds naturally make infants cringe and shudder with fear. Sure enough, Albert showed signs of fear when the bar was struck—crying and burying his face in the mattress. Watson and Rayner then repeatedly paired the rat and the loud sound, which resulted in Albert's developing a fear response to the sight of the rat alone. Such an acquired fear response is called a **conditioned emotional reaction (CER)**. Later experiments showed that Albert's fear response had generalized to other furry stimuli, including a dog, a rabbit, and even a Santa Claus mask that Watson had worn.

Let us examine the Watson and Rayner study by applying what we know about classical conditioning. Before conditioning, Albert showed no fear of the white rat; it was a neutral stimulus. The unconditioned stimulus (US) was the loud banging sound, a stimulus that naturally elicits a fear response (UR) in young children. Through repeated pairings of the white rat and the banging sound (US), the white rat alone (CS) came to elicit a fear response (CR).

Though the Little Albert experiment is among the most famous studies in psychology, it would not pass muster with the stricter ethical standards in place today. Exposing a child to intense fear, even with the parents' permission, fails to adhere to the responsibility that investigators have to safeguard the welfare of their research subjects. In addition, Watson and Rayner made no attempt to undo or extinguish Albert's fear of white rats, as present ethical codes would require, although they did discuss techniques they might use to do so.

Stimulus Generalization and Discrimination In one example, a man became trapped behind a refrigerator while he was helping a friend move and nearly suffocated. He developed a fear of tight, enclosed spaces that generalized to riding on small, crowded elevators. As the result of stimulus discrimination, however, he showed no fear of riding on larger, uncrowded elevators.

conditioned emotional reaction (CER)
An emotional response to a particular stimulus acquired through classical conditioning.

THE PIONEERS | Mr. Watson Goes to Madison Avenue

John Watson

It didn't matter on that September day in 1920 that John B. Watson was a prominent psychologist and educator, as well as the founder of a new school of psychology called behaviorism. The only thing that mattered to the president of Johns Hopkins University, where Watson was a professor, was that Watson, a married man, was having an illicit affair with Rosalie Rayner, his young assistant with whom he had conducted the now-famous study of "Little Albert." Watson was forced to resign his academic appointment. Just as the movement he had founded was gathering steam in academic circles, Watson, at the age of forty-two, found his academic career abruptly ended (Hunt, 1993). After his divorce from his first wife became final, Watson married Rosalie and had two children with her. Sadly, Rosalie died in her mid-thirties of complications from dysentery.

After leaving academia, Watson found a job as a psychological consultant to a large advertising firm, the J. Walter Thompson Agency. Relying on his knowledge of psychology and his personal salesmanship, he went on to develop some of the firm's most successful advertising campaigns. His work with the Maxwell House Coffee account helped make the "coffee break" an American institution.

Although it may seem surprising that the father of behaviorism found a niche in the world of advertising, Watson's success in this field rested on his application of the principles of classical conditioning (Buckley, 1989). He suggested that manufacturers pair the presentation of their products in print advertisements with emotionally arousing cues, such as sexual stimuli. His advertising campaign for a popular toothpaste of the time, Pebeco, featured a seductively dressed young woman smoking a cigarette. In conditioning terms, the toothpaste represents the CS and the attractive young woman, the US. Today, thanks in part to Mr. Watson, we are bombarded with advertisements and television commercials that pair products with sexual cues and other emotionally arousing stimuli. Advertisers hope their products will elicit sexual arousal and positive emotions that will in turn spur sales.

Many **phobias**, or excessive fears, such as Albert's fear of white rats or the fear of dentistry, may be acquired through classical conditioning. In one example, a 34-year-old woman had been terrified of riding on elevators ever since a childhood incident in which she and her grandmother were trapped on an elevator for hours. For her, the single pairing of previously neutral stimuli (cues associated with riding on elevators) and a traumatic experience was sufficient to produce an enduring phobia (fear of elevators). In some cases, the original conditioning experiences may be lost to memory, or they may have occurred even before language developed (as in Albert's case).

Early work on the conditioning of fear responses set the stage for the development of a model of therapy called **behavior therapy**, which is the systematic application of the principles of learning to help people overcome phobias and other problem behaviors, including addictive behaviors, sexual dysfunctions, and childhood behavior problems. We discuss specific applications of behavior therapy in Chapter 14.

Classical Conditioning of Positive Emotions   It's not just negative emotions like fear that can be classically conditioned. Perhaps you've had the experience of suddenly smiling or feeling cheerful, or experiencing a tinge of sexual arousal, when you hear a certain song on the radio. Chances are the song evoked past experiences associated with pleasant emotions or sexual arousal. Similarly, feelings of nostalgia may represent classically conditioned responses elicited by stimuli associated with pleasant experiences in the past—a whiff of perfume or perhaps even the mist in the air on a spring day.

💡 **CONCEPT 5.9**
Feelings of nostalgia may be conditioned responses elicited by stimuli that were associated with pleasant experiences in the past.

phobias   Excessive fears of particular objects or situations.

behavior therapy   A form of therapy that involves the systematic application of the principles of learning.

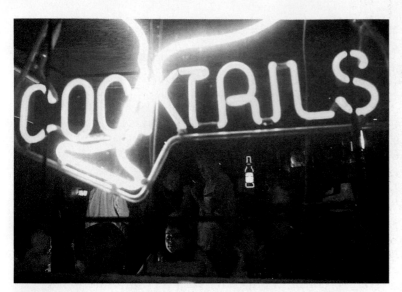

Drug Cravings as Conditioned Responses Drug cravings may be conditioned responses elicited by exposure to cues (conditioned stimuli) associated with drug-using behavior.

💡 **CONCEPT 5.10**
Drug cravings and taste aversions may be acquired through classical conditioning.

🌟 *Online Study Center*
Improve Your Grade
Tutorials: Classical Conditioning in the Development of Taste Aversions

conditioned taste aversions Aversions to particular tastes acquired through classical conditioning.

Classical Conditioning of Drug Cravings People with chemical dependencies frequently encounter drug cravings, especially when they undergo drug withdrawal or go "cold turkey." Though cravings may have a physiological basis (they constitute part of the withdrawal syndrome for addictive drugs), classical conditioning can also contribute to these strong desires. Cravings may be elicited by cues in the environment that were associated with previous drug use (O'Brien et al., 1992). A person battling alcoholism who goes "on the wagon" may experience strong cravings for a drink whenever he or she passes a familiar "watering hole" or socializes with former "drinking buddies." Cravings may represent conditioned responses that continue to be elicited long after the physiological signs of withdrawal have passed.

The conditioning model of drug cravings is supported by research showing that people with alcoholism salivate more at the sight and odor of alcohol than do nonalcoholic subjects (Monti et al., 1987). Salivating to the sound of a tone may be harmless enough, but salivating when looking at a picture of a Scotch bottle in a magazine can be dangerous to a person struggling with alcoholism. Not surprisingly, drug counselors encourage recovering drug and alcohol abusers to avoid cues associated with their former drug-use patterns.

Classical Conditioning of Taste Aversions The principles of classical conditioning can also be used to explain **conditioned taste aversions**, such as my disgust for eggs (Limebeer & Parker, 2000). Psychologist John Garcia was the first to demonstrate experimentally the role of classical conditioning in the acquisition of taste aversions. Garcia and his colleague Bob Koelling noticed something interesting in the behavior of rats that had been exposed to nausea-inducing radiation (Garcia & Koelling, 1966). The rats developed an aversion or "conditioned nausea" to flavored water sweetened with saccharine when the water was paired with the nausea-producing radiation. In classical conditioning terms, the radiation is the US; the nausea it produces is the UR; the flavored water is the CS; and the aversion (nausea) the CS elicits on its own is the CR.

In related work, Garcia was able to demonstrate that an aversion to a particular food could also be classically conditioned by administering a nausea-inducing drug after the rats ate the food (Garcia & Koelling, 1971). Moreover, taste aversions can be acquired even when the CS (the taste of the food) is presented a few hours before the US (the nausea-inducing stimulus) is administered (Domjan, 2005). This discovery shocked many experimenters in the field, who had long believed that classical conditioning could only occur when the CS is followed almost immediately by the US. Moreover, Garcia and his colleagues were able to demonstrate that conditioned taste aversions could be acquired on the basis of a single pairing of the flavor of a food or drink with a nausea-inducing stimulus.

Like other forms of classical conditioning, conditioned taste aversions have clear survival benefits. Our ancestors lived without the benefit of refrigeration or preservatives. Acquiring an aversion to foods whose rancid smells and tastes sickened them would have helped them avoid such foods in the future.

In a classic study that literally applied the principles of classical conditioning on the range, John Garcia and his colleagues came up with an ingenious way to help sheep ranchers protect their sheep from coyotes (Gustavson & Garcia, 1974; Gustavson et al., 1974). At the time of the study, free-ranging coyotes were killing thousands of sheep, and ranchers seeking to protect their flocks were killing so

Conditioned Taste Aversion in Coyotes Experimenters left sheep carcasses on the range after injecting them with a nausea-producing chemical. Shortly after eating the meat from one of these carcasses, a coyote would fall to the ground with extreme nausea.

John Garcia

💡 **CONCEPT 5.11**
Investigators have found that even immune-system responses can be classically conditioned.

many coyotes that their survival as a species was endangered. It was therefore important to find a way of stopping the coyotes' destructive behavior without killing them. As an experiment, the researchers injected sheep carcasses with a poison that would sicken but not kill the coyotes and scattered the carcasses over the range. Not only did sheep killings drop; some coyotes developed such an aversion to the taste of the sheep meat that they ran away just at the sight or smell of sheep. The Thinking Critically section at the end of the chapter asks you to break down this experiment in classical conditioning terms.

Conditioning the Immune System

In a landmark study, Robert Ader and Nicholas Cohen (1982) showed that classical conditioning extends even to the workings of the **immune system**. The immune system is the body system that protects us from disease-causing organisms. These researchers simultaneously gave rats saccharin-sweetened water (CS) and a drug (US) that suppresses immune-system responses (the UR). After several pairings, immune suppression (CR) occurred in response to drinking the sweetened water alone. Other investigators have found that conditioned immune suppression occurs with different conditioned stimuli, such as odors and sounds, as well as in different species, including guinea pigs, mice, and even humans (Kusnecov, 2001).

The ability to learn an immune-suppressant response through classical conditioning may have important health implications for humans. In people who receive organ transplants, the immune system attacks the transplanted organs as foreign objects. Perhaps classical conditioning can be used to suppress the tendency of the body to reject transplanted organs, lessening the need for immune-suppressant drugs. This hope was bolstered by findings that classical conditioning of immune suppression increased the survival rate of mice that had undergone heart-tissue transplants (Grochowicz et al., 1991). Whether similar procedures can be used successfully with humans who undergo organ transplants remains to be seen. We may also be able to use classical conditioning to give the immune system a boost in its fight against disease, perhaps even strengthening the body's ability to defend itself against cancer (Hollis, 1997). One intriguing possibility involves pairing odors and other conditioned stimuli with drugs that enhance the functioning of the immune system. These stimuli might be used to trigger an immune-system response on their own, lessening the need for drugs that may have adverse side effects.

immune system   The body's system of defense against disease.

MODULE 5.1 REVIEW

Classical Conditioning: Learning Through Association

RECITE IT

What is learning?

- Psychologists generally define learning as a relatively permanent change in behavior that results from experience.

What is classical conditioning?

- Classical conditioning is a process of learning in which the pairing of two stimuli leads to a response to one stimulus that is the same as or similar to the response previously elicited by the other stimulus.

What roles do extinction, spontaneous recovery, stimulus generalization, discrimination, and higher-order conditioning play in classical conditioning?

- Extinction is the process by which learned responses gradually weaken and eventually disappear when the conditioned stimulus (CS) is presented repeatedly in the absence of the unconditioned stimulus (US).

- Spontaneous recovery is the return of the conditioned response some time after extinction.

- Stimulus generalization refers to the tendency of stimuli that are similar to the conditioned stimulus to elicit a conditioned response.

- Through stimulus discrimination, organisms learn to differentiate among stimuli so that stimuli that are related to the conditioned stimulus, but not identical to it, fail to elicit a conditioned response.

- Higher-order conditioning refers to learning in which a new stimulus acquires the ability to elicit a conditioned response after it is paired with an established conditioned stimulus that already produces the conditioned response.

What stimulus characteristics strengthen conditioned responses?

- Factors related to the strength of conditioned responses include the frequency of the pairings of the conditioned stimulus and unconditioned stimulus, the timing of the presentation of the two stimuli, and the intensity of the unconditioned stimulus.

What is the cognitive perspective on classical conditioning?

- Developed by Robert Rescorla, the cognitive perspective on classical conditioning holds that conditioning depends on the informational value that the conditioned stimulus acquires in predicting the occurrence of the unconditioned stimulus. According to this model, humans and other animals actively seek information that helps them make predictions about important events in their environment; conditioned stimuli are cues that they use to make these predictions.

What are some examples of classical conditioning in daily life?

- Examples of classical conditioning in daily life include the acquisition of fear responses and taste aversions. Classical conditioning also plays a role in positive emotions and drug cravings.

RECALL IT

1. The process by which conditioned responses occur in response to stimuli that are similar to conditioned stimuli is called _____.

2. Which of the following does *not* affect the strength of conditioned responses?
   a. frequency of pairings of the CS with the US
   b. timing of the presentation of the CS and US
   c. intensity of the US
   d. alternation of a US-CS presentation with a CR-UR presentation

3. In John Garcia's study of conditioned taste aversions, nausea-inducing radiation was the
   a. UR.   b. CS.   c. US.   d. CR.

4. Robert Rescorla formulated a cognitive model of classical conditioning that views learning as a process in which animals learn to respond to stimuli that have _____ value.

5. In Watson and Rayner's study of "Little Albert," the child became frightened of a white rat and similar stimuli because
   a. children are naturally afraid of white rats.
   b. a loud noise occurred whenever the rat was in Albert's presence.
   c. the rat was repeatedly paired with a neutral stimulus.
   d. Albert had a traumatic experience with a rat.

THINK ABOUT IT

- Can you think of any examples of classical conditioning in your daily life? For example, some people experience emotional reactions when they hear certain music or sounds or get a whiff of certain odors. How might you explain the origins of these responses in classical conditioning terms?

- Have you developed any fears you find troubling or that interfere with your daily life? Based on your reading of the chapter, what do you think might be the origin of these fears? How are you coping with them? Have you talked to anyone about them? Is there anyone you might contact to help you overcome them, such as a college health official or a health care provider or clinic in your area?

MODULE 5.2

Operant Conditioning: Learning Through Consequences

- What is Thorndike's Law of Effect?
- What is operant conditioning?
- What are the different types of reinforcers?
- What are schedules of reinforcement, and how do they differ?
- How are schedules of reinforcement related to learning?
- What are the differences in the effects of reinforcement and punishment?
- What are some applications of operant conditioning?

Online Study Center
Improve Your Grade
Tutorials: Reinforcement and Punishment in Operant Conditioning

Classical conditioning can explain how we learn relatively simple, reflexive responses, such as salivation and eye-blinks, as well as emotional responses associated with fear and disgust. But classical conditioning cannot explain how we learn the more complex behaviors that are part and parcel of our daily experiences. You get up in the morning, dress, go to work or school, prepare meals, take care of household chores, run errands, socialize with friends, and perhaps have an hour or two to relax at the end of the day. To account for such behaviors, we need to consider a form of learning called *operant conditioning*. With classical conditioning, we examined learning that results from the association between stimuli before a response occurs. With operant conditioning, we explore learning that results from the association of a response with its consequences, such as rewards and punishments. In this form of learning, responses are acquired and strengthened by the effects they have in the environment.

Though classical and operant conditioning clearly represent different forms of learning, they appear to be related at a more basic level. Both involve learning relationships between predictors and outcomes (Brembs, 2003). In classical conditioning, the organism learns that a certain stimulus, called a conditioned stimulus, predicts the occurrence of another stimulus, the unconditioned stimulus. In operant conditioning, the predictor is the organism's own behavior, or *operant response*. The organism learns to reliably predict the occurrence of a particular consequence (reward or punishment) based on its own behavior.

In our survey of operant conditioning, we focus on the contributions of two American psychologists: Edward Thorndike, whose Law of Effect was the first systematic attempt to describe how behavior is affected by its consequences, and B. F. Skinner, whose experimental work laid out many of the principles of operant conditioning.

Thorndike and the Law of Effect

Edward Thorndike (1874–1947) used animals in his studies of learning because he found them easier to work with than people (Hunt, 1993). He constructed a device called a "puzzle box": a cage in which the animal (usually a cat) had to perform a simple act (such as pulling a looped string or pushing a pedal) in order to make its escape and reach a dish of food placed within its view just outside the cage (see Figure 5.7). The animal would first engage in seemingly random behaviors until it accidentally performed the response that released the door. Thorndike argued that the animals did not employ reasoning, insight, or any other form of higher intelligence to find their way to the exit. Rather, it was through a random process of *trial and error* that they gradually eliminated useless responses and eventually

Figure 5.7 Thorndike's Puzzle Box
Cats placed in Thorndike's puzzle box learned to make their escape through a random process of trial and error.

CONCEPT 5.12
According to Thorndike's Law of Effect, we are more likely to repeat responses that have satisfying effects and are less likely to repeat those that lead to discomfort.

CONCEPT 5.13
B. F. Skinner believed that human behavior is completely determined by environmental and genetic influences and that the concept of free will is an illusion or myth.

Law of Effect Thorndike's principle that responses that have satisfying effects are more likely to recur, while those that have unpleasant effects are less likely to recur.

radical behaviorism The philosophical position that free will is an illusion or myth and that human and animal behavior is completely determined by environmental and genetic influences.

reinforcer A stimulus event that strengthens the response it follows.

operant conditioning The process of learning in which the manipulation of the consequences of a response influences the likelihood or probability of the response occurring.

chanced upon the successful behavior. Successful responses were then "stamped in" by the pleasure they produced and became more likely to be repeated in the future.

Based on his observations, Thorndike (1905) proposed a principle that he called the **Law of Effect**, which holds that the tendency for a response to occur depends on the effects it has on the environment. More specifically, Thorndike's Law of Effect states that responses that have satisfying effects are strengthened and become more likely to occur again in a given situation, while responses that lead to discomfort are weakened and become less likely to recur. Modern psychologists call the first part of the Law of Effect *reinforcement* and the second part, *punishment* (L. T. Benjamin, 1988).

Thorndike went on to study how the principles of animal learning that he formulated could be applied to human behavior and especially to education. He believed that while human behavior is certainly more complex than animal behavior, it, too, can be explained on the basis of trial-and-error learning in which accidental successes become "stamped in" by positive consequences.

B. F. Skinner and Operant Conditioning

Thorndike laid the groundwork for an explanation of learning based on the association between responses and their consequences. It would fall to another American psychologist, B. F. Skinner (1904–1990), to develop a more formal model of this type of learning, which he called *operant conditioning*.

Skinner was arguably not only the most famous psychologist of his time, but also the most controversial. What made him famous was his ability to bring behaviorist principles into the public eye through his books, articles in popular magazines, and public appearances. What made him controversial was his belief in **radical behaviorism**, which holds that behavior, whether animal or human, is completely determined by environmental and genetic influences. Free will, according to Skinner, is but an illusion or a myth. Though the staunch behaviorism he espoused was controversial in his own time and remains so today, there is no doubt that his concept of operant conditioning alone merits him a place among the pioneers of modern psychology.

Like Watson, Skinner was a strict behaviorist who believed that psychologists should limit themselves to the study of observable behavior. Because "private events," such as thoughts and feelings, cannot be observed, he believed they have no place in a scientific account of behavior. For Skinner, the mind was a "black box" whose contents cannot be illuminated by science.

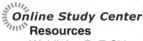
Online Study Center
Resources
Weblinks: B. F. Skinner Foundation

Skinner allowed that some responses occur reflexively, as Pavlov had demonstrated. But classical conditioning is limited to explaining how new stimuli can elicit existing behaviors, such as salivation. It cannot account for new behaviors, such as the behavior of the experimental animals in Thorndike's puzzle box. Skinner found in Thorndike's work a guiding principle that behavior is shaped by its consequences. However, not wanting to speculate about internal mental states, he rejected Thorndike's concept that consequences influence behavior because they produce "satisfying" effects. Skinner used a more objective term, **reinforcer**, to describe any stimulus event that increases the likelihood that the behavior it follows will be repeated.

We identify reinforcers based on the effects they have on strengthening the responses they follow—that is, increasing the frequency or likelihood of occurrence of these responses. If praising a child for saying "please" before making a request makes the response (saying please) more likely to occur again, then praise is a reinforcer.

💡 **CONCEPT 5.14**

Skinner developed the principles of operant conditioning, a form of learning in which organisms learn responses that lead to positive or rewarding effects.

Skinner coined the term **operant conditioning** to describe the process of learning by which responses are strengthened through manipulating the effects or consequences that follow them. Through this form of learning, organisms learn responses that produce positive or rewarding effects. The responses themselves are called *operants* because they operate on, or act upon, the environment. Over time, a well-trained operant response, such as saying please before making a request, becomes a habit (Staddon & Cerutti, 2003). Similarly, if teachers respond to questions in class only when students first raise their hands, students may quickly develop the habit of raising their hands before asking questions.

Skinner focused much of his experimental work on manipulating reinforcers to observe the effects they had on animal behavior (see the Pioneers box). He used

THE PIONEERS   The Making of a Behaviorist

B. F. Skinner

Burrhus Frederic Skinner was raised in a small town in Pennsylvania. Something of a tinkerer as a boy, he was fond of building things—especially elaborate contraptions (Hunt, 1993). Later, as a psychologist, he used his mechanical aptitude to construct laboratory equipment for studying the behavior of animals (including the now-famous "Skinner box"). Skinner did not set out to become a psychologist. He majored in English in college and upon graduating tried his hand at writing. He gave up a writing career after a year because he realized he had nothing to say about human behavior. Instead, he turned to psychology, believing that the understanding of human behavior is best approached by scientific study.

Skinner worked mostly with rats and pigeons. He first focused his research on classically conditioned responses, but he soon began to explore the role of reinforcement—the environmental consequences that serve to strengthen behaviors. He charted the principles of reinforcement, a body of work that continues to inform our understanding of how behavior is shaped by its consequences. Ironically, in 1948, the would-be writer who turned to psychology produced one of the most widely read novels of its time: *Walden Two*, a fictional account of a utopian society in which principles of reinforcement help people lead happier and more productive, fulfilling lives. *Walden Two* gave millions of college students their first exposure to the principles of operant conditioning. In a self-deprecating way, Skinner later minimized his impact on the world, telling an interviewer that he had more of an effect on rats and pigeons than he had on people (cited in Hunt, 1993).

CONCEPT 5.15
Skinner showed how superstitious behavior can be learned through the coincidental pairing of responses and reinforcement.

REALITY CHECK

THE CLAIM Skinner raised his daughter in a Skinner box.

THE EVIDENCE This widely circulated claim is akin to many urban myths, such as the belief that alligators live in the New York subways. Though Skinner fabricated a temperature-controlled crib for his infant daughter Deborah to keep her warm during cold Minnesota winters, he never placed her in a Skinner box, the laboratory apparatus used to conduct studies of operant conditioning with pigeons and other animals (Mikkelson & Mikkelson, 2004).

THE TAKE-AWAY MESSAGE Skinner did not use a Skinner box to raise his daughter or to conduct experiments on her. Following publication of a new book that rekindled these old rumors, Deborah Skinner wrote a newspaper article to set the record straight. About putting her in a Skinner box, Deborah wrote, "My father did nothing of the sort" (Buzan, 2004).

Skinner box An experimental apparatus developed by B. F. Skinner for studying relationships between reinforcement and behavior.

superstitious behavior In Skinner's view, behavior acquired through coincidental association of a response and a reinforcement.

a device we now call a **Skinner box**. The Skinner box is a cage that contains a food-release mechanism that the animal activates when it responds in a certain way—for example, by pressing a lever or pushing a button. In a typical experiment, a pigeon would be deprived of food and placed in the cage. Whenever the pigeon pecked a button at the side of the cage, a food pellet would drop into its food tray (Skinner, 1938). It usually took a while before the pigeon, by trial and error, happened to peck the button that released the food pellet. But after a few repetitions of the behavior followed by the reinforcer, the pigeon would peck fast and furiously until it had had its fill. The rate of response was recorded on a mechanical device so the experimenter did not have to be present to observe the responses.

Skinner observed that the longer reinforcement is delayed, the weaker its effects will be. An animal in the Skinner box or a child in the classroom will learn the correct responses faster when reinforcement follows the response as quickly as possible. In general, learning progresses more slowly as the delay between response and reinforcement increases.

Skinner also showed how operant conditioning could explain some forms of **superstitious behavior**. Consider a baseball player who hits a home run after a long slump and then wears the same pair of socks he had on at the time for good luck in every remaining game of the season. What is the basis of such superstitious behavior? An intriguing experiment performed by Skinner provides an answer.

Skinner (1948) set up the feeding mechanism in the Skinner box to deliver a food pellet to a pigeon's feeding tray every fifteen seconds regardless of the bird's behavior. He soon noticed that the feeding schedule led to the development of some peculiar behaviors. One pigeon kept bobbing its head up and down, while another spun around and around in a counterclockwise direction. Another kept flapping its wings. As Skinner explained it, these were the behaviors the pigeons happened to be performing when reinforcement was delivered to them. In other words, these useless behaviors were coincidentally reinforced. The birds acted as though it was the behavior—the bobbing, spinning, and wing flapping—that brought about the food reward.

Skinner's experiment showed that superstitious behavior can be acquired through the coincidental association of a response and a reinforcement (A. P. White & Liu, 1995). The superstitious behavior of the baseball player can be understood in terms of mistaking a mere coincidence between a response (wearing a particular pair of socks) and a reinforcement (the home run) for a connection between the two.

Many commonly held superstitions, from not stepping on cracks in the sidewalk to throwing salt over one's shoulder for good luck, are part of our cultural heritage, handed down from generation to generation. Perhaps there was a time when these behaviors were accidentally reinforced, but they have become so much a part of our cultural tradition that people no longer recall their origins.

In the next sections, we review the basic principles of operant conditioning. Before proceeding, you may wish to review Table 5.1, which compares classical and operant conditioning.

TABLE 5.1   Comparison of Classical and Operant Conditioning

Type of Conditioning	Basis of Learning	Adaptive Value
Classical conditioning	Association between stimuli	Provides a means of learning to respond to stimuli that signal the occurrence of other stimuli
Operant conditioning	Association between behavior and consequences	Provides a means of learning behaviors that have rewarding outcomes or that avoid pain or other aversive stimuli

Figure 5.8   Discriminative Stimulus in a Skinner Box
Here we see a rat in a Skinner box, an apparatus used to study operant conditioning. When the rat presses the bar, it receives a pellet of food or a drop of water as a reinforcer. The light is a discriminative stimulus, a cue that signals that the reinforcer is available. The rat learns to press the lever only when the light is on.

Red Light, Green Light
A green light is a discriminative stimulus signaling that driving a car through an intersection is likely to be reinforced by a safe passage through the intersection.

 CONCEPT 5.16
Discriminative stimuli set the stage for reinforcement—a useful thing to know if you want to ask someone for a favor.

CONCEPT 5.17
In positive reinforcement, a response is strengthened when it is followed by the introduction of a stimulus, such as a reward, whereas in negative reinforcement, a response is strengthened when it leads to the removal of an unpleasant or aversive stimulus.

discriminative stimulus   A cue that signals that reinforcement is available if the subject makes a particular response.
positive reinforcement   The strengthening of a response through the introduction of a stimulus following the response.
negative reinforcement   The strengthening of a response through the removal of a stimulus after the response occurs.

Principles of Operant Conditioning

Experimental work by Skinner and other psychologists established the basic principles of operant conditioning, including those we consider here: discriminative stimuli, positive and negative reinforcement, primary and secondary reinforcers, shaping, and extinction.

Discriminative Stimuli   Put a rat in a Skinner box and reinforce it with food when it presses a bar, but only if it makes that response when a light is turned on. When the light is off, it receives no reinforcement no matter how many times it presses the bar. How do you think the rat will respond? Clearly, the rate of response will be much higher when the light is on than when it is off. The light is an example of a **discriminative stimulus**, a cue that signals that reinforcement is available if the subject makes a particular response (see Figure 5.8).

Our physical and social environment is teeming with discriminative stimuli. When is the better time to ask someone for a favor: when the person appears to be down in the dumps or is smiling and appears cheerful? You know the answer. The reason you know is that you have learned that a person's facial cues serve as discriminative stimuli that signal times when requests for help are more likely to be positively received. A green traffic light is another type of discriminative stimulus: it signals that driving a car through an intersection is likely to be reinforced by a safe passage through the intersection.

Positive and Negative Reinforcement   Skinner distinguished between two types of reinforcement, *positive reinforcement* and *negative reinforcement*. Both positive and negative reinforcement strengthen behavior. In **positive reinforcement**, a response is strengthened by the introduction of a stimulus after the response occurs. This type of stimulus is called a *positive reinforcer* or *reward* (see Figure 5.9). Examples of positive reinforcers include food, money, and social approval. You are more likely to continue working at your job if you receive a steady paycheck (a positive reinforcer) than if the checks stop coming. You are more likely to study hard for exams if your efforts are rewarded with good grades (another positive reinforcer) than if you consistently fail.

In **negative reinforcement**, a response is strengthened when it leads to the removal of an "aversive" (unpleasant or painful) stimulus. Negative reinforcers are aversive stimuli such as loud noise, cold, pain, nagging, or a child's crying. We are more likely to repeat behaviors that lead to their removal. A parent's behavior in picking up a crying baby to comfort it is negatively reinforced when the baby stops crying; in this case, the aversive stimulus of crying has been removed.

Figure 5.9   Types of Reinforcers
Behavior is strengthened through both positive and negative reinforcement. Can you think of examples of how your behavior has been influenced by positive and negative reinforcement?

Type of Reinforcer		Behavior	Reinforcer	Effect: Frequency of Behavior Increases
	Positive reinforcer	Child brushes teeth before sleep	Parent praises child	Likelihood of tooth-brushing increases
	Negative reinforcer	You take an aspirin when you have a headache	The headache pain disappears	You become more likely to take aspirin in the future when you have a headache

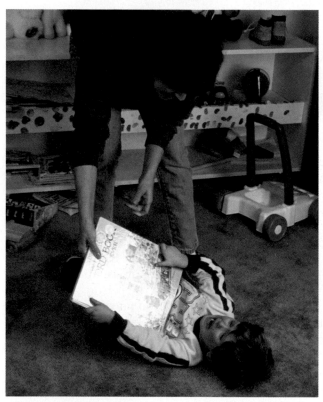

Who Is Reinforcing Whom?   Reinforcement is not a one-way street. Children and parents continually reinforce each other. By stopping a tantrum when she gets her way, the child negatively reinforces the parent. Unwittingly, perhaps, the parent positively reinforces tantrum-throwing behavior by giving in. How would you suggest the parent change these reinforcement patterns?

primary reinforcers   Reinforcers, such as food or sexual stimulation, that are naturally rewarding because they satisfy basic biological needs or drives.

secondary reinforcers   Learned reinforcers, such as money, that develop their reinforcing properties because of their association with primary reinforcers.

Note that both forms of reinforcement—positive and negative—strengthen responses. The difference is that in positive reinforcement, behaviors are strengthened when they are followed by the *introduction* of a stimulus, whereas in negative reinforcement, behaviors are strengthened when they lead to the *removal* of a stimulus.

Negative reinforcement can be a "two-way street." Crying is the only means infants have of letting us know when they are hungry or wet or have other needs. It is also an aversive stimulus to anyone within earshot. It is a negative reinforcer because parents will repeat behaviors that succeed in stopping the infant's crying. The baby's crying is positively reinforced by the parents' responses. (Like Skinner's pigeons, parents may need to do some "pecking around" to find out what Junior wants: "Let's see, he's not wet, so he must be hungry.")

Negative reinforcement may have undesirable effects in some situations. Consider a child who throws a tantrum in a toy store when the parent refuses the child's request for a particular toy. The child may have learned from past experience that tantrums get results. In operant conditioning terms, when a tantrum does get results, the child is positively reinforced for throwing the tantrum (because the parent "gives in"), while the parent is negatively reinforced for complying with the child's demands (because the tantrum, an aversive stimulus, stops). Unfortunately, this pattern of reinforcement only makes the recurrence of tantrums more likely.

Primary and Secondary Reinforcers   At sixteen months of age, my daughter Daniella became intrigued with the contents of my wallet. It wasn't those greenbacks with the pictures of Washington and Lincoln that caught her eye. No, she ignored the paper money but was fascinated with the holograms on the plastic credit cards. The point here is that some stimuli, called **primary reinforcers**, are intrinsically rewarding because they satisfy basic biological needs or drives. Their reward or reinforcement value does not depend on learning. Primary reinforcers include food, water, sleep, relief from pain or loud noise, oxygen, sexual stimulation, and novel visual stimuli, such as holograms.

Other reinforcers, called **secondary reinforcers**, acquire their reinforcement value through a learning process by which they become associated with primary reinforcers. Money is a secondary reinforcer (also called a *conditioned reinforcer*). It acquires reinforcement value because we learn it can be exchanged for more basic reinforcers, such as food or clothing. Other types of secondary reinforcers include

CONCEPT 5.18

Some reinforcers are rewarding because they satisfy basic biological needs; other reinforcers acquire reward value as the result of experience.

CONCEPT 5.19

Organisms can learn complex behaviors through a process of shaping, or reinforcement of successive approximations to the desired behaviors.

CONCEPT 5.20

In operant conditioning, extinction is the weakening and eventual elimination of a response that occurs when the response is no longer reinforced.

CONCEPT 5.21

The schedule by which reinforcements are dispensed influences the rate of learning and resistance to extinction.

shaping A process of learning that involves the reinforcement of increasingly closer approximations of the desired response.

method of successive approximations The method used to shape behavior that involves reinforcing ever-closer approximations of the desired response.

schedules of reinforcement Predetermined plans for timing the delivery of reinforcement.

schedule of continuous reinforcement A system of dispensing a reinforcement each time a response is produced.

schedule of partial reinforcement A system of dispensing a reinforcement for only a portion of responses

good grades, awards, and praise. Much of our daily behavior is influenced by secondary reinforcers in the form of expressions of approval from others.

Shaping   Rats don't naturally press levers or bars. If you place a rat in a Skinner box, it may eventually happen upon the correct response through trial and error. The experimenter can help the animal learn the correct response more quickly through a process called **shaping**. Shaping is an application of the **method of successive approximations**. In this method, the experimenter reinforces a series of responses that represent ever-closer approximations of the correct response. The experimenter may at first reinforce the rat when it moves to the part of the cage that contains the bar. Once this behavior is established, reinforcement occurs only if the animal moves closer to the bar, then closer still, then touching the bar with its paw, and then actually pressing the bar. If you have ever observed animal trainers at work, you will recognize how shaping is used to train animals to perform a complex sequence of behaviors.

We put the method of successive approximations into practice in our daily lives when we attempt to teach someone a new skill, especially one involving a complex set of behaviors. When teaching a child to swim, the instructor may deliver verbal reinforcement (telling the child he or she is doing "great") each time the child successfully performs a new step in the series of steps needed to develop proper form.

Extinction   You'll recall from Module 5.1 that extinction of classically conditioned responses occurs when the conditioned stimulus is repeatedly presented in the absence of the unconditioned stimulus. Similarly, in operant conditioning, extinction is the process by which responses are weakened and eventually eliminated when the response is repeatedly performed but is no longer reinforced. Thus, the bar-pressing response of a rat in the Skinner box will eventually be extinguished if reinforcement (food) is withheld. If you repeatedly raise your hand in class but aren't called upon, you will probably in time stop raising your hand.

Schedules of Reinforcement

In the Skinner box, an animal can be reinforced for each peck or bar press, or for some portion of pecks or bar presses. One of Skinner's major contributions was to show how these different **schedules of reinforcement**—predetermined plans for timing the delivery of reinforcement—influence learning.

In a **schedule of continuous reinforcement**, reinforcement follows each instance of the operant response. The rat in the Skinner box receives a food pellet every time it presses the lever. Similarly, if a light comes on every time you flick a light switch, you will quickly learn to flick the switch each time you enter a darkened room. Operant responses are learned most rapidly under a schedule of continuous reinforcement. However, continuous reinforcement also leads to rapid extinction when reinforcement is withheld. How long will it take before you stop flicking the light switch if the light fails to come on because the bulb needs replacing? Just one or two flicks of the switch without results may be sufficient to extinguish the response. But extinction does not mean the response is forgotten or lost to memory (Baeyens, Eelen, & Crombez, 1995). It is likely to return quickly once reinforcement is reinstated, that is, once you install a new bulb.

Responses are more resistant to extinction under a **schedule of partial reinforcement** than under a schedule of continuous reinforcement (Rescorla, 1999). In a schedule of partial reinforcement, only a portion of responses is reinforced. Because this makes it more unlikely that an absence of reinforcement will be noticed, it takes a longer time for the response to fade out.

Schedules of partial reinforcement are much more common than schedules of continuous reinforcement in daily life. Think what it would mean to be reinforced

CONCEPT 5.22
There are four types of partial-reinforcement schedules: fixed-ratio, variable-ratio, fixed-interval, and variable-interval schedules.

on a continuous basis. You would receive a reinforcer (reward) each time you came to class, cracked open a textbook, or arrived at work on time. However desirable this rate of reinforcement might seem, it is no doubt impossible to achieve in daily life. Fortunately, partial-reinforcement schedules produce overall high response rates and have the added advantage of greater resistance to extinction.

Partial reinforcement is administered under two general kinds of schedules: *ratio schedules* and *interval schedules*. In ratio schedules, reinforcement is based on the *number* of responses. In interval schedules, reinforcement is based on the *timing* of responses. Within each type, reinforcement can be administered on either a *fixed* or *variable* basis.

Figure 5.10 shows typical rates of response under different schedules of partial reinforcement. Notice how much faster response rates are in ratio schedules than in interval schedules. In accounting for this difference, we should remember that in ratio schedules, reinforcement depends on the number of responses and not on the length of time elapsed since the last reinforcement, as is the case with interval schedules.

Fixed-Ratio (FR) Schedule   In a fixed-ratio (FR) schedule, reinforcement is given after a specified number of correct responses. For example, in an "FR-6" schedule, reinforcement is given after each sixth response. The classic example of fixed-ratio schedules is piecework, in which workers are paid according to the number of items they produce. Fixed-ratio schedules produce a constant, high level of response, with a slight dip in responses occurring after each reinforcement (see Figure 5.10). On fixed-ratio schedules, the faster people work, the more items they produce and the more money they earn. However, quality may suffer if quantity alone determines how reinforcements are dispensed.

Variable-Ratio (VR) Schedule   In a variable-ratio (VR) schedule, the number of correct responses needed before reinforcement is given varies around some average number. For example, a "VR-20" schedule means that reinforcement is ad-

Figure 5.10   Rates of Response Under Different Schedules of Partial Reinforcement
Here we see rates of response we typically find under different schedules of partial reinforcement. The diagonal lines that intersect with these response curves show the times at which reinforcement is given. Notice how ratio schedules produce much faster response rates than interval schedules. In addition, with fixed schedules there is a pause following each reinforcement: short pauses in the fixed-ratio schedule, as shown in the indentions ("teeth"); and long pauses in the fixed-interval schedule, as shown in the "scalloped" effect. In contrast, both types of variable schedules show steady rates of response.

Source: Adapted from Skinner, 1961.

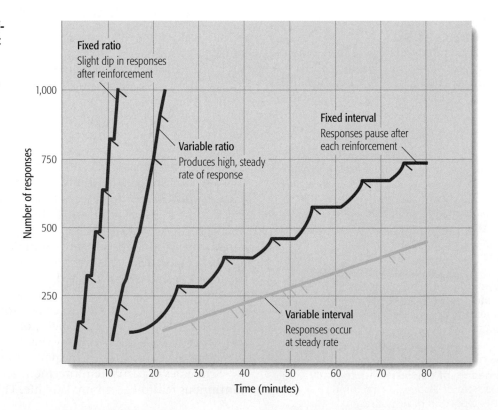

Gambling, a Variable-Ratio Problem
Gambling behavior is maintained on a variable-ratio schedule of reinforcement. Gamblers never know how many more throws of the dice or tries on a slot machine will result in a payoff. But while they are waiting for "lady luck" to strike, they are piling up losses.

ministered after an average of every twenty responses. In some instances, reinforcement may be delivered after only two, five, or ten responses; at other times, thirty or forty responses may be required. Gambling is an example of behavior that is reinforced on a variable-ratio schedule. With a slot machine, for instance, a win (reinforcement) may occur after perhaps one, two, ten, or fifty or more tries. (No wonder it's called a one-armed bandit.)

Variable-ratio schedules typically produce high, steady rates of response (see Figure 5.10). They are also more resistant to extinction than fixed-ratio schedules since one cannot reliably predict whether a given number of responses will be rewarded. Perhaps this explains why many people routinely buy state lottery tickets even though they may win only piddling amounts every now and then. As an advertisement for one state lottery puts it, "Hey, you never know."

Fixed-Interval (FI) Schedule   In a fixed-interval (FI) schedule, reinforcement is given only for a correct response made after a fixed amount of time has elapsed since the last reinforcement. On an "FI-30" schedule, for example, an animal in a Skinner box receives a food pellet if it makes the required response after an interval of thirty seconds has elapsed since the last food pellet was delivered, regardless of the number of responses it made during the thirty-second interval. Fixed-interval schedules tend to produce a "scalloped" response pattern in which the rate of response typically dips just after reinforcement and then increases as the end of the interval approaches (see Figure 5.10). Workers who receive monthly performance reviews may show more productive behaviors in the days leading up to their evaluations than immediately afterward.

Variable-Interval (VI) Schedule   In a variable-interval (VI) schedule, the amount of time that must elapse before reinforcement can be given for a correct response is variable rather than fixed. A "VI-60" schedule, for example, means that the period of time that must elapse before reinforcement may be given varies around an average of sixty seconds across occasions (trials). On any given occasion, the interval could be as short as one second or as long as one hundred and twenty seconds, but the average across all occasions must be sixty seconds. Variable-interval schedules tend to produce a slow but steady rate of response (see Figure 5.10). Because reinforcement doesn't occur after predictable intervals on such a schedule, responses tend to be more resistant to extinction than on a fixed-interval schedule.

Teachers may employ variable-interval schedules when they use surprise ("pop") quizzes to encourage regular studying behavior. Because students never know the exact day on which a quiz will be given, they are more likely to receive reinforcement (good grades) if they study regularly from day to day. With scheduled tests, reinforcement is based on a fixed-interval schedule; that is, rewards for studying become available only at the regular times the tests are given. In this case, we would expect to find the scalloped rate of response that is typical of fixed-interval reinforcement: an increased rate of studying, or perhaps even cramming, just before the test and a decline afterward.

Escape Learning and Avoidance Learning

> **CONCEPT 5.23**
> In escape learning, organisms learn responses that allow them to escape aversive stimuli, whereas in avoidance learning, they learn responses that allow them to avoid aversive stimuli.

In **escape learning**, an organism learns to *escape* an aversive stimulus by performing an operant response. The escape behavior is negatively reinforced by the removal of the aversive stimulus. A rat may be taught to press a bar to turn off an electric shock. We may learn to escape from the heat of a summer day by turning on a fan or air conditioner.

In **avoidance learning**, the organism learns to perform a response that *avoids* an aversive stimulus. The rat in a Skinner box may receive a signal (e.g., a tone) that a shock is about to be delivered. The animal learns to avoid the shock by performing the correct response, such as pressing a bar. You open an umbrella before stepping out in the rain to avoid the unpleasant experience of being drenched.

Like other forms of learning, escape learning and avoidance learning may be adaptive in some circumstances but not in others. We learn to apply sunscreen to avoid sunburn, which is adaptive. But skipping regular dental visits to avoid unpleasant or painful dental procedures is not, as it can lead to more serious dental problems or even tooth loss. People may turn to alcohol or other drugs to escape from their problems or troubling emotions. But the escape is short-lived, and problems resulting from drug or alcohol abuse can quickly compound the person's initial difficulties. At this point you may wish to review the key concepts in operant conditioning outlined in Concept Chart 5.2.

Punishment

Skinner observed that behaviors that are not reinforced or that are punished are less likely to be repeated. **Punishment** is the flip side of reinforcement. It involves the introduction of an aversive stimulus (e.g., physical pain or harsh criticism) or the removal of a reinforcing stimulus (e.g., turning off the TV) after a response, which leads to the weakening or suppression of the response (see Figure 5.11). In

Figure 5.11 Types of Punishment
Punishment involves the introduction of an aversive stimulus or the removal of a reinforcing stimulus to weaken or suppress a behavior.

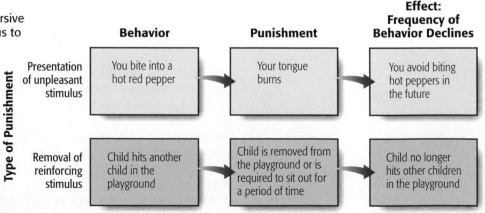

escape learning The learning of behaviors that allow an organism to escape from an aversive stimulus.

avoidance learning The learning of behaviors that allow an organism to avoid an aversive stimulus.

punishment The introduction of an aversive stimulus or the removal of a reinforcing stimulus after a response occurs, which leads to the weakening or suppression of the response.

physical punishment—spanking, for example—an aversive stimulus (pain) is applied following an undesirable behavior. Other forms of punishment include imposing monetary penalties (e.g., parking or traffic tickets), taking away privileges (e.g., grounding teenagers), or removing a misbehaving child from a reinforcing environment ("time-out"). Later in the module we explore the concerns that psychologists and other professionals have raised about the use of punishment as a method of discipline.

Punishment is often confused with negative reinforcement, since both rely on aversive stimuli. But here's the difference: with punishment, the *introduction* of an aversive stimulus or negative consequence (e.g., a time-out) after a behavior occurs *weakens* or *suppresses* the behavior (hitting other children in the playground). With negative reinforcement, the *removal* of an aversive stimulus (a

CONCEPT CHART 5.2   Key Concepts in Operant Conditioning

Concept	Description	Example
Nature of operant conditioning	A form of learning in which responses are strengthened by the effects they have in the environment	If students receive answers to their questions only when they raise their hands before asking them, hand-raising behavior is strengthened.
Discriminative stimulus	A stimulus that indicates that reinforcement will be available if the correct response is made	A child learns to answer the phone when it rings and to wait for a dial tone before dialing.
Positive reinforcer	A stimulus event whose introduction strengthens the behavior it follows	Praising children for picking up their clothes increases the likelihood that they will repeat the behavior.
Negative reinforcer	An aversive or unpleasant stimulus whose removal strengthens the preceding behavior	The annoying sound of a buzzer on an alarm clock increases the likelihood that we will get out of bed to turn it off.
Primary reinforcer	A stimulus that is innately reinforcing because it satisfies basic biological needs or drives	Food, water, and sexual stimulation are primary reinforcers.
Secondary reinforcer	A stimulus whose reinforcement value derives from its association with primary reinforcers	Money, which can be exchanged for food and clothing, is a secondary reinforcer.
Shaping	A process of learning that involves the reinforcement of increasingly closer approximations to the desired response	A boy learns to dress himself when the parent reinforces him for accomplishing each small step in the process.
Extinction	The gradual weakening and elimination of an operant response when it is not reinforced	A girl stops calling out in class without first raising her hand when the teacher fails to respond to her.
Schedule of continuous reinforcement	A schedule for delivering reinforcement every time a correct response is produced	A girl receives praise each time she puts her clothes away.
Schedule of partial reinforcement (fixed-ratio, variable-ratio, fixed-interval, or variable-interval schedule)	A schedule of delivering reinforcement in which only a portion of responses is reinforced	A boy receives praise for putting his clothes away every third time he does it (fixed-ratio schedule).
Escape learning	Learning responses that result in escape from an aversive stimulus	A motorist learns detours that provide an escape from congested traffic.
Avoidance learning	Learning responses that result in avoidance of an aversive stimulus	A person leaves for work an hour early to avoid heavy traffic.

TABLE 5.2 Comparing Reinforcement and Punishment

	What Happens?	**When Does This Occur?**	**Example**	**Consequence on Behavior**
Positive reinforcement	A positive event or stimulus is introduced.	After a response	Your instructor smiles at you (a positive stimulus) when you answer a question correctly.	You become more likely to answer questions in class.
Negative reinforcement	An aversive stimulus is removed.	After a response	Buckling the seat belt turns off the annoying buzzer.	You become more likely to buckle your seat belt before starting the engine.
Punishment (application of aversive stimulus)	An aversive stimulus is applied.	After a response	A parent scolds a child for slamming a door.	The child becomes less likely to slam doors.
Punishment (removal of a reinforcing stimulus)	A reinforcing stimulus is removed.	After a response	A child loses TV privileges for hitting a sibling.	The child becomes less likely to engage in hitting.

baby's crying) after a behavior occurs *strengthens* the behavior (picking up the baby). Before going further, you may wish to review Table 5.2, which compares reinforcement and punishment.

Applications of Operant Conditioning

> **CONCEPT 5.24**
> Principles of operant conditioning are used in biofeedback training, behavior modification, and programmed instruction.

In many ways, the world is like a huge Skinner box. From the time we are small children, reinforcements and punishments mold our behavior. We quickly learn which behaviors earn approval and which incur disapproval. How many thousands upon thousands of reinforcements have shaped your behavior over the years? Would you be taking college courses today were it not for the positive reinforcement you received from an early age for paying attention in class, doing your homework, studying for exams, and getting good grades? Who were the major reinforcing agents in your life? Your mother or father? A favorite uncle or aunt? Your teachers or coaches? Yourself? Psychologists have developed a number of applications of operant conditioning, including biofeedback training, behavior modification, and programmed instruction.

Biofeedback Training: Using Your Body's Signals as Reinforcers Chapter 3 introduced the topic of biofeedback training, a technique for learning to change certain bodily responses, including brain wave patterns and heart rate. Biofeedback training relies on operant conditioning principles. Physiological monitoring devices record changes in bodily responses and transmit the information to the user, typically in the form of auditory signals that provide feedback regarding desirable changes in these responses. The feedback reinforces behaviors (e.g., thinking calming thoughts) that bring about these desirable changes.

Behavior Modification: Putting Learning Principles into Practice **Behavior modification (B-mod)** is the systematic application of learning principles to strengthen adaptive behavior and weaken maladaptive behavior. Various learning-based methods are used, especially operant conditioning techniques.

Skinner and his colleagues applied operant conditioning principles in a real-world setting by establishing the first **token economy program** in a mental hospital. In a token economy program, patients receive tokens, such as plastic chips, for performing desired behaviors, such as dressing and grooming themselves, making

behavior modification (B-mod) The systematic application of learning principles to strengthen adaptive behavior and weaken maladaptive behavior.

token economy program A form of behavior modification in which tokens earned for performing desired behaviors can be exchanged for positive reinforcers.

their beds, or socializing with others. The tokens are exchangeable for positive reinforcers, such as extra privileges. Token economy programs continue to be used in mental hospitals, where they have been successful in improving social functioning and reducing aberrant behavior (Mueser & Liberman, 1995).

Behavior modification programs are also applied in the classroom, where they have produced measurable benefits in academic performance and social interactions and reductions in aggressive and disruptive behaviors and truancy. Teachers may use tokens or gold stars to reward students for appropriate classroom behavior and academic achievement. Children can use the tokens or gold stars at a later time to "purchase" small prizes or special privileges, such as more recess time.

Parent training programs have helped bring behavior modification into the home (Kazdin, 1997). After training in using B-mod techniques, parents implement them with their children, rewarding appropriate behaviors and punishing, when necessary, noncompliant and aggressive behaviors through the use of "time-outs" and loss of privileges or rewards.

Programmed Instruction   Skinner applied operant conditioning to education in the form of **programmed instruction**. In programmed instruction, the learning of complex material is broken down into a series of small steps. The learner proceeds to master each step at his or her own pace. Skinner even designed a "teaching machine" that guided students through a series of questions of increasing difficulty. After the student responded to each question, the correct response would immediately appear. This provided immediate reinforcement for correct responses and allowed students to correct any mistakes they had made. Since questions were designed to build upon each other in small steps, students would generally produce a high rate of correct responses and thus receive a steady stream of reinforcement. Teaching machines have since given way to computerized forms of programmed instruction, called **computer-assisted instruction**, in which the computer guides the student through an inventory of increasingly more challenging questions (Bostow, Kritch, & Tompkins, 1995; Tudor, 1995).

EXPLORING PSYCHOLOGY
Should Parents Use Punishment as a Method of Discipline?

Psychologists and pediatricians advise parents not to rely on punishment in disciplining their children; instead, they recommend reinforcing desirable behaviors (American Academy of Pediatrics, 1998; Gershoff, 2002a, 2002b). Punishment may temporarily suppress undesirable behavior, but it doesn't eliminate it. The punished behavior often returns when the punishing stimulus is withdrawn. For example, the child who is punished for misbehavior may perform the undesirable behavior when the parents aren't looking. Punishment, especially physical or *corporal* punishment, has other drawbacks, including the following:

- *Punishment does not teach new behaviors.* Punishment may suppress an undesirable behavior, but it does not help the child acquire a more appropriate behavior in its place.

- *Punishment can have undesirable consequences.* Punishment, especially physical punishment, can lead to strong negative emotions in children, such as anger, hostility, and fear directed toward the parent or other punishing agent. Fear may also generalize. Children repeatedly punished for poor performance in school may lose confidence in themselves or develop a fear of failure that handicaps their academic performance. They may begin cutting classes, withdraw from challenging courses, or even drop out of school.

CONCEPT 5.25
Though punishment may suppress or weaken behavior, psychologists generally advise parents not to rely on punishment as a means of disciplining their children.

programmed instruction   A learning method in which complex material is broken down into a series of small steps that learners master at their own pace.

computer-assisted instruction   A form of programmed instruction in which a computer is used to guide a student through a series of increasingly difficult questions.

- *Punishment may become abusive.* Stopping a child's undesirable behavior, at least temporarily, may reinforce the parents for using spankings or other forms of physical punishment. This may lead to more frequent physical punishment that crosses the line between discipline and abuse (Gershoff, 2002a, 2002b). Another type of abusive situation occurs when parents turn to ever-harsher forms of punishment when milder punishments fail. Abused children may harbor intense rage or resentment toward the punisher, which they may vent by responding aggressively against that person or other less physically imposing targets, such as peers or siblings.

- *Punishment may represent a form of inappropriate modeling.* When children observe their parents resorting to physical punishment to enforce compliance with their demands, the lesson they learn is that using force is an acceptable way of resolving interpersonal problems.

Is punishment always bad? The occasional use of mild punishment may be appropriate as a method of discipline when it is used in combination with positive methods, such as use of praise for desirable behaviors. For example, parents may need to use punishment to stop their children from harming themselves or others (e.g., by running into the street or hitting other children in the playground). But parents should avoid using harsh physical punishment (Foote, 2000). Examples of milder punishments include (1) *verbal reprimand* ("No, Johnny, don't do that. You can get hurt that way"); (2) *removal of a reinforcer,* such as grounding teenagers or taking away a certain number of points or tokens that children receive each week that are exchangeable for tangible reinforcers (toys, special activities); and (3) *time-out,* or temporary removal of a child from a reinforcing environment following misbehavior.

Parents who use punishment should help the child understand why he or she is being punished. Children may think they are being punished because they are "bad." They may think negatively of themselves or fear that Mommy and Daddy no longer love them. Parents need to make clear exactly what behavior is being punished and what the child can do differently in the future. In this way, parents can help children learn more desirable behaviors. Punishment is more effective when it is combined with positive reinforcement for desirable alternative behaviors.

Punishment vs. Reinforcement
Psychologists advocate the use of positive reinforcement rather than punishment when disciplining children. Scolding, a form of punishment, may temporarily suppress an undesirable behavior, but it does not help the child acquire more adaptive behaviors in its place.

MODULE 5.2 REVIEW

Operant Conditioning: Learning Through Consequences

RECITE IT

What is Thorndike's Law of Effect?

- Edward Thorndike's Law of Effect holds that responses that have satisfying effects will be strengthened while those that lead to discomfort will be weakened.

What is operant conditioning?

- Operant conditioning is a form of learning in which the consequences of behavior influence the likelihood or probability that the behavior will be repeated.

What are the different types of reinforcers?

- Positive reinforcers are stimuli whose introduction following a response strengthens the response.
- Negative reinforcers are aversive stimuli whose removal following a response strengthens the response.
- Primary reinforcers, such as food and water, are stimuli that are naturally reinforcing because they satisfy basic biological needs.
- Secondary reinforcers, such as money and social approval, acquire reinforcing value because of their association with primary reinforcers.

What are schedules of reinforcement, and how do they differ?

- Schedules of reinforcement are predetermined plans for timing the delivery of reinforcement. In a schedule of continuous reinforcement, reinforcement is given after every correct response. In a partial-reinforcement schedule, only a portion of correct responses is reinforced.
- Partial reinforcement is administered under ratio or interval schedules.

- In a fixed-ratio schedule, reinforcement follows a specified number of correct responses.
- In a variable-ratio schedule, the number of correct responses needed before reinforcement is given varies around some average number.
- In a fixed-interval schedule, a specified period of time must pass before a correct response can be reinforced.
- In a variable-interval schedule, the period of time that must elapse before a response can be reinforced varies around some average interval.

How are schedules of reinforcement related to learning?

- A schedule of continuous reinforcement produces the most rapid learning but also the most rapid extinction of a response when reinforcement is withheld.
- Response rates in partial-reinforcement schedules vary, as does the resistance of responses to extinction.

What are the differences in the effects of reinforcement and punishment?

- Reinforcement and punishment affect behavior, but in opposite ways. Whereas reinforcement strengthens the response it follows, punishment weakens or suppresses the preceding response.

What are some applications of operant conditioning?

- Principles of operant conditioning are used in biofeedback training, behavior modification, and programmed instruction.

RECALL IT

1. In operant conditioning, responses are learned and strengthened by the effects they have in the _____.

2. B. F. Skinner's belief that all behavior is determined by environmental and genetic influences and that free will is an illusion or myth is called _____.

3. Skinner demonstrated that superstitious behavior can be acquired through the coincidental pairing of a(n) _____ with a(n) _____.

4. In negative reinforcement, a behavior is strengthened by the
   a. introduction of a negative reinforcer.
   b. extinction of a positive stimulus.
   c. introduction of a positive reinforcer.
   d. removal of an aversive stimulus.

5. Operant responses are learned most rapidly under a schedule of _____ reinforcement; responses are most resistant to extinction under a schedule of _____ reinforcement.
   a. continuous; continuous
   b. partial; partial
   c. continuous; partial
   d. partial; continuous

THINK ABOUT IT

- B. F. Skinner believed that free will is but an illusion. Do you agree? Explain.
- The parents of a 13-year-old boy would like him to help out more around the house, including doing his share of the dishes. After a meal at which it is his turn to do the dishes, he first refuses, pleading that he has other things to do that are more important. Frustrated with his refusal, his parents start yelling at him and continue until he complies with their request. But as he washes the dishes, his mother notices that he is doing a very poor job, so she relieves him of his duty and finishes the job herself. What type of reinforcement did the parents use to gain the boy's compliance? What behaviors of the parents did the boy reinforce by complying with their request? What behavior did the mother inadvertently strengthen by relieving the boy of his chores? Based on your reading of the text, how would you suggest this family change these reinforcement patterns?

MODULE 5.3

Cognitive Learning

- What is cognitive learning?
- What is insight learning?
- What is latent learning?
- What is observational learning?

Let's say you wanted to learn the way to drive to your friend's new house. You could stumble about like Thorndike's laboratory animals until you happened upon the correct route by chance. Then again, you could ask for directions and form a mental image of the route ("Let's see, you make a left at the blue house on the corner, then a right turn at the stop sign, and then . . ."). Forming a mental roadmap, or mental representation of getting from point A to point B, allows you to perform a new behavior (driving to your friend's house) even before you have had the opportunity to be reinforced for it. Many psychologists believe that we need to go beyond classical and operant conditioning to explain this type of learning, which is called **cognitive learning**. Cognitive learning involves mental processes that cannot be directly observed—processes like thinking, information processing, problem solving, and mental imaging. Psychologists who study cognitive learning maintain that humans and other animals are, at least to a certain extent, capable of new behaviors without actually having had the chance to perform them or being reinforced for them.

In Chapter 7, we elaborate on cognitive processes involved in information processing, problem solving, and creativity. Here we focus on three types of cognitive learning: insight learning, latent learning, and observational learning.

Insight Learning

In the 1930s, Wolfgang Köhler (1887–1967), a German psychologist and one of the pioneers of Gestalt psychology, put himself in great personal danger by openly protesting the Nazi regime and helping Jewish friends escape from Germany. He later left Nazi Germany himself and eventually moved to the United States.

In an early experiment with a chimp named Sultan, Köhler (1927) placed a bunch of bananas outside the animal's cage beyond its reach. Sultan, who was obviously hungry, needed to use a nearby object, a stick, as a tool to obtain the fruit. Before long, the chimp succeeded in using the stick to pull in the bananas. Köhler then moved the bananas farther away from Sultan, beyond the reach of the stick, but made a longer stick available to him. Sultan looked at the two sticks and held

cognitive learning Learning that occurs without the opportunity of first performing the learned response or being reinforced for it.

insight learning The process of mentally working through a problem until the sudden realization of a solution occurs.

them in his hands. He tried reaching the bananas with one of the sticks and then the other, but to no avail. The bananas were too far away. He again held the two sticks, tinkered with them a bit, then attached one to the other to form a longer stick (the sticks were attachable), and *voilà*—the problem was solved. Sultan used the longer stick to pull the bananas into the cage. Unlike the animals in Thorndike's or Skinner's operant conditioning studies, Sultan did not gradually happen upon the reinforced response through an overt process of trial and error. Köhler believed Sultan had solved the problem on the basis of *insight*, the sudden flash of inspiration that reveals the solution to a problem.

Insight learning is the process of mentally working through a problem until the sudden realization of a solution occurs (the "Aha!" phenomenon) (Jones, 2003). But insight learning does not depend on waiting for a flash of inspiration to arise "out of the blue." To work through a problem mentally, you restructure or reorganize the problem in your mind until you see how its various parts fit together to form a solution.

Some critics, especially behaviorists, remain unconvinced by demonstrations of insight learning. They argue that "insight" is neither sudden nor free of prior reinforcement (Windholz & Lamal, 1985). They suggest that what you don't see is the history of reinforced behavior leading to an apparently sudden flash of "insight." In the behaviorist's view, insight learning is nothing more than the chaining of previously reinforced responses (Epstein et al., 1984). Perhaps there is room for compromise between these positions. Insight learning may arise from a *mental* process of trial and error—the working out in your mind of possible solutions to a problem based on responses that were reinforced in the past.

💡 **CONCEPT 5.26**

By reworking a problem in your mind, you may come to see how the various parts fit together to form a solution.

Latent Learning

💡 **CONCEPT 5.27**

Latent learning occurs without apparent reinforcement and is not displayed until reinforcement is provided.

In an early study of the role of cognitive processes in learning, Edward Tolman and C. H. Honzik (1930) trained rats to run a maze. Some rats were rewarded with food placed in goal boxes at the end of the maze; others went unrewarded for their efforts. Each day for ten days, the rats were put in the maze and the experimenters counted the number of wrong turns they made (see Figure 5.12). The rewarded rats quickly learned the maze, but the unrewarded rats did not. They seemed to wander aimlessly through the maze, making many wrong turns.

Figure 5.12 Tolman and Honzik's Study of Latent Learning
Notice the sharp reduction in errors that occurred among the rats that had not previously received reinforcement when on the eleventh day they were reinforced for reaching the goal. Tolman argued that learning had occurred in these rats during the previous trials but that it had remained hidden until rewarded.

On the eleventh day, food was placed in the goal boxes of some of the previously unrewarded rats. The next day, these rats ran the maze with even fewer errors than the rats that had been rewarded during the previous ten days. The investigators argued that a single reinforced trial could not account for this dramatic improvement in performance. These rats must have learned the maze earlier, without reinforcement, but only demonstrated what they had learned when they were reinforced for doing so. This type of learning is called **latent learning**—a kind of "hidden" learning that occurs without apparent reinforcement and that is not revealed in performance at the time it occurs. The learned behavior is only displayed when it is reinforced. But what had the rats learned? The lead investigator, psychologist Edward Tolman (1886–1959), believed he had an answer. He argued that the rats had developed a **cognitive map**—a mental representation of the maze that allowed them to find their way to the goal box.

Tolman's research laid a foundation for the view that humans and other animals create mental representations of the world around them. In Chapter 7, we explore the mental representations people use to gain knowledge about the world. Recent interest in **implicit learning**, or learning without conscious awareness, also owes a debt to Tolman. In implicit learning, people acquire new behaviors without making a conscious effort to do so and cannot even verbally articulate what they have learned (Frensch & Rünger, 2003). For example, we learn to speak grammatically correct sentences even before we take grammar classes in school. We also learn to speak grammatically correct sentences even though we cannot explain many of the rules of grammar we follow when speaking.

Observational Learning

In preschool, Jenny sees that the teacher praises Tina for picking up the blocks after playing with them. Tina's behavior provides Jenny with a cue that she can use to guide her own behavior. In **observational learning** (also called *vicarious learning* or

💡 **CONCEPT 5.28**
In observational learning, behaviors are acquired by observing and imitating the behaviors of others.

Next Time We'll Do a Soufflé   We can learn a wide range of skills by carefully observing and imitating the behavior of others. But practice and aptitude also count in developing skilled behaviors.

latent learning   Learning that occurs without apparent reinforcement and that is not displayed until reinforcement is provided.

cognitive map   A mental representation of an area that helps an organism navigate its way from one point to another.

implicit learning   Learning without conscious awareness of what is learned.

observational learning   Learning by observing and imitating the behavior of others (also called *vicarious learning* or *modeling*).

TRY THIS OUT

The Fine Art of Observing Others

How might you use modeling to expand your social skills? Here's an example. If you're at a loss to know what to say to someone you meet at a party, observe how others interact with each other, especially people you believe are socially skillful. What do you notice about their body language, facial expressions, and topics of conversation that could be helpful to you? Begin practicing these behaviors yourself. Note how other people respond to you. Fine-tune your skills to produce a more favorable response. With some practice and fine-tuning, the behaviors are likely to become part of your regular behavioral repertoire.

modeling), we acquire new behaviors by imitating behaviors we observe in others. The person whose behavior is observed is called a *model*.

Through observational learning, we become capable of behaviors even before we have had the chance to perform them ourselves. I have never fired a gun, but I expect I can do so because of having observed countless gun battles on television and in the movies. I expect I could even learn the basics of making a soufflé by watching a chef demonstrate each step in the process. Whether you'd want to eat it is another matter, which only goes to underscore a limitation of learning by observation—practice and aptitude also count in developing and refining skilled behavior.

Modeling influences a wide range of behaviors, from learning what outfit to wear at a social occasion to how to change a tire. Adolescents and adults may develop styles of dealing with conflicts in their intimate relationships based on their observations during childhood of how their mothers and fathers resolved their marital disagreements (Reese-Weber & Marchand, 2002). For example, young people may learn to imitate an attack style for handling disputes that they have observed in the relationship between their parents or between their parents and themselves (Reese-Weber, 2000).

The effects of modeling are generally stronger when the model is similar to the learner and when the behavior is reinforced. In other words, we are more likely to imitate models with whom we can identify and who receive rewards for performing the observed behavior (see Try This Out). For example, a fearful child who observes a model petting a small dog will be more likely to imitate the behavior if the model is similar to the child in age and if the animal responds in a friendly (reinforcing) way.

Does the idea of holding a rat make you squirm? Does the sight of a crab on the beach make you want to run in the other direction? How about touching an insect? Many of us have fears of various creatures even though we have never had any negative experience with them. These fears may be acquired by modeling—that is, by observing other people squirm or show fright when confronted with them (Merckelbach et al., 1996). In a study of forty-two people with a phobia about spiders, modeling experiences were a greater contributor to acquisition of the phobia than direct conditioning experiences (Merckelbach, Arntz, & de Jong, 1991). Concept Chart 5.3 provides an overview of the three types of cognitive learning.

CONCEPT CHART 5.3   Types of Cognitive Learning

Type of Learning	Description	Example
Insight learning	The process of mentally dissecting a problem until the pieces suddenly fit together to form a workable solution	A person arrives at a solution to a problem after thinking about it from a different angle.
Latent learning	Learning that occurs but remains "hidden" until there is a reward for performing the learned behavior	A person learns the words of a song playing on the radio but doesn't sing them until friends at a party begin singing.
Observational learning	Learning by observing and imitating the behavior of others	Through observation, a child learns to imitate the gestures and habits of older siblings.

MODULE 5.3 REVIEW

Cognitive Learning

RECITE IT

What is cognitive learning?

• In cognitive learning, an organism learns a behavior before it can perform the behavior or be reinforced for it. Cognitive learning depends on mental processes such as thinking, problem solving, and mental imaging.

What is insight learning?

• Insight learning is a mental process in which the restructuring of a problem into its component parts leads to the sudden realization of a solution to the problem.

What is latent learning?

• Latent learning is a kind of "hidden" learning that occurs without apparent reinforcement and is not displayed until reinforcement is provided.

What is observational learning?

• In observational learning, behaviors are acquired by observing and imitating the behaviors of others.

RECALL IT

1. The type of learning that involves thinking, information processing, mental imaging, and problem solving is called _____ learning.

2. The chimp named Sultan learned to reach bananas by attaching two sticks together. This type of learning is called _____ learning.

3. The type of learning that occurs without any apparent reinforcement and that is not displayed at the time it is acquired is called _____ learning.

4. Observational learning (does or does not) involve acquiring new behaviors by imitating the behavior of others.

THINK ABOUT IT

• Do you believe that learning can occur by insight alone? Why or why not?

• Who were the major modeling influences in your life? What behaviors, positive or negative, did you acquire by observing these models?

APPLICATION MODULE 5.4
Putting Reinforcement into Practice

CONCEPT 5.29
To modify behavior through reinforcement, it is important to establish a clear connection, or contingency, between the desired behavior and the reinforcement.

When you smile at someone who compliments you or thank someone for doing you a favor, you are applying positive reinforcement, one of the principles of operant conditioning. Showing appreciation for desired behavior increases the likelihood that the behavior will be repeated.

To modify behavior through reinforcement, it is important to establish a clear *contingency,* or connection, between the desired behavior and the reinforcement. For example, making a child's weekly allowance of spending money contingent on certain behaviors (e.g., cleaning up after meals) will be far more effective than granting the allowance irrespective of behavior. *Contingency contracting,* which involves an exchange of desirable reinforcers, is a more formal way of establishing a contingency. In contingency contracting, each person in a relationship lists the behaviors of the other that he or she would like changed. The two people then agree to reinforce each other for carrying out making the desired behavioral changes by making a quid pro quo contract, as in this example between two college roommates:

Carmen: I agree to keep the stereo off after 8:00 P.M. every weekday evening if you agree to forbid your friends to smoke in the apartment.

Lukisha: I agree to replace the toilet paper when we run out if you, in return, clean your hair out of the bathroom sink.

Applying Reinforcement

As noted in our earlier discussion of behavior modification programs, teachers and parents apply reinforcement to help children develop more appropriate behaviors. Here are some guidelines for enhancing the effectiveness of reinforcement (adapted from Eberlein, 1997; Samalin & Whitney, 1997):

1. *Be specific.* Identify the specific behavior you want to increase, such as having 5-year-old Johnny put the blocks back on the shelf after playing with them.

2. *Use specific language.* Rather than saying, "Johnny, I'd like you to clean your room when you finish playing," say, "Johnny, when you finish with the blocks, you need to put them back on the shelf."

3. *Select a reinforcer.* Identify a reinforcer that the child values, such as access to TV or gold stars the child can accumulate and later redeem for small gifts. The reinforcer should be one that is readily available and that can be used repeatedly.

4. *Explain the contingency.* "Johnny, when you put back all of the blocks on the shelf, you'll get a gold star."

5. *Apply the reinforcer.* Reinforce the child immediately after each occurrence of the desired behavior. If the child cannot achieve the desired standard of behavior (e.g., a few blocks are left on the floor), demonstrate how to do so and give the child the opportunity to perform the behavior satisfactorily. Pair the reinforcer with praise: "Johnny, you did a great job putting those blocks away."

6. *Track the frequency of the desired behavior.* Keep a running record of the behavior in terms of how often it occurs each day.

Hugs as Reinforcers Hugs are a form of positive reinforcement when they follow desirable behavior.

7. *Wean the child from the reinforcer.* After the desired response is well established, gradually eliminate the reinforcer but continue using social reinforcement (praise) to maintain the behavior: "Johnny, I think you did a good job in putting the blocks where they belong."

Giving Praise

Praise can be a highly effective reinforcer in its own right. Here are some guidelines for using praise to strengthen desirable behavior in children:

- *Make eye contact with the child and smile when giving praise.*

- *Use hugs.* Combine physical contact with verbal praise.

- *Be specific.* Connect praise with the desired behavior (Belluck, 2000). Rather than offering vague praise—"You're a great older brother"—connect it with the noteworthy effort or accomplishment. Say, for example, "Thanks for watching your little brother while I was on the phone. It was a big help."

- *Be sincere.* Children are more likely to perceive praise as sincere when it is given honestly, when it is given soon after evidence of achievements or desirable behaviors, and when it is consistent with the person's nonverbal behavior (Henderlong & Lepper, 2002). Insincere praise may actually do more harm than good.

- *Avoid empty flattery.* Children can see through empty flattery. Empty flattery may prompt them to think, why do people need to make up stuff about me? What is so wrong with me that people feel they need to cover up? (Henderlong & Lepper, 2002). Indiscriminant praise can also have the unfortunate effect of leading to an inflated sense of self-importance (Baumeister et al., 2003).

- *Reward the effort, not the outcome.* Instead of saying, "I'm so proud of you for getting an A in class," say, "I'm so proud of you for how well you prepared for the test." Praising the accomplishment, not the effort, may convey the message that the child will be prized only if he or she continues to get As.

- *Avoid repeating yourself.* Avoid using the same words each time you praise the child. If you tell Timmy he's terrific each time you praise him, the praise will soon lose its appeal.

- *Don't end on a sour note.* Don't say, "I'm proud of how you cleaned your room by yourself, but next time I think you can do it faster."

TYING IT TOGETHER

Our capacity to learn, or change our behavior as the result of experience, helps us adapt to the demands of the environment. Whether we are learning to garner rewards and avert punishments or simply to dress warmly in cold weather, we are continually modifying and adjusting our behavior in light of environmental demands. The modules in this chapter focus on three major types of learning. Classical conditioning, or learning by association, is a form of learning in which the repeated pairing of two stimuli leads to a response to one stimulus that was previously elicited by the other stimulus (Module 5.1). Whereas classical conditioning explains the development of relatively simple, reflexive responses, operant conditioning, or learning by consequences, focuses on the development of more complex behaviors (Module 5.2). The third major form of learning is cognitive learning, which involves mental processes that cannot be directly observed (Module 5.3). Teachers and parents apply reinforcement, a principle of operant conditioning, to help children develop more appropriate behaviors (Module 5.4).

Thinking Critically About Psychology

Based on your reading of this chapter, answer the following questions. Then, to evaluate your progress in developing critical thinking skills, compare your answers to the sample answers found in Appendix A.

Recall the experiment described on page 190 in which psychologist John Garcia and his colleagues left sheep carcasses on the open range that were laced with a poison that sickened coyotes when they ate the tainted meat. Apply your critical thinking skills in breaking down this study in classical conditioning terms.

1. **What was the unconditioned stimulus in this example?**
2. **What was the conditioned stimulus?**
3. **What was the unconditioned response?**
4. **What was the conditioned response?**

Key Terms

learning *(p. 182)*
classical conditioning *(p. 182)*
unconditioned response (UR) *(p. 183)*
unconditioned stimulus (US) *(p. 183)*
neutral stimulus (NS) *(p. 183)*
conditioned response (CR) *(p. 184)*
conditioned stimulus (CS) *(p. 184)*
extinction *(p. 184)*
spontaneous recovery *(p. 184)*
reconditioning *(p. 184)*
stimulus generalization *(p. 184)*
stimulus discrimination *(p. 185)*
higher-order conditioning *(p. 185)*
conditioned emotional reaction (CER) *(p. 188)*
phobias *(p. 189)*
behavior therapy *(p. 189)*

conditioned taste aversions *(p. 190)*
immune system *(p. 191)*
Law of Effect *(p. 194)*
radical behaviorism *(p. 194)*
reinforcer *(p. 195)*
operant conditioning *(p. 195)*
Skinner box *(p. 196)*
superstitious behavior *(p. 196)*
discriminative stimulus *(p. 197)*
positive reinforcement *(p. 197)*
negative reinforcement *(p. 197)*
primary reinforcers *(p. 198)*
secondary reinforcers *(p. 198)*
shaping *(p. 199)*
method of successive approximations *(p. 199)*
schedules of reinforcement *(p. 199)*

schedule of continuous reinforcement *(p. 199)*
schedule of partial reinforcement *(p. 199)*
escape learning *(p. 202)*
avoidance learning *(p. 202)*
punishment *(p. 202)*
behavior modification (B-mod) *(p. 204)*
token economy program *(p. 204)*
programmed instruction *(p. 205)*
computer-assisted instruction *(p. 205)*
cognitive learning *(p. 208)*
insight learning *(p. 209)*
latent learning *(p. 210)*
cognitive map *(p. 210)*
implicit learning *(p. 210)*
observational learning *(p. 210)*

ANSWERS TO RECALL IT QUESTIONS

Module 5.1: 1. stimulus generalization; 2. d; 3. c; 4. predictive; 5. b.
Module 5.2: 1. environment; 2. radical behaviorism; 3. response, reinforcement; 4. d; 5. c.
Module 5.3: 1. cognitive; 2. insight; 3. latent; 4. does.

6

Memory

DID YOU KNOW THAT . . .

■ A man was able to memorize lists of hundreds of meaningless syllables and recite them again fifteen years later? (p. 217)

■ Some research subjects did better on a memory test when they were submerged in water? (p. 219)

■ The World Wide Web was modeled on the way the human brain works? (p. 226)

■ You may be a skilled typist but not be able to name the keys in each row of the keyboard from memory? (p. 227)

■ It may seem that memories of traumatic events like 9/11 are seared in our brains as exact records of these experiences, but evidence shows they are not any more accurate than ordinary memories? (p. 230)

■ People can be misled into believing they saw a yield sign at an accident scene when they actually saw a stop sign? (p. 231)

■ Fewer than half of the people tested in a research study could pick out the correct drawing of a penny? (p. 239)

■ If your hippocampus were removed, each new experience would come and go without any permanent trace left in your brain that the event ever happened? (p. 245)

We are a nation that loves competitions. We watch or engage in competitions of all kinds, from sporting contests and tractor-pulls to the perennial game shows and award ceremonies on TV. But memory competitions? These are one of the newest entries in the competitive field. In the U.S. and world memory championships, experts compete in various challenges, such as recalling long lists of words or random numbers, or matching names to the faces of people they've seen in photographs. Some recent champions have demonstrated amazing feats of memory. The U.S. record holder in 1997 succeeded in memorizing in a mere 34.03 seconds each card (suit and number) in the order in which it appeared in a shuffled deck of fifty-two cards ("Instant Recall," 2000). But none of the feats of the recent champions can hold a candle to those of a Russian known only by his first initial, S., who had perhaps the most prodigious memory ever studied. He could repeat seventy randomly selected numbers in the precise order in which he had just heard them (Luria, 1968). Even more amazingly, he could memorize lists of hundreds of meaningless syllables and recite them not only immediately after studying them, but also when tested again some fifteen years later. He memorized long mathematical formulas that were utterly meaningless to him except as an enormously long string of numbers and symbols. After but a single reading, he could recite stanza after stanza of Dante's *Divine Comedy* in Italian, even though he could not speak the language (Rupp, 1998).

Imagine what it would be like to have such an extraordinary memory—to be able to remember everything you read word for word or to recall lists of facts you learned years ago. Yet if S.'s life story is any indication, it may be just as well you don't possess such a prodigious memory. S. didn't have an easy time of it. His mind was so crammed with meaningless details that he couldn't see the forest for the trees. He had difficulty distinguishing between the trivial and the significant (Turkington, 1996). He even had difficulty holding conversations, since individual words opened a floodgate of associations that distracted him from what the other person was saying. He was also unable to shift gears when new information conflicted with fixed images he held in memory. For example, he had difficulty recognizing people who had changed small details of their appearance, such as by getting a haircut or wearing a new suit. Unfortunately, S.'s life didn't end well. He spent the last years of his life confined to a mental hospital.

Most of us will probably never possess the memory of someone like S., nor would we even want to. Yet learning how our memory works and what we can do to improve it can help us meet many of life's challenges, from performing better in school or on the job to remembering to water the plants before leaving the house.

Our study of memory begins with a discussion of the underlying processes that make memory possible. We then consider the loss of information that results from forgetting and the role of the brain in creating and storing memories. We end with some practical suggestions for improving your memory. ■

MODULE 6.1

Remembering

- **What are the basic processes and stages of memory?**
- **What is the constructionist theory of memory?**
- **What are flashbulb memories?**
- **What factors influence the accuracy of eyewitness testimony?**

In Chapter 5, we defined learning as a relatively permanent change in behavior that occurs as the result of experience. But learning could not occur without memory. **Memory** is the system by which we retain information and bring it to mind. Without memory, experience would leave no mark on our behavior; we would be unable to retain the information and skills we acquire through experience. In this module, we focus on the factors that make memory possible.

Human Memory as an Information Processing System

CONCEPT 6.1
The three basic processes that make memory possible are encoding, storage, and retrieval.

Many psychologists conceptualize human memory as a type of information processing system that has three basic processes: *encoding, storage,* and *retrieval.* These processes allow us to take information from the world, encode it in a form that can be stored in memory, and later retrieve it when it is needed (see Figure 6.1). As we shall see, these underlying processes work through a sequence of stages leading to the formation of enduring memories.

Memory Encoding: Taking in Information   Information about the outside world comes to us through our senses. But for this information to enter memory, it must undergo a process of **memory encoding**, or conversion into a form we can store in memory. We encode information in different ways, including *acoustically* (coded by sound), *visually* (coded by forming a mental picture), and *semantically* (coded by meaning). We encode information acoustically by converting auditory signals into strings of recognizable sounds. For example, you use acoustic coding when trying to keep a phone number in mind by repeating it to yourself. Or you might encode this information visually by picturing a mental image of the digits of the telephone number. But visual coding tends to fade more quickly than auditory coding, so it is generally less efficient for remembering strings of numbers. We encode information semantically when we transform sounds or visual images into recognizable words.

Encoding information semantically—by meaning—helps preserve information in memory. You're more likely to remember material when you make a conscious effort to understand what the material means than when you rely on rote memorization (just repeating the words). We tend to use visual coding when forming memories of people's faces. We use acoustic codes to retain melodies and familiar rhymes or catch phrases, such as "M'm! M'm! Good!" Advertisers introduce such catch phrases because their meter or rhyme is easily remembered (see Try This Out).

TRY THIS OUT

Visual vs. Acoustic Coding

How do visual and acoustic coding of the same information compare? Picture in your mind a visual image of the following sequence of numbers: 4-2-6-9. Did you find the image faded within a few seconds? Now try repeating the numbers to yourself and see how much longer you can retain them in memory.

Memory Storage: Retaining Information in Memory   **Memory storage** is the process of retaining information in memory. Some memories—your first kiss or your wedding, for example—may last a lifetime. But not all information becomes an enduring or long-term memory. As we shall see when we discuss the stages of memory, some information is retained for only a fraction of a second.

memory   The system that allows us to retain information and bring it to mind.

memory encoding   The process of converting information into a form that can be stored in memory.

memory storage   The process of retaining information in memory.

Figure 6.1   Three Basic Processes of Memory
Human memory can be represented as an information processing system consisting of three basic processes: encoding, storage, and retrieval of information.

Memory Retrieval: Accessing Stored Information   **Memory retrieval** is the process of accessing stored information to make it available to consciousness. Retrieving long-held information is one of the marvels of the human brain. At one moment, we can summon to mind the names of the first three presidents of the United States, and at the next moment, recall our Uncle Roger's birthday. But memory retrieval is far from perfect ("Now, when is Uncle Roger's birthday anyway?"). Though some memories seem to be retrieved effortlessly, others depend on the availability of **retrieval cues**, cues associated with the original learning, to jog them into awareness.

Police detectives often take victims back to the scene of the crime to help jog their memories of the crime. You may perform better on an examination you take in the classroom where you originally learned the material. The question is, *why?* The most widely held explanation invokes the **encoding specificity principle** (Tulving, 1983). According to this principle, retrieval of particular memories will be more successful when cues available during recall are similar to those that were present when the information was originally encoded. The tendency for information to be better recalled in the context in which it was originally learned is called a **context-dependent memory effect**. Researchers believe that stimuli present in settings in which material is originally learned may be encoded along with the material itself. These stimuli may then serve as retrieval cues that help people access the learned material (Tulving & Thompson, 1973).

Consider a classic experiment that literally went underwater to demonstrate a context-dependent memory effect. Duncan Godden and Alan Baddeley (1975) had members of two university swim clubs learn a list of words. Members of one club learned the words on the beach; those in the other club learned them while submerged in water. The "beach group" showed better recall when they were tested on the beach than when immersed in water. The other group also showed a context-dependent effect; their retention was better when they were again submerged in water (see Figure 6.2).

memory retrieval   The process of accessing and bringing into consciousness information stored in memory.

retrieval cues   Cues associated with the original learning that facilitate the retrieval of memories.

encoding specificity principle   The belief that retrieval will be more successful when cues available during recall are similar to those present when the material was first committed to memory.

context-dependent memory effect   The tendency for information to be better recalled in the same context in which it was originally learned.

Figure 6.2
Context-Dependent Memory Effect
Students who originally learned material on the beach recalled the material better when they were tested on the beach. Similarly, students who originally learned material under water performed better on a recall test when they were again immersed in water.

Source: Adapted from Godden & Baddeley, 1975.

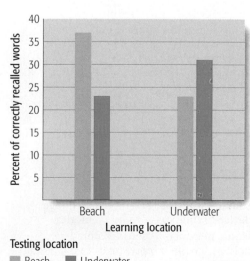

Bodily or psychological states may also serve as retrieval cues. A **state-dependent memory effect** occurs when people have better recall of information when they are in the same physiological or psychological state as when they first encoded or learned the information. Investigators Schramke and Bauer (1997) manipulated research participants' physiological states by having them either rest or exercise immediately before learning a list of twenty words. They found that recall after twenty minutes was better under the condition that prevailed in the original learning (rest or exercise). Similarly, people are generally better able to recall information when they are in the same mood (happy or sad) as when they learned the information (Bower, 1992). However, context- and state-dependent memory effects are not always observed, and when they are found, they often turn out to be rather weak (Eich, 1989).

Memory Stages

Some memories are fleeting; others are more enduring. The **three-stage model** of memory proposes three distinct stages of memory that vary with the length of time information is stored: *sensory memory, short-term memory,* and *long-term memory* (Atkinson & Shiffrin, 1971).

Sensory Memory: Getting to Know What's Out There   **Sensory memory** is a storage system that holds sensory information in memory for a very short time. Visual, auditory, and other sensory stimuli constantly strike your sensory receptors, forming impressions you briefly hold in sensory memory in a kind of temporary storage device called a **sensory register**. This information lasts in memory for perhaps a fraction of a second to as long as three or four seconds. The sensory impression then disappears and is replaced by the next one.

Visual stimuli encoded in the form of mental images enter a sensory register called **iconic memory**. Iconic memory is a type of photographic memory that allows us to hold an image of a visual stimulus in sensory memory for a fraction of a second. A visual image held in iconic memory is so clear and accurate that people can report exact details of the image.

Landmark research by psychologist George Sperling (1960) showed that people store more of the iconic image than they are able to report. Sperling presented research participants with a visual stimulus consisting of three rows of four letters, similar to the following, which was flashed on a screen for one-twentieth of a second:

RCBT

BNKH

PCLW

When the research participants were asked to report all the letters they had seen (called the *full-report technique*), they could report no more than about four of the twelve letters, or 33 percent of the stimulus array.

Did this mean that iconic memory is limited to a maximum of four stimuli? To find out, Sperling devised an ingenious method called the *partial-report technique*. He again flashed an array of three rows of four letters, but in this case, he followed the array by a tone indicating which of the three rows of letters he wanted subjects to recall. A high tone indicated the top row; a medium tone, the middle row; and the low tone, the bottom row. Subjects did not know ahead of time which row of letters they would be instructed to recall. Sperling found that if he presented the tone within a fraction of a second after the flash, people could recall about three of the four letters in the designated row. This result suggests that the subjects had registered about nine of twelve letters in iconic memory. However, these images faded so quickly that subjects could report only about a third of them. Sperling also reported that when the tone was delayed for more than one-quarter of a

---

CONCEPT 6.3
The three-stage model of memory proposes three stages of memory organized around the length of time that information is held in memory: sensory memory, short-term memory, and long-term memory.

state-dependent memory effect   The tendency for information to be better recalled when the person is in the same psychological or physiological state as when the information was first learned.

three-stage model   A model of memory that posits three distinct stages of memory: sensory memory, short-term memory, and long-term memory.

sensory memory   The storage system that holds memory of sensory impressions for a very short time.

sensory register   A temporary storage device for holding sensory memories.

iconic memory   A sensory store for holding a mental representation of a visual image for a fraction of a second.

second, subjects could recall only an average of one letter per row. This indicates that the visual image is held in iconic storage for but a fraction of a second before it fades away.

Some people can recall a visual image in such vivid detail it is as if they are still looking at it. This form of visual memory is called **eidetic imagery**, or *photographic memory*. (The term *eidetic* is derived from the Greek term *eidos,* meaning "image.") Eidetic images may be quite vivid, but they are not perceived as clearly as actual photographs (Jahnke & Nowaczyk, 1998). Eidetic imagery is rare in adults, but it occurs in about 5 percent of young children (Haber, 1979). It typically disappears before the age of ten.

Auditory stimuli encoded as mental representations of sounds are held in a sensory register called **echoic memory**. The memory traces of auditory stimuli create the impression of hearing a sound "echo" in your mind for a few seconds after you hear it. Although sounds held in echoic memory fade quickly, they last about two or three seconds longer than visual images.

Short-Term, or Working, Memory: The Mind's Blackboard   Many sensory impressions don't just fade away into oblivion. They are transferred into **short-term memory (STM)** for further processing. Short-term memory is a storage system that permits you to retain and process sensory information for a maximum of about thirty seconds. Short-term memory relies on both visual and acoustic coding, but mostly on acoustic coding. For example, you attempt to keep a phone number in mind long enough to dial it by verbally repeating it to yourself.

Suppose that you multiply 43 by 6 in your head and you get the right answer: 258. How did you do it? Did you multiply 40 by 6 to get 240, then multiply 6 by 3 to get 18, and then add 240 and 18 to get 258? Or did you use some other form of mental arithmetic? However you performed this task, you engaged **working memory**: the memory system that allows you to hold and mull over information in your mind for brief periods of time (Jonides, Lacey, & Nee, 2005). Many memory scientists equate short-term memory with *working memory* because information held in short-term memory is actively "worked on," or processed, by the brain (Baddeley, 2001; Barch et al., 2002).

Working memory is a kind of mental workspace or blackboard for holding information in mind long enough to process it and act upon it (MacAndrew et al., 2002). We engage working memory whenever we perform mental arithmetic, engage others in conversation, or hold an image of a person's face in memory for the time it takes the brain to determine whether it is the face of someone we know. During a conversation, working memory allows us to retain memory of sounds long enough to convert them into recognizable words.

In the 1950s, psychologist George Miller performed a series of landmark studies in which he sought to determine the storage capacity of short-term memory. Just how much information can most people retain in short-term memory? The answer, Professor Miller determined, was about seven items, plus or minus two (Cowan, Chen, & Rouder, 2004; Kareev, 2000). Miller referred to the limit of seven as the "Magic 7."

The magic number seven appears in many forms in human experience, including the "seven ages of man" in Shakespeare's *As You Like It,* the Seven Wonders of the World, the Seven Deadly Sins, and even the seven dwarfs of Disney fame. People can normally repeat a maximum of six or seven single-syllable words they have just heard. Think about the "Magic 7" in the context of your daily experiences. Telephone numbers are seven-digit numbers, which means you can probably retain a telephone number in short-term memory just long enough to dial it.

People vary in their working memory capacities, with some people having greater capacity than others (Barrett, Tugade, & Engle, 2004; Bayliss et al., 2003; Kane & Engle, 2003). Despite these differences, we can all boost our capacity to keep information in mind by using certain memory techniques. One such tech-

The Magic 7   Most of us can retain about seven bits of information in short-term memory, plus or minus two. You probably are able to retain in memory a seven-digit telephone number you were just given by an operator, at least for the few seconds it takes to dial it. Adding an unfamiliar area code to the number, however, might just stretch your short-term memory beyond its limit.

CONCEPT 6.4

People can normally retain a maximum of about seven items in short-term memory at any one time.

eidetic imagery   A lingering mental representation of a visual image (commonly called *photographic memory*).

echoic memory   A sensory store for holding a mental representation of a sound for a few seconds after it registers in the ears.

short-term memory (STM)   The memory storage system that allows for short-term retention of information before it is either transferred to long-term memory or forgotten.

working memory   The memory system that enables you to hold and manipulate information in your mind for brief periods of time.

nique is **chunking**, the process of breaking a large amount of information into smaller chunks to make it easier to recall (Cowan et al., 2004). For example, children learn the alphabet by chunking series of letters. That's why they often say the letters *lmnop* as if they were one word (Rupp, 1998).

Most information that passes through short-term memory fades away after a few seconds or is transferred to long-term memory. You can extend short-term memory beyond thirty seconds by engaging in **maintenance rehearsal**, the conscious rehearsal of information by repeating it over and over again in your mind. You practice maintenance rehearsal whenever you try to remember a person's name by rehearsing it again and again in your mind. But when your rehearsal is interrupted, even for just a few seconds, the contents of short-term memory quickly fade away. This is why it is difficult to keep a particular thought in mind and at the same time follow what someone is saying in conversation.

Memory theorists have developed a number of models to explain how working memory functions. The leading model, called the *three-component model*, was formulated by Alan Baddeley and Graham Hitch (1974; Baddeley, 1996). They proposed that working memory consists of three components (sometimes called *subsystems*): the *phonological loop*, the *visuospatial sketchpad*, and the *central executive* (see Figure 6.3).

1. The **phonological loop** is the speech-based, or verbal, part of working memory. It is a storage device or buffer that holds numbers and words we rehearse or mull over in our minds at any given moment, such as telephone numbers, people's names, or plans for dinner.

2. The **visuospatial sketchpad** is a storage buffer for visual and spatial material. Think of it as a kind of drawing pad in the brain (Logie, 1996). You engage your visuospatial sketchpad whenever you picture in your mind an object, pattern, or image—the face of your significant other, the map of your home state, or the arrangement of the furniture in your living room.

3. The **central executive** is the control unit of working memory. It doesn't store information. Rather, it receives input from the other two components and coordinates the working memory system. It also receives and processes information from long-term memory and filters out distracting thoughts so we can focus our attention on information we hold in mind at any given moment. The other components—the phonological loop and the visuospatial sketchpad—are called "slaves" because they do the bidding of the central executive (Willingham, 2001).

CONCEPT 6.5
The major contemporary model of working memory holds that it consists of three components, or subsystems: the phonological loop, the visuospatial sketchpad, and the central executive.

chunking The process of enhancing retention of a large amount of information by breaking it down into smaller, more easily recalled chunks.

maintenance rehearsal The process of extending retention of information held in short-term memory by consciously repeating the information.

phonological loop The speech-based part of working memory that allows for the verbal rehearsal of sounds or words.

visuospatial sketchpad The storage buffer for visual-spatial material held in short-term memory.

central executive The component of working memory responsible for coordinating the other subsystems, receiving and processing stored information, and filtering out distracting thoughts.

Figure 6.3 Three-Component Model of Working Memory
According to the three-component model, working memory consists of three subsystems: (1) a phonological loop for storing speech-based, or verbal, material; (2) a visuospatial sketchpad for storing visual and spatial material; and (3) a central executive for coordinating the other two subsystems, receiving and processing information retrieved from long-term memory, and filtering out distracting thoughts.

Since the two "slaves" work independently, they can operate at the same time without interfering with one another. When you drive an automobile, visual images of the road are temporarily stored in the visuospatial sketchpad. At the same time, your phonological loop allows you to carry on a conversation with a passenger or sing along with a song on the radio. However, as we noted in Chapter 4, it can be dangerous to engage in a complex conversation while you are driving.

Conflicts can arise when two or more simultaneous demands are placed on either component. It is difficult, as well as dangerous, to drive and read a roadmap at the same time. It is also difficult to hold two conversations at the same time.

Long-Term Memory: Preserving the Past   **Long-term memory (LTM)** is a storage system that allows you to retain information for periods of time beyond the capacity of short-term memory. Though some information may remain in long-term memory for only days or weeks, other information may remain for a lifetime. Whereas the storage capacity of short-memory is limited, long-term memory is virtually limitless in what it can hold. We may never reach a point at which we can't squeeze yet one more experience or fact into long-term memory.

Consolidation is the process by which the brain converts unstable, fresh memories into stable, long-term memories (Dudai, 2004). The first twenty-four hours after information is acquired is critical for consolidation to occur. Scientists believe that both REM sleep and deep, slow-wave sleep play important roles in consolidating daily experiences into long-term memories (Ribeiro et al., 2003; Wixted, 2004). This means that if you are studying for a test you have the next day and want to increase your chances of retaining the information you've just learned, you should make sure you get a good night's sleep.

Whereas short-term memory relies largely on acoustic coding, long-term memory depends more on semantic coding, or coding by meaning. One way of transferring information from short-term to long-term memory is to use maintenance rehearsal, which, as we've noted, is the repeated rehearsal of words or sounds. But a better way is through **elaborative rehearsal**, a method of rehearsal in which you focus on the *meaning* of the material. A friend of mine has a telephone number that ends with the digits 1991, a year I remember well because it was the year my son Michael was born. I have no trouble remembering my friend's number because I associate it with something meaningful (my son's birth year). But I need to mentally rehearse other friends' numbers that end in digits that have no personal significance for me (or look them up in my electronic directory).

Why should elaborative rehearsal (rehearsal by meaning) result in better transfer of information from short-term to long-term memory than maintenance rehearsal (rehearsal by repetition)? One explanation, called the **levels-of-processing theory**, holds that the level at which information is encoded or processed determines how well or how long information is stored in memory (Craik & Lockhart, 1972). In this view, information is better retained when it is processed more "deeply," which means when it is encoded on the basis of its meaning. For example, you're more likely to remember the principles of classical conditioning if you think of meaningful examples of each of these principles in real life (see Chapter 5).

In general, the levels-of-processing theory is correct in its view that information is better retained when it is processed more deeply in terms of its meaning. However, the model doesn't hold up as well when we consider memory tasks in which retrieval is pegged to shallow levels of processing or rote memorization (Jahnke & Nowaczyk, 1998). Rhyming, for example, is a shallow level of processing. We may enhance memory of rhyming words when we instruct people who are asked to learn a list of such words to focus on the sounds the words make rather than their meaning. Simple repetition or rote memorization may also be effective for remembering simple number sequences that lack meaningful associations, like

---

💡 **CONCEPT 6.6**
According to the levels-of-processing theory, information is better retained in memory when it is encoded or processed at a "deeper" level.

long-term memory (LTM)   The memory subsystem responsible for long-term storage of information.

consolidation   The process of converting short-term memories into long-term memories.

elaborative rehearsal   The process of transferring information from short-term to long-term memory by consciously focusing on the meaning of the information.

levels-of-processing theory   The belief that how well or how long information is remembered depends on the depth of encoding or processing.

TRY THIS OUT

The Name Game

The "name game" helps strangers in a group remember each other's names (Morris & Fritz, 2000). One member of the group begins by announcing his or her full name. Then the next member repeats the first person's name and adds his or her own name. Then the next person repeats the names of the first two people as well as his or her own name. This process is repeated for each member of the group, up to a maximum of perhaps 10 or 11 members. After all the names are announced, the first person then repeats the full set of names. If any group member stumbles when recalling the names, the other group members supply the missing names. Researchers believe that the active effort each member expends in retrieving the names during the game boosts retrieval. You can put this technique into practice the next time you need to remember a set of new names. With each introduction, repeat all the names of the people in the group and encourage others to do the same.

telephone numbers, or even names of people you meet for the first time (see the "Name Game" in the nearby Try This Out).

How do we manage to organize our long-term memory banks so we can retrieve what we want to know when we want to know it? Imagine being in a museum where bones, artifacts, and other holdings were strewn about without any organization. It would be difficult, perhaps impossible, to find the exhibit you were looking for. Now imagine how difficult it would be to retrieve specific memories if they were all scattered about in LTM without any rhyme or reason. Fortunately, LTM is organized in ways that provide relatively quick access to specific memories.

The leading conceptual model of how LTM is organized is called the **semantic network model** (Collins & Quillian, 1969). This model proposes that information is held in networks of interlinking concepts. We understand the meaning of something by linking it to related things. For example, the concept of "animal" might

CONCEPT 6.7

According to the semantic network model, when you think of a particular concept, it causes a ripple effect to occur within the network of interlinking concepts, triggering memory of related concepts.

Figure 6.4   Semantic Network
The semantic network model posits that information in long-term memory is held in networks of inter-linking concepts.

Source: Adapted from A. M. Collins & Quillian, 1969.

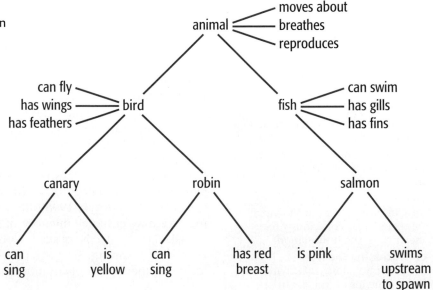

semantic network model   A representation of the organizational structure of long-term memory in terms of a network of associated concepts.

💡 CONCEPT CHART 6.1   Stages and Processes of Memory

Memory Stage	Memory Process		
	Encoding	Storage	Retrieval
Sensory memory	Iconic and echoic	Very brief, from a fraction of a second to three or four seconds	No retrieval. Information is either lost or transferred to short-term memory.
Short-term memory	Acoustic and visual, but primarily acoustic	A maximum of about thirty seconds, but maintenance rehearsal or elaborative rehearsal can maintain the memory longer or convert it into long-term memory	No retrieval. Information is either lost or transferred to long-term memory.
Long-term memory	Acoustic, visual, and semantic, but primarily semantic	Long-term, possibly lifelong	Retrieval is assisted by retrieval retrieval cues and activation of semantic networks.

be linked to related concepts of "fish" and "bird," which in turn might be linked to associated concepts, such as "salmon" and "robin," respectively (see Figure 6.4). As the Pioneers box on the next page explains, this simple idea is the basis for the World Wide Web.

Thinking about a concept causes a ripple effect throughout the semantic network. This rippling effect, called *spreading activation*, triggers recall of related concepts (Nelson, McEvoy, & Pointer, 2003). In other words, you think "fish" and related concepts suddenly spring to mind, such as "salmon" or "cod," which in turn trigger other associations such as "is pink," "tastes fishy," and so on.

We began our discussion of how memory works by recognizing that memory depends on underlying processes (encoding, storage, retrieval) that proceed through a series of stages (sensory memory, short-term memory, long-term memory). Concept Chart 6.1 summarizes these processes and stages; Figure 6.5 shows the three stages in schematic form. Through them, we come to form long-term memories that we can recall at will or with some help (retrieval cues). Next we focus on the contents of long-term memory—the kinds of memories that enrich our lives.

Figure 6.5   Three-Stage Model of Memory
Although human memory is more complex than the three-stage model would suggest, the model does provide a useful framework for understanding relationships among the three memory storage systems. *Sensory input* (visual images, sounds, etc.) creates impressions that are held briefly in temporary storage buffers called sensory registers. If we attend to this information, it may enter *short-term memory*. We can use active rehearsal strategies (maintenance rehearsal and elaborative rehearsal) to transfer information from short-term memory into *long-term memory*. Once information is stored in long-term memory, it must be retrieved and enter short-term memory again before it can be used.

THE PIONEERS

Tim Berners-Lee: Weaving the Web

Tim Berners-Lee

You may have never heard of Tim Berners-Lee, but you certainly have heard of his invention. At first he thought of calling it "Mesh" because he wanted the name to reflect the new kind of computer structure it represented. But *Mesh* sounded too much like *mess*. He then went through other possible names, including the *Information Mine,* before settling on what would soon become a household name: the *World Wide Web.*

Berners-Lee is a physicist, not a psychologist, but his design of the World Wide Web (WWW) was modeled on the workings of the human brain. As discussed in the text, the brain links information in networks of interlinking concepts. For example, when we think of the word *canary,* other linked concepts come to mind, such as "can sing" and "is yellow."

Berners-Lee modeled the WWW on the same principle. He later said, "I liked the idea that a piece of information is really defined only by what it's related to, and how it's related. . . . The structure is everything. There are billions of neurons in our brains, but what are neurons? Just cells. The brain has no knowledge until connections are made between neurons. All that we know, all that we are, comes from the way our neurons are connected" (Berners-Lee, 1999, p. 12).

Berners-Lee was a child of two highly accomplished mathematicians who were involved in the early development of the modern computer. As a child, he came home one day from school to find his father reading books on the human brain, looking for clues for making computers more intuitive by forming links in much the same way that the brain connects bits and pieces of information. Berners-Lee would go on to use this idea in developing a system, the WWW, for linking information stored in different computers. As he wrote in his memoir, "Suppose all the information stored on computers everywhere were linked, I thought. Suppose I could program my computer to create a space in which anything could be linked to anything. All the bits of information in every computer . . . on the planet . . . would be available to me and to anyone else . . . here would be a single, global information space" (Berners-Lee, 1999, p. 4). Few inventions in the past fifty or even one hundred years have had such a profound impact on our daily lives as the WWW, which Berners-Lee introduced in 1991. Today, whenever you go surfing in cyberspace by clicking on one link after another, you are modeling what your brain does naturally when it creates meaning by linking related concepts to each other.

What We Remember: The Contents of Long-Term Memory

 CONCEPT 6.8
The two major types of long-term memory are declarative memory ("knowing that") and procedural memory ("knowing how").

 CONCEPT 6.9
Declarative memory consists of semantic memory (memory of facts) and episodic, or autobiographical, memory (memory of life events and experiences).

declarative memory Memory of facts and personal information that requires a conscious effort to bring to mind (also called *explicit memory*).

semantic memory Memory of facts.

What types of memories are stored in long-term memory? At the broadest level, we can distinguish between two types of long-term memory, *declarative memory,* or "knowing that," and *procedural memory,* or "knowing how" (Eichenbaum, 1997; Rupp, 1998).

Declarative Memory: "Knowing That" Declarative memory (also called *explicit memory*) is memory of facts and personal information that requires a conscious effort to bring to mind. Declarative memory is memory for specific information (Ojemann, Schoenfield-McNeill, & Corina, 2002). It allows us to know "what" and "that." We know that there are fifty states in the United States, that we live on such-and-such a street, and that water and oil don't mix. We know what elements are found in water and what colors are in the American and Canadian flags. We can group declarative memories into two general categories organized according to (1) type of memory (*semantic* or *episodic memory*) and (2) time frame (*retrospective* or *prospective memory*).

Semantic memory is memory of facts, general knowledge, and beliefs (Dixon & Cohen, 2003). We can compare semantic memory to a mental encyclopedia or

What Was I Supposed to Do Today?
Rather than relying entirely on prospective memory, many people use such aids as electronic organizers and Post-It® notes to remind them of things they need to do.

CONCEPT 6.10
Prospective memory, or remembering to remember, has important applications in daily life, involving such mental activities as remembering appointments and remembering to call people on their birthdays.

CONCEPT 6.11
We can distinguish between two types of memory, implicit and explicit memory, that differ in terms of whether we make a conscious effort to bring information to mind.

episodic memory   Memory of personal experiences.

retrospective memory   Memory of past experiences or events and previously acquired information.

prospective memory   Memory of things one plans to do in the future.

procedural memory   Memory of how to do things that require motor or performance skills.

implicit memory   Memory accessed without conscious effort.

explicit memory   Memory accessed through conscious effort.

priming task   An experimental task in which subjects are presented with a stimulus that primes them to respond in a certain way to subsequent stimuli.

storehouse of information we carry around in our heads. It allows us to remember who wrote *The Grapes of Wrath,* which film won the Academy Award for best picture last year, how to spell the word *encyclopedia,* and what day Japan attacked Pearl Harbor. Semantic memories are not indelibly imprinted in our brains, which is why you may no longer remember last year's Oscar winner or the author of *The Grapes of Wrath* (John Steinbeck). Semantic memories are better remembered when they are retrieved and rehearsed from time to time. So if you stumbled when it came to remembering the name of the author of *The Grapes of Wrath,* reminding you of it today will probably help you remember it tomorrow.

Episodic memory (also called *autobiographical memory*) is memory of personal experiences that constitute the story of your life—everything from memories of what you had for dinner last night to the time you fell from a tree when you were ten years old and needed fifteen stitches. Episodic memory is like a personal diary of one's life experiences, whereas semantic memory is like an encyclopedia of general facts and information (Baddeley, Conway, & Aggleton, 2002; Tulving, 2002). Another difference between semantic and episodic memory is the context in which the event or experience occurred. Knowing that the United States was attacked by terrorists on September 11, 2001, is a semantic memory. Knowing where you were at the time you heard the news of the tragedy is an episodic memory.

Retrospective memory is memory of past experiences or events and previously acquired information. **Prospective memory** is remembering to do something in the future (McDaniel et al., 2004; Smith & Bayen, 2004). You rely on prospective memory when remembering to take your medication, pay your phone bill on time, or call your mother on her birthday. It is remembering to remember. Some of our most embarrassing lapses of memory involve forgetting to do things ("Sorry, I forgot to call the restaurant for reservations. It just slipped my mind.").

Procedural Memory: "Knowing How"   **Procedural memory** is memory of how to do things, such as how to ride a bicycle, climb stairs, tie shoelaces, perform mathematical operations, or play a musical instrument. Declarative memory is brought to mind by conscious effort ("Let's see, what year was it that the Berlin Wall fell?"). But procedural memory operates largely unconsciously (Eichenbaum, 2003). We don't think about how to walk down the stairs before doing so. It's a good thing procedural memory operates automatically without conscious thought, since we'd likely trip over ourselves if we needed to think through every step.

Another difference between these two forms of memory is that declarative memory involves information that can be verbalized, whereas procedural memory involves motor or performance skills that cannot be explained in words, at least not easily. Try, for example, to describe how you move your muscles when riding a bicycle. Touch typing is a skill requiring procedural memory of how keys are arranged on a keyboard, even though you may not be able to name the keys in each row of the keyboard from memory.

Implicit memory—memory evoked without any deliberate effort to remember—is closely related to procedural memory and is perhaps even a form of procedural memory. Hearing a familiar song on the radio may evoke pleasant feelings associated with past experiences, even though you make no conscious attempt to bring these memories to mind. We know that odors, for instance, can elicit implicit memories (Stevenson & Boakes, 2003). A fragrance or cooking odors may elicit memories of earlier experiences without a conscious attempt to recall them. In contrast, **explicit memory** requires that we make an *explicit* or conscious effort to bring the information to mind ("Hmm, what is the capital of Finland?") (Thompson, 2005).

Implicit memory can be demonstrated through the use of a **priming task** (Bodenhausen, Macrae, & Hugenberg, 2003; Fazio & Olson, 2003). A priming task exposes individuals to a word or concept that sensitizes, or "primes," them to respond in a particular way to subsequent stimuli. For example, subjects who first

Muscle Memory New York Yankees' manager Joe Torre once referred to the ability to throw a baseball accurately as "muscle memory." We rely on muscle memory, or procedural memory, whenever we perform complex motor skills, such as riding a bike, dancing, typing, climbing stairs, hitting or throwing a baseball, or dribbling or shooting a basketball.

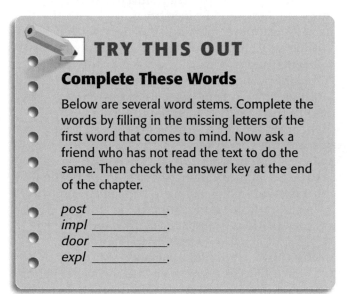

TRY THIS OUT

Complete These Words

Below are several word stems. Complete the words by filling in the missing letters of the first word that comes to mind. Now ask a friend who has not read the text to do the same. Then check the answer key at the end of the chapter.

post _____.
impl _____.
door _____.
expl _____.

read the word *elephant* in a text passage are more likely to complete the word when presented with it in fragmented form, such as E_E_ _A_T, than are others who were not exposed to this priming stimulus (E. R. Smith, 1998). Priming effects may occur even though subjects are unaware of having been exposed to the priming stimulus and make no conscious effort to recall it (see Try This Out).

The Reliability of Long-Term Memory: Can We Trust Our Memories?

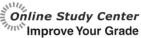

CONCEPT 6.12
The constructionist theory holds that memory is a process of reconstructing past events and experiences, not of replaying them exactly as they occurred.

Online Study Center
Improve Your Grade
Tutorials: Constructionist Theory of Memory

constructionist theory A theory that holds that memory is not a replica of the past, but a representation, or *reconstruction,* of the past.

We might like to think our memories accurately reflect events we've witnessed or experienced. But evidence shows that recollections may not be as reliable as we believe them to be. Contemporary memory researchers reject the view that long-term memory works like a video camera that records exact copies of experience. Rather, they believe it is a representation, or *reconstruction,* of the past. This view is generally called **constructionist theory**. We stitch together bits and pieces of information stored in long-term memory to form a coherent explanation or account of past experiences and events. Reconstruction, however, can lead to distorted memories of events and experiences.

According to constructionist theory, memories are not carbon copies of reality. From this vantage point, it is not surprising that people who witness the same event or read the same material may have very different memories of the event or of the passage they read. Nor is it surprising if recollections of your childhood are not verbatim records of what actually occurred, but rather reconstructions based on pieces of information from many sources—old photographs, what your mother told you about the time you fell from the tree when you were 10, and so on.

Constructionist theory leads us to expect that memories may be distorted. These distortions can range from simplifications, to omissions of details, to outright fabrications (Koriat & Goldsmith, 1996). Even so, we shouldn't presume that all memories are distorted. Some may be more or less accurate reflections of events. Others, perhaps most, can be likened more to impressionist paintings than to mental snapshots of experiences.

TRY THIS OUT

What's in the Photograph?

Look briefly at the photograph of a professor's office that appears in Figure 6.6. Then continue with your reading of the chapter. After a few minutes, return here and, without looking at the photo again, list all the objects you saw in the office.

_____

_____

_____

_____

Now look again at the photo. Did you list any objects not actually present in the office but that may have fit your concept, or schema, of what a professor's office looks like, like filing cabinets and bookshelves? Investigators who used this photograph in a similar experiment found that many subjects remembered seeing such objects, demonstrating that their memories were affected by their existing schemas (W. F. Brewer & Treyens, 1981).

Figure 6.6   Professor's Office

Racial Biases in Memory Schemas   The constructionist account of memory provides an interesting perspective on how *negative stereotyping*—ascribing negative traits to people of certain groups—can influence perceptions and attitudes of people subjected to stereotyping. Given the long history of exclusion, prejudice, and discrimination on the basis of skin color, it is not surprising that members of the dominant culture often perceive African Americans with darker skin tones more negatively—as less intelligent, less attractive, and less successful—than African Americans with lighter skin tones. Since African Americans are raised in the same culture, we should not be surprised if they, too, hold these negative stereotypes, at least to a certain degree. Psychologists, leading African American writers, other scholars, and even artists, including the filmmaker Spike Lee, have examined the effects of racist attitudes in the general society on skin color prejudice among African Americans. Researchers have extended this line of research to examine skin color prejudice in other cultures as well, including Brazil (Bianchi et al., 2002).

Cara Averhart and Rebecca Bigler (1997) examined the influence of racial stereotypes on memory in African American children of elementary school age. They used a memory test in which the children recalled information embedded in stories in which light- and dark-complexioned African American characters were associated with either positive ("nice") or negative ("mean") attributes. The results showed that children had better memory for stories in which more favorable attributes were associated with light-complexioned characters and more negative characteristics were associated with dark-complexioned characters. The memory bias was even greater among children who rated themselves as having light skin tones. The results support a constructionist view that people are better able to recall information that is consistent with their existing *memory schemas*, even when these schemas are grounded in prejudice. A **memory schema** is an organized knowledge structure, such as a set of beliefs, that reflects one's past experiences, expectations, and knowledge about the world (Neath, 1998) (see Try This Out). The study also highlighted the need for multicultural education programs to

CONCEPT 6.13

People are generally better able to recall information that is consistent with their existing schemas, even when such schemas are rooted in prejudice.

memory schema   An organized knowledge structure, such as a set of beliefs, that reflects one's past experiences, expectancies, and knowledge about the world.

address racial prejudices within racial and ethnic groups as well as between groups.

Constructionist theory leads us to recognize that long-term memories are not necessarily accurate. In the next sections, we take a look at two controversial issues that call into question the credibility of long-term memory: eyewitness testimony and recovery of repressed memories. These issues place memory research squarely in the public eye. First, however, we examine another type of long-term memory: flashbulb memories, which, regardless of their accuracy, seem indelibly etched in the brain.

CONCEPT 6.14

Emotionally arousing events may leave vivid, lasting impressions in memory, called flashbulb memories, that seem permanently etched into our brains.

Flashbulb Memories: What Were You Doing When . . . ? Extremely stressful or emotionally arousing personal or historical events may leave vivid, lasting, and highly detailed memories called **flashbulb memories** (Tekcan & Peynircioglu, 2002). They are called flashbulb memories because they seem to have been permanently seared into the brain by the pop of the flashbulb on an old-fashioned camera. Many of us share a flashbulb memory of the World Trade Center disaster. We remember where we were and what we were doing at the time we heard of the attack, just as though it had happened yesterday. Many baby-boomers share the flashbulb memory of the assassination of President John Kennedy in 1963.

Despite the vividness of flashbulb memories, they may be as inaccurate and prone to distortion as other forms of long-term memory (Hertel, 1996). A recent study of flashbulb memories of the terrorist attacks of September 11, 2001 showed that they were not any more accurate than ordinary memories (Talarico & Rubin, 2003).

I wonder what flashbulb memories of dramatic historical events will be etched into your brain by the time this book reaches your hands. I wonder, too, how accurate your memory will be.

CONCEPT 6.15

Memory reports of eyewitnesses may be flawed, even when eyewitnesses are convinced of the accuracy of their recollections.

Eyewitness Testimony: "What Did You See on the Day in Question?" In reaching a verdict, juries give considerable weight to eyewitness testimony. Yet memory researchers find that eyewitness testimony can be as flawed and strewn with error as other forms of memory. Psychologist Elizabeth Loftus points out that many people have been wrongly convicted of crimes because of faulty eyewitness testimony (Loftus, 2004).

Frozen in Memory? Emotionally charged experiences such as the horrific events of 9/11 can create "flashbulb memories" that seem indelibly etched in our brains. Yet such memories may not be as accurate as we think they are.

flashbulb memories Enduring memories of emotionally charged events that seem permanently seared into the brain.

Figure 6.7   Misinformation Effect
Subjects saw a film of a car accident at an intersection marked by a stop sign. Some were then given the false information that they had seen a yield sign at the intersection. If you were one of these subjects, would your memory be based on what you had seen or on what you were told afterward?

Elizabeth Loftus

One source of distortions in eyewitness testimony is the **misinformation effect** (Chambers & Zaragoza, 2001; Loftus, 2003). These distortions are caused by events that occur in the interval between the event and recall of the event. In one early study, Loftus and her colleagues had subjects view a film of a car accident that occurred at an intersection with a stop sign (Loftus, Miller, & Burns, 1978). Some subjects were then given misleading information telling them that the traffic sign was a yield sign. When subjects were later asked what traffic sign they saw at the intersection, subjects given the false information tended to report seeing the yield sign (see Figure 6.7). Subjects who were not given the false information were much more likely to recall the correct traffic sign. In later research, Loftus and her colleagues showed that giving people misinformation can cause them to make various memory mistakes—for example, recalling that they saw a white car at a crime scene when in actuality it was a blue car or that they saw Minnie Mouse when they actually saw Mickey Mouse (Loftus, 2003).

False memories of events that never occurred have also been induced experimentally (Gleaves et al., 2004; Kihlstrom, 2004; Loftus, 2003). In some cases, experimenters have planted false memories from childhood of having been hospitalized overnight or having been involved in an unfortunate accident at a family wedding (Loftus, 2004). Some people exposed to a false ad showing Bugs Bunny at Disneyland later recalled that they too had met Bugs at Disneyland, and some even remembered hugging him (Loftus, 2004). Such a meeting is of course impossible, because the Bugs Bunny character is owned by Disney rival Warner Brothers.

Even when participants in memory studies are warned that they were misled, they are still vulnerable to saying they saw events or items that had only been suggested to them (Chambers & Zaragoza, 2001). False memories become stronger when people receive confirmation from others that their recollection is correct (Zaragoza et al., 2001). Research on false or distorted memories calls into question the credibility of eyewitness testimony, especially when witnesses are subject to

misinformation effect   A form of memory distortion that affects eyewitness testimony and that is caused by misinformation provided during the retention interval.

Me at Disneyland? What's Up with That, Doc?   About one in three people who were shown a phony ad featuring a picture of Bugs Bunny just outside the Magic Kingdom at Disneyland later said they believed or remembered that they had once met Bugs at Disneyland. But such meetings could never have occurred because the character of Bugs is owned by the Disney rival Time Warner. These findings suggest how easy it can be to create false memories in the minds of some people.

leading or suggestive questioning that might "plant" ideas in their heads (Begley, 2001d).

Imagination and visualization can also play tricks on your memory. Simply imagining a past experience can induce a false memory of an event that actually occurred (Mazzoni & Memom, 2003). Other investigators had laboratory participants visualize certain objects in their minds while their brain activity was monitored by functional MRI (Gonsalves et al., 2004). Later, participants sometimes claimed to have seen photos of objects that they had only visualized. Interestingly, these false memories were more likely to occur when brain areas that are engaged during visual imagery were more strongly activated during the visualizing task. These results suggest that activating areas of the brain involved in visual imagery can lead to false memories of having seen something that was merely visualized in one's mind.

Accuracy of eyewitness testimony is one thing. But accuracy of juror memory for information presented at trial is quite another. Evidence from studies of mock juries indicates that jurors often do not remember accurately the information presented at trial (Pritchard & Keenan, 1999, 2002). Given this evidence, it makes sense to encourage jurors to review trial information during their deliberations rather than rely solely on memory.

Since eyewitness testimony may often be flawed, should we eliminate it from court proceedings? Loftus (1993b) argues that if we dispensed with eyewitness testimony, many criminals would go free. As an alternative, we can attempt to increase the accuracy of eyewitness testimony. One way of boosting accuracy is to find corroborating evidence or independent witnesses who can back up each other's testimony. Another way is to ensure that fair and unbiased procedures are followed for administering police lineups to witnesses (Devenport et al., 2002). The accuracy of eyewitness testimony also involves the following factors:

1. *Ease of recall.* People who take longer to answer questions in giving testimony are less likely to be accurate in their recall than those who respond without hesitation (Robinson, Johnson, & Herndon, 1997). Similarly, eyewitnesses who are quicker in making identifications of a perpetrator from a lineup tend to be more accurate than those who take longer (Dunning & Perretta, 2002; Weber et al., 2004; Wells, Olson, & Charman, 2002).

2. *Degree of confidence.* Confidence in memory is only modestly associated with better accuracy (Fruzzetti et al., 1992). People who say with solid certainty, "That's the person who did it," are not necessarily more accurate than those who admit they could be mistaken. However, many juries are swayed by eyewitnesses who express confidence in their memories.

3. *General knowledge about a subject.* People who are knowledgeable about a subject are more likely than those who know less about the subject to be reliable witnesses. For example, when asked by a police officer to identify a motor vehicle involved in a crime, a person familiar with the various makes and models of automobiles will be better equipped to give a reliable answer than one who knows little or nothing of the subject (Davies et al., 1996).

4. *Ethnic/racial identification.* People are generally better able to recognize faces of people of their own racial/ethnic group (H. D. Ellis & Shepherd, 1992). Thus, eyewitnesses are more likely to make mistakes when identifying members of other racial/ethnic groups (Egeth, 1993).

5. *Types of questions.* Leading or suggestive questions by investigators can result in the misidentification of perpetrators (Loftus, 1997). Open-ended questions— for example, "What did you see?"—tend to increase the accuracy of eyewitness testimony (Fruzzetti et al., 1992). However, open-ended questions tend to elicit fewer details from witnesses.

6. *Facial characteristics.* Faces with distinctive features are much more likely to be accurately recognized than nondistinctive faces (Wells & Olson, 2003). Also, highly attractive or highly unattractive faces are more likely to be accurately identified than are those of average attractiveness.

EXPLORING PSYCHOLOGY
Are Recovered Memories Credible?

A high-level business executive's comfortable life fell apart one day when his 19-year-old daughter accused him of having repeatedly molested her throughout her childhood. The executive lost his marriage as well as his $400,000-a-year job. But he fought back against the allegations, which he insisted were untrue. He sued his daughter's therapists, who had helped her recover these memories. A jury sided with the businessman, awarding him $500,000 in damages from the two therapists.

This case is but one of many involving adults who claim to have only recently become aware of memories of childhood sexual abuse. Hundreds of people throughout the country have been brought to trial on the basis of recovered memories of childhood abuse, with many of these cases resulting in convictions and long jail sentences, even in the absence of corroborating evidence. Such recovered memories often occur following suggestive probing by a therapist or hypnotist (Loftus, 1993a, 1993b). The issue of recovered memories continues to be hotly debated in psychology and the broader community. At the heart of the debate is the question "Are recovered memories believable?" No one doubts that childhood sexual abuse is a major problem confronting our society. But should recovered memories be taken at face value?

Several lines of evidence lead us to question the validity of recovered memories. Experimental evidence shows that false memories can be created, especially under the influence of leading or suggestive questioning (Gleaves et al., 2004; Kihlstrom, 2004; Zoellner et al., 2000). Memory for events that never happened may be created, and they may seem just as genuine as memories of real events, (Zola, 1999). Moreover, although people who have experienced actual abuse in childhood may be somewhat sketchy on the details, a total lack of memory of traumatic childhood events is rare (Bradley & Follingstad, 2001). Loftus (1996, p. 356), writes of the dangers of taking recovered memories at face value:

After developing false memories, innumerable "patients" have torn their families apart, and more than a few innocent people have been sent to prison. This is not to say that people cannot forget horrible things that have happened to them; most certainly they can. But there is virtually no support for the idea that clients presenting for therapy routinely have extensive histories of abuse of which they are completely unaware, and that they can be helped only if the alleged abuse is resurrected from their unconscious.

Should we conclude, then, that recovered memories are bogus? Not necessarily. Both false memories and recovered true memories may exist. It is possible for adults to suddenly recover memories of long-forgotten childhood experiences, including memories of abuse (Chu et al., 1999). All in all, some recovered memories may be true; others may not be (Gleaves et al., 2004; Rubin, 1996).

In sum, we shouldn't think of the brain as a kind of mental camera that stores snapshots of events as they actually happened in the form of memories. Memory is more of a reconstructive process in which bits of information are pieced together in ways that can sometimes lead to a distorted recollection of events, even though the person may be convinced the memory is accurate. Unfortunately, we don't have the tools to distinguish the true memory from the false one (Cloitre, 2004; Loftus, 1993b).

MODULE 6.1 REVIEW

Remembering

RECITE IT

What are the basic processes and stages of memory?

- The three basic memory processes are encoding (converting stimuli into a form that can be stored in memory), storage (retaining them in memory), and retrieval (accessing stored information).

- We encode information by means of acoustic codes (coding by sounds), visual codes (coding by mental imaging), and semantic codes (coding by meaning). Though we often encode auditory information acoustically, semantic coding typically leads to more enduring memories.

- The three stages of memory are sensory memory (momentary storage of sensory impressions), short-term memory (working memory of information held in awareness for up to about thirty seconds), and long-term memory (long-term or permanent storage of information).

- The three-component model holds that working memory consists of three subsystems: (1) the speech-based phonological loop; (2) the visuospatial sketchpad for holding visual or spatial information; and (3) the central executive, which coordinates the other subsystems, processes material held in working memory, and filters out distracting thoughts.

- The semantic network model posits that information is held in long-term memory in networks of interlinking concepts. Through a process of spreading activation, thinking of one concept brings related concepts within that semantic network to mind.

- The two major types of long-term memory are declarative memory ("knowing what or that") and procedural memory ("knowing how").

- Declarative memory is brought to mind by conscious effort, whereas procedural memory is engaged without any conscious effort.

What is the constructionist theory of memory?

- Constructionist theory holds that memory is a representation, or reconstruction, of past events or experiences.

What are flashbulb memories?

- Flashbulb memories are vivid, highly detailed, and long-lasting memories of emotionally charged personal or historical events.

What factors influence the accuracy of eyewitness testimony?

- Factors affecting the accuracy of eyewitness testimony include ease of recall, confidence in memory, general knowledge about the subject, same-race identification, and occurrence of leading or suggestive questioning.

RECALL IT

1. Psychologists generally think of memory as a(n) _____ processing system.

2. The _____ principle holds that retrieval of a memory will be more successful when cues available during recall are similar to those present when the material was first committed to memory.

3. Which of the following is *not* correct? Constructionist theory suggests that
   a. memory recall may not be accurate.
   b. information is best recalled when it is consistent with a person's memory schemas.
   c. eyewitness testimony may be influenced by misinformation.
   d. flashbulb memories are immune to distortion.

4. The type of memory that corresponds to "knowing how" is called _____.

5. Match the concepts with their descriptions below:
   i. sensory; ii. short-term memory; iii. consolidation; iv. elaborative rehearsal

   a. process by which short-term memory is converted to long-term memory
   b. also known as "working" memory
   c. process that uses semantic coding to transfer short-term memory to long-term memory
   d. storage system for fleeting iconic and echoic memories

THINK ABOUT IT

- Why is it incorrect to say that memory works like a mental camera?

- What factors influence the accuracy of eyewitness testimony?

MODULE 6.2
Forgetting

- What are the major theories of forgetting?
- How is recall related to the methods used to measure it?
- What is amnesia, and what causes it?

Everyone is forgetful. Some of us are more forgetful than others. But why do we forget? Is it simply a matter of memories fading over time? Or are there other factors that account for forgetfulness? Degenerative brain diseases, such as Alzheimer's disease, are one cause of forgetfulness; another is amnesia, a memory disorder we discuss at the end of this module. Our main focus here, however, is on normal processes of forgetting. We recount several leading theories of forgetting and highlight the role of factors that make it easier or harder to remember information. We begin with decay theory.

CONCEPT 6.18
The oldest theory of forgetting, decay theory, may explain memory loss that occurs because of the passage of time, but it fails to account for why some memories endure better through time than others.

Figure 6.8 **Ebbinghaus Forgetting Curve**
As Ebbinghaus showed, forgetting occurs most rapidly shortly after learning and then gradually declines over time.

decay theory   A theory of forgetting that posits that memories consist of traces laid down in the brain that gradually deteriorate and fade away over time (also called *trace theory*).

savings method   A method of testing memory retention by comparing the numbers of trials needed to learn material with the number of trials needed to relearn the material at a later time.

massed vs. spaced practice effect The tendency for retention of learned material to be greater with spaced practice than with massed practice.

Decay Theory: Fading Impressions

The belief that memories consist of traces in the brain that gradually deteriorate and fade away over time dates back to the writings of the Greek philosopher Plato some 2,500 years ago. This theory of forgetting, now known as **decay theory** (also called *trace theory*), was bolstered by early experimental studies conducted by one of the founders of experimental psychology, Hermann Ebbinghaus (1850–1909 (see the Pioneers box on the following page). An interesting aspect of Ebbinghaus's experimental work on forgetting is that the only subject in his early studies was himself.

To study the processes of memory and forgetting, Ebbinghaus knew he had to eliminate any earlier associations to the material to be remembered. He devised a method for testing memory that used nonsense syllables (combinations of letters that don't spell out anything), such as *nuz* and *lef* (Ebbinghaus, 1885). He presented these lists of syllables to himself and determined the number of trials it took for him to recall them perfectly. He then tested himself again at different intervals to see how much he would forget over time. The results showed a decline in memory that has since become known as the *Ebbinghaus forgetting curve* (see Figure 6.8). Forgetting occurred rapidly in the first few hours after learning but then gradually declined. It seemed as though memories simply faded over time. By the end of the first day, 66 percent of the information had been lost, and after a month, nearly 80 percent was gone (Rupp, 1998).

Ebbinghaus also employed a **savings method** to test his memory retention. He first counted the number of times needed to rehearse a list of nonsense syllables in order to commit it to memory. Then he counted the number of times it took to relearn the list after a period of time had elapsed. If it took ten repetitions to learn the list the first time and five the second, the savings would be 50 percent.

Memory researchers recognize that when people attempt to memorize information, they generally retain more information when they space their study sessions than when they cram them together (Payne & Wenger, 1996). One reason for this effect, called the **massed vs. spaced practice effect**, is that massed, or crammed, practice causes mental fatigue that interferes with learning and retention. A practical implication of this effect should be obvious: When studying for exams, don't cram; space out your study sessions.

One major weakness of the decay theory of forgetting is that it fails to account for the unevenness with which memory decays over time. Some memories remain well preserved over time, whereas others quickly fade. Decay theory may account for memory loss due to the passage of time, but other factors, including the meaningfulness of the material, also influence forgetting. Ebbinghaus had studied retention

THE PIONEERS | A Chance Encounter?

Hermann Ebbinghaus

A chance encounter in a second-hand bookstore in Paris seems an unlikely beginning for a young man who was about to carve out a significant niche in the annals of scientific psychology (Boring, 1950; R. I. Watson, 1971). But there among the stacks of used books was a copy of Fechner's *Elements of Psychophysics*. Upon reading it, the young man, Hermann Ebbinghaus, was immediately captivated by the advances that Fechner's experimental approach to psychology had made toward understanding the processes of sensation. Some contemporary historians of psychology consider the story of Ebbinghaus's accidental discovery of a used copy of Fechner's book to be far-fetched and perhaps even fictional (Hogan, 2001). Yet there is no doubt that Ebbinghaus determined to bring Fechner's experimental method to bear on the higher mental processes of learning and memory. The only problem was that Ebbinghaus had no teacher, no university, no laboratory, and no professional appointment. For the next several years, he painstakingly pursued the scientific study of memory processes entirely on his own and with himself as his only subject. Ebbinghaus's life story demonstrates that adoption of the scientific method, not one's professional affiliations or appointments, is the key to expanding scientific knowledge.

Online Study Center
Improve Your Grade
Tutorials: Interference Theory of Forgetting

💡 **CONCEPT 6.19**
Interference theory posits that memories held in short-term or long-term memory may be pushed aside by other memories.

interference theory   The belief that forgetting is the result of the interference of memories with each other.

retroactive interference   A form of interference in which newly acquired information interferes with retention of material learned earlier.

proactive interference   A form of interference in which material learned earlier interferes with retention of newly acquired information.

of meaningless syllables. But if we examine the retention of more meaningful information, such as poetry or prose, we find a more gradual loss of memory over time. For other meaningful information, such as important historic events, specific job-related knowledge, and personal data like birth dates and schools attended, little if any forgetting occurs over time. Another factor to help explain forgetting is interference (Wixted, 2005).

Interference Theory: When Learning More Leads to Remembering Less

Chances are you have forgotten what you ate for dinner a week ago Wednesday. The reason for your forgetfulness, according to **interference theory**, is interference from memories of dinners that preceded and followed that particular dinner. On the other hand, you are unlikely to forget your wedding day because it is so unlike any other day in your life (except for those, perhaps, who have taken many walks down the aisle). Interference theory helps explain why some events may be easily forgotten while others remain vivid for a lifetime. The greater the similarity between events, the greater the risk of interference. There are two general kinds of interference, *retroactive interference* and *proactive interference*.

Interference occurring after material is learned but before it is recalled is called **retroactive interference**. Perhaps you have found that material you learned in your 9:00 A.M. class, which seemed so clear when you left the classroom, quickly began to fade once you started soaking in information in the next class. One reason that new memories retroactively interfere with unstable earlier memories is that they are still undergoing the process of memory consolidation (Wixted, 2004).

Proactive interference is caused by the influence of previously learned material. Because of proactive interference, you may have difficulty remembering a new area code (you keep dialing the old one by mistake). Or you may forget to advance the year when writing checks early in a new year. Figure 6.9 illustrates retroactive and proactive interference.

Figure 6.9 Retroactive and Proactive Interference
In retroactive interference, new learning (psychology in the first example) interferes with recall of previously learned material (philosophy). In proactive interference, previously learned material (philosophy in the second example) interferes with recall of new material (psychology).

REALITY CHECK

THE CLAIM Once you learn something, you never forget it.

THE EVIDENCE You may sometimes have the experience of remembering something you thought you had forgotten. However, this doesn't mean that everything you've ever learned is permanently etched in your brain. Ebbinghaus showed that most of the nonsense syllables he had learned were forgotten within the span of one day. Much of what we learn in our daily experiences, especially the insignificant details, is quickly forgotten as the result of ineffective encoding of information, fading or decay of memory traces, or interference from other learning.

THE TAKE-AWAY MESSAGE
Memories may last a lifetime, but much of what we learn is soon forgotten.

 CONCEPT 6.20
The serial position effect explains why we are more likely to forget the middle items in a list than those at the beginning or end.

overlearning Practice repeated beyond the point necessary to reproduce material without error.

serial position effect The tendency to recall items at the start or end of a list better than items in the middle of a list.

Though some interference is unavoidable, we can take steps to minimize its disruptive effects:

- *Sleep on it.* Sleeping is an activity that is minimally disruptive of newly learned material. In fact, as noted in Module 6.1, REM sleep may help consolidate new memories into lasting ones. Studying material directly before sleep may help you retain what you learn.

- *Rehearse fresh memories.* New long-term memories are fragile. Practicing or rehearsing fresh memories aloud or silently can strengthen them, making them more resistant to the effects of interference. Practice repeated beyond the point necessary to reproduce material without error is called **overlearning**. Apply the principle of overlearning to ensure retention by repeating newly learned material at least two times beyond the point of minimal competence.

- *Give yourself a break.* Try not to schedule one class directly after another. Give your recent memories time to consolidate in your brain.

- *Avoid sequential study of similar material.* Try not to study material that is similar in content in back-to-back fashion. For example, avoid scheduling a French class right after a Spanish one.

Interference may help explain the **serial position effect**, the tendency to recall the first and last items in a list, such as a shopping list, better than those in the middle of the list. The unfortunate items in the middle are often forgotten. Researchers find that when people are asked to name the last seven U.S. presidents in order, they are more likely to make mistakes in the middle of the list than at either the beginning or end (Storandt, Kaskie, & Von Dras, 1998). Serial position effects influence both short-term and long-term memory.

Interference is the likely culprit in serial position effects. Items compete with one another in memory and interference is greatest in the middle of a list than at either end of the list. For example, in a list of seven items, the fourth item may interfere with the item that it follows and the item that it precedes. But interference is least for the first and last items in the list—the first, because no other item

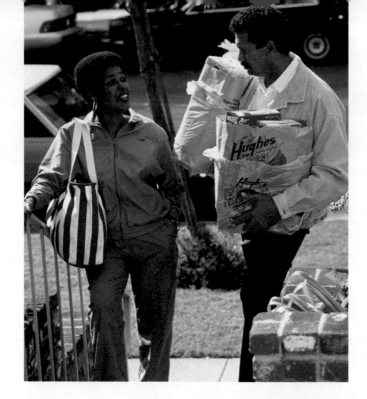

But I Remembered the Broccoli! This man remembered the broccoli his wife asked him to pick up at the store, but not the tuna fish. Based on your knowledge of the serial position effect, why do you suppose he remembered the broccoli and not the tuna fish?

precedes it; the last, because no other item follows it. The tendency to recall items better when they are learned first is called the **primacy effect**. The tendency to recall items better when they are learned last is called the **recency effect** (Davelaar et al., 2005). As the delay between a study period and a test period increases, primacy effects become stronger, whereas recency effects become weaker (Knoedler, Hellwig, & Neath, 1999). This recency-primacy shift means that as time passes after you committed a list to memory, it becomes easier to remember the early items but harder to remember those that appeared later in the list.

In sum, evidence shows that both the passage of time and interference contribute to forgetting. But neither decay theory nor interference theory can determine whether forgotten material becomes lost to memory or just more difficult to retrieve. Some forgotten material can be recovered if subjects are given retrieval cues to jog their memory, such as exposure to stimuli associated with the original situations in which the memories were formed. This brings us to a third model of forgetting, retrieval theory.

Retrieval Theory:
Forgetting as a Breakdown in Retrieval

According to **retrieval theory**, forgetting is the result of a failure to access stored memories (Koriat, 1993; Rovee-Collier, 1996). Let us consider two principal ways in which the retrieval process can break down, *encoding failure* and *lack of retrieval cues*.

Encoding Failure: What Image Is on the Back Side of a Nickel? Memories cannot be retrieved if they were never encoded in the first place. The failure to encode information may explain why people often cannot recall details about common objects they use every day. For example, do you know what image appears on the back of a nickel? Before you rummage through your pockets, let me tell you it is an image of Monticello, the home of Thomas Jefferson, whose image is on the front of the coin. You may have glanced at this image of Monticello countless times but never brought it into memory because you failed to encode it. We tend to encode only as much information as we need to know. Since we don't need to encode more specific details of a coin to recognize one or use it correctly, such information may not be encoded and thus cannot be retrieved (see Try This Out).

Online Study Center
Improve Your Grade
Tutorials: Memories Are Made of This—Primacy and Recency Effect

CONCEPT 6.21
Memory retrieval may be impaired by a failure to encode information and by a lack of retrieval cues to access stored memories.

primacy effect The tendency to recall items better when they are learned first.
recency effect The tendency to recall items better when they are learned last.
retrieval theory The belief that forgetting is the result of a failure to access stored memories.

TRY THIS OUT

What Does a Penny Look Like?

How well do you remember the features of a penny, the most commonplace of coins? Researchers Raymond Nickerson and Marilyn Jager Adams (1979) decided to find out. They showed subjects an array of drawings of a penny, only one of which was correct. Fewer than half of their subjects were able to pick out the correct one. Without looking at the coins in your pocket, can you tell which drawing of a penny in Figure 6.10 is the correct one? The answer appears on page 251.

Figure 6.10   What Image Appears on the Front of a Penny?

CONCEPT 6.22

A common problem with memory retrieval involves the tip-of-the-tongue phenomenon, the experience of sensing you know something but just can't seem to bring it to mind.

Events that stand out tend to be better remembered. You are more likely to remember your first date than your twenty-third one. You are also more likely to remember events that occur irregularly (e.g., visits to a doctor because of an injury) than regularly occurring events (visits to an allergist) (Means & Loftus, 1991). Events that are similar are generally encoded in terms of their common features rather than their distinctive characteristics (Conrad & Brown, 1996). Because similar events tend to be encoded in similar ways, it becomes more difficult to retrieve memories of the specific events.

Lack of Retrieval Cues: What's His Name?   Information may be encoded in memory but remain inaccessible because of a lack of appropriate retrieval cues. A common and often embarrassing difficulty with memory retrieval is recalling proper names. Proper names have no built-in associations, no convenient retrieval cues or "handles" that can be used to distinguish among the many Jennifers, Susans, Davids, and Johns of the world. Unusual names may be more easily recalled, since we are more likely to remember information that stands out from the pack. The Gertrudes and Oscars of the world may not be pleased to carry such monikers, but people may be more likely to remember their names.

A lack of retrieval cues may account for a common experience called the **tip-of-the-tongue (TOT) phenomenon**, in which the information seems to be at the tip of one's tongue but just outside reach. If you've ever felt frustrated trying to recall something you're certain you know but just can't seem to bring to mind, you've experienced the TOT phenomenon. People who experience it may have partial recall of the information they are trying to retrieve, which is why they feel so certain the information is stored somewhere in memory (Schwartz & Smith, 1997). They may recall the first few letters or sounds of the word or name ("I know it

tip-of-the-tongue (TOT) phenomenon
An experience in which people are sure they know something but can't seem to bring it to mind.

starts with a *B*"), or perhaps a similar-sounding word comes to mind. TOTs may result not only from a lack of available retrieval cues, but also from more general difficulties with word retrieval. They tend to increase in later life, when word retrieval typically becomes more difficult (Burke & Shafto, 2004).

TOTs appear to be very common. A recent diary study revealed that, among a sample of undergraduate students, individuals averaged slightly more than one TOT experience per week (Schwartz, 2002). Most of the TOTs involved common nouns, such as people's names, and nearly 90 percent were successfully resolved, though it sometimes took more than twenty-four hours for the memory to be retrieved.

What can you do if you experience the TOT phenomenon? First, try using any available retrieval cues, such as situational associations; also, try to draw upon phonological cues—words you believe sound like the target word (L. E. James & Burke, 2000; White & Abrams, 2002). Imagine you see someone you've met before but can't quite remember the person's name. You might say to yourself, "Let's see, I think I met him at the party last month. A friend of Jill. Plays basketball on weekends. I think his name sounded something like Terry. No, it was Kerry. Yes, that's it." You might also try talking to the person for a while until an association comes up that jogs your memory. If you find yourself stuck, perhaps the best advice is to give it a rest. The answer may eventually "pop" into your mind if you put it aside for a while and try again later in a different context (P. T. Smith, 1997).

Motivated Forgetting: Memories Hidden from Awareness

Sigmund Freud believed that certain memories are not forgotten but are kept hidden from awareness by **repression**, or motivated forgetting. In Freud's view, repression is a psychological defense mechanism that protects the self from awareness of threatening material, such as traumatic sexual experiences, aggressive impulses, and unacceptable sexual desires (e.g., incestuous wishes). Were it not for repression, Freud believed, we would be flooded with overwhelming anxiety whenever threatening material entered consciousness. Repression, or motivated forgetting, is not simple forgetting; the repressed contents do not disappear but remain in the unconscious mind, hidden from awareness.

Freud's concept of repression does not account for ordinary forgetting—the kind that occurs when you try to retain information you read in your psychology textbook, to use a convenient example. Another problem with this concept is that people who are traumatized by rape, combat, or natural disasters, such as earthquakes or floods, tend to retain vivid if somewhat fragmented memories of these experiences. They often find it difficult to put such anxiety-evoking events out of their minds, which is the opposite of what we might expect from Freud's concept of repression. Moreover, since repression operates unconsciously, we may lack direct means of testing it scientifically. Nonetheless, many memory researchers, including a panel of experts appointed by the American Psychological Association, believe that repression can occur (Alpert, Brown, & Courtois, 1998; Willingham, 2001).

Measuring Memory: How It Is Measured May Determine How Much Is Recalled

Students who are given the choice generally prefer multiple-choice questions to questions that require a written essay. Why? The answer has to do with the different ways in which memory is measured.

The methods used to measure memory can have an important bearing on how well you are able to retrieve information stored in memory. In a **recall task**, such as an essay or fill-in-the-blank question, you are asked to recall previously learned information with minimal cues available to jog your memory. There are three basic types of recall task. In *free recall,* you are asked to recall as much information as you can in any order you wish (e.g., randomly naming starting players on your college's basketball team). In a *serial recall* task, you are asked to recall a series of items or numbers in a particular order (e.g., reciting a telephone number). In *paired-associates recall,* you are first asked to memorize pairs of items, such as pairs of unrelated words like *shoe-crayon* and *cat-phone.* You are then presented with one item in each pair, such as the word *shoe,* and asked to recall the item with which it was paired (*crayon*). If you've ever taken a foreign language exam in which you were presented with a word in English and asked to produce the foreign word for it, you know what a paired-associates recall task is.

In a **recognition task**, you are asked to pick out the correct answer from among a range of alternative answers. Tests of recognition memory, such as multiple-choice tests, generally produce much better retrieval than those of recall memory, largely because recognition tests provide more helpful retrieval cues, such as seeing the correct answer among a choice of alternative answers. You're more likely to remember the name of the author of *Moby Dick* if you see the author's name among a group of authors' names on a multiple-choice test than if you are asked to complete a recall task, such as a fill-in-the-blank item in which you are required to insert the author's name (Herman Melville, in case you're stumped).

Amnesia: Of Memories Lost or Never Gained

A medical student is brought by ambulance to the hospital after falling from his motorcycle and suffering a blow to his head. His parents rush to his side, keeping a vigil until he regains consciousness. Fortunately, he is not unconscious for long. As his parents are explaining what has happened to him, his wife suddenly bursts into the hospital room, throwing her arms around him and expressing her great relief that he wasn't seriously injured or killed. When his wife, whom he had married only a few weeks earlier, leaves the room, the medical student turns to his mother and asks, "Who is she?" (cited in Freemon, 1981, p. 96).

How can we explain this severe memory loss? The medical student suffered from a type of **amnesia**, or memory loss. The term *amnesia* is derived from the Greek roots *a* ("not") and *mnasthai* ("to remember").

Amnesia Amnesia is often caused by a traumatic injury to the brain, such as a blow to the head. This football player was knocked unconscious and may not remember anything about the play in which he was injured or other events preceding the play.

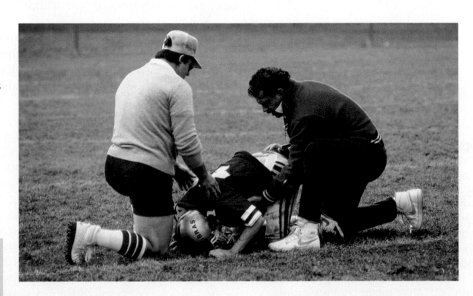

recognition task A method of measuring memory retention that assesses the ability to select the correct answer from among a range of alternative answers.

amnesia Loss of memory.

CONCEPT 6.25

There are two general types of amnesia, retrograde amnesia (loss of memory of past events) and anterograde amnesia (loss or impairment of the ability to form or store new memories).

Types of Amnesia The medical student suffered from **retrograde amnesia**, or loss of memory of events occurring prior to a traumatic injury (Riccio, Millin, & Gisquet-Verrier, 2003). A football player knocked unconscious by a blow to the head during a game may remember nothing beyond suiting up in the locker room. A boxer knocked cold in the ring may not remember the fight. A blow to the head can interfere with *memory consolidation,* which, as noted in Module 6.1, is the process of converting unstable, short-term memories into stable and enduring ones. When this process is disrupted, memories of events occurring around the time of the disruption may be lost permanently. Sometimes the memory loss extends further back in time, as in the case of the medical student. In some cases, whole chunks of memory are lost. Nonetheless, recent memories are generally more susceptible to retrograde amnesia than remote events (James & MacKay, 2001). In another form of amnesia, **anterograde amnesia**, people cannot form or store new memories or life experiences or have difficulty doing so.

Amnesia typically involves impairment of episodic memory: memory of personal experiences. Amnesic patients generally retain procedural memory, the automatic memory we call upon when performing mechanical tasks such as tying our shoes or frying an egg (Cavaco et al., 2004). The retention of procedural memory in the face of loss of episodic memory in amnesic patients leads us to think that different memory systems in the brain are responsible for these two types of memory.

Let's ask a more personal question. What is your earliest memory? Your fifth or sixth birthday party? The day your parents took you to the circus when you were four or five? Before the age of three or four, people can recall virtually no memories (Fivush & Nelson, 2004; Weigle & Bauer, 2000). Failure to recall early life experiences, which Freud called *infantile amnesia,* is a perfectly normal process of development. **Childhood amnesia** may be a more accurate term than *infantile amnesia* because memory loss extends beyond infancy into early childhood. Numerous theories have been proposed to explain childhood amnesia. Freud explained it in terms of repression, or motivated forgetting of disturbing sexual or aggressive material. One problem with Freud's account is that it fails to explain why all memories of early childhood are lost, not just potentially troubling memories.

One contemporary view of childhood amnesia suggests that preverbal memories—memories formed before language develops—are not well organized in the brain. They are thus difficult to retrieve through the word-based, or verbal, memory system that typically develops between the second and third years of life (Pillemer, 1999). Another view is that the brain structures needed to form lasting memories do not mature until a child is about 2 or 3 years of age.

Causes of Amnesia The causes of amnesia may be physical or psychological. Physical causes include blows to the head, degenerative brain diseases (such as Alzheimer's disease; see Chapter 10), blockage of blood vessels to the brain, infectious diseases, and chronic alcoholism. Early detection and treatment of the underlying physical condition are critical, as many of these forms of amnesia can be corrected with proper treatment.

Amnesia resulting from psychological causes is called **dissociative amnesia**. *Dissociation* means "splitting off." Memories of a traumatic experience may become "dissociated" (split off) from consciousness, producing a form of amnesia for events occurring during a specific time (see Chapter 13). These events may be too emotionally troubling—provoking too much anxiety or guilt—to be consciously experienced. A soldier may have at best a dim memory of the horror he experienced on the battlefield and remember nothing of his buddy's being killed; yet his memory of other past events remains intact. Rarely is dissociative amnesia of the type that has fueled many a daytime soap opera, the type in which people forget their entire lives—who they are, where they live, and so on. Concept Chart 6.2 provides an overview of the key concepts of forgetting.

retrograde amnesia Loss of memory of past events.

anterograde amnesia Loss or impairment of the ability to form or store new memories.

childhood amnesia The normal occurrence of amnesia for events occurring during infancy and early childhood.

dissociative amnesia A psychologically based form of amnesia involving the "splitting off" from memory of traumatic or troubling experiences.

CONCEPT CHART 6.2   Forgetting: Key Concepts

	Concept	Description	Example
Theories of Forgetting	Decay theory	Gradual fading of memory traces as a function of time	Facts you learned in school gradually fade out of memory over time.
	Interference theory	Disruption of memory caused by interference of previously learned material or newly learned material	After sitting through your biology lecture, you forget what you learned in chemistry class the hour before.
	Retrieval theory	Failure to access material stored in memory because of encoding failure or lack of retrieval cues	You have difficulty remembering something you know is stored in memory.
	Repression	Motivated forgetting of anxiety-provoking material	You cannot remember a traumatic childhood experience.
Measuring Methods	Recall tasks	Test of the ability to reproduce information held in memory with only minimal cues available	You recite a phone number or the capital cities of the United States or provinces of Canada.
	Recognition tasks	Test of the ability to recognize material held in memory	You recognize the correct answer in a multiple-choice question.
Types of Amnesia	Retrograde amnesia	Loss of memory of past events	After suffering a blow to the head in a car accident, you are unable to remember details of the accident itself.
	Anterograde amnesia	Loss or impairment of the ability to form or store new memories	Because of a brain disorder, you find it difficult to retain new information.

MODULE 6.2 REVIEW

Forgetting

RECITE IT

What are the major theories of forgetting?

- Decay theory holds that forgetting results from the gradual deterioration of memory traces in the brain.

- Interference theory is the belief that forgetting results from the interference of memories with each other. In retroactive interference, newly acquired information interferes with retention of material learned earlier. In proactive interference, material learned earlier interferes with retention of newly acquired information.

- Retrieval theory holds that forgetting is the result of a failure to access stored memories.

- According to Freudian belief, repression, or motivated forgetting, happens when people banish emotionally troubling events, impulses, and wishes from conscious awareness.

How is recall related to the methods used to measure it?

- Recognition tasks (such as multiple-choice questions) generally produce better memory retrieval than recall tests (free recall, serial recall, or paired-associates recall) because they provide more retrieval cues that help jog specific memories.

What is amnesia, and what causes it?

- Amnesia, or memory loss, may be caused by psychological factors or by physical factors such as degenerative brain diseases and brain trauma. There are two general types of amnesia: retrograde amnesia, or loss of memory of past events; and anterograde amnesia, or inability to form and store new memories.

RECALL IT

1. According to the decay theory of memory, memory _____ in the brain fade or disappear over time.

2. The type of interference that accounts for why you may forget to advance the year when writing checks early in a new year is called _____.

3. The tip-of-the-tongue phenomenon may result from a lack of _____ cues.

4. _____ amnesia is memory loss for past life events.

5. Which of the following is *not* a helpful way to reduce the effects of interference on memory?
   a. Follow the principle of "massed practice" when studying or memorizing.
   b. Study material just before going to bed.
   c. Rehearse or practice material repeatedly.
   d. Avoid studying similar content simultaneously.

THINK ABOUT IT

- Have you had any tip-of-the-tongue experiences? Were you eventually able to retrieve the memory you were searching for? If so, how were you able to retrieve it?

- Why is it not a good idea to apply the principle of "massed practice" when preparing for exams? What study techniques are likely to be more effective?

- What suggestions would you offer to a fellow student to help him or her avoid the disruptive effects on memory of retroactive and proactive interference?

MODULE 6.3

The Biology of Memory

- **Where are memories stored in the brain?**
- **What is the role of the hippocampus in memory?**
- **What is LTP, and what role do scientists believe that it plays in memory formation?**
- **What have scientists learned about the genetic basis of memory?**

How are memories formed in the brain? Where are they stored? Breakthrough research is beginning to answer these and other questions that probe the biological underpinnings of memory. In this module, we examine what is presently known about those underpinnings.

Brain Structures in Memory: Where Do Memories Reside?

Psychologist Karl Lashley (1890–1958) spent much of his career attempting to track down the elusive **engram**, the term he used to describe a physical trace or etching in the brain where he believed a memory is stored. A rat that learns to run a maze, for example, should have an engram somewhere in its brain containing a memory trace of the correct route leading to the exit or goal box.

Lashley spent years training rats to run mazes, then surgically removing parts of their cerebral cortexes, and testing them again to see if their memories for mazes remained intact. He reasoned that if removal of a part of the cortex wiped away a given memory, that part must be where the particular memory was stored. Despite years of painstaking research, he found that rats continued to run mazes they had learned previously regardless of the parts of the cortex he removed. The rats simply did not forget. He concluded that memories are not housed in any specific brain structure but must be scattered about the brain.

Neuronal Networks: The Circuitry of Memory   Leading investigators today believe that memories are not etched into particular brain cells. Rather, they are coded, stored, and retrieved by complex circuits of neurons in the brain, called **neuronal networks** (also called *neural networks*) (Matsumoto, Suzuki, & Tanaka, 2003; Ojemann et al., 2002). The biochemical bases for how these circuits create memories are beyond our present understanding (Thompson, 2005). We can think of memory as the form in which information is encoded, stored, and retrieved by these circuits or neuronal networks. In simplest terms, the circuit is the memory (Thompson, 2005).

CONCEPT 6.26
Memories are stored in complex networks of interconnected brain cells called neuronal networks.

engram   Lashley's term for the physical trace or etching of a memory in the brain.
neuronal networks   Memory circuits in the brain that consist of complicated networks of nerve cells.

Figure 6.11   Brain Structures in Memory
There is no single memory center in the brain. Among the structures that work in coordination with the cerebral cortex in memory processes are the hippocampus, amygdala, and thalamus.

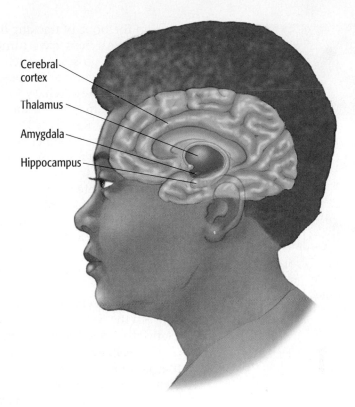

Cerebral cortex
Thalamus
Amygdala
Hippocampus

The Hippocampus: Where New Memories Are Formed   Scientists believe that the hippocampus, a structure in the brain's limbic system, plays a key role in turning short-term memories into long-term declarative memories—that is, into memories of facts (semantic memory) and life experiences (episodic memory) (Eichenbaum, 2003; Jacobs & Schenk, 2003; Leutgeb et al., 2004; Yasuno et al., 2003). But the hippocampus doesn't appear to play a role in procedural memory, the kind of memory we use when riding a bicycle or using tools. Nor does it appear that the hippocampus is the final destination for new declarative memories. Rather, it appears to be a temporary storage bin for holding new memories, perhaps for weeks or even months, before they are transferred for long-term storage to the cerebral cortex and other parts of the brain.

If you suffered extensive damage to your hippocampus, you might develop anterograde amnesia and be unable to form new memories (Thompson, 2005; Wixted, 2004). Depending on the extent of the damage, you might retain earlier memories but each new experience would fail to leave any mark in your memory (Dingfelder, 2004b). It would seem as if the new event had never happened.

Memory also depends on other brain structures, including the thalamus and the amygdala. We know, for example, that damage to the thalamus can result in amnesia. The amygdala plays an important part in encoding emotional experiences, such as fear and anger. Scientists believe that the amygdala and hippocampus become especially active during emotionally charged experiences, helping to strengthen and preserve memories of meaningful events (Adelson, 2004a; Hassert, Miyashita, & Williams, 2004). All in all, a number of different structures in the brain work in coordination in forming and storing memories (see Figure 6.11).

Strengthening Connections Between Neurons: The Key to Forming Memories

Locating neuronal networks corresponding to particular memories makes finding the proverbial needle in the haystack seem like child's play. The human brain contains billions of neurons and trillions of synapses among them. Any individual neuron in the brain may have some 10,000 synaptic connections with other neu-

CONCEPT 6.27
Damage to the hippocampus could prevent you from forming new memories, so that you might be unable to remember someone you've just met.

CONCEPT 6.28
The key to forming memories may lie in strengthening the interconnections between the neurons that form neuronal networks in the brain.

The Biology of Memory Nobel Prize winner Erik Kandel holding an *Aplysia,* the sea snail he used to study the biological bases of memory.

CONCEPT 6.29
Scientists suspect that long-term potentiation (LTP) may be needed for long-term memory to occur.

CONCEPT 6.30
Scientists have begun to unravel the genetic bases of memory, which may lead to the development of safe drugs that can help preserve or restore memory functioning.

long-term potentiation (LTP) The long-term strengthening of neural connections as the result of repeated stimulation.

rons. In the hope of tracking down specific networks of cells where memories are formed, researchers have turned to a relatively simple animal, a large sea snail (*Aplysia*) that possesses a mere 20,000 neurons but that may help us understand how memory works at the biochemical level (Carmichael, 2004).

Landmark research by Nobel laureate Erik Kandel, a molecular biologist, on *Aplysia* was a major step forward in unraveling the biological bases of memory (Kandel, 1995; Kandel & Hawkins, 1993). Since learning results in the formation of new memories, Kandel needed to demonstrate that these animals were capable of learning new responses. To accomplish this, he and his colleagues first desensitized the snails to receiving a squirt of water. After a number of trials, the animals became habituated to the water squirt so that it no longer caused them to budge. In the second phase of the experiment, the researchers paired the squirt with a mild electric shock. The animals showed they could learn a simple conditioned response—reflexively withdrawing their gills (their breathing apparatus) when squirted with water alone. This self-defensive maneuver was the equivalent of the snails battening down the hatches in anticipation of impending shock (Rupp, 1998).

Kandel observed that the amount of neurotransmitter released into synapses between the nerve cells that control the withdrawal reflex increased as the animals learned the conditioned response. The added neurotransmitter kicked the reflex into overdrive, making it more likely to fire. In effect, these synapses became stronger—that is, more capable of transmitting neural messages. Kandel had shown that memory formation involves biochemical changes occurring at the synaptic level.

Synaptic connections can also be strengthened by repeated electrical stimulation of brain cells. Moreover, they remain strengthened for a period of time. The long-lasting increase in the strength of the synaptic connections between neurons is called **long-term potentiation (LTP)**. *Potentiation* simply means "strengthening." Strengthened synaptic connections are more efficient in transmitting messages between neurons (Wixted, 2005).

Many memory scientists today believe that the conversion of short-term memory into long-term memory depends on the production of LTP within complex neuronal networks in the brain (Hoelscher, 2001; Martin, Grimwood, & Morris, 2000). LTP may result from the repeated stimulation of nerve cells within these neuronal networks that occurs as we learn to retain new information through repeated rehearsal or practice.

Genetic Bases of Memory

Promising research with genetic engineering is offering new insights into how memory works. The transformation of short-term memory into long-term memory depends on the production of certain proteins. The production of these proteins is regulated by certain genes. Scientists have found that manipulation of a particular gene in fruit flies can enhance learning and memory ability, producing a kind of "smart fly" (S. S. Hall, 1998). Perhaps a similar gene might one day be found in humans.

Scientists hope that knowledge gained about the role of brain proteins in memory and the genes that help regulate their production may eventually lead to the development of drugs to treat or even cure Alzheimer's disease and other memory disorders (S. S. Hall, 1998). Someday we may also have drugs that boost the memory functioning of the average person. In the meantime, think critically if you encounter claims about so-called memory-enhancing drugs. Though many companies are on the hunt for a memory-enhancing drug, at present we have no available drugs or supplements that have been shown to improve memory in normal individuals (e.g., Carmichael, 2004). Concept Chart 6.3 summarizes some of the key concepts relating to the biology of memory.

CONCEPT CHART 6.3   Biology of Memory: Key Concepts

Concept	Description
Lashley's engram	Despite years of research, Karl Lashley failed to find evidence of an engram, his term for a physical trace or etching in the brain where he believed a memory is stored.
Neuronal networks	Memory scientists believe that memories may "reside" in complex networks of neurons distributed across different parts of the brain.
Biological underpinnings of memory	The hippocampus is a key brain structure in converting short-term memory into long-term memory. A leading contemporary view of the conversion of short-term to long-term memory holds that it depends on long-term potentiation, the strengthening of synaptic connections between neurons.
Genetic factors in memory	Conversion of short-term memory to long-term memory depends on brain proteins whose production is regulated by certain genes. Advances in genetic engineering show that it is possible to enhance learning and memory ability in nonhuman organisms by genetic manipulation.

MODULE 6.3 REVIEW

The Biology of Memory

RECITE IT

Where are memories stored in the brain?

- Memories are stored within neuronal networks, the circuitry of nerve cells in the brain.

What is the role of the hippocampus in memory?

- The hippocampus appears to play a key role in the formation and temporary storage of declarative memory, such as memory of events and daily experiences.

What is LTP, and what role do scientists believe that it plays in memory formation?

- LTP (long-term potentiation) is the biochemical process by which repeated stimulation strengthens the synaptic connections between nerve cells.

- Scientists suspect that the conversion of short-term memory into long-term memory may depend on the LTP process.

What have scientists learned about the genetic basis of memory?

- Scientists have identified genes that appear to play important roles in biochemical processes needed for long-term memory.

RECALL IT

1. Lashley's search for the elusive _____ led him to recognize that memories are not localized in one part of the brain.

2. Researchers today believe that memories are stored in constellations of brain cells known as _____.

3. The strengthening of synaptic connections that may underlie the conversion of short-term memory into long-term memory is called _____.

4. Researchers are finding genetic influences in memory. How do genes influence memory functioning?
   a. They regulate the production of certain proteins that are critical to long-term memory.
   b. A memory gene leads to the production of specialized neurotransmitters involved in learning and memory.
   c. Genes regulate the production of a memory molecule that allows new memories to form.
   d. Memories are directly encoded in genes, which are then passed from one generation to the next.

THINK ABOUT IT

- Why did Lashley's search for engrams prove elusive?

- Suppose memory boosters are found that would allow you to preserve perfect memories of everything you read and experience. Though memory pills might help you around

exam time, would you really want to retain crystal-clear memories of every personal experience, including disappointments, personal tragedies, and traumatic experiences? What do you think?

APPLICATION MODULE 6.4
Powering Up Your Memory

CONCEPT 6.31
You can boost your memory power in many ways, such as by using mnemonics, focusing your attention, practicing repeatedly, taking care of your health, and adopting effective study habits.

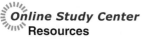
Online Study Center
Resources
Weblinks: Mind Tools for Improving Memory; Mnemonics and Memory Techniques

Even if you never compete in a memory championship, you can learn to boost your memory power. Techniques specifically aimed at enhancing memory are called *mnemonics,* some of which have been practiced since the time of the ancient Greeks. Yet perhaps the most important ways to power up your memory are to take care of your health and to adopt more effective methods of studying, such as the SQ3R+ system (see "To the Student" in the preface of the text).

Using Mnemonics to Improve Memory

A **mnemonic** is a device for improving memory. The word *mnemonic* is derived from the name of the Greek goddess of memory, Mnemosyne, and is pronounced neh-MAHN-ik (the first *m* is silent). Here are some of the most widely used mnemonic devices.

Acronyms and Acrostics   The method of acronyms (also called the *first-letter system*) is among the easiest and most widely used mnemonic devices. An **acronym** is a word composed of the first letters of a series of words. The acronym HOMES can help you remember the names of the Great Lakes (Huron, Ontario, Michigan, Erie, and Superior). In Chapter 3, you learned the acronym Roy G. Biv, which spells out the first letters of the colors of the spectrum. You might try devising some acronyms to help you retain information you learned in class.

An **acrostic** is a verse or saying in which a letter of each word, usually the first letter, stands for something else. Generations of musicians have learned the lines of the treble clef staff (E, G, B, D, and F) by committing to memory the acrostic "*Every Good Boy Does Fine.*"

Popular Sayings and Rhymes   Popular sayings and poems help us remember a variety of things, including when to turn the clock forward or back ("Fall back, spring forward"). Rhymes can be used as a mnemonic for remembering specific information. A common example is the rhyme for remembering the number of days in each month: "Thirty days hath September, April, June, and November . . ."

Visual Cues and Visual Imagery   Visual cues can help us remember to remember. When you need to remember to do something, pin a reminder note where you will be most likely to notice it, such as on your shoes, the front door, or the steering wheel of your car.

Figure 6.12
Funny, It Doesn't Look Like a Hippopotamus
You may be better able to remember the word *hippocampus* if you link it to a visual image of a hippopotamus.

Hippocampus

?

Hippopotamus

mnemonic   A device for improving memory.
acronym   A word composed of the first letters of a series of words.
acrostic   A verse or saying in which the first or last letter of each word stands for something else.

Visual imagery can help us remember new words, names, and word combinations. For example, to remember the word *hippocampus,* think of an associated image, such as the image of a hippopotamus (see Figure 6.12). To remember the name Bill Smith, picture a blacksmith who has a mouth shaped like a duck's bill (Turkington, 1996). The well-known memory expert Harry Lorayne (2002) recommended linking imagery to tasks that need to be remembered. For example, if you want to remember to mail a letter, picture the letter on the handle of the front door. Seeing the front door handle may cue you to take the letter to the mailbox.

Online Study Center
Improve Your Grade
Tutorials: A Chunk of Pie

Chunking   Chunking, which we discussed in Module 6.1, is one of the easiest ways to remember a series of numbers. To use it, break down a number series into more easily remembered bits. For example, the number 7362928739 may be difficult to remember as one long series. The task becomes easier when the digits are chunked like a telephone number into three bits: 736-292-8739. Learning the zip code 10024 becomes easier when it is chunked into 100-24.

General Suggestions for Improving Memory

Though mnemonic devices can help you remember bits and pieces of information, they are of little use when it comes to remembering more complex material, like the content of your college courses. But following the guidelines offered below and adopting good study habits will help you keep your learning and memory processes as sharp as possible (Herrmann & Palmisano, 1992; Turkington, 1996).

Pay Attention   One of the best ways to boost your learning or memory ability is to pay close attention. Paying attention means not only focusing more closely on the material at hand; it also means placing yourself in a quiet area that is conducive to studying and free of distractions (no TV, radio, phone, etc.).

Practice, Practice, Practice   You may have heard the old saw that the way to get to Carnegie Hall is to practice. Well, a good way to retain information is to rehearse it, and then rehearse it some more. Repeating information out loud or silently can help convert it from a short-term memory into a more enduring long-term memory. Make it a practice to "overlearn" material by repeating it two or more times beyond the point necessary for minimal proficiency.

You can also use "elaborative rehearsal" to strengthen retention of material you want to remember. One way of doing this is to relate the material to your personal experiences. For example, find examples in your own life of the concepts discussed in this chapter, such as declarative memory, procedural memory, implicit memory, and the tip-of-the-tongue phenomenon.

Spaced practice is more effective than massed practice at boosting retention. Spacing study sessions throughout the semester is a better strategy for preparing for exams than cramming at the end. Moreover, don't try to retain all the material in a chapter at one time. Break it down by sections or parts and rehearse your knowledge of each part. Then rehearse how the parts relate to each other as a whole.

Use External Memory Aids   Our daily lives are so packed with bits and pieces of information to be remembered that it makes sense to use whatever resources we can. Yes, you could use a mnemonic device to remember to tell your roommate that her mother called. But writing a reminder note to yourself will allow you to expend your mental efforts more profitably on something else. Other types of notes, such as class notes, are tools that you can use to retain more information. External memory aids, such as electronic organizers and computerized to-do lists, may also be helpful. You might even try putting objects, such as your key ring, in conspicuous places (thereby reducing occurrences of the common cry, "Now, where did I leave those keys?").

Link Time-Based Tasks to External Cues   Linking time-based tasks to external cues or activities can help boost prospective memory (Marsh, Hicks, & Cook, 2005). For example, if you need to take medication at 6:00 P.M., link it with having dinner (Einstein & McDaniel, 1996). Setting an alarm to go off at a certain time may prompt you to take your medicine or to make an important phone call. Even the time-honored tradition of tying a string around your finger may be helpful.

Mentally Rehearse What You Intend to Do   Rehearsing what you plan to do may increase the likelihood of performing the intended action (Chasteen, Park, & Schwarz, 2001). Before leaving the house in the morning, practice saying to yourself the intended action, as for example, "I intend to pick up my clothes from the dry cleaners today." Or form a mental image of yourself performing the intended action.

Enhance Context-Dependent Memory Effects   Create a studying environment as similar as possible to the testing situation. For example, if you are likely to be tested in a quiet setting, avoid studying with music or other distracting sounds in the background.

Control Stress   Though we may need some level of stress to remain active and alert, prolonged or intense stress can interfere with the transfer of new learning into long-term memory (LeDoux, 1996). The stress management techniques discussed in Chapter 15 can help you keep stress within manageable levels.

Adopt Healthy Habits   Adopting a healthy diet and a regular exercise program can enhance memory performance (Herrmann & Palmisano, 1992). You should also avoid eating a large meal before cracking open your textbook, since consumption of large amounts of food puts your body in a restful mood that facilitates digestion, not mental alertness. On the other hand, avoid studying on an empty stomach, as hunger pangs make it more difficult to concentrate and retain new information. Bear in mind that use of alcohol and other drugs does not mix with the mental alertness needed to learn and retain information. Finally, make sure to get enough sleep. Skipping sleep to cram for exams may make it more difficult for you to retain the information you've learned.

TYING IT TOGETHER

Without memory, experiences would leave no mark on our behavior. Memory permits us to retain and recall what we have learned through experience. Psychologists study the processes that make it possible for us to remember and that explain why we forget. We can conceptualize memory in terms of three underlying processes (encoding, storing, and retrieving information) occurring across three stages of memory (sensory memory, short-term memory, and long-term memory) (Module 6.1). Decay of memory traces, interference, retrieval failure, and repression may each play a role in forgetting (Module 6.2). By exploring the biological bases of memory, we may come to a better understanding of how memories are formed and how they are lost (Module 6.3). Even as memory scientists continue to explore the foundations of memory, we can apply the knowledge we have acquired about how memory works to boost our memory power (Module 6.4).

Thinking Critically About Psychology

Based on your reading of this chapter, answer the following questions. Then, to evaluate your progress in developing critical thinking skills, compare your answers to the sample answers found in Appendix A.

1. **Two men observe an accident in which a car hits a pedestrian and speeds away without stopping. They both are alert enough to glance at the car's license plate before it disappears around the corner. Later, when interviewed by the police, the first man says, "I only got a glimpse of it but tried to picture it in my**

mind. I think it began with the letters QW." The second man chimes in, "Yes, but the whole plate number was QW37XT." Why do you think the second man was able to remember more details of the license plate than the first man?

2. An English-speaking singer gives a concert in Italy and includes a popular Italian folk song in her repertoire. Her rendition is so moving that an Italian woman from the audience later comes backstage to congratulate the singer, telling her, "That song was one of my favorites as a little girl. I've never heard it sung so beautifully. But when did you learn to speak Italian so

well?" The singer thanks her for the compliment but tells her she doesn't speak a word of Italian. Drawing on your knowledge of memory processes, explain how the woman was able to learn a song in a language she couldn't speak.

3. Here let us perform a little experiment (Kirsch & Lynn, 1999; Reason, 1992):
a. First, pronounce the word formed by the letters S-H-O-P.
b. Now, answer this question: "What do you do when you come to a green light?"

Key Terms

memory (p. 218)
memory encoding (p. 218)
memory storage (p. 218)
memory retrieval (p. 219)
retrieval cues (p. 219)
encoding specificity principle (p. 219)
context-dependent memory effect (p. 219)
state-dependent memory effect (p. 220)
three-stage model (p. 220)
sensory memory (p. 220)
sensory register (p. 220)
iconic memory (p. 220)
eidetic imagery (p. 221)
echoic memory (p. 221)
short-term memory (STM) (p. 221)
working memory (p. 221)
chunking (p. 222)
maintenance rehearsal (p. 222)
phonological loop (p. 222)
visuospatial sketchpad (p. 222)
central executive (p. 222)
long-term memory (LTM) (p. 223)

consolidation (p. 223)
elaborative rehearsal (p. 223)
levels-of-processing theory (p. 223)
semantic network model (p. 224)
declarative memory (p. 226)
semantic memory (p. 226)
episodic memory (p. 227)
retrospective memory (p. 227)
prospective memory (p. 227)
procedural memory (p. 227)
implicit memory (p. 227)
explicit memory (p. 227)
priming task (p. 227)
constructionist theory (p. 228)
memory schema (p. 229)
flashbulb memories (p. 230)
misinformation effect (p. 231)
decay theory (p. 235)
savings method (p. 235)
massed vs. spaced practice effect (p. 235)
interference theory (p. 236)
retroactive interference (p. 236)
proactive interference (p. 236)

overlearning (p. 237)
serial position effect (p. 237)
primacy effect (p. 238)
recency effect (p. 238)
retrieval theory (p. 238)
tip-of-the-tongue (TOT) phenomenon (p. 238)
repression (p. 240)
recall task (p. 240)
recognition task (p. 241)
amnesia (p. 241)
retrograde amnesia (p. 242)
anterograde amnesia (p. 242)
childhood amnesia (p. 242)
dissociative amnesia (p. 242)
engram (p. 244)
neuronal networks (p. 244)
long-term potentiation (LTP) (p. 246)
mnemonic (p. 248)
acronym (p. 248)
acrostic (p. 248)

ANSWERS TO RECALL IT QUESTIONS

Module 6.1: 1. information; 2. encoding specificity; 3. d; 4. procedural memory; 5. i. d; ii. b; iii. a; iv. c.

Module 6.2: 1. traces; 2. proactive interference; 3. retrieval; 4. retrograde; 5. a.

Module 6.3: 1. engram; 2. neuronal networks; 3. long-term potentiation (LTP); 4. a.

ANSWER TO TRY THIS OUT (P. 228)

This exercise tests whether your reading of the text primed you to respond to certain highlighted words. A priming effect would be shown if you completed the second and fourth items in the list as *implicit* and *explicit,* respectively, and your friend completed them in some other way, such as *implement* and *explode.* The words *implicit* and *explicit* are highlighted as key terms in the text that preceded this test. Forming an implicit memory of these words may have primed you to produce them even if you made no conscious effort to recall them. The first and third items in the list are filler items, with no particular significance.

ANSWER TO TRY THIS OUT (P. 239)

Drawing (h) shows the correct image of a penny in Figure 6.10.

Thinking, Language, and Intelligence

DID YOU KNOW THAT . . .

■ Albert Einstein used visual imagery in developing his theory of relativity? (p. 256)

■ People clearly recognize that an apple is a fruit, but they are more hazy when it comes to identifying what makes a fruit a fruit? (p. 257)

■ Alexander Graham Bell used an analogy based on the human ear in developing the design for the first telephone? (p. 260)

■ A commonly used rule of thumb could lead you to make a bad decision about which college to attend? (pp. 262–263)

■ Creativity is not limited to a few creative geniuses, but is an ability we all possess to one degree or another? (p. 264)

■ A gorilla used sign language to signal she had a toothache? (p. 272)

■ A psychological test can be reliable but not valid? (p. 278)

■ A leading psychological theory of intelligence proposes not one, but many different intelligences? (p. 281)

■ The closer the genetic relationship between two people, the closer their IQ scores are likely to be? (p. 285–286)

W hile working on adhesives, Arthur Fry, a chemist for the 3M Company, came upon an unusual compound: an adhesive that could be used to stick paper to other objects. It was not nearly as strong as other adhesives then available, such as the adhesive in Scotch Tape (Bellis, 2001), and the 3M Company did not at first see any commercial use for it. Nothing more might have been made of the new compound had Fry not had a recurring problem finding his place in his church hymnal. The slips of paper he used as bookmarks often fell to the floor, leaving him scrambling to find his place. Then it dawned on him that the unusual compound he had developed in the lab might be of help in keeping bookmarks in place. What product that many people now use in their daily lives is based on Fry's adhesive?

Here's another story about a sticky invention (Bellis, 2001). In 1948, a man in Switzerland took his dog out for a nature walk. Both returned covered with burrs, the plant seed sacs that stick to clothing and animal fur. The man decided to inspect the burrs under a microscope to determine what made them so sticky. It turned out that they contained tiny hooks that grabbed hold of small loops in the fabric of his clothing. The man, George de Mestral, looked up from the microscope and a knowing smile crossed his face. He knew in a flash what he must do. What do you think de Mestral did with his discovery of how burrs stick to fabrics? What widely used product resulted from this discovery?

You may never have heard of Arthur Fry and George de Mestral. But chances are you make use of their discoveries in your daily life. Arthur Fry's sticky compound is the adhesive in the stick-it pads that people use to post reminder notes. George de Mestral's discovery led him to develop the fastening fabric we now call Velcro®.

The insights of Fry and de Mestral are examples of the creative mind at work. Creativity is a form of thinking in which we combine information in new ways that provide useful solutions to problems. Creative thought is not limited to a few creative geniuses. It is a basic mental capability available to nearly all of us. This chapter focuses on creativity and other forms of thinking, including concept formation, problem solving, and decision making.

Thinking, or *cognition*, is a major focus of study in *cognitive psychology*, the branch of psychology that explores how we acquire knowledge about the world. Cognitive psychologists investigate how we think, process information, use language, and solve problems. The first module in the chapter looks at various forms of thinking, starting with ways we represent information in our minds. In Module 7.2, we examine how we develop language and how language affects our thinking. We also venture into the controversy about whether humans are the only species to use language. Module 7.3 focuses on the nature and measurement of intelligence—the mental ability or abilities allowing us to solve problems, learn from our experiences, and adapt to the demands of the environment. ■

MODULE 7.1
Thinking

- **What is cognitive psychology?**
- **What is thinking?**
- **What are the major types of concepts people use, and how are they organized?**
- **What can we do to solve problems more efficiently?**
- **How do cognitive biases influence decision making?**
- **What cognitive processes underlie creative thinking?**

American psychology was not always receptive to the study of thinking, or cognition. Throughout much of the twentieth century, the behaviorism of John Watson and B. F. Skinner dominated psychology and discouraged studies of mental activities that could not be directly observed. Studying the mind was the stuff of philosophy, not something a respectable experimental psychologist should endeavor to do. It was not until the 1960s that **cognitive psychology** began to make significant inroads within the broader discipline of psychology. It was then that many experimental psychologists who had been trained to perform experiments on learning in animals began shifting their interests to the study of higher mental processes in humans. By the 1970s, this movement had grown so strong that it was known as the "cognitive revolution." The study of cognition is now an area of respected scientific inquiry that crosses disciplinary lines, drawing upon experimental psychology, computer science, mathematics, neuroscience, and linguistics (Ingram & Siegle, 2001; Pitt, Myung, & Zhang, 2002). Considering that psychology as a scientific discipline began with the study of mental experience, the rise of cognitive psychology in the mid-twentieth century was a little like coming home again.

Psychologists generally define **thinking** as the mental representation and manipulation of information. We represent information in our minds in the form of images, words, and concepts (such as truth and beauty). We manipulate informa-

A Sticky Invention If you are wandering through the woods, you might come home with a few burrs sticking to your clothing. These seed vessels have hooks or teeth that stick to clothing or fur. Inventor George de Mestral adapted the properties of the burr in creating a fastening device used today by millions of people: Velcro®.

cognitive psychology The branch of psychology that focuses on such mental processes as thinking, problem solving, decision making, and use of language.

thinking The process of mentally representing and manipulating information.

Figure 7.1 Mental Rotation
Are the objects in each pair the same or different? Answering this question depends on your ability to rotate objects in your mind's eye.*

(a)

(b)

(c)

tion in our minds when we solve problems, make decisions, and engage in creative pursuits. Let us first examine the ways in which we mentally represent and act upon information.

Mental Images: In Your Mind's Eye

When we think, we represent information in our minds in the form of images, words, or concepts. Some information is better represented by words and concepts than by images. Abstractions like justice, honor, liberty, and respect fall into this category. After all, we may be able to describe in words what we mean by the term *justice,* but what sort of mental image would represent what justice looks like? On the other hand, nonabstract objects in the "real world" are generally better represented by mental pictures. If, for example, you were asked whether a rhino has one horn or two, you would most likely try to picture a rhino in your mind. You may more readily bring to mind an image of a flower than a memory of one (Tracy, Fricano, & Greco, 2001).

A **mental image** is a mental picture or representation of an object or event. People form mental images of many different objects—faces of familiar people, the layout of the furniture in their homes, the letters of the alphabet, a graduation or religious ceremony. A mental image is not an actual or photographic representation of an object. Rather, it is a reconstruction of the object or event from memory.

Researchers find that the parts of the visual cortex we use when we form mental images are very similar to the parts we use when we actually observe the objects themselves (Kosslyn, 1994). Yet there is a difference between an image imagined and an image seen: the former can be manipulated, but the latter cannot. For example, we can manipulate imagined images in our minds by rotating them or perusing them from different angles. Figure 7.1 provides an opportunity to test your ability to manipulate mental images.

CONCEPT 7.1
When we think, we represent information in our minds in the form of images, words, and concepts and manipulate that information to solve problems, make decisions, and engage in creative pursuits.

CONCEPT 7.2
Mental images help us perform cognitive functions, such as remembering directions and finding creative solutions to problems.

What Does Justice Look Like? What do you picture in your mind when you think of the concept of justice? Visual imagery is generally better suited for representing objects in the real world than for representing abstract concepts like justice, which are better described in words.

*Answer: The objects in pairs *a* and *b* are the same; those in pair *c* are different.

mental image A mental picture or representation of an object or event.

The ability to hold and manipulate mental images helps us perform many cognitive tasks, including remembering directions. You could use verbal representations ("Let's see, that was two lefts and a right, right?"). But forming a mental image—for example, by picturing the church where you make a left turn and the gas station where you make a right—may work better.

Mental imaging can also lead to creative solutions to puzzling problems. For example, when the famed physicist Albert Einstein was developing his breakthrough theory of relativity, he found it helpful to visualize himself traveling along a beam of light (Finke, Ward, & Smith, 1992). In writing to a friend, Einstein commented that words did not play any role in his creative thought. They came only after he was able to reproduce mental images of the new ideas he had formulated.

Investigators find gender differences in mental imagery. In one study, women reported more vivid images of past experiences and greater use of imagery to remember past experiences than men did, but men more often reported using imagery to solve problems (Harshman & Paivio, 1987). Women also tend to outperform men in forming still images of objects. Perhaps that's why husbands seem so often to ask their wives where they have put their keys or their glasses. Women may be better at recalling where things are placed because of their greater skill in visually scanning an image of a particular location in their minds. As we'll see later in the chapter, men generally have the edge when it comes to mentally rotating objects or visualizing moving objects (Voyer, Voyer, & Bryden, 1995).

Mental imagery is not limited to visual images. Most people can experience mental images of other sensory experiences, such as "hearing" in their minds the rousing first chords of Beethoven's Fifth Symphony, or recalling the taste of a fresh strawberry or the feel of cotton brushing lightly against the cheek. Some (but not all) people say they can create mental imagery of different odors, such as the smell of freshly cut grass (Djordjevic et al., 2004). Yet people generally have an easier time forming visual images than images of other sensory experiences.

Concepts: What Makes a Bird a Bird?

Not only do we form representations of objects in our mind's eye; we also represent objects in terms of the mental categories in which we place them. You see objects moving along a road and think of them as "trucks" or "cars." Trucks and cars are examples of **concepts**, the mental categories we use to group objects, events, and ideas according to their common features. Forming concepts helps us develop a sense of order in the world and allows us to distinguish threatening from harmless stimuli. For example, classifying a slithering creature in the road as a snake prompts us to keep a respectful distance, a response that could be a lifesaver. Think how differently you react to an approaching animal if you classify it as a skunk rather than a rabbit. If you were unable to form any concepts, each time you encountered a four-legged furry creature in the street that went "woof" you would have no idea whether to pet it or to run from it. Nor would you know whether a spherical object placed before you is one to be eaten (a meatball) or played with (a ball). Any species that failed to differentiate between something poisonous and something nutritious, or between a harmless creature or a predator, would quickly become extinct (Ashby & Maddox, 2005).

Concepts also help us respond more quickly to events by reducing the need for new learning each time we encounter a familiar object or event. Having acquired the concept *ambulance,* we immediately know how to respond when we see one pulling up behind us on the road.

Types of Concepts   Concepts can be classified as *logical concepts* or *natural concepts* (Jahnke & Nowaczyk, 1998). **Logical concepts** are those that have clearly defined rules for determining membership. Schoolchildren learn that the concept of a tri-

CONCEPT 7.3

Forming concepts or mental categories for grouping objects, events, and ideas helps bring a sense of order and predictability to the world.

CONCEPT 7.4

Cognitive psychologists classify concepts in two general categories, logical concepts and natural concepts.

concepts   Mental categories for classifying events, objects, and ideas on the basis of their common features or properties.

logical concepts   Concepts with clearly defined rules for membership.

Is a Penguin a Bird? Although a penguin doesn't fly, it is classified as a bird. Yet people may not recognize it as a bird if it does not closely resemble the model of a bird they have in mind, such as a robin.

Online Study Center
Improve Your Grade
Tutorials: Cognitive Psychologists and the Hierarchy of Concepts

 CONCEPT 7.5

People form their judgments of whether objects belong to particular categories by comparing them with models or examples of category members.

 CONCEPT 7.6

We organize our concepts within hierarchies of broad to narrow categories.

natural concepts Concepts with poorly defined or fuzzy rules for membership.
superordinate concepts The broadest concepts in a three-level hierarchy of concepts.
basic-level concepts The middle level of concepts in a three-level hierarchy of concepts, corresponding to the categories we most often use in grouping objects and events.
subordinate concepts The narrowest level of concepts in a three-level hierarchy of concepts.

angle applies to any three-sided form or figure. If a figure has three sides, it must be a triangle. However, most of the concepts we use in everyday life are **natural concepts**, in which the rules for determining how they are applied are poorly defined or fuzzy.

Natural concepts include various *objects,* such as furniture, mammals, and fruit; *activities,* such as games, work, and sports; and *abstractions,* such as justice, honor, and freedom (Jahnke & Nowaczyk, 1998). A botanist may use a logical concept (one having fixed rules) for classifying objects as fruits or as vegetables, but most people use natural concepts for classifying these and other objects, even if they are hazy about the rules they use in applying their concepts. For example, most people have an imprecise idea about what makes a fruit a "fruit." They might readily agree that an apple is a fruit, but they may not be sure about an avocado, a pumpkin, or an olive.

How do people apply natural concepts? How do they determine whether a particular animal, say an ostrich or a penguin, is a bird? Cognitive psychologists believe we base these judgments on the *probability* that objects are members of particular categories (Willingham, 2001). In other words, we decide whether an object is more or less likely to belong to a particular category by comparing its characteristics with a mental representation of a model or example of a category member (Jahnke & Nowaczyk, 1998; Minda & Smith, 2001). For instance, if we pictured a robin as a model or "best example" of a bird, we would more readily classify a sparrow as a bird than we would an ostrich or a penguin because the sparrow has more robinlike features (sparrows fly; ostriches and penguins don't).

Hierarchies of Concepts Cognitive psychologists find that people order their concepts within hierarchies of broad to narrow categories. One commonly used hierarchy has three levels of concepts: *superordinate,* basic-level, and *subordinate* concepts (Rosch et al., 1976). **Superordinate concepts** are broad categories, such as vehicle, animal, and furniture. Within these categories are **basic-level concepts**, such as car, dog, and chair, and within these categories are **subordinate concepts**, which are even more specific, such as sedan, standard poodle, and rocking chair.

People are more likely to use basic-level concepts than superordinate or subordinate ones when identifying objects (e.g., calling an object a "car" rather than a "vehicle" or a "sedan") (Rosch et al., 1976). Children also more readily acquire words representing basic-level concepts than those representing superordinate or subordinate concepts. Moreover, people are faster at recognizing an object as an example of a basic-level concept (like "apple") than as an example of a superordinate one (like "fruit") (E. E. Smith, Balzano, & Walker, 1978).

Why do people gravitate toward basic-level concepts? The answer may be that basic-level concepts provide the most useful information about the objects we encounter (Guenther, 1998). Categorizing an object as a piece of furniture tells us little about its specific features. (Is it something to sit on? To lie on? To eat on?) The features associated with a basic-level concept like "chair" give us more useful information. Subordinate concepts, like "rocking chair," are more specific and limited in range, and they may give us more information than we need.

As children, we learn to narrow and refine the concepts we use through exposure to *positive instances* and *negative instances* of concepts. A **positive instance** exemplifies the concept, whereas a **negative instance** is one that doesn't fit the concept. A parent of a toddler identifies dogs in the street as "bow-wows," a positive instance. At first, the child may overextend the concept of "dog" (or bow-wow), calling all animals "bow-wows," even cats. But after repeated experience with positive and negative instances of "dogs," "cats," and the like, children learn to fine-tune their concepts. They identify features that distinguish different concepts and begin calling dogs *dogs* and cats *cats*. On the other hand, logical concepts are usually acquired by learning formal definitions rather than through direct experience. We might say to a child each time we see a square figure, "Hey, look at the square here. And, look, there's another one over there." But the child will acquire the concept more rapidly by learning the rule that any four-sided figure with sides of equal length is classified as a square.

We now turn to considering ways in which we act upon the information we represent in our minds, beginning with problem solving. Before going any further, try answering the following questions, which are intended to probe the way you think through problems. The answers are provided in various places throughout the chapter.

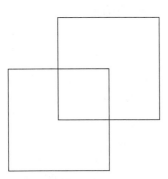

Figure 7.2
Two Interlocking Squares?

Source: Adapted from de Bono, 1970.

1. Do you perceive two interlocking squares in Figure 7.2? Or might this figure represent something else?

2. Jane and Sue played six games of chess, and each of them won four. There were no ties. How was that possible (adapted from Willingham, 2001)?

3. An airliner from France crashed just off the coast of New Jersey within the territorial waters of the United States. Although all of the passengers and crew were French citizens, none of the survivors was returned to France for burial. Why not?

4. A man used a key that allowed him to enter but could not be used to open any locks. What kind of key was it?

Figure 7.3
The Nine-Dot Problem

5. Figure 7.3 shows a classic problem called the nine-dot problem. Your task is to draw no more than four lines that connect all the dots without lifting your pen or pencil from the paper.

 CONCEPT 7.7

Algorithms, heuristics, analogies, and incubation periods are problem-solving strategies that can help you solve problems more efficiently.

positive instance An object that fits a particular concept (e.g., a terrier is a positive instance of dog).

negative instance An object that does not fit a particular concept (e.g., a calico kitten is a negative instance of dog but a positive instance of cat).

problem solving A form of thinking focused on finding a solution to a particular problem.

Problem Solving: Applying Mental Strategies to Solving Problems

Problem solving is a cognitive process in which we employ mental strategies to solve problems. As you may recall from Chapter 5, psychologist Edward Thorndike observed that animals placed in his puzzle box used trial and error to solve the problem of escaping from the enclosed compartment. The animals would try one response after another until they stumbled upon the action that activated the escape mechanism. Solving a problem by trial and error is a "hit-or-miss" approach in which one tries one solution after another until the correct one is found.

Some people arrive at solutions to problems by trial and error, while others report "Eureka-type" experiences in which solutions seem to just suddenly "pop"

Figure 7.4   An Insight Problem
Your task here is to move only three of the dots to make a downward-facing triangle. You can try it using a stack of poker chips. If you get stuck, see Figure 7.5 on page 260 for the answer.

Source: Metcalfe, 1986.

into their minds. You'll recall from Chapter 5 that the Gestalt psychologist Wolfgang Köhler referred to this sudden awareness of a solution to a problem as *insight.* Cognitive psychologists believe that insight results from restructuring a problem so that its elements suddenly fit together to render a solution. Restructuring may occur when the person sees the problem from a different perspective, notices new information, or recognizes connections between elements of the problem that were previously overlooked. Recall the question of how Jane and Sue could each win four games of chess if they played six games and there were no ties. The answer is that Jane and Sue did not play against each other. The solution comes from restructuring the problem so that it does not depend on their playing each other. Figure 7.4 shows another type of insight problem.

Though we sometimes arrive at correct solutions through trial and error or insight, these approaches to problem solving have certain drawbacks. Trial and error is tedious. You must try one solution after another until you happen upon the right one. And mulling over a problem while waiting for a sudden flash of insight to occur may require quite a long wait. How might we approach problem solving more efficiently? Here we consider some useful problem-solving strategies: *algorithms, heuristics, analogies,* and *incubation periods.* We also explore common pitfalls that can impede our problem-solving efforts.

Algorithms   An **algorithm** is a step-by-step set of rules for solving a problem. You probably first became acquainted with algorithms when you learned the basic rules (algorithms) of arithmetic, such as carrying the number to the next column when adding columns of numbers. The major drawback to algorithms is that none may precisely apply to a particular problem. Lacking a precise algorithm, you might still boost your chances of solving a problem by following an imprecise algorithm, or general set of guidelines. For example, a general set of guidelines for achieving a good grade in introductory psychology would be to set aside a certain number of hours to study the text and other readings each week, attend class regularly, and participate in a study group. Will this guarantee success? Perhaps not. But the odds are in your favor.

Heuristics   A rule of thumb used as an aid in solving problems or making judgments or decisions is called a **heuristic.** Heuristics do not guarantee a solution, but they may help you arrive at one more quickly. In using a *backward-working* heuristic, we start with a possible solution and then work backward to see if the data support the solution. A psychologist seeking the causes of schizophrenia might approach the problem by proposing a model (schizophrenia as a genetic disease) and then examine whether the available data fit the model. Using the *means-end heuristic,* we evaluate our current situation and compare it to the end result we want to achieve. Then we develop a step-by-step procedure to reduce the distance between the two. Another heuristic, *creating subgoals,* involves breaking the problem down into smaller, more manageable problems. Scientists use this strategy when they assign different teams to work on different parts of a problem. In AIDS research, for example, one team might work on how HIV penetrates the cell, another on how it reproduces, and so on. Solving the riddle of HIV may depend on knowledge gained from achieving each of the subgoals.

algorithm   A step-by-step set of rules that will always lead to a correct solution to a problem.

heuristic   A rule of thumb for solving problems or making judgments or decisions.

Problem
Move only three of these dots to
make a downward-facing triangle

Solution

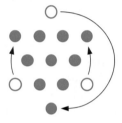

Figure 7.5 Solution to the Insight Problem in Figure 7.4
Assuming you solved the problem, did you rely on the trial-and-error method—moving the dots (or chips) around until you chanced upon the correct solution? Or did you mull the problem over in your mind until a moment of illumination, or insight, arrived? If so, what do you think accounted for this sudden awareness?

Online Study Center
Improve Your Grade
Tutorials: The Yuks and the Nerds

💡 **CONCEPT 7.8**
Mental set and functional fixedness are examples of cognitive tendencies that can impede problem solving.

analogy In problem-solving, a strategy based on using similarities between the properties of two things or applying solutions to past problems to the problem at hand.
incubation period A respite from active problem-solving efforts, which may facilitate a solution.
mental set The tendency to rely on strategies that worked in similar situations in the past but that may not be appropriate to the present situation.

Using Analogies to Solve Problems Alexander Graham Bell used the workings of the human ear as an analogy in his design of the first telephone. Have you ever drawn upon an analogy to develop a creative solution to a problem?

Analogies When we use an **analogy** to solve a problem, we apply knowledge gained from solving similar problems in the past. Many people fail to recognize how solutions to one problem can be modified or adapted to solve new problems (Guenther, 1998). Analogies are most useful when similarities exist between old problems and new ones. Consider the analogy used by Alexander Graham Bell, the inventor of the telephone. In studying the human ear, Bell had noticed how sounds were transmitted when the membrane known as the eardrum vibrated. He applied this idea of a membrane that vibrates in response to sounds in his design of the telephone (Levine, 1994). Though analogies can be useful in problem solving, they may lead to faulty solutions if the present and past situations are less similar than they initially seem (Holyoak & Thagard, 1995).

Incubation Periods It often helps to take a break from a problem, especially when you reach an impasse. Researchers find that people are sometimes better able to solve problems when they put them aside for a while and return to them later (Houtz & Frankel, 1992). Such a respite is called an **incubation period** because it is assumed that the passage of time helps the person develop a fresh perspective on the problem, which may lead to a sudden realization of the solution. The person may also better understand which pieces of information are relevant to solving the problem and which are not.

Mental Roadblocks to Problem Solving Chris is sitting in the front passenger seat of a car waiting for the driver to return when the car suddenly begins to roll backward down a hill. In panic, he tries to climb over the gearshift lever, clumsily reaching with his foot for the brake pedal to stop the car. Unfortunately, he can't reach the brake pedal in time to prevent the car from slamming into a pole. What could he have done differently in this situation? Why do you think he responded the way he did (adapted from Levine, 1994)?

Perhaps Chris should have realized that a much simpler solution was available: pulling the emergency brake. Yet Chris was locked into a preconceived way of solving the problem: depressing the brake pedal. This solution works well if you're sitting in the driver's seat but may not be effective if you need to climb over from the passenger side. The tendency to rely on strategies that worked well in similar situations in the past is called a **mental set** (Greeno & Simon, 1991).

Figure 7.6   The Box-Candle Problem
Using only the material you see on the table, figure out a way to mount a candle on the wall so that it doesn't drip wax on the floor when it burns. The answer is shown in Figure 7.9 on page 262.

Source: Adapted from Duncker, 1945.

CONCEPT 7.9
We may think we approach decision making in a logical way, but underlying biases in our thinking often hamper our ability to make rational decisions.

Figure 7.7   The Two-String Problem
Two strings hang from the ceiling but are too far apart to be touched at the same time. The task is to tie them together. Except for the string and the pliers on the table, the room is empty. How would you tie the strings together? The solution is shown in Figure 7.8 on page 262.

functional fixedness   The tendency to perceive objects as limited to the customary functions they serve.
decision making   A form of problem solving in which one must select a course of action from among the available alternatives.
confirmation bias   The tendency to maintain allegiance to an initial hypothesis despite strong evidence to the contrary.

In some instances, as when a new problem is similar to an old one, a mental set may help you reach an appropriate solution more quickly (Luchins & Luchins, 1994). But a mental set can be an impediment to problem solving if a new problem requires a solution different from an old one, as the example of Chris illustrates.

Another impediment to problem solving is **functional fixedness**, the inability to see how familiar objects can be used in new ways (German & Barrett, 2005). Suppose you're working at your desk and a sudden wind blows in from an open window, scattering your papers about (Levine, 1994). Would functional fixedness prevent you from recognizing new uses for familiar objects? Or would you reach for objects that don't ordinarily serve as paperweights, such as your eyeglasses or wallet, and use them to hold down your papers long enough for you to get up and close the window? The box-candle problem and the two-string problem are classic examples of functional fixedness (see Figures 7.6 and 7.7).

Yet another impediment to problem solving is the tendency to allow irrelevant information to distract your attention from the relevant information needed to solve the problem. Recall the problem on page 258, which stated that none of the survivors of the crash of the French airliner were buried in France. Did the geographical details distract you so that you overlooked the statement that no *survivors* were returned for burial?

Mental Roadblocks in Decision Making   We constantly face the need to make decisions, ranging from everyday ones ("What should I wear?" "What should I have for dinner?") to important life decisions ("What should I major in?" "Should I get married?" "Should I take this job or stay in college?"). **Decision making** is a form of problem solving in which we must select a course of action from among the available alternatives.

We may think we approach decision making logically, but researchers find that underlying biases in thinking often hamper our ability to make rational choices (Kahneman, 1991; Kahneman & Tversky, 1973). One example is the **confirmation bias**—the tendency to stick to an initial hypothesis even in the face of strong evi-

Figure 7.8 Solution to the Two-String Problem in Figure 7.7
The solution? Think of an alternate use for the pliers. By attaching them as a weight to the end of one of the strings, you can swing the string as a pendulum. Then move to the other string and wait for the swinging string to come close enough to catch it so that you can tie the two strings together.

Source: Adapted from Maier, 1931.

Figure 7.9 Solution to the Box-Candle Problem in Figure 7.6
Most people fail to solve the problem because they fail to recognize that the thumbtack box can be used as a candle holder.

dence that is inconsistent with it. The confirmation bias leads us to place greater weight on information confirming our prior beliefs and expectations than on contradictory evidence. An example would be a juror who decides whether a defendant is guilty based on the preliminary evidence and then fails to reconsider that decision even when strong contradictory evidence presents itself.

Though heuristics may help us solve problems, they can sometimes lead to bad decisions. For instance, the **representativeness heuristic** may lead us to make more of something than we should. In using this heuristic, we assume that a given sample is representative of a larger population (Kahneman & Tversky, 1973). The representativeness heuristic can lead us to base our decision on which movie to attend on the opinion of someone we just happened to overhear talking about it. We might thus wind up seeing a bad movie or passing up a good one. Or we might decide to attend a particular college because the few people we met on a campus

💡 **CONCEPT 7.10**
The confirmation bias, the representativeness heuristic, the availability heuristic, and framing are examples of biases in thinking that can lead us to make bad decisions.

Guilty or Not Guilty? The confirmation bias can lead jurors to develop a fixed concept of the guilt or innocence of a defendant early in the trial proceedings and then discount any contradictory evidence presented later at trial.

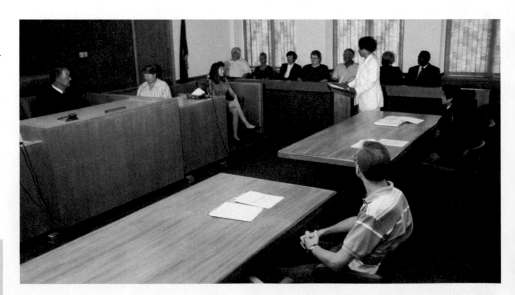

representativeness heuristic A rule of thumb for making a judgment that assumes a given sample is representative of the larger population from which it is drawn.

TRY THIS OUT

A Farmer or a Librarian?

You can see the representativeness heuristic in action by first looking at the man in the photograph. Do you think he is more likely to be a farmer or a librarian?

If you said librarian, as many people do, your judgment was probably influenced by the representativeness heuristic: that is, you assumed that a thin man with glasses is more representative of the population of librarians than of the population of farmers.

tour seemed friendly, a decision we may later come to regret. The representativeness heuristic also comes into play in judging people on the basis of first impressions. We might reject a potential romantic partner on the basis of a two-minute conversation or even how the person dressed on a particular occasion. We infer that the sample of behavior we observe is representative of the person's behavior in general, which may not be the case. The two nearby Try This Out features offer examples of how the representativeness heuristic may bias your thinking.

The **availability heuristic** is the tendency to base decisions on information that readily comes to mind (Kahneman & Tversky, 1973). Consider the many uncertainties we face in life. Driving to work, flying on an airplane, eating a fat-filled dessert—all entail some degree of risk. Even getting out of bed in the morning is somewhat risky (you could fall). The availability heuristic may lead us to make errors in assessing relative risk. For instance, vivid images of a plane crash on a television news program may stick in our minds, leading us to overestimate the risk we face in flying on a commercial airliner.

How a problem is described may also affect the decisions we make. For example, imagine you are told that a disease is expected to kill 600 people but that two programs are available that could save some or all of the people (Willingham, 2001). Program A has a 100 percent chance of saving 200 people. Program B has a one-third chance of saving all 600 people and a two-thirds chance of saving none. Which program would you choose?

Now let's suppose you are told that if you select program A, 400 people will die, but if you select program B, there will be a one-third chance that no one will

Online Study Center
Improve Your Grade
Tutorials: The Missing Dollar Problem

TRY THIS OUT

The Coin Toss

A quarter is tossed six times. It lands heads up three times and tails up three times. Which of the sequences at the right was most likely to have occurred?

Did you select the last sequence? Many people do. Yet each of these sequences is equally likely to have occurred. The representativeness heuristic leads people to judge the irregular sequence in the last item to be more representative of a random order than the others.

1. HHHTTT
2. HTHTHT
3. TTTHHH
4. HTTHHT

availability heuristic The tendency to judge events as more likely to occur when information pertaining to them comes readily to mind.

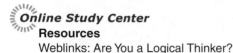

CONCEPT 7.11
Creativity is a cognitive ability found in varying degrees in most people.

framing   The tendency for decisions to be influenced by how potential outcomes are phrased.

creativity   Originality of thought associated with the development of new, workable products or solutions to problems.

divergent thinking   The ability to conceive of new ways of viewing situations and new uses for familiar objects.

convergent thinking   The attempt to narrow down a range of alternatives to converge on the one correct answer to a problem.

metaphor   A figure of speech used to represent an object or concept by comparing it to another.

conceptual combinations   Combinations of two or more concepts into one concept, resulting in the creation of a novel idea or application.

conceptual expansion   The expansion of familiar concepts into new uses.

die and a two-thirds chance that all 600 people will die. Which of these programs would you choose?

About three out of four people given the first set of choices select program A. But when people are given the second set of choices, about three out of four choose program B. The question is, why? Examine the two sets of choices more closely. *Notice that the outcomes are exactly the same.* The only difference is whether the problem is framed in terms of potential gains or potential losses. Psychologists believe that people tend to be more conservative when deciding between two potential gains, as in the first example, but more willing to take risks when choosing between two potential losses, as in the second example (Willingham, 2001). The tendency for decisions to be influenced by how potential outcomes are phrased is called **framing**. Framing can lead us to make decisions that are not based on a purely rational appraisal of the facts.

Creativity: Not Just for the Few

Creativity is thinking in ways that lead to original, practical, and meaningful solutions to problems or that generate new ideas or forms of artistic expression. The creation of a new product, for example, may solve a problem in a novel and useful way.

Creativity is not limited to a few creative geniuses in the arts or sciences. Psychologists recognize that virtually all of us have the ability to be creative and to apply creativity to many aspects of our daily life (Runco, 2004; Simonton, 2000). For example, a parent who invents a new activity for a 4-year-old, a chef who combines ingredients in innovative ways, a worker who improves on a production method—all demonstrate creativity. Creativity researcher Keith Simonton identifies three qualities associated with creative works: they are novel, useful, and aren't simply an obvious extension of what others have done before (Kersting, 2003).

Though most of us have the potential to be creative, some people are clearly more creative than others. Most creative people typically have at least an average to high-average IQ. However, there doesn't seem to be any relationship between creativity and IQs in the high range (above 120) (Csikszentmihalyi, 1996). As psychologist Robert Sternberg (2001) notes, products developed by highly intelligent people may be of high quality, but they are not necessarily novel. Creativity goes beyond general intelligence.

Creativity is measured in different ways but most commonly through tests that tap *divergent thinking*. **Divergent thinking** is the wellspring of invention; it is the ability to conceive of new ways of viewing situations and new uses for familiar objects. By contrast, **convergent thinking** is the attempt to find the one correct answer to a problem. Refer back to problem 1 on page 258. The answer (two interlocking squares) seems so obvious we may not think of any alternatives. Yet by thinking divergently we can find other answers: three squares (note the one in the area of intersection), two L-shaped pieces separated by a square (see Figure 7.10), and a rectangle divided into two pieces that have been pushed askew.

Figure 7.10   Divergent Thinking
Compare Figure 7.2 on page 258 with the cutout shown here. Now imagine these two L-shaped figures pushed together so that they are separated by a square.

TRY THIS OUT

Alternate Uses Test

The Alternate Uses Test is widely used to measure creativity. Before reading the next paragraph, write down all the uses you can think of for the following objects: brick, newspaper, coffee mug, hanger.

Most people start off with conventional uses, such as using bricks to build a house, a barbecue, or a patio. How many of your uses fall within a traditional category? How many represent innovative uses, such as using a brick as a doorstop, a paperweight, or a tool in weight-lifting exercises?

Source: Adapted from Levine, 1994.

CONCEPT 7.12
Creativity involves using cognitive processes to manipulate or act upon stored knowledge.

Psychologist J. P. Guilford and his colleagues were the originators of tests that tap divergent thinking. One widely used measure, the Alternate Uses Test, has subjects list possible uses for a common object, such as a newspaper (Guilford et al., 1978). The person's score is based on the number of acceptable responses the person is able to generate (see Try This Out).

When we think creatively, we use cognitive processes to manipulate or act upon stored knowledge. Investigators identify a number of cognitive processes that underlie creative thinking, including the use of *metaphor* and *analogy, conceptual combination,* and *conceptual expansion* (Ward, Smith, & Vaid, 1997):

1. *Metaphor and analogy.* Metaphor and analogy are creative products in their own right; they are also devices we use to generate creative solutions to puzzling problems. A **metaphor** is a figure of speech for likening one object or concept to another. In using metaphor, we speak of one thing as if it were another. For example, we might describe love as a candle burning bright. An analogy is a comparison between two things based on their similar features or properties—for example, likening the actions of the heart to those of a pump. Consider again Bell's use of analogy of the human ear in the design of the first telephone.

2. *Conceptual combination.* Combining two or more concepts into one can result in novel ideas or applications that reflect more than the sum of the parts (Costello & Keane, 2001). Examples of **conceptual combinations** include "cell phones," "veggie burgers," and "home page." Can you think of other ways in which concepts can be creatively combined?

3. *Conceptual expansion.* One way of developing novel ideas is to expand familiar concepts. Examples of **conceptual expansion** include an architect's adaptation of an existing building to a new use, a writer's creation of new scenes using familiar characters, and a chef's variation on a traditional dish that results in a new culinary sensation (Ward et al., 1997).

Have you noticed that aliens depicted in movies and TV shows tend to have features that resemble those of animals on earth—symmetrical appendages (arms and legs), a round if somewhat enlarged head with two eyes, a nose, and two ears? Even people who claim to have been abducted by aliens describe their features in much the same way. Is there any reason to believe that if aliens existed, they would look like animals on earth? Why not three headlike protrusions or no heads at all?

When asked to draw species that might exist on other planets—and to use their wildest imaginations—college students also typically produced creatures that

TRY THIS OUT

Thinking Creatively

You can test your creativity by thinking of a new product, such as a watch that keeps track of one's emotional states or a website that people would use regularly. Then try your idea out on some friends and note their reactions. Are they telling you what they honestly feel or just trying to be polite? If you think your idea has potential, work on developing it further.

Source: Adapted from Levine, 1994.

Figure 7.11   Do Aliens Look Like This?
When college students were asked to draw pictures of what aliens might look like, the figures they produced typically had features similar to those of animals on earth.

Source: Ward, 1994.

CONCEPT 7.13
When people approach creative tasks, they tend to expand on what is familiar to them.

resembled animals on earth (see Figure 7.11). The figures they drew had symmetrical features with ordinary appendages and sense organs (Ward, 1994, 1995). These drawings teach us something about the creative process (whether they teach us anything about aliens is another matter). We learn that when people approach creative tasks, they rely on what is familiar to them. They tend to expand their existing concepts rather than invent entirely new ones. Creativity typically springs from the expansion or modification of familiar categories or concepts. The ability to take what is given in our knowledge structures and modify and expand on it is one of the basic processes of creative thinking. Before going further, you may wish to review the cognitive processes involved in thinking, which are outlined in Concept Chart 7.1.

CONCEPT CHART 7.1   Cognitive Processes in Thinking

Cognitive Process	Definition	Description
Mental imaging	Forming mental representations of objects or events	Images can be formed based on various sensory experiences, including vision, hearing, taste, and touch. Mental images can be manipulated to help us solve certain kinds of problems.
Concept formation	Grouping objects, events, and ideas on the basis of their common features	Most concepts are natural concepts, which have fuzzy or imprecise rules for membership. Logical concepts are those that have strict rules for membership. People tend to use basic-level concepts more often than superordinate (more general) or subordinate (more specific) concepts.
Problem solving	The process of arriving at a solution to a given problem	Strategies include the use of algorithms, heuristics, analogies, and incubation periods. Pitfalls include mental set and functional fixedness.
Decision making	The process of deciding which of two or more courses of action to take	Decision making is often influenced by errors in thinking associated with the confirmation bias, the representativeness heuristic, the availability heuristic, and framing.
Creativity	The generation of novel, workable products or ideas	When we think creatively, we use divergent thinking to act upon or manipulate stored knowledge. The cognitive processes used include metaphor and analogy, conceptual combination, and conceptual expansion.

MODULE 7.1 REVIEW

Thinking

RECITE IT

What is cognitive psychology?

- Cognitive psychology is the study of thinking and other mental processes, including problem solving, language use, and information processing.

What is thinking?

- Thinking is the creation of mental representations of the external world and the manipulation of these representations.

What are the major types of concepts people use, and how are they organized?

- The major types of concepts are logical concepts, which have clearly defined rules for membership, and natural concepts, in which the rules for determining how they are applied are poorly defined.

- People apply natural concepts probabilistically by judging whether something is likely to belong to a certain category.

- Concepts are organized in hierarchies composed of broad to narrow categories.

- One commonly used hierarchy has three levels of concepts: superordinate, basic-level, and subordinate concepts.

What can we do to solve problems more efficiently?

- Rather than relying on trial and error or a sudden insight, we can use such problem-solving strategies as algorithms, heuristics, analogies, and incubation periods.

- We can also remove impediments to problem solving, such as mental set and functional fixedness.

How do cognitive biases influence decision making?

- The confirmation bias leads people to discount evidence that contradicts their prior beliefs and expectations.

- The representativeness heuristic leads people to make more of a given sample of data than they should.

- The availability heuristic leads people to make snap decisions based on whatever information comes most readily to mind.

- Framing leads people to base decisions on how a problem is phrased rather than on the facts at hand.

What cognitive processes underlie creative thinking?

- Cognitive processes involved in creative thinking include the use of metaphor and analogy, conceptual combination, and conceptual expansion.

RECALL IT

1. Psychologists generally define _____ as the mental representation and manipulation of information.

2. Match the terms with their descriptions below:
   i. logical concept; ii. natural concept; iii. superordinate concept; iv. basic-level concept

   a. broadest mental category in a three-level conceptual hierarchy
   b. mental category most often used when identifying objects
   c. mental category with clearly defined rules for membership
   d. mental category with poorly defined rules for membership

3. One mental roadblock to problem solving is the inability to see how a familiar object can be used in new ways. This impediment is known as
   a. a mental set.
   b. functional fixedness.
   c. an incubation period.
   d. confirmation bias.

4. A(n) _____ is a problem-solving strategy that draws on past experience with similar problems, whereas a(n) _____ is a set of step-by-step rules for solving problems.

5. Merging two or more concepts to produce novel ideas or applications is called
   a. conceptual expansion.
   b. creative combination.
   c. divergent thinking.
   d. conceptual combination.

THINK ABOUT IT

- Have you ever used mental imagery to find a creative solution to a problem? Might you use it in the future? Why or why not?

- How might you apply the concepts of metaphor and analogy, conceptual combination, and conceptual expansion to develop a novel idea, application, or service? Think of at least one example.

MODULE 7.2

Language

- **What are the major components of language?**
- **How does language develop?**
- **What is the linguistic relativity hypothesis?**
- **Can nonhuman animals use language?**

anguage is a system of communication composed of symbols—words or hand signs (as in the case of American Sign Language)—that are arranged according to a **grammar**, a set of rules governing the proper use of words, phrases, and sentences, to express meaning. Language is so tightly woven into the human experience, says prominent linguist Steven Pinker (1994, p. 17), that "it is scarcely possible to imagine life without it. Chances are that if you find two or more people together anywhere on earth they will soon be exchanging words. When there is no one to talk with, people talk to themselves, to their dogs, even to their plants."

In this module, we examine the remarkable capacity of humans to communicate through language. We consider the basic components of language, developmental milestones in language acquisition, and leading theories of language acquisition. We also consider the question of whether language is a uniquely human characteristic.

Components of Language

Concept 7.14

Language consists of four basic components: phonemes, morphemes, syntax, and semantics.

The basic units of sound in a spoken language are called **phonemes**. English has about forty phonemes to sound out the 500,000 or so words found in modern unabridged English dictionaries. The word *dog* consists of three phonemes: "d," "au," "g." From this example, you can see that phonemes in English correspond both to individual letters and to letter combinations, including the "au" in *dog* and the sounds "th" and "sh." The same letter can make different sounds in different words. The "o" in the word *two* is a different phoneme from the one in the word *one*. Changing one phoneme in a word can change the meaning of the word. Changing the "r" sound in *reach* to a "t" sound makes it *teach*. Different languages have different phonemes. In some African languages, various clicking sounds are phonemes. Hebrew has a guttural "chhh" phoneme, as in the expression *l'chaim* ("to life").

Phonemes are combined to form **morphemes**, the smallest units of meaning in a language. Simple words such as *car, ball,* and *time* are morphemes, but so are other linguistic units that convey meaning, such as prefixes and suffixes. The prefix *un*, for example, means "not," and the suffix *ed* following a verb means that the action expressed by the verb occurred in the past. More complex words are composed of several morphemes. The word *pretested* consists of three morphemes: "pre," "test," and "ed."

Language requires more than phonemes and morphemes. It also requires **syntax**, the rules of grammar that determine how words are ordered within sentences and phrases to form meaningful expressions, and **semantics**, the set of rules governing the meaning of words. The sentence "buy milk I" sounds odd to us because it violates a basic rule of English syntax—that the subject ("I") must precede the verb ("buy"). We follow rules of syntax in everyday speech even if we are not aware of them or cannot verbalize them. But even when our speech follows proper syntax, it may still lack meaning. The famed linguist Noam Chomsky, to whose work we will turn shortly, illustrated this point with the example "Colorless green ideas sleep furiously." The sentence may sound correct to our ears since it follows the

language A system of communication composed of symbols (words, hand signs, etc.) that are arranged according to a set of rules (grammar) to form meaningful expressions.

grammar The set of rules governing how symbols in a given language are used to form meaningful expressions.

phonemes The basic units of sound in a language.

morphemes The smallest units of meaning in a language.

syntax The rules of grammar that determine how words are ordered within sentences or phrases to form meaningful expressions.

semantics The set of rules governing the meaning of words.

CONCEPT CHART 7.2   Milestones in Language Acquisition

Age (Approximate)	Vocal Activity	Description
Birth	Crying	Crying expresses distress.
2 months	Cooing	Infant begins making cooing sounds (e.g., "aah" and "oooh").
6 to 12 months	Babbling	Phonemes, the basic units of sound, appear.
12 months	One-word phrases	Baby imitates sounds and can understand some words; begins to say single words.
18 to 24 months	Two-word phrases or sentences	Vocabulary grows to about fifty words, and the baby emits two-word phrases or sentences.
24 to 36 months	Complex speech	Sentences become longer and more complex and include plurals and past tense; speech shows elements of proper syntax.

rules of English syntax, but it doesn't convey any meaning. The same word may convey very different meanings depending on the context in which it is used. "Don't *trip* going down the stairs" means something very different from "Have a good *trip*."

Language Development

CONCEPT 7.15
Young children pass through a series of milestones of language acquisition, from crying and cooing to babbling, to one- and two-word phrases, and then to more complex speech.

Children the world over develop language in basically the same stages, which unfold at basically the same ages. Until about 6 months of age, infants are limited to nonlinguistic forms of communication—crying and cooing. At around that time, the first sounds resembling human speech appear in the form of babbling. The child then progresses through stages of one- and two-word phrases, and between the ages of 2 and 3 begins developing more complex speech patterns (see Concept Chart 7.2 and Try This Out).

The similar course of language development across cultures and the ease with which children naturally acquire language suggest that language depends on an innate mechanism that may be "prewired" in the human brain. Noam Chomsky (1965) called this mechanism the **language acquisition device**. We acquire the ability to speak, much as we do the ability to walk and jump, because we have an inborn propensity to develop it. As Steven Pinker (1994) has put it, "We don't teach our children to sit, stand, and walk, and they do it anyway." Children learn

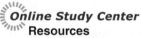
Online Study Center
Resources
Weblinks: Psychology of
Language Page

language acquisition device Chomsky's concept of an innate, prewired mechanism in the brain that allows children to acquire language naturally.

TRY THIS OUT
From the Mouths of Babes

If you have the opportunity to observe an infant over time, keep a running record of the infant's verbalizations, jotting down the types produced at different ages. Compare the chronology of these verbalizations with the one presented in Concept Chart 7.2: neonatal crying that progresses to cooing at about 2 months and is followed by babbling (starting at about 6 months), one-word speech (starting at around 12 months), two-word speech (starting at around 18 months), and more complex speech (between 24 and 36 months). Keep track of the infant's vocabulary, noting the rapid increase beginning at around 18 months.

Noam Chomsky

CONCEPT 7.16
Language development depends on both a biological capacity for language production and experience with the sounds, meanings, and structures of human speech.

to use the rules of grammar without any formal instruction. In English-speaking cultures, they begin placing the subject before the verb long before they learn what the terms *subject* and *verb* mean. According to Chomsky and Pinker, children are able to learn grammatical structures as rapidly and easily as they do because the human brain contains the basic blueprints or neural circuitry for using grammar.

Critics point out that Chomsky's language acquisition device is not an actual physical structure in the brain, but a hypothesis—an abstract concept of how language centers in the brain work—and that it does not explain the mechanisms by which language is produced. In fairness to Chomsky, we should point out that brain mechanisms responsible for language are extremely complex, consisting of complicated circuits in many areas of the brain that link together to produce language in ways we don't yet understand (Lieberman, 1998). Yet the pieces of the puzzle may be starting to fall into place. Scientists have discovered the first gene linked to the development of the brain mechanisms responsible for speech and language (Balter, 2001; Lai et al., 2001).

Regardless of the exact mechanisms involved in language production, there is little question that both nature and nurture are necessary for language to develop (Mayberry et al., 2002). Our ability to use language depends not only on a biological capacity for language production, but also on experience with the sounds, meanings, and structures of human speech. Children may have a natural capacity for language, but they learn grammar by listening to the speech of others, and they enlarge their vocabularies by imitating the words others use to refer to particular objects (Pinker, 1994). Parents can help children develop language skills by talking and reading to them frequently. They can also use principles of operant conditioning and observational learning (discussed in Chapter 5) by modeling proper language use and rewarding children for imitating it.

However language develops, it is clear that language and thinking are closely intertwined. As discussed in the next section, some theorists even propose that language determines how we think.

Culture and Language: Does the Language We Use Determine How We Think?

Does the language we speak affect how we think? Might French Canadians, Chinese, and Africans see the world differently because of the vocabulary and syntax of their native languages? According to the **linguistic relativity hypothesis**, the an-

The Whorfian Hypothesis Eleanor Rosch's research findings ran contrary to the Whorfian hypothesis. Members of a New Guinea tribe, even though they used only two words to distinguish among different colors, were just as able as English-speaking subjects to identify different colors.

linguistic relativity hypothesis The proposition that the language we use determines how we think and how we perceive the world (also called the *Whorfian hypothesis*).

Fireman or Firefighter? Language influences thinking in many ways. Traditional gender constructions of occupational titles that embody maleness, such as *policeman* and *fireman,* may lead young women to think that such careers are not available to them.

CONCEPT 7.17
The belief that the language we speak determines how we think and perceive the world is a controversial viewpoint that has not been supported by research evidence.

CONCEPT 7.18
Though research findings have not supported the original form of the linguistic relativity hypothesis, a weaker version that holds that culture and language influence thinking may have merit.

swer is yes. This hypothesis—also called the *Whorfian hypothesis* after Benjamin Whorf, the amateur linguist who developed it—holds that the language we use determines how we think and how we perceive reality. Whorf (1956) pointed out that some cultures have many different words for colors, whereas others have only a few. English has eleven words for basic colors: *black, white, red, green, yellow, blue, brown, purple, pink, orange,* and *gray* (Adelson, 2005). At the other end of the spectrum is the Navajo language, which has no separate words for blue and green.

Does a lack of color vocabulary determine the ability to perceive colors? Apparently not, according to landmark research by Eleanor Rosch (Rosch-Heider & Olivier, 1972). Rosch and her colleagues showed that members of a preliterate tribe in New Guinea, whose language contained but two color names, were just as capable as English-speaking subjects in recognizing different colors.

Overall, evidence fails to support the original version of the Whorfian hypothesis, which held that language *determines* how we think and perceive the world (Pinker, 2002, 2003; Siegal, Varley, & Want, 2001). But a weaker version of the theory does have merit, a version that proposes that the culture in which we are raised, and the language we use, are important *influences* on how we think and how we perceive the world (Adelson, 2005; Özgen, 2004; Özgen & Davies, 2002; Roberson et al., 2004). For example, while English speakers perceive blue- and green-colored objects as representing different color categories, speakers of African languages who use only a single term to describe the colors blue and green tend to perceive these hues as belonging to the same category (Özgen, 2004).

Psychologist Richard Nisbett presents evidence that people from different cultures tend to think differently (Nisbett, 2003; Nisbett et al., 2001). For example, he argues that East Asians have a more "holistic" style of thinking than Americans, who tend to be "analytic" in their thinking. Holistic thinkers have a greater appreciation of context and complexity and are less bound in their thinking to strict rules of logic. Analytic thinkers rely more heavily on principles of logic and are less accepting of contradictions.

Another way in which language can influence thinking is illustrated by this sentence: "A person should always be respectful of *his* parents." If the very concept of personhood embodies maleness, where does that leave females? As *non*persons? Not surprisingly, investigators find that women feel excluded when they read texts that use the generic *he* to represent a person (Romaine, 1994). If Sally sees that *he* is almost always used when referring to professionals like doctors, engineers, or scientists, might she get the idea that such careers are not as available to her as they are to her brother?

Is Language Unique to Humans?

Can nonhuman animals, such as apes, communicate through language? Apes lack the vocal apparatus needed to form human sounds, so researchers have turned to nonverbal means of expression to try to communicate with them, such as sign language and artificial languages (manipulation of signs and symbols). Chimpanzees, gorillas, and orangutans have been taught to use a simple form of sign language (Corballis, 2003). For example, Beatrice and Allen Gardner trained a chimpanzee named Washoe to use about 160 signs, including signs for "apple," "tickle," "flower," and "more" (Gardner & Gardner, 1969, 1978). Washoe learned to combine signs into simple phrases, such as "more fruit" and "gimme flower."

Is This Language? Questions remain about whether an ape's ability to manipulate symbols on a keyboard as seen here, or to use sign language, is tantamount to human language.

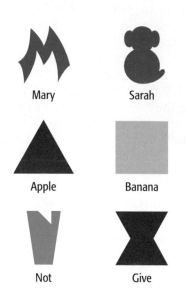

Mary

Sarah

Apple

Banana

Not

Give

Figure 7.12   Examples of Materials Used in Premack's Study

CONCEPT 7.19
Whether humans are unique in possessing the ability to communicate through language remains a controversial question.

She even displayed a basic grammar by changing the position of the subject and object in her signing to reflect a change in meaning. For example, when she wanted her trainer to tickle her, she would sign, "You tickle Washoe." But when she wanted to do the tickling, she would sign, "Washoe tickle you" (Gardner & Gardner, 1978).

Psychologist David Premack developed an artificial language in which plastic chips of different sizes, colors, and shapes symbolize different words (see Figure 7.12). Using shaping and reinforcement techniques, he trained a chimp named Sarah to communicate by placing the chips on a magnetic board. Sarah learned to form simple sentences. For example, she would request food by putting together a sequence of chips that signaled, "Mary give apple Sarah" (Premack, 1971).

A yet more compelling demonstration of simian communication occurred in 2004 with a gorilla named Koko, who had been trained in the use of American Sign Language (ASL). When Koko flashed the ASL sign for pain and pointed to her mouth, several dentists sprung into action and extracted a decayed tooth, thus relieving the pain ("Koko the Gorilla," 2004).

If apes can communicate through use of symbols, should we conclude that they are capable of acquiring and using language? Critics claim that Washoe, Sarah, Koko, and others merely learned to imitate gestures and other responses for which they were reinforced, rather than learning the complex syntax and morphemes of a true human language like ASL (Pinker, 1994; Terrace, 1980). A chimp signing "me cookie" is no different, critics say, than a pigeon learning to perform a series of responses to obtain a food pellet.

Perhaps the question of whether apes can use language depends on how broadly we define language. If our definition hinges on the ability to communicate through the use of symbols, then we can say that apes can indeed use language (Hillix & Rumbaugh, 2004; Rumbaugh & Washburn, 2003). But if our definition hinges on the use of complex syntax and grammatical structures, then the ability to use language may be unique to humans. Some commentators believe that the language abilities of Koko and other language-trained apes are no more advanced that those of human infants or toddlers (Corballis, 2003; Seyfarth & Cheney, 2003). Moreover, the number of words used by a human child dwarfs those of even the best language-trained ape (Hauser & Fitch, 2003).

Apart from whether apes can learn human language, it is clear that many animal species have communication systems of their own (Seyfarth & Cheney, 2003). They use grunts, squeals, growls, and other sounds—their own "native tongues"—as well as facial expressions to communicate emotional states like anger and sexual arousal, to gather their young, and to warn others of approaching predators. If the roles of experimenter and subject were reversed, it is unlikely that we could measure up to their standards of communication. By the same token, it's unreasonable to expect them to measure up to ours. According to Noam Chomsky, trying to teach animals to use language is as irrational as trying to teach people to flap their arms and fly (cited in G. Johnson, 1995).

MODULE 7.2 REVIEW

Language

RECITE IT

What are the major components of language?

- The major components of language are phonemes (basic units of sounds), morphemes (basic units of meaning), syntax (the rules of grammar that determine how words are ordered in sentences and phrases to express meaning), and semantics (the set of rules governing the meaning of words).

How does language develop?

- According to Noam Chomsky, language development depends on an innate mechanism that is "prewired" in the human brain.
- Language development also depends on exposure to the speech of others. Thus, both nature and nurture are necessary.

What is the linguistic relativity hypothesis?

- In its original form, this hypothesis holds that language determines how we think and how we perceive the world. Research findings fail to support this version of the hypothesis, but a weaker version, which holds that culture and language influence thinking, has some merit.

Can nonhuman animals use language?

- Scholars continue to debate the question of whether animals other than humans can use language. The answer may hinge on how we define language.
- Research with chimps and gorillas has shown that these primates are capable of learning elementary forms of communication—for example, manipulation of symbols to request food—but questions remain about whether these communication skills are equivalent to human language.

RECALL IT

1. The set of rules governing the proper use of words, phrases, and sentences is called
   a. language.
   b. grammar.
   c. cultural determinism.
   d. syntax.

2. The basic units of sounds in a language are called
   a. phonemes.
   b. morphemes.
   c. semantics.
   d. syntax.

3. The belief that language determines how we think and perceive reality is called the linguistic _____ hypothesis.

4. Some people believe that chimps and gorillas can use language because they have been able to manipulate _____.

THINK ABOUT IT

- In what ways are sexist biases reflected in the language we use in ordinary speech?

- Do you believe that chimps that learn to use signs are capable of communicating through language? Why or why not?

MODULE 7.3

Intelligence

- What is intelligence, and how is it measured?
- What constitutes a good intelligence test?
- What are some examples of the misuse of intelligence tests?
- What are some of the major theories of intelligence?
- Is intelligence determined by heredity or environment?

Perhaps no subject in psychology has sparked as much controversy as intelligence. Psychologists have long argued about how to define it, how to measure it, what factors govern it, whether different racial and ethnic groups have more or less of it, and if so, what accounts for these differences. These debates are still very much at the forefront of contemporary psychology.

What Is Intelligence?

Just what is **intelligence**? Is it the ability to acquire knowledge from books or formal schooling? Or might it be "street smarts"—practical intelligence of the kind we see in people who survive by their wits rather than by knowledge acquired in school? Is it the ability to solve problems? Or is it the ability to adapt to the demands of the environment? Psychologists believe intelligence may be all these things and more. Though definitions of intelligence vary, a central belief of each is that intelligence is the ability to adapt to the environment. Perhaps the most widely used definition of intelligence is the one offered by psychologist David Wechsler (1975): "Intelligence is the global capacity of the individual to act purposefully, to think rationally, and to deal effectively with the environment."

Some theorists believe there are many different forms of intelligence, perhaps even multiple intelligences. Before we explore theories of intelligence, let us consider the history and nature of intelligence testing in modern times and also discuss the extremes of intelligence.

How Is Intelligence Measured?

The earliest attempts at measuring intelligence in the modern age were undertaken by Sir Francis Galton (1822–1911), an Englishman of many talents. Galton, a cousin of naturalist Charles Darwin, was a successful inventor, geographer, meteorologist, and mathematician (Hunt, 1993). He also was an amateur psychologist and the originator of mental tests of ability. He believed that intelligence was largely hereditary and could be measured by tests of reaction time, hand-eye coordination, and other psychophysical responses. Though we no longer use his tests of intelligence, Galton remains well known to us as an early proponent of the genetic basis of intelligence. His reputation was tarnished by his support of **eugenics**, a term he coined to describe societal efforts to "improve the human stock" by encouraging breeding among people with desirable traits while discouraging breeding among those without such traits (Lykken, 2004). This view was taken up by others who believed that selective breeding would eliminate "feeble-mindedness" and reduce crime, poverty, and other social ills. Less than three decades after Galton's death, eugenics was taken to horrendous ends by the Nazis, who attempted to "purify" the human race by encouraging people they felt were true "Aryans" to have families and exterminating Jews, Gypsies, and others whom they considered human vermin (Hunt, 1993).

CONCEPT 7.20

Though theorists define intelligence in different ways, one widely used definition holds that intelligence is the capacity to act purposefully, think rationally, and deal effectively with the environment.

Online Study Center
Improve Your Grade
Tutorials: Test Your Intelligence

---

intelligence The capacity to think and reason clearly and to act purposefully and effectively in adapting to the environment and pursuing one's goals.

eugenics Attempts to improve the human genetic stock by encouraging breeding among intellectually superior people.

THE PIONEERS | The Birth of the Modern Intelligence Test

Alfred Binet

In Alfred Binet's time, many scientists believed that brain size determined intelligence. Evidence from the scientific measurement of the skull was used to support the belief that members of the lower classes, notably Blacks and Native Americans, had smaller brains than upper-class Whites and were therefore inferior in intelligence. Some scientists even measured the brains of corpses to get more direct measurements of brain size. Scientists conveniently ignored evidence that many prominent Whites had small heads. Though subsequent research debunked claims about group differences in brain sizes, they were very much in vogue when Binet began his work on intelligence. He wrote, "I began with the idea impressed upon me by the studies of so many other scientists, that intellectual superiority is tied to superiority of cerebral volume" (1900, p. 427). But Binet soon rejected these beliefs, as his own measurements of children's skulls showed differences between the head sizes of good and poor students that were much too small and variable to matter.

Binet believed that a better way was needed to measure intelligence. He decided to turn away from physical measurement of skull size to psychological measurement of intellectual ability.

💡 **CONCEPT 7.21**

Alfred Binet and Theodore Simon developed the type of intelligence test in use today. Their work led to the concept of an intelligence quotient (IQ).

mental age A representation of a person's intelligence based on the age of people who are capable of performing at the same level of ability.

intelligence quotient (IQ) A measure of intelligence based on performance on tests of mental abilities, expressed as a ratio between one's mental age and chronological age or derived from the deviation of one's scores from the norms for those of one's age group.

The type of intelligence test in use today originated with the work of a Frenchman, Alfred Binet (1857–1911). Binet started out doing what many other scientists of his time did to measure mental abilities: he measured heads (see the Pioneers box). But he soon turned from physical measurement to psychological measurement.

In 1904, school officials in Paris commissioned Binet to develop methods of identifying children who were unable to cope with the demands of regular classroom instruction and who required special classes to meet their needs. Today, we might describe such children as having learning disabilities or mild mental retardation. To measure the mental abilities of these children, Binet and a colleague, Theodore Simon, developed an intelligence test, which they began using in 1905 (R. B. Evans, 1999a). It consisted of memory tasks and other short tasks representing the kinds of everyday problems children might encounter, such as counting coins. By 1908, Binet and Simon had decided to scale the tasks according to the age at which a child should be able to perform them successfully. A child began the testing with tasks scaled at the lowest age and then progressed to more difficult tasks, stopping at the point at which he or she could no longer perform them. The age at which the child's performance topped off was considered the child's **mental age**.

Binet and Simon calculated intelligence by subtracting the child's mental age from his or her chronological (actual) age. Children whose mental ages sufficiently lagged behind their chronological ages were considered in need of special education. In 1912, a German psychologist, William Stern, suggested a different way of computing intelligence, which Binet and Simon adopted. Stern divided mental age by chronological age, yielding a "mental quotient." It soon was labeled the **intelligence quotient (IQ)**. IQ is given by the following formula, in which MA is mental age and CA is chronological age:

$$IQ = \frac{MA}{CA} \times 100$$

Thus, if a child has a mental age of 10 and a chronological age of 8, the child's IQ would be 125 (10 ÷ 8 = 1.25 × 100 = 125). A child with a mental age of 10 who is 12 years of age would have an IQ of 83 (10 ÷ 12 = .8333 × 100 = 83).

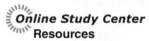

CONCEPT 7.22
The Stanford-Binet Intelligence Scale and the Weschler scales of intelligence are the major tests of intelligence in use today.

Online Study Center
Resources
    Weblinks: History of Intelligence
    Theory and Testing

CONCEPT 7.23
Like all psychological tests, intelligence tests must be standardized, reliable, and valid if we are to be confident of the results.

norms   The standards used to compare an individual's performance on a test with the performance of others.

standardization   The process of establishing norms for a test by administering the test to large numbers of people who constitute a standardization sample.

Researchers following in Binet's footsteps developed intelligence tests that could be used with groups other than French schoolchildren. Henry Goddard (1865–1957), a research director at a school for children with mental retardation, brought the Binet-Simon test to the United States and translated it into English for use with American children. The U.S. Army developed group-administered intelligence tests to screen millions of recruits during World War I.

Stanford University psychologist Lewis Terman (1877–1956) adapted the Binet-Simon test for American use, adding many items of his own and establishing criteria, or **norms**, for comparing an individual's scores with those of the general population. The revised test, known as the Stanford-Binet Intelligence Scale (SBIS), was first published in 1916.

The Stanford-Binet Intelligence Scale is still commonly used to measure intelligence in children and young adults. However, tests developed by David Wechsler (1896–1981) are today the most widely used intelligence tests in the United States and Canada. Wechsler, a psychologist at Bellevue Hospital in New York, developed tests of intelligence for preschool children (Wechsler Preschool and Primary Scales of Intelligence—Revised, or WPPSI-R), for school-age children (Wechsler Intelligence Scale for Children, now in a third edition called WISC-III), and for adults (Wechsler Adult Intelligence Scale, now in a third edition called WAIS-III). The Wechsler scales introduced the concept of the *deviation IQ*—an IQ score based on the deviation, or difference, of a person's test score from the norms for the person's age group, rather than on the ratio of mental age to chronological age. The Wechsler scales are standardized in such a way that an average score is set at 100. The contemporary version of the Stanford-Binet Intelligence Scale also uses the deviation method to compute IQ scores.

Wechsler believed that intelligence consists of various mental abilities, and he designed his tests to measure these abilities. The WAIS-III contains various subtests, which are organized in two groupings. "Verbal subtests" focus on comprehension, vocabulary, and the like, whereas "performance subtests" assess one's skill at block design, picture arrangement, object assembly, and similar tasks (see Figure 7.13). The person who completes the test receives an IQ score on overall performance, an IQ score on the verbal subtests, and an IQ score on the performance subtests. By examining how well the person does overall and on each of the subtests, the test administrator can assess the person's general level of intelligence and the areas in which the person is relatively strong or weak.

What Are the Characteristics of a Good Test of Intelligence?

Like all psychological tests, tests of intelligence must be standardized, reliable, and valid. If they do not meet these criteria, we cannot be confident of the results.

Standardization   **Standardization** is the process of establishing norms for a test by administering it to large numbers of people. These large numbers make up the *standardization sample*. The standardization sample must be representative of the population for whom the test is intended. As noted earlier, norms are the criteria, or standards, used to compare a person's performance with the performance of others. You can determine how well you do on an intelligence test by comparing your scores with the norms for people in your age group in the standardization sample.

As noted above, IQ scores are based on the difference, or deviation, of a person's score from norms for others of the same age, and the mean (average) score is set at 100. IQ scores are distributed around the mean in such a way that two-thirds of the scores in the general population fall within an "average" range of 85 to 115. Figure 7.14 shows that the distribution of IQ scores follows a bell-shaped curve. As

Figure 7.13   Examples of Items Similar to Those on the WAIS-III

Verbal Subtests

Comprehension
Why do people need to obey traffic laws? What does the saying, "The early bird catches the worm," mean?

Vocabulary
What does *capricious* mean?

Arithmetic
John wanted to buy a shirt that cost $31.50, but only had 17 dollars. How much more money would he need to buy the shirt?

Similarities
How are a stapler and a paper clip alike?

Digit Span
Listen to this series of numbers and repeat them back to me in the same order:
6 4 5 2 7 3

Listen to this series of numbers and then repeat them backward:
9 4 2 5 8 7

Letter-Number Sequencing
Listen to this series of numbers and letters and repeat them back, first saying the numbers from least to most, and then saying the letters in alphabetical order:
S-2-C-1

Performance Subtests

Digit Symbol
Fill in as many boxes as you can with the correct symbol in the time allowed.

Picture Completion
What's missing from this picture?

Block Design
Using these blocks, match the design shown.

Picture Arrangement
Arrange the pictures in the correct order to tell a story.

Object Assembly
Arrange the pieces of the puzzle so that they form a meaningful object.

Completed form

you can see from the figure, relatively few people score at either the very high or very low end of the curve.

Standardization has another meaning in test administration. It also refers to uniform procedures that must be followed to ensure that the test is used correctly.

Reliability   **Reliability** refers to the consistency of test scores over time. You wouldn't trust a bathroom scale that gave you different readings each time you used it. Nor would you trust an IQ test that gave you a score of 135 one day, 75 the next, and 105 the day after that. A reliable test is one that produces similar results over time. One way of assessing reliability is the *test-retest method*. With this method, the subject takes the same test again after a short interval. Because familiarity with the test questions can result in consistent performance, psychologists

reliability   The stability of test scores over time.

Figure 7.14 Normal Distribution of IQ Scores
The average (mean) IQ score is 100, plus or minus 15 points.
The percentages shown are rounded off.

sometimes use the *alternate-forms method*. When this method is used, subjects are given a parallel form of the test.

Validity **Validity** is the degree to which a test measures what it purports to measure. A test may be reliable—producing consistent scores over time—but not valid. For example, a test that measures head size may be reliable, yielding consistent results over time, but invalid as a measure of intelligence.

There are several types of validity. One type is **predictive validity**, the degree to which test scores accurately predict future behavior or performance. IQ tests are good predictors of academic achievement and performance on general aptitude tests, such as the Scholastic Aptitude Test (SAT) and the Graduate Record Examination (GRE) (Neisser et al., 1996; Wadsworth et al., 1995). Recent evidence shows that IQ scores predict not only academic success but also long-term health and even longevity (Gottfredson & Deary, 2004), perhaps because people who do well on IQ tests have the kinds of learning and problem-solving skills needed to acquire and practice healthier behaviors.

Misuses of Intelligence Tests Even Binet, the father of the modern IQ test, was concerned that intelligence tests may be misused if teachers or parents lose interest or hope in children with low IQ scores and set low expectations for them. Low expectations can in turn become self-fulfilling prophecies, as children who are labeled as "dumb" may give up on themselves and become underachievers.

Misuse also occurs when too much emphasis is placed on IQ scores. Though intelligence tests do predict future academic performance, they are far from perfect predictors, and they should not be used as the only basis for placing children in special education programs. Some children who test poorly may be able to benefit from regular classroom instruction. Placement decisions should be based on a comprehensive assessment—one that takes into account not only the child's performance on intelligence tests, but also the child's cultural and linguistic background and ability to adapt to the academic environment.

In addition, intelligence tests may be biased against children who are not part of the White majority culture. Children from different cultural backgrounds may not have had any exposure to the types of information assessed by standard IQ tests, such as knowledge of vocabulary words. Several **culture-fair tests**—tests designed to eliminate cultural biases—have been developed. They consist of nonverbal tasks that measure visual-spatial abilities and reasoning skills (see Figure 7.15). However, these tests are not widely used, largely because they don't predict aca-

Online Study Center
Improve Your Grade
Tutorials: Test Your Mental
Rotation Ability

CONCEPT 7.24
Intelligence tests are misused when children with low scores are labeled as innately incapable or inferior, when too much emphasis is placed on IQ scores, and when cultural biases in the tests put children at a disadvantage.

validity The degree to which a test measures what it purports to measure.
predictive validity The degree to which test scores accurately predict future behavior or performance.
culture-fair tests Tests designed to eliminate cultural biases.

Figure 7.15 The Analogic Reasoning Test: A Culture-Fair Intelligence Test
The Analogic Reasoning Test is a nonverbal measure of symbolic reasoning. The subject must use skills of analogical reasoning to select the missing item from a set of four options. Though the test may be culture-fair in the sense that it does not presuppose competence in a particular language, it is not culture-free. Choosing the correct item requires knowledge of how canoes are used and how airplanes work—knowledge that may not be available to people from some preliterate societies.

Source: Universal Nonverbal Intelligence Test (UNIT), The Riverside Publishing Company .

demic performance as well as standard tests. This is not surprising, since academic success in the United States and other Western countries depends heavily on the types of linguistic and knowledge-acquisition skills reflected in standard IQ tests. It may be impossible to develop a purely culture-free IQ test because the skills that define intelligence depend on the values of the culture in which the test is developed (Benson, 2003b).

Extremes of Intelligence: Mental Retardation and Giftedness

Low IQ scores alone are not sufficient to determine **mental retardation**, a psychological disorder in which there is a general delay in the development of intellectual and social skills. In addition to having an IQ score of approximately 70 or below, the person must have difficulty coping with the tasks appropriate to his or her age and life situation (Robinson, Zigler, & Gallaher, 2001). The kinds of educational and support services needed by children with mental retardation depend to a large extent on the severity of the retardation. Table 7.1 shows the capabilities of school-age children according to levels of mental retardation. Most individuals with mental retardation fall in a mild range of severity and are capable of meeting basic educational challenges, such as reading and solving arithmetic problems. Many children with mild retardation are placed in regular classrooms, a practice called **mainstreaming**. Those with severe intellectual deficits require more supportive programs, which may include institutional placement, at least until the person can function in less restrictive settings in the community.

The causes of mental retardation can be biological, environmental, or both. Biological factors include genetic or chromosomal disorders, brain damage, and exposure to lead (Canfield et al., 2003). Environmental factors include a deprived family environment, one that is lacking in verbal interactions between the child and parents or in intellectually stimulating play activities.

People at the upper end of the IQ spectrum (typically about 130 or higher) are generally classified as intellectually gifted (Winner, 2000). As children, they may benefit from enriched educational programs that allow them to progress at a faster pace than standard programs. Today, the concept of giftedness includes not only children with high IQ scores, but also those with special talents, such as musical or artistic ability—skills not typically assessed by standard IQ tests. Gifted children

CONCEPT 7.25
Most people with mental retardation are able to acquire basic reading and arithmetic skills and can learn to function relatively independently and perform productive work.

mental retardation A generalized deficit or impairment in intellectual and social skills.

mainstreaming The practice of placing children with special needs in a regular classroom environment.

TABLE 7.1 **Levels of Mental Retardation and Capabilities of School-Age Children**

Level of Mental Retardation (IQ Range)	Percentage of Cases at Each Level	Capabilities of School-Age Children
Mild (50–70)	85%	Able to acquire reading and arithmetic skills to about a sixth-grade level and can later function relatively independently and engage in productive work
Moderate (35–49)	10%	Able to learn simple communication and manual skills, but have difficulty acquiring reading and arithmetic skills
Severe (20–34)	3–4%	Capable of basic speech and may be able to learn repetitive tasks in supervised settings
Profound (below 20)	1–2%	Severe delays in all areas of development, but some may learn simple tasks in supervised settings

Source: Adapted from American Psychiatric Association, 2000.

CONCEPT 7.26
The long-term study of intellectually gifted children begun by psychologist Lewis Terman shows that achievement in life is not based on intelligence alone.

may play musical instruments as well as highly trained adults or solve algebra problems at an age when their peers have not yet learned to carry numbers in addition.

The systematic study of intellectually gifted children began with the work of Lewis Terman, the developer of the Stanford-Binet Intelligence Scale (see nearby Pioneers box). Many of the intellectually gifted children he studied—the "little geniuses," as they were originally called—became successful executives and professionals and are credited with authoring ninety books and holding more than one hundred patents (Feldhusen, 2004). But others worked as sales clerks and in other occupations far below their intellectual potential (Goleman, 1995a). When investigators compared the high- and low-achievement groups, they found that, from childhood, the high achievers were more likely than the low achievers to have shown such personality traits as persistence in pursuing goals and a desire to excel. The lesson we can draw from this is that while intelligence may contribute to success, other factors enter the equation.

Theories of Intelligence

CONCEPT 7.27
Psychologists have been debating the nature of intelligence ever since intelligence tests were first introduced.

Does intelligence consist of one general ability or a cluster of different abilities? Might there be different forms of intelligence or even different intelligences? Throughout the history of modern psychology, theorists have been attempting to explain intelligence. Here we consider several major theories.

Spearman's "g": In Search of General Cognitive The British psychologist Charles Spearman (1863–1945) observed that people who scored well on one test of mental ability tended to score well on other tests (Spearman, 1927). He reasoned that there must be an underlying general factor of intelligence that allows people to do well on mental tests, a factor he labeled "g" for general intelligence. However, he believed that mental tests also measure specific abilities that are unique to each test. Thus, a person's performance on any given mental test is a function of both "g" and a specific factor, or "s." So, for instance, a person's performance on an arithmetic test might be determined by both general intelligence and specific

THE PIONEERS | Till Death Do Us Part

Lewis Terman

For most of his professional life, Lewis M. Terman (1877–1956) was fascinated by extremes in intelligence. Even his doctoral dissertation in 1905 contrasted the abilities of people at opposite ends of the intellectual spectrum. But it wasn't until 1921 that he began the study in which he tried to answer some of his most basic questions: What are intellectually gifted people like? Do they retain their intellectual superiority in later life?

The common wisdom of the time was that people with high intelligence were bookish, sickly individuals who burned out early. Terman thought otherwise. He realized that the only proper way to answer this question was through a longitudinal study—that is, to follow the same individuals over a significant part of their life spans.

His sample consisted of 1,528 men and women with IQs of 135 and higher. Their average age at the beginning of the study was 11. The preliminary results of the study were quite clear. On average, members of Terman's gifted sample were superior to the general population in many ways. Not only were they more successful academically; they were also bigger, stronger, healthier, and more social. They even excelled at extracurricular activities.

Terman's study was not only the first longitudinal study in the social sciences; it also became the longest. Almost certainly, it has gathered more data than any other study. Its subjects are still being studied today, some fifty years after Terman's death. To date, it has resulted in the publication of five volumes, the latest in 1995. The study is expected to continue until every member of the original subject pool is gone.

—John Hogan

---

mathematical ability. Intelligence tests, such as the SBIS and the Wechsler scales, were developed to measure Spearman's concept of general intelligence, or "g," which is expressed as an IQ score.

CONCEPT 7.28
Though IQ tests were developed to measure Spearman's concept of general intelligence, or "g," theorists like Thurstone believed that intelligence consists of a range of mental abilities that cannot be measured by one general IQ score.

Thurstone's Primary Mental Abilities: Not Two Factors, but Seven   Psychologist Louis L. Thurstone (1887–1955) did not believe that any one large, dominating factor like "g" could account for intelligence. Rather, his studies pointed to a set of seven **primary mental abilities**: verbal comprehension, numerical ability, memory, inductive reasoning, perceptual speed, verbal fluency, and spatial relations (Thurstone & Thurstone, 1941). Though Thurstone did not deny the existence of "g," he argued that a single IQ score does not hold much value in assessing intelligence. He and his wife, Thelma Thurstone, developed a test called the *Primary Mental Abilities Test* to measure the seven primary abilities they believed constitute intelligence.

CONCEPT 7.29
According to Gardner's model of multiple intelligences, we possess separate intelligences that we rely on to perform different types of tasks.

primary mental abilities   Seven basic mental abilities that Thurstone believed constitute intelligence.

multiple intelligences   Gardner's term for the distinct types of intelligence that characterize different forms of intelligent behavior.

Gardner's Model of Multiple Intelligences   Psychologist Howard Gardner (b. 1943) rejects the view that there is a single entity called "intelligence" (Gardner & Traub, 1999). Rather, he believes there exist different types of intelligence, called **multiple intelligences**, that vary from person to person. Gardner identifies eight different intelligences: linguistic, logical-mathematical, musical, spatial, bodily-kinesthetic, interpersonal, intrapersonal, and naturalist (Gardner, 1993, 1998) (see Figure 7.16 and Table 7.2). These separate intelligences are believed to be independent of one another. Thus, a person could be high in some intelligences but low in others (Gardner & Traub, 1999). For example, you might have a high level of linguistic, or verbal, intelligence but a lower level of intelligence in mathematics, music, or spatial relationships. Some people have good "people

Linguistic Intelligence

Musical Intelligence

Figure 7.16 Gardner's Model of Multiple Intelligences

Gardner conceptualizes intelligence in terms of distinct intelligences that vary from person to person. Some people may be strong in musical intelligence, while others may be gifted in bodily-kinesthetic or linguistic intelligence. What types of intelligence best represent your strengths or abilities?

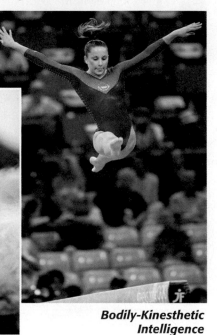

Interpersonal Intelligence

Bodily-Kinesthetic Intelligence

skills" (interpersonal intelligence) but may not be highly skilled at mathematical and logical tasks.

Gardner's model has had enormous influence, especially in educational settings. It has prompted schools to enrich their programs by cultivating specific intelligences in children rather than focusing just on verbal and mathematical abilities. Yet critics of his model point out that it fails to account for how multiple intelligences interact with one another (Guenther, 1998). Most cognitive activities involve an interaction of multiple abilities, not just one type of intelligence. For example, the ability to relate effectively to others (interpersonal intelligence) depends in part on the linguistic skills needed to express oneself clearly (linguistic intelligence). Other critics claim that Gardner's theory provides no firm evidence supporting the existence of multiple intelligences (Gustafsson & Undheim, 1996).

An even broader concern is where to draw the line in deciding how many different intelligences are needed to account for the full range of mental abilities. Why eight intelligences (Gardner now believes there may be nine) and not ten, fifteen, or twenty or more (Gardner & Traub, 1999)? Why musical intelligence but not, say, culinary intelligence or practical intelligence (common sense, or "street smarts")?

Sternberg's Triarchic Theory of Intelligence Whereas Gardner focuses on different types of intelligence, psychologist Robert Sternberg (b. 1949) emphasizes how we bring together different aspects of our intelligence to meet the demands we face in our daily lives. Sternberg (1994a, 1994b, 1997) proposes a **triarchic theory of intelligence**, which holds that intelligence has three aspects: analytic, creative, and practical (see Figure 7.17).

💡 **CONCEPT 7.30**
Sternberg's triarchic theory of intelligence focuses on how we bring together the analytic, creative, and practical aspects of our intelligence to solve the range of problems we face in everyday situations.

triarchic theory of intelligence
Sternberg's theory of intelligence that posits three aspects of intelligence: analytic, creative, and practical.

Practical Intelligence

Figure 7.17   Sternberg's Triarchic Model of Intelligence

Practical intelligence
Applying
Using
Doing

Analytic intelligence
Analyzing
Comparing
Evaluating

Creative intelligence
Creating
Inventing
Designing

Analytic Intelligence

Creative Intelligence

TABLE 7.2   Gardner's Multiple Intelligences

Type of Intelligence	Description	Groups with High Levels
Linguistic	Ability to understand and use words	Writers, poets, effective public speakers
Logical-mathematical	Ability to perform mathematical, computational, or logical operations	Scientists, engineers, computer programmers
Musical	Ability to analyze, compose, or perform music	Musicians, singers, composers
Spatial	Ability to perceive spatial relationships and arrange objects in space	Painters, architects, sculptors
Bodily-kinesthetic	Ability to control bodily movements and manipulate objects effectively	Dancers, athletes, race-car drivers, mechanics
Interpersonal	Ability to relate effectively to others and to understand others' moods and motives	Industrial and political leaders, effective supervisors
Intrapersonal	Ability to understand one's own feelings and behavior (self-perception)	Psychologically well-adjusted people
Naturalist	Ability to recognize objects and patterns in nature, such as flora and fauna	Botanists, biologists, naturalists

Sternberg believes that people with high levels of intelligence are better able to integrate or organize these three aspects of intelligence in their daily lives. *Analytic intelligence* is the kind of intelligence measured by traditional intelligence tests. It comes into play when you analyze and evaluate familiar problems, break them down into their component parts, and develop strategies to solve them. *Creative intelligence* allows us to invent new ways of solving unfamiliar problems. *Practical intelligence* is the ability to apply what we know to everyday life—the common sense, or "street smarts" that traditional intelligence tests fail to measure. Sternberg argues that we need all three types of intelligence to succeed in life. He also believes we need to supplement standard intelligence tests with measures of creative intelligence and practical intelligence.

Overview of Theories of Intelligence   Conventional views of intelligence, as represented by Spearman's and Thurstone's theories, focus on the structure of intelligence and ways of measuring the amount of intelligence a person possesses. Recent evidence supports the importance of a general factor of intelligence, or "g," in predicting not only school performance but job performance as well (Greer, 2004a; Kuncel, Hezlett, & Ones, 2004). Yet scientists continue to debate how much importance to place on "g" in explaining cognitive ability (see Flynn, 2003; Gottfredson, 2004; Grigorenko, 2002; Jensen, 2002).

Gardner's and Sternberg's models of intelligence take us in a different direction (Benson, 2003c). They raise our awareness that whereas traditional intelligence tests measure "g," they fail to capture other types of intelligences, such as how people use their intelligence to meet the challenges and demands they face in everyday contexts. Yet, here too, controversy continues to brew, as some critics contend that we lack sufficient evidence to support the existence of separate types of intelligence, such as Gardner's multiple intelligences or Sternberg's practical intelligence (Goode, 2001c). Though both Gardner's and Sternberg's theories are prompting renewed interest in the nature of intelligence, they have yet to be thoroughly evaluated through scientific tests (e.g., Gottfredson, 2003a, 2003b).

What can we conclude about these various theories of intelligence? First, it is clear that human intelligence consists of multiple abilities (Lubinski, 2004), perhaps even multiple intelligences (Horn & Noll, 1997). Second, we need to take into account the cultural contexts in which intelligent behavior occurs. The abilities a society values determine how it defines and measures intelligence. Our society

CONCEPT CHART 7.3   Theories of Intelligence

Theorist	Major Concepts	Comments
Spearman	Intelligence involves general cognitive ability, or "g."	Traditional intelligence tests are designed to measure "g" in the form of an IQ score.
Thurstone	Intelligence consists of seven primary mental abilities.	Thurstone argued that a single IQ score cannot capture the broad range of mental abilities that constitutes intelligence.
Gardner	Multiple intelligences are needed to account for the range of mental abilities.	Gardner's theory has popular appeal but does not account for the interrelationships among the different intelligences. It also does not draw the line in determining how many separate intelligences are needed to account for the full range of mental abilities.
Sternberg	Sternberg's triarchic theory proposes three aspects of intelligence: analytic, creative, and practical.	The triarchic theory is important because it provides a much-needed focus on how people use their intelligence in everyday life.

places a high value on verbal, mathematical, and spatial skills, so it is not surprising that conventional IQ tests measure these abilities and little else. Perhaps, as Sternberg argues, we need to think about measuring intelligence more broadly to assess the wider range of abilities that may constitute human intelligence. Concept Chart 7.3 offers an overview of the major theories of intelligence.

Intelligence and the Nature-Nurture Question

Scientists have long sought to answer the question of whether intelligence is primarily the result of nature (genetics) or nurture (environment). A heated focus of the nature-nurture debate is whether genetic factors or environmental ones are responsible for racial/ethnic differences in IQ scores.

Separating the Effects of Nature and Nurture A large body of evidence supports the belief that intelligence has a strong genetic component (e.g., Bishop et al., 2003; Malykh, Iskoldsky, & Gindina, 2005; Petrill & Deater-Deckard, 2004; Petrill et al., 2004). The closer the genetic relationship between two people, the closer their IQ scores tend to be. Consider Figure 7.18, which is based on evidence from over one hundred kinship studies of more than 100,000 pairs of relatives (Plomin & Petrill, 1997). Notice that the statistical association (correlation) between IQs of twins raised together is greater among monozygotic (MZ), or identical, twins than among dizygotic (DZ), or fraternal, twins. Since MZ twins share 100 percent of their genes in common whereas DZ twins, like other siblings, have only a 50 percent genetic overlap, this finding suggests that heredity helps account for intelligence as measured by IQ.

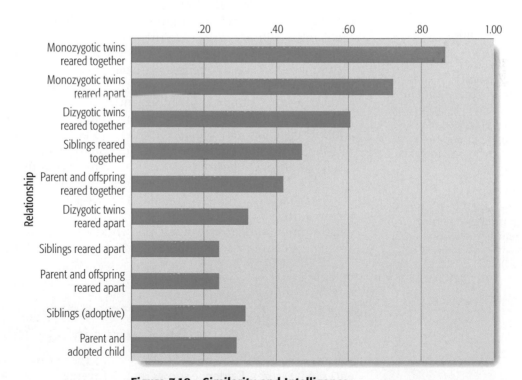

Figure 7.18   Similarity and Intelligence
Here we see the average correlations of IQ scores of people in different family relationships. The closer the genetic and environmental similarity between family members, the closer their IQ scores tend to be.
Source: Adapted from Plomin & Petrill, 1997.

But we need to note, as we did in Chapter 2, that kinship studies are limited because closely related people are very often raised in the same environment. MZ twins not only share the same genes; they may also be treated more alike than are DZ twins or other siblings. Thus, we need to look to other sources of evidence to better separate the contributions of genetics and environment to intelligence. One compelling piece of evidence favoring the role of genetic factors, also shown in Figure 7.18, is that the IQ scores of MZ twins who are raised in separate households are more similar than the IQ scores of DZ twins who are raised together.

Adoptee studies provide yet more evidence of the role of genetics in determining IQ. Studies consistently show IQ scores of adopted children to be closer to those of the children's biological parents than those of their adoptive parents (Bishop et al., 2003; Garlick, 2003).

Yet heredity doesn't tell the whole story. Refer again to Figure 7.18. Notice that the correlation for the IQ scores of MZ twins raised together is greater than the correlation for the IQ scores of MZ twins raised apart. Since MZ twins share the same genes, the difference in these correlations is evidence that the environment also plays a role in determining IQ. Environmental influences also contribute to intellectual development. A home environment that emphasizes verbal interaction, reading, and exploration can foster children's intellectual development.

Taken together, the evidence makes a compelling case that both genetic and environmental factors interact in complex ways in determining intelligence (Dickens & Flynn, 2001; Garlick, 2003). We also have learned that heredity helps shape intelligence throughout the life span, not just during early development (e.g., McGue & Christensen, 2001). Studies of twins in their eighties show similarities in intelligence virtually identical to those among adolescent twins (McClearn et al., 1997).

But just how much of intelligence is explained by genetics and how much by the environment? The **heritability** of a trait is the degree to which genetic factors explain the variability within the population on the trait (Benson, 2004b; Merikangas & Risch, 2003). A heritability estimate of 50 percent for intelligence—at least intelligence as measured by IQ tests—would mean that genetics accounts for 50 percent of the differences (variability) among people in IQ scores; the environment or other unspecified factors would account for the rest.

Heritability estimates of intelligence vary, typically ranging from about 50 to 75 percent (Gottesman, 1997; Scarr, Weinberg, & Waldman, 1993). However, although genetics may account for 50 to 75 percent of variability of IQ scores in the population, we cannot conclude that 50 to 75 percent of a given person's IQ results from genetic factors and the rest from environmental or other influences. Heritability estimates apply to differences among people in the population in general, not to the role that genetics plays in any given individual. Complicating the picture further is recent evidence that heredity plays a larger and stronger role in determining differences in IQ among children from more affluent families than among those from poorer families (Turkheimer et al., 2003).

CONCEPT 7.31

Evidence indicates that genetic and environmental factors interact in complex ways in shaping intelligence.

REALITY CHECK

THE CLAIM IQ is determined at birth.

THE EVIDENCE Evidence supports roles for both heredity and environment in determining intelligence or IQ. Environmental factors, such as an intellectually stimulating home environment, a healthy diet, and formal enrichment programs like Head Start, can foster intellectual development and help children achieve higher IQ scores than they might otherwise.

THE TAKE-AWAY MESSAGE Intelligence, as measured by IQ, is not fixed at birth but is determined by an interplay of genetic and environmental influences.

heritability The degree to which heredity accounts for variations on a given trait within a population.

EXPLORING PSYCHOLOGY
Racial/Ethnic Differences in IQ

Controversy continues to swirl concerning the meaning of racial/ethnic differences in IQ scores. Evidence shows that, on average, White Americans of European descent (Euro-Americans) score higher on IQ tests than African Americans—about 15 points higher (Fagan & Holland, 2002). This gap in IQ scores exists even when differences in income levels are taken into account (Cowley, 1994). African American students also tend to lag behind Euro-American students in scores on reading

CONCEPT 7.32

A gap between the IQ scores of African Americans and Euro-Americans provoked a heated controversy over the meaning of these differences and whether the gap can be closed.

tests (Zernike, 2000). But are racial/ethnic differences on tests of intellectual ability *genetic* or *environmental* in origin?

In a highly controversial 1994 book, *The Bell Curve,* psychologist Robert Herrnstein and political scientist Charles Murray argued that low IQ is associated with a greater risk of many social ills, including poverty, welfare dependence, illegitimacy, and crime. Further, they contended that IQ is largely determined by genetics and that social and educational programs were therefore unlikely to narrow the racial/ethnic gap in IQ scores. They perceived a widening gap between the socioeconomic status of an "IQ elite" and that of a growing underclass of low-IQ groups consisting mainly of African Americans, Hispanic Americans, and recent immigrants.

Evidence does not square with this pessimistic outlook. Social scientists point out that early intervention can improve later performance on intelligence tests to a greater extent than the authors of *The Bell Curve* supposed (Barnett & Camilli, 2002). Nor is IQ fixed at birth; early enrichment can make a difference. Young children exposed to an intellectually enriched environment, in which parents frequently talk with them, read to them, and provide them with stimulating activities and age-appropriate play materials, typically achieve higher IQ scores than children raised in intellectually impoverished conditions. Formal enrichment programs that provide young children from low-income families with exposure to books and puzzles, such as the Head Start program for preschoolers, also produce measurable gains in IQ scores (Zigler & Styfco, 1994).

Perhaps the most telling argument against the claims made in *The Bell Curve* is that group differences in IQ tell us nothing about individual potential. Any group, no matter what its average IQ scores may be, can produce its share of intellectually gifted people. Critics of the book also point to the fact that differences in IQ scores between African Americans and Euro-Americans have actually narrowed over the past few decades, possibly owing to increased educational spending that benefits historically disadvantaged groups (Ceci, Rosenblum, & Kumpf, 1998; W. M. Williams, 1998). Moreover, investigators have found that group differences in knowledge of word meanings can be eliminated when African American students are given equal opportunities to be exposed to the information to be tested (Fagan & Holland, 2002).

IQ scores also appear to be more malleable than *The Bell Curve* would suggest. For example, average IQ scores in the United States and many other countries have been rising steadily for several generations, at a rate of about 3 points a decade (Blair et al., 2005; Dickens & Flynn, 2001; Kanaya, Scullin, & Ceci, 2003). In fact, IQ scores have been rising slightly more rapidly among African Americans than among White Americans, perhaps because educational opportunities for African Americans have been increasing (Flynn, 1999). IQ scores are also observed to be rising in developing countries, such as in rural Kenya (Daley et al., 2003).

The reasons IQ scores are on the rise aren't clear, but investigators suspect that increased access to schooling and more challenging math curricula may help account for the increase (Blair et al., 2005). Then, too, increased availability of word games with tasks similar to those on IQ tests and of materials that challenge young minds to perform visual-spatial tasks, such as Legos and perhaps even some computer games, may also play a role (Begley, 2001a). In Kenya, rising IQ scores are attributed to such factors as increased literacy and improvements in children's nutrition and health (Daley et al., 2003).

Other evidence against the so-called IQ gap is that IQ scores of African American and interracial children who are adopted and raised by upper-middle-class White American families are about 15 points higher than those expected of the average child in the African

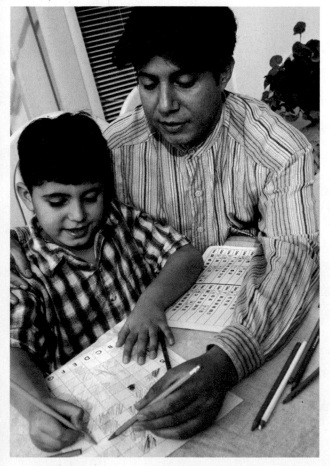

Emphasizing Education Parental emphasis on education can have an important bearing on a child's intellectual development.

CONCEPT 7.33

Most investigators attribute racial differences in IQ scores to environmental factors.

American community (Waldman, Weinberg, & Scarr, 1994). This finding seems to cancel out the oft-cited 15-point gap between the IQ scores of African Americans and those of Whites. The investigators in this study attributed the better performance of the African American adoptees to the sociocultural effects of being raised in a cultural framework that places a strong value on educational achievement.

We also need to consider cultural factors in test-taking situations that can negatively affect how members of particular groups perform. For example, children from some cultural groups may misunderstand test instructions or fail to take them seriously. Because African Americans and members of some other cultural groups place a value on creative expression, children from these groups may not give the obvious answers to questions on IQ tests. Psychologist Janet Helms (1992) suggests that test administrators talk to subjects who give incorrect answers to determine whether a "wrong" answer is the result of cultural differences. She notes that if people use reasoning strategies that differ from those that members of the majority group use to solve a problem, their doing so does not necessarily mean they are any less intelligent.

We still have much to learn about the role of genetics in intelligence. As psychologist Robert Sternberg and his colleagues argue, present evidence does not allow us to determine the role that genetic factors may play in determining racial or ethnic differences in intelligence (Sternberg, Grigorenko, & Kidd, 2005). All in all, however, the evidence we do have points to environmental factors as playing the determining role in accounting for group differences in IQ scores (e.g., Neisser et al., 1996; Waldman et al., 1994; Weinberg, Scarr, & Waldman, 1992).

MODULE 7.3 REVIEW

Intelligence

RECITE IT

What is intelligence, and how is it measured?

- Though theorists define intelligence in different ways, one widely used definition holds that intelligence is the capacity to act purposefully, think rationally, and deal effectively with the environment.

- Standardized intelligence tests, such as the Stanford-Binet Intelligence Scale and the Wechsler scales of intelligence, are generally used to measure intelligence.

- The IQ, or intelligent quotient, is a measure of general intelligence. The Stanford-Binet Intelligence Scale and the Wechsler scales compute IQ on the basis of the deviation of a person's test score from the norms for the person's age group.

What constitutes a good intelligence test?

- The basic requirements of a good intelligence test are standardization (generation of norms based on samples representative of the population), reliability (stability of test scores over time), and validity (the test's ability to measure what it purports to measure).

What are some examples of the misuse of intelligence tests?

- Intelligence tests are misused when children with low scores are labeled as innately incapable or inferior, when too much emphasis is placed on IQ scores, and when cultural biases in the tests put children from diverse cultural backgrounds at a disadvantage.

What are some of the major theories of intelligence?

- Major theories of intelligence include Spearman's concept of general intelligence, or "g," Thurstone's theory of primary mental abilities, Gardner's model of multiple intelligences, and Sternberg's triarchic theory. Some theorists favor the view that intelligence consists of a general cognitive ability, while others favor a model based on multiple abilities or even multiple intelligences.

Is intelligence determined by heredity or environment?

- Most authorities believe that intelligence is based on a complex interaction of nature (genetic influences) and nurture (environmental influences).

RECALL IT

1. The first modern intelligence test was developed by Alfred _____ and Theodore _____.

2. Match the terms with the definitions below:
   i. standardization; ii. validity;
   iii. mainstreaming; iv. Spearman's "g"

   a. a test's ability to measure what it is designed to measure
   b. the practice of placing children with mild mental retardation in regular classrooms
   c. an underlying general factor of intelligence
   d. the generation of test norms based on representative samples of the population

3. The theory of intelligence that emphasizes how we integrate various aspects of intelligence in meeting the challenges and demands of everyday life is called
   a. Sternberg's triarchic theory of intelligence.
   b. Gardner's model of multiple intelligences.
   c. Thurstone's theory of primary mental abilities.
   d. Spearman's theory of "g."

4. The authors of *The Bell Curve* argued that
   a. social and educational programs are unlikely to close the racial gap in IQ scores.
   b. genetics plays only a minor role in intelligence.
   c. the racial gap in IQ scores is due largely to socioeconomic factors.
   d. low IQ is not linked to social problems, such as poverty and crime.

THINK ABOUT IT

- Do you believe that conventional intelligence tests are culturally biased? Why or why not?
- In what ways are intelligence tests useful? In what ways might they be misused?

- Have you ever taken an intelligence test? Did you think it was a fair appraisal of your intelligence? How were the results used? Do you feel you benefited from the experience? If so, how? What would you do differently if you were called upon to develop a new intelligence test?

APPLICATION MODULE 7.4
Becoming a Creative Problem Solver

CONCEPT 7.34

Creative problem solvers challenge preconceptions and consider as many alternative solutions to a problem as possible.

The range of problems we face in our personal lives is virtually limitless. Consider some common examples: getting to school or work on time; helping a friend with a personal problem; resolving disputes; juggling school, work, and family responsibilities. Creative problem solvers challenge preconceptions and consider as many alternative solutions to a problem as possible. Were you stumped by the problem on page 258 about the key that opened no locks but allowed the man to enter? Perhaps it was because you approached the problem from only one vantage point—that the key was a door key. Solving the problem requires that you consider an alternative that may not have seemed obvious at first—that the key was an Enter key on a keyboard. Speaking of keys, here are some key steps toward becoming a creative problem solver.

Adopt a Questioning Attitude

Finding creative solutions to problems begins with adopting a questioning attitude. The creative problem solver asks, "What alternatives are available? What has worked in the past? What hasn't worked? What can I do differently?"

Gather Information

Creative problem solvers acquire the information and resources they need to explore possible solutions. People today have a wider range of information resources available than ever before, including newspapers and magazines, college courses, and, of course, the Internet. Want to know more about combating a common problem like insomnia? Why not search the Internet to see what information is available? However, think critically about the information you find.

Avoid Getting Stuck in Mental Sets

Here's a question: "If there were three apples and you took two away, how many would you have?" If you answered one, chances are you had a mental set to respond to this type of problem as a subtraction problem. But the question did not ask how many apples were left. The answer is that you would have two apples—the two you took away.

To avoid slipping into a mental set that impairs problem-solving efforts, think through each question carefully. Ask yourself:

- What am I required to do?
- What type of problem is this?
- What problem-solving strategy would work best for this type of problem?

Put these skills into practice by responding to a few brainteasers (the answers are given on page 293) (*Brainteaser Quizzes*, 2001):

1. How many two-cent stamps are there in a dozen?
2. You are holding two U.S. coins that total 55 cents. One of the coins is not a nickel. What are the coins you are holding?
3. A farmer had 18 cows and all but 11 of them died. How many were left?

Be on guard against the destructive side of mental set—the tendency to apply a "tried and true" solution even when it no longer applies. The major danger is not the mental set itself, but failing to realize when one is trapped in a fixed way of doing things (Luchins & Luchins, 1994). By remaining aware of this tendency, you can stop yourself every now and then to reflect on whether the strategies you are using are working for or against you.

Generate Alternatives

Creative problem solvers generate as many alternative solutions to a problem as possible. They may then decide to return to their original solution. Or they may decide that one of the alternatives works best. Sifting through alternatives can help you rearrange your thinking so that a more workable solution becomes obvious. Here are a few suggestions for generating alternatives:

1. *Practice personal brainstorming.* Alex Osborne (1963) introduced the concept of brainstorming to help business executives and engineers solve problems more creatively. The basic idea is to encourage divergent thinking. **Brainstorming** encourages people to propose as many solutions to a problem as possible without fear of being judged negatively by others, no matter how far-fetched their proposals may seem. There are four general rules for brainstorming:

   Rule 1: Write down as many solutions to the problem as you can think of. Quantity counts more than quality.

   Rule 2: Suspend judgment. Don't evaluate any of the possible solutions or strike them off your list.

   Rule 3: Seek unusual, remote, or even weird ideas. Today's strange or oddball idea may turn into tomorrow's brilliant solution.

brainstorming A method of promoting divergent thinking by encouraging people to propose as many solutions to a problem as possible without fear of being judged negatively by others, no matter how far-fetched their proposals may be.

Rule 4: After generating your list, put it aside for a few days. When you return to it, ask yourself which solutions are worth pursuing. Take into account the resources or additional information you will need to put these solutions into practice.

2. *Find analogies.* Finding a situation analogous to the present problem can lead to a creative solution. Ask yourself how the present problem is similar to problems you've encountered before. What strategies worked in the past? How can they be modified to fit the present problem? This is constructive use of mental set—using past solutions as a guide, not an impediment, to problem solving.

3. *Think outside the box.* Recall the nine-dot problem in Figure 7.3 (p. 258). People have difficulty with this problem because of their tendency to limit the ways they think about it. If you didn't solve the nine-dot problem, you're in good company. In a laboratory test, none of the research participants who were given several minutes to solve the problem were able to do so (MacGregor, Ormerod, & Chronicle, 2001). The problem is solvable only if you think "outside the box"—literally, as shown in Figure 7.19. Creative problem solvers make an effort to conceptualize problems from different perspectives, steering their problem-solving efforts toward finding new solutions (Ormerod, MacGregor, & Chronicle, 2002).

Figure 7.19
Two Solutions to the Nine-Dot Problem in Figure 7.3

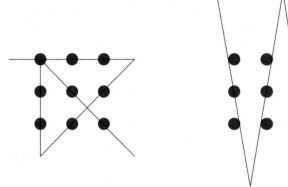

Sleep on It

In cases where people are faced with difficult problems, evidence supports the age-old wisdom of "sleeping on it." For example, some investigators found that research subjects who were challenged with solving challenging math problems did better after they slept (Wagner et al., 2004). Indeed, the cognitive benefits of getting a good night's sleep may account for the experiences of many famous scientists and artists whose inspired ideas occurred shortly upon awakening (Komaroff, 2004).

If you are unable to find a solution to a problem, take time away from thinking about it. Allow the problem to "incubate" in your mind. When you return to it, you may have a fresh perspective that will help you discover a workable solution.

Try It Out

Try out possible solutions to see how they work. Gather information that will help you evaluate what you need to do differently to achieve a better solution.

However you arrive at a possible solution, test it out to see how it works. Even if it doesn't succeed, you may be able to gather additional information that can help you evaluate what you need to do differently to achieve a better solution.

TYING IT TOGETHER

Cognitive psychology focuses on how we acquire knowledge about the world, communicate with others, and solve problems we face in daily life. Through the cognitive process of thinking, we acquire knowledge of the world by mentally representing and manipulating information in our minds (Module 7.1). But to share information with others we need to use a shared system of communication called language (Module 7.2). Understanding how people acquire knowledge, solve problems, and adapt to their environments leads us to consider individual differences in intelligence (Module 7.3). Psychologists are interested in studying the nature of intelligence and ways of measuring it. We can apply knowledge gained from studies of problem solving to become more creative problem solvers, such as by challenging preconceptions and generating as many possible solutions to a problem as possible (Module 7.4).

Thinking Critically About Psychology

Based on your reading of this chapter, answer the following questions. Then, to evaluate your progress in developing critical thinking skills, compare your answers to the sample answers found in Appendix A.

An ambulance is heading toward the hospital on a country road, carrying an injured man who needs emergency surgery. When the ambulance comes around a bend, the driver notices a large flock of sheep blocking the road. The driver starts pounding on the horn and sounding the siren to part the sheep, but to no effect. A medical technician jumps out of the ambulance and tries to shove the rearmost sheep out of the way, hoping the others will follow. The driver starts screaming at the shepherd, imploring him to clear the road. The shepherd also starts screaming, but the sheep just keep on bleating. Suddenly, the shepherd raises his hand to signal the ambulance to stop. He then succeeds in clearing a path ahead for the ambulance, but not by parting the sheep or by guiding the ambulance past them (adapted from Levine, 1994).

1. a. **How did the shepherd clear the road for the ambulance?**

   b. **What impediment to problem solving does the behavior of the medical technician represent?**

John receives an inheritance, which he decides to invest in the stock market. Like many other investors today, he decides to open an online trading account. At first, he does well. Then he begins to trade more actively, buying and selling stocks almost daily. His losses soon begin to mount. Concerned, he consults a financial adviser, who asks him about his trading strategy. John recounts that he buys stocks in companies he hears positive things about and sells stocks in companies whenever he notices negative news items.

2. a. **What cognitive error(s) in decision making might explain John's losses in the stock market?**

   b. **How would you advise him to avoid such errors in the future?**

Key Terms

cognitive psychology *(p. 254)*
thinking *(p. 254)*
mental image *(p. 255)*
concepts *(p. 256)*
logical concepts *(p. 256)*
natural concepts *(p. 257)*
superordinate concepts *(p. 257)*
basic-level concepts *(p. 257)*
subordinate concepts *(p. 257)*
positive instance *(p. 258)*
negative instance *(p. 258)*
problem solving *(p. 258)*
algorithm *(p. 259)*
heuristic *(p. 259)*
analogy *(p. 260)*
incubation period *(p. 260)*
mental set *(p. 260)*
functional fixedness *(p. 261)*
decision making *(p. 261)*

confirmation bias *(p. 261)*
representativeness heuristic *(p. 262)*
availability heuristic *(p. 263)*
framing *(p. 264)*
creativity *(p. 264)*
divergent thinking *(p. 264)*
convergent thinking *(p. 264)*
metaphor *(p. 265)*
analogy *(p. 265)*
conceptual combinations *(p. 265)*
conceptual expansion *(p. 265)*
language *(p. 268)*
grammar *(p. 268)*
phonemes *(p. 268)*
morphemes *(p. 268)*
syntax *(p. 268)*
semantics *(p. 268)*
language acquisition device *(p. 269)*
linguistic relativity hypothesis *(p. 270)*

intelligence *(p. 274)*
eugenics *(p. 274)*
mental age *(p. 275)*
intelligence quotient (IQ) *(p. 275)*
norms *(p. 276)*
standardization *(p. 276)*
reliability *(p. 277)*
validity *(p. 278)*
predictive validity *(p. 278)*
culture-fair tests *(p. 278)*
mental retardation *(p. 279)*
mainstreaming *(p. 279)*
primary mental abilities *(p. 281)*
multiple intelligences *(p. 281)*
triarchic theory of intelligence *(p. 282)*
heritability *(p. 286)*
brainstorming *(p. 290)*

ANSWERS TO RECALL IT QUESTIONS

Module 7.1: 1. thinking; 2. i. c, ii. d, iii. a, iv. b; 3. b; 4. analogy, algorithm; 5. d.

Module 7.2: 1. b; 2. a; 3. relativity; 4. symbols.

Module 7.3: 1. Binet, Simon; 2. i. d, ii. a, iii. b, iv. c; 3. a; 4. a.

ANSWERS TO BRAINTEASERS *(page 290)*

1. There are 12 two-cent stamps, since a dozen of anything is 12.

2. You are holding a fifty-cent piece and a nickel. One of the two coins (the fifty-cent piece) is not a nickel.

3. There are 11 cows left. All but 11 died.

Motivation and Emotion

DID YOU KNOW THAT . . .

- The founding father of American psychology believed there is a human instinct for cleanliness? (p. 297)
- Obese people typically have more fat cells than do people of normal weight? (p. 309)
- One in seven college women are embarrassed to buy a chocolate bar in a store? (p. 312)
- Practicing smiling can lift your mood? (p. 319)
- There is no one emotion center in the brain? (p. 321)
- Responding without thinking can be a lifesaver in some situations? (p. 324)
- Money is not the key to happiness? (p. 325)
- According to a leading psychologist, happiness comes from what we do with our lives, not what we have? (p. 327)

Imagine you came into a windfall of an enormous amount of money—let's say $10 million. How would you spend your days? Would you continue pursuing your college degree, or would you just lounge about in luxury? Perhaps you'd relax on a tropical beach for a few weeks, maybe even a few months. But sooner or later, you'd probably want to do something more meaningful. Perhaps you'd devote your time and energy to philanthropy. Or start a new business in the hope of accumulating even more wealth. Or perhaps pursue a career you would enjoy for reasons other than financial rewards. In any event, you wouldn't crawl into a ball and remain motionless for the rest of your life. You would be motivated to do something and get on with your life.

Although few people ever attain great wealth, we might learn something about human motivation from someone who became so wealthy that the sheer size of his fortune boggles the imagination. Bill Gates—co-founder of Microsoft, the world's leading software company—remains the world's richest person, with a net worth valued at a whopping $46.5 billion according to recent estimates (Kroll & Goldman, 2005). Windows, Microsoft's flagship operating system, is used in more than 90 percent of the world's personal computers. Yet Gates is still plugging away, though perhaps not at the frenetic pace of his youth.

What motivates someone like Bill Gates? After all, he has more money than he or anyone could spend in a dozen lifetimes, short of buying half a dozen small countries. Evidently, his motivation has to do with sources of gratification that cannot be deposited in a bank account. He once told an interviewer that life for him is a continuous process of challenge and achievement. For Gates and others like him, there are always more mountains to climb, more challenges to test one's mettle. Such people prize wealth not for what it can buy, but for what it represents—winning.

What about you? What drives your behavior? Is it the desire to satisfy your biological needs—to have sufficient food, water, sexual gratification, and protection from the elements? Or are you, like Bill Gates, driven by a need to achieve, succeed, and prove something about yourself to the world? What is it that starts your engine and keeps it going?

In this chapter, we explore the factors that energize and direct human behavior—not just motivation, but also emotion. Both words—*motivation* and *emotion*—are derived from the Latin *movere*, meaning "to move." Like motivation, emotion moves us to act. The emotion of fear, for instance, can motivate us to act defensively to escape a threatening situation. The emotion of anger can motivate us to act aggressively to rectify an injustice. The emotion of happiness inspires us to repeat the behavior that creates it. Throughout the ages, love has been considered a prime motivator, the emotion that "makes the world go round."

We begin by considering the sources of motivation that prompt behavior and keep it going. We then focus on one of the most basic motives, hunger, and examine in depth the problems of obesity and eating disorders. Finally, we explore the complex phenomenon of emotion. ■

MODULE 8.1
Motivation: The "Whys" of Behavior

- What is motivation?
- What is instinct theory?
- What is drive theory?
- How does arousal theory account for differences in motivational states?
- How does incentive theory differ from drive theory?
- What is cognitive dissonance theory?
- What are psychosocial needs?
- What is Maslow's hierarchy of needs?

CONCEPT 8.1
Motivation refers to the "whys" of behavior—factors that activate, direct, and sustain goal-directed behavior.

Online Study Center
Improve Your Grade
Tutorials: What is Motivation?

Motivation refers to factors that *activate, direct,* and *sustain* goal-directed behavior. If after a few hours of not eating, you get up from your chair and go to the kitchen to fix yourself a snack, we might infer that the *motive* for your behavior is hunger. The hunger motive activates your behavior (causing you to stand), directs it (moving you toward the kitchen), and sustains it (as you make yourself a snack and consume it) until you've achieved your goal (satisfying your hunger). **Motives** are the "whys" of behavior—the needs or wants that drive behavior and explain why we do what we do. We don't actually observe a motive; rather, we infer that one exists based on the behavior we observe.

In this module, we focus on the biological and psychological sources of motivation and the various theories psychologists have constructed to explain motivated behavior. None of these theories offers a complete explanation of motivated behavior, but each contributes something to our understanding of the "whys" of behavior.

Biological Sources of Motivation

We need oxygen to breathe, food for energy, water to drink, and protection from the elements. These basic biological needs motivate much of our behavior. Biological needs are inborn. We don't learn to breathe or to become hungry or thirsty. Nonetheless, learning and experience influence how we satisfy our biological needs, especially our need for food. Eating tamales or mutton stew might satisfy our

What Makes Bill Run? For more than a decade, Bill Gates has been America's wealthiest individual. What drives his behavior? What drives your behavior?

motivation Factors that activate, direct, and sustain goal-directed behavior.
motives Needs or wants that drive goal-directed behavior.

hunger, but whether we choose to eat tamales or mutton stew, as well as how we prepare it, often depends on our cultural background and learning experiences.

Biological sources of motivation include instincts and drives, which are inborn mechanisms for satisfying basic survival needs. But as you'll see, theorists believe that some biologically based needs, such as the need to maintain an optimal level of arousal, are not directly tied to survival.

Instincts: Behavior Programmed by Nature   Birds build nests, and salmon return upstream to their birthplaces to spawn. They do not acquire these behaviors through experience or by attending nest-building or spawning schools. These are **instinctive behaviors**—fixed, inborn patterns of response that are specific to members of a particular species. **Instinct theory** holds that behavior is motivated by instincts.

Though we can find examples of instinctive behaviors in other species, do instincts motivate human behavior? One theorist who thought so was Sigmund Freud, who believed that human behavior is motivated primarily by sexual and aggressive instincts (see Chapter 12). Another was William James (1890/1970), the father of American psychology, who compiled a list of thirty-seven instincts that he believed could explain much of human behavior. His list included physical instincts, such as sucking, and mental instincts, such as curiosity, jealousy, and even cleanliness. (Yes, cleanliness.) Other early psychologists, notably William McDougall (1908), expanded on James's list. The list kept growing and growing, so much so that by the 1920s it had ballooned to some ten thousand instincts covering a wide range of human behavior (Bernard, 1924).

The instinct theory of human motivation has long been out of favor. One reason for its decline is that the list of instincts simply grew too large to be useful. Another is that explaining behavior on the basis of instincts is merely a way of describing it, not explaining it (Gaulin & McBurney, 2001). For example, saying a person is lazy because of a laziness instinct or stingy because of a stinginess instinct doesn't really explain the person's behavior. It merely attaches a label to it. Perhaps most important, psychologists recognized that human behavior is much more variable and flexible than would be the case if it were determined by instinct. Moreover, instinct theory fails to account for the important roles of culture and learning in determining human behavior. Though instincts may account for some stereotypical behavior in other animals, most psychologists reject the view that instincts motivate complex human behavior.

Needs and Drives: Maintaining a Steady Internal State   By the early 1950s, **drive theory** had replaced instinct theory as the major model of human motivation. Its foremost proponent, psychologist Clark Hull (1943, 1952), believed we have biological needs that demand satisfaction, such as the needs for food, water, and sleep. A **need** is a state of deprivation or deficiency. A **drive** is a state of bodily tension, such as hunger or thirst, that arises from an unmet need. The satisfaction of a drive is called **drive reduction**.

Drive theory is based on the principle of *homeostasis*, the tendency of the body to maintain a steady internal state (see Chapter 2). Homeostatic mechanisms in the body monitor temperature, oxygen, and blood sugar and maintain them at a steady level. According to drive theory, whenever homeostasis is disturbed, drives activate the behavior needed to restore a steady balance. For example, when our blood sugar level drops because we haven't eaten in a while, we become hungry. Hunger is the drive that motivates us to seek nourishment, which restores homeostasis. Although drive theory focuses on biological needs, some needs, such as the needs for comfort and safety, have a psychological basis that cannot be explained by homeostasis.

Though needs and drives are related, they are distinct from each other. We may have a bodily need for a certain vitamin but not become aware of it until we develop a vitamin deficiency disorder. In other words, the need may exist in the

---

CONCEPT 8.2

Instinct theorists believe that humans and other animals are motivated by instincts—fixed, inborn patterns of response that are specific to members of a particular species.

CONCEPT 8.3

Drive theorists maintain that we are motivated by drives that arise from biological needs that demand satisfaction.

---

instinctive behaviors   Genetically programmed, innate patterns of response that are specific to members of a particular species.

instinct theory   The belief that behavior is motivated by instinct.

drive theory   The belief that behavior is motivated by drives that arise from biological needs that demand satisfaction.

need   A state of deprivation or deficiency.

drive   A state of bodily tension, such as hunger or thirst, that arises from an unmet need.

drive reduction   Satisfaction of a drive.

absence of a corresponding drive. Moreover, the strength of a need and the drive to satisfy it may differ. People who fast for religious or other reasons may find they are less hungry on the second or third day of a fast than on the first, even though their need for food is even greater.

Unlike instinct theory, drive theory posits an important role for learning, especially operant conditioning (discussed in Chapter 5). We learn responses (like ordering a pizza when we're hungry) that are reinforced by drive reduction. A behavior that results in drive reduction is more likely to be repeated the next time the need arises. Drives may also be acquired through experience. Biological drives, such as hunger, thirst, and sexual desire, are called **primary drives** because they are considered inborn; drives that are the result of experience are called **secondary drives**. For example, a drive to achieve monetary wealth is not something we are born with; we acquire it as a secondary drive because we learn that money can be used to satisfy many primary and other secondary drives.

Optimal Level of Arousal: What's Optimal for You? Drive theory focuses on drives that satisfy survival needs, such as needs for food and water. But classic experiments by psychologist Harry Harlow and his colleagues challenged the notion that all drives satisfy basic survival needs. When they placed a mechanical puzzle in a monkey's cage, they found that the monkey began manipulating it and taking it apart, even though the animal didn't receive any food or other obvious reinforcement for its efforts (Harlow, Harlow, & Meyer, 1950). Human babies, too, manipulate objects placed before them. They shake rattles, turn knobs, push buttons on activity toys, and mouth new objects, even though none of these behaviors is connected with satisfaction of their basic survival needs.

The work of Harlow and others suggests that humans and many other animals have innate, biologically based needs for exploration and activity. These needs, which prod organisms to explore their environments and manipulate objects—especially unusual or novel objects—are called **stimulus motives**. Stimulus motives don't disappear as we get older. As adults, we still want to touch and manipulate interesting objects, as witnessed by the many grown-ups who try their hand at the latest gizmos displayed at stores like The Sharper Image.

Drive theory leads us to expect that organisms are motivated to reduce *states of arousal*—that is, states of general alertness and nervous system activation. For example, when we are hungry, we experience a state of heightened arousal until we eat; after eating, we may feel tranquil or even sleepy. But with stimulus motives, motivated behavior leads to increased arousal—not decreased arousal, as drive theory would suggest. In other words, even when our basic needs for food and water are met, we seek out stimulation that heightens our level of arousal.

Some theorists believe that stimulus motives serve a biologically based need to maintain an *optimal* level of arousal (Hebb, 1955; Zuckerman, 1980). According to **arousal theory**, whenever the level of stimulation dips below an organism's optimal level, the organism seeks out stimulation. When stimulation exceeds an optimal level, the organism seeks ways of toning down stimulation.

The optimal level of arousal varies from person to person. Some people require a steady diet of highly stimulating activities, such as mountain climbing, snowboarding, bungee jumping, or parasailing. Others are satisfied to spend quiet evenings at home, curled up with a good book or relaxing by watching TV.

People with a high need for arousal see life as an adventure. To maintain their optimal level of stimulation, they seek exciting experiences and thrills. Psychologist Marvin Zuckerman (1996) calls such people sensation-seekers. Sensation-seekers tend to get bored easily and may have difficulty restraining their impulses. Some get into trouble because their desire for stimulation leads them to take undue risks; for example, they may experiment with illicit drugs or engage in other illegal activities (Roberti, 2004). Yet many sensation-seekers limit sensation seeking to sanctioned, reasonably safe activities. Not surprisingly, surfers tend to score higher on

---

💡 **CONCEPT 8.4**
Stimulus motives prod organisms to explore their environments and manipulate objects.

💡 **CONCEPT 8.5**
Arousal theory postulates a biologically based need to maintain stimulation at an optimal level.

primary drives Innate drives, such as hunger, thirst, and sexual desire, that arise from basic biological needs.

secondary drives Drives that are learned or acquired through experience, such as the drive to achieve monetary wealth.

stimulus motives Internal states that prompt inquisitive, stimulation-seeking, and exploratory behavior.

arousal theory The belief that whenever the level of stimulation dips below an organism's optimal level, the organism seeks ways of increasing it.

Yerkes-Dodson law The proposition that the relationship between arousal and performance involves an inverted U-shaped function, with better performance occurring at moderate levels of arousal.

TRY THIS OUT

Are You a Sensation-Seeker?

Do you pursue thrills and adventure? Or do you prefer quiet evenings at home? To evaluate whether you fit the profile of a sensation-seeker, circle the number on each line that best describes you.

Interpreting your responses. Responses above five indicate a high level of sensation seeking; those five or below indicate a low level. On which side of the continuum do your responses lie? Draw a line connecting your responses. The further to the right the line falls, the stronger your personality fits the profile of a sensation-seeker.

Prefer a job in one location	1 2 3 4 5 6 7 8 9 10	Prefer a job with lots of travel
Prefer staying out of the cold	1 2 3 4 5 6 7 8 9 10	Enjoy a brisk walk on a cold day
Prefer being with familiar people	1 2 3 4 5 6 7 8 9 10	Prefer meeting new people
Like to play it safe	1 2 3 4 5 6 7 8 9 10	Like living "on the edge"
Would prefer not to try hypnosis	1 2 3 4 5 6 7 8 9 10	Would like to try hypnosis
Would prefer not to try parachute jumping	1 2 3 4 5 6 7 8 9 10	Would like to try parachute jumping
Prefer quiet evenings at home	1 2 3 4 5 6 7 8 9 10	Prefer going out dancing at night
Prefer a safe and secure life	1 2 3 4 5 6 7 8 9 10	Prefer experiencing as much as possible
Prefer calm and controlled people	1 2 3 4 5 6 7 8 9 10	Prefer people who are a bit wild
Like to sleep in a comfortable room with a good bed	1 2 3 4 5 6 7 8 9 10	Enjoy camping out
Prefer avoiding risky activities	1 2 3 4 5 6 7 8 9 10	Like to do things that are a little dangerous

Source: Adapted from Zuckerman, 1980.

CONCEPT 8.6
The Yerkes-Dodson law specifies that people perform best under moderate levels of arousal.

sensation-seeking than do golfers (Diehm & Armatas, 2004). Sensation-seeking appears to have a strong genetic component—the taste for thrills may be something we are born with.

At what level of arousal do you perform at your peak? Are you more likely to perform your best on a test when (1) you are so unconcerned about doing well that you can barely keep your eyes open, (2) you hope to do well and are mentally alert but not unduly anxious, or (3) you are convinced this is a life-or-death situation and are so anxious you can't think straight? It's a safe bet you'd do best under condition 2, the condition of moderate arousal.

The relationship between arousal and performance generally takes the form of an inverted U-shaped curve (see Figure 8.1). This relationship, known as the **Yerkes-Dodson law**, states that people perform best under conditions of moderate

Figure 8.1
Yerkes-Dodson Law
According to the Yerkes-Dodson law, the relationship between performance and arousal (motivational) level can be represented as an inverted U-shaped curve. The point at which performance begins to decline becomes lower as task difficulty increases.

arousal. The point at which the curve turns downward depends on the complexity of the task. For relatively simple tasks, the optimal point of arousal is relatively high. But for more difficult tasks, the optimal level is relatively low. Thus, a high level of arousal will impair your performance more when you are trying to perform a difficult task, such as trying to get your tennis serve in the box, than when you are performing a more routine task, such as mowing the lawn.

Psychological Sources of Motivation

If motivation were simply a matter of maintaining homeostasis in our bodies, we would rest quietly until prompted again by hunger, thirst, or some other biological drive. But we don't sit idly by when our bellies are full and our other biological needs are met. We are also motivated by psychological needs, such as the need for friendship or achievement. We perceive certain goals as desirable or rewarding even though attaining them will not satisfy any biological needs. We may also be motivated to change our attitudes and behaviors to make them consistent with each other. Clearly, such motivated behaviors are best addressed by considering the role of psychological factors in motivation. These factors include incentives, cognitive dissonance, and psychosocial needs.

Incentives: The "Pull" Side of Motivation   According to **incentive theory**, our attraction to particular goals or objects motivates much of our behavior. **Incentives** are rewards or other stimuli that motivate us to act. The attraction, or "pull," exerted by an incentive stems from our perception that it can satisfy a need or is in itself desirable.

In contrast to drive theory, which explains how unmet biological needs push us in the direction of satisfying them, incentive theory holds that incentives motivate us by pulling us toward them. Incentive theory thus focuses on the lure, or "pull," of incentives in motivating behavior, rather than the "push" of internal need states or drives. You may crave a scrumptious-looking dessert even though you've just eaten a full meal and no longer feel "pushed" by the drive of hunger. You may feel drawn to buy the latest fashions or technological gizmos even though obtaining these objects will not satisfy any biological need.

The strength of the "pull" that a goal or reward exerts on our behavior is its **incentive value**. Incentive values are influenced by many factors, including an individual's learning experiences and expectancies. We place more value on a goal if we have learned from past experience to associate it with pleasure and if we expect it will be rewarding when we obtain it. Many employers spur productivity in their employees by offering them incentives in the form of bonuses.

Cultural influences play a large part in determining incentive values. Some cultures place great value on individual achievement and accumulation of wealth. Others place a premium on meeting obligations to one's family, religious group, employer, or community. What incentives motivate your behavior—a college diploma, wealth, the man or woman of your dreams, status, or the respect of your family or community? Which of these incentives has the strongest "pull" on your behavior?

Cognitive Dissonance: Maintaining Consistency in Attitudes and Behavior
Psychologists recognize that people are motivated to maintain consistency in their attitudes and behavior. In a classic study, Leon Festinger and J. Merrill Carlsmith (1959) had two groups of college students complete an extremely boring task. They then paid one group $1 and the other group $20 to persuade other students that the task was exciting and interesting. Afterward, the subjects were asked to express their attitude toward the task—how much they liked it or disliked it. Curiously, those who received the lower payment expressed greater enthusiasm for the task than those in the higher-paid group. *Why?*

CONCEPT 8.7
Incentives motivate us by exerting a pull on our behavior; their strength varies in relation to the value we place on them.

---

incentive theory   The belief that our attraction to particular goals or objects motivates much of our behavior.

incentives   Rewards or other stimuli that motivate us to act.

incentive value   The strength of the "pull" of a goal or reward.

cognitive dissonance   A state of internal tension brought about by conflicting attitudes and behavior.

cognitive dissonance theory   The belief that people are motivated to resolve discrepancies between their behavior and their attitudes or beliefs.

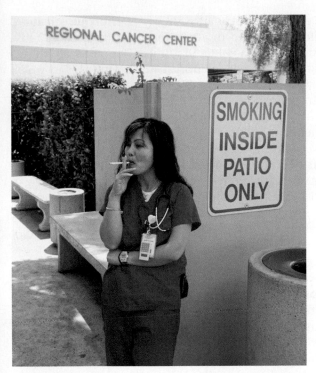

Cognitive Dissonance? Can you think of examples in which your behavior was inconsistent with your deeply held attitudes or beliefs? Were you motivated to reconcile these differences? Or did you ignore them?

Both groups had engaged in behavior (telling others the task was exciting) that was presumably incompatible with their underlying attitude (disliking the task because it was boring). Festinger and Carlsmith theorized that when attitudes are inconsistent with behavior, people are likely to experience an unpleasant state of tension called **cognitive dissonance**. They reasoned that this uncomfortable state motivates efforts to bring attitudes and behavior in line with each other. Subjects in the higher-paid group apparently were able to resolve their dissonance by telling themselves they had been paid handsomely for telling an untruth. Those in the lower-paid group could not use this justification, so they presumably had to resolve their dissonance by changing how they felt about the task.

The theory that attempts to explain Festinger and Carlsmith's finding is called **cognitive dissonance theory**. It holds that people are motivated to resolve discrepancies between their behavior and their attitudes or beliefs by making them more compatible. There are several ways to reduce cognitive dissonance (Matz & Wood, 2005). People can change their behavior to fit their attitudes or beliefs, change their attitudes or beliefs to fit their behavior, attempt to explain away any inconsistencies between their behavior and their attitudes or beliefs, or simply ignore any discrepancies. As an example, smokers who believe that smoking causes cancer but continue to smoke may reduce cognitive dissonance by altering their behavior (quitting smoking), altering their belief (adopting the belief that smoking isn't really all that harmful), or using a form of rationalization to explain away the inconsistency ("Cancer doesn't run in my family"). Yet perhaps the most common ways of reducing dissonance are not to change either beliefs or behavior but simply to ignore inconsistencies until they fade away ("I'll worry about my smoking when I get older") or engage in distracting tasks that take your mind off of it (Newby-Clark, McGregor, & Zanna, 2002). Figure 8.2 illustrates some ways of reducing cognitive dissonance.

Figure 8.2
Ways of Reducing Cognitive Dissonance

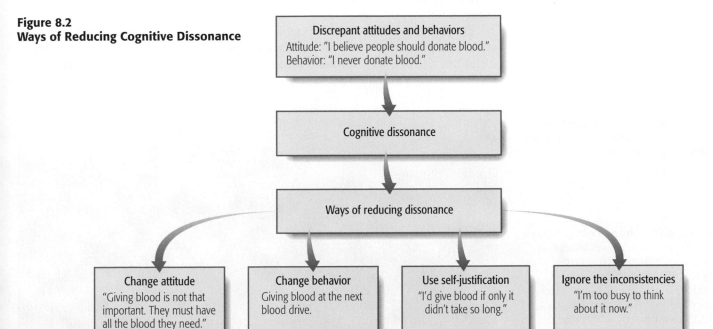

An important concept in cognitive dissonance theory is **effort justification**, the tendency to justify the effort expended in attaining difficult goals. Suppose you had to wait in line for four hours on a cold and rainy day to purchase tickets for a concert or sporting event. The concept of effort justification leads us to expect that you would rate the event as more enjoyable than you would if the tickets had been easy to come by. In other words, the harder we have to work to attain a goal or object, the more highly we tend to value it.

By and large, research evidence supports cognitive dissonance theory. Studies show that inconsistencies between attitudes and behavior create emotional distress and that changing these beliefs or attitudes can help reduce or eliminate this discomfort (Aronson, Wilson, & Akert, 2004; Jones, 1998; Petty, Wegener, & Fabrigar, 1997). As we'll see in Chapter 16, salespersons, advertisers, fundraisers, and others who try to influence us often use strategies that take advantage of our need for consistency in behavior and belief.

Psychosocial Needs   Although fulfilling biological needs is necessary for survival, human beings seek more out of life than mere survival. We are social creatures who are motivated to satisfy **psychosocial needs** (also called *interpersonal needs*), such as the need for social relationships (also called the *need for affiliation*) and the need to achieve. Here we focus on the most widely studied of these needs—the need to excel at what we do, which is known as the **need for achievement**.

Some people strive relentlessly to get ahead, to earn vast sums of money, to invent, to create—in short, to achieve. People with a high need for achievement are found in many walks of life, from business and professional sports to academia and the arts. Like Bill Gates, they have a strong desire to excel at what they do. They are hard-driving and ambitious and take pride in accomplishing their goals.

Harvard psychologist David McClelland found that the goals that people with a high need for achievement set for themselves are challenging but realistic (McClelland, 1958, 1985; McClelland et al., 1953). Goals that are too easily achieved are of no interest to them, nor are goals that are patently unobtainable. Such people may not always succeed, but they take failure in stride and keep pushing ahead. By contrast, people with a low need for achievement are motivated by a desire to avoid failure. They set goals either so low that anyone can achieve them or so unrealistically high that no one can achieve them. If the bar is set too high, who can blame them if they fail? When they meet with failure, they are more likely to quit than to persevere.

People with a high need for achievement typically receive higher grades and earn more promotions and money than people with similar abilities and opportunities but a lower need for achievement. They generally seek positions that offer moderate levels of risk, opportunities for decision making, and a chance at be-

💡 **CONCEPT 8.8**
Many psychologists believe we are motivated to satisfy not only biological needs, but also psychosocial needs, such as the need for achievement.

Need for Achievement   How strong is your need for achievement—your need not just to succeed, but to excel?

effort justification   The tendency to place greater value on goals that are difficult to achieve in order to justify the effort expended in attaining them.

psychosocial needs   Needs that reflect interpersonal aspects of motivation, such as the need for friendship or achievement.

need for achievement   The need to excel in one's endeavors.

coming highly successful (McClelland, 1965). They often pursue careers as entrepreneurs or in business management or sales.

The need for achievement is driven by *extrinsic motivation, intrinsic motivation,* or both (Ryan & Deci, 2000). **Extrinsic motivation** reflects a desire for external rewards, such as money or the respect of one's peers or family. **Intrinsic motivation** reflects a desire for internal gratification, such as the self-satisfaction or pleasure derived from accomplishing a particular goal or performing a certain task. In other words, extrinsic motivation is a "means to an end," whereas intrinsic motivation is an "end in itself" (Pittman, 1998). The level of enjoyment associated with activities we perform for their own sake (intrinsic motivation), as well as our performance in these activities, tends to increase in situations requiring competition *and* cooperation, such as when participating in team sports (Tauer & Harackiewicz, 2004).

In achievement situations, we may be pulled in opposite directions by two kinds of motives: **achievement motivation** (the desire to achieve success) and **avoidance motivation** (the desire to avoid failure). Achievement motivation leads us to undertake challenges that run the risk of failure but that may also lead to success. Avoidance motivation leads us to avoid taking chances that could result in failure; it prompts us to stick with the sure and safe path. Although avoidance motivation may reduce the chance of failure, it also reduces the likelihood of success. One study found that students with a lower level of avoidance motivation did better in their courses and showed higher levels of emotional well-being than those with a higher level of avoidance motivation (Elliot & Sheldon, 1997).

Achievement motivation develops early in life and is strongly influenced by parents. Parents of children with a high need for achievement typically encourage them to be independent and to attempt difficult tasks. They reward them for their persistence at difficult tasks with praise and other reinforcements and encourage them to attempt even more challenging tasks (Dweck, 1997; McClelland, 1985).

The Hierarchy of Needs: Ordering Needs from the Basement to the Attic of Human Experience

We have seen that both biological and psychological needs play important roles in human motivation. But how do these needs relate to each other? We now consider a model that bridges both sources of motivation—the **hierarchy of needs** developed by humanistic psychologist Abraham Maslow (1970).

As Figure 8.3 shows, Maslow's hierarchy has five levels: (1) *physiological needs,* such as hunger and thirst; (2) *safety needs,* such as the need for secure housing;

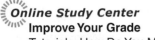
Online Study Center
Improve Your Grade
Tutorials: How Do You Motivate Others?

CONCEPT 8.9
According to Maslow, human needs are organized in a hierarchy that ranges from biological needs at the base to the need for self-actualization at the top.

extrinsic motivation Motivation reflecting a desire for external rewards, such as wealth or the respect of others.

intrinsic motivation Motivation reflecting a desire for internal gratification, such as the self-satisfaction derived from accomplishing a particular goal.

achievement motivation The motive or desire to achieve success.

avoidance motivation The motive or desire to avoid failure.

hierarchy of needs Maslow's concept that there is an order to human needs, which starts with basic biological needs and progresses to self-actualization.

Figure 8.3
Maslow's Need Hierarchy

CONCEPT CHART 8.1 Sources of Motivation

	Source	Description
Biological Sources	Instincts	Instincts are fixed, inborn response patterns that are specific to members of a particular species. However, they are not considered useful for explaining complex human behavior.
	Needs and drives	Unmet needs create internal drive states, which motivate behavior that leads to drive reduction.
	Stimulus motives and optimal level of arousal	Stimulus motives arise from biologically based needs to be curious and active and to explore the environment. Arousal theory holds that we are motivated to maintain a level of stimulation that is optimal for us. The Yerkes-Dodson law states that we perform best under conditions of moderate arousal.
Psychological Sources	Incentives	The value we place on goals or objects creates a lure, or "pull," to obtain them.
	Cognitive dissonance	Inconsistency in attitudes and behavior induces cognitive dissonance, an unpleasant emotional state that motivates efforts to reconcile the inconsistency.
	Psychosocial needs	These reflect psychosocial (interpersonal) needs, such as the needs for achievement and social relationships.

Note: According to Maslow, human needs are organized within a hierarchy that ranges from basic biological needs at the base to the need for self-actualization at the pinnacle.

Online Study Center
Improve Your Grade
Tutorials: Gender Expectations as
Motivators?

self-actualization The motive that drives individuals to express their unique capabilities and fulfill their potentials.

(3) *love and belongingness needs,* such as the need for intimate relationships; (4) *esteem needs,* such as the need for the respect of one's peers; and (5) *the need for self-actualization,* which is the need that motivates individuals to fulfill their unique potentials and become all they are capable of being. In Maslow's view, our needs are ordered in such a way that we are motivated to meet basic needs before moving upward in the hierarchy. In other words, once we fill our bellies, we strive to meet higher-order needs, such as our needs for security, love, achievement, and **self-actualization**. Maslow believed that achieving a full measure of psychological integration and well-being depends on meeting all five levels of need.

Since no two people are perfectly alike, the drive for self-actualization leads people in different directions. For some, self-actualization may involve creating works of art, but for others it may mean striving on the playing field, in the classroom, or in a corporate office. Not all of us climb to the top of the hierarchy; we don't all achieve self-actualization.

Maslow's hierarchical model of needs has intuitive appeal. We generally seek satisfaction of our basic needs for food, drink, and shelter before concerning ourselves with psychologically based needs like belongingness. But critics point out that our needs may not be ordered in as fixed a manner as Maslow's hierarchy suggests. An artist might go for days with little if any nourishment in order to complete a new work. People may forgo seeking satisfaction of their need for intimate relationships to focus their energies on career aspirations. Maslow might counter that eventually the emptiness of their emotional lives would motivate them to fill the gap.

Another problem with Maslow's model is that the same behavior may reflect multiple needs. For example, you might be attending college to satisfy physiological and safety needs (to prepare for a career so that you can earn money to live comfortably and securely), love and belongingness needs (to form friendships and social ties), esteem needs (to achieve status or approval), and self-actualization needs (to fulfill your intellectual or creative potential). Despite its limitations, Maslow's model leads us to recognize that human behavior is motivated by higher pursuits as well as satisfaction of basic needs.

Before going forward, you may wish to review the sources of motivation outlined in Concept Chart 8.1.

MODULE 8.1 REVIEW

Motivation: The "Whys" of Behavior

RECITE IT

What is motivation?

- Motivation consists of the factors or internal processes that activate, direct, and sustain behavior toward the satisfaction of a need or attainment of a goal.

What is instinct theory?

- Instinct theory proposes that behavior is motivated by genetically programmed, species-specific, fixed patterns of responses called instincts. While this model may have value in explaining some forms of animal behavior, human behavior is too complex to be explained by instincts.

What is drive theory?

- Drive theory asserts that animals are driven to satisfy unmet biological needs, such as hunger and thirst. The theory is limited, in part because it fails to account for motives involving the desire to increase states of arousal.

How does arousal theory account for differences in motivational states?

- According to arousal theory, the optimal level of arousal varies from person to person. To maintain arousal at an optimal level, some people seek exciting, even potentially dangerous, activities, while others seek more tranquil ones.

How does incentive theory differ from drive theory?

- Incentive theory focuses on the "pull," or lure, of goals or objects that we perceive as attractive, whereas drive theory focuses on the "push" of unmet biological needs.

What is cognitive dissonance theory?

- Cognitive dissonance theory holds that inconsistencies between our behavior and our attitudes, beliefs, or perceptions produce a state of psychological tension (dissonance) that motivates efforts to reconcile these inconsistencies.

What are psychosocial needs?

- Psychosocial needs are distinctly human needs that are based on psychological rather than biological factors. They include the need for social relationships and the need for achievement.

- People with a high need for achievement are hard-driving and ambitious. They set challenging but realistic goals for themselves. They accomplish more than people with similar abilities and opportunities but a lower need for achievement.

What is Maslow's hierarchy of needs?

- Maslow believed we are motivated to meet basic biological needs, such as hunger and thirst, before fulfilling our psychological needs. His hierarchy has five levels, ranging from physiological needs at the base to self-actualization at the top.

RECALL IT

1. Motivation refers to factors that activate, direct, and sustain _____-directed behavior.

2. Fixed, inborn patterns of response that are specific to members of a particular species are called
   a. reinforcers.
   b. instincts.
   c. drives.
   d. self-actualization.

3. Match these terms with the definitions below:
   i. primary drive; ii. secondary drive; iii. need; iv. homeostasis
   a. a drive acquired through experience
   b. the tendency to maintain a steady internal state
   c. a state of deprivation or deficiency
   d. an innate biological drive

4. _____ theory helps explain individual differences in the need for sensation, as well as the relationship between arousal and performance.

5. Discrepancies between one's attitudes and behavior can create _____ _____, an unpleasant emotional state that motivates efforts to reduce the discrepancies.

6. At the top of Maslow's hierarchy of needs is self-_____, the need that motivates people to fulfill their unique potentials and become all they are capable of being.

THINK ABOUT IT

- Do you believe that human behavior is motivated by instinct? Why or why not?

- Are you a self-actualizer? Upon what evidence do you base your judgment? What steps could you take to become a self-actualizer?

MODULE 8.2
Hunger and Eating

- How are hunger and appetite regulated?
- What causes obesity?
- What is anorexia nervosa?
- What is bulimia nervosa?
- What are the causes of eating disorders?

Obese Rat Destroying the ventromedial hypothalamus of laboratory rats induces insatiable eating, which leads to severe obesity.

 CONCEPT 8.10

The hypothalamus detects decreases in blood sugar levels and depletion of fat from fat cells, which leads to the feelings of hunger that motivate eating.

 CONCEPT 8.11

Neurotransmitters and hormones play important roles in regulating hunger.

fat cells Body cells that store fat.
lateral hypothalamus A part of the hypothalamus involved in initiating, or "turning on," eating.
ventromedial hypothalamus A part of the hypothalamus involved in regulating feelings of satiety.

Here is one of the most basic drives—and one of the most difficult to ignore. If your stomach is growling at this moment, you are unlikely to pay close attention to what you are reading. But is hunger a product of a grumbling stomach? Or does it arise in the brain?

Psychologists have long sought to understand the physiological basis of hunger and the role it plays in behavior. As a drive state, hunger motivates efforts to obtain and consume food, which satisfies an underlying biological need for nourishment. But why do so many of us become obese? And why do some of us develop eating disorders characterized by self-starvation or by repetitive cycles of binge eating and purging? In this module, we examine these problems and ways of helping people who struggle with them.

What Makes Us Hungry?

It may seem that pangs of hunger arise from the grumblings of an empty stomach, but it is the brain, not the stomach, that controls hunger. Here's how it works: When we haven't eaten for a while, our blood sugar levels drop. When this happens, fat is released from **fat cells**—body cells that store fat—to provide fuel that cells use until we are able to eat again. The hypothalamus, a small structure in the forebrain that helps regulate hunger and many other bodily processes (discussed in Chapter 2), detects these changes and triggers a cascading series of events, leading to the feelings of hunger that motivate us to eat (Campfield et al., 1995). Eating restores an internally balanced state, or homeostasis, by bringing blood sugar levels back into balance and replenishing fat cells.

Different parts of the hypothalamus play different roles in regulating hunger and eating (see Figure 8.4). Stimulating the **lateral hypothalamus** causes a laboratory animal to start eating even if it has just consumed a full meal. If the lateral hypothalamus is surgically destroyed, the animal will stop eating and eventually starve to death. Thus, we know that the lateral hypothalamus is involved in initiating, or "turning on," eating.

Another part of the hypothalamus, the **ventromedial hypothalamus**, acts as an off-switch that signals when it is time to stop eating. When this area is destroyed, animals will overeat and eventually become severely obese.

A mixture of chemicals in our bodies, including neurotransmitters and hormones, also play important roles in regulating hunger (Cummings, Braungart-Rieker, & Du Rocher-Schudlich, 2003; Underwood & Adler, 2004). One of these chemicals, the neurotransmitter neuropeptide Y, works on the hypothalamus to stimulate appetite and eating. When we haven't eaten in a while, the brain releases additional amounts of neuropeptide Y (Siegel, 2004).

Other brain chemicals work to curb appetite and eating (Batterham et al., 2003; Korner & Leibel, 2003). For example, the hormone *leptin* (from the Greek word *leptos,* meaning "thin") helps put the brakes on hunger by acting upon the hypothalamus when we've had enough to eat (Bouret, Draper, & Simerly, 2004; Grady, 2002). One way leptin works is by reducing the brain's production of neuropeptide Y.

Figure 8.4   Parts of the Hypothalamus Involved in Hunger and Eating
The parts of the hypothalamus involved in regulating hunger and eating include the lateral hypothalamus and the ventromedial hypothalamus. What roles do these structures play?

Location of the Hypothalamus

Cross-section Showing Parts of the Hypothalamus

Online Study Center
Improve Your Grade
Tutorials: Parts of the Brain Involved in Hunger and Eating

Other brain chemicals, including dopamine and endorphins, appear responsible for the feelings of pleasure associated with eating (Wang et al., 2001). Consuming food may increase the concentration of these chemicals in the brain, which in turn stimulates the brain's reward or pleasure circuits. Yet another brain chemical, the neurotransmitter serotonin, may be responsible for regulating feelings of satiety, the sensations associated with having had enough to eat.

The full story of the biological underpinnings of hunger and appetite is still being written. Further study of the brain chemicals involved in hunger and appetite and the brain structures they act upon may lead to better ways of helping people with weight problems. For example, this research may lead to the development of effective antiobesity drugs that work on the brain to control hunger directly (Kolata, 2003).

Obesity: A National Epidemic

Obesity, a state of excess body fat, is a national epidemic. We Americans are fatter than ever before. About two out of three U.S. adults are overweight, as compared to fewer than one in four in the early 1960s ("CDC Chief," 2003; Manson & Bassuk, 2003). Nearly one in three Americans is clinically obese (Vastag, 2004).

Moreover, the problem of overweight is rising rapidly among U.S. children and young adults, which has important implications for their health and longevity. The proportions of overweight young Americans doubled over the past twenty-five years (Dietz, 2004; Hedley et al., 2004). Even among children 2 to 5 years of age, one in ten is now overweight, a rise of nearly 50 percent since the mid-1990s ("Obesity Rising," 2004). Health experts believe that obesity may cut the life expectancy of today's children by as much as two to five years as compared to their parents' generation (Olshansky et al., 2005; Preston, 2003).

The problem doesn't stop at national borders. For the first time in history, as many people worldwide may be overweight (more than a billion) as are underfed (Bazell, 2002). Yet the American diet may be especially hazardous to the waistline. Evidence shows that rates of obesity are more than double among immigrants

obesity   A state of excess body fat.

Figure 8.5 Body Mass Index (BMI)
To determine your BMI, first find your height in inches and then move across the table to find your weight. Which weight group do you fall into?

Source: Report of the Dietary Guidelines Advisory Committee on the Dietary Guidelines for Americans, 2000, United States Department of Agriculture, Agriculture Research Service, Beltsville, MD.

Healthy Weight BMI from 18.5 up to 25 refers to a healthy weight.

Overweight BMI from 25 to 30 refers to overweight.

Obese BMI 30 or higher refers to obesity. Obese persons are also overweight.

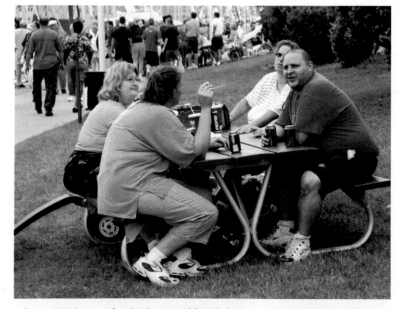

Obese Nation Obesity is an epidemic in our society and poses a significant health risk, cutting life expectancy by an average of six to seven years.

body mass index (BMI) A standard measure of obesity based on body weight adjusted for height.

who have resided in the United States for more than fifteen years, as compared to newly arrived immigrants (Goel et al., 2004).

Why should it matter if we weigh too much? It matters because obesity is a major health risk. Obese people stand an increased risk of developing many serious and even life-threatening diseases, including heart disease, hypertension, severe respiratory disorders, stroke, diabetes, and certain types of cancer (Carmichael, 2003b; Mokdad et al., 2003; Schwartz & Porte, 2005). According to the latest available estimates, obesity accounts for more than 100,000 extra deaths per year in the United States (Kolata, 2005). Not surprisingly, obesity cuts life expectancy markedly, by about six to seven years on the average (Fontaine et al., 2003).

Why is obesity on the rise? Health experts cite two main factors: too many calories consumed and too little exercise (Pollan, 2003). On the average, Americans consume 530 more calories today than they did thirty years ago (Gorman, 2003). Many of us have become "couch potatoes" and "cyberslugs" who sit around too much, exercise too little, and eat way too much high-fat, high-calorie foods (Levine et al., 2005; Mitka, 2003). We have also become increasingly dependent on the automobile rather than foot power to get from place to place, especially those of us living in the increasingly sprawling suburban areas (Ewing et al., 2003; McKee, 2003). Finally, portion sizes in restaurants are way up.

Are you obese? Scientists use a yardstick called the **body mass index (BMI)** (see Figure 8.5). The BMI takes height into account in determining whether body

All in the Family? We've learned from studies of twins and adoptees that genetics plays an important role in obesity.

weight falls within a healthy or obese range. According to the standards of the National Institutes of Health, people with a BMI of 30 or more are classified as obese. Those with a BMI of 25 to 29.9 are considered overweight.

CONCEPT 8.12
Obesity is a complex health problem in which behavioral patterns, genetics, and environmental and emotional factors may all play a role.

Causes of Obesity Obesity occurs when energy intake in the form of calories exceeds energy output (calories expended through bodily processes and physical activity) (Levine et al., 2005). Excess calories are converted into body fat, adding both weight and girth to the body (Pi-Sunyer, 2003).

Research points to the large role that genetics plays in obesity (Farooqi et al., 2003). Obese people may have a genetic predisposition to gain weight more readily than lean people. Body weight is influenced by *basal metabolic rate* (also called *basal metabolism*), the rate at which the body burns calories while at rest. The slower the body's metabolic rate, the more likely the person is to gain weight easily. Heredity may explain why some people have slower metabolic rates than others.

According to **set point theory**, the brain regulates body weight around a genetically predetermined level or "set point." This theory proposes that when weight gain or loss occurs, the brain adjusts the basal metabolic rate to keep body weight around its set point (Pinel, Assanand, & Lehman, 2000). When people lose weight, the brain slows the body's metabolic rate, and as this rate slows, the body conserves stores of fat. This perhaps explains why dieters often find it hard to continue losing weight or even to maintain their weight loss. The body's ability to adjust its metabolic rate downward when caloric intake falls off is a bane to many dieters today, but it may have helped ancestral humans survive times of famine (Grady, 2002).

The number of fat cells in one's body is also a factor in obesity. Obese people typically have more fat cells than do average adults, billions more (Underwood & Adler, 2004). We noted earlier that depletion of fat cells is a factor in triggering hunger. Since obese people typically have more fat cells than normal-weight individuals, they may feel hungry sooner after eating than do people with fewer fat cells.

The human body is designed as a kind of fat-storage machine that retains its fat cells to provide reserves of energy (stored fat) through lean times. Although genetics plays a role in determining the numbers of fat cells we have, early dietary patterns, such as excessive eating in childhood, may also play a role.

However, whatever roles behavioral patterns and genetics play in obesity, they don't tell the whole story. Environmental factors certainly contribute to the problem (Hill et al., 2003). We are constantly bombarded with food cues—TV commercials showing displays of tempting foods, aromas permeating the air as we walk by the bakery in the supermarket, and on and on. Consider that among

set point theory The belief that brain mechanisms regulate body weight around a genetically predetermined "set point."

children, Ronald McDonald is the second most widely recognized figure, after Santa Claus (Parloff, 2003). Ads for fast-food restaurants typically feature burgers, shakes, and other high-calorie, high-fat items; more nutritious items, such as salads, are notably missing. Environmental cues can trigger cravings for food even when our bodies are not registering hunger.

Emotional states, such as anger, fear, and depression, can prompt excessive eating. Many of us overeat in anger, or when we're feeling lonely, bored, or depressed. Have you ever tried to quell anxiety over an upcoming examination by finishing off a carton of ice cream? We may find we can soothe our negative feelings, at least temporarily, by treating ourselves to food.

What's the bottom line (or curve) on the causes of obesity? Behavioral patterns, genetics, environmental factors, and emotional cues all play a role. Yet even people whose genes predispose them to weight problems can achieve and maintain a healthy body weight by eating sensibly and exercising regularly.

Health experts recognize that "quickie" diets are not the answer to long-term weight management. More than 90 percent of people regain the weight they lose on a diet (Kolata, 2000a). Diet (antiobesity) drugs offer at best only temporary benefit and may carry serious side effects. Experts doubt that we will find a safe and effective antiobesity drug anytime soon (Stafford & Radley, 2003; Stipp, 2003). Moreover, despite images of smiling, thin people in television commercials, scientists find virtually no credible evidence that commercial weight loss programs help people lose weight and keep it off (Tsai & Wadden, 2005).

The best advice for managing your weight remains the traditional advice: eat less and exercise more (Underwood & Adler, 2004). Long-term success in fighting the "battle of the bulge" requires a lifelong commitment to regular exercise and to following a sensible low-calorie, low-fat diet plan (Irwin et al., 2002; Manson et al., 2004). Regular physical activity not only burns calories; it also increases the metabolic rate because it builds muscles, and muscle tissue burns more calories than fatty tissue. Thus, regular exercise combined with gradual weight reduction can help offset the reduction in the body's metabolic rate that may occur when we begin losing weight. Though we can expect to gain a modest amount of weight as we age, obesity is neither a natural nor an inevitable consequence of aging.

We also need to become more calorie conscious and check nutritional labels more carefully. For example, we need to recognize that "low fat" does not necessarily mean "low calorie." Even if obesity is not a current concern in your life, adopting healthy eating and exercise habits can help you avoid weight problems in the future. Table 8.1 offers suggestions for maintaining a healthy weight.

CONCEPT 8.13
Effective weight management requires a lifelong commitment to healthy eating and exercise habits that balance caloric intake with energy output.

TABLE 8.1 Suggestions for Maintaining a Healthy Weight

- *Limit fat intake.* The number of calories you need to maintain a healthy weight depends on many factors, including your body size, metabolic rate, and activity level. Health officials recommend eating more whole grain foods (as opposed to processed grain), as well as fruits and vegetables, and limiting high-fat foods (Zamiska, 2004).

- *Control portion size.* The major factor in controlling weight is striking a balance between calories consumed and calories expended. Controlling portion size can help you maintain this caloric balance.

- *Slow down the pace of eating.* It takes about fifteen minutes for your brain to register that your stomach feels full. Give it a chance to catch up with your stomach.

- *Beware of hidden calories.* Some fruit drinks and other beverages are loaded with calories, so be sure to check the product label. Try diluting fruit drinks with water, or substitute the actual fruit itself. Also be aware that many processed foods, especially baked goods, contain a lot of sugar and fat.

- *Make physical activity a part of your lifestyle.* Health experts recommend thirty minutes a day of moderate physical activity—activity equivalent in strenuousness to walking three to four miles per hour (Fogelholm et al., 2000). This doesn't mean you must work out in a gym or jog around a park every day. Taking a brisk walk from your car to your office or school, climbing stairs, or doing vigorous work around the house can help you meet your daily exercise needs. But additional aerobic exercise—like running, swimming, or using equipment specially designed for aerobic exercise—may help even more. Before starting any exercise program, discuss your health needs and concerns with a health care provider.

Eating Disorders

Karen, the 22-year-old daughter of a famed English professor, felt her weight was "just about right" (Boskind-White & White, 1983). But at seventy-eight pounds on a five-foot frame, she looked more like a prepubescent 11-year-old than a young adult. Her parents tried to persuade her to seek help with her eating behavior, but she continually denied she had a problem. Ultimately, however, after she lost yet another pound, her parents were able to convince her to enter a residential treatment program where her eating could be closely monitored. Another young woman, Nicole, wakes up each morning hoping this will be the day she begins living normally—that today she'll avoid gorging herself and inducing herself to vomit. But she doesn't feel confident that her eating behavior and purging are under her control. The disordered eating behaviors of Karen and Nicole are characteristic of the two major types of eating disorders: *anorexia nervosa* and *bulimia nervosa*, respectively.

Anorexia Nervosa   **Anorexia nervosa** (AN) is a form of self-starvation that results in an unhealthy and potentially dangerously low body weight. It is characterized by both an intense fear of becoming fat and a distorted body image. More than 95 percent of cases are found among women, typically adolescents or young adults. About 0.5 percent of women (one in two hundred) develop AN at some point in their lives (American Psychiatric Association, 2000; Lamberg, 2003). The young woman with anorexia is convinced she is too fat, even though others see her as little more than "skin and bones."

Anorexia is a dangerous medical condition and poses serious risks, including cardiovascular problems, such as irregular heartbeat and low blood pressure; gastrointestinal problems, such as chronic constipation and abdominal pain; loss of menstruation; and even death, caused by suicide or by medical complications associated with severe weight loss.

In a typical case, the young woman begins to notice some weight gain in adolescence. She becomes overly concerned about getting fat. She resorts to extreme dieting and perhaps excessive exercise to reduce her weight to a prepubescent level. She denies that she is too thin or losing too much weight, despite the concerns of others. In her mind's eye, she is heavier than she actually is.

Do You See What I See? Young women with anorexia have a distorted body image. They perceive themselves as fat even though others see them as just "skin and bones."

Bulimia Nervosa   **Bulimia nervosa** (BN) is a disorder in which episodes of binge eating are followed by purging. The purging is accomplished through self-induced vomiting or other means, such as excessive use of laxatives. Some bulimic individuals purge regularly after meals, not just after binges. Some engage in excessive, even compulsive, exercise regimens to try to control their weight. Like those with anorexia, people with bulimia are obsessed with their weight and are unhappy with their bodies (Heatherton et al., 1997). But unlike those with anorexia, they typically maintain a relatively normal weight. Estimates of the prevalence of BN among women vary from 1 percent to 3 percent (American Psychiatric Association, 2000); among men, the lifetime rates are estimated at less that 0.3 percent (three men in a thousand) (Lamberg, 2003).

Bulimia usually begins in late adolescence following a period of rigid dieting to lose weight. Binging may alternate with strict dieting. The binge itself usually occurs in secret. During the binge, the person consumes enormous amounts of foods that are sweet and high in fat. Bulimia can lead to many medical complications, including potentially dangerous potassium deficiencies and decay of tooth enamel from frequent vomiting, and severe constipation from overuse of laxatives.

Causes of Eating Disorders   Scholars believe that multiple causes are at work in explaining eating disorders (Polivy & Herman, 2002). One prominent factor is the preoccupation with thinness in our society and the consequent social pressure on

anorexia nervosa An eating disorder involving a pattern of self-starvation that results in an unhealthy and potentially dangerous low body weight.

bulimia nervosa An eating disorder involving recurrent episodes of binge eating followed by purging.

Barbie: An Impossible Standard If a slender woman like the one on the left had the same proportions as a Barbie doll, she would look like the woman on the right. To achieve this, she would need to grow nearly a foot in height, increase her bust size by four inches, and reduce her waist by five inches. What message do you think the Barbie doll sends to the average young woman?

On a Binge People with bulimia nervosa engage in cycles of binge eating and purging but typically maintain a relatively normal weight.

Online Study Center
Resources
Weblinks: Mirror, Mirror

young women to conform to an idealized thin body shape (McKnight Investigators, 2003; Stice, 2001). As many as 50 to 75 percent of adolescent girls are dissatisfied with their weight and their body shape (Rubinstein & Caballero, 2000). Even in children as young as 8, more girls are dissatisfied with their bodies than are boys (Ricciardelli & McCabe, 2001).

Young women are continually bombarded with images of slender, often emaciated-looking female models and actresses who personify the contemporary ideal of the ultrathin feminine form. It's no wonder that many women in our culture are preoccupied with what they eat and what they buy. A recent study found that about one in seven female college students said they would be embarrassed to buy a chocolate bar in a store (Rozin, Bauer, & Catanese, 2003). When college men in a recent study were asked at what weight they would consider a 5'8" woman to be overweight, the answers they gave averaged 159 pounds, a weight that actually falls in the normal weight category by BMI standards (Oakes, Slotterback, & Mecca, 2003). But women's answers averaged 175 pounds, a level that falls in the overweight BMI category.

The slenderizing of the ideal feminine form is even reflected in an analysis of the body mass index of winners of the Miss America pageant (see Figure 8.6). Regular exposure to these ultrathin images may lead young girls to develop a negative image of their own bodies and encourage them to adopt drastic measures in the pursuit of thinness, such as excessive dieting and purging. Body dissatisfaction (not liking your body) and peer pressure to become thin emerge as strong predictors of bulimic behavior in young women (Johnson & Wardle, 2005; Young, Clopton, & Bleckley, 2004).

Although social pressure to achieve and maintain a slender figure falls most heavily on women in our society, especially young women, the gender gap in obesity is actually quite small. Overall, 27 percent of women are obese, as compared with 24 percent of men. Moreover, gender differences in the percentage of overweight adults do not develop until late middle-age (see Figure 8.7).

Figure 8.6   The Thinning of the Ideal Feminine Figure
The slenderizing of the ideal feminine form in our society may account for the declining BMIs of winners of the Miss America pageant in recent years. The dots represent the BMIs of the winners, and the darkened line represents the trend over time.

Source: Data based on Rubinstein & Caballero, 2000.

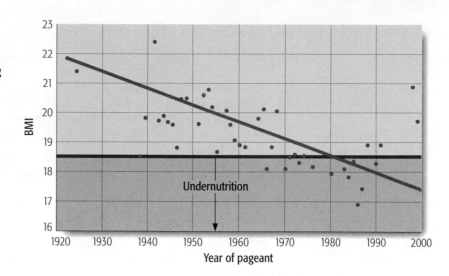

Figure 8.7   Gender Differences in Overweight Adults
The percentages of overweight men and women are virtually identical until around age 55. Yet our culture imposes greater pressures on younger women to lose weight.

Source: National Heart, Lung, and Blood Institute, National Institutes of Health, 1993.

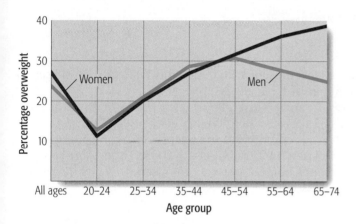

Online Study Center
Improve Your Grade
Tutorials: Planting the Seeds of Eating Disorders

Eating disorders are far less common, even rare, in non-Western countries, where a cultural emphasis on thinness is lacking. These disorders also occur less commonly among African American women and women from other minority groups for whom body image is not as closely tied to body weight as it is among non-Hispanic White women (Lamberg, 2003; Striegel-Moore et al., 2003). However, rates of eating disorders among women of color can be expected to rise as a function of increased identification with mainstream culture and greater exposure to a Eurocentric ideal of feminine beauty (Gilbert, 2003).

Although cultural pressures that emphasize thinness clearly play a major role in fostering eating disorders, the great majority of young women who are exposed to these pressures do not develop these disorders. Other factors also play a part. For example, many young women with eating disorders have issues relating to perfectionism and control. They place unreasonable pressures on themselves to achieve a "perfect body" and feel that the only part of their lives they can control is their dieting (Cockell et al., 2002; Shafran & Mansell, 2001). Eating disorders also frequently develop in young women with histories of childhood sexual or physical abuse or whose families are wracked by conflict (Jacobi et al., 2004; Kent & Waller, 2000). From a psychodynamic perspective, anorexia may represent an unconscious wish in developing young women to remain little girls.

Biological factors, such as genetics and disturbances in brain mechanisms that control hunger and satiety, are also believed to contribute to eating disorders (Lamberg, 2003; Strober et al., 2000). Irregularities in the activity of serotonin, a neurotransmitter involved in regulating feelings of satiety, may prompt bulimic binges. Antidepressant drugs that boost the availability of serotonin in the brain can help reduce binges (Walsh, Wheat, & Freund, 2000).

Eating disorders disproportionately affect young women, but clinicians have recently noted an increasing number of young men with these problems ("Officials See," 2004). One of the factors associated with disordered eating behaviors in young men is participation in sports that place a value on leanness (Cafria et al., 2005; Ricciardelli & McCabe, 2004). Media exposure to lean but muscular male models in advertisements can contribute to body dissatisfaction in young men, in much the same way that idealized female images may come to affect body image in young women (Agliata & Tantleff-Dunn, 2004; Jones, 2004). "Muscle

CONCEPT CHART 8.2   Hunger, Obesity, and Eating Disorders

Hunger and Appetite	Obesity	Eating Disorders
The hypothalamus's detection of decreases in blood sugar levels and depletion of fat in fat cells prompts hunger, which motivates eating. Hormones and neurotransmitters also play important roles in regulating hunger and appetite.	Causes of obesity are genetic, psychological, and environmental. They include metabolic rate, number of fat cells in the body, behavioral patterns (such as an unhealthy diet and lack of exercise), and emotional and environmental cues that prompt eating.	Cultural pressure to achieve unrealistic standards of thinness is a major factor in fostering anorexia (self-starvation) and bulimia (binge eating followed by purging). Psychological causes of eating disorders may include issues of control and perfectionism, sexual or physical abuse during childhood, family conflicts, and, for anorexia, underlying fears of adulthood and sexual maturity. Biological factors that may be implicated in eating disorders include abnormalities in brain mechanisms controlling feelings of hunger and satiation, genetics, and irregularities in serotonin activity.

belittlement" (believing one is less muscular than one truly is) is strongly linked to body dissatisfaction in men (Olivardia et al., 2004).

Although promising results in treating eating disorders with psychological and drug therapies have been reported (e.g., Walsh et al., 2004; Wilson et al., 2002), recovery is typically a long-term process and relapses and continuing symptoms are common (Fairburn et al., 2003; Halmi et al., 2003; Thompson-Brenner, Glass, & Westen, 2003). Concept Chart 8.2 presents an overview of our discussion of hunger, obesity, and eating disorders.

MODULE 8.2 REVIEW

Hunger and Eating

RECITE IT

How are hunger and appetite regulated?

- Homeostatic processes in the brain regulate hunger and appetite. The hypothalamus plays a pivotal role. It senses changes in blood sugar levels and depletion of fat from fat cells, which leads to the feelings of hunger that motivate eating. Neurotransmitters and hormones also play important roles in regulating hunger and appetite.

What causes obesity?

- Obesity is a complex problem that has multiple causes, including behavioral patterns, genetics, metabolic factors, and environmental and emotional factors.

What is anorexia nervosa?

- Anorexia nervosa is an eating disorder in which people starve themselves because of exaggerated concerns about weight gain.

What is bulimia nervosa?

- Bulimia nervosa is an eating disorder characterized by episodes of binge eating followed by purging. Purging is accomplished through self-induced vomiting or other means, such as excessive use of laxatives.

What are the causes of eating disorders?

- Many factors are implicated in eating disorders. They include cultural pressure on young women to achieve unrealistic standards of thinness, issues of control and perfectionism, childhood abuse, family conflicts, and possible disturbances in brain mechanisms that control hunger and satiety.

RECALL IT

1. Which of the following does *not* describe what happens physiologically after a person has not eaten for a while?
   a. Blood sugar level drops.
   b. Fat is released from fat cells.
   c. The ventromedial hypothalamus signals that it is time to start eating.
   d. The brain releases more neuropeptide Y.

2. If the lateral hypothalamus in a laboratory animal is stimulated, it
   a. stops eating.
   b. starves to death.
   c. begins to eat even if it has just consumed a full meal.
   d. becomes obese.

3. Match the terms with the definitions below:
   i. leptin; ii. BMI; iii. basal metabolic rate; iv. set point
   a. the rate at which the body at rest burns calories
   b. a hormone that reduces production of neuropeptide Y
   c. a genetically predetermined range for weight
   d. a measure of body weight used to determine obesity

4. Which of the following factors is *not* linked to the development of eating disorders?
   a. relatively high levels of serotonin in the brain
   b. unrealistic cultural standards of thinness
   c. issues of control and perfectionism
   d. childhood abuse

THINK ABOUT IT

• What would you say to someone who claims that people become obese because they lack willpower?

• How much should you weigh? Has your answer to this question changed as a result of our discussion of obesity? Are you aware of your daily calorie intake? If not, should you be? Do you have any unhealthy eating habits you would like to change? If so, how might you change them?

MODULE 8.3

Emotions

- What are the three components of emotions?
- Are facial expressions of emotion universal?
- What role do brain structures play in emotions?
- What are the major theories of emotions?
- What factors are associated with personal happiness?
- What are the three components of love in Sternberg's model of love?
- What is the polygraph?

From the joy we feel at graduating from college or landing a desirable job, to the sadness we feel at the loss of a loved one, to the ups and downs we experience in everyday life, our lives are filled with emotions. **Emotions** infuse our lives with color. We commonly say we are "red" with anger, "green" with envy, and "blue" with sadness.

Imagine how colorless life would be without emotions. But what are emotions? How do we recognize emotions in others? Are emotional expressions recognized universally or only by members of the same culture? What is the physiological basis of emotions?

We then explore the physiological and cognitive bases of emotions and take a closer look at two primary emotional states, happiness and love.

emotions Feeling states that psychologists view as having physiological, cognitive, and behavioral components.

CONCEPT 8.15
To psychologists, emotions are more than just feelings; they have physiological, cognitive, and behavioral components.

What Are Emotions?

Most people think of emotions simply as feelings, such as feelings of joy or anger. But psychologists view emotions as more complex feeling states that have three basic components: *bodily arousal* (nervous system activation), *cognition* (subjective, or conscious, experience of the feeling, as well as the thoughts or judgments we have about the people or situations that evoke the feeling), and *expressed behavior* (outward expression of the emotion, such as approaching a love object or avoiding a feared one).

When you experience fear, your body is in a heightened state of arousal (e.g., your heart races, your palms sweat). The cognitive component of fear includes the subjective experience of feeling afraid, as well as the judgment that the situation is threatening. (If someone tosses a rubber snake at your feet, it may startle you, but it will not evoke fear when you appraise it as a fake.) The cognitive component of anger includes the judgment (cognitive appraisal) that events or the actions of others are unjust.

The behavioral expression of emotions generally takes two forms. We tend to approach objects or situations associated with pleasant emotions, such as joy or love, and to avoid those associated with fear, loathing, or disgust. When afraid, we approach the feared object in the hope of fighting it off, or we try to flee from it. Similarly, when angry, we tend to attack (approach) the object of our anger or to withdraw from it (i.e., keep it at a distance). The behavioral component of emotions also encompasses ways in which we express emotions through facial features and other outward behaviors, such as gestures, tone of voice, and bodily posture.

Emotional Expression: Read Any Good Faces Lately?

CONCEPT 8.16
Though we may say that people wear their hearts on their sleeves, it is more accurate to say that they wear their emotions on their faces.

Charles Darwin (1872) believed that emotions evolved because they have an adaptive purpose in helping species survive and flourish. Fear mobilizes animals to take defensive action in the face of a threatening predator; anger can be adaptive in provoking aggression that helps secure territory, resources, or mating partners. Darwin also recognized that the expression of emotions has communication value. For example, an animal displaying fear through its bodily posture or facial expression may signal others of its kind that danger lurks nearby. Darwin was the first to link specific facial expressions to particular emotions.

We can see the evolutionary roots of emotional expression in the similarity of the facial expressions of humans and nonhuman primates, such as gorillas. You don't need instructions to interpret the emotion expressed by the bared teeth of the ape and human shown in Figure 8.8. This cross-species similarity in facial expression supports Darwin's view that human modes of emotional expression evolved from nonhuman primate ancestors (Chevalier-Skolnikoff, 1973).

Figure 8.8 Cross-Species Similarity in Facial Expression
The bared teeth of both ape and human signal readiness to defend or to attack.

Facial Expressions of Emotion: Are They Universal? Cross-cultural studies show that people from many different cultures can accurately identify six basic emotions from facial expressions: anger, fear, disgust, sadness, happiness, and surprise (Edwards, Jackson, & Pattison, 2002; Ekman, 2003; Matsumoto, 2004). In one intriguing study, researchers had American students watch Japanese soap operas. Although the students didn't speak a word of Japanese, they recognized the emotions displayed by the characters simply by observing the facial expressions of the actors (Krauss, Curran, & Ferleger, 1983). The evidence thus supports the view that six basic emotional expressions are universally recognized (see Try This Out).

CONCEPT 8.17
Evidence supports the view that facial expressions of at least six basic emotions are recognized universally.

Does the ability to recognize six emotional expressions mean that there are only six basic emotions? Psychologists continue to debate how many different emotions there may be (Hess, 2003). Psychologist Robert Plutchik (1980) recognizes

TRY THIS OUT

Reading Emotions in Facial Expressions

The same emotional expressions found in the streets of Chicago are found in the distant corners of the world. The photographs accompanying this exercise show a man from a remote area of New Guinea. You'll probably have little difficulty recognizing the emotions he is portraying. Before reading further, match the following emotions to the numbers on the photos: (a) disgust, (b) sadness, (c) happiness, and (d) anger.

The man was asked to make faces as he was told stories involving the following: "Your friend has come and you are happy"; "Your child has died"; "You are angry and about to fight"; and "You see a dead pig that has been lying there a long time." So the correct answers are 1 (c), 2 (b), 3 (d), and 4 (a).

1. _____   2. _____   3. _____   4. _____

Source: Ekman, 1980.

the six basic emotions but adds two more: anticipation and acceptance. Where does that leave other emotions, such as disappointment, awe, and love? Plutchik believes these are more complex emotions that are formed by the combination of the basic emotions, just as the melding of primary colors forms many different hues. He uses a color wheel of emotions to represent how the basic, or "primary," emotions merge to form the more complex emotions surrounding them. As you can see in the depiction of Plutchik's wheel in Figure 8.9, a combination of the primary emotions anger and disgust produces the secondary emotion contempt. The combination of the primary emotions acceptance and joy produces the secondary emotion love.

Cultural and Gender Differences in Emotions   Though people the world over may recognize the same basic facial expressions of emotions, subtle differences exist across cultures in the appearance of these expressions (Marsh, Elfenbein, & Ambady, 2003). Such cultural differences in facial expressions may be likened to nonverbal accents.

Researchers have also uncovered cultural differences in how accurately emotions are recognized and how they are experienced and displayed (Mesquita & Walker, 2003; Tsai et al., 2002). For example, people are generally more accurate when recognizing facial expressions of emotions in people of their own national, ethnic, and regional groups (Elfenbein & Ambady, 2002a, 2002b). In addition, certain emotions are more common in some cultures than in others, or perhaps even unique to a particular culture. For example, Japanese people commonly report such emotions as *fureai* (feeling closely linked to others) and *oime* (an unpleasant feeling of indebtedness to others, similar to our feeling of being "beholden") (Ellsworth, 1994; Markus & Kitayama, 1991). These emotions are not unknown in

Figure 8.9 Plutchik's Color Wheel of Emotions
Robert Plutchik proposes that people experience eight primary emotions, represented by the segments within the circle, and that combinations of these primary emotions produce the more complex secondary emotions represented outside the circle.

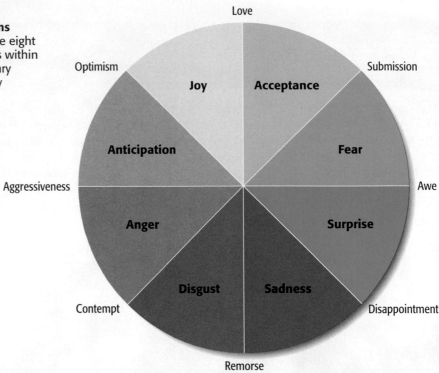

the United States, but they are not as central to our lives as they are in Japan, where there is a greater cultural emphasis on communal values and mutual obligations.

Nonetheless, there is a degree of universality in how certain emotions are experienced. For instance, researchers have reported considerable agreement in how individuals in thirty different countries described the experience of fear, anger, joy, and sadness (Wallbott & Scherer, 1989). Sadness, for example, was associated with crying; fear was associated with feeling cold and having a faster heartbeat.

Cultures also differ in how, or even whether, emotions are expressed. We use the term **display rules** to describe the cultural customs and norms that regulate the display of particular emotions (Matsumoto et al., 2005). For example, Asian cultures tend to frown on public displays of emotion (Tsai et al., 2002). In these cultures, people are generally expected to suppress their feelings in public; a failure to keep their feelings to themselves reflects poorly on their upbringing (Huang, 1994). Display rules are learned as part of the socialization process and become so ingrained that they occur automatically among members of the same culture.

Cultural differences in emotional expression extend to gestures and bodily movements. In some cultures, it is customary to embellish speech, especially emotional speech, with gestures of the hands or arms. In other cultures, such gestures are considered rude. In Latin American cultures, there is typically more hugging and kissing among friends upon greeting or leaving each other than there is in the United States or Canada.

Cultures also have rules for governing the appropriate display of emotions by men and women. In many cultures, women are given greater latitude than men in expressing certain emotions, such as joy, love, fear, and sadness. This may explain why women, on average, are more likely to express their emotions in both words and facial expressions and to recognize and recall feelings in others (DePaulo & Friedman, 1998: Ripley, 2005). A woman's brain may also be wired differently than a man's, allowing her to better perceive and recall emotional cues (Canli et al., 2002).

One form of emotional expression in which Western cultures give men more latitude is anger. Men are taught that anger is "masculine" and that acting out

CONCEPT 8.18
Each culture has display rules that determine how emotions are expressed and how much emotion it is appropriate to express.

CONCEPT 8.19
Evidence supports the view that practicing or mimicking the facial movements associated with particular emotions can produce corresponding emotional states.

display rules Cultural customs and norms that govern the display of emotional expressions.

TRY THIS OUT

The Facial-Feedback Effect

Hold a pencil between your teeth for about a minute. Notice any change in your mood? Now hold the pencil between your lips. Notice any change in your mood now?

Holding a pencil between your teeth engages facial muscles used for smiling, whereas holding a pencil between your lips activates muscles used in frowning. According to the facial-feedback hypothesis, you should find your mood cheerier after holding the pencil between your teeth than after holding it between your lips. In one study, investigators found that subjects who held a pencil between their teeth rated cartoons as funnier than those who were instructed to hold a pencil between their lips (Strack, Martin, & Stepper, 1988).

REALITY CHECK

THE CLAIM Women are more emotional than men.

THE EVIDENCE A common gender stereotype is that women are more emotional than men. Evidence from a recent cross-cultural study does show that women tend to report certain emotional states, such as affection, joy, fear, and sadness, more often than men (Brebner, 2003). But support for the stereotype must be tempered by the fact that these gender differences range from small to extremely small. Moreover, men typically express and experience another emotion—anger—more often than women (Fischer et al., 2004).

THE TAKE-AWAY MESSAGE Women may experience certain emotions more than men, but not all emotions. Moreover, gender differences tend to be small and are likely to reflect cultural expectations about the gender appropriateness of displaying certain emotions.

facial-feedback hypothesis The belief that mimicking facial movements associated with a particular emotion will produce the corresponding emotional state.
Duchenne smile A genuine smile that involves contraction of a particular set of facial muscles.

anger physically, even through physical aggression, is "manly." But, says anger researcher Sandra Thomas of the University of Tennessee, Knoxville, "for girls, acting out in that way is not encouraged. . . . Women usually get the message that anger is unpleasant and unfeminine" (cited in Dittmann, 2003b). Yet women may learn to express anger through more indirect channels, such as by gossiping or "writing off" people who have offended them by never intending to speak to them again.

In Western cultures men aren't supposed to cry or show their emotions, or even to smile very much. Not surprisingly, evidence shows that women in these cultures tend to smile more than men (LaFrance, Hecht, Paluck, & 2003). However, the ideal of the stoic unemotional male epitomized by Hollywood action heroes may be giving way to a new ideal: the "sensitive" male character.

The Facial-Feedback Hypothesis: Putting on a Happy Face Can practicing smiling lift your mood? According to the **facial-feedback hypothesis**, mimicking the facial movements associated with an emotion will induce the corresponding emotional state (Izard, 1990a). Consistent with this hypothesis, researchers find that practicing smiling can induce more positive feelings (Soussignan, 2002). Doing this several times a day may lift your spirits, at least temporarily, perhaps because it prompts you to recall pleasant experiences (see the two Try This Out features on the facial-feedback effect and on making positive and negative faces).

However, a put-on smile is not the equivalent of real one. With insincere smiles, "something just doesn't look right" (Harrigan & Taing, 1997). There's a good reason for this: the two types of smiles flex different facial muscles (Lemonick, 2005b). A genuine smile is called a **Duchenne smile**, named after Guillaume Duchenne de Boulogne (1806–1875), the French physician who discovered the facial muscles used to produce a genuine smile. You can see the difference between a genuine smile and a phony one in the photographs of researcher Paul Ekman in Figure 8.10.

Emotions conveyed by facial expressions may be catching (Goleman, 1991a). Evidence suggests that people tend to experience the emotions they observe in others. Have you ever broken into a laugh when you've seen someone else laughing? Does a person's cheery disposition lift your mood? Does a dour face in someone else bring you down? Some people are better than others at transmitting their moods, and some are more susceptible to other people's moods. This transfer of emotions may result from the unconscious mimicry of facial expressions,

TRY THIS OUT

Putting on a Sad Face

You can put the facial-feedback hypothesis to work by imitating facial features associated with particular emotions. This exercise may be especially helpful if you are involved in acting and need to project a particular emotion, such as sadness, to an audience (Ekman, 2003). Try imitating the facial features of sadness identified below. Then examine how you felt. It may help to use a mirror to check that you are practicing the facial movements correctly.

- Drop your mouth open.
- Pull the corners of your lips down.
- While holding your lip corners down, try to raise your cheeks, as if you are squinting. This pulls against the lip corners.
- Maintain this tension between the raised cheeks and the lip corners pulling down.
- Let your eyes look downward and your upper eyelids droop.

Figure 8.10   In Which Photo Is Paul Really Smiling?
As you probably guessed, the photo on the right shows a genuine smile; the smile in the photo on the left is simulated. One way to tell the difference is to look for crow's feet around the eyes, a characteristic associated with genuine smiles.

gestures, and movements. Someone smiles—you smile back; someone laughs—you begin mimicking the facial and vocal expressions, which brings you to laughter as well.

Listening to music can also affect our emotions, quite apart from the lyrics that accompany music (Collier, 2002). Certain music may lead you to feel cheerful whereas other music may leave you feeling sad or sorrowful. In movies, music is often used to elicit unpleasant emotions, such as fear (Stratton & Zalanowski, 1997).

Brain Structures in Emotions: Where Do Emotions Reside?

There is a certain truth to the belief that we feel with our hearts. Strong emotions, such as fear and anger, are accompanied by activation of the sympathetic branch of the autonomic nervous system (ANS). As we noted in Chapter 2, activation of the sympathetic nervous system prompts the adrenal glands to release epinephrine and norepinephrine—the stress hormones that speed up bodily processes, such as heart rate and breathing rate. By increasing the flow of oxygen and nutrient-rich blood to our muscles and internal organs, these bodily events enable us to re-

Figure 8.11   Activation of the Amygdala in Response to a Fearful Face
Here we see functional MRI images of the amygdala in response to viewing a fearful face. Areas of the amygdala that show greater levels of activation are displayed with more intense yellow and reddish colors. Slice 24 shows the forward part of the amygdala, whereas Slice 25 shows the back part. The image is viewed as though the person were looking out from the page.
Source: NIMH, 2001.

spond more quickly to the situation at hand and, if necessary, either to fight or flee from a threat. (This bodily response to a threat—the *fight-or-flight* mechanism—is discussed further in Chapter 15.) An opposing series of bodily changes, orchestrated by the parasympathetic branch of the ANS, returns the body to a calm, relaxed state when the threat has passed.

The *limbic system* (discussed in Chapter 2), which includes the amygdala and the hippocampus, plays an important role in emotional processing (Hariri et al., 2002; Skipper, 2002). The almond-shaped amygdala works like an "emotional computer" by sizing up and responding to objects or stimuli we encounter that may pose a threat (LeDoux, 2000; Öhman & Mineka, 2001). We know from laboratory studies that the amygdala becomes active in response to threatening or fearful stimuli (Carlsson et al., 2004; Whalen et al., 2004). We also know that when we electrically stimulate the amygdala in people, the most common emotional reaction is one of fear or worry (Davis & Lang, 2003). In Figure 8.11 we see activation of the amygdala to viewing a fearful face (NIMH, 2001).

From an evolutionary perspective, it makes sense that we would be equipped with an internal alarm system that signals the presence of threat or danger. The amygdala is the place where threatening stimuli that induce fear do their triggering. But the amygdala also appears to play a role in processing other emotional cues, including images of grief and despair, as well as positive emotions (Mather et al., 2004; Pearson, 2004; Wang et al., 2005). In a recent brain-imaging study, bursts of activity in the amygdala occurred when men and women were exposed to erotic photographs (Hamann et al., 2003; O'Connor, 2004a).

What of the role of the cerebral cortex itself, the "thinking center" of the brain? The cortex plays several key roles in the processing of emotions. For one thing, it evaluates the meaning of emotionally arousing stimuli and then plans and directs how to respond to them. It determines whether we should approach stimuli (as in the case of a love interest or a pleasurable event) or avoid them (as in the case of a threat). It also processes the felt experience of emotions and controls the facial expression of emotion. As we consider later in this module, evidence also points to differences in how the right and left cerebral hemispheres process emotions.

CONCEPT 8.20
Although the cerebral cortex and the brain structures that make up the limbic system play key roles in regulating emotional responses, there is no one seat of emotions in the brain.

Where then do emotions reside in the brain? Actually, no one center in the brain is solely responsible for emotions. Structures in the limbic system play important roles, as do higher brain regions in the cerebral cortex to which they connect (Davidson, Putnam, & Larson, 2000; Fischer et al., 2002).

Theories of Emotion: Which Comes First—the Thought or the Feeling?

One night while I was driving home, my car hit an icy patch in the road and went out of control. The car spun completely around twice and wound up facing oncoming traffic. At that instant, I felt the way a deer must feel when it is caught in the headlights of a car bearing down on it—terrified and helpless. Fortunately, the cars coming toward me stopped in time, and I was able to regain control of my car. I arrived home safely but still shaking in fear. At the time, I didn't stop to consider the question pondered by many psychologists: Did my awareness of my fear precede or follow my bodily response (shaking, sweating, heart pounding)? The *commonsense* view of emotion is that we first perceive a stimulus (the car spinning out of control), then feel the emotion (fear), then become physiologically aroused (heart pounding), and then take action (grip the steering wheel). Yet one of the more enduring debates in psychology concerns which comes first—the subjective experience of the emotion or the physiological or behavioral response.

James-Lange Theory William James (1890/1970) argued that bodily reactions or sensations precede emotions. Because Carl Georg Lange, a Danish physiologist, postulated similar ideas independently, this view is called the **James-Lange theory**. James used the now-classic example of confronting a bear in the woods. James asked the question, "Do we run from the bear because we are afraid, or do we become afraid because we run?" He answered this question by proposing that the response of running comes first. We see the bear. We run. Then we become afraid. We become afraid because we sense the particular pattern of bodily arousal associated with running, such as a pounding heart, rapid breathing, and muscular contractions. Thus, emotions *follow* bodily reactions. In this view, we experience fear because we tremble; we experience the emotion of sadness because we cry. If this theory is correct, then my body would have reacted first when my car spun out of control. Only when I sensed my body's reaction would I have become consciously aware of fear.

James argued that distinct bodily changes are associated with each emotion. This is why fear feels different from other emotions, such as anger or love.

Cannon-Bard Theory In the 1920s, physiologist Walter Cannon (1927) proposed a second major theory of emotions. He based his theory on research conducted by his laboratory assistant, Philip Bard. This theory, called the **Cannon-Bard theory**, challenged the James-Lange theory. It holds that the same bodily changes that result from the activation of the sympathetic nervous system accompany different emotions. Sympathetic activation makes our hearts race, our breathing quicken, and our muscles contract whether we experience anger, fear, or sexual arousal. How could these common responses in the body evoke different emotions, as the James-Lange theory suggests? The Cannon-Bard theory proposes that the subjective experience of an emotion and the bodily reactions associated with it occur virtually simultaneously. In other words, our emotions accompany our bodily responses but are not caused by them. In simplest terms, the Cannon-Bard theory postulates that we see the bear, we experience fear and a pounding heart, and then we run.

Two-Factor Model Let us turn to the **two-factor model**, which holds that emotions depend on two factors: (1) a state of general arousal and (2) a cognitive interpretation, or *labeling* (Schachter & Singer, 1962; Schachter, 1971). According to this model, when we experience states of bodily arousal, we look for cues in the environment to explain why we feel aroused or excited. Your heart may race when you see a monster in the latest sci-fi thriller jump onto the movie screen; it may also race when your car spins out of control. Your arousal in the safe confines of the movie theater is likely to be labeled and experienced as "pleasurable excitement." But the same pattern of arousal experienced in the spinning car will probably be labeled and experienced as "sheer terror."

The two-factor model continues to generate interest, but it fails to account for the distinctive physiological features associated with different emotions. Anger may feel different from fear not merely because of how we label our arousal, but also because it is associated with different bodily responses.

CONCEPT 8.21
The James-Lange theory proposes that emotions follow bodily reactions to triggering stimuli.

CONCEPT 8.22
The Cannon-Bard theory proposes that the subjective experience of an emotion and the bodily reactions associated with it occur virtually simultaneously.

CONCEPT 8.23
The two-factor model proposes that the combination of physiological arousal and cognitive appraisal (labeling) of the source of the arousal produces the specific emotional state.

James-Lange theory The belief that emotions occur after people become aware of their physiological responses to the triggering stimuli.

Cannon-Bard theory The belief that emotional and physiological reactions to triggering stimuli occur almost simultaneously.

two-factor model The theory that emotions involve two factors: a state of general arousal and a cognitive interpretation (or labeling) of the causes of the arousal.

Figure 8.12   LeDoux's Dual-Pathway Model of Fear
Joseph LeDoux posits that fear messages are processed at
two levels. A "low road" bypasses the higher cognitive centers
of the brain so that a faster response to a potentially threatening stimulus can occur. A "high road" leads to the cerebral
cortex, where the message is interpreted more carefully.

Source: Adapted from LeDoux, 1996.

CONCEPT 8.24
The dual-pathway model suggests two
pathways for processing fear stimuli in
the brain: a "high road" leading to the
cerebral cortex and a "low road"
leading to the amygdala.

dual-pathway model of fear   LeDoux's
theory that the brain uses two pathways
(a "high road" and a "low road") to process
fear messages.

Experimental evidence also casts doubt on whether we must label the state of
arousal in order to experience an emotion. Psychologist Robert Zajonc (1980,
1984) exposed subjects to brief presentations of Japanese ideographs (written symbols). Later, he found that subjects preferred particular characters they had seen,
even if they had no recall of ever having seen these stimuli. Zajonc believes that
some emotional responses, such as liking and disliking, may not involve any cognitive appraisal—that they may occur through mere exposure to a stimulus.

Dual-Pathway Model of Fear   According to the **dual-pathway model of fear** formulated by psychologist Joseph LeDoux (1994, 2000), the brain uses two pathways to process fear messages (see Figure 8.12). Stimulus information from the
environment ("seeing a car barreling down on you") is first processed by the thalamus. From there the information branches off, with one pathway (the "high

road") leading to the cerebral cortex, where it can be processed more carefully. Another pathway (the "low road") leads directly to the amygdala, where the information can be acted upon more quickly than if it had first passed through the cortex. The "low road" thus allows a faster response to danger cues.

Suppose you are walking in the woods and see a curved object in the bush. This visual image is first processed by the thalamus, which makes a rough appraisal of the object as potentially dangerous (possibly a snake). The thalamus transmits this information directly to the amygdala via the "low road," which prompts an immediate bodily response. Heart rate and blood pressure jump, and muscles throughout the body contract as the body prepares to respond quickly to a possible threat. The cortex, slower to respond, processes the information further ("No, that's not a snake. It's just a stick."). From the standpoint of survival, it is better to act quickly on the assumption that the suspicious object is a snake and to ask questions later. Responding without thinking can be a lifesaver. As LeDoux puts it, "The time saved by the amygdala in acting on the thalamic information, rather than waiting for the cortical input, may be the difference between life and death. It is better to have treated a stick as a snake than not to have responded to a possible snake" (1994, p. 270). Depending on whether the cortex interprets the object as a "snake" or a "stick" determines whether a fear response continues or is quickly quelled. It is in the cortex that the subjective experience of fear arises.

What Does This All Mean?　Where do these various theories of emotions, as represented in Figure 8.13, leave us? The James-Lange theory implies that distinctive bodily responses are associated with each emotion, whereas the Cannon-Bard theory postulates that a similar pattern of bodily responses accompanies different emotions. Both views may be at least partially correct. There certainly are common physiological responses associated with such emotions as fear, anger, and love, as the Cannon-Bard theory proposes. We feel our hearts beating faster when

Online Study Center
Improve Your Grade
Tutorials: LeDoux's Dual Pathway Model of Fear

Figure 8.13　Theoretical Models of Fear

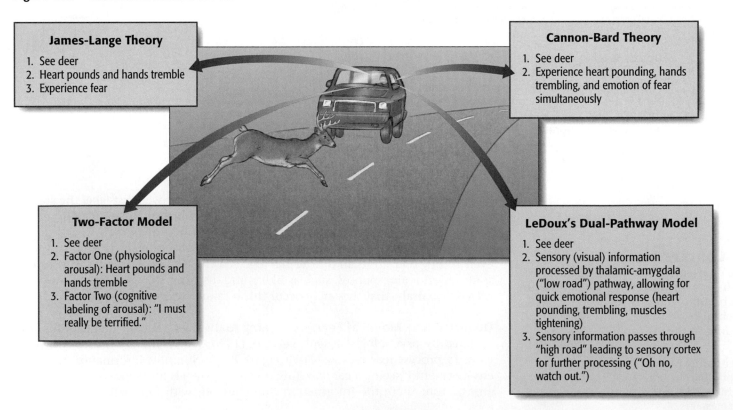

James-Lange Theory
1. See deer
2. Heart pounds and hands tremble
3. Experience fear

Cannon-Bard Theory
1. See deer
2. Experience heart pounding, hands trembling, and emotion of fear simultaneously

Two-Factor Model
1. See deer
2. Factor One (physiological arousal): Heart pounds and hands tremble
3. Factor Two (cognitive labeling of arousal): "I must really be terrified."

LeDoux's Dual-Pathway Model
1. See deer
2. Sensory (visual) information processed by thalamic-amygdala ("low road") pathway, allowing for quick emotional response (heart pounding, trembling, muscles tightening)
3. Sensory information passes through "high road" leading to sensory cortex for further processing ("Oh no, watch out.")

we are in the presence of a new love and when we are faced with an intruder in the night. Yet, as the James-Lange theory proposes, there are also distinctive bodily reactions associated with different emotions. Less blood flows to our extremities during states of fear than of anger, which is why we may experience a sensation of "cold feet" when we are afraid but not when we are angry (Levenson, 1994). Anger is accompanied by a dramatic rise in skin temperature, which may explain why people who are angry are often described as "hot under the collar."

Different emotions are also connected with different facial expressions. Blushing, for instance, is a primary characteristic of embarrassment. James considered facial expressions to be among the bodily responses that distinguish one emotion from another. Evidence favoring the facial-feedback hypothesis lends at least partial support to the James-Lange theory, because it shows that our response to muscular cues associated with certain emotions can influence our feeling states (Izard, 1990b).

Emotions may precede cognitions under some conditions, as suggested by Zajonc's studies and by the dual-pathway model proposed by LeDoux. That emotions may occur before cognitions does not dismiss the important role that cognitions play in emotions. Whether you are angered when an instructor springs an unexpected assignment on you or frightened when a doctor points to a spot on your X-ray depends on the appraisal of the situation made in the cerebral cortex, not on automatic processing of stimuli by lower brain structures.

How we appraise events also depends on what the events mean to us personally. The same event, such as a pregnancy or a change of jobs, can lead to feelings of joy, fear, or even anger depending on the meaning the event has for the individual and its perceived importance.

The final chapter in the debate about how emotions are processed in the brain is still to be written. Yet the belief that distinctive bodily changes are associated with different emotions has had at least one practical implication. It is the basis of a method of lie detection, which is discussed later in this module.

Happiness: What Makes You Happy?

What would make you truly happy? Great wealth? A good marriage? Love and companionship? Owning the house of your dreams? Status or recognition in your chosen field?

Happiness is a primary human emotion, but it has long been neglected by psychologists, who have focused mostly on understanding negative emotions, such as fear, anger, and sadness. However, with the emergence of positive psychology in the past ten years, the field has begun to balance out as more investigators have begun to focus on the positive attributes of the human condition, including happiness. Investigators are examining human happiness from different vantage points. Some focus on factors associated with happiness, others on measuring happiness, and still others on comparing happiness levels of people in different countries. Let's have a look at what they are finding and what it may mean in terms of achieving happiness in your own life.

What makes people happy? It's not money, researchers tell us. Such things as wealth, marriage, and even health make but a small contribution to explaining differences in happiness among people (Diener, Oishi, & Lucas, 2003). Yes, coping with severe poverty can dampen happiness, but investigators find very little increase in personal happiness or well-being as income rises above a subsistence level of about ten or twelve thousand dollars a year (Diener, 2005; Diener & Seligman, 2004; Helliwell, 2003). Even members of the vaunted *Forbes 400*—the nation's wealthiest individuals—are but a tiny bit happier than the public on the whole (Easterbrook, 2005).

Does Money Breed Happiness?   Many people think so, but greater wealth makes only a small contribution to explaining differences among people in personal happiness. Even the emotional boost from winning the lottery tends to be short-lived. Personal happiness has more to do with how people lead their lives than with what they own.

CONCEPT 8.25
People seem to have a particular "set point" for happiness that remains fairly constant throughout life.

In fact, people in many poorer countries, including Colombia and Costa Rica, are actually happier on the average than are those in wealthier countries such as Japan, Canada, and the United States (Altman, 2004). Evidence also shows that while lottery winners may get an emotional boost shortly after their windfalls, within a year their happiness levels tend to return to earlier levels (Corliss, 2003).

Just as wealth does not necessarily lead to happiness, neither does great misfortune necessarily bestow misery (Rowe, 2001). People who have suffered personal crises, such as developing cancer or losing a loved one, eventually bounce back (Corliss, 2003). But multiple life crises that pile on top of each other can alter a person's basic outlook. As positive psychology pioneer Martin Seligman observed, "On average, people with one life-threatening disease are not more unhappy than the rest of the population. Of course, a cascade of bad things happening can make a difference" (as quoted in Corliss, 2003). What about marriage? Is it the key to happiness? Generally speaking, married people tend to be happier than singles (Gallup Organization, 2005). But cause and effect may be muddled; it may be that happier people are more likely to get married or stay married (Stein, 2005; Wallis, 2005). This latter view is supported by evidence from a recent survey of more than 24,000 newly married people (Lucas et al., 2003). The results showed the bounce in happiness reported by many newlyweds tended to be short-lived

What is it that women report makes them happy in their daily experiences? In a recent survey of 900 working women in Texas, women rated "intimate relationships" high, even higher than time spent with children (Carey, 2004; Kahneman et al., 2004). Not surprisingly, commuting, grocery shopping, and cleaning fall at the bottom of the list.

Other factors linked to personal happiness are having friends (a big plus) and religious faith (Paul, 2005; Wallis, 2005). With respect to religion, we don't know whether it is the sense of purpose and meaning associated with religious belief, the social participation in the communal aspects of the religion, or a combination of factors relating to religious commitment that contributes to happiness.

A leading theory of happiness posited by psychologist David Lykken is that people have a particular "set point" for happiness, a level around which their general level of happiness tends to settle (Wallis, 2005). We don't yet understand how happiness set points are determined, but evidence points to genetics playing an important role (Rowe, 2001). Even so, our general sense of well-being or life satisfaction can change and often does change over the course of our lifetime (Fujita & Diener, 2005). There's also much we can do to boost our level of happiness. Before we consider these suggestions, let's take a closer look at what researchers have discovered about the physiological and psychological bases of happiness.

Physiological Factors: Searching for the Hard Wiring of Human Happiness
University of Wisconsin psychologist Richard Davidson points to the prefrontal cortex in the left hemisphere as the prime locus for human happiness (Lemonick, 2005a). Davidson and others find that positive emotions, including happiness, are associated with increased activity in the prefrontal cortex of the left cerebral hemisphere, whereas negative emotions, such as disgust, are associated with increased activity in the right prefrontal cortex (Davidson et al., 2000, 2002; Goleman, 2003; Harmon-Jones & Sigelman, 2001). The prefrontal cortex, as you may remember from Chapter 2, is the part of the frontal lobe that lies in front of the motor cortex. It is the brain's executive center—the problem-solving, decision-making, and planning center of the brain.

The ratio between the levels of activation in the two hemispheres may reveal a person's general disposition. Davidson showed that the more the ratio shifts in favor of the left hemisphere, the happier and more enthusiastic people tend to be (Davidson et al., 2002). People in whom the balance shifts furthest to the right are most likely to suffer from depression or anxiety.

Although differences in levels of activation between the two hemispheres may be genetically determined, it may be possible through certain types of training to shift the balance more to the left. Davidson shows that people who practice the Buddhist style of mindfulness meditation (discussed in Chapter 4) develop a leftward shift in their brain activation patterns after training (Goleman, 2003). Davidson finds that Buddhists—whom he calls "gold medalists" of meditation—have high levels of left, prefrontal activation ("Buddhists Are Happier," 2003). Meditative practices, such as those practiced by Buddhist monks, may induce physical changes in the brain that lead to happiness.

Psychological Factors   Research on human happiness also points to the importance of cognitive factors. It turns out that what you think is more important than what you have. Happy people, for instance, tend to appreciate what they have, rather than dwelling on what they don't have or on how much better off other people are (Sheldon & King, 2001). Abraham Lincoln expressed this view when he said, "Most people are about as happy as they make up their minds to be" (cited in Lyubormirsky, 2001).

Martin Seligman (2003) notes that people who are happier aren't any richer, better looking, or even healthier, on the average, than are less happy people. But they do tend to be more sociable, very sociable in fact (Neto, 2001). Sociability is a defining feature of *extraversion,* a personality trait strongly linked to personal happiness, so it is not surprising that sociability is also connected with happiness (Dieneret al., 2003). (Extraversion is discussed further in Chapter 12.) Since links between sociability and happiness are based on correlational evidence, we should be careful about drawing causal connections. But it stands to reason that becoming more socially active can increase opportunities for participating in rewarding activities with others. This in turn may help bolster positive moods, which is likely to translate into higher levels of life satisfaction and personal happiness.

CONCEPT 8.26
Proponents of positive psychology believe that it is possible to increase happiness by making changes in our daily behavior.

Positive Psychology: Using Science to Help People Become Happier   If differences in happiness are largely a function of how our brains are wired, does it mean that happiness cannot be changed? Are we stuck with what we've got? Not necessarily so, says a leading expert on emotions, Mike Csikszentmihalyi, who argues that it is possible to boost personal happiness (Lykken & Csikszentmihalyi, 2001). Martin Seligman (2003) agrees and believes that the mission of positive psychology is to increase human happiness.

For Seligman, happiness stems from the things we do, such as participating in pleasurable activities, becoming fully absorbed and engaged in our daily experiences, and finding a sense of meaning or fulfillment in our lives. Seligman (2003) offers a number of suggestions to help people increase their personal happiness, including the following:

- *Gratitude visits.* Seligman believes that expressing gratitude is a key component of personal happiness. Pay a visit to someone who has had a large impact on your life but whom you never really thanked. First write a testimonial of thanks to this person. When you arrive, read your testimonial and discuss the importance of this person to your life. Gratitude visits can be infectious in a positive way. The recipients begin to think about people *they* haven't thanked. They then make their own pilgrimage of thanks, which in turn leads to a kind of daisy chain of gratitude (Pink, 2003).

- *Three blessings.* Every night, before going to bed, think of three things that went well during the day. Write them down and reflect on them.

- *Savorings.* Plan a perfect day. But be sure to share it with another person.

All in all, happiness is not so much a function of what you've got as what you make of it.

Love: The Deepest Emotion

Notions about love have long intrigued and puzzled poets and philosophers. Only recently, however, have psychologists applied the scientific method to the study of love. Psychologists consider love to be both a motive (a need or want that drives us) and an emotion (or feeling state).

The ancient Greeks taught that there are several kinds of love, including love between parents and children and love between close friends. But it is **romantic love** that is idealized in countless songs, poems, and books, not to mention daytime soap operas. Nor is the worship of romantic love limited to Western culture. The great majority of cultures studied by anthropologists, even many preliterate societies, have a concept of romantic love (Jankowiak & Fischer, 1992).

Psychologist Robert Sternberg's (1988) **triangular model of love** conceptualizes love in terms of three basic components (see Figure 8.14):

1. *Intimacy,* the close bond and feeling of attachment between two people, including their desire to share their innermost thoughts and feelings

2. *Passion,* an intense sexual desire for the other person

3. *Decision/commitment,* the recognition that one loves the other person (decisional component) and is committed to maintaining the relationship through good times and bad (commitment component)

Decision and commitment need not go hand in hand. A person may acknowledge being in love but not be ready or willing to make a lasting commitment.

Sternberg believes that different combinations of these three basic components characterize different types of loving relationships (see Table 8.2). In his view, *romantic love* combines intimacy and passion but is lacking in decision/commitment. Romantic love may burn brightly but soon flicker out. On the other hand, it may develop into a more abiding form of love called *consummate love,* which combines all three components: intimacy, passion, and decision/commitment. Consummate love may be more of an ideal for many couples than an enduring reality. In *companionate love,* the type of love found in many long-term marriages, intimacy and commitment remain strong even though passion has ebbed.

CONCEPT 8.27
Though we generally think of love in terms of romantic love, it has been recognized since the time of the ancient Greeks that there are different kinds of love.

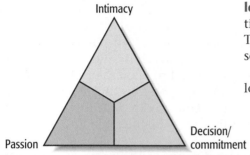

Figure 8.14   Sternberg's Triangular Model of Love
Sternberg conceptualizes love as a triangle with three components: intimacy, passion, and decision/commitment.

CONCEPT 8.28
Sternberg's triangular model of love proposes that different types of loving relationships can be characterized by different combinations of three basic components of love: intimacy, passion, and decision/commitment.

Consummate Love   In Sternberg's model, consummate love combines intimacy, passion, and decision/commitment. Consummate love may not be as enduring as companionate love, which combines intimacy and decision/commitment but lacks passion. But even couples for whom the flames of passion have ebbed may occasionally stir the embers.

romantic love   Love involving strong erotic attraction and desire for intimacy.
triangular model of love   Sternberg's concept of love as a triangle with three components: intimacy, passion, and decision/commitment.

TABLE 8.2   Types of Love According to Sternberg's Triangular Model

Nonlove	A relationship in which all three components of love are absent. Most of our personal relationships are of this type—casual acquaintanceships that do not involve any elements of love.
Liking	Friendship in which intimacy is present but passion and decision/commitment are not.
Infatuation	A kind of "love at first sight," in which one experiences passionate desire for another person but in which there is neither intimacy nor decision/commitment.
Fatuous (foolish) love	The type of love associated with whirlwind romances and "quicky marriages," in which both passion and decision/commitment are present but intimacy is not.
Empty love	Love characterized by a commitment to maintain the relationship but lacking passion and intimacy. Stagnant relationships that no longer have the intimacy or physical attraction that once characterized them are of this type.
Romantic love	Love characterized by the combination of passion and intimacy but that lacks decision/commitment.
Consummate love	The complete measure of love, which combines passion, intimacy, and decision/commitment. Many of us strive to attain this type of love in our romantic relationships. Maintaining it is often harder than achieving it.
Companionate love	A kind of love that combines intimacy with decision/commitment. This kind of love often occurs in marriages in which passionate attraction between the partners has died down and been replaced by a kind of committed friendship.

Source: Adapted from Sternberg, 1988.

Is This Woman Lying? The polygraph is widely used to detect lying, but scientific evidence demonstrating its reliability is lacking.

CONCEPT 8.29

The polygraph is widely used, even though scientists remain skeptical of its ability to detect lying.

polygraph   A device used for lie detection that records differences in physiological responses to control questions and test questions.

Sternberg proposes that relationships are balanced when the love triangles of both partners are well matched or closely overlapping. But relationships may fizzle, rather than sizzle, when partners differ in these components. For example, one partner may want to make a lasting commitment to the relationship, while the other's idea of making a commitment is deciding to stay the night.

The Polygraph: How Credible Is It?

Let us end this module by commenting on the use of the **polygraph**, a device used to detect whether people are lying based on their responses to control (neutral) and test questions about the crime in question. It is based on the assumption that there are distinctive patterns of physiological activity that polygraph experts can use to tell whether someone is lying. The polygraph measures physiological signs of arousal, as registered by changes in sweating of the skin, breathing, and heart rates. Thus the polygraph measures bodily arousal, not lying per se. Critics contend that it is often inaccurate and cannot distinguish between lying and generalized arousal that might be brought about by anxiety or guilt (e.g., Iacono & Lykken, 1997). Many innocent people react strongly to test questions, perhaps out of fear that they could be accused of the crime in question. Critics also point out that some (perhaps many) people, especially those who are seasoned liars, can lie without any telltale physiological reactions.

Unfortunately, the false findings of polygraphs have damaged the lives of many innocent people. Though the polygraph may occasionally catch a person in a lie, it is not reliable enough to pass scientific muster (Adelson, 2004b, 2004c). More sophisticated methods of detecting lying are currently under study, but none are ready for "prime time" use. Concept Chart 8.3 provides an overview of the major concepts of emotion discussed in this module.

CONCEPT CHART 8.3 Major Concepts of Emotion

Concept	Description
Facial expressions of emotion	Evidence from cross-cultural studies supports universal recognition of the facial expressions of six basic emotions: anger, fear, disgust, sadness, happiness, and surprise.
Facial-feedback hypothesis	According to this hypothesis, mimicking facial movements associated with an emotion can produce the corresponding emotional state.
Physiological bases of emotions	Emotions are accompanied by activation of the sympathetic branch of the autonomic nervous system. Emotions are processed by the structures of the limbic system (the amygdala, hippocampus, and parts of the hypothalamus) and by the cerebral cortex.
James-Lange theory of emotions	Emotions follow our bodily reactions to triggering stimuli—we become afraid because we run; we feel sad because we cry.
Cannon-Bard theory of emotions	Emotions accompany bodily responses to triggering stimuli but are not caused by them.
Two-factor model of emotions	The combination of physiological arousal and cognitive appraisal (labeling) of the source of the arousal produces the emotional state.
LeDoux's dual-pathway model of fear	A pathway leads from the thalamus to the amygdala, which produces the initial fear response (bodily arousal), while a second pathway leads to the cortex, which further processes the fear stimulus and produces the conscious awareness of fear.
Happiness	Happiness is a basic human emotion. Researchers suspect there is a set point around which our general level of happiness varies throughout life.
Love	In Sternberg's model, different types of love can be characterized on the basis of different combinations of three basic components: intimacy, passion, and decision/commitment.
Polygraph	A device used to detect lying based on analysis of differences in physiological responses to control questions and relevant questions.
Emotional intelligence	According to this concept, the ability to manage emotions effectively is a form of intelligent behavior.

 EXPLORING PSYCHOLOGY
Emotional Intelligence:
How Well Do You Manage Your Emotions?

 CONCEPT 8.30
The ability to recognize emotions in yourself and others and to regulate your emotions effectively is a form of intelligent behavior called emotional intelligence.

emotional intelligence The ability to recognize emotions in oneself and others and to manage one's own emotions effectively.

Some theorists believe that a person's ability to manage emotions represents a form of intelligent behavior, called **emotional intelligence** (Goleman, 1995c; Salovey & Mayer, 1990). Emotional intelligence is difficult to define precisely, but it can be generally described in terms of five main characteristics:

1. *Knowing your emotions.* Self-awareness, or knowing your true feelings, is a core feature of emotional intelligence.

2. *Managing your emotions.* Emotionally intelligent people are able to handle their emotions in appropriate ways. They can soothe themselves in difficult times, and they bounce back quickly from disappointments and setbacks.

3. *Motivating yourself.* People with a high level of emotional intelligence can marshal their emotions to pursue their goals. They approach challenges with enthusiasm, zeal, and confidence and thus are better equipped to attain high levels of achievement and productivity. They also are able to delay gratification and constrain their impulses as they pursue long-term goals.

TRY THIS OUT

Taking Stock of Your Emotional Intelligence

Though we lack a validated self-report scale of emotional intelligence, the following questions should give you some insight into how you measure up on the construct. Your answers are not for public consumption, so answer them as honestly as you can in terms of your real self, not your imagined or ideal self.

1. Would you say (honestly now) that
   a. you generally go through the day without paying attention to your emotions, OR
   b. you are generally attuned to your feelings?

2. Would you say that
   a. your emotions tend to get all lumped together, OR
   b. you are able to clearly discriminate one emotion from another?

3. Would you say that
   a. you seldom if ever experience negative emotions, such as anger or fear, OR
   b. you are able to recognize these emotions when you experience them?

4. Would you say that
   a. you deny feeling strong positive emotions, such as love or joy, OR
   b. you recognize these feelings when they occur?

5. Would you say that
   a. you are able to recognize emotions in others, OR
   b. you have a hard time reading emotions in other people?

6. Would you say that
   a. you try to understand what people are feeling, OR
   b. you would rather not deal with that mushy stuff?

7. Would you say that
   a. you tend to focus on what people say, not what they must be feeling, OR
   b. you tend to focus on both what people say and what they must be feeling?

8. If someone starts crying or gets angry, do you
   a. just want to leave the scene, OR
   b. seek to calm or comfort the person?

9. If you get into an argument with your partner or a family member, do you
   a. just try to stop the argument by becoming silent, OR
   b. try to focus on the issues and resolve them?

10. If someone has a gripe with you, do you
    a. immediately jump to defend yourself, OR
    b. try to understand the situation from the other person's perspective?

Did you detect a pattern? These items are scaled such that (b) responses are keyed to be reflective of emotional intelligence. How did you do? Would you consider yourself to be emotionally intelligent or emotionally challenged? Do you think you can change how you deal with your own emotions and how you respond to emotions in others? How would you go about it?

Source: Adapted from Nevid & Rathus, 2005. Reprinted with permission of John Wiley & Sons, Inc.

4. *Recognizing emotions in others.* Empathy, the ability to perceive emotions in others, is an important "people skill." It not only helps build strong relationships, but it also contributes to success in teaching, sales, management, and the helping professions.

5. *Helping others handle their emotions.* The ability to help others deal with their feelings is an important factor in maintaining meaningful relationships.

There is only a slight correlation between IQ and emotional intelligence. Perhaps you know brilliant people who seem to be clueless about deciphering other people's emotions or even their own. But we do have evidence linking emotional intelligence to better academic performance in school, at least among some groups of high school students (e.g., Parker et al., 2004; Petrides, Frederickson, & Furnham, 2004). Emotional intelligence may help students cope better with the challenges they face in school. However, it does not appear to be a strong predictor of academic performance in college, at least as measured by GPAs (O'Connor & Little, 2003).

Online Study Center
Resources
Weblinks: What's Your Emotional Intelligence Quotient?

Research on emotional intelligence shows that it is also linked to such positive outcomes as emotional well-being and life satisfaction (Gannon & Ranzijn, 2005; Spence, Oades, & Caputi, 2004) as well as marital success (Ciarrochi et al., 2001; Fitness, 2001). However, we await direct evidence that it can do a better job of predicting successful outcomes than more general measures of intelligence and personality (Brody, 2004). You may gain a better appreciation of your own emotional intelligence by completing the accompanying Try This Out exercise on the previous page.

MODULE 8.3 REVIEW

Emotions

RECITE IT

What are the three components of emotions?

- Psychologists conceptualize emotions as having a physiological component (heightened bodily arousal), a cognitive component (a feeling state, as well as thoughts and judgments about experiences linked to the feeling state), and a behavioral component (approach or avoidance behaviors).

Are facial expressions of emotion universal?

- Evidence from cross-cultural studies supports the view that facial expressions of six basic emotions—anger, fear, disgust, sadness, happiness, and surprise—are universal.

- There are both differences and similarities in how emotions are experienced in different cultures. Each culture has rules, called display rules, that determine how emotions are expressed and how much emotion is appropriate to express. Gender differences in emotional expression may reflect cultural expectations.

What role do brain structures play in emotions?

- Parts of the limbic system, especially the amygdala, play key roles in emotional processing.

- The cerebral cortex interprets stimuli and plans strategies for either approaching or avoiding stimuli, depending on whether they are perceived as "friend" or "foe." The cortex also controls facial expression of emotions and is responsible for processing the felt experience of emotions.

What are the major theories of emotions?

- The major theories of emotions are the James-Lange theory (emotions occur after people become aware of their physiological responses to the triggering stimuli), the Cannon-Bard theory (emotional and physiological reactions to triggering stimuli occur almost simultaneously), the two-factor model (emotions depend on an arousal state and a labeling of the causes of the arousal), and LeDoux's dual-pathway model of fear (the amygdala responds to fear stimuli before the cerebral cortex gets involved).

What factors are associated with personal happiness?

- The major factors identified by researchers include more activation of the left cerebral cortex, a cognitive decision to be happy, and sociability. Wealth has but a modest relationship with personal happiness or life satisfaction. Happiness may also vary around a genetically influenced set point.

What are the three components of love in Sternberg's model of love?

- According to Sternberg's triangular model, the components of love are intimacy, passion, and decision/commitment.

What is the polygraph?

- The polygraph is a device used to detect physiological response patterns believed to indicate when a person is lying. However, scientific evidence does not support the utility of the polygraph in detecting lying.

RECALL IT

1. All of the following are basic components of emotion *except*
   a. bodily arousal.　　c. production of neuropeptide Y.
   b. cognition.　　　　 d. expressed behavior.

2. The belief that the subjective experience of an emotion and the bodily response that accompanies it occur at virtually the same time is the
   a. James-Lange theory.　c. two-factor model.
   b. Cannon-Bard theory.　d. dual-pathway model of fear.

3. Facial expressions of six basic emotions are recognized universally. What are these six emotions?

4. The component in Sternberg's triangular model of love that corresponds to the desire to share one's personal feelings with another person is labeled _____.

5. The ability to manage emotions effectively can be conceptualized as a form of intelligent behavior, called _____ _____.

THINK ABOUT IT

- How is emotional intelligence different from general intelligence? In what ways might it become more important for success in life than general intelligence?

- Apply Sternberg's triangular model to a current or past intimate relationship. How are (were) you and your partner alike in the three components of love? How are (were) you different? How important are (were) these differences?

APPLICATION MODULE 8.4

Managing Anger:
What Can You Do to Control Your Anger?

CONCEPT 8.31

By identifying and correcting anger-inducing thoughts, people can gain better control over their anger and develop more effective ways of handling conflicts.

Do you know people who have problems controlling their temper? Do you yourself do things in anger that you later regret? Anger can be a catalyst for physical or verbal aggression. But even if you never express your anger through aggression, frequent episodes of anger can take a toll on your health, putting you at increased risk of cardiovascular disorders, such as hypertension and heart disease (see Chapter 15). Anger floods the body with stress hormones that may eventually damage the cardiovascular system.

Cognitive theorists recognize that anger is prompted by a person's reactions to frustrating or provocative situations, not by the situations themselves. Though people often blame the "other guy" for making them angry, people make themselves angry by thinking angry thoughts or making anger-inducing statements to themselves. To gain better control over their anger, people need to identify and correct such thoughts and statements. By doing so, they can learn to avoid hostile confrontations and perhaps save wear and tear on their cardiovascular systems. Here are some suggestions psychologists offer for identifying and controlling anger:

Anger and Aggression   Anger is frequently the catalyst for physical or verbal aggression.

- *Become aware of your emotional reactions in anger-provoking situations.* When you notice yourself getting "hot under the collar," take this as a cue to calm yourself down and think through the situation. Learn to replace anger-arousing thoughts with calming alternatives.

- *Review the evidence.* Might you be overreacting to the situation by taking it too personally? Might you be jumping to the conclusion that the other person means you ill? Are there other ways of viewing the person's behavior?

- *Practice more adaptive thinking.* For example, say to yourself, "I can handle this situation without getting upset. I'll just calm down and think through what I want to say."

- *Engage in competing responses.* You can disrupt an angry response by conjuring up soothing mental images, by taking a walk, or by practicing self-relaxation. The time-honored practice of counting to ten when you begin to feel angry may also help defuse an emotional response. If it doesn't, you can follow Mark Twain's advice and count to a hundred instead. While counting, try to think calming thoughts.

- *Don't get steamed.* Others may do dumb or hurtful things, but you make yourself angry by dwelling on them. Take charge of your emotional responses by not allowing yourself to get steamed. When someone treats you unfairly, tell yourself that the other person may be a jerk but that he or she is not worth getting upset about. Or better yet, think through alternative, assertive responses or plans of action to resolve the conflict. You should also avoid discussions that simply lead to pointless arguments.

- *Oppose anger with empathy.* Try to understand what the other person is feeling. Rather than saying to yourself, "He's a miserable so-and-so who deserves to be punished," say, "He must really have difficulties at home to act like this. But that's his problem. I won't take it personally."

- *Congratulate yourself for responding assertively rather than aggressively.* Give yourself a mental pat on the back when you handle stressful situations with equanimity rather than with anger.

- *Scale back your expectations of others.* Perceptions of unfairness may result from the expectation that others "should" or "must" fulfill your needs or expectations. By scaling back your expectations, you're less likely to get angry with others when they disappoint you.

- *Modulate verbal responses.* Avoid raising your voice or cursing. Stay cool, even when others do not.

- *Learn to express positive feelings.* Expressing positive feelings can help diffuse negative emotions. Tell others you love them and care about them. They are likely to reciprocate in kind.

Think about situations in which you have felt angry or have acted in anger. How might you handle these situations differently in the future? What coping responses can you use to help you keep your cool? Table 8.3 offers some calming alternatives to thoughts that trigger anger. Before ending, let us note that people with anger management problems can also benefit from psychological interventions specifically designed to help people control anger (e.g., DelVecchio & O'Leary, 2004; DiGiuseppe & Tafrate, 2003; Holloway, 2003a).

TABLE 8.3 Anger Management: Replacing Anger-Inducing Thoughts with Calming Alternatives

Situation	Anger-Inducing Thoughts	Calming Alternatives
A provocateur says, "So what are you going to do about it?"	"That jerk. Who does he think he is? I'll teach him a lesson he won't forget!"	"He must really have a problem to act the way he does. But that's his problem. I don't have to respond at his level."
You get caught in a monster traffic jam.	"Why does this always happen to me? I can't stand this."	"This may be inconvenient, but it's not the end of the world. Don't blow it out of proportion. Everyone gets caught in traffic every now and then. Just relax and listen to some music."
You're in a checkout line at the supermarket, and the woman in front of you is cashing a check. It seems as if it's taking hours.	"She has some nerve holding up the line. It's so unfair for someone to make other people wait. I'd like to tell her off!"	"It will take only a few minutes. People have a right to cash their checks in the market. Just relax and read a magazine while you wait."
You're looking for a parking spot when suddenly another car cuts you off and seizes a vacant space.	"No one should be allowed to treat me like this. I'd like to punch him out."	"Don't expect people always to be considerate of your interests. Stop personalizing things." Or "Relax, there's no sense going to war over this."
Your spouse or partner comes home several hours later than expected, without calling to let you know he or she would be late.	"It's so unfair. I can't let him (her) treat me like this."	Explain how you feel without putting your spouse or partner down.
You're watching a movie in a theater, and the people sitting next to you are talking and making a lot of noise.	"Don't they have any regard for others? I'm so angry with these people I could tear their heads off."	"Even if they're inconsiderate, it doesn't mean I have to get angry about it or ruin my enjoyment of the movie. If they don't quiet down when I ask them, I'll just change my seat or call the manager."
A person insults you or treats you disrespectfully.	"I can't just walk away from this as if nothing happened."	"I can just let this drop. When did anger ever settle anything? There are better ways of handling this than getting steamed."

Source: Adapted from Nevid, Rathus, & Greene, 2003.

TYING IT TOGETHER

Motivation and emotion are processes that move us to action. Motives are the "whys" of behavior—the factors that drive goal-directed behavior and explain why we do what we do (Module 8.1). Hunger is a major source of motivation—a drive that motivates us to seek nourishment to satisfy a basic biological need for food (Module 8.2). Emotions are complex feeling states, but like motives, they also have a behavioral component—tendencies to approach or avoid particular objects or situations (Module 8.3). Anger is a negative emotion that can cause serious health problems. People can gain better control over their anger by identifying and correcting anger-inducing thoughts (Module 8.4).

Thinking Critically About Psychology

Based on your reading of this chapter, answer the following questions. Then, to evaluate your progress in developing critical thinking skills, compare your answers to the sample answers found in Appendix A.

Amanda and Craig are at a crossroads in their relationship. The two 20-year-olds have been dating for six months, and the relationship has gotten to a stage Amanda describes as "almost serious." She feels she loves Craig but is concerned that he does not seem to open up to her. Craig says he would like to date Amanda exclusively, but she is unsure. They both say they are strongly attracted to each other and get excited whenever they see each other.

1. **Apply Sternberg's triangular model of love to Amanda and Craig's relationship. Which components of love appear to be present in the relationship? Which appear to be absent or mismatched?**

2. **If they wish to bring their love triangles into a closer match, what advice would you give them?**

Key Terms

motivation (p. 296)
motives (p. 296)
instinctive behaviors (p. 297)
instinct theory (p. 297)
drive theory (p. 297)
need (p. 297)
drive (p. 297)
drive reduction (p. 297)
primary drives (p. 298)
secondary drives (p. 298)
stimulus motives (p. 298)
arousal theory (p. 298)
Yerkes-Dodson law (p. 299)
incentive theory (p. 300)
incentives (p. 300)
incentive value (p. 300)

cognitive dissonance (p. 301)
cognitive dissonance theory (p. 301)
effort justification (p. 301)
psychosocial needs (p. 302)
need for achievement (p. 302)
extrinsic motivation (p. 303)
intrinsic motivation (p. 303)
achievement motivation (p. 303)
avoidance motivation (p. 303)
hierarchy of needs (p. 303)
self-actualization (p. 304)
fat cells (p. 306)
lateral hypothalamus (p. 306)
ventromedial hypothalamus (p. 307)
obesity (p. 307)
body mass index (BMI) (p. 308)

set point theory (p. 309)
anorexia nervosa (p. 311)
bulimia nervosa (p. 311)
emotions (p. 315)
display rules (p. 318)
facial-feedback hypothesis (p. 319)
Duchenne smile (p. 319)
James-Lange theory (p. 322)
Cannon-Bard theory (p. 322)
two-factor model (p. 322)
dual-pathway model of fear (p. 323)
romantic love (p. 328)
triangular model of love (p. 328)
polygraph (p. 329)
emotional intelligence (p. 330)

ANSWERS TO RECALL IT QUESTIONS

Module 8.1: 1. goal; 2. b; 3. i. d, ii. a, iii. c, iv. b; 4. Arousal; 5. cognitive dissonance; 6. actualization.

Module 8.2: 1. c; 2. c; 3. i. b, ii. d, iii. a, iv. c; 4. a.

Module 8.3: 1. c; 2. b; 3. anger, fear, disgust, sadness, happiness, and surprise; 4. intimacy; 5. emotional intelligence.

Child Development

DID YOU KNOW THAT . . .

- A fertilized egg cell is not yet attached to the mother's body during the first week or so after conception? (p. 343)
- Pregnant women cannot assume it is safe to drink even one or two alcoholic beverages per week? (p. 346)
- A newborn can distinguish the breast pad worn by its mother from those worn by other women? (p. 351)
- By 1 year of age, infants have already mastered the most difficult balancing problems they will ever face in life? (p. 352)
- Baby geese followed a famous scientist around as if he were their mother? (p. 357)
- According to theorist Erik Erikson, the development of a sense of trust begins before the infant speaks its first word? (p. 363)
- It is normal for a 4-year-old to believe the moon has feelings? (p. 371)
- One out of four children in the United States under the age of 2 now has a TV set in his or her room? (p. 377)

One of the things parents learn when they have a second child is the everyday meaning of the concept of equality. They learn that whatever they give to one child they must give to the other in equal measure. Parents learn to buy in twos. If they give one child a present, they match it by giving the same present or one quite similar to the other child. This lesson in parenting was driven home for me one day when we sat down at the dinner table to share a pizza we had had delivered. Everything was fine until we divided the last two slices between Daniella, then age 5, and Michael, who was then 11. I noticed Daniella's eyes beginning to well up with tears. I asked her what was wrong. She pointed to Michael's slice and said that his was bigger. Michael had already begun eating his slice, so it was clear that pulling a last-minute switch wouldn't ease her concern, let alone be fair to Michael. It was then that the heavy hammer of equality came down squarely on my head.

To resolve the situation, I drew upon a principle you'll read about in this chapter: the principle of *conservation*. This is the principle that the amount or size of a substance does not change merely as the result of a superficial change in its outward appearance. You don't increase the amount of clay by merely flattening or stretching it out. Neither do you increase the amount of a liquid by pouring it from a wider container into a narrower one, even though the liquid rises to a higher level in the narrower container. Although the principle of conservation may seem self-evident to an adult or older child, the typical child of 5 years of age has not mastered this concept. Knowing this, I quickly took a pizza slicer and divided Daniella's slice into two. "There," I said, "now you have twice as many slices as Michael." Michael gave me a quizzical look, as if he was wondering who on Earth would fall for such an obvious trick. Daniella, on the other hand, looked at the two slices and quite happily starting eating them, the tears receding. Peace at the Nevid dining table was restored, at least for the moment.

The pizza experience illustrates a theme that carries throughout our study of human development. It's not about applying principles of child psychology to keep peace at the dinner table. Rather, it's about recognizing that the world of the child is very different from the world of the adolescent or adult. Children's cognitive abilities and ways of understanding the world change dramatically during childhood. Moreover, as we shall see in the next chapter, many adolescents see themselves and the world quite differently than do their parents and other adults. Even in adulthood, people of 20-something or 30-something years see themselves and their place in the world quite differently than do those of more advanced years.

In this chapter and the next, we trace the developmental changes that occur from birth through advanced age. Though this chapter focuses on child development, our story would be incomplete without considering the important events that occur well before a child takes its first breath. Our investigation starts, however, by looking at the questions psychologists seek to answer as they study development and some of the methods they use. ■

Key Questions and Methods of Study

- What major questions underlie the study of human development?
- How do developmental psychologists study age-related changes?

CONCEPT 9.1

The study of human development has been shaped by four major questions: nature versus nurture, continuity versus discontinuity, universality, and stability.

We can think of development progressing chronologically in terms of the stages shown in Table 9.1. The branch of psychology that studies the systematic changes that occur during the life span is called **developmental psychology**. Developmental psychologists gather data on the kinds of changes that occur during development. But they also use this information to help answer larger questions about human development. In this section, we first consider four of these major questions: the nature versus nurture question, the continuity versus discontinuity question, the universality question, and the stability question. Then we examine the major methods developmental psychologists use in their studies.

The Nature Versus Nurture Question

One of the oldest controversies in psychology is the **nature-nurture debate**. Is our behavior governed by nature (genetics) or nurture (environment and culture)? In the early twentieth century, the debate between opposing sides was more clearly drawn. Behaviorists such as John Watson maintained that behavior is determined by learning and experience. As explained in Chapter 1, Watson even boasted that he could take healthy, "well-formed" infants and, by controlling their environment, turn them into doctors, lawyers, or even beggars or thieves. Another early theorist, psychologist Arnold Gesell (1880–1961), emphasized the role of biological processes in human development. Gesell was heavily influenced by Darwin's theory of evolution and believed that child development proceeds through a series of genetically determined changes that unfold according to nature's plan.

Though the nature-nurture debate continues, psychologists recognize that human behavior is influenced by a combination of genes and the environment (Cacioppo et al., 2000; Plomin et al., 2003). The contemporary version of the nature-nurture debate is more about the relative contributions of nature *and* nurture to particular behaviors than it is about nature *or* nurture (Bouchard, 2004). In

TABLE 9.1   Stages of Development Through the Life Span

Stage	Approximate Ages
Prenatal period	Conception to birth
Infancy period	Birth to 1 year
Toddler period	2 to 3 years
Preschool period	3 to 6 years
Middle childhood	6 to 12 years
Adolescence	12 to 18 years
Young adulthood	18 to 40 years
Middle adulthood	40 to 65 years
Late adulthood	65 years and older

developmental psychology The branch of psychology that explores physical, emotional, cognitive, and social aspects of development.

nature-nurture debate The debate in psychology over the relative influences of genetics (nature) and environment (nurture) in determining behavior.

other words, scientists recognize that biology and experience work together to enhance the organism's ability to adapt successfully to its environment (Gottesman & Hanson, 2005).

Developmental psychologists seek to determine how much of development can be attributed to nature, or genes, and how much to nurture, or the environment. For example, evidence shows that genes account for about half of the variability in personality traits among people (Bouchard, 2004). But although our genetic make-up influences the development of behavioral patterns, whether these patterns emerge depends in large part on the cultural and family environment in which the child is reared (Cravchik & Goldman, 2000; Li, 2003). Some physical traits, such as hair color, are determined by a single gene, but complex behavioral traits are influenced by multiple genes interacting with environmental factors (Plomin & McGuffin, 2003). Development is best understood in terms of a continuous interplay of biology and experience (Lickliter & Honeycutt, 2003).

As discussed in Chapter 2, researchers use kinship studies (familial association studies, twin studies, and adoptee studies) to help determine the relative contributions of nature and nurture to particular traits.

The Continuity Versus Discontinuity Question

Another question that has aroused debate among developmentalists is whether development progresses continuously in a series of small changes or discontinuously in abrupt steps. According to the **continuity model**, the changes children undergo at various ages are *quantitative* in nature: they occur in small steps rather than in major leaps. Stage theorists, most notably the Swiss developmentalist Jean Piaget, subscribe to a **discontinuity model**, the view that development progresses in stages that are *qualitative* in nature. Development occurs as sudden transformations or abrupt leaps in the child's abilities and ways of interacting with the world. These theorists believe that development remains relatively stable within each stage but then suddenly jumps to the next stage.

Most developmentalists take a middle position: they believe development involves both quantitative and qualitative changes. On the one hand, no amount of practice crawling or "taking steps" will lead to walking until the infant reaches a stage of readiness in terms of physical maturation. Nor will coaxing an infant to speak produce recognizable words until the child reaches the stage at which language use first appears. On the other hand, many skills, such as vocabulary and arithmetical abilities, develop gradually through practice and experience. Even for these skills, however, we could argue that the child must reach a stage of developmental readiness for training and experience to matter.

The Universality Question

Does development follow a universal course that is essentially the same for children the world over, or does development depend more on culture and experience? Once again, most developmental psychologists take a compromise position (Overton, 1997). As we will see, there is strong evidence that children progress through a series of stages of cognitive development. Yet cultural differences exist in the ages at which children reach certain stages. Developmental psychologists take into account many social and cultural influences on development, including factors such as ethnicity, socioeconomic status, lifestyle, and diet.

The Stability Question

Developmental psychologists are also interested in the degree to which temperaments and personality traits are stable over the life span. Do traits or temperaments observed in infancy or early childhood endure throughout life, or

continuity model   The model proposing that development involves quantitative changes that occur in small steps over time.

discontinuity model   The model proposing that development progresses in discrete stages that involve abrupt, qualitative changes in cognitive ability and ways of interacting with the world.

might people change over time? Some theorists, such as Sigmund Freud, have argued that our personalities are generally fixed in early childhood, typically by age 6 or so. Today Freud's position is considered too limiting; even some of his own followers, such as the theorist Erik Erikson, recognized that our personality continues to develop as we age and face new life challenges. Even so, we will see that researchers find certain consistencies in behavior across time, especially in temperament.

Methods of Study

💡 **CONCEPT 9.2**

Developmental psychologists use different research strategies to study age-related differences, most commonly longitudinal studies and cross-sectional studies.

Developmental psychologists employ a range of research strategies to study developmental changes. The two methods used most frequently are the *longitudinal method* and the *cross-sectional method*.

Longitudinal Method   A **longitudinal study** observes the same people repeatedly over time. Longitudinal studies may last years or decades. Investigators conduct longitudinal studies to examine how personality and behavior change over time (Warner et al., 2004). These studies may address such questions as "Do shy children become shy adults?" or "Is temperament stable or does it change over time?" In Chapter 7 we discussed results from the first and longest-running longitudinal study. Begun in 1921 by psychologist Louis Terman, the study tracked the life course of a group of intellectually gifted children from middle childhood into old age.

The major strength of longitudinal research is that it allows investigators to examine developmental processes by observing changes in the same individuals over time. However, the method has some major limitations. It is time-consuming and may require a continuing commitment of resources that only the best-funded research programs can afford. Moreover, research participants may drop out of the study for various reasons, such as death, disability, or relocation. In addition, the study sample may not be representative of the larger population, which limits the ability to generalize the results beyond the study group.

Cross-Sectional Method   Because of the limitations of the longitudinal method, developmental psychologists more often use an alternative approach, called the cross-sectional method, to study developmental changes. A **cross-sectional study** observes people of different ages at the same point in time. Thus, researchers can compare groups of people who are similar in background characteristics (income level, ethnicity, etc.) but differ in age. Differences among the groups on the variables of interest, such as shyness or temperament, will then presumably reflect age-related developmental processes.

The cross-sectional method has several advantages. Compared to the longitudinal method, it is much less expensive and time-consuming, since participants need to be tested at only one point in time. However, it too has drawbacks (P. S. Kaplan, 2000a; Kraemer et al., 2000). In particular, investigators cannot be sure that the comparison groups are comparable with respect to every important characteristic except age. It remains possible that some unrecognized variable other than age per se caused the observed differences among the groups.

Another problem with the cross-sectional method is the possibility of a **cohort effect**, a limitation which results from research participants being members of a particular generation or being raised at a certain time in history (P. S. Kaplan, 2000b; Twenge, 2000). The term *cohort* describes a group of people who were born about the same time and so may share many historical and social background characteristics. Thus, differences among groups of people of different ages may be generationally or historically related rather than age related. A child born today may have different experiences than children from prior generations and therefore may see the world through different eyes. Children today may have no concept of the world earlier generations knew—a world without computers, microwave

longitudinal study   Study that compares the same individuals at periodic intervals over an extended period of time.

cross-sectional study   Study that compares individuals of different ages or developmental levels at the same point in time.

cohort effect   Differences between age groups as a function of historical or social influences affecting those groups rather than age per se.

CONCEPT CHART 9.1   Major Methods of Studying Human Development

	Longitudinal Method	Cross-sectional Method
Method	Repeated study of the same individuals over time to track developmental changes	Comparison of individuals from different age groups or developmental stages at the same time
Study plan	Study the same group of individuals at 20 years of age, at 40 years, and at 60 years	Study three groups of participants at the same time: a group of 20-year-olds, a second group of 40-year-olds, and a third group of 60-year-olds
Strengths and weaknesses	Permits study of the same individuals over time, but is costly, time-consuming, and may be limited in the generalizability of the findings beyond the original study group	Less costly and more efficient than longitudinal studies, but subject to unrecognized factors that may distinguish the groups (other than age) and cohort effects (differences between groups reflecting historical rather than developmental factors)

ovens, cell phones, or even TVs. Access to video and computer games and to the Internet may also give contemporary children an advantage in developing certain visual-spatial skills compared to earlier cohorts of children. Longitudinal studies, which track the same individuals over time, help disentangle such historical effects from age-related effects. Concept Chart 9.1 compares the longitudinal and cross-sectional methods.

MODULE 9.1 REVIEW

Key Questions and Methods of Study

RECITE IT

What major questions underlie the study of human development?

- The nature versus nurture question refers to the relative contributions of heredity and environment to development.

- The continuity versus discontinuity question refers to the debate about whether development progresses continuously in a series of small changes or discontinuously in abrupt steps.

- The universality question deals with whether developmental changes are universal or variable across cultures.

- The stability question refers to whether traits and behaviors are consistent over time or change across the life span.

How do developmental psychologists study age-related changes?

- The longitudinal approach involves studying the same groups of individuals repeatedly over time.

- The cross-sectional approach involves comparing people of different ages at the same point in time.

RECALL IT

1. If we believe that development progresses in abrupt steps, leading to qualitatively different changes, our view holds to the _____ model of development.
   a. continuity
   b. discontinuity
   c. disparity
   d. variability

2. What does the universality question address?

3. In cross-sectional research,
   a. the same group of individuals are studied for many years, even decades.
   b. people of the same age are studied repeatedly over time.
   c. there may be problems with cohort effects.
   d. is typically more expensive and time-consuming than longitudinal studies.

THINK ABOUT IT

- How do present investigators reframe the traditional "nature-nurture" question?

- An investigator compared groups of older adults and younger adults on a memory task to study developmental changes in memory functioning. What type of study method (longitudinal or cross-sectional) did the investigator use?

- What are the advantages and disadvantages of the longitudinal and the cross-sectional methods of studying human development?

MODULE 9.2

Prenatal Development: A Case of Nature and Nurture

- What are the major stages of prenatal development?
- What are some major threats to prenatal development?
- What types of tests are used to detect chromosomal and genetic defects?

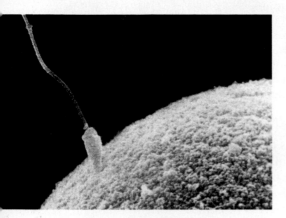

Dance of Life In this remarkable photograph, a single sperm is attempting to penetrate the egg covering. If it succeeds, the genetic material from both parents will combine into a single cell that marks the beginning of a new life.

Scientists believe that sexual reproduction began some 240 to 320 million years ago, long before humans ever strode upon the Earth (Lahn & Page, 1999). They believe it began with a single chromosome that mutated to form the X and Y sex chromosomes that determine sex in mammals, including humans. The male of the species carries both an X and a Y chromosome, whereas the female carries two X chromosomes. Each reproductive cell, or germ cell—the **sperm** in males and the **ovum** (egg cell) in females—contains only one sex chromosome. All other body cells have two sex chromosomes. Thus, a sperm cell carries either one X or one Y sex chromosome, and an ovum carries only one X. During **ovulation**, an ovum is released from an ovary and then begins a slow journey through a **fallopian tube** (see Figure 9.1). If **fertilization** (the uniting of a sperm and an ovum) occurs, the resulting combination (XX for females or XY for males) of the sex chromosomes in the fertilized ovum determines the baby's sex.

The fertilized ovum is a single cell, called a **zygote**, that soon undergoes cell division. First, it divides into two cells; then each of these two cells divides, forming four cells; each of these four cells divides, resulting in eight cells; and so on. In the months that follow, organ systems form as the developing organism increasingly takes on the form and structure of a human being.

Figure 9.1 The Journey Begins
A mature egg cell (ovum) is released during ovulation by either the left or right ovary. It slowly travels to the opening of a fallopian tube and then inches down the tube. Fertilization, the union of sperm and ovum, usually takes place in a fallopian tube. The fertilized ovum, or zygote, makes its way to the uterus, where it becomes implanted within the uterine wall.

Fertilization

Implantation

Fallopian tube

Ovulation

Ovary

Interior of the uterus

Cervix

Vagina

sperm The male reproductive cell.

ovum An egg cell (pl: ova).

ovulation The release of an ovum from an ovary.

fallopian tube A strawlike tube between an ovary and the uterus through which an ovum passes after ovulation.

fertilization The union of a sperm with an ovum during sexual reproduction.

zygote A fertilized egg cell.

(a)

(b)

Figure 9.2   Prenatal Development
Dramatic changes in shape and form occur during prenatal development. Compare the embryo (a) at about six to seven weeks of development with the fetus (b) at approximately sixteen weeks. The fetus has already taken on a clearly recognizable human form.

germinal stage The stage of prenatal development that spans the period from fertilization through implantation.

uterus The female reproductive organ in which the fertilized ovum becomes implanted and develops to term.

embryonic stage The stage of prenatal development from implantation through about the eighth week of pregnancy during which the major organ systems begin to form.

embryo The developing organism at an early stage of prenatal development.

neural tube The area in the embryo from which the nervous system develops.

amniotic sac The uterine sac that contains the fetus.

placenta The organ that provides for the exchange of nutrients and waste materials between mother and fetus.

fetal stage The stage of prenatal development in which the fetus develops, beginning around the ninth week of pregnancy and lasting until the birth of the child.

fetus The developing organism in the later stages of prenatal development.

A pregnancy typically lasts 280 days, or about nine months, which are commonly divided into three trimesters, or three-month periods. From the standpoint of prenatal development, we can also identify three major prenatal stages or periods: the germinal stage, which corresponds to roughly the first two weeks after conception; the embryonic stage, which spans the period of about two weeks to about eight weeks after conception; and the fetal stage, which continues until birth (see Figure 9.2).

The **germinal stage** spans the time from fertilization to implantation in the wall of the **uterus**. For the first three or four days following conception, the mass of dividing cells moves about the uterus before implantation. The process of implantation is not completed for perhaps another week or so.

The **embryonic stage** spans the period from implantation to about the eighth week of pregnancy. The major organ systems begin to take shape in the developing organism, which we now call the **embryo**. About three weeks into pregnancy, two ridges fold together to form the **neural tube**, from which the nervous system will develop. The head and blood vessels also begin to form at this time. By the fourth week, a primitive heart takes shape and begins beating. It will normally continue beating without a break (hopefully) for at least the next eighty or ninety years.

The embryo is suspended in a protective environment within the mother's uterus called the **amniotic sac** (see Figure 9.3). Surrounding the embryo is amniotic fluid, which acts as a kind of shock absorber to cushion the embryo and later the fetus from damage that could result from the mother's movements. Nutrients and waste materials are exchanged between the mother and embryo (and fetus) through the **placenta**, which is connected to the embryo (and fetus) by the umbilical cord. The placenta allows nutrients and oxygen to pass from mother to fetus. Their blood streams do not mix.

The **fetal stage**, or stage of the **fetus**, begins around the ninth week of pregnancy and continues until the birth of the child. All of the major organ systems, as well as the fingers and toes, are formed by about the twelfth week of prenatal development, which roughly corresponds to the end of the first trimester. They continue to develop through the course of the pregnancy. The fetus increases more than thirtyfold in weight during the second trimester of pregnancy, from about one ounce to about two pounds. It grows from about four inches in length

Figure 9.3 Structures in the Womb
During prenatal development, the embryo lies in a protective enclosure within the uterus called the amniotic sac. Nutrients and waste materials are exchanged between mother and embryo/fetus through the placenta. The umbilical cord connects the embryo and fetus to the placenta.

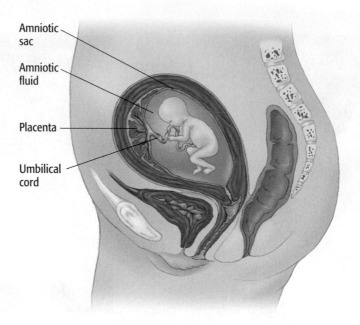

Amniotic sac

Amniotic fluid

Placenta

Umbilical cord

to about fourteen inches. Typically the mother will feel the first fetal movements around the middle of the fourth month. By the end of the second trimester, the fetus approaches the *age of viability,* the point at which it becomes capable of sustaining life on its own. However, fewer than half of infants born at the end of the second trimester weighing less than two pounds will survive on their own, even with the most intense medical treatment.

Threats to Prenatal Development

💡 **CONCEPT 9.3**
The developing fetus faces many risks, including maternal malnutrition and teratogens.

A pregnant woman requires adequate nutrition for the health of the fetus as for her own. Maternal malnutrition is associated with a greater risk of premature birth (birth prior to thirty-seven weeks of gestation) and low birth weight (less than 5 pounds, or about 2,500 grams). Preterm and low-birth-weight babies face a higher risk of infant mortality and later developmental problems, including cognitive deficits and attention difficulties (Lemons et al., 2001; Marcus et al., 2001; Peterson et al., 2000).

Women may receive prescriptions from their obstetricians for multivitamin pills to promote optimal fetal development. The federal government recommends that all women of childbearing age take four hundred micrograms daily of the B vitamin *folic acid* and that pregnant women take eight hundred micrograms (Williams, 2000). Folic acid greatly reduces the risk of neural tube defects such as **spina bifida**, but only if it is taken early in pregnancy (Brent, Oakley, & Mattison, 2000; Stevenson et al., 2000). The U.S. government also requires that certain foods (e.g., enriched bread) be fortified with folic acid ("Folic Acid," 2004).

💡 **CONCEPT 9.4**
Certain environmental influences or agents, called teratogens, may harm the developing embryo or fetus.

The word **teratogen** is derived from the Greek root *teras,* meaning "monster." Teratogens include certain drugs taken by the mother, X-rays, environmental contaminants such as lead and mercury, and infectious organisms capable of passing through the placenta to the embryo or fetus. The risks posed by teratogens are greatest during certain critical periods of development. For example, teratogens that may damage the arms and legs are most likely to have an effect during the fourth through eighth weeks of development (see Concept Chart 9.2). Let us now consider several of the more dangerous teratogens.

spina bifida A neural tube defect in which the child is born with a hole in the tube surrounding the spinal cord.

teratogen An environmental influence or agent that may harm the developing embryo or fetus.

rubella A common childhood disease that can lead to serious birth defects if contracted by the mother during pregnancy (also called *German measles*).

Infectious Diseases **Rubella** (also called *German measles*) is a common childhood disease that can lead to serious birth defects, including heart disease, deafness, and mental retardation, if contracted during pregnancy. Women exposed to

CONCEPT CHART 9.2   Critical Periods in Prenatal Development

Germinal stage	Embryonic stage					Fetal stage				Full term
Weeks 1, 2	3	4	5	6	7	8	12	16	20 – 36	38

Period of dividing zygote and implantation

Implantation of embryo

Dividing zygote

Labels indicate common sites of action of teratogen

Central nervous system — Eye — Heart — Eye — Heart — Teeth — Ear — Palette — Ear — Brain

Heart — Leg — Arm — Leg — Arm — Palette — External genitalia — External genitalia

Central nervous system

Heart

Ears

Arms

Eyes

Legs

Risk of major structural abnormalities

Risk of minor structural abnormalities

Teeth

Palate

External genitalia

Source: Adapted from Berger & Thompson, 1995.

CONCEPT 9.5
Genetic and chromosomal testing techniques can detect the presence of many fetal abnormalities.

rubella in childhood acquire immunity to the disease. Those who lack immunity may be vaccinated before becoming pregnant to protect their future offspring.

Some sexually transmitted infections, such as HIV/AIDS and syphilis, may be transmitted from mother to child during pregnancy. Fortunately, aggressive treatment of HIV-infected mothers with the antiviral drug AZT greatly reduces the risk of maternal transmission of the virus to the fetus (Mofenson & McIntyre, 2000). Children born with congenital syphilis may suffer liver damage, impaired hearing and vision, and deformities in their teeth and bones. The risk of transmission can be reduced if the infected mother is treated effectively with antibiotics prior to the fourth month of pregnancy.

Smoking   Maternal smoking can lead to miscarriage (spontaneous abortion), premature birth, low birth weight, and increased risk of infant mortality (Ebrahim et al., 2000; Haslam & Draper, 2001). The more the mother smokes, the greater the risks. Maternal smoking during pregnancy is also linked to increased risks of **sudden infant death syndrome (SIDS)** and childhood asthma, as well as developmental problems such as reduced attention span, lower IQ, and hyperactivity.

Alcohol and Drugs   Fetal alcohol syndrome **(FAS)**, which affects as many as 40,000 babies in the United States, is the leading preventable cause of mental retardation (Springen & Kantrowitz, 2004). FAS results from the mother's use of

sudden infant death syndrome (SIDS) The sudden and unexplained death of infants that usually occurs when they are asleep in their cribs.

fetal alcohol syndrome (FAS)   A syndrome caused by maternal use of alcohol during pregnancy in which the child shows developmental delays and facial deformities.

Fetal Alcohol Syndrome FAS, a leading cause of mental retardation, is characterized by facial features such as an underdeveloped upper jaw, a flattened nose, and widely spaced eyes.

alcohol during pregnancy and is associated not just with mental retardation but also with facial deformities such as a flattened nose, an underdeveloped upper jaw, and widely spaced eyes (Wood, Vinson, & Sher, 2001). Through the risk of FAS is greater in cases of heavy maternal use of alcohol during pregnancy, it is even found among children of mothers who drank as little as a drink and a half per week (Carroll, 2003). Moreover, heavy use of alcohol can also lead to miscarriage, premature delivery, or stillbirth.

Any drug used during pregnancy, whether legal or not, or any medication, whether prescribed or bought over the counter, is potentially harmful to the fetus. For example, heavy maternal use of cocaine or opiates can damage the fetal brain (Lester et al., 2003). Prenatal exposure to maternal cocaine use is also linked to problems with attention and cognitive functioning during childhood (Peterson, Burns, & Widmayer, 1995; Singer et al., 2004).

Prenatal Testing

Various methods are used to detect fetal abnormalities during prenatal development. In **amniocentesis**, generally performed between weeks sixteen and eighteen of pregnancy, a syringe is inserted into the amniotic sac and fluid containing fetal cells is extracted (Brody, 2001b). The fetal cells are cultured and then analyzed for biochemical and chromosomal abnormalities. Another technique, **chorionic villus sampling (CVS)**, may be performed several weeks earlier than amniocentesis (Kuliev et al., 1999). A small amount of tissue from the **chorion**, the membrane that holds the amniotic sac and fetus, is analyzed. Both amniocentesis and CVS can detect a wide range of fetal abnormalities, including **Down syndrome**, a chromosomal disorder that results in mental retardation and physical abnormalities. This disorder, which occurs in about one in every seven hundred live births, occurs when three chromosomes are present on the twenty-first pair of chromosomes instead of the normal two (Nelson & Gibbs, 2004). The risk of Down syndrome increases with the mother's age (see Table 9.2).

Ultrasound imaging is also used to detect fetal abnormalities. High-pitched sound waves are (harmlessly) bounced off the fetus, revealing an image of the fe-

amniocentesis A technique for diagnosing fetal abnormalities involving examination of extracted fetal cells.

chorionic villus sampling (CVS) A technique of detecting fetal abnormalities that involves examination of fetal material extracted from the chorion.

chorion The membrane that contains the amniotic sac and fetus.

Down syndrome A chromosomal disorder characterized by mental retardation and certain facial abnormalities.

ultrasound imaging A technique for using high-pitched sound waves to form an image of the fetus in the womb.

Ultrasound Image You may be able to make out the ultrasound image of the author's son Michael at twelve weeks of development. Michael's father notes that he was handsome even then!

REALITY CHECK

THE CLAIM Women may safely consume alcoholic beverages during pregnancy so long as they do so in moderation.

THE EVIDENCE Though fetal alcohol syndrome (FAS) is more likely to occur with heavy maternal drinking, there is actually no established safe limit for alcohol use in pregnancy. According to the American College of Obstetricians and Gynecologists (2000), even a few drinks every so often can put the baby at risk for fetal alcohol syndrome. Alcohol use can also damage the developing fetus in other ways.

THE TAKE-AWAY MESSAGE We do not know at what level of alcohol intake damaging effects to the fetus may occur. Lacking any recognized safe level of alcohol use during pregnancy, it is prudent for pregnant women not to drink at all.

TABLE 9.2   Risk of Giving Birth to an Infant with Down Syndrome

Age of Mother	Probability of Down Syndrome
30	1 in 885
35	1 in 365
40	1 in 109
45	1 in 32
49	1 in 11

tus and amniotic sac that can be displayed on a TV-type monitor. In addition to using these tests, parents can have their blood tested to determine whether they are carriers of genetic disorders such as sickle cell anemia or Tay-Sachs disease. Still other tests examine fetal DNA to reveal other genetic disorders. Perhaps in the future we will have the means to correct genetic defects to prevent them from being passed from generation to generation. At present, expectant couples facing this agonizing situation may rely upon genetic counselors, psychologists, and other health professionals for information and support.

MODULE 9.2 REVIEW

Prenatal Development

RECITE IT

What are the major stages of prenatal development?

- The germinal stage is the period from conception to implantation.
- The embryonic stage begins with implantation and extends to about the eighth week of development; it is characterized by differentiation of the major organ systems.
- The fetal stage begins around the ninth week and continues until birth; it is characterized by continued maturation of the fetus's organ systems and dramatic increases in size.

What are some major threats to prenatal development?

- Threats include maternal diet, maternal diseases and disorders, and use of certain medications and drugs.
- Exposure to particular teratogens causes the greatest harm during critical periods of vulnerability.

What types of tests are used to detect chromosomal and genetic defects?

- Tests include amniocentesis, chorionic villus sampling (CVS), ultrasound imaging, and parental blood tests.

RECALL IT

1. When a sperm unites with an egg, a process known as *fertilization,* the result is a single cell called a(n)
   a. zygote.
   b. blastocyst.
   c. embryo.
   d. fetus.

2. Name two major risks to the developing embryo or fetus.

3. Match the following terms to their descriptions:
   i. neural tube; ii. amniotic sac; iii. placenta; iv. germinal stage
   a. the first stage of pregnancy
   b. a protective environment
   c. the organ in which nutrients and wastes are exchanged within the uterus
   d. a structure in the developing organism from which the nervous system develops

THINK ABOUT IT

- Based on your reading of the text, what advice might you give someone about the risks posed by drinking alcohol or smoking during pregnancy?

- Would you want to know if you or your partner was at risk for carrying a genetic abnormality? Why or why not? How would such knowledge affect your decisions about having children?

MODULE 9.3

Infant Development

- ■ What reflexes do newborn babies show?
- ■ How does the infant develop physically during the first year of life?
- ■ What abilities do infants possess with respect to sensory functioning, perception, and learning?
- ■ How do the infant's motor abilities develop during the first year?

It may seem that newborns do little more than sleep and eat, but they actually come into the world with a wider range of responses than you might think. Even more remarkable are the changes that take place during development in the first two years of life. Let us enter the world of the infant and examine these remarkable changes.

Reflexes

A reflex is an unlearned, automatic response to a particular stimulus. Babies are born with a number of basic reflexes (see Figure 9.4). For example, if you lightly touch a newborn's cheek, the baby will reflexively turn its head in the direction of the tactile (touch) stimulation. This is the **rooting reflex**, which, like many basic reflexes, has important survival value. It helps the baby obtain nourishment by orienting its head toward the breast or bottle. Another reflex that has survival value is the **eyeblink reflex**, the reflexive blinking of the eyes that protects the baby from bright light or foreign objects. Another is the **sucking reflex**, the rhythmic sucking action that enables the infant to obtain nourishment from breast or bottle. It is prompted whenever an object like a nipple or a finger is placed in the mouth.

Some reflexes appear to be remnants of our evolutionary heritage that may no longer serve any adaptive function. For example, if the infant is exposed to a loud noise, or if its head falls backward, the **Moro reflex** is elicited: the infant extends its arms, arches its back, and then brings its arms toward each other as if attempting to grab hold of someone. The **palmar grasp reflex**, or curling of the fingers around an object that touches the palm, is so strong that the infant can literally be lifted by its hands. In ancestral times, these reflexes may have had survival value by preventing infants from falling as their mothers carried them around all day. The **Babinski reflex** involves fanning out and curling the toes and twisting the foot inward when the sole of the foot is stroked.

Most newborn reflexes disappear within the first six months of life. The presence and later disappearance of particular reflexes at expected periods of time are taken as signs of normal neurological development.

Physical Development and Brain Size

Maturation, the biological unfolding of an organism according to its underlying genetic blueprint, largely determines how organisms, including humans, grow and develop physically. It explains why children of tall parents tend to be tall themselves. Development also depends on environmental factors, such as nutrition (Lipsitt, 1993). Improved nutrition largely explains why children today are generally taller than children of a century ago. Children whose growth is slowed by a temporary period of malnutrition may catch up by experiencing a later growth spurt that allows them to overcome any growth deficits (Tanner, 1990). However, prolonged malnutrition, especially during the first five years, can lead to permanent

Concept 9.6
Infants enter the world with some motor reflexes that may have had survival value among ancestral humans.

rooting reflex The reflexive turning of the newborn's head in the direction of a touch on its cheek.

eyeblink reflex The reflexive blinking of the eyes that protects the newborn from bright light and foreign objects.

sucking reflex Rhythmic sucking in response to stimulation of the tongue or mouth.

Moro reflex An inborn reflex, elicited by a sudden noise or loss of support, in which the infant extends its arms, arches its back, and brings its arms toward each other as though attempting to grab hold of someone.

palmar grasp reflex The reflexive curling of the infant's fingers around an object that touches its palm.

Babinski reflex The reflexive fanning out and curling of an infant's toes and inward twisting of its foot when the sole of the foot is stroked.

maturation The biological unfolding of the organism according to the underlying genetic code.

(a) Palmar grasp reflex

(b) Rooting reflex

c) Moro reflex

Figure 9.4   Infant Reflexes
The palmar grasp reflex (a) is so strong that the infant can literally be lifted by its hands. In the rooting reflex (b), the infant turns its head in the direction of a touch to its check. In the Moro reflex (c), when the infant is exposed to a noise or loss of support, it arches its back, extends its arms outward, and then brings the arms toward each other. What survival functions might these reflexes serve?

CONCEPT 9.7

Physical development is controlled by the process of maturation, the biological unfolding of the organism according to the programmed set of instructions contained in the genes.

deficits in physical stature and brain development. As a result, many malnourished children develop mental retardation or fail to achieve normal adult size.

During the first year of life, infants on average triple their birth weight from about seven pounds to about twenty-one or twenty-two pounds. They also grow in height from about twenty inches to around thirty inches. Between birth and adulthood, the brain quadruples in volume (Johnson, 1997). Most, though not all, of the many billions of neurons in the human brain are formed before birth. The increase in brain volume during development is largely due to the formation of trillions of synaptic connections between neurons. As the infant develops, these complex linkages of neurons make learning, memory, and perceptual and motor processes possible. Brain development continues throughout childhood as the child becomes capable of more complex mental tasks, such as language use and reading (Schlaggar et al., 2002). Adding further to brain size is the formation of the fatty myelin sheath that covers axons, resulting in speedier and more efficient transmission of nerve signals. Myelination is necessary for performing skilled motor responses such as grasping objects, crawling, and, eventually, walking.

Sensory, Perceptual, and Learning Abilities in Infancy

Infants are capable of sensing a wide range of sensory stimuli and of learning simple responses and retaining them in memory.

Figure 9.5 Newborn Vision and Face Recognition
To a newborn, mother's face may appear as blurry as the photograph on the left. But a newborn can still recognize its mother's
face and shows a preference for her face over other faces.

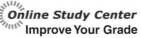
CONCEPT 9.8
Shortly after birth, the infant is able to
discern many different stimuli,
including the mother's odor, face, and
voice, as well as different tastes.

Sensory and Perceptual Ability Vision is the slowest of the senses to develop.
Infants have blurry vision at birth, but their visual world is not a complete blur.
(see Figure 9.5). They can see closer objects more clearly and can discern meaningful patterns. For example, newborns show preferences for looking at facelike
patterns over nonfacelike patterns (Gauthier & Curby, 2005; Turati, 2004). They
can even recognize their own mother's face and show a preference for looking at
her face over other faces (Raymond, 2000a).

One-month-old infants can visually track a moving object (Von Hofsten &
Rosander, 1996). Basic color vision develops by about 8 weeks, and depth perception develops by around 6 months (Raymond, 2000b). Using a *visual cliff apparatus*
consisting of a glass panel that covers an apparent sudden drop-off, Eleanor Gibson
and Richard Walk (1960) showed that most infants about 6 months or older will
hesitate and then refuse to crawl across to the deep side, indicating they have
developed depth perception (see Figure 9.6).

Newborns can hear many different types of sounds. They are particularly sensitive to sounds falling within the frequency of the human voice. In fact, they can
discern their mother's voice from other voices. Even fetuses respond more strongly

Figure 9.6 The Visual Cliff
The visual cliff apparatus consists of a
glass panel covering what appears to be a
sudden drop-off. An infant who has developed depth perception will crawl toward a
parent on the opposite end but will hesitate
and refuse to venture into the "deep" end
even if coaxed by the parent.

Online Study Center
Improve Your Grade
 Tutorials: Development Psychologists
 and Depth Perception

Figure 9.7   Infant Learning
Infants as young as 2 months can learn and remember simple responses, such as performing a kicking response that activates the movement of a crib mobile.

CONCEPT 9.9
Infants may seem to do little more than eat and sleep, but a closer look reveals they are both active learners and active perceivers of their environment.

CONCEPT 9.10
Motor development in infancy progresses rapidly through a series of steps from near immobility to coordinated running by around 18 months of age.

(show greater heart rate responses) to their mother's voice than to the voices of female strangers (Kisilevsky et al., 2003). By several months of age, infants can differentiate among various speech sounds, such as distinguishing "ba" from "ma." This ability helps prepare them for the development of language. Infants as young as 2 to 4 months can also distinguish components of music such as pitch and tempo (Begley, 2000d).

At 5 to 6 days of age, infants can detect their mother's odor (Lipsitt, 1993). Neonates can even discriminate between breast pads worn by their mothers and those worn by other women (Macfarlane, 1975). The smell of rotten eggs elicits a frown, whereas a whiff of chocolate or bananas results in a positive facial expression (Steiner, 1979). Newborns can also discriminate among different tastes and show preferences for sweetness (no surprise!) (Raymond, 2000b). They will suck faster and longer if given sweetened liquids than if given bitter, salty, or plain-water solutions.

The perceptual world of the infant is not a blooming, buzzing confusion of meaningless stimuli as people once believed. Rather, infants begin making meaningful discriminations among stimuli shortly after birth. For example, newborns are extremely sensitive to a soothing voice and to the way in which they are held.

By the age of 4 to 6 months, babies can discriminate among happy, angry, and neutral facial expressions (Pascalis, de Haan, & Nelson, 2002; Saxe, Carey, & Kanwisher, 2004). What we don't know is what, if anything, different facial expressions mean to infants. We might think, "Mom looks mad," but what infants make of Mom's expression remains open to conjecture.

Learning Ability   Infants are capable of learning simple responses and retaining memories of these learned behaviors for days or even weeks. For example, infants as young as 2 to 6 months can learn and remember a kicking response that activates a crib mobile (Rovee-Collier & Fagen, 1981) (see Figure 9.7). They can remember this response for several days at 2 months of age and for as long as several weeks at 6 months (Hartshorn & Rovee-Collier, 1997). Infants as young as 6 or 7 months can also retain memories for faces (Pascalis et al., 1998) and for the sounds of particular words one day after hearing them (Houston & Jusczyk, 2003). Learning even occurs prenatally, as shown by newborns' preference for their mother's voice and for sounds reflecting their native language (Moon, Cooper, & Fifer, 1993).

Motor Development

Newborns' motor skills are not limited to simple reflexes. They can engage in some goal-directed behaviors, such as bringing their hands to their mouths to suck their thumbs, an ability that first appears prenatally during the third trimester (Bertenthal & Clifton, 1997). Just minutes after birth, newborns can imitate their parents' facial expressions (Gopnik, 2000). Such imitative behavior may be the basis for shared communication between the infant and others. The infant and caregiver begin imitating each other's facial expressions in a kind of nonmusical duet (Trevarthen, 1995) (see Figure 9.8).

During the first three months, infants slowly begin replacing reflexive movements with voluntary, purposive movements. By the second or third month, they begin bringing objects to their mouths. By 4 or 5 months of age, infants seem to prefer bringing objects into their fields of view—to have a first look at them—before bringing them to their mouths (Rochat, 1993). By about 6 months, they can reliably grasp stationary objects and begin catching moving objects.

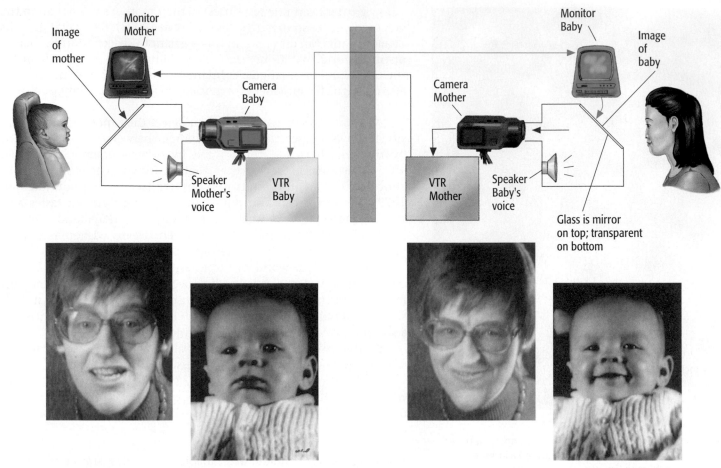

Figure 9.8   Infant Imitative Behavior
This experimental setup separates caregiver and infant but uses two cameras that allow each to see the other on a monitor. Notice how infant and caregiver imitate each other's facial expressions in a kind of nonmusical duet.

Source: Trevarthen, 1995.

Online Study Center
Improve Your Grade
Tutorials: Milestones of Motor Development

By 2 months of age, infants can lift their chins; by 5 months, they can roll over; and by 9 months, they can sit without support. By the end of the first year, infants will master the most difficult balancing problem they'll ever face in life: standing without support (Rader, 1997). Why is standing alone so difficult? A 1-year-old sways about 40 percent more while standing than does an adult; consequently the 1-year old has less time to respond to balance disturbances in order to maintain itself in an upright position. To appreciate the challenge the 1-year-old faces in attempting to stand, imagine trying to keep your balance while standing on a bridge that is constantly swaying. The development of motor skills, as outlined in Concept Chart 9.3, occurs in the same sequence among nearly all infants at about the same ages and in all cultures.

CONCEPT CHART 9.3   Milestones in Infant Development

Approximate Ages	Sensory Skills and Learning Abilities	Motor Skills
Birth to 1 month	• Has blurry vision, but sees more clearly at short distances • Can visually track a moving object • Is sensitive to sounds within range of human voice • Shows preference for mother's voice and native language sounds (develops prenatally) • Can detect mother's odor • Can discern certain pleasant or unpleasant basic odors • Shows taste preference for sweetness • Responds to a soothing voice • Can discern differences in how he/she is held • Shows preferences for facelike stimuli and responds to certain facial features	• Basic reflexes • Thumb sucking • Mimicking facial acts
2–3 months	• Can discriminate direction of a moving object • Has developed basic color vision • Can discern differences in the tempo (beat) of a pattern of sounds • Can discriminate among faces of different people • Can learn simple responses and remember them for several days (at 2 months) to several weeks (at 6 months)	• Lifts chin • Brings objects to mouth
4–6 months	• Depth perception develops • Can discern differences among certain facial expressions • Can retain memory for certain faces	• Grasp stationary objects • Catches moving objects • Brings objects into field of view • Able to roll over
7–9 months	Further development of depth perception and visual acuity	• Sits without support • Stands holding on
10–12 months	Shows improved visual acuity, to near normal vision	• Walks holding on • Stands without support

MODULE 9.3 REVIEW

Infant Development

RECITE IT

What reflexes do newborn babies show?

• Reflexes include the rooting, eyeblink, sucking, Moro, palmar grasp, and Babinski reflexes.

How does the infant develop physically during the first year of life?

• The weight of the average infant increases threefold in the first year, from about seven pounds to about twenty-one or twenty-two pounds. Height increases by about 50 percent, from around twenty inches to about thirty inches. By adulthood, the brain will have quadrupled in volume.

What abilities do infants possess with respect to sensory functioning, perception, and learning?

• The newborn can detect objects visually, despite blurry vision, and can discriminate among different sounds, odors, and tastes.

• The ability to respond to depth cues and to discern facial expressions develops within the first six months.

• Infants are also capable of learning simple responses and retaining memories of those responses.

How do the infant's motor abilities develop during the first year?

• During the first year, the infant acquires the ability to move its body, sit without support, turn over, crawl, and begin to stand and walk on its own.

RECALL IT

1. Match the following reflexes to the appropriate description: i. rooting reflex; ii. eyeblink reflex; iii. sucking reflex; iv. Moro reflex

   a. a rhythmic action that enables an infant to take in nourishment
   b. a reflex action protecting one from bright lights and foreign objects
   c. a grabbing movement, often in response to a loud noise
   d. turning in response to a touch on the cheek; helps the baby find breast or bottle

2. The process of physical growth and development as directed by the organism's genetic code is known as _____.

3. Babies seem to learn even while still in the womb. What evidence (based on the sense of hearing) do we have to support this notion?

THINK ABOUT IT

• What is the adaptive value of certain basic infant reflexes?

• Why is it incorrect to say that the world of the infant is merely a jumble of disconnected stimuli?

MODULE 9.4

Emotional and Social Development

■ **What are the three basic types of infant temperament identified in the New York Longitudinal Study, and what are the major differences among them?**

■ **What are the three types of attachment styles identified by Ainsworth?**

■ **What are the three major styles of parenting in Baumrind's model, and how do they differ?**

■ **What roles do peer relationships play in children's emotional and social development?**

■ **What are the stages of psychosocial development during childhood according to Erikson?**

Childhood is a period of wonderment, discovery, and, most of all, change. Here we examine the world of the growing child from the standpoint of its emotional and social development. Earlier we noted how infants the world over develop motor skills in the same sequence at about the same ages. But with emotional and social development, we see a wider range of expression of different behaviors, ways of relating to others, and emerging personalities in infants and young children. The influences on children's emotional and social development reflect roles for nature (genetics) and for nurture (environmental influences, including parents, peers, and the media).

In this section, we examine temperamental differences among infants, development of secure attachments, parenting styles, and peer relationships. We also introduce a key theory proposed by psychoanalyst Erik Erikson that represents a milestone in our understanding of psychosocial development. In the application section at the end of the chapter, we examine an area of concern to many parents: the influence of television viewing on children's development.

Temperament: The "How" of Behavior

Janet was talking about her two daughters, Tabitha (7) and Alicia (2½). "They're like day and night. Tabitha is the sensitive type. She's very tentative about taking chances or joining in with the other children. She can play by herself for hours.

Just give her a book to read and she's in heaven. What can I say about Alicia? Where Tabitha would sit at the top of the slide and have to be coaxed to come down, Alicia goes down head first. Most kids her age stay in the part of the playground for the toddlers, but Alicia is off running to the big climbing equipment. She even thinks she's one of the older kids and tries to join them in their games. Can you picture that? Alicia is running after a baseball with the 6- and 7-year-olds." Ask parents who have two or more children and you're likely to hear a similar refrain: "They're just different. I don't know why they're different, but they just are."

We may attempt to explain these differences in terms of the construct of **temperament**. A temperament is a characteristic style of behavior, or disposition. Some theorists refer to temperament as the "how" of behavior—the characteristic way in which behavior is performed (Chess & Thomas, 1996). One child may display a cheerful temperament in approaching new situations, whereas another may exhibit a fearful or apprehensive temperament.

The most widely used classification of temperaments is based on a study of middle-class and upper-middle-class infants from the New York City area: the New York Longitudinal Study (NYLS) (Chess & Thomas, 1996). The investigators identified three general types of temperament that could be used to classify about two out of three of the children in the study group:

1. *Easy children.* These children are playful and respond positively to new stimuli. They adapt easily to changes; display a happy, engaging mood; and are quick to develop regular sleeping and feeding schedules. About 40 percent of the NYLS children were classified in this category.

2. *Difficult children.* These children react negatively to new situations or people, have irritable dispositions, and have difficulty establishing regular sleeping and feeding schedules. About 10 percent of the group fell into this category.

3. *Slow-to-warm-up children.* These children (called "inhibited children" by others) have low activity levels; avoid novel stimuli; require more time to adjust to new situations than most children; and typically react to unfamiliar situations by becoming withdrawn, subdued, or mildly distressed. This category described about 15 percent of the group.

The remaining 35 percent of the children studied represented a mixed group who could not be easily classified.

Subsequent research has found that the three distinct types of temperament observed in infancy predict later differences in adjustment (Rothbart & Bates, 1997). The easy infant is generally better adjusted as an adult than infants with other temperaments (Chess & Thomas, 1984). The slow-to-warm-up infant is more likely to experience anxiety or depression in childhood than other infants. The difficult infant is at higher risk for developing acting-out or other problem behaviors in childhood. Of the three temperament groups, the difficult infants are most likely to develop psychiatric problems in later childhood (Kagan, 1997). However, they may also have positive qualities, such as being high-spirited and not being a "pushover."

In other recent work relating temperament to behavioral differences in childhood, investigators examined peer interactions in play situations among a sample of African American preschoolers (Mendez, Fantuzzo, & Cicchetti, 2002). Children with more adaptable or flexible temperaments interacted more effectively and cooperatively with their peers than did children with less adaptable temperaments. In another study, investigators showed that toddlers with more difficult temperaments showed more aggressive and other undesirable behaviors as preschoolers (Rubin, Burgess, & Dwyer, 2003). It is important to note, however, that this was especially the case for toddlers whose mothers were punitive and unresponsive. Toddlers with difficult temperaments whose mothers were responsive and sensitive to their needs were not aggressive as preschoolers.

CONCEPT 9.11
Many psychologists believe that children differ in their basic temperaments and that these differences are at least partially determined by genetic factors.

temperament   A characteristic style of behavior or disposition.

Temperament is also linked to other aspects of development, including early language acquisition. Investigators found that toddlers with more adaptable and easygoing temperaments showed better early language development than did those with moodier temperaments (Dixon & Smith, 2000).

Developmental psychologists believe that temperament is shaped by both nature and nurture, that is, by genetics as well as by environmental influences (Kagan, 2003; Rothbart, Ahadi, & Evans, 2000). But the question of whether it is possible to change basic temperament remains unanswered. Even if basic temperament can't be changed, however, children are better able to adapt successfully to their environment when parents, teachers, and other caregivers take their underlying temperaments into account. For example, the difficult or slow-to-warm-up child may need more time and gentle encouragement when adjusting to new situations such as beginning school, making friends, or joining in play activities with other children. Kagan (1997) found that mothers whose infants show signs of inhibited temperament but who relate to them in nurturing but not overly protective ways can help them overcome fearfulness of new experiences.

Attachment: Binding Ties

In human development, **attachment** is the enduring emotional bond that infants and older children form with their caregivers. This is not the same as **bonding**, which is the parent's tie to the infant that may form in the hours following birth. Rather, attachment develops over time during infancy. As attachment develops, infants may crawl to be near their caregivers, pull or grab at them to maintain contact, and cry and show other signs of emotional distress when separated from them, even if only momentarily.

Attachment Behaviors in Other Animal Species   Many species exhibit attachment behaviors. Baby chimpanzees, tigers, and lions will cling for dear life to their mothers' fur. The famed scientist Konrad Lorenz (1903–1989) studied imprinting in geese and other species. **Imprinting** is the formation of a strong bond of attachment to the first moving object seen after birth. A gosling (baby goose) will instinctively follow its

Online Study Center
Improve Your Grade
Tutorials: Baby's First Love Affair

💡 **CONCEPT 9.12**
Attachment behaviors are found in a wide range of species, from ducks to humans.

Attachment   Attachment behaviors are the ties that bind infants to their caregivers.

Father Goose
Goslings that had imprinted on scientist Konrad Lorenz followed him everywhere.

attachment   The enduring emotional bond that infants and older children form with their caregivers.
bonding   The process by which parents develop strong ties to their newborns, which may form in the first few hours following birth.
imprinting   The formation of a strong bond of the newborn animal to the first moving object seen after birth.

Contact Comfort   Harry Harlow showed that baby monkeys preferred contact with a "cloth mother," even though a "wire mother" fed them.

CONCEPT 9.13

Using a laboratory method for measuring attachment behavior in infants, investigators can classify infants according to their basic attachment style.

Online Study Center
Resources
   Weblinks: Forming Secure Attachments

Strange Situation   Ainsworth's method for assessing infant attachment to the mother, based on a series of brief separations and reunions with the mother in a playroom situation.

mother wherever she goes. But goslings hatched in incubators will imprint on objects that happen to be present at their birth, including humans (Lorenz was one) and even mechanical toys. The goslings that imprinted on Lorenz followed him everywhere, even to the point of ignoring adult female geese.

In landmark research, psychologists Harry and Marguerite Harlow showed that baby monkeys developed attachment behaviors to inanimate objects placed in their cages (Harlow & Harlow, 1966). Newborn rhesus monkeys were separated from their mothers within hours of birth and raised in experimental cages in which various objects served as surrogate (substitute) mothers. In one study, infant monkeys were raised in cages containing two types of surrogate mothers: a wire cylinder or a soft, terry-cloth-covered cylinder (Harlow & Zimmermann, 1959). The infants showed clear preferences for the cloth mother, even when they were fed by an apparatus containing a bottle attached to the wire mother. Contact comfort apparently was a stronger determinant of attachment than food.

Attachment in Human Infants   Psychiatrist John Bowlby (1908–1990) was among the first theorists to focus on attachment in human infants (Bowlby, 1969, 1980). To Bowlby, people have an innate predisposition to attach themselves to caregivers. However, he believed the quality of the attachment an infant forms with its parent depends on the sensitivity and quality of care the parent provides during the infant's first year of life.

Psychologist Mary Ainsworth developed a laboratory method for measuring attachment behavior, which she called the Strange Situation (see the nearby Pioneers box). In the **Strange Situation**, a child of about 12 months of age and its mother enter a playroom filled with attractive toys. The mother periodically leaves the room and returns shortly afterward. On some occasions, an unfamiliar adult is present in the room either with or without the mother. Trained observers rate the child's exploration of the room, its wariness of the stranger, and its response to the brief separations and reunions with the mother. These responses are used to determine the infant's style of attachment to its mother. The quality of the greeting the mother receives during reunions tells more about the infant's attachment than the child's behavior during separations. Using this method, Ainsworth and colleagues (Ainsworth, 1979; Ainsworth et al., 1978) noted three basic attachment styles, one characterized by secure attachments and the other two by insecure attachments:

1. *Secure type (Type B).* These infants used their mothers as a secure base for exploring the environment, periodically looking around to check on her whereabouts and limiting exploration when she was absent. They sometimes cried when the mother left but warmly greeted her and were easily soothed by her when she returned. Soon they began exploring again. About 65 to 70 percent of middle-class samples of infants were classified as having secure attachments (Seifert & Hoffnung, 2000; Thompson, 1997). Cross-cultural studies indicate that most infants show a secure pattern of attachment (Main, 1996).

2. *Insecure-avoidant type (Type A).* These infants paid little attention to the mother when she was in the room and separated easily from her to explore the environment. They showed little distress when the mother departed and ignored her when she returned. About 20 percent of the infants in the typical sample fit this type (Thompson, 1997).

3. *Insecure-resistant type (Type C).* These infants clung to the mother and were reluctant to explore the environment despite the presence of desirable toys. They showed a high level of distress when the mother departed and continued to experience some distress despite her attempts to comfort them when she returned. They also showed ambivalence or resistance toward the mother, reaching out to her to be picked up one moment and rebuffing her the next by pushing her away or twisting their bodies to get free of her. About 10 percent of the infants showed this attachment pattern.

THE PIONEERS | A Secure Base

Mary Ainsworth

Mary Salter Ainsworth (1913–1999) shared with Bowlby the view that the parent-infant relationship is crucial to the development of secure attachments. She was first introduced to attachment theory in her graduate studies at the University of Toronto just prior to World War II. In her dissertation study, she expressed one of the core ideas of attachment theory: that infants and young children need to use their parents as a "secure base" to venture into unfamiliar situations (Bretherton, 1992). Ainsworth spent several years working with John Bowlby in London, but it was in a remote Uganda village in the early 1950s where Ainsworth was first to leave her mark on attachment theory (Ainsworth, 1967).

In Uganda, Ainsworth observed how infants interacted with their mothers. Infants whose mothers were more sensitive to their babies' behavior were securely attached, whereas those with less sensitive mothers tended to be insecurely attached. From this early work, Ainsworth recognized that individual differences in attachment are linked to maternal sensitivity (Thompson, 1997). To Ainsworth, attachment behavior arises from the countless hours of interaction between infant and caregiver and is influenced by the quality of that interaction.

In later studies, researchers identified a fourth type of attachment style, labeled *Type D* for *disorganized/disoriented* attachment (Cassidy, 2003; Main & Solomon, 1990). These infants appeared to lack a consistent or organized strategy for responding to separations and reunions. They seemed confused and were unable to approach the mother directly for support even when they were very distressed.

The infant's development of secure attachments is influenced by the quality of maternal care (Posada et al., 2004). For example, infants are more likely to develop secure attachments when their mothers are high in *maternal sensitivity,* or ability to respond appropriately to the infant's needs and cues (Atkinson et al., 2000; Cummings et al., 2003; Thompson, Easterbooks, & Padilla-Walker, 2003). Investigators also find that mothers often recreate with their own children the kinds of attachment relationships they had with their mothers and caregivers during childhood (Kretchmar & Jacobvitz, 2002).

One area of debate in the field is whether attachment is best conceptualized in terms of discrete categories, such as Types A, B, C, and D, or by a dimensional approach in which attachment behaviors are represented as points on a continuum along which children vary (Fraley & Spieker, 2003b; Sroufe, 2003). For example, attachment styles may be better represented in terms of young children's relative degree of insecurity or avoidance in relating to their mothers than by categorizing children into particular attachment types (Cummings, 2003). Early evidence supports the dimensional view of attachment styles (e.g., Fraley & Spieker, 2003a), but it's still too early to tell whether this approach will come to replace the Ainsworth typology.

The Ainsworth method may not be appropriate for assessing attachment behaviors in children from cultures with different child-rearing practices. For example, Japanese cultural practices emphasize mother-infant closeness and interdependence, which may make it more difficult for these infants to manage brief separations from their mothers (Takahashi, 1990). More broadly, we need to recognize that substantial variations exist in attachment behavior across cultures (Rothbaum et al., 2000). For example, Americans place a greater emphasis on exploration and independence in young children than do the Japanese.

CONCEPT 9.14
Attachment patterns formed in infancy may set the stage for attachment styles in adolescence and adulthood.

CONCEPT 9.15
A more securely attached infant is likely to be better adjusted in childhood and adolescence than a less securely attached infant.

CONCEPT 9.16
The quality of parenting is an important influence on children's intellectual, emotional, and social development.

Attachment and Later Development Attachment behaviors do not end in infancy; they affect development throughout life. Attachment behaviors span the first love relationships in adolescence, marital and loving relationships and long-term friendships in adulthood, and bonds formed between friends in the retirement years (Crowell, Treboux, & Waters, 2002; Field, 1996). A lack of solid attachments in adult life is linked to poorer physical and emotional health (Baumeister & Leary, 1995; Goodwin, 2003). Longitudinal studies generally find a correspondence between the attachment styles shown in infancy and those shown in later development (Main, 1996).

Bowlby believed that attachment patterns formed in infancy are carried forward into childhood and adult life in the form of generalized expectancies about how others are likely to respond in close relationships. These expectancies, called **internal working models**, become a guide for future relationships through childhood, adolescence, and adulthood. Children who form secure attachments in infancy will develop an internal working model of others as basically dependable and trustworthy and of themselves as deserving of love and capable of developing caring relationships. Those with insecure attachments may have difficulty trusting others in close relationships or expecting others to meet their needs.

The more securely attached infant is also likely to be better adjusted in childhood and adolescence than the less securely attached infant (Belsky & Cassidy, 1994; Scarr & Eisenberg, 1993). For example, the more securely attached infant is likely to have higher self-esteem (degree of liking for oneself), to show greater cooperativeness and independence, to have fewer problem behaviors (such as aggressiveness or withdrawal), to have better relationships with peers and teachers, and to exhibit better overall emotional health (Schneider, Atkinson, & Tardif, 2001; Thompson, Easterbrooks, & Padilla-Walker, 2003).

We also have learned that mothers with more secure attachment styles typically have infants who develop more secure attachments (Benoit & Parker, 1994; van Ijzendoorn, 1995). Fathers' attachment styles tend to be less strongly related to the security of attachments formed with their infants, perhaps because fathers tend to spend less time with infants than mothers do. Before we move on, you may want to review the differences in infant temperaments and attachment styles as shown in Concept Chart 9.4.

Child-Rearing Influences

Many factors influence a child's intellectual, emotional, and social development, including genetics, peer group influences, and the quality of parenting (Brazelton & Greenspan, 2000; Li, 2003; Vandell, 1999). Good parenting encompasses many behaviors, including spending time with children (plenty of time!), modeling appropriate behaviors, helping children acquire skills to develop healthy peer relationships, stating rules clearly, setting limits, being consistent in correcting inappropriate behavior and praising good behavior, and providing a warm, secure environment. Explaining to children how their behavior affects others can also help them develop more appropriate social behaviors (P. M. Kaplan, 2000a). Children whose parents use discipline inconsistently, rely on harsh punishment, and are highly critical are more likely than others to develop problem behaviors at home and school and less likely to develop healthy peer relationships (Baumrind, Larzelere, & Cowan, 2002; Kilgore, Snyder, & Lentz, 2000).

Father's Influence Though much research on parent-child relationships has focused on children and their mothers, we shouldn't lose sight of the importance of fathers in child development. Children whose fathers share meals with them, spend leisure time with them, and assist them with schoolwork tend to perform better academically than those with less engaged fathers (Cooksey & Fondell, 1996). Researchers also find that children in two-parent, mother-father house-

internal working models Generalized expectations, developed in early childhood, about how others are likely to respond in close relationships.

CONCEPT CHART 9.4 Differences in Temperaments and Attachment Styles

	Source	Major Types	General Characteristics
Temperaments	New York Longitudinal Study	Easy child	Playful; shows interest in new situations or novel stimuli; quickly develops regular sleeping and eating patterns
		Difficult child	Irritable; has difficulty adjusting to new situations or people and establishing regular sleeping and feeding schedules
		Slow-to-warm-up child	Shows low activity levels; becomes inhibited, withdrawn, or fretful when exposed to new situations
Attachment styles	Ainsworth's research using the Strange Situation	Secure type (Type B)	Uses mother as a secure base to explore the environment while frequently checking on her whereabouts; may cry when mother leaves, but quickly settles down and warms up to her when she returns and then begins exploring again
		Insecure-avoidant type (Type A)	Pays little attention to mother when she is present and shows little distress when she leaves
		Insecure-resistant type (Type C)	Clings to mother, avoiding venturing into unfamiliar situations; becomes very upset when mother leaves and fails to be comforted completely when she returns; shows some ambivalence or resistance toward mother
		Disorganized/disoriented type (Type D, from later research)	Lacks a consistent or organized strategy for responding to separations and reunions; seems confused and unable to approach mother directly for support even when very distressed

holds tend to fare better academically and socially than those in mother-partner or single-mother households, even after accounting for differences in income levels (Thomson, Hanson, & McLanahan, 1994).

Mothers and fathers tend to differ in their parenting behavior. Fathers are more likely than mothers to encourage children to be independent and assertive and to take risks (Fitzgerald et al., 2003). Compared to mothers, fathers typically provide less basic care (changing, feeding, bathing, etc.) but engage in more physically active play with their children (Parke & Buriel, 1997). For example, a father might zoom the baby in the air ("play airplane"), whereas a mother might engage in more physically restrained games like peek-a-boo and talk and sing soothingly to the infant (Berger, 1998). However, greater physical play with fathers is not characteristic of all cultures. In Chinese, Malaysian, and Indian cultures, for example, fathers and mothers rarely engage in physical play with their children (Parke & Buriel, 1997).

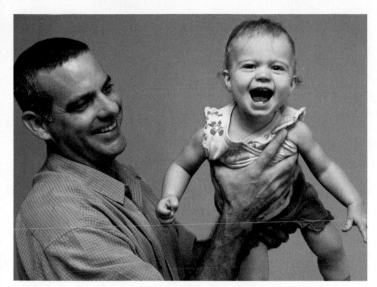

Dads Make A Difference   What does research evidence teach us about the influence of fathers on children's development? How do mothers and fathers tend to differ in their parenting behavior?

Taking Responsibility   In some cultures, children are expected to perform responsible roles needed to ensure the survival of the family and community.

Online Study Center
Resources
Weblinks: Parenthood

Cultural Differences in Parenting   Cultural learning has a strong bearing on child rearing, leading to variations across cultures in the ways that children are raised. African American families, for example, tend to have strong kinship bonds and to distribute childcare responsibilities among different family members (Nevid, Rathus, & Greene, 2006). The grandmother in such families often assumes direct parenting responsibilities and is often referred to as "mother." In traditional Hispanic families, the father is expected to be the provider and protector of the female, whereas the mother assumes full responsibility for childcare (De La Cancela & Guzman, 1991). These traditional gender roles are changing, however, as more Hispanic women are entering the work force and pursuing advanced educational opportunities. Hispanic families also tend to adopt strict disciplinary standards and to place a high value on children's development of a proper demeanor and respect toward adults (P. M. Kaplan, 2000a). Likewise, Asian cultures emphasize respect for parental authority, especially the father's, and warm maternal relationships (Berk, 2000; Nevid & Sta. Maria, 1999). All cultures help children move from a state of complete dependency in infancy toward assuming more responsibility for their own behavior. However, they vary in the degree to which they promote early independence in children and expect them to assume responsible roles within the family and community.

CONCEPT 9.17
Diana Baumrind identified three different parenting styles: authoritative, authoritarian, and permissive.

Parenting Styles   An important investigation into parenting influences on children's development focuses on differences in parenting styles. Diana Baumrind, a leading researcher in this area, identified three basic parenting styles: authoritative, authoritarian, and permissive (Baumrind, 1971, 1991):

1. *Authoritative style.* Authoritative parents set reasonable limits for their children but are not overcontrolling. The parent is the authority figure, firm but understanding, willing to give advice, but also willing to listen to children's concerns. Parents explain the reasons for their decisions rather than just "laying down the law." To Baumrind, authoritative parenting is the most successful parenting style. Evidence shows that children of authoritative parents tend to achieve the most positive outcomes in childhood and adolescence (Baumrind, 1971, 1991). They tend to have high self-esteem and to be popular with peers, self-reliant, and competent (Parke & Buriel, 1997). The flexible but firm child-

TABLE 9.3 Keys to Becoming an Authoritative Parent

Authoritative parents set firm limits but take the time to explain their decisions and to listen to their children's point of view. They also help children develop a sense of competence by setting reasonable demands for mature behavior. Here are suggestions for becoming an authoritative parent:

- *Rely on reason, not force.* Explain the rules, but keep explanations brief. When the child throws food against the wall, you can say, "We don't do that. That makes a mess, and I'll have to clean it up."

- *Show warmth.* Children's self-esteem is molded by how others, especially their parents, relate to them. Express your feelings verbally by using praise and physically by means of hugs, kisses, and holding hands when walking together. Praise the child for accomplishing tasks, even small ones.

- *Listen to your children's opinions.* Encourage the child to express his or her opinions and feelings, but explain why it is important to follow the rules.

- *Set mature but reasonable expectations.* Encourage children to adopt more mature behaviors in line with their developmental level. If a child requires assistance, demonstrate how to perform the expected behavior, and give the child encouragement and feedback when he or she attempts it independently.

rearing approach of authoritative parents encourages children to be independent and assertive but also respectful of the needs of others. Table 9.3 outlines some key steps in becoming an authoritative parent.

2. *Authoritarian style.* Authoritarian parents are rigid and overcontrolling. They expect and demand unquestioned obedience from their children. If children dare to ask why they are being told to do something, the answer is likely to be "Because I say so." Authoritarian parents are unresponsive to their children's needs and rely on harsh forms of discipline while allowing their children little control over their lives. Children of authoritarian parents tend to be inhibited, moody, withdrawn, fearful, and distrustful of others. The most negative outcomes in adolescence are found in boys with authoritarian parents. They typically perform poorly in school; lack initiative and self-confidence; and tend to be conflicted, unhappy, and unfriendly toward peers (Baumrind, 1991; Olson, Bates, & Kaskie, 1992).

3. *Permissive style.* Permissive parents have an "anything goes" attitude toward raising their children. They may respond affectionately to children but are extremely lax in setting limits and imposing discipline. Children with permissive parents tend to be impulsive and lacking in self-control. They lack the experience of conforming to other people's demands, which is important in developing effective interpersonal skills (Parke & Buriel, 1997).

Table 9.4 summarizes these three parenting styles. However, we need to take sociocultural realities into account when applying Baumrind's parenting styles. It may be unfair or misleading to apply the same categories in classifying parenting styles in other cultures that have different child-rearing traditions. For example, some cultures emphasize authoritarian styles of parenting more than others do. Within our own society, authoritarian styles in lower socioeconomic status (SES) families may represent a type of adaptation to stresses that families in poorer, more dangerous neighborhoods might face, such as heightened risks of violence and drug abuse. In these circumstances, it may be an adaptive strategy for parents to enforce stricter obedience and to set stricter limits to protect children from outside threats (Parke, 2004). Parents in poorer families may also relate warmly to their children but become frustrated in the parenting role because they lack the psychological and economic resources needed to meet the many challenges they face (Weis, 2002).

We should also recognize that while parenting styles may affect children's adjustment, children's behaviors may influence how their parents relate to them.

TABLE 9.4   Baumrind's Styles of Parenting

	Authoritative Style	Authoritarian Style	Permissive Style
Limit setting	High	High	Low
Style of discipline	Reasonable	Forceful	Lax
Maturity expectations	High	High	Low
Communications with children	High	Low	Moderate
Warmth and support	High	Low	High

In other words, both parent-to-child and child-to-parent effects need to be considered (Kerr et al., 2003).

Peer Relationships

CONCEPT 9.18

Peer relationships provide opportunities for children to develop social competencies and establish feelings of closeness and loyalty that can serve as the basis for later relationships.

As children venture into the world, the relationships they form with peers affect many aspects of their development (McCrae et al., 2000). Peer relationships provide the child with opportunities to develop socially competent behaviors in relating to others outside the family and as a member of a group. The acceptance and approval of peer group members help shape the child's developing self-esteem and sense of competence.

Friendships provide opportunities for children to learn prosocial behaviors such as sharing, cooperating, and resolving conflicts. Children with friends tend to have higher self-esteem and are perceived by others as more sensitive and caring (Vaughn et al., 2000). On the other hand, peer-rejected kindergartners tend to feel lonelier, more often want to avoid school, and do more poorly on achievement measures than their more accepted peers (Buhs & Ladd, 2001). Older peer-rejected children tend to show higher levels of antisocial behavior, such as aggressiveness or social withdrawal (Rodkin et al., 2000). Having friends can also help protect children from physical or verbal abuse from other children (Schwartz et al., 2000). Friends may become allies or help defend children from bullies (Hodges et al., 1999).

Peer relationships can also have negative consequences. Children and adolescents have a strong need for peer acceptance and may be influenced by peers to engage in deviant activities they might never attempt on their own.

Erikson's Stages of Psychosocial Development

CONCEPT 9.19

Erik Erikson described four stages of psychosocial development in childhood, each characterized by a particular life crisis or challenge: trust versus mistrust, autonomy versus shame and doubt, initiative versus guilt, and industry versus inferiority.

Erik Erikson (1902–1994), a prominent psychodynamic theorist, emphasized the importance of social relationships in human development (Erikson, 1963). In his view, psychosocial development progresses through a series of stages that begin in early childhood and continue through adulthood. He believed our personalities are shaped by how we deal with a series of psychosocial crises or challenges during these stages. In this section, we focus on the four stages of psychosocial development that occur during childhood.

Trust Versus Mistrust   The first psychosocial challenge the infant faces is the development of a sense of trust toward its social environment. When parents treat the infant warmly and are responsive to its needs, a sense of trust develops. But if the parents are seldom there when the infant needs them, or if they are detached or respond coldly, the infant develops a basic mistrust of others. The world may seem a cold and threatening place.

Autonomy Versus Shame and Doubt   Erikson believed that the central psychosocial challenge faced during the second and third years of life concerns autonomy. The child is now becoming mobile within the home and is "getting into everything." Parents may warmly encourage the child toward greater independence and nurture this newly developed sense of autonomy. However, if they demand too much too soon or make excessive demands that the child cannot meet (such as in the area of toilet training), the child may become riddled with feelings of self-doubt and shame that come to pervade later development, even into adulthood.

Initiative Versus Guilt   This stage, corresponding to the preschool years of 3 to 6, is a time of climbing gyms and play dates, a time at which the child is challenged to initiate actions and carry them out. Children who largely succeed in their efforts and are praised for their accomplishments will come to develop a sense of initiative and competence. In contrast, children who frequently fail to accomplish tasks and can't seem to "get things right" may develop feelings of guilt and powerlessness, especially if they are ridiculed or harshly criticized for their awkwardness or missteps.

Developing Self-Confidence   Erikson believed that children of 6 to 12 years of age face the central challenge of developing industriousness and self-confidence. Performing competently in the classroom and the playing field enhances their self-confidence and willingness to apply themselves.

Industry Versus Inferiority   At this stage, which corresponds to the elementary school period of 6 to 12 years, the child faces the central challenge of developing industriousness and self-confidence. If children believe they perform competently in the classroom and on the playing field, they will likely become industrious by taking an active role in school and extracurricular activities. But if the pendulum swings too far in the other direction and failure outweighs success, feelings of inadequacy or inferiority may develop, causing the child to become withdrawn and unmotivated.

Table 9.5 provides an overview of Erikson's stages of psychosocial development in childhood. Though Erikson believed that childhood experiences can

TABLE 9.5   Erik Erikson's Stages of Psychosocial Development in Childhood

Approximate Ages	Life Crisis	Major Challenge in Psychosocial Development
Infancy (birth to 1 year)	Trust versus mistrust	Developing a basic sense of trust in the caregiver and the environment
Toddlerhood (1 to 3 years)	Autonomy versus shame and doubt	Building a sense of independence and self-control
Preschool period (3 to 6 years)	Initiative versus guilt	Learning to initiate actions and carry them out
Elementary school period (6 to 12 years)	Industry versus inferiority	Becoming productive and involved

Source: Adapted from Erikson, 1963.

have lasting effects on the individual's psychological development, he emphasized that later experiences in life may counter these earlier influences and lead eventually to more successful resolutions of these life challenges.

EXPLORING PSYCHOLOGY
Does Day Care Affect Attachment?

CONCEPT 9.20

Evidence shows that placing infants in day care does not prevent the development of secure attachments to their mothers.

Today, there are more mothers of preschool children employed in the labor force than there are stay-at-home moms (Lewin, 2001) (see Figure 9.9). Also, more children under 5 are cared for during the day in organized day-care centers than in their own homes or their relatives' homes (Greenberg & Springen, 2000). Might infants who are placed in day-care centers become less attached to their mothers than those of stay-at-home mothers? The answer, investigators tell us, is no. A number of studies find no harmful effects of day care on the strength or security of infant-mother attachments (NICHD Early Child Care Research Network, 1997; Sandlin-Sniffen, 2000).

Actually, evidence points to some benefits of high-quality day care. High-quality center-based day care has positive effects on cognitive and social development because it fosters independence, language development, and cooperative play (Greenberg & Springen, 2000; Marshall, 2004; McNamar, 2004). Not surprisingly, children show greater cognitive growth when caregivers are responsive and sensitive to their needs (Loeb et al., 2004). That said, a recent study showed that kindergartners who had spent long hours in day care were more aggressive, on the average, than their peers (Stolberg, 2001a). The causes for the link remain under study, but investigators suspect that a lack of high-quality day care may be to blame (J. M. Love, as cited in Gilbert, 2003).

Professionals recognize that the quality of day care makes a difference in the infant's emotional and cognitive development. But choosing a childcare center is no easy task. Since licensing regulations and standards vary widely, parents need to weigh the alternatives carefully. Here are some questions parents might ask in evaluating the quality of day-care centers:

- *General Questions.* Is the center licensed? By whom? How long has it been providing care? Does it carry liability insurance? How does it handle emergencies? What is the ratio of childcare workers to children? Can the center provide a list

Figure 9.9   Working Mothers
The percentage of mothers of preschool children in the labor force has been rising steadily.

Source: Adapted from Lewin, 2001.

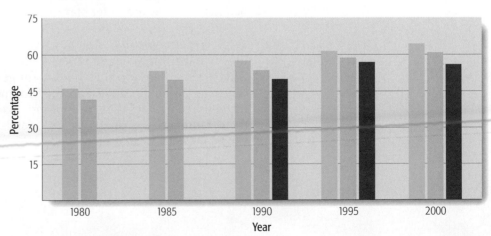

Working mothers with children under the age of

■ 6   ■ 3   ■ 1*

*Data not available before 1990.

Does Day Care Affect Attachment Behaviors? Evidence from carefully conducted studies showed that day care did not affect the strength or security of infant-mother attachments. What are some of the questions parents need to ask when selecting a day-care center?

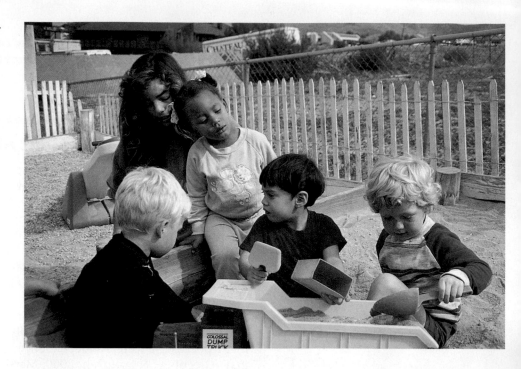

of references? What is its illness policy? Are its fees reasonable for the area and services it provides? Are the hours suitable to your needs? Does the center encourage parents to stop by to visit at almost any time?

- *Questions About the Facility.* Is the facility clean and cheerful? Is it safe for young children (covered outlets, no dangerous objects within reach, gates at the top and bottoms of stairs, no furniture with sharp corners, window guards on all windows, etc.)? Is there sufficient play space? Are the toys and equipment in good condition? Is the food nutritious and appealing? Are there separate cribs and sheets for each child? Are there ample supplies of diapers and other baby supplies? Do infants have opportunities to crawl about and explore safely? Are there toys, games, books, and structured activities that would engage your child's interest? Are there secure outside facilities? Is climbing equipment available to help promote motor development? Are children well supervised when using play equipment and walking up and down stairs? Does the schedule allow periods of active and quiet play? Is there a quiet area for napping?

- *Questions About the Staff.* Are they warm and responsive to the child's needs? Do they avoid using harsh commands or reprimands? Do they interact verbally with the children? Do they hold them gently? Do they encourage children toward exploration, creativity, and development of language skills? Do they engage the children in ways that are appropriate to their developmental levels? What is their training background and experience? Do they seem to enjoy their work? What is the turnover rate?

MODULE 9.4 REVIEW

Emotional and Social Development

RECITE IT

What are the three basic types of infant temperament identified in the New York Longitudinal Study, and what are the major differences among them?

- The three types are the easy child, the difficult child, and the slow-to-warm-up child.

- Easy children have generally positive moods, react well to changes, and quickly develop regular feeding and sleep schedules.

- Difficult children have largely negative moods and have difficulty reacting to new situations and people and developing regular feeding and sleep schedules.

- Slow-to-warm-up children tend to become withdrawn when facing new situations and experience mild levels of distress.

What are the three types of attachment styles identified by Ainsworth?

- The secure type of infant attaches to the mother and uses her as a secure base to explore the environment.

- The insecure-avoidant type freely explores the environment but tends to ignore the mother.

- The insecure-resistant type clings excessively to the mother but shows ambivalence or resistance toward her.

- Securely attached infants tend to show better social and emotional adjustment in later development than insecurely attached infants.

What are the three major styles of parenting in Baumrind's model, and how do they differ?

- Authoritative parenting involves setting maturity expectations, using reasoning, and setting firm limits.

- Authoritarian parenting also involves setting firm limits but is overly controlling and relies on harsh styles of discipline.

- Permissive parenting involves an "anything goes" style characterized by a lax approach to limit setting.

- Authoritative parenting is generally associated with better emotional and social adjustment in children than the other parenting styles.

What roles do peer relationships play in children's emotional and social development?

- Peers are important influences on children's psychosocial adjustment, especially on self-esteem and development of social competencies.

- Peer relationships may also set the stage for deviant behavior.

What are the stages of psychosocial development during childhood according to Erikson?

- Erikson's stages are (1) the stage of trust versus mistrust (birth to 1 year), (2) the stage of autonomy versus shame and doubt (ages 1 to 3), (3) the stage of initiative versus guilt (ages 3 to 6), and (4) the stage of industry versus inferiority (ages 6 to 12).

RECALL IT

1. Researchers identify three basic infant temperament types: easy children, difficult children, and _____-to-warm-up children.

2. Match the following types of attachment identified by Ainsworth and other researchers to the appropriate descriptions below: i. secure; ii. insecure-avoidant; iii. insecure-resistant; iv. disorganized/disoriented

   a. child clings to mother, yet shows signs of ambivalence or negativity
   b. mother is an important "base" for exploration; child is happy in mother's presence
   c. child appears confused; seems unable to utilize mother for any support
   d. child ignores mother when she is present and is unaffected by her departure or return

3. Parenting style is an important influence on children's development. Which of the following terms describes a parent who is warm, supportive, and consistent; understands the child's point of view; and communicates well?
   a. permissive
   b. authoritarian
   c. authoritative
   d. laissez-faire

4. In which of the following stages in Erikson's theory of psychosocial development do children compare their abilities to those of their friends and classmates?
   a. trust versus mistrust
   b. autonomy versus shame and doubt
   c. initiative versus guilt
   d. industry versus inferiority

THINK ABOUT IT

- Based on your reading of Baumrind's work on parent-child relationships, what do you think you need to do to become a better parent now or in the future?

- Think of a child or young adult you know well. How do Erikson's stages of psychosocial development relate to this person's development in childhood? Which outcomes (trust versus mistrust, autonomy versus shame and doubt, initiative versus guilt, and industry versus inferiority) best describe the person's psychosocial development?

MODULE 9.5

Cognitive Development

- How do assimilation and accommodation differ?
- What are the major features associated with Piaget's stages of cognitive development?
- What is the basic theme in Vygotsky's theory of cognitive development?

Seven-year-old Jason is upset with his younger brother Scott, age 3. Scott just can't seem to get the basic idea of hide-and-go-seek. Every time Scott goes off to hide, he curls up in the corner of the room in plain sight of Jason. "You're supposed to hide where I can't see you," Jason complains. So Scott goes off and hides in the same spot, but now he covers his eyes. "Now you can't see me," he calls back to Jason. Though they live in the same home and share many family outings together, the world of a 3-year-old like Scott is very different from that of a 7-year-old like Jason. Let's consider how different by examining the changes in the way children think and reason as they progress through childhood. We begin with the work of the most influential theorist on cognitive development, Jean Piaget.

Piaget's Theory of Cognitive Development

CONCEPT 9.21

To Piaget, a schema is an action strategy or a mental representation that helps people understand and interact with the world.

Jean Piaget (1896–1980) is arguably the most important developmental theorist of all time—a "giant with a giant theory," to borrow a phrase from the social historian Morton Hunt (1993) (see the nearby Pioneers box). Piaget believed the best way to understand how children think is to observe them closely as they interact with objects and solve problems. In attempting to understand how children think, Piaget was less concerned with whether children answered questions correctly

---

THE PIONEERS | A Pattern of Errors

Jean Piaget

It would have been difficult to predict that Jean Piaget would become one of the world's leading psychologists, at least from his early years. He certainly was bright enough: he published his first professional paper when only 10 years old and was an authority on mollusks and the author of almost two dozen papers while still in his teens. But he was primarily a naturalist with a strong interest in philosophy. He received a Ph.D. in natural history when he was 22, never having taken a formal course in psychology.

Piaget's first opportunity to study children came about through a chance meeting with Theodore Simon, a former associate of the late Alfred Binet, the originator of the modern intelligence test (see Chapter 7). Simon offered Piaget a job administering intelligence tests to develop more useful norms. At first, the task bored Piaget. But then he began to notice a consistent pattern of errors in the children's thinking: the children confused part-whole relationships, and they were unable to classify objects correctly. That intrigued Piaget. Could it be that what he thought were errors were really qualitative differences in the way children think?

In a few years Piaget's own three children were born, and he studied them intensely. His children showed the same patterns of thinking he had observed earlier. Before long, Piaget had developed the most comprehensive theory of intellectual development ever proposed, a qualitative approach that revolutionized the way we think about children. Today his contributions are considered among the most important in all of psychology.

—John Hogan

than with the reasoning children used to arrive at their answers (Feldman, 2003). Much of his work was based on his observations of his own three children.

To understand Piaget's theory of cognitive development, we must look at what he means by the term *schema*. To Piaget, a **schema** is an organized system of actions or a mental representation that people use to understand the world and interact with it (Piaget, 1952). The child is born with simple schemas comprising basic reflexes such as sucking. This schema obviously has adaptive value, since the infant needs to obtain nourishment from its mother's breast or the bottle by sucking.

Eventually the infant discovers that the schema works more effectively for some objects than for others. For my daughter Daniella, the sucking schema crashed the day we introduced her to an infant cup. Her dad demonstrated how to tip the cup at an angle to draw the liquid into the mouth. Daniella was unimpressed and continued to hold the cup upright and suck on its lip, which unhappily failed to produce the desired result.

Eventually schemas change as the child adapts to new challenges and demands. According to Piaget, **adaptation** is a process by which people adapt or change to meet challenges in the environment more effectively. Through adaptation, we adjust our schemas to meet the changing demands the environment imposes on us. Adaptation, in turn, consists of two complementary processes: *assimilation* and *accommodation*.

Assimilation is the process of incorporating new objects or situations into existing schemas. For example, newborns will reflexively suck any object placed in their mouths, such as a finger or even a piece of cloth. Daniella applied her sucking schema to an infant cup by attempting to suck on its lip. Older children develop classification schemas, which consist of mental representations of particular classes of objects. When Daniella was a toddler, she applied her "dog schema" to any nonhuman animal, including cats, horses, sheep, and even fish. To her, all were "bow-wows."

Assimilation is adaptive when new objects fit existing schemas, as when the infant sucks on the nipple of a baby bottle for the first time rather than the mother's breast. But horses and fish are not dogs, and infant cups cannot be sucked to draw liquid into the mouth. **Accommodation** is the process of altering existing schemas or creating new ones to deal with objects or experiences that don't fit readily into existing schemas. Eventually Daniella developed a new "tipping schema" for using an infant cup: tipping it in her mouth so the contents would drip in.

Stages of Cognitive Development   In Piaget's view, the processes of assimilation and accommodation are ongoing throughout life. However, he held that the child's cognitive development progresses through a series of stages that occur in an ordered sequence at about the same ages in all children. Children at the different stages of cognitive development differ in how they view and interact with the world. Here we take a closer look at Piaget's four stages of cognitive development: the sensorimotor, preoperational, concrete operational, and formal operational stages.

Sensorimotor Stage: Birth to 2 Years   The sensorimotor stage spans a period of momentous growth in the infant's cognitive development. During this stage, which actually consists of six substages, the child becomes increasingly capable of performing more complex behaviors and skills. Piaget used the term *sensorimotor* because the infant explores its world by using its senses and applying its developing motor skills (body movement and hand control). The infant's intelligence is expressed through action and purposeful manipulation of objects.

At birth through 1 month, the infant's behaviors are limited to inborn reflexes, such as grasping and sucking. From months 1 through 8, the infant gains increasing voluntary control over some of its movements, such as grasping objects placed above its crib. The infant is now beginning to act on the world and to repeat actions that have interesting effects, such as repeatedly squeezing a rubber

---

CONCEPT 9.22
In Piaget's view, adaptation to the environment consists of two complementary processes, assimilation and accommodation.

Online Study Center
Improve Your Grade
    Tutorials: Piaget's Stages of
    Cognitive Development

CONCEPT 9.23
Piaget proposed that children progress at about the same ages through a series of four stages of cognitive development: the sensorimotor, preoperational, concrete operational, and formal operational stages.

schema   In Piaget's theory, a mental framework for understanding or acting on the environment.

adaptation   In Piaget's theory, the process of adjustment that enables people to function more effectively in meeting the demands they face in the environment.

assimilation   In Piaget's theory, the process of incorporating new objects or situations into existing schemas.

accommodation   In Piaget's theory, the process of creating new schemas or modifying existing ones to account for new objects or experiences.

Object Permanence Infants who have not yet developed object permanence act as though objects that have disappeared from sight no longer exist.

duck to produce a squealing sound. By 8 to 12 months, the infant's actions are intended to reach a particular goal. The child will perform purposeful actions such as crawling to the other side of the room to open the bottom drawers of cabinets where toys are kept.

Early in the sensorimotor stage, infants are aware of an object's existence only if it is physically present. Out of sight is, quite literally, out of mind. If you block a 4-month-old's view of an object that he or she has been looking at, the child will immediately lose interest and begin looking at other objects. By about 8 months, the child will begin looking for a hidden object. Now, if you place a pillow over a teddy bear, she or he will push the pillow out of the way to get the toy. By this age, the child has begun to develop a concept of **object permanence**, or the recognition that objects continue to exist even if they have disappeared from sight (Cohen & Cashon, 2003).

Piaget believed that object permanence is not yet complete at this point. It reaches a mature level toward the end of the sensorimotor stage when the child begins to acquire the ability to form a mental representation of an object that is not visibly present. One sign that 22-month-old Daniella had acquired object permanence was that she began asking for her brother Michael upon awakening. She apparently was able to retain a mental representation of Michael. Her parents tried not to take it personally that she always asked for Michael first.

Preoperational Stage: 2 to 7 Years Piaget used the term *preoperational* to describe the cognitive abilities of children roughly ages 2 to 7 years because they lacked the ability to perform basic logical operations—to apply basic principles of logic to their experiences. During this period, however, extraordinary growth occurs in the ability to form mental or **symbolic representations** of the world, especially with the use of language. Specifically, a child forms symbolic representations of objects and experiences by naming or describing them in words. Language makes the child's thinking processes far more expansive and efficient than was possible in the sensorimotor stage.

Another form of representational thinking is make-believe or pretend play. In pretend play, children form mental representations that allow them to enact scenes with characters that are not physically present. Pretend play becomes increasingly complex as children progress through the preoperational stage. By age 5 or 6, children are creating scenes with imagined characters or reenacting scenes they have seen on TV or in movies.

object permanence The recognition that objects continue to exist even if they have disappeared from sight.

symbolic representations Symbols that stand for names and experiences; specifically, the words in a language.

TRY THIS OUT

Learning Through Observation

You may be able to acquire more direct knowledge of children's cognitive development by serving as a volunteer in a nursery or preschool setting. To what extent does the cognitive development of preschoolers correspond to Piaget's concepts of egocentrism, animistic thought, centration, and irreversibility?

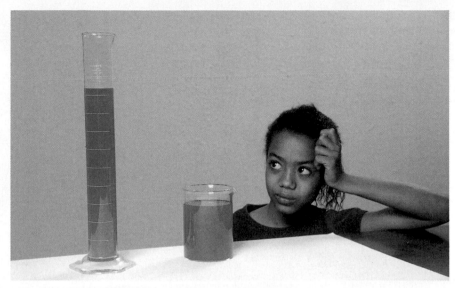

Which Beaker Holds More Juice? Preoperational children fail to recognize that the quantity of an object remains the same when placed in a different-size container.

Though cognitive abilities expand dramatically during the preoperational stage, Piaget noted that the child's thinking processes are still quite limited. For example, the preoperational child demonstrates **egocentrism**, the tendency to view the world only from one's own point of view. Egocentric thinking doesn't mean the child is selfish or unconcerned about others; rather, the child at this stage lacks the cognitive ability to take another person's point of view or perspective. In the child's mind, he or she is the center of the universe. For example, 5-year-old Michelle wants to play with Mommy but doesn't understand that Mommy is tired and needs to rest. When Michelle feels like playing, she thinks Mommy should feel like playing too. In our earlier example, 3-year-old Scott is unable to take his brother's perspective when playing hide-and-go-seek. He doesn't realize that his hiding place is in plain view of his brother. He also assumes that since he can't see his brother when he covers his own eyes, his brother can't see him either.

Egocentrism leads to another type of thinking typical of the preoperational child: **animistic thinking**. The child believes that inanimate objects like the moon, the sun, and the clouds have living qualities such as wishes, thoughts, and feelings just as she or he does. A 4-year-old, for instance, may think the moon is his friend and follows him as he walks home with his parents at night.

Two other limitations of the preoperational child's thinking are irreversibility and centration. **Irreversibility** is the inability to reverse the direction of a sequence of events to their starting point. **Centration** is the tendency to focus on only one aspect of a situation at a time to the exclusion of all other aspects.

Piaget illustrated these principles through his famous **conservation** tasks (see Figure 9.10). (Conservation, the hallmark of the concrete operational stage, is discussed in the next section.) In a volume conservation task, the child is shown two identical glasses of water. Once the child agrees that the glasses contain the same amounts of water, the water in one glass is poured into a shorter, wider glass, which causes the water to come to rest at a lower level in the shorter glass than in the taller one. The preoperational child now insists that the taller, narrower glass contains more water. Because of centration, the child focuses on only one thing: the height of the column of water. Because of irreversibility, the child fails to recognize that the process can be reversed to its starting point—that pouring the water back into its original container would restore it to its original state.

egocentrism In Piaget's theory, the tendency to see the world only from one's own perspective.

animistic thinking In Piaget's theory, the child's belief that inanimate objects have living qualities.

irreversibility In Piaget's theory, the inability to reverse the direction of a sequence of events to their starting point.

centration In Piaget's theory, the tendency to focus on only one aspect of a situation at a time.

conservation In Piaget's theory, the ability to recognize that the quantity or amount of an object remains constant despite superficial changes in its outward appearance.

Figure 9.10 Examples of Piaget's Conservation Tasks

Source: Adapted from Berger & Thompson, 1995.

Type of Conservation	Initial Presentation	Transformation	Question	Preoperational Child's Answer
Liquids	Two equal glasses of liquid	Pour one into a taller, narrower glass	Which glass contains more?	The taller one
Number	Two equal lines of checkers	Increase spacing of checkers in one line	Which line has more checkers?	The longer one
Mass	Two equal balls of clay	Squeeze one ball into a long, thin shape	Which piece has more clay?	The long one
Length	Two sticks of equal length	Move one stick	Which stick is longer?	The one that is farther to the right

Concrete Operational Stage: 7 to 11 Years   The stage of concrete operations is marked by the development of conservation. To Piaget, conservation is the ability to recognize that the amount or quantity of a substance does not change if its outward appearance is changed, so long as nothing is either added to it or subtracted from it. The kinds of conservation tasks that stymied the 6-year-old become mere "child's play" to the average 7- or 8-year-old. The child at the concrete operational stage is able to mentally reverse the process in the conservation task and recognize that the amount of water doesn't change when poured into a container of a different shape. The child also becomes capable of decentered thinking, the ability to take into account more than one aspect of a situation at a time. The child now recognizes that a rise in the water level in the narrower container is offset by a change in the width of the column of water.

The child's thinking at this stage also becomes much less egocentric. The child recognizes that other people's thoughts and feelings may differ from his or her own. The child can also perform simple logical operations, but only when they are tied to concrete examples. Seven-year-old Timmy can understand that if he has more baseball cards than Sally and Sally has more than Sam, then he also has more than Sam. But Timmy would have great difficulty understanding the question if it were posed abstractly, such as "If A is greater than B and B is greater than C, is A greater than C?"

Formal Operational Stage   The stage of **formal operations** is the final one in Piaget's theory—the stage of full cognitive maturity. In Western societies, formal operational thought tends to begin at around puberty, at about age 11 or 12. However, not all children enter this stage at this time, and some never do even as adults. Formal operations are characterized by the ability to think logically about abstract ideas, generate hypotheses, and think deductively. The person with formal operations can think through hypothetical situations, including the "A is greater than B" example earlier. He or she can follow arguments from their premises to their conclusions and back again. We will return to this stage of cognitive development when we consider the thinking processes of the adolescent.

formal operations   The level of full cognitive maturity in Piaget's theory, characterized by the ability to think in abstract terms.

Piaget's Shadow: Evaluating His Legacy   Piaget is a luminous figure in the annals of psychology who left a rich legacy. Concepts such as schemas, assimilation and accommodation, egocentricity, conservation, and reversibility, among others, provide a strong basis for understanding cognitive processes in children and how they change during development. Piaget encouraged us to view children not as passive responders to stimuli but as natural scientists who seek to understand the world and to operate on it. Although Piaget's theory of cognitive development offers many insights into the mental abilities of children, a number of criticisms of his theory have emerged.

Challenges to the Stage Model   Some theorists challenge Piaget's basic premise that cognitive development unfolds in stages. They believe a child's cognitive abilities develop through a more continuous process of gradual change over time (e.g., Bjorklund, 1995).

Underestimation of Children's Abilities   Critics also contend that Piaget underestimated the abilities of young children (Haith & Benson, 1997; Meltzoff & Gopnik, 1997). Infants clearly know more about the world and act on it in more meaningful ways than Piaget believed. We noted, for example, that even newborns can imitate facial expressions. Piaget believed this ability doesn't develop until late in the first year. Evidence suggests that children may begin to develop object permanence and ability to view events from other people's perspectives at earlier ages than Piaget's model would suppose (Aguiara & Baillargeon, 2002; Munakata et al., 1997).

Lack of Attention to Cultural Influences   Piaget believed the stages of cognitive development unfold naturally as the result of underlying maturational processes as long as the child has opportunities to interact with objects in the external world. However, critics claim he failed to account for cultural differences in the timing by which these stages unfold. In some respects, Piaget was right: cross-cultural studies shows that children do progress through the stages of cognitive development in the order he described (Dasen, 1994). But, cross-cultural evidence also shows that the ages at which children pass through these stages do differ across cultures.

The anthropologist Pierre Dasen studied with Piaget and later tested Piaget's theory in different cultures. In one study, he tested aborigine children in Australia on the conservation of liquid task in which water is transferred from a shorter, wider glass to a taller, narrower glass. He found that aborigine children developed conservation between ten and thirteen years of age, some three years or more later, on the average, than Swiss children. Moreover, some adolescents and even some adults failed to demonstrate conservation on several different types of conservation tasks.

On the other hand, the aborigine children found spatial reasoning tasks easier to master than conservation tasks, just the opposite of what was found in Swiss children. In one spatial task, a landscape model is rotated by 180 degrees. The child is asked to find an object (such as a toy sheep) on one model and then locate it on the same spot on the rotated model. We shouldn't be surprised that aborigine children do better on spatial tasks than quantification tasks. The ability to locate objects in the rugged landscape in which the aborigines live—to find fresh water and wild game—is crucial to their survival. The meat from the hunt is not divided evenly by weight but is allocated by pieces, with each particular part of the animal going to a designated person according to kinship relationships. The need for counting is minimal; in fact, the aborigine language contains words for numbers only through *five;* any quantity above that is simply "many." The message here is that the child's cultural experiences may affect both the rate of cognitive development and the eventual level of cognitive development.

Despite these challenges, Piaget's observations and teachings about how children develop have provided a guiding framework for researchers' study and exploration, and they will likely continue to do so for future generations.

CONCEPT 9.24
Though Piaget continues to have an enormous impact on the field of developmental psychology, a number of challenges to his theory have surfaced.

Vygotsky's Sociocultural Theory of Cognitive Development

CONCEPT 9.25
Vygotsky's theory of cognitive development emphasizes the role of social and cultural factors.

The Russian psychologist Lev Vygotsky was born in the same year (1896) as Piaget, but he died of tuberculosis in 1934 at age 38. Whereas Piaget focused on children's understanding of their physical environment—the world of objects and things—Vygotsky (1978, 1986) was concerned primarily with how children come to understand their social world. He believed that cultural learning is acquired through a gradual process of social interactions between children and parents, teachers, and other members of the culture. These interactions provide the basis for acquiring the knowledge that children need to solve everyday challenges and to meet the demands the culture imposes on them. In Vygotsky's view, the adult is the expert and the child is the novice, and the relationship between them is one of tutor and student.

Vygotsky developed a cognitive developmental theory that emphasizes the role of culture as the framework through which the child's understanding of the world develops. To Vygotsky, children are born as cultural blank slates (Zukow-Goldring, 1997). They must learn the skills, values, and behaviors valued by the given culture (Feldman, 2003). In American culture, this social knowledge includes such everyday behaviors as using the proper eating utensils, brushing teeth before bed, saying "excuse me" after sneezing, and waiting in line patiently.

Vygotsky emphasized that social learning occurs within a **zone of proximal development (ZPD)** (also called the *zone of potential development*). The ZPD refers to the range between the skills children can currently perform and those they could perform if they received proper guidance and instruction from people with greater expertise. Working in the zone means providing less experienced individuals, or novices, with the instruction they need to surpass what they would otherwise be able to accomplish on their own (Zukow-Goldring, 1997).

Followers of Vygotsky believe that parents and educators should use the technique of scaffolding to help children acquire new skills (Rogoff, 1997). In **scaffolding**, the parent or instructor scales the degree and type of instruction to the child's current level of ability or knowledge. For example, in early picture book reading, the parent of a 12-month-old will read the book aloud and point to the figures in the pictures. With a 15- or 18-month-old, the parent may identify the subject in a pic-

Passing on Knowledge Vygotsky emphasized social interactions as the basis for children's acquisition of knowledge about the world.

zone of proximal development (ZPD)
In Vygotsky's theory, the range between children's present level of knowledge and their potential knowledge state if they receive proper guidance and instruction.

scaffolding In Vygotsky's theory, tailoring the degree and type of instruction to the child's current level of ability or knowledge.

TRY THIS OUT

Using Scaffolding to Teach Skills

Apply the principle of scaffolding to help a child acquire a particular skill. Select a skill the child can potentially acquire with some instruction and practice. Begin by providing direct guidance and instruction, and gradually taper off the amount of direct support as the child achieves mastery. Afterward, review what you learned. Did you provide clear direction at a level the child could understand? Did you gradually withdraw support to allow the child to master the skill increasingly on his or her own? How might you do things differently in the future?

ture by saying, "Is that a tiger?" or use "What's that?" types of questions. The parent of a 2- or 3-year-old may use a picture book as a platform for introducing other learning, perhaps by posing questions such as "What does a bee make?" (Zukow-Goldring, 1997). The scaffolding agent (parent or teacher) needs to be sensitive to signals from the novice (child) indicating the child's level of competence and readiness to progress to a higher level. Using such cues leads the agent to phase in or withdraw direct support as needed. As the child's competencies develop, less direct guidance and instruction become necessary. Vygotsky's work continues to have a major influence not only in developmental psychology but also in education. Concept Chart 9.5 provides an overview of the major theories of cognitive development reviewed in this module.

CONCEPT CHART 9.5   Theories of Cognitive Development

Theory	Overview	
Piaget's theory of cognitive development	Piaget emphasized the role of adaptation in cognitive development, which he believed consists of two complementary processes: assimilation (incorporation of unfamiliar objects or situations into existing schemas) and accommodation (modification of existing schemas or creation of new ones to take into account new objects and situations).	
Piaget's stages of cognitive development	The child progresses through a fixed sequence of stages involving qualitative leaps in ability and ways of understanding and interacting with the world.	
	Sensorimotor stage (birth to 2 years)	The child uses its senses and developing motor skills to explore and act upon the world. Begins to develop a concept of object permanence, which is the recognition that objects continue to exist even if they are not presently in sight.
	Preoperational stage (2 to 7 years)	The child acquires the ability to use language to symbolize objects and actions in words. Yet the child's thinking is limited by egocentrism, animistic thought, centration, and irreversibility.
	Concrete operational stage (7 to 11 years)	The child becomes capable of performing simple logical operations as long as they're tied to concrete problems. A key feature of this stage is the acquisition of the principle of conservation, or ability to recognize that the amount of a substance does not change if its shape or size is rearranged.
	Formal operational stage (begins around puberty, age 11 or 12)	The child becomes capable of abstract thinking. Yet not all children, nor all adults, progress to this stage.
Critique of Piaget's theory	Piaget's observations and teachings remain a guiding framework for understanding cognitive development, but his theory has been challenged on some grounds, including the ages at which he believed children acquire certain abilities and his lack of attention to cultural factors in development.	
Vygotsky's sociocultural theory	Vygotsky emphasizes the social interaction between children and adults as the basis for the child's acquisition of the skills, values, and behaviors needed to meet the demands imposed by the particular culture.	

MODULE 9.5 REVIEW

Cognitive Development

RECITE IT

How do assimilation and accommodation differ?

- Assimilation is the process of incorporating new stimuli within existing schemas.

- Accommodation involves altering existing schemas or developing new ones to account for new stimuli that present schemas cannot handle effectively.

What are the major features associated with Piaget's stages of cognitive development?

- During the sensorimotor stage, from birth to about 2 years, children explore their world through their senses, motor responses, and purposeful manipulation of objects.

- During the preoperational stage, from about 2 to 7 years of age, the child's thinking is more representational but is limited by centration, egocentricity, animistic thinking, and irreversibility.

- The concrete operational stage, beginning around age 7 in Western cultures, is characterized by development of the principles of conservation and reversibility and the ability to draw logical relationships among concrete objects or events.

- The formal operational stage, the most advanced stage of cognitive development according to Piaget, is characterized by the ability to engage in deductive thinking, generate hypotheses, and engage in abstract thought.

What is the basic theme in Vygotsky's theory of cognitive development?

- Vygotsky focused on how children acquire knowledge of their social world. He believed this knowledge is achieved through the interaction of the child (novice) with the parent (expert) within a zone of proximal development that takes into account the child's present and potentially realizable knowledge structures.

RECALL IT

1. In which stage does Piaget suggest a child learns by interacting with the environment through using his or her senses and developing motor skills?
   a. sensorimotor
   b. preoperational
   c. concrete operational
   d. formal operational

2. Piaget believed that adaptation consists of two complementary cognitive processes, _____ and _____.

3. Anthropologist Pierre Dasen found that aborigine children in Australia are better able to master spatial skills than quantification skills than were Swiss children How might you explain this finding?

4. Russian psychologist Lev Vygotsky emphasized the role of _____ interactions and cultural learning in shaping the child's cognitive development.

THINK ABOUT IT

- Drawing upon Piaget's theory of cognitive development, how is the world of the child different from that of the adult?

- Think of examples of assimilation and accommodation in your own thinking. In which situations were you able to assimilate new information into existing schemas? In which situations did you need to alter your schemas or form new ones?

APPLICATION MODULE 9.6
TV and Kids

CONCEPT 9.26
Though violence on TV and in other media may foster aggressive behavior in children, there is evidence that viewing certain types of children's programs may improve the preacademic skills of preschoolers.

The box. The tube. Is it a window to the world or, as one critic put it, a "vast wasteland"? Love it or hate it, it's here to stay—right smack in your living room. Your TV set.

How much TV should children be allowed to watch? The American Academy of Pediatrics recommends a maximum of one to two hours of quality programming daily for children 2 years of age or older (Miller, 1999). Yet the average 2-year-old spends nearly four hours a day in front of the TV, about the same amount as the average 10-year-old (Leland, 1997; Liebert, Sprafkin, & Davidson, 1989). Young children under 6 spend roughly three times as much time watching television, playing video games, or using a computer as they do reading or being read to ("Kids' TV," 2003). Even infants are immersed in television viewing, to such as extent that one-fourth of children under the age of 2 now have TV sets in their rooms (Lewin, 2003).

We tend to think of TV only in terms of its possible negative effects on children's development. However, researchers believe that watching TV—at least some types of programs—may actually have some benefits. For example, programs such as *Sesame Street* and even *Barney* have been found to contribute to preacademic skills in preschoolers (Huston & Wright, 1996). Hispanic parents may use programs such as *Sesame Street* to help increase their children's, and possibly their own, proficiency in English. However, we need to recognize that most children's programs do not attempt to teach useful skills.

Is TV viewing harmful to a child's psychological and physical development? Many people certainly think so. Let's turn to the evidence to evaluate some widely touted claims about the negative effects of TV viewing.

Watching TV takes time away from important intellectual and leisure activities. Henry Shapiro of the American Academy of Pediatrics states the issue quite plainly: "Watching TV is far inferior to playing with toys, being read to or playing with adults or talking with parents" ("Kids' TV," 2003). Few authorities would argue Shapiro's point, but we should caution that there is little reason to assume that time not spent watching TV would be spent in imaginal play and other meaningful activities. For many children, TV viewing is a kind of default activity that fills time when there are few structured opportunities for other activities. The lesson

What's Billy Learning?   Evidence indicates that exposure to violent programming on television and in other media contributes to aggressive behavior in children.

for parents is to become involved in helping to structure the child's time in more meaningful ways—through reading, physical activities, imaginal play, and adventure trips—and not to use the TV as a default activity or electronic babysitter.

TV viewing is responsible for poor school performance. A small negative relationship exists between amount of TV viewing and children's school grades during late childhood and early adolescence (Huston & Wright, 1996). That is, older children and younger adolescents who watch more TV tend to have somewhat lower grades than those who watch less. Other evidence shows that young children from homes in which the TV is on most of the time have more trouble learning how to read than those from homes in which the TV is on less often ("Kids' TV," 2003). Children who spend more time watching television are also more likely than their peers to be judged by their teachers to have attentional difficulties in school (Levine & Waite, 2000). Researchers also find that the amount of early television viewing in infancy and early childhood predicts later development of attentional problems (Bertholf et al., 2004; Christakis et al., 2004; "TV May Cause," 2004).

Overall, relationships between TV viewing and academic performance appear to be small in magnitude. Though many people blame American TV for the inferior performance of U.S. children compared to Japanese children on math and science tests, in fact children in both countries spend about the same amount of time watching TV (Murray, 1997).

TV viewing fosters violent or aggressive behavior. TV is permeated with violent content, and not just during prime-time viewing hours. By the time the average child completes elementary school, he or she has been exposed to some 8,000 murders and 100,000 acts of violence on television (Eron, 1993).

TV characters in hero roles commit much of the violence, particularly in cartoons pitched at young boys. The hero typically prevails against the "bad guys" through violence but always comes out unscathed. The resulting message is that violence on the side of right is not only acceptable but heroic and carries minimal risk to the self.

Relationships between media exposure to violence and aggressive behavior in children are complex, in large part because more aggressive youngsters tend to select more violent programming. However, a large body of evidence supports the belief that exposure to violent media does contribute to aggressive behavior in children and adolescents (Bushman & Anderson, 2001; Huesmann et al., 2003; Uhlmann & Swanson, 2004). That said, the question of whether exposure to media violence on TV and in the movies contributes to actual criminal behavior remains unsettled (Savage, 2004).

Social-cognitive theorists such as psychologist Albert Bandura (1973, 1986) believe that children learn to imitate aggressive behavior they observe in the home, in the schoolyard, and on television. In classic research, Bandura and his colleagues showed how children imitated aggressive behavior of characters they observed on television, even cartoon characters (Bandura, Ross, & Ross, 1963). Figure 9.11 illustrates children imitating an adult model shown striking a toy doll (the "Bobo doll"). Other studies point to the same conclusion: children and adults responded more aggressively in laboratory-based studies after exposure to violence on television or other media (DeAngelis, 1993).

Investigators have also turned to examining another form of media exposure to violence: violent video games. A growing body of evidence links playing violent video games to an increased likelihood of aggressive behavior responses (Anderson, 2004; Anderson, Funk, & Griffiths, 2004; Gentile et al., 2004). Other forms of media violence, even violent comic books, may affect how we perceive aggressive situations. In one study, investigators found that following exposure to violent comic books, students tended to perceive more hostile intent in the actions of a provocateur in an ambiguous hypothetical story and to impose harsher retaliation toward that character than did other students exposed to nonviolent comic books (Kirsh & Olczak, 2002).

Online Study Center
Resources
Weblinks: Children and Television Violence

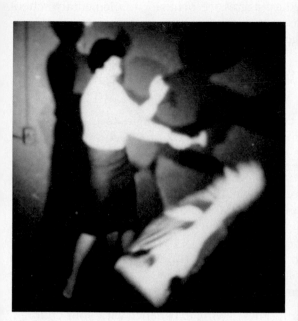

Figure 9.11   Imitation of Aggressive Models
Research by psychologist Albert Bandura and his colleagues shows that children will display aggressive behavior after exposure to aggressive models. Here we see a boy and girl striking a toy "Bobo" doll after observing an adult model strike the doll.

Media violence may foster aggressive behavior in a number of ways, including the following (Anderson et al., 2004; Uhlmann & Swanson, 2004):

1. It *models* aggressive ways of resolving conflicts that children learn to imitate.

2. It *kindles* or primes aggressive thoughts.

3. It *lessens inhibitions* against violence by showing that characters who use violence not only get away with it but are often rewarded for it.

When children are regularly exposed to TV violence, they come to believe violence is an effective way to resolve conflicts. Repeated exposure to televised violence may also lead to a kind of emotional numbing or *habituation effect,* desensitizing viewers to real-world acts of violence and to the plight of victims. However, viewing violence on television is not nearly as strong a predictor of aggressive behavior as violence observed in the home, the schools, or the community (Gunter & McAleer, 1990).

Heavy TV viewing fosters childhood obesity. TV viewing may also affect children's physical development. Researchers point to strong links between heavy TV viewing and poorer dietary habits in children, including consumption of more snack foods and fewer fruits and vegetables (Coon et al., 2001; Etheridge, 2001). Not surprisingly, children who watch more TV and those who have a TV in their rooms stand a greater risk of childhood obesity (Dennison, Erb, & Jenkins, 2002). Time spent in front of the TV may limit opportunities to burn off excess calories through physical activity. Moreover, children who are glued to the TV are likely to add unneeded calories by munching on the high-calorie snacks and treats so heavily advertised during children's programs.

There is good news to report on the intervention front. School-based programs designed to reduce television and video viewing, as well as video game playing, promote weight loss and reduce aggressive behavior in elementary school children (Nagourney, 2001; Robinson et al., 2001). Other research shows that overweight children typically lose weight as they reduce their TV viewing (Miller, 1999).

Responsible Television Viewing: What Parents Can Do

Short of pulling the plug, parents can use a number of strategies to encourage more responsible television viewing in their children (Berk, 1997; Huston & Wright, 1996):

1. *Screen violent or sexually provocative programming.* Television programs are rated by the TV industry for violence and sexual content. Parents may use the ratings to weed out shows they believe are inappropriate for their children. Today's television sets also come equipped with a V-chip to block out shows containing unwanted programming (Rutenberg, 2001). Parents can also explain differences between violence in the media and real-world violence. They can point out that actors on TV shows are able to wipe away fake blood and go home to their families unharmed, unlike the victims of actual violence.

2. *Watch TV with your kids.* Sharing the viewing experience with your children, or *coviewing,* can help them better understand what they are watching. Parents of young children can use shows such as *Sesame Street* as a kind of moving picture book by labeling and pointing out the characters on the screen. For older children, coviewing allows the parent to help diffuse any fear or anxiety the child might experience while viewing disturbing material.

3. *Don't use television as a baby-sitter.* Planting a child in front of a TV screen is no substitute for actively engaging the child in stimulating activities.

4. *Set limits.* Parents should establish clear limits for TV viewing, such as an hour or two a day, and stick to the rules themselves to model appropriate behavior. Parents may also limit the kinds of shows children watch and steer them away from violent programming and toward more educational programs.

5. *Encourage children to regulate their own television viewing.* Children can be taught to regulate their own viewing behavior. They can learn to identify and select only those shows that are appropriate for them. Younger children can be taught what to do when scary scenes are shown, such as covering their eyes and ears, quickly changing the channel, or turning the set off. Older children (age 8 or older) can be helped to distinguish between fiction and reality so they understand that not everything they see on TV is real.

6. *Monitor the news.* Some of the most disturbing content on TV today is found on the evening news, especially local news shows that seem to follow the motto "If it bleeds, it leads." Parents of younger children can control their children's exposure to news programs and reality-based "cop shows." With older children, parents can explain that television news gives an unbalanced view of society by emphasizing the most sensationalistic crimes.

7. *Limit snacking while watching TV.* Restrict—or, better, avoid—snacking or having family meals in front of the TV.

8. *Encourage children to develop other interests.* Get children to participate in other activities besides watching TV, such as reading, sports, play-dates with friends (minus TV), and outdoor play.

There is little doubt that TV and other media can influence children and that the effects are neither all good nor all bad. By becoming more involved in their children's television viewing, parents can help shape how their children use and react to TV.

TYING IT TOGETHER

Childhood is a period of wonderment, discovery, and—most of all—change. We began our study of childhood development by focusing on the general types of questions developmental psychologists seek to answer and the two major methods they use to study developmental changes, the cross-sectional and longitudinal methods (Module 9.1). Next, we looked at the changes that occur during prenatal development (Module 9.2). We continued our study with exploration of the rapid, dramatic changes that occur in the child's sensory, motor, and learning abilities during the first two years of life (Module 9.3). We then examined how infants and young children vary in their temperaments and attachment styles and how their behavior is influenced by their parents and peers (Module 9.4). In the next module, we turned to the cognitive changes that occur as children mature. We looked particularly at the contributions of Jean Piaget, who studied how children of different ages think and solve problems, as well as the work of Lev Vygotsky (Module 9.5). In the application module, we examined how exposure to television programming may influence children's cognitive, social, and even physical development (Module 9.6).

Thinking Critically About Psychology

Based on your reading of the chapter, answer the following question. Then, to evaluate your progress in developing critical thinking skills, compare your answer with the sample answer found in Appendix A.

One evening after the sun sets, Nick asks his 3-year-old son Trevor, "Where did the sun go?" Trevor responds, "It went to sleep." Nick then asks, "Why did it go to sleep?" Trevor answers, "Because it was sleepy."

1. **Based on your understanding of Piaget's theory of cognitive development, explain why Trevor believes that the sun went to sleep because it was sleepy.**

Key Terms

developmental psychology (p. 338)
nature-nurture debate (p. 338)
continuity model (p. 339)
discontinuity model (P. 339)
longitudinal study (p. 340)
cross-sectional study (p. 340)
cohort effect (p. 340)
sperm (p. 342)
ovum (p. 342)
ovulation (p. 342)
ovary (p. 342)
fallopian tube (p. 342)
fertilization (p. 342)
zygote (p. 342)
germinal stage (p. 343)
uterus (p. 343)
embryonic stage (p. 343)
embryo (p. 343)
neural tube (p. 343)
amniotic sac (p. 343)
placenta (p. 343)

fetal stage (p. 343)
fetus (p. 343)
spina bifida (p. 344)
teratogen (p. 344)
rubella (p. 344)
sudden infant death syndrome (SIDS) (p. 345)
fetal alcohol syndrome (FAS) (p. 345)
amniocentesis (p. 346)
chorionic villus sampling (CVS) (p. 346)
chorion (p. 346)
Down syndrome (p. 346)
ultrasound imaging (p. 346)
rooting reflex (p. 348)
eyeblink reflex (p. 348)
sucking reflex (p. 348)
Moro reflex (p. 348)
palmar grasp reflex (p. 348)
Babinski reflex (p. 348)
maturation (p. 348)
temperament (p. 355)

attachment (p. 356)
bonding (p. 356)
imprinting (p. 356)
Strange Situation (p. 357)
internal working models (p. 359)
schema (p. 369)
adaptation (p. 369)
assimilation (p. 369)
accommodation (p. 369)
object permanence (p. 370)
symbolic representations (p. 370)
egocentrism (p. 371)
animistic thinking (p. 371)
irreversibility (p. 371)
centration (p. 371)
conservation (p. 371)
formal operations (p. 372)
zone of proximal development (ZPD) (p. 374)
scaffolding (p. 374)

ANSWERS TO RECALL IT QUESTIONS

Module 9.1: 1. b; 2. the degree to which developmental changes occur universally across cultures; 3. c.

Module 9.2: 1. a; 2. maternal malnutrition, teratogens; 3. i. d, ii. b, iii. c, iv. a.

Module 9.3: 1. i. d, ii. b, iii. a, iv. c; 2. maturation; 3. Newborns show preferences for their mothers' voices and sounds reflecting their native languages.

Module 9.4: 1. slow; 2. i. b, ii. d, iii. a, iv. c; 3. c; 4. d.

Module 9.5: 1. a; 2. assimilation, accommodation; 3. The cultural experiences of aborigine children emphasize the importance of spatial skills rather than quantification skills; 4. social.

Adolescence and Adulthood

DID YOU KNOW THAT . . .

- Early-maturing girls tend to have poorer self-esteem, a more negative body image, and more symptoms of depression than later-maturing girls. (p. 386)
- Many adolescents see themselves as being continually on stage? (p. 386)
- Adolescents typically love and respect their parents? (p. 391)
- An identity crisis is considered a normal part of adolescent development? (p. 392)
- Since like generally marries like, stories like Cinderella remain by and large fairy tales? (p. 402)
- People in the United States are getting married later than ever? (p. 402)
- Dementia is not a normal consequence of aging? (p. 408)
- Older people usually lead better lives when they do more rather than less? (p. 413)

What am I like as a person? Complicated! I'm sensitive, friendly, outgoing, popular, and tolerant, though I can also be shy, self-conscious, and even obnoxious. Obnoxious! I'd like to be friendly and tolerant all the time. That's the kind of person I want to be, and I'm disappointed when I'm not. I'm responsible—even studious every now and then, but on the other hand I'm a goof-off too, because if you're too studious, you won't be popular. I don't usually do that well at school. I'm a pretty cheerful person, especially with my friends, where I can even get rowdy. At home I'm more likely to be anxious around my parents. They expect me to get all As. It's not fair! I worry about how I probably should get better grades. But I'd be mortified in the eyes of my friends. So I'm usually pretty stressed-out at home, or sarcastic, since my parents are always on my case. But I really don't understand how I can switch so fast. I mean, how can I be cheerful one minute, anxious the next, and then be sarcastic? Which one is the real me?

Sometimes I feel phony, especially around boys. Say I think some guy might be interested in asking me out. I try to act different, like Madonna. I'll be flirtatious and fun-loving. And then everybody, I mean everybody else is looking at me like they think I'm totally weird! Then I get self-conscious and become radically introverted. I don't know who I really am. Am I just trying to impress them or what? But I don't really care what they think anyway. I don't want to care, that is. I just want to know what my close friends think.

I can be my true self with my close friends. I can't be my real self with my parents. They don't understand me. What do they know about what it's like to be a teenager? They treat me like I'm still a kid. At least at school people treat you more like you're an adult. That gets confusing, though. I mean, which am I, a kid or an adult? It's scary, too, because I don't have any idea what I want to be when I grow up. I mean, I think about it a lot, but I can't resolve it. There are days when I wish I could become immune to myself. (Harter, 1990, pp. 352–353)

This self-portrait by a 15-year-old girl illustrates a key developmental challenge of adolescence: the attempt to answer the question "Who am I?" Part of her seeks to piece together her seemingly contradictory traits to find out which of them make up the current "real me." Another part of her is preoccupied with what she wishes to become in future years.

As we will see in this chapter, development does not end when we enter adulthood. Physical, cognitive, and emotional and social changes are hallmarks of development throughout the life span. In this chapter we proceed through the major periods of development during adolescence and adulthood, focusing on the changes that occur in each stage of life. We begin with the period of adolescence, a time of momentous developmental changes, both physical and psychological. ■

MODULE 10.1

Adolescence

- What is puberty?
- What changes in cognitive development occur during adolescence?
- What are Kohlberg's levels of moral reasoning?
- Why did Gilligan criticize Kohlberg's theory?
- What did Erikson believe is the major developmental challenge of adolescence?

During **adolescence**, the young person's body may seem to be sprouting in all directions at once. Adolescents may wonder what they will look like next year or even next month—who and what they will be. Intellectually they may feel they are suddenly grown-ups, or expected to act as though they are, as they tackle more demanding subjects in middle school and high school and are expected to begin thinking seriously about what lies ahead for them when they leave high school. Yet their parents and teachers may continue to treat them as children—children masquerading in adult bodies who often must be restrained for their own good. Adolescents may find themselves in constant conflict with their parents over issues such as dating, using the family car, spending money, and _____ (you fill in the blank). At a time when young people are stretching their wings and preparing to fly on their own, they remain financially, and often emotionally, dependent on their parents. No wonder the early psychologist and founder of the American Psychological Association, G. Stanley Hall, characterized adolescence as a time of *sturm und drang,* or "storm and stress." Contemporary research bears out the belief that many, though certainly not all, young people experience adolescence as a turbulent, pressure-ridden period (Arnett, 1999). Table 10.1 offers a snapshot of today's teenagers.

Let us now consider the physical, cognitive, social, and emotional changes that occur during the years when many young people feel they are betwixt and between—no longer children but not quite adults.

Physical Development

After the rapid growth that takes place during infancy, children typically gain two to three inches and four to six pounds a year until the growth spurt of adolescence. The spurt lasts for two to three years, during which time adolescents may

TABLE 10.1   A Snapshot of Today's Teens

A *Newsweek* poll offers the following snapshot of teens:	
70%	say they face more stress than their parents did as teens
48%	say they use a computer almost every day at home
21%	say they have looked at something on the Internet that they wouldn't want their parents to know about
59%	worry about violence in society
56%	worry about sexually transmitted diseases
54%	worry about the cost of a college education
43%	worry about their future job opportunities
69%	say they would rather accomplish something outstanding than fit in with their friends
24%	say they spend too little time with their parents, 15% say they spend too much time, while 61% say they spend enough time

Source: Newsweek, May 8, 2000, p. 56.

Figure 10.1   Physical Changes Occurring During Puberty
This graph illustrates a number of changes occurring during puberty in boys and girls. Note how the growth spurt begins sooner in girls than boys. Note too that the graph represents the average ages at which these changes occur and that growth patterns in individuals often vary from these averages.

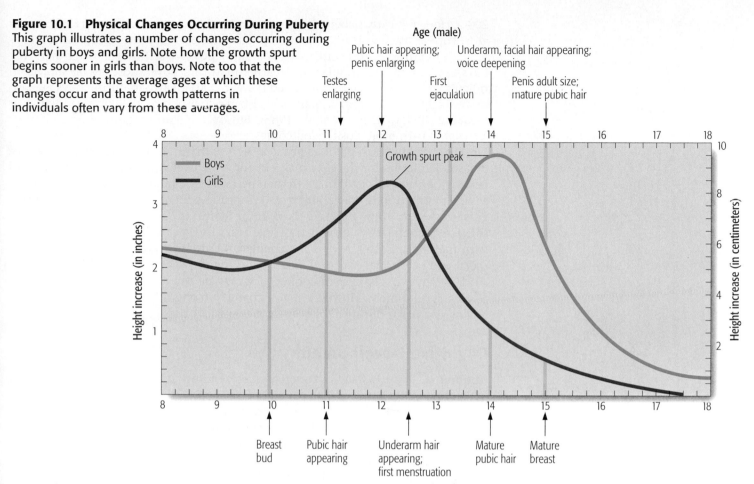

Source: Adapted from Seifert, Hoffnung, & Hoffnung, 2000.

CONCEPT 10.1

The major event in physical development in adolescence is puberty, the period of physical growth and sexual maturation during which we attain full sexual maturity.

adolescence   The period of life beginning at puberty and ending with early adulthood.

puberty   The stage of development at which individuals become physiologically capable of reproducing.

secondary sex characteristics   Physical characteristics that differentiate males and females but are not directly involved in reproduction.

primary sex characteristics   Physical characteristics, such as the gonads, that differentiate males and females and play a direct role in reproduction.

menarche   The first menstruation.

shoot up eight inches to one foot or more. Girls experience their growth spurt earlier than boys, so the average girl may be taller than the average boy, at least for a while (Susman, Dorn, & Schiefelbein, 2003). But boys, on the average, eventually surpass girls in both height and body weight. Boys also develop greater upper-body musculature.

The major landmark of physical development during adolescence is **puberty**, the period in which young people reach full sexual maturity (see Figure 10.1). Puberty begins with the appearance of **secondary sex characteristics**, physical characteristics that differentiate men and women but are not directly involved in reproduction, such as pubic hair, breast development, and deepening of the voice. **Primary sex characteristics** also emerge; these are changes in sex organs directly involved in reproduction, such as enlargement of the testes and penis in boys and of the uterus in girls. Puberty typically lasts about three to four years and ends when bone growth stops, usually about the age of 16 in girls and 17.5 in boys (Schneider, 2004). By the end of puberty, adolescents have become physically capable of reproduction.

Girls today enter puberty and experience **menarche**, the beginning of menstruation, at much earlier ages than did girls in previous generations, most likely as the result of improved nutrition and health care (Anderson et al., 2003). They typically show breast development and other signs of puberty by age 10, as compared to age 15 at the beginning of the twentieth century. The average age today of menarche is about 12.1 years for African American girls and about 12.6 years for European American girls (Anderson et al., 2003).

The timing of puberty and the unfolding of physical changes during puberty are strongly influenced by genetic factors (Beier & Dluhy, 2003; Mustanski et al.,

2004). However, early puberty is associated with different consequences for boys and girls. For earlier-maturing boys, their greater size and strength gives them an advantage in athletics and contributes to a more positive self-image. Later-maturing boys tend to be less popular than earlier-maturing boys and may be subject to ridicule or become socially ostracized (Berger, 2001). Early-maturing boys are also more likely to engage in deviant social behavior such as drinking, smoking, or breaking the law (Duncan et al., 1985). But overall, earlier maturation in boys is associated with more positive outcomes.

For girls, the most obvious physical sign of maturation is the development of breasts. Earlier-maturing girls may encounter unwelcome sexual attention and believe they no longer "fit in" with their peers. They tend to have lower self-esteem, a more negative body image, and more symptoms of depression than later-maturing girls (Caspi & Moffitt, 1991; Ge et al., 2003; Stattin & Magnusson, 1990). Research suggests that the ways in which people react to the physical changes associated with maturation, rather than the changes themselves, are what account for the social and emotional effects of pubertal timing.

The physical changes of adolescence may be the most obvious signs of adolescent development. However, major changes in cognitive abilities and social behavior also occur during adolescence. We consider these developments next.

Cognitive Development

Children at Piaget's stage of concrete operations stick to the facts at hand. They make judgments based on the concrete evidence available to them. They are unable to think abstractly or construct hypothetical situations that are not tied to those facts. But adolescents who reach the stage of formal operations can recognize relationships among propositions and concepts and can speculate about "what might be," not simply "what is."

Piaget noted that not all adolescents, or even adults, reach the stage of formal operations in which they are capable of abstract thinking. Evidence from a sample of about 1,800 college students at a college in Pennsylvania showed that the percentages of students reaching formal operations increased over the four years of college (Anderson, 2003). We can't say whether particular experiences at college or perhaps just maturation best explains these changes.

People who develop formal operational thought become capable of creating hypothetical situations and scenarios and playing them through in their minds. They can mount an argument in favor of something that runs counter to their own views (Flavell, Miller, & Miller, 2002). They are also able to use deductive reasoning in which one derives conclusions about specific cases or individuals based on a set of premises. For example, they may deduce "who-done-it" from the facts of a crime long before the guilty party in the television drama is revealed.

The ability to think abstractly doesn't mean adolescents are free from egocentric thinking. As Piaget noted, preschoolers are egocentric in the sense that they have difficulty seeing things from other people's points of view. Psychologist David Elkind (1985) believes that adolescent egocentrism basically reveals itself in two ways: through the imaginary audience and the personal fable.

The **imaginary audience** describes the adolescent's belief that other people are as keenly interested in his or her concerns and needs as the adolescent is. Adolescents may feel as though they are always on stage, as though all eyes are continually scrutinizing how they look, what they wear, and how they act (Frankenberger, 2000). They view themselves as the center of attention and feel extremely self-conscious and overly concerned about the slightest flaw in their appearance ("How could they not notice this blemish? Everybody will notice!").

The **personal fable** is an exaggerated sense of one's uniqueness and invulnerability. Adolescents may believe their life experiences or personal feelings are so unique that no one could possibly understand them, let alone have experienced

CONCEPT 10.2
Adolescents who develop formal operational thinking become capable of solving abstract problems.

CONCEPT 10.3
Adolescents often show a form of egocentric thinking in which they believe their concerns and needs should be as important to others as they are to themselves.

imaginary audience The common belief among adolescents that they are the center of other people's attention.
personal fable The common belief among adolescents that their feelings and experiences cannot possibly be understood by others and that they are personally invulnerable to harm.

them. When parents try to relate to what their adolescent is experiencing, they may be summarily rebuffed: "You can't possibly understand what I'm going through!" Another aspect of the personal fable is the belief that "Bad things can't happen to me." This sense of personal invulnerability may underlie risky behavior patterns such as reckless driving, unsafe sex, and use of drugs and alcohol (Arnett, 1992). Indeed, teenagers tend to underestimate the dangers posed by such behaviors, and so they may engage in riskier behaviors than they might otherwise had they judged risks more accurately. Factors such as poor school performance, having close friends who engage in risky behavior, impulsivity, lack of capacity to regulate one's emotions, attention and behavior, and strained family relationships are also linked to riskier health behaviors, including drinking, smoking, unsafe sex, and suicide attempts (Blum et al., 2000; Carpenter, 2001a; Cooper et al., 2003; Raffaelli & Crockett, 2003). (Adolescent suicide is discussed further in Chapter 13.)

The developing cognitive abilities of adolescents change the way they see the world, including themselves, family and friends, and broad social and moral issues. These changes influence the ways people form judgments about questions of right and wrong, as we will see next.

Kohlberg's Stages of Moral Reasoning

How Could They Not Notice? Adolescents may constantly scrutinize their appearance and become overly concerned about the slightest flaw.

Psychologist Lawrence Kohlberg (1927–1987) was a pioneer in studying how individuals make moral judgments about conflict-laden issues (see the nearby Pioneers box). He was interested in the process by which people arrive at moral choices—what makes something right or wrong—rather than in the particular choices they make. He developed a methodology in which he presented subjects

THE PIONEERS | Following His Conscience

Lawrence Kohlberg

Lawrence Kohlberg was not your average student. If he had written an essay on "How I Spent My Summer Vacation," it would not have been about going to the beach or getting a summer job to help put himself through college. Instead, at the end of World War II, he helped smuggle shiploads of displaced European Jews past the British blockade into what was then called Palestine.

Kohlberg spent his early years in the wealthy New York City suburb of Bronxville. He went to high school at the elite Phillips Academy in Andover, Massachusetts. The doors to the nation's best colleges were open to Kohlberg, but he delayed attending college so that he could follow the dictates of his conscience.

Kohlberg's moral sense required self-sacrifice. It also required that he act in opposition to British rule of Palestine. (British rule ended in 1948 with the founding of the state of Israel.) While other 18-year-olds were packing for college, Kohlberg felt the bitter spray of the Mediterranean Sea against his face and was held captive by the British in a prison camp in Cyprus. There he contracted a painful parasitic infection that plagued him for the rest of his life.

Following his release from the prison camp and his return to the United States, Kohlberg studied psychology at the University of Chicago, where John Watson had studied many years before. But Kohlberg was not a behaviorist. He was interested in people's cognitive development, especially as it concerned moral issues. He believed moral judgments are connected with moral behavior, just as he believed his own placement of the highest value on the lives of the individuals who had managed to escape from Europe compelled him to oppose the British. His research later showed, however, that at best only a modest relationship exists between moral reasoning and moral behavior.

CONCEPT 10.4
Psychologist Lawrence Kohlberg explored how individuals make moral judgments; his theory of moral development consists of a sequence of six stages organized in terms of three levels of moral reasoning.

Online Study Center
Improve Your Grade
Tutorials: Kohlberg's Stages of Moral Development

Online Study Center
Improve Your Grade
Tutorials: Developing Morals

with hypothetical situations involving conflicting moral values, or moral dilemmas. Let's look at his most famous example:

> *In Europe, a woman lies near death from a certain type of cancer. Only one drug that might save her is available, from a druggist in the same town who is charging ten times what it costs him to make it. Lacking this sum, the woman's husband, Heinz, attempts to borrow money from everyone he knows but can raise only about half the amount. Heinz tells the druggist his wife is dying and pleads with him to sell it for less so he can buy it now or allow him to pay for it later. The druggist refuses. Desperate, Heinz breaks into the druggist's store and steals the drug to give to his wife.* (Adapted from Kohlberg, 1969)

Now Kohlberg poses the questions: "Should Heinz have stolen the drug? Why or why not?" Here we have the making of a moral dilemma, a situation that pits two opposing moral values against each other—in this case, the moral injunction against stealing versus the human value of attempting to save the life of a loved one. Kohlberg believed that one's level of moral development is reflected in the way one reasons about the moral dilemma, not on whether one believes the behavior in question was right or wrong.

Based on his studies of responses to these types of hypothetical situations, Kohlberg determined that moral development progresses through a sequence of six stages organized into three levels of moral reasoning: the preconventional level, the conventional level, and the postconventional level.

Preconventional Level   Children at the *preconventional level* base their moral judgments on the perceived consequences of behavior. Kohlberg divided preconventional moral reasoning into two stages. Stage 1 is characterized by an *obedience and punishment orientation:* Good behavior is defined simply as behavior that avoids punishment by an external authority. In our example, we might reason that Heinz should take the drug because if he does not, he may be blamed for his wife's death; or he shouldn't take the drug because he could get caught and sent to jail. Stage 2 represents an *instrumental purpose orientation:* A behavior is judged good when it serves the person's needs or interests. Thus, we might reason that Heinz should have taken the drug because, by saving his wife, he would ensure that she'd be available to meet his needs for companionship, love, and support; or Heinz shouldn't have taken the drug because if he were caught and sent to jail, he would have done neither himself nor his wife any good.

Conventional Level   At the *conventional level,* moral reasoning is based on conformity with conventional rules of right and wrong. Individuals at this level recognize that the purpose of social rules is to preserve the social order and ensure harmonious relationships among people.

Stage 3 is characterized by a *"good boy–good girl" orientation:* Individuals believe that conformity with rules and regulations is important because of the need to be perceived by others as a "good boy" or a "good girl." They value the need to do the "right thing" in the eyes of others. Thus, Heinz should steal the drug because others would be displeased with him for failing to help save his wife's life; or Heinz should not steal the drug because if he is caught, he will bring dishonor on himself and his family.

Stage 4 has an *authority* or *law-and-order orientation.* Moral reasoning now goes beyond the need to gain approval from others: Rules must be obeyed and applied evenhandedly because they are needed for the orderly functioning of society. Each of us has a duty to uphold the law, simply because it is the law. Heinz should steal the drug because it is a husband's duty to protect his wife's life, but he must repay the druggist as soon as he is able and accept responsibility and punishment for breaking the law. Or Heinz should not steal the drug because although we may sympathize with his wish to save his wife's life, people cannot be permitted to break the law even when they face such dire circumstances.

Postconventional Level Individuals generally reach the *postconventional level* of moral reasoning during adolescence, if they reach it at all. Postconventional reasoners apply their own moral standards or principles rather than relying on those of authority figures or blindly adhering to social rules or conventions. The postconventional thinker believes that when laws are unjust, a moral person is bound to disobey them. Kohlberg's own protest against the British is an example of postconventional reasoning, of putting principle first (see the Pioneers box on page 367). In Kohlberg's (1969) studies, only about one in four people had reached the postconventional level by age 16. Even in adulthood, most people remain at the level of conventional moral reasoning.

Kohlberg identified two stages of postconventional moral reasoning. Stage 5, the *social contract orientation,* involves the belief that laws are based on mutual agreement among members of a society, but they are not infallible. They should be open to question rather than followed blindly out of respect for authority. Stage 5 reasoners weigh the rights of the individual against the rights of society. They might argue that although laws should be obeyed, protection of a life is a more important value than protection of property, and so an exception should be made in Heinz's case. Or they might reason that individuals must obey the law because the common good takes precedence over the individual good and that the ends, no matter how noble they may be, do not justify the means.

Stage 6 thinking involves adoption of *universal ethical principles,* an underlying set of self-chosen, abstract ethical principles that serve as a guiding framework for moral judgments. Beliefs in the sanctity of human life or in the "Golden Rule" exemplify such universal ethical principles. People at this stage are guided by their own internal moral compass, regardless of the dictates of society's laws or the opinions of others. They may believe that if laws devalue the sanctity of human life, it becomes *immoral* to obey them. Hence it would be immoral for Heinz to obey laws that would ultimately devalue the sanctity of his wife's life. Kohlberg believed that very few people, even those within the postconventional level, reach Stage 6. Concept Chart 10.1 summarizes the six stages of moral reasoning in Kohlberg's model.

Kohlberg's model of moral development continues to foster understanding of how people develop a sense of morality. But does moral reasoning dictate moral behavior? Do people who achieve higher levels of moral reasoning in Kohlberg's system actually practice what they preach? The answer seems to be that although there is some overlap between moral reasoning and moral behavior, situational factors are more likely to determine how people act when confronted by ethical or moral dilemmas (Bandura, 1986).

Moral reasoning also appears to be linked to self-esteem. A recent study of middle-school children showed that children with *higher* levels of self-esteem were more likely to make a moral choice when presented with situations that challenged their values (e.g., whether to look at another student's answer sheet during a test when the teacher is looking away) (Dai, Nolan, & White, 2002).

CONCEPT 10.5
Though evidence generally supports Kohlberg's stage model of moral reasoning, critics contend that his model may contain cultural and gender biases.

Cross-Cultural and Gender-Based Research on Kohlberg's Model Evidence supports the view that children and adolescents progress through the stages Kohlberg suggested, even if they may not reach the level of postconventional reasoning (Flavell, Miller, & Miller, 2002). Moreover, Kohlberg's own studies of people in other countries led him to believe in the universality of his first four stages, a belief that was later supported by a review of forty-four studies conducted in twenty-seven countries (Snarey, 1985). Nevertheless, critics have challenged Kohlberg's model for both cultural and gender biases.

💡 **CONCEPT CHART 10.1   Kohlberg's Levels and Stages of Moral Development**

	Stage of Moral Reasoning	Arguments Favoring Heinz Stealing the Drug	Arguments Against Heinz Stealing the Drug
LEVEL I Preconventional Level	Stage 1: Obedience and punishment orientation; behavior is judged good if it serves to avoid punishment	Heinz should steal the drug to avoid being blamed if his wife dies.	Heinz shouldn't steal the drug because he would be punished for stealing it if he were caught and would be sent to jail.
	Stage 2: Instrumental purpose orientation; behavior is judged good when it serves personal needs or interests	Heinz should steal the drug because he needs his wife and she might die without it.	Heinz would likely be sent to prison and his wife would probably die before he gets out, so it wouldn't do her or himself any good to steal the drug.
LEVEL II Conventional Level	Stage 3: "Good boy–nice girl" orientation; conforming with rules to impress others	People would lose respect for Heinz if he didn't at least try to save his wife by stealing the drug.	Heinz shouldn't take the drug because others will see him as a criminal, and that would bring shame and dishonor to his family.
	Stage 4: Authority or law-and-order orientation; obeying rules and laws because they are needed to maintain social order	Heinz must steal the drug because he has a duty to protect his wife. People need to do their duty even if they might get punished for it.	People should not be permitted to break the law under any circumstances. The law must be respected.
LEVEL III Postconventional Level	Stage 5: Social contract orientation; viewing rules and laws as based on mutual agreement in the service of the common good	While laws should be obeyed to maintain order in society, an exception should be made in Heinz's case because a law should not take precedence over protecting a human life.	Though Heinz faces a difficult choice, he reasons that respect for the law outweighs individual needs no matter what the circumstances.
	Stage 6: Universal ethical principle orientation; adopting an internal moral code based on universal values that takes precedence over social rules and laws	Heinz would be morally wrong not to steal the drug because it would violate his belief in the absolute value of a human life.	Sometimes doing what we believe is right requires personal sacrifice. If Heinz truly feels that stealing is worse than letting his wife die, he must not steal the drug.

Source: Adapted from Kohlberg, 1981.

Critics contend that Kohlberg's model may be culturally biased because it emphasizes ideals found primarily in Western cultures, such as individual rights and social justice (Shweder, 1994). A cross-cultural study comparing moral reasoning among people in the United States and India found cultural differences in the priorities placed on justice and interpersonal values (Miller & Bersoff, 1992). Americans placed greater value than did Indians on a justice orientation in determining morally correct choices—believing that what is just or fair governs what is right. Indians placed a greater weight on interpersonal responsibilities, such as upholding one's obligations to others and being responsive to other people's needs.

Harvard psychologist Carol Gilligan addressed the issue of gender bias in Kohlberg's work. Earlier research applying Kohlberg's model suggested that men attained higher levels of moral reasoning than women did. Gilligan did not believe women are less capable of developing moral reasoning; rather, she argued that Kohlberg's model was gender-biased because it had been derived entirely from studies of male subjects. The voices of girls and women had not been heard.

Gilligan began listening to women's views and soon discovered that women applied a different moral standard than men (Gilligan, 1982). She found that females adopted a *care orientation,* whereas males applied a *justice orientation.* Young men appealed to abstract principles of justice, fairness, and rights in making moral judgments of right and wrong. They would argue, for example, that Heinz should steal the drug because the value of life supersedes that of property. Young women sought solutions that responded both to the druggist's needs to protect his property and to Heinz's need to save his wife—solutions that expressed a caring attitude and the need to preserve the relationship between them. However, because young women are less willing to apply abstract moral principles when facing ethical situations like that of Heinz, they may be classified at lower levels in Kohlberg's system. Gilligan argued that the moral standards of men and women represent two different ways of thinking about moral behavior, with neither way standing on higher moral ground than the other.

Researchers find partial support for Gilligan's belief in gender differences in moral reasoning (e.g., Jaffee & Hyde, 2000; Walker, 1997). Females do place somewhat more emphasis on the care orientation, whereas males place somewhat greater stress on the justice orientation. However, there is little support for the view that men adopt primarily a justice orientation in making moral judgments or that women adopt primarily a care orientation (Jaffee & Hyde, 2000). Nor is there much evidence of systematic biases against females in how they are classified according to Kohlberg's model. On the whole, however, Gilligan's work remains influential, partly because it encourages investigators to listen to female voices and partly because it encourages young women to find and develop their own voices.

Psychosocial Development

In this section we examine the psychosocial development of adolescents as they negotiate the transition from childhood to young adulthood. Throughout we focus on their relationships with parents and peers and the challenges adolescents face in establishing a clear psychological identity of their own. We also consider an aspect of psychosocial development that often takes center stage during adolescence: sexuality.

CONCEPT 10.6

Issues relating to independence come to the fore in the adolescent's social and personality development, but these issues often bring adolescents into conflict with their parents.

Adolescent-Parent Relationships   Adolescent yearnings for independence often lead to some degree of withdrawal from family members and to arguments with parents over issues of autonomy and decision making. Such distancing may be healthy during adolescence, as young people need to form meaningful relationships outside the family and develop a sense of independence and social competence. Yet research indicates that adolescents and their parents typically express love and respect for each other and agreement on many of the principal issues in life (Arnett, 2004). It may surprise you to learn that nearly three out of four high school students surveyed in a recent national poll said that they got along very well or extremely well with their parents or guardians ("Teens Say," 2003). Though disagreements with parents are not uncommon, serious conflict is neither normal nor helpful for adolescents. Parents also influence their adolescents in more subtle ways, and not always for the better. Adolescents tend to mimic their parents' health-related behaviors, for better or sometimes for worse. Consider, for example, that one of the strongest predictors of adolescent smoking is having a parent who smokes (Kodl & Mermelstein, 2004).

By psychologically separating from their parents, adolescents begin to grapple with the major psychosocial challenge they face: developing a clear sense of themselves and of their future direction in life. As we will see next, the theorist Erik Erikson believed that the process of coming to terms with the question "Who am I?" represents the major life challenge of adolescence.

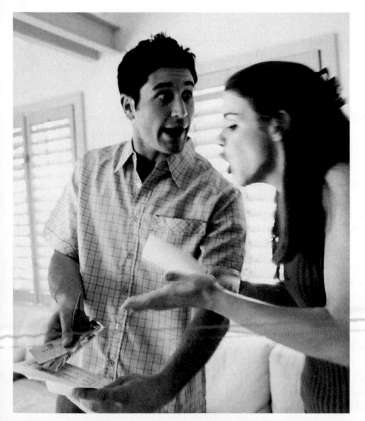

Conflicts with Parents   Though conflicts between adolescents and parents are common, most adolescents say they have good relationships with their parents.

THE PIONEERS — "Who Am I, Really?"

Erik Erikson

We shouldn't be surprised that Erik Erikson devoted much of his professional life to the study of identity. Erikson didn't learn until he was an adolescent that the father who had raised him, a physician named Theodor Homburger, was actually his stepfather (Erikson, 1975). His biological father had abandoned his mother while she was pregnant with Erik, and she remarried shortly after his birth. His mother and stepfather kept the secret about his parentage because they did not want him to feel strange or different. Yet he did feel different. With blond hair and blue eyes, he physically resembled his biological father, a Dane. But his stepfather and mother were Jewish. People at his stepfather's synagogue considered him a Gentile, yet his classmates considered him a Jew. He would later recount that the question "Who am I, really?" dominated his struggle for personal identity in his youth.

Questions about his professional ambitions took center stage as he matured. For several years he traveled about Europe, eking out a meager existence as a struggling artist. Yet this time was also a period of serious soul searching about his direction in life, an experience he later characterized as an "identity crisis." He emerged from his identity crisis with a resolve to become a psychoanalyst. He met Sigmund Freud and immersed himself in psychoanalytic training. He eventually married and moved with his wife to the United States, where he continued to produce scholarly works until his death in 1994 at age 92. Though he never graduated from college or was awarded any university degrees, Erikson achieved worldwide recognition both as a psychoanalyst and a theorist.

Ironically, this man whose name is most closely connected with the concept of identity was named Erik Homburger until he became a U.S. citizen in 1939 at age 37. He believed he had found a "loving stepfather" in his adopted country and wanted a new name to use in his new home. He adopted the last name Erikson, which may have represented his identification with the early Norwegian explorer of America, Leif Erikson (Roazen, 1976).

CONCEPT 10.7

To Erik Erikson, the major life challenge adolescents face is the development of a sense of ego identity, a coming to terms with the fundamental question "Who am I?"

ego identity In Erickson's theory, the attainment of a psychological sense of knowing oneself and one's direction in life.

identity crisis In Erikson's theory, a stressful period of serious soul searching and self-examination of issues relating to personal values and one's direction in life.

Identity Versus Role Diffusion: Who Am I? Earlier we saw that the theorist Erik Erikson believed children progress through a series of four stages of psychosocial development. Erikson's fifth stage of psychosocial development occurs during adolescence: the stage of *identity versus role diffusion.*

Ego identity is the attainment of a firm sense of self—who one is, where one is headed in life, and what one believes in. People who achieve ego identity clearly understand their personal needs, values, and life goals. Erikson coined the term **identity crisis** to describe the stressful period of soul searching and serious self-examination that many adolescents experience when struggling to develop a set of personal values and direction in life. As you'll see in the Pioneers box, Erikson's own early life mirrored this quest for identity. Although Erikson believed that an identity crisis is a normal part of the development of the healthy personality, some contemporary scholars use the term *exploration* rather than *crisis* to avoid implying that the process of examining oneself is inherently fraught with anguish and struggle (Arnett, 2004).

Adolescents who successfully resolve an identity crisis emerge as their own persons, as people who have achieved a state of ego identity. Ego identity, however, continues to develop throughout life. Our occupational goals and our political, moral, and religious beliefs often change over time. Therefore, we may experience many identity crises in life.

Many adolescents or adults never grapple with an identity crisis. They may develop a firm sense of ego identity by modeling themselves after others, espe-

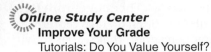

💡 **CONCEPT 10.8**
Peer pressure is an important influence in the social and emotional development of adolescents.

cially parents, without undergoing any type of identity crisis. Others may fail to develop a clear sense of ego identity. They stay at sea, aimlessly taking each day as it comes without any clear values or goals. This state, called **role diffusion**, is characterized by a lack of direction in life. Adolescents who fail to achieve ego identity may be especially vulnerable to negative peer influences such as illicit drug use. They may also become intolerant of people who differ from themselves for fear of shattering their own fragile identities, and they have difficulty forging or maintaining close personal relationships with others. Evidence supports Erikson's view that people who successfully negotiate earlier psychosocial crises, including the ego identity challenge, are generally better able to resolve later psychosocial crises in life (Whitbourne, Elliot, & Waterman, 1992).

Peer Relationships As adolescents experiment with greater independence, peer relationships become increasingly important influences in their psychosocial development. "Fitting in" or belonging comes to play an even greater role in determining their self-esteem and emotional adjustment. Friendships help ease adjustment into adolescence and middle school (Dittmann, 2004a; Wentzel, Barry, & Caldwell, 2004).

On the other hand, parents are often concerned that their teenagers may "run with the wrong crowd." They tend to perceive their teens as being subject to a greater amount of peer pressure to engage in negative behaviors such as stealing or using alcohol or drugs than do the teens themselves (see Table 10.2). Evidence bears out at least some parental concerns, since exposure to deviant peer groups is an important factor in early substance abuse (Walden et al., 2004). However, studies with Hispanic and African American teens support the view that parents can be an "antidrug" influence: strong parental support reduces the negative influence of drug-using peers on the teen's use of tobacco and other drugs (Farrell & White, 1998; Frauenglass et al., 1997). We also have evidence that teens who share five or more dinners a week with their parents are less likely to use drugs than their peers who dine together fewer than twice a week (Radsch, 2004). Close relationships between teens and parents can also help protect against other problem behaviors, such as suicidal and violent behavior (Resnick et al., 1997).

Let us turn to consider the topic that is often foremost in the minds of many adolescents: sexuality.

TABLE 10.2 Teens and Peer Pressure

"How much peer pressure from friends do you feel (does your teen feel) today to do the following?"		
Those Responding "a lot"	Teens	Parents
Have sex	10%	20%
Grow up too fast	16	34
Steal or shoplift	4	18
Use drugs or abuse alcohol	10	10
Defy parents or teachers	9	16
Be mean to kids who are different	11	14

Source: Newsweek poll, based on a national sample of teens 13 to 19 years of age and 509 parents of these teens. Results reported in *Newsweek*, May 8, 2000, p. 56.

role diffusion In Erikson's model, aimlessness or a lack of direction with respect to one's role in life or public identity

CONCEPT 10.9
Sexual maturation occurring during puberty leads to reproductive capability, whether or not youngsters are psychologically prepared for it.

Online Study Center
Improve Your Grade
Tutorials: When Conformity Leads to Danger

Adolescent Sexuality   Adolescents may be more than just "hormones with feet," as one observer put it, but sexual thoughts and interests often do take center stage during this period. However, despite the common perception that sexual activity among young people is rising rapidly, rates of sexual intercourse among teens as well as the teenage birth rate have actually been on the decline in recent years (Arnett, 2004; Rosenberg, 2002). The efforts of schools and parents to educate young people about the risks of teenage pregnancy appear to be yielding dividends. Officials also credit the decline in teenage pregnancies to increased use of contraception (Ali & Scelfo, 2002). Despite these declines, about half of American high school students report they have engaged in sexual intercourse (Centers for Disease Control and Prevention, 2001), and about 3 million cases of sexually transmitted diseases among 10- to 19-year-olds are reported annually in the United States (Dittmann, 2003d). Increasing numbers of teens are also experimenting with other forms of sexual contact as an alternative to vaginal intercourse, including oral and anal sex.

The teenage birth rate in the United States far exceeds those in other Western, industrialized countries. About 500,000 American teenagers give birth each year (Centers for Disease Control, 2000a). Although some teen mothers become pregnant to fill an emotional void or to rebel against their families, most teenage pregnancies result from failure to use contraceptives reliably. Many sexually active teenagers get caught up in their own personal fables that lead them to believe pregnancy is something that could not happen to them.

Unwed teenage mothers face serious obstacles to their educational and social development. They are more likely than other girls to live below the poverty level, to quit school, and to depend on public assistance (Arnett, 2004; Desmond, 1994). Although the father (usually a teenager himself) is equally responsible for the pregnancy, he is usually absent or incapable of contributing to the child's support.

Why do some teens become sexually active whereas others abstain? Peer pressure, whether real or imagined, can either promote or restrain sexual activity. Those who abstain may also do so for moral reasons, or they may be concerned about getting caught, becoming pregnant, or contracting a sexually transmitted disease. Other factors linked to teens' sexual restraint include the following (Carvajal et al., 1999; Hardy & Raffaelli, 2003; McBride, Paikoff, & Holmbeck, 2003):

• Living in an intact family

• Having a family with low levels of conflict

• Having at least one parent who graduated from college

• Placing importance on religion and attending religious services frequently

• Being able to communicate openly with parents

Many gay adolescents face the challenge of coming to terms with their sexuality against the backdrop of social condemnation and discrimination against gays in the broader culture (Meyer, 2003). Their struggle for self-acceptance often requires stripping away layers of denial about their sexuality. Some gay men and lesbians fail to achieve a "coming out" to themselves—that is, a personal acceptance of their sexual orientation—until young or middle adulthood. The process of achieving self-acceptance can be so difficult that many gay adolescents consider or even attempt suicide (Bagley & D'Augelli, 2000).

Before we leave our discussion of adolescence, it's important to note that most adolescents are generally happy and optimistic about their futures (Arnett, 2004). Though they may have wider and more frequent changes in moods than adults, most of their mood swings fall within a mild range. However, adolescents who undergo more intense negative events, such as peer rejection, school problems, a failed romantic relationship, or serious conflicts with parents, are more likely than others to experience significant psychological distress, especially depression (Buchanan, Eccles, & Becker, 1992; Monroe et al., 1999).

MODULE 10.1 REVIEW

Adolescence

RECITE IT

What is puberty?

• Puberty spans the period of physical development that begins with the appearance of secondary sex characteristics and ends with the attainment of full sexual maturity.

What changes in cognitive development occur during adolescence?

• Adolescents may progress to the stage of formal operations, which, according to Piaget, is denoted by the ability to engage in abstract thinking and reasoning.

• According to Elkind, egocentricity in adolescence involves concepts of the imaginary audience (believing everyone else is as concerned about us as we are ourselves) and the personal fable (an exaggerated sense of uniqueness and perceptions of personal invulnerability).

What are Kohlberg's levels of moral reasoning?

• At the preconventional level, moral judgments are based on the perceived consequences of behavior. Behaviors that avoid punishment are good; those that incur punishment from an external authority are bad.

• At the conventional level, conformity with conventional rules of right and wrong is valued because of the need to do what others expect or because one has an obligation to obey the law.

• At the postconventional level, moral judgments are based on the value systems the individual develops through personal reflection, such as the importance of human life and the concept of justice above that of the law. Postconventional thinking does not develop until adolescence, if ever.

Why did Gilligan criticize Kohlberg's theory?

• Gilligan pointed out that Kohlberg's model was based only on the responses of males and did not take female voices into account.

• Through her own research, Gilligan concluded that females tend to adopt a care orientation, whereas males tend to adopt a justice orientation. Other researchers have found that differences in moral reasoning between men and women are less clear-cut, although women have a greater tendency to adopt a care orientation.

What did Erikson believe is the major developmental challenge of adolescence?

• Erikson believed the achievement of a sense of who one is and what one stands for (ego identity) is the major developmental challenge of adolescence.

• Erikson coined the term *identity crisis* to describe a period of serious soul searching in which adolescents attempt to come to terms with their underlying beliefs and future direction in life.

RECALL IT

1. The physical growth period during which young people mature sexually and reach their full reproductive capacity is known as _____.

2. The average age at which girls begin menstruating [rose or dropped?] sharply during the twentieth century.

3. What are two ways in which egocentric thinking becomes expressed during adolescence?

4. Lawrence Kohlberg posed moral dilemmas to children and then classified their responses. Children whose responses indicated that they based their moral judgments on the perceived consequences of actions were classified at the _____ level of moral reasoning.
   a. preconventional
   b. conventional
   c. concrete operational
   d. postconventional

5. Cite two types of biases that critics have leveled at Kohlberg's theory.

THINK ABOUT IT

• Was your adolescence a period of *sturm und drang* (storm and stress), or was it relatively peaceful? Why do you suppose some teenagers move through adolescence with relative ease, whereas others find it a difficult period? What made adolescence easy or difficult for you?

• Describe two types of biases critics have leveled at Kohlberg's theory. Do you believe these criticisms are well grounded?

MODULE 10.2
Early and Middle Adulthood

- What cognitive and physical changes take place as people age?
- How do theorists conceptualize social and personality development during early and middle adulthood?
- What are the major variations in adult lifestyles today?

Who's Middle Aged? Veteran rock stars like Madonna have led to a blurring of generational lines.

CONCEPT 10.10
Though many cognitive abilities reach a peak in early adulthood, declines in memory functioning that normally occur with age may not interfere with occupational or social functioning.

fluid intelligence A form of intelligence associated with the ability to think abstractly and flexibly in solving problems.
crystallized intelligence A form of intelligence associated with the ability to use accumulated knowledge.

Development doesn't stop with the end of puberty. Physical and psychological development is a continuing process that lasts a lifetime. When does adolescence end and adulthood—in the psychological, not the legal sense—begin? As we'll see in this module, we can think of the transition from adolescence to adulthood as a process that occurs over a period of years from the late teens through the middle twenties. It is not any particular date, like your eighteenth birthday, that you can mark on a calendar.

When does middle adulthood or *middle age* begin? When does it end? The most common conception of middle age is that it begins at age 40 and ends at age 60 or 65 with the beginning of late adulthood or old age (Lachman, 2004). But for many people, age is more a state of mind than a matter of years. A survey of 1,200 Americans asked people when they thought middle age begins. Nearly half (46 percent) claimed that middle age begins when you come to realize you no longer know the names of the new musical groups (Beck, 1992). Forty-two percent stated that it begins when the last child leaves home. Because these markers can occur at very different times—no doubt some older people can still identify the new music groups—it's difficult to identify precisely when middle age begins. Many of the so-called baby boomers, now in their fifties and early sixties, act younger than their parents did at the same age, or at least believe they do. The middle years can be a time to reflect upon what we have done (or haven't done) and determine what remains to be done (Lachman, 2004).

In this module, we continue our journey through human development by examining the changes in our physical and psychological development that occur as we progress from early adulthood through middle age.

Physical and Cognitive Development

In many respects, physical and cognitive development reach a peak in early adulthood. During their twenties, most people are at their height in terms of memory functioning, ability to learn new skills, sensory acuteness, muscle strength, reaction time, and cardiovascular condition.

By and large, people also perform best on standardized intelligence tests during early adulthood. Some declines in mental functioning can be expected as people age during middle and late adulthood. The greatest declines occur in **fluid intelligence**, or mental flexibility, the type of intelligence needed to solve problems quickly, perceive relationships among patterns, remember newly acquired information, form and recognize concepts, and reason abstractly and rapidly (Lachman, 2004; Salthouse, 2004). Another form of intelligence, **crystallized intelligence**, represents the person's accumulated knowledge, vocabulary, numerical ability, and ability to apply acquired knowledge. It shows little decline with age and may even improve in certain respects, such as through increased vocabulary size (Mayr & Kliegl, 2000; Verhaeghen, 2003) (see Figure 10.2).

As people age, they typically experience declines in some types of memory functioning, especially working memory, memory for recent experiences, word lists, and people's names (DeDe et al., 2004; Henry et al., 2004). Although we may not be able to solve problems as quickly as we age and may occasionally fumble

Figure 10.2   Age-Related Changes in Intellectual Ability
Crystallized intelligence, which includes abilities such as verbal meaning (vocabulary comprehension) and numerical skills, remains relatively stable or may even improve as we age. The sharpest declines occur with fluid intelligence, the kind of intelligence needed for abstract reasoning skills, such as inductive reasoning, and spatial orientation.

Source: Schaie, 1996.

Fluid Intelligence

Crystallized Intelligence

over people's names, the experience and knowledge we've gained may offset the gradual declines in cognitive abilities associated with normal aging.

Beginning in their late twenties, people start losing lean body tissue, especially muscle. With each passing decade, they tend to lose about seven pounds of lean body mass as more and more lean tissue turns to fat. From ages twenty to seventy, people are likely to lose as much as 30 percent of their muscle cells. Even so, most physical changes in middle adulthood occur gradually and the rates at which changes occur vary among individuals (Connell & Janevic, 2003).

Loss of muscle tissue is associated with a gradual decline of muscle strength. A person can help offset this loss, however, by following a regular weight-bearing exercise program. Regular exercise, in combination with a proper diet, can also help prevent significant gains in weight. Major weight gains are neither a normal nor an inevitable consequence of aging (Williamson et al., 1990).

The most dramatic physical change during middle age is the cessation of menstruation and reproductive capability in women. This biological event, called **menopause**, typically occurs in a woman's late forties or early fifties. With menopause, the ovaries no longer ripen egg cells or produce the sex hormones estrogen and progesterone.

A persistent stereotype about menopause is that it signals the end of the woman's sexual appetite or drive. In fact, a woman's sex drive is fueled by the small amounts of male sex hormones (androgens) produced by her adrenal glands, not by estrogen. Still, the meaning menopause holds for the individual woman can have a strong bearing on her adjustment. Women who have been raised to believe menopause is connected with a loss of femininity may lose sexual interest or feel less sexually desirable. Others may actually feel liberated by the cutting of ties between sex and reproduction. Table 10.3 lists some common myths and corresponding facts about menopause.

Unlike women, men can maintain fertility well into later adulthood. Men do experience a gradual decline in testosterone as they age, in contrast to the sharp decline in estrogen production that occurs in women during menopause.

💡 **CONCEPT 10.11**
Menopause is a major life event for most women and may symbolize other issues they may face in middle adulthood, including changes in appearance, health, and sexuality.

💡 **CONCEPT 10.12**
Men experience a gradual decline in production of the male sex hormone testosterone as they age, but unlike women they may maintain reproductive capability well into late adulthood.

menopause   The time of life when menstruation ends.

TABLE 10.3 Myths Versus Facts About Menopause

Myth	Fact
A woman's body no longer produces estrogen after menopause.	Though estrogen production falls off, some estrogen continues to be produced by the adrenal glands and fatty tissue.
Women normally become depressed or anxious during menopause as a result of hormonal changes.	Researchers have found no overall relationship between menopausal status and depression or anxiety (Dennerstein et al., 2002; Jackson, Taylor, & Pyngolil, 1991; Matthews et al., 1990). Of course, women who had psychological problems before menopause may continue to have difficulties following menopause.
Menopause is a physical event, not a psychological event.	Though physical changes occur in the woman's body during menopause, the meaning she applies to these changes has a determining effect on her emotional response. If the woman considers menopause to be the beginning of the end of her life, she may develop a sense of hopelessness that can lead to depression. Investigators also have linked psychological factors such as marital dissatisfaction to greater menopausal symptoms (Kurpius, Nicpon, & Maresh, 2001).
Women can expect to experience severe hot flashes during menopause.	Many women experience mild flashes or no flashes at all.
Women lose all desire for sexual activity after menopause.	Not true. Sexual interest and capability may continue throughout the woman's life span.

Source: Adapted from Nevid & Rathus, 2005.

Psychosocial Development

The challenges of young adulthood have largely to do with sorting out adult roles and relationships (Zucker, Ostrove, & Stewart, 2002). Yet for many young adults today, the twenties may be an extended adolescence, with age 30 becoming the threshold of full-fledged adulthood (Grigoriadis, 2003).

Psychologist Jeffrey Arnett coined the term **emerging adulthood** to describe the transition from adolescence to adulthood that occurs roughly from age 18 to age 25 (Arnett, 2000, 2004). Arnett uses the word *roughly* because the process varies among individuals. Some people, perhaps by dint of their personality or the circumstances they face, emerge into adulthood earlier, whereas others take longer to move out of adolescence and into adulthood.

Arnett (2004) conceptualizes emerging adulthood as a distinct period of development that can be distinguished from other periods of life by five key characteristics:

1. *The age of identity exploration.* Emerging adulthood is a period of sorting who we are, what we believe in, and where we are headed in life. It is also a time for exploration of romantic partners and career alternatives in preparation for making lasting choices and commitments.

2. *The age of instability.* Exploring different possibilities in love and work entails a good deal of instability. The young person may switch majors or career objectives and move from one relationship to another or from one residence to another.

3. *The self-focused age.* Emerging adults become focused on themselves in terms of developing the skills, knowledge, and self-understanding that will help prepare them for meeting the responsibilities of adult life.

4. *The age of feeling in between.* We noted earlier how adolescents feel betwixt and between the worlds of children and adults. But emerging adults also have feelings of being in between, of feeling not quite adolescents but not quite full

CONCEPT 10.13
Psychosocial development in early adulthood often centers on establishing intimate relationships and finding a place in the world.

emerging adulthood In some cultures, the period of psychosocial development roughly spanning ages 18 to 25 during which the person makes the transition from adolescence to adulthood.

Figure 10.3   Are You an Adult?
Respondents were asked, "Do you feel that you have reached adulthood?" A majority of respondents did not perceive themselves to be adults until their late twenties or early thirties.

Source: Reprinted with permission from Arnett (2004); based on data from Arnett, 2000.

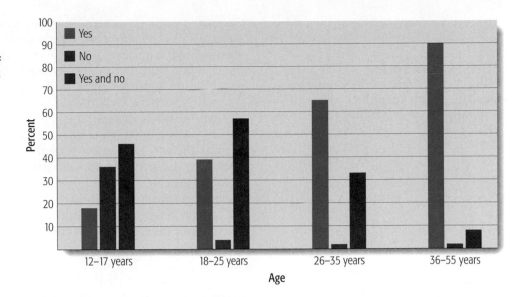

CONCEPT 10.14
Arnett's concept of emerging adulthood recognizes that in some cultures the transition from adolescence to adulthood involves a distinct period of development between the late teens and early to mid-twenties.

independent adults. As you can see in Figure 10.3, it isn't until the late twenties or early thirties that most people say they feel they have reached full adulthood.

5. *The age of possibilities.* Emerging adulthood is a period of possibilities, not certainties, a time when one holds great hopes and expectations for a future life that hasn't yet been realized.

Emerging adult is not found in all cultures. Arnett believes that it exists only in those cultures that allow a gradual transition from adolescence to adulthood (Arnett, 2004). In many cultures, young people are expected to assume the roles of full adulthood, such as marriage and parenthood, at earlier ages than is true of contemporary Western society. Cultural factors also come into play in our own society in determining when young adults set out on their own. For example, the sense of familial duty is especially strong among Filipino and Latino young adults, which may explain their tendency to continue to live with their families and contribute financially to them (Fuligni & Pedersen, 2002).

Arnett follows in the tradition of other theorists, most notably Erik Erikson (1963), in emphasizing the importance of identity formation in development. Erikson characterized the major identity challenge (crisis) of young adulthood as one of *intimacy versus isolation,* of forming intimate relationships versus remaining lonely and isolated.

In Erikson's view, earlier difficulties navigating life challenges can affect the resolution of later-occurring challenges. For example, young adults who forged a strong ego identity or a commitment to a stable life role during adolescence may be prepared in early adulthood to form intimate attachments, to "fuse" their identities with others in marriage and in lasting friendships. Those who fail to establish intimate relationships may retreat into isolation and loneliness. People who did not learn a basic sense of trust early in life may also have a greater fear of intimacy in adulthood (Terrell, Terrell, & Von Drashek, 2000) and so may experience more loneliness and difficulties establishing close relationships.

Some gender differences in social and personality development emerge in early and middle adulthood. Men often appear more oriented toward becoming their own person: separating from parents and other authority figures and establishing their own independent identities (Guisinger & Blatt, 1994). Women, especially college women, may share this goal but also seem more strongly oriented toward developing social and intimate relationships (Gilligan, Lyons, & Hanmer, 1990).

CONCEPT 10.15
Erikson characterized the challenge faced by people in midlife as one of generativity versus stagnation.

REALITY CHECK

THE CLAIM Most people in middle adulthood experience a midlife crisis.

THE EVIDENCE Actually, evidence fails to bear out the commonly held belief that a midlife crisis is a widespread occurrence (Lachman, 2004). It may actually be more the exception than the rule.

THE TAKE-AWAY MESSAGE Most people navigate through middle adulthood without a significant midlife crisis.

CONCEPT 10.16
Although some people experience a midlife crisis, most appear to weather the changes in their middle years without a period of personal upheaval or crisis.

midlife crisis   A state of psychological crisis, often occurring during middle adulthood, in which people grapple with the loss of their youth.

empty nest syndrome   A cluster of negative emotions, involving a loss of purpose and direction, that can occur when one's children have grown and left home.

Compared to men, women seem to experience more conflict with respect to career plans, which may reflect the difficulties they face in combining outside work with motherhood in a society where women remain the primary caregivers.

Middle adulthood may be characterized by a loosening of traditional gender roles (Helson & Wink, 1992). Middle-age women may become more assertive and competitive, whereas middle-age men may become more nurturing and emotionally expressive. To Erikson, the key psychosocial challenge faced by adults in midlife pits *generativity versus stagnation*. By "generativity," he meant efforts directed at shaping the new generation or generations to come. Shaping may include raising one's own children or helping to make the world a better place for other children or future generations of children, such as by transmitting one's values or mentoring younger workers (Lachman, 2004). A failure to achieve generativity leads to stagnation, a kind of self-absorption in which people indulge themselves as though they themselves were "their one and only child" (Erikson, 1980). Research evidence supports Erikson's view that generativity is primarily a task of midlife (Zucker et al., 2002).

To Erikson, each stage of adult life presents unique challenges that can either strengthen and enrich us or weaken or diminish us. Other investigators and social observers focus less on stages of adult development and more on how people cope with the transitions they face during the course of their lives. For example, psychologist Daniel Levinson and his colleagues (1978) suggested that a midlife transition begins at about age 40. To Levinson, this age is a time of reckoning when we assess our lives in terms of whether or not we have reached the dreams we held in our youth. We may feel life is starting to slip away and realize we are now a full generation older than the youngest of the young adults. We may start to wonder whether we have more to look back on than forward to. Many middle-age adults compare their accomplishments to their earlier dreams they held as youths and may despair if they find they have fallen short.

This midlife transition can trigger a **midlife crisis**: a sense of entrapment from the closing down of future options, of feeling that life is open-ended no more, of a loss of purpose or a sense of failure from not having fulfilled one's youthful ambitions or aspirations. Some people may respond to the midlife crisis by attempting to recover their lost youth. Such behavior may include an extramarital affair to prove that one is still sexually desirable to others, increased risk taking, or perhaps the purchase of a two-seater sports car (in red, of course). However, a midlife crisis is far from inevitable and is less common than many people believe.

In actuality, many people in middle adulthood today are focusing on what they believe will be another three to four decades of promise rather than decline. On this assumption, they are switching careers and aspiring to new dreams and goals. They feel that it is perhaps now that they will make their greatest contributions to the next generation. This concept resonates with Erikson's concept of generativity.

Another commonly held belief is that people in their forties and fifties, especially women, are likely to experience depression and loss of purpose and direction when their children leave home. This crisis, labeled the **empty nest syndrome**, was probably fairly common in the days when a woman's identity centered on childbearing and child rearing. But though there may be understandable concerns about letting go of one's children, research shows many parents—fathers as well as mothers—experience the period of life after raising children as a time of reconnecting with each other and pursuing their own interests (Clay, 2003; Fingerman, 2002). However, many empty nests are refilling these days as increasing numbers of adult children are returning home (or deciding not to leave in the first place) because of a tough job market and high housing costs (Belkin, 2003; Clay, 2003). Concept Chart 10.2 provides an overview of development during young and middle adulthood.

CONCEPT CHART 10.2   Development in Young and Middle Adulthood

Physical Development	People tend to reach their physical and mental peaks in early adulthood. Declines in lean body tissue and muscle mass begin in the twenties. In middle age, women experience menopause, the cessation of menstruation, which is accompanied by a sharp drop in estrogen production. Men encounter a more gradual reduction in testosterone as they age.
Cognitive Development	While fluid intelligence tends to decline during middle and late adulthood, crystallized intelligence shows little, if any, decline and may actually improve in some respects. Memory skills, such as the ability to memorize lists of words or names, may show the greatest age-related declines but typically do not have a significant impact on the person's social and occupational functioning.
Psychosocial Development	Arnett described *emerging adulthood* (18 to 25 years) as a period in which a person gradually assumes the more independent roles associated with full adulthood; this lengthy period of transition is not found in all cultures. Erikson proposed two stages of psychosocial development in young and middle adulthood, respectively: *intimacy* versus *isolation* and *generativity* versus *stagnation.* Levinson and colleagues focused on the important transitions that occur during adulthood. One of these, the *midlife crisis,* is not as common as most people believe.

Marriage, American Style

Half of adults age 15 and older in our society (53 percent of men and 49.5 percent of women) are married and living with their spouses (U.S. Census Bureau, 2003). Marriage is a universal societal institution that is found in every human culture, from the industrialized societies of North America and Europe to the farthest reaches of Micronesia (Ember & Ember, 2004). Most people in all human societies—in some cases, nearly all—marry at least once. More than 95 percent of Americans marry by age 60 (U.S. Census Bureau, 2003).

CONCEPT 10.17

Despite the wider range of lifestyles available to adults today, marriage remains the most common lifestyle in the United States.

Why People Marry   Marriage is popular worldwide because it meets many personal and social needs. It legitimizes and provides opportunities for regular sexual relations and offers a family structure to raise children within a stable home environment. It is an institution in which children are supported and socialized into adopting the values of the family and of the culture at large. Marriage also permits the orderly transmission of wealth from one family to another and from one generation to the next.

Does marriage bring happiness? The results of a recent survey of 24,000 people showed that marriage tends to give a small boost to personal happiness, but the effects are typically short-lived (Lucas et al., 2003; Salleh, 2003). As people get accustomed to married life, happiness levels generally return to their earlier levels. As noted in Chapter 8, personal happiness may have more do with one's general disposition than with marital status.

Most people today become sexually active long before they march down the wedding aisle. Since marriage is no longer the point of entry for sexual relations for most couples, its continuing appeal primarily reflects other factors, such as providing a sense of security, offering opportunities for raising children within a family unit, providing opportunities for companionship and intimacy, and fulfilling a desire to travel with a partner down life's road. The majority of Americans—86 percent according to a recent survey—believe marriage is "for keeps:" once you get married, you expect to stay married for the rest of your life ("Intimacies," 2000).

Who We Marry   People today generally say they marry for love, but it wasn't always so. As late as the seventeenth and eighteenth centuries, most European marriages were arranged by parents to enhance the family's financial stability. Though parents in Western societies may no longer arrange marriages, they may still encourage their children to date the wonderful sons and daughters of those solid churchgoing couples who live down the block. The principle of **homogamy**, or "like marrying like," continues to hold true. People in our society tend to marry others from the same geographical area, race, educational level, religion, and social class. Stories like Cinderella's by and large remain fairy tales. That being said, interracial marriages in the United States have been on the rise and now number some 1.5 million marriages (Kennedy, 2003; Kristof, 2002). A recent study of Mexican American/European American marriages showed that these interethnic couples were similar to European American couples in measures of relationship satisfaction (Negy & Snyder, 2000).

Generally speaking, people also marry others who are similar to themselves in physical and psychological characteristics—even in height, weight, personality traits, and general intelligence (Buss, 1994; Lamanna & Riedmann, 1997).

Singlehood An increasing number of young people are choosing to remain single as a way of life, not just as a way station while awaiting the arrival of Mr. or Ms. Right. As you'll see in the nearby "Exploring Psychology" feature, more couples are also choosing to live together—to *cohabit*—without getting married. Attitudes have changed along with the times. A generation or two ago, people living together out of wedlock were branded as "shacking up" or "living in sin." Today we are more apt to hear more descriptive terms—such as "living together" or the more official-sounding "cohabiting" rather than terms carrying a social stigma.

Marriages may be made in heaven, but many people are saying heaven can wait. Singlehood is the most common lifestyle among adults in their early twenties. Single people living alone constitute one out of four of all U.S. households and now outnumber households consisting of married couples with children (Lewin, 2003). The proportions of people in their late twenties and early thirties who remain single have more than doubled since 1970 (Edwards, 2000). At the same time, the average age of first marriage has risen to its highest level ever, to 27 for men and 25 for women (U.S. Census Bureau, 2003). Figure 10.4 shows the increasing percentages of adults in the United States who have yet to take that walk down the aisle of matrimony.

Why are more adults remaining single? One reason is that more people are postponing marriage or commitment to a life partner to pursue their own educational and career goals. More young people today are also choosing to cohabit, at least temporarily, rather than get married. The high incidence of divorce also swells the ranks of single adults.

No one specific pattern fits all singles. Many single adults are not sexually active, either by choice or through lack of opportunity. Some choose to remain celibate to focus more energy on their careers or interests. Many others practice *serial monogamy,* becoming involved in a series of exclusive relationships rather than having simultaneous sexual relationships. Some, but certainly not most, singles fit the stereotype of the "swinging single" in pursuing a series of casual sexual encounters or "one-night stands." Similar variations exist in the lifestyles of both gay and heterosexual singles and couples.

Of course, many older people are single because they are widowed. Because they tend to live longer than men, women are five times more likely than men to be widowed. The adjustment of widows depends on many factors, including health, financial security, and social relationships with children, grandchildren, and peers (DeSpelder & Strickland, 1999).

Divorce About 40 percent of first marriages (and about 65 percent of second marriages) in the United States end in divorce (Kaslow, 2001). The divorce rate doubled from 1960 to 1990 but leveled off and then dipped slightly in the 1990s. The increased acceptability of divorce as an alternative to a troubled marriage, the

💡 **CONCEPT 10.18**
Though marriage remains our most popular lifestyle overall, singlehood is the most common lifestyle among people in their early twenties.

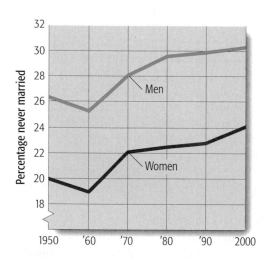

Figure 10.4 Percentages of Adults (age 15+) in the U.S. Who Have Never Married The percentages of adults in the United States who have yet to take that walk down the wedding aisle have been rising steadily since the 1950s.

Source: U.S. Census Bureau, *Marital Status of the Population 15 Years Old and Over, by Sex, Age, Race, and Hispanic Origin; Census 2000 Special Tabulation.*

homogamy The tendency for people to marry others who are similar to themselves.

"Good evening, I am Martha's son by a previous marriage."

CONCEPT 10.19

Factors contributing to the rising divorce rates in recent years include changing attitudes toward the acceptability of divorce, the loosening of divorce laws, and the increased economic independence of women.

loosening of divorce laws, and the increased economic independence of women were major contributors to the higher divorce rate.

Divorce is often associated with financial and emotional problems. The splitting up of a household's resources often leaves both partners with a lower standard of living. The financial burdens are not evenly distributed, however. Women typically experience a drop of about 25 percent in household income after divorce, compared to about 6 percent for men (Bianchi & Spain, 1997).

Couples coping with divorce often experience emotional difficulties such as depression, loneliness, and lingering fears about what the future may bring. They may feel a sense of personal failure as a spouse and parent. However, for those leaving failed marriages, divorce may offer opportunities for a new, more rewarding life.

The children of divorce may also suffer (Wolchik et al., 2002). Children's adjustment to divorce depends on many factors, including circumstances, age, and gender. Still, children from divorced families tend to fare more poorly in school and to have more behavioral problems, often including substance abuse (O'Connor et al., 2000). Children of divorced parents may appear to be well adjusted in childhood but experience problems in later development (Wallerstein, Lewis, & Blakeslee, 2000). For example, as adults they may have difficulty trusting that lovers or spouses will remain committed to them.

Divorce is difficult for children in the best of circumstances and is made worse when marital problems and conflicts spill over into parent-child relationships. Conflict between ex-spouses can easily lead to a decline in the quality of parenting. Children of divorce fare better when their parents do the following:

- Try, in spite of their differences, to agree on how to handle the children

- Help each other maintain important roles in the children's lives

- Refrain from disparaging or criticizing each other in front of the children

Most divorced people eventually remarry. You might expect divorced people to be seasoned by their earlier experience to "get it right" this time, but later marriages are more likely than first marriages to end in divorce. One reason may be that people who divorce from their first spouses are less likely than others to stick it out when they encounter marital problems the second time around. Another may be the toll on the marital relationship resulting from conflicts over stepchildren (Golish, 2003; Hofferth & Anderson, 2003), such as favoring one's own biological children, or the financial strain of supporting children from two (or more) marriages.

EXPLORING PSYCHOLOGY
Cohabitation: Trial Marriage or Marriage Alternative?

Mark and Nancy live together with their 7-year-old daughter, Janet. Why are they not married? Mark says, "We feel we are not primarily a couple but rather primarily individuals who happen to be *in* a couple. It allows me to be a little more at arm's length. Men don't like committing," he then admits, "so maybe this is just some sort of excuse" (cited in Steinhauer, 1995).

Some social scientists argue that cohabitation has now become accepted within the mainstream of contemporary society (Bumpass, 1995). Whether or not

CONCEPT 10.20

For many couples, cohabitation is an alternative both to living alone and to marriage.

this is true, the fact is that the numbers of cohabiting couples increased by 72 percent in just the period from 1990 to 2000, to about 5.5 million couples today (Marquis, 2003). More than half of contemporary marriages in the United States were preceded by a period of living together (Smock, 2000).

For Mark, as for many other adults, *cohabitation* is an alternative both to living alone and to marriage. Some partners have deep feelings for each other but are not ready to get married. Some prefer cohabitation because of its relative lack of legal and economic entanglements (Steinhauer, 1995). Some view cohabitation as a type of trial marriage, an opportunity to give living together a trial run before deciding to "tie the knot." Cohabitation is not limited to heterosexual couples. In a recent research sample, adult gay men and lesbians in cohabiting couples expressed as much overall satisfaction with their relationships as unmarried, cohabiting heterosexual couples (Means-Christensen, Snyder, & Negy, 2003).

Many cohabiting couples believe that cohabitation is a trial marriage that will strengthen their eventual marriage. Living together, they say, helps them iron out the kinks in their relationship. But the evidence suggests otherwise. It turns out that cohabiting couples who later marry are more likely to divorce than couples who did not cohabit before marriage (Cohan & Kleinbaum, 2002; Holman, 2000). We should be cautious about making causal inferences, however. People who cohabit prior to marriage may be less committed to traditional values associated with the institution of marriage, such as the commitment to "sticking it out through thick and thin." Differences in attitudes or values, rather than cohabitation per se, may account for the higher rates of divorce among people who had cohabited before marriage. In any event, about four in ten young cohabiting couples do marry eventually (Laumann et al., 1994). Most other cohabiting couples break up within three years. Overall, cohabiting couples are more likely to break apart than join together in marriage (Willis & Michael, 1994).

MODULE 10.2 REVIEW

Early and Middle Adulthood

RECITE IT

What cognitive and physical changes take place as people age?

- Beginning in their twenties, people start to experience a gradual decline in lean body mass and muscle tissue.

- Fluid intelligence—including rapid problem-solving ability and memory for lists of words, names, or text—tends to decline with increasing age during middle and late adulthood

- Crystallized intelligence remains relatively intact and may actually improve in some respects.

- Menopause, the cessation of menstruation, is the major physical marker of middle adulthood in women. Menopause is associated with a dramatic decline in estrogen production.

- Testosterone production in men also declines with age, but more gradually.

How do theorists conceptualize social and personality development during early and middle adulthood?

- Arnett defined a stage called emerging adulthood (ages 18 to 25) in some cultures that is a transition between adolescence and adulthood.

- Erikson focused on the stages of psychosocial development: intimacy versus isolation (forming intimate, stable relationships versus remaining emotionally detached) during early adulthood and generativity versus stagnation (making meaningful contributions to the future generation or generations versus becoming stagnant and self-absorbed) during middle adulthood.

- Theorist Daniel Levinson focuses on the transitions through which people may need to navigate as they age.

What are the major variations in adult lifestyles today?

- Though marriage remains the most common lifestyle, the proportion of single people has risen sharply during the past twenty years or so.

- The divorce rate, after rising dramatically from 1960 to 1990, dipped slightly in the 1990s. Eventually, most divorced people remarry.

RECALL IT

1. In general, people perform best on standardized tests of intelligence
   a. in middle childhood.
   b. in adolescence.
   c. in early adulthood.
   d. in middle adulthood.

2. Evidence supports the linkage between menopause and depression. True or false?

3. The transition from adolescence to adulthood can be described as a period of _____ adulthood.

4. The major psychosocial challenge of early adulthood, according to Erikson, is that of
   a. role identity versus confusion.
   b. intimacy versus isolation.
   c. generativity versus stagnation.
   d. ego integrity versus despair.

5. The relationship pattern among single adults that is characterized by a series of exclusive relationships rather than simultaneous sexual relationships is called _____ monogamy.

THINK ABOUT IT

- What is your current "stage" of psychosocial development? Does your life reflect the issues and challenges framed by Erikson and Levinson? If so, in what respects?

- The principle of homogamy suggests that "like marries like." How well does this principle apply to people you know, including yourself if you happen to be married or engaged?

- Do you believe cohabitation is an acceptable lifestyle choice? Do your views differ from those of your parents or friends? If so, what do you suppose may account for these differences?

MODULE 10.3

Late Adulthood

- **What physical and cognitive changes occur in late adulthood?**
- **What is Alzheimer's disease?**
- **How do theorists characterize the psychosocial challenges of late adulthood?**
- **How do our emotions change as we age?**
- **What qualities are associated with successful aging?**
- **What are the stages of dying as identified by Kübler-Ross?**

CONCEPT 10.21

On average, Americans are living longer than ever before.

If you are fortunate enough, you may one day join the ranks of the fastest-growing segment of the population: people ages 65 and older. We are in the midst of a "graying of America," an aging of the population that has already begun to have profound effects on our society (Libow, 2005). As you can see in Figure 10.5, life expectancy has been rising steadily, but is expected to level off in the years ahead. So many people are living longer today that the overall age of the population has risen sharply. By the year 2050, more than one in five Americans— approximately 74 million people—will be in the 65-plus age group (Clements, 2003) (see Figure 10.6). The percentage of Americans over age 75 is expected to nearly double by the next half-century, from 5.9 percent in 2000 to 11.4 percent in 2050 (Kawas & Brookmeyer, 2001). These facts are amazing when we consider that throughout human history until about the beginning of the nineteenth century, only a small minority of people lived to the "grand old age" of 50! (Freund & Riediger, 2003).

One major reason for increased life expectancy is that many infectious diseases that took the lives of millions of people in the early twentieth century, especially children, have been largely controlled or even eliminated through the

Figure 10.5 Increasing Life Expectancy
Life expectancy in the United States increased sharply in the early to mid twentieth century and is expected to increase slightly more through the first half of the twenty-first century.

Figure 10.6 The Aging of America
The "graying of America" is in full stride. The percentage of the population over age 65 is projected to continue to increase through the first half of the twenty-first century.

Source: Data from U.S. Census Bureau, 1995.

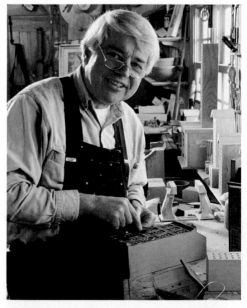

Remembering Mr. Carpenter, but Forgetting His Name Research participants were shown faces of people identified by name and occupation. Older participants had a more difficult time than young adults remembering the names associated with the faces they'd seen, but were not more forgetful when it came to remembering occupations (James, 2004).

introduction of vaccination programs, development of antibiotics, and creation of public health efforts to ensure safer water supplies. Other factors contributing to increased longevity are improvements in health care and reductions in the number of Americans who smoke (see Chapter 15).

Physical and Cognitive Development

As people age, they experience a general decline in sensory and motor abilities. They continue to lose bone density as well as muscle mass, and their senses become less acute. The skin loses elasticity, and wrinkles and folds appear. Night vision fades and joints stiffen. In addition, declines in the functioning of the immune system, the body's system of defense against disease-causing agents, makes older people more susceptible to illness, including life-threatening illnesses such as cancer.

We noted in Module 10.2 that performance on tasks requiring fluid intelligence tends to decline as people age. Older people typically require more time to solve problems and have greater difficulties with tasks involving pattern recognition, such as piecing together jigsaw puzzles (Jenkins et al., 2000). In addition, they may encounter more difficulties with memory for new information, such as remembering people's names, and with working memory—keeping information briefly in mind while mulling it over (MacPherson, Phillips, & Della Sala, 2002; Rypma et al., 2001). Some decline in mental processing speed can also be expected as people age (Braver et. al., 2001; Zimprich & Martin, 2002). Since older people take longer to respond to stimuli, older drivers may require more time to respond to other cars and traffic signals. On the other hand, performance on tasks involving crystallized intelligence, such as vocabulary skills, remains relatively intact as people age. Our fund of knowledge actually increases across much of the life span and only begins to decline around the advanced age of 90 (Park et al., 2002; Singer et al., 2003).

Older people often have trouble recalling names of common objects or occasionally may call a familiar person by the wrong name. Nevertheless, declines in memory functioning generally do not significantly impair daily functioning (Burke, 1992; Hertzog & Dunlosky, 1996). In one study of 397 people age 55 and over, fewer than 3 percent reported that their memory posed major problems for them (Smith, Goldman, Greenbaum, & Christiansen, 1996).

Nor are slight changes in memory, such as occasionally forgetting where one put one's glasses, signs of dementia or Alzheimer's disease. People should not get

TRY THIS OUT

Examining Your Attitudes Toward Aging

What are your assumptions about growing old? Do you see older people as fundamentally different from younger people in their behavior and outlook, or just as more mature? To evaluate the accuracy of your attitudes toward aging, mark each of the following items true (T) or false (F). Then turn to the answer key at the end of the chapter.

True False

___ ___ 1. By age sixty, most couples have lost their capacity for satisfying sexual relations.
___ ___ 2. Older people cannot wait to retire.
___ ___ 3. As individuals age, they become less able to adapt satisfactorily to a changing environment.
___ ___ 4. General satisfaction with life tends to decrease as people become older.
___ ___ 5. Most older people are depressed much of the time.
___ ___ 6. Church attendance increases with age.
___ ___ 7. The occupational performance of the older worker is typically less effective than that of the younger adult.
___ ___ 8. Most older people are unable to learn new skills.
___ ___ 9. Compared to younger adults, older people tend to think more about the past than the present or the future.
___ ___ 10. Most people in later life are unable to live independently and reside in nursing home–like institutions.

Source: Adapted from Rathus & Nevid, 1995.

alarmed at these normal age-related memory lapses, since everyone has them. Still, older adults may need more time or repeated exposure to new material to commit information to memory and to later recall it. Preserved intellectual ability in later life is associated with such factors as general physical health, engagement in stimulating activities, and openness to new experiences (Schaie, 1996).

Creativity, too, is not time-limited. The great architect Frank Lloyd Wright worked on the famed Guggenheim Museum until this death at the age of 91 (Springen & Seibert, 2005). Benjamin Franklin invented bifocals at the age of 78 to help with his own poor vision, and Michelangelo was still painting frescoes well into his seventies.

Keeping the Mind Sharp Remaining open to new experiences and challenges can help keep the mind sharp in later life.

Alzheimer's Disease: The Long Goodbye

CONCEPT 10.22

In older adults, declines in cognitive and memory performance are typically not significant enough to impair daily functioning and are largely offset by use of acquired knowledge and skills.

CONCEPT 10.23

Alzheimer's disease is a degenerative brain disease and is not a consequence of normal aging.

TRY THIS OUT

Getting Involved

You can acquire firsthand knowledge about the devastating effects of memory loss and help those suffering with Alzheimer's disease and related conditions by serving as a volunteer. Many communities have Alzheimer's support groups you can contact to offer assistance. Ask your family physician or college health office for help if you have trouble locating local support groups.

Most people retain the bulk of their mental abilities throughout their lives and can compensate for gradual losses in memory and mental processing speed by applying acquired knowledge and skills to the demands they face (Freund & Riediger, 2003). However, some people develop **dementia** (sometimes called senility) in late adulthood. Dementia is characterized by a sharp decline in mental abilities, especially memory and reasoning ability. Dementia is *not* a normal consequence of aging (Butler, 2001).

Dementia has many causes, including brain infections, tumors, Parkinson's disease, brain injuries, strokes, and chronic alcoholism. But the most common cause is Alzheimer's disease (Coyle, 2003) (see Figure 10.7).

Alzheimer's disease, or AD, is an irreversible brain disease with a gradual onset and a slow but progressive course toward inevitable deterioration of mental functioning (Hurley & Volicer, 2002). At first there are only subtle changes in cognition and personality. People may have trouble recalling recent events and managing their financial affairs. As the disease progresses, people require help selecting clothes, driving, recalling names and addresses, and maintaining personal hygiene. They may start wandering and even become lost in familiar environments (Ryan et al., 1995). They may no longer be able to recognize family and friends or speak coherently. Even those who had the most easygoing temperaments may become depressed, agitated, or aggressive. In the final stages, there is a loss of speech and ability to control body movement (Fuchs, 2001). The person may become incontinent and be unable to walk or even sit up. At the end, seizures, coma, and death result.

Alzheimer's disease affects about 4 million Americans and is among the leading causes of death among older adults in the United States (Blakey, 2002; Brookmeyer et al., 2002; Grady, 2004). Risk of the disease increases dramatically in later life (L. S. Schneider, 2004). One in ten people over age 65 suffers from Alzheimer's, a proportion that rises to nearly one in two after age 85 (Lemonick & Park, 2001;

dementia A condition involving a major deterioration or loss of mental abilities involved in memory, reasoning, judgment, and capacity to carry out purposeful behavior.

Alzheimer's disease An irreversible brain disease characterized by progressive deterioration of mental functioning.

Do You Know My Name? The man shown here can sometimes recall the names of his loved ones when he is prompted by viewing old photographs.

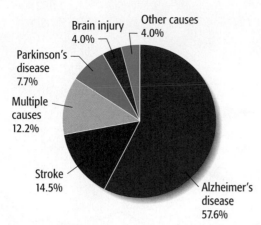

Figure 10.7   Prevalence and Causes of Dementia
Alzheimer's disease is the leading cause of dementia, accounting for more than half of the cases.

Source: Tune, 1998.

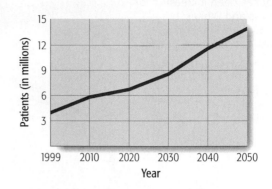

Figure 10.8   Projections of Numbers of Alzheimer's Patients Through 2050
The number of Alzheimer's patients is expected to soar through at least the first half of the twenty-first century.

Source: Cowley, 2000c.

Online Study Center
Resources
Weblinks: Alzheimer's Disease
Education

Sommerfeld, 2002). As the U.S. population continues to age, cases of AD are expected to nearly quadruple by the middle of the twenty-first century, to about 14 million (Kawas & Brookmeyer, 2001) (see Figure 10.8). The disease can also affect younger people, but it is rare in those under 65.

Alzheimer's disease is associated with progressive death of brain cells in many parts of the brain (Thompson, Hayashi, et al., 2003). The causes of AD remain unknown, but scientists suspect that genetic factors play important roles (Mattson, 2003; Small et al., 2004). Scientists believe that different genes are involved in different forms of the disease (Nussbaum & Ellis, 2003; Pastor & Goate, 2004; Plomin & McGuffin, 2003). Although there is no cure for AD, drugs are available that can produce some modest benefits in slowing cognitive decline or boosting memory functioning in AD patients (AD 2000 Collaborative Group, 2004; Grady, 2004; Trinh et al., 2003). Hopes for the future lie with the development of an effective vaccine (Check, 2003).

Gender and Ethnic Differences in Life Expectancy

CONCEPT 10.24
Gender and ethnic factors play important roles in determining which Americans live longest and how well they live.

While longevity has been rising across the board, not every group has benefited equally. The gender gap in longevity has narrowed in recent years, but women in the United States still outlive men on the average by about seven years (Laino, 2002). There are many reasons for the discrepancy. One is that women are protected from heart disease by estrogen to some degree, so their risk for heart disease does not begin to approach men's until after menopause, when estrogen production falls off sharply. Men also are more likely than women to die from crimes of violence, accidents, cirrhosis of the liver (related to alcoholism), AIDS, suicide, and most forms of cancer (Hayflick, 1994).

Women may outlive men, but older men tend to live *better.* Older women are more likely than their male counterparts to be widowed and to live alone. They are also more likely to live in poverty and to have chronic health problems.

White (non-Hispanic) Americans tend to live longer than African Americans, Asian Americans, Hispanic Americans, and Native Americans. Figure 10.9 shows the changes in life expectancies for Blacks and Whites in the United States since 1950. One reason for ethnic differences in life expectancy is socioeconomic level (Siegler, Bosworth, & Poon, 2003). Members of ethnic minority groups are more

Figure 10.9   Life Expectancy at Birth
Life expectancy has been increasing for African Americans and Whites, but Whites still tend to live longer than African Americans of the same gender.

Source: National Center for Health Statistics, 2004.

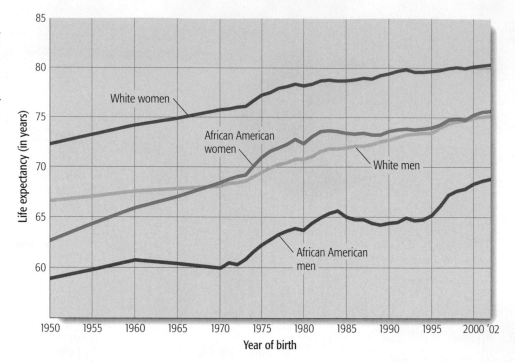

likely to live below the poverty line, and people living in poverty have life spans that are about seven years shorter on the average than those of more affluent people (Nevid, Rathus, & Rubenstein, 1998). Several lifestyle factors associated with lower socioeconomic level may be responsible for the life expectancy gap between the rich and poor. Poor people are more likely to smoke and have high-fat diets, are less likely to exercise regularly, and are less likely to have access to regular health care. Genetic differences may also play a role in ethnic differences in longevity.

Psychosocial Development

A major determinant of psychological adjustment in later life is physical health status. For older adults in good health, reaching age 65 is experienced more as an extension of middle age than of entry into old age, particularly if they continue to work. In this section, we chronicle how theorists conceptualize the social and personal challenges often encountered in later adulthood. We also examine the major emotional problem older adults face: depression.

Psychosocial Theories of Adjustment in Late Adulthood   To Erik Erikson, the central challenge of psychosocial development in late adulthood is one of *ego integrity versus despair.* He believed that if people in late adulthood feel good about their lives and their accomplishments, they experience a sense of ego integrity. People who achieve ego integrity are able to come to terms with their lives: to accept the joys and sorrows, and the successes and failures, that make up the totality of their life experiences. But people who look back with a sense of disappointment and regret can drift into a state of despair and bitterness. Erickson also believed that later adulthood involves a struggle to maintain a sense of meaning and satisfaction in life. Erikson himself lived and worked productively into his nineties. He was basically an optimist, believing we can remain fulfilled and maintain a sense of purpose at any stage of life and avoid falling into despair. Though Erikson is recognized for being among the first theorists to develop a model of lifelong development, his theory has been criticized for relying too much on the life experiences of highly educated males and failing to consider differences that may

CONCEPT 10.25
Erikson believed the major psychosocial challenge of late adulthood involves maintaining a sense of ego integrity or meaningfulness even as one approaches the end of life.

TABLE 10.4   Erikson's Stages of Psychosocial Development During Adolescence and Adulthood

Life Period	Life Crisis	Major Challenge in Psychosocial Development
Adolescence	Identity versus role diffusion	To develop a sense of who one is and what one stands for; commitment to an occupational choice and adoption of a set of firmly held personal beliefs
Early adulthood	Intimacy versus isolation	To develop close, abiding relationships and friendships with others, including intimate relationships
Middle adulthood	Generativity versus stagnation	To contribute to the development and well-being of young people and future generations
Late adulthood	Integrity versus despair	To maintain one's sense of dignity and psychological integrity as one approaches the final years of life

Source: Adapted from Erikson, 1963.

Aging and Sexuality   People who enjoy reasonably good physical health can expect to remain sexually active throughout their lives.

CONCEPT 10.26

Though there are age-related changes in sexuality, social stereotypes underlie perceptions that older adults who maintain an active sexual life are somehow abnormal or deviant.

exist in the developmental trajectories of women and people from non-Western cultures (Bertrand & Lachman, 2003). Table 10.4 offers an overview of Erikson's stages of psychosocial development from adolescence through late adulthood.

Other theorists, such as Daniel Levinson and Robert Havighurst, also recognize that late adulthood is characterized by increasing awareness of the psychological and physical changes and challenges that accompany aging and the need to come to terms with death. Havighurst outlined a number of developmental tasks people face in their later years, including adjusting to physical changes and retirement, coping with the loss of friends and loved ones, and establishing new relationships with aging peers. Levinson points out that among the life tasks older adults face is the need to rediscover the self—to understand who one is and find meaningful activities that continue to fill life with meaning and purpose—as well as to maintain connections to families and friends. Lacking connections to others and engagement in meaningful activities that imbue life with purpose can set the stage for depression, as we shall see next.

Aging and Sexuality

The stereotype that older adults with sexual interests are abnormal ("dirty old men") is a form of **ageism**, or prejudice against older people. Even older people themselves may buy into the myth and believe they should withdraw from sexual activity as they surpass middle age. However, older adults are not asexual. Continued sexual activity in later adulthood is not only normal but can also represent a source of gratification and self-esteem. Yes, people do need to adjust to physical changes in sexuality as they age. Men may take longer to achieve erections, and their erections may not be as firm as when they were young (Perry et al., 2001). Women may experience reduced vaginal lubrication, or dryness, as estrogen production falls off after menopause. The muscle contractions of orgasm may be less intense for both men and women. In addition, sexual interest and level of activity may decline to some extent. Yet despite these age-related changes, sexual relations in older adults can remain sexually fulfilling (Trudel, Turgeon, & Piche, 2000). Any change in sexual responsiveness may be offset by the years of sexual experience older adults bring to their intimate relationships.

Emotional Development in Late Adulthood

There's good news to report about how our emotions change as we age. Evidence from a long-term longitudinal study showed that negative emotions tended to decline as people aged, whereas positive emotions tended to hold fairly steady

ageism   Prejudice and discrimination directed at older persons.

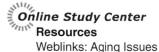

CONCEPT 10.27
Depression is a significant mental health problem affecting many older adults, though medical caregivers often overlook it.

Depression in Late Adulthood
Depression is a common emotional problem in late adulthood. What factors contribute to depression among older adults?

Online Study Center
Resources
Weblinks: Aging Issues

CONCEPT 10.28
Developmental psychologists have identified certain behavior patterns associated with successful aging, including selective optimization and compensation, optimism, and self-challenge.

(Charles, Reynolds, & Gatz, 2001). Nonetheless, many older adults, perhaps as many as 15 percent, experience some form of depression (Beekman et al., 2002; Charney et al., 2003; Pear, 1999). Unfortunately, depression among older adults often goes undiagnosed and untreated (Bruce et al., 2002, 2004). Signs of depression are often overlooked by medical caregivers because they may be so absorbed with older people's physical problems that they ignore their emotional difficulties. The tendency to downplay depression in elderly people comes at a significant risk, since the prevalence of suicide is much higher in later adulthood, especially in older White males (Bruce et al., 2004; Szanto et al., 2003).

Older adults may become vulnerable to depression because of the particular stressors they face, such as loss of lifelong friends and loved ones; disability or infirmity; placement in a nursing care facility; and the burdens of caring for spouses in declining health (Cole & Dendukuri, 2003; Meeks, Murrell, & Mehl, 2000; Siegler, Bosworth, & Poon, 2003). Retirement, whether voluntary or forced, may sap the sense of meaning and purpose in life and lead to a loss of role identity that can foster depression. Among the groups of older adults at greater risk for depression are those living alone and those lacking social support. Social support helps buffer the effects of stress that older adults encounter and thus may help reduce the risk of health problems as well as depression (Volz, 2000).

The deaths of close friends and relatives may deal a double blow, not only by removing important sources of social support but also by reminding the bereaved of their own advancing age. The older adult may also have a difficult time forming new friends or finding new life goals to give the later years a sense of meaning and purpose. Yet we should bear in mind that depression only affects a minority of older adults. In addition, those affected can benefit from available treatments for depression, including antidepressant medication and psychotherapy (Ciechanowski et al., 2004; Schneider et al., 2003; Wei et al., 2005).

Successful Aging: Will You Become a Successful Ager?

Despite the challenges faced by older adults, most people in their seventies report they are generally satisfied with their lives (Margoshes, 1995). Moreover, the great majority of participants in one sample of married older adults reported they were satisfied with their marriages and had relatively few marital problems (Clements & Swensen, 2000). Recent evidence shows that self-esteem, an important component of psychological adjustment, tends to rise throughout much of adulthood before declining in old age (Robins et al., 2002). Not surprisingly, income level and social contacts (quality more than quantity) are associated with better psychological well-being in late adulthood (Pinquart & Sörensen, 2000). Happiness may even increase with age, along with perceptions of having greater control over such areas of life as work, finances, and marriage (Lachman & Weaver, 1998).

There is much we can do to preserve our mental health as we age, such as coping with the loss of a spouse or other loved one by increasing our contacts with existing friends and seeking out new friends. Developmental psychologists highlight the importance of several key characteristics associated with more successful aging:

1. *Selective optimization and compensation.* Successful aging is associated with the ability to optimize one's time and use available resources to compensate for shortcomings in physical energy, memory, or fluid intelligence (Dixon & Cohen, 2003; Freund & Baltes, 1999). Rather than compete on the athletic field or in the business arena where younger people may have the advantage,

CONCEPT CHART 10.3   Development in Late Adulthood

Physical Development	With aging, sensory acuity declines; muscles and bones lose mass; skin loses elasticity, causing wrinkles; reaction times increase; immune functioning declines; and sexual responsiveness is reduced, though not necessarily sexual satisfaction.
Cognitive Development	Declines are noted in learning and memory, especially recall of word lists or names, and in fluid intelligence. Crystallized intelligence—general verbal ability and accumulated knowledge—tends to remain stable or even improve in certain respects as we age. Dementias such as Alzheimer's disease are not normal aspects of aging but result from brain diseases or abnormalities.
Psychosocial Development	Erikson postulated that adults in later life face a psychosocial crisis of ego integrity versus despair. Theorists such as Havighurst and Levinson focused on the tasks that accompany advancing age, such as maintaining meaningful connections to families and activities that continue to imbue life with meaning. Depression is a major emotional concern faced by many older adults.

older people may optimize their time by focusing on things that are more meaningful and important, such as visiting with family and friends more often—activities that allow them to pursue emotional goals that afford satisfaction. They may compensate for declining functioning by writing notes to jog their memories; giving themselves more time to learn; and using mechanical devices, such as hearing aids or canes, to compensate for loss of sensory or motor ability (Greenberg & Springen, 2001).

2. *Optimism.* Maintaining an optimistic frame of mind is linked to higher levels of life satisfaction and lower levels of depressive symptoms in later life (Chang & Sanna, 2001). Optimistic people are better able to meet the challenges of aging. They assume they will be able to surmount obstacles or live with them if necessary, including health problems.

3. *Self-challenge.* Seeking new challenges is a primary feature of successful adjustment at any age. The key for most older people, as for younger people, is not to do less but to do more of the things that matter. Maintaining an engaged lifestyle is also associated with better-preserved verbal intellectual ability (Pushkar et al., 1999).

Concept Chart 10.3 summarizes developmental changes in late adulthood.

Death and Dying: The Final Chapter

Now let us turn to a topic many of us would rather not think about: life's final transition, the one leading to death. When young, we may feel immortal. Our bodies may be strong and flexible, and our senses and minds sharp. We parcel thoughts about death and dying into a mental file cabinet to be opened much later in life, along with items like retirement, social security, and varicose veins. But death can occur at any age—by accident, violence, or illness. Death can also affect us deeply at any stage of life through the loss of loved ones. The issue of death raises questions well worth thinking about at any age, questions such as: Should I be an organ donor? How can I best leave my assets to those I care about? Shall I be buried or cremated? Shall I donate my body to science? Should I prepare a living will so that doctors will not need to use heroic measures to prolong my life when things are beyond hope?

Elisabeth Kübler-Ross

CONCEPT 10.29

Elisabeth Kübler-Ross described the psychological experience of dying in terms of five identifiable stages: denial, bargaining, anger, depression, and final acceptance.

CONCEPT 10.30

Coping with the loss of a loved one typically involves a process of grief that parallels in certain ways the stages of confronting death identified by Kübler-Ross.

bereavement A psychological state of deprivation involving feelings of grief and loss resulting from the death of a loved one or close friend.

mourning The expression of sorrow or grief in accordance with a set of customs, such as wearing black clothing.

Psychiatrist Elisabeth Kübler-Ross (1969) focused on how people cope with impending death. Based on her interviews with terminally ill people, she observed some common themes and identified five stages of dying through which many people pass:

1. *Denial.* At first, the person thinks, "It can't be me. I'm not really dying. The doctors made a mistake."

2. *Anger.* Once the reality of impending death is recognized, feelings of anger and resentment take center stage. Anger may be directed at younger or healthier people or toward the physicians who cannot save the person.

3. *Bargaining.* By the next stage, the person attempts to make a deal with God, such as promising to do good deeds in exchange for a few more months or years.

4. *Depression.* Depression reflects the growing sense of loss over leaving behind loved ones and losing life itself. A sense of utter hopelessness may ensue.

5. *Final acceptance.* As the person works through the earlier stages, he or she eventually achieves some degree of inner peace and acceptance. The person may still fear death, but comes to accept it with a kind of quiet dignity.

Kübler-Ross believed family members and health professionals can help dying people by understanding the stages through which they are passing and helping them attain a state of final acceptance. Many dying people have experiences similar to those Kübler-Ross observed, but not necessarily all of them and not always in the order she proposed (Schneidman, 1983). Some dying people do not deny the inevitable but arrive at a rapid though painful acceptance of death. Some become hopelessly depressed, others experience mainly fear, and still others have rapidly shifting feelings.

The death of a close friend or family member is often a traumatic experience. It typically leads to a state of **bereavement**, which is characterized by feelings of grief and a sense of loss. **Mourning** is the term used to describe the culturally prescribed manner of displaying grief. Various cultures prescribe different periods of mourning and different rituals for expressing grief. Religious and cultural traditions prescribe methods of mourning to help people express their grief and receive social support. For example, it is customary for Jewish families to "sit *shivah*" for seven days after the funeral. In sitting *shivah,* mourners customarily remain at home and receive a stream of visitors. Rituals include sitting on the floor or on wooden crates, covering mirrors, and wearing a shred of fabric from the deceased's clothing.

Though people may grieve in different ways, we can identify some common patterns, or stages of grief and mourning (Parkes & Weiss, 1983). These stages parallel in some respects the stages of dying identified by Kübler-Ross. The first stage is characterized by feelings of numbness and shock. In the days, and perhaps weeks, following the death, bereaved people may find it difficult to accept the reality of the loss and feel dazed or detached from their surroundings. They may need others to take responsibility for making burial arrangements and attending to other necessities. During the next stage, they become preoccupied with thoughts about the deceased person and consumed with feelings of grief. Finally, the grief begins to resolve and they are able to accept the loss and return to a normal level of functioning.

MODULE 10.3 REVIEW

Late Adulthood

RECITE IT

What physical and cognitive changes occur in late adulthood?

- In late adulthood, the skin wrinkles, hair grays, and the senses become less acute. Reaction time increases, and lean body mass, bone density, and strength decline. Other physical processes, including immune system functioning, decline.

- People generally experience a decline in some aspects of learning and memory, especially ability to learn or recall lists of words or names, and in fluid intelligence.

- Crystallized intelligence remains relatively stable and may even increase in some respects with age.

What is Alzheimer's disease?

- Alzheimer's disease (AD) is a form of dementia (loss of mental abilities) that is progressive and irreversible. It is characterized by memory problems, confusion, and eventually death. Though no one knows what causes AD, genetic factors are believed to be involved.

How do theorists characterize the psychosocial challenges of late adulthood?

- To Erikson, late adulthood is characterized by the psychosocial crisis of ego integrity versus despair (remaining meaningfully engaged in life while coming to terms with one's life versus despairing over the approaching finality of life).

- Other theorists, such as Havighurst and Levinson, focus on the developmental tasks and challenges that older adults are likely to face.

How do our emotions change as we age?

- Negative emotions tend to decline, whereas positive emotions tend to hold fairly steady. Still, many older adults suffer from emotional problems, especially depression.

What qualities are associated with successful aging?

- Successful aging is associated with the ability to concentrate on what is important and meaningful, to maintain a positive outlook, and to continue to challenge oneself.

What are the stages of dying as identified by Kübler-Ross?

- Kübler-Ross proposed that terminally ill people experience five stages of dying: denial, anger, bargaining, depression, and final acceptance. However, not all dying people experience these stages, and those who do may experience them in different orders.

RECALL IT

1. Which of the following cognitive skills is *not* likely to show a substantial decline as people age?
   a. rapid problem solving
   b. memory for new information
   c. speed at pattern recognition
   d. ability to apply acquired knowledge

2. List several factors that may help preserve intellectual functioning in later life.

3. Which of the following is closest in meaning to Erikson's term *ego integrity?*
   a. focusing attention on oneself
   b. achieving a sense of meaningfulness and satisfaction with one's life
   c. the development of generativity, or the ability to give of oneself to the next generation
   d. living an honest life

4. According to Kübler-Ross's model, which stage of dying immediately precedes final acceptance?
   a. depression   c. anger
   b. bargaining   d. denial

THINK ABOUT IT

- What key features of successful aging are highlighted in the text? How might you put this information to use in your own life?

- What changes in your current behavior can you make to improve your chances of living a longer and healthier life?

- Examine your own attitudes toward aging. How are your attitudes toward older adults affected by stereotypical perceptions?

APPLICATION MODULE 10.4
Living Longer, Healthier Lives

Longevity is partly determined by genes, a factor that lies beyond our control, at least for now (Hasty et al., 2003; Hekimi & Guarente, 2003). Looking ahead, scientific advances in gene alteration techniques during the twenty-first century may allow people to extend their lives by perhaps fifty or more years (Bulluck, 2000).

But for now, the way in which we live—our behaviors and habits—are important determinants of longevity we can control. Lifestyle factors such as exercise and dietary habits contribute not only to longevity but also to the quality of life as we age, improving our vitality. Young people who believe aging is a concern only for older people should note that the earlier they establish healthier habits, the greater their chances of living a longer and healthier life. In this section, we look at some guidelines for acquiring healthier behaviors.

CONCEPT 10.31
Longevity is partly determined by genetic inheritance and partly by factors people can directly control, such as a healthy diet, regular exercise, avoidance of harmful substances, and an active, involved lifestyle.

Developing Healthy Exercise and Nutrition Habits

Ponce de León, the Spanish explorer who searched for the mythical *Fountain of Youth*, might have been more successful had he just stayed home and built a gym. Exercise at any age is healthful, but especially as we age (Adler & Raymond, 2001; Fukukawa et al., 2004; O'Neil, 2003).

Mounting evidence points to the role of physical exercise in slowing effects of aging such as loss of lean body mass, bone, and muscle strength. Regular exercise is also associated with a lower risk of certain cancers, such as cancer of the colon, and with other major killers such as heart disease, stroke, and diabetes, as well as the potentially disabling bone disorder **osteoporosis** (NIH Consensus Development Panel, 2001). Weight-bearing exercise that requires working against gravity

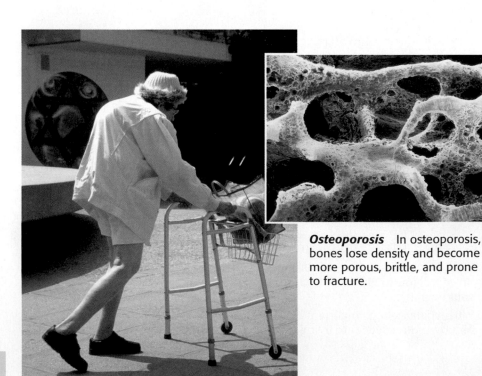

Osteoporosis In osteoporosis, bones lose density and become more porous, brittle, and prone to fracture.

osteoporosis A bone disease characterized by a loss of bone density in which the bones become porous, brittle, and more prone to fracture.

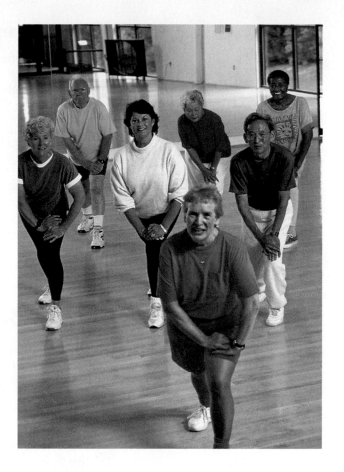

Exercise: Not Just for the Young Regular exercise in late adulthood can enhance longevity and physical health, as well as maintain mental sharpness.

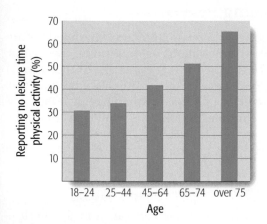

Figure 10.10   Lack of Leisure-Time Physical Activity in Relation to Age
Although regular exercise can help improve health and may combat the effects of aging, the percentages of people reporting no leisure-time physical activity increases with age.

Source of data: U.S. Department of Health and Human Services, 2000.

helps build bone density and keeps bones and muscles strong (Adler & Raymond, 2001; Nelson, 2000).

Regular exercise is associated with increased life expectancy (Gregg et al., 2003). It also helps preserve mental sharpness in later life as well as combat depression (Colcombe & Kramer, 2003; O'Neil, 2003; Underwood & Watson, 2001; Weuve et al., 2004). Evidence also links regular walking as a form of exercise to a reduced risk of developing dementia (Abbott et al., 2004).

People of any age can benefit from physical exercise, especially muscle-strengthening exercise (working out with weights), stretching, and aerobic exercise such as brisk walking, swimming, bicycling, or jogging. Unfortunately, people tend to grow more sedentary as they age (see Figure 10.10).

People contemplating beginning an exercise program should first consult with their personal physicians to ensure that the exercise routine they choose is healthy for them. The exercise program should also be phased in gradually to allow the body to adjust to the increased demands placed on it (Maron, 2000).

Following a nutritious, balanced diet is another key factor in promoting health and longevity. Adopting a low-fat diet rich in fruits, vegetables, and whole grains can help reduce the risks of potentially life-shortening diseases, such as coronary heart disease.

Staying Involved

Staying actively involved in meaningful activities and personal projects can contribute not only to preserving mental sharpness but also to emotional well-being (Lawton et al., 2002). Older adults who remain productive and participate in active leisure activities and in social or volunteer organizations are less likely than their less involved counterparts to encounter depression (Herzog et al., 1998).

Lending a Hand

Recent evidence gives credence to the familiar adage that it is better to give than to receive. A study of older adults showed that giving support to others was associated with a higher survival rate and was more strongly linked to extending longevity than receiving support (Brown et al., 2003).

Thinking Positively About Aging

Think positively—you just might live longer if you do. In one study, investigators found that people with more positive attitudes about aging lived an average of 7.5 years longer than those with less positive attitudes (Levy et al., 2002). According to the lead researcher in the study, Beca Levy of Yale University, how a person feels about aging is a more powerful predictor of longevity than having either low blood pressure or cholesterol ("Think Positive," 2002). In a similar vein, older adults in a Dutch sample were less likely to die within a nine-year span of the study if they held more optimistic attitudes in general (Giltay et al., 2004).

Avoiding Harmful Substances

Tobacco use, illicit drug use, and excessive use of alcohol can lead to physical health problems that can cut life expectancy significantly. Moreover, many lives, both young and old, have been lost to drug overdoses.

Maintaining a Healthy Weight

In Chapter 8 we noted that obesity is a major risk factor for several life-threatening and life-shortening diseases, such as coronary heart disease, diabetes, and some forms of cancer. Since metabolism tends to slow down with age, maintaining a healthy weight in middle and late adulthood requires compensating accordingly by curtailing calorie intake and exercising regularly to burn off excess calories.

Managing Stress

In Chapter 15, you will learn how stress impairs physical health and emotional well-being. Prolonged or intense stress can impair the immune system, the body's line of defense against disease-causing organisms and damaged cells. In turn, a weakened immune system makes people more likely to develop infectious diseases and less able to protect themselves from chronic diseases associated with aging

Making a Difference A key factor in psychological well-being at any age is engaging in meaningful activities.

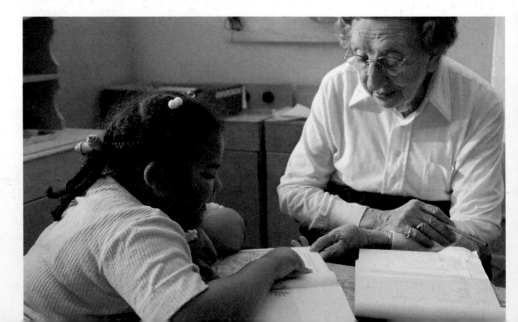

Exercise for the Mind The mind, not just the body, needs to be continually stimulated to remain sharp. Older adults who regularly exercise their minds by playing games such as chess, checkers, backgammon, or cards have a lower risk of developing dementia.

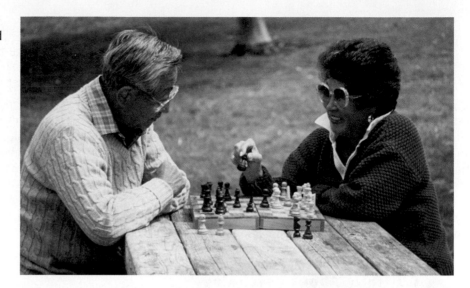

such as hypertension, cancer, and heart disease. The stress management techniques described in Chapter 15 can help take the distress out of stress and hopefully reduce the risk of developing stress-related disorders.

Exercising the Mind, Not Just the Body

When it comes to preserving higher mental functions, there appears to be some truth to the adage, "use it or lose it" (Cassel, 2002). Researchers find that intellectually stimulating activities and participation in memory training programs can help preserve cognitive functioning in later life, including memory ability (Ball et al., 2002; Carmichael, 2002; Kramer & Willis, 2002). Holding a mentally challenging job and engaging in mentally stimulating leisure activities are also linked to reduced risks of developing Alzheimer's disease (Hopkin, 2004; Smyth et al., 2004; Wilson et al., 2002; Wilson & Bennett, 2003).

Among the intellectual activities that can help preserve mental sharpness are mentally challenging games (such as chess), crossword or jigsaw puzzles, reading, writing, painting, and sculpting, to name but a few (Susman, 2000; Verghese et al., 2003). Older adults who regularly exercise their minds by playing board games show lower rates of developing dementia (Coyle, 2003).

Do Healthy Habits Pay Off?

People who adopt healthier habits (avoiding smoking, remaining physically and socially active, following a healthy diet, controlling excess body weight, and avoiding excessive drinking) and who maintain favorable levels of blood cholesterol and blood pressure are more likely to live longer, healthier lives than those with unhealthier habits (Hu et al., 2000; Stamler et al., 1999).

Critical thinkers recognize that we cannot draw a cause-and-effect relationship between healthy habits and longevity based simply on a statistical relationship. Since longevity researchers may not be able to control whether people adopt healthier habits, they are generally limited to studying differences in outcomes between those who do and those who do not. Still, correlations can point to possible causal relationships, and it stands to reason that the adoption of healthier habits may help extend life.

All in all, it is wise to take stock of your health habits sooner rather than later. It is like salting away money for your later years: developing healthy habits now and maintaining them throughout life are likely to boost your chances of living a longer and healthier life.

TYING IT TOGETHER

This chapter picks up from the preceding chapter by focusing on the changes in human development that occur through the course of adolescence and adulthood. Adolescence, a time of significant physical, cognitive, social, and emotional changes, covers the period of development spanning the end of childhood and the beginning of adulthood (Module 10.1). As adolescence passes and people progress through early and middle adulthood, they face major life challenges in establishing independent identities, assuming an occupational role, forming intimate relationships, and making lifestyle choices (Module 10.2). The major life challenges that people face as they progress through late adulthood typically revolve around keeping active and involved and coping with age-related physical and mental changes (Module 10.3). We may increase our chances of living longer and healthier lives by developing healthier habits early in life and maintaining those habits as we age (Module 10.4).

Thinking Critically About Psychology

Based on your reading of the chapter, answer the following questions. Then, to evaluate your progress in developing critical thinking skills, compare your answer with the sample answer found in Appendix A.

This critical thinking exercise asks you to apply Erikson's model of psychosocial development to yourself. Erikson believed that an identity crisis is a normal part of the development of the healthy personality. He viewed it as a time of serious soul searching or self-exploration in which we strive to achieve ego identity. By *ego identity*, he meant the adoption of a firm set of beliefs about who we are, what we believe, and where we are headed in life. Many college-age students are in the process of creating their ego identities. But creation takes time, and the process need not be completed by graduation. Psychologist James Marcia (Marcia, 1966, 1980; Marcia et al., 1993) identified four identity statuses that describe where people stand in their ego identities at any given time:

> *Identity achievement* describes people who have emerged from an identity crisis (a period of serious self-reflection) with a commitment to a relatively stable set of personal beliefs and to a course of action in pursuing a particular career. An example of a career commitment would be pursuing a course of study in engineering in preparation for becoming an engineer.

Foreclosure describes people who have adopted a set of beliefs or a course of action, though with no period of serious self-exploration or self-examination. They did not go through an identity crisis to arrive at their beliefs and occupational choices. Most base their commitments on what others, especially their parents, instilled in them.

Moratorium is a state of identity crisis concerning one's beliefs or career choices. People in moratorium are currently working through their personal beliefs or struggling to determine which career course to pursue.

Identity diffusion is the status describing people who are not yet committed to a set of personal beliefs or career choices and show no real interest in developing these commitments. Issues of ego identity have not yet taken center stage in their lives.

1. **What evidence would you need to determine your identity status in areas such as occupational choice and personal (political and moral) beliefs? Bear in mind that you may have a different identity status in each area.**

2. **Now apply these criteria to yourself. Based on this self-appraisal, which identity status best describes your ego identity at this point in time in the areas of career choice and personal (moral, religious, and political) beliefs?**

Key Terms

adolescence *(p. 384)*

puberty *(p. 385)*

secondary sex characteristics *(p. 385)*

primary sex characteristics *(p. 385)*

menarche *(p. 385)*

imaginary audience *(p. 386)*

personal fable *(p. 386)*

ego identity *(p. 392)*

identity crisis *(p. 392)*

role diffusion *(p. 393)*

fluid intelligence *(p. 396)*

crystallized intelligence *(p. 396)*

menopause *(p. 397)*

emerging adulthood *(p. 398)*

midlife crisis *(p. 400)*

empty nest syndrome *(p. 400)*

homogamy *(p. 402)*

dementia *(p. 408)*

Alzheimer's disease *(p. 408)*

ageism *(p. 411)*

bereavement *(p. 414)*

mourning *(p. 414)*

osteoporosis *(p. 416)*

ANSWERS TO RECALL IT QUESTIONS

Module 10.1: 1. puberty; 2. dropped; 3. imaginary audience and personal fable; 4. a; 5. gender and cultural biases.

Module 10.2: 1. c; 2. false; 3. emerging; 4. b; 5. serial.

Module 10.3: 1. d; 2. good general physical health, involvement in stimulating activities, openness to new experiences; 3. b; 4. a.

ANSWERS TO TRY THIS OUT *(P. 407)*

1. **False.** Most healthy couples continue to engage in satisfying sexual activities into their seventies and eighties.

2. **False.** This statement is too general. Those who find their work satisfying are less willing to retire.

3. **False.** *Adaptability* remains reasonably stable throughout adulthood.

4. **False.** Age itself is not linked to noticeable declines in life satisfaction. Of course, we may respond negatively to disease and losses, such as the death of a spouse.

5. **False.** Only a minority are depressed.

6. **False.** Actually, church attendance declines, but not verbally expressed religious beliefs.

7. **False.** Although reaction time may decrease and general learning ability may undergo a slight decline, older adults usually have little or no difficulty at familiar work tasks. In most jobs, experience and motivation are more important than age.

8. **False.** Learning may just take a bit longer.

9. **False.** Older adults do not direct a higher proportion of thoughts toward the past than do younger people. Regardless of our age, we may spend more time daydreaming if we have more time on our hands.

10. **False.** Fewer than 10 percent of older adults require some form of institutional care.

11

Gender and Sexuality

DID YOU KNOW THAT . . .

- Some people feel trapped in the body of the opposite gender by a mistake of nature? (p. 425)

- The gender gap in math skills that traditionally favored boys has narrowed considerably in recent years? (p. 430)

- Women tend to be better at remembering where things are placed? *(Now, where are those car keys?)* (p. 431)

- When it comes to using computers, men show greater confidence in their skills than do women of the same level of math ability? (p. 432)

- Only women have a sex organ whose sole known function is to produce sexual pleasure? (p. 436)

- Gay males and lesbians have the same levels of sex hormones circulating in their bodies as heterosexual men and women? (p. 441)

- The male sex hormone testosterone energizes sexual drives in women as well as men? (p. 451)

- College women are much more likely to be raped by someone they know than by a stranger? (p. 455)

Sonya, 19, faces a dilemma. Raised in a traditional household, she has been taught to preserve her virginity until marriage. Yet she sees most of her friends at college having intimate relationships and wonders whether she is too old-fashioned.

Daniel and Lisa are both 20 and have been dating for several months. They are strongly attracted to one other but have held off becoming sexually intimate because of concerns about AIDS. Daniel wants both of them to be tested for HIV. Lisa has refused to be tested, partly because she feels insulted that Daniel thinks she might have HIV and partly out of fear of the test results. She wonders whether she might have become infected by one of the men with whom she had sex during what she calls her "wild period" when she was 18.

Chanya and Janet have lived a secret life for six years, maintaining a pretense of being just "roommates"—just two 30-something career women splitting the rent in the big city. Yet each time they move the twin beds apart when either of their parents visit, they find it ever more difficult to maintain the illusion that they are just friends and not lovers.

"It's kind of funny," Stewart said, "not ha-ha funny but ironic, really. The last thing I expected at my age (twenty-seven) was to have trouble getting erections." Since his divorce two years earlier, he has been unable to perform sexually. Failing to achieve erections has been so humiliating that he has given up trying. He makes excuses for avoiding sexual intimacy in new relationships, but his explanations have begun to sound hollow.

The concerns expressed by these young people touch upon a number of issues about sexuality addressed in this chapter, such as sexual morality, fear of sexually transmitted diseases, sexual orientation, and sexual response (or lack of response).

Our sexuality encompasses the many ways in which we experience ourselves as sexual beings. It includes our capacity to experience sexual thoughts, interests, and desires and to express ourselves through sexual behaviors.

Sex is important biologically, psychologically, and socially. It is nature's way of ensuring that we perpetuate our species, it shapes our behavior and our motives, and it influences our personality—the qualities that make us unique. For example, our gender identity (sense of maleness or femaleness) and our sexual orientation (direction of erotic attraction) are essential parts of our self-identity. Our sexual behavior is shaped by family influences and the society in which we live. We learn that social rules and customs govern how we are permitted to express our sexuality. For many of us, what we learned from our elders can be expressed in one word: "Don't." Others were brought up with more relaxed or flexible sexual standards, or perhaps with little or no guidance at all.

Each society imposes not only rules for governing sexual conduct but also a set of expectations, or *gender roles,* that designate the behaviors it deems appropriate for men and women to perform.

In this chapter we explore many facets of our sexuality, beginning with our gender identity, the psychological sense of being male or female. ■

MODULE 11.1
Gender Identity and Gender Roles

- What accounts for gender identity?
- What are the major theories of gender-role behavior?
- What gender differences exist in cognitive abilities, personality, and leadership style?

Before proceeding, let's define some terms. In this text, *sex* refers to the biological division between males and females. So when we identify anatomical differences between men and women, we are speaking about *sexual organs*, not *gender organs*. **Gender** is a psychosocial concept that distinguishes masculinity from femininity. Thus, we use the term **gender roles** to refer to the set of behaviors that a particular culture deems acceptable for men or women. The psychological experience of being male or female is called **gender identity**.

In this module we examine gender identity and gender roles and how they develop. In particular, we will consider evidence of biological and psychosocial influences in determining our sense of ourselves as male or female and the roles we play in society.

Gender Identity: Our Sense of Maleness or Femaleness

CONCEPT 11.1
Children early in life develop a firm gender identity, or psychological sense of being male or female.

By the age of 3, most children have acquired a firm sense of their gender identity, of being either male or female. But what determines gender identity? The answer is not yet clear. Some research points to biological influences. Investigators suspect that prenatal hormones sculpt the developing brain in ways that influence the later development of gender identity (Dingfelder, 2004a; Reiner & Gearhart, 2004). But research suggests that gender identity is not fully stamped in at birth. In this research, children who were born with ambiguous genitalia because of

Gender Reassignment Police officer Tom Ashton (left) underwent gender reassignment surgery and hormonal replacement, becoming Claire Ashton (right).

gender The state of maleness or femaleness.

gender roles The cultural expectations imposed on men and women to behave in ways deemed appropriate for their gender.

gender identity The psychological sense of maleness or femaleness.

CONCEPT 11.2

While researchers continue to explore the underpinnings of gender identity, both biological (hormonal) and environmental (rearing) influences may be involved.

CONCEPT 11.3

Transsexuals have a gender identity that is at odds with their anatomic sex; they often undergo gender-reassignment surgery to correct what they perceive to be a mistake of nature.

congenital birth defects developed a gender identity that was consistent with the gender to which they were assigned and raised accordingly, even when the assigned gender conflicted with their chromosomal (XY or XX) sex (Slijper, Drop, & Molenaar, 1998). All in all, most scientists believe that gender identity arises from a complex interaction of nature (biology) and nurture (rearing influences) (e.g., Berenbaum & Bailey, 2003).

Whatever the determinants of gender identity may be, it is almost always consistent with one's chromosomal sex. But for a few individuals gender identity and chromosomal sex are mismatched. These individuals have the gender identity of one gender but the chromosomal sex and sexual organs of the other.

Transsexualism: A Mismatch of Identity and Biology People with **transsexualism** feel trapped in the body of the opposite gender by a mistake of nature. A transsexual man is anatomically a man but has the gender identity of a woman. A transsexual woman is anatomically a woman but possesses a male gender identity. Myths around transsexualism abound. Table 11.1 exposes some of the more common myths.

Transsexual men and women may be repulsed by the sight of their own genitals. To correct what they see as nature's mistake, many undergo gender reassignment surgery to surgically alter their genitals. Gender reassignment surgery transforms the genitalia to a workable likeness of those of the opposite gender. But since it cannot transplant the internal reproductive organs that produce the germ cells—the testes in the man and the ovaries in the woman—reproduction is impossible. Thus, surgery does not change a man into a woman or a woman into a man, if what it means to be a man or a woman depends on having the internal reproductive organs of their respective sex. Nonetheless, gender reassignment surgery generally permits the individual to perform sexual intercourse. Hormonal replacement therapy is used to foster growth of the beard and body hair in female-to-male cases and of the breasts in male-to-female cases.

The causes of transsexualism remain unclear (van Goozen et al., 2002). Scientists suspect that a combination of sex hormones and other factors, such as genetic influences, act on the architecture of the developing brain during prenatal development (Gooren & Kruijver, 2002). The result may be a mismatch of mind and body in which the brain becomes sexually differentiated in one direction during prenatal development even as the genitals become sculpted in the other.

TABLE 11.1   Myths vs. Facts About Transsexualism

Myth	Fact
Only people who have sex-change operations are transsexuals.	Many transsexual men and women do not have gender reassignment surgery because they want to avoid post-surgical pain and complications or because the costs are prohibitive.
Men who wear women's clothes are transsexuals.	Some are. But others cross-dress to become sexually aroused, not because they are transsexual. Also, some gay males known as "drag queens" dress in women's clothing but are not transsexual.
Transsexualism is just a form of homosexuality.	People with a gay male or lesbian sexual orientation have a gender identity consistent with their anatomic sex. A gay male perceives himself to be a man who is sexually attracted to other men, not a woman trapped in a man's body. Gay males or lesbians would no more want to rid themselves of their own genitals than would a heterosexual man or woman.

transsexualism A mismatch in which one's gender identity is inconsistent with one's chromosomal and anatomic sex.

Gender Roles and Stereotypes: How Society Defines Masculinity and Femininity

The cultural expectations imposed on men and women to behave in ways deemed appropriate for their gender are called *gender roles*. Fixed, conventional views of "masculine" and "feminine" behavior are called *gender-role stereotypes*. In our culture, the stereotypical female is perceived as nurturing, gentle, dependent, warm, emotional, kind, helpful, patient, and submissive. The stereotypical male, personified by the ruggedly masculine characters in countless movies, is tough, self-reliant, and independent, but also dominant and protective.

Yet gender roles have changed and are changing still. Most women today work outside the home, and many are pursuing careers in traditionally male domains like law, medicine, and engineering. Some command naval vessels or pilot military helicopters. And in the legal profession, women now constitute 29 percent of lawyers as compared to only 15 percent in the 1980s ("A Growing Gender Gap," 2000). Nevertheless, many traditional gender roles remain much as they were several generations ago. Women currently constitute 93 percent of registered nurses (only a slight decrease from 96 percent in 1983) and 84 percent of flight attendants (an increase from 74 percent in 1983). Household and childcare responsibilities still fall more heavily on women, even on those who work in full-time jobs outside the home.

But what accounts for the acquisition of gender roles? In other words, why do boys and girls act like, well, boys and girls? Is it simply a matter of cultural learning—the imparting to children of how men and women are expected to act and the roles they are expected to play? Or might there be biological origins for these behaviors? Here we consider several major theories that seek to account for the acquisition of gender-typed behaviors.

CONCEPT 11.4
Each society defines masculinity and femininity by imposing a set of gender-based expectations about behavior and personality.

CONCEPT 11.5
Though gender roles in our society have changed and are changing still, housekeeping and childcare roles still fall disproportionately on women.

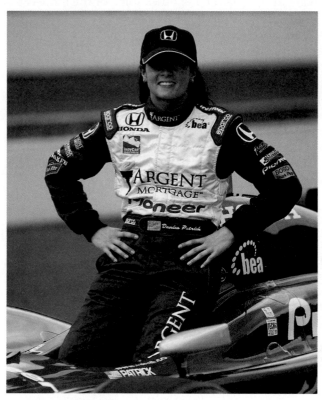

Changing Gender Roles Gender roles in our society have changed and are changing still.

CONCEPT 11.6
Social-cognitive theorists emphasize the roles of observational learning and reinforcement in the development of gender-typed behavior.

Social-Cognitive Theory: Learning What Others Expect of You
Social-cognitive theorists, such as Albert Bandura (1986) and Walter Mischel (1970), emphasize the roles of observational learning and reinforcement in the development of gender-role behaviors. Children are natural observers—taking in what they observe in other people's behavior and what they see on television and in the movies. And parents are important modeling influences (Leaper, 2000). If children see Dad and Mom and sister and brother dressing differently and performing different roles in the family, they begin to learn what is expected of males and females and to conduct themselves accordingly.

Parents use rewards and punishments (praise and criticism) to shape children's gender-role behavior. During infancy, parents may talk more to girls and engage in more physical or rough-housing play with boys. Later they may encourage sons to play tough on the athletic field and to hold back tears when they get hurt or feel upset. They may praise girls when they engage in cooperative play or help out in the kitchen. They may also punish or ignore gender-inappropriate behavior.

The toys that parents give their children also mirror the gender-role expectations of the society in which they live. Girls are given dolls and encouraged to practice caretaking behaviors in pretend play that prepares them for traditional feminine roles. Boys receive "action figures" (a euphemism for male dolls), which they use in pretend play to enact aggressive scripts that are characteristic of the traditional male role.

The popular media—TV, movies, books, and magazines—also model traditional gender-role expectations by depicting men and women in stereotypical

Modeling and Gender Roles Modeling is an important influence in the development of gender-typed behavior.

roles (Bryant & Check, 2000). As one critic noted, "Women are often still depicted on television as half-clad and half-witted, and needing to be rescued by quick-thinking, fully clothed men" (Adelson, 1990, p. C18). Though some people might argue that the media merely reflect the society they seek to depict, the continuing portrayals of men and women in stereotypical roles only serve to reinforce these stereotypes.

Gender-role expectations are changing as broader social changes occur in society. Daughters today are more likely than not to have a mother who works outside the home. And many young girls today are encouraged to develop interests in competitive sports and to follow career paths in fields traditionally reserved for men. Yet changes are slow (relatively few stockbrokers or computer programmers are women, for instance). Though many boys are exposed to fathers who do their share of the household tasks, a study of male college students in the United States and China showed that they continue to hold more stereotypical views of gender roles than female college students (Chia et al., 1994).

CONCEPT 11.7
Gender-schema theory holds that children form mental representations, or schemas, of the attributes and behaviors associated with masculinity and femininity, and then begin acting in ways that are consistent with these schemas.

Gender-Schema Theory: What Does It Mean to Be a Girl (or Boy)? **Gender-schema theory** emphasizes the importance of cognitive factors in the development of gender-role behavior. It holds that children form mental representations, or *schemas*, of masculinity and femininity (Bem, 1993; Fagot, 1995). A schema is a way of organizing knowledge about the world, a kind of lens through which one sees the world. Gender schemas incorporate the dress, toys, behaviors, and social roles considered appropriate for boys and men and for girls and women. By the age of 3, children typically have developed a gender schema for toys such that they recognize that trucks are boys' toys and dolls are girls' toys. Gender schemas influence what children are likely to recall. For example, children are better able to remember gender-linked objects and activities they have seen previously. Boys are better able to recall cars and trucks they were shown earlier, whereas girls are better at recalling dolls (Bradbard & Endsley, 1983).

Once children acquire gender-role schemas, they begin using them as ways of organizing their behavior and as frames of reference for evaluating their self-worth. They begin acting in ways that reflect their concepts of how boys or girls are expected to act. They also begin judging themselves positively when they feel they measure up to the traits they deem important to their gender. Young boys may hitch their self-esteem to how well they compare to other boys in masculine traits such as body strength and aggressiveness. Young girls may judge themselves according to whether they perceive themselves as beautiful or their physical skills

gender-schema theory The belief that children form mental representations or schemas of masculinity and femininity, which they then use as a basis for organizing their behavior and evaluating their self-worth.

as graceful. Evidence shows that, among preadolescents, perceiving oneself as being typical of one's gender is associated with better psychological adjustment (Yunger, Carver, & Perry, 2004).

CONCEPT 11.8
According to evolutionary psychologists, men and women may be genetically predisposed to develop gender-typed traits, such as aggressiveness and nurturance, respectively.

Evolutionary Theory: It's Nature's Way   Evolutionary psychologists speculate that genetic predispositions may shape gender-typed behavior (Buss, 1996; Buss & Kenrick, 1998). They note that in ancestral hunter-gatherer societies, men and women typically lived in small bands in which the men hunted and went to war and the women remained close to home, tending the children and gathering edible fruits and vegetables. This strict division of roles continues to be observed in many (but not all) preliterate societies today.

Evolutionary psychologists argue that men's greater upper-body strength makes them more likely than women to succeed as hunters and warriors. Their physical attributes enable them to spear fleeing game and overpower adversaries. Men, on average, also possess better visual-spatial skills, such as being able to mentally rotate objects and track movement through three-dimensional space (Halpern, 2004). These skills may give them additional advantages in hunting or warfare, such as the ability to accurately aim bows and arrows. On the other hand, women may be genetically predisposed to develop empathic and nurturant traits that allow them to sense the needs of infants before they can speak. These traits may have increased the chances that the children of ancestral humans would survive and carry forward their genetic legacy. Evolutionary psychologists speculate that gender-linked traits that proved adaptive in the struggle of ancestral humans to survive may have been passed down through the generations to modern humans.

In the context of evolutionary theory, the existence of stereotypical gender roles—men as breadwinners and women as homemakers—merely reflects the natural order of things. Modern gender roles are merely modern adaptations of the traditional roles of men as hunters and warriors and women as gatherers and nurturers.

Evolutionary psychologists buttress their claims by pointing to evidence that boys and men, by most any gauge, are more physically aggressive than girls and women (Archer, 2004; Kimura, 2002). Boys are also more likely than girls to get into trouble for fighting. Our prisons are largely populated by men who have committed violent crimes. Violent sexual offenders are also almost exclusively male. Notable gender differences have even been found in patterns of play. Observations in the playground reveal that boys are typically more active and show more aggressive behavior, including more rough-and-tumble play (Kimura, 2002; Martin & Fabes, 2001). Boys' play also tends to be more competitive, while girls tend toward a cooperative or taking-turns style of play (Cohen, 2001).

We should be careful not to overgeneralize, however. Evidence shows that both males and females engage in aggressive behavior, but its form differs along gender lines. For example, studies of children indicate that boys more often engage in physical or overt aggression, whereas girls more often engage in *relational aggression,* in which relationships are used as a means of inflicting harm (Crick & Rose, 2000; Roecker-Phelps, 2001). Relational aggression includes behaviors such as excluding others from the friendship circle or "group" and starting rumors.

But the question remains: Are men more physically aggressive and women gentler and more cooperative by *nature?* Perhaps testosterone plays a role. Although much higher levels of the male sex hormone are produced in men than in women, evidence links testosterone levels to more aggressive behavior in both men and women (Rubinow & Schmidt,

Aggression and Gender   Are all forms of aggression more common in boys than in girls?

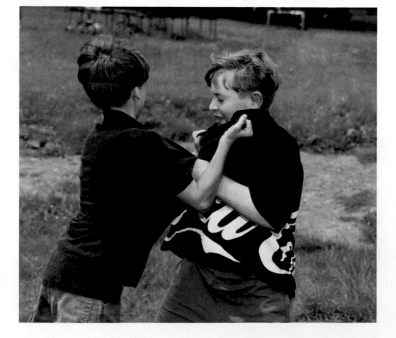

1996). But connections between testosterone and aggressive behavior are complex; testosterone is not a kind of on-off switch for aggression (Sullivan, 2000).

Cultural influences also play important roles in accounting for male-female differences in aggression. For example, young boys are exposed to male action heroes who routinely use their fists or weapons to kill, dismember, and overpower their opponents. And physically aggressive play among boys and men in sporting events is encouraged by coaches and richly rewarded in the professional ranks. We can't offer any final answer here. Scientists continue to grapple with the difficult challenge of sorting out the respective roles of biology and environment.

Sociocultural Theory: Gender Roles as Cultural Adaptations   Margaret Mead (1935), the famed anthropologist, emphasized the importance of cultural influences in gender-role behaviors. In one New Guinea culture she studied, both men and women shared childcare responsibilities. In another, stereotypical gender roles were reversed: women were reared to be hunters and food gatherers while men stayed close to home and tended the children. Mead's evidence suggests that gender roles may have more to do with how societies adapt to the environmental demands they face than to biology.

What can we conclude about the determinants of gender-typed behavior? Many investigators believe that biological and social-environmental factors interact in determining a child's gender-specific behavior (Bryant & Check, 2000; Wood & Eagly, 2002). Biological influences may create behavioral dispositions toward stereotypical gender-role behaviors, such as greater preferences among young boys for rough-and-tumble play and aggressive behavior (Collaer & Hines, 1995). Yet biology is not destiny. Gender-role behaviors are neither universal nor fixed by nature. *How* children are socialized into particular gender roles is an important influence in itself (Bryant & Check, 2000).

Masculinity and Femininity: Opposite Poles or Different Dimensions?   Conventionally we tend to think of masculinity and femininity as opposite poles of a single continuum. The more masculine traits you hold, the fewer feminine traits you're likely to possess. But must we assume that masculinity and femininity represent mutually exclusive categories? Why couldn't you have masculine traits such as independence and assertiveness *and* feminine traits such as nurturance and empathy? Psychologist Sandra Bem believes you could (Bem, 1993). Using a gender-role inventory she developed that includes separate measures of masculinity and femininity, she found that men and women could be either high or low in either masculine traits or feminine traits. The category of psychological **androgyny** was used to type people who had high levels of both masculine and feminine traits (see Figure 11.1). Others who were low on both dimensions were classified as "undifferentiated." The androgynous person may have the best of both worlds—able to draw upon "masculine" assertiveness or independence in business dealings

CONCEPT 11.9
According to sociocultural theorists, gender roles may be cultural adaptations that have helped societies adapt to the demands of their environments.

CONCEPT 11.10
According to psychologist Sandra Bem, people can be psychologically androgynous in the sense of possessing high levels of both masculine and feminine traits.

Figure 11.1   Gender-Role Identification
How would you classify yourself in terms of gender-role identification—as masculine, feminine, undifferentiated, or psychologically androgynous?

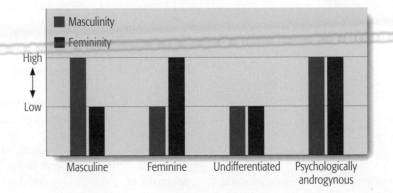

androgyny   A type of gender-role identification that characterizes people who possess high levels of both masculine and feminine traits.

CONCEPT CHART 11.1 Gender Identity and Gender Roles

Concept	Description	Additional Comments
Gender identity	The psychological sense of being male or female	The determinants of gender identity remain under study, but both biological influences (prenatal shaping of the brain along gender-specific lines) and environmental influences (being raised as a boy or girl) may be involved.
Gender roles	Cultural expectations of the behaviors and social roles deemed appropriate for men and women	Theoretical views on the acquisition of gender roles include social-cognitive theory (observational learning and reinforcement), gender-schema theory (gender schemas as ways of organizing behavior and as frameworks for self-evaluation), evolutionary theory (gender roles representing genetic predispositions), and sociocultural theory (gender roles as cultural adaptations).

and upon "feminine" nurturance and sensitivity when interacting with a child or baby animal.

The concept of androgyny has been criticized, especially by feminists, on the grounds that it perpetuates a belief that masculinity and femininity are attributes of people rather than reflections of society's differential treatment of men and women. Many feminists argue that people should be treated as individuals, not as exemplars of gender stereotypes (Matlin, 1999). Even Bem (1993) recognizes that the concept of androgyny diverts attention away from examining gender inequalities in society. But many scholars, including Bem, believe that androgyny remains a useful construct for describing people who combine "masculine" and "feminine" traits in their personalities and behavior and cannot be easily classified on the basis of traditional gender roles (Arnett, 2004).

Investigators find that androgyny is useful in predicting a range of behaviors. For example, androgynous people tend to be more creative than people with a masculine or feminine gender-role orientation (Norlander, Erixon, & Archer, 2000). Other researchers find that men and women prefer androgynous partners as dates and as mates (Green & Kenrick, 1994). Basically, they prefer partners who are both *expressive* (a feminine trait) and *instrumental* (capable of acting effectively in the world, a masculine trait). Before going further, you may wish to review Concept Chart 11.1, which provides an overview of gender identity and gender roles.

Gender Differences: How Different Are We?

We have already examined gender differences in aggressiveness. Let us now consider gender differences in other areas: cognitive abilities, personality, and leadership style.

CONCEPT 11.11
Researchers find that, on average, girls outperform boys on some verbal skills whereas boys typically do better on some visual-spatial tasks.

Gender Differences in Cognitive Abilities Who's smarter—men or women? Before you jump to defend your gender, note that the evidence teaches us that men and women perform similarly on tests of both general intelligence (IQ) and problem-solving ability. As former APA president Diane Halpern points out, "there is no evidence that one sex is smarter than the other" (Halpern, 2004, p. 139). However, girls do hold an edge in verbal skills such as reading, writing, and spelling (Applebome, 1997). Boys are more likely to have problems in reading that range from reading below grade level to more severe disabilities such as **dyslexia** (Rutter et al., 2004).

Boys, on the other hand, typically show better performance, on the average, in math skills (Beller & Gafni, 2000; Halpern & LaMay, 2000). However, this gender gap has narrowed considerably in recent years. Today the average scores of boys and girls on standardized math tests are quite close (Ripley, 2005). Still, a greater proportion of boys is found at both the high end and the low end of the spectrum of math ability (Hedges & Nowell, 1995; Murray, 1995).

dyslexia A learning disorder characterized by impaired ability to read.

Males, on average, continue to outperform females in some visual-spatial skills, such as map reading and the ability to mentally rotate a three-dimensional figure (see Figure 11.2) (e.g., Grön et al., 2000; Liben et al., 2002). The ability to perceive relationships among three-dimensional objects may explain why boys and men tend to excel in certain skills, such as playing chess, solving geometry problems, and finding embedded shapes within geometric figures.

Women, again on average, are better skilled at remembering where objects are located, which may explain why women seem to have a keener ability to find lost keys (Azar, 1996b). But notice the use of the qualifying term *on average*. Many individuals exhibit abilities in which the opposite gender tends to excel: many women excel in math and science, and many men shine in writing and verbal skills. In fact, greater variations in cognitive abilities exist within genders than between genders. The differences between males and females in cognitive ability are overshadowed by the similarities.

Researchers have also noted gender differences in spatial navigation: when asked to give directions, men are more likely than women to use compass directions (north, south, east, west), whereas women are more likely to navigate by landmarks (Lawton, 2001).

What accounts for gender differences in cognitive ability? Some researchers suspect that the brains of boys and men are more highly specialized for certain kinds of visual-spatial skills. Male fetuses are exposed to higher levels of testosterone, which scientists suspect may spur the development of neural connections in the brain responsible for performing certain spatial tasks (McGuffin & Scourfield, 1997).

Consider the contribution of psychosocial factors to explaining gender differences in cognitive skills. Parents who hold a stereotypical view that "girls are not good at math and science" may fail to encourage their daughters to develop math skills or take science courses. They may come to believe that daughters will find science less interesting and more difficult than will their sons (Tenenbaum & Leaper, 2003). Even when men and women perform equally well on science tests, women tend to underestimate their ability in comparison to men (Ehrlinger & Dunning, 2003). It's as though our culture trains women to perform a simple

Figure 11.2   Gender Differences in Abilities

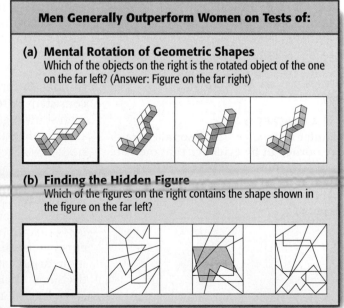

Source: Kimura, 1992.

Who's Smarter—Men or Women? Let's call this age-old battle a draw, since evidence shows that men and women perform similarly on tests of general intelligence and problem-solving ability. However, gender differences do emerge on some specific cognitive abilities.

REALITY CHECK

THE CLAIM Girls are not good at math.

THE EVIDENCE The widely held stereotype that girls are not good at math is not backed up by evidence. On average, boys and girls obtain similar scores on standardized math tests. However, expectations that girls can't do math can become a self-fulfilling prophecy if parents and counselors discourage young women from pursuing courses in math or science or if girls themselves doubt their abilities to succeed in these areas.

THE TAKE-AWAY MESSAGE Girls certainly can do math, but negative expectations can lead them to avoid taking challenging math courses or pursuing careers in scientific or technical fields.

CONCEPT 11.12

Gender differences in personality traits are borne out by evidence that men are generally more aggressive and have higher self-esteem while women tend to be more nurturant and emotionally expressive.

deduction based on a faulty premise that math is "masculine": Math = Male, Me = Female, Therefore Math ≠ Me (Nosek, Banaji, & Greenwald, 2003).

Evidence also shows that college men tend to overestimate their math ability more than do college women (Beyer, 2002). Women, by contrast, are more likely to doubt their math and computer skills. In a recent study of male and female college students of the same level of quantitative ability, men expressed greater confidence in using computers (Beyer et al., 2003). Moreover, female computer science majors expressed less confidence in their computer skills than did male nonmajors!

The narrowing of gender differences in math and science in recent years lends further credence to the influence of social or cultural factors. In all likelihood, a combination of biological and psychosocial factors accounts for gender differences in cognitive abilities. Indeed, the shrinking gender gap in math skills suggests we are making progress in encouraging our daughters to develop their abilities in math and science.

Gender Differences in Personality and Leadership Style Evidence points to consistent differences in personality traits between men and women. In general, men show higher levels of self-esteem and assertiveness, whereas women tend to show more extraversion, warmth, openness to feelings, and emotional expressiveness (Costa, Terracciano, & McCrae, 2002; Feingold, 1994; Ripley, 2005).

Despite the common stereotype that men make better leaders, experimental studies show that women are at least the equal of men in managerial and leadership ability (Eagly, Karau, & Makhijani, 1995). Yet because of prevailing sexist attitudes, effective leadership behavior may be evaluated more negatively when the behavior is enacted by women than by men (Eagly & Karau, 2002). There are also differences between men and women in leadership styles. Women leaders tend to be more democratic—more inclined to seek opinions of subordinates when making decisions. Their male counterparts tend to adopt a more autocratic or domineering style, leading more by command than by consensus building (Eagly & Johnson, 1990). Table 11.2 summarizes the key findings on gender differences in cognitive abilities, personality, and leadership ability.

TABLE 11.2   Gender Differences

Skill or Trait	Research Findings	Additional Comments
Cognitive abilities	Girls generally perform better than boys in certain verbal skills, while boys generally perform better in specific visual-spatial skills and in math skills.	Differences within genders are greater than those between genders. Gender differences in abilities may reflect both biological and psychosocial factors.
Personality	Males are generally higher in aggressiveness and self-esteem. Females tend to be higher in extraversion, trust, nurturance, and emotional expressiveness.	Personality traits, cognitive abilities, and play behaviors are closely linked to gender-role expectations, so it may be impossible to separate the effects of culture from biological differences.
Leadership ability	Women and men are equally effective as leaders, but leadership styles typically vary in relation to gender.	Women leaders tend to focus more on seeking cooperation, whereas male leaders are more likely to lead by command or direction.

MODULE 11.1 REVIEW

Gender Identity and Gender Roles

RECITE IT

What accounts for gender identity?

- Gender identity may arise from a complex interaction of biological (genetic) and environmental (rearing) influences. Though the brain becomes sexually differentiated before birth, our gender identity continues to be shaped by experiences during early childhood.

- In transsexualism a person's gender identity is inconsistent with his or her chromosomal sex and sexual organs.

What are the major theories of gender-role behavior?

- Biological models based on evolutionary theory propose that the acquisition of gender-role behaviors is a product of our genetic heritage, whereas psychosocial and cultural models (social-cognitive theory, gender-schema theory, sociocultural theory) focus on such factors as socialization, gender schemas, and cultural adaptation.

What gender differences exist in cognitive abilities, personality, and leadership style?

- Girls tend to outperform boys on some verbal skills, such as reading, writing, and spelling. Boys hold an edge in some visual-spatial tasks and in math skills, though the gap in math abilities is narrowing. However, boys and girls perform similarly on tests of general intelligence and problem-solving skills.

- Males tend to be more aggressive and have higher self-esteem, while females are generally higher in extraversion, trust, and nurturance.

- Women leaders tend to be more democratic in their leadership style, while male leaders tend to adopt a more autocratic or domineering style.

RECALL IT

1. Our sense of maleness or femaleness is our
   a. sexual orientation.
   b. gender roles.
   c. gender identity.
   d. androgyny.

2. The condition experienced by individuals who possess the genitalia of one sex but the psychological identity of the other is called _____.

3. Which hormone have scientists linked to aggression in *both* males and females?

4. According to social-cognitive theory, gender-typed behavior is acquired through all of the following *except*
   a. observational learning and reinforcement.
   b. modeling of television and magazine content and adults' behavior.
   c. praise given for gender-appropriate behavior.
   d. genetically transmitted gender-based traits.

5. Boys have the upper hand in certain _____-spatial skills, such as mental _____ of objects in three-dimensional space.

THINK ABOUT IT

- Do you believe that gender-typed behavior is a product of our evolutionary history? Why or why not?

- Who, or what, were the major influences on your development of gender-specific behaviors? On your concepts of what it means to be a man or a woman?

MODULE 11.2

Sexual Response and Behavior

- **What are the phases of the sexual response cycle?**
- **What are the origins of sexual orientation?**
- **How do attitudes toward homosexuality vary across cultures?**
- **What are paraphilias?**

Our sexuality is a natural or biological function—indeed, a necessary function to perpetuate the species. Yet our sexual behavior is influenced by many factors, not simply by our biological drives. These include cultural learning, individual experiences, and perhaps most importantly, personal values. Similarly, sexual gratification is not the only source of motivation for sexual behavior. Other motives, such as procreation and expression of emotional intimacy, are also important.

Each society establishes rules or codes of behavior that govern sexual conduct. We may not always follow the rules we were taught, but we learn from an early age what is acceptable behavior and what is not. Our values are shaped by our parents, teachers, religious leaders, and also—for better or worse—our peer groups.

Though sexuality is a natural function, there is great variability in the types and frequencies of sexual practices. The largest national study of sexual practices in the United States showed that about one in four men (27 percent), but less than one in ten women (7.6 percent), reported masturbating at least once a week (Laumann, Paik, & Rosen, 1994). (Many more probably did so but failed to report it.) Among married couples, 80 percent of the men and 71 percent of the women reported performing oral sex on their partners; 80 percent of the men and 74 percent of the women reported receiving oral sex. Much lower percentages of people surveyed—26 percent of men and 20 percent of women—reported engaging in anal intercourse at some point in their lives. On the average, married couples report having intercourse slightly more than once a week (Deveny, 2003). Here again, variability is the norm, as you can see in the reported frequency of sexual intercourse in marriage (see Figure 11.3).

In this module we consider the capacity of our bodies to respond to sexual stimulation and the variations in sexual behavior that exist with respect to sexual orientation and atypical forms of sexual arousal. First, however, let us examine cultural and gender differences in sexuality.

Figure 11.3
Frequency of Marital Sexual Relations During the Past Year

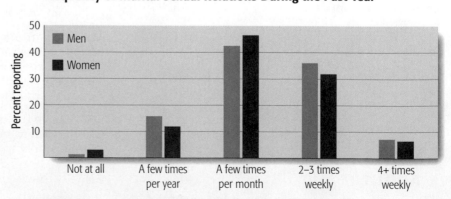

Source: Adapted from Laumann et al., 1994.

Cultural and Gender Differences

CONCEPT 11.13
The human body is sensitive to many forms of sexual stimulation, but how we express ourselves sexually has more to do with our cultural learning and personal values than with the capacity of our bodies for sexual pleasure.

Cultures vary widely in sexual values and practices. Some cultures are more permissive with respect to such sexual practices as oral sex, anal sex, and masturbation, whereas others are more restrictive. Even in our culture, we gain a clearer understanding of variations in sexual values and behavior when we take into account cultural and gender differences. Hispanic Americans, for example, tend to hold conservative sexual values. But a recent study of Hispanic college students in a southern Texas university revealed that men expressed more permissive attitudes toward some sexual practices, such as oral sex and masturbation, and more disapproving attitudes toward homosexuality, than did female students (Dantzker & Eisenman, 2003).

From the perspective of evolutionary psychology, tendencies for men to have roving eyes and for women to be less inclined to seek a variety of sexual partners may have evolutionary roots. Women are limited biologically to having a few potential offspring in their lifetimes, but men can sire a great many children, even thousands in the case of some tribal chieftains. Thus, women need to be careful about safeguarding their limited reproductive opportunities by seeking partners who would be most likely to support their offspring and help ensure their survival. They cannot afford to waste their precious reproductive opportunities on whatever Tom, Dick, or Harry happens along. On the other hand, men may be more reproductively successful—that is, able to spread their seed as widely as possible—if they seek multiple partners. Might these gender differences in desire for sexual variety be imprinted in our genes as a legacy of our evolutionary past? We do have evidence from a survey of more than 16,000 people from different cultures across the world that supports the universality of these gender differences (Schmitt, 2003). However, the question of whether these differences are based in our genes or in the messages ingrained in young people in cultures throughout the world remains a point of continuing controversy in the field.

Psychologist Letitia Peplau (2003) recently reviewed scientific evidence on gender differences in sexual behavior. Here are her major conclusions:

- *Men show greater sexual desire than women.* Several lines of evidence support the view that men show greater interest in sex than women. Men tend to want to have sex more frequently than women. They are also more likely to engage in masturbation and to masturbate more often. Men also tend to fantasize more often about sex and to have more frequent sexual desires (Baumeister, Catanese, & Vohs, 2001).

Intimacy Is More Than Skin Deep   For many couples, sexual activity provides a way of sharing emotional, not just physical, intimacy.

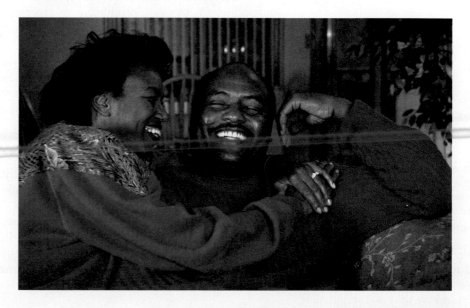

- *Women place greater emphasis on commitment as a context for sexual intimacy.* Women are more likely to limit sexual intimacy to committed relationships. Men tend to have more permissive attitudes toward casual sex and extramarital sex than women.

- *Sexual aggression is more strongly linked to sexuality in men.* Men are more likely to use physical force to compel someone to engage in a sexual act.

In drawing attention to gender differences in sexual behavior, we should be careful not to overgeneralize. For example, not all men hold permissive attitudes toward premarital sex. Nor do all women seek to limit sexual activity to committed relationships. There is a range of variation in sexual interest, desire, and activity both within and across genders.

The Sexual Response Cycle: How Your Body Gets Turned On

What happens within your body when you are sexually aroused? Some of the changes may be obvious—penile erection in the male and vaginal lubrication in the female, for example. But are the bodily responses of men and women as different as they may seem? Or might there be some similarities in how our bodies respond sexually?

Much of what we've learned about the physical response of the body to sexual stimulation comes from the pioneering research of William Masters and Virginia Johnson. They demonstrated that the body responds to sexual stimulation with a characteristic pattern of changes, which they called the **sexual response cycle**. They divided the sexual response cycle into four phases: *excitement, plateau, orgasm,* and *resolution* (Masters & Johnson, 1966). Figure 11.4 shows the levels of sexual arousal during the phases of the sexual response cycle in men and women, respectively. Below, we consider the changes in the body that occur during these phases according to Masters and Johnson's research. These changes are summarized in Table 11.3.

Excitement Phase   There are obvious gender differences in how our bodies respond to sexual stimulation. The penis in males becomes erect; the vagina in women becomes moist through a process called *vaginal lubrication.* Yet both of these markers of sexual excitement reflect the same underlying biological process: **vasocongestion**, or pooling of blood in bodily tissues. When we are sexually stimulated, blood rushes to our genitals. In males, the pooling of blood in the penis causes it to swell, producing an erection. The penis consists of spongy tissue, not bone. These spongy masses soak up blood when the man becomes sexually aroused and thus become enlarged and stiff.

In females, vasocongestion causes the walls of the vagina to swell, which forces moisture through the lining of the vagina (vaginal lubrication). The testes in men expand, as do the earlobes in both genders and the breasts in women. The testes and scrotum begin to elevate and the skin covering the scrotum tenses and thickens.

Vasocongestion causes the vaginal walls to thicken and the inner two-thirds of the vagina to expand. The uterus becomes elevated. The nipples may become erect in both men and women, especially if they are directly stimulated. Both men and women experience increased muscle tension throughout the body, as well as increased heart rate and blood pressure.

The **clitoris** in the female, composed of tissue that is similar to the penis in males, also enlarges and becomes erect in response to vasocongestion. The clitoris is a unique organ, the only organ in either gender devoted exclusively to sexual pleasure. (The penis serves multiple functions—not just sexual pleasure but also passage of urine and sperm.) The clitoris is tightly packed with nerve endings and

CONCEPT 11.14
Landmark research by Masters and Johnson showed that the body's response to sexual stimulation can be characterized in terms of a sexual response cycle consisting of four phases: excitement, plateau, orgasm, and resolution.

sexual response cycle   The term used by Masters and Johnson to refer to the characteristic stages of physiological response to sexual stimulation.

vasocongestion   Swelling of tissues with blood, a process that accounts for penile erection and vaginal lubrication during sexual arousal.

clitoris   A sex organ in the female that is highly sensitive to sexual stimulation.

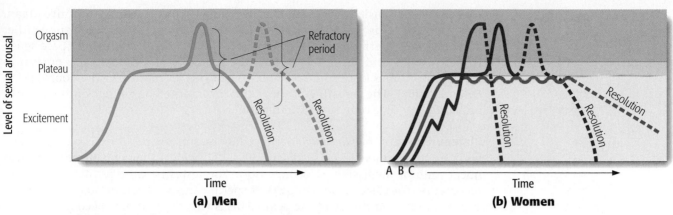

Figure 11.4   The Sexual Response Cycle
Here we see the level of sexual arousal across the four phases of the cycle. Men enter a refractory period after orgasm in which they become unresponsive to sexual stimulation. But as indicated by the broken line, men may become rearoused to the point of orgasm once the refractory period is past. Women do not enter a refractory period. Pattern A shows a woman's cycle with multiple orgasms, as indicated by the dotted line. Pattern B shows a response cycle in which the woman reaches the plateau stage but does not achieve orgasm. Pattern C shows a pattern leading to orgasm in which the woman quickly passes through the plateau phase.

TABLE 11.3   Sexual Response Cycle: How Our Bodies Respond to Sexual Stimulation

Phase of Sexual Response	In Males	In Females	In Both Genders
Excitement Phase	Vasocongestion results in erection. The testes begin to elevate. Skin on the scrotum tenses and thickens.	Vasocongestion swells the vaginal tissue, the clitoris, and the area surrounding the opening of the vagina. Vaginal lubrication appears. The inner two-thirds of the vagina expand, and the vaginal walls thicken and turn a deeper color.	Vasocongestion of the genital tissues occurs. Heart rate, muscle tension (*myotonia*), and blood pressure increase. Nipples may become erect.
Plateau Phase	The tip of the penis turns a deep reddish-purple. The testes become completely elevated. Droplets of semen may be released from the penile opening before ejaculation.	The inner two-thirds of the vagina expand fully. The outer third of the vagina thickens. The clitoris retracts behind its hood, and the uterus elevates and increases in size.	Vasocongestion increases. Myotonia, heart rate, and blood pressure continue to increase.
Orgasm Phase	Sensations of impending ejaculation lasting 2 to 3 seconds precede the ejaculatory reflex. Orgasmic contractions propel semen through the penis and out of the body.	Contractions of the pelvic muscles surrounding the vagina occur.	Orgasmic release of sexual tension occurs, producing intense feelings of pleasure. Muscle spasms occur throughout the body; blood pressure, heart rate, and breathing rate reach a peak.
Resolution Phase	Men become physiologically incapable of achieving another orgasm or ejaculation for a period of time called the refractory period.	Multiple orgasms may occur if the woman desires it and sexual stimulation continues.	Lacking continued sexual stimulation, myotonia and vasocongestion lessen and the body gradually returns to its prearoused state.

so is extremely sensitive to touch. It is the woman's most erotically sensitive organ, which explains why women typically masturbate through clitoral stimulation rather than vaginal penetration. The vagina also contains nerve endings that are sensitive to sexual stimulation. But most of the sensory input that triggers orgasm in the woman comes from stimulation of the clitoris, even during intercourse (Mah & Binik, 2001). The thrusting of the penis during intercourse tugs on the clitoris, providing a source of indirect stimulation.

Plateau Phase   The *plateau phase* precedes orgasm. Sexual arousal "plateaus" at a fairly high but stable level (see Figure 11.4). The tip of the penis turns a purplish hue, a sign of increasing vasocongestion. The testes become further elevated in preparation for ejaculation. Droplets of sperm-carrying seminal fluid are secreted and accumulate at the tip of the penis. This is why women may become pregnant even if the man doesn't fully ejaculate.

Vasocongestion in women leads to greater swelling of the tissues in the outer vagina and around the vaginal opening. The inner part of the vagina expands fully. The uterus reaches its full elevation and increases in size. The clitoris withdraws beneath a flap of tissue called the *clitoral hood*.

Increased **myotonia** (muscle tension) may cause the face to grimace and muscles in the hands and feet to contract in spasms. Heart rate and breathing rate increase further in both genders, as does blood pressure.

Orgasmic Phase   Orgasm, like erection and lubrication, is a reflex. In the orgasm reflex, rhythmic contractions of the pelvic muscles occur, resulting in a release of sexual tension and feelings of intense pleasure (Meston & Frohlich, 2000). In both genders, orgasm is accompanied by muscle spasms throughout the body. Blood pressure and heart rate reach their peaks. The heart beats up to 180 times a minute. In the female, the pelvic muscles around the vagina contract rhythmically. Women typically experience between three and fifteen contractions in total.

In the male, orgasm occurs in two stages of muscular contractions. In the first stage, pelvic contractions cause seminal fluid to collect in a small tube at the base of the penis. Muscles close off the urinary bladder to prevent urine from mixing with semen. This pooling of semen produces the feeling that nothing will stop the ejaculate from "coming"—a sensation, called *ejaculatory inevitability,* lasting perhaps two to three seconds. In the second stage, contractions of pelvic muscles propel the ejaculate through the penis and out of the body. Sensations of pleasure are typically associated with the strength of the contractions and the amount of semen. The first few contractions are most intense.

Resolution Phase   The resolution phase follows orgasm. The body now returns to its prearoused state. Following ejaculation, the man loses his erection. The testes and scrotum return to normal size. The scrotum regains its wrinkled appearance.

In women, blood is released from engorged areas. The nipples return to normal size. The clitoris, vagina, and surrounding tissue shrink to their prearoused sizes. Most muscle tension disappears within five minutes after orgasm in both men and women. Blood pressure, heart rate, and respiration return to normal within a few minutes. Both men and women may feel relaxed and satisfied.

Despite these similarities, the resolution phase is characterized by an important gender difference. Unlike women, men enter a *refractory period.* During this period, they cannot experience another orgasm or ejaculation. The refractory period of adolescent males may last only minutes. In men aged 50 and above, it may last from several minutes to a day. Women do not experience a refractory period. With continued stimulation they are capable of becoming quickly re-aroused to the point of repeated (multiple) orgasms.

Now that we've examined how the body responds to sexual stimulation, let us consider the variations that exist in the directionality of sexual attraction.

myotonia   A state of muscle tension or rigidity.

sexual orientation   The directionality of one's erotic interests.

Sexual Orientation

Sexual orientation refers to the direction of one's erotic attraction and romantic interests—whether one is attracted to members of one's own sex, the opposite sex, or both sexes. Heterosexuals are sexually attracted to members of the opposite sex. Gay males and lesbians are attracted to members of their own sex. And bisexuals are attracted to members of both sexes. Yet the boundaries between these different sexual orientations may not be as clearly drawn as you might think.

In the 1930s and 1940s, the famed sex researcher Alfred Kinsey and his associates challenged the widely held assumption that homosexuality and heterosexuality are mutually exclusive categories—that a person is either homosexual or heterosexual and never anything in between (see the nearby Pioneers box). Kinsey and his colleagues conducted the first large-scale survey of sexual practices by interviewing nearly 12,000 people in the United States about their sexual behaviors, including homosexual behavior. Though most people said they were exclusively heterosexual or homosexual, many reported sexual attraction to both sexes or felt they were primarily but not exclusively homosexual or heterosexual. "The world," Kinsey and his colleagues wrote, "is not to be divided into sheep and goats. . . . Only the human mind invents categories and tries to force facts into separated pigeonholes. The living world is a continuum in each and every one of its aspects" (Kinsey, Pomeroy, & Martin, 1948, p. 639). Kinsey represented sexual orientation on a continuum extending from exclusive heterosexuality on one end to exclusive homosexuality on the other. Like Kinsey, many investigators today conceptualize sexual orientation as a continuum with many gradations, much like the colors in the spectrum of a rainbow (DeAngelis, 2001).

CONCEPT 11.15
Sexual orientation refers to the direction of one's erotic and romantic attraction: toward members of one's own gender, the opposite gender, or both genders.

Online Study Center
Improve Your Grade
Tutorials: Myths and Facts About Homosexuality

THE PIONEERS "A Quiet Man Who Ignited a Storm of Controversy"

Alfred Kinsey

Alfred Kinsey (1894–1956) was a controversial figure in his own time and remains so today. Controversy arose when Kinsey, a zoologist, decided to study intimate sexual behavior in humans. He and his associates conducted the first large-scale survey of sexual behavior in the United States—who was doing what with whom. At the time, America was rather close-lipped about sexuality, and even many scientists did not consider it a topic fit for scientific study. Kinsey believed that any topic, especially one as important to people as their sexuality, was open to scientific exploration. Kinsey and his research team conducted detailed interviews, asking people the kinds of questions no one had ever asked before—questions about how many sexual partners they had before marriage, whether they masturbated, whether they had extramarital affairs, and so on.

Kinsey published his findings in two books, *Sexual Behavior in the Human Male* (Kinsey et al., 1948) and *Sexual*

Behavior in the Human Female (Kinsey et al., 1953). Though his books seem rather tame by today's standards (no explicit pictures, no racy dialogue, just reams of statistical tables), many people branded Kinsey and his work immoral and obscene. He was called a pervert, a menace, and accused of being a communist (Crain, 2004). A committee of Congress charged him with undermining the nation's moral fiber and making the country more vulnerable to a communist takeover (Gebhard, 1977). Kinsey died a few years later in 1956. Colleagues felt that his death at age 62 may have been hastened by the emotional stress he endured in his final years (Gagnon, 1990; Reinisch, 1990). Even today, controversy over Kinsey continues, although the focus has shifted to Kinsey's personal life. Two biographies and a recent film have probed the intimate aspects of Kinsey's own sexual life, including claims that he was bisexual and had sexual relations with some of his graduate students (Crain, 2004; Gathorne-Hardy, 2000; Jones, 1997). Whatever the facts of his personal life may be, his work helped establish the study of sexuality as a legitimate domain of scientific research (Bullough, 2004).

Variations in Sexual Orientation   Kinsey proposed that sexual orientation varies along a continuum from exclusive heterosexuality to exclusive homosexuality.

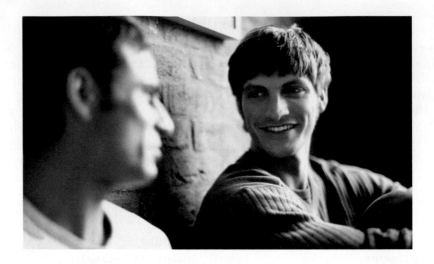

CONCEPT 11.16
The boundaries between different sexual orientations are not as clearly drawn as many people may believe.

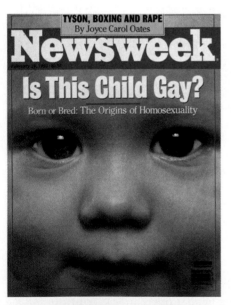

Genes and Sexual Orientation   Are we born gay or heterosexual? Though evidence points to roles for genetic factors, we still have much to learn about the origins of sexual orientation.

How many people identify themselves as gay? Surveys in the United States and Europe find that about 1 to 3 percent of men, and about 1 to 2 percent of women, identify themselves as exclusively gay (Billy et al., 1993; Laumann et al., 1994; Reinisch, 1990). Higher percentages (about 20 to 25 percent of men; about 17 percent of women) report having had some same-sex sexual contact during adolescence or adulthood. In addition, investigators classify 1 to 4 percent of the general population as bisexual (Gabriel, 1995). Census figures indicate that about 600,000 households in the United States are headed by same-sex partners ("Gay Couples," 2001).

Psychological Theories of Sexual Orientation   Why do some people have a gay male or lesbian sexual orientation, whereas others are bisexual or heterosexual? Why are you the way you are? Though the causes of sexual orientation remain under study, one thing is clear: people don't consciously choose to be gay or straight. We don't make a conscious decision to adopt a particular sexual orientation, as we might select a college major or a life partner.

Freud (1922/1959) believed that heterosexuality develops from a "normal" process of identification with the parent of the same sex. In contrast, he believed that homosexuality results from an overidentification with the parent of the opposite sex—boys with their mothers, girls with their fathers. In men, this reversal of identification reflects a "classic pattern" of childrearing characterized by an emotionally "close binding" mother and a "detached hostile" father. As a result, the boy identifies more strongly with his mother than with his father. In this view, gay men would be expected to be effeminate and to disdain traditional masculine interests. The reverse is true of lesbians, who would be expected to identify more with their fathers than with their mother, and to show tomboyish, masculine interests.

Freud's views have been provocative, but evidence does not support his view that sexual orientation stems from family relationship patterns. Investigators find such great variation among families of gay males, lesbians, and heterosexuals that no one pattern applies in all cases (Isay, 1990).Many gay males had close relationships with their fathers, while many heterosexual males had closer relationships with their mothers.

Evidence does show that gay males and lesbians typically recall more cross-gender behavior in childhood than their heterosexual counterparts (Dawood et al., 2000; Bailey & Zucker, 1995; Rahman & Wilson, 2002). Gay males are more likely to have preferred "girls' toys" and to have enjoyed playing with girls more than playing with the trucks or guns, or engaging in the rough-and-tumble games, that young boys favored—preferences that led them to be called "sissies" (Bell, Weinberg,

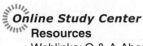

& Hammersmith, 1981; Green, 1987). Investigators believe that genetic factors play an important role in explaining cross-gender behaviors in children (Bailey, Dunne, & Martin, 2000; Knafo, Iervolino, & Plomin, 2005). We should note, however, that many gay males and lesbians report interest patterns in childhood that are typical of their own gender. Moreover, gay males are found among the ranks of even the most "macho" football and hockey players.

Many gay males report childhood recollections of feeling and acting "different" than their peers at a very young age—often as early as 3 or 4 (Isay, 1990). Gay men are more likely than heterosexual comparison groups to recall being more sensitive than other boys and having fewer male buddies (Bailey & Zucker, 1995). Perhaps, as these boys mature, feelings of differentness become transformed into erotic attractions. As psychologist Darryl Bem (1996) put it, what was exotic now becomes erotic. A similar process may occur in girls who develop a lesbian sexual orientation.

CONCEPT 11.17
While the underlying causes of sexual orientation continue to be debated, contemporary theorists focus on the interplay of biological and environmental factors.

Biological Theories of Sexual Orientation   Identical (MZ) twins are more likely to share their sexual orientation in common than fraternal (DZ) twins, a finding that supports a genetic contribution (Bailey, 2003; Rahman & Wilson, 2002). This pattern is found even among twins who were separated shortly after birth and raised in different families. But the fact that one identical twin is gay or heterosexual doesn't necessarily mean that the other will follow suit. Life experiences and environmental influences also contribute to the development of sexual orientation (Kendler, et al., 2000d). Moreover, genetic factors appear to play a larger role in determining homosexuality in men as compared to women (LeVay, 2003).

What about the role of sex hormones? Most studies fail to find differences in circulating sex hormones in adult gay males and lesbians in comparison with their heterosexual counterparts (LeVay, 2003). However, scientists speculate that the male sex hormone testosterone plays a pivotal role in sculpting the developing brain during prenatal development in ways that later affect sexual orientation (T. J. Williams et al., 2000; LeVay, 2003). Recent evidence even raises the possibility that maternal use of certain prescription drugs during pregnancy may influence sex hormone levels during prenatal development, affecting the later development of sexual orientation (Ellis & Hellberg, 2005).

In sum, research on the origins of sexual orientation remains inconclusive (Gooren & Kruijver, 2002). Most experts believe that sexual orientation is explained not by any single factor but rather by a combination of genes, hormones, and the environment interacting throughout the life span (Bailey, Dunne, & Martin, 2000; Jones & Yarhouse, 2001). Since it is possible to arrive at the same destination via different routes, we should allow for the possibility that multiple pathways are involved in explaining how people develop their sexual orientations (Garnets, 2002). Table 11.4 explores some common myths about sexual orientation.

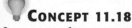

CONCEPT 11.18
In some cultures, an accepted social role is accorded to men who adopt female social and sexual roles.

Cultural Differences in Attitudes Toward Homosexuality   Attitudes toward homosexuality vary widely across cultures. Some condemn it; others accept it (Broude & Greene, 1976; Ford & Beach, 1951). In some tribal societies, male homosexuality is practiced as a rite of passage for males into adulthood. In others, homosexual men are accorded an acceptable social role in which they are permitted to dress like women, perform women's tasks, and take the receptive (female) sexual role in sexual contacts with other men (Ford & Beach, 1951).

We know little about lesbianism in non-Western cultures. The available evidence indicates that lesbianism is less common, or at least less commonly reported, than male homosexuality (Ford & Beach, 1951). This cross-cultural evidence is consistent with findings from our own culture indicating that homosexual interest and activity are less common among women (Laumann et al., 1994; Sell et al., 1995).

Why do some cultures have more tolerant attitudes toward homosexuality than others? Perhaps the answer has to do with the need to either limit or expand

TABLE 11.4   Myths vs. Facts About Sexual Orientation

Myth	Fact
A person's sexual orientation is a matter of choice.	Sexual orientation is not a matter of personal choice. One does not choose to be homosexual any more than one chooses to be heterosexual.
Children raised by gay or lesbian parents will turn out to be maladjusted or become gay themselves.	Children raised by gay or lesbian couples turn out to be as well adjusted as other children (Allen & Burrell, 1996; Victor & Fish, 1995). Nor is there any evidence that children raised by gay parents are more likely than other children to become gay themselves (Bailey et al., 1995; Victor & Fish, 1995).
You are either completely homosexual or completely heterosexual.	Since the time of Kinsey, investigators have classified sexual orientation on the basis of a continuum between exclusive homosexuality and exclusive heterosexuality.
Rates of homosexuality have increased sharply in recent years.	Though homosexuality is more openly discussed today, there is no evidence that underlying rates of homosexuality have changed in a significant way.
Gay males are responsible for most cases of sexual abuse of young boys.	Not true. The great majority of molesters of young boys and young girls are heterosexual men.
Gay males and lesbians really would prefer to be members of the opposite sex.	No, gay males and lesbians have a gender identity that is consistent with their anatomic gender.
Homosexuality is mostly about sex.	Not so. Homosexuality, like heterosexuality, is about patterns of sexual attraction, not how often—or even if—one engages in sexual relationships.

the population. Anthropologists find intolerance toward homosexuality to be more common in cultures in which there is a perceived need to increase the size of the population (Ember & Ember, 1990). On the other hand, cultures that experience periodic famines appear to be more tolerant of homosexuality since it may help limit population growth.

Negative attitudes toward gay males and lesbians are widespread in the United States and many other Western cultures. **Homophobia** is a persistent, irrational fear of gay males or lesbians. Many people with homophobic attitudes feel justified in treating gay men and lesbians rudely, discriminating against them, or even acting violently toward them (Freiberg, 1995; Katz, 1995). Homophobic individuals typically have rigid personalities and attitudes and cannot tolerate any deviation from their views of what is normal or appropriate behavior (Kantor, 1998). Interestingly, many homophobic people claim to have had no direct contact with gay people, so their beliefs are not based on actual experience (Herek, 1996). The harm that homophobia can cause, ranging from insults directed toward gay men and lesbians to discrimination to outright physical attacks ("gay bashing"), highlights the importance of understanding the roots of the problem and developing ways of increasing tolerance (Nevid, Rathus, & Greene, 2006).

Atypical Sexual Variations: The Case of Paraphilias

The word **paraphilia** is derived from the Greek roots *para*, meaning "to the side of," and *philia*, meaning "love." People with paraphilias are sexually attracted to stimuli or situations that are "to the side of" the normal range of sexual variation (see Table 11.5). They may be sexually excited by caressing objects such as women's shoes, as in **fetishism**; wearing clothing of the opposite sex, as in **transvestism**; watching unsuspecting others disrobe or engage in sexual activities, as in

CONCEPT 11.19
Some forms of paraphilia are illegal and for good reason—they are associated with acts that cause harm to others.

homophobia   Unreasoning fear and loathing of people with a homosexual sexual orientation.

paraphilia   A psychological disorder involving atypical or deviant patterns of sexual attraction.

fetishism   A type of paraphilia involving use of objects as sources of sexual arousal.

transvestism   A type of paraphilia involving cross-dressing for purposes of sexual arousal.

TABLE 11.5 Paraphilias: Examples of Atypical Patterns of Sexual Attraction

Paraphilia	Related Behavior	Associated Features
Fetishism	Manipulating or caressing objects for sexual gratification	The person may masturbate while rubbing or fondling the object or smelling it. Women's undergarments, leather boots, high-heeled shoes, and other articles made of rubber, leather, silk, or furs are commonly used as fetishistic objects.
Transvestism	Cross-dressing for sexual arousal and gratification	Transvestism represents a type of fetishism in which the fetishistic object is worn rather than handled. Transvestites are almost always heterosexual men. They may cross-dress in private while masturbating and imagining themselves as women whom they are stroking. Some frequent transvestite clubs or become involved in a transvestic subculture.
Exhibitionism ("flashing")	Exposing one's genitals to unsuspecting strangers for sexual gratification	Exhibitionists seek to elicit a reaction of surprise or shock from their victims, perhaps to buttress their flagging sense of masculinity.
Voyeurism	"Peeping" at unsuspecting persons who are nude, disrobing, or engaging in sexual activity	Voyeurs may masturbate while peeping but typically do not seek any direct contact with their victims.
Sexual masochism and sexual sadism	Acts in which the individual is subject to pain or humiliation (masochism) or inflicts pain or humiliation on others (sadism) for purposes of sexual gratification	Sexual masochists and sadists may engage in mutually gratifying, consensual interactions—called *sadomasochism* (S & M)—to satisfy each other's sexual needs. The pain involved is usually mild or simulated (as when felt whips are used) and is incorporated within elaborate sexual rituals. In a few cases, sexual sadists commit sexual assaults on nonconsenting victims.
Pedophilia	Sexual contact with children	Most people with pedophilia do not fit the stereotype of a man in a trenchcoat lurking around the playground or schoolyard. Rather, most are otherwise law-abiding men, often married with children of their own. In most cases, they are either friends or relatives of the victim or victim's family.

voyeurism; or displaying their genitals to shock strangers, as in **exhibitionism**. Some behaviors associated with paraphilia are illegal, and for good reason: they cause harm to others. For example, acting upon exhibitionistic and voyeuristic urges violates the rights of others and can have damaging psychological effects on victims. **Pedophilia**, in which adults are sexually attracted to children, can cause severe psychological and physical harm when these urges are expressed in the form of child molestation. In **sexual sadism,** a person desires to inflict pain or humiliation on others for purposes of sexual gratification. Paraphilias are believed to occur almost exclusively among men, with one exception: **sexual masochism**, in which the person desires to experience pain or humiliation during sexual contacts (Seligman & Hardenburg, 2000). Even sexual masochism predominantly involves men. Not all cases of paraphilia involve overt acts. In some cases, people have paraphilic urges but do not act upon them.

People develop paraphilias for different reasons. For example, exhibitionists may be shy and socially awkward (Dwyer, 1988); flashing their genitals may be a substitute for the adult relationships they find too frightening or threatening to develop. A response of shock or surprise from their victims may reinforce their flagging sense of masculinity. Men with pedophilia may feel secure only in sexual relationships with children whom they can easily master. Or they may have been abused themselves as children and feel compelled to reverse the situation with themselves in the aggressor's role.

voyeurism A type of paraphilia that involves watching unsuspecting others as they disrobe or engage in sexual activities.

exhibitionism A type of paraphilia characterized by exposing one's genitals to unsuspecting others for purposes of sexual arousal.

pedophilia A type of paraphilia involving sexual attraction to children.

sexual sadism A type of paraphilia involving the infliction of physical suffering or humiliation on another person for purposes of sexual gratification.

sexual masochism A type of paraphilia involving the receipt of painful or humiliating experiences as part of a sexual act.

Exhibitionism
Exhibitionists gain sexual satisfaction by provoking a shocked expression in their unsuspecting victims.

Some Touch Is Good

Some Touch Is Bad

Author
James Molnar

Art Direction
David Palmer

Illustrator
Matthew Bendel

Child Molestation Most child molesters are not strangers but, rather, members or friends of the child's own family.

Psychoanalytic theorists posit that men with paraphilias may have a deep-seated fear of sexual relations with adult partners because of unresolved castration anxiety (unconscious fear of castration). They manage this anxiety by finding safer means of satisfying their sexual urges—for example, by watching others disrobe, caressing undergarments, or molesting children. Learning theorists believe that conditioning may account for paraphilic behavior. For example, people with rubber fetishes (sexual interest in touching or fondling rubber clothing) may have had experiences dating back to infancy in which erections were associated with contact with rubber pants or diapers (Reinisch, 1990). Such experiences might then have led to a conditioned response (sexual arousal) connected with touching the object. Concept Chart 11.2 reviews key concepts relating to sexual response and behavior.

CONCEPT CHART 11.2 Sexual Response and Behavior

Concept	Description	Additional Comments
Sexual response cycle	The characteristic pattern of bodily responses to sexual stimulation	According to Masters and Johnson, the sexual response cycle consists of four phases: excitement, plateau, orgasm, and resolution.
Sexual orientation	The direction of sexual attraction toward one's own gender, toward the opposite gender, or toward both genders	The roots of sexual orientation remain obscure, but interest among investigators and theorists has focused on biological factors (genetics, prenatal sex hormones) and psychosocial factors (self-perceptions in childhood of differentness, relationship patterns with parents).
Sexual behavior	Includes masturbation, sexual intercourse, oral sex, and anal sex	Though the human body can respond to many forms of sexual stimulation, sexual behavior is strongly influenced by cultural learning, personal values, and individual experiences, not simply by biological drives or capacities for sexual response.
Paraphilias	Atypical or deviant patterns of sexual attraction	Some forms of paraphilia are associated with behaviors that are illegal because of the harm these behaviors cause to others.

EXPLORING PSYCHOLOGY

AIDS and Other STDs: Is Your Behavior Putting You at Risk?

AIDS (acquired immune deficiency syndrome) has become one of history's worst epidemics. More than 40 million people worldwide are infected with HIV *(human immunodeficiency virus),* the virus that causes AIDS, and more than 20 million have died of the disease (National Women's Health Information Center, 2005; Stephenson, 2004).

The majority of cases of HIV transmission worldwide result from heterosexual intercourse. In the United States, the federal Centers for Disease Control and Prevention (CDCP) estimate that heterosexual intercourse accounts for about one in three cases of HIV transmission (CDCP, 2004a). Among cases of heterosexual transmission in the United States, two-thirds are found among women and about three-fourths among African Americans.

Nowhere has the impact of HIV/AIDS been greater than in sub-Saharan Africa. So many adults have been annihilated by this devastating disease that nearly an entire generation of children are now without parents—some 11 million orphans by some estimates (National Women's Health Information Center, 2005).

HIV is transmitted by contact with infected bodily fluids, generally through intimate sexual contact or needle-sharing (Steinbrook, 2004). HIV attacks and disables the body's immune system, making the person vulnerable to other infections the body is normally able to fend off.

HIV/AIDS is the most threatening **sexually transmitted disease (STD)** (also called a *sexually transmitted infection* or STI). Bacterial STDs (e.g., chlamydia, syphilis, and gonorrhea) and viral STDs (e.g., HIV/AIDS, herpes, and HPV infection) constitute the two major classes of STDs. HIV/AIDS is the most threatening STD, but it is far from the most common one. Whereas nearly 1 million Americans are infected with HIV, more than one in five adolescents and adults in the United States—an estimated 45 million people—are infected with HSV-2, the virus that causes genital herpes (Tuller, 2001). *Human papillomaviruses (HPVs)* are a group of viruses that cause warts to appear in different parts of the body, including the genitals. HPV is found in at least one in five Americans over the age of 12 (Baer, Allen, & Braun, 2000; Rubin, 2003). Chlamydia, the most common bacterial type of STD, affects an estimated 4 percent of young adults in this country (W. C. Miller et al., 2004). All told, some 3 million cases of sexually transmitted disease occur annually among preteens and teens in the United States (Dittmann, 2003b).

Many STDs, not just HIV/AIDS, pose serious threats to our health. Many strains of HPV cause cervical cancer in women, a potential killer (Muñoz et al., 2003). Untreated gonorrhea and chlamydia can lead to pelvic inflammatory disease and infertility in women (W. C. Miller et al., 2004) and can reduce male fertility ("Chlamydia," 2004), and untreated gonorrhea in men can lead to a serious infection of the internal reproductive system, which can cause fertility problems. Another bacterial disease, syphilis, can damage the heart and brain if left untreated. Genital herpes can cause serious complications, especially in women, including increased risks of miscarriage and cervical cancer (Nevid, 1998).

Prevention and Treatment   Though antibiotics can cure bacterial forms of STD, they are of no use against viral STDs. Antiviral drugs may help control viral STDs, such as HIV/AIDS and genital herpes, but they cannot eliminate the infectious organisms from the body. The advent of a new generation of antiviral drugs does raise hopes that HIV infection may become a chronic but manageable disease (e.g., Wainberg, 2005; Yeni et al., 2004). However, hopes are tempered by evidence

CONCEPT 11.20
Many STDs, not just HIV/AIDS, pose serious threats to our health.

sexually transmitted disease (STD)
A disease caused by an infectious agent that is spread by sexual contact.

that many patients fail to benefit from existing treatments and that drug-resistant strains of the virus are emerging (Grant et al., 2002; Lawrence et al., 2003).

The lack of a cure for viral STDs, as well as awareness of the risks posed by untreated bacterial STDs, underscores the importance of prevention and early treatment. Arming yourself with information about how these diseases are transmitted, early signs of infection, and available treatments (see Table 11.6) is an important step in protecting yourself from STDs. But information alone does not reduce the risks of transmitting STDs: it must be put into practice through changes in behavior (Carey et al., 2004; DiClemente et al., 2004; Greer, 2004b). The following section lists suggestions for safer sexual practices and medical screening.

TABLE 11.6 Major Types of STDs

	Mode of Transmission	Symptoms	Treatment
Bacterial STDs			
Gonorrhea	Sexual contact (vaginal, oral, or anal intercourse); from mother to newborn during childbirth	Men may have a yellowish, thick penile discharge and burning urination; though most women do not show early symptoms, some have increased vaginal discharge, burning urination, and irregular menstrual bleeding.	Antibiotics
Syphilis	Sexual contact; by touching an infectious chancre (sore)	A round, painless but hard chancre develops at the site of infection within 2 to 4 weeks; symptoms progress through additional stages if left untreated.	Antibiotics
Chlamydia in women, or nongonococcal urethritis (NGU) in men	Sexual contact; touching an eye after contact with genitals of an infected partner; from infected mother to newborn during childbirth	Most women are symptom-free, but some have frequent and painful urination, lower abdominal pain and inflammation, and vaginal discharge. Men, too, are generally symptom-free but may have gonorrhea-like symptoms.	Antibiotics
Viral STDs			
HIV/AIDS	Sexual contact; injection-sharing; receiving contaminated blood; from mother to fetus during pregnancy or during childbirth or breast-feeding	Infected persons may be initially symptom-free or have mild flulike symptoms, but may progress to develop full-blown AIDS.	Antiviral drugs may help control the virus but do not cure the disease.
Genital herpes	Sexual contact	Painful, reddish bumps appear around the genitals, thighs, buttocks, or in the vagina or on the cervix in women. The bumps may develop into blisters or sores that fill with pus and break open before healing over.	Antiviral drugs can help control outbreaks but do not rid the body of the virus.
Viral hepatitis	Sexual contact, especially anal contact in the case of hepatitis A; contact with infected fecal matter; transfusion of contaminated blood (especially for hepatitis B and C)	Symptoms range from absence of symptoms to mild flulike symptoms to more severe symptoms, such as fever, abdominal pain, vomiting, and "jaundiced" (yellowish) skin and eyes.	Bed rest and possible use of the drug alpha interferon in cases of hepatitis C
Genital warts	Sexual contact; contact with infected towels or clothing	Painless warts resembling cauliflowers may develop on the genitals, the internal reproductive organs, around the anus, or in the rectum.	Warts may be removed, but the virus (HPV) remains in the body.

CONCEPT 11.21
Modifiable behaviors such as unprotected sex and needle-sharing are major risk factors for transmission of sexually transmitted diseases, including HIV/AIDS.

Protecting Yourself and Your Partners from STDs   The only sure way to prevent the sexual transmission of STDs is to practice lifelong abstinence or maintain a monogamous relationship with an uninfected partner who is also monogamous. Short of that, you can reduce the risk from sexual contact rather than eliminate it entirely, that is, practice *safer* sex rather than *safe* sex. Here are some guidelines that can lower the risk of contracting an STD or suffering the consequences of an untreated STD (adapted from Nevid, Rathus, & Greene, 2006):

1. *Be careful in your choice of sex partners.* Get to know the person's sexual background before engaging in sexual activity. (Even so, getting to know someone is no guarantee that the person is not carrying HIV or some other infectious agent.)

2. *Avoid multiple partners, especially partners who themselves may have multiple partners.*

3. *Communicate your concerns.* Be assertive with your partner. Openly state your concerns about the risks of AIDS and other STDs and the need to practice safer sex.

4. *Avoid engaging in sexual contact with anyone with a sore or blister around the genitals.* Inspect your partner's sex organs before any sexual contact. Rashes, blisters, chancres, discharges, warts, disagreeable odors, and so on should be treated as warning signs of a possible infection. But be aware that some STDs, including HIV infection, do not have any obvious signs.

5. *Avoid unprotected sexual contact.* Latex condoms (not "natural" condoms, which are more porous) offer the most reliable protection against the spread of HIV during sexual contact. Spermicides should be used along with latex condoms, not as a substitute for them. Be aware that condoms may not protect against some STDs, such as genital herpes and HPV (Morse, 2002; Wingert, 2002).

6. *Obtain a medical evaluation if you suspect that you may have been exposed to a sexually transmitted disease.*

7. *Get regular medical checkups to detect and treat disorders you may not be aware you have.*

8. *When in doubt, don't.* Abstain from intimate sexual contact if you have any doubts about whether it is potentially harmful. Your safety and that of your partner should be your top priority.

Online Study Center
Resources
Weblinks: Fact Sheets on STDs

MODULE 11.2 REVIEW

Sexual Response and Behavior

RECITE IT

What are the phases of the sexual response cycle?

- The excitement phase is characterized by erection in the male and vaginal lubrication in the female.
- The plateau phase is an advanced state of arousal that precedes orgasm.
- The orgasmic phase is characterized by orgasmic contractions of the pelvic musculature.
- During the resolution phase, the body returns to its prearoused state.

What are the origins of sexual orientation?

- The origins remain unknown. Psychological theories attempt to explain sexual orientation in terms of patterns of child rearing and early childhood experiences. Biological theories note possible roles for genetics and prenatal sex hormones.

How do attitudes toward homosexuality vary across cultures?

- Variations in cultural attitudes range from condemnation in some cultures to legitimization of a homosexual social role in others.

What are paraphilias?

- Paraphilias are atypical or deviant patterns of sexual attraction or arousal, such as fetishism (sexual arousal connected with inanimate objects such as shoes) and exhibitionism (sexual arousal from exposing one's genitals to unsuspecting strangers).

RECALL IT

1. Regarding the human sexual response cycle, match the following terms with their descriptions:
   i. excitement phase; ii. plateau phase;
   iii. orgasmic phase; iv.resolution phase

   a. sexual release, intense pleasure
   b. body returns to prearoused state
   c. increased myotonia and further increases in vasocongestion
   d. initial response to sexual stimulation

2. All of the following are sexual orientations *except*
   a. transsexuality.   c. homosexuality.
   b. bisexuality.   d. heterosexuality.

3. A paraphilia in which one dresses in clothing of the opposite sex for purposes of sexual gratification is known as _____.

4. Bacterial forms of STDs include
   a. HIV/AIDS.   c. genital herpes.
   b. HPV.   d. chlamydia.

THINK ABOUT IT

• How do your sexual practices reflect your personal values? Which people have been the major influences on your sexual personal values?

• Are you struggling with issues concerning your sexual orientation? Do you know someone who is? Are there resources on your campus or in your community that provide counseling services to people with these types of questions? How can you find out more about these services?

• What are you doing to protect yourself from STDs? What—if anything—might you do differently?

MODULE 11.3

Sexual Dysfunctions

- **What are sexual dysfunctions?**
- **What are the causes of sexual dysfunctions?**
- **What are the general aims of sex therapy?**

Although our bodies are capable of responding to many types of sexual stimulation, problems do occasionally arise. Some people experience a lack of sexual desire or interest; others have difficulties becoming aroused or reaching orgasm. Occasional problems with sexual interest or response are quite common and may affect virtually everyone at one time or another. Men may occasionally have difficulty achieving erections or may ejaculate sooner than they desire. Women may occasionally have difficulty becoming sexually aroused or reaching orgasm. When such problems become persistent and cause distress, they are considered psychological disorders and are classified as **sexual dysfunctions**.

Sexual dysfunctions are quite common, affecting 43 percent of women and 31 percent of men at some points in their lives, according to evidence from a national survey (Laumann , Paik, & Rosen, 1999; Rosen & Laumann, 2003). Concept Chart 11.3 lists the major types of sexual dysfunctions. Women are more likely to experience a lack of interest in sex, lack of sexual pleasure, and inability to reach orgasm (see Table 11.7). Men more often report performance-related anxiety and reaching orgasm too soon. In the following sections we discuss several major types of sexual dysfunctions and the methods of therapy that are available to help people overcome them.

sexual dysfunctions Persistent or recurrent problems with sexual interest, arousal, or response.

CONCEPT CHART 11.3   Sexual Dysfunctions

	Disorder	What It Is	Associated Features/Treatments
Sexual Desire Disorders	Hypoactive sexual desire disorder	Abnormally low level of sexual interest or drive	May occur in response to hormone deficiencies, relationship problems, depression, or other causes
	Sexual aversion disorder	Revulsion or strong aversion to genital contact	Typically represents a fear of sexual contact that may develop in the aftermath of sexual trauma
Sexual Arousal Disorders	Male erectile disorder	Persistent difficulty achieving or maintaining erections	May be due to psychological causes (e.g., self-doubts, performance-related anxiety), physical causes (e.g., diabetes, neurological problems), or a combination of causes
	Female sexual arousal disorder	Failure to become adequately sexually aroused in response to sexual stimulation	May be caused by underlying health problems, a sexually repressive cultural or family background, or relationship problems
Orgasmic Disorders	Female orgasmic disorder	Difficulty achieving orgasm in response to adequate levels of sexual stimulation	Treatment techniques focus on helping women learn more about their sexual responsiveness (through directed masturbation) and transferring this learning to their relationship with their partners
	Male orgasmic disorder	Delay or inability to ejaculate	Relatively uncommon, but may stem from excessive anxiety, neurological problems, sexual guilt, or hostility toward the partner
	Premature ejaculation	Ejaculation occurring with a minimum of sexual stimulation and before the man desires it	Affects men who have difficulty keeping the level of stimulation from rising to the point that the ejaculatory reflex is triggered

TABLE 11.7   Percentages of Adults in the United States Reporting Sexual Problems Occurring Within the Past Year

	Men	Women
Sex not pleasurable	8	21
Unable to reach orgasm	8	24
Lack of interest in sex	16	33
Anxiety about performance*	17	12
Reaching climax too early	29	10
Unable to keep an erection	10	—
Having trouble lubricating	—	19

*Though performance-related anxiety is not a sexual dysfunction in itself, it is a common feature of sexual dysfunctions.

Source: Adapted from Laumann et al., 1994.

CONCEPT 11.22
Though occasional problems with sexual interest or response may affect virtually everyone, people with sexual dysfunctions have persistent difficulties with sexual interest, arousal, or response.

hypoactive sexual desire disorder
A type of sexual desire disorder characterized by an absence or lack of sexual interest or desire.

sexual aversion disorder   A type of sexual desire disorder involving repulsion or strong aversion to genital sexual contact.

male erectile disorder   A type of sexual arousal disorder in men characterized by difficulty achieving or maintaining erections sufficient to engage in sexual intercourse.

female sexual arousal disorder   A type of sexual arousal disorder in women involving difficulties in becoming sexually aroused.

female orgasmic disorder   A type of orgasmic disorder in women characterized by a lack of orgasm, or persistent difficulties in achieving orgasm, following a normal phase of sexual excitement.

male orgasmic disorder   A type of orgasmic disorder in men characterized by a lack of orgasm, or persistent difficulties in achieving orgasm, following a normal phase of sexual excitement.

premature ejaculation (PE)   A type of orgasmic disorder in men characterized by rapid ejaculation following sexual stimulation.

Types of Sexual Dysfunctions

Many different types of sexual problems are classified as sexual dysfunctions. Here we focus on three major classes of sexual dysfunctions: sexual desire disorders, sexual arousal disorders, and orgasmic disorders.

Sexual Desire Disorders   Individuals with these disorders experience a lack of sexual desire or an aversion to genital sexual contact. **Hypoactive sexual desire disorder**, one of the most frequently diagnosed sexual dysfunctions, is characterized by little or no sexual interest or desire. It occurs more frequently in women (Bancroft, Loftus, & Long, 2003), but the belief that all men are eager and willing to engage in sex is a myth. People with **sexual aversion disorder** have a strong aversion to genital sexual contact. They may enjoy other forms of affectionate contact, so long as it does not involve the genitals. Sexual aversion disorder often involves a fear of sexual contact that arises in individuals who have suffered some form of sexual trauma, such as childhood sexual abuse or rape.

Sexual Arousal Disorders   These disorders include **male erectile disorder** (also known as *erectile dysfunction,* or *ED*) and **female sexual arousal disorder**. Men with erectile disorder encounter persistent problems achieving or maintaining erections sufficient to engage in sexual intercourse. Women with sexual arousal disorder have persistent difficulty becoming sexually aroused or adequately lubricated.

Orgasmic Disorders   Women with **female orgasmic disorder** and men with **male orgasmic disorder** have problems reaching orgasm or cannot reach orgasm at all. In cases where the individual can achieve orgasm through masturbation but not through sexual relations with a partner, a clinician needs to determine whether there is adequate stimulation during sexual relations for orgasm to occur. However, experts continue to debate how to define sexual dysfunctions, especially in women (Fishman & Mamo, 2001; D. Smith, 2003b). For example, do women have a sexual dysfunction if they can achieve orgasm reliably through masturbation but not with their partners? Might their difficulty result from a lack of effective stimulation (especially clitoral stimulation) from their partners rather than an orgasmic disorder?

Premature ejaculation (PE), the most common type of sexual dysfunction in males, is characterized by rapid ejaculation with minimal stimulation (Byers & Grenier, 2003). Research indicates that about three men in ten suffer from PE (Laumann et al., 1994).

Causes of Sexual Dysfunctions

There are many causes of sexual dysfunctions, including biological and psychosocial factors.

Biological Causes   Most cases of erectile dysfunction are traced to biological factors, with circulatory problems topping the list (Bivalacqua et al., 2000; Kleinplatz, 2003). For example, diabetes can damage the blood vessels and nerves that service the penis, leading to erectile problems. You probably knew that obesity is a major risk factor for many serious, chronic diseases, including heart disease and diabetes. But recently we've learned that obesity also increases the risk of erectile dysfunction (Saigal, 2004). The good news is that investigators find that health interventions that help obese men lose weight and increase their activity levels lead to improved erectile functioning (Esposito et al., 2004).

Neurological or circulatory conditions or diseases can also interfere with sexual interest, arousal, or response. These include multiple sclerosis, spinal-cord injuries, epilepsy, complications from surgery (such as prostate surgery in men), side effects of certain medications, and hormonal problems. Psychoactive drugs such as cocaine, alcohol, and narcotics may also dampen sexual interest or impair sexual responsiveness.

Although testosterone is a male sex hormone produced in a man's testes, it is also produced in smaller amounts in a woman's ovaries and in the adrenal glands of both men and women (Guzick & Hoeger, 2000; Shifren & Ferrari, 2004). You may be surprised to learn that the male sex hormone testosterone energizes sexual desire or drive in both men and women, and that deficiencies of the hormone can dampen sexual desire in both sexes (Apperloo et al., 2003; Bachmann et al., 2002). That being said, most men and women with sexual dysfunctions have normal sex hormone levels.

Psychosocial Causes   Sexual dysfunctions are often rooted in psychological or cultural factors, such as relationship problems, performance-related anxiety, or repressive attitudes in the family toward sexuality. Children reared in homes where negative attitudes toward sexuality prevail may encounter anxiety, guilt, or shame when they become sexually active, rather than sexual arousal and pleasure. This is especially true of young women who have been exposed to sexually repressive cultural attitudes and to a sexual double-standard which permits greater sexual expression in men than women. These women may learn that sex is a marital duty to be performed for reproduction purposes or to satisfy their husband's sexual cravings, not for their own sexual pleasure—a cultural framework that discourages them from learning about their sexual responsiveness or inhibits them from asserting their sexual needs with their partners.

Some couples fall into a sexual routine, perhaps even a rut. Couples who fail to communicate their sexual preferences or to regularly invigorate their lovemaking routines may find themselves losing interest. Relationship problems can also impair a couple's sexual responsiveness, especially when conflicts and long-simmering resentments are carried into bed.

Survivors of rape and other sexual traumas, such as childhood sexual abuse, often develop deep feelings of disgust or revulsion toward sex (Bean, 2002). Not surprisingly, they often have difficulty responding sexually, even with loving partners. Other emotional factors—especially anxiety, depression, and anger—can also lessen sexual interest or responsiveness (Frohlich & Meston, 2002; Mah & Binik, 2001).

Anxiety, especially **performance anxiety**, plays a key role in many cases of sexual dysfunction. Performance anxiety is an excessive concern about how well one is performing. Anxiety may make it impossible for a man to achieve or sustain an erection or for a woman to become adequately lubricated or achieve orgasm. Failure

Online Study Center
Resources
Weblinks: Online Sexual Disorders Screening

CONCEPT 11.23
The underlying causes of sexual dysfunctions include biological factors, such as neurological or circulatory problems, and psychosocial factors, such as performance anxiety.

Communication Problems and Sexual Dysfunctions   Sexually dysfunctional couples often have difficulty communicating their sexual needs and interests.

performance anxiety   Anxiety experienced in performance situations (including sexual acts) stemming from a fear of negative evaluation of one's ability to perform.

to perform then fuels self-doubts and fears of repeated failure, which in turn heighten anxiety on subsequent occasions, leading to yet more failure experiences—and so on and on in a vicious cycle.

Performance anxiety leads people to become spectators of their own performance. Rather than immersing themselves in the sexual act, they mentally scrutinize how their bodies are responding. It is little wonder they have difficulty responding sexually. A man with erectile dysfunction said that on dates leading up to sexual relations he kept picturing his partner's face and how disappointed she'd be if he failed to perform. He went on to say, "By the time we did go to bed, I was paralyzed with anxiety" (cited in Nevid, Rathus, & Greene, 2006). In our culture there is such a deep-rooted connection between the man's ability to perform sexually and his sense of manhood that repeated failure experiences might lead him to feel he is no longer a man. He may consequently suffer a severe loss of self-esteem or become depressed. Performance anxiety may also contribute to male orgasmic disorder, especially in cases where men have difficulty achieving orgasm with a partner. Male orgasmic disorder may also arise from underlying neurological problems, sexual guilt, or hostility toward the partner. Although performance anxiety primarily affects men, women, too, may be burdened with performance anxiety about achieving orgasm.

Premature ejaculation may arise from a failure to keep the level of stimulation below the man's ejaculatory threshold or "point of no return." Though ejaculation is a reflex, men need to learn (usually through trial and error) to gauge their level of stimulation so that it does not exceed their ejaculatory threshold. In particular, they need to signal their partners to stop stimulation before this point so that their sensations can subside before resuming again.

Sex Therapy

CONCEPT 11.24
Sex therapy is a problem-focused form of therapy that aims to reduce performance anxiety and foster sexual skills and competencies.

Sex therapy is a set of relatively brief, problem-focused therapeutic techniques for treating sexual dysfunctions. In sex therapy, people—usually couples—meet with a therapist or a pair of male and female therapists and undergo behavioral techniques specifically designed to help them overcome their sexual difficulties. Sex therapy attempts to eliminate performance anxiety by removing pressures to perform. Even in cases where biological causes are suspected, people with sexual dysfunctions tend to achieve better results when they participate in sex therapy along with medical treatment (Carey, Wincze, & Meisler, 1998).

Sex therapy was pioneered by William Masters and Virginia Johnson (1970). They treated couples in an intensive, two-week program that consisted of daily treatment sessions and nightly sexual homework assignments. An important part of their treatment method was **sensate-focus exercises**, in which partners massaged each other in nongenital areas of the body while relaxing in the nude. These exercises provided a source of pleasurable stimulation without the performance demands associated with sexual intercourse. Indeed, couples were instructed to postpone having intercourse until their confidence levels were restored. They were also helped to open channels of communication about the types of stimulation they found arousing and to gently guide or direct one another in providing effective stimulation.

A wide range of other techniques are employed in sex therapy. For example, therapists may use a program of directed masturbation to help women who have never been able to achieve an orgasm by themselves or with their partners (Leiblum & Rosen, 2000). Reported success rates from such programs are in the 70 to 90 percent range. The treatment itself typically consists of a therapist directing the woman to practice a series of masturbation exercises in the privacy of her own home. The purpose is to help the woman explore her body's sexual response and learn the skills needed to bring about an orgasm. Women are then guided to transfer this learning to their relationships with their partners. Another example is the

sensate-focus exercises A technique used in sex therapy that consists of nongenital massage to lessen the anxiety associated with sexual interactions.

stop-start method, the most common treatment for premature ejaculation. In this method, a couple practices suspending sexual stimulation before the man reaches the level at which his ejaculation reflex is triggered. The two partners then resume stimulation once his sensations subside, continuing to practice these start-stop cycles until the man gains better control. Overall, most people with sexual dysfunctions benefit from some form of sex therapy.

Biological therapies are also available to help people with sexual dysfunctions. Testosterone therapy may be helpful in treating problems of low sexual interest or desire (Goldstat et al., 2003; Wang et al., 2004). The drug Viagra and other similar drugs are effective in producing erections in the majority of men suffering from erectile disorder (Naughton, 2004; Walker, 2004). They work by relaxing blood vessels in the penis, allowing them to expand and carry more blood. We still lack safe and effective pharmacological treatments for female sexual dysfunction, though testing of Viagra and other drugs is ongoing (e.g., Modelska & Cumming, 2003).

Some drugs commonly used to treat depression, such as certain antidepressants like Paxil, have been successful in treating premature ejaculation (Waldinger et al., 2001, 2002). Delayed ejaculation appears to be a common side effect of these drugs, which may be a benefit to men suffering from premature ejaculation.

Most cases of sexual dysfunction can be treated successfully through either biological or psychological interventions or a combination of both. This finding is especially encouraging when we consider that only a generation or two ago there were no effective treatments available for sexual disorders.

MODULE 11.3 REVIEW

Sexual Dysfunctions

RECITE IT

What are sexual dysfunctions?

- Sexual dysfunctions are persistent and distressing problems in sexual interest, arousal, or response. They include sexual desire disorders, sexual arousal disorders, and orgasmic disorders.

What are the causes of sexual dysfunctions?

- Sexual dysfunctions can have biological causes, such as declining hormone levels and health problems, and psychosocial causes, such as sex-negative attitudes, communication problems, sexually traumatic experiences, and performance anxiety.

What are the general aims of sex therapy?

- The general aims are to reduce performance anxiety, foster sexual skills or competencies, and improve communication between sexual partners.

RECALL IT

1. The term *sexual dysfunction* refers to problems with
   a. sexual response only.
   b. sexual interest or response only.
   c. sexual arousal or response only.
   d. sexual interest, arousal, or response.

2. Match the following sexual dysfunction terms with the appropriate descriptions: i. sexual desire disorders; ii. sexual arousal disorders; iii. orgasmic disorders; iv. premature ejaculation

   a. may include aversion to genital sexual contact
   b. may occur in response to only minimal stimulation
   c. difficulty experiencing sexual climax
   d. includes erectile dysfunction (males) and insufficient lubrication (females)

3. Timothy has virtually no interest in sexual activity. Only rarely does he experience sexual fantasies or desires. Though he doesn't have any problems achieving erections, he wonders why so many people seem so interested in sex. Which type of sexual dysfunction would most probably apply in his case?
   a. sexual aversion disorder
   b. male sexual interest disorder
   c. male orgasmic disorder
   d. hypoactive sexual desire disorder

4. List one or more of the *psychosocial* causes of sexual dysfunctions.

THINK ABOUT IT

- How are sexual dysfunctions in men and women similar? How are they different?

- Have you experienced a problem with sexual arousal or performance? How did it affect you? What did you do about it? Did the information in this chapter raise your awareness about factors that may have contributed to your problem or about ways of dealing with it?

APPLICATION MODULE 11.4
Combating Rape and Sexual Harassment

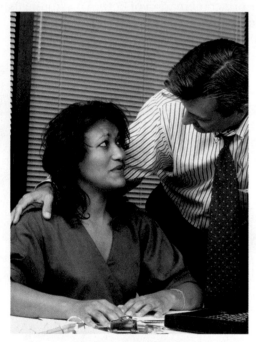

Is This Sexual Harassment?   What defines sexual harassment? Based on research evidence, do men and women tend to perceive behaviors that constitute sexual harassment in the same way?

rape   The use or threat of force to compel a person into having sexual intercourse.

statutory rape   Sexual intercourse with a person who is under the legal age of consent, even if the person is a willing participant.

sexual harassment   A form of sexual coercion involving unwelcome sexual comments, jokes, overtures, demands for sexual favors, or outright physical contact.

Acts of sexual coercion represent a broad continuum ranging from sexual taunts and insults to outright sexual assault and rape. Rape and sexual harassment are two major forms of sexual coercion. **Rape** is the use or threat of force to compel a person into having sexual intercourse. In cases of **statutory rape**, sexual intercourse occurs with a person who is under the legal age of consent, even if the person willingly cooperates. **Sexual harassment** is any act in which a person subjects someone else to unwanted sexual remarks, gestures, touching, overtures, or demands for sexual favors in exchange for favored treatment or as a condition of employment or advancement (see Table 11.8).

How Common Is Rape and Sexual Harassment?

Incidents of rape and sexual harassment are, unfortunately, far too common in our society. The federal government estimates that 75,000 rapes and 62,000 attempted rapes occur annually in the United States (U.S. Department of Justice, 2003). The actual numbers are undoubtedly far greater because the great majority of rapes and attempted rapes go unreported (Fisher et al., 2003; Watts & Zimmerman, 2002).

The prevalence of rape is shocking. Between 15 and 25 percent of American women are likely to be raped at some point in their lives (Brener, McMahon, Warren, & Douglas, 1999; Koss & Kilpatrick, 2001). Approximately 3 percent of college women suffer a rape or attempted rape each year (Fisher et al., 2003). According to surveys conducted in Massachusetts and Minnesota, between 10 and 20 percent of high school girls report that they have been physically or sexually assaulted by a dating partner (Silverman et al., 2001; Stenson, 2001b).

Though the majority of rapes are committed against young women, women of all ages, races, and economic classes are at risk. The incidence of rape is much higher in the United States than in other industrialized societies such as Canada, Great Britain, and Japan.

Men, too, may be raped, although legally the act may be classified as sexual assault because it involves forced anal intercourse or anal penetration by objects rather than vaginal intercourse. Most but certainly not all of these attacks occur in prison settings. Researchers estimate that perhaps one in ten survivors of rape are male (Gibbs, 1991). Contrary to the commonly held belief that men who rape other men are gay, most assailants are heterosexual men who commit rape as a form of retaliation, humiliation, or domination and control.

The prevalence of sexual harassment is difficult to pin down because, as with rape, the great majority of women who experience sexual harassment do not file formal complaints. Yet sexual harassment is believed to be so widespread that it is

TABLE 11.8   Types of Sexual Harassment

Type of Harassment	Description	Examples
Gender harassment	Making statements or displaying behaviors that are insulting or degrading to women in general	Sexual insults, obscene jokes or humor, offensive graffiti
Seductive behavior	Making unwelcome, inappropriate, and offensive sexual advances	Making repeated, unwanted sexual overtures or requests for dates; sending repeated letters or making repeated phone calls to offer sexual invitations
Sexual bribery	Soliciting sexual activity by promising rewards	Offering to advance someone's career for sexual favors
Sexual coercion	Coercing someone into sexual activity by threat of punishment	Threatening negative job evaluations, job termination, or withholding of promotions for failure to comply with sexual requests
Sexual imposition	Unwelcome sexual contact	Any form of unwelcome touching, including grabbing or fondling, or outright sexual assault

Note: The key feature of sexual harassment is that it is unwanted. Gender harassment is far and away the most common form of sexual harassment, followed by seductive behavior. Sexual bribery and coercion are relatively uncommon, but sexual imposition occurs more often than many people believe.

Source: Adapted from *Sexual Harassment: Myths and Realities,* American Psychological Association, Office of Public Affairs, 1996.

regarded as the most common form of sexual victimization in the United States (Fitzgerald, 1993b). Though either men or women may suffer sexual harassment, in nearly all cases women are harassed and men are the harassers (Mansnerus & Kocieniewski, 2004; Stockdale et al., 2004). Estimates are that about 50 percent of women suffer sexual harassment in school or on the job (Fitzgerald, 1993a, 1993b). A recent national survey found that about 80 percent of teenage boys and girls reported being sexually harassed by their peers (Smith, 2001a). Women in traditionally male-dominated work settings, such as construction sites or firehouses, face an especially high risk of sexual harassment.

Women tend to perceive a wider range of behaviors as sexual harassment than do men, especially behaviors that involve derogatory remarks, dating pressures, and direct sexual contact such as kissing or fondling (Rotundo, Nguyen, & Sackett, 2001). Men and women agree more strongly on whether such extreme behaviors as rape, requests for sexual involvement as a condition of employment or promotion, and unwanted pressure or requests for sexual involvement constitute harassment.

Acquaintance Rape—the Most Common Type

Most rapes, about two-thirds, are committed not by strangers but by men with whom the women are acquainted, such as dates, husbands, family members, and friends of the family (U.S. Department of Justice, 2003). A large-scale survey of college men and women found that only 11 percent of rapes were committed by strangers (Koss, Gidycz, & Wisniewski, 1987) (see Figure 11.5). Women who are sexually assaulted also stand an increased risk of future sexual assaults (Breitenbecher, 2001).

Ten to 20 percent of women report being raped by a man they were dating (Tang, Critelli, & Porter, 1995). The date rapist may mistake a woman's interest as willingness to engage in sexual intercourse, believing that even if she says "no," she is merely being coy (Monson, Langhinrichsen-Rohling, & Binderup, 2000; Osman, 2003). He may erroneously believe that women who accompany men home or who frequent singles bars or attend parties are "just asking for it." Sexually aggressive men often endorse myths about rape, such as the belief that women secretly desire to be raped or overpowered. In their minds they may not believe they

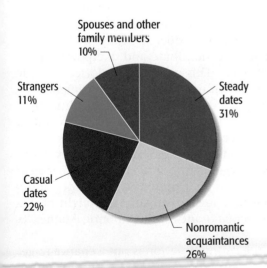

Figure 11.5   Relationships Between Rapists and their Victims
According to a leading national survey of college women, only a relatively small percentage of rapes were committed by strangers. Most were committed by nonromantic acquaintances (26 percent) or steady or casual dates (53 percent).

Source: Adapted from Koss, 1988.

are actually committing rape, but they are. To set the record straight, when a woman fails to consent or says "no," she means "no."

What Motivates Rape and Sexual Harassment?

Though rape is a sexual act, make no mistake: it is fundamentally a crime of sexual violence. Complex motives underlie rape, including power, anger, revenge, and intentional cruelty, intermingled with sexual desire (Barbaree & Marshall, 1991; Baumeister et al., 2002; Bushman et al., 2003; Hall & Hirschman, 1991). For some rapists, it is a means of controlling and dominating women; for others, it is a way of exacting revenge against women because of a history of perceived mistreatment and humiliation by them. Similarly, sexual harassment is a means by which the harasser seeks to dominate and control someone who holds a subordinate position. In traditional male bastions, it also becomes a tactic of social control, of keeping "women in their place" by treating them as sexual objects or by making them feel uncomfortable and unwelcome. Many harassers trivialize their own behavior, sometimes claiming they were only "kidding around" when accused of a pattern of sexual taunts, gestures, or unwelcome overtures. Efforts must be made to raise people's awareness of the types of behaviors that may be experienced by recipients as harassment.

What Are We Teaching Our Sons?

Though some rapists have antisocial personalities, many others appear perfectly normal except for their sexual violence. Not every young man becomes a rapist, but a surprising number of college men, about one in thirteen in the aforementioned large-scale college survey, reported committing rape or attempted rape. The sheer ordinariness of the great majority of rapists surely prompts the question "What are we teaching our sons?"

The answer may lie in the stereotypical messages conveyed by the media and the community to young men from an early age. These messages can have the effect of socializing young men into sexually aggressive roles (Davis & Liddell, 2002; Holcomb et al., 2002). Consider the example that is set when we teach our sons to dominate and overpower opponents on the playing fields. This culturally endorsed attitude may be carried over into their relationships with women. They may adopt the cultural stereotype that a masculine man should be sexually assertive and be able to overcome a woman's resistance. Objectification of women in films and other media also affects male attitudes. Experimental evidence shows that exposing college men to R-rated movies that treat women as sexual objects or that present them in degrading ways leads men to become less sensitive to the plight of victims in depictions of acquaintance rape (Milburn, Mather, & Conrad, 2000).

For some men, the dating situation is not a chance to get to know their partners but, rather, an opportunity for sexual conquest in which the object is to overcome a woman's resistance—to "score"—by whatever means it may take. Adding alcohol to the mix only increases the likelihood that this underlying attitude will become expressed in sexually aggressive behavior. As noted in Chapter 4, alcohol has the effect of disinhibiting (releasing) impulsive behavior as well as clouding one's judgment and making it more difficult to weigh the consequences of one's behavior.

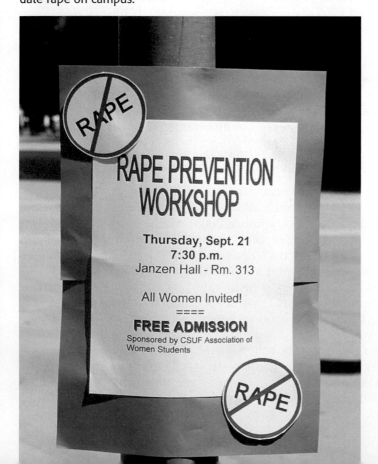

Rape Awareness Workshop Many colleges have instituted rape awareness workshops to help combat the problem of date rape on campus.

Preventing Rape and Sexual Harassment

Efforts to prevent rape and sexual harassment need to begin at the societal level. Education programs that expose young men to feminist and multicultural viewpoints may help promote more respectful attitudes toward women (Hall & Barongan, 1997; O'Donohue et al., 2003). So, too, might rape-prevention workshops, many of which have sprung up on college campuses and are sometimes incorporated into the college orientation process. Generally speaking, these programs help change student attitudes toward rape, but questions remain about whether they reduce the incidence of sexual assault (Breitenbecher, 2000). On a broader level, we need to adopt a public policy that sends a clear and consistent message that sexual coercion of any kind will not be tolerated.

At the individual level, too, we may take steps, such as those listed below, to prevent sexual victimization (Boston Women's Health Book Collective, 1992; Powell, 1991, 1996; Rathus, Nevid, & Fichner-Rathus, 2005). But focusing on ways of protecting ourselves does not mean that the responsibility for acts of sexual coercion falls on the victim. The assailant or the harasser is always the one responsible for the act.

Here are some suggestions that may help prevent rape:

- *Have your keys handy when opening the car, or, if possible, equip your car with a keyless entry system.*

- *Secure your front door with dead-bolt locks and lock all windows.* Secure first-floor windows with iron gates.

- *List your first name by its initial on your mailbox and in the phone directory.*

- *Keep hallways and entrances around doorways well lit.*

- *Avoid walking alone at night or walking in deserted areas.*

- *Meet first dates in a common place.* Avoid getting into a car with a new date.

- *Remain sober in dating situations.* Many date rapes occur when alcohol or other drugs are used. Date rapists may also take advantage of women they perceive as vulnerable because of their use of alcohol.

- *Check the credentials of any service people who request to enter your home.* Ask to call their dispatcher or supervisor to ensure that they are legitimate.

- *Drive with your doors locked and your windows up.* Make sure no one is lurking in the back seat of the car upon entering. Don't pick up any hitchhikers.

- *Carry a loud alarm that can be sounded in the event of attack.*

- *Take rape-prevention courses or workshops offered by your college or community organizations.*

- *Establish clear limits in dating situations.* Tell your date what you are willing to do and not willing to do.

- *Be firm when refusing sexual overtures.* The more clearly you state where the boundaries are, the less likely your date will misinterpret your wishes. If your date doesn't seem to take "no" for an answer, consider it a signal to end the relationship.

- *Trust your feelings.* If you have a strange feeling about your date or acquaintance, pay attention to it. Don't assume you're merely imagining things.

Women react to sexual harassment in different ways. Some confront the harasser, whereas others ignore, avoid, or attempt to appease the harasser (Magley, 2002). There is no one correct way to respond to sexual harassment. However, the following suggestions may be helpful in the event that you or someone close to you is subjected to sexual harassment:

- *Adopt a professional attitude.* Conveying a businesslike but courteous attitude may stop harassment dead in its tracks.

- *Avoid meeting with the harasser behind closed doors.* If you need to interact with the person, make sure others are present or insist on meeting in a public place or leaving the office door open so that others can see you.

- *Keep a journal.* If you are being harassed, keep a journal, noting what happened in each incident, where and when it occurred, and the names of any witnesses who were present.

- *Put the harasser on notice.* Let the harasser know that you find his or her behavior unwelcome and will not tolerate it. Provide the harasser with a copy of your journal record of the harassing behavior. If you feel uncomfortable approaching the harasser directly, ask a friend to accompany you or write the harasser a letter detailing your complaints.

- *Speak to your supervisor or to the company or school official responsible for handling sexual harassment complaints.* Inquire about the company grievance procedure and protection of confidentiality. Most college campuses have designated individuals for handling sexual harassment complaints; ask your adviser or college dean for their names.

- *Consider legal actions.* Sexual harassment is legally actionable. Consult an attorney familiar with the law in this area, or contact the Equal Employment Opportunity Commission (listed in the government section of your phonebook).

TYING IT TOGETHER

Our sexuality comprises many ways of experiencing ourselves as sexual beings. It includes not only our gender identity, or psychological sense of being male or female, but also the gender roles that are impressed upon us in the cultural environment in which we are raised (Module 11.1). In addition, our sexuality embraces the capacity of our bodies to respond to sexual stimulation and the different ways in which we may seek sexual gratification (Module 11.2). However, many of us experience sexual dysfunctions, or problems relating to sexual interest, arousal, or response. Fortunately, treatment alternatives are available to help people overcome these sexual problems (Module 11.3). One major problem we need to combat is sexual coercion in the form of rape and sexual harassment. We can act both collectively, by examining how we as a society are raising our sons, and individually, by taking steps to prevent sexual victimization (Module 11.4).

Thinking Critically About Psychology

Based on your reading of the chapter, answer the following questions. Then, to evaluate your progress in developing critical thinking skills, compare your answers to the sample answers found in Appendix A.

1. **How is homosexuality different from transsexualism?**

2. **John, a 29-year-old information technology manager, has been dating Jessica, a 25-year-old biology graduate student, for the past few months. They recently began having sexual relations, but John has been unable to achieve an erection each time. On each sexual occasion, he has tried to free his mind of other concerns and to focus all of his attention on achieving an erection. But it doesn't seem to be working. What do you think he might be doing wrong?**

Key Terms

gender *(p. 424)*
gender roles *(p. 424)*
gender identity *(p. 424)*
transsexualism *(p. 425)*
gender-schema theory *(p. 427)*
androgyny *(p. 429)*
dyslexia *(p. 430)*
sexual response cycle *(p. 436)*
vasocongestion *(p. 436)*
clitoris *(p. 436)*
myotonia *(p. 438)*
sexual orientation *(p. 439)*

homophobia *(p. 442)*
paraphilia *(p. 442)*
fetishism *(p. 442)*
transvestism *(p. 442)*
voyeurism *(p. 443)*
exhibitionism *(p. 443)*
pedophilia *(p. 443)*
sexual sadism *(p. 443)*
sexual masochism *(p. 443)*
sexually transmitted disease (STD) *(p. 448)*
sexual dysfunctions *(p. 448)*

hypoactive sexual desire disorder *(p. 450)*
sexual aversion disorder *(p. 450)*
male erectile disorder *(p. 450)*
female sexual arousal disorder *(p. 450)*
female orgasmic disorder *(p. 450)*
male orgasmic disorder *(p. 450)*
premature ejaculation (PE) *(p. 450)*
performance anxiety *(p. 451)*
sensate-focus exercises *(p. 452)*
rape *(p. 454)*
statutory rape *(p. 454)*
sexual harassment *(p. 454)*

ANSWERS TO RECALL IT QUESTIONS

Module 11.1: 1. c; 2. transsexualism; 3. testosterone; 4. d; 5. visual, rotation.

Module 11.2: 1. i. d, ii. c, iii. a, iv. b; 2. a; 3. transvestism; 4. d.

Module 11.3: 1. d; 2. i. a, ii. d, iii. c, iv. b; 3. d; 4. performance anxiety, guilt, exposure to sexually repressive cultural attitudes.

12

Personality

Know thyself.
—Socrates

Who is that person who stares back at you in the bathroom mirror? Do you know the person well, or is she or he still something of a mystery? How would you describe the person you see? What is special or unique about the person? How is the person similar to other people you know? How is the person different? Do you like the person you see? What would you like to change about the person you see?

This chapter is about the person in the mirror—you. It is also about every other human. Specifically, we are interested in *personality,* the relatively stable set of psychological characteristics and behavior patterns that make individuals unique and account for the consistency of their actions over time. Personality is a composite of the ways in which individuals relate to others and adapt to the demands placed on them by the environment.

The study of personality involves the attempt to describe and explain the characteristics that make each of us unique as individuals. Psychologists seek to understand these characteristics by drawing upon knowledge from the many other areas of psychology discussed elsewhere in the text. They consider how learning experiences, biological factors, social and cultural influences, and cognitive and developmental processes shape the persons we become.

In this chapter we consider the views of several leading personality theorists. Each brings a different perspective to bear on the study of personality (Funder, 2001). Some, including Sigmund Freud, the originator of psychodynamic theory, emphasize unconscious influences on personality. They believe that our personalities are shaped by a struggle between opposing forces within the mind that occurs outside the range of ordinary consciousness.

Other theorists, called trait theorists, view personality as composed of a set of underlying traits that account for the consistencies in behavior from one situation to another. Social-cognitive theorists view personality in terms of the individual's learning history and ways of thinking. To humanistic psychologists, such as Carl Rogers and Abraham Maslow, our personalities are expressed through our efforts to actualize our unique potential as human beings. We explore these different perspectives and examine what each has to say about personality, beginning with the psychodynamic model of personality espoused by Freud and his followers. ■

DID YOU KNOW THAT . . .

■ According to the originator of psychodynamic theory, Sigmund Freud, slips of the tongue may reveal hidden motives and wishes of which we are unaware? (p. 465)

■ According to Carl Gustav Jung, another psychodynamic theorist, we inherit a shared unconscious mind containing images that can be traced to ancestral times? (p. 469)

■ Research evidence suggests that even if you don't think of yourself as an extravert, you can benefit from enacting the role of an extraverted person? (p. 476)

■ According to a leading personality theorist, extraverted people may require more stimulating activities than introverted people to maintain an optimal level of arousal? (p. 476)

■ The "Big Five" is not the name of a new NCAA basketball conference but the label used to describe the leading trait theory of personality today? (p. 476–477)

■ A leading humanistic theorist, Carl Rogers, believed that children should receive love and approval unconditionally from their parents regardless of their behavior at any particular point in time? (p. 486)

■ Despite the negative effects of discrimination and prejudice, African Americans show higher levels of self-esteem, on average, than White Americans? (p. 488)

■ According to a widely held view in the nineteenth century, you can learn about a person's character and mental abilities by examining the pattern of bumps on the person's head? (p. 492)

MODULE 12.1
The Psychodynamic Perspective

- What is personality?
- In Freud's theory, what are the three levels of consciousness that exist in the human mind?
- What are the structures of personality in Freud's theory?
- What are psychological defense mechanisms?
- What are the five stages of psychosexual development in Freud's theory?
- What are some of the major contributions of other psychodynamic theorists?

CONCEPT 12.1
Your personality is the sum total of the psychological characteristics and behavior patterns that define you as a unique individual and characterize the ways in which you relate to the world and adapt to demands placed upon you.

CONCEPT 12.2
Freud developed the first psychodynamic theory of personality, the belief that personality is shaped by underlying conflicts between opposing forces within the mind.

CONCEPT 12.3
Freud believed that the mind consists of three levels of consciousness: the conscious, the preconscious, and the unconscious.

personality   The relatively stable constellation of psychological characteristics and behavioral patterns that account for our individuality and consistency over time.

psychoanalytic theory   Freud's theory of personality, which holds that personality and behavior are shaped by unconscious forces and conflicts.

Psychodynamic theory began with Freud and continues to be influenced heavily by Freudian concepts. Yet it is also an evolving tradition that continues to be shaped by the unique vision of theorists who have followed in Freud's footsteps.

Sigmund Freud was the architect of the first major theory of **personality**, called **psychoanalytic theory**. The central idea underlying his theory is the belief that a dynamic struggle takes place within the human psyche (mind) between unconscious forces. For this reason, Freud's views and those of his followers are often called *psychodynamic theory*. The turning point in Freud's early professional life came when he journeyed to Paris to study with a famous neurologist, Jean Martin Charcot (1825–1893). It was from this experience, discussed in the nearby Pioneers box, that he derived the kernel of the idea that would underlie his theory of personality—the belief that unconscious forces in our personalities influence our motives and behavior.

Though Freud's beliefs were controversial in his own time and remain so today, the theory of personality he developed continues to provide fertile ground for study and debate among scientists and scholars. In this module, we first discuss Freud's ideas and then describe the contributions of other psychodynamic theorists who followed in Freud's footsteps.

Sigmund Freud: Psychoanalytic Theory

In the tradition of Darwin, Freud recognized that we share with nonhuman animals certain common processes that have *survival* as their aim. We need to breathe, feed, and eliminate bodily wastes. And to survive as a species, we need to reproduce. Freud believed we are endowed with a sexual instinct that has as its purpose the preservation of the species. He later would add an aggressive instinct to explain human aggression. Yet Freud believed that giving free rein to these instincts might tear apart the very fabric of society and of the family unit itself. To live in an ordered society, Freud maintained, humans need to control their primitive sexual and aggressive impulses. In other words, humans need to channel their sexual and aggressive instincts in socially appropriate ways so as to live harmoniously with one another. We need to learn that aggression and sexual touch are unacceptable except in socially acceptable contexts, such as the football field in the case of aggression and the marital bed in the case of sexual contact.

Freud developed psychoanalytic theory to account for how the human mind balances these conflicting demands of instinct and social acceptability. Freud's theory of personality is complex, but it can be represented in terms of four major concepts: levels of consciousness, structure of personality, defense mechanisms, and stages of psychosexual development.

The Levels of Consciousness: The Conscious, the Preconscious, and the Unconscious   Freud compared the human mind to a giant iceberg. Like an iceberg, which has much of its mass hidden below the surface of the water, most of the

THE PIONEERS | Freud is Spellbound

Sigmund Freud

The son of an impoverished Jewish wool merchant, Sigmund Freud was born in 1856 in a small village in Moravia, which is now part of the Czech Republic. Upon seeing that the baby had a shock of black hair, a local woman foretold that he would become a great man. Though soothsayers are likely to fare better when they foretell good news rather than bad news, the woman's revelation proved prescient. The child would one day become a man whose views on human nature would have an enormous influence on psychology, the arts, and the broader society.

Freud's family moved to Vienna when he was a boy. He was a brilliant student and entered the medical school at the University of Vienna at the age of 17. Yet because he was a Jew, he felt he was an alien, an outsider in anti-Semitic Vienna. The sense of being an outsider would pervade his professional life, especially since the theory of personality he went on to espouse was roundly criticized by the scientific establishment of his time. He had hoped to pursue an academic career in physiological research, but Jews at the time were afforded few opportunities in academia. So after medical school he set up a private medical practice, where he began treating people with nervous disorders.

As a young physician, Freud traveled to Paris to study with Jean Martin Charcot, a prominent French neurologist who had begun to use hypnosis in his studies of hysteria, a disorder in which patients lost or experienced a change in a physical function that could not be explained by physical causes. Freud was spellbound by what he observed. Here were patients with paralysis of an arm or loss of feeling in the hands that could not be explained as the result of known trauma or disease. The thinking at the time was that they must have an affliction of the nervous system that caused their symptoms. Yet Charcot and his associates demonstrated that these symptoms could be removed in hysterical patients or actually induced in normal patients by means of hypnotic suggestion (Ellenberger, 1965). Freud reasoned that if hysterical symptoms could be made to disappear or appear by the mere "suggestion of ideas" during hypnosis, they must be psychological in origin (Jones, 1953). He concluded that whatever the psychological factors were that gave rise to hysteria, they must lie outside of awareness. Freud later wrote of his experience with Charcot: "I received the proudest impression of the possibility that there could be powerful mental processes which nevertheless remained hidden from the consciousness of men" (cited in Sulloway, 1983, p. 32).

Though he never practiced his religion, Freud was forced to flee Vienna in 1938 because as a Jew he faced almost certain death at the hands of the Nazis. He moved to England but died a year later from cancer of the mouth and jaw that had first developed in 1923, caused by his many years of cigar smoking. Ironically, this man who introduced the idea of "oral fixation" continued to smoke his beloved cigars even after he developed oral cancer and despite his doctor's urgings to quit. In the years before his death he underwent thirty operations to remove cancerous growths caused by cigar smoking.

conscious In Freudian theory, the part of the mind corresponding to the state of present awareness.

preconscious To Freud, the part of the mind whose contents can be brought into awareness through focused attention.

unconscious In Freudian theory, the part of the mind that lies outside the range of ordinary awareness and that contains primitive drives or instincts and unacceptable urges, wishes, or ideas.

human mind lies below the surface of conscious awareness (see Figure 12.1). Freud represented the human mind as consisting of three levels of consciousness: the **conscious**, the **preconscious**, and the **unconscious**. The conscious is the tip of the iceberg. It is the level of consciousness that corresponds to our present awareness—what we are thinking or feeling at any given moment in time. The preconscious holds information we've stored from past experience or learning. This information can be retrieved from memory and brought into awareness at any time. Your telephone number, for example, is information stored in the preconscious that you can bring into awareness when needed.

The unconscious is like the large mass of the iceberg lying under the surface of the water. It contains primitive sexual and aggressive impulses as well as memories of troubling emotional experiences (e.g., traumatizing events) and unacceptable sexual or aggressive wishes or ideas. The contents of the unconscious cannot be brought directly into consciousness simply by focusing on them; they are brought

Figure 12.1 Levels of Consciousness in Freud's Theory
The human mind in Freudian theory can be likened to an iceberg in which only the tip rises above the level of conscious awareness. While information held in the preconscious can be brought into the conscious mind at any time, a substantial portion of the mind—including many of our deepest wishes, ideas, and urges—remains mired in the dark recesses of the unconscious.

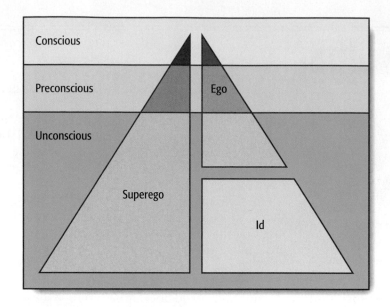

CONCEPT 12.4
Freud believed that personality consists of three mental entities: the id, the ego, and the superego.

id Freud's term for the psychic structure existing in the unconscious that contains our basic animal drives and instinctual impulses.

ego Freud's term for the psychic structure that attempts to balance the instinctual demands of the id with social realities and expectations.

superego Freud's term for the psychic structure that corresponds to an internal moral guardian or conscience.

pleasure principle In Freud's theory, a governing principle of the id that is based on demand for instant gratification without regard to social rules or customs.

reality principle In Freudian theory, the governing principle of the ego that takes into account what is practical and acceptable in satisfying basic needs.

into consciousness only with great difficulty, if at all. With so much of the contents of the mind mired in the unconscious, we remain unaware of our deepest wishes, ideas, and urges.

The Structure of Personality: Id, Ego, and Superego Freud proposed that personality consists of three mental entities called **id**, **ego**, and **superego**. The balance and interactions of these three parts of the personality largely determine our behavior and our ability to meet the life challenges we face. Freud did not consider these mental entities to be actual structures we could locate in the brain. Rather, he conceived of them as hypothetical concepts that represent the opposing forces within the personality.

As Figure 12.1 shows, the id (literally, "it") operates only in the unconscious. The id contains our basic animal drives or instinctual impulses, including hunger, thirst, elimination, sex, and aggression. The id stirs us to action to ensure that our basic biological needs are met. It is the only psychic structure present at birth, and it follows what Freud called the **pleasure principle**, the demand for instant gratification without regard to social rules or customs. In essence, the id wants what it wants when it wants it. Think of the infant. When a need arises, such as hunger or elimination, the infant demands immediate satisfaction of that need. It doesn't wait patiently until an appropriate time comes to feed or to move its bowels. However, according to Freud, when the desired object (mother's nipple, for example) is not available, the id is able to achieve some partial gratification by forming a mental image of the desired object.

The infant soon finds that not every instinctual demand is instantly gratified. It also learns that conjuring a mental image of the desired object is a poor substitute for the real thing. It finds it must cope with frustration and learn to delay gratification. So a second part of the mind forms during the first year of life that is responsible for organizing ways to handle delays of gratification. Freud called this entity the ego. The ego represents "reason and good sense" (Freud, 1964, p. 76).

The ego operates according to the **reality principle**, the governing dictate by which the ego seeks to satisfy instinctual demands in ways that are practical and socially acceptable. The ego seeks ways to satisfy the demands of the id without incurring social disapproval. The id may motivate you to rise from your chair and seek nourishment when you are hungry. But the ego enables you to make a sandwich and keeps you from grabbing food from someone else's plate.

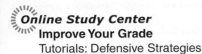

CONCEPT 12.5

Freud believed that the ego uses defense mechanisms as a means of preventing anxiety that would result from conscious awareness of disturbing impulses, wishes, or ideas arising from the id.

defense mechanisms In Freudian theory, the reality-distorting strategies of the ego to prevent awareness of anxiety-evoking or troubling ideas or impulses.

repression In Freudian theory, a type of defense mechanism involving motivated forgetting of anxiety-evoking material.

denial In Freudian theory, a defense mechanism involving the failure to recognize a threatening impulse or urge.

reaction formation In Freudian theory, a defense mechanism involving behavior that stands in opposition to one's true motives and desires so as to prevent conscious awareness of them.

rationalization In Freudian theory, a defense mechanism involving the use of self-justification to explain away unacceptable behavior, impulses, or ideas.

projection In Freudian theory, a defense mechanism involving the projection of one's own unacceptable impulses, wishes, or urges onto another person.

sublimation In Freudian theory, a defense mechanism involving the channeling of unacceptable impulses into socially sanctioned behaviors or interests.

regression In Freudian theory, a defense mechanism in which an individual, usually under high levels of stress, reverts to a behavior characteristic of an earlier stage of development.

displacement In Freudian theory, a defense mechanism in which an unacceptable sexual or aggressive impulse is transferred to an object or person that is safer or less threatening than the original object of the impulse.

erogenous zones Parts of the body that are especially sensitive to sexual or pleasurable stimulation.

The superego is our internal moral guardian or conscience. By 3 to 5 years of age, during middle childhood, it splits off from the ego and develops by internalizing the moral teachings of parents or other significant figures. Part of the superego may be available to consciousness, the part that corresponds to our moral convictions—our personal beliefs about right and wrong. But much of the superego operates in the unconscious, standing in judgment of whether the actions of the ego are morally right or wrong. When they are not, the superego can impose self-punishment in the form of guilt or shame.

The ego is the great compromiser. It stands between the superego and the id. It seeks to satisfy the demands of the id without offending the moral standards of the superego. Our behavior is a product of the dynamic struggles among the id, the ego, and the superego. These conflicts take place outside of conscious awareness, on the stage of the unconscious mind. Part of the ego rises to the level of consciousness, such as when we consciously seek to fix ourselves a sandwich in response to hunger pangs. But much of the ego operates below the surface of consciousness, where it employs strategies called *defense mechanisms* to prevent awareness of unacceptable sexual or aggressive impulses or wishes.

Defense Mechanisms In Freud's view, the ego uses **defense mechanisms** to prevent the anxiety that would result if troubling desires and memories residing in the unconscious were fully realized in conscious awareness (Murray, Kilgour, & Wasylkiw, 2000). The major defense mechanism—**repression**, or motivated forgetting—involves the ejection of threatening desires, impulses, and emotionally troubling memories from awareness into the depths of the unconscious.

Repression permits people to remain outwardly calm and controlled even though they harbor hateful or lustful urges under the surface of awareness. Yet repressed desires or memories may become revealed in disguised forms, such as in dream symbols and in slips of the tongue (so-called *Freudian slips*) (Freud, 1938). To Freud, slips of the tongue may reveal underlying motives and wishes kept hidden by repression. If a friend intended to say "I know what you're saying," but it comes out as "I hate what you're saying," perhaps the friend is expressing a repressed feeling (Nevid, Rathus, & Greene, 2006). Other defense mechanisms identified by Freud include **denial**, **reaction formation**, **rationalization**, **projection**, **sublimation**, **regression**, and **displacement** (see Table 12.1).

Though defense mechanisms may be a normal process of adjusting to the unreasonable demands of the id, they can give rise to abnormal behavior. For example, a man who sexually assaults a woman may rationalize to himself that "she had it coming" rather than directly confronting his aggressive urges. A person who regresses to a dependent infantile-like state during times of extreme stress may be shielded from the anxiety of facing the stressful situation but is also unable to function effectively.

Stages of Personality Development In Freud's view, personality develops through five psychosexual stages of development. These stages are considered psychosexual in nature because they are characterized by changes in how the child seeks physical pleasure from sexually sensitive parts of the body, called **erogenous zones**. He further believed that physical activities connected to basic life functions, such as feeding, elimination, and reproduction, are basically "sexual" because they are inherently pleasurable. So the infant sucking at the mother's breast or eliminating bodily wastes is performing acts that are sexual in Freud's view. And why are these activities pleasurable? The answer, Freud believed, is clear: they are essential to survival. The infant needs to suck to obtain nourishment. If sucking weren't pleasurable, the infant wouldn't do it and would likely die. As the child progresses through the stages of psychosexual development, the primary erogenous zone shifts from one part of the body to another.

TABLE 12.1   Major Defense Mechanisms in Psychodynamic Theory

Type of Defense Mechanism	Description	Example
Repression	Expulsion from awareness of unacceptable ideas or motives	A person remains unaware of harboring hateful or destructive impulses toward others.
Regression	The return of behavior that is typical of earlier stages of development	Under stress, a college student starts biting his nails or becomes totally dependent on others.
Displacement	The transfer of unacceptable impulses away from their original objects onto safer or less threatening objects	A worker slams a door after his boss chews him out.
Denial	Refusal to recognize a threatening impulse or desire	A person who nearly chokes someone to death acts afterward like it was "no big deal."
Reaction formation	Behaving in a way that is the opposite of one's true wishes or desires in order to keep these repressed	A sexually frustrated person goes on a personal crusade to stamp out pornography.
Rationalization	The use of self-justifications to explain away unacceptable behavior	When asked why she continues to smoke, a woman says, "Cancer doesn't run in my family."
Projection	Imposing one's own impulses or wishes onto another person	A sexually inhibited person misinterprets other people's friendly approaches as sexual advances.
Sublimation	The channeling of unacceptable impulses into socially constructive pursuits	A person channels aggressive impulses into competitive sports.

CONCEPT 12.6

Freud believed that personality develops through five stages of psychosexual development: the oral, anal, phallic, latency, and genital stages.

Psychological conflicts may emerge during each psychosexual stage of development. These conflicts, which often arise from receiving too much or too little gratification, can lead to the development of **fixations**—personality traits or behavior patterns characteristic of the particular stage. It's as though one's personality gets "stuck" at an early level of development. Let us briefly consider these five stages and the conflicts that may emerge during each one.

Oral Stage   The **oral stage** spans the period of birth through about 12 to 18 months of age. During this stage the primary erogenous zone is the mouth. The infant seeks sexual pleasure by sucking at its mother's breast and mouthing (taking into the mouth) or, later, biting objects that happen to be nearby, including nibbling at the parents' fingers. Whatever fits into the mouth goes into the mouth. Too much gratification in the oral stage may lead to oral fixations in adulthood such as smoking, nail biting, alcohol abuse, and overeating. Too little gratification, perhaps from early weaning, may lead to the development of traits suggesting that one did not have one's needs for nurturance met during infancy, such as passivity, clinging dependence, and a pessimistic outlook.

Anal Stage   By about the age of 18 months, the child has entered the **anal stage**. The anal cavity becomes the primary erogenous zone as the child develops the ability to control elimination by contracting and releasing the sphincter muscles at will. Yet this stage, which lasts until about age 3, is set for conflict between the parents and the child around the issue of toilet training. To earn the parents' approval and avoid their disapproval, the child must learn to "go potty" at the appropriate time and to delay immediate gratification of the need to eliminate whenever the urge is felt.

fixations   Constellations of personality traits characteristic of a particular stage of psychosexual development, resulting from either excessive or inadequate gratification at that stage.

oral stage   In Freudian theory, the first stage of psychosexual development, during which the infant seeks sexual gratification through oral stimulation (sucking, mouthing, and biting).

anal stage   In Freudian theory, the second stage of psychosexual development, during which sexual gratification is centered on processes of elimination (retention and release of bowel contents).

An Oral Fixation? Freud believed that insufficient or excessive gratification in the oral stage can lead to the development of an oral fixation that becomes a feature of the individual's personality.

anal-retentive personality In Freudian theory, a personality type characterized by perfectionism and excessive needs for self-control as expressed through extreme neatness and punctuality.

anal-expulsive personality In Freudian theory, a personality type characterized by messiness, lack of self-discipline, and carelessness.

phallic stage In Freudian theory, the third stage of psychosexual development, marked by erotic attention on the phallic region (penis in boys, clitoris in girls) and the development of the Oedipus complex.

Oedipus complex In Freudian theory, the psychological complex in which the young boy or girl develops incestuous feelings toward the parent of the opposite gender and perceives the parent of the same gender as a rival.

Electra complex The term given by some psychodynamic theorists to the form of the Oedipus complex in young girls.

castration anxiety In Freudian theory, unconscious fear of removal of the penis as punishment for having unacceptable sexual impulses.

penis envy In Freudian theory, jealousy of boys for having a penis.

In Freud's view, anal fixations reflect either too harsh or too lenient toilet training. Training that is too harsh may lead to traits associated with the so-called **anal-retentive personality**, such as perfectionism and extreme needs for self-control, orderliness, cleanliness, and neatness. Extremely lax training may lead to an opposite array of traits associated with the **anal-expulsive personality**, such as messiness, lack of self-discipline, and carelessness.

Phallic Stage   During the **phallic stage**, which roughly spans the ages of 3 to 6, the erogenous zone shifts to the phallic region—the penis in males and the clitoris in females. Conflicts with parents over masturbation (self-stimulation of the phallic area) may emerge at this time. But the core conflict of the phallic stage is the **Oedipus complex**, which involves the development of incestuous desires for the parent of the opposite sex that lead to rivalry with the parent of the same sex. Freud named the Oedipus complex after the ancient Greek myth of Oedipus the King—the tragic story of Oedipus who unwittingly slew his father and married his mother. He believed that this ancient tale revealed a fundamental human truth about psychosexual development. Some of Freud's followers dubbed the female version of the Oedipus complex the **Electra complex**, after another figure in ancient Greek tragedy, Electra, who avenged her father's death by killing his murderers—her own mother and her mother's lover.

In Freud's view, boys normally resolve the conflict by forsaking their incestuous wishes for their mother and identifying with their rival—their father. Girls normally surrender their incestuous desires for their father and identify with their mother. Identification with the parent of the same sex leads to the development of gender-based behaviors. Boys develop aggressive and independent traits associated with masculinity, and girls develop nurturant and demure traits associated with femininity. Another by-product of the Oedipus complex is the development of the superego—the internalization of parental values in the form of a moral conscience.

Freud believed that the failure to successfully resolve Oedipal conflicts may cause boys to become resentful of strong masculine figures, especially authority figures. For either boys or girls, failure to identify with the parent of the same gender may lead to the development of gender-nonconforming behavior and later homosexuality.

Freud believed that young boys develop **castration anxiety**, the fear that their father will retaliate against their sexual desires for their mother by removing the organ that has become the primary erogenous zone. It is this fear of castration that motivates boys to forsake their incestuous desires for their mother and to identify with their father. Girls lack a penis and so don't develop castration anxiety. Rather, they experience **penis envy**, or jealousy of boys for having a penis. Penis envy, in Freud's view, leads girls to feel inferior or inadequate in relation to boys and to unconsciously blame their mother for bringing them into the world so "ill-equipped." The young girl sexually desires her father so that she can possess his penis as a substitute for her own missing one. However, fear of losing her mother's love and protection because of her incestuous desires prompts the girl to forsake her sexual desires for her father and to identify with her mother. As the girl becomes sexually mature, she forsakes her wish to have a penis of her own (to "be a man") for a desire to have a baby—that is, as a kind of substitute for her missing penis. Women who opt for professional or business careers over motherhood are

TABLE 12.2 Freud's Psychosexual Stages of Development

Psychosexual Stage	Approximate Age	Erogenous Zone	Source of Sexual Pleasure	Source of Conflict	Adult Characteristics Associated with Conflicts at This Stage
Oral	Birth to 12 to 18 months	Oral cavity	Sucking, biting, and mouthing	Weaning	Oral behaviors such as smoking, alcohol use, nail-biting; dependency; passivity; pessimism
Anal	18 months to 3 years	Anal region	Retention and release of feces	Toilet training	Anal-retentive vs. anal-expulsive traits
Phallic	3 to 6 years	Penis in boys; clitoris in girls	Masturbation	Masturbation; Oedipus complex	Homosexuality; resentment of authority figures in men; unresolved penis envy in women
Latency	6 years to puberty	None	None (focus on play and school activities)	None	None
Genital	Puberty to adulthood	Genitals (penis in men; vagina in women)	Return of sexual interests expressed in mature sexual relationships	None	None

seen as having unresolved penis envy—a lingering desire to "be a man." Bear in mind that Freud believed that the Oedipus complex, with its incestuous desires, rivalries, and castration anxiety and penis envy, largely occurs at an unconscious level. On the surface, all may seem quiet, masking the turmoil occurring within.

Latency Stage The turbulent psychic crisis of the phallic period gives way to a period of relative tranquility—the **latency stage**, spanning the years between about 6 and 12. The latency stage is so named because of the belief that sexual impulses remain latent (dormant) during this time—a time when the child's psychological energies are focused on other pursuits such as school and play activities, making friendships, and acquiring skills.

Genital Stage The child enters the final stage of psychosexual development, the **genital stage**, at about the time of puberty. The forsaken incestuous desires for the parent of the opposite sex give rise to yearnings for more appropriate sexual partners of the opposite gender. Girls may be attracted to boys who resemble "dear old Dad" while boys may seek "the kind of girl who married dear old Dad." Sexual energies seek expression through mature (genital) sexuality in the form of sexual intercourse in marriage and the bearing of children. See Table 12.2 for a summary of Freud's psychosexual stages of development.

Other Psychodynamic Approaches

Though Freud's theories were not embraced by the scientific establishment of his day, he did attract a host of followers, many of whom are recognized as important personality theorists in their own right. These followers retained certain central tenets of psychodynamic theory, especially the belief that behavior is influenced by unconscious conflicts within the personality, yet their views also differed in certain respects from Freud's. As a group, the theorists who followed in Freud's footsteps (often called *neo-Freudians*) placed less emphasis on sexual and aggressive motivations and more emphasis on social relationships and the workings of

latency stage In Freudian theory, the fourth stage of psychosexual development, during which sexual impulses remain latent or dormant.

genital stage In Freudian theory, the fifth and final stage of psychosexual development, which begins around puberty and corresponds to the development of mature sexuality and emphasis on procreation.

CONCEPT 12.7

As a group, neo-Freudians placed less emphasis on sexuality than did Freud and more emphasis on the roles of conscious choice, self-direction, and ways of relating to others.

the ego, especially the development of a concept of the self. Here we discuss the major ideas of several leading neo-Freudians: Carl Jung, Alfred Adler, and Karen Horney. The contributions of another neo-Freudian, Erik Erikson, were discussed in Chapter 9.

Carl Jung: Analytical Psychology   Carl Gustav Jung (1875–1961) was once part of Freud's inner circle, but he broke with Freud as he developed his own distinctive views of personality. Jung shared with Freud the beliefs that unconscious conflicts influence human behavior and that defense mechanisms distort or disguise people's underlying motives. However, he placed greater emphasis on the present than on infantile or childhood experience (Kirsch, 1996), and he emphasized conscious processes, such as self-awareness and pursuit of self-directed goals, more than unconscious processes (Boynton, 2004; Kirsch, 1996).

Jung believed that people possess both a **personal unconscious**, which consists of repressed memories and impulses, and a **collective unconscious**, or repository of accumulated ideas and images in the unconscious mind that is shared among all humans and passed down genetically through the generations (Neher, 1996). The collective unconscious contains primitive images called **archetypes** that reflect the ancestral or universal experiences of humans, including images such as an omniscient and all-powerful God, the young hero, and the fertile and nurturant mother figure. Jung believed that while these images remain unconscious, they influence our dreams and waking thoughts and emotions. It is the collective unconscious, Jung maintained, that explains similarities among cultures in dream images, religious symbols, and artistic expressions (such as movie heroes and heroines).

Alfred Adler: Individual Psychology   Alfred Adler (1870–1937) was another member of Freud's inner circle who broke away to develop his own theory of personality. Adler called his theory **individual psychology** because of its emphasis on the unique potential of each individual. He believed that conscious experience plays a greater role in our personalities than Freud had believed. The **creative self** is what he called the part of the personality that is aware of itself and organizes goal-seeking behavior. As such, our creative self strives toward overcoming obstacles that lie in the path of pursuing our potential, of becoming all that we seek to become.

Adler is perhaps best known for his concept of the **inferiority complex**. He believed that because of their small size and limited abilities, all children harbor feelings of inferiority to some degree. How they compensate for these feelings influences their emerging personalities. Feelings of inferiority lead to a desire to compensate, which Adler called the **drive for superiority** or *will-to-power*. The drive for superiority may motivate us to try harder and achieve worthwhile goals, such as professional accomplishments and positions of prominence. Or it may lead us to be domineering or callous toward others, to perhaps step on or over people as we make our way up the professional or social ladder.

Adler himself was a sickly child who was crippled by rickets (a vitamin D deficiency). His notion that we all possess a drive to overcome, a drive for superiority, may have derived from his own childhood strivings to overcome physical difficulties. Many other personal stories attest to the will to overcome physical adversity. Athlete Wilma Rudolph, for instance, suffered polio as a child and fought back to become one of the greatest track stars in history, capturing three gold medals in the 1960 Olympic games.

Karen Horney: An Early Voice in Feminine Psychology   One of the staunchest critics of Freud's views on female development was one of his own followers, Karen Horney (1885–1952) (pronounced *HORN-eye*), a German physician and early

personal unconscious   Jung's term for an unconscious region of mind comprising a reservoir of the individual's repressed memories and impulses.

collective unconscious   In Jung's theory, a part of the mind containing ideas and archetypal images shared among humankind that have been transmitted genetically from ancestral humans.

archetypes   Jung's term for the primitive images contained in the collective unconscious that reflect ancestral or universal experiences of human beings.

individual psychology   Adler's theory of personality, which emphasizes the unique potential of each individual.

creative self   In Adler's theory, the self-aware part of personality that organizes goal-seeking efforts.

inferiority complex   In Adler's theory, the feelings of inadequacy or inferiority in young children that influence their developing personalities and create desires to overcome.

drive for superiority   Adler's term for the motivation to compensate for feelings of inferiority. Also called the *will-to-power*.

Karen Horney

psychoanalyst who became a prominent theorist in her own right. Horney accepted Freud's belief that unconscious conflicts shape personality, but she focused less on sexual and aggressive drives and more on the roles of social and cultural forces. She also emphasized the importance of parent-child relationships. When parents are harsh or uncaring, children may develop a deep-seated form of anxiety she called **basic anxiety**, which is associated with the feeling of "being isolated and helpless in a potentially hostile world" (cited in Quinn, 1987, p. 41). Children may also develop a deep form of resentment toward their parents, which she labeled **basic hostility**. Horney believed, as did Freud, that children repress their hostility toward their parents out of fear of losing them or suffering their reprisals. Yet repressed hostility generates more anxiety and insecurity.

Horney accepted the general concept of penis envy in girls, but she believed that the development of young women must be understood within a social context as well. For example, she rejected Freud's belief that a female's sense of inferiority derives from penis envy. She argued that if women feel inferior, it is because they envy men their social power and authority, not their penises (Stewart & McDermott, 2004). Horney even raised the possibility that men may experience "womb envy" over the obvious "physiological superiority" of women with respect to their biological capacity for creating and bringing life into the world.

Evaluating the Psychodynamic Perspective

Psychodynamic theory remains the most detailed and comprehensive theory of personality yet developed. Many of the terms Freud introduced—such as *ego, superego, repression, fixation,* and *defense mechanisms*—are used today in everyday language, although perhaps not precisely in the ways that Freud defined them.

Perhaps the major contribution of Freud and later psychodynamic thinkers was to increase our awareness that unconscious drives and impulses may motivate our behavior. To know oneself, Freud believed, means to plumb the depths of our unconscious mind. As we shall see in Chapter 14, Freud developed a method of psychotherapy, called *psychoanalysis,* that focuses on helping people gain insight into the unconscious motives and conflicts that he believed were at the root of their problems.

Psychodynamic theory has had its critics, however. Many, including some of Freud's own followers, believe Freud placed too much importance on sexual and aggressive drives and too little emphasis on the role of social relationships in the development of personality. Other psychodynamic thinkers, including Horney, did place greater emphasis on social influences in personality development. Another challenge to Freud is the lack of evidence to support many of the principles on which his theory is based, including his beliefs in castration anxiety and penis envy and the universality of the Oedipus complex. Some critics even question whether the Oedipus complex exists at all (see Kupfersmid, 1995).

Other critics challenged the progression and timing of Freud's psychosexual stages of development. Still others challenged psychodynamic theory itself as resting almost entirely on evidence gathered from a relatively few case studies. Case studies may be open to varied interpretations. Moreover, the experiences of the few individuals who are the subjects of case studies may not be representative of people in general. Yet perhaps the greatest limitation of the psychodynamic approach is the difficulty of putting many of its concepts, especially unconscious phenomena, to more formal scientific tests. The scientific method requires that theories lend themselves to testable hypotheses. But by their nature, unconscious processes are not open to direct observation or scientific measurement, which makes them difficult—some would say impossible—to study scientifically. Still, we find

💡 **CONCEPT 12.8**
Although the psychodynamic perspective has had a major impact on psychology and beyond, critics contend that it lacks support from rigorous scientific studies for many of its key concepts.

basic anxiety   In Horney's theory, a deep-seated form of anxiety in children that is associated with feelings of being isolated and helpless in a world perceived as potentially threatening and hostile.

basic hostility   In Horney's theory, deep feelings of resentment that children may harbor toward their parents.

today a number of investigators attempting to objectively test certain aspects of psychodynamic theory, including Freud's beliefs about repression. A growing body of evidence from different areas of research in psychology supports the existence of psychological functioning outside of awareness, including defense mechanisms (Cramer, 2000; Westen & Gabbard, 2002).

Concept Chart 12.1 provides an overview of the psychodynamic perspective on personality. In subsequent modules, we will consider other leading perspectives on personality—namely, the trait, social-cognitive, and humanistic approaches.

CONCEPT CHART 12.1   Major Concepts in Psychodynamic Theory

	Concept	Description	Summary
Freud's Psychoanalytic Theory	Levels of consciousness	The mind consists of three levels of consciousness: the conscious, the preconscious, and the unconscious.	Only a small part of the mind is fully conscious. The unconscious mind, the largest part of the mind, contains our baser drives and impulses.
	Structure of personality	Id, ego, and superego	The id, which exists only in the unconscious, represents a repository of instinctual impulses and wishes that demand instant gratification. The ego seeks to satisfy the demands of the id through socially acceptable channels without offending the superego, the moral guardian of the personality.
	Governing principles	Pleasure principle and reality principle	The id follows the pleasure principle, the demand for instant gratification regardless of social necessities. The ego follows the reality principle by which gratification of impulses must be weighed in terms of social acceptability and practicality.
	Defense mechanisms	The ego uses defense mechanisms to conceal or distort unacceptable impulses, thus preventing them from rising into consciousness.	The major defense mechanisms include repression, regression, projection, rationalization, denial, reaction formation, sublimation, and displacement.
	Stages of psychosexual development	Sexual motivation is expressed through stimulation of different body parts or erogenous zones as the child matures.	The five stages of psychosexual development are oral, anal, phallic, latency, and genital. Overgratification or undergratification at any stage can lead to personality features or fixations characteristic of that stage.
Jung	Collective unconscious	All people share an inherited unconscious that contains universal symbols, or archetypes.	The collective unconscious, like the personal unconscious, is buried in the self but surfaces in dreams, religious symbols, and artistic expressions.
Adler	The creative self	The creative self is the part that consciously organizes goal-seeking behavior.	Alfred Adler's individual psychology emphasized self-awareness, goal-striving, and ways in which people compensate for underlying feelings of inadequacy or inferiority.
Horney	Basic anxiety and basic hostility	If parents are uncaring, children develop a deep distrust of the world and hatred toward the parents.	Karen Horney focused on ways in which people relate to each other and the importance of parent-child relationships.

MODULE 12.1 REVIEW

The Psychodynamic Perspective

RECITE IT

What is personality?

- Psychologists generally speak of personality in terms of the relatively stable constellation of traits, thoughts, feelings, and behaviors that make individuals unique and that account for the ways in which they relate to others and adapt to the environment.

In Freud's theory, what are the three levels of consciousness that exist in the human mind?

- According to Freud, the three levels of consciousness are the conscious, the preconscious, and the unconscious.

- The conscious represents your present awareness, the preconscious represents the region of the mind that contains information you can readily retrieve from memory, and the unconscious represents a darkened region of mind that contains primitive urges, wishes, and troubling memories that cannot be directly summoned to consciousness.

What are the structures of personality in Freud's theory?

- Freud represented personality as composed of three mental structures: the id, the ego, and the superego.

- The ego attempts to satisfy the sexual and aggressive urges of the id in ways that avoid social disapproval or condemnation from the superego, the internal moral guardian or conscience.

What are psychological defense mechanisms?

- Psychological defense mechanisms are strategies used by the ego, such as repression, displacement, and projection, to prevent awareness of troubling desires and memories.

What are the five stages of psychosexual development in Freud's theory?

- Freud believed that psychological development is influenced by changes in the sexually sensitive areas of the body, or erogenous zones, during early childhood.

- The stages of psychosexual development parallel these changes in erogenous zones and are ordered as follows: oral, anal, phallic, latency, and genital.

What are some of the major contributions of other psychodynamic theorists?

- Jung believed in both a personal unconscious and a shared unconscious he called the collective unconscious.

- Adler developed the concept of the "inferiority complex," the tendency to compensate for feelings of inferiority by developing a drive to excel ("drive for superiority").

- Horney believed that unmet emotional needs in childhood can lead to basic anxiety and basic hostility, which in turn cause more insecurity.

RECALL IT

1. Psychoanalytic theory attempts to explain how humans balance
   a. sexual instincts and social standards.
   b. demands for productivity with demands for leisure.
   c. desire for wealth with desire for sexual reproduction.
   d. basic biological needs with self-actualization needs.

2. To Freud, the part of the mind that organizes efforts to satisfy basic impulses in ways that avoid social condemnation is the _____.

3. Match the following terms with their descriptions:
   i. defense mechanisms; ii. repression; iii. Freudian slip; iv. projection
   a. motivated forgetting
   b. accidentally reveals underlying thought
   c. protect the self from anxiety
   d. imposing one's own impulses or desires on others

4. According to Freud, the psychosexual developmental stage during which a young boy experiences the Oedipus complex is the _____ stage.

5. Which of the following psychodynamic theorists emphasized the creative aspects of the self which strive toward achieving our individual potential?
   a. Alfred Adler
   b. Karen Horney
   c. Erik Erikson
   d. Carl Jung

THINK ABOUT IT

- Underlying the psychodynamic perspective is the belief that we are not aware of our deeper motives and impulses that drive our behavior. Do you agree? Why or why not?

- Can you identify any of your behaviors that might be examples of defense mechanisms? How would you even know?

MODULE 12.2
The Trait Perspective

- What are the three types of traits in Allport's trait model?
- What was Cattell's view on the organization of traits?
- What three traits are represented in Eysenck's model of personality?
- What is the "Big Five" trait model of personality?
- What role do genes play in personality?

Like psychodynamic theorists, trait theorists look within the personality to explain behavior. But the structures of personality they bring into focus are not opposing mental states or entities. Rather, they believe that personality consists of a distinctive set of relatively stable or enduring characteristics or dispositions called **traits**. They use personality traits to predict how people are likely to behave in different situations. For example, they may describe Rosa as having personality traits such as cheerfulness and outgoingness. Based on these traits, they might predict that she is likely to be involved in many social activities and to be the kind of person people describe as always having a smile on her face. They might describe Derek, however, as having traits such as suspiciousness and introversion. Based on these traits, they might expect Derek to shun social interactions and to feel that people are always taking advantage of him.

Trait theorists are interested in learning how people differ in their underlying traits. They are also interested in measuring traits and understanding how traits are organized or structured within the personality. Some trait theorists believe that traits are largely innate or inborn; others argue that traits are largely acquired through experience. In this module, we focus on the contributions of several prominent trait theorists, beginning with an early contributor to the trait perspective, Gordon Allport.

Gordon Allport: A Hierarchy of Traits

To Gordon Allport (1897–1967), personality traits are physical entities embedded in the brain that come to influence our behavior. He believed that traits are inherited but are influenced by experience. He also claimed that traits could be ranked within a hierarchy in terms of the degree to which they influence behavior (Allport, 1961). At the highest level are **cardinal traits**—pervasive characteristics that influence a person's behavior in most situations. For example, we might describe the cardinal trait in Martin Luther King's personality as the commitment to social justice. Yet Allport believed that relatively few people possess such dominant traits. More common but less wide-reaching traits are **central traits**, the basic building blocks of personality that influence behavior in many situations. Examples of central traits are characteristics such as competitiveness, generosity, independence, arrogance, and fearfulness—the kinds of traits you would generally use when describing the general characteristics of other people's behavior. At a more superficial level are **secondary traits**, such as preferences for particular styles of clothing or types of music, which affect behavior in fewer situations.

Raymond Cattell: Mapping the Personality

Trait theorist Raymond Cattell (1905–1998) believed that there are two basic levels of traits (Cattell, 1950, 1965). **Surface traits** lie on the "surface" of personality. They are characteristics of personality that can be inferred from observations of behavior. Surface traits are associated with adjectives commonly used to describe

CONCEPT 12.9
Allport believed that personality traits are ordered in a hierarchy of importance from cardinal traits at the highest level through central traits and secondary traits at the lower levels.

traits   Relatively enduring personal characteristics.

cardinal traits   Allport's term for the more pervasive dimensions that define an individual's general personality.

central traits   Allport's term for personality characteristics that have a widespread influence on the individual's behavior across situations.

secondary traits   Allport's term for specific traits that influence behavior in relatively few situations.

surface traits   Cattell's term for personality traits at the surface level that can be gleaned from observations of behavior.

TRY THIS OUT

Sizing Up Your Personality

You can use the personality traits found in Cattell's 16PF to compare your personality with those of the occupational groups shown in Figure 12.2. Place a mark at the point on each dimension that you feel best describes your personality. Connect the points using a black pen. Then examine your responses in relation to those of the other groups. Which of these groups most closely matches your perceptions of your own personality? Were you surprised by the results? Did you learn anything about yourself by completing this exercise?

CONCEPT 12.10

Cattell believed that the structure of personality consists of two levels of traits, surface traits that correspond to ordinary descriptions of personality, and a deeper level of more general traits, called source traits, that give rise to these surface traits.

personality, such as *stubbornness, emotionality,* and *carelessness.* Cattell observed that surface traits often occur together. A person whom people perceive as stubborn also tends to be perceived as rigid and foul-tempered. These linkages suggested that there is a deeper level of personality consisting of more general, underlying traits that give rise to surface traits. To explore this deeper level, Cattell used statistical techniques to analyze the relationships among surface traits and thereby map the underlying structure of personality (Horn, 2001). Through this work, he derived a set of more general factors of personality, which he called **source traits.** Cattell went on to construct a paper-and-pencil personality scale to measure sixteen source traits, which he called the Sixteen Personality Factor Questionnaire, or 16PF. Each trait on the 16PF is represented on a continuum, such as "reserved vs. outgoing." Figure 12.2 compares the 16PF scores for writers, airline pilots, and creative artists (see Try This Out above).

Figure 12.2 Cattell's 16PF

The 16PF is a personality test that compares individuals on sixteen source traits or key dimensions of personality, each of which is represented on a continuum ranging from one polar extreme to the other. Here we see the average scores of samples composed of three occupational groups: creative artists, airline pilots, and writers. Notice the differences in the personalities in these groups. For example, compared to the other groups, airline pilots tend to be more controlled, self-assured, and relaxed—traits that should help put airline passengers at ease.

Source: Adapted from Cattell, Eber, & Tatsuoka, 1970.

source traits Cattell's term for traits at a deep level of personality that are not apparent in observed behavior but must be inferred based on underlying relationships among surface traits.

Hans Eysenck: A Simpler Trait Model

In contrast to Cattell's model, which organized personality traits into a complex hierarchy, Hans Eysenck (1916–1997) constructed a simpler model of personality. This model describes personality using three major traits (Eysenck, 1981):

1. **Introversion-Extraversion**. People who are introverted are solitary, reserved, and unsociable, whereas those who are extraverted are outgoing, friendly, and people-oriented.

2. **Neuroticism**. People who are high on neuroticism, or emotional instability, tend to be tense, anxious, worrisome, restless, and moody. Those who are low on neuroticism tend to be relaxed, calm, stable, and even-tempered. Neuroticism is linked both to poorer self-esteem and lower levels of life satisfaction (Heller, Watson, & Ilies, 2004; Watson, Suls, & Haig, 2002).

3. **Psychoticism**. People who are high on psychoticism are perceived as cold, antisocial, hostile, and insensitive. Those who are low on psychoticism are described as warm, sensitive, and concerned about others.

Eysenck developed an inventory, called the Eysenck Personality Inventory (EPI), to measure where people place on these traits. Using this instrument, he was able to classify people according to four basic personality types based on the combination of these traits: extraverted-neurotic, extraverted-stable, introverted-stable, and introverted-neurotic (Eysenck, 1982). Figure 12.3 shows these four types, as represented by the four quadrants of the chart, along with the observed characteristics identified with each type.

Eysenck believed that biological differences are responsible for variations in personality traits from person to person. He argued that introverts inherit a nervous system that operates at a higher level of arousal than does that of extraverts. Consequently, introverts require less stimulation to maintain an optimal level of arousal. An introvert would be most comfortable enjoying quiet activities.

CONCEPT 12.11
Eysenck believed that the combinations of three general traits of introversion-extraversion, neuroticism, and psychoticism could be used to classify basic personality types.

Figure 12.3   Eysenck's Personality Types
Combining the dimensions of introversion-extraversion and emotional instability in Eysenck's model of personality yields four basic personality types as represented by these four quadrants: extraverted-neurotic, extraverted-stable, introverted-stable, and introverted-neurotic. Personality traits associated with these personality types are shown within each quadrant.

Source: Adapted from Eysenck, 1982.

introversion-extraversion   One of the three underlying dimensions of personality in Eysenck's model, referring to tendencies toward being solitary and reserved on the one end or outgoing and sociable on the other end.

neuroticism   One of the three underlying dimensions of personality in Eysenck's model, referring to tendencies toward emotional instability, anxiety, and worry.

psychoticism   One of the three underlying dimensions of personality in Eysenck's model, referring to tendencies to be perceived as cold and antisocial.

TRY THIS OUT

Not an Extravert?
Why Not Just Try the Part on for Size?

Psychologist William Fleeson and his colleagues at Wake Forest University find that even introverted people feel happier when they are enacting the part of an extraverted person than when they are acting introverted (Dittmann, 2003c; Fleeson, Malanos, & Achille, 2002). Even if you don't think of yourself as an extravert, you can benefit from pretending you are. Acting the part of an extravert involves such expressive behaviors as being talkative and energetic when interacting with others. With repeated practice in the role, the lines between acting the part of an extravert and becoming one may begin to blur. After a time, it may begin to feel natural to be more outgoing in your behavior.

Need for a higher level of stimulation? Extraversion is linked to needs for higher levels of stimulation, which sometimes involve risk-taking activities. The actor Jason Priestly's thrill-seeking activities include racing cars and boats. He reported suffering fourteen concussions in his life and nearly died when the race car he was driving at 186 miles per hour crashed into a wall at the track.

CONCEPT 12.12
The five-factor model of personality—the "Big Five"—identifies the five most common personality factors derived from research on personality.

five-factor model (FFM) The dominant contemporary trait model of personality, consisting of five broad personality factors: neuroticism, extraversion, openness, agreeableness, and conscientiousness.

Extraverts may require more stimulation to raise their arousal to optimal levels, which could explain why they are drawn to more exciting activities, perhaps including risk-taking adventures such as mountain climbing and sky diving. For example, the actor Jason Priestly nearly died when the racing car he was driving at 186 miles per hour crashed into a wall of a racetrack. Priestly, whose interests in thrill-seeking extended to motorcycles, racing boats, and bungee jumping, said he has always liked to challenge himself ("Jason Priestly," 2003).

It would come as no surprise to Eysenck that a group of mountain climbers who were attempting to scale Mt. Everest, the world's tallest peak, scored high on extraversion (Egan & Stelmack, 2003). They were also low on neuroticism (emotional instability), which is a good thing if you happen to be climbing the face of a mountain. Extraversion is also positively correlated with other characteristics, such as self-esteem (Watson, Suls, & Haig, 2002) and even firefighting ability among professional firefighters (Fannin & Dabbs, 2003). If you want to practice being more extraverted, see Try This Out above.

The Five-Factor Model of Personality: The "Big Five"

The most widely adopted trait model of personality today is the **five-factor model (FFM)**, or "Big Five" model (McCrae, 2004). This model captures the five broad factors that are found most consistently in research on personality traits (Gosling, Rentfrow, & Swann, 2003; Hofstee, 2003; Widiger, 2005). The "Big Five" isn't so much a new set of personality traits as it is a consolidation and integration of traits previously identified by Cattell, Eysenck, and other trait theorists. In fact, the first two traits, *neuroticism* and *extraversion,* parallel those in Eysenck's model. The three other factors making up the "Big Five" are *openness, agreeableness,* and *conscientiousness* (see Table 12.3).

Researchers believe that the "Big Five" factors have a substantial genetic component (McCrae et al., 2000). Moreover, cross-cultural studies show that personality traits resembling the "Big Five" emerge in many different cultures, both Western and non-Western, among men as well as women, among people of different races, and when measured in different ways and by instruments in different languages and different language groups (Egger et al., 2003; McCrae et al., 2004; Paunonen, 2003).

TABLE 12.3   The "Big Five" Trait Model

Personality Factor	Description
Neuroticism	Prone to anxiety, worry, guilt, emotional instability vs. relaxed, calm, secure, emotionally stable
Extraversion	Outgoing, friendly, enthusiastic, fun-loving vs. solitary, shy, serious, reserved
Openness	Imaginative, curious, intellectual, open to nontraditional values vs. conforming, practical, conventional
Agreeableness	Sensitive, warm, tolerant, easy to get along with, concerned with other's feelings and needs vs. cold, suspicious, hostile, callous
Conscientiousness	Reliable, responsible, self-disciplined, ethical, hard-working, ambitious vs. disorganized, unreliable, lax, impulsive, careless

Sources: Adapted from Costa & McCrae, 1992a, 1992b; Goldberg, 1993; McCrae & Costa, 1986, 1996.

The "Big Five" is useful in predicting many behaviors, including how well students do in college. Neuroticism, for example, is linked to lower final exam grades, whereas conscientiousness predicts higher grades and performance motivation (setting goals and pursuing them) (Chamorro-Premuzic & Furnham, 2003; Judge & Ilies, 2002). Not surprisingly, conscientiousness tends to increase during young adulthood and middle age, the times in life when people typically take on more career and family responsibilities (Caspi, Roberts, & Shiner, 2005).

Conscientiousness is also linked to living longer and happier lives, perhaps because it is associated with lower rates of reckless behavior, such as unsafe driving, with better diets, and with lower use of alcohol and drugs (Bogg & Roberts, 2004; Kersting, 2003a; Markey, Markey, & Tinsley, 2003). Agreeableness has also been linked to indices of safer driving, such as lower numbers of tickets and accidents (Cellar, Nelson, & Yorke, 2000). Perhaps more agreeable drivers are less likely to drive aggressively.

Other investigators link the "Big Five" to the level of satisfaction that college students report in their intimate relationships, with neuroticism associated with less relationship satisfaction and agreeableness and extraversion associated with greater satisfaction (White, Hendrick, & Hendrick, 2004). Perhaps we should not be surprised that personality traits and relationship factors are closely intertwined.

Investigators are also actively exploring links between the personality traits represented by the "Big Five" and psychological disorders such as mood disorders and attention-deficit hyperactivity disorder (ADHD) in adults (Duberstein et al., 2000; Nigg et al., 2002).

However, the "Big Five" is not the final word on describing the structure of personality. For one thing, the "Big Five" factors may not be as independent of each other as many investigators believe (Blackburn et al., 2004). Or perhaps more factors (a *Big Seven?*) may provide a better approximation of how people describe personalities. Some researchers also question whether any model that reduces personality to only a few broadly defined categories can capture the richness and uniqueness of personality or account for an individual's behavior in specific contexts (Epstein, 1996; Paunonen, 1998).

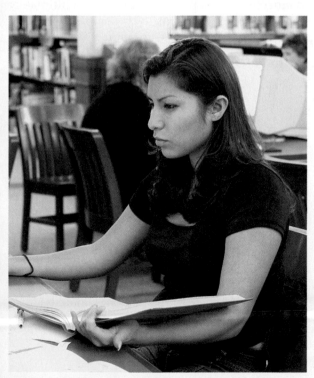

One of the "Big Five" Conscientiousness is one of the five major traits that make up the "Big Five" model of personality. People who are conscientious are reliable, hard-working, and self-disciplined. Where do you think you stand on each of the "Big Five" traits?

CONCEPT 12.13

Psychologists are moving beyond the nature-nurture debate to examine how heredity and environment interact in the development of personality.

The Genetic Basis of Traits: Moving Beyond the Nature-Nurture Debate

How much of our personality is inherited? Evolutionary psychologists (see Chapter 1) have brought genetic contributions to personality into sharper focus, and increasing evidence points to the important role that heredity plays in shaping our personalities (Bouchard, 2004). Evidence has shown that genetics accounts for between 40 and 60 percent of the variability (differences among people) on many psychological traits, including shyness, aggressiveness, neuroticism, and novelty-seeking, with the rest of the variability accounted for by environmental factors such as early learning experiences (e.g., Arbelle et al., 2003; Johnson & Krueger, 2004; Livesley, Jang, & Vernon, 2003; Sen et al., 2003).

Scientists have also begun exploring the role of specific genes in shaping personality. For example, Israeli researchers found that people with high levels of novelty-seeking often have a specific form of a gene known to play a role in regulating the neurotransmitter dopamine (Ebstein et al., 1996). People who are high on the trait of novelty-seeking are typically described by others as exploratory, impulsive, fickle, excitable, and quick-tempered. They tend to do things just for thrills or "kicks." Dopamine helps regulate exploratory behavior in other animals, so perhaps it has a similar function in humans.

Researchers today are moving beyond the old nature-nurture debate. They recognize that genes create a *predisposition* or *likelihood* for certain personality traits to develop, not a certainty. Whether these traits actually do emerge depends on the interaction of genetic factors with environmental and social influences, including learning experiences (Frank & Kupfer, 2000; Plomin, 2000; Sapolsky, 2000). Early life experiences can also affect how the brain develops, which in turn affects later personality development.

How research into the interconnections of nature and nurture will ultimately play out in explaining personality development remains to be seen. In the meantime, you can refer to Concept Chart 12.2 to review the major trait models of personality.

CONCEPT CHART 12.2   Trait Models of Personality

Trait Theorist/Model	Traits	Summary
Gordon Allport	Cardinal traits, central traits, and secondary traits	Allport believed that traits were physical entities that influenced behavior. Relatively few people possess cardinal traits, the more encompassing traits that determine behavior across most situations.
Raymond Cattell	Surface traits and source traits	Surface traits are clusters of observed behaviors. More general traits, called source traits, account for relationships among surface traits.
Hans Eysenck	Three major traits: introversion-extraversion, neuroticism, and psychoticism	Organized personality into simpler structure consisting of these three major traits and emphasized the role of biological differences in explaining variations in these traits among people.
Five-Factor Model (FFM): The "Big Five"	Neuroticism, extraversion, openness, agreeableness, and conscientiousness	The most widely accepted trait model today, the FFM is based on five trait factors that have most consistently emerged in research on personality. Yet critics contend that such broad factors cannot explain the richness or uniqueness of personality.

CONCEPT 12.14

Though trait theories provide convenient ways of describing personality features, they have been criticized on grounds of circular reasoning and failure to account for the effects of different situations on behavior.

Is Personality Research Going to the Dogs? Many dog owners and cat owners believe their pets have distinct personalities. Recent evidence indicates that judgments of personality traits in dogs achieve as much agreement among raters as judgments of traits in humans. Do other animals have personalities? What do you think?

Evaluating the Trait Perspective

Let us note on the positive side of the ledger that the trait perspective has intuitive appeal. We commonly use trait terms when describing our own and other people's personalities (Fleeson, 2004). For example, we might describe Samantha as cold or callous, while we might think of Li Ming as kind and compassionate.

Trait theories also led to the development of personality tests, including Cattell's 16PF and the Eysenck Personality Inventory, which psychologists use to compare how people score on different traits. Childhood personality traits do tend to be associated with adult personality traits, as reported by a recent study that showed similar traits, such as negative emotionality, in children aged 8 to 12 years and then again ten years later at ages 17 to 23 (Shiner, Masten, & Tellegen, 2002).

But trait theories have their drawbacks. Perhaps the major challenge is that they simply attach a label to behavior rather than explaining it. Consider the following example:

1. You can always count on Mary. She's very reliable.

2. Why is Mary reliable? Because she is a conscientious person.

3. How do you know she is a conscientious person? Because she's reliable.

This is *circular reasoning*—explaining Mary's behavior in terms of a trait ("conscientiousness") whose existence is based on observing the very same behavior. Traits may be nothing more than shorthand descriptions of the apparent behaviors of people, with little to offer in terms of explaining the underlying causes of the behaviors. Even as descriptions, trait theories are based on broadly defined traits, such as the "Big Five," that may fail to capture the unique characteristics of individuals (Epstein, 1996; McAdams, 1992).

Another argument against trait theories is that behavior may not be as stable across time and situations as trait theorists suppose. How you act with your boss, for example, may be different from how you act around the house. How you relate to people today may be very different from how you related to people in the past. Learning theorists argue that we need to take into account environmental or situational factors, such as stimulus cues and reinforcements, in order to more accurately predict behavior.

Some personality theorists, such as Walter Mischel, whose own contributions will be discussed in the next module, argue that behavior depends more on situational factors than trait theorists would suppose. Mischel contends that people act consistently when the situations they face, and the meanings these situations hold for them, are similar (Mischel, 2004; Mischel & Shoda, 1999). But Mischel recognizes that individual differences in trait dimensions do exist. As he wrote recently, "On the whole, some people are more sociable than others, some are more open-minded, some are more punctual, and so on" (Mischel, 2004).

A developing consensus in the field is emerging around the concept of *interactionism*—the belief that behavior reflects an interaction between trait tendencies and situational factors (Reynolds & Karraker, 2003; Tett & Burnett, 2003; Wu & Clark, 2003). Situational factors clearly affect behavior in that people act differently in different situations depending upon the particular demands they face (Furr & Funder, 2004). But we also need to account for the fact that people have typical ways of acting that cut across various situations (Fleeson, 2004).

Personality factors tend to be relatively stable over time (e.g., McCrae et al., 2002; Shiner, Masten, & Tellegen, 2002; Trzesniewski, Donnellan, & Robins, 2003). That said, we should not think of personality as fixed in childhood or young adulthood. Evidence shows that personality is not "set like plaster" by early adulthood; it continues to develop and change throughout adult life (Helson, Jones, & Kwan, 2002). For example, investigators report increasing levels of "Big Five" factors of conscientiousness and agreeableness among men and women after age 30

(Srivastava et al., 2003). These changes suggest that people become better adapted to their environment as they get older, at least well into middle adulthood.

Measurement of personality traits in humans is well established, but can we assess personality traits in other animals, such as dogs? Some investigators have found that judgments of personality traits of dogs achieved as much consensus among raters as personality judgments of humans (Gosling, Kwan, & John, 2003). These findings suggest that personality differences can be measured in other animals as well. Do you believe that dogs have personality traits? Why or why not?

MODULE 12.2 REVIEW
The Trait Perspective

RECITE IT

What are the three types of traits in Allport's trait model?

• The three types of traits are cardinal traits (pervasive characteristics that govern behavior), central traits (more commonly found general characteristics around which behavior is organized), and secondary traits (interests or dispositions that influence behavior in specific situations).

What was Cattell's view on the organization of traits?

• Cattell believed that traits are organized in terms of surface traits (consistencies in a person's observed behavior) and source traits (general, underlying traits that account for relationships among surface traits).

What three traits are represented in Eysenck's model of personality?

• Eysenck believed that variations in personality could generally be explained in terms of three major traits: introversion-extraversion, neuroticism, and psychoticism.

What is the "Big Five" trait model of personality?

• The "Big Five" (neuroticism, extraversion, openness, agreeableness, conscientiousness) are five broad dimensions or traits that have consistently emerged in personality research, especially in factor-analytic studies.

What role do genes play in personality?

• Genetic influences are implicated in many personality traits, including neuroticism, shyness, aggressiveness, and novelty-seeking. Scientists today are exploring how genes interact with environmental influences in the development of personality.

RECALL IT

1. In the field of personality, "relatively stable or enduring characteristics or dispositions" are referred to as _____.

2. In Gordon Allport's view, the most common characteristics that form the basic building blocks of personality are
   a. cardinal traits.
   b. central traits.
   c. secondary traits.
   d. universal traits.

3. Among the personality psychologists discussed in this module, who described personality on the basis of three major traits?

4. The 16PF Questionnaire, developed by Raymond Cattell, is designed to measure
   a. source traits.
   b. surface traits.
   c. introversion-extraversion.
   d. psychoticism traits.

5. The most prominent contemporary trait model is based on a set of _____ broadly defined personality factors.

6. Name some of the personality characteristics for which a genetic link has been supported.

THINK ABOUT IT

• What psychological traits would you use to describe your personality? What traits do you believe others might use to describe you? How do you account for any differences?

• Do you believe that your personality traits are fixed or unchangeable? Or might your personality be open to adjustment here and there? What would you like to change about yourself and how you relate to others? Are you willing to see whether or not you're a leopard who can change its spots?

MODULE 12.3
The Social-Cognitive Perspective

- **What are expectancies and subjective values?**
- **What is reciprocal determinism?**
- **What are situation and person variables?**

CONCEPT 12.15
To behaviorists, the concept of personality refers to the sum total of an individual's learned behavior.

CONCEPT 12.16
Social-cognitive theorists expanded traditional learning theory by focusing on the cognitive and social learning aspects of behavior.

CONCEPT 12.17
Social-cognitive theorists believe that personality consists of the individual's repertoire of behavior and ways of thinking about the self and the world.

social-cognitive theory A contemporary learning-based model that emphasizes the roles played by both cognitive factors and environmental or situational factors in determining behavior.

expectancies In social-cognitive theory, personal predictions about the outcomes of behavior.

subjective value In social-cognitive theory, the importance that individuals place on desired outcomes.

Some psychologists developed models of personality that were quite different from the models of Freud and the trait theorists. Behaviorists such as John Watson and B. F. Skinner believed that personality is shaped by environmental influences (rewards and punishments), not by unconscious influences, as in Freud's theory, or by underlying traits, as the trait theorists believed. The behaviorists believed that personality consists of the sum total of an individual's learned behavior. Consider your own personality as a behaviorist might view it. Others may see you as friendly and outgoing; but to a behaviorist, terms like *friendly* and *outgoing* are merely labels describing a set of behaviors, such as showing an interest in others and participating in a wide range of social activities.

Behaviorists believe that behavior is learned on the basis of classical and operant conditioning. Rather than probe the depths of your unconscious to understand the roots of your behavior, behaviorists might explore how you were reinforced in the past for displaying friendly and outgoing behaviors. People with different histories of rewards and punishments develop different patterns of behavior. If Maisha is respectful and conscientious in her work habits, it is because she has been rewarded for this kind of behavior in the past. If Tyler spends more time socializing than studying, it is likely he has been reinforced more for social interactions than for academic performance.

Many learning theorists today adopt a broader view of learning than did the traditional behaviorists, such as Watson and Skinner. This contemporary model, called **social-cognitive theory**, maintains that to explain behavior we need to take into account cognitive and social aspects of behavior, not just the rewards and punishments to which we are exposed in the environment. These social and cognitive variables include expectancies we hold about the outcomes of our behavior, the values we place on rewards, and the learning that occurs when we imitate the behavior of others we observe interacting in social situations. To social-cognitive theorists, personality comprises not only learned behavior but also the ways that individuals think about themselves and the world. They believe that humans act upon the environment in pursuing their goals, not just react to it (Bandura, 2001). The three primary contributors to social-cognitive theory are the psychologists Julian Rotter, Albert Bandura, and Walter Mischel.

Julian Rotter: The Locus of Control

To Julian Rotter (1990), explaining and predicting behavior involves knowing an individual's reinforcement history as well as the person's expectancies and subjective values. **Expectancies** are your personal predictions of the outcomes of your behavior. For example, students who hold a positive expectancy about schoolwork believe that studying will improve their chances of getting good grades. **Subjective value** is the worth you place on desired outcomes. A dedicated student will place a high subjective value on getting good grades. In this instance, a student with high positive expectancy and high subjective value would be more likely to study for a forthcoming exam than someone who does not link studying with grades or who does not care about grades.

CONCEPT 12.18
Rotter believed that our ability
to explain and predict behavior
depends on knowing an individual's
reinforcement history as well as the
person's expectancies and subjective
values.

Rotter also believed that people acquire general expectancies about their ability to obtain reinforcements in their lives. Some, for example, have an internal **locus of control** (*locus* is the Latin word for "place"). They believe they can obtain reinforcements through work and effort. Others feel that reinforcements are largely controlled by external forces beyond their control, such as luck or fate. They have an external locus of control. Rotter (1966) developed a psychological inventory, called the Internal-External (I-E) Scale, to measure an individual's locus of control. Researchers have found that locus of control is linked to various outcomes. For example, people with an internal locus of control ("internals") are more likely than "externals" to succeed in school (Hackett et al., 1992; Kalechstein & Nowicki, 1997) and, among overweight individuals, to make changes in diet and exercise patterns (Holt, Clark, & Kreuter, 2001).

Albert Bandura: Reciprocal Determinism and the Role of Expectancies

CONCEPT 12.19
Bandura's model of reciprocal
determinism holds that cognitions,
behaviors, and environmental factors
mutually influence each other.

Albert Bandura's (1986) model of **reciprocal determinism** holds that cognitions, behaviors, and environmental factors influence each other (see Figure 12.4). Bandura focuses on the interaction between what we do (our behavior) and what we think (our cognitions). For example, suppose a motorist is cut off by another motorist on the road. The first motorist may think angering thoughts, such as "I'm going to teach that guy a lesson." These thoughts or cognitions increase the likelihood of aggressive behavior (e.g., cutting in front of the other motorist). The aggressive behavior, in turn, affects the social environment (the other motorist responds aggressively). The other motorist's actions then lead the first to have even more angering thoughts ("I can't let him get away with that!"), which, in turn, lead to more aggressive behavior. This vicious cycle of escalating aggressive behavior and angering thoughts may result in an incident of *road rage,* which can have tragic consequences.

Bandura (1997, 2004) emphasizes the role of *observational learning,* or learning by observing and imitating the behavior of others in social contexts. He believes that people learn from role models to whom they are exposed in their families and

Figure 12.4   Bandura's Model of Reciprocal Determinism
Bandura's model holds that cognitions, behaviors, and environmental factors mutually influence each other.
Source: Adapted from Bandura, 1986.

locus of control   In Rotter's theory, one's general expectancies about whether one's efforts can bring about desired outcomes or reinforcements.

reciprocal determinism   Bandura's model in which cognitions, behaviors, and environmental factors both influence and are influenced by each other.

"I Can Do This"   Bandura's social-cognitive model of personality emphasizes the importance of cognitive factors such as self-efficacy—the belief in our ability to accomplish tasks we set out to do.

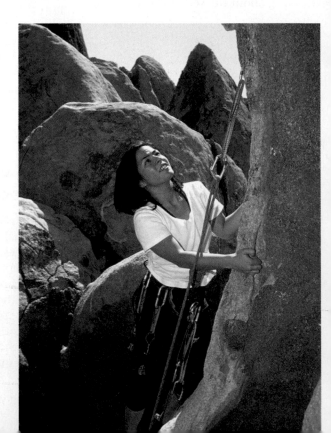

communities, as well as in the media. Bandura's social-cognitive theory has been put into practice in Third World countries (D. Smith, 2002). In Mexico and Tanzania, for example, "entertainment-education" programs are televised to millions that feature characters modeling desirable behaviors, such as taking concrete steps to overcome literacy in Mexico and practicing safer sex to reduce the risk of transmission of HIV/AIDS in Tanzania. The modeling has worked. In Tanzania, safer sex and family planning practices increased following exposure to televised programs featuring actors modeling these behaviors.

Bandura also distinguishes between two types of expectancies: outcome expectations and efficacy expectations. **Outcome expectations** are predictions of the outcomes of behavior. You are more likely to drink alcohol in a social situation if you believe it will be a pleasant experience and perhaps increase your self-confidence than if you think it will make you sick or act silly. **Efficacy expectations** are predictions about your personal ability to perform the behaviors you set out to accomplish. People with high *self-efficacy,* or beliefs in their personal effectiveness, are generally more likely to undertake challenges, such as academic and social challenges, and persevere to see them through.

Self-efficacy is associated with better health outcomes in which adherence to medical directives is important, such as with diabetic patients (Johnston-Brooks, Lewis, & Garg, 2002). People with higher levels of self-efficacy are also more likely to persevere and accomplish tasks they undertake. For example, they are less likely to relapse after quitting smoking and more likely to maintain ongoing physical activity (Motl et al., 2002; Shiffman et al., 2000). Self-efficacy is also associated with better recovery following traumatic events; people who are high in self-efficacy take a direct hand in mending their lives in the face of calamitous events, such as natural disasters and terrorist attacks (Benight & Bandura, 2004). We also have learned that self-efficacy is related to many aspects of achievement, including achievement motivation, academic performance, and persistence in pursuing academic pursuits (Harris & Halpin, 2002).

Yet success also boosts efficacy expectations. This is one reason that success experiences are so important to children and adults alike. Self-efficacy is generally an asset in performance situations (Bandura & Locke, 2003). However, in some cases it can lead to overconfidence, which in turn can handicap performance (Vancouver et al., 2002).

Walter Mischel: Situation Versus Person Variables

Walter Mischel's (1973) theoretical model overlaps to a large extent with Rotter's and Bandura's. Mischel argues that behavior is influenced by both **situation variables**, which are environmental factors such as rewards and punishments, and **person variables**, or internal personal factors. Two of these person variables, *expectancies* and *subjective values,* have the same meaning as in Rotter's model. But Mischel adds other person variables, including (1) *competencies,* or the knowledge and skills we possess, such as the ability to play an instrument or to speak a foreign language; (2) *encoding strategies,* or personal perceptions of events, such as whether we see a sudden gift of a basket of flowers as a gesture of love or as a way of making amends; and (3) *self-regulatory systems and plans,* or the ability to plan courses of action to achieve our goals and to reward ourselves for accomplishing them. In Mischel's view, as in Bandura's, environmental and personal factors interact to produce behavior. In predicting a specific person's behavior, we need to take into account what we know about the person as well as the situation at hand.

In his more recent work, Mischel focuses on the interactions of emotions (affects) and person variables. One example he considers is how negative feeling states such as depression cast a dim outlook on the ways that people encode experiences and form expectancies about future outcomes (Mischel & Shoda, 1995).

outcome expectations   Bandura's term for our personal predictions about the outcomes of our behavior.

efficacy expectations   Bandura's term for the expectancies we have regarding our ability to perform behaviors we set out to accomplish.

situation variables   Mischel's term for environmental influences on behavior, such as rewards and punishments.

person variables   Mischel's term for internal personal factors that influence behavior, including competencies, expectancies, and subjective values.

But Mischel also recognizes that our emotional reactions, in turn, depend on how we interpret and label experiences, a point to which we shall return when we consider cognitive theories of depression in Chapter 13.

Evaluating the Social-Cognitive Perspective

Learning theorists have increased our understanding of how behavior is influenced by environmental factors, such as a history of rewards and punishments. Reinforcement principles are now applied in a wide range of programs, including those designed to help parents learn better parenting skills and to help children learn more effectively in the classroom. Learning theory has also given rise to a major contemporary model of psychotherapy, *behavior therapy,* in which learning principles are applied to help people deal with emotional and behavioral problems (see Chapter 14).

Social-cognitive theorists broadened the scope of learning theory to include cognitive influences on learning and the recognition that much of what we learn occurs by observing others in social contexts. Today, many behavior therapists subscribe to a broader treatment model, called *cognitive-behavioral therapy,* or *CBT* (see Chapter 14), which incorporates cognitive as well as behavioral approaches to therapy and mirrors the teachings of the social-cognitive theorists. But perhaps the most important influence of the social-cognitive theorists is that they have presented us with a view of people as active seekers and interpreters of information, not just responders to environmental influences. Indeed, many psychologists have come to believe that behavior is best explained by the reciprocal interactions between the person and the environment.

To some of its critics, social-cognitive theory presents a limited view of personality because it fails to account for the roles of unconscious influences and heredity. To others, specifically trait theorists, social-cognitive theorists fail to take personality traits into account when attempting to explain underlying consistencies in behavior across situations. Social-cognitive theorists would counter that traits don't explain behavior but merely attach labels to behavior—and, moreover, that behavior is not as consistent across situations as trait theorists may suppose. Finally, social-cognitive theory is criticized by those who believe that it focuses too little on subjective experience, such as self-awareness and the flow of consciousness. Social-cognitive theorists may believe that the emphasis they place on cognitive factors, such as expectancies and subjective values, addresses these concerns. As you'll see next, subjective experience takes center stage in another perspective on personality, the humanistic approach. But first you may want to review Concept Chart 12.3, which summarizes the major concepts associated with the behavioral and social-cognitive perspectives on personality.

CONCEPT 12.21

Though social-cognitive theories broadened traditional learning theory, critics claim that they don't account for unconscious processes and genetic factors in personality.

CONCEPT CHART 12.3 **Behavioral and Social-Cognitive Perspectives on Personality**

Traditional Behaviorism	Social-Cognitive Theory
Behaviorists believe that personality is the sum total of an individual's learned behavior and that distinctive patterns of behavior are determined by differences between people in their learning experiences.	To social-cognitive theorists, personality consists of both learned behaviors and ways of thinking. They believe that we need to attend to the role of cognitions and observational learning in explaining and predicting behavior, not just to the role of environmental influences such as rewards and punishments.

MODULE 12.3 REVIEW

The Social-Cognitive Perspective

RECITE IT

What are expectancies and subjective values?

• Rotter believed that to explain and predict behavior we need to take into account a person's expectancies (personal predictions about the outcomes of events) and subjective values (worth placed on particular goals).

What is reciprocal determinism?

• Reciprocal determinism refers to Bandura's belief that cognitions, behaviors, and environmental factors mutually influence each other.

What are situation and person variables?

• Mischel proposed that both situation variables (environmental influences such as rewards and punishments) and person variables (factors relating to the person such as competencies, expectancies, encoding strategies, subjective values, and self-regulatory systems and plans) are needed to explain and predict behavior.

RECALL IT

1. Unlike Freudian and trait theorists, behaviorists believe that personality is due to
   a. deep, underlying unconscious conflicts.
   b. the sum total of a person's history of reinforcements and punishments.
   c. ways we think about ourselves and the world.
   d. ways we think about others in the world.

2. According to Julian Rotter, the individual who expects a good outcome from hard work and effort has a(n) _____ locus of control.

3. Describe Albert Bandura's concept of *reciprocal determinism*.

4. Match the following terms with the appropriate descriptions: i. self-efficacy; ii. situation variables; iii. competencies; iv. encoding strategies

   a. personal perceptions of events
   b. belief in personal effectiveness
   c. personal knowledge and skills
   d. environmental influences

THINK ABOUT IT

• How does social-cognitive theory represent a shift in learning-based theories of personality?

• Do you believe the roots of personality lie more in the environment or in the person? Explain.

• How is your behavior influenced by your outcome and efficacy expectations? your subjective values?

MODULE 12.4

The Humanistic Perspective

■ **What is self-theory?**

■ **What role does unconditional positive regard play in the development of self-esteem?**

Humanistic psychology departed from the psychodynamic and behaviorist schools in proposing that conscious choice and personal freedom are central features of what it means to be a human being (Bargh & Chartrand, 1999). Humanistic psychology arose as a "third force" in psychology that countered the determinism of psychodynamic and behavioral theories (Clay, 2002). To humanistic psychologists, we are not puppets whose movements are controlled by strings pulled by the unconscious mind or the environment; rather, we are endowed with the ability to make free choices that give meaning and personal direction to our lives. Two of the major contributors to humanistic thought were the American psychologists Carl Rogers (1902–1987) and Abraham Maslow (1908–1970).

Concept 12.22
Rogers's theory of personality emphasizes the importance of the self, the sense of the "I" or "me" that organizes how you relate to the world.

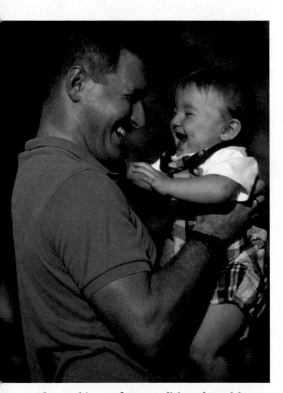

The Makings of Unconditional Positive Regard? Rogers emphasized the importance of unconditional positive regard in the development of self-esteem.

self-theory Rogers's model of personality, which focuses on the importance of the self.

unconditional positive regard Valuing another person as having intrinsic worth, regardless of the person's behavior at the particular time.

conditional positive regard Valuing a person only when the person's behavior meets certain expectations or standards.

self-ideals Rogers's term for the idealized sense of how or what we should be.

Carl Rogers: The Importance of Self

Rogers (1961, 1980) believed that each of us possesses an inner drive that leads us to strive toward *self-actualization*—toward realizing our own unique potentials. The roadway toward self-actualization is an unfolding process of self-discovery and self-awareness, of tapping into one's true feelings and needs, accepting them as our own, and acting in ways that genuinely reflect them. To Rogers and other humanists, personality is expressed through the conscious experience of directing ourselves toward fulfilling our unique potentials as human beings.

Rogers believed that the self is the center of the human experience. Thus it is no surprise that he referred to his theory of personality as **self-theory**. To Rogers, the self is the executive part of your personality that organizes how you relate to the world. It is the sense of being "I" or "me"—the person who looks back at you in the mirror, the sense of being a distinct individual with your own likes, dislikes, needs, and values. The self also includes the impressions you have of yourself, impressions that constitute your *self-concept*. As was the case in his own life, the theory of personality Rogers developed reflects the importance of coming to know yourself and being true to yourself, regardless of what others might think or say. (See the Pioneers box for more on this subject.)

One of the primary functions of the self, as Rogers viewed it, is the development of self-esteem, or the degree of liking we have for ourselves. Humans the world over appear to have a need to feel good about themselves (DuBois & Flay, 2004; Sheldon, 2004).

Rogers noted that self-esteem at first mirrors how other people value us, or fail to value us. For this reason, he believed it is crucial for parents to bestow on their children **unconditional positive regard**, or acceptance of a person's basic worth regardless of whether their behavior pleases or suits us. In other words, Rogers believed that parents should prize their children regardless of their behavior at any particular moment in time. In this way, children learn to value themselves as having intrinsic worth, rather than judging themselves as either good or bad depending on whether they measure up to other people's expectations or demands. Rogers didn't mean that parents should turn a blind eye toward undesirable behavior. Parents do not need to accept all of their children's behavior; they can correct their children's poor behavior without damaging their self-esteem. However, parents need to clarify that it is the *behavior* that is undesirable, not the child.

Unfortunately, many parents show **conditional positive regard** toward their children. They bestow approval only when the children behave "properly." Children given conditional positive regard may learn to think of themselves as being worthwhile only when they are behaving in socially approved ways. Their self-esteem may become shaky, as it comes to depend on what other people think of them at a particular moment in time. To maintain self-esteem, they may need to deny their genuine feelings, interests, and desires. They learn to wear masks or to don social facades to please others. Their sense of themselves, or self-concept, may become so distorted that they feel like strangers to themselves. They may come to question who they really are.

Our self-esteem is ultimately a function of how close we come to meeting our **self-ideals**—our idealized sense of who or what we should be. When these ideals are shaped by what others expect of us, we may have a hard time measuring up to them. Our self-esteem may plummet. The model of therapy Rogers developed, called *client-centered therapy* (discussed in Chapter 14), helps people get in touch with their true feelings and come to value and prize themselves.

Rogers was an optimist who believed in the essential worth and goodness of human nature. He believed that people become hurtful toward each other only when their own pathways toward self-actualization are blocked or stymied by obstacles. Parents can help their children in this personal voyage of discovery by

THE PIONEERS

To Thine Own Self Be True

Carl Rogers

Carl Rogers, the fourth of six children, was born in 1902 in Oak Park, Illinois, just outside Chicago. When he was 12, his parents bought a farm some thirty miles to the west of Chicago, where he spent much of his adolescence. His parents encouraged independent thinking in their children. Looking back, Rogers could never recall being given a direct command by his parents on any matter of importance (Rogers, 1967). This early encouragement of thinking for himself may have had a formative influence on the direction his professional life was to take.

Rogers was a gifted student who balanced his farm chores with his schoolwork. During his college years at the University of Wisconsin, he became active in Christian youth groups, which led him toward a career in the ministry. He started training for the ministry at Union Theological Seminary in New York but, during his second year, began to have doubts about becoming a minister. He decided that working in the ministry with its set of prescribed teachings would not be a good fit with his personality because it would not allow him the freedom of thought he was seeking.

During his time at Union he began taking courses in psychology at neighboring Teachers College of Columbia University. Before long he decided to make psychology his life's work and enrolled in the clinical psychology program at Teachers College. He graduated with a Ph.D. in 1928 and went on to a distinguished career as a clinical psychologist and personality theorist.

bestowing on them unconditional approval, even if the children's developing interests and values differ from their own.

As you reflect on the importance of self-esteem, recall from Chapter 1 the 1939 study by Kenneth and Mamie Clark on the self-esteem of African American preschool children. They discovered that the children preferred playing with a white doll over a black one and attributed more positive characteristics to the white doll—a result they believed reflected the negative effects of segregation on self-esteem. In the intervening years, many other researchers have examined self-esteem in African American children using a number of different methods. They

How Do You See Yourself?
Do you like yourself? Why or why not?

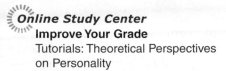
Online Study Center
Improve Your Grade
Tutorials: Theoretical Perspectives on Personality

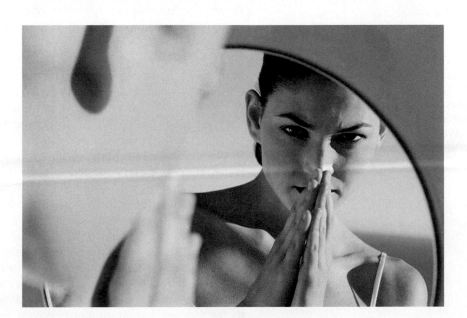

have found that African American children, adolescents, and adults actually show higher levels of self-esteem, on average, than their White counterparts (Gray-Little & Hafdahl, 2000; Hafdahl & Gray-Little, 2002; Twenge & Crocker, 2002a, 2002b).

One explanation of the self-esteem advantage among young African Americans is that they tend to have a stronger sense of ethnic identity than young Whites. Ethnic identity is a strong predictor of self-esteem among African Americans and Hispanic Americans (Gray-Little & Hafdahl, 2000; Umaña-Taylor, 2004).

The nearby Try This Out feature gives you the opportunity to evaluate how well your self-concept measures up with your concept of an ideal self. If your self-esteem is lagging, don't give up hope. The application module at the end of the chapter focuses on ways of enhancing self-esteem.

Abraham Maslow: Scaling the Heights of Self-Actualization

CONCEPT 12.23
Whereas Freud was primarily concerned with our baser instincts, Maslow focused on the highest reaches of human endeavor, the process of realizing our unique potentials.

Like Rogers, Maslow believed in an innate human drive toward self-actualization—toward becoming all that we are capable of being (Maslow, 1970, 1971). To Maslow, this drive toward self-actualization shapes our personality by motivating us to develop our unique potentials as human beings. He believed that if people were given the opportunity, they would strive toward self-actualization. Yet he recognized that few of us become fully self-actualized. In the humanistic view, personality is perhaps best thought of as a continuing process of personal growth and realization—more a road to be followed than a final destination.

Evaluating the Humanistic Perspective

Humanistic psychologists, following the principles established by Maslow and Rogers, note that each of us has unique feelings, desires, and needs. Therefore, we cannot completely abide by the wishes of others and still be true to ourselves. The path to psychological health is paved with awareness and acceptance of *all* parts of ourselves, warts and otherwise.

The humanistic perspective provided much of the impetus for the broad social movement of the 1960s and 1970s in which many people searched inside themselves to find direction and meaning in their lives. It renewed the age-old debate about free will and determinism and focused attention on the need to understand the subjective or conscious experiences of individuals (Bargh & Chartrand, 1999). Rogers's method of therapy, *client-centered therapy,* remains highly influential. And perhaps most important of all, humanistic theorists helped restore to psychology the concept of self—that center of our conscious experience of being in the world.

CONCEPT 12.24
The humanistic perspective focuses on the need to understand conscious experience and one's sense of self, but difficulties exist in studying private, subjective experiences and in measuring such core concepts as self-actualization.

Yet the very strength of the humanistic viewpoint, its focus on conscious experience, is also its greatest weakness when approached as a scientific endeavor. Ultimately your conscious experience is known or knowable only to an audience of one—you. As scientists, how can humanistic psychologists ever be certain that they are measuring with any precision the private, subjective experience of another person? Humanistic psychologists might answer that we should do our best to study conscious experience scientifically, for to do less is to ignore the very subject matter—human experience—we endeavor to know. Indeed, they have been joined by cognitive psychologists in developing methods to study conscious experience, including rating scales and thought diaries that allow people to make public their private experiences—to report their thoughts, feelings, and attitudes in systematic ways that can be measured reliably.

Critics also contend that the humanistic approach's emphasis on self-fulfillment may lead some people to become self-indulgent and so absorbed with themselves that they develop a lack of concern for others. Even the concept of self-actualization poses challenges. For one thing, humanistic psychologists consider self-actualization to be a drive that motivates behavior toward higher purposes. Yet how do we

TRY THIS OUT

Examining Your Self-Concept

What do you *really* think of yourself? Are you pleased with the person you see in the mirror? Or do you put yourself down at every opportunity?

One way to measure your self-concept is to evaluate yourself on the dimensions listed below. Add other dimensions that are important to you. Circle the number that corresponds to your concept of yourself along each dimension.

Now consider your self-ratings. Did you rate yourself toward the positive or negative end of these dimensions? People with higher self-esteem tend to rate themselves more positively than those with lower self-esteem. Some dimensions, such as "wise-foolish," may have a greater bearing on your self-esteem than other dimensions. The general pattern of your ratings should give you insight into your overall self-concept and how it affects your self-esteem.

Next, repeat the exercise with a marker of a different color. But this time indicate where you think you *ought* to be according to each dimension by marking the space above the corresponding number. Ignore your original ratings during this step. (Ratings for some dimensions might overlap, indicating a match between your self-concept and your ideal self.)

Now consider the *differences* between your ratings of your present self and your ideal self on each dimension. Pay particular attention to dimensions you consider most important. The higher the *differences* between your actual self and your ideal self, the *lower* your self-esteem is likely to be. The *closer* your self-perceptions are to your ideal self, the *higher* your self-esteem is likely to be.

What aspects of your personality show the greatest discrepancies? Which, if any, of these characteristics would you like to change in yourself? Do you think it is possible to move closer to your desired self? How would you do it? What would you need to change about yourself and how you relate to others?

	Extremely	Mostly	Somewhat	In between	Somewhat	Mostly	Extremely	
Fair	1	2	3	4	5	6	7	Unfair
Independent	1	2	3	4	5	6	7	Dependent
Creative	1	2	3	4	5	6	7	Uncreative
Unselfish	1	2	3	4	5	6	7	Selfish
Self-Confident	1	2	3	4	5	6	7	Lacking Confidence
Competent	1	2	3	4	5	6	7	Incompetent
Important	1	2	3	4	5	6	7	Unimportant
Attractive	1	2	3	4	5	6	7	Unattractive
Educated	1	2	3	4	5	6	7	Uneducated
Sociable	1	2	3	4	5	6	7	Unsociable
Kind	1	2	3	4	5	6	7	Cruel
Wise	1	2	3	4	5	6	7	Foolish
Graceful	1	2	3	4	5	6	7	Awkward
Intelligent	1	2	3	4	5	6	7	Unintelligent
Artistic	1	2	3	4	5	6	7	Unartistic

Add other traits of importance to you:

	Extremely	Mostly	Somewhat	In between	Somewhat	Mostly	Extremely	
_____	1	2	3	4	5	6	7	_____
_____	1	2	3	4	5	6	7	_____
_____	1	2	3	4	5	6	7	_____

Source: Adapted from Nevid, Rathus, & Rubenstein, 1998.

CONCEPT CHART 12.4 The Humanistic Perspective: Key Points

Concept	Summary	Key Principle
Rogers's self-theory	The self is the executive or organizing center of the personality—the "I" that determines how we relate to the world and pursue our goals.	People who are not encouraged in their upbringing to develop their individuality and uniqueness—but instead are valued only when they meet other people's expectations—tend to develop distorted self-concepts.
Maslow's concept of self-actualization	Self-actualization is a key element of personality and human motivation.	If given the chance, people will strive toward achieving self-actualization, a goal that is better thought of as a continuing journey rather than as a final destination.

CONCEPT 12.25

Whether we define ourselves in terms of our individuality or the social roles that we perform, our personality is influenced by the values of the culture in which we are raised.

collectivistic culture A culture that emphasizes people's social roles and obligations.

individualistic culture A culture that emphasizes individual identity and personal accomplishments.

know that this drive exists? If self-actualization means different things to different people—one person may become self-actualized by pursuing an interest in botany, another by becoming a skilled artisan—how can we ever measure self-actualization in a standardized way? To this, humanistic psychologists might respond that because people are unique, we should not expect to apply the same standard to different people. Concept Chart 12.4 provides a summary of some of the major concepts in the humanistic perspective on personality.

EXPLORING PSYCHOLOGY
Culture and Self-Identity

Let's not leave our discussion of humanistic concepts of the self without acknowledging the important role that culture plays in the development of our self-concepts. Before reading on, take a moment to complete this sentence, "I am _____." (Don't fill in your name, but describe some aspect of who you are.)

How you define yourself may depend on the culture in which you were raised. If you were raised in a **collectivistic culture**, you might define yourself in terms of the social roles you assume or the groups to which you belong (Markus & Kitayama, 1991; Triandis & Suh, 2002). You might say, "I am a Korean American" or "I am Jonathan's father." By contrast, if you were raised in an **individualistic culture**, you are likely to define yourself in terms of your unique individuality (the characteristics that distinguish you from others) and your personal accomplishments. You might say, "I am a systems analyst" or "I am a caring person." (Of course, these descriptions represent general cultural trends; differences certainly exist among individuals within cultures as well as between cultures themselves.)

Many cultures in Asia, Africa, and Central and South America are considered collectivistic, whereas those of the United States, Canada, and many Western European countries are characterized as individualistic (Rhee, Uleman, & Lee, 1996; Robinson, 1996; Triandis & Gelfand, 1998). Most of the world's population—80 percent according to a recent estimate—live in collectivistic cultures (Dwairy, 2002).

Collectivistic cultures value the group's goals over the individual's. They emphasize communal values such as harmony, respect for authority and for one's elders, conformity, cooperation, interdependence, and avoiding conflicts with others (Markus & Kitayama, 1991; Nisbett, 2003). For example, traditional Filipino culture emphasizes deference to elders at any cost (Nevid & Sta. Maria, 1999). Filipino children are taught to never disrespect their older siblings, no matter how small the age difference and, in many cases, regardless of who is "right." Individualistic cultures, by contrast, emphasize values relating to independence and self-sufficiency. They idealize rugged individualism as personified in tales of the nineteenth-century

REALITY CHECK

THE CLAIM Your personality is determined by the stars.

THE EVIDENCE No scientific evidence supports beliefs that our personalities are governed by astrological signs (Clarke, Gabriels, & Barnes, 1996; Crowe, 1990; Dean, Mather, & Kelly, 1996). Yet, despite the lack of scientific evidence, popular beliefs in astrology remain strong.

THE TAKE-AWAY MESSAGE Knowing whether you are a Leo, Scorpio, or Capricorn tells us nothing about your personality.

American West. However, despite general differences between individualistic and collectivistic cultures, the human mind possesses the ability to think both individualistically and collectivistically depending on the circumstances (Oyserman, Coon, & Kemmelmeier, 2002; Oyserman, Kemmelmeier, & Coon, 2002).

Differences in cultural values also affect how people attain status. In individualistic cultures, status is associated with individual accomplishment or the accrual of wealth: how much money you earn, the kind of house you own, the car you drive, the awards you receive, and the individual goals you've achieved or failed to achieve. In collectivistic cultures, status is achieved by placing the needs of the group above your own and being willing to sacrifice your needs for the welfare of the group or society.

One aspect of collectivism is the value placed on acting honorably in meeting one's social obligations, even to the extent of turning in cash someone dropped on a sidewalk (Onishi, 2004). In Tokyo, for example, $23 million in cash was turned into lost-and-found centers in 2002, of which 72 percent was returned to owners who were able to persuade authorities that the money was theirs. A 24-year-old woman, Hitomi Sasaki, found $250 lying next to a plant outside the restaurant where she worked, and she promptly turned it in. Probably not many New Yorkers would follow Ms. Sasaki's lead if they happened upon a wad of cash lying in the street. Would you?

Extremes of either individualism or collectivism can have undesirable outcomes. Excessive collectivism may stifle creativity, innovation, and personal initiative, whereas excessive individualism may lead to unmitigated greed and exploitation.

MODULE 12.4 REVIEW

The Humanistic Perspective

RECITE IT

What is self-theory?

- In Rogers' view, the self is the organized center of our experience. The self naturally moves toward self-actualization, or development of its unique potential.

What role does unconditional positive regard play in the development of self-esteem?

- Carl Rogers, a leading humanistic theorist, believed that unconditional positive regard (noncontingent approval) from significant others underpins the development of self-esteem. By contrast, when approval is contingent on "proper" behavior, people may develop a distorted self-concept to maintain self-esteem and disown the parts of themselves that meet with disapproval.

RECALL IT

1. "Free will" is considered by behaviorists to be _____; to humanists it is _____.
   a. easy to achieve; difficult to achieve
   b. difficult to achieve; easy to achieve
   c. central to being human; an illusion
   d. an illusion; central to being human

2. What did Rogers believe was the center of our experience of being human?

3. Describe the relationship between Rogers's own early experiences and his psychological theory.

4. Defining oneself in terms of the roles one plays within the group or society is most likely to occur in
   a. a collectivist culture.
   b. an individualistic culture.
   c. Western European cultures.
   d. the traditional U.S. culture.

THINK ABOUT IT

- How has your cultural background affected your goals and ambitions? Your values? Your self-identity? Your relationships with others? Do you think you would have developed a different personality had you been raised in another culture? Why or why not?

- Do you consider yourself more of an individualist or a collectivist? How are your views of yourself connected with your cultural background?

MODULE 12.5

Personality Tests

- **What are self-report personality inventories?**
- **What are projective tests of personality?**

Let us now move from attempts to describe or explain personality to ways of measuring it. What does it mean to measure personality? Attempts to measure personality actually have a long history. In the eighteenth and nineteenth centuries, many well-respected scientists believed one could make reasonable judgments about a person's character and mental abilities by examining the bumps on the person's head, or even the shape of the person's nose. Such beliefs very nearly derailed Charles Darwin's momentous journey around the world that led him to develop the theory of evolution. Darwin's appointment as the naturalist on the British ship the *Beagle* was nearly scuttled because Robert Fitz-Roy, the ship's captain, thought the shape of Darwin's nose indicated he lacked the energy and determination needed for such an arduous voyage. As Darwin later wrote,

> He [Fitz-Roy] was . . . convinced that he could judge a man's character by the outline of his features; and doubted whether anyone with my nose could possess sufficient energy and determination for the voyage. But I think he was afterwards well satisfied that my nose had spoken falsely. (Darwin, 1892/1958)

Darwin thus embarked in 1831 on a remarkable five-year journey during which he gathered samples of the plant and animal species he encountered along the way—evidence that would form the foundation of his theory of evolution.

According to **phrenology**, a popular view in the nineteenth century, you could judge people's character and mental abilities from the pattern of bumps on their heads. The physician Franz Joseph Gall (1758–1828) made many early contributions to the understanding of brain anatomy, but he is best known to us as the

Phrenology Phrenology is based on a misconception that one can determine mental abilities and personality traits by examining the bumps or indentations on a person's skull.

phrenology The now-discredited view that one can judge a person's character and mental abilities by measuring the bumps on his or her head.

personality tests Structured psychological tests that use formal methods of assessing personality.

self-report personality inventories Structured psychological tests in which individuals are given a limited range of response options to answer a set of questions about themselves.

objective tests Tests of personality that can be scored objectively and that are based on a research foundation.

standard scores Scores that represent an individual's relative deviation from the mean of the standardization sample.

leading proponent of phrenology (Hunt, 1993). He argued that specific areas of the brain were responsible for different character traits and that the contours of the skull in these areas indicated the degree to which the person possessed such traits. We now know that you cannot assess people's personality traits by their superficial biological characteristics, such as bumps on the head or the shape of a person's nose or of a person's body.

Today, investigators no longer measure bumps on people's heads or the shapes of their noses to learn about their personalities. The methods used by psychologists today include case studies, interviews, observational techniques, and experimental studies (see Chapter 1). But the most widely used method for learning about personality is based on the use of formal **personality tests**. The two major types of personality tests are self-report personality inventories and projective tests.

Self-Report Personality Inventories

CONCEPT 12.26
Self-report personality inventories are widely used measures of personality in which a person's response options are limited so that scoring can be objective.

Self-report personality inventories are structured psychological tests in which individuals are given a set of questions to answer about themselves in the form of "yes-no" or "true-false" or "agree-disagree" types of response formats. Self-report personality inventories are also called **objective tests**. They are not objective in the same sense that your bathroom scale is an objective measure of your weight. Unlike scales of weight, they rely on people's opinions or judgments as to whether they agree or disagree with particular statements. The tests are objective in the sense that they can be scored objectively because the responses they require are limited to a few choices, such as true or false. They are also considered objective because they were constructed from evidence gathered from research studies. Some self-report personality tests measure single dimensions of personality, such as assertiveness or hostility. Others attempt to capture multiple dimensions of personality. A leading example of a multidimensional personality test is the Minnesota Multiphasic Personality Inventory (MMPI), the most widely used self-report personality inventory in the world (Camara, Nathan, & Puente, 2000).

Minnesota Multiphasic Personality Inventory (MMPI)   Do you like fashion magazines? Are you frequently troubled by feelings of anxiety or nervousness? Do you feel that others "have it in for you"? What might your answers to questions such as these tell us about your underlying personality or mental health?

These questions model the items found in the MMPI, now in a revised edition called the MMPI-2 (Butcher, 2000). The MMPI-2 consists of 567 true-false items that yield scores on ten clinical scales (see Table 12.4) and additional scales measuring other personality dimensions and response tendencies.

The MMPI was constructed to help clinicians diagnose mental disorders. Items are grouped on particular scales if they tended to be answered differently by particular diagnostic groups than by normal reference groups. For example, an item such as "I feel moody at times" would be placed on the depression scale if it tended to be endorsed more often by people in a depressed group than by normal controls. The more items a person endorses in the same direction as the diagnostic group, the higher the score the person receives on the scale.

When scoring the MMPI, one converts raw scores (number of items scored in the same direction as the diagnostic group) into **standard scores**, which are then plotted on a graph similar to the one shown in Figure 12.5. Scores of 65 or higher on the clinical scales are considered clinically elevated or abnormally high. Examiners take into account the elevations on individual scales and

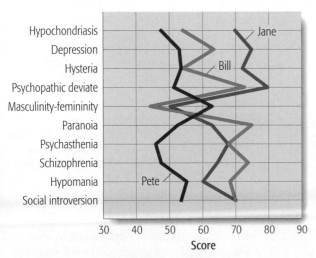

Figure 12.5   Sample MMPI-2 Profiles
(a) Jane is a 21-year-old woman who was admitted to a psychiatric facility following a suicide attempt; (b) Bill is a 34-year-old schizophrenia patient; and (c) Pete is a well-adjusted, 25-year-old editor.

Note: Scores of 50 are average. Scores on masculinity-femininity are keyed here in the masculine direction for females and in the feminine direction for males.

the pattern of relationships among the scale scores to form impressions of individuals' personality characteristics and their possible psychological problems.

Evaluation of Self-Report Personality Tests A large body of evidence supports the validity of the MMPI and other self-report personality inventories (e.g., Garb, 2003; Graham, 2000; Greene et al., 2003; Robin et al., 2003). The MMPI provides a wealth of information about a person's interests, areas of concern, needs, and

TABLE 12.4   Clinical Scales of The MMPI

Scale Number and Label	Items Similar to Those Found on MMPI Scale	Sample Traits of High Scorers
1 Hypochondriasis	I am frequently bothered by an upset stomach. At times, my body seems to ache all over.	Many physical complaints, cynical defeatist attitudes, often perceived as whiny, demanding
2 Depression	Nothing seems to interest me anymore. My sleep is often disturbed by worrisome thoughts.	Depressed mood; pessimistic, worrisome, despondent, lethargic
3 Hysteria	I sometimes become flushed for no apparent reason. I tend to take people at their word when they're trying to be nice to me.	Naive, egocentric, little insight into problems, immature; develops physical complaints in response to stress
4 Psychopathic deviate	My parents often disliked my friends. My behavior sometimes got me into trouble at school.	Difficulties incorporating values of society; rebellious, impulsive, antisocial tendencies; strained family relationships; poor work and school history
5 Masculinity-femininity*	I like reading about electronics. (M) I would like to work in the theater. (F)	Males endorsing feminine attributes: have cultural and artistic interests, effeminate, sensitive, passive. Females endorsing male interests: aggressive, masculine, self-confident, active, assertive, vigorous
6 Paranoia	I would have been more successful in life but people didn't give me a fair break. It's not safe to trust anyone these days.	Suspicious, guarded, blames others, resentful, aloof, may have paranoid delusions
7 Psychasthenia	I'm one of those people who have to have something to worry about. I seem to have more fears than most people I know.	Anxious, fearful, tense, worried, insecure, difficulties concentrating, obsessional, self-doubting
8 Schizophrenia	Things seem unreal to me at times. I sometimes hear things that other people can't hear.	Confused and illogical thinking, feels alienated and misunderstood, socially isolated or withdrawn, may have blatant psychotic symptoms such as hallucinations or delusional beliefs, or may lead a detached lifestyle
9 Hypomania	I sometimes take on more tasks than I can possibly get done. People have noticed that my speech is sometimes pressured or rushed.	Energetic, possibly manic, impulsive, optimistic, sociable, active, flighty, irritable, may have overly inflated or grandiose self-image or unrealistic plans
10 Social introversion*	I don't like loud parties. I was not very active in school activities	Shy, inhibited, withdrawn, introverted, lacks self-confidence, reserved, anxious in social situations

*The construction of these scales was based on nonclinical comparison groups.
Source: Adapted from Nevid, Rathus, & Greene, 2006.

CONCEPT 12.27
Projective tests are based on the belief that the ways in which people respond to ambiguous stimuli are determined by their underlying needs and personalities.

projective tests Personality tests in which ambiguous or vague test materials are used to elicit responses that are believed to reveal a person's unconscious needs, drives, and motives.

ways of relating to others, and it helps clinicians diagnose psychological or mental disorders. However, it should not be used by itself to make a diagnosis. A high score on the depression scale does not necessarily mean that a person has a depressive disorder, for example, only that the person may share certain personality traits or complaints in common with people who do.

Self-report personality inventories have several strengths. They are relatively inexpensive to administer and score—in fact, many can be machine-scored and interpreted by computer. People may also be more willing to disclose personal information on paper-and-pencil tests than when facing an interviewer. Most important, the results of these tests may be used to predict a wide range of behaviors, including the ability to relate effectively to others and to achieve positions of leadership or dominance (see Try This Out).

Reliance on self-report data in personality tests, such as the MMPI, can introduce potential biases, however. Some responses may be outright lies. Others may be prone to more subtle distortions, such as tendencies to respond in a socially desirable direction—in other words, to put one's best foot forward. Still others may reflect a "yea-saying" or "nay-saying" response style—tending toward either agreement or disagreement with items regardless of their content. The more sophisticated self-report scales, including the MMPI, have validity scales that help to identify response biases. Yet even these scales may not be able to eliminate all sources of bias (McGovern & Nevid, 1986; Nicholson et al., 1997).

Projective Tests

In **projective tests**, people are presented with a set of unstructured or ambiguous stimuli, such as inkblots, that can be interpreted in various ways. Projective tests are based on the belief in psychodynamic theory that people transfer, or "project," their unconscious needs, drives, and motives onto their responses to unstructured or vague stimuli. Unlike objective tests, projective tests have a response format that is not restricted to "yes-no" or multiple-choice answers or other limited response options. Therefore, an examiner must interpret the subject's responses, thus bringing more subjectivity to the procedure. Here we focus on the two most widely used projective tests, the Rorschach test and the TAT (Camara et al., 2000).

Rorschach Test   As a child growing up in Switzerland, Hermann Rorschach (1884–1922) amused himself by playing a game of dripping ink and folding the paper to make symmetrical inkblot figures. He noticed that people would perceive the same blots in different ways and came to believe that their responses revealed something about their personalities. His fascination with inkblots earned him the nickname *Klex*, which means "inkblot" in German. Rorschach, who went on to become a psychiatrist, turned his childhood pastime into the psychological test that bears his name. Unfortunately, Rorschach did not live to see how popular and influential his inkblot test would become. He died at the age of 37 from complications following a ruptured appendix, only months after the publication of his test (Exner, 2002).

The Rorschach test consists of ten cards similar to the one appearing in Figure 12.6. Five have splashes of color and the others are in black and white and shades of gray. Subjects are asked what each blot looks like. After the responses to each card are obtained, the examiner conducts a follow-up inquiry to probe more deeply into the person's responses.

Scoring Rorschach responses is a complex task. The scoring is based on such features as content (what the blot looked like—a "bat," for example) and form level (consistency of the response with the actual shape of the blot). The examiner notes whether the subject tends to use the whole blot or details of the blot. An overattention to detail may indicate obsessional or compulsive tendencies. Poor form level may indicate problems with perceiving reality clearly or perhaps an

Figure 12.6   Inkblot Similar to Rorschach Inkblot
What do you think this looks like? The Rorschach test is based on the assumption that people project aspects of their own personalities onto their responses to ambiguous figures.

Figure 12.7   TAT Drawing
What is happening here? What led up to this scene? What do you think will happen next? What might your responses to these types of questions reveal about your own personality?

overly fertile imagination. Those who see formless figures dominated by color—who see reddened areas as "blood," for instance—may have difficulty controlling their emotions. The content of the response may indicate underlying conflicts with others. For example, someone who sees only animal figures and no human forms may have difficulties relating to other people.

Thematic Apperception Test (TAT)   Harvard psychologist Henry Murray developed the Thematic Apperception Test (TAT) in the 1930s (Murray, 1938). The test consists of a set of pictures depicting ambiguous scenes that may be interpreted in different ways (see Figure 12.7). The subject is asked to tell a story about the scene, what led up to these events, and what the eventual outcome will be. Murray believed that the stories people tell reveal aspects of their own personalities, or projections of their own psychological needs and conflicts into the events they describe. For example, people whose stories consistently touch upon themes of parental rejection may be saying something about their own underlying psychological issues.

Evaluation of Projective Tests   One drawback of projective tests is that the scoring is largely based on the examiner's subjective impressions. Two examiners may disagree on the scoring of the form level of a particular Rorschach response, for example. Psychologist John Exner (1993) tried to standardize the scoring of the Rorschach by introducing a comprehensive scoring system. Yet concerns about reliability, including those directed at Exner's scoring system, persist (e.g., Wood et al., 2001). Even if projective tests can be scored reliably, are they valid? Do they measure what they purport to measure?

One problem with projective tests is *stimulus pull*. Despite efforts to make stimuli ambiguous, they often contain cues, such as sad-looking faces in the TAT, that may elicit (pull for) certain types of responses. In such cases, responses may involve reactions to the stimulus properties of the test materials themselves rather than projections of one's underlying personality (Murstein & Mathes, 1996).

CONCEPT 12.28
Though projective tests are widely used by psychologists, controversy over their validity and clinical utility persists.

Online Study Center
Improve Your Grade
Tutorials: Personality Testing in the Workplace

Although the validity of the Rorschach continues to be debated (Kubiszyn et al., 2000; Wood et al., 2001), recent evidence supports the validity of at least some Rorschach interpretations (Garb et al., 2005; Meyer et al., 2001; Perry, 2003). For example, certain Rorschach responses can help predict success in psychotherapy (Meyer, 2000), distinguish between different types of mental disorders (Kubiszyn et al., 2000), and detect underlying needs for dependency (Garb et al., 2005). Yet critics claim that the overall validity and utility of the Rorschach in particular and projective tests in general remain to be demonstrated (Hunsley & Bailey, 2001; Lilienfeld, Wood, & Garb, 2000). Proponents of projective testing argue that in skilled hands these tests can yield valuable information about personality that cannot be gleaned from self-report tests or interviews (Stricker & Gold, 1999).

Let us end this section by noting that psychological tests fare rather well in comparison to medical tests in their ability to make accurate predictions (Daw, 2001b; Meyer et al., 2001, 2002). For example, the MMPI is able to detect underreported psychopathology about as well an ultrasound can detect endometrial cancer in postmenopausal women.

Concept Chart 12.5 compares the methods of assessment and forms of therapy associated with each of the major perspectives on personality covered in this chapter.

CONCEPT CHART 12.5   Overview of Theoretical Perspectives on Personality

Theoretical Model	Key Theorists	Major Concepts	Assessment Techniques	Associated Therapy
Psychoanalytic	Freud	Personality is influenced by an unconscious dynamic struggle among the id, the ego, and the superego.	Interviews, projective techniques	Psychoanalysis (discussed in Chapter 14)
Psychodynamic (neo-Freudians)	Adler, Jung, Horney, Erikson	Social factors and development of self are more important influences on personality than sexual motivation.	Interviews, projective techniques	Psychodynamic therapy (discussed in Chapter 14)
Trait	Allport, Cattell, Eysenck	Personality consists of a set of underlying traits that account for the characteristic ways people act in different situations.	Self-report personality inventories, such as Cattell's 16PF and the Eysenck Personality Inventory (EPI)	None
Behaviorism	Watson, Skinner	Personality consists of learned behavior acquired through classical and operant conditioning.	Behavioral observation	Behavior therapy (discussed in Chapter 14)
Social-cognitive	Rotter, Bandura, Mischel	Personality consists of the individual's repertoire of behavior and ways of thinking about the world.	Behavioral observation, interviewing, self-report measures, thought checklists	Cognitive-behavioral therapy (discussed in Chapter 14)
Humanistic	Rogers, Maslow	Personality consists of the subjective experience of being in the world, organized around a concept of the self.	Interviews, self-concept measures	Rogers's client-centered therapy (discussed in Chapter 14)

MODULE 12.5 REVIEW

Personality Tests

RECITE IT

What are self-report personality inventories?

• Self-report personality tests are psychological tests that consist of sets of questions that people answer about themselves by using limited response options. They are classified as objective tests because they use objective methods of scoring and are based on research foundations.

What are projective tests of personality?

• Projective tests use ambiguous test materials that are answered in ways believed to reflect projections of the person's unconscious needs, drives, and motives.

RECALL IT

1. Why was Darwin's position as naturalist aboard the *Beagle* temporarily in jeopardy?
   a. There was insufficient funding to make the trip.
   b. Phrenologists objected to Darwin as the ship's naturalist.
   c. The captain of the *Beagle* thought Darwin's nose made him unsuitable.
   d. The theory of evolution was a controversial topic.

2. Unlike the MMPI, projective tests
   a. make use of limited response options.
   b. are capable of providing a clear interpretation.
   c. are most closely associated with the behaviorist perspective.
   d. are used to reveal unconscious desires and motives.

3. Two general types of tests are _____, such as the MMPI, and _____, such as the Rorschach and TAT.

4. The greatest concern about projective tests is
   a. that pictures in the TAT resemble known historical figures.
   b. that the interpretation of subjective responses is invalid.
   c. that they were developed from a psychodynamic perspective.
   d. that people may reveal their inner needs and desires in their responses.

THINK ABOUT IT

• Have you ever taken a personality test? What, if anything, do you believe you learned about your personality?

• Consider the debate over the validity of projective tests. Do you believe that people reveal underlying aspects of their personality in their responses to unstructured stimuli, such as inkblots? Why or why not?

APPLICATION MODULE 12.6

Building Self-Esteem

Humanistic psychologists Carl Rogers and Abraham Maslow recognized the importance of self-esteem in developing a healthy personality. The need to feel a sense of self-worth is a universal human striving (Sheldon, 2004). Self-esteem is associated with better health and psychological well-being (DuBois & Flay, 2004). It also predicts more successful adjustment to the transition to college (Paul & Brier, 2001) and higher grade point averages in college (Di Paula & Campbell, 2002; Robins, Hendin, & Trzesniewski, 2001; Taylor et al., 2003).

When self-esteem is low, it is usually because we see ourselves as falling short of some ideal. Yet self-esteem is not a fixed quality; it goes through ups and downs throughout the course of life (Robins et al., 2002). Self-esteem is not a product of simply telling ourselves how wonderful we are. Rather, our sense of self-worth develops naturally as we pursue and achieve the goals we set for ourselves. Achieving goals requires development of competencies, such as skills and abilities. But self-esteem also hinges on challenging perfectionistic expectations that can lead us to get down on ourselves when we inevitably fall short of idealized standards.

Acquire Competencies: Become Good at Something

CONCEPT 12.29
Self-esteem, rather than being a fixed quality, can be enhanced by developing competencies and adopting more realistic goals and expectations.

Social-cognitive theorists recognize that our self-esteem is related to the skills or competencies we can marshal to meet the challenges we face. Competencies include academic skills such as reading, writing, and math; artistic skills such as drawing and playing the piano; athletic skills such as walking a balance beam and throwing a football; social skills such as knowing how to start conversations; and job or occupational skills. The more competencies we possess, especially in areas that matter most to us, the better we feel about ourselves.

We develop competencies through training and practice. You may not be able to throw a baseball at ninety miles per hour unless you possess genetic advantages in arm strength and coordination. However, most skills we use in daily life can be developed within a normal range of genetic variation. Most of us can learn to play the piano fairly well, although only a few will ever grace the concert stage with our virtuosity. Indeed, most of the skills valued in our society are achievable by most people.

Online Study Center
Improve Your Grade
Tutorials: Online Self-Esteem Test

Set Realistic, Achievable Goals

Part of boosting self-esteem is setting realistic goals. This does not mean that you should not strive to be the best that you can be. It does mean that you may find it helpful to evaluate your goals in light of your true needs and capabilities.

Enhance Self-Efficacy Expectations

Success breeds success. You can enhance your self-efficacy expectations by choosing tasks that are consistent with your interests and abilities and working at them. Start with smaller, clearly achievable goals. Meeting these challenges will boost your self-confidence and encourage you to move toward more challenging goals. Regard the disappointments that life inevitably has in store as opportunities to learn from your mistakes, not as signs of ultimate failure.

Create a Sense of Meaningfulness in Your Life

To psychologically healthy individuals, life is not just a matter of muddling through each day. Rather, each day provides opportunities to pursue higher purposes. There are many different kinds of meaning in life, many different purposes. Some people find meaning in connecting themselves spiritually to something larger—whether it be a specific religion or the cosmos. Other people find meaning in community, among those who share a common ethnic identity and cultural heritage. Still others find meaning in love and family. Their spouses and their children provide them with a sense of fulfillment. People may also find meaning in their work.

Challenge Perfectionistic Expectations

Many of us withdraw from life challenges because of the unreasonable demands we impose on ourselves to be perfect in everything we attempt. If you place perfectionistic demands on yourself, consider an attitude shift. Try lightening up on yourself and adopting more realistic expectations based on a fair-minded appraisal of your strengths and weaknesses. You may not measure up to an idealized image of perfection, but chances are you already have some abilities and talents you can cultivate, thus bolstering your self-esteem.

Challenge the Need for Constant Approval

The psychologist Albert Ellis believed that an excessive need for social approval is a sure-fire recipe for low self-esteem (Ellis, 1977; Ellis & Dryden, 1987). Inevitably we will all encounter the disapproval of people who are important to us. But Ellis asks us to consider whether encountering disapproval is truly as awful as we might imagine. Replacing irrational needs for approval with more rational expectations can help bolster our self-esteem, especially when we run into people who fail to appreciate our finer points.

TYING IT TOGETHER

In this chapter we have explored different models of personality and ways of measuring it. The psychodynamic perspective focuses on how conflicts between opposing forces or mental states shape our personalities and behaviors (Module 12.1). The trait perspective also looks inward, but not to sources of inner conflict. Rather, trait theorists conceptualize personality in terms of a set of traits that predispose people to act in characteristic ways (Module 12.2). The social-cognitive perspective looks both inward and outward by focusing, respectively, on the roles of cognitive variables and the environment in shaping behavior (Module 12.3). The

humanistic perspective rejects the deterministic viewpoints of both the psychodynamic and behaviorist perspectives by arguing that conscious choice and personal freedom are core features of what it means to be human (Module 12.4). Psychologists are concerned not only with understanding personality but also with measuring it. Two commonly used test forms are self-report personality inventories and projective tests (Module 12.5). Self-esteem is an important part of our personalities, and one that we can bolster by developing competencies and learning to accept ourselves (Module 12.6).

Thinking Critically About Psychology

Read the following discussion. Then, based on your reading of this chapter, answer the question at the end. To evaluate your progress in developing critical thinking skills, compare your answer to the sample answer found in Appendix A.

Personality and Astrology: Is Your Personality All in the Stars? What's in store for you? Let's see what the stars say about "Geminis" and "Scorpios:"

Gemini (May 21–June 20). It is now time to focus on meeting your personal needs. Your energy level is high, and you can make the best use of your personal resources. There are many creative opportunities available to you, but you will need to apply yourself to take full advantage of them. You are the type of person who can go beyond what others expect of you. You are facing an important financial decision that can have a great impact on your future. But allow others to counsel you in reaching the best decision. All in all, now is the time to fully enjoy the many blessings in your life.

Scorpio (October 23–November 21). Your best-laid plans may need to be altered because of an unforeseen development. This can cause stress with others, but you will be able to use your sense of humor to ease the situation. You are a caring person whose concern for others shines through. Even though the next month or two may be unsettled, it is best to stay calm. Pursue what it is that is important to you and take advantage of the romantic

opportunities you may find or discover. Above all, maintain that sense of humor through trying times and don't accept more responsibilities than you can handle.

Believers in astrology hold that our personalities and destinies are fixed at the time of our birth by the positions of the sun, the moon, and the planets in the zodiac. Do you believe your personality was determined by the alignment of the heavens at the time of your birth? Do you read the astrology charts in your local newspaper? Do you believe them?

Astrology can be traced back thousands of years and still attracts many adherents, even among people with advanced education. More than 30 percent of college students polled in one survey expressed beliefs in astrology (Duncan, Donnelly, & Nicholson, 1992). Despite the fact that there is no scientific basis for astrology, it remains popular? Why?

One reason may be the *Barnum effect*—the tendency to believe overgeneralized descriptions of personality as accurate descriptions of oneself. The "Barnum" after whom the effect is named was the famous nineteenth-century circus showman P. T. Barnum, who once said, "There's a sucker born every minute." The next time you glance at an astrology forecast in your local paper, notice how often the statements are phrased in general terms that can apply to just about anyone (e.g., "Now is the time to focus on your personal needs . . . ," "Even though the next month or two may be unsettled . . . ."). Look again at the astrological readings for

"Geminis" and "Scorpios" given above. Chances are that you will identify with characteristics found in both descriptions, regardless of your particular date of birth.

The Barnum effect may also explain the continued popularity of other pseudosciences, such as psychic reading and fortune-telling. The special "insights" into our futures that psychics and fortune-tellers claim they have are based on general characteristics that fit just about everyone ("You are likely to encounter some financial difficulty . . ."). In addition, they tend to be good observers who notice subtle cues in their clients' attire, gestures, or responses to leading questions that they can use to personalize their predictions.

Another contributor to beliefs in astrology and other pseudosciences is the tendency for people to filter information about themselves in terms of how it reflects upon them. For instance, we tend to give greater credence to information that confirms a positive image of ourselves than to information that casts us in a negative light. Notice that the astrology readings shown above contained many positive attributes (e.g., "caring person," "sense of humor"). The tendency to place greater emphasis on information that bolsters a positive self-image is called the *self-serving bias*—a bias that also accounts for the tendency of people to take credit for their successes and to explain away their failures or disappointments (see Chapter 16).

Now it's your turn to try a little critical thinking. Explain how another type of cognitive bias, the *confirmation bias* (see Chapter 7), contributes to beliefs in astrology.

Key Terms

personality *(p. 462)*
psychoanalytic theory *(p. 462)*
conscious *(p. 463)*
preconscious *(p. 463)*
unconscious *(p. 463)*
id *(p. 464)*
ego *(p. 464)*
superego *(p. 464)*
pleasure principle *(p. 464)*
reality principle *(p. 464)*
defense mechanisms *(p. 465)*
repression *(p. 465)*
denial *(p. 465)*
reaction formation *(p. 465)*
rationalization *(p. 465)*
projection *(p. 465)*
sublimation *(p. 165)*
regression *(p. 465)*
displacement *(p. 465)*
erogenous zones *(p. 465)*
fixations *(p. 466)*
oral stage *(p. 466)*
anal stage *(p. 466)*
anal-retentive personality *(p. 467)*

anal-expulsive personality *(p. 467)*
phallic stage *(p. 467)*
Oedipus complex *(p. 467)*
Electra complex *(p. 467)*
castration anxiety *(p. 467)*
penis envy *(p. 467)*
latency stage *(p. 468)*
genital stage *(p. 468)*
personal unconscious *(p. 469)*
collective unconscious *(p. 469)*
archetypes *(p. 469)*
individual psychology *(p. 469)*
creative self *(p. 469)*
inferiority complex *(p. 469)*
drive for superiority *(p. 469)*
basic anxiety *(p. 470)*
basic hostility *(p. 470)*
traits *(p. 473)*
cardinal traits *(p. 473)*
central traits *(p. 473)*
secondary traits *(p. 473)*
surface traits *(p. 473)*
source traits *(p. 473)*
introversion-extraversion *(p. 475)*

neuroticism *(p. 475)*
psychoticism *(p. 475)*
five-factor model (FFM) *(p. 476)*
social-cognitive theory *(p. 481)*
expectancies *(p. 481)*
subjective value *(p. 481)*
locus of control *(p. 482)*
reciprocal determinism *(p. 482)*
outcome expectations *(p. 483)*
efficacy expectations *(p. 483)*
situation variables *(p. 483)*
person variables *(p. 483)*
self-theory *(p. 486)*
unconditional positive regard *(p. 486)*
conditional positive regard *(p. 486)*
self-ideals *(p. 486)*
collectivistic culture *(p. 490)*
individualistic culture *(p. 490)*
phrenology *(p. 492)*
personality tests *(p. 493)*
self-report personality inventories *(p. 493)*
objective tests *(p. 493)*
standard scores *(p. 494)*
projective tests *(p. 495)*

ANSWERS TO RECALL IT QUESTIONS

Module 12.1: 1. a; 2. ego; 3. i. c, ii. a, iii. b, iv. d; 4. phallic; 5. a.

Module 12.2: 1. traits; 2. b; 3. Eysenck; 4. a; 5. five; 6. shyness, neuroticism, aggressiveness, novelty-seeking.

Module 12.3: 1. b; 2. internal; 3. Our thoughts, behaviors, and environmental factors mutually influence each other; 4. i. b, ii. d, iii. c, iv. a.

Module 12.4: 1. d; 2. the self; 3. His parents encouraged him to think things through for himself but gave him no direct commands on matters of importance—hence his belief that we must each think for ourselves and be self-determining; 4. a.

Module 12.5: 1. c; 2. d; 3. self-report personality inventories; projective tests; 4. b.

13

Psychological Disorders

It was about 2 A.M. when the police brought Claire to the emergency room. She seemed to be about 45; her hair was matted, her clothing disheveled. Her face was expressionless, fixed in a blank stare. She clutched a clove of garlic in her right hand. She did not respond to the interviewer's questions: "Do you know where you are? Can you tell me your name? Can you tell me if anything is bothering you?"

The police officers filled in the details. Claire had been found meandering along the painted line that divided the main street through town, apparently oblivious to the cars swerving around her. She was waving the clove of garlic in front of her. She said nothing to the officers when they arrived on the scene, but she offered no resistance.

Claire was admitted to the hospital and taken to the psychiatric ward. The next morning, she was brought before the day staff, still clutching the clove of garlic, and interviewed by the chief psychiatrist. She said little but her intentions could be pieced together from mumbled fragments. Claire said something about "devils" who were trying to "rob" her mind. The garlic was meant to protect her. She had decided that the only way to rid the town of the "devils" that hounded her was to walk down the main street, waving the garlic in front of her. Claire would become well known to the hospital. This was but one of a series of such episodes.

Phil was 42, a police photographer. It was his job to take pictures at crime scenes. "Pretty grisly stuff," he admitted, "corpses and all." Phil was married and had two teenage sons. He sought a psychological consultation because he was bothered by fears of being confined in enclosed spaces. Many situations evoked his fears. He was terrified of becoming trapped in an elevator and took the stairs whenever possible. He felt uncomfortable sitting in the back seat of a car. He had lately become fearful of flying, although in the past he had worked as a news cameraperson and would often fly to scenes of news events at a moment's notice—usually by helicopter.

"I guess I was younger then and more daring," he related. "Sometimes I would hang out of the helicopter to shoot pictures with no fear at all. But now, just thinking about flying makes my heart race. It's not that I'm afraid the plane will crash. I just start trembling when I think of them closing that door, trapping us inside. I can't tell you why."

In this chapter we examine the behavior of people like Claire and Phil—behavior that psychologists would consider abnormal. Let us begin by examining the criteria that psychologists use to determine when behavior crosses the line between normal and abnormal. Later we will explore different kinds of abnormal behavior patterns that psychologists and other professionals classify as psychological or mental disorders.

The descriptions in this chapter may raise your awareness about psychological problems of people you know, or perhaps even problems you've faced yourself. But it is not intended to make you a diagnostician. If the problems touched upon in the chapter hit close to home, it makes sense to discuss your concerns with a qualified professional. ■

MODULE 13.1

What Is Abnormal Behavior?

- What criteria are used to determine whether behavior is abnormal?
- What are the major models of abnormal behavior?
- What are psychological disorders?

Determining whether behavior is abnormal is a more complex problem than it may seem at first blush. Most of us get anxious or depressed from time to time, but our behavior is not abnormal. The same behavior may be deemed normal under some circumstances but abnormal in others. For example, anxiety during a job interview is normal, but anxiety experienced whenever you board an elevator is not. Deep feelings of sadness are appropriate when you lose a loved one, but not when things are going well or following a mildly upsetting event that others take in stride.

Charting the Boundaries Between Normal and Abnormal Behavior

Where, then, might we draw the line between normal and abnormal behavior? Psychologists typically identify abnormal behavior based on a combination of the following criteria (Nevid, Rathus, & Greene, 2006):

💡 **CONCEPT 13.1**
Psychologists use several criteria in determining whether behavior is abnormal, including unusualness, social deviance, emotional distress, maladaptive behavior, dangerousness, and faulty perceptions of reality.

1. *Unusualness.* Behavior that is unusual, or experienced by only a few, may be abnormal—but not in all cases or situations. Surely it is unusual for people to report "hearing voices" or, like Claire, to walk through town warding off demons. Yet uncommonness, by itself, is not sufficient to be deemed abnormal. Exceptional behavior, such as the ability to hit a three-point jump shot with some regularity or to become a valedictorian, is also unusual; but it is not abnormal.

2. *Social deviance.* All societies establish standards or social norms that define socially acceptable behaviors. Deviation from these norms is often used as a criterion for labeling behavior as abnormal. The same behavior might be considered abnormal in some contexts but perfectly acceptable in others. For example, we might consider it abnormal to shout vulgarities at strangers in the street. Yet shouting vulgarities at an umpire or referee who misses an important call in a ballgame may fall within the range of acceptable social norms, however offensive it might be.

3. *Emotional distress.* States of emotional distress, such as anxiety or depression, are considered abnormal when inappropriate, excessive, or prolonged relative to the person's situation.

4. *Maladaptive behavior.* Behavior is maladaptive when it causes personal distress, is self-defeating, or is associated with significant health, social, or occupational problems. For example, abuse of alcohol or other drugs may threaten an individual's health and ability to function in meeting life's responsibilities.

5. *Dangerousness.* Violent or dangerous behavior is another criterion for which we need to examine the social context. For example, engaging in behavior that is dangerous to oneself or others may be an act of bravery in times of war, but not in peacetime. Hockey players and football players regularly engage in physically aggressive behavior that may be dangerous to themselves or their opponents, but their (controlled) violent behavior is often rewarded with lucrative contracts and endorsement deals. Outside the sanctioned contexts of warfare and sports, however, violent behavior is likely to be considered abnormal.

Is This Man Abnormal? Abnormality must be judged in relation to cultural standards. The behavior and style of dress of this football fan may be in bad taste but would probably not be considered abnormal in a contemporary context.

6. *Faulty perceptions or interpretations of reality.* **Hallucinations** ("hearing voices" or seeing things that are not there) involve distorted perceptions of reality. Similarly, fixed but unfounded beliefs, called **delusions**, such as believing that FBI agents are listening in on your phone conversations, represent faulty interpretations of reality (unless of course the FBI really is tapping your phone).

As we shall see next, the cultural context in which behavior occurs must also be evaluated when making judgments about whether behavior is abnormal.

Cultural Bases of Abnormal Behavior   Psychologists take into account the cultural context when making judgments about abnormal behavior (Arrindell, 2003; Dana, 2000). They realize that the same behavior can be normal in one culture but abnormal in another. For example, in the majority American culture, "hearing voices" is deemed abnormal. Yet among some Native American peoples, it is considered normal for individuals to hear voices of their recently deceased relatives. They believe that the voices of the departed call out as their spirit ascends to the afterworld (Kleinman, 1987). Such behavior, because it falls within the normal spectrum of the culture in which it occurs, is not deemed abnormal—even if it may seem so to people from other cultures.

Abnormal behavior patterns may be expressed differently in different cultures. For example, people in Western cultures may experience anxiety in the form of excessive worries about financial, health, or job-related concerns. Among some native African peoples and Australian aboriginal peoples, anxiety may be expressed in the form of fears of witchcraft or sorcery. Among the Chinese, depression is experienced more in terms of physical than psychological symptoms. Rather than report feeling sad, many depressed Chinese people report feeling headaches, fatigue, weakness, and even dizziness (Draguns & Tanaka-Matsumi, 2003; Kleinman 2004).

Forms of abnormal behavior in one culture may have no direct counterparts in another culture. Psychological disorders occurring in only one or a few cultures are called **culture-bound syndromes** (American Psychiatric Association, 2000; Osborne, 2001). One example is **Dhat syndrome**, a culture-bound syndrome found primarily in India that characterizes men who have intense fears of losing semen during nocturnal emissions. Culture-bound syndromes often reflect exaggerated forms of commonly held superstitions and folk beliefs of a particular culture. In Indian culture, there is a popular folk belief that loss of semen is harmful because it depletes the man's body of its vital natural energy (Chadda & Ahuja, 1990).

Culture-Bound Syndromes   Culture-bound syndromes are found in only one culture, or perhaps a few, and may represent exaggerated forms of commonly held superstitions and beliefs.

hallucinations   Perceptions experienced in the absence of external stimuli.
delusions   Fixed but patently false beliefs, such as believing that one is being hounded by demons.
culture-bound syndromes   Psychological disorders found in only one or a few cultures.
Dhat syndrome   A culture-bound syndrome found in India in which men develop intense fears about losing semen.

Alternatively, the same behavior may be judged abnormal at some points in time but not at others. For example, although the American Psychiatric Association once classified homosexuality as a type of mental disorder, it no longer does so. Many professionals today consider homosexuality a variation of sexual behavior rather than an abnormal behavior pattern.

Applying the Criteria Reconsider the examples of Claire and Phil described at the start of this chapter. Is their behavior abnormal? Claire's behavior certainly met several of the criteria of abnormal behavior. It was clearly unusual as well as socially deviant, and it represented what most people would take to be a delusion—believing you are protecting the community from demons. It was also clearly maladaptive and dangerous, because it put at risk not only Claire herself but also the drivers who were forced to swerve out of the way to avoid hitting her.

Phil, on the other hand, had good contact with reality. He understood that his fears exceeded the dangers he faced. Yet his phobia was a source of considerable emotional distress and was maladaptive because it impaired his ability to carry out his occupational and family responsibilities. We might also employ a criterion of unusualness here. Relatively few people have such fears of confinement that they avoid flying or taking elevators. Yet, as we have noted, unusualness alone is not a sufficient criterion for abnormality.

The behavior of these individuals could be considered abnormal, although they invoke different criteria. Overall, professionals apply multiple criteria when making judgments about abnormality.

Models of Abnormal Behavior

Abnormal behavior has existed in all societies, even though the view of what is or is not abnormal varies from culture to culture and has changed over time. In some cases, these explanations have led to humane treatment of people with abnormal behavior, but more frequently, people deemed to be "mad" or mentally ill were treated cruelly or harshly.

Early Beliefs Throughout much of Western history, from ancient times through the Middle Ages, people thought that those displaying abnormal behavior were controlled by supernatural forces or possessed by demonic spirits. Beliefs in supernatural causes of abnormal behavior, especially the doctrine of demonic possession, held sway until the rise of scientific thinking in the seventeenth and eighteenth centuries. The treatment of choice for demonic possession—*exorcism*—was used to ferret out satanic forces or the Devil himself from the afflicted person's body. If that didn't work, there were even more forceful "remedies," such as the torture rack. Not surprisingly, many recipients of these "cures" attempted to the best of their ability to modify their behavior to meet social expectations.

The Medical Model The eighteenth and nineteenth centuries were times of rapid advances in medical science. Among the more notable advances were the development of a vaccine against the ancient scourge of smallpox, the discovery of the bacterial causes of diseases such as anthrax and leprosy, and the introduction of antiseptics in surgery to prevent infections. It was against this backdrop of medical discovery and shifts from religious dogma to scientific or naturalistic explanations of human behavior that the first modern model of abnormal behavior was developed, the **medical model**. The medical model is based on the belief that abnormal behavior patterns represent *mental illnesses* that have a biological, not demonic, basis and can be classified by their particular characteristics, or symptoms.

Psychological Models Even as the medical model was taking shape, theorists were actively developing psychological models of abnormal behavior. The first

Exorcism Exorcism was used in medieval times to expel evil spirits from people believed to be possessed.

CONCEPT 13.3
Throughout much of Western history, the prevailing view of abnormal behavior was based on a concept of demonic possession.

CONCEPT 13.4
With the rise of scientific thought, attention began to shift from religious dogma to scientific or naturalistic explanations of human behavior.

medical model A framework for understanding abnormal behavior patterns as symptoms of underlying physical disorders or diseases.

CONCEPT 13.5

Psychodynamic, behavioral, humanistic, and cognitive models focus on the psychological roots of abnormal behavior.

Online Study Center
Improve Your Grade
Tutorials: One Disorder—Many Causes

major psychological model of abnormal behavior was the psychodynamic model developed by Sigmund Freud. Freud believed that abnormal behavior arises from unconscious conflicts during childhood that remain unresolved. These conflicts result from the need to control primitive sexual and aggressive impulses or to channel them into socially acceptable outlets. Psychological symptoms (a phobia, for example) are merely the outward expressions of inner turmoil. The person may be aware of the symptom (the phobia) but not of the unconscious conflicts that gave rise to it. Contemporary psychodynamic theorists differ from Freud in some respects, but they retain the central belief that unconscious conflicts are at the root of abnormal behavior patterns.

At about the time that Freud was plumbing the depths of the unconscious, behaviorists were exploring the role of learning in the development of abnormal behavior. Pavlov's discovery of the conditioned response gave the early behaviorist movement a model for studying how maladaptive behaviors, such as phobias, could be learned or acquired through experience. The behavioral model is based on the belief that most forms of abnormal behavior are learned in the same ways that normal behavior is learned. Among the early demonstrations of the role of learning in the development of abnormal behavior was the experiment with "Little Albert" (discussed in Chapter 5). In this experiment, John B. Watson and his colleague Rosalie Rayner (1920) induced a fear of white rats in a young boy by presenting a noxious stimulus (a loud banging sound) whenever a rat was brought close to the child. The repeated pairing of the conditioned stimulus (rat) and unconditioned stimulus (loud banging) instilled a conditioned response (fear evoked by the rat itself).

The humanistic model offers another psychological perspective on abnormal behavior. Humanistic theorists such as Carl Rogers and Abraham Maslow rejected the belief that human behavior is the product of either unconscious processes or simple conditioning. Human beings, they argued, possess an intrinsic ability to make conscious choices and to strive toward self-actualization. Abnormal behavior develops when people encounter roadblocks on the path toward personal growth or self-actualization. To satisfy the demands of others to think, feel, and act in certain ways, people may become detached from their true selves and develop a distorted self-image that can lead to emotional problems such as anxiety and depression. Humanistic theorists believe that people with psychological problems need to become more aware of their true feelings and come to accept themselves for who they truly are.

Cognitive theorists, such as Albert Ellis and Aaron Beck, believe that irrational or distorted thinking leads to emotional problems and maladaptive behavior. Examples of faulty styles of thinking include magnifying or exaggerating the consequences of negative events ("making mountains out of molehills") and interpreting events in an overly negative way, as though one were seeing things through blue-colored glasses.

CONCEPT 13.6

The sociocultural model views abnormal behavior in terms of the social and cultural contexts in which it occurs.

The Sociocultural Model The sociocultural model views the causes of abnormal behavior within the broader social and cultural contexts in which the behavior develops. Theorists in this tradition believe that abnormal behavior may have more to do with social ills or failures of society than with problems within the individual. Accordingly, they examine a range of social and cultural influences on behavior, including social class, poverty, ethnic and cultural background, and racial and gender discrimination. Sociocultural theorists believe that the stress of coping with poverty and social disadvantage can eventually take its toll on mental health. This view receives support from a study showing that severe forms of abnormal behavior, such as schizophrenia and depression, occur proportionately more often among poor and socially disadvantaged groups (Ostler et al., 2001). Recent evidence also connects perceptions of discrimination to increased risk of drug use among African Americans (Gibbons et al., 2004).

Sociocultural theorists also focus on the effects of labeling people as mentally ill. They recognize that because of social prejudices, people who are labeled mentally ill are often denied job or housing opportunities and become stigmatized or marginalized in society. These theorists join with other professionals in arguing for greater understanding and support for people with mental health problems.

The Biopsychosocial Model Today we have many different models to explain abnormal behavior. Indeed, because there are different ways of looking at a given phenomenon, we can't conclude that one particular model is necessarily right and all the others wrong. Each of these models—medical, psychological, and sociocultural—has something unique to offer our understanding of abnormal behavior. None offers a complete view.

CONCEPT 13.7
Today there is increasing convergence toward a biopsychosocial model of abnormal behavior, which focuses on the contributions and interactions of biological and psychosocial influences.

Abnormal behavior presents us with many puzzles as we attempt to unravel its causes. How is mental functioning affected by biology—by genes, brain structures, and neurotransmitter systems? What psychological factors are involved, such as underlying motives or conflicts, personality traits, cognitions, and learned behaviors? And how is our behavior affected by society and culture? Many psychologists today subscribe to the view that most forms of abnormal behavior are not simply products of biology or environment alone; rather, they result from complex interactions of biological, psychological, and sociocultural factors (Andreasen, 2003). The view that multiple factors representing these different domains interact in the development of abnormal behavior is called the **biopsychosocial model**. We are only beginning to put together the pieces of what has turned out to be a very complicated puzzle—the subtle and often complex patterns of underlying factors that give rise to abnormal behavior patterns. Where genes are involved, they create a *predisposition* of *likelihood* for the development of the disorder under certain conditions, but whether the disorder emerges depends on many other factors, including environmental influences.

A prominent example of the biopsychosocial model is the **diathesis-stress model**. According to this model, certain people have a vulnerability or predisposition, called a **diathesis**, which increases their risks of developing a particular disorder. Though usually genetic in nature, the diathesis may include other biological factors, such as complications during pregnancy and childbirth, and psychological factors such as maladaptive personality traits or dysfunctional thinking patterns (Harris & Curtin, 2002; Just, Abramson, & Alloy, 2001; Zvolensky et al., 2005).

In the diathesis-stress model, the question of whether a person with a diathesis goes on to develop the disorder depends on the level of stress he or she experiences. Stressors may include complications during pregnancy or childbirth, family conflict, prolonged unemployment, loss of loved ones, physical or sexual abuse, brain trauma, or infectious illness (Jablensky et al., 2005). If the person encounters a low level of stress or has effective skills for handling stress, the disorder may never emerge even if a diathesis is present. But the stronger the diathesis, the less stress is typically needed to produce the disorder (see Figure 13.1). In some cases, the diathesis may be so strong that the disorder develops even under the most benign life circumstances.

biopsychosocial model An integrative model for explaining abnormal behavior patterns in terms of the interactions of biological, psychological, and sociocultural factors.

diathesis-stress model A type of biopsychosocial model that relates the development of disorders to the combination of a diathesis, or predisposition, usually genetic in origin, and exposure to stressful events or life circumstances.

diathesis A vulnerability or predisposition to developing a disorder.

psychological disorders Abnormal behavior patterns characterized by disturbances in behavior, thinking, perceptions, or emotions that are associated with significant personal distress or impaired functioning. Also called *mental disorders* or *mental illnesses*.

What Are Psychological Disorders?

Distinctive patterns of abnormal behavior are classified as **psychological disorders**—also known as *mental disorders* or *mental illnesses* within the medical model. Psychological disorders involve disturbances of mood, behavior, thought processes, or perception that result in significant personal distress or impaired functioning. Examples of psychological disorders include schizophrenia, anxiety disorders such as phobias and panic disorder, and mood disorders such as major depression.

Figure 13.1 The Diathesis-Stress Model
The diathesis-stress model posits that the development of particular disorders involves an interaction of a predisposition (diathesis), usually genetic in nature, and exposure to life stress.

Source: Nevid, Rathus, & Greene, 2003.

Diathesis
A predisposition or vulnerability

Inherited predisposition to develop the disorder

Stress
Environmental stressors

• Prenatal trauma
• Childhood sexual or physical abuse
• Family conflict
• Significant life changes

Development of the Disorder
The stronger the diathesis, the less stress is necessary to produce the disorder

Psychological disorder

CONCEPT 13.8

Psychological disorders are patterns of disturbed behavior, mood, thinking, or perception that cause personal distress or impaired functioning.

CONCEPT 13.9

The DSM, the diagnostic system used most widely for classifying psychological or mental disorders, consists of five dimensions or axes of evaluation.

How Many Are Affected? Psychological disorders are far more common than many people think. You may not have had contact with people severely impaired by psychological disorders, but chances are that either you or someone you know will be affected by a psychological disorder at one time or another. Investigators find that about one in two adult Americans (46 percent) develops a diagnosable psychological disorder at some point in her or his lifetime (Kessler et al., 2005a; see Figure 13.2). About one in four adults (26 percent) experiences a psychological disorder in any given year (Kessler et al., 2005b; The WHO World Mental Health Survey Consortium, 2004). If we also take into account the economic costs of diagnosing and treating these disorders, and the lost productivity and wages that result from them, it is fair to say that virtually everyone is affected by psychological disorders.

How Are Psychological Disorders Classified? One reference book found on the shelves of virtually all mental health professionals and probably dog-eared from repeated use is the *Diagnostic and Statistical Manual of Mental Disorders,* or DSM—currently in a fourth, text-revised edition, the DSM-IV-TR (American Psychiatric Association, 2000). The manual contains descriptions and diagnostic criteria for all recognized psychological disorders, which in the manual are called *mental disorders.*

The DSM classifies mental disorders on the basis of their distinctive features or symptoms. But the DSM goes beyond merely classifying various disorders. It represents a multiaxial system consisting of multiple axes or dimensions that help the examiner conduct a comprehensive evaluation of a person's mental health (see

REALITY CHECK

THE CLAIM Psychological disorders affect relatively few people.

THE EVIDENCE About one in two adult Americans suffers from a diagnosable psychological disorder at some point in his or her lifetime. In any given year, about one in four adults is affected by a psychological disorder. Moreover, the economic and social burdens of caring for people with these disorders impact virtually all of us.

THE TAKE-AWAY MESSAGE Psychological disorders affect nearly all of us to one degree or another.

Figure 13.2 Prevalence of Psychological Disorders
These data were drawn from a representative survey of the U.S. population of people 18 years of age and older. Nearly 50 percent suffered from a diagnosable psychological or mental disorder at some point in their lives. About one in four suffered from a disorder in the past year.

Source: National Comorbidity Survey Replication (NCS-R); Kessler et al., 2005a, 2005b.

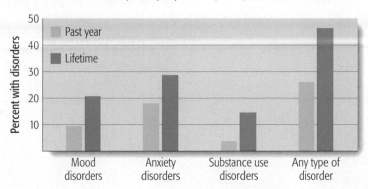

TABLE 13.1   The Multiaxial DSM System

Axis	Type of Information	Brief Description
Axis I	Clinical disorders	Mental disorders that impair functioning or cause distress, including anxiety disorders, mood disorders, dissociative and somatoform disorders, schizophrenia, eating disorders, sleep disorders, and disorders usually first diagnosed in infancy, childhood, or adolescence
	Other conditions that may be a focus of clinical attention	Problems that may warrant attention but do not represent diagnosable mental disorders, such as academic, vocational, or social problems affecting daily functioning
Axis II	Personality disorders	A class of mental disorders characterized by excessively rigid, enduring, and maladaptive ways of relating to others and adjusting to external demands
	Mental retardation	A generalized delay or impairment in the development of intellectual and adaptive skills or abilities
Axis III	General medical conditions	Illnesses and other medical conditions that may be important to the understanding or treatment of the person's psychological disorder
Axis IV	Psychosocial and environmental problems	Problems in the person's social or physical environment that may affect the diagnosis, treatment, and outcome of mental disorders
Axis V	Global assessment of functioning	Overall judgment of the person's level of functioning in meeting the responsibilities of daily life

Source: Adapted from the DSM-IV-TR (American Psychiatric Association, 2000).

Table 13.1). Axis I and Axis II comprise the diagnostic classifications. The DSM classifies mental disorders into several major groupings, including *anxiety disorders, mood disorders, eating disorders,* and *personality disorders.*

Axis III lists general medical conditions and diseases, such as cancer and AIDS, which can affect a person's mental health. Axis IV allows the examiner to note psychosocial and environmental problems that impair the person's ability to function, such as stressful life events, homelessness, and lack of social support. Finally, Axis V allows the examiner to make a global assessment of the person's overall level of functioning in meeting life responsibilities.

Though the DSM is the most widely used diagnostic system, it is not without its critics. Questions remain about the reliability and validity of certain diagnostic classifications (Kendell & Jablensky, 2003; Widiger & Clark, 2000). Some mental health professionals say that the system is based too heavily on the medical model in which abnormal behaviors are assumed to be symptoms of underlying disorders or mental illnesses. Yet many clinicians find the system useful in providing designated criteria to help them formulate diagnostic impressions. Perhaps it is best to think of the DSM as a work in progress rather than as a finished product.

Let us next consider several of the major classes of psychological disorders. The following modules discuss major classes or types of psychological disorders and describe the prominent symptoms of specific disorders represented within each class, the rates of occurrence of these disorders, and theories about their underlying causes. See Concept Chart 13.1 for a listing of the major contemporary models of abnormal behavior.

💡 **CONCEPT CHART 13.1 Contemporary Models of Abnormal Behavior**

Model	Focus	Key Questions
Medical model	Biological underpinnings of abnormal behavior	What role is played by neurotransmitters in abnormal behavior? By genetics? By brain abnormalities?
Psychodynamic model	Unconscious conflicts and motives underlying abnormal behavior	How do particular symptoms represent or symbolize unconscious conflicts? What are the childhood roots of a person's problem?
Behavioral model	Learning experiences that shape the development of abnormal behavior	How are abnormal patterns of behavior learned? What role does the environment play in explaining abnormal behavior?
Humanistic model	Roadblocks that hinder self-awareness and self-acceptance	How do a person's emotional problems reflect a distorted self-image? What roadblocks did the person encounter in the path toward self-acceptance and self-realization?
Cognitive model	Faulty thinking underlying abnormal behavior	What styles of thinking characterize people with particular types of psychological disorders? What role do personal beliefs, thoughts, and ways of interpreting events play in the development of abnormal behavior patterns?
Sociocultural model	Social ills contributing to the development of abnormal behavior, such as poverty, racism, and prolonged unemployment; relationships between abnormal behavior and ethnicity, gender, culture, and socioeconomic level	What relationships exist between social-class status and risks of psychological disorders? Are there gender or ethnic group differences in various disorders? How are these explained? What are the effects of stigmatization of people who are labeled mentally ill?
Biopsychosocial model	Interactions of biological, psychological, and sociocultural factors in the development of abnormal behavior	How might genetic or other factors predispose individuals to psychological disorders in the face of life stress? How do biological, psychological, and sociocultural factors interact in the development of complex patterns of abnormal behavior?

MODULE 13.1 REVIEW

What Is Abnormal Behavior?

RECITE IT

What criteria are used to determine whether behavior is abnormal?

- Several criteria are used, including unusualness, social deviance, emotional distress, maladaptive behavior, dangerousness, and faulty perceptions or interpretations of reality.

What are the major models of abnormal behavior?

- The major contemporary models are the medical, psychological, sociocultural, and biopsychosocial (integrative) models.

What are psychological disorders?

- Varying in symptoms and severity, psychological disorders (also called *mental disorders*) are disturbances in behavior, thought processes, or emotions that are associated with significant personal distress or impaired functioning. About one person in two in the United States develops a diagnosable psychological disorder at some point in life.

- The DSM (*Diagnostic and Statistical Manual of Mental Disorders*) is the American Psychiatric Association's diagnostic manual for classifying mental disorders.

RECALL IT

1. List the six criteria for defining abnormal behavior discussed in the text.

2. _____ are distorted perceptions of reality; _____ are fixed but unfounded beliefs.
   a. delusions; hallucinations
   b. dreams; fantasies
   c. fantasies; dreams
   d. hallucinations; delusions

3. The explanation for abnormal behavior during much of the history of Western civilization was
   a. brain malfunction or chemical disorder.
   b. harsh and cruel treatment by close family members.
   c. possession by demons or supernatural forces.
   d. falsehoods or other retaliation spread by a sufferer's enemies.

4. Match the following psychological models for abnormal behavior with the appropriate descriptions: i. psychodynamic; ii. behavioral; iii. humanistic; iv. cognitive
   a. distorted self-image, loss of sense of true self
   b. faulty styles of thinking, exaggeration of negative aspects of events
   c. learned patterns of behavior
   d. unresolved unconscious conflicts dating from childhood

5. The _____ model is a leading example of the biopsychosocial model.

THINK ABOUT IT

- Where should we draw the line between normal and abnormal behavior? Is heavy use of body-piercing abnormal or simply a fashion statement? Is excessive shopping behavior, or even excessive use of the Internet, a form of mental illness? Is bullying a feature of a psychological disorder or simply "bad behavior"?

- What criteria do you use to distinguish between normal and abnormal behavior? How do the criteria you use stack up against those described in the text?

MODULE 13.2

Anxiety Disorders

- **What are anxiety disorders?**
- **What causal factors are implicated in anxiety disorders?**

CONCEPT 13.10
An anxiety disorder is a psychological disorder characterized by excessive or inappropriate anxiety reactions.

CONCEPT 13.11
The major types of anxiety disorders are phobias, panic disorder, generalized anxiety disorder, obsessive-compulsive disorder, and posttraumatic stress disorder.

anxiety disorders A class of psychological disorders characterized by excessive or inappropriate anxiety reactions.

There is much we might be anxious about—our health, our jobs, our families, the hole in the ozone layer, the state of the nation and the world. Indeed, anxiety can be an adaptive response in some situations. It can motivate us to study before an exam and to seek regular medical checkups, for example. But when anxiety is excessive in a given situation or interferes with the ability to function, it can become abnormal. *Fear* is the term we use to describe anxiety experienced in specific situations, as when boarding an airplane or taking a final exam.

Types of Anxiety Disorders

Anxiety disorders are among the most commonly experienced psychological disorders among adults. Formerly called *neuroses* in earlier diagnostic manuals, these disorders are characterized by excessive or inappropriate anxiety reactions. The major types of anxiety disorders are phobias, panic disorder, generalized anxiety disorder, and obsessive-compulsive disorder. A fifth major type, posttraumatic stress disorder, is discussed in Chapter 15.

Panic Attack   The symptoms associated with a panic attack, such as shortness of breath and a pounding heart, may lead people to think they are having a heart attack and are about to die.

Phobias   **Phobias** are irrational or excessive fears of particular objects or situations. The DSM classifies three types of phobic disorders: *social phobia, specific phobia,* and *agoraphobia.* People with **social phobia** have intense fears of social interactions, such as meeting others, dating, or giving a speech or presentation in class. People with **specific phobia** have excessive fears of specific situations or objects, such as animals, insects, heights (**acrophobia**), or enclosed spaces (**claustrophobia**). People with **agoraphobia** fear venturing into open places or going out in public.

People with claustrophobia may refuse to use elevators despite the inconvenience of climbing many flights of stairs several times a day. Those with agoraphobia may become literally housebound, unable even to go to the local store to buy a quart of milk. And those with social phobia may have difficulty maintaining a normal social life. People with phobias usually recognize that their fears are irrational or excessive but they still avoid the objects or situations they fear.

Panic Disorder   People with **panic disorder** experience sudden episodes of sheer terror called *panic attacks.* Panic attacks are characterized by intense physical symptoms: profuse sweating, nausea, numbness or tingling, flushes or chills, trembling, chest pain, shortness of breath, and pounding of the heart. These symptoms may lead people to think they are having a heart attack, "going crazy," or losing control. A specific attack can last anywhere from a few minutes to more than an hour. One person recounted the experience by saying "All of a sudden, I felt a tremendous wave of fear for no reason at all. My heart was pounding, my chest hurt, and it was getting harder to breathe. I thought I was going to die."

Panic attacks initially seem to come "out of the blue." Yet they can later become connected with the situations in which they occur, such as shopping in a crowded department store or riding on a train. Agoraphobia, too, sometimes develops in people with panic disorder when they begin avoiding public places out of fear of having panic attacks while away from the security of their homes.

phobias   Excessive fears of particular objects or situations.

social phobia   A type of anxiety disorder involving excessive fear of social situations.

specific phobia   Phobic reactions involving specific situations or objects.

acrophobia   Excessive fear of heights.

claustrophobia   Excessive fear of enclosed spaces.

agoraphobia   Excessive, irrational fear of being in public places.

panic disorder   A type of anxiety disorder involving repeated episodes of sheer terror called panic attacks.

generalized anxiety disorder (GAD)   A type of anxiety disorder involving persistent and generalized anxiety and worry.

obsessive-compulsive disorder (OCD)   A type of anxiety disorder involving the repeated occurrence of obsessions and/or compulsions.

Generalized Anxiety Disorder   People with **generalized anxiety disorder (GAD)** experience persistent anxiety that is not tied to any particular object or situation. In such cases the anxiety has a "free-floating" quality, as it seems to travel with the person from place to place. The key feature of GAD is excessive worry. People with the disorder tend to worry over just about everything. They are seldom if ever free of worry. Other characteristics of GAD include shakiness, inability to relax, fidgeting, and feelings of dread and foreboding (Fricchione, 2004).

Obsessive-Compulsive Disorder   Have you ever had a thought you couldn't shake off? Have you ever felt compelled to repeat the same behavior again and again? People with **obsessive-compulsive disorder (OCD)** experience persistent obsessions and/or compulsions. Obsessions are nagging, intrusive thoughts the person feels unable to control. Compulsions are repetitive behaviors or rituals the person feels compelled to perform again and again. Some people with this disorder are obsessed with the thought that germs contaminate their skin, spending hours each day compulsively washing their hands or showering. Others repeatedly perform checking rituals upon leaving the house to ensure that the doors and windows are securely locked and the gas jets on the stove are turned off.

CONCEPT 13.12
Both biological factors, such as disturbed neurotransmitter functioning, and psychological factors, such as learning experiences, are implicated as causal influences in anxiety disorders.

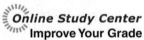
Online Study Center
Improve Your Grade
Tutorials: What's Your Anxiety Level?

Online Study Center
Improve Your Grade
Tutorials: The Case of the Confused Clerk

anxiety sensitivity Fear of fear, involving excessive concern that anxiety symptoms will spin out of control.

Causes of Anxiety Disorders

Nearly everyone experiences anxiety from time to time, but only some people develop anxiety disorders. Although we don't know precisely why these disorders develop, we can identify biological and psychological factors that contribute to them, and surmise that an interaction of these factors affects their development.

Biological Factors   Evidence from studies of twins and adoptees supports a role for heredity in the development of many anxiety disorders, including panic disorder, generalized anxiety disorder, obsessive-compulsive disorder, and phobic disorders (Hettema et al., 2003; Kendler, 2005; Rapee & Spence, 2004).

Other biological causes have also been implicated. Regarding panic disorder, for example, one possibility is that biochemical changes in the brain involving neurotransmitter imbalances trigger a kind of internal alarm system that induces feelings of panic in susceptible people (Glass, 2000; Klein, 1993). In people with OCD, evidence also points to overactivity in the parts of the brain involved in states of worry and anxiety (e.g., Mataix-Cols et al., 2004; Szeszko et al., 2004). The brains of people with this disorder may be continually sending messages that something is terribly wrong and requires immediate attention—a situation that then leads to obsessional, worrisome thoughts. The compulsive aspect of OCD may result from disturbances in brain circuits that normally curtail repetitive behaviors.

Psychological Factors   Some phobias may be learned through classical conditioning in which a previously neutral or benign stimulus becomes paired with an aversive stimulus. A person bitten by a dog during childhood may come to develop a fear of dogs or other small animals; a person trapped in an elevator for hours may acquire a fear of elevators or of confinement in other enclosed spaces. The previously neutral stimulus is the conditioned stimulus (CS), the aversive stimulus is the unconditioned stimulus (US), and the acquired fear response is the conditioned response (CR).

Operant conditioning may help account for avoidance behavior. Avoidance of the phobic object or situation (as when a person with an elevator phobia takes the stairs instead of the elevator) is negatively reinforced by relief from anxiety. However, though avoiding a fearful situation may offer short-term relief from anxiety, it doesn't help people overcome their fears. (The principle of negative reinforcement is discussed in Chapter 5.)

Negative reinforcement (relief from anxiety) may also contribute to obsessive-compulsive disorder. People with OCD often become trapped in a repetitive cycle of obsessive thinking and compulsive behavior. Obsessive thoughts ("my hands are covered with germs") trigger anxiety, which, in turn, is partially relieved through performance of a compulsive ritual (repetitive hand-washing). But since relief from the obsessive thoughts is incomplete or fleeting, the thoughts soon return, prompting yet more compulsive behavior—and so on in a continuing cycle.

Cognitive models of panic disorder focus on the interrelationship between biological and psychological factors. One leading cognitive model holds that people with panic attacks misinterpret minor changes in bodily sensations (e.g., sudden light-headedness or dizziness) as signs of an imminent catastrophe, such as an impending heart attack or loss of control (Clark, 1986). These misinterpretations generate symptoms of anxiety (sweating, racing heart), which, like falling dominoes, lead to more catastrophic thinking, then to more anxiety symptoms, and so on in a cycle that may quickly spiral into a full-blown panic attack (see Figure 13.3). Internal cues (dizziness, heart palpitations) and external cues (boarding a crowded elevator) that were connected with panic attacks in the past may also become conditioned stimuli (CSs) that elicit anxiety or panicky symptoms when the person encounters them (Bouton, Mineka, & Barlow, 2001).

Other cognitive factors also play key roles in anxiety disorders. Social phobias, for example, can arise from excessive concerns about social embarrassment or being judged negatively by others. People with high levels of **anxiety sensitivity**, or fear of fear itself, may overreact to anxiety symptoms, which in turn can lead to escalating anxiety that culminates in a full-fledged panic attack (Zinbarg et al., 2001). A recent study of high school students over a four-year period showed that

Figure 13.3   Cognitive Model of Panic
Cognitive theorists conceptualize panic disorder in terms of a panic cycle that involves an interaction of physiological and cognitive factors. A triggering stimulus, such as sudden light-headedness or boarding a crowded train, sets the cycle in motion. The stimulus is perceived as threatening, leading to feelings of apprehension (anxiety and worry), which in turn lead to bodily sensations associated with anxiety, such as a tightening feeling in the chest. These sensations are misconstrued as signs of an impending catastrophe—a heart attack, for example. Perceptions of threat are increased, further raising the level of anxiety, and so on in a vicious cycle that can quickly spiral into a full-fledged panic attack.

Source: Adapted from Clark, 1986.

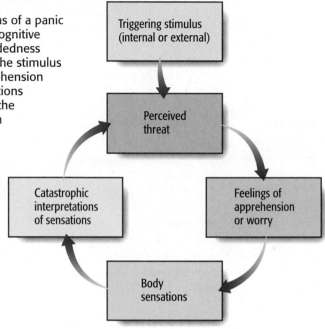

CONCEPT CHART 13.2   Anxiety Disorders

Type of Disorder	Lifetime Prevalence in Population (%)	Symptoms	Associated Features
Social phobia	3 to 13.3	Fear and avoidance of social situations	Social phobia is characterized by an underlying fear of rejection, humiliation, or embarrassment in social situations.
Specific phobia	7 to 13	Fear and avoidance of specific objects or situations	Avoidance of the phobic object or situation is negatively reinforced by relief from anxiety.
Agoraphobia	6 to 7	Fear and avoidance of public places	Agoraphobia often develops secondarily to panic disorder, as the person attempts to avoid situations in which attacks have occurred or in which help might be unavailable in the event of an attack.
Panic disorder	1 to 4	Repeated panic attacks accompanied by persistent concern about future attacks	Panic attacks have strong physiological symptoms; beginning attacks occur without warning.
Generalized anxiety disorder	About 5	Persistent, excessive levels of anxiety and worry	Anxiety has a free-floating quality in that it is not tied to particular objects or situations.
Obsessive-compulsive disorder	2 to 3	Recurrent obsessions and/or compulsions	A repetitive cycle may ensue in which obsessive thoughts engender anxiety that, in turn, is partially relieved (negatively reinforced) by performing the compulsive ritual.

Note: Another type of anxiety disorder, posttraumatic stress disorder, is discussed in Chapter 15.
Sources: American Psychiatric Association, 2000; Furmark, 2002; Magee et al., 1996; Rapee & Spence, 2004; USDHHS, 1999.

those with high levels of anxiety sensitivity had an increased risk of experiencing panic attacks (Weems et al., 2002).

Compulsive checkers may have difficulty remembering whether they have completed the task correctly, such as turning off the toaster oven before leaving for the day. Evidence shows that compulsive checkers tend to underperform on many types of memory tasks (Woods et al., 2002). The degree to which impaired memory may contribute to compulsive checking remains for future researchers to determine.

In sum, anxiety disorders reflect the interplay of biological and psychological factors. Before going further, you may wish to review the summary of anxiety disorders presented in Concept Chart 13.2.

MODULE 13.2 REVIEW

Anxiety Disorders

RECITE IT

What are anxiety disorders?

- Anxiety disorders are characterized by excessive or inappropriate anxiety reactions.
- Anxiety disorders include phobias, panic disorder, generalized anxiety disorder, obsessive-compulsive disorder, and posttraumatic stress disorder.

What causal factors are implicated in anxiety disorders?

- These include psychological factors, such as prior learning experiences and thinking patterns, and biological factors, such as genetic influences, imbalances of neurotransmitters in the brain, and underlying brain abnormalities.

RECALL IT

1. An intense anxiety reaction in which people may think they are suffering a heart attack is called a _____ attack.

2. Acrophobia and claustrophobia are two examples of _____ phobia.

3. Match the following anxiety disorders with the appropriate descriptions: i. specific phobia; ii. panic disorder; iii. generalized anxiety disorder; iv. obsessive-compulsive disorder

   a. sudden onset; intense fear and dread
   b. excessive, persistent worry
   c. irrational, extreme fear of a particular object or situation
   d. repeated, uncontrollable thoughts or behaviors

THINK ABOUT IT

- Apply learning principles to explain the development of specific types of anxiety disorders, including specific fears and obsessive-compulsive disorder.

- Is anxiety normal? What might evolutionary psychologists say about the survival value of anxiety? When does a normal response become abnormal?

- Have you ever "panicked"? Do you think you suffered a true panic attack? Why or why not?

MODULE 13.3
Dissociative and Somatoform Disorders

- What are dissociative disorders and somatoform disorders?
- What causal factors are implicated in dissociative and somatoform disorders?

Among the most puzzling psychological disorders are the **dissociative disorders** and **somatoform disorders**. People with dissociative disorders may show multiple personalities, have amnesia that cannot be explained by a physical cause, or even assume a completely new self-identity. The dissociative disorders are fodder for countless television melodramas and soap operas. In real life they are relatively uncommon, even rare. Indeed, there is controversy among professionals as to whether multiple personality (now called *dissociative identity disorder*) even exists.

Although they have different symptoms or characteristics, dissociative disorders and somatoform disorders are often grouped together because of the classic view that they involve psychological defenses against anxiety. Here we examine several of these mystifying disorders, beginning with dissociative disorders.

Dissociative Disorders

Dissociative disorders involve problems with memory or changes in consciousness or self-identity that fracture the continuity or wholeness of an individual's personality. Normally we know who we are and where we've been. We may forget how we spent last weekend, but we don't suddenly lose the capacity to remember whole chunks of our lives or abruptly shift back and forth between very different personalities. Dissociative disorders, however, affect the ability to maintain a cohesive sense of self or unity of consciousness, resulting in unusual, even bizarre behavior. Let us consider two major types of dissociative disorders: dissociative identity disorder and dissociative amnesia.

Dissociative Identity Disorder   Consider the following case history:

> [Margaret explained that] she often "heard a voice telling her to say things and do things." It was, she said, "a terrible voice" that sometimes threatened to "take over completely." When it was finally suggested to [Margaret] that she let the voice "take over," she closed her eyes, clenched her fists, and grimaced for a few moments during which she was out of contact with those around her. Suddenly she opened her eyes and one was in the presence of another person. Her name, she said, was "Harriet." Whereas Margaret had been paralyzed, and complained of fatigue, headache and backache, Harriet felt well, and she at once proceeded to walk unaided around the interviewing room. She spoke scornfully of Margaret's religiousness, her invalidism, and her puritanical life, professing that she herself liked to drink and "go partying" but that Margaret was always going to church and reading the Bible. "But," she said impishly and proudly, "I make her miserable— I make her say and do things she doesn't want to." At length, at the interviewer's suggestion, Harriet reluctantly agreed to "bring Margaret back," and after more grimacing and fist clenching, Margaret reappeared, paralyzed, complaining of her headache and backache, and completely amnesiac for the brief period of Harriet's release from prison. (Adapted from Nemiah, 1978, pp. 179–180)

In **dissociative identity disorder (DID)**, commonly called *multiple personality* or *split personality,* two or more distinct personalities exist within the same individual. Each of the personalities has its own distinctive traits, manner of speech, and memories—even, in some cases, its own eyeglass prescription (S. D. Miller et al.,

---

CONCEPT 13.13
In dissociative identity disorder, the personality is split into two or more distinct alternate personalities residing within the same individual.

---

dissociative disorders A class of psychological disorders involving changes in consciousness, memory, or self-identity.

somatoform disorders A class of psychological disorders involving physical ailments or complaints that cannot be explained by organic causes.

dissociative identity disorder (DID) A type of dissociative disorder characterized by the appearance of multiple personalities in the same individual.

1991). The different personalities may also exhibit varying allergic reactions and responses to medication (Braun, 1986). In some cases, there is a core personality that is generally known to the outside world and hidden *alternate personalities* that reveal themselves at certain times or in certain situations. Sometimes alternate personalities compete for control. The alternate personalities may represent different genders, ages, sexual orientations, or—as in the case of Margaret—conflicting sexual urges. One personality may be morally upright, another licentious; one a heterosexual, another homosexual. The dominant personality may be unaware of the existence of these alternates or of events experienced by other identities (Huntjens et al., 2005). Women with the disorder tend to have fifteen or more identities, whereas men average about eight (American Psychiatric Association, 2000).

CONCEPT 13.14

In dissociative amnesia, people experience a loss of memory for personal information that cannot be explained by a blow to the head or some other physical cause.

Dissociative Amnesia People with *dissociative amnesia* (first discussed in Chapter 6) experience a loss of memory for information about themselves or their life experiences. The absence of any physical cause for their amnesia (a blow to the head, neurological condition, drug or alcohol abuse) suggests that the disorder is psychological in nature. The information lost to memory is usually a traumatic or stressful experience that the person may be motivated to forget. A soldier returning from the battlefield or a survivor of a serious accident may have no memory of the battle or the accident. These memories sometimes return, perhaps gradually in bits and pieces, or suddenly all at once. Much less common, except in the imaginations of soap opera writers, is *generalized amnesia* in which people forget their entire lives. They forget who they are, what they do for a living, and whom they are married or related to. More typically, the amnesia is limited to memories associated with traumatic events that generated strong negative emotions.

Causes of Dissociative Disorders

CONCEPT 13.15

The formation of alternate personalities in dissociative identity disorder may represent a psychological defense against trauma or unbearable abuse.

Dissociative amnesia may represent an attempt to disconnect or dissociate one's conscious state from awareness of traumatic experiences or other sources of psychological pain or conflict (Dorahy, 2001). Dissociative symptoms may protect the self from anxiety that might occur if these memories and experiences became fully conscious. Similarly, individuals with dissociative identity disorder may split off parts of themselves from consciousness. Severe, repetitive physical or sexual abuse in childhood, usually beginning before the age of 5, figures prominently in case histories of people with dissociative identity disorder (Burton & Lane, 2001).

Many people with DID were highly imaginative as children, often creating games of make-believe. In these early years, they may have used their fertile imaginations to split off parts of themselves to distance themselves psychologically from the abusive situations they faced. Over time, these parts may have become consolidated as distinct personalities. And in adulthood, they may continue to use their alternate personalities to block out memories of childhood trauma and of the conflicting emotions that these experiences evoked. The alternate personalities themselves may represent a psychological means of expressing the deep-seated hatred and anger they are unable to integrate within their primary personalities.

Some psychologists believe that DID is a rare but genuine disorder that arises in a few individuals as a way of coping with terrible physical or sexual abuse dating back to childhood. But there are dissenting voices. Among these are authorities who doubt the existence of DID, ascribing the behavior to a form of attention-seeking role playing (Lilienfeld et al., 1999; Spanos, 1994). Perhaps troubled individuals with a history of abuse might inadvertently be cued by their therapists to enact alternate personalities that help them make sense of the confusing and conflicting emotions they experience, eventually identifying so closely with the role they are performing that it becomes a reality to them. This description is not

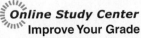

meant to suggest that people with DID are faking their alternate selves, any more than we would suggest that you are faking your behavior whenever you adopt the role of a student, spouse, or worker. Whatever the underlying process in DID may be, authorities agree that people with the disorder need help dealing with the underlying traumas they have experienced and working through the often-conflicting emotions and impulses these brutal experiences evoked.

Somatoform Disorders

People with somatoform disorders have physical ailments or complaints that cannot be explained medically (Creed & Barsky, 2004; Rief & Sharpe, 2004). Or they may hold the belief that they are gravely ill, despite reassurances from their doctors to the contrary. One type of somatoform disorder, **conversion disorder**, figured prominently in the history of psychology. It was conversion disorder—called *hysteria* or *hysterical neurosis* at the time—that attracted a young physician named Sigmund Freud to study the psychological bases of abnormal behavior.

CONCEPT 13.16
People with conversion disorder experience a loss of a physical function that defies medical explanation.

Conversion Disorder   In conversion disorder, a person suffers a loss of physical function, such as loss of movement in a limb (hysterical paralysis), loss of vision (hysterical blindness), or loss of feeling in a hand or arm (anesthesia) (Sar et al., 2004). Yet there is no physical cause that can account for these symptoms. Conversion disorder or hysteria appears to have been much more common in Freud's day but is relatively rare today. In Freud's time, hysteria was considered a female problem; however, experience with male soldiers in combat who experience a loss of function (blindness or paralysis) that cannot be explained medically has taught us that the disorder can affect both men and women.

If you suddenly lost feeling in your hand, you would probably be quite upset. But curiously, some people with conversion symptoms appear indifferent to their situations—a phenomenon called *la belle indifférence* ("beautiful indifference"). This lack of concern suggests that the symptoms may be of psychological value to the individual, perhaps representing a way of avoiding anxiety associated with painful or stressful conflicts or situations.

Let us note that many cases, perhaps as many as four out of five, that initially appear to be conversion disorders turn out upon further testing to be unrecognized medical conditions (Fishbain & Goldberg, 1991). In other cases, the causes remain obscure and are believed to be psychological in nature.

CONCEPT 13.17
People with hypochondriasis mistakenly believe that their minor physical complaints are signs of serious underlying illness.

Hypochondriasis   People with **hypochondriasis** are preoccupied with the idea that there is something terribly wrong with their health. They attribute their physical complaints or symptoms to a serious underlying disease, perhaps cancer or heart disease (Barsky & Ahem, 2004). Though they may receive assurances from their doctors that their concerns are groundless, they believe the doctors are wrong or may have missed something. They may not realize how their anxiety about their symptoms contributes to their physical complaints—for example, by leading to sweating, dizziness, rapid heartbeat, and other signs of sympathetic nervous system arousal. Not surprisingly, they have more health worries and more psychological problems than do other people.

Causes of Somatoform Disorders

To Freud, the hysterical symptom (loss of movement in a limb) is the outward sign of an unconscious dynamic struggle between opposing motives. On the one side are the sexual or aggressive impulses of the id seeking expression. On the other side are the forces of restraint, marshaled by the ego. The ego seeks to protect the self from the flood of anxiety that would occur if these unacceptable impulses

conversion disorder   A type of somatoform disorder characterized by a change or a loss of a physical function that cannot be explained by medical causes.

hypochondriasis   A somatoform disorder in which there is excessive concern that one's physical complaints are signs of underlying serious illness.

CONCEPT CHART 13.3 Dissociative and Somatoform Disorders

	Type of Disorder	Lifetime Prevalence	Features	Comments
Dissociative Disorders	Dissociative identity disorder	Rare	Development of multiple personalities within the same individual	May represent a type of psychological defense against trauma or unbearable abuse from childhood
	Dissociative amnesia	Rare	Loss of memory that cannot be explained as the result of head trauma or other physical cause	Typically involves loss of memories associated with specific traumatic events
Somatoform Disorders	Conversion disorder	Rare	A loss or change of physical function that cannot be explained by a medical condition	Appears to have been much more common in Freud's day than our own
	Hypochondriasis	Unknown	Preoccupation with fear of having a serious illness	May have features similar to those of anxiety disorders

CONCEPT 13.18

Though Freudian and learning theory explanations of somatoform disorders differ, they both focus on the anxiety-reducing role of somatoform symptoms.

were to become fully conscious. It employs defense mechanisms, especially repression, to keep these impulses buried in the unconscious. The leftover energy from these impulses becomes "strangulated," or cut off from its source, and is then converted into physical symptoms like paralysis or blindness. One problem with Freud's view, however, is that it doesn't explain how conversion occurs—that is, how leftover sexual or aggressive energy becomes channeled into particular physical symptoms (Miller, 1987).

Freud also believed that the symptom serves an underlying hidden purpose. For instance, hysterical paralysis of the arm serves the purpose of preventing the person from using the arm to act out an unacceptable sexual (e.g., masturbatory) or aggressive (e.g., murderous) impulse. The symptom has yet another function, called **secondary gain**. It can prevent the individual from having to confront stressful or conflict-laden situations. If Freud was correct in his belief that conversion symptoms serve hidden purposes, it may explain why many people with conversion appear strangely unconcerned or untroubled about their symptoms.

Learning theorists, too, recognize that conversion symptoms may serve a secondary role of helping the individual avoid painful or anxiety-evoking situations. (The bomber pilot who develops hysterical night blindness may avoid the danger of night missions, for example.) People with conversion disorders may also be reinforced by others for adopting a "sick role," drawing sympathy and support from them and being relieved of ordinary work or household responsibilities. This is not to suggest that such individuals are consciously faking their symptoms. Perhaps they are deceiving themselves, but they do not appear to be deliberately faking.

Cognitive theorists focus on cognitive biases associated with somatoform disorders (e.g., Cororve & Gleaves, 2001; Salkovskis & Clark, 1993). People with hypochondriasis, for example, may "make mountains out of molehills" by misinterpreting bodily sensations as signs of underlying catastrophic causes (cancer, heart disease, etc.). In this respect they may resemble people with panic disorder, who tend to misinterpret their bodily sensations as signs of an impending catastrophe. Dissociative and somatoform disorders are summarized in Concept Chart 13.3.

secondary gain The reward value of having a psychological or physical symptom, such as release from ordinary responsibilities.

MODULE 13.3 REVIEW

Dissociative and Somatoform Disorders

RECITE IT

What are dissociative disorders and somatoform disorders?

- Dissociative disorders involve disturbances in memory, consciousness, or identity that affect the ability to maintain an integrated sense of self. These disorders include dissociative identity disorder and dissociative amnesia.

- People with somatoform disorders either exaggerate the meaning of physical complaints (hypochondriasis) or have physical complaints that cannot be accounted for by underlying medical or organic causes (conversion disorder).

What casual factors are implicated in dissociative and somatoform disorders?

- Exposure to childhood abuse figures prominently in the backgrounds of people with dissociative identity disorder, leading theorists to believe the disorder may represent a psychological defense that protects the self from troubling memories or feelings. Avoidance of painful or troubling memories is also implicated in dissociative amnesia.

- Freud believed that conversion disorder represents the transformation of inner psychological conflicts into physical symptoms. Learning theorists focus on the anxiety-reducing roles of somatoform symptoms, while cognitive theorists focus on underlying cognitive biases.

RECALL IT

1. Another term often used to describe dissociative identity disorder is
   a. intermittent neurotic disorder.
   b. multiple personality.
   c. obsessive-compulsive personality.
   d. amnesiac identity disorder.

2. Dissociative amnesia
   a. involves a clear physical underlying cause.
   b. does not seem to be related to a particular traumatic event.
   c. involves extensive and permanent memory loss.
   d. has no apparent neurological cause.

3. Dissociative identity disorder is strongly linked to a history of severe childhood _____ and may represent a form of psychological _____ against unbearable trauma.

4. Which of the following is *not* correct? Conversion disorder
   a. is classified as one of the somatoform disorders.
   b. was known as hysteria in earlier times.
   c. involves loss of a physical function.
   d. is caused by underlying physical problems.

THINK ABOUT IT

- Do you believe that dissociative identity disorder is a true disorder? Or do you think it is an exaggerated form of role playing? Explain your answer.

- People are sometimes labeled as hypochondriacs when others don't believe their physical complaints are genuine. Based on your reading of the text, does the diagnosis of hypochondriasis hinge on whether the physical symptoms are real? If not, what criteria do apply?

MODULE 13.4

Mood Disorders

- **What are mood disorders?**
- **What causal factors are implicated in mood disorders?**

mood disorders A class of psychological disorders involving disturbances in mood states, such as major depression and bipolar disorder.

Most people have occasional ups and downs, but those with **mood disorders** have more severe or persistent disturbances of mood. These mood disturbances limit their ability to function and may even sap their will to live. It is normal to feel sad when unfortunate events occur and to be uplifted when fortune shines on us. But people with mood disorders often feel down when things are going right. Or they remain down following a disappointing experience long after others would have snapped back. Some people with mood disorders have exaggerated mood swings. Their moods may alternate between dizzying heights and abysmal depths.

Types of Mood Disorders

There are two general types of mood disorders: *depressive disorders* and *bipolar disorders*.

Depressive Disorders   Depressive disorders are often called *unipolar disorders* because they involve only the depressive end (or pole) of a spectrum of moods. The most common type of depressive disorder is **major depressive disorder** (also called *major depression*). People with major depression typically feel sad or "down in the dumps" and may experience feelings of worthlessness, changes in sleep or appetite, lethargy, and loss of interest in pleasurable activities. When left untreated, major depressive episodes can last months, even a year or more (Kessler et al., 2003). Some people experience a single episode with a full return to previous levels of functioning. However, the great majority of people who develop major depressive disorder have repeated occurrences (Kennedy, Abbott, & Paykel, 2003).

People with major depression may feel they cannot get out of bed to face the day. They may be unable to make decisions, even about small things, such as what to have for dinner. They may be unable to concentrate. They may feel helpless or say that they don't "care" anymore. They may have recurrent thoughts of suicide or attempt suicide. To help you become more aware of the warning signs of depression, see the Try This Out feature on the next page.

Major depressive disorder affects about 16 percent of adults at some point in their lives (Duenweld, 2003; Kessler et al., 2003). Women in the United States are about twice as likely as men to develop the disorder—5 to 12 percent of men versus 10 to 25 percent of women (NIMH, 2000). Recent evidence shows that the gender difference exists in many countries, including Canada, Brazil, Germany, and Japan (Gilbert, 2004).

Gender differences in depression begin to emerge during adolescence (Consolacion, Russell, & Sue, 2004; Twenge & Nolen-Hoeksema, 2002). Although hormonal or other biological differences between men and women may play a role in explaining the gender gap in depression (Davis, 2002), we also need to consider the greater levels of stress experienced by many women today. Women are more likely to encounter such stressors as physical and sexual abuse, poverty, single parenthood, and sexism. Even when both spouses work, women typically shoulder the bulk of household and childcare chores. Women are also more likely than men to provide support for aging family members or those coping with disabling medical conditions. These additional caregiving burdens add to the stress that women endure.

Differences in how men and women cope with depression may also come into play. Researchers find that men are more likely to distract themselves when they are feeling depressed, whereas women are more likely to ruminate about their problems, which may only worsen their depression (Nolen-Hoeksema et al., 1993, Nolen-Hoeksema & Girgus, 1994). Ruminating or dwelling on one's problems may only worsen depression, whereas distraction may blunt the emotional effects of disappointments and setbacks (Gilbert, 2004). Among both men and women, those who ruminate more when feeling down or sad are more likely to become depressed than those who ruminate less (Just & Alloy, 1997; Nolen-Hoeksema, 2000).

Seasonal affective disorder (SAD) is a type of major depression in which people experience a repeated pattern of severe depression in the fall and winter, followed by elevated moods during the spring and summer. SAD has been treated successfully with exposure to bright artificial light as a kind of substitute for natural sunlight (Terman, Terman, & Cooper, 2001).

💡 **CONCEPT 13.19**
The two major types of mood disorders are depressive (unipolar) disorders and bipolar (mood swing) disorders.

💡 **CONCEPT 13.20**
Depressive disorders include major depressive disorder, a relatively severe form of depression, and dysthymic disorder, a chronic but milder form of depression.

Gender Differences in Depression   Many psychologists believe that the stressors faced by many women today contribute to their increased risk of depression.

major depressive disorder   The most common type of depressive disorder, characterized by periods of downcast mood, feelings of worthlessness, and loss of interest in pleasurable activities.

seasonal affective disorder (SAD)   A type of major depression that involves a recurring pattern of winter depressions followed by elevations of mood in the spring and summer.

TRY THIS OUT

Self-Screening for Depression

Many people suffer depression in silence out of ignorance or shame. They believe that depression is not a real problem because it doesn't show up on an X-ray or CT scan. They think it's just all in their heads. Or they may feel that asking for help is an admission of weakness and that they should bear it on their own.

The following test, developed by the organizers of the National Depression Screening Day, is widely used to help people become more aware of the warning signs of depression. The test is not meant to provide a diagnosis of a depressive disorder; rather, its purpose is to raise awareness of problems that should be evaluated further by a mental health professional.

YES	NO	
☐	☐	1. I feel downhearted, blue, and sad.
☐	☐	2. I don't enjoy the things that I used to.
☐	☐	3. I feel that others would be better off if I were dead.
☐	☐	4. I feel that I am not useful or needed.
☐	☐	5. I notice that I am losing weight.
☐	☐	6. I have trouble sleeping through the night.
☐	☐	7. I am restless and can't keep still.
☐	☐	8. My mind isn't as clear as it used to be.
☐	☐	9. I get tired for no reason.
☐	☐	10. I feel hopeless about the future.

Scoring key: If you answered "yes" to at least five of the statements, including either the first or second one, and if these complaints have persisted for at least two weeks, then professional help is strongly recommended. If you answered "yes" to the third statement, we suggest that you immediately consult a health professional. Contact your college or university counseling or health center. Or talk to your instructor.

Source: Adapted from Brody, 1992.

Online Study Center
Improve Your Grade
Tutorials: Cognitive Distortions Linked to Depression

dysthymic disorder A type of psychological disorder characterized by mild but chronic depression.

bipolar disorder A type of mood disorder characterized by mood swings from extreme elation (mania) to severe depression.

manic episodes Periods of mania, or unusually elevated mood and extreme restlessness.

Dysthymic disorder (also called *dysthymia*) is a relatively mild but chronic form of depression. Although the symptoms of dysthymic disorder are less severe than those of major depressive disorder, people with dysthymia tend to be dispirited or "down in the dumps" for long periods of time, typically for five years or longer. About 6 percent of people in the general population develop dysthymic disorder at some point in their lives (American Psychiatric Association, 2000). Like major depression, dysthymic disorder is more common in women.

Bipolar Disorders Bipolar disorders (also called *mood swing disorders*) are characterized by alternating moods that shift between euphoric feelings and depression. There are two major types of bipolar disorders: *bipolar disorder* and *cyclothymic disorder.*

People with **bipolar disorder** (formerly called *manic-depression*) experience mood swings that shift between periods of euphoric or elevated mood, or **manic episodes** (mania), and periods of depression (Das et al., 2005). They may have intervening periods of normal moods. During a manic episode, people may feel unusually euphoric or become extremely restless, excited, talkative, and argumentative (Tohen et al., 2003). They may spend lavishly, drive recklessly, destroy property, or become involved in sexual escapades that appear out of character with their usual personalities. Even those who care about such individuals may find

CONCEPT 13.21
People with bipolar disorders experience mood swings between euphoric and depressed states.

Online Study Center
Resources
Weblinks: NYU Medical School Online Depression Screening

CONCEPT 13.22
Psychological causes implicated in mood disorders include changes in reinforcement levels, distorted ways of thinking, depressive attributional style, and stress.

cyclothymic disorder A mood disorder characterized by a chronic pattern of relatively mild mood swings.

---

them abrasive. Other symptoms are *pressured speech* (talking too rapidly), *flight of ideas* (jumping from topic to topic), and an inflated sense of self-worth (grandiosity). During manic episodes, people may become delusional—believing, for example, that they have a special relationship with God. They may undertake tasks beyond their abilities, such as writing a symphony, or show poor judgment, such as giving away their life savings. They may have boundless energy and little need for sleep. Then, when their moods sink into depression, they may feel hopelessness and despair. Some people with bipolar disorder commit suicide on the way down, apparently wanting to avoid the depths of depression they have learned to expect. About 1 percent of the adult U.S. population suffers from some sort of bipolar disorder (USDHHS, 1999).

Cyclothymic disorder (the word *cyclothymia* is derived from the Greek roots *kyklos,* meaning "circle," and *thymos,* or "spirit") is a mood disorder characterized by a pattern of milder mood swings than those seen in bipolar disorder. Among the general population, an estimated four to ten persons in a thousand (0.4 to 1 percent) develop the disorder at some point in their lives. It usually develops during late adolescence or early adulthood and lasts for years (American Psychiatric Association, 2000). Unlike unipolar depression, which is more common in women, both bipolar disorder and cyclothymic disorder affect about as many men as women.

Causes of Mood Disorders

Like anxiety disorders, mood disorders are believed to have both psychological and biological causes.

Psychological Factors Several psychological models of depression have been proposed. The classic psychodynamic theory espoused by Freud (1917/1957) and his followers (e.g., Abraham, 1916/1948) held that depression involves anger turned inward against the self. By contrast, the behavioral model attempts to account for depression in terms of changes in reinforcement levels (e.g., Lewinsohn, 1974). In order to maintain motivation, one needs a balance between output and input, between the effort one expends and the reinforcement one receives. A shortfall in reinforcement, especially social reinforcement, may occur for many reasons: the loss of a loved one removes that person as a potential reinforcing agent; attending college away from home may limit opportunities for reinforcement from friends at home; a disabling injury may cut a person off from the usual sources of reinforcement. In addition, we may find it difficult to make new friends or develop new social networks that provide opportunities for reinforcement. According to this model, loss of reinforcement saps motivation and induces depression. The more depressed we become, the less motivated we feel to make the effort to find new sources of reinforcement. In the manner of a vicious cycle, the less reinforcement we receive, the more we withdraw, and so on. In some cases, reinforcement opportunities abound but the individual needs to develop more effective social skills to establish and maintain relationships that can lead to a continuing flow of reinforcements.

Cognitive theorists focus on how our thoughts and interpretations of events contribute to emotional disorders such as depression. One of the most influential cognitive theorists is the psychiatrist Aaron Beck, the developer of cognitive therapy (discussed in Chapter 14). Beck and his colleagues (Beck et al., 1979; Beck & Young, 1985) believe that people who adopt a negatively biased or distorted way of thinking become prone to depression when they encounter disappointing or unfortunate life events. Negative thinking becomes a kind of mental filter that puts a slant on how people interpret their life experiences, especially disappointments such as getting a bad grade or losing a job. A minor disappointment is blown out of proportion—experienced more as a crushing blow than as a mild set-

TABLE 13.2 Cognitive Distortions Linked to Depression

Type of Cognitive Distortion	Description	Example
All-or-nothing thinking	Viewing events in black or white terms, as either all good or all bad	Do you view a relationship that ended as a total failure? Do you consider any less-than-perfect performance as a total failure?
Misplaced blame	Tendency to blame or criticize yourself for disappointments or setbacks while ignoring external circumstances	Do you automatically assume when things don't go as planned that it's your fault?
Misfortune telling	Tendency to think that one disappointment will inevitably lead to another	If you get a rejection letter from a job you applied for, do you assume that all the other applications you sent will meet the same fate?
Negative focusing	Focusing your attention only on the negative aspects of your experiences	When you get a job evaluation, do you overlook the praise and focus only on the criticism?
Dismissing the positives	Snatching defeat from the jaws of victory by trivializing or denying your accomplishments; minimizing your strengths or assets	When someone compliments you, do you find some way of dismissing it by saying something like "It's no big deal" or "Anyone could have done it"?
Jumping to conclusions	Drawing a conclusion that is not supported by the facts at hand	Do you usually or always expect the worst to happen?
Catastrophizing	Exaggerating the importance of negative events or personal flaws (making mountains out of molehills)	Do you react to a disappointing grade on a particular examination as though your whole life is ruined?
Emotion-based reasoning	Reasoning based on your emotions rather than on a clear-headed evaluation of the available evidence	Do you think that things are really hopeless because it feels that way?
Shouldisms	Placing unrealistic demands on yourself that you *should* or *must* accomplish certain tasks or reach certain goals	Do you feel that you *should* be further along in your life than you are now? Do you feel you *must* ace this course *or else*? (Not that it wouldn't be desirable to ace the course, but is it really the case that you *must*?)
Name calling	Attaching negative labels to yourself or others as a way of explaining your own or others' behavior	Do you label yourself *lazy* or *stupid* when you fall short of reaching your goals?
Mistaken responsibility	Assuming that you are the cause of other people's problems	Do you automatically assume that your partner is depressed or upset because of something you said or did (or didn't say or do)?

Source: Adapted from Burns, 1980; Nevid, Rathus, & Rubenstein, 1998.

back. Beck and his colleagues have identified a number of faulty thinking patterns, called *cognitive distortions,* that they believe increase one's vulnerability to depression following negative life events. The more these distorted thinking patterns dominate a person's thinking, the greater the vulnerability to depression. Table 13.2 lists the cognitive distortions most closely associated with depression.

Another psychological model of depression, the **learned helplessness model,** suggests that people become depressed when they come to believe that they are helpless to control the reinforcements in their lives. The concept, developed by psychologist Martin Seligman (1973, 1975), is based on experiments showing that

learned helplessness model The view that depression results from the perception of a lack of control over the reinforcements in one's life that may result from exposure to uncontrollable negative events.

What's Wrong with Me? How Could I Have Missed That Tackle? Cognitive theorists believe that the ways in which we interpret events have an important bearing on our proneness to depression in the face of disappointing life experiences.

laboratory animals who were exposed to inescapable shocks failed to learn to avoid the shocks when the conditions changed in such a way as to make escape possible. The animals seemed to give up trying, becoming lethargic and unmotivated—behaviors that resembled depression in people. Seligman proposed that exposure to uncontrollable situations may induce a learned helplessness effect in humans, leading to depression. In essence, when repeated efforts prove futile, the person may eventually give up trying and sink into a state of depression.

Seligman and his colleagues later revised the helplessness model to include cognitive factors (Abramson et al., 1978). In particular, they borrowed from social psychology the concept of **attributional style**, which refers to the characteristic ways in which individuals explain the causes of events that happen to them. The reformulated helplessness model proposes that attributions vary along three dimensions: *internal vs. external, global vs. specific,* and *stable vs. unstable.*

Consider a negative event, such as receiving a poor grade on a math test. An internal attribution fixes blame on oneself ("I screwed up"), while an external attribution places responsibility on external factors ("The exam was too hard"). A global attribution treats the cause as reflecting generally on one's underlying personality or abilities ("I'm really not very good at math"), while a specific attribution knocks it down to size ("I tripped up on the equations"). A stable attribution treats the cause as more or less permanent ("I'll never be able to learn this stuff"), while an unstable attribution views it as changeable ("Next time I'll be better prepared"). Seligman and his colleagues posit that a **depressive attributional style** consisting of *internal, global,* and *stable* attributions for disappointments and failure experiences predisposes individuals to become depressed following exposure to negative or disappointing life events.

We have evidence linking negative or distorted thinking to depression, just as Beck's model would suppose (McDermut, Haaga, & Bilek, 1997; Riso et al., 2003). Similarly, we have evidence that people who attribute their failures and disappointments to internal, stable, and global factors stand a greater risk of developing major depression, just as the reformulated helplessness theory would predict (Alloy et al., 2000). Yet questions remain about whether distorted thinking or attributional styles are causes or effects of depression. Perhaps depression leads people to develop negative, distorted thoughts and to adopt a depressive attributional style, rather than the other way around. Or perhaps the causal linkages work both ways, such that thinking styles affect moods and moods affect thinking styles. Complicating the picture further is that low levels of serotonin activity in the brain may lead to the distorted, pessimistic thinking associated with depression (Meyer et al., 2003).

Stress also contributes to depression (Dougherty, Klein, & Davila, 2004). Among the stressful factors most closely linked to vulnerability to depression are loss of a loved one, prolonged unemployment, serious physical illness, marital problems, pressures at work, and financial hardship (Burton, Stice, & Seeley, 2004; Kendler, Kuhn, & Prescott, 2004).

Biological Factors Biological factors play important roles in depression, including irregularities in neurotransmitter functioning, abnormalities in neural pathways, and genetics. Scientists have tied depression to irregularities in neurotransmitter functioning, especially the neurotransmitter serotonin, a key brain chemical in regulating mood (Bremner et al., 2003; Harmer et al, 2003; Meyer et al., 2003). Recently, scientists using an advanced MRI scanner found a kind of chemical signature associated with bipolar disorder ("Imaging Helps Diagnose," 2004). They observed differences in the levels of brain chemicals in different regions between bipolar patients and normal controls (Raeburn, 2005). With further advances in neuroscience, it may be possible for clinicians to use brain-scanning techniques to shed light on the underlying biological factors in psychological disorders and even help diagnose them.

attributional style A person's characteristic way of explaining outcomes of events in his or her life.

depressive attributional style A characteristic way of explaining negative events in terms of internal, stable, and global causes.

Drugs that help relieve depression, called antidepressants, increase the availability in the brain of serotonin and other neurotransmitters, such as norepinephrine. Prozac, a widely used antidepressant, boosts levels of serotonin by interfering with the reabsorption (reuptake) of this mood-regulating chemical by the transmitting neuron (Gupta, 2003; Jacobs, 2004).

We need to learn more about the specific role of serotonin in depression. Irregularities in the numbers or sensitivity of serotonin receptors may be involved. Evidence also points to lower production of the chemical in brain pathways (Rosa-Neto et al., 2004). We also have evidence that people with mood disorders have brain abnormalities in the dense networks of neurons involved in controlling feeling states and memory (Davidson et al., 2002; Schatzberg, 2002; Videbech & Ravnkilde, 2004).

Studies of twins point to an important role of heredity in mood disorders, and especially in bipolar disorder (Green et al., 2005; Kieseppä et al., 2004; McGuffin et al., 2003). Researchers are now zeroing in on several chromosomes they believe may carry genes that increase susceptibility to mood disorders, especially genes involved in neurotransmitter functioning and basic cellular processes (Bonham et al., 2005; Konradi et al., 2004; Ryu et al., 2004).

Whatever the role of biological factors in mood disorders may be, they don't tell the whole story. Psychological factors also play important roles. All told, mood disorders are complex phenomena in which a number of factors interact in complex ways (Kendler, Gardner, & Prescott, 2002). Different causal pathways may be involved. For example, genetic vulnerability may predispose people to the effects of stressful life events, such as loss of a loved one or prolonged illness, perhaps by affecting neurotransmitter functioning (NIMH, 2003). Other factors, such as a distorted, pessimistic way of thinking and lack of positive reinforcement, may further increase vulnerability in the face of negative life events. Concept Chart 13.4 reviews factors linked to mood disorders.

CONCEPT 13.23

Biological causes implicated in mood disorders include disturbances in neurotransmitter functioning in the brain and genetic influences.

CONCEPT CHART 13.4   Mood Disorders

	Type of Disorder	Lifetime Prevalence (%)	Features	Comments
Depressive Disorders	Major depression	10 to 25 in women; 5 to 12 in men	Downcast mood, feelings of hopelessness and worthlessness, changes in sleep patterns or appetite, loss of motivation, loss of pleasure in pleasant activities	Following a depressive episode, the person may return to his or her usual state of functioning, but recurrences are common. Seasonal affective disorder (SAD) is a type of major depression.
	Dysthymic disorder	Approximately 6	A chronic pattern of mild depression	Person feels "down in the dumps" most of the time, but is not as severely depressed as in major depression.
Bipolar Disorders	Bipolar disorder	About 1	Periods of shifting moods between mania and depression, perhaps with intervening periods of normal mood	Manic episodes are characterized by pressured speech, flight of ideas, poor judgment, high levels of restlessness and excitability, and inflated mood and sense of self.
	Cyclothymic disorder (cyclothymia)	0.4 to 1 (4 to 10 people in 1,000)	Mood swings that are milder in severity than those in bipolar disorder	Cyclothymia usually begins in late adolescence or early adulthood and tends to persist for years.

Sources: American Psychiatric Association, 2000; Kessler et al., 2003; USDHHS, 1999.

EXPLORING PSYCHOLOGY

The Personal Tragedy of Suicide

Nearly a half million Americans each year make suicide attempts that are serious enough to require medical treatment (Duryea, 2000), and about 30,000 people in the United States commit suicide each year (Mokdad et al., 2004). In fact, suicide is the third leading cause of death (after accidents and homicides) among people 15 to 24 years of age (Winerman, 2004b). A national survey showed that about 10 percent of college students had seriously thought of killing themselves during the preceding year (Brener, Hassan, & Barrios, 1999). In a representative U.S. sample of 15- to 54-year-olds, nearly one in twenty adult Americans (4.6 percent) reported making a prior suicidal attempt (Kessler, Borges, & Walters, 1999).

Who Is Most at Risk? Suicide cuts across every stratum of our society. Yet certain factors are related to an increased risk:

Starry, Starry Night The artist Vincent Van Gogh suffered from terrible bouts of depression that eventually led to his suicide at the age of 37 from a self-inflicted gunshot wound. In this melancholy self-portrait, his eyes and facial countenance reveal the despair with which he struggled through much of his life.

- *Age.* Though much attention is focused on adolescent suicides, suicide rates are greater among older adults, especially White males aged 75 and above (Pearson & Brown, 2000; Szanto et al., 2003) (see Figure 13.4). Yet we shouldn't ignore the fact that the risk of suicide in young men and women also remains a major concern (Kopper, Osman, & Barrios, 2001).

- *Gender.* More women attempt suicide, but about four times as many men complete the act (Cochran & Rabinowitz, 2003; Miller et al., 2004). Why do more women attempt suicide but more men succeed? The primary reason is that men typically use more lethal means, especially firearms. Women are more apt to use pills, poison, or other methods that may be less lethal.

- *Race/Ethnicity.* White (non-Hispanic) Americans and Native Americans are more likely to take their own lives than African Americans and Hispanic Americans (Garlow, Purselle, & Heninger, 2005; Gone, 2004). Young Native Americans living on reservations are at especially high risk. The widespread sense of hopelessness among Native Americans arising from lack of opportunities and segregation from the dominant culture helps set the stage for alcohol and drug abuse, which are often preludes to depression and suicide. Figure 13.5 also shows differences in the overall suicide rates between African Americans and White (non-Hispanic) Americans.

Why Do People Commit Suicide? Many myths about suicide abound, including the belief that people who threaten suicide are only seeking attention (see Table 13.3). Suicide is not a psychological or mental disorder in itself. But it is closely

Figure 13.4 Suicide Rates in Relation to Age As you can see, the risk of suicide is greatest among older adults.

Source: Statistical Abstracts of the United States, U.S. Bureau of the Census, 2000.

TABLE 13.3   Myths About Suicide

Myth	Fact
People who threaten suicide are only seeking attention.	Not so. Researchers report that most people who commit suicide gave prior indications of their intentions or consulted a health provider beforehand (Luoma, Martin, & Pearson, 2002).
A person must be insane to attempt suicide.	Most people who attempt suicide may feel hopeless, but they are not insane (i.e., out of touch with reality).
Talking about suicide with a depressed person may prompt the person to attempt it.	An open discussion of suicide with a depressed person does not prompt the person to attempt it. In fact, extracting a promise that the person will not attempt suicide before calling or visiting a mental health worker may well *prevent* a suicide.
People who attempt suicide and fail aren't serious about killing themselves.	Most people who commit suicide have made previous unsuccessful attempts.
If someone threatens suicide, it is best to ignore it so as not to encourage repeated threats.	Though some people do manipulate others by making idle threats, it is prudent to treat every suicidal threat as genuine and to take appropriate action.

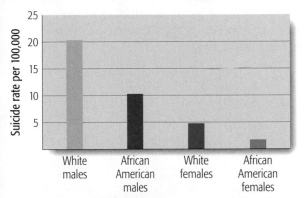

Figure 13.5   Suicide Rates in Relation to Gender and Ethnicity
Rates of completed suicide are highest among males in general and White males in particular. Though more women attempt suicide, they tend to use less lethal means.

Source: Statistical Abstracts of the United States, U.S. Bureau of the Census, 2000.

CONCEPT 13.24
Most suicides are linked to depression and, especially, to feelings of utter hopelessness.

disinhibition effect   The removal of normal restraints or inhibitions that serve to keep impulsive behavior in check.

linked to mood disorders, especially major depression and bipolar disorder, and to the deep feelings of hopelessness and helplessness that often accompany depression (Kaslow et al., 2002). The belief that things are hopeless and that one is helpless to change them can lead to the overwhelming feelings of distress that many suicidal individuals experience. Like depression, suicide is linked to biochemical factors, including reduced utilization of serotonin in the brain, and to genetic factors, possibly involving genes that play a role in regulating serotonin functioning (Dwivedi et al., 2003; Joiner, Brown, & Wingate, 2005; Lemonde et al., 2003). Serotonin is important not only because it helps regulate mood states, but also because it functions to curb or inhibit excess nervous system activity. Thus, irregularities in serotonin functioning can result in a **disinhibition effect**—the removal of inhibitions that might otherwise constrain impulsive behavior, including impulses to commit suicide.

Drug or alcohol dependence is an important risk factor in suicide, as is alcohol intoxication itself (Preuss et al., 2003). Use of alcohol may lead people to act impulsively, with the result that suicidal thoughts are carried over into action. Other factors, such as severe forms of posttraumatic stress disorder (PTSD) or other anxiety disorders, prolonged unemployment, and serious medical illness also figure in many suicides (Ben-Ya'acov & Amir, 2004; Oquendo et al., 2003; Qin, Agerbo, & Mortensen, 2003; Roy, 2003).

Suicide expert Edwin Shneidman (1987) points to a lack of coping responses among people who attempt or commit suicide. Suicidal people may see no other way of resolving their problems or ending their unendurable psychological or physical pain. In addition, suicide is linked to *exit events,* or losses of supportive persons through death, divorce or separation, or family separations. Exit events leave vulnerable people feeling stripped of crucial sources of social support.

Teenagers have been known to commit copycat suicides in the wake of widely publicized suicides in their communities. The sensationalism that attends a teenage suicide may make it seem a romantic or courageous statement to impressionable young people with problems of their own. Researchers find that adolescents who

Suicide Hotline Suicide hotlines are available in many communities to provide immediate support to people experiencing suicidal thoughts and to assist them in getting help.

have a friend who attempted suicide are more likely than their peers to attempt suicide themselves (Blum et al., 2000).

It is clear that many suicides could be prevented if people received effective treatment for the disorders that give rise to suicidal behavior, especially depression and alcohol and substance abuse. As we explore in the concluding module in this chapter, knowing what to say and do if someone is threatening suicide may also help prevent this personal tragedy from occurring.

MODULE 13.4 REVIEW

Mood Disorders

RECITE IT

What are mood disorders?

• Mood disorders are disturbances in mood that are unusually severe or prolonged. The two major types of mood disorder are depressive (unipolar) disorders and bipolar (mood swing) disorders.

What causal factors are implicated in mood disorders?

• Suspected causes include genetic factors, heredity, biochemical imbalances in neurotransmitter activity in the brain, self-directed anger, changes in reinforcement patterns, and dysfunctional thinking.

RECALL IT

1. A depressive disorder characterized by lingering states of mild depression is _____ disorder .

2. What factors may explain the greater prevalence of depression in women than in men? (Identify at least one factor.)

3. Using an MRI scanner, scientists were able to find differences in levels of brain chemicals between _____ patients and normal controls.

4. Suicide is closely linked to depression and deep feelings of _____ and _____.

THINK ABOUT IT

• Which, if any, of the errors in thinking and negative attributions described in the text describe how you typically explain disappointing events in your life? How do your thinking patterns affect your moods? your motivation? your feelings about yourself? How might you change your ways of thinking about negative experiences in the future?

• How do bipolar disorders differ from the ordinary "ups and downs" of everyday life?

MODULE 13.5

Schizophrenia

- What is schizophrenia?
- What are the three specific types of schizophrenia?
- What causal factors are implicated in schizophrenia?
- What is the diathesis-stress model of schizophrenia?

Online Study Center
Improve Your Grade
Tutorials: Schizophrenia: Thoughts and Talks

CONCEPT 13.25
Schizophrenia is a puzzling and disabling disorder that fills the mind with distorted perceptions, false ideas, and loosely connected thoughts.

schizophrenia A severe and chronic psychological disorder characterized by disturbances in thinking, perception, emotions, and behavior.

psychotic disorder A psychological disorder, such as schizophrenia, characterized by a "break" with reality.

thought disorder A breakdown in the logical structure of thought and speech, revealed in the form of a loosening of associations.

chizophrenia is the disorder that most closely corresponds to popular concepts of insanity, madness, or lunacy. The word *schizophrenia* comes from Greek roots meaning "split brain." In cases of schizophrenia, the mind is stripped of the intimate connections among thoughts, perceptions, and feelings. Individuals with this disorder may giggle in the face of disaster, hear or see things that aren't physically present, or firmly maintain beliefs that are patently false.

Schizophrenia affects about one adult in a hundred (Freedman, 2003). The disorder is characterized by bizarre, irrational behavior; recall the case of Claire, who was convinced she was protecting the populace from demons. In the United States, an estimated 2.5 million people are diagnosed with schizophrenia, and about a third of these individuals require hospitalization (McGuire, 2000). Treatment of schizophrenia accounts for 75 percent of the nation's mental health expenditures.

Schizophrenia is somewhat more common in men than in women (Aleman, Kahn, & Selten, 2003; NCA, 2005). Men also tend to develop the disorder somewhat earlier than women and to experience a more severe course of the disorder. Schizophrenia follows a lifelong course and typically develops in late adolescence or early adulthood, at about the time that people are beginning to make their way in the world (Cowan & Kandel, 2001; Harrop & Trower, 2001). It affects about 24 million people worldwide and occurs about as frequently in other cultures as in our own, although the particular symptoms may vary from culture to culture (Jablensky et al., 1992; Olson, 2001).

Symptoms of Schizophrenia

Schizophrenia is a **psychotic disorder**—that is, a disorder in which an individual confuses reality with fantasy, seeing or hearing things that aren't there (hallucinations) or holding fixed but patently false beliefs (delusions). *Hallucinations* are perceptions that occur in the absence of external stimuli. They may affect different senses. Auditory hallucinations ("hearing voices") are most common, affecting between half and three-quarters of schizophrenia patients (Goode, 2003a). Visual hallucinations (seeing things that are not there) and other sensory hallucinations (sensing odors or having taste sensations without any physical stimulus) are much less common. *Delusions* may represent many different themes, but the most common are themes of persecution, such as the belief that demons or "the Devil" is trying to harm the person.

People with schizophrenia may exhibit bizarre behavior, incoherent speech, and illogical thinking. They may not know the time of day, or what day or year it is. Or where they are. Or *who* they are. Not all of these symptoms must be present for a diagnosis of schizophrenia to be given.

Many people with schizophrenia exhibit a **thought disorder**, a breakdown in the logical structure of thinking and speech characterized by *loose associations* between expressed ideas (Docherty et al., 2003). Normally, our thoughts are tightly connected or associated; one thought follows another in a logical sequence. But in schizophrenia, there may be an absence of logical connections between thoughts.

The ideas expressed are strung loosely together or jumbled in such a way that the listener is unable to follow the person's train of thought. In severe cases, speech becomes completely incoherent or incomprehensible. The person may begin to form meaningless words or mindless rhymes.

The more flagrant signs of schizophrenia, such as hallucinations, delusions, bizarre behavior, and thought disorder, are behavioral excesses classified as **positive symptoms**. Yet people with schizophrenia may also have behavioral deficits or **negative symptoms**, such as extreme withdrawal or social isolation, apathy, and absent or blunted emotions (Roth et al., 2004; Walker et al., 2004). Positive symptoms may fade after acute episodes, but negative symptoms are typically more enduring, making it difficult for the person to meet the demands of daily life.

Types of Schizophrenia

Different types of schizophrenia can been identified on the basis of their distinctive symptoms or characteristics. Here we discuss the three specific types identified in the DSM system.

Disorganized Type   The **disorganized type** of schizophrenia is characterized by confused behavior, incoherent speech, vivid and frequent hallucinations, inappropriate emotions or lack of emotional expression, and disorganized delusions that often have religious or sexual themes. People with this form of schizophrenia may giggle inappropriately, act silly, or talk nonsensically. They tend to neglect their personal hygiene, may have difficulty controlling their bladders or bowels, and have significant problems relating to others.

Catatonic Type   People with the **catatonic type** of schizophrenia show bizarre movements, postures, or grimaces. Some persist in a motionless or stuporous state for hours and then abruptly switch into a highly agitated state. Others display highly unusual body movements or positions, such as holding a fixed posture for hours. They may be mute or uncommunicative during these episodes, showing no evidence of responding to the environment. Later, however, they may report that they heard what others were saying at the time. Less commonly they may show **waxy flexibility**, a behavior pattern in which their body position can be molded by others (like wax) into unusual, even uncomfortable positions that they then hold for hours at a time. The catatonic type is a rare form of schizophrenia.

Paranoid Type   The most common form of schizophrenia, the **paranoid type**, is characterized by delusions that are accompanied by frequent auditory hallucinations. The delusions often have themes of grandeur (e.g., believing that one is Jesus or has superhuman abilities), persecution (e.g., believing that one is being persecuted by demons or by the Mafia), or jealousy (e.g., believing that one's spouse or lover is unfaithful despite a lack of evidence).

Causes of Schizophrenia

Schizophrenia remains a puzzling, indeed mystifying disorder. Though we have not solved the puzzle, researchers have made substantial progress in putting many of the pieces into place (Walker et al., 2004).

Genetic Factors   Genetic factors play important roles in determining the risk of developing schizophrenia (Bouchard, 2004; Gottesman & Hanson, 2005; Tienari et al., 2003). The closer the genetic relationship a person shares with someone with schizophrenia, the greater the likelihood the person will also develop the disorder (Walker et al., 2004). Consistent with a genetic contribution, twin studies show a higher concordance rate (percentage of cases in which both twins share a

CONCEPT 13.26
There are three distinct types of schizophrenia: the disorganized, catatonic, and paranoid types.

positive symptoms   Symptoms of schizophrenia involving behavioral excesses, such as hallucinations and delusions.

negative symptoms   Behavioral deficits associated with schizophrenia, such as withdrawal and apathy.

disorganized type   A subtype of schizophrenia characterized by confused behavior and disorganized delusions, among other features.

catatonic type   A subtype of schizophrenia characterized by bizarre movements, postures, or grimaces.

waxy flexibility   A feature of catatonic schizophrenia in which people rigidly maintain the body position or posture in which they were placed by others.

paranoid type   The most common subtype of schizophrenia, characterized by the appearance of delusional thinking accompanied by frequent auditory hallucinations.

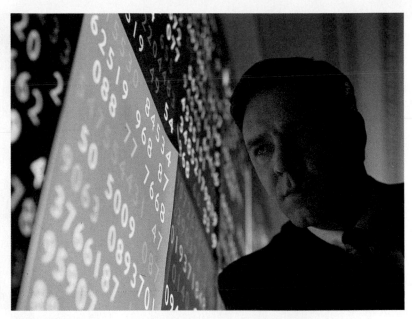

Catatonic Type   The body position of some persons with catatonic schizophrenia can be molded by others into unusual postures that they then hold for hours at a time.

Paranoid Type   Paranoid schizophrenia, the most common subtype, is characterized by delusional thinking and auditory hallucinations. John Nash, played by Russell Crowe in the movie *A Beautiful Mind,* is a brilliant mathematician who was diagnosed with paranoid schizophrenia.

CONCEPT 13.27

Though the causes of schizophrenia remain a mystery, scientists suspect that a combination of biological factors, including heredity, biochemical imbalances, and structural abnormalities in the brain, together with stressful life experiences contributes to its development.

common disorder or trait) among monozygotic twins (about 45 to 50 percent) than among dizygotic twins (about 17 percent) (see Figure 2.21 in Chapter 2).

Adoptee studies add further evidence of a genetic predisposition (Conklin & Iacono, 2002). A classic study that investigated adopted children whose biological parents had schizophrenia showed that these children were more likely to develop schizophrenia than were adopted-away children of parents who were free of schizophrenia (Rosenthal et al., 1968, 1975). Investigators are making progress tracking down specific genes associated with a vulnerability to schizophrenia (e.g., Williams et al., 2004). Investigators believe that multiple genes play important roles in the development of the disorder (Berry, Jobanputra, & Pal, 2003; Bunney et al., 2003).

Though heredity clearly plays an important role in the development of schizophrenia, genes alone do not tell the whole story. For one thing, only about 13 percent of people who have a parent with schizophrenia develop the disorder themselves. Moreover, if one identical twin has schizophrenia, the other twin, though genetically identical, has less than a 50 percent chance of having the disorder as well. If only genetics were involved, we would expect 100 percent concordance among monozygotic twins. In short, genetic vulnerability is not genetic inevitability (Sapolsky, 2000). Though we can't yet specify the specific causes of schizophrenia, in all likelihood a combination of influences involving both biological factors (e.g., genes, early brain trauma) and psychosocial factors (e.g., life stress, childhood abuse or deprivation) are involved.

Biochemical Imbalances   Researchers suspect that biochemical imbalances in nerve pathways in the brain that utilize the neurotransmitter dopamine contribute to the development of schizophrenia (McGowan et al., 2004). Dopamine is suspected largely because *antipsychotic drugs* that help quell hallucinations and delusions, such as Thorazine and Mellaril, work on the brain to reduce dopamine activity by blocking dopamine receptors (Gründer, Carlsson, & Wong, 2003). Yet the brains of schizophrenia patients do not appear to produce too much dopamine. Rather, they may have an excess number of dopamine receptors (Walker et al.,

Figure 13.6 Brain Images of Schizophrenia Patients Versus Normal Controls
Here we see PET scan (positron emission tomography) images showing metabolic activity in the brains of schizophrenia patients versus normal controls. Note the lower level of activity in the frontal lobes of the brains of schizophrenia patients (denoted by less yellow and red in the upper part of the brain images in the lower row). This evidence supports the belief that schizophrenia involves abnormalities in the frontal lobes of the brain, and more specifically, in the prefrontal cortex.

Source: Monte Buchsbaum, M.D., Mount Sinai School of Medicine, New York.

Normal controls

Schizophrenia patients

2004). Or perhaps their dopamine receptors are overly sensitive to the chemical. Hopefully, future research will clarify these underlying mechanisms.

Brain Abnormalities   Recent work with brain-imaging techniques shows evidence of brain abnormalities in many schizophrenia patients (e.g., Bagary et al., 2003; Callicott et al., 2003; Csernansky et al., 2004; Kasai et al., 2003; Kuperberg et al., 2003) (see Figure 13.6). These abnormalities may develop during critical prenatal periods when brain structures are first forming or during early childhood when they are developing further (Walker et al., 2004).

The areas of the brain that seem to be most affected in schizophrenia are the *prefrontal cortex* and the *limbic system* (Gaser et al., 2004; Hugdahl et al., 2004; Ragland et al., 2004; Winterer et al., 2004). The prefrontal cortex is the part of the brain responsible for the ability to keep information in mind (working memory), to organize our thoughts and behavior, and to allow us to formulate and carry out goals and plans—the very functions that are often disrupted in schizophrenia (Silver et al., 2003). The limbic system plays key roles in memory formation and the processing of emotional experiences.

TRY THIS OUT

Exploring the Human Side of Abnormal Behavior

One of the formative experiences of my college years was the opportunity I had to volunteer in a state psychiatric hospital. I had been interested in psychology and was eager to learn firsthand about the types of disorders I read about in textbooks. Once a week I would take a twenty-minute drive to the nearby state hospital and spend several hours just talking to a resident who seemed to enjoy just talking to me. He was a man in his early thirties who had been diagnosed with schizophrenia and had lived in a locked, inpatient unit for about three years. We sometimes played cards or watched TV, but mostly we just talked. The most important lesson I learned is that the individuals I met were human beings with unique personalities, experiences, interests, and needs—not simply "cases" I had read about in a textbook. If you would like to explore the human side of abnormal behavior, a good place to start would be the volunteer office at a local psychiatric facility. Keep a journal of your experiences and evaluate how your experiences either confirm or disconfirm your prior expectations about people with psychological disorders.

CONCEPT CHART 13.5   Schizophrenia

What It Is	Symptoms	Probable Causes
A chronic psychotic disorder affecting about 1 percent of the population	Delusions, hallucinations, bizarre behavior, incoherent or loosely connected speech, inappropriate emotions or lack of emotional expression, social withdrawal, and apathy	An interaction of a genetic predisposition and life stress; underlying brain abnormalities

CONCEPT 13.28

The diathesis-stress model holds that schizophrenia results from the interaction of a genetic predisposition and stressful life events or trauma.

Psychosocial Influences and Stress   Psychosocial influences may also be part of the matrix of causes of schizophrenia. For example, life stress may interact with genetic vulnerability in leading to schizophrenia (Byrne et al., 2003; Walker et al., 2004). The belief that schizophrenia results from the interaction of a genetic predisposition (diathesis) and stressful life experiences is expressed in the form of a diathesis-stress model, discussed earlier in the chapter (Zubin & Spring, 1977) (again, see Figure 13.1). The sources of stress are varied and may include biological influences, such as prenatal or early brain trauma; psychosocial influences, such as being raised in an abusive family environment or experiencing disturbed patterns of communication in the family; and negative life events, such as the loss of a loved one or failure in school. Though we lack a precise understanding of how these factors fit together, one possibility is that genetic and stressful influences combine to produce abnormalities in the brain that interfere with thinking, memory, and perceptual processes, leading eventually to the welter of confusing thoughts and perceptions that we see in people with schizophrenia. The symptoms and suspected causes of schizophrenia are summarized in Concept Chart 13.5.

MODULE 13.5 REVIEW

Schizophrenia

RECITE IT

What is schizophrenia?

- Schizophrenia is a psychotic disorder, meaning that it is characterized by a break with reality. Gross confusion, delusions, and hallucinations may be present in individuals with this disorder.

What are the three specific types of schizophrenia?

- The three specific types of schizophrenia are the disorganized type, the catatonic type, and the paranoid type. The paranoid type is the most common.

What causal factors are implicated in schizophrenia?

- Precise causes are unknown, but suspected causes include biological factors such as a genetic predisposition, disturbed neurotransmitter activity in the brain, brain abnormalities, and life stress.

What is the diathesis-stress model of schizophrenia?

- The diathesis-stress model refers to the belief that schizophrenia arises from an interaction of a genetic predisposition and stressful life experiences.

RECALL IT

1. Regarding schizophrenia, which of the following is *not* true?
   a. Schizophrenia is classified as a psychotic disorder.
   b Schizophrenia is much more prevalent in our own culture than in other cultures throughout the world.
   c. More males than females are affected by the disorder.
   d. The onset of schizophrenia most frequently occurs during late adolescence or early adulthood.

2. About how many people will develop schizophrenia if they have an identical (MZ) twin with this disorder?
   a. 10 to 15 percent   c. 45 to 50 percent
   b. 20 to 25 percent   d. more than 50 percent

3. Scientists believe that abnormalities involving the neurotransmitter _____ are closely linked to the development of schizophrenia.
   a. serotonin   c. epinephrine
   b. dopamine   d. acetylcholine

4. Match the following terms with the appropriate descriptions: i. catatonic schizophrenia; ii. paranoid schizophrenia; iii. disorganized schizophrenia; iv. hallucinations
   a. the most common type of schizophrenia
   b. perceiving things that are not really there
   c. confused behavior, incoherent speech, neglect of personal hygiene
   d. holding a fixed posture for hours

THINK ABOUT IT

- In what sense does schizophrenia correspond to the Greek roots from which it derives its name?

- Have you known anyone who was diagnosed with schizophrenia? How did the disorder affect the person's behavior and ability to function? How is the person functioning now?

MODULE 13.6
Personality Disorders

- **What are personality disorders?**
- **What characteristics are associated with antisocial personality disorder?**
- **What causal factors are implicated in antisocial personality disorder?**

CONCEPT 13.29

People with personality disorders exhibit excessively rigid patterns of behavior that make it difficult for them to relate to others or meet the demands that are placed upon them.

personality disorders A class of psychological disorders characterized by rigid personality traits that impair people's ability to adjust to the demands they face in the environment and that interfere with their relationships with others.

narcissistic personality disorder A type of personality disorder characterized by a grandiose sense of self.

paranoid personality disorder A type of personality disorder characterized by extreme suspiciousness or mistrust of others.

schizoid personality disorder A type of personality disorder characterized by social aloofness and limited range of emotional expression.

Personality disorders are a cluster of psychological disorders characterized by excessively rigid patterns of behavior. These behavioral patterns become self-defeating because they make it difficult for people to adjust to external demands and interfere with their relationships with others. People with personality disorders have maladaptive personality traits that become so deeply ingrained that they are highly resistant to change. In many cases, such people believe that others should change to accommodate them, not the reverse.

People with **narcissistic personality disorder** have an inflated or grandiose sense of self. Those with **paranoid personality disorder** show an extreme degree of suspiciousness or mistrust of others. Those with **schizoid personality disorder** have little if any interest in social relationships, display a limited range of emotional expression, and are perceived as distant and aloof. And those with **borderline personality disorder** tend to have stormy relationships with others, dramatic mood swings, and an unstable self-image. In all, the DSM identifies ten personality disorders (see Concept Chart 13.6). The most widely studied of these is **antisocial personality disorder (APD)**, which is the focus of our attention here.

CONCEPT CHART 13.6   Personality Disorders

Type of Disorder	Major Features or Symptoms
Paranoid personality disorder	High levels of suspiciousness of the motives and intentions of others but without the outright paranoid delusions associated with paranoid schizophrenia
Schizoid personality disorder	Aloof and distant from others, with shallow or blunted emotions
Schizotypal personality disorder	Persistent difficulties establishing close social relationships; holding beliefs or showing behaviors that are odd or peculiar but not clearly psychotic
Antisocial personality disorder	A pattern of antisocial and irresponsible behavior, callous treatment of others, and lack of remorse for wrongdoing
Borderline personality disorder	A failure to develop a stable self-image, together with a pattern of tumultuous moods and stormy relationships with others and lack of impulse control
Histrionic personality disorder	Dramatic and emotional behavior; excessive demands to be the center of attention; excessive needs for reassurance, praise, and approval
Narcissistic personality disorder	Grandiose self-image and excessive needs for admiration
Avoidant personality disorder	Pattern of avoiding social relationships out of fear of rejection
Dependent personality disorder	Pattern of excessive dependence on others and difficulty making independent decisions
Obsessive-compulsive personality disorder	Excessive needs for orderliness and attention to detail, perfectionism, and rigid ways of relating to others

CONCEPT 13.30

Antisocial personality disorder is characterized by a blatant disregard for social rules and regulations, antisocial behavior, impulsivity, irresponsibility, lack of remorse for wrongdoing, and a tendency to take advantage of others.

CONCEPT 13.31

Evidence points to an interaction of environmental and biological factors in the development of antisocial personality disorder.

borderline personality disorder   A type of personality disorder characterized by unstable emotions and self-image.

antisocial personality disorder (APD)   A type of personality disorder characterized by callous attitudes toward others and by antisocial and irresponsible behavior.

Symptoms of Antisocial Personality Disorder

People with antisocial personalities (sometimes called *psychopaths* or *sociopaths*) show a flagrant disregard for the rules of society and a lack of concern for the welfare of others. They are not psychotic; they maintain contact with reality. But they tend to act on impulse—doing what they want, when they want. They are typically irresponsible and take advantage of other people for their own needs or personal gain. They lack remorse for their misdeeds or mistreatment of others and appear to be untroubled by anxiety or undeterred by the threat of punishment or by punishment itself.

Some people with antisocial personalities engage in criminal behavior, but most are law-abiding. They may display a high level of intelligence and a superficial charm that attracts others. APD is found more often among men than women (Cale & Lilienfeld, 2002), with estimates of lifetime rates of 3 to 6 percent in men and 1 percent in women (American Psychiatric Association, 2000; Kessler et al., 1994).

Causes of Antisocial Personality Disorder

Men with APD may have brain abnormalities that may make it difficult for them to restrain their impulses and aggressive behavior (Damasio, 2000). Evidence from brain-imaging studies shows that many men with APD have lower levels of activity in the frontal lobes of the cerebral cortex, the area of the brain responsible for inhibiting impulsive behavior (Deckel, Hesselbrock, & Bauer, 1996). Other investigators find evidence of structural damage in the frontal lobes of APD patients (Raine et al., 2000).

An Antisocial Personality Serial killer Henry Lee Lucas was a career drifter who fits the stereotype of the antisocial personality. Many people with antisocial personalities do not run afoul of the law, but they do show antisocial characteristics, such as irresponsibility, callousness in the treatment of others, and lack of remorse for misdeeds.

Still other research points to a genetic contribution to the development of antisocial behavior (Caspi et al., 2002; Rhee & Waldman, 2002). We also have evidence showing that many people with antisocial personalities have exaggerated cravings for stimulation (Arnett, Smith, & Newman, 1997). They may need higher-than-normal levels of stimulation to maintain an optimum state of arousal. These findings may explain why such individuals seem to become quickly bored with routine activities and turn to more dangerous activities that provide immediate thrills, such as alcohol and drug use, racing cars or motorcycles, high-stakes gambling, or risky sexual encounters.

What role does the environment play? Research shows that many people with APD were raised in families characterized by lack of parental warmth, neglect, rejection, and use of harsh punishment (Luntz & Widom, 1994). A history of emotional or physical abuse in childhood may lead to a failure to develop a sense of empathy or concern for the welfare of others. It may also lead to a failure to develop a moral compass or sense of conscience. This lack of empathy and moral values may explain why people with APD act in a callous way toward others. In all likelihood, then, both genetic and environmental factors contribute to the development of APD, as is the case with many forms of abnormal behavior (Gabbard, 2005).

MODULE 13.6 REVIEW

Personality Disorders

RECITE IT

What are personality disorders?

- Personality disorders are deeply ingrained patterns of behavior that become maladaptive because they either cause personal distress or impair the person's ability to relate to others.

- Personality disorders include narcissistic personality disorder, paranoid personality disorder, schizoid personality disorder, borderline personality disorder, and antisocial personality disorder.

What characteristics are associated with antisocial personality disorder?

- The characteristics associated with antisocial personality disorder include impulsivity, irresponsibility, a callous disregard for the rights and feelings of others, and antisocial behavior.

What causal factors are implicated in antisocial personality disorder?

- A number of causal factors are implicated, including environmental factors, such as a family environment characterized by a lack of parental warmth, neglect, rejection, and use of harsh punishment, and biological factors, such as a genetic predisposition, abnormalities in higher brain centers that control impulsive behavior, and a greater need for stimulation.

RECALL IT

1. What are some of the characteristics of individuals with personality disorders?

2. Investigators find that people with antisocial personality disorder are more likely than others to have damage in which part of the brain?

3. Match the following types of personality disorder with the appropriate descriptions: i. paranoid personality disorder; ii. schizoid personality disorder; iii. narcissistic personality disorder; iv. borderline personality disorder
   a. stormy interpersonal relationships, unstable self-image
   b. distant, aloof, limited emotional and social interaction
   c. inflated, grandiose sense of self
   d. extreme suspiciousness and distrust of others

THINK ABOUT IT

- What are the differences between criminality and antisocial personality? Or are they one and the same? Explain.

- Have you known anyone with a personality disorder? What factors might have led to the development of these problem personality traits? How did these personality traits affect the person's relationships with others? with you?

APPLICATION MODULE 13.7
Suicide Prevention

"I don't believe it. I saw him just last week and he looked fine."

"She sat here just the other day, laughing with the rest of us. How were we to know what was going on inside her?"

"I knew he was depressed, but I never thought he'd do something like this. I didn't have a clue."

"Why didn't she just call me?"

W e may respond to the news of a suicide of a friend or family member with shock or with guilt that we failed to pick up any warning signs. Even professionals have difficulty predicting whether someone is likely to commit suicide. But when signs are present, the time to take action is now. Encourage the person, calmly but firmly, to seek professional assistance. Offer to accompany the person to a helping professional—or make the first contact yourself.

Facing the Threat

Suppose a friend confides in you that he or she is contemplating suicide. You know your friend has been going through a difficult time and has been depressed. You didn't think it would come to this, however. You want to help but are unsure about what to do. It's normal to feel frightened, even flustered. Here are some suggestions to consider if you ever face this situation. They are offered as general guidelines, not as direct instructions, since the situation at hand may call for specific responses:

1. *Recognize the seriousness of the situation.* Don't fall for the myth of thinking that people who talk about suicide are not truly serious. Treat any talk of suicide as a clear warning sign.

2. *Take implied threats seriously.* Some suicidal people don't come right out and say they are planning to kill themselves. They might say something like "I just don't feel I can go on anymore."

3. *Express understanding.* Engage the person in conversation to allow his or her feelings to be expressed. Show that you understand how troubled the person is. Don't dismiss his or her concerns by saying something like "Everyone feels like this from time to time. It'll pass."

4. *Focus on alternatives.* Tell the person that other ways of dealing with his or her problems may be found, even if they are not apparent at the moment.

5. *Assess the immediate danger.* Ask the person whether he or she has made a specific plan to commit suicide. If the person plans to use guns or drugs kept at home, prevent the person from returning home alone.

6. *Enlist the person's agreement to seek help.* Insist that the person accompany you to a health professional or nearby hospital emergency room. If that's not immediately possible, call a health professional or suicide prevention hotline. Help is available by calling the national suicide hotline at 1-800-SUICIDE or a local crisis center or health center.

7. *Accompany the person to seek help.* Above all, don't leave the person alone. If you do get separated for any reason, or if the person refuses help and leaves, call a mental health professional, suicide hotline service, or the police for assistance.

CONCEPT 13.32
A suicide threat should be taken seriously and the immediacy of the threat should be assessed; but above all, professional help should be sought at the first opportunity.

Online Study Center
Improve Your Grade
Tutorials: How Much Do You Know About Suicide?

TYING IT TOGETHER

Psychologists apply multiple criteria in determining when behavior crosses the line between normal and abnormal (Module 13.1). Mental or psychological disorders are patterns of abnormal behavior associated with significant personal distress or impaired functioning. This chapter reviews several examples of psychological disorders, including anx-

iety disorders (Module 13.2), dissociative and somatoform disorders (Module 13.3), mood disorders (Module 13.4), schizophrenia (Module 13.5), and personality disorders (Module 13.6). It ends with a discussion of suicide and steps we can take to help someone who may be contemplating suicide (Module 13.7).

Thinking Critically About Psychology

Based on your reading of this chapter, answer the following questions. Then, to evaluate your progress in developing critical thinking skills, compare your answers to the sample answers found in Appendix A.

Ron, a 22-year-old stock clerk in an auto parts store, sought a consultation with a psychologist because he was feeling "down in the dumps." He explained that he was involved in a three-year relationship with Katie. The relationship followed a seesawing pattern of numerous breakups and brief reconciliations. Most of the breakups occurred after incidents in which Ron became angry when he felt Katie was becoming distant from him. On one occasion, he accused her of sitting too far away from him in the car. If she was in a bad mood, he assumed it was because she didn't really want to be with him. The relationship meant everything to him, he told the psychologist, and he added, "I don't know what I'd do if she left me, you know, for good. I've got to figure out how to make this relationship work" (adapted from Nevid, Rathus & Greene, 2003).

1. **Review the characteristic errors in thinking associated with depression, which are listed in Table 13.2. Give some examples of these cognitive errors in Ron's thinking.**

Lonnie, a 38-year-old chemical engineer for a large pharmaceutical company, sought a consultation at the urging of his wife, Maria. He told the psychologist that Maria had grown exasperated over "his little behavioral quirks." It seems that Lonnie was a compulsive checker. Whenever the two of them would leave their apartment, he would insist on returning to check and recheck that the gas jets were turned off, the windows were shut, the door was securely locked, and the refrigerator door was tightly shut. Sometimes he'd get as far as the garage before the compulsion to return to the apartment would strike. He would apologize to Maria and leave her fuming. When retiring to bed at night, he performed an elaborate ritual of checking and rechecking to see that everything was secure. But even then, he would often bolt out of bed to check everything again, which would disturb Maria's sleep. Leaving for vacation was especially troublesome, as it required checking rituals that consumed the better part of the morning. Yet he would still be bothered by nagging doubts that would plague him throughout his trip. Lonnie recognized that his compulsive behavior was wrecking his marriage and causing him emotional distress. However, he feared that giving them up would leave him defenseless against the anxieties they helped to ease (adapted from Nevid, Rathus, & Greene, 2006).

2. **Review the six criteria used to define abnormal behavior. Which of these criteria do you think would apply to Lonnie's case? Which wouldn't apply?**

Key Terms

hallucinations *(p. 505)*
delusions *(p. 505)*
culture-bound syndromes *(p. 505)*
Dhat syndrome *(p. 505)*
medical model *(p. 506)*
biopsychosocial model *(p. 508*
diathesis-stress model *(p. 508)*
diathesis *(p. 508)*
psychological disorders *(p. 508)*
anxiety disorders *(p. 512)*
phobia *(p. 513)*
social phobia *(p. 513)*
specific phobia *(p. 513)*
acrophobia *(p. 513)*
claustrophobia *(p. 513)*
agoraphobia *(p. 513)*
panic disorder *(p. 513)*
generalized anxiety disorder (GAD)
  (p. 513)

obsessive-compulsive disorder (OCD)
  (p. 513)
anxiety sensitivity *(p. 515)*
dissociative disorders *(p. 517)*
somatoform disorders *(p. 517)*
dissociative identity disorder (DID)
  (p. 517)
conversion disorder *(p. 519)*
hypochondriasis *(p. 519)*
secondary gain *(p. 520)*
mood disorders *(p. 521)*
major depressive disorder *(p. 522)*
seasonal affective disorder (SAD) *(p. 522)*
dysthymic disorder *(p. 523)*
bipolar disorder *(p. 523)*
manic episodes *(p. 523)*
cyclothymic disorder *(p. 524)*
learned helplessness model *(p. 525)*
attributional style *(p. 526)*

depressive attributional style *(p. 526)*
disinhibition effect *(p. 529)*
schizophrenia *(p. 531)*
psychotic disorder *(p. 531)*
thought disorder *(p. 531)*
positive symptoms *(p. 532)*
negative symptoms *(p. 532)*
disorganized type *(p. 532)*
catatonic type *(p. 532)*
waxy flexibility *(p. 532)*
paranoid type *(p. 532)*
personality disorders *(p. 536)*
narcissistic personality disorder *(p. 536)*
paranoid personality disorder *(p. 536)*
schizoid personality disorder *(p. 536)*
borderline personality disorder *(p. 536)*
antisocial personality disorder (APD)
  (p. 536)

ANSWERS TO RECALL IT QUESTIONS

Module 13.1: 1. unusualness, social deviance, emotional distress, maladaptive behavior, dangerousness, faulty perceptions or interpretations of reality; 2. d; 3. c; 4. i. d, ii. c, iii. a, iv. b; 5. diathesis-stress.

Module 13.2: 1. panic; 2. specific; 3. i. c, ii. a, iii. b, iv. d.

Module 13.3: 1. b; 2. d; 3. abuse, defense; 4. d.

Module 13.4: 1. dysthymic; 2. Women appear to be exposed to greater stress and are more likely to ruminate or dwell on their problems; 3. bipolar; 4. hopelessness; helplessness.

Module 13.5: 1. b; 2. c; 3. b; 4. i. d, ii. a, iii. c, iv. b.

Module 13.6: 1. excessively rigid patterns of behavior, difficulty adjusting to external demands and relating to other people; 2. frontal lobes; 3. i. d, ii. b, iii. c, iv. a.

Methods of Therapy

"They're talking about us in the hall," Amanda explained. "Who?" I asked. She replied: "Well, you know, the voices. They're saying you think I'm cute or something." "What else are the voices telling you, Amanda?" "The usual stuff, you know. That FBI agents are hiding in the bushes outside my house. But I'm too smart for them. I always enter through the back of the house." Amanda went on: "Yesterday on TV, this reporter was sending me secret messages. My mother couldn't hear them. Nobody could hear them except me. He was telling me to watch out for my next-door neighbor, that he's doing something with the wiring in my house."

Amanda, 23, was diagnosed with schizophrenia. She was first hospitalized at age 20, shortly after she began hearing voices and wouldn't leave her college dorm out of fear that something terrible would happen to her. This interview occurred during Amanda's third hospitalization in the past year.

In this chapter, we discuss ways of helping people like Amanda who suffer from psychological disorders. As we shall see in Modules 14.2 and 14.3, help takes many forms, including psychotherapy and such biomedical therapies as drug therapy and electroconvulsive therapy (ECT). Not only are there many different forms of treatment available to help people with psychological disorders, but there are many different types of mental health professionals offering these services, including clinical and counseling psychologists, psychiatrists, social workers, and nurses.

Let us begin our exploration of ways of helping people with psychological disorders by reviewing in Module 14.1 the history of therapy and the role of the contemporary mental health system in meeting the needs of people like Amanda who have persistent and severe disorders. We will then explore the major forms of psychotherapy and biomedical approaches to treatment in use today. Finally, we will review the information that informed consumers need to know—and the questions they need to ask—when seeking the assistance of mental health professionals. ■

DID YOU KNOW THAT . . .

- According to government estimates, about one out of three homeless adults in the United States suffers from a severe psychological disorder? (p. 545)

- Sigmund Freud believed that clients bring into the therapeutic relationship the conflicts they have had with important persons in their lives? (p. 550–551)

- Gestalt therapists have their clients talk to an empty chair? (p. 553)

- Cognitive therapists believe that emotional problems, such as anxiety and depression, are caused not directly by the troubling events we experience but by the ways in which we interpret these events? (p. 556)

- Behavior therapists have used virtual reality to help people overcome fear of heights? (p. 568)

- Antidepressant drugs have been used to treat not only depression but other disorders as well, such as panic disorder and even bulimia? (p. 571)

- Stimulant drugs are widely used to reduce hyperactive behavior in children and adolescents? (p. 571)

- Sending jolts of electricity through a person's head can help relieve severe depression? (p. 572–573)

- In some states, anyone can practice psychotherapy? (p. 576)

MODULE 14.1

Pathways to the Present: A Brief History of Therapy

- How has the treatment of people with disturbed behavior changed over time?
- What are community-based mental health centers?
- How successful is the policy of deinstitutionalization?

Throughout much of Western history, society's treatment of people with severe emotional or behavioral problems was characterized more by neglect and harsh remedies than by compassion and humane care. Even today, many people with serious and persistent mental health problems, such as schizophrenia, are essentially left to fend for themselves on city streets. In this module, we briefly explore the history of society's treatment of mentally disturbed people from the beginnings of more humane forms of treatment to the community mental health movement of today.

The Rise of Moral Therapy

CONCEPT 14.1

The rise of moral therapy in the late eighteenth and early nineteenth centuries was a major step toward humanizing the treatment of mental patients.

The philosophy of treatment called **moral therapy** emerged in large measure from the efforts of two eighteenth-century Frenchmen, Jean-Baptiste Pussin and Philippe Pinel. They believed that mentally disturbed people suffer from diseases and should be treated with compassion and humane care. Their views were unpopular at the time, since deranged people were viewed as threats to society, not as sick people who required treatment. Based on the belief that humane treatment could help restore disturbed people to normal functioning, moral therapy led to similar reforms in mental health treatment in England and the United States.

In 1784, Pussin (1746–1811), though not a medical doctor, was placed in charge of a ward for the "incurably insane" at La Bicêtre, a large mental hospital in Paris. It was Pussin, not Pinel as many people believe, who first unchained mental patients in the hospital. He believed that if they were treated with kindness, they would not need to be chained. He also insisted that staff members treat the inmates with respect and compassion.

Pinel (1745–1826) became the medical director of the ward at La Bicêtre in 1793 and continued Pussin's humane philosophy of treatment, including unchain-

Pinel Unchaining Inmates at La Bicêtre

moral therapy A philosophy of treatment that emphasized treating mentally ill people with compassion and understanding, rather than shackling them in chains.

ing inmates. He eliminated harsh treatments, such as bleeding and purging, and had patients moved out of darkened dungeons into sunny, well-ventilated rooms.

A leading nineteenth-century proponent of moral therapy was Dorothea Dix (1802–1887), a Boston schoolteacher who brought attention to the plight of the mentally ill in the United States. She crusaded for kinder treatment of mentally disturbed people, who at the time were often housed under deplorable conditions in jails and almshouses. In Massachusetts, she found them locked away in jails or poorhouses, where they were "chained, naked, beaten with rods and lashed into obedience!" (cited in Winerip, 1999, p. 47). Dix found similarly dreadful conditions in her travels elsewhere in the country. Her efforts helped lead to the establishment of thirty-two mental hospitals throughout the United States.

Moral therapy fell out of favor in the latter half of the nineteenth century as it became clear that this technique failed to restore severely disturbed people to normalcy. In the absence of effective alternative treatments, the ensuing years were a period of apathy characterized by the "warehousing" of patients in the back wards of large state hospitals (Grob, 1996). Patients were largely neglected and left with little hope or expectation of returning to the community. Little if any "therapy" was offered long-term patients, and the majority of facilities were dreadful places.

Though more humane exceptions existed, conditions in state mental hospitals through the middle part of the twentieth century were often deplorable. Patients were typically crowded together in locked wards, some lacking even basic sanitation. At the time, social observers described many state-run mental hospitals as "human snakepits."

The Movement Toward Community-Based Care

By the 1950s the public outcry over deplorable conditions in mental hospitals led to a call for reform. The result was the community mental health system, which began to take shape in the 1960s. The hope was that community-based facilities would provide people suffering from schizophrenia or other severe and persistent psychological disorders with alternatives to long-term hospitalization. The advent of antipsychotic drugs, which helped control the flagrant symptoms of schizophrenia, was an additional impetus for the massive exodus of chronic mental patients from state institutions that began in earnest during the 1960s.

The social policy that redirected care of persons with severe mental disorders from state mental hospitals toward community-based treatment settings is called **deinstitutionalization**. As a result of this policy, the back wards of many mental hospitals were largely vacated. Many state mental hospitals were closed entirely and were replaced by community mental health centers and residential treatment facilities. The state hospital census in the United States dropped from about 550,000 in 1955 to fewer than 130,000 by the late 1980s (Braddock, 1992).

Today, community-based mental health centers offer a variety of services, including outpatient care, day treatment programs, and crisis intervention. Many operate supervised residential facilities, such as halfway houses, that help formerly hospitalized patients make the transition to community life. The contemporary mental hospital now exists as a resource to provide patients with more structured treatment alternatives that may be needed during times of crisis and a protective living environment for long-term patients who are unable to manage the challenges of life in the community. However, critics claim that mental hospitals today are like revolving doors, repeatedly admitting patients and then rapidly discharging them once they become stabilized. Discharged patients are often returned to communities that are ill-prepared to provide them with adequate housing and other forms of support. Many wind up homeless (Folsom et al., 2005). The U.S. government estimates that about one out of three homeless adults in the United States suffers from a severe psychological disorder (National Institutes of Health, 2003).

CONCEPT 14.2
The community mental health movement offers the hope that mental patients can be reintegrated into society, but in far too many cases it remains a hope as yet unfulfilled.

deinstitutionalization A policy of reducing the population of mental hospitals by shifting care from inpatient facilities to community-based outpatient facilities.

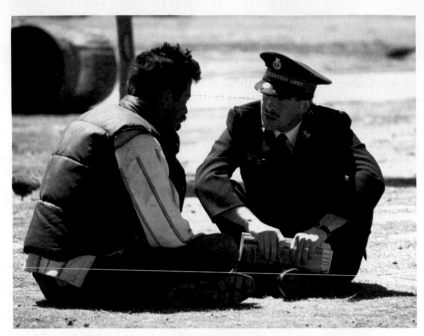

Psychiatric Homelessness Meeting the multifaceted needs of the psychiatric homeless population challenges the mental health system and the broader society.

The objectives of deinstitutionalization are certainly laudable. But the question remains: Has it succeeded in its goal of reintegrating mental patients into their communities?

Deinstitutionalization receives at best a mixed grade. Though the community mental health movement has had some successes, far too many patients fail to receive the comprehensive range of psychological and support services they need to adapt successfully to community living (Rosenheck et al., 2003). Many simply fall through the cracks of the mental health system and are left to fend for themselves. Many homeless people seen wandering about or sleeping in bus terminals have unrecognized mental health and substance-abuse problems and are not receiving the help they need. Understaffed and underfunded, community mental health facilities continue to struggle to meet the demands of a generation of people with severe mental health problems who have come of age during the era of deinstitutionalization.

Not surprisingly, more intensive community-based programs that match services to the needs of people with severe and persistent mental health problems generally achieve better results (Rosenheck, 2000; Tolomiczenko, Sota, & Goering, 2000). Aggressive outreach efforts are especially important if we are to reach the large numbers of psychiatric homeless people who fail to seek out mental health services on their own. All in all, perhaps it is best to think of deinstitutionalization as a work in progress rather than a failed policy. Concept Chart 14.1 reviews the history of therapy discussed in this module.

CONCEPT CHART 14.1 From Institutional Care to Community-Based Care

Type of Institution	When It Operated	Comments
State hospital system	19th century through mid-20th century	Large state institutions that provided little more than custodial care. Conditions in some institutions were so deplorable they were sometimes called "human snakepits."
Modern state hospitals	1955 to present	Significantly downsized institutions that provide more humane care than earlier institutions. Yet critics claim that some institutions function as little more than revolving doors for chronic patients who are repeatedly shuttled back and forth between the hospital and the community.
Community mental health centers	1960s to present	Comprehensive treatment facilities in the community that offer alternatives to hospitalization, including outpatient treatment, day hospital programs, and transitional treatment facilities such as halfway houses. However, many marginally functioning mental patients have been released to the community without access to adequate housing and other necessary support. Meanwhile, more intensive community-based programs are beginning to show better outcomes in helping patients adjust more successfully to community living.

TRY THIS OUT

"Hello, Can I Help You?"

Many campuses and local communities have telephone hotlines that people who are distressed or suicidal can call for immediate assistance, day or night. The volunteers who staff these call centers receive specialized training in crisis intervention services. The staffers field phone calls, provide emotional support to people in crisis, and make referrals to mental health agencies or counseling centers in the area. Serving as a volunteer for a hotline service can be a formative experience in helping you prepare for a career in the helping professions, including psychology, counseling, or social work. The work can be rewarding but also very challenging. Make sure the hotline is well supervised and provides the support and guidance you will need to handle the responsibilities of providing help to people in crisis. Keep a journal to document your experiences, noting how they shape your views of psychology and, more important, of yourself.

MODULE 14.1 REVIEW

Pathways to the Present: A Brief History of Therapy

RECITE IT

How has the treatment of people with disturbed behavior changed over time?

- In the late eighteenth century, a more humane approach to the treatment of mental patients, called "moral therapy," began to gain prominence.

- As this movement declined, a state of apathy ensued and the focus shifted from therapy to custodial treatment in large, forbidding state mental institutions.

- Pressures to reform the mental health system in the United States led to the creation of a nationwide network of community mental health centers in the 1960s. The community mental health movement shifted the delivery of care from large inpatient facilities to community-based facilities.

What are community-based mental health centers?

- Community-based mental health centers are treatment facilities that provide a comprehensive range of mental health services and other supportive services to psychiatric patients in the communities in which they reside.

How successful is the policy of deinstitutionalization?

- Deinstitutionalization remains a promise not yet fulfilled, as many patients fail to receive the services they need to adjust successfully to the community.

RECALL IT

1. The eighteenth-century Frenchmen Jean-Baptiste Pussin and Philippe Pinel adopted a more humane approach to the treatment of mental patients, called _____ therapy.

2. The nineteenth-century American reformer who campaigned for more compassionate care of the mentally ill was _____.

3. Why did moral therapy eventually fall out of favor?

4. The policy of _____ greatly reduced the census of state mental hospitals and shifted treatment of people with severe psychological disorders largely to community-based programs.

THINK ABOUT IT

- How has society's treatment of people with mental health problems changed over time? Are we more tolerant and understanding today? What do you think?

- What should be done about the problem of psychiatric homelessness?

- If you or someone you know needed mental health services, where would you turn? How might you find out what types of mental health services are available in your college and your community?

MODULE 14.2

Types of Psychotherapy

- What is psychotherapy?
- What are the major types of mental health professionals?
- What are the major forms of psychotherapy?
- Is psychotherapy effective?
- What cultural factors do therapists need to consider when working with members of diverse groups?

CONCEPT 14.3

Psychotherapy consists of one or more verbal interactions between a therapist and a client and is used to help people understand and resolve their psychological problems.

CONCEPT 14.4

Mental health services are offered by different types of professionals who vary in their training backgrounds and areas of competence.

CONCEPT 14.5

Psychodynamic therapy is based on the belief that insight into unresolved psychological conflicts originating in childhood can help people overcome psychological problems.

psychotherapy A verbal form of therapy derived from a psychological framework that consists of one or more treatment sessions with a therapist.

psychoanalysis Freud's method of psychotherapy; it focuses on uncovering and working through the unconscious conflicts he believed were at the root of psychological problems.

psychoanalysts Practitioners of psychoanalysis who are schooled in the Freudian tradition.

Psychotherapy is a psychologically based form of treatment used to help people better understand their emotional or behavioral problems and resolve them. It consists of a series of verbal interactions between a therapist and a client, which is why it is often referred to as "talk therapy." In some forms of psychotherapy, there is an ongoing back-and-forth dialogue between the therapist and client, whereas in others, especially in classical psychoanalysis, the client does most or virtually all of the talking. There are many different types of psychotherapy, literally hundreds of types, but the most widely used ones have been derived from the major psychological models of abnormal behavior reviewed in Module 13.1: the psychodynamic, behavioral, humanistic, and cognitive models. Although most forms of psychotherapy focus on the individual, some therapists extend their model of treatment to couples, families, and groups of unrelated individuals. Let us consider the major forms of psychotherapy used today. Before we do so, you may wish to review the training backgrounds and areas of expertise of the types of mental health professionals who provide psychotherapy and other mental health services, as shown in Table 14.1.

Psychodynamic Therapy

What comes to mind when you think of psychotherapy? If you picture a person lying on a couch and talking about the past, especially early childhood, you are probably thinking of **psychoanalysis**, the first form of *psychodynamic therapy* to be developed. Psychodynamic therapies share in common the belief that psychological problems are rooted in unconscious psychological conflicts dating from childhood. They also assume that gaining insight into these conflicts and working them through in the light of the individual's adult personality are the key steps toward restoring psychological health.

Traditional Psychoanalysis: Where Id Was, Ego Shall Be Psychoanalysis, the form of psychotherapy developed by Sigmund Freud, is based on the belief that abnormal behavior arises from unconscious conflicts originating in childhood of which we are unaware. Practitioners of psychoanalysis are called **psychoanalysts**, or *analysts* for short. Recall from Chapter 12 that Freud believed that conflicts over primitive sexual or aggressive impulses cause the ego to employ *defense mechanisms,* especially *repression,* to keep these impulses out of conscious awareness. In some instances, these unconscious impulses threaten to leak into consciousness, resulting in feelings of anxiety. The person may report feeling anxious or experience a sense of dread or foreboding but have no idea about its cause. In other instances, the energy attached to the impulse is channeled or converted into a physical symptom, as in cases of hysterical blindness or paralysis. The symptom itself, such as inability to move an arm, serves a hidden purpose: it prevents the person from acting upon the underlying impulse. Thus, for example, the person with hysterical paral-

TABLE 14.1   Major Types of Mental Health Professionals

Clinical psychologists

Clinical psychologists have earned a doctoral degree in clinical psychology (either a Ph.D., Doctor of Philosophy; a Psy.D., Doctor of Psychology; or an Ed.D., Doctor of Education) and have passed a licensing examination. Clinical psychologists specialize in administering psychological tests, diagnosing psychological disorders, and practicing psychotherapy. Until recently, they were not permitted to prescribe psychiatric drugs. By 2004, however, two states (New Mexico and Louisiana) had enacted laws to grant prescription privileges to psychologists who complete specialized training programs (Holloway, 2004; Murray, 2003; Practice Directorate Staff, 2005). Whether other states will follow suit remains to be seen. Moreover, the granting of prescription privileges to psychologists remains a hotly contested issue between psychologists and psychiatrists and within the field of psychology itself (see Heiby, DeLeon, & Anderson, 2004; McGrath et al., 2004; Welsh, 2003; Willis, 2003).

Counseling psychologists

Counseling psychologists hold doctoral degrees in counseling psychology and have passed a licensing examination. They typically provide counseling to people with psychological problems falling within a milder range of severity than those treated by clinical psychologists, such as difficulties adjusting to college or uncertainties regarding career choices. Many counseling psychologists in college settings are also involved in providing appropriate services to students covered by the Americans with Disabilities Act (ADA).

Psychiatrists

Psychiatrists have earned a medical degree (M.D.) and completed residency training programs in psychiatry, which usually are three years in length. They are physicians who specialize in the diagnosis and treatment of psychological disorders. As licensed physicians, they can prescribe psychiatric drugs and may employ other medical techniques, such as electroconvulsive therapy (ECT). Many also practice psychotherapy based on training they receive during their residency programs or in specialized training institutes.

Clinical or psychiatric social workers

Clinical or psychiatric social workers have earned a master's degree in social work (M.S.W.) and use their knowledge of community agencies and organizations to help people with severe mental disorders receive the services they need. Many clinical social workers practice psychotherapy or specific forms of therapy, such as marital or family therapy.

Psychoanalysts

Psychoanalysts are typically either psychiatrists or psychologists who have completed extensive additional training in psychoanalysis. They are required to undergo psychoanalysis themselves as part of their training.

Counselors

Counselors have typically earned a master's degree and work in settings such as public schools, college testing and counseling centers, and hospitals and health clinics. Many specialize in vocational evaluation, marital or family counseling, or substance abuse counseling. Counselors may focus on providing psychological assistance to people with milder forms of disturbed behavior or those struggling with a chronic or debilitating illness or recovering from a traumatic experience.

Psychiatric nurses

Psychiatric nurses are typically R.N.'s who have completed a master's program in psychiatric nursing. They may work in a psychiatric facility or in a group medical practice where they treat people suffering from severe psychological disorders.

ysis becomes unable to use the arm to engage in unacceptable sexual acts such as masturbation. Similarly, the person with a fear of heights may harbor unconscious self-destructive impulses that are kept in check by avoiding height situations in which the person might lose control over the impulse to jump. The task of therapy, Freud believed, was to help people gain insight into their unconscious conflicts and work them through—to allow the conscious light of the ego to shine on the darkest reaches of the id. With self-insight, the ego would no longer need to maintain defensive behaviors or psychological symptoms that shield the self from the inner turmoil lying within. The ego would then be free to focus its efforts on pursuing more constructive interests, such as work and love relationships.

Freud used psychoanalysis to probe the unconscious mind for these inner conflicts, a lengthy process that typically would take years. He believed that unconscious conflicts are not easily brought into consciousness, so he devised several techniques to help clients gain awareness of them, including free association, dream analysis, and interpretation.

CONCEPT 14.6
Freud devised a number of techniques, including free association, dream analysis, and interpretation, to help clients gain awareness of their unconscious conflicts.

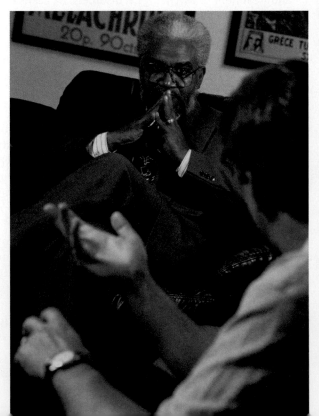

Online Study Center
Resources
   Weblinks: American Psychoanalytic
   Association

Free Association   In **free association**, the client is instructed to say anything that crosses his or her mind, no matter how trivial or irrelevant it may seem. Freud believed these free associations would eventually work their way toward uncovering deep-seated wishes and desires that reflect underlying conflicts. In classical psychoanalysis, the client lies on a couch with the analyst sitting off to the side, out of the client's direct view, saying little. By remaining detached, the analyst hopes to create an atmosphere that encourages the client to focus inwardly on his or her own thoughts.

Dream Analysis   In **dream analysis**, the analyst helps the client gain insight into the symbolic or *latent* content of dreams, as opposed to the overt or manifest content (see Chapter 4). Freud called dreams the "royal road to the unconscious." He encouraged clients to freely associate to the manifest content of their dreams, hoping that doing so would lead to a better understanding of the dreams' hidden meanings.

Interpretation   **Interpretation** is an explanation of the connections between the client's behavior and verbal expressions—how the client acts and what the client says—and the client's unconscious motives and conflicts. By offering interpretations, the analyst helps the client gain **insight** into the unconscious origins of the problem.

   Interpretation of the client's **resistance** plays an important role in psychoanalysis. Resistance is the blocking that occurs when the analyst touches upon anxiety-evoking thoughts or feelings. The client may suddenly draw a blank when free associations touch upon sensitive areas, or suddenly "forget" to show up for an appointment when deeper issues are being discussed. Psychoanalysts see resistance as a tactic used by the ego to prevent awareness of unconscious material, interpreting signs of resistance as clues to important underlying issues that need to be addressed in therapy.

   The most important use of interpretation, in Freud's view, is analysis of the **transference relationship**. Freud believed that clients reenact troubled, conflicted relationships with others in the context of the relationship they develop with the

Contemporary Psychoanalysis
Many modern psychoanalysts have replaced the traditional couch with more direct, face-to-face verbal interactions with clients.

free association   A technique in psychoanalysis in which the client is encouraged to say anything that comes to mind.

dream analysis   A technique in psychoanalysis in which the therapist attempts to analyze the underlying or symbolic meaning of the client's dreams.

interpretation   In psychoanalysis, the attempt by the therapist to explain the connections between the material the client discloses in therapy and his or her unconscious conflicts.

insight   In Freud's theory, the awareness of underlying, unconscious wishes and conflicts.

resistance   In psychoanalysis, the blocking that occurs when therapy touches upon anxiety-evoking thoughts or feelings.

transference relationship   In therapy, the tendency of clients to reenact earlier conflicted relationships in the relationship they develop with their therapists.

CONCEPT 14.7
Freud believed that the ability to understand the transference relationship is essential to the client's success in psychoanalysis.

analyst. A female client may respond to the analyst as a "father figure," perhaps transferring her ambivalent feelings of love and hate toward her own father onto the therapist. A young man may view the analyst as a competitor or rival, reenacting an unresolved Oedipal conflict from his childhood. By interpreting the transference relationship, the analyst raises the client's awareness about how earlier conflicted relationships intrude upon the client's present relationships. Freud believed that the client's ability to come to an understanding of the transference relationship is an essential ingredient in a successful analysis.

Transference is a two-way street. Freud himself recognized that he sometimes responded to clients in ways that carried over from his relationships with others. He called this process **countertransference** and believed that it damaged the therapeutic relationship. A male therapist, for example, may react to a male client as a competitor or rival or to a female client as a rejecting love interest.

CONCEPT 14.8
Compared to traditional psychoanalysis, modern forms of psychodynamic therapy are briefer, allow for more interaction between therapist and client, and focus more on the ego.

Modern Psychodynamic Approaches: More Ego, Less Id Traditional psychoanalysis is a lengthy, intensive process. It may require three to five sessions a week for many years. Some contemporary psychoanalysts continue to practice in much the same way as Freud did. However, many psychodynamic therapists today focus less on sexual issues than on the adaptive functioning of the ego. They may also focus more on the client's present relationships than on the remote past. Moreover, because many modern analysts adopt a briefer therapy format, they tend to take a more direct approach to exploring how client's defenses and transference relationships cause difficulties in their relationships with others (Messer, 2001). One obvious difference is that many analysts today prefer to have their clients sit facing them, rather than lying on a couch. There is also more dialogue between analyst and client, and clients typically come to only one or two sessions a week (Grossman, 2003).

Here we see an example of the give-and-take between a contemporary psychoanalyst and a young adult patient. The analyst focuses on the client's competitiveness with him. In an analytic framework, this competitiveness represents a transference of the client's unresolved Oedipal rivalry with his own father:

> Client: . . . I continue to have success, but I have been feeling weak and tired. I saw my doctor yesterday and he said there's nothing organically wrong.
>
> Analyst: Does anything come to mind in relation to weak and tired feelings?
>
> Client: I'm thinking of the way you looked last year after you came out of the hospital. (The patient was referring to a hospitalization that, in fact, I had the previous year during which time our treatment sessions were suspended.)
>
> Analyst: Do you recall how you felt when you saw me looking that way?
>
> Client: It made me upset, even guilty.
>
> Analyst: But why guilty?
>
> Client: I'm not sure why I said that. There was nothing to feel guilty about.
>
> Analyst: Perhaps you had some other feelings.
>
> Client: Well, it's true that at one point I felt faintly pleased that I was young and vigorous and you seemed to be going downhill. . . .
>
> Analyst: . . . Clearly you're not very comfortable when you contrast your state with mine—to your advantage.
>
> Client: Well, you know, I've never felt comfortable when thinking of myself outdoing you in any way. . . .
>
> Analyst: . . . Perhaps your weak and tired feelings represent an identification with me brought on by your feeling guilty about your successes, since that implies that you are outdoing me. . . . Your discomfort with feeling that in certain respects you're surpassing me is posing a problem for you.

Source: Silverman, 1984, pp. 226–227

countertransference The tendency for therapists to relate to clients in ways that mirror their relationships with important figures in their own lives.

Humanistic Therapy

Humanistic therapists believe that human beings possess free will and can make conscious choices that enrich their lives. The methods of therapy developed within the humanistic tradition emphasize the client's subjective, conscious experiences. Humanistic therapists focus on what the individual is experiencing at the particular moment in time, rather than on the distant past. It's not that they view the past as unimportant; they believe that past experiences do affect present behavior and feelings. But they emphasize that change must occur in the present, in the *here-and-now*. The two major forms of humanistic therapy are *client-centered therapy*, developed by Carl Rogers, and *gestalt therapy*, developed by Fritz Perls.

Client-Centered Therapy   Rogers (1951) believed that when children are valued only when they behave in ways that please others, they may become psychologically detached from parts of themselves that meet with disapproval or criticism. They may become so good at playing the "good boy" or "good girl" role that they develop a distorted self-concept—a view of themselves that does not reflect who they really are and what they truly feel. Well-adjusted people make choices that are consistent with their own unique selves, needs, and values. But people with a distorted self-concept remain largely strangers to themselves.

As the name *client-centered* therapy implies, Rogerian therapy focuses on the person. Client-centered therapists strive to achieve a warm and accepting therapeutic atmosphere in which clients feel safe to explore their innermost feelings and become accepting of their true selves. Client-centered therapists take a *nondirective* approach to therapy by allowing the client to take the lead and set the tone. The therapist's role is to *reflect back* the client's feelings so as to encourage self-exploration and self-acceptance (Hill & Nakayama, 2000). Here, Rogers illustrates how a client-centered counselor uses reflection to help a client clarify and further explore her feelings:

> *Client: Now—one of the things that . . . had worried me was . . . living at the dorm, it's hard—not to just sort of fall in with a group of people . . . that aren't interesting, but just around. . . . So, now I find that I'm . . . getting away from that group a little bit . . . and being with a group of people . . . I really find I have more interests in common with.*
>
> *Counselor: That is, you've really chosen to draw away from the group you're just thrown in with by chance, and you pick people whom you want more to associate with. Is that it?*
>
> *Client: That's the idea. . . . They [my roommates] . . . had sort of pulled me in with a group of their friends that I wouldn't have picked myself, especially. And . . . so that I found that all my time was being taken up with these people, and now I'm beginning to seek out people that I prefer myself . . . rather than being drawn in with the bunch.*
>
> *Counselor: You find it a little more possible, I gather, to express your real attitudes in a social situation . . . [to] make your own choice of friends. . . .*
>
> *Client: . . . I tried to see if I was just withdrawing from this bunch of kids I'd been spending my time with. . . . It's not a withdrawal, but it's more of an assertion of my real interest.*
>
> *Counselor: M-hm. In other words, you've tried to be self-critical in order to see if you're just running away from the situation, but you feel really, it's an expression of your positive attitudes.*
>
> *Client: I–I think it is.*

Source: Rogers, 1951, pp. 154–155.

CONCEPT 14.10

Carl Rogers believed that for therapists to be effective, they must demonstrate empathy and unconditional positive regard for their clients as well as genuineness in their expression of feelings.

Rogers believed that effective therapists display three qualities that are necessary to create the atmosphere of emotional support needed for clients to benefit from therapy:

1. *Unconditional positive regard.* The therapist is unconditionally accepting of the client as a person, even though he or she may not approve of all of the client's choices or behaviors.

2. *Empathy.* The therapist demonstrates *empathy,* the ability to accurately mirror or reflect back the client's experiences and feelings—to see the world through the client's eyes or frames of reference. By entering the client's subjective world, the therapist encourages the client to do likewise—to get in touch with deeper feelings of which he or she may be only dimly aware.

3. *Genuineness.* The therapist is able to express genuine feelings and demonstrates that one's feelings and actions can be congruent or consistent. Even when the therapist is feeling bored or down, it is best to express these feelings, so as to encourage the client to do the same, rather than distorting true feelings or concealing them.

CONCEPT 14.11

Fritz Perls, who developed gestalt therapy, believed that therapists should help clients blend the conflicting parts of their personalities into an integrated whole or "gestalt."

Gestalt Therapy   Fritz Perls (1893–1970), the originator of gestalt therapy, was trained as a psychoanalyst but became dissatisfied with the lack of emphasis on the client's subjective experiences in the present. Perls was influenced by Gestalt psychology and believed that it was important to help clients blend the conflicting parts of their personalities into an integrated whole or "gestalt." Unlike client-centered therapists, who attempt to create a warm and accepting atmosphere, gestalt therapists take a direct and even confrontational approach in helping clients get in touch with their underlying feelings. They repeatedly challenge clients to express how they are feeling at each moment in time—in the here-and-now. They don't let them off the hook by allowing them to slide into discussing events from their past or to ramble in general, abstract terms about their feelings or experiences. They also attend to the client's facial expressions and other body cues to help the client identify underlying feelings.

Gestalt therapists use role-playing exercises to help clients integrate their inner feelings into their conscious experience. In the *empty chair* technique, therapists place an empty chair in front of the clients (Greenberg & Malcolm, 2002). Clients are told to imagine that someone with whom they have had a troubled relationship (mother, father, spouse, boss) is sitting in the chair and to express their feelings toward that person. They can feel safe to express their innermost feelings and unmet needs without fear of criticism from the other person and work through unfinished "business" with these significant figures in their lives (Wagner-Moore, 2004).

Perls also had clients role-play different parts of their own personalities. One part might bark a command, like "Take chances. Get involved." A more restrained part might bark back, "Play it safe. Don't risk it." By helping the individual become more aware of these opposing parts, gestalt therapists hope to bring about an integration of the client's personality that may take the form of a compromise between opposing parts.

Behavior Therapy

CONCEPT 14.12

Behavior therapy involves the systematic application of learning principles to weaken undesirable behaviors and strengthen adaptive behaviors.

behavior therapy A form of therapy that involves the systematic application of the principles of learning.

In **behavior therapy** (also called *behavior modification*), therapists systematically apply principles of learning to help individuals make adaptive changes in their behavior. Behavior therapists believe that psychological problems are largely learned and thus can be unlearned. Like humanistic therapies, behavior therapy addresses the client's present situation, not the distant past. But behavior therapy focuses directly on changing problem behaviors, rather than on exploring the

THE PIONEERS | Little Peter

Mary Cover Jones

At a time when Freud's psychoanalytic theory was establishing a foothold in the United States, psychologists steeped in the behaviorist tradition were beginning to apply learning theory to clinical problems. Mary Cover Jones (1896–1987) was among the first of these pioneers. Having studied with Watson, she was familiar with the case of Little Albert in which Watson and Rayner demonstrated the acquisition of a fear response (to a white rat) using Pavlovian (classical) conditioning (see Chapter 5). She thought to herself, "If fears could be built in by conditioning, as Watson demonstrated, could they not also be removed by similar procedures?" (Jones, 1924, p. 581).

In 1924 Jones reported what might well be the first case study of behavior therapy (Jones, 1924). It involved a nearly 3-year-old boy, Little Peter, who had a fear of white rabbits. Jones directly taught him to unlearn his fear. She used a variety of behavioral treatment techniques, but she is best known for using a direct conditioning technique in which she associated foods Peter liked with the gradual presentation of a white rabbit. Each day the rabbit was brought closer and closer while he was eating in his high chair. Peter's fear of rabbits gradually disappeared, as did his fear of other animals and objects that were similar in appearance. Jones reasoned that the fear was unlearned through the process of pairing the feared object with pleasurable stimuli associated with eating.

CONCEPT 14.13
To help people overcome phobic responses, behavior therapists use learning-based techniques such as systematic desensitization, gradual exposure, and modeling.

systematic desensitization A behavior therapy technique for treating phobias through the pairing of exposure in imagination to fear-inducing stimuli and states of deep relaxation.

fear hierarchy An ordered series of increasingly fearful objects or situations.

gradual exposure A behavior therapy technique for treating phobias based on direct exposure to a series of increasingly fearful stimuli. Also called *in-vivo ("real-life") exposure.*

client's feelings. Behavior therapy is relatively brief, usually lasting weeks or months rather than years.

Behavior therapy has its origins in the behaviorism of John Watson. One of its early developers was a student of Watson's, Mary Cover Jones (see the Pioneers box).

Methods of Fear Reduction Behavior therapists use several techniques to treat phobias, including systematic desensitization, gradual exposure, and modeling. In **systematic desensitization**, the client is first taught skills of deep muscle relaxation, typically using a relaxation technique that consists of tensing and relaxing selected muscle groups in the body (Wolpe, 1958). An ordered series of fear-inducing stimuli, called a **fear hierarchy**, is then constructed, scaled from the least to the most fearful stimulus. The therapist then guides the client in practicing deep relaxation. Once a state of deep relaxation is achieved, the client is instructed to imagine confronting the first stimulus in the fear hierarchy (or perhaps views the stimulus, as through a series of slides). If anxiety occurs, the client stops imagining the feared stimulus and restores deep relaxation before trying the exercise again. When the client can remain relaxed during the imagined exposure to the first stimulus on several trials, he or she then moves to the next stimulus in the hierarchy. This procedure is repeated for each step in the hierarchy. The objective is to use relaxation as an incompatible response to fear in order to weaken the bonds between frightening stimuli and the fear they evoke.

Behavior therapists also use **gradual exposure** (alternately called *in-vivo exposure,* meaning exposure in "real life") to help people overcome phobias. In this technique, people gradually expose themselves to a hierarchy of increasingly fearful stimuli. By progressing at their own pace through the hierarchy, they learn to tolerate these fearful situations or stimuli. Clients may first be taught self-relaxation skills that they can use during their exposure trials. They are also trained to use calming coping statements to help them through these encounters—statements

Gradual Exposure   Through gradual exposure, the client confronts increasingly fearful stimuli or situations, sometimes assisted by the therapist or supportive others.

they can repeat to themselves under their breath, like "I can do this. Just take a few deep breaths and the fear will pass."

A sample hierarchy for a person with an elevator phobia might include the following steps:

1. Standing outside the elevator.
2. Standing in the elevator with the door open.
3. Standing in the elevator with the door closed.
4. Taking the elevator down one floor.
5. Taking the elevator up one floor.
6. Taking the elevator down two floors.
7. Taking the elevator up two floors.
8. Taking the elevator down two floors and then up two floors.
9. Taking the elevator down to the basement.
10. Taking the elevator up to the highest floor.
11. Taking the elevator all the way down and then all the way up.

Gradual exposure is used to help people overcome not only specific types of fears, such as a fear of snakes or insects, or riding on trains or elevators, but also social phobias, such as a fear of meeting new people or of speaking in public (e.g., Davidson et al., 2004; Hoffman, 2000). For example, people with a social phobia might be instructed to create a hierarchy of fearful social situations. They would then be trained in relaxation skills and begin a series of exposure encounters starting with the least socially stressful situation and working their way up to the most stressful. Gradual exposure can also help people with posttraumatic stress disorder or PTSD confront their fears of stimuli or situations associated with the trauma they experienced (Bradley et al., 2005; Gray & Acierno, 2002). (See Chapter 15 for further discussion of PTSD.)

A form of observational learning known as **modeling** is often used to help people overcome fears and acquire more adaptive behaviors (Braswell & Kendall, 2001). Specifically, individuals acquire desirable behaviors by observing and imitating others whom they observe performing the behaviors. Psychologist Albert Bandura (Bandura, Blanchard, & Ritter, 1969) pioneered the use of modeling as a therapeutic technique to help people overcome phobias, such as fears of snakes, dogs, and other small animals.

Aversive Conditioning   In **aversive conditioning**, a form of classical conditioning, stimuli associated with an undesirable response are paired with aversive stimuli, such as an electric shock or a nausea-inducing drug. The idea is to make these stimuli elicit a negative response (fear or nausea) that would discourage the person from performing the undesirable behavior. For example, adults who are sexually attracted to children might receive a mild but painful electric shock when they view sexually provocative pictures of children. Or in alcoholism treatment, a nausea-inducing drug could be paired with sniffing or sipping an alcoholic beverage. In conditioning terms, the nausea-inducing drug is the unconditioned stimulus (US) and nausea is the unconditioned response (UR). The alcoholic beverage becomes a conditioned stimulus (CS) that elicits nausea (CR) when it is paired repeatedly with the US (see Figure 14.1). Unfortunately, the effects of aversive conditioning are often temporary; outside the treatment setting, the aversive stimulus no longer accompanies the undesirable behavior. Partly for this reason, aversive conditioning has not achieved widespread use (Kadden, 1994), but it may be useful as a component of a broader treatment program.

Operant Conditioning Methods   Behavior therapists apply operant principles of reinforcement and punishment to help strengthen desirable behavior and weaken undesirable behavior. For example, therapists may train parents to reward children

💡 **CONCEPT 14.14**
Aversive conditioning is used to create an unpleasant response to stimuli associated with undesirable behaviors.

Online Study Center
Improve Your Grade
Tutorials: Classical and Adversive Conditioning

modeling   A behavior therapy technique for overcoming phobias and acquiring more adaptive behaviors, based on observing and imitating models.

aversive conditioning   A form of behavior therapy in which stimuli associated with undesirable behavior are paired with aversive stimuli to create a negative response to these stimuli.

Figure 14.1 Model of Aversive Conditioning
After repeated pairing of a nausea-inducing drug and sniffing or sipping an alcoholic beverage, exposure to the alcoholic beverage alone elicits nausea, which discourages drinking.

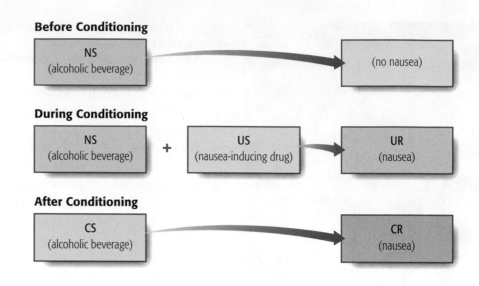

Before Conditioning

NS
(alcoholic beverage) → (no nausea)

During Conditioning

NS
(alcoholic beverage) + US
(nausea-inducing drug) → UR
(nausea)

After Conditioning

CS
(alcoholic beverage) → CR
(nausea)

CONCEPT 14.15
Behavior therapists apply operant conditioning principles to strengthen desirable behavior and weaken or eliminate undesirable behavior.

for appropriate behavior and to withdraw attention (a social reinforcer) following problem behavior in order to weaken or eliminate it. Or they may train parents to use mild forms of punishment, such as a time-out procedure in which children are removed from a rewarding environment when they misbehave and "sit out" for a prescribed period of time before resuming other activities.

In Chapter 5 you were introduced to another operant conditioning technique, the *token economy,* a behavior modification program used in mental hospitals and other settings such as schools. For example, residents of mental hospitals may receive tokens, or plastic chips, as positive reinforcers for performing certain desirable behaviors such as grooming themselves, tidying their rooms, and socializing appropriately with others. Tokens can then be exchanged for tangible reinforcers such as extra privileges or candy. Token economy programs have been used successfully in mental hospitals, institutions and group homes for people with mental retardation, and residential treatment facilities for delinquents.

CONCEPT 14.16
Many behavior therapists subscribe to a broader concept of behavior therapy called cognitive-behavioral therapy, which focuses on changing maladaptive thoughts and beliefs as well as problem behaviors.

Cognitive-Behavioral Therapy   **Cognitive-behavioral therapy (CBT)** combines behavioral techniques, such as gradual exposure, with cognitive techniques that focus on challenging and correcting faulty patterns of thinking (Dobson & Dozois, 2001; McGinn & Sanderson, 2001). Many therapists recognize the value of combining behavioral and cognitive techniques in therapy, so much so that cognitive-behavioral therapy has become the most widely endorsed training orientation in clinical psychology training programs in the United States (Nevid, Lavi, & Primavera, 1986, 1987). Cognitive-behavioral therapists draw upon the principles and techniques of cognitive models of therapy, such as those pioneered by psychologist Albert Ellis and psychiatrist Aaron Beck, whose work we consider in the next section.

Cognitive Therapies

Cognitive therapists focus on helping people change how they think. Their techniques are based on the view that distorted or faulty ways of thinking underlie emotional problems (e.g., anxiety disorders and depression) as well as self-defeating or maladaptive behavior. In short, they argue that emotional problems are caused not by external events or life experiences but, rather, by the ways people interpret them.

CONCEPT 14.17
Cognitive therapists help clients challenge maladaptive thoughts and beliefs and replace them with more adaptive ways of thinking.

Cognitive therapies are relatively brief forms of treatment (involving months rather than years). Like the humanistic approach, they focus more on what is happening in the present than on what happened in the distant past. Clients are

cognitive-behavioral therapy (CBT)
A form of therapy that combines behavioral and cognitive treatment techniques.

THE PIONEERS

Using His Head

Albert Ellis

Ellis claimed that as early as age 4 he began to develop beliefs that would later inform his views on psychology—beliefs such as "Life is full of hassles you can't control or eliminate" and "Hassles are never terrible unless you make them so" and "Use your head in reactions as well as your heart" (cited in Wiener, 1988, p. 18). He began acting on these principles at a young age, taking life as it came and never allowing himself to feel upset or angry for very long. He reasoned that it doesn't make sense to spend your time feeling miserable when you could be enjoying yourself. His early professional training was in psychoanalysis, which at the time was the only major school of therapy. But the slow pace of the therapy and the passive role of the therapist didn't suit his personality. He soon began to experiment, taking a more active therapeutic role and developing a direct and pointed way of questioning clients. He formulated his model of therapy based on the assumption that irrational or illogical thinking is at the root of emotional problems. To cure these problems, he believed, the therapist must teach the client to recognize irrational beliefs and replace them with more logical, self-enhancing beliefs. He viewed this process as a kind of "pounding-away" at the client's irrational beliefs until the client is persuaded to change these beliefs and adopt more logical ways of thinking.

given homework assignments to help them not only identify and challenge distorted thoughts as they occur but also adopt more adaptive behaviors and rational ways of thinking. The two major cognitive therapies are *rational emotive behavior therapy*, which was developed by Ellis, and *cognitive therapy*, which was developed by Beck.

CONCEPT 14.18
Rational emotive behavior therapy is based on the view that irrational beliefs cause people to suffer emotional distress in the face of disappointing life experiences.

Online Study Center
Resources
Weblinks: Albert Ellis Institute

rational emotive behavior therapy (REBT)
Developed by Albert Ellis, a form of psychotherapy based on identifying and correcting irrational beliefs that are believed to underlie emotional and behavioral difficulties.

Rational Emotive Behavior Therapy: The Importance of Thinking Rationally
Albert Ellis (b. 1913) developed **rational emotive behavior therapy (REBT)** based on his view that irrational or illogical thinking is at the root of emotional problems (Dryden & Ellis, 2001; Ellis, 1991, 2001). To cure these problems, he believed the therapist must teach the client to recognize these irrational beliefs and replace them with logical, self-enhancing beliefs. He viewed this process as a kind of "pounding-away" at the client's irrational beliefs until the client is persuaded to change these beliefs and adopt more logical ways of thinking in their place.

Ellis contends that irrational beliefs often take the form of *shoulds* and *musts*, such as the belief that one must always have the approval of the important people in one's life. Ellis notes that while the desire for approval is understandable, it is irrational to believe that one will always receive approval or that one couldn't possibly survive without it. REBT encourages clients to replace irrational beliefs (such as those listed in Table 14.2) with rational alternatives, and to face their problems rationally. As described in the Pioneers box above, the early experiences in Ellis's own life set the stage for the psychological theory he later developed.

To Ellis, negative emotional reactions, such as anxiety and depression, are not produced directly by life experiences. Rather, they stem from the irrational beliefs that we hold about life experiences. Irrational beliefs are illogical because they are based on a distorted, exaggerated appraisal of the situation, not on the facts at hand. Ellis uses an "ABC" approach to explain the causes of emotional distress. This model can be diagrammed as follows:

Activating event → Beliefs → Consequences

Consider a person who feels worthless and depressed after getting a poor grade on a college exam (see Figure 14.2). The poor grade is the *activating event* (A). The

TABLE 14.2 Examples of Irrational Beliefs According to Ellis

- You absolutely must have love and approval from virtually all the people who are important to you.
- You must be completely competent in all your activities in order to feel worthwhile.
- It is awful and catastrophic when life does not go the way you want it to go. Things are awful when you don't get your first choices.
- People must treat each other fairly, and it is horrible when they don't.
- It's awful and terrible when there is no clear or quick solution to life's problems.
- Your past must continue to affect you and determine your behavior.

Source: Adapted from Ellis, 1991.

Figure 14.2 The Ellis "ABC" Model

consequences (C), or outcomes, are feelings of depression. But the activating event (A) does not lead directly to the emotional consequence (C). Rather, the event is filtered through the person's *beliefs* (B) ("I'm just a complete jerk. I'll never succeed"). People often have difficulty identifying their beliefs (B)—in part, because they are generally more aware of what they are feeling than of what they are thinking in response to the activating event (A) and, in part, because the event (A) and the emotional consequence (C) occur so closely together that the event seems to be the cause of the emotion. They may have difficulty stopping themselves in the middle of a situation and asking, "What am I saying to myself that is causing this distress?"

Ellis recognizes that disappointment is a perfectly understandable reaction in the face of upsetting or frustrating events. But when people exaggerate the consequences of negative events, they convert disappointment into depression and despair.

Consider the case of Jane, a shy and socially inhibited 27-year-old woman (Ellis & Dryden, 1987, p. 69). Jane's therapist first helped her identify her underlying irrational beliefs, such as the belief that if she became anxious and tongue-tied when speaking to people at a social gathering, it would mean she was a stupid, inadequate person. Her therapist helped her replace this irrational belief with a rational alternative: "If people do reject me for showing them how anxious I am, that will be most unfortunate, but I can stand it." Jane also rehearsed more rational beliefs several times a day, as in these examples:

"I would like to speak well, but I never have to."

"When people I favor reject me, it often reveals more about them and their tastes than about me."

REBT has a strong behavioral component as well. Therapists help clients develop more effective interpersonal behaviors to replace self-defeating or maladaptive behavior. They give clients specific tasks or homework assignments, like disagreeing with an overbearing relative or asking someone for a date. They also help them practice or rehearse more adaptive behaviors.

CONCEPT 14.19
Cognitive therapy focuses on helping clients identify and correct distorted thoughts and beliefs that have no basis in reality.

Cognitive Therapy: Correcting Errors in Thinking As a psychiatrist, Albert Beck (b. 1921) found that his work with depressed clients mirrored personal experiences of his own in which he found that his emotional reactions to events were rooted in distorted thinking (see nearby Pioneers box). The form of therapy he de-

THE PIONEERS | "Doctor, Heal Thyself"

Aaron Beck

Like Ellis, Beck was trained as a psychoanalyst, but his early life experiences impressed upon him the value of using more direct approaches to overcoming psychological problems. As a child, he had several operations that left him with a severe phobia of blood (Hunt, 1993). The very sight of blood would make him faint. One reason he decided to attend medical school was to overcome his blood phobia. As a first-year medical student,

he forced himself to watch bloody operations. In his second year, he elected to work as a surgical assistant. By directly confronting the stimuli that evoked his fear and learning that he could handle them, he found that his fear gradually disappeared. Beck used a cognitive technique to overcome another childhood phobia that continued to plague him as an adult: a fear of tunnels. He attributed the phobia to a fear of suffocation he had developed as a child following a severe case of whooping cough. He overcame this phobia by repeatedly pointing out to himself that his expectations of danger had no basis in reality.

veloped, **cognitive therapy**, helps clients identify and correct errors in thinking and to replace them with rational alternatives (Beck, 2005; Beck et al., 1979).

Beck used cognitive techniques on himself long before he developed cognitive therapy (see nearby Pioneers box). Beck refers to errors in thinking as "cognitive distortions." For example, Beck believes that depressed people tend to magnify or exaggerate the consequences of negative events and to blame themselves for disappointments in life while ignoring the role of external circumstances. Table 13.2 in Chapter 13 lists the common types of cognitive distortions.

Cognitive therapists also give clients homework assignments in which they are to record the distorted thoughts that accompany their negative emotional responses and practice substituting rational alternative thoughts (The Try This Out on the following page lists a number of distorted thoughts associated with proneness to depression. See if you can generate some rational alternatives to these thoughts.)

Another type of homework assignment is *reality testing,* in which clients are encouraged to test out their negative beliefs to determine if they are valid. For example, a depressed client who feels unwanted by everyone might be asked to call two or three friends on the phone to gather data about how the friends react to the calls. The therapist might then ask the client to report on the assignment: "Did they immediately hang up the phone? Or did they seem pleased that you called? Did they express any interest at all in talking to you again or getting together sometime? Does the evidence support the conclusion that *no one* has any interest in you?"

In the following case example, Beck and his colleagues illustrate how a cognitive therapist challenges the distortions in a client's thinking—in this instance, all-or-nothing thinking that leads the client to judge herself as completely lacking in self-control:

> Client: I don't have any self-control at all.
>
> Therapist: On what basis do you say that?
>
> Client: Somebody offered me candy and I couldn't refuse it.
>
> Therapist: Were you eating candy every day?
>
> Client: No, I just ate it this once.
>
> Therapist: Did you do anything constructive during the past week to adhere to your diet?

cognitive therapy Developed by Aaron Beck, a form of therapy based on a collaborative effort between clients and therapists that helps clients recognize and correct distorted patterns of thinking believed to underlie their emotional problems.

Client: Well, I didn't give in to the temptation to buy candy every time I saw it at the store. . . . Also, I did not eat any candy except that one time when it was offered to me and I felt I couldn't refuse it.

Therapist: If you counted up the number of times you controlled yourself versus the number of times you gave in, what ratio would you get?

Client: About 100 to 1.

Therapist: So if you controlled yourself 100 times and did not control yourself just once, would that be a sign that you are weak through and through?

Client: I guess not—not through and through [smiles].

Source: Adapted from Beck et al., 1979, p. 68.

REBT and cognitive therapy are similar in many respects. Both focus primarily on helping people replace dysfunctional thoughts and beliefs with more adaptive, rational ones. The major difference may be one of therapeutic style: the REBT therapist typically adopts a more direct and sometimes confrontational approach in disputing the client's irrational beliefs (Dryden, 1984; Ellis, Young, & Lockwood, 1989), whereas the cognitive therapist usually takes a gentler, more collaborative approach to help clients identify and correct the distortions in their thinking.

The differences between specific psychotherapies are not as clear-cut as they may seem. On the one hand, there is a blurring of lines between cognitive and behavioral therapies in the sense that we can classify the cognitive therapies of Ellis and Beck as forms of cognitive-behavioral therapy. Both rely on behavioral and cognitive techniques to help people develop more adaptive behaviors and to change dysfunctional thinking patterns. Many therapists identify themselves with an even broader eclectic approach, as we see next.

TRY THIS OUT

Replacing Distorted Thoughts with Rational Alternatives

For each of the automatic thoughts listed below, fill in a rational alternative response. If necessary, refer again to Table 13.2 for a listing of the common types of cognitive distortions. Sample rational alternatives can be found in the key at the end of the chapter.

Automatic Thought	Type of Cognitive Distortion	Rational Alternative
1. This relationship is a disaster, a complete disaster.	All-or-nothing thinking	_____
2. I'm falling apart. I can't handle this.	Catastrophizing	_____
3. Things must really be awful for me to feel this way.	Emotion-based reasoning	_____
4. I know I'm going to flunk this course.	Jumping to conclusions	_____
5. _____'s problems are really my fault.	Mistaken responsibility	_____
6. I'm just a loser.	Name calling	_____
7. Someone my age should be further along than I am.	Shouldism	_____
8. It would be awful if I don't get this job.	Catastrophizing	_____
9. I know that if _____ got to know me, he/she would not like me.	Jumping to conclusions	_____
10. All I can think about are the negatives.	Negative focusing	_____

Eclectic Therapy

Therapists who practice **eclectic therapy** look beyond the theoretical barriers that divide one school of psychotherapy from another. They seek common ground among the different schools and integrate principles and techniques representing these different approaches (Beutler, Harwood, & Caldwell, 2001; Stricker & Gold, 2001). In a particular case, an eclectic therapist might use behavior therapy to help the client change problem behaviors and psychodynamic approaches to help the client develop insight into underlying conflicts. A recent survey of two hundred practitioners showed that about half used a combination of cognitive-behavioral and psychodynamic techniques in their practices (Holloway, 2003b).

Eclecticism is the most widely endorsed theoretical orientation among clinical and counseling psychologists today (Bechtoldt et al., 2001; see Figure 14.3). Eclectic therapists tend to be older and more experienced than other therapists (Beitman, 1989). Perhaps they have learned through experience about the value of drawing upon diverse points of view.

Not all therapists subscribe to an eclectic approach. Many believe that the differences between schools of therapy are so compelling that therapeutic integration is neither desirable nor achievable. Trying to combine them, they argue, leads to a veritable hodgepodge of techniques that lack a cohesive conceptual framework. Nevertheless, the movement toward eclecticism continues to grow within the therapeutic community.

Group, Family, and Couple Therapy

Group therapy brings people together in small groups to help them explore and resolve their problems. Compared to individual therapy, it offers several advantages. For one thing, because the therapist treats several people at a time, group therapy may yield savings in terms of therapists' time and patients' costs compared to individual therapy (Dugas et al., 2003). For another, it may be particularly helpful for people experiencing interpersonal problems such as loneliness, shyness, and low self-esteem. These individuals often benefit from interacting with supportive others in a group treatment program. The give-and-take within the group may help improve a member's social skills. In addition, clients in group therapy can learn how others in the group have coped with similar problems in their lives.

Group therapy may not be for everyone. Some clients prefer the individual attention of a therapist. They may feel that one-on-one therapy provides an opportunity for a deeper exploration of their emotions and experiences. They may also be reluctant to disclose their personal problems to other members of a group. Or they may feel too inhibited to relate comfortably to others in a group, even if they themselves are perhaps the ones for whom group interaction is most beneficial.

Group therapists can offset some of these drawbacks by creating an atmosphere that promotes trust and self-exploration. In particular, they require that information disclosed by group members is kept in strict confidence, ensure that group members relate to each other in a supportive and nondestructive fashion, and prevent any single member from monopolizing their attention or dominating the group. In short, effective group therapists attempt to provide each member with the attention he or she needs.

Family therapy helps troubled families learn to communicate better and resolve their differences. The family, not the individual, is the unit of treatment. Most family therapists view the family unit as a complex social system in which

CONCEPT 14.20
Many therapists identify with an eclectic orientation in which they adopt principles and techniques from different schools of therapy.

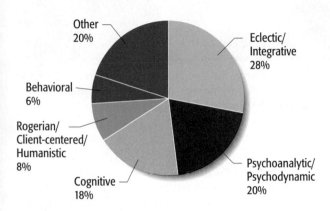

Figure 14.3   Therapeutic Orientations of Clinical and Counseling Psychologists
According to a recent survey, the eclectic or integrative orientation has the greatest number of adherents.

Source: Adapted from Bechtoldt et al., 2001.

CONCEPT 14.21
Therapists often treat individuals in group settings, where the "group" may be a collection of unrelated persons, a family, or a couple.

eclectic therapy   A therapeutic approach that draws upon principles and techniques representing different schools of therapy.
group therapy   A form of therapy in which clients are treated within a group format.
family therapy   Therapy for troubled families that focuses on changing disruptive patterns of communication and improving the ways in which family members relate to each other.

Group Therapy Group therapy brings together small groups of people to help them explore and work through their psychological problems.

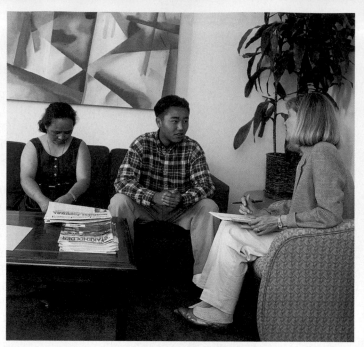

Family Therapy Family therapy provides opportunities for family members to develop more effective ways of communicating and relating to each other.

individuals play certain roles. In many cases there is one family member whom the family brands as the source of the family's problems. Effective family therapists demonstrate how the problems of this individual are symptomatic of larger problems in the family involving a breakdown in the family system, not in the individual per se. They help dysfunctional families change how family members interact and relate to one another so that members can become more accepting and supportive of each other's needs and differences.

In **couple therapy** (often called marital therapy when applied to married couples), the couple is the unit of the treatment. Couple therapy builds healthier relationships by helping couples acquire more effective communication and problem-solving skills (Christensen et al., 2004). Couple therapists identify power struggles and lack of communication as among the typical problems faced by troubled couples seeking help. Their aim is to help open channels of communication between partners and encourage them to share personal feelings and needs in ways that do not put each other down.

Is Psychotherapy Effective?

Yes, psychotherapy works. A wealth of scientific findings supports the effectiveness of psychotherapy. Yet questions remain about whether some forms of therapy are more effective than others.

Measuring Effectiveness The strongest body of evidence supporting the effectiveness of psychotherapy comes from controlled studies in which people who received psychotherapy are compared with those who received control treatments or were placed in waiting-list control groups. Investigators commonly use a statistical technique called **meta-analysis** to average the results across a large number of such studies.

An early but influential meta-analysis was conducted by Mary Lee Smith, Gene Glass, and Thomas Miller (1980). From an analysis of more than four hundred controlled studies comparing particular types of therapy (psychodynamic, behavioral, humanistic, etc.) against control groups, they reported that the average person receiving psychotherapy achieved better results on outcome measures

couple therapy Therapy that focuses on helping distressed couples resolve their conflicts and develop more effective communication skills.

meta-analysis A statistical technique for averaging results across a large number of studies.

than did 80 percent of the people placed in waiting-list control groups (see Figure 14.4). More recent meta-analyses also point to better outcomes for people treated with psychotherapy than for those placed in control groups (e.g., McLeod & Weisz, 2004). Meta-analysis also supports the effectiveness of marital, family, and group therapy techniques (McDermut, Miller, & Brown, 2001; Shadish et al., 1993; Shadish & Baldwin, 2005).

The greatest gains in therapy are typically achieved during the first few months of treatment. About half of the people who participate in psychotherapy show significant improvement within the first twenty-one sessions (Anderson & Lambert, 2001; Lambert, Hansen, & Finch, 2001). Many other patients respond with additional treatment. But not everyone benefits from therapy, and some people even deteriorate. Then too, individuals receiving other forms of treatment, such as drug therapy, sometimes have negative outcomes.

Which Therapy Is Best?   To say that therapy overall is effective does not mean that all therapies are equally effective, or that one form of therapy is as good as any other for a particular problem. Studies using meta-analysis show little difference in the magnitude of the outcomes achieved when comparing different forms of therapy against control groups or even against each other (Luborsky et al., 2002; Nathan, Stuart, & Dolan, 2000; Wampold et al., 1997).

Does this mean that different therapies are about equally effective? Not necessarily. Therapies often differ with respect to the types of problems they treat and the ways in which they measure outcomes. In other words, we need to know which therapy works best for which particular type of problem when outcomes are measured in the same way.

For example, behavior therapy and cognitive-behavioral therapies have produced impressive results in treating a range of disorders, including anxiety disorders such as panic disorder, generalized anxiety disorder, social phobia, posttraumatic stress disorder (PTSD, which is discussed in Chapter 15), agoraphobia, and obsessive-compulsive disorder, as well as other disorders, such as bulimia, depression, and personality disorders (see, for example, Addis et al., 2004; Bryant et al., 2003; Clark, 2004; Ehlers et al., 2005; Foa et al., 2005; Hamilton & Dobson, 2002; Heimberg, Turk, & Mennin, 2004; Leichsenring & Leibing, 2003).

Other behavioral approaches, such as the token economy, help improve social functioning of patients in institutional settings. Evidence also supports a role for cognitive-behavioral therapy in the treatment of schizophrenia (Rector & Beck, 2001; Wiersma et al., 2001).

REALITY CHECK

THE CLAIM Psychological disorders are best treated with drugs.

THE EVIDENCE Evidence shows that psychological forms of treatment are at least as effective as drug therapy in treating many types of anxiety and mood disorders. Moreover, psychotherapy does not carry the risk of side effects associated with drug therapy and often leads to more lasting effects. However, severe and persistent psychological disorders such as schizophrenia, bipolar disorder, and some forms of major depression typically require biomedical therapies or a combination of biomedical and psychological approaches.

THE TAKE-AWAY MESSAGE Psychotherapy is effective in treating a wide range of psychological disorders. Some people respond better to psychological approaches, others to psychiatric drugs, and still others to a combination of approaches.

CONCEPT 14.22
A wealth of scientific findings supports the effectiveness of psychotherapy, but questions remain about whether some forms of therapy are more effective than others.

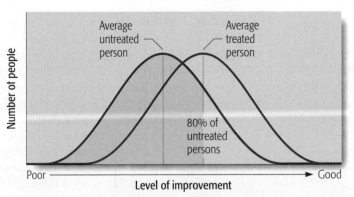

Figure 14.4   Effectiveness of Psychotherapy
A meta-analysis of more than 400 outcome studies showed that the average therapy client achieved greater improvement than 80 percent of untreated controls.
Source: Adapted from Smith, Glass, & Miller, 1980.

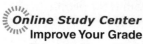

TABLE 14.3 **Examples of Empirically Supported Treatments (ESTs)**

Treatment	Effective in Treating
Cognitive therapy	Depression
Behavior therapy	Depression Persons with developmental disabilities Enuresis ("bed-wetting") Headache Agoraphobia and specific phobia Obsessive-compulsive disorder
Cognitive-behavioral therapy (CBT)	Panic disorder Generalized anxiety disorder Bulimia Smoking cessation
Interpersonal psychotherapy (a structured brief form of psychodynamic therapy)	Depression

Source: Adapted from Chambless et al., 1998.

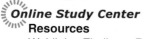

Although psychodynamic therapy no longer dominants the field the way it once did, many therapists continue to draw upon psychodynamic principles and techniques. In a recent survey of 177 practicing psychologists, 45 percent described their approach to clinical practice as involving a combination of psychodynamic and cognitive-behavioral techniques (PracticeNet, 2003).

Some structured forms of psychodynamic therapy show good results in treating certain disorders, including depression, borderline personality disorder, and bulimia (see, for example, DeRubeis et al., 2005; Leichsenring et al., 2004; Mufson et al., 2004; Wilson et al., 2002). Humanistic therapies may have the greatest benefits in helping individuals develop a more cohesive sense of self, connect with their innermost feelings, and mobilize their efforts toward self-actualization.

Recently, a task force of psychologists developed a list of psychological treatments whose effectiveness has been demonstrated in scientifically based studies (Addis, 2002; Chorpita et al., 2002). They identified a number of such treatments, called *empirically supported treatments* or ESTs, that they believed met the grade (Chambless & Ollendick, 2001; Deegear & Lawson, 2003; Table 14.3). Since the process of identifying empirically supported treatments is an ongoing effort, other therapies may be added to the list as clear evidence supporting their effectiveness becomes available.

CONCEPT 14.23
Evidence points to both specific and nonspecific factors in accounting for the benefits of psychotherapy.

What Accounts for the Benefits of Therapy? Might the benefits of therapy have to do with the common characteristics shared by different therapies? These common characteristics are called **nonspecific factors** because they are not limited to any one therapy (Hanna, 2003; Norcross, 2002). They include aspects of the interpersonal relationship between the client and therapist such as the *therapeutic alliance*—that is, the attachment the client feels toward the therapist and the therapy. The therapeutic relationship between the client and therapist may have beneficial effects quite apart from the effects of specific techniques themselves (Norcross, 2002). For example, the strength of the therapeutic alliance is linked to better outcomes in therapy (Ackerman & Hilsenroth, 2003; Martin, Garske, & Davis, 2000). Another nonspecific factor is the expectation of improvement (Perlman, 2001). Positive expectancies of change can become a type of self-fulfilling prophecy by motivating clients to mobilize their efforts to overcome their problems (Meyer et al.,

nonspecific factors General features of psychotherapy, such as attention from a therapist and mobilization of positive expectancies or hope.

2002). Responses to positive expectancies are called **placebo effects** or *expectancy effects*. Investigators believe that the effectiveness of psychotherapy may be based on a combination of nonspecific factors and factors that are specific to particular forms of therapy (Ilardi & Craighead, 1994).

Multicultural Issues in Treatment

In our multicultural society, therapists treat people from diverse ethnic and racial groups. Members of ethnic and racial minorities may have different customs, beliefs, and philosophies than members of the dominant majority culture, and therapists must be aware of these differences to provide successful treatment (James & Prilleltensky, 2002). They need to be able to relate to the client's world and adjust their treatment approaches to the cultural and social realities of clients from diverse backgrounds (Barry & Bullock, 2001; Cardemil & Battle, 2003; Wong et al., 2003). For example, with African American clients, therapists need to understand the long history of extreme racial discrimination and oppression to which African Americans have been exposed in our society. This history of negative treatment and cultural oppression may lead African Americans to develop a heightened sense of suspiciousness or reserve toward Whites, including White therapists, as a type of coping skill—a defense against exploitation. They may thus be hesitant to disclose personal information in therapy, especially during the early stages. Therapists should not press for disclosure or confuse culturally laden suspiciousness with paranoid thinking.

In working with Asian clients, therapists need to understand that many Asian cultures discourage public displays of emotion, a cultural practice that may conflict with the emphasis in Western models of psychotherapy on the open expression of emotions. Indeed, the failure of Asian Americans to keep their feelings to themselves may be interpreted within the culture as reflecting poorly on their upbringing (Huang, 1994). Traditional Asian cultures also emphasize collective values, such as regarding the importance of the group as greater than that of the individual. By contrast, therapists in Western cultures often emphasize the importance of individuality and self-determination.

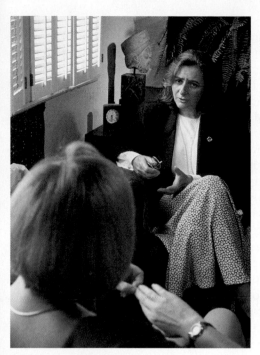

The Therapeutic Alliance The development of a strong working relationship, or therapeutic alliance, between the client and therapist is an important element in the effectiveness of psychotherapy.

CONCEPT 14.24
Therapists are trained to be sensitive to cultural differences among the different groups of people who seek their help.

Culturally Sensitive Therapy Culturally sensitive therapy is structured to create a more receptive therapeutic environment for people from varied cultural backgrounds.

placebo effects Positive outcomes of an experiment resulting from participants' expectations about the effects of a treatment rather than from the experimental treatment itself.

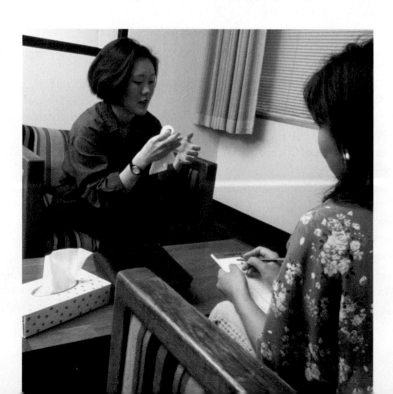

Value conflicts may also come into play in therapeutic situations involving Latinos from traditional Hispanic backgrounds. Latino or Hispanic cultures place a strong value on interdependency among family members—a value that may clash with the emphasis on independence and self-reliance in mainstream U.S. culture. Treatment providers need to be respectful of this difference and avoid imposing their own values on Latino clients. Therapists also need to understand the strongly held spiritual beliefs of many Latino clients (Zea, Mason & Murguía, 2000).

In some situations, therapists can incorporate the customs, cultures, and values of their clients into the therapeutic setting (Rice & O'Donohue, 2002). In working with Native Americans, for example, they may find it helpful to bring elements of tribal culture into the therapy setting, such as healing ceremonies that are part of the client's cultural or religious traditions (Rabasca, 2000a). They also need to be aware that Native American clients may expect therapists to do most of the talking, consistent with the traditional healer role within their culture.

Culturally sensitive therapists recognize that just because a particular therapy works well with one population group doesn't mean it necessarily works with all groups (Hall, 2003; Sue, 2003). Therefore, they need to consider evidence supporting a particular therapy with the particular population with which they are working In working with Latinos as well as other ethnic groups, therapists must also be sensitive to the linguistic preferences of the people they serve (Biever et al.,

TABLE 14.4   Disparities in Mental Health Care: Culture, Race, and Ethnicity

Disparities

As compared to other groups, racial or ethnic minorities have less access to mental health care and receive lower-quality care.

Causes

• Minority-group members are more likely to lack health insurance.

• Minority-group members lack access to treatment providers who are similar in ethnicity or who possess appropriate language skills.

• The lingering stigma about mental illness discourages help-seeking.

• There are few treatment providers in rural or isolated locations where minority-group members, especially Native Americans, may reside.

Vision for the future

• Expand the scientific base to better understand relationships between mental health and sociocultural factors such as acculturation, stigma, and racism.

• Improve access to treatment, such as by improving language access and geographic availability of mental health services.

• Reduce barriers to mental health care, such as costs of services and societal stigma toward mental illness.

• Improve quality of care, such as by individualizing treatment to the person's age, gender, race, ethnicity, and culture.

• Increase minority representation among mental health treatment providers.

• Promote mental health by strengthening supportive families and working to eradicate contributors to mental health problems, such as poverty, community violence, racism, and discrimination.

Source: U.S. Department of Health and Human Services, 2001b.

2002). Finally, they need to be aware of their own cultural biases to avoid stereo-typing clients from other cultural groups (Stuart, 2004). When a therapist's own cultural biases are left unexamined, these biases can quickly damage the therapeutic relationship.

The mental health system also needs to do a better job of providing quality care to all groups. A 2001 report by the U.S. Surgeon General concluded that minority-group members typically receive lower-quality care and have less access to care than other Americans (U.S. Department of Health and Human Services, 2001b; see Table 14.4). Consequently, minority-group members shoulder a greater mental health burden because of mental disorders that go undiagnosed and untreated (Stenson, 2001a). Concept Chart 14.2 summarizes the differences among the types of psychotherapy discussed in this module.

CONCEPT CHART 14.2   Major Types of Psychotherapy: How They Differ

Type of Therapy	Focus	Length	Therapist's Role	Techniques
Classical psychoanalysis	Insight into unconscious causes of behavior	Long, at least several years	Passive, interpretive	Free association, dream analysis, interpretation
Modern psychodynamic approaches	Insight-oriented, but focuses more on ego functioning and current relationships than is the case in Freudian analysis	Briefer than traditional analysis	Probing, engaging client in back-and-forth discussion	More direct analysis of client's defenses and transference relationships; less use of free association
Humanistic, client-centered therapy	Promotes self-growth by helping clients become more aware of, and accepting of, their inner feelings, needs, and interests	Varies	Nondirective; allows client to lead, with therapist serving as an empathic listener	Demonstrating empathy, unconditional positive regard, and genuineness to create a warm and accepting therapeutic atmosphere
Humanistic, gestalt therapy	Helps clients develop a unified sense of self by bringing into present awareness their true feelings and conflicts with others	Brief, sometimes only a few sessions	Directive, engaging, even confrontational	Empty chair technique and other role-playing exercises
Behavior therapy	Changes problem behavior through use of learning-based techniques tailored to the specific problem	Brief, lasting perhaps 10 to 20 sessions	Direct, active problem solving	Systematic desensitization, exposure therapy, aversion therapy, operant conditioning techniques
Cognitive-behavioral therapy	Focuses on changing both maladaptive cognitions and overt behaviors	Brief, usually lasting 10 to 20 sessions	Direct, active problem solving	Combines cognitive and behavioral techniques
Rational-emotive behavior therapy	Helps clients replace irrational beliefs with more adaptive, logical alternatives	Brief, typically 10 to 20 sessions	Directive, challenging, sometimes confrontational	Identifying and disputing irrational beliefs, with behavioral homework assignments
Cognitive therapy	Helps clients identify and correct faulty styles of thinking	Brief, typically 10 to 20 sessions	Collaborative process of engaging client in an effort to logically examine beliefs and find evidence to support or refute them	Identifying and correcting distorted thoughts; specific homework assignments including thought recording and reality testing

EXPLORING PSYCHOLOGY
Virtual Reality Therapy, the Next Best Thing to Being There

You may recall the movie *The Matrix*, in which the lead character played by Keanu Reeves learns that the world he believes is real is merely an illusion, a virtual environment so lifelike that people take it to be real. Though the movie is science fiction, the use of virtual reality as a therapeutic tool has become science fact.

Behavior therapists have adapted the technology of virtual reality to create simulated environments they can use as therapeutic tools. In **virtual reality therapy (VRT)**, people with phobias can gradually expose themselves to increasingly fearful "virtual" stimuli. Clients wear a specialized helmet and gloves that are connected to a computer to create these virtual environments. For example, a person with a fear of heights can experience a simulation of riding on a glass-enclosed virtual elevator or peering out over a virtual balcony in a high-rise building. Through a process of gradual exposure to a series of increasingly frightening virtual stimuli, while progressing only when fear at each step diminishes, people can learn to overcome fears in virtual reality in much the same way they would had they followed a program of gradual exposure in real-life situations.

Through VRT, therapists can simulate real-life environments that would be difficult to arrange in reality, such as simulated airplane takeoffs. Virtual therapy offers other potential advantages, such as permitting the client to control the intensity and range of stimuli presented during virtual exposure sessions (Zimand et al., 2003). Participants may also be more willing to attempt certain fearful tasks in virtual reality than they would in real life.

Advances in virtual reality technology make it possible to create simulated virtual environments that are indeed convincing enough to produce intense anxiety in fearful people (Lubell, 2004). Consider this comment by Dr. Barbara Rothbaum, the psychologist who pioneered virtual therapy: "If the first person had put the helmet on and said, 'This isn't scary,' it wouldn't have worked. But you get the same physiological changes—the racing heart, the sweat—that you would in the actual place" (cited in Goleman, 1995d, p. C11). Virtual therapy has been shown to be effective in treating a wide range of phobias, including fear of heights and fear of flying (Botella et al., 2004; Kamphuis, Emmelkamp, & Krijn, 2002). The results of a recent study showed that VRT for fear of flying was just as effective as real-life exposure, with both treatments demonstrating better results than an untreated (waiting list) control (Rothbaum et al., 2002). Ninety-two percent of the clients treated with VRT were able to fly on a commercial airliner within the year following treatment.

We have virtually only scratched the surface that this new technology has to offer as a therapeutic tool. Today, therapists are expanding the application of VRT to include treatment of many other phobias, such as fear of public speaking and agoraphobia. There are even attempts to create "virtual bars" and "virtual crack houses" to help people with substance abuse problems develop more effective coping skills for resisting drugs (Lubell, 2004). In yet another possible use, VRT may help troubled families by permitting family members to confront virtual representations of one another while receiving guidance and feedback from the therapist (Steven, 1995).

Virtual Reality Therapy Virtual reality therapy has been used to help people overcome a fear of heights by guiding them through a series of virtual reality encounters with height situations.

virtual reality therapy A form of behavior therapy in which virtual reality is used to simulate real-world environments that can be used as therapeutic tools.

MODULE 14.2 REVIEW

Types of Psychotherapy

RECITE IT

What is psychotherapy?

- Psychotherapy is a verbal form of therapy intended to help people overcome psychological or personal problems.

What are the major types of mental health professionals?

- The major types of professionals who provide mental health services are clinical and counseling psychologists, psychiatrists, clinical or psychiatric social workers, psychoanalysts, counselors, and psychiatric nurses. They vary in their training backgrounds as well as in the services they provide.

What are the major forms of psychotherapy?

- Psychodynamic therapy is an insight-oriented approach to therapy based on the Freudian model. The psychodynamic therapist helps clients uncover and work through unconscious conflicts dating from childhood that are believed to be at the root of their problems. Traditional psychoanalysts used free association, dream analysis, interpretation, and analysis of the transference relationship to help the client gain insight into underlying conflicts from the past involving sexual and aggressive instincts. By contrast, modern psychodynamic approaches tend to be more focused on the workings of the ego than on the role of the id and on problems in the client's present relationships.

- Humanistic therapists focus primarily on the client's subjective, conscious experience in the here-and-now. Rogers's client-centered therapy and Perls's gestalt therapy are two examples.

- Behavior therapy is the systematic application of learning principles to help people unlearn maladaptive behaviors and acquire more adaptive behaviors.

- The techniques of behavior therapy include systematic desensitization, gradual exposure, modeling, aversive conditioning, and methods based on operant conditioning.

- Cognitive-behavioral therapy is a broader form of behavior therapy that incorporates both behavioral and cognitive techniques in treatment.

- Cognitive therapies, such as rational emotive behavior therapy (REBT) and cognitive therapy, focus on modifying the individual's maladaptive thoughts and beliefs that are believed to underlie emotional problems such as anxiety and depression and self-defeating or maladaptive forms of behavior.

- In eclectic therapy, the therapist adopts principles or techniques from different schools of therapy.

- Forms of therapy that extend treatment to more than one individual at a time include group therapy, family therapy, and couple therapy.

Is psychotherapy effective?

- The answer is yes. Meta-analyses show that people who participate in psychotherapy are more likely to achieve a good outcome than those who remain untreated.

- There is a continuing debate about whether some forms of therapy are better than others.

What cultural factors do therapists need to consider when working with members of diverse groups?

- The cultural factors to be considered include differences in cultural beliefs, customs, values, and linguistic preferences, as well as the therapists' own cultural biases and stereotyping tendencies.

RECALL IT

1. Match the following concepts from psychodynamic therapy with the appropriate descriptions: i. free association; ii. insight; iii. resistance; iv. transference relationship
   a. understanding the unconscious origins of a problem
   b. responding to the analyst as a "father figure"
   c. blocking that occurs when emotionally sensitive topics arise
   d. saying whatever comes to mind

2. Name three important qualities shown by an effective client-centered therapist.

3. Jonathan's therapist trains him to use deep muscle relaxation and helps him construct a fear hierarchy. Which behavior therapy technique is this therapist likely to be using?

4. The form of therapy that holds that irrational beliefs underlie the development of psychological problems is

   _____.

5. List two advantages and two disadvantages of group therapy.

THINK ABOUT IT

- Which approach to therapy would you prefer if you were seeking help for a psychological problem? Why would you prefer this approach?

- What would you say to someone who claims that psychotherapy is useless? What evidence would you use to support your views?

- What cultural factors should therapists take into account when providing services to members of diverse cultural or racial groups?

MODULE 14.3
Biomedical Therapies

- What are the major types of psychotropic or psychiatric drugs?
- What are the advantages and disadvantages of psychiatric drugs?
- What is ECT, and how is it used?

Remarkable gains have been made in treating a wide range of psychological disorders with biomedical therapies, especially *drug therapy*, the most widely used form of biomedical treatment. Despite their success, psychiatric drugs have limitations, including unwelcome side effects and potential for abuse. Other forms of biomedical treatment, such as electroconvulsive therapy (ECT) and psychosurgery, are more controversial.

Drug Therapy

As discussed in Chapter 2, neurotransmitters ferry nerve impulses from one neuron to another. But imbalances in the levels of neurotransmitters in the brain or irregularities in how they function are implicated in a wide range of psychological disorders, including anxiety disorders, mood disorders, eating disorders, and schizophrenia. Scientists have developed a range of **psychotropic drugs** (also called *psychiatric* or *psychotherapeutic drugs*) that influence the delicate balance of neurotransmitter activity in the brain in ways that offer relief from troubling symptoms ranging from anxiety to to depression to hallucinations and delusions (Snyder, 2002). However, these drugs are not cures. There are three major groupings of psychotropic drugs: antianxiety drugs, antidepressants, and antipsychotics.

Antianxiety Drugs   **Antianxiety drugs** (sometimes called *minor tranquilizers*) help quell anxiety, induce calmness, and reduce muscle tension. The most widely used antianxiety drugs are minor tranquilizers such as *diazepam* (Valium), *chlordiazepoxide* (Librium), and *alprazolam* (Xanax). They act on the neurotransmitter *gamma-aminobutyric acid*—or GABA for short (first discussed in Chapter 2). GABA is an inhibitory neurotransmitter, which means that it inhibits the flow of nerve impulses and thus prevents neurons in the brain from overly exciting their neighbors. The major types of antianxiety drugs, including Valium, Librium, and Xanax, make GABA receptors more sensitive, thereby enhancing the chemical's calming (inhibitory) effects.

Antidepressants   **Antidepressants** increase the availability in the brain of the neurotransmitters norepinephrine and serotonin (Cryan et al., 2004). There are three major types of antidepressants: **tricyclics**, **monoamine oxidase (MAO) inhibitors**, and **selective serotonin-reuptake inhibitors (SSRIs)**. The tricyclics, such as *imipramine* (Tofranil), *amitriptyline* (Elavil), and *doxepin* (Sinequan), raise brain levels of norepinephrine and serotonin by interfering with the reuptake process by which these chemical messengers are reabsorbed by the transmitting cells. MAO inhibitors such as *phenelzine* (Nardil) and *tranylcypromine* (Parnate) inhibit the action of the enzyme *monoamine oxidase,* which normally breaks down (degrades) these neurotransmitters in the synapse. SSRIs, such as *fluoxetine* (Prozac) and *sertraline* (Zoloft), are a newer generation of drugs that have more specific effects on raising levels of serotonin in the brain by interfering with its reuptake (Jacobs, 2004). Though antidepressants are known to increase the availability of key neurotransmitters at the synaptic level in the brain, the precise mechanisms by which they help relieve depression remain unclear (Lucassen, Fuchs, & Czeh, 2004).

CONCEPT 14.25
Psychotropic drugs work on neurotransmitter systems in the brain to help regulate moods and thinking processes.

CONCEPT 14.26
Three major classes of psychotropic drugs are antianxiety drugs, antidepressants, and antipsychotics.

psychotropic drugs Psychiatric drugs used in the treatment of psychological or mental disorders.

antianxiety drugs Drugs that combat anxiety.

antidepressants Drugs that combat depression by affecting the levels or activity of neurotransmitters in the brain.

tricyclics A class of antidepressant drugs that increase the availability of neurotransmitters in the brain by interfering with the reuptake of these chemicals by transmitting neurons.

monoamine oxidase (MAO) inhibitors A class of antidepressant drugs that increase the availability of neurotransmitters in the brain by inhibiting an enzyme, monoamine oxidase, that breaks down or degrades them in the synapse.

selective serotonin-reuptake inhibitors (SSRIs) A class of antidepressant drugs that work specifically on increasing availability of the neurotransmitter serotonin by interfering with its reuptake.

Use of antidepressant medication in outpatient treatment has risen sharply in recent years (Olfson et al., 2002). Antidepressants help relieve depression in perhaps 50 to 70 percent of cases (Leon et al., 2003; USDHHS, 1999). But even in these instances, depression is not necessarily eliminated; improvement appears to be modest at best (Kirsch, Moore, Scoboria, & Nicholls, 2002). Though tricyclics and SSRIs are about equally effective, the SSRIs generally produce less severe side effects and are less dangerous in an overdose situation.

You may know that antidepressants are helpful in treating depression. But perhaps you didn't know that they also have therapeutic benefits in treating anxiety disorders such as panic disorder, social phobia, posttraumatic stress disorder (PTSD), generalized anxiety disorder, and obsessive-compulsive disorder, as well as bulimia (e.g., Allgulander et al., 2004; Flynn & Chen, 2003; Hudson et al., 2003; Liebowitz, Gelenberg, & Munjack, 2005).

Why do antidepressants have such broad-ranging effects? One reason is that neurotransmitters, especially serotonin, are implicated in the regulation of emotional states, including anxiety and depression. Another, as noted in Chapter 8, is that serotonin plays a key role in controlling appetite; perhaps the antidepressants reduce the incidence of binges because of their effects on this particular neurotransmitter (Walsh et al., 2004).

Antipsychotics   Antipsychotics (sometimes called *major tranquilizers*) are powerful drugs used to treat schizophrenia and other psychotic disorders. The first class of antipsychotic drugs to be developed were the *phenothiazines,* which includes the drugs Thorazine, Mellaril, and Prolixin. The introduction of these drugs in the 1950s revolutionized the treatment of schizophrenia, making it possible to control the more flagrant symptoms of the disorder, such as hallucinations and delusions (Essock et al., 2000). With their symptoms largely controlled on maintenance doses of these drugs, many schizophrenia patients were able to leave the confines of state hospitals and return to their families and communities.

Phenothiazines and newer types of antipsychotic drugs block the action of the neurotransmitter dopamine at receptor sites in the brain (Davis, Chen, & Glick, 2003). Though the underlying causes of schizophrenia remain unknown, researchers suspect that the disorder arises from disturbances in neural pathways that utilize dopamine (Haber & Fudge, 1997; see also Chapter 13).

Other Psychiatric Drugs   Mood-stabilizing drugs, such as the powdered form of the metallic element *lithium,* help stabilize mood swings in people with bipolar disorder and reduce the risks of recurrent manic episodes (Baldessarini & Tondo, 2003; Geddes et al., 2004). Other mood stabilizers include anticonvulsant drugs that are also used in the treatment of epilepsy (Ruvas-Vazquez et al., 2002).

Certain stimulant drugs, such as *methylphenidate* (Ritalin), are widely used to improve attention spans and reduce disruptive behavior in hyperactive children (Biederman, 2003; Pelham et al., 2002). These drugs appear to work by increasing activity of the neurotransmitter dopamine in the frontal lobes of the cerebral cortex, the parts of the brain that regulate attention and control impulsive behavior (Faraone, 2003; Volkow et al., 2004).

Evaluating Psychotropic Drugs   Though psychiatric drugs may reduce or control symptoms of many psychological disorders, they are not panaceas; none can produce a cure. Not all patients respond well to psychiatric drugs. Nor do drugs teach people how to resolve their problems or develop the skills needed to relate more effectively with others or manage the challenges of daily life.

Another limitation of psychiatric drugs is the risk of adverse side effects, including drowsiness (from antianxiety drugs), dry mouth and problems with sexual response (from antidepressants), and muscular tremors, rigidity, and even severe movement disorders (from antipsychotic drugs) (Minkin, 2002; Nurnberg et al.,

Psychotropic Drugs   Though psychotropic drugs like Prozac are not a cure, they often help relieve symptoms associated with psychological disorders.

CONCEPT 14.27
Psychotropic drugs help control symptoms of psychological disorders, but they do not cure the disorders.

antipsychotics   Drugs used in the treatment of psychotic disorders that help alleviate hallucinations and delusional thinking.

2003; Richardson et al., 2003). The drug lithium needs to be closely monitored because of potential toxic effects. It can also produce mild impairments in memory.

A new generation of antipsychotic drugs, including *clozapine* (Clozaril), *risperidone* (Risperdal), and *olanzapine* (Zyprexa) , appear to be at least as effective as conventional antipsychotics in controlling symptoms of schizophrenia—but with fewer troubling neurological side effects than the earlier antipsychotics (Davis, Chen, & Glick, 2003; Lindenmayer & Khan, 2004). Still unclear, however, is whether these newer drugs reduce the risk of the most serious side effect associated with the use of antipsychotic drugs, an often irreversible and potentially disabling movement disorder called **tardive dyskinesia (TD)** (Correll, Leucht, & Kane, 2004; Rosenheck et al., 2003). The symptoms of TD include involuntary lip smacking, chewing, and facial grimacing.

Some drugs, such as the antianxiety drug Valium, can lead to psychological and physical dependence (addiction) if used regularly over time. Valium can also be very dangerous, even deadly, in overdoses or if mixed with alcohol or other drugs. Some people come to depend on antianxiety drugs to cope with life's troubles rather than confronting the sources of their anxiety or relationship problems.

Relapses are common when people stop taking psychiatric drugs (Spiegel & Bruce, 1997). Relapses also occur among 15 to 20 percent of schizophrenia patients who take their medications reliably (Kane, 1996).

Psychiatric drugs are widely used in treating psychological disorders in children, including Ritalin for attention-deficit hyperactivity disorder (ADHD) and antidepressants for childhood depression (Abikoff et al., 2004; Wagner et al., 2004). Yet critics argue that mental health professionals and parents may be too eager to find a "quick fix" for complex emotional or behavioral problems, rather than expending the effort needed to more fully explore the bases of problem behaviors and pursue other treatment alternatives.

Complicating the picture is evidence that antidepressants can have the unintended consequence of increasing risks of suicidal thinking and behavior in children and adolescents (Glass, 2004; Jick, Kaye, & Jick, 2004; Wessely & Kerwin, 2004). In late 2004, the U.S. Food and Drug Administration issued an order requiring makers of antidepressants to include a strong warning that the drugs may increase the risk of suicidal thoughts and behaviors in children and adolescents (Harris, 2004). On the other hand, advocates of drug therapy point to the benefits of using medication to treat serious behavioral and emotional problems in children and to the risks of leaving these problems untreated or undertreated (Kluger, 2003).

Psychiatric drugs can be used to provide patients with temporary relief. But many health care providers use psychiatric drugs in tandem with psychotherapy or skills-building approaches, such as social skills training, which help individuals acquire more adaptive behaviors. Indeed, research evidence indicates that a combination of psychiatric drugs and psychotherapy may be more effective in some cases than either treatment alone in treating disorders such as major depression in adults and adolescents, panic disorder, and social phobia (e.g., Barlow et al., 2000; Fava et al., 2004; Feldman & Rivas-Vazquez, 2003; Harris, 2004).

Electroconvulsive Therapy

Electroconvulsive therapy (ECT) sounds barbaric. A jolt of electricity is passed through the head. It is strong enough to cause convulsions similar to those of a grand mal epileptic seizure. Yet it often produces dramatic relief from severe depression and can be a lifesaver for people who are suicidally depressed. When receiving ECT, the patient is first anesthetized to prevent any pain or discomfort. Muscle relaxants are used to prevent injuries that may result from the convulsive jerking that follows. The person awakens shortly afterward, with no memory of the procedure. ECT typically involves a series of six to twelve treatments over several weeks.

tardive dyskinesia (TD) A potentially disabling motor disorder that may occur following regular use of antipsychotic drugs.

electroconvulsive therapy (ECT) A form of therapy for severe depression that involves the administration of an electrical shock to the head.

Electroconvulsive Therapy   In ECT, an electric current is passed through the head while the patient is anesthetized. It often produces dramatic relief from severe depression, but relapses are common.

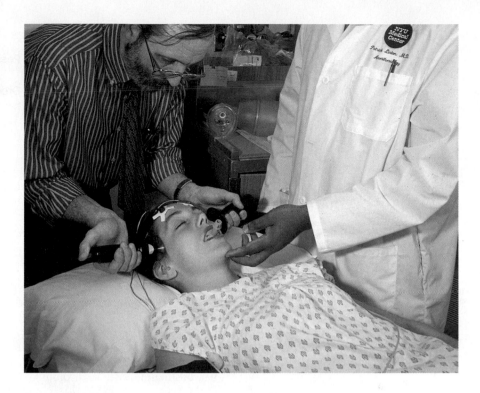

ECT is used almost exclusively in the treatment of severe depression, especially in cases that are unresponsive to other forms of treatment. Though it can help people suffering from severe depression (Sanacora et al., 2003; UK ECT Review Group, 2003), no one knows for certain how it works. Most probably it helps regulate levels of neurotransmitters in brain circuits that control moods.

ECT may be effective, but investigators are concerned about the high rate of relapse in the weeks and months following a course of treatment (Prudic et al., 2004). ECT may also produce permanent memory losses for some events happening in the months preceding treatment and for several weeks afterward (Glass, 2001). In light of these concerns, it is not surprising that many health professionals view ECT as a treatment of last resort.

Psychosurgery

Psychosurgery is a procedure in which the brain is surgically altered to control deviant or violent behavior. The most widely practiced form of psychosurgery in the past was the **prefrontal lobotomy**, developed in the 1930s by Portuguese neurologist António Egas Moniz. In a prefrontal lobotomy, nerve pathways between the frontal lobe and lower brain centers are severed to control a patient's violent or aggressive behavior. More than one thousand patients underwent the procedure before it was eliminated because of serious complications, including death in some cases. Meanwhile, the introduction of psychiatric drugs offered a less radical alternative to controlling aberrant behavior. A sad footnote to this story was that one of Moniz's own patients (for whom the treatment failed) later shot him, leaving his legs paralyzed.

More sophisticated psychosurgery techniques have been introduced in recent years, involving surgical alterations that are limited to smaller areas of the brain. These procedures are used rarely—and, again, only as a treatment of last resort—in some cases of severe obsessive-compulsive behavior (Irle et al., 1998; Sachdev & Hay, 1996). Concerns remain about the potential long-term complications of such procedures. Concept Chart 14.3 summarizes the major types and uses of the psychotropic drugs discussed in this module.

CONCEPT 14.28
Many health professionals view electroconvulsive therapy as a treatment of last resort for severe depression in cases where less invasive treatments have failed.

psychosurgery   Brain surgery used to control violent or deviant behavior.

prefrontal lobotomy   A surgical procedure in which neural pathways in the brain are severed in order to control violent or aggressive behavior.

💡 **CONCEPT CHART 14.3 Major Types and Uses of Psychotropic Drugs**

	Generic Name	Brand Name	Clinical Uses	Possible Side Effects or Complications
Antianxiety Drugs	Diazepam Chlordiazepoxide Lorazepam Alprazolam	Valium Librium Ativan Xanax	Treatment of anxiety and insomnia	Drowsiness, fatigue, impaired coordination, nausea
Antidepressant Drugs	**Tricyclics** Imipramine Desipramine Amitriptyline Doxepin	Tofranil Norpramin Elavil Sinequan	Depression, bulimia, panic disorder	Changes in blood pressure, heart irregularities, dry mouth, confusion, skin rash
	MAO Inhibitors Phenelzine Tranylcypromine	Nardil Parnate	Depression	Dizziness, headache, sleep disturbance, agitation, anxiety, fatigue
	Selective Serotonin-Reuptake Inhibitors Fluoxetine Sertraline Paroxetine Citalopram	Prozac Zoloft Paxil Celexa	Depression, bulimia, panic disorder, obsessive-compulsive disorder, posttraumatic stress disorder (Zoloft), social anxiety (Paxil)	Nausea, diarrhea, anxiety, insomnia, sweating, dry mouth, dizziness, drowsiness
	Other Antidepressant Drugs Bupropion Venlafaxine	Wellbutrin, Zyban Effexor	Depression, nicotine dependence Depression	Dry mouth, insomnia, headaches, nausea, constipation, tremors Nausea, constipation, dry mouth, drowsiness, insomnia, dizziness, anxiety
Antipsychotic Drugs	**Phenothiazines** Chlorpromazine Thioridazine Trifluoperazine Fluphenazine	Thorazine Mellaril Stelazine Prolixin	Schizophrenia and other psychotic disorders	Movement disorders (e.g., tardive dyskinesia), drowsiness, restlessness, dry mouth, blurred vision, muscle rigidity
	Other Antipsychotic Drugs Haloperidol Clozapine Risperidone Olanzapine	Haldol Clozaril Risperdal Zyprexa	Schizophrenia and other psychotic disorders	Similar to phenothiazines Potentially lethal blood disorder, seizures, fast heart rate, drowsiness, dizziness, nausea Feeling unable to sit still, constipation, dizziness, drowsiness, weight gain Low blood pressure, dizziness, drowsiness, heart palpitations, fatigue, constipation, weight gain
Antimanic Drugs	Lithium carbonate Divalproex sodium	Eskalith Depakote	Manic episodes and stabilization of mood swings associated with bipolar disorder	Tremors, thirst, diarrhea, drowsiness, weakness, lack of coordination Nausea, vomiting, dizziness, abdominal cramps, sleeplessness
Stimulant Drugs	Methylphenidate Amphetamine with dextroamphetamine	Ritalin Concerta Adderall	Childhood hyperactivity	Nervousness, insomnia, nausea, dizziness, heart palpitations, headache; may temporarily retard growth

MODULE 14.3 REVIEW

Biomedical Therapies

RECITE IT

What are the major types of psychotropic or psychiatric drugs?

- The major classes of psychiatric drugs are antianxiety agents (e.g., Valium, Xanax), antidepressants (e.g., Elavil, Prozac), and antipsychotics (e.g., Thorazine, Clozaril).

- Other drugs, such as lithium and Ritalin, are used to treat specific disorders.

What are the advantages and disadvantages of psychiatric drugs?

- Psychiatric drugs can help relieve or control symptoms of many psychological disorders, including anxiety disorders, mood disorders, and schizophrenia.

- The major disadvantages of these drugs are the occurrence of troubling side effects, high relapse rates following discontinuance, and, in some cases, possible chemical dependence.

What is ECT, and how is it used?

- ECT (electroconvulsive therapy) involves the administration of brief pulses of electricity to the brain. It is used to treat severe depression, especially in cases that do not respond to other treatments.

RECALL IT

1. The most widely used biomedical form of therapy is
   a. psychosurgery.
   b. electroconvulsive therapy.
   c. drug therapy.
   d. psychiatric hospitalization.

The drugs Valium and Xanax are examples of _____ drugs.
   a. antianxiety
   b. antidepressant
   c. antipsychotic
   d. antisocial

3. Childhood hyperactivity is typically treated by the use of
   a. extensive psychotherapy.
   b. a stimulant drug.
   c. lithium.
   d. gamma-aminobutyric acid.

4. Electroconvulsive therapy (ECT) is often used
   a. only after successful treatment with antidepressant drugs.
   b. in treating severe cases of schizophrenia as well as depression.
   c. in combination with antidepressants in cases of mild to moderate depression.
   d. as a treatment of last resort in cases of severe depression.

THINK ABOUT IT

- Do you know children who have been treated with stimulant medication for hyperactivity and attentional problems? What were the outcomes? Do you believe that stimulant medication is used too often or not often enough?

- What are the advantages and disadvantages of psychotropic drugs? Would you consider using psychotropic drugs if you developed an anxiety disorder or a mood disorder? Why or why not?

APPLICATION MODULE 14.4
Getting Help

CONCEPT 14.29
Though consumers face a bewildering array of mental health services providers, there are a number of things they can do to ensure that they receive quality care.

In most areas in the United States and Canada, there are pages upon pages of clinics and health professionals in the telephone directory. Many people have no idea whom to call for help. If you don't know where to go or whom to see, there are a number of steps you can take to ensure that you receive appropriate care:

1. *Seek recommendations from respected sources, such as your family physician, course instructor, clergyperson, or college health service.*

2. *Seek a referral from a local medical center or local community mental health center.* When making inquiries, ask about the services that are available or about opportunities for referral to qualified treatment providers in the area.

3. *Seek a consultation with your college counseling center or health services center.* Most colleges and universities offer psychological assistance to students, generally without charge.

4. *Contact professional organizations for recommendations.* Many local or national organizations maintain a referral list of qualified treatment providers in your area. If you would like to consult a psychologist, contact the American Psychological Association in Washington, D.C. (by telephone at 202-336-5650, or on the Web at www.apa.org), and ask for local referrals in your area. Alternatively, you can call your local or state psychology association in the United States or your provincial or territorial psychological association in Canada.

5. *Let your fingers do the walking—but be careful!* Look under "Psychologists," "Physicians," "Social Workers," or "Social and Human Services" in your local Yellow Pages. However, be wary of professionals who take out large ads and claim to be experts in treating many different kinds of problems.

6. *Make sure the treatment provider is a licensed member of a recognized mental health profession, such as psychology, medicine, counseling, or social work.* In many states, anyone can set up practice as a "therapist," even as a "psychotherapist." These titles may not be limited by law to licensed practitioners. Licensed professionals clearly display their licenses and other credentials in their offices, usually in plain view. If you have any questions about the licensure status of a treatment provider, contact the licensing board in your state, province, or territory.

7. *Inquire about the type of therapy being provided (e.g., psychoanalysis, family therapy, behavior therapy).* Ask the treatment provider to explain how his or her particular type of therapy is appropriate to treating the problems you are having.

8. *Inquire about the treatment provider's professional background.* Ask about the person's educational background, supervised experience, and credentials. An ethical practitioner will not hesitate to provide this information.

9. *Inquire whether the treatment provider has had experience treating other people with similar problems.* Ask about their results and how they were measured.

10. *Once the treatment provider has had the opportunity to conduct a formal evaluation of your problem, discuss the diagnosis and treatment plan before making any commitments to undertake treatment.*

11. *Ask about costs and insurance coverage.* Ask about what types of insurance are accepted by the provider and whether co-payments are required on your part. Ask whether the provider will adjust his or her fees on a sliding scale that takes your income and family situation into account. If you are eligible for Medicaid or Medicare, inquire whether the treatment provider accepts these types of coverage. College students may also be covered by their parents' health insurance plans or by student plans offered by their colleges. Find out if the treatment provider participates in any health maintenance organization to which you may belong.

12. *Find out about the treatment provider's policies regarding charges for missed or canceled sessions.*

13. *If medication is to be prescribed, find out how long a delay is expected before it starts working.* Also inquire about possible side effects, and about which side effects should prompt you to call with questions. Don't be afraid to seek a second opinion before undergoing any course of medication.

14. *If the treatment recommendations don't sound quite right to you, discuss your concerns openly.* An ethical professional will be willing to address your concerns rather than feeling insulted.

15. *If you still have any doubts, request a second opinion.* An ethical professional will support your efforts to seek a second opinion. Ask the treatment provider to recommend other professionals—or select your own.

16. *Be wary of online therapy services.* The use of online counseling and therapy services is growing rapidly, even as psychologists and other mental health professionals raise the yellow flag of caution (Jacobs et al., 2001; Reed, McLaughlin, & Milholland, 2000; Taylor & Luce, 2003). Because we lack a system for ensuring that online therapists have the appropriate credentials and licensure to practice, unqualified practitioners can take advantage of unwary consumers. We also lack evidence that therapy can be effective when people interact with a therapist they never meet in person. Despite these concerns, many psychologists believe that online therapy services have potential value if proper safeguards are established (e.g, Glueckauf et al., 2003; Palmiter & Renjilian, 2003; Taylor & Luce, 2003).

TYING IT TOGETHER

The history of treatment of people with mental disorders is characterized more by harsh treatment and neglect than by humane treatment. Today, a wide range of services are available to help people with severe and persistent mental health problems, yet many people in need still fail to receive the services they require to adjust successfully to community life (Module 14.1). Today mental health problems are generally treated through psychotherapy or talk therapy, through use of psychiatric drugs, or through a combination of both psychotherapy and drug therapy. Psychotherapy is a psychologically based form of treatment that helps individuals understand and resolve their problems. Each of the major theoretical models of abnormal behavior—the psychody-namic, behavioral, humanistic, and cognitive models—has spawned its own form of psychotherapy (Module 14.2). Many therapists adopt an eclectic approach in which they draw from different therapeutic orientations or approaches. Biomedical therapies are biologically based forms of treatment that derive from the medical model of abnormal behavior. The principal form of biomedical therapy is drug therapy; electroconvulsive therapy and psychosurgery are more controversial (Module 14.3). By becoming informed consumers of psychological services, people in need of psychological help can ensure that they receive appropriate care (Module 14.4).

Thinking Critically About Psychology

Based on your reading of this chapter, answer the essay question at the end of the example. Then, to evaluate your progress in developing critical thinking skills, compare your answer to the sample answer found in Appendix A.

Lauren has been depressed since the breakup of her relationship with her boyfriend two months ago. She is crying frequently, has difficulty getting out of bed in the morning, and has been losing weight. She claims she doesn't feel like eating. She tells the psychologist that she hasn't ever felt like hurting herself, but wavers when asked if she feels she might reach a point where she would consider ending her life. She says she feels like a failure and that no one will ever want her. Looking down at the floor, she tells the psychologist, "Everyone's always rejected me. Why should this be any different?"

Review the major approaches to therapy (psychodynamic, humanistic, behavioral, cognitive) and biomedical treatments discussed in this chapter. Then briefly describe how each might be used to help someone like Lauren.

Key Terms

moral therapy *(p. 544)*
deinstitutionalization *(p. 545)*
psychotherapy *(p. 548)*
psychoanalysis *(p. 548)*
psychoanalysts *(p. 548)*
free association *(p. 550)*
dream analysis *(p. 550)*
interpretation *(p. 550)*
insight *(p. 550)*
resistance *(p. 550)*
transference relationship *(p. 550)*
countertransference *(p. 551)*
behavior therapy *(p. 553)*
systematic desensitization *(p. 554)*
fear hierarchy *(p. 554)*

gradual exposure *(p. 554)*
modeling *(p. 555)*
aversive conditioning *(p. 555)*
cognitive-behavioral therapy (CBT)
 (p. 556)
rational emotive behavior therapy
 (REBT) *(p. 557)*
cognitive therapy *(p. 559)*
eclectic therapy *(p. 561)*
group therapy *(p. 561)*
family therapy *(p. 562)*
couple therapy *(p. 562)*
meta-analysis *(p. 562)*
nonspecific factors *(p. 564)*
placebo effects *(p. 565)*

virtual reality therapy *(p. 568)*
psychotropic drugs *(p. 570)*
antianxiety drugs *(p. 570)*
antidepressants *(p. 570)*
tricyclics *(p. 570*
monoamine oxidase (MAO) inhibitors
 (p. 570)
selective serotonin-reuptake inhibitors
 (SSRIs) *(p. 570)*
antipsychotics *(p. 571)*
tardive dyskinesia (TD) *(p. 572)*
electroconvulsive therapy (ECT) *(p. 572)*
psychosurgery *(p. 573)*
prefrontal lobotomy *(p. 573)*

ANSWERS TO RECALL IT QUESTIONS

Module 14.1: 1. moral; 2. Dorothea Dix; 3. Compassionate care of severely disturbed people was not sufficient to restore them to normalcy; 4. deinstitutionalization.

Module 14.2: 1. i. d, ii. a, iii. c, iv. b; 2. unconditional positive regard, empathy, genuineness; 3. systematic desensitization; 4. rational emotive behavior therapy; 5. The advantages of group therapy include its lower cost and the fact that clients can gain experience relating to others and learn from others how to cope with problem situations; its disadvantages include a lower level of individual attention and clients' potential fear of revealing very personal matters to other members of the group.

Module 14.3: 1. c; 2. a; 3. b; 4. d.

KEY TO SAMPLE RATIONAL ALTERNATIVES IN TRY THIS OUT *(P. 560)*

1. We've got problems, but it's not a complete disaster. It's better to think of ways of making it better than thinking the worst.

2. I sometimes feel overwhelmed, but I've handled things like this before. I need to take things a step at a time to get through this.

3. Just because it feels that way doesn't make it so.

4. Focus on getting through this course, not on jumping to conclusions.

5. Stop taking the blame for other people's problems. There are many reasons why _____ has these problems that have nothing to do with me.

6. Stop dumping on yourself. Focus on what you need to do.

7. It doesn't help to compare myself to others. All I can expect of myself is to do the best I can.

8. It would be upsetting, but it wouldn't be the end of the world. It's awful only if I make it so.

9. What evidence do I have for believing that? People who get to know me like me more often than not.

10. Putting everything in context, it's really not so bad.

Psychology and Health

DID YOU KNOW THAT . . .

- Happy or joyous events can be a source of stress? (p. 583)

- As many as 90 percent of doctor visits are linked to stress-related problems? (p. 596)

- The emotional stress of divorce or even college examinations may damage your health? (p. 596)

- Writing about traumatic or stressful experiences in your life can be good for your mental and physical health? (p. 597)

- Optimistic people have fewer postoperative complications following coronary artery bypass surgery than pessimistic people? (p. 599)

- Unhealthy behaviors are among the major risk factors for the leading causes of death of Americans? (p. 602)

- Regular exercise can reduce your risk of heart disease? (p. 603)

- Chronic anger may be harmful to your heart? (p. 604)

T he Paris morgue is a strange place for a famous philosopher to be rummaging about. But there among the corpses was the seventeenth-century French philosopher René Descartes (1596–1650) (Searle, 1996). You probably know Descartes for his famous statement "I think, therefore I am." Descartes believed that the mind and the body are two fundamentally different entities. But if the mind and body are separate, there must be some connection between them. For example, if you decide to raise your arm and a fraction of a second later your arm moves up, the mind must have had an effect on the body. By examining corpses, Descartes hoped to find the part of the brain where the mind connected to the body. Modern science teaches that the mind and body, the psychological and the physical, are more closely intertwined than Descartes would ever have imagined (Damasio, 1994; Kendler, 2001; Lemonick, 2003b). The mind affects the body, and the body affects the mind. There is no single point in the brain where the mind and body intersect.

In previous chapters we focused on how the workings of the body, especially the brain, affect mental experiences such as sensations, perceptions, emotions, and thinking. Here we look at the other side of the coin by considering how the mind affects the body—how psychological factors, especially stress, affect our health and well-being. We also discuss how we can moderate the impact of stress. We then examine psychological factors that affect such major health problems as heart disease and cancer, the two leading killers in America. We will see that unhealthy behaviors and lifestyles, such as smoking and consumption of a high-fat diet, are linked to the risk of developing these life-threatening diseases. By better understanding the psychological links to physical illness, psychologists can develop health promotion programs to help people make healthful changes in their behaviors and lifestyles. Finally, we consider how each of us can apply psychological techniques and principles to better manage the stress we face in our daily lives. ■

MODULE 15.1

Stress: What It Is and What It Does to the Body

- What is health psychology?
- What is stress, and what are the major sources of stress?
- How does the body respond to stress?
- How does stress affect the immune system?
- What psychological factors buffer the effects of stress?

CONCEPT 15.1

When the level of stress in our lives overtaxes our ability to cope, we may experience distress in the form of psychological and physical health problems.

The study of interrelationships between psychology and physical health is called **health psychology** (Revenson & Baum, 2001). Health psychologists work in universities, hospitals, and government agencies conducting research and using the knowledge they gain to develop health promotion and disease prevention programs (Schneiderman et al., 2001).

Health psychologists are especially concerned with the effects of stress on physical health. But what is stress, and how does it affect our health?

Psychologists use the term **stress** to describe pressures or demands placed upon an organism to adjust or adapt to its environment. Stress is a fact of life. We may even need a certain amount of stress to remain active, alert, and energized. But when the stress we face in our lives increases to a level that taxes our ability to cope, we may experience **distress**, which is an internal state of physical or mental pain or suffering. Distress may take the form of psychological problems, especially anxiety and depression, or physical health problems, including headaches, digestive problems, even heart conditions such as irregular heart rhythms (see Table 15.1). Though most people are remarkably resilient to stress, we all have our limits.

In this module, we discuss the sources of stress and examine how stress affects us. Some readers might be surprised to learn that not all sources of stress arise from negative life events or circumstances.

Online Study Center
Improve Your Grade
Tutorials: How We Kill Ourselves

health psychology The specialty in psychology that focuses on the interrelationships between psychological factors and physical health.

stress Pressure or demand placed on an organism to adjust or adapt.

distress A state of emotional or physical suffering, discomfort, or pain.

TABLE 15.1 Examples of Stress-Related Health Problems

Biological Problems	
Tension or migraine headaches	Nausea and vomiting
Allergic reactions	Upset stomach or indigestion
Back pain, especially low back pain	Ulcers
High blood pressure	Frequent urination or diarrhea
Skin inflammations (such as hives and acne)	Skin rashes
Rheumatoid arthritis (painful inflammation of the joints)	Fatigue
	Asthma
Regional enteritis (inflammation of the intestine, especially the small intestine)	**Psychological Problems**
Ulcerative colitis (inflammation and open sores of the colon, or large intestine)	Depression
	Anger
Heart disease and cardiac irregularities such as arrhythmias (irregularities in the rhythm of the heart)	Irritability
	Anxiety
	Difficulty concentrating
Sleep problems	Feeling overwhelmed
	Alcohol or substance abuse

Source: Adapted from Nevid, Rathus, & Rubenstein, 1998.

What Are the Sources of Stress in Your Life?

💡 **CONCEPT 15.2**
Stressors are sources of stress, such as hassles, life changes, frustration, and conflict.

Sources of Stress

If you had to identify the sources of stress in your life, what would you list? School or work demands, relationship problems, traffic jams, or such daily sources of stress as preparing meals, shopping, and doing household chores? Sources of stress are called **stressors**. We face many stressors in our lives. In this section we examine a number of stressors, including daily hassles, life events or life changes, frustration, conflict, trauma, Type A behavior pattern, and pressure to adjust to a new culture, which is a stressor faced by immigrant groups.

Positive as well as negative experiences can be sources of stress. Happy or joyous events, such as having a baby, getting married, or graduating from college, are stressors because they impose demands on us to adjust or adapt. Positive changes in our lives, like negative ones, can tax our ability to cope, as any new parent will attest. How well we are able to cope with the stress we experience in our daily lives plays a key part in determining our mental and physical well-being.

Hassles   **Hassles** are annoyances we commonly experience in our daily lives. Examples include traffic jams, household chores, coping with inclement weather, and balancing job demands and social relationships. Few, if any, of us are immune from daily hassles. Table 15.2 lists the ten most common hassles reported by a sample of college students.

We may experience some hassles on a daily basis, such as hunting for a parking spot in overcrowded parking lots. Others occur irregularly or unexpectedly, such as getting caught in a downpour without an umbrella. A single hassle may not amount to much in itself. But the accumulation of daily hassles can contribute to the general level of **chronic stress** in our lives. Chronic stress is a state of persistent tension or pressure that can lead us to feel exhausted, irritable, and depressed. Sources of chronic stress include ongoing financial problems, job-related problems, marital or relationship conflicts, and persistent or recurrent pain or other chronic medical conditions.

Life Events   Stress can also result from major changes in life circumstances, which psychologists call *life events*. These may be negative events, such as the loss of a

💡 **CONCEPT 15.3**
Sources of chronic stress in our lives include daily annoyances, or hassles, financial problems, job-related problems, relationship problems, and persistent pain or other medical problems.

stressors   Sources of stress.
hassles   Annoyances of daily life that impose a stressful burden.
chronic stress   Continuing or persistent stress

TABLE 15.2   The Ten Most Common Hassles Reported by College Students

Hassle	Students Reporting (%)
1. Troubling thoughts about the future	77
2. Not getting enough sleep	72.5
3. Wasting time	71
4. Inconsiderate smokers	71
5. Physical appearance	70
6. Too many things to do	69
7. Misplacing or losing things	67
8. Not enough time to do the things you need to do	66
9. Concerns about meeting high standards	64
10. Being lonely	61

Source: Kanner et al., 1981.

CONCEPT 15.4
People experiencing a greater number of life change events are at increased risk of physical health problems, but questions of cause and effect remain open to debate.

loved one or a job termination, or positive events, such as getting married, receiving a promotion, or having a baby. In other words, changes for better or for worse can impose stressful burdens that require adjustment. Unlike daily hassles, life events occur irregularly and sometimes unexpectedly.

Data suggest that people who experience many life changes are more likely to suffer from physical health problems (Smith, Smoll, & Ptacek, 1990; Stewart et al., 1994). We need to observe some cautions when interpreting these data, however. For one thing, relationships between life changes and later problems are typically small. For another, links between life events and health problems are correlational. As you may recall from Chapter 1, a correlation is a statistical association between two variables (in this case, level of stress and poor health) and, as such, does not necessarily reflect a causal linkage. It is possible that exposure to life events causes or aggravates physical or health problems. But it is also possible that health problems disrupt people's lives, leading them to encounter more life change events, such as job relocations or conflicts with family members. In the final analysis, relationships between life events and our physical health likely cut both ways.

Although everyone experiences hassles and life changes, some people are less vulnerable to these types of stressors than are others. They may have higher thresholds for coping with daily annoyances and are not as rattled by them. Others may lack the skills needed to adjust to new circumstances, such as those needed to make new friends when relocating to a new community. Then too, some hold more optimistic attitudes than others and believe they can control the future course of their lives. These people may be better able to meet the challenges posed by various stressors.

How we appraise or evaluate a life event also has an important bearing on how stressful it becomes for us. The same event may hold different meanings for different people. A life event like a pregnancy is probably less stressful to people who welcome the pregnancy and believe they can cope with the changes that the birth of a child will bring. Similarly, whether or not you find work demands to be stressful may depend on whether or not you like your job and feel in control of how and when you do your work.

Frustration   Another major source of stress is **frustration**, the negative emotional state that occurs when our efforts to pursue our goals are blocked or thwarted. Adolescents may feel frustrated when they want to drive, date, or drink alcoholic beverages but are told they are too young. People desiring higher education may be frustrated when they lack the financial resources to attend the college of their choice. We may frustrate ourselves when we set unrealistically high goals that we are unable to achieve.

frustration   A negative emotional state experienced when one's efforts to pursue one's goals are thwarted.

TRY THIS OUT

How Stressful Is Your Life?

The College Life Stress Inventory was designed to measure the amount of life stress experienced by college students. Circle the items in the inventory that you have experienced during the past year. Then compute your stress level by adding the stress ratings of the circled items. Use the scoring key to help you interpret your score.

Stress Rating	Event
100	Being raped
100	Finding out that you are HIV-positive
98	Being accused of rape
97	Death of a close friend
96	Death of a close family member
94	Contracting a sexually transmitted disease (other than AIDS)
91	Concerns about being pregnant
90	Finals week
90	Concerns about your partner being pregnant
89	Oversleeping for an exam
89	Flunking a class
85	Having a boyfriend or girlfriend cheat on you
85	Ending a steady dating relationship
85	Serious illness in a close friend or family member
84	Financial difficulties
83	Writing a major term paper
83	Being caught cheating on a test
82	Drunk driving
82	Sense of overload in school or work
80	Two exams in one day
77	Cheating on your boyfriend or girlfriend
76	Getting married
75	Negative consequences of drinking or drug use
73	Depression or crisis in your best friend
73	Difficulties with parents
72	Talking in front of a class
69	Lack of sleep
69	Change in housing situation (hassles, moves)
69	Competing or performing in public
66	Getting in a physical fight
66	Difficulties with a roommate
65	Job changes (applying, new job, work hassles)
65	Declaring a major or concerns about future plans
62	A class you hate
61	Drinking or use of drugs
60	Confrontations with professors
58	Starting a new semester
57	Going on a first date
55	Registration
55	Maintaining a steady dating relationship
54	Commuting to campus or work, or both
53	Peer pressures
53	Being away from home for the first time
52	Getting sick
52	Concerns about your appearance
51	Getting straight A's
48	A difficult class that you love
47	Making new friends; getting along with friends
47	Fraternity or sorority rush
40	Falling asleep in class
20	Attending an athletic event (e.g., football game)

Scoring Key: You can gauge your overall level of stress by comparing your total score with the scores obtained by the developers of the scale based on a sample of 257 introductory psychology students. The average (mean) score was 1,247, and approximately two out of three students obtained scores ranging from 806 to 1,688. Though your total score may give you insight into how high your level of stress is, it does not reveal how stress may be affecting you. Some people thrive on higher levels of stress than others. They may possess the coping skills and social support that they need to handle stress more effectively. But anyone can become overstressed as pressures and life changes continue to pile up. If you are facing a high level of stress in your life, perhaps you can reduce some of these sources of stress. You might also benefit by learning effective ways of handling stressors you can't avoid. Module 15.3 at the end of the chapter offers some guidelines for managing stress that you may find helpful.

Source: Renner & Mackin, 1998.

CONCEPT 15.5
In a state of psychological conflict a person may vacillate between two or more competing goals.

CONCEPT 15.6
The four major types of psychological conflict are approach-approach, avoidance-avoidance, approach-avoidance, and multiple approach-avoidance conflict.

Conflict **Conflict** is a state of tension resulting from the presence of two or more competing goals that demand resolution. People in conflict often vacillate, or shift back and forth, between competing goals. The longer they remain in conflict, the more stressed and frustrated they feel. Psychologists identify four major types of conflicts. Let us consider each in turn.

Approach-Approach Conflict In an approach-approach conflict (see Figure 15.1a), you feel drawn toward two positive but mutually exclusive goals at the same time. You may need to decide between taking a vacation in the mountains or at the beach, or dating Taylor or Alex this weekend, or choosing between two attractive job offers. Though you may initially vacillate between the two goals, an approach-approach conflict is generally resolved by deciding on one course of action or another. The approach-approach conflict is generally considered the least stressful type of conflict.

Avoidance-Avoidance Conflict In avoidance-avoidance conflicts, you face two opposing goals, both of which are unpleasant (see Figure 15.1b). Moreover, avoiding one of these undesirable goals requires approaching the other. You may want to avoid a painful dental procedure, but you also want to prevent tooth loss. You may avoid taking a less demanding major because of your strong tendency to avoid failure, but you also want to avoid settling for a lesser job or career (Elliot & Sheldon, 1997). If there is no obvious resolution, you may put off dealing with the conflict, at least for a period of time. In cases where the conflict is highly stressful, you could become virtually immobilized and unable to attend to your usual responsibilities.

Approach-Avoidance Conflict In approach-avoidance conflicts, you face a goal that has both positive and negative qualities (see Figure 15.1c). You may want to ask someone for a date, but you feel panic-stricken by fears of rejection. You may want to attend graduate school, but you fear incurring heavy loans. Resolution of the conflict seems possible if you compare the relative pluses and minuses and then decide to commit yourself to either pursuing the goal or abandoning it.

Figure 15.1 Types of Conflicts
In an approach-approach conflict (a), the person (P) is motivated (M) to pursue two goals (G) but cannot pursue both of them at the same time. In an avoidance-avoidance conflict (b), the person is motivated to avoid each of two undesirable goals. In an approach-avoidance conflict (c), the same goal has both positive and negative qualities. And in a multiple approach-avoidance conflict (d), the person faces two or more goals, each with positive and negative features.

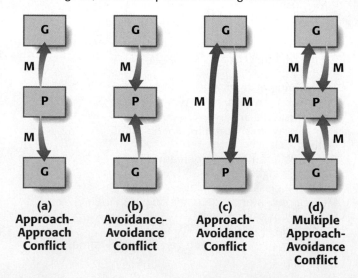

conflict A state of tension brought about by opposing motives operating simultaneously.

But like a piece of metal within proximity of a magnet's two opposing poles, you may at first feel pulled toward the goal by its desirable qualities, only to be repelled by its unattractive qualities as you get closer to it.

Multiple Approach-Avoidance Conflict   The most complex type of conflict, this one involves two or more goals, each with compelling positive and negative characteristics (see Figure 15.1d). You may want to pursue further training after graduation because it will expand your career options, but you are put off by the expense and additional time commitments involved. On the other hand, you may have a job opportunity waiting for you that will get you started in a career, but you worry that you'll come to regret not having gone further with your education. Such conflicts can sometimes be resolved by combining both goals (getting started at the new job while taking night courses). At other times, the resolution comes from making a commitment to a course of action, even though it may entail nagging concerns about "the road not taken."

Conflicts are most easily resolved and least stressful when one goal is decidedly more attractive than another or when the positive qualities of a goal outweigh the negative. But when two goals pull you in opposite directions, or when the same goal both strongly attracts and repels you, you may experience high levels of stress and confusion about which course of action to pursue.

Traumatic Stressors   Traumatic stressors are potentially life-threatening events. Included in this category are natural or technological disasters (hurricanes, tornadoes, floods, nuclear accidents, etc.); combat experiences; serious accidents; physical or sexual assaults; a diagnosis of cancer, AIDS, or other life-threatening illness; and terrorist attacks, such as the devastating attack on September 11.

Exposure to traumatic stress may lead to the development of a psychological disorder called **posttraumatic stress disorder (PTSD)**. PTSD is characterized by a maladaptive reaction to traumatic events or stressors. People with PTSD encounter lingering problems in adjustment, often for years after the traumatic event has passed. They may show the following symptoms:

- *Avoidance of cues associated with the trauma.* People with PTSD may avoid situations or cues that may be reminders of the traumatic experience. The rape survivor may avoid traveling in the same part of town in which she was attacked. The combat veteran may avoid viewing war movies or socializing with service buddies.

- *Reexperiencing the traumatic event.* Such people may experience intrusive memories, images, or dreams of the traumatic experience. They may even have flashbacks of the traumatic experience, as with combat veterans who momentarily have the feeling of being back on the battlefield.

- *Impaired functioning.* People with PTSD may experience depression or anxiety that interferes with the ability to meet ordinary responsibilities as workers, students, parents, or family members.

- *Heightened arousal.* They may be unusually tense or keyed-up, find it difficult to relax or fall asleep, or have a heightened heart rate (Bryant et al., 2000). They may also appear to be constantly on guard and show an exaggerated startle response to sudden noises.

- *Emotional numbing.* They may experience a numbing of emotional responses and find it difficult to feel love or other strong emotions.

Though people commonly link PTSD to exposure to the trauma of combat, experts find that the traumas most often connected with PTSD are serious motor vehicle accidents (Blanchard & Hickling, 2004). Exposure to violence is another major source of trauma leading to PTSD (Norris et al., 2003).

CONCEPT 15.7
Traumatic events can be sources of intense stress that, in turn, can have profound, enduring effects on our psychological adjustment.

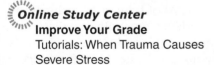
Online Study Center
Improve Your Grade
Tutorials: When Trauma Causes Severe Stress

posttraumatic stress disorder (PTSD)
A psychological disorder involving a maladaptive reaction to traumatic stress.

TABLE 15.3 **Warning Signs of Trauma-Related Stress**

The American Psychological Association recommends that people who experience the following symptoms for more than a month should continue consulting a mental health professional. Help is available through your college health services or through mental health care providers in your community. For more information or to arrange a referral with a local health care provider, you may contact your local American Red Cross chapter or the American Psychological Association at (202) 336-5800.

- Experiencing frequent nightmares or intrusive thoughts about the traumatic event.
- Experiencing difficulty sleeping or changes in appetite.
- Feeling anxious or fearful, especially when exposed to stimuli associated with the traumatic experience.
- Being easily startled or unusually alert or vigilant.
- Having little energy or feeling depressed or sad.
- Having memory problems, including memory for events linked to the trauma.
- Having difficulty making decisions or focusing on your work or daily activities; feeling "scattered."
- Feeling unusually jumpy, irritable, or angry; becoming easily agitated.
- Feeling "numb" emotionally or becoming withdrawn or disconnected from others.
- Having spontaneous crying spells or feelings of hopelessness or despair.
- Becoming extremely protective of your loved ones or fearful about their safety.
- Avoiding activities, situations, or contact with people that remind you of the traumatic event.

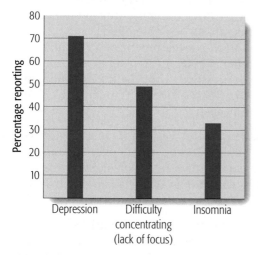

Figure 15.2 Stress-Related Symptoms Reported by Americans in the Week Following the Terrorists Attacks of September 11, 2001
Most Americans reported some form of emotional distress or difficulty functioning normally in the days following the terrorist attacks of 9/11/01.

Source: Pew Research Center (2002, September 20), *American psyche reeling from terror attacks.* people-press.org/reports/display.php3?ReportID=3.

Not everyone who experiences a traumatic event develops PTSD. Overall, though about half of adults experience traumatic events, only about 7 percent develop PTSD at some point in their lives (Ozer & Weiss, 2004). Symptoms of PTSD may not develop until months or years after exposure to a traumatic stressor (Zlotnick et al., 2001). As Figure 15.2 shows, seven out of ten people reported depression in the week following the terrorist attacks of September 11, 2001, and substantial proportions of people suffered from insomnia and difficulty concentrating. We can't yet say how many people developed PTSD in the wake of the World Trade Center and Pentagon attacks, but high levels of initial symptoms were observed (Simeon et al., 2003). A survey of New Yorkers taken two years after the attacks showed that many people were still suffering emotional strain from the tragedy and nearly a third felt their lives had not yet returned to normal (Kleinfield & Connelly, 2003).

As we try to adapt to a world in which the horrors of terrorism may come to affect us directly, we need to be able to recognize signs of trauma-related stress in ourselves and our loved ones. It is normal to experience psychological distress in the face of trauma. In fact, remaining blasé at times of crisis or disaster would likely be deemed abnormal. But traumatic stress reactions become cause for concern when they linger for months at a time or significantly interfere with our ability to meet our usual responsibilities. The American Psychological Association offers some suggestions that may help us identify the warning signs of trauma-related stress (see Table 15.3).

PTSD is not limited to Western cultures. Researchers have found high rates of PTSD among earthquake survivors in India and China, hurricane survivors in Nicaragua, Khmer refugees who survived the "killing fields" of the Pol Pot War in Cambodia from 1975 to 1979, survivors of the Balkan conflicts of the 1990s, and Afghans displaced by more than twenty years of conflict in Afghanistan (Cardozo et al., 2004; Goenjian et al., 2001; Mitka, 2000; Mollica, Henderson, & Tor, 2002; Wang et al., 2000). Culture plays a role in determining not only the ways in which people manage and cope with traumatic experiences but also the extent of their vulnerability to PTSD and other psychological disorders arising from stress (de Silva, 1993).

TRY THIS OUT

Are You Type A?

Check the appropriate column to indicate whether or not the item is generally true of you. Then consult the scoring key below to determine whether you fit the Type A profile.

YES NO   Do You . . .

☐ ☐ 1. Walk briskly from place to place or from meeting to meeting?

☐ ☐ 2. Strongly emphasize important words in your ordinary speech?

☐ ☐ 3. Think that life is by nature dog-eat-dog?

☐ ☐ 4. Get fidgety when you see someone complete a job slowly?

☐ ☐ 5. Urge others to complete what they're trying to express?

☐ ☐ 6. Find it exceptionally annoying to get stuck in line?

☐ ☐ 7. Envision all the things you have to do even when someone is talking to you?

☐ ☐ 8. Eat while you're getting dressed, or jot down notes while you're driving?

☐ ☐ 9. Catch up on work during vacations?

☐ ☐ 10. Direct the conversation to things that interest you?

☐ ☐ 11. Feel as if things are going to pot because you're relaxing for a few minutes?

☐ ☐ 12. Get so wrapped up in your work that you fail to notice beautiful scenery passing by?

YES NO   Do You . . .

☐ ☐ 13. Get so wrapped up in money, promotions, and awards that you neglect expressing your creativity?

☐ ☐ 14. Schedule appointments and meetings back to back?

☐ ☐ 15. Arrive early for appointments and meetings?

☐ ☐ 16. Make fists or clench your jaws to drive home your views?

☐ ☐ 17. Think that you've achieved what you have because of your ability to work fast?

☐ ☐ 18. Have the feeling that uncompleted work must be done *now* and fast?

☐ ☐ 19. Try to find more efficient ways to get things done?

☐ ☐ 20. Struggle always to win games instead of having fun?

☐ ☐ 21. Interrupt people who are talking?

☐ ☐ 22. Lose patience with people who are late for appointments and meetings?

☐ ☐ 23. Get back to work right after lunch?

☐ ☐ 24. Find that there's never enough time?

☐ ☐ 25. Believe that you're getting too little done, even when other people tell you that you're doing fine?

Scoring Key: "Yes" answers suggest a Type A behavior pattern—and the more items to which you answered "yes," the stronger your TABP. You should have little difficulty determining whether you are strongly or moderately inclined toward this behavior pattern—that is, if you are honest with yourself.

Source: Adapted from Nevid, Rathus, & Greene, 2003.

CONCEPT 15.8

The Type A behavior pattern is a source of stress that can pose a risk to one's health, perhaps even to one's life.

Type A behavior pattern (TABP)
A behavior pattern characterized by impatience, time urgency, competitiveness, and hostility.

Type A Behavior Pattern   Are you the type of person whom others would describe as hard-driving, competitive, impatient, and ambitious? Do you seem to take life at a faster pace than others? Does the idea of waiting in line or being stuck in traffic make you want to pull out your hair or pound your fists? If these characteristics ring true, your personality style probably fits the **Type A behavior pattern (TABP)** (Friedman & Rosenman, 1974).

People with the Type A behavior pattern are impatient, competitive, and aggressive. They are constantly in a rush and have a strong sense of time urgency. They feel pressured to get the maximum amount done in the shortest possible amount of time. They tend to do everything fast; they talk fast, walk fast, even eat fast. They quickly lose patience with others, especially those who move or work more slowly than they would like. They may become hostile and prone to anger when others fail to meet their expectations. They are intense even at play. While others are content to bat the ball around on the tennis court, people with the Type A behavior pattern play to win at all costs. By contrast, those with the opposite personality style, sometimes called the Type B behavior pattern, take a slower, more relaxed pace in life. The Try This Out feature above can help you determine whether you fit the Type A profile.

Type A Behavior Pattern Does your personality style contribute to the level of stress in your life?

People with the Type A behavior pattern stand a modestly higher risk of coronary heart disease (CHD) (Donker, 2000; Smith & Gallo, 2001). Hostility (quickness to anger) is the component of the Type A profile most strongly connected to increased cardiac risk (Eckhardt, Norlander, & Deffenbacher, 2004; Niaura et al., 2002). Hostile people tend to be quick to anger and to experience anger much of the time.

We also have evidence linking other negative emotions, especially anxiety and depression, to increased risk of coronary heart disease and other health problems (Frasure-Smith & Lespérance, 2005; Kiecolt-Glaser et al., 2002; Underwood,

CONCEPT CHART 15.1   Sources of Stress

Source	Description	Key Points
Hassles	Common annoyances of everyday life	The accumulation of a large number of daily hassles may contribute to chronic stress, which can impair psychological and physical well-being.
Life events	Changes in life circumstances, either positive or negative, that place demands on us to adjust	A greater number of life change events is associated with poorer psychological and physical health outcomes, but cause-and-effect relationships are difficult to tease out.
Frustration	A state of negative arousal brought about by the thwarting of one's efforts to attain personal goals	We feel frustrated when obstacles placed in our path prevent us from achieving our goals or when we set unattainable goals for ourselves.
Conflict	The state of tension that occurs when we feel torn between two opposing goals	Conflicts are most stressful when opposing goals are equally strong and no clear resolution appears in sight.
Traumatic stressors	Sudden, life-threatening events such as natural or technological disasters, combat experiences, accidents, or physical or sexual assault	Traumatic events can tax our coping abilities to the limit. Many survivors of trauma go on to develop a type of psychological disorder called posttraumatic stress disorder (PTSD).
Type A behavior pattern (TABP)	A behavior pattern characterized by impatience, competitiveness, aggressiveness, and time urgency	The TABP is linked to a higher risk of coronary heart disease. While Type A "hares" are not likely to become "tortoises," they can learn to reduce their Type A behavior.
Acculturative stress	Pressures imposed on immigrant people to adapt to the cultural and linguistic demands of the host country	Complex relationships exist between acculturation status and psychological adjustment. Adjustment depends on many factors, including economic opportunities, language proficiency, ethnic identification, and a supportive social network.

2004; Yan et al., 2003). Investigators also speculate that what puts people at increased disease risk are tendencies toward strong negative emotions in general, rather than any specific negative emotion (anger, anxiety, depression) (Suls & Bunde, 2005).

Whether other features of the Type A behavior pattern, such as the hurried pace of life, directly contribute to health problems remains open to further study. Nonetheless, this behavior pattern is a modifiable source of stress. If you are seeking to reduce the level of stress in your life, a good place to start might be with modifying Type A behavior. Module 15.3 contains suggestions for reducing Type A behavior that you might find helpful. Before reading further, you may wish to review the sources of stress outlined in Concept Chart 15.1.

EXPLORING PSYCHOLOGY
Making It in America:
The Challenge of Acculturative Stress

> **CONCEPT 15.9**
> Acculturative stress is a source of stress faced by immigrants struggling to meet the demands of adjusting to a new culture.

Adjusting to a New Culture Should immigrant groups adapt to their new culture or retain their identification with their traditional cultures? Or should they attempt both?

acculturative stress Demands faced by immigrants in adjusting to a host culture.

For immigrants, the demands of adjusting to a new culture can be a significant source of stress. Establishing a new life in an adopted country can be a difficult adjustment under the best of circumstances, but all the more difficult when immigrants don't speak the language of the host culture and when there are few available jobs or training opportunities. How do these demands to adjust—to become *acculturated*—affect the mental health of immigrant groups?

Acculturative stress refers to pressure to adapt to the values, linguistic preferences, and customs of a host or dominant culture. Relationships between acculturation and psychological adjustment are complex (Escobar & Vega, 2000). Most of this research has focused on Latinos. Consider, for example, evidence that more acculturated Latinos (Hispanic Americans) are more likely to develop psychological disorders than their less acculturated counterparts (Ortega et al., 2000). Others find that Mexican Americans born in the United States show higher rates of psychological problems than recent immigrants from Mexico (Escobar, Hoyos-Nervi, & Gara, 2000). Taken together, these findings suggest that acculturation might prove dangerous to one's mental health. But other researchers link *lower* acculturation status among Latinos to higher risks of depression and anxiety (e.g., Neff & Hoppe, 1993; Zamanian et al., 1992).

In attempting to understand these mixed findings, we should note that the process of adjusting successfully to a new society depends on a number of factors. For Latinos, pressure to adjust to an English-speaking culture emerges as perhaps the predominant source of acculturative stress (Rodriguez et al., 2002). Lack of acculturation is often associated with economic hardship, or lower socioeconomic status (SES) (Negy & Woods, 1992). Stress associated with economic hardship is a major contributor to adjustment problems in immigrant groups, as it is for members of the host culture. So it is not surprising that difficulties faced by poorly acculturated immigrants in gaining an economic foothold in the host country may lead to emotional difficulties, such as anxiety and depression. A study of immigrant Chinese children in the United States also showed more adjustment problems among those living in more economically stressful situations (Short & Johnston, 1997). But the downside of acculturation is that it can lead to an erosion of traditional family networks, which in turn may increase vulnerability to psychological disorders in the face of stress (Ortega et al., 2000).

All in all, factors such as economic opportunity, language proficiency in the host language, connections to a social network of people with whom one can identify, and maintaining one's ethnic identity may help buffer the effects of acculturative stress faced by immigrant groups (Kim et al., 2003; Ryder, Alden, & Paulhus, 2000). We also have evidence from studies of Asian Americans that establishing contacts with the majority culture while maintaining one's ethnic identity

Ethnic Pride A strong sense of ethnic identity can contribute to psychological health and help buffer stress resulting from prejudice and racism.

generates less stress than withdrawal and separation (Huang, 1994). Withdrawal fails to prepare the individual to make the necessary adjustments to function effectively in a multicultural society.

The leading theory of acculturative stress, generally called the *bicultural theory,* posits that immigrants fare better psychologically when they maintain their identity with their traditional values and beliefs while also making efforts to adapt to the host culture. That is, adaptability combined with a supportive cultural tradition and a sense of ethnic identity fosters psychological health. Evidence shows that maintaining strong ethnic identification is linked to better psychological health in many groups, including Asian American adolescents and Navajo youth (Phinney & Alipuria, 1990; Huang, 1994; Rieckmann, Wadsworth, & Deyhle, 2004).

Racism and prejudice are also significant sources of stress for immigrant groups and for native-born ethnic minority-group members (Clark et al., 1999). Not surprisingly, investigators find that exposure to racism is linked to poorer psychological well-being and self-concept (Utsey et al., 2002). Yet investigators point out that ethnic identity and pride in one's own culture can bolster the person's ability to cope with the effects of racism and prejudice (Thompson, Anderson, & Bakeman, 2000).

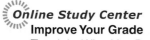

Online Study Center

Improve Your Grade

Tutorials: What You Don't Know Can Hurt You

The Body's Response to Stress

Much of what we know about the body's response to stress is the result of pioneering research by Hans Selye (1907–1982), the famed stress researcher known affectionately as "Dr. Stress" (see the Pioneers box).

The General Adaptation Syndrome Selye recognized that specific stressors, such as an invading virus, elicit specific reactions in the body. But layered over these specific reactions is a more general stress response that represents the body's attempt to adapt to intense or persistent stress. He called this adaptive response the **general adaptation syndrome (GAS)**. Many different kinds of stressors can activate the GAS, including an ominous physical threat, excessive noise, infectious agents, job pressures, or even mental stress in the form of nagging worries or anxiety. The general adaptation syndrome consists of three stages, each of which we consider below.

CONCEPT 15.10

The general adaptation syndrome (GAS), the body's adaptive response to stress, comprises three stages: the alarm reaction, , the resistance stage, and the exhaustion stage.

general adaptation syndrome (GAS)

Selye's term for the three-stage response of the body to persistent or intense stress.

THE PIONEERS

"Dr. Stress"

Hans Selye

Hans Selye ("Dr. Stress") first became interested in the effects of stress while he was a student in medical school (Selye, 1976). Like most medical students, Selye was eager to start seeing patients. He had completed his preclinical studies in the basic sciences but had only a vague idea about how to treat patients. During the first lecture he attended on internal medicine, the professor brought in several patients suffering from various infectious diseases. Each patient was carefully questioned and examined in an effort to find the distinguishing symptoms or features that would lead to a diagnosis. But what intrigued Selye most was the commonality of the patients' symptoms. They all felt and looked ill and had general aches and pains, intestinal distress, and a loss of appetite. Most also had fever and general signs of infection, including inflamed tonsils. Selye began to wonder whether the body responds similarly to different kinds of stressors, including different infectious agents. Ten years later, he had an opportunity to pursue his interest in stress by conducting medical research at McGill University in Montreal, Canada. There he observed the same physiological response pattern when laboratory animals were exposed to a variety of stressors, including injections of hormonal extracts, freezing cold, x-rays, and toxic chemicals. He concluded that the body reacts to different types of stressors with a general or nonspecific adaptive response, which he called the *general adaptation syndrome (GAS)*. Investigating this syndrome further led him to believe that the way the body responds to persistent stress is much like an alarm clock that does not shut off until its energy becomes dangerously depleted.

CONCEPT 15.11

During the alarm reaction stage of the GAS, the body's mobilizes its resources in the face of stress, preparing to fend off a threat by either fighting or fleeing.

alarm reaction The first stage of the general adaptation syndrome, involving mobilization of the body's resources to cope with an immediate stressor.

fight-or-flight response The body's built-in alarm system that allows it to quickly mobilize its resources to either fight or flee when faced with a threatening stressor.

Alarm Reaction   The **alarm reaction** is the body's first stage of response to a stressor, during which it mobilizes it defenses to prepare for action. Suppose a car ahead of you on the road suddenly veers out of control. This is an immediate stressful event. Your heart starts pounding faster, speeding the flow of blood to your extremities and providing muscles with the oxygen and fuel they need to take swift action, such as performing an emergency maneuver to avoid a collision. The alarm reaction is also called the **fight-or-flight response** because it prepares the body to deal with threatening stressors by either fleeing from them or fending them off.

The alarm reaction is accompanied by strong physiological and psychological arousal. Our hearts pound, our breathing quickens, sweat pours down our foreheads, and we are flooded with strong emotions such as terror, fright, anxiety, rage, or anger.

Different stressful events may trigger the alarm reaction stage of the GAS. The threat may be physical, as in an attack by an assailant, or psychological, as in an event that induces fear of failure (a professor handing out an examination, for example). In people who are fearful of rejection, the alarm can be triggered whenever they meet a new person at a social gathering. They may find themselves sweating heavily, feeling anxious, and becoming tongue-tied. In some people, the body's alarm system may be activated whenever they visit the dentist. Whether the perceived threat is physical or psychological, the body's response is the same.

The alarm reaction is like a "call to arms" that is prewired into the nervous system. This wiring is a legacy inherited from our earliest ancestors, who faced many potential threats in their daily lives. A glimpse of a suspicious-looking object or a rustling sound in the bush might have cued them to the presence of a predator, triggering the fight-or-flight response, which helped them defend themselves against a threat. But the fight-or-flight response didn't last long. If they survived the immediate threat, their bodies returned to their normal state. If they failed, they simply perished.

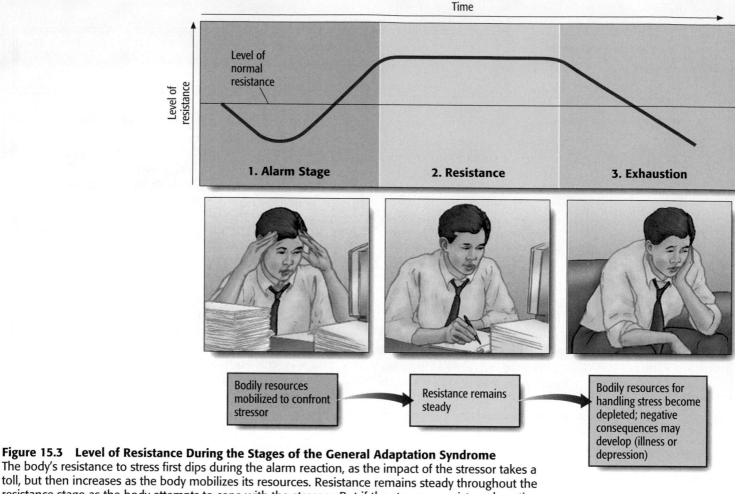

Figure 15.3 **Level of Resistance During the Stages of the General Adaptation Syndrome**
The body's resistance to stress first dips during the alarm reaction, as the impact of the stressor takes a toll, but then increases as the body mobilizes its resources. Resistance remains steady throughout the resistance stage as the body attempts to cope with the stressor. But if the stressor persists, exhaustion eventually sets in as bodily reserves needed to resist stress become dangerously depleted.

CONCEPT 15.12
During the resistance stage of the GAS, the body conserves its resources to adapt to the effects of enduring stress.

CONCEPT 15.13
During the exhaustion stage of the GAS, continuing stress can lead to severe depletion of bodily resources and development of stress-related diseases.

resistance stage The second stage of the general adaptation syndrome, characterized by the body's attempt to adjust or adapt to persistent stress.
exhaustion stage The third stage of the general adaptation syndrome, characterized by depletion of bodily resources and a lowered resistance to stress-related disorders or conditions.

Resistance Stage Death may occur within the first few hours or days of exposure to a stressor that is so damaging (such as extreme cold) that its persistence is incompatible with life. But if survival is possible and the stressor continues, the body attempts to adapt to it as best it can. Selye called this part of the GAS the **resistance stage** (also called the *adaptation stage*). During this stage, the body attempts to return to a normal biological state by restoring spent energy and repairing damage. Yet arousal remains high, though not as high as during the alarm reaction. This prolonged bodily arousal may be accompanied by such emotional reactions as anger, fatigue, and irritability.

Exhaustion Stage If the stressor persists, the body may enter the final stage of the GAS—the **exhaustion stage**. Heart rate and respiration now *decrease* to conserve bodily resources. Yet with continued exposure to stress, the body's resources may become seriously depleted and the individual may develop what Selye called "diseases of adaptation"—stress-related disorders such as kidney disease, heart disease, allergic conditions, digestive disorders, and depression. Some people are hardier than others, but relentless, intense stress can eventually exhaust anyone. Figure 15.3 shows the changes that occur in the body's level of resistance across the three stages of the GAS.

A sensitive alarm system may have helped our ancient ancestors survive many of the physical threats they faced. Yet the alarm reaction was designed not to last very long. Our ancestors either escaped a predator or fought it off; within seconds, minutes perhaps, the threat was over and their bodies returned to their normal, prearoused state. The stresses of contemporary life are more persistent. Our ancestors didn't need to juggle school and jobs, fight daily traffic jams, or face the daily grind of working a double shift to make ends meet. The reality for many of us today is that the stressful demands of everyday life may repeatedly activate our alarm reaction day after day, year after year. Over time, persistent stress may overtax the body's resources to the point where we become more susceptible to stress-related disorders (Kemeny, 2003).

Psychologists have found behavioral differences in how men and women respond to stress. Women tend to engage in more nurturing behaviors during times of stress than do men, such as by comforting and soothing infants and children, and befriending others who might help protect them and their children from threats. Women's stress-related behavior may be described as a "tend and befriend" pattern, which may be influenced by female reproductive and maternal hormones (Taylor et al., 2000). Among males, stressful experiences are more likely to lead to aggressive responses, possibly because of the influence of the male sex hormone testosterone.

Stress and the Endocrine System

The endocrine system is a system of ductless glands throughout the body that release secretions, called *hormones,* directly into the bloodstream (see Chapter 2). The hypothalamus, a small endocrine gland located in the midbrain, coordinates the endocrine system's response to stress. Like a series of falling dominoes, the chain reaction it sets off leads other glands to release their hormones.

Let's look closer at the falling dominoes. Under stress, the hypothalamus secretes **corticotrophin-releasing hormone (CRH)**, which in turn stimulates the pituitary gland to secrete **adrenocorticotrophic hormone (ACTH)**. ACTH travels through the bloodstream to the **adrenal glands**, the pair of small endocrine glands located just above the kidneys. There it stimulates the **adrenal cortex**, the outer layer of the adrenal glands, to release stress hormones called **corticosteroids** (or *cortical steroids*). These hormones help the body resist stress by making stored nutrients more available to meet the demands for energy that may be required to cope with stressful events.

The sympathetic branch of the autonomic nervous system triggers the **adrenal medulla**, the inner layer of each adrenal gland, to secrete the stress hormones *epinephrine* and *norepinephrine*. These hormones make the heart pump faster, allowing more oxygen and nutrient-rich blood to reach the muscles where it is needed to allow the organism to either flee from a threatening stressor or fight it off. The experience of a "racing heart" during times of stress is explained by the surge of these stress hormones (Sternberg, 2000). The body's response to stress is depicted in Figure 15.4.

Stress and the Immune System

The **immune system** is the body's primary system of defense against infectious diseases and worn-out or diseased cells (Delves & Roitt, 2000). The immune system fights disease in several ways. It dispatches billions of specialized white blood cells called **lymphocytes**. Lymphocytes constantly circulate throughout the body and remain on alert to the presence of foreign agents or **antigens** (literally *anti*body *gen*erators). An antigen is any substance recognized as foreign to the body, such as a bacterium, virus, foreign protein, or a body cell that has turned cancerous. As the term's literal meaning suggests, antigens activate the immune system to produce **antibodies**, which are specialized protein molecules that fit the invading antigen like a key fitting a lock. When antibodies lock into position on an antigen, they mark it for destruction by specialized "killer" lymphocytes.

Some lymphocytes hold a "memory" of specific antigens to which the body has been exposed, allowing the immune system to render a quick blow the next time

---

CONCEPT 15.14
The endocrine system plays a key role in the body's response to stress.

corticotrophin-releasing hormone (CRH) A hormone released by the hypothalamus that induces the pituitary gland to release adrenocorticotrophic hormone.

adrenocorticotrophic hormone (ACTH) A pituitary hormone that activates the adrenal cortex to release corticosteroids (cortical steroids).

adrenal glands A pair of endocrine glands located just above the kidneys that produce various stress-related hormones

adrenal cortex The outer layer of the adrenal glands that secretes corticosteroids (cortical steroids).

corticosteroids Adrenal hormones that increase the body's resistance to stress by increasing the availability of stored nutrients to meet the increased energy demands of coping with stressful events. Also called *cortical steroids.*

adrenal medulla The inner part of the adrenal glands that secretes the stress hormones epinephrine (adrenaline) and norepinephrine (noradrenaline).

immune system The body's system of defense against disease.

lymphocytes White blood cells that protect the body against disease-causing organisms.

antigens Substances, such as bacteria and viruses, that are recognized by the immune system as foreign to the body and that induce it to produce antibodies to defend against them.

antibodies Protein molecules produced by the immune system that serve to mark antigens for destruction by specialized lymphocytes.

Figure 15.4 The Body's Response to Stress
Under stress, the body responds by releasing stress hormones (epinephrine and norepinephrine) from the adrenal medulla and corticosteroids from the adrenal cortex. These substances help the body prepare to cope with an immediate stressor. Stress hormones increase heart rate, respiration, and blood pressure, and secretion of corticosteroids leads to the release of stored reserves of energy.

CONCEPT 15.15

Evidence suggests that stress can increase vulnerability to physical illness by impairing the functioning of the body's immune system.

vaccination A method of acquiring immunity by means of injecting a weakened or partial form of an infectious agent that can induce production of antibodies but does not produce a full-blown infection.

the invader appears. Thus we may develop immunity or resistance to many disease-causing antigens—which is why we do not contract certain illnesses, such as chicken pox, more than once. We may also acquire immunity through **vaccination** (also called *immunization*). A vaccination involves the administration of dead or weakened infectious agents that will not cause an infection themselves but can stimulate the body's natural production of antibodies to the particular antigen.

Health experts estimate that between 60 and 90 percent of all doctor visits involve stress-related problems (Benson, Corliss, & Cowley, 2005). Occasional stress may not be harmful, but chronic stress can weaken the immune system, making us more vulnerable to disease (Epstein, 2003; Kemeny, 2003; Segerstrom & Miller, 2004). The kinds of stressors most often linked to health problems include divorce; chronic illness; prolonged unemployment; persistent lack of sleep; loss of loved ones; exposure to trauma such as hurricanes, other natural or technological disasters, or acts of violence; and college examination periods.

Investigators are actively studying the cellular mechanisms by which stress affects vulnerability to disease (Bierhuas et al., 2003). One way that chronic stress damages the body's immune system is by increasing levels of a chemical called *interleukin-6* (Kiecolt-Glaser et al., 2003a). Heightened levels of this chemical are associated with increased vulnerability to disease. Chronic stress is also linked to lower numbers of the body's natural killer cells, the immune system's attack cells that help combat infection (Dougall & Baum, 2003). Chronic stress and worry can even increase the length of time it takes for wounds to heal (Kiecolt-Glaser et al., 2002).

Perhaps you've noticed you become more vulnerable to catching a cold during times of stress, such as around final exams. The reason may be that exposure to stress is linked to lower production of *immunoglobulin A,* an antibody that helps protect us against cold viruses (Stone et al., 1994). Chronic stress can also lead to reactivation of latent or dormant viruses in the body, such as the herpes simplex virus and the Epstein-Barr virus (Dougall & Baum, 2003). Epstein-Barr virus is linked to chronic fatigue syndrome.

💡 **CONCEPT 15.16**
Social support, self-efficacy, perceptions of control and predictability, psychological hardiness, and optimism are psychological factors that moderate or buffer the effects of stress.

Helping Hands Social support is an important buffer against the effects of stress associated with negative life circumstances or physical illness.

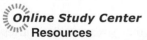
Online Study Center
Resources
  Weblinks: Stress: How and When to Get Help

Stress and physical illness are also linked through the actions of corticosteroids. These adrenal hormones are released as part of the body's reaction to stress. While they initially help the body cope with stress, their continued secretion dampens the ability of immune-system cells to respond to invading microbes (Sternberg, 2000). (Immune functioning also can be impaired by the use of synthetic steroids, such as those taken by some body builders and wrestlers.)

Stress hormones may even affect our relationship health. Recent evidence shows that newlyweds whose bodies pumped out more stress hormones during the first year of marriage were more likely to get divorced within ten years than were newlyweds with a lower stress response (Kiecolt-Glaser et al., 2003b).

Psychological techniques can help combat stress and may improve immunological functioning. For example, researchers find that people who are instructed to express their emotions by writing about traumatic or stressful life experiences show fewer psychological and physical symptoms than control participants (Frisina, Borod & Lepore, 2004; Pennebaker, 2004; Sloan & Marx, 2004). Cancer patients who were instructed to write about their cancer in a journal reported sleeping better than those who wrote about neutral topics (de Moor et al., 2003).

The health benefits of expressive writing may even extend to writing about intensely positive experiences as well as negative experiences. Recently, investigators at Southern Methodist University had undergraduate students write about intensely positive experiences or control topics for twenty minutes each day for three consecutive days (Burton & King, 2004). Writing about positive experiences was associated with enhanced mood and fewer medical visits to the campus health center in the months following the study.

Though expressive writing appears to have health benefits, we should add that more research is needed to confirm the causal effect (Miller & Cohen, 2001).

Psychological Buffers to Stress

Stress may affect us all, but how we cope with stress has an important bearing on how stress affects us. Here we examine psychological moderators that may lessen the impact of stress, including social support, self-efficacy, perceptions of control and predictability, psychological hardiness, and optimism (see Figure 15.5).

Social Support   Social support plays a major role in determining how well people cope with stress. In pioneering studies with medical students and dental stu-

Figure 15.5 Psychological Moderators of Stress
Social support, self-efficacy, perceptions of control and predictability, psychological hardiness, and optimism are psychological moderators that help us better withstand the effects of stress.

Psychological Moderators
- Social support
- Self-efficacy
- Perceptions of control/predictability
- Psychological hardiness
- Optimism

Factors that may buffer or lessen negative effects of stress

Stressor
- Final exams
- Unemployment
- Serious illness
- Relocation
- Financial hardship
- Job or family-related conflicts

Negative Effects of Stress
Psychological effects
- Negative emotional states like anxiety, depression, and anger
- Development of psychological disorders
- Withdrawal or aggressive behavior

Physical effects
- Nervous system arousal
- Development of stress-related physical illness

Online Study Center
Improve Your Grade
Tutorials: Coping with Stress

dents, two highly stressed groups, researchers showed that students with a wide range of friends had better immune-system functioning than those with fewer friends (Jemmott et al., 1983; Kiecolt-Glaser et al., 1984). And in other research, people with a wider social network were shown to be more resistant to infection when intentionally exposed to a common cold virus than were others with a more limited social network (Cohen et al., 1997). This same research group also showed that more sociable, people-oriented individuals were more resistant to developing the common cold after voluntarily receiving injections of a cold virus than were less sociable volunteers (Cohen et al., 2003). The mechanism through which social networks and sociability affect vulnerability to illness remains to be determined.

Self-Efficacy You may recall from Chapter 12 that *self-efficacy* is the belief that we are capable of accomplishing what we set out to do. High levels of self-efficacy are linked to an increased ability to withstand stress (Bandura, 1997). People with high levels of self-efficacy tend to view stressful situations more as challenges to be met than as obstacles to overcome. Self-confidence in their abilities leads them to tackle stressors head-on and persevere, even when they confront barriers in their path.

Predictability and Controllability The impact of particular stressors also varies with how *predictable* and *controllable* they seem. Stressful events that seem more predictable and controllable, such as school assignments, have less impact on us than other events, such as hurricanes and fluctuations in the stock market, that seem to lie beyond our ability to predict or control them (Lazarus & Folkman, 1984). Interestingly, even stressful events that are not in fact controllable tend to have this lesser impact when viewed as controllable (Thompson et al., 1993).

People also vary in the degree to which they perceive themselves as capable of controlling events. Those with an *internal locus of control* believe that rewards or reinforcements are a direct consequence of their actions (Wallston, 2001; see Chapter 12). Those with an *external locus of control* believe that their fate is determined by external factors or blind luck, not by their own efforts. "Internals" may be better able to marshal their efforts to cope with stressful events because of their belief that they can control them. "Externals," on the other hand, may feel helpless and overwhelmed in the face of stressful events.

Psychological Hardiness   An internal locus of control is also a defining characteristic of **psychological hardiness**, a cluster of personality traits associated with an increased resilience to stress. This term was introduced by psychologist Suzanne Kobasa (1979), based on her studies of business executives who maintained their physical health despite the high levels of stress they endured. She and her colleagues identified three key traits associated with psychological hardiness (Kobasa, Maddi, & Kahn, 1982):

- *Commitment.* The hardy executives had a strong commitment to their work and a belief that what they were doing was important.

- *Openness to challenge.* The hardy executives viewed the stressors they faced as challenges to be met, not as overwhelming obstacles. They believed that change is a normal part of life and not something to be dreaded.

- *Internal locus of control.* The hardy executives believed that they could control the future direction of their lives, for better or for worse.

In short, people with psychological hardiness accept stress as a normal challenge of life. They feel in control of the stress they encounter and believe that the challenges they face make life more interesting. They seek to solve problems, not avoid them.

Psychologically hardy people report fewer physical symptoms and less depression in times of stress (Maddi & Khoshaba, 1994; Ouellette & DiPlacido, 2001; Pengilly & Dowd, 2000). They also show stronger immune system responses than less hardy people (Dolbier et al., 2001).

Optimism   Another buffer to stress is optimism. Optimism is a key concept in the developing movement in psychology called *positive psychology* (see Chapter 1 and Chapter 8). People with more optimistic attitudes tend to be more resilient to the effects of stress. For example, optimism is associated with lower levels of emotional distress in heart disease patients and with less perceived pain and emotional distress in cancer patients (Bjerklie, 2005; Shnek et al., 2001; Trunzo & Pinto, 2003). Among pregnant women, optimism is linked with better birth outcomes, such as higher infant birth weights (Lobel et al., 2000). Among coronary artery bypass surgery patients, those with more optimistic attitudes before surgery experienced fewer serious postoperative complications (Scheier et al., 1999). In contrast, holding pessimistic attitudes is linked to greater emotional distress, such as depression and social anxiety (Hardin & Leong, 2005).

Evidence tying optimism to better outcomes is correlational, so we should be careful not to draw a causal link. Still, doesn't it make sense to take an optimistic approach toward the stressors you face, seeing the glass as half-full rather than half-empty?

Let's turn the discussion around to you. What about your own outlook on life? Do you tend to be an optimist or a pessimist? The Try This Out feature on the next page can help you evaluate your outlook on life.

Burnout

Are you so consumed by work that you neglect other aspects of your life, such as social relationships and leisure activities? People who have overextended themselves may develop a stress-related condition called **burnout**, a state of physical

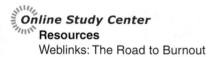
Online Study Center
Resources
Weblinks: The Road to Burnout

CONCEPT 15.17
Burnout, a state of physical and emotional exhaustion, may result when we overextend ourselves in our work, caregiving responsibilities, or other commitments.

psychological hardiness   A cluster of traits (commitment, openness to challenge, internal locus of control) that may buffer the effects of stress.

burnout   A state of physical and mental fatigue caused by excessive stress relating to work or other commitments.

CONCEPT 15.18
Vulnerability to burnout may be affected by role conflict, role overload, and role ambiguity.

Burnout Burnout does not arise from hard work per se, but from an imbalance between work and other activities.

and emotional exhaustion resulting from excessive demands on the job, in the home, and in other stressful situations in life (Maslach, 2003; Peeters et al., 2005).

Burnout can leave people feeling apathetic toward their work and the people they serve (Spector, 2003). It is also linked to increased risk of stress-related health problems such as headaches, stomach distress, sleep problems, and hypertension (Leiter & Maslach, 2001). Nurses and teachers are among the occupational groups at highest risk of burnout (Sternberg, 2000). Many factors are linked to the potential for burnout. For example, a recent study showed that poor working conditions was a strong predictor of burnout among teachers in both rural and urban settings (Abel & Sewell, 1999).

It is not hard work per se that causes burnout. Rather, burnout results from an imbalance between work and other life activities. Vulnerability to burnout is influenced by factors such as role conflict, role overload, and role ambiguity. *Role conflict* occurs when people face competing demands for their time. They may feel as if they are being pulled in several directions at once. Repeated, unsuccessful attempts to reconcile these competing demands may eventually lead to burnout. People with *role overload* have a hard time saying no to others. They just keep accepting additional responsibilities until they burn out. People who experience *role ambiguity* are unsure about what others expect of them. They continually seek ways to be "all things to all people" and may eventually suffer burnout as a result. Table 15.4 lists some warning signs of burnout.

▶ TRY THIS OUT

Are You an Optimist or a Pessimist?

Do you tend to look on the bright side of things? Or do you usually expect the worst? The following scale, called the Life Orientation Test, can help raise your awareness about whether you are the type of person who tends to see the proverbial glass as half-full or half-empty (Scheier & Carver, 1985).

Instructions: Answer the following questions about yourself by indicating the extent of your agreement using the following scale:

    0 = strongly disagree
    1 = disagree
    2 = neutral
    3 = agree
    4 = strongly agree

Be as honest as you can throughout, and try not to let your responses to one question influence your response to other questions. There are no right or wrong answers.

_____ 1. In uncertain times, I usually expect the best.

_____ 2. It's easy for me to relax.

_____ 3. If something can go wrong for me, it will.

_____ 4. I'm always optimistic about my future.

_____ 5. I enjoy my friends a lot.

_____ 6. It's important for me to keep busy.

_____ 7. I hardly ever expect things to go my way.

_____ 8. I don't get upset too easily.

_____ 9. I rarely count on good things happening to me.

_____ 10. Overall, I expect more good things to happen to me than bad.

Scoring Key: 1. Reverse the scoring for items 3, 7, and 9; that is, change 0 to 4, 1 to 3, 3 to 1, and 4 to 0. Keep 2 as 2. 2. Sum items 1, 3, 4, 7, 9, and 10 to obtain an overall score.*

*Note: Items 2, 5, 6, and 8 are filler items only. They are not included in your score. The revised scale was constructed in order to eliminate two items from the original scale, which dealt more with coping style than with positive expectations for future outcomes. The correlation between the revised scale and the original scale is 0.95.

Source: Based on Scheier, Carver, & Bridges, 1994.

TABLE 15.4   Warning Signs of Burnout

Burnout develops slowly over time. Here are some warning signs:

- Mental and physical fatigue or loss of energy
- Increased irritability and proneness to anger
- Development of stress-related problems such as headaches, backaches, general malaise, or depression
- Problems with concentration at work
- Changes in one's feelings toward work in someone who was previously highly committed and enthusiastic, as evidenced by feelings of detachment, loss of motivation, or lack of concern about the quality of one's work
- Loss of satisfaction or of a sense of accomplishment in performing work
- Feeling that one lacks the energy or will to remain committed to one's work or causes

MODULE 15.1 REVIEW

Stress: What It Is and What It Does to the Body

RECITE IT

What is health psychology?

- Health psychology is the branch of psychology that studies interrelationships between psychological factors and health.

What is stress, and what are the major sources of stress?

- The term *stress* refers to pressures and demands to adjust or adapt.
- The major sources of stress include daily hassles, life changes, frustration, conflict, Type A behavior pattern, traumatic events, and, for immigrant groups, pressures of acculturation.

How does the body respond to stress?

- Stress activates a general pattern of physiological responses, described by Selye as the general adaptation syndrome, or GAS. GAS consists of three stages: the alarm reaction, the resistance stage, and the exhaustion stage.

How does stress affect the immune system?

- Persistent or severe stress can impair the functioning of the immune system, leaving us more susceptible to many illnesses, including the common cold.

What psychological factors buffer the effects of stress?

- Psychological buffers against stress include social support, self-efficacy, perceptions of controllability and predictability, psychological hardiness, and optimism.

RECALL IT

1. (a) Give a psychological definition of stress.
   (b) At what point does stress lead to distress?

2. Match the following types of stressors with the appropriate descriptions: i. hassles; ii. life events; iii. conflict; iv. traumatic stressors
   a. two or more competing goals where a choice must be made
   b. common annoyances such as traffic jams and balancing work and social demands
   c. major changes in life circumstances
   d. potentially life-threatening events

3. Psychological moderators of stress include social support and _____-_____, the belief we hold about our ability to accomplish tasks we set out to perform.

4. The stage of the GAS characterized by the fight-or-flight response is the _____ stage.

5. A state of physical and emotional exhaustion often accompanied by a sense of apathy toward one's work and the people one serves is called _____.

THINK ABOUT IT

- What is the role of the nervous system in the general adaptation syndrome? What is the role of the endocrine system?
- Agree or disagree and support your answer: Stress can be healthy or unhealthy.

- Do you show any signs of suffering burnout? If so, what can you do about it?

MODULE 15.2

Psychological Factors in Physical Illness

- How are psychological factors linked to the health of our heart and circulatory system?
- What roles do psychological factors play in the development of cancer?
- What roles do psychological factors play in other health conditions, such as asthma, headaches, and ulcers?

Our physical health depends on many influences, including heredity and exposure to infectious organisms, such as bacteria and viruses. But to a surprising degree, our health depends on psychological factors, such as behaviors, emotional states, and exposure to psychological sources of stress. Our health and longevity can be affected by what we eat, whether we use tobacco and alcohol, whether we exercise regularly, and whether we experience persistent negative emotions, such as anger and anxiety. We'll see that unhealthy behaviors such as smoking and poor diet are major risk factors for the three leading killers of Americans: heart disease, cancer, and stroke (Holloway, 2004; Mokdad, Marks, & Stroup, 2004). Figure 15.6 shows the leading causes of death in the United States based on the most recently available statistics.

Coronary Heart Disease

CONCEPT 15.19
Health-related behaviors, such as diet, exercise, and smoking, affect a person's risk of developing many physical disorders, including coronary heart disease.

The heart is composed of muscle tissue, which, like other body tissue, requires oxygen and nutrients carried through blood vessels called **arteries**. **Coronary heart disease (CHD)** is a disorder in which the flow of blood to the heart becomes insufficient to meet its needs. In most cases, the underlying cause is **atherosclerosis**, the narrowing of arteries that results from a buildup of fatty deposits called **plaque** along artery walls (Stoney, 2003). Atherosclerosis impairs circulation of blood to the heart. It is the major form of **arteriosclerosis**, or "hardening of the arteries," a condition in which artery walls become thicker, harder, and less elastic.

Blood clots are more likely to become lodged in arteries narrowed by atherosclerosis. If a blood clot forms in a coronary artery (an artery that brings oxygen

Figure 15.6 America's Leading Killers
Unhealthy behaviors, such as smoking, poor diet, and inactivity, are major risk factors for many of America's leading killer diseases, including heart disease, cancer, and stroke.
Source: Anderson & Smith, 2005.

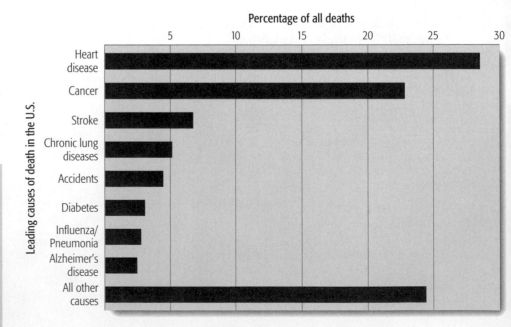

arteries Blood vessels that carry oxygen-rich blood from the heart through the circulatory system.

coronary heart disease (CHD) The most common form of heart disease, caused by blockages in coronary arteries, the vessels that supply the heart with blood.

atherosclerosis A form of arteriosclerosis involving the narrowing of artery walls resulting from the buildup of fatty deposits or plaque.

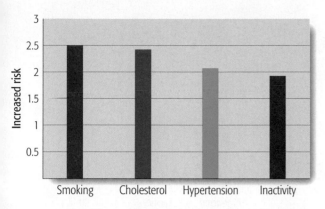

Figure 15.7   Risk Factors for Coronary Heart Disease
Shown here is the increased risk of CHD associated with several leading risk factors: smoking, cholesterol, hypertension, and inactivity. For example, people who smoke are 2.5 times more likely to develop CHD than are nonsmokers.
Source: Based on data from the American Heart Association.

CONCEPT 15.20
Risk factors for coronary heart disease include some factors you can't control, such as heredity, and some you can, such as hypertension, physical activity, and tobacco use.

plaque   In the circulatory system, fatty deposits that accumulate along artery walls.

arteriosclerosis   A condition in which artery walls become thicker and lose elasticity. Commonly called *hardening of the arteries*.

heart attack   A potentially life-threatening event involving the death of heart tissue due to a lack of blood flow to the heart. Also called *myocardial infarction*.

and nutrients to the heart), it may nearly or fully block the flow of blood to a part of the heart, causing a **heart attack** or *myocardial infarction (MI)*. Factors other than blocked arteries are also involved in triggering heart attacks, such as inflammation in the walls of arteries, which can cause built-up plaque to burst and form blood clots that block the flow of blood to the heart (Levine, 2005; Underwood & Adler, 2004).

During a heart attack, heart tissue literally dies from lack of oxygenated blood. Whether or not one survives a heart attack depends on the extent of damage to heart tissue and to the electrical system of the body that controls the heart rhythm.

Heart disease claims about 700,000 lives annually in the United States, with most deaths resulting from heart attacks (Nabel, 2003). The good news, as we shall see next, is that people can take steps to greatly reduce their risk of developing CHD.

Risk Factors for CHD   The risk of developing CHD varies with the number of risk factors an individual possesses. The most prominent risk factors include age (CHD increases with age after about age 40), gender (men are at greater risk until about age 65), family history (heredity), hypertension (high blood pressure), smoking, obesity, diabetes, lack of physical activity, and high cholesterol level (e.g., Chobanian et al., 2003; Hajjar & Kotchen, 2003; Tarkan, 2003; Winslow, 2004). These factors also increase the risk of stroke, the third leading killer of Americans after heart disease and cancer. Several leading risk factors for CHD are shown in Figure 15.7.

Note that some of these risk factors cannot be controlled. You can't choose your parents or your gender; nor can you stop aging. Others, such as hypertension, smoking, obesity, diabetes, and cholesterol level, *can* be controlled through either behavioral changes (diet and exercise) or appropriate medical treatment. A study of more than 84,000 nurses showed that those who followed a healthy lifestyle comprising regular exercise, adopting a diet low in saturated fat and cholesterol, and avoiding smoking—had a much lower than average risk of developing CHD (Stampfer et al., 2000).

Inactivity or following a sedentary lifestyle is a prominent risk factor for CHD (Manson et al., 2004). The good news is that making behavioral changes, such as adopting a program of regular exercise, even moderate exercise such as brisk walking, can lower your risk of heart disease (Kalb, 2003a; Pickering, 2003a; Writing Group, 2003). Not surprisingly, evidence shows that people who exercise regularly tend to live longer than their more sedentary counterparts (Gregg et al., 2003).

Smoking, another behavioral factor, doubles the risk of heart attacks and is linked to more than one in five deaths from CHD. Quitting smoking, however, can significantly reduce the risks of premature deaths from heart disease and cancer. (Some suggestions for quitting smoking are provided in the Try This Out feature on page 605.) Many Americans have heeded the health message and quit smoking. The percentage of Americans who smoke has dropped from 42 percent in 1966 to about 22 percent today (CDC, 2005a). Unfortunately, however, risk factors for CHD remain uncontrolled in many cases. A recent study showed that only about one-quarter of adults with hypertension were taking medications that controlled their blood pressure (Hyman & Pavlik, 2001). Clearly more needs to be done to help people reduce their risks of developing CHD.

Heart disease is not an equal opportunity destroyer. Black (non-Hispanic) Americans have a much higher death rate due to coronary heart disease than (non-Hispanic) White Americans and people of other ethnicities in the United States (Freeman & Payne, 2000; see Figure 15.8). One factor explaining this difference is that African Americans overall have higher rates of three key risk factors for heart disease: hypertension, obesity, and diabetes (Jones et al., 2002; Shields et al., 2005).

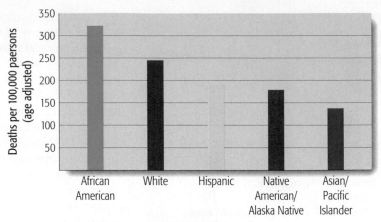

Figure 15.8   Ethnicity and Heart Disease
Death rates from diseases of the heart are higher among Black (non-Hispanic) Americans than among (non-Hispanic) White Americans and people of other ethnicities in the United States. What factors might account for these differences?
Source: Centers for Disease Control and Prevention, 2005b 2001.

CONCEPT 15.21
Negative emotions, such as anger, anxiety, and depression, may have damaging effects on the cardiovascular system.

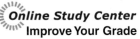

Online Study Center
Improve Your Grade
Tutorials: Chronic Hostility and Heart Disease

Another factor is that African American heart patients and heart attack victims typically receive less aggressive treatments than do Whites (Chen et al., 2001; Stolberg, 2001b). This dual standard of care may reflect unequal access to quality health care and discrimination by health care providers.

Emotions and Your Heart   As noted earlier, hostility is the component of the Type A behavior profile most strongly linked to an increased risk of coronary heart disease. Hostile people are angry much of the time, and chronic anger appears to be the culprit in explaining their increased risk of hypertension and CHD (Contrada & Guyll, 2001; Kiecolt-Glaser et al., 2002; Rutledge & Hogan, 2002).

Persistent emotional arousal, whether in the form of anger or anxiety, may damage the cardiovascular system because of the effects of the stress hormones epinephrine (adrenaline) and norepinephrine (noradrenaline) that accompany these emotional states (Melani, 2001). These hormones accelerate the heart rate, raise blood pressure, and increase the strength of heart contractions, resulting in a greater burden on the heart and circulatory system. These increased demands may eventually compromise the cardiovascular system, especially in vulnerable people. Stress hormones (primarily epinephrine) also increase the stickiness of blood clotting factors, which in turn may heighten the risk of potentially dangerous blood clots that can lead to heart attacks or strokes.

We have also learned that people who anger easily also stand a greater chance of developing two of the major risk factors for CHD and early death: high blood cholesterol levels and high blood pressure (Richards, Hof, & Alvarenga, 2000; Smith, 2003a). People who experience persistent anxiety also face an increased risk of heart disease (Smith & Gallo, 2001). Yet more evidence links other forms of emotional distress, such as depression and marital conflict, to increased risk of heart disease (Orth-Gomér et al., 2000; Winslow, 2004; Yusuf et al., 2004). Even exposure to the stress of traffic jams is linked to an increased risk of heart attacks in susceptible people in the hour following the exposure (Peters et al., 2004).

Psychologists are developing ways of helping chronically angry or anxious people learn to control their emotional responses. These programs have helped lower blood pressures and reduce risks of recurrent heart attacks leading to death in coronary heart disease patients (e.g., Gidron, Davidson, & Bata, 1999). The question of whether people without established heart disease also benefit remains to be answered.

TRY THIS OUT

Suggestions for Quitting Smoking

If you are a smoker, the first step toward becoming a non-smoker is making the decision to quit. Many smokers quit on their own. But many others seek help from health professionals or organizations, like the American Lung Association, that offer smoking cessation programs either free of charge or at modest costs. If you decide to quit on your own, you may find the following suggestions helpful:

• *Set a quit date.* Set a date several weeks ahead when you intend to quit smoking completely. Tell your friends and family of your commitment to quit smoking by that date. Publicly announcing your intentions will increase the likelihood that you'll stick to your plan of action.

• *Taper off.* Begin reducing the number of cigarettes you smoke daily in anticipation of your quitting date. A typical schedule to follow is cutting back the number of cigarettes you smoke daily by 25 percent each week for three weeks before quitting completely during the fourth week. Lengthen the interval between cigarettes to keep your smoking rate down to your daily limit.

• *Limit exposure to smoking environments.* Restrict the locations in which you smoke. Limit smoking to one particular room in your house, or outside on your porch, terrace, or deck. Break the habit of smoking while watching TV or conversing on the phone.

• *Increase exposure to nonsmoking environments.* Spend more time in settings where smoking isn't permitted or customary, such as the library. Also, socialize more with nonsmokers and, to the extent possible, avoid socializing with friends who smoke. What other smoke-free settings can you think of?

• *Limit the availability of cigarettes.* Carry only as many cigarettes as you need to meet your daily limit. Never buy more than a pack at a time.

• *Practice competing responses when tempted to smoke.* Preceding and following your quit date, substitute responses that are incompatible with smoking whenever you feel the urge to smoke. Delay reaching for a cigarette. Practice relaxation exercises. Exercise instead of smoking until the urge passes. Take a bath or a walk around the block (without your cigarettes). Use sugar-free mints or gum as substitutes whenever you feel the urge to smoke.

• *Mentally rehearse the benefits of not smoking.* Imagine yourself living a longer, healthier, noncoughing life.

• *Learn to cope, not smoke.* Learn healthier ways of coping with negative feelings, such as anxiety, sadness, and anger, than reaching for a cigarette.

Once you have quit smoking completely, remove all smoking-related paraphernalia from your house, including ashtrays and lighters. Remove as many cues as possible that were associated with your smoking habit. Establish a nonsmoking rule in your house, and request that friends and family members respect it. Ask others to be especially patient with you in the days and weeks following your quit date. Ask others not to smoke in your presence (explain that you have recently quit and would appreciate their cooperation). If you should lapse, don't despair. Make a commitment then and there not to have another cigarette. Many people succeed completely after a few prior unsuccessful attempts.

Cancer

The word *cancer* may strike more fear in people's hearts than any other word in the English language. The fear is understandable. Each year, more than 1.4 million Americans receive the dreaded diagnosis of cancer and nearly half a million die from it (Andersen, Golden-Kreutz, & DiLillo, 2001). The good news is that deaths from both cancer and heart disease have been declining in recent years.

Cancer is a disease in which body cells exhibit uncontrolled growth. The body normally manufactures new cells only when they are needed. The genes in our cells direct them to replicate in orderly ways. But in cancer, cells lose the ability to regulate their growth. They multiply even when they are not needed, eventually forming masses of excess body tissue called **malignant tumors**. Malignant or cancerous tumors may spread to other parts of the body, where they invade healthy tissue. Cancerous tumors damage vital body organs and systems, leading to death in many cases. Cancers can form in any body tissue or organ.

malignant tumors   Uncontrolled growths of body cells that invade surrounding tissue and spread to other parts of the body.

TABLE 15.5 Behaviors That Can Help Prevent Cancer

- If people protected themselves from the sun, more than 1 million cases of skin cancer would be prevented.
- If people avoided tobacco use, 172,000 fewer people would die of cancer.
- If people avoided excessive alcohol use, 19,000 fewer people would die of cancer.
- If people had their cancers detected in an early stage, 100,000 fewer people would die of cancer.

Source: American Cancer Society, 2001.

CONCEPT 15.22

Two out of three cancer deaths in the United States are accounted for by two modifiable behaviors: smoking and diet.

CONCEPT 15.23

If everyone practiced cancer-preventive behaviors, hundreds of thousands of lives would be saved each year.

There are many causes of cancer, including heredity, exposure to cancer-causing chemicals, and even exposure to some viruses, such as some strains of human papillomavirus virus (HPV) (Levy-Lahad & Plon, 2003; Lynch et al., 2004; Samuels et al., 2004). Yet two of three cancer deaths in this country are attributable to two modifiable behaviors: smoking and diet. Other modifiable behaviors, such as alcohol consumption and excess sun exposure, also contribute to the development of cancer. The good news is that these behaviors can be controlled.

As with CHD, African Americans have a higher death rate from cancer than Euro Americans (Freeman & Payne, 2000). The factors accounting for this difference, investigators believe, have more to do with the relative lack of access to quality health care and the stage at which cancer is diagnosed in African Americans than to differences in the biology of cancer (Bach et al., 2002; Meyerowitz et al., 1998).

Risk Factors for Cancer   Some risk factors, like family history and age (older people are at greater risk), are unavoidable. Others, including the factors we now review, can be controlled through lifestyle changes. If everyone practiced these cancer-preventive behaviors, hundreds of thousands of lives would be saved each year (see Table 15.5).

Smoking   You probably know that smoking causes lung cancer, the leading cancer killer of men and women. Nearly 90 percent of lung cancer deaths are directly attributable to smoking. It may surprise you to learn that lung cancer has overtaken breast cancer as the leading cause of cancer deaths among women (see Figure 15.9). Lung cancer is also the leading cancer killer among men.

Smoking is also linked to many other cancers, including colorectal (colon or rectal) cancer. Overall, cigarette smoking accounts for about one-third of all cancer deaths in the United States. Other means of using tobacco, such as pipe and cigar smoking, as well as smokeless tobacco, can also cause cancer.

Diet and Alcohol Consumption   High consumption of saturated fat, the type of fat found in meat and dairy products, is linked to two leading cancer killers: prostate cancer in men, and colorectal cancer. All told, dietary patterns may account for about 30 percent of cancer deaths. Obesity, which we know is also linked to a high-fat diet, is associated with an increased risk of some types of cancer, including colorectal cancer, endometrial cancer, and kidney cancer (Calle et al., 2003; Hellmich, 2003a, 2003b; "Obesity Hikes Risk," 2004).

Figure 15.9 Breast vs. Lung/Bronchus Cancer Deaths in Women
Cancer of the lungs and bronchial tubes has replaced breast cancer as the leading cause of cancer death among women in the United States. Here we see the rising numbers of deaths due to lung and bronchus cancer among women in the United States.

Source: National Cancer Institute, 2005.

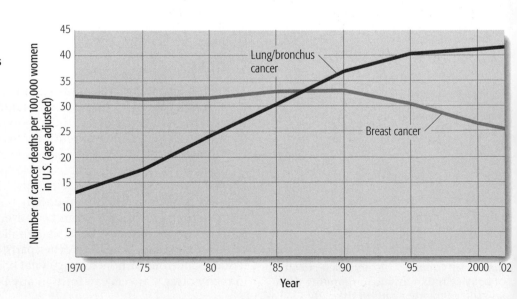

Smoking and diet are not the only forms of behavior linked to cancer risk. Heavy alcohol consumption raises the risk of several cancers, including those of the mouth, pharynx, and esophagus. Alcohol is also implicated in a wide range of other health problems, especially diseases of the liver, the organ responsible for alcohol metabolism (see Chapter 4).

Sun Exposure   Prolonged sun exposure can lead to **basal cell carcinoma**, the most common type of skin cancer but also the least dangerous. This form of cancer, which accounts for 75 percent of skin cancers, typically appears on the head, neck, and hands—areas of the body frequently exposed to the sun. It is readily curable so long as it is detected at an early stage and removed surgically. Severe sunburns early in life increase the risk of developing the least common but most deadly form of skin cancer, **melanoma**, which accounts for about 5 percent of skin cancers and claims about 8,000 lives in the United States annually (Kalb, 2001c). To protect ourselves from skin cancer, we need to limit our exposure to the sun and use a sunscreen whenever this exposure exceeds a few minutes.

Stress   The scientific verdict on the role of stress in cancer is yet to be determined (Delahanty & Baum, 2001; Dougall & Baum, 2001). It is possible that by weakening the immune system, persistent stress diminishes the body's ability to rid itself of cancerous cells. However, research evidence on the links between stressful events, such as the loss of loved ones, and the risk of cancer has yielded inconsistent results (e.g., McKenna et al., 1999). The best we can say at the present time is that connections between stress and cancer require further study.

Some psychologists counsel cancer patients and their families to help them cope with the devastating emotional effects of cancer, especially feelings of depression and hopelessness. Psychological assistance, which may include group support programs for cancer patients and their families, boosts the psychological adjustment and well-being of cancer patients (DeAngelis, 2002; Tyre, 2004). But psychological techniques have not been shown to increase the length of survival (e.g., Taylor, Lamdan, et al., 2003). Nor do we have any solid evidence that adopting particular way of coping with cancer, such as maintaining a "fighting spirit," improves the odds of survival (Bjerklie, 2005; Verghese, 2004). We have learned, however, that the ability to find a hidden benefit in something as devastating as a cancer diagnosis is associated with less depression at follow-up (Carver & Antoni, 2004).

Psychologists can help cancer patients cope with the effects of cancer treatments, such as chemotherapy. For example, health psychologists use psychological techniques such as relaxation training and hypnosis to reduce the nausea and vomiting that often accompany chemotherapy (Redd & Jacobsen, 2001).

The fact that psychological techniques may be of value to people with serious health conditions such as cancer does not mean that psychological techniques should be used in place of established methods of medical treatment for these health problems. Rather, psychological techniques should be considered adjunctive (additional) therapies. There is no persuasive evidence that psychological techniques in themselves can cure cancer or other physical diseases.

Stress and Other Physical Disorders

Stress is implicated in many physical disorders, including asthma, headaches, and possibly peptic ulcers.

Asthma   **Asthma** is a chronic lung disease in which the tubes in the lungs needed for breathing—the bronchial airways or *bronchi*—become obstructed or blocked. This blockage makes breathing difficult during acute attacks and can be life-threatening in some cases. The Centers for Disease Control (CDC) estimates that some

---

Online Study Center
Resources
Weblinks: Therapy and Cancer

basal cell carcinoma   A form of skin cancer that is easily curable if detected and removed early.

melanoma   A potentially lethal form of cancer that develops in melanin-forming cells, generally in the skin but sometimes in other parts of the body that contain these cells, such as the eye. *Melanin* is the pigment that gives color to the skin, hair, eyes, and some other body parts.

asthma   A chronic lung disease characterized by temporary obstruction of the breathing tubes, leading to attacks of wheezing and difficulty breathing.

14 million adults and 5 million children in the United States are affected by asthma (CDC, 2001). Rates of asthma are increasing and have doubled since 1980.

Asthma has many causes, including underlying allergic reactions, respiratory infections (such as bronchitis or pneumonia), exposure to environmental pollutants (such as soot and cigarette smoke), and genetic and immunological factors (Van Eerdewegh et al., 2002). Psychological factors such as stress, depression, and anxiety do not cause asthma, but they can increase susceptibility to attacks (Lehrer et al., 2002). Training asthma patients to use relaxation skills helps them improve their breathing during times of stress (Lehrer et al., 1994).

Headaches Does your head ache or throb when you are under stress? Millions of people suffer from stress-related headaches. When we are under stress, the muscles in our scalp, face, neck, and shoulders may tense up, leading to a muscle-tension headache, the most common type of headache. Muscle-tension headaches typically involve dull, steady pain experienced on both sides of the head along with feelings of pressure or tightness.

Stress plays a role in another type of headache that affects about one in ten Americans, the **migraine headache**. A migraine is a severe type of headache that can last for hours or even days and involves piercing or throbbing sensations (usually on one side of the head) that may become so intense they seem intolerable (Lipton et al., 2000). It results from changes in blood flow to the brain, which may be caused by imbalances in the neurotransmitter serotonin. Serotonin plays a role in many bodily processes, including the regulation of the size of blood vessels in the brain, which in turn affects the amount of blood flow. Differences in the amount of blood flowing to different parts of the brain may account for the throbbing, piercing sensations associated with migraine attacks.

Other factors besides stress are linked to migraines, including genetic factors (Estevez & Gardner, 2004). Migraines can be triggered by such factors as hormonal fluctuations, fatigue, use of certain drugs or chemicals, foods such as ripened cheese or chocolate, and even exposure to glaring lights or changes in barometric pressure.

Pain relievers such as aspirin and ibuprofen (including the brand-names Advil, Nuprin, and Motrin) are widely used in treating headache pain. Drugs that constrict blood vessels in the brain or that regulate serotonin levels can help relieve migraine headache pain (Lipton et al., 2000; Lohman, 2001). Psychological treatment, including stress-reduction techniques such as relaxation training and biofeedback, can also help reduce pain associated with muscle-tension and migraine headaches (Gatchel, 2001; Holroyd, 2002; Holroyd et al., 2001).

Peptic Ulcers About one in ten people in the United States suffers from **peptic ulcers**, which are sores that form on the lining of the stomach or small intestine. The great majority of cases are caused by a bacterium, *H. pylori*. The bacterium damages the protective lining of the stomach or intestines, leading to ulcers. Peptic ulcers can be cured in many cases with antibiotics that directly attack *H. pylori*. Still, it is puzzling that only about 10 to 20 percent of people who harbor *H. pylori* in their stomachs develop ulcers. This finding leads scientists to suspect that psychological factors, such as stress, and behaviors such as smoking and alcohol abuse, increase susceptibility to ulcers (Levenstein et al., 1999). In particular, stress may increase the release of stomach acid, which together with *H. pylori* may cause ulcers to form on the linings of the stomach or small intestine.

In the following module we will examine ways of handling stress so that it does not lead to distress. But first you may want to review Concept Chart 15.2, which highlights some key points about psychological risk factors in physical disorders.

💡 **CONCEPT 15.24**

Stress plays a role in many physical disorders, including asthma, headaches, and possibly peptic ulcers.

---

migraine headache An intense, prolonged headache brought on by changes in blood flow in the brain's blood vessels.

peptic ulcers Sores that form on the lining of the stomach or small intestine.

CONCEPT CHART 15.2   Psychological Risk Factors in Physical Disorders

Health Problem	Psychological or Behavioral Risk Factors	Healthier Habits
Coronary heart disease	Smoking, unhealthy diet, lack of physical activity, chronic anger or anxiety	Avoiding tobacco use, exercising regularly, controlling anger and anxiety, limiting dietary fat, reducing excess weight, practicing stress-management techniques
Cancer	Smoking, high-fat diet, heavy alcohol consumption, unsafe sun exposure, inactivity, possible role of stress	Avoiding tobacco use and excessive alcohol consumption, exercising regularly, using sunscreens, reducing excess weight, practicing stress-management techniques
Asthma	Stress can trigger asthma attacks in vulnerable individuals.	Practicing stress-management and relaxation techniques
Headaches	Stress can contribute to muscle-tension headaches and migraines.	Practicing relaxation techniques or biofeedback
Ulcers	Stress may increase susceptibility to *H. pylori* or exacerbate the condition.	Keeping stress at tolerable levels to reduce the risk of developing or aggravating peptic ulcers

MODULE 15.2 REVIEW

Psychological Factors in Physical Illness

RECITE IT

How are psychological factors linked to the health of our heart and circulatory system?

- Unhealthy behaviors such as smoking, inactivity, and adopting an unhealthy diet and persistent negative emotions, such as anger and anxiety, are associated with an increased risk of heart disease.

What roles do psychological factors play in the development of cancer?

- Unhealthy behaviors, such as smoking and consumption of a high-fat diet, are linked to an increased risk of various forms of cancer.

What roles do psychological factors play in other health conditions, such as asthma, headaches, and ulcers?

- Psychological sources of stress are implicated in many health conditions, including asthma, ulcers, and headaches.

- Stress-management techniques, such as training in muscle relaxation and biofeedback, are useful in helping people with asthma and chronic headaches cope with these conditions.

RECALL IT

1. Match the following terms with the appropriate descriptions: i. arterioscloerosis; ii. myocardial infarction (MI); iii. plaque; iv. atherosclerosis

   a. narrowing of vessels carrying blood to the heart
   b. fatty deposits on artery walls
   c. a heart attack (blood clot blocks blood flow in a coronary artery)
   d. thicker, harder, and less elastic artery walls

2. (a) List some of the major risk factors for coronary heart disease. (b) Which of these are we able to control?

3. Two modifiable forms of behavior, _____ and diet, account for two of three cancer deaths.

4. The type of headache that results from changes in blood flow to the brain is the _____ headache.

THINK ABOUT IT

- What risk factors do you have for cardiovascular disease that you can control? What steps do you need to take to control these factors?

- What steps are you taking to protect yourself from the risk of cancer? What steps are you taking to ensure early detection of cancer?

APPLICATION MODULE 15.3

Taking the Distress Out of Stress

W̱e may not be able to eliminate all stress from our lives—indeed, a certain amount of stress might be good for us. But we can learn to cope more effectively with stress so that stress doesn't lead to distress. Here let us summarize some of the basic skills needed to manage stress more effectively (adapted from Nevid, Rathus, & Rubenstein, 1998).

Maintain Stress at a Tolerable Level

CONCEPT 15.25

Though stress may be an unavoidable part of life, how we cope with stress lies within our control.

Examine your daily life. Are you constantly running from place to place just to keep up with all the demands on your time? Is it difficult to find time just to relax? Following are some suggestions for keeping stress within a manageable level:

- *Reduce daily hassles.* What can you do to reduce the stressful burdens of daily hassles? Might you rearrange your school or work schedule to avoid morning traffic jams? How about joining a car pool? You might still be stuck in traffic, but you can use that time to catch up on your reading rather than fighting traffic.

- *Know your limits.* Don't bite off more than you can chew. Avoid taking on more tasks than you can reasonably accomplish. Whenever possible, delegate responsibilities to others.

- *Follow a reasonable schedule.* Learn to schedule tasks so they don't pile up. In this way you break down stressful tasks into more manageable doses. If stressful demands become too taxing, try to extend some deadlines to give yourself added time to finish your work.

- *Take frequent breaks.* When working on an assignment, take frequent breaks to refresh your mind and body.

- *Develop more effective time-management skills.* Use a monthly calendar to organize your activities and tasks. Schedule as many of your activities as you can in advance to ensure that you have enough time to accomplish your goals. But don't overschedule yourself. Allow yourself some free, unstructured time.

- *Learn to prioritize.* Use a monthly calendar to list the tasks you must accomplish each day. Prioritize your daily goals. Assign the number 1 to tasks you must accomplish, the number 2 to those you'd like to accomplish but are less essential, and the number 3 to tasks you'd like to accomplish if time permits. Then arrange your daily schedule to progress downward in your list.

Develop Relaxation Skills

Tone down your body's response to stress by learning to relax. Some people find that listening to music helps them unwind at the end of the day. Some like to curl up with a book (not a textbook—not even this one). Others use more formal relaxation techniques, such as biofeedback training (see Chapter 3), meditation (see Chapters 3 and 4), and deep breathing exercises. To practice deep breathing, breathe only through your nose. Take about the same amount of time breathing in as breathing out, and pace yourself by silently repeating a resonant-sounding word like *relax* on each outbreath. Elongating the *x*-sound can help you lengthen each breath to ensure that you breathe deeply and evenly. Many colleges offer seminars or workshops in stress-management techniques where students can learn to develop relaxation skills. Why not check them out?

Online Study Center
Improve Your Grade
Tutorials: Living Well Is the Best Revenge

Take Care of Your Body

Prepare your body to cope more effectively with stress by getting enough sleep, following a nutritionally balanced diet, exercising regularly, obtaining regular medical check-ups, and avoiding harmful substances such as drugs. Evidence indicates that regular exercise increases resilience to stress, reduces risks of heart disease, and lessens the emotional consequences of stress, such as anxiety (Gaulin & McBurney, 2001; Salmon, 2001; Tanasescu et al., 2002).

Gather Information

People facing a serious illness may cope more effectively if they obtain information about their underlying condition rather than keeping themselves in the dark. Whether you are facing an illness or the stress of adjusting to life in a new town or city, gather the information you need to adjust more effectively.

Expand Your Social Network

Social support helps people cope better during times of stress. You can expand your social network by forming relationships with others through participation in clubs and organizations sponsored at your college. The office of student life or counseling services at your college should be able to advise you about the availability of these resources.

Prevent Burnout

Set reasonable goals and limits for yourself. Establish personal goals that are attainable, and don't push yourself beyond your limits. Learn to say "no" when people make excessive demands on you. Start delegating responsibilities, and learn to cut back on low-priority tasks when commitments begin piling up.

Replace Stress-Inducing Thoughts with Stress-Busting Thoughts

What you say to yourself under your breath about stressful events can influence your adjustment to them. Do you react to disappointing events by blowing them out of proportion—treating them as utter disasters rather than as mere setbacks? Do you see events only in all-or-nothing, black-and-white terms—as either total

The Basics Simple steps, such as eating healthful foods, exercising moderately, and getting enough sleep, go a long way toward combating stress.

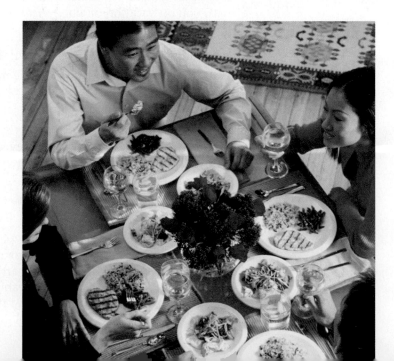

successes or total failures? Do you place unrealistic expectations on yourself and then hold yourself accountable for failing to measure up? If you have thought patterns like these, you may benefit from replacing them with rational alternatives. Examples include: "This is a problem, not a catastrophe. I am a good problem-solver. I can find a solution to this problem."

We are better able to withstand stressful demands when we believe we are capable of handling them. If your self-confidence has been shaky, try to boost it by setting achievable goals for yourself and taking steps to accomplish them. Remind yourself to respond to disappointments as opportunities to learn from your mistakes, not as signs of inevitable failure.

Don't Keep Upsetting Feelings Bottled Up

Keeping disturbing thoughts and feelings under wraps may place stressful demands on your autonomic nervous system, which in turn may weaken your immune system and make you more vulnerable to physical illness. Expressing your feelings about stressful or traumatic events may have positive effects on your emotional and physical health. In particular, consider writing down your feelings in a journal or sharing them with a trusted person or a helping professional.

Control Type A Behavior

People with the Type A behavior pattern place additional stressful demands on themselves by attempting to accomplish as much as possible in as little time as possible. Though it may not be feasible (or even desirable) to turn "hares" into "tortoises," researchers find that people can learn to modify their Type A behavior, such as by reducing their sense of time urgency (Friedman & Ulmer, 1984). Here are some behavioral changes that may prove helpful, even to people who are not bona fide Type As:

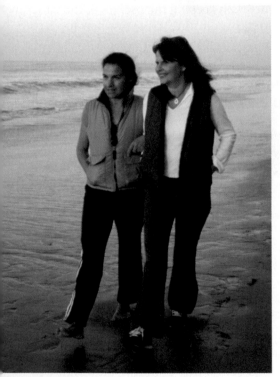

Reducing Type A Behavior   What can you do to reduce Type A behavior?

- *Take things slower.* Slow down your walking pace. Enjoy looking at your surroundings rather than rushing past them. Bear in mind that posted speed limits are the maximum speeds you are permitted to drive, not the minimum.

- *Read books for enjoyment.* Spend time reading enjoyable books—perhaps that latest techno-thriller or romance novel, but not one designed to help you climb the corporate ladder.

- *Leave your computer at home.* Don't bring a laptop or other work-related gadgets with you on vacation or when visiting friends.

- *Avoid rushing through your meals.* Don't wolf down your food. Take time to talk to your family members or dining companions.

- *Engage in enjoyable activities.* Go to the movies, visit art galleries and museums, or attend the theater or concerts. Give yourself a break from the stressful demands of daily life.

- *Develop relaxing interests.* Daily stress is more manageable when you make it a practice to engage in some pleasant events every day. Choose activities you truly enjoy, not simply those that are preferred by others. Take up a hobby or pursue an interest that can help you unwind.

- *Set realistic daily goals.* Don't overschedule your activities or impose unrealistic demands on yourself. Lighten up.

Hostility, a component of the Type A behavior profile, is associated with quickness to anger. Suggestions for controlling anger are discussed in Chapter 8.

In sum, stress is an inescapable part of life. But handling stress more effectively can help you keep it at a manageable level and tone down your body's alarm reaction. Stress may be a fact of life, but it is a fact you can learn to live with.

TYING IT TOGETHER

Health psychology is the study of interrelationships between psychology and physical health. Stress is a psychological factor that investigators link to a wide range of physical and mental health problems (Module 15.1). But stress is not the only psychosocial variable linked to physical health problems; connections have also been found between unhealthy behaviors or lifestyles (e.g., smoking, high-fat diets, excessive sun exposure, and lack of physical activity) and risks of serious, chronic diseases such as heart disease and cancer (Module 15.2). By learning stress-management skills, we can learn to keep stress at a manageable level and take the distress out of stress (Module 15.3).

Thinking Critically About Psychology

Based on your reading of this chapter, do the following exercise. Then, to evaluate your progress in developing critical thinking skills, compare your answers to the sample answers found in Appendix A.

Every now and then we hear claims touting some miracle drug, vitamin, hormone, or alternative therapy that promises to enhance health and vitality, cure or prevent disease, or even reverse the effects of aging. Some of these claims are outright hoaxes. Others take promising scientific leads and exaggerate or distort the evidence. Still others tout psychological therapies as cures for medical conditions on the basis of unsupported testimonials. Although the federal watchdog agency, the Food and Drug Administration (FDA), regulates health claims for drugs and medications, many of the substances found in your health-food store or neighborhood supermarket purporting to have disease-preventive or antiaging effects are classified as foods and are not regulated as drugs. It's basically a case of "buyer beware."

Critical thinkers do not take health claims at face value. They recognize that alternative therapies and health care products may not work as promised and could even be harmful. Another concern is that people advocating particular therapies may have a vested interest in getting consumers to try their services or use their products, and may play fast and loose with the truth. Use your critical thinking skills to read between the lines in evaluating health claims.

What do you think these claims for products found in your neighborhood health store actually mean?

- **Designed to enhance vitality and well-being.**
- **Promotes muscle growth.**
- **Recommended by leading physicians.**
- **Backed by advanced research.**
- **Supercharge your metabolism!**

Key Terms

health psychology (p. 582)
stress (p. 582)
distress (p. 582)
stressors (p. 583)
hassles (p. 583)
chronic stress (p. 583)
frustration (p. 584)
conflict (p. 586)
posttraumatic stress disorder (PTSD) (p. 587)
Type A behavior pattern (TABP) (p. 589)
acculturative stress (p. 591)
general adaptation syndrome (GAS) (p. 592)
alarm reaction (p. 593)

fight-or-flight response (p. 593)
resistance stage (p. 594)
exhaustion stage (p. 594)
corticotrophin-releasing hormone (CRH) (p. 595)
adrenocorticotrophic hormone (ACTH) (p. 595)
adrenal glands (p. 595)
adrenal cortex (p. 595)
corticosteroids (p. 595)
adrenal medulla (p. 595)
immune system (p. 595)
lymphocytes (p. 595)
antigens (p. 595)
antibodies (p. 595)

vaccination (p. 596)
psychological hardiness (p. 599)
burnout (p. 599)
arteries (p. 602)
coronary heart disease (CHD) (p. 602)
atherosclerosis (p. 602)
plaque (p. 602)
arteriosclerosis (p. 602)
heart attack (p. 603)
malignant tumors (p. 605)
basal cell carcinoma (p. 607)
melanoma (p. 607)
asthma (p. 607)
migraine headache (p. 608)
peptic ulcers (p. 608)

ANSWERS TO RECALL IT QUESTIONS

Module 15.1: 1. (a) pressures or demands placed upon an organism to adjust or adapt to its environment, (b) when stress reaches a level that taxes our ability to cope effectively; 2. i. b, ii. c, iii. a, iv. d; 3. self-efficacy; 4. alarm; 5. burnout.

Module 15.2: 1. i. d, ii. c, iii. b, iv. a; 2. (a) age, gender, heredity, lack of physical activity, smoking, obesity, high cholesterol, diabetes, high blood pressure, (b) all but the first three can potentially be controlled; 3. smoking; 4. migraine.

Social Psychology

Astranger faints on a crowded street as you pass by. Several people gather about the fallen person. Do you offer assistance or continue on your way?

You participate in a psychology experiment in which you and other members of a group are asked to determine which of two lines is longer. One person after another chooses the line that looks shorter to you. Now comes your turn. Do you go along with the crowd or stand your ground and select the line you think is longer?

A man and a woman are standing on a street corner speaking privately in Italian. The man hands the woman an envelope, which she puts in her handbag. What do you make of this interaction? Do you suppose it was a lover's note that was passed between them? Or do you think it was an exchange related to Mafia business?

You volunteer for a psychology experiment on the effects of electric shock on learning. You are instructed to administer to another participant what you are told are painful shocks each time the other person gives a wrong answer. At first you refuse. But the experimenter insists you continue and tells you the shocks will cause no serious harm to the other participant. You would still refuse such an unreasonable demand, wouldn't you?

These questions fall within the domain of *social psychology,* the branch of psychology that deals with how our thoughts, feelings, and behaviors are influenced by our social interactions with others and the culture in which we live. In this chapter we explore how we perceive others in our social environment, how we relate to them, and how we are influenced by them. We consider what social psychologists have learned about these social processes, beginning with how we perceive others and how our perceptions of others influence our behavior. ■

DID YOU KNOW THAT . . .

■ Revealing too much about yourself when first meeting someone can convey a negative impression? (p. 616)

■ Japanese people are more likely than Americans to attribute their successes to luck or fate than to themselves? (p. 619)

■ People are more likely to marry others whose first or last names resemble their own? (p. 625)

■ Waitresses who write helpful messages on the backs of customer's checks tend to get larger tips? (pp. 627–628)

■ At least thirty-eight people in a quiet urban neighborhood heard the screams of a woman who was viciously attacked by a knife-wielding assailant but did nothing? (pp. 628)

■ The origins of prejudice may be traced back to ancestral times? (p. 632)

■ Most people who participated in a famous psychology experiment administered what they believed to be painful and dangerous electric shocks to other participants simply because they were told to so by an experimenter? (pp. 644–646)

MODULE 16.1
Perceiving Others

- What is social perception?
- What are the major influences on first impressions, and why do first impressions often become lasting impressions?
- What role do cognitive biases play in the judgments we make about the causes of behavior?
- What are attitudes, and how are they acquired?
- How are attitudes related to behavior, and how do they change in response to persuasive appeals?

In Chapter 3 we explored the ways in which we perceive the physical world of objects and shapes. As we turn to the study of **social psychology**, we focus on the ways in which we perceive the social world, composed of the people whom we see and with whom we interact in our daily lives. **Social perception** is the process by which we come to form an understanding of our social environment based on observations of others, personal experiences, and information we receive. In this section we examine three major aspects of social perception: forming impressions of others, making sense of the causes of our own and other people's behaviors, and developing attitudes that incline us to respond to people, issues, and objects in positive or negative ways.

Impression Formation: Why First Impressions Count So Much

Impression formation is the process by which we form an opinion or impression of another person. We tend to form first impressions quickly. First impressions count so much because they tend to be long-lasting and difficult to change; they also affect how we relate to people who are the objects of these impressions. Suppose you meet a number of people at a party or social gathering. Within the first few minutes of talking to them—perhaps even the first few seconds—you begin forming impressions that will be hard to change. Even before you begin talking to someone, you have already started to size up their surface characteristics, such as how they look and how they dress. Let us examine some of the factors that influence impression formation, including personal disclosure, social schemas, stereotyping, and self-fulfilling prophecies.

Personal Disclosure: Going Beyond Name, Rank, and Serial Number We generally form more favorable impressions of people who are willing to disclose personal information about themselves. But revealing too much too soon can lead to a negative impression. People who disclose too much about themselves in the first stages of a social relationship tend to be perceived as less secure, less mature, and more poorly adjusted than those who are more restrained regarding what they say about themselves. Cultural differences also come into play in determining how much disclosure is deemed acceptable. People in East Asian societies, such as China and Japan, tend to disclose less about themselves than do people in Western cultures (Nevid & Sta. Maria, 1999).

Impressions as Social Schemas: Why Early Impressions Are Hard to Budge
An impression is a type of **social schema**, a mental image or representation we use to understand our social environment. We filter information about others through these schemas. One reason that first impressions tend to be long-lasting is that we

CONCEPT 16.1
We begin sizing people up on the basis of surface characteristics, such as their manner of dress even before we meet them.

CONCEPT 16.2
The amount of personal information we disclose affects the impressions that other people form of us.

social psychology The subfield in psychology that deals with how our thoughts, feelings, and behaviors are influenced by our social interactions with others.

social perception The processes by which we form impressions, make judgments, and develop attitudes about the people and events that constitute our social world.

impression formation The process of developing an opinion or impression of another person.

social schema A mental image or representation that we use to understand our social environment.

CONCEPT 16.3
Because we filter new information through existing social schemas, first impressions can become lasting impressions.

filter new information about people through the earlier impressions or social schemas we formed about them (Hamilton & Sherman, 1994). So if someone about whom we hold a favorable impression (schema) does something to upset us, we're more likely to look for extenuating factors that explain the person's behavior ("He must be having a bad day") than to alter our existing impression. Likewise, when we hold a negative impression of someone, we're more likely to ignore or explain away any positive information we receive about that person.

Stereotyping: Judging Groups, Not Individuals   We all have preconceived ideas about groups of people, called **stereotypes**, that influence our first impressions (Aronson et al., 2004). Stereotypes are sets of beliefs about the characteristics, attributes, and behaviors of members of a particular group or category. For example, we might hold a stereotype that fraternity members are big drinkers or that people who wear glasses are intelligent.

Stereotypes influence first impressions. Recall the couple speaking in Italian on the street corner. Did you think they were engaged in a romantic exchange or in illegal, Mafia-related activities? Both interpretations are based on stereotypes of Italians as romantic people or crooks (Lepore & Brown, 1997). As the example suggests, stereotypes may include positive attributes (romantic in this case) or negative attributes (criminal). However, stereotypes about members of other social or ethnic groups are usually more negative than those about members of one's own group.

Stereotyping is not limited to race or gender. A recent study showed that people stereotyped fans of rap music as dangerous to others, whereas they stereotyped heavy metal fans as dangerous to themselves (Fried, 2003). People tend to stereotype obese people in negative ways—as lazy, unproductive, and unattractive (Polinko & Popovich, 2001). These negative attitudes can translate into overt discrimination in cases where obese persons are rejected for jobs, especially more active jobs (Popovich et al., 1997). Social psychologists believe that stereotyping is a normal cognitive tendency, a kind of cognitive shorthand that simplifies the process of making social judgments (Nelson, 2002). Upon meeting someone for the first time, we automatically classify the person as belonging to particular groups on the basis of general categories such as race, gender, and age (Blair, Judd, & Fallman, 2004). Stereotypes allow us to more efficiently use stored information about other groups instead of expending cognitive resources to evaluate each individual member of the groups we encounter (Hilton & von Hippel, 1996). Efficient, perhaps—but not necessarily accurate.

Stereotyping on the basis of race, ethnicity, gender, age, disability, body weight, or sexual orientation leads us to make inferences about people that may prove to be unfounded as we get to know them as individuals. Yet there may be a "kernel of truth" in some commonly held stereotypes (e.g., that Mexicans enjoy spicy food) (Gordon, 2000; Judd & Park, 1993). Still, stereotypes are exaggerated and overgeneralized concepts that fail to take individual differences into account. Moreover, once stereotypes are formed, they are resistant to change in the face of new information.

Stereotyping can damage group relations and be used to justify social inequities. For example, beliefs that Blacks lack the ability to govern themselves were long used as a justification for colonial rule in Africa by European powers. And stereotypes of obese people as lazy and undisciplined may lead employers to pass over them for jobs or promotions.

Cultural Differences in Self-Disclosure
People from East Asian cultures are typically more reserved about disclosing personal information when meeting new people.

stereotypes   Oversimplified generalizations about the characteristics, attributes, and behaviors of members of a particular group or category.

self-fulfilling prophecy   An expectation that helps bring about the outcome that is expected.

Self-Fulfilling Prophecies: What Goes Around Comes Around   When you form an initial impression of someone, you may act toward the person in a way that mirrors your impression. Let's say you form an impression of someone as unfriendly. This belief can become a type of **self-fulfilling prophecy** if it leads you to be somewhat standoffish when interacting with the person and he or she responds in kind. Self-fulfilling prophecies may also lead to underperformance in school. Teachers who expect students to do poorly may convey their lower expectations to their students. Expecting less of themselves, the students may apply less than their best efforts, leading them to underperform.

Attributions: Forming Personal Explanations of Events

The pizza guy delivers your pizza thirty minutes late. Do you believe the guy was loafing on the job or that some external influence (traffic, orders backing up) caused the delay? What about the times *you* arrive late? Are you likely to reach the same judgments about your own behavior as you do when explaining the behavior of others?

An **attribution** is a personal explanation that we form about the causes of behavior or events. When interpreting our social world, we act like personal scientists who seek to understand the underlying causes of the events we observe. We tend to explain these events by attributing them to either dispositional causes or situational causes. **Dispositional causes** are internal factors, such as internal traits, needs, or personal choices of the person ("actor"). **Situational causes** are external or environmental factors, such as pressures or demands imposed upon the actor. Saying that the pizza guy is late because he is a loafer invokes a dispositional cause. Saying he is late because several other pies were in the oven at the time invokes a situational cause. Social psychologists have found that attributions can be affected by certain cognitive biases, such as the *fundamental attribution error,* the *actor-observer effect,* and the *self-serving bias.*

Fundamental Attribution Error Social psychologist Fritz Heider (1958) proposed that people tend to focus more on the behavior of others than on the circumstances in which the behavior occurs. Consequently, they tend to overlook situational influences when explaining other people's behavior. The **fundamental attribution error** is a term that social psychologists use to describe our tendency to attribute behavior to internal traits or causes, without regard to situational influences that come to bear on people. The waiter is slow to bring our food and we conclude that he is lazy or incompetent (Riggs & Gumbrecht, 2004). We tend to overlook situational factors that might explain his behavior, such as being overburdened by having too many tables to handle.

The fundamental attribution error does not apply to all attributions of observed behavior. When judging the causes of emotional displays, people tend to assume they are evoked by situational forces rather than internal dispositions (Krull, Segere, & Silvera, 2001). For example, if you see Monica pacing and nervously wringing her hands, you will likely assume that she is responding to situational influences (such as an impending final exam), even if the situation is not obvious at the time.

Let us also note a cross-cultural difference. Recent evidence indicates that people in collectivist cultures such as China and Japan are less likely to commit fundamental attribution errors than are people in individualistic cultures in the West (Kitayama et al., 2003). Collectivist cultures tend to emphasize external causes of behavior that stem from the social environment, such as the obligations imposed on people (Choi et al., 2003). Individualistic cultures, by contrast, emphasize individuality and autonomy of the self. People from these cultures are quicker to assume that behavior results from something inside us—our individual personalities, attitudes, or motives.

The Actor-Observer Effect When people commit the fundamental attribution error, they ignore the external circumstances that influence the behavior of others. But apparently we do not commit the same error when explaining our own behavior. In these situations, social psychologists have identified another type

---

CONCEPT 16.4
We tend to explain events by attributing them to either dispositional or situational causes; that is, to factors either within the individual or within the environment.

CONCEPT 16.5
People tend to overemphasize internal causes and to overlook situational influences when explaining other people's behavior.

CONCEPT 16.6
The actor-observer effect leads us to attribute the behavior of others to dispositional internal causes but to explain our own behavior in terms of the situational demands we face in the environment.

attribution An assumption about the causes of behavior or events.
dispositional causes Causes relating to the internal characteristics or traits of individuals.
situational causes Causes relating to external or environmental events.

CONCEPT 16.7
Another type of cognitive bias, the self-serving bias, comes into play in accounting for the tendency of people to take credit for their successes but to explain away their failures.

CONCEPT 16.8
The self-serving bias is widespread in Western cultures but virtually absent in some Eastern cultures.

fundamental attribution error   The tendency to attribute behavior to internal causes without regard to situational influences.

actor-observer effect   The tendency to attribute the causes of one's own behavior to situational factors while attributing the causes of other people's behavior to internal factors or dispositions.

self-serving bias   The tendency to take credit for our accomplishments and to explain away our failures or disappointments.

attitude   A positive or negative evaluation of persons, objects, or issues.

of cognitive bias that comes into play, the **actor-observer effect**. The actor-observer effect is the tendency to attribute the causes of one's own behavior to external factors, such as situational demands, while attributing other people's behavior to internal causes or dispositions (Jones & Nisbett, 1971; Pronin, Gilovich, & Ross, 2004). If you do poorly on an exam, you're likely to attribute your poor performance to external causes—the exam wasn't fair, you didn't have time to study, the material you studied wasn't on the exam, and so on. But when someone else does poorly, you're more likely to think the person lacked the ability to do well or was too lazy to study.

Heider (1958) attributed the actor-observer effect to differences in perspective. As an actor, you look outward to the environment, so the situation engulfs your view. But your perspective as an observer is engulfed by your view of the actor within the situation.

The actor-observer effect does not occur under all conditions (Robins, Spranca, & Mendelsohn, 1996). It can be eliminated or even reversed by changes in the relevant factors, as when possible causal factors in the situation are made more prominent. The effect also appears to be strongest when people are merely observing other people's behavior. When they interact with them, they come to better appreciate the situational factors that influence their behavior.

Self-Serving Bias   A specific type of attributional bias occurring in performance situations is the **self-serving bias**—the tendency to attribute our personal successes to internal or dispositional causes and personal failures to external or situational causes (Mezulis et al., 2004). In other words, people tend to take credit for their successes but to disclaim responsibility for their failures. If you achieve a good grade on an exam, you are likely to attribute it to your ability or talent (an internal attribution). Yet you are likely to attribute a poor grade to an external cause beyond your control, such as too little time to study or unfair questions on the exam. Self-serving biases buttress our self-esteem (Kitayama et al., 1997).

The self-serving bias is stronger in Western cultures, such as the United States and Canada, than it is in East Asian cultures, such as Japan, China, and Taiwan (DeAngelis, 2003a; Mezulis et al., 2004). Unlike Americans, the Japanese tend to attribute their successes to luck and their failures to lack of ability or talent. The self-serving bias may be embedded within a cultural ethic in the United States and other individualistic Western cultures that value the protection of self-esteem (Chang & Asakawa, 2003). The opposite tendency (valuing self-criticism and humility) is found more often in collectivist cultures, such as China or Japan (Oyserman, Coon, & Kemmelmeier, 2002). In these cultures, people are more attuned to their responsibilities to the group than to themselves or to their need to enhance their own self-esteem. Blaming oneself for personal failure affirms one's responsibility to the social group and the need to work harder to improve one's performance in the future (Nisbett, 2003).

Self-enhancement exists in collectivistic cultures, but it tends to be organized around fulfillment of group obligations rather than individual achievement, such as being a good son or good daughter, a good worker, and the like (Sedikides, Gaertner, & Toguchi, 2003). People in individualistic Western cultures value individual accomplishment and expect to be credited for their personal successes. In other words, self-enhancement may be a universal human attribute, but the form that it takes depends on the values the individual deems important.

Attitudes: How Do You Feel About . . . ?

What are your attitudes toward gun control laws, sport utility vehicles (SUVs), and vegetarian diets? An **attitude** is an evaluation or judgment of either liking or disliking a person, object, or social issue (Olson & Maio, 2003). Social psychologists conceptualize attitudes as consisting of three components: (1) *cognitions* (sets of

Figure 16.1 Attitudes
The attitudes we hold consist of cognitive, emotional, and behavioral components.

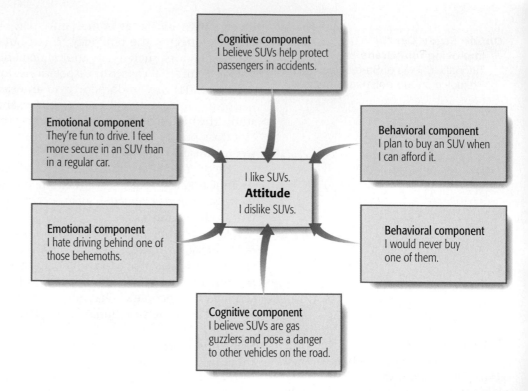

Cognitive component
I believe SUVs help protect passengers in accidents.

Emotional component
They're fun to drive. I feel more secure in an SUV than in a regular car.

Behavioral component
I plan to buy an SUV when I can afford it.

I like SUVs.
Attitude
I dislike SUVs.

Emotional component
I hate driving behind one of those behemoths.

Behavioral component
I would never buy one of them.

Cognitive component
I believe SUVs are gas guzzlers and pose a danger to other vehicles on the road.

CONCEPT 16.9
To social psychologists, attitudes are judgments of liking or disliking that can be conceptualized in terms of three components: cognitions, emotions, and behaviors.

CONCEPT 16.10
Our social environments shape the attitudes we develop, but research points to possible genetic influences as well.

CONCEPT 16.11
Though attitudes predispose us to act in certain ways, they are not very strong predictors of behavior.

beliefs), (2) *emotions* (feelings of liking or disliking), and (3) *behaviors* (inclinations to act positively or negatively) (Crites, Fabrigar, & Petty, 1994). For example, you may hold favorable or unfavorable views about SUVs, feel positively or negatively toward them, and be either inclined or disinclined to purchase one if you were shopping for a vehicle (see Figure 16.1).

The importance we ascribe to attitudes is a function of their personal relevance. Our attitudes toward sport utility vehicles (love them, hate them) will be more important to us if we happen to be considering buying one. Yet it's also true that the more often we express a particular attitude, the more important it is likely to become to us (Roese & Olson, 1994).

Sources of Attitudes   Our attitudes are acquired from many sources in our social environment—our parents, teachers, peers, personal experiences, and media sources such as newspapers, television, and movies. Not surprisingly, people from similar backgrounds tend to hold similar attitudes. Yet evidence also points to a role for genetic factors in shaping attitudes (Abrahamson, Baker, & Caspi, 2002; Olson & Maio, 2003). Studies of twins reared apart show a surprising degree of shared attitudes on a range of issues that cannot be explained by shared environmental influences. People do not inherit a gene or genes for a particular attitude, such as liking or disliking SUVs. Rather, heredity may indirectly come to influence attitudes by affecting intelligence and personality traits that make people more or less likely to develop certain attitudes (Petty, Wegener, & Fabrigar, 1997). Yet evidence suggests that genetic factors are less important determinants of attitudes than environmental influences (DeAngelis, 2004a).

Attitudes and Behavior: Not as Strong a Link as You Might Expect   Attitudes are not as closely linked to behavior as you might think. You may hold favorable attitudes toward environmental issues but still purchase a high-performance car that guzzles gas. You may dislike someone but smile and say hello to the person because of social norms of politeness that influence your behavior (Olson & Maio, 2003). Or you may hold a positive attitude toward a specific charity but be unable to make a contribution to the latest fund drive because you are short of cash or need the money for another important purpose. Attitudes, overall, are only modestly related to behavior (Eagly & Chaiken, 1998). Under some conditions, attitudes are more strongly linked to behavior—such as when the attitudes are more stable and held with a greater degree of confidence or certainty, when they relate specifically to the behavior at hand, when the person is free to perform or not perform the behavior, and when the attitude can be more readily recalled from memory (e.g., Kraus, 1995; Olson & Maio, 2003; Petty & Wegener, 1998).

Persuasion: The Fine Art of Changing People's Minds

We are constantly bombarded with messages attempting to persuade us to change our attitudes. Commercials on radio and TV, and advertisements in newspapers and magazines, attempt to persuade us to adopt more favorable attitudes toward advertised products and to purchase them. Political candidates and political action groups seek to sway us to support their candidacies and causes. Doctors, religious leaders, teachers, friends, and family members regularly urge us to change our behaviors, beliefs, and attitudes in ways they believe would be beneficial to us.

Short of secluding ourselves in an isolated cabin in the woods, we can hardly avoid persuasive appeals. But how do such appeals lead to attitude change? And what factors are likely to increase their effectiveness?

A leading model of attitude change is the **elaboration likelihood model (ELM)** (Petty & Wegener, 1998; Petty, Wheeler, & Tormala, 2003). According to this model, people are more likely to carefully evaluate ("elaborate") a persuasive message when their motivational state is high (i.e., when the message is personally meaningful or important to them) and when they possess the skills or knowledge needed to evaluate the information (see Figure 16.2).

When evaluation likelihood is high, attitude change occurs via a *central route* of processing information, whereby people carefully evaluate the content of the message. When elaboration likelihood is low, attitude change occurs through a *peripheral route* of cognitive processing, whereby people focus on cues not centrally related to the content of the message. Consider a televised political debate. Assume that viewers are alert, well informed about the issues, and interested in the views held by the candidates. Under these conditions, elaboration likelihood is high and attitude change is likely to occur through a central processing route by which the viewers carefully evaluate the arguments made by the respective candidates. Conversely, if the viewers are distracted, fatigued, or uninterested in the issues, they are not likely to carefully evaluate each candidate's message. Attitude

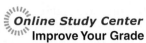

Online Study Center
Improve Your Grade
Tutorials: Elaboration Likelihood Model
of Attitude Change

CONCEPT 16.12
According to the elaboration likelihood model, attitude change occurs through either a central processing route or a peripheral processing route.

Figure 16.2   Elaboration Likelihood Model
According to the elaboration likelihood model, attitude change occurs through one of two routes of cognitive processing—a central route or a peripheral route. When elaboration likelihood is high, we attend more carefully to the content of the message itself. When it is low, as when we are distracted or disinterested, we attend to peripheral cues unrelated to the content of the message.

elaboration likelihood model (ELM)
A theoretical model that posits two channels by which persuasive appeals lead to attitude change: a central route and a peripheral route.

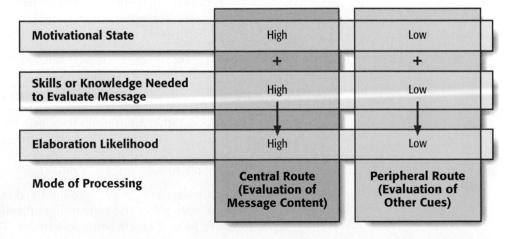

Motivational State	High	Low
	+	+
Skills or Knowledge Needed to Evaluate Message	High	Low
Elaboration Likelihood	High	Low
Mode of Processing	Central Route (Evaluation of Message Content)	Peripheral Route (Evaluation of Other Cues)

Figure 16.3   Getting Your Message Across: Factors in Persuasive Appeals
The effectiveness of persuasive appeals depends upon characteristics of the source of the message, the message itself, and the recipient of the message.

change occurring under these conditions is likely to be based on peripheral cues that are not directly related to the content of the candidate's message, such as the physical attractiveness of the candidate. In other words, the viewers may be persuaded to endorse candidates on the basis of how they look in the debate rather than how they stand on the issues.

Advertisers often take advantage of the peripheral route of attitude change by using leading sports stars as commercial spokespersons. Celebrity endorsers needn't even mention the distinctive qualities of the product. Just using the product or wearing it may be sufficient to convey the message that the advertiser wants to get across.

CONCEPT 16.13
The effectiveness of persuasive appeals is influenced by variables relating to the source, the message itself, and the recipient.

Variables Influencing Persuasion   Some persuasive appeals are more effective than others. Persuasion is influenced by many variables, including those relating to the source, the message, and the recipient (see Figure 16.3) (Petty & Wegener, 1998):

- *Source variables*. Source variables are features of the communicator who presents the message. Communicators are generally more persuasive when they are perceived as *credible* (knowledgeable and trustworthy), *likable* (attractive and personable), and *similar* to the receiver in key respects (e.g., a former substance abuser may be more successful in persuading current substance abusers to accept treatment than a person who has never abused drugs).

- *Message variables*. First, presenting both sides of an argument is generally more effective than presenting only one side, so long as the communicator refutes the other side. Second, messages that run counter to the perceived interests of the communicator tend to be perceived as more credible. Not surprisingly, people paid great attention a few years ago when a member of the R. J. Reynolds family of tobacco growers spoke out on the dangers of smoking. Third, the more often we are exposed to a message, the more favorably we are likely to evaluate it, but only up to a point (Petty, Wheeler, & Tormala, 2003). When the message is repeated often enough, people may come to believe it, whether or not it is true. But with further repetition, irritation and tedium begin to set in and acceptance of the message begins to decline.

- *Recipient variables*. Though nobody is immune to persuasive appeals, some people are easier to persuade than others. Those of low intelligence or low self-confidence are generally more susceptible to persuasive appeals. People also tend to be more receptive to persuasive messages when they are in a positive mood rather than a negative one (Park & Banaji, 2000). Evidence shows that putting people in a good mood increases the likelihood that they will help worthy causes (Batson, Daniel, & Powell, 2003). A good mood may also motivate people to see things in a more positive light.

People also tend to be less convinced by a persuasive appeal when they receive a prior warning of the impending appeal (Wood & Quinn, 2003). In other words, being forewarned is being forearmed. The major influences on social perception are summarized in Concept Chart 16.1.

💡 **CONCEPT CHART 16.1   Perceiving Others**

Topic	What It Is	Influences on Social Perception
Initial impressions	Initial evaluation (liking or disliking) of others	Initial impressions are influenced by physical appearance, attire, preexisting stereotypes, and degree of personal disclosure. They are difficult to dislodge because we tend to filter new information through them and because they may become self-fulfilling prophecies.
Attributions	Personal explanations of the causes of behavior	Attributional biases that affect social perception include the fundamental attribution error (the tendency to overemphasize internal or dispositional causes and to overlook external causes), the actor-observer effect (the tendency to explain other people's behavior in terms of their underlying personalities while explaining our own behavior in terms of situational demands), and the self-serving bias (the tendency to explain away our failures but take credit for our accomplishments).
Attitudes	Judgments of liking or disliking persons, objects, and issues	Attitudes are influenced by our social environment and possibly by genetic factors. They do not necessarily predict behavior. According to the elaboration likelihood model, attitude change occurs through either a central or peripheral route of processing, depending on the degree to which the message is elaborated. The effectiveness of persuasive appeals depends on source variables, recipient variables, and message variables.

MODULE 16.1 REVIEW

Perceiving Others

RECITE IT

What is social perception?

- Social perception is the process of forming impressions of others and attitudes about people, objects, and issues in our social environment.

What are the major influences on first impressions, and why do first impressions often become lasting impressions?

- First impressions are influenced by surface characteristics, such as physical appearance and attire, and by stereotypes and personal disclosures.

- A modest amount of self-disclosure is associated with a more favorable impression. However, self-disclosure is generally looked upon more favorably in Western cultures than in Eastern cultures.

- First impressions may become lasting impressions when people reconcile discrepant information with their existing impressions, or social schemas. Impressions may also become self-fulfilling prophecies.

What role do cognitive biases play in the judgments we make about the causes of behavior?

- The fundamental attribution error is an overemphasis on internal or dispositional causes of behavior to the exclusion of situational factors.

- The actor-observer effect is the tendency to explain our own behavior in terms of the demands of the situation while explaining the behavior of others in terms of internal or dispositional causes.

- The self-serving bias bolsters self-esteem in that it involves attributing personal success to one's talents or abilities while explaining personal failure in terms of external causes.

What are attitudes, and how are they acquired?

- Attitudes are evaluations or judgments of liking or disliking people, objects, or issues. Psychologists conceptualize attitudes as having three components: cognitions, emotions, and behaviors.

- The social environment, which encompasses our relationships and experiences with others as well as our exposure to mass media, is the learning ground for the acquisition of attitudes. Genetic factors may also play a role.

How are attitudes related to behavior, and how do they change in response to persuasive appeals?

- Attitudes are related to behavior only modestly at best. Our behavior is influenced by many factors, not just our attitudes.

- According to the elaboration likelihood model, attitudes may be altered by persuasive messages that are processed through either a central route (careful evaluation of the content of the message) or a peripheral route (focusing on cues that are peripheral to the content of the message).

RECALL IT

1. Which of the following statements about first impressions is *incorrect?*
   a. First impressions are generally replaced by later in-depth, more accurate judgments.
   b. Preconceived ideas or stereotypes influence how we perceive others.
   c. Culture has an important bearing on how much information people disclose about themselves to others.
   d. Our behavior may elicit expected behaviors in others.

2. Social perception is also influenced by the types of _____ we make about the causes of other people's behavior and our own.

3. When we interpret a behavior or event, we usually see it as due to either _____ or _____ causes.

4. The fundamental attribution error refers to
   a. underestimation of the influence of internal factors.
   b. underestimation of the influence of external factors.
   c. the tendency to attribute personal failure to external factors.
   d. the tendency to misinterpret the motives of others.

5. Match the following terms with the appropriate descriptions: i. peripheral processing route; ii. source variable(s); iii. message variable(s); iv. recipient variable(s)
   a. the tendency of repetition to lead to more favorable evaluations
   b. when people are not likely to carefully evaluate message contents
   c. the relationship between low self-confidence and greater susceptibility to persuasion
   d. credibility, similarity, and likability

THINK ABOUT IT

- Why do first impressions tend to become lasting impressions?
- How do you account for findings that the self-serving bias is stronger in Western cultures than Eastern cultures?

- Do you have a tendency to take credit for your successes and explain away your failures? How might the self-serving bias prevent you from learning from your mistakes and taking appropriate steps to prevent them in the future?

MODULE 16.2
Relating to Others

- **What are the major determinants of attraction?**
- **What factors are linked to helping behavior?**
- **What is prejudice, and how does it develop?**
- **What can be done to reduce prejudice?**
- **What factors contribute to human aggression?**

Social psychologists are interested in how individuals relate to each other in their social environments. We may categorize ways of relating to others in terms of positive and negative interactions. Attraction and helping are two types of positive interactions. Negative ways of relating include prejudiced behavior and aggression. In this module we examine what psychologists have learned about these positive and negative ways of relating to others.

CONCEPT 16.14
Attraction is influenced by similarity, physical attractiveness, proximity, and reciprocity.

attraction Feelings of liking for others, together with having positive thoughts about them and inclinations to act toward them in positive ways.

Attraction: Getting to Like You

In nature, attraction is the tendency for two objects or bodies to be drawn toward each other, like the opposite poles of a magnet. In psychology, **attraction** describes feelings of liking others as well as having positive thoughts about them and inclinations to act positively toward them (Berscheid & Reis, 1998).

Though we usually think of attraction in terms of romantic or erotic attraction (attraction toward a love interest), social psychologists use the term more broadly to include other kinds of attraction as well, such as feelings of liking toward friends. Psychologists have identified several key determinants of attraction, including similarity, physical attractiveness, proximity, and reciprocity.

Similarity   Like birds of a feather, we are generally attracted to people with whom we share similar values and attitudes (Angier, 2003; Buston & Emlen, 2003). We tend to like people who are similar to ourselves in characteristics ranging from physical appearance to social class to race, height, musical tastes, intelligence, and even clothing. People also tend to select mates who are similar to themselves on attitudes, religious views, and values (Luo & Klohnen, 2005). People are even more likely to marry others whose first or last names resemble their own (Jones et al., 2004).

Why are people attracted to similar others? One widely held view is that similarity is gratifying because each person in the relationship serves to validate, reinforce, and enhance the other's self-concept. If you echo my sentiments about movies, politics, and the like, I might feel better about myself.

However, this does not mean that relationships are doomed to fail if two people (roommates, friends, or lovers) differ in their attitudes, interests, or tastes. For one thing, no two people are identical in all respects (fortunately so!). At least some common ground is necessary to anchor a relationship, but every successful relationship still requires compromise and accommodation to keep it afloat. Not surprisingly, the attitudes of dating partners tend to become more closely aligned over time (Davis & Rusbult, 2001).

Bear in mind that it is the *perception* of people's personalities, not their actual personalities, that determines attraction (Dittmann, 2003d; Klohen & Luo, 2003). For example, we may be attracted to people whom we perceive as secure and confident in their relationships, even if in actuality they are somewhat insecure.

Physical Attractiveness   We might think we are attracted romantically to people because of their inner qualities. However, evidence shows that it is the outer packaging, not the inner soul, that is the major determinant of initial attraction (Berscheid & Reis, 1998). When investigators set up contrived dating situations in which male and female college students were randomly paired off and later asked to rate how attracted they were to their assigned partners, it turned out that partner physical attractiveness was the key reason for both attraction and interest in future dates (Hatfield & Sprecher, 1986). Men typically place greater emphasis than women do on the physical attractiveness of potential partners (Buss, 1994; Feingold, 1991; Nevid, 1984).

REALITY CHECK

THE CLAIM Opposites attract.

THE CLAIM Evidence strongly links attraction to similarity in attitudes and interests. We tend to like others who agree with us. Similarity of attitudes and interests is a key factor not only in initial attraction but also in friendships and romantic relationships.

THE TAKE-AWAY MESSAGE When it comes to attraction, evidence more strongly supports the "birds of a feature" hypothesis than the "opposites attract" hypothesis.

It Pays to Be Tall   Researchers find that taller people tend to earn more than shorter workers. How might you explain this finding?

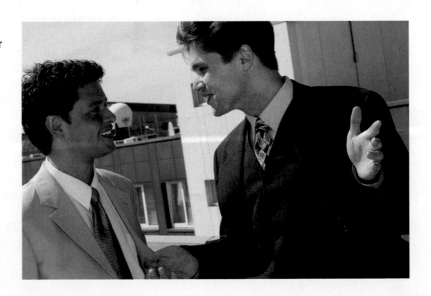

Sorry, Arnold When rating male faces, both men and women tend to rate those having more feminine features, such as the refined and delicate features of Leonardo DiCaprio, as more attractive than those with more masculinized, Arnold Schwarzenegger-type features.

Not only do people tend to be attracted to pretty packages, but they also tend to adopt the stereotype that "what is beautiful is also good" (Berscheid & Reis, 1998), judging attractive people more favorably on many personality traits such as sociability, popularity, intelligence, persuasiveness, and psychological health (Eagly & Wood, 1991; Feingold, 1992; Langlois et al., 2000). Yet there are exceptions to the "beautiful is good" stereotype: attractive people are typically judged as more vain and less modest than their less attractive peers (Feingold, 1992).

Our physical appearance affects how others perceive us. In our society, it pays to be tall—literally (Dittmann, 2004b). Evidence shows that height is associated with higher incomes. The reason, investigators suspect, is that taller workers tend to be favored for sales and executive positions (Judge & Cable, 2004).

You may not be able to change your height, but evidence suggests that smiling often improves the odds you'll be judged by others as more sociable and independent (e.g., Borkenau & Liebler, 1992). Moreover, people who wear glasses tend to be perceived as less attractive but as more intelligent, honest, and reliable (McKelvie, 1997; Terry & Macy, 1991). Suppose you wear contact lenses and want to create a favorable impression about your intelligence in a job interview. If so, it might be wise to leave the contacts at home and wear your glasses.

Beauty may be in the eye of the beholder, but beholders tend to view beauty in highly similar ways. We tend to agree on whom we find attractive or not attractive. For example, faces with a clear complexion are universally perceived as more attractive (Fink & Penton-Voak, 2002).

Evidence also exists showing little variation in the characteristics of the ideal female face (Langlois et al., 2000). In one study, investigators asked groups of White, Euro-American students and recently arrived Asian and Hispanic students to judge the attractiveness of photographs of Asian, Hispanic, Black, and White women (Cunningham et al., 1995). Judgments of physical beauty were generally consistent for photographs of members of different groups. Faces rated as more attractive typically had such features as high cheekbones and eyebrows, widely spaced eyes, a small nose, thin cheeks, a large smile, a full lower lip, a small chin, and a fuller hairstyle.

Both male and female raters tended to judge the same faces as attractive; they also tended to agree that faces of women with more feminine features were more attractive than those with more masculine features (Angier, 1998b). Yet perhaps surprisingly, both male and female raters generally found male faces with *more feminine features* to be more attractive. The more refined and delicate features of a Leonardo DiCaprio, for example, are preferred over the more squared-jawed, masculinized features of an Arnold Schwarzenegger (Angier, 1998b). On the other hand, evidence also shows that babyish facial features, as denoted by larger eyes and lips, tend to diminish perceptions of sexiness of male faces more than female faces (Keating, 2002).

Although some features of physical beauty appear to be universal, cultural differences certainly exist (Buss & Kenrick, 1998). In certain African cultures, for example, feminine beauty is associated with such physical features as long necks and round, disklike lips (Ford & Beach, 1951). Female plumpness is valued in some societies, whereas in others, including our own, the female ideal is associated with thinness, indeed an unrealistic standard of thinness (see Chapter 8). Women themselves tend to associate curvaceousness with female attractiveness, but only so long as the curvaceous figure is lean and does not have large hips (Forestell, Humphrey, & Stewart, 2004). Slenderness in men is also valued in Western society, but social pressures to be thin are placed disproportionately on women.

What if you don't happen to meet standards of physical perfection? Don't give up hope. The correlations between physical attractiveness and measures of mental ability and personality are generally small (Feingold, 1992). Moreover, only small relationships are found between physical attractiveness and feelings of well-being, and between attractiveness and income (Diener, Wolsic, & Fujita, 1995).

Another explanation for why people who fall short of a physical ideal are likely to be saved from a lifetime of dinners-for-one is the **matching hypothesis**, the prediction that people will seek partners who are similar to themselves in physical attractiveness. Evidence generally supports the matching hypothesis and also shows that in mismatches, the less attractive partner usually compensates by having greater wealth or social position than the more attractive partner (Berscheid & Reis, 1998). The matching hypothesis applies to other characteristics as well. We tend to be attracted to mates who are similar to ourselves in personality, attitudes, and even body weight (Angier, 2003; Buss, 1984; Schafer & Keith, 1990).

Proximity   Friendship patterns are strongly influenced by physical **proximity**. If you live in a college dormitory, your friends are more likely to live down the hall than across campus. Your earliest friends were probably children who lived next door or down the block from you.

We might also expect that Emily Ang would be more likely to make friends in school with Maria Arnez and Jessica Arnold than Sally Smith. Why? In many schools, children are assigned seats in alphabetical order, so they're more likely to sit near students whose last names are close in the alphabet to their own. A study of police trainees showed this effect. Friendships were more likely to be formed between trainees whose last names started with the same letter of the alphabet or an adjacent letter (Segal, 1994).

Proximity increases the chances of interacting with others and getting to know them better, thus providing a basis for developing feelings of attraction toward them. Another explanation for the positive effects of proximity on attraction is the tendency for people to have more in common with people who live nearby or attend the same classes. Similarity in attitudes and background can increase feelings of liking.

Of course, proximity can also increase negative attraction, or dislike. Repeated contact with someone you dislike may intensify negative feelings.

Reciprocity   **Reciprocity** is the tendency to like others who like us back. We typically respond in kind to people who compliment us, do us favors, or tell us how much they like us (Nowak, Vallacher, & Miller, 2003). Reciprocal interactions build upon themselves, leading to feelings of liking. Yet we may be wary of people who compliment us too quickly or seem to like us too much before they get to know us. We may suspect that they want something from us or are not very discriminating.

The principle of reciprocity comes into play in many aspects of social behavior, including, researchers find, tipping behavior (Cialdini & Goldstein, 2004). Investigators found that when waitresses wrote helpful messages on the back of

matching hypothesis   The belief that people tend to pair off with others who are similar to themselves in physical attractiveness and other characteristics.

proximity   Nearness or propinquity.

reciprocity   The principle that people tend to like others who like them back.

the customers' checks, or when they gave customers a small piece of chocolate along with their checks, patrons tended to reciprocate by leaving larger tips (Rind & Strohmetz, 1999; Strohmetz et al., 2002).

Next we turn to another positive way of relating to others—helping others in time of need. We begin with a tragic story of nonhelping in which a young woman was brutally attacked and people who heard her agonizing screams did nothing to help her.

Helping Behavior: Lending a Hand to Others in Need

💡 **CONCEPT 16.15**

Helping may be motivated by both altruistic and self-centered motives.

Online Study Center

Improving Your Grade

Tutorials: Helping Others

Even now, some forty years after the 1964 murder of 28-year-old Kitty Genovese on a quiet street in Queens, New York, the shock remains. Kitty screamed for help as she was viciously attacked by an assailant who repeatedly stabbed her until she lay dying from her wounds. According to media reports at the time, thirty-eight people living in nearby apartment buildings heard her screams for help and did nothing. None came to her aid and only one person called the police some thirty minutes later, but too late to help her. Some witnesses reportedly looked out their windows in the direction of the commotion, but then went back to their dinners and television shows.

Why had no one helped? Though later reports suggested that there were far fewer individuals who saw what was happening to Kitty and did nothing than the thirty-eight reported in newspaper accounts (Rasenberger, 2004), the Kitty Genovese case raises deeper questions about our willingness to intervene to help someone in distress. Is there something so callous in human nature that we would turn our backs on someone in desperate need of assistance? If so, how are we to explain the countless acts of simple kindness of people who selflessly help people in need, let alone the heroic acts of people who risk their lives in emergency situations to save others? Consider the heroic efforts of the firefighters and police officers who responded to the terrorist attack at the World Trade Center, many of whom lost their lives in a valiant attempt to save others. Many civilians at this site of tragedy also lost their lives as they stopped to help others escape the inferno. Consider too the courageous resistance shown in the selfless behavior of people who risked their lives to rescue Jews during the Holocaust, those who blew the whistle on corporate corruption knowing their jobs and livelihoods were imperiled, and those who protested and resisted repressive political regimes at the risk of imprisonment and even death (Becker & Eagly, 2004; Shepela et al., 1999). Clearly, the question is not whether people will help others in need, but under what conditions they will help.

Helping is a form of **prosocial behavior**, or behavior that is beneficial to others. Psychologist C. Daniel Batson, a leading authority on helping, distinguishes between two types of motives that underlie helping behavior (Batson et al., 2002; Batson & Powell, 2003). One type of helping arises from *altruistic* motives—the desire to help others without expecting anything in return. But another type is based on self-centered motives, such as the desire to help someone in order to make oneself look good in the eyes of others or to avoid feeling guilty from failing to help. One factor influencing altruistic helping is the helper's identification or empathy with the victim (Batson et al., 2002; Penner et al., 2005). By putting ourselves in the victim's position, we are able to empathize with the suffering of that person, which prompts us to take action. Batson's belief in pure altruism is not universally accepted by social psychologists. Some believe that all forms of helping benefit the helper to a certain extent.

💡 **CONCEPT 16.16**

According to one decision-making model, bystander intervention depends on a series of five decisions.

prosocial behavior Behavior that benefits others.

bystander intervention Helping a stranger in distress.

Bystander Intervention: Deciding to Get Involved—Or Not The decision-making model of helping behavior proposed by Bibb Latané & John Darley (1970) explains **bystander intervention** in terms of a decision-making process that can be broken down into a series of five decisions (see Figure 16.4). First, people must decide that a need for help exists. Second, they must decide that the situation is a clear emergency. Third, they must decide to assume personal responsibility for providing assistance. Fourth, they must decide what kind of help to give. Fifth, they must decide to implement this course of action.

Consider again the thirty-eight people who witnessed Kitty Genovese's murder but did nothing. Why didn't they help? The critical thinking exercise at the end of the chapter poses this question for you to answer. For now, however, let us examine what social psychologists have learned about the factors that affect helping behavior. Some of these factors may shed light on the inaction of those thirty-eight witnesses.

Influences on Helping   Many factors influence people's willingness to help, including the ambiguity of the situation, perceived cost, diffusion of responsibility, similarity, facial features, mood and gender, attributions of the causes of need, and social norms.

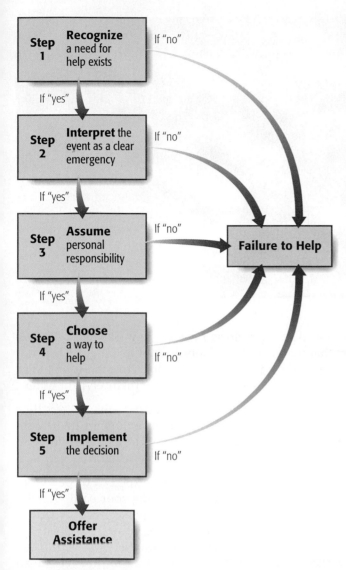

Figure 16.4   A Decision-Making Model of Bystander Intervention
The decision-making model of bystander intervention identifies five decision-making steps that precede either helping or failing to offer help.

Source: Latané & Darley, 1970.

CONCEPT 16.17
Helping behavior is influenced by situational and individual factors and by social norms.

- *Situational ambiguity.* People who fail to assist others in need may not be apathetic or cold-hearted, but they may be confused and uncertain (Rasenberger, 2004). In ambiguous situations, as Latané and Darley would predict, people are much less likely to offer assistance than in situations involving a clear-cut emergency (Shotland & Heinold, 1985). They are also less likely to help in unfamiliar environments than in familiar ones (e.g., when they are in strange cities rather than in their hometowns).

- *Perceived cost.* The likelihood of helping increases as the perceived cost to ourselves declines (Simmons, 1991). We are more likely to lend our class notes to someone whom we believe will return them than to a person who doesn't appear trustworthy.

- *Diffusion of responsibility.* The presence of others may *diffuse* the sense of individual responsibility (Garcia et al., 2002). It follows that if you suddenly felt faint and were about to pass out on the street, you would be more likely to receive help if there were only a few passers-by present than if the street were crowded with pedestrians. With fewer people present, it becomes more difficult to point to the "other guy" as the one responsible for taking action. If everyone believes the other guy will act, then no one acts.

- *Similarity.* People are more willing to help others whom they perceive to be similar to themselves—people who share a common background and beliefs. They are even more likely to help others who dress the way they do than those in different attire (Cialdini & Trost, 1998). People also tend to be more willing to help their kin than to help nonkin (Gaulin & McBurney, 2001).

- *Facial features.* People with baby-faced features are more likely to elicit help than people with more mature facial features (Keating et al., 2003).

- *Mood.* People are generally more willing to help others when they are in a good mood (Batson & Powell, 2003).

- *Gender and race.* Despite changes in traditional gender roles, women in need are more likely than men in need to receive assistance from strangers. Racism and prejudice enter the picture when the person needing help is Black. Evidence shows that Blacks are less likely to receive help than Whites under certain conditions, such as when helping requires more time, when it entails more risk or

Would You Help This Man? What influences the decision to help a person in need?

effort, and when the person needing help is further away (Saucier, Miller, & Doucet, 2005). It appears that having other reasons for not helping, such as not having enough time to render assistance, allows individuals to express prejudice without having to acknowledge their racial biases to either themselves or others.

- *Attributions of the cause of need.* People are much more likely to help others they judge to be innocent victims than those they believe have brought their problems on themselves (Batson, 1998). Thus, they may fail to lend assistance to homeless people and drug addicts whom they feel "deserve what they get."

- *Social norms.* **Social norms** prescribe behaviors that are expected of people in social situations (Batson, 1998). The social norm of "doing your part" in helping a worthy cause places a demand on people to help, especially in situations where their behavior is observed by others (Gaulin & McBurney, 2001). For example, people are more likely to make a charitable donation when they are asked to do so by a co-worker in full view of others than when they receive an appeal in the mail in the privacy of their own homes.

Let us now explore negative ways of relating to others, including prejudice and discrimination as well as human aggression.

Prejudice: Attitudes That Harm

Prejudice is a preconceived attitude, usually unfavorable, that is formed without critical thought or evaluation of the facts. Some prejudices reflect positive biases, such as when we prejudge members of our own ethnic or religious group more favorably than members of other groups. But most prejudices reflect negative biases against other groups or categories based on race, ethnicity, social class, gender, age, and occupational, disability, or social status.

Prejudice, like other attitudes, consists of cognitive, emotional, and behavioral components. The cognitive component is the set of biased beliefs and stereotypes that a person holds about other groups. The emotional component consists of feelings of dislike that the person has toward members of these groups. And the behavioral component is the person's inclination to discriminate against them. **Discrimination** is unfair or biased treatment of people based on group membership. Examples of discrimination include denial of housing or job opportunities, exclusion from social clubs, and increased scrutiny by police officers or department-store security guards. Social psychologists note that people often fail to acknowledge

CONCEPT 16.18
Social psychologists conceptualize prejudice, as they do other types of attitudes, as consisting of cognitive, emotional, and behavioral components.

social norms Standards that define what is socially acceptable in a given situation.

prejudice A preconceived opinion or attitude about an issue, person, or group.

discrimination Unfair or biased treatment of people based on their membership in a particular group or category.

their racial biases and may not even be aware of them (Banaji & Greenwald, 1995; Macrae, Stangor, & Milne, 1994).

Stereotypes and prejudices are generally resistant to change. Social psychologists find that Whites who hold stereotypical views of Blacks may perceive them as "lazy" even when they perform exactly the same as the Whites (Hilton & von Hippel, 1996). This belief demonstrates the difficulty of dislodging negative stereotypes, since what you see is often determined by what you *expect* to see. A woman executive may have to work harder than any of her male peers to prove she deserves her position. S. L. Carter wrote in his 1993 book, *Reflections of an Affirmative Action Baby,* "Our parents' advice was true: We really do have to work twice as hard to be considered half as good [as Whites]" (p. 58). Individuals from groups stereotyped as inferior may find it difficult—even impossible—to prove that the stereotype is not deserved (Biernat & Kobrynowicz, 1997).

Social scientists have long observed that prejudice and discrimination typically increase during times of social upheaval and increased competition among groups. Competition over jobs and scarce economic opportunities can strain intergroup relationships. It comes as no surprise, then, that acts of racial hatred tend to increase during economic downturns, when unemployment is high. Members of ethnic minority groups may become convenient scapegoats when the economic security of the majority is threatened.

CONCEPT 16.19

Prejudice develops as an outgrowth of negative stereotypes and is acquired in the same way that other attitudes are learned.

How Does Prejudice Develop?   Prejudice arises as an outgrowth of negative stereotypes of other groups as lazy, dishonest, violent, dumb, and so on (Hilton & von Hippel, 1996). These stereotypes are learned or acquired. Children may start forming negative attitudes toward other groups by imitating the prejudiced attitudes they see modeled by parents, teachers, and peers. Prejudices may also be acquired through repeated exposure to negative, stereotypical depictions of other groups, especially ethnic minorities, in the media. We are repeatedly exposed to television and movie depictions of ethnic minorities in negative roles—as criminals, gang members, abusers, drug pushers, and so on. Repeated exposure alone may be sufficient to instill prejudiced attitudes without any conscious effort on the perceiver's part (Hilton & von Hippel, 1996).

Prejudices may also be acquired through direct experience. If a person has a few experiences with members of a particular group who are cold or nasty, he or she may overgeneralize and develop a stereotyped belief that all members of the particular group share these characteristics.

Though we may differ in the prejudices we acquire, we all harbor some prejudices. The universality of prejudice points to a basic cognitive tendency we may have to parse our social environment into two general categories: people who are like us and people who are different from us. Social psychologists describe these social categories as **in-groups** (one's own social, religious, ethnic, and national groups) and **out-groups** (all other groups).

CONCEPT 16.20

The cognitive bases of prejudice reflect tendencies to separate people into two basic categories, in-groups and out-groups, and to attribute more negative characteristics to out-group members and more positive characteristics to in-group members.

Prejudice develops when our thinking becomes biased in such a way that we attribute more negative characteristics to members of out-groups and more positive characteristics to members of in-groups. These two biased ways of thinking are called **out-group negativism** (also called *out-group prejudice*) and **in-group favoritism** (or *in-group bias*), respectively (Aboud, 2003; Dovidio et al., 2003; Hewstone, Rubin, & Willis, 2002). Negative stereotypes of out-groups—beliefs that "we" are better than "they"—bolster the self-esteem of in-group members. Labeling other groups as dumb, lazy, dishonest, and so on makes us feel good in comparison.

in-groups   Social, religious, ethnic, or national groups with which one identifies.

out-groups   Groups other than those with which one identifies.

out-group negativism   A cognitive bias involving the predisposition to attribute more negative characteristics to members of out-groups than to those of in-groups.

in-group favoritism   A cognitive bias involving the predisposition to attribute more positive characteristics to members of in-groups than to those of out-groups.

out-group homogeneity   A cognitive bias describing the tendency to perceive members of out-groups as more alike than members of in-groups.

Another type of biased thinking associated with prejudice is **out-group homogeneity**. This is the tendency to perceive members of out-groups as all alike or *homogeneous,* whereas people in our own groups are as "different as snowflakes" (Nelson, 2002). Whites are more likely to believe that Blacks are more similar to each other than are Whites, and vice versa. One prominent explanation of out-group homogeneity is based on the *exemplar model* (Linville & Fischer, 1993). It holds that people are likely to know more in-group members than out-group members and so can more easily recall differences among people within their own groups who are different from each other.

The roots of prejudice may run deep into our evolutionary past. Psychologist Martin Fishbein (1996) argues that ancestral humans organized themselves into tribal groups that shared a common language and culture, and they needed to keep their guard up against threats posed by outsiders—people from other groups who might harm them or kill them. Stereotyping other groups as "dangerous" or "evil" may have served an adaptive function to these early humans, who had good reason to fear outsiders. In the multicultural society of today, however, the adaptive demands we face are very different. We need to learn to get along with people of diverse backgrounds and to avoid branding people who are different from ourselves with unwarranted stereotypes.

CONCEPT 16.21
Individual differences in prejudice may be explained by learning experiences, personality traits, and the tendency to emphasize either similarities or differences between people.

Why Are Some People More Prejudiced than Others? Why are some people highly prejudiced and others low in prejudice? Learning experiences play a key role in explaining these differences. Children exposed to the teachings of less prejudiced parents are likely to develop less prejudiced attitudes than are children of more intolerant parents. Low-prejudiced individuals also tend to differ in their cognitive style. They tend to look more at the similarities among people than at their differences, a cognitive framework that psychologists call a *universalist orientation* (Phillips & Ziller, 1997). By contrast, people with more prejudiced attitudes emphasize differences among people and use ethnicity as a basis for judging people.

The presence of an underlying personality type called the **authoritarian personality** may also contribute to the development of highly prejudiced attitudes. Theodore Adorno and his colleagues (1950) coined this term to describe a cluster of personality traits that included rigidity and excessive concern with obedience and respect for authority. Individuals with authoritarian personalities are prone to hate people who are different from themselves and those they perceive as weak or downtrodden. What can be done to counter stereotypes and prejudices more generally? Social psychologists suggest some possible remedies.

CONCEPT 16.22
According to Allport, intergroup contact can help reduce prejudice, but only under conditions of social and institutional support, acquaintance potential, equal status, and intergroup cooperation.

What Can We Do to Reduce Prejudice? The most widely cited model for reducing prejudice, the **contact hypothesis**, was formulated in 1954 by psychologist Gordon Allport. He proposed that the best way to reduce prejudice and intergroup tension was to bring groups into closer contact with each other. But he recognized that intergroup contact alone was not sufficient. Under some conditions, intergroup contact may increase negative attitudes by making differences between groups more apparent. Allport outlined four conditions that must be met in order for intergroup contact to have a desirable effect on reducing prejudice and intergroup tension (Brewer & Brown, 1998):

- *Social and institutional support.* People in positions of authority must be clearly behind the effort to bring groups closer together. For example, school integration is more likely to facilitate race relations if it is fully supported by teachers, school administrators, and public officials.

- *Acquaintance potential.* Opportunities must exist for members of different groups to become better acquainted with each other. With opportunities for more face-to-face interaction, members of different groups have a better chance of finding common ground. They may also discover evidence that refutes negative stereotypes they hold about each other. Even knowing that a member of one's own group has a close relationship with a member of another group can promote more positive attitudes toward the other group (Wright et al., 1997).

- *Equal status.* Increased opportunities for contact with members of other groups who occupy subordinate roles may actually reinforce existing stereotypes and

authoritarian personality A personality type characterized by rigidity, prejudice, and excessive concerns with obedience and respect for authority.

contact hypothesis Allport's belief that under certain conditions, increased intergroup contact helps reduce prejudice and intergroup tension.

prejudices. When opportunities exist for members of different groups to meet on an equal footing, it becomes more difficult to maintain prejudiced beliefs.

- *Intergroup cooperation.* Working cooperatively to achieve a common goal can help reduce intergroup bias by bringing members of different groups closer together (Gaertner et al., 1999). Whether it involves a baseball team, a work team in the office, or citizens banding together to fight a common cause, cooperation can foster feelings of friendliness and mutual understanding.

Combating prejudice and discrimination begins with the lessons we teach our children in the home and at school. Teaching empathy and modeling tolerance in the home can help counter the development of prejudiced attitudes. Empathy is the ability to take the perspective of other people and understand their feelings. Popular movies that allow us to share emotional experiences of members of stigmatized groups—films such as *Rain Man, Schindler's List,* and *The Color Purple*—may be useful in promoting more accepting, prosocial attitudes. Enforcing laws against discrimination and strengthening a cultural climate that encourages tolerance are societal measures that help combat prejudice and discrimination.

We as individuals can also take steps to counter prejudiced thinking. However, trying to consciously suppress stereotypes or push them out of awareness may actually make them more likely to come to mind (Bodenhausen et al., 2003).

Though we automatically or unconsciously form stereotypes, investigators find that it is possible to change them or, at the very least, not act upon them (Ashburn-Nardo, Voils, & Monteith, 2001; Dasgupta & Greenwald, 2001). For example, we can make a conscious attempt not to apply stereotypes when forming judgments of others (Kunda & Spencer, 2003). Other suggestions include rehearsing positive mental images of out-group members, taking part in cooperative works or projects in which we get to interact with people of different backgrounds, and participating in diversity education, such as workshops or seminars on prejudice and intergroup conflict (Blair, Ma, & Lenton, 2001; Nelson, 2002; Rudman, Ashmore, & Gary, 2001).

Human Aggression: Behavior That Harms

CONCEPT 16.23
Like other forms of human behavior, aggression is too complex to be reduced to the level of instinct.

Stereotyping and prejudice are negative ways of relating to people who are different from ourselves. Far too often in human history these negative attitudes toward members of other groups have set the stage for violent behavior in the form of killing and warfare. What are we to make of this all? Are human beings inherently aggressive? Or is aggression a form of learned behavior that can be modified by experience? There are many opinions among psychologists and other scientists about the nature of human aggression. Let us consider what the major perspectives in psychology might teach us about our capacity to harm one another.

Is Human Aggression Instinctual?   Some theorists believe that aggression in humans and other species is based on instinct. For example, the famed ethologist Konrad Lorenz (1966) believed that the fighting instinct is a basic survival mechanism in many animal species. Predators need to survive by instinctively attacking their prey. The more fortunate animals on which they prey survive by either instinctively fleeing from these attacks or fighting them off. In Lorenz's view, aggression can be an adaptive response that increases the chances of survival of predator and prey.

Aggression among members of the same animal species may also have survival value. It usually occurs among males and is used to establish dominance, defend territory, and lay claim to food, mates, or other valuable resources. Aggressiveness in males may increase their chances of surviving and producing offspring that carry their genes, presumably including genes that control aggressive behavior. Again, aggression may prove adaptive under some circumstances—adaptive to the survival of the individual's genes, that is. But what of human aggression? Might it also be explained by instinct?

Contemporary theorists believe that human aggression is far too complex to be based on instinct. Human aggression takes many forms, from organized warfare and acts of terrorism to interpersonal forms of violent behavior such as muggings, spousal abuse, and sexual assaults. These different forms of aggression reflect a variety of political, cultural, and psychological motives. Moreover, instinct theories fail to account for the important roles that learning and culture play in shaping behavior, nor do they explain the diversity that exists in human aggression. Violence is unusual in some cultures but all too common in others, unfortunately including our own.

Theorists today believe that human aggression cannot be explained by any one cause. Next we consider the multiple factors that contemporary theorists believe contribute to human aggression, including biological influences, learning influences, sociocultural influences, use of alcohol, emotional states, and environmental influences (Anderson & Bushman, 2002, 2003; Geen, 1998).

> **CONCEPT 16.24**
> The biological underpinnings of aggression reflect genetic, hormonal, and neurotransmitter influences.

Biological Influences   Though human aggression may not be explained by instinct, evidence points to other biological influences that appear to play a role. Researchers have focused on the neurotransmitter serotonin, since this chemical is implicated in brain circuits that curb impulsive behavior. Serotonin can be likened to a "behavioral seat belt" because of the role it seems to play in curbing impulsive behavior (Davidson, Putnam, & Larson, 2000; Zuckerman, 2003). Lower levels of serotonin in the brains of aggressive men may create a predisposition that makes them more likely to respond aggressively to social provocation (Bjork et al., 2000). But more research is needed to form any definitive conclusions about the role that serotonin may play in human aggression.

The male sex hormone testosterone is also linked to aggressive behavior, especially in men (Zuckerman, 2003). Men have higher levels of testosterone than women, and compelling evidence from cross-cultural studies shows that men

Violence in America   These empty shoes of gunshot victims in the United States provide a poignant reminder of the consequences of violent behavior.

typically engage in more aggressive and violent behavior than women (Bennett, Farrington, & Huesmann, 2005; Buss & Kenrick, 1998; Felson, 2002). That said, not all aggressive or violent men have high testosterone levels, nor do all—or even most—men with high testosterone levels engage in violent behavior. Clearly, other factors are involved in aggression that are more complex.

Evolutionary psychologists suggest that among ancestral humans, aggression may have benefited men in their primary role as hunters. Ancestral women, so far as we know, primarily engaged in food gathering and childcare roles in which aggressiveness may have been counterproductive. Perhaps the greater aggressiveness we find in males today is explained in part by inherited tendencies passed down through generations from ancestral times.

CONCEPT 16.25
Social-cognitive theorists view aggression as learned behavior that is acquired through observational learning and reinforcement.

Learning Influences   According to social-cognitive theorists, such as psychologist Albert Bandura (1973, 1986), aggression is a learned behavior that is acquired through the same principles of learning as other learned behaviors. Bandura highlights the role of observational learning. He notes that children learn to imitate aggressive behavior that they observe in the home, the schools, and the media, especially television (see Module 9.6 in Chapter 9). Young boys, for example, may learn by observing their peers or by watching male characters on television that conflicts are to be settled with fists or weapons, not with words. Researchers find that aggressive or violent children often come from homes in which aggression was modeled by parents and other family members ("Risk Factors," 2000).

Reinforcement also contributes to the learning of aggressive behavior. If children are rewarded for aggressive behavior, such as by receiving approval or respect from peers, or by getting their way, they are more likely to repeat the same behavior. Indeed, people in general are more likely to resort to aggressive behavior if they have failed to learn alternative ways of resolving conflicts. Violent behavior may be perpetuated from generation to generation as children who are exposed to violence in the home learn that violent behavior is an acceptable way to settle disagreements.

CONCEPT 16.26
Sociocultural theorists explore the social stressors that contribute to aggressive behavior, including poverty, child abuse and neglect, family breakdown, and exposure to violence.

Sociocultural Influences   Sociocultural theorists encourage us to consider the broader social contexts in which aggression takes place. Interpersonal violence often occurs against a backdrop of social stressors such as poverty, prolonged unemployment, lack of opportunity, child abuse and neglect, family breakdown, and exposure to violence in the family and community. Children who are abused by their parents may fail to develop the secure loving attachments to their parents that would otherwise provide the basis for acquiring empathy and concern for others. Not surprisingly, abused children often display violent behavior in childhood and adulthood. Aggressive or violent behavior in childhood is a risk factor for poor school performance and even long-term unemployment in adulthood (Kokko & Pulkkinen, 2000).

Social psychologists recognize that violence may also be used as a social influence tactic—a means of coercion by which individuals seek to compel others to comply with their wishes. We need only consider such examples as the "mob enforcer" who uses strong-arm tactics to obtain compliance or the abusive spouse who uses physical force or threat of force to get his wife to accede to his demands.

CONCEPT 16.27
Use of alcohol may be linked to aggressive behavior because it loosens inhibitions, impairs the ability to weigh the consequences of behavior and interpret social cues, and reduces sensitivity to punishment-related cues.

Alcohol Use   Investigators find strong links between alcohol use and violent behaviors, including domestic violence, homicide, and rape (Boles & Miottoa, 2003; Fals-Stewart, 2003; Marshal, 2003). Alcohol loosens inhibitions or restraints on impulsive behavior, including acts of impulsive violence. It also impairs our ability to weigh the consequences of our actions, reduces our sensitivity to cues that signal the threat of punishment, and leads us to misperceive other people's motives as malevolent (Giancola & Zeichner, 1997; Ito, Miller, & Pollock, 1996). Not everyone who drinks becomes aggressive, of course. Relationships between alcohol use and aggression may be influenced by the user's biological sensitivity to alcohol as well as by the social demands of the situation in which provocation occurs, such as a bar versus the family home.

Emotional Influences   Psychologists have long recognized that certain negative emotions, especially frustration and anger, may trigger aggression. **Frustration** is a negative emotional state that is induced when our efforts to reach a goal are thwarted or blocked. Though frustration often leads to aggression, other outcomes are possible. You may feel frustrated when someone behind you in a movie theater talks throughout the picture, prompting a *state of readiness* to respond aggressively either verbally or physically (Berkowitz, 1993). But whether you actually respond aggressively may depend on your expectation that an aggressive response will yield a positive outcome and your history of aggressive behavior, among other factors. Questions remain about whether aggression is necessarily preceded by frustration. The cool, premeditated aggression of a mob "hit man" does not fit the pattern of frustration-induced aggression.

Anger is a strong negative emotion that can incite aggressive responses in some individuals. We might think of the husband who strikes out violently at his wife when she says something that angers him or the child abuser who lashes out angrily when a child is slow to comply with a demand. People who think angering thoughts ("I can't let him/her get away with this . . .") or who blow minor provocations out of proportion are more likely to respond aggressively in conflict situations than others who think calmer thoughts. Recently, investigators found that men who reported committing a physically violent act toward a female dating partner showed more intense levels of anger than did nonviolent men (Eckhardt, Jamison, & Watts, 2002). Still, we should recognize that many acts of aggression occur without anger as a catalyst (DeAngelis, 2003b).

Environmental Influences   People may get hot under the collar as the outdoor temperature rises, but are they more likely to become aggressive? Indeed they are. Environmental psychologists find that aggressive behavior increases with rising temperatures, although it may begin to decline at very high temperatures (Anderson & DeNeve, 1992; Sundstrom et al., 1996).

According to social-cognitive theorists, hot temperatures incite aggression by inducing angry, hostile thoughts and feelings, which in turn increase the readiness to respond aggressively to social provocations (Geen, 1998). Supportive evidence for this belief comes from findings that higher outdoor temperatures are associated with a greater frequency of hostile thoughts and feelings (Anderson, Deuser, & DeNeve, 1995). Links between rising temperature and aggression raise some interesting questions that might be pursued through more formal study: Might the use of air conditioning in prisons reduce the problems of inmate violence? Might air conditioning have a similar effect in reducing aggression in the workplace or in schools? Before reading further, you may want to review the positive (helping) and negative ways of relating to others outlined in Concept Chart 16.2.

CONCEPT 16.28
Anger and frustration are negative emotions that may serve as triggers for aggression.

CONCEPT 16.29
High temperatures are linked to aggressive behavior, perhaps because they induce angry, hostile thoughts and feelings that become expressed in aggressive behavior.

frustration   A negative emotional state experienced when one's efforts to pursue one's goals are thwarted.

CONCEPT CHART 16.2   Relating to Others

	Concept	Description	More About It
Determinants of Helping	Decision-making processes	The decision-making model proposed by Latané and Darley consists of the following steps: (1) recognizing that a need for help exists, (2) interpreting the situation as an emergency, (3) assuming personal responsibility for helping, (4) determining the type or kind of help needed, and (5) deciding to implement a course of action.	Helping is not an automatic response in situations of need but, rather, is based on a decision-making process in which one appraises the situation at hand as well as one's personal responsibility and resources to deal with it.
	Influences on helping	Influences include situational ambiguity, perceived cost, diffusion of responsibility, similarity, facial features, mood, gender and race effects, attributions of the cause of need, and social norms.	Whether people help others in need depends on a combination of personal and situational factors.
Negative Ways of Relating	Prejudice	A cluster of (mostly) negative beliefs, feelings, and behavioral tendencies toward members of other social groups (e.g., ethnic or religious minorities) or categories (e.g., people with disabilities).	Efforts to reduce prejudice can be directed at increasing intergroup contacts under conditions of social and institutional support, acquaintanceship potential, equal status, and cooperativeness. Individuals can practice non-stereotyped ways of thinking and seek opportunities for contact with people of other social groups. Parents can help instill in their children nonprejudiced attitudes through what they teach them and by setting an example of tolerance.
	Discrimination	Unfair or biased treatment of people on the basis of their membership in particular social groups that reflects underlying prejudices.	Programs designed to reduce prejudice may also have the benefit of reducing discrimination. Moreover, laws against discrimination in housing, education, and employment need to be enforced.
	Aggression	Human aggression takes many forms, from organized warfare to interpersonal violence, such as assaults, rapes, and partner abuse.	Many factors are implicated in human aggression, including biological, learning, sociocultural, emotional, and environmental influences, as well as use of alcohol.

EXPLORING PSYCHOLOGY
How Does Racism and Stereotyping Affect Stereotyped Groups?

Racism is unfortunately a part of the everyday experience of many minority-group members in our society who are targets of stereotyping. Here we examine the toll that racism and stereotyping exacts on members of stereotyped groups.

Exposure to racism is a significant source of environmental stress for many African Americans and is linked to feelings of alienation from the mainstream culture, to a lower self-concept, and to poorer mental and physical health (Thompson et al., 2000; Utsey et al., 2002). Other research with Puerto Rican children shows that exposure to discrimination and even worrying about discrimination are linked to mental health problems, such as depression (Szalacha et al., 2003).

Stereotyping itself can have many negative effects, including lowered expectations. Stereotypical beliefs that "girls can't do math" may discourage young women from pursuing promising career opportunities in engineering and the sciences. Negative stereotypes may also become internalized by members of stereotyped

CONCEPT 16.30
As a result of being subjected to stereotyping and prejudice, stereotyped groups may internalize the negative stereotypes and have lower expectations of themselves.

racism   Negative bias held toward others based on their ethnicity or racial identification.

groups, leading them to perceive themselves as dumb or inferior. These negative beliefs may lead to underperformance in school, sap motivation to succeed, and lower self-esteem (e.g., Pungello et al., 1996). Underperformance of negatively stereotyped groups supports the existing stereotype, which thus may become a self-fulfilling prophecy (Pratto et al., 1997).

Psychologist Claude Steele coined the term **stereotype threat** to apply to the "threat in the air" that exists when members of stereotyped groups are aware of how negatively others may view them because they belong to a stereotyped group (Steele, 1997). Stereotype threat can lead people to perform more poorly than they would otherwise (Steele, Spencer, & Aronson, 2002).

In one study, Steele and his colleague Joshua Aronson had Black and White Stanford University students take a test consisting of the most difficult items from the verbal section of the SAT (Steele & Aronson, 1995). Some of the students were informed beforehand that the test measured intellectual ability. Others were told it was a laboratory problem-solving task unrelated to intellectual ability. Black students underperformed White students of equal aptitude when the task was defined as a measure of intelligence but equaled them in the laboratory problem-solving condition.

Steele believes that identifying the test as a measure of intellectual ability activated stereotype threat in the Black students, which in turn impaired their performance. In a related experiment, women underperformed relative to *equally skilled* men on a test meant to evoke a gender-linked negative stereotype (a difficult math test), but not on a test that stereotypically favored women (a difficult literature test) (Spencer, Steele, & Quinn, 1999). In yet another study, White students underperformed in a golf task under a condition in which they were told the task tapped "natural athletic ability," whereas Black students underperformed when they were led to believe the golf task measured "sports intelligence" (Stone et al., 1999). The underperformance of the stereotyped group members does not seem to come from a reduction of effort; rather, stereotype threat appears to impair performance by acting both as a source of distraction and additional pressure (Dion, 2003). Steele believes that the damaging effects of stereotype threat can sap motivation to achieve in competitive situations (cited in Benson, 2003a). For example, exposure to stereotypical depictions of women and ethnic minorities in the media may lead young women with good math ability to opt out of science and math courses or influence Blacks to drop out of college.

The effects of stereotype threat and exposure to racism may also take a toll on the physical health of targeted groups. Investigators showed that exposing African Americans in a laboratory setting to a high stereotype threat condition led to a rise in blood pressure (Blascovich et al., 2002). No changes in blood pressure were found among African Americans exposed to a low stereotype threat condition or among European Americans in either condition. It is conceivable that daily exposure to stereotype threat may contribute to the higher rates of hypertension we find within the African American community. Moreover, as a source of chronic stress, exposure to racism may also increase the risks of other cardiovascular problems (Troxel et al., 2003).

What can be done to counter the effects of stereotype threat? Steele suggests that stereotype threat may be reduced if teachers hold genuinely optimistic beliefs about the potentials of all their students. We may also be able to counter stereotype threat by conveying the message that intelligence is not a fixed quantity (Aronson, Fried, & Good, 2002).

stereotype threat A sense of threat evoked in members of stereotyped groups when they believe they may be judged or treated stereotypically.

MODULE 16.2 REVIEW

Relating to Others

RECITE IT

What are the major determinants of attraction?

- The major determinants of attraction include similarity, physical attractiveness, proximity, and reciprocity.

What factors are linked to helping behavior?

- The decision-making model holds that bystander intervention is based on a series of decisions that must be made before helping occurs.

- Factors that influence helping behavior include the ambiguity of the situation, perceived cost, diffusion of responsibility, social norms, similarity, facial features, mood, gender and race, and attributions of the causes of need.

What is prejudice, and how does it develop?

- Prejudice is a preconceived attitude or bias, usually unfavorable, that is formed without critical thought or evaluation.

- Prejudice derives from negative group stereotypes to which people are exposed in their social environment. The development of prejudice may also reflect basic cognitive processes that evolved over thousands of generations.

- Individual differences in prejudice may be explained by differences in learning experiences, authoritarian personality traits, and adoption of a universalist orientation.

What can be done to reduce prejudice?

- Prejudice may be reduced by creating opportunities for intergroup contacts that have strong social and institutional support, are based on equal-status relationships, allow acquaintanceships to develop, and emphasize cooperation rather than competition.

What factors contribute to human aggression?

- Contemporary theorists attempt to explain human aggression on the basis of biological influences, learning influences, sociocultural influences, alcohol use, emotional states, and environmental influences.

RECALL IT

1. Name several key factors that determine attraction.

2. One reason _____ of attitudes is important in interpersonal attraction is that we tend to feel better about ourselves when others validate our views.

3. What is the order of steps in the decision-making model of helping proposed by Latané and Darley?
   a. Assume personal responsibility for helping.
   b. Determine that the situation is a true emergency.
   c. Implement the chosen course of action.
   d. Determine that a true need for help exists.
   e. Choose what kind of help to provide.

4. Prejudice, like other attitudes, consists of (a) cognitive, (b) emotional, and (c) behavioral components. What are these components?

5. What are the four conditions that Allport said must be met in order for intergroup contact to reduce prejudice?

THINK ABOUT IT

- To what extent was your attraction to your friends and romantic partners a function of similarity of attitudes, backgrounds, physical attractiveness, proximity, and reciprocity?

- Do you believe that people can be completely altruistic or selfless? Or might there be underlying self-serving motives even in acts of kindness and self-sacrifice? Explain.

- Suppose you were asked to develop a proposal to improve intergroup relations among students of different ethnic groups on campus by bringing them together. What factors do you think would determine whether your efforts are successful?

MODULE 16.3
Group Influences on Individual Behavior

- What is social identity?
- What was the significance of the Asch study on conformity?
- What factors influence conformity?
- What principles are compliance techniques based upon?
- Why were Milgram's findings so disturbing, and why were his methods so controversial?
- How does the presence of others affect individual performance?
- What are deindividuation, group polarization, and groupthink?

T he view that humans are social creatures was expressed perhaps most clearly by the sixteenth-century English poet John Donne, who wrote *"no man is an island, sufficient unto himself."* We influence others and are influenced in turn by them. In this module we consider ways in which others influence our behavior and even our self-concepts. We examine the tendency to conform our behavior to social pressure, even when we consider such demands unreasonable or immoral. We examine situations where the presence of others may enhance our performance and those where it may not. We also consider destructive group influences in the form of mob behavior. Finally, we explore how group influences may affect decision making and sometimes lead to bad decisions.

Our Social Selves: "Who Are We?"

CONCEPT 16.31
Our social or group identity is an important part of our psychological identity or self-concept.

Many social psychologists separate psychological identity or self-concept into two parts: **personal identity** (individual identity) and **social identity** (group identity) (Brewer & Brown, 1998; Ellemers, Spears, & Doosje, 2002; Verkuyten, 2005). Your personal identity ("Who am I?") is the part of your psychological make-up that distinguishes you as a unique individual. You might think of yourself as a caring, creative person who likes pepperoni pizza, jazz, and sci-fi movies. Your social identity ("Who are we?") refers to your sense of yourself as a member of the various family, kinship, religious, national, and social groups to which you belong. You might refer to this part of your identity by saying, "I am a Catholic . . . I am a software developer . . . I am a Mexican American . . . I am Jonathan's dad."

Our social identity converts the "I" to the "we." Social psychologists believe that humans have a fundamental need to be members of groups, in other words, to belong (Baumeister & Leary, 1995). Our social identity tends to rub off on our self-esteem. We are likely to feel better about ourselves when someone of the same ethnicity, religion, or even locality accomplishes something special.

Social identity is generally a more prominent part of one's psychological identity in collectivist cultures, such as those in the Far East, than it is in individualistic societies in the West (Fiske et al., 1998; Markus & Kitayama, 1991; Triandis & Gelfand, 1998). As already discussed, in collectivist cultures, individuals have a stronger desire to fulfill their social obligations to the group, whereas Western societies emphasize a more individualistic or autonomous sense of self. People in Western cultures tend to define themselves less by what they share in common with others and more in terms of their unique abilities, interests, and attributes. They expect to stand out from the crowd—being themselves means becoming unique individuals. Yet there are variations within Western cultures. Women tend to place a greater emphasis on an interdependent sense of self—defining themselves more in terms of their roles as mothers, wives, daughters, and so on, while men tend to have a more independent sense of self (Cross & Madson, 1997).

personal identity The part of our psychological identity that involves our sense of ourselves as unique individuals.

social identity The part of our psychological identity that involves our sense of ourselves as members of particular groups. Also called *group identity*.

Figure 16.5 What Does it Mean to Be an American?
What it means to be an American varies with the ethnicity of the respondent. In this study, Chinese American students mentioned customs and traditions more often, and ethnic diversity less often, than European American students.

Source: Adapted from Tsai et al., 2002.

Online Study Center
Improve your Grade
Tutorials: Common Sense Test—Conformity

Social identity also varies along ethnic lines. Recently, investigators posed the question, "What does it mean to be an American?" to groups of Chinese American and European American students in the San Francisco Bay area (Tsai et al., 2002). As seen in Figure 16.5, Chinese Americans referred to customs and traditions more and to ethnic diversity less than did European Americans. No group differences emerged for the dimension of political ideology.

We can also distinguish in our own culture between the collectivist and family-centered tendencies of African Americans and the individualistic tendencies of White European Americans (Gaines et al., 1997; Oyserman, Gant, & Ager, 1995). African Americans and other ethnic minorities in the United States, such as Hispanic Americans and Asian Americans, tend to endorse more of a "we-orientation" in contrast to the "me-orientation" that is prominent among European Americans. These differences reflect distinctions between the cultures from which we trace our heritage, such as the traditional individualistic cultures of Western Europe versus the more communalistic cultures of Africa, Latin America, and Asia. The traditional African cultural heritage, for instance, emphasizes social connectedness and responsibility to others, and it promotes interdependence among members of the same group or tribe (Boykin & Ellison, 1995). Yet some observers believe that the history of oppression and discrimination faced by ethnic minority groups in the United States has led them to form stronger psychological, political, and economic bonds to members of their own groups—to find "strength in numbers" in order to survive in a culture that has traditionally mistreated and abused them.

CONCEPT 16.32
When we conform, we behave in ways that adhere to social norms.

Conformity: Bending the "I" to Fit the "We"

You would not get arrested if you arrived at work in your pajamas, but you probably would hear some snickering comments or be asked to go home and change. We are expected to conform our behavior to prevailing social standards or norms. Though social norms don't carry the force of law, violation of these standards can incur social disapproval. If we deviate too far from social standards, we might even lose our friends or jobs or alienate our family members.

Conformity affects many aspects of our daily behavior, from the clothes we wear for specific occasions, to the custom of covering our mouths and saying "excuse me" when we sneeze, to choosing a college to attend ("You're going to State, like your brother, right?"). Conformity pressures may also lead us to date or even marry the kinds of persons whom others deem acceptable.

We conform not only to general social norms but also to group or peer norms. Young people who color their hair purple may not be conforming to the standards of mainstream society, but they are conforming to those of their peer group—just as their parents are to their own.

conformity The tendency to adjust one's behavior to actual or perceived social pressures.

Participant in Asch Experiment The person third from the right in the photograph is the actual participant. The other individuals are confederates of the experimenter. The participant is asked to indicate which of three lines matches a standard line after the others in the room have unanimously given the wrong response.

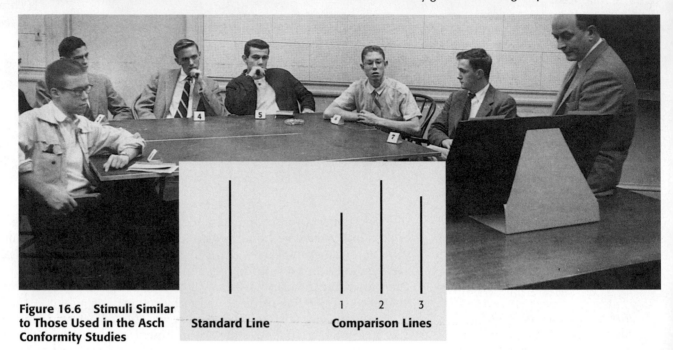

Figure 16.6 Stimuli Similar to Those Used in the Asch Conformity Studies

Standard Line   Comparison Lines

1   2   3

CONCEPT 16.33
People are more likely to conform than they might think, even to the extent of claiming that something is true when they know it to be false.

We might consider ourselves to be free thinkers who can resist pressures to conform when we don't see eye-to-eye with others. But the results of a classic study by psychologist Solomon Asch (1956) lead us to recognize that we may conform more than we think. Asch set out to study independence, not conformity. He believed that if participants in the study were faced with a unanimous group judgment that was obviously false, they would stick to their guns, resist pressures to conform, and report the correct information. He was wrong.

Asch placed individuals in a group consisting of people who were actually in league with the experimenter. The group was presented with the task of choosing the one line among a group of three that was the same length as a test line (see Figure 16.6). But the twist was that the other group members—all confederates of the experimenter—unanimously made the wrong choice. Now it was the individual's turn. Would the person go along with the group and make an obviously incorrect choice? Asch was surprised by the results. Bowing under the pressure to conform, the college students who participated in Asch's studies followed the incorrect majority by giving wrong answers more than one-third of the time.

CONCEPT 16.34
Many factors influence conformity, including personal and situational characteristics.

Why Do Some People Conform More than Others? Why were people so willing to conform in the Asch experiment, even to the extent of claiming that something was true when it was obviously false? Subsequent research has established at least three reasons: (1) people assume the majority must be correct; (2) they are so concerned about being liked by the group that they don't care whether their judgments were correct; (3) they feel it is easier to go along with the group than to risk ridicule by disagreeing (Cialdini & Trost, 1998; Nowak et al., 2003). Even so, some groups of people are more susceptible to pressures to conform than others (Cialdini & Trost, 1998). Women, by a small margin, are more likely to conform than men. People from collectivist cultures such as China tend to conform more than people from individualistic cultures such as the United States, Canada, and Great Britain. And conformity is greater among people with low self-esteem, social shyness, and a strong desire to be liked by the group. More generally, conformity tends to decline with age from childhood through older adulthood (Pasupathi, 1999).

Conformity is also influenced by situational factors. In the Asch paradigm, people were more likely to conform when they were required to disclose their responses publicly rather than privately, when the size of the group increased to about four or five people (beyond that number, conformity leveled off with increasing group size), and when more ambiguous stimuli were used (Bond & Smith, 1996; Cialdini & Trost, 1998). Yet just one dissenting voice in the group—one fellow traveler down the road of defection—can override group influence, regardless of the size of the group (Morris, Miller, & Spangenberg, 1977).

Asch believed that conformity can stifle individuality and independence. Yet some degree of conformity may help groups to function more smoothly. After all, sneezing on someone might be taken as a social affront; covering our noses and mouths and saying "excuse me" afterward shows respect for other people's rights.

Compliance: Doing What Others Want You to Do

Compliance is the process of acceding to the requests or demands of others (Cialdini & & Goldstein, 2004). One factor influencing compliance is authority. Appeals from a recognized authority figure are often extremely influential. You may be more willing to follow your doctor's advice about making changes in your diet than advice from your next-door neighbor. Another factor is **social validation**. We tend to use the actions of others as a standard or social norm for judging the appropriateness of our own behavior (Cialdini & & Goldstein, 2004). Thus, we are more likely to donate to a charity appeal if we find out that other people in the office are giving than if they are not. The desire for consistency is another important determinant of compliance. Salespeople, advertisers, fundraisers, and others try to get us to comply with their requests by using consistency to their advantage.

Several market-honed techniques succeed because they first obtain a person's commitment to a particular course of action that is consistent with a later requested action Here are three examples.

1. *Foot-in-the-door technique.* In the **foot-in-the door technique**, the person making an appeal first asks for a small favor that will almost certainly be granted. After obtaining initial compliance, the person raises the ante by asking for a larger, related favor. Evidence shows that people who agree to smaller requests are more likely to comply with larger ones, apparently because of the desire for consistency (Cialdini & Trost, 1998). In an early example, Patricia Pliner and her colleagues (1974) showed that people who agreed to wear a lapel pin promoting a local charity were subsequently more willing to make a monetary

---

CONCEPT 16.35
The need for social validation and the need for consistency are important determinants of compliance.

compliance   The tendency to accede to the requests or demands of others.
social validation   The tendency to use other people's behavior as a standard for judging the appropriateness of one's own behavior.
foot-in-the-door technique   A compliance technique based on securing compliance with a smaller request as a prelude to making a larger request.

donation to the charity. Yet investigators find that only those people with a strong preference for consistency show evidence of the foot-in-the-door effect (Cialdini, Trost, & Newsom, 1995).

2. *Bait-and-switch technique.* In the **bait-and-switch technique**, a marketer advertises merchandise at an usually low price. When people come to buy the merchandise, they learn that it is actually of inferior quality or is sold out or back-ordered. Then comes the switch, as they are shown more expensive merchandise for sale. Here again the person making the pitch capitalizes on the desire for consistency. Prospective buyers who expressed an initial interest in the merchandise are often more receptive to buying more expensive merchandise than they would be otherwise (Joule, Gouilloux, & Weber, 1989).

3. *Low-ball technique.* A car salesperson offers you an attractive price, only to pull the offer minutes later, claiming the sales manager couldn't approve it or the allowance offered for your trade-in came in lower than expected. You are then offered a higher price, which the salesperson swears is the best possible price. This is the **low-ball technique** at work. Committing yourself to the prior action of accepting a lower price may make you more likely to follow through on the subsequent, more costly action.

Another tactic designed to gain compliance is the **door-in-the-face technique** (Cialdini & Goldstein, 2004). First comes a large unreasonable request, which is rejected out of hand. Then the person making the request offers a lesser alternative in the form of a smaller request, which is actually what the person wanted in the first place. This smaller request is more likely to be accepted following rejection of the larger, unreasonable request than it would be had it been presented first. Why? Recall the concept of *reciprocity*. When requesters appear willing to compromise by withdrawing the original request in favor of a smaller one, people receiving the request may feel obliged to reciprocate by becoming more accommodating themselves. The Try This Out feature on the following page invites you to find ways to combat these various manipulative sales techniques.

Obedience to Authority: When Does It Go Too Far?

The study of **obedience** to authority has implications that go far beyond psychology. The atrocities of the Nazi regime in Germany preceding and during World War II raised disturbing questions about the tendency of soldiers and even ordinary citizens to obey authority figures in the commission of horrific acts. Many individuals, including civilians, participated in the Holocaust—the systematic genocide of the Jewish population of Europe. When later called to account for their deeds, many Nazis claimed they were "only following orders." Years afterward, American soldiers who participated in a massacre of civilians in the village of My Lai during the Vietnam War would offer a similar defense.

Yale University psychologist Stanley Milgram developed a unique and controversial research program to find out whether ordinary Americans would perform clearly immoral actions if they were instructed to do so. Participants in these studies were residents of New Haven, Connecticut, and surrounding areas who answered newspaper ads requesting participants for studies on learning and memory. They ranged in age from 20 to 50 and included teachers, engineers, salespeople, and laborers. Some were college graduates; others had not even completed elementary school. When they arrived at the lab, they were told that they would be participating in a study designed to test the effects of punishment on learning, based on the theory that people learn to perform correct responses when they are punished for making a mistake (Blass, 2004). They would play the role of a "teacher." Another person to whom they were introduced would be the "learner."

Online Study Center
Improve Your Grade
Tutorials: Your Grade: How Far Would You Go?

bait-and-switch technique A compliance technique based on "baiting" an individual by making an unrealistically attractive offer and then replacing it with a less attractive offer.

low-ball technique A compliance technique based on obtaining a person's initial agreement to purchase an item at a lower price before revealing hidden costs that raise the ultimate price.

door-in-the-face technique A compliance technique in which refusal of a large unreasonable request is followed by a smaller, more reasonable request.

obedience Compliance with commands or orders issued by others, usually persons in a position of authority.

TRY THIS OUT

What Do You Say Now?

You are in the market for a new car. The salesperson shows you a model you like, and after haggling for a while, you settle on a price that seems fair to you. The salesperson then says, "Let me get this approved by my manager and I'll be right back." What would you say to protect yourself against the types of influence tactics described in the text? For each of the following examples, write your response in the column provided below. Then compare your answers with some sample responses you'll find at the end of the chapter.

Type of Tactic	What the Salesperson Says	What Do You Say Now?
Low-ball technique	"I'm sorry. He says we can't let it go for this amount. It has nothing to do with you, but he's getting more pressure from the boss. Maybe if we went back to him with another two or three hundred dollars, he'd accept it."	_____ _____ _____
Bait-and-switch technique	"My manager tells me that we're having difficulty placing orders for that model. Something to do with a strike in Osaka. We can definitely get the LX version, however. It's got some great features."	_____ _____ _____
Foot-in-the-door technique	"Okay, we can get you the car." After completing some of the paperwork, the salesman slips in the following comment: "You know, you really should think about this factory-installed security system. You can never be too safe these days."	_____ _____ _____

CONCEPT 16.36

In the classic Milgram studies of obedience, ordinary people were willing to obey the dictates of an external authority even to the extent of inflicting what they believed were serious and even dangerous shocks to other supposed participants.

The learner was seated in one room, the teacher in an adjoining room. The teacher was placed in front of a console that was described as a device for administering electric shocks to the learner. The console consisted of a series of levers with labels indicating increasingly intense shock levels. The highest levels were labeled simply but ominously as "XXX" (Blass, 2004). The learner was presented with a list of word pairs to memorize. Then one word in each pair was presented and the learner's task was to respond with the correct word with which it had been paired in the list. The teacher was instructed that following each incorrect response from the learner, he was to deliver an electric shock. With each additional error, the voltage of the shock was to increase to the next shock level. To persuade teachers that the shock machine was genuine, they were administered a mild electric shock.

Unbeknown to the teachers, the learners were confederates of the experimenter. It was all part of an elaborate ruse. The experiment was not actually intended to study learning. What it tested was the teacher's willingness to inflict pain on another person when instructed to do so. No actual shocks were given, other than the sample shock the teacher received. The learner's incorrect responses were all predetermined. But to the "teachers," it was all too real.

Each teacher was informed that while the shocks might be extremely painful they would cause "no permanent tissue damage" to the learner. As the number of errors mounted, the teacher was instructed to increase the voltage until it reached the "danger" level. Most teachers were visibly upset when given the order to raise the shock level to apparently hazardous levels. When they hesitated, the experimenter used a series of prompts, including "Please go on," "The experiment requires that you go on" and, "You have no other choice, you *must* go on."

"Learner" in Milgram Experiment
The participant is led to believe that the "learner," as shown here, receives actual electric shocks following each wrong answer. If you were a participant, would you have obeyed the experimenter even as the learner cried out for help?

The results were disturbing (Milgram, 1963, 1974). Of the forty original participants, twenty-six out of forty (65 percent) obeyed every order, including the one to deliver the highest voltage shocks—the ones labeled "XXX" (Blass, 2004).

In a variation in which participants themselves did not throw the switch activating the shock but instructed others (actually confederates) to do so, the rate of obedience rose to 92.5 percent (Meeus & Raaijmakers, 1995). Placing the learner in the same room as the participant reduced obedience, but 40 percent still obeyed. Milgram later obtained similar results with female participants and groups of college undergraduates (Milgram, 1974).

Some commentators believe that Milgram's findings reveal something about the potential in ordinary people for a type of behavior akin to that of the Nazis, the soldiers who were "only following orders" when they committed the My Lai massacre, even the mass suicides at the behest of cult leaders (Elms, 1995; Miller, Collins, & Brief, 1995). Perhaps Milgram's studies teach us how good people can commit bad deeds in situations where they are led to blindly follow authority. In fact, Milgram conducted his study because he wanted to better understand the Holocaust (see the Pioneers box on the following page). Yet critics question the relevance of applying Milgram's findings on obedience of laboratory participants to explaining the kind of destructive obedience found in Nazi Germany and other real-life atrocities (Mastroianni, 2002).

Milgram's studies provoked controversy on other grounds as well, much of it concerning the ethics of deceiving participants in research studies and the emotional aftereffects of raising people's awareness that they were capable of such behavior (Goode, 2000d; Jones, 1998). Ethical issues raised by the Milgram experiments played a large part in the American Psychological Association's adoption of a set of ethical guidelines to protect the welfare of participants in psychological research. (See Chapter 1 for a discussion of ethical principles.)

CONCEPT 16.37
The willingness to obey immoral commands may arise from the legitimization of authority.

legitimization of authority The tendency to grant legitimacy to the orders or commands of persons in authority.

Why Do People Obey Immoral Commands? The **legitimization of authority** is one explanation for the behavior of participants in Milgram's studies. We are taught from an early age to obey authority figures such as parents and teachers and not to question or second-guess them. This early socialization prepares us to comply when directed to do so by a legitimate authority figure, be it a police officer, government or military official, or a scientist. Another likely reason for obedience is *social comparison*. Milgram's participants may have lacked any basis for knowing what other people would do in a similar situation. The only basis for social com-

THE PIONEERS | The Man Who Shocked the World

Stanley Milgram

Stanley Milgram was born in the Bronx, New York, in 1933, the son of Jewish immigrants from Eastern Europe. Stanley excelled in school and achieved an IQ score of 158, the highest score among his high school schoolmates. He went on to attend Harvard University, where he studied with the famed personality theorist Gordon Allport (see Chapter 12) and with a visiting professor, the social psychologist Solomon Asch. Asch's work on conformity had a profound influence on the young Milgram, who devoted his dissertation study to studying national differences in conformity between people from Norway and France. But when Milgram graduated and embarked upon an academic career in the early 1960s, he knew he needed to develop an important and distinctive research program to call his own. His decision to study obedience was rooted in his Jewish heritage and his de-termination to better understand the atrocities of the Holocaust. Milgram later wrote,

> [My] laboratory paradigm . . . gave scientific expres-sion to a more general concern about authority, a concern forced upon members of my generation, in particular upon Jews such as myself, by the atrocities of World War II. . . . The impact of the Holocaust on my own psyche energized my interest in obedience and shaped the particular form in which it was examined. (quoted in Blass, 2004, p. 62)

Milgram developed an experimental paradigm in which ordinary people were prodded by an experimenter to in-flict on others what they were led to believe were painful electric shocks. The fundamental question Milgram would ask was, "Just how far *would* a person go under the ex-perimenter's orders? (Blass, 2004, p. 62).

Source: Adapted from The Man Who Shocked the World by Thomas Blass (Basic Books, 2004).

parison was the example set by the experimenter. For people in Nazi Germany, seeing respected others perform atrocities may have served to legitimize their activities not only as socially acceptable but, more disturbingly, as admirable. The foot-in-the-door effect may also apply. People are generally more willing to comply with more extreme requests once they have shown a willingness to comply with lesser requests. Once participants began to deliver shocks to "learners," they may have found it increasingly difficult to stop—just as soldiers who have been trained to respond unstintingly to commands may not hesitate to follow orders, even immoral ones.

Evaluating Milgram's Legacy   The scientific jury is still out regarding the ultimate significance of Milgram's findings. Ethical concerns about his procedure make it virtually impossible for similar research to be performed in any educational or re-search institution, at least in the United States. His findings stand etched in time as a reminder to us to look inward to our capacity for blind and destructive obedi-ence. As some have observed, the Milgram studies may indicate that we do *too good* a job at socializing young people to be obedient to authority (Vecchio, 1997). Per-haps more emphasis should be placed on personal responsibility for one's actions, a teaching that might go a long way toward preventing destructive obedience.

Now we consider ways in which the presence of groups may influence indi-vidual performance—for better or worse.

Social Facilitation and Social Loafing: When Are You Most Likely to Do Your Best?

social facilitation   The tendency to work better or harder in the presence of others than when alone.

Do you perform better when you work in front of others? **Social facilitation** refers to the tendency for people to work better or harder when they work in the pres-

The presence of others may enhance individual performance on simple tasks but impair performance on more complex tasks.

ence of others than when they work alone. The presence of others might be perceived as a threat or a challenge, which in turn may energize one to perform better (Blascovich, Mendes, Hunter, & Saloman,1999). But the presence of others does not necessarily *improve* performance. The presence of others typically enhances performance of overlearned, familiar tasks (Nowak, Vallacher, & Miller, 2003). But it can decrease performance on novel or difficult tasks. So, if you are a good typist, you may type faster when others are present than when you are alone. But if you need to solve complex math problems, having an audience would likely slow your performance.

Bernd Schmitt and his colleagues (1986) had participants perform either a simple typing task (typing their own names) or a complex typing task (typing their names backward while inserting numbers in ascending order between every two letters). As expected, the presence of others during completion of the task was associated with faster performance of the simple task but slower performance of the more difficult task (see Figure 16.7).

CONCEPT 16.39
In social loafing, people fail to pull their own weight because they believe others will pick up the slack.

Social loafing is the tendency for people to apply less effort when they work as members of a group than when they work on their own. Perhaps you have observed social loafing in work that you did as part of a team effort. Did one or more members of the team fail to apply themselves as much as they could?

Underlying social loafing is the tendency for people to conserve individual effort when they expect that other team members will pick up the slack (Plaks & Higgins, 2000). But social loafing is not inevitable. It is more likely to occur when individual performance is not evaluated. It can be reduced in several ways, including the following (Kerr & Tindale, 2004; Levine & Moreland, 1998; Nowak, Vallacher, & Miller, 2003):

- Making tasks more interesting or challenging
- Making each member's contribution more visible
- Increasing one's responsibility to the group
- Holding each member accountable for his or her own contributions
- Giving public feedback of individual performance.

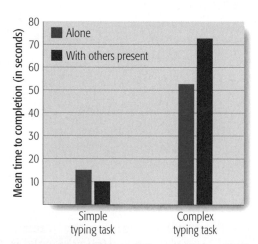

Figure 16.7 Effects of the Presence of Others
The presence of others facilitated the performance of a simple typing task, but it interfered with the performance of a complex typing task.

Source: Schmitt et al., 1986.

The Presence of Others: A Help or a Hindrance? The presence of others may impair performance of complex tasks but facilitate performance of simple or well-learned tasks.

social loafing The tendency to expend less effort when working as a member of a group than when working alone.

Mob Behavior: The Dangers of Losing Yourself in a Crowd

CONCEPT 16.40
People who are caught up in a mob may engage in behavior they might not otherwise commit.

Have you ever been so swept up in the actions of a crowd that you felt as though you'd momentarily lost your sense of individuality? This sense of losing self-awareness ("being lost in a crowd") is called **deindividuation**. Perhaps you experienced it while attending a football or baseball game and became part of a human "wave" that undulated through the spectators, or when everyone rose in unison when a football player on the home team made a diving catch in the end zone.

Deindividuation may be destructive when it loosens inhibitions that normally constrain deviant or reckless behavior and lead to mob behavior. We see the tragic results of mob behavior in race-related lynchings and looting during urban riots. Hate groups capitalize on deindividuation, even augmenting it by having members wear the same outfits or uniforms. The white sheets worn by members of the Ku Klux Klan promote a loss of individual identity and diffusion of responsibility that can foster unrestrained moblike behavior. Deindividuation appears to result from many factors, including *anonymity* (becoming part of a large, unstructured group), *shifting attention* from one's own thoughts and personal standards to the actions of the group, and *conforming* one's behavior to the social norms of the group or mob (Cialdini & Goldstein, 2004; Nowak, Vallacher, & Miller, 2003).

We can resist destructive forms of deindividuation by stopping to focus on our internal standards when we are caught up in the actions of a crowd and by taking steps to maintain our individuality, such as refusing to hide our personal identities.

Group Decision Making: A Help or a Hindrance?

CONCEPT 16.41
Group biases arising from group decision-making processes, such as group polarization and groupthink, may foster more extreme views among group members.

Are decisions made by groups such as committees, councils, and executive boards more level-headed than those made by individuals? In some circumstances, group members can bounce ideas off each other (a form of group brainstorming) that may energize creative thinking and enhance problem solving (Brown & Paulus, 2002; Paulus &Yang, 2000) (see Try This Out below). Group discussion may also lead group members to think more alike about issues similar to those that are discussed (Stasson & Hawkes, 1995). And group decision making may avoid the pitfalls of

Online Study Center
Improve Your Grade
Tutorials: Group Processes

TRY THIS OUT

Brainwriting

We noted how group brainstorming may energize creative thinking by providing a forum in which people can bounce ideas off each other. But some people hesitate to express themselves openly in a group out of fear of negative evaluation. Brainwriting is a written form of brainstorming that eliminates the need for speaking up in the group. First a problem or question is put to a group of people. Each member of the group is instructed to write down an idea on a piece of paper and pass the paper along to the next group member, who in turn adds an additional idea and then passes it on to the next member in a round-robin fashion. Then all the ideas are read and discussed. Findings from a recent study showed that brainwriting resulted in more unique ideas than did individual writing (Paulus & Yang, 2000). Perhaps you can suggest this technique if you have the opportunity to participate in a problem-solving group.

deindividuation   The loss of self-awareness that may occur when one acts in concert with the actions of a crowd.

relying on any one individual's judgment. However, two types of group biases, *group polarization* and *groupthink,* may lead groups to make bad decisions.

Group Polarization: Going to Extremes   **Group polarization** is the tendency for group members to adopt views that are more extreme but in the same direction as their original views. Members who were slightly in favor of a particular point of view become more strongly committed to their original views; those who originally opposed a particular course of action become more committed in their opposition. Depending on the group's original orientation, the adoption of more extreme views may lead to riskier actions, a tendency called the **risky-shift phenomenon**. Or it may lead to more staunchly conservative actions. In either case, initial opinions may be hardened and alternative points discouraged.

Why does group polarization occur? One common reason is *social validation*. Since groups are often composed of people holding similar views, interactions with like-minded people allow individuals to express attitudes or arguments that echo their own, thus strengthening the confidence they have in their own attitudes. Another explanation is based on normative influences. Groups define the appropriate (or normative) level of strength that an attitude should have. When individuals discover that their own attitudes are less extreme than the group norm, they may strengthen their attitudes to conform to that norm.

CONCEPT 16.42
When groups tackle a problem, they may become so focused on reaching a consensus that they fail to critically examine the issues before them.

Groupthink: How Can Smart People Make Dumb Decisions?   This was the question President John Kennedy asked his advisers in the aftermath of the disastrous invasion of Cuba at the Bay of Pigs in 1961, when Cuban forces easily defeated a brigade of U.S.-backed Cuban exiles. Yale psychologist Irving Janis (1982, 1997) believed that stupidity wasn't the explanation. To Janis, the fault lay in a flawed approach to group decision making that he termed **groupthink**. Groupthink is the tendency for members of a group to become so concerned with reaching a consensus that they lose the ability to critically evaluate the problem before them. Groupthink can be likened to a kind of "tunnel vision" in which the group's perspective is limited to a single point of view (Nowak, Vallacher, & Miller, 2003).

In groupthink, the pressure to conform to majority opinion squelches any serious debate. Janis believed that groupthink is more likely to occur (1) when members are strongly attached to the group, (2) when an external threat is present, and (3) when there is a strong-minded leader directing the group. Group members may not want to "rock the boat" by expressing a dissenting opinion, or they may have a misplaced confidence that the leader and other group members must be right. Critics point out that research evidence supporting the groupthink model is mixed (Kerr & Tindale, 2004). Others question whether the groupthink model can account for high-level foreign policy decisions (Tetlock, 1998). But Janis's recommendations for avoiding the negative effects of groupthink are well worth considering at any level of decision making:

- Group members should be encouraged to consider all alternatives and carefully weigh the evidence on all sides of an issue.
- The group leader should avoid stating preferences as the group begins its work.
- Outsiders should be called upon to offer their opinions and analyses.
- Group members or outsiders should be encouraged to play the role of "devil's advocate."
- The group should be subdivided into smaller groups to independently review the issues that are before the larger group.
- Several group meetings should be held to reassess the situation and evaluate any new information before final decisions are reached.

Concept Chart 16.3 summarizes the group influences on behavior discussed in the text.

group polarization   The tendency for members of decision-making groups to shift toward more extreme views in whatever direction they were initially leaning.

risky-shift phenomenon   A type of group polarization effect in which group discussion leads to the adoption of a riskier course of action than the members would have endorsed initially.

groupthink   Janis's term for the tendency of members of a decision-making group to be more focused on reaching a consensus than on critically examining the issues at hand.

CONCEPT CHART 16.3   Group Influences on Identity and Behavior

Sources of Group Influence	Description
Conformity	Adherence to social standards or norms
Compliance	Acceding to demands or requests from others
Obedience	Adherence to the commands of external authority
Social facilitation	The improvement in performance that occurs when we perform in front of others
Social loafing	The impaired performance that occurs when our individual effort is obscured by a group effort
Deindividuation	The temporary loss of self-awareness in members of a crowd or mob, which may lead to a loosening of ordinary restraints on deviant conduct
Group polarization	The tendency for group members to adopt more extreme versions of their original views
Groupthink	The tendency for groups to emphasize consensus-building rather than thoughtful consideration of the issues

MODULE 16.3 REVIEW

Group Influences on Individual Behavior

RECITE IT

What is social identity?

• Social identity (also called group identity) is our social self—that part of our self-concept that relates to our family and social roles and the collective identities we share with members of our own religious, ethnic, fraternal, or national groups.

What was the significance of the Asch study on conformity?

• Asch showed that people often conform to group judgments, even when those judgments are obviously false.

What factors influence conformity?

• Factors influencing conformity include gender, cultural background, self-esteem, social shyness, desire to be liked by the group, age, and situational features such as public disclosure, group size, and stimulus ambiguity.

What principles are compliance techniques based upon?

• The foot-in-the-door technique, bait-and-switch technique, and low-ball technique are based on the desire for consistency. The door-in-the-face technique is based on reciprocity.

Why were Milgram's findings so disturbing, and why were his methods so controversial?

• Milgram found that people from various walks of life could be induced to obey unreasonable or even immoral commands given by an authority figure.

• The use of deception, as well as the potential emotional aftereffects of raising participants' awareness of their capabilities for such behavior, led to a storm of controversy over Milgram's methods.

How does the presence of others affect individual performance?

• The presence of others may improve performance in simple, well-learned tasks but impair performance in more complex tasks.

• People may also exert less than their best effort in a group task when they know others will pick up the slack and their performance will not be individually evaluated.

What are deindividuation, group polarization, and groupthink?

• Deindividuation, the loss of self-awareness that occurs when one becomes swept up in a crowd, can lead to diffusion of responsibility and loss of individuality, resulting in a loosening of constraints on reckless or deviant behavior.

• Group polarization and groupthink are sources of biases that affect group decision making. In group polarization, group members adopt more extreme versions of their original views. In groupthink, decisions derive from a desire for consensus rather than from a critical evaluation of the issues.

RECALL IT

1. Social identity is an important aspect of our psychological identity, but it is generally stronger in _____ cultures than in _____ cultures.

2. Match the following compliance techniques with the appropriate descriptions: i. foot-in-the-door; ii. bait-and-switch; iii. low-ball; iv. door-in-the-face
   a. Low price prompts consumer initial interest.
   b. Initial low price is later retracted by seller.
   c. Simple initial request is followed by related greater request.
   d. Initial substantial request is followed by lesser, more reasonable request.

3. The _____ of authority and the _____-in-the-door effect may help account for destructive obedience.

4. Social facilitation is likely to lead to _____ performance on simpler, well-known tasks and _____ performance on less familiar or more difficult tasks.
   a. enhanced, impaired   c. enhanced, enhanced
   b. impaired, enhanced   d. impaired, impaired

5. The experience of losing our individuality when we become part of a human "wave" at a sporting event is called
   a. deindividuation.   c. groupthink
   b. group polarization.   d. playing "devil's advocate."

THINK ABOUT IT

• Agree or disagree with this statement, and support your answer: "Had I been a participant in the Milgram study, I would have refused to comply with the experimenter's demands."

• Have you ever been subject to a manipulative sales tactic? Based on your reading of the text, how might you handle the situation differently if it should happen again?

APPLICATION MODULE 16.4
Psychology Goes to Work

CONCEPT 16.43
Industrial/organizational (I/O) psychology is the branch of psychology that studies people at work and the organizational structures in which they work.

Many of us spend more time interacting with others in the workplace than we do with our families or friends. *Industrial/organizational (I/O) psychology* is the branch of psychology that studies people at work and the organizations in which they work. I/O psychologists develop tests to find the most suitable workers for particular jobs, design equipment for optimum efficiency and safety, overcome obstacles to successful employment of workers with disabilities, and help companies develop management structures to maximize productivity and worker satisfaction. Have you worked in a job in which you received incentives or bonuses for meeting certain goals? How did these incentives motivate your work behavior? Answers to questions like these were provided by I/O psychologists who assisted companies in designing incentive programs to motivate workers (Society for Industrial and Organizational Psychology, 2001).

Here, let us examine two key areas of interest to I/O psychologists today: job satisfaction and adjustment to a changing workplace.

Understanding Job Satisfaction: It's Not Just About the Job

Job satisfaction—the degree to which workers have positive feelings toward their jobs—depends not only on the job itself but also on the personalities of the workers themselves (Gerhart, 2005; Staw & Cohen-Charash, 2005). Certainly some job-related characteristics have a bearing on job satisfaction, such as job status, good pay and fringe benefits, availability of childcare facilities, and opportunities to perform interesting and personally fulfilling work (e.g., Kossek & Ozeki, 1998; London-Vargas, 2001). But we've also learned that people with more cheerful dispositions tend to be happier with their jobs than are other people (Thoresen et al.,

2003). Moreover, people who are unhappy at one job tend to be unhappy at whatever job they hold (Judge & Hulin, 1993).

Personality traits such as self-esteem, self-efficacy, and emotional stability are associated with greater job satisfaction, whereas other traits, such as neuroticism, are associated with lower job satisfaction (Judge & Bono, 2001; Judge, Heller, & Mount, 2002). Investigators even find similar levels of job satisfaction among sets of identical twins raised apart (Keller et al., 1992). This evidence suggests that genetic influences may be at work in determining whether people like their jobs.

Job satisfaction may also depend on the fit between attributional style (a cognitive factor) and the amount of control people have at work (Hewlett, 2001). For many workers, the ability to have some control over the work they do reduces job-related stress and contributes to a more positive work experience. Having control over the job is also linked to better overall health and well-being (Spector, 2003). But a recent study shows that a subgroup of workers prefer not having control (Schaubroeck, Jones, & Xie, 2001). These workers possess a negative attributional style—namely, the tendency to blame themselves when things go wrong at work. They generally prefer jobs in which they lack control and so can avoid blaming themselves for negative work outcomes.

This research illustrates once again how important it is to think critically and avoid overgeneralizing. Recall our earlier discussion of the self-serving bias, which is the tendency of people to take credit for their successes and explain away their disappointments and failures. The self-serving bias protects self-esteem because disappointments are blamed on external factors rather than the self. Yet research on job satisfaction indicates that the self-serving bias isn't true of everyone. Some people have the opposite tendency, a negative attributional style in which they minimize their accomplishments and blame themselves for negative outcomes. In Chapter 13 we learned that people with a negative attributional style are also more likely than others to have low self-esteem and a greater proneness to depression. On the job, they tend to view negative outcomes as being their fault, especially when they control the work they do. For these people, investigators believe that having control on the job may actually create unhealthy levels of stress (Schaubroeck , Jones, & Xie, 2001). Research along these lines may have practical applications. Companies may find it useful to train workers for specific types of jobs on the basis of their attributional styles (Hewlett, 2001).

In a broader context, research on job satisfaction links different areas of research in psychology, including studies of personality, emotional well-being, genetic influences on behavior, and attributional styles. But does the psychological factor of job satisfaction have a bearing on traditional measures of work behavior? Job satisfaction is linked to lower rates of absenteeism, less employee turnover, and lower employee intentions of leaving their present jobs (e.g., Hellman, 1997; Sagie, 1998). But job satisfaction has only a modest relationship with job performance and worker productivity (e.g., Judge et al., 2001). Perhaps we shouldn't be surprised. Factors other than job satisfaction may play a more important role in determining job performance, such as fear of losing one's job or future raises or bonuses if one's performance begins to slide.

Psychologist Nashá London-Vargas (2001) suggests that our career choices have the potential to help us fulfill our basic values and life goals. Connecting work with our interests, passions, personal fulfillment, and need for challenges can help add meaning and value to our lives and those of others (see Table 16.1).

TABLE 16.1   Finding Your Dream Job

Is your work personally fulfilling? Does it allow you to pursue your dreams? Industrial-organizational psychologist Nashá London-Vargas (2001) offers some self-study questions to help determine whether your present (or perhaps future) job meets your personal needs, not just your financial obligations:

- Is your work connected to your interests or passions in life?

- Is it a vehicle to pursue your dreams?

- Do you have a passion about your work?

- How did you get to this job at this point in your life? Did you seek it, or did it find you?

- Are you satisfied each day from a job well done, or does your job leave you feeling unfulfilled or depressed?

Meeting the Challenges of a Changing Workplace

We have entered a new century that promises to bring major changes to the workplace. One likelihood is that the workplace will be less secure than in past generations. Even now, fewer companies are offering workers the long-term job security that their parents and grandparents enjoyed (McGuire, 1998). Rapid changes in technology may mean that jobs will be created and redesigned with dizzying speed. Advances in technology already allow workers to interact electronically with their home offices through e-mail, video conferencing, and wireless telephony.

Many work-related changes involve the way we work. Where is it written that people always perform best on a traditional nine-to-five schedule? Companies are increasingly restructuring the workday to allow more flextime (flexible work shifts) and increased off-site work, such as **telecommuting** (working at home) or working in customer worksites (Spector, 2003). An estimated 28 million Americans are telecommuters—people whose only office is at home (Belkin, 2003). The number of telecommuters has been rising rapidly and is expected to continue to rise in the years ahead. Many companies provide satellite offices or telework centers where telecommuting workers can drop in to perform work they cannot complete at home. One work model provides temporary office space in a central office for workers only as needed—much as they would check into a hotel when traveling (Pfeffer, 1998).

I/O psychologists can assist companies in shaping their organizational culture in ways that help them adapt to the changing workplace. **Organizational culture** is the system of shared values (what the organization deems important) and norms (rules and regulations for acceptable behavior) that exists within the organization (O'Reilly & Chatman, 1996). Though relationships between organizational culture and company performance are complex, I/O psychologists recognize that no one culture fits the needs of all organizations. Aware that companies must also adapt to the trend toward globalization and the need to interact with suppliers, manufacturers, and customers in many other cultures, I/O psychologists are helping companies develop a greater sensitivity to cultural differences and ways of working more effectively in today's global business environment.

The twenty-first-century workplace promises to become more entrepreneurial as well. Workers who succeed in the changing workplace will need to take increasing responsibility for their own career development (McGuire, 1998). Even workers who staff corporate offices and keep assembly lines humming will need continuing training to keep pace with changes in technology and job responsibilities. With populations continuing to age, we will also need to provide wider opportunities for older workers who are interested in working after retirement, including job-training programs that help them update their skills; for such older workers, we also need to redesign jobs to allow for more flexible work schedules (August & Quintero, 2001). I/O psychologists can help companies identify individuals who can work best in this changing work environment; they can also redesign that environment to best suit the needs of workers and employers in the new millennium.

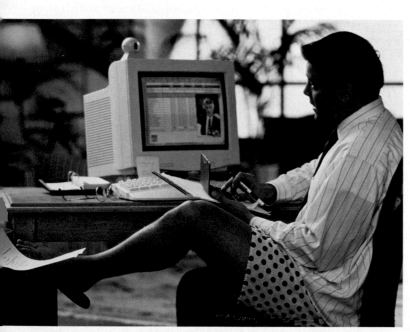

Pants Optional Advances in computer systems and telecommunications have enabled millions of American workers to able to work at home one or more days a week. Pants are optional.

telecommuting A form of working at home in which people communicate with their home office and clients via computer or telecommunications.

organizational culture The system of shared values and norms within an organization.

TYING IT TOGETHER

Social psychologists study how we relate to others in our social environment. They are concerned with how we perceive others and how our perceptions of others affect how we act toward them (Module 16.1). They are also concerned with positive forms of relating, such as attraction and helping, and negative forms of relating, such as prejudice and aggression (Module 16.2). The study of social psychology also encompasses how people are influenced by the groups with which they interact (Module 16.3). We influence others and are influenced in turn by them. For many of us, the groups with which we interact the most consist of people with whom we work. The study of people at work and the organizations in which they work is the province of the applied area of psychology called industrial/organizational (I/O) psychology (Module 16.4).

Thinking Critically About Psychology

Based on your reading of the chapter, answer the following question. Then, to evaluate your progress in developing critical thinking skills, compare your answer with the sample answer found in Appendix A.

Why didn't they help? Thirty-eight people reportedly witnessed Kitty Genovese being stabbed to death but did nothing. Based on your reading of the factors influencing helping behavior, speculate on the reasons why these bystanders failed to help.

Key Terms

social psychology *(p. 616)*
social perception *(p. 616)*
impression formation *(p. 616)*
social schema *(p. 616)*
stereotypes *(p. 617)*
self-fulfilling prophecy *(p. 617)*
attribution *(p. 618)*
dispositional causes *(p. 618)*
situational causes *(p. 618)*
fundamental attribution error *(p. 618)*
actor-observer effect *(p. 619)*
self-serving bias *(p. 619)*
attitude *(p. 619)*
elaboration likelihood model (ELM) *(p. 621)*
attraction *(p. 624)*
matching hypothesis *(p. 627)*
proximity *(p. 627)*
reciprocity *(p. 627)*

prosocial behavior *(p. 628)*
bystander intervention *(p. 628)*
social norms *(p. 630)*
prejudice *(p. 630)*
discrimination *(p. 630)*
in-groups *(p. 631)*
out-groups *(p. 631)*
out-group negativism *(p. 631)*
in-group favoritism *(p. 631)*
out-group homogeneity *(p. 631)*
authoritarian personality *(p. 632)*
contact hypothesis *(p. 632)*
frustration *(p. 636)*
racism *(p. 637)*
stereotype threat *(p. 638)*
personal identity *(p. 640)*
social identity *(p. 640)*
conformity *(p. 641)*
compliance *(p. 643)*

social validation *(p. 643)*
foot-in-the-door technique *(p. 643)*
bait-and-switch technique *(p. 644)*
low-ball technique *(p. 644)*
door-in-the-face technique *(p. 644)*
obedience *(p. 644)*
legitimization of authority *(p. 646)*
social facilitation *(p. 647)*
social loafing *(p. 648)*
deindividuation *(p. 649)*
group polarization *(p. 650)*
risky-shift phenomenon *(p. 650)*
groupthink *(p. 650)*
telecommuting *(p. 654)*
organizational culture *(p. 654)*

ANSWERS TO RECALL IT QUESTIONS

Module 16.1: 1. a; 2. attributions; 3. dispositional, situational; 4. b; 5. i. b, ii. d, iii. a, iv. c.

Module 16.2: 1. similarity, physical attractiveness, proximity, reciprocity; 2. similarity; 3. The correct order is d, b, a, e, c; 4. (a) biased beliefs and stereotypes, (b) feelings of dislike toward target, (c) discrimination; 5. social and institutional support, acquaintance potential, equal status, intergroup cooperation.

Module 16.3: 1. collectivistic, individualistic; 2. i. c, ii. a, iii. b, iv. d; 3. legitimatization, foot; 4. a; 5. a.

SAMPLE RESPONSES TO TRY THIS OUT *(P. 645)*

• *Low-ball technique:* You might say, "Sorry, that's my best offer. We agreed on a price and I expect you to stick to it."

• *Bait-and-switch technique:* You might say, "If I wanted the LX version I would have asked for it. If you're having difficulty getting the car I want, then it's your problem. Now, what are you going to do for me?"

• *Foot-in-the-door technique:* You might say, "If you want to lower the price of the car, we can talk about it. But the price I gave you is all I can afford to spend."

Appendix A
Sample Answers to Thinking Critically About Psychology Questions

Chapter 1 Introduction to Psychology and Methods of Research

1. Unfortunately, a basic flaw in the research design casts serious doubt on the experimenter's conclusions. The experimenter did not use random assignment as the basis for assigning subjects to the experimental (sleep learning) or control (nonparticipating) groups. Rather, students who responded to the invitation to participate constituted the experimental group, and the control group was selected from nonparticipating students from the same class. Lacking random assignment, we have no way of knowing whether differences between the two groups were due to the independent variable (sleep learning) or to the characteristics of subjects comprising these groups.

2. In the absence of random assignment, it is conceivable that the more motivated and committed students opted to participate and that these students would have achieved higher test grades than the nonparticipating students, whether they had participated in the sleep learning study or not.

3. To provide a fairer test of the sleep learning method, the experimenter should have randomly assigned students to experimental and control groups. Experimenters use random assignment to equate groups on differences that may exist among individuals in level of ability or other subject characteristics.

Chapter 2 Biological Foundations of Behavior

1. Fortunately for Gage, the rod that penetrated his skull did not damage structures in the brainstem that control basic bodily processes, such as breathing and heart rate. However, the rod did damage the prefrontal cortex, the part of the brain responsible for personality and other higher mental functions.

2. The prefrontal cortex, which was damaged in the accident, helps us weigh the consequences of our actions and inhibit impulsive behaviors, including aggressive behaviors.

Chapter 3 Sensation and Perception

1. The woman located an area on the map where the missing man might be found. But her success at locating the missing man could be explained in a number of ways other than ESP. It could have been a lucky guess. Or perhaps the woman used the process of elimination to systematically narrow the possible search areas by ruling out those in which the police had already focused their efforts. Or perhaps she arrived at a possible location by identifying areas where a person would be likely to have wandered off. What other explanations can you generate that do not rely on positing the existence of ESP?

2. To evaluate whether the woman's predictions were likely to have been mere chance events, we would need to know how often her predictions turn out to be right. In other words, we'd need to know whether her success rate significantly exceeds chance expectations. But even if she turned out to be right more often than you would expect by chance alone, we still couldn't conclude that her success was attributable to ESP rather than to more conventional explanations.

Chapter 4 Consciousness

1. No, the evidence does not directly demonstrate that ethnicity or race is the differentiating factor in rates of drug use. Statistics comparing rates of drug use in ethnic or racial groups may be misleading if they fail to take into account possible confounding factors, such as differences between groups in education and income levels or characteristics of the neighborhoods in which people of different ethnic or racial groups may live.

2. African Americans have disproportionately high rates of unemployment, and people who are unemployed tend to abuse drugs more often. Blacks and other ethnic minorities are also more likely than Whites to be poor and to live in socially distressed neighborhoods. People living under such conditions are more likely to use drugs than are more affluent people who live in more secure neighborhoods. Investigators who controlled for differences in types of neighborhoods found that African Americans are no more likely than (non-Hispanic) Whites to use crack cocaine (USDHHS, 1999). Moreover, investigators who controlled for education and income level found that Black Americans are actually less likely than White Americans to develop alcohol or drug dependence problems (Anthony, Warner, & Kessler, 1994).

Chapter 5 Learning

1. the poison; 2. the sheep meat; 3. nauseating sickness; 4. taste aversion to sheep meat

Chapter 6 Memory

1. It is likely that the second man rehearsed the information by repeating the license plate number to himself a number of times. Acoustic rehearsal is generally a more efficient method of holding information in short-term memory and transferring it to long-term memory than trying to retain a visual image of the stimulus in mind.

2. The woman apparently had memorized the song phonologically (by sound) rather than semantically (by meaning).

3. Pronouncing the letters comprising the word S-H-O-P serves as a priming stimulus that increases the likelihood of responding with the similar sounding word STOP, even though it is an incorrect response to the question.

Chapter 7 Thinking, Language, and Intelligence

1a. The shepherd led the sheep to reverse direction and move back behind the ambulance, thus freeing the ambulance to move ahead without obstruction.

1b. The medical technician relied on a mental set for making one's way past a crowd.

2a. The availability heuristic and the representativeness heuristic may help explain John's poor investment decisions. The availability heuristic applies when we base our decisions on whatever happens to come most readily to mind—in John's case, the news reports of the day or comments he hears from others. When using the representativeness heuristic, we treat small samples of occurrences as though they were representative of occurrences in general. An individual news report about a company may be a poor indication of the company's overall financial health or future prospects. Comments from others may be even less trustworthy as a basis for making sound investment decisions.

2b. As John's investment adviser, you should probably recommend that he adopt a sound investment strategy and stick to it rather than basing his investment decisions on daily news reports or passing comments from others.

Chapter 8 Motivation and Emotion

1. Sternberg's model conceptualizes love as having three basic components: intimacy, passion, and decision/commitment. Amanda's and Craig's love components are both high in passion (strong sexual desire for one another), but they're mismatched on intimacy and decision/commitment. Amanda desires more intimacy (emotional disclosure) but Craig seems to hold back. At the same time, Craig is ready to make a commitment to date Amanda exclusively, but she remains unsure.

2. This relationship appears to be shaky because of differences in intimacy and decision/commitment. By discussing the parts of the relationship they feel are working (passionate component) and those that are not (intimacy and decision/commitment), Amanda and Craig may be able to explore ways of meeting each other's needs to bring their love triangles closer together.

Chapter 9 Child Development

1. Three-year-old children like Trevor show a type of thinking pattern that Piaget called animistic thinking—the tendency to attribute human qualities to inanimate objects, such as the sun and the clouds. To Trevor, the sun has feelings ("gets sleepy") and engages in behaviors ("goes to sleep"), just as people do.

Chapter 10 Adolescence and Adulthood

1. To determine your identity status, you first need to decide whether you have achieved a commitment in each area (i.e., occupational choice, political and moral beliefs). A commitment represents either the adoption of a relatively firm set of beliefs or the pursuit of a course of action consistently over time. Critical thinkers weigh the validity of claims in terms of the evidence at hand—in this case, claims of achieving a commitment. What evidence would you seek to support these claims? Here are some examples of the types of criteria you may wish to apply:

- Showing evidence in your actions and pronouncement to others of a relatively permanent or unswerving commitment to an occupational choice, political philosophy, or set of moral values.

- Being able to describe your beliefs or actions in an organized and meaningful way.

- Pursuing a course of action consistent with your career choice and your political and moral beliefs or values.

2. Now you need to carefully evaluate whether you experienced an identity crisis to arrive at any of the commitments you have achieved. Bearing in mind, again, that critical thinkers weigh the evidence at hand, consider that evidence of an identity crisis might be based on meeting the following criteria:

- Having undergone a serious examination of alternatives before arriving at a commitment (or are now undergoing this serious examination).

- Having devoted a serious effort to arriving at a commitment (or are now devoting a serious effort).

- Having gathered information (or are now gathering information) to seriously evaluate different points of view or courses of action.

Classify yourself in the *identity achievement* status in a given area (career choice, political and moral beliefs) if you have developed a commitment to a set of beliefs or a course of action and underwent an identity crisis to arrive at this commitment. Place yourself in the *moratorium* status if you are presently in a state of identity crisis and are making active efforts to arrive at a commitment. Place yourself in the *foreclosure* category if you arrived at a commitment without having experienced an identity crisis. Classify yourself in the *identity diffusion* category if you have neither achieved a commitment (i.e., currently lack a clear career course or a firmly held set of beliefs or values) nor are currently struggling to arrive at one.

Chapter 11 Gender and Sexuality

1. Homosexuality is a type of sexual orientation in which one's erotic attraction and choice of partners are directed toward members of one's own sex. It is not a statement about one's gender identity, or sense of maleness or femaleness. In transsexualism, by contrast, there is a mismatch between one's gender identity and one's anatomic sex. Gay males and lesbians prefer having partners of the same gender as themselves, but their gender identity is consistent with their anatomic sex.

2. Since an erection is an involuntary reflex, it cannot be forced or willed. Thus John may be making it more difficult to achieve an erection by focusing his attention on his penis rather than on his partner. As a result, he is likely to become less aroused and more anxious.

Chapter 12 Personality

The confirmation bias leads us to give credence to information that confirms our preexisting beliefs and to ignore contrary evidence. Thus, for example, we are more likely to believe astrological readings when they conform to beliefs we already hold about ourselves than when they provide contrary information. Since astrological readings contain general personality descriptions that apply to a wide range of people, it's not surprising that many individuals believe these descriptions are true of themselves.

Chapter 13 Psychological Disorders

1. Ron's thought patterns illustrate several cognitive distortions or errors in thinking, including mistaken responsibility (assuming his girlfriend's bad moods were a response to him), catastrophizing (exaggerating the consequences of breaking off the relationship), and jumping to conclusions (assuming that when his girlfriend sat farther away from him in the car it meant she was trying to distance herself emotionally).

2. Lonnie's behavior appears to meet four of the six listed criteria: (1) unusualness (relatively few people are troubled by such obsessive concerns or compulsive rituals); (2) social deviance (repeated checking may be considered socially unacceptable behavior); (3) emotional distress (his compulsive behavior was a source of emotional distress), and (4) maladaptive behavior (his checking rituals were damaging his marital relationship). His behavior does not meet the criterion of dangerousness, since it did does not appear to have posed any danger to himself or others. Nor does he exhibit faulty perceptions or interpretations of reality, such as experiencing hallucinations or holding delusional beliefs.

Chapter 14 Methods of Therapy

A psychodynamic therapist might help Lauren explore how her present relationships and feelings of rejection are connected with disappointments she may have experienced in other relationships, including her early relationships with her parents. A humanistic therapist might help Lauren learn to accept and value herself for who she is, regardless of how others respond to her, and not to judge herself by other people's expectations. A cognitive-behavioral therapist might help Lauren increase reinforcing or pleasurable activities in her life and identify and correct distorted thinking patterns ("No one will ever want me . . . I'm just a complete failure"). Biomedical treatment might involve antidepressant medication, or perhaps even electroconvulsive therapy if her depression deepens and fails to respond to other treatment approaches.

Chapter 15 Psychology and Health

The claims may mean the following:

- We may have designed our product to enhance vitality and well-being, but we can't claim that it actually accomplishes this purpose.

- Our product contains amino acids that the body uses to build muscle, but so do many other sources of protein, including meat and dairy products.

- We hired a few physicians with respectable credentials who said they would recommend our product, and we paid them for their endorsements.

- By *backed*, we mean that we conducted research on our product. We're not saying what our research actually found or whether the studies were well designed or carried out by impartial investigators. And when we say *advanced*, we're referring to research methods that went beyond just asking people if they liked our product.

- We're not really sure what we mean by *supercharge*, but it sounded good in the advertising copy.

Chapter 16 Social Psychology

Why didn't they help? Though we will never know for certain, several hypotheses can be offered based on factors known to influence bystander behavior:

- *Situational ambiguity.* It was dark, and observers may not have had a direct view of the situation. Perhaps they were confused or uncertain about what was happening and whether it was a true emergency.

- *Diffusion of responsibility.* Even if they recognized the situation as an emergency, perhaps they weren't willing to assume personal responsibility for getting involved. Or perhaps they thought others would act, so they didn't need to. Or perhaps they thought it was "none of their business."

- *Perceived cost.* Perhaps they believed the costs of helping would be too great—including possible injury or loss of their own lives. But what about the minimal costs involved in calling the police? Perhaps they didn't want to accept a personal role in the incident and become involved in a lengthy court case.

- *Attributions of cause of need.* Perhaps they reasoned that the victim deserved what she got. Perhaps they figured the assailant was her boyfriend or husband and that she shouldn't have chosen such a partner.

What do you think is the likely explanation? What do you think *you* would do in a similar situation?

Appendix B
Statistics in Psychology

Dennis Hinkle Towson University   **Leping Liu** Towson University

The word *statistics* means different things to different people. Weatherpersons report daily weather statistics, such as high and low temperatures, amount of rainfall, and the average temperatures recorded for this day in history. Sportscasters flood us with statistics that include players' batting averages, fielding percentages, and ratios of home runs to times at bat. And in televised football games, commentators give half-time statistics that include total yards rushing and total yards passing.

Psychologists, too, use statistics. But to them, statistics are procedures for analyzing and understanding the results of research studies. For example, in Chapter 4 you read about studies showing that night-shift workers in sensitive positions tend to be sleepier and less alert than day-shift workers. Investigators in these studies used statistical techniques to determine whether the two groups of workers—night-shift and day-shift workers—differed from each other, *on the average*, on measures of sleepiness and alertness, among other variables. Psychologists also use statistics for describing the characteristics of particular groups of people, including themselves. In Chapter 1, for example, you learned about the characteristics of psychologists with respect to their ethnicities and places of employment.

Fundamental theories in modern psychology would not exist without the application of statistics in psychological research. Psychologists rely on statistics to explain the results of their research studies, as well as to provide empirical evidence to support or refute particular theories or beliefs. For example, investigators used statistical techniques to refute the original version of the *linguistic relativity hypothesis*, which was based on the theory that language determines how we think (see Chapter 7). In this case, statistical analysis of the research findings supported an alternative theory—that cultural factors influence how we think. We all need to understand statistics in order to become more knowledgeable consumers of psychological research. For example, we need to understand how the IQ scores of people in the general population are distributed in order to determine the relative standing of a particular score (again, see Chapter 7). And when seeking psychological assistance, we need to know which forms of therapy have been shown through methods of statistical analysis to be effective for which types of psychological problems (see the discussion in Chapter 14 about *empirically supported treatments*). Whatever the reason for using statistics, researchers and consumers alike should understand the information that statistics provide and the conclusions that can be drawn from them.

Populations and Samples

The terms *population* and *sample* are used frequently in psychological research involving statistical analysis. By definition, a *population* includes all members of a specified group, such as "all residents living in Washington, D.C.," "all patients in a psychiatric hospital at a specified time who are being treated for various psychological disorders," or "all students enrolled in an introductory psychology class in a particular university during the fall semester." In many research situations, however, it is not feasible to include all members of a given population. In such instances, a subset or segment of the population, called a *sample,* is selected to participate, and only the members of that sample are included in the research study.

Descriptive Statistics and Inferential Statistics

The study of statistics can be divided into two broad categories: descriptive statistics and inferential statistics. Investigators use **descriptive statistics** to describe data (i.e., to classify and summarize information expressed in numerical form), and they use

descriptive statistics Procedures used for classifying and summarizing information in numerical form—in short, for describing data.

TABLE 1 Final Examination Scores for Freshman Psychology Students

68	52	69	51	43	36	44	35	54	57	55	56
55	54	54	53	33	48	32	47	47	57	48	56
65	57	64	49	51	56	50	48	53	56	52	55
42	49	41	48	50	24	49	25	53	55	52	56
64	63	63	64	54	45	53	46	50	40	49	41
45	54	44	55	63	55	62	56	50	46	49	47
56	38	55	37	68	46	67	45	65	48	64	49
59	46	58	47	57	58	56	59	60	62	59	63
56	49	55	50	43	45	42	46	53	40	52	41
42	33	41	34	56	32	55	33	40	45	39	46
38	43	37	44	54	56	53	57	57	46	56	45
50	40	49	39	47	55	46	54	39	56	38	55
37	29	36	30	37	49	36	50	36	44	35	45
42	43	41	42	52	47	51	46	63	48	62	49
53	60	52	61	49	55	48	56	38	48	37	47

TABLE 2 Frequency Distribution of Final Examination Scores Using Class Intervals

Class Interval	f
65–69	6
60–64	15
55–59	37
50–54	30
45–49	42
40–44	22
35–39	18
30–34	7
25–29	2
20–24	1

inferential statistics Procedures for making generalizations about a population by studying the characteristics of samples drawn from the population.

frequency distribution A tabulation that indicates the number of times a given score or group of scores occurs.

histogram A graph that depicts the frequencies of individual scores or categories of scores, using bars of different lengths.

frequency polygon A graph on which the frequencies of class intervals are at their midpoints, which are then connected with straight lines.

central tendency A central point on a scale of measurement around which scores are distributed.

inferential statistics to make generalizations about a population by studying results based on a sample drawn from the population.

Descriptive and inferential statistics have three main purposes in scientific inquiry:

1. *To describe*
2. *To relate*
3. *To compare*

These approaches form a general framework for applying statistical procedures that allow researchers to interpret the results of a study, draw conclusions, make generalizations and inferences from samples to populations, and provide a focus for future studies. In the remainder of this appendix, we provide an overview of these three approaches to statistical analysis.

Using Statistics to Describe

The simplest application of statistics involves describing a distribution of scores collected from a group of individuals. Suppose, for example, that we have the final examination scores for 180 freshman psychology students, as shown in Table 1. In order to describe this distribution of scores, we must (1) identify the shape of the distribution, (2) compute the "average" score, and (3) determine the variability of the scores.

Frequency Distribution The first step in describing a distribution of scores is to develop a **frequency distribution** for individual scores or categories of scores.

Table 2 shows a frequency distribution constructed by combining our 180 scores into categories, called *class intervals*, beginning with the category of scores 20–24 and ending with the category of scores 65–69. Note that the categories with the most scores are 45 to 49, which contains 42 scores, and 55–59, which contains 37 scores. We can depict this frequency distribution using a type of bar graph, called a **histogram**. As shown in Figure 1, a histogram depicts the frequencies of class intervals of scores using bars of different lengths. Thus, for example, the class interval of 45–49 is represented by a bar with a value of 42.

Another way of graphing a frequency distribution is to use a **frequency polygon**, as shown in Figure 2. Here, the frequencies of class intervals are plotted at the intervals' midpoints, which are then connected with straight lines.

Measures of Central Tendency The second step in describing a distribution of scores is to compute the **central tendency** of the scores. Central tendency is an indicator of the average score in a distribution of scores. Three different statistical meas-

Figure 1   Histogram of Final Examination Scores

Figure 2   Frequency Polygon of Final Examination Scores

ures of central tendency are available. The researcher can determine the **mode** (most frequent score), the **median** (middle score), or the **mean** (arithmetic average).

As an example, consider the following distribution: 2, 5, 9, 10, 12, 13, 13. The mode is 13, which is the score that occurs most often. The median is the score that slices the distribution of scores in half (half of the scores fall above the median and half fall below). The median is 10, since three scores fall above this value and three fall below.

The mean is the most often used measure of central tendency. To find the mean ($\overline{X}$), sum all the scores (X) and then divide the sum by the number of scores. Symbolically,

$$\overline{X} = \Sigma X/n,$$

where ΣX is the sum of all the scores and n is the total number of scores. For the above distribution of scores, the mean would be computed as follows:

$$\overline{X} = 64/7 = 9.14$$

As you can see, the mode, median, and mean sometimes represent different values.

Similarly, for the final examination scores for the 180 freshman psychology students, the mean would be computed as follows:

$$\overline{X} = 8860/180 = 49.22$$

In other cases, such as the distribution shown in Figure 3(a), the mean, median, and mode are represented by the same value. But when the distribution is skewed ("tilted" to the right or left), as in Figure 3(b), the mean, median, and mode do not coincide.

What is the best measure of central tendency? The answer depends on what we want to know. If we're interested in finding out what score has been received most often on an examination, we would use the mode. But the most frequently occurring score may not be the best representation of how the class performed on the average.

Figure 3   Comparisons of the Mode, Median, and Mean in Two Distributions

mode   The most frequent score in a distribution of scores.

median   The middle score in a distribution, above and below which half of the scores fall.

mean   The arithmetic average of the scores in a distribution.

For that determination, we could use the median, which indicates the middle score in the distribution—that is, the score below which half of the scores fall and above which half of the scores fall. By knowing the median, we could specify which score separates the top half of the class from the bottom half.

We could also use the mean, which provides us with the arithmetic average of the whole class. But one limitation of the mean is that it is greatly influenced by extreme scores. Consider the following example of the distribution of salaries for employees in a small manufacturing company:

Position	Number of Employees	Salary	Measure of Central Tendency
President/CEO	1	$350,000	
Executive vice president	1	120,000	
Vice presidents	2	95,000	
Controller	1	60,000	
Senior salespeople	3	58,000	Mean
Junior salespeople	4	40,000	
Foreman	1	36,000	Median
Machinists	12	30,000	Mode

In this example, the mean is greatly influenced by one very high score—the salary of the president/CEO. If you were the chairperson of the local machinists' union, which measure of central tendency would you use to negotiate a new wage agreement? Alternatively, which would you use if you represented management's position in the negotiations?

Another consideration in choosing the best measure concerns how it is to be used. If we wish to generalize from samples to populations, the mean has a distinct advantage. It can be manipulated mathematically in ways that are inappropriate for the median or the mode. But if the purpose is primarily descriptive, then the measure that best characterizes the data should be used. In general, reporting all three measures of central tendency provides the most accurate description of a given distribution.

Measures of Variability   The final step in describing a distribution of scores is to compute the **variability** of the scores. Variability is the spread of scores throughout the distribution of scores. One measure of variability is the **range** of scores, or the difference between the highest and lowest scores in the distribution. The final examination scores for the 180 freshman psychology students range from a low of 24 to a high of 69, so the range would be $69 - 24 = 45$.

Another, more commonly used measure of variability is the **standard deviation (SD)**, conceptually defined as the average difference between each individual score and the mean of all scores in the data set. A large standard deviation suggests considerable variability (spread) of scores around the mean, whereas a small standard deviation indicates little variability. Table 3 illustrates the computations involved in calculating the standard deviation based on a hypothetical data set. (The standard deviation of the 180 final examination scores is 8.98.)

TABLE 3   Calculation of a Standard Deviation

Score	Deviation from Mean (D)	Deviation Squared (D^2)
3	$3 - 9 = -6$	36
5	$5 - 9 = -4$	16
6	$6 - 9 = -3$	9
9	$9 - 9 = 0$	0
12	$12 - 9 = 3$	9
13	$13 - 9 = 4$	16
15	$15 - 9 = 6$	36
$\bar{X} = 63/7 = 9$		$\Sigma D^2 = 122$

Standard Deviation $= \sqrt{\Sigma D^2 / n} = \sqrt{122/7} = \sqrt{17.43} = 4.17$

variability   In statistics, the spread or dispersion of scores throughout the distribution.

range   A measure of variability that is given by the difference in value between the highest and lowest scores in a distribution of scores.

standard deviation (SD)   A measure of variability defined as the average difference between each individual score and the mean of all scores in the data set.

Figure 4   A Normal Distribution, Showing the Approximate Percentages of Cases Falling Within One and Two Standard Deviations from the Mean

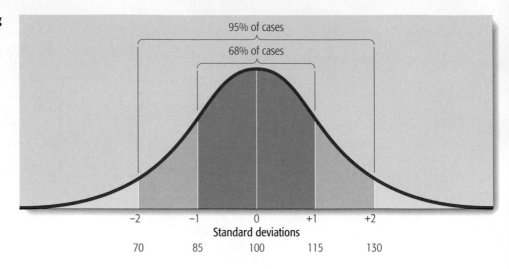

The Normal Distribution   The histogram for the 180 final examination scores in Figure 1 illustrates a commonly observed phenomenon in psychological data—namely, that the majority of scores tend to fall in the middle of the distribution, with fewer scores in the extreme categories. For many measures used in psychological research, score distributions have this general shape and are said to resemble a "bell-shaped curve," which is otherwise known as a "normal curve" or "normal distribution." In statistics, the true normal distribution is a mathematical model. However, when the shape of a particular score distribution closely aligns with a normal distribution, we can use the general properties of the normal distribution to describe the distribution of actual scores under study. The normal distribution provides a good description of the distribution of many sets of data, such as measures of intelligence and achievement. Moreover, in a normal distribution, the mean, median, and mode all have the same value, so we can use the standard deviation to describe a particular score in the distribution relative to all scores in the distribution.

In a normal distribution, such as the one shown in Figure 4, half of all cases fall above the mean and half fall below. Based on the properties of the normal distribution, we can determine the percentages of cases that fall within each segment of the distribution. For example, approximately 68 percent of cases fall within one standard deviation above and below the mean (between −1.0 and +1.0), and approximately 95 percent of cases fall within two standard deviations above and below the mean (between −2.0 and +2.0).

The properties of the normal distribution can also be used to describe the distance between a score and the mean. Scores on most IQ tests, for example, are distributed with a mean of 100 and a standard deviation of 15. Thus, an IQ score of 115 would be about one standard deviation above the mean. We use the term **standard score** (also called a *z-score*) to refer to a transformed score that indicates how many standard deviations the actual (raw) score is above or below the mean. For example, the standard score corresponding to a raw score of 115, based on a mean of 100 and a standard deviation of 15, would be +1.0. Similarly, we could say that a score of 70 is two standard deviations below the mean; in this case, the standard score would be −2.0. These standard score properties of the normal distribution are critical in applying inferential statistical procedures in psychological research.

Using Statistics to Relate

A second application of statistics involves determining the relationship between two variables. As an example, let's say we want to determine the relationship between quantitative SAT scores and final examination scores, using the data for fifteen introductory psychology students shown in Table 4.

standard score   A transformed score that indicates the number of standard deviations a corresponding raw score is above or below the mean. Also called a *z-score*.

scatterplot   A graph in which pairs of scores are plotted for each research participant on two variables.

TABLE 4 Quantitative SAT Scores and Final Examination Scores for Fifteen Introductory Psychology Students

Student	Quantitative SAT Score (X)	Final Examination Score (Y)
1	595	68
2	520	55
3	715	65
4	405	42
5	680	64
6	490	45
7	565	56
8	580	59
9	615	56
10	435	42
11	440	38
12	515	50
13	380	37
14	510	42
15	565	53
Σ	8,010	772

$$\overline{X} = 534.00 \qquad \overline{Y} = 51.47$$
$$s_X = 96.53 \qquad s_Y = 10.11$$

Figure 5
Scatterplot Illustrating the Relationship Between Final Examination Scores (Y) and Quantitative SAT Scores (X)

The Scatterplot: Plotting the Data Our first step would be to enter these data in a **scatterplot**, a type of graph that represents the "scatter" of scores obtained by plotting each individual's scores on two variables. The two variables can be symbolized by the terms X and Y.

In Figure 5, each point represents the paired measurements for each of the fifteen students, three of whom—Students 1, 8, and 13—are labeled specifically. (For example, the point for Student 1 represents the paired scores "SAT = 595" and "Final Score = 68.") Notice that these points form a pattern that starts in the lower-left corner and ends in the upper-right corner of the scatterplot. This pattern occurs when there is a positive relationship, or *positive correlation*, between the two variables. A positive correlation between two variables means that higher scores on one variable are associated with higher scores on the other variable. The pattern shown in Figure 5 thus illustrates that students with higher SAT scores tend to have higher final examination scores, and vice versa.

Different scatterplot patterns emerge as a result of different types of relationships between two variables. Three of these patterns are illustrated in Figure 6. Pattern A depicts a positive correlation between two variables. Pattern B depicts a negative correlation—a relationship in which higher scores on one variable are associated with lower scores on the other variable. And Pattern C is a scatterplot in which the points have neither an upward nor a downward trend. This last pattern occurs in situations where there is a zero correlation (no relationship) between the two variables.

Figure 6
Scatterplots Illustrating Varying Degrees of Relationship Between X and Y

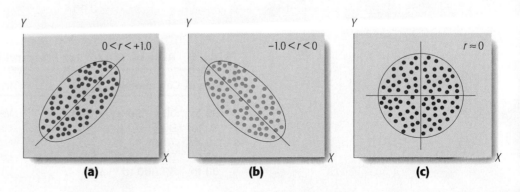

The Correlation Coefficient: Calculating the Relationship Between Two Variables   The scatterplot gives us a visual representation of the relationship between two variables. But researchers also use a statistical measure that provides a more precise indication of both the magnitude (strength) and direction of the relationship (positive or negative). The statistical measure of the relationship between two variables is called the *correlation coefficient* (expressed by the letter *r*). The range of values for positive correlation coefficients is from 0 (minimum) to +1.0 (maximum); the range of values for negative correlation coefficients is from 0 (minimum) to −1.0 (maximum).

Table 5 shows a worked-out example of the computations involved in calculating a correlation coefficient based on the data presented in Table 4. The correlation coefficient is found to be +0.90, which represents a very high, positive relationship between SAT scores and final examination scores. In other words, as we saw earlier, freshmen with higher SAT scores tend to achieve higher scores in their psychology exams.

Table 6 provides some rules of thumb for interpreting the magnitude of a correlation coefficient.

TABLE 5   Calculation of Correlation Coefficient Between Quantitative SAT Scores and Final Examination Scores

Quantitative SAT Scores		Final Exam Scores		
X	X^2	Y	Y^2	XY
595	354,025	68	4,624	40,460
520	270,400	55	3,025	28,600
715	511,225	65	4,225	46,475
405	164,025	42	1,764	17,010
680	462,400	64	4,096	43,520
490	240,100	45	2,025	22,050
565	319,225	56	3,136	31,640
580	336,400	59	3,481	34,220
615	378,225	56	3,136	34,440
435	189,225	42	1,764	18,270
440	193,600	38	1,444	16,720
515	265,225	50	2,500	25,750
380	144,400	37	1,369	14,060
510	260,100	42	1,764	21,420
565	319,225	53	2,809	29,945
8,010	4,407,800	772	41,162	424,580

$$\text{Raw Score Formula} = \frac{n\Sigma XY - \Sigma X \Sigma Y}{\sqrt{n\Sigma X^2 - (\Sigma X)^2}\ \sqrt{n\Sigma Y^2 - (\Sigma Y)^2}}$$

$$= \frac{15(424,580) - (8,010)(772)}{\sqrt{15(4,407,800) - (8,010)^2}\ \sqrt{15(41,162) - (772)^2}}$$

$$= 0.90$$

TABLE 6   Rule of Thumb for Interpreting the Size of a Correlation Coefficient

Size of Correlation	Interpretation
.90 to 1.00 (−.90 to −1.00)	Very high positive (negative) correlation
.70 to .90 (−.70 to −.90)	High positive (negative) correlation
.50 to .70 (−.50 to −.70)	Moderate positive (negative) correlation
.30 to .50 (−.30 to −.50)	Low positive (negative) correlation
.00 to .30 (.00 to −.30)	Little if any correlation

Using One Variable to Predict Another   An important use of correlational statistics is prediction. If two variables are correlated, we can predict scores on one variable based upon scores on the other variable. For example, after determining the relationship between SAT scores and final examination scores for our fifteen introductory psychology students, let's suppose that we want to predict the final examination scores of similar students based upon our knowledge of their SAT scores. The process of prediction involves developing a mathematical equation that incorporates the paired sets of scores on the two variables obtained in the study. This equation can then be used to predict final examination scores based on SAT scores for comparable groups of students. The accuracy of the prediction reflects the magnitude of the correlation between the variables: The higher the correlation, the better the prediction. If a strong relationship exists between the two variables, knowing how students score on the SAT would allow us to make fairly accurate predictions about how they will perform in their psychology courses.

Using Statistics to Compare

A third application of statistics involves comparing two or more groups. Let's say, for example, that an educational psychologist is interested in examining the effects of computerized instruction on the mathematics achievement of fourth-grade students. The psychologist's first step would be to assign participants to either an experimental group or a control group based on the technique of *random assignment* (discussed in Chapter 1). The experimental group would use a computer program that allows them to acquire mathematical concepts through interactive on-screen exercises, whereas the control group would receive standard classroom instruction. Then, at the conclusion of the study, both groups would be tested on a mathematics achievement test.

Let's further suppose that the results of the initial descriptive data analysis are as follows:

	Control Group	Experimental Group
Mean ($\bar{X}$)	62.4	77.6
Standard Deviation (SD)	15.8	16.3

Using these data, the educational psychologist would be able to describe the performance of the two groups by examining their means and standard deviations. Note, however, that for drawing conclusions and making generalizations from these data, inferential statistical procedures would also be needed.

Beyond Description: Using Inferential Statistics   Descriptive statistics allow us to summarize data, but the meaning of these statistical measures cannot be fully understood through descriptive statistics alone. In psychological research, it is important to determine whether the size of a correlation coefficient, or the difference between the means of two groups, is statistically significant. As discussed in Chapter 1 of the text, *statistical significance* indicates that the results obtained from a study are unlikely to have been due to chance or to the random fluctuations that would be expected to occur among scores in the general population.

Statistical significance can be determined only through the use of statistical techniques, called inferential statistics, that enable us to draw conclusions from our data and to make inferences and generalizations from samples to the populations from which they are drawn.

Stating the Null Hypothesis   The first step in using inferential statistics is to state a **null hypothesis** for the study in question. Defined literally, the word *null* refers to something of no value or significance. By the same token, a null hypothesis is a prediction that a given finding has no value or significance. For the study of the relationship between SAT scores and final examination scores, we can state the following null hypothesis: "There is *no relationship* between the two variables." And for the study of the difference between experimental and control groups on the question of

null hypothesis   A prediction of no difference between groups or no relationship between variables.

computerized versus standard instruction, we can offer this null hypothesis: "There is *no difference* between the two groups."

Testing the Null Hypothesis   The main purpose of inferential statistics is to test the null hypothesis. Using these techniques, scientific investigators can apply principles of probability to determine whether relationships between variables or differences between groups are large enough to be unlikely to be due to chance. In the process, they typically apply a criterion by which an outcome is judged to be significant when its likelihood of arising from chance is less than 5 percent. In other words, if the probability that an outcome would occur by chance alone is less than 5 percent, they would say that the finding is statistically significant. Depending on the nature of the research, researchers may set either more stringent or more liberal criteria for determining the threshold at which they would represent a given finding as statistically significant.

Let's return to our example of the fifteen introductory psychology students. First, if the correlation coefficient between their SAT scores and final examination scores is high enough to reach a level of statistical significance, we would reject the null hypothesis of "no relationship." In other words, we would conclude that the correlation is significantly different from zero (which in itself means "no relationship"). Second, in applying inferential statistics to the prediction of scores on one variable from scores on another, we would say that the null hypothesis is that SAT scores do not predict final examination scores. But since there *is* a statistically significant relationship between these two variables, our conclusion (based on probability theory) would be that SAT scores are a significant predictor of final examination scores.

Inferential statistics are used in a similar way when investigating differences between two or more groups. These statistical techniques involve mathematical constructs based on probability theory for determining whether differences between sample means are large enough to reject the null hypothesis of "no difference." If the difference between the means of the computer instruction group and the classroom instruction group are large enough to meet the threshold of statistical significance, we would reject the null hypothesis and conclude that the difference between the groups is statistically significant. The underlying rationale is that when group differences between samples of research participants on measures of interest meet the threshold for statistical significance, they are unlikely to reflect chanceful variations that would be expected to occur on these measures in the population in general.

Summing Up

In this brief introduction to statistics, we have provided some basic terminology, identified several approaches to using statistics in psychological research, and discussed descriptive and inferential statistics as well as their general application in research studies. We have also offered a convenient way of categorizing the main purposes of statistics: (1) to describe, (2) to relate, and (3) to compare. An understanding of all these aspects of statistics is necessary not only for researchers in psychology but also for consumers of research results.

Glossary

absolute threshold The smallest amount of a given stimulus a person can sense. *(p. 94)*

accommodation (1) The process by which the lens changes its shape to focus images more clearly on the retina. (2) In Piaget's theory, the process of creating new schemas or modifying existing ones to account for new objects or experiences. *(pp. 98 and 369)*

acculturative stress Demands faced by immigrants in adjusting to a host culture. *(p. 591)*

achievement motivation The motive or desire to achieve success. *(p. 303)*

acronym A word composed of the first letters of a series of words. *(p. 248)*

acrophobia Excessive fear of heights. *(p. 513)*

acrostic A verse or saying in which the first or last letter of each word stands for something else. *(p. 248)*

action potential An abrupt change from a negative to a positive charge of a nerve cell, also called a *neural impulse*. *(p. 49)*

activation-synthesis hypothesis The proposition that dreams represent the brain's attempt to make sense of the random discharges of electrical activity that occur during REM sleep. *(p. 147)*

actor-observer effect The tendency to attribute the causes of one's own behavior to situational factors while attributing the causes of other people's behavior to internal factors or dispositions. *(p. 619)*

acupuncture An ancient Chinese practice of inserting and rotating thin needles in various parts of the body in order to release natural healing energy. *(p. 116)*

adaptation In Piaget's theory, the process of adjustment that enables people to function more effectively in meeting the demands they face in the environment. *(p. 369)*

adolescence The period of life beginning at puberty and ending with early adulthood. *(p. 384)*

adoptee studies Studies that examine whether adoptees are more similar to their biological or adoptive parents with respect to their psychological traits or the disorders they develop. *(p. 87)*

adrenal cortex The outer layer of the adrenal glands that secretes corticosteroids (cortical steroids). *(p. 595)*

adrenal glands A pair of endocrine glands located just above the kidneys that produce various stress-related hormones. *(pp. 81 and 595)*

adrenal medulla The inner part of the adrenal glands that secretes the stress hormones epinephrine (adrenaline) and norepinephrine (noradrenaline). *(p. 595)*

adrenocorticotrophic hormone (ACTH) A pituitary hormone that activates the adrenal cortex to release corticosteroids (cortical steroids). *(p. 595)*

afterimage The visual image of a stimulus that remains after the stimulus is removed. *(p. 102)*

ageism Prejudice and discrimination directed at older persons. *(p. 411)*

agonists Drugs that either increase the availability or effectiveness of neurotransmitters or mimic their actions. *(p. 52)*

agoraphobia Excessive, irrational fear of being in public places. *(p. 513)*

alarm reaction The first stage of the general adaptation syndrome, involving mobilization of the body's resources to cope with an immediate stressor. *(p. 593)*

alcoholism A chemical addiction characterized by impaired control over the use of alcohol and physiological dependence on it. *(p. 162)*

algorithm A step-by-step set of rules that will always lead to a correct solution to a problem. *(p. 259)*

all-or-none principle The principle by which neurons will fire only when a change in the level of excitation occurs that is sufficient to produce an action potential. *(p. 49)*

altered states of consciousness States of awareness that differ from one's usual waking state. *(p. 140)*

Alzheimer's disease An irreversible brain disease characterized by progressive deterioration of mental functioning. *(p. 408)*

amnesia Loss of memory. *(p. 241)*

amniocentesis A technique for diagnosing fetal abnormalities involving examination of extracted fetal cells. *(p. 346)*

amniotic sac The uterine sac that contains the fetus. *(p. 343)*

amphetamines A class of synthetically derived stimulant drugs, such as methamphetamine or "speed." *(p. 52)*

amygdala A set of almond-shaped structures in the limbic system believed to play an important role in aggression, rage, and fear. *(p. 62)*

anal-expulsive personality In Freudian theory, a personality type characterized by messiness, lack of self-discipline, and carelessness. *(p. 467)*

analogy In problem-solving, a strategy based on using similarities between the properties of two things or applying solutions to past problems to the problem at hand. *(p. 260)*

anal-retentive personality In Freudian theory, a personality type characterized by perfectionism and excessive needs for self-control as expressed through extreme neatness and punctuality. *(p. 467)*

anal stage In Freudian theory, the second stage of psychosexual development, during which sexual gratification is centered on processes of elimination (retention and release of bowel contents). *(p. 466)*

androgyny A type of gender-role identification that characterizes people who possess high levels of both masculine and feminine traits. *(p. 429)*

animistic thinking In Piaget's theory, the child's belief that inanimate objects have living qualities. *(p. 371)*

anorexia nervosa An eating disorder involving a pattern of self-starvation that results in an unhealthy and potentially dangerous low body weight. *(p. 311)*

antagonists Drugs that block the actions of neurotransmitters by occupying the receptor sites in which the neurotransmitters dock. *(p. 51)*

anterograde amnesia Loss or impairment of the ability to form or store new memories. *(p. 242)*

antianxiety drugs Drugs that combat anxiety. *(p. 570)*

antibodies Protein molecules produced by the immune system that serve to mark antigens for destruction by specialized lymphocytes. *(p. 595)*

antidepressants Drugs that combat depression by affecting the levels or activity of neurotransmitters in the brain. *(pp. 52 and 570)*

antigens Substances, such as bacteria and viruses, that are recognized by the immune system as foreign to the body and that induce it to produce antibodies to defend against them. *(p. 595)*

antipsychotics Drugs used in the treatment of psychotic disorders that help alleviate hallucinations and delusional thinking. *(p. 571)*

antisocial personality disorder (APD) A type of personality disorder characterized by callous attitudes toward others and by antisocial and irresponsible behavior. *(p. 536)*

anxiety disorders A class of psychological disorders characterized by excessive or inappropriate anxiety reactions. *(p. 512)*

anxiety sensitivity Fear of fear, involving excessive concern that anxiety symptoms will spin out of control. *(p. 515)*

aphasia Loss or impairment of the ability to understand or express language. *(p. 72)*

applied research Research that attempts to find solutions to specific problems. *(p. 18)*

archetypes Jung's term for the primitive images contained in the collective unconscious that reflect ancestral or universal experiences of human beings. *(p. 469)*

arousal theory   The belief that whenever the level of stimulation dips below an organism's optimal level, the organism seeks ways of increasing it. (*p. 298*)

arteries   Blood vessels that carry oxygen-rich blood from the heart through the circulatory system. (*p. 602*)

arteriosclerosis   A condition in which artery walls become thicker and lose elasticity. Commonly called *hardening of the arteries*. (*p. 609*)

assimilation   In Piaget's theory, the process of incorporating new objects or situations into existing schemas. (*p. 369*)

association areas   Parts of the cerebral cortex that piece together sensory information to form meaningful perceptions of the world and perform higher mental functions. (*p. 65*)

asthma   A chronic lung disease characterized by temporary obstruction of the breathing tubes, leading to attacks of wheezing and difficulty breathing. (*p. 607*)

atherosclerosis   A form of arteriosclerosis involving the narrowing of artery walls resulting from the buildup of fatty deposits or plaque. (*p. 602*)

attachment   The enduring emotional bond that infants and older children form with their caregivers. (*p. 356*)

attitude   A positive or negative evaluation of persons, objects, or issues. (*p. 619*)

attraction   Feelings of liking for others, together with having positive thoughts about them and inclinations to act toward them in positive ways. (*p. 624*)

attribution   An assumption about the causes of behavior or events. (*p. 618*)

attributional style   A person's characteristic way of explaining outcomes of events in his or her life. (*p. 526*)

audition   The sense of hearing. (*p. 105*)

auditory nerve   The nerve that carries neural impulses from the ear to the brain, which gives rise to the experience of hearing. (*p. 107*)

authoritarian personality   A personality type characterized by rigidity, prejudice, and excessive concerns with obedience and respect for authority. (*p. 632*)

autonomic nervous system   The part of the peripheral nervous system that automatically regulates involuntary bodily processes, such as breathing, heart rate, and digestion. (*p. 57*)

availability heuristic   The tendency to judge events as more likely to occur when information pertaining to them comes readily to mind. (*p. 263*)

aversive conditioning   A form of behavior therapy in which stimuli associated with undesirable behavior are paired with aversive stimuli to create a negative response to these stimuli. (*p. 555*)

avoidance learning   The learning of behaviors that allow an organism to avoid an aversive stimulus. (*p. 202*)

avoidance motivation   The motive or desire to avoid failure. (*p. 303*)

axon   The tubelike part of a neuron that carries messages away from the cell body toward other neurons. (*p. 46*)

Babinski reflex   The reflexive fanning out and curling of an infant's toes and inward twisting of its foot when the sole of the foot is stroked. (*p. 348*)

bait-and-switch technique   A compliance technique based on "baiting" an individual by making an unrealistically attractive offer and then replacing it with a less attractive offer. (*p. 644*)

basal cell carcinoma   A form of skin cancer that is easily curable if detected and removed early. (*p. 607*)

basal ganglia   An assemblage of neurons lying in the forebrain that is important in controlling movement and coordination. (*p. 61*)

basic anxiety   In Horney's theory, a deep-seated form of anxiety in children that is associated with feelings of being isolated and helpless in a world perceived as potentially threatening and hostile. (*p. 470*)

basic hostility   In Horney's theory, deep feelings of resentment that children may harbor toward their parents. (*p. 470*)

basic-level concepts   The middle level of concepts in a three-level hierarchy of concepts, corresponding to the categories we most often use in grouping objects and events. (*p. 257*)

basic research   Research focused on acquiring knowledge even if such knowledge has no direct practical application. (*p. 18*)

basilar membrane   The membrane in the cochlea that is attached to the organ of Corti. (*p. 106*)

behavior modification (B-mod)   The systematic application of learning principles to strengthen adaptive behavior and weaken maladaptive behavior. (*p. 204*)

behavior therapy   A form of therapy that involves the systematic application of the principles of learning. (*pp. 10, 189, and 553*)

behavioral perspective   An approach to the study of psychology that focuses on the role of learning in explaining observable behavior. (*p. 10*)

behaviorism   The school of psychology that holds that psychology should limit itself to the study of overt, observable behavior. (*p. 7*)

bereavement   A psychological state of deprivation involving feelings of grief and loss resulting from the death of a loved one or close friend. (*p. 414*)

binocular cues   Cues for depth that involve both eyes, such as retinal disparity and convergence. (*p. 124*)

biofeedback training (BFT)   A method of learning to control certain bodily responses by using information transmitted by physiological monitoring equipment. (*p. 134*)

biopsychosocial model   An integrative model for explaining abnormal behavior patterns in terms of the interactions of biological, psychological, and sociocultural factors. (*p. 508*)

bipolar cells   A layer of interconnecting cells in the eye that connect photoreceptors to ganglion cells. (*p. 99*)

bipolar disorder   A type of mood disorder characterized by mood swings from extreme elation (mania) to severe depression. (*p. 523*)

blind spot   The area in the retina where the optic nerve leaves the eye and that contains no photoreceptor cells. (*p. 100*)

body mass index (BMI)   A standard measure of obesity based on body weight adjusted for height. (*p. 308*)

bonding   The process by which parents develop strong ties to their newborns, which may form in the first few hours following birth. (*p. 356*)

borderline personality disorder   A type of personality disorder characterized by unstable emotions and self-image. (*p. 536*)

bottom-up processing   A mode of perceptual processing by which the brain recognizes meaningful patterns by piecing together bits and pieces of sensory information. (*p. 120*)

brain   The mass of nerve tissue encased in the skull that controls virtually everything we are and everything we do. (*p. 46*)

brainstem   The "stalk" in the lower part of the brain that connects the spinal cord to higher regions of the brain. (*p. 59*)

brainstorming   A method of promoting divergent thinking by encouraging people to propose as many solutions to a problem as possible without fear of being judged negatively by others, no matter how far-fetched their proposals may be. (*p. 290*)

brightness constancy   The tendency to perceive objects as retaining their brightness even when they are viewed in dim light. (*p. 123*)

Broca's area   An area of the left frontal lobe involved in speech. (*p. 72*)

bulimia nervosa   An eating disorder involving recurrent episodes of binge eating followed by purging. (*p. 311*)

burnout   A state of physical and mental fatigue caused by excessive stress relating to work or other commitments. (*p. 599*)

bystander intervention   Helping a stranger in distress. (*p. 628*)

Cannon-Bard theory   The belief that emotional and physiological reactions to triggering stimuli occur almost simultaneously. (*p. 322*)

cardinal traits   Allport's term for the more pervasive dimensions that define an individual's general personality. (*p. 473*)

carpentered-world hypothesis   An attempt to explain the Müller-Lyer illusion in terms of the cultural experience of living in a carpentered, right-angled world like our own. (*p. 128*)

case study method   An in-depth study of one or more individuals. (*p. 29*)

castration anxiety   In Freudian theory, unconscious fear of removal of the penis as punishment for having unacceptable sexual impulses. (*p. 467*)

cataplexy   Sudden, involuntary loss of muscular tone or control. (*p. 150*)

catatonic type   A subtype of schizophrenia characterized by bizarre movements, postures, or grimaces. (*p. 532*)

central executive   The component of working memory responsible for coordinating the other subsystems, receiving and processing stored information, and filtering out distracting thoughts. (*p. 222*)

central nervous system   The part of the nervous system that consists of the brain and spinal cord. (*p. 54*)

central tendency   A central point on a scale of measurement around which scores are distributed. (*p. A-5*)

central traits   Allport's term for personality characteristics that have a widespread influence on the individual's behavior across situations. (*p. 473*)

centration   In Piaget's theory, the tendency to focus on only one aspect of a situation at a time. (*p. 371*)

cerebellum   A structure in the hindbrain involved in controlling coordination and balance. (*p. 60*)

cerebral cortex   The wrinkled, outer layer of gray matter that covers the cerebral hemispheres; controls higher mental functions, such as thought and language. (*p. 62*)

cerebral hemispheres   The right and left masses of the cerebrum, which are joined by the corpus callosum. (*p. 62*)

cerebrum   The largest mass of the forebrain, consisting of two cerebral hemispheres. (*p. 62*)

childhood amnesia   The normal occurrence of amnesia for events occurring during infancy and early childhood. (*p. 242*)

chorion   The membrane that contains the amniotic sac and fetus. (*p. 346*)

chorionic villus sampling (CVS)   A technique of detecting fetal abnormalities that involves examination of fetal material extracted from the chorion. (*p. 346*)

chromosomes   Rodlike structures in the cell nucleus that house the individual's genes. (*p. 83*)

chronic stress   Continuing or persistent stress. (*p. 583*)

chunking   The process of enhancing retention of a large amount of information by breaking it down into smaller, more easily recalled chunks. (*p. 222*)

circadian rhythm   The pattern of fluctuations in bodily processes that occur regularly each day. (*p. 143*)

clairvoyance   The ability to perceive objects and events without using the known senses. (*p. 130*)

classical conditioning   The process of learning by which a previously neutral stimulus comes to elicit an identical or similar response to one originally elicited by another stimulus as the result of the pairing of the two stimuli. (*p. 182*)

claustrophobia   Excessive fear of enclosed spaces. (*p. 513*)

clinical psychologists   Psychologists who use psychological techniques to evaluate and treat individuals with mental or psychological disorders. (*p. 20*)

clitoris   A sex organ in the female that is highly sensitive to sexual stimulation. (*p. 436*)

closure   The perceptual principle that people tend to piece together disconnected bits of information to perceive whole forms. (*p. 122*)

cochlea   The snail-shaped organ in the inner ear that contains sensory receptors for hearing. (*p. 106*)

cognitive-behavioral therapy (CBT)   A form of therapy that combines behavioral and cognitive treatment techniques. (*p. 556*)

cognitive dissonance   A state of internal tension brought about by conflicting attitudes and behavior. (*p. 301*)

cognitive dissonance theory   The belief that people are motivated to resolve discrepancies between their behavior and their attitudes or beliefs. (*p. 301*)

cognitive learning   Learning that occurs without the opportunity of first performing the learned response or being reinforced for it. (*p. 208*)

cognitive map   A mental representation of an area that helps an organism navigate its way from one point to another. (*p. 210*)

cognitive perspective   An approach to the study of psychology that focuses on the processes by which we acquire knowledge. (*p. 12*)

cognitive psychology   The branch of psychology that focuses on such mental processes as thinking, problem solving, decision making, and use of language. (*p. 254*)

cognitive therapy   Developed by Aaron Beck, a form of therapy based on a collaborative effort between clients and therapists that helps clients recognize and correct distorted patterns of thinking believed to underlie their emotional problems. (*p. 559*)

cohort effect   Differences between age groups as a function of historical or social influences affecting those groups rather than age per se. (*p. 340*)

collective unconscious   In Jung's theory, a part of the mind containing ideas and archetypal images shared among humankind that have been transmitted genetically from ancestral humans. (*p. 469*)

collectivistic culture   A culture that emphasizes people's social roles and obligations. (*p. 490*)

color constancy   The tendency to perceive an object as having the same color despite changes in lighting conditions. (*p. 123*)

comparative psychologists   Psychologists who study behavioral similarities and differences among animal species. (*p. 18–19*)

compliance   The tendency to accede to the requests or demands of others. (*p. 643*)

computer-assisted instruction   A form of programmed instruction in which a computer is used to guide a student through a series of increasingly difficult questions. (*p. 205*)

concepts   Mental categories for classifying events, objects, and ideas on the basis of their common features or properties. (*p. 256*)

conceptual combinations   Combinations of two or more concepts into one concept, resulting in the creation of a novel idea or application. (*p. 265*)

conceptual expansion   The expansion of familiar concepts into new uses. (*p. 265*)

concordance rates   In twin studies, the percentages of cases in which both members of twin pairs share the same trait or disorder. (*p. 86*)

concussion   A jarring of the brain caused by a blow to the head. (*p. 75*)

conditional positive regard   Valuing a person only when the person's behavior meets certain expectations or standards. (*p. 486*)

conditioned emotional reaction (CER)   An emotional response to a particular stimulus acquired through classical conditioning. (*p. 188*)

conditioned response (CR)   An acquired or learned response to a conditioned stimulus. (*p. 184*)

conditioned stimulus (CS)   A previously neutral stimulus that comes to elicit a conditioned response after it has been paired with an unconditioned stimulus. (*p. 184*)

conditioned taste aversions   Aversions to particular tastes acquired through classical conditioning. (*p. 190*)

conduction deafness   A form of deafness, usually involving damage to the middle ear, in which there is a loss of conduction of sound vibrations through the ear. (*p. 109*)

cones   Photoreceptors that are sensitive to color. (*p. 99*)

confirmation bias   The tendency to maintain allegiance to an initial hypothesis despite strong evidence to the contrary. (*p. 261*)

conflict   A state of tension brought about by opposing motives operating simultaneously. (p. 586)

conformity   The tendency to adjust one's behavior to actual or perceived social pressures. (p. 641)

connectedness   The principle that objects positioned together or moving together will be perceived as belonging to the same group. (p. 122)

conscious   In Freudian theory, the part of the mind corresponding to the state of present awareness. (p. 463)

consciousness   A state of awareness of ourselves and of the world around us. (p. 138)

conservation   In Piaget's theory, the ability to recognize that the quantity or amount of an object remains constant despite superficial changes in its outward appearance. (p. 371)

consolidation   The process of converting short-term memories into long-term memories. (p. 223)

constructionist theory   A theory that holds that memory is not a replica of the past, but a representation, or *reconstruction*, of the past. (p. 228)

consumer psychologists   Psychologists who study why people purchase particular products and brands. (p. 21)

contact hypothesis   Allport's belief that under certain conditions, increased intergroup contact helps reduce prejudice and intergroup tension. (p. 632)

context-dependent memory effect   The tendency for information to be better recalled in the same context in which it was originally learned. (p. 219)

continuity   The principle that a series of stimuli will be perceived as representing a unified form. (p. 122)

continuity model   The model proposing that development involves quantitative changes that occur in small steps over time. (p. 339)

control groups   Groups of research participants in an experimental study who do not receive the experimental treatment or intervention. (p. 33)

convergence   A binocular cue for distance based on the degree of tension required to focus two eyes on the same object. (p. 124)

convergent thinking   The attempt to narrow down a range of alternatives to converge on the one correct answer to a problem. (p. 264)

conversion disorder   A type of somatoform disorder characterized by a change or a loss of physical function that cannot be explained by medical causes. (p. 519)

cornea   A transparent covering on the eye's surface through which light enters. (p. 98)

coronary heart disease (CHD)   The most common form of heart disease, caused by blockages in coronary arteries, the vessels that supply the heart with blood. (p. 602)

corpus callosum   The thick bundle of nerve fibers that connects the two cerebral hemispheres. (p. 62)

correlational method   A research method that examines relationships between variables. (p. 31)

correlation coefficient   A statistical measure of association between variables that can vary from −1.00 to +1.00. (p. 31)

corticosteroids   Adrenal hormones that increase the body's resistance to stress by increasing the availability of stored nutrients to meet the increased energy demands of coping with stressful events. Also called *cortical steroids*. (p. 595)

corticotrophin-releasing hormone (CRH)   A hormone released by the hypothalamus that induces the pituitary gland to release adrenocorticotrophic hormone. (p. 595)

counseling psychologists   Psychologists who help people clarify their goals, make life decisions, and overcome problems they face in their lives. (p. 20)

countertransference   The tendency for therapists to relate to clients in ways that mirror their relationships with important figures in their own lives. (p. 551)

couple therapy   Therapy that focuses on helping distressed couples resolve their conflicts and develop more effective communication skills. (p. 562)

creative self   In Adler's theory, the self-aware part of personality that organizes goal-seeking efforts. (p. 469)

creativity   Originality of thought associated with the development of new, workable products or solutions to problems. (p. 264)

critical thinking   The adoption of a skeptical, questioning attitude and careful scrutiny of claims or arguments. (p. 40)

cross-sectional study   Study that compares individuals of different ages or developmental levels at the same point in time. (p. 340)

crystallized intelligence   A form of intelligence associated with the ability to use accumulated knowledge. (p. 396)

CT (computed tomography) scan   A computer-enhanced imaging technique in which an X-ray beam is passed through the body at different angles to generate a three-dimensional image of bodily structures (also called a *CAT* scan, short for *computed axial tomography*). (p. 67)

culture-bound syndromes   Psychological disorders found in only one or a few cultures. (p. 505)

culture-fair tests   Tests designed to eliminate cultural biases. (p. 278)

cyclothymic disorder   A mood disorder characterized by a chronic pattern of relatively mild mood swings. (p. 524)

daydreaming   A form of consciousness during a waking state in which one's mind wanders to dreamy thoughts or fantasies. (p. 139)

decay theory   A theory of forgetting that posits that memories consist of traces laid down in the brain that gradually deteriorate and fade away over time (also called *trace theory*). (p. 235)

decision making   A form of problem solving in which one must select a course of action from among the available alternatives. (p. 261)

declarative memory   Memory of facts and personal information that requires a conscious effort to bring to mind (also called *explicit memory*). (p. 226)

defense mechanisms   In Freudian theory, the reality-distorting strategies of the ego to prevent awareness of anxiety-evoking or troubling ideas or impulses. (p. 465)

deindividuation   The loss of self-awareness that may occur when one acts in concert with the actions of a crowd. (p. 649)

deinstitutionalization   A policy of reducing the population of mental hospitals by shifting care from inpatient facilities to community-based outpatient facilities. (p. 545)

delirium   A mental state characterized by confusion, disorientation, difficulty in focusing attention, and excitable behavior. (p. 169)

delusions   Fixed but patently false beliefs, such as believing that one is being hounded by demons. (pp. 51 and 505)

dementia   A condition involving a major deterioration or loss of mental abilities involved in memory, reasoning, judgment, and capacity to carry out purposeful behavior. (p. 408)

dendrites   Treelike structures projecting from the soma that receive neural messages from neighboring neurons. (p. 47)

denial   In Freudian theory, a defense mechanism involving the failure to recognize a threatening impulse or urge. (p. 465)

deoxyribonucleic acid (DNA)   The basic chemical material in chromosomes that carries the individual's genetic code. (p. 83)

dependent variables   The effects or outcomes of an experiment that are believed to be dependent on the values of the independent variables. (p. 33)

depolarization   A positive shift in the electrical charge in the neuron's resting potential, making it less negatively charged. (p. 49)

depressants   Drugs, such as alcohol and barbiturates, that dampen central nervous system activity. (p. 161)

depressive attributional style   A characteristic way of explaining negative events in terms of internal, stable, and global causes. (p. 526)

descriptive statistics   Procedures used for classifying and summarizing information in numerical form—in short, for describing data. (p. A-4)

detoxification A process of clearing drugs or toxins from the body. (p. 174)

developmental psychologists Psychologists who focus on processes involving physical, cognitive, social, and personality development. (p. 20)

developmental psychology The branch of psychology that explores physical, emotional, cognitive, and social aspects of development. (pp. 338)

Dhat syndrome A culture-bound syndrome found in India in which men develop intense fears about losing semen. (p. 505)

diabetes A metabolic disease involving the insufficient production of insulin or failure to efficiently use the insulin that is produced. (p. 80)

diathesis A vulnerability or predisposition to developing a disorder. (p. 508)

diathesis-stress model A type of biopsychosocial model that relates the development of disorders to the combination of a diathesis, or predisposition, usually genetic in origin, and exposure to stressful events or life circumstances. (p. 508)

dichromats People who can see some colors but not others. (p. 103)

difference threshold The minimal difference in the magnitude of energy needed for people to detect a difference between two stimuli. (p. 94)

discontinuity model The model proposing that development progresses in discrete stages that involve abrupt, qualitative changes in cognitive ability and ways of interacting with the world. (p. 339)

discrimination Unfair or biased treatment of people based on their membership in a particular group or category. (p. 630)

discriminative stimulus A cue that signals that reinforcement is available if the subject makes a particular response. (p. 197)

disinhibition effect The removal of normal restraints or inhibitions that serve to keep impulsive behavior in check. (p. 529)

disorganized type A subtype of schizophrenia characterized by confused behavior and disorganized delusions, among other features. (p. 532)

display rules Cultural customs and norms that govern the display of emotional expressions. (p. 318)

displacement In Freudian theory, a defense mechanism in which an unacceptable sexual or aggressive impulse is transferred to an object or person that is safer or less threatening than the original object of the impulse. (p. 465)

dispositional causes Causes relating to the internal characteristics or traits of individuals. (p. 618)

dissociative amnesia A psychologically based form of amnesia involving the "splitting off" from memory of traumatic or troubling experiences. (p. 242)

dissociative disorders A class of psychological disorders involving changes in consciousness, memory, or self-identity. (p. 517)

dissociative identity disorder (DID) A type of dissociative disorder characterized by the appearance of multiple personalities in the same individual. (p. 517)

distress A state of emotional or physical suffering, discomfort, or pain. (p. 582)

divergent thinking The ability to conceive of new ways of viewing situations and new uses for familiar objects. (p. 264)

divided consciousness A state of awareness characterized by divided attention to two or more tasks or activities performed at the same time. (p. 139)

door-in-the-face technique A compliance technique in which refusal of a large unreasonable request is followed by a smaller, more reasonable request. (p. 644)

double-blind studies In drug research, studies in which both participants and experimenters are kept uninformed about which participants receive the active drug and which receive the placebo. (p. 33)

Down syndrome A chromosomal disorder characterized by mental retardation and certain facial abnormalities. (p. 346)

dream analysis A technique in psychoanalysis in which the therapist attempts to analyze the underlying or symbolic meaning of the client's dreams. (p. 550)

drifting consciousness A state of awareness characterized by drifting thoughts or mental imagery. (p. 139)

drive A state of bodily tension, such as hunger or thirst, that arises from an unmet need. (p. 297)

drive for superiority Adler's term for the motivation to compensate for feelings of inferiority. Also called the *will-to-power*. (p. 469)

drive reduction Satisfaction of a drive. (p. 297)

drive theory The belief that behavior is motivated by drives that arise from biological needs that demand satisfaction. (p. 297)

drug abuse Maladaptive or dangerous use of a chemical substance. (p. 160)

drug addiction Drug dependence accompanied by signs of physiological dependence, such as the development of a withdrawal syndrome. (p. 160)

drug dependence A severe drug-related problem characterized by impaired control over the use of a drug. (p. 160)

dual-pathway model of fear LeDoux's theory that the brain uses two pathways (a "high road" and a "low road") to process fear messages. (p. 323)

Duchenne smile A genuine smile that involves contraction of a particular set of facial muscles. (p. 319)

dyslexia A learning disorder characterized by impaired ability to read. (p. 430)

dysthymic disorder A type of psychological disorder characterized by mild but chronic depression. (p. 523)

eardrum A sheet of connective tissue separating the outer ear from the middle ear that vibrates in response to auditory stimuli and transmits sound waves to the middle ear. (p. 106)

echoic memory A sensory store for holding a mental representation of a sound for a few seconds after it registers in the ears. (p. 221)

eclectic therapy A therapeutic approach that draws upon principles and techniques representing different schools of therapy. (p. 561)

educational psychologists Psychologists who study issues relating to the measurement of intelligence and the processes involved in educational or academic achievement. (p. 20)

EEG (electroencephalograph) A device that records electrical activity in the brain. (p. 66)

efficacy expectations Bandura's term for the expectancies we have regarding our ability to perform behaviors we set out to accomplish. (p. 483)

effort justification The tendency to place greater value on goals that are difficult to achieve in order to justify the effort expended in attaining them. (p. 302)

ego Freud's term for the psychic structure that attempts to balance the instinctual demands of the id with social realities and expectations. (p. 464)

egocentrism In Piaget's theory, the tendency to see the world only from one's own perspective. (p. 371)

ego identity In Erickson's theory, the attainment of a psychological sense of knowing oneself and one's direction in life. (p. 392)

eidetic imagery A lingering mental representation of a visual image (commonly called *photographic memory*). (p. 221)

elaboration likelihood model (ELM) A theoretical model that posits two channels by which persuasive appeals lead to attitude change: a central route and a peripheral route. (p. 621)

elaborative rehearsal The process of transferring information from short-term to long-term memory by consciously focusing on the meaning of the information. (p. 223)

Electra complex The term given by some psychodynamic theorists to the form of the Oedipus complex in young girls. (p. 467)

electrical recording   As a method of investigating brain functioning, a process of recording the electrical changes that occur in a specific neuron or groups of neurons in the brain in relation to particular activities or behaviors. (p. 69)

electrical stimulation   As a method of investigating brain functioning, a process of electrically stimulating particular parts of the brain to observe the effects on behavior. (p. 70)

electroconvulsive therapy (ECT)   A form of therapy for severe depression that involves the administration of an electrical shock to the head. (p. 572)

electromyographic (EMG) biofeedback   A form of biofeedback training that involves feedback about changes in the level of muscle tension in the forehead or elsewhere in the body. (p. 134)

embryo   The developing organism at an early stage of prenatal development. (p. 343)

embryonic stage   The stage of prenatal development from implantation through about the eighth week of pregnancy during which the major organ systems begin to form. (p. 343)

emerging adulthood   In some cultures, the period of psychosocial development roughly spanning ages 18 to 25 during which the person makes the transition from adolescence to adulthood. (p. 398)

emotional intelligence   The ability to recognize emotions in oneself and others and to manage one's own emotions effectively. (p. 330)

emotions   Feeling states that psychologists view as having physiological, cognitive, and behavioral components. (p. 315)

empirical approach   A method of developing knowledge based on evaluating evidence gathered from experiments and careful observation. (p. 25)

empty nest syndrome   A cluster of negative emotions, involving a loss of purpose and direction, that can occur when one's children have grown and left home. (p. 400)

encoding specificity principle   The belief that retrieval will be more successful when cues available during recall are similar to those present when the material was first committed to memory. (p. 219)

endocrine system   The body's system of glands that release their secretions, called hormones, directly into the bloodstream. (p. 79)

endorphins   Natural chemicals released in the brain that have pain-killing and pleasure-inducing effects. (p. 52)

engram   Lashley's term for the physical trace or etching of a memory in the brain. (p. 244)

environmental psychologists   Psychologists who study relationships between the physical environment and behavior. (p. 21)

enzymes   Organic substances that produce certain chemical changes in other organic substances through a catalytic action. (p. 51)

epilepsy   A neurological disorder characterized by seizures marked by sudden, violent discharges of electrical activity in the brain. (p. 76)

episodic memory   Memory of personal experiences. (p. 227)

erogenous zones   Parts of the body that are especially sensitive to sexual or pleasurable stimulation. (p. 465)

escape learning   The learning of behaviors that allow an organism to escape from an aversive stimulus. (p. 202)

ethics review committees   Committees that evaluate whether proposed studies meet ethical guidelines. (p. 34)

eugenics   Attempts to improve the human genetic stock by encouraging breeding among intellectually superior people. (p. 274)

evolutionary psychology   A branch of psychology that focuses on the role of evolutionary processes in shaping behavior. (p. 11)

exhaustion stage   The third stage of the general adaptation syndrome, characterized by depletion of bodily resources and a lowered resistance to stress-related disorders or conditions. (p. 594)

exhibitionism   A type of paraphilia characterized by exposing one's genitals to unsuspecting others for purposes of sexual arousal. (p. 443)

expectancies   In social-cognitive theory, personal predictions about the outcomes of behavior. (p. 481)

experimental method   A method of scientific investigation involving the manipulation of independent variables and observation or measurement of their effects on dependent variables under controlled conditions. (p. 33)

experimental psychologists   Psychologists who apply experimental methods to the study of behavior. (p. 18)

explicit memory   Memory accessed through conscious effort. (p. 227)

extinction   The gradual weakening and eventual disappearance of a conditioned response. (p. 184)

extrasensory perception (ESP)   Perception that occurs without benefit of the known senses. (p. 130)

extrinsic motivation   Motivation reflecting a desire for external rewards, such as wealth or the respect of others. (p. 303)

eyeblink reflex   The reflexive blinking of the eyes that protects the newborn from bright light and foreign objects. (p. 348)

facial-feedback hypothesis   The belief that mimicking facial movements associated with a particular emotion will produce the corresponding emotional state. (p. 319)

Fallopian tube   A strawlike tube between an ovary and the uterus through which an ovum passes after ovulation. (p. 342)

familial association studies   Studies that examine the degree to which disorders or characteristics are shared among family members. (p. 84)

family therapy   Therapy for troubled families that focuses on changing disruptive patterns of communication and improving the ways in which family members relate to each other. (p. 561)

fat cells   Body cells that store fat. (p. 306)

fear hierarchy   An ordered series of increasingly fearful objects or situations. (p. 554)

feature detectors   Specialized neurons in the visual cortex that respond only to particular features of visual stimuli, such as horizontal or vertical lines. (p. 101)

female orgasmic disorder   A type of orgasmic disorder in women characterized by a lack of orgasm, or persistent difficulties in achieving orgasm, following a normal phase of sexual excitement. (p. 450)

female sexual arousal disorder   A type of sexual arousal disorder in women involving difficulties in becoming sexually aroused. (p. 450)

fertilization   The union of a sperm with an ovum during sexual reproduction. (p. 342)

fetal alcohol syndrome (FAS)   A syndrome caused by maternal use of alcohol during pregnancy in which the child shows developmental delays and facial deformities. (p. 345)

fetal stage   The stage of prenatal development in which the fetus develops, beginning around the ninth week of pregnancy and lasting until the birth of the child. (p. 343)

fetishism   A type of paraphilia involving use of objects as sources of sexual arousal. (p. 442)

fetus   The developing organism in the later stages of prenatal development. (p. 343)

fight-or-flight response   The body's built-in alarm system that allows it to quickly mobilize its resources to either fight or flee when faced with a threatening stressor. (p. 593)

five-factor model (FFM)   The dominant contemporary trait model of personality, consisting of five broad personality factors: neuroticism, extraversion, openness, agreeableness, and conscientiousness. (p. 476)

fixations   Constellations of personality traits characteristic of a particular stage of psychosexual development, resulting from either excessive or inadequate gratification at that stage. (p. 466)

flashbulb memories   Enduring memories of emotionally charged events that seem permanently seared into the brain. (p. 230)

fluid intelligence   A form of intelligence associated with the ability to think abstractly and flexibly in solving problems. (*p. 396*)

focused awareness   A state of heightened alertness in which one is fully absorbed in the task at hand. (*p. 138*)

foot-in-the-door technique   A compliance technique based on securing compliance with a smaller request as a prelude to making a larger request. (*p. 643*)

forebrain   The largest and uppermost part of the brain; contains the thalamus, hypothalamus, limbic system, basal ganglia, and cerebral cortex. (*p. 61*)

forensic psychologists   Psychologists involved in the application of psychology to the legal system. (*p. 22*)

formal operations   The level of full cognitive maturity in Piaget's theory, characterized by the ability to think in abstract terms. (*p. 372*)

fovea   The area near the center of the retina that contains only cones and that is the center of focus for clearest vision. (*p. 100*)

framing   The tendency for decisions to be influenced by how potential outcomes are phrased. (*p. 264*)

fraternal twins   Twins who developed from separate zygotes and so have 50 percent of their genes in common (also called *dizygotic*, or *DZ*, twins). (*p. 86*)

free association   A technique in psychoanalysis in which the client is encouraged to say anything that comes to mind. (*p. 550*)

frequency distribution   A tabulation that indicates the number of times a given score or group of scores occurs. (*p. A-5*)

frequency polygon   A graph on which the frequencies of class intervals are at their midpoints, which are then connected with straight lines. (*p. A-5*)

frequency theory   The belief that pitch depends on the frequency of vibration of the basilar membrane and the volley of neural impulses transmitted to the brain via the auditory nerve. (*p. 108*)

frontal lobes   The parts of the cerebral cortex, located at the front of the cerebral hemispheres, that are considered the "executive center" of the brain because of their role in higher mental functions. (*p. 63*)

frustration   A negative emotional state experienced when one's efforts to pursue one's goals are thwarted. (*pp. 584 and 636*)

functional fixedness   The tendency to perceive objects as limited to the customary functions they serve. (*p. 261*)

functionalism   The school of psychology that focuses on the adaptive functions of behavior. (*p. 6*)

fundamental attribution error   The tendency to attribute behavior to internal causes without regard to situational influences. (*p. 618*)

ganglion cells   Nerve cells in the back of the eye that transmit neural impulses in response to light stimulation, the axons of which make up the optic nerve. (*p. 100*)

Ganzfeld procedure   A method of studying telepathy in which a sender attempts to mentally transmit information to a receiver who is in a sensory-restricted environment in another room. (*p. 131*)

gate-control theory of pain   The belief that a neural gate in the spinal cord opens to allow pain messages to reach the brain and closes to shut them out. (*p. 115*)

gender   The state of maleness or femaleness. (*p. 424*)

gender identity   The psychological sense of maleness or femaleness. (*p. 424*)

gender roles   The cultural expectations imposed on men and women to behave in ways deemed appropriate for their gender. (*p. 424*)

gender-schema theory   The belief that children form mental representations or schemas of masculinity and femininity, which they then use as a basis for organizing their behavior and evaluating their self-worth. (*p. 427*)

general adaptation syndrome (GAS)   Selye's term for the three-stage response of the body to persistent or intense stress. (*p. 592*)

generalized anxiety disorder (GAD)   A type of anxiety disorder involving persistent and generalized anxiety and worry. (*p. 513*)

genes   Basic units of heredity that contain the individual's genetic code. (*p. 83*)

genital stage   In Freudian theory, the fifth and final stage of psychosexual development, which begins around puberty and corresponds to the development of mature sexuality and emphasis on procreation. (*p. 468*)

genotype   An organism's genetic code. (*p. 83*)

germ cells   Sperm and egg cells from which new life develops. (*p. 81*)

germinal stage   The stage of prenatal development that spans the period from fertilization through implantation. (*p. 343*)

geropsychologists   Psychologists who focus on psychological processes involved in aging. (*p. 22*)

gestalt   A German word meaning "unitary form" or "pattern." (*p. 8*)

Gestalt psychology   The school of psychology that holds that the brain structures our perceptions of the world in terms of meaningful patterns or wholes. (*p. 8*)

glands   Body organs or structures that produce secretions. (*p. 47*)

glial cells   Small but numerous cells in the nervous system that support neurons and that form the myelin sheath found on many axons. (*p. 48*)

gonads   Sex glands (testes in men and ovaries in women) that produce sex hormones and germ cells (sperm in the male and egg cells in the female). (*p. 81*)

gradual exposure   A behavior therapy technique for treating phobias based on direct exposure to a series of increasingly fearful stimuli. Also called *in-vivo* ("real-life") *exposure.* (*p. 554*)

grammar   The set of rules governing how symbols in a given language are used to form meaningful expressions. (*p. 268*)

group polarization   The tendency for members of decision-making groups to shift toward more extreme views in whatever direction they were initially leaning. (*p. 650*)

group therapy   A form of therapy in which clients are treated within a group format. (*p. 561*)

groupthink   Janis's term for the tendency of members of a decision-making group to be more focused on reaching a consensus than on critically examining the issues at hand. (*p. 650*)

habituation   Reduction in the strength of a response to a constant or repeated stimulus. (*p. 119*)

hair cells   The auditory receptors that transform vibrations caused by sound waves into neural impulses that are then transmitted to the brain via the auditory nerve. (*p. 107*)

hallucinations   Perceptions experienced in the absence of external stimuli. (*pp. 51 and 505*)

hallucinogens   Drugs that alter sensory experiences and produce hallucinations. (*p. 168*)

hassles   Annoyances of daily life that impose a stressful burden. (*p. 583*)

health psychologists   Psychologists who focus on the relationship between psychological factors and physical health. (*p. 21*)

health psychology   The specialty in psychology that focuses on the interrelationships between psychological factors and physical health. (*p. 582*)

heart attack   A potentially life-threatening event involving the death of heart tissue due to a lack of blood flow to the heart. Also called *myocardial infarction.* (*p. 603*)

heritability   The degree to which heredity accounts for variations on a given trait within a population. (*p. 286*)

heuristic   A rule of thumb for solving problems or making judgments or decisions. (*p. 259*)

hidden observer   Hilgard's term for a part of consciousness that remains detached from the hypnotic experience but aware of everything that happens during it. (*p. 156*)

hierarchy of needs   Maslow's concept that there is an order to human needs, which starts with basic biological needs and progresses to self-actualization. *(p. 303)*

higher-order conditioning   The process by which a new stimulus comes to elicit a conditioned response as a result of its being paired with a conditioned stimulus that already elicits the conditioned response. *(p. 185)*

hindbrain   The lowest and, in evolutionary terms, oldest part of the brain; includes the medulla, pons, and cerebellum. *(p. 59)*

hippocampus   A structure in the limbic system involved in memory formation. *(p. 62)*

histogram   A graph that depicts the frequencies of individual scores or categories of scores, using bars of different lengths. *(p. A-5)*

homeostasis   The tendency of systems to maintain a steady, internally balanced state. *(p. 80)*

homogamy   The tendency for people to marry others who are similar to themselves. *(p. 402)*

homophobia   Unreasoning fear and loathing of people with a homosexual sexual orientation. *(p. 442)*

hormones   Secretions from endocrine glands that help regulate bodily processes. *(p. 47)*

humanistic perspective   An approach to the study of psychology that applies the principles of humanistic psychology. *(p. 11)*

humanistic psychology   The school of psychology that holds that free will and conscious choice are essential aspects of the human experience. *(p. 10)*

hypnosis   An altered state of consciousness characterized by focused attention, deep relaxation, and heightened susceptibility to suggestion. *(p. 155)*

hypnotic age regression   A hypnotically induced experience that involves reexperiencing past events in one's life. *(p. 155)*

hypnotic analgesia   A loss of feeling or responsiveness to pain in certain parts of the body during hypnosis. *(p. 155)*

hypoactive sexual desire disorder   A type of sexual desire disorder characterized by an absence or lack of sexual interest or desire. *(p. 450)*

hypochondriasis   A somatoform disorder in which there is excessive concern that one's physical complaints are signs of underlying serious illness. *(p. 519)*

hypothalamus   A small, pea-sized structure in the forebrain that helps regulate many vital bodily functions, including body temperature and reproduction, as well as emotional states, aggression, and response to stress. *(p. 61)*

hypothesis   A precise prediction about the outcomes of an experiment. *(p. 28)*

iconic memory   A sensory store for holding a mental representation of a visual image for a fraction of a second. *(p. 220)*

id   Freud's term for the psychic structure existing in the unconscious that contains our basic animal drives and instinctual impulses. *(p. 464)*

identical twins   Twins who developed from the same zygote and so have identical genes (also called *monozygotic*, or *MZ*, twins). *(p. 86)*

identity crisis   In Erikson's theory, a stressful period of serious soul searching and self-examination of issues relating to personal values and one's direction in life. *(p. 392)*

imaginary audience   The common belief among adolescents that they are the center of other people's attention. *(p. 386)*

immune system   The body's system of defense against disease. *(pp. 191 and 595)*

implicit learning   Learning without conscious awareness of what is learned. *(p. 210)*

implicit memory   Memory accessed without conscious effort. *(p. 227)*

impression formation   The process of developing an opinion or impression of another person. *(p. 616)*

imprinting   The formation of a strong bond of the newborn animal to the first moving object seen after birth. *(p. 356)*

in-group favoritism   A cognitive bias involving the predisposition to attribute more positive characteristics to members of in-groups than to those of out-groups. *(p. 631)*

in-groups   Social, religious, ethnic, or national groups with which one identifies. *(p. 631)*

incentives   Rewards or other stimuli that motivate us to act. *(p. 300)*

incentive theory   The belief that our attraction to particular goals or objects motivates much of our behavior. *(p. 300)*

incentive value   The strength of the "pull" of a goal or reward. *(p. 300)*

incubation period   A respite from active problem-solving efforts, which may facilitate a solution. *(p. 260)*

independent variables   Factors that are manipulated in an experiment. *(p. 33)*

individualistic culture   A culture that emphasizes individual identity and personal accomplishments. *(p. 490)*

individual psychology   Adler's theory of personality, which emphasizes the unique potential of each individual. *(p. 469)*

industrial/organizational (I/O) psychologists   Psychologists who study people's behavior at work. *(p. 21)*

inferences   Conclusions drawn from observations. *(p. 26)*

inferential statistics   Procedures for making generalizations about a population by studying the characteristics of samples drawn from the population. *(p. A-5)*

inferiority complex   In Adler's theory, the feelings of inadequacy or inferiority in young children that influence their developing personalities and create desires to overcome. *(p. 469)*

informed consent   Agreement to participate in a study following disclosure of information about the purposes and nature of the study and its potential risks and benefits. *(p. 34)*

insight   In Freud's theory, the awareness of underlying, unconscious wishes and conflicts. *(p. 550)*

insight learning   The process of mentally working through a problem until the sudden realization of a solution occurs. *(p. 209)*

insomnia   Difficulty falling asleep, remaining asleep, or returning to sleep after nighttime awakenings. *(p. 150)*

instinctive behaviors   Genetically programmed, innate patterns of response that are specific to members of a particular species. *(p. 297)*

instinct theory   The belief that behavior is motivated by instinct. *(p. 297)*

intelligence   The capacity to think and reason clearly and to act purposefully and effectively in adapting to the environment and pursuing one's goals. *(p. 274)*

intelligence quotient (IQ)   A measure of intelligence based on performance on tests of mental abilities, expressed as a ratio between one's mental age and chronological age or derived from the deviation of one's scores from the norms for those of one's age group. *(p. 275)*

interference theory   The belief that forgetting is the result of the interference of memories with each other. *(p. 236)*

internal working models   Generalized expectations, developed in early childhood, about how others are likely to respond in close relationships. *(p. 359)*

interneurons   Nerve cells in the central nervous system that connect neurons to neurons; in the brain, they are involved in processing information. *(p. 47)*

interpretation   In psychoanalysis, the attempt by the therapist to explain the connections between the material the client discloses in therapy and his or her unconscious conflicts. *(p. 550)*

intoxicant   A chemical substance that induces a state of drunkenness. *(p. 161)*

intrinsic motivation   Motivation reflecting a desire for internal gratification, such as the self-satisfaction derived from accomplishing a particular goal. *(p. 303)*

introspection Inward focusing on mental experiences, such as sensations or feelings. *(p. 5)*

introversion-extraversion One of the three underlying dimensions of personality in Eysenck's model, referring to tendencies toward being solitary and reserved on the one end or outgoing and sociable on the other end. *(p. 475)*

ions Electrically charged chemical particles. *(p. 48)*

iris The pigmented, circular muscle in the eye that regulates the size of the pupil to adjust to changes in the level of illumination. *(p. 98)*

irreversibility In Piaget's theory, the inability to reverse the direction of a sequence of events to their starting point. *(p. 371)*

James-Lange theory The belief that emotions occur after people become aware of their physiological responses to the triggering stimuli. *(p. 322)*

jet lag A disruption of sleep-wake cycles caused by the shifts in time zones that accompany long-distance air travel. *(p. 143)*

kinesthesis The sense that keeps us informed about movement of the parts of the body and their position in relation to each other. *(p. 116)*

laceration A type of brain trauma in which a foreign object, such as a bullet or a piece of shrapnel, pierces the skull and injures the brain. *(p. 75)*

language A system of communication composed of symbols (words, hand signs, etc.) that are arranged according to a set of rules (grammar) to form meaningful expressions. *(p. 268)*

language acquisition device Chomsky's concept of an innate, prewired mechanism in the brain that allows children to acquire language naturally. *(p. 269)*

latency stage In Freudian theory, the fourth stage of psychosexual development, during which sexual impulses remain latent or dormant. *(p. 468)*

latent learning Learning that occurs without apparent reinforcement and that is not displayed until reinforcement is provided. *(p. 210)*

lateral hypothalamus A part of the hypothalamus involved in initiating, or "turning on," eating. *(p. 306)*

lateralization The specialization of the right and left cerebral hemispheres for particular functions. *(p. 71)*

Law of Effect Thorndike's principle that responses that have satisfying effects are more likely to recur, while those that have unpleasant effects are less likely to recur. *(p. 194)*

laws of perceptual organization The principles identified by Gestalt psychologists that describe the ways in which the brain groups bits of sensory stimulation into meaningful wholes or patterns. *(p. 120)*

learned helplessness model The view that depression results from the perception of a lack of control over the reinforcements in one's life that may result from exposure to uncontrollable negative events. *(p. 525)*

learning A relatively permanent change in behavior acquired through experience. *(p. 182)*

legitimization of authority The tendency to grant legitimacy to the orders or commands of persons in authority. *(p. 646)*

lens The structure in the eye that focuses light rays on the retina. *(p. 98)*

lesioning In studies of brain functioning, the intentional destruction of brain tissue in order to observe the effects on behavior. *(p. 69)*

levels-of-processing theory The belief that how well or how long information is remembered depends on the depth of encoding or processing. *(p. 223)*

limbic system A formation of structures in the forebrain that includes the hippocampus, amygdala, and parts of the thalamus and hypothalamus; is involved in memory and emotional processing. *(p. 62)*

linguistic relativity hypothesis The proposition that the language we use determines how we think and how we perceive the world (also called the *Whorfian hypothesis*). *(p. 270)*

locus of control In Rotter's theory, one's general expectancies about whether one's efforts can bring about desired outcomes or reinforcements. *(p. 482)*

logical concepts Concepts with clearly defined rules for membership. *(p. 256)*

longitudinal study Study that compares the same individuals at periodic intervals over an extended period of time. *(p. 340)*

long-term memory (LTM) The memory subsystem responsible for long-term storage of information. *(p. 223)*

long-term potentiation (LTP) The long-term strengthening of neural connections as the result of repeated stimulation. *(p. 246)*

low-ball technique A compliance technique based on obtaining a person's initial agreement to purchase an item at a lower price before revealing hidden costs that raise the ultimate price. *(p. 644)*

lucid dreams Dreams in which the dreamer is aware that he or she is dreaming. *(p. 149)*

lymphocytes White blood cells that protect the body against disease-causing organisms. *(p. 595)*

mainstreaming The practice of placing children with special needs in a regular classroom environment. *(p. 279)*

maintenance rehearsal The process of extending retention of information held in short-term memory by consciously repeating the information. *(p. 222)*

major depressive disorder The most common type of depressive disorder, characterized by periods of downcast mood, feelings of worthlessness, and loss of interest in pleasurable activities. *(p. 522)*

male erectile disorder A type of sexual arousal disorder in men characterized by difficulty achieving or maintaining erections sufficient to engage in sexual intercourse. *(p. 450)*

male orgasmic disorder A type of orgasmic disorder in men characterized by a lack of orgasm, or persistent difficulties in achieving orgasm, following a normal phase of sexual excitement. *(p. 450)*

malignant tumors Uncontrolled growths of body cells that invade surrounding tissue and spread to other parts of the body. *(p. 605)*

manic episodes Periods of mania, or unusually elevated mood and extreme restlessness. *(p. 523)*

mantra A sound or phrase chanted repeatedly during transcendental meditation. *(p. 154)*

massed vs. spaced practice effect The tendency for retention of learned material to be greater with spaced practice than with massed practice. *(p. 235)*

matching hypothesis The belief that people tend to pair off with others who are similar to themselves in physical attractiveness and other characteristics. *(p. 627)*

maturation The biological unfolding of the organism according to the underlying genetic code. *(p. 348)*

mean The arithmetic average of the scores in a distribution. *(p. A-6)*

median The middle score in a distribution, above and below which half of the scores fall. *(p. A-6)*

medical model A framework for understanding abnormal behavior patterns as symptoms of underlying physical disorders or diseases. *(p. 506)*

meditation A process of focused attention that induces a relaxed, contemplative state. *(p. 134)*

medulla A structure in the hindbrain involved in regulating basic life functions, such as heartbeat and respiration. *(p. 59)*

melanoma A potentially lethal form of cancer that develops in melanin-forming cells, generally in the skin but sometimes in other parts of the body that contain these cells, such as the eye. *Melanin* is the pigment that gives color to the skin, hair, eyes, and some other body parts. *(p. 607)*

memory   The system that allows us to retain information and bring it to mind. *(p. 218)*

memory encoding   The process of converting information into a form that can be stored in memory. *(p. 218)*

memory retrieval   The process of accessing and bringing into consciousness information stored in memory. *(p. 219)*

memory schema   An organized knowledge structure, such as a set of beliefs, that reflects one's past experiences, expectancies, and knowledge about the world. *(p. 229)*

memory storage   The process of retaining information in memory. *(p. 218)*

menarche   The first menstruation. *(p. 385)*

menopause   The time of life when menstruation ends. *(p. 397)*

mental age   A representation of a person's intelligence based on the age of people who are capable of performing at the same level of ability. *(p. 275)*

mental image   A mental picture or representation of an object or event. *(p. 255)*

mental retardation   A generalized deficit or impairment in intellectual and social skills. *(p. 279)*

mental set   The tendency to rely on strategies that worked in similar situations in the past but that may not be appropriate to the present situation. *(p. 260)*

meta-analysis   A statistical technique for averaging results across a large number of studies. *(p. 562)*

metaphor   A figure of speech used to represent an object or concept by comparing it to another. *(p. 265)*

method of successive approximations   The method used to shape behavior that involves reinforcing ever-closer approximations of the desired response. *(p. 199)*

midbrain   The part of the brain that lies on top of the hindbrain and below the forebrain. *(p. 60)*

midlife crisis   A state of psychological crisis, often occurring during middle adulthood, in which people grapple with the loss of their youth. *(p. 400)*

migraine headache   A prolonged, intense headache brought on by changes in blood flow in the brain's blood vessels. *(pp. 134 and 608)*

mindfulness meditation   A form of meditation in which one adopts a state of nonjudgmental attention to the unfolding of experience on a moment-to-moment basis. *(p. 154)*

misinformation effect   A form of memory distortion that affects eyewitness testimony and that is caused by misinformation provided during the retention interval. *(p. 231)*

mnemonic   A device for improving memory. *(p. 248)*

mode   The most frequent score in a distribution of scores. *(p. A-6)*

modeling   A behavior therapy technique for overcoming phobias and acquiring more adaptive behaviors, based on observing and imitating models. *(p. 555)*

monoamine oxidase (MAO) inhibitors   A class of antidepressant drugs that increase the availability of neurotransmitters in the brain by inhibiting an enzyme, monoamine oxidase, that breaks down or degrades them in the synapse. *(p. 570)*

monochromats   People who have no color vision and can see only in black and white. *(p. 103)*

monocular cues   Cues for depth that can be perceived by each eye alone, such as relative size and interposition. *(p. 124)*

mood disorders   A class of psychological disorders involving disturbances in mood states, such as major depression and bipolar disorder. *(p. 521)*

moral therapy   A philosophy of treatment that emphasized treating mentally ill people with compassion and understanding, rather than shackling them in chains. *(p. 544)*

Moro reflex   An inborn reflex, elicited by a sudden noise or loss of support, in which the infant extends its arms, arches its back, and brings its arms toward each other as though attempting to grab hold of someone. *(p. 348)*

morphemes   The smallest units of meaning in a language. *(p. 268)*

motivation   Factors that activate, direct, and sustain goal-directed behavior. *(p. 296)*

motives   Needs or wants that drive goal-directed behavior. *(p. 302)*

motor cortex   A region of the frontal lobes involved in regulating body movement. *(p. 65)*

motor neurons   Neurons that convey nerve impulses from the central nervous system to muscles and glands. *(p. 47)*

mourning   The expression of sorrow or grief in accordance with a set of customs, such as wearing black clothing. *(p. 414)*

MRI (magnetic resonance imaging)   A technique that uses a magnetic field to create a computerized image of internal bodily structures. *(p. 67)*

multiple intelligences   Gardner's term for the distinct types of intelligence that characterize different forms of intelligent behavior. *(p. 281)*

multiple sclerosis (MS)   A disease of the central nervous system in which the myelin sheath that insulates axons is damaged or destroyed. *(p. 48)*

myelin sheath   A layer of protective insulation that covers the axons of certain neurons and helps speed transmission of nerve impulses. *(p. 48)*

myotonia   A state of muscle tension or rigidity. *(p. 438)*

narcissistic personality disorder   A type of personality disorder characterized by a grandiose sense of self. *(p. 536)*

narcolepsy   A disorder characterized by sudden unexplained "sleep attacks" during the day. *(p. 150)*

narcotics   Addictive drugs that have pain-relieving and sleep-inducing properties. *(p. 164)*

natural concepts   Concepts with poorly defined or fuzzy rules for membership. *(p. 257)*

naturalistic observation method   A method of research based on careful observation of behavior in natural settings. *(p. 30)*

natural selection   The evolutionary process by which individuals of a species that are best adapted to their environments are the ones most likely to survive and pass along their traits to succeeding generations. *(p. 7)*

nature-nurture   The debate in psychology over the relative influences of genetics (nature) and environment (nurture) in determining behavior. *(p. 338)*

need   A state of deprivation or deficiency. *(p. 297)*

need for achievement   The need to excel in one's endeavors. *(p. 302)*

negative instance   An object that does not fit a particular concept (e.g., a calico kitten is a negative instance of dog but a positive instance of cat). *(p. 258)*

negative reinforcement   The strengthening of a response through the removal of a stimulus after the response occurs. *(p. 197)*

negative symptoms   Behavioral deficits associated with schizophrenia, such as withdrawal and apathy. *(p. 532)*

neodissociation theory   A theory of hypnosis based on the belief that hypnosis represents a state of dissociated (divided) consciousness. *(p. 156)*

nerve   A bundle of axons from different neurons that transmit nerve impulses. *(p. 47)*

nerve deafness   Deafness associated with nerve damage, usually involving damage to the hair cells or to the auditory nerve itself. *(p. 109)*

nervous system   The network of nerve cells for communicating and processing information from within and outside the body. *(p. 54)*

neural tube   The area in the embryo from which the nervous system develops. *(p. 343)*

neuromodulators   Chemicals released in the nervous system that influence the sensitivity of the receiving neuron to neurotransmitters. *(p. 51)*

neuronal networks   Memory circuits in the brain that consist of complicated networks of nerve cells. *(p. 244)*

neurons   Nerve cells. *(p. 46)*

neuropsychologists Psychologists who study relationships between the brain and behavior. *(p. 21)*

neuroticism One of the three underlying dimensions of personality in Eysenck's model, referring to tendencies toward emotional instability, anxiety, and worry. *(p. 475)*

neurotransmitters Chemical messengers that transport nerve impulses from one nerve cell to another. *(p. 47)*

neutral stimulus (NS) A stimulus that before conditioning does not produce a particular response. *(p. 183)*

nightmare disorder A sleep disorder involving a pattern of frequent, disturbing nightmares. *(p. 150)*

nodes of Ranvier Gaps in the myelin sheath that create noninsulated areas along the axon. *(p. 48)*

nonspecific factors General features of psychotherapy, such as attention from a therapist and mobilization of positive expectancies or hope. *(p. 564)*

norms The standards used to compare an individual's performance on a test with the performance of others. *(p. 276)*

null hypothesis A prediction of no difference between groups or no relationship between variables. *(p. A-11)*

obedience Compliance with commands or orders issued by others, usually persons in a position of authority. *(p. 644)*

obesity A state of excess body fat. *(p. 307)*

objective tests Tests of personality that can be scored objectively and that are based on a research foundation. *(p. 493)*

object permanence The recognition that objects continue to exist even if they have disappeared from sight. *(p. 370)*

observational learning Learning by observing and imitating the behavior of others (also called *vicarious learning* or *modeling*). *(p. 210)*

obsessive-compulsive disorder (OCD) A type of anxiety disorder involving the repeated occurrence of obsessions and/or compulsions. *(p. 513)*

occipital lobes The parts of the cerebral cortex, located at the back of both cerebral hemispheres, that process visual stimuli. *(p. 63)*

Oedipus complex In Freudian theory, the psychological complex in which the young boy or girl develops incestuous feelings toward the parent of the opposite gender and perceives the parent of the same gender as a rival. *(p. 467)*

olfaction The sense of smell. *(p. 111)*

olfactory bulb The area in the front of the brain above the nostrils that receives sensory input from olfactory receptors in the nose. *(p. 112)*

olfactory nerve The nerve that carries impulses from olfactory receptors in the nose to the brain. *(p. 111)*

operant conditioning The process of learning in which the manipulation of the consequences of a response influences the likelihood or probability of the response occurring. *(p. 195)*

opponent-process theory A theory of color vision that holds that the experience of color results from opposing processes involving two sets of color receptors, red-green receptors and blue-yellow receptors, and that another set of opposing receptors, black-white, is responsible for detecting differences in brightness. *(p. 102)*

optic nerve The nerve that carries neural impulses generated by light stimulation from the eye to the brain. *(p. 100)*

oral stage In Freudian theory, the first stage of psychosexual development, during which the infant seeks sexual gratification through oral stimulation (sucking, mouthing, and biting). *(p. 466)*

organizational culture The system of shared values and norms within an organization. *(p. 654)*

organ of Corti A gelatinous structure in the cochlea containing the hair cells that serve as auditory receptors. *(p. 107)*

ossicles Three tiny bones in the middle ear (the hammer, anvil, and stirrup) that vibrate in response to vibrations of the eardrum. *(p. 106)*

osteoporosis A bone disease characterized by a loss of bone density in which the bones become porous, brittle, and more prone to fracture. *(p. 416)*

outcome expectations Bandura's term for our personal predictions about the outcomes of our behavior. *(p. 483)*

out-group homogeneity A cognitive bias describing the tendency to perceive members of out-groups as more alike than members of in-groups. *(p. 631)*

out-group negativism A cognitive bias involving the predisposition to attribute more negative characteristics to members of out-groups than to those of in-groups. *(p. 631)*

out-groups Groups other than those with which one identifies. *(p. 631)*

oval window The membrane-covered opening that separates the middle ear from the inner ear. *(p. 106)*

ovaries The female gonads, which secrete the female sex hormones estrogen and progesterone and produce mature egg cells. *(p. 81)*

overlearning Practice repeated beyond the point necessary to reproduce material without error. *(p. 237)*

ovulation The release of an ovum from an ovary. *(p. 342)*

ovum An egg cell (pl: ova). *(p. 342)*

palmar grasp reflex The reflexive curling of the infant's fingers around an object that touches its palm. *(p. 348)*

pancreas An endocrine gland located near the stomach that produces the hormone insulin. *(p. 80)*

panic disorder A type of anxiety disorder involving repeated episodes of sheer terror called panic attacks. *(p. 513)*

paranoid personality disorder A type of personality disorder characterized by extreme suspiciousness or mistrust of others. *(p. 536)*

paranoid type The most common subtype of schizophrenia, characterized by the appearance of delusional thinking accompanied by frequent auditory hallucinations. *(p. 532)*

paraphilia A psychological disorder involving atypical or deviant patterns of sexual attraction. *(p. 442)*

parapsychology The study of paranormal phenomena. *(p. 130)*

parasympathetic nervous system The branch of the autonomic nervous system that regulates bodily processes, such as digestion, that replenish stores of energy. *(p. 57)*

parietal lobes The parts of the cerebral cortex, located on the side of each cerebral hemisphere, that process bodily sensations. *(p. 63)*

Parkinson's disease A progressive brain disease involving destruction of dopamine-producing brain cells and characterized by muscle tremors, shakiness, rigidity, and difficulty in walking and controlling fine body movements. *(p. 51)*

pedophilia A type of paraphilia involving sexual attraction to children. *(p. 443)*

penis envy In Freudian theory, jealousy of boys for having a penis. *(p. 467)*

peptic ulcers Sores that form on the lining of the stomach or small intestine. *(p. 608)*

perception The process by which the brain integrates, organizes, and interprets sensory impressions to create representations of the world. *(p. 118)*

perceptual constancy The tendency to perceive the size, shape, color, and brightness of an object as remaining the same even when the image it casts on the retina changes. *(p. 122)*

perceptual set The tendency for perceptions to be influenced by one's expectations or preconceptions. *(p. 119)*

performance anxiety Anxiety experienced in performance situations (including sexual acts) stemming from a fear of negative evaluation of one's ability to perform. *(p. 451)*

peripheral nervous system The part of the nervous system that connects the spinal cord and brain with the sensory organs, muscles, and glands. *(p. 56)*

person variables Mischel's term for internal personal factors that influence behavior, including competencies, expectancies, and subjective values. *(p. 483)*

personal fable   The common belief among adolescents that their feelings and experiences cannot possibly be understood by others and that they are personally invulnerable to harm. *(p. 386)*

personal identity   The part of our psychological identity that involves our sense of ourselves as unique individuals. *(p. 640)*

personal unconscious   Jung's term for an unconscious region of mind comprising a reservoir of the individual's repressed memories and impulses. *(p. 469)*

personality   The relatively stable constellation of psychological characteristics and behavioral patterns that account for our individuality and consistency over time. *(p. 462)*

personality disorders   A class of psychological disorders characterized by rigid personality traits that impair people's ability to adjust to the demands they face in the environment and that interfere with their relationships with others. *(p. 536)*

personality psychologists   Psychologists who study the psychological characteristics and behaviors that distinguish us as individuals and lead us to act consistently over time. *(p. 20)*

personality tests   Structured psychological tests that use formal methods of assessing personality. *(p. 493)*

PET (positron emission tomography) scan   An imaging technique in which a radioactive sugar tracer is injected into the blood stream and used to measure levels of activity of various parts of the brain. *(p. 67)*

phallic stage   In Freudian theory, the third stage of psychosexual development, marked by erotic attention on the phallic region (penis in boys, clitoris in girls) and the development of the Oedipus complex. *(p. 467)*

phenotype   The observable physical and behavioral characteristics of an organism, representing the influences of the genotype and environment. *(p. 84)*

pheromones   Chemical substances that are emitted by many species and that have various functions, including sexual attraction. *(p. 112)*

phobias   Excessive fears of particular objects or situations. *(pp. 189 and 513)*

phonemes   The basic units of sound in a language. *(p. 268)*

phonological loop   The speech-based part of working memory that allows for the verbal rehearsal of sounds or words. *(p. 222)*

photoreceptors   Light-sensitive cells (rods and cones) in the eye upon which light registers. *(p. 99)*

phrenology   The now-discredited view that one can judge a person's character and mental abilities by measuring the bumps on his or her head. *(p. 492)*

physiological dependence   A state of physical dependence on a drug caused by repeated usage that changes body chemistry. *(p. 160)*

physiological perspective   An approach to the study of psychology that focuses on the relationships between biological processes and behavior. *(p. 11)*

physiological psychologists   Psychologists who focus on the biological underpinnings of behavior. *(p. 19)*

pineal gland   A small endocrine gland in the brain that produces the hormone melatonin, which is involved in regulating sleep-wake cycles. *(p. 81)*

pitch   The highness or lowness of a sound that corresponds to the frequency of the sound wave. *(p. 106)*

pituitary gland   An endocrine gland in the brain that produces various hormones involved in growth, regulation of the menstrual cycle, and childbirth. *(p. 81)*

placebo   An inert substance or experimental condition that resembles the active treatment. *(p. 33)*

placebo effects   Positive outcomes of an experiment resulting from participants' expectations about the effects of a treatment rather than from the experimental treatment itself. *(pp. 33 and 565)*

placenta   The organ that provides for the exchange of nutrients and waste materials between mother and fetus. *(p. 343)*

place theory   The belief that pitch depends on the place along the basilar membrane that vibrates the most in response to a particular auditory stimulus. *(p. 108)*

plaque   In the circulatory system, fatty deposits that accumulate along artery walls. *(p. 602)*

plasticity   The ability of the brain to adapt itself after trauma or surgical alteration. *(p. 74)*

pleasure principle   In Freud's theory, a governing principle of the id that is based on demand for instant gratification without regard to social rules or customs. *(p. 464)*

polyabusers   People who abuse more than one drug at a time. *(p. 160)*

polygenic traits   Traits that are influenced by multiple genes interacting in complex ways. *(p. 84)*

polygraph   A device used for lie detection that records differences in physiological responses to control questions and test questions. *(p. 329)*

pons   A structure in the hindbrain involved with sleep and wakefulness. *(p. 59)*

population   All the individuals or organisms that constitute particular groups. *(p. 30)*

positive instance   An object that fits a particular concept (e.g., a terrier is a positive instance of dog). *(p. 258)*

positive psychology   A contemporary movement within psychology that emphasizes the study of human virtues and assets rather than weaknesses and deficits. *(p. 15)*

positive reinforcement   The strengthening of a response through the introduction of a stimulus following the response. *(p. 197)*

positive symptoms   Symptoms of schizophrenia involving behavioral excesses, such as hallucinations and delusions. *(p. 532)*

posthypnotic amnesia   An inability to recall what happened during hypnosis. *(p. 156)*

posthypnotic suggestion   A hypnotist's suggestion that the subject will respond in a particular way following hypnosis. *(p. 156)*

posttraumatic stress disorder (PTSD)   A psychological disorder involving a maladaptive reaction to traumatic stress. *(p. 587)*

precognition   The ability to foretell the future. *(p. 130)*

preconscious   To Freud, the part of the mind whose contents can be brought into awareness through focused attention. *(p. 463)*

predictive validity   The degree to which test scores accurately predict future behavior or performance *(p. 278)*

prefrontal cortex   The area of the frontal lobe that lies in front of the motor cortex and that is involved in higher mental functions, including thinking, planning, impulse control, and weighing the consequences of behavior. *(p. 75)*

prefrontal lobotomy   A surgical procedure in which neural pathways in the brain are severed in order to control violent or aggressive behavior. *(p. 573)*

prejudice   A preconceived opinion or attitude about an issue, person, or group. *(p. 630)*

premature ejaculation (PE)   A type of orgasmic disorder in men characterized by rapid ejaculation following sexual stimulation. *(p. 450)*

premenstrual syndrome (PMS)   A cluster of physical and psychological symptoms occurring in the few days preceding the menstrual flow. *(p. 82)*

primacy effect   The tendency to recall items better when they are learned first. *(p. 238)*

primary drives   Innate drives, such as hunger, thirst, and sexual desire, that arise from basic biological needs. *(p. 298)*

primary mental abilities   Seven basic mental abilities that Thurstone believed constitute intelligence. *(p. 281)*

primary reinforcers   Reinforcers, such as food or sexual stimulation, that are naturally rewarding because they satisfy basic biological needs or drives. *(p. 198)*

primary sex characteristics   Physical characteristics, such as the gonads, that differentiate males and females and play a direct role in reproduction. *(p. 385)*

priming task An experimental task in which subjects are presented with a stimulus that primes them to respond in a certain way to subsequent stimuli. *(p. 227)*

proactive interference A form of interference in which material learned earlier interferes with retention of newly acquired information. *(p. 236)*

problem solving A form of thinking focused on finding a solution to a particular problem. *(p. 258)*

procedural memory Memory of how to do things that require motor or performance skills. *(p. 227)*

programmed instruction A learning method in which complex material is broken down into a series of small steps that learners master at their own pace. *(p. 205)*

projection In Freudian theory, a defense mechanism involving the projection of one's own unacceptable impulses, wishes, or urges onto another person. *(p. 465)*

projective tests Personality tests in which ambiguous or vague test materials are used to elicit responses that are believed to reveal a person's unconscious needs, drives, and motives. *(p. 495)*

prosocial behavior Behavior that benefits others. *(p. 628)*

prospective memory Memory of things that one plans to do in the future. *(p. 227)*

proximity The principle that objects that are near each other will be perceived as belonging to a common set. *(p. 121)*

psychiatrists Medical doctors who specialize in the diagnosis and treatment of mental or psychological disorders. *(p. 20)*

psychoactive drugs Chemical substances that affect a person's mental or emotional state. *(p. 158)*

psychoanalysis Freud's method of psychotherapy; it focuses on uncovering and working through the unconscious conflicts he believed were at the root of psychological problems. *(pp. 9 and 548)*

psychoanalysts Practitioners of psychoanalysis who are schooled in the Freudian tradition. *(p. 548)*

psychoanalytic theory Freud's theory of personality, which holds that personality and behavior are shaped by unconscious forces and conflicts. *(p. 462)*

psychodynamic perspective The view that behavior is influenced by the struggle between unconscious sexual or aggressive impulses and opposing forces that try to keep this threatening material out of consciousness. *(p. 9)*

psychokinesis The ability to move objects by mental effort alone. *(p. 130)*

psychological dependence A pattern of compulsive or habitual use of a drug to satisfy a psychological need. *(p. 160)*

psychological disorders Abnormal behavior patterns characterized by disturbances in behavior, thinking, perceptions, or emotions that are associated with significant personal distress or impaired functioning. Also called *mental disorders* or *mental illnesses*. *(p. 508)*

psychological hardiness A cluster of traits (commitment, openness to challenge, internal locus of control) that may buffer the effects of stress. *(p. 599)*

psychology The science of behavior and mental processes. *(p. 4)*

psychophysics The study of the relationship between features of physical stimuli, such as their intensity, and the sensations we experience in response to them. *(pp. 5 and 94)*

psychosocial needs Needs that reflect interpersonal aspects of motivation, such as the need for friendship or achievement. *(p. 302)*

psychosurgery Brain surgery used to control violent or deviant behavior. *(p. 573)*

psychotherapy A verbal form of therapy derived from a psychological framework that consists of one or more treatment sessions with a therapist. *(p. 548)*

psychotic disorder A psychological disorder, such as schizophrenia, characterized by a "break" with reality. *(p. 531)*

psychoticism One of the three underlying dimensions of personality in Eysenck's model, referring to tendencies to be perceived as cold and antisocial. *(p. 475)*

psychotropic drugs Psychiatric drugs used in the treatment of psychological or mental disorders. *(p. 570)*

puberty The stage of development at which individuals become physiologically capable of reproducing. *(p. 385)*

punishment The introduction of an aversive stimulus or the removal of a reinforcing stimulus after a response occurs, which leads to the weakening or suppression of the response. *(p. 202)*

pupil The black opening inside the iris that allows light to enter the eye. *(p. 98)*

questionnaire A written set of questions or statements to which people reply by marking their responses on an answer form. *(p. 30)*

racism Negative bias held toward others based on their ethnicity or racial identification. *(p. 636)*

radical behaviorism The philosophical position that free will is an illusion or myth and that human and animal behavior is completely determined by environmental and genetic influences. *(p. 194)*

random assignment A method of randomly assigning research participants to experimental or control groups. *(p. 33)*

range A measure of variability that is given by the difference in value between the highest and lowest scores in a distribution of scores. *(p. A-8)*

random sampling A method of sampling in which each individual in the population has an equal chance of being selected. *(p. 30)*

rape The use or threat of force to compel a person into having sexual intercourse. *(p. 454)*

rapid-eye-movement (REM) sleep The stage of sleep that involves rapid eye movements and that is most closely associated with periods of dreaming. *(p. 145)*

rational-emotive behavior therapy (REBT) Developed by Albert Ellis, a form of psychotherapy based on identifying and correcting irrational beliefs that are believed to underlie emotional and behavioral difficulties. *(p. 557)*

rationalization In Freudian theory, a defense mechanism involving the use of self-justification to explain away unacceptable behavior, impulses, or ideas. *(p. 465)*

reaction formation In Freudian theory, a defense mechanism involving behavior that stands in opposition to one's true motives and desires so as to prevent conscious awareness of them. *(p. 465)*

reality principle In Freudian theory, the governing principle of the ego that takes into account what is practical and acceptable in satisfying basic needs. *(p. 464)*

recall task A memory task, such as an essay test, requiring retrieval of stored information with minimal cues available. *(p. 240)*

recency effect The tendency to recall items better when they are learned last. *(p. 238)*

receptor site A site on the receiving neuron in which neurotransmitters dock. *(p. 50)*

reciprocal determinism Bandura's model in which cognitions, behaviors, and environmental factors both influence and are influenced by each other. *(p. 482)*

reciprocity The principle that people tend to like others who like them back. *(p. 627)*

recognition task A method of measuring memory retention that assesses the ability to select the correct answer from among a range of alternative answers. *(p. 241)*

reconditioning The process of relearning a conditioned response following extinction. *(p. 184)*

reflex An automatic, unlearned response to particular stimuli. *(p. 55)*

refractory period A temporary state in which a neuron is unable to fire in response to continued stimulation. *(p. 49)*

regression In Freudian theory, a defense mechanism in which an individual, usually under high levels of stress, reverts to a behavior characteristic of an earlier stage of development. *(p. 465)*

reinforcer   A stimulus event that strengthens the response it follows. (p. 195)

reliability   The stability of test scores over time. (p. 277)

replication   The attempt to duplicate findings. (p. 29)

representativeness heuristic   A rule of thumb for making a judgment that assumes a given sample is representative of the larger population from which it is drawn. (p. 262)

repression   In Freudian theory, a type of defense mechanism involving motivated forgetting of anxiety-evoking material. (pp. 240 and 465)

resistance   In psychoanalysis, the blocking that occurs when therapy touches upon anxiety-evoking thoughts or feelings. (p. 550)

resistance stage   The second stage of the general adaptation syndrome, characterized by the body's attempt to adjust or adapt to persistent stress. (p. 594)

resting potential   The electrical potential across the cell membrane of a neuron in its resting state. (p. 48)

reticular formation   A weblike formation of neurons involved in regulating states of attention, alertness, and arousal. (p. 61)

retina   The light-sensitive layer of the inner surface of the eye that contains photoreceptor cells. (p. 98)

retinal disparity   A binocular cue for distance based on the slight differences in the visual impressions formed in both eyes. (p. 124)

retrieval cues   Cues associated with the original learning that facilitate the retrieval of memories. (p. 219)

retrieval theory   The belief that forgetting is the result of a failure to access stored memories. (p. 238)

retroactive interference   A form of interference in which newly acquired information interferes with retention of material learned earlier. (p. 236)

retrograde amnesia   Loss of memory of past events. (p. 242)

retrospective memory   Memory of past experiences or events and previously acquired information. (p. 227)

reuptake   The process by which neurotransmitters are reabsorbed by the transmitting neuron. (p. 50)

risky-shift phenomenon   A type of group polarization effect in which group discussion leads to the adoption of a riskier course of action than the members would have endorsed initially. (p. 650)

rods   Photoreceptors that are sensitive only to the intensity of light (light and dark). (p. 99)

role diffusion   In Erikson's model, aimlessness or a lack of direction with respect to one's role in life or public identity. (p. 393)

romantic love   Love involving strong erotic attraction and desire for intimacy. (p. 328)

rooting reflex   The reflexive turning of the newborn's head in the direction of a touch on its cheek. (p. 348)

rubella   A common childhood disease that can lead to serious birth defects if contracted by the mother during pregnancy (also called *German measles*). (p. 344)

samples   Subsets of a population. (p. 30)

savings method   A method of testing memory retention by comparing the numbers of trials needed to learn material with the number of trials needed to relearn the material at a later time. (p. 235)

scaffolding   In Vygotsky's theory, tailoring the degree and type of instruction to the child's current level of ability or knowledge. (p. 374)

scatterplot   A graph in which pairs of scores are plotted for each research participant on two variables. (p. A-9)

schedule of continuous reinforcement   A system of dispensing a reinforcement each time a response is produced. (p. 199)

schedule of partial reinforcement   A system of dispensing a reinforcement for only a portion of responses. (p. 199)

schedules of reinforcement   Predetermined plans for timing the delivery of reinforcement. (p. 199)

schema   In Piaget's theory, a mental framework for understanding or acting on the environment. (p. 369)

schizoid personality disorder   A type of personality disorder characterized by social aloofness and limited range of emotional expression. (p. 536)

schizophrenia   A severe and chronic psychological disorder characterized by disturbances in thinking, perception, emotions, and behavior. (pp. 51 and 531)

school psychologists   Psychologists who evaluate and assist children with learning problems or other special needs. (p. 20)

scientific method   A method of inquiry involving careful observation and use of experimental methods. (p. 28)

seasonal affective disorder (SAD)   A type of major depression that involves a recurring pattern of winter depressions followed by elevations of mood in the spring and summer. (p. 522)

secondary drives   Drives that are learned or acquired through experience, such as the drive to achieve monetary wealth. (p. 298)

secondary gain   The reward value of having a psychological or physical symptom, such as release from ordinary responsibilities. (p. 520)

secondary reinforcers   Learned reinforcers, such as money, that develop their reinforcing properties because of their association with primary reinforcers. (p. 198)

secondary sex characteristics   Physical characteristics that differentiate males and females but are not directly involved in reproduction. (p. 385)

secondary traits   Allport's term for specific traits that influence behavior in relatively few situations. (p. 473)

selective attention   The process by which we attend to meaningful stimuli and filter out irrelevant or extraneous stimuli. (p. 119)

selective serotonin-reuptake inhibitors (SSRIs)   A class of antidepressant drugs that work specifically on increasing availability of the neurotransmitter serotonin by interfering with its reuptake. (p. 570)

self-actualization   The motive that drives individuals to express their unique capabilities and fulfill their potentials. (p. 304)

self-fulfilling prophecy   An expectation that helps bring about the outcome that is expected. (p. 617)

self-ideals   Rogers's term for the idealized sense of how or what we should be. (p. 486)

self-report personality inventories   Structured psychological tests in which individuals are given a limited range of response options to answer a set of questions about themselves. (p. 493)

self-serving bias   The tendency to take credit for our accomplishments and to explain away our failures or disappointments. (p. 619)

self-theory   Rogers's model of personality, which focuses on the importance of the self. (p. 486)

semantic memory   Memory of facts. (p. 226)

semantic network model   A representation of the organizational structure of long-term memory in terms of a network of associated concepts. (p. 224)

semantics   The set of rules governing the meaning of words. (p. 268)

semicircular canals   Three curved, tube-like canals in the inner ear that are involved in sensing changes in the direction and movement of the head. (p. 116)

sensate-focus exercises   A technique used in sex therapy that consists of nongenital massage to lessen the anxiety associated with sexual interactions. (p. 452)

sensation   The process by which we receive, transform, and process stimuli from the outside world to create sensory experiences of vision, touch, hearing, taste, smell, and so on. (p. 94)

sensory adaptation   The process by which sensory receptors adapt to constant stimuli by becoming less sensitive to them. (p. 96)

sensory memory   The storage system that holds memory of sensory impressions for a very short time. (p. 220)

sensory neurons   Neurons that transmit information from sensory organs, muscles, and inner organs to the spinal cord and brain. (p. 47)

sensory receptors   Specialized cells that detect sensory stimuli and convert them into neural impulses. *(p. 94)*

sensory register   A temporary storage device for holding sensory memories. *(p. 220)*

serial position effect   The tendency to recall items at the start or end of a list better than items in the middle of a list. *(p. 237)*

set point theory   The belief that brain mechanisms regulate body weight around a genetically predetermined "set point." *(p. 309)*

sexual aversion disorder   A type of sexual desire disorder involving repulsion or strong aversion to genital sexual contact. *(p. 450)*

sexual dysfunctions   Persistent or recurrent problems with sexual interest, arousal, or response. *(p. 448)*

sexual harassment   A form of sexual coercion involving unwelcome sexual comments, jokes, overtures, demands for sexual favors, or outright physical contact. *(p. 454)*

sexual masochism   A type of paraphilia involving the receipt of painful or humiliating experiences as part of a sexual act. *(p. 443)*

sexual orientation   The directionality of one's erotic interests. *(p. 439)*

sexual response cycle   The term used by Masters and Johnson to refer to the characteristic stages of physiological response to sexual stimulation. *(p. 436)*

sexual sadism   A type of paraphilia involving the infliction of physical suffering or humiliation on another person for purposes of sexual gratification. *(p. 443)*

sexually transmitted disease (STD)   A disease caused by an infectious agent that is spread by sexual contact. *(p. 445)*

shape constancy   The tendency to perceive an object as having the same shape despite differences in the images it casts on the retina as the viewer's perspective changes. *(p. 123)*

shaping   A process of learning that involves the reinforcement of increasingly closer approximations of the desired response. *(p. 199)*

short-term memory (STM)   The memory storage system that allows for short-term retention of information before it is either transferred to long-term memory or forgotten. *(p. 221)*

signal-detection theory   The belief that the detection of a stimulus depends on factors such as the intensity of the stimulus, the level of background stimulation, and the biological and psychological characteristics of the perceiver. *(p. 95)*

similarity   The principle that objects that are similar will be perceived as belonging to the same group. *(p. 121)*

single-blind studies   In drug research, studies in which research participants are kept uninformed about whether they are receiving the experimental drug or a placebo. *(p. 33)*

situational causes   Causes relating to external or environmental events. *(p. 618)*

situation variables   Mischel's term for environmental influences on behavior, such as rewards and punishments. *(p. 483)*

size constancy   The tendency to perceive an object as having the same size despite changes in the images it casts on the retina as the viewing distance changes. *(p. 123)*

skin senses   The senses of touch, pressure, warmth, cold, and pain that involve stimulation of sensory receptors in the skin. *(p. 114)*

Skinner box   An experimental apparatus developed by B. F. Skinner for studying relationships between reinforcement and behavior. *(p. 196)*

sleep apnea   Temporary cessation of breathing during sleep. *(p. 150)*

sleep terror disorder   A sleep disorder involving repeated episodes of intense fear during sleep, causing the person to awake abruptly in a terrified state. *(p. 150)*

sleepwalking disorder   A sleep disorder characterized by repeated episodes of sleepwalking. *(p. 151)*

social-cognitive theory   A contemporary learning-based model that emphasizes the roles played by both cognitive factors and environmental or situational factors in determining behavior. *(pp. 10 and 481)*

social desirability bias   The tendency to respond to questions in a socially desirable manner. *(p. 30)*

social facilitation   The tendency to work better or harder in the presence of others than when alone. *(p. 647)*

social identity   The part of our psychological identity that involves our sense of ourselves as members of particular groups. Also called *group identity*. *(p. 640)*

social loafing   The tendency to expend less effort when working as a member of a group than when working alone. *(p. 648)*

social norms   Standards that define what is socially acceptable in a given situation. *(p. 630)*

social perception   The processes by which we form impressions, make judgments, and develop attitudes about the people and events that constitute our social world. *(p. 616)*

social phobia   A type of anxiety disorder involving excessive fear of social situations. *(p. 513)*

social psychologists   Psychologists who study group or social influences on behavior and attitudes. *(p. 20)*

social psychology   The subfield in psychology that deals with how our thoughts, feelings, and behaviors are influenced by our social interactions with others. *(p. 616)*

social schema   A mental image or representation that we use to understand our social environment. *(p. 616)*

social validation   The tendency to use other people's behavior as a standard for judging the appropriateness of one's own behavior. *(p. 643)*

sociocultural perspective   An approach to the study of psychology that emphasizes the role of social and cultural influences on behavior. *(p. 12)*

soma   The cell body of a neuron; contains the nucleus of the cell and carries out the cell's metabolic functions. *(p. 46)*

somatic nervous system   The part of the peripheral nervous system that transmits information between the central nervous system and the sensory organs and muscles; also controls voluntary movements. *(p. 56)*

somatoform disorders   A class of psychological disorders involving physical ailments or complaints that cannot be explained by organic causes. *(p. 517)*

somatosensory cortex   The part of the parietal lobe that processes information about touch and pressure on the skin, as well as the position of the parts of our bodies as we move about. *(p. 63)*

source traits   Cattell's term for traits at a deep level of personality that are not apparent in observed behavior but must be inferred based on underlying relationships among surface traits. *(p. 474)*

specific phobia   Phobic reactions involving specific situations or objects. *(p. 513)*

sperm   The male reproductive cell. *(p. 342)*

spina bifida   A neural tube defect in which the child is born with a hole in the tube surrounding the spinal cord. *(p. 344)*

spinal cord   The column of nerves that transmits information between the brain and the peripheral nervous system. *(p. 54)*

spinal reflex   A reflex controlled at the level of the spinal cord that may involve as few as two neurons. *(p. 55)*

spine   The protective bony column that houses the spinal cord. *(p. 55)*

split-brain patients   Persons whose corpus callosum has been surgically severed. *(p. 76)*

spontaneous recovery   The spontaneous return of a conditioned response following extinction. *(p. 184)*

sport psychologists   Psychologists who apply psychology to understanding and improving athletic performance. *(p. 22)*

standardization   The process of establishing norms for a test by administering the test to large numbers of people who constitute a standardization sample. *(p. 276)*

standard deviation (SD)   A measure of variability defined as the average difference between each individual score and the mean of all the scores in the data set. *(p. A-8)*

standard scores   (1) Scores that represent an individual's relative deviation from the mean of the standardization sample. (2) A transformed score that indicates the number of standard deviations a corresponding raw score is above or below the mean. Also called a *z-score*. *(pp. 493 and A-8)*

state-dependent memory effect   The tendency for information to be better recalled when the person is in the same psychological or physiological state as when the information was first learned. (p. 220)

states of consciousness   Levels of consciousness ranging from alert wakefulness to unconsciousness during deep sleep. (p. 138)

statistical significance   A term representing that a finding is unlikely to have been due to chance or random fluctuations. (p. 29)

statistics   The branch of mathematics involving the tabulation, analysis, and interpretation of numerical data. (p. 29)

statutory rape   Sexual intercourse with a person who is under the legal age of consent, even if the person is a willing participant. (p. 454)

stereotypes   Oversimplified generalizations about the characteristics, attributes, and behaviors of members of a particular group or category. (p. 617)

stereotype threat   A sense of threat evoked in members of stereotyped groups when they believe they may be judged or treated stereotypically. (p. 637)

stimulant   A drug that activates the central nervous system, such as cocaine or nicotine. (pp. 52 and 164)

stimulus discrimination   The tendency to differentiate among stimuli so that stimuli that are related to the original conditioned stimulus, but not identical to it, fail to elicit a conditioned response. (p. 185)

stimulus generalization   The tendency for stimuli that are similar to the conditioned stimulus to elicit a conditioned response. (p. 184)

stimulus motives   Internal states that prompt inquisitive, stimulation-seeking, and exploratory behavior. (p. 298)

Strange Situation   Ainsworth's method for assessing infant attachment to the mother, based on a series of brief separations and reunions with the mother in a playroom situation. (p. 357)

stream of consciousness   The continuous flow of conscious thoughts. (p. 7)

stress   Pressure or demand placed on an organism to adjust or adapt. (p. 582)

stressors   Sources of stress. (p. 583)

stroboscopic movement   A type of apparent movement based on the rapid succession of still images, as in motion pictures. (p. 127)

stroke   The sudden loss of consciousness and resulting paralysis, loss of sensation, and other disability or death resulting from blockage of blood to a part of the brain or from bleeding in the brain. (p. 74)

structuralism   The school of psychology that attempts to understand the structure of the mind by breaking it down into its component parts. (p. 6)

structured interview   An interview in which a set of specific questions is asked in a particular order. (p. 30)

subjective value   In social-cognitive theory, the importance that individuals place on desired outcomes. (p. 481)

sublimation   In Freudian theory, a defense mechanism involving the channeling of unacceptable impulses into socially sanctioned behaviors or interests. (p. 465)

subliminal perception   Perception of stimuli that are presented below the threshold of conscious awareness. (p. 130)

subordinate concepts   The narrowest level of concepts in a three-level hierarchy of concepts. (p. 257)

sucking reflex   Rhythmic sucking in response to stimulation of the tongue or mouth. (p. 348)

sudden infant death syndrome (SIDS)   The sudden and unexplained death of infants that usually occurs when they are asleep in their cribs. (p. 345)

superego   Freud's term for the psychic structure that corresponds to an internal moral guardian or conscience. (p. 464)

superordinate concepts   The broadest concepts in a three-level hierarchy of concepts. (p. 257)

superstitious behavior   In Skinner's view, behavior acquired through coincidental association of a response and a reinforcement. (p. 196)

surface traits   Cattell's term for personality traits at the surface level that can be gleaned from observations of behavior. (p. 473)

survey method   A research method that uses structured interviews or questionnaires to gather information about groups of people. (p. 30)

symbolic representations   Symbols that stand for names and experiences; specifically, the words in a language. (p. 370)

sympathetic nervous system   The branch of the autonomic nervous system that accelerates bodily processes and releases the stores of energy needed to meet increased physical demands. (p. 57)

synapse   The small fluid-filled gap between neurons through which neurotransmitters carry neural impulses. (p. 47)

syntax   The rules of grammar that determine how words are ordered within sentences or phrases to form meaningful expressions. (p. 268)

systematic desensitization   A behavior therapy technique for treating phobias through the pairing of exposure in imagination to fear-inducing stimuli and states of deep relaxation. (p. 554)

tardive dyskinesia (TD)   A potentially disabling motor disorder that may occur following regular use of antipsychotic drugs. (p. 572)

taste buds   Pores or openings on the tongue containing taste cells. (p. 113)

taste cells   Nerve cells that are sensitive to tastes. (p. 113)

telecommuting   A form of working at home in which people communicate with their home office and clients via computer or telecommunications. (p. 654)

telepathy   Communication of thoughts from one mind to another that occurs without using the known senses. (p. 130)

temperament   A characteristic style of behavior or disposition. (p. 355)

temporal lobes   The parts of the cerebral cortex lying beneath and somewhat behind the frontal lobes that are involved in processing auditory stimuli. (p. 65)

teratogen   An environmental influence or agent that may harm the developing embryo or fetus. (p. 344)

terminal buttons   Swellings at the tips of axons from which neurotransmitters are dispatched into the synapse. (p. 47)

testes   The male gonads, which produce sperm and secrete the male sex hormone testosterone. (p. 81)

thalamus   A structure in the forebrain that serves as a relay station for sensory information and that plays a key role in regulating states of wakefulness and sleep. (p. 61)

theories   Formulations that account for relationships among observed events or experimental findings in ways that make them more understandable and predictable. (p. 26)

thermal biofeedback   A form of biofeedback training that involves feedback about changes in temperature and blood flow in selected parts of the body; used in the treatment of migraine headaches. (p. 134)

thinking   The process of mentally representing and manipulating information. (p. 254)

thought disorder   A breakdown in the logical structure of thought and speech, revealed in the form of a loosening of associations. (p. 531)

three-stage model   A model of memory that posits three distinct stages of memory: sensory memory, short-term memory, and long-term memory. (p. 220)

thyroid gland   An endocrine gland in the neck that secretes hormones involved in regulating metabolic functions and physical growth. (p. 81)

tip-of-the-tongue (TOT) phenomenon   An experience in which people are sure they know something but can't seem to bring it to mind. (p. 238)

token economy program A form of behavior modification in which tokens earned for performing desired behaviors can be exchanged for positive reinforcers. (p. 204)

tolerance A form of physical habituation to a drug in which increased amounts are needed to achieve the same effect. (p. 160)

top-down processing A mode of perceptual processing by which the brain identifies patterns as meaningful wholes rather than as piecemeal constructions. (p. 120)

traits Relatively enduring personal characteristics. (p. 473)

transcendental meditation (TM) A form of meditation in which practitioners focus their attention by repeating a particular mantra. (p. 154)

transference relationship In therapy, the tendency of clients to reenact earlier conflicted relationships in the relationship they develop with their therapists. (p. 550)

transsexualism A mismatch in which one's gender identity is inconsistent with one's chromosomal and anatomic sex. (p. 425)

transvestism A type of paraphilia involving cross-dressing for purposes of sexual arousal. (p. 442)

triangular model of love Sternberg's concept of love as a triangle with three components: intimacy, passion, and decision/commitment. (p. 328)

triarchic theory of intelligence Sternberg's theory of intelligence that posits three aspects of intelligence: analytic, creative, and practical. (p. 282)

trichromatic theory A theory of color vision that posits that the ability to see different colors depends on the relative activity of three types of color receptors in the eye (red, green, and blue-violet). (p. 102)

trichromats People with normal color vision who can discern all the colors of the visual spectrum. (p. 103)

tricyclics A class of antidepressant drugs that increase the availability of neurotransmitters in the brain by interfering with the reuptake of these chemicals by transmitting neurons. (p. 570)

twin studies Studies that examine the degree to which concordance rates between co-twins for particular disorders or characteristics vary in relation to whether the twins are identical or fraternal. (p. 86)

two-factor model The theory that emotions involve two factors: a state of general arousal and a cognitive interpretation (or labeling) of the causes of the arousal. (p. 322)

Type A behavior pattern (TABP) A behavior pattern characterized by impatience, time urgency, competitiveness, and hostility. (p. 589)

ultrasound imaging A technique for using high-pitched sound waves to form an image of the fetus in the womb. (p. 346)

unconditional positive regard Valuing another person as having intrinsic worth, regardless of the person's behavior at the particular time. (p. 486)

unconditioned response (UR) An unlearned response to a stimulus. (p. 183)

unconditioned stimulus (US) A stimulus that elicits an unlearned response. (p. 183)

unconscious In Freudian theory, the part of the mind that lies outside the range of ordinary awareness and that contains primitive drives or instincts and unacceptable urges, wishes, or ideas. (pp. 8 and 463)

unconsciousness In ordinary use, a term referring to lack of awareness of one's surroundings or to loss of consciousness. (p. 140)

uterus The female reproductive organ in which the fertilized ovum becomes implanted and develops to term. (p. 343)

vaccination A method of acquiring immunity by means of injecting a weakened or partial form of an infectious agent that can induce production of antibodies but does not produce a full-blown infection. (p. 596)

validity The degree to which a test measures what it purports to measure. (p. 278)

variability In statistics, the spread or dispersion of scores throughout the distribution. (p. A-8)

variables Factors or measures that vary within an experiment or among individuals. (p. 27)

vasocongestion Swelling of tissues with blood, a process that accounts for penile erection and vaginal lubrication during sexual arousal. (p. 436)

ventromedial hypothalamus A part of the hypothalamus involved in regulating feelings of satiety. (p. 306)

vestibular sacs Organs in the inner ear that connect the semicircular canals. (p. 116)

vestibular sense The sense that keeps us informed about balance and the position of our body in space. (p. 116)

virtual reality therapy A form of behavior therapy in which virtual reality is used to simulate real-world environments that can be used as therapeutic tools. (p. 568)

visual illusions Misperceptions of visual stimuli. (p. 125)

visuospatial sketchpad The storage buffer for visual-spatial material held in short-term memory. (p. 222)

volley principle The principle that relates the experience of pitch to the alternating firing of groups of neurons along the basilar membrane. (p. 108)

volunteer bias The type of bias that arises when people who volunteer to participate in a survey or research study have characteristics that make them unrepresentative of the population from which they were drawn. (p. 30)

voyeurism A type of paraphilia that involves watching unsuspecting others as they disrobe or engage in sexual activities. (p. 443)

waxy flexibility A feature of catatonic schizophrenia in which people rigidly maintain the body position or posture in which they were placed by others. (p. 532)

Weber's law The principle that the amount of change in a stimulus needed to detect a difference is given by a constant ratio or fraction, called a constant, of the original stimulus. (p. 95)

Wernicke's area An area of the left temporal lobe involved in processing written and spoken language. (p. 72)

withdrawal syndrome A cluster of symptoms associated with abrupt withdrawal from a drug. (p. 160)

working memory The memory system that enables you to hold and manipulate information in your mind for brief periods of time. (p. 221)

Yerkes-Dodson law The proposition that the relationship between arousal and performance involves an inverted U-shaped function, with better performance occurring at moderate levels of arousal. (p. 299)

zone of proximal development (ZPD) In Vygotsky's theory, the range between children's present level of knowledge and their potential knowledge state if they receive proper guidance and instruction. (p. 374)

zygote A fertilized egg cell. (pp. 86 and 342)

References

A growing gender gap (and it's not what you think). (2000, June 14). *New York Times*, p. G1.

Abbott, R. D., White, L. R., Ross, G. W., Masaki, K. H., Curb, J. D., & Petrovitch, H. (2004). Walking and dementia in physically capable elderly men. *Journal of the American Medical Association, 292*, 1447–1453.

Abel, M., & Sewell, J. (1999). Stress and burnout within rural and secondary school teachers. *Journal of Educational Research, 92*, 287–293.

Abikoff, H., Hechtman, L., Klein, R. G., Weiss, G., Fleiss, K., Etcovitch, J., et al. (2004). Symptomatic improvement in children with ADHD treated with long-term methylphenidate and multimodal psychosocial treatment. *Journal of the American Academy of Child and Adolescent Psychiatry, 43*, 802–811.

Aboud, F. E. (2003). The formation of in-group favoritism and out-group prejudice in young children: Are they distinct attitudes? *Developmental Psychology, 39*, 48–60.

Abraham, K. (1948). The first pregenital stage of the libido (1916). In D. Bryan & A. Strachey (Eds.), *Selected papers of Karl Abraham, M. D.* London: Hogarth Press.

Abrahamson, A. C., Baker, L. A., & Caspi, A. (2002). Rebellious teens? Genetic and environmental influences on the social attitudes of adolescents. *Journal of Personality and Social Psychology, 83*, 1392–1408.

Abramson, L. T., Seligman, M. E. P., & Teasdale, J. D. (1978). Learned helplessness in humans: Critique and reformulation. *Journal of Abnormal Psychology, 87*, 49–74.

Ackerman, S. J., & Hilsenroth, M. J. (2003). A review of therapist characteristics and techniques positively impacting the therapeutic alliance. *Clinical Psychology Review, 23*, 1–33.

AD 2000 Collaborative Group. (2004). Long-term donepezil treatment in 565 patients with Alzheimer's disease (AD2000): Randomised double-blind trial. *Lancet, 363*, 2105–2015.

Addis, M. E. (2002). Methods for disseminating research products and increasing evidence-based practice: Promises, obstacles, and future directions. *Clinical Psychology: Science and Practice, 9*, 367–378.

Addis, M. E., Hatgis, C., Krasnow, A. D., Jacob, K., Bourne, L., & Mansfield, A. (2004). Effectiveness of cognitive-behavioral treatment for panic disorder versus treatment as usual in a managed care setting. *Journal of Consulting and Clinical Psychology, 72*, 625–635.

Adelson, A. (1990, November 19). Study attacks women's roles in TV. *New York Times*, p. C18.

Adelson, R. (2002, June). Figure this: Deciding what's figure, what's ground. *Monitor on Psychology, 33*, 44–45.

Adelson, R. (2004a, April). Stimulating the vagus nerve: Memories are made of this. *Monitor on Psychology, 35*, 36–38.

Adelson, R. (2004b, July). Detecting deception. *Monitor on Psychology, 35*, 70–73.

Adelson, R. (2004c, July). The polygraph in doubt. *Monitor on Psychology, 35*, 71.

Adelson, R. (2005, February). Hues and views. *Monitor on Psychology, 36*, 26–29.

Ader, R., & Cohen, N. (1982). Behaviorally conditioned immunosuppression and murine systemic lupus erythematosus. *Science, 215*, 1534–1536.

Adler, J. (2003, October 20). In the grip of a deeper pain. *Newsweek*, pp. 48–49.

Adler, J. (2004, March 8). The war on strokes. *Newsweek*, pp. 42–48.

Adler, J., & Raymond, J. (2001, Fall/Winter). Fight back, with sweat. *Newsweek Special Issue*, pp. 35–41.

Adorno, T. W., Frenkel-Brunswik, E., Levinson, D., & Sanford, R. N. (1950). *The authoritarian personality*. New York: Harper.

Agliata, D., & Tantleff-Dunn, S. (2004). The impact of media exposure on males' body image. *Journal of Social and Clinical Psychology, 23*, 7–22.

Aguiara, A., & Baillargeon, R. (2002). Developments in young infants' reasoning about occluded objects. *Cognitive Psychology, 45*, 267–336.

Ainsworth, M. D. S. (1967). *Infancy in Uganda: Infant care and the growth of love*. Baltimore, MD: John Hopkins University Press.

Ainsworth, M. D. S. (1979). Infant-mother attachment. *American Psychologist, 34*, 932–937.

Ainsworth, M. D. S., Blehar, M. C., Waters, E., & Wall, S. (1978). *Patterns of attachment: A psychological study of the Strange Situation*. Hillsdale, NJ: Erlbaum.

Aldrich, M. S. (1992). Narcolepsy. *Neurology, 42*(7, Suppl. 6), 34–43.

Aleman, A., Kahn, R. S., & Selten, J.-P. (2003). Sex differences in the risk of schizophrenia: Evidence from meta-analysis. *Archives of General Psychiatry, 60*, 565–571.

Alexander, C. N., Robinson, P., & Rainforth, M. (1995). "Treating and preventing alcohol, nicotine, and drug abuse through transcendental meditation: A review and statistical meta-analysis": Errata. *Alcoholism Treatment Quarterly, 13*(4), 97.

Alexander, E. N., & Bowen, A. M. (2004). Excessive drinking in college: Behavioral outcome, not binge, as a basis for prevention. *Addictive Behaviors, 29*, 1199–1205.

Ali, L, & Scelfo, J. (2002, December 9). Choosing virginity. *Newsweek*, pp. 61–66.

Allen, G., & Courchesne, E. (2003). Differential effects of developmental cerebellar abnormality on cognitive and motor functions in the cerebellum: An fMRI study of autism. *American Journal of Psychiatry, 160*, 262–273.

Allen, M., & Burrell, N. (1996). Comparing the impact of homosexual and heterosexual parents on children: Meta-analysis of existing research. *Journal of Homosexuality, 32*(2), 19–35.

Allgulander, C., Dahl, A. A., Austin, C., Morris, P. L. P., Sogaard, J. A., Fayyad, R., Kutcher, S. P., et al. (2004). Efficacy of sertraline in a 12-week trial for generalized anxiety disorder. *American Journal of Psychiatry, 161*, 1642–1649.

Alloy, L. B., Abramson, L. Y., Hogan, M. E., Whitehouse, W. G., Rose, D. T., Robinson, M. S., et al. (2000). The Temple-Wisconsin cognitive vulnerability to depression project: Lifetime history of Axis I psychopathology in individuals at high and low cognitive risk for depression. *Journal of Abnormal Psychology, 109*, 403–418.

Allport, G. W. (1954). *The nature of prejudice*. Reading, MA: Addison-Wesley.

Allport, G. W. (1961). *Pattern and growth in personality*. New York: Holt, Rinehart & Winston.

Alpert, J. L., Brown, L. S., & Courtois, C. A. (1998). *Working group on investigation of memories of childhood abuse: Final report*. Washington, DC: American Psychological Association.

Alterman, A. I., Cacciola, J. S., Mulvaney, F. D., Rutherford, M. J., & Langenbucher, J. (2002). Alcohol dependence and abuse in three groups at varying familial alcoholism risk. *Journal of Consulting and Clinical Psychology, 70*, 336–343.

Altman, D. (2004, June). The dismal science measures the meaning of life. *Business 2.0.*, p. 56.

Altman, L. K. (2001, January 30). The AIDS questions that linger. *New York Times*, pp. F1, F6.

American Academy of Pediatrics, Committee on Psychosocial Aspects of Child and Family Health. (1998). Guidance for effective discipline. *Pediatrics, 101*(4), 723.

American Cancer Society. (2001). *Cancer facts and figures 2001*. Atlanta, GA: Author.

American College of Obstetricians and Gynecologists. (2000). *Alcohol and pregnancy* (ACOG Education Pamphlet AP132). Retrieved October 12, 2004, from www.medem.com/medlb/article_detaillb.cfm?article_ID=ZZZQJ1NS77C&sub_cat=3.

American dream: Live long and prosper. (2001, June 13). Retrieved June 15, 2001, from www.cnn.com/2001/HEALTH/06/13/living.longer/index.html.

American Psychiatric Association. (2000). *DSM-IV-TR: Diagnostic and statistical manual of mental disorders* (Text Revision). Washington, DC: Author.

American Psychological Association (APA). (2002). Ethical principles of psychologists and code of conduct. *American Psychologist, 57*, 1060–1073.

American Psychological Association. (2003a, July*). Employment settings for PhD psychologists: 2001*. Washington, DC: APA Research Office.

American Psychological Association. (2003b, September). *Demographic shifts in psychology*. Washington, DC: APA Research Office.

American Psychological Association. (2004, April). *Current major fields of APA membership by membership status, 2002*. Washington, DC: APA Research Office.

Americans Axel, Buck win Nobel for medicine (2004, October 4). *Wall Street Journal Online*. Retrieved October 4, 2004, from online.wsj.com/article/0,,SB109688300056835177,00.html?mod=home_whats_news_us.

Andersen, B. L., Golden-Kreutz, D. M., & DiLillo, V. (2001). Cancer. In A. Baum, T. A. Revenson, & J. E. Singer (Eds.), *Handbook of health psychology* (pp. 709–726). Mahwah, NJ: Lawrence Erlbaum Associates.

Anderson, C. A. (2004). Video games and public health. *Journal of Adolescence, 27,* 113–122.

Anderson, C. A., Berkowitz, L., Donnerstein, E., Huesmann, L. R., Johnson, J. D., Linz, D., et al. (2004). The influence of media violence on youth. *Psychological Science in the Public Interest, 4,* 81–110.

Anderson, C. A., & Bushman, B. J. (2002). Human aggression. *Annual Review of Psychology, 53,* 27–51.

Anderson, C. A., & DeNeve, K. M. (1992). Temperature, aggression, and the negative affect escape model. *Psychological Bulletin, 111,* 347–351.

Anderson, C. A., Deuser, W. E., & DeNeve, K. M. (1995). Hot temperatures, hostile affect, hostile cognition, and arousal: Tests of a general model of affective aggression. *Personality and Social Psychology Bulletin, 21,* 434–448.

Anderson, C. A., Funk, J. B., & Griffiths, M. D. (2004). Contemporary issues in adolescent video game playing: Brief overview and introduction to the special issue. *Journal of Adolescence, 27,* 1–3.

Anderson, D. E. (2003, August). *Longitudinal study of formal operations in college students.* Paper presented at the meeting of the American Psychological Association, Toronto, CA.

Anderson, E. M., & Lambert, M. J. (2001). A survival analysis of clinically significant change in outpatient psychotherapy. *Professional Psychology: Research and Practice, 57,* 875–888.

Anderson, N. B., & Nickerson, K. J. (2005). Genes, race, and psychology in the genome era: An introduction. *American Psychologist, 60,* 5–8.

Anderson, R. N., & Smith, B. L. (2005, March 7). Deaths: Leading causes for 2002. *National Vital Statistics Reports, 53*(17). Retrieved July 3, 2005, from www.cdc.gov/nchs/data/nvsr/nvsr53/nvsr53_17.pdf.

Anderson, S. E., Dallal, G. E., & Must, A. (2003). Relative weight and race influence average age at menarche: Results from two nationally representative surveys of US girls studied 25 years apart. *Pediatrics, 111,* 844–850.

Anderson, S. W., Bechara, A., Damasio, H., Tranel, D., & Damasio, A. R. (1999). Impairment of social and moral behavior related to early damage in human prefrontal cortex. *Nature Neuroscience, 2,* 1032–1037.

Andreasen, A. (2003). From molecule to mind: Genetics, genomics, and psychiatry. *American Journal of Psychiatry, 160,* 613. [Editorial]

Angier, N. (1998a, February 8). Separated by birth? *New York Times Book Review,* p. 9.

Angier, N. (1998b, September 1). Nothing becomes a man more than a woman's face. *New York Times,* p. F3.

Angier, N. (2003, July 8). Opposites attract? Not in real life. *New York Times,* pp. F1, F6.

Ansorge, U., & Heumann, M. (2003). Top-down contingencies in peripheral cuing: The roles of color and location. *Journal of Experimental Psychology: Human Perception and Performance, 29,* 937–948.

Appelloo, M. J., Van Der Stege, J. G., Hoek, A., & Weijmar Schultz, W. C. (2003). In the mood for sex: The value of androgens. *Journal of Sex and Marital Therapy, 29,* 87–102.

Applebome, P. (1997, May 7). Gender gap in testing narrower than believed, study finds. *New York Times,* p. A16.

Arbelle, S., Benjamin, J., Golin, M., Kremer, I., Belmaker, R. H., & Ebstein, R. P. (2003). Relation of shyness in grade school children to the genotype for the long form of the serotonin transporter promoter region polymorphism. *American Journal of Psychiatry, 160,* 671–676.

Archer, J. (2004). Sex differences in aggression in real-world settings: A meta-analytic review. *Review of General Psychology, 8,* 291–322.

Arnett, J. (1992). Reckless behavior in adolescence: A developmental perspective. *Developmental Review, 12,* 339–373.

Arnett, J. J. (1999). Adolescent storm and stress, reconsidered. *American Psychologist, 54,* 317–26.

Arnett, J. J. (2000). Emerging adulthood: A theory of development from the late teens through the twenties. *American Psychologist, 55,* 469–480.

Arnett, J. J. (2004). *Adolescence and emerging adulthood: A cultural approach* (2nd ed.). Upper Saddle River, NJ: Pearson/Prentice Hall.

Arnett, P. A., Smith, S. S., & Newman, J. P. (1997). Approach and avoidance motivation in psychopathic criminal offenders during passive avoidance. *Journal of Personality and Social Psychology, 72,* 1413–1428.

Arnold, D. H., & Doctoroff, G. L. (2003). The early education of socioeconomically disadvantaged children. *Annual Review of Psychology, 54,* 517–545.

Aronson, E., Wilson, T. D., & Akert, R. M. (2004). *Social psychology: Media and research update.* (5th ed.). Upper Saddle River, NJ: Prentice Hall.

Aronson, J., Fried, C. B., & Good, C. (2002). Reducing the effects of stereotype threat on African American college students by shaping theories of intelligence. *Journal of Experimental Social Psychology, 38,* 113–125.

Arrindell, W. A. (2003). Cultural abnormal psychology. *Behaviour Research & Therapy, 41,* 749–753.

Asch, S. E. (1956). Studies of independence and conformity: I. A minority of one against a unanimous majority. *Psychological Monographs, 70,* 70.

Ashburn-Nardo, L., Voils, C. I., & Monteith, M. J. (2001). Implicit associations as the seeds of intergroup bias: How easily do they take root? *Journal of Personality and Social Psychology, 81,* 789–799.

Ashby, F. G., & Maddox, W. T. (2005). Human category learning. *Annual Review of Psychology, 56,* 149–178.

Ashmore, J. (2004). Hearing: Channel at the hair's end. *Nature, 432,* 685–686.

Asian Americans and Census 2000 results. (2003, September 13). *AsiaSource Web Posting.* Retrieved September 13, 2003, from http://www.asiasource.org/news/at_mp_02.cfm?newsid=53011.

Atkinson, L., Paglia, A., Coolbear, J., Niccols, A., Parker, K. C. H., & Buger, S. (2000). Attachment security: A meta-analysis of maternal mental health correlates. *Clinical Psychology Review, 20,* 1019–1040.

Atkinson, R. C., & Shiffrin, R. M. (1971). The control of short-term memory. *Scientific American, 225,* 82–90.

August, R. A., & Quintero, V. C. (2001). The role of opportunity structures in older women workers' careers. *Journal of Employment Counseling, 38,* 62–81.

Averhart, C. J., & Bigler, R. S. (1997). Shades of meaning: Skin tone, racial attitudes, and constructive memory in African American children. *Journal of Experimental Child Psychology, 67,* 363–388.

Azar, B. (1996a, April). Musical studies provide clues to brain functions. *APA Monitor, 27*(4), 1, 24.

Azar, B. (1996b, August). Why men lose keys—and women find them. *APA Monitor, 27*(8), 32.

Azar, B. (1998a, January). What predicts which foods we eat? *APA Monitor, 29*(1), 13.

Azar, B. (1998b, September). Of Zajonc's ever-changing focus, friends joke 'What about Bob?' *APA Monitor, 29*(9), 12.

Bach, P. B., Schrag, D., Brawley, O. W., Galaznik, A., Yakren, S., & Begg, C. B. (2002). Survival of Blacks and Whites after a cancer diagnosis. *Journal of the American Medical Association, 287,* 2106–2113.

Bachmann, G., Bancroft, J., Braunstein, G., Burger, H., Davis, S., Dennerstein, L., Goldstein, I., et al. (2002). Female androgen insufficiency: The Princeton consensus statement on definition, classification, and assessment. *Fertility and Sterility, 77,* 660–665.

Baddeley, A. D. (1996). *Human memory: Theory and practice* (2nd ed.). Hove, England: Psychology Press.

Baddeley, A. D. (2001). Levels of working memory. In M. Naveh-Benjamin, M. Moscovitch, & H. L. Roediger (Eds.), *Perspectives on human memory and cognitive aging: Essays in honor of Fergus Craik.* Hove, England: Psychology Press.

Baddeley, A., Conway, M., & Aggleton J. (Eds.). (2002). *Episodic memory: New directions in research.* Oxford, England: Oxford University Press.

Baddeley, A. D., & Hitch, G. J. (1974). Working memory. In G. Bower (Ed.), *The psychology of learning and motivation* (Vol. 8, pp. 47–90). New York: Academic Press.

Baer, H., Allen, S., & Braun, L. (2000). Knowledge of human papillomavirus infection among young adult men and women: Implications for health education and research. *Journal of Community Health, 25,* 67–78.

Baer, R. A. (2003). Mindfulness training as a clinical intervention: A conceptual and empirical review. *Clinical Psychology: Science and Practice, 10,* 125–143.

Baeyens, F., Eelen, P., & Crombez, G. (1995). Pavlovian associations are forever: On classical conditioning and extinction. *Journal of Psychophysiology, 9,* 127–141.

Bagary, M. S., Symms, M. R., Barker, G. J., Mutsatsa, S. H., Joyce, E. M., & Ron, M. A. (2003). Gray and white matter brain abnormalities in first-episode schizophrenia inferred from magnetization transfer imaging. *Archives of General Psychiatry, 60,* 779–788.

Bagley, C., & D'Augelli, A. R. (2000). Suicidal behaviour in gay, lesbian, and bisexual youth. *British Medical Journal, 320,* 1617–1618.

Bailar, J. C., III. (2001). The powerful placebo and the wizard of Oz. *New England Journal of Medicine, 344,* 1630–1632.

Bailey, J. M. (2003). *The man who would be queen: The science of gender-bending and transsexualism.* Washington, DC: Joseph Henry Press.

Bailey, J. M., Bobrow, D., Wolfe, M., & Mikach, S. (1995). Sexual orientation of adult sons of gay fathers. *Developmental Psychology, 31,* 124–129.

Bailey, J. M., Dunne, M. P., & Martin, N. G. (2000). Genetic and environmental influences on sexual orientation and its correlates in an Australian twin sample. *Journal of Personality and Social Psychology, 78,* 524–536.

Bailey, J. M., & Zucker, K. J. (1995). Childhood sex-typed behavior and sexual orientation: A conceptual analysis and quantitative review. *Developmental Psychology, 31,* 43–55.

Baldessarini, R. J., & Tondo, M. D. (2003). Suicide risk and treatments for patients with bipolar disorder. *Journal of the American Medical Association, 290,* 1517–1519.

Balkin, T. J., Braun, A. R., Wesensten, N. J., Jeffries, K., Varga, M., et al. (2002). The process of awakening: A PET study of regional brain activity patterns mediating the re-establishment of alertness and consciousness. *Brain, 125,* 2308–2319.

Ball, K., Berch, D. B., Helmers, K. F., Jobe, J. B., Leveck, M. D., Marsiske, M., et al. (2002). Effects of cognitive training interventions with older adults. A randomized controlled trial. *Journal of the American Medical Association, 288,* 2271—2281.

Balter, M. (2001, October 5). First gene linked to speech identified. *Science, 294,* 32.

Banaji, M. R., & Greenwald, A. G. (1995). Implicit gender stereotyping in judgments of fame. *Journal of Personality and Social Psychology, 68,* 181–198.

Bancroft, J., Loftus, J., & Long, J. S. (2003). Distress about sex: A national survey of women in heterosexual relationships. *Archives of Sexual Behavior, 32,* 193–208.

Bandura, A. (1973). *Aggression: A social learning analysis.* Englewood Cliffs, NJ: Prentice-Hall.

Bandura, A. (1986). *Social foundations of thought and action: A social-cognitive theory.* Englewood Cliffs, NJ: Prentice-Hall.

Bandura, A. (1997). *Self-efficacy: The exercise of control.* New York: Freeman.

Bandura, A. (2001). Social cognitive theory: An agentic perspective. *Annual Review of Psychology, 52,* 1–26.

Bandura, A. (2004). Swimming against the mainstream: The early years from chilly tributary to transformative mainstream. *Behaviour Research and Therapy, 42,* 613–630.

Bandura, A., Blanchard, E. B., & Ritter, B. (1969). The relative efficacy of desensitization and modeling approaches for inducing behavioral, affective, and cognitive changes. *Journal of Personality and Social Psychology, 13,* 173–199.

Bandura, A., & Locke, E. A. (2003). Negative self-efficacy and goal effects revisited. *Journal of Applied Psychology, 88,* 87–89.

Bandura, A., Ross, S. A., & Ross, D. (1963). Imitation of film-mediated aggressive models. *Journal of Abnormal Psychology, 66,* 3–11.

Barbaree, H. E., & Marshall, W. L. (1991). The role of male sexual arousal in rape: Six models. *Journal of Consulting and Clinical Psychology, 59,* 621–630.

Barber, T. X. (1999). A comprehensive three-dimensional theory of hypnosis. In I. Kirsch et al. (Eds.), *Clinical hypnosis and self-regulation: Cognitive-behavioral perspectives* (pp. 21–48). Washington, DC: American Psychological Association.

Barch, D. M., Csernansky, J. G., Conturo, T., & Snyder, A. Z. (2002). Working and long-term memory deficits in schizophrenia: Is there a common prefrontal mechanism? *Journal of Abnormal Psychology, 111,* 478–494.

Bargh, J. A., & Chartrand, T. L. (1999). The unbearable automaticity of being. *American Psychologist, 54,* 462–279.

Barinaga, M. (2002). How the brain's clock gets daily enlightenment. *Science, 295,* 955–957.

Barlow, D. H., Gorman, J. M., Shear, M. K., & Woods, S. W. (2000). Cognitive-behavioral therapy, imipramine, or their combination for panic disorder: A randomized controlled trial. *Journal of the American Medical Association, 283,* 2529–2536.

Barnes, V. A., Treiber, F. A., & Johnson, M. H. (2004). Impact of transcendental meditation on ambulatory blood pressure in African-American adolescents. *American Journal of Hypertension, 17,* 366–369.

Barnett, W. S., & Camilli, G. (2002). Compensatory preschool education, cognitive development, and "race." In J. M. Fish (Ed.), *Race and intelligence: Separating science from myth* (pp. 369–406). Mahwah, NJ: Lawrence Erlbaum Associates.

Barrett, D. (1996). Fantasizers and dissociaters: Two types of high hypnotizables, two different imagery styles. In R. G. Kunzeorf, N. P. Spanos, & B. Wallace (Eds.), *Hypnosis and imagination* (pp. 123–135). Amityville, NY: Baywood Publishing.

Barrett, L. F., Tugade, M. M., & Engle, R. (2004). Individual differences in working memory capacity and dual-process theories of the mind. *Psychological Bulletin, 130,* 553–573.

Barry, D. T., & Bullock, W. A. (2001). Culturally creative psychotherapy with a Latino couple by an Anglo therapist. *Journal of Family Psychotherapy, 12,* 15–30.

Bartho, P., Hirase, H., Monconduit, L., Zugaro, M., Harris, K. D., & Buzsaki, G. (2004). Characterization of neocortical principal cells and interneurons by network interactions and extracellular features. *Journal of Neurophysiology, 92,* 600–608.

Bartholet, J. (2000, January 17). The plague years. *Newsweek,* pp. 32–37.

Bartoschuk, L. M., & Beauchamp, G. K. (1994). Chemical senses. *Annual Review of Psychology, 45,* 419–449.

Basic Behavioral Science Task Force of the National Advisory Mental Health Council. (1996a). Basic behavioral science research for mental health: Perception, attention, learning, and memory. *American Psychologist, 51,* 133–142.

Basic Behavioral Science Task Force of the National Advisory Mental Health Council. (1996b). Basic behavioral science research for mental health: Sociocultural and environmental practices. *American Psychologist, 51,* 722–731.

Batson, C. D. (1998). Altruism and prosocial behavior. In D. T. Gilbert, S. T. Fiske, & G. Lindzey (Eds.), *The handbook of social psychology* (4th ed., Vol. 2, pp. 282–316). Boston: McGraw-Hill.

Batson, C. D., Ahmad, N., Lishner, D. A., & Tsang, J. (2002). Empathy and altruism. In C. R. Snyder & S. J. Lopez (Eds.), *Handbook of positive psychology* (pp. 485–498). New York: Oxford University Press.

Batson, C. Daniel, & Powell, A. A. (2003). Altruism and prosocial behavior. In T. Millon & M. J. Lerner (Eds.), *Handbook of psychology: Personality and social psychology* (Vol. 5, pp. 463–484). New York: Wiley.

Batterham, R. L., Cohen, M. A., Ellis, S. M., Le Roux, C. W., Withers, D. J., et al. (2003). Inhibition of food intake in obese subjects by Peptide YY3–36. *New England Journal of Medicine, 349,* 941–948.

Baumeister, R. F. (2000). Gender differences in erotic plasticity: The female sex drive as socially flexible and responsive. *Psychological Bulletin, 126,* 347–374.

Baumeister, R. F., Campbell, J. D., Krueger, J. I., & Vohs, K. D. (2003). Does high self-esteem cause better performance, interpersonal success, happiness, or healthier lifestyle? *Psychological Science in the Public Interest, 4,* 1–44.

Baumeister, R. F., Catanese, K. R., & Vohs, K. D. (2001). Is there a gender difference in strength of sex drive? Theoretical views, conceptual distinctions, and a review of relevant evidence. *Personality & Social Psychology Review, 5,* 242–273.

Baumeister, R. F., Catanese, K. R., & Wallace, H. M. (2002). Conquest by force: A narcissistic reactance theory of rape and sexual coercion. *Review of General Psychology, 6,* 92–135.

Baumeister, R. F., & Leary, M. R. (1995). The need to belong: Desire for interpersonal attachments as a fundamental human motivation. *Psychological Bulletin, 117,* 497–529.

Baumrind, D. (1971). Current patterns of parental authority. *Developmental Psychology, 4*(1), Part 2, 1–103.

Baumrind, D. (1991). Parenting styles and adolescent development. In J. Brooks-Gunn, R. Lerner, & A. C. Petersen (Eds.), *Encyclopedia of adolescence, II.* New York: Garland.

Baumrind, D., Larzelere, R. E., & Cowan, P. A. (2002). Ordinary physical punishment: Is it harmful? Comment on Gershoff (2002). *Psychological Bulletin, 128,* 580–589.

Baylis, G. C., & Cale, E. M. (2001). The figure has a shape, but the ground does not: Evidence from a priming paradigm. *Journal of Experimental Psychology: Human Perception and Performance, 27,* 633–643.

Bayliss, D. M., Jarrold, C., Gunn, D. M., & Baddeley, A. D. (2003). The complexities of complex span: Explaining individual differences in working memory in children and adults. *Journal of Experimental Psychology-General, 132,* 71–92.

Bazell, R. (2002, August 7). Hunger hormone may fight obesity: Natural chemical shown to make people feel full in buffet experiment. *MSNBC.com.* Retrieved August 9, 2002, from www.msnbc.com/news/791118.asp.

Bean, J. L. (2002). Expressions of female sexuality. *Journal of Sex & Marital Therapy, 28*(Suppl.), 29–38.

Bechtoldt, H., Norcross, J. C., Wyckoff, L. A., Pokrywa, M. L., Campbell, L. F., et al. (2001, Winter). Theoretical orientations and employment settings of clinical and counseling psychologists: A comparative study. *Clinical Psychologist, 54,* 3–6.

Beck, A. T., & Young, J. E. (1985). Depression. In D. H. Barlow (Ed.), *Clinical handbook of psychological disorders* (pp. 206–244). New York: Guilford Press.

Beck, A. T., Rush, A. J., Shaw, B. F., & Emery, G. (1979). *Cognitive therapy of depression.* New York: Guilford Press.

Beck, A. T. (2005). The current state of cognitive therapy: A 40-year retrospective. *Archives of General Psychiatry, 62,* 953–959.

Beck, M. (1992, December 7). The new middle age. *Newsweek,* pp. 50–56.

Becker, S. W., & Eagly, A. H. (2004). The heroism of women and men. *American Psychologist, 59,* 163–178.

Beekman, A. T. F., Geerlings, S. W., Deeg, D. J. H., Smit, J. H., Schoevers, R. S., de Beurs, E., et al. (2002). The natural history of late-life depression: A 6-year prospective study in the community. *Archives of General Psychiatry, 59,* 605–611.

Begley, S. (2000a, October 9). The science of laughs. *Newsweek*, pp. 75–76.

Begley, S. (2000b, Fall/Winter). Tuning up the brain. *Newsweek Special Issue*, p. 28.

Begley, S. (2001a, April 23). Are we getting smarter? *Newsweek*, pp. 50–51.

Begley, S. (2001b, July 16). Memory's mind games. *Newsweek*, pp. 52–53.

Beier, D. R., & Dluhy, R. G. (2003). Bench and bedside — the g protein--coupled receptor GPR54 and puberty. *New England Journal of Medicine, 349*, 1589–1592.

Beilock, S. L., Carr, T. H., MacMahon, C., & Starkes, J. L. (2002). When paying attention becomes counterproductive: Impact of divided versus skill-focused attention on novice and experienced performance of sensorimotor skills. *Journal of Experimental Psychology-Applied, 8*, 6–16.

Beins, B. (2002, November). Reducing student beliefs in the paranormal. *Monitor on Psychology, 33*, pp. 44–45.

Beitman, B. D. (1989). Why I am an integrationist (not an eclectic). *British Journal of Guidance and Counseling, 17*(3), 259–273.

Belkin, L. (2003a, May 25). In tough times, graduates slink back home. *New York Times*, Section 10, p. 1.

Belkin, L. (2003b, October 26). How to make your telecommute work. *New York Times*, Section 10, p. 1.

Beller, M., & Gafni, N. (2000). Can item format (multiple choice vs. open-ended) account for gender differences in mathematics achievement? *Sex Roles, 42*, 1–21.

Bellis, M. (2001, April 14). Your about.com guide to inventors. *About.com*. Retrieved May 7, 2001, from http://inventors.about.com/science/inventors/library/bl/bl12_2a_u.htm.

Belluck, P. (2000, October 18). New advice for parents: Saying "That's great!" may not be. *New York Times*, p. A18.

Belluck, P. (2003, February 9). Methadone, once the way out, suddenly grows as a killer drug. *New York Times*, pp. A1, A30.

Belsky, J., & Cassidy, J. (1994). Attachment: Theory and evidence. In M. Rutter (Ed.), *Development through life: A handbook for clinicians* (pp. 373–402). Boston: Blackwell Scientific Publications.

Bem, D. J. (1996). Exotic becomes erotic: A developmental theory of sexual orientation. *Psychological Review, 103*, 320–335.

Bem, D. J., & Honorton, C. (1994). Does Psi exist? Replicable evidence for an anomalous process of information transfer. *Psychological Bulletin, 115*, 4–18.

Bem, S. L. (1993). *The lenses of gender*. New Haven: Yale University Press.

Benight, C. C., & Bandura, A. (2004). Social cognitive theory of posttraumatic recovery: The role of perceived self-efficacy. *Behaviour Research and Therapy, 10*, 1129–1148.

Benjamin, L. T. (1988). *A history of psychology: Original source and contemporary research*. New York: McGraw-Hill.

Benjamin, L. T. (1997). The origin of psychological species: History of the beginnings of American Psychological Association divisions. *American Psychologist, 51*, 725–732.

Benjamin, L. T. (2000). The psychology laboratory at the turn of the 20th century. *American Psychologist, 55*, 318–321.

Bennett, S., Farrington, D. P., & Huesmann, L. R. (2005). Explaining gender differences in crime and violence: The importance of social cognitive skills. *Aggression and Violent Behavior, 10*, 263–288.

Benoit, D., & Parker, K. C. H. (1994). Stability and transmission of attachment across three generations. *Child Development, 65*, 1444–1456.

Benotsch, E. G., Kalichman, S., & Weinhardt, L. S. (2004). HIV–AIDS patients' evaluation of health information on the Internet: The digital divide and vulnerability to fraudulent claims. *Journal of Consulting and Clinical Psychology, 72*, 1004–1011.

Benson, E. (2003a, February). Breaking new ground. *Monitor on Psychology, 34*, 52–54.

Benson, E. (2003b, February). Intelligence across cultures. *Monitor on Psychology, 34*, 56–58.

Benson, E. (2003c, February). Intelligent intelligence testing. *Monitor on Psychology, 34*, 48–51.

Benson, E. (2003d, March). Even hands-free cell phones may impair driving. *Monitor on Psychology, 34*, 15.

Benson, E. (2003e, April). Both halves of brain process emotional speech. *Monitor on Psychology, 34*, 12.

Benson, E. S. (2004a, April). Behavioral genetics: Meet molecular biology. *Monitor on Psychology, 35*, 42–45.

Benson, E. S. (2004b, April). Heritability: It's all relative. *Monitor on Psychology, 35*, 44.

Benson, H., Corliss, J., & Cowley, G. (2005, September 27). Brain check. *Newsweek Health Online*, http://www.msnbc.msn.com/id/6038621/site/newsweek/.

Ben-Ya'acov, Y., & Amir, M. (2004). Posttraumatic symptoms and suicide risk. *Personality and Individual Differences, 36*, 1257–1264.

Berenbaum, S. A., & Bailey, J. M. (2003). Effects on gender identity of prenatal androgens and genital appearance: Evidence from girls with congenital adrenal hyperplasia. *Journal of Clinical Endocrinology and Metabolism, 88*, 1102 1106.

Berger, K. S. (1998). *The developing person through the life span* (4th ed.). New York: Worth Publishers.

Berger, K. S. (2001). *The developing person through the life span* (5th ed.). New York: Worth Publishers.

Berger, K. S., & Thompson, R. A. (1995). *The developing person through childhood and adolescence* (4th ed.). New York: Worth Publishers.

Berger, R. J., & Phillips, N. H. (1995). Energy conservation and sleep. *Behavioural Brain Research, 69*, 65–73.

Berk, L. E. (1997). *Child development* (4th ed.). Needham Heights, MA: Allyn & Bacon.

Berk, L. E. (2000). *Child development* (5th ed.). Needham Heights, MA: Allyn & Bacon.

Berkowitz, L. (1993). *Aggression: Its causes, consequences, and control*. New York: McGraw-Hill.

Berland, G. K., Elliott, M. N., Morales, L. S., Algazy, J. I., Kravitz, R. L., Broder, M. S., et al. (2001). Information on the Internet: Accessibility, quality, and readability in English and Spanish. *Journal of the American Medical Association, 285*, 2612–2621.

Bernard, L. L. (1924). *Instinct*. New York: Holt, Rinehart & Winston.

Berners-Lee, R. (with Fischetti, M.). (1999, October 24). Weaving the Web: The original design and ultimate destiny of the World Wide Web by its inventor. In K. Hafner (Ed.), Putting the W's in www. *New York Times Book Review*, p. 20.

Berry, N., Jobanputra, V., & Pal, H. (2003). Molecular genetics of schizophrenia: A critical review. *Journal of Psychiatry and Neuroscience, 28*, 415–429.

Berscheid, E., & Reis, H. T. (1998). Attraction and close relationships. In D. T. Gilbert, S. T. Fiske, & G. Lindzey (Eds.), *The handbook of social psychology* (4th ed., Vol. 2, pp. 193–281). Boston: McGraw-Hill.

Berson, D. M., Dunn, F. A., & Takao, M. (2002). Phototransduction by retinal ganglion cells that set the circadian clock. *Science, 295*, 1070–1073.

Bertenthal, B. I., & Clifton, R. K. (1997). Perception and action. In W. Damon (Series Ed.), D. Kuhn, & R. Siegler (Vol. Eds.), *Handbook of child psychology: Vol. 2. Cognition, perception, and language* (5th ed., pp. 52–102). New York: John Wiley & Sons.

Bertholf, R. L., Goodison, S., Christakis, D. A., & Zimmerman, F. J. (2004). Television viewing and attention deficits in children. *Pediatrics, 114*, 511–512.

Berthoz, S., Artiges, E., Van de Moortele, P.-F., Poline, J.-B., Rouquette, S., Consoli, S. M., et al. (2002). Effect of impaired recognition and expression of emotions on frontocingulate cortices: An fMRI study of men with alexithymia. *American Journal of Psychiatry, 159*, 961–967.

Bertrand, R. M., & Lachman, M. E. (2003). Personality development in adulthood and old age. In R. M. Lerner, M. A. Easterbrooks, & J. Mistry (Eds.), *Handbook of psychology: Developmental psychology* (Vol. 6, pp. 463–486). New York: John Wiley & Sons.

Beutler, L. E., Harwood, T. M., & Caldwell, R. (2001). Cognitive-behavioral therapy and psychotherapy integration. In K. S. Dobson (Ed.), *Handbook of cognitive-behavioral therapies* (2nd ed., pp. 138–170). New York: Guilford Press.

Beyer, S. (2002). The effects of gender, dysphoria, and performance feedback on the accuracy of self-evaluations. *Sex Roles, 47*, 453–464.

Beyer, S., Rynes, K., Perrault, J., Hay, K., & Haller, S. (2003). Gender differences in computer science students. *Proceedings of the Thirty-Fourth SIGCSE Technical Symposium on Computer Science Education*, pp. 49–53.

Beyerstein, B. (1999). *Mind-myths: Exploring everyday mysteries of the mind and brain*. New York: John Wiley.

Bianchi, F. T., Zea, M. C., Belgrave, F. Z., Echeverry, J. J. (2002). Racial identity and self-esteem among black Brazilian men: Race matters in Brazil too! *Cultural Diversity and Ethnic Minority Psychology, 8*, 157–169.

Bianchi, S. M., & Spain, D. (1977). *Women, work and family in America*. Washington, DC: Population Reference Bureau.

Biederman, J. (2003, August). *Current concepts on the pharmacotherapy of ADHD*. Paper presented at the meeting of the American Psychological Association, Toronto, CA.

Bierhaus, A., Wolf, J., Andrassy, M., Rohleder, N., Humpert, P. M., Petrov, D., et al. (2003). A mechanism converting psychosocial stress into mononuclear cell activation. *Proceedings of the National Academy of Sciences, 100*, 1920–1925.

Biernat, M., & Kobrynowicz, D. (1997). Gender- and race-based standards of competence: Lower minimum standards but higher ability standards for devalued groups. *Journal of Personality and Social Psychology, 72,* 544–557.

Biever, J. L., Castaño, M. T., de las Fuentes, C., González, C., Servín-López, S., Sprowls, C., et al. (2002). The role of language in training psychologists to work with Hispanic clients. *Professional Psychology: Research and Practice, 33,* 330–336.

Billy, J. O. G., Tanfer, K., Grady, W. R., & Klepinger, D. J. (1993). The sexual behavior of men in the United States. *Family Planning Perspectives, 25,* 52–60.

Binet, A. (1900). Reserches sur la technique de la mensuration de la tete vivante, plus other memoirs on cephalometry. *L'Année psychologique, 7,* 314–429.

Bingham, R. P., Porche-Burke, L., James, S., Sue, D. W., & Vasquez, M. J. T. (2002). Introduction: A report on the National Multicultural Conference and Summit II. *Cultural Diversity and Ethnic Minority Psychology, 8,* 75–87.

Bishop, E. G., Cherny, S. S., Corleya, R., Plomin, R., DeFriesa, J. C., & Hewitt, J. K. (2003). Developmental genetic analysis of general cognitive ability from 1 to 12 years in a sample of adoptees, biological siblings, and twins. *Intelligence, 31,* 31–49.

Bivalacqua, T. J, Champion, H. C., Hellstrom, W. J. G., &. Kadowitz, P. J. (2000). Pharmacotherapy for erectile dysfunction. *Trends in Pharmacological Sciences, 21,* 484–489.

Bjerklie, D. (2005, January 17). Can sunny thoughts halt cancer? *Time Magazine,* p. A14.

Bjork, J. M., Dougherty, D. M., Moeller, F. G., & Swann, A. C. (2000). Differential behavioral effects of plasma tryptophan depletion and loading in aggressive and nonaggressive men. *Neuropsychopharmacology, 22,* 357–359.

Bjorklund, D. F. (1995). *Children's thinking* (2nd ed.). Pacific Grove, CA: Brooks/Cole.

Bjorklund, D. F. (2003). Evolutionary psychology from a developmental systems perspective: Comment on Lickliter and Honeycutt (2003). *Psychological Bulletin, 129,* 836–841.

Blackburn, R., Renwick, S. J. D., Donnelly, J. P., & Logana, C. (2004). Big five or big two? Superordinate factors in the NEO Five Factor Inventory and the Antisocial Personality Questionnaire. *Personality and Individual Differences, 37,* 957–970.

Blackman, M. R. (2000). Age-related alterations in sleep quality and neuroendocrine function: Interrelationships and implications [Editorial]. *Journal of the American Medical Association, 284,* 879–881.

Blair, C., Gamson, D., Thorne, S., & Baker, D. (2005). Rising mean IQ: Cognitive demand of mathematics education for young children, population exposure to formal schooling, and the neurobiology of the prefrontal cortex. *Intelligence, 33,* 93–106.

Blair, I. V., Judd, C. M., & Fallman, J. L. (2004). The automaticity of race and afrocentric facial features in social judgments. *Journal of Personality and Social Psychology, 87,* 763–778.

Blair, I. V., Ma, J. E., & Lenton, A. P. (2001). Imagining stereotypes away: The moderation of implicit stereotypes through mental imagery. *Journal of Personality and Social Psychology, 81,* 828–841.

Blakeslee, S. (2003, November 11). How does the brain work? *New York Times,* Section F, p. 4.

Blakey, R. (2002, July). Advances in Alzheimer's research. *Cable News Network.* Retrieved August 14, 2002, from http://www.cnn.com/2002/HEALTH/conditions/07/18/blakey.alzheimers.otsc/index.html.

Blanchard, E. B., & Diamond, S. (1996). Psychological treatment of benign headache disorders. *Professional Psychology, 27,* 541–547.

Blanchard, E. B., & Hickling, E. J. (2004). *After the crash: Psychological assessment and treatment of survivors of motor vehicle accidents* (2nd ed.). Washington, DC: American Psychological Association.

Blascovich, J., Mendes, W. B., Hunter, S. B., & Salomon, K. (1999). Social "facilitation" as challenge and threat. *Journal of Personality and Social Psychology, 77,* 68–77.

Blascovich, J., Spencer, S. J., Quinn, D., & Steele, C. (2002). African Americans and high blood pressure: The role of stereotype threat. *Psychological Science, 12,* 225–229.

Blass, T. (2004). *The man who shocked the world.* New York: Basic Books.

Blum, R. W., Beuhring, T., Shew, M. L., Bearinger, L. H., Sieving, R. E., & Resnick, M. D. (2000). The effects of race/ethnicity, income, and family structure on adolescent risk behaviors. *American Journal of Public Health, 90,* 1879–1884.

Bodenhausen, G. V., Macrae, C. N., & Hugenberg, K. (2003). Social cognition. In T. Millon & M. J. Lerner (Eds.), *Handbook of psychology: Personality and social psychology* (Vol. 5, pp. 257–282). New York: John Wiley & Sons.

Bogg, T., & Roberts, B. W. (2004). Conscientiousness and health-related behaviors: A meta-analysis of the leading behavioral contributors to mortality. *Psychological-Bulletin, 130,* 887–919.

Boles, S. M., & Miottoa, K. (2003). Substance abuse and violence: A review of the literature. *Aggression and Violent Behavior, 8,* 155–174.

Bond, R., & Smith, P. B. (1996). Culture and conformity: A meta-analysis of studies using Asch's (1952b, 1956) line judgment task. *Psychological Bulletin, 119,* 111–137.

Bonham, V. L., Warshauer-Baker, E., & Collins, F. S. (2005). Race and ethnicity in the genome era: The complexity of the constructs. *American Psychologist, 60,* 9–15.

Bonifati,V., Rizzu, P., van Baren, M. J., Schaap, O., Breedveld, G. J., Krieger, E., et al. (2003). Mutations in the DJ-1 gene associated with autosomal recessive early-onset Parkinsonism. *Science, 299,* Issue 5604, 256–225.

Bonné, J. (2001, February 6). Meth's deadly buzz. *MSNBC.* Retrieved February 8, 2001, from http://www.MSNBC.com/news/510835.asp?bt=nm&btu=http://www.msnbc.com/tools/newstools/d/news_menu.asp&cp1=1.

Boring, E. G. (1950). *A history of experimental psychology.* New York: Appleton-Century-Crofts.

Borkenau, P., & Liebler, A. (1992). Trait inferences: Sources of validity at zero acquaintance. *Journal of Personality and Social Psychology, 62,* 645–657.

Boskind-White, M., & White, W. C. (1983). *Bulimarexia: The binge-purge cycle.* New York: W. W. Norton.

Boston Women's Health Book Collective. (1992). *The new our bodies, ourselves.* New York: Simon & Schuster.

Bostow, D. E., Kritch, K. M., & Tompkins, B. F. (1995). Computers and pedagogy: Replacing telling with interactive computer-programmed instruction. *Behavior Research Methods, Instruments and Computers, 27,* 297–300.

Botella, C., Osma, J., Garcia_Palacios, A., Quero, S., & Banos, R. M. (2004). Treatment of flying phobia using virtual reality: Data from a 1-year follow-up using a multiple baseline design. *Clinical Psychology and Psychotherapy, 11,* 311–323.

Bouchard, T. J., Jr. (2004). Genetic influence on human psychological traits. *Current Directions in Psychological Science, 13,* 148–151.

Bouret, S. G., Draper, S. J., & Simerly, R. B. (2004). Trophic action of leptin on hypothalamic neurons that regulate feeding. *Science, 304,* 108–110.

Bouton, M. E., Mineka, S., & Barlow, D. H. (2001). A modern learning theory perspective on the etiology of panic disorder. *Psychological Review, 108,* 4–32.

Bower, G. H. (1992). How might emotions affect learning? In S. A. Christianson (Ed.), *Handbook of emotions and memory* (pp. 3–31). Hillsdale, NJ: Erlbaum.

Bowlby, J. (1969). *Attachment and loss* (2nd ed.). New York: Basic Books.

Bowlby, J. (1980). *Attachment and loss / John Bowlby* (3rd ed.). New York: Basic Books.

Bowman, L. (2000, November 21). *Sleep on it for long-term memory.* Retrieved November 23, 2000, from http://www.psycport.com/news/2000/11/21/a/0000–0002-sleeplearn.html.

Boykin, A. W., & Ellison, C. M. (1995). The multiple ecologies of Black youth socialization: An Afrographic analysis. In R. L. Taylor (Ed.), *African American youth: Their social and economic status in the United States.* Westport, CT: Praeger.

Boynton, R. S. (2004, January 11). In the Jung archives. *New York Times Book Review,* p. 8.

Brackett, M. A., Mayer, J. D., & Warner, R. M. (2004). Emotional intelligence and its relation to everyday behaviour. *Personality and Individual Differences, 36,* 1387–1402.

Bradbard, M. R., & Endsley, R. C. (1983). The effects of sex-typed labeling on preschool children's information-seeking and retention. *Sex Roles, 9,* 247–261.

Braddock, D. (1992). Community mental health and mental retardation services in the United States: A comparative study of resource allocation. *American Journal of Psychiatry, 149,* 175–183.

Bradley, R. G., & Follingstad, D. R. (2001). Utilizing disclosure in the treatment of the sequelae of childhood sexual abuse. A theoretical and empirical review. *Clinical Psychology Review, 21,* 1–32.

Bradley, R., Greene, J., Russ, E., Dutra, L., & Westen, D. (2005). A multidimensional meta-analysis of psychotherapy for PTSD. *American Journal of Psychiatry, 162,* 214–227.

Bradsher, K. (2000, July 17). Was Freud a minivan or S.U.V. kind of guy? *New York Times,* pp. A1, A16.

Brain scans suggest people feel emotions through effect on body. (2000, September 20). *Cable News Network.* Retrieved September 22, 2000, from http://www.cnn.com/2000/HEALTH/09/20/brain.emotions.ap/index.html.

Brainteaser quizzes. (2001). National Institute of Environment Health Sciences, National Institutes of Health. Retrieved January 13, 2002, from http://www.niehs.nih.gov/kids/questionstx.htm.

Braswell, L., & Kendall, P. C. (2001). Cognitive-behavioral therapy with youth. In K. S. Dobson (Ed.), *Handbook of cognitive-behavioral therapies* (2nd ed., pp. 246–294). New York: Guilford Press.

Braun, B. G. (Ed.). (1986). *Treatment of multiple personality disorder.* Washington, DC: American Psychiatric Press.

Braver, T. S., Barch, D. M., Keys, B. A., Carter, C. S., Cohen, J. D., Kaye, J. A., et al. (2001). Context processing in older adults: Evidence for a theory relating cognitive control to neurobiology in healthy aging. *Journal of Experimental Psychology: General, 130,* 746–763.

Brazelton, T. B., & Greenspan, S. (2000, Fall/Winter). Our window to the future. *Newsweek Special Issue,* pp. 34–36.

Brebner, J. (2003). Gender and emotions. *Personality and Individual Differences, 34,* 387–394.

Breitenbecher, K. H. (2000). Sexual assault on college campuses: Is an ounce of prevention enough? *Applied and Preventive Psychology, 9,* 23–52.

Breitenbecher, K. H. (2001). Sexual revictimization among women. A review of the literature focusing on empirical investigations. *Aggression and Violent Behavior, 6,* 415–432.

Brembs, B. (2003). Operant reward learning in Aplysia. *Current Directions in Psychological Science, 12,* 218–221.

Bremner, J. D., Vythilingam, M., Ng, C. K., Vermetten, E., Nazeer, A., Oren, D. A., et al. (2003). Regional brain metabolic correlates of -methylparatyrosine–induced depressive symptoms: Implications for the neural circuitry of depression. *Journal of the American Medical Association, 289,* 3125–3134.

Brener, N. D., Hassan, S. S., & Barrios, L. C. (1999). Suicidal ideation among college students in the United States. *Journal of Consulting and Clinical Psychology, 67,* 1004–1008.

Brener, N. D., McMahon, P. M., Warren, C. W., & Douglas, K. A. (1999). Forced sexual intercourse and associated health-risk behaviors among female college students in the United States. *Journal of Consulting and Clinical Psychology, 67,* 252–259.

Brent, R. L., Oakley, G. P., Jr., & Mattison, D. R. (2000). The unnecessary epidemic of folic acid-preventable spina bifida and anencephaly. *Pediatrics, 106,* 825–827.

Bretherton, I. (1992). The origins of attachment theory: John Bowlby and Mary Ainsworth. *Devleopmental Psychology, 28,* 759–775.

Brewer, M. B., & Brown, R. J. (1998). Intergroup relations. In D. T. Gilbert, S. T. Fiske, & G. Lindzey (Eds.), *The handbook of social psychology* (4th ed., Vol. 2, pp. 554–594). Boston: McGraw-Hill.

Brewer, W. F., & Treyens, J. C. (1981). Role of schemata in memory for places. *Cognitive Psychology, 13,* 207–230.

Britt, T. W., Adler, A. B., & Bartone, P. T. (2001). Deriving benefits from stressful events: The role of engagement in meaningful work and hardiness. *Journal of Occupational Health Psychology, 6,* 53–63.

Brody, J. E. (1992, September 30). Myriad masks hide an epidemic of depression. *New York Times,* p. C12.

Brody, J. E. (2001a, January 2). Sometimes, good health tastes bad. *New York Times,* p. F6.

Brody, J. E. (2001b, January 23). Experts explore safer tests for Down syndrome. *New York Times,* p. F6.

Brody, N. (2004). Emotional intelligence: Science and myth. *Intelligence, 32,* 109–111.

Brookmeyer, R., Corrada, M. M., Curriero, F. C., & Kawas, C. (2002). Survival following a diagnosis of Alzheimer disaease. *Archives of Neurology, 59,* 1764–1767.

Brown, K. W., & Ryan, R. M. (2003). The benefits of being present: Mindfulness and its role in psychological well-being. *Journal of Personality and Social Psychology, 84,* 822–848.

Brown, S. L., Nesse, R. M., Vinokur, A. D., & Smith, D. M. (2003). Providing social support may be more beneficial than receiving it: Results from a prospective study of mortality. *Psychological Science, 14,* 320–327.

Brown, V. R., & Paulus, P. B. (2002). Making group brainstorming more effective: Recommendations from an associative memory perspective. *Current Directions in Psychological Science, 11,* 208–212.

Bruce, M. L., McAvay, G. J., Raue, P. J., Brown, E. L., Meyer, B. S., & Keohane, D. J. (2002). Major depression in elderly home health care patients. *American Journal of Psychiatry, 159,* 1367–1374.

Bruce, M. L., Ten Have, T. R., Reynolds, C. F., III, Katz, I. I., Schulberg, H. C., Mulsant, B. H., Brown, G. K., et al. (2004). Reducing suicidal ideation and depressive symptoms in depressed older primary care patients: A randomized controlled trial. *Journal of the American Medical Association, 291,* 1081–1091.

Brundtland, G. H. (2000). Achieving worldwide tobacco control [Editorial]. *Journal of the American Medical Association, 284,* 751–751.

Bruner, J. S., & Minturn, A. L. (1955). Perceptual identification and perceptual organization. *Journal of General Psychology, 53,* 21–28.

Bryant, A., & Check, E. (2000, Fall/Winter). How parents raise boys and girls: A sense of self. *Newsweek Special Issue,* pp. 64–65.

Bryant, R. A., Harvey, A. G., Guthrie, R. M., & Moulds, M. L. (2000). A prospective study of psychophysiological arousal, acute stress disorder, and posttraumatic stress disorder. *Journal of Abnormal Psychology, 109,* 341–344.

Bryant, R. A., & Mallard, D. (2002). Hypnotically induced emotional numbing: A real simulating analysis. *Journal of Abnormal Psychology, 111,* 203–207.

Bryant, R. A., Moulds, M. L., Guthrie, R. M., Dang, S. T., & Nixon, R. D. V. (2003). Imaginal exposure alone and imaginal exposure with cognitive restructuring in treatment of posttraumatic stress disorder. *Journal of Consulting and Clinical Psychology, 71,* 706–712.

Buchanan, C. M., Eccles, J. S., & Becker, J. B. (1992). Are adolescents the victims of raging hormones? Evidence for activational effects of hormones on moods and behavior at adolescence. *Psychological Bulletin, 111,* 62–107.

Buchert, R., Thomasius, R., Wilke, F., Petersen, K., Nebeling, B., Obrocki, J., et al. (2004). A voxel-based pet investigation of the long-term effects of "ecstasy" consumption on brain serotonin transporters. *American Journal of Psychiatry, 161,* 1181–1189.

Buckley, K. W. (1989). *Mechanical man: John Broadus Watson and the beginnings of behaviorism.* New York: Guilford Press.

Buddhists are happier. (2003, May 22). *Cable News Network.*. Retrieved May 23, 2003, from http://www.cnn.com/2003/HEALTH/05/22/buddhist.happiness.reut/index.html.

Budney, A. J., Hughes, J. R., Moore, B. A., & Vandrey, R. (2004). Review of the validity and significance of cannabis withdrawal syndrome. *American Journal of Psychiatry, 161,* 1967–1977.

Buhs, E. S., & Ladd, G. W. (2001). Peer rejection as an antecedent of young children's school adjustment: An examination of mediating processes. *Developmental Psychology, 37,* 550–560.

Bullough, V. L., (2004). Sex will never be the same: The contributions of Alfred C. Kinsey. *Archives of Sexual Behavior, 33,* 277–286.

Bulluck, P. (2000, January 1). Will longer lives be different lives? And better ones? *New York Times,* p. E7.

Bumpass, L. (1995, July 6). Cited in J. Steinhauer, "No marriage, no apologies." *New York Times,* pp. C1, C7.

Bunney, W. E., Bunney, B. G., Vawter, M. P., Tomita, H., Li, J., Evans, S. J., et al. (2003). Microarray technology: A review of new strategies to discover candidate vulnerability genes in psychiatric disorders. *American Journal of Psychiatry, 160,* 657–666.

Burke, D. M. (1992). Memory and aging. In M. Gruneberg & P. Morris (Eds.), *Aspects of memory: Vol. 1. The practical aspects* (2nd ed., pp. 124–146). London: Routledge.

Burke, D. M., & Shafto, M. A. (2004). Aging and language production. *Current Directions in Psychological Science, 13,* 21–24.

Burns, D. D. (1980). *Feeling good: The new mood therapy.* New York: Morris.

Burton, C. M., & King, L. A. (2004). The health benefits of writing about intensely positive experiences. *Journal of Research in Personality, 38,* 150–163.

Burton, E., Stice, E., & Seeley, J. R. (2004). A prospective test of the stress-buffering model of depression in adolescent girls: No support once again. *Journal of Consulting and Clinical Psychology 72,* 689–697.

Burton, N., & Lane, R. C. (2001). The relational treatment of dissociative identity disorder. *Clinical Psychology Review, 21,* 301–320.

Bushman, B. J., & Anderson, C. A. (2001). Media violence and the American public: Scientific facts versus media misinformation. *American Psychologist, 56,* 477–489.

Bushman, B. J., Bonacci, A. M., van Dijk, M., & Baumeister, R. F. (2003). Narcissism, sexual refusal, and aggression: Testing a narcissistic reactance model of sexual coercion. *Journal of Personality and Social Psychology, 84,* 1027–1040.

Buss, D. M. (1984). Marital assortment for personality dispositions: Assessment with three different data sources. *Behavior Genetics, 14,* 111–123.

Buss, D. M. (1994). *The evolution of desire: Strategies of human mating.* New York: Basic Books.

Buss, D. M., & Kenrick, D. T. (1998). Evolutionary social psychology. In D. T. Gilbert, S. T. Fiske, & G. Lindzey (Eds.), *The handbook of social psychology* (4th ed., Vol. 2, pp. 982–1026). Boston: McGraw-Hill.

Buss, D. (1996). The evolutionary psychology of human social strategies. In E. T. Higgins & A. W. Kruglanski (Eds.), *Social psychology: Handbook of basic principles* (pp. 3–38). New York: Guilford Press.

Buston, P. M., & Emlen, S. T. (2003). Cognitive processes underlying human mate choice: The relationship between self-perception and mate preference in Western society. *Proceedings of the National Academy of Sciences, 100,* 8805–8810.

Butcher, J. N. (2000). Revising psychological tests: Lessons learned from the revision of the MMPI. *Psychological Assessment, 12,* 263–271.

Butler, R. N. (2001, Fall/Winter). The myth of old age. *Newsweek Special Issue,* p. 33.

Buzan, D. (2004, March 12). I was not a lab rat. *The Guardian Online.* Retrieved August 22, 2004, from books.guardian.co.uk/departments/health-mindandbody/story/0.6000.1168052.00.html.

Byers, E. S., & Grenier, G. (2003). Premature or rapid ejaculation: Heterosexual couples_ perceptions of men_s ejaculatory behavior. *Archives of Sexual Behavior, 32*(3), 261–270.

Byrne, M., Clafferty, B. A., Cosway, R., Grant, E., Hodges, A, Whalley, H. C., Lawrie, S. M., et al. (2003). Neuropsychology, genetic liability, and psychotic symptoms in those at high risk of schizophrenia. *Journal of Abnormal Psychology, 112,* 38–48.

Cacioppo, J. T., Berntson, G. G., Sheridan, J. F., & McClintock, M. K. (2000). Multilevel integrative analyses of human behavior: Social neuroscience and the complementing nature of social and biological approaches. *Psychological Bulletin, 126,* 829–843.

Caetano, R. (1987). Acculturation and drinking patterns among U.S. Hispanics. *British Journal of Addiction, 82,* 789–799.

Cafria, G., Thompson, J. K., Ricciardelli, L., McCabe, M., Smolak, L., & Yesalis, C. (2005). Pursuit of the muscular ideal: Physical and psychological consequences and putative risk factors. *Clinical Psychology Review, 25,* 215–239.

Cale, E. M., & Lilienfeld, S. O. (2002). Sex differences in psychopathy and antisocial personality disorder. A review and integration. *Clinical Psychology Review, 22,* 1179–1207.

Calle, E. E., Rodriguez, C., Walker-Thurmond, K., & Thun, M. J. (2003). Overweight, obesity, and mortality from cancer in a prospectively studied cohort of U.S. adults. *New England Journal of Medicine, 348,* 1625–1638.

Callicott, J. H., Egan, M. F., Mattay, V. S., Bertolino, A., Bone, A. D., Verhcinski, B., et al. (2003). Abnormal fMRI response of the dorsolateral prefrontal cortex in cognitively intact siblings of patients with schizophrenia. *American Journal of Psychiatry, 160,* 709–719.

Camara, W. J., Nathan, J. S., & Puente, A. E. (2000). Psychological test usage: Implications in professional psychology. *Professional Psychology: Research and Practice, 31,* 141–154.

Campfield, L. A., Smith, F. J., Guisez, Y., Devos, R., et al. (1995). Recombinant mouse OB protein: Evidence for a peripheral signal linking adiposity and central neural networks. *Science, 269,* 546–549.

Cancer now top killer of younger Americans. (2005, January 20). The Associated Press.

Canfield, R. L., Henderson, C. R., Cory-Slechta, A. A., Cox, C., Jusko, T. A., & Lanphea, B. P. (2003). Intellectual impairment in children with blood lead concentrations below 10 µg per deciliter. *New England Journal of Medicine, 348,* 1517–1526.

Canli, T., Desmond, J. E., Zhao, Z., & Gabrieli, J. D. E. (2002). Sex differences in the neural basis of emotional memories. *Proceedings of the National Academy of Sciences, 99*(16), 10789–10794.

Cannon, W. (1927). The James-Lange theory of emotions: A critical examination as an alternative theory. *American Journal of Psychology, 39,* 106–112.

Cardemil, E. V., & Battle, C. L. (2003). Guess who's coming to therapy? Getting comfortable with conversations about race and ethnicity in psychotherapy. *Professional Psychology: Research and Practice, 34,* 278–286.

Cardozo, B. L., Bilukha, O. O., Crawford, C. A. G., Shaikh, I., Wolfe, M. I., Gerber, M. L., & Anderson, M. (2004). Mental health, social functioning, and disability in postwar Afghanistan. *Journal of the American Medical Association, 292,* 575–584.

Carey, B. (2004, December 3). TV time, unlike child care, ranks high in mood study. *New York Times,* p. A22.

Carey, M. P., Carey, K. B., Maisto, S. A., Gordon, C. M., Schroder, K. E. E., & Vanable, P. A. (2004). Reducing HIV-risk behavior among adults receiving outpatient psychiatric treatment: Results from a randomized controlled trial. *Journal of Consulting and Clinical Psychology, 72,* 252–268.

Carey, M. P., Wincze, J. P., & Meisler, A. W. (1998). Sexual dysfunction: Male erectile disorder. In D. H. Barlow (Ed.), *Clinical handbook for psychological disorders* (pp. 442–480). New York: Guilford Press.

Carlsson, K., Petersson, K. M., Lundqvist, D., Karlsson, A., Ingvar, M., & Öhman, A. (2004). Fear and the amygdala: Manipulation of awareness generates differential cerebral responses to phobic and fear-relevant (but nonfeared) stimuli. *Emotion, 4,* 340–353.

Carmichael, M. (2002, December 2). Ginkgo on your mind? *Newsweek,* p. 59.

Carmichael, M. (2003a, January 20). Rx: Two martinis a day. *Newsweek,* p. 48.

Carmichael, M. (2003b, May 5). The fat factor. *Newsweek,* p. 69.

Carmichael, M. (2004a, March 8). How a brain heals. *Newsweek,* p. 49.

Carmichael, M. (2004b, December 6). Medicine's next level. *Newsweek,* pp. 45–50.

Carpenter, S. (2000a, October). Research confirms the virtues of "sleeping on it." *Monitor on Psychology, 31,* 49–50.

Carpenter, S. (2000b, October). A taste expert sniffs out a long-standing measurement oversight. *Monitor on Psychology, 31*(10), 20–21.

Carpenter, S. (2001a, February). Teens' risky behavior is about more than race and family resources. *Monitor on Psychology, 32,* 47–48.

Crpenter, S. (2001b, May). Stimulants boost achievement in ADHD teens. *Monitor on Psychology, 32,* 26–27.

Carroll, L. (2003, November 4). Fetal brains suffer badly from effects of alcohol. *New York Times Online.* Retrieved November 4, 2003, from http://www.nytimes.com/2003/11/04/health/04FETA.html?th.

Carroll., L. (2004, February 10). Parkinson's research focuses on links to genes and toxins. *New York Times,* p. F5.

Carter, S. L. (1993). *Reflections of an affirmative action baby.* New York: Basic Books.

Carvajal, S. C., Parcel, G. S., Basen-Engquist, K., Banspach, S. W., Coyle, K. K., Kirby, D., et al. (1999). Psychosocial predictors of delay of first sexual intercourse by adolescents. *Health Psychology, 18,* 443–452.

Carver, C. S., & Antoni, M. H. (2004). Finding benefit in breast cancer during the year after diagnosis predicts better adjustment 5 to 8 years after diagnosis. *Health Psychology, 23,* 595–598.

Caspi, A., Roberts, B. W., & Shiner, R. L. (2005). Personality development: Stability and change. *Annual Review of Psychology, 56,* 453–484.

Caspi, A., & Moffitt, T. E. (1991). Individual differences are accentuated during periods of social change: The sample case of girls at puberty. *Journal of Personality and Social Psychology, 61,* 157–168.

Caspi, A., et al. (2002). Role of genotype in the cycle of violence in maltreated children. *Science, 297,* 851—854.

Cassel, C. K. (2002). Use it or lose it: Activity may be the best treatment for aging. *Journal of the American Medical Association, 288*(18), 2333–2335.

Cassidy, J. (2003). Continuity and change in the measurement of infant attachment: Comment on Fraley and Spieker (2003). *Developmental Psychology, 39,* 409–412.

Cattell, R. B., Eber, H. W., & Tatsuoka, M. M. (1970). *Handbook for the Sixteen Personality Factor Questionnaire (16PF).* Champaign, IL: Institute for Personality and Ability Testing.

Cavaco, S., et al. (2004). The scope of preserved procedural memory in amnesia. *Brain, 127,* 1853–1867.

CDC chief: Obesity top health threat. (2003, October 29). *CNN Web Posting.* Retrieved October 29, 2003, from http://www.cnn.com/2003/HEALTH/diet.fitness/10/29/obesity.threat.reut/index.html.

Ceci, S. J., Rosenblum, T. B., & Kumpf, M. (1998). The shrinking gap between high- and low-scoring groups: Current trends and possible causes. In U. Neisser (Ed.), *The rising curve: Long-term gains in IQ and related measures* (pp. 287–302). Washington, DC: American Psychological Association.

Cellar, D. F., Nelson, Z. C., & Yorke, C. M. (2000). The five-factor model and driving behavior: Personality and involvement in vehicular accidents. *Psychological Reports, 86*(2), 454–456.

Centers for Disease Control (CDC). (2000a, June 9). National and state-specific pregnancy rates among adolescents—United States, 1995–1997. *Morbidity and Mortality Weekly Report, 49*(27).

Centers for Disease Control (CDC). (2000b, June 9). Youth risk behavior surveillance—United States, 1999. *Morbidity and Mortality Weekly Report, 49*(SS05), 1–96.

Centers for Disease Control (CDC). (2001). Self-reported asthma prevalence among adults: United States, 2000. *Morbidity and Mortality Weekly Report, 50,* 682–686.

Centers for Disease Control and Office of Minority Health (2001). *Race and health: Cardiovascular disease: Statistics and data charts.* Retrieved October 7, 2001 from http://raceandhealth.hhs.gov/3rdpgblue/cardio/k11.gif.

Centers for Disease Control and Prevention (CDC). (2001). *Adolescent and school health: Programs that work.* Atlanta, GA: Author.

Centers for Disease Control and Prevention (CDC). (2004a, October 12). Deaths: Final data for 2002. *National Vital Statistics Reports, 53*(5).

Centers for Disease Control and Prevention (CDC). (2004b). Morbidity and Mortality Weekly Report, *Journal of the American Medical Association, 291,* 1317–1318.

Centers for Disease Control and Prevention (CDC). (2004c, March). *Report to Congress: Prevention of genital human papillomavirus infection.* Retrieved March 25, 2004, from http://www.cdc.gov/std/HPV/2004HPV%20Report.pdf.

Centers for Disease Control and Prevention (CDC). (2005a, May 27). Cigarette smoking among adults—United States, 2003. *Morbidity and Mortality Weekly Report, 52.* Retrieved June 28, 2005, from http://www.cdc.gov/mmwr/preview/mmwrhtml/mm5420a3.htm.

Centers for Disease Control and Prevention (CDC). (2005b). *The burden of chronic diseases and their risk factors: National and state perspectives 2004.* Retrieved July 6, 2005, from http://www.cdc.gov/nccdphp/burdenbook2004/.

Chadda, R. K., & Ahuja, N. (1990). Dhat syndrome: A sex neurosis of the Indian subcontinent. *British Journal of Psychiatry, 156,* 577–579.

Chambers, K. L., & Zaragoza, M. S. (2001). Intended and unintended effects of explicit warnings. *Memory & Cognition, 29,* 1120–1129.

Chambless, D. L., & Ollendick, T. H. (2001). Empirically supported psychological interventions: Controversies and evidence. *Annual Review of Psychology, 52,* 685–716.

Chambless, D. L., et al. (1998, Winter). Update on empirically validated therapies, II. *Clinical Psychologist, 51,* 3–16.

Chamorro-Premuzic, T., & Furnham, A. (2003). Personality predicts academic performance: Evidence from two longitudinal university samples. *Journal of Research in Personality, 37,* 319–338.

Chang, E. C., & Asakawa, K. (2003). Cultural variations on optimistic and pessimistic bias for self versus a sibling: Is there evidence for self-enhancement in the West and for self-criticism in the East when the referent group is specified? *Journal of Personality and Social Psychology, 84,* 569–581.

Chang, E. C., & Sanna, L. J. (2001). Optimism, pessimism, and positive and negative affectivity in middle-aged adults: A test of a cognitive-affective model of psychological adjustment. *Psychology and Aging, 16,* 524–531.

Charles, S. T., Reynolds, C. A., & Gatz, M. (2001). Age-related differences and change in positive and negative affect over 23 years. *Journal of Personality and Social Psychology, 80,* 136–151.

Charney, D. S., Nemeroff, C. B., Lewis, L., Laden, S. K., Gorman, J. M., & Laska, E. M. (2002). National depressive and manic-depressive association consensus statement on the use of placebo in clinical trials of mood disorders. *Archives of General Psychiatry, 59,* 262–270.

Charney, D. S., Reynolds, C. F., III, Lewis, L., Lebowitz, B. D., Sunderland, T., Alexopoulos, G. S., et al. (2003). Depression and bipolar support alliance consensus statement on the unmet needs in diagnosis and treatment of mood disorders in late life [Review]. *Archives of General Psychiatry, 60,* 664–672.

Chassin, L., Flora, D. B., & King, K. M. (2004). Trajectories of alcohol and drug use and dependence from adolescence to adulthood: The effects of familial alcoholism and personality. *Journal of Abnormal Psychology, 113,* 483–498.

Chassin, L., Pitts, S. C., & Prost, J. (2002). Binge drinking trajectories from adolescence to emerging adulthood in a high-risk sample: Predictors and substance abuse outcomes. *Journal of Consulting and Clinical Psychology, 70,* 67–78.

Chassin, L., Presson, C. C., Sherman, S. J., & Kim, K. (2003). Historical changes in cigarette smoking and smoking-related beliefs after 2 decades in a Midwestern community. *Health Psychology, 22,* 347–353.

Chasteen, A. L., Park, D. C., & Schwarz, N. (2001). Implementation intentions and facilitation of prospective memory. *Psychological Science, 12,* 457–461.

Check, E. (2003). Battle of the mind. *Nature, 422,* 370–372.

Chen, J., Rathore, S. S., Radford, M. J., Wang, Y., Krumholz, H. M., et al. (2001). Racial differences in the use of cardiac catheterization after acute myocardial infarction. *New England Journal of Medicine, 344,* 1443–1449.

Chess, S., & Thomas, A. (1984). *Origins and evolution of behavior disorders: From infancy to early adult life.* Cambridge, MA: Harvard University Press.

Chess, S., & Thomas, A. (1996). *Temperament: Theory and practice.* New York: Brunner/Mazel.

Chevalier-Skolnikoff, S. (1973). Facial expression of emotion in nonhuman primates. In P. Ekman (Ed.), *Darwin and facial expression: A century of research in review* (pp. 11–82). New York: Academic Press.

Chia, R. C., Moore, J. L., Lam, K-N., Chuang, C. J., et al. (1994). Cultural differences in gender role attitudes between Chinese and American students. *Sex Roles, 31,* 23–30.

Chih, B., Engelman, H., & Scheiffele, P. (2005). Control of excitatory and inhibitory synapse formation by neuroligins. *Science, 307,* 1324–1328.

Chlamydia can reduce male fertility. (2004, May 3). *MSNBC.com.* Retrieved May 5, 2004, from http://www.msnbc.msn.com/id/4862414/.

Chobanian, A. V., Bakris, G. L., Black, H. R., Cushman, W. C., Green, L. A., Izzo, J. L., Jr., et al. (2003). The seventh report of the Joint National Committee on Prevention, Detection, Evaluation, and Treatment of High Blood Pressure: The JNC 7 report. *Journal of the American Medical Association, 289,* 2560–2572.

Choi, I., Dalal, R., Kim-Prieto, C., & Park, H. (2003). Culture and judgment of causal relevance. *Journal of Personality and Social Psychology, 84,* 46–59.

Chomsky, N. (1965). *Aspects of the theory of syntax.* Cambridge, MA: MIT Press.

Chorpita, B. F., Yim, L. M., Donkervoet, J. C., Arensdorf, A., Amundsen, M. J., McGee, C., Serrano, A., et al. (2002). Toward large-scale implementation of empirically supported treatments for children: A review and observations by the Hawaii Empirical Basis to Services Task Force. *Clinical Psychology: Science and Practice, 9,* 165–190.

Chrisler, J. C., & Johnston-Robledo, I. (2002). Raging hormones? Feminist perspectives on premenstrual syndrome and postpartum depression. In M. Ballou & L. S. Brown (Eds.), *Rethinking mental health and disorder* (pp. 174–197). New York: Guilford Press.

Christakis, D. A., Zimmerman, F. J., DiGiuseppe, D. L., & McCarty, C. A. (2004). Early television exposure and subsequent attentional problems in children. *Pediatrics, 113,* 708–713.

Christensen, A., Atkins, D. C., Berns, S., Wheeler, J., Baucom, D. H., & Simpson, L. E. (2004). Traditional versus integrative behavioral couple therapy for significantly and chronically distressed married couples. *Journal of Consulting and Clinical Psychology, 72,* 176–191.

Chu, J. A., Frey, L. M., Ganzel, B. L., & Matthews, J. A. (1999). Memories of childhood abuse: Dissociation, amnesia, and corroboration. *American Journal of Psychiatry, 156,* 749–755.

Cialdini, R. B., & Goldstein, N. J. (2004). Social influence: Compliance and conformity. *Annual Review of Psychology, 55,* 591–621.

Cialdini, R. B., & Trost, M. R. (1998). Social influence: Social norms, conformity, and compliance. In D. T. Gilbert, S. T. Fiske, & G. Lindzey (Eds.), *The handbook of social psychology* (4th ed., Vol. 2, pp. 151–192). Boston: McGraw-Hill.

Cialdini, R. B., Trost, M. R., & Newsom, J. T. (1995). Preference for consistency: The development of a valid measure and the discovery of surprising behavioral implications. *Journal of Personality and Social Psychology, 69,* 318–328.

Ciarrochi, J., Chan, A., Caputi, P., & Roberts, R. (2001). Measuring emotional intelligence. In J. Ciarrochi & J. P. Forgas, et al. (Eds.), *Emotional intelligence in everyday life: A scientific inquiry* (pp. 25–45). Philadelphia: Psychology Press.

Ciechanowski, P., Wagner, E., Schmaling, K., Schwartz, S., Williams, B., Diehr, P., et al. (2004). Community-integrated home-based depression treatment in older adults: A randomized controlled trial. *Journal of the American Medical Association, 291,* 1569–1577.

Clark, D. A., (2004). *Cognitive-behavioral therapy for OCD.* New York: Guilford Press.

Clark, D. M. (1986). A cognitive approach to panic. *Behaviour Research and Therapy, 24,* 461–470.

Clark, K. B., & Clark, M. P. (1939). The development of self and the emergence of racial identification in Negro preschool children. *Journal of Social Psychology, 10,* 591–599.

Clark, R., Anderson, N. B., Clark, V. R., & Williams, D. R. (1999). Racism as a stressor for African Americans: A biopsychological model. *American Psychologist, 54,* 805–816.

Clarke, D., Gabriels, T., & Barnes, J. (1996). Astrological signs as determinants of extroversion and emotionality: An empirical study. *Journal of Psychology, 130,* 131–140.

Clay, R. (2002, September). A renaissance for humanistic psychology. *Monitor on Psychology, 33,* 42–43.

Clay, R. A. (2003, April). An empty nest can promote freedom, improved relationships. *Monitor on Psychology, 34,* 40–41.

Clay, R. A. (2005, February). On the practice horizon. *Monitor on Psychology, 36*(2), 48–50.

Clements, J. (2003, March 5). Working late: Your friends won't retire at age 65, but here's how you can. *Wall Street Journal,* p. D1.

Clements, R., & Swensen, C. H. (2000, Summer). Commitment to one's spouse as a predictor of marital quality among older couples. *Current Psychology: Development, Learning, Personality, Social, 19,* 110–119.

Clemetson, L. (2003, January 21). Hispanics now largest minority, census shows. *New York Times,* pp. A1, A17.

Cloitre, M. (2004). Aristotle revisited: The case of recovered memories. *Clinical Psychology: Science and Practice, 11,* 42–46.

Cnattingius, S. S., Signorello, L. B., Anneren, G., Clausson, B., Ekbom, A., Ljunger, E., et al. (2000). Caffeine intake and the risk of first-trimester spontaneous abortion. *New England Journal of Medicine, 343,* 1839–1845.

Cocaine impairs brain's "pleasure circuits." (2003, January 1). *CNN Web Posting.* Retrieved January 2, 2003, from http://www.cnn.com/2003/HEALTH/01/01/cocaine.brain.ap/index.html.

Cochran, S. V., & Rabinowitz, F. E. (2003). Gender-sensitive recommendations for assessment and treatment of depression in men. *Professional Psychology: Research and Practice, 34,* 132–140.

Cockell, S. J., Hewitt, P. L., Seal, B., Sherry, S., Goldner, E. M., Flett, G. L., et al. (2002). Trait and self-presentational dimensions of perfectionism among women with anorexia nervosa. *Cognitive Therapy and Research, 26,* 745–758.

Coderre, T. J., Mogil, J. S., & Bushnell, M. C. (2003). The biological psychology of pain. In M. Gallagher & R. J. Nelson (Eds.), *Handbook of psychology: Vol. 3. Biological psychology* (pp. 237–268). New York: John Wiley & Sons.

Cohan, C. L., & Kleinbaum, S. (2002). Toward a greater understanding of the cohabitation effect: Premarital cohabitation and marital communication. *Journal of Marriage and the Family, 64,* 180–192.

Cohen, J. (2001, July/August). Time spent playing with peers influences gender-typed behaviors in young children. *Monitor on Psychology, 32,* 17.

Cohen, L. B., & Cashon, C. H. (2003). Infant perception and cognition. In R. M. Lerner, M. A. Easterbrooks, & J. Mistry (Eds.), *Handbook of psychology: Vol. 6. Developmental psychology* (pp. 65–90). New York: John Wiley & Sons.

Cohen, L. G., Ceinik, P., Pascual-Leone, A., Corwell, B., Faiz, L., Dambrosi, J., et al. (1997). Functional relevance of cross-modal plasticity in blind humans. *Nature, 389,* 180–183.

Cohen, L. J., Celnik, P., Pascual-Leone, A., Corwell, B., Faiz, L., & Dambrosia, J. (1997). Separate neural bases of two fundamental memory process in the human medial temporal lobe. *Science, 276,* 264–266.

Cohen, S., Doyle, W. J., Skoner, D. P., Rabin, B. S., Gwaltney, J. M., Jr., et al. (1997). Social ties and susceptibility to the common cold. *Journal of the American Medical Association, 277,* 1940–1944.

Cohen, S., Doyle, W. J., Turner, R., Alper, C. M., & Skoner, D. P. (2003). Sociability and susceptibility to the common cold. *Psychological Science, 14,* 389–395.

Cohen, S., Frank, E., Doyle, W. J., Skoner, D. P., Rabin, B. S., & Gwaltney, J. M., Jr. (1998). Types of stressors that increase susceptibility to the common cold in healthy adults. *Health Psychology, 17,* 214–223.

Colcombe, S, & Kramer, A. F. (2003). Fitness effects on the cognitive function of older adults: A meta-analytic study. *Psychological Science, 14,* 125–130.

Cole, M. G., & Dendukuri, N. (2003). Risk factors for depression among elderly community subjects: A systematic review and meta-analysis. *American Journal of Psychiatry, 160,* 1163–1168.

Collaer, M. L., & Hines, M. (1995). Human behavioral sex differences: A role for gonadal hormones during early development? *Psychological Bulletin, 118,* 55–107.

Collier, G. L. (2002). Why does music express only some emotions?A test of a philosophical theory. *Empirical Studies of the Arts, 20,* 21–31.

Collins, A. M., & Quillian, M. R. (1969). Retrieval times from semantic memory. *Journal of Verbal Learning and Verbal Behavior, 8,* 240–247.

Collins, J. J., & Messerschmidt, P. M. (1993). Epidemiology of alcohol-related violence. *Alcohol Health and Research World, 17,* 93–100.

Collins, K. (2005, February 11). It's all in the taste buds . . . *MSNBC.Com/ American Institute for Cancer Research.* Retrieved February 11, 2005 from http://www.msnbc.msn.com/id/6949085/.

Conklin, H. M., & Iacono, W. G. (2002). Schizophrenia: A neurodevelopmental perspective. *Current Directions in Psychological Science, 11,* 33–37.

Connell, C. M., & Janevic, M. R. (2003). Health and human development. In R. M. Lerner, M. A. Easterbrooks, & J. Mistry (Eds.), *Handbook of psychology: Vol. 6. Developmental psychology* (pp. 579–600). New York: John Wiley & Sons.

Conrad, F. G., & Brown, N. R. (1996). Estimating frequency: A multiple-strategy perspective. In D. Herrmann, C. McEvoy, C. Hertzog, P. Hertel, & M. K. Johnson (Eds.), *Basic and applied memory research: Practical applications* (Vol. 2., pp. 166–178). Mahwah, NJ: Lawrence Erlbaum Associates.

Consolacion, T. B., Russell, S. T., & Sue, S. (2004). Sex, race/ethnicity, and romantic attractions: multiple minority status adolescents and mental health. *Cultural Diversity and Ethnic Minority Psychology, 10,* 200–214.

Contrada, R. J., & Guyll, M. (2001). On who gets sick and why: The role of personality and stress. In A. Baum, T. A. Revenson, & J. E. Singer (Eds.), *Handbook of health psychology* (pp. 59–84). Mahwah, NJ: Lawrence Erlbaum Associates.

Cooksey, E. C., & Fondell, M. M. (1996). Spending time with his kids: Effects of family structure on fathers' and children's lives. *Journal of Marriage and the Family, 58,* 693–707.

Coon, K. A., Goldberg, J., Rogers, B. L., & Tucker, K. L. (2001). Relationships between use of television during meals and children's food consumption patterns. *Pediatrics, 107,* 7.

Cooper, M. L. (1992). Alcohol and increased behavioral risk for AIDS. *Alcohol World: Health and Research, 16,* 64–72. (National Institute on Alcohol Abuse and Alcoholism, NIH Publication No. 93–3466).

Cooper, M. L., Wood, P. K., Orcutt, H. K., & Albino, A. (2003). Personality and the predisposition to engage in risky or problem behaviors during adolescence. *Journal of Personality and Social Psychology, 84,* 390–410.

Corballis, M. C. (2001). Is the handedness gene on the X chromosome? Comment on Jones and Martin (2000). *Psychological Review, 108,* 805–810.

Corballis, M. C. (2003). From hand to mouth: The gestural origins of language. In M. H. Christiansen & S. Kirby (Eds.), *Language evolution* (pp. 201–218). New York: Oxford University Press.

Coren, S. (1992). *The left-hander syndrome: The causes and consequences of left-handedness.* New York: Free Press.

Corliss, R. (2003, January 20). Is there a formula for joy? *Time Magazine,* pp. 44–46.

Cororve, M. B., & Gleaves, D. H. (2001). Body dysmorphic disorder: A review of conceptualizations, assessment, and treatment strategies. *Clinical Psychology Review, 21,* 949–970.

Correll, C. U., Leucht, S., &. Kane, J. M. (2004). Lower risk for tardive dyskinesia associated with second-generation antipsychotics: a systematic review of 1-year studies. *American Journal of Psychiatry, 161,* 414–425.

Correll, J., Park, B., Judd, C. M., & Wittenbrink, B. (2002). The police officer's dilemma: Using ethnicity to disambiguate potentially threatening individuals. *Journal of Personality and Social Psychology, 83,* 1314–1329.

Costa, G. (1996). The impact of shift and night work on health. *Applied Ergonomics, 27*(1), 9–16.

Costa, P. T., & McCrae, R. R. (1992a). Four ways five factors are basic. *Personality and Individual Differences, 13,* 653–665.

Costa, P. T., & McCrae, R. R. (1992b). Normal personality assessment in clinical practice: The NEO Personality Inventory. *Psychological Assessment, 4,* 5–13.

Costa, P., Jr., Terracciano, A., & McCrae, R. R. (2002). Gender differences in personality traits across cultures: Robust and surprising findings. *Journal of Personality and Social Psychology, 81,* 322–331.

Costello, F. J., & Keane, M. T. (2001). Testing two theories of conceptual combination: Alignment versus diagnosticity in the comprehension and production of combined concepts. *Journal of Experimental Psychology: Learning, Memory, and Cognition, 27,* 255–271.

Council of Economic Advisers for the President's Initiative on Race. (1998). *Changing America: Indicators of social and economic well-being by race and Hispanic origin.* Washington, DC: U.S. Government Printing Office.

Cowan, N., Chen, Z., & Rouder, J. N. (2004). Constant capacity in an immediate serial-recall task: A logical sequel to Miller (1956). *Psychological Science, 15,* 634–640.

Cowan, W. M., & Kandel, E. R. (2001). Prospects for neurology and psychiatry. *Journal of the American Medical Association, 285,* 594–600.

Cowley, G. (1994, October 24). Testing the science of intelligence. *Newsweek,* pp. 56–60.

Coyle, J. T. (2003). Use it or lose it—do effortful mental activities protect against dementia? *New England Journal of Medicine, 348,* 2489–2490.

Crabbe, J. C. (2002). Genetic contributions to addiction. *Annual Review of Psychology, 53,* 435–462.

Craik, F. I. M., & Lockhart, R. S. (1972). Levels of processing: A framework for memory research. *Journal of Verbal Learning and Verbal Behavior, 11,* 671–684.

Crain, C. (2004, October 3). Doctor Strangelove. *New York Times,* Section 2, pp. 1, 20.

Cramer, P. (2000). Defense mechanisms in psychology today: Further processes for adaptation. *American Psychologist, 55,* 637–646.

Cravchik, A., & Goldman, D. (2000). Neurochemical individuality: Genetic diversity among human dopamine and serotonin receptors and transporters. *Archives of General Psychiatry, 57,* 1105–1114.

Crick, N. R., & Rose, A. J. (2000). Toward a gender-balanced approach to the study of social-emotional development: A look at relational aggression. In P. H. Miller & E. Kofsky Scholnick (Eds.), *Toward a feminist developmental psychology* (pp. 153–168). Florence, KY: Taylor & Francis/Routledge.

Crites, S. L., Jr., Farbrigar, L. R., & Petty, R. E. (1994). Measuring the affective and cognitive properties of attitudes: Conceptual and methodological issues. *Personality and Social Psychology Bulletin, 20,* 619–634.

Cross, S. E., & Madson, L. (1997). Models of the self: Self-construals and gender. *Psychological Bulletin, 122,* 89–103.

Crowe, R. A. (1990). Astrology and the scientific method. *Psychological Reports, 67,* 163–191.

Crowell, J. A., Treboux, D., & Waters, E. (2002). Stability of attachment representations: The transition to marriage. *Developmental Psychology, 38,* 467–479.

Cryan, J. F., O'Leary, O. F., Jin, S. H., Friedland, J. C., Ouyang, M., Hirsch, B. R., et al. (2004). Norepinephrine-deficient mice lack responses to antidepressant drugs, including selective serotonin reuptake inhibitors. *Proceedings of the National Academy of Science, 101,* 8186–8191.

Csernansky, J. G., Schindler, M. K., Splinter, N. R., Wang, L., Gado, M., Selemon, L. D., et al. (2004). Abnormalities of thalamic volume and shape in schizophrenia. *American Journal of Psychiatry, 161,* 896–902.

Csicsvari, J., Henze, D. A., Jamieson, B., Harris, K. D., Sirota, A., Bartho, P., Wise, K. D., & Buzsaki, G. (2003). Massively parallel recording of unit and local field potentials with silicon-based electrodes. *Journal of Neurophysiology, 90,* 1314–1323.

Csikszentmihalyi, M. (1996). *Creativity: Flow and the psychology of discovery and invention.* New York: Harper Perennial.

Cummings, E. M. (2003). Toward assessing attachment on an emotional security continuum: comment on Fraley and Spieker (2003). *Developmental Psychology, 39,* 405–408.

Cummings, E. M., Braungart-Rieker, J. M., & Du Rocher-Schudlich, T. (2003). Emotion and personality development in childhood. In R. M. Lerner, M. A. Easterbrooks, & J. Mistry (Eds.), *Handbook of psychology: Vol. 6. Developmental psychology* (pp. 211–240). New York: John Wiley & Sons.

Cunningham, J. A., & Breslin, F. C. (2004). Only one in three people with alcohol abuse or dependence ever seek treatment. *Addictive Behaviors, 29,* 221–223.

Cunningham, M. R., Roberts, A. R., Barbee, A. P., Druen, P. B., et al. (1995). "Their ideas of beauty are, on the whole, the same as ours": Consistency and variability in the cross-cultural perception of female physical attractiveness. *Journal of Personality and Social Psychology, 68,* 261–279.

Curtin, J. J., Patrick, C. J., Lang, A. R., Cacioppo, J. T., & Birbaumer, N. (2001). Alcohol affects emotion through cognition. *Psychological Science, 12,* 527–531.

Dai, Y., Nolan, R. F., & White, B. (2002). Response to moral choices as a function of self-esteem. *Psychological Reports, 90,* 907–912.

Daley, T. C., Whaley, S. E., Sigman, M. D., Espinosa, M. P., & Neumann, C. (2003). IQ on the rise: The Flynn Effect in rural Kenyan children. *Psychological Science, 14,* 215–219.

Damasio, A. R. (1994). *Descartes' error: Emotion, reason, and the human brain.* New York: Putnam.

Damasio, A. R. (2000). A neural basis for sociopathy. *Archives of General Psychiatry, 57,* 128–129.

Damasio, A. R., & Damasio, H. (1992, September). Brain and language. *Scientific American, 267,* 62–71.

Damasio, A. R., Grabowski, T. J., Bechara, A., Damasio, H., Ponto, L. L. B., Parvizi, J., et al. (2000). Subcortical and cortical brain activity during the feeling of self-generated emotions. *Nature Neuroscience, 3,* 1049–1056.

Dana, J. (2000, December 6). *Athletes use mind games to improve on the field.* Retrieved December 14, 2000, from http://www.psycport.com/news/2000/12/06/Uwire/harvest_Uwire97608326578915265.html.

Dantzker, M. L., & Eisenman, R. (2003). Sexual attitudes among Hispanic college students: Differences between males and females. *International Journal of Adolescence and Youth, 11,* 79–89.

Darwin, C. A. (1872). *The expression of the emotions in man and animals.* London: J. Murray.

Darwin, F. (Ed.). (1958). *The autobiography of Charles Darwin and selected letters.* New York: Dover. (Original work published 1892.)

Das, A. K., Olfson, M., Gameroff, M. J., Pilowsky, D. J., Blanco, C., Feder, A., et al. (2005). Screening for bipolar disorder in a primary care practice. *Journal of the American Medical Association, 293,* 956–963.

Dasen, P. R. (1994). Culture and cognitive development from a Piagetian perspective. In W. J. Lonner & R. Malpass (Eds.), *Psychology and culture.* Boston: Allyn & Bacon.

Dasgupta, N., & Greenwald, A. G. (2001). On the malleability of automatic attitudes: Combating automatic prejudice with images of admired and disliked individuals. *Journal of Personality and Social Psychology, 81,* 800–814.

Davelaar, E. J., Goshen-Gottstein, Y., Ashkenazi, A., Haarmann, H. J., & Usher, M. (2005). The demise of short-term memory revisited: Empirical and computational investigations of recency effects. *Psychological Review, 112,* 3–42.

Davidson, J. R. T., Foa, E. B., Huppert, J. D., Keefe, F. J., Franklin, M. E., Compton, J. S., et al. (2004). Fluoxetine, comprehensive cognitive behavioral therapy, and placebo in generalized social phobia. *Archives of General Psychiatry, 61,* 1005–1013.

Davidson, R. J., Marshall, J. R., Tomarken, A. J., & Henriques, J. B. (2000). While a phobic waits: Regional brain electrical and autonomic activity in social phobics during anticipation of public speaking. *Biological Psychiatry, 47,* 85–95.

Davidson, R. J., Pizzagalli, D., Nitschke, J. B., & Putnam, K. (2002). Depression: Perspectives from affective neuroscience. *Annual Review of Psychology, 53,* 545–574.

Davidson, R. J., Putnam, K. M., & Larson, C. L. (2000). Dysfunction in the neural circuitry of emotion regulation—A possible prelude to violence. *Science, 289,* 591–594.

Davies, G., et al. (1996). Memory for cars and their drivers: A test of the interest hypothesis. In D. Herrmann, C. McEvoy, C. Hertzog, P. Hertel, & M. K. Johnson (Eds.), *Basic and applied memory research: Practical applications* (Vol. 2, pp. 37–50). Mahwah, NJ: Lawrence Erlbaum Associates.

Davis, J. L. (2002, November 4). Depression: Genetic or environmental? Genetics plus temperament affect mood disorders. *WebMD Medical News.* Retrieved November 9, 2002, from http://my.webmd.com/content/article/53/61257.htm?z=1663_00000_2409_f1_05.

Davis, J. L., & Rusbult, C. E. (2001). Attitude alignment in close relationships. *Journal of Personality and Social Psychology, 81,* 65–84.

Davis, J. M., Chen, N., & Glick, I. D. (2003). A meta-analysis of the efficacy of second-generation antipsychotics. *Archives of General Psychiatry, 60,* 553–564.

Davis, M., & Lang, P. J. (2003). Emotion. In M. Gallagher & R. J. Nelson (Eds.), *Handbook of psychology: Vol. 3. Biological psychology* (pp. 405440). New York: John Wiley & Sons.

Davis, T. L., & Liddell, D. L. (2002). Getting inside the house: The effectiveness of a rape prevention program for college fraternity men. *Journal of College Student Development, 43,* 35–50.

Daw, J. (2001, July/August). Psychological assessments shown to be as valid as medical tests. *Monitor on Psychology, 32,* 46–47.

Dawood, K., Pillard, R. C., Horvath, C., Revelle, W., & Bailey, J. M. (2000). Familial aspects of male homosexuality. *Archives of Sexual Behavior, 29,* 155–163.

de Bono, E. (1970). *Lateral thinking: Creativity step by step.* New York: Harper & Row.

De La Cancela, V., & Guzman, L. P. (1991). Latino mental health service needs: Implications for training psychologists. In H. F. Myers, L. P. Guzman, & R. J. Echemendia (Eds.), *Ethnic minority perspectives on clinical training and services in psychology* (pp. 59–64). Washington, DC: American Psychological Association.

de Moor, C., Sterner, J., Hall, M., Warneke, C., Gilani, Z., Amato, R., et al. (2003). A pilot study of the effects of expressive writing on psychological and behavioral adjustment in patients enrolled in a Phase II trial of vaccine therapy for metastatic renal cell carcinoma. *Health Psychology, 21,* 615–619.

De Silva, P. (1993). Post-traumatic stress disorder: Cross-cultural aspects. *International Review of Psychiatry, 5,* 217–229.

de Waal, F. B. M. (2002). Evolutionary psychology: The wheat and the chaff. *Current Directions in Psychological Science, 11,* 187–191.

Dean, G., Mather, A., & Kelly, I. W. (1996). Astrology. In G. Stein (Ed.), *The encyclopedia of the paranormal.* Buffalo, NY: Prometheus.

DeAngelis, T. (1993). It's back: TV violence, concern for kid viewers. *APA Monitor, 24*(8), 16.

DeAngelis, T. (2000, September). School psychologists: In demand and expanding their reach. *Monitor on Psychology, 31*(9), 30–32.

DeAngelis, T. (2001, April). Our erotic personalities are as unique as our fingerprints. *Monitor on Psychology, 32,* 25.

DeAngelis, T. (2002, June). How do mind-body interventions affect breast cancer? *Monitor on Psychology, 33,* 51–53.

DeAngelis, T. (2003a, February). Why we overestimate our competence. *Monitor on Psychology, 34,* 60–62.

DeAngelis, T. (2003b, March). When anger's a plus. *Monitor on Psychology, 34,* 44–45.

DeAngelis, T. (2004a, April). Are beliefs inherited? *Monitor on Psychology, 35,* 50–51.

DeAngelis, T. (2004b, June). Too many choices? *Monitor on Psychology, 35,* 56–57.

Deckel, A. W., Hesselbrock, V., & Bauer, L. (1996). Antisocial personality disorder, childhood delinquency, and frontal brain functioning: EEG and neuropsychological findings. *Journal of Clinical Psychology, 52,* 639–650.

DeDe, G., Caplan, D., Kemtes, K., & Waters, G. (2004). The relationship between age, verbal working memory, and language comprehension. *Psychology and Aging, 19,* 601–616.

Deegear, J., & Lawson, D. M. (2003). The utility of empirically supported treatments. *Professional Psychology: Research and Practice, 34,* 271–277.

Del Boca, F. K., Darkes, J., Greenbaum, P. E., & Goldman, M. S. (2004). Up close and personal: Temporal variability in the drinking of individual college students during their first year. *Journal of Consulting and Clinical Psychology, 72,* 155–164.

Delahanty, D. L., & Baum, A. (2001). Stress and breast cancer. In A. Baum, T. A. Revenson, & J. E. Singer (Eds.), *Handbook of health psychology* (pp. 747–756). Mahwah, NJ: Lawrence Erlbaum Associates.

Delfino, R. J., Jamner, L. D., & Whalen, C. K. (2001). Temporal analysis of the relationship of smoking behavior and urges to mood states in men versus women. *Nicotine and Tobacco Research, 3,* 235–248.

DelVecchio, T., & O'Leary, K. D. (2004). Effectiveness of anger treatments for specific anger problems: A meta-analytic review. *Clinical Psychology Review, 24,* 15–34.

Delves, P. J., & Roitt, I. M. (2000). Advances in immunology: The immune system. *New England Journal of Medicine, 343,* 37–39.

Denizel-Lewis, B. (2005, January 9). Ban of brothers. *New York Times Magazine,* pp. 32–39, 52, 73, 74.

Dennerstein, L., Randolph, J., Taffe, J., Dudley, E., & Burger, H. (2002). Hormones, mood, sexuality, and the menopausal transition. *Fertility and Sterility, 77,* 42–48.

Dennison, B. A., Erb, T. A., & Jenkins, P. L. (2002). Television viewing and television in bedroom associated with overweight risk among low-income preschool children. *Pediatrics, 109,* 1028–1035.

DePaulo, B. M., & Friedman, H. S. (1998). Nonverbal communication. In D. T. Gilbert, S. T. Fiske, & G. Lindzey (Eds.), *The handbook of social psychology* (4th ed., Vol. 2, pp. 3–40). Boston: McGraw-Hill.

Derlega, V., Winstead, B. A., & Jones, W. H. (Eds.). (1999). *Personality: Contemporary theory and research* (2nd ed.). Nelson-Hall series in psychology (pp. 3–26). Chicago: Nelson-Hall Publishers.

Derrington, A. M. (2004). Visual mechanisms of motion analysis and motion perception. *Annual Review of Psychology, 55,* 181–205.

DeRubeis, R. J., Hollon, S. D., Amsterdam, J. D., Shelton, R. C., Young, P. R., Salomon, R. M., et al. (2005). Cognitive therapy vs medications in the treatment of moderate to severe depression. *Archives of General Psychiatry, 62,* 409–416.

DeRubeis, R. J., Tang, T. Z., & Beck, A. T. (2001). Cognitive therapy. In K. S. Dobson (Ed.), *Handbook of cognitive-behavioral therapies* (2nd ed., pp. 349–392). New York: Guilford Press.

Desmond, A. M. (1994). Adolescent pregnancy in the United States: Not a minority issue. *Health Care for Women International, 15*(4), 325–331.

DeSpelder, L. A., & Strickland, A. L. (1999). *The last dance* (5th ed.). Mountain View, CA: Mayfield.

Devenport, J. L., Stinson, V., Cutler, B. L., & Kravitz, D. A. (2002). How effective are the cross-examination and expert testimony safeguards? Jurors' perceptions of the suggestiveness and fairness of biased lineup procedures. *Journal of Applied Psychology, 87,* 1042–1054.

Deveny, K. (2003, June 30). We're not in the mood. *Newsweek,* pp. 41–46.

Dewsbury, D. A. (1997). In celebration of the centennial of Ivan P. Pavlov's (1897/1902) *The Work of the Digestive Glands. American Psychologist, 52,* 933–935.

Dewsbury, D. A. (2000). Issues in comparative psychology at the dawn of the 20th century. *American Psychologist, 55,* 750–753.

Di Paula, A., & Campbell, J. D. (2002). Self-esteem and persistence in the face of failure. *Journal of Personality and Social Psychology, 83,* 711–724.

Diamond, L. M., (2003). Was it a phase? Young women's relinquishment of lesbian/bisexual identities over a 5-year period. *Journal of Personality and Social Psychology, 84,* 352–364.

Dick, D. M., & Foroud, T. (2003). Genetic strategies to detect genes involved in alcoholism and alcohol-related traits. *Alcohol Research & Health, 26,* 172–180.

Dickens, W. T., & Flynn, J. R. (2001). Heritability estimates versus large environmental effects: The IQ paradox resolved. *Psychological Review, 108,* 346–369.

DiClemente, R. J., Wingood, G. M., Harrington, K. F., Lang, D. L., Davies, S. L., Hook, E. W. III. (2004). Efficacy of an HIV prevention intervention for African American adolescent girls: A randomized controlled trial. *Journal of the American Medical Association, 292,* 171–179.

Diehm, R., & Armatas, C. (2004). Surfing: An avenue for socially acceptable risk-taking, satisfying needs for sensation seeking and experience seeking. *Personality and Individual Differences, 36,* 663–677.

Diener, E. (2005, April). Income and happiness. *APS Observer, 18*(4), p. 35.

Diener, E., Oishi, S., & Lucas, R. E. (2003). Personality, culture, and subjective well-being: Emotional and cognitive evaluations of life. *Annual Review of Psychology, 54,* 403–425.

Diener, E., & Seligman, M. E. P. (2004). Beyond money: Toward an economy of well-being. *Psychological Science in the Public Interest, 5,* 1–32.

Diener, E., Wolsic, B., & Fujita, F. (1995). Physical attractiveness and subjective well-being. *Journal of Personality and Social Psychology, 69,* 120–129.

Dietz, W. H. (2004). Overweight in childhood and adolescence. *New England Journal of Medicine, 350,* 855–857.

DiGiuseppe, R., & Tafrate, R. C. (2003). Anger treatment for adults: A meta-analytic review. *Clinical Psychology: Science and Practice, 10,* 70–84.

Dijksterhuis, A., & Smith, P. K. (2002). Affective habituation: Subliminal exposure to extreme stimuli decreases their extremity. *Emotion, 2,* 203—214.

DiLorenzo, P. M. & Youngentob, S. L. (2003). Olfaction and taste. In M. Gallagher & R. J. Nelson (Eds.), *Handbook of psychology: Biological psychology, Vol. 3.* (pp. 269–298). New York: John Wiley & Sons.

Dingfelder, S. F. (2004a, April. Gender bender. *Monitor on Psychology,35,* pp. 48–49.

Dingfelder, S. F. (2004b, July/August). Gateways to memory. *Monitor on Psychology,* pp. 22–23.

Dingfelder, S. (2004c, September). Clark honored for desegregation influence, life's work. *Monitor on Psychology,* p. 59.

Dinh, K. T., Sarason, I. G., Peterson, A. V., & Onstad, L. E. (1995). Children's perceptions of smokers and nonsmokers: A longitudinal study. *Health Psychology, 14,* 32–40.

Dion, K. L. (2003). Prejudice, racism, and discrimination. In T. Millon, M. J. Lerner, & E. B. Weiner (Eds.), *Handbook of psychology, Vol. 2: Personality and social psychology* (pp. 507–536). New York: Wiley.

Dittmann, M. (2003a, February). Psychology's first prescribers. *Monitor on Psychology, 34,* 36–37.

Dittmann, M. (2003b, March). Anger across the gender divide. *Monitor on Psychology, 34,* 52–53.

Dittmann, M. (2003c, April). Acting extraverted spurs positive feelings, study finds. *Monitor on Psychology, 34,* 17.

Dittmann, M. (2003d, April). Worth the risk? *Monitor on Psychology, 34,* 58–60.

Dittmann, M. (2003e, November). Compassion is what most find attractive in mates. *Monitor on Psychology, 34,* 12.

Dittmann, M. (2004a, July/August). Friendships ease middle school adjustment. *Monitor on Psychology, 35,* 18.

Dittmann, M. (2004b, July/August). Standing tall pays off, study finds. *Monitor on Psychology, 35,* 14.

Dixon, R. A., & Cohen, A.-L. (2003). Cognitive development in adulthood. In R. M. Lerner, M. A. Easterbrooks, & J. Mistry (Eds.), *Handbook of psychology: Vol. 6. Developmental psychology* (pp. 423–442). New York: John Wiley & Sons.

Dixon, W. E., Jr., & Smith, P.-H. (2000). Links between early temperament and language acquisition. *Merrill Palmer Quarterly, 46,* 417–440.

Djordjevic, J., Zatorre, R. J., Petrides, M., & Jones-Gotman, M. (2004). The mind's nose. *Psychological Science, 15,* 143–148.

Dobson, K. S., & Dozois, D. J. A. (2001). Historical and philosophical bases of the cognitive-behavioral therapies. In K. S. Dobson (Ed.), *Handbook of cognitive-behavioral therapies* (2nd ed., pp. 3–40). New York: Guilford Press.

Docherty, N. M., Cohen, A. S., Nienow, T. M., Dinzeo, T. J., & Dangelmaier, R. E. (2003). Stability of formal thought disorder and referential communication disturbances in schizophrenia. *Journal of Abnormal Psychology, 112,* 469–475.

Dodd, P. R., Foley, P. F., Buckley, S. T., Eckert, A. L., & Innes, D. J. (2004). Genes and gene expression in the brain of the alcoholic. *Addictive Behaviors, 29,* 1295–1309.

Dolbier, C. L., Cocke, R. R., Leiferman, J. A., Steinhardt, M. A., Schapiro, S. J., Nehete, P. N., et al. (2001). Differences in functional immune responses of high vs. low hardy healthy individuals. *Journal of Behavioral Medicine, 24,* 219–229.

Domjan, M. (2005). Pavlovian conditioning: A functional perspective. *Annual Review of Psychology, 56,* 179–206.

Donker, F. J. S. (2000). Cardiac rehabilitation: A review of current developments. *Clinical Psychology Review, 20,* 923–943.

Dorahy, M. J. (2001). Dissociative identity disorder and memory dysfunction: The current state of experimental research and its future directions. *Clinical Psychology Review, 21,* 771–795.

Doty, R. L. (2001). Olfaction. *Annual Review of Psychology, 52,* 423–452.

Dougall, A. L., & Baum, A. (2001). Stress, health, and illness. In A. Baum, T. A. Revenson, & J. E. Singer (Eds.), *Handbook of health psychology* (pp. 339–348). Mahwah, NJ: Lawrence Erlbaum Associates.

Dougall, A. L., & Baum, A. (2003). Stress, coping, and immune function. In M. Gallagher & R. J. Nelson (Eds.), *Handbook of psychology: Vol. 3. Biological psychology* (pp. 441–456). New York: John Wiley & Sons.

Dougherty, L. R., Klein, D. N., & Davila, J. (2004). A growth curve analysis of the course of dysthymic disorder: The effects of chronic stress and moderation by adverse parent–child relationships and family history. *Journal of Consulting and Clinical Psychology, 72,* 1012–1021.

Dovidio, J. F., Gaertner, S. L., Esses, V. M., & Brewer, M. B. (2003). Social conflict, harmony, and integration. In T. Millon & M. J. Lerner (Eds.), *Handbook of psychology: Vol. 5. Personality and social psychology* (pp. 485–506). New York: John Wiley & Sons, Inc.

Draguns, J. G., & Tanaka-Matsumi, J. (2003). Assessment of psychopathology across and within cultures: Issues and findings. *Behaviour Research and Therapy, 41,* 755–776.

Driver study: Cell phones not major distraction. (2003, August 6). *CNN Web Posting*. Retrieved August 17, 2003, from http://www.cnn.com/2003/TRAVEL/08/06/distracted.driving.ap/index.html.

Droomers, M., Schrijvers, C. T. M., & Mackenbach, J. P. (2002). Why do lower educated people continue smoking? Explanations from the longitudinal GLOBE study. *Health Psychology, 21,* 263–272.

Drucker, J. (2004, September 24). Headset phones may still pose risks for drivers. *Wall Street Journal Online*. Retrieved September 24, 2004, from http://online.wsj.com/article/0,,SB109599238867526997,00.html?mod=gadgets%5Flead%5Fstory%5Fcol.

Druckman, D., & Bjork, R. A. (Eds.). (1991). *In the mind's eye: Enhancing human performance*. Washington, DC: National Academy Press.

Dryden, W. (1984). *Rational-emotive therapy: Fundamentals and innovations*. London: Croom Helm.

Dryden, W., & Ellis, A. (2001). Rational emotive behavior therapy. In K. S. Dobson (Ed.), *Handbook of cognitive-behavioral therapies* (2nd ed., pp. 295–348). New York: Guilford Press.

Duberstein, P. R., et al. (2000). Personality traits and suicidal behavior and ideation in depressed inpatients 50 years of age and older. *Journals of Gerontology: Series B: Psychological Sciences & Social Sciences, 55B*(1), P18–P26.

DuBois, D. L., & Flay, B. R. (2004). The healthy pursuit of self-esteem: Comment on and alternative to the Crocker and Park (2004) formulation. *Psychological Bulletin, 130,* 415–420.

Dudai, Y. (2004). The neurobiology of consolidations, or, how stable is the engram? *Annual Review of Psychology, 55,* 51–86.

Duenweld, M. (2003, June 18). More Americans seeking help for depression. *New York Times*, pp. A1, A22.

Dugas, M. L., Ladouceur, R., Léger, E., Freeston, M. H., Langlis, F., Provencher, M. D., et al. (2003). Group cognitive–behavioral therapy for generalized anxiety disorder: Treatment outcome and long-term follow-up. *Journal of Consulting and Clinical Psychology, 71,* 821–825.

Dugger, C. W. (2003, November 30). Rural Haitians are vanguard in AIDS battle. *New York Times*, pp. A1, A20.

Duncan, D. F., Donnelly, J. W., & Nicholson, T. (1992). Belief in the paranormal and religious belief among American college students. *Psychological Reports, 70,* 15–18.

Duncan, J., Seitz, R. J., Kolodny, J., Bor, D., Herzog, H., Ahmed, A., et al. (2000). A neural basis for general intelligence. *Science, 289,* 457–460.

Duncan, P. D., Ritter, P., Dornbush, S. K., Gross, P., & Carlsmith, J. (1985). The effects of pubertal timing on body image, school behavior, and deviance. *Journal of Youth and Adolescence, 14,* 227–235.

Duncker, K. (1945). On problem-solving. *Psychological Monographs, 58* (Whole No. 270).

Dunning, D., & Perretta, S. (2002). Automaticity and eyewitness accuracy: A 10- to 12-second rule for distinguishing accurate from inaccurate positive identifications. *Journal of Applied Psychology, 87,* 951–962.

Durham, P. L. (2004). CGRP-receptor antagonists—a fresh approach to migraine therapy? *New England Journal of Medicine, 350,* 1073–1075.

Durrant, R., & Ellis, B. J. (2003). Evolutionary psychology. In M. Gallagher & R. J. Nelson (Eds.), *Handbook of psychology: Vol. 3. Biological psychology* (pp. 1–33). New York: John Wiley & Sons.

Duryea, B. (2000, July 21). Illuminating the reasons for suicide. *St. Petersburg Times*. Retrieved July 21, 2000, from http://www.sptimes.com/News/072100/Floridian/Illuminating_the_reas.s.html.

Dwairy, M. (2002). Foundations of psychosocial dynamic personality theory of collective people. *Clinical Psychology Review, 22,* 343–360.

Dweck, C. (1997, June). Cited in B. Murray, "Verbal praise may be the best motivator of all." *APA Monitor, 28,* 26.

Dwivedi, Y., Rizavi, H. S., Conley, R. R., Roberts, R. C., Tamminga, C. A., & Pandey, G. N. (2003). Altered gene expression of brain-derived neurotrophic factor and receptor tyrosine kinase b in postmortem brain of suicide subjects. *Archives of General Psychiatry, 60,* 804–815.

Dwyer, M. (1988). Exhibitionism/voyeurism. *Journal of Social Work and Human Sexuality, 7,* 101–112.

Eagly, A. H., & Chaiken, S. (1998). Structure and function. In D. T. Gilbert, S. T. Fiske, & G. Lindzey (Eds.), *The handbook of social psychology* (4th ed., Vol. 1, pp. 269–322). Boston: McGraw-Hill.

Eagly, A. H., & Johnson, B. T. (1990). Gender and leadership style: A meta-analysis. *Psychological Bulletin, 108,* 233–256.

Eagly, A. H., & Karau, S. J. (2002). Role congruity theory of prejudice toward female leaders. *Psychological Review, 109,* 573–598.

Eagly, A. H., Karau, S. J., & Makhijani, M. G. (1995). Gender and the effectiveness of leaders: A meta-analysis. *Psychological Bulletin, 117,* 125–145.

Eagly, A. H., & Wood, W. (1991). Explaining sex differences in social behavior: A meta-analytic perspective. *Personality and Social Psychology Bulletin, 17,* 306–315.

Easterbrook, G. (2005, January 17). The real truth about money. *Time*, pp. A32–A34.

Ebbinghaus, H. (1885). *Über das Gedachtnis*. Leipzig: Duncker & Humblot.

Eberlein, T. (1997). *Child magazine's guide to whining*. New York: Pocket Books.

Ebrahim, S. H., Floyd, R. L., Merritt, R. K., II, Decoufle, P., & Holtzman, D. (2000). Trends in pregnancy-related smoking rates in the U.S., 1987–1996. *Journal of the American Medical Association, 283,* 361–266.

Ebstein, R. P., Novick, O., Umansky, R., Priel, B., Osher, Y., Blaine, D., et al. (1996). Dopamine D4 receptor (D4DR) exon III polymorphism associated with the human personality trait of novelty seeking. *Nature Genetics, 12,* 78–80.

Eckhardt, C., Jamison, T. R., & Watts, K. (2002). Anger experience and expression among male dating violence perpetrators during anger arousal. *Journal of Interpersonal Violence, 17,* 1102–1114.

Eckhardt, C., Norlander, B., & Deffenbacher, J. (2004). The assessment of anger and hostility: A critical review. *Aggression and Violent Behavior, 9,* 17–43.

Edinger, J. D., Wohlgemuth, W. K., Radtke, R. A., Marsh, G. R., & Quillian, R. E. (2001). Cognitive behavioral therapy for treatment of chronic primary insomnia: A randomized controlled trial. *Journal of the American Medical Association, 285,* 1856–1864.

Edwards, J., Jackson, H. R., & Pattison, P. E. (2002). Emotion recognition via facial expression and affective prosody in schizophrenia: A methodological review. *Clinical Psychology Review, 22,* 789–832.

Edwards, T. M. (2000, August 28). Single by choice. *Time online, 156*(9).

Egan, S., & Stelmack, R. M. (2003). A personality profile of Mount Everest climbers. *Personality and Individual Differences, 34,* 1491–1494.

Egeth, H. E. (1993). What do we not know about eyewitness identification? *American Psychologist, 48,* 577–580.

Egger, J. I. M., De Mey, H. R. A., Derksen, J. J. L., & van der Staak, C. P. F. (2003). Cross-cultural replication of the five-factor model and comparison of the NEO-PI-R and MMPI-2 PSY-5 scales in a Dutch psychiatric sample. *Psychological Assessment, 15,* 81–88.

Ehlers, A., Clark, D. M., Hackmann, A., McManus, G., & Fennell, M. (2005). Cognitive therapy for post-traumatic stress disorder: Development and evaluation. *Behaviour Research and Therapy, 43,* 413–431.

Ehrlinger, J., & Dunning, D. (2003). How chronic self-views influence (and potentially mislead) estimates of performance. *Journal of Personality and Social Psychology, 84,* 5–17.

Eich, F. (1989). Theoretical issues in state-dependent memory. In H. L. Roediger III and I. M. Fergus (Eds.), *Varieties of memory and consciousness: Essays in honour of Edel Tulving*. Hillsdale, NJ: Erlbaum.

Eichenbaum, H. (1997). How does the brain organize memories? *Science, 277,* 330–332.

Eichenbaum, H. (2003). Memory systems. In M. Gallagher & R. J. Nelson (Eds.), *Handbook of psychology: Vol. 3. Biological psychology* (pp. 543–560). New York: John Wiley & Sons.

Einstein, G. O., & McDaniel, M. A. (1996). Remembering to do things: Remembering a forgotten topic. In D. Herrmann, C. McEvoy, C. Hertzog, P. Hertel, & M. K. Johnson (Eds.), *Basic and applied memory research: Practical applications* (Vol. 2, pp. 79–94). Mahwah, NJ: Lawrence Erlbaum Associates.

Eisner, R. (2005, January). Study suggests cognitive deficits in MDMA-only drug abusers. *NIDA Notes, 19*(5). Retrieved February 9, 2005, from http://www.nida.nih.gov/NIDA_notes/NNvol19N5/Study.html.

Ekman, P. (1980). Biological and cultural contributions to body and facial movement in the expression of emotions. In A. O. Rorty (Ed.), *Explaining emotions* (pp. 73–101). Berkeley: University of California Press.

Ekman, P. (2003). *Emotions revealed: Recognizing faces and feeling to improve communication and emotional life*. New York: Times Books.

El Nasser, H. (2004, March 18). Census projects growing diversity. *USA Today*, p. A1.

Elfenbein, H. A., & Ambady, N. (2002a). Is there an in-group advantage in emotion recognition? *Psychological Bulletin, 128,* 243–249.

Elfenbein, H. A., & Ambady, N. (2002b). On the universality and cultural specificity of emotion recognition: A meta-analysis. *Psychological Bulletin, 128,* 203–235.

Elkind, D. (1985). Egocentrism redux. *Developmental Review, 5,* 218–226.

Ellemers, N., Spears, R., & Doosje, B. (2002). Self and social identity. *Annual Review of Psychology, 53,* 161–186.

Ellenberger, H. F. (1965). Charcot and the Salpetriere school. *American Journal of Psychotherapy, 19,* 253–267.

Elliot, A. J., & Sheldon, K. M. (1997). Avoidance achievement motivation: A personal goals analysis. *Journal of Personality and Social Psychology, 73,* 171–185.

Ellis, A. (1977). The basic clinical theory of rational-emotive therapy. In A. Ellis & R. Grieger (Eds.), *Handbook of rational-emotive therapy.* New York: Springer Publishing Company.

Ellis, A. (1991). *Reason and emotion in psychotherapy.* New York: Carol Publishing.

Ellis, A. (2001). *Overcoming destructive beliefs, feelings, and behaviors: New directions for rational emotive behavior therapy.* Amherst, NY: Prometheus Books.

Ellis, A., & Dryden, W. (1987). *The practice of rational emotional therapy.* New York: Springer Publishing Company.

Ellis, A., Young, J., & Lockwood, G. (1989). Cognitive therapy and rational-emotive therapy: A dialogue. *Journal of Cognitive Psychotherapy, 1,* 205–256.

Ellis, H. D., & Shepherd, J. W. (1992). Face memory: Theory and practice. In M. Gruneberg & P. Morris (Eds.), *Aspects of memory: Second Edition, Volume 1: The practical aspects* (pp. 18–85). London: Routledge.

Ellis, L., & Bonin, S. L. (2003). Genetics and occupation-related preferences. Evidence from adoptive and non-adoptive families. *Personality and Individual Differences, 35,* 929–937.

Ellis, L., & Hellberg, J. (2005). Fetal exposure to prescription drugs and adult sexual orientation. *Personality and Individual Differences, 38,* 225–236.

Ellsworth, P. C. (1994). Sense, culture, and sensibility. In S. Kitayama & H. R. Markus (Eds.), *Emotion and culture: Empirical studies of mutual influence* (pp. 23–50). Washington, DC: American Psychological Association.

Elms, A. C. (1995). Obedience in retrospect. *Journal of Social Issues, 51,* 21–31.

Ember, C., & Ember, M. (2004). *Cultural anthropology* (11th ed.). Upper Saddle River, NJ: Prentice Hall.

Epstein, H. (2003, October 12). Enough to make you sick? *New York Times Magazine,* pp. 75–81, 98, 102–108.

Epstein, R., Kirshnit, C. E., Lanza, R. P., & Rubin, L. C. (1984). "Insight" in the pigeon: Antecedents and determinants of an intelligent performance. *Nature, 308,* 61–62.

Epstein, S. (1996). Commentary: Recommendations for the future development of personality psychology. *Journal of Research in Personality, 30,* 435–446.

Erikson, E. H. (1963). *Childhood and society* (2nd ed.). New York: Norton.

Erikson, E. H. (1975). *Life history and the historical moment.* New York: Norton.

Erikson, E. H. (1980). *Identity and the life cycle.* New York: Norton.

Eron, L. D. (1993, August). Cited in DeAngelis, T. (1993). It's back: TV violence, concern for kid viewers. *APA Monitor, 24*(8), 16.

Escobar, J. I., Hoyos-Nervi, C., & Gara, M. (2000). Immigration and mental health: Mexican-Americans in the United States. *Harvard Review of Psychiatry, 8,* 64–72.

Escobar, J. I., & Vega, W. A. (2000). Commentary: Mental health and immigration's AAAs: Where are we and where do we go from here? *Journal of Nervous and Mental Disease, 188,* 736–740.

Espenshade, T. (1993, April 25). Cited in F. Barringer, "Polling on sexual issues has its drawbacks." *New York Times,* p. A23.

Espie, C. A. (2002). Insomnia. *Annual Review of Psychology, 53,* 215–243.

Esposito, K., Giugliano, F., Di Palo, C., Giugliano, G., Marfella, R., D'Andrea, F., et al. (2004). Effect of lifestyle changes on erectile dysfunction in obese men: A randomized controlled trial. *Journal of the American Medical Association, 291,* 2978–2984.

Essock, S. M., Frisman, L. K., Covell, N. H., & Hargreaves, W. A. (2000). Cost-effectiveness of clozapine compared with conventional antipsychotic medication for patients in state hospitals. *Archives of General Psychiatry, 57,* 987–994.

Estevez, M., & Gardner, K. L. (2004). Update on the genetics of migraine. *Human Genetics, 114,* 225–235.

Etheridge, P. (2001, January 8). *Kids' TV watching linked to unhealthy eating habits.* Retrieved January 10, 2001, from http://www.cnn.com/2001/HEALTH/children/01/08/tv.eating/index.html.

Evans, R. B. (1999a, December). Controversy follows psychological testing. *APA Monitor, Online, 30*(11). Retrieved December 3, 2001, from http://www.apa.org/monitor/dec99/ss4.html.

Evans, R. B. (1999b, December). Behaviorism: the rise and fall of a discipline. *APA Monitor, 30*(11). Retrieved December 3, 2001, from http://www.apa.org/monitor/dec99/ss6.html.

Evans, R. B. (1999c, December). Once behind the scenes, now in the fore. *APA Monitor, 30*(11). Retrieved December 3, 2001, from http://www.apa.org/monitor/dec99/ss10.html.

Evans, R. B. (1999d, December). The long road to diversity. *APA Monitor, 30* (11). Retrieved December 3, 2001, from http://www.apa.org/monitor/dec99/ss11.html.

Ewing, R., Schmid, T., Killingsworth, R., Zlot, A., & Raudenbush, S. (2003). Relationship between urban sprawl and physical activity, obesity and morbidity. *American Journal of Health Promotion, 18,* 47–57.

Exner, J. E. (1993). *The Rorschach: A comprehensive system: Vol. 1. Basic foundations* (3rd ed.). New York: Wiley.

Exner, J. E., Jr. (2002). Early development of the Rorschach test. *Academy of Clinical Psychology Bulletin, 8,* 9–24.

Eysenbach, G., Powell, J., Kuss, O., & Sa, E-R. (2003). Empirical studies assessing the quality of health information for consumers on the World Wide Web: A systematic review. *Journal of the American Medical Association, 287,* 2691–2700.

Eysenck, H. J. (1982). *Personality, genetics, and behavior.* New York: Praeger.

Eysenck, H. J. (Ed.). (1981). *A model for personality.* New York: Springer Publishing Company.

Fagan, J. F., & Holland, C. R. (2002). Equal opportunity and racial differences in IQ. *Intelligence, 30,* 361–387.

Fagot, B. J. (1995). Psychosocial and cognitive determinants of early gender-role development. *Annual Review of Sex Research, 6,* 1–31.

Fairburn, C. G., Stice, E., Cooper, Z., Doll, H. A., Norman, P. A., & O'Connor, E. E. (2003). Understanding persistence in bulimia nervosa: A 5-year naturalistic study. *Journal of Consulting and Clinical Psychology, 71,* 103–109.

Fals-Stewart, W. (2003). The occurrence of partner physical aggression on days of alcohol consumption: A longitudinal diary study. *Journal of Consulting and Clinical Psychology, 71,* 41–52.

Fannin, N., & Dabbs, J. M, Jr. (2003). Testosterone and the work of firefighters: Fighting fires and delivering medical care. *Journal of Research in Personality, 37,* 107–115.

Faraone, S. V. (2003, August). *ADHD: Facts and fiction.* Paper presented at the meeting of the American Psychological Association, Toronto, CA.

Farberman, R. K. (2003, April). Preparing for the "minority majority." *Monitor on Psychology, 34,* 42–43.

Farooqi, I. S., Keogh, J. M., Yeo, G. S. H., Lank, E. J., Cheetham, T., et al. (2003). Clinical spectrum of obesity and mutations in the melanocortin 4 receptor gene. *New England Journal of Medicine, 348,* 1085–1095.

Farrell, A. D., & White, K. S. (1998). Peer influences and drug use among urban adolescents: Family structure and parent/adolescent relationship as protective factors. *Journal of Consulting and Clinical Psychology, 66,* 248–258.

Fava, G. A., Ruini, C., Rafanelli, C., Finos, L., Conti, S., & Grandi, S. (2004). Six-year outcome of cognitive behavior therapy for prevention of recurrent depression. *American Journal of Psychiatry,161,* 1872–1876.

Fazio, R. H., & Olson, M. A. (2003). Implicit measures in social cognition research: Their meaning and use. *Annual Review of Psychology, 54,* 297–327.

Feingold, A. (1991). Sex differences in the effects of similarity and physical attractiveness on opposite-sex attraction. *Basic and Applied Social Psychology, 12,* 357–367.

Feingold, A. (1992). Good-looking people are not what we think. *Psychological Bulletin, 111,* 304–341.

Feingold, A. (1994). Gender differences in personality: A meta-analysis. *Psychological Bulletin, 116,* 429–456.

Feldhusen, J. F. (2004). Can we be intelligent and creative simultaneously? *Contemporary Psychology: APA Review of Books, 49,* 616–617.

Feldman, D. H. (2003). Cognitive development in childhood. In R. M. Lerner, M. A. Easterbrooks, & J. Mistry (Eds.), *Handbook of psychology: Vol. 6. Developmental psychology* (pp. 195–210). New York: John Wiley & Sons.

Feldman, L. B., & Rivas-Vazquez, R. A. (2003). Assessment and treatment of social anxiety disorder. *Professional Psychology: Research and Practice, 34,* 396–405.

Felson, R. B. (2002). *Violence and gender reexamined.* Washington, DC: American Psychological Association.

Feng, Y., Niu, T., Xing, H., Xu, X., Chen, C., Peng, S., et al. (2004). A common haplotype of the nicotine acetylcholine receptor alpha 4 subunit gene is associated with vulnerability to nicotine addiction in men. *American Journal of Human Genetics, 75,* 112–121.

Festinger, L., & Carlsmith, J. M. (1959). Cognitive consequences of forced compliance. *Journal of Abnormal and Social Psychology, 58,* 203–210.

Field, T. (1996). Attachment and separation in young children. *Annual Review of Psychology, 47,* 541–561.

Fierros-Gonzalez, R., & Brown, J. M. (2002). High-risk behaviors in a sample of Mexican-American college students. *Psychological Reports, 90,* 117–130.

Fingerman, K. L. (2002). *Mothers and their adult daughters: Mixed emotions, enduring bonds.* New York: Prometheus Books.

Fink, B., & Penton-Voak, I. (2002). Evolutionary psychology of facial attractiveness. *Current Directions in Psychological Science, 11,* 154–158.

Finke, R. A., Ward, T. B., & Smith, S. M. (1992). *Creative cognition: Theory, research, and applications.* Cambridge, MA: MIT Press.

Fischer, A. H., Mosquera, P. M. R., van Vianen, A. E. M., & Manstead, A. S. R. (2004). Gender and culture differences in emotion. *Emotion, 4,* 87–94.

Fischer, H., Jesper, L. R., Furmark, T., Wik, G. , & Fredrikson, M. (2002). Right-sided human prefrontal brain activation during acquisition of conditioned fear. *Emotion, 2,* 233–241.

Fishbain, D. A., & Goldberg, M. (1991). The misdiagnosis of conversion disorder in a psychiatric emergency service. *General Hospital Psychiatry, 13,* 177–181.

Fishbein, M. D. (1996). *Peer prejudice and discrimination: Evolutionary, cultural, and developmental dynamics.* Boulder, CO: Westview Press.

Fisher, B. S., Daigle, L. E., Cullen, F. T., & Turner, M. G. (2003). Reporting sexual victimization to the police and others: Results from a national-level study of college women. *Criminal Justice and Behavior, 30,* 6–38.

Fisher, S., & Greenberg, R. (Eds.). (1978). *The scientific evaluation of Freud's theories and therapy: A book of readings.* New York: Basic Books.

Fishman, J. R., & Mamo, L. (2001). What's in a disorder: A cultural analysis of medical and pharmaceutical constructions of male and female sexual dysfunction. *Women and Therapy, 24,* 179–193.

Fiske, A. P., Kitayama, S., Markus, H. R., & Nisbett, R. E. (1998). The cultural matrix of social psychology. In D. T. Gilbert, S. T. Fiske, & G. Lindzey (Eds.), *The handbook of social psychology* (4th ed., Vol. 2, pp. 915–981). Boston: McGraw-Hill.

Fitness, J. (2001). Emotional intelligence and intimate relationships. In J. Ciarrochi & J. P. Forgas et al. (Eds.), *Emotional intelligence in everyday life: A scientific inquiry* (pp. 98–112). Philadelphia: Psychology Press.

Fitzgerald, H. E., Mann, T., Cabrera, N., & Wong, M. M. (2003). Diversity in caregiving contexts. In R. M. Lerner, A. Easterbrooks, & I. Mistry (Eds.), *Comprehensive handbook of psychology, Vol. 6: Developmental psychology* (pp. 135–167). New York: Wiley.

Fitzgerald, L. F. (1993a). *Sexual harassment in higher education: Concepts and issues.* Washington, DC: National Education Association.

Fitzgerald, L. F. (1993b). Sexual harassment: Violence against women in the workplace. *American Psychologist, 48,* 1070–1076.

Fitzpatrick, O. D., Jr., & Shook, S. L. (1994). Belief in the paranormal: Does identity development during the college years make a difference? An initial investigation. *Journal of Parapsychology, 58,* 315–329.

Fivush, R., & Nelson, K. (2004). Culture and language in the emergence of autobiographical memory. *Psychological Science, 15,* 573–000.

Flavell, J. H. (1992). Cognitive development: Past, present, and future. *Developmental Psychology, 28,* 998–1005.

Flavell, J. H., Miller, P. H., & Miller, S. A. (2002). *Cognitive development* (4th ed.). Upper Saddle River, NJ: Prentice Hall.

Fleeson, W. (2004). Moving personality beyond the person-situation debate: The challenge and the opportunity of within-person variability. *Current Directions in Psychological Science, 13,* 83–87.

Fleeson, W., Malanos, A. B., & Achille, N. M. (2002). Intraindividual process approach to the relationship between extraversion and positive Affect: Is acting extraverted as "good" as being extraverted? *Journal of Personality and Social Psychology, 83,* 1409–1422.

Flynn, C. A., & Chen, Y. C. C. (2003). Antidepressants for generalized anxiety disorder. *American Family Physician, 68,* 1757–1758.

Flynn, J. R. (1999). Searching for justice: The discovery of IQ gains over time. *American Psychologist, 54,* 5–20.

Flynn, J. R. (2003). Movies about intelligence: The limitations of g. *Current Directions in Psychological Science, 12,* 95–98.

Foa, E. G., et al. (2005). Randomized, placebo-controlled trial of exposure and ritual prevention, clomipramine, and their combination in the treatment of obsessive-compulsive disorder. *American Journal of Psychiatry, 162,* 151–161.

Fogel, J. (2003). Use of the Internet for health information and communication. *Journal of the American Medical Association, 290,* 2256. [Letter]

Fogelholm, M., Kukkonen-Harjual, K., Nenonen, A., & Pasenen, M. (2000). Effects of walking training on weight maintenance after a very-low-energy diet in premenopausal obese women: A randomized controlled trial. *Archives of Internal Medicine, 160,* 2177–2184.

Folic acid behind birth defect decline (2004, May 7). *CNN Web Posting.* Retrieved May 8, 2004, from http://www.cnn.com/2004/HEALTH/05/07/birth.defects.reut/index.html.

Folsom, D. P., Hawthorne, W., Lindamer, L.,Gilmer, T., Bailey, A., Golshan, S., Garcia, P., et al. (2005). Prevalence and risk factors for homelessness and utilization of mental health services among 10,340 patients with serious mental illness in a large public mental health system. *American Journal of Psychiatry, 162,* 370–376.

Fontaine, K. R., Redden, D. T., Wang, C., Westfall, A. O, & Allison, D. B. (2003). Years of life lost due to obesity. *Journal of the American Medical Association, 289,* 187–193.

Foote, D. (2000, Fall/Winter). The war of the wills. *Newsweek Special Issue,* pp. 64–65.

Ford, C. S., & Beach, F. A. (1951). *Patterns of sexual behavior.* New York: Harper & Row.

Forestell, C. A., Humphrey, T. M., & Stewart, S. H. (2004). Involvement of body weight and shape factors in ratings of attractiveness by women: a replication and extension of Tassinary and Hansen (1998). *Personality and Individual Differences, 36,* 295–305.

Foster, R., & Kreitzman, L. (2004). *Rhythms of life.* London: Profile Books.

Fowler, R. D. (1992, June). Solid support needed for animal research. *APA Monitor, 23*(6), 2.

Foxhall, K. (2000a, January). Bringing law and psychology together. *Monitor on Psychology, 31*(1), 38–39.

Foxhall, K. (2000b, October). Dispatches from the prescription privileges fronts. *Monitor on Psychology, 31*(10), 30–31.

Foxhall, K. (2000c, October). Platform for a long-term push. *Monitor on Psychology, 31*(10), 30.

Fraley, R. C., & Spieker, S. J. (2003a). What are the differences between dimensional and categorical models of individual differences in attachment? Reply to Cassidy (2003), Cummings (2003), Sroufe (2003), and Waters and Beauchaine (2003). *Developmental Psychology, 39,* 423–429.

Fraley, R. C., & Spieker, S. J. (2003b). Are infant attachment patterns continuously or categorically distributed? A taxometric analysis of strange situation behavior. *Developmental Psychology, 39,* 387–404.

Frank, E., & Kupfer, D. J. (2000). Peeking through the door to the 21st century. *Archives of General Psychiatry, 57,* 83–85.

Frankenberger, K. D. (2000). Adolescent egocentrism: A comparison among adolescents and adults. *Journal of Adolescence, 23,* 343–354.

Frasure-Smith, N., & Lespérance, F. (2005). Reflections on depression as a cardiac risk factor. *Psychosomatic Medicine, 67* (Suppl 1), S19-S25.

Frauenglass, S., Routh, D. K., Pantin, H. M., & Mason, C. A. (1997). Family support decreases influence of deviant peers on Hispanic adolescents' substance use. *Journal of Clinical Child Psychology, 26,* 15–23.

Freedman, R. (2003). Schizophrenia. *New England Journal of Medicine, 349,* 1738–1749.

Freeman, H. P., & Payne, R. (2000). Racial injustice in health care. *New England Journal of Medicine, 342,* 1045–1047.

Freeman, M. S., Spence, M. J., & Oliphant, C. M. (1993, June). *Newborns prefer their mothers' low-pass filtered voices over other female filtered voices.* Paper presented at the annual meeting of the American Psychological Society, Chicago.

Freemon, F. R. (1981). *Organic mental disease.* Jamaica, NY: Spectrum.

Frensch, P. A., & Rünger, D. (2003). Implicit learning *Current Directions in Psychological Science, 12,* 13–18.

Freud, S. (1900). The interpretation of dreams. In J. Strachey (Ed.), *The standard edition of the complete psychological works of Sigmund Freud: Vol. 8.* London: Hogarth Press.

Freud, S. (1922/1959). Analysis of a phobia in a 5-year-old boy. In A. & J. Strachey (Eds. & Trans.), *Collected papers* (Vol. 3). New York: Basic Books. (Original work published 1909.)

Freud, S. (1938). *The psychopathology of everyday life.* Hammondsworth: Pelican Books.

Freud, S. (1957). Mourning and melancholia (1917). In J. Rickman (Ed.), *A general selection from the works of Sigmund Freud.* Garden City, NY: Doubleday.

Freud, S. (1964). New introductory lectures. In *Standard edition of the complete psychological works of Sigmund Freud* (Vol. 22). London: Hogarth. (Original work published 1933.)

Freund, A. M., & Baltes, P. B. (1999). Selection, optimization, and compensation as strategies of life management: Correction to Freund and Baltes (1998). *Psychology and Aging, 14,* 700–702.

Freund, A. M., & Riediger, M. (2003). Successful aging. In R. M. Lerner, M. A. Easterbrooks, & J. Mistry (Eds.), *Handbook of psychology: Vol. 6. Developmental psychology* (pp. 601–628). New York: John Wiley & Sons.

Fricchione, G. (2004). Generalized anxiety disorder. *New England Journal of Medicine, 351,* 675–682.

Fried, C. B. (2003). Stereopytes of music fans: Are rap and heavy metal fans a danger to themselves or others? *Journal of Media Psychology, 8,* Fall 2003 online. Retrieved from http://www.calstatela.edu/faculty/sfischo/Fried%20rev.pdf.

Friedman, M., & Rosenman, R. H. (1974). *Type A behavior and your heart.* New York: Knopf.

Friedman, M., & Ulmer, D. (1984). *Treating Type A behavior and your heart.* New York: Fawcett Crest.

Friedman, R. A. (2002, December 31). Born to be happy, through a twist of human hard wire. *New York Times,* p. F5.

Frisina, P. G., Borod, J. C., & Lepore, S. J. (2004). A meta-analysis of the effects of written emotional disclosure on the health outcomes of clinical populations. *Journal of Nervous and Mental Disease, 192,* 629–634.

Frohlich, P., & Meston, C. (2002). Sexual functioning and self-reported depressive symptoms among college women. *Journal of Sex Research, 39*(4), 321–325.

Fruzzetti, A. E., Toland, K., Teller, S. A., & Loftus, E. F. (1992). Memory and eyewitness testimony. In M. M. Gruneberg & P. E. Morris (Eds.), *Aspects of memory: Vol. 1. The practical aspects* (2nd ed., pp. 18–50). Florence, KY: Taylor & Francis/Routledge.

Fuchs, M. (2001, June 9). For Alzheimer's patients, some solace, if not hope. *New York Times,* pp. B1, B6.

Fujita, F., & Diener, E. (2005). Life satisfaction set point: stability and change. *Journal of Personality and Social Psychology, 88,* 158–164.

Fukukawa, Y., Nakashima, C., Tsuboi, S., Kozakai, R., Doyo, W., Niino, N., et al. (2004). Age differences in the effect of physical activity on depressive symptoms. *Psychology and Aging, 19,* 346–351.

Fuligni, A., & Pedersen, S. (2002). Family obligation and the transition to young adulthood. *Developmental Psychology, 38,* 856–868.

Funder, D. C. (1994). Explaining traits. *Psychological Inquiry, 5,* 125–127.

Furmark, T. (2002). Social phobia: Overview of community surveys. *Acta Psychiatrica Scandinavica, 105,* 84–93.

Furr, R. M., & Funder, D. C. (2004). Situational similarity and behavioral consistency: Subjective, objective, variable-centered, and person-centered approaches. *Journal of Research in Personality, 38,* 421–447.

Furumoto, L. (1992). Joining separate spheres—Christine Ladd-Franklin, woman-scientist. *American Psychologist, 47,* 175–182.

Gabbard, G. O. (2005). Mind, brain, and personality disorders. *American Journal of Psychiatry, 162,* 648–655.

Gabriel, T. (1995, June 12). A new generation seems ready to give bisexuality a place in the spectrum. *New York Times,* p. A12.

Gaertner, S. L., Dovidio, J. F., Rust, M. C., Nier, J. A., Banker, B. S., Ward, C. M., et al. (1999). Reducing intergroup bias: Elements of intergroup cooperation. *Journal of Personality and Social Psychology, 76,* 388–402.

Gagnon, J. H. (1990). Gender preferences in erotic relations: The Kinsey scale and sexual scripts. In D. P. McWhirter, S. A. Sanders, & J. M. Reinisch (Eds.), *Homosexuality/heterosexuality: concepts of sexual orientation* (pp. 177–207). New York: Oxford University Press.

Gaines, S. O., Jr., Marelich, W. D., Bledsoe, K. L., Steers, W. N., et al. (1997). Links between race/ethnicity and cultural values as mediated by racial/ethnic identity and moderated by gender. *Journal of Personality and Social Psychology, 72,* 1460–1476.

Gais, S., & Born, J. (2004). Declarative memory consolidation: Mechanisms acting during human sleep. *Learning and Memory, 11,* 679–685.

Galanter, E. (1962). Contemporary psychophysics. In R. Brown, E. Galanter, H. Hess, & G. Mandler (Eds.), *New directions in psychology.* New York: Holt, Rinehart & Winston.

Gallup Organization. (2005). *Americans' personal satisfaction.* Retrieved April 20, 2005, from http://www.gallup.com/poll/content/default.aspx?ci=14506.

Gannon, N., & Ranzijn, R. (2005). Does emotional intelligence predict unique variance in life satisfaction beyond IQ and personality? *Personality and Individual Differences, 38,* 1353–1364.

Garb, H. N. (2003). Incremental validity and the assessment of psychopathology in adults. *Psychological Assessment, 15,* 508–520,

Garb, H. N., Wood, J. M., Lilienfeld, S. O., & Nezworski, M. T. (2005). Roots of the Rorschach controversy. *Clinical Psychology Review, 25,* 97–118.

Garcia, J., & Koelling, R. A. (1966). Relation of cue to consequence in avoidance learning. *Psychonomic Science, 4,* 123–124.

Garcia, J., & Koelling, R. A. (1971). The use of ionizing rays as a mammalian olfactory stimulus. In H. Autrum et al. (Eds.), *Handbook of sensory physiology: Vol. 4. Chemical senses* (Part 1). New York: Springer-Verlag.

Garcia, S. M., Weaver, K., Moskowitz, G. B., & Darley, J. M. (2002). Crowded minds: The implicit bystander effect. *Journal of Personality and Social Psychology, 83,* 843–853.

Gardner, H. (1993). Intelligence in seven phases. In H. Gardner (Ed.), *Multiple intelligences: The theory in practice* (pp. 213–230). New York: Basic Books.

Gardner, H. (1998). Are there additional intelligences? The case for naturalist, spiritual, and existential intelligences. In J. Kane (Ed.), *Education information, and transformation.* Upper Saddle River, NJ: Prentice Hall.

Gardner, H., & Traub, J. (1999, Fall). Debate on "multiple intelligences." *Cerebrum, 1,* 2.

Gardner, R. A., & Gardner, B. T. (1969). Teaching sign language to a chimpanzee. *Science, 165,* 664–672.

Gardner, R. A., & Gardner, B. T. (1978). Comparative psychology and language acquisition. *Annals of the New York Academy of Science, 309,* 37–76.

Garlick, D. (2003). Integrating brain science research with intelligence research. *Current Directions in Psychological Science, 12,* 185–189.

Garlow, S. J., Purselle, D., & Heninger, M. (2005). Ethnic differences in patterns of suicide across the life cycle. *American Journal of Psychiatry, 162,* 319–323.

Garnets, L. D. (2002). Sexual orientations in perspective. *Cultural Diversity and Ethnic Minority Psychology, 8,* 115–129.

Garwood, S. G., et al. (1980). Beauty is only "name deep": The effect of first name in ratings of physical attraction. *Journal of Applied Social Psychology, 10,* 431–435.

Gaser, C., Nenadic, I., Buchsbaum, B. R., Hazlett, E. A., & Buchsbaum, M. S. (2004). Ventricular enlargement in schizophrenia related to volume reduction of the thalamus, striatum, and superior temporal cortex. *American Journal of Psychiatry, 161,* 154–156.

Gatchel, R. J. (2001). Biofeedback and self-regulation of physiological activity: A major adjunctive treatment modality in health psychology. In A. Baum, T. A. Revenson, & J. E. Singer (Eds.), *Handbook of health psychology* (pp. 95–104). Mahwah, NJ: Lawrence Erlbaum Associates.

Gathorne-Hardy, J. (2000). *Sex, the measure of all things: A life of Alfred C. Kinsey.* Bloomington: Indiana University Press.

Gaulin, S. J. C., & McBurney, D. H. (2001). *Psychology: An evolutionary approach.* Upper Saddle River, NJ: Prentice Hall.

Gauthier, I., & Curby, K. M. (2005). A perceptual traffic jam on highway N170 interference between face and car expertise. *Current Directions in Psychological Science, 14,* 30–33.

Gay couples found to head more homes. (2001, August 22). *New York Times,* p. A16.

Gazzaniga, M. S. (1992). *Nature's mind.* New York: Basic Books.

Gazzaniga, M. S. (1995). Consciousness and the cerebral hemispheres. In M. S. Gazzaniga (Ed.), *The cognitive neurosciences* (pp. 1391–1400). Cambridge, MA: MIT Press.

Gazzaniga, M. (1999). The interpreter within: The glue of conscious experience. *Cerebrum, 1*(1), 68–78.

Ge, X., Kim, I. J, Brody, G. H., Conger, R. D., Simons, R. L., Gibbons, F. X., & Cutrona, C. E. (2003). It's about timing and change: Pubertal transition effects on symptoms of major depression among African American youths. *Developmental Psychology, 39,* 430–439.

Gebhard, P. H. (1977). *Memorandum on the incidence of homosexuals in the United States.* Bloomington: Indiana University Institute for Sex Research.

Geddes, J. R., Burgess, S., Hawton, K., Jamison, K., & Goodwin, G. M. (2004). Long-term lithium therapy for bipolar disorder: Systematic review and meta-analysis of randomized controlled trials. *American Journal of Psychiatry, 161,* 217–222.

Geen, R. G. (1998). Aggression and antisocial behavior. In D. T. Gilbert, S. T. Fiske, & G. Lindzey (Eds.), *The handbook of social psychology* (4th ed., Vol. 2, pp. 317–356). Boston: McGraw-Hill.

Gentile, D. A., Lynch, P. J., Linder, J. R., & Walsh, D. A. (2004). The effects of violent video game habits on adolescent hostility, aggressive behaviors, and school performance. *Journal of Adolescence, 27,* 5–22.

Gerhart, B. (2005). The (affective) dispositional approach to job satisfaction: Sorting out the policy implications. *Journal of Organizational Behavior, 26,* 79–97.

German, T. P., & Barrett, H. C. (2005). Functional fixedness in a technologically sparse culture. *Psychological Science, 16,* 1–5.

Gershoff, E. T. (2002a). Corporal punishment by parents and associated child behaviors and experiences: A meta-analytic and theoretical review. *Psychological Bulletin, 128,* 539–579.

Gershoff, E. T. (2002b). Corporal punishment, physical abuse, and the burden of proof: Reply to Baumrind, Larzelere, and Cowan (2002), Holden (2002), and Parke (2002). *Psychological Bulletin, 128,* 602–611.

Giancola, P. R., & Zeichner, A. (1997). The biphasic effects of alcohol on human physical aggression. *Journal of Abnormal Psychology, 106,* 598–607.

Gibbons, F. X., Gerrard, M., Cleveland, M. J., Wills, T. A., & Brody, G. (2004). Perceived discrimination and substance use in African American parents and their children: A panel study. *Journal of Personality and Social Psychology, 86,* 517–529.

Gibbs, N. (1991, June 3). When is it rape? *Time,* pp. 48–54.

Gibson, E. J., & Walk, R. D. (1960, April). The visual cliff. *Scientific American,* pp. 64–71.

Gidron, Y., Davidson, K., & Bata, I. (1999). The short-term effects of a hostility-reduction intervention on male coronary heart disease patients. *Health Psychology, 18,* 416–420.

Gil, K. M., Williams, D. A., Keefe, F. J., & Beckham, J. C. (1990). The relationship of negative thoughts to pain and psychological distress. *Behavior Therapy, 21,* 349–362.

Gilbert, S. (2004, March 16). New clues to women veiled in black. *New York Times, Science Times,* pp. F1, F7.

Gilbert, S. C. (2003). Eating disorders in women of color. *Clinical Psychology: Science and Practice, 10,* 444–455.

Gilligan, C. (1982). *In a different voice: Psychological theory and women's development.* Cambridge, MA: Harvard University Press.

Gilligan, C., Lyons, P., & Hanmer, T. J. (Eds.). (1990). *Making connections.* Cambridge, MA: Harvard University Press.

Giltay, E. J., et al. (2004). Dispositional optimism and all-cause and cardiovascular mortality in a prospective cohort of elderly Dutch men and women. *Archives of General Psychiatry, 61,* 1126–1135.

Glass, R. M. (2000). Panic disorder: It's real and it's treatable [Editorial]. *Journal of the American Medical Association, 283,* 2573–2574.

Glass, R. M. (2001). Electroconvulsive therapy: Time to bring it out of the shadows [Editorial]. *Journal of the American Medical Association, 285,* 1346–1348.

Glass, R. M. (2004). Treatment of adolescents with major depression: Contributions of a major trial. *Journal of the American Medical Association, 292,* 861–863.

Gleaves, D. H., Smith, S. M., Butler, L. D., & Spiegel, D. (2004). False and recovered memories in the laboratory and clinic: a review of experimental and clinical evidence. *Clinical Psychology: Science and Practice, 11,* 3–28.

Glueckauf, R. L., Pickett, T. C., Ketterson, T. U., Loomis, J. S., & Rozensky, R. H. (2003). Preparation for the delivery of telehealth services: A self-study framework for expansion of practice. *Professional Psychology: Research and Practice, 34,* 159–163.

Goddard, A. W., Mason, G. F., Almai, A., Rothman, D. L., Behar, K. L., Petroff, O. A., et al. (2001). Reductions in occipital cortex GABA levels in panic disorder detected with sup-1H-magnetic resonance spectroscopy. *Archives of General Psychiatry, 58,* 556–561.

Godden, D. R., & Baddeley, A. D. (1975). Context-dependent memory in two natural environments: On land and underwater. *British Journal of Psychology, 66,* 325–331.

Goel, M. S., McCarthy, E. P., Phillips, R. S., & Wee, C. C. (2004). Obesity among US immigrant subgroups by duration of residence. *Journal of the American Medical Association, 292,* 2860–2867.

Goenjian, A. K., Molina, L., Steinberg, A. M., Fairbanks, L. A., Alvarez, M. L., Goenjian, H. A., & Pynoos, R. S. (2001). Posttraumatic stress and depressive reactions among Nicaraguan adolescents after Hurricane Mitch. *American Journal of Psychiatry, 158,* 788–794.

Goff, D. C., & Coyle, J. T. (2001). The emerging role of glutamate in the pathophysiology and treatment of schizophrenia. *American Journal of Psychiatry, 158,* 1367–1377.

Goldberg, I. J., Mosca, L., Piano, M. R., & Fisher, E. A. (2001). AHA Science Advisory: Wine and your heart. *Circulation, 103,* 472–475.

Goldberg, L. R. (1993). The structure of phenotypic personality traits. *American Psychologist, 48,* 26–34.

Goldstat, R., et al. (2003). Transdermal testosterone therapy improves well-being, mood, and sexual function in premenopausal women. *Menopause, 10,* 390–398.

Goldstein, A. (1994). *Addiction: From biology to drug policy.* New York: W. H. Freeman and Company.

Goleman, D. (1991a, October 15). Happy or sad, a mood can prove contagious. *New York Times,* pp. C1, C8.

Goleman, D. (1991b, October 22). Sexual harassment: It's about power, not lust. *New York Times,* pp. C1, C12.

Goleman, D. (1995a, March 8). 75 years later, study still tracking geniuses. *New York Times,* pp. C1, C9.

Goleman, D. (1995b, March 28). The brain manages happiness and sadness in different centers. *New York Times,* pp. C1, C9.

Goleman, D. (1995c). *Emotional intelligence.* New York: Bantam Books.

Goleman, D. (2003, February 4). Finding happiness: Cajole your brain to lean to the left. *New York Times,* p. F5.

Golish, T. D. (2003). Stepfamily communication strengths: Understanding the ties that bind. *Human Communication Research, 29,* 41–80.

Gone, J. (2004). Mental health services for Native Americans in the 21st century United States. *Professional Psychology: Research and Practice, 35,* 10–18.

Gonsalves, B., Reber, P. J., Gitelman, D. R., Parrish, T. B., Mesulam, M.-M., & Paller, K. A. (2004). Neural evidence that vivid imagining can lead to false remembering. *Psychological Science, 15,* 655–660.

Goode, E. (2000, August 27). Hey, what if contestants give each other shocks? *New York Times Week in Review,* p. 2.

Goode, E. (2001a, January 2). Researcher challenges a host of psychological studies. *New York Times,* pp. F1, F7.

Goode, E. (2001b, January 25). Rats may dream, it seems, of their days at the mazes. *New York Times,* pp. A1, A16.

Goode, E. (2001c, April 3). Scientist at work: Robert Sternberg. His goal: Making intelligence tests smarter. *New York Times,* pp. F1, F7.

Goode, E. (2003). Experts see mind's voices in new light. *New York Times,* pp. F1, F6.

Goodwin, I. (2003). The relevance of attachment theory to the philosophy, organization, and practice of adult mental health care. *Clinical Psychology Review, 23,* 35–56.

Gooren, L. J. G., & Kruijver, P. M. (2002). Androgens and male behavior. *Molecular and Cellular Endocrinology, 198,* 31–40.

Gopnik, A. (2000, December 24). Children need childhood, not vocational training. *New York Times Week in Review,* p. 6.

Gordon, R. A. (2000). Stereotype measurement and the "kernel of truth' hypothesis." In M. E. Ware & D. E. Johnson (Eds.). (2000). *Handbook of demonstrations and activities in the teaching of psychology, Vol. III: Personality, abnormal, clinical-counseling, and social* (2nd ed.). Mahwah, NJ: Lawrence Erlbaum Associates.

Gorman, C. (2003, October 20). How to eat smarter. *Time,* pp. 48–59.

Gosling, S. D., Kwan, V. S. Y., & John, O. P. (2003). A dog's got personality: A cross-species comparative approach to personality judgments in dogs and humans. *Journal of Personality and Social Psychology, 85,* 1161–1169.

Gosling, S. D., Rentfrow, P. J., & Swann, W. B., Jr. (2003). A very brief measure of the Big-Five personality domains. *Journal of Research in Personality, 37,* 504–528.

Gottesman, I. I. (1997). Twins: En route to QTLs for cognition. *Science, 276,* 1522–1523.

Gottesman, I. I., & Gould, T. D. (2003). The endophenotype concept in psychiatry: Etymology and strategic intentions. *American Journal of Psychiatry, 160,* 636–645.

Gottesman, I. I., & Hanson, D. R. (2005). Human development: Biological and genetic processes. *Annual Review of Psychology, 56,* 263–286.

Gottesman, I. I., McGuffin, P., & Farmer, A. E. (1987). Clinical genetics as clues to the "real" genetics of schizophrenia. *Schizophrenia Bulletin, 13,* 23–47.

Gottfredson, L. S. (2003a). Dissecting practical intelligence theory: Its claims and evidence. *Intelligence, 31,* 343–397.

Gottfredson, L. S. (2003b). Discussion on Sternberg's "Reply to Gottfredson." *Intelligence, 31,* 415–424.

Gottfredson, L. S. (2004). Intelligence: Is it the epidemiologists' elusive "fundamental cause" of social class inequalities in health? *Journal of Personality and Social Psychology, 86,* 174–199.

Gottfredson, L. S., & Deary, I. J. (2004). Intelligence predicts health and longevity, but why? *Current Directions in Psychological Science, 13,* 1–4.

Grady, D. (2002, November 26). Why we eat (and eat and eat). *New York Times,* pp. F1, F4.

Grady, D. (2004, April 7). Minimal benefit is seen in drugs for Alzheimer's. *New York Times,* pp. A1, A16.

Graham, J. R. (2000). *MMPI-2: Assessing personality and psychopathology* (3rd ed.). New York: Oxford University Press.

Grant, B. F., Stinson, F. S., Dawson, D. A., Chou, P., Dufour, M. C., Compton, W., et al. (2004). Prevalence and co-occurrence of substance use disorders and independent mood and anxiety disorders: Results from the National Epidemiologic Survey on Alcohol and Related Conditions. *Archives of General Psychiatry, 61,* 807–816.

Grant, R. M., Hecht, F. M., Warmerdam, M., Liu, L., Liegler, T., Petropoulos, C. J., Hellmann, N. S., Chesney, M., et al. (2002). Time trends in primary HIV-1 drug resistance among recently infected persons. *Journal of the American Medical Association, 288,* 181–188.

Gray, M. J., & Acierno, R. (2002). Posttraumatic stress disorder. In M. Hersen (Ed.), *Clinical behavior therapy: Adults and children* (pp. 106–124). New York: John Wiley & Sons.

Gray, R. (2002). "Markov at the bat": A model of cognitive processing in baseball batters. *Psychological Science, 13,* 542–547.

Gray-Little, B., & Hafdahl, A. R. (2000). Factors influencing racial comparisons of self-esteem: A quantitative review. *Psychological Bulletin, 126,* 26–54.

Green, B. L., & Kenrick, D. T. (1994). The attractiveness of gender-typed traits at different relationship levels: Androgynous characteristics may be desirable after all. *Personality and Social Psychology Bulletin, 20*(3), 244–253.

Green, E., Elvidge, G., Jacobsen, N., Glaser, B., Jones, I., O'Donovan, M. C., et al. (2005). Localization of bipolar susceptibility locus by molecular genetic analysis of the chromosome 12q23-q24 region in two pedigrees with bipolar disorder and Darier's disease. *American Journal of Psychiatry, 162,* 35–42.

Greenberg, L. S., & Malcolm, W. (2002). Resolving unfinished business: Relating process to outcome. *Journal of Consulting and Clinical Psychology, 70,* 406–416.

Greenberg, S. H., & Springen, K. (2000, October 16). Back to day care. *Newsweek,* pp. 61–62.

Greenberg, S. H., & Springen, K. (2001, Fall/Winter). Keeping hope alive. *Newsweek Special Issue*, pp. 60–63.

Greene, R. L., Robin, R. W., Albaugh, B., Caldwell, A., & Goldman, D. (2003). Use of the MMPI-2 in American Indians: II. Empirical correlates. *Psychological Assessment, 5*, 360–369.

Greeno, J. G., & Simon, H. A. (1991). Problem solving and reasoning. In R. C. Atkinson, R. J. Hernstein, G. Lindzey, & R. D. Luce (Eds.), *Smith's handbook of experimental psychology: Vol. 2. Learning and cognition* (pp. 589–672). New York: Wiley.

Greenwald, A. G., Abrams, R. L., Naccache, L, & Dehaene, S. (2003). Long-term semantic memory versus contextual memory in unconscious number processing. *Journal of Experimental Psychology-Learning, Memory, and Cognition, 29*, 235–247.

Greenwald, A. G., & Draine, S. G. (1997). Do subliminal stimuli enter the mind unnoticed? Tests with a new method. In J. D. Cohen & J. W. Schooler (Eds.), *Scientific approaches to consciousness* (pp. 83–108). Mahwah, NJ: Lawrence Erlbaum Associates.

Greer, M. (2004a, April). General cognition also makes the difference on the job, study finds. *Monitor on Psychology, 35*, 12.

Greer, M. (2004b, May). Intervention helps reduce HIV risk. *Monitor on Psychology, 35*, 23.

Greer, M. (2004c, July). Strengthen your brain by resting it. *Monitor on Psychology, 35*(7), 60–61.

Gregg, E. W., Cauley, J. A., Stone, K., Thompson, T. J., Bauer, D. C. , Cummings, S. R., et al. (2003). Relationship of changes in physical activity and mortality among older women. *Journal of the American Medical Association, 289*, 2379–2386.

Grigorenko, E. L. (2002). Other than g: The value of persistence. In R. J. Sternberg & E. L. Grigorenko (Eds.), *The general factor of intelligence: How general is it?* (pp. 299–327). Mahwah, NJ: Lawrence Erlbaum Associates.

Grigoriadis, V. (2003, July 20). Smiling through the 30th, a birthday once apocalyptic. *New York Times*, Section 9, pp. 1, 8.

Grob, G. N. (1996). *The mad among us: A history of the care of America's mentally ill.* Cambridge, MA: Harvard University Press.

Grochowicz, P. M., Schedlowski, M., Husband, A. J, King, M. G., Hibberd, A. D., & Bowen, K. M. (1991). Behavioral conditioning prolongs heart allograft survival in rats. *Brain, Behavior, and Immunity, 5*, 349–356.

Grön, G., Wunderlich, A. P., Spitzer, M., Tomczak, R., & Riepe, M. W. (2000). Brain activation during human navigation: Gender-different neural networks as substrate of performance. *Nature Neuroscience, 3*(4), 404–408.

Grossman, L. (2003, January 20). Can Freud get his job back? *Time*, pp. 48–51.

Grossman, P., Niemann, L., Schmidt, S., & Walach, H. (2004). Mindfulness-based stress reduction and health benefits: A meta-analysis. *Journal of Psychosomatic Research, 57*, 35–43.

Gründer, G., Carlsson, A., & Wong, D. F. (2003). Mechanism of new antipsychotic medications occupancy is not just antagonism. *Archives of General Psychiatry, 60*, 974–977.

Guenther, R. K. (1998). *Human cognition.* Englewood Cliffs, NJ: Prentice Hall.

Guilford, J. P., Christensen, P. R., Merrifield, P. R., & Wilson, R. C. (1978). *Alternate uses: Form B, Form C.* Orange, CA: Sheridan Psychological Services.

Guisinger, S., & Blatt, S. J. (1994). Individuality and relatedness: Evolution of a fundamental dialectic. *American Psychologist, 49*, 104–111.

Gunter, B., & McAleer, J. (1990). *Children and television: The one-eyed monster?* London: Routledge.

Gupta, S. (2003, January 20). If everyone were on Prozac. *Time*, p. 49.

Gustafsson, J. E., & Undheim, J. O. (1996). Individual differences in cognitive functions. In D. C. Berliner & R. C. Calfee (Eds.), *Handbook of educational psychology* (pp. 186–242). New York: Macmillan Library Reference.

Gustavson, C. R., & Garcia, J. (1974). Aversive conditioning: Pulling a gag on the wily coyote. *Psychology Today, 8*, 68–72.

Gustavson, C. R., Garcia, J., Hawkins, W. G., & Rusiniak, K. W. (1974). Coyote predation control by aversive conditioning. *Science, 184*, 581–583.

Guzick, D. S., & Hoeger, K. (2000). Sex, hormones, and hysterectomies. *New England Journal of Medicine, 343*, 730–731.

Gyatso, T. (2003, April 26). The monk in the lab. *New York Times*, p. A29.

Haber, R. N. (1979). Twenty years of haunting eidetic imagery: Where's the ghost? *Behavioral and Brain Sciences 2*, 583–629.

Haber, S. N., & Fudge, J. L. (1997). The interface between dopamine neurons and the amygdala: Implications for schizophrenia. *Schizophrenia Bulletin, 23*, 471–482.

Hacker, C. M. (2002). United States Women's National Soccer Team: Psychological skills training program and history. *Exercise and Sport Psychology Newsletter, 16*, 4–6.

Hackett, G., Betz, N. E., Casas, J. M., & Rocha Singh, I. A. (1992). Gender, ethnicity, and social cognitive factors predicting the academic achievements of students in engineering. *Journal of Counseling Psychology, 39*, 527–538.

Hackett, T. A., & Kaas, J. H. (2003). Auditory processing in the primate brain. In M. Gallagher & R. J. Nelson (Eds.), *Handbook of psychology: Vol. 3. Biological psychology* (pp. 187–210). New York: John Wiley & Sons.

Hafdahl, A. R., & Gray-Little, B. (2002). Explicating methods in reviews of race and self-esteem: Reply to Twenge and Crocker (2002). *Psychological Bulletin, 128*, 409–416.

Hafner, K. (2000, November 2). Working at home today? *New York Times*, pp. G1, G8.

Hafner, K., & George, J. (2005, March 3). For drivers, a traffic jam of distractions. *New York Times, Circuits*, pp. G1, G7.

Haith, M. M., & Benson, J. B. (1997). Infant cognition. In W. Damon (Editor-in-Chief), D. Kuhn, & R. Siegler (Vol. Eds.), *Handbook of child psychology: Vol. 2. Cognition, perception and language* (5th ed., pp. 199–254). New York: John Wiley & Sons.

Hajjar, I., & Kotchen, T. A. (2003). Trends in prevalence, awareness, treatment, and control of hypertension in the United States, 1988–2000. *Journal of the American Medical Association, 290*, 199–206.

Hakim, D. (2003, October 25). New luxury-car specifications: Styling. Performance. Aroma. *New York Times*, pp. A1, C2.

Hall, G. C., & Barongan, C. (1997). Prevention of sexual aggression: Sociocultural risk and protective factors. *American Psychologist, 52*, 5–14.

Hall, G. C. N., & Hirschman, R. (1991). Toward a theory of sexual aggression: A quadripartite model. *Journal of Consulting and Clinical Psychology, 59*, 662–669.

Hall, G. N. (2003). Cultural competence in clinical psychology research. *Clinical Psychologist, 56*, 11–16.

Hall, S. S. (1998, February 15). Our memories, our selves. *New York Times Magazine*, 26–33, 49, 56–57.

Halmi, K., Agras, W. S., Mitchell, J., Wilson, G. T., Crow, S., Bryson, S. W., & Kraemer, H. (2003). Relapse predictors of patients with bulimia nervosa who achieved abstinence through cognitive behavioral therapy. *American Journal of Psychiatry, 59*, 1105–1109.

Halpern, D. F. (2004). A cognitive-process taxonomy for sex differences in cognitive abilities. *Current Directions in Psychological Science, 13*, 135–139.

Halpern, D. F., & LaMay, M. L. (2000). The smarter sex: A critical review of sex differences in intelligence. *Educational Psychology Review, 12*(2), 229–246.

Ham, L. S., & Hope, D. A. (2003). College students and problematic drinking: A review of the literature. *Clinical Psychology Review, 23*, 719–759.

Ham, L. S., & Hope, D. A. (2005). Incorporating social anxiety into a model of college student problematic drinking. *Addictive Behaviors, 30*, 127–150.

Hamann, S. B., Ely, T. D., Hoffman, J. M., & Kilts, C. D. (2003). Ecstasy and agony: Activation of the human amygdala in positive and negative emotion. *Psychological Science, 13*, 135–141.

Hamilton, D., L., & Sherman, J. W. (1994). Stereotypes. In R. S. Wyer, Jr., & T. K. Srull (Eds.), *Handbook of social cognition* (2nd ed., Vol. 2, pp. 1–68). Hillsdale, NJ: Lawrence Erlbaum Associates.

Hamilton, K. E., & Dobson, K. S. (2002). Cognitive therapy of depression: Pretreatment patient predictors of outcome. *Clinical Psychology Review, 22*, 875–893.

Hanna, F. J. (2003). Confronting the controversy. *Contemporary Psychology: APA Review of Books, 48*, 835–836.

Hardin, E. E., & Leong, F. T. L. (2005). Optimism and pessimism as mediators of the relations between self-discrepancies and distress among Asian and European Americans. *Journal of Counseling Psychology, 52*, 25–35.

Hardy, S. A., & Raffaelli, M. (2003). Adolescent religiosity and sexuality: An investigation of reciprocal influences. *Journal of Adolescence, 26*, 731–739.

Hariri, A. R., Mattay, V. S., Tessitore, A., Kolachana, B., Fera, F., Goldman, D., & Egan, M. F. (2002). Serotonin transporter genetic variation and the response of the human amygdala. *Science 297*, 400–403.

Harlow, H. F., & Harlow, M. K. (1966). Learning to love. *American Scientist, 54*, 244–272.

Harlow, H. F., Harlow, M. K., & Meyer, D. R. (1950). Learning motivated by a manipulation drive. *Journal of Experimental Psychology, 40*, 228–234.

Harlow, H. F., & Zimmermann, R. R. (1959). Affectional responses in the infant monkey. *Science, 130*, 421–432.

Harmer, D. J., Bhagwagar, Z., Perrett, D. I., Vollm, B. A., Cowen, P. J., & Goodwin, G. M. (2003). Acute SSRI administration affects the processing of social cues in healthy volunteers. *Neuropsychopharmacology, 28*, 148–152.

Harmon-Jones, E., & Sigelman, J. (2001). State anger and prefrontal brain activity: Evidence that insult-related relative left-prefrontal activation is associated with experienced anger and aggression. *Journal of Personality and Social Psychology, 80,* 797–803.

Harrigan, J. A., & Taing, K. T. (1997). Fooled by a smile: Detecting anxiety in others. *Journal of Nonverbal Behavior, 21,* 203–221.

Harris, A. E., & Curtin, L. (2002). Parental perceptions, early maladaptive schemas, and depressive symptoms in young adults. *Cognitive Therapy and Research, 26,* 405–416.

Harris, G. (2004, June 2). Antidepressants seen as effective for adolescents. *New York Times,* pp. A1, A16.

Harris, S. M., & Halpin, G. (2002). Development and validation of the Factors Influencing Pursuit of Higher Education Questionnaire. *Educational and Psychological Measurement, 62,* 79–96.

Harrison, Y., & Horne, J. A. (2000). The impact of sleep deprivation on decision making: A review. *Journal of Experimental Psychology: Applied, 6,* 236–249.

Harrop, C., & Trower, P. (2001). Why does schizophrenia develop at late adolescence? *Clinical Psychology Review, 20,* 823–851, 241–266.

Harshman, R. A., & Paivio, A. (1987). Paradoxical sex differences in self-reported imagery. *Canadian Journal of Psychology, 41,* 287–302.

Harter, S. (1990). Self and identity development. In S. S. Feldman & G. R. Elliott (Eds.), *At the threshold: The developing adolescent* (pp. 352–387). Cambridge, MA: Harvard University Press.

Hartshorn, K., & Rovee-Collier, C. (1997). Infant learning and long-term memory at 6 months: A confirming analysis. *Developmental Psychobiology, 30,* 71–85.

Haslam, C. & Draper, E. S. (2001). A qualitative study of smoking during pregnancy. *Psychology, Health and Medicine, 6,* 95–99.

Hassert, D. L., Miyashita, T., Williams, C. L. (2004). The effects of peripheral vagal nerve stimulation at a memory-modulating intensity on norepinephrine output in the basolateral amygdala. *Behavioral Neuroscience, 118,* 79–88.

Hasty, P, Campisi, J., Hoeijmakers, J., van Steeg, H., & Vijg, J. (2003). Aging and genome maintenance: Lessons from the mouse? *Science, 299,* 1355–1359.

Hatfield, E., & Sprecher, S. (1986). Measuring passionate love in intimate relationships. *Journal of Adolescence, 9,* 383–410.

Hauser, M. D., & Fitch, W. T. (2003). What are the uniquely human components of the language faculty? In M. H. Christiansen and S. Kirby (Eds.), *Language evolution* (pp. 158–181). New York: Oxford University Press.

Haydel, M. J., Preston, C. A., Mills, T. J., Luber, S., Blaudeau, E., & Deblieux, P. M. (2000). Indications for computed tomography in patients with minor head injury. *New England Journal of Medicine, 343,* 100–105.

Hayes, S. C., & Wilson, K. G. (2003). Mindfulness: Method and process. *Clinical Psychology: Science and Practice, 10,* 161–165.

Hayflick, L. (1994). *How and why we age.* New York: Ballantine Books.

Hays, K. F. (2002, Fall). Giving sport psychology away. *Exercise and Sport Psychology Newsletter, 16,* 1, 2.

He, S., Don, W., Deng, Q., Weng, S., & Sun, W. (2002). Seeing more clearly: Recent advances in understanding retinal circuitry. *Science, 302,* 408–411.

Heatherton, T. F., Mahamedi, F., Striepe, M., Field, A. E., et al. (1997). A 10-year longitudinal study of body weight, dieting, and eating disorder symptoms. *Journal of Abnormal Psychology, 106,* 117–125.

Hebb, D. O. (1955). Drive and the CNS (central nervous system). *Psychological Review, 62,* 243–254.

Hedges, L. V., & Nowell, A. (1995, July). Sex differences in mental test scores, variability, and numbers of high-scoring individuals. *Science, 269,* 41–45.

Hedley, A. A., Ogden, C. L., Johnson, C. L., Carroll, M. D., Curtin, L. R., & Flegal, K. M. (2004). Prevalence of Overweight and obesity among US children, adolescents, and adults, 1999–2002. *Journal of the American Medical Association, 291,* 2847–2850.

Heider, F. (1958). *The psychology of interpersonal relations.* New York: Wiley.

Heimberg, R. G., Turk, C. L., & Mennin, D. S. (2004). (Eds). *Generalized anxiety disorder.* New York: Guilford Press.

Hekimi, S., & Guarente, L. (2003). Genetics and the specificity of the aging process. *Science, 299,* 1351—1354.

Helby, E. M., DeLeon, P. H., & Anderson, T. (2004). A debate on prescription privileges for psychologists. *Professional Psychology: Research and Practice, 35,* 336–344.

Heller, D., Watson, D., & Ilies, R. (2004). The role of person versus situation in life satisfaction: a critical examination. *Psychological Bulletin, 130,* 574–600.

Helliwell, J. F. (2003). How's life? Combining individual and national variables to explain subjective well-being. *Economic Modelling, 20,* 331–360.

Hellman, C. M. (1997). Job satisfaction and intent to leave. *Journal of Social Psychology, 137,* 677–689.

Hellmich, N. (2003a, January 7). Extra weight shaves years off lives. *USA Today,* p. A1.

Hellmich, N. (2003b, April 24). Being overweight linked to dying of cancer. *USA Today,* p. 1A.

Helms, J. E. (1992). Why is there no study of culture equivalence in standardized cognitive ability testing? *American Psychologist, 47,* 1083-1101.

Helms, J. E., Jernigan, M., & Mascher, J. (2005). Meaning of race in psychology and how to change it: A methodological perspective. *American Psychologist, 60,* 27–36.

Helmuth, L. (2001, January 26). Glia tell neurons to build synapses. *Science, 291,* 569–570.

Helson, R., Jones, C., & Dwan, V. (2002). Personality change over 40 years of adulthood: Hierarchical linear modeling analyses of two longitudinal samples. *Journal of Personality and Social Psychology, 83,* 752–766.

Helson, R., & Wink, R. (1992). Personality change in women from the early 40s to the early 50s. *Psychology and Aging, 7,* 46–55.

Henderlong, J., & Lepper, M. R. (2002). The effects of praise on children's intrinsic motivation: A review and synthesis. *Psychological Bulletin, 128,* 774–795.

Henry, J. D., MacLeod, M. S., Phillips, L. H., & Crawford, J. R. (2004). A meta-analytic review of prospective memory and aging. *Psychology and Aging, 19,* 27–39.

Hepper, P. G., Shahidullah, S., & White, R. (1990). Origins of fetal handedness. *Nature, 347,* 431.

Hergenhahn, B. R. (1997). *An introduction to the history of psychology* (3rd ed.). Pacific Grove, CA: Brooks/Cole.

Hergovich, A. (2004). The effect of pseudo-psychic demonstrations as dependent on belief in paranormal phenomena and suggestibility. *Personality and Individual Differences, 36,* 365–380.

Herrmann, D. J., & Palmisano, M. (1992). The facilitation of memory performance. In M. Gruneberg & P. Morris (Eds.), *Aspects of memory: 2nd ed.: Vol. 1. The practical aspects* (pp. 147–167). London: Routledge.

Herrnstein, R., & Murray, C. (1994). *The bell curve.* New York: Free Press.

Hertel, P. T. (1996). Practical aspects of emotion and memory. In D. Herrmann, C. McEvoy, C. Hertzog, P. Hertel, & M. K. Johnson (Eds.), *Basic and applied memory research: Theory in context* (Vol. 1, pp. 317–336). Mahwah, NJ: Lawrence Erlbaum Associates.

Hertzog, C., & Dunlosky, J. (1996). The aging of practical memory: An overview. In D. Herrmann et al. (Eds.), *Basic and applied memory research: Theory in context* (Vol. 1., pp. 337–358). Mahwah, NJ: Lawrence Erlbaum Associates.

Herzog, A. R., Franks, M. M., Markus, H. R., & Holmberg, D. (1998). Activities and well-being in older age: Effects of self-concept and educational attainment. *Psychology and Aging, 13,* 179–185.

Hess, U. (2003). Now you see it, now you don't—the confusing case of confusion as an emotion: Commentary on Rozin and Cohen (2003). *Emotion, 3,* 76–78.

Hettema, J. M., Annas, P., Neale, M. C., Kendler, K. S., & Fredrikson, M. (2003). A twin study of the genetics of fear conditioning. *Archives of General Psychiatry, 60,* 702–708.

Hewlett, K. (2001, July/August). Can low self-esteem and self-blame on the job make you sick? *Monitor on Psychology, 32,* 58–60.

Hewstone, M., Rubin, M., & Willis, H. (2002). Intergroup bias. *Annual Review of Psychology, 53,* 575–604.

Hilgard, E. R. (1977). *Divided consciousness: Multiple controls in human thought and action.* New York: Wiley.

Hilgard, E. R. (1994). Neodissociation theory. In S. Lynn & J. W. Rhue (Eds.), *Dissociation: Clinical and theoretical perspectives.* New York: Guilford Press.

Hilgard, E. R., Morgan, A. H., & Macdonald, H. (1975). Pain and dissociation in the cold pressor test: A study of "hidden reports" through automatic key-pressing and automatic talking. *Journal of Abnormal Psychology, 84,* 280–289.

Hill, C. E., & Nakayama, E. Y. (2000). Client-centered therapy: Where has it been and where is it going? A comment on Hathaway (1948). *Journal of Clinical Psychology, 56,* 861–873.

Hill, J. O., Wyatt, H. R., Reed, G. W., & Peters, J. C. (2003). Obesity and the environment: Where do we go from here? [Editorial]. *Science, 299,* 853–855.

Hillix, W. A., & Rumbaugh, D. M. (2004). *Animal bodies, human minds: Ape, dolphin, and parrot language skills.* New York: Kluwer/Plenum.

Hilton, J. L., & von Hippel, W. (1996). Stereotypes. In J. T. Spence, J. M. Darley, & D. J. Foss (Eds.), *Annual review of psychology* (Vol. 47, pp. 237–271). Palo Alto, CA: Annual Reviews.

Hingson, R. W., Heeren, T., Jamanka, A., & Howland, J. (2000). Age of drinking onset and unintentional injury involvement after drinking. *Journal of the American Medical Association, 284,* 1527–1533.

Hobson, J. A. (2002). *Dreaming: An introductory to the science of sleep*. Oxford, England: Oxford University Press.

Hobson, J. A., & McCarley, R. W. (1977). The brain as a dream state generator: An activation-synthesis hypothesis of the dream process. *American Journal of Psychiatry, 134*, 1335–1348.

Hodges, E. V. E., Boivin, M., Vitaro, F., & Bukowski, W. M. (1999). The power of friendship: Protection against an escalating cycle of peer victimization. *Developmental Psychology, 35*, 94–101.

Hodson, D. S., & Skeen, P. (1994). Sexuality and aging: The hammerlock of myths. *Journal of Applied Gerontology, 13*, 219–235.

Hoelscher, C. (Ed.). (2001). *Neuronal mechanisms of memory formation: Concepts of long-term potentiation and beyond*. New York: Cambridge University Press.

Hoff, E. (2003). Language development in childhood. In R. M. Lerner, M. A. Easterbrooks, & J. Mistry (Eds.), *Handbook of psychology: Vol. 6. Developmental psychology* (pp. 171–194). New York: John Wiley & Sons.

Hofferth, D. G., & Anderson, K. G. (2003). Are all dads equal? Biology versus marriage as a basis for paternal investment. *Journal of Marriage and the Family, 65*, 213–232.

Hoffman, S. G. (2000a). Self-focused attention before and after treatment of social phobia. *Behavior Research and Therapy, 38*, 717–725.

Hoffman, S. G. (2000b). Treatment of social phobia: Potential mediators and moderators. *Clinical Psychology: Science and Practice, 7*(1), 3–16.

Hofstee, W. K. B. (2003). Structures of personality traits. In T. Millon & M. J. Lerner (Eds.), *Handbook of psychology: Vol. 5. Personality and social psychology* (pp. 231–256). New York: John Wiley & Sons.

Hogan, J. (2001, May 2). Personal communication.

Holahan, C. J., Moos, R. H., Holahan, C. K., Cronkite, R. C., & Randall, P. K. (2004). Unipolar depression, life context vulnerabilities, and drinking to cope. *Journal of Consulting and Clinical Psychology, 72*, 269–275.

Holcomb, D. R., Savage, M. P., Seehafer, R., & Waalkes, D. M. (2002). A mixed-gender date rape prevention intervention targeting freshman college athletes. *College Student Journal, 36*, 165–179.

Holland, P. C., & Ball, G. F. (2003). The psychology and ethnology of learning. In M. Gallagher & R. J. Nelson (Eds.), *Handbook of psychology: Vol. 3. Biological psychology* (pp. 457–498). New York: John Wiley & Sons.

Hollis, K. L. (1997). Contemporary research on Pavlovian conditioning: A "new" functional analysis. *American Psychologist, 52*, 956–965.

Holloway, J. D. (2003a, March). Advances in anger management. *Monitor on Psychology, 34*, 54–55.

Holloway, J. D. (2003b, December). Snapshot from the therapy room. *Monitor on Psychology, 34*, 31.

Holloway, J. D. (2004, June). Gaining prescriptive knowledge. *Monitor on Psychology, 35*, 22–24.

Holman, B. (2000, August 2). Experts doubt value of living together before marriage. *Star Tribune Company*. Retrieved August 23, 2000, from http://www.psycport.com/news/2000/08/02/eng-startribune_variety/eng-startribune_variety_090918_169_044099028688.html.

Holroyd, K. A. (2002). Assessment and psychological management of recurrent headache disorders. *Journal of Consulting and Clinical Psychology, 70*, 656–677.

Holroyd, K. A., O'Donnell, F. J., Stensland, M., Lipchik, G. L., Cordingley, G. E., & Carlson, B. W. (2001). Management of chronic tension-type headache with tricyclic antidepressant medication, stress management therapy, and their combination: A randomized controlled trial. *Journal of the American Medical Association, 285*, 2208–2215.

Holt, C. L., Clark, E. M., & Kreuter, M. W. (2001). Weight locus of control and weight-related attitudes and behaviors in an overweight population. *Addictive Behaviors, 26*, 329–340.

Holyoak, K. J., & Thagard, P. (1995). *Mental leaps: Analogy in creative thought*. Cambridge, MA: MIT Press/Bradford Books.

Hopkin, M. (2004, August 10). Alzheimer's linked to lowbrow jobs. *Nature.com*. Retrieved August 11, 2004, from http://www.nature.com/news/2004/040809/full/040809-3.html.

Horn, J. (2001). Raymond Bernard Cattell (1905–1998). *American Psychologist, 56*, 71–72.

Horn, J. L., & Noll, J. (1997). Human cognitive capabilities: Gf-Gc theory. In D. P. Flanagan, J. L. Genshaft, & P. L. Harrison (Eds.), *Contemporary intellectual assessment: Theories, tests, and issues* (pp. 53–91). New York: Guilford Press.

Houston, D. M., & Jusczyk, P. W. (2003). Infants' long-term memory for the sound patterns of words and voices. *Journal of Experimental Psychology: Human Perception and Performance, 29*, 1143–1154.

Houtz, J. C., & Frankel, A. D. (1992). Effects of incubation and imagery training on creativity. *Creativity Research Journal, 5*, 183–189.

Hrobjartsson, A., & Gotzsche, P. C. (2001). Is the placebo powerless? An analysis of clinical trials comparing placebo with no treatment. *New England Journal of Medicine, 344*, 1594–602.

Hu, F. B., Stampfer, M. J., Manson, J. E., Grodstein, F., Colditz, G. A., Speizer, F. E., et al. (2000). Trends in the incidence of coronary heart disease and changes in diet and lifestyle in women. *New England Journal of Medicine, 343*, 530–537.

Huang, L. H. (1994). An integrative approach to clinical assessment and Intervention with Asian-American adolescents. *Journal of Clinical Child Psychology, 23*, 21–31.

Hubel, D. H. (1988). *Eye, brain, and vision*. New York: Scientific American Library.

Hubel, D. H., & Wiesel, T. N. (1979). Brain mechanisms of vision. *Scientific American, 241*, 130–144.

Huber, R., Ghilardi, M. F., Massimini, M., & Tononi, G. (2004). Local sleep and learning. *Nature, 430*, 78–81.

Hublin, C., Kaprio, J., Partinen, M., & Koshenvuo, M. (1998). Sleeptalking in twins: Epidemiology and psychiatric comorbidity. *Behavior Genetics, 28*, 289–298.

Hudson, J. I., Mangweth, B., Pope, H. G., Jr., De Col, C., Hausmann, A., Gutweniger, S., et al. (2003). Family study of affective spectrum disorder. *Archives of General Psychiatry, 60*, 170–177.

Huesmann, L. R., Moise-Titus, J., Podolski, C.-L., & Eron, L. D. (2003). Longitudinal relations between children's exposure to TV violence and their aggressive and violent behavior in young adulthood: 1977–1992. *Developmental Psychology, 39*, 201–221.

Hugdahl, K., Rund, B. R., Lund, A., Asbjørnsen, A., Egeland, J., Ersland, L, et al. (2004). Brain activation measured with fMRI during a mental arithmetic task in schizophrenia and major depression. *American Journal of Psychiatry, 161*, 286–293.

Hull, C. L. (1943). *Principles of behavior*. New York: Appleton-Century-Crofts.

Hull, C. L. (1952). *A behavior system*. New Haven: Yale University Press.

Hull, J. G., Slone, L. B., Meteyer, K. B., & Matthews, A. R. (2002). The non-consciousness of self-consciousness. *Journal of Personality and Social Psychology, 83*, 406–424.

Hunsley, J., & Bailey, J. M. (2001). Whither the Rorschach? An analysis of the evidence. *Psychological Assessment, 13*, 472–485.

Hunt, M. (1993). *The story of psychology*. New York: Anchor Books.

Huntjens, R. J. C., Peters, M. L., Postma, A., Woertman, L., Effting, M., & van der Hart, O. (2005). Transfer of newly acquired stimulus valence between identities in dissociative identity disorder (DID). *Behaviour Research and Therapy, 43*, 243–255.

Hurley, A. C., & Volicer, L. (2002). "It's okay, mama, if you want to go, it's okay." *Journal of the American Medical Association, 288*, 2324–2331.

Huston, A. C., &. Wright, J. C. (1996). Television and socialization of young children. In T. M. MacBeth (Ed.), *Tuning in to young viewers: Social science perspectives on television* (pp. 37–60). Thousand Oaks, CA: Sage.

Hyman, D. J., & Pavlik, V. N. (2001). Characteristics of patients with uncontrolled hypertension in the United States. *New England Journal of Medicine, 345*, 479–486.

Iacono, W. G., & Lykken, D. T. (1997). The validity of the lie detector: Two surveys of scientific opinion. *Journal of Applied Psychology, 82*, 426–433.

Ilardi, S. S., & Craighead, W. E. (1994). The role of nonspecific factors in cognitive-behavior therapy for depression. *Clinical Psychology: Science and Practice, 1*, 138–156.

Imaging helps diagnose bipolar disease. (2004, December 1). *Daily Bulletin*, Radiological Society of North America. Retrieved February 22, 2005, from http://www.rsna.org/daily/wednesday/bipolar.html.

Ingram, R. E., & Siegle, G. J. (2001). Cognition and clinical science: From revolution to evolution. In K. S. Dobson (Ed.), *Handbook of cognitive-behavioral therapies* (2nd ed., pp. 111–137). New York: Guilford Press.

Instant recall. (2000, February 14). *Newsweek*, p. 8.

Intimacies. (2000, May 7). *New York Times Magazine*, p. 76.

Ioannidis, J. P. A., Haidich, A. B., Pappa, M., Pantazis, N., Kokori, S. I., Tektonidou, M. G., et al. (2001). Comparison of evidence of treatment effects in randomized and nonrandomized studies. *Journal of the American Medical Association, 286*, 821–830.

Irle, E., Exner, C., Thielen, K., Weniger, G., & Ruether, E. (1998). Obsessive-compulsive disorder and ventromedial frontal lesions: Clinical and neuropsychological findings. *American Journal of Psychiatry, 155*, 255–263.

Irwin, C. E., Jr., Burg, S. J., & Cart, C. U. (2002). America's adolescents: Where have we been, where are we going? *Journal of Adolescent Health, 31*, 91–121.

Irwin, M. L., Yasui, Y., Ulrich, C. M., Bowen, D., Rudolph, R. E., Schwartz, R. S., et al. (2002). Effect of exercise on total and intra-abdominal body fat in postmenopausal women: A randomized controlled trial. *Journal of the American Medical Association, 289*, 323–330.

Isay, R. A. (1990). Psychoanalytic theory and the therapy of gay men. In D. P. McWhirter, S. A. Saers, & J. M. Reinisch (Eds.), *Homosexuality/Heterosexuality: Concepts of sexual orientation* (pp. 283–303). New York: Oxford University Press.

Ito, T. A., Miller, N., & Pollock, V. E. (1996). Alcohol and aggression: A meta-analysis on the moderating effects of inhibitory cues, triggering events, and self-focused attention. *Psychological Bulletin, 120*, 60–82.

Iversen, L. L. (2000). *The science of marijuana.* New York: Oxford University Press.

Izard, C. E. (1990a). Facial expression and the regulation of emotions. *Journal of Personality and Social Psychology, 58*, 487–498.

Izard, C. E. (1990b). The substrates and functions of emotion feelings: William James and current emotion theory. *Personality and Social Psychology Bulletin, 16*, 626–635.

Jablensky, A. V., Morgan, V., Zubrick, S. R., Bower, C., & Yellachich, L.-A. (2005). Pregnancy, delivery, and neonatal complications in a population cohort of women with schizophrenia and major affective disorders. *American Journal of Psychiatry, 162*, 79–91.

Jablensky, A., Sartorius, N., Ernberg, G., & Anker, M. (1992). Schizophrenia: Manifestations, incidence and course in different cultures: A World Health Organization ten-country study [Monograph Suppl.]. *Psychological Medicine, 20*, 1–97.

Jackson, B. B., Taylor, J., & Pyngolil, M. (1991). How age conditions the relationship between climacteric status and health symptoms in African American women. *Research in Nursing and Health, 14*, 1–9.

Jacob, S., Garcia, S., Hayreh, D., & McClintock, M. K. (2002). Psychological effects of musky compounds: Comparison of androstadienone with androstenol and muscone. *Hormones and Behavior, 42*, 274–283.

Jacobi, C., Hayward, C., de Zwaan, M., Kraemer, H. C., & Agras, W. S. (2004). Coming to terms with risk factors for eating disorders: application of risk terminology and suggestions for a general taxonomy. *Psychological Bulletin, 130*, 19–65.

Jacobs, B. L. (2004). Depression: The brain finally gets into the act. *Current Directions in Psychological Science, 13*, 103–106.

Jacobs, L. D., Munschauer, F. E., & Pullicino, P. (2000). Intramuscular interferon beta-1a therapy initiated during a first demyelinating event in multiple sclerosis. *New England Journal of Medicine, 13*, 898–904.

Jacobs, L .F., & Schenk, F. (2003). Unpacking the cognitive map: The parallel map theory of hippocampal function. *Psychological Review, 110*, 285–315.

Jacobs, M. K., Christensen, A., Snibbe, J. R., Dolezal-Wood, S., Huber, A., & Polterok, A. (2001). A comparison of computer-based versus traditional individual psychotherapy. *Professional Psychology: Research and Practice, 32*, 92–96.

Jaffe, E. (2004, December). At the height of its game. *APS Observer, 17*, 25–27.

Jaffee, S., & Hyde, J. S. (2000). Gender differences in moral orientation: A meta-analysis. *Psychological Bulletin, 126*, 703–726.

Jahnke, C. J., & Nowaczyk, R. H. (1998). *Cognition.* Upper Saddle River, NJ: Prentice Hall.

James, L. E., & Burke, D. M. (2000). Phonological priming effects on word retrieval and tip-of-the-tongue experiences in young and older adults. *Journal of Experimental Psychology: Learning, Memory, and Cognition, 26*, 1378–1391.

James, L. E., & MacKay, D. G. (2001). H. M., word knowledge and aging: Support for a new theory of long-term retrograde amnesia. *Psychological Science, 12*, 485–492.

James, S., & Prilleltensky, I. (2002). Cultural diversity and mental health: Towards integrative practice. *Clinical Psychology Review, 22*, 1133–1154.

James, W. (1890/1970). *The principles of psychology* (Vol. 1). New York: Holt.

Janis, I. L. (1982). *Groupthink* (2nd ed.). Boston: Houghton Mifflin.

Janis, I. L. (1997). Groupthink. In R. P. Vecchio (Ed.), *Leadership: Understanding the dynamics of power and influence in organizations* (pp. 163–176). Notre Dame: University of Notre Dame Press.

Jankowiak, W. R., & Fischer, E. F. (1992). A cross-cultural perspective on romantic love. *Ethnology, 31*, 149–155.

Jason Priestley: Q & A. (2003, November 1). *Newsweek*, p. 73.

Jemmott, J. B., III, Borysenko, J. Z., Borysenko, M., McClelland, D. C., Chapman, R., et al. (1983, June 25). Academic stress, power motivation, and decrease in secretion rate of salivary secretory immunoglobulin A. *Lancet*, 1400–1402.

Jenkins, L., Myerson, J., Joerding, J. A., & Hale, S. (2000). Converging evidence that visuospatial cognition is more age-sensitive than verbal cognition. *Psychology and Aging, 15*, 157–175.

Jennings, C. (1999, October 19). The neurobiology of morals. *Nature News Service.* Retrieved December 23, 1999, from http://www.nature.com/nsu/991021/991021-6.html.

Jensen, A. R. (2002). Psychometric g: Definition and substantiation. In R. J. Sternberg & E. L. Grigorenko (Eds.), *The general factor of intelligence: How general is it?* (pp. 39–53). Mahwah, NJ: Lawrence Erlbaum Associates.

Jick, H., Kaye, J. A., & Jick, S. S. (2004). Antidepressants and the risk of suicidal behaviors. *Journal of the American Medical Association, 292*, 338–343.

Johns, A. (2001). Psychiatric effects of cannabis. *British Journal of Psychiatry, 178*, 116–122.

Johnson, F., & Wardle, J. (2005). Dietary restraint, body dissatisfaction, and psychological distress: A prospective analysis. *Journal of Abnormal Psychology, 114*, 119–125.

Johnson, G. (1994, October 23). Learning just how little is known about the brain. *New York Times*, p. E5.

Johnson, G. (1995, June 6). Chimp talk debate: Is it really language? *New York Times*, pp. C1, C10.

Johnson, G. (2000, October 15). The Nobels: Dazzled by the digital light. *New York Times Week in Review*, p. 4.

Johnson, I. M. (1993). Complementary medicine: Acupuncture has weak scientific foundations. *British Medical Journal, 307*, 624–627.

Johnson, M. H. (1997). The neural basis of cognitive development. In W. Damon (Editor-in-Chief), D. Kuhn, & R. Siegler (Vol. Eds.), *Handbook of child psychology: Vol. 2. Cognition, perception, and language* (5th ed., pp. 1–50). New York: John Wiley & Sons.

Johnson, T. J. (2002). College students' self-reported reasons for why drinking games end. *Addictive Behaviors, 27*, 145–153.

Johnson, T. J., Wendel, J., & Hamilton, S. (1998). Social anxiety, alcohol expectancies, and drinking-game participation. *Addictive Behaviors, 23*, 65–79.

Johnson, W., & Krueger, R. F. (2004). Genetic and environmental structure of adjectives describing the domains of the Big Five Model of personality: A nationwide US twin study. *Journal of Research in Personality, 38*, 448–472.

Johnson, W., McGue, M., Krueger, R. J., & Bouchard, T. J., Jr. (2004). Marriage and personality: A genetic analysis. *Journal of Personality and Social Psychology, 86*, 285–294.

Johnston, L. D., O'Malley, P. M., & Bachman, J. G. (2001). *Monitoring the Future National Survey Results on Drug Use, 1975–2000. Vol. II: College student and adults ages 19–40.* (NIH Publication No. 01–4925). Bethesda, MD: National Institute on Drug Abuse.

Johnston-Brooks, C. H., Lewis, M. A., & Garg, S. (2002). Self-efficacy impacts self-care and HbA1c in young adults with Type I Diabetes. *Psychosomatic Medicine, 64*, 43–51.

Joiner, T. E., Jr., Brown, J. S., & Wingate, L. R. (2005). The psychology and neurobiology of suicidal behavior. *Annual Review of Psychology, 56*, 287–314.

Jones, D. C. (2004). Body image among adolescent girls and boys: A longitudinal study. *Developmental Psychology, 40*, 823–835.

Jones, D. W., Chambless, L. E., Folsom, A. R., Heiss, G., Hutchinson, R. G., Sharrett, A. R., et al. (2002). Risk factors for coronary heart disease in African Americans: The atherosclerosis risk in communities study, 1987–1997. *Archives of Internal Medicine, 162*, 2565–2571.

Jones, E. (1953). *The life and work of Sigmund Freud.* New York: Basic Books.

Jones, E. E. (1998). Major developments in five decades of social psychology. In D. T. Gilbert, S. T. Fiske, & G. Lindzey (Eds.), *The handbook of social psychology* (4th ed., Vol. 1, pp. 1–57). Boston: McGraw-Hill.

Jones, E. E., & Nisbett, R. E. (1971). The actor and the observer: Divergent perceptions of the causes of behavior. In E. E. Jones, D. E. Kanouse, H. H. Kelley, R. E. Nisbett, S. Valins, & B. Weiner (Eds.), *Attribution: Perceiving the causes of behavior.* Morristown, NJ: General Learning Press.

Jones, G. (2003). Testing two cognitive theories of insight. *Journal of Experimental Psychology-Learning, Memory, and Cognition, 29*, 1017–1027.

Jones, G. V., & Martin, M. (2001). Confirming the X-linked handedness gene as recessive, not additive: Reply to Corballis (2001). *Psychological Review, 108*, 811–813.

Jones, J. H. (1997). *Alfred C. Kinsey: A public/private life.* New York: W. W. Norton, 1997.

Jones, J. M. (1997). *Prejudice and racism* (2nd ed.). New York: McGraw-Hill.

Jones, J. T., Pelham, B. W., Carvallo, M., & Mirenberg, M. C. (2004). How do I love thee? Let me count the Js: Implicit egotism and interpersonal attraction. *Journal of Personality and Social Psychology, 87*, 665–683.

Jones, M. C. (1924). The elimination of children's fears. *Journal of Experimental Psychology, 7*, 382–390.

Jones, S. L., & Yarhouse, M. A. (2001). *Homosexuality: The use of scientific research in the Church's moral debate.* Downers Grove, IL: InterVarsity Press.

Jonides, J., Lacey, S. C., & Nee1, D. E. (2005). Processes of working memory in mind and brain. *Current Directions in Psychological Science, 14*, 2–5.

Joule, R. V., Gouilloux, F., & Weber, F. (1989). The lure: A new compliance procedure. *Journal of Social Psychology, 129,* 741–749.

Judd, C. M., & Park, B. (1993). Definition and assessment of accuracy in social stereotypes. *Psychological Review, 100,* 109–128.

Judge, T. A., & Bono, J. E. (2001). Relationship of core self-evaluations traits—self-esteem, generalized self-efficacy, locus of control, and emotional stability—with job satisfaction and job performance: A meta-analysis. *Journal of Applied Psychology, 86,* 80–92.

Judge, T. A., & Cable, D. M. (2004). Income: Preliminary test of a theoretical model. *Journal of Applied Psychology, 89,* 428–441.

Judge, T. A., Heller, D., & Mount, M. K. (2002). Five-Factor Model of personality and job satisfaction: A meta-analysis. *Journal of Applied Psychology, 87,* 530–541.

Judge, T. A., & Hulin, C. L. (1993). Job satisfaction as a reflection of disposition: A multiple-source causal analysis. *Organizational Behavior and Human Decision Processes, 56,* 388–421.

Judge, T. A., & Ilies, R. (2002). Relationship of personality to performance motivation: A meta-analytic review. *Journal of Applied Psychology, 87,* 797–807.

Judge, T. A., Thoresen, C. J., Bono, J. E., & Patton, G. K. (2001). The job satisfaction–job performance relationship: A qualitative and quantitative review. *Psychological Bulletin, 127,* 376–407.

Just, N., Abramson, L. Y., & Alloy, L. B. (2001). Remitted depression studies as tests of the cognitive vulnerability hypotheses of depression onset. A critique and conceptual analysis. *Clinical Psychology Review, 21,* 63–83.

Just, N., & Alloy, L. B. (1997). The response styles theory of depression: Tests and an extension of the theory. *Journal of Abnormal Psychology, 106,* 221–229.

Kabat-Zinn, J. (2003). Mindfulness-based interventions in context: Past, present, and future. *Clinical Psychology: Science and Practice, 10,* 144–156.

Kadden, R. M. (1994). Cognitive-behavioral approaches to alcoholism treatment. *Alcohol Health and Research World, 18,* 279–286.

Kagan, J. (1997). Biology and the child. In W. Damon (Editor-in-Chief) & N. Eisenberg (Vol. Ed.), *Handbook of child psychology: Vol. 3. Social, emotional, and personality development* (5th ed., pp. 177–236). New York: John Wiley & Sons.

Kagan, J. (2003). Biology, context, and developmental inquiry. *Annual Review of Psychology 54,* 1–23.

Kahler, C. W., Read, J. P., Wood, M. D., & Palfai, T. P. (2003). Social environmental selection as a mediator of gender, ethnic, and personality effects on college student drinking. *Psychology of Addictive Behaviors, 17,* 226–234.

Kahneman, D. (1991). Judgment and decision making: A personal view. *Psychological Science, 2,* 142–145.

Kahneman, D., & Tversky, A. (1973). On the psychology of prediction. *Psychological Review, 80,* 237–251.

Kahneman, D., Krueger, A. B., Schkade, D. A., Schwarz, N., & Stone, A. A. (2004). A survey method for characterizing daily life experience: The Day Reconstruction Method. *Science, 306,* 1776—1780.

Kalb, C. (2001a, January 22). Seeing a virtual shrink. *Newsweek,* pp. 34–38.

Kalb, C. (2001b, February 12). Can this pill stop you from hitting the bottle? *Newsweek,* pp. 48–51.

Kalb, C. (2001c, August 20). Overexposed. *Newsweek,* pp. 34–38.

Kalb, C. (2003a, January 20). Get up and get moving. *Newsweek,* pp. 60–64.

Kalb, C. (2003b, May 19). Taking a new look at pain. *Newsweek,* pp. 45–52.

Kalechstein, A. D., & Nowicki, S., Jr. (1997). A meta-analytic examination of the relationship between control expectancies and academic achievement: An 11-year follow-up. *Genetic, Social, and General Psychology Monographs, 123,* 27–56.

Kamei, Y., Ishizuka, Y., Usui, A., Okado, T., et al. (1994). Bright light improves self-evaluation for day-time sleep in nurses after night work. *Journal of Mental Health, 40,* 49–54.

Kamphuis, J. H., Emmelkamp, P. M. G., & Krijn, M. U. (2002). Specific phobia. In M. Hersen (Ed.), *Clinical behavior therapy: Adults and children* (pp. 75–89). New York: John Wiley & Sons.

Kanaya, T., Scullin, M. H., & Ceci, S. J. (2003). The Flynn effect and U.S. policies: The impact of rising IQ scores on American society via mental retardation diagnoses. *American Psychologist, 58,* 778–790.

Kandel, D. B. (2003). Does marijuana use cause the use of other drugs? *Journal of the American Medical Association, 289,* 482–483.

Kandel D. B. (Ed.). (2002). *Stages and pathways of drug involvement: Examining the gateway hypothesis.* Cambridge, England: Cambridge University Press.

Kandel, E. R. (1995). Cellular mechanisms of learning and memory: Synaptic integration. In E. R. Kandel, J. H., Schwartz, & T. M. Jessel (Eds.), *Essentials of neural science and behavior.* Norwalk, CT: Appleton & Lange.

Kandel, E. R., & Hawkins, R. D. (1993). The biological basis of learning and individuality. In *Mind and brain: Readings from Scientific American Magazine* (pp. 40–53). New York: W. H. Freeman.

Kane, J. M. (1996). Drug therapy: Schizophrenia. *New England Journal of Medicine, 334,* 34–41.

Kane, M. J., & Engle, R. W. (2003). Working-memory capacity and the control of attention: The contributions of goal neglect, response competition, and task set to Stroop interference. *Journal of Experimental Psychology–General, 132,* 47–70.

Kanner, A. D., Coyne, J. C., Schaefer, C., & Lazarus, R. S. (1981). Comparison of two modes of stress measurement: Daily hassles and uplifts versus major life events. *Journal of Behavioral Medicine, 4,* 1–39.

Kantrowitz, B., & Springen, K. (2003, September 22). Why sleep matters. *Newsweek,* pp. 75–77.

Kaplan, P. M. (2000). Two pathways to prevention. *American Psychologist, 55,* 382–396.

Kaplan, P. S. (2000a). *A child's odyssey: Child and adolescent development* (3rd ed.). Belmont, CA: Wadsworth.

Kaplan, P. S. (2000b, April). *The cohort effect and the teaching of psychology.* Paper presented at the 14th annual Teaching of Psychology Conference, Ellenville, NY.

Kaptchuk, R., Eisenberg, D., & Komaroff, A. (2002a, December 2). Pondering the placebo effect. *Newsweek,* pp. 71–73.

Kaptchuk, R., Eisenberg, D., & Komaroff, A. (2002b, December 2). Finding out what works. *Newsweek,* p. 73.

Kareev, Y. (2000). Seven (indeed, plus or minus two) and the detection of correlations. *Psychological Review, 107,* 397–402.

Kasai, K., Shenton, M. E., Salisbury, D. F., Hirayasu, Y., Lee, C.-U., Ciszewski, A. A., et al. (2003). Gray matter volume in patients with first-episode schizophrenia. *American Journal of Psychiatry, 160,* 156–164.

Kaslow, F. W. (2001). Families and family psychology at the millennium: Intersecting crossroads. *American Psychologist, 56,* 37–46.

Kaslow, N. J., Thompson, M. P., Okun, A., Price, A., Young, S., Bender, M., et al. (2002). Risk and protective factors for suicidal behavior in abused African American Women. *Journal of Consulting and Clinical Psychology, 70,* 311–319.

Kauer, J. A. (2003). Addictive drugs and stress trigger a common change at VTA synapses. *Neuron, 37,* 549–550.

Kawas, C. H., & Brookmeyer, R. (2001). Aging and the public health effects of dementia [Editorial]. *New England Journal of Medicine, 344,* 1160–1161.

Kazdin, A. E. (1997). Parent management training: Evidence, outcomes, and issues. *Journal of the American Academy of Child and Adolescent Psychiatry, 36,* 1349–1356.

Keating, C. F., Randall, D., Kendrick, T., & Gutshall, K. (2003). Do babyfaced adults receive more help? The (cross-cultural) case of the lost resume. *Journal of Nonverbal Behavior, 27,* 89–109.

Keating, C. R. (2002). Charismatic faces: Social status cues put face appeal in context. In G. Rhodes & L. A. Zebrowitz (Eds.), *Facial attractiveness: Evolutionary, cognitive, and social perspectives* (pp. 153–192). Westport, CT: Ablex Publishing.

Keefe, F. J., Abernethy, A. P., & Campbell, L. C. (2005). Psychological approaches to understanding and treating disease-related pain. *Annual Review of Psychology, 56,* 601–630.

Keller, L. M., Bouchard, T. J., Arvey, R. D., Segal, N. L., et al. (1992). Work values: Genetic and environmental influences. *Journal of Applied Psychology, 77,* 79–88.

Keller, S. N., & Brown, J. D. (2002). Media interventions to promote responsible sexual behavior. *Journal of Sex Research, 39,* 1–6.

Kelley, B. B. (1997, May/June). Running on empty. *Health,* pp. 64–68.

Kemeny, M. E. (2003). The psychobiology of stress. *Current Directions in Psychological Science, 12,* 124–129.

Kendell, R., & Jablensky, A. (2003). Distinguishing between the validity and utility of psychiatric diagnoses. *American Journal of Psychiatry, 160,* 4–12.

Kendler, K. S. (2005). Psychiatric genetics: A methodologic critique. *American Journal of Psychiatry, 162,* 3–11.

Kendler, K. S. (2001). A psychiatric dialogue on the mind-body problem. *American Journal of Psychiatry, 158,* 989–1000.

Kendler, K. S., Bulik, C. M., Silberg, J., Hettema, J. M., Myers, J., & Prescott, C. A. (2000). Childhood sexual abuse and adult psychiatric and substance use disorders in women: An epidemiological and cotwin control analysis. *Archives of General Psychiatry, 57,* 953–959.

Kendler, K. S., Gardner, C. O., & Prescott, C. A. (2002). Toward a comprehensive developmental model for major depression in women. *American Journal of Psychiatry, 159,* 1133–1145.

Kendler, K. S., Jacobson, K. C., Prescott, C. A., & Neale, M. C. (2003). Specificity of genetic and environmental risk factors for use and abuse/dependence of cannabis, cocaine, hallucinogens, sedatives, stimulants, and opiates in male twins. *American Journal of Psychiatry, 160,* 687–695.

Kendler, K. S., Kuhn, J., & Prescott, C. A. (2004). The interrelationship of neuroticism, sex, and stressful life events in the prediction of episodes of major depression. *American Journal of Psychiatry,161,* 631–636.

Kennedy, M. B. (2000). Signal-processing machines at the postsynaptic density. *Science, 290,* 750–754.

Kennedy, N., Abbott, R., & Paykel, E. S. (2003). Remission and recurrence of depression in the maintenance era: Long-term outcome in a Cambridge cohort. *Psychological Medicine, 33,* 827–838.

Kennedy, R. (2003). *Interracial intimacies: Sex, marriage, identity, and adoption.* New York: Knopf.

Kenrick, D. T., Li, N. P., & Butner, J. (2003). Dynamical evolutionary psychology: Individual decision rules and emergent social norms. *Psychological Review, 110,* 3–28.

Kent, A., & Waller, G. (2000). Childhood emotional abuse and eating psychopathology. *Clinical Psychology Review, 20,* 887–903.

Keppel, B. (2002). Kenneth B. Clark in the patterns of American culture. *American Psychologist, 57,* 29–37.

Kerr, M., Stattin, H., Biesecker, G., & Ferrer-Wreder, L. (2003). Relationships with parents and peers in adolescence. In R. M. Lerner, M. A. Easterbrooks, & J. Mistry (Eds.), *Handbook of psychology: Vol. 6. Developmental psychology* (pp. 395–422). New York: John Wiley & Sons.

Kerr, N. H., & Homhoff, G. W. (2004). Do the blind literally "see" in their dreams? A critique of a recent claim that they do. *Dreaming, 14,* 230–233.

Kerr, N. L., & Tindale, R. S. (2004). Group performance and decision making. *Annual Review of Psychology, 55,* 623–655.

Kersting, K. (2003a, November). What exactly is creativity? *Monitor on Psychology, 34,* 40–41.

Kersting, K. (2003b, December). Turning happiness into economic power. *Monitor on Psychology, 34,* 26–27.

Kessler, R. C. (1994). The National Comorbidity Survey: Preliminary results and future directions. *International Journal of Methods in Psychiatric Research, 4,* 114.1–114.13.

Kessler, R. C., Berglund, P., Demler, O., Jin, R., Koretz, D., Merikangas, K. R., et al. (2003). The epidemiology of major depressive disorder: Results from the National Comorbidity Survey Replication (NCS-R). *Journal of the American Medical Association, 289,* 3095–3105.

Kessler, R. C., Berglund, P. A., Demler, O., Jin, R., & Walters, E. E. (2005). Lifetime prevalence and age-of-onset distributions of DSM-IV disorders in the National Comorbidity Survey Replication (NCS-R). *Archives of General Psychiatry, 62,* 593–602.

Kessler, R. C., Borges, G., & Walters, E. E. (1999). Prevalence of and risk factors for lifetime suicide attempts in the National Comorbidity Survey. *Archives of General Psychiatry, 56,* 617–626. Kessler, R. C., Chiu, W. T., Demler, O., & Walters, E. E. (2005). Prevalence, severity, and comorbidity of 12-month DSM-IV disorders in the National Comorbidity Survey Replication. *Archives of General Psychiatry, 62,* 617–627.

Kessler, R. C., McGonagle, K. A., Zhao, S., & Nelson, C. B. (1994). Lifetime and 12–month prevalence of DSM-III-R psychiatric disorders in the United States: Results from the National Comorbidity Survey. *Archives of General Psychiatry, 51,* 8–19.

Khamsi, R. (2004, December 22). Shops must mix festive scents and sounds to tempt the buyer. *News@Nature.com.* Retrieved December 29, 2004, from http://www.nature.com/news/2004/041220/full/041220–10.html.

Kids' TV use may impact reading. (2003, October 28). *MSNBC Web Posting.* Retrieved October 29, 2003, from http://www.msnbc.com/news/986121.asp?0dm=C11PH.

Kiecolt-Glaser, J. K., Bane, C., Glaser, R., & Malarkey, W. B. (2003). Love, marriage, and divorce: Newlyweds' stress hormones foreshadow relationship changes. *Journal of Consulting and Clinical Psychology, 71,* 176–188.

Kiecolt-Glaser, J. K., Marucha, P. T., Atkinson, C., & Glaser, R. (2001). Hypnosis as a modulator of cellular immune dysregulation during acute stress. *Journal of Consulting and Clinical Psychology, 69,* 674–682.

Kiecolt-Glaser, J. K., McGuire, L., Robles, T. F., & Glaser, R. (2002). Emotions, morbidity, and mortality: New perspectives from psychoneuroimmunology. *Annual Review of Psychology, 53,* 83–107.

Kiecolt-Glaser, J. K., Preacher, K. J., MacCallum, R. C., Atkinson, C., Malarkey, W. B., & Glaser, R. (2003). Chronic stress and age-related increases in the proinflammatory cytokine IL-6. *Proceedings of the National Academy of Sciences, 100* (15), 9090–9095.

Kiecolt-Glaser, J. K., Speicher, C. E., Holliday, J. E., & Glaser, R. (1984). Stress and the transformation of lymphocytes in Epstein-Barr virus. *Journal of Behavioral Medicine, 7,* 1–12.

Kiefer, F., Jahn, H., Tarnaske, T., Helwig, H., Briken, P., Holzbach, R., et al. (2003). Comparing and combining naltrexone and acamprosate in relapse prevention of alcoholism: A double-blind, placebo-controlled study. *Archives of General Psychiatry, 60,* 92–99.

Kieseppä, T., Partonen, T., Haukka, J., Kaprio, J., & Lönnqvist, J. (2004). High concordance of Bipolar I disorder in a nationwide sample of twins. *American Journal of Psychiatry, 161,* 1814–1821.

Kihlstrom, J. F. (2004). An unbalanced balancing act: Blocked, recovered, and false memories in the laboratory and clinic. *Clinical Psychology: Science and Practice, 11,* 34–39.

Kilgore, K., Snyder, J., & Lentz, C. (2000). The contribution of parental discipline, parental monitoring, and school risk to early-onset conduct problems in African American boys and girls. *Developmental Psychology, 36,* 835–845.

Kim, B. S. K., Brenner, B. R., Liang, C. T. H., & Asay, P. A. (2003). A qualitative study of adaptation experiences of 1.5-generation Asian Americans. *Cultural Diversity and Ethnic Minority Psychology, 9,* 156–170.

Kim, U., Jorgenson, E., Coon, H., Leppert, M., Risch, N., & Drayna1, D. (2003). Positional cloning of the human quantitative trait locus underlying taste sensitivity to phenylthiocarbamide. *Science, 299,* 1221–1225.

Kimura, D. (1992). Sex differences in the brain. *Scientific American, 267*(3), 118–125.

Kimura, D. (2002, May 13). Sex differences in the brain. *Scientific American Online.* Retrieved June 23, 2002, from http://www.sciam.com/article.cfm?articleID=00018E9D-879D-1D06–8E49809EC588EEDF.

Kinsey, A. C., Pomeroy, W. B., & Martin, C. E. (1948). *Sexual behavior in the human male.* Philadelphia: W. B. Saunders.

Kinsey, A. C., Pomeroy, W. B., Martin, C. E., & Gebhard, P. H. (1953). *Sexual behavior in the human female.* Philadelphia: W. B. Saunders.

Kirsch, I. (1994). Clinical hypnosis as a nondeceptive placebo: Empirically derived techniques. *American Journal of Clinical Hypnosis, 37,* 95–106.

Kirsch, I. (1996). Hypnotic enhancement of cognitive-behavioral weight loss treatments: Another meta-reanalysis. *Journal of Consulting and Clinical Psychology, 64*(3), 517–519.

Kirsch, I. (2004). Conditioning, expectancy, and the placebo effect: Comment on Stewart-Williams and Podd (2004). *Psychological Bulletin,* 130, 341–343.

Kirsch, I., Moore, T. J., Scoboria, A., & Nicholls, S. S. (2002, July 15). The emperor's new drugs: An analysis of antidepressant medication data submitted to the U.S. Food and Drug Administration. *Prevention & Treatment, 5.* Retrieved July 16, 2003, from http://journals.apa.org/prevention/volume5/pre0050023a.html.

Kirsch, I., Scoboria, A., & Moore, T. J. (2002). Antidepressants and placebos: Secrets, revelations, and unanswered questions. *Prevention and Treatment, 5.* Retrieved August 8, 2005, from http://www.journals.apa.org/prevention/volume5/pre0050033r.html.

Kirsch, J. F., & Lynn, S. J. (1998). Dissociation theories of hypnosis. *Psychological Bulletin, 123,* 100–115.

Kirsch, J. F., Silva, C. E., Comey, G., & Reed, S. (1995). A spectral analysis of cognitive and personality variables in hypnosis: Empirical disconfirmation of the two-factor model of hypnotic responding. *Journal of Personality and Social Psychology, 69,* 167–175.

Kirsh, S. J., & Olczak, P. V. (2002). The effects of extremely violent comic books on social information processing. *Journal of Interpersonal Violence, 17,* 1160–1178.

Kisilevsky, B. S., Hains, S. M. J., Lee, K., Xie, X., Huang, H., Ye, H-H., et al. (2003). Effects of experience on fetal voice recognition. *Psychological Science, 14,* 220–224.

Kitayama, S., Duffy, S., Kawamura, T., & Larsen, J. T. (2003). Perceiving an object and its context in different cultures: A cultural look at new look. *Psychological Science, 14,* 201–206.

Kitayama, S., Markus, H. R., Matsumoto, H., & Norasakkunkit, V. (1997). Individual and collective processes in the construction of the self: Self-enhancement in the United States and self-criticism in Japan. *Journal of Personality and Social Psychology, 72,* 1245–1267.

Klar, A. J. S. (2003). Human handedness and scalp hair whorl direction develop from a common genetic mechanism. *Genetics, 165,* 269–276.

Klein, D. F. (1993). False suffocation alarms, spontaneous panics, and related conditions: An integrative hypothesis. *Archives of General Psychiatry, 50,* 306–317.

Kleinfield, N. R., & Connelly, M. (2003, September 8). 9/11 still strains New York psyche. *New York Times,* pp. A1, A22.

Kleinman, A. (1987). Anthropology and psychiatry: The role of culture in cross-cultural research on illness. *British Journal of Psychiatry, 151,* 447–454.

Kleinman, A. (2004). Culture and depression. *New England Journal of Medicine, 351,* 951–953.

Kleinplatz, P. J. (2003). What's new in sex therapy? From stagnation to fragmentation. *Sexual and Relationship Therapy, 18*(1), 95–106.

Klinger, E. (1987, October). The power of daydreams. *Psychology Today,* pp. 37–44.

Klohen, E. C., & Luo, S. (2003). Interpersonal attraction and personality: What is attractive—self similarity, ideal similarity, complementarity, or attachment security? *Journal of Personality and Social Psychology, 85,* 709–722.

Kluger, J. (2001, June 18). How to manage teen drinking (the smart way). *Time,* pp. 42–44.

Kluger, J. (2003, October 26). Medicating young minds. *Time Magazine Online.* Retrieved October 27, 2003, from http://www.time.com/time/magazine/article/0,9171,1101031103–526331,00.html.

Knafo, A., Iervolino, A. C., & Plomin, R. (2005). Masculine girls and feminine boys: Genetic and environmental contributions to atypical gender development in early childhood. *Journal of Personality & Social Psychology, 88,* 400–412.

Knoedler, A. J., Hellwig, K. A., & Neath, I. (1999). The shift from recency to primacy with increasing delay. *Journal of Experimental Psychology: Learning, Memory, and Cognition, 25,* 474–487.

Kobasa, S. C. (1979). Stressful life events, personality, and health: An inquiry into hardiness. *Journal of Personality and Social Psychology, 37,* 1–11.

Kobasa, S. C., Maddi, S. R., & Kahn, S. (1982). Hardiness and health: A prospective study. *Journal of Personality and Social Psychology, 42,* 168–177.

Kodl, M. M., & Mermelstein, R. (2004). Beyond modeling: Parenting practices, parental smoking history, and adolescent cigarette smoking. *Addictive Behaviors, 29,* 17–32.

Kogan, M. (2001, January). Where happiness lies. *Monitor on Psychology, 32*(1), 74–76.

Kohlberg, L. (1969). *Stages in the development of moral thought and action.* New York: Holt, Rinehart & Winston.

Kohlberg, L. (1981). *The philosophy of moral development.* San Francisco: Harper & Row.

Köhler, W. (1927). *The mentality of apes.* New York: Harcourt Brace.

Kohout, J. (2001, February). Who's earning those psychology degrees? *Monitor on Psychology,* 42.

Kokko, K., & Pulkkinen, L. (2000). Aggression in childhood and long-term unemployment in adulthood: A cycle of maladaptation and some protective factors. *Developmental Psychology, 36,* 463–472.

Koko the gorilla calls for the dentist. (2004, August 8). *Cable News Network..* Retrieved August 9, 2004, from http://www.cnn.com/2004/US/West/08/08/koko.health.ap/index.html.

Kolata, G. (2000a, October 17). How the body knows when to gain or lose. *New York Times,* pp. F1, F8.

Kolata, G. (2000b, October 18). Days off are not allowed, experts argue. *New York Times,* pp. A1, A20.

Kolata, G. (2003, September 4). Study finds appetites reduced by hormone. *New York Times,* p. A16.

Kolata, G. (2005, April 20). Some extra helft may be helpful, new study says. *New York Times,* pp. A1, A22.

Komaroff, A. L. (2004, March 25). Sleep improves insight. *Journal Watch Psychiatry.* Retrieved March 25, 2004, from http://psychiatry.jwatch.org/cgi/content/full/2004/325/10?q=etoc.

Konradi, C., Eaton, M., MacDonald, M. L., Walsh, J., Benes, F. M., & Heckers, S. (2004). Molecular evidence for mitochondrial dysfunction in bipolar disorder. *Archives of General Psychiatry, 61,* 300–308.

Kopper, B. A., Osman, A., & Barrios, F. X. (2001). Assessment of suicidal ideation in young men and women: The incremental validity of the MMPI-2 content scales. *Death Studies, 25,* 593–607.

Koriat, A. (1993). How do we know that we know? The accessible model of the feeling of knowing. *Psychological Review, 100,* 609–639.

Koriat, A., & Goldsmith, M. (1996). Memory as something that can be counted versus memory as something that can be counted on. In D. Herrmann, C. McEvoy, C. Hertzog, P. Hertel, & M. K. Johnson (Eds.), *Basic and applied memory research: Practical applications* (Vol. 2, pp. 3–18). Mahwah, NJ: Lawrence Erlbaum Associates.

Korner, J., & Leibel, R. L. (2003). To eat or not to eat—how the gut talks to the brain. *New England Journal of Medicine, 349,* 926–928.

Koss, M. P. (1988). Stranger and acquaintance rape: Are there differences in the victim's experience? *Psychology of Women Quarterly, 12,* 1–24.

Koss, M. P., Gidycz, C. A., & Wisniewski, N. (1987). The scope of rape: Incidence and prevalence of sexual aggression and victimization in a national sample of higher education students. *Journal of Consulting and Clinical Psychology, 55,* 162–170.

Koss, M. P., & Kilpatrick, D. G. (2001). Rape and sexual assault. In E. Gerrity et al. (Eds.), *The mental health consequences of torture. Plenum series on stress and coping* (pp. 177–193). Dordrecht, Netherlands: Kluwer Academic Publishers.

Kossek, F. E., & Ozeki, C. (1998). Work-family conflict, policies, and the job-life satisfaction relationship: A review and directions for organizational behavior-human resources research. *Journal of Applied Psychology, 83,* 139–149.

Kosslyn, S. M. (1994). *Image and brain: The resolution of the imagery debate.* Cambridge, MA: MIT Press.

Kosslyn, S. M., Thompson, W. L., Costantini-Ferrando, M. F., Alpert, N. M., & Spiegel, D. (2000). Hypnotic visual illusion alters color processing in the brain. *American Journal of Psychiatry, 157,* 1279–1284.

Kraemer, H. C., Yesavage, J. A., Taylor, J. L., & Kupfer, D. (2000). How can we learn about developmental processes from cross-sectional studies, or can we? *American Journal of Psychiatry, 157,* 163–171.

Krahn, L. E., & Gonzalez-Arriaza, H. L. (2004). Narcolepsy with cataplexy. *American Journal of Psychiatry, 161,* 2181–2184.

Kramer, A. F., & Willis, S. L. (2002). Enhancing the cognitive vitality of older adults. *Current Directions in Psychological Science, 11,* 173–177.

Kraus, S. J. (1995). Attitudes and the prediction of behavior: A meta-analysis of the empirical literature. *Personality and Social Psychology Bulletin, 21,* 58–75.

Krauss, R. M., Curran, N. M., & Ferleger, N. (1983). Expressive conventions and the cross-cultural perception of emotion. *Basic and Applied Social Psychology, 4,* 295–305.

Kretchmar, M. D., & Jacobvitz, D. B. (2002). Observing mother-child relationships across generations: Boundary patterns, attachment, and the transmission of caregiving. *Family Process, 41,* 351–374.

Kristof, N. D. (2002, December 5). Love and race. *New York Times Online.* Retrieved July 23, 2003, from http://www.racematters.org/loveandrace.htm.

Kroll, L., & Goldman, L. (Eds.). (2005, March 28). The richest people on earth. *Forbes, 175,* 125.

Kros, C. (2005). Hearing: Aid from hair force. *Nature, 433,* 810–811.

Kruger, T. E., & Jerrells, T. R. (1992). Potential role of alcohol in human immunodeficiency virus infection. *Alcohol World: Health and Research, 16* (NIH Publication No. 93–3466, pp. 57–63). Washington, DC: National Institute on Alcohol Abuse and Alcoholism.

Krull, D. S., Segere, C. R., & Silvera, D. H. (2001). On the profits and perils of guessing right: Effects of situational expectations for emotions on the correspondence of inferences. *Journal of Experimental Social Psychology, 37,* 413–418.

Kubey, R. W., Lavin, M. J., & Barrows, J. R. (2001). Internet use and collegiate academic performance decrements: Early findings. *Journal of Communication, 51,* 366–382.

Kubiszyn, T. W., Meyer, G. J., Finn, S. E., Eyde, L. D., Kay, G. G., Moreland, K. L., et al. (2000). Empirical support for psychological assessment in clinical health care settings. *Professional Psychology: Research and Practice, 31,* 119–130.

Kuliev, A., Rechitsky, S., Verlinsky, O., Ivakhnenko, V., Cieslak, J., Evsikov, S., et al. (1999). Evaluation of chorionic villus sampling safety: WHO/PAHO consultation on CVS. *Prenatal Diagnosis, 19,* 97–99.

Kuncel, N. R., Hezlett, A. A., & Ones, D. S. (2004). Academic performance, career potential, creativity, and job performance: Can one construct predict them all? *Journal of Personality and Social Psychology, 86,* 148–161.

Kunda, Z., & Spencer, S. J. (2003). When do stereotypes come to mind and when do they color judgment? A goal-based theoretical framework for stereotype activation and application. *Psychological Bulletin, 129,* 522–544.

Kuperberg, G. R., Broome, M. R., McGuire, P. K., David, A. S., Eddy, M., Ozawa, F., et al. (2003). Regionally localized thinning of the cerebral cortex in schizophrenia. *Archives of General Psychiatry, 60,* 878–888.

Kupfersmid, J. (1995). Does the Oedipus complex exist? *Psychotherapy, 32,* 535–547.

Kurpius, S. E. R., Nicpon, M. F., &. Maresh, S. E. (2001). Mood, marriage, and menopause. *Journal of Counseling Psychology, 48,* 77–84.

Kusnecov, A. W. (2001). Behavioral conditioning of the immune system. In A. Baum, T. A. Revenson, & J. E. Singer (Eds.), *Handbook of health psychology* (pp. 105–116). Mahwah, NJ: Lawrence Erlbaum Associates.

Kyle, T. (2000, February). Minorities and women in undergraduate psychology: Where are we? *Monitor on Psychology, 31*(2), 15.

LaBerge, S. (2003). Paradoxes of dreaming consciousness: The need to examine our assumptions about dreaming. *Contemporary Psychology: APA Review of Books, 48,* 621–624.

Lachman, M. E. (2004). Development in midlife. *Annual Review of Psychology, 55,* 305–331.

Lachman, M. E., & Weaver, S. L. (1998). Sociodemographic variations in the sense of control by domain: Findings from the MacArthur Studies of Midlife. *Psychology and Aging, 13,* 553–562.

Lackner, J. R., & DiZio, P. (2005). Vestibular, proprioceptive, and haptic contributions to spatial orientation. *Annual Review of Psychology, 56,* 115—147.

LaFrance, M., Hecht, M. A., & Paluck, E. L. (2003). The contingent smile: A meta-analysis of sex differences in smiling. *Psychological Bulletin, 129,* 305–334.

Lahn, B. T., & Page, D. C. (1999). Four evolutionary strata on the human X chromosome. *Science, 286,* 964–967. Lai, C. S. L., Fisher, S. E., Hurst, J. A., Vargha-Khadem, F., & Monaco, A. P. (2001). A forkhead-domain gene is mutated in a severe speech and language disorder. *Nature, 413,* 519–523.

Laino, C. (2002, April 25). Gender gap in longevity narrowing. *MSNBC Web Posting.* Retrieved May 5, 2002, from http://www.msnbc.com/news/743069.asp.

Lallemant, M., Jourdain, G., Le Coeur, S., Kim, S., Koetsowang, S., Comeau, A. M., et al. (2000). A trial of shortened zidovudine regimens to prevent mother-to-child transmission of human immunodeficiency virus type 1. Perinatal HIV Prevention Trial (Thailand) Investigators. *New England Journal of Medicine, 343,* 982–991.

Lamanna, M. A., & Riedmann, A. (1997). *Marriages and families* (6th ed.). Belmont, CA: Wadsworth.

Lamberg, L. (2003). Advances in eating disorders offer food for thought. *Journal of the American Medical Association, 290,* 1437–1442.

Lambert, M. J., Hansen, N. B., & Finch, A. E. (2001). Patient-focused research: Using patient outcome data to enhance treatment effects. *Journal of Consulting and Clinical Psychology, 69,* 159–172.

Langlois, J. H., Kalakanis, L., Rubenstein, A. J., Larson, A., Hallam, M., & Smoot, M. (2000). Maxims or myths of beauty? A meta-analytic and theoretical review. *Psychological Bulletin, 126,* 390–423.

Latané, B., & Darley, J. M. (1970). *The unresponsive bystander: Why doesn't he help?* New York: Appleton-Century-Crofts.

Latta, F., & Van Cauter, E. (2003). Sleep and biological clocks. In M. Gallagher & R. J. Nelson (Eds.), *Handbook of psychology: Vol. 3. Biological psychology* (pp. 355–378). New York: John Wiley & Sons.

Laumann, E. O., Gagnon, J. H., Michael, R. T., & Michaels, S. (1994). *The social organization of sexuality: Sexual practices in the United States.* Chicago: University of Chicago Press.

Laumann, E. O., Paik, A., & Rosen, R. C. (1999). Sexual dysfunction in the United States. Prevalence and predictors. *Journal of the American Medical Association, 281*(6), 537–544.

Lavie, P. (2001). Sleep-wake as a biological rhythm. *Annual Review of Psychology, 52,* 607–628.

Lawrence, J., Mayers, D. L, Hullsiek, K. H., Collins, G., Abrams, D. I., Reisler, R. B., et al. (2003). Structured treatment interruption in patients with multidrug-resistant Human Immunodeficiency Virus. *New England Journal of Medicine, 349,* 837–846.

Lawton, C. A. (2001). Gender and regional differences in spatial referents used in direction giving. *Sex Roles, 44,* 321–337.

Lawton, M. P., Moss, M. S., Winter, L., & Hoffman, C. (2002). Motivation in later life: Personal projects and well-being. *Psychology and Aging, 17,* 539–547.

Lazarus, R. S., & Folkman, S. (1984). *Stress, appraisal, and coping.* New York: Springer Publishing Company.

Leaper, C. (2000). Gender, affiliation, assertion, and the interactive context of parent-child play. *Developmental Psychology, 36,* 381–393.

Lear, J. (2000, February 27). Freud's second thoughts. *New York Times Book Review,* p. 39.

Leary, W. E. (1996, December 18). Responses of alcoholics to therapies seem similar. *New York Times,* p. A17.

Leber, P. (2000). Placebo controls: No news is good news. *Archives of General Psychiatry, 57,* 319–320.

LeDoux, J. E. (1994, June). Emotion, memory, and the brain. *Scientific American, 270,* 32–39.

LeDoux, J. E. (1996). *The emotional brain.* New York: Touchstone.

LeDoux, J. E. (2000). Emotion circuits in the brain. *Annual Review of Neuroscience, 23,* 155–184.

Lehrer, P., Feldman, J., Giardino, N., Song, H.-S., & Schmaling, K. (2002). Psychological aspects of asthma. *Journal of Consulting and Clinical Psychology, 70,* 691–711.

Lehrer, P. M., Hochron, S. M., Mayne, T., Isenberg, S., et al. (1994). Relaxation and music therapies for asthma among patients prestabilized on asthma medication. *Journal of Behavioral Medicine, 17,* 1–24.

Leiblum, S. R., & Rosen, R. C. (Ed.). (2000). *Principles and practice of sex therapy* (3rd ed.). New York: Guilford Press.

Leibowitz, H. W. (1971). Sensory, learned, and cognitive mechanisms of size perception. *Annals of the New York Academy of Sciences, 1988,* 47–62.

Leichsenring, F., et al. (2004). The efficacy of short-term psychodynamic psychotherapy in specific psychiatric disorders: A meta-analysis. *Archives of General Psychiatry, 61,* 1208–1216.

Leichsenring, F., & Leibing, E. (2003). The effectiveness of psychodynamic therapy and cognitive behavior therapy in the treatment of personality disorders: A meta-analysis. *American Journal of Psychiatry, 160,* 1223–1232.

Leiter, M. P., & Maslach, C. (2001). Burnout and health. In A. Baum, T. A. Revenson, & J. E. Singer (Eds.), *Handbook of health psychology* (pp. 415–426). Mahwah, NJ: Lawrence Erlbaum Associates.

Leland, J. (1997, Spring/Summer). The magnetic tube. *Newsweek (Special Edition: Your Child from Birth to Three),* pp. 89–90.

Lemonde, S., Turecki, G., Bakish, D., Du, L., Hrdina, P. D., Bown, C. D., Sequeira, A., et al. (2003). Impaired repression at a 5-hydroxytryptamine 1A receptor gene polymorphism associated with major depression and suicide. *Journal of Neuroscience, 23,* 8788–8799.

Lemonick, M. C. (2003a, January 20). The power of mood. *Time,* pp. 36–41.

Lemonick, M. D. (2003b, January 20). Your mind your body. *Time,* p. 35.

Lemonick, M. D. (2005a, January 17). The biology of joy. *Time,* pp. A12–A17.

Lemonick, M. D. (2005b, January 17). A smile doesn't always mean happy. *Time,* p. A29.

Lemonick, M. D., & Park, A. (2001, May 14). Alzheimer's: The Nun study. *Time,* pp. 54–64.

Lemons, J. A., Baur, C. R., Oh, W., Korones, S. B., Stoll, B. J., Verter, J., et al. (2001). Very low birth weight outcomes of the National Institute of Child Health and Human Development neonatal research network, January 1995 through December 1996. *Pediatrics, 107,* 1.

Leon, A. C. (2000). Placebo protects subjects from nonresponse: A paradox of power. *Archives of General Psychiatry, 57,* 329–330.

Leon, A. C., Solomon, D. A., Mueller, T. L., Endicott, J., Rice, J. P., Maser, J. D., et al. (2003). A 20-year longitudinal observational study of somatic antidepressant treatment effectiveness. *American Journal of Psychiatry, 160,* 727–733.

Lepore, L., & Brown, R. (1997). Category and stereotype activation: Is prejudice inevitable? *Journal of Personality and Social Psychology, 72,* 275–287.

Lester, B. M., et al. (2003). The Maternal Lifestyle Study (MLS): Effects of prenatal cocaine and/or opiate exposure on auditory brain response at one month. *Journal of Pediatrics, 142,* 279–285.

Leutgeb, S., Leutgeb, J. K., Treves, A., Moser, M.-B., & Moser, E. I. (2004). Distinct ensemble codes in hippocampal areas CA3 and CA1. *Science, 305,* 1295–1298.

LeVay, S. (2003). *The biology of sexual orientation.* Retrieved December 19, 2003, from http://members.aol.com/slevay/page22.html.

Levenson, R. W. (1994). The search for autonomic specificity. In P. Ekman & R. J. Davidson (Eds.), *The nature of emotion: Fundamental questions* (pp. 252–257). New York: Oxford University Press.

Levenstein, S., Ackerman, S., Kiecolt-Glaser, J. K., & Dubois, A. (1999). Stress and peptic ulcer disease. *Journal of the American Medical Association, 281,* 10–11.

Levine, H. (2005, January 17). Another culprit to watch. *Newsweek,* p. 48.

Levine, J. A., Lanningham-Foster, L. M., McCrady, S. K., Krizan, C., Olson, L. R., Kane, P. H., et al. (2005). Interindividual variation in posture allocation: Possible role in human obesity. *Science, 307,* 584–586.

Levine, J. M., & Moreland, R. L. (1998). Small groups. In D. T. Gilbert, S. T. Fiske, & G. Lindzey (Eds.), *The handbook of social psychology* (4th ed., Vol. 2, pp. 415–469). Boston: McGraw-Hill.

Levine, L. E., & Waite, B. M. (2000). Television viewing and attentional abilities in fourth and fifth grade children. *Journal of Applied Developmental Psychology, 21,* 667–679.

Levine, M. (1994). *Effective problem solving* (2nd ed.). Englewood Cliffs, NJ: Prentice Hall.

Levinson, D. J., with Darrow, C. N., Klein, E. R., Levinson, M. H., & McKee, B. (1978). *The seasons of a man's life.* New York: Knopf.

Levy, B. R, Slade, M. D., Kunkel, S. R., & Kasl, S. V. (2002). Longevity increased by positive self-perceptions of aging. *Journal of Personality and Social Psychology, 83,* 261–270.

Levy-Lahad, E., & Plon, S. E. (2003). A risky business—assessing breast cancer risk. *Science, 302,* 574–575.

Lewin, T. (2001, September 10). Study finds little change in working mothers debate. *New York Times,* p. A26.

Lewin, T. (2003, November 23). For better or worse: Marriage's stormy future. *New York Times Week in Review,* pp. 1, 4.

Lewinsohn, P. M. (1974). A behavioral approach to depression. In R. J. Friedman & M. M. Katz (Eds.), *The psychology of depression: Contemporary theory and research.* Washington, DC: Winston-Wiley.

Leyton, M., Boileau, I., Benkelfat, C., Diksic, M., Baker, G., & Dagher, A. (2002). Amphetamine-induced increases in extracellular dopamine, drug wanting, and novelty seeking: A PET/[11C]raclopride study in healthy men. *Neuropsychopharmacology, 27,* 1027–35.

Li, S.-C. (2003). Biocultural orchestration of developmental plasticity across levels: the interplay of biology and culture in shaping the mind and behavior across the life span. *Psychological Bulletin, 129,* 171–194.

Liben, L. W., Susman, E. J., Finkelstein, J. W., Chinchilli, V. M., Kunselman, S., Schwab, J., et al. (2002). The effects of sex steroids on spatial performance: A review and an experimental clinical investigation. *Developmental Psychology, 38,* 236–253.

Libkuman, T. M., Love, K. G., & Donn, P. D. (1998). An empirically based selection and evaluation system for collegiate football. *Journal of Sport Management, 12,* 220–241.

Libow, L. S. (2005). Geriatrics in the United States — Baby Boomers' boon? *New England Journal of Medicine, 352,* 750–752.

Lickliter, R., & Honeycutt, H. (2003). Developmental dynamics: Toward a biologically plausible evolutionary psychology. *Psychological Bulletin, 129,* 819–835.

Lieberman, P. (1998). *Eve spoke: Human language and human evolution.* New York: Norton.

Liebert, R. M., Sprafkin, J. N., & Davidson, E. S. (1989). *The early window: Effects of television on children and youth* (3rd. ed.). New York: Pergamon.

Liebowitz, M. R., Gelenberg, A. J., & Munjack, D. (2005). Venlafaxine extended release vs placebo and paroxetine in social anxiety disorder. *Archives of General Psychiatry, 62,* 190–198.

Lilienfeld, S. O., Kirsch, I., Sarbin, T. R., Lynn, S. J., Chaves, J. F., Ganaway, G. K., et al. (1999). Dissociative identity disorder and the sociocognitive model: Recalling the lessons of the past. *Psychological Bulletin, 125,* 507–523.

Lilienfeld, S. O., Wood, J. M., & Garb, H. N. (2000). The scientific status of projective techniques. *Psychological Science in the Public Interest, 1,* 27–66.

Limebeer, C. L., &. Parker, L. A. (2000). The antiemetic drug ondansetron interferes with lithium-induced conditioned rejection reactions, but not lithium-induced taste avoidance in rats. *Journal of Experimental Psychology-Animal Behavior Processes, 26,* 371–384.

Lindeman, B., Libkuman, T., King, D., & Kruse, B. (2000). Development of an instrument to assess jump-shooting form in basketball. *Journal of Sport Behavior, 23,* 336–348.

Lindenmayer, J. P., & Khan, A. (2004). Pharmacological treatment strategies for schizophrenia. *Expert Review of Neurotherapeutics, 4,* 705–723.

Linville, P. W., & Fischer, G. W. (1993). Exemplar and abstraction models of perceived group variability and stereotypicality. *Social Cognition, 11,* 92–125.

Lipsitt, L. P. (1993). Early experience and nutritional factors in infant learning, cognition, and behavior. In J. Dobbing (Ed.), *Lipids, learning, and the brain: Fats in infant formulas* (pp. 50–68). Columbus, OH: Ross Laboratories.

Lipton, R. B., Stewart, W. F., Stone, A. M., Láinez, M. J., & Sawyer, J. P. (2000). Stratified care vs. step care strategies for migraine: The disability in strategies of Care (DISC) Study: A randomized trial. *Journal of the American Medical Association, 284,* 2599–2605.

Litt, M. D., Kadden, R. M., Cooney, N. L, & Kabela, E. (2003). Coping skills and treatment outcomes in cognitive–behavioral and interactional group therapy for alcoholism. *Journal of Consulting and Clinical Psychology, 71,* 118–128.

Liu, I.-C., Blacker, D. L., Xu, R., Fitzmaurice, G., Lyons, M. J., & Tsuang, M. T. (2004). Genetic and environmental contributions to the development of alcohol dependence in male twins. *Archives of General Psychiatry, 61,* 897–903.

Livesley, W. J., Jang, K. L., & Vernon, P. A. (2003). Genetic basis of personality structure. In M. J. Lerner & T. Millon (Eds.), *Handbook of psychology: Personality and social psychology* (Vol. 5, pp. 59–83). New York: Wiley.

Lobel, M., DeVincent, C. J., Kaminer, A., & Meyer, B. A. (2000). The impact of prenatal maternal stress and optimistic disposition on birth outcomes in medically high-risk women. *Health Psychology, 19,* 544–553.

Lockley, S. W., Cronin, J. W., Evans, E. E., Cade, B. E., Lee, C. J., Landrigan, C. P., et al. (2004). Effect of reducing interns' weekly work hours on sleep and attentional failures. *New England Journal of Medicine, 351,* 1829–1837.

Loeb, S., Fuller, B., Kagan, S. L., & Carrol, B. (2004). Child care in poor communities: Early learning effects of type, quality, and stability. *Child Development, 75,* 47–65.

Loftus, E. F. (1993a). Psychologists in the eyewitness world. *American Psychologist, 48,* 550–552.

Loftus, E. F. (1993b). The reality of repressed memories. *American Psychologist, 48,* 518–537.

Loftus, E. F. (1996). The myth of repressed memory and the realities of science. *Clinical Psychology: Science and Practice, 3,* 356–365.

Loftus, E. F. (1997, September). Creating false memories. *Scientific American,* pp. 71–75.

Loftus, E. F. (2003). Make-believe memories. *American Psychologist, 58,* 867–873.

Loftus, E. F. (2004). Memories of things unseen. *Current Directions in Psychological Science, 13,* 145–147.

Loftus, E. F., Miller, D. G., & Burns, H. J. (1978). Semantic integration of verbal information into a visual memory. *Journal of Experimental Psychology: Human Learning and Memory, 4,* 19–31.

Logan, G. D. (2003). Executive control of thought and action: In search of the wild homunculus. *Current Directions in Psychological Science, 12,* 45–48.

Logie, R. H. (1996). The seven ages of working memory. In J. T. E. Richardson et al. (Eds.), *Working memory and human cognition* (pp. 31–65). New York: Oxford University Press.

Logsdon-Conradsen, S. (2002). Using mindfulness meditation to promote holistic health in individuals with HIV/AIDS. *Cognitive and Behavioral Practice, 9,* 67–71.

Lohman, J. J. H. M. (2001). Treatment strategies for migraine headache. *Journal of the American Medical Association, 285,* 1014.

London-Vargas, N. (2001, July). Organizing a life's work: Finding your dream job. *TIP: The Industrial-Organizational Psychologist, Vol. 39*(1). Retrieved August 23, 2001, from http://www.siop.org/TIP/backissues/TipJul01/Jul01TOC.htm.

Lorayne, H. (2002). *The complete guide to memory mastery.* Hollywood, FL: Fell Publishers.

Lorenz, K. (1966). *On aggression.* New York: Harcourt Brace Jovanovich.

Love, J. M., as cited in Gilbert, S. (2003, July 22). Turning a mass of data on child care into advice for parents: Four views. *New York Times,* p. F5.

Lowrey, V. (2004, May 11). It's fizzy and the can is nice, but coffee may be cheaper. *New York Times,* p. F5.

Lubell, S. (2004, February 19). On the therapist's couch, a jolt of virtual reality. *New York Times,* p. G5.

Lubinski, D. (2004). Introduction to the special section on cognitive abilities: 100 Years After Spearman's (1904) "'General intelligence,' objectively determined and measured." *Journal of Personality and Social Psychology, 86,* 96–111.

Luborsky, L., Rosenthal, R., Digue, L., Andrusyna, T. P., Berman, J. S., Levitt, J. T., et al. (2002). The Dodo bird verdict is alive and well—mostly. *Clinical Psychology: Science and Practice, 9,* 2–12.

Lucas, R. E., Clark, A. E., Georgellis, Y., & Diener, E. (2003). Reexamining adaptation and the set point model of happiness: Reactions to changes in marital status. *Journal of Personality and Social Psychology, 84,* 527–539.

Lucassen, P. J., Fuchs, E., & Czeh, B. (2004). Antidepressant treatment with tianeptine reduces apoptosis in the hippocampal dentate gyrus and temporal cortex. *Biological Psychiatry, 55,* 789–796.

Luchins, A. S., & Luchins, E. H. (1994). The water jar experiments and Einstellung effects: II. Gestalt psychology and past experience. *Gestalt Theory, 16*(4), 205–259.

Luna, T. D., French, J., & Mindtcha, J. L. (1997). A study of USAF air traffic controller shiftwork: Sleep, fatigue, activity, and mood analyses. *Aviation, Space, and Environmental Medicine, 68,* 18–23.

Luntz, B. K., & Widom, C. S. (1994). Antisocial personality disorder in abused and neglected children grown up. *American Journal of Psychiatry, 151,* 670–674.

Luo, S., & Klohnen, E. C. (2005). Assortative mating and marital quality in newlyweds: A couple-centered approach. *Journal of Personality and Social Psychology, 88,* 304–326.

Luoma, J. B., Martin, C. E., & Pearson, J. L. (2002). Contact with mental health and primary care providers before suicide: A review of the evidence. *American Journal of Psychiatry, 159,* 909–916.

Luria, A. R. (1968). *The mind of a mnemonist.* New York: Basic Books.

Lykken, D. (1999). *Happiness: What studies on twins show us about nature, nurture, and the happiness set-point.* New York: Golden Books.

Lykken, D. (2004). The new eugenics. *Contemporary Psychology: APA Review of Books, 49,* 670–672.

Lykken, D., & Csikszentmihalyi, M. (2001). Happiness—stuck with what you've got? *Psychologist, 14,* 470–472.

Lynch, H. T., Coronel, S. M., Okimoto, R., Hampel, H., Sweet, K., Lynch, J. F., et al. (2004). A founder mutation of the MSH2 gene and hereditary nonpolyposis colorectal cancer in the United States. *Journal of the American Medical Association, 291,* 718–724.

Lyubomirsky, S. (2001). Why are some people happier than others? The role of cognitive and motivational processes in well-being. *American Psychologist, 56,* 239–249.

MacAndrew, D. K., Katzky, R. J., Fiez, J. A., McClelland, J. L., & Becker, J. T. (2002). The phonological-similarity effect differentiates between two working memory tasks. *Psychological Science, 13,* 465–467.

MacDonald, T. K., MacDonald, G., Zanna, M. P., & Fong, G. (2000). Alcohol, sexual arousal, and intentions to use condoms in young men: Applying alcohol myopia theory to risky sexual behavior. *Health Psychology, 19,* 290–298.

Mace, B. L., Bell, P. A., & Loomis, R. J. (1999). Aesthetic, affective, and cognitive effects of noise on natural landscape assessment. *Society & Natural Resources, 12,* 225–242.

Mace, B. L., Clark, S., Bell, P. A., Loomis, R. J., Yafee, J., & Haas, G. (2000, April). *Even rescuing Bambi doesn't help: Helicopter noise degrades evaluation of park scenery.* Paper presented at the meeting of the Rocky Mountain Psychological Association, Tucson, AZ.

Macfarlane, J. A. (1975). Olfaction in the development of social preferences in the human neonate. In M. A. Hofer (Ed.), *Parent-infant interaction.* Amsterdam: Elsevier.

MacGregor, J. N., Ormerod, T. C., & Chronicle, E. P. (2001). Information processing and insight: A process model of performance on the nine-dot and related problems. *Journal of Experimental Psychology: Learning, Memory, and Cognition, 27,* 176–201.

MacPherson, S. E., Phillips, L. H., & Della Sala, S. (2002). Age, executive function, and social decision making: A dorsolateral prefrontal theory of cognitive aging. *Psychology and Aging, 17,* 598–609.

Macrae, C. N., Stangor, C., & Milne, A. B. (1994). Activating social stereotypes: A functional analysis. *Journal of Experimental Social Psychology, 30,* 370–389.

Maddi, S. R., & Khoshaba, D. M. (1994). Hardiness and mental health. *Journal of Personality Assessment, 63,* 265–274.

Magee, W. J., Eaton, W. W., Wittchen, H. U., McGonagle, K. A., & Kessler, R. C. (1996). Agoraphobia, simple phobia, and social phobia in the National Comorbidity Survey. *Archives of General Psychiatry, 53,* 159–168.

Magley, V. J. (2002). Coping with sexual harassment: Reconceptualizing women's resistance. *Journal of Personality and Social Psychology, 83,* 930–946.

Mah, K., & Binik, Y. M. (2001). The nature of human orgasm: A critical review of major trends. *Clinical Psychology Review, 21,* 823–856.

Maier, N. R. F. (1931). Reasoning in humans: II. The solution of a problem and its appearance in consciousness. *Journal of Comparative Psychology, 12,* 181–194.

Main, M. (1996). Introduction to the special section on attachment and psychopathology: 2. Overview of the field of attachment. *Journal of Consulting and Clinical Psychology, 64,* 237–243.

Main, M., & Soloman, J. (1990). Procedures for identifying infants as disorganized/disoriented during the Ainsworth Strange Situation. In M. T. Greenberg, D. Cicchetti, & E. M. Cummings (Eds.), *Attachment in the preschool years: Theory, research, and intervention* (pp. 121–160). Chicago: University of Chicago Press.

Malykh, S. B., Iskoldsky, N. V., & Gindina, E. D. (2005). Genetic analysis of IQ in young adulthood: a Russian twin study. *Personality and Individual Differences, 38,* 1475–1485.

Mansnerus, L., & Kocieniewski, D. (2004, August 14). Ex-aide says he was victim of McGreevey. *New York Times Online.* Retrieved August 18, 2004, from www.nytimes.com/2004/08/14/nyregion/14jersy.html.

Manson, J. E., & Bassuk, S. S. (2003). Obesity in the United States: A fresh look at its high toll. *Journal of the American Medical Association, 289,* 229–230.

Manson, J. E., Skerrett, P. J., Greenland, P., & VanItallie, T. B. (2004). The escalating pandemics of obesity and sedentary lifestyle a call to action for clinicians. *Archives of Internal Medicine, 164,* 249–258.

Marcia, J. E. (1966). Development and validation of ego-identity status. *Journal of Personality and Social Psychology, 3,* 551–558.

Marcia, J. E. (1980). Identity in adolescence. In J. Adelson (Ed.), *Handbook of adolescent psychology* (pp. 159–187). New York: Wiley.

Marcia, J. E., Waterman, A. S., Matteson, D. R., Archer, S. L., & Orlofsky, J. L. (Eds.). (1993). *Ego identity: A handbook for psychosocial research.* New York: Springer-Verlag.

Marcus, R., Hardy, R., Kuh, D., & Wadsworth, M. E. J. (2001). Birth weight and cognitive function in the British 1946 birth cohort: Longitudinal population-based study. *British Medical Journal, 322,* 199–203.

Margoshes, P. (1995, May). For many, old age is the prime of life. *APA Monitor, 26,* 36–37.

Markel, H. (2003, September 3). Lack of sleep takes it toll on student psyches. *New York Times, Science Times,* p. F6.

Markey, C. N., Markey, P. M., & Tinsley, B. J. (2003). Personality, puberty, and preadolescent girls' risky behaviors: Examining the predictive value of the Five-Factor Model of personality. *Journal of Research in Personality, 37,* 405–419.

Markus, H. R., & Kitayama, S. (1991). Culture and the self: Implications for cognition, emotion, and motivation. *Psychological Review, 98,* 224–253.

Maron, B. J. (2000). The paradox of exercise [Editorial]. *New England Journal of Medicine, 343,* 1409–1410.

Marquis, C. (2003, March 16). Living in sin. *New York Times,* p. WK2.

Marsh, A. A., Elfenbein, H. A., & Ambady, N. A. (2003). Nonverbal "accents": Cultural differences in facial expressions of emotion. *Psychological Science, 14,* 373–376.

Marsh, R. L., Hicks, J. L., & Cook, G. I. (2005). On the relationship between effort toward an ongoing task and cue detection in event-based prospective memory. *Journal of Experimental Psychology: Learning, Memory, and Cognition, 31,* 68–75.

Marshal, M. P. (2003). For better or for worse? The effects of alcohol use on marital functioning. *Clinical Psychology Review, 23,* 959–997.

Marshall, N. J. (2004). The quality of early child care and children's development. *Current Directions in Psychological Science, 13,* 165–168.

Martin, C. L., & Fabes, R. A. (2001). The stability and consequences of young children's same-sex peer interactions. *Developmental Psychology, 37,* 431–446.

Martin, D. J., Garske, J. P., & Davis, M. K. (2000). Relation of the therapeutic alliance with outcome and other variables: A meta-analytic review. *Journal of Consulting and Clinical Psychology, 68,* 438–450.

Martin, S. E. (1992). The epidemiology of alcohol-related interpersonal violence. *Alcohol, Health and Research World, 16,* 230–237.

Martin, S. J., Grimwood, P. D., & Morris, R. G. M. (2000). Synaptic plasticity and memory: An evaluation of the hypothesis. *Annual Review of Neuroscience, 23,* 649–711.

Martindale, C. (2001). Oscillations and analogies: Thomas Young, MD, RFS, genius. *American Psychologist, 56,* 342–345.

Maslach, C. (2003). Job burnout: New directions in research and intervention. *Current Directions in Psychological Science, 12,* 189–192.

Maslow, A. H. (1970). *Motivation and personality* (2nd ed.). New York: Harper & Row.

Maslow, A. H. (1971). *Farther reaches of human nature.* New York: Viking Penguin.

Masters, W. H., & Johnson, V. E. (1966). *Human sexual response.* Boston: Little, Brown.

Masters, W. H., & Johnson, V. E. (1970). *Human sexual inadequacy.* Boston: Little, Brown.

Mastroianni, G. R. (2002). Milgram and the Holocaust: A reexamination. *Journal of Theoretical and Philosophical Psychology, 22,* 158–173.

Mataix-Cols, D., Wooderson, S., Lawrence, N., Brammer, M. J., Speckens, A., & Phillips, M. L. (2004). Distinct neural correlates of washing, checking, and hoarding symptom dimensions in obsessive-compulsive disorder. *American Journal of Psychiatry, 61,* 564–576.

Mather, J., Canli, T., English, T., Whitfield, S., Wais, P., Ochsner, K., et al. (2004). Amydala responses to emotionally valuenced stimuli in older and young adults. *Psychological Science, 15,* 259–263.

Matlin, M. (1999). *The psychology of women.* New York: Harcourt-Brace Jovanovich.

Matsumoto, D. (2004). Paul Ekman and the legacy of universals. *Journal of Research in Personality, 38,* 45–51.

Matsumoto, D., Yoo, S. H., Hirayama, S., & Petrova, G. (2005). Development and validation of a measure of display rule knowledge: The display rule assessment inventory. *Emotion, 5,* 23–40.

Matsumoto, K., Suzuki, W., & Tanaka, K. (2003). Neuronal correlates of goal-based motor selection in the prefrontal cortex. *Science, 301,* 229–232.

Matthews, K. A., Wing, R. R., Kuller, L. H., Meilahn, E. N., et al. (1990). Influences of natural menopause on psychological characteristics and symptoms of middle-aged healthy women. *Journal of Consulting and Clinical Psychology, 58,* 345–351.

Mattson, M. P. (2003). Neurobiology: Ballads of a protein quartet. *Nature, 422,* 385–387.

Matz, D. C., & Wood, W. (2005). Cognitive dissonance in groups: The consequences of disagreement. *Journal of Personality and Social Psychology, 88,* 22–37.

Maxson, S. C. (2003). Behavioral genetics. In M. Gallagher & R. J. Nelson (Eds.), *Handbook of psychology: Vol. 3. Biological psychology* (pp. 35–46). New York: John Wiley & Sons.

Mayberry, R. I., Lock, E., & Kazmi, H. (2002). Linguistic ability and early language exposure. *Nature, 417,* 38.

Mayr, U., & Kliegl, R. (2000). Complex semantic processing in old age: Does it stay or does it go? *Psychology and Aging, 15,* 29–43.

Mays, V. M. (2003, August). *Psychology and America's changing demographics.* Paper presented at the meeting of the American Psychological Association, Toronto, CA.

Mazzoni, G., & Memom, A. (2003). Imagination can create false autobiographical memories. *Psychological Science, 14,* 186–188.

McAdams, D. P. (1992). The five-factor model in personality. *Journal of Personality, 60,* 329–361.

McAndrew, F. T., & Milenkovic, M. A. (2002). Of tabloids and family secrets: The evolutionary psychology of gossip. *Journal of Applied Social Psychology, 32,* 1–20.

McBride, C. K., Paikoff, R. L., & Holmbeck, G. N. (2003). Individual and familial influences on the onset of sexual intercourse among urban African American adolescents. *Journal of Consulting and Clinical Psychology, 71,* 159–167.

McClearn, G. E., Johansson, B., Berg, S., Pedersen, N. L., et al. (1997). Substantial genetic influence on cognitive abilities in twins 80 or more years old. *Science, 276,* 1560–1563.

McClelland, D. C. (1958). Risk-taking in children with high and low need for achievement. In J. W. Atkinson (Ed.), *Motives in fantasy, action, and society.* Princeton, NJ: Van Nostrand.

McClelland, D. C. (1965). Achievement and entrepreneurship: A longitudinal study. *Journal of Personality and Social Psychology, 1,* 389–392.

McClelland, D. C. (1985). *Human motivation.* Glenview, IL: Scott, Foresman.

McClelland, D. C., Atkinson, J. W., Clark, R. A., & Lowell, E. L. (1953). *The achievement motive.* New York: Appleton-Century-Crofts.

McCoy, N. L., & Pitino, L. (2002). Pheromonal influences on sociosexual behavior in young women. *Physiology and Behavior, 75,* 367–375.

McCrady, B. S., & Epstein, E. E. (2004). Alcoholics Anonymous and relapse prevention as maintenance strategies after conjoint behavioral alcohol treatment for men: 18-Month outcomes. *Journal of Consulting and Clinical Psychology, 72,* 870–878.

McCrae, R. R. (2004). Human nature and culture: A trait perspective. *Journal of Research in Personality, 38,* 3–14.

McCrae, R. R., & Costa, P. T., Jr. (1986). Clinical assessment can benefit from recent advances in personality psychology. *American Psychologist, 41,* 1001–1003.

McCrae, R. R., & Costa, P. T., Jr. (1996). Toward a new generation of personality theories: Theoretical contexts for the five-factor model. In J. S. Wiggins (Ed.), *The five-factor model of personality: Theoretical perspectives.* New York: Guilford Press.

McCrae, R. R., Costa, P. T., Jr. Martin, T. A., Oryol, V. E., Rukavishnikov, A. A., Senin, I. G., et al. (2004). Consensual validation of personality traits across cultures. *Journal of Research in Personality, 38,* 179–201.

McCrae, R. R., Costa, P. T., Jr., Ostendorf, F., Angleitner, A., Hrebickova, M., Avia, M., et al. (2000). Nature over nurture: Temperament, personality, and life span development. *Journal of Personality and Social Psychology, 78,* 173–186.

McCrae, R. R., Costa, P. T., Jr., Terracciano, A., Parker, W. D., Mills, C. J. De Fruyt, F., et al. (2002). Personality trait development from age 12 to age 18: longitudinal, cross-sectional, and cross-cultural analyses. *Journal of Personality and Social Psychology, 83,* 1456–1468.

McDaniel, M. A., Guynn, M. J., Einstein, G. O., & Breneiser, J. (2004). Cue-focused and reflexive-associative processes in prospective memory retrieval. *Journal of Experimental Psychology: Learning, Memory, and Cognition, 30,* 605–614.

McDermut, J. F., Haaga, D. A. F., & Bilek, L. A. (1997). Cognitive bias and irrational beliefs in major depression and dysphoria. *Cognitive Therapy and Research, 21,* 459–476.

McDermut, W., Miller, I. W., & Brown, R. A. (2001). The efficacy of group psychotherapy for depression: A meta-analysis and review of the empirical research. *Clinical Psychology: Science and Practice, 8,* 98–116.

McDougall, W. (1908). *An introduction to social psychology.* New York: Methuen.

McGinn, L. K., & Sanderson, W. C. (2001). What allows cognitive behavioral therapy to be brief: Overview, efficacy, and crucial factors facilitating brief treatment. *Clinical Psychology: Science and Practice, 8,* 23–37.

McGovern, F. J., & Nevid, J. S. (1986). Evaluation apprehension on psychological inventories in a prison-based setting. *Journal of Consulting and Clinical Psychology, 54,* 576–578.

McGowan, S., Lawrence, A. D., Sales, T., Quested, D., & Grasby, P. (2004). Presynaptic Dopaminergic dysfunction in schizophrenia: A positron emission tomographic [18f]fluorodopa study. *Archives of General Psychiatry, 61,* 134–142.

McGrath, R. E., Wiggins, J. G., Sammons, M. T., Levant, R. F., Brown, A., & Stock, W. (2004). Professional issues in pharmacotherapy for psychologists. *Professional Psychology: Research and Practice, 35,* 158–163,

McGreal, D., & Evans, B. J. (1994). Recall during hypnosis. *Australian Journal of Clinical and Experimental Hypnosis, 22,* 177–180.

McGue, M., & Christensen, K. (2001). The heritability of cognitive functioning in very old adults: Evidence from Danish twins aged 75 years and older. *Psychology and Aging, 16,* 272–280.

McGuffin, P., Rijsdijk, F., Andrew, M., Sham, P., Katz, R., & Cardno, A. (2003). The heritability of bipolar affective disorder and the genetic relationship to unipolar depression. *Archives of General Psychiatry, 60,* 497–502.

McGuffin, P., & Scourfield, J. (1997). A father's imprint on his daughter's thinking. *Nature, 387,* 652–653.

McGuire, P. A. (1998, July). Wanted: Workers with flexibility for 21st century jobs. *APA Monitor, 29*(7), 7.

McGuire, P. A. (2000, February). New hope for people with schizophrenia. *Monitor on Psychology, 31*(2), 24–28.

McKee, B. (2003, September 4). As suburbs grow, so do waistlines. *New York Times,* pp. F1, F13.

McKelvie, S. J. (1997). Perception of faces with and without spectacles. *Perceptual and Motor Skills, 84,* 497–498.

McKenna, M. C., Zevon, M. A., Corn, B., & Rounds, J. (1999). Psychosocial factors and the development of breast cancer: A meta-analysis. *Health Psychology, 18,* 520–531.

McKnight Investigators, The. (2003). Risk factors for the onset of eating disorders in adolescent girls: Results of the McKnight Longitudinal Risk Factor Study. *American Journal of Psychiatry, 160,* 248–254.

McLeod, B. D., & Weisz, J. R. (2004). Using dissertations to examine potential bias in child and adolescent clinical trials. *Journal of Consulting and Clinical Psychology, 72,* 235–251.

McNamar, M. P. (2004, February 10). Research on day care finds few time-outs. *New York Times,* p. F7.

Mead, M. (1935). *Sex and temperament in three primitive societies.* New York: Dell.

Meagher, M. W., Arnau, R. C., & Rhudy, J. L. (2001). Pain and emotion: Effects of affective picture modulation. *Psychosomatic Medicine, 63,* 79–90.

Means, B., & Loftus, E. (1991). When personal history repeats itself: Decomposing memories for recurring events. *Applied Cognitive Psychology, 5,* 297–318.

Means-Christensen, A. J., Snyder, D. K., & Negy, C. (2003). Assessing nontraditional couples: Validity of the Marital Satisfaction Inventory-Revised with gay, lesbian, and cohabiting heterosexual couples. *Journal of Marital and Family Therapy, 29,* 69–83.

Meeks, S., Murrell, S. A., & Mehl, R. C. (2000). Longitudinal relationships between depressive symptoms and health in normal older and middle-aged adults. *Psychology and Aging, 15,* 100–109.

Meeus, W. H. J., & Raaijmakers, Q. A. W. (1995). Obedience in modern society: The Utrecht studies. *Journal of Social Issues, 51,* 155–175.

Melani, D. (2001, January 17). Emotions can pull trigger on heart attack. *Evansville Courier and Press, Scripps Howard News Service.* Retrieved February 20, 2001, from http://www.psycport.com/news/2001/01/17/eng-courierpress.

Meltzoff, A. N., & Gopnik, A. (1997). *Words, thoughts, and theories.* Cambridge, MA: MIT Press.

Melzack, R., & Wall, P. D. (1965). Pain mechanisms: A new theory. *Science, 150,* 971–979.

Melzack, R., & Wall, P. D. (1983). *The challenge of pain.* New York: Basic Books.

Men, muscles and body image. (2000, July 27). Retrieved July 31, 2000, from http://www.cnn.com/2000/HEALTH/mayo/07/27/men.muscles/index.html.

Mendez, J. L., Fantuzzo, J., & Cicchetti, D. (2002). Profiles of social competence among low-income African American preschool children. *Child Development, 73,* 1085–1100.

Merckelbach, H., Arntz, A., & de Jong, P. (1991). Conditioning experiences in spider phobics. *Behaviour Research and Therapy, 29,* 301–304.

Merckelbach, H., de Jong, P. J., Muris, P., & van den Hout, M. A. (1996). The etiology of specific phobias: A review. *Clinical Psychology Review, 16,* 337–361.

Merikangas, K. R., & Risch, N. (2003). Will the genomics revolution revolutionize psychiatry? *American Journal of Psychiatry, 160,* 625–635.

Mesquita, B., & Walker, R. (2003). Cultural differences in emotions: A context for interpreting emotional experiences. *Behaviour Research and Therapy, 41,* 777–793.

Messer, S. B. (2001). What makes brief psychodynamic therapy time efficient? *Clinical Psychology: Science and Practice, 8,* 5–22.

Meston, C. M., & Frohlich, P. F. (2000). The neurobiology of sexual function. *Archives of General Psychiatry, 57,* 1012–1030.

Metcalfe, J. (1986). Feelings of knowing in memory and problem solving. *Journal of Experimental Psychology: Learning, Memory, and Cognition, 12,* 288–294.

Meyer, B., Pilkonis, P. A., Krupnick, J. L., Egan, M. K., Simmens, S. J., & Sotsky, S. M. (2002). Treatment expectancies, patient alliance, and outcome: Further analyses from the national institute of mental health treatment of depression collaborative research program. *Journal of Consulting and Clinical Psychology, 70,* 1051–1055.

Meyer, G. J. (2000). Incremental validity of the Rorschach Prognostic Rating Scale over the MMPI Ego Strength Scale and IQ. *Journal of Personality Assessment, 74,* 365–370.

Meyer, G. J., Finn, S. E., Eyde, L. D., Kay, G. G., Dies, R. R., Eisman, E. J., et al. Amplifying issues related to psychological testing and assessment [Letter]. *American Psychologist, 57,* 140–141.

Meyer, G. J., Finn, S. E., Eyde, L. D., Kay, G. G., Moreland, K. L., Dies, R. R., et al. (2001). Psychological testing and psychological assessment: A review of evidence and issues. *American Psychologist, 56,* 128–165.

Meyer, I. H. (2003). Prejudice, social stress, and mental health in lesbian, gay, and bisexual populations: Conceptual issues and research evidence. *Psychological Bulletin, 129,* 674–697.

Meyer, J. H., McMain, S., Kennedy, S. H., Korman, L., Brown, G. M., DaSilva, J. N., et al. (2003). Dysfunctional attitudes and 5-HT2 receptors during depression and self-harm. *American Journal of Psychiatry, 160,* 90–99.

Meyerowitz, B. E., Richardson, J., Hudson, S., & Leedham, B. (1998). Ethnicity and cancer outcomes: Behavioral and psychosocial considerations. *Psychological Bulletin, 123,* 47–70.

Meyers, A. W., Coleman, J. K., Whelan, J. P., & Mehlenbeck, R. S. (2001). Examining careers in sport psychology: Who is working and who is making money? *Professional Psychology: Research and Practice, 32,* 5–11.

Mezulis, A. H., Abramson, L. Y., Hyde, J. S., & Hankin, B. L. (2004). Is there a universal positivity bias in attributions? A meta-analytic review of individual, developmental, and cultural differences in the self-serving attributional bias. *Psychological Bulletin, 130,* 711–747.

Mignot, E., & Thorsby, E. (2001). Narcolepsy and the HLA System. *New England Journal of Medicine, 344,* 692.

Mikkelson, B., & Mikkelson, D. P. (2004). One man and a baby box. *Urban Legends Reference Pages.* Retrieved September 12, 2004, from www.snopes.com/science/skinner.asp.

Milburn, M. A., Mather, R., & Conrad, S. D. (2000). The effects of viewing R-rated movie scenes that objectify women on perceptions of date rape. *Sex Roles, 43,* 645–664.

Milgram, S. (1963). Behavioral study of obedience. *Journal of Abnormal and Social Psychology, 67,* 371–378.

Milgram, S. (1974). *Obedience to authority.* New York: Harper & Row.

Miller, A. G., Collins, B. E., & Brief, D. E. (1995). Perspectives on obedience to authority: The legacy of the Milgram experiments. *Journal of Social Issues, 51,* 1–19.

Miller, D. (1999, August 20). Television's effects on kids: It can be harmful. *Cable News Network.*. Retrieved July 25, 2005, from http://www.cnn.com/HEALTH/9908/20/kids.tv.effects/.

Miller, E. (1987). Hysteria: Its nature and explanation. *British Journal of Clinical Psychology, 26,* 163–173.

Miller, G. E., & Cohen, S. (2001). Psychological interventions and the immune system: A meta-analytic review and critique. *Health Psychology, 20,* 47–63.

Miller, J. G., & Bersoff, D. M. (1992). Culture and moral judgment: How are conflicts between justice and interpersonal responsibilities resolved? *Journal of Personality and Social Psychology, 62,* 541–554.

Miller, M. (2000, August 10). He just said no to the drug war. *New York Times Magazine,* pp. 32–35.

Miller, S. D., Blackburn, R., Scholes, G., White, G. L., & Mamalis, N. (1991). Optical differences in multiple personality disorder: A second look. *Journal of Nervous and Mental Disease, 179,* 132–135.

Miller, W. C., Ford, C. A., Morris, M., Handcock, M. S., Schmitz, J. L., Hobbs, M. M., et al. (2004). Prevalence of chlamydial and gonococcal infections among young adults in the United States. *Journal of the American Medical Association, 291,* 2229–2236.

Miller, W. R., & Brown, S. A. (1997). Why psychologists should treat alcohol and drug problems. *American Psychologist, 52,* 1269–1279.

Milton, J., & Wiseman, R. (2001). Does Psi exist? Reply to Storm and Ertel (2001). *Psychological Bulletin, 127,* 434–438.

Minda, J. P., & Smith, J. D. (2001). Prototypes in category learning: The effects of category size, category structure, and stimulus complexity. *Journal of Experimental Psychology: Learning, Memory, and Cognition, 27,* 775–799.

Minkin, M. J. (2002, November). "Where'd my sex drive go?" *Prevention, 54* (11), 164–166.

Mischel, W. (1970). Sex-typing and socialization. In P. H. Mussen (Ed.), *Carmichael's manual of child psychology* (3rd ed.). New York: Wiley.

Mischel, W. (1973). Toward a cognitive social learning reconceptualization of personality. *Psychological Review, 80,* 252–283.

Mischel, W. (2004). Toward an integrative science of the person. *Annual Review of Psychology, 55,* 1–22.

Mischel, W., & Shoda, Y. (1995). Cognitive-affective system theory of personality: Reconceptualizing situations, dispositions, dynamics, and invariance in personality structure. *Psychological Review, 102,* 246–268.

Mitka, M. (2000). Psychiatrists help survivors in the Balkans. *Journal of the American Medical Association, 283,* 1277–1228.

Mitka, M. (2003). Economist takes aim at "big fat" US lifestyle. *Journal of the American Medical Association, 289,* 33–34.

Modelska, K., & Cumming, S. (2003). Female sexual dysfunction in postmenopausal women: Systematic review of placebo-controlled trials. *American Journal of Obstetrics and Gynecology, 188,* 286–293.

Mofenson, L. M., & McIntyre, J. A. (2000). Advances and research directions in the prevention of mother-to-child HIV-1 transmission. *Lancet, 355,* 2237, 2244.

Mokdad, A. H., Ford, E. S., Bowman, B. A., Dietz, W. H., Vinicor, F., Bales, V. S., et al. (2003). Prevalence of obesity, diabetes, and obesity-related health risk factors. *Journal of the American Medical Association, 289,* 76–79.

Mokdad, A. H., Marks, J. S., & Stroup, D. F. (2004). Modifiable behavioral factors as causes of death—reply. *Journal of the American Medical Association, 291,* 2942–2943.

Mokdad, A. H., Marks, J. S., Stroup, D. F., & Gerberding, J. L. (2004). Actual causes of death in the United States, 2000. *Journal of the American Medical Association, 291,* 1238, 1241.

Mollica, R. F., Henderson, D. C., & Tor, S. (2002). Psychiatric effects of traumatic brain injury events in Cambodian survivors of mass violence. *British Journal of Psychiatry, 181,* 339–347.

Monroe, S. M., Rohde, P., Seeley, J. R., & Lewinsohn, P. M. (1999). Life events and depression in adolescence: Relationship loss as a prospective risk factor for first onset of major depressive disorder. *Journal of Consulting and Clinical Psychology, 108,* 606–614.

Monson, C. M., Langhinrichsen-Rohling, J., & Binderup, T. (2000). Does "no" really mean "no" after you say "yes"? Attributions about date and marital rape. *Journal of Interpersonal Violence, 15*(11), 1156–1174.

Montgomery, R. L., & Haemmerlie, F. M. (1993). Undergraduate adjustment to college, drinking behavior, and fraternity membership. *Psychological Reports, 73,* 801–802.

Monti, P. M., Binkoff, J. A., Abrams, D. B., & Zwick, W. R. (1987). Reactivity of alcoholics and nonalcoholics to drinking cues. *Journal of Abnormal Psychology, 96,* 122–126.

Moon, C., Cooper, R. P., & Fifer, W. P. (1993). Two-day-olds prefer their native language. *Infant Behavior and Development, 16,* 495–500.

Mooney, M., White, T., & Hatsukami, D. (2004). The blind spot in the nicotine replacement therapy literature: Assessment of the double-blind in clinical trials. *Addictive Behaviors, 29,* 673–684.

Moos, R. H., & Moos, B. S. (2004). Long-term influence of duration and frequency of participation in alcoholics anonymous on individuals with alcohol use disorders. *Journal of Consulting and Clinical Psychology, 72,* 81–90.

Morawska, A., & Oei, T. P. S. (2005). Binge drinking in university students: A test of the cognitive model. *Addictive Behaviors, 30,* 203–218.

Morin, C. M. (2000). The nature of insomnia and the need to refine our diagnostic criteria. *Psychosomatic Medicine, 62,* 483–485.

Morris, P. E., & Fritz, C. O. (2000). The name game: Using retrieval practice to improve the learning of names. *Journal of Experimental Psychology—Applied, 6,* 124–129.

Morris, W. N., Miller, R. S., & Spangenberg, S. (1977). The effects of dissenter position and task difficulty on conformity and response conflict. *Journal of Personality, 45,* 251–256.

Morse, J. (2002, October 7). An Rx for teen sex. *Time,* pp. 64–65.

Motl, R. W., Dishman, R. K., Saunders, R. P., Dowda, M., Felton, G., Ward, D. S., et al. (2002). Examining social–cognitive determinants of intention and physical activity among Black and White adolescent girls using structural equation modeling. *Health Psychology, 21,* 459–467.

Mueser, K. T., & Liberman, R. P. (1995). Behavior therapy in practice. In B. Bongar & L. E. Beutler (Eds.), *Comprehensive textbook of psychotherapy: Theory and practice* (pp. 84–110). New York: Oxford University Press.

Mufson, L., Dorta, K. P., Wickramaratne, P., Nomura, Y., Olfson, M., & Weissman, M. M. (2004). A randomized effectiveness trial of interpersonal psychotherapy for depressed adolescents. *Archives of General Psychiatry, 61,* 577–584.

Mukamal, K. J., Conigrave, K. M., Mittleman, M. A., Camargo, C. A., Jr., Stampfer, M. J., Willett, W. C., et al. (2003). Roles of drinking pattern and type of alcohol consumed in coronary heart disease in men. *New England Journal of Medicine, 348,* 109–118.

Munakata, Y., McClelland, J. L., Johnson, M. H., & Siegler, R. S. (1997). Rethinking infant knowledge: Toward an adaptive process account of successes and failures in object permanence tasks. *Psychological Review, 104,* 686–713.

Muñoz, N., Bosch, X., de Sanjosé, S., Herrero, R., Castellsagué, X., Shah, K. V., Snijders, P. J. F., et al. (2003). Epidemiologic classification of human papillomavirus types associated with cervical cancer. *New England Journal of Medicine, 348,* 518–527.

Murphy, S. T., & Zajonc, R. B. (1993). Affect, cognition, and awareness: Affective priming with optimal and suboptimal stimulus exposures. *Journal of Personality and Social Psychology, 64,* 723–739.

Murray, B. (1995, November). Gender gap in math scores is closing. *APA Monitor, 26*(11), 43.

Murray, B. (1997, January). America still lags behind in mathematics test scores. *APA Monitor, 28*(1), 44.

Murray, B. (2003, October). The seven sins of memory. *Monitor on Psychology, 34,* 28.

Murray, D. J., Kilgour, A. R., & Wasylkiw, L. (2000). Conflicts and missed signals in psychoanalysis, behaviorism, and Gestalt psychology. *American Psychologist, 55,* 422–426.

Murray, H. A. (1938). *Explorations in personality.* New York: Oxford University Press.

Murstein, B. I., & Mathes, S. (1996). Projection on projective techniques pathology: The problem that is not being addressed. *Journal of Personality Assessment, 66,* 337–349.

Mustanski, B. S., Viken, R. J., Kaprio, J., Pulkkinen, L., & Rose, R. J. (2004). Genetic and environmental influences on pubertal development: Longitudinal data from Finnish twins at ages 11 and 14. *Developmental Psychology, 40,* 1188–1198.

Nabel, E. G. (2003). Cardiovascular disease. *New England Journal of Medicine, 349,* 60–72.

Nagourney, E. (2001, January 23). Curbing aggression with the off switch. *New York Times,* p. F7.

Nagourney, E. (2003). Cellphone peril, hands on or off. *New York Times,* p. F6.

Naimi, T. S., Brewer, R. D., Mokdad, A., Denny, C., Serdula, M. K., & Marks, J. S. (2003). Binge drinking among US adults. *Journal of the American Medical Association, 289,* 70–75.

Nash, M. (1987). What, if anything, is regressed about hypnotic age regression? A review of the empirical literature. *Psychological Bulletin, 102,* 42–52.

Nathan, P. E., Stuart, S. P., & Dolan, S. L. (2000). Research on psychotherapy efficacy and effectiveness: Between Scylla and Charybdis? *Psychological Bulletin, 126,* 964–981.

National Cancer Institute. (2005). *Surveillance, Epidemiology, and End Results (SEER) Program.* National Cancer Institute, DCCPS, Surveillance Research Program, Cancer Statistics Branch, released April 2005. Retrieved July 6, 2005, from www.seer.cancer.gov.

National Center for Health Statistics. (2004). *Deaths: Final data for 2002* (Vol. 53, No. 5). Retrieved June 16, 2005, from www.cdc.gov/nchs/data/nvsr/nvsr53/nvsr53_05acc.pdf.

National Heart, Lung, and Blood Institute, National Institutes of Health (1993, March). *Data fact sheet: Obesity and cardiovascular disease.* Bethesda, MD: Author.

National Institute of Mental Health (NIMH). (2000). *Depression research at the National Institute of Mental Health* (NIH Publication No. 00–4501). Retrieved from http://www.nimh.nih.gov/publicat/depresfact.cfm.

National Institute on Alcohol Abuse and Alcoholism. (1996, September). *State trends in alcohol-related mortality, 1979–92. U.S. Alcohol Epidemiologic Data Reference Manual, Vol. 5* (NIH Publication No. 96–4174). Rockville, MD: Author.

National Institutes of Health (NIH) (2003). *HIV/AIDS, severe mental illness and homelessness.* Retrieved March 24, 2004, from http://grants.nih.gov/grants/guide/pa-files/PA-04-024.html.

National Science Foundation. (2004, April). *Science and engineering degrees, by race/ethnicity of recipients: 1992–2001* (NSF 04–318, Division of Science Resources Statistics). Arlington, VA: Author.

National Sleep Foundation. (2005). *Sleep in America.* Retrieved March 30, 2005, from http://www.sleepfoundation.org/hottopics/index.php?secid=16.

National Women's Health Information Center, U.S. Department of Health and Human Services. (2005, April). *AIDS worldwide.* Retrieved July 1, 2005, from http://www.4woman.gov/HIV/world.cfm.

Naughton, K. (2004, February 2). The soft sell. *Newsweek,* pp. 46–47.

Navarro, M. (2000, November 9). Going beyond black and white, Hispanics in Census pick "other." *New York Times,* pp. A1, A27.

Nawrot, M., Nordenstrom, B., & Olson, A. (2004). Disruption of eye movements by ethanol intoxication affects perception of depth from motion parallax. *Psychological Science, 15,* 858–865.

NCA (2005). Vulnerability to mental illnesses: Gender makes a difference, and so does providing good psychiatric care. *American Journal of Psychiatry, 162,* 211–213.

Neath, I. (1998). *Human memory: An introduction to research, data, and theory.* Pacific Grove, CA: Brooks/Cole.

Neff, J. A., & Hoppe, S. K. (1993). Race/ethnicity, acculturation, and psychological distress: Fatalism and religiosity as cultural resources. *Journal of Community Psychology, 21,* 3–20.

Negy, C., & Snyder, D. K. (2000). Relationship satisfaction of Mexican American and non-Hispanic white American interethnic couples: Issues of acculturation and clinical intervention. *Journal of Marital and Family Therapy, 26,* 293–304.

Negy, C., & Woods, D. J. (1992). A note on the relationship between acculturation and socioeconomic status. *Hispanic Journal of Behavioral Sciences, 14,* 248–251.

Neher, A. (1996). Jung's theory of archetypes: A critique. *Journal of Humanistic Psychology, 36*(2), 61–91.

Neisser, U., Boodoo, G., Bouchard, T. J., Jr., Boykin, A. W., Brody, N., Ceci, S. J., et al. (1996). Intelligence: Knowns and unknowns. *American Psychologist, 51,* 77–101.

Neitz, M., & Neitz, J. (1995). Numbers and ratios of visual pigment genes for normal red-green color vision. *Science, 267,* 1013–1016.

Nelson, D. L., & Gibbs, R. A. (2004). The critical region in trisomy 21. *Science, 306,* 619–621.

Nelson, D. L., McEvoy, C. L., & Pointer, L. (2003). Spreading activation or spooky action at a distance? *Journal of Experimental Psychology: Learning, Memory, and Cognition, 29,* 42–52.

Nelson, N. J. (2000). Do follow-up tests actually help detect recurrent disease? *Journal of the National Cancer Institute, 92,* 1798–1800.

Nelson, T. D. (2002). The psychology of prejudice. Needham Heights, MA: Allyn & Bacon.

Nemiah, J. C. (1978). Psychoneurotic disorders. In A. M. Nicholi, Jr. (Ed.), *The new Harvard guide to psychiatry* (pp. 234–258). Cambridge, MA: Belknap Press.

Neto, F. (2001). Personality predictors of happiness. *Psychological Reports, 88,* 817–824.

Nevid, J. S. (1984). Sex differences in factors of romantic attraction. *Sex Roles, 11*(5/6), 401–411.

Nevid, J. S. (1998). *Choices: Sex in the age of STDs* (2nd ed.). Needham Heights, MA: Allyn & Bacon.

Nevid, J. S., Lavi, B., & Primavera, L. H. (1986). Cluster analysis of training orientations in clinical psychology. *Professional Psychology: Research and Practice, 17,* 367–370.

Nevid, J. S., Lavi, B., & Primavera, L. H. (1987). Principal components analysis of therapeutic orientations of doctoral programs in clinical psychology. *Journal of Clinical Psychology, 43,* 723–729.

Nevid, J. S., & Rathus, S. A. (2005). *Psychology and the challenges of life: Adjustment in the new millennium* (9th ed.). New York: Wiley.

Nevid, J. S., Rathus, S. A., & Greene, B. A. (2006). *Abnormal psychology in a changing world* (6th ed.). Upper Saddle River, NJ: Prentice-Hall.

Nevid, J. S., Rathus, S. A., & Greene, B. A. (2003). *Abnormal psychology in a changing world* (5th ed.). Upper Saddle River, NJ: Prentice Hall.

Nevid, J. S., Rathus, S. A., & Rubenstein, H. R. (1998). *Health in the new millennium.* New York: Worth.

Nevid, J. S., & Sta. Maria, N. (1999). Multicultural issues in qualitative research. *Psychology and Marketing, 16,* 305–325.

New method helps map women's happiness. (2004, December 3). *MSNBC.com.* Retrieved December 3, 2004, from http://www.msnbc.msn.com/id/6640833/.

New studies define cell-phone hazards. (2003, May). *Consumer Reports,* p. 8.

Newby-Clark, I. R., McGregor, I., & Zanna, M. P. (2002). Thinking and caring about cognitive inconsistency: When and for whom does attitudinal ambivalence feel uncomfortable? *Journal of Personality and Social Psychology, 82,* 157–166.

Niaura, R., Todaro, J. F., Stroud, L., Spiro, A., III, Ward, K. D., & Weiss, S. (2002). Hostility, the metabolic syndrome, and incident coronary heart disease. *Health Psychology, 21,* 588–593.

NICHD Early Child Care Research Network. (1997). The effects of infant child care on infant-mother attachment security: Results of the NICHD study of early child care. *Child Development, 68,* 860–879.

Nicholson, R. A., Mouton, G. J., Bagby, R. M., Buis, T., Peterson, S. A., & Buigas, R. A. (1997). Utility of MMPI-2 indicators of response distortion: Receiver operating characteristic analysis. *Psychological Assessment, 9,* 471–479.

Nickerson, R. A., & Adams, M. J. (1979). Long-term memory for a common object. *Cognitive Psychology, 11,* 287–307.

NIDA Notes (2004, December). 2003 survey reveals increase in prescription drug abuse, sharp drop in abuse of hallucinogens. *NIDA Notes, 19*(4), 14.

Nieto, F. J., Young, T. B., Lind, B. K., Shahar, E., Samet, J. M., Redline S., et al. (2000). Association of sleep-disordered breathing, sleep apnea, and hypertension in a large community-based study. *Journal of the American Medical Association, 283,* 1829–1836.

Nigg, J. T., John, O. P., Blaskey, L. G., Huang-Pollock, C. L., Willcut, E. G., Hinshaw, S. P., & Pennington, B. (2002). Big five dimensions and ADHD symptoms: Links between personality traits and clinical symptoms. *Journal of Personality and Social Psychology, 83,* 451–469.

NIH Consensus Development Panel on Osteoporosis Prevention, Diagnosis, and Therapy. (2001). Osteoporosis prevention, diagnosis, and therapy. *Journal of the American Medical Association, 285,* 785–795.

NIMH (National Institute of Mental Health). (2001). *Seeing our feelings: Imaging emotion in the brain* (NIH Publication No. 01–460). Bethesda, MD: Author.

NIMH (National Institute of Mental Health). (2003, July 17). Gene more than doubles risk of depression following life stresses. *NIMH Press Office.* Retrieved July 19, 2003, from http://www.nih.gov/news/pr/jul2003/nimh-17.htm.

Nisbett, R. E. (2003). *The geography of thought: How Asians and Westerners think differently . . . and why.* New York: Free Press.

Nisbett, R., Peng, K., Choi, I., & Norenzayan, A. (2001). Culture and systems of thought: Holistic versus analytic cognition. *Psychological Review, 108,* 291–310.

Nolen-Hoeksema, S. (2000). The role of rumination in depressive disorders and mixed anxiety/depressive symptoms. *Journal of Abnormal Psychology, 109,* 504–511.

Nolen-Hoeksema, S., & Girgus, J. S. (1994). The emergence of gender differences in depression during adolescence. *Psychological Bulletin, 115,* 424–443.

Norcross, J. C. (2002). (Ed.). *Psychotherapy relationships that work: Therapist contributions and responsiveness to patients.* London: Oxford University Press.

Norlander, T., Erixon, A., & Archer, T. (2000). Psychological androgyny and creativity: Dynamics of gender-role and personality trait. *Social Behavior and Personality, 28*(5), 423–435.

Norris, F. N., Murphy, A. D., Baker, C. K., Perilla, J. L., Rodriguez, F. G, & Rodriguez, J. D. (2003). Epidemiology of trauma and posttraumatic stress disorder in Mexico. *Journal of Abnormal Psychology, 112,* 646–656.

Nosek, B. A., Banaji, M. R., & Greenwald, A. G. (2003). Math = male, me = female, therefore math ≠ me. *Journal of Personality and Social Psychology, 83,* 44–59.

Nowak, A., Vallacher, R. R., & Miller, M. E. (2003). Social influence and group dynamics. In T. Millon & M. J. Lerner (Eds.), *Handbook of psychology: Vol. 5. Personality and social psychology* (pp. 383–418). New York: John Wiley & Sons.

NSAID use may help prevent Parkinson's. (2003, August 19). *USA Today,* p. 7D.

Nuland, S. (2003, May 19). "Where doesn't it hurt." *Newsweek,* p. 62.

Nurnberg, H. G., Hensley, P. L., Gelenberg, A. J., Fava, M., Lauriello, J., & Paine, S. (2003). Treatment of antidepressant-associated sexual dysfunction with sildenafil. *Journal of the American Medical Association, 289,* 56–64.

Nussbaum, R. L., & Ellis, C. E. (2003). Alzheimer's disease and Parkinson's disease. *New England Journal of Medicine, 348,* 1356–1364.

Oakes, M. E., Slotterback, C. S., & Mecca, E. K. (2003). Gender differences in acceptable body weights. *Current Psychology, 22,* 93–99.

Oberauer, K., & Kliegl, R. (2004). Simultaneous cognitive operations in working memory after dual-task practice. *Journal of Experimental Psychology-Human Perception and Performance, 30,* 689–707.

Obesity hikes risk for nine types of cancers. (2004, August 23). *MSNBC Web Posting.* Retrieved August 24, 2004, from http://www.usatoday.com/news/health/2004–08-23-obesity-cancer_x.htm.

Obesity rising sharply among U.S. preschoolers. (2004, December 30). *Cable News Network..* Retrieved December 31, 2004, from http://www.cnn.com/2004/HEALTH/conditions/12/30/childhood.obesity.index.html.

O'Brien, C. P., Childress, A. R., Mclellan, A. T., & Ehrman, R. (1992). Classical conditioning in drug-dependent humans. *Annals of the New York Academy of Sciences, 654,* 400–415.

O'Connor, A. (2004a, March 16). In sex, brain studies show, 'la difference' still holds. *New York Times, Science Times,* p. F5.

O'Connor, A. (2004b, March 23). Dreams ride on Freud's royal road, study finds. *New York Times,* p. F5.

O'Connor, A. (2005, Feburary 8). Really? *New York Times,* p. F5.

O'Connor, R. M., & Little, I. S. (2003). Revisiting the predictive validity of emotional intelligence: Self-report versus ability-based measures. *Personality and Individual Differences, 35,* 1893–1902.

O'Connor, T. G., Caspi, A., DeFries, J. C., & Plomin, R. (2000). Are associations between parental divorce and children's adjustment genetically mediated? An adoption study. *Developmental Psychology, 36,* 429–437.

O'Donnell, J. (2003, April 24). Traffic deaths rise to 12-year high. *USA Today,* p. 1D.

O'Donohue, W., Yeater, E. A., & Fanetti, M. (2003). Rape prevention with college males: The roles of rape myth acceptance, victim empathy, and outcome expectancies. *Journal of Interpersonal Violence, 18,* 513–531.

Officials see more eating disorders in men. (2004, September 21). *Associated Press Online.* Retrieved September 24, 2004, from http://www.psycport.com/showArticle.cfm?xmlFile=ap%5F2004%5F09%5F21%5F%2D%2D%2D%2D%2D%5F5574%2D4541%2DMale%2DEating%2DDis%2E%2Exml&provider=Associated%20Press.

Öhman, A., & Mineka, S. (2001). Fears, phobias, and preparedness: Toward an evolved module of fear and fear learning. *Psychological Review, 108,* 483–522.

Ojemann, G. A., Schoenfield-McNeill, J., & Corina, D. P. (2002). Anatomic subdivisions in human temporal cortical neuronal activity related to recent verbal memory. *NatureNeuroscience, 5,* 64–71.

Olfson, M., Marcus, S. C., Druss, B., Elinson, L., Tanielian, T., & Pincus, H. A. (2002). National trends in the outpatient treatment of depression. *Journal of the American Medical Association, 287,* 203–209.

Olivardia, R., Pope, H. G., Jr., Borowiecki, J. J., III, & Cohane, G. H. (2004). Biceps and body image: The relationship between muscularity and self-esteem, depression, and eating disorder symptoms. *Psychology of Men and Masculinity, 5* (2), 112–120.

Olkin, R. (2002). Could you hold the door for me? Including disability in diversity. *Cultural Diversity and Ethnic Minority Psychology, 8,* 130–137.

Olshansky, S. J., Passaro, D. J., Hershow, R. C., Layden, J., Carnes, B. A., Brody, J., et al. (2005). A potential decline in life expectancy in the United States in the 21st Century. *New England Journal of Medicine, 352,* 1138–1145.

Olson, E. (2001, October 7). Countries lag in treating mental illness, W. H. O. says. *New York Times,* p. A24.

Olson, J. M., & Maio, G. R (2003). Attitudes in social behavior. In T. Millon & M. J. Lerner (Eds.), *Handbook of psychology: Vol. 5. Personality and social psychology* (pp. 299–326). New York: John Wiley & Sons.

Olson, S. L., Bates, J. E., & Kaskie, B. (1992). Caregiver-infant interaction antecedents of children's school-age cognitive ability. *Merrill-Palmer Quarterly, 38,* 309–330.

O'Neil, J. (2003, February 4). Job your memory? At the gym? *New York Times,* p. F6.

Onion, A. (2000, September 12). Mind games: Subliminal ads mostly ineffective, but Americans think otherwise. *ABC News.com.* Retrieved September 19, 2000, from http://abcnews.go.com/sections/science/Daily News/subliminal000912.html.

Onishi, N. (2004, January 8). Never lost, but found daily: Japanese honesty. *New York Times,* pp. A1, A4.

Oquendo, M. A., Friend, J. M., Halberstam, B., Brodsky, B. S., Burke, A. K., Grunebaum, M. F., Malone, K. M., & Mann, J. J. (2003). Association of comorbid posttraumatic stress disorder and major depression with greater risk for suicidal behavior. *American Journal of Psychiatry, 160,* 580–582.

O'Reilly, C. A., & Chatman, J. A. (1996). Culture as social control: Corporations, cults, and commitment. In B. M. Staw & L. L. Cummings (Eds.), *Research in organizational behavior: An annual series of analytical essays and critical reviews* (Vol. 18, pp. 157–200). Stamford, CT: JAI Press.

Ormerod, T. C., MacGregor, J. N., & Chronicle, E. P. (2002). Dynamics and constraints in insight problem solving. *Journal of Experimental Psychology: Learning, Memory, and Cognition, 28,* 791–799.

Ortega, A. N., Rosenheck, R., Alegria, M., & Desai, R. A. (2000). Acculturation and the lifetime risk of psychiatric and substance use disorders among Hispanics. *Journal of Nervous and Mental Disease, 188,* 728–735.

Orth-Gomer, K., Wamala, S. P., Horsten, M., Schenck-Gustafsson, K., Schneiderman, N., & Mittleman, M. A. (2000). Marital stress worsens prognosis in women with coronary heart disease: The Stockholm Female Coronary Risk Study. *Journal of the American Medical Association, 284,* 3008–3014.

Osborne, A. F. (1963). *Applied imagination: Principles and procedures of creative problem solving.* New York: Scribners.

Osborne, L. (2001, May 6). Regional disturbances. *New York Times,* pp. 98–102.

Osman, S. L. (2003). Predicting men's rape perceptions based on the belief that "No" really means "Yes." *Journal of Applied Social Psychology, 33,* 683–692.

Ostler, K., Thompson, C., Kinmonth, A. L. K., Peveler, R. C., Stevens, L., & Stevens, A. (2001). Influence of socio-economic deprivation on the prevalence and outcome of depression in primary care: The Hampshire Depression Project. *British Journal of Psychiatry, 178,* 12–17.

Otto, R. K., & Heilbrun, K. (2002). The practice of forensic psychology: A look toward the future in light of the past. *American Psychologist, 57,* 5–18.

Ouellette, S. C., & DiPlacido, J. (2001). Personality's role in the protection and enhancements of health: Where the research has been, where it is stuck, how it might move. In A. Baum, T. A. Revenson, & J. E. Singer (Eds.), *Handbook of health psychology* (pp. 175–194). Mahwah, NJ: Lawrence Erlbaum Associates.

Overton, W. F. (1997). *Developmental psychology: Philosophy, concepts, and methodology.* New York: Oxford University Press.

Oyserman, D., Coon, H. M., & Kemmelmeier, M. (2002). Rethinking individualism and collectivism: evaluation of theoretical assumptions and meta-analyses. *Psychological Bulletin, 128,* 3–72.

Oyserman, D., Gant, L., & Ager, J. (1995). A socially contextualized model of African American identity: Possible selves and school persistence. *Journal of Personality and Social Psychology, 69,* 1216–1232.

Oyserman, D., Kemmelmeier, M., & Coon, H. M., (2002). Cultural psychology, A New Look: Reply to Bond (2002), Fiske (2002), Kitayama (2002), and Miller (2002). *Psychological Bulletin, 128,* 110–117.

Oz, M. (2003, January 20). Say "om" before surgery. *Time,* p. 43.

Ozegovic, J. J., Bikos, L. H., & Szymanski, D. M. (2001). Trends and predictors of alcohol use among undergraduate female students. *Journal of College Student Development, 42,* 1–9.

Ozer, E. J., & Weiss, D. S. (2004). Who develops posttraumatic stress disorder? *Current Directions in Psychological Science, 13,* 169–172.

Özgen, E. (2004). Language, learning, and color perception. *Current Directions in Psychological Science, 13,* 95–102.

Özgen, E., & Davies, I. R. L. (2002). Acquisition of categorical color perception: A perceptual learning approach to the linguistic relativity hypothesis. *Journal of Experimental Psychology: General, 131,* 477–493.

Pallesen, S., Hilde, I. N., Havik, O. E., & Nielsen, G. H. (2001). Clinical assessment and treatment of insomnia. *Professional Psychology: Research and Practice, 32,* 115–124.

Palmiter, D., Jr., & Renjilian, D. (2003). Clinical Web pages: Do they meet expectations? *Professional Psychology: Research and Practice, 34,* 164–169.

Park, D. C., Lautenschlager, G., Hedden, T., Davidson, N. S., Smith, A. D., & Smith, P. K. (2002). Models of visuospatial and verbal memory across the adult life span. *Psychology and Aging, 17,* 299–320.

Park, J., & Banaji, M. R. (2000). Mood and heuristics: The influence of happy and sad states on sensitivity and bias in stereotyping. *Journal of Personality and Social Psychology, 78,* 1005–1023.

Parke, R. D. (2004). Development in the family. *Annual Review of Psychology, 55,* 365–399.

Parke, R. D., & Buriel, R. (1997). Socialization in the family: Ethnic and ecological perspectives. In W. Damon (Editor-in-Chief) & N. Eisenberg (Vol. Ed.), *Handbook of child psychology: Vol. 3. Social, emotional, and personality development* (5th ed., pp. 463–552). New York: John Wiley & Sons.

Parker, J. D. A., Creque, R. E., Sr., Barnhart, D. L., Harris. J.-I., Majeski, S. A., et al. (2004). Academic achievement in high school: Does emotional intelligence matter? *Personality and Individual Differences, 37,* 1321–1330.

Parkes, C. M., & Weiss, R. S. (1983). *Recovery from bereavement.* New York: Basic Books.

Parloff, R. (2003, February 3). Is fat the next tobacco? *Fortune,* pp. 51–54.

Pascalis, O., de Haan, M., & Nelson, C. A. (2002). Is face processing species-specific during the first year of life? *Neuroscience, 296,* 1321–1323.

Pascalis, O., de Haan, M., Nelson, C. A., & de Schonen, S. (1998). Long-term recognition memory for faces assessed by visual paired comparison in 3- and 6-month-old infants. *Journal of Experimental Psychology: Learning, Memory, and Cognition, 24,* 249–260.

Pasternak, T., Bisley, J. W., & Calkins, D. (2003). Visual processing in the primate brain. In M. Gallagher & R. J. Nelson (Eds.), *Handbook of psychology: Vol. 3. Biological psychology* (pp. 139–186). New York: John Wiley & Sons.

Pastor, P., & Goate, A. M. (2004). Molecular genetics of Alzheimer's disease. *Current Psychiatry Reports, 6,* 125–133.

Pasupathi, M. (1999). Age differences in response to conformity pressure for emotional and nonemotional material. *Psychology and Aging, 14,* 170–174.

Pate, J. L. (2000). Psychological organizations in the United States. *American Psychologist, 55,* 1139–1143.

Patrick, A., & Durndell, A. (2004). Lucid dreaming and personality: A replication. *Dreaming, 14,* 234–239.

Patterson, D. R. (2004). Treating pain with hypnosis. *Current Directions in Psychological Science, 13,* 252–255.

Patterson, D. R., & Jensen, M. P. (2003). Hypnosis and clinical pain. *Psychological Bulletin, 129,* 495–521.

Patton, G. C., Coffey, C., Carlin, J. B., Degenhardt, L., Lynskey, M., & Hall, W. (2002). Cannabis use and mental health in young people: Cohort study. *British Medical Journal, 325,* 1195–1198.

Paul, E. L., & Brier, S. (2001). Friendsickness in the transition to college: Pre-college predictors and college adjustment correlates. *Journal of Counseling and Development, 79*(1), 77–89.

Paul, P. (2005, January 17). The power to uplift. *Time,* pp. A46–A48.

Paulus, P. B., & Yang, H.-C. (2000). Idea generation in groups: A basis for creativity in organizations. *Organizational Behavior and Human Decision Processes, 82,* 76–87.

Paunonen, S. V. (1998). Hierarchical organization of personality and prediction of behavior. *Journal of Personality and Social Psychology, 74,* 538–556.

Paunonen, S. V. (2003). Big Five Factors of personality and replicated predictions of behavior. *Journal of Personality and Social Psychology, 84,* 411–424.

Payne, D. G., & Wenger, M. J. (1996). Practice effects in memory: Data, theory, and unanswered questions. In D. Herrmann, C. McEvoy, C. Hertzog, P. Hertel, & M. K. Johnson (Eds.), *Basic and applied memory research: Practical applications* (Vol. 2, pp. 123–138). Mahwah, NJ: Lawrence Erlbaum Associates.

Pear, R. (1999, December 13). Mental disorders common, U.S. says; many not treated. *New York Times,* pp. A1, A30.

Pearson, H. (2003, September 4). Handedness equals hairstyle. *Nature Science Update.* Retrieved September 12, 2002, from http://www.nature.com/nsu/030901/030901–7.html.

Pearson, H. (2004, January 21). Brain size matters for sex: The fear centre finds a role in arousal. *Nature News Service Online.* Retrieved February 22, 2004, from http://cmbi.bjmu.edu.cn/news/0401/78.htm.

Pearson, J. L., & Brown, G. K. (2000). Suicide prevention in late life: Direction for science and practice. *Clinical Psychology Review, 20,* 685–705.

Pedersen, D. M., & Wheeler, J. (1983). The Mueller-Lyer illusion among Navajos. *Journal of Social Psychology, 121,* 3–6.

Peeters, M. C., Bakker, A. B., Schaufeli, W. B., & Wilmar, B. (2005). Balancing work and home: How job and home demands are related to burnout. *International Journal of Stress Management, 12,* 43–61.

Pelham, W. E., Hoza, B., Pillow, D. R., Gnagy, E. M., Kipp, H. L., Greiner, A. R., et al. (2002). Effects of methylphenidate and expectancy on children with ADHD: Behavior, academic performance, and attributions in a summer treatment program and regular classroom settings. *Journal of Consulting and Clinical Psychology, 70,* 320–335.

Pengilly, J. W., & Dowd, E. T. (2000). Hardiness and social support as moderators of stress. *Journal of Clinical Psychology, 56,* 813–820.

Pennebaker, J. W. (2004). Theories, therapies, and taxpayers: On the complexities of the expressive writing paradigm. *Clinical Psychology: Science and Practice, 11,* 138–142.

Penner, L. A., Dovidio, J. F., Piliavin, J. A., & Schroeder, D. A. (2005). Prosocial behavior: Multilevel perspectives. *Annual Review of Psychology, 56,* 365–392.

Peplau, L. A. (2003). Human sexuality: How do men and women differ? *Current Directions in Psychological Science, 12,* 37–40.

Pepper, T. (2005, February 21). Inside the head of an applicant. *Newsweek,* pp. E24–E26.

Peretz, I., & Zatorre, R. J. (2005). Brain organization for music processing. *Annual Review of Psychology, 56,* 89–114.

Perlman, L. M. (2001). Nonspecific, unintended, and serendipitous effects in psychotherapy. *Professional Psychology: Research and Practice, 32,* 283–288.

Perry, P. J., Lund, B. C., Arndt, S., Holman, T., Bever-Stille, K. A., Paulsen, J., et al. (2001). Bioavailable testosterone as a correlate of cognition, psychological status, quality of life, and sexual function in aging males: Implications for testosterone replacement therapy. *Annals of Clinical Psychiatry, 13,* 75–80.

Perry, W. (2003). Let's call the whole thing off: A response to Dawes (2001). *Psychological Assessment, 15,* 582–585.

Pert, C. B., & Snyder, S. H. (1973). Opiate receptor: Demonstration in nervous tissue. *Science, 179,* 1011–1014.

Pesant, N., & Zadra, A. (2004). Working with dreams in therapy: What do we know and what should we do? *Clinical Psychology Review, 24,* 489–512.

Peters, A., von Klot, S., Heier, M., Trentinaglia, I., Hörmann, A., Wichmann, E., et al. (2004). Exposure to traffic and the onset of myocardial infarction. *New England Journal of Medicine, 351,* 1721–1730.

Peterson, B. S., Vohr, B., Staib, L. H., Cannistraci, C. J., Dolberg, A., & Schneider, K. C. (2000). Regional brain volume abnormalities and long-term cognitive outcome in pre-term infants. *Journal of the American Medical Association, 284,* 1939–1947.

Peterson, L. M., Burns, W. J., & Widmayer, S. M. (1995). Developmental risk for infants of maternal cocaine abusers: Evaluation and critique. *Clinical Psychology Review, 15,* 739–776.

Petrides, K. V., Frederickson, N., & Furnham, A. (2004). The role of trait emotional intelligence in academic performance and deviant behavior at school. *Personality and Individual Differences, 36,* 277–293.

Petrill, S. A., & Deater-Deckard, K. (2004). The heritability of general cognitive ability: A within-family adoption design. *Intelligence, 32,* 403–409.

Petrill, S. A., Lipton, P. A., Hewitt, J. K., Plomin, R., Cherny, S. S., Corley, R., et al. (2004). Genetic and environmental contributions to general cognitive ability through the first 16 years of life. *Developmental Psychology, 40,* 805–812.

Petty, R. E., & Wegener, D. T. (1998). Multiple roles for persuasion. In D. T. Gilbert, S. T. Fiske, & G. Lindzey (Eds.), *The handbook of social psychology* (4th ed., Vol. 1, pp. 323–390). Boston: McGraw-Hill.

Petty, R. E., Wegener, D. T., & Fabrigar, L. R. (1997). Attitudes and attitude change. *Annual Review of Psychology, 48,* 609–647.

Petty, R. E., Wheeler, S. C., & Tormala, Z. L. (2003). Persuasion and attitude change. In T. Millon & M. J. Lerner (Eds.), *Handbook of psychology: Vol. 5. Personality and social psychology* (pp. 353–382). New York: John Wiley & Sons.

Pfeffer, J. (1998). Understanding organizations: Concepts and controversies. In D. T. Gilbert, S. T. Fiske, & G. Lindzey (Eds.), *The handbook of social psychology* (4th ed., Vol. 2, pp. 733–777). Boston: McGraw-Hill.

Phillips, S. T., & Ziller, R. C. (1997). Toward a theory and measure of the nature of nonprejudice. *Journal of Personality and Social Psychology, 72,* 420–434.

Phinney, J., & Alipuria, L. (1990). Ethnic identity in older adolescents from four ethnic groups. *Journal of Adolescence, 13,* 171–183.

Piaget, J. (1952). *The origins of intelligence in children.* New York: International Universities Press.

Pickering, T. G. (2003). Lifestyle modification and blood pressure control: Is the glass half full or half empty? *Journal of the American Medical Association, 289,* 2131–2132.

Pihl, R. O., Peterson, J., & Finn, P. (1990). Inherited predisposition to alcoholism: Characteristics of sons of male alcoholics. *Journal of Abnormal Psychology, 99,* 291–301.

Pilcher, H. R. (2003, May 28). Men's underarms may hold clue to new fertility drug. *Nature Science Update.* Retrieved June 10, 2003, from http://www.nature.com/nsu/030527/030527-2.html.

Pillemer, D. B. (1999). What is remembered about early childhood events? *Clinical Psychology Review, 19,* 895–913.

Pinel, J. P. J., Assanand, S., & Lehman, D. R. (2000). Hunger, eating, and ill health. *American Psychologist, 55,* 1105–1116.

Pink, D. (2003, December 14). Gratitude visits. *New York Times Magazine,* p. 73.

Pinker, S. (1994). *The language instinct.* New York: William Morrow.

Pinker, S. (2002). *The blank slate: The modern denial of human nature.* New York: Viking.

Pinquart, M., & Soerensen, S. (2000). Influences of socioeconomic status, social network, and competence on subjective well-being in later life: A meta-analysis. *Psychology and Aging, 15,* 187–224.

Pi-Sunyer, X. (2003). A clinical view of the obesity problem [Editorial]. *Science, 299,* 859–860.

Pitt, M. A., Myung, I. J., & Zhang, S. (2002). Toward a method of selecting among computational models of cognition. *Psychological Review, 109,* 472–491.

Pittman, T. S. (1998). Motivation. In D. T. Gilbert, S. T. Fiske, & G. Lindzey (Eds.), *The handbook of social psychology* (4th ed., Vol. 1, pp. 549–590). Boston: McGraw-Hill.

Plaks, J. E., & Higgins, E. T. (2000). Pragmatic use of stereotyping in teamwork: Social loafing and compensation as a function of inferred partner-situation fit. *Journal of Personality and Social Psychology, 79,* 962–974.

Pliner, P. H., Hart, H., Kohl, J., & Saari, D. (1974). Compliance without pressure: Some further data on the foot-in-the door technique. *Journal of Experimental Social Psychology, 10,* 17–22.

Plomin, R. (2000). Behavioural genetics in the 21st century. *International Journal of Behavioral Development, 24*(1), 30–34.

Plomin, R., & Crabbe, J. (2000). DNA. *Psychological Bulletin, 126,* 806–828.

Plomin, R., DeFries, J. C., Craig, I. W., & McGuffin, P. (Eds.). (2003). *Behavioral genetics in the postgenomic era.* Washington, DC: APA Books.

Plomin, R., & McGuffin, P. (2003). Psychopathology in the postgenomic era. *Annual Review of Psychology, 54,* 205–228.

Plomin, R., & Petrill, S. A. (1997). Genetics and intelligence: What's new. *Intelligence, 24,* 53–57.

Plous, S. (1996). Attitudes toward the use of animals in psychological research and education. *American Psychologist, 51,* 1167–1180.

Plutchik, R. (1980). *Emotion: A psychoevolutionary synthesis.* New York: Harper & Row.

Polinko, N. K., & Popovich, P. M. (2001). Evil thoughts but angelic actions: Responses to overweight job applicants. *Journal of Applied Social Psychology, 31,* 905–924.

Polivy, J., & Herman, C. P. (2002). Causes of eating disorders. *Annual Review of Psychology, 53,* 187–213.

Pollack, A. (2004a, January 13). Sleep experts debate root of insomnia: Body, mind or a little of each. *New York Times,* p. F8.

Pollack, A. (2004b, January 13). Putting a price on a good night's sleep. *New York Times,* pp. CF1, F8.

Pollan, M. (2003, October 12). The (Agri)cultural contradictions of obesity. *New York Times Magazine,* pp. 41, 48.

Pollock, V. E. (1992). Meta-analysis of subjective sensitivity to alcohol in sons of alcoholics. *American Journal of Psychiatry, 149,* 1534–1538.

Pope, H. G., Kouri, E. M., & Hudson, J. I. (2000). Effects of supraphysiologic doses of testosterone on mood and aggression in normal men: A randomized controlled trial. *Archives of General Psychiatry, 57,* 133–140.

Popovich, P. M., Everton, W. J., Campbell, K., Godinho, R. M., Kramer, K. M., & Mangan, M. R. (1997). Criteria used to judge obese persons in the workplace. *Perceptual and Motor Skills, 85,* 859–866.

Posada, G., Carbonell, O. A., Alzate, G., & Plata, S. J. (2004). Through Colombian lenses: Ethnographic and conventional analyses of maternal care and their associations with secure base behavior. *Developmental Psychology, 40,* 508–518.

Powell, E. (1991). *Talking back to sexual pressure.* Minneapolis: CompCare Publishers.

Powell, E. (1996). *Sex on your terms.* Boston: Allyn & Bacon.

Practice Directorate Staff. (2005, February). Prescription for success. *Monitor on Psychology, 36,* 25.

PracticeNet (2003, Summer). Survey results—clinical practice patterns. *American Psychological Association Online.* Retrieved December 11, 2003, from www.apapracticenet.net/results/Summer2003/13.asp.

Pratkanis, A. R. (1992). The cargo-cult science of subliminal persuasion. *Skeptical Inquirer, 16,* 260–272.

Pratto, F., Stallworth, L. M., Sidanius, J., Siers, B., et al. (1997). The gender gap in occupational role attainment: A social dominance approach. *Journal of Personality and Social Psychology, 72,* 37–53.

Premack, D. (1971). Language in chimpanzees. *Science, 172,* 808–822.

Preston, S. H. (2005). Deadweight? The influence of obesity on longevity. *New England Journal of Medicine, 352,* 1135–1137.

Preti, G., Wysocki, C. J., Barnhart, K. T., Sondheimer, S. J., & Leyden, J. J. (2003). Male axillary extracts contain pheromones that affect pulsatile secretion of luteinizing hormone and mood in women recipients. *Biology of Reproduction, 68,* 2107–2103.

Preuss, U. W., Schuckit, M. A., Smith, T. L., Danko, G. P., Bucholz, K. K., Hesselbrock, M. N., et al. (2003). Predictors and correlates of suicide attempts over 5 years in 1,237 alcohol-dependent men and women. *American Journal of Psychiatry, 160,* 56–63.

Pritchard, M. E., & Keenan, J. M. (1999). *Journal of Experimental Psychology: Applied, 5,* 152–168.

Pritchard, M. E., & Keenan, J. M. (2002). Does jury deliberation really improve jurors' memories? *Applied Cognitive Psychology, 16,* 589–601.

Pronin, E., Gilovich, T., & Ross, L. (2004). Objectivity in the eye of the beholder: Divergent perceptions of bias in self versus others. *Psychological Review, 111,* 781–799.

Provine, R. R. (2004). Laughing, tickling and the evolution of speech and self. *Current Directions in Psychological Science, 13,* 215–218.

Prudic, J., et al. (2004). Effectiveness of electroconvulsive therapy in community settings. *Biological Psychiatry, 55,* 301–312.

Pungello, E. P., Kupersmidt, J. B., Burchinal, M. R., & Patterson, C. J. (1996). Environmental risk factors and children's achievement from middle childhood to early adolescence. *Developmental Psychology, 32,* 755–767.

Pushkar, D., Etezadi, J., Andres, D., Arbuckle, T., Schwartzman, A. E., & Chaikelson, J. (1999). Models of intelligence in late life: Comment on Hultsch et al. (1999). *Psychology and Aging, 14,* 520–527.

Qin, P., Agerbo, E., & Mortensen, P. B. (2003). Suicide risk in relation to socioeconomic, demographic, psychiatric, and familial factors: A national register–based study of all suicides in Denmark, 1981–1997. *American Journal of Psychiatry, 160,* 765–772.

Quesnel, C., Savard, J., Simard, S., Ivers, H., & Morin, C. M. (2003). Efficacy of cognitive–behavioral therapy for insomnia in women treated for nonmetastatic breast cancer. *Journal of Consulting and Clinical Psychology, 71,* 189–200.

Quinn, K. P., & McDougal, J. L. (1998). A mile wide and a mile deep: Comprehensive interventions for children and youth with emotional and behavioral disorders and their families. *School Psychology Review, 27,* 191–203.

Quinn, S. (1987). *A mind of her own: The life of Karen Horney.* New York: Summit Books.

Rabasca, L. (2000a, March). Listening instead of preaching. *Monitor on Psychology, 31*(3), 50–51.

Rabasca, L. (2000b, July/August). Therapy that starts online but aims to continue in the psychologist's office. *Monitor on Psychology, 31,* 15.

Rader, N. (1997). Change and variation in responses to perceptual information. In C. Dent-Read & P. Zukow-Goldring (Eds.), *Evolving approaches to organism-environment systems* (pp. 129–158). Washington, DC: American Psychological Association.

Radsch, C. (2004, August 20). Teenagers' sexual activity is tied to drugs and drink. *New York Times on the Web.* Retrieved August 21, 2002, from http://www.nytimes.com/2004/08/20/politics/20drugs.html.

Raeburn, P. (2005, February 20). The therapeutic mind scan. *New York Times Magazine,* pp. 20–21.

Raffaelli, M., & Crockett, L. J. (2003). Sexual risk raking in adolescence: The role of self-regulation and attraction to risk. *Developmental Psychology, 39,* 1–11.

Ragland, J. D., Gur, R. C., Valdez, J., Turetsky, B. I., Elliott, M., Kohler, C., et al. (2004). Event-related fMRI of frontotemporal activity during word encoding and recognition in schizophrenia. *American Journal of Psychiatry, 161,* 1004–1015.

Rahman, Q., & Wilson, G. D. (2002). Born gay? The psychobiology of human sexual orientation. *Personality and Individual Differences, 34,* 1337–1382.

Raine, A., Lencz, T., Bihrle, S., LaCasse, L., & Colletti, P. (2000). Reduced prefrontal gray matter volume and reduced autonomic activity in antisocial personality disorder. *Archives of General Psychiatry, 57,* 119–127.

Rapee, R. M., & Spence, S. H. (2004). The etiology of social phobia: Empirical evidence and an initial model. *Clinical Psychology Review, 24,* 737–767.

Rasenberger, J. (2004, February 8). Kitty, 40 years later. *New York Times,* Section 14, pp. 1, 9.

Rathus, S. A., & Nevid, J. S. (1995). *Adjustment and growth: The challenges of life* (6th ed.). Ft. Worth: Harcourt Brace.

Rathus, S. A., Nevid, J. S., & Fichner-Rathus, L. (2005). *Human sexuality in a world of diversity* (6th ed.). Boston: Allyn & Bacon.

Ratiu, P., & Talos, I.-F. (2004). The tale of Phineas Gage, digitally remastered. *New England Journal of Medicine, 351,* e21.

Ray, O., & Ksir, C. (1990). *Drugs, society, and human behavior* (5th ed.). St. Louis: Times Mirror/Mosby.

Raymond, J. (2000a, Fall/Winter). Kids, start your engines. *Newsweek Special Issue,* pp. 8–11.

Raymond, J. (2000b, Fall/Winter). The world of the senses. *Newsweek Special Issue,* pp. 16–18.

Read, J. P., Wood, M. D., Kahlera, C. W., Maddock, J. E., & Palfaid, T. P. (2003). Examining the role of drinking motives in college student alcohol use and problems. *Psychology of Addictive Behaviors, 17,* 13–23.

Reason, J. T. (1992). Cognitive underspecification: Its variety and consequences. In B. J. Baars (Ed.), *Experimental slips and human error* (pp. 71–91). New York: Plenum.

Recarte, M. A., & Nunes, L. M. (2003). Mental workload while driving: Effects on visual search, discrimination, and decision making. *Journal of Experimental Psychology: Applied, 9,* 119–137.

Rector, N. A., & Beck, A. T. (2001). Cognitive behavioral therapy for schizophrenia: An empirical review. *Journal of Nervous and Mental Disease, 189,* 278–287.

Redd, W. H. (1995). Behavioral research in cancer as a model for health psychology. *Health Psychology, 14,* 99–100.

Redd, W. H., & Jacobsen, P. (2001). Behavioral intervention in comprehensive cancer care. In A. Baum, T. A. Revenson, & J. E. Singer (Eds.), *Handbook of health psychology* (pp. 757–776). Mahwah, NJ: Lawrence Erlbaum Associates.

Redelmeier, D. A., & Tibshirani, R. J. (1997). Association between cellular-telephone calls and motor vehicle collisions. *New England Journal of Medicine, 336,* 453–458.

Reed, G. M., McLaughlin, C. J., & Milholland, K. (2000). Psychology. *Professional Psychology: Research and Practice, 31,* 170–178.

Reese-Weber, M. (2000). Middle and late adolescents' conflict resolution skills with siblings: Associations with interparental and parent-adolescent conflict resolution. *Journal of Youth and Adolescence, 29,* 697–711.

Reese-Weber, M., & Marchand, J. E. (2002). Family and individual predictors of late adolescents' romantic relationships. *Journal of Youth and Adolescence, 31,* 197–206.

Refinetti, R. (2000). *Circadian physiology.* Boca Raton, FL: CRC Press.

Reid, P. T. (2002). Multicultural psychology: Bringing together gender and ethnicity. *Cultural Diversity and Ethnic Minority Psychology, 8,* 103–114.

Reiner, W. G., & Gearhart, J. P. (2004). Discordant sexual identity in some genetic males with cloacal exstrophy assigned to female sex at birth. *New England Journal of Medicine, 350,* 333–341.

Reinisch, J. M. (1990). *The Kinsey Institute new report on sex: What you must know to be sexually literate.* New York: St. Martin's Press.

Reiss, D., Neiderhiser, J. M., Hetherington, E. M., & Plomin, R. (2000). *The relationship code: Deciphering genetic and social influences on adolescent development.* Cambridge, MA: Harvard University Press.

Renner, M. J., & Mackin, R. S. (1998). A life stress instrument for classroom use. *Teaching of Psychology, 25,* 46–48.

Rescorla, R. A. (1967). Pavlovian conditioning and its proper control procedures. *Psychological Review, 74,* 71–80.

Rescorla, R. A. (1988). Pavlovian conditioning: It's not what you think it is. *American Psychologist, 43,* 151–160.

Rescorla, R. A. (1999). Partial reinforcement reduces the associative change produced by nonreinforcement. *Journal of Experimental Psychology: Animal Behavior Processes, 25,* 403–414.

Resnick, M. D., Bearman, P. S., Blum, R. W., Bauman, K. E., Harris, K. M., Jones, J., et al. (1997). Protecting adolescents from harm: Findings from the National Longitudinal Study on Adolescent Health. *Journal of the American Medical Association, 278,* 823–832.

Revenson, T. A., & Baum, A. (2001). Introduction. In A. Baum, T. A. Revenson, & J. E. Singer (Eds.), *Handbook of health psychology* (pp. xv–xx). Mahwah, NJ: Lawrence Erlbaum Associates.

Rey, J. M., & Tennant, C. C. (2002). Cannabis and mental health: More evidence establishes clear link between use of cannabis and psychiatric illness. *British Medical Journal, 325,* 1183–1184.

Reynolds, B., & Karraker, K. (2003). A Big Five model of disposition and situation interaction: Why a "helpful" person may not always behave helpfully. *New Ideas in Psychology, 21,* 1–13.

Rhee, E., Uleman, J. S., & Lee, H. K. (1996). Variations in collectivism and individualism by ingroup and culture: Confirmatory factor analyses. *Journal of Personality and Social Psychology, 71,* 1037–1054.

Rhee, S. H., & Waldman, I. D. (2002). Genetic and environmental influences on antisocial behavior: A meta-analysis of twin and adoption studies. *Psychological Bulletin, 128,* 490–529.

Ribeiro, S., Gervasoni, D., Soares, E. S., Zhou, Y., Lin, S., et al. (2003). Long-lasting novelty-induced neuronal reverberation during slow-wave sleep in multiple forebrain areas. *Public Library of Science, 2*(1), e24 DOI: 10.1371/journal.pbio.0020024.

Ribeiro, S., & Nicolelis, M. (2004). Reverberation, storage, and postsynaptic propagation of memories during sleep. *Learning and Memory, 11,* 686–696.

Ricciardelli, L. A., & McCabe, M. P. (2004). A biopsychosocial model of disordered eating and the pursuit of muscularity in adolescent boys. *Psychological Bulletin, 130,* 179–205.

Ricciardelli, L. A., & McCabe, M. P. (2001). Children's body image concerns and eating disturbance: A review of the literature. *Clinical Psychology Review, 21,* 325–344.

Riccio, D. C., Millin, P. M., & Gisquet-Verrier, P. (2003). Retrograde amnesia: Forgetting back. *Current Directions in Psychological Science, 12,* 41–44.

Rice, N., & O'Donohue, W. (2002). Cultural sensitivity: A critical examination. *New Ideas in Psychology, 20,* 35–48.

Richards, J. C., & Hof, A., & Alvarenga, M. (2000). Serum lipids and their relationships with hostility and angry affect and behaviors in men. *Health Psychology, 19,* 393–398.

Richards, R. J. (2002, October 13). The evolutionary war. *New York Times Book Review,* p. 9.

Richardson, M. A., Bevans, M. L., Read, L. L., Chao, H. M., Clelland, J. D., et al. (2003). Efficacy of the branched-chain amino acids in the treatment of tardive dyskinesia in men. *American Journal of Psychiatry, 160,* 1117–1124.

Ridley, M. (2003). *Nature via nurture genes, experience, and what makes us human.* New York: HarperCollins.

Rieckmann, T. R., Wadsworth, M. E., & Deyhle, D. (2004). Cultural identity, explanatory style, and depression in Navajo adolescents. *Cultural Diversity and Ethnic Minority Psychology, 10,* 365–382.

Riggs, J. M., & Gumbrecht, L. B. (2005). Correspondence bias and American sentiment in the wake of September 11, 2001. *Journal of Applied Social Psychology, 35,* 15–28.

Rilling, J. K., Gutman, D. A., Zeh, T. R., Pagnoni, G., Berns, G. S., & Kilts, C. D. (2002). CD: A neural basis for social cooperation. *Neuron, 35,* 395–405.

Rilling, M. (2000). John Watson's paradoxical struggle to explain Freud. *American Psychologist, 55,* 301–312.

Rind, B., & Strohmetz, D. (1999). Effect on restaurant tipping of a helpful message written on the back of customers' checks. *Journal of Applied Social Psychology, 29*, 139–144.

Ripley, A. (2005, March 7). Who says a woman can't be Einstein? *Time,* pp. 51–60.

Risk factors help ID violence-prone youths, psychiatrists say. (2000, May 16). In *Risk factors for heart disease. A publication of the American Heart Association.*

Riso, L. P., duToit, P. L., Blandino, J. A., Penna, S., Dacey, S., Duin, J. S., et al. (2003). Cognitive aspects of chronic depression. *Journal of Abnormal Psychology, 112*, 72–80.

Roazen, P. (1976). *Erik H. Erikson: The power and limits of a vision.* New York: Free Press.

Roberson, D., Davidoff, J., Davies, I. R. L., & Shapiro, L. R., (2004). The development of color categories in two languages: A longitudinal study. *Journal of Experimental Psychology: General, 133*, 554–571.

Roberti, J. W. (2004). A review of behavioral and biological correlates of sensation seeking. *Journal of Research in Personality, 38*, 256–279.

Roberts, T. A., & Ryan, S. A. (2002). Tattooing and high-risk behavior in adolescents. *Pediatrics, 110*, 1058–1063.

Robin, R. W., Greene, R. L., Albaugh, B., Caldwell, A., & Goldman, D. (2003). Use of the MMPI-2 in American Indians: I. Comparability of the MMPI-2 between two tribes and with the MMPI-2 normative group. *Psychological Assessment, 15*, 351–359.

Robins, R. W., Hendin, H. M., & Trzesniewski, K. H. (2001). Measuring global self-esteem: Construct validation of a single-item measure and the Rosenberg Self-Esteem Scale. *Personality and Social Psychology Bulletin, 27*(2), 151–161.

Robins, R. W., Spranca, M. D., & Mendelsohn, G. A. (1996). The actor-observer effect revisited: Effects of individual differences and repeated social interactions on actor and observer attributions. *Journal of Personality and Social Psychology, 71*, 375–389.

Robins, R. W., Trzesniewski, K. H., Tracy, J. L., Gosling, S. D., & Potter, J. (2002). Global self-esteem across the life span. *Psychology and Aging, 17*, 423–434.

Robinson, C. (1996). Asian culture: The marketing consequences. *Journal of the Market Research Society, 38*(1), 55–62.

Robinson, M. D., Johnson, J. T., & Herndon, F. (1997). Reaction time and assessments of cognitive effort as predictors of eyewitness memory accuracy and confidence. *Journal of Applied Psychology, 82*, 416–425.

Robinson, N. M., Zigler, E., & Gallagher, J. J. (2001). Two tails of the normal curve: Similarities and differences in the study of mental retardation and giftedness. *American Psychologist, 55*, 1413–1424.

Rochat, P. (1993). Hand-mouth coordination in the newborn: Morphology, determinants, and early development of a basic act. In G. J. P. Savelsbergh (Ed.), *The development of coordination in infancy* (pp. 265–288). Amsterdam, Netherlands: North-Holland.

Rodkin, P. C., Farmer, T. W., Pearl, R., & Van Acker, R. (2000). Heterogeneity of popular boys: Antisocial and prosocial configurations. *Developmental Psychology, 36*, 14–24.

Rodriguez, I., Greer, C. A., Mok, M. Y., & Mombaerst, P. (2000). A putative pheromone receptor gene expressed in human olfactory mucosa. *Nature and Genetics, 26*, 18–19.

Rodriguez, N., Myers, H. F., Mira, C. B., Flores, T., & Garcia-Hernandez, L. (2002). Development of the Multidimensional Acculturative Stress Inventory for adults of Mexican origin. *Psychological Assessment, 14*, 451–461.

Roecker-Phelps, C. E. (2001). Children's responses to overt and relational aggression. *Journal of Clinical Child Psychology, 30*, 240–252.

Roemer, L., & Orsillo, S. M. (2003). Mindfulness: A promising intervention strategy in need of further study. *Clinical Psychology: Science and Practice, 10*, 172–178.

Roese, N. J., & Olson, J. M. (1994). Attitude importance as a function of repeated attitude expression. *Journal of Experimental Social Psychology, 30*, 39–51.

Rogers, C. R. (1951). *Client-centered therapy: Its current practice, implications, and theory.* Boston: Houghton Mifflin.

Rogers, C. R. (1961). *On becoming a person.* Boston: Houghton Mifflin.

Rogers, C. R. (1967). Autobiography. In E. G. Boring & G. Lindzey (Eds.), *A history of psychology in autobiography* (Vol. 5, pp. 343–384). New York: Appleton-Century-Croft.

Rogers, C. R. (1980). *A way of being.* Boston: Houghton Mifflin.

Rogoff, B. (1997). Cognition as a collaborative process. In W. Damon (Editor-in-Chief), D. Kuhn, & R. Siegler (Vol. Eds.), *Cognition, perception and language: Vol. 2. Theoretical models of human development* (5th ed., pp. 679–744). New York: John Wiley & Sons.

Romaine, S. (1994). *Language in society: An introduction to sociolinguistics.* Oxford, England: Oxford University Press.

Rosa-Neto, P., Diksic, M., Okazawa, H., Leyton, M., Ghadirian, N., Mzengeza, S., et al. (2004). Measurement of brain regional -[11c]methyl-l-tryptophan trapping as a measure of serotonin synthesis in medication-free patients with major depression. *American Journal of Psychiatry, 61*, 556–563.

Rosch, E., et al. (1976). Basic objects in natural categories. *Cognitive Psychology, 8*, 382–439.

Rosch-Heider, E., & Olivier, D. C. (1972). The structure of the color space in naming and memory for two languages. *Cognitive Psychology, 3*, 337–354.

Rosen, R. C., & Laumann, E. O. (2003). The prevalence of sexual problems in women: How valid are comparisons across studies? Commentary on Bancroft, Loftus, and Long's (2003) "Distress about sex: A national survey of women in heterosexual relationships." *Archives of Sexual Behavior, 32*(3), 209–211.

Rosenbaum, D. E. (2000, May 16). On left-handedness, its causes and costs. *New York Times,* pp. E1, E8.

Rosenberg, D. (2002, December 9). The battle over abstinence. *Newsweek,* pp. 67–71.

Rosenberg, L., Palmer, J. R., & Shapiro, S. (1990). A decline in the risk of myocardial infarction among women who stop smoking. *New England Journal of Medicine, 322*, 213–219.

Rosenheck, R. (2000). Cost-effectiveness of services for mentally ill homeless people: The application of research to policy and practice. *American Journal of Psychiatry, 157*, 1563–1570.

Rosenheck, R., Kasprow, W., Frisman, L., & Liu-Mares, W. (2003). Cost-effectiveness of supported housing for homeless persons with mental illness. *Archives of General Psychiatry, 60*, 940–951.

Rosenthal, D., Wender, P. H., Keyt, S. S., Schulsinger, F., Welner, J., & Ostergaard, L. (1968). Schizophrenics' offspring reared in adoptive homes. In D. Rosenthal & S. S. Kety (Eds.), *The transmission of schizophrenia.* Oxford, England: Pergamon Press.

Rosenthal, D., Wender, P. H., Kety, S. S., Schulsinger, F., Welner, J., & Rieder, R. O. (1975). Parent-child relationships and psychopathological disorder in the child. *Archives of General Psychiatry, 32*, 466–476.

Roth, R. M., Flashman, L. A., Saykin, A. J., McAllister, T. W., & Vidaver, R. (2004). Apathy in schizophrenia: Reduced frontal lobe volume and neuropsychological deficits. *American Journal of Psychiatry, 161*, 157–159.

Rothbart, M. K., Ahadi, S. A., & Evans, D. E. (2000). Temperament and personality. Origins and outcomes. *Journal of Personality and Social Psychology, 78*, 122–135.

Rothbart, M. K., & Bates, J. E. (1997). Temperament. In W. Damon (Editor-in-Chief) & N. Eisenberg (Vol. Ed.), *Handbook of child psychology: Vol. 3. Social, emotional, and personality development* (5th ed., pp. 105–176). New York: John Wiley & Sons.

Rothbaum, B. A., Hodges, L., Smith, S., Lee, J. H., & Price, L. (2000). A controlled study of virtual reality exposure therapy for the fear of flying. *Journal of Consulting and Clinical Psychology, 68*, 1020–1026.

Rothbaum, B. O., Hodges, L., Anderson, P. L., Price, L., & Smith, S. (2002). Twelve-month follow-up of virtual reality and standard exposure therapies for the fear of flying. *Journal of Consulting and Clinical Psychology, 70*, 428–432.

Rotter, J. B. (1966). Generalized expectancies for internal versus external control of reinforcement. *Psychological Monographs, 80* (Whole No. 609).

Rotter, J. B. (1990). Internal versus external control of reinforcement: A case history of a variable. *American Psychologist, 45*, 489–493.

Rotundo, M., Nguyen, D.-H., & Sackett, P. R. (2001). A meta-analytic review of gender differences in perceptions of sexual harassment. *Journal of Applied Psychology, 86*, 914–922.

Rovee-Collier, C. (1996). Measuring infant memory: A critical commentary. *Developmental Review, 16*, 301–310.

Rovee-Collier, C., & Fagen, J. W. (1981). The retrieval of memory in early infancy. *Advances in Infancy Research, 1*, 225–254.

Rowe, D. C. (2001). Do people make environments or do environments make people? In A. Damasio, A. Harrington, et al. (Eds), *Unity of knowledge: The convergence of natural and human science.* Annals of the New York Academy of Sciences, vol. 935 (pp. 62–74). New York: New York Academy of Sciences.

Roy, A. (2003). Characteristics of HIV patients who attempt suicide. *Acta Psychiatrica Scandinavica, 107*, 41–44.

Rozin, P., Bauer, R., & Catanese, D. (2003). Food and life, pleasure and worry, among American college students: Gender differences and regional similarities. *Journal of Personality and Social Psychology, 85*, 132–141.

Rubin, K. H., Burgess, K. B., & Dwyer, K. M. (2003). Predicting preschoolers' externalizing behaviors from toddler temperament, conflict, and maternal negativity. *Developmental Psychology, 39*, 164–176.

Rubin, L. J. (1996). Childhood sexual abuse: False accusations of "false memory"? *Professional Psychology: Research and Practice, 27*, 447–451.

Rubin, R. (2003, April 3). Newly approved HPV test must be used wisely, experts say. *USA Today*, p. 10D.

Rubinow, D. R., & Schmidt, P. J. (1995). The treatment of premenstral syndrome—Forward into the past. *New England Journal of Medicine, 332,* 1574–1575.

Rubinow, D. R., & Schmidt, P. J. (1996). Androgens, brain, and behavior. *American Journal of Psychiatry, 153,* 974–984.

Rubinow, D. R., Schmidt, P. J., & Roca, C. A. (1998). Estrogen-serotonin interactions: Implications for affective regulation. *Biological Psychiatry, 44,* 839–850.

Rubinstein, J. S., Meyer, D. E., & Evans, J. E. (2001). Executive control of cognitive processes in task switching. *Journal of Experimental Psychology: Human Perception and Performance, 27,* 763–797.

Rubinstein, S., & Caballero, B. (2000). Is Miss America an undernourished role model? *Journal of the American Medical Association, 283,* 1569.

Rudman, L. A., Ashmore, R. D., & Gary, M. L. (2001). "Unlearning" automatic biases: The malleability of implicit prejudice and stereotypes. *Journal of Personality and Social Psychology, 81,* 856–868.

Rumbaugh, D. M., & Washburn, D. A. (2003). *Intelligence of apes and other rational beings.* New Haven, CT: Yale University Press.

Runco, M. A. (2004). Creativity. *Annual Review of Psychology, 55,* 657–687.

Rupp, R. (1998). *Committed to memory: How we remember and why we forget.* New York: Crown.

Rutenberg, J. (2001, July 25). Survey shows few parents use TV V-Chip to limit children's viewing. *New York Times*, pp. E1, E7.

Rutledge, T., & Hogan, B. E. (2002). A quantitative review of prospective evidence linking psychological factors with hypertension development. *Psychosomatic Medicine, 64,* 758–766.

Rutter, M., Caspi, A., Fergusson, D., Horwood, L. J., Goodman, R., Maughan, B., et al. (2004). Sex differences in developmental reading disability: New findings from 4 epidemiological studies. *Journal of the American Medical Association, 291,* 2007–2012.

Ruvas-Vazquez, R. A., Johnson, S. L., Rey, G. J., Blais, M. A., & Rivas-Vazquez, A. (2002). Current treatments for bipolar disorder: A review and update for psychologists. *Professional Psychology: Research and Practice, 33,* 212–223.

Ryan, J. P., McGowan, J., McCaffrey, N., Ryan, T., Zandi, T., et al. (1995). Graphomotor perseveration and wandering in Alzheimer's disease. *Journal of Geriatric Psychiatry and Neurology, 8,* 209–212.

Ryan, R. M., & Deci, E. L. (2000). Self-determination theory and the facilitation of intrinsic motivation, social development, and well-being. *American Psychologist, 55,* 68–78.

Rybarczyk, B., Lopez, M., Benson, R., Alsten, C., & Stepanski, E. (2002). Efficacy of two behavioral treatment programs for comorbid geriatric insomnia. *Psychology and Aging, 17,* 288–298.

Ryder, A. G., Alden, L. E., & Paulhus, D. L. (2000). Is acculturation unidimensional or bidimensional? A head-to-head comparison in the prediction of personality, self-identity, and adjustment. *Journal of Personality and Social Psychology, 79*(1), 49–65.

Rypma, B., Prabhakaran, V., Desmond, J. E., & Gabrieli, J. D. E. (2001). Age differences in prefrontal cortical activity in working memory. *Psychology and Aging, 16,* 371–384.

Ryu, S. H., Lee, S. H., Lee, H. J., Cha, J. H., Ham, B. J., Han, C. S., et al. (2004). Association between transporter gene polymorphism and major depression. *Neuropsychobiology, 49,* 74–77.

Saal, D., Dong, Y., Bonci, A., & Malenka, R. (2003). Drugs of abuse and stress trigger a common synaptic adaptation in dopamine neurons. *Neuron, 37,* 577–582.

Sachdev, P., & Hay, P. (1996). Site and size of lesion and psychosurgical outcome in obsessive-compulsive disorder: A magnetic resonance imaging study. *Biological Psychiatry, 39,* 739–742.

Sacks, O. (1985). *The man who mistook his wife for a hat and other clinical tales.* New York: Summit.

Saffran, E. M., & Schwartz, M. F. (2003). Language. In M. Gallagher & R. J. Nelson (Eds.), *Handbook of psychology: Vol. 3. Biological psychology* (pp. 595–636). New York: John Wiley & Sons.

Sage, C., Huang, M., Karimi, K., Gutierrez, G., Vollrath, M. A., Zhang, D.-S., et al. (2005). *Science, 307,* 1114–1118.

Sagie, A. (1998). Employee absenteeism, organizational, and job satisfaction: Another look. *Journal of Vocational Behavior, 52,* 156–171.

Saigal, C. S. (2004). Obesity and erectile dysfunction: Common problems, common solution? *Journal of the American Medical Association, 291,* 3011–3012.

Salkovskis, P. M., & Clark, D. M. (1993). Panic disorder and hypochondriasis. *Advances in Behaviour Research and Therapy, 15,* 23–48.

Salleh, A. (2003, March 17). Marriage makes you a bit happier—for a while. *ABC Science Online.* Retrieved November 13, 2003, from http://www.abc.net.au/science/news/stories/s807111.htm.

Salmon, P. (2001). Effects of physical exercise on anxiety, depression, and sensitivity to stress. A unifying theory. *Clinical Psychology Review, 21,* 33–61.

Salovey, P., & Mayer, J. D. (1990). Emotional intelligence. *Imagination, Cognition, and Personality, 9,* 185–211.

Salthouse, T. A. (2004). What and when of cognitive aging. *Current Directions in Psychological Science, 13,* 140–144.

Samalin, N., & Whitney, C. (1997, December). When to praise. *Parents Magazine*, pp. 51–55.

Samuels, Y., Wang, Z., Bardelli, A., Silliman, N., Ptak, J., Szabo, S., et al. (2004). High frequency of mutations of the PIK3CA gene in human cancers. *Science, 23,* 554.

Sanacora, G., Mason, G. F., Rothman, D. L., Hyder, F., Ciarcia, J. J., Ostroff, R. B., et al. (2003). Increased cortical GABA concentrations in depressed patients receiving ECT. *American Journal of Psychiatry, 160,* 577–579.

Sandlin-Sniffen, C. (2000, November 2). How are we raising our children? *St. Petersburg Times.* Retrieved November 5, 2000, from http://www.psycport.com/news/2000/11/02/eng-sptimes_floridian/eng-sptimes_floridian_071015_110_905256867409.html.

Sapolsky, R. (2000, April 10). It's not "all in the genes." *Newsweek*, pp. 43–44.

Sapolsky, R. M. (2003). Gene therapy for psychiatric disorders. *American Journal of Psychiatry, 160,* 208–220.

Sar, V., Akyuz, G., Kundakci, T., Kiziltan, E., & Dogan, O. (2004). Childhood trauma, dissociation, and psychiatric comorbidity in patients with conversion disorder. *American Journal of Psychiatry, 161,* 2271–2276.

Saucier, D. A., Miller, C. T., & Doucet, N. (2005). Differences in helping Whites and Blacks: A meta-analysis. *Personality and Social Psychology Review,9,* 2–16.

Savage, J. (2004). Does viewing violent media really cause criminal violence? A methodological review. *Aggression and Violent Behavior, 10,* 99–128.

Saxe, R., Carey, S., & Kanwisher, N. (2004). Understanding other minds: Linking developmental psychology and functional neuroimaging. *Annual Review of Psychology, 55,* 87–124.

Scarr, S., & Eisenberg, M. (1993). Child care research: Issues, perspectives, and results. *Annual Review of Psychology, 44,* 613–644.

Scarr, S., Weinberg, R. A., & Waldman, I. D. (1993). IQ correlations in transracial adoptive families. *Intelligence, 17,* 541–555.

Schachter, S. (1971). *Emotion, obesity, and crime.* New York: Academic Press.

Schachter, S., & Singer, J. E. (1962). Cognitive, social, and physiological determinants of emotional state. *Psychological Review, 69,* 377–399.

Schafer, R. B., & Keith, P. M. (1990). Matching by weight in married couples: A life cycle perspective. *Journal of Social Psychology, 130,* 657–664.

Schaie, K. W. (1996). *Intellectual development in adulthood: The Seattle Longitudinal Study.* Cambridge, England: Cambridge University Press.

Schatzberg, A. F. (2002). Brain imaging in affective disorders: More questions about causes versus effects. *American Journal of Psychiatry, 159,* 1807–1808.

Schaubroeck, J., Jones, J. R., & Xie, J. L. (2001). Individual differences in utilizing control to cope with job demands: Effects on susceptibility to infectious disease. *Journal of Applied Psychology, 86,* 265–278.

Scheier, M. F., & Carver, C. S. (1985). Optimism, coping, and health: Assessment and implications of generalized outcome expectancies. *Health Psychology, 4,* 219–247.

Scheier, M. F., Carver, C. S., & Bridges, M. W. (1994). Distinguishing optimism from neuroticism (and trait anxiety, self-mastery, and self-esteem): A re-evaluation of the Life Orientation Test. *Journal of Personality and Social Psychology, 67,* 1063–1078.

Scheier, M. F., Matthews, K. A., Owens, J. F., Schulz, R., Bridges, M. W., Magovern, G. J., et al. (1999). Optimism and rehospitalization after coronary artery bypass graft surgery. *Archives of Internal Medicine, 159,* 829–935.

Schlaggar, B. L., Brown, T. T., Lugar, H. M., Visscher, K. M., Miezin, F. M., & Petersen, S. E. (2002). Functional neuroanatomical differences between adults and school-age children in the processing of single words. *Science, 296,* 1476–1479.

Schmitt, B., Gilovich, T., Goore, H., & Joseph, L. (1986). Mere presence and social facilitation: One more time. *Journal of Experimental Psychology, 22,* 242–248.

Schmitt, D. P. (2003). Universal sex differences in the desire for sexual variety: Tests from 52 nations, 6 continents, and 13 islands. *Journal of Personality and Social Psychology, 85,* 85–104.

Schmitt, E. (2001a, March 8). New census shows Hispanics are even with Blacks in U.S. *New York Times*, pp. A1, A21.

Schmitt, E. (2001b, March 13). For 7 million people in census, one race category isn't enough. *New York Times*, pp. A1, A14.

Schmitt, E. (2001c, April 1). U.S. now more diverse, ethnically and racially. *New York Times*, p. A20.

Schneider, A. (2004, December 3). Early sleep marks the end of adolescence. *News@Nature.com*. Retrieved December 31, 2004, from http://www.nature.com/news/2004/041229/full/041229-5.html.

Schneider, B. H., Atkinson, L, & Tardif, C. (2001). Child-parent attachment and children's peer relations: A quantitative review. *Developmental Psychology, 37*, 86–100.

Schneider, L. S. (2004). Estrogen and dementia: Insights from the Women's Health Initiative Memory Study. *Journal of the American Medical Association, 291*, 3005–3007.

Schneider, L. S., Nelson, J. C., Clary, C. M., Newhouse, P., Krishnan, K. R. R., Shiovitz, T., Weihs, K., et al. (2003). An 8-week multicenter, parallel-group, double-blind, placebo-controlled study of sertraline in elderly outpatients with major depression. *American Journal of Psychiatry, 160*, 1277–1285.

Schneiderman, N. (2004). Psychosocial, behavioral, and biological aspects of chronic diseases. *Current Directions in Psychological Science, 13*, 247–251.

Schneiderman, N., Antoni, M. H., Saab, P. G., & Ironson, G. (2001). Health psychology: Psychosocial and biobehavioral aspects of chronic disease management. *Annual Review of Psychology, 52*, 555–580.

Schneidman, E. S. (1983). On abolishing "death": An etymological note. *Suicide and Life Threatening Behavior, 13*, 176–178.

Schramke, C. J., & Bauer, R. M. (1997). State-dependent learning in older and younger adults. *Psychology and Aging, 12*, 255–262.

Schwartz, B. L. (2002). The phenomenology of naturally occurring tip-of-the-tongue states: A diary study. In S. P. Shohov (Ed.), *Advances in psychology research* (Vol. 8, pp. 73–84). Huntington, NY: Nova Science Publishers.

Schwartz, B. L., & Smith, S. M. (1997). The retrieval of related information influences tip-of-the-tongue states. *Journal of Memory and Language, 36*, 68–86.

Schwartz, C. E., Wright, C. I., Shin, L. M., Kagan, J., & Rauch, S. L. (2003). Inhibited and uninhibited infants "grown up": Adult amygdalar response to novelty. *Science, 300*, 1952–1953.

Schwartz, D., Dodge, K. A., Pettit, G. S., & Bates, J. E. (2000). Friendship as a moderating factor in the pathway between early harsh home environment and later victimization in the peer group: The Conduct Problems Prevention Research Group. *Developmental Psychology, 36*, 646–662.

Schwartz, M. W., & Porte, D., Jr. (2005). Diabetes, obesity, and the brain. *Science, 307*, Issue 5708, 375–379.

Searle, J. R. (1996). *Dualism: Descartes' legacy. The philosophy of mind: The Superstar Teachers Series* [Audiotape]. Springfield, VA: The Teaching Company.

Sedikides, C., Gaertner, L, & Toguchi, Y. (2003). Pancultural self-enhancement. *Journal of Personality and Social Psychology, 84*, 60–79.

Segall, M. H. (1994). A cross-cultural research contribution to unraveling the nativist/empiricist controversy. In J. Lonner & R. Malpass (Eds.), *Psychology and culture* (pp. 135–138). Boston: Allyn & Bacon.

Segall, M. H., Campbell, D. T., & Herskovits, M. J. (1963). Culture differences in the perception of geometric illusions. *Science, 139*, 769–771.

Segall, M. H., Campbell, D. T., & Herskovits, M. J. (1966). *The influence of culture on visual perception*. Indianapolis: Bobbs-Merrill.

Segerstrom, S. C., & Miller, G. E. (2004). Psychological stress and the human immune system: A meta-analytic study of 30 years of inquiry. *Psychological Bulletin, 130*, 601–630.

Seifert, K. L., Hoffnung, R. J., & Hoffnung, M. (2000). *Lifespan development* (2nd ed.). Boston: Houghton Mifflin.

Sekuler, A. B., & Bennett, P. J. (2001). Generalized common fate: Grouping by common luminance changes. *Psychological Science, 12*, 437–444.

Seligman, L., & Hardenburg, S. A. (2000). Assessment and treatment of paraphilias. *Journal of Counseling and Development, 78*, 107–113.

Seligman, M. E. P. (1973). Fall into helplessness. *Psychology Today, 7*, 43–48.

Seligman, M. E. P. (1975). *Helplessness: On depression, development, and death*. San Francisco: Freeman.

Seligman, M. E. P. (2003, August). *Positive psychology: Applications to work, love, and sports*. Paper presented at the meeting of the American Psychological Association, Toronto, CA.

Seligman, M. E. P., & Csikszentmihalyi, M. (2000). Positive psychology: An introduction. *American Psychologist, 55*, 5–14.

Seligman, M. E. P., & Csikszentmihalyi, M. (2001). Reply to comments. *American Psychologist, 56*, 89–90.

Selye, H. (1976). *The stress of life* (rev. ed.). New York: McGraw-Hill.

Sen, S., Nesse, R. M., Stoltenberg, S. F., Li, S., Gleiberman, L., Chakravarti, A., et al. (2003). A BDNF coding variant is associated with the NEO Personality Inventory domain neuroticism, a risk factor for depression. *Neuropsychopharmacology, 28*, 397–401.

Seyfarth, R. M., & Cheney, D. L. (2003). Signalers and receivers in animal communication. *Annual Review of Psychology 54*, 145–173.

Shadish, W. R., & Baldwin, S. A. (2005). Effects of behavioral marital therapy: A meta-analysis of randomized controlled trials. *Journal of Consulting and Clinical Psychology, 73*, 6–14.

Shadish, W. R., Montgomery, L. M., Wilson, P., & Wilson, M. R. (1993). Effects of family and marital psychotherapies: A meta-analysis. *Journal of Consulting and Clinical Psychology, 61*, 992–1002.

Shafran, R., & Mansell, W. (2001). Perfectionism and psychopathology: A review of research and treatment. *Clinical Psychology Review, 21*, 879–906.

Sheets, V., & Ajmere, K. (2005). Are romantic partners a source of college students' weight concern? *Eating Behaviors, 6*, 1–9.

Sheldon, K. M. (2004). The benefits of a "sidelong" approach to self-esteem need satisfaction: Comment on Crocker and Park (2004). *Psychological Bulletin, 130*, 421–424.

Sheldon, K. M., & King, L. (2001). Why positive psychology is necessary. *American Psychologist, 56*, 216–217.

Shellenbarger, S. (2003a, February 27). Multitasking makes you stupid: Studies show pitfalls of doing too much at once. *Wall Street Journal*, p. D1.

Shellenbarger, S. (2003b, March 20). Female rats are better multitaskers; with humans, the debate rages on. *Wall Street Journal*, p. D1.

Shepela, S. T., with J. Cook, E. Horlizt, R. Leal, S. Luciano, & E. Lutfy et al. (1999). Courageous resistance: A special case of altruism. *Theory and Psychology, 9*, 787–805.

Shields, A. E., Fortun, M., Hammonds, E. M., King, P. A., Lerman, C., Rapp, R. et al. (2005). The use of race variables in genetic studies of complex traits and the goal of reducing health disparities: A transdisciplinary perspective. *American Psychologist, 60*, 77–103.

Shiffman, H. R. (2000). *Sensation and perception: An integrated approach* (5th ed.). New York: John Wiley & Sons.

Shiffman, S., Balabanis, M. H., Paty, J. A., Engberg, J., Gwaltney, C. J., Liu, K. S., et al. (2000). Dynamic effects of self-efficacy on smoking lapse and relapse. *Health Psychology, 19*, 315–323.

Shifren, J., & Ferrari, N. A. (2004, May 10). A better sex life. *Newsweek*, pp. 86–87.

Shiner, R. L., Masten, A. S., & Tellegen, A. (2002). A developmental perspective on personality in emerging adulthood: Childhood antecedents and concurrent adaptation. *Journal of Personality and Social Psychology, 83*, 1165–1177.

Shneidman, E. S. (1987). A psychological approach to suicide. In G. R. Vanderbos & B. K. Bryant (Eds.), *Cataclysms, cries, and catastrophes: Psychology in action* (Master Lecture Series, Vol. 6, pp. 151–183). Washington, DC: American Psychological Association.

Shnek, Z. M., Irvine, J., Stewart, D., & Abbey, S. (2001). Psychological factors and depressive symptoms in ischemic heart disease. *Health Psychology*, 141–145.

Short, K. H., & Johnston, C. (1997). Stress, maternal distress, and children's adjustment following immigration: The buffering role of social support. *Journal of Consulting and Clinical Psychology, 65*, 494–503.

Shotland, R., L., & Heinold, W. D. (1985). Bystander response to arterial bleeding: Helping skills, the decision-making process, and differentiating the helping response. *Journal of Personality and Social Psychology, 49*, 347–356.

Shweder, R. A. (1994). Liberalism as destiny. In B. Puka (Ed.), *The great justice debate: Kohlberg criticism. Moral development: A compendium* (Vol. 4, pp. 71–74). New York: Garland Publishing.

Siegal, M., Varley, R., & Want, S. C. (2001). Mind over grammar: Reasoning in aphasia and development. *Trends in Cognitive Sciences, 5*, 296–301.

Siegel, J. M. (2004). Hypocretin (orexin): Role in normal behavior and neuropathology. *Annual Review of Psychology, 55*, 125–148.

Siegler, I., Bosworth, H. B., & Poon, L. W. (2003). Disease, health, and aging. In R. M. Lerner, M. A. Easterbrooks, & J. Mistry (Eds.), *Handbook of psychology: Vol. 6. Developmental psychology* (pp. 423–442). New York: John Wiley & Sons.

Silver, H., Feldman, P., Bilker, W., & Gur, R. C. (2003). Working memory deficit as a core neuropsychological dysfunction in schizophrenia. *American Journal of Psychiatry, 160*, 1809–1816.

Silverman, J. G., Raj, A., Mucci, L. A., & Hathaway, J. E. (2001). Dating violence against adolescent girls and associated substance use, unhealthy weight control, sexual risk behavior, pregnancy, and suicidality. *Journal of the American Medical Association, 286*, 572–579.

Silverman, L. H. (1984). Beyond insight: An additional necessary step in redressing intrapsychic conflict. *Psychoanalytic Psychology, 1*, 215–234.

Simeon, D., Greenberg, J., Knutelska, M., Schmeidler, J., & Hollander, E. (2003). Peritraumatic reactions associated with the World Trade Center disaster. *American Journal of Psychiatry, 160*, 1702–1705.

Simmons, R. G. (1991). Presidential address on altruism and sociology. *Sociological Quarterly, 46,* 36–46.

Simonton, D. K. (2000). Creativity: Cognitive, personal, developmental, and social aspects. *American Psychologist, 55,* 151–158.

Singer, L. T., Minnes, S., Short, E., Arendt, R., Farkas, K., Lewis, B., et al. (2004). Cognitive outcomes of preschool children with prenatal cocaine exposure. *Journal of the American Medical Association, 291,* 2448–2456.

Singer, R. N. (2003). Creating an identity for sport psychology. *APS Observer, 16*(5), 14, 19.

Singer, T., Verhaeghen, P., Ghisletta, P., Lindenberger, U., & Baltes, P. B. (2003). The fate of cognition in very old age: Six-year longitudinal findings in the Berlin Aging Study (BASE). *Psychology and Aging, 18,* 318–331.

Sink, M. (2004, November 9). Drinking deaths draw attention to old campus problem. *New York Times,* p. A16.

Skinner, B. F. (1938). *The behavior of organisms.* New York: Appleton.

Skinner, B. F. (1961). *Cumulative record* (3rd ed.) Englewood Cliffs, NJ: Prentice-Hall.

Skipper, M. (2002). It's all in the mind. *Nature Reviews Genetics, 3,* 650.

Slijper, F. M., Drop, S. L. S., Molenaar, J. C., & de Muinck Keizer Schrama, S. M. P. F. (1998). Long-term psychological evaluation of intersex children. *Archives of Sexual Behavior, 27,* 125–144.

Sloan, D. M., & Marx, B. P. (2004). A closer examination of the structured written disclosure procedure. *Journal of Consulting and Clinical Psychology, 72,* 165–175.

Slutske, W. S., Hunt-Carter, E. E., Nabors-Oberg, R. E., Sher, K .J., Bucholz, K. K., Madden, P. A. F., et al. (2004). Do college students drink more than their non-college-attending peers? Evidence from a population-based longitudinal female twin study? *Journal of Abnormal Psychology, 113,* 530–540.

Small, B. J., Rosnick, C. B., Fratiglioni, L, & Bäckman, L. (2004). Apolipoprotein E and cognitive performance: A meta-analysis. *Psychology and Aging, 19,* 592–600.

Smedley, A., & Smedley, B. D. (2005). Race as biology is fiction, racism as a social problem is real: Anthropological and historical perspectives on the social construction of race. *American Psychologist, 60,* 16–26.

Smith, D. (2001a, September). Harassment in the hallways. *Monitor on Psychology, 32,* 38–40.

Smith, D. (2001b, October). Sleep psychologists in demand. *Monitor on Psychology, 32,* 36–38.

Smith, D. (2002, October). The theory heard "round the world." *Monitor on Psychology, 33,* 30–32.

Smith, D. (2003a, March). Hostility associated with immune function. *Monitor on Psychology, 34,* 47.

Smith, D. (2003b, April). Women and sex: What is "dysfunctional"? *Monitor on Psychology, 34,* 54–56.

Smith, E. E., Balzano, G. J., & Walker, J. H. (1978). Nominal, perceptual, and semantic codes in picture categorization. In J. W. Cotton & R. L. Klatzky (Eds.), *Semantic factors in cognition* (pp. 137–168). Hillsdale, NJ: Erlbaum.

Smith, E. R. (1998). Mental representation and memory. In D. T. Gilbert, S. T. Fiske, & G. Lindzey (Eds.), *The handbook of social psychology* (4th ed., Vol. 1, pp. 391–445). Boston: McGraw-Hill.

Smith, G. E., Petersen, R. C., Ivnik, R. J., Malec, J. F., & Tangalos, E. G. (1996). Subjective memory complaints, psychological distress, and longitudinal change in objective memory performance. *Psychology and Aging, 11,* 272–279.

Smith, G. T., Goldman, M. S., Greenbaum, P. E., & Christiansen, B. A. (1995). Expectancy for social facilitation from drinking: The divergent paths of high-expectancy and low-expectancy adolescents. *Journal of Abnormal Psychology, 104,* 32–40.

Smith, K. H., & Rogers, M. (1994). Effectiveness of subliminal messages in television commercials: Two experiments. *Journal of Applied Psychology, 79,* 866–874.

Smith, M. L., Glass, G. V., & Miller, T. I. (1980). *The benefits of psychotherapy.* Baltimore: Johns Hopkins University Press.

Smith, P. T. (1997). Constraint satisfaction models, and their relevance to memory, aging and emotion. In M. A. Conway (Ed.), *Cognitive models of memory* (pp. 341–364). Cambridge, MA: MIT Press.

Smith, R. E., & Bayen, U. J. (2004). A multinomial model of event-based prospective memory. *Journal of Experimental Psychology: Learning, Memory, and Cognition, 30*(4), 756–777.

Smith, R. E., Smoll, F. L., & Ptacek, J. T. (1990). Conjunctive moderator variables in vulnerability and resiliency research: Life stress, social support and coping skills, and adolescent sport injuries. *Journal of Personality and Social Psychology, 58,* 360–370.

Smith, T. W., & Gallo, L. C. (2001). Personaltiy traits as risk factors for physical illness. In A. Baum, T. A. Revenson, & J. E. Singer (Eds.), *Handbook of health psychology* (pp. 139–174). Mahwah, NJ: Lawrence Erlbaum Associates.

Smock, P. J. (2000). *Annual Review of Sociology.* Cited in Nagourney, E. (2000, February 15). Study finds families bypassing marriage. *New York Times,* p. F8.

Smyth, K. A., Fritsch, T., Cook, T. B., McClendon, M. J., Santillan, C. E., & Friedland R. P. (2004). Worker functions and traits associated with occupations and the development of AD. *Neurology, 63,* 498–503.

Snarey, J. R. (1985). Cross-cultural universality of social-moral development: A critical review of Kohlbergian research. *Psychological Bulletin, 97,* 202–232.

Snibbe, A. C. (2004, November). Taking the "vs." out of nature vs. nurture. *Monitor on Psychology, 35*(10), 22–25.

Snyder, S. H. (2002). Forty years of neurotransmitters: A personal account. *Archives of General Psychiatry, 59,* 983–994.

Society for Industrial and Organizational Psychology. (2001). *Motivation and performance.* Retrieved October 13, 2001, from http://www.siop.org/Instruct/Motivate/MotivIntro.htm.

Solowij, N., Stephens, R. S., Roffman, R. A., Babor, T., Kadden, R., Miller, M., et al. (2002). Cognitive functioning of long-term heavy cannabis users seeking treatment. *Journal of the American Medical Association, 287,* 1123–1131.

Sommerfeld, J. (2002, August 25). Simple test may predict Alzheimer's. *MSNBC Web Posting.* Retrieved August 26, 2002, from http://www.msnbc.com/news/797904.asp.

Soussignan, R. (2002). Duchenne smile, emotional experience, and autonomic reactivity: A test of the facial feedback hypothesis. *Emotion, 2,* 52–74.

Spanos, N. P. (1994). Multiple identity enactments and multiple personality disorder: A sociocognitive perspective. *Psychological Bulletin, 116,* 143–165.

Spearman, C. (1927). *The abilities of man.* New York: Macmillan.

Spector, P. E. (2003). *Industrial and organizational psychology: Research and practice* (3rd ed.). New York: John Wiley & Sons.

Spence, G., Oades, L. G., & Caputi, P. (2004). Trait emotional intelligence and goal self-integration: Important predictors of emotional well-being? *Personality and Individual Differences, 37,* 449–461.

Spencer, S. J., Steele, C. M., & Quinn, D. M. (1999). Stereotype threat and women's math performance. *Journal of Experimental Social Psychology, 35,* 4–28.

Sperling, G. (1960). The information available in brief visual presentation. *Psychological Monographs, 74* (Whole No. 11).

Sperry, R. W. (1982). Some effects of disconnecting the cerebral hemispheres. *Science, 217,* 1223–1226.

Spiegel, D. A., & Bruce, T. J. (1997). Benzodiazepines and exposure based cognitive behavior therapies for panic disorder: Conclusions from combined treatment trials. *American Journal of Psychiatry, 154,* 773–781.

Springen, K. (2003, May 19). Small patients, big pain. *Newsweek,* pp. 54–61.

Springen, K. (2004, May 10). Women, cigarettes and death. *Newsweek,* p. 69.

Springen, K., & Kantrowitz, B. (2004, May 10). Alcohol's deadly triple threat. *Newsweek,* pp. 90–92.

Springen, K., & Seibert, S. (2005, January 17). Artful aging. *Newsweek,* pp. 56–65.

Springer, S. P., & Deutsch, G. (1993). *Left brain, right brain* (4th ed.). New York: Freeman.

Squier, L. H., & Domhoff, G. W. (1998). The presentation of dreaming and dreams in introductory psychology textbooks: A critical examination with suggestions for textbook authors and course instructors. *Dreaming, 8,* 149–168.

Srivastava, S., John, O. P., Gosling, S. D., & Potter, J. (2003). Development of personality in early and middle adulthood: Set like plaster or persistent change? *Journal of Personality and Social Psychology, 84,* 1041–1053.

Sroufe, L. A. (2003). Attachment categories as reflections of multiple dimensions: Comment on Fraley and Spieker (2003). *Developmental Psychology, 39,* 413–416.

Staddon, J. E., R., & Cerutti, D. T. (2003). Operant conditioning. *Annual Review of Psychology 54,* 115–144.

Stafford, R. S., & Radley, D. C. (2003). National trends in antiobesity medication use. *Archives of Internal Medicine, 163,* 1046–1050.

Stamler, J., Stamler, R., Neaton, J. D., Wentworth, D., Daviglus, M. L., Garside, D., et al. (1999). Low risk-factor profile and long-term cardiovascular and noncardiovascular mortality and life expectancy: Findings for 5 large cohorts of young adult and middle-aged men and women. *Journal of the American Medical Association, 282,* 2012–2018.

Stampfer, M. J., Hu, F. B., Manson, J. E., Rimm, E. B., & Willett, W. C. (2000). Primary prevention of coronary heart disease in women through diet and lifestyle. *New England Journal of Medicine, 343,* 16–22.

Stasson, M. F., & Hawkes, W. G. (1995). Effect of group performance on subsequent individual performance: Does influence generalize beyond the issues discussed by the group? *Psychological Science, 6,* 305–307.

Statistics Canada. 2001 Census: Analysis series. *Canada's ethnocultural portrait: The changing mosaic* (2003). Retrieved May 24, 2005, from www.gov.on.ca/FIN/english/demographics/cenhi6e.htm.

Stattin, H., & Magnusson, D. (1990). *Pubertal maturation in female development.* Hillsdale, NJ: Lawrence Erlbaum Associates.

Staw, B. M., & Cohen-Charash, Y. (2005). The dispositional approach to job satisfaction: More than a mirage, but not yet an oasis. *Journal of Organizational Behavior, 26,* 59–78.

Steele, C. M. (1997). A threat in the air: How stereotypes shape intellectual identity and performance. *American Psychologist, 52,* 613–629.

Steele, C. M., & Aronson, J. (1995). Stereotype threat and the actual test performance of African Americans. *Journal of Personality and Social Psychology, 69,* 797–811.

Steele, C. M., Spencer, S. J., & Aronson, J. (2002). Contending with group image: The psychology of stereotype and social identity threat. In M. P. Zanna (Ed.), *Advances in experimental social psychology* (Vol. 34, pp. 379–440). San Diego, CA: Academic Press.

Stein, J. (2005, January 17). Is there a hitch? *Time,* pp. A37–A40.

Steinbrook, R., (2004). The AIDS epidemic in 2004. *New England Journal of Medicine, 351,* 115–117.

Steiner, J. E. (1979). Human facial expression in response to taste and smell stimulation. In H. W. Reese & L. P. Lipsittt (Eds.), *Advances in child development and behavior* (Vol. 13, pp. 257–295). New York: Academic Press.

Steinhauer, J. (1995, July 6). No marriage, no apologies. *New York Times,* pp. C1, C7.

Stenson, J. (2001a, August 26). Burden of mental illness in America falls on minorities. *MSNBC.com.* Retrieved August 26, 2001, from http://www.msnbc.com/news/619545.asp.

Stenson, J. (2001b, August 26). Many teens abused by dating partners. *MSNBC.* Retrieved August 27, 2001, from http://www.msnbc.com/news/619696.asp.

Stenson, J. (2001c, August 27). Breaking down a male myth: Men not "emotional mummies," suggests new research. *MSNBC.* Retrieved August 28, 2001, from http://www.msnbc,com/news/620211.asp.

Stephenson, J. (2004). Global AIDS epidemic worsens. *Journal of the American Medical Association, 291,* 31–32.

Sternberg, E. M. (2000). *The balance within: The science connecting health and emotions.* New York: W. H. Freeman.

Sternberg, R. J. (1988). Triangulating love. In R. J. Sternberg & M. J. Barnes (Eds.), *The psychology of love.* New Haven: Yale University Press.

Sternberg, R. J. (1994a). Intelligence. In R. J. Sternberg (Ed.), *Thinking and problem solving* (pp. 263–288). San Diego: Academic Press.

Sternberg, R. J. (1994b). *In search of the human mind.* Forth Worth: Harcourt Brace College Publishers.

Sternberg, R. J. (1997). The triarchic theory of intelligence. In D. P. Flanagan, J. L. Genshaft, & P. L. Harrison (Eds.), *Contemporary intellectual - assessment: Theories, tests, and issues* (pp. 92–104). New York: Guilford Press.

Sternberg, R. J. (2001). What is the common thread of creativity? Its dialectical relation to intelligence and wisdom. *American Psychologist, 56,* 360–362.

Sternberg, R. J., Grigorenko, E. L., & Kidd, K. K. (2005). Intelligence, race, and genetics. *American Psychologist, 60,* 46–59.

Steven, J. E. (1995, January 30). Virtual therapy. *Boston Globe,* pp. 25, 29.

Stevenson, R. E., Allen, W. P., Pai, G. S., Best, R., Seaver, L. H., Dean, J., et al. (2000). Decline in prevalence of neural tube defects in a high-risk region of the United States. *Pediatrics, 106,* 677–683.

Stevenson, R. J., & Boakes, R. A. (2003). A mnemonic theory of odor perception. *Psychological Review, 110,* 340–364.

Stewart, A. J., & McDermott, C. (2004). Gender in psychology. *Annual Review of Psychology, 55,* 519–544.

Stewart, M. W., et al. (1994). Differential relationships between stress and disease activity for immunologically distinct subgroups of people with rheumatoid arthritis. *Journal of Abnormal Psychology, 1103,* 251–258.

Stice, E. (2001). A prospective test of the dual-pathway model of bulimic pathology: Mediating effects of dieting and negative affect. *Journal of Abnormal Psychology, 110,* 124–135.

Stickgold, R., Hobson, J. A., Fosse, R., & Fosse, M. (2001). Sleep, learning, and dreams: Off-line memory reprocessing. *Science, 294,* 1052–1057.

Stickgold, R., LaTanya, J., & Hobson, J. A. (2000). Visual discrimination learning requires sleep after training. *Nature Neuroscience, 3,* 1237–1238.

Stickgold, R., Malia, A., Fosse, R., Hobson, J. A. (2001a). Brain-mind states: I. Longitudinal field study of sleep/wake factors influencing mentation report length. *Sleep 24,* 171–179.

Stipp, D. (2003, February). The quest for the antifat pill. *Fortune,* pp. 66–67.

Stockdale, M. S., Gandolfo Berry, C., Schneider, R. W., & Cao, F. (2004). Perceptions of the sexual harassment of men. *Psychology of Men and Masculinity, 5,* 158–167.

Stolberg, S. G. (2001a, April 22). Science, studies and motherhood. *New York Times Week in Review,* p. 3.

Stolberg, S. G. (2001b, May 10). Blacks found on short end of heart attack procedure. *New York Times,* p. A20.

Stolberg, S. G. (2001c, June 2). In AIDS war, new weapons and new victims. *New York Times,* pp. A1, A24.

Stone, A. A., Neale, J. M., Cox, D. S., Napoli, A., et al. (1994). Daily events are associated with a secretory immune response to an oral antigen in men. *Health Psychology, 13,* 440–446.

Stone, J., Lynch, C. I., Sjomeling, M., & Darley, J. M. (1999). Stereotype threat effects on Black and White athletic performance. *Journal of Personality and Social Psychology, 77,* 1213–1227.

Stoney, C. M. (2003). Gender and cardiovascular disease: a psychobiological and integrative approach. *Current Directions in Psychological Science, 12,* 129–133.

Storandt, M., Kaskie, B., & Von Dras, D. D. (1998). Temporal memory for remote events in healthy aging and dementia. *Psychology and Aging, 13,* 4–7.

Strack, F., Martin, L. L., & Stepper, S. (1988). Inhibiting and facilitating conditions of the human smile: A non-obtrusive test of the facial-feedback hypothesis. *Journal of Personality and Social Psychology, 54,* 768–777.

Stratton, V. N., & Zalanowski, A. H. (1997). The relationships between characteristic moods and most commonly listened to types of music. *Journal of Music Therapy, 34,* 129–140.

Strayer, D. L., & Johnston, W. A. (2001). Driven to distraction: Dual-task studies of simulated driving and conversing on a cellular telephone. *Psychological Science, 12,* 462–466.

Stricker, G., & Gold, J. R. (1999). The Rorschach: Toward a nomothetically based, idiographically applicable configurational model. *Psychological Assessment, 11,* 240–250.

Stricker, G., & Gold, J. R. (2001, January). An introduction to psychotherapy integration. *NYS Psychologist, 13,* 7–12.

Striegel-Moore, R. H., Dohm, F. A., Kraemer, H. C., Taylor, C. B.,Daniels, S. D., Crawford, P. B., et al. (2003). Eating disorders in white and black women. *American Journal of Psychiatry, 160,* 1326–1331.

Strillacci, L. (2003, July 8). 10 most dangerous foods to eat on the road. *MSN.com,* reprinted from Insure.com. Retrieved January 8, 2005, from http://moneycentral.msn.com/content/Insurance/P51290.asp.

Strober, M., Freeman, R., Lampert, C., Diamond, J., & Kaye, W. (2000). Controlled family study of anorexia nervosa and bulimia nervosa: Evidence of shared liability and transmission of partial syndromes. *American Journal of Psychiatry, 157,* 393–401.

Strohmetz, D. B., Rind, B., Fisher, R., & Lynn, M. (2002). Sweetening the till: The use of candy to increase restaurant tipping. *Journal of Applied Social Psychology, 32,* 300–309.

Strote, J. L., & Wechsler, H. (2002). Increasing MDMA use among college students: Results of a national survey. *Journal of the American Academy of Child & Adolescent Psychiatry, 41,* 1215.

Stuart, R. B. (2004). Twelve practical suggestions for achieving multicultural competence. *Professional Psychology: Research and Practice, 35,* 3–9.

Substance Abuse and Mental Health Services Administration (SAMHSA). (2005). *Overview of findings from the 2002 National Survey on Drug Use and Health* (Office of Applied Studies, NHSDA Series H-21 DHHS Publication No. MA 03–3774). Rockville, MD. Retrieved February 9, 2005, from http://www.nida.nih.gov/NIDA_notes/NNvol19N5/Study.html

Sue, S. (2003). In defense of cultural competency in psychotherapy and treatment. *American Psychologist, 58,* 964–970.

Sullivan, M. P. (2000). Preventing the downward spiral. *American Journal of Nursing, 100,* 26–32.

Sullivan, R. (1998, February). Like you, I haven't been sleeping well. *Life,* pp. 56–66.

Sulloway, F. J. (1983). *Freud: Biologist of the mind.* New York: Basic Books.

Suls, J., & Bunde, J., (2005). Anger, anxiety, and depression as risk factors for cardiovascular disease: The problems and implications of overlapping affective dispositions. *Psychological Bulletin, 13,* 260–300.

Sundstrom, E., Bell, P. A., Busby, P. L., & Asmus, C. (1996). Environmental psychology: 1989–1994. *Annual Review of Psychology, 47,* 485–512.

Surgeon General warns of other cancers, pneumonia, cataracts and more. (2004, May 27). *MSNBC.com.* Retrieved May 29, 2004, from http://www.msnbc.msn.com/id/5077308/.

Susman, E. (2000, May 4). Researchers say it's never too late to start exercising the mind with activities like crossword puzzles. *MSNBC.* Retrieved May 6, 2000, from http://www.msnbc.com.

Susman, E. J., Dorn, L. D., & Schiefelbein, V. L. (2003). Puberty, sexuality, and health. In R. M. Lerner, M. A. Easterbrooks, & J. Mistry (Eds.), *Handbook of psychology: Vol. 6. Developmental psychology* (pp. 211–240). New York: John Wiley & Sons.

Suzuki, K. (1991). Moon illusion simulated in complete darkness: Planetarium experiment reexamined. *Perception and Psychophysics, 49,* 349–354.

Szalacha, L. A., Erkut, S., Coll, C. G., Alarcón, O, Fields, J. P., Ceder, I., et al. (2003). Discrimination and Puerto Rican children's and adolescents' mental health. *Cultural Diversity and Ethnic Minority Psychology, 9,* 141–155.

Szanto, K., Mulsant, B. H., Houck, P., Dew, M. A., & Reynolds, C. F. (2003). Occurrence and course of suicidality during short-term treatment of late-life depression. *Archives of General Psychiatry, 60,* 610–617.

Szeszko, P. R., MacMillan, S., McMeniman, M., Chen, S., Baribault, K., Lim, K. O., et al. (2004). Brain structural abnormalities in psychotropic drug-naive pediatric patients with obsessive-compulsive disorder. *American Journal of Psychiatry, 161,* 1049–1056.

Takahashi, C. (2001, April 8). Selling to Gen Y: A far cry from Betty Crocker. *New York Times Week in Review,* p. 3.

Takahashi, Y. (1990). Separation distress of Japanese infants in the strange situation. *Research and Clinical Center for Child Development, 12,* 141–150.

Talan, J. (1998, February 3). The power of dreams: It's all in understanding them. *Newsday,* pp. B15, B16.

Talarico, J. M., & Rubin, D. C. (2003). Confidence, not consistency, characterizes flashbulb memories. *Psychological Science, 14,* 455–461.

Tanasescu, M., Leitzmann, M. F., Rimm, E. B., Willett, W. C., Stampfer, M. J., & Hu, F. B. (2002). Exercise type and intensity in relation to coronary heart disease in men. *Journal of the American Medical Association, 288,* 1994–2000.

Tang, C. S., Critelli, J. W., & Porter, J. F. (1995). Sexual aggression and victimization in dating relationships among Chinese college students. *Archives of Sexual Behavior, 24,* 47–53.

Tanner, J. M. (1990). *Foetus into man* (2nd ed.). Cambridge, MA: Harvard University Press.

Tapert, S. F., Brown, G. G., Baratta, M. V., & Brown, S. A. (2004). fMRI BOLD response to alcohol stimuli in alcohol dependent young women. *Addictive Behaviors, 29,* 33–50.

Tarkan, L. (2003, April 22). New test for hearts at risk: What it can and can't do. *New York Times,* p. F5.

Tauer, J. M., & Harackiewicz, J. M. (2004). The effects of cooperation and competition on intrinsic motivation and performance. *Journal of Personality and Social Psychology, 86,* 849–861.

Taylor, C. B., & Luce, K. H. (2003). Computer- and Internet-based psychotherapy interventions. *Current Directions in Psychological Science, 12,* 18–22.

Taylor, E. (2000). Psychotherapeutics and the problematic origins of clinical psychology in America. *American Psychologist, 55,* 1029–1033.

Taylor, K. L., Lamdan, R. M., Siegel, J. E., Shelby, R., Moran-Klimi, K., & Hrywna, M. (2003). Psychological adjustment among African American breast cancer patients: One-year follow-up results of a randomized psychoeducational group intervention. *Health Psychology, 22,* 316–323.

Taylor, S. E., Klein, L. C., Lewis, B. P, Gruenewald, T. L., Gurung, R. A., & Updegraff, J. A. (2000). Biobehavioral responses to stress in females: Tend-and-befriend, not fight-or-flight. *Psychological Review, 7,* 411–429.

Tecott, L. H. (2003). The genes and brains of mice and men. *American Journal of Psychiatry, 160,* 646–656.

Teen drug use, smoking up slightly. (2003, September 4). *CNN Web Posting.* Retrieved September 6, 2003, from http://www.cnn.com/2003/HEALTH/parenting/09/04/drug.survey.ap/index.html.

Teens say they get along with parents. (2003, August 5). *Associated Press, MSNBC.com.* Retrieved August 8, 2003, from http://www.msnbc.com/news/948480.asp.

Teens see little risk in ecstasy. (2003, February 11). *Cable News Network..* Retrieved February 15, 2003, from http://www.Cable News Network.com/2003/HEALTH/parenting/02/11/drug.survey.ap/index.html.

Tekcan, A. I., & Peynircioglu, Z. F. (2002). Effects of age on flashbulb memories. *Psychology and Aging, 17,* 416–422.

Tellegen, A., Lykken, D. T., Bouchard, T. J., & Wilcox, K., J. (1988). Personality similarity in twins reared apart and together. *Journal of Personality and Social Psychology, 54,* 1031–1039.

Tenenbaum, H. R., & Leaper, C. (2003). Parent–child conversations about science: The socialization of gender inequities? *Developmental Psychology, 39,* 34–47.

Terman, J. S., Terman, M., Lo, E. S., & Cooper, T. B. (2001). Circadian time of morning light administration and therapeutic response in winter depression. *Archives of General Psychiatry, 58,* 69–75.

Terrace, H. S. (1980). *Nim.* New York: Knopf.

Terrell, F., Terrell, I. S., & Von Drashek, S. R. (2000). Loneliness and fear of intimacy among adolescents who were taught not to trust strangers during childhood. *Adolescence, 35,* 611–617.

Terry, R. L., & Macy, R. J. (1991). Children's social judgments of other children who wear glasses. *Journal of Social Behavior and Personality, 6,* 965–974.

Tetlock, P. E. (1998). Social psychology and world politics. In D. T. Gilbert, S. T. Fiske, & G. Lindzey (Eds.), *The handbook of social psychology* (4th ed., Vol. 2, pp. 868–914). Boston: McGraw-Hill.

Tett, R. P., & Burnett, D. D. (2003). A personality trait-based interactionist model of job performance. *Journal of Applied Psychology, 88,* 500–517.

Think positive, live longer (2002, July 28). *MSNBC.com.* Retrieved July 30, 2002, from http://www.msnbc.com/news/786749.asp.

Thompson, C. P., Anderson, L. P., & Bakeman, R. A. (2000). Effects of racial socialization and racial identity on acculturative stress in African American college students. *Cultural Diversity and Ethnic Minority Psychology, 6*(2), 196–210.

Thompson, P. M., Hayashi, K. M., de Zubicaray, G., Janke, A. L., Rose, S. E., Semple, J., et al. (2003). Dynamics of gray matter loss in Alzheimer's Disease. *Journal of Neuroscience, 23,* 994.

Thompson, P. M., Hayashi, K. M., Simon, S. L., Geaga, J. A., Hong, M. S., Sui, Y., et al. (2004). Structural abnormalities in the brains of human subjects who use methamphetamine. *Journal of Neuroscience, 30,* 6028–6036.

Thompson, R. A. (1997). Early sociopersonality development. In W. Damon (Editor-in-Chief) & N. Eisenberg (Vol. Ed.), *Handbook of child psychology: Vol. 3. Social, emotional, and personality development* (5th ed., pp. 25–104). New York: John Wiley & Sons.

Thompson, R. A., Easterbrooks, M. A., & Padilla-Walker, L. M. (2003). Social and emotional development in infancy. In R. M. Lerner, M. A. Easterbrooks, & J. Mistry (Eds.), *Handbook of psychology: Vol. 6. Developmental psychology* (pp. 91–112). New York: John Wiley & Sons.

Thompson, R. R. (2005). In search of memory traces. *Annual Review of Psychology, 56,* 1–23.

Thompson, S. C., Sobolew-Shubin, A., Galbraith, M. E., Schwankovsky, L., et al. (1993). Maintaining perceptions of control: Finding perceived control in low control circumstances. *Journal of Personality and Social Psychology, 64,* 293–304.

Thompson-Brenner, H., Glass, S., & Westen, D. (2003). A multidimensional meta-analysis of psychotherapy for bulimia nervosa. *Clinical Psychology: Science and Practice, 10,* 269–287.

Thomsen, D. K., Mehlsen, M. Y., Christensen, S., & Zachariae, R. (2003). Rumination—relationship with negative mood and sleep quality. *Personality and Individual Differences, 34,* 1293–1301.

Thomson, E., Hanson, T. L., & McLanahan, S. S. (1994). Family structure and child well-being: Economic resources vs. parental behaviors. *Social Forces, 73,* 221–242.

Thoresen, C. J., Kaplan, S. A., Barsky, A. P., Warren, C. R., & de Chermont, K. (2003). The affective underpinnings of job perceptions and attitudes: A meta-analytic review and integration. *Psychological Bulletin, 129,* 914–945.

Thorndike, E. L. (1905). *The elements of psychology.* New York: Seiler.

Thornhill, R., & Palmer, C. T. (2000). *A natural history of rape.* Cambridge, MA: MIT Press.

Thulborn, K. R. (2003). Clinical fMRI at 3.0 Tesla: "Watching Thoughts," University of Illinois at Chicago, Center for MR Research. Retrieved January 17, 2005, from www.uic.edu/com/mrc. *14,* 30–33.

Thurstone, L. L., & Thurstone, T. G. (1941). Factorial studies of intelligence. *Psychometric Monographs, 94*(2).

Tienari, P., Wynne, L. C., Läksy, K., Moring, J., Nieminen, P., Sorri, A., et al. (2003). Genetic boundaries of the schizophrenia spectrum: Evidence from the Finnish adoptive family study of schizophrenia. *American Journal of Psychiatry, 160,* 1587–1594.

Tohen, M., Zarate, C. A., Hennen, J., Khalsa, H.-M. K., Strakowski, S. M., Gebre-Medhin, P., et al. (2003). The McLean-Harvard First-Episode Mania Study: Prediction of recovery and first recurrence. *American Journal of Psychiatry, 160,* 2099–2107.

Tolman, E. C., & Honzik, C. H. (1930). Introduction and removal of reward, and maze performance in rats. *University of California Publications in Psychology, 4,* 257–275.

Tolomiczenko, G. S., Sota, T., & Goering, P. N. (2000). Personality assessment of homeless adults as a tool for service planning. *Journal of Personality Disorders, 14,* 152–161.

Tomes, H. (2004, June). The case—and the research—that forever connected psychology and policy. *Monitor on Psychology, 35,* 28.

Toomey, R., Lyons, M. J., Eisen, S. A., Xian, H., Chantarujikapong, S., Seidman, L. J., et al. (2003). A twin study of the neuropsychological consequences of stimulant abuse. *Archives of General Psychiatry, 60,* 303–310.

Tracy, R. J., Fricano, G., & Greco, N. (2000–2001). Images can be more powerful than memories. *Imagination, Cognition and Personality, 20,* 3–19.

Trevarthen, C. (1995). Mother and baby—Seeing artfully eye to eye. In R. L. Gregory et al. (Eds.), *The artful eye* (pp. 157–200). New York: Oxford University Press.

Triandis, H. C., & Gelfand, M. J. (1998). Converging measurement of horizontal and vertical individualism and collectivism. *Journal of Personality and Social Psychology, 74,* 118–128.

Triandis, H. C., & Suh, E. M. (2002). Cultural influences on personality. *Annual Review of Psychology, 53,* 133–160.

Trinh, N. H., Hoblyn, J., Mohanty, S., & Yaffe, K. (2003). Efficacy of cholinesterase inhibitors in the treatment of neuropsychiatric symptoms and functional impairment in Alzheimer disease: A meta-analysis. *Journal of the American Medical Association, 289,* 210–216.

Troxel, W. M., Matthews, K. A., Bromberger, J. T., & Sutton-Tyrrell, K. (2003). Chronic stress burden, discrimination, and subclinical carotid artery disease in African American and Caucasian women. *Health Psychology, 22,* 300–309.

Trudel, G., Turgeon, L., & Piche, L. (2000). Marital and sexual aspects of old age. *Sexual and Relationship Therapy, 15,* 381–406.

Trunzo, J. J., & Pinto, B. M. (2003). Social support as a mediator of optimism and distress in breast cancer survivors. *Journal of Consulting and Clinical Psychology, 71,* 805–811.

Trzesniewski, K. H., Donnellan, M. B., & Robins, R. W. (2003). Stability of self-esteem across the life span. *Journal of Personality and Social Psychology, 84,* 205–220.

Tsai, A G., & Wadden, T. A. (2005). Systematic review: An evaluation of major commercial weight loss programs in the United States. *Annals of Internal Medicine, 142,* 56–66.

Tsai, J. L., Chentsova-Dutton, Y., Freire-Bebeau, L., & Przymus, D. E. (2002). Emotional expression and physiology in European Americans and Hmong Americans. *Emotion, 2,* 380–397.

Tsai, J. L., Mortensen, H., Wong, Y., & Hess, D. (2002). What does "being American" mean? A comparison of Asian American and European American young adults. *Cultural Diversity and Ethnic Minority Psychology, 8,* 257–273.

Tudor, R. M. (1995). Isolating the effects of active responding in computer-based instruction. *Journal of Applied Behavior Analysis, 28,* 343–344.

Tuller, D. (2001, May 8). Experts voice new alarm on herpes. *New York Times,* p. F1, F6.

Tulving, E. (1983). *Elements of episodic memory.* Oxford, England: Oxford University Press.

Tulving, E. (2002). Episodic memory: From mind to brain. *Annual Review of Psychology, 53,* 1–25.

Tulving, E., & Thompson, D. M. (1973). Encoding specificity and retrieval processes in episodic memory. *Psychological Review, 80,* 352–373.

Tune, L. (1998). Treatments for dementia. In P. E. Nathan & J. M. Gorman (Eds.), *A guide to treatments that work* (pp. 90–126). New York: Oxford University Press

Turati, C. (2004). Why faces are not special to newborns: An alternative account of the face preference. *Current Directions in Psychological Science, 13,* 5–8.

Turkheimer, E., Haley, A., Waldron, M., D'Onofrio, B., & Gottesman, I. I. (2003). Socioeconomic status modifies heritability of IQ in young children. *Psychological Science, 14,* 623–628.

Turkington, C. (1996). *12 steps to a better memory.* New York: MacMillan.

Turnbull, C. (1961). *The forest people.* New York: Simon & Schuster.

TV may cause attention deficit. (2004, April 5). *Cable News Network..* Retrieved April 7, 2004, from http://www.cnn.com/2004/HEALTH/parenting/04/05/toddler.tv.ap/index.html.

Tweney, R. D., & Budzynski, C. A. (2000). The scientific status of American psychology in 1900. *American Psychologist, 55,* 1014–1017.

Twenge, J. M. (2000). The age of anxiety? Birth cohort change in anxiety and neuroticism, 1952–1993. *Journal of Personality and Social Psychology, 79,* 1007–1021.

Twenge, J. M., & Crocker, J. (2002a). Race and self-esteem: Meta-analyses comparing whites, Blacks, Hispanics, Asians, and American Indians and comment on Gray-Little and Hafdahl (2000). *Psychological Bulletin, 128,* 371–408.

Twenge, J. M., & Crocker, J. (2002b). Race and self-esteem revisited: Reply to Hfdahl and Gray-Little (2002). *Psychological Bulletin, 128,* 417–420.

Twenge, J. M., & Nolen-Hoeksema, S. (2002). Age, gender, race, socioeconomic status, and birth cohort differences on the children's depression inventory: A meta-analysis. *Journal of Abnormal Psychology, 111,* 578–588.

Tyre, P. (2004, October 4). Combination therapy. *Newsweek Online.* Retrieved July 2, 2005, from msnbc.msn.com/id/6100257/site/newsweek/.

U.S. Bureau of the Census. (2000). *Statistical abstract of the United States* (120th ed.). Washington, DC: U.S. Government Printing Office.

U.S. Census Bureau. (2000). *Marital status of the population 15 years old and over, by sex, age, race, and Hispanic origin.* Washington, DC: U.S. Government Printing Office.

U.S. Census Bureau (2003, October). *Marital status 2000.* Retrieved November 15, 2003, from www.census.gov/prod/2003pubs/c2kbr-30.pdf.

U.S. Census Bureau. (2005). Population Division, Population Projections Branch.

U.S. Department of Agriculture. (2000). *Report of the Dietary Guidelines Advisory Committee on the dietary guidelines for Americans, 2000.* Beltsville, MD: Agriculture Research Service.

U.S. Department of Health and Human Services (USDHHS). (1990). *The health benefits of smoking cessation: A report of the Surgeon General.* (DHHS Pub. No CDC 90–8416). Rockville, MD: Centers for Disease Control, Office on Smoking and Health.

U.S. Department of Health and Human Services (USDHHS). (1991a). *Healthy people 2000: National health promotion and disease prevention objectives* (DHHS Pub. No. PHS 91–50212). Washington, DC: Public Health Service.

U.S. Department of Health and Human Services (USDHHS). (1991b). *NIDA capsules: Summary of findings from the 1991 National Household Survey on Drug Abuse* (No. 20). Public Health Service, Alcohol Drug Abuse and Mental Health Administration, National Institute on Drug Abuse. Rockville, MD: National Institute on Drug Abuse. U.S. Department of Health and Human Services (USDHHS). (2000). *Healthy people 2010: Understanding and improving health* (2nd ed.). Washington, DC: U.S. Government Printing Office.

U.S. Department of Health and Human Services (USDHHS). (2001). *National Household Survey on Drug Abuse: Highlights 2000.* Retrieved March 28, 2001, from www.samhsa.gov.

U.S. Department of Health and Human Services, Substance Abuse and Mental Health Services Administration, Center for Mental Health Services, National Institutes of Health, National Institute of Mental Health. (1999). *Mental health: A report of the Surgeon General.* Rockville, MD: Author.

U.S. Department of Health and Human Services, Substance Abuse and Mental Health Services Administration, Center for Mental Health Services, National Institutes of Health, National Institute of Mental Health. (2001). *Mental health: Culture, race, and ethnicity: A supplement to mental health: A report of the Surgeon General—Executive summary.* Rockville, MD: Author.

U.S. Department of Justice, Bureau of Justice Statistics. (2003). *Crime and victim statistics.* Retrieved November 30, 2003, from http://www.ojp.usdoj.gov/bjs/cvict.htm.

Uhl, G. R., & Grow, R. W. (2004). The burden of complex genetics in brain disorders. *Archives of General Psychiatry, 61,* 223–229.

Uhlmann, E., & Swanson, J. (2004). Exposure to violent video games increases automatic aggressiveness. *Journal of Adolescence, 27,* 41–52.

UK ECT Review Group. (2003). Efficacy and safety of electroconvulsive therapy in depressive disorders: A systematic review and meta-analysis. *Lancet, 361,* 799–808.

Umaña-Taylor, A. J. (2004). Ethnic identity and self-esteem: examining the role of social context. *Journal of Adolescence, 27,* 139–146.

Underwood, A. (2004, October 11). We've got rhythm. *Newsweek Online.* Retrieved October 14, 2004, from http://www.msnbc.msn.com/id/6161341/site/newsweek/.

Underwood, A., & Adler, J. (2004, August 23). What you don't know about fat. *Newsweek,* pp. 40–47.

Underwood, A., & Watson, R. (2001, Fall/Winter). Keeping hope alive. *Newsweek Special Issue,* pp. 55–58.

Utsey, S. O., Chae, M. H., Brown, C. F., & Kelly, D (2002). Effect of ethnic group membership on ethnic identity, race-related stress, and quality of life. *Cultural Diversity and Ethnic Minority Psychology, 8,* 366–377.

Van Eerdewegh, P. P., Little, R. D., Dupuis, J., Del Mastro, R. G., Falls, K., Simon, J., et al. (2002). Association of the ADAM33 gene with asthma and bronchial hyperresponsiveness. *Nature, 418,* 426–430.

van Goozen, S. H. M., Slabbekoorn, D., Gooren, L. J. G., Sanders, G., & Cohen-Kettenis, P. T. (2002). Organizing and activating effects of sex hormones in homosexual transsexuals. *Behavioral Neuroscience, 116,* 982–988.

van Ijzendoorn, M. (1995). Adult attachment representations, parental responsiveness, and infant attachment: A meta-analysis on the predictive validity of the Adult Attachment Interview. *Psychological Bulletin, 117,* 387–403.

Van Raalte, J. L., & Brewer, B. W. (2002). *Exploring sport and exercise psychology* (2nd ed.). Washington, DC: American Psychological Association.

Van-Cauter, E., Leproult, R., & Plat, L. (2000). Age-related changes in slow-wave sleep and REM sleep and relationship with growth hormone and cortisol levels in healthy men. *Journal of the American Medical Association, 284*, 861–868.

Vancouver, J. B., Thompson, C. M., Tischner, E. C., & Putka, D. J. (2002). Two studies examining the negative effect of self-efficacy on performance. *Journal of Applied Psychology, 87*, 506–516.

Vandell, D. L. (1999). Parents, peer groups, and other socializing influences. *Developmental Psychology, 36*, 699–710.

Vastag, B. (2001). Multiple sclerosis report released by IOM. *Journal of the American Medical Association, 285*, 874.

Vastag, B. (2004). Obesity is now on everyone's plate. *Journal of the American Medical Association, 291*, 1186–1188.

Vaughn, B. E., Azria, M. R., Krzysik, L., Caya, L. R., Bost, K. K., Newell, W., et al. (2000). Friendship and social competence in a sample of preschool children attending Head Start. *Developmental Psychology, 36*, 326–338.

Vecchio, R. P. (1997). *Leadership: Understanding the dynamics of power and influence in organizations.* Notre Dame: University of Notre Dame Press.

Vecera, S. P., Vogel, E. K., & Woodman, G. F. (2002). Lower region: A new cue for figure-ground assignment. *Journal of Experimental Psychology: General, 131*, 194–205.

Verghese, A. (2004, February 22). Hope and clarity: Is optimism a cure? *New York Times Magazine*, pp. 11–12.

Verghese, J., Lipton, R. B., Katz, M. J., Hall, C. B., Derby, C. A., Kuslansky, G., et al. (2003). Leisure activities and the risk of dementia in the elderly. *New England Journal of Medicine, 348*, 2508–2516.

Verhaeghen, P. (2003). Aging and vocabulary scores: A meta-analysis. *Psychology and Aging, 18*, 332–339.

Verhovek, S. H. (2000). What is the matter with Mary Jane? *New York Times Week in Review*, p. 3.

Verkuyten, M. (2005). Ethnic group identification and group evaluation among minority and majority groups: Testing the multiculturalism hypothesis. *Journal of Personality and Social Psychology, 88*, 121–138.

Vickers, A. J., Rees, R. W., Zollman, C. E., McCarney, R., Smith, C. M., Ellis, N., et al. (2004). Acupuncture for chronic headache in primary care: Large, pragmatic, randomised trial. *British Medical Journal, 328*, 744–747.

Victor, S. B., & Fish, M. C. (1995). Lesbian mothers and the children: A review for school psychologists. *School Psychology Review, 24*(3), 456–479.

Videbech, P., & Raynkilde, B. (2004). Hippocampal volume and depression: A meta-analysis of MRI studies. *American Journal of Psychiatry, 161*, 1957–1966.

Volkow, N. D., Wang, G.-J., Fowler, J. S., Telang, F., Maynard, L., Logan, J., et al. (2004). Evidence that methylphenidate enhances the saliency of a mathematical task by increasing dopamine in the human brain. *American Journal of Psychiatry, 161*, 1173–1180.

Volz, J. (2000, January). Successful aging: The second 50. *Monitor on Psychology, 31*, 24–38.

von Békésy, G. (1957, August). The ear. *Scientific American*, pp. 66–78.

Von-Hofsten, C., & Rosander, K. (1996). The development of gaze control and predictive tracking in young infants. *Vision Research, 36*, 81–96.

Voyer, D., Voyer, S., & Bryden, M. P. (1995). Magnitude of sex differences in spatial abilities: A meta-analysis and consideration of critical variables. *Psychological Bulletin, 117*, 250–270.

Vygotsky, L. S. (1978). *Mind in society: The development of higher psychological processes.* Cambridge, MA: Harvard University Press.

Vygotsky, L. S. (1986). *Thought and language.* Cambridge, MA: MIT Press. (Original work published 1934.)

Wade, N. (2003a, April 15). Once again, scientists say human genome is complete. *New York Times*, p. F1.

Wade, N. (2003b, June 3). Gene sweepstakes ends, but winner may well be wrong. *New York Times*, pp. F1, F2.

Wadsworth, S. J., DeFries, J. C., Fulker, D. W., & Plomin, R. (1995). Cognitive ability and academic achievement in the Colorado Adoption Project: A multivariate genetic analysis of parent/offspring and sibling data. *Behavior Genetics, 25*, 1–15.

Wagner, U., Gais, S., Haider, H., Verleger, R., & Born, J. (2004). Sleep inspires insight. *Nature, 427*, 352–355.

Wagner-Moore, L. E. (2004). Gestalt therapy: Past, present, theory, and research. *Psychotherapy: Theory, Research, Practice, Training, 41*, 180–189.

Wainberg, M. A. (2005). Generic HIV drugs — enlightened policy for global health. *New England Journal of Medicine, 352*, 747–750.

Walden, B., McGue, M., Iacono, W. G., Burt, S. A., & Elkins, I. (2004). Identifying shared environmental contributions to early substance use: The respective roles of peers and parents. *Journal of Abnormal Psychology, 113*, 440–450.

Waldinger, M. D., van De Plas, A., Pattij, T., van Oorschot, R., Coolen, L. M., Veening, J. G., et al. (2002). The selective serotonin re-uptake inhibitors fluvoxamine and paroxetine differ in sexual inhibitory effects after chronic treatment. *Psychopharmacology, 160*(3), 283–289.

Waldinger, M. D., Zwinderman, A. H., & Olivier, B. (2001). Antidepressants and ejaculation: A double-blind, randomized, placebo-controlled, fixed-dose study with paroxetine, sertraline and nefazodone. *Journal of Clinical Psychopharmacology, 21*(3), 293–297.

Waldman, I. D., Weinberg, R. A., & Scarr, S. (1994). Racial-group differences in IQ in the Minnesota Transracial Adoption Study: A reply to Levin and Lynn. *Intelligence, 19*, 29–44.

Walker, E., Kestler, L., Bollini, A., & Hochman, K. M. (2004). Schizophrenia: Etiology and course. *Annual Review of Psychology, 55*, 401–430.

Walker, L. J. (1997). Is morality gendered in early parent-child relationships? A commentary on the Lollis, Ross, and Leroux study. *Merrill-Palmer Quarterly, 43*, 148–159.

Walker, R. (2004, February 8). Cialis. *New York Times Magazine*, p. 26.

Wall, T. L., Carr, L. G., & Ehlers, C. L. (2003). Protective association of genetic variation in alcohol dehydrogenase with alcohol dependence in Native American Mission Indians. *American Journal of Psychiatry, 160*, 41–46.

Wallerstein, J., Lewis, J., & Blakeslee, S. (2000). *The unexpected legacy of divorce: A 25-year landmark study.* New York: Hyperion.

Wallis, C. (2005, January 17). The new science of happiness. *Time*, pp. A3–A9.

Wallston, K. A. (2001). Conceptualization and operationalization of perceived control. In A. Baum, T. A. Revenson, & J. E. Singer (Eds.), *Handbook of health psychology* (pp. 49–58). Mahwah, NJ: Lawrence Erlbaum Associates.

Walsh, B. T., Fairburn, C. G., Mickley, D., Sysko, R., & Parides, M. K. (2004). Treatment of bulimia nervosa in a primary care setting. *American Journal of Psychiatry, 161*, 556–561.

Walsh, J. M., Wheat, M. E., & Freund, K. (2000). Detection, evaluation, and treatment of eating disorders: The role of the primary care physician. *Journal of General Internal Medicine, 15*, 577–579.

Wampold, B. E., Mondin, G. W., Moody, M., Stich, F., Benson, K., & Ahn, H. (1997). A meta-analysis of outcome studies comparing bona fide psychotherapies: Empirically, "All must have prizes." *Psychological Bulletin, 122*, 203–215.

Wang, C., Cunningham, G., Dobs, A., Iranmanesh, A., Matsumoto, A. M., Snyder, P. J., et al. (2004). Long-term testosterone gel (AndroGel) treatment maintains beneficial effects on sexual function and mood, lean and fat mass, and bone mineral density in hypogonadal men. *Journal of Clinical Endocrinology and Metabolism, 89*, 2085–2098.

Wang, G., Volkow, N. D., Logan, J., Pappas, N. R., Wang, C. T., Zhu, W., et al. (2001). Brain dopamine and obesity. *Lancet, 357*, 354–358.

Wang, L., McCarthy, G., Song, A. W., & LaBar, K. S. (2005). Amygdala activation to sad pictures during high-field (4 tesla) functional magnetic resonance imaging. *Emotion, 5*, 12–22.

Wang, X., Gao, L., Shinfuku, N., Zhang, H., Zhao, C., & Shen, Y. (2000). Longitudinal study of earthquake-related PTSD in a randomly selected community sample in North China. *American Journal of Psychiatry, 157*, 1260–1266.

Ward, T. B. (1994). Structured imagination: The role of conceptual structure in exemplar generation. *Cognitive Psychology, 27*, 1–40.

Ward, T. B. (1995). What's old about new ideas? In S. M. Smith, T. B. Ward, & R. A. Finke (Eds.), *The creative cognition approach* (pp. 157–178). Cambridge, MA: MIT Press.

Ward, T. B., Smith, S. M., & Vaid, J. (1997). Conceptual structures and processes in creative thought. In T. B. Ward, S. M. Smith, & J. Vaid (Eds.), *Creative thought: An investigation of conceptual structures and processes* (pp. 1–30). Washington, DC: American Psychological Association.

Warner, M. B., Morey, L. C., Finch, J. F., Gunderson, J. G., Skodol, A. E., et al. (2004). The longitudinal relationship of personality traits and disorders. *Journal of Abnormal Psychology, 113*, 217–227.

Waterworth, D. M., Bassett, A. S., & Brzustowicz, L. M. (2002). Recent advances in the genetics of schizophrenia. *Cellular and Molecular Life Sciences, 59*, 331–348.

Watkins, L. R., & Maier, S. F. (2003). Gila: A novel drug discovery target for clinical pain. *Nature Reviews: Drug Discovery, 2*, 973–985.

Watson, D., Suls, J., & Haig, J. (2002). Global self-esteem in relation to structural models of personality and affectivity. *Journal of Personality and Social Psychology, 83*, 185–197.

Watson, J. B. (1913). Psychology as the behaviorist views it. *Psychological Bulletin, 20*, 158–177.

Watson, J. B. (1924). *Behaviorism.* New York: W. W. Norton.

Watson, J. B., & Rayner, R. (1920). Conditioned emotional reactions. *Journal of Experimental Psychology, 3,* 1–14.

Watson, R. I. (1971). *The great psychologists* (3rd ed.). Philadelphia: J. B. Lippincott.

Watts, C., & Zimmerman, C. (2002). Violence against women: Global scope and magnitude. *Lancet, 359*(9313), 1232–1237.

Weber, N., Brewer, N., Wells, G. L., Semmler, C., & Keast, A. (2004). Eyewitness identification accuracy and response latency: The unruly 10–12-second rule. *Journal of Experimental Psychology-Applied, 10,* 139–147.

Webster, A., & Beveridge, M. (1997). The role of educational psychologists in educational research: Some implications for professional training. *Educational Psychology in Practice, 13,* 155–164.

Wechsler, D. (1975). Intelligence defined and undefined: A relativistic appraisal. *American Psychologist, 34,* 135–139.

Weed, W. S. (2003, December 14). Questions for Raymond Damadian: Scanscam? *New York Times Online.* Retrieved January 8, 2004, from www.nytimes.com/2003/12/14/magazine/14QUESTIONS.html.

Weems, C. F., Hayward, C., Killen, J., & Taylor, C. B. (2002). A longitudinal investigation of anxiety sensitivity in adolescence. *Journal of Abnormal Psychology, 111,* 471–477.

Wegner, D. M., Wenzlaff, R. M., & Kozak, M. (2004). Dream rebound: The return of suppressed thoughts in dreams. *Psychological Science, 15,* 232–236.

Wei, W., Sambamoorthi, U., Olfson, M., Walkup, J. T., & Crystal, S. (2005). Use of psychotherapy for depression in older adults. *American Journal of Psychiatry, 162,* 711–717.

Weigle, T. W., & Bauer, P. J. (2000). Deaf and hearing adults' recollections of childhood and beyond. *Memory, 8,* 293–310.

Weinberg, R. A., Scarr, S., & Waldman, I. D. (1992). The Minnesota Transracial Adoption Study: A follow-up of IQ test performance at adolescence. *Intelligence, 16,* 117–135.

Weis, R. (2002). A parenting dimensionality and typology in a disadvantaged, African American sample: A cultural variance perspective. *Journal of Black Psychology, 28,* 142–173.

Wells, G. L., & Olson, E. A. (2003). Eyewitness testimony. *Annual Review of Psychology, 54,* 277–295.

Wells, G. L., Olson, E. A., & Charman, S. D. (2002). The confidence of eyewitnesses in their identifications from lineups. *Current Directions in Psychological Science, 11,* 151–154.

Welsh, R. S. (2003). Prescription privileges: Pro or con [Letter]. *Clinical Psychology: Science and Practice, 10,* 371–372. Wentzel, K. R., Barry, C. M., & Caldwell, K. A. (2004). Friendships in middle school: Influences on motivation and school adjustment. *Journal of Educational Psychology, 96,* 195–203.

Wessely, S., & Kerwin, M. A. (2004). Suicide risk and the SSRIs. *Journal of the American Medical Association, 292,* 379–381.

Westen, D., & Gabbard, G. O. (2002). Developments in cognitive neuroscience: 1. Conflict, compromise, and connectionism. *Journal of the American Psychoanalytic Association, 50,* 53–98.

Weuve, J., Kang, J. H., Manson, J. E., Breteler, M. M. B., Ware, J. H., & Grodstein, F. (2004). Physical activity, including walking, and cognitive function in older women. *Journal of the American Medical Association, 292,* 1454–1461.

Whalen, P. J., Kagan, J., Cook, R. G., Davis, C., Kim, H., Polis, S., et al. (2004). Human amygdala responsivity to masked fearful eye whites. *Science, 306,* 2061.

Whitbourne, S. K., Elliot, L. B., & Waterman, A. S. (1992). Psychosocial development in adulthood: A 22-year sequential study. *Journal of Personality and Social Psychology, 63,* 260–271.

White, J. K., Hendrick, S. S., & Hendrick, C. (2004). Big five personality variables and relationship constructs. *Personality and Individual Differences, 37,* 1519–1530.

White, K. K., & Abrams, L. (2002). Does priming specific syllables during tip-of-the-tongue states facilitate word retrieval in older adults? *Psychology and Aging, 17,* 226–235.

WHO World Mental Health Survey Consortium, The. (2004). Prevalence, severity, and unmet need for treatment of mental disorders in the World Health Organization World mental health surveys. *Journal of the American Medical Association, 29,* 2581–2590.

Whorf, B. L. (1956). Science and linguistics. In J. B. Carrroll (Ed.), *Language, thought, and reality: Selected writings of Benjamin Lee Whorf.* Cambridge, MA: MIT Press.

Widiger, T. A. (2005). Five factor model of personality disorder: Integrating science and practice. *Journal of Research in Personality, 39,* 67–83.

Widiger, T. A., & Clark, L. A. (2000). Toward DSM-V and the classification of psychopathology. *Psychological Bulletin, 126,* 946–963.

Wiener, D. N. (1988). *Albert Ellis: Passionate skeptic.* New York: Praeger.

Wiers, R. W., & Kummeling, R. H. C. (2004). An experimental test of an alcohol expectancy challenge in mixed gender groups of young heavy drinkers. *Addictive Behaviors, 29,* 215–220.

Wiersma, D., Jenner, J. A., van de Willige, G., Spakman, M., & Nienhuis, F. J. (2001). Cognitive behaviour therapy with coping training for persistent auditory hallucinations in schizophrenia: A naturalistic follow-up study of the durability of effects. *Acta Psychiatrica Scandinavica, 103,* 393–399.

Wilcox, L. M., & Duke, P. A. (2003). Stereoscopic surface interpolation supports lightness constancy. *Psychological Science, 14,* 525–530.

Williams, N. M., Preece, A., Morris, D. W., Spurlock, G., Bray, N. J., Stephens, D. M, Norton, N., et al. (2004). Identification in 2 independent samples of a novel schizophrenia risk haplotype of the Dystrobrevin Binding Protein Gene (DTNBP1). *Archives of General Psychiatry, 61,* 336–344.

Williams, S. M., & Templeton, A. R. (2003). Race and genomics. *New England Journal of Medicine, 348,* 2581–2582.

Williams, S. P. (2000, Fall/Winter). The new face of nutrition. *Newsweek Special Issue,* pp. 42–45.

Williams, T. J., Pepitone, M. E., Christensen, S. E., Cooke, B. M., Huberman, A. D., Breedlove, N. J., et al. (2000, April). Finger length patterns and human sexual orientation. *Nature, 404,* 455–456.

Williams, T., & Underwood, J. (1970). *The science of hitting.* New York: Simon & Schuster.

Williams, W. M. (1998). Are we raising smarter children today? School- and home-related influences on IQ. In U. Neisser (Ed.), *The rising curve: Long-term gains in IQ and related measures* (pp. 125–154). Washington, DC: American Psychological Association.

Williamson, D. F., Kahn, H. S., Remington, P. L., & Anda, R. F. (1990). The 10-year incidence of overweight and major weight gain in U.S. adults. *Archives of Internal Medicine, 150,* 665–672.

Willingham, D. B. (2001). *Cognition: The thinking animal.* Upper Saddle River, NJ: Prentice Hall.

Willis, D. J. (2003, Fall). The case for prescription privileges. *Clinical Psychologist, 56,* 1–4.

Willis, R. J., & Michael, R. T. (1994). Innovation in family formation: Evidence on cohabitation in the United States. In J. Eruisch & K. Ogawa (Eds.), *The family, the market and the state in aging societies.* London, England: Oxford University Press.

Wilson, G. T., Fairburn, C. C., Agras, W. S., Walsh, B. T., & Kraemer, H. (2002). Cognitive behavioral therapy for bulimia nervosa: Time course and mechanisms of change. *Journal of Consulting and Clinical Psychology, 70,* 267–274.

Wilson, R. S., & Bennett, D. A. (2003). Cognitive activity and risk of Alzheimer's disease. *Current Directions in Psychological Science, 12,* 87–91.

Wilson, R. S., Bennett, D. A., Bienias, J. L., Aggarwal, N. T., Mendes de Leon, C. F., Morris, M. C., et al. (2002). Cognitive activity and incident AD in a population-based sample of older persons. *Neurology, 59,* 1910–1914.

Windholz, G. (1997). Ivan P. Pavlov: An overview of his life and psychological work. *American Psychologist, 52,* 941–946.

Windholz, G., & Lamal, P. A. (1985). Koehler's insight revisited. *Teaching of Psychology, 12,* 165–167.

Winerip, M. (1999, May 23). Bedlam on the streets. *New York Times Magazine,* pp. 42–49.

Winerman, L. (2004a, April). A second look at twin studies. *Monitor on Psychology, 35*(4), 46–47.

Winerman, L. (2004b, May). Panel stresses youth suicide prevention. *Monitor on Psychology, 35,* 18.

Winerman, L. (2004c, July/August). Sleep deprivation threatens public health, says research award winner. *Monitor on Psychology, 35,* 61.

Wingert, P. (2002, December 9). Some basic truths about teen sex. *Newsweek,* pp. 67–71.

Winner, E. (2000). The origins and ends of giftedness. *American Psychologist, 55,* 159–169.

Winslow, R. (2004, August 29). Study finds common threads in global risks for heart attack. *Wall Street Journal Online.* Retrieved September 2, 2004, from http://online.wsj.com/article/0,,SB109378959028403743,00.html?mod=home_whats_news_us.

Winterer, G., Coppola, R., Goldberg, T. E., Egan, M. F., Jones, D. W., et al. (2004). Prefrontal broadband noise, working memory, and genetic risk for schizophrenia. *American Journal of Psychiatry, 161,* 490–500.

Wixted, J. T. (2004). The psychology and neuroscience of forgetting. *Annual Review of Psychology, 55,* 235–269.

Wixted, J. T. (2005). A theory about why we forget what we once knew. *Current Directions in Psychological Science, 14,* 6–9.

Wolchik, S. A., Sandler, I. N., Millsap, R. E., Plummer, B. A., Greene, S. M., Anderson, E. R., et al. (2002). Six-year follow-up of preventive interventions for children of divorce: A randomized controlled trial. *Journal of the American Medical Association, 288,* 1874–1881.

Wolpe, J. (1958). *Psychotherapy by reciprocal inhibition*. Stanford, CA: Stanford University Press.

Wong, E. C., Kim, B. S. K., Zane, N. W. S., Kim, I. J., & Huang, J. S. (2003). Examining culturally based variables associated with ethnicity: Influences on credibility perceptions of empirically supported interventions. *Cultural Diversity and Ethnic Minority Psychology, 9*, 88–96.

Wood, J. M., Lilienfeld, S. O., Nezworski, M. T., & Garb, H. N. (2001). Coming to grips with negative evidence for the comprehensive system for the Rorschach: A comment on Gacono, Loving, and Bodholdt; Ganellen; and Bornstein. *Journal of Personality Assessment, 77*, 48–70.

Wood, M. D., Vinson, D. C., & Sher, K. J. (2001). Alcohol use and misuse. In A. Baum, T. A. Revenson, & J. E. Singer (Eds.), *Handbook of health psychology* (pp. 280–320). Mahwah, NJ: Lawrence Erlbaum Associates.

Wood, W., & Eagly, A. H. (2002). A cross-cultural analysis of the behavior of women and men: Implications for the origins of sex differences. *Psychological Bulletin, 128*, 699–727.

Wood, W., & Quinn, J. M. (2003). Forewarned and forearmed? Two meta-analytic syntheses of forewarnings of influence appeals. *Psychological Bulletin, 129*, 119–138.

Woods, C. M., Vevea, J. L., Chambless, D. L., & Bayen, U. J. (2002). Are compulsive checkers impaired in memory? A meta-analytic review. *Clinical Psychology: Science and Practice, 9*, 353–366.

Wren, C. S. (2001, June 26). Powell, at U.N., asks for war on AIDS. *New York Times*, pp. A1, A4.

Wright, S. C., Aron, A., McLaughlin-Volpe, R., & Ropp, S. A. (1997). The extended contact effect: Knowledge of cross-group friendships and prejudice. *Journal of Personality and Social Psychology, 73*, 73–90.

Writing Group of the PREMIER Collaborative Research Group. (2003). Effects of comprehensive lifestyle modification on blood pressure control: Main results of the PREMIER Clinical Trial. *Journal of the American Medical Association, 289*, 2083–2093.

Wu, K. D., & Clark, L. A. (2003). Relations between personality traits and self-reports of daily behavior. *Journal of Research in Personality, 37*, 231–256.

Xu, K., Lichtermann, D., Lipsky, R. H., Franke, P., Liu, X., Hu, Y., et al. (2004). Association of specific haplotypes of D2 dopamine receptor gene with vulnerability to heroin dependence in 2 distinct populations. *Archives of General Psychiatry, 61*, 597–606.

Yali, A. M, & Revenson, T. A. (2004). How changes in population demographics will impact health psychology: Incorporating a broader notion of cultural competence into the field. *Health Psychology, 23*, 147–155.

Yamaguchi, S., Isejima, H., Matsuo, T., Okura, R., Yagita, K., Kobayashi, M., et al. (2003). Synchronization of cellular clocks in the suprachiasmatic nucleus. *Science, 302*, 1408–1412.

Yan, L. L., Liu, K., Matthews, K. A., Daviglus, M. L., Ferguson, F., & Kiefe, C. I. (2003). Psychosocial factors and risk of hypertension: The Coronary Artery Risk Development in Young Adults (CARDIA) Study. *Journal of the American Medical Association, 290*, 2138–2148.

Yasuno, F., Suhara, T., Nakayama, T., Ichimiya, T., Okubo, Y., Takano, A., et al. (2003). Inhibitory effect of hippocampal 5-HT1A receptors on human explicit memory. *American Journal of Psychiatry, 160*, 334–340.

Yeni, P. G., Hammer, S. M., Hirsch, M. S., Saag, M. S., Schechter, M., Carpenter, C. C. J., et al. (2004). Treatment for Adult HIV Infection: 2004 Recommendations of the International AIDS Society-USA Panel. *Journal of the American Medical Association, 292*, 251–265.

Young, E. A., Clopton, J. R., & Bleckley, M. K. (2004). Perfectionism, low self-esteem, and family factors as predictors of bulimic behavior. *Eating Behaviors, 5*, 273–283.

Yunger, J. L., Carver, P. R., & Perry, D. G. (2004). Does gender identity influence children's psychological well-being? *Developmental Psychology, 40*, 572–582.

Yusuf, S., Hawken, S., Ôunpuu, S., Dans, T., Avezum, A., Lanas, F., et al. (2004). Effect of potentially modifiable risk factors associated with myocardial infarction in 52 countries (the INTERHEART study): Case-control study. *Lancet, 364*, 937–952.

Zajonc, R. B. (1980). Feeling and thinking: Preferences need no inferences. *American Psychologist, 35*, 151–175.

Zajonc, R. B. (1984). On the primacy of affect. *American Psychologist, 39*, 117–123.

Zamanian, K., Thackrey, M., Starrett, R. A., Brown, L. G., et al. (1992). Acculturation and depression in Mexican-American elderly. *Gerontologist, 11*, 109–121.

Zamiska, N. (2004, August 12). U.S. diet advisory panel to urge eating more fish, whole grain. *Wall Street Journal*, p. D3.

Zaragoza, M. S., Payment, K. E., Ackil, J. K., Drivdahl, S. B., & Beck, M. (2001). Interviewing witnesses: Forced confabulation and confirmatory feedback increase false memories. *Psychological Science, 12*, 473–477.

Zea, M. C., Mason, M., & Murguia, A. (2000). Psychotherapy with members of Latino/Latina religions and spiritual traditions. In P. S. Richards & A. E. Bergin (Eds.), *Handbook of psychotherapy and religious diversity* (pp. 397–419). Washington, DC: American Psychological Association.

Zernicke, K. (2005, March 12). A 21st-birthday drinking game can be a deadly rite of passage. *New York Times*, pp. A1, A13.

Zernike, K. (2000, August 25). Gap widens again on tests given to Blacks and Whites. *New York Times*. Retrieved September 13, 2000, from http://www.nytimes.com/library/national/082500race-tests-edu.html.

Zigler, E., & Styfco, S. J. (1994). Head Start: Criticisms in a constructive context. *American Psychologist, 49*, 127–132.

Zimand, E., Rothbaum, B., Tannenbaum, L., Ferrer, M., & Hodges, L. (2003). Technology meets psychology: Integrating virtual reality into clinical practice. *Clinical Psychologist, 56*, 5–11.

Zimprich, D., & Martin, M. (2002). Can longitudinal changes in processing speed explain longitudinal age changes in fluid intelligence? *Psychology and Aging, 17*, 690–695.

Zinbarg, R. E., Brown, T. A., Barlow, D. H., & Rapee, R. M. (2001). Anxiety sensitivity, panic, and depressed mood: A reanalysis teasing apart the contributions of the two levels in the hierarchical structure of the Anxiety Sensitivity Index. *Journal of Abnormal Psychology, 110*, 372–377.

Zinser, O., Freeman, J. E., & Ginnings, D. K. (1999). A comparison of memory for and attitudes about alcohol, cigarette, and other product advertisements in college students. *Journal of Drug Education, 29*, 175–185.

Zlotnick, C., Bruce, S. E., Shea, M. T., & Keller, M. B. (2001). Delayed posttraumatic stress disorder (PTSD) and predictors of first onset of PTSD in patients with anxiety disorders. *Journal of Nervous and Mental Disease, 189*, 404–406.

Zoellner, L. A., Foa, E. B., Brigidi, B. D., & Przeworski, A. (2000). Are trauma victims susceptible to "false memories"? *Journal of Abnormal Psychology, 109*, 517–524.

Zola, S. M. (1999). Memory, amnesia, and the issue of recovered memory: Neurobiological aspects. *Clinical Psychology Review, 19*, 915–932.

Zubin, J., & Spring, B. (1977). Vulnerability—A new view of schizophrenia. *Journal of Abnormal Psychology, 86*, 103–126.

Zucker, A. N., Ostrove, J. M., & Stewart, A. J. (2002). College-educated women's personality development in adulthood: Perceptions and age differences. *Psychology and Aging, 2*, 236–244.

Zuckerman, M. (1980). Sensation seeking. In H. London & J. Exner (Eds.), *Dimensions of personality*. New York: John Wiley & Sons.

Zuckerman, M. (1996). The psychobiological model for impulsive unsocialized sensation seeking: A comparative approach. *Neuropsychobiology, 34*, 125–129.

Zuckerman, M. (2003). Biological bases of personality. In T. Millon & M. J. Lerner (Eds.), *Handbook of psychology: Vol. 5. Personality and social psychology* (pp. 85–116). New York: John Wiley & Sons.

Zuger, A. (1997, August 19). Removing half of brain improves young epileptics' lives. *New York Times*, p. C4.

Zukow-Goldring, P. (1997). A social ecological realist approach to the emergence of the lexicon: Educating attention to amodal invariants in gesture and speech. In C. Dent-Read & P. Zukow-Goldring (Eds.), *Evolving explanations of development: Ecological approaches to organism-environment systems* (pp. 199–250). Washington, DC: American Psychological Association.

Zvolensky, M. J., Kotov, R., Antipova, A. V., & Schmidt, N. B. (2005). Diathesis stress model for panic-related distress: A test in a Russian epidemiological sample. *Behaviour Research and Therapy, 43*, 521–532.

Credits

Photo Credits

Chapter opener photos: Ch. 1, p. 2: © Gary Buss/Taxi/Getty Images; Ch. 2, p. 44: © Lester Lefkowitz/CORBIS; Ch. 3, p. 92: © LWA-Dann Tardif / CORBIS; Ch. 4, p. 136: © Chris Lisle/CORBIS; Ch. 5, p. 180: © Paul Barton/CORBIS; Ch. 6, p. 216: © Richard Lord/The Image Works; Ch. 7, p. 252: © Ariel Skelley/CORBIS; Ch. 8, p. 294: © Bob Daemmrich/PhotoEdit; Ch. 9, p. 336: © David Young-Wolff/PhotoEdit; Ch. 10, p. 382: © Ephraim Ben-Shimon/Corbis; Ch. 11, p. 422: © Stockbyte/Getty Images; Ch. 12, p. 460: © Stockbyte/Getty Images; Ch. 13, p. 502: © John Lamb/Taxi/Getty Images; Ch. 14, p. 542: © Bruce Ayres/Stone/Getty Images; Ch. 15, p. 580: © Bob Daemmrich/PhotoEdit; Ch. 16, p. 614: © David Grossman/The Image Works.

Chapter 1: p. 4: © Michael Keller/CORBIS. p. 6: Archives of the History of American Psychology-The University of Akron. p. 7: © J.P. Laffont/Sygma/CORBIS. p. 9: Archives of the History of American Psychology-The University of Akron. p. 12: © David Madison/CORBIS. p. 13: © Chuck Savage/CORBIS. p. 15: *(left)* © Topham/The Image Works; *(middle)* AP/Wide World Photos; *(right)* © Reuters/Corbis. p. 21: © Richard T. Nowitz/Photo Researchers. p. 23: *(top left)* Wellesley College Archives, photo by Partridge; *(top middle)* Archives of the History of American Psychology-The University of Akron; *(top right)* Courtesy of Wilberforce University, Archives and Special Collections; *(bottom)* Library of Congress. p. 29: © Brand X Pictures/Getty Images. p. 31: © Karl Ammann/CORBIS. p. 32: © David Young-Wolff/PhotoEdit. p. 36: © Bill Bachmann/PhotoEdit. p. 41: © Spencer Grant/PhotoEdit.

Chapter 2: p. 51: © Scott Nelson/AFP/Getty Images. p. 64: © The Natural History Museum, London. p. 67: © Richard Nowitz/Photo Researchers. p. 68: *(top)* © Syracuse Newspapers/The Image Works; *(bottom)* © Pascal Goetgheluck/Science Photo Library/Photo Researchers. p. 69: *(left)* © Scott Grafton MD/Visuals Unlimited; *(right)* © Lilly Dong/Botanica/Getty Images. p. 70: Courtesy of Dr. Keith Thulborn. p. 72: © Leland Bobbé/CORBIS. p. 73: © Neil Bromhall/Science Photo Library/Photo Researchers. p. 74: © CNRI/Photo Researchers. p. 75: "The Tale of Phineas Gage, Digitally Remastered," by Peter Ratiu, M.D. and Ion-Florin Talos, M.D., *New England Journal of Medicine*, Vol. 351, No. 23, 12/ 2/04, p. e21. Copyright © 2004 Massachusetts Medical Society. All rights reserved. p. 89: *(puppy)* © Jeanne White/Photo Researchers; *(man)* © RubberBall Productions/Getty Images; *(MRIs)* © Neil Borden/Photo Researchers.

Chapter 3: p. 99: © Ralph C. Eagle/Photo Researchers. p. 103: Used with permission of Richmond Products. p. 112: *(top)* © Rolf Bruderer / CORBIS; *(bottom)* © David Young-Wolff/PhotoEdit. p. 115: © Lon C. Diehl/PhotoEdit. p. 116: *(top)* © TEK Image/Science Photo Library/Photo Researchers; *(bottom)* © Royalty-Free/CORBIS. p. 120: © John Chiasson/Getty Images. p. 124: © Susan Van Etten/PhotoEdit. p. 125: *(top left)* © Royalty-Free/Corbis; *(top middle)* © David Stoecklein/CORBIS; *(top right)* © Art Wolfe/Stone/Getty Images; *(bottom left)* ©John Harris/Report Digital-REA/Redux; *(bottom middle)* © Momatiuk - Eastcott/CORBIS. p. 127: *(top)* © James Blank/Taxi/Getty Images; *(bottom)* © Abe Rezny/The Image Works. p. 128: © Peter Menzel/Stock Boston. p. 133: © Will & Deni McInyre/Photo Researchers. p. 134: © Grace/zefa/CORBIS.

Chapter 4: p. 138: © Artiga Photo/CORBIS. p. 139: Archives of the History of American Psychology-The University of Akron. p. 140: Images.com/CORBIS. p. 152: © Tony Anderson/FPG International/Getty Images. p. 154: © Bill Aron/PhotoEdit. p. 155: © Patrick ALLARD/REA/Redux. p. 160: *(left)* © Don Mason/CORBIS; *(right)* © Karen Moskowitz/Stone/Getty Images. p. 163: © Ariel Skelley/CORBIS. p. 166: © Mark Richards/PhotoEdit. p. 167: © David Young-Wolff/Photo Edit. p. 168: © Michael Newman/PhotoEdit. p. 169: © R. Flynt/The Image Works. p. 172: *(top)* © Royalty-Free/CORBIS; *(bottom)* © David Young-Wolff/PhotoEdit. p. 173: *(all)* Reprinted from *Addictive Behaviors*, Vol. 29, "fMRI BOLD response to alcohol stimuli in alcohol dependent young women" by Susan F. Tapert et al, pp. 43-50, copyright 2004, with permission from Elsevier. p. 175: Photo provided by the Sam Spady Foundation, www.samspadyfoundation.org. p. 177: © T. Petillot/Explorer/Photo Researchers.

Chapter 5: p. 183: © Bettmann/CORBIS. p. 188: *(top)* Archives of the History of American Psychology-The University of Akron; *(bottom)* © Andrew Yates Productions/The Image Bank/Getty Images. p. 189: Archives of the History of American Psychology-The University of Akron. p. 190: © Mark Peterson/Redux. p. 191: *(top)* © Tom Stack & Associates; *(bottom)* Courtesy of Dr. John Garcia. p. 195: Nina Leen/Time & Life Pictures/Getty Images. p. 197: © L. Clarke/CORBIS. p. 198: © Bob Daemmrich/The Image Works. p. 201: © Michelle Gabel/Syracuse Newspapers/The Image Works. p. 206: © Tony Freeman/PhotoEdit. p. 210: AP/Wide World Photos. p. 214: © Thinkstock/Getty Images.

Chapter 6: p. 221: © David Young-Wolff/PhotoEdit. p. 226: AP/Wide World Photos. p. 227: © Gaetano/CORBIS. p. 228: © Greg Flume/NewSport/CORBIS. p. 229: Courtesy of W. F. Brewer, from Brewer, W. F. and Treyens, J. C. (1981), "Role of Schemata in Memory of Places," *Cognitive Psychology*, 13, 207-230. p. 230: © Allan Tannenbaum/The Image Works. p. 231: © Siner Jeff/CORBIS SYGMA. p. 232: Everett Collection. p. 236: Archives of the History of American Psychology-The University of Akron. p. 238: © Dana White/PhotoEdit. p. 241: © Jeff Persons/Stock Boston. p. 246: Courtesy of Eric Kandel.

Chapter 7: p. 254 *(top)* © Laura Dwight/CORBIS; *(bottom)* © Topham/The Image Works. p. 255: © Bob Daemmrich/The Image Works. p. 257: © T. Brakefield/The Image Works. p. 260: © CORBIS. p. 262: © Dennis MacDonald/PhotoEdit. p. 263: © Lawrence Migdale/Stock Boston. p. 270: *(top)* © Rick Friedman/CORBIS; *(bottom)* © Art Wolfe/Stone/Getty Images. p. 271: © Spencer Grant/Photo Researchers. p. 272: Courtesy of Great Ape Trust of Iowa, www.greatapetrust.org. p. 275: © Bettmann/CORBIS. p. 281: Archives of the History of American Psychology-The University of Akron. p. 282: *(left)* © Robert Brenner/PhotoEdit; *(top)* © Bob Daemmrich/The Image Works; *(bottom)* © Tim Pannell/CORBIS; *(right)* © Michael Mulvey/Dallas Morning News/CORBIS. p. 283: *(top)* © Michael Newman/PhotoEdit; *(bottom left)* © Stephen Collins/Photo Researchers; *(bottom right)* © Mike Greenlar/The Image Works. p. 287: © Don Smetzer/PhotoEdit.

Chapter 8: p. 296: © Reuters/CORBIS. p. 301: © Spencer Grant/PhotoEdit. p. 302: © Fabian Falcon/Stock Boston. p. 306: Courtesy of Neal E. Miller, Dept. of Psychology, Yale University. p. 308: © Dennis MacDonald/PhotoEdit. p. 309: © Joel Gordon Photography p. 311: © Tony Freeman/PhotoEdit. p. 312: *(top left and right)* © Jill Greenburg; *(bottom)* © David Young-Wolff/PhotoEdit. p. 317: *(all)* Paul Ekman, from *The face of man: Expression of universal emotions in a New Guinea Village*, 1980. p. 319: *(all)* © Tony Freeman/PhotoEdit. p. 320: Paul Ekman, from *Telling Lies*, 1975. p. 321: NIMH (National Institute of Mental Health), 2001. p. 328: © George Shelley/CORBIS. p. 329: © Willie L. Hill, Jr./Stock Boston. p. 333: © Bob Daemmrich/Stock Boston. p. 334: © Reuters/CORBIS.

Chapter 9: p. 342: © D.W. Fawcett/SS/Photo Researchers. p. 343: *(all)* © Petit Format/Nestle/Photo Researchers. p. 346: *(top)* © David H. Wells/CORBIS; *(bottom)* Jeffrey Nevid. p. 349: *(left)* © Charles Gupton/Stock Boston; *(middle)* © J.daCunha/Petit Format/Photo Researchers; *(right)* © Elizabeth Crews. p. 350: *(top left and right)* © 2007 PhotoDisc; *(bottom)* © Mark Richards/PhotoEdit. p. 351: *(all)* Courtesy of Carolyn Rovee-Collier. p. 352: Courtesy of Prof. Colwyn Trevarthen. p. 356: *(left)* © Jose Luis Pelaez, Inc./CORBIS; *(right)* Thomas McAvoy/Time & Life Pictures/Getty Images. p. 357: Harlow Primate Laboratory, University of Wisconsin. p. 358: Courtesy of Robert Marvin. p. 361: *(left)* © Tony Freeman/PhotoEdit; *(right)* © Strauss/Curtis/CORBIS. p. 364: © Cindy Charles/PhotoEdit. p. 366: © Myrleen F. Cate/PhotoEdit. p. 368: © Bill Anderson/Photo Researchers. p. 370: *(all)* Doug Goodman/Photo Researchers. p. 371: © Lew Merrim/Science Source/Photo Researchers. p. 374: © Tony Freeman/PhotoEdit. p. 377: © Peter Byron/Photo Researchers. p. 379: *(all)* Courtesy of Albert Bandura.

Chapter 10: p. 387: *(top)* © Michael Newman/PhotoEdit; *(bottom)* Harvard Graduate School of Education. p. 391: © David Young-Wolff/PhotoEdit. p. 392: © Ted Streshinsky/COEBIS. p. 396: © Topham/The Image Works. p. 406: © Don Mason/CORBIS. p. 407: © Paul Thomas/The Image Bank/Getty Images. p. 408: © Laura Dwight/PhotoEdit. p. 411: © Stockbyte/Getty Images. p. 412: © Jon Feingersh/zefa/CORBIS. p. 414: © Jack Moebes/CORBIS. p. 416: *(left)* © Barbara Stitzer/PhotoEdit; *(right)* © Prof. P. Motta/Dept. of Anatomy/University "La Sapienza," Rome/Science Photo Library/Photo

Researchers. p. 417: © Chuck Savage/CORBIS. p. 418: © Owen Franken/CORBIS. p. 419: © David Young-Wolff/PhotoEdit.

Chapter 11: p. 424: *(all)* © David Burges/FSP/Gamma. p. 426: © Donald Miralle/Getty Images Sport/Getty Images. p. 427: © Gary Salter/zefa/CORBIS. p. 428: © Ellen Senisi/The Image Works. p. 432: © Photodisc/Getty Images. p. 435: © Myrleen F. Cate/PhotoEdit. p. 439: © Topham/The Image Works. p. 440: *(top)* © M. Thomsen/zefa/CORBIS; *(bottom)* © 1992 Newsweek, Inc. All rights reserved. Reprinted by permission. Photo © Penny Gentieu. p. 444: *(left)* Courtesy of Broken Hearts Foundation at www.brokenhearts.org; *(right)* © Beryl Goldberg. p. 451: © Teo Lannie/PhotoAlto/Getty Images. p. 454: © Bob Daemmrich/The Image Works. p. 456: © Tony Freeman/PhotoEdit.

Chapter 12: p. 463: Hulton Archive/Getty Images. p. 467: © altrendo images/Getty Images. p. 470: © Bettmann/CORBIS. p. 476: AP/Wide World Photos. p. 477: © Bonnie Kamin/PhotoEdit. p. 479: © Renee Lynn/CORBIS. p. 482: © Davis Barber/PhotoEdit. p. 486: © Myrleen F. Cate/PhotoEdit. p. 487: *(top)* © Roger Ressmeyer/CORBIS; *(bottom)* © Royalty-Free/CORBIS. p. 492: © The Image Works Archive. p. 496: © Charlotte Miller.

Chapter 13: p. 504: © G. D. T./Stone/Getty Images. p. 505: © Michele Burgess/Stock Boston. p. 506: The Granger Collection, New York. p. 513: © Jim Whitmer. p. 522: © Royalty-Free/CORBIS. p. 526: © David Madison/zefa/CORBIS. p. 528: © Burstein Collection/CORBIS. p. 530: © Mary Kate Denny/PhotoEdit. p. 533: *(left)* © Grunnitus/Photo Researchers; *(right)* Photofest. p. 534: Courtesy of Monte Buchsbaum, M.D./Mount Sinai School of Medicine, New York, NY; p. 538: AP/Wide World Photos.

Chapter 14: p. 544: © Bettmann/CORBIS. p. 546: © David Young-Wolff/PhotoEdit. p. 550: © Zigy Kaluzny/Stone/Getty Images. p. 554: Archives of the History of American Psychology-The University of Akron. p. 555: © Jim Whitmer. p. 557: Courtesy of Albert Ellis Institute. p. 559: Aaron T. Beck, MD, Professor of Psychiatry, University of Pennsylvania. p. 562: *(left)* © Ken Whitmore/Stone/Getty Images; *(right)* © Michael Newman/PhotoEdit. p. 565: *(top)* © Zigy Kaluzny/Stone/Getty Images; *(bottom)* © Michael Newman/PhotoEdit. p. 568: Georgia Tech Photo-Stanley Leary. p. 571: © Paul S. Howell/Getty Images. p. 573: © Najlah Feanny/Stock Boston.

Chapter 15: p. 583: *(left)* © Phil Martin/PhotoEdit; *(right)* © Robert Brenner/PhotoEdit. p. 590: © Rob Van Petten/The Image Bank/Getty Images. p. 591: © Ronnie Kaufman/CORBIS. p. 592: © Lon C. Diehl/PhotoEdit. p. 593: © Bettmann/CORBIS. p. 597: © Ansgar Photography/zefa/CORBIS. p. 600: © Tony Savino/The Image Works. p. 611: © John Henley Photography/CORBIS. p. 612: © Felicia Martinez/PhotoEdit.

Chapter 16: p. 617: © Tomas del Amo/Index Stock. p. 625: © Royalty-Free/CORBIS. p. 626: *(left)* © Vince Bucci/Liaison/Getty Images; *(right)* © Frank Trapper/Corbis Sygma. p. 630: © Bill Aron/PhotoEdit. p. 634: © Sygma/CORBIS. p. 642: Photo by William Vandivert; courtesy of Susan Vandivert. p. 646: From the Film Obedience. © 1965 by Stanley Milgram and distributed by Penn State Media Sales. p. 647: © 1981 by Eric Kroll. p. 648: © Michael Doolittle/The Image Works. p. 654: © Daniel Bosler/Stone/Getty Images.

Text Credits

Chapter 1: p. 26: *Excerpt:* From *Abnormal Psychology in a Changing World,* 5/e by Nevid/Rathus/Green, © 2003. Reprinted by permission of Prentice-Hall, Inc., Upper Saddle River, NJ.

Chapter 2: p. 58: *Figure 2.6:* From *Newsweek,* February 21, 2005, © 2005 Newsweek, Inc. All rights reserved. Reprinted by permission.

Chapter 3: p. 120: *Figure 3.19:* From H. R. Schiffman, *Sensation and Perception: An Integrated Approach.* Copyright © 2000 by John Wiley & Sons, Inc. Reprinted with permission of John Wiley & Sons, Inc.

Chapter 4: p. 141: *Table 4.1:* From "Behavior effects of blood alcohol levels" by O. Ray & C. Ksir, *Drugs, society, & human behavior,* 5/e. Copyright © 1990 Times Mirror/Mosby College Publishing. Used with permission of Worth Publishers.

Chapter 6: p. 229: *Try This Out:* Reprinted from *Cognitive Psychology,* Vol. 13, No. 3, W. F. Brewer and J. C. Treyens, "Role of Schemata in Memory for Places," pp. 207-230. Copyright © 1981 with permission from Elsevier. p. 239: *Try This Out:* Reprinted from *Cognitive Psychology,* Vol. 11, No. 3, Nickerson and Adams, "What Does a Penny Look Like?" pp. 287-307. Copyright © 1979 with permission from Elsevier.

Chapter 7: p. 266: *Figure 7.11:* Drawing based on Ward, *What's odd about new ideas?* In Smith, Ward, & Finke (Eds.), *The creative cognition approach* (pp. 157-178). Figure 6.10 on p. 128, Copyright © 1995 MIT Press. Reprinted with permission. p. 272: *Figure 7.12:* From D. Premack, "Language in Chimpanzee?" *Science,* Vol. 172, pp. 808-822, 1971. p. 279: *Figure 7.15:* Copyright © 1998 by The Riverside Publishing Company. "Analogic Reasoning Sample" from the Universal Nonverbal Intelligence Test(tm) (UNIT(tm)) reproduced with permission of the publisher. All rights reserved. p. 281: *Pioneers box:* Reprinted with permission. John Hogan, St. John's University. p. 285: *Figure 7.18:* Adapted from *Journal of Intelligence,* Vol. 24, pp. 53-57, Plomin et al., "Genetics and intelligence: What's new?" Copyright © 1997, with permission from Elsevier Science.

Chapter 8: p. 310: *Table 8.1:* From J. S. Nevid, S. A. Rathus, and H. R. Rubenstein, *Health in the New Millennium,* 1998. Reprinted with permission of Worth Publishers. p. 323: *Figure 8.12:* Figure adapted from "The Emotional Brain: The Mysterious Underpinnings of Emotional Life" by J. E. LeDoux. Copyright © 1996 Brockman, Inc. Reprinted with permission. p. 328: *Figure 8.14:* From Sternberg and Barnes, *The Psychology of Love,* Copyright © 1998. Reprinted with permission from Yale University Press. p. 329: *Table 8.2:* Figure adapted from S. A. Rathus, J. S. Nevid, & L. Fichner-Rathus, *Human Sexuality in a World of Diversity,* 3/e, p. 202: Copyright © Allyn & Bacon 1997. Reprinted with permission. p. 331: *Try This Out:* From Nevid and Rathus, *Psychology and the Challenges of Life,* 9th Edition. Copyright © 2005 by John Wiley & Sons, Inc. Reprinted with permission of John Wiley & Sons, Inc. p. 334: *Table 8.3:* From Jeffrey S. Nevid, Spence A. Rathus, and Beverly Greene, *Abnormal Psychology in a Changing World with CD-ROM,* 5th edition. Copyright © 2003. Electronically reproduced by permission of Pearson Education, Inc., Upper Saddle River, NJ.

Chapter 9: p. 352: *Figure 9.8:* Adapted from R. L. Gregory et al., *The Artful Eye,* 1995, p. 166. Reprinted with permission of Oxford University Press. p. 365: *Figure 9.9:* From "At Issue: Work Force Moms," *New York Times,* September 10, 2001. Copyright © 2001 by The New York Times Co. Reprinted with permission. p. 368: *Pioneers box:* Reprinted with permission. John Hogan, St. John's University. p. 372: *Figure 9.10:* From *The Developing Person Through Childhood and Adolescence,* 2/e by Kathleen Berger. Copyright © 1995, 2000 Worth Publishers. Used with permission.

Chapter 10: p. 383: *Excerpt:* Adapted from "Self and Identity Development," by Susan Harter, from S. S. Feldman & G. R. Elliot (Eds.), *At the Threshold: The Developing Adolescent,* pp. 352-353. Copyright © 1990. Reprinted with permission. p. 384: *Table 10.1:* From *Newsweek,* May 8, 2000, © 2000 Newsweek, Inc. All rights reserved. Reprinted by permission. p. 385: *Figure 10.1:* Adapted from *Lifespan Development,* by K.L. Seifert, R.J. Hoffnung, and M. Hoffnung. Copyright © 2000 by Houghton Mifflin Company. Reprinted with permission of Houghton Mifflin Company. p. 393: *Table 10.2:* From *Newsweek,* May 8, 2000, © 2000 Newsweek, Inc. All rights reserved. Reprinted by permission. p. 398: *Table 10.3:* Adapted from S.A. Rathus, J.S. Nevid, & L. Fichner-Rathus, *Human Sexuality in a World of Diversity,* 3/e, pp. 96-97. Copyright © Allyn & Bacon 1995. Reprinted with permission. p. 399: *Figure 10.3:* From Jeffrey Jenson Arnett, *Adolescence and Emerging Adulthood: A Cultural Approach,* 2nd Edition, © 2004, p. 15. Reprinted by permission of Pearson Education, Inc., Upper Saddle River, NJ. p. 409: *Figure 10.7:* From *Newsweek,* May 8, 2000, © 2000 Newsweek, Inc. All rights reserved. Reprinted by permission.

Chapter 11: p. 431: *Figure 11.2:* Adapted from Kimura, D. (September 1992). "Sex differences in the brain." *Scientific American,* pp. 120-121. Reprinted by permission of Jared Schneidman Design. p. 434: *Figure 11.3:* From Laumann, Gagnon, Michael & Michaels, *The Social Organization of Sexuality.* Reprinted with permission of The University of Chicago Press. p. 449: *Table 11.7:* From Laumann, Gagnon, Michael & Michaels, *The Social Organization of Sexuality.* Reprinted with permission of The University of Chicago Press.

Chapter 12: p. 474: *Figure 12.2:* Data derived from Cattell, Eber, and Tatsuoka: *Handbook for the Sixteen Personality Factor Questionnaire* (16PF(r)),

Name Index

Subject Index

Pages on which key terms appear are indicated in boldface.

CONTENTS

CONCEPT MAPS FOR PSYCHOLOGY:
Visualizing Concepts and Connections

A Note to Students . . .

This booklet contains a visual learning tool called a *concept map*. A concept map helps you visualize key concepts and ideas and the connections between them.

WHAT ARE CONCEPT MAPS?

Concept maps are visual diagrams that allow you to see at a glance how key concepts or ideas are linked together. Each map starts with a central idea or concept in psychology, such as "Motivation" or "Conditioning." Related concepts emanate from the central concept, forming a kind of organized knowledge structure. As you leaf through this booklet, you'll see that each map consists of two key elements:

1. NODES These are concepts or ideas. Nodes are placed within the concept map in different colored shapes such as squares and ellipses.

2. LINKS These are the connectors between nodes. Links explain the relationships between concepts and ideas and help you see the relational connections between them. You'll recognize a connector because it is italicized and placed outside of a colored shape. The direction of the relationship between the nodes is indicated by an arrow symbol.

HOW TO USE THIS BOOKLET

The concept maps in this booklet correspond to particular chapters in the text. All of the information in these maps is extracted directly from the textbook. This booklet is a supplement to the text, but it is not a substitute for reading the text assignments.

A distinctive feature of the concept map is that it is can be read either top-to-bottom or side-to-side, much like a sentence. Read each of the links and nodes to visualize how key concepts in psychology are linked together.

To make these maps an even more effective learning tool, they are accompanied by two types of questions that appear at the end of the booklet:

Study Questions help you review your knowledge of the concepts represented in the maps.

Thought Questions encourage you to think more deeply about these concepts by relating the material to your personal experiences. Deeper processing is a key feature of effective learning and leads to more enduring memories.

I hope you find these concept maps to be a helpful aid in your study of psychology.

Jeff Nevid
New York, New York

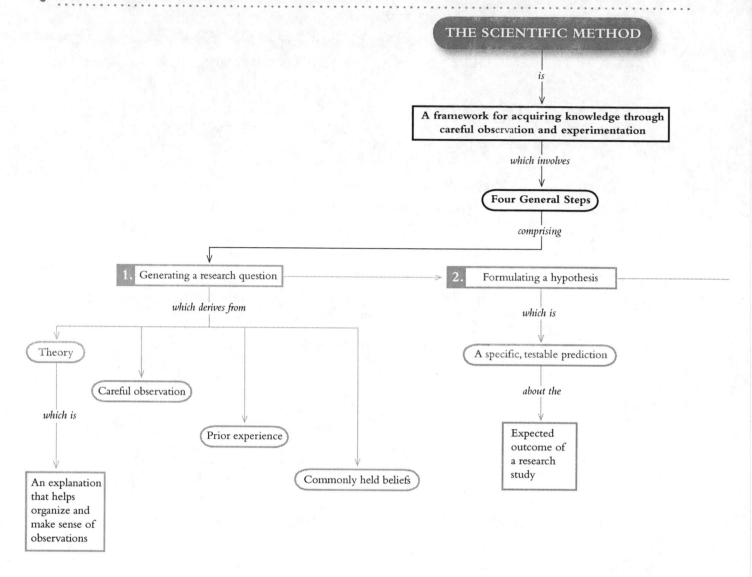

Sharpen your skills by completing the Concept Map Study Questions and Thought Questions at the end of this booklet.

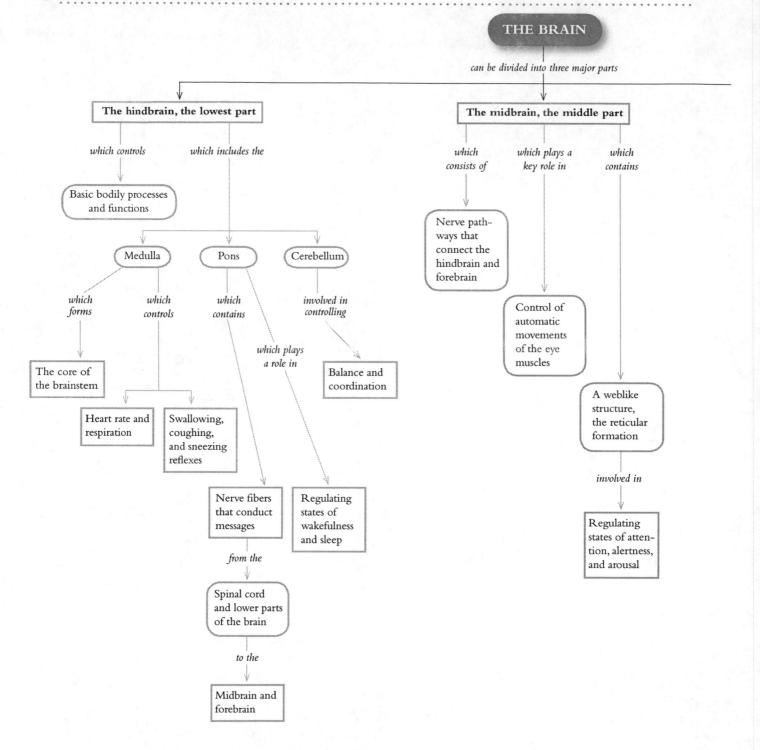

THE BRAIN

can be divided into three major parts

The hindbrain, the lowest part

which controls

Basic bodily processes and functions

which includes the

Medulla   Pons   Cerebellum

which forms   *which controls*   *which contains*   *involved in controlling*

The core of the brainstem

Heart rate and respiration

Swallowing, coughing, and sneezing reflexes

which plays a role in

Balance and coordination

Nerve fibers that conduct messages

Regulating states of wakefulness and sleep

from the

Spinal cord and lower parts of the brain

to the

Midbrain and forebrain

The midbrain, the middle part

which consists of   *which plays a key role in*   *which contains*

Nerve pathways that connect the hindbrain and forebrain

Control of automatic movements of the eye muscles

A weblike structure, the reticular formation

involved in

Regulating states of attention, alertness, and arousal

Sharpen your skills by completing the Concept Map Study Questions and Thought Questions at the end of this booklet.

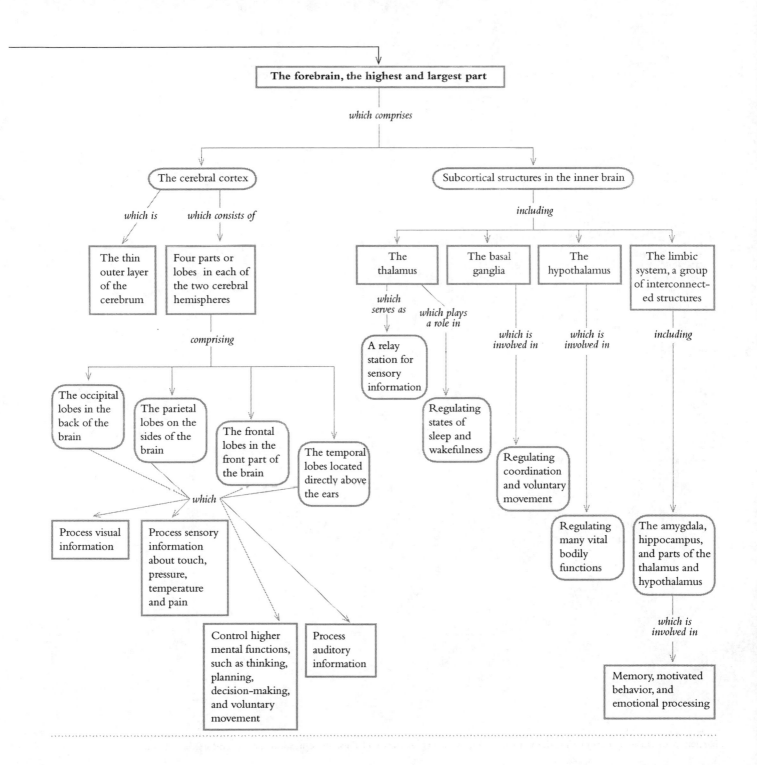

The forebrain, the highest and largest part

which comprises

The cerebral cortex

which is

which consists of

The thin outer layer of the cerebrum

Four parts or lobes in each of the two cerebral hemispheres

comprising

The occipital lobes in the back of the brain

The parietal lobes on the sides of the brain

The frontal lobes in the front part of the brain

The temporal lobes located directly above the ears

which

Process visual information

Process sensory information about touch, pressure, temperature and pain

Control higher mental functions, such as thinking, planning, decision-making, and voluntary movement

Process auditory information

Subcortical structures in the inner brain

including

The thalamus

The basal ganglia

The hypothalamus

The limbic system, a group of interconnected structures

which serves as

which plays a role in

which is involved in

which is involved in

including

A relay station for sensory information

Regulating states of sleep and wakefulness

Regulating coordination and voluntary movement

Regulating many vital bodily functions

The amygdala, hippocampus, and parts of the thalamus and hypothalamus

which is involved in

Memory, motivated behavior, and emotional processing

BASIC CONCEPTS OF SENSATION AND PERCEPTION

How We Form Sensations

involves

A process of transforming physical energy

into

which is accomplished by

Neural impulses the brain processes

Sensory receptors

which give rise to

that convert

examples of which include

Sensations of vision, hearing, smell, taste, touch, and so on

Stimulation into neural impulses

Rods and cones in the retina for vision

Hair cells in the inner ear for hearing

Taste cells for the sense of taste

Odor receptors for smell

Skin receptors for skin senses

What We Sense

depends on

The absolute threshold

The difference threshold

Sensory adaptation

Signal detection

which is

which is determined by

The minimum amount of a stimulus that can be reliably detected

The minimal difference between two stimuli that can be reliably detected

The ability of sensory systems to adapt to constant stimuli by becoming less sensitive to them

Characteristics of the perceiver, the background, and the stimulus itself

Sharpen your skills by completing the Concept Map Study Questions and Thought Questions at the end of this booklet.

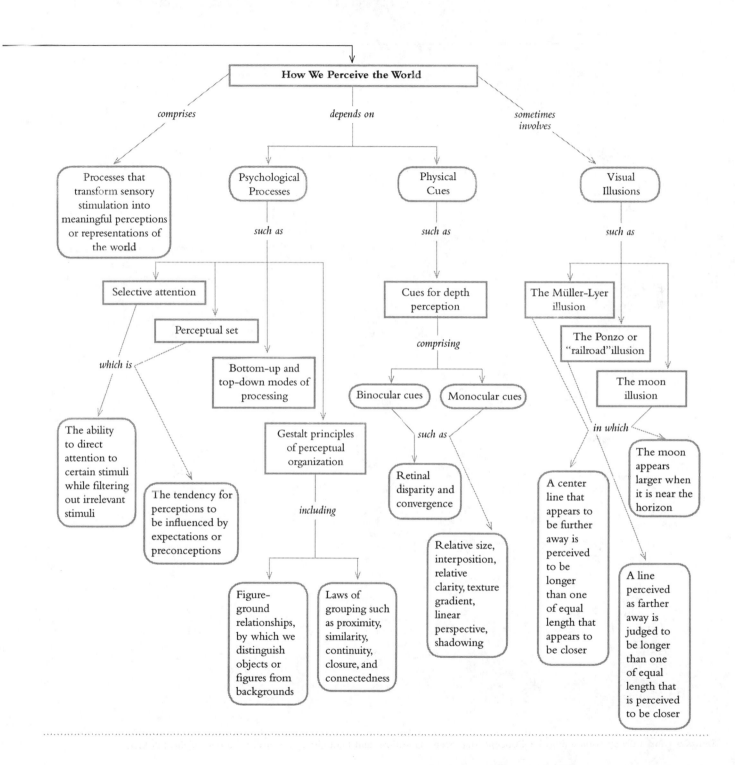

How We Perceive the World

comprises → Processes that transform sensory stimulation into meaningful perceptions or representations of the world

depends on → Psychological Processes

sometimes involves → Visual Illusions

such as (Psychological Processes) → Selective attention

Perceptual set

which is → The ability to direct attention to certain stimuli while filtering out irrelevant stimuli

The tendency for perceptions to be influenced by expectations or preconceptions

Bottom-up and top-down modes of processing

Gestalt principles of perceptual organization

including →

Figure-ground relationships, by which we distinguish objects or figures from backgrounds

Laws of grouping such as proximity, similarity, continuity, closure, and connectedness

Physical Cues

such as → Cues for depth perception

comprising → Binocular cues / Monocular cues

such as → Retinal disparity and convergence

Relative size, interposition, relative clarity, texture gradient, linear perspective, shadowing

Visual Illusions

such as → The Müller-Lyer illusion

The Ponzo or "railroad" illusion

The moon illusion

in which →

A center line that appears to be further away is perceived to be longer than one of equal length that appears to be closer

The moon appears larger when it is near the horizon

A line perceived as farther away is judged to be longer than one of equal length that is perceived to be closer

KEY CONCEPTS OF CONSCIOUSNESS

Consciousness

is conceptualized as

shifts

The state of present awareness of yourself and the world around you

During the day among different states of awareness

including

Focused Awareness

Drifting Consciousness

Divided Consciousness

in which

Unconsciousness

which is characterized by

Complete absorption in an activity or task

Drifting thoughts and daydreams

Attention is focused on two or more tasks at the same time

which occurs during

Sleep and dreaming states

or during

States of deep unconsciousness associated with coma

Sleeping and Dreaming

Sleep-wake cycles

Sleep involves four distinct stages

Sleep may serve several functions

Theories of dreaming

are regulated by the

occurring prior to

including a

include

SCN

which is a

Clockwork mechanism in the hypothalamus

that stimulates

The pineal gland to secrete the hormone melatonin

which induces

Feelings of drowsiness leading to sleep

REM sleep, the stage of sleep

in which

Most dreams occur

Protective function

Energy conservation function

Memory consolidation function

Restorative function

Hartmann's problem-solving theory

Activation-synthesis hypothesis

Freud's wish-fulfillment theory

Sharpen your skills by completing the Concept Map Study Questions and Thought Questions at the end of this booklet.

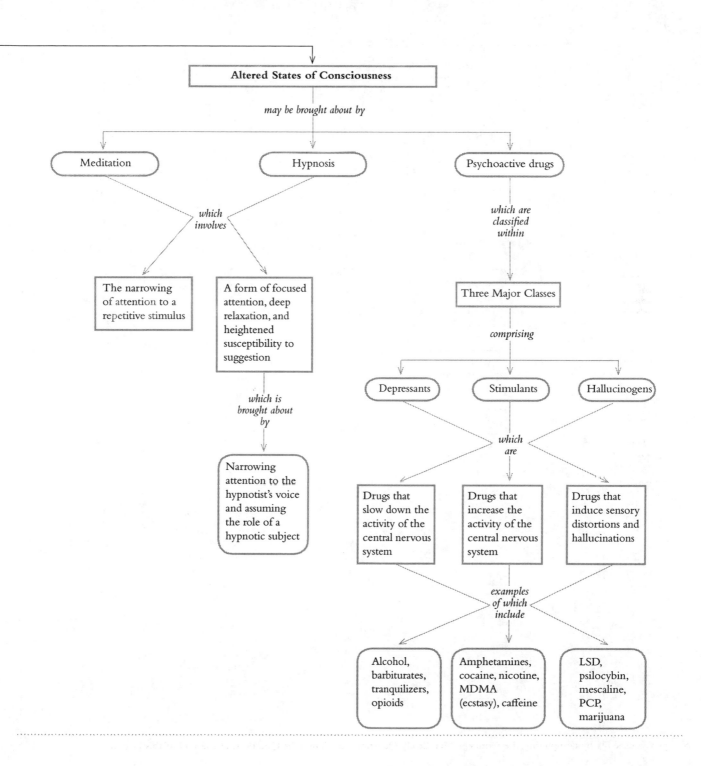

Altered States of Consciousness

may be brought about by

Meditation | Hypnosis | Psychoactive drugs

which involves

The narrowing of attention to a repetitive stimulus

A form of focused attention, deep relaxation, and heightened susceptibility to suggestion

which is brought about by

Narrowing attention to the hypnotist's voice and assuming the role of a hypnotic subject

which are classified within

Three Major Classes

comprising

Depressants | Stimulants | Hallucinogens

which are

Drugs that slow down the activity of the central nervous system

Drugs that increase the activity of the central nervous system

Drugs that induce sensory distortions and hallucinations

examples of which include

Alcohol, barbiturates, tranquilizers, opioids

Amphetamines, cocaine, nicotine, MDMA (ecstasy), caffeine

LSD, psilocybin, mescaline, PCP, marijuana

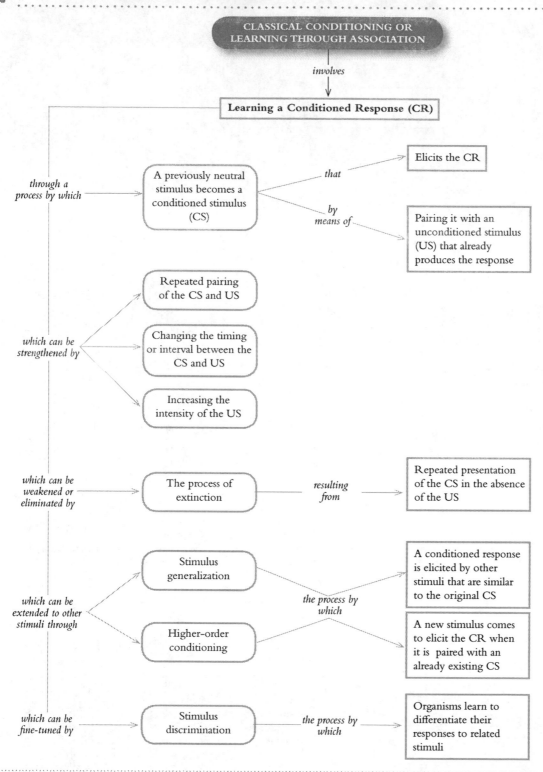

CLASSICAL CONDITIONING OR
LEARNING THROUGH ASSOCIATION

involves

Learning a Conditioned Response (CR)

*through a
process by which*

A previously neutral stimulus becomes a conditioned stimulus (CS)

that → Elicits the CR

*by
means of* → Pairing it with an unconditioned stimulus (US) that already produces the response

*which can be
strengthened by*

Repeated pairing of the CS and US

Changing the timing or interval between the CS and US

Increasing the intensity of the US

*which can be
weakened or
eliminated by* → The process of extinction → *resulting
from* → Repeated presentation of the CS in the absence of the US

*which can be
extended to other
stimuli through*

Stimulus generalization

Higher-order conditioning

*the process by
which* → A conditioned response is elicited by other stimuli that are similar to the original CS

*the process by
which* → A new stimulus comes to elicit the CR when it is paired with an already existing CS

*which can be
fine-tuned by* → Stimulus discrimination → *the process by
which* → Organisms learn to differentiate their responses to related stimuli

Sharpen your skills by completing the Concept Map Study Questions and Thought Questions at the end of this booklet.

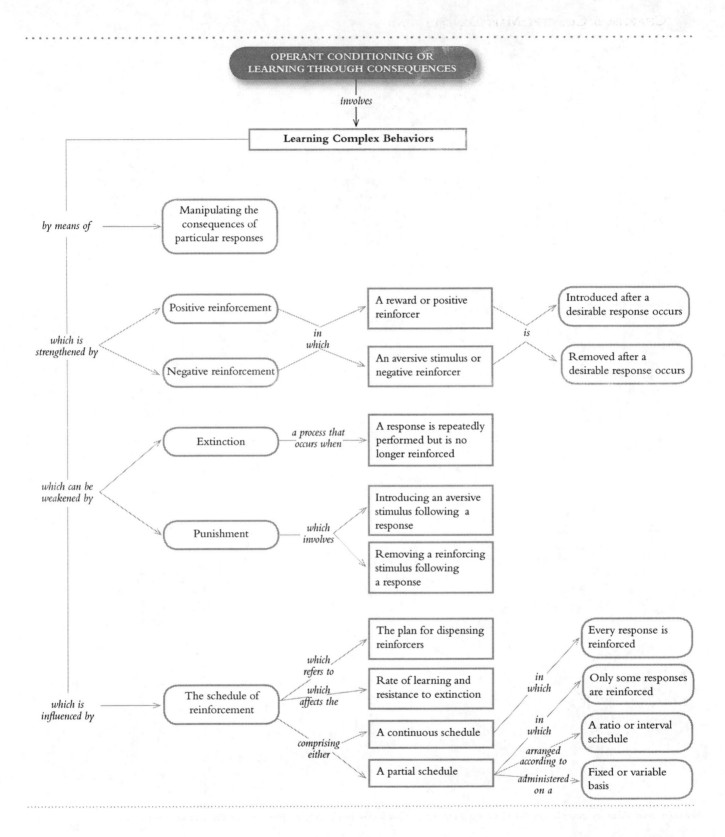

OPERANT CONDITIONING OR LEARNING THROUGH CONSEQUENCES

involves

Learning Complex Behaviors

by means of → Manipulating the consequences of particular responses

which is strengthened by

Positive reinforcement

Negative reinforcement

in which

A reward or positive reinforcer

An aversive stimulus or negative reinforcer

is

Introduced after a desirable response occurs

Removed after a desirable response occurs

which can be weakened by

Extinction

a process that occurs when

A response is repeatedly performed but is no longer reinforced

Punishment

which involves

Introducing an aversive stimulus following a response

Removing a reinforcing stimulus following a response

which is influenced by →

The schedule of reinforcement

which refers to

The plan for dispensing reinforcers

which affects the

Rate of learning and resistance to extinction

comprising either

A continuous schedule

A partial schedule

in which

Every response is reinforced

in which

Only some responses are reinforced

arranged according to

A ratio or interval schedule

administered on a

Fixed or variable basis

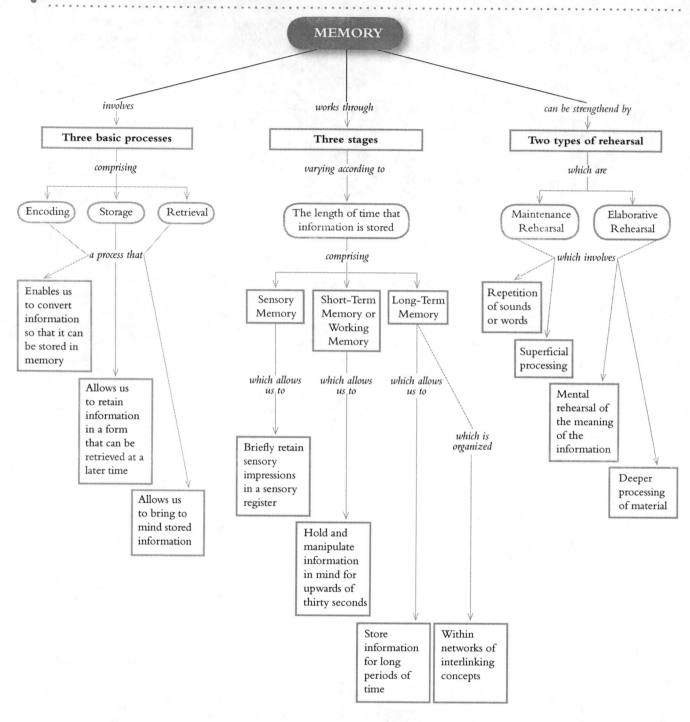

Sharpen your skills by completing the Concept Map Study Questions and Thought Questions at the end of this booklet.

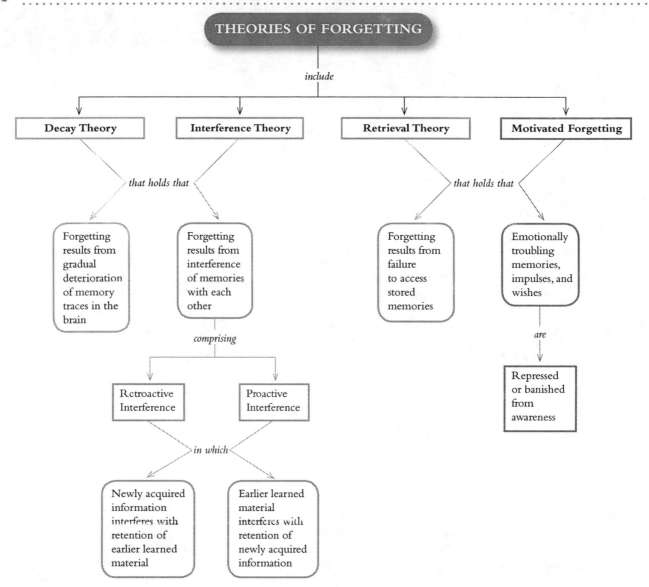

THEORIES OF FORGETTING

include

Decay Theory   **Interference Theory**   **Retrieval Theory**   **Motivated Forgetting**

that holds that   *that holds that*

Forgetting results from gradual deterioration of memory traces in the brain

Forgetting results from interference of memories with each other

Forgetting results from failure to access stored memories

Emotionally troubling memories, impulses, and wishes

comprising

are

Retroactive Interference

Proactive Interference

Repressed or banished from awareness

in which

Newly acquired information interferes with retention of earlier learned material

Earlier learned material interferes with retention of newly acquired information

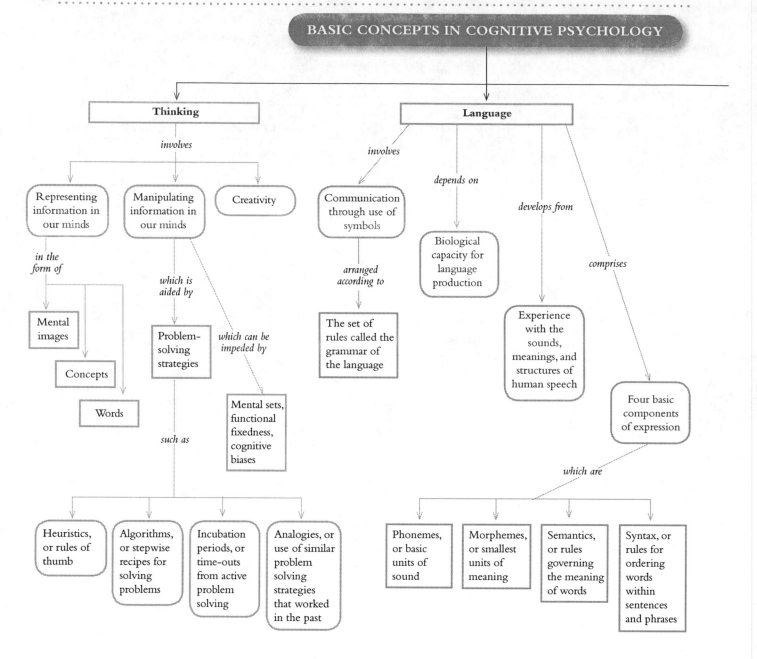

Sharpen your skills by completing the Concept Map Study Questions and Thought Questions at the end of this booklet.

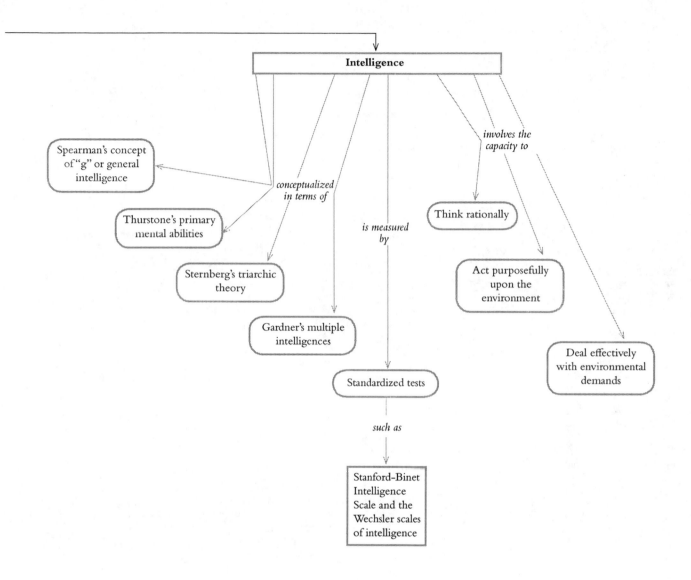

Intelligence

Spearman's concept of "g" or general intelligence

Thurstone's primary mental abilities

Sternberg's triarchic theory

conceptualized in terms of

Gardner's multiple intelligences

is measured by

Standardized tests

such as

Stanford–Binet Intelligence Scale and the Wechsler scales of intelligence

involves the capacity to

Think rationally

Act purposefully upon the environment

Deal effectively with environmental demands

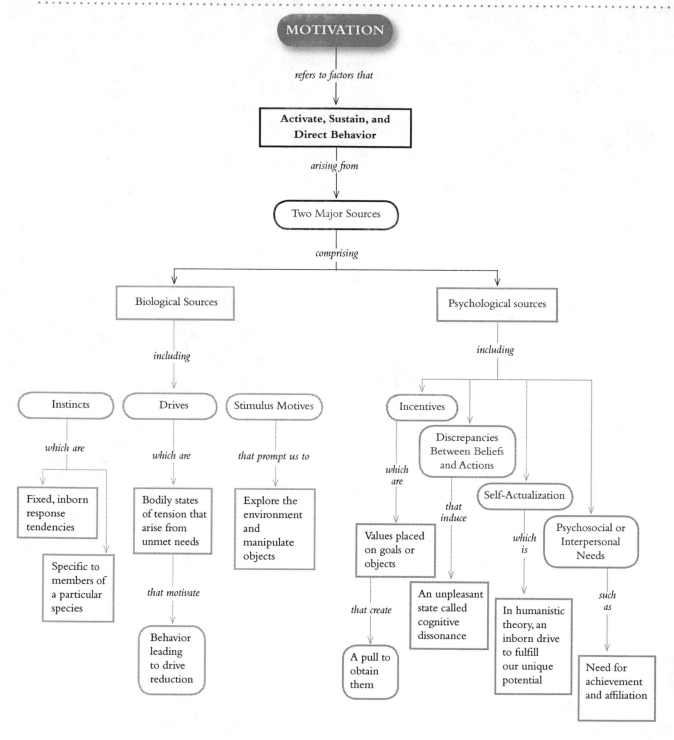

MOTIVATION

refers to factors that

Activate, Sustain, and Direct Behavior

arising from

Two Major Sources

comprising

Biological Sources

including

Instincts

which are

Fixed, inborn response tendencies

Specific to members of a particular species

Drives

which are

Bodily states of tension that arise from unmet needs

that motivate

Behavior leading to drive reduction

Stimulus Motives

that prompt us to

Explore the environment and manipulate objects

Psychological sources

including

Incentives

which are

Values placed on goals or objects

that create

A pull to obtain them

Discrepancies Between Beliefs and Actions

that induce

An unpleasant state called cognitive dissonance

Self-Actualization

which is

In humanistic theory, an inborn drive to fulfill our unique potential

Psychosocial or Interpersonal Needs

such as

Need for achievement and affiliation

Sharpen your skills by completing the Concept Map Study Questions and Thought Questions at the end of this booklet.

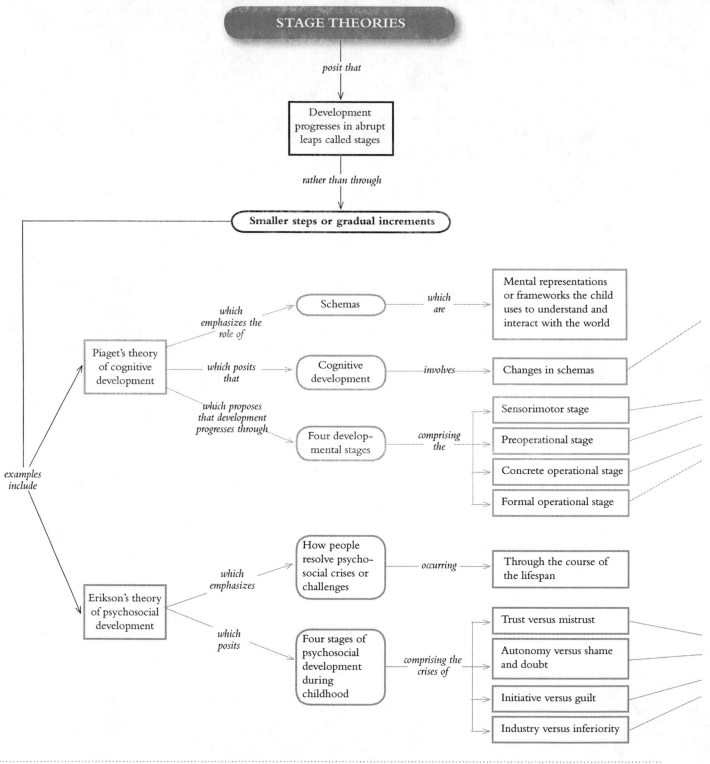

STAGE THEORIES

posit that

Development progresses in abrupt leaps called stages

rather than through

Smaller steps or gradual increments

examples include

Piaget's theory of cognitive development

which emphasizes the role of → Schemas → *which are* → Mental representations or frameworks the child uses to understand and interact with the world

which posits that → Cognitive development → *involves* → Changes in schemas

which proposes that development progresses through → Four developmental stages → *comprising the* →
- Sensorimotor stage
- Preoperational stage
- Concrete operational stage
- Formal operational stage

Erikson's theory of psychosocial development

which emphasizes → How people resolve psychosocial crises or challenges → *occurring* → Through the course of the lifespan

which posits → Four stages of psychosocial development during childhood → *comprising the crises of* →
- Trust versus mistrust
- Autonomy versus shame and doubt
- Initiative versus guilt
- Industry versus inferiority

Sharpen your skills by completing the Concept Map Study Questions and Thought Questions at the end of this booklet.

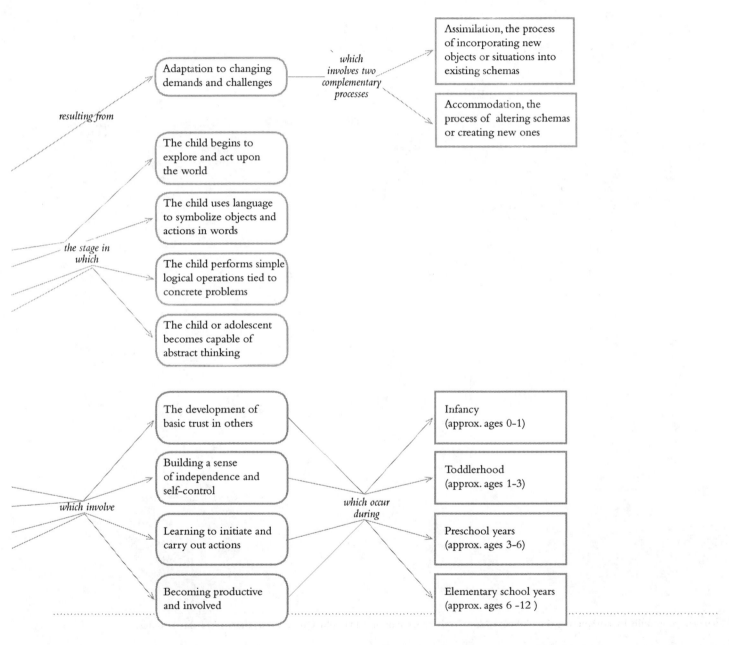

Adaptation to changing demands and challenges

resulting from

which involves two complementary processes

Assimilation, the process of incorporating new objects or situations into existing schemas

Accommodation, the process of altering schemas or creating new ones

The child begins to explore and act upon the world

The child uses language to symbolize objects and actions in words

The child performs simple logical operations tied to concrete problems

The child or adolescent becomes capable of abstract thinking

the stage in which

The development of basic trust in others

Building a sense of independence and self-control

Learning to initiate and carry out actions

Becoming productive and involved

which involve

which occur during

Infancy (approx. ages 0–1)

Toddlerhood (approx. ages 1–3)

Preschool years (approx. ages 3–6)

Elementary school years (approx. ages 6 –12)

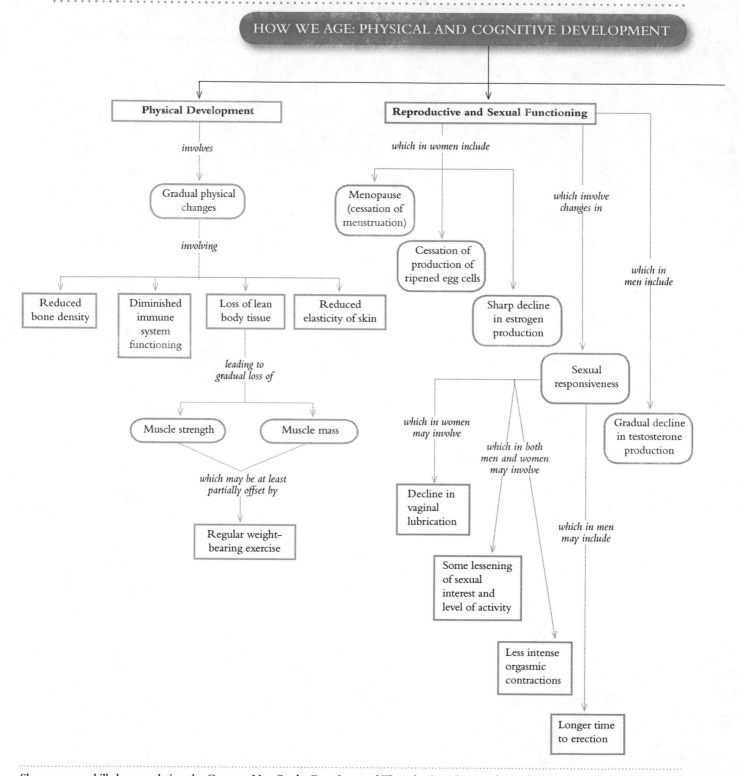

HOW WE AGE: PHYSICAL AND COGNITIVE DEVELOPMENT

Physical Development

involves

Gradual physical changes

involving

Reduced bone density

Diminished immune system functioning

Loss of lean body tissue

Reduced elasticity of skin

leading to gradual loss of

Muscle strength

Muscle mass

which may be at least partially offset by

Regular weight-bearing exercise

Reproductive and Sexual Functioning

which in women include

Menopause (cessation of menstruation)

Cessation of production of ripened egg cells

Sharp decline in estrogen production

which involve changes in

which in men include

Sexual responsiveness

Gradual decline in testosterone production

which in women may involve

Decline in vaginal lubrication

which in both men and women may involve

Some lessening of sexual interest and level of activity

which in men may include

Less intense orgasmic contractions

Longer time to erection

Sharpen your skills by completing the Concept Map Study Questions and Thought Questions at the end of this booklet.

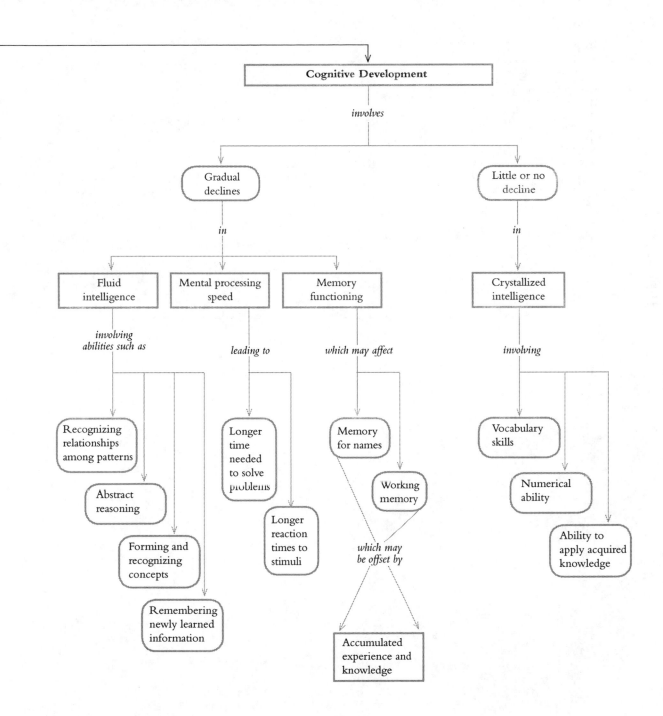

Cognitive Development

involves

Gradual declines

Little or no decline

in

in

Fluid intelligence

Mental processing speed

Memory functioning

Crystallized intelligence

involving abilities such as

leading to

which may affect

involving

Recognizing relationships among patterns

Abstract reasoning

Forming and recognizing concepts

Remembering newly learned information

Longer time needed to solve problems

Longer reaction times to stimuli

Memory for names

Working memory

which may be offset by

Accumulated experience and knowledge

Vocabulary skills

Numerical ability

Ability to apply acquired knowledge

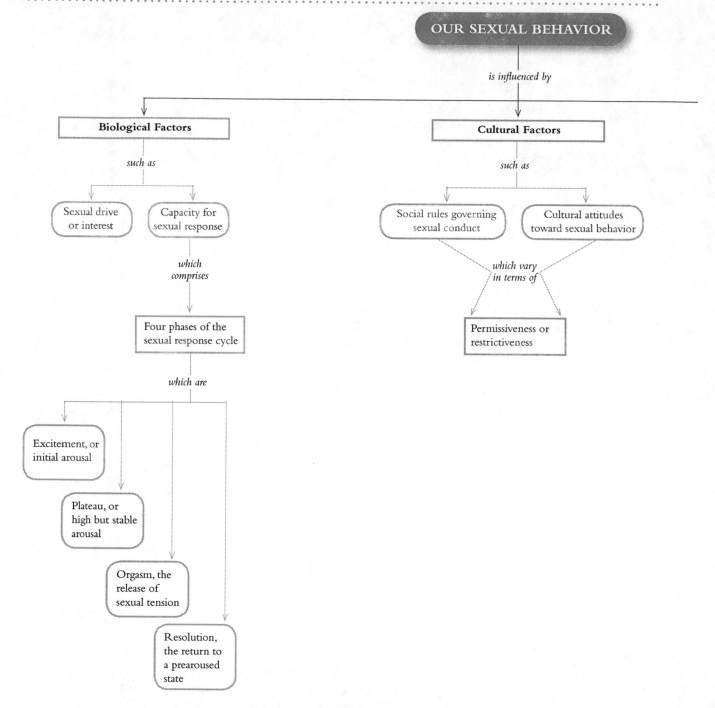

OUR SEXUAL BEHAVIOR

is influenced by

Biological Factors

such as

Sexual drive or interest

Capacity for sexual response

which comprises

Four phases of the sexual response cycle

which are

Excitement, or initial arousal

Plateau, or high but stable arousal

Orgasm, the release of sexual tension

Resolution, the return to a prearoused state

Cultural Factors

such as

Social rules governing sexual conduct

Cultural attitudes toward sexual behavior

which vary in terms of

Permissiveness or restrictiveness

Sharpen your skills by completing the Concept Map Study Questions and Thought Questions at the end of this booklet.

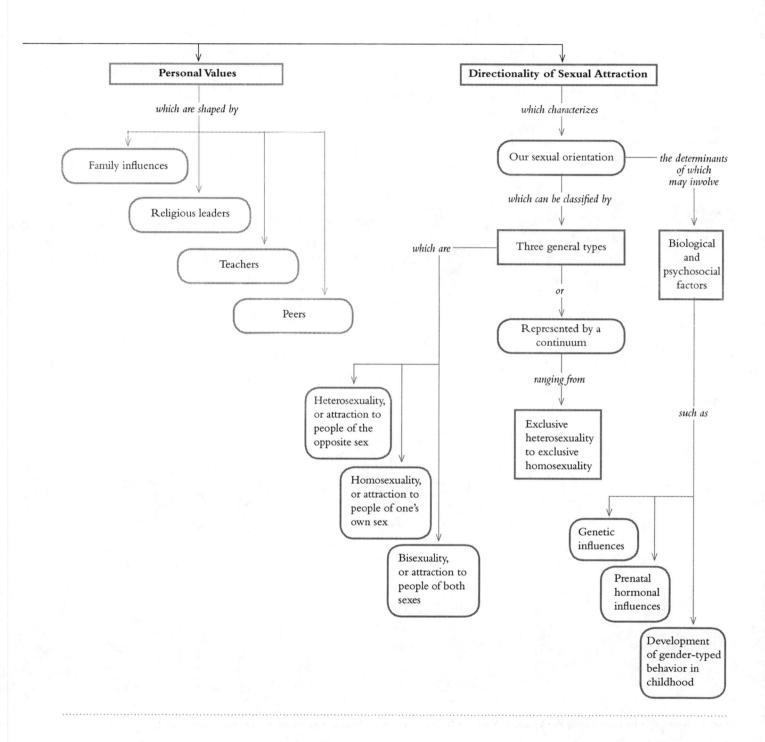

Personal Values

which are shaped by

Family influences

Religious leaders

Teachers

Peers

Directionality of Sexual Attraction

which characterizes

Our sexual orientation

which can be classified by

which are

Three general types

or

Represented by a continuum

ranging from

Exclusive heterosexuality to exclusive homosexuality

Heterosexuality, or attraction to people of the opposite sex

Homosexuality, or attraction to people of one's own sex

Bisexuality, or attraction to people of both sexes

the determinants of which may involve

Biological and psychosocial factors

such as

Genetic influences

Prenatal hormonal influences

Development of gender-typed behavior in childhood

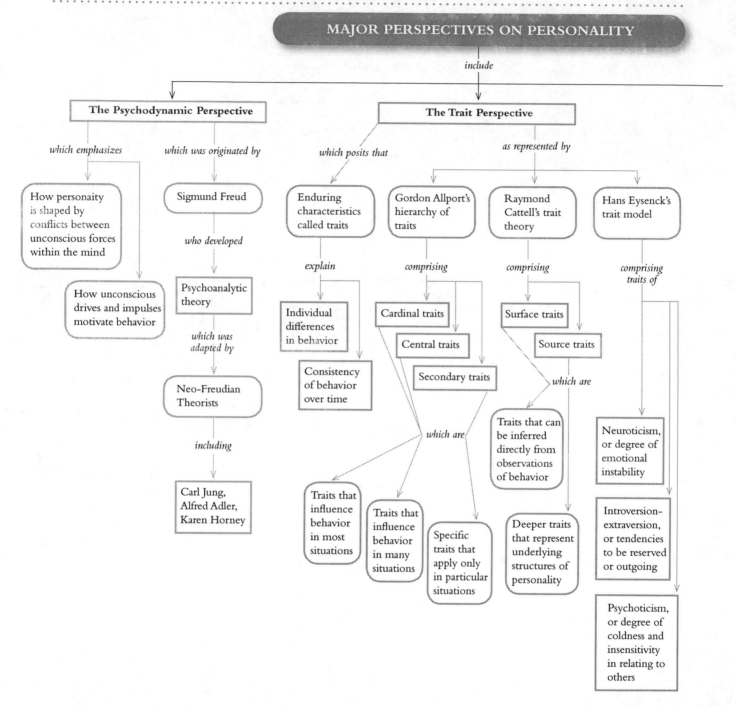

MAJOR PERSPECTIVES ON PERSONALITY

include

The Psychodynamic Perspective

which emphasizes

How personality is shaped by conflicts between unconscious forces within the mind

How unconscious drives and impulses motivate behavior

which was originated by

Sigmund Freud

who developed

Psychoanalytic theory

which was adapted by

Neo-Freudian Theorists

including

Carl Jung, Alfred Adler, Karen Horney

The Trait Perspective

which posits that

Enduring characteristics called traits

explain

Individual differences in behavior

Consistency of behavior over time

as represented by

Gordon Allport's hierarchy of traits

comprising

Cardinal traits

Central traits

Secondary traits

which are

Traits that influence behavior in most situations

Traits that influence behavior in many situations

Specific traits that apply only in particular situations

Raymond Cattell's trait theory

comprising

Surface traits

Source traits

which are

Traits that can be inferred directly from observations of behavior

Deeper traits that represent underlying structures of personality

Hans Eysenck's trait model

comprising traits of

Neuroticism, or degree of emotional instability

Introversion-extraversion, or tendencies to be reserved or outgoing

Psychoticism, or degree of coldness and insensitivity in relating to others

Sharpen your skills by completing the Concept Map Study Questions and Thought Questions at the end of this booklet.

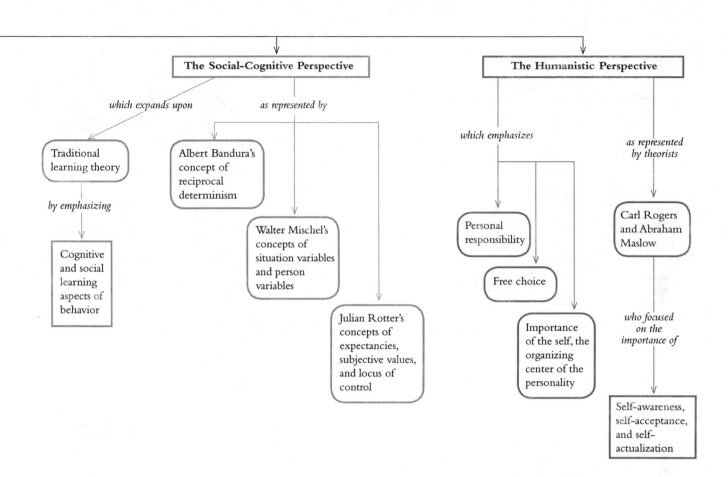

The Social-Cognitive Perspective

which expands upon

as represented by

Traditional learning theory

by emphasizing

Cognitive and social learning aspects of behavior

Albert Bandura's concept of reciprocal determinism

Walter Mischel's concepts of situation variables and person variables

Julian Rotter's concepts of expectancies, subjective values, and locus of control

The Humanistic Perspective

which emphasizes

as represented by theorists

Personal responsibility

Free choice

Importance of the self, the organizing center of the personality

Carl Rogers and Abraham Maslow

who focused on the importance of

Self-awareness, self-acceptance, and self-actualization

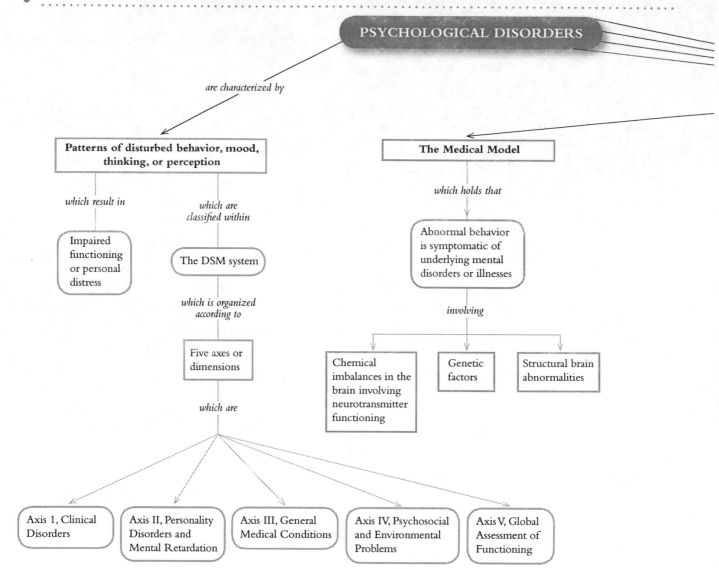

PSYCHOLOGICAL DISORDERS

are characterized by

Patterns of disturbed behavior, mood, thinking, or perception

which result in

Impaired functioning or personal distress

which are classified within

The DSM system

which is organized according to

Five axes or dimensions

which are

Axis 1, Clinical Disorders

Axis II, Personality Disorders and Mental Retardation

Axis III, General Medical Conditions

Axis IV, Psychosocial and Environmental Problems

Axis V, Global Assessment of Functioning

The Medical Model

which holds that

Abnormal behavior is symptomatic of underlying mental disorders or illnesses

involving

Chemical imbalances in the brain involving neurotransmitter functioning

Genetic factors

Structural brain abnormalities

Sharpen your skills by completing the Concept Map Study Questions and Thought Questions at the end of this booklet.

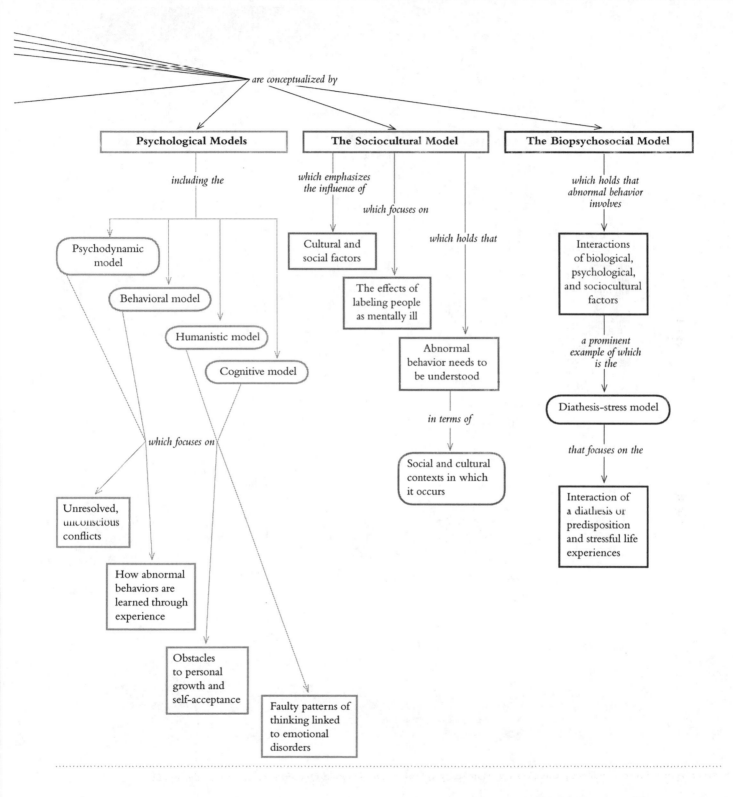

are conceptualized by

Psychological Models

The Sociocultural Model

The Biopsychosocial Model

including the

which emphasizes the influence of

which focuses on

which holds that

which holds that abnormal behavior involves

Psychodynamic model

Behavioral model

Humanistic model

Cognitive model

Cultural and social factors

The effects of labeling people as mentally ill

Abnormal behavior needs to be understood

Interactions of biological, psychological, and sociocultural factors

a prominent example of which is the

Diathesis-stress model

that focuses on the

which focuses on

in terms of

Unresolved, unconscious conflicts

How abnormal behaviors are learned through experience

Obstacles to personal growth and self-acceptance

Faulty patterns of thinking linked to emotional disorders

Social and cultural contexts in which it occurs

Interaction of a diathesis or predisposition and stressful life experiences

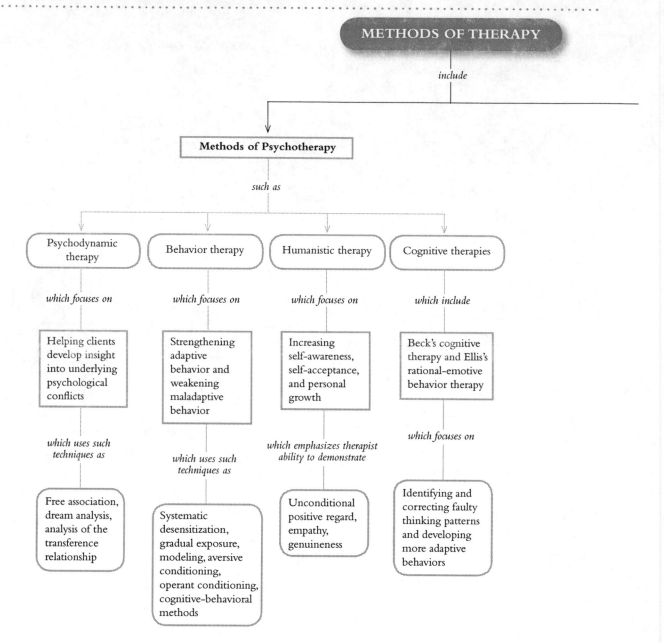

METHODS OF THERAPY

include

Methods of Psychotherapy

such as

Psychodynamic therapy	Behavior therapy	Humanistic therapy	Cognitive therapies

which focuses on | *which focuses on* | *which focuses on* | *which include*

Helping clients develop insight into underlying psychological conflicts

Strengthening adaptive behavior and weakening maladaptive behavior

Increasing self-awareness, self-acceptance, and personal growth

Beck's cognitive therapy and Ellis's rational-emotive behavior therapy

which uses such techniques as

which uses such techniques as

which emphasizes therapist ability to demonstrate

which focuses on

Free association, dream analysis, analysis of the transference relationship

Systematic desensitization, gradual exposure, modeling, aversive conditioning, operant conditioning, cognitive-behavioral methods

Unconditional positive regard, empathy, genuineness

Identifying and correcting faulty thinking patterns and developing more adaptive behaviors

Sharpen your skills by completing the Concept Map Study Questions and Thought Questions at the end of this booklet.

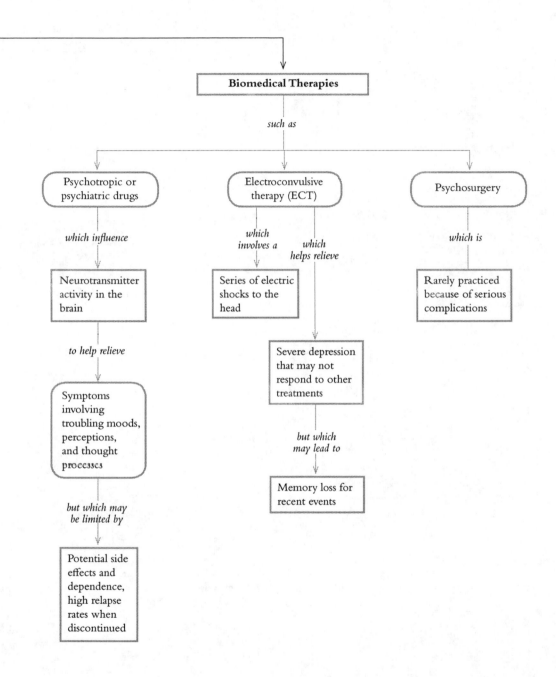

Biomedical Therapies

such as

Psychotropic or psychiatric drugs

Electroconvulsive therapy (ECT)

Psychosurgery

which influence

Neurotransmitter activity in the brain

to help relieve

Symptoms involving troubling moods, perceptions, and thought processes

but which may be limited by

Potential side effects and dependence, high relapse rates when discontinued

which involves a

Series of electric shocks to the head

which helps relieve

Severe depression that may not respond to other treatments

but which may lead to

Memory loss for recent events

which is

Rarely practiced because of serious complications

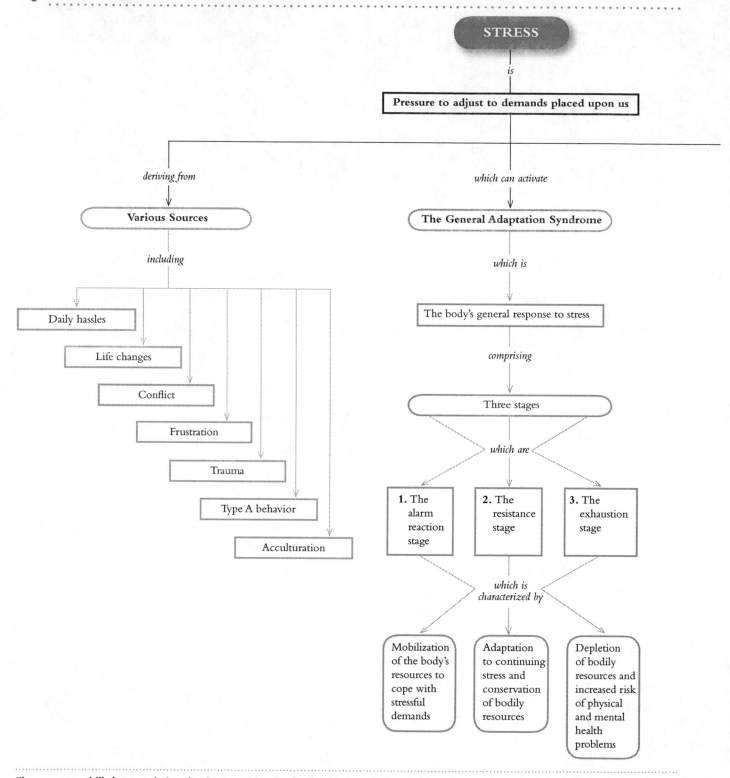

STRESS

is

Pressure to adjust to demands placed upon us

deriving from — Various Sources

which can activate — The General Adaptation Syndrome

including

Daily hassles

Life changes

Conflict

Frustration

Trauma

Type A behavior

Acculturation

which is

The body's general response to stress

comprising

Three stages

which are

1. The alarm reaction stage

2. The resistance stage

3. The exhaustion stage

which is characterized by

Mobilization of the body's resources to cope with stressful demands

Adaptation to continuing stress and conservation of bodily resources

Depletion of bodily resources and increased risk of physical and mental health problems

Sharpen your skills by completing the Concept Map Study Questions and Thought Questions at the end of this booklet.

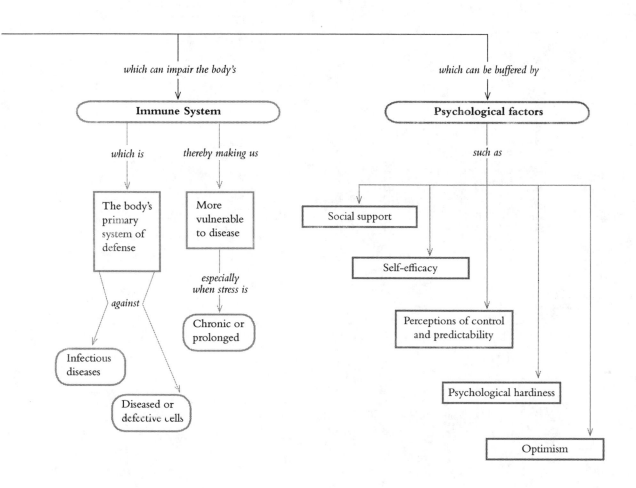

which can impair the body's

which can be buffered by

Immune System

Psychological factors

which is

thereby making us

such as

The body's primary system of defense

More vulnerable to disease

Social support

Self-efficacy

against

especially when stress is

Perceptions of control and predictability

Infectious diseases

Chronic or prolonged

Psychological hardiness

Diseased or defective cells

Optimism

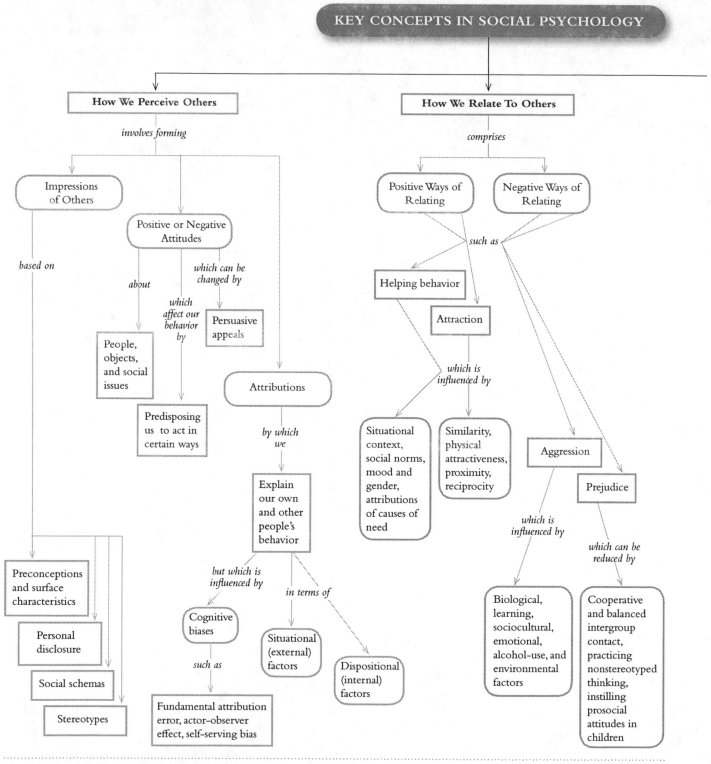

KEY CONCEPTS IN SOCIAL PSYCHOLOGY

How We Perceive Others

involves forming

Impressions of Others

based on

Positive or Negative Attitudes

about

which can be changed by

which affect our behavior by

Persuasive appeals

People, objects, and social issues

Predisposing us to act in certain ways

Attributions

by which we

Explain our own and other people's behavior

but which is influenced by

in terms of

Cognitive biases

such as

Situational (external) factors

Dispositional (internal) factors

Fundamental attribution error, actor-observer effect, self-serving bias

Preconceptions and surface characteristics

Personal disclosure

Social schemas

Stereotypes

How We Relate To Others

comprises

Positive Ways of Relating

Negative Ways of Relating

such as

Helping behavior

Attraction

which is influenced by

Situational context, social norms, mood and gender, attributions of causes of need

Similarity, physical attractiveness, proximity, reciprocity

Aggression

Prejudice

which is influenced by

which can be reduced by

Biological, learning, sociocultural, emotional, alcohol-use, and environmental factors

Cooperative and balanced intergroup contact, practicing nonstereotyped thinking, instilling prosocial attitudes in children

Sharpen your skills by completing the Concept Map Study Questions and Thought Questions at the end of this booklet.

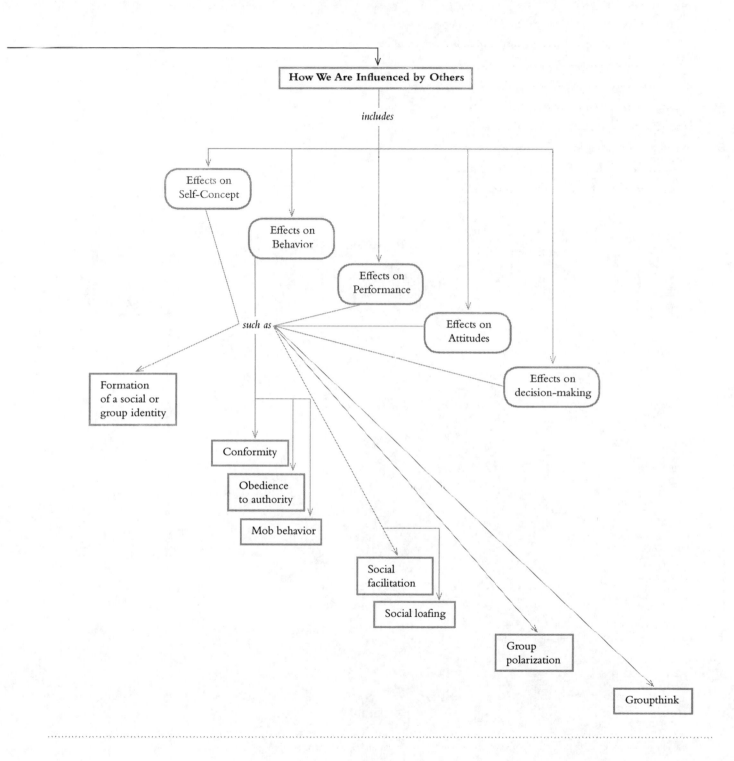

How We Are Influenced by Others

includes

Effects on Self-Concept

Effects on Behavior

Effects on Performance

Effects on Attitudes

Effects on decision-making

such as

Formation of a social or group identity

Conformity

Obedience to authority

Mob behavior

Social facilitation

Social loafing

Group polarization

Groupthink

Use the **Study Questions** on the following pages to review your knowledge of the key concepts in the concept maps. Then use the **Thought Questions** to reflect upon how the concepts relate to your own experiences. Reflection makes the material more personally meaningful and fosters more effective learning. Additional pages are provided in the **Notes** section at the back of the booklet, if you need more space for your answers to the **Thought Questions**.

Please note that the answers to the **Study Questions** are provided at the end of the booklet.

1. The scientific method involves all of the following steps except
   a. developing a research question.
   b. relying on expert opinion.
   c. formulating a hypothesis.
   d. gathering evidence.

2. When investigators apply the scientific method to generate research questions, they draw upon each of the following except
   a. theory.
   b. prior experience.
   c. careful observation.
   d. reductive reasoning.

3. A hypothesis is best described as a(n)
   a. statistically significant result.
   b. experimental manipulation.
   c. testable prediction.
   d. manipulation of an independent variable.

4. The research method best designed to demonstrate cause-and-effect relationships is the
   a. intensive case study method.
   b. naturalistic observation method.
   c. experimental method.
   d. causal inference method.

5. The research method used to examine relationships between variables is the
   a. experimental method.
   b. correlational method.
   c. naturalistic observation method.
   d. survey method.

💡 THOUGHT QUESTIONS

1. Think of a situation in which you have casually observed other people's behavior, such as the behavior of fans in a sports stadium, of people riding on a bus or train, or of children in a playground or schoolyard. What biases or errors might arise from such casual observations? For example, were the people you observed representative of people in general in this setting? How would scientific observation differ from casual observation in this situation?

2. Think of an example of an advertising claim you have read in a newspaper or magazine or have seen in a television commercial. What evidence, if any, was given to support the claim? What evidence would you need to critically evaluate the claim?

1. The part of the brain that controls vital bodily processes is the
   a. hindbrain.
   b. midbrain.
   c. limbic system.
   d. reticular formation.

2. The parts (or part) of the brain that control(s) balance and coordination are/is the
   a. reticular formation.
   b. medulla.
   c. cerebellum.
   d. occipital lobes.

3. The cerebral cortex consists of each of the following parts or lobes except the
   a. parietal lobes.
   b. frontal lobes.
   c. temporal lobes.
   d. reticular lobes.

4. The parts of the cerebral cortex that process visual stimuli are the
   a. parietal lobes.
   b. occipital lobes.
   c. temporal lobes.
   d. frontal lobes.

5. The parts of the cerebral cortex that control higher thinking processes are the
   a. parietal lobes.
   b. occipital lobes.
   c. temporal lobes.
   d. frontal lobes.

THOUGHT QUESTIONS

1. Do you know someone (or have you heard about someone) who suffered brain damage? What part of the brain was affected? What functions were affected?

2. If you were struck in the back of the head, you might have the experience of seeing stars. Drawing upon your knowledge of the organization of the brain, explain why you might have this symptom.

1. *Sensation is the process that allows us to*
   a. convert physical energy into sense impressions.
   b. make sense of sense impressions.
   c. convert neural impulses into meaningful impressions of the world.
   d. form perceptions.

2. *Which of the following is not a Gestalt principle of perceptual organization?*
   a. proximity
   b. continuity
   c. closure
   d. perceptual set

3. *Which of the following is a monocular cue for depth perception?*
   a. retinal disparity
   b. texture gradient
   c. convergence
   d. continuity

4. *Which of the following is a binocular cue for depth perception?*
   a. retinal disparity
   b. texture gradient
   c. linear perspective
   d. interposition

5. *Jonathan fails to notice the hum of the air conditioner a few minutes after he enters a room. This is an example of*
   a. sensory adaptation.
   b. perceptual set.
   c. selective attention.
   d. texture gradient.

THOUGHT QUESTIONS

1. Describe an experience of sensory adaptation in which you noticed a stimulus when you were first exposed to it, but then, after a period of time had elapsed, you were no longer aware of it.

2. The ability to detect a signal (stimulus) in your environment varies with the characteristics of the stimulus, the background, and your own characteristics, such as your level of alertness, general fatigue, or states of motivation, such as hunger. Describe an experience in which your mental state or motivational state made you either more or less sensitive to noticing a particular stimulus (a sound or an odor, for example) in your environment.

1. Ripley was texting her friend while listening to some music. We can best characterize her state of consciousness as
   a. drifting consciousness.
   b. focused awareness.
   c. divided consciousness.
   d. meditative consciousness.

2. Shepala becomes so absorbed in the novel she is reading that she becomes unaware of her surroundings. Her state of consciousness is best described as
   a. selective attention.
   b. focused awareness.
   c. divided consciousness.
   d. dissociative consciousness.

3. The hormone melatonin plays a key role in
   a. inducing drowsiness.
   b. restoring wakefulness.
   c. transitioning from light to deep sleep.
   d. stimulating the pituitary gland.

4. Hypnosis involves each of the following except
   a. heightened susceptibility to suggestions.
   b. a state of deep relaxation.
   c. focused attention.
   d. release of melatonin in the brain.

5. Depressant drugs
   a. induce feelings of depression.
   b. increase activity of the central nervous system.
   c. include opioids.
   d. include MDMA (ecstasy).

THOUGHT QUESTIONS

1. Think of a situation in which you experienced states of drifting consciousness. Give an example of one such experience, briefly describing where and when it occurred and what you were doing at the time. What was the experience like? For example, did your thoughts simply wander or did you experience full-fledged daydreams?

2. Do you believe dreams have meaning? Why or why not?

1. *In classical conditioning, a previously neutral stimulus is paired with a(n)*
   a. higher-order stimulus.
   b. unconditioned stimulus.
   c. unconditioned response.
   d. conditioned response.

2. *Each of the following could be used to strengthen a conditioned response except*
   a. repeatedly pairing the CS and the US.
   b. changing the interval between the CS and the US.
   c. changing the interval between the CS and the CR.
   d. increasing the intensity of the US.

3. *Stimulus generalization is to stimulus discrimination as*
   a. broadening is to narrowing.
   b. narrowing is to broadening.
   c. intensifying is to weakening.
   d. weakening is to intensifying.

4. *In operant conditioning, extinction*
   a. is the same as punishment.
   b. is the same as negative reinforcement.
   c. involves withdrawal of a reinforcer.
   d. involves withdrawal of a punisher.

5. *In a ratio schedule of partial reinforcement, reinforcement is based on*
   a. the ratio between reinforcers and punishments.
   b. a portion of responses.
   c. the amount of time elapsed since the last reinforcer.
   d. the ratio of time between reinforcers.

THOUGHT QUESTIONS

1. Think of an example of how classical conditioning comes into play in your life, such as feeling anxious or fearful when entering a dentist's office, developing an aversion to a particular food, or feeling positive emotions upon hearing a particular song or sensing a particular aroma. Describe this experience in terms of the principles of conditioning. In other words, what was the conditioned stimulus? The unconditioned stimulus? The unconditioned response? The conditioned response?

2. Observational learning or modeling involves learning from others. Describe an experience in which you learned a new behavior by observing the behavior of others in your daily life or of actors on TV or in the movies.

1. *Each of the following is a basic memory process except*
   a. encoding.
   b. rehearsal.
   c. storage.
   d. retrieval.

2. *Taking information and converting it into a form that can be stored in memory describes the process of*
   a. encoding.
   b. rehearsal.
   c. storage.
   d. retrieval.

3. *Each of the following represents a stage of memory except*
   a. sensory memory.
   b. encoding memory.
   c. short-term memory.
   d. long-term memory.

4. *The stages of memory are based on which of the following?*
   a. the amount of information that is retained in memory
   b. the type of information that is held in memory
   c. the length of time information is held in memory
   d. the part of the brain that is involved in forming memories

5. *Leisha is studying for a Spanish midterm and feels well prepared. She then switches to studying French for an hour. When she returns to reviewing her Spanish, she forgets the meaning of many words she had learned earlier. This is most likely an example of*
   a. encoding errors.
   b. proactive interference.
   c. retroactive interference.
   d. motivated forgetting.

THOUGHT QUESTIONS

1. Detectives often take a victim back to the scene of the crime in order to jog the person's memory about the details of the crime. The crime scene may contain retrieval cues that help jog the victim's memory. Briefly describe an experience in your life in which a cue in the environment triggered the recall of a particular memory.

2. We can strengthen memory of newly learned information through two forms of rehearsal: maintenance rehearsal (rote memorization of words and sounds) and elaborative rehearsal (rehearsal by meaning). Give an example from your own experience in which you used rote memorization, such as remembering strings of numbers that had no intrinsic meaning. Then give an example of deeper processing through elaborative rehearsal, such as relating a psychological concept to a particular experience in your life.

1. Which of the following is likely to enhance our ability to solve problems?
   a. mental set
   b. cognitive bias
   c. analogies
   d. functional fixedness

2. Which of the following is likely to impede rather than enhance our ability to solve new problems?
   a. algorithms
   b. heuristics
   c. analogies
   d. functional fixedness

3. Javier applies a rule of thumb he has found useful in solving problems. This is an example of a(n)
   a. heuristic.
   b. analogy.
   c. mental set.
   d. algorithm.

4. The basic units of meaning in a language are called
   a. phonemes.
   b. morphemes.
   c. syntax.
   d. semantics.

5. Which of the following theorists is associated with the concept of primary mental abilities?
   a. Spearman
   b. Thurstone
   c. Gardner
   d. Sternberg

THOUGHT QUESTIONS

1. Think of a physical object, like a palm tree or piano. When you represent this object in your mind, do you use mental imagery or words? Now think about an abstract concept, such as freedom. What comes to mind— a mental picture or a word description? What accounts for these differences?

2. An algorithm is a step-by-step recipe for solving a problem. Think of a problem you face from day to day and describe an algorithm, or step-by-step set of rules you have found useful, though perhaps not perfect, in solving the problem (e.g. steps you take to beat traffic during your morning commute).

1. *Each of the following represents a biological source of motivation except*

a. instincts.

b. incentives.

c. stimulus motives.

d. drives.

2. *Nadia believes that smoking is unhealthy, but she continues to smoke herself. This inconsistency creates an unpleasant state of tension called*

a. cognitive dissonance.

b. drive reduction.

c. attitude readjustment.

d. cognitive adjustment.

3. *The theoretical perspective identified with the concept of self-actualization is*

a. psychodynamic theory.

b. behavioral theory.

c. humanistic theory.

d. the biopsychosocial model.

4. *Which of the following is not a basic component of emotions?*

a. behavioral

b. cognitive

c. physiological

d. developmental

5. *Which parts (or part) of the brain regulate(s) emotions?*

a. the limbic system

b. the cerebral cortex

c. networks of brain structures

d. all of the above

Thought Questions

1. Are you the type of person who craves highly stimulating or thrill-seeking activities to maintain your optimal level of arousal, or do you generally prefer quieter, more restrained activities? Or, are you somewhere in-between?

2. Do you consider yourself to be high or low in achievement motivation? How does achievement motivation affect your behavior?

1. *Piaget's concept of a schema is best described as*
   a. specific facts or knowledge about the world.
   b. a schematic diagram of a knowledge structure.
   c. a knowledge structure that serves as a guide for action.
   d. a hierarchy of interlinking concepts in the brain.

2. *Two-year-old Jonathan sees a squirrel in the park and says "woof-woof". This is an example of*
   a. accommodation.
   b. assimilation.
   c. schematic overload.
   d. complementary processing.

3. *Each of the following represents a stage of cognitive development in Piaget's theory except the*
   a. sensorimotor stage.
   b. preoperational stage.
   c. latency stage.
   d. formal operational stage.

4. *In Erikson's view, the central psychosocial challenge or crisis faced by a child in the first year of life is*
   a. development of a sense of autonomy.
   b. development of a basic sense of competence.
   c. development of basic trust.
   d. development of a budding sense of independence.

5. *In Erikson's view, the major challenge faced by children in the elementary school years is*
   a. development of trust in others.
   b. development of ability to initiate and carry out actions.
   c. development of a sense of self-control.
   d. becoming productive and involved in activities.

THOUGHT QUESTIONS

1. Describe an example of a schema in your daily life—a mental framework for acting upon or understanding your physical and social environment. Examples include parallel parking, reading a book from left to right, and knowing how to act in a restaurant or in a classroom. Briefly describe the schema and how you use it in your daily life.

2. Erikson emphasized the challenge the infant faces in developing a sense of basic trust in others. If you were to give advice to a new parent about instilling a sense of trust in an infant, what general suggestion would you offer?

1. *Each of the following represents an expected change in physical functioning as we age except*
   a. decreased lean body tissue.
   b. reduced immune system functioning.
   c. increased bone density.
   d. reduced elasticity of skin.

2. *Each of the following represents an age-related change in sexual functioning except*
   a. less intense orgasmic contractions.
   b. reduced vaginal lubrication.
   c. longer time to erection.
   d. loss of sexual drive.

3. *Each of the following changes is associated with age-related changes in sexual and reproductive functioning in women except*
   a. loss of sexual functioning.
   b. cessation of menstruation.
   c. drop in estrogen production.
   d. cessation of production of ripened egg cells.

4. *Which of the following represents fluid intelligence?*
   a. vocabulary skills
   b. numerical skills
   c. forming and recognizing concepts
   d. applying knowledge to solving problems

5. *Which aspect of cognitive functioning is most likely to decline with increasing age?*
   a. vocabulary skills
   b. working memory
   c. ability to apply stored knowledge
   d. numerical ability

THOUGHT QUESTIONS

1. Describe one or two behaviors you have incorporated in your life or could incorporate in your life that might improve your health or increase your longevity.

2. List one or two cognitive abilities you expect will show the greatest declines as you age. How might you compensate for these age-related changes?

1. *Each of the following is a phase in the sexual response cycle except*
   a. attraction.
   b. plateau.
   c. excitement.
   d. resolution.

2. *During which stage of the sexual response cycle does the body return to its prearoused state?*
   a. excitement
   b. plateau
   c. orgasm
   d. resolution

3. *Which stage of the sexual response cycle is characterized by high but stable levels of arousal?*
   a. excitement
   b. plateau
   c. orgasm
   d. resolution

4. *Each of the following is implicated as a causal factor in determining sexual orientation except*
   a. genetic influences.
   b. harsh discipline in childhood.
   c. hormonal influences in prenatal development.
   d. gender-typed behavior in childhood.

5. *Henry is sexually attracted to both men and women. Which of the following best describes his sexual orientation?*
   a. heterosexuality
   b. bisexuality
   c. ambisexuality
   d. homosexuality

THOUGHT QUESTIONS

1. Who, or what, were the major influences on your sexual values? Explain.

2. Do you believe that sexual orientation is a matter of personal choice? Why or why not?

1. *Dr. Hogwood is studying relationships between central traits and success in marriage. Dr. Hogwood's research is likely to be based on which theorist's work?*
   a. Sigmund Freud
   b. Raymond Cattell
   c. Gordon Allport
   d. Walter Mischel

2. *Which of the following theorists is considered a neo-Freudian?*
   a. Alfred Adler
   b. Albert Bandura
   c. Raymond Cattell
   d. Abraham Maslow

3. *Dr. Acumen is studying personality traits that people can directly infer from observing the behavior of others. Which type of trait is Dr. Acumen most likely to be studying?*
   a. cardinal traits
   b. surface traits
   c. source traits
   d. secondary traits

4. *Which trait characterizes emotional instability in Eysenck's trait model?*
   a. neuroticism
   b. psychoticism
   c. introversion
   d. source traits

5. *Each of the following theorists is classified as a social-cognitive theorist except*
   a. Albert Bandura
   b. B. F. Skinner
   c. Julian Rotter
   d. Walter Mischel

THOUGHT QUESTIONS

1. Do you consider yourself to be an introverted or extraverted person? Briefly explain your answer.

----

2. Do you believe your behavior is determined by underlying traits you possess or by situational factors you face in your everyday life? Briefly explain your answer.

----

1. John is suffering from a disorder that is coded on Axis II of the DSM. Which type of disorder is he likely to have?
   a. a clinical disorder
   b. a medical disorder
   c. a personality disorder
   d. a general medical condition

2. The medical model conceptualizes patterns of abnormal behaviors as
   a. signs of stunted development.
   b. symbols of unconscious conflicts.
   c. symptoms of underlying disorders.
   d. learned behaviors.

3. Dr. Gomez, a psychologist who treats people with psychological disorders, identifies with the psychodynamic model. Dr. Gomez most likely subscribes to the belief that psychological disorders involve
   a. learned behavior patterns.
   b. unresolved, unconscious conflicts.
   c. distorted thinking patterns.
   d. interactions of stress and underlying predispositions.

4. Dr. Mustafa believes that we need to take into account the contexts in which abnormal behavior arises, such as times of unemployment and economic hardship. Dr. Mustafa most likely adopts which of the following conceptual models?
   a. the psychodynamic model
   b. the behavioral model
   c. the sociocultural model
   d. the medical model

5. The concept of a diathesis is closest in meaning to a(n)
   a. symptom profile.
   b. faulty style of thinking.
   c. obstacle to personal growth.
   d. predisposition.

THOUGHT QUESTIONS

1. Think of someone you have known or have heard about who suffered from a psychological or mental disorder. Which theoretical model or models do you believe best explains the development of the person's disorder? Why?

2. When is anxiety normal and when does it become abnormal? How does your answer relate to the criteria given in the textbook for distinguishing normal from abnormal behavior?

1. The method of psychotherapy that focuses on correcting errors in thinking is
   a. behavior therapy.
   b. psychodynamic therapy.
   c. cognitive therapy.
   d. humanistic therapy.

2. Dr. Canuba is a therapist who uses techniques such as interpretation of the transference relationship and free association. Which method of psychotherapy is Dr. Canuba most likely to practice?
   a. behavior therapy
   b. psychodynamic therapy
   c. cognitive therapy
   d. humanistic therapy

3. Humanistic therapists emphasize the importance of therapists demonstrating each of the following qualities except
   a. empathy.
   b. unconditional positive regard.
   c. genuineness.
   d. ability to accurately interpret dreams.

4. A psychiatrist, Dr. Rubles, prescribes the drug Clozapine for a new patient. The patient most likely suffers from a(n)
   a. anxiety disorder.
   b. mood disorder.
   c. psychotic disorder.
   d. manic disorder.

5. Which of the following statements is false?
   a. Relapses are common following the termination of drug therapy.
   b. Some psychiatric drugs can lead to dependence.
   c. Psychiatric drugs create new nerve pathways in the brain.
   d. Psychiatric drugs sometimes have troubling side effects.

THOUGHT QUESTIONS

1. If someone you knew were interested in seeking help for a psychological disorder, which form of treatment would you recommend? Why?

2. Would you recommend that this person consider using psychiatric drugs? Why or why not?

1. *Each of the following is a source of stress except*
   a. conflict.
   b. transference.
   c. Type A behavior.
   d. life changes.

2. *The stage of the general adaptation syndrome describing the body's attempts to adapt to continuing stress is called the*
   a. alarm stage.
   b. resistance stage.
   c. exhaustion stage.
   d. replenishment stage.

3. *Omar holds a high-pressured job and is experiencing persistent, intense stress in his daily life. Lately he has been suffering digestive problems, which his doctor believes are stress-related. Which stage of the general adaptation syndrome is he most likely experiencing?*
   a. the alarm stage
   b. the resistance stage
   c. the exhaustion stage
   d. the replenishment stage

4. *Psychological hardiness represents a(n)*
   a. buffer to stress.
   b. psychological source of stress.
   c. predisposing or triggering factor in stress.
   d. an ineffective coping strategy.

5. *Each of the following represents a psychological buffer to stress except*
   a. self-efficacy.
   b. self-determination.
   c. social support.
   d. optimism.

THOUGHT QUESTIONS

1. What are two sources of stress in your life? How are you coping with them?

2. What advice would you give to someone experiencing a high level of stress? Offer two or three suggestions you believe would be helpful.

1. *Deirdre asks her classmate Nya for help with her homework, but Nya declines, saying she doesn't have any extra time. Deirdre believes that Nya refused to help because she is selfish. Deirdre's belief is an example of which type of attribution?*
   a. situational attribution
   b. external attribution
   c. dispositional attribution
   d. self-serving attribution

2. *All of the following are examples of how attributions may be influenced by cognitive biases except the*
   a. fundamental attribution error.
   b. actor–observer effect.
   c. self-serving bias.
   d. reciprocity bias.

3. *Which of the following factors directly influences helping behavior?*
   a. actor–observer effect
   b. fundamental attribution error
   c. group identity
   d. social norms

4. *Each of the following is a factor that influences attraction except*
   a. actor–observer effect.
   b. reciprocity.
   c. similarity.
   d. proximity.

5. *Which of the following is an example of a group influence on performance?*
   a. group polarization
   b. deindividuation
   c. social compliance
   d. social facilitation

THOUGHT QUESTIONS

1. Suppose you were driving and noticed a motorist who was stranded on the side of the road. What factors would influence your decision to either stop and help the person or just pass by?

2. How do these factors relate to those listed in the Chapter 16 concept map?

Chapter 1: 1. b; 2. d; 3. c; 4. c; 5. b

Chapter 2: 1. a; 2. c; 3. d; 4. b; 5. d

Chapter 3: 1. a; 2. d; 3. b; 4. a; 5. a

Chapter 4: 1. c; 2. b; 3. a; 4. d; 5. c

Chapter 5: 1. b; 2. c; 3. a; 4. c; 5. b

Chapter 6: 1. b; 2. a; 3. b; 4. c; 5. c

Chapter 7: 1. c; 2. d; 3. a; 4. b; 5. b

Chapter 8: 1. b; 2. a; 3. c; 4. d; 5. d

Chapter 9: 1. c; 2. b; 3. c; 4. c; 5. d

Chapter 10: 1. c; 2. d; 3. a; 4. c; 5. b

Chapter 11: 1. a; 2. d; 3. b; 4. b; 5. b

Chapter 12: 1. c; 2. a; 3. b; 4. a; 5. b

Chapter 13: 1. c; 2. c; 3. b; 4. c; 5. d

Chapter 14: 1. c; 2. b; 3. d; 4. c; 5. c

Chapter 15: 1. b; 2. b; 3. c; 4. a; 5. b

Chapter 16: 1. c; 2. d; 3. d; 4. a; 5. d

Contents

To the Student

Welcome to the Study Guide that accompanies the Second Edition of *Psychology: Concepts and Applications*. This Study Guide supplements the text but does not replace it. If used properly, it should help you to understand and master key facts, concepts, and issues discussed in the text.

The approach of this study guide is to parallel the material as it is presented to you in your textbook. Because the chapters in your textbook are divided into modules and each module presents a cohesive unit of information, the information included in this study guide has also been organized according to those units within each chapter. In other words, each chapter and module (modules are the subsections within each chapter) in this study guide corresponds to the relevant chapter and module in your text. Study guide modules are broken down into sections that will help you focus more specifically on different segments of the material presented. Within each module you will find the following features:

1. Learning Objectives

2. Outline

3. Summary of the module's contents

4. Key Terms

5. Self-Test Practice Quiz, which will help you assess your understanding of what you have learned in each module

This format is used for all study guide modules except those that correspond to the text's Application modules, which appear at the end of each chapter in your textbook. The Application modules in your textbook present helpful information primarily for you to try out and make use of in your own life. However, an objective, outline, and summary of each Application module are provided in this study guide as well. In a few cases, Key Terms and Self-Test Practice Quiz sections are also included in the study guide, depending upon the material presented in the textbook Application module. At the end of each chapter of the study guide, you will find an Application Exercise. This exercise, provided as part of your study guide review, is again geared toward not just conveying information to you but helping you take what you are learning and apply it to your own life.

Among the invaluable features of your textbook are the many opportunities for review. This *Study Guide* has been developed to complement those features. Following are some suggested procedures for making the best use of both your textbook and this study guide.

RECOMMENDED APPROACH FOR STUDY

Read the Textbook

It is recommended that you read through your assigned textbook material at least once before you begin to use this study guide. The study guide will be most effective if you already have some understanding of the material you will review. The study guide in no way incorporates every bit of information in the textbook, nor is it intended to. Rather, it is geared for your review once you have had some exposure to the textbook material. Nothing precludes or substitutes for a thorough reading and mastery of the textbook material itself. Your greatest success will come in using the textbook and the study guide in combination.

Highlight Important Features of the Textbook

As you read your textbook, take note of the most important information that it presents to you. What are the main concepts that are discussed? You will find these key concepts carefully presented and numbered in the margins of your textbook. However, restating all main concepts presented in the text in your own words will help with your understanding. The Recall It and Review It sections in the textbook summarize and test the module material, but again, doing this on your own further facilitates retention of the material. You may want to take notes from the textbook, highlighting particularly important passages in the text. Stop and ask yourself periodically what you have learned. Finally, you may do your own "self-test" by closing the book, taking a blank piece of paper, and writing down what you have learned so far. Writing information down from memory at this point will help you be clear on what you understand, what you did not retain, and what you need to look at further. Read and review the material presented in the textbook until you feel you have at least a basic grasp and understanding of the textbook information. You need not study a full chapter or even a full module's material at one time. Instead, use whatever units of textbook information you find you can comfortably master. As you progress with your studying, you will find you can review and retain larger and larger chunks of textbook material as you become increasingly familiar with the information through your efforts.

Turn to the Study Guide

At this point, you are ready to turn to this study guide for further help in mastering what is in your textbook. The study guide presents no additional information beyond what is in the textbook; rather, it reviews the material you have already read, conveys it to you in several different ways (module outline, module summary, and chapter overview), and helps you evaluate your level of understanding. The study guide is intended to strengthen your comprehension as well as aid you in assessing what you have mastered and what material needs further review.

Following is a more detailed description of each segment you will find for the modules in this study guide. As mentioned earlier, each module of the study guide corresponds to the same-numbered module in your text. Thus, you will want to read the material assigned in your textbook at least once, and then turn to the corresponding module in this study guide and begin to review further. Remember that the study guide is not a substitute for reading your textbook material. For the maximum benefit from your study, it is recommended that you read the textbook material no fewer than three times over. Each time you read the textbook material, you will gain something further from it, and your understanding will be enhanced. When you feel that you have a sufficient level of mastery of the textbook material, turn to the appropriate module(s) in the study guide and begin to review further. Listed below are the features presented in the study guide for each module, along with a description of how best to use each of these features.

FEATURES WITHIN EACH MODULE OF THIS STUDY GUIDE

Learning Objectives

The learning objectives listed in each module of your study guide are derived from the survey questions highlighted in your textbook at the beginning of each module. There are usually three to five or six main topic areas that will be addressed throughout a particular module in your textbook. Keep these survey questions in mind as you read your textbook material. The learning objectives in the study guide reiterate the focus on these main topic areas. After you have read the information in the textbook, see if you can answer the textbook survey questions. The study guide will assist you in mastering the information corresponding to each learning objective. As with your textbook study, once you have finished reviewing the material in the study guide, go back to the learning objectives. Can you address each topic or area of focus emphasized by a particular learning objective?

Outline

Each module in your study guide contains a complete, detailed outline of the corresponding textbook module material. After you have read the textbook, go over the information in the study guide outline. What points do you remember accurately from having read the textbook? What points have you not remembered or do you remember incorrectly? Make note of the points that you have not fully mastered. These sections of information will need further review.

Note the format of the overall presentation of the material as evident in the organization of the module outline. What sections of information are presented together? What is the common theme in each section? Try, initially, to remember all the main points given in the outline for each module. Once you have mastered these, try to remember the sub-points presented under each main heading. When you find a unit of material in the module outline of which you do not feel confident, go back to the corresponding portion of the textbook and read the material again. Return to the study guide module outline once more and try to mentally list the points made under each heading. Follow this procedure until all information presented in the module outline is familiar to you.

Summary

Each module in this study guide includes a brief summary of information presented in the corresponding textbook module. Read the summary once when you first begin your review of the textbook material, using this book as your guide. When you have finished using this book for study, read the study guide module summary again. Does the information in the summary now seem much more familiar? Be sure to read and review the module and chapter summaries presented in your textbook as well.

Key Terms

Each module in this study guide lists all the Key Terms given in the textbook for the material presented in the corresponding module. After you have read the textbook material, review the list of Key Terms, either at the back of your textbook chapter or in this study guide. Try to define each Key Term as you go through the list, and try to think of an example for each one. Clarify differences among related Key Terms. Which Key Terms are not familiar? Note the ones you cannot define and use accurately, and go back to the textbook and re-read the information related to those Key Terms. Again review the Key Term list, making sure you can define and appropriately apply each one.

Self-Test Practice Quiz

The objective of the Self-Test Practice Quiz in each study guide module is to allow you to evaluate your level of comprehension and mastery regarding the information presented in the corresponding module of the textbook. As such, you may wish to save the Self-Test Practice Quiz portion of your study guide review until you feel you have a good understanding of the material you have been studying. The Self-Test Practice Quiz will help you discover objectively just how complete your understanding of that relevant material is. For best results, it is recommended that you take the Self-Test Practice Quiz under the same conditions as if you were taking a real exam on the textbook material. That is, avoid looking at either the textbook or the related material in the study guide while you take the Self-Test Practice Quiz. If you find you are having difficulty with a number of the questions in the quiz, you may need more review and study. Rather than complete the Self-Test Practice Quiz at that time, return to the text and other portions of the study guide and review further. When you reach the point that you feel you have a very good mastery of the information for a given module, go back to the corresponding Self-Test Practice Quiz. With your additional review and study you should be able to answer most, if not all, of the questions successfully. If not, this again is an indication that more review of the original material is needed. Continue this procedure until you can answer all or nearly all the Self-Test Practice Quiz questions correctly without referring either to the book or to other portions of the study guide.

The Self-Test Practice Quiz in each module of this study guide consists of matching and multiple-choice questions. Match each alternative given in Question #1 of the Self-Test Practice Quiz with the appropriate Key Term given in the section preceding it. *Please note!* For most study guide modules, matching alternatives for every Key Term are provided. However, where there are a very large number of Key Terms in a module, not every Key Term in that module has a corresponding matching definition. Some, but not all, of the Key Terms are used. In that case, please remember that, although not every Key Term is used in the Self-Test Practice Quiz, you do want to be sure that you can define, understand, and apply each Key Term listed. For any Key Term or matching item where you find you are uncertain regarding the meaning or definition, return to the corresponding portion of the textbook and read and study that material one more time.

For the multiple-choice questions in the Self-Test Practice Quiz, please choose the one alternative out of the four given that best completes or answers each question. Again, if you find you are having trouble with a number of the multiple-choice questions, stop and return to the textbook and other portions of the study guide for further review. Resume answering questions when you feel you have a very good mastery of the corresponding information. Evaluate how well you do on the Self-Test Practice Quiz. How many questions can you answer correctly (without looking at either the textbook or the related portions in the study guide)? Which questions were most difficult? Use these results as an indication of your level of mastery and as an indication of what areas in the corresponding textbook material you need to study further.

Essay Questions

In nearly all of the study guide modules, one or more essay questions relating to broader aspects of that module's information are provided. These are just sample essay questions; there may be more broad topics in the module you are studying that are suitable for essay-type questions as well. You might want to consider thinking up your own essay questions to prepare for in addition to studying for and answering the essay questions provided in this study guide.

Essay questions, of course, involve a different kind of testing and recollection than do multiple-choice questions. With essay questions, you bring information up from memory rather than having the correct alternative presented as one of four choices before you. Essay questions can often test deeper, more integrated and more comprehensive levels of understanding. Follow the same procedures for answering essay questions as for answering the Self-Test Practice Quiz. Try to write a response to the essay question(s) without looking at either the textbook or related material in the study guide. If you find you are really stumped, consider going back to the textbook and other portions of the relevant material in the study guide and reviewing further before you continue. When you feel you have understood the essay question material in depth and have written a sufficiently complete short essay, evaluate the quality of the response you have written. Does it answer all portions of the essay question that was asked? Is your response clear and cohesive? Compare it to the sample answers to essay questions provided in the study guide module. How comprehensively were you able to answer the question? What points are made in the sample essay provided that you would like to include in your own response?

Answer Key

Answers to the Key Term matching questions, the multiple-choice questions, and the essay questions are provided at the end of each study guide module. As mentioned above, not every Key Term is used in the matching questions, so be sure to review and master all Key Terms not used in the exercise as well as all of those that are. Check your answers against the answers to questions provided in the Answer Key. How well are you learning the material? Is the correct answer to most study guide questions fairly readily apparent to you? The Answer Key will help you objectively evaluate the degree to which you are absorbing and retaining the information presented in the text and study guide. If, when you go to check your answers, you find that more than a few of your responses are not correct, consider going back and studying the textbook material again more thoroughly before you continue. Once you have done further review, again look at the study guide questions and reflect on the answers you have given. Are there any you would like to change in light of the more extensive information you have obtained? Evaluate your answers against those provided in the Answer Key. You will gain a fairly clear indication of how well you are mastering information provided in the textbook and study guide.

Sample Answers To Essay Questions

Nearly all study guide modules offer one or more essay questions to test your knowledge in addition to the matching and multiple-choice questions. Essay questions are always geared towards broader topics and more integrated and comprehensive responses. Be sure to write your answer to the essay question out first before you read the sample response given at the end of the study guide module. Evaluate what you have written in comparison to the sample answer provided in the study guide. How much is included in the same answer that you also incorporated in your own essay? What did you include that is not included in the study guide answer? While the sample answers to essay questions provided in this study guide are quite comprehensive, a good essay response does not have to precisely duplicate the sample answers you are given here. You may write your essay differently and include other points in addition to the necessary basic information and this would constitute a very good response. Always refer back to the appropriate section of the textbook to evaluate your answers and to ensure that they are accurate and complete.

A Final Word

Learning is an opportunity and a great joy, and learning can change your life. There are few, if any, fields of study more relevant to many aspects of your life than psychology. The earnest wish of your study guide author is that you find this course in psychology an exciting adventure with endless possibilities for the application of what you learn in order to enhance your understanding and your experience as you journey through life.

CHAPTER 1

Introduction to Psychology and Methods of Research

In Chapter 1 you are introduced to the field of psychology. Although the term *psychology* has been around for centuries, modern-day psychology (beginning in the year 1879) is different in that it is much more scientific. Psychology traces its roots thousands of years back to the Greek philosophers, including Socrates, Plato, and Aristotle. Socrates, you may recall, is famous for the adage "know thyself." In psychology today we are still trying!

Perhaps humans have always wondered who we are, what human nature is like, and what our relationship is to this world we live in. Wise people throughout history have dwelled on such philosophical questions, and Greek philosophers are not the only source of influence on psychology as we know it today. Thinkers elsewhere, such as Confucius in the Far East, concerned themselves with the nature of the human too. Confucius thought the human being was not evil, but good. It was his view that a poor environment or lack of education led basically good individuals to do bad things.

These early thinkers not only addressed fundamental questions regarding human nature, they also had opinions as to how knowledge regarding these issues could and should be obtained. Though Aristotle, for example, did not have the scientific tools we have today, it was his belief that we should let experience and careful examination teach us answers to questions we have. Many philosophers historically have relied on pure thought and reasoning, but Aristotle opposed this approach. Though there is always room for both, modern psychology has cast its lot with the views advocated by Aristotle.

Psychology as a modern scientific discipline is concerned with behavior and mental processes. The year 1879 is particularly important, and generally marks the start of psychology as we know it today because it is then Wilhelm Wundt began the first true psychological laboratory in Leipzig, Germany. Though now still a relatively young science, psychology has evolved rapidly and grown tremendously.

In this chapter you will learn that there is not just one "psychology" but many and that there are also many approaches to researching psychological questions. These varying explanations have gone in and out of popularity through the years as the field of psychology has evolved and also as society itself constantly changes. Why are there so many different ways to study humans and so many ideas about what human nature is like? You are an exceedingly complex creature! Your environment can influence you to the extent that you may seem like a different person day to day—or even hour to hour! Different thoughts in your head and chemicals in your body can also influence your behavior. Other people standing right next to you may be different yet again from you. No wonder we have such a challenging and exciting task ahead of us as we begin our study of psychology!

MODULE 1.1 FOUNDATIONS OF MODERN PSYCHOLOGY

LEARNING OBJECTIVES

After you have mastered the information in this unit, you will be able to:

- Define psychology

- Discuss the origins of psychology

- Outline the major early schools of psychology

- Discuss the major contemporary perspectives in psychology

OUTLINE

I. Origins of Psychology
    A. Roots in ancient philosophy
        1. Socrates—"know thyself"
        2. Plato—rely on thought and reason
        3. Aristotle—rely on experience, observation
        4. Confucius—concerned with the nature of the human
    B. Influences on modern psychology (nineteenth-century German physiologists)
        1. Fechner—psychophysics
        2. Helmholtz—perceiving color
    C. Wilhelm Wundt—1879—transition from philosophy to science
        1. Founder of modern psychology
        2. First true psychological laboratory
        3. Leipzig, Germany
II. Major Early Schools of Psychology
    A. Structuralism
        1. Introspection
        2. Components or building blocks of the mind
    B. Functionalism
        1. William James—United States
        2. The mind adapts us to our environment
        3. Understand the mind by understanding how it functions
    C. Behaviorism
        1. John Watson—early 1900s
        2. Study only overt behavior
        3. Experience, environment mold us
        4. B. F. Skinner—operant conditioning—consequences are crucial to learning
    D. Reinforcer—pleasant consequence; increases behavior
    E. Punishment—unpleasant consequence; decreases behavior
    F. Gestalt psychology
        1. Max Wertheimer—contemporary of Watson
        2. Unified, organized patterns
        3. "Whole is greater than the sum of the parts"
    G. Sigmund Freud and psychoanalysis
        1. Austrian physician (early 1900s)
        2. Focus on the unconscious
        3. Sexual and aggressive impulses motivate

4. Importance of early childhood experience
5. Dynamic conflict between unconscious desires and acceptable behavior
6. Psychoanalysis developed—"talk therapy"

III. Contemporary Perspectives in Psychology
    A. Behavioral perspective
        1. Modeled after school of behaviorism
        2. Observable behavior; emphasis on experience and learning
        3. Broader variation: social-cognitive theory
        4. Environment and cognitive factors
        5. Values, goals, and expectations important
        6. Social cognitive theory: psychology should include study of mental processes, not only behavior itself
        7. Behavior therapy—applying learning principles to treat psychological problems
    B. Psychodynamic perspective
        1. Neo-Freudians include emphasis on self-awareness and choices
        2. Focus remains on unconscious drives and early childhood experience
        3. Criticized because scientific study difficult
    C. Humanistic perspective
        1. Known as "third force" in psychology (besides psychodynamic and behavioral)
        2. Each human has unique abilities and potential
        3. Free will, personal choice: crucial aspects of this perspective
    D. Physiological perspective
        1. Biological processes influence behavior
        2. Nervous system (especially brain) and body chemicals at root of human functioning
        3. Heredity an important consideration
        4. Subfield: Evolutionary psychology
            a) Study non-human species as well as humans
            b) Genetic programming creates behavioral tendencies, predispositions
    E. Cognitive perspective
        1. *Cognitio* means knowledge
        2. Study of mental processes; acquiring knowledge of ourselves and the world
        3. How we learn, think, reason, remember, and use language
        4. Criticized by behaviorists as beyond scientific study
    F. Sociocultural perspective
        1. Behavior and attitudes are influenced by culture
        2. Social and economic experiences have impact
        3. Ethnicity, age, gender, sexual orientation, and disability are considered
        4. Increasing diversity of contemporary society
            a) Whites no longer such a majority
            b) "Race" not a very useful concept
            c) Blurring racial boundaries
        5. Good research includes sociocultural aspects—can't generalize from limited samples
    G. Summary of contemporary perspectives
        1. No one perspective is the "correct" one
            a) Each focuses on different aspects of behavior and functioning
            b) None is complete; each has something unique to offer
        2. Positive psychology—a growing movement
            a) Emphasis on human virtues and strengths

SUMMARY

In this module, you learn how psychology began. The earliest concern with psychological issues was nearly 2,500 years ago. Greek philosophers examined questions regarding human nature, the mind, behavior, and our experience with life. Confucius, in the Far East, believed human nature was basically good. These philosophers varied in how they thought such questions should be addressed: just think and reason about them? Or rely on scrutiny of real-life experiences?

The psychological laboratory established by Wilhelm Wundt in 1879 in Leipzig, Germany, marks the beginning of modern psychology. Psychology today is scientific, which is why we distinguish it from its philosophical origins. Wundt's school became known as structuralism, looking at the mind and conscious experience. Functionalism, introduced by William James, expanded structuralism to look at how the mind adapts us to our environment. Sigmund Freud, originally trained as a physician in Austria, believed psychological issues stemmed from unconscious desires and conflicts within the human. He created the therapy known as psychoanalysis.

The early 1900s in America marked a shift in psychology—behaviorists insisted only observable behavior and experience were suitable for study. At about the same time, the school of Gestalt psychology was introduced, which has much to do with how we perceive the world. Both of these schools objected to the structuralists' approach of studying the mind and its component parts.

Contemporary perspectives in psychology include behaviorism and the Freudian or psychodynamic approach, modified somewhat from their earlier forms. Added to this list are humanism, with a focus on discovering one's true inner self, and the cognitive perspective, looking at how thoughts and mental processes influence our behavior. Lastly in our contemporary perspectives are the physiological approach (considering the brain and nervous system's influence on behavior) and the sociocultural view, reminding us that life experiences differ depending on the culture in which we are raised. In addition, positive psychology is a growing movement within psychology. Its emphasis is on the positive aspects of the human behavior, such as love, optimism, creativity, and altruism.

KEY TERMS

Psychology

Psychophysics

Introspection

Structuralism

Functionalism

Natural selection

Stream of consciousness

Behaviorism

Gestalt psychology

Gestalt

Unconscious

Psychodynamic perspective

Psychoanalysis

Behavioral perspective

Social-cognitive theory

Behavior therapy

Humanistic psychology

Humanistic perspective

Physiological perspective

Evolutionary psychology

Cognitive perspective

Sociocultural perspective

Positive psychology

SELF-TEST PRACTICE QUIZ

From the Key Terms select that which best matches the following (Note: Not every Key Term will be used.):

1. _____ An approach within psychology that focuses on the impact of human thought, reasoning, intelligence, and memory

2. _____ Part of Wundt's research methodology; involves "looking within"

3. _____ An approach within psychology based on the work of Sigmund Freud, emphasizing unconscious conflict, primitive sexual instinct and early childhood experiences

4. _____ A perspective within psychology that emerged as a reaction to the psychodynamic and behavioral approaches; emphasizes the uniqueness and self-awareness of every individual

5. _____ One of the more recently developed perspectives in psychology; it recognizes the influence of cultural heritage, ethnic background, economic status, and lifestyle factors

6. _____ A psychological school of thought that emerged in the early 1900s, suggesting that measurable overt behavior and experience were the only appropriate topics for study

7. _____ The study of behavior and of mental processes

a. Psychology
b. Psychophysics
c. Introspection
d. Structuralism
e. Positive psychology
f. Functionalism
g. Natural selection
h. Stream of consciousness
i. Behaviorism
j. Gestalt psychology
k. Gestalt
l. Unconscious
m. Psychodynamic perspective
n. Psychoanalysis
o. Behavioral perspective
p. Social-cognitive theory
q. Behavior therapy
r. Humanistic psychology
s. Humanistic perspective
t. Physiological perspective
u. Evolutionary psychology

8. _____ A school of psychology that examines how the brain interprets and organizes our experiences in the world so that what we perceive is a unified whole or pattern

9. _____ A contemporary perspective in psychology that advocates an expanded view of the principles that are the foundation of the school of behaviorism

10. _____ A contemporary movement within psychology that emphasizes the study of human virtues and assets, rather than weaknesses and deficits

11. _____ A movement within psychology based on the views of Charles Darwin, recognizing that genetic influences on behavior may serve to aid in the survival of the species

12. _____ A relatively recent expansion within the behavioral perspective, emphasizing that cognitions in addition to environmental experience shape behavior

13. _____ According to Freud, a region of the mind consisting of primitive urges and conflicts and of which we are not aware

14. _____ A perspective within psychology where genetic, neurological, and in particular brain functioning influences are researched

15. _____ An approach to psychological therapy developed by Sigmund Freud

16. _____ A psychological treatment approach based on the belief that maladaptive behaviors are learned

v. Cognitive perspective

w. Sociocultural perspective

17. Which psychologist argued that mental experiences should be examined in terms of their purposes, not broken down into their component parts?
    a. Max Wertheimer
    b. Wilhelm Wundt
    c. William James
    d. Gustav Fechner

18. The "third force" in contemporary psychology (in addition to the behavioral and psychodynamic perspectives) is the
    a. sociocultural perspective.
    b. humanistic perspective.
    c. cognitive perspective.
    d. physiological perspective.

19. In what way is psychology still like philosophy? Both fields
    a. study questions related to behavior and the nature of the human being.
    b. take a scientific approach.
    c. research biological and genetic bases for behavior.
    d. are relatively new disciplines.

20. What was one criticism directed towards the school of behaviorism?
    a. There was too much emphasis on thought and inner experience.
    b. Animals were not believed to be useful research subjects.
    c. Psychology does not really fit the "scientific" model.
    d. Behaviorism did not deem the mind as appropriate for study.

21. Psychologists from the _____ perspective examine the role of biological factors such as heredity and drugs on human behavior and functioning.
    a. behavioral
    b. cognitive
    c. physiological
    d. sociocultural

22. Freud was trained as a
    a. psychologist.
    b. physiologist.
    c. philosopher.
    d. physician.

23. Behavior therapy applies _____ principles to help individuals discover more adaptive ways to live.
    a. cognitive
    b. psychodynamic
    c. learning
    d. introspective

24. Which contemporary perspective is generally considered to be the most accurate?
    a. Cognitive perspective
    b. Physiological perspective
    c. Sociocultural perspective
    d. Behavioral perspective
    e. None of them—each contributes to our knowledge in unique ways

ESSAY QUESTIONS

1. Trace the history of psychology, from its earliest origins to the state of the discipline today.

2. Why do we have multiple explanations regarding the nature of the human? Is one perspective more correct than another?

ANSWER KEY

1.   Cognitive perspective

2.   Introspection

3.   Psychodynamic perspective

4.   Humanistic perspective

5.   Sociocultural perspective

6.   Behaviorism

7.   Psychology

8.   Gestalt psychology

9.   Behavioral perspective

10.   Developmental psychology

11.   Evolutionary psychology

12.   Social-cognitive theory

13.   Unconscious

14.   Physiological perspective

15.   Psychoanalysis

16.   Behavior therapy

17.   c

18.   b

19.   a

20.   b

21.   c

22.   d

23.   c

24.   e

SAMPLE ANSWERS TO ESSAY QUESTIONS

1.   The questions studied by psychologists have been around probably as long as thinking human beings have been around. Thus, the early Greeks, Confucius, and other ancients wondered about the inner nature of the human being and how we might best learn more about ourselves, our world, and how we function in our world. These questions have been around literally for millennia; however, they were not subjected to truly scientific study until the time of Fechner and Wundt, in the latter half of the nineteenth century. Fechner studied psychophysics, and Wundt brought his scientific training as a physiologist to the long-standing questions about human nature. In 1879, he established what is recognized as the first scientific laboratory in Leipzig, Germany. Wundt took a very rigorous approach to learning about the human mind by using introspection. His school of thought became known as structuralism. William James looked at how the mind functioned to help us adapt to our environment, and behaviorists, beginning in the 1920s,

promoted the idea that psychology is best served by concentrating on observable, measurable behavior. Sigmund Freud, in Austria, was a contemporary of most of the other pioneers in psychology. His emphasis, however, was quite unlike that of the other psychologists of his day. Freud believed the source of influence on our behavior lay out of our awareness, in the unconscious mind. A major contribution from Freud was the development of a treatment method for psychological disorders. The humanistic school emerged in the mid-twentieth century and emphasized the uniqueness and self-determination of the human. Recent additions to the field of psychology include the cognitive, physiological, evolutionary, and sociocultural perspectives.

2. It is true that there are a number of approaches regarding human psychological functioning. Each perspective has a different emphasis, such as a focus on human thought or on behavior or on unconscious influences or on our genetic heritage. The human being is quite a complex creature. Thus, it is no wonder that there are a variety of approaches utilized when examining human behavior and the human psyche. All of these aspects are influences as to why we behave the way we do, and each perspective makes a contribution towards human understanding. Each perspective has valuable information to offer; yet no one approach seems to adequately explain everything about human functioning. In addition, the various psychological perspectives really do not have distinct divisions. Social-cognitive theory, for example, is based on behavioral principles but adds considerations related to human thought and interpretation. Because the human being is so complex, we need a variety of different approaches that may focus on different aspects of the human. Together they begin to provide us with a clearer understanding about the nature, and actions, of the human being.

MODULE 1.2 PSYCHOLOGISTS: WHO THEY ARE AND WHAT THEY DO

LEARNING OBJECTIVES

After you have mastered the information in this unit, you will be able to:

* Describe the two general types of research that psychologists conduct

* Define the various specialties in psychology

* Discuss the changes that have occurred in the ethnic and gender characteristics of psychologists over time

OUTLINE

I. Types of Research
    A. Basic—expanding our knowledge
    B. Applied—research for a specific objective
II. Traditional Major Specialty Areas of Psychology
    A. Experimental psychologists—use the experimental research method (to establish cause and effect) for study of behavior and mental processes
    B. Comparative—study animals and their behavior
    C. Physiological—study biological processes related to behavior
    D. Clinical psychologists—study individuals with psychological disorders
    E. Counseling psychologists—treat individuals with less severe psychological disorders
    F. School psychologists—work directly with children to aid in their school experience
    G. Educational psychologists—research and/or apply learning and instructional advances
    H. Developmental psychologists—study human growth and changes over the entire lifespan
    I. Personality psychologists—study unique personal characteristics and behaviors

J. Social psychologists—focus on the individual as a member of a group

K. Environmental psychologists—study the relationship between people's behavior and their physical environment

L. Industrial/Organizational (I/O) psychologists—research and/or apply ways to improve the work setting

M. Health psychologists—study the relationship between psychological factors and physical well-being

N. Consumer psychologists—investigate people's purchases and reactions to advertising

III. Emerging Specialty Areas in Psychology

A. Neuropsychologists—study the brain specifically for its relationship to behavior

B. Geropsychologists—investigate the psychological impact of aging

C. Forensic psychologists—work with individuals involved in the legal system

D. Sport psychologists—study competition and ways to maximize athletic performance

IV. Professional Psychology: Becoming More Diverse

A. Early psychologists (nineteenth century)

1. White male, European background

2. Women and minorities faced many barriers

3. Ph.D. not awarded to women, though doctoral work may be completed

4. 1920: first Ph.D. awarded to African-American

B. Current demographics among psychologists

1. Women now majority of recipients of psychology degrees

2. Ethnic minorities in psychology slowly increasing

SUMMARY

Once psychology appeared in its modern, more scientific form, the field grew and expanded rapidly. Many psychologists conduct research: either basic, simply to expand our knowledge of a particular aspect within psychology, or applied, to determine new or better methods to address a particular problem. There are now many subfields, or specializations, within the profession of psychology. Individuals in these subfields may or may not conduct research as part of their day-to-day activities, but all attempt to stay current regarding research on relevant psychological topics. In addition, regardless of specialization, professionals within the field of psychology usually have adopted one or more of the psychological perspectives, such as cognitive, behavioral, humanistic, and the like. The perspective (or eclectic approach if a number of perspectives are utilized) tends to be reflected to an extent in how each professional undertakes his or her occupational activity.

Traditional specialty areas in psychology include experimental (always do research), clinical (use psychotherapy), counseling (treat less severe disorders), school (work directly with children), educational (try to improve teaching and learning), developmental (study whole lifespan), and personality (study unique human nature). Ongoing specialty areas also include environmental, I/O, health, and consumer psychology. New areas in psychology include research on the brain, aging, sports, and legal concerns. Many more women now participate in psychology, and the role of ethnic minorities is increasing.

KEY TERMS AND CONCEPTS

Basic research

Applied research

Experimental psychologists

Comparative psychologists

Physiological psychologists

Clinical psychologists

Psychiatrists

Counseling psychologists

School psychologists

Educational psychologists

Developmental psychologists

Personality psychologists

Social psychologists

Environmental psychologists

Industrial/Organizational (I/O) psychologists

Health psychologists

Consumer psychologists

Neuropsychologists

Geropsychologists

Forensic psychologists

Sport psychologists

SELF-TEST PRACTICE QUIZ

From the Key Terms select that which best matches the following (Note: Not every Key Term will be used.):

1. _____ Psychologists who study human growth and changes over the life span

2. _____ Research aimed simply at furthering our knowledge and understanding

3. _____ Psychologists who study the relationship between psychological patterns and physical health

4. _____ Individuals with a medical degree who specialize in treating mental health disorders

5. _____ Psychologists who research criminal behavior and are involved with other aspects of the legal system

6. _____ Psychologists who research matters dealing with aging and the elderly

a. Basic research

b. Applied research

c. Experimental psychologists

d. Comparative psychologists

e. Physiological psychologists

f. Clinical psychologists

g. Psychiatrists

h. Counseling psychologists

i. School psychologists

j. Educational psychologists

k. Developmental psychologists

l. Personality psychologists

m. Social psychologists

n. Environmental psychologists

7. _____ Psychologists who conduct controlled research to establish cause and effect; usually carried out in a laboratory setting

8. _____ Psychologists who investigate genetic and other biological influences on behavior

9. _____ Research conducted in order to learn more about or solve a particular problem

10. _____ Psychologists who study brain structures, neurotransmitters, and the like with regard to their impact on human functioning

11. _____ Psychologists involved in business or other organizational settings with the objective of optimizing the work experience for employees and administrators

12. _____ Psychologists investigating the influence of interpersonal contact and the actions of others on the behavior of individuals

13. _____ Psychologists who treat mental disorders by means of psychotherapy

14. _____ Psychologists involved with evaluating academic abilities and optimizing the learning experience

15. _____ Psychologists who study many other species besides the human to investigate similarities and differences

16. _____ Psychologists interested in the functioning of the individual and how individuals differ from one another

o. Industrial/Organizational (I/O) psychologists

p. Health psychologists

q. Consumer psychologists

r. Neuropsychologists

s. Geropsychologists

t. Forensic psychologists

u. Sport psychologists

17. As the baby boomer population ages and more and more adults live longer, what type of psychologist will be increasingly in demand as a result?
    a. Geropsychologist
    b. Forensic psychologist
    c. Experimental psychologist
    d. Comparative psychologist

18. _____ psychologists study the relationship between the brain and behavior.

    a. Clinical
    b. Social
    c. Neuro
    d. Developmental

19. The subfield, or specialization, in psychology that has the greatest number of people working in it is _____ psychology.

    a. personality
    b. educational
    c. clinical
    d. industrial/organizational

20. A psychologist who does _____ research wants to help resolve a particular psychological issue.

    a. basic
    b. applied
    c. grant-funded
    d. humane

21. Unlike earlier years, _____ now make up the largest group of degree recipients in the field of psychology.

    a. men
    b. women
    c. African Americans
    d. Native Americans

22. Dr. Hawkins is conducting research to determine how to best motivate overweight adults to start (and stick with) an exercise program. Dr. Hawkins is most likely a _____ psychologist.

    a. clinical
    b. social
    c. developmental
    d. health

23. A personality psychologist is one who

    a. studies the impact of the environment on health and behavior.
    b. treats psychological disorders, such as anxiety and depression.
    c. investigates the unique characteristics of an individual.
    d. studies any of the above psychological topics.

24. If you were feeling dissatisfied and unclear as to where you should be going with your life, most likely you would be advised to see a _____ psychologist.

    a. counseling
    b. forensic
    c. developmental
    d. consumer

25. A psychologist who works with a corporation to improve employee morale is most likely a(n) _____ psychologist.

    a. developmental
    b. experimental
    c. educational
    d. industrial/organizational

26. If you investigate such matters as interpersonal attraction, attitudes, aggression, and conformity, most likely you are a _____ psychologist.
    a. social
    b. clinical
    c. developmental
    d. comparative
27. Though psychologists work in many settings, the greatest number of psychologists are employed
    a. in colleges and universities.
    b. at private for-profit organizations.
    c. for government agencies.
    d. in schools.

ESSAY QUESTIONS

1. If you were to choose a profession within the field of psychology, which area of specialization appeals most to you? Why?
2. What value or usefulness can there be in carrying out basic research?
3. How has the composition of people who become psychologists changed over the years?
4. What is the difference between clinical and counseling psychology?
5. Is someone who does research always an experimental psychologist? Explain.

ANSWER KEY

1. Developmental psychologists
2. Basic research
3. Health psychologists
4. Psychiatrists
5. Forensic psychologists
6. Geropsychologists
7. Experimental psychologists
8. Physiological psychologists
9. Applied research
10. Neuropsychologists
11. Industrial/organizational psychologists
12. Social psychologists
13. Clinical psychologists
14. Educational psychologists
15. Comparative psychologists
16. Personality psychologists
17. a
18. c

19. c

20. b

21. b

22. d

23. c

24. a

25. d

26. a

27. a

SAMPLE ANSWERS TO ESSAY QUESTIONS

1. Describe the psychology subfield that most interests you, and explain why it interests you.

2. Basic research explores psychological issues for the sake of knowledge. Of course, simply gaining that knowledge is useful. It may help expand our general understanding of human psychological functioning, and it may be interesting in its own right. Since funding sources are limited, however, we may not think of purely basic research as deserving of too much in the way of financial support. However, there is another advantage to basic research. Even though it may have no apparent immediate application, it is entirely possible that at some time in the future the knowledge will help address a particular problem, or clarify advances we have made in related lines of research.

3. We are seeing more diversity among psychology professionals. Originally, all psychologists were white males of European descent. With time, however, the composition of people in psychology has changed. There has been a great increase in women taking professional roles in the field of psychology, and there has been some increase in the number of minorities. Presently, the greatest number of new Ph.D. degrees are awarded to women (about 70 percent). The first female president of the American Psychological Association (APA) was Mary Whiton Calkins, in 1905, followed by the second woman president, Margaret Floy Washburn, in 1921. Gilbert Haven Jones was the first African American to receive a doctorate in psychology (in Germany, in 1909). Kenneth Clark was the first African American elected president of APA, in 1971.

4. There are some similarities between clinical psychologists and counseling psychologists because professionals in both specializations treat individuals with psychological disorders. However, clinical psychologists treat fairly serious mental health problems such as schizophrenia and bi-polar disorder. Counseling psychologists treat the more everyday problems that people have. These more common problems include issues such as adjustment disorders, marital difficulties, and the considerations involved when making career decisions.

5. Psychological research may be carried out by almost any kind of psychologist. However, research does not always involve the procedures utilized by an experimental psychologist. Experimental psychologists always conduct research and often on the same topics as Wundt and the other structuralists investigated in their early laboratories. Experimental psychologists also are more likely to carry out research with animals. Conducting experimental research (as opposed to other kinds of research) involves utilizing a very specific set of procedures that are particular to the experimental method. All experimentation, then, is a form of scientific research, but scientific research may involve methodologies in addition to those used by experimental psychologists. Other disciplines within psychology (social, developmental, educational, or clinical, for example), may conduct research using the experimental methodology or other methodologies. Psychologists try to stay informed regarding current research findings even if they do not carry out the work themselves.

MODULE 1.3 RESEARCH METHODS IN PSYCHOLOGY

LEARNING OBJECTIVES

After you have mastered the information in this unit, you will be able to:

*   Describe the major objectives of science

*   Define the scientific method and identify its four general steps

*   Describe the major research methods used by psychologists

*   Discuss the ethical guidelines psychologists must follow in their research

*   Provide an example of a specific ethical guideline

OUTLINE

I.   Objectives of Science
    A.   Description—clear, accurate and objective information; based on observation
    B.   Explanation—tying information together to make sense of it (such as with theories)
    C.   Prediction—understanding and expectation regarding future events
    D.   Control—managing events and circumstances for human well-being
II.   The Scientific Method
    A.   Develop a research question
    B.   Frame the research question in the form of a testable hypothesis
    C.   Gather evidence to test the hypothesis
    D.   Draw conclusions regarding the outcome
III. Research Methods
    A.   Case study—thorough, careful study of one or a few individuals
        1.   Advantage: detailed and extensive information
        2.   Disadvantage: not necessarily representative of others
    B.   Survey
        1.   Information from a sample to reveal features of a population
        2.   Interviews or questionnaires most often used
        3.   To generalize accurately, sample must be representative
            a)   A few thousand people may sufficiently represent U.S. trends
        4.   Advantage: broad range of information if done correctly
        5.   Disadvantage: may be biases in responses

      C.   Naturalistic observation
          1.   Studying humans (or animals) in familiar, everyday environment
          2.   Researcher observing must be inconspicuous
          3.   Advantage: greatest likelihood of genuine, authentic behavior
          4.   Disadvantage: least amount of control over events that will take place
      D.   Correlational—relationship between two variables, represented mathematically
          1.   Advantage: helpful for prediction, suggests further study
          2.   Disadvantage: does not establish causality, though may be (wrongly) interpreted as such
          3.   Correlation coefficients range from -1.00 to +1.00
              a)   The farther the value is from 0, the stronger the relationship
      E.   Experimental
          1.   Can truly establish cause and effect
          2.   Involves independent and dependent variables
          3.   Control group helps establish causality
          4.   Random assignment helps assure no pre-existing differences
          5.   Advantages and disadvantages
              a)   Advantage: learn why an effect actually happens
              b)   Disadvantage: expectations (e.g., placebo effect) may influence results

IV.   Ethical Principles in Psychological Research
      A.   Ethical standards protect research participants
      B.   Review committees at institutions verify ethical procedures
      C.   Some basic ethical guidelines for research
          1.   Informed consent
               a)   Research participant knows what will happen in study
               b)   Willingly agrees, based on explanation given, to be part of study
               c)   Aware can withdraw from study at any time
          2.   Confidentiality—keep records on clients and research participants private
      D.   Animal research—protect animal from harm unless no other research alternative
          1.   Ethics review panel must give permission
          2.   Benefits from such research must be substantial

V.   Exploring Psychology: Anatomy of a Research Study: Shooter Bias
      A.   Question: Will race or ethnicity of a target figure affect a police officer's decision to shoot a suspect?
      B.   Procedure: Experimental method
          1.   Pictures of targets flashed on a screen; participants had to decide which ones were armed and shoot only those
      C.   Results: Officers were quicker to shoot armed African American targets than armed Whites, and they were more likely to mistakenly shoot unarmed African Americans than unarmed Whites

SUMMARY

Because modern psychology is a science, information we gain in the field is through research. Researchers follow the scientific method. The objective of the scientific method is to obtain useful information and avoid bias.

There are many different ways of conducting research in psychology. Each method has its particular advantages—but there are disadvantages too. Participants in psychological research are now protected by ethical guidelines. Foremost among these guidelines are the notion of informed consent (the individual knows what he or she is about to experience and willingly agrees to participate) and confidentiality. Though less stringent, animals used in research are protected by ethical guidelines also.

The simplest research method is naturalistic observation. Naturalistic observation involves studying the research target in its familiar, everyday environment. This is an important methodology because we are most likely to get genuine, authentic behavior this way. When we utilize the case study methodology we are investigating one, or only a few, individuals. We learn much about these few individuals through case study research, but they may not represent the population we are truly interested in. Nor can we assume they are representative of humanity in general. Correlation is a mathematical calculation showing that there is a link between two variables, or measures. Just because two factors are related, however, does not mean one causes the other. Surveys can collect large amounts of information but the sample surveyed must be representative. Obtaining a truly representative sample is difficult and usually expensive. The experimental methodology may be the most highly regarded research procedure. With it (and only with experimentation) we can establish the cause of some psychological phenomena. This is a very important achievement.

KEY TERMS

Empirical approach

Inferences

Theories

Variables

Scientific method

Hypothesis

Theory

Statistic

Statistical significance

Replication

Case study method

Survey method

Structured interview

Questionnaire

Population

Samples

Random sampling

Social desirability bias

Volunteer bias

Naturalistic observation method

Correlational method

Correlation coefficient

Experimental method

Independent variables

Dependent variables

Control groups

Random assignment

Placebo

Placebo effects

Single-blind studies

Double-blind studies

Ethics review committees

Informed consent

SELF-TEST PRACTICE QUIZ

From the Key Terms select that which best matches the following (Note: Not every Key Term will be used.):

1. _____ A prediction about the anticipated relationship between cause and effect in an empirical study

2. _____ A subset from the population used to test questions related to the entire population—for quality research, it must be representative of the entire population

3. _____ A research methodology, which, through the use of a control group, can establish a causal relationship between independent and dependent variables

4. _____ Where there may be an effect from an intervention, but the effect is due to participants' hopes or expectations and not the treatment administered

5. _____ A critical component in ethical research; the participant is aware of what he or she will experience as part of a research study, and willingly agrees to participate

6. _____ The result of many studies in a particular research area; the various confirmed and disconfirmed hypotheses are unified to provide a framework for understanding, interpretation, and direction for future research

a. Empirical approach

b. Inferences

c. Theories

d. Variables

e. Scientific method

f. Hypothesis

g. Statistic

h. Statistical significance

i. Replication

j. Case study method

k. Survey method

l. Structured interview

m. Questionnaire

n. Population

o. Samples

p. Random Sampling

q. Social desirability bias

r. Volunteer bias

s. Naturalistic observation method

t. Correlational method

u. Correlation coefficient

7. _____ An important component in research; involves assuring that research findings are the result of direct observation and precise measurement

8. _____ All of the people about whom a research question is concerned (usually too many to test in their entirety, and subsets are used)

9. _____ An important research procedure that helps to control for possible preexisting differences among participants; each participant has equal likelihood of being placed in any of the study research conditions

10. _____ The suspected causes (can be proposed by the researcher) in an experimental study

11. _____ Drawing conclusions from observation or research that may not be entirely based on the evidence in the study

12. _____ The determination that research findings are highly likely to be real results, not due to chance

13. _____ A set of steps or criteria for research that help assure that the findings in the study were obtained objectively

14. _____ An important criterion in scientific research; similar results to a study are found when using the same methodology but conducted by a different researcher, with different participants, and often in a different location

15. _____ A research methodology where there is no intervention whatsoever by the researcher; participants are simply watched, without their awareness, in their familiar, comfortable, everyday environment

16. _____ A research methodology aimed at assessing the views of large numbers of people with regard to broad, general questions; to be done correctly a representative sample is crucial

v.   Experimental method

w.   Independent variables

x.   Dependent variables

y.   Control groups

z.   Random assignment

aa.   Placebo

bb.   Placebo effects

cc.   Single-blind studies

dd.   Double-blind studies

ee.   Ethics review committees

ff.   Informed consent

17. _____   Components in a research study whose quantitative values can change (and these changes can be measured)

18. _____   The suspected effects (due to the independent variable) in an experimental research design

19. _____   A research methodology that indicates the degree to which measured behavior on one variable for individuals is related to scores obtained for those individuals on another variable

20. _____   A research methodology used in psychology where only one or a few individuals are studied, but they are researched in great depth

21. If you wrote the conclusion "the little boy really wanted the cookie" you would be making a(n)
    a. observation.
    b. inference.
    c. prediction.
    d. hypothesis.
22. "Children who take afternoon naps will perform better in school than children who do not take afternoon naps." This is an example of a(n)
    a. hypothesis.
    b. case study.
    c. theory.
    d. objective.
23. A researcher wishes to determine which high school students are at greatest risk of dropping out. This goal illustrates the scientific objective of
    a. control.
    b. description.
    c. explanation.
    d. prediction.
24. An important aspect of the scientific method is
    a. test every member of the relevant population.
    b. gather objective evidence with which to evaluate the hypothesis.
    c. use correlational findings to establish causality.
    d. All of the above are correct.
25. Clear description is an important component of science because
    a. published findings can be read more easily by individuals who speak other languages.
    b. it makes the process of arriving at inferences easier.
    c. accurate, precise reporting helps us to remain objective.
    d. it helps us write up our findings for others' use in the fewest words possible.

26. Determining statistical significance is important because it allows researchers to
    a. determine how likely it is that a given outcome occurred by chance.
    b. calculate correlation coefficients between two individuals.
    c. help assure that our observations are collected objectively.
    d. help assure that all research participants are treated ethically.

27. Questionnaires and interviews are part of the
    a. survey method.
    b. formation of the hypothesis.
    c. double-blind procedure.
    d. random sampling procedure.

28. What is a disadvantage of case study research?
    a. Memories of participants may have become distorted with the passage of time.
    b. The researcher may become biased from knowing the participant so well.
    c. We cannot legitimately generalize findings to other individuals.
    d. All of the above are correct.

29. Why is it important to use control groups in experiments?
    a. They ensure that the sample is representative.
    b. They provide a basis for comparison when exploring the effects of the independent variable.
    c. They prevent volunteer bias.
    d. This is necessary to comply with ethics guidelines.

ESSAY QUESTIONS

1. How does the experimental method help determine the true cause of a psychological phenomenon?

2. What is the advantage for research in modern psychology to be scientific?

3. Why is it so important that sample groups studied via the survey method be representative of the larger population in which we are interested?

4. Discuss the term *ethics*. What are some ethical guidelines we have for research in psychology?

5. Explain the idea of random assignment. How does this practice help us have more control in our psychological research (especially with regard to the experimental method)?

6. Why must we use statistics in order to conclude that our study yielded a meaningful finding?

7. Why are there so many ways of doing research in psychology?

8. What are some ways a researcher conducting a naturalistic observation study can assure that he or she is unobtrusive? Why is this step so important?

ANSWER KEY

1. Hypothesis

2. Samples

3. Experimental method

4. Placebo

5. Informed consent

6. Theories

7. Empirical approach

8.   Population

9.   Random assignment

10.   Independent variables

11.   Inferences

12.   Statistical significance

13.   Scientific method

14.   Replication

15.   Naturalistic observation method

16.   Survey method

17.   Variables

18.   Dependent variables

19.   Correlational method

20.   Case study method

21.   b

22.   a

23.   d

24.   b

25.   c

26.   a

27.   a

28.   d

29.   b

SAMPLE ANSWERS TO ESSAY QUESTIONS

1.   With the experimental research method, all conditions are kept the same between research groups except that which is expected to be the cause of some phenomena (this suspected cause is called *the independent variable*). If there is a difference in the dependent variable (that which is used to assess any effects of the independent variable), then that effect must be due to the independent variable; e.g., what was suspected by the researchers as the likely cause. Because of control in the experimental methodology procedures, there was no other difference between the two groups.

2.   When we are scientific, we remain objective, and we do not allow our biases or expectations to enter into our investigating a research question. We attempt to carry out first-hand, empirical research, and we let our experience and the objective evidence answer our research questions. It is thought, through being scientific, that psychologists are much more likely to discover real, unbiased truth rather than being affected by expectations or preconceived notions.

3. A sample group must be representative of the population in which we are interested. That is, the small group we actually test with our research question(s) must be perfectly proportional to the larger population with whom we are actually concerned. Thus, the sample group must share proportionally the same socioeconomic, political, religious, educational, ideological and so forth characteristics as in the relevant population. Only when a sample is representative does it truly tell us what is going on with regard to the population.

4. "Ethics" conveys the notion that we should never put any other individual or group at risk or in jeopardy, and certainly not simply to further our own ends. Important ethical guidelines include:

   - No harm may come to participants, physically, psychologically, or in any other way.

   - A participant must give *informed consent;* that is, the participant knows the general nature of the study and willingly agrees to participate.

   - The participant is aware he or she is free to withdraw at any time.

   - All identities and information gained from the research study are kept anonymous and confidential.

5. Random assignment means any individual participating in a research study has equal likelihood of being put in any of the groups involved in the study. Thus, there is no pre-existing bias as to how the groups getting either the treatment or the control condition are formed. We assume any variation among humans participating in the study, which cannot be controlled for in any other way, is evened out through the random assignment. Such a practice is useful in experimental research. With sufficient numbers in each group, it is likely that research groups are fairly homogenous at the onset of a study. Any differences between groups at the conclusion of a study, then, would be due to the treatment variable (the independent variable), as all other features of the study were held constant.

6. The use of statistics allows us to determine what the likelihood is that we obtained our finding simply due to chance. If statistical analysis shows that it is very unlikely that our result occurred by chance, then we can conclude that the experimental variable (the independent variable) is what caused the result.

7. There are many ways of doing research in psychology because (1) human beings are complicated and complex; (2) different perspectives may address different kinds of research question more effectively depending on the nature of the question; and (3) we look for convergence among different research methods, which collectively help strengthen our confidence in our findings.

8. A researcher can be unobtrusive in naturalistic observation research by (1) using a one-way mirror; (2) blending into or hiding among surroundings; or (3) through time and exposure becoming a very familiar part of the surroundings, and thus inconspicuous.

   It is important to be unobtrusive because we do not want our observation targets to be aware they are being watched and/or to feel self-conscious. If they are aware of an observer, then their behavior may not necessarily be what they would naturally or ordinarily do. If the behavior exhibited by participants is not representative of what they typically do, then findings based on such research are in essence meaningless.

MODULE 1.4 APPLICATION: BECOMING A CRITICAL THINKER

LEARNING OBJECTIVE

After you have mastered the information in this unit, you will be able to:

- Outline the key features of critical thinking

OUTLINE

I.   Background Factors in Critical Thinking
    A.   How do we determine what is really the truth?
    B.   Critical thinking—adopting a questioning attitude, willingness to challenge conventional thinking of the day
    C.   Base beliefs on reasons, not on "gut feelings"
II. Features of Critical Thinking
    A.   Question everything
        1.   Do not blindly accept claims
        2.   Keep an open mind, weigh the evidence
    B.   Look for clarification of terms
    C.   Avoid oversimplifying
    D.   Avoid overgeneralizing
    E.   Maintain distinction between correlation and causality
    F.   Consider assumptions on which claims are based
    G.   Carefully examine all sources for timeliness, credibility
    H.   Question evidence—is it sound, rational, objective?
    I.   As a precaution, think of other ways the findings might be interpreted besides the one presented
III. Thinking Critically About Online Information
    A.   Anyone can create or post to Internet sites
    B.   Not all information is accurate; retain critical thinking approach
    C.   Best sources still scientific journals, credible and respected agencies and organizations

SUMMARY

In this applications model you learn about important critical thinking skills. Especially in this information age, there are untold numbers of sources where you can obtain opinions and findings on almost any topic. It is wonderful that we have access to so very much information, almost instantaneously. But now, perhaps more than ever, we need to be particularly wary about what we believe. Anyone can post just about any information or views to Internet sites. Just because something is presented in written form, even if it is presented repeatedly, does not make it true. For our own benefit, we can adopt critical thinking skills that will help us evaluate information. We can use these guides to critical thinking to evaluate the accuracy of information presented to us from any source.

A critical thinker keeps an open mind and a questioning attitude. Critical thinkers choose to be skeptical and avoid rushing to judgment. The objective is to wait until the facts and convincing evidence lead us to understand what is truly accurate. There may be times when the evidence that seems most legitimate does not correspond to existing popular views. A critical thinker needs to be comfortable challenging, if necessary, conventionally held beliefs.

Steps involved in critical thinking include questioning everything that comes your way. Keep an open mind, regardless of the sources of claims that you hear. When investigating, look for clarification of terms. Make sure you and the communicator are in accord with regard to the meanings of terminology. Avoid claims that oversimplify or overgeneralize, and refrain from doing these things yourself with information you have obtained. Remember the distinction between correlation and causality. Just because there is a relationship between changes in one variable and changes in another does not mean that one variable causes another. These concepts are two entirely different things.

Clarify the assumptions made in the sources that you read or listen to. If the assumptions are inaccurate, then so are conclusions drawn from them. Check for the sources of the information you obtain. Are credible sources for all pertinent facts listed (such as in a citation)? Take note of dates of publication of all sources. Even once-accurate information may no longer be correct or relevant if considerable time has lapsed since the original investigation. Verify that claims are made on replicable, objective evidence. As a check for yourself, when you read an interpretation of some finding, try to think up alternate explanations. Focusing on alternative explanations at least long enough to come up with some will help you keep the claims you read or hear of in perspective. Despite the easy access to unlimited sources of information, it is probably best to rely on the most credible sources you can find wherever possible.

CHAPTER 1 APPLICATION EXERCISE

Choose an article reporting some new phenomena, either from an Internet resource or from a popular publication to which you have access.

Critique that article in terms of its scientific value. What findings does it report? How was the research carried out? Did the investigator(s) attempt to follow the scientific method? What are the differences between many popular publications and the way psychological research is carried out?

CHAPTER 2

Biological Foundations of Behavior

In Chapter 2 you are introduced to the biological processes that underlie much of human behavior. While we often think of behavior in a global sense (how your friend was acting yesterday afternoon, the excitement of spending a weekend at the beach), closer examination reveals that behaviors can be broken down to very small, physiologically based increments of activity. In fact, in this chapter we look at behavior beginning with the unit of a single cell, the neuron. Perhaps if just a few cells or cell clusters fired differently in your brain, you would feel differently. Perhaps even just finding yourself experiencing different surroundings would lead to differing operations within your brain! Indeed, it is possible that all behavior can be traced to the firing of one nerve cell, eliciting a particular synapse, and then affecting one other neuron. As we will learn, the knee-jerk reflex is a visible behavior that involves just two cells in your nervous system.

Your nervous system, including your brain, is composed of nerve cells, also known as neurons. Neurons are cells that are specialized for rapid communication. You need communication both within your body to inform the brain and relevant organs of various body conditions and with the outside world to allow you to absorb, process, and react to environmental events. The nervous system communicates quickly because it is predominantly electrical in nature. Neural impulses traveling within a nerve cell are electrical, but impulses must switch to chemical form in order to reach adjoining neurons. The tiny gap between nerve cells and the process of a neural message traveling through it, is known as the synapse. Because transmission from cell to cell is chemical, neural messages at any time may be modified, depending on the chemicals present in the region of the synapse. Your body contains billions and billions of neurons, most of them located in the brain. Think of all of these nerve cells firing many times a second and interconnecting with thousands of other neurons—it is a process that is almost impossible to comprehend. However, in this chapter, at least we will begin to try!

Your body has another internal communication system, one that is slower than the nervous system and strictly chemical in nature. This is your system of glands, known collectively as the endocrine system. Your endocrine system is not independent of your nervous system, of course, and in fact the two work quite closely together. Workings of the brain determine to a great extent what happens with regard to glandular activity and hormones that are secreted. The hypothalamus is one of the most important brain structures to influence the endocrine system. Secretions from the hypothalamus (a part of the large brain structure known as the forebrain) stimulate the pituitary gland, which in turn secretes hormones affecting activity in many other glands.

The brain is so complicated—how can we study it? Because of technological advances, we now have a number of strategies available for brain research. Nearly all of these brain research techniques can be classified as noninvasive procedures. We are learning more about the role of genes and hereditary influences on behavior as well.

The nervous system has two divisions: the central and the peripheral. The central nervous system (CNS) consists of the brain and spinal cord. The peripheral nervous system has further divisions with networks running throughout the body. Some networks bring information in, while others put responses from the brain into action. The entire nervous system is composed of nerve cells. A neuron is not a nerve; a nerve is made up of many, many nerve cells bundled together. Lucky for you, much of it operates without you having to think about it!

A tip as you start your travel through the wonder that is your brain: Keep in mind a small segment of your behavior—say perhaps just a few minutes' worth. When you finish reading the chapter, think back on that slice of behavior. What brain and peripheral nervous system components were involved in the activity? How much of the endocrine system was involved, if any? Were muscles activated? Were cognitions processed? The neurons in your body have been busy, indeed!

MODULE 2.1 NEURONS: THE BODY'S WIRING

LEARNING OBJECTIVES

After you have mastered the information in this unit, you will be able to:

- Define a neuron

- Identify the parts of a neuron

- Identify the types of neurons and the other types of cells in the nervous system

- Describe how a neural impulse is generated and transmitted from one neuron to another

- Discuss the roles of neurotransmitters in psychological functioning

OUTLINE

I.   The Structure of the Neuron
   A.   Basic building block of the nervous system
   B.   Cells specialized for rapidly communicating information
   C.   Neuron parts and functions
      1.   Dendrites—receive information from adjoining neurons (or sensory receptors)
      2.   Soma (cell body)—receives and stores information within the cell
      3.   Nucleus—governs and directs action of the cell
      4.   Axon—transmits neural impulse down length of cell
      5.   Terminal buttons—branching at end of axon; contain neurotransmitters
   D.   Types of neurons
      1.   Sensory neurons—bring information from outside world to your brain
      2.   Motor neurons—transmit responses from brain to muscles and glands
      3.   Interneurons
         a)   Connect neurons to other neurons
         b)   Join sensory and motor neurons in spinal cord
   E.   Synapses—chemical (neurotransmitter) connections between all neurons
II. Glial Cells
   A.   Most numerous cells within the nervous system
   B.   "Glue" to help hold neurons together
   C.   Assist and support activity of neurons
   D.   Form myelin sheath
      1.   Fatty, protective covering on many neuron axons
      2.   Forms over time, usually by age of 12
      3.   Nodes of Ranvier (gaps in myelin sheath)—neural impulse may jump from node to node
      4.   Multiple sclerosis (MS)—destruction of myelin sheath
III. How Neurons Communicate
   A.   Ions involved: sodium, potassium, and chloride
   B.   Resting potential—neuron not activated; cell has slightly negative charge

      C.   Depolarization—stimulation leads sodium to enter cell; electrical charge now changed from negative to positive

      D.   Action potential—neuron fires down length of axon; called a neural impulse

IV. Neurotransmitters

      A.   Synapse is tiny gap between one neuron and the next

      B.   At synapse, the impulse changes from electrical to chemical

      C.   Neurotransmitters are these chemical messengers across synapse

      D.   Chemicals from adjacent neurons may either excite or inhibit cell firing

      E.   Some important neurotransmitters

           1.   Acetylcholine—for muscle contractions, and learning and memory

           2.   Dopamine—related to muscle activity, also involved in emotional functioning

           3.   Glutamate—keeps central nervous system aroused

           4.   Serotonin—regulates emotion, satiety, and sleep

           5.   Endorphins—body's natural painkillers; similar chemically to narcotic drugs

SUMMARY

In this module you learn about the structure and function of the neuron and accompanying glial cells. The neuron is one type of body cell that is specialized for the very rapid communication of information. This information may be from the outside world (conducted to your spinal cord and brain by sensory neurons), from your brain back to your muscles and glands to help you act upon the world (via motor neurons), or completely within your body (most often conducted by interneurons). Glial cells support and nourish the activity of neurons.

The neuron is comprised of important components. The dendrites receive incoming information, and this is passed to the soma (cell body). The nucleus, in the center of the cell body, regulates the activity of the neuron, as it does in any of your body cells. Action potentials travel the length of the axon—that is when the nerve cell fires. Terminal buttons contain chemicals, the neurotransmitters. Axons may eventually become wrapped in the myelin sheath (composed of glial cells); this sheath speeds neural transmissions. Nerves are not neurons; nerves are bundles of many, many axons.

The neural impulse causes the release of chemicals into the synapse. When the neurotransmitters reach adjoining neurons, the impulse reverts to electrical form. Important neurotransmitters include acetylcholine, dopamine, serotonin, norepinephrine, GABA, and the endorphins. Problems with the neurotransmitters and/or sending and receiving sites in the brain can be related to serious diseases such as multiple sclerosis, schizophrenia, and Parkinson's disease.

KEY TERMS

Neurons

Brain

Soma

Axon

Terminal buttons

Neurotransmitters

Synapse

Dendrite

Sensory neurons

Motor neurons

Glands

Hormones

Interneurons

Nerve

Glial cells

Myelin sheath

Nodes of Ranvier

Multiple sclerosis (MS)

Ions

Resting potential

Depolarization

Action potential

All-or-none principle

Refractory period

Receptor site

Reuptake

Enzymes

Neuromodulators

Antagonists

Schizophrenia

Hallucinations

Delusions

Parkinson's disease

Agonists

Stimulant

Amphetamine

Antidepressants

Endorphins

SELF-TEST PRACTICE QUIZ

From the Key Terms select that which best matches the following (Note: Not every Key Term will be used.):

1. _____ The fact that neurons fire down the complete length of the cell if a sufficient level of excitatory impulses are received

2. _____ The cell body containing the nucleus

3. _____ Chemicals present in the brain that allow for message transmission among nerve cells

4. _____ Brain chemicals that moderate pain messages and produce feelings of pleasure

5. _____ Nerve cells

6. _____ Fibers extending out from the soma of the neuron; receive incoming messages from adjoining neurons

7. _____ Neurons in the peripheral nervous system that transport messages from spinal cord to muscles and glands

8. _____ Tiny gaps within the myelin sheath covering a nerve cell; may help speed impulses

9. _____ The connection between neurons where neural message becomes chemical (carried by neurotransmitters)

10. _____ The part of the neuron conducting messages down the length of the cell toward connections with other neurons; usually the longest part of a neuron

11. _____ A fatty protective layer that covers the axons of some nerve cells and helps speed transmission of neural impulses

12. _____ Chemical secretions from the endocrine system that regulate many body functions

a. Neurons

b. Brain

c. Soma

d. Axon

e. Terminal buttons

f. Neurotransmitters

g. Synapse

h. Dendrite

i. Sensory neurons

j. Motor neurons

k. Glands

l. Hormones

m. Interneurons

n. Nerve

o. Glial cells

p. Myelin sheath

q. Nodes of Ranvier

r. Multiple sclerosis (MS)

s. Ions

t. Resting potential

u. Depolarization

v. Action potential

w. All-or-none principle

x. Refractory period

y. Receptor site

z. Reuptake

aa. Enzymes

bb. Neuromodulators

cc. Antagonists

13. _____ Neurons that receive messages from sensory receptors and transmit that information to the spinal cord

14. _____ Knobs on the ends of axon terminal branches that contain neurotransmitters

15. _____ Locations on neurons receiving incoming messages; neurotransmitters fit into these sites

16. _____ A number of axon fibers that are bunched together and relay neural information

dd. Schizophrenia

ee. Hallucinations

ff. Delusions

gg. Parkinson's disease

hh. Agonists

ii. Stimulant

jj. Amphetamine

kk. Antidepressants

ll. Endorphins

17. The part of the neuron that receives incoming messages is the
    a. dendrites.
    b. axon.
    c. terminal buttons.
    d. myelin sheath.

18. Axons are often covered with a layer called the _____ that contain the nodes of Ranvier.
    a. dendrites
    b. nucleus
    c. myelin sheath
    d. neurilemma

19. Transmission of a neural impulse travels from _____ at the receiving end of the cell to _____ at the other end of the cell (which will transmit message to adjoining neurons).
    a. dendrites; terminal buttons
    b. terminal buttons; nucleus
    c. axon; terminal buttons
    d. axon hillock; myelin sheath

20. Neural messages become chemical in nature and are transmitted by neurotransmitters across the
    a. nodes of Ranvier.
    b. synapse.
    c. receptor site.
    d. terminal buttons.

21. _____ carry messages away from the spinal cord and brain.
    a. Sensory neurons
    b. Glial cells
    c. Endorphins
    d. Motor neurons

22. Multiple sclerosis is a disease that attacks the
    a. soma of a nerve cell.
    b. myelin sheath.
    c. glands.
    d. ions around a nerve cell.

23. When a cell is stimulated, positively charged sodium ions rush in, causing the area to become less negatively charged. This process is called
   a.   an action potential.
   b.   a differential gradient.
   c.   depolarization.
   d.   a refractory period.
24. Which neurotransmitter acts as a painkiller?
   a.   Endorphins
   b.   Acetylcholine
   c.   Antigens
   d.   Antagonists

ESSAY QUESTION

1.   How do neurons communicate with one another?

ANSWER KEY

1.   All-or-none principle

2.   Soma

3.   Neurotransmitters

4.   Endorphins

5.   Neurons

6.   Dendrites

7.   Motor neurons

8.   Nodes of Ranvier

9.   Synapse

10. Axon

11. Myelin sheath

12. Hormones

13. Sensory neurons

14. Terminal buttons

15. Receptor site

16. Nerve

17. a

18. c

19. a

20. b

21. d

22. b

23. c

24. a

SAMPLE ANSWER TO ESSAY QUESTION

1.   Neurons communicate with each other by means of neurotransmitters. Neurotransmitters are chemicals that travel across the synapse to adjoining neurons. Dendrites on receiving neurons have neurotransmitter receptor sites. Neurotransmitters bring either excitatory ("fire") or inhibitory ("don't fire") messages to a neuron. When the neuron is not active, the condition is known as the resting potential. During this time, sodium and potassium ions tend to be outside of the neuron, and chloride ions tend to be within it. When depolarization occurs (the electrical charge within a neuron shifts to become positive) and reaches a certain threshold, then the neuron fires. This is known as the action potential. The impulse within a neuron is electrical, but the transmission between neurons is chemical. The nucleus monitors nerve cell activity and makes the decision as to whether the cell will fire or not. Especially within the brain, a single neuron may exchange messages with thousands of other neurons.

MODULE 2.2 THE PERIPHERAL NERVOUS SYSTEM: YOUR BODY'S INFORMATION SUPERHIGHWAY

LEARNING OBJECTIVES

After you have mastered the information in this unit, you will be able to:

*   Detail the organization of the nervous system

*   Describe spinal reflexes

*   Describe the autonomic nervous system

*   Explain the relationship between the sympathetic and parasympathetic divisions of the autonomic nervous system

OUTLINE

I.   Central Nervous System
     A.   Consists of brain and spinal cord
          1.   Spinal cord is a column of nerves about as thick as one's thumb, encased in the spine
               a)   Transmits information between brain and peripheral nervous system
               b)   Spinal reflexes are the quickest possible response to stimuli, bypassing the brain and involving only two or three neurons
     B.   Peripheral nervous system—components of nervous system other than brain and spinal cord
II. Peripheral Nervous System:
     A.   Somatic nervous system
          1.   Comprised of sensory and motor neurons
          2.   Links communication between central nervous system and sense organs, muscles
     B.   Autonomic nervous system—two further divisions
          1.   Sympathetic nervous system
               a)   Prepares body to meet physical demands or stress
               b)   Increases heart rate, breathing, blood sugar
          2.   Parasympathetic nervous system
               a)   Slows bodily activity, conserves energy
               b)   Fosters bodily processes, such as digestion

SUMMARY

Module 2.2 discusses the basic organization of the human nervous system. Your nervous system has two major divisions: the central and the peripheral nervous systems. The central nervous system is composed of the brain and spinal cord. The spinal cord runs through your spine (bony tissue that protects it), connecting your peripheral nervous system to the brain. All of your body's actions involve the brain except, at the time it occurs, the spinal reflex. The peripheral nervous system is everything else in your body's nervous system other than the brain and spinal cord.

The peripheral nervous system has two major divisions: the somatic nervous system, and the autonomic nervous system. Much of the somatic nervous system was discussed in Module 2.1—the somatic nervous system is made up of sensory and motor neurons. Thus, the somatic nervous system allows you to grasp, through your senses, what is going on in the world and respond to it via motor neurons that activate muscles and/or glands.

The autonomic nervous system has two further divisions: the sympathetic and the parasympathetic nervous systems. They act somewhat in concert with each other. The sympathetic nervous system prepares you for stress or physical demands by speeding up your bodily systems and giving you increased fuel in your bloodstream. The parasympathetic nervous system slows the body down again and allows for bodily activities that replenish your store of energy.

KEY TERMS

Nervous system

Central nervous system

Spinal cord

Spine

Reflex

Spinal reflex

Peripheral nervous system

Somatic nervous system

Autonomic nervous system

Sympathetic nervous system

Parasympathetic nervous system

SELF-TEST PRACTICE QUIZ

From the Key Terms select that which best matches the following (Note: Not every Key Term will be used.):

1. _____ A part of the peripheral nervous system that regulates bodily processes such as breathing, heart rate, and digestion

2. _____ An immediate response to external stimuli directed at the level of the spinal cord

3. _____ A part of the peripheral nervous system that works in tandem with the sympathetic nervous system to restore the body's energy sources once they have been depleted

4. _____ A branch of the human nervous system that includes all components except the brain and spinal cord

5. _____ Nerves that form the connections between the brain and the peripheral nervous system and are encased in the spine

6. _____ The part of the peripheral nervous system that controls voluntary movements

7. _____ The part of the human nervous system that encompasses the brain and spinal cord

8. _____ A branch of the autonomic nervous system that helps an organism respond to demands the organism faces from the environment

a. Nervous system

b. Central nervous system

c. Spinal cord

d. Spine

e. Reflex

f. Spinal reflex

g. Peripheral nervous system

h. Somatic nervous system

i. Autonomic nervous system

j. Sympathetic nervous system

k. Parasympathetic nervous system

9. The _____ nervous system is made up of sensory and motor neurons.
   a. autonomic
   b. somatic
   c. central
   d. parasympathetic

10. The peripheral nervous system has two divisions, the _____ and _____.
   a. central; autonomic
   b. sympathetic; parasympathetic
   c. brain; spinal cord
   d. somatic; autonomic

11. Which part of your nervous system would be activated if you were walking down the street and realized that a truck was headed straight for you?
    a. Central
    b. Somatic
    c. Sympathetic
    d. Parasympathetic

ESSAY QUESTION

1. Trace the pathway of neural communication within your body from the instant an event occurs in your external environment until you have completed whatever response you will make to that event.

ANSWER KEY

1. Autonomic nervous system

2. Spinal reflex

3. Parasympathetic nervous system

4. Peripheral nervous system

5. Spinal cord

6. Somatic nervous system

7. Central nervous system

8. Sympathetic nervous system

9. b

10. d

11. c

SAMPLE ANSWER TO ESSAY QUESTION

1. An event in the environment is detected by the sensory nervous system. The sensory nervous system is one of the two main divisions of the somatic nervous system, which in turn is a division within the peripheral nervous system. The sensory nervous system transmits the detected information to the spinal cord where it is passed up to the brain. The brain and the spinal cord make up the central nervous system. The brain processes the environmental event and determines a response (if one is to be made). The message conveying the response travels outward from the brain, down the spinal cord, and to the motor nervous system (the other division in the somatic nervous system). The motor nervous system then activates muscles in the body, allowing you to make a physical response to the environmental event. If the event was at all threatening, the autonomic nervous system could be activated also. The sympathetic branch of the autonomic nervous system prepares you for meeting demanding challenges in the environment by increasing heart and breathing rates and the like. When danger has passed, the parasympathetic branch allows the body to be restored to normal functioning levels and replace energy reserves within the body that have been used.

MODULE 2.3 THE BRAIN: YOUR CROWNING GLORY

LEARNING OBJECTIVES

After you have mastered the information in this unit, you will be able to:

- Discuss how the brain is organized and how its various parts function

- Describe the organization of the cerebral cortex

- Identify the major function associated with each of the four lobes of the cerebral cortex

OUTLINE

I. The Brain
   A. Hindbrain—lowest part of brain
      1. Evolutionarily the "oldest"
      2. Medulla—breathing, heart rate, swallowing
      3. Pons—conducts information; influences wakefulness and sleep
      4. Cerebellum—controls balance and coordination
   B. Midbrain—above the hindbrain
      1. Connects hindbrain with forebrain
      2. Reticular formation
         a) Neural network that connects to thalamus
         b) Involved in attention, alertness and arousal
         c) Filters out irrelevant information
   C. Forebrain—largest part of the brain, located at top and front
      1. Thalamus—relay station, routes information to appropriate brain area
      2. Basal ganglia—control movement and coordination
      3. Hypothalamus
         a) Under the thalamus; size of a pea
         b) Regulates hunger, thirst, body temperature
         c) Involved in reproduction, emotional states
         d) Directs activity of the endocrine system
      4. Limbic system—memory and emotional processing
         a) Amygdala—aggression, rage and fear
         b) Hippocampus—important role in formation of memories
II. Cerebral cortex
   A. Part of the forebrain
   B. Thin outer layer of cerebrum
   C. Two cerebral hemispheres (connected by corpus callosum)
   D. Each hemisphere—four lobes
      1. Occipital lobes—vision
      2. Parietal lobes
         a) Includes somatosensory cortex
         b) Touch, pressure, pain, temperature
         c) Area proportional to sensitivity of skin tissue
      3. Frontal lobes
         a) "Executive center"
         b) Accesses stored memories
         c) Used to solve problems, reason, carry out coordinated activities
         d) Involved in emotional states

    e) Motor cortex—voluntary movement
   4. Temporal lobes—hearing
  E. Consists largely of association areas—higher mental functions

SUMMARY

In this module you learn about the brain.

The brain is divided into three major parts: the hindbrain, midbrain, and forebrain. The hindbrain includes the medulla, pons, and cerebellum and is responsible for the most basic life functions. The cerebellum is involved in controlling balance and coordination. The midbrain connects the hindbrain to the forebrain. The reticular formation runs from the hindbrain to the forebrain; it is responsible for filtering information and for alertness and arousal. The forebrain is the largest part of the brain. Parts of the forebrain include the thalamus (routes information) and the hypothalamus (hunger and thirst, reproductive processes, internal body temperature, emotions). The amygdala (rage and fear) and the hippocampus (memories) are part of the limbic system. The cerebrum in the forebrain is covered with a thin layer known as the cerebral cortex. This cortex is divided into two hemispheres, and information passes between the two hemispheres by means of a thick connecting band of fibers called the corpus callosum. Each hemisphere is divided into four lobes; the function of the lobes differs somewhat depending on which of the two hemispheres they are located in. The occipital lobes are involved in vision, the parietal lobes process sensory information, the frontal lobes are the "executive center," and the temporal lobes are involved in processing sound. Association areas in the cerebral cortex perform higher mental functions such as thinking and learning.

KEY TERMS

Hindbrain

Medulla

Pons

Brainstem

Cerebellum

Midbrain

Reticular formation

Forebrain

Thalamus

Basal ganglia

Hypothalamus

Limbic system

Amygdala

Hippocampus

Cerebral cortex

Cerebrum

Cerebral hemispheres

Corpus callosum

Occipital lobes

Parietal lobes

Somatosensory cortex

Frontal lobes

Motor cortex

Temporal lobes

Association areas

SELF-TEST PRACTICE QUIZ

From the Key Terms select that which best matches the following (Note: Not every Key Term will be used.):

1. _____ A network of neurons involved in regulating attention, alertness, and arousal

2. _____ A set of structures in the brain especially involved in the experience of emotion

3. _____ The lobes at the back of the head that process visual stimuli

4. _____ The part of the hindbrain involved in regulating vital life functions

5. _____ The lobes located at the top and front of the brain, most involved in higher-order functions

6. _____ The portion of the forebrain divided into two hemispheres

7. _____ The part of the limbic system most involved in the formation of memories

8. _____ A brain structure in the limbic system involved in many functions, including sexual reproduction, emotional reactions, and maintaining internal body temperature

9. _____ Lobes located in the upper back of the head; process information relating to touch, pressure, external temperature

10. _____ One component of the limbic system; particularly involved in the experiences of fear, aggression

a. Hindbrain

b. Medulla

c. Pons

d. Brainstem

e. Cerebellum

f. Midbrain

g. Reticular formation

h. Forebrain

i. Thalamus

j. Basal ganglia

k. Hypothalamus

l. Limbic system

m. Amygdala

n. Hippocampus

o. Cerebral cortex

p. Cerebrum

q. Cerebral hemispheres

r. Corpus callosum

s. Occipital lobes

t. Parietal lobes

u. Somatosensory cortex

v. Frontal lobes

w. Motor cortex

x. Temporal lobes

11. _____ A forebrain structure that relays information on to different parts of the brain

12. _____ Lobes located on the sides of the head near the ear; primary function involves processing speech, sound

13. _____ The outer covering of the cerebrum

14. _____ A brain structure located in the back of the head; vital for balance and coordination

y.   Association areas

15. The part of the brain that joins the cerebral hemispheres is the
    a. cerebrum.
    b. thalamus.
    c. corpus callosum.
    d. reticular formation.

16. The amygdala, hippocampus, and parts of the thalamus and hypothalamus make up the
    a. limbic system.
    b. reticular activating system.
    c. executive center.
    d. cerebral cortex.

17. Which lobe of the brain is responsible for hearing?
    a. Frontal
    b. Occipital
    c. Parietal
    d. Temporal

18. The _____ makes up 80 percent of the brain's total mass.
    a. corpus callosum
    b. cerebral cortex
    c. medulla
    d. hippocampus

ESSAY QUESTION

1. Explain the functions of association cortex.

ANSWER KEY

1. Reticular formation
2. Limbic system
3. Occipital lobes
4. Medulla
5. Frontal lobes
6. Cerebrum
7. Hippocampus
8. Hypothalamus

9. Parietal lobes

10. Amygdala

11. Thalamus

12. Temporal lobes

13. Cerebral cortex

14. Cerebellum

15. c

16. a

17. d

18. b

SAMPLE ANSWER TO ESSAY QUESTION

1. Association cortex is found in every lobe of the brain. These areas allow us to put together the different types of information we take in so that we can form meaningful perceptions of the world. They allow us to think, plan, solve problems, be creative, and function socially. For example, if you are walking down the street, you need to be able to see where you're going, move your body in such a way that you don't fall over or bump into things, plan the most efficient route to reach your destination, and perhaps hold a conversation at the same time (which involves hearing, language, memory, and social skills). If a new shape enters your field of vision, you need to not only see it, but also recognize it ("Hey, that's a person! And it's a friend of mine!") and respond accordingly ("Hi there!").

MODULE 2.4 METHODS OF STUDYING THE BRAIN

LEARNING OBJECTIVES

After you have mastered the information in this unit, you will be able to:

• Describe the various recording and imaging techniques used to study brain functioning

• Discuss the experimental methods used to study brain functioning

OUTLINE

I. Methods of Studying the Brain
   A. Recording and imaging techniques
      1. EEG (electroencephalograph)—records electrical activity in the brain
      2. CT (computed tomography) scan—measures reflection of an X-ray beam passing through body
      3. PET (positron emission tomography) scan—radioactive isotope reveals more active parts of brain
      4. MRI (magnetic resonance imaging)—gives picture of body's soft matter; disrupted atoms give signals as they realign
   B. Experimental methods
      1. Lesioning
         a) Part of experimental animal's brain is destroyed
         b) Researcher investigates effects of the brain tissue loss

2.   Electrical recording—electrodes in neurons/brain tissue reveal changes
3.   Electrical stimulation—observe results of mild electric current passed through brain

SUMMARY

In this module you learn about methods for studying the brain. Initially, most of what we knew about the brain was due to natural occurrences. That is, individuals who suffered brain injury or disease showed corresponding losses in physical, mental, and psychological functioning. We learned, for example, that the left side of the brain controls the right side of the body and vice versa.

Today we have additional, often less invasive techniques. Researchers may use either recording and imaging techniques or experimental methods. Technologies used include the EEG (to record brain waves), CT scans (X-ray beam reflection is measured), PET scans (reveals concentrations of radioactive isotope tracer), and MRI (magnetic field aligns brain atoms that are then disrupted). Experimental methods include lesioning (cutting out part of research animal's brain and observing results), electrical recording of neural activity, or electrical stimulation.

KEY TERMS

EEG (electroencephalograph)

CT (computed tomography) scan

PET (positron emission tomography) scan

MRI (magnetic resonance imaging)

Lesioning

Electrical recording

Electrical stimulation

SELF-TEST PRACTICE QUIZ

From the Key Terms select that which best matches the following (Note: Not every Key Term will be used.):

1. _____ Equipment that measures brain waves

2. _____ Electrodes in brain reveal brain changes

3. _____ Used to see the results of a radioactive isotope tracer

4. _____ Measures the reflection of an X-ray beam

5. _____ Passing a mild current through the brain

6. _____ Measures atoms as they realign

a.   EEG (electroencephalograph)

b.   CT (computed tomography) scan

c.   PET (positron emission tomography) scan

d.   MRI (magnetic resonance imaging)

e.   Lesioning

f.   Electrical recording

g.   Electrical stimulation

7. Which of the following brain research techniques involves the use of X-rays?
    a. CT scan
    b. PET scan
    c. Lesioning
    d. MRI

ESSAY QUESTION

1. How does MRI (magnetic resonance imaging) produce an image of the brain?

ANSWER KEY

1. EEG (electroencephalograph)

2. Electrical recording

3. PET (positron emission tomography) scan

4. CT (computed tomography) scan

5. Electrical stimulation

6. MRI (magnetic resonance imaging)

7. a

SAMPLE ANSWER TO ESSAY QUESTION

1. Magnetic resonance imaging is conducted by having the brain placed within a device that creates a strong magnetic field. The magnetic field aligns atoms in the brain. These atoms are disrupted by radio waves, and the atoms again realign. The MRI is the result of signals the atoms emit while they are realigning. With computer technology these signals can be put together to form an image of the brain.

MODULE 2.5 THE DIVIDED BRAIN: SPECIALIZATION OF FUNCTION

LEARNING OBJECTIVES

After you have mastered the information in this unit, you will be able to:

*   Discuss the major differences between the left and right hemispheres

*   Describe how handedness is determined

*   Discuss the main causes of brain damage and the effects of such damage on psychological functioning

*   Explain the use of "split-brain" patients to learn about brain lateralization

OUTLINE

I. The Brain at Work: Lateralization and Integration
    A. Lateralization
        1. Division of functions between left and right hemispheres
        2. Left brain: language, logical analysis, mathematical computations
            a) Broca's area: production of speech
            b) Wernicke's area: understanding meaning in language
            c) Aphasia: loss or impairment in language communication

3.   Right brain: spatial relations, recognizing faces, emotional expression
    B.   Integration: Both hemispheres share work in performing most tasks
II.   Handedness—hand dominance related to hemispheric specialization
    A.   Left-handers may not follow typical pattern
    B.   Genetic factors seem to play a role
    C.   Prenatal hormones may also influence
    D.   Twice as many males as females left-handed
III.   Brain Damage and Psychological Functioning
    A.   Head trauma—laceration or concussion
    B.   Stroke
       1.   Flow of blood to brain is blocked
       2.   Cerebral hemorrhage—bleeding into the brain
    C.   Brain plasticity—healthy part of brain may take over lost function
IV.   Exploring Psychology: Research on Split-Brain Patients: Does the Left Hand Know What the Right Hand is Doing?
    A.   Corpus callosum may be severed as a treatment for severe epilepsy
    B.   Patient holds a familiar object in the left hand—can use it but not name it
       1.   The left hand connects to the right hemisphere, which lacks language capabilities
    C.   Perception studies—researchers flash pictures to either left or right visual field
       1.   Patients can only describe the picture if flashed to the right visual field (which connects to the left hemisphere)
    D.   Split-brain patients appear quite normal in everyday behavior

SUMMARY

In this module you learn more about the two hemispheres of the brain. The hemispheres are connected by the thick band of nerve fibers known as the corpus callosum. In split-brain patients, however, the corpus callosum has been severed by physicians as a last resort treatment for brain diseases such as epilepsy. Thus, the two halves can no longer directly communicate. We have been able to learn more about specialization in the brain hemispheres in part due to research with split-brain individuals.

The left brain hemisphere is usually the logical and analytical side, including processing for language functions and for mathematical computations. The right brain typically is more involved with communicating expression and emotion, with grasping spatial relations, and in appreciating music and art. It is important to note, however, that the hemispheres in most humans are highly integrated; that is, they have overlapping functions and share in most brain activities. The left side of the brain controls functioning in the right side of the body, and the right side of the brain controls the left side of the body.

Language functions are related to handedness. Nearly all right-handers have the language centers in the left brain; however, only about 70 percent of the left-handers do. The two vital language areas in the brain are Broca's (for speech production), in the frontal lobe, and Wernicke's area (for understanding word meanings), in the temporal lobe.

Though the brain may experience trauma, such as concussions, stroke, and even the removal in extreme cases of an entire hemisphere, it often can adapt and reorganize itself remarkably well. This is due to brain plasticity—the ability for brain cells that are still healthy to take over functions of brain tissue that has been injured or destroyed.

KEY TERMS

Lateralization

Broca's area

Wernicke's area

Aphasia

Plasticity

Stroke

Prefrontal cortex

Laceration

Concussion

Epilepsy

Split-brain patients

SELF-TEST PRACTICE QUIZ

From the Key Terms select that which best matches the following (Note: Not every Key Term will be used.):

1. _____ Individuals for whom the corpus callosum has been severed due to brain illness

2. _____ A part of the brain, located on the temporal lobe, utilized in the processing of the meanings of speech

3. _____ Where the brain hemispheres have specialized with different functions

4. _____ The ability of other brain cells to take over functions of damaged or destroyed brain tissue

5. _____ The part of the brain in front of the motor cortex; involved in judgments, reasoning, and decision-making

6. _____ Loss or impairment of language function

7. _____ A part of the brain involved in the production of speech; located on the frontal lobe

8. _____ When brain tissue has been damaged due to cerebral bleeding or a blockage

a. Lateralization

b. Broca's area

c. Wernicke's area

d. Aphasia

e. Plasticity

f. Stroke

g. Prefrontal cortex

h. Laceration

i. Concussion

j. Epilepsy

k. Split-brain patients

9. _____ When brain tissue has been damaged due to a blow to the head

10. _____ A neurological disorder involving tremendous bursts of electrical activity in the brain

11. _____ Injury to the brain or other part of the body due to being cut and pierced

12. Which statement about brain lateralization is correct?
    a. Most people are clearly "left-brained" or "right-brained."
    b. On most tasks, the two hemispheres work together.
    c. Language is centered exclusively in the left hemisphere.
    d. The left hemisphere contains specialized areas for face recognition.

13. Why is there some hope for recovery after strokes or other brain damage?
    a. Brain grafts are becoming increasingly successful.
    b. Dead brain cells can usually be revived.
    c. Spinal cord tissue takes over lost functions.
    d. Healthy brain cells may eventually assume some of lost functions.

14. An individual suffers from a severe brain disease, and as a last resort physicians sever the corpus callosum. Which of the following is NOT a likely characteristic of this individual after surgery?
    a. The individual will become one of the split-brain patients.
    b. The two hemispheres in his brain will be unable to communicate directly.
    c. When blindfolded, he will not be able to name an object in his left hand.
    d. He will be unable ever to function effectively.

ESSAY QUESTION

1. Tell the story of Phineas Gage. In what ways was he different after his accident? What does this tell you about functions of the brain?

ANSWER KEY

1. Split-brain patients
2. Wernicke's area
3. Lateralization
4. Plasticity
5. Prefrontal cortex
6. Aphasia
7. Broca's area
8. Stroke
9. Concussion
10. Epilepsy
11. Laceration

12. b

13. d

14. d

SAMPLE ANSWER TO ESSAY QUESTION

1. In the 1800s, while working on a railroad track, an inch-thick metal rod shot through Gage's brain, exiting out the top of his head. Despite the severity of his injuries, he survived, and his wounds healed in about two months. Gage was able to function; however, his personality was forever changed. One area of Gage's brain that was damaged in the blast was the prefrontal cortex. This region of the frontal lobe is responsible for reasoning, judgment, and maintaining appropriate restraints on impulsive behavior. Though Gage could speak and move (there was no damage to language or motor portions of his brain), he exhibited different personality characteristics than before the accident. Thus the brain is involved not only in physical and cognitive activities, but determines our personality and ability to make moral and social judgments.

MODULE 2.6 THE ENDOCRINE SYSTEM: THE BODY'S OTHER COMMUNICATION SYSTEM

LEARNING OBJECTIVES

After you have mastered the information in this unit, you will be able to:

*   Identify the major endocrine glands

*   Explain the role of hormones in behavior

OUTLINE

I.   The Endocrine System
    A.   A grouping of glands
    B.   Glands release secretions called hormones
    C.   Regulates bodily processes such as growth, reproduction, and metabolism
    D.   Maintains homeostasis—an internally balanced state
II. Important Glands
    A.   Hypothalamus—secretes releasing factors that act on pituitary gland
    B.   Pituitary gland
        1.   "Master gland"—influences hormone activity of other glands
        2.   Also promotes physical growth via GH (growth hormone)
    C.   Pancreas
        1.   Produces the hormone insulin
        2.   Regulates amount of glucose in the blood
    D.   Pineal gland
        1.   Secretes melatonin
        2.   Regulates sleep-wake cycles
    E.   Adrenal glands
        1.   Lie above the kidneys
        2.   Adrenal cortex
            a)   Secretes hormones that promote muscle development
            b)   Stimulates liver to release sugar in times of stress
        3.   Adrenal medulla—releases epinephrine and norepinephrine to deal with stress

    F.   Gonads—sex glands
       1.   Ovaries in women
          a)   Produce egg cells for reproduction
          b)   Secrete female hormones estrogen and progesterone
       2.   Testes in men
          a)   Produce sperm
          b)   Secrete male sex hormone testosterone

III. Hormones and Behavior
    A.   Testosterone is linked to aggressive behavior
    B.   Thyroid hormones—influence metabolism; related to behavior
    C.   PMS—hormone sensitivity appears to play a role

SUMMARY

In this module you learn about the human endocrine system. The endocrine system is composed of glands that are distributed throughout the body. It is closely related to our nervous system and, like the nervous system, is a means for the body to communicate. Communication is slower than that of the nervous system because glands communicate chemically through the secretion of hormones. The hormones are released directly into the bloodstream. They lock into receptor sites, just like neurotransmitters do.

Endocrine activity is under the control of the brain, particularly the autonomic nervous system. In addition, the hypothalamus secretes hormones that influence the "master gland," the pituitary gland. The pituitary is so-named because it influences, through hormones, the activity of many other glands. The pituitary gland also secretes the hormone promoting growth.

Other important glands include the pancreas (regulating blood sugar concentration), the pineal (important to sleep-wake cycles), the adrenal glands (help us face stress), and the gonads (promote sexual characteristics and capability for reproduction). The thyroid gland regulates metabolism, the rate at which the body turns our food into energy. Variations in thyroid hormone levels are associated with different behavioral patterns.

KEY TERMS

Endocrine system

Pancreas

Diabetes

Homeostasis

Pituitary gland

Pineal gland

Adrenal gland

Gonads

Ovaries

Testes

Germ cells

Thyroid gland

Premenstrual syndrome (PMS)

SELF-TEST PRACTICE QUIZ:

From the Key Terms select that which best matches the following (Note: Not every Key Term will be used):

1. _____ A system for regulating activities in the body by means of glandular secretions

2. _____ A medical condition resulting when the pancreas produces insufficient amounts of the hormone insulin

3. _____ Glands in the body that secrete stress hormones

4. _____ Female reproductive gonads that secrete estrogen and produce egg cells

5. _____ Regulates body metabolism; different hormone levels associated with differing behavioral characteristics

6. _____ The cells that unite to create a new human organism

7. _____ An organ in the body that regulates blood sugar concentration

8. _____ Releases serotonin; involved in sleep-wake cycles

9. _____ The "master gland"—secretes hormones that impact the functioning of other glands

10. _____ Glands related to sexual characteristics and the processes involved in reproduction

11. _____ A balanced internal body state

12. _____ Male reproductive gonads that secrete testosterone and produce sperm

13. _____ A period of psychological and hormonal changes that occur a few days before the onset of the menstrual cycle

a. Endocrine system

b. Pancreas

c. Diabetes

d. Homeostasis

e. Pituitary gland

f. Pineal gland

g. Adrenal gland

h. Gonads

i. Ovaries

j. Testes

k. Germ cells

l. Thyroid gland

m. Premenstrual syndrome (PMS)

14. An effective communication system within the body, the _____ system utilizes the secretion of chemicals (hormones).

   a. nervous
   b. respiratory
   c. circulatory
   d. endocrine

15. Hormones that promote muscle development are secreted by the
  a. hypothalamus.
  b. pineal gland.
  c. adrenal glands.
  d. pancreas.
16. Homeostasis means
  a. the body maintains a balanced internal state.
  b. there is a shortage of insulin and excessive blood sugar.
  c. the quantity of chemicals secreted is equaled by the quantity of chemicals absorbed.
  d. endocrine glands are distributed rather uniformly throughout the body.

ESSAY QUESTION

1. Discuss the relationship between hormones and behavior.

ANSWER KEY

1. Endocrine system

2. Diabetes

3. Adrenal glands

4. Ovaries

5. Thyroid gland

6. Germ cells

7. Pancreas

8. Pineal gland

9. Pituitary gland

10. Gonads

11. Homeostasis

12. Testes

13. Premenstrual syndrome

14. d

15. a

16. c

SAMPLE ANSWER TO ESSAY QUESTION

1. Hormones do appear to influence human behavior. We know that variations in levels of thyroid hormones are related to different kinds of behavior. Excess levels of thyroid hormones are associated with anxiety; whereas deficient levels of the hormones are associated with sluggishness, weight gain, and retarded intellectual development in children. Hormones seem to play a role in premenstrual syndrome (PMS); levels of estrogen and progesterone change dramatically in the days just preceding the start of a woman's period. In addition, testosterone may be one factor associated with aggression, and low levels of testosterone lead to loss of sexual desire for both males and females.

MODULE 2.7 GENES AND BEHAVIOR: A CASE OF NATURE *AND* NURTURE

LEARNING OBJECTIVES

After you have mastered the information in this unit, you will be able to:

• Discuss the role of genetic factors in human behavior

• Describe the methods used to study genetic influences on behavior

OUTLINE

I. Genes
   A. Composed of deoxyribonucleic acid (DNA)
   B. Linked together on long strands called chromosomes
   C. Found in cell nucleus
   D. A child receives 23 chromosomes from each parent
   E. Human genome mapped in year 2000
   F. Only twins share identical genetic code
II. Genetic Influences on Behavior
   A. Genotype is the genetic code; phenotype is the gene's physical or behavioral expression
      1. Phenotype depends on complex interaction of genes and environment
   B. Many psychological characteristics may be polygenic traits
   C. Genetic factors establish a predisposition; characteristics may not necessarily appear
III. Kinship Studies
   A. Familial association studies
      1. Closer genetic links related to more similar traits and behaviors
      2. Higher incidence of schizophrenia as genetic commonality increases
      3. Limitation: people sharing close genetic links often share similar environment
   B. Twin studies
      1. Monozygotic (identical) twins—identical genetic inheritance
      2. Dizygotic (fraternal) twins—genetic commonality like siblings
      3. Concordance rates suggest genetic contribution
      4. Identical twins more similar than fraternals on sociability, some psychological disorders
      5. Limitation: identical twins may share greater environmental similarity
   C. Adoptee studies
      1. Adopted children compared to biological and adoptive parents
      2. Shyness in children more likely to resemble biological parent
      3. Genetically identical (monozygotic) twins, reared apart
         a) Rare event, but a natural experiment
         b) Heredity seems to play major role in personality development

SUMMARY

In this module you learn of the genetic influences on behavior. *Nature* refers to what we have inherited (the genetic code); *nurture* means our experiences as a result of our environment. Genes are composed of DNA and are linked together on chromosomes. This genetic information is carried in the nucleus of every typical body cell. Mapping of the human genome was completed in 2000, which was a huge scientific breakthrough. The genetic code (genotype) is the basic blueprint of the characteristics a human may have. However, traits included in the genotype do not necessarily manifest themselves unless they become part of the phenotype—the features and traits we actually see in a person. The phenotype is the result not only of genetic inheritance but also of other factors, such as environmental experiences. Many psychological characteristics are probably polygenic; that is, they result from a cluster of genes.

How can we study genetic influence more precisely? We use kinship studies, and we especially use studies involving individuals with an identical genetic heritage (monozygotic twins, triplets, and so forth). Familial association studies do tell us that the more genes there are in common, such as among close family members, the more similar traits and behaviors are likely to be. It is true, however, that close family members usually share the same or similar environment as well. Children who have been adopted are compared with both their adoptive and their biological parents. In the rare case where identical twins have been raised apart, evidence suggests that many personality characteristics and traits have a genetic basis.

KEY TERMS

Genotype

Genes

Deoxyribonucleic acid (DNA)

Chromosomes

Phenotype

Polygenic traits

Familial association studies

Identical twins

Zygote

Fraternal twins

Twin studies

Concordance rates

Adoptee studies

SELF-TEST PRACTICE QUIZ

From the Key Terms select that which best matches the following (Note: Not every Key Term will be used.):

1. _____ An organism's observable traits

2. _____ Twins produced when one fertilized egg splits

3. _____ Comparing adopted children with biological and adoptive parents

4. _____ Underlying set of instructions determining organism's possible characteristics

5. _____ The chemicals within chromosomes that determine genetic heritage

6. _____ A single-celled organism resulting from the union of an egg and a sperm

7. _____ The percentage of cases where both twins share the same trait or disorder

8. _____ Basic units of heredity; composed of DNA

9. _____ The genetic source for many psychological characteristics

10. _____ Twins who develop from different eggs fertilized by different sperm; no more genetically alike than other siblings

11. _____ Long strands of genetic instructions found in the nuclei of cells

12. _____ Genetic commonality is compared with exhibited traits

13. _____ Investigating behavioral similarities between twins

14. In the year 2000, scientists completely mapped the
    a. human cerebral cortex.
    b. human genetic code.
    c. nature-nurture problem.
    d. locations of monozygotic twins.

a. Genotype

b. Genes

c. Deoxyribonucleic acid (DNA)

d. Chromosomes

e. Phenotype

f. Polygenic traits

g. Familial association studies

h. Identical twins

i. Zygote

j. Fraternal twins

k. Twin studies

l. Concordance rates

m. Adoptee studies

15. Examining the relationship between close family members and their common behaviors is involved in
    a. human genome mapping.
    b. polygenetic traits.
    c. familial association studies.
    d. predisposition studies.

ESSAY QUESTIONS

1. Why is it helpful to study identical twins raised separately when investigating genetic influences on behavior?

2. When examining genetic influences on behavior (e.g., by looking at family members, identical and fraternal twins), what is a problem we nearly always encounter?

ANSWER KEY

1. Phenotype

2. Identical twins

3. Adoptee studies

4. Genotype

5. Deoxyribonucleic acid (DNA)

6. Zygote

7. Concordance rates

8. Genes

9. Polygenic traits

10. Fraternal twins

11. Chromosomes

12. Familial association studies

13. Twin studies

14. b

15. c

SAMPLE ANSWERS TO ESSAY QUESTIONS

1. It is helpful to study identical twins, especially those reared apart, because monozygotic twins share an identical genetic heritage. If they are raised in different environments, it is assumed that behaviors that remain similar or alike in both twins must be due to heredity. Anything influenced by environment would theoretically be different because each twin experienced a different environment. It should be remembered, however, that even though twins have been separated from birth or shortly thereafter and not raised in the same environment, the individual environments that they did experience may not have been that fundamentally different after all.

2. We examine genetic influence on behavior by looking at various family members. Family members, of course, share many of the same genes. Thus, we look for similar behavior traits where there are many genes in common. The problem that we encounter, however, is that very often genetically close family members reside in the same, or similar, environments. Once again, it becomes difficult to separate nature from nurture.

MODULE 2.8 APPLICATION: LOOKING UNDER THE HOOD: SCANNING THE HUMAN BRAIN

LEARNING OBJECTIVES

After you have mastered the information in this unit, you will be able to:

- Describe some cutting-edge applications of brain scanning

OUTLINE

I. Memory and Cognitive Research
   A. Specific brain circuits may relate to specific memories
II. Personality Research
   A. Different patterns of brain activity in people who are more or less extraverted or neurotic
III. Personnel Selection
   A. Scans may indicate suitability for particular types of tasks
IV. Diagnosing Psychological Disorders
   A. Scans may be used to detect signs of schizophrenia, bipolar disorder, and ADHD

SUMMARY

In this Application module, you learn about some of the newest advances in brain scanning. Researchers are exploring ways in which specific patterns of brain activity might reveal the presence of mental disorders, differences in personality and job suitability, or particular memories. Although these applications are very much in the experimental stage, they may soon be in common use.

CHAPTER 2 APPLICATION EXERCISE

Take a five-minute slice of time from your day during waking hours. Write down everything that you do for those five minutes. Now, analyze the components of your body utilized during each of the activities you listed. (It might almost be easier to list the components not used! You can see how very integrated our whole physiological system is.) What part of your nervous system was involved? What particular brain structures were used? Do you think your glandular system was part of your activity for those five minutes? If so, how? Can you think of any neurotransmitters that might have been particularly involved? What pathways and what directions did your neural transmissions travel?

CHAPTER 3

Sensation and Perception

In Chapter 3 you are introduced to the basic concepts that comprise the processes of sensation and perception. Sensation and perception are two different things: Sensation occurs at the level of your senses and includes all the information impinging on your sensory receptors. Note that there are very many stimuli in the world that can constantly bombard you—triggering reactions in your eyes, ears, nose, and skin for example. Suppose all of this information traveled all the way to the cerebral cortex in your brain. You would indeed be on overload!

Fortunately, much of the information that your senses can detect is filtered out, and only a small portion is transmitted to your brain where it can be further processed. Perception occurs in the brain, and the process of perception involves the brain receiving the incoming stimuli then organizing and making meaningful interpretations of it. The brain may process in either a top-down or a bottom-up fashion. Gestalt principles are important in perception, and help us understand how the brain can determine what we perceive as meaningful wholes. Clearly, the brain's understanding of current phenomena has much to do with information stored from prior experiences.

Information about the world is transmitted via your sensory nervous system. This process begins with your sensory receptors, the nerve cells specialized to detect stimuli in the environment. For vision, the retina of the eye contains the rods and cones. These sensory receptors (called rods and cones because that is what each looks like) detect wavelengths of light energy that enter the eye. Each wavelength corresponds to what we would perceive as a color. It is important that the wavelengths land directly on the fovea in the retina. This aids in color vision and visual acuity. For the sense of hearing, wavelengths create vibrations in the ear, which, like visual input, are converted to neural signals. These impulses are transmitted by the auditory nerve to the brain. Several theories exist for how we detect color and how we determine the pitch of a sound. It seems to take more than one theory to explain how both processes occur.

Smell and taste are both conveyed by means of chemical molecules. A chemical molecule from the environment must fit one of the sensory receptors in the nose or tongue region—otherwise the stimulus is not detected. Skin sense receptors are distributed throughout your body. Your skin responds not only to touch but to pressure, pain, cold, and warmth. The human body is very sensitive to all of your senses—but only to a certain range of stimuli. For example, there are many electromagnetic energy frequencies zipping around in your world. Your vision receptors, however, can detect only a certain number of these. For color as conveyed by light, the wavelengths to which we are sensitive make up the visible spectrum. Our sensory receptors simply cannot detect other wavelengths in the environment. This phenomenon is true for all your senses. Unless a receptor exists for a certain wavelength (vibration, chemical molecule, or the like), you will not be able to detect that stimulus. It's a little spooky to consider that there are things in our environment we cannot perceive!

All stimuli impinging on your senses must reach a certain minimum threshold in order to be detected. This minimum is somewhat affected by how alert and attuned an organism is. Once sensory information is received, we use perceptual cues to organize and interpret this information. Visual perception, for example, utilizes both monocular (one eye is sufficient) and binocular cues from the environment. Monocular cues include linear perspective and relative size. Binocular cues usually incorporate the phenomenon known as retinal disparity—the fact that each eye sends the brain a slightly differing image. The brain then integrates and interprets this information.

Sometimes the perceptual cues we rely on mislead us, as in the case of visual illusions. Scientists have studied subliminal perception and paranormal phenomena such as ESP. There is some evidence that subliminal perception does indeed occur. On the other hand, reliable and replicable scientific evidence does not yet exist for extrasensory perception. At least at present it's likely no one can read your mind!

MODULE 3.1 SENSING OUR WORLD: BASIC CONCEPTS OF SENSATION

LEARNING OBJECTIVES:

After you have mastered the information in this unit, you will be able to:

- Describe sensation

- Explain the difference between absolute thresholds and difference thresholds

- Discuss the factors that contribute to signal detection

- Define sensory adaptation

OUTLINE

I.   Sensation
    A.   Process by which we receive, transform, and process stimuli presented to sensory organs
    B.   Sensory receptors—in sensory organs
        1.   Detect stimuli from the outside world
        2.   Very sensitive to certain types of stimuli
        3.   Form of light, sound, odors, etc.
    C.   Psychophysics—how we experience such stimuli
II. Absolute and Difference Thresholds
    A.   Absolute threshold
        1.   Smallest amount of stimulus reliably detected
        2.   Variation in sensitivity among individuals
    B.   Difference threshold
        1.   Just-noticeable difference (jnd)
        2.   Weber's law—must change stimulus by a constant proportion for change to be detected
        3.   Constants are given for various senses
III. Signal Detection
    A.   Signals are stimuli such as sounds or tastes
    B.   Detection depends on
        1.   Intensity of signal
        2.   Background factors
        3.   Attention and motivation of receiver
        4.   Physical condition of organism
IV. Sensory Adaptation—becoming less sensitive to unchanging stimuli

SUMMARY

In this module you learn how the process of detecting what is going on in the outside world actually begins. First, information must be sensed; that is, information must be received by sensory receptors within our sense organs. Our sense organs are eyes, ears, nose, mouth, and so forth. Sensory receptors receive physical inputs from the world and convert them into a form your body can use—into the neural impulses (electrochemical in nature) with which your brain and the rest of your nervous system communicates. Thus, once converted, your nervous system can use this information.

Not all stimuli in the world can be detected. A stimulus must be present in a sufficient amount to reach the absolute threshold for detection relevant to that particular sense. This minimum amount that can be reliably detected is known as the absolute threshold. There also must be a sufficient increase or decrease in the amount of stimulus presented in order for an individual to determine that there has been a change. This amount for detection of change is known as the just-noticeable difference (jnd), and for each sense it is a constant proportion (Weber's law). Detection of signals (sensory stimuli) is governed not only by stimulus intensity, but also by background factors and how alert and attuned the receiving individual is. Repeated presentations of unchanging stimuli can lead to sensory adaptation where sensitivity decreases.

KEY TERMS

Sensation

Sensory receptors

Psychophysics

Absolute threshold

Difference threshold

Weber's law

Signal-detection theory

Sensory adaptation

SELF-TEST PRACTICE QUIZ

From the Key Terms select that which matches the following (Note: Not every Key Term will be used.):

1. _____ The amount of stimulus change that can be detected is a constant

2. _____ The process by which we receive, transform, and process impinging stimuli

3. _____ Factors related to the human's ability to detect a stimulus

4. _____ The minimum amount of stimulus we can reliably detect

5. _____ Nervous system cells specialized to detect outside stimuli

a. Sensation
b. Sensory receptors
c. Psychophysics
d. Absolute threshold
e. Difference threshold
f. Weber's law
g. Signal-detection theory
h. Sensory adaptation

6. _____ Reduced sensitivity to an unchanging stimulus

7. _____ The minimum amount of stimulus we can reliably detect

8. The very first step in understanding behavior and mental processes is understanding the process of
   a. sensory adaptation.
   b. signal detection.
   c. perception.
   d. sensation.

9. _____ is the study of how we experience physical stimulation.
   a. Weber's law
   b. Psychophysics
   c. Sensory adaptation
   d. Neurometrics

10. What does Weber's Law explain?
    a. The accuracy of signal-detection theory
    b. The minimum amount of stimulus that can be noticed
    c. The amount that a stimulus must change before you can notice the difference
    d. Variations in sensitivity between different people

11. Physical stimuli impinging upon our senses are first detected by
    a. sensory receptors.
    b. perceptual mechanisms in the brain.
    c. sensory adaptation mechanisms.
    d. the visual and auditory channels.

12. When you travel to a new place, you may at first notice some unusual smells. But you will generally get used to those smells quickly, and you won't notice them anymore. What principle does this illustrate?
    a. Sensory adaptation
    b. Signal detection
    c. The jnd
    d. Psychophysics

ESSAY QUESTION

1. Certainly, how intense a stimulus is and how frequently it is presented to you are factors related to whether you will detect that stimulus or not. Based on signal-detection theory, what other considerations are there with regard to the human detection of physical energies?

ANSWER KEY

1. Weber's law
2. Sensation
3. Signal-detection theory
4. Absolute threshold
5. Sensory receptors
6. Sensory adaptation
7. Difference threshold

8. d

9. b

10. b

11. a

12. a

SAMPLE ANSWER TO ESSAY QUESTION

1. Signal-detection theory also considers other features in the process of sensation. These features include characteristics of the background such as how noisy and/or distracting the setting is. Whether or not a stimulus is detected also depends on physical and psychological characteristics of the receiver: general health, the acuity of the sense organ, state of alertness, and degree of motivation.

MODULE 3.2 VISION: SEEING THE LIGHT

LEARNING OBJECTIVES

After you have mastered the information in this unit, you will be able to:

- Explain how the eye processes light

- Identify feature detectors and describe their role in visual processing

- Discuss the two major theories of color vision

- Identify the two major forms of color blindness

OUTLINE

I. Light: The Energy of Vision
   A. Physical energy
   B. Electromagnetic radiation
      1. Visible spectrum is small portion of entire spectrum
      2. Wavelengths correspond to the experience of different colors
II. The Eye: The Visionary Sensory Organ
   A. Contains the sensory receptors to detect light
   B. Parts of the eye
      1. Cornea—transparent covering on the surface of the eye
      2. Iris—muscle surrounding pupil
         a) Adjusts reflexively to permit entry of light
         b) Colored part of eye, usually blue or brown
      3. Pupil—size of opening is controlled by iris
      4. Lens—changes shape to adjust to distance of object (accommodation)
      5. Retina
         a) Receives the image created by light striking it
         b) Contains photoreceptors—rods and cones
      6. Bipolar cells—interconnecting cells
      7. Ganglion cells—each projecting axon is one nerve fiber
      8. Optic nerve
         a) Large bundle of ganglion nerve fibers
         b) Transmits visual information to the brain
         c) Creates blind spot

         9.   Fovea—part of the retina
            a)   Contains only cones
            b)   Site for sharpest vision
III.   Feature Detectors: Getting Down to Basics
    A.   Nerve cells in visual cortex
    B.   Respond to specific features of the visual stimulus
IV.   Color Vision: Sensing a Colorful World
    A.   Color receptors (cones) transmit different messages to the brain
    B.   Hermann von Helmholtz—trichromatic theory
        1.   Three types of color receptors—for red, green, and blue-violet
        2.   Other colors result from combinations of these three
    C.   Ewald Hering—opponent-process theory
        1.   Afterimages—image seen on neutral surface after other visual stimulation
        2.   Three sets of color receptors that work in either-or pairs

SUMMARY

In this module you are presented with basic information regarding how the process of vision works. Vision begins with light, which occurs in our environment in the form of electromagnetic energy.

This energy enters our eyes as wavelengths. Not all of electromagnetic radiation is visual information we can detect; only a small portion of these wavelengths (those ranging from 300 to 750 nanometers) falls within the visible spectrum. The shortest wavelength we can detect corresponds to what we see as violet; the longest wavelength corresponds to what we see as red. The Roy G. Biv acronym we may have learned refers to the colors of the visible spectrum arranged in order of decreasing wavelength.

Light enters the eye through the pupil, the diameter of which is controlled by the iris. If light is very bright, the iris makes the pupil small; conversely, when there is little light the iris widens the pupil, which allows us to see more clearly. The lens changes shape in order to best direct incoming light to the retina where it will be processed by photoreceptors. Cones can detect color and provide acuity but need bright light to work well. Rods, the other photoreceptors, function well in dim light but cannot process color. Rods also provide our peripheral vision. Very specific features of a visual stimulus are conveyed by neurons known as feature detectors. The visual cortex in the brain combines incoming information to yield meaningful visual patterns.

There are two theories explaining how a human detects color, and both seem to account for parts of this process of vision. Helmholtz's trichromatic theory proposes that three different types of photoreceptors (cones) process one of three basic colors: red, green, and blue-violet. According to this theory, all other colors result from combinations of these three. The opponent-process theory, proposed by Hering, suggests that there are three photoreceptors in the retina but each works as a pair of receptors—when "on" for one color in the pair, the receptor is "off" for the other. These theories help explain some visual phenomena such as afterimages. Color blindness is caused by a genetic defect where one or more type of photoreceptor is lacking.

KEY TERMS

Cornea

Iris

Pupil

Lens

Accommodation

Retina

Photoreceptors

Rods

Cones

Bipolar cells

Ganglion cells

Optic nerve

Blind spot

Fovea

Feature detectors

Trichromatic theory

Afterimage

Opponent-process theory

Trichromats

Monochromats

Dichromats

SELF-TEST PRACTICE QUIZ

From the Key Terms select that which best matches the following (Note: Not every Key Term will be used.):

1. _____ Part of the retina with a concentration of cone cells; color processing and acuity most effective here

2. _____ Color vision theory proposing that each photoreceptor processes one basic color; other colors are combination of these three

3. _____ Photoreceptors that process color and provide sharpness of image

4. _____ A transparent covering on the eye's surface

5. _____ The changing of the shape of the lens to help direct an incoming image onto the retina

6. _____ Hering's view that the three photoreceptors are pairs of receptors; stimulation of one color in a pair leads to inhibition of processing of the other color

a. Cornea

b. Iris

c. Pupil

d. Lens

e. Accommodation

f. Retina

g. Photoreceptors

h. Rods

i. Cones

j. Bipolar cells

k. Ganglion cells

l. Optic nerve

m. Blind spot

n. Fovea

7. _____ The black opening in the center of the iris; light enters the eye this way

8. _____ Neural mechanism that transmits visual information from the retina to the brain; creates blind spot on retina

9. _____ The eye structure which, using the process of accommodation, helps incoming light to land on the retina

10. _____ Individuals lacking one of the three types of cones used in visual color processing

11. _____ Specialized neurons in the visual cortex; they respond to very specific visual stimuli

12. _____ Colored muscle surrounding the pupil; adjusts to amount of available light

13. _____ The lining on the back inner surface of the eye; contains photoreceptors

14. _____ Photoreceptors for peripheral vision and visual activity in dim light

15. _____ Axons of these cells are the nerve fibers in the optic nerve

16. _____ Specialized cells in the eyes retina which are sensitive to light

o. Feature detectors

p. Trichromatic theory

q. Afterimage

r. Opponent-process theory

s. Trichromats

t. Monochromats

u. Dichromats

17. How much electromagnetic radiation can we see?
    a. All of it
    b. Most of it
    c. Some of it
    d. None of it

18. Wavelengths entering our eyes are measured in terms of
    a. nanometers.
    b. feet.
    c. inches.
    d. centimeters.

19. The objective of accommodation, performed by the lens in the eye, is to
    a. prevent nearsightedness.
    b. prevent farsightedness.
    c. cast the light image onto the retina.
    d. reduce the size of the pupil.

20. The blind spot in our vision occurs because
    a. receptors cannot work in very dim light.
    b. the wavelengths we are processing have landed on the fovea.
    c. there are no receptors in the visual cortex.
    d. it corresponds to the position of the optic nerve in the retina.
21. If you're trying to see an object in dim light, which method will work best?
    a. Look directly at the object so that you'll use mostly cones.
    b. Use your peripheral vision because that's where the most rods are.
    c. Stare straight at the object because that way you'll use mostly rods.
    d. It doesn't matter how you look at the object—you'll see it equally well from any angle.
22. When the eyeball is too long or the cornea is very curved an individual experiences
    a. tunnel vision.
    b. nearsightedness.
    c. farsightedness.
    d. monochromatism.
23. Which theory of color vision explains the phenomenon of afterimages?
    a. Opponent-process theory
    b. Trichromatic theory
    c. Helmholtz-Young theory
    d. All of the above

ESSAY QUESTIONS

1. Briefly explain how feature detectors work. Where are they located?

2. Compare and contrast the two theories of color vision. Give at least one example of visual phenomena that support each point of view.

ANSWER KEY

1. Fovea

2. Trichromatic theory

3. Cones

4. Cornea

5. Accommodation

6. Opponent-process theory

7. Pupil

8. Optic nerve

9. Lens

10. Dichromats

11. Feature detectors

12. Iris

13. Retina

14. Rods

15. Ganglion cells

16. Photoreceptors

17. c

18. a

19. c

20. d

21. b

22. b

23. a

SAMPLE ANSWERS TO ESSAY QUESTIONS

1. Feature detectors are specialized neurons within the visual cortex in the brain. They respond to very specific features of visual stimuli such as particular angles, various orientations of lines, and stimuli following particular patterns of movement. These neurons respond only when the specific stimulus characteristics are presented.

2. One theory of color vision, proposed by Helmholtz, says that there are three photoreceptors (cones) and each cone responds to a particular color wavelength. These colors are red, green, and blue-violet, and all other detected colors result from combinations of these three. This view proposed by Helmholtz is known as the trichromatic theory. A second theory of color vision, suggested by Hering, again confirms that there are three photoreceptors to process stimuli for color. However, this second theory, called the opponent-process theory, proposes that each photoreceptor has two components. Color processing occurs as the photoreceptor components work in pairs—when a receptor for one color is active, the paired receptor is inhibited. Suggested color pairings are red-green, blue-yellow, and black-white. Hering devised his theory in part as a consequence of his research on afterimages.

MODULE 3.3 HEARING: THE MUSIC OF SOUND

LEARNING OBJECTIVES

After you have mastered the information in this unit, you will be able to:

• Discuss how the ear enables us to hear sound

• Explain what determines our perception of pitch

• Describe the main types and causes of deafness

OUTLINE

I. Sound: Sensing Waves of Vibrations
   A. Energy that travels in waves (vibrations)
   B. Must have a medium in order to exist
   C. Characteristics
      1. Amplitude (loudness)—the height of a wave
      2. Frequency—number of complete waves, or cycles, per second
      3. Travels much more slowly than light
      4. Measured in decibels (dB), an indication of perceived loudness
      5. Perception of pitch is related to wave frequency

II. The Ear: A Sound Machine
    A. Sound waves are captured and converted to neural form
    B. Ear components
        1. Eardrum—membrane that vibrates in response to sound waves
        2. Ossicles—three tiny bones in middle ear
            a) Hammer (*malleus*)
            b) Anvil (*incus*)
            c) Stirrup (*stapes*)
        3. Oval window—membrane connecting to inner ear
        4. Cochlea—fluid-filled snail-shaped bony tube
        5. Basilar membrane—vibrates within the cochlea
        6. Organ of Corti—gelatinous structure lined with hair cells
        7. Hair cells—auditory receptors
        8. Auditory nerve—transmits auditory messages to brain
    C. Location of sound determined by disparity between two ears' messages
III. Perception of Pitch: Perceiving the Highs and Lows
    A. Place theory
        1. Developed by Hermann von Helmholtz
        2. Perceived sound related to vibration location on basilar membrane
        3. High frequencies—vibration near oval window
        4. Low frequencies—further down basilar membrane
    B. Frequency theory
        1. May best account for perception of lowest-frequency sounds
        2. Basilar membrane vibrates at same frequency as sound wave
    C. Volley principle—helps explain how mid-range sounds are detected
IV. Hearing Loss
    A. Conduction deafness
        1. Damage to middle ear—eardrum or ossicles
        2. Hearing aids may help this problem
    B. Nerve deafness—damage to hair cells or to auditory nerve
    C. For protection avoid excessive noise, wear earplugs

SUMMARY

In this module you learn about the sense of hearing. Sound, like light, travels in the form of waves, though sound travels much more slowly. Unlike the process of vision, however, sound must have a medium through which to travel. Characteristics of a sound wave include amplitude, which conveys loudness, and frequency—how many complete waves, or cycles, per second. These waves must be converted into neural impulses in order to be used by your body.

The outer ear is shaped to help capture sound waves. Waves next go to the eardrum, which vibrates and passes the message to the ossicles. These little bones vibrate in turn, and the last passes the vibration on to the oval window. The cochlea, basilar membrane, organ of Corti, and auditory nerve complete the chain for the transmission of sound. Both place theory and frequency theory help explain the perception of pitch, along with a combination of the two called the volley principle. Deafness is due either to middle ear damage, which can be rectified somewhat, or to more serious damage, such as to the auditory nerve.

KEY TERMS

Audition

Pitch

Eardrum

Ossicles

Oval window

Cochlea

Basilar membrane

Organ of Corti

Hair cells

Auditory nerve

Place theory

Frequency theory

Volley principle

Conduction deafness

Nerve deafness

SELF-TEST PRACTICE QUIZ

From the Key Terms select that which best matches the following (Note: Not every Key Term will be used.):

1. _____ Auditory receptors triggered by basilar membrane vibration

2. _____ A bony tube in the inner ear, filled with fluid

3. _____ The neural mechanism by which auditory messages are transmitted to the brain

4. _____ How high or low a sound is (related to frequency)

5. _____ The process of hearing

6. _____ The little bones in the middle ear: the hammer, anvil, and stirrup

7. _____ A structure within the cochlea

8. _____ The belief that pitch depends on which part of the basilar membrane vibrates the most in response to an auditory stimulus

a. Audition

b. Pitch

c. Eardrum

d. Ossicles

e. Oval window

f. Cochlea

g. Basilar membrane

h. Organ of Corti

i. Hair cells

j. Auditory nerve

k. Place theory

l. Frequency theory

m. Volley principle

n. Conduction deafness

9. _____   A gelatinous structure, lined   o.   Nerve deafness
    with hair cells

10. _____   The membrane to which the
    stirrup is attached

11. _____   A tight membrane receiving
    sound waves from the outer ear

12. The hammer, anvil, and stirrup together make up the

    a.   organ of Corti.
    b.   oval window.
    c.   ossicles.
    d.   basilar membrane.

13. In what way is audition much like the process of vision?

    a.   Information is transmitted by means of wavelengths.
    b.   Information travels at about the same rate.
    c.   A unified theory explains how each sense operates.
    d.   Both need a medium in which to exist.

14. The frequency of a sound wave determines its

    a.   loudness.
    b.   pitch.
    c.   amplitude.
    d.   speed.

15. The absolute threshold for hearing

    a.   is zero decibels.
    b.   is 20 decibels.
    c.   is 100 decibels.
    d.   cannot be determined from information given.

16. A sound of 20 decibels is _____ louder than a sound of 10 decibels.

    a.   two times
    b.   five times
    c.   ten times
    d.   twenty times

17. Loss of hearing due to damage to the eardrum or ossicles

    a.   is known as nerve deafness.
    b.   cannot be remedied through the use of hearing aids.
    c.   leads to greater vibration in the oval window.
    d.   is known as conduction deafness.

18. What term is used to describe the fact that pitch is related to the alternating firing of groups of
    neurons along the basilar membrane?

    a.   Place theory
    b.   Volley principle
    c.   Frequency theory
    d.   The Helmholtz principle

ESSAY QUESTIONS

1. Put the following in order to reflect the sequence in which a sound vibration is transmitted: organ of Corti, eardrum, ossicles, outer ear, oval window, hair cells, basilar membrane

2. Why are women's voices perceived as higher in pitch than men's?

3. What form must sound take in order to be utilized by your nervous system?

ANSWER KEY

1. Hair cells
2. Cochlea
3. Auditory nerve
4. Pitch
5. Audition
6. Ossicles
7. Basilar membrane
8. Place theory
9. Organ of Corti
10. Oval window
11. Eardrum
12. c
13. a
14. b
15. a
16. c
17. d
18. b

SAMPLE ANSWERS TO ESSAY QUESTIONS

1. The order in which these organs in the ear will experience income sound waves is: Outer ear, eardrum, ossicles, oval window, basilar membrane, organ of Corti, hair cells.

2. Women's vocal cords are shorter and thus vibrate at a greater frequency. The frequency of the occurrence of sound waves entering the ear is related to the pitch that is perceived by a listener. In general, the greater the frequency, the higher the pitch that a listener hears. Since women have shorter vocal cords and shorter vocal cords have a higher frequency of vibration, women's voices are perceived as having a higher pitch.

3. Like light for vision, sound waves must be converted from physical energy to neural impulses. The actual location where incoming sound waves are converted to usable neural form is in the organ of Corti. The organ of Corti is lined with hair cells. When sound wavelengths enter the ear, these hair cells are set in motion in a pattern that corresponds to characteristics of the incoming waves. Neurons then pick up the action of the hair cells and transmit that information to the brain.

MODULE 3.4 OUR OTHER SENSES: CHEMICAL, SKIN, AND BODY SENSES

LEARNING OBJECTIVES

After you have mastered the information in this unit, you will be able to:

- Explain how odors and tastes are sensed

- Discuss the skin senses

- Describe the kinesthetic and vestibular senses

OUTLINE

I.   Olfaction: What Your Nose Knows
   A.   Chemicals in the air that the nose can respond to
   B.   Lock-and-key fitting of molecules into odor receptors
   C.   Olfactory nerve—transmits odor information to brain
   D.   Olfactory bulb—brain destination; odor information does not travel through thalamus
   E.   Pheromones—chemical substances that play a role in behavior

II. Taste: The Flavorful Sense
   A.   Four basic tastes: sweet, sour, salty, and bitter
   B.   Flavors are a result of combinations of tastes
   C.   Taste cells—taste receptors
   D.   Taste buds—pores or openings on tongue (and surrounding area)
   E.   Taste sensitivity partly genetic
   F.   Supertasters—very dense network of tastebuds

III. The Skin Senses: Your Largest Sensory Organ
   A.   Code information regarding touch, pressure, warmth, cold, and pain
   B.   Sensory receptors distributed throughout body
   C.   Somatosensory cortex—brain region processing skin sense information
   D.   Specific receptors for warmth and cold
   E.   Gate-control theory of pain—pain messages may be regulated via a neural gateway
   F.   Acupucture may release endorphins—natural painkillers

IV. The Kinesthetic and Vestibular Senses: Of Grace and Balance
   A.   Kinesthesis tells us about body position and body movement
   B.   Vestibular sense monitors body position in space
      1.   Aids in keeping one's balance
      2.   Informs whether we are moving quickly, slowly
      3.   The ear's semicircular canals—movement of fluid relates body position information
      4.   Dizziness: semicircular canal fluid still moving though we have stopped

SUMMARY

In this module you learn about your other body senses: the sense of smell, of taste, and your skin senses. Your skin sense conveys more that just touch—it also relays information about pain, pressure, warmth, and cold. Senses discussed in this module include the kinesthetic and vestibular senses, which tell you about your body movement, direction, speed, and balance.

The senses of smell and taste are both based on chemical molecules, which may or may not fit into receptors in your nose and mouth. We can only sense, in terms of taste or smell, what we have receptors for. Odor receptors are located in the nose. Taste receptors are imbedded within the taste buds, most of which are on the tongue but that also can be found in mouth regions near the tongue.

Detecting a taste or an odor depends on whether the chemical molecule fits, like a key into a lock, the sensory receptor it reaches. If so, then information about that particular molecule is passed on to the brain. Information about odors is relayed directly to the olfactory bulb; unlike other sensory input this information does not first pass through the thalamus.

The skin is your body's largest organ; and information from skin receptors is processed in the brain's somatosensory cortex. You have sensory receptors for skin information distributed throughout your body. Pain messages in the body may be monitored via the gate-control theory, suggesting that factors influence whether the pain message is relayed or not. The body produces endorphins, which are natural painkillers. The vestibular sense helps you keep your balance, know where your body is in space, and if and how it is moving through space. Your kinesthetic sense helps you know about movement of your various body parts and what position they are in relative to one another. Your sense of balance is related to the movement of fluid in the semicircular canals within your inner ear.

KEY TERMS

Olfaction

Olfactory nerve

Olfactory bulb

Pheromones

Taste cells

Taste buds

Skin senses

Gate-control theory of pain

Acupuncture

Kinesthesis

Vestibular sense

Semicircular canals

Vestibular sacs

SELF-TEST PRACTICE QUIZ

From the Key Terms select that which best matches the following (Note: Not every Key Term will be used.):

1. _____   Sensory receptors for taste

2. _____   Chemical substances that may play a role in human behavior

3. _____   Inserting thin needles into the body and rotating them—to aid healing

a.   Olfaction

b.   Olfactory nerve

c.   Olfactory bulb

d.   Pheromones

4. _____ Transmits information about odors to the brain

5. _____ Fluid-filled portion of inner ear; relay information about movement

6. _____ Receptors that convey information about touch, pressure, warmth, cold, and pain

7. _____ A sense that monitors position and movement of the body in space; aids balance

8. _____ Openings in the tongue; contain taste cells

9. _____ The sense of smell

10. _____ Structures in the ear that connect the semicircular canals; also relay information about head position and movement

11. _____ A brain structure that processes information about odors

12. _____ The sense of body movement and interrelation of body parts and positions

13. _____ The notion that neural messages from the spinal cord may not be passed on to brain

e. Taste cells

f. Taste buds

g. Skin senses

h. Gate-control theory of pain

i. Acupuncture

j. Kinesthesis

k. Vestibular sense

l. Semicircular canals

m. Vestibular sacs

14. Which is the only sensory information that does NOT first travel through the thalamus on the way to the cortex?
    a. Kinesthetic
    b. Vestibular
    c. Olfactory
    d. Taste

15. Which is the largest sense organ in your body?
    a. Skin
    b. Kinesthetic
    c. Vestibular
    d. Visual

16. People who suffer from inner ear disorders may have difficulty keeping their balance. Which sense is being affected?
    a. Kinesthetic
    b. Olfactory
    c. Pheromonal
    d. Vestibular

ESSAY QUESTIONS

1. How do we detect odors and tastes to which we are exposed?

2. What are pheromones, and what role might they play in human and animal behavior?

3. Briefly explain the gate-control theory of pain.

ANSWER KEY

1. Taste cells

2. Pheromones

3. Acupuncture

4. Olfactory nerve

5. Semicircular canals

6. Skin senses

7. Vestibular sense

8. Taste buds

9. Olfaction

10. Vestibular sacs

11. Olfactory bulb

12. Kinesthesis

13. Gate-control theory of pain

14. c

15. a

16. d

SAMPLE ANSWERS TO ESSAY QUESTIONS

1. Odors, and tastes, are both transmitted by means of chemical molecules. We have sensory receptors for only some of the chemical molecules to which we are exposed. If a chemical molecule fits one of our sensory receptor sites, its presence is then detected and such information is relayed to the brain.

2. Pheromones are chemical substances that species emit, which may then play a role in behaviors exhibited among members of that species. Pheromones emitted by animals are involved in mating behavior, marking territory, obtaining food, establishing dominance, and managing aggression. There is ongoing debate over whether humans possess an organ for pheromone detection and what role (if any) pheromones play in human sexual behavior.

3. The gate-control theory of pain suggests that we may or may not feel all the pain messages that are produced in our nervous system. Nerve fibers that conduct pain messages through neural gateways in the spinal cord are thinner and slower than other nerve fibers, which conduct messages about touch, or warmth and cold. Thus, the signals carried on the thicker, faster nerve fibers may block the gate, helping to inhibit neural messages about pain.

MODULE 3.5 PERCEIVING OUR WORLD: PRINCIPLES OF PERCEPTION

LEARNING OBJECTIVES

After you have mastered the information in this unit, you will be able to:

- Define perception

- Discuss how perception is influenced by attention and perceptual set

- Describe the two general modes of processing visual stimuli

- Discuss the Gestalt principles of perceptual organization

- Define perceptual constancy and discuss the cues we use to perceive depth and motion

- Describe visual illusions

- Discuss the possible existence of subliminal perception

- Discuss the various forms of ESP and what evidence, if any, supports its existence

OUTLINE

I.   Perception—the Brain Organizes and Interprets Sensations
II.   Attention: Did You Notice That?
        A.   Attention—the first step in perception
        B.   Selective attention—limit attention to certain stimuli
        C.   Habituation—results from exposure to a constant stimulus
III.   Perceptual Set: Seeing What You Expect to See
        A.   Ambiguous stimuli interpreted differently based on expectations and preconceptions
IV.   Modes of Visual Processing
        A.   Bottom-up processing—begin with specific features of shapes in environment
        B.   Top-down processing—begin with knowledge and experience about patterns
V.   Gestalt Principles of Perceptual Organization
        A.   Figure and ground—figures have shapes; ground does not
        B.   Gestalt laws of grouping: proximity, similarity, continuity, closure, connectedness
VI.   Perceptual Constancies
        A.   Shape constancy—shape seen as the same across various perspectives
        B.   Size constancy—size perceived as same regardless of distance from perceiver
        C.   Color constancy—color perceived the same despite changes in lighting
        D.   Brightness constancy—brightness seen as the same though illumination may change
VII.   Cues to Depth Perception
        A.   Binocular cues—need both eyes
             1.   Retinal disparity—slightly differing image relayed to brain from each eye
             2.   Convergence—based on degree of muscular tension needed to focus on an object
        B.   Monocular cues—one eye sufficient
             1.   Relative size: larger objects perceived as closer
             2.   Interposition: obscured object perceived as farther away
             3.   Relative clarity: distant objects are blurrier
             4.   Texture gradient: closer objects appear coarser
             5.   Linear perspective: parallel lines appear to converge in distance
             6.   Shadowing: light and dark are cues to projections and indentations

VIII. Motion Perception
    A.   Projected image of object moves across retina
    B.   Changing size of object
IX.   Visual Illusions: Do Your Eyes Deceive You?
    A.   Perceptual cues may lead to misinterpretation
    B.   Stroboscopic movement—apparent movement
X.   Cultural Differences in Perceiving Visual Illusions
    A.   Experience plays a role in visual perception
    B.   Carpentered-world hypothesis—an environment dominated by straight lines and angles
XI.   Exploring Psychology: Controversies in Perception
    A.   Subliminal perception
        1.   Perception of stimuli below the level of conscious awareness
        2.   Two-thirds of Americans believe subliminal suggestions do work
        3.   Does seem to occur in some cases; influence is subtle
    B.   Extrasensory perception
        1.   Perception that occurs without benefit of the known senses
        2.   A major focus of study in parapsychology
            a)   Telepathy—the ability to exchange thoughts without use of the senses
            b)   Clairvoyance—the perception of events that are not available to the senses
            c)   Precognition—the ability to foretell the future
            d)   Psychokinesis—the ability to move objects without touching them
            e)   Ganzfeld procedure—way of testing for ESP
        3.   As yet no reliable, replicable findings of ESP that have withstood scientific scrutiny

SUMMARY

In this module you are introduced to basic concepts regarding perception. Perception is different from sensation, in that perception occurs in the brain. With perception, sensory information transmitted to the brain is interpreted; that is, it is compared to past experience and given meaning. With visual illusions, such as presented in this module, interpretation is difficult because perceptual cues may be conflicting.

The process of perception begins with giving our attention to some stimulus. Selective attention means we are limiting ourselves to certain stimuli and not attending to others. Thus we are able to focus our attention and avoid being bombarded by the many events and distractions in our environment. Past experience very much directs how we tend to interpret certain situations. Our expectancies (perceptual set) regarding what we are going to see or hear may shape our actual experience of these, focus our attention, and avoid being bombarded by the many events and distractions in the events.

Visual processing may be top-down (the brain is aware of meaningful wholes and does not first process individual parts) or bottom-up (the brain begins by attending to specific features in the environment). We organize what we see—by grouping and determining what is figure and what is ground. Both monocular (one eye needed) and binocular (two eyes needed) cues help us interpret depth. Perceptual constancy means objects continue to appear the same to us even though they may change in orientation, illumination, and proximity. Visual illusions help us learn more about how the process of perception works. Studies have shown that there are cultural differences in perception. Once again, past experience plays a role. Perceptual experience in differing environments leads members of various cultures to perceive the world differently.

Two controversies within the field of perception involve whether subliminal perception and extrasensory perception (ESP) exist. Subliminal perception is the perception of stimuli presented below the threshold for conscious awareness. Extrasensory perception is the ability to perceive without using any of the known senses. It is easier to test for the effects of subliminal perception than for ESP.

Laboratory researchers can test for the presence of subliminal perception by exposing individuals to a stimulus at such a rapid rate that these individuals are not consciously aware the stimulus was present. Yet, a subtle influence due to such exposure can sometimes be found. Researchers testing paranormal phenomena—telepathy, clairvoyance, psychokinesis, and precognition—have yet to come up with reliable, replicable scientific evidence that convincingly supports the existence of ESP.

KEY TERMS

Perception

Selective attention

Habituation

Perceptual set

Bottom-up processing

Top-down processing

Laws of perceptual organization

Proximity

Similarity

Continuity

Closure

Connectedness

Perceptual constancy

Shape constancy

Size constancy

Color constancy

Brightness constancy

Binocular cues

Retinal disparity

Convergence

Monocular cues

Visual illusions

Stroboscopic movement

Carpentered-world hypothesis

Subliminal perception

Extrasensory perception

Parapsychology

Telepathy

Clairvoyance

Precognition

Psychokinesis

Ganzfeld procedure

SELF-TEST PRACTICE QUIZ

From the Key Terms select that which best matches the following (Note: Not every Key Term will be used.):

1. _____ Perceptual grouping based on how alike stimuli are

2. _____ The brain attends to specific features in order to yield an overall pattern

3. _____ Limiting attention to certain stimuli and filtering out other stimuli

4. _____ Information from both eyes is needed to interpret stimuli

5. _____ An object is perceived as the same size even though the image on the retina changes

6. _____ The ability to perceive information without using the known senses

7. _____ The ability to foretell the future

8. _____ The brain receives slightly differing image from each eye

9. _____ Features of a stimulus are perceived as remaining the same even though sensory input changes

10. _____ Perceptual grouping based on how near stimuli are to each other

11. _____ Becoming accustomed to constant exposure to a stimulus

12. _____ The study of events that cannot be explained by known physical, psychological, or biological mechanisms

13. _____ A way of testing for ESP

14. _____ Perceiving stimuli presented below the level of conscious awareness

15. _____ Expectations or preconceptions that influence what we perceive

16. _____ How people assemble bits of sensory stimuli into meaningful wholes

a. Perception

b. Selective attention

c. Habituation

d. Perceptual set

e. Bottom-up processing

f. Top-down processing

g. Laws of perceptual organization

h. Proximity

i. Similarity

j. Continuity

k. Closure

l. Connectedness

m. Perceptual constancy

n. Shape constancy

o. Size constancy

p. Color constancy

q. Brightness constancy

r. Binocular cues

s. Retinal disparity

t. Convergence

u. Monocular cues

v. Visual illusions

w. Stroboscopic movement

x. Carpentered-world hypothesis

y. Subliminal perception

z. Extrasensory perception

aa. Parapsychology

bb. Telepathy

cc. Clairvoyance

17. _____   Muscular tension produced by both eyes turning inward

dd. Precognition

ee. Psychokinesis

ff. Ganzfeld procedure

18. With _____, the image presented to the brain from each eye differs slightly.
    a. binocular cues
    b. monocular cues
    c. perceptual set
    d. retinal disparity
19. When you see a person walking toward you, the retinal image grows, yet you perceive that the person remains the same height. This illustrates the principle of
    a. constancy.
    b. retinal disparity.
    c. stroboscopic movement.
    d. bottom-up processing.
20. Bottom-up processing is directed mostly by
    a. patterns existing in the brain.
    b. specific features of the stimulus.
    c. visual illusions.
    d. all of the above.
21. A stimulus is perceived as _____ when it is perceived as having a shape.
    a. converging
    b. figure
    c. ground
    d. constant
22. Perception differs from sensation in that perception
    a. occurs in the brain, where information about stimuli are interpreted.
    b. consists of all information transmitted by sensory receptors.
    c. necessitates binocular cues, while monocular cues are sufficient for sensation.
    d. does not utilize cues such as linear perspective and interposition.
23. Texture gradient is a
    a. perceptual set.
    b. monocular cue.
    c. binocular cue.
    d. constancy cue.
24. Clairvoyance is the ability to
    a. read another's mind.
    b. perceive objects and events without using the known senses.
    c. predict the future.
    d. move objects with one's mind.
25. What does research on subliminal perception indicate?
    a. Participants in subliminal perception studies often become ill.
    b. Research on subliminal perception has been discontinued.
    c. There is some scientific evidence to suggest the phenomenon does exist.
    d. Subliminal perception cannot be tested scientifically.
26. Generally speaking, do Americans believe that subliminal perception can occur?

ESSAY QUESTIONS

1. How do we perceive motion, such as when we watch movies?

2. Explain visual illusions. Why do they occur?

3. What is the Ganzfeld procedure? How is it carried out?

ANSWER KEY

1. Similarity

2. Bottom-up processing

3. Selective attention

4. Binocular cues

5. Size constancy

6. Extrasensory perception

7. Precognition

8. Retinal disparity

9. Perceptual constancy

10. Proximity

11. Habituation

12. Parapsychology

13. Ganzfeld procedure

14. Subliminal perception

15. Perceptual set

16. Laws of perceptual organization

17. Convergence

18. d

19. a

20. b

21. b

22. a

23. b

24. b

25. c

26. Yes, about two-thirds of Americans believe in the phenomenon of subliminal perception.

SAMPLE ANSWERS TO ESSAY QUESTIONS

1. We perceive motion various ways. One way is simply that the image moves across the retina corresponding to how the stimuli move in our field of vision. Another way is that objects change size, and, for example, we perceive that an object has moved away from us if the retinal image grows smaller. Motion that appears to occur (as in motion pictures), but actually does not, is stroboscopic motion. Here, illuminated images that are projected are still. However, they are presented in a progression and at such a rapid rate that they are perceived as displaying movement.

2. We cannot fully explain why visual illusions occur. However, it is probably related to our reliance on perceptual cues. These cues come from our experience with the environment. The cues may trigger one perception. Actual objective measurement of the stimuli involved, however, may produce different, and more accurate, information.

3. The Ganzfeld procedure is used to test for extrasensory perception. Two participants are involved in the study—one is the "sender," and one is the "receiver." Each is placed in a separate, sound-proof room and the receiver's eyes and ears are blocked from receiving stimuli. The sender must then mentally transmit a randomly selected visual image to the receiver. To verify that ESP has actually occurred, the receiver must identify the correct visual image at a higher than chance (25 percent) rate. Some studies do report a higher-than-chance rate, but other studies refute this finding.

MODULE 3.6 APPLICATION: THE PSYCHOLOGY OF PAIN MANAGEMENT

LEARNING OBJECTIVE

After you have mastered the information in this unit, you will be able to:

*   Describe research on pain management

OUTLINE

I.   Gaining Control Over Pain
    A.   Pain does protect us from danger
    B.   Endorphins produced by body can help diminish experience of pain
II. Pain management strategies
    A.   Distraction—directing attention away from pain
    B.   Bottleneck pain at neurological gate—rubbing, heat and cold may block gateway
    C.   Do something enjoyable—priming positive emotions reduces pain intensity
    D.   Changing thoughts and attitudes—remain positive, focus on what can help
    E.   Obtaining accurate information—about pain source and treatment
    F.   Meditation—focused attention yields a relaxed, contemplative state
    G.   Biofeedback training—learning to control tension and other responses by the body

MODULE 3.6 SUMMARY

In this Application module, you learn what psychologists have discovered about pain. True, pain does help us in that it makes us aware of harm. The body has some defense against pain; this is the naturally occurring production of endorphins. Pain management strategies include maintaining positive and informed thoughts and a relaxed state, directing attention to other activities, and some physiological activities that may block the pain message or help us lessen tension and stress.

CHAPTER 3 APPLICATION EXERCISE

Which of your senses do you tend to rely on the most? That is, which one seems to provide you with the most information during the course of a typical day? How does that information come into your awareness? Can you distinguish the sensory information from what you then perceive? How much different is what you sensed from how your mind later interpreted it? What do you think influenced those interpretations?

How do your thoughts and feelings affect what you perceive? Can you think of an example where you were processing information from the environment? It is happening all the time, of course! How did the stimuli from the environment catch your attention? What frame of mind were you in? Evaluate how, if at all, your mental set and/or emotional state affected what it was that you perceived.

CHAPTER 4

Consciousness

In Chapter 4 you learn about the many different states of consciousness a human being can experience, sometimes all within a day's time. These states range from being alert and aware (perhaps particularly focused) to sleeping and dreaming, which are altered states of awareness. Another state is deep unconsciousness due to brain injury or anesthesia. Much of our state of consciousness is in our own hands—either through where we choose to focus our attention, when we decide to lie down and sleep, or when we induce altered mental functioning through meditation or the use of drugs.

Some states of consciousness can be helpful. We can prime our minds to be particularly alert and aware, absorbing the maximum amount of information from whatever stimuli we have chosen to attend to. We can allow ourselves sufficient time to sleep thus increasing the likelihood that we will awake alert, refreshed, and most able to do our best. Drifting consciousness (the mind is free to wander) or meditation both provide opportunities for the mind to contemplate new ideas, and the body is likely to be in a natural, more relaxed state. Hypnosis, again an altered state where no drugs are used, may be of therapeutic value in treating physical or psychological disorders and in helping an individual adopt more desirable behavior patterns such as losing weight or stopping smoking.

We not only must sleep to allow the body to restore and replenish itself, but we must also dream. Individuals who obtain enough sleep but who are prevented from dreaming show learning and memory impairments even though they may not experience fatigue. We can tell when an individual is dreaming during sleep by observing that individual's eyes. The state of dreaming is associated with REM sleep—that is, rapid-eye-movement sleep, where the eyes are moving under the eyelids as if the person were actually watching a movie. Everyone dreams every night, though the dreams may not be remembered. Sleeping during the night tends to occur in stages with Stages 1 and 2 being associated with lighter sleep and Stages 3 and 4 with deeper sleep. Dreaming tends not to occur during any of these stages but rather usually after an individual has been in Stage 4 sleep and is cycling out of it (reversing through Stage 3 and then Stage 2, respectively). Each stage of sleep corresponds to a different pattern of brain waves, which can be measured electrically. Waking states are associated with beta waves, early phases of relaxation with alpha waves, and the deepest stages of sleep with delta waves. Influences on when we sleep include the amount of available light hitting our eyes, regular bodily patterns for activity and rest known as circadian rhythms, and a brain structure that secretes the hormone melatonin making us feel sleepy.

Our state of consciousness may also be altered through the use of chemical substances. These chemicals include the most widely used and abused drug, alcohol, and also include a number of other legal and illegal substances. All of the mind-altering substances are classified according to the effect they have on the body. Depressants lower the activity of the central nervous system. An individual will feel relaxed, calm, and may experience a sense of euphoria. Depressants include alcohol, barbiturates, tranquilizers, and opioids (also called opiates). Some of these have legitimate uses in the medical field. Stimulants make us more alert and aware since they increase the activity level of the central nervous system. Stimulants include amphetamines, cocaine, MDMA (Ecstasy), nicotine, and caffeine. Stimulants may be sought after because they can produce a "rush" or a psychological "high." They may create intense feelings of pleasure that, once a user is hooked, become hard to resist. These feelings of pleasure drive the user to desire more and more of the drug, and oftentimes a user then becomes addicted. Addictions may be psychological, physiological, or both. Physiological dependency means the mental chemistry of the brain actually has been changed due to repeated use of the drug. A third class of mind-altering drugs is the hallucinogens, which include marijuana (the most widely used illicit drug), LSD, PCP, and similar drugs. Mind-altering drugs may be naturally-occurring or may be synthesized in a laboratory-type setting. Many have serious consequences from their prolonged use, and many can and do result in death.

MODULE 4.1 STATES OF CONSCIOUSNESS

LEARNING OBJECTIVE

After you have mastered the information in this unit, you will be able to:

- Identify and provide examples of states of consciousness

OUTLINE

I.   Consciousness—whatever you are aware of at any point in time
II.   States of Consciousness
     A.   Focused awareness
         1.   Consciousness is selective
         2.   We choose to direct our attention and effort
         3.   Extraneous information is filtered out
     B.   Drifting consciousness
         1.   Focused awareness difficult to maintain long term
         2.   Mind may start to drift from thought to thought
         3.   Daydreaming—a waking state but of dreamy thoughts
     C.   Divided consciousness
         1.   We may perform two different tasks simultaneously
         2.   We perform best on routine tasks when we don't pay too much attention
         3.   Automatic pilot—performing mechanical tasks that do not require focused awareness
     D.   States of unconsciousness
         1.   Relatively unaware of our external surroundings—as in sleeping and dreaming
         2.   Still responsive to personally meaningful stimuli
         3.   Deep unconsciousness—as from anesthesia or coma
         4.   Altered states
            a)   State of awareness unlike normal waking state
            b)   Daydreaming, meditation, hypnosis, influence of mind-altering drugs
            c)   Also may result from repetitive physical activity
III.   Exploring Psychology: Driving While Distracted
     A.   Driving while using a cell phone carries the same risk as driving drunk
         1.   Using a hands-free device does *not* lower this risk
     B.   Other serious distractions include eating, putting on makeup, and attending to children

SUMMARY

In this module you learn about states of consciousness. In the early history of psychology, both Wilhelm Wundt and William James were interested in studying consciousness, but the behaviorists who followed them suggested this effort be abandoned. Among other things it was thought that studying something so unobservable and subjective was simply too difficult. However, recently, especially with advances in technological equipment, studying varying types of consciousness is back in the fore.

Consciousness is a state of awareness of ourselves and of the world around us. Consciousness can shift from alert arousal to a deep unconsciousness as in sleep. Focused awareness is a heightened state of alert wakefulness where extraneous stimuli are filtered out. Drifting consciousness means the mind moves away from focused awareness to a mental wandering from thought to thought. Drifting consciousness can lead to daydreaming. Divided consciousness involves doing more than one mental activity at a time. Often one of the activities is a mechanical one, which when well learned frees us to simultaneously contemplate something else such as meeting a friend for a baseball game or ruminating about a romantic relationship. If we are driving during a state of divided consciousness, we may arrive at our destination with no clear recollection of how we got there—we were on automatic pilot. Dividing our attention in this fashion works to an extent, but it presents hazards if the second task (cell phones, children who need attention, heated discussions or arguments) becomes too distracting.

Unconsciousness means we are relatively unaware of our surroundings such as during sleep or when dreaming. When we are in states of awareness unlike our typical waking state, these are known as altered states of awareness. They are likely to occur when we daydream, meditate, or as a result of using mind-altering drugs.

KEY TERMS

Consciousness

States of consciousness

Focused awareness

Drifting consciousness

Daydreaming

Divided consciousness

Unconsciousness

Altered states of consciousness

SELF-TEST PRACTICE QUIZ

From the Key Terms select that which best matches the following (Note: Not every Key Term will be used.):

1. _____ Attention given to two tasks at the same time

2. _____ When the mind wanders to dreamy states or fantasies

3. _____ Heightened alertness; full attention directed to task at hand

4. _____ A state of awareness of ourselves and of the world around us

5. _____ Range of consciousness from alert wakefulness to unconsciousness

6. _____ States of awareness that are unlike the typical waking state

a. Consciousness

b. States of consciousness

c. Focused awareness

d. Drifting consciousness

e. Daydreaming

f. Divided consciousness

g. Unconsciousness

h. Altered states of consciousness

7. _____   When thoughts meander from one to the next

8. _____   A lack of awareness

9. William James felt that consciousness was

    a.   similar to being on automatic pilot.
    b.   where the mind drifts from thought to thought.
    c.   a continuous process of thinking like water flowing down a river.
    d.   mental states not typical of our every day wakefulness.

10. In which state of consciousness is daydreaming most likely?

    a.   Unconsciousness
    b.   Focused awareness
    c.   Drifting consciousness
    d.   Divided consciousness

11. When we are asleep, we

    a.   are at the lowest levels of consciousness.
    b.   are functioning outside of conscious awareness.
    c.   are in a state of deep unconsciousness.
    d.   may still be responsive to some kinds of stimuli.

12. The state of deep unconsciousness may be induced by

    a.   repetitive physical activities.
    b.   trauma to the head or by general anesthesia.
    c.   prolonged meditation or by hypnosis.
    d.   mind-altering drugs such as alcohol or marijuana.

ESSAY QUESTIONS

1.   Why did the behaviorists object to studying consciousness? Give some pros and cons with regard to the study of this subject.

2.   Discuss situations where our use of divided consciousness can be an advantage. Discuss situations where its use can become hazardous.

ANSWER KEY

1.   Divided consciousness

2.   Daydreaming

3.   Focused awareness

4.   Consciousness

5.   States of consciousness

6.   Altered states of consciousness

7.   Drifting consciousness

8.   Unconsciousness

9.   c

10. c

11. d

12. b

SAMPLE ANSWERS TO ESSAY QUESTIONS

1.   The behaviorists objected to studying consciousness because it involved internal and subjective phenomena, which was therefore quite difficult to measure. What would study of such a vague concept accomplish? Behaviorists' research focus was simply on observable behavior, and they believed that all human characteristics were derived solely from the environment and experience. An advantage to studying consciousness is that at least some of the human psyche can be traced to inner, rather than external, workings. A disadvantage is that consciousness is more difficult to measure—but innovations in research methodology are helping with that problem.

2.   Dividing the focus of our attention, as in divided consciousness, can be helpful in that we can accomplish more than one task at a time. In addition, devoting our full attention to a task that is easy and/or that we know well often is not necessary and may in fact lead to feelings of boredom. Conversely, if we are attempting more than one task at a time, such as driving while using a cell phone, eating, or putting on makeup, and that secondary task becomes demanding of more and more of our attention, we put ourselves (and others) at serious risk.

MODULE 4.2 SLEEPING AND DREAMING

LEARNING OBJECTIVES

After you have mastered the information in this unit, you will be able to:

*   Explain how our sleep-wake cycles are regulated

*   Describe the stages and functions of sleep

*   Explain why we dream

*   Describe the various sleep disorders

OUTLINE

I.   Sleep and Wakefulness: A Circadian Rhythm
    A.   One-third of human life is spent sleeping
    B.   Circadian rhythm—daily pattern for sleep-wake cycles
    C.   Suprachiasmatic nucleus (SCN) in hypothalamus regulates sleep
    D.   Melatonin is hormone that makes us feel sleepy
    E.   Human eye is sensitive to light, even in blind individuals
    F.   Jet lag—local time conflicts with internal body clock
II. Stages of Sleep
    A.   Stage 1
        1.   Brain waves small and irregular, varying frequencies
        2.   Light sleep; sleeper is easily awakened
    B.   Stage 2
        1.   Onset two minutes after Stage 1 sleep
        2.   Bursts of brain wave activity: sleep spindles
    C.   Stage 3—Deep sleep; 50 percent or fewer of brain wave patterns are delta waves
    D.   Stage 4—Deep sleep; 50 percent or more of brain wave patterns are delta waves
    E.   REM (rapid-eye-movement) sleep
        1.   Stage of sleep associated with dreaming
        2.   Follows Stages 3 and 2 after reverting from deep sleep
        3.   High level of brain activity, body movement blocked

III. Why We Sleep
   A. Species' average length of sleep time varies
   B. Universal need for sleep suggests survival necessity
   C. Sleep serves a variety of functions—protection, restoration, energy conservation, knowledge consolidation, disease prevention
IV. Dreams and Dreaming
   A. Why do we dream?
      1. Dreams may help us find solutions to problems
      2. Activation-synthesis hypothesis—cerebral cortex tries to integrate experiences generated by random electrical brain impulses
      3. Brain area for logical thought less active during dream state
      4. Sigmund Freud: dreams are wish fulfillment
         a) Dreams represent unconscious wishes, usually sexual or aggressive
         b) The "royal road" to the unconscious
         c) Manifest content—events that actually occur in a dream
         d) Latent content—what the dream really means, since dreams are symbolic
         e) Difficult to verify empirically
   B. Lucid dreams: dreamer is aware of dreaming
V. Sleep Disorders
   A. Insomnia
      1. Most common sleep disorder
      2. Inability to fall asleep, remain asleep, or return to sleep after being awakened
      3. Array of causes
         a) Substance abuse, physical illness
         b) Psychological disorders—depression, worry
         c) Sleep cannot be forced
   B. Narcolepsy—falling asleep suddenly during the day
   C. Sleep apnea—frequently stopping breathing during sleep
   D. Nightmare disorder—frequent, disturbing nightmares
   E. Sleep terror disorder
      1. More likely to affect children, especially boys
      2. More intense than nightmares
      3. Does not occur during REM sleep—occurs during deep sleep period
   F. Sleepwalking
      1. Also more often in children than adults
      2. Sleeping individual walks about, eyes open
      3. No harm in wakening sleepwalker
VI. Sleep Deprivation
   A. Normally need 7 to 9 hours sleep per day
   B. Infants and children: more time proportionally in REM sleep
   C. Insufficient sleep
      1. Slows reaction times
      2. Impairs concentration, memory, and problem-solving ability
      3. Harder to retain newly acquired information
      4. Impairs academic performance
      5. Common cause of highway accidents
      6. Weakens body's immune system
   D. Need sufficient REM sleep as well

SUMMARY

In this module you learn about our remarkable experiences of sleeping and dreaming. Sleep appears to be fundamentally necessary both to our physical well-being and survival and for our effective mental functioning. Most people need between seven and nine hours of sleep a night in order to feel truly refreshed and alert. Though sleep deprivation endangers our health and impairs our functioning in many ways, once an individual has the opportunity to "catch up" on sleep, there seem to be no lasting consequences of the former sleep deprivation period.

Why do we sleep? There are a variety of reasons. Circadian rhythms direct many body patterns of activity, and the sleep-wake cycle is one of them. The human sleep cycle corresponds roughly to the 24-hour clock. The eye is sensitive to the presence or absence of light, and that plus the production of melatonin in our body (the hormone that makes us feel sleepy) together help explain why we sleep and wake when we do. Of course, sleep time is an opportunity for our body to restore itself. Energy in our cells can be replenished, and some wear-and-tear in the body and brain can be repaired. Insufficient sleep appears to suppress the immune system. Animal species (probably true for our forebears also) are afforded protection by sleeping at night when predators roam.

Sleep is not a consistent state—our sleep time goes through cycles from very light sleep (Stage 1, where we may not even realize we are asleep) to the deep sleep of Stage 4. Brain wave patterns change with each sleep stage, and humans typically experience four or five sleep cycles during a night. Most of our sleep time is spent in Stage 2 sleep during which the brain experiences bursts of wave activity known as sleep spindles.

We not only need to sleep, but we need to dream as well although the actual purpose of dreaming is not entirely known. We do know that individuals who get enough sleep in terms of hours still are cognitively impaired if they are deprived of REM sleep. REM (rapid-eye-movement) sleep occurs when an individual is dreaming—the eyes are actually moving under the eyelids as if the individual were watching a movie. REM sleep is usually a separate period of sleep not corresponding to any of the sleep stages and usually occurring after an individual is reversing the sleep stages following the deep sleep period. The majority of dreams are about our day's activities. These dreams may help us consolidate into the brain what we have learned during the day and/or help us work on various solutions to problems we face. Sigmund Freud was one of the first to extensively discuss and utilize dream interpretation.

Not everyone goes to sleep easily or sleeps soundly at night. There are various sleep disorders, including narcolepsy, where individuals will fall asleep suddenly even though they have just been actively involved in daytime events. Insomnia may be caused by substance abuse or physical pain; other possible causes are psychological disorders and simple worry. We can even become anxious about not sleeping, and that keeps us awake more!

It is most often children who have nightmares and also a more severe form of nightmare called night terrors. Nightmares occur during REM sleep; night terrors occur during a deep sleep phase. Usually most of a nightmare can be remembered, but conversely with the more intense night terror little is usually remembered. Children also are more prone to sleepwalking. Fortunately, most of these disorders lessen as a child grows older.

KEY TERMS

Circadian rhythm

Jet lag

Rapid-eye-movement (REM) sleep

Activation-synthesis hypothesis

Lucid dreams

Insomnia

Narcolepsy

Cataplexy

Sleep apnea

Nightmare disorder

Sleep terror disorder

Sleepwalking disorder

SELF-TEST PRACTICE QUIZ

From the Key Terms select that which best matches the following (Note: Not every Key Term will be used.):

1. _____ The stage of sleep most closely associated with dreaming

2. _____ Temporary cessation of breathing during sleep

3. _____ A disruption of sleep-wake cycles due to long-distance air travel

4. _____ The notion that the brain creates dreams to help make sense of random electrical brain activity during sleep

5. _____ Difficulty falling asleep, remaining asleep, or returning to sleep after being awakened

6. _____ A disorder involving frequent, disturbing nightmares

7. _____ Walking about while sound asleep

8. _____ Fluctuations in bodily processes that occur regularly each day

9. _____ Dreams in which the dreamer is aware that he or she is dreaming

10. _____ Repeated episodes of intense fear during sleep

11. _____ Sudden, unexplainable "sleep attacks" that occur during the day

a. Circadian rhythm

b. Jet lag

c. Rapid-eye-movement (REM) sleep

d. Activation-synthesis hypothesis

e. Lucid dreams

f. Insomnia

g. Narcolepsy

h. Cataplexy

i. Sleep apnea

j. Nightmare disorder

k. Sleep terror disorder

l. Sleepwalking disorder

12. Why do some people have difficulty falling or staying asleep?

    a. They may be suffering from psychological problems, such as depression.
    b. They have worries or concerns, which they take to bed with them.
    c. They may be experiencing pain.
    d. All of the above are correct.

13. The hormone secreted by our body that tends to make us feel sleepy is

    a. dopamine.
    b. serotonin.
    c. acetylcholine.
    d. melatonin.

14. The part of the hypothalamus in the brain that helps regulate sleep-wake cycles is the

    a. ventromedial lobe.
    b. superior olive.
    c. suprachiasmatic nucleus (SCN).
    d. reticular formation.

15. How can we tell when individuals are dreaming?

    a. They tend to thrash about and talk in their sleep.
    b. They exhibit REM sleep where their eyes under the eyelid are moving.
    c. They tend to get up and walk around the room or house.
    d. Any of the above indicate that an individual is dreaming.

16. What do we call the pattern that tends to regulate many of our daily bodily processes?

    a. Circadian rhythms
    b. Biological predispositions
    c. Parental regulations
    d. The alarm clock

17. How do we explain the fact that even blind individuals tend to follow the typical human sleep-wake cycles?

    a. They have been taught since childhood to follow daily patterns of other humans.
    b. They always have access to Braille watches or other indicators of the time.
    c. Their eyes, like those of sighted individuals, are sensitive to light and changes in light.
    d. Blind individuals have a great deal of difficulty with sleep-wake cycles.

18. We spend most of our time in

    a. Stage 1 sleep.
    b. Stage 2 sleep.
    c. Stage 3 sleep.
    d. Stage 4 sleep.

19. According to the activation-synthesis model, dreams are

    a. the "royal road to the unconscious."
    b. a means of allowing us to think more creatively while asleep.
    c. a representation of unconscious wishes, desires, and fears.
    d. simply a way for the brain to make sense of random electrical discharges.

20. About how long does the typical human sleep cycle last?

    a. 20 minutes
    b. 40 minutes
    c. 60 minutes
    d. 90 minutes

21. What brain wave patterns are most typical of our brain activity when we are awake?

    a. Alpha waves
    b. Beta waves
    c. Delta waves
    d. Spindle-shaped brain wave bursts

22. People who are chronically sleep deprived

    a. may have problems with psychological well-being but not physical health.
    b. can often get used to it without any ill effects.
    c. are happier than those who sleep too much.
    d. are more likely to get into car accidents.

23. During a night's sleep, the amount of time we spend in Stage 4 (deep sleep)

    a. increases.
    b. decreases.
    c. stays the same.
    d. essentially reduces to nothing.

24. REM sleep is called paradoxical sleep because

    a. our dreams may be disturbing or difficult to interpret.
    b. though we are asleep, we are getting very little actual rest.
    c. the brain is very active but muscles are essentially paralyzed.
    d. dreaming is not really helpful if the dreamer experiences nightmares.

25. Which statement about night terrors is correct?

    a. They are the same thing as nightmares.
    b. They are more common in boys than in girls.
    c. They occur only during REM sleep.
    d. It is more common in adults than in children.

ESSAY QUESTIONS

1. Briefly describe the typical sleep pattern of a human during the night. What sleep stages does this individual go through? How does the sleep cycle change? When do we dream?

2. In what ways does sleeping help our body function?

3. What are some causes of insomnia? How might it be treated?

4. What were some of Freud's views on dreaming?

ANSWER KEY

1. Rapid-eye-movement (REM) sleep

2. Sleep apnea

3. Jet lag

4. Activation-synthesis hypothesis

5. Insomnia

6. Nightmare disorder

7. Sleepwalking disorder

8. Circadian rhythm

9. Lucid dreams

10.   Sleep terror disorder

11.   Narcolepsy

12.   d

13.   d

14.   c

15.   b

16.   a

17.   c

18.   b

19.   d

20.   d

21.   b

22.   d

23.   d

24.   c

25.   b

SAMPLE ANSWERS TO ESSAY QUESTIONS

1.   Sleep begins with our relaxation, and the beta brain waves shift to slower alpha waves. We slip into Stage 1 sleep where brain waves become small, irregular, and of varying frequencies. All these brain wave patterns may be measured by an electroencephalograph (EEG). In Stage 1, we may not even realize we are sleeping. Stage 2 sleep begins two minutes after Stage 1, and brain wave patterns are characterized by bursts of activity known as sleep spindles. In both Stage 1 and Stage 2 sleep we can easily be awakened. In deeper sleep (Stages 3 and 4) the brain exhibits a large, slow (delta) wave pattern. In Stage 3 sleep, delta waves constitute 50 percent or less of the brain wave pattern; in Stage 4 sleep delta waves comprise more than 50 percent. REM sleep is not associated with any of these sleep stages; generally it occurs as a person is coming out of deep sleep, reversing the pattern through Stages 3 and 2; what follows then is the REM sleep period. These sleep cycles typically last about 90 minutes, and an individual probably experiences four or five of these cycles each night. As our sleep period continues, Stage 4 sleep basically disappears, so we reach the REM sleep phase more quickly.

2.   It is apparent that sleep is necessary to preserve and protect our body. During sleep, our body restores and replenishes itself. Wear and tear from daily experiences and activity can be repaired. Research on individuals deprived of sleep shows that they experience impairment in both cognitive and motor functions. Obviously, then, sleep helps keep our body, particularly the brain and the rest of the nervous system, in top working order. Lack of sleep also weakens our immune system, so sleeping helps protect our health as well. We not only need to sleep, but we need to be able to experience REM sleep as needed through the night.

3. Insomnia may have physical or psychological causes, or it may simply result from poor sleeping habits. Substance abuse or physical pain may inhibit our ability to relax and to sleep. Psychological depression is known to be associated with sleep problems.

    To treat insomnia, an individual would need to treat the underlying cause. Once pain is controlled, an individual learns to disengage himself from worries and concerns, and then healthier sleep patterns should reappear. Sleep must come naturally and cannot be forced.

4. Freud was one of the first major figures in psychology to study and write extensively about dreams and dream interpretation. In keeping with his other views on the human psyche, Freud believed that dreaming was symbolic. Dreams represent wishes that we would like to have come true in our lives. Most of these wishes, according to Freud, dealt with sexual or aggressive desires.

    Dreaming, to Freud, had two layers: the outer layer (the manifest content), which was what the dream appeared to be, and the inner layer (latent content), which represented the true underlying meaning of the dream. The true meaning of the dream was hidden to disguise our perhaps unacceptable desires even to ourselves. Freud believed that dreaming helped us remain asleep. By disguising our underlying feelings through the use of symbols, our sleep would not be disturbed. If the actual content of our inner desires was apparent in our dreams, it might be sufficiently emotionally upsetting to awaken us.

MODULE 4.3 ALTERING CONSCIOUSNESS THROUGH MEDITATION AND HYPNOSIS

LEARNING OBJECTIVES

After you have mastered the information in this unit, you will be able to:

- Define meditation

- Define hypnosis

- Discuss the major theories of hypnosis

OUTLINE

I. Meditation
    A. Focused attention; relaxed, contemplative state
    B. Narrow attention to a single object or thought
    C. Transcendental meditation—repeat a phrase or sound (mantra)
    D. Mindfulness meditation—focus on moment-to-moment thoughts and sensations
    E. Relaxed but still alert
    F. May help
        1. Expand consciousness
        2. Achieve a state of inner peace
        3. Relieve stress and chronic pain
        4. Treat psychological disorders
II. Hypnosis
    A. An altered state of consciousness
    B. Focused attention, deep relaxation, heightened susceptibility to suggestion
    C. Experiences under hypnosis:
        1. Hypnotic age regression—reliving past events (usually childhood)
        2. Hypnotic analgesia—loss of awareness of pain
        3. Posthypnotic amnesia—inability to recall what happened during hypnosis

4.   Posthypnotic suggestion—planting a suggestion during hypnosis that individual follows (usually without awareness) after trance

III.   Theories of Hypnosis
- A.   No consensus as to what hypnosis is or does
- B.   Possibly a trance state
- C.   Possibly just role-playing (but evidence does not support this notion)
- D.   Ernest Hilgard: neodissociation theory
    1.   Altered state of consciousness—consciousness splits or divides
    2.   Split off portion follows hypnotist's suggestions
    3.   "Hidden observer" part of mind still monitors all events
    4.   Cold pressor test—shows hypnotic influence

SUMMARY

In this module you learn about states of consciousness that are unlike our typical everyday awareness. Meditation and hypnosis are both altered states of consciousness brought about through focusing attention and no other (chemical, for example) means. In meditation, the individual focuses his or her attention on a single object, spoken word, or thought. All other thoughts are removed from consciousness, and the result is a relaxed, contemplative state. Unlike hypnosis, the meditative individual is still alert and aware. Meditation is thought to be helpful in expanding awareness, achieving a state of inner peace, relieving stress, and aiding in the treatment of physical and psychological disorders.

Hypnosis comes from the Greek word for sleep, although hypnotized individuals are not actually sleeping. Researchers are still not quite certain what hypnosis is, how to define it, or indeed how it works. Also, not everyone is susceptible to being hypnotized. As with meditation, hypnosis involves focusing attention but usually on the hypnotist's voice. When the individual is deeply relaxed, the hypnotist gives suggestions. These suggestions may guide the individual through unusual experiences (age regression, distortions of reality), reduce awareness of pain, or lead to certain responses once the individual reawakens.

Theories about the nature of hypnosis include that it is a trance state where the individual is particularly susceptible to suggestion. Others believe hypnosis is simply role-playing—the individual is not really affected or "under" hypnosis at all. Since patterns of brain activity differ between those who are acting and those who really have been hypnotized, evidence supports the notion that hypnosis is more than just pretense. Ernest Hilgard has proposed the neodissociation theory regarding hypnosis. According to this theory, hypnosis is an altered state of consciousness, and the hypnotized individual splits off part of the consciousness. It is this part that is impacted by the hypnotist's suggestion. Another part of the brain remains detached from the experience but monitors what is going on. In Hilgard's cold pressor test, differences were found between the experiences of those who were hypnotized versus those who were not. Though the actual nature of hypnosis still remains unclear, it has established itself as useful in treating a range of physical and psychological problems.

KEY TERMS

Transcendental meditation (TM)

Mantra

Mindfulness meditation

Hypnosis

Hypnotic age regression

Hypnotic analgesia

Posthypnotic amnesia

Posthypnotic suggestion

Neodissociation theory

Hidden observer

SELF-TEST PRACTICE QUIZ

From the Key Terms select that which best matches the following (Note: Not every Key Term will be used.):

1. _____ Loss of feeling or responsiveness to pain as a result of hypnosis

2. _____ According to Hilgard, the part of consciousness that is detached from hypnotic influence

3. _____ Re-experiencing past events in one's life due to hypnosis

4. _____ A form of meditation practiced by repeating a mantra

5. _____ An inability to recall what happened during hypnosis

6. _____ Belief that hypnosis is a state of divided consciousness

7. _____ A hypnotic suggestion about behavior once an individual reawakens

8. _____ A sound or phrase chanted repeatedly

9. _____ An altered state of consciousness involving focused attention, deep relaxation, and heightened susceptibility to suggestion

a. Transcendental meditation (TM)

b. Mantra

c. Mindfulness meditation

d. Hypnosis

e. Hypnotic age regression

f. Hypnotic analgesia

g. Posthypnotic amnesia

h. Posthypnotic suggestion

i. Neodissociation theory

j. Hidden observer

10. A state where an individual remains alert and awake but is focused, relaxed, and contemplative is known as

    a. hypnosis.
    b. neodissociation.
    c. meditation.
    d. hypnotic stupor.

11. In mindfulness meditation, the goal is to focus on

    a. sensations as they occur.
    b. a mantra.
    c. posthypnotic suggestions.
    d. a lamp or candle.

12. In hypnosis,

    a. one is asleep.
    b. one is susceptible to suggestion.
    c. one is alert and focused.
    d. the hypnotist directs all behavior of the hypnotized individual.

13. Evidence regarding hypnosis

    a. verifies that it really is just role-playing.
    b. has demonstrated that hypnotized individuals share the same experiences as non-hypnotized individuals.
    c. shows that it has no lasting therapeutic value.
    d. does not substantiate any of the above.

14. In Hilgard's cold pressor test,

    a. subjects had one hand submerged in ice water.
    b. subjects reported excruciating pain.
    c. only hypnotized individuals were used as participants.
    d. hypnotism had no impact on individuals in the study.

15. Which statement about hypnosis is correct?

    a. It can be used to reduce pain.
    b. Some people are more hypnotizable than others.
    c. People may, as a result of suggestion, later be unable to recall what occurred while they were hypnotized.
    d. All of the above are correct.

ESSAY QUESTIONS

1. What have we learned regarding the value of meditation?

2. What are some experiences one may have while under hypnosis?

ANSWER KEY

1. Hypnotic analgesia

2. Hidden observer

3. Hypnotic age regression

4. Transcendental meditation

5. Posthypnotic amnesia

6. Neodissociation theory

7. Posthypnotic suggestion

8. Mantra

9. Hypnosis

10. c

11. a

12. b

13. d

14. a

15. d

SAMPLE ANSWERS TO ESSAY QUESTIONS

1.   Meditation, unlike hypnosis, is something everyone can do. Also, unlike hypnosis, meditation does not take the presence of another individual (the hypnotist) in order to be practiced, and the phenomenon is fairly well understood. Meditation involves deep relaxation combined with focused attention and an alert awareness. There are distinct physiological changes that accompany meditation—the individual is clearly experiencing a reduced state of arousal. Such complete relaxation is generally considered to have health benefits both physically and psychologically. In addition, meditation aids in reducing the experience of pain and stress and in treating psychological disorders such as anxiety and some addictions. As is often cited with regard to meditation, it is credited with expanding awareness and creating a state of inner peace.

2.   Hypnosis is an altered state of consciousness where the individual is very relaxed, is focused on the hypnotist's voice, and is more susceptible to suggestion. Not everyone can be hypnotized, but those who are can be helped with physical or psychological problems they are facing. Under hypnosis, an individual may experience an age regression (going back to re-live earlier childhood events) or hypnotic analgesia (reducing experience of pain). Hypnotic suggestion combined with other forms of therapy helps individuals who wish to quit smoking or lose weight. It has also been shown to help our immune system function better during stress.

MODULE 4.4 ALTERING CONSCIOUSNESS THROUGH DRUGS

LEARNING OBJECTIVES

After you have mastered the information in this unit, you will be able to:

*   Differentiate between drug use and drug dependence

*   Discuss the different types of psychoactive drugs and their effects

*   Explain the factors that contribute to alcohol and drug abuse problems

*   Discuss the treatment alternatives for people with drug problems

OUTLINE

I.   Use of Drugs
     A.   To change state of waking consciousness
     B.   Psychoactive drugs—chemical substances that act on brain (mental state is affected)
          1.   Includes both legal and illegal drugs
II. Drug Abuse
     A.   Repeated use causes or aggravates personal, occupational, or health-related problems
     B.   Maladaptive or dangerous use of a chemical substance
     C.   Impairs one's ability to function effectively
III. Drug Dependence
     A.   Individual compelled to use or unable to resist drug despite harm that it causes
     B.   Physiological (chemical) dependence—body chemistry has been changed due to repeated use
          1.   Withdrawal syndrome—painful symptoms when drug use abruptly stopped
          2.   Tolerance—need to increase the amount of drug taken to achieve same effect

      3.   Drug addiction—chemical addiction; physiological dependence involved
   C.   Psychological dependence—individual unable to control reliance on drug, but no physiological dependence involved
IV.   Depressants—reduce activity of central nervous system
   A.   Alcohol
      1.   Most widely used and abused depressant
      2.   Intoxicant—chemical substance that produces drunkenness
      3.   Impairs judgment, ability to concentrate, ability to evaluate consequences of behavior
      4.   Disinhibits—undesirable behaviors no longer blocked
      5.   Alcoholism—chemical dependence on alcohol
         a)   Few alcoholics fit "skid-row bum" stereotype
         b)   Very heavy use—body, especially liver, severely damaged
         c)   Moderate use of alcohol appears to have health benefits
   B.   Barbiturates
      1.   Calming or sedating drugs
      2.   Legitimate medical uses such as managing high blood pressure and epilepsy
      3.   Highly addictive: street drugs that induce state of euphoria, relaxation
      4.   Include pentobarbital, phenobarbital; (Quaalude is similar)
      5.   Induce drowsiness, slurred speech; impair motor activity and judgment
   C.   Tranquilizers
      1.   Depressants used to treat anxiety, insomnia
      2.   Less toxic than barbiturates
      3.   Dangerous in high doses, especially when combined with alcohol, other drugs
      4.   Include Valium, Xanax, Halcion
      5.   Potentially physiologically and psychologically addictive
   D.   Opioids (narcotics)
      1.   Highly addictive drugs; have pain-relieving and sleep-inducing properties
      2.   Include morphine, heroin, codeine, Demerol, Percodan
      3.   Produce a "rush" of euphoria; reduce awareness of problems
      4.   Legitimate medical use to treat pain
      5.   Similar to endorphins naturally produced by body
V.   Stimulants—heighten activity of central nervous system
   A.   Amphetamines
      1.   Synthetic chemical form only
      2.   Increase heart rate, breathing, blood pressure
      3.   Low doses: heighten alertness, reduce feelings of fatigue
      4.   High doses: intense, pleasurable rush
      5.   Boost brain neurotransmitters dopamine and norepinephrine
      6.   Include Benzedrine, methamphetamine, Dexedrine
      7.   High doses may cause amphetamine psychosis, coma, death
   B.   Cocaine
      1.   Natural stimulant from coca plant
      2.   Increases brain levels of norephinephrine and dopamine
      3.   Increases arousal, feelings of extreme pleasure
      4.   High is shorter than that produced by amphetamines
      5.   Regular use damages heart, other organs
      6.   Highly physically and psychologically addictive; produces intense cravings
   C.   MDMA (Ecstasy)
      1.   Produces mildly euphoric and hallucinogenic state
      2.   Increases bodily arousal; undesirable psychological and cognitive effects
      3.   Physical consequences; high doses may cause death

    D.   Nicotine
       1.   Mild stimulant, highly addictive
       2.   Increases physiological arousal but also feelings of calmness and relaxation
       3.   Physiological and psychological dependence
       4.   Smoking is the major preventable cause of death in the US and the world
    E.   Caffeine
       1.   Mild stimulant, found in coffee, tea, chocolate
       2.   Physiological dependence, but most can be controlled
       3.   Enhances alertness; may increase risk of miscarriage

VI. Hallucinogens
    A.   Alter sensory perceptions (psychedelics)
    B.   May induce relaxation but also paranoia or panic in others
    C.   Psychological but not physical dependence
    D.   LSD—"trip" produces vivid hallucinations and other sensory distortions
    E.   Mescaline, Psilocybin, PCP
    F.   Marijuana
       1.   Most widely used illicit drug in Western world
       2.   Alters perceptions; may induce hallucinations
       3.   Can lead to psychological dependence; possibly physical dependence as well
       4.   Lower doses: relaxation, heightened awareness of bodily sensations
       5.   Higher doses: nausea, disorientation, paranoia

VII. Understanding Drug Abuse
    A.   Social and behavioral context
       1.   Peer pressure
       2.   Unemployment
       3.   Cultural norms and attitudes
    B.   Physical factors
       1.   Genetics
       2.   Neurotransmitters
    C.   Psychological factors
       1.   Hopelessness, sensation-seeking
       2.   Self-medication, to relieve anxiety
    D.   Cognitive factors: positive expectations and attitudes

VIII. Drug Treatment
    A.   Most effective programs use a variety of approaches
    B.   Detoxification—eliminating chemical dependency
    C.   Confront underlying psychological problems
    D.   May use therapeutic drugs (such as methadone) as well

IX. Exploring Psychology: Binge Drinking
    A.   Large quantity of alcohol consumed on one occasion
    B.   Strong predictor of later alcoholism
    C.   Individual at risk of death from overdose

SUMMARY

In this module you learn of other ways our consciousness may be altered—in this case via chemical means by using legal and illegal drugs. Most drugs do not affect our mental state; however, psychoactive drugs do. These are chemicals that literally act on the brain and change how it functions. Psychoactive drugs affect neurotransmitter activity in the brain. They may also occupy or otherwise impact the neurotransmitter sending and receiving sites.

Essentially everyone uses drugs—we drink coffee, tea, or colas, and many individuals still smoke despite the demonstrated health risks. Alcohol, of course, is very widely used. Some drugs are vital to the treatment of physical disorders. They may control pain, treat epilepsy, or anesthetize a patient during surgery. Drug use becomes drug abuse when obtaining and using a drug becomes the focus of one's existence. All other aspects of one's life—occupation, personal health, relationships with loved ones—take second place. At this point the individual is physically or psychologically addicted. Physiological dependency means the body's chemistry and chemical functioning literally have been changed as a result of repeated use of a drug. Psychological dependency means an individual is unable to cope with life without relying on the drug, though no true chemical dependency is present. Some drugs are strictly psychologically addictive; others have both physiologically and psychologically addicting capacities. Drug addiction means an individual is both compulsive about obtaining and using a drug and is chemically dependent upon it.

Legal and illegal drugs are categorized in various classifications depending upon the effect the particular drug has. Some drugs decrease arousal; these are classified as depressants. Some drugs increase arousal and activity—these are known as stimulants. A third category of drug classification is that of hallucinogens. Hallucinogens change sensory perceptions. They will create, as the name implies, hallucinations—the world perceived by the individual using these drugs is not as it actually exists. Sensory input is distorted

Depressants include alcohol, barbiturates, tranquilizers, and opioids. They reduce the activity of your central nervous system; in other words, your body slows down. Depressants typically have a calming effect, inducing feelings of relaxation and perhaps relief. Heart rate, breathing, and other bodily activities are reduced. These drugs can be quite dangerous because, in sufficient quantity, vital bodily processes are halted altogether. Depressants typically are highly addictive. They also are especially lethal when combined with other drugs. Drug users are drawn to depressants because they calm an individual and may create feelings of euphoria.

Stimulants arouse the body, and increase the rate of physiological processes. The appeal of stimulants is that they create a "rush." The individual using stimulants may feel a physiological "high"—they feel particularly alert, focused, and unusually sharp or perceptive. Interestingly, others around a drug user may not share this view! The class of stimulants includes amphetamines (methamphetamine or "speed" is one example), cocaine, and MDMA (Ecstasy). Legal stimulants include both nicotine (found in tobacco products) and caffeine, which is found in coffee, tea, cola, and chocolate foods and drinks.

Hallucinogens include LSD, marijuana, and PCP. These drugs may create states of delirium or vivid hallucinations. Hallucinogens are also known as psychedelic drugs because the user feels particularly attuned to what is perceived as revealing sensory phenomena. These drugs can definitely be psychologically addicting; there is some evidence that they may also be physically addictive. They often create sensations of calmness and relaxation, but the use of hallucinogens is also associated with feelings of paranoia or panic. Marijuana is the most widely used illicit drug in the Western world. Cocaine is the second most frequently used.

There are many problems associated with drug use beyond the fact that many mentioned here are illegal and are controlled substances. Chronic drug use plays havoc with the body, disrupting and harming physiological organs and processes. It impacts the very functioning of the brain, changing the levels of naturally occurring neurotransmitters and affecting neural transmissions. High doses of drugs, and/or drugs taken in combination with other substances, can lead to permanent physical damage, coma, or death. There are psychological effects as well. Drug use may produce feelings of anxiety or paranoia. Users of LSD report flashbacks sometimes many years later. Because the human body develops a tolerance when drugs are used regularly, increasing amounts of the drug must be taken in order to achieve the same effect. Drug use can easily result in dependency, which disrupts the functioning of all other facets in one's life.

It is thought that drug dependency is the result of a number of factors. Some of these include genetic predisposition, social pressures, and self-medication. Very often substance abuse is a symptom of more serious underlying difficulties. To treat the drug abuse problem, the psychological precipitating factors must be addressed. Typically, a chemically dependent individual must undergo detoxification (addictive drugs are cleared from the body) before other therapies are undertaken. Drugs are addictive, sometimes highly addictive. The potential for physical and psychological harm is great.

KEY TERMS

Psychoactive drugs

Drug abuse

Polyabusers

Drug dependence

Physiological dependence

Withdrawal syndrome

Tolerance

Drug addiction

Psychological dependence

Depressants

Intoxicant

Alcoholism

Narcotics

Stimulants

Hallucinogens

Delirium

Detoxification

SELF-TEST PRACTICE QUIZ

From the Key Terms select that which best matches the following (Note: Not every Key Term will be used.):

1. _____ Clearing drugs or toxins from the body

2. _____ Chemicals that reduce the activity of the central nervous system; induce relaxation and euphoria

3. _____ A severe drug-related problem involving compulsive use of and reliance on a drug

4. _____ Drugs that alter or distort sensory input

a. Psychoactive drugs

b. Drug abuse

c. Polyabusers

d. Drug dependence

e. Physiological dependence

f. Withdrawal syndrome

g. Tolerance

h. Drug addiction

5. _____ Drugs that increase the activity of the central nervous system; increase alertness and arousal

6. _____ Lack of control over use of and physiological dependence on alcohol

7. _____ Body adjusts to regular drug use; increasing amounts of drug are needed to achieve same effect

8. _____ Maladaptive or dangerous use of a chemical substance; causes physical or personal harm

9. _____ Painful symptoms associated with abrupt cessation of use of a drug

10. _____ People who abuse more than one drug at a time

11. _____ Physical dependence on a drug due to repeated use that changes body chemistry

12. _____ Chemical substances that affect functioning of the brain; change mental state

13. _____ Confusion, disorientation, inability to focus attention; may result from use of a hallucinogen

14. _____ Chemical substance that induces a state of drunkenness

15. _____ Compulsive use of and reliance on a drug; no physiological dependency is apparent

16. _____ Addictive drugs that relieve pain, induce feelings of drowsiness; also called opioids

17. _____ Drug use involving both physiological and psychological dependency; cessation would result in withdrawal symptoms

i. Psychological dependence

j. Depressants

k. Intoxicant

l. Alcoholism

m. Narcotics

n. Stimulants

o. Hallucinogens

p. Delirium

q. Detoxification

18. Heroin, morphine, Demerol, and Percodan are in the class of
   a. stimulants.
   b. depressants.
   c. barbiturates.
   d. hallucinogens.

19. Which of the following is *not* a stimulant?

    a. Alcohol
    b. Cocaine
    c. Caffeine
    d. Nicotine

20. Psychoactive drugs are

    a. illegal substances.
    b. legal medications.
    c. street drugs.
    d. drugs that act on the brain, affecting moods of the user.

21. The difference between drug use and drug abuse is that in drug abuse, use of substances

    a. interferes with the ability to function effectively.
    b. causes physical damage to the user's body.
    c. puts one's employment and/or emotional relationships in jeopardy.
    d. does all of the above.

22. Chemical dependence is also known as

    a. psychological dependence.
    b. physiological dependence.
    c. chemical addiction.
    d. drug addiction.

23. Compulsive behaviors such as gambling, sexual addiction, and the like are known as _____ dependencies.

    a. disruptive
    b. non-chemical
    c. behavioral
    d. abusive

24. The most widely used and abused depressant is

    a. marijuana.
    b. caffeine.
    c. alcohol.
    d. cocaine.

25. Drugs that increase central nervous system activity are called

    a. stimulants.
    b. depressants.
    c. hallucinogens.
    d. barbiturates.

26. Which of the following is a risk associated with binge drinking?

    a. Higher risk of later alcoholism
    b. Unsafe or unplanned sexual activity
    c. Coma or dose from alcohol overdose
    d. All of the above

27. One problem with alcohol is that it has a(n) _____ effect, meaning that the user is more likely to exhibit foolish, reckless, or impulsive behavior.

    a. disorienting
    b. impairment
    c. disinhibiting
    d. aggressiveness

28. Depressants can kill because in high doses they
    a. destroy large areas of brain tissue.
    b. can stop functioning of vital bodily processes altogether.
    c. lead to aggressive behavior where an individual is likely to be physically attacked.
    d. lead to the use of other substances in large quantities.

29. The chronic use of chemical substances, especially in high doses, leads to
    a. physical problems such as cirrhosis of the liver.
    b. psychological problems such as paranoia and anxiety.
    c. social and emotional problems such as job loss or difficulties with loved ones.
    d. all of the above.

30. An individual may use stimulants because of chemical properties that
    a. provide a sense of relaxation and relief.
    b. increase a sense of alertness or euphoria.
    c. decrease levels of dopamine and epinephrine in the brain.
    d. numb the awareness of pain or grief.

31. The most widely used illicit substance in the Western world is
    a. marijuana.
    b. cocaine.
    c. heroin.
    d. methamphetamine

32. Max used to drink one cup of coffee every morning, and that was enough to keep him awake. Lately, though, he has been finding he needs two cups of coffee to get the same effect. Max is experiencing
    a. psychological dependence.
    b. tolerance.
    c. withdrawal.
    d. drug abuse.

33. Which of the following is *not* a risk factor for drug abuse?
    a. Being unemployed
    b. Inherited tendency
    c. Negative expectations about drug effects
    d. High need for sensation-seeking

34. Caffeine is in the same class of mind-altering substances as
    a. nicotine.
    b. LSD.
    c. alcohol.
    d. phenobarbital.

35. Narcotics occupy the same brain receptor sites as
    a. dopamine.
    b. acetylcholine.
    c. endorphins.
    d. all of the above.

ESSAY QUESTIONS

1. Why are individuals drawn to use and abuse mind-altering substances?

2. What are some of the harmful effects of drug abuse and dependency?

3. What are the most effective methods we have for treating drug addictions?

ANSWER KEY

1. Detoxification
2. Depressants
3. Drug dependence
4. Hallucinogens
5. Stimulants
6. Alcoholism
7. Tolerance
8. Drug abuse
9. Withdrawal syndrome
10. Polyabusers
11. Physiological dependence
12. Psychoactive drugs
13. Delirium
14. Intoxicant
15. Psychological dependence
16. Narcotics
17. Drug addiction
18. b
19. a
20. d
21. d
22. b
23. b
24. c
25. a
26. d
27. c
28. b
29. d
30. b
31. a
32. b

33. c

34. a

35. c

SAMPLE ANSWERS TO ESSAY QUESTIONS

1. Individuals may be drawn to drug use for a variety of reasons. Depending in part on the individual's physiological and psychological characteristics, drug use may turn into drug abuse and dependency. The initial pull to try drugs or continue to use them may be social: If one's peers use drugs then such use may help make one more a part of the group. Drugs are often used as an escape to provide relief from psychological or emotional problems. They may help reduce feelings of anxiety and in fact help one feel more at ease and socially adept. Because drugs not only relieve pain, dull awareness of problems, create a "rush" or a "high," induce temporary feelings of euphoria, and yield the perception of heightened awareness—once used, the desire to experience again such feelings may become quite strong. In addition, it appears that there is a genetic predisposition regarding substances. Some individuals are more likely than others to become compulsive about drug use and exhibit addictive behaviors and patterns of use.

2. Drug use and dependency can negatively impact every facet of a person's life. Chronic drug use causes physical harm to the user's body, affecting bodily organs (such as the liver or heart) and various life-sustaining systems such as respiration. Brain functioning also is affected, and physiological dependency means that literally one's brain chemistry has been changed. Should an individual try to stop using drugs, there may be a period of severe withdrawal where the body, which has grown used to the presence of the chemical(s), readjusts to functioning without such drugs. When one becomes addicted, obtaining and using the drug(s) of choice becomes the focus of existence. Personal integrity and values, employment obligations, family and social matters, and even physical health take a back seat to compulsive behavior regarding the drug. Thus, all of these latter issues are neglected and tend to suffer. Drug use itself can cause death either directly through very high doses or via drugs that become lethal in combination with other drugs—or indirectly, in that functioning is impaired and one is more at risk for automobile accidents and the like. Also, when one is addicted, such an individual engages in behaviors (stealing, prostitution, and worse) where there is a high risk of physical harm or consequences.

3. To treat individuals with drug addiction, usually the most important first step is detoxification; that is, getting rid of all drugs that may be present in the user's system. Since this process is difficult and painful, often it takes place in an institution such as a hospital. Though chemical dependency may be the most obvious problem, typically there are underlying psychological difficulties that must be addressed if the individual is to become truly well. Following detoxification, persons with addictions usually begin therapy with professional counselors. The objective is not simply to get off drugs but to stay off drugs. Therapy is intended to help the individual face the psychological problems leading to drug use and drug abuse; psychological difficulties often involve problems with depression and self-esteem. In some cases, therapeutic drugs (like methadone for heroin users) may be used in combination with psychological counseling to help individuals resist falling back into old patterns of drug use.

MODULE 4.5 APPLICATION: GETTING YOUR Z'S

LEARNING OBJECTIVE

After you have mastered the information in this unit, you will be able to:

- Outline the steps you can take to combat insomnia

OUTLINE

I.   Suggestions for Developing Healthier Sleep Habits Include
    A.   Adopt a regular sleep schedule (go to bed and get up at about the same time every day)
    B.   Allow yourself to wind down naturally before trying to sleep
    C.   Have a routine before going to bed
    D.   Use your bed primarily for sleeping; not, for example, for reading or studying
    E.   If you can't sleep, get up and go somewhere else to relax
    F.   Avoid daytime naps if you miss sleep at night
    G.   Don't bring problems to bed
    H.   Use relaxing mental imagery
    I.   Engage in regular exercise during the day
    J.   Avoid caffeine and nicotine, especially in the afternoon
    K.   Think positively about your ability to sleep and to cope

SUMMARY

In this Application module, you learn about ways to combat insomnia and get a restful night's sleep. We must remember that sleep cannot be forced. It is helpful to engage in sufficient exercise during the day and avoid napping so we will be more prone to sleep at night. Following a routine before bedtime and reserving our bed primarily for sleep will help make sleep come more naturally. We can create a good sleep habit by going to bed and getting up at approximately the same time each day. It is important not to bring worries and concerns to bed and, if one cannot sleep, it is better to get up, go elsewhere to relax, then return to bed when relaxed and try again. Caffeine and nicotine are stimulants so they are to be avoided if one has sleep problems. We need a positive attitude about sleeping and our ability to sleep. Above all, worrying about lack of sleep only makes the condition worse. It is important to remember that we can get through a day and function, whether or not we have been able to get all the sleep we would like.

CHAPTER 4 APPLICATION EXERCISE

Observe a television, theatre, Internet, or video production where one or more characters in the cast have drug addictions. What are some of the behaviors they exhibit? Has their substance abuse been long-term and chronic, or has it begun recently? Briefly describe the setting of the program you have viewed, and then consider the following:

1.   Is the drug use or abuse glamorized?

2.   What seem to be precipitating factors leading to the drug use?

3.   Do cultural or social norms in the setting seem to support, tolerate, or frown upon the substance use and abuse?

4.   Is the user seeking treatment? If so, what does that treatment consist of?

5.   If you have a friend with a substance abuse problem, how might you help him or her?

CHAPTER 5

Learning

In Chapter 5 you are introduced to processes that are vital to human, and animal survival. These processes involve the ability to learn. If humans were not able to learn from experience—to assess, contemplate, adapt to, and make best use of our environment—our time on this planet would be short indeed!

Learning involves a relatively permanent change in behavior due to experience. Usually learning is adaptive; that is, it makes our behavior and existence more conducive to survival. However, this beneficial end product of learning is not always the case. We may learn things that are not helpful, but are, in fact, detrimental. Why would we learn such things when they are not truly productive? Probably because there is some stimulus, some reinforcer in the environment that can keep even maladaptive behaviors going. If we learn about learning, we can think more in depth about what we do and why we do it. If learning comes from experience, we can learn better ways to function in our world. Perhaps we behave in some ways that truly are not helpful. Learning why this behavior occurs can help us alter or eliminate it. Since much of learning does enhance and improve our well-being, understanding how the processes occur will help us maximize the experience.

Learning is generally thought to come from three basic sources. Fundamental to our understanding of learning is the premise that environment and experience play a tremendous role. In fact, early well-known psychologists, such as John Watson and B. F. Skinner, insisted that only observable behaviors should be studied. They chose to disregard any processes that were not visible to the eye. Not surprisingly, then, two of the three major categories regarding learning deal strictly with experiences relating to the external environment. These two categories are classical conditioning and operant conditioning. A third source for learning is that due to cognitive processes. The first two sources are, of course, easier to study. The impact of experience with the environment is clear. The latter process, cognitive learning, is harder to study because such learning takes place almost entirely within the head. Some behaviorists argue that cognitive learning does not really occur. The debate continues and is difficult to settle. This state of affairs is likely to continue since, at least at present, we cannot see the actual process that is the subject of contention!

Classical conditioning was first discovered and introduced by Ivan Pavlov. He was not a psychologist and was not researching learning—but he found that dogs used in his digestion studies secreted saliva when he did not expect them to. Why would they salivate when no food was actually present? Pavlov's work is a fine example of how some of our most worthwhile advances are discovered by accident. The animals had learned (just like you and your pets might!) that a food dish, or the handler, or even certain sounds, were associated with the presence of food, which they could eat. The neutral stimulus (the dish, or a tone) was perceived as having characteristics like the unconditioned stimulus (the food), and thus, with time, came to elicit a response from the organism.

Operant conditioning is best known as the work of B. F. Skinner. Skinner built upon the earlier findings of Edward Thorndike. In operant conditioning, consequences of behavior have everything to do with whether that behavior will be learned. Simply put, we adopt and exhibit behaviors that (based on past experience) we know will lead to pleasant outcomes. We minimize the appearance of behaviors when we have learned they likely will have unpleasant consequences. Note that classical conditioning tends to be built upon reflexive, or wired-in, behaviors. It deals predominantly with the learning of feelings and emotions. Operant conditioning is a more conscious experience; the learner here is more actively and intentionally involved. Through operant conditioning we learn a huge array of different skills. In general the voluntary, motor nervous system is involved.

Cognitive learning, mentioned above, deals with unseen mental processes. These include such activities as thinking, problem solving, and mental imagery. Human beings are able to learn much both from experience and from reasoning. How very fortunate we are that we have this great capacity to learn! How fortunate, also, that so many enriching learning opportunities come our way.

MODULE 5.1 CLASSICAL CONDITIONING: LEARNING THROUGH ASSOCIATION

LEARNING OBJECTIVES

After you have mastered the information in this unit, you will be able to:

- Define learning

- Describe classical conditioning

- Discuss the roles of extinction, spontaneous recovery, stimulus generalization, discrimination, and higher-order conditioning in classical conditioning

- Explain the stimulus characteristics that strengthen conditioned responses

- Discuss the cognitive perspective on classical conditioning

- Provide some examples of classical conditioning in daily life

OUTLINE

I. Principles of Classical Conditioning
    A. Unconditioned stimulus (US)—stimulus that elicits a response from an organism with no learning needed
    B. Unconditioned response (UR)—a response by an organism to a stimulus that is based on reflexive behavior (no learning is needed)
    C. Neutral stimulus (NS)—a stimulus from the environment around the organism that does not initially elicit the response in question
    D. Conditioned stimulus (CS)—a previously neutral stimulus; through pairing with unconditioned stimulus comes to elicit conditioned response
    E. Conditioned response (CR)—a learned response; through pairing of CS with US becomes the reaction to an initially neutral stimulus
    F. Extinction—conditioned (learned) response disappears when CS repeatedly presented without pairing with the US
    G. Spontaneous recovery—conditioned response (CR) may reappear briefly if CS again presented at a later time
    H. Reconditioning—the quicker relearning of a conditioned response after extinction
    I. Stimulus generalization—CR elicited; is in response to stimuli similar to CS
    J. Stimulus discrimination—CR not elicited; stimuli presented are unlike CS
    K. Higher-order conditioning—previously neutral stimulus comes to elicit CR (after being paired with a CS that elicits the CR)
    L. Strengthening conditioned responses
        1. Frequency of pairings—the more often the CS is paired with the US, the stronger the CR will be

2. Timing—for strongest CR, CS must be presented first and remain during entire presentation of US
3. Intensity of US—stronger level of US will result in quicker conditioning than weak presentation of US

II. Cognitive Perspective on Classical Conditioning
   A. Learning not just via CS/US pairing
   B. Rescorla's research shows CS must be able to reliably predict occurrence of US (thus a cognitive component in classical conditioning)

III. Examples of Classical Conditioning
   A. Study of "Little Albert" (conditioning of fear response)
      1. Eleven-month-old boy used as subject (Watson & Rayner, 1920)
      2. Initially not afraid of a white rat presented to him
      3. Did respond naturally with fear to a loud noise
      4. Rat (CS) presented with loud noise (US)—eventually Albert feared the white rat
      5. Albert's fear generalized to other furry stimuli
   B. Phobias
      1. Excessive fears
      2. May be due to classical conditioning
      3. Behavior therapy—psychological treatment (such as for phobias) based on classical conditioning principles
   C. Positive emotions—these also may be learned via association (classical conditioning)
   D. Drug cravings—environment (such as a bar, party, or drug-using friends) may trigger desire for drug due to learned association
   E. Taste aversions—learned avoidance (such as of a food) due to prior unpleasant experience with it (e.g., nausea or vomiting)

IV. Conditioning the Immune System—animals' immune systems were suppressed (CR) when they drank a CS previously paired with an immune response suppressing drug (US)

SUMMARY

In this module you learn one of the ways our environment teaches us through pairings of neutral stimuli with things that we naturally (usually reflexively) already respond to. Your pets are a perfect example. Does your cat know where you keep the can opener? Does your dog respond to his leash or when you tear open a package that sounds like his dinner or the dog treat bag? Notice these learnings (these responses) did not occur initially. Your dog or cat first was enthusiastic just about the food itself. However, after repeated pairings (the can opener is always kept in the same drawer; you have to open the drawer to open the food tin; to your dog the leash comes to mean "Hurray! We are going out!"), these originally neutral stimuli come to signify the unconditioned stimulus—the food your pet will eat or the wonderful walk in the park. These are learnings of positive emotions. Classical conditioning can teach us both positive or negative associations. Your dog or cat may usually be very enthusiastic about the car (the car has come to signify an exciting trip with you, which may include many marvelous smells!). However, once that car is used to take the pet to the vet, where your pet may receive a shot or experience perhaps painful surgery—the car is no longer exciting. In fact, at least for a few trips, you might have to work hard to coax your pet back into the car. The car, a conditioned stimulus (CS), now has come to represent something unpleasant (the pain of a veterinarian visit) rather than something pleasant (you, that trip, and those wonderful smells…!).

Humans also learn much through classical conditioning. Typically, classical conditioning involves the learning of feelings or emotions. Generally it involves our autonomic nervous system—responses or reflexes that are already "wired in" to our functioning. The conditioning occurs when these naturally-eliciting stimuli are paired (usually repeatedly) with a stimulus to which at first we have a different, or no, reaction to. However, when the naturally-eliciting stimulus (maybe a very good meal, or social pleasures shared with warm and wonderful friends) is paired repeatedly with this neutral stimulus—eventually the neutral stimulus becomes a conditioned stimulus (CS)—it takes on the characteristics of the unconditioned stimulus (US). The unconditioned stimulus is the one to which we responded from the beginning. No learning was necessary. Notice that learning (experiencing the association of the CS with the US) is necessary for classical conditioning to occur. We may come to respond to the sight of that restaurant that serves such delicious meals or is the place where we always congregate with friends very dear to us. Advertising tries to sell us on products by combining a given product or logo with something we already like. Do you respond with feelings of interest and anticipation when you simply see the box from your favorite pizza shop?

The terms needed to understand classical conditioning are (1) the US (a stimulus from the environment around the organism which elicits a naturally-occurring reaction); (2) the UR (a naturally-occurring response from the organism; the response is to the presentation of the US); (3) the CS (a stimulus from the environment where the reaction of the learning organism was initially neutral); and (4) the CR—a learned response that now is elicited by the CS, though this reaction was not present prior to the CS/US experience.

We become classically conditioned to many things. If your room is a place where you are comfortable and experience many pleasant things, you have a positive response to it now (a CR) even though you may not have felt that way originally. If your sweetheart broke up with you on a warm summer evening in June down by the ocean, you may feel more despondent than charmed for a while by your summer ocean experiences. With time (due to the classical conditioning phenomenon known as extinction) the seashore and summer evenings will come to entrance you again. Phobias (excessive fears) may have their roots in classical conditioning, in that an early terrifying experience may become associated with the setting where the experience occurred. If you were in a serious car accident, for example, you may forever feel tense and clammy when you pass the location where that accident occurred.

It is important to remember that the environment and experience do teach us. For example, if you offer a baby a cookie or a bottle of juice or milk—the baby will take the food that is in your one hand rather than the $100 bill in your other hand! Notice our response to money (or even the sight of it) is learned, through classical conditioning. Fortunately, what we know about classical conditioning also helps us undo learned behaviors that actually are detrimental to us. Understanding the factors that cause us to learn by means of classical conditioning also helps us understand influences on our behavior. If we choose to, we can eliminate or change these behaviors.

KEY TERMS

Learning

Extinction

Conditioned emotional reaction (CER)

Classical conditioning

Spontaneous recovery

Unconditioned response (UR)

Reconditioning

Phobias

Unconditioned stimulus (US)

Stimulus generalization

Behavior therapy

Neutral stimulus (NS)

Stimulus discrimination

Conditioned taste aversions

Conditioned response (CR)

Higher-order conditioning

Immune system

Conditioned stimulus (CS)

SELF-TEST PRACTICE QUIZ

Matching Questions

From the Key Terms, select that which best matches the following (Note: Not every Key Term will be used.):

1. _____ Excessive fears of objects or situations

2. _____ A previously neutral stimulus is paired with a conditioned stimulus; comes to elicit the conditioned response

3. _____ The quicker relearning of a conditioned response following extinction

4. _____ A relatively permanent change in behavior due to experience

5. _____ Aversions to particular tastes; acquired via classical conditioning

6. _____ A learned response to an originally neutral stimulus (which has been paired with an unconditioned stimulus)

7. _____ A previously neutral stimulus; comes to elicit a learned response due to repeated pairing with an unconditioned stimulus

8. _____ The diminishing and disappearance of a conditioned response when the CS is no longer ever paired with the US

9. _____ An emotional response to a particular stimulus resulting from classical conditioning

a. Learning

b. Extinction

c. Conditioned emotional reaction (CER)

d. Classical conditioning

e. Spontaneous recovery

f. Unconditioned response (UR)

g. Reconditioning

h. Phobias

i. Unconditioned stimulus (US)

j. Stimulus generalization

k. Behavior therapy

l. Neutral stimulus (NS)

m. Stimulus discrimination

n. Conditioned taste aversions

o. Conditioned response (CR)

p. Higher-order conditioning

q. Immune system

r. Conditioned stimulus (CS)

10. _____ A stimulus that elicits a response from an organism where no learning or conditioning is necessary

11. _____ The spontaneous return of a conditioned response following extinction

12. _____ A therapeutic application of principles regarding conditioning and learning

13. _____ Learning, usually involving affective states, due to the pairing of a neutral stimulus with an unconditioned stimulus

14. _____ A response by an organism to an unconditioned stimulus

15. _____ The ability to differentiate, and not respond to, stimuli that are unlike a conditioned stimulus

16. _____ A stimulus that initially does not elicit a response; one may be learned later through conditioning

17. _____ An organism responds to a stimulus because it is similar to the original conditioned stimulus

18. _____ The system that protects the body from disease

19. Part of the concept of learning is that any change in behavior resulting from it is
    a. adaptive.
    b. relatively permanent.
    c. innovative.
    d. healthful.

20. Classical conditioning was first discovered by
    a. B. F. Skinner.
    b. John Watson.
    c. Sigmund Freud.
    d. Ivan Pavlov.

21. A response (where none exists initially) to a certain stimulus that is learned due to the pairing of that stimulus with one that reliably produces the response is
    a. a conditioned stimulus.
    b. a conditioned response.
    c. an unconditioned response.
    d. vicarious learning.

22. Your dog is very fond of Eatitall dog food. You typically feed your pet late in the afternoon and prepare her dish in the kitchen. If your pet starts hanging around in the kitchen in the late afternoon, you can assume that _____ is a conditioned stimulus.

    a. Eatitall dog food
    b. the kitchen
    c. saliva
    d. time

23. The love of your life drives a silver Volkswagen. Prior to meeting her you could care less about Volkswagens no matter what color they were. Now when you see a silver Volkswagen, your pulse quickens and your heart leaps. Your positive feelings for silver Volkswagens are

    a. conditioned stimuli.
    b. conditioned responses.
    c. unconditioned responses.
    d. foolishness.

24. Which of the following could be an example of a US-UR pairing?

    a. A man smiles whenever he thinks of his wife.
    b. A girl runs away when she sees the school bully.
    c. A woman gets drunk after consuming a lot of alcohol.
    d. A little boy gets excited when he hears the words *ice cream.*

25. The stimulus that becomes the CS was initially a(n)

    a. unconditioned stimulus.
    b. conditioned stimulus.
    c. neutral stimulus.
    d. random behavior.

26. One reason a stimulus from the environment around the organism is called an unconditioned stimulus is because

    a. it reliably produces a response.
    b. no learning is necessary for the organism to emit the response.
    c. the response elicited is in the organism's repertoire of behaviors.
    d. it has been repeatedly paired with a conditioned stimulus.

27. Ever since she watched a movie about a man-eating shark, Alisha has become afraid of all fish. This is because of

    a. stimulus discrimination.
    b. spontaneous recovery.
    c. higher-order conditioning.
    d. stimulus generalization.

28. Research by Robert Rescorla (1967, 1988) demonstrates that there is a cognitive component to classical conditioning. That is, not just any stimulus can be paired with a US and come to elicit a conditioned response. Rescorla's findings indicate that the CS must

    a. be familiar to the learning organism.
    b. be easy to discriminate.
    c. reliably predict the US.
    d. exhibit all of the above.

ESSAY QUESTIONS

1. Briefly explain how the process of classical conditioning works.

2. From each of the following two episodes, pick out the US, the UR, the CS, and the CR. For each episode, explain why you made the choices that you did:

   a. Every summer, Alan went up to the lake cottage with his family and friends. He left his work and worries at home. He and his friends would often fish, swim, or go boating. They had many good times and many good meals at the cottage. Alan has taken pictures of the lake and cottage and has them posted around his office. Whenever he looks at the pictures, he feels peaceful and happy.

   b. Your mother was quite sick during much of your childhood. She often was hospitalized, and you would visit her there. Your mother was uncomfortable in the hospital and many pieces of medical equipment were in the room and attached to her body. Eventually, she died while she was at the hospital. To this day you despise hospitals, and feel sick and full of dread whenever you go near one.

3. There are several features of the classical conditioning process that can help speed up or strengthen the learning of the conditioned response. What are these? Explain each.

ANSWER KEY

1. Phobias

2. Higher-order conditioning

3. Reconditioning

4. Learning

5. Conditioned taste aversions

6. Conditioned response

7. Conditioned stimulus

8. Extinction

9. Conditioned emotional reaction (CER)

10. Unconditioned stimulus

11. Spontaneous recovery

12. Behavior therapy

13. Classical conditioning

14. Unconditioned response

15. Stimulus discrimination

16. Neutral stimulus

17. Stimulus generalization

18. Immune system

19. b

20. d

21. b

22. d

23. b

24. c

25. c

26. b

27. d

28. c

SAMPLE ANSWERS TO ESSAY QUESTIONS

1. In classical conditioning, we learn to have an affective response of some kind to a stimulus that did not elicit that type of response earlier. The response (a conditioned response) is learned because the one stimulus, originally known as the neutral stimulus, comes to represent the unconditioned stimulus because the two have been paired. We learn to associate the conditioned stimulus (CS) with the unconditioned stimulus (US), since they have occurred together. Such learning, or classical conditioning, takes place best if the CS and US are paired together repeatedly. This learning may happen to us (as in the learning of phobic reactions) without our intentionally taking part in the process. If the CS is presented many times without being combined with the US, extinction will occur—that is, the learned response (CS) will eventually disappear. We may respond also to stimuli similar to the CS (stimulus generalization), and not respond to stimuli that are sufficiently unlike the CS (stimulus discrimination).

2.

   a. US: good food, pleasant social times; UR: happiness and peace in response to the good food and pleasant social times; CS: pictures of the lake and cottage where the pleasant times occurred; CR: happiness and peace in response to looking at the lake and cottage pictures.

   b. US: Suffering, death and loss of mother; UR: child's unhappiness in response to this loss; CS: Hospital where death and loss took place; CR: unhappiness now experienced in response to seeing the hospital.

3. Classically conditioned responses may be strengthened by (a) frequent pairings of US and CS, (b) timing, and (c) using a greater intensity of US. In other words, the more often an organism experiences the pairing of a US with a CS, the stronger the learning (as evidenced by the CR) will be. Also, it is quite important that the CS be presented first and followed rather promptly by the US. The CS must be present during the entire time the US is administered in order for maximal learning to take place. The stronger the intensity of the US presented, the more quickly classical conditioning will take place.

MODULE 5.2 OPERANT CONDITIONING: LEARNING THROUGH CONSEQUENCES

LEARNING OBJECTIVES

After you have mastered the information in this unit, you will be able to:

- Explain Thorndike's Law of Effect

- Describe operant conditioning

- Discuss the different types of reinforcers

- Compare and contrast the schedules of reinforcement

- Explain how schedules of reinforcement are related to learning

- Discuss differences in the effects of reinforcement and punishment

- Describe applications of operant conditioning

OUTLINE

I.   Thorndike and the Law of Effect
    A.   Used animals for research because they were easier to study
    B.   Was a student of William James at Harvard
    C.   Learning occurs through trial and error
    D.   No cognitive component; consequences "stamped in" successful responses
    E.   Law of Effect: pleasant consequence increases likelihood behavior will be repeated; unpleasant consequence decreases

II.   B. F. Skinner and Operant Conditioning
    A.   Limit study to observable behavior
    B.   Radical behaviorism—all behavior (human and animal) determined by genetics and environment
    C.   Free will is an illusion, myth
    D.   Operant conditioning (also called instrumental learning)—consequences of a behavior determine probability of its recurrence
    E.   Reinforcer—pleasant/desirable outcome; increases likelihood behavior will occur again
    F.   Skinner box—for testing operant conditioning principles with animals
    G.   Superstitious behavior—learned when random behavior is accidentally paired with a reinforcing consequence

III. Principles of Operant Conditioning
    A.   Discriminative stimuli—signals reinforcement is available if correct response produced by organism
    B.   Positive reinforcement—desirable stimulus introduced after response occurs
    C.   Negative reinforcement—undesirable stimulus removed after response occurs
    D.   Primary reinforcer—intrinsically reinforcing; satisfies a basic need
    E.   Secondary reinforcer—reinforcing value (such as money) learned through association
    F.   Shaping—application of successive approximations method
    G.   Method of successive approximations—reinforcing broad or general attempts first; then reinforcing closer and closer steps toward ultimate desired behavior
    H.   Extinction—learned behaviors (responses) disappear if not ever paired with a reinforcer

IV. Schedules of Reinforcement
    A. Continuous reinforcement
      1. Every desired response is followed by a reinforcer
      2. Behaviors are learned most quickly with continuous reinforcement
      3. Learned behaviors also most quick to extinguish this way
    B. Partial reinforcement (ratio = number of responses; interval = passage of time)
      1. Fixed-ratio (FR) schedule—reinforcement given after a set number of responses (after every third, or sixth, or the like)
      2. Variable-ratio (VR) schedule
        a) Reinforcement based on number of responses; actual number varies
        b) Targeted number of responses is an average
        c) Example of VR schedule: slot machine
      3. Fixed-interval (FI) schedule—reinforcement given for desired response produced after a set amount of time has passed
      4. Variable-interval (VI) schedule
        a) Reinforcement based on passage of time; actual length of time varies
        b) Targeted passage of time is an average
        c) Example of VI schedule: "pop" quizzes in class
V. Escape Learning—organism learns a behavior in order to escape an aversive stimulus
VI. Avoidance Learning—organism learns a behavior in order to avoid an aversive stimulus
VII. Punishment
    A. Something unpleasant follows a behavior
    B. Introduce an aversive stimulus or remove a pleasant one
    C. Objective: decrease occurrence of undesirable behavior(s)
VIII. Applications of Operant Conditioning
    A. Biofeedback training
    B. Behavior modification—target desired behaviors; strengthen through operant conditioning (may use a token economy program)
    C. Programmed instruction—reinforce each step in a learning task
IX. Exploring Psychology: Should Parents Use Punishment as a Method of Discipline?
    A. Drawbacks of punishment
      1. May suppress but does not eliminate undesirable behavior
      2. Does not teach more preferable behavior
      3. Can create anger, fear, lowered self-esteem
      4. Used frequently, may become out of control
      5. Does not model desirable behaviors for children (teaches might makes right)
    B. Best approach is to reinforce desirable behaviors

SUMMARY

In this module you learn about another kind of conditioning—operant conditioning. Whereas classical conditioning involves mostly reflexive, "wired-in" behaviors, operant conditioning involves learning where the organism is much more an active and knowing participant. Operant conditioning includes the very many behaviors we as humans have learned in order to navigate our way through the world. These behaviors range from the simplest, such as tying a shoe or jotting down notes, to more complex such as a complicated dance step, driving a car, building a house, or preparing for your Ph.D. Your ability to speak, feed and dress yourself, ride a bike, use the microwave, participate in a classroom, study for an exam, behave in social settings, find your way to Paris or the movie theater—these behaviors and many more were learned predominantly through operant conditioning. Notice these behaviors almost entirely involve motor skills. Thus, operant conditioning makes extensive use of the voluntary nervous system.

Animals, too, learn by the same means as you, and they were the most used research subject when early studies on operant conditioning began.

Edward Thorndike (1874–1947) was the first to study operantly-learned responses. He used animals for his research because they were less complex than humans. Based on his work with animals, Thorndike concluded that all learning was trial and error. When an organism happened to stumble upon an appropriate behavioral response (such as running the correct pathway in a maze), the animal was more likely to utilize that behavior in the future because it met with a desirable outcome (the food reward at the end of the maze). Thorndike did not believe that the animals had any insight or cognitions regarding this learning process. Rather, it was his view that the pleasurable outcome "stamped" the behavior pattern into the brain.

To fully understand operant conditioning, you must be aware of the great impact of consequences. Behaviors (conditioned responses) learned through classical conditioning depend mostly upon how frequently the CS is paired with the US. This pairing comes before the learned response is made. For responses learned through operant conditioning, the outcome of any behavior (even if the behavior is random) influences heavily whether that response will be made again. Psychologically well-adjusted people generally like pleasant outcomes and much prefer them to other, more unpleasant outcomes. We learn from our earliest days to perform or exhibit the behaviors that have pleasurable consequences for us. These consequences might be a smile, praise, or a cookie when we've managed to say the word correctly. A behavior that we learn leads to something unpleasant is not a behavior we are likely to repeat any time soon. Thus, via experiences with our environment, much of our long-term behavior is shaped. It should be noted that in the ideal world, "good" behaviors would result in positive outcomes, and poor or harmful behaviors would result in unpleasant consequences. That is the ideal world. However, in our world, unfortunately sometimes good behavior, or even very good behavior, goes unnoticed and unappreciated. In contrast, undesirable behavior (disrupting class, knocking over a lamp, bombing innocent people) may inadvertently be encouraged due to all the attention it receives.

B. F. Skinner built upon Thorndike's ideas and noted that the organism *operates* on the environment; hence, the term *operant conditioning*. Good outcomes are called reinforcers because they literally strengthen a behavior (like reinforced concrete). Where the consequence of a response is pleasant, the response is more likely to occur again. Both positive and negative reinforcers increase the likelihood that a behavior will occur again. Whenever you see the word "reinforcer," keep in mind that that is the case. However, a positive reinforcer is better! Positive reinforcers mean something good is introduced into the environment for you. A negative reinforcer is still a good thing to have—it is removing something from your environment that has been unpleasant for you. *Punishment* is a term with which you are already familiar, and its meaning in operant conditioning is similar to what you already know. Punishment is an unpleasant consequence, and its intended impact is to reduce the likelihood that the behavior it follows will occur again. We must be careful in our use of punishment. Also, reinforcers are most effective if, once a response is learned, they occur on a partial, rather than a continuous, schedule. Behavior modification is one very useful application of operant conditioning.

KEY TERMS

Law of Effect

Negative reinforcement

Schedule of partial reinforcement

Radical behaviorism

Primary reinforcers

Operant conditioning

Secondary reinforcers

Escape learning

Operant response

Shaping

Avoidance learning

Reinforcer

Method of successive approximations

Punishment

Skinner box

Behavior modification

Superstitious behavior

Schedules of reinforcement

Token economy program

Discriminative stimulus

Schedule of continuous reinforcement

Programmed instruction

Positive reinforcement

Computer-assisted instruction

SELF-TEST PRACTICE QUIZ

From the Key Terms, select that which best matches the following (Note: Not every Key Term will be used.):

1. _____ Increases the likelihood that a behavior will occur again by removing an unpleasant stimulus

2. _____ A process of learning where consequences are crucial in determining whether or not a response will occur again

3. _____ A system of reinforcement where some, but not all, responses are reinforced

4. _____ A kind of programmed instruction, guiding and reinforcing the student step by step

5. _____ Reinforcers that gain their reinforcing power through being associated with a reinforcer that meets a basic need

a. Law of Effect

b. Negative reinforcement

c. Schedule of partial reinforcement

d. Radical behaviorism

e. Primary reinforcers

f. Operant conditioning

g. Secondary reinforcers

h. Escape learning

i. Operant response

j. Shaping

k. Avoidance learning

l. Reinforcer

6. _____ Behavior acquired because a random act was accidentally reinforced by a pleasant outcome

7. _____ A consequence designed to decrease the likelihood that the behavior it follows will occur again

8. _____ Increases the likelihood that a behavior will occur again by introducing a desirable stimulus following the emitted response

9. _____ Thorndike's principle regarding why learned behaviors reoccur

10. _____ Reinforcing increasingly more accurate manifestations of a learned response

11. _____ Applying operant conditioning principles in a systematic fashion to help improve behaviors

12. _____ A reinforcement schedule where every desired response from an organism is reinforced

13. _____ Responses an organism learns in order to avoid experiencing an unpleasant stimulus

14. _____ The belief that only environment and genetics determine behavior

15. _____ An apparatus designed by B. F. Skinner in order to study and test the impact of operant conditioning principles on learning

m. Method of successive approximations

n. Punishment

o. Skinner box

p. Behavior modification

q. Superstitious behavior

r. Schedules of reinforcement

s. Token economy program

t. Discriminative stimulus

u. Schedule of continuous reinforcement

v. Programmed instruction

w. Positive reinforcement

x. Computer-assisted instruction

16. What kind of learning is NOT explained by classical conditioning?
    a. The learning of modern-day musical themes
    b. The learning of voluntary responses such as motor skills
    c. The learning of feelings and affective responses
    d. Various responses elicited by a conditioned stimulus

17. Which psychologist coined the Law of Effect?
    a. Thorndike
    b. Pavlov
    c. Skinner
    d. Watson

18. Watson and Skinner both believed that

    a. vicarious conditioning was best researched by neurological lesioning.
    b. cognitive influences were the most complete explanation for instrumental learning.
    c. if a behavior could not be seen by the human eye, it was not appropriate for study.
    d. behaviors were often likely to reappear even though no reinforcer was administered.

19. Positive and negative reinforcers

    a. increase and decrease, respectively, the responses they follow.
    b. are both means to increase the likelihood that a behavior will occur again.
    c. involve the presentation of a desirable stimulus.
    d. involve the presentation of an undesirable stimulus.

20. Which of the following is an example of negative reinforcement?

    a. Studying hard earns you an A in your psychology course.
    b. Drinking too much leads to a hangover.
    c. Doing well at work earns you a bonus on your paycheck.
    d. Hitting the snooze button on your alarm clock makes the annoying noise go away.

21. When an organism is first learning a response, it is most effective if that organism is reinforced under a _____ schedule of reinforcement.

    a. fixed-interval
    b. fixed-ratio
    c. partial
    d. continuous

22. When a young child is first learning language, parents tend to respond with delight every time their little one makes a sound remotely like the family's native tongue. However, with time, a parent will repeat the proper pronunciation of a word and only respond as the child's pronunciation comes increasing close to the sound the parent modeled. What learning system is being utilized here?

    a. Foreign language learning principles
    b. Classical conditioning of operant events
    c. The method of successive approximations
    d. The neurological-maturation advancement system

23. Extinction in operant conditioning is likely to occur when

    a. a CS is promptly followed by a US.
    b. learned behaviors no longer have a reinforcer as a consequence.
    c. the CS is rarely or never paired with the US.
    d. a species has experienced no learning for a considerable length of time.

24. When an organism is reinforced after 3 minutes, 8 minutes, 4½ minutes, and so forth, and the average time span between reinforcers is 4 minutes, this is a_____ schedule of reinforcement.

    a. fixed-ratio (FR)
    b. variable-ratio (VR)
    c. fixed-interval (FI)
    d. variable-interval (VI)

25. Joel responded to an ad in the paper that promised he could make tons of money stuffing envelopes. Unfortunately, he only gets paid after every batch of one million envelopes. Joel will get paid (eventually) on a _____ reinforcement schedule.
    a.   variable interval
    b.   variable ratio
    c.   fixed ratio
    d.   fixed interval

26. A reinforcer that is effective without any prior learning by the organism is known as a _____ reinforcer.
    a.   positive
    b.   negative
    c.   primary
    d.   secondary

27. Behavior modification programs
    a.   utilize operant conditioning strategies.
    b.   identify desirable behaviors that will be strengthened through reinforcement.
    c.   may make use of a token economy system.
    d.   do all of the above.

28. A problem with fixed-ratio schedules of reinforcement for piecework (e.g., as in a factory) is
    a.   workers are not very motivated to produce.
    b.   quality may suffer if only quantity is rewarded.
    c.   absenteeism rates are likely to increase.
    d.   the very high level of resistance to extinction.

ESSAY QUESTIONS

1.   How does a negative reinforcer influence the occurrence of a behavior? Give an example.

2.   Why is a Skinner box particularly useful for studying operant conditioning?

3.   Why do positive reinforcers tend to increase the likelihood that a behavior will occur again?

4.   What are some concerns we have regarding the use of punishment?

ANSWER KEY

1.   Negative reinforcement

2.   Operant conditioning

3.   Schedule of partial reinforcement

4.   Computer-aided instruction

5.   Secondary reinforcers

6.   Superstitious behavior

7.   Punishment

8.   Positive reinforcement

9.   Law of Effect

10. Shaping

11. Behavior modification

12. Schedule of continuous reinforcement

13. Avoidance learning

14. Radical behaviorism

15. Skinner box

16. b

17. a

18. c

19. b

20. d

21. d

22. c

23. b

24. d

25. c

26. c

27. d

28. b

SAMPLE ANSWERS TO ESSAY QUESTIONS

1. A negative reinforcer influences behavior the same way any reinforcer would. A reinforcer is a stimulus that follows an organism's response, increasing the likelihood that this response will occur again. Both positive and negative reinforcers strengthen (that is, increase the likelihood of future occurrence) learned behaviors. Any reinforcer is considered a desirable outcome. This is the fundamental notion of operant conditioning—that consequences shape what we do and how we do it. Unlike a positive reinforcer, however, a negative reinforcer influences the occurrence of future behavior by taking away something unpleasant. A rather gruesome example would be an individual who is confined or beaten until he reveals national secrets. The behavior that is desired from the organism is giving up the information. The negative reinforcer is that the unpleasant experience will be removed as soon as this occurs. Such behavioral responses (revealing the secret information) are likely to increase due to the available negative reinforcer.

2. A Skinner box is particularly useful for studying operant conditioning phenomena because the environment in the box can be almost completely controlled by a researcher. All other stimuli except for the intended reinforcer(s) may be eliminated from the chamber. The organism in the box has no other access to food (the typical reinforcer used in a Skinner box), and probably is hungry. There is little else in the apparatus except the mechanism (usually a lever or bar) allowing for the learned behavioral response. With no other distractions, the animal is bound to soon exhibit the desired behavior (in this case, bar-pressing) even if purely by accident. The organism's response rate to the bar can be precisely measured. A researcher can vary reinforcement schedules easily in this highly structured environment. In the real world there would be too many other uncontrollable events taking place.

3.   A positive reinforcer increases the likelihood that the response it follows will occur again because gaining a positive reinforcer is a pleasant experience. The notion of working extra hard to experience something pleasant, and discontinuing a behavior if it leads to an unpleasant consequence, forms the very basis of Thorndike's Law of Effect. Humans (and animals) like pleasurable things. Once we learn that that pleasant outcome is a possibility, we will do what is within our means to make that experience occur again.

4.   Punishment is an aversive or unpleasant consequence to a behavior. It is administered with the intention of decreasing that behavior's occurrence. The organism being punished has an unpleasant experience following a response. It is true that the behavioral concept of punishment does have some usefulness in the shaping of how organisms act.

Problems with the use of punishment include that it doesn't really eliminate undesirable behavior. Nor does it teach an individual what behavior is more preferred. Parents who punish, especially with physical punishment, are modeling aggressive behavior. They are conveying to their children that "might makes right" and that the bully wins. The child who is punished may come to resent the parent who is punishing her. And, a frequently punished child starts to feel that he is not good or worthwhile. Anger and fear may be created, and the child's level of self-esteem is lowered.

MODULE 5.3 COGNITIVE LEARNING

LEARNING OBJECTIVES

After you have mastered the information in this unit, you will be able to:

- Define cognitive learning
- Define insight learning
- Define latent learning
- Define observational learning

OUTLINE

I.   Cognitive Learning
    A.   Mental processes that cannot be directly observed
    B.   Involves thinking, problem solving, mental imaging
    C.   Learning without the experience of direct reinforcement
II.   Types of Cognitive Learning
    A.   Insight learning
        1.   Kohler's (1927) research with chimpanzee Sultan—Sultan joins sticks to reach bananas
        2.   Problem solving did not occur with step-by-step approximations
        3.   Involves the sudden realization of the solution to a problem ("Aha!") while the matter is being reworked mentally
    B.   Latent learning
        1.   Tolman and Honzik (1930) for 10 days do not reward some rats placed in a maze
        2.   Eleventh day: now with a food reward, these rats run the maze with even fewer errors than rewarded rats
        3.   Apparent that unrewarded rats learned even though not reinforced
        4.   Learning only evident when reinforcement provided later

> 5. Cognitive map—mental representation of surrounding world (formed without actual reinforcement)
> 6. Implicit learning—new behaviors are learned without conscious effort
> C. Observational learning (vicarious learning)
>   1. Learn from simply watching the behavior (and consequences) of others
>   2. Practice and aptitude still very important
>   3. Learning most likely to occur when model is similar to learner
>   4. Learning most likely to occur when learner witnesses model's behavior being reinforced

SUMMARY

In this module you learn about a learning process that seems to take place almost entirely within the head. That is, no direct or overt interaction with the environment appears necessary. With operant conditioning, the learner absorbs and uses behaviors because the environment directs that he should do so. The learned behaviors are manifested because they lead rather reliably to pleasurable outcomes. Other behaviors are suppressed or not manifested because in the past they have been ignored—or worse, they met with consequences that were unpleasant. Thus, with operant conditioning, experience with and feedback from the environment is crucial. Cognitive learning is different, in that the learner comes up with or adopts new behaviors without any apparent direct reinforcement. Cognitive learning involves a learning process that is not outwardly visible. The results of the learning may, of course, be visible, but the process itself is not.

Cognitive learning consists of three basic types. The first is insight learning—the individual (or organism) may work and work with a problem, and no solution is immediately available. However, eventually there is a flash of understanding (of insight), and the solution to the problem comes to the individual all at once. The problem has perhaps been restructured in the head, and the learner suddenly comes to look at it in a different way. The second type of learning, latent learning, occurs where it seems the individual is making no effort to learn whatsoever. This type of learning was well demonstrated by Tolman and Honzik (1930). Rats placed in a maze where no reinforcer (food reward) was provided for 10 days in a row ran the maze better than rats who had been rewarded during those 10 days, once a reinforcer was provided to the previously non-rewarded rats. Tolman suggested that individuals create cognitive maps—a representation of the surrounding world created in the head of the organism. The last type of cognitive learning discussed in this section involves observational learning—that is, learning simply by watching the behavior (and behavior outcomes) of others. This is also known as vicarious learning (or modeling), and those whom we learn from are models. We are most likely to model the behaviors of individuals to whom we can relate and where we can see that given behaviors result in (at least for our model) desirable consequences.

KEY TERMS

Cognitive learning

Insight learning

Latent learning

Cognitive map

Implicit learning

Observational learning

SELF-TEST PRACTICE QUIZ

From the Key Terms, select that which best matches the following (Note: Not every Key Term will be used.):

1. _____ A mental representation of our surroundings that helps us find our way

2. _____ Learning by an organism that occurs without apparent direct reinforcement

3. _____ Mentally working through a problem until the solution suddenly comes to us

4. _____ Also known as vicarious learning, it is learning through watching the behavior (and behavioral consequences) of others

5. _____ Learning that occurs without reinforcement or apparent intent; the learning is only evident when reinforcement for it is provided later

a. Cognitive learning

b. Insight learning

c. Latent learning

d. Cognitive map

e. Implicit learning

f. Observational learning

6. The type of learning that seems to take place entirely in the head and involves reasoning, information processing, problem solving, and mental imagery is

   a. active intellectual contemplation.
   b. classical conditioning.
   c. operant conditioning.
   d. cognitive learning.

7. When Sultan the chimp was faced with bananas outside of his cage that he could not reach with his stick, he

   a. signed to his keeper that he needed the bananas.
   b. tried repeatedly and unsuccessfully with the stick to reach the bananas.
   c. combined his stick with another stick, thereby reaching the bananas.
   d. ate the apples and mangoes that were already available in his cage.

8. The type of learning evidenced by the chimp Sultan when he wanted the bananas he could not reach with his stick, is

   a. latent learning.
   b. observational learning.
   c. insight learning.
   d. rational learning.

9. How does cognitive learning differ from classical and operant conditioning?

   a. Cognitive learning involves processes that cannot be directly observed.
   b. Cognitive learning deals strictly with physiological responses to stimuli.
   c. Cognitive learning involves reinforcements but not punishments.
   d. Cognitive learning requires that you perform a behavior in order to learn it.

10. You have been invited to dinner with the governor of your state. You have no idea how to act, so you watch what other attendees around you do. The type of learning you are utilizing is
    a. latent learning.
    b. observational learning.
    c. insight learning.
    d. etiquette learning.
11. What is one argument that behaviorists present to dispute the existence of insight learning?
    a. The past history of reinforcement relative to the new learning must be considered.
    b. Insight learning really is another form of observational learning.
    c. Insight learning really is another form of latent learning.
    d. Insight learning does not involve trial and error in the head.
12. In interacting with others, all of us follow rules about how close we should stand to the other person. We do this even though we've never been formally taught any such rules, and most of us are not consciously aware of them. This is an example of
    a. latent learning.
    b. observational learning.
    c. insight learning.
    d. rational learning.

ESSAY QUESTIONS

1. A key feature to cognitive learning is that if the process truly exists, it involves learning by an organism without first having the experience of performing the learned behaviors (perhaps randomly or inadvertently) and/or being reinforced for them. What evidence can you think of that supports the notion that cognitive learning is a genuine phenomenon? What evidence can you think of that refutes this concept?

2. What is the most helpful thing you have learned through observational learning? Have you experienced insight or latent learning in your life? If so, relate what you learned and how you learned it.

ANSWER KEY

1. Cognitive map
2. Cognitive learning
3. Insight learning
4. Observational learning
5. Latent learning
6. d
7. c
8. c
9. a
10. b
11. a
12. a

SAMPLE ANSWERS TO ESSAY QUESTIONS

1. Evidence in support of cognitive learning includes the studies reported in this module (Kohler reporting Sultan's insight to combine both sticks; Tolman and Honzik's research with rewarded and unrewarded rats in a maze). Evidence also includes the many things we learn simply through thought or mental analysis. Behaviorists argue that the insight is not really a learning process in and of itself. Rather, they point out that the "insight" may be nothing more than the final step in a long process of trial-and-error efforts (with consequences for each). Behaviors leading up to the "insight" are the cumulative product of previous reinforcement and punishment.

    Cognitive learning really does exist, although it is not, of course, independent of past experience. Those of us who have labored long to arrive at a solution (and the solution is just not presenting itself at the time) know that there is a difference between having all the pieces of the puzzle and grasping how that puzzle fits together. Further trial and error simply does not help, though knowing what has worked in the past does. The mind reorganizes and reworks relevant aspects. Nothing new is added; rather, what is needed is a different or fresh way of looking at the same information. This new understanding is appropriately termed *insight*. Unlike operant conditioning, a solution gained through insight may mentally appear even when we are not actively working on the problem. Latent and observational learning, too, occur without any particular effort on the part of the learner. This is in contrast to operant conditioning where the learner *operates* on the environment. With latent and observational learning, we may not even know we have gained new information until the opportunity to use it presents itself later. Ultimately, much of learning is not a discrete experience. All components mentioned in this chapter play a part.

2. The student may relate important personal examples of each of the three cognitive learning types. Experiences that fit insight, latent, and observational learning categories must be distinguished from each other.

MODULE 5.4 APPLICATION: PUTTING REINFORCEMENT INTO PRACTICE

LEARNING OBJECTIVE

After you have mastered the information in this unit, you will be able to:

*   Outline the steps involved in putting reinforcement into practice

OUTLINE

I. Applying Reinforcement—the following are useful steps when trying to influence behavior
    A. Identify specifically the target behavior you wish to strengthen
    B. Make sure requests and instructions are clear
    C. Choose a reinforcer that is meaningful to the individual you are working with
    D. Explain how the reinforcer (contingency) will be used once the behavior occurs
    E. Administer the reinforcer
        1. If the desired behavior appears, reward it immediately
        2. If the individual does not perform the behavior, demonstrate and help
        3. Pair the reinforcer with praise
    F. Track the pattern of the desired behavior—how often does it occur?
    G. Gradually wean the individual from the reinforcer, but continue to give praise
II. Tips for Giving Praise Effectively to Children—(Praise is a powerful social reinforcer)
    A. Make eye contact, smile, give hugs

B.   Connect praise to specific behavior; praise effort
C.   Be sincere and avoid empty flattery
D.   Avoid using same words each time
E.   Keep statements positive, don't end with a negative comment

SUMMARY

In this Application module you learn how to shape and influence the behavior of others, especially children. Though intentional application of learning principles may seem manipulative, in fact the environment gives such encouraging or discouraging feedback to us hundreds of times each day. In addition, children (and adults!) function much better when their efforts are noticed and appreciated. We feel more capable of performing a behavior if we have received praise and recognition for it previously. Much of our ability to learn is, indeed, related to our beliefs and expectations regarding our abilities. Those beliefs predominantly come from feedback from the environment. The conscientious and effective application of reinforcement principles can do much to optimize the behaviors of individuals with whom you come in contact.

CHAPTER 5 APPLICATION EXERCISE

Is there a behavior you would like to change about yourself? Why do you think this behavior occurs? Where did it come from? What seems to keep the behavior going (what reinforces it)?

What would work for you as a different effective reinforcer? We have discussed conditioning others—it is possible to condition oneself! See if you can alter your own behavior using principles discussed here. Set up a reinforcement schedule, and give yourself two or three weeks to change.

CHAPTER 6

Memory

In Chapter 6 you are introduced to the many facets of memory. There is much that we know about memory and much we still have to learn. Memory can be compared to an information processing system. We need to get information in (encoding), store it (the specific phases of memory), and then get the information back out again when we need it (retrieval). Have you ever tried hard to learn something, but didn't? Did you ever think you'd never forget something—but you did? Certainly our memory is far from perfect! But, considering how complex and comprehensive our memory system is, it is remarkable that it works as well as it does!

Memory is the system by which we are able to retain information and bring it to mind. Encoded information comes from any of our senses, but most typically it takes the form of visual or auditory representations. The first stage of memory is the sensory storage phase. Here all input is kept very briefly in the sensory register. Sensory memory is fleeting—visual mental images last a fraction of a second. The auditory stimuli input (echoes) may last as long as 3 or 4 seconds. Though much information in sensory storage is transmitted no further, some is moved on into short-term memory (STM). Short-term memory is often also referred to as *working memory* because information in STM includes things we are "working on." These are things the brain is actively processing, mulling over, and so forth. Capacity in STM is actually rather limited. Research indicates we can retain about seven items, plus or minus two. We say *items* or *units* with regard to STM storage capacity, rather than a more specific term (like *words*), because information in STM can be chunked. That is, larger amounts of information may be broken up into convenient, perhaps more familiar units (chunks), and thus more information may be retained. For example, perhaps you had to remember the numbers: 0-7-8-1-2-1-9-0-7-6-3-7. That's more than seven, and looks a little cognitively demanding. How about if you recoded these numbers—into, let's say, 1776, 1987, 2003. Does this make things a little easier for you?

The duration for short-term memories is also rather brief, although it is longer than sensory memory. STM information may be retained typically up to about 30 seconds unless one begins to practice the information (called maintenance rehearsal) by repeating it over and over again (what you do when you've just looked up a telephone number, or the correct spelling of a word you need to use).

Most information, even if initially visual, is retained in STM in auditory form. Notice that the telephone number or word that you looked up was presented to you in the visual channel. Yet, to retain it in STM, you repeat the word or number to yourself (an auditory function). Converting even visual information to auditory form means we can recreate the stimuli for ourselves (we can repeat it) aiding our memory. Information is moved from short-term memory to long-term memory by a process called consolidation. Consolidation seems to occur in or be regulated by the brain structure known as the hippocampus. Memories are stored in brain cell units called neural networks.

Long-term memory (LTM) has features unlike either sensory storage or STM. Obviously, duration is much different—long-term memories can last a lifetime. Capacity is different as well, and it is believed that LTM capacity is essentially unlimited. We store many different kinds of information in LTM such as how to do things (procedural memory), who and what we know (declarative memory), and our own personal story (episodic memory). Information in LTM tends to be retained on the basis of semantics or meaning. (Note in STM it was on the basis of sound.)

Maybe it is easier to get information into LTM than to get it back out again. We have an array of theories regarding forgetting, among them decay theory, which suggests that we forget because information has not been used for some time. There is evidence for this theory, but there also is substantial evidence for interference theory—that other information, particularly if it is similar to what was originally learned, makes remembering more difficult. A lack of retrieval cues or failure to actually encode the original information also are some of the explanations for forgetting. One important thing to remember about memory is that our recollections may not be exact. This fact must be considered when evaluating eyewitness testimony or recovered repressed childhood memories.

MODULE 6.1 REMEMBERING

LEARNING OBJECTIVES

After you have mastered the information in this unit, you will be able to:

- Describe the basic processes and stages of memory

- Explain the constructivist theory of memory

- Describe flashbulb memories

- Discuss the factors that influence the accuracy of eyewitness testimony

- Discuss the controversy regarding recovered memories of childhood sexual abuse

OUTLINE

I.   Human Memory as an Information Processing System
    A.   Memory—the system by which we retain information and bring it to mind
    B.   Memory encoding—taking information in
        1.   Converting information into a form we can store
        2.   Acoustically—encoded by sound
        3.   Visually—encoded by mental image
        4.   Semantically—encoded by meaning
    C.   Memory storage—retaining information in memory (see Memory Stages, below)
    D.   Memory retrieval
        1.   Accessing stored information to make it available to our consciousness
        2.   Availability may be a function of retrieval cues
        3.   Encoding specificity principle—retrieval better when surrounding cues similar to those present when information learned (Tulving, 1983)
        4.   Context-dependent memory effect—retrieval best when in same setting
        5.   State-dependent memory effect—retrieval best when in same physiological or psychological condition
II.   Memory Stages—Three-Stage Model
    A.   Sensory memory
        1.   Very brief sensory information storage (few seconds at most)
        2.   Sensory register—temporary storage device for sensations
        3.   Iconic memory
            a)   Holds sensory visual images
            b)   Lasts fraction of a second
        4.   Eidetic imagery (photographic memory)
        5.   Echoic memory
            a)   Holds sensory auditory input
            b)   Lasts three or four seconds maximum

B. Short-term (working) memory—STM
   1. Holds information up to 30 seconds
   2. Most information stored acoustically
   3. "Working memory" because we are actively processing
   4. "Magic number": 7 (plus or minus 2) units can be stored
   5. Chunking—more remembered when restructured into units
   6. Maintenance rehearsal—repeating information to keep longer in STM
   7. Three-component model of memory
      a) Phonological loop—stores verbal/speech-based information
      b) Visuospatial sketchpad—stores visual and spatial information
      c) Central executive—coordinates both and interfaces with LTM
C. Long-term memory (LTM)
   1. Retains information for a longer period of time
   2. Essentially unlimited in capacity
   3. Consolidation
      a) Converting less stable STM information into LTM
      b) Needs at least twenty-four hours after learning to occur
      c) Both REM sleep and slow-wave sleep crucial to this process
   4. Information stored on basis of meaning (semantically)
   5. Elaborative rehearsal—focus is on meaning of material
   6. Semantic network model
      a) Leading model regarding LTM organization
      b) Information held via interlinking concepts
      c) Spreading activation—one concept triggers recall of related others
   7. Levels-of-processing theory
      a) Information held best depending on depth of level at which it is encoded or processed
      b) Elaborative rehearsal more effective than maintenance rehearsal
III. The Contents of Long-Term Memory
   A. Declarative memory (explicit memory)
      1. "Knowing that"
      2. Takes conscious effort to bring to mind
      3. Categories (organized by type or time frame)
         a) Semantic memory—compare to our storehouse of information
         b) Episodic memory—personal experiences, personal "story"
         c) Retrospective memory—memory of past events
         d) Prospective memory—keeping in mind future events
   B. Procedural memory
      1. "Knowing how"
      2. Engaged without conscious effort
      3. Less easy to explain verbally
      4. Involves motor or performance skills
      5. Types of procedural memory
         a) Implicit memory—memory evoked without intentional effort (e.g., pleasant memories when hearing a favorite song)
         b) Explicit memory—intentional effort needed to bring it to mind (e.g., remembering the capital of a state or country)
IV. The Reliability of Long-Term Memory
   A. Constructionist theory
      1. Memories not a perfect copy of past experience
      2. Memories created from integrated pieces of stored information

3.   Possibility that memories can be distorted
   B.   Flashbulb memories
      1.   Vivid, lasting, highly detailed memories
      2.   Derived from extremely salient past events
      3.   Also may be inaccurate, distorted (like other LTM)
   C.   Eyewitness testimony
      1.   Possible that it is inaccurate, distorted
      2.   Misinformation effect—suggestions lead to inaccuracies in recall
      3.   Accuracy involves the following factors:
         a)   Ease of recall—slower response indicates less accurate
         b)   Degree of confidence—more confident eyewitness not necessarily more accurate
         c)   General knowledge about a subject—more knowledgeable witness is more accurate regarding that particular subject
         d)   Racial identification—more errors made when identification crosses racial lines
         e)   Types of questions—leading, suggestive questions result in more errors from witnesses than open-ended questions
V.   Exploring Psychology: Are Recovered Memories Credible?
   A.   Often a lack of corroborating evidence
   B.   Some memories may be genuine; some surely are false or distorted
   C.   Very difficult to differentiate between false vs. true

SUMMARY

In this module you learn about remembering. All that we learn would not be very helpful to us if we could not retain it, retrieve it, and use it over time. This is the role of memory.

There seem to be different kinds of memory. You yourself know that some things you forget instantly, while others you remember seemingly forever. In fact, our memory does have stages—there are different kinds of memory storage, and each has its own characteristics and properties.

Before we can store information, we first must get it into our awareness. This is known as encoding. Our ability to remember is much like an information processing system. Sensations from the world (transmitted to us by our sensory receptors, thus providing sensory input) must be encoded before they can become a part of our memory. Once information is encoded, if it is processed further then it is stored (this is the memory phase) and then, in order to use it again, information must be retrieved. If no information was ever stored (there is, in fact, no memory), it can never be retrieved.

Our memory storage also has three phases, or components. The first, corresponding to the encoding process mentioned above, is sensory memory. All our sensory input arrives here. Most information is in the form of visual (iconic) or auditory (echoic) memory. Visual memory lasts a fraction of a second, and auditory input lasts no more than three or four seconds. It is a good thing that auditory memory lasts as long as it does! Because we speak in sentences (and thus information enters our brain in a linear fashion, one auditory unit after another), we need to be able to retain earlier tidbits of information while continuing to process current input. If our auditory memory were not three or four seconds long, we would forget the beginning of a sentence before our speaker arrived at the end! Notice that with visual input this longer storage capacity is not necessary. Visual images are presented all at once.

The second phase of memory storage is short-term memory, often abbreviated as STM. Short-term memory is also known as *working memory* because it is what we are actively using or working on. It contains everything we are conscious of at the moment—but we may be attending to only a small portion of all that is available. This ability to selectively attend to what we will process keeps us from being overloaded by all the sensory input coming our way. Short-term memory lasts, obviously, longer than sensory memory—about 30 seconds, unless we use maintenance rehearsal to keep information in storage longer. Capacity for STM is not large—about seven units of information, give or take. Seven units is so typical of regular STM storage that it is known as the "magic number," or "Magic 7." We say *units* rather than, for example, *words*, because information may be chunked. That is, we may take a larger amount of information and recode it into units (U-T-A-A-S-W may be recoded as USA TWA, for example), and thus we can retain much more in STM. Information in short-term memory tends to be stored on the basis of sound. While there are a number of suggested explanations for how STM works, the leading model is the three-component model. This model proposes that one part of short-term memory simply monitors, coordinates, and integrates two other facets, which process auditory and visual information, respectively.

The third and last phase of memory storage is long-term memory, abbreviated LTM. Long-term memory again has its own very unique characteristics. While STM memory capacity is very limited, LTM storage capacity is essentially unlimited. STM information tends to be stored acoustically; in LTM, it is stored semantically (on the basis of meaning). STM storage is brief; LTM information may be stored indefinitely. Information moves from STM to LTM by a process known as consolidation. Interestingly, consolidation occurs some time after (as much as 24 hours or more) the information is first learned. Both REM (rapid-eye-movement) sleep and slow-wave sleep seem to play a very important role in the consolidation process. Elaborative rehearsal (practicing information by focusing on its meaning) seems a better strategy than maintenance rehearsal to move information from STM to LTM.

There are many aspects of long-term memory. It stores all kinds of things—from what we know (declarative memory) to knowing how to do things (procedural memory). We may have to work to invoke certain memory processes (such as semantic or explicit memory), but others may happen effortlessly (such as procedural or implicit memory). Though our long-term memory is remarkable, as is indeed the entire memory process, LTM is not entirely flawless. Research suggests that rather than being a precise, exact record of all we have experienced, LTM is more piece-meal in how information is stored. When we want to retrieve information (call upon a memory), research suggests the LTM information is *reconstructed.* That is, the bits and pieces are recalled, and in remembering we integrate these pieces to form a coherent whole. According to research, the whole that is remembered is not necessary exactly what happened during the actual event or experience remembered. Thus, because of this research, eyewitness accounts and recovered repressed childhood memories can be fallible. Both, for example, may be influenced by how requests for the remembered information may be phrased. If the request contains some cues suggesting either directly or indirectly what happened, these suggestions can and do impact what is recalled.

KEY TERMS

Memory

Memory encoding

Memory storage

Memory retrieval

Retrieval cues

Encoding specificity principle

Context-dependent memory effect

State-dependent memory effect

Three-stage model

Sensory memory

Sensory register

Iconic memory

Eidetic memory

Echoic memory

Short-term memory (STM)

Working memory

Chunking

Maintenance rehearsal

Phonological loop

Visuospatial sketchpad

Central executive

Long-term memory (LTM)

Consolidation

Elaborative rehearsal

Semantic network model

Levels-of-processing theory

Declarative memory

Semantic memory

Episodic memory

Retrospective memory

Prospective memory

Procedural memory

Implicit memory

Explicit memory

Priming task

Constructionist theory

Memory schema

Flashbulb memories

Misinformation effect

SELF-TEST PRACTICE QUIZ

From the Key Terms select that which best matches the following (Note: Not every Key Term will be used.):

1. _____ Storage phase of memory that holds initial input when first encoded; very brief

2. _____ A belief that how well information is stored is a function of the mental depth at which it is processed

3. _____ Possible memory distortion due to suggestions made during retention interval

4. _____ STM information retained longer because the information is intentionally repeated

5. _____ A view that memory retrieval will be more successful when the environment is like that when information was first stored

6. _____ Sensory storage component that very briefly holds visual images

7. _____ Also called *working memory;* holds 7 (plus or minus 2) units of information

8. _____ Information stored on the basis of meaning

9. _____ The memory phase where an unlimited amount of information may be stored, perhaps indefinitely

10. _____ The system that allows us to retain information and bring it to mind

11. _____ Sensory storage component that very briefly holds auditory input

12. _____ Retaining more information in STM by recoding it into manageable units

13. _____ Recalling information better because one is in the same environment as where the experience occurred

14. _____ Recalling information better because one feels physiologically or psychologically much like one did when the experienced occurred

a. Memory
b. Memory encoding
c. Memory storage
d. Memory retrieval
e. Retrieval cues
f. Encoding specificity principle
g. Context-dependent memory effect
h. State-dependent memory effect
i. Three-stage model
j. Sensory memory
k. Sensory register
l. Iconic memory
m. Eidetic memory
n. Echoic memory
o. Short-term memory (STM)
p. Working memory
q. Chunking
r. Maintenance rehearsal
s. Phonological loop
t. Visuospatial sketchpad
u. Central executive
v. Long-term memory (LTM)
w. Consolidation
x. Elaborative rehearsal
y. Semantic network model
z. Levels-of-processing theory
aa. Declarative memory
bb. Semantic memory
cc. Episodic memory
dd. Retrospective memory

15. _____ Transferring information from STM to LTM by focusing on the meaning of the information

16. _____ The view that LTM is not infallible; memory is only a representation of the past

17. _____ The process of accessing information stored in memory and bringing it into conscious awareness

18. _____ Converting short-term information into LTM; takes twenty-four hours or more after learning

19. _____ Our memory of how to do things—involves motor or performance skills

20. _____ The process of converting information from the environment into a form that can be stored in memory

ee. Prospective memory

ff. Procedural memory

gg. Implicit memory

hh. Explicit memory

ii. Priming task

jj. Constructionist theory

kk. Memory schema

ll. Flashbulb memories

mm. Misinformation effect

21. The representation of our memory system as consisting of sensory, short-term, and long-term memory storage phases is known as the

    a. semantic-state model of memory.
    b. three-stage model.
    c. constructionist model.
    d. reconstructionist model.

22. The ability to _____ is crucial to learning.

    a. remember
    b. reconstruct
    c. perceive auditory information
    d. perceive visual information

23. In order for information to enter our memory storage, it first must be

    a. encoded.
    b. selectively attended to.
    c. retrieved.
    d. recalled.

24. If you restructure information so that it consists of fewer units, you are engaging in

    a. consolidation.
    b. retrieval.
    c. chunking.
    d. elaborative rehearsal.

25. We are better able to recall information when we are in the same type of mood as when the experience happened to us. This phenomenon is known as the _____ effect.

    a. context-dependent memory
    b. state-dependent memory
    c. three-stage memory
    d. affective-state memory

26. Though some memories come to mind spontaneously, others are helped by
    a. hypnotic suggestion.
    b. eidetic imagery.
    c. retrieval cues.
    d. the central executive.

27. Short-term memory
    a. consists of auditory and visual input.
    b. stores information on the basis of meaning.
    c. holds approximately seven units.
    d. exhibits all of the above.

28. Research by George Sperling (1960) indicated that
    a. people mentally store more of an iconic display than they can report.
    b. auditory memory is more efficient than visual memory.
    c. mnemonic devices are most helpful with spatial memory tasks.
    d. most people utilize the partial-report-technique.

29. In the sensory memory phase of memory storage, which type of information is retained the longest?
    a. Visual imagery
    b. Semantic input
    c. Echoes
    d. Procedural input

30. Eidetic imagery means
    a. stored on the basis of sound.
    b. stored on the basis of meaning.
    c. stored on the basis of visual sensory input (icons).
    d. photographic memory.

31. According to the working memory model proposed by Baddeley and Hitch (1974), the subsystem that holds verbal or speech-based information is the
    a. phonological loop.
    b. visuospatial sketchpad.
    c. central executive.
    d. auditory processing center.

32. Consolidation is
    a. a type of mnemonic device.
    b. a part of the phonological loop.
    c. the process of converting unstable STM into more stable LTM.
    d. none of the above.

33. The semantic network model regarding LTM organization suggests that
    a. information must first be stored in STM before it can be moved to LTM.
    b. maintenance rehearsal is crucial to LTM processes.
    c. there are links between all phases of memory storage.
    d. thinking of one concept causes a ripple effect involving related concepts.

34. The part of our long-term memory that contains our personal story, like an autobiography, is _____ memory.
    a. semantic
    b. episodic
    c. retrospective
    d. implicit

35. Knowledge of how to play the piano or how to drive a stick shift car would be stored in _____ memory.
    a. procedural
    b. declarative
    c. flashbulb
    d. echoic

36. Which statement about flashbulb memories is TRUE?
    a. They are very vivid.
    b. They are subject to the same inaccuracies as other memories.
    c. They derive from highly intense experiences.
    d. All of the above are correct.

37. Regarding eyewitness testimony, which of the following is correct?
    a. People who take longer to answer questions are more accurate.
    b. People who appear confident about their answers are usually correct.
    c. People with general knowledge about the topic are no more accurate than other witnesses.
    d. People who take less time to answer questions are more accurate.

ESSAY QUESTIONS

1. What is the misinformation effect? How can it impact the testimony of eyewitnesses?

2. What are repressed memories? How accurate can we assume recovered repressed memories to be?

ANSWER KEY

1. Sensory memory

2. Levels-of-processing theory

3. Misinformation effect

4. Maintenance rehearsal

5. Encoding specificity principle

6. Iconic memory

7. Short-term memory (STM)

8. Semantic memory

9. Long-term memory (LTM)

10. Memory

11. Echoic memory

12. Chunking

13. Context-dependent memory effect

14. State-dependent memory effect

15. Elaborative rehearsal

16. Constructionist theory

17. Memory retrieval

18. Consolidation

19. Procedural memory

20. Memory encoding

21. b

22. a

23. a

24. c

25. b

26. c

27. c

28. a

29. c

30. d

31. a

32. c

33. d

34. b

35. a

36. d

37. d

SAMPLE ANSWERS TO ESSAY QUESTIONS

1. The misinformation effect occurs when an individual is trying to recall a past experience. It can happen, actually, any time between when the experience occurred and when the individual attempts to recall it some time later. The misinformation effect involves the introduction, intentionally or accidentally, of features or characteristics that were not actually present when the event or experience occurred. These features may be introduced (usually through the use of words) by an interviewer or other person who asks questions about the remembered experience. Research by Loftus and her colleagues (1978, 1997) revealed that when individuals are given misleading information (such as whether a yield sign is present at an intersection), this misinformation tends to create distortions in the memories later recalled. When an incorrect feature or descriptor is suggested, that feature may find its way into the recalled memories. Thus, at least portions of recalled information can be false. Although eyewitness testimony is often viewed as highly credible, we must remember that errors and mistakes in such memories can occur.

2. Repressed memories are usually memories of traumatic childhood events. However, the early experiences may have been so painful that the experience is no longer actually remembered. It is thought that very disturbing memories are too emotionally disruptive to keep in conscious awareness. Thus, the individual represses the memory—he or she "forgets" that the events ever occurred. With time, especially as the individual gets older, the individual may experience flashbacks—brief glimpses or recollections of these painful past events. A psychotherapist or hypnotist may be consulted to help gain more information about these flashbacks. In this setting many more repressed memories may be recovered. On the basis of these recovered memories, sometimes with no other corroborating evidence, a person may be accused and convicted of

serious sexual crimes. It is true that at least some recovered repressed memories are accurate, and we want the perpetrator of such crimes to be appropriately punished. As with eyewitness testimony, however, we must remember that distorted and false memories can be created. Investigators and interviewers must be careful to ask only open-ended questions and not plant suggestions through either words or nonverbal behavior.

MODULE 6.2 FORGETTING

LEARNING OBJECTIVES

After you have mastered the information in this unit, you will be able to:

- Discuss the major theories of forgetting

- Explain how recall is related to the methods used to measure it

- Discuss amnesia and its causes

OUTLINE

I. Why Do We Forget?
    A. Some people more forgetful than others
    B. Variety of explanations for normal forgetting
II. Decay Theory
    A. Belief that memory is a trace that fades over time
    B. Hermann Ebbinghaus (1885) used nonsense syllables to test himself and memory
    C. Ebbinghaus forgetting curve—most information lost shortly after learning (66 percent in first day)
    D. Savings method—much less time to relearn forgotten information
    E. Massed vs. spaced practice effect—more information retained when learning sessions spread out over time
    F. Weakness in decay theory:
        1. Forgetting over time is quite uneven
        2. Seems to be related to meaningfulness of original material
III. Interference Theory
    A. Belief that memory loss is due to occurrence of other similar events
    B. Retroactive interference—what learned now interferes with previous learning
    C. Proactive interference—what learned now interferes with what will be learned in the future
    D. Steps to minimize memory disruption from interference:
        1. Sleep after learning
        2. Practice (repeat) new information when first learned (may want to overlearn)
        3. Schedule breaks between learning sessions (such as between classes)
        4. Avoid studying similar topics in close succession
    E. Serial position effect
        1. Tendency to recall first and last items in a list best
        2. Interference most likely to occur with items in middle
        3. Primacy effect—recalling items best when they are given first
        4. Recency effect—recalling items best when they are given last
IV. Retrieval Theory
    A. Forgetting results from breakdown in retrieving stored memories
    B. Encoding failure
        1. Memory cannot be retrieved because information was never originally stored (never encoded)

     2.   We encode only as much information as we need

     3.   Distinct, unique events tend to be remembered

     4.   Similar events tend to be encoded as a group (based on common features) so more difficult to distinguish among these

  C.   Lack of retrieval cues

     1.   Information encoded but not accessible

     2.   Insufficient distinctive cues to help us retrieve

     3.   Tip-of-the-tongue phenomenon—partial recall; may be associated with general word retrieval difficulty

V.   Motivated Forgetting

  A.   Sigmund Freud—memories are not forgotten, just kept hidden (repression)

  B.   Repressed information is threatening or unpleasant

  C.   Repression—defense mechanism that helps protect from overwhelming anxiety

  D.   Concept is controversial since there is evidence that refutes

VI.   Measuring Memory

  A.   What is remembered may in part depend on how it is assessed

  B.   Recall task—reproduce information that has been stored in memory

     1.   Free recall—remember as much as possible; order does not matter

     2.   Serial recall—recall items or numbers in a particular order

     3.   Paired-associates recall—after word pairs are memorized, one word is presented (must retrieve associated word)

  C.   Recognition task

     1.   Select correct answer from among choices given (like a multiple-choice test)

     2.   Recognition memory nearly always better than recall

VII. Amnesia—Severe Type of Memory Loss

  A.   Types of amnesia

     1.   Retrograde amnesia

        a)   Loss of memory regarding past events

        b)   May involve disruption of consolidation process

        c)   Loss is greatest for more recent events

     2.   Anterograde amnesia—difficulty or inability to store new memories

     3.   Childhood amnesia

        a)   No recollection of earliest childhood years

        b)   May be due to lack of sufficient organization of pre-verbal memories in the brain or immature brain structures for LTM

  B.   Causes of amnesia—physical or psychological

     1.   Physical causes

        a)   Blows to the head, degenerative brain diseases (such as Alzheimer's)

        b)   Blood vessel blockage, infectious diseases, alcoholism

        c)   Early detection critical to successful treatment

     2.   Psychological causes (dissociative amnesia)—memory is traumatic, too disturbing for conscious awareness (condition may be reversed)

SUMMARY

In this module, you learn about the various theories for forgetting. Everyone forgets things at one time or another, though there is wide variation among human beings of all ages as to how often this experience occurs. Several explanations for forgetting have been proposed. The first seems like an obvious one—decay theory. This theory suggests that we forget information we once knew simply because we have not used it in so long. The view is derived from the notion that memories leave a trace in the brain. If left dormant, or unused, this trace will fade and eventually disappear.

Though the decay theory of forgetting seems to have many obvious applications, there are some phenomena that it does not explain well. For example, information we have had in our memory at one time may be forgotten very quickly, while other tidbits or recollections stay with us essentially indefinitely. It appears that not just frequency of use but meaningfulness of information affects memory. Secondly, if we go to relearn "forgotten" information, much less time is needed to relearn in comparison to time needed in our first attempt. So information we thought had decayed and was no longer there—actually is.

A remarkable person in the history of psychology provided much of what we know about memory and forgetting. This individual was Hermann Ebbinghaus (1850–1909), and what is perhaps more remarkable is that he used only himself as his research subject! Ebbinghaus would study and memorize information. He would investigate how long it took him to learn information to the point where it could be recalled perfectly. He also gave us what is now known as the Ebbinghaus forgetting curve. He recorded how much information, once memorized, he forgot, and over what span of time the forgetting of learned material occurred. Most information, he discovered, is forgotten rather promptly, beginning immediately after it is learned. Wisely, Ebbinghaus knew he could not use ordinary words and concepts as memorization material. There would be too many associations relating to familiarity with words; thus he could not be sure he was truly testing pure memory. Instead, Ebbinghaus cleverly devised three-letter nonsense syllables (such as *lef* and *nuz*). Because they were not true words, no prior associations or familiarity with these terms existed to confound memory research.

A second explanation for forgetting is interference theory. This theory proposes that we forget because we are exposed to massive amounts of other information as well. The more this information is similar to what we have already learned, or memorized, the more it is likely to cause problems (interfere) with our attempts at recollection. Retroactive interference means what we learn now makes it harder to remember information learned earlier. Proactive interference means what we learn now will likely make it more difficult to absorb and remember information presented in the future. Though we can do things to combat the effects of interference, it is clear that this phenomenon can "get" us coming and going! Actively practicing (repeating) learned material, sleeping after studying, and spacing learning and study times can help us retain more of the material we have learned.

A third possible explanation for why we forget is retrieval theory. This theory places emphasis on our attempts to get information back out of memory (to retrieve it). One reason we may not be able to get information back out of our memory is that it was never entered into memory storage in the first place! This is known as encoding failure. We all have had this experience. We may stare and stare at the printed words on the page. We may be staring at those words for some length of time! But unless we are actually attending to the words, actively processing them and their meanings, the information is not really going into our heads. We have stared at the words, but the material does not get encoded. Come test time, we cannot bring the information back out for our use. Why? It never entered our memory in the first place! Another component in retrieval theory is noting that lack of helpful, distinctive cues is a factor in forgetting. Memories are triggered by cues that bring them to mind. If there is a dearth of such retrieval cues, it is much harder to bring information out of our memory store. Certainly, how questions are asked (e.g., there are more cues in a recognition task than in memory recall) is related to what and how much we can remember. Physical and/or psychological trauma also impacts our ability to remember.

KEY TERMS

Decay theory

Savings method

Massed vs. spaced practice effect

Interference theory

Retroactive interference

Proactive interference

Overlearning

Serial position effect

Primacy effect

Recency effect

Retrieval theory

Tip-of-the-tongue (TOT) phenomenon

Repression

Recall task

Recognition task

Amnesia

Retrograde amnesia

Anterograde amnesia

Childhood amnesia

Dissociative amnesia

SELF-TEST PRACTICE QUIZ

From the Key Terms select that which best matches the following (Note: Not every Key Term will be used.):

1. _____ The view that forgetting is due to similar memories that interfere with each other

2. _____ Loss of memory of past events

3. _____ A defense mechanism proposed by Freud; threatening information is kept out of conscious awareness

4. _____ The tendency for better recall for items learned first

5. _____ Information is retained better when learning sessions are spread out over time

6. _____ An explanation for forgetting based on the notion that information in memory will fade and disappear if not used for an extended period of time

a. Decay theory

b. Savings method

c. Massed vs. spaced practice effect

d. Interference theory

e. Retroactive interference

f. Proactive interference

g. Overlearning

h. Serial position effect

i. Primacy effect

j. Recency effect

k. Retrieval theory

l. Tip-of-the-tongue (TOT) phenomenon

m. Repression

7. _____   What we learn now will interfere with information we store from future learning

8. _____   The normal lack of recollection of very early childhood experiences

9. _____   What we learn now interferes with information we have stored in memory earlier

10. _____   A memory task where an individual must choose the correct answer among alternatives

11. _____   The tendency to recall items at the beginning and ending of a list; memory is less good for items in the middle of the list

12. _____   The theory that forgetting occurs because there is difficulty in accessing stored memories

13. _____   Loss of memory due to traumatic psychological experiences; no underlying physical cause

14. _____   Practice continued beyond what is needed to remember information completely; helps with memory recollection in future

15. _____   The time and effort needed to relearn material in comparison to what was needed when information first learned

n.   Recall task

o.   Recognition task

p.   Amnesia

q.   Retrograde amnesia

r.   Anterograde amnesia

s.   Childhood amnesia

t.   Dissociative amnesia

16. The theory of forgetting that involves the inability to access information because it was never really encoded into memory is the _____ theory.
    a.   decay
    b.   interference
    c.   retrieval
    d.   proactive

17. Much of what we know about remembering and forgetting was made available through research conducted by
    a.   Hermann Ebbinghaus.
    b.   Ivan Pavlov.
    c.   Sigmund Freud.
    d.   Carl Jung.

18.   Ari used to play the clarinet quite well, but then he learned to play the oboe (a similar instrument), and now he can't remember how to play the clarinet anymore. Ari is experiencing

    a.   the serial position effect.
    b.   context-dependent learning.
    c.   proactive interference.
    d.   overlearning.

19.   In order to study memory and avoid prior associations due to familiarity with words, Ebbinghaus used

    a.   family names.
    b.   nonsense syllables.
    c.   words that were all of equal difficulty.
    d.   words that all contained the same number of vowels and consonants.

20.   One way to help reduce the effects of interference on our ability to remember is to

    a.   avoid studying topics in close succession, especially when they are very similar to each other.
    b.   try to sleep for some length of time soon after a period of studying.
    c.   practice or repeat newly memorized information, perhaps to the point of overlearning.
    d.   make use of all of the tips above.

21.   The tendency to best remember words at the beginning and end of a list and remember less well the words in the middle of a list is known as

    a.   the primacy effect.
    b.   the recency effect.
    c.   the serial position effect.
    d.   proactive interference.

22.   One reason that decay theory is an incomplete explanation for forgetting is that

    a.   the more that time passes, the more information we tend to forget.
    b.   how meaningful information is to us is related to how long we remember it.
    c.   we tend to remember the words in the middle of a list less well than other words at the beginning or end.
    d.   failure to remember information may occur because it was never encoded.

23.   When events occur regularly in our lives, it is harder to distinguish among them because

    a.   repetitiveness of these events makes us less alert and aware.
    b.   information is lost due to the serial position effect.
    c.   such events tend to be encoded on the basis of common features.
    d.   there is a greater likelihood for retrograde amnesia.

24.   It may be particularly difficult to remember the names of people whom we do not know well because

    a.   there often is a lack of distinctive retrieval cues.
    b.   their names may be the same as those of other individuals whom we know.
    c.   social settings are normally noisy and it is difficult to hear names clearly.
    d.   typically we hear a name only once, the first time we are introduced.

25.   According to Freud, repression can be beneficial by

    a.   freeing up space in long-term memory so we can learn new information.
    b.   protecting us from traumatic or disturbing memories.
    c.   providing retrieval cues for later recall.
    d.   preventing retroactive interference.

26. A memory task where an individual must remember, in order, information that has been presented to him is a _____ task.

  a. free recall
  b. serial recall
  c. paired-associates recall
  d. recognition

27. On some intelligence tests, the researcher may recite a list of numbers and ask the test-taker to recite those numbers in order. This is an example of a _____ task.

  a. free recall
  b. paired-associates
  c. recognition
  d. serial recall

28. The type of amnesia that does not have a physiological basis for its occurrence is _____ amnesia.

  a. retrograde
  b. anterograde
  c. childhood
  d. dissociative

ESSAY QUESTIONS

1. It is important to keep in mind that how much an individual shows he or she can remember is in part a function of how memory is measured. In most cases, an individual is more successful (that is, the person remembers more) using recognition memory than at free recall tasks. Why would this be? Can you think of any instance where a recognition task might lead to lesser amounts of information remembered in comparison to a recall task on the same material?

2. What is the massed vs. spaced practice effect? Apply this concept to how you have scheduled your classes and the pattern you typically follow when you study.

ANSWER KEY

1. Interference theory

2. Retrograde amnesia

3. Repression

4. Primacy effect

5. Massed vs. spaced practice effect

6. Decay theory

7. Proactive interference

8. Childhood amnesia

9. Retroactive interference

10. Recognition task

11. Serial position effect

12. Retrieval theory

13. Dissociative amnesia

14. Overlearning

15. Savings method

16. c

17. a

18. b

19. b

20. d

21. c

22. b

23. c

24. a

25. b

26. b

27. d

28. d

SAMPLE ANSWERS TO ESSAY QUESTIONS

1. Recognition tasks are almost always easier than recall tasks when people are being tested for what they remember. A main reason for the greater success rate at recognition tasks is that many retrieval cues are present—indeed, they are right before your eyes. The recognition task is easier, in that the test-taker simply must choose the response that has the most (and the most relevant) retrieval cues of all. The only real difficulty is selecting which set of retrieval cues is most complete and relevant, including eliminating choices where the retrieval cues do not apply. With recognition memory it is not necessary to generate a response entirely out of the head, as is the case with any of the different recall tasks. Recall tasks have fewer or no retrieval cues available. Serial recall tasks have the added demand that, not only must the information itself be remembered, but the order in which it was presented must be remembered as well.

   An exception to the above may be when plausible suggestions are made, either before or during the recognition task session, that are closely related or similar to information already in memory storage. As with eyewitness testimony, for example, plausible suggestions may create their own mental images, which possibly are integrated when memories are reconstructed. Unless information is extremely well-learned and in great detail (such as with overlearning), these inaccurate but plausible features may be incorporated into what an individual thinks he or she remembers. Thus, due to the power of suggestion, a recognition memory task may become more difficult than a recall task. In the latter there are few retrieval cues, but on the other hand, the individual is free to pull from memory what the experience or information was. With typical recall-type questions, at least no distracting or misleading information is given.

2. The massed vs. spaced practice effect relates to the fact that trying to cram much information into memory, especially within a very short period of time, creates mental fatigue. This fatigue interferes with the ability to learn and remember. Research has shown (Payne & Wenger, 1996) that more information is retained when sessions for learning are spaced over time. We learn and remember better when the mind is fresh and rested. In addition, as we have seen, the process of consolidation (moving information from STM to LTM) takes some time to complete. It is suggested that at least twenty-four hours, at a minimum, is necessary. Thus, studying large amounts of information in a short period of time and with insufficient opportunity to make the

information really a part of long-term memory is less effective! It produces undue mental strain and is necessarily less successful for true learning.

At this point, the student should reflect on his or her schedule and study patterns. How effective are they, in light of what we know about memory and forgetting?

MODULE 6.3 THE BIOLOGY OF MEMORY

LEARNING OBJECTIVES

After you have mastered the information in this unit, you will be able to:

- Describe where memories are stored in the brain

- Discuss the role of the hippocampus in memory

- Define LTP, and explain its possible role in memory formation

- Explain what scientists have learned about the genetic basis of memory

OUTLINE

I. Brain Structure in Memory: Where Do Memories Reside?
    A. Karl Lashley (early twentieth century)—search for engram
        1. Believed to be the physical trace or record of a memory (in the brain)
        2. Research on rats—removing portions of cortex
        3. Rats still retained memory, regardless of what removed
        4. Conclusion is memory is stored throughout brain
    B. Neuronal networks—current technology reveals memory stored in intricate circuitry of neural constellations (in brain)
    C. Hippocampus
        1. Portion of limbic system in brain
        2. Responsible for converting STM into long-term declarative (semantic, episodic) memory
        3. Is not involved in procedural memory processes
        4. Temporary storage only of new declarative memories
    D. Other brain structures
        1. Thalamus—if damaged, results in amnesia
        2. Amygdala—helps encode emotional experiences
II. Strengthening Connections Between Neurons: The Key to Forming Memories
    A. Research on sea snail (*Aplysia*) by Eric Kandel (1995)
    B. Shows memory formation involves biochemical changes (at level of synapse, the connection between neurons)
    C. Long-term potentiation (LTP)
        1. Connections between nerve cells (e.g., in brain) become stronger as a result of repeated stimulation
        2. Stronger synaptic connections mean neuron communication easier
        3. LTP believed to be a factor in STM to LTM conversion
III. Genetic Bases of Memory
    A. STM-LTM transformation in brain requires various proteins
    B. Production of these proteins regulated by certain genes

SUMMARY

In this module you are learning about structures in the brain that are related to the processes of memory. Since technology allowing us to investigate these questions is quite new, we have by no means learned everything there is to know about how the brain functions during learning, remembering, and forgetting. Research is ongoing and much more will be added to our store of knowledge. We continue to study and investigate further these fascinating processes.

The earliest notion about memory was that there must be a physical trace (called *an engram*) in the brain that corresponds to the memories an individual has. Karl Lashley investigated this concept in the early twentieth century. Laboratory rats were first trained to run a maze; thus, they would have a memory for the layout of the maze and how most rapidly to get to the food reward. Lashley then surgically removed a portion of a research rat's brain in the region of the cortex. The cortex is responsible for higher function activities, which would include learning and memory. The rat was again put in the maze and tested. Lashley did his work with a variety of rats and removed different portions of the cortical region in each rat. No matter what portion of the cortex Lashley removed from a rat—the rat still showed memory for the maze. Lashley had to conclude (we now know correctly) that there was no specific region in the brain corresponding to memory.

Happily, we have become more sophisticated in our research on the brain. Modern technology can show us exactly what regions in the brain are active at any given time and to what extent. We have learned that any memory does not reside in one or a few particular brain cells. Rather, it is believed that memories are stored in constellations of neurons, which then are connected in a very elaborate circuitry. The circuits are known as neural (or neuronal) networks.

Certain brain structures are clearly involved in memory. The brain structure studied for the longest period of time is the hippocampus, one component of our limbic system. The most crucial role of the hippocampus seems to be in the transfer of information from STM to LTM. We learn much about brain functioning when an area of brain damage or destruction corresponds to a loss in how a human functions. Damage to the hippocampus interferes with, or prevents, the formation of long-term memories. Thus it is reasonably conclusive that this STM-LTM movement is carried out by the hippocampus. However, the hippocampus is involved in the transfer of declarative memory information only, not procedural. And, it appears that storage at the site of the hippocampus is temporary. Probably, long-term storage of declarative memories occurs elsewhere. In addition, other brain structures have a role in memory. We know that, if the thalamus in the brain is damaged, amnesia can result. The amygdala is involved in the storage of emotional experiences related to fear and rage.

It cannot be overstated that we still have much to learn regarding the brain's functioning. Neural activity is exceedingly complex. However, we have discovered (through research with a large sea snail, *Aplysia)* that memory involves clusters of neurons that act more or less as a unit. Research by Eric Kandel (1995) on these sea snails revealed that when learning occurs, the connections among a unit of brain cells are strengthened. This is known as long-term potentiation (LTP). Synapses (these chemical connections between neurons) occur more easily and more quickly when the neural network has undergone potentiation. It is suspected that once a neural network is so strengthened, it is therefore more easily stimulated into action in the future. We have also learned that contrary to longstanding belief, the brain actually can create new brain cells. Knowledge about these new brain cells allows for the possibility that they are created in response to, or in a manner related to, learning.

Lastly, genetic research has impacted what we know about memory because certain genes regulate the production of brain proteins. Some of these proteins are utilized in various memory activities. By the insertion or altering of genes, learning and memory processes necessarily can be influenced. We are only beginning to scratch the surface as to what future impact genetic engineering will have on human memory.

KEY TERMS

Engram

Neuronal networks

Long-term potentiation (LTP)

SELF-TEST PRACTICE QUIZ

From the Key Terms select that which best matches the following:

1. _____ Strengthening neural connections within a neural network; occurs as a result of repeated stimulation

2. _____ The term for the original idea that memories would have a corresponding physical trace in the brain

3. _____ Our current view of memory in the brain, consisting of units of neurons combined into neural circuits

a. Engram

b. Neuronal networks

c. Long-term potentiation (LTP)

4. Lashley researched the brain site for memories by
   a. training rats on increasingly complex mazes.
   b. removing portions of a rat's cortex to see if memory had disappeared.
   c. conducting microscopic examination of rat brain tissue.
   d. comparing tissue from rat cortexes to that of other organisms.

5. Which part of the brain appears to be involved with encoding intense emotional experiences?
   a. Amygdala
   b. Thalamus
   c. Hippocampus
   d. Hypothalamus

6. The current belief about memory is
   a. memories are etched into particular brain cells.
   b. learning and memory processes are unrelated.
   c. the hippocampus is responsible for procedural memory processes.
   d. memory storage is in clusters of brain cells known as neuronal networks.

7. The hippocampus appears to play a key role in memory by
   a. preventing dissociative amnesia.
   b. converting STM into LTM.
   c. enhancing eidetic memory.
   d. creating additional brain cells as needed.

8. Research with the sea snail *Aplysia* revealed that
   a. memory storage is closely related to memory capacity.
   b. memory was better for fish than for scorpions.
   c. synaptic connections can be strengthened through repeated stimulation.
   d. all of the above are correct.

9. Long-term potentiation (LTP) occurs because

    a. synaptic connections are flooded with greater amounts of relevant neurotransmitters.
    b. neural connections cannot really function well as a unit.
    c. training in mazes is only partially reinforced.
    d. salt water is most conducive to the transmission of neural (electrical) impulses.

10. New neurons grew in the brains of adult research monkeys, specifically in the region(s) of

    a. the cerebral cortex.
    b. the hippocampus.
    c. the amygdala.
    d. both the amygdala and the thalamus.

11. Why might an altered gene produce a smarter mouse?

    a. Intelligence increases as the number of genes increases.
    b. Altered genes increase the occurrence of LTP.
    c. Genes produce the proteins that are involved in learning and memory.
    d. The altered gene allowed for the introduction of human cortical tissue.

ESSAY QUESTIONS

1. Why was Lashley unable to find the brain site for memories?

2. How is long-term potentiation (LTP) related to research on the sea snail *Aplysia?*

ANSWER KEY

1. Long-term potentiation (LTP)

2. Engram

3. Neuronal networks

4. b

5. a

6. d

7. b

8. c

9. a

10. a

11. c

SAMPLE ANSWERS TO ESSAY QUESTIONS

1. Lashley conducted his research believing that there would be a trace, or engram, in the brain where memory was located. As such, his approach was to remove various portions of the brain (in the cortex) and see if research rats then lost their memory of a maze on which they had been trained. No matter what portion of the rat's brain Lashley removed, the rats never lost their memory for the maze. Because Lashley was looking for a specific location for memory, his endeavors were unsuccessful. However, his research has led us to understand that memory does, indeed, occur in clusters of cells and networks throughout the brain.

2.   The *Aplysia* is a small enough and simple enough animal that its neurological processes can be studied. It has a few simple reflexes (such as withdrawing gills) that can be trained through simple conditioning procedures. Thus, the sea snail is able to "learn" to respond to a conditioned stimulus (a squirt of water in the research by Kandel). Kandel noted that the quantity of neurotransmitter increased as the animal learned the response. Synaptic connections were strengthened (LTP) as a result, and the strengthening lasted for at least several months.

MODULE 6.4 APPLICATION: POWERING UP YOUR MEMORY

LEARNING OBJECTIVE

After you have mastered the information in this unit, you will be able to:

- Discuss ways in which you can improve your memory

OUTLINE

I.   Using Mnemonics to Improve Memory
    A.   Mnemonic—device for improving memory
    B.   Types of mnemonics
        1.   Acronyms and acrostics—use first letter of a series of words to form a word or a verse
        2.   Popular sayings and rhymes (such as "30 days hath September…")
        3.   Visual cues, visual imagery—leave a visual note or create an associated visual image
        4.   Chunking—recombine larger amounts of information into a useable or familiar unit
II.   General Suggestions for Improving Memory
    A.   Pay attention—focus on task, have quiet surroundings
    B.   Practice—especially with elaborative rehearsal
    C.   Use external memory aids—a reminder note is fine!
    D.   Link time-based tasks to external cues
    E.   Mentally rehearse—plan and visualize your tasks in advance
    F.   Enhance context-dependent effects
    G.   Control stress
    H.   Adopt healthy habits—healthy diet and exercise help memory

SUMMARY

In this Application module you learn very helpful ways to improve your memory. These range from simple specific memory strategies, known as mnemonics, to more general tips like keeping the mind healthy and focusing attention. Practice, whether it is repeating information or visualizing in advance what one will do, is crucial to effective memory. Making use of the many simple mnemonics (acronyms, everyday rhymes, and sayings) is an easy way to help improve memory.

KEY TERMS

Mnemonic

Acronym

Acrostic

SELF-TEST PRACTICE QUIZ

From the Key Terms select that which best matches the following:

1. _____ A verse or saying that helps with memory, such as "Every good boy does fine" for musical notes

2. _____ A device or strategy for improving memory

3. _____ A word made up of the first letters of words one needs to remember

    a.   Mnemonic

    b.   Acronym

    c.   Acrostic

4. The mnemonic where one takes larger amounts of information and recasts them into more familiar, manageable units is known as

    a.   the method of loci.
    b.   chunking.
    c.   rehearsal.
    d.   using an acrostic.

5. Many people use sentences such as "My Very Educated Mother Just Served Us Nine Pies" to remember the names of the planets (Mercury, Venus, Earth, etc). This is an example of a(n)

    a.   acrostic.
    b.   acronym.
    c.   visual cue.
    d.   pegword.

ESSAY QUESTION

1. What are some general things you can do to help improve your memory?

ANSWER KEY

1. Acrostic

2. Mnemonic

3. Acronym

4. b

5. a

ANSWER TO SAMPLE ESSAY QUESTION

1. There are many general things we can do to help our ability at memory tasks—and many of them can help our lives overall as well! The first is to adopt a healthy life-style, which includes sufficient exercise and an appropriate, nutritious diet. Diet and exercise are closely related to the functioning of the mind overall. In addition, we need to manage the stress in our lives so that it is not excessive. We certainly can make use of the many memory aids available. There is a lot to remember these days, and much of it is more complicated than our forebears had to deal with. There is no embarrassment in making use of prominently displayed sticky notes, hand-held memory devices, writing things down, and so forth. For memory, we usually need all the help we can get. We certainly need to pay attention to important events or information and mentally practice or rehearse what we will do or what we need to remember. Lastly, we can be forgiving of

ourselves if we cannot remember everything all of the time. We can be equally forgiving of others who may forget things on occasion too. By this point we know that memory is a complex process.

CHAPTER 6 APPLICATION EXERCISES

1. Recall the clever work Hermann Ebbinghaus did regarding memory and how much we have learned from his work.

    Take on the role of Hermann Ebbinghaus. Make up for yourself lists of nonsense syllables, and see how long it takes you to memorize them all. How many words can you remember easily in short-term memory? How long can you remember all the words in your list perfectly? When do you start to forget, and how much do you forget? Are there some syllables that you remember longer than others?

2. Think of an occasion when you forgot something—something really important. What was it that you forgot? Why do you think you forgot it? Did situational cues (the context) help you remember, or not? What was the frame of mind you were in? How were you feeling physically?

    At what point did you remember what you had forgotten? How did you feel at that time? What do you think triggered that memory?

CHAPTER 7

Thinking, Language, and Intelligence

In Chapter 7 you are introduced to the ways humans (and maybe some animals) think, use language, and demonstrate intelligence. Study on this whole realm within psychology did not really begin until the 1960s because prior to that time anything "inside the head" was not considered acceptable subject matter by many psychologists. Because it was necessarily more vague, with a process not immediately visible, cognition and related topics were not viewed as sufficiently scientifically rigorous. You may remember that beginning with the early twentieth century, the behavioral perspective was a dominant force within the field of psychology. Behaviorism would deal only with observable behavior. Behaviorists thought that everything anyone learned and manifested was directly due to reinforcement (a consequence that involved a pleasant or desirable outcome) or punishment (a consequence that involved a painful or unpleasant outcome).

Research began in earnest on mental processes in part because we gained the technological resources needed for in-depth and accurate study. In addition, psychologists acknowledged that not everything important in human functioning dealt just with observable environmental factors or behavior. Cognitive psychology has become a substantial scientific discipline.

How do we think? An important component to thinking is creating mental representations of objects and/or experiences from the environment. We form concepts regarding our mental representations—these are mental categories to which we believe the object or experience belongs. Because we can manipulate these representations and manipulate concepts, we can turn these things and ideas about in our heads. We can try physical, intellectual, or other rotations of these ideas mentally, very quickly, and without the tedious stimuli needed were we to actually try them out in the environment. Concepts may be logical (category membership is clear) or natural (we seem to know what fits in a category, and the associated probability that it does, but we cannot actually state clearly what the rules of category membership are). We learn concepts through experience with the environment. Problem solving is an important part of thinking. By using algorithms (standard step-by-step procedures), heuristics (handy rules of thumb), or analogies (drawing on experience with previous similar situations), we may solve a problem more quickly or effectively. Creativity is one kind of thinking, but high creativity does not necessarily mean an individual is highly intelligent or vice versa. Everyone has some creative ability. Intelligence, though difficult to define, is certainly related to thinking processes. Both heredity and environment are important factors in intelligence.

Could we think if we did not have language? There are varying opinions on this question. While language tremendously advances and streamlines our ability to think, it is apparent that our thinking may take effective forms that are other than language-based. Einstein reported that his creativity was visually based. Language clearly greatly increases our ability to communicate with each other.

What makes a true language? The most basic unit of sound in a language is a phoneme. Phonemes are combined to make morphemes, the most basic unit of meaning in a language. Not just any morphemes or words can be strung together. Word order is governed by syntax—the proper ordering to give an utterance meaning. Also, the meaning of words (referred to as *semantics*) can change depending upon how words are used in a sentence. Rules of grammar govern how all of this language composition takes place. Whether animals can acquire language is still under debate.

Children learn language so quickly, so easily, and when they are very young—it seems as if they come into the world "prewired" to absorb the components necessary to communicate—whatever language it is that they are exposed to. This notion was given a name by a well-known linguist, Noam Chomsky. He called this innate ability a *language acquisition device*. It does not really exist, neurologically (as far as we know), but it represents the recognition that the language process is very fast, and it is universal in sequence and timing among the world's children. Language, thinking, and intelligence certainly do much to make us human and add to the marvel of life.

MODULE 7.1 THINKING

LEARNING OBJECTIVES

After you have mastered the information in this unit, you will be able to:

- Define cognitive psychology

- Define thinking

- Describe the major types of concepts that people use and explain how they are organized

- Discuss how we can solve problems more efficiently

- Explain how cognitive biases influence decision making

- Discuss the cognitive processes that underlie creative thinking

OUTLINE

I.   Cognitive Psychology
    A.   How we acquire knowledge about the world
    B.   How we think, form concepts, use language, process information, solve problems
    C.   Not considered appropriate for study in psychology until 1960s
II.   Thinking
    A.   The mental representation and manipulation of information
    B.   Solving problems, making decisions, engaging in creativity
III. Mental Images
    A.   We represent information in the mind as images, words, or concepts
    B.   Mental image
        1.   Mental picture (representation) of an object or event
        2.   A reconstruction of the object or event from memory
        3.   Uses similar parts of visual cortex as those for actually seeing the object
        4.   Advantage is mental representation can be manipulated—allows for many cognitive tasks
        5.   Gender differences in mental imagery abilities
            a)   Women—more vivid imagery; better representations of still objects
            b)   Men—greater use in problem solving; better at visualizing moving objects
IV.   Concepts
    A.   Mental categories used to group objects, events, and ideas
    B.   Categorization based upon common features or properties
    C.   Types of concepts
        1.   Logical concepts—clearly defined rules for membership
        2.   Natural concepts
            a)   Include objects (such as fruit), activities, and abstractions
            b)   Rules for membership understood and applied, but less clear

        c)   Membership for category based on *probability* that item fits

    D.   Hierarchies of concepts—ordered from broad to narrow

        1.   Superordinate—broadest category (e.g., vehicle, animal, furniture)

        2.   Basic-level

            a)   Most frequently used concept category

            b)   Examples are car (in vehicle category), dog (in animal category), and chair (in furniture category)

            c)   Basic-level concepts probably provide most useful information

        3.   Subordinate

            a)   Very specific regarding features

            b)   Examples are sedan, cocker spaniel, beach chair

        4.   Understanding of concepts refined through use

            a)   Positive instance—concept is exemplified

            b)   Negative instance—experience does not fit concept

V.   Problem Solving

    A.   A cognitive process—mental strategies are used to solve problems

    B.   Previously discussed methods are insight, trial and error

    C.   Useful problem-solving strategies

        1.   Algorithms

            a)   Step-by-step set of rules for solving a problem

            b)   None may apply specifically to given problem

        2.   Heuristics

            a)   A rule of thumb that aids in problem solving and decision making

            b)   Backward-working heuristic—start from solution and see if it fits problem

            c)   Means-end heuristic—compare current situation and desired end result; create steps to connect or resolve difference

            d)   Creating subgoals heuristic—divide objective into smaller units and solve each individually

        3.   Analogies

            a)   Use and apply knowledge from similar problems solved in the past

            b)   Effective unless past and present problems not really very similar

        4.   Incubation periods

            a)   Take a break from attempting to solve problem

            b)   Passage of time may actually help in seeing problem clearly

    D.   Mental roadblocks to problem solving

        1.   Mental set

            a)   Relying on strategies that worked well in previous situations

            b)   May lead to quick solution to current problem

            c)   Hinders ability to find solution when prior method not effective

        2.   Functional fixedness—inability to see how familiar objects can be used in new ways

        3.   Irrelevant information—attending to this distracts from truly relevant factors

    E.   Mental roadblocks in decision making

        1.   Decision making—problem solving where one course of action is selected from among alternatives

        2.   Examples of decision-making roadblocks:

            a)   Confirmation bias—sticking to initial approach despite evidence that does not support (preference is to confirm existing belief, ignore facts that might necessitate reconsideration)

            b)   Representativeness heuristic—assuming given sample is like all other cases; no true basis for believing this is so

          c)   Availability heuristic—basing decision on information that most readily comes to mind

          d)   Framing—decisions are made based on how alternatives are described

VI.   Creativity

    A.   Thinking that leads to original, practical, meaningful solutions

    B.   Thinking that generates new ideas or artistic expressions

    C.   Everyone has potential for creativity; some show more than others

    D.   Creativity associated with higher levels of intelligence

    E.   Most intelligent not necessarily more creative; creativity extends beyond intelligence

    F.   Measuring creativity

        1.   Variety of tests (one is Alternate Uses Test)

        2.   Most typically measure *divergent thinking* (finding new ways to view situations or objects)

        3.   *Convergent thinking* not considered a measure of creativity (looks at finding the one "correct" solution only)

    G.   Cognitive processes that underlie creative thinking

        1.   Metaphor and analogy

           a)   Metaphor—one object or concept is seen as like another

           b)   Analogy—comparing two things having similar properties

        2.   Conceptual combination—uniting two or more concepts into one novel result

        3.   Conceptual expansion—extending a familiar concept to novel application

SUMMARY

In this module you learn about the incredible process of human thinking. The study of thinking is part of the endeavors of the branch of psychology known as cognitive psychology. Cognition, of course, means thinking. Though much research currently is carried out by cognitive psychologists, it was not always so. For the greater part of the twentieth century (when a dominant force in psychology was that of the behaviorists), anything going on inside the head—whether it be thought or, worse, emotion!—was not considered appropriate subject matter for study. Such topics were considered soft, not scientific or rigorous. However, as time went on (and the technology allowing more study of the brain and mental functioning was developed) cognition eventually became a suitable and respectable research area. In part, we were beginning to be aware of the incredible role thinking and other mental processes had with regard to behavior. In part, too, by the 1960s behaviorism had been around for some forty years. Despite behaviorists' tremendous contributions to psychology and our understanding of behavior, the limitations of the field (ignoring what was going on within the human psyche) were becoming apparent.

How do we think? Most thinking is done by creating mental representations (of objects, events, concepts) in the head, then mentally moving them around, sometimes with an objective (such as problem solving) in mind. Interestingly, mental images (that mental picture we have) use about the same parts of the visual cortex in the brain as actually viewing the object does. Though mental images typically are of visual stimuli, other representations (such as of smells or auditory experiences) may be formed also. The concepts in our head seem to be organized into hierarchies. There are broad categories (called superordinate concepts), everyday categories (known as basic-level concepts), which tend to be the most often used, and subordinate concepts, which contain very specific detail. We learn about concepts through experience with the world as we are growing up. We learn what fits into a category—and what doesn't.

A major goal of thinking is to solve problems, big and small, which arise in our lives every day (and sometimes, it seems, all the time!). We also are faced with various avenues and alternatives, and we must arrive at decisions by choosing from among these. Both activities take mental work. Though trial and error and insight as methods of problem solving have already been discussed, other problem-solving strategies are presented in this unit that we also rely on for effective solutions. These include the use of algorithms (a set of step-by-step rules), heuristics (standard rule-of-thumb guidelines), analogies (considering solutions from prior similar situations), and an incubation period (taking a break to allow inspiration or a fresh look).

Roadblocks to good problem solving include being unable to move beyond an existing mental set (a past successful way of approaching a problem), functional fixedness (the inability to see new uses for familiar objects), and being distracted by irrelevant stimuli or information. Roadblocks to successful decision making include having a confirmation bias (a preference for prior notions despite new, perhaps disconfirming information), relying too much on heuristics (believing whatever is handy or most obvious without more thorough examination), and being swayed by how various outcomes are described instead of considering the deeper meanings and implications.

Lastly, this module deals with one application of thinking, which is creativity. There is some relation between creativity and intelligence, in that creative individuals typically have average or higher levels of intelligence. However, there is no correspondence between high levels of intelligence and high levels of creativity—having one is unrelated to whether an individual has the other. Creative people seem to possess the ability for divergent thinking—being able to see and use every day items and experiences in new ways. All people have the potential for creativity, at least to some extent.

KEY TERMS

Cognitive psychology

Thinking

Mental image

Concepts

Logical concepts

Natural concepts

Superordinate concepts

Basic-level concepts

Subordinate concepts

Positive instance

Negative instance

Problem solving

Algorithm

Heuristic

Analogy

Incubation period

Mental set

Functional fixedness

Decision-making

Confirmation bias

Representativeness heuristic

Availability heuristic

Framing

Creativity

Divergent thinking

Convergent thinking

Metaphor

Conceptual combinations

Conceptual expansion

SELT-TEST PRACTICE QUIZ

From the Key Terms select that which best matches the following (Note: Not every Key Term will be used.):

1. _____ A problem-solving strategy where knowledge gained from solving prior similar problems is applied to the current situation

2. _____ Mental categories for classifying events, objects, and ideas on the basis of their common features

3. _____ A rule of thumb for making a decision based on the assumption that the given sample is representative of all cases

4. _____ The ability to come up with new ways of viewing familiar situations and objects

5. _____ A branch of psychology that focuses on thinking, problem solving, use of language, and the like

6. _____ An experience that teaches that a given object does belong to a particular concept

7. _____ A set of step-by-step rules for solving a problem

8. _____ Taking a break from problem-solving attempts, may allow for a fresh perspective

9. _____ The process of mentally representing information and manipulating these representations

10. _____ The broadest category for classifying concepts

a. Cognitive psychology

b. Thinking

c. Mental image

d. Concepts

e. Logical concepts

f. Natural concepts

g. Superordinate concepts

h. Basic-level concepts

i. Subordinate concepts

j. Positive instance

k. Negative instance

l. Problem solving

m. Algorithm

n. Heuristic

o. Analogy

p. Incubation period

q. Mental set

r. Functional fixedness

s. Decision-making

t. Confirmation bias

u. Representativeness heuristic

v. Availability heuristic

w. Framing

11. _____   The tendency to rely on past successful strategies that worked in prior situations but that may not be effective in current situation

12. _____   A mental picture or representation, usually visual

13. _____   Concepts with clearly defined rules for membership

14. _____   Combinations of two or more concepts, resulting in one novel idea or application

15. _____   A type of thinking where the attempt is simply to find the "correct answer"

16. _____   An inability to conceive of novel uses for familiar objects

17. _____   Originality in thinking that tends to result in new, practical, and useful solutions or approaches

18. _____   The type of problem solving where one must choose a course of action from among the available alternatives

19. _____   The middle level in concept classification, tends to be the most frequently used

x.   Creativity

y.   Divergent thinking

z.   Convergent thinking

aa.   Metaphor

bb.   Conceptual combinations

cc.   Conceptual expansion

20. The form of thinking where we come up with original ways of conceiving of objects or concepts that result in useful solutions or applications is
    a.   convergent thinking.
    b.   creativity.
    c.   analogy.
    d.   mental imagery.

21. The study of cognition in the field of psychology did not really begin until the 1960s because
    a.   we lacked the techniques to study mental processes.
    b.   other issues in psychology had not been fully investigated.
    c.   reinforcers for thinking and problem solving were not well defined.
    d.   the topic was not considered sufficiently scientific.

22. When we represent information in our heads so we can make use of it, we form a(n)
    a.   analogy.
    b.   metaphor.
    c.   mental image.
    d.   heuristic.

23. Most people would feel more positively about a medical treatment with a 60 percent chance of success than one with a 40 percent chance of failure, even though that is the same thing. This illustrates the concept of

    a. negative instances.
    b. divergent thinking.
    c. heuristics.
    d. framing.

24. As we learn more about the world, we classify information into categories based on commonalities. These classifications are known as

    a. concepts.
    b. algorithms.
    c. mental images.
    d. heuristics.

25. A method of problem solving where we work at a mental task then leave it for a while during which we may develop a fresh perspective is known as using a(n)

    a. availability heuristic.
    b. representativeness heuristic.
    c. incubation period.
    d. conceptual combination.

26. The manipulation of information in our heads, such as of images and concepts, is known as

    a. cognitive psychology.
    b. thinking.
    c. functional fixedness.
    d. positive instances.

27. The type of category most easily grasped by children as they are learning language is that of _____ concepts.

    a. natural
    b. superordinate
    c. basic-level
    d. subordinate

28. With regard to mental imagery, men show a superiority for

    a. mentally rotating or visualizing moving objects.
    b. vividness of images of past experiences.
    c. greater use of imagery in recalling past experiences.
    d. forming mental representations of still objects.

29. With regard to mental imagery, women show a superiority for

    a. mentally rotating objects or visualizing moving objects.
    b. greater and more vivid use of imagery when recalling past experiences.
    c. images of auditory, olfactory, and tactile stimuli.
    d. speed in creating visual images.

30. Even though we all know what the word *love* means, there are no hard and fast rules to define what love actually is. "Love" is therefore a _____ concept.

    a. superordinate
    b. natural
    c. logical
    d. basic-level

31. In problem solving, when we break a task into smaller units and then work to solve each smaller unit, this is known as using a _____ heuristic.
     a. means-end
     b. sub-concept
     c. backward-working
     d. creating subgoals

32. A method of problem solving where we rely on a standard rule of thumb is known as using
     a. analogies.
     b. heuristics.
     c. algorithms.
     d. incubation periods.

33. A disadvantage in using trial and error or insight for problem solving is that both
     a. are relatively inefficient and take a fair amount of time.
     b. cancel out the beneficial effects of other problem solving methodologies.
     c. make creativity in thought and divergent solutions less likely.
     d. There are no disadvantages to using trial and error and insight.

34. Sue needed to buy a new car. All the car magazines said that Zippy cars were the most reliable and efficient cars on the market. But Sue remembered that her friend had a Zippy that turned out to be a real lemon. Because this one incident stuck out in her mind, Sue did not buy a Zippy. She had fallen victim to
     a. confirmation bias.
     b. the representativeness heuristic.
     c. the availability heuristic.
     d. functional fixedness.

ESSAY QUESTIONS

1. What are some characteristics of creative people? Use Arthur Fry and George deMestral as examples. Does everyone have the potential to be creative, or is it limited to a select few?

2. Why are mental representations important in effective thinking processes?

ANSWER KEY

1. Analogy

2. Concepts

3. Representativeness heuristic

4. Divergent thinking

5. Cognitive psychology

6. Positive instance

7. Algorithm

8. Incubation period

9. Thinking

10. Superordinate concepts

11. Mental set

12. Mental image

13. Logical concepts

14. Conceptual combinations

15. Convergent thinking

16. Functional fixedness

17. Creativity

18. Decision making

19. Basic-level concepts

20. b

21. d

22. c

23. d

24. a

25. c

26. b

27. c

28. a

29. b

30. b

31. d

32. b

33. a

34. c

SAMPLE ANSWERS TO ESSAY QUESTIONS

1. Anyone can be a creative person, and all individuals possess some creative ability. Intelligence is related to creativity to an extent, in that creative people typically have at least average levels of intelligence. Highly intelligent people, however, are no more likely to be highly creative than any other individuals possessing reasonable intelligence.

    Both Arthur Fry and George deMestral show a creative mind at work. Fry had developed a compound through his research that was only mildly adhesive, and his company, 3M, saw no immediate use for it. However, Fry had a problem that needed a solution—pieces of paper, which he used to mark his place in his hymnal, tended to fall out from among the pages. He was able to take a new compound, which had no apparent use, and apply it (literally!) to solve his problem in a way that had not been done before. This is evidence, among other things, of conceptual combination. DeMestral took an everyday, and annoying, experience of getting burrs stuck to his clothing and his dog, and applied these long-known circumstances to a new and very beneficial use (Velcro). Both individuals show divergent thinking—coming up with fresh new ways of seeing events, objects, and components that already existed. The ingredients for deMestral's creative breakthrough have been around as long as there have been burrs, dogs, and outdoor clothing. However, it took deMestral's ability to look further (in this case, he examined the phenomenon microscopically) and see a new application for a very familiar experience that led to the now widespread use of his creative insight. For both Fry and DeMestral, the tools they utilized in their creativity were already available (for a short time and a long time, respectively). The spark of creativity was all in how these individuals viewed already-existing phenomena.

2. Mental representations make our thinking process far more efficient and quick. We are able to create representations in our mind, which we then can manipulate, unlike the ponderous task of manipulating actual objects and situations in the real world. By using mental representations, too, we are able to attempt solutions or recombinations that might not even be possible in our current environment. Mental representations allow us to play out possible new applications (divergent thinking), draw on past similar experiences (analogies), and extend existing concepts (conceptual expansion) without the time and materials needed to actually try these out. We can come up with helpful new solutions that, for the time being, may exist in a world we can only imagine.

MODULE 7.2 LANGUAGE

LEARNING OBJECTIVES

After you have mastered the information in this unit, you will be able to:

- Describe the major components of language

- Explain how language develops

- Discuss the linguistic relativity hypothesis

- Discuss the controversy regarding whether nonhuman animals can use language

OUTLINE

I. Language
    A. A system of communication composed of symbols
    B. Symbols are arranged according to a grammar
II. Grammar—a set of rules governing the proper use of words, phrases, and sentences to express meaning
III. Components of Language
    A. Phonemes—basic units of sounds in a language
    B. Morphemes
        1. Formed by combinations of phonemes
        2. Smallest units of meaning in a language
        3. Include simple words (car, ball) but also prefixes and suffixes
    C. Syntax—rules of grammar that determine how words are ordered in a sentence (or phrase) to form meaningful expressions
    D. Semantics—the set of rules governing the meaning of words
IV. Language Development
    A. Children develop language in the same stages, at the same ages, universally
    B. Language acquisition in young children usually occurs very easily and naturally
    C. "Language acquisition device"—suggested by Chomsky; human is "prewired" to acquire a language
    D. Both nature and nurture necessary to learn language
    E. Close relationship between language and thought
V. Culture and Language
    A. Is the language one speaks related to how one thinks?
    B. Linguistic relativity hypothesis (Whorfian hypothesis)

1.   Proposes that language we use determines how we think
2.   Proposes that language we use determines how we perceive reality
3.   Research (e.g., by Rosch et al., 1972) does not support this notion
4.   Dani tribe just as capable as English-speaking participants at distinguishing colors
5.   There is support for notion that language influences how we think

VI.   Is Language Unique to Humans?
    A.   Communication is via American Sign Language (ASL) or another artificial language
    B.   Simian communication gives evidence of a basic grammar
    C.   Debate is whether true "language" or just product of imitation, reinforcement
    D.   Ultimate conclusion depends on how "language" defined
    E.   Animals do communicate among themselves with vocalizations and facial expression

SUMMARY

In this module you learn about the fascinating concept of language. Although language generally makes us think of speech, communication may take other forms as well (such as sign language). Language is a communication system based on symbols. These symbols must be used and arranged in a certain way to allow for meaningful exchange. Rules guiding this use and arrangement are known as grammar.

The most basic units in language are phonemes. These are the simplest, single sounds a language has. Morphemes, the smallest units of meaning in a language, are made up of phonemes. Syntax involves the rules of grammar that govern how words are sequenced in order to create meaningful expressions. Semantics relates to the actual meaning of words—the meaning of the same word can change, depending upon how it is used in a communication.

People learn language universally, and children learn language remarkably easily. Children grasp the same concepts, at the same ages, worldwide. Why might this be? Noam Chomsky, a famous linguist, suggests that humans come into the world "prewired"—the brain, due to its structure, is already prepared to adopt a language. Experience just needs to supply what the specific words are to be. In other words, according to Chomsky, the neural circuitry for language already exists. He calls this particular readiness for language the *language acquisition device*. The device is not an actual brain structure—the term represents the notion of the prewired readiness. Since language acquisition in children does occur so easily, readily, consistently, and universally, some explanation for this phenomenon seems desirable. There is opposition to Chomsky's viewpoint, however. Predominantly this opposition emphasizes that no real brain structure exists precisely corresponding to the language acquisition device.

The linguistic relativity hypothesis (also called the Whorfian hypothesis) proposes that our language determines how we think and how we perceive the world. If we lack the term for a certain concept in the world—can we then truly know and contemplate that concept? In fact, research (Rosch et al., 1972) does not provide much support for the linguistic relativity hypothesis. The Dani tribe, with almost no words in their language for color, were just as able to distinguish among plastic chips of different colors as were English-speaking participants (with 11 different terms for color). Our language may to an extent *influence* how we think; there is some evidence that people from different cultures do think differently (Goode, 2000).

For several decades researchers have been investigating human-animal communication. Gorillas and other apes do show some facility for human language. Since apes lack the vocal structures needed to form human sounds, sign language (ASL, for example) or other artificial languages are taught. Koko (a female gorilla), Washoe (a chimpanzee), and Sarah (a chimpanzee) all seemed to grasp the notion of the language they were taught, including something of a basic grammar. They were able to create sentences for communication and put the subject, verb and object of their communication in the proper order to reflect what they wanted to convey. (Washoe, for instance, knew the difference between "Washoe tickle you" and "You tickle Washoe," depending upon how she wanted the tickling to occur.) There is criticism regarding simian-human communication that is mostly from members of the behavioral perspective in psychology. Behaviorists believe that all we learn is due to modeling and reinforcement. It is difficult, fundamentally, to make a clear distinction as to whether the animals truly use and understand language, or whether they are simply repeating actions of their trainers that they have seen and have been reinforced for. We do know that animals communicate among themselves, with various vocalizations and facial expressions that have meaning, at least, within a given species.

KEY TERMS

Language

Grammar

Phonemes

Morphemes

Syntax

Semantics

Language acquisition device

Linguistic relativity hypothesis

SELF-TEST PRACTICE QUIZ

From the Key Terms select that which best matches the following:

1. _____ The notion of an inborn neural preparedness, suggested by Noam Chomsky, which explains why children learn language so easily and in a universal pattern

2. _____ The smallest units of meaning in a language

3. _____ A system of communication involving symbols that are arranged according to a set of rules to yield meaningful expressions

4. _____ Rules of grammar that govern how words are sequenced within sentences or phrases in order to result in meaningful communications

5. _____ The view that the language we use determines how we think and how we perceive the world

6. _____ The most basic units of sounds within a language

7. _____ Rules that govern the meaning of words

a. Language

b. Grammar

c. Phonemes

d. Morphemes

e. Syntax

f. Semantics

g. Language acquisition device

h. Linguistic relativity hypothesis

8. _____   The set of rules regarding how symbols within a given language are to be used in order to form meaningful expressions

9. A system of communication using symbols whose ordering is governed by a grammar is known as

   a. linguistics.
   b. language.
   c. syntax.
   d. semantics.

10. Language is absorbed and used so easily by children and in a pattern that is universal across all cultures, that Noam Chomsky has suggested the existence of

   a. private speech.
   b. one innate universal language.
   c. a language acquisition device.
   d. neural prewiring that is identical in apes and humans.

11. How many morphemes are in the word *unhappy*?

   a. One
   b. Two
   c. Three
   d. Four

12. When we put words in the correct order in a sentence so that the sentence is meaningful, we are using rules of grammar called

   a. syntax.
   b. semantics.
   c. morphemes.
   d. linguistic relativity.

13. The sentence "Colorless green ideas sleep furiously" does not convey anything to us because it violates rules regarding

   a. morphemes.
   b. semantics.
   c. syntax.
   d. language universals.

14. "I apples like to eat" is a sentence that violates the English rules of

   a. syntax.
   b. semantics.
   c. linguistic relativity.
   d. phonemes.

15. Evidence regarding the linguistic relativity hypothesis leads us to conclude that

   a. language precedes thought.
   b. thought precedes language.
   c. language determines how we perceive the world.
   d. language influences how we think.

16. _____ are formed from combinations of _____.
    a. Syllables; vowels
    b. Universals; constants
    c. Phonemes; morphemes
    d. None of the above is correct.

17. When Rosch (1972) tested members of the Dani tribe of New Guinea, who have only two words in their language for all colors, she found that
    a. the Dani tribe members could distinguish among many colors as well as English-speaking study participants could.
    b. the Dani tribe members used either one of their words or the other to describe all colors presented to them in the study.
    c. English-speaking study participants had considerable difficulty in distinguishing among some of the colors presented to them in the study.
    d. the English-speaking participants showed a superiority for purple, pink and black, while the Dani showed a superiority for blues, greens, and yellows.

18. One argument against the idea that chimpanzees and gorillas can communicate with humans using a version of our language is that
    a. American sign language (ASL) is not a true language.
    b. trainers tend to be biased, due to their emotional attachment to their animals.
    c. gorillas and other apes do not have the vocal structures necessary to use our language.
    d. simian "communication" with humans is really just imitating behaviors that they have seen their trainers do; apes repeat the behaviors because they have been reinforced for doing so.

ESSAY QUESTIONS

1. Discuss the concept of the linguistic relativity hypothesis (the Whorfian hypothesis) and the evidence presented in the text for and against it. How is the former use of the pronoun *he* in language (to represent all humans) a way that language can influence thinking?

2. It is difficult to conclude whether animals can communicate using language because ultimately the answer lies with how "language" is defined. What are some ways we can define language? Evaluate the findings regarding animal communication in light of these definitions.

ANSWER KEY

1. Language acquisition device

2. Morphemes

3. Language

4. Syntax

5. Linguistic relativity hypothesis

6. Phonemes

7. Semantics

8. Grammar

9. b

10. c

11. b

12. a

13. b

14. a

15. d

16. d

17. a

18. d

SAMPLE ANSWERS TO ESSAY QUESTIONS

1. The linguistic relativity hypothesis suggests that language determines both how we think and how we perceive the world. Despite some logic in this approach (if a word does not exist for a concept, how can we think about it?), evidence does not fully support Benjamin Whorf's view. Research by Rosch on distinguishing colors, for example, found no differences between results from study participants who did and did not have words for many different colors. Research by Goode (2000) and Nisbett (2000, 2001) support the notion that there is cultural variation in how people think, and language, while not a total determinant, does have some influence. Using a term such as *he,* even for all speakers of the same language, can impact how such a communication is perceived. Though intended, in its past use, to represent all humans, still *he* conveys that the information presented really relates more to, or is more appropriate for, males.

2. If a definition of language includes the concept simply of communication by means of symbols, then Washoe, Sarah, and other animals indeed are communicating effectively. If our definition of language includes an understanding and use of complex syntax and grammatical structures, then the animal communication reported in the text is not sufficient to meet these criteria. Children, it should be pointed out, do not show a use and awareness of sophisticated language features in their earliest years, yet they are viewed as having a language and using it for communication. If this standard is acceptable for children, should it not indicate an acceptable level for animals as well? Trainers believe animal communication falls into this category—primitive, but still as much a language as that used by young children.

MODULE 7.3 INTELLIGENCE

LEARNING OBJECTIVES

After you have mastered the information in this unit, you will be able to:

*   Define intelligence, and discuss how it is measured

*   Explain what constitutes a good intelligence test

*   Describe some examples of the misuse of intelligence tests

*   Discuss the major theories of intelligence

*   Discuss whether intelligence is determined by heredity or environment

*   Discuss intelligence and the nature-nurture question, and discuss racial/ethnic differences in IQ

OUTLINE

I.   Intelligence
    A.   Difficult to define
    B.   David Wechsler (1975): "…the global capacity of the individual to act purposefully, to think rationally, and to deal effectively with the environment"
    C.   May be multiple intelligences or many different forms of intelligence
    D.   Alfred Binet (French)
        1.   Commissioned (1904) by school officials in Paris to identify intellectually at-risk children
        2.   Binet and Theodore Simon developed an intelligence test (1905)
        3.   Test items scaled to what typical child of a given age could do
        4.   Mental age—age level of work a child could do (derived from Binet and Simon's intelligence test)
    E.   IQ (Intelligence Quotient—suggested by William Stern, 1912)
    F.   Lewis Terman (at Stanford University, USA)
        1.   Adapted Binet-Simon test for use in United States
        2.   Added many test items
        3.   Established norms for comparison of scores
        4.   Revised test known as the Stanford-Binet Intelligence Scale (SBIS, 1916)
    G.   Most widely used intelligence tests today: created by David Wechsler
        1.   Developed for pre-school children, school age children, and adults
        2.   Test based on idea that intelligence is a variety of abilities
        3.   Score consists of a deviation IQ (how different from norm for that age group)
        4.   Test includes verbal and performance subtests
II.   Characteristics of Good Intelligence Tests
    A.   Standardization
        1.   Establishing norms by administering test to large numbers of people (standardization sample)
        2.   Sample must be representative of population to which it refers
        3.   IQ score is based on difference (deviation) from norm
        4.   Mean (average score) is 100
        5.   2/3 of scores from general population range from 85 to 115
        6.   Uniform procedures must be followed when administering test
    B.   Reliability—consistency of test scores over time
    C.   Validity—when a test measures what it is supposed to test (e.g., a math test does test math ability not verbal or mechanical ability or ability to follow directions)
    D.   Misuses of intelligence tests
        1.   Parents and teachers may lose hope for children with low IQ scores
        2.   Low expectations can become self-fulfilling prophecies
        3.   Children may give up on themselves; accept label
        4.   Too much emphasis may be placed on IQ scores—other measures of assessment should also be considered
        5.   Tests may be biased against those not in majority culture
        6.   Culture-fair tests have been developed, but not as good predictors of academic performance
III. Extremes of Intelligence
    A.   Mental retardation
        1.   IQ score of 70 or below
        2.   Difficulty in coping with age-appropriate tasks and life situations

          3.   Causes may be biological, environmental, or both

    B.   Mainstreaming—children with mild retardation are placed in regular classrooms

    C.   Intellectual giftedness

          1.   IQ of 130 or higher (98th percentile)

          2.   May benefit from enriched, faster-paced academic programs

          3.   Category also includes musical, artistic ability

          4.   Research shows persistence, motivation always important

IV. Theories of Intelligence

    A.   Spearman's "g"—idea that there is a general underlying factor (ability in one area often correlated with ability in other areas)

    B.   Thurstone's primary mental abilities (7): verbal comprehension, numerical ability, memory, inductive reasoning, perceptual speed, verbal fluency, spatial relations

    C.   Gardner's model of multiple intelligences (8): linguistic, logical-mathematical, musical, spatial, bodily-kinesthetic, interpersonal, intrapersonal, naturalist

    D.   Sternberg's triarchic theory of intelligence

          1.   Bringing together different aspects of our intelligence

          2.   Intelligence has three aspects: analytic, creative, and practical

          3.   More intelligent individuals integrate these aspects better

    E.   Overview

          1.   Traditional view is that people vary in "amount" of intelligence they have

          2.   Clear that human intelligence involves multiple abilities, perhaps multiple intelligences (lack of data in support of latter)

          3.   Cultural context is always important (e.g., societies vary in what they value as intelligence, and what they measure for)

V.   Intelligence and the Nature-Nurture Question

    A.   Distinguishing between the influences of each

    B.   Closer genetic tie corresponds to closer intellectual similarity (MZ twins more similar than DZ twins)

    C.   Problem with kinship studies—close relatives tend to be raised in similar environments

    D.   IQ scores of adopted children closer to that of biological parents

    E.   Yet MZ twins raised together have more similar IQ than MZ twins raised apart (thus environment plays a role here too)

    F.   Conclusion is environment and genetics influence together in complex ways

    G.   Heritability of a trait—the degree to which genetic factor is a contributor

VI. Exploring Psychology: Racial/Ethnic Differences in IQ

    A.   Racial disparity in scores even when income level accounted for

    B.   *The Bell Curve*—proposed a widening gap between people with high and low IQ, with African Americans and recent immigrants have lower IQ than whites

    C.   Early intervention can make a difference (IQ is not fixed at birth)

    D.   Individual potential always unique

    E.   IQ scores have been rising in recent generations, especially among African Americans (relative to Euro-Americans)

SUMMARY

In this module you learn about human intelligence and the attempts we have made to define it and measure it. It is difficult to measure something when you are not even sure what it is. Various theories regarding what intelligence is and how to measure it continue to emerge. However, unlike past views, researchers are moving away from the idea of one notion of intelligence and toward the belief that there may be many intelligences, or at least many abilities, which comprise the notion of intelligence.

The earliest specific work evaluating intelligence began in France about 100 years ago. Alfred Binet was asked by Paris school officials to test children in the Paris system. The objective was to determine who might have difficulty with the existing school program and need special classrooms. Binet, along with assistance from Theodore Simon, developed an intelligence test based on the notion that brighter children would show abilities more typical of children older than they. Children of lesser ability would not be able to accomplish all the tasks that other children their age could. The intelligence test yielded, then, a mental age. This approach evolved into determining an intelligence quotient (IQ). The term is still used today, though it more often refers to Wechsler tests than the one developed by Binet). The intelligence quotient resulted from dividing a child's mental age (the score on the intelligence test) by that child's actual chronological age (how old he or she actually was, in years, at the time of taking the test), and multiplying by 100. Lewis Terman at Stanford University adapted Binet's test, and it became known as the Stanford-Binet Intelligence Scale (1916). More recently, David Wechsler created intelligence tests that include not only verbal tasks but also "performance" tasks, assessing abilities such as for picture arrangement, object assembly, and so forth. These have been created for different age groups. The IQ score derived from the test indicates how different the test-taker is from the typical score (the norm).

What makes a good intelligence test? First, the test must be standardized; that is, we must have results from testing large numbers of individuals with which we determine typical (average) scores and deviations. The mean (average) IQ score is set at 100, and approximately two-thirds of all people taking the intelligence test fall between the scores of 85 and 115. Second, a test must be reliable. That means that each time it is given, it must yield a similar type of result. Last, a test must have validity. This is a very important criterion. Validity comes from the word *valid*, meaning "true." A valid test measures what it says it measures. One of our concerns with intelligence testing is that the tests are culture-fair. In other words, if someone taking the test is not familiar either with the words or the concepts used in the test, is it a test of that person's intelligence? Or is it a test of the ability to understand, let's say, a foreign language or objects (and concepts) common to a foreign culture.

Binet's intention when he developed the first intelligence test was that it would be helpful and allow for earlier identification of and intervention for children who needed special assistance in learning. We hope that that does occur with the intelligence tests in use today. However, such tests can be and are misused. A child scoring low on the test may be thought of as less capable, and thus less energy and enthusiasm are expended on such an individual. Children themselves may adopt a more helpless attitude and may approach their learning tasks with less confidence and few expectations. No intelligence test is a perfect predictor of a child's future achievements. Certainly that and other assessment measures must be considered.

Though we are not quite sure what intelligence is, results of intelligence tests do reveal that individuals who perform at scores of 70 and below are likely to show developmental delays (mental retardation) if they have difficulty with everyday life tasks as well. Mental retardation may be a result of biological or environmental factors. Intellectual giftedness (an IQ score at 130 or higher) is the other end of the spectrum. Giftedness now also means exceptional artistic or musical ability. Though intelligence is important, persistence and motivation are crucial to one's overall success.

Because we are not sure what intelligence is, there are a number of theories. The oldest theory is Charles Spearman's (1927), who thought that there is one general ("g") intelligence factor. Spearman noted that many people who show intelligence in one area show similar ability in other areas as well. Louis Thurstone, a bit later in the twentieth century, had a different view, and proposed seven basic mental abilities. These abilities (such as memory, verbal fluency and comprehension, spatial and numerical ability) are what we have traditionally thought of as indicating "intelligence." Howard Gardner expanded Thurstone's approach, suggesting that in fact there are multiple intelligences. These include not only the traditional intellectual abilities (e.g., verbal and mathematical skill) but also things like musical, kinesthetic, and interpersonal intelligence. Sternberg (1994) suggests intelligence is more how we pull our skills together to meet daily challenges. His theory is the triarchic theory of intelligence, and its three components are analytic, creative, and practical intelligence. More intelligent people, Sternberg says, are able to integrate these three skills better to manage everyday tasks.

It is difficult to tell which contributes more to intelligence—nature (genes/heredity) or nurture (environment/how one is raised). The reason there is such difficulty is that people who share a common genetic heritage almost always share the same (or same type of) living environment as well. Teasing apart this question is next to impossible. To help address the task, we look at kinship studies (studies on sets of relatives). Identical (monozygotic, or MZ) twins have a more similar intelligence than do fraternal (dizygotic, or DZ) twins. This finding suggests that genetics is an important factor. Yet, identical twins raised together are more similar in their intelligence than identical twins raised apart. What would account for this latter difference? It must be environmental experience. The conclusion is that both genetic heritage and environmental experience are of great importance in determining intellectual ability. And, these two factors intimately interact, or influence each other, as a child grows and matures.

Intelligence tests traditionally have shown a higher level of ability for Euro-American white test-takers than for African Americans. Some (see Herrnstein and Murray, *The Bell Curve,* 1994) have suggested this difference is genetic, and social and educational intervention would not be productive. However, when existing research is considered as a whole, it does appear that the racial gap in intelligence is due to environment, and not heredity. Most likely, it is important that children are exposed to a culture of books and learning in order to strengthen abilities and excel in these areas.

KEY TERMS

Intelligence

Eugenics

Mental age

Intelligence quotient (IQ)

Norms

Standardization

Reliability

Validity

Predictive validity

Culture-fair tests

Mental retardation

Mainstreaming

Primary mental abilities

Multiple intelligences

Triarchic theory of intelligence

Heritability

SELF-TEST PRACTICE QUIZ

From the Key Terms select that which best matches the following:

1. _____ Standards used to compare one's test results with those of others

2. _____ A view on intelligence proposed by Robert Sternberg suggesting that intelligence is the ability to successfully integrate analytical, creative, and practical skills

3. _____ Tests that eliminate potential bias due to lack of prior experience with the dominant culture

4. _____ The ability to think and reason clearly and act purposefully in order to live effectively

5. _____ The degree to which genetic influence accounts for the manifestation of a trait within a population

6. _____ Seven basic factors constituting intelligence, as proposed by Thurstone

7. _____ The result of a formula indicating degree of intelligence, based on score (mental age) derived from an intelligence test

8. _____ A desirable test feature wherein the test yields similar results when administered over time

9. _____ Experiencing developmental delays in both intellectual and social functioning

10. _____ An important feature of a test, wherein the test measures accurately the abilities it is designed to measure

11. _____ A concept, introduced by Howard Gardner, suggesting that there are a variety of intelligences (including social and kinesthetic skills) that give evidence of intelligent human behavior

12. _____ A score derived from an intelligence test, where ability is related to success at tasks typical for other individuals of a comparable age

a. Intelligence
b. Eugenics
c. Mental age
d. Intelligence quotient (IQ)
e. Norms
f. Standardization
g. Reliability
h. Validity
i. Predictive validity
j. Culture-fair tests
k. Mental retardation
l. Mainstreaming
m. Primary mental abilities
n. Multiple intelligences
o. Triarchic theory of intelligence
p. Heritability

13. _____   Placing children who have some intellectual deficit or impairment in a regular school classroom

14. _____   The extent to which a test accurately indicates the test-taker's future ability at the skill or area of knowledge being tested

15. _____   Establishing norms for a test, derived from administering the test to a large representative sample from the relevant population

16. _____   Encouraging breeding among the intelligent to improve the human stock

17. Central to the definition of intelligence is the belief that it involves the ability to

    a.   excel academically.
    b.   adapt to the environment.
    c.   survive on the streets.
    d.   show exceptional social or analytical skills.

18. Binet and Simon developed the first intelligence test because they wanted to

    a.   identify the most capable among French children.
    b.   exclude children of low abilities from further education.
    c.   conduct a longitudinal study on children who were classified as gifted.
    d.   discover children with learning difficulties who would need extra help.

19. On an IQ test, a child's mental age is

    a.   the same as his chronological age.
    b.   calculated by multiplying chronological age by 100.
    c.   an indication of the individual's mental ability relative to tasks others the same age can achieve.
    d.   within 15 points of the norm calculated for that child's age group.

20. Why is it important to standardize a test? Standardization

    a.   allows test developers to establish accurate norms.
    b.   lets test givers accurately measure children's mental ages.
    c.   gives an indication of how much of intelligence is due to genetics.
    d.   establishes a test's level of predictive validity.

21. The most widely used intelligence test in the United States is the

    a.   Stanford-Binet Intelligence Scale (SBIS).
    b.   series of tests developed by Wechsler.
    c.   Object Assembly Test.
    d.   Primary Mental Abilities Test.

22. Professor Meeny has a nasty habit of giving tests that have nothing to do with the class. The tests are so difficult that everybody fails them every time. Professor Meeny's tests are

    a.   high in both validity and reliability.
    b.   low in both validity and reliability.
    c.   low in validity, but high in reliability.
    d.   high in validity, but low in reliability.

23. A major difference between the tests created by Binet and Terman and those developed by Wechsler are that the Wechsler tests
    a. lead to consistently higher IQ scores achieved by test-takers.
    b. have components that include tests of nonverbal (e.g., performance) abilities.
    c. are a more modern version of the Stanford-Binet test with more modern terminology.
    d. are based on a ratio score rather than a deviation score.
24. What is one drawback of using intelligence tests to classify individuals in terms of mental ability?
    a. Individuals who do not perform well may be labeled and treated with lower expectations.
    b. Children who do not score highly may give up on themselves and simply not try to learn.
    c. Other criteria, besides scores on an intelligence test, are indicators of how likely a person is to achieve.
    d. All of the above are correct.
25. Cultural background is an important consideration when administering intelligence tests. An intelligence test is NOT an indicator of ability when it
    a. tests familiarity with a language rather than the concepts it was designed to evaluate.
    b. is given to individuals from a variety of different cultures.
    c. is given to children of just one age group.
    d. shows an unusually high level of predictive validity.
26. In Terman's study of gifted children (the "little geniuses"), he found that
    a. individuals who were quite bright as children lost this superiority once they entered adulthood.
    b. more intelligent children were also more at risk for physical and psychological disorders.
    c. personality characteristics such as persistence and motivation were also important in achievement.
    d. the children categorized as "gifted" were really no different from other children.
27. Which statement best describes Spearman's view of intelligence?
    a. There are many intelligences including linguistic, naturalist, and intrapersonal.
    b. Intelligence is determined entirely by genetics.
    c. There is one general intelligence that underlies all abilities.
    d. Intelligence is composed of seven primary mental abilities.
28. Which of the following is a potential cause of mental retardation?
    a. Genetics
    b. Lack of environmental stimulation
    c. Lead exposure
    d. All of the above
29. A problem with kinship studies, such as researching the factors involved in intelligence, is that
    a. nature and nurture are not the real issues with regard to intellectual functioning.
    b. it is difficult to get all members of a large family unit to participate.
    c. the closer the genetic link among family members, the closer (usually) are the environmental experiences as well.
    d. we cannot distinguish the heritability of traits between monozygotic (MZ) and dizygotic (DZ) twins.
30. The approach that considered intelligence to consist of seven components—such as verbal comprehension and fluency, memory, and inductive reasoning—is known as
    a. Spearman's Theory of General Cognitive Ability.
    b. Thurstone's Primary Mental Abilities approach.
    c. Gardner's Model of Multiple Intelligences.
    d. Sternberg's Triarchic Theory of Intelligence.

31. Studies that compare the intelligence of adopted children with the intelligence of both their biological and their adoptive parents find
     a. no differences between the intelligence of the adopted children and that of their adoptive parents.
     b. no differences between the intelligence of the adopted children and that of their biological parents.
     c. the intelligence of adopted children to be more like that of their biological parents.
     d. the intelligence of adopted children to be more like that of their adoptive parents.

32. Results of adoption studies tend to provide evidence in support of
     a. a genetic explanation for intelligence.
     b. an environmental explanation for intelligence.
     c. quality of the school system as the determinant of intelligence.
     d. age of parents at time of adoption as the determinant of intelligence.

33. One source of evidence that counters the notion proposed in Herrnstein and Murray's *The Bell Curve* that intellectual differences are racially based is the finding that
     a. IQ scores among African Americans have been rising slightly more quickly than those of Euro-Americans.
     b. African Americans score as high on intelligence tests as do Euro-Americans when socioeconomic factors are taken into account.
     c. IQ scores among African Americans have been declining more slowly than those of Euro-Americans.
     d. children adopted by African American parents score higher on intelligence tests than do children adopted by non-Hispanic white parents.

34. When the intelligence of monozygotic (MZ) twins is compared to that of dizygotic (DZ) twins, we find that the greatest similarity in intelligence is between
     a. identical twins raised together.
     b. identical twins raised apart.
     c. fraternal twins raised together.
     d. fraternal twins raised apart.

35. Which of these is NOT one of the three aspects of intelligence proposed by Sternberg?
     a. creative
     b. analytic
     c. mathematical
     d. practical

36. Regarding the notion of multiple intelligences,
     a. increasing amounts of evidence reveal support for this view.
     b. there are no more than seven or eight basic types of intelligence.
     c. evidence suggests that there are many factors contributing to intelligence, but support for multiple intelligences has not yet been widely found.
     d. there appears to be one pervasive underlying factor for cognitive ability.

ESSAY QUESTIONS

1. Explain how the first IQ (intelligence quotient) was computed. How is a deviation score different from an intelligence score computed this way?

2. Why is it difficult to develop a truly culture-free intelligence test?

3. How can kinship and adoptee studies help us learn more about influences on intelligence? What are some findings we have from these studies?

ANSWER KEY

1. Norms
2. Triarchic theory of intelligence
3. Culture-fair tests
4. Intelligence
5. Heritability
6. Primary mental abilities
7. Intelligence quotient (IQ)
8. Reliability
9. Mental retardation
10. Validity
11. Multiple intelligences
12. Mental age
13. Mainstreaming
14. Predictive validity
15. Standardization
16. Eugenics
17. b
18. d
19. c
20. a
21. b
22. c
23. b
24. d
25. a
26. c
27. c
28. d
29. c
30. b
31. c
32. a
33. a
34. a

35. c

36. c

SAMPLE ANSWERS TO ESSAY QUESTIONS

1. The first IQ score was indeed a quotient—the result of the mathematical process of division. A child was given an intelligence test. This test was composed of tasks that could be accomplished by typical children of various ages. The level of tasks the child taking the test was able to accomplish successfully yielded a mental age. For example, a child may be 10 years old (her chronological age). However, if she is able to accomplish all the tasks of the typical 9-year-old, 10-year-old, 11-year-old, and even some of those typical for a 12-year-old, she may have a mental age of, let's say, 11.7 years. In other words, she can accomplish tasks that normally a child would need to be 11.7 years old in order to carry out successfully. This mental age (MA) is then divided by her chronological or actual age in years (CA), and multiplied by 100 (to standardize so that scores have a mean or average of 100). This child's score would be 117. Since most intelligence test-takers (more than two-thirds) score at or below an IQ of 115—this test-taker is above average. The traditional IQ (an example of which is computed here) is based on a ratio. More recent versions of intelligence tests use deviation scores. The deviation score just means it is an indication of how different the test-taker's score is from the norm, or arithmetic average.

2. Although it is important to have culture-free tests, they are difficult to develop. A culture-free test is one where a test-taker from any culture and environmental experience has equal familiarity with the concepts and objects used in the questions (and tasks) actually assessing intellectual ability. Thus, there is no bias against (no disadvantage for) a test-taker who may be unfamiliar, or less familiar, with the language in which the intelligence test is written, the tools (objects, concepts) by which intelligence is probed, or both. If a test is given to someone less familiar or unfamiliar with these aspects, the test is not really a test of intelligence but rather a test of familiarity with the test items.

    The problem with creating a culture-free test is that (a) the ones that have been created are not as good predictors of future achievement, and (b) all tests must be grounded in some form of common understanding and reflect what is valued and desired as showing intelligence. Thus, the very definition of intelligence, and what shows intelligent behavior, may vary from culture to culture. In the predominant culture in the United States, for example, intelligence is very much tied to linguistic and mathematical ability. Where children of any race are exposed to books, mathematical games, and an emphasis on learning, they perform better on typical American intelligence tests than do children without these environmental experiences.

3. The two main accepted sources of influence on intelligence are nature (the genetic code that an individual inherits) and nurture (the experiences an individual has with his or her environment). Adopted children tend to be more similar in IQ to their biological parents than to their adopted parents, which suggests a genetic basis of intelligence. Kinship studies can also help distinguish between the influences of nature and nurture, as there is a varying amount of genetic similarity among members of the same family unit. Indeed, kinship studies have shown that the more family members are alike in terms of genetic inheritance, the more alike they are in terms of exhibited intelligence. This finding then suggests a strong genetic source for intelligence. However, it should be remembered that nearly all closely-related family members also often share a similar, or in fact the same, environment. Thus, with kinship studies alone, we cannot completely distinguish between influences from nature vs. nurture.

    One kind of kinship study is with twins, and identical twins are of particular interest since they share exactly the same genetic code. Studies with identical twins are the most convincing with regard to a hereditary influence on intelligence; identical twins show the greatest intellectual similarity of all. However, our research with monozygotic (identical) twins has also revealed that MZ twins raised together are more similar than MZ twins raised apart. Why the difference in intelligence findings here? Clearly, it must be differing environmental experiences that account for the difference among twins where the genetic heritage is identical.

MODULE 7.4 APPLICATION: BECOMING A CREATIVE PROBLEM SOLVER

LEARNING OBJECTIVES

After you have mastered the information in this unit, you will be able to:

- Outline the keys to becoming a creative problem solver

OUTLINE

I.   Keys to Becoming a Creative Problem Solver
   A.   Adopt a questioning attitude—be aware of various alternatives and their potential
   B.   Gather information—use the many information sources available
   C.   Avoid getting stuck in mental sets
      1.   Mental sets can impair problem-solving efforts (cannot see real problem)
      2.   Examine what the real requirement is of a question or challenge
   D.   Generate alternatives
      1.   Best to come up with many possible solutions, not just grasp the first one
      2.   Try brainstorming
         a)   Write down as many solutions to problem as can be come up with
         b)   Don't prejudge your list of solutions
         c)   Seek all ideas, no matter how "off the wall"
         d)   Let list sit a few days before contemplating
         e)   Think of analogies—a prior problem related to what you are facing now
         f)   Think "outside the box"
   E.   Sleep on it—sleep enhances insight and creative thinking
   F.   Test it out
      1.   Try out your possible solutions
      2.   Let situation "incubate" if necessary
      3.   Remember danger of mental set—the tendency to stick with traditional solution

SUMMARY

In this module you learn about applying what we know about intelligence, thinking, and creativity with regard to problem solving. We all have problems to face. The key is in not avoiding the problem (this is an unhealthy approach) but in finding an effective, practical, and relatively timely solution.

The most important thing to remember in solving problems is to avoid the allure of sticking with the same solutions just because they are the ones you have tried in the past. If you think of an analogous situation and the previous approach works, fine. But that is not likely to be the case. If so, we need to be open-minded and allow ourselves to come up with a variety of other possible solutions, no matter how "wild" they may seem. As we know, finding fresh ways to view traditional (and perhaps previously unresolved) problems can lead to revolutionary breakthroughs for ourselves and perhaps for others. These breakthroughs may even affect large numbers of the human population.

A good way to come up with creative solutions to problems is to allow yourself to brainstorm. In brainstorming, you let whatever solutions come to your mind enter the realm of consideration. Write them all down, and avoid making decisions at the time you are coming up with potential solutions. Ideally, let your list of possible solutions rest for a bit of time. You will come back to the list later with perhaps a fresher and even more objective perspective. Remember that the key to creative solutions is not just a matter of problems and ideas but also how you look at them. Try your solutions out, unless one is so wacky it may pose harm to someone. You never know where your innovative approach to problems in your life will lead you.

KEY TERM

Brainstorming—a technique for coming up with novel effective solutions to problems,by allowing the mind to generate as many potential solutions as possible, without prejudgment, and considering all of them after a period of rest or incubation.

SELF-TEST PRACTICE QUIZ

1.   Which of the following is NOT helpful with respect to creative problem solving?
   a.   Allow yourself to generate many possible solutions no matter how "weird" they may seem at the outset.
   b.   Think of past experiences, and consider what worked for you before in similar situations.
   c.   Try out some of your potential solutions, assuming it is safe to do so.
   d.   Try to come up with an answer or solution as quickly as possible.

ANSWER KEY

1.   d

CHAPTER 7 APPLICATION EXERCISES

1.   What do you think intelligence is? Write down three or four characteristics that you have found indicate intelligent thinking or behavior. How well do they correspond with the concepts presented in this chapter? Do you think intelligence can change? If not, why not? If so, how? Do you think your own intelligence is fixed, or can it change? Has it changed?

2.   What kinds of problems have you had in your life recently? Have you solved them? How? What problem-solving strategies do you typically use? Which of the suggestions given in Module 7.4 might you add to your problem-solving techniques? In what way might they be helpful; that is, in what way would they be an improvement compared to the processes you use now? Choose one or two of the techniques listed—and try them out.

CHAPTER 8

Motivation and Emotion

In Chapter 8 you learn about the more subtle sources of energy that are the impetus behind what we do and why we do it. Motivation, of course, is related to our emotions because much of what prompts us to do things is a function of that which we find to be personally meaningful. Some sources of motivation are purely for survival. These are inborn biological needs such as the need to obtain food. The experience of hunger seems to involve both the stomach and various parts of the brain. Eating, while physiologically based, has social and behavioral aspects as well. It is the social and behavioral aspects that have most led to current problems with various eating disorders.

While nearly all inborn needs are for survival, we also have needs for exploration and activity. Though apparently not necessary to keep us alive, these stimulus motives seem to be programmed in to human and animal functioning. Arousal theory proposes that there is an optimal level of stimulation, which can vary from individual to individual, and from time to time. Moderate levels of arousal are best for performing most routine tasks. In addition to biological sources of motivation, there are psychological ones as well. Abraham Maslow proposed the hierarchy of needs, which incorporates both physiological and psychological needs as an individual strives towards self-actualization. Self-actualization is maximizing our unique potential—being all that we can be.

Instincts have little, if any, role in human motivation. Rather, physiological needs (a physical lack) create drives (such as hunger), and drive theory is now the prevailing view in explaining motivation. The drive creates action, to satisfy the need (resulting in drive reduction). Drive theory is oriented around the notion of homeostasis. Homeostasis is a steady bodily state—it is thought that the body functions best at, and seeks, an optimal level of fluid, sustenance, oxygen, and so forth. When the body is depleted of one or more of these biological necessities, the organism is motivated to act, obtain what is lacking, and restore homeostasis. Can everything be explained in terms of the disruption and subsequent restoration of homeostasis? No. In fact, humans sometimes deliberately upset homeostasis—in your latest rugby game or track and field match, for example. Psychological (interpersonal) motives include the need for affiliation and the need for achievement. People vary in their need to excel. For some, achievement is very important, and opportunities for it are sought. For others, presumably with a low need for achievement, there is little desire to find opportunities to excel and the objective, rather, seems to be to avoid failure. Both of these components are factors in psychological sources of motivation. We also have a need for our thoughts and behaviors to be consistent (if not, we experience cognitive dissonance, and we will work to resolve that inconsistency). Factors that motivate behavior from outside an organism are incentives. Instead of motivation being a "push" from within, incentives (goals or rewards we want) pull us from without.

We do not have the full or final picture on emotions other than to say the experience of emotion is complex and appears to involve many parts of the brain. Emotions are considered to be feeling states and to be comprised of physiological (activation of the nervous system), cognitive, and behavioral components. Emotions typically are expressed through our faces and how we act, though there are cultural norms (display rules) that direct more specifically how this is done within a given culture. There are six basic emotions that are universally recognized: happiness, sadness, anger, fear, surprise, and disgust. Other, more complex emotions are thought to be blends of these basic ones.

Debate continues as to how emotions are experienced and how that experience is tied to situational factors. Must emotion always have a cognitive component? Must our cognitions about what is going on with us precede determining how we feel emotionally? Do we respond first and then use our body's behavior as an indicator of the emotion we are feeling? All of these views regarding emotional experience have been proposed and are still being considered. Love, a fundamental emotion, has been researched, and the triangular model of love is one way of contemplating this concept. Without doubt, emotions are vitally important in our everyday functioning. The gift of emotional intelligence helps us use the motivation and energy in emotions wisely.

MODULE 8.1 MOTIVATION: THE "WHY'S" OF BEHAVIOR

LEARNING OBJECTIVES

After you have mastered the information in this unit, you will be able to:

- Define motivation

- Discuss instinct theory

- Discuss drive theory

- Explain how arousal theory accounts for differences in motivational states

- Explain how incentive theory differs from drive theory

- Discuss cognitive dissonance theory

- Define psychosocial needs

- Discuss Maslow's hierarchy of needs

OUTLINE

I.   Motivation
    A.   Involves factors that initiate, direct and sustain goal-directed behavior
    B.   Motives—what drives behavior and accounts for why we do what we do
II.   Biological Sources of Motivation
    A.   Involves inborn needs (such as for food, water, oxygen)
    B.   Needs are predominantly those necessary for survival
    C.   Instincts
        1.   Behaviors programmed by nature (nest-building, salmon going upriver to spawn)
        2.   Instinctive behaviors
            a)   Fixed, inborn patterns of response
            b)   Specific to members of a particular species
        3.   Instinct theory—view that all behavior is motivated by instinct
        4.   Do humans have instincts?
            a)   Sigmund Freud (sexual and aggressive instincts), William James (37 different instincts; including curiosity, cleanliness)—proponents
            b)   Current view of motivation does not support notion of instincts (too many, not a useful approach)
    D.   Needs and drives
        1.   Drive theory
            a)   Became model for human motivation beginning in 1950s
            b)   Idea is biological needs demand satisfaction (Clark Hull)
        2.   Need—state of deprivation or deficiency (usually biological)

3. Drive—bodily tension or unease arising from an unmet need (e.g., hunger, thirst)
4. Drive reduction—satisfaction of a drive
5. Homeostasis
   a) Basis for drive theory
   b) Idea is body tends to maintain a steady internal state
   c) Disruption (e.g., drop in temperature, blood sugar) prompts behavior to restore homeostasis (steady state)
6. Needs and drives differ
   a) Bodily need may exist but without corresponding drive
   b) Strength of need vs. drive may differ (e.g., when fasting, may feel less hungry on second day than on first)
7. Drive theory incorporates important role for learning
   a) We learn responses that are reinforced by drive reduction
   b) Primary drives are inborn; however, we may learn some drives as a result of experience (secondary drives)

E. Optimum level of arousal
1. Harry Harlow—not all drives are to satisfy biological needs
2. Humans (and other animals) may have innate needs for exploration, activity
3. Stimulus motives—needs to investigate environment, manipulate (especially novel stimuli)
4. Arousal theory
   a) Notion that there is an optimal level of arousal
   b) This level can vary from individual to individual, and from time to time
   c) Sensation-seekers—high need for arousal
   d) Moderate level of arousal best for most tasks
   e) More difficult tasks—lower levels of arousal needed
   f) Yerkes-Dodson law (inverted U) represents this relationship between arousal and quality of performance

III. Psychological Sources of Motivation
A. We are not idle even when homeostasis level is perfect
B. Incentive theory—attraction to particular goals or objects motivates much of our behavior (a drive is a "push," an incentive is a "pull")
1. Incentives—rewards or other stimuli which motivate us to act
2. Incentive value
   a) The strength of the pull, or lure, a goal or object has
   b) Culture, experience are important determining factors
C. Cognitive dissonance—when thoughts and behaviors are incongruent
1. People are motivated to maintain consistency between thoughts, behaviors
2. Festinger and Carlsmith (1959) study—boring task
   a) One group paid $20.00 to lie, say task was interesting (to other students)
   b) Second group paid $1.00 to do the same
   c) Attitude towards boring task evaluated for both—$1.00 group had more positive feelings towards task; why?
   d) Explanation: $1.00 not sufficient to justify lying (telling other students task was interesting); thoughts/beliefs adjusted to fit behavior/actions
3. Can adjust thought, adjust behavior, rationalize (explain away), or ignore incongruence in order to reduce dissonance
4. Effort justification—we like objective more if we had to work harder for it (keeps behavior and belief consistent)
D. Psychosocial needs (interpersonal needs)
1. Need for affiliation—need for social contact with others

     2.   Need for achievement
       a)   High need for achievement—strong desire to excel
       b)   Low need for achievement—objective is to avoid failure
     3.   Sources of motivation
       a)   Extrinsic—desire is for external rewards (money, praise)
       b)   Intrinsic—effort is expended just for personal satisfaction or pleasure
     4.   Goals regarding achievement may be in opposition
       a)   Achievement motivation—take on challenges in order to gain success
       b)   Avoidance motivation—avoid challenges in order to avoid failure
     5.   Achievement motivation strongly influenced by experience (parents and others)

IV.   Hierarchy of Needs
   A.   Proposed by Abraham Maslow (1970)
   B.   Incorporates both biological and psychological needs
   C.   Basic needs
     1.   Physiological, safety
     2.   According to theory these must be met first
   D.   Higher-order needs—love and belongingness, esteem, and self-actualization
   E.   Self-actualization
     1.   Knowing one's abilities, strengths, talents
     2.   Putting one's unique potential to best use
   F.   View has intuitive appeal
   G.   Criticisms of Maslow's model:
     1.   Needs may not always follow order as proposed in theory
     2.   Same behavior may fit several of the levels (e.g., both nourishment and esteem)

SUMMARY

In this module you learn some of the basics regarding motivation. Most of motivation theory discussed in this unit has to do with human motivation. Motivation is incredibly important, in that it is what gets us involved in a behavior and maintains our interest and effort at it. Nearly always our motivated behavior has some end objective—even if that final objective is simply the fun or learning gained from carrying out the actions. Motivation comprises the factors that activate, direct, and sustain goal-directed behavior. Motives, the objectives prompting us to do what we do, are the explanation, the answer to "Why?" regarding our behavior.

A major motivating force, of course, has always been survival. Thus, we are motivated to meet certain needs—e.g., for food, water, oxygen—that are fundamentally biologically based. A question examined regarding human behavior is that of the role of instincts. Instincts are "wired-in" behavior patterns particular to a given species. Is human behavior, or any part of it, governed by instinctual reactions? The early view (especially as proposed by Sigmund Freud and William James) was that instincts are a substantial component in human motivation. The current thinking, however, does not attribute much, if any, human behavior to instincts. Rather, the view is that humans have needs. Most needs, as implied above, are biologically based. A need (for example, lack of sustenance in the body, low blood sugar levels) creates a drive (hunger). The drive is an uncomfortable or unsettled bodily state, which motivates us to seek its satisfaction or resolution (in other words, drive reduction). These views, together known as drive theory, are based on the concept of homeostasis. Homeostasis suggests that the body functions best when it is at a kind of physiological equilibrium. The body has sufficient nourishment, fluid, rest, and so forth. Disruption to the ideal levels of homeostasis motivates us to restore these optimal levels again. Thus, we eat until we are full, rest until we feel restored—and so forth.

Though much of motivation can be traced to these biological survival needs, not all behavior has such as its driving force. Harry Harlow, who did extensive research with monkeys, noted that animals will explore and manipulate the environment—whether or not reinforcers for doing so are present. Thus, there may be stimulus motives as well. Stimulus motives are also, it is believed, innate and biologically based, though apparently not necessary for survival. Arousal theory is related to the stimulation that we seek or experience, and it is thought that there is an optimal level of arousal for various tasks we need to perform. The relationship between task complexity and ideal level of arousal is represented as an inverted U-shape and is described by the Yerkes-Dodson law. Simple and/or routine tasks can be performed well even at fairly high levels of arousal. The more difficult a task, however, the lower the level of arousal at which we will have the most success in completing the task effectively. Thus, an unfamiliar or complicated task is made more difficult by becoming anxious (raising one's level of arousal) about it.

Notice that needs and drives are related (usually), but they are different as well. A need is something the body lacks—sustenance, oxygen, or even the opportunity to try out and explore, as with the stimulus motives. A need may exist, but it is not always translated into a drive—that uncomfortable or unsettled bodily state that heads us toward whatever objective will resolve that unsettled feeling. Our blood sugar level may have dropped, for example, but if we are so intensely involved in an activity that we are not aware of this need, we may not feel hungry and not act to bring sustenance our way. Physically or mentally we may really need some stimulation or a change of scene—but on the other hand, we just can't seem to get ourselves out of the chair or out of the house. There is a need, but the drive is not accompanying it, or is not sufficiently strong.

Though most of the motivation factors we have discussed have been primary drives (innate, biologically based), there are psychological factors that motivate us as well. Our goals or objectives tempt us, or draw us, because they have incentive value. Thus, some behavior may not be based on a biological drive (a "push," from the drive) but rather we feel the "pull"—the lure, emanating from the objective or goal that we seek. Some objectives, of course, can be very good things—getting that degree, earning the paycheck. But, for example, we may eat—even though we are not hungry, and even though in fact more food will make us feel uncomfortable—because that barbeque smells so good or the strawberry shortcake and chocolate torte look irresistible. Incentives can be powerful!

We also have the psychological need to keep our behaviors and our thoughts/beliefs consistent. When they are inconsistent, we feel cognitive dissonance. Thoughts and behaviors that contradict each other leave us with a sense of disharmony or inner unrest. Research by Festinger and Carlsmith (1959) revealed that when beliefs and behaviors are in opposition and cannot otherwise be explained away, we adjust one or the other until they are again consonant. In their classic study, Festinger and Carlsmith had all participants carry out a very boring task. Then, half the participants were each paid $1.00 to go out to other students and tell them the task they just completed was interesting. The remaining half of the participants were paid $20.00 each to do the same thing. Later, all participants were asked how well they had liked the task (the very boring one). Surprisingly, the students paid $1.00 to lie reported that they liked the task significantly more than the participants paid $20.00 to lie. Why would this be? Apparently, the participants paid $20.00 each to lie could justify their behavior—they didn't like the task, they told other students the task was interesting—but for $20.00, the lying behavior was worth it. What was going on with the $1.00 participants? Presumably, none of them believed they would lie for only $1.00; thus, obviously, their behavior of lying could not have been from the money ($1.00 was not enough of an incentive). The $1.00 participants did not approve of lying (we assume), yet they lied; beliefs and behaviors are inconsistent here. This should (and did, in Festinger and Carlsmith's study) create cognitive dissonance, and individuals experiencing this needed to resolve this disparity. Cognitive dissonance can be resolved by changing a behavior, changing a belief, rationalizing ("I did it for the money"), or ignoring the discrepancy. In the case of the $1.00 Festinger and Carlsmith participants, they changed their beliefs to fit the behaviors they had exhibited. Their thinking was, "I didn't like the task, I told other people I did like it; I wouldn't lie for just $1.00—I must have liked it (the task)!"

Effort justification, one component of cognitive dissonance, leads to some rather notable beliefs and behaviors. Research shows that, when we have worked extremely hard for an objective (even if this effort involved unpleasant or distasteful activities), we tend to like that objective more than goals we obtained with far less effort. Why? Again it is a resolution of conflict between behaviors and beliefs. Why would we endure or work so hard for an objective? Why would we put up with an experience that was really unpleasant? Only, of course, if the outcome were truly terrific! Effort expended (behavior) should match our appraisal of the goal (a thought or belief).

Psychosocial needs also motivate behavior. We have a need for affiliation, for example, which leads us to associate with others and seek social contact. We have, as well, a need for achievement. Achievement motivation varies among individuals. Some people have a very high need to achieve. These individuals seek out numerous reasonable opportunities and challenges, ones that will allow them to apply themselves and excel. They take on tasks with enthusiasm and a positive attitude, even though it is true they don't meet with success every time. Others may be motivated more by a fear of failure or simply have low achievement needs. In these latter cases, opportunities may be passed up unless the tasks are quite easy. Avoidance motivation leads such individuals to evade opportunities unless success is assured.

A theory proposed by Abraham Maslow helps incorporate both the biological and the psychological needs driving behavior. Maslow proposed the hierarchy of needs where lower level needs (which first demand our attention) are biological in nature. If these (basic) needs are satisfied, we then can go on to higher-order needs; higher-order needs are more psychological in nature. These include needs for love and belongingness, esteem, and ultimately, self-actualization. Self-actualization involves knowing oneself and one's abilities and putting these abilities to best use. Utilizing our potential fully leads to the state of self-actualization. Since everyone (according to Maslow's view) is unique and has a different set of talents, becoming self-actualized is a different experience and process for every person.

KEY TERMS

Motivation

Motives

Instinctive behaviors

Instinct theory

Drive theory

Need

Drive

Drive reduction

Primary drives

Secondary drives

Stimulus motives

Arousal theory

Yerkes-Dodson law

Incentive theory

Incentives

Incentive value

Cognitive dissonance

Cognitive dissonance theory

Effort justification

Psychosocial needs

Need for achievement

Extrinsic motivation

Intrinsic motivation

Achievement motivation

Avoidance motivation

Hierarchy of needs

Self-actualization

SELF-TEST PRACTICE QUIZ

From the Key Terms select that which best matches the following (Note: Not every Key Term will be used.):

1. _____   The view that the body needs an optimal level of stimulation; if stimulation drops below this level the organism will act to restore it

2. _____   Motivation stemming from one's own interest in a goal and the knowledge or pleasure gained from achieving it

3. _____   Valuing an objective more when we have had to work very hard or suffer much to achieve it

4. _____   Relating to the factors that initiate, direct, and sustain goal-directed behavior

5. _____   "Prewired," innate patterns of behavior that are particular to a given species

6. _____   The view that motivation stems from the pull, or lure, of a goal or objective

7. _____   The unsettled feeling when one's thoughts/beliefs and one's behaviors are contradictory

a.   Motivation

b.   Motives

c.   Instinctive behaviors

d.   Instinct theory

e.   Drive theory

f.   Need

g.   Drive

h.   Drive reduction

i.   Primary drives

j.   Secondary drives

k.   Stimulus motives

l.   Arousal theory

m.   Yerkes-Dodson law

n.   Incentive theory

o.   Incentives

p.   Incentive value

q.   Cognitive dissonance

r.   Cognitive dissonance theory

8. _____ A theory proposed by Abraham Maslow, which incorporates both biological (basic) and psychological (higher-order) needs, culminating in self-actualization

9. _____ Interpersonal needs that motivate us; they include a need for social contact and a need for achievement

10. _____ A state (usually physiological) where there is a deficiency or lack

11. _____ Needs or wants that prompt behavior aimed at achieving them

12. _____ Innate, biologically based motives that lead an organism to explore and manipulate the environment; probably not necessary for survival

13. _____ Basic, inborn, biologically based drives (such as hunger, thirst)

14. _____ A representation of the relationship between arousal level and quality of performance; relationship is roughly an inverted U-shape

15. _____ An unsettled or uncomfortable bodily condition resulting from an unmet need

16. _____ The need to excel, experience success

17. _____ The view that behavior is motivated by a desire to satisfy unmet biological needs

18. Instincts are
    a. the same in every species.
    b. learned behaviors.
    c. programmed by nature.
    d. none of the above

19. When our body is lacking in something biologically fundamental, such as appropriate sustenance or sufficient fluid, we experience a(n)
    a. need.
    b. drive.
    c. instinct.
    d. incentive.

s. Effort justification

t. Psychosocial needs

u. Need for achievement

v. Extrinsic motivation

w. Intrinsic motivation

x. Achievement motivation

y. Avoidance motivation

z. Hierarchy of needs

aa. Self-actualization

20. William James and Sigmund Freud both believed that much of human behavior could be attributed to

    a. needs.
    b. drives.
    c. instincts.
    d. incentives.

21. The major model for human motivation is

    a. arousal theory.
    b. drive theory.
    c. incentive theory.
    d. Maslow's hierarchy of needs.

22. A need is different from a drive, in that a drive

    a. is based on a fundamental biological lack.
    b. prompts behavior, but a need may not.
    c. does not necessarily motivate behavior, but a need does.
    d. is closely related to incentive value.

23. Homeostasis means

    a. a balance between biological and psychological needs.
    b. that one or more primary drives have been triggered.
    c. that the body seeks, and functions best at, a state of biological equilibrium.
    d. a balance between arousal levels for both needs and drives.

24. The Yerkes-Dodson law explains

    a. the human drive toward self-actualization.
    b. why some people are greater sensation-seekers than others.
    c. how instincts and learned behaviors interact.
    d. the relationship between task difficulty and optimal levels of arousal.

25. Motives that seem to be inborn, but are not necessary for survival, are called _____ motives.

    a. arousal
    b. stimulus
    c. optimal
    d. incentive

26. Sensation-seekers

    a. have a high need for arousal.
    b. are more likely to fill their lives with many stimulating activities and thrills.
    c. may pose some risk to themselves because they may have difficulty restraining impulsive behavior.
    d. exhibit all of the above characteristics.

27. Incentive theory suggests that

    a. we act because we have an unmet need.
    b. we act because we have an unmet drive.
    c. the "pull" or lure of a goal or objective motivates us.
    d. the desire for money motivates all of human behavior.

28. Our need for stimulation may vary, based upon

    a. the amount of activity we have engaged in previously.
    b. the difficulty of the task we are about to undertake.
    c. restrictions in place regarding exploration and investigation.
    d. culturally-established guidelines for activity.

29. In his research with monkeys, Harry Harlow discovered that

    a.   even animals are attracted to financial rewards.
    b.   monkeys seem to grasp their own version of self-actualization.
    c.   monkeys would play with a mechanical puzzle just because it was there.
    d.   there is no real evidence for stimulus motivation.

30. Which of the following is NOT a determinant of incentive value?

    a.   Experience
    b.   Culture
    c.   Expectations
    d.   Stimulus motivation

31. Simon went to "make millions the easy way" seminar, only to find out that the seminar was a waste of time. Unfortunately, though, he spent a huge amount of money on this seminar. According to the effort justification effect, Simon will probably

    a.   tell his friends how horrible the seminar was.
    b.   insist that it wasn't a *complete* waste.
    c.   take the seminar again.
    d.   none of the above

32. The discomfort experienced when attitudes and behaviors are inconsistent is known as

    a.   arousal disequilibrium.
    b.   homeostasis.
    c.   cognitive dissonance.
    d.   dissociation.

33. Maria enjoys crossword puzzles simply because she likes the mental challenge. Maria is experiencing _____ motivation.

    a.   extrinsic
    b.   stimulus
    c.   dissonant
    d.   intrinsic

34. When thoughts and behaviors are in conflict, we may

    a.   adjust a behavior to fit our attitude or belief.
    b.   adjust a belief to fit our behaviors or actions.
    c.   ignore, or rationalize away, the disparity.
    d.   do all of the above.

35. Someone who is not interested in a goal because it appears to them to be too easy probably is

    a.   high in achievement motivation.
    b.   high in avoidance motivation.
    c.   best classified as a sensation-seeker.
    d.   motivated by extrinsic factors.

36. Individuals who set predominantly learning goals for themselves probably are

    a.   most interested in the approval of others.
    b.   motivated more by extrinsic factors.
    c.   motivated more by intrinsic factors.
    d.   afraid of very high levels of achievement.

37. According to Abraham Maslow, the ultimate goal of human behavior is

    a.   self-actualization.
    b.   extrinsic motivation.
    c.   effort justification.
    d.   belongingness.

ESSAY QUESTIONS

1. What are instincts? What are some of the criticisms of instinct theory?
2. Explain Maslow's hierarchy of needs. How does Maslow's theory explain motivation? In particular, discuss the concept of self-actualization.

ANSWER KEY

1. Arousal theory
2. Intrinsic motivation
3. Effort justification
4. Motivation
5. Instinctive behaviors
6. Incentive theory
7. Cognitive dissonance
8. Hierarchy of needs
9. Psychosocial needs
10. Need
11. Motives
12. Stimulus motives
13. Primary drives
14. Yerkes-Dodson law
15. Drive
16. Need for achievement
17. Drive theory
18. c
19. a
20. c
21. b
22. b
23. c
24. d
25. b
26. d
27. c
28. a
29. c
30. d

31. b

32. c

33. d

34. d

35. a

36. c

37. a

SAMPLE ANSWERS TO ESSAY QUESTIONS

1. Instincts are reasons for behavior that are completely programmed into the functioning of a species. We do find instinctual behavior in animals. For example, spiders spin webs, birds build nests, salmon swim upriver to spawn—these occur in a species without prior training or even exposure to the behaviors. Thus, these behaviors are prompted by instincts.

    Since instincts so clearly exist in animals, it was assumed that human behavior was governed by instinct also. Sigmund Freud believed much of human behavior was motivated by sexual or aggressive instincts. William James listed many instincts which he proposed accounted for much of human behavior.

    Over time, support for instinct theory has all but disappeared. Attributing a behavior to an instinct does not really explain why the behavior occurs; in that sense, the notion of instincts is just not very useful. Most important, human behavior tends to be quite complex and can vary greatly from situation to situation. Since this is the case, how can human behavior be instinctual? Behavior governed by instincts should be consistent across humans and across time. As individual and unique as human behavior can be, it is unlikely that instincts have much to do with why human behavior occurs.

2. Maslow's hierarchy of needs is an explanation of motivation that proposes we need to get our basic (physiological and safety) needs satisfied first before we can meet what are called higher-order needs. Higher-order needs include the need for love and a sense of belonging, a need for esteem (regard for self and others), and the need for self-actualization. Self-actualization is a very important feature in Maslow's theory. In Maslow's view, all human beings have unique talents and potential. The key to a fulfilling life is discovering these abilities and putting them to best use. Making full use of our abilities, consistently, is being self-actualized.

    The hierarchy explains motivation because our fundamental desire is to achieve self-actualization, and this motivation propels us, so to speak, through the lower levels in the hierarchy. We are not always aware of this desire, and certainly not everyone achieves it. Lack of satisfaction of a lower-level need prohibits, according to Maslow's theory, movement up towards any of the higher needs. This view certainly makes sense, at least to a degree. Most of us, if starving or in danger for our lives, are not concerning ourselves with discovering our unique potential and putting it to best use.

    While Maslow's view is intuitively appealing, it has been criticized on several accounts. Among other things, there are too many examples where people are addressing a higher-order need, though lower (biological) levels have not been met. Sometimes great works, and great deeds materialize under circumstances that may include severe deprivation. In addition, we may be motivated towards activities that fulfill two or more levels of needs (based on the hierarchy) at the same time. Most of us when we work are working to provide food, shelter, and clothing. But there may be little satisfaction in spending eight or ten hours a day just for these goals, important as they are. Simultaneously, our occupations may also provide us with companionship and a sense of belonging, with esteem for others and ourselves—and, we hope, with a lasting sense of self-actualization as well.

MODULE 8.2 HUNGER AND EATING

LEARNING OBJECTIVES

After you have mastered the information in this unit, you will be able to:

- Describe how hunger and appetite are regulated

- Discuss the causes of obesity

- Describe anorexia nervosa

- Describe bulimia nervosa

- Discuss the causes of eating disorders

OUTLINE

I. What Makes Us Hungry?
    A. The brain controls hunger, not the stomach
    B. Fat cells—release fat for fuel when blood sugar level drops
    C. Hypothalamus (a brain structure)
        1. Regulates hunger (and many other bodily processes)
        2. Lateral hypothalamus—initiates ("On" switch for) eating
        3. Ventromedial hypothalamus—stops ("Off" switch for) eating
    D. Brain chemicals
        1. Neuropeptide Y—stimulates hypothalamus to trigger appetite and eating
        2. Leptin—hormone that conveys when enough food has been consumed
        3. Dopamine and endorphins—probably responsible for pleasurable feelings associated with eating
        4. Serotonin—may regulate feelings of satiation
II. Obesity: A National Epidemic
    A. Obesity—state of excess body fat
    B. Two-thirds of American adults are overweight
    C. One-third of American adults are obese
    D. Obesity—a major health risk worldwide
    E. Body mass index (BMI)—used to determine obesity
    F. Causes of obesity
        1. Behavioral patterns
            a) Too many calories consumed
            b) Too little exercise
        2. Heredity
            a) Metabolism rate related to weight gain
            b) Set point theory—brain regulates body weight around a genetically predetermined level (set point)
            c) Number of fat cells (obese people have more)
        3. Environmental factors
            a) Constant advertising of food, restaurants
            b) Food served is often higher calorie, higher fat
            c) Attractive, appetizing food harder to resist
        4. Emotional states

          a)   Anger, fear, depression, loneliness may lead to excess eating
          b)   Food is a natural tranquilizer; mood elevator

  G.   Losing excess weight
      1.   Objective is to use up more calories a day than are consumed
      2.   Healthy eating, regular exercise are crucial
      3.   Diet drugs, "quickie" diets and the like not usually successful long term, may have serious side effects

III. Eating Disorders
  A.   Anorexia nervosa
      1.   Self-starvation resulting in dangerously low body weight
      2.   Involves an intense fear of gaining weight, being fat
      3.   Most cases teenage or young adult female
      4.   Physical risks: cardiovascular, gastrointestinal, suicide

  B.   Bulimia nervosa
      1.   Characterized by binge eating (maybe several thousand calories at one sitting) followed by purging (vomiting, laxatives) to rid body of food
      2.   May include excessive, compulsive exercise regimen
      3.   Bulimics typically maintain normal weight
      4.   Physical complications: nutrient deficiencies, deterioration of tooth enamel, gastrointestinal problems

  C.   Causes of eating disorders
      1.   Cultural pressures, particularly on young women
      2.   Societal standards for unrealistic thinness
      3.   Negative body image for majority of young girls, women
      4.   Some cases among males (young), especially those in sports (e.g., wrestling)
      5.   Eating disorders rare in non-Western cultures
      6.   May involve issues of control, perfectionism
      7.   Possibly disturbances in brain mechanisms (e.g., serotonin levels)

SUMMARY

In this module you learn about a major motivator in our lives—hunger and eating. There is debate regarding what actually makes us hungry. Anyone with a stomach who has gone too long without eating knows how the stomach can "growl." However, research has shown that the brain, not the stomach, controls hunger—specifically, the structure in the forebrain known as the hypothalamus. The lateral hypothalamus seems to regulate "turning on" the act of eating; the ventromedial hypothalamus turns this action off again. Brain chemicals such as neuropeptide Y, leptin, dopamine, endorphins, and serotonin appear to be related to the regulation of eating, to feelings of satiation and to the pleasure and comfort that often accompany eating.

Many people, especially in America, eat too much. Attractive, appetizing food, heavy in calories, is very easy to come by. Fast food menus usually consist of items that are high in calories and high in fat. Americans are leading more and more sedentary lives—the calories consumed are not being burned off by physical activity. Metabolism (how fast caloric intake is used up by the body) varies somewhat among individuals, and thus the genetic heritage involved in the regulation of metabolism can play a role in weight gain. There are no "quick fixes" regarding having and maintaining an appropriate body weight. Long-term adherence to a healthy lifestyle—eating reasonable amounts of nutritious foods, engaging in regular exercise—is the only established way to promote good physical health and keep our weight within appropriate boundaries.

With a huge everyday emphasis on eating (the many ads we are exposed to that deal with food, cooking, eating, and restaurants), all the while accompanied by our society's desire for ever-diminishing levels of thinness (especially in women), it is no wonder that there are problems with eating that plague some members of our society. Obesity is just one of these problems. We also have the serious eating disorders such as anorexia nervosa (eating little or nothing out of a fear of being fat) and bulimia nervosa (eating huge amounts at one sitting, followed by episodes of purging to rid the body of the food consumed). These eating disorders are thought to be related to the unrealistic standards of thinness, combined with psychological factors such as control, perfectionism, and/or a history of abuse or family conflict. Eating disorders have medical complications, and in severe cases can result in death.

KEY TERMS

Fat cells

Lateral hypothalamus

Ventromedial hypothalamus

Obesity

Body mass index (BMI)

Set point theory

Anorexia nervosa

Bulimia nervosa

SELF-TEST PRACTICE QUIZ

From the Key Terms select that which best matches the following:

1. _____ The notion that the brain adjusts bodily processes to keep weight approximately at a level determined by genetics

2. _____ The "on" switch triggering the start of hunger and eating

3. _____ An eating disorder where large quantities of food are ingested, followed by self-induced vomiting or excessive use of laxatives (to rid body of the consumed food)

4. _____ Body cells that store fat

5. _____ An indicator of body fat based on body weight relative to height

6. _____ The "off" switch regulating cessation of eating

7. _____ A state of excess body fat

a. Fat cells

b. Lateral hypothalamus

c. Ventromedial hypothalamus

d. Obesity

e. Body mass index (BMI)

f. Set point theory

g. Anorexia nervosa

h. Bulimia nervosa

8.   _____   An eating disorder
characterized by self-starvation; serious
medical side effects

9.   Approximately how many American adults are obese?

   a.   67 percent
   b.   50 percent
   c.   25 percent
   d.   33 percent

10.   According to set point theory,

   a.   each person has a particular weight that the body strives to maintain.
   b.   hunger is the result of stomach contractions.
   c.   a diet low in fat is the best method for weight loss.
   d.   None of the above

11.   The ventromedial hypothalamus acts as the

   a.   "on" switch for eating.
   b.   "off" switch for eating.
   c.   regulator of fat cell content.
   d.   regulator of feelings of satiety.

12.   When we are hungry and blood sugar level has dropped, a substance is released from
_____, which we will utilize for energy until we again ingest food.

   a.   the hypothalamus
   b.   dopamine receptors
   c.   fat cells
   d.   neurotransmitter sites

13.   The lateral hypothalamus acts as the

   a.   "on" switch for eating.
   b.   "off" switch for eating.
   c.   regulator of fat cell content.
   d.   regulator of feelings of satiety.

14.   Neuropeptide Y

   a.   triggers the release of leptin.
   b.   stimulates activity of the lateral hypothalamus.
   c.   decreases the brain's production of dopamine.
   d.   reduces neural levels of available serotonin.

15.   The rate at which the body burns available calories is known as

   a.   set point rate.
   b.   body mass index (BMI).
   c.   metabolism.
   d.   energy activity level.

16.   Research indicates that obese people have _____ fat cells in comparison to people of
normal weight.

   a.   the same number of
   b.   fewer
   c.   more
   d.   an undetermined number of

17. Which of the following has been proposed as a potential cause of eating disorders such as anorexia?
    a. Cultural pressure to be thin
    b. Neurotransmitter imbalances
    c. Perfectionism
    d. All of the above
18. The best way to take and keep excess weight off is to
    a. follow new diets as soon as they are introduced.
    b. rely on diet and antiobesity drugs.
    c. eat reasonable portions of healthy food and get regular exercise.
    d. avoid worrying and fretting about excess weight.

ESSAY QUESTIONS

1. Why are so many Americans overweight or even obese?

2. Discuss set point theory. According to this theory, how is the body's weight maintained? How might features suggested in this approach aid in human survival?

3. Discuss eating disorders and their causes. How are eating disorders treated?

ANSWER KEY

1. Set point theory

2. Lateral hypothalamus

3. Bulimia nervosa

4. Fat cells

5. Body mass index (BMI)

6. Ventromedial hypothalamus

7. Obesity

8. Anorexia nervosa

9. d

10. a

11. b

12. c

13. a

14. b

15. c

16. c

17. b

18. c

SAMPLE ANSWERS TO ESSAY QUESTIONS

1. A large number of Americans are overweight for many reasons. Large quantities of food are readily available, and we are assaulted with attractive advertising for foods, restaurants, and the like. Thus, since food has incentive value, particularly when it is presented to us in an appealing fashion, we can be drawn to it even when we are not hungry. Fast food and other restaurant food typically is high in calories and high in fat. Second, more Americans are leading sedentary lives. Many people have desk jobs and may sit in front of the television or computer for hours on end as well. Our survival no longer mandates years of toiling in fields to produce crops. Last, food has comfort value. Eating brings pleasurable feelings, which we are especially likely to seek if we are feeling depressed, lonely, or bored. Since the number of overweight and obese children is increasing, too, this adds to the number of overweight adults. A child or teen who is overweight is much more likely than their normal-weight counterpart to become an overweight or obese adult.

2. Set point theory proposes that the brain acts to maintain body weight at a level that is fairly consistent over time. That level, or appropriate weight, is known as the set point and is believed to be genetically determined. A body's rate of metabolism, it is proposed, is a function of how close, or how distant, actual body weight is relative to this set point. If there is weight gain, then (according to set point theory) metabolism speeds up. Food will be burned more quickly since the body has more fat in storage than required by genetic guidelines. However, if an individual begins to consume less food than is burned in a typical day and begins to lose weight—such as when on a diet—the process acts in reverse. Metabolism, according to the theory, will slow down, as part of the body's effort to conserve food. Thus, in times of food shortages, a body is protected, at least to an extent, since metabolic rates can be adjusted and energy can be conserved. However, if one wishes to lose weight, it may take extra effort to get past the body's efforts to maintain the customary set point.

3. There are a number of eating disorders. The two major ones discussed in this module are anorexia nervosa, and bulimia nervosa. Individuals with anorexia nervosa often look emaciated. They try to eat very little food, or none at all. Though they are dangerously thin, in their eyes they are fat. Anorexics typically have a profound fear of gaining weight and of becoming fat or being fat. They tend to have a distorted body image: they see their bodies as overweight when in fact they are severely underweight. Anorexic individuals may have psychological issues relating to control or perfectionism. Since food intake is so greatly reduced, an anorexic is medically at risk. Health risks most typically a consequence of anorexia are irregular heartbeat, low blood pressure, gastrointestinal problems, and suicide.

    Bulimics tend to gorge on food then rid their body of it (by various means) shortly afterward. There are often psychological factors in the backgrounds of individuals suffering from bulimia nervosa, including a history of abuse or family conflict. Both anorexics and bulimics tend to be teenage or young adult females and of white, non-Hispanic origin.

    Causes for eating disorders center around societal standards for thinness, though biological and psychological factors (as mentioned above) also play a role. As the quantity and availability of food has increased, and excessive weight and obesity among Americans has increased, proportions for the "ideal" female body have decreased. The current standard for the female body is at an unrealistic level for thinness. It does not reflect the body proportions of a typical, healthy female. Yet, this ultrathin image is what is projected as most desirable for the female body. Females are much more likely to be dissatisfied with their bodies than are males. There is pressure, then, to take even drastic measures (such as anorexic or bulimic behavior) to achieve and maintain these idealized levels of thinness.

Eating disorders are treated by both psychological and chemical means. An individual with an eating disorder likely will be placed in therapy, and antidepressant drugs may help. Recovery, however, is usually a lengthy process.

MODULE 8.3 EMOTIONS

LEARNING OBJECTIVES

After you have mastered the information in this unit, you will be able to:

- Describe the three components of emotions

- Discuss whether facial expressions of emotion are universal

- Explain the role that brain structures play in emotions

- Discuss the three major theories of emotions

- Discuss the factors associated with personal happiness

- Describe the three components of love in Sternberg's triarchic model

- Describe the polygraph

OUTLINE

I.   Emotions: Feeling States with Three Components
    A.   Bodily arousal—nervous system is activated
    B.   Cognition—subjective experience and evaluation
    C.   Expressed behavior—what happens outwardly, on face or in actions
II.   Emotional Expression
    A.   Charles Darwin: emotions evolved because they are adaptive
    B.   Universal facial expressions of emotion
        1.   Six basic emotional expressions universally identified (Ekman, 1989)
        2.   Anger, fear, disgust, sadness, happiness, surprise
        3.   May be more than six (e.g., Plutchik, 1980: add anticipation, acceptance)
        4.   Other emotions are complex; are combinations of the simpler basic emotions
    C.   Cultural differences in emotions
        1.   Some emotions may be more common in some cultures than in others
        2.   Japanese: *fureai* (being closely linked to others), *oime* (beholden)—common in Japan, uncommon in U.S.
        3.   Rules for displaying emotions do vary by culture (e.g., Asian cultures discourage displays of emotion in public)
        4.   Cultural differences involve gestures and bodily movements also
        5.   Rules for male vs. female expressiveness may differ
    D.   Facial-feedback hypothesis—mimicking the movements that comprise an emotion will lead to feeling that emotion
        1.   But a "put-on" smile not the same emotion as a genuine smile
        2.   Duchenne smile—a genuine smile (named after French physician who discovered the facial muscles used to produce)
        3.   Emotions "catchy" because we mildly imitate the expression we see
III. Brain Structures Involved in Emotions
    A.   We do feel with our hearts to an extent (autonomic nervous system is aroused, increasing heart and breathing rates)
    B.   Limbic system (in brain) important in emotions

       1.   Amygdala—evaluates whether stimulus is a threat
       2.   Role of cerebral cortex
          a)   Evaluates meaning of emotionally arousing stimuli
          b)   Plans/directs response to these stimuli
          c)   Processes subjective experience of emotion
          d)   Controls accompanying facial expression

IV. Theories of Emotion
    A.   Which comes first—cognitive awareness or emotional response?
    B.   James-Lange theory
       1.   Emotions follow bodily reactions (bear in the woods)
       2.   "I am afraid because I ran and because my heart is pounding"
       3.   William James: distinct bodily changes are associated with each emotion
    C.   Cannon-Bard theory
       1.   Challenges view of James-Lange theory
       2.   Notes common bodily response (due to activation of sympathetic nervous system) regardless of emotion experienced
       3.   Proposes that physical reaction and subjective experience of emotion occur simultaneously
       4.   Emotions accompany bodily reaction, but are not caused by them
    D.   Two-factor model—Schachter and Singer
       1.   Proposes emotions depend on (1) physiological arousal and (2) cognitive interpretation of that arousal
       2.   Cues in environment explain why we feel aroused (allow us to label emotion)
       3.   Problems with Schachter and Singer's view:
          a)   Doesn't account for distinctive physiological patterns that accompany various emotions
          b)   Other research (Zajonc, 1980, 1984) demonstrates that feelings may occur without cognitive awareness or labeling
    E.   Dual-pathway model of fear (LeDoux, 1994, 1996)
       1.   Proposes that brain processes incoming environmental information two ways (at same time), beginning with thalamus
       2.   "High road"—information then goes to cerebral cortex (processed carefully)
       3.   "Low road"—information goes directly to amygdala (quick emotional reaction; body is prepared to respond if necessary)
       4.   Allows quick response due to amgydala, in case there is danger; cortex can address with more cognitive analysis, which takes more time
       5.   May make difference between life and death
    F.   Conclusions and interpretation
       1.   General common physiological response (e.g., increased heart and breathing rate), but also differences among experienced emotions (e.g., blood flow, skin temperature)
       2.   Facial expression can lead to certain feeling states (thus partial support for James-Lange theory)
       3.   Though emotional reaction may precede cognition, cognitive appraisal still vitally important
       4.   Personal meaning of experience also crucial
       5.   Still much to learn regarding emotion and brain's processing

V. Happiness
    A.   Psychologists have historically focused on negative emotions
    B.   With emergence of positive psychology movement has come renewed interest in positive human experiences
    C.   What makes people happy?

        1.   Money makes little difference as long as above subsistence level
        2.   Misfortune doesn't necessarily lead to unhappiness, although multiple misfortunes might
        3.   Married people generally happier than singles—but this relationship is correlational
        4.   Having friends, being religiously active also correlated with happiness
   D.   Physiological factors
        1.   Happiness associated with increased activity in left prefrontal cortex
        2.   May be possible to "train" the brain to be more active in this region
   E.   Psychological factors
        1.   It doesn't matter what you have—just how happy you are with what you have
        2.   Sociability is a key component of extraversion—strongly linked to happiness
   F.   Positive psychology
        1.   Suggestions for increasing happiness include counting your blessings (literally!), thanking people who've made a difference in your life, and savoring life's "perfect moments"

VI. Love
   A.   Both a motive and an emotion
   B.   As Greeks proposed, there are several kinds of love (e.g., among friends, family members)
   C.   Romantic love—components idealized in Western culture
   D.   Sternberg—love can consist of three components
        1.   Intimacy—close attachment and sharing
        2.   Passion—strong sexual desire
        3.   Decision/commitment—awareness of love for the other will preserve relationship
   E.   Sternberg—different combinations yield different types of love relationships
        1.   Romantic love—intimacy and passion
        2.   Consummate love—intimacy, passion, and decision/commitment
        3.   Companionate love—intimacy and decision/commitment
        4.   Relationships are balanced when both partners share similar view regarding type of love

VII. The Polygraph (Lie Detector)
   A.   Insufficient scientific evidence that polygraph results accurate, credible
   B.   Polygraph based on assumption that different emotions (lying vs. telling the truth) have different physiological characteristics
   C.   Measures used: skin reactivity, respiration, heart rate
   D.   Problems with current polygraph test
        1.   Measures physiological arousal, not lying per se
        2.   Objection is there is no truly distinctive physiological pattern for lying
        3.   Innocent may react strongly to relevant questions out of nervousness or fear
        4.   Seasoned liars can respond with complete physiological control
        5.   False findings do much damage

VIII. Exploring Psychology: Emotional Intelligence: How Well Do You Manage Your Emotions?
   A.   Emotional intelligence—ability to manage one's emotions
   B.   Probably five main characteristics:
        1.   Self-awareness; knowing true inner feelings
        2.   Can manage own emotions effectively—not usually overwhelmed, can bounce back reasonably well from disappointment (emotions are not out of control)
        3.   Can delay gratification, utilize emotional energy to reach goals
        4.   Have empathy (perceive and feel emotions of others)
        5.   Helping others deal with their emotions
   C.   Essentially independent of IQ-type intelligence
   D.   Goleman believes more important to success in life than IQ-type intelligence

SUMMARY

In this module you learn about emotions—what we think they are, how they occur, and why. Emotions seem to involve many parts of the brain. The basic view of emotions (or feeling states) is that they have three components, consisting of (1) bodily arousal, due to nervous system activation, (2) cognition, and (3) expressed behavior. Charles Darwin (1872) believed emotions evolved because they are adaptive—they help us function and survive in our environment.

The expression and interpretation of basic emotions seems to be universal. Research involving many unrelated cultures has indicated that six emotions (anger, happiness, fear, sadness, surprise, and disgust) are both facially manifested and interpreted as having the same meaning. When and how emotions are displayed, however, is more determined by culture and varies among cultures. For example, Americans are more likely to display emotions in public than are members of Asian cultures. Traditionally, females have been given more latitude in emotional range and display than have males.

There is a relationship between the expression displayed (on the face) and the emotion felt. Different psychologists (Zajonc, 1989; Izaard, 1990; Ekman, 1993) have shown that moving facial muscles to result in a certain facial array (for example, holding a pencil between your teeth) elicits a corresponding emotion. The emotion stems from the facial array, not (in this case) the other way around. This finding is known as the facial-feedback hypothesis.

The brain and nervous system are involved in emotional communication. When emotionally aroused, our nervous system directs the release of epinephrine and norepinephrine, and when the situation has passed the parasympathetic branch of the autonomic nervous system calms us down again. Brain structures comprising the limbic system (the amygdala, hippocampus, and hypothalamus) are all involved in processing and responding to emotion. The cerebral cortex gives a cognitive evaluation of the process going on, as well as being responsible for the actual subjective feeling of emotion. Negative and positive emotions seem to activate different parts of the prefrontal cortex.

We are unsure as to the actual process involved in experiencing and responding to emotion; thus, a number of theories have been proposed. The first is the James-Lange theory, which states that we react first and then, based on our reaction, interpret how we must feel (I ran, I must be afraid). The Cannon-Bard theory challenges this notion, and its proponents pointed out that bodily reactions tend to be rather similar (increased heart and breathing rates, perspiration) regardless of the particular emotion experienced. Since there is this similarity, how then can different emotional interpretations result? The Cannon-Bard theory proposes instead that physical reaction and emotional experience occur independently but simultaneously. Schachter and Singer theorized that arousal differently based on the situational cues provided to them. Thus, this two-factor model suggests that arousal occurs first, and then it is labeled (as a function of environmental features). The dual-pathway model of fear (proposed by LeDoux, 1994, 1996) suggests that the brain processes emotional information from the environment two ways at once beginning with the thalamus. The incoming information is then sent to the amygdala, which reacts in an emotional way immediately including being prepared for a response (as to a threat). The incoming information also goes to the cerebral cortex where it is processed more slowly but more thoroughly. The cortex is responsible for a more cognitive evaluation of the events plus the actual experience of the associated emotion. The immediate reaction (or readiness for) governed by the amygdala is for our preservation. The cognitive appraisal that follows later gives us the true state of affairs.

We are still researching emotion, so we have no final conclusions regarding the above theories. We do know that there are distinctive physiological patterns accompanying various emotions and that we need not necessarily have a cognitive awareness of phenomena in order to experience it emotionally (Zajonc, 1980, 1984). We know that many different parts of the brain are involved. We also know that the personal meaningfulness of a given experience has much to do with our emotional response and interpretation of it.

Although psychology has focused historically on negative emotions, recent years have seen renewed attention to the determinants of happiness. Contrary to what many people think, money is not correlated with happiness. Lottery winners, for example, experience an initial thrill but quickly return to their normal levels of happiness (or unhappiness). Being sociable, married, and religious are all correlated with happiness. The level of activity in the left prefrontal cortex is correlated with happiness; although people may have a genetic predisposition toward more or less activity in this area, they can train themselves to become happier over time. Overall, people can become happier by taking active steps to think about what they are grateful for and to enjoy life's pleasures.

Romantic love is one emotion that has been researched to an extent. Sternberg (1988) has proposed the triangular model of love involving the components of intimacy, passion, and decision/commitment. Different kinds of love, according to Sternberg, result from different combinations of the above three components.

Lastly, information is presented in this module on the polygraph, also known as the lie detector. The objective of the polygraph is to detect emotional changes in test-takers, which reveal who is telling the truth and who is lying. In fact, the polygraph simply reports differences in physiological responses. Skin reactivity, heart rate, and breathing are the physiological measures most often recorded during a polygraph test. The polygraph cannot really detect truth vs. lying; its credibility has not been established and indeed the issue is quite controversial. Since the lie detector can really just measure level of arousal, someone anxious about taking the test or fearful that they will be wrongly convicted will show higher levels of arousal that may be misinterpreted as revealing guilt. Conversely, truly cold and calculating liars often can mask their feelings entirely, regardless of degree of guilt or involvement. Thus, the prohibiting feature of the lie detector test is that it may wrongly implicate the innocent while failing to detect the guilty.

Goleman (1995) has proposed that one kind of intelligence is emotional intelligence. Emotional intelligence constitutes the ability to understand emotions in oneself and others and regulate and utilize them effectively. It is Goleman's view that this type of intelligence is more important to successful and fulfilling living than is the more traditional IQ-type of intelligence. There is little, if any, relationship between emotional intelligence and the traditional IQ-type of intelligence.

KEY TERMS

Emotions

Display rules

Facial-feedback hypothesis

Duchenne smile

James-Lange theory

Cannon-Bard theory

Two-factor model

Dual-pathway model of fear

Romantic love

Triangular model of love

Polygraph

Emotional intelligence

SELF-TEST PRACTICE QUIZ

From the Key Terms select that which best matches the following:

1. _____ A theory proposed by Schachter and Singer that we experience arousal first then label it

2. _____ Equipment intended to test for individuals who are lying; measures physiological responses indicating arousal

3. _____ Norms and customs that vary from culture to culture regarding when, where, and to what extent emotions are expressed

4. _____ The view that emotional experience and physiological response occur simultaneously but independently

5. _____ The model of love proposed by Sternberg where different types of love are composed of various combinations of intimacy, passion, and decision/commitment

6. _____ Named after the physician who determined the facial muscles involved in a genuine smile

7. _____ Intelligence involving the ability to detect, regulate, and effectively utilize emotions

8. _____ A model of brain processing of emotion proposed by Joseph LeDoux, where two different parts of the brain process the same information in different ways

9. _____ Feeling states having physiological, cognitive, and behavioral components

10. _____ Love involving sexual attraction and intimacy

11. _____ The perspective that we have a bodily response to a situation first, then emotions follow once we are aware of this bodily response

a. Emotions

b. Display rules

c. Facial-feedback hypothesis

d. Duchenne smile

e. James-Lange theory

f. Cannon-Bard theory

g. Two-factor model

h. Dual-pathway model of fear

i. Romantic love

j. Triangular model of love

k. Polygraph

l. Emotional intelligence

12. _____ The view that arranging one's
facial features in an array corresponding
to what is typical for a given emotional
expression will result in the experience of
that emotion

13. Writing a letter back to someone you cherish is the _____ component of an emotion.
    a. physiological
    b. cognitive
    c. behavioral
    d. communication

14. According to Charles Darwin, humans and animals convey emotional expression because it is
    a. adaptive.
    b. enjoyable.
    c. intellectually stimulating.
    d. genetically programmed behavior.

15. The six basic emotional expressions, as proposed by Ekman (1989) are happiness, sadness, fear, surprise, disgust and
    a. anticipation.
    b. anxiety.
    c. acceptance.
    d. anger.

16. Asians are much less likely to exhibit emotions in public in comparison to Americans. This is an example of
    a. universal exceptions.
    b. display rules.
    c. cognitive intervention.
    d. affective parameters.

17. The part of the brain that appears to process positive emotions is the
    a. amygdala.
    b. hippocampus.
    c. left prefrontal cortex.
    d. right prefrontal cortex.

18. According to the Cannon-Bard theory of emotions,
    a. physical reactions accompany emotions but do not cause them.
    b. emotions depend on how people interpret physical arousal.
    c. each emotion produces a distinct pattern of bodily changes.
    d. none of the above

19. Research by Zajonc (1980, 1984) has revealed that
    a. emotion and cognition actually occur simultaneously.
    b. individuals receiving an injection of epinephrine labeled the accompanying emotion according to available environmental cues.
    c. an emotional reaction may not necessarily have a cognitive component.
    d. more thorough processing of emotional experiences is carried out by the cerebral cortex.

20. Romantic love, according to Sternberg (1988), consists of
    a. intimacy only.
    b. passion only.
    c. intimacy and passion.
    d. intimacy, passion, and commitment.

21. A problem with the two-factor model of emotional experience is
    a. we must cognitively identify our emotional state in order to experience it.
    b. different emotions have correspondingly different physiological characteristics.
    c. it is unethical to give study participants injections of epinephrine.
    d. we are more likely to feel frightened when in real danger than when in a movie theatre.
22. Which statement about happiness is INCORRECT?
    a. Married people tend to be happier than single people.
    b. People may have a "set point" for happiness just as they do for weight.
    c. Extraversion is strongly correlated with happiness.
    d. People in wealthier countries are typically happier than people in poorer countries.

ESSAY QUESTIONS

1. What is the facial-feedback hypothesis? How can emotions be "catching"?

2. What is emotional intelligence? What are some characteristics of people who exhibit emotional intelligence?

ANSWER KEY

1. Two-factor model

2. Polygraph

3. Display rules

4. Cannon-Bard theory

5. Triangular model of love

6. Duchenne smile

7. Emotional intelligence

8. Dual-pathway model of fear

9. Emotions

10. Romantic love

11. James-Lange theory

12. Facial-feedback hypothesis

13. c

14. a

15. d

16. b

17. c

18. a

19. c

20. c

21. b

22. d

SAMPLE ANSWERS TO ESSAY QUESTIONS

1.   The facial-feedback hypothesis is the belief that mimicking facial movements associated with a particular emotion will produce the corresponding emotional state. That is, if one arranges one's face in the expression pattern that typifies a certain emotion, that emotion at least to an extent will also be experienced. This emotional experience, then, is happening more or less from the "outside" in. We usually think of facial expression as the result of emotion. The facial-feedback hypothesis gives evidence that emotion can result from facial expression as well. Thus, contorting one's face while in a difficult situation may make one feel even more anxious or upset. Attempting to smile even when things look grim may help a bad situation seem a little bit better.

    Emotions can be "catching" in that we tend to imitate, at least slightly, the emotional expression we see on another person's face. If we see someone laughing or smiling broadly we unconsciously play out that expression on our face. We become, then, more susceptible to laughing or smiling ourselves. And, keeping the facial-feedback hypothesis in mind, with our facial features arrayed in a manner that imitates the expression on our social partner's face, soon we too are feeling a bit of that emotion he or she is presumably experiencing. This phenomenon is helpful not only in smoothing and easing emotional communication, but also in promoting empathy among those with whom we have social contact.

2.   Emotional intelligence is the ability to perceive our own and others' emotions accurately and to utilize this information wisely and well. Characteristics of emotional intelligence include the ability to (1) know ourselves well and fully and accurately grasp what we are feeling; (2) regulate and manage our emotions effectively—to not fly off the handle, to be able to weather difficult experiences and recover from them within a reasonable amount of time, to allow ourselves to express joy and happiness in appropriate ways and in appropriate settings, to be able to communicate our emotions successfully; (3) harness and use the energy from our emotions in appropriate ways, in order to achieve meaningful goals; (4) accurately detect emotions in others, and be able to share in and understand what others are feeling (e.g., have empathy); and (5) apply what we know about our own and others' feelings to our relationships, so that these relationships are strengthened, enhanced, and fulfilling for all parties involved. Research indicates that there is little, if any, correlation between emotional intelligence and the traditional type of intelligence evidenced in standard IQ tests. It is food for thought that, between the two, emotional intelligence may be the more vital for happy and successful life experiences.

MODULE 8.4 APPLICATION: MANAGING ANGER: WHAT CAN YOU DO TO CONTROL YOUR ANGER?

LEARNING OBJECTIVE

After you have mastered the information in this unit, you will be able to:

- Outline steps you can take to control your anger

OUTLINE

I.   Problems in controlling anger
    A.   Behaviors may occur that have undesirable and unproductive consequences
    B.   Frequent or chronic anger damages health
II.   Cognitive approach to anger
    A.   Anger and blame are responses to a situation, not the situation itself
    B.   Better to recognize influences on anger and take steps to manage effectively
III. Anger management strategies

A.   Be aware of own emotional reactions
B.   Review evidence objectively
C.   Try adaptive approaches; think positively
D.   Focus on soothing thoughts; relax
E.   Try not to lose control
F.   Try to understand other's perspective
G.   Praise self for assertive (not aggressive) responses
H.   Consider altering expectations of others
I.   Stay calm; use moderate verbal responses
J.   Try to express positive feelings

SUMMARY

In this module you learn helpful anger management strategies. Anger is not only harmful to our social or other relationships, if prolonged it can be harmful to our health. It is important to remember that our behavior may have consequences we don't really want when we speak or act in the heat of anger. We may further antagonize others rather than promote solutions. Though we may have a tendency to blame others, whether or not we respond in anger is our choice. Even in anger-provoking situations, it is best if we remember what is really important in that situation and act accordingly.

Effective anger management tips include being attuned to our emotional reaction, evaluating factors objectively, and trying to think of effective ways to work through a problem. It is important not to lose control ourselves even though others may be doing so. We can think of things that help us stay calm and keep our tone and our word choice within reasonable limits. Perhaps we are expecting too much of others. We need to consider the other person's point of view as well as our own. We can express positive feelings about others, which may help them calm down and think better of us. We need to try assertive, but not aggressive, approaches, and congratulate ourselves for using them.

CHAPTER 8 APPLICATION EXERCISE

What motivates you? Think of all the activities you are involved in at this stage of your life. They may be family-or work-related, they may involve academics (probably!) or sports, or they may be primarily social in nature. Some activities involve others; some are more often carried out alone such as artistic endeavors. Make a list of the major activities in which you are currently involved.

What is the source of motivation for each of these activities? Which meet primary or biological needs? Which seem to satisfy secondary or stimulus motives? How much of your behavior is motivated by a need for affiliation or achievement? Is some of your behavior prompted simply by the incentives presented to you? Does striving for self-actualization play a role in your activities?

Analyze your behavior and motives in light of what you have learned in this chapter.

CHAPTER 9

Child Development

Chapter 9 deals with human development from the moment of conception up through the elementary school years. Human development includes physical, social, emotional, and cognitive growth and change. We keep some questions in mind when studying human growth: Which is the greater influence, nature or nurture? What is development like—is it a continuous, steady process, or is it characterized by stable periods interspersed with rapid, qualitative changes? To answer questions with regard to developmental psychology, we often use longitudinal (one large group of individuals is studied over a very long period of time) or cross-sectional (different groups of people, of different ages, are studied at one time) research methods.

Development begins with an ovum (mother's egg) fertilized by a sperm (father's reproductive cell), resulting in a zygote. The zygote is a single-celled organism, but cells begin to multiply and the organism grows rapidly. Fertilization is not the only component in the creation of a new offspring. Conception occurs in the Fallopian tubes but the organism must implant successfully in the uterus in order to grow further and to thrive. There are three stages of pregnancy, and birth occurs approximately 280 days after conception. The mother's physical health, before and during pregnancy, is crucial to the baby's development before and after birth.

The newborn infant is quite small, but it is not at all incapable of dealing with its environment. A newborn has surprisingly good sensory capabilities, with hearing being the best-developed sense, and vision the least well-developed. Infants are born with basic reflexes, most of which are, or at least were (in an evolutionary sense), adaptive in aiding the baby's survival. Babies can discriminate sounds, tastes, and other stimuli from birth, and they show a preference for the human face and for the voice and smells associated with their mother. Development is rapid, and most evident is motor development. Whereas at birth an infant cannot move to speak of and can do little for himself, a mere 12 months later that little one is crawling, walking, and perhaps running from place to place (usually with glee!). The physical adjustments associated with maintaining one's balance are particularly noteworthy, and it is remarkable that a child can manage this feat so soon after entering the world.

Children's emotional and social development is very much a function of the environment into which the child is born. Children do show evidence of a temperament at birth—they may be more mellow and laid-back (an "easy" child), or be more irritable (a "difficult" child), or have difficulty adjusting to changes (a "slow-to-warm-up" child). Much of a child's emotional and social behavior, however, is related to how that child is treated. The more successful child is the one who is securely emotionally attached to a parent. The quality of this attachment is most related to how perceptive and responsive a parent is with regard to his or her child's cues. Parents who are not particularly loving and responsive to their child's needs tend to have an insecurely attached child, and these early emotional experiences are related to how the individual deals with emotional relationships later in life. The warm, consistent, authoritative parent is likely to have offspring who can relate more effectively with others and who show higher levels of self-esteem. Authoritarian parents insist on their own rules, without explanation, and rarely if ever consider a child's point of view or feelings. Permissive parents may or may not show affection, but otherwise are not involved in establishing and maintaining guidelines for their children's appropriate behavior.

Cognitive development is also rapid during childhood. Most of what we know about cognitive development is from the work of Jean Piaget, who believed children develop in qualitatively different stages. Piaget's stages correspond to the child's facility at what he called *mental operations*. The very young child interacts with the world primarily in a sensorimotor fashion. An older child develops through preoperational and then concrete operational thought. Piaget believed children were capable of entering the last stage, formal operational, by about the age of 12 years. He also proposed that children develop schemas for interacting with the world and these schemas are modified and expanded through experience. Vygotsky emphasized social and cultural influences on cognition.

MODULE 9.1 KEY QUESTIONS AND METHODS OF STUDY

LEARNING OBJECTIVES

After you have mastered the information in this unit, you will be able to:

- Discuss the major questions that underlie the study of human development

- Explain how developmental psychologists study age-related changes

OUTLINE

I.   Developmental Psychology—study of growth and change over the life span
II. The Nature Versus Nurture Question
    A.   How much of human development occurs due to nature (biology, genetic inheritance)?
    B.   How much of human development occurs due to nurture (environment, experiences)?
    C.   Early view: quite polarized
    D.   Current view: nature and nurture both crucial; one influences manifestation of the other
III. The Continuity Versus Discontinuity Question
    A.   In what pattern does development occur?
    B.   Continuity model—quantitative changes; steady pattern of small, fairly regular steps
    C.   Discontinuity model (main proponent was Jean Piaget)—qualitative changes, in stages; fairly stable within a stage, then rather dramatic shift in abilities
    D.   Current view: development involves both
IV. The Universality Question
    A.   Does developmental pattern occur universally, or are there cultural differences?
    B.   Basic pattern seems to occur universally
    C.   Cultural differences in what stages experienced and when
V.   The Stability Question—how consistent are personality features over the life span?
VI. Methods of Study
    A.   Longitudinal studies
        1.   Studies of same very large group of people over a long, or very long, period of time
        2.   Allow study of developmental changes (e.g., personality, behavior) in the same people over time
        3.   Drawbacks: expensive, very time-consuming, lose participants over time, may not be representative
    B.   Cross-sectional studies
        1.   Involve study of different age groups of people, at same time
        2.   Objective is same as with longitudinal, just easier and less expensive
        3.   Drawbacks:
            a)   Cannot be certain of all comparisons, since age groups are different people as well
            b)   Cohort effects—function of being born at a particular time in history, among members of a particular generation

SUMMARY

In this module, you learn about the field of developmental psychology and what the basic questions are when we consider the process of human development. The nature-nurture question involves the source of human growth and change. "Nature" means the source is due to heredity, the genetic code we are born with. "Nurture" means development is due to the experiences we have once we are born into our environment. We also ask what the pattern of development is like. Those who take the continuity view see development as a rather steady, quantitative series of changes. Those who take the discontinuity view find development consisting of stages where behavior is rather stable and interspersed with developmental changes between stages that are qualitative and rather dramatic.

Developmental psychologists usually take the middle ground with regard to both of these questions. We also ask if developmental patterns are universal or a function of culture and whether personality features change or remain the same over the life span. Among the methodologies used to investigate these questions are longitudinal research (the same group of people is studied for a very long period of time) and cross-sectional research (different age groups are studied at the same time, again to look at developmental trends). Both of these research methods provide helpful information, although both have drawbacks.

KEY TERMS

Developmental psychology

Nature-nurture debate

Continuity model

Discontinuity model

Longitudinal study

Cross-sectional study

Cohort effects

SELF-TEST PRACTICE QUIZ

From the Key Terms select that which best matches the following (Note: Not every Key Term will be used.):

1. _____ The view that development occurs in a steady, quantitative fashion

2. _____ The branch of psychology that looks at patterns of change and growth over time

3. _____ Studies that compare different individuals, of different ages, at the same time

4. _____ Effects due to being a member of a particular group born during a particular era

a. Developmental psychology

b. Nature-nurture debate

c. Continuity model

d. Discontinuity model

e. Longitudinal study

f. Cross-sectional study

g. Cohort effects

5. _____ The view, particularly promoted by Jean Piaget, that development occurs in qualitatively different, distinct stages

6. _____ Studies involving a large group of the same individuals where data are collected at various intervals over a long period of time

7. The conclusion regarding the nature versus nurture question is that
   a. heredity is the greatest influence on human development.
   b. environmental experiences are the greatest influence on human development.
   c. both heredity and environment are crucial to development, and each influences the manifestation of the other.
   d. emotion and cognition, rather than nature or nurture, are most crucial to human development.

8. Whether or not developmental patterns vary substantially due to cultural influences is known as the _____ question.
   a. nature vs. nurture
   b. continuity vs. discontinuity
   c. universality
   d. stability

9. A researcher wants to study developmental changes in memory, so she studies three groups of people (ages 10, 20, and 30) all at once. She is using a _____ research method.
   a. longitudinal
   b. cross-sectional
   c. correlational
   d. experimental

ESSAY QUESTIONS

1. How does conception occur?

2. Compare and contrast the continuity and discontinuity views regarding human development.

ANSWER KEY

1. Continuity model

2. Developmental psychology

3. Cross-sectional studies

4. Cohort effects

5. Discontinuity model

6. Longitudinal study

7. c

8. c

9. b

SAMPLE ANSWERS TO ESSAY QUESTIONS

1.   Conception begins first with the act of intercourse where no physical or chemical barriers impede the journey of sperm from the vagina through the uterus to the Fallopian tubes. Most sperm do not complete the trip. Since typically only one egg (ovum) is released from one of the two female ovaries each month during ovulation, about half the sperm will travel up one of the two Fallopian tubes where no mature egg is present. Sperm and egg usually meet in the Fallopian tube, and that is where fertilization (the penetration of the egg by one sperm cell) occurs. The fertilized egg is called a zygote. With normal conception this new organism continues to travel down the remainder of the Fallopian tube, finds a receptive site on the uterine wall, implants successfully, and begins to grow and flourish. If all goes well, about nine months later the result will be a marvelous new human being.

2.   Humans, of course, grow and change over the course of the lifespan. The issue that forms the basis of the continuity versus discontinuity question has to do with just how that growth and change occurs. Developmental psychologists who take the continuity view advocate that human growth is basically additive, involving quantitative changes only. That is, the human being is the same person he or she was; the person just adds to the skills and characteristics that were present in earlier developmental stages. Continuity theorists do not propose that there are dramatic shifts in development; human growth and change tends to be steady and rather orderly.

Discontinuity theorists take a different position. Jean Piaget was the leading developmental psychology figure advocating the discontinuity view. Piaget's developmental focus was primarily in the cognitive domain. The discontinuity approach to development proposes that, as humans grow older, they become qualitatively, not just quantitatively, different. Whereas a continuity theorist would say that a child who can now speak is the same child he or she was previously, just with the addition of language, a discontinuity theorist would state that the acquisition of language has such an impact on development, that the child is now qualitatively different from what he or she was before. The child is now, in a sense, a different person. In addition, discontinuity proponents do not see development as stable and steady. Rather, they point out the dramatic spurts in development, interspersed with plateaus where growth and change are somewhat quiescent. In physical growth, for example, there are periods when a child will grow many inches in a year. In other years, the child may growth very little in height. Thus, the physical dimension of growth and change regarding height is not steady and consistent. Currently, most developmental psychologists advocate that human growth and change occurs in both a continuous and a discontinuous manner.

MODULE 9.2 PRENATAL DEVELOPMENT: A CASE OF NATURE AND NURTURE

LEARNING OBJECTIVES

After you have mastered the information in this unit, you will be able to:

- Discuss the major stages of prenatal development

- Describe some threats to prenatal development

- Explain the types of tests used to detect chromosomal and genetic defects

OUTLINE

I.   Stages of Pregnancy (about 280 days total)
    A.   Germinal
        1.   Approximately the first two weeks after conception
        2.   Spans from moment of fertilization to complete implantation within the uterine lining
    B.   Embryonic (organism is an embryo)
        1.   Period from two weeks to eight weeks after conception
        2.   Basics of major organ systems develop
        3.   Baby is cushioned by amniotic fluid; nutrients, oxygen and wastes are exchanged via placenta
    C.   Fetal—from ninth week of pregnancy until birth (organism is a fetus)

II.   Threats to Prenatal Development
    A.   Adequate nutrition important, including sufficient folic acid (reduces risk of neural tube defects if taken during and preferably before first trimester of pregnancy)
    B.   Teratogens (cause harm to developing baby)
        1.   Infectious diseases
            a)   Rubella (German measles)—can cause heart disease, deafness, mental retardation
            b)   Sexually transmitted diseases (HIV, syphilis)
        2.   Smoking—increases risk for miscarriage, premature birth, low birth weight, infant mortality, SIDS, respiratory problems, hyperactivity
        3.   Alcohol and drugs—increase risk of birth defects, infant mortality, mental retardation

III.   Prenatal Testing (testing for fetal abnormalities)
    A.   Amniocentesis—extract amniotic fluid (which contains fetal cells)
    B.   Chorionic villus sampling (CVS)—chorion membrane tissue is analyzed
    C.   Ultrasound imaging—gives picture of fetus and amniotic sac
    D.   Parental blood tests—detects if parents are carriers of genetic disorders

SUMMARY

In this module you learn about the earliest stages of life—prenatal development. Once a zygote is created, development occurs very rapidly. Pregnancy is divided into three stages: the germinal (first two weeks), embryonic (two weeks to eight weeks after conception), and fetal (eight weeks after conception up until birth). The first stage corresponds to the newly-formed organism completing the trip down the Fallopian tube and successfully implanting into the uterine environment. The second stage is marked by the preliminary development of the organism's basic body systems (respiratory, circulatory, and so forth). The last stage covers all final development leading up to birth.

Though nearly all births occur successfully, it is important that an expectant mother get adequate nutrition and avoid harmful substances (teratogens) that could permanently harm her baby. Alcohol, drugs, smoking, and infectious diseases all can lead to birth defects, mental retardation, or even death for the fetus. Chromosomal and genetic defects can be tested for by means of amniocentesis, chorionic villus sampling, ultrasound, and blood tests for the parents.

KEY TERMS

Ovum

Ovulation

Fallopian tube

Zygote

Germinal stage

Fertilization

Uterus

Embryonic stage

Embryo

Neural tube

Amniotic sac

Placenta

Fetal stage

Fetus

Spina bifida

Teratogen

Rubella

Sudden infant death syndrome (SIDS)

Fetal alcohol syndrome (FAS)

Amniocentesis

Chorionic villus sampling (CVS)

Chorion

Down syndrome

Ultrasound imaging

SELF-TEST PRACTICE QUIZ

From the Key Terms select that which best matches the following (Note: Not all Key Terms will be used.):

1. _____ A disorder in newborns where the baby suffers physical deformities and mental retardation due to the mother's excessive drinking of alcoholic beverages during pregnancy

2. _____ A neural tube defect; appears to be related to insufficient levels of folic acid in the diet of the mother before and during pregnancy

3. _____ The first stage of development for the organism during pregnancy—covers the period of about the first two weeks (from conception to complete implantation within the uterus)

a. Ovum

b. Ovulation

c. Fallopian tube

d. Zygote

e. Germinal stage

f. Fertilization

g. Uterus

h. Embryonic stage

i. Embryo

j. Neural tube

4. _____   Also called German measles; normally harmless if contracted during childhood but can cause serious birth defects in baby if contracted by mother while she is pregnant

5. _____   Term describing the developing organism during the second through eighth weeks of prenatal development

6. _____   A technique where high-pitched sound waves are "bounced off" the abdominal region of the mother providing a picture of the developing organism

7. _____   A large membrane that develops within the uterus during pregnancy; allows the exchange of nutrients and oxygen from mother to baby and carbon dioxide and wastes from baby to mother (which will be expelled by her system)

8. _____   The term given to the developing organism covering the span of prenatal development from the third month of pregnancy up until birth

9. _____   A fertilized egg

10. _____   The female reproductive organ (also known as the womb) where the fertilized egg implants and develops until birth

11. _____   A chromosomal disorder characterized by mental retardation and physical abnormalities

12. _____   The removal of amniotic fluid to check for fetal abnormalities

13. _____   Also known as conception—the union of a mature egg and sperm

14. The newly developing organism, created by the union of one sperm cell from the father and one egg cell from the mother, is completely attached to the mother's body by about _____ after conception.
    a. one hour
    b. one day
    c. one week
    d. two weeks

k. Amniotic sac

l. Placenta

m. Fetal stage

n. Fetus

o. Spina bifida

p. Teratogen

q. Rubella

r. Sudden infant death syndrome (SIDS)

s. Fetal alcohol syndrome (FAS)

t. Amniocentesis

u. Chorionic villus sampling (CVS)

v. Chorion

w. Down syndrome

x. Ultrasound imaging

15. The second period of prenatal development, which lasts from about the second through eighth weeks of pregnancy, is the _____ stage.
    a. fetal
    b. germinal
    c. embryonic
    d. zygotic
16. Use of alcohol or drugs by the mother during pregnancy can cause _____ in her unborn infant.
    a. birth defects
    b. mental retardation
    c. miscarriage or death
    d. all of the above

ESSAY QUESTION

1. What are some problems a baby is more likely to have if the mother smokes or does not adhere to proper nutrition standards during pregnancy?

ANSWER KEY

1. Fetal alcohol syndrome (FAS)

2. Spina bifida

3. Germinal stage

4. Rubella

5. Embryo

6. Ultrasound imaging

7. Placenta

8. Fetus

9. Zygote

10. Uterus

11. Down syndrome

12. Amniocentesis

13. Fertilization

14. d

15. c

16. d

SAMPLE ANSWER TO ESSAY QUESTION

1. While not every woman who smokes (or uses drugs or alcohol) during her pregnancy causes lasting harm to her unborn baby, the likelihood for problems is greater. As smoking (or amount of alcohol/drug use) increases, the risk for subsequent harm increases. The mother who smokes during pregnancy increases the likelihood that her baby will be born pre-term, of lower birth weight, and with a greater risk for respiratory problems. There is a greater risk of miscarriage and a higher incidence of infant mortality and of sudden infant death syndrome (SIDS). Last, developmental problems such as hyperactivity and a lower IQ are more common among offspring

of mothers who smoked during pregnancy. Poor nutrition on the part of a mother-to-be, whether due to scarcity or the mother's inappropriate eating habits, is associated with a higher incidence of premature birth, low birth weight, birth defects such as spina bifida, cognitive deficits, and other deficiencies. Some birth problems cannot be detected in advance or avoided. Those due to smoking, poor eating habits, and substance abuse are, in contrast, completely preventable.

MODULE 9.3 INFANT DEVELOPMENT

LEARNING OBJECTIVES

After you have mastered the information in this unit, you will be able to:

- Describe the reflexes that newborn babies show

- Outline infant physical development during the first year of life

- Discuss the abilities infants possess with respect to sensory functioning, perception, and learning

- Explain how the infant's motor abilities develop during the first year

OUTLINE

I. Reflexes—unlearned, automatic responses to stimuli (usually have survival value; most disappear after a few months)
    A. Rooting reflex—turn head in direction of stroke to cheek
    B. Eyeblink reflex—protects from bright light, foreign objects
    C. Sucking reflex—enables baby to get nourishment
    D. Moro reflex (startle reflex)—response to being frightened (e.g., loud noise)
    E. Palmar grasp reflex—curling fingers tightly around an object
    F. Babinski reflex—toes fan out and curl when sole of foot stroked
II. Physical Development and Brain Size
    A. Maturation—underlying blueprint directing much of emerging characteristics, patterns of growth
    B. Role of environment—better nutrition has produced larger infants, children
    C. Weight usually triples during first year
    D. Brain quadruples in volume from birth to adulthood
        1. Most of neurons in brain formed before birth
        2. Increase in volume is due to
            a) Creation of synapses (neural interconnections)
            b) Formation of myelin sheath covering axons (allows for quicker, more efficient neural communication)
III. Sensory, Perceptual, and Learning Abilities in Infancy
    A. Sensory ability
        1. Vision
            a) Least well-developed sense
            b) Can recognize (and prefer) mother's face; track moving objects
        2. Depth perception
            a) Studied using visual cliff apparatus
            b) Depth perception apparent by age of six months
        3. Hearing
            a) Well developed at birth; know and prefer mother's voice
            b) Babies especially responsive to sounds corresponding to range of human verbal expression

        c)   By three months of age can distinguish among some speech sounds
    4.   Odors and tastes—newborns can differentiate among both, show preferences
  B.   Perceptual ability
    1.   Infants born with many perceptual abilities
    2.   Can differentiate among meaningful stimuli shortly after birth
    3.   Show a preference for faces among visual stimuli
    4.   Differentiate among facial expressions by four to six months of age
  C.   Learning ability
    1.   Can learn some simple (e.g., operantly conditioned) responses
    2.   Retain this learning for at least several weeks
    3.   Show prenatal learning in preference for mother's voice
IV. Motor Development
  A.   Many universal features in pattern of development
  B.   Goal-directed behaviors evidenced early on (e.g., bringing fist to mouth)
  C.   Early reflexive behavior slowly replaced by intentional, voluntary movements
  D.   Sitting alone, standing, and walking usually mastered by one year of age

SUMMARY

In this module you learn about the incredible, and incredibly fast, early development in a human. Babies are not born helpless, but rather bring many rudimentary behaviors and perceptual abilities into the world. Babies are born with many reflexes (sucking, rooting, eyeblink), which help them get their start and help them survive. Most reflexes are soon replaced with intentional, more complex behaviors. Babies usually triple their weight during the first year of life, and by adulthood the size of the brain has quadrupled. Though nearly all neurons in the brain exist at birth, much of the brain size increase is due to the formation of trillions of synapses (nerve cell interconnections) and of myelin coating neural axons that helps speed impulse transmission. These increasingly sophisticated neural interconnections allow the baby to progress rapidly. Although vision is the least well-developed sense at birth, hearing is quite well developed, and there is evidence for discriminations among stimuli for the remaining senses as well. The baby's rapid growth is perhaps most obvious with regard to motor development. Newborns typically have little mobility, but they soon can lift their heads, roll over, and by nine months of age sit without support. Amazingly, usually around one year of age, the little one can stand alone, walk, and may even run—at least, after a fashion!

KEY TERMS

Rooting reflex

Eyeblink reflex

Sucking reflex

Moro reflex

Palmar grasp reflex

Babinski reflex

Maturation

SELF-TEST PRACTICE QUIZ

From the Key Terms select that which best matches the following:

1. _____ A reflex where the baby startles in response to a loud noise or loss of support

2. _____ An automatic turning of the head by a baby in response to her cheek being stroked

3. _____ An unlearned response by a baby, occurring when the bottom of the foot is stroked

4. _____ A pattern of growth and development in a human infant that is largely determined by heredity

5. _____ A reflex where the baby's fingers curl tightly around an object placed in his palm

6. _____ A repeated response by the baby's lips when the tongue or mouth is stimulated

7. _____ A reflex that protects the baby from foreign objects and bright lights

a. Rooting reflex

b. Eyeblink reflex

c. Sucking reflex

d. Moro reflex

e. Palmar grasp reflex

f. Babinski reflex

g. Maturation

8. The great increase in human brain size during the course of development occurs because
   a. many and more elaborate neural cells have been created.
   b. interconnections among neurons in the brain have been streamlined.
   c. the myelin sheath and axons have relocated to the cortex.
   d. synapses among neurons have been greatly increased.

9. Regarding perceptual abilities in newborn infants,
   a. babies are remarkably prepared to absorb from and interact with their environment.
   b. hearing is not well developed, but a baby's vision is much like that of an adult.
   c. babies begin to discriminate among speech sounds at about one year of age.
   d. babies are easily upset because the world is unfamiliar and confusing.

10. Why is the process of myelination so important to a child's development?
    a. It allows nerve signals to be transmitted more quickly and efficiently.
    b. It causes a growth in the number of neurons in the brain.
    c. It stimulates growth of brain synapses.
    d. It allows the infant to engage in reflexive behavior.

11. Infants show a preference for visual stimuli that resemble
    a. colors.
    b. faces.
    c. toys.
    d. mobiles.

12. The pattern of physical development in humans is most determined by
  a.   nutrition.
  b.   sleep.
  c.   maturation.
  d.   cultural affiliations.
13. Most motor activity in the baby's first year of life consists of
  a.   Babinski reflexes.
  b.   sucking reflexes.
  c.   mimicry of facial expressions.
  d.   intentional, voluntary movements.

ESSAY QUESTIONS

1.   Briefly trace the motor development of an infant from birth through one year of age.

2.   Which reflexes serve to help a baby with his or her survival? Which reflexes may have had historical significance but seem to serve no purpose now?

ANSWER KEY

1.   Moro reflex

2.   Rooting reflex

3.   Babinski reflex

4.   Maturation

5.   Palmar grasp reflex

6.   Sucking reflex

7.   Eyeblink reflex

8.   d

9.   a

10. a

11. b

12. c

13. d

SAMPLE ANSWERS TO ESSAY QUESTIONS

1.   Babies have little in the way of motor development when they are born, other than reflexes. They are not really mobile; that is, they are essentially unable to move themselves from place to place. They have very simple goal-directed behaviors, such as the ability to suck their thumbs (a behavior they exhibit even before birth). Newborns can respond to and imitate facial expressions. However, brain growth, physical growth, sensory gains, and motor development all occur rather rapidly and dramatically after birth. These developments are interrelated. The reflexes babies use initially are gradually replaced by more complex and more intentional motor behaviors. Babies can reach for things and eventually grasp them, and much ends up in the baby's mouth (intentionally). Muscles strengthen, and the baby can first lift the chin, then the entire upper body, roll over, and eventually creep and sit up. By the baby's first birthday, standing alone has usually been mastered, followed quickly by the ability to walk, and even to run.

2. Reflexes are crucial to a baby's survival at birth. Most important would be the sucking reflex (the ability of the baby to use her lips in the movements necessary to get nourishment from breast or bottle). Also of great importance is the rooting reflex (when an infant's cheek is stroked, he will turn his head in that direction—this helps with finding the breast or bottle), and the eyeblink reflex (the eyes will shut very quickly if the baby is exposed to very bright light, or if a potentially harmful object seems to be coming towards the eyes—you do the same!). Babies show other reflexes (automatic, unlearned responses to stimuli), even though now they do not seem to have any survival value. One typical reflex is the Moro, or startle, reflex, where in response to a loud noise or sense of loss of support the baby's arms fly out quickly while the back arches, then the arms fold back in again over the chest. Other reflexes include the palmar grasp reflex, and the Babinski reflex. Possibly the palmar grasp reflex (where the baby appears to grab on to whatever is placed on his or her palm) aided our prehistoric ancestors in holding on to a parent's fur or hair covering.

MODULE 9.4 EMOTIONAL AND SOCIAL DEVELOPMENT

LEARNING OBJECTIVES

After you have mastered the information in this unit, you will be able to:

- Compare and contrast the three basic types of infant temperament identified in the New York Longitudinal Study

- Describe the three types of attachment styles identified by Ainsworth

- Compare and contrast the three major styles of parenting in Baumrind's model

- Explain the roles that peer relationships play in children's emotional and social development

- Outline Erikson's childhood stages of psychosocial development

OUTLINE

I. Temperament
   A. More variation in social and emotional development (in comparison to development of physical abilities)
   B. Types of temperament (based on New York Longitudinal Study [NYLS])
      1. Easy children—40 percent of children in study; playful, adaptive
      2. Difficult children—10 percent of children in study; negative, irritable
      3. Slow-to-warm-up children—15 percent of children in study; "inhibited," need more time to adjust
      4. 35 percent of children in study could not be classified
   C. Temperament in childhood predicts adjustment as an adult
   D. Both nature and nurture are influences
   E. Children can learn to adapt successfully to environment, regardless of temperament
II. Attachment—enduring emotional bond, develops over time
   A. Attachment behaviors in other species
      1. Attachment found in many other species
      2. Konrad Lorenz—studied ducks, geese, other fowl
      3. Imprinting—following behavior; occurs in response to first moving object seen (shortly after birth)
      4. Harry and Marguerite Harlow—rhesus monkeys prefer soft, cuddly surrogate "mother," even when other surrogate has food

B. Attachment in human infants
   1. John Bowlby (1908-1990)
      a) Attachment biologically based, necessary for survival
      b) Quality of attachment related to sensitivity, degree of care from parent
   2. Mary Ainsworth—developed methodology to assess attachment (Strange Situation) and identified three basic types
      a) Secure attachment (Type B)—65 to 70 percent of children show; rely on parent, warm reunion when mother returns
      b) Insecure-avoidant attachment (Type A)—about 20 percent of children show; child has little interest, little distress with regard to parent
      c) Insecure-resistant attachment (Type C)—about 10 percent of children show; emotionally erratic, ambivalent or may rebuff mother
      d) Fourth type of attachment identified later—disorganized/disoriented (Type D)—child seems confused, unable to make effective use of available support, unable to approach parent directly even when in need
      e) Conclusion: responding promptly, appropriately to infant's signals leads to secure attachment
   3. Criticisms of Strange Situation research method
      a) Attachment measured in too limited a period
      b) Method may not take cultural differences into account
C. Attachment and later development
   1. Early attachment styles affect later emotional relationships
   2. Poor adult attachment patterns correlated with poorer physical and emotional health
   3. Early attachment experiences result in internal working models—expectations for what emotional relationships are like
   4. More securely attached infant more likely to later exhibit: better adjustment, higher self-esteem, greater cooperativeness, greater independence, fewer behavioral problems, better peer relationships, better overall emotional health

III. Child-Rearing Influences
A. Characteristics of good parenting
   1. Many factors influence child's emotional, intellectual, and social development
   2. Factors include genetics, peer groups, quality of parenting
   3. Quality parenting: spending much time with children; sensitive to their needs and cues; modeling and reinforcing appropriate behaviors; setting and explaining clear rules, establishing limits; consistency in standards and interaction; providing warm, loving environment
B. Father's influence
   1. Involved fathers have children who perform better academically
   2. Two-parent (mother, father) families have children with greater academic and social success
   3. Fathers (in western societies) engage in more active physical play with children, less basic care giving, relative to mothers
C. Cultural differences in parenting
   1. African American
      a) Strong kinship bonds; parenting is shared among family members
      b) Grandmother may assume most important role
   2. Hispanic
      a) Father is traditional provider, protector
      b) Mother usually assumes full child-care responsibility
      c) Fairly strict discipline standards; emphasis on demeanor, respect towards adults

            d)   Currently changing as cultural characteristics change
     3.   Asian cultures
            a)   Emphasize respect for parental authority, particularly that of father
            b)   Usually warm relationship with mother
     4.   All cultures move child from dependency to independence

D.   Parenting styles (Baumrind, 1971, 1991)
     1.   Three basic types of parenting styles identified
            a)   Authoritative—reasonable, consistent limits; loving; listen; explain
            b)   Authoritarian—rigid, demand unquestioning obedience; disregard for child's feelings or point of view
            c)   Permissive—little involvement on part of parent as far as establishing guidelines, rules; little follow-through
     2.   Critique
            a)   Need to consider environment when evaluating effectiveness of parenting style (e.g., high-risk may necessitate different parenting tactics in comparison to low-risk environment)
            b)   Cultural influences may vary with regard to what are considered desirable parenting qualities
            c)   Some influence from child's personality

IV. Peer Relationships
  A.   Peer relationships affect much of child's development
  B.   Provide opportunities to develop social competencies, self-esteem, emotional understanding
  C.   Peer-rejected children are at greater risk (lower academic performance, poorer social and psychological adjustment)
  D.   Some peer influence undesirable (e.g., learning deviant behaviors)

V.   Erikson's Stages of Psychosocial Development
  A.   Emphasized importance of social relationships (1963)
  B.   Personalities shaped by psychosocial challenges
  C.   Stages that cover childhood development period:
     1.   Trust vs. mistrust
            a)   First year of life—creates view of people, world in general
            b)   Trust develops when infant treated with warmth, responsiveness
            c)   Mistrust develops when child not attended to
     2.   Autonomy vs. shame and doubt
             a)   One through three years of age
            b)   Child's greater mobility, inquisitiveness, toilet training are major features
            c)   Shame and doubt if child criticized, given tasks beyond his abilities
     3.   Initiative vs. guilt
             a)   Includes child's ages of four and five years
            b)   Children come up with own ideas, not just adopting those of others
            c)   When praised, gain sense of confidence, competence
            d)   When criticized, feel inept, incapable, awkward
     4.   Industry vs. inferiority
             a)   Includes elementary school ages (approximately six to twelve years)
            b)   Not only initiate own tasks, interests, but much more likely to follow them through
            c)   Very many skills and areas of knowledge gained (academic, social, physical/motor)
            d)   Much comparison by children among themselves, in addition to feedback from parents, teachers
  D.   Experiences later in life can alter impact of earlier stages

VI. Exploring Psychology: Does Day Care Affect Attachment?
  A. More preschoolers now in day-care centers than at home, or in relative's home
  B. Apparently no differences in attachment patterns for children experiencing full-time day-care setting
  C. High-quality care can have positive effects on cognitive and social development
  D. Possibly long hours of day care associated with more aggressiveness
  E. Effects on child development related to *quality* of care, whether day-care setting or at home
    1. Parents should ask about licensure; facilities; policies; staff attitudes, morale, and qualifications; types of toys/activities available to children.

SUMMARY

In this module you learn about emotional and social development of the human during childhood. Emotional attachment is crucial to a child's survival in that babies and young children cannot fulfill their own needs and are dependent upon others to care enough to provide for them. In this sense, attachment behaviors on the part of parents and children may be genetically predetermined. We see examples of attachment in other species—Lorenz's research with geese and other fowl (for example, the phenomenon of imprinting, a following behavior) and the work of the Harlows with rhesus monkeys (baby monkeys prefer to be with a soft, cuddly surrogate mother rather than a wire surrogate equipped with a source of food). The formation of attachment in humans is most dependent upon characteristics exhibited by the parent. Parents who are warm, loving, consistent, responsive, and perceptive regarding their child's needs and cues will have the most securely attached children. A secure attachment in childhood is associated with higher self-esteem, better psychological adjustment, and better social and emotional relationships throughout life. The child's temperament is somewhat related to the quality of attachment with the caregiver.

Mary Ainsworth developed the Strange Situation, a laboratory method for assessing attachment in very young children (typically carried out when the youngster is about 12 months of age). The quality of attachment is determined most by how the child responds when the mother returns after having left the little one for a brief period of time. Children who respond immediately to the parent's return, have a warm reunion, and show clear evidence of relying upon the mother for emotional support are classified as exhibiting secure attachment. Most children are in this category. Children who show no real reaction to the mother's return and who seem little disturbed by her disappearance or absence are classified as having an insecure-avoidant type of attachment. Children who seem excessively emotionally dependent upon the parent and somewhat uncertain (perhaps even anxious or angry) about the nature of the relationship are classified as having an insecure-resistant type of attachment. These children have an erratic response to their mother's return—they may quickly seek her out yet appear to fight her overtures once she reaches for the child. A fourth type of attachment has been added by later researchers, and that is the disorganized/disoriented category of attachment. Children with this classification seem emotionally confused and do not have an effective way for dealing with emotional difficulties. Attachment to fathers seems less related to the father's behavior, in part perhaps because fathers typically spend less time with their children than mothers do.

Three basic styles of parenting have been identified (Baumrind, 1971, 1991). These are (1) authoritative, (2) authoritarian, and (3) permissive. Parents who raise their children using the authoritative style tend to have the most successful and most well-adjusted offspring. The authoritative parent is consistent, has clear rules that are explained and modeled, and shows a great deal of love, caring, and respect for her child. Authoritative parents listen to their children, support and believe in their children, and show interest in their child's friends and activities. The authoritarian parent is rigid, demands unquestioning obedience, and relies on discipline and punishment to mold children's behavior. The child's point of view is not considered, nor, usually, are the child's feelings. Children raised in this manner may be withdrawn and somewhat inhibited in their behavior; they tend to have lower self-esteem. The permissive parent may show affection towards the child, but is not involved with regard to setting reasonable parameters for behavior, establishing and explaining rules, and following through to assure that desired behaviors and guidelines are met.

Erik Erikson has proposed stages for human psychosocial development, and four of these stages fall within the childhood years. Erikson's view is that an individual's development is heavily influenced by social experiences from parents and also from others. At each stage, the individual is faced with a psychosocial challenge, and one outcome is preferred over the other (trust is preferred to mistrust, for example). During the first year of life, the psychosocial issue most crucial is whether the baby develops a sense of trust or a sense of mistrust. As indicated in the Ainsworth model for attachment, whether trust is established depends most upon how the child is treated, and this is predominantly in the hands of the parents. Caregivers who respond promptly and appropriately to the child's needs and signals help the child develop a sense of security and trust and the belief that the world is a welcoming place. The second psychosocial stage is autonomy vs. shame and doubt; the third, initiative vs. guilt, and the fourth (spanning the elementary school years of about six to twelve years of age) involves industry vs. inferiority. A successful outcome in each case is related to the feedback a child receives. When the child is praised and supported for his attempts, the child tends to develop a sense of competence. By the fourth stage (industry vs. inferiority), feedback from peers also becomes crucial. Of course, this feedback is related to the child's already existing sense of self-worth, which is a function of previous stages.

Though most American children are in some kind of day-care setting during the preschool years, children in day care show little difference regarding attachment patterns when compared with children raised entirely at home. The quality of day care (or home care) seems more important to a child's development than the setting in which this care occurs. There are cultural differences in parenting styles and parenting standards, and these variations need to be taken into consideration when evaluating parenting success. Hispanic cultures, for example, place a greater emphasis on respect and traditional discipline, so a parent who exhibits these characteristics may be reflecting cultural patterns and not necessarily an individual parenting style. Fathers interact differently with their children than mothers do in that fathers tend to involve their children in more active and more physical play. Mothers' behaviors tend to involve the basic caregiving procedures—feeding, bathing, and so forth. Though most research on parenting, attachment, and child development has focused on the mother-child relationship, research does show that where fathers are present and are involved with their children, children show higher levels of academic, and perhaps social, abilities.

KEY TERMS

Temperament

Attachment

Bonding

Imprinting

Strange Situation

Internal working models

SELF-TEST PRACTICE QUIZ

From the Key Terms select that which best matches the following:

1. _____ Attachment behavior exhibited by an animal (typically a gosling or other fowl) where it follows the first moving object it is exposed to after birth

2. _____ A laboratory method developed by Mary Ainsworth to assess the quality of attachment between mother and child

3. _____ Expectations, resulting from early childhood attachment experiences, regarding what emotional relationships should be like

4. _____ An enduring emotional bond between parent and child; forms over time and with extended contact

5. _____ The close tie established between parent and newborn due to contact in the first few hours after birth

6. _____ Typical personality or disposition characteristics, thought to be inborn

a. Temperament
b. Attachment
c. Bonding
d. Imprinting
e. Strange Situation
f. Internal working models

7. A child who needs a little extra time to get used to changes and who exhibits a somewhat lower activity level is classified as having a(n) _____ temperament.
   a. easy
   b. difficult
   c. slow-to-warm-up
   d. passive

8. If basic temperament cannot be changed,
   a. difficult and slow-to-warm-up children have a poor prognosis for future relationships.
   b. caregivers can work with children and help them find more effective adaptive strategies.
   c. children with less desirable temperaments can be sent to special schools.
   d. genetic alteration may be one solution.

9. Using the Strange Situation for evaluation, children who are unresponsive when a mother returns after an absence and who seem little concerned when she is not with them are classified as having a(n) _____ type of attachment.
   a. secure (Type B)
   b. insecure-avoidant (Type A)
   c. insecure-resistant (Type C)
   d. disorganized/disoriented (Type D)

10. Studies regarding the formation of attachment for children who attend full-time day care reveal that
    a. full-time day-care children are likely to be somewhat less securely attached to their mothers than are other same-age children.
    b. full-time day-care children are likely to be much less securely attached to their mothers than are other same-age children.
    c. full-time day-care children are most likely to show a secure attachment to the day-care center regular attendant.
    d. there are no appreciable differences in attachment between children enrolled in full-time day care and other same-age children.

11. Ducks, geese, and other fowl that follow the first moving object to which they are exposed after birth are exhibiting a behavior known as
    a. imprinting.
    b. attachment.
    c. bonding.
    d. an internal working model.

12. Based on Harlow's work, when baby monkeys had both a terry-cloth-covered surrogate mother and a wire surrogate mother in the cage with them, the baby monkeys tended to spend most of their time with
    a. "wire mama," provided she had food.
    b. "soft mama," whether or not she had food.
    c. "soft mama," provided she had food.
    d. "wire mama," whether or not she had food.

13. As a parent, Jeffrey is very strict with his children. When they question his rules, his typical response is, "Because I'm your father, that's why!" Based on this, Jeffrey is a(n) _____ parent.
    a. authoritarian
    b. authoritative
    c. permissive
    d. totalitarian

14. Regardless of culture, all families
    a. give a prominent role and much authority to the maternal grandmother.
    b. cast fathers in the role of primary provider and protector.
    c. place a high value on warm maternal relationships.
    d. move children from a state of relative dependency to a state of relative independence.

15. Peer group relationships are important because
    a. young children who are not accepted by peers tend to score lower on achievement tests and often do not look forward to going to school.
    b. children with friendships learn prosocial behaviors and tend to have higher self-esteem.
    c. older children who are not accepted by peers show more aggressive and antisocial behavior.
    d. they fulfill all of the above roles.

16. Juan is 2-1/2 years old. A typical toddler, he loves to assert his independence by shouting "No!" and often insists on dressing himself (even though that takes a long time). Juan is in Erikson's stage of
    a. trust vs. mistrust.
    b. initiative vs. guilt.
    c. autonomy vs. shame and doubt.
    d. industry vs. inferiority.

ESSAY QUESTIONS

1.   Discuss how attachments are formed between parents and children. How is early experience with attachment related to interpersonal relationships for the individual as an older child and as an adult?

2.   Briefly discuss the three basic parenting styles as identified by Baumrind and note the differences among them. What do children tend to be like when raised with the authoritative parenting style, and why is that parenting style the most preferred?

ANSWER KEY

1.   Imprinting

2.   Strange Situation

3.   Internal working models

4.   Attachment

5.   Bonding

6.   Temperament

7.   c

8.   b

9.   b

10.   d

11.   a

12.   b

13.   a

14.   d

15.   d

16.   a

SAMPLE ANSWERS TO ESSAY QUESTIONS

1.   According to research by Bowlby, Ainsworth, and others, attachment is a process that occurs over an extended period of time (from birth on) and is most linked to the behavior and responsiveness of the mother. It is likely that the formation of attachments is biologically-based in that attachment between the infant and some older caregiver is vital to that infant's survival. Attachment is not the same as bonding; bonding is the tie connecting parent to infant in the hours shortly after birth. Attachment is the result of many hours, days, and months of contact between the baby and the parent. The parent who is consistently available to the infant, discerns the infant's needs and cues accurately, and responds promptly and appropriately encourages the establishment of a secure attachment with her baby.

Based on Ainsworth's research utilizing the Strange Situation, about two-thirds of all children show signs of a secure attachment by the end of their first year. Securely attached children seek their parent's presence, feel comfortable leaving the parent for a brief period of time in order to explore or play, and clearly rely on the parent as an emotional base. A secure attachment not only provides a baby with emotional stability, which includes a sense of freedom and opportunity to explore and learn more about his environment, but it has consequences for later childhood and adulthood as well. Securely attached children show better psychological adjustment, higher self-esteem, and more effective social relationships. In adulthood, the type of childhood attachment is related to later emotional relationships. It appears that the emotional pattern established in childhood leads to behaviors and expectations regarding what adult relationships should be like.

2. In the authoritative parenting style, parents are consistent, warm and loving; this is combined with clear rules and expectations that are carefully explained and modeled in the adults' behavior. Parents retain their authority in the home but treat their children with respect and regard. In the authoritarian parenting style, parents are rigid, inflexible, and emphasize obedience and punishment. The child's point of view, and usually the child's feelings, are not considered. The atmosphere is one of "might makes right." In the permissive parenting style, parents usually have abdicated their authority and their responsibility to parent and do not get involved with regard to establishing and enforcing reasonable rules and boundaries. They may or may not show affection to the child, but the child is otherwise left free to determine whatever behaviors he or she will engage in. Offspring raised with the authoritative parenting style have the greatest likelihood for success in all avenues of their lives. They are emotionally secure enough to feel confident venturing into new things since they feel loved and accepted unconditionally. They are well adjusted and have mastered effective prosocial skills. Because emotional relationships are stable and not draining, these individuals have the energy and confidence to apply the best of their abilities to the task at hand. Thus, the authoritative parenting style is the most preferred.

MODULE 9.5 COGNITIVE DEVELOPMENT

LEARNING OBJECTIVES

After you have mastered the information in this unit, you will be able to:

- Compare and contrast assimilation and accommodation

- Describe Piaget's stages of cognitive development

- Discuss the basic theme in Vygotsky's theory of cognitive development

OUTLINE

I. Piaget's Theory of Cognitive Development
   A. Basics of Piaget's theory
      1. Best way to learn about children is to observe them carefully
      2. Schema—organizational system used by individuals to interact with the world
      3. Adaptation—changing in order to better meet challenges in the world
      4. Assimilation—adding a new item to an existing schema
      5. Accommodation—modifying an existing schema (or creating a new one) to account for phenomena that do not fit in existing schemas
      6. Stage approach to cognitive development
         a) Assimilation and accommodation processes are lifelong
         b) Cognitive development progresses through stages—universal pattern for all children; each stage qualitatively different from others
   B. Sensorimotor stage
      1. Birth to two years of age
      2. Gain object permanence (traditional test) by about eight months of age
      3. Learn about world through motor actions; sensory system detects result
   C. Preoperational stage
      1. Two to seven years of age
      2. Still do not have logical cognitive ability

        3.   Gain ability for symbolic representations (one is language)

        4.   Piaget's view—child egocentric until end of stage; uses animistic thinking

        5.   Do not yet understand principles of conservation (of number, area, volume)

  D.   Concrete operational stage

        1.   Seven to eleven years of age

        2.   Gain understanding of conservation—when nothing added or subtracted, quantity does not change though form or appearance might

        3.   Can perform simple logical operations provided they deal with real-world examples (e.g., do not involve abstract or hypothetical thinking)

  E.   Formal operational stage

        1.   Last stage—begins at about eleven or twelve years of age

        2.   Full cognitive maturity—but not everyone reaches this level

        3.   Can manage deductive, abstract, and hypothetical thinking

  F.   Critique of Piaget's theory

        1.   Challenges to the stage model of development

            a)   Another view is that development is quantitative and continuous

        2.   Underestimation of children's abilities

            a)   More recent research—children more capable, earlier than Piaget realized

            b)   Tasks may be too difficult to show what children know

        3.   Lack of attention to cultural influences on cognitive development

            a)   Cross-cultural studies confirm order of stages of development, not timing

II.   Vygotsky's Sociocultural Theory of Cognitive Development

  A.   A Russian psychologist (1896–1934); social interactions are vehicle for learning

  B.   Zone of proximal development—what child can learn, with guidance, help

  C.   Scaffolding—scale instruction to level of child; adjust as child progresses

SUMMARY

In this module you learn about the dramatic increases in cognitive functioning that are evident in children as they grow older. The prevailing view regarding cognitive development is that proposed by Jean Piaget. Piaget believed cognitive growth occurred in stages and that each stage was qualitatively different from the previous one. A child who can use language, for example, is qualitatively different from the one who cannot yet speak. Piaget's theory of cognitive development involves four stages with the last stage beginning at about eleven or twelve years of age.

Piaget believed individuals develop, through their experience with the world, schemas, which are a sense of what a concept or notion is and how one would use it. You may have a schema for, let's say, "ball" or "mother" or "classroom." Why is a soccer ball a ball, but a grapefruit is not? You didn't always know this! But you have learned through your interactions and your experience with the environment. Much of this learning begins in the first stage Piaget proposes—the sensorimotor stage. In this stage, children act upon the world with even the simplest of motor skills. The world responds, and the child is aware of this reaction from the world via his sensory system. Gradually, the child learns what actions go with what consequences, and the child builds on this learning. We add to our knowledge either through assimilation (where a new item fits into an existing schema) or through accommodation (no current schema fits the new knowledge; either an existing schema is modified [why is a football still a ball?] or we create a new schema).

In Piaget's second stage (preoperational, covering ages two to seven years), much cognitive development occurs. Most importantly, the child acquires the ability for symbolic representations, and the number one symbol system we acquire is language. According to Piaget, the child during this stage is still egocentric; that is, she is unable to grasp anyone else's perspective but her own. Later research, however, has disputed the belief that a child is egocentric all the way up until seven years of age. As with other of Piaget's findings, the critique is that his tasks are too difficult for the children to show us what they know. More recent research has found evidence for object permanence (which, using Piaget's tasks, occurs around eight months of age) as early as 3-1/2 or 4 months of age. Still, the information Piaget has provided us with has been extremely helpful.

The third stage of Piaget's theory is the concrete operational stage. It is only at this stage that children truly begin to think, said Piaget, because it is the first time youngsters can be truly logical and contemplate concepts (do mental "operations") in their heads. Concrete operational children gain the notion of reversibility and conservation—that the quantity of matter remains the same, even if the shape or other appearance of it changes. They are no longer egocentric, even by Piaget's standards. However, their logical thought must involve real-world (e.g., "concrete") objects and situations—the one thing concrete operational children still lack is the ability for abstract and hypothetical thinking. This last ability is the distinctive feature of Piaget's fourth and final stage of cognitive development, formal operational thought. Though we have learned now that even Piaget underestimated what children can do, we can appreciate the understanding his research has brought, and can appreciate his effective research method itself—observing children closely, first-hand.

Some cognitive developmental researchers disagree with Piaget's view beginning with the notion that development occurs in stages. Development, some experts say, does not occur in so neat and tidy a fashion, nor does progression from one phase in life to the next necessarily involve only qualitative differences. Development can be more steady, continuous, and can involve quantitative changes. Piaget's stage theory suggests a much more absolute, complete, and rather sudden shift from one stage to the next. In addition, though Piaget's approach seems to be correct across cultures regarding the order in which children go through stages, more recent research has shown there are cultural influences on the timing of these stages.

Lev Vygotsky presented another view of cognitive advancement. Vygotsky's emphasis is on the importance of social experiences and social exchange in the process of learning. He made the point, basically, that children do not learn in a vacuum. Parents are parents, but they are also teachers as are others with whom the child comes in contact. According to Vygotsky, there is a zone of proximal development, that is a realm (a "zone") of things that children have not yet mastered but can learn if they have a little help. We are constantly helping children learn how to speak, dress themselves, and behave with others. Children, of course, learn these things more quickly and more successfully with help from a knowledgeable other person rather than from attempting to learn on their own. Tasks or knowledge far beyond the child's current level are beyond the zone of proximal development. However, knowledge that the child shows a readiness for, such as understanding new concepts and learning new behaviors, are within her reach and can be acquired, provided that an individual who already has the skill or knowledge helps with the acquisition. Vygotsky felt that much of what a child needs to learn has to do with cultural information because that is the environment within which the child will need to function.

KEY TERMS

Schema

Adaptation

Assimilation

Accommodation

Object permanence

Symbolic representations

Egocentrism

Animistic thinking

Irreversibility

Centration

Conservation

Formal operations

Zone of proximal development (ZPD)

Scaffolding

SELF-TEST PRACTICE QUIZ

From the Key Terms choose that which best matches the following:

1. _____ An infant's understanding that objects or people still exist even though the person or object is not visible at the moment

2. _____ Piaget's fourth and final stage of cognitive development; the individual now exhibits abstract and hypothetical thinking

3. _____ The process of adjustment, according to Piaget, where people learn ways to function more effectively in their environment

4. _____ The ability to use something else (such as a word) to stand for something allowing for easier mental operations

5. _____ A hypothetical area, described by Vygotsky, that includes what children have not yet learned but which they can learn with some assistance

6. _____ The tendency for children, according to Piaget, to contemplate and refer to inanimate things as if they had properties of living organisms

7. _____ The understanding, most likely gained during the concrete operational period, where children grasp that quantity of matter remains the same even if its shape or arrangement has been altered

8. _____ The tendency for younger children to focus on only one aspect of an object or situation

a. Schema

b. Adaptation

c. Assimilation

d. Accommodation

e. Object permanence

f. Symbolic representations

g. Egocentrism

h. Animistic thinking

i. Irreversibility

j. Centration

k. Conservation

l. Formal operations

m. Zone of proximal development (ZPD)

n. Scaffolding

9. _____ A framework we develop, according to Piaget, as we experience the world where we come to understand what an object or concept is and how to appropriately deal with it

10. _____ According to Piaget's theory, the inability to understand that doing the same process in reverse does not change the substance of that process

11. _____ Vygotsky's view that we teach a child best by presenting or conceptualizing information at the level where the child can best understand it

12. _____ Adding information to a schema where the schema must be modified or a new schema created in order to properly categorize the new information

13. _____ The tendency, according to Piaget, for a young child to be unable to grasp any point of view other than his own

14. _____ Adding a new item to an existing schema; the schema as it currently exists is adequate

15. The stage where a child develops symbolic representation, has not yet mastered reversibility, and is, according to Piaget, still egocentric is the _____ stage of cognitive development.
    a. sensorimotor
    b. preoperational
    c. concrete operational
    d. formal operational

16. Despite the many advances and understandings Piaget provided us through his research, a criticism of his theory is that he
    a. underestimated children's actual abilities.
    b. overestimated children's actual abilities.
    c. relied on hypothetical rather than real-world evidence.
    d. emphasized quantitative rather than qualitative change.

17. A child who believes she now has more pizza because her slice has been cut into many small pieces is showing evidence of
    a. scaffolding.
    b. concrete operational thinking.
    c. egocentrism.
    d. centration.

18. Lily understands the concept of "table," and knows that's where she sits to eat dinner and to color in her coloring book. When she goes to school, she is given a desk. She comes to understand that "desk" does not fit with her previous schema for "table," and she develops a new schema for "desk." Lily is showing evidence of the process of

    a.   animistic thinking.
    b.   reversibility.
    c.   assimilation.
    d.   accommodation.

19. Which of the following statements about the formal operational stage is TRUE, according to Piaget?

    a.   Children in this stage can think logically but not in the abstract.
    b.   It usually starts about age 7.
    c.   Not everybody reaches this stage, even in adulthood.
    d.   None of the above are true.

20. When Piaget's ideas regarding cognitive developmental stages are tested cross-culturally, we find that

    a.   Piaget's work has relevance for Swiss children only.
    b.   Piaget's work has universal application.
    c.   the order of stages may vary, depending on culture, but the timing is consistent.
    d.   the timing of the appearance of stages may vary, but the order of stages is consistent.

21. Vygotsky emphasized the _____ context as relevant to a child's cognitive development.

    a.   academic
    b.   emotional
    c.   sociocultural
    d.   economic

22. When children learn to ride a bike, they often start with tricycles and then with training wheels before progressing to a standard two-wheeler. This illustrates the concept of

    a.   formal operations.
    b.   scaffolding.
    c.   centration.
    d.   animistic thinking.

ESSAY QUESTIONS

1. Trace the process of cognitive development in children, according to Jean Piaget.

2. How is Vygotsky's approach to cognitive development different from that of Piaget?

ANSWER KEY

1. Object permanence

2. Formal operations

3. Adaptation

4. Symbolic representations

5. Zone of proximal development (ZPD)

6. Animistic thinking

7. Conservation

8.   Centration

9.   Schema

10. Irreversibility

11. Scaffolding

12. Accommodation

13. Egocentrism

14. Assimilation

15. b

16. a

17. d

18. d

19. c

20. d

21. c

22. b

SAMPLE ANSWERS TO ESSAY QUESTIONS

1.   Piaget believes that children's cognitive development begins with simple reflexes. His first stage of development is the sensorimotor stage where children are basically nonverbal and are involved in much physical interaction with their environment. Children utilize their motor abilities and experience the consequences of their actions by means of their sensory system. In this way children begin to put together a picture of this world. Much of this picture, according to Piaget, involves the development of schemas. Our earliest schemas are quite simple. As we experience the world more, we add to our schemas (an understanding of a what an object or concept is and how to interact with it) either through assimilation, where a new item fits well into an existing schema, or accommodation, where the new item really does not fit and the schema must be modified or a new schema must be created. Piaget's second stage for a child's cognitive development is the preoperational stage. This covers ages 2 to 7, and the most important advancement during this stage is the child's acquisition of symbol systems (language being preeminent). According to Piaget, the child is still egocentric; that is, he is still unable to perceive anyone else's view other than his own. A preoperational child also has not yet mastered conservation principles. The preoperational child believes that, if the appearance of something has changed (for example, a ball of clay is rolled out into a long, thin piece) then the quantity has changed also—even when in fact it has not (in the example above, it is the same amount of clay, but a preoperational child will perceive the longer piece as "more"). During the concrete operational period (ages 7 to 11 years) children do gain these concepts, and are able, according to Piaget, to think logically for the first time. It is not until Piaget's last stage of cognitive development, the formal operations stage, that he believes children can think deductively and grasp abstract and hypothetical notions. Piaget was a stage theorist; that is, he believed cognitive development occurred in distinct stages, and the child's abilities in one stage were qualitatively different from abilities in another stage.

2. Perhaps Piaget did not realize it, but he conceived of children's cognitive development more or less devoid of surrounding situational input. His theory of cognitive development presents the changes that occur in children's thinking as rather regular and universal, regardless of social and cultural influences on the child and regardless of the child's actual experience with the environment. Piaget has greatly advanced our understanding of children's cognitive growth, and that fact should not be overlooked. However, cross-cultural studies have indicated, for example, that there is variation as to when cognitive developmental stages occur depending upon the cultural environment. Lev Vygotsky, in contrast, heavily emphasized the social and cultural context in which a child's learning occurs. And it was Vygotsky's view that much of what a child needs to learn is, in fact, cultural and social information since it is that environment within which a child will need to function. Vygotsky stressed the role of parents and others as teachers. Instead of children's learning unfolding automatically, Vygotsky noted that much of what a child learns is due to a parent's (or other more skill individual's) willingness to teach this information.

MODULE 9.6 APPLICATION: TV AND KIDS

LEARNING OBJECTIVE

After you have mastered the information in this unit, you will be able to:

*   Explain how TV viewing influences children's development

OUTLINE

I. Possible Physical and Psychological Drawbacks to Children's Viewing Television
    A. Television takes away from other important activities—keep in mind that children are not always engaged in "constructive" activities
    B. It is because of television that children do poorly in school—there is a slight but consistent negative correlation between television viewing and performance in school (e.g., as hours of television viewing increase among children, academic achievement decreases)
    C. Watching television fosters violence and aggressive behavior in children
        1. Even children's programs have much violent content
        2. Heroes often win with violence—sends the message that violence is acceptable
        3. Violence on television increases aggressive behavior; aggressive individuals select more violent programming
        4. Research by Albert Bandura—children exhibit more aggressive behavior when they see it modeled
        5. Habituation effects—viewers become sensitized to real-life violence
    D. TV viewing is related to obesity in children
II. Parent's Role in Responsible Television Viewing for Children
    A. Screen programs children will watch
    B. Join child in television viewing, explain
    C. Avoid using television as a baby-sitter
    D. Limit hours of TV viewing (recommended is one to two hours a day at most)
    E. Encourage children to limit viewing, choose programs wisely
    F. News programs may be very inappropriate for young children
    G. Avoid eating in front of the television (for anyone)
    H. Encourage other interests on the part of the child

SUMMARY

In this module, you learn about the effects of television viewing on children's development. Though the belief is widespread that television viewing is harmful, that is probably not entirely true. If a parent chooses carefully, some programming can be helpful for children, and it is best if the amount a child watches is not excessive (an hour or two a day is plenty). Parents can watch television with their children, help children learn to regulate what and how much they watch, and help children realize there are many other interesting and worthwhile activities to be involved in as well. Though television viewing by young children is probably not all bad, there is some association between aggressive behavior and level of violence in programs watched.

CHAPTER 9 APPLICATION EXERCISE

Reflect back on your childhood (you may want to contemplate the experiences of young children you know currently as well). What was most important to you as a child? What did you most enjoy? Were there any events or developments that at the time you thought were absolutely crucial? Were any experiences you had particularly traumatic or particularly meaningful? How do you think these experiences have affected you in the long run?

What were your favorite possessions? What were your favorite pastimes? Why were they important to you? What parenting style would you say was most typical of how you were raised? Compare what was important to you as a child with the perspective that you have now as an adult. What has changed? What has remained the same? If you had to do it over again, how would you like your childhood to be different (or would you keep it exactly as it was)? What approaches and behaviors do you think are most important relative to how you (will) raise your own children?

CHAPTER 10

Adolescence and Adulthood

In Chapter 10 you learn about the physical, cognitive, social and emotional issues that face us as we move out of childhood and into the remaining years of our lives. At every stage there are challenges we must meet, and these challenges are always formidable. We will see that at all stages, attitude is everything. Also, warm and loving relationships help us weather whatever storms face us and help us stay involved in life and function at our best.

Adolescence is a time of many challenges, though not of the same nature as those in middle and older adulthood. The task of adolescence is making the transition from being a rather dependent, immature child to becoming an independent, fully functioning and autonomous adult. This is a daunting undertaking. One of the most challenging features of being an adolescent is that one is thrust into the world of adulthood with absolutely no prior experience! Teenagers seem to have the understanding that the family will not always be their reference group and that in fact their peers will be. Thus, there is a gradually breaking away from the family, especially the parents, and the continued strengthening of ties with friends and other peers. This loosening of ties with the family may be traumatic for both parents and child, or it may be a welcome relief! Often it is some of both.

For adolescents, sexual development and sexual relationships become a major focus. The body of the teenager is changing and goes from physical immaturity to eventual full sexual maturity and the ability to reproduce the species. As with so many other aspects of adolescence, the ability may appear prior to a full understanding of related consequences. Cognitively, too, the adolescent is changing. The stage of cognitive development that, according to Jean Piaget, is associated with adolescence and adulthood is formal operational thinking. Here, the teen can now contemplate not just real-life issues but those that involve abstract and hypothetical reasoning and concepts. Adolescents begin to form an identity—a sense of who they are and where (at least, as it seems at the time) they are going. In order to form an identity, the teen must "try on" many things, whether these are clothing styles, personal or political philosophies, or interpersonal behaviors and standards. The teen continues to add and strengthen many cognitive skills, and considers moral issues as well. Adolescents have gained the capability to see and consider others' points of view. By any standard, they are no longer egocentric except that they do tend to feel the world is watching them closely. As is true throughout human life, loving, supportive, close relationships (with both family and friends) help the transitions of adolescence go more smoothly.

Young and middle adulthood is also a time of great activity and many challenges. Most skills and abilities peak in young adulthood including body strength and agility and many cognitive functions such as memory, mental quickness, and mental flexibility. Tasks of young adulthood include establishing a meaningful and lasting emotional relationship (Erikson termed the psychosocial challenge of young adulthood as intimacy vs. isolation), establishing one's career and one's place in the community, and often bringing children into the world and raising them. Most individuals marry at some time or another, but they do not necessarily stay married. Divorce is prominent in American society, and it involves much physical, emotional, financial, and psychological readjustment for all concerned. Middle adulthood may involve what is called a midlife crisis; but a true crisis at this time of life is the exception rather than the rule. Often, adults in their middle years find the new opportunities facing them refreshing and inviting. Children may be grown and out of the house, often middle-aged individuals still experience very good physical health, and thus the future still seems open-ended and full of promise. This may be a time to try new ideas, switch to a more satisfying career, return for more education, or just completely review one's philosophy and approach to life.

For the older adult, the recognition that life must be, sooner or later, coming to an end presents a great deal of challenge in and of itself. The overriding task is to continue to find life meaningful and rewarding. Fortunately for older individuals, while they may not have quite the acuity of earlier years, they have gained immeasurably in experience. Older adults can live longer and better lives.

MODULE 10.1 ADOLESCENCE

LEARNING OBJECTIVES

After you have mastered the information in this unit, you will be able to:

- Define puberty

- Describe the changes in cognitive development that occur during adolescence

- Explain Kohlberg's levels of moral reasoning

- Discuss Gilligan's criticisms of Kohlberg's theory

- Explain what Erikson believed to be the major developmental challenge

OUTLINE

I.   Physical Development
    A.   Adolescent growth spurt
    B.   Puberty—reaching full sexual maturity
        1.   Secondary sex characteristics (pubic hair, voice changes)
        2.   Primary sex characteristics—directly involved in reproduction
        3.   Menarche—onset of menstruation in females
    C.   Timing of puberty has social and emotional effects—based on people's reactions to puberty, not the physical changes themselves
II. Cognitive Development
    A.   Piaget's formal operational stage
    B.   Adolescent egocentrism
        1.   Imaginary audience—adolescents believe others are keenly interested in themselves and their concerns
        2.   Personal fable—exaggerated sense of own uniqueness and invulnerability
III. Kohlberg's Theory of Moral Development
    A.   Methodology—present participants with vignettes; ask why behavior seen as right or wrong
    B.   Levels of moral reasoning (based on these responses)
        1.   Preconventional—only concerned with consequences
            a)   Stage 1: obedience and punishment
            b)   Stage 2: instrumental purpose
        2.   Conventional—conformity with rules as they currently exist
            a)   Stage 3: "good boy–good girl"
            b)   Stage 4: authority or law-and-order
        3.   Postconventional
            a)   Not everyone reaches
            b)   Applying one's own moral principles
            c)   Stage 5: social contract
            d)   Stage 6: universal ethical principles

    C.   Note: moral reasoning not necessarily related to moral behavior

    D.   Cross-cultural and gender-based research on Kohlberg's model

        1.   Children do tend to follow these stages, and there is evidence for universality of findings

        2.   Criticism: morality associated with Western and male values

        3.   Carol Gilligan's research (some evidence for these views)

           a)   Females have a care orientation

           b)   Males have a justice orientation

IV. Psychosocial Development

    A.   Adolescent-parent relationships

        1.   Children need to pull away somewhat in order to become independent

        2.   Close ties, secure emotional base with parents still crucial

        3.   Distance part of teen's effort to discover own individual identity

    B.   Erikson's view of adolescence

        1.   Answering "Who am I?"

        2.   Psychosocial challenge of adolescence is ego identity vs. role diffusion

        3.   Ego identity—clear, stable sense of self

        4.   Role diffusion—uncertainty regarding identity, lack of sense of direction

    C.   Identity crisis—represents intense self-examination, need for knowing self

    D.   Peer relationships

        1.   Become increasingly important

        2.   Parental closeness can ameliorate undesirable peer influences

    E.   Adolescent sexuality

        1.   Much interest during adolescence regarding sexuality

        2.   Rate of intercourse slightly lower than ten years ago

        3.   Teen pregnancy rate also has dropped

        4.   Sexual activity related to peer pressure, personal values, goals

SUMMARY

In this module you learn about the physical, cognitive, social and emotional growth of the teenager. Adolescence has long been considered a time of turbulence and stress, and, although not every teen has this experience, there is probably good reason for that view. Very many changes face adolescents. Their bodies are changing, and sexual characteristics and feelings are emerging. Physically the teen becomes quite interested in sexual activity, and this interest also usually prompts an examination of personal sexual standards, goals, and values.

Adolescence is characterized by self-examination on all fronts. Erik Erikson proposed that the most overriding challenge of the teenage years is exploring and attempting to determine one's identity. The choice during adolescence, according to Erikson, is between ego identity and role diffusion. One can have an identity in many different facets of one's life—the sexual identity, for example, as referred to above. The teen also needs to establish his or her identity in terms of morals and principles, career goals, as a social and community member, and the like. An individual with a firm identity, according to Erikson, knows who she is, where she is headed, and that sense of self and of direction does not waiver a great deal. The teen caught in role diffusion does not have a focus and may seem to drift. She does not have a plan and is confused about who she is. Erikson created the *term identity* crisis to describe the uncomfortable state associated with not having a clear sense of who one is.

Cognitively, teenagers may be, but are not necessarily, in Piaget's last stage of cognitive development, formal operational. An adolescent at this level can reason abstractly and can speculate about things that do not and even cannot exist. Piaget noted that even some adults never reach this last stage, at least according to the Piagetian tasks used to evaluate for formal operational reasoning. Though teenagers have moved out of childhood egocentrism, they show signs of an adolescent egocentrism. David Elkind (1985) proposed the notion of the imaginary audience—the idea that everyone is looking at the teen and is exceedingly interested in the teen's concerns. Elkind has also proposed that during adolescence a teen develops a personal fable. This is an exaggerated sense of uniqueness on the part of the teen and a sense of invulnerability. The cognitive changes during adolescence, taken together, do lead a teen to consider world issues, intellectual controversies, personal relationships, and the like differently than in the past.

Moral values also become a particular focus during the teenage years. How might we assess an individual for type of moral reasoning? A methodology was developed by Lawrence Kohlberg in which brief stories are presented to the listener, who is then asked about behavior that occurred in the story. A classic story involves Heinz, his wife who is dying of cancer, and a drugstore owner. The individual is asked whether the behavior was right or wrong, and then the question of greatest interest to Kohlberg is asked—why? Why was the behavior seen as the right thing to do or not? Responses to this last question are classified as indicating a level of moral reasoning. Individuals who are just concerned with the end result of the behavior (would Heinz get in trouble?) are classified as preconventional reasoners. People who are concerned with rules and regulations as they currently exist are said to be reasoning at the conventional level, and individuals who apply their own, personally developed set of principles (which may transcend existing law and order) are classified as postconventional reasoners. Carol Gilligan has challenged Kohlberg's interpretations noting that differences in the classification of female respondents may well be due to women's care orientation rather than the justice orientation, which may be more typical of males. It should be noted that though we have developed several ways of evaluating moral reasoning, the ability to reason about the moral components of an issue does not necessarily result in corresponding evidence of moral behavior.

KEY TERMS

Adolescence

Puberty

Secondary sex characteristics

Primary sex characteristics

Menarche

Imaginary audience

Personal fable

Ego identity

Identity crisis

Role diffusion

SELF-TEST PRACTICE QUIZ

From the Key Terms select that which best matches the following:

1. _____ Sexual characteristics emerging during adolescence that are not directly related to reproduction

2. _____ A term created by Erikson to describe the discomfort of not having a clear sense of identity and the stress involved in the effort to establish that identity

3. _____ A belief among adolescents that their life and experiences are incredibly unique

4. _____ The period in life that spans moving out of childhood and into full adulthood

5. _____ The preferred outcome for the challenge facing adolescents, according to psychosocial theory

6. _____ Sexual characteristics developing during adolescence that are directly related to reproduction

7. _____ The less desired outcome of the adolescent psychosexual stage—a lack of clear understanding regarding oneself and a lack of sense of direction

8. _____ A stage of physical, sexual development occurring during adolescence when one reaches the level of becoming capable of reproduction

9. _____ The onset of the menstrual cycle

10. _____ The feeling adolescents have that everyone is watching them and is quite interested in their concerns

a. Adolescence
b. Puberty
c. Secondary sex characteristics
d. Primary sex characteristics
e. Menarche
f. Imaginary audience
g. Personal fable
h. Ego identity
i. Identity crisis
j. Role diffusion

11. Adolescence tends to be a time of greater conflict with parents, especially since the teen desires adult-level freedom and behaviors. Regarding their relationship with parents, teens report
    a. they really would rather not be around their parents.
    b. that oftentimes parents would rather not be around the teen.
    c. generally a good relationship with parents and a sense of love and respect.
    d. stronger and warmer bonds than at any time since birth.

12. Maturity in sexual organs directly related to reproduction (enlargement of testes and penis, and of the uterus, for example) is known as the development of
    a. primary sex characteristics.
    b. secondary sex characteristics.
    c. menarche.
    d. reproductive capability.

13. Earlier physical development seems to be related to greater _____ in males, though this is not usually the case with females.
    a. intelligence
    b. self-esteem
    c. emotional maturity
    d. leadership qualities

14. Jamie, age 14, is too embarrassed to walk into her classroom because she has a big pimple on her nose. Since she's been thinking a lot about this pimple, she just assumes that everybody else will be thinking about it too. This illustrates the principle of _____.
    a. the personal fable.
    b. concrete operations.
    c. role diffusion.
    d. the imaginary audience.

15. When asked if it's ever acceptable to tell a lie, little Joey answers, "No, it's not. Lying's just wrong. You should never ever lie because that's the rule." Based on this answer, which of Kohlber's levels of moral reasoning is Joey in?
    a. Preconventional
    b. Postconventional
    c. Ponventional
    d. Unconventional

16. A criticism of Kohlberg's research on moral reasoning is that
    a. stages are portrayed that most individuals actually do not go through.
    b. cross-cultural studies do not support his conclusions.
    c. values associated with higher levels of moral reasoning reflect male, Western standards.
    d. the approach shows severe and systematic bias against women.

17. The psychosocial challenge facing teenagers, according to Erikson, is that of
    a. trust vs. mistrust.
    b. autonomy vs. shame and doubt.
    c. identity vs. role diffusion.
    d. intimacy vs. isolation.

ESSAY QUESTIONS

1. Trace the history of Erik Erikson. Why did the period of adolescence and of discovering one's identity have such particular meaning for Erikson?

2. Discuss the role of peer relationships in adolescence (you may draw on your own experiences if you like). In what ways can peer relationships be helpful? In what ways might they be harmful?

ANSWER KEY

1. Secondary sex characteristics

2. Identity crisis

3. Personal fable

4. Adolescence

5. Ego identity

6. Primary sex characteristics

7. Role diffusion

8. Puberty

9. Menarche

10. Imaginary audience

11. c

12. a

13. b

14. d

15. c

16. c

17. c

SAMPLE ANSWERS TO ESSAY QUESTIONS

1. Erik Erikson was of Danish heritage, and he felt out of place because he did not look at all like his father, who was small of stature, dark, and of Jewish heritage. Erikson was considered a Gentile at the family synagogue because of his appearance, but classmates regarded him as a Jew. Erikson did not learn until adolescence that in fact he had been adopted, and the man he grew up with was his stepfather not his biological father. Thus, from the beginning, Erikson did not have a clear familial identity nor a religious or cultural one. This presented additional disruption to his adolescence when the period of adolescence already has sufficient challenges in and of itself. Erikson also was unsure as to what he would do regarding a career. He traveled, and he tried out a number of occupations and living experiences. He gave much thought regarding who he was, and where he wanted to be headed—a struggle he called an identity crisis. Ultimately, he changed his last name (he initially was Erik Homburger, *Homburger* being the surname of his adoptive father), which reflected perhaps a final resolution regarding the determination of his identity. Most of his career, then, involved studying and writing about the issues facing adolescents and beyond. He certainly could speak from experience!

2. As teens mature, they necessarily draw away somewhat from their parents and typically form strong, important relationships with peers. The adolescent is becoming mature in many ways and soon will need to function as an adult. He will need to function much more independently from the parents than in the past when he was a child. Thus, peers become a very important reference group and a powerful source of influence. Because acceptance from peers becomes crucial, adolescents are prone to doing whatever they can to fit in with the group. They are likely to conform with group standards whether or not these standards reflect personal or family values. The need is to be accepted by the peer group and thus adhering to group norms helps with this acceptance. Peer relationships are beneficial in that they provide social and emotional ties outside the family as well as additional perspectives. Peer groups may have negative impact, however, if a teen is persuaded to engage in activities that are unhealthful simply out of a desire to conform. Fortunately, adolescents who have close, warm ties with their parents carry that sense of love and acceptance over to their peer relationships. Emotional stability on the part of the teen helps her make a better choice of friends and keeps peer influence from becoming excessive.

MODULE 10.2 EARLY AND MIDDLE ADULTHOOD

LEARNING OBJECTIVES

After you have mastered the information in this unit, you will be able to:

- Discuss the cognitive and physical changes that occur as people age

- Explain how theorists conceptualize social and personality development during early and middle adulthood

- Describe the major variations in adult lifestyles today

OUTLINE

I. Early and Middle Adulthood
    A. Human development is a lifelong process
    B. Early adulthood encompasses age range of twenties and thirties
    C. Middle adulthood encompasses age range of forty to sixty-five
    D. Markers for start of middle adulthood ("middle age") vary widely

II. Cognitive and Physical Development
    A. Both peak in early adulthood
    B. Greatest declines in fluid intelligence; crystallized intelligence is stable or may improve
    C. Physical issues
        1. Decline in muscle mass and strength—can be offset by weight-bearing exercise
        2. Menopause
            a) May have some physiological side effects
            b) Woman's attitude is most important determinant of adjustment
        3. Osteoporosis—loss of bone density

III. Psychosocial Development
    A. Arnett—Five key characteristics of emerging adulthood
        1. Age of identity exploration
        2. Age of instability
        3. Self-focused age
        4. Age of feeling in-between
        5. Age of possibilities
    B. Erikson's stage for early adulthood: intimacy vs. isolation
    C. Ability to establish intimate relationships related to earlier formation of identity
    D. Middle adulthood—loosening of traditional gender roles
    E. Erikson's stage for middle adulthood: generativity vs. stagnation
        1. Generativity—fostering the well-being of next generation
        2. Stagnation—continued self-absorption; inability to move ahead with psychosocial issues and development
    F. Levinson—midlife transition begins around age 40
    G. Midlife crisis
        1. Concern that options in life are disappearing
        2. True crisis more the exception than the rule
        3. Many believe middle adulthood is time of new opportunities, perspectives
        4. May be period of greatest productivity
    H. Empty nest syndrome
        1. Sense of loss of purpose once children leave the home
        2. Not typical for women today, especially those with careers
        3. Many adult children either don't leave home or later return

IV. Lifestyles in Adulthood
    A. Marriage
        1. A universal societal institution
        2. Most people marry, at least once
        3. Sexual activity no longer tied to marriage
        4. Marriage for stability, to create a family unit (raising children), for lasting companionship and intimacy, to have a life partner
        5. Homogamy—like marry like
    B. Singlehood
        1. May be chosen as permanent, not temporary, style of life
        2. Most adults in twenties are not married
        3. May not be married, but may choose to live with another
    C. Divorce
        1. 40 percent of first marriages, 65 percent of second marriages end in divorce
        2. Divorce laws have been liberalized; divorce viewed as more acceptable
        3. Women more economically independent
        4. Associated with emotional and financial difficulties
        5. Children tend to suffer during divorce because of instability and parental trauma, hostility towards each other
V. Exploring Psychology: Cohabitation: Trial Marriage or Marriage Alternative?
    A. In over half of contemporary marriages, couples cohabited first
    B. Some couples prefer cohabitation to marriage for emotional, legal, and/or economic reasons
    C. Other couples view cohabitation as a "trial run" for marriage
    D. Cohabiting couples are more likely to break up than to marry
    E. Divorce rate higher among those who cohabitate first (but this relationship is correlational, not necessarily causal)

SUMMARY

In this module, you learn about changes and issues facing young and middle-age adults. Human development is life long, and there still are many opportunities for growth and productivity across the life span. Physical and cognitive abilities tend to peak in the young adult years. Young adults typically experience their greatest levels of strength, agility, and cardiovascular health. Young adults tend to perform best on IQ-type tests and show the greatest ability for memory, learning new skills, and sensory acuteness. Middle-age adults usually show the beginnings of some memory loss. By the middle adult years, both men and women begin to lose muscle tissue and experience an accompanying loss of muscle strength. More lean tissue turns to fat, although substantial weight gain is not at all necessarily a part of growing older. Women experience a more dramatic physical change, and that is menopause, the cessation of the menstrual cycle and loss of ability to bear children. A healthy diet and regular exercise both help to delay and offset the effects of aging.

There are psychosocial issues that relate to the young and middle adult years of development as well. Erikson believed the most important challenge for the young adult was the establishment of intimate relationships. Erikson believed that the more effective the preceding psychosocial stage (where the formation of a stable identity is paramount), the greater the likelihood for a successful emotional relationship in young adulthood. Isolation is the consequence when a young adult is unable or unwilling to establish an intimate relationship. Other psychosocial researchers emphasize the many developmental tasks facing the young adult such as settling down with an emotional partner, finding one's place in the occupational and social community, and raising children. For the middle-age adult, the psychosocial issue is generativity vs. stagnation. Generativity refers to promoting the well-being of the next generation—bringing children into the world and raising them effectively, and/or helping with the development and environment of children elsewhere. The individual trapped in the outcome of stagnation remains concerned with his or her own issues only.

The traditional notion of the middle adult years was that it signaled the beginning of deterioration and loss. Instead (perhaps very much due to the influence of maturing baby boomers) it is now viewed as a time of new opportunity, new freedom, and a loosening of traditional gender roles. Women may become more assertive; men may feel comfortable getting involved in "gentler" roles, such as gardening and cooking. There are few true midlife crises, and the empty nest resulting from the independence of even the most loved children allows parents the opportunity to engage more in activities of their own choosing. With a healthy lifestyle, adults in their middle years may remain young much longer than in preceding generations. Though most adults marry, they may not stay married, and singlehood and cohabitation are lifestyles that now are acceptable.

KEY TERMS

Fluid intelligence

Crystallized intelligence

Menopause

Emerging adulthood

Midlife crisis

Empty nest syndrome

Homogamy

SELF-TEST PRACTICE QUIZ

From the Key Terms select that which best matches the following:

1. _____ The practice of marrying someone who is like you in terms of culture, appearance, education, socioeconomic status

2. _____ Concerns that tend to occur during the middle adulthood years regarding potential loss of abilities and recognition that life and the future have a finite end point

3. _____ A form of intelligence that tends to remain stable, or even improve, during the middle adulthood years

4. _____ The cessation of the menstrual cycle in a female

5. _____ A sense of depression, loss, and lack of purpose that may occur once one's children have moved away from home

a. Fluid intelligence

b. Crystallized intelligence

c. Menopause

d. Emerging adulthood

e. Midlife crisis

f. Empty nest syndrome

g. Homogamy

6. _____ Mental flexibility, including the ability to retain new information and detect patterns, solve problems quickly

7. _____ The period roughly spanning ages eighteen to twenty-five during which the person makes the transition from adolescence to adulthood

8. Which statement best describes how parents react when their children leave home?
    a. Mothers typically experience an emotional crisis while fathers are unaffected.
    b. Both mothers and fathers typically experience an emotional crisis.
    c. Mothers typically adjust well, but only if their identity revolves around child rearing.
    d. Both mothers and fathers often view this as a time to reconnect with each other.

9. The type of intelligence involving accumulated knowledge and the ability to apply it
    a. deteriorates after peaking in young adulthood.
    b. is known as crystallized, rather than fluid, intelligence.
    c. is not involved in social or occupational functioning.
    d. All of the above are correct.

10. The experience of menopause
    a. results in the cessation of estrogen production.
    b. is mostly related to how a woman thinks about it.
    c. involves the loss of the female sexual drive.
    d. tends to cause lasting emotional and psychological difficulties.

11. According to Erikson, the psychosocial challenge facing individuals in the young adult years is
    a. initiative vs. guilt.
    b. identity vs. role diffusion.
    c. intimacy vs. isolation.
    d. generativity vs. stagnation.

12. Which of the following is NOT a characteristic of emerging adulthood, according to Arnett?
    a. It is a time for individuals to focus on marrying and settling down.
    b. It is a period of instability in people's lives.
    c. It is a time for people to solidify their identities.
    d. It is a time of possibilities rather than certainties.

13. As men age, they
    a. tend to become more openly assertive and competitive.
    b. place greater emphasis on masculinity and masculine activities.
    c. are more likely than women to experience a midlife crisis.
    d. become more comfortable with non-traditional gender roles.

14. Which of the following is NOT correct? Increasing numbers of young adults are remaining single because
    a. singlehood is recognized as an acceptable lifestyle choice.
    b. emotional and sexual companionship is desired, but marriage may be too big a step.
    c. parents of young adults exert less pressure to have grandchildren.
    d. the opportunity for a demanding career may preclude serious intimate relationships.

15. Daniel Levinson (1978, 1996) characterizes the middle adult years as a time when we
    a. evaluate whether or not we have achieved the dreams of our younger adulthood.
    b. face a series of transitions through adult life stages.
    c. are more or less likely to be involved in the well-being of the next generation.
    d. have a series of developmental tasks to master.

ESSAY QUESTIONS

1. Are physical and cognitive losses inevitable as one ages? Discuss and cite examples to support your response.

2. Why is there a high rate of divorce in the United States? How can the impact of divorce be lessened for children whose parents are involved in the process?

ANSWER KEY

1. Homogamy
2. Midlife crisis
3. Crystallized intelligence
4. Menopause
5. Empty nest syndrome
6. Fluid intelligence
7. Emerging adulthood
8. d
9. b
10. b
11. c
12. a
13. d
14. c
15. a

SAMPLE ANSWERS TO ESSAY QUESTIONS

1. Physical and cognitive losses are not inevitable as one ages. The key to maintaining physical and cognitive strengths is adhering to a healthy diet and participating in physical (and mental!) exercise. Physical and cognitive prowess peaks in the young adulthood years after which there is a tendency for these attributes to decline. Muscle tissue tends to diminish, and the body can develop an increasing store of fat tissue. Though cumulative intelligence, such as vocabulary and knowledge gained from experience with the world, may remain at young adult levels or even improve, mental agility overall tends to decline. There is a greater difficulty with tasks involving memory and with the learning of new and unfamiliar skills.

    Physical ability can be maintained and enhanced, however, by engaging in strength-training exercises such as appropriate lifting of weights. Other regular exercise is helpful as well. Since metabolism slows somewhat as an individual grows older, there is a tendency to put on weight, but this need not occur if a proper diet is observed along with sufficient exercise. While menopause in women is unavoidable, how a woman thinks about the experience seems to have the greatest impact as to what extent she is affected. Cognitive activity helps maintain mental agility, and even unavoidable losses in mental quickness may be offset by greater life experience and accumulated knowledge. Also, cognitive changes in the middle adult years do not necessarily intrude on one's ability to function effectively in social and occupational realms.

Ultimately, as research by Sheehy (1995) and others has indicated, middle age is very much a state of mind. Instead of the middle adult years being a time of loss (loss of physical abilities, loss of cognitive dexterity, and loss of children and perhaps purpose in the home), most individuals in the middle adult years see the time as one of great opportunity. Often, the middle adult years are the most productive of one's life.

2.   Divorce occurs at a fairly high rate in the United States because (1) divorce has become more socially acceptable, (2) laws regulating the process of obtaining a divorce have been liberalized, and (3) marriage partners (usually the woman) are no longer completely financially dependent on the other for their livelihood and subsistence. Divorce can improve an acrimonious situation.

Nonetheless, there are consequences to divorce, most especially if the divorce involves children of the divorcing couple. In addition, there are financial repercussions since now two households must be maintained. Usually women suffer the greater loss in financial standing. Children tend to suffer because the parents may be experiencing great sadness or a sense of failure over the broken marriage. The child, of course, is experiencing loss and instability. Parents may not have the full complement of emotional resources to deal effectively with the normal problems and challenges of their children. One or both parents may be preoccupied with increased financial stress. The impact of divorce on children can be lessened if parents, regardless of their feelings for each other, try to keep the focus on what is best for their children. It is important that parents not disparage each other and certainly not within the presence or hearing of the children. Each parent needs to help and encourage the other to maintain a substantial and vital role in the children's lives. It is preferable that the parents talk and agree on major issues relating to the children. A child should not suffer for a decision made by the parent.

MODULE 10.3 LATE ADULTHOOD

LEARNING OBJECTIVES

After you have mastered the information in this unit, you will be able to:

- Describe the physical and cognitive changes that occur in late adulthood

- Discuss Alzheimer's disease

- Explain how theorists characterize the psychosocial challenges of late adulthood

- Describe how our emotions change as we age

- Discuss the qualities associated with successful aging

- Describe the stages of dying identified by Kübler-Ross

OUTLINE

I.   Over 65—the Fastest Growing Segment of the Population
    A.   Life expectancy is continuing to increase
    B.   Again, age is a state of mind, and "old" partly a function of current age
    C.   Many infectious diseases have been controlled; smoking is less prevalent
II.   Physical Development
    A.   General decline in sensory and motor abilities
    B.   General decline in immune system functioning
III.   Cognitive Development
    A.   Performance on tasks requiring fluid intelligence tends to decline
    B.   Older individuals need more time to solve problems, grasp new information

    C.   Increasing difficulty with memory tasks, pattern recognition
        1.   Usually has no significant impact on daily functioning
    D.   Bulk of mental abilities are retained throughout life (dementia is the exception)
    E.   Crystallized intelligence (a store of knowledge gained from experience)
        1.   Often more crucial to functioning than fluid intelligence
        2.   Tends to be maintained or even enhanced into old age
        3.   Helps the individual deal with real problems he or she is likely to encounter
    F.   Alzheimer's disease
        1.   Irreversible brain disease leading to inevitable mental functioning deterioration and death
        2.   Characterized by progressive death of brain cells
        3.   Genetic, neurochemical factors appear to play a role
        4.   No cure, but some symptoms may be slowed by medications
    G.   Gender and ethnic differences
        1.   Women outlive men by about seven years
        2.   Older men more likely to have a spouse, financial stability, good health
        3.   White non-Hispanic Americans tend to live longer than other ethnic groups
        4.   Socioeconomic status related to longevity
            a)   More ethnic minorities live below poverty line
            b)   Lower socioeconomic status associated with less healthy lifestyles
IV. Psychosocial Development
    A.   Psychosocial theories of late adulthood
        1.   Erikson's stage for older adulthood: ego integrity versus despair
            a)   Important issue is maintaining a sense of meaning
            b)   Possible to remain satisfied and fulfilled throughout life
        2.   Views of Daniel Levinson and Robert Havighurst
            a)   Recognized need is to accept physical and psychological realities
            b)   Havighurst listed older adult's developmental tasks—adjusting to loss of loved ones, to physical changes and to retirement
            c)   Levinson emphasizes older adult can rediscover self, meaningful activities that maintain connections with others
    B.   Aging and sexuality
        1.   Ageism—prejudice against older individuals
        2.   Sexual activity normal and healthy for older adults
        3.   Older adults report high level of sexual satisfaction
    C.   Depression in late adulthood
        1.   The most common emotional problem faced by older adults (as many as 15 percent of older population)
        2.   Concern with physical problems may overshadow awareness of depression
        3.   Suicide rate higher among older adults, especially white males
        4.   Reasons for depression
            a)   Loss of longtime friends and loved ones
            b)   Move to nursing home or assisted living
            c)   Loss of meaning, purpose, sense of worth due to retirement
            d)   Health problems and care of self, aging spouse
    D.   Successful aging
        1.   Most people in their seventies are satisfied with their lives
        2.   Income level, social contact are important factors
        3.   Happiness may increase with age along with greater control over important life factors (work, finances, marriage)
        4.   Keys to successful aging

a) Be selective in use of time, choose activities that maximize one's abilities
b) Support and maintain an optimistic outlook; assume success is likely and all challenges can be met
c) Remain involved in activities, or better yet, begin new ones that are appropriate (do more of the things that matter)

V. Death and Dying
   A. Death in fact can occur at any age
   B. Though young, we may be severely affected by death of others (e.g., loved ones)
   C. Kübler-Ross's stages of dying
      1. Denial—refuse to believe
      2. Anger—resentment towards others not in same predicament
      3. Bargaining—attempting to make a deal with God
      4. Depression—hopelessness in face of reality of situation
      5. Final acceptance—end result is inevitable, retain dignity and peace
   D. Bereavement—intense feeling of grief and loss following death of a loved one
   E. Mourning—culturally established ways of dealing with death and loss
   F. Patterns of grief similar to Kübler-Ross's stages of dying

SUMMARY

In this module you learn of the many changes and challenges facing the older adult. Aging adults usually are aware of their decreasing ability with regard to their physical and cognitive attributes. These physical and cognitive challenges mean psychological issues come to the fore as well. The older adult must find a way to accept the physical and cognitive changes while maintaining an optimistic outlook and continuing to find meaning in life. As individuals get older, too, they tend to experience the death and loss of loved ones. The loss of close friends and family members not only reminds the aging adult of his or her advancing years, but also removes sources of social and emotional support that would help the older adult cope with the many life changes that have to be faced. Because of these many challenges, plus the recognition that life has a finite end point, there is a fairly high incidence of depression among older adults. Suicide rates are higher in older adulthood especially among white males.

One may be getting older, but now there are lots more people one can get older with! The over-65 population is the fastest growing segment in the United States. Females tend to outlive males, but older males tend to have better health and a greater likelihood of emotional and financial stability. Individuals of higher socioeconomic status tend to live longer as do white, non-Hispanic Americans.

The older adult faces very many physical and cognitive changes, including increasing loss of muscle tissue, sensory capabilities, and cognitive agility. Still, older people often can function well as far as managing their own daily lives. Many tasks still can be accomplished, especially if the older adult has a bit more time to grasp the situation, to process information, or to react. Most of the challenges faced by the older individual involve crystallized intelligence, dealing with matters with which the individual is already familiar and experienced. As mentioned previously, accumulated knowledge and expertise may actually improve intellectual functioning in these areas as an individual grows older. Contrary to some stereotypes, healthy older adults maintain their sexuality and are capable of satisfying sexual experiences.

Some memory difficulty and loss are expected in older adults, but normally basic mental functioning remains intact throughout life. The exception is the development of dementia (also known as senility), which occurs among some members of the older population. Dementia involves substantial loss in mental capability and may be caused by alcoholism, brain injuries, stroke, or disease. The leading cause in the United States, however, is Alzheimer's disease. This disease is characterized by increasing loss in the most basic mental processes, and personality changes may be evident as well. Physically,

Alzheimer's causes progressive death of neurons in the brain. There is no cure but steps can be taken to slow the course of the disease.

Psychosocial researchers agree that the issue for individuals in late adulthood is managing the physical and cognitive limitations while continuing to find meaning and purpose in life. Erikson characterized the challenge as one of ego integrity vs. despair. Despite the many challenges faced by the older adult, most individuals in their seventies report being satisfied with their lives. The experience of happiness may even increase, and one may gain greater control over financial, work, or relationship aspects of one's life. Successful aging involves maintaining a positive outlook, making the most of opportunities where one can compensate for possible deficiencies, and seeking challenges where one can continue to be fulfilled and grow. However, it is probably best if death is recognized as inevitable. Elisabeth Kübler-Ross (1969) delineated five stages that individuals facing death are likely to go through, beginning with denial and ending with a final resignation and acceptance.

KEY TERMS

Dementia

Alzheimer's disease

Ageism

Bereavement

Mourning

SELF-TEST PRACTICE QUIZ

From the Key Terms select that which best matches the following (Note: Not every Key Term will be used.):

1. _____ The practice of treating older individuals with prejudice or disregard because of their age

2. _____ The culturally established manner for dealing with grief and loss

3. _____ The experience of grief and great loss due to the death of a close friend or family member

4. _____ A brain disorder where there are substantial losses in mental functioning due to injury or disease; may be accompanied by personality changes

a. Dementia

b. Alzheimer's Disease

c. Ageism

d. Bereavement

e. Mourning

5. A factor involved in how an individual defines "old age" is
   a. the number of living older relatives the individual has.
   b. the extent of exposure the individual has had to gerontology.
   c. the age of the individual at the time he or she is asked for the definition.
   d. unrelated to the amount of experience an individual has had with aging issues.

6. The most important determinant of how an individual copes with growing older is
   a. financial status.
   b. physical health.
   c. level of education.
   d. social and emotional sources of support.

7. One area of cognitive functioning that remains stable or even improves in older adult years is
   a. working memory.
   b. pattern recognition.
   c. knowledge related to our career or specialization.
   d. quickness of response.

8. Among individuals studied who were age 55 and older, _____ reported that memory difficulties created major problems in their lives.
   a. 3 percent
   b. 10 percent
   c. 15 percent
   d. 21 percent

9. Which of the following people is likely to live the longest?
   a. a Black woman
   b. an Asian man
   c. an African American man
   d. a White, non-Hispanic woman

10. Which statement about Alzheimer's disease is NOT true?
    a. It can be cured by brain surgery.
    b. Both genetic and neurochemical factors appear to play a role in causing it.
    c. It is one of the leading causes of death among older American adults.
    d. Medications may help slow the memory declines associated with Alzheimer's.

11. The psychosocial challenge for individuals in late adulthood, according to Erikson, is
    a. industry vs. inferiority.
    b. intimacy vs. isolation.
    c. ego integrity vs. despair.
    d. ego identity vs. role diffusion.

12. The psychosocial focus for older adults, according to Levinson, involves
    a. rediscovering oneself and continuing with meaningful activities and emotional contacts.
    b. becoming involved in activities that increase the well-being of future generations.
    c. accomplishing tasks of aging such as managing retirement and adjusting to physical changes.
    d. recognizing that death is inevitable, and planning accordingly.

13. Which of the following is NOT a factor that has been found to be associated with more successful aging?
    a. Income level
    b. Extent of contact with friends and family members
    c. Longevity of one or both parents
    d. Becoming involved with new goals or projects

14. In the stages of dying, as proposed by Elisabeth Kübler-Ross, the experience that immediately precedes the stage of final acceptance is
    a. bargaining.
    b. depression.
    c. anger.
    d. denial.

ESSAY QUESTIONS

1. What, based on the research we have so far, are some ways an older adult can maintain and preserve cognitive functioning?

2. Why might older adults be more prone to depression? What are some suggestions for successful aging that will help protect against and diminish the experience of depression?

ANSWER KEY

1. Ageism

2. Mourning

3. Bereavement

4. Dementia

5. c

6. b

7. c

8. a

9. d

10. a

11. c

12. a

13. c

14. b

SAMPLE ANSWERS TO ESSAY QUESTIONS

1. Some loss of cognitive functioning as we age cannot be avoided. Skills related to fluid intelligence are the ones most likely to be affected by aging. Older adults can take steps to help maintain and preserve cognitive functioning, however. For tasks involving fluid intelligence, it is not that older adults cannot do these tasks; rather, they simply need a bit more time—to be exposed to information (it may take an extra repetition or two), to grasp and process information, and to carry out their response. Thus, older adults can expect satisfactory cognitive functioning if they try to stick to matters that involve crystallized intelligence and seek opportunities where they will be provided with extra time if they need to call upon fluid intelligence skills in order to successfully complete a task.

 Higher levels of cognitive functioning in later years have been associated with general physical health, involvement in stimulating activities, and openness to new experiences. General physical health is somewhat in response to what we do with our lives, and the latter two factors are completely under our control. General physical health, as has been mentioned previously, is related to diet, exercise, and lifestyle choices. Older adults can help keep the mind active by staying involved with mentally stimulating activities. This course of action is much more promising than choosing to withdraw from social contacts and live in relative isolation. Housing communities for senior citizens are springing up around academic institutions; often older adults can take college courses for free or at a greatly reduced price. An older adult need not be afraid to consider taking on new challenges and experiences, regardless of how advanced in age the individual may be. Social exchange and support, new learnings, and new experiences help keep even the aging mind sharp.

2. Older adults are more prone to depression because (1) their abilities are deteriorating in comparison to when they were young; (2) the possibility of death is a reality and they realize their life has an end point; (3) there is a concern that life now has less meaning, in that these adults are

no longer raising children, have retired, and do not have an unlimited future before them; (4) long-time friends and loved ones die, reminding the older individual that she too will die, and not only bringing feelings of grief and loss, but removing people who could help the individual with those painful feelings. Problems with physical health can bring on depression, and if the elderly person is isolated from others or has financial difficulties, these factors too are associated with the incidence of depression.

Evidence shows (Margoshes, 1995) that we can be happy even in our most advanced years, and in fact happiness can increase over time. By late adulthood, many major features of an individual's life should be settled (work, relationships, finances), and thus not be a source of upset or concern. Cumulative life experience may help an individual live not just longer, but better. Tips for successful aging include: (1) making the best use of one's time—with physical and cognitive changes, we can choose activities that make best use of our talents and that provide the opportunity (for example, where time for completion would not a be a criterion) for us to compensate for any decrements we have experienced; (2) adopting and maintaining an attitude of optimism—for older adults, like everyone else, attitude is everything; believing that one can succeed and can meet the demands of any reasonable challenge goes a long ways towards making that view manifest in reality; and (3) continuing to take on reasonable challenges—establish new goals, make the most of new opportunities that are presented, and continue to form and to nurture social contacts. Erikson worked happily and productively until his death in his early nineties. Levinson suggests that older adulthood (as at any other times in our lives) is an opportunity to rediscover who we are. Always, we need to find ways to make life meaningful, stay mentally and physically involved with life, and do those things that matter most to us.

MODULE 10.4 APPLICATION: LIVING LONGER, HEALTHIER LIVES

LEARNING OBJECTIVE

After you have mastered the information in this unit, you will be able to:

*   Summarize some of the ways people can live longer and healthier lives

OUTLINE

I.   Living Longer
    A.   Genetic heritage one factor in longer life
    B.   Another factor is under our control—lifestyle choices, habits and behaviors
II. Steps We Can Take to Increase the Likelihood of a Longer and Healthier Life
    A.   Developing healthy exercise and nutrition habits
        1.   Physical exercise slows effects of aging, reduces risk for some diseases, aids in mental acuity
        2.   A nutritious, balanced diet helps reduce risk of disease
    B.   Staying involved
        1.   Keeps mind sharp
        2.   Reduces risk of depression
        3.   Associated with longevity
    C.   Lend a hand—giving support to others is associated with longer life
    D.   Think positively about aging
    E.   Avoiding harmful substances—tobacco, illicit drugs, excessive alcohol all related to health problems
    F.   Maintaining a healthy weight
        1.   Obesity is a major health risk
        2.   Adjust diet and exercise to compensate for slight slowing of metabolism rate

  G. Managing stress—stress impairs physical and psychological well-being

  H. Exercising the mind—intellectually stimulating activities help preserve cognitive functioning

III. Do Healthy Habits Pay Off?

  A. People who adopt healthier life habits (as listed above) are more likely to live longer, healthier lives

  B. One experimental study (Diabetes Prevention Program Research Group, 2002) provided evidence that individuals randomly assigned to a weight loss and exercise program have less incidence of Type 2 diabetes, in comparison to a control group without this intervention

SUMMARY

In this module, you learn of diet and exercise habits that, at any age, can help promote health and longevity. Things we can do to help extend the quantity and the quality of our years include being involved in regular exercise and eating healthy foods, such as those that are low fat. A diet that includes many whole grains, fruits, and vegetables also has been shown to reduce the risk for some diseases. Exercise and sufficient calcium in our diet help reduce the risk of osteoporosis. It is important to stay mentally and physically involved with life, which helps us maintain our cognitive abilities, helps guard against depression, and helps us continue to find meaning in what we do. As is true at any time in our lives, tobacco, illicit drugs, and excessive consumption of alcohol are all associated with a greater risk for health problems.

Though metabolism tends to slow somewhat as individuals get older, that does not mean that weight gain is unavoidable, and certainly excessive weight gain is not healthy for individuals of any age. A healthy diet will help us manage our weight and keep it within reasonable limits. Also, exercise, which has other benefits as mentioned above, helps in keeping our weight at an appropriate level.

Excessive amounts of stress, of course, are not healthy for us at any age, and this remains true for older adults as well. Stress reduces the functioning of our immune system and makes us less resistant to many kinds of diseases. Again, a healthy lifestyle, including exercise, can help us reduce stress and reduce the impact of stress.

There is no guarantee that following these suggestions will lead to a longer life, and perhaps we do not really want to live forever. However, people who have adopted these habits and maintain them, live not only longer, but healthier (and probably happier) lives.

KEY TERMS

Osteoporosis

CHAPTER 10 APPLICATION EXERCISE

Do you know an older individual? Think of an elderly family member or an older person as portrayed in a television program or a movie.

How is that person characterized? If it is a real person, what are his or her personality characteristics? How do others react to the elderly person? What do others seem to think of this older individual?

How does this older person live in terms of exercise, healthy habits, and mental outlook? Do you see a relationship between lifestyle choices and functioning as an older adult?

Lastly, list what you think are keys to healthy, and happy, living at any age.

CHAPTER 11

Gender and Sexuality

In Chapter 11 you learn about factors that are basic to our survival as a species and also play an important physical, emotional, and social role in our everyday lives. These factors are our sexual (and gender) identity and our sexual behaviors. Though nearly always consistent (that is, someone with a sexual identity as determined by genetics is comfortable with the gender roles associated with that sex), sexual identity and gender identity are two different things. Humans are born with two different chromosomal patterns that result in one's biological sex. The chromosomal pattern of XX means we have a biologically female individual; the chromosomal pattern of XY means we have a biologically male individual. There are behaviors, of course, that go along with being "female" or being "male." How comfortable are we with the traditional characteristics of behavior that go along with one sex or another? The adoption of a set of behavioral characteristics typical of one sex or the other is one's gender identity. Thus, when one is born male and is comfortable with the typical "male" attributes and behaviors, sexual identity and gender identity are the same. In the rare case where biological sex is not compatible with gender identity, we have what is called transsexualism.

It is not clear where our understanding and our manifestation of gender-based behavior comes from. The evolutionary perspective suggests that typical male behaviors (such as aggressiveness) and typical female behaviors (such as nurturance and empathy) are genetically based, biologically adaptive, and the "natural way." These behaviors are necessary for the survival of the species. Other theories suggest that gender behaviors are learned through modeling and reinforcement or are cognitively arrived at via the development of schemas (mental representations of what it means to be a boy or a girl), which are then played out in overt actions. Probably gender behaviors are derived from all three of these sources with an interacting influence that is next to impossible to fully differentiate. Anthropological studies do reveal that there are many cross-cultural variations in what are deemed to be appropriate behaviors for males and females. Within our own society, androgyny (comfort with exhibiting both traditionally male and traditionally female characteristics) is becoming widespread, and what were thought to be biologically based differences in cognitive abilities (mathematical superiority for males, verbal superiority for females) are narrowing to the point of nonexistence.

Because humans are sexual beings, in most cases we become involved in sexual behavior. This is not true for every one, and the form and frequency of sexual behavior varies widely. The biological experience of sexual arousal and resolution is fairly consistent. The sex research team of Masters and Johnson divided the human sexual response cycle into four phases: the excitement phase, the plateau phase, the orgasmic phase, and the resolution phase. Though male and female sexual organs are quite different, there are some underlying similarities in sexual response. Sexual orientation has to do with the type of recipient we prefer to meet our sexual desires. Individuals who are heterosexual are sexually attracted to members of the opposite sex; homosexual individuals are attracted to members of the same sex. Bisexuals are aroused by, and attracted to, both sexes. Individuals may experience different kinds of sexual attraction, of course, but not act upon these desires. Alfred Kinsey suggested that homosexuality and heterosexuality are not mutually exclusive; that is, just because one is predominantly heterosexual does not mean that a person might not have an occasional homosexual interest, and vice versa. As with gender-based differences, we cannot confirm where sexual orientation comes from. Research has indicated that causes include genetic, hormonal, and socio-environmental factors, again most likely in combination and over the life span.

Sexual behavior and experiences may not always go smoothly. When a sexual difficulty occurs over a prolonged period of time, it becomes classified as a sexual dysfunction. Fortunately, many effective biological and psychological treatments exist for sexual disorders. Aberrant sexual behavior may include offenses that are legally punishable since they cause harm to victims. With regard to sexual behavior, we need to know how to protect ourselves from sexually transmitted diseases (STDs) and from sexual coercion, which includes rape and sexual harassment.

MODULE 11.1 GENDER IDENTITY AND GENDER ROLES

LEARNING OBJECTIVES

When you have mastered the information in this unit, you will be able to:

- Discuss the development of gender identity

- Describe the major theories of gender-role behavior

- Discuss gender differences in cognitive abilities, personality, and leadership styles

OUTLINE

I.   Gender Identity: Our Sense of Maleness or Femaleness
    A.   Chromosomal patterns
        1.   Chromosomes (XX, XY) determine biological sex
        2.   Gender is a psychosocial concept
        3.   Gender roles—acceptable behaviors for males and females
        4.   Gender identity
            a)   Psychological experience of being male or female
            b)   Individuals born with ambiguous genitalia tend to adopt identity of gender by which they were raised
            c)   Usually gender identity consistent with biological sex
    B.   Transsexualism
        1.   Feel trapped in body of wrong gender
        2.   Genitalia seen as a mistake by nature
        3.   Surgery for gender reassignment changes appearance but does not make opposite-gender reproduction capabilities possible
II.   Gender Roles and Stereotypes: How Society Defines Masculinity and Femininity
    A.   Gender roles determined by culture
    B.   Gender-role stereotypes—fixed, conventional views regarding gender-appropriate behavior
    C.   Gender roles can change
    D.   Social-cognitive theory
        1.   Emphasizes role of observational learning and reinforcement
        2.   Parents are important modeling influences
        3.   Parents may treat male and female children differently
        4.   Parents (and others) praise desired behavior, discourage or punish undesired
        5.   Toys may mirror gender expectations
        6.   Media tends to portray, promote traditional gender behavior
    E.   Gender-schema theory
        1.   Emphasizes the importance of cognitive factors
        2.   Children form mental representations (schemas) of masculinity and femininity
        3.   Children then act in ways that are in accord with their schemas (i.e., how a boy or girl should behave)
        4.   Children judge themselves according to how well they measure up to their schemas

    F.   Evolutionary theory
- 1. View is that genetic predispositions shape behavior
- 2. Male aggressiveness is an adaptive trait (protection, hunting)
- 3. Nurturance and empathy in females support birth and growth of offspring
- 4. View is that gender roles reflect natural order of things
- 5. Men engage in more physical aggression; women engage in more relational aggression
- 6. Testosterone is linked to level of aggression

    G.   Sociocultural theory
- 1. Does not rule out that culture shapes behavior from earliest days (e.g., research by Margaret Mead)
- 2. Most likely gender identity an interaction of both biological and social-environmental sources

    H.   Masculinity and femininity: opposite poles or different dimensions?
- 1. Traditionally perceived as opposite poles
- 2. "Masculine" and "feminine" behaviors need not be mutually exclusive
- 3. Androgyny—comfortable with, and show evidence of, both "male" and "female" behaviors
- 4. Men and women both prefer androgynous partners

III.   Gender Differences: How Different Are We?
    A.   Gender differences in cognitive abilities
- 1. Far more similarities than differences
- 2. No differences in general intelligence, ability to learn, or problem-solving ability
- 3. Female cognitive characteristics
  - a) Some superiority in verbal skills (reading, writing, spelling)
  - b) Less evidence of reading difficulties, dyslexia
  - c) Better ability for remembering where things located
- 4. Male cognitive characteristics
  - a) Better performance in math skills
  - b) Greater ability in some visual-spatial skills such as map reading
- 5. More variation within genders than between genders
- 6. Gender differences may be related to brain specialization
- 7. Psychosocial factors may shape cognitive abilities
- 8. Overall, gender gap shrinking

    B.   Gender differences in personality and leadership style
- 1. Consistent differences in personality traits
  - a) Males—more aggressive, higher levels of self-esteem
  - b) Females—more extraverted, trusting, nurturing, emotionally expressive
- 2. Stereotype that men make better leaders not borne out by research; women at least as good with regard to managerial and leadership ability
- 3. Difference in male and female leadership styles
  - a) Females—democratic, more likely to seek opinions of subordinates
  - b) Males—more autocratic, lead by command rather than consensus
- 4. Unresolved as to source of difference between leadership styles

SUMMARY

In this module, you learn about how we define "male" and "female" and that chromosomal sexual characteristics and gender identity are not always the same thing. One's sex is biologically determined. The XX chromosome pair from our genetic heritage results in a female organism; if the organism receives an XY chromosome pair, the result then is a male. Usually, though not always, external genitalia reflect that chromosomal arrangement. In cases where genitalia are unclear, there is evidence both that the individual will develop an identity consistent with the chromosome pattern, and that the individual will develop an identity consistent with how he or she was raised, regardless of underlying chromosomal pattern.

Gender identity is a psychological, not a biological, concept. Usually, one's gender identity is consistent with that of the biological heritage. Gender identity consists of whether one regards oneself as male or female. Transsexuals have the sexual organs of one gender, but they feel the identity of the other. The conflict between sexual identity and gender identity may be so great that the individual seeks surgery to create sexual organs more consistent with the psychological orientation.

How do we come to adopt and identify with gender roles? Gender roles are the behaviors seen as appropriate for either a male or a female. Happily, gender roles are blurring with time, and andryogynous behavior (manifesting and being comfortable with both traditional "male" and traditional "female" behaviors) is now usually accepted and often preferred. In other words, it is all right if females want to be assertive, choose careers that have been traditionally in the male realm, work outside the home, and share childcare responsibilities with others. Similarly, males do not always have to be aggressive, stoic, and take responsibility for the entire "breadwinner" role. They can and do share in child raising responsibilities and find the nurturance of and influence on their young children extremely rewarding. Males can feel comfortable sharing in the responsibilities for maintaining the home (including cleaning, laundry, and what is often a male favorite—cooking).

Still, there are differences between the ways males and females behave, and we have not totally answered the question as to why this is so. Some explanations (the social-cognitive theory) point to the modeling of male/female behaviors on the part of parents and that parents reinforce, perhaps even inadvertently, what they expect as far as appropriate behavior from their sons and daughters, respectively. Most children's toys and programs in the media continue to enforce and promote the more traditionally masculine and feminine roles. The gender-schema theory proposes a cognitive explanation for gender-role behavior in that boys and girls develop a representation (a schema) in their heads as to what it means to be a male or a female. The schema, it is suggested, develops from experience with the world especially with toys, clothing, and what are seen as gender-specific social roles and behaviors. Children acquire these schemas at a relatively young age (perhaps as young as 3 years), and then exhibit the behaviors that are in accord with their schema. A third explanation for gender-role behavior is derived from evolutionary theory. This theory recognizes the genetic heritage we all have, and that traditionally male and traditionally female behaviors have had long-term adaptive value. The male trait of aggressiveness is useful, for example, in providing protection and obtaining food. The female characteristic of nurturance helps ensure that offspring conceived by the female will be born, survive, be cared for, and reach adulthood. The evolutionary theory still cannot be entirely supported because children from birth are exposed to family and cultural influences, and this influence cannot be discounted. Research by the anthropologist Margaret Mead (1935) reported that there are cultures where females are the hunters and food gatherers, and the males stay home and raise children. With such evidence, we cannot conclude that traditional male behaviors appear strictly because of a genetic inheritance.

Though male and female cognitive abilities are much more alike than different, males continue to show a superiority for mathematical tasks and for visual-spatial skills. Females, on the other hand, continue to show greater aptitude for the verbal category skills—memory, reading, writing, spelling. Again, we are not sure why this difference exists, and the possibility is that it is due to socialization.

The reason why such differences may be due to cultural and social influences is that the gap between these gender variations is growing smaller. We continue to find differences in personality between males and females and in how males and females perform leadership roles. Males do tend to be more aggressive and to show higher levels of self-esteem. Females tend to be more extraverted, trusting, nurturing, and emotionally expressive. Women, contrary to prior beliefs, are just as capable as men in managerial and leadership roles. However, how they carry out these roles again is a function of gender difference. A woman tends to lead by consensus—consulting the subordinates with whom she works and gaining their input before arriving at a decision and course of action. In contrast, males still tend to lead more autocratically, arriving at their own view and then imposing it on others.

Though gender differences are becoming less polarized, they still exist. Are they due to nature? Are these differences due to nurture? Do we arrive at our gender identity due to a combination and interaction of both? The latter is probably most likely, although we may not ever answer the question with complete certainty.

KEY TERMS

Gender

Gender roles

Gender identity

Transsexualism

Gender-schema theory

Androgynous

Dyslexia

SELF-TEST PRACTICE QUIZ

From the Key Terms select that which best matches the following:

1. _____ A cognitive explanation for gender roles based on the notion that children form schemas as a result of their experience with the world and align their behavior to conform to these schemas

2. _____ Behavior considered appropriate for males and females, respectively, as determined by cultural standards

3. _____ An individual who is comfortable exhibiting traditional "female" and traditional "male" behaviors, regardless of his or her own gender identity

4. _____ The psychological state of being a male or being a female

5. _____ A state where an individual has the chromosomal pattern typical of one biological sex but whose gender identity is that of the other sex

6. _____ A learning disability where difficulties are with the ability to read

a. Gender

b. Gender roles

c. Gender identity

d. Transsexualism

e. Gender-schema theory

f. Androgynous

g. Dyslexia

7. _____ The psychological awareness of whether one is more comfortable with typical female characteristics or typical male characteristics

8. If you have the chromosome pair of XY, this determines your

   a. sexual identity.
   b. gender identity.
   c. sexual orientation.
   d. gender orientation.

9. When an individual's gender identity is different from that person's biological sex, that person is a

   a. homosexual.
   b. transsexual.
   c. transvestite.
   d. pedophile.

10. Having the rather inflexible view that males must be invincible without emotions such as compassion or grief and must be a dominant force in all situations is known as

    a. gender identity.
    b. transsexualism.
    c. pervasive stoicism.
    d. gender-role stereotyping.

11. The view that we learn how to behave as males or females because praise or other reinforcers from our environment shaped this behavior is a component of

    a. social-cognitive theory.
    b. gender-schema theory.
    c. evolutionary theory.
    d. psychosocial theory.

12. The fact that aggressiveness in males helps them protect their home and family, and nurturance in females helps ensure the procreation and survival of offspring is evidence for the _____ theory regarding gender identity and behavior.

    a. social-cognitive
    b. gender-schema
    c. evolutionary
    d. psychosocial

13. When boys and girls learn how to behave (as a function of gender) by watching and imitating the behavior of males and females to whom they are exposed, this supports the _____ explanation for gender role behavior.

    a. social-cognitive
    b. gender-schema
    c. evolutionary
    d. psychosocial

14. Extensive research supports the notion that males are always more physically aggressive than females. Jails are populated predominantly with males, males are much more likely to respond aggressively to social provocations, and even a children's playground reveals that boys are more aggressive than girls and tend to be more competitive. We should hesitate to conclude, however, that males are more aggressive overall, because

    a. gender role behavior has been changing rapidly.
    b. females also engage in aggression, but it is less obvious (e.g., relational aggression).
    c. little substantive research has been conducted on female aggression.
    d. females also produce testosterone, and testosterone is linked to aggression.

15. Regarding typically masculine and typically feminine behaviors,

    a. the more traditionally male-type behaviors one exhibits, the fewer traditionally female behaviors one exhibits.
    b. the more traditionally female-type behaviors one exhibits, the fewer traditionally male behaviors one exhibits.
    c. individuals who are androgynous show impaired levels of psychological functioning.
    d. both sexes prefer partners who are expressive (a feminine trait) and instrumental (a masculine trait).

16. Which of the following abilities tends to be better in males than in females?

    a. mentally rotating three-dimensional figures
    b. remembering where objects are located
    c. reading
    d. general intelligence

17. Women's ability in leadership and managerial roles is _____ men's ability in leadership and managerial roles.

    a. inferior to
    b. the same as
    c. superior to
    d. a duplication of

ESSAY QUESTION

1. What evidence do we have that gender differences are biologically (genetically) based? What evidence do we have that gender differences are due to sociocultural influences?

ANSWER KEY

1. Gender-schema theory

2. Gender roles

3. Androgynous

4. Gender

5. Transsexualism

6. Dyslexia

7. Gender identity

8. a

9. a

10. d

11. a

12. c

13. a

14. b

15. d

16. d

17. b

SAMPLE ANSWER TO ESSAY QUESTION

1. To date, we have been unable to truly distinguish what in gender behavior is dictated by genetic inheritance and what is the result of social or cultural environmental experience. Perhaps the ultimate answer is that both are influential and the impact is due to an interaction between these two factors. Biological evidence includes the prevalence for physical aggression among males and the relationship of testosterone to levels of aggression. Sociocultural evidence includes Margaret Mead's research where traditional gender roles were reversed. Additional sociocultural evidence is that the previous gap between men and women with regard to math and science skills is rapidly diminishing. Still, some gender differences (such as in personality characteristics) do remain. That gender roles are changing, and males and females today both prefer partners with a blend of traditional traits, suggests much gender difference is due to psychosocial factors.

MODULE 11.2 SEXUAL RESPONSE AND BEHAVIOR

LEARNING OBJECTIVES

After you have mastered the information in this unit, you will be able to:

*   Identify the phases of the sexual response cycle

*   Discuss the origins of sexual orientation

*   Describe how attitudes toward homosexuality vary across cultures

*   Define paraphilias

*   Discuss the various sexually transmitted diseases and how we can protect ourselves from them

OUTLINE

I.   Sexual Behavior
    A.   Sexuality is necessary to ensure reproduction of the species
    B.   Motives are gratification, procreation, intimacy
    C.   Rules for sexual behavior vary (e.g., among cultures)
    D.   Forms and frequency of sexual behavior vary
II. Cultural and Gender Differences
    A.   Some cultures are more permissive than others with regard to different sexual behaviors
    B.   Men tend to want more partners than women—may be an evolutionary basis for this
    C.   Men generally exhibit more sexual desire than women
    D.   Women place more emphasis than men on commitment as a context for sex
    E.   Men more likely than women to link aggression with sexuality
III. The Sexual Response Cycle
    A.   Phases of the sexual response cycle
        1.   Much of our knowledge from research by William Masters and Virginia Johnson
        2.   Sexual response cycle is a characteristic pattern of changes for both males and females
    B.   Excitement phase
        1.   Vasocongestion—pooling of blood in bodily tissues
            a)   Penis becomes erect
            b)   Vagina swells, produces lubrication
            c)   Testes expand
            d)   Muscle tension, heart rate increase
        2.   Clitoris
            a)   Female sexual organ composed of tissue like penis

b)   Only organ (in either gender) whose function is exclusively pleasure
c)   Sensory input that triggers orgasm is mostly from clitoris
C. Plateau phase
   1. Precedes orgasm
   2. Increasing vasocongestion in both sexes
   3. Further changes in sex organs
   4. Myotonia (muscle tension) continues to increase
   5. Heart rate, breathing, blood pressure increase further
D. Orgasmic phase
   1. Orgasm is a reflex
   2. Involves rhythmic contractions of the pelvic muscles
   3. Blood pressure, heart rate reach peaks
   4. Sexual tension released, feelings of intense pleasure
   5. Two stages of muscular contractions for male
E. Resolution phase
   1. Body returns to prearoused state
   2. Sexual tissues in men and women return to normal size
   3. Heart rate, muscle tension, breathing become normal within a few minutes
   4. One difference between genders
      a)   Males—refractory period; another ejaculation not possible at least for a few minutes
      b)   Females—no refractory period; continued stimulation may produce further orgasms

IV. Sexual Orientation
A. Factors relating to sexual orientation
   1. Definition: the direction of one's erotic attraction and romantic interests
   2. Types of attraction
      a)   Heterosexual—attraction to opposite sex
      b)   Homosexual—attraction to members of same sex
      c)   Bisexual—attraction to both sexes
   3. Research by Alfred Kinsey
      a)   Homosexuality and heterosexuality may not be mutually exclusive
      b)   Proposed notion that sexual orientation is a continuum between these two end points
   4. Current research on sexual orientation in the United States and Europe
      a)   Orientation may not be as fixed or as varied as most people think
      b)   A few percent of men and women exclusively homosexual
      c)   More (perhaps one-fifth) report some same-sex sexual contact
      d)   A few percent of U.S. and European population bisexual
B. Origins of sexual orientation
   1. Sigmund Freud
      a)   Heterosexuality results from normal identification with same-sex parent
      b)   Homosexuality results from over-identification with opposite-sex parent
      c)   Too much variation in families of homosexual individuals to support one explanation
      d)   Is evidence of more cross-gender behavior among homosexuals in childhood
   2. Perspective of Darryl Bem—what was exotic becomes erotic
   3. Genetic influence
      a)   Monozygotic (identical) twins more similar in sexual orientation than dizygotic (fraternal) twins, even when identical twins raised in different environments
      b)   Genetic similarity not always a predictor; must be other influences

4. Hormonal influences
   a) Rats given sex hormones during prenatal period show changes in their behaviors (e.g., females given testosterone attempt to mount females)
   b) No clear evidence yet regarding humans
5. Conclusions
   a) Results currently inconclusive
   b) Likely that sexual orientation results from combination of factors (genetic, hormonal, and environmental)

V. Atypical Sexual Variations—Paraphilia (sexual attraction that is out of mainstream)
   A. Fetishism—attracted to objects (e.g., women's shoes)
   B. Transvestism—wearing clothing of opposite sex
   C. Voyeurism—watching unsuspecting individuals disrobe or engage in sexual activities
   D. Exhibitionism—quick display of genitals
   E. Pedophilia—sexual attraction to children
   F. Sexual masochism—desire pain along with sexual experience
   G. Paraphilias may develop to compensate for sexual fears, inadequacies
   H. Occur almost always exclusively among males

VI. Exploring Psychology: AIDS and other STDs: Is Your Behavior Putting You at Risk?
   A. AIDS
      1. One of history's worst epidemics
      2. Most transmission is from heterosexual sex
      3. Greatest impact in sub-Saharan Africa
   B. STDs—sexually transmitted diseases
      1. Viral STDs
         a) HIV/AIDS—disables immune system
         b) HSV-2—genital herpes virus
         c) HPV—human papillomaviruses
      2. Bacterial STDs
         a) Chlamydia—most common bacterial STD
         b) Gonorrhea—can lead to infertility
         c) Syphilis—damages heart and brain if untreated
   C. Treatment of STDs
      1. Antibiotics can cure bacterial STDs
      2. Antiviral drugs control but do not cure viral STDs
      3. Early treatment is crucial
   D. Prevention of STDs
      1. Complete prevention not possible unless practice abstinence or maintain monogamous relationship with an uninfected monogamous partner
      2. Tips for safer sex
         a) Be careful in choosing sexual partner (know background)
         b) Avoid multiple partners; be assertive about STD prevention
         c) Talk to your partner about your concerns
         d) Avoid relations with anyone with genital sore, blister
         e) Avoid unprotected sexual contact
         f) Get regular medical checkups and medical attention if exposed
         g) When in doubt, don't

SUMMARY

In this module, you learn about sexual behavior, sexual orientations, and risks accompanying sexual activity. Sexuality is fundamental to the human being as it is to other species. Powerful desires and the pleasure associated with sexual gratification ensure that the human species will reproduce itself. As such, sexuality is necessary for our collective survival. Sexual behavior offers the opportunity for gratification, for procreation, and for a very close form of intimacy. Cultures vary widely in terms of their sexual practices and values.

Though we think of males and females as sexually different because their sexual organs and uses for the sexual organs are different, still there are a number of underlying similarities in human sexual response. Both males and females respond to sexual stimulation. There are four phases of the sexual response cycle. The first phase, the excitement phase, is characterized by our initial response to sexual stimulation—for both sexes, blood rushes to the genital area and collects there, which is a process known as *vasocongestion*. It is blood filling spongy tissue in the penis that causes it to become erect. Similarly, blood collecting around the vagina in the female causes the walls of the vagina to expand, moisture to appear (serves as lubrication), tissue around the vagina to expand, and the uterus to elevate. Muscle tension, heart rate, respiration, and blood pressure all increase for both males and females. The clitoris, in the female, is unique in that it has no other apparent function except that of sexual pleasure. The tissue comprising the clitoris is similar to that of the penis, and the clitoris also enlarges and becomes erect in response to stimulation.

The second phase of the sexual response cycle is the plateau phase. This immediately precedes orgasm, and at this point the individual has become highly sexually aroused. Physiological changes, which began in the excitement phase, continue and heighten. Even though ejaculation on the part of the male has not yet occurred, there are droplets of semen (carrying sperm) that issue from the penis; thus, a woman can become pregnant (from this semen) even if the male does not ejaculate inside her.

The third phase of the sexual response cycle is the orgasmic phase where the individual experiences orgasm. Orgasm involves muscle contractions for both the male and female, and this is the point of ejaculation for the male. It is accompanied by a sense of release and also by intense feelings of pleasure. Because of the great pleasure of the sexual experience, it is no wonder that the continued reproduction of our species seems assured!

The fourth and last phase of the sexual response cycle is the resolution phase, and at this time, within a few minutes, the physiological state of both men and women returns to much like their pre-aroused condition. Males will not be able to experience another erection for at least a few minutes. There is no refractory (resting) period for women, and thus they can experience multiple orgasms in relatively quick succession.

Sexual orientation is the direction of one's erotic and romantic interests. Most humans have a heterosexual orientation—they desire and are sexually attracted to members of the opposite sex. A smaller number of humans have a homosexual orientation—they are sexually attracted to members of their own sex. A few humans are bisexual (attracted to both males and females), although perhaps a fifth of humans surveyed (in the United States and Europe) report some same-sex contact at some point in their lives. The well-known sex researcher, Alfred Kinsey, suggested that homosexuality and heterosexuality are not mutually exclusive categories—that one may be predominantly heterosexual, for example, but have occasional homosexual feelings, and vice versa.

The question of what determines whether one is heterosexual, homosexual, or of another sexual orientation remains not fully answered. Several explanations have been provided, by Freud (that normal identification with the same-sex parent leads to heterosexual relations; aberrations in the identification process lead to a homosexual orientation), by geneticists, and by researchers examining the influences of sex hormones. Genetic evidence is somewhat convincing, in that there is a fairly high concordance rate regarding sexual orientation among identical (monozygotic) twins, even when raised in separate environments, compared to fraternal (dizygotic) twins. Research on the influence of sex hormones has been conducted only with animals, so as yet we cannot make any interpretations regarding hormones and human sexual orientation. In laboratory rats, when a female rat is given testosterone (the male sex hormone) during prenatal development, that rat exhibits masculine-type behaviors at maturity. That is, such female rats tend to attempt to mount other females and resist mating attempts from males. There are so many different factors and influences in the backgrounds of gay and lesbian individuals who have been studied that it is impossible to draw any final conclusions or point to a single determining source. It is expected that sexual orientation is a result of genetic, hormonal, and environmental influences interacting over the life span.

There are some variations of sexual behavior that are considered outside the normal range, and some are unlawful because they cause harm to their victims. These paraphilias include fetishism (being sexually aroused by an object such as women's shoes or underwear), transvestism (wearing clothing of the opposite sex), voyeurism (watching the nude or sexual behavior of others without their awareness) and exhibitionism (exposing one's sexual organs momentarily in the presence of strangers). Pedophilia is the sexual attraction of adults to children, and sexual masochism is desiring the experience of pain along with sexual activity. Individuals exhibiting paraphilias are almost always male, and it is thought that these avenues for sexuality compensate for fears and inadequacies relative to the more typical (and acceptable) forms of sexual behavior.

Along with sexual behavior comes sexual risks, and a serious risk is that of contracting an STD (sexually transmitted disease). Some STDs have been known for some time, such as the bacterial infections of syphilis and gonorrhea. Chlamydia is the most widespread bacterial STD. Untreated bacterial STDs can result in serious infections, fertility problems, an increased risk for cancer and, in the case of syphilis, life-threatening damage to the heart and brain. Usually, bacterial STDs can be treated with antibiotics. Genital herpes and HIV/AIDS are the well-known viral STDs, and as yet there are treatments but no cures for these virus-based disorders. AIDS, which suppresses the functioning of the immune system, has reached epidemic proportions world-wide. In order to prevent contracting a sexually transmitted disease, it is important that you take steps to protect yourself or abstain altogether. These include being careful in whom you choose as a sexual partner, being aware of the risk of STDs, and using protection (a latex condom is usually considered the most effective barrier), seeing a physician on a regular basis and immediately if there is a possibility you have been exposed to an STD, and avoiding sexual contact if there appears to be risk involved.

KEY TERMS

Sexual response cycle

Vasocongestion

Clitoris

Myotonia

Sexual orientation

Paraphilia

Fetishism

Transvestism

Voyeurism

Exhibitionism

Pedophilia

Sexual masochism

Sexually transmitted disease (STD)

SELF-TEST PRACTICE QUIZ

From the Key Terms select that which best matches the following (Note: Not every Key Term will be used.):

1. _____ A type of paraphilia where adults are sexually attracted to children (also a legal offense)

2. _____ Sexual orientations and behaviors that are considered outside of the normal range

3. _____ A female sex organ that functions exclusively for sexual pleasure

4. _____ Bacterial and viral diseases such as HIV, genital herpes, and chlamydia that are transmitted through sexual contact

5. _____ A description conveying the objective of one's sexual and romantic interests

6. _____ The paraphilia where an individual is sexually aroused by watching others disrobe or engage in sexual activity (without the others' awareness, also a legal offense)

7. _____ A term utilized by Masters and Johnson to characterize the various stages in human sexual behavior in response to sexual stimulation

8. _____ The paraphilia where an individual is particularly sexually aroused by the inclusion of painful experiences as part of sexual activities

9. _____ Pooling of blood within the sexual tissues causing further sexual response

10. _____ The paraphilia where an individual is aroused by contact with objects that he finds erotic (women's shoes, intimate apparel, rubber objects)

a. Sexual response cycle

b. Vasocongestion

c. Clitoris

d. Myotonia

e. Sexual orientation

f. Paraphilia

g. Fetishism

h. Transvestism

i. Voyeurism

j. Exhibitionism

k. Pedophilia

l. Sexual masochism

m. Sexually transmitted disease (STD)

11. _____ The paraphilia where an individual is sexually aroused by quickly exposing his sexual organs to unsuspecting strangers (also a legal offense)

12. _____ The paraphilia where an individual is particularly sexually aroused by dressing in clothing of the opposite gender (usually males dressing in women's clothing)

13. _____ A state of muscle tension, accompanies several phases of the human sexual response

14. The only organ in either the male or female body whose sole purpose is pleasure is the

    a. clitoris.
    b. vagina.
    c. penis.
    d. testes.

15. In the human sexual response cycle, the phase shortly before orgasm, where both partners are fully aroused and ejaculation is imminent, is the _____ phase.

    a. excitement
    b. plateau
    c. orgasmic
    d. resolution

16. Alfred Kinsey characterized exclusive heterosexuality and exclusive homosexuality as

    a. polar opposites.
    b. anchor points on a continuum.
    c. essentially the same thing.
    d. an outward manifestation of good and evil.

17. If one is sexually attracted to members of both sexes, one is classified as having a _____ sexual orientation.

    a. heterosexual
    b. homosexual
    c. bisexual
    d. monogamous

18. According to Sigmund Freud, when a child experiences the normal identification process with the same-sex parent, that child will become

    a. heterosexual.
    b. homosexual.
    c. bisexual.
    d. monogamous.

19. When gay males and lesbians recall childhood experiences,

    a. gay males report feeling "different," and exhibiting more sensitivity than other male children.
    b. gay males were more interested in female-type activities, and lesbians were more interested in typically masculine behaviors and activities.
    c. some gay males and lesbians exhibited behavior patterns in childhood that were like other members of their gender.
    d. they report all of the above.

20. Regarding the determination of one's sexual orientation, which of the following is NOT correct as a source identified thus far by research?

    a. Genetics
    b. Sex hormones
    c. Sociocultural experiences
    d. A self-selected pattern of behavior

21. The most common STD in the United States is

    a. chlamydia.
    b. gonorrhea.
    c. Human papillovirus (HPV).
    d. HIV/AIDS.

22. Being sexually aroused by and desiring sexual contact with children is classified as

    a. fetishism.
    b. voyeurism.
    c. pedophilia.
    d. sexual masochism.

23. A learning theory explanation for paraphilia would include

    a. unconscious motives and desires driving the behavior.
    b. earlier experiences where sexual pleasure was associated with a behavior or inanimate object.
    c. a predisposition for sexual deviance due to genetic heritage.
    d. all of the above.

24. What is the most common method of HIV transmission?

    a. intravenous drug use
    b. heterosexual sex
    c. homosexual sex
    d. blood transfusions

25. Which of the following CANNOT be treated, and usually cured, by use of antibiotics?

    a. Syphilis
    b. Gonorrhea
    c. Chlamydia
    d. Genital herpes

26. The only sure way to prevent contracting an STD is

    a. caution in whom one chooses as a sexual partner.
    b. regular checkups with a physician.
    c. abstinence or monogamous relations with a monogamous STD-free partner.
    d. use of a latex condom and spermicide.

27. Based on current research, which statement about sexual orientation is *correct*?

  a. Bisexuality is a myth—people are either heterosexual or homosexual not in between.
  b. All people who engage in same-sex sexual contact are homosexual.
  c. Sexual orientation can change over time.
  d. None of the above are correct.

ESSAY QUESTIONS

1. Nearly all individuals with paraphilias are male. What are some of the explanations given as to why this might be so?

2. What is HIV and AIDS? How are they transmitted? How is AIDS treated? Is it possible to die from this disorder?

ANSWER KEY

1. Pedophilia

2. Paraphilia

3. Clitoris

4. Sexually transmitted disease (STD)

5. Sexual orientation

6. Voyeurism

7. Sexual respose cycle

8. Sexual masochism

9. Vasocongestion

10. Fetishism

11. Exhibitionism

12. Transvestism

13. Myotonia

14. a

15. b

16. b

17. c

18. a

19. d

20. d

21. c

22. c

23. b

24. b

25. d

26. c

27. c

SAMPLE ANSWERS TO ESSAY QUESTIONS

1. Nearly all people with paraphilias are male. Reasons that this might be so include that males may find normal sexual relationships threatening or frightening, and they turn to other alternatives in order to satisfy their sexual urges. An exhibitionist may actually be shy and feel sexually awkward—the shocked response his behavior of exposing himself elicits may help the exhibitionist feel more exciting, powerful, and masculine. Similarly, a pedophile may not feel comfortable in normal sexual relationships or may have experienced an abusive relationship himself as a child. Since a sexual relationship with a child is unbalanced, and the adult has the greater power and control, this may become an alluring avenue for a male with strong sexual desires but with difficulty engaging in the acceptable avenues for sexual gratification.

2. AIDS can be treated, and perhaps controlled, but not cured. It develops from HIV, a virus that disables our immune system. HIV is most often transmitted through sexual intercourse with an infected partner or through sharing infected needles. Treatment of AIDS is expensive and time-consuming. Most importantly, the end result is not guaranteed. Today one may still die of AIDS.

MODULE 11.3 SEXUAL DYSFUNCTIONS

LEARNING OBJECTIVES

After you have mastered the information in this unit, you will be able to:

- Discuss sexual dysfunctions

- Explain the causes of sexual dysfunctions

- Describe the general aims of sex therapy

OUTLINE

I. Types of Sexual Dysfunctions (three major classes)
   A. Sexual desire disorders
      1. Hypoactive sexual desire disorder
         a) One of most frequently occurring dysfunctions
         b) More often a problem for women than men
         c) Little or no sexual desire, interest
      2. Sexual aversion disorder
         a) Comfortable with other forms of physical contact, but strong resistance, fear, dislike of genital contact
         b) May be related to history of child abuse or trauma
   B. Sexual arousal disorders
      1. Male erectile disorder (ED)—difficulty in achieving or maintaining an erection
      2. Female sexual arousal disorder—frequent difficulty becoming sexually aroused, sufficiently lubricated
   C. Orgasmic disorders
      1. Female orgasmic disorder and male orgasmic disorder
         a) In both cases, difficult or impossible to reach orgasm
      2. Premature ejaculation (PE)
         a) Most common sexual dysfunction in males
         b) Ejaculation occurs after only minimal stimulation, before man wants it to occur

II.   Causes of Sexual Dysfunctions
    A.   Biological causes
        1.   Obesity
        2.   Neurological and circulatory diseases (diabetes, spinal-cord injury, epilepsy, complications from surgery, hormonal problems)
        3.   Psychoactive drugs
        4.   Regular cocaine use
        5.   Low levels of testosterone
    B.   Psychosocial causes
        1.   Raised with negative attitudes towards sexuality—inhibits
        2.   Routine behavior, failure to communicate with partner
        3.   Rape or other sexual trauma survivor
        4.   Performance anxiety
            a)   Usually among males (may be a factor in ED)
            b)   Can create a cycle of failure leading to anxiety, which then further inhibits
III. Sex Therapy
    A.   Basic approach of sex therapy
        1.   Makes use of behavioral techniques
        2.   Remove anxiety by removing pressures to perform
    B.   Sex therapies introduced by Masters and Johnson (1970)
        1.   Daily treatment sessions, nightly sexual homework
        2.   Sensate-focus exercises—relaxation, massage involving, non-genital areas
        3.   Encourage open channels of communication between partners
    C.   Techniques developed by other sex therapists
        1.   Directed masturbation—to help woman with orgasm
        2.   Stop-start method—to help with premature ejaculation
    D.   Biological therapies
        1.   Testosterone therapy—for low sexual interest or desire
        2.   Viagra—helps produce erections for men with ED
        3.   Antidepressants help with premature ejaculation

SUMMARY

In this module you learn about sexual dysfunctions, which are not uncommon in adult sexual behavior. Although there are many types of sexual dysfunctions, the three main categories discussed in this unit are sexual desire disorders, sexual arousal disorders, and orgasmic disorders. Though not every problem involving sexual dysfunction can be completely eliminated, in most cases at least some help can be offered. A combination of biological and psychological approaches in therapy seems to be the most effective in bringing about desired results.

Both males and females may experience all the categories of sexual dysfunction discussed in this module, but sexual desire disorder is more common among women. Sexual desire disorder involves a lack of interest in sexual activities, and sometimes a strong aversion to any kind of sexual or genital contact. *Hypoactive sexual desire* disorder is the term for low or non-existent levels of interest in sex. *Sexual aversion disorder* is the term for the disorder where individuals are repulsed by any kind of genital contact. Childhood experiences of incest or other sexual abuse or trauma may be a factor in sexual aversion disorder.

Sexual arousal disorders involve a failure by men to achieve and maintain an erection (known as ED, erectile disorder) and difficulties among women to become aroused or to become sufficiently lubricated. Orgasmic disorders occur when either a male or a female cannot reach orgasm. Premature ejaculation, the most common type of sexual dysfunction in males, involves ejaculating too soon and is classified as an orgasmic disorder.

Sexual dysfunction disorders have both biological and psychological causes. Biological causes include obesity, which is associated with erectile dysfunction. Others include consequences of surgery (prostate surgery, for example), and illnesses such as epilepsy, diabetes, or multiple sclerosis. Spinal-cord injuries, of course, impair sexual functioning since nerve damage is involved in the injury. Some medications have sexual side effects, and low levels of important sexual hormones may be a factor. Psychoactive drugs also can impair sexual functioning.

Psychosocial causes include a negative attitude towards sex, possibly as a consequence of being raised in an environment where sex was considered "dirty" or simply a duty. Feelings of guilt or shame can inhibit normal sexual responsiveness. A major cause for sexual dysfunction is performance anxiety. This can be a problem for women, but is much more common among men, especially when a man (or his partner) defines masculinity in terms of the ability to achieve and maintain erections. Performance anxiety occurs when the focus shifts from the desires and pleasure involved in the sexual activity to attending to how one's body is functioning. Any anxiety associated with this misplaced attention can impede the very process the individual is concerned about. Another psychosocial source of sexual dysfunction occurs when sexual partners have fallen into a rut, and the sexual act becomes a routine. The partners may not be communicating or not communicating well with each other.

Although a few decades ago there was no treatment for sexual dysfunction, Masters and Johnson contributed pioneering work in this area. Sex therapies are directed at helping individuals learn more about their bodies and their sexual responsiveness (this is primarily useful for women), eliminating performance anxiety (this is more useful for men), and opening channels of communication between partners. Premature ejaculation is most often treated by what is called the stop-start method. This involves sexual stimulation up to a certain level, having partners stop (so that the man does not ejaculate), then begin again—to help the man gain more control over his sexual arousal and responses. Since antidepressants can have sexual impairment as a side effect, this feature becomes useful in treating premature ejaculation since the drugs will help slow the sexual arousal and response process. Performance anxiety is treated usually through sensate-focus exercises where sexual partners relax unclothed with each other and massage non-genital body parts. Partners avoid intercourse until both are feeling confident (and not anxious) about the act. The sex hormone testosterone may help where there are low levels of sexual interest, and Viagra has been shown to be useful for men with erectile dysfunction (but does not seem to help women with sexual disorders). Even where causes of sexual dysfunction are biological, psychological therapies along with medical treatment seem to be the most helpful.

KEY TERMS

Sexual dysfunctions

Hypoactive sexual desire disorder

Sexual aversion disorder

Male erectile disorder

Female sexual arousal disorder

Female orgasmic disorder

Male orgasmic disorder

Premature ejaculation

Performance anxiety

Sensate-focus exercises

SELF-TEST PRACTICE QUIZ

From the Key Terms select that which best matches the following:

1. _____ A sexual dysfunction in a woman where she is unable to experience orgasm though she has responded to sexual stimulation leading up to that point

2. _____ A sexual desire disorder, more typical in females, where there is a lack of interest in or desire for sexual activity

3. _____ Concern for and focus on how the body is responding (including in sexual situations), leading to a sense of anxiety that may impair performance

4. _____ A sex therapy created by Masters and Johnson where partners relax with each other and massage non-genital body parts, the objective being to remove feelings of anxiety from sexual behavior

5. _____ A sexual dysfunction in men where males are unable to consistently achieve and experience orgasm

6. _____ A common sexual dysfunction in men where they are unable to achieve or maintain penile erection sufficient for intercourse

7. _____ A sexual desire disorder, more common in women, where the individual fears, resists, and does not enjoy any kind of genital sexual contact

8. _____ A class of disorders characterized by difficulties in feeling interest or desire for sexual relations or difficulties related to the actual processes involved in sexual activity

9. _____ A sexual dysfunction in women where a woman is consistently unable to become sexually aroused, even though she is experiencing what are typically effective types of sexual stimulation

a. Sexual dysfunctions

b. Hypoactive sexual desire disorder

c. Sexual aversion disorder

d. Male erectile disorder

e. Female sexual arousal disorder

f. Female orgasmic disorder

g. Male orgasmic disorder

h. Premature ejaculation

i. Performance anxiety

j. Sensate-focus exercises

10. _____ A common sexual dysfunction in men where males consistently experience ejaculation before they would like in the sexual relations process

11. Most everyone experiences sexual problems at some time or other in their lives. These problems are not considered sexual dysfunctions until

    a. one's sexual partner makes frequent mention of the issue.
    b. they occur persistently over time and cause distress.
    c. males cannot achieve an erection at every sexual encounter.
    d. sexual partners are unable to conceive a child.

12. Lately, Fran has been having a problem—she simply has no interest in sex. She's not physically ill, but sex just holds no appeal for her. Based on this description, which sexual dysfunction does Fran probably suffer from?

    a. sexual aversion disorder.
    b. female orgasmic disorder.
    c. hypoactive sexual disorder.
    d. female sexual arousal disorder.

13. The most common sexual dysfunction in males is

    a. sexual desire disorder.
    b. sexual aversion disorder.
    c. male erectile disorder (ED).
    d. premature ejaculation (PE).

14. The hormone involved in the sexual arousal and activity of both men and women is

    a. testosterone.
    b. estrogen.
    c. progesterone.
    d. serotonin.

15. A problem that occurs more often with men but that can also occur in the sexual activity of women is performance anxiety. Sensate-focus exercises are used to treat this disorder, and the objective is to

    a. use the naturally-occurring side effects of psychoactive drugs to slow sexual response.
    b. use the naturally-occurring side effects of psychoactive drugs to calm sexually active individuals.
    c. relieve and eliminate the anxiety that has become associated with sexual behavior.
    d. help partners find other sources of gratification that lessen their reliance on sexual intercourse.

16. Which of the following may be a cause of erectile dysfunction in men?

    a. performance anxiety
    b. obesity
    c. alcohol
    d. all of the above

17. Testosterone is produced in males' testes, in females' ovaries, and in

    a. the male penis and the female clitoris.
    b. pancreatic glands of both males and females.
    c. adrenal glands of both males and females.
    d. the hypothalamus in the brain of both males and females.

ESSAY QUESTIONS

1. Though psychoactive drugs may be used to treat sexual dysfunction, they also can impair sexual performance. Discuss the psychoactive drugs mentioned in this module, and briefly explain their impact on sexual functioning.

2. Even where the suspected cause of a sexual disorder is biological, psychological therapies still often prove helpful. Why might this be?

ANSWER KEY

1. Female orgasmic disorder

2. Hypoactive sexual desire disorder

3. Performance anxiety

4. Sensate-focus exercises

5. Male orgasmic disorder

6. Male erectile disorder

7. Sexual aversion disorder

8. Sexual dysfunctions

9. Female sexual arousal disorder

10. Premature ejaculation (PE)

11. b

12. c

13. d

14. a

15. c

16. d

17. c

SAMPLE ANSWERS TO ESSAY QUESTIONS

1. The psychoactive drugs (both legal and illegal) mentioned in this module are antidepressants, cocaine, alcohol, and narcotics. All of these drugs tend to suppress sexual arousal and response.

    If a sexual dysfunction involves the sexual experience occurring too quickly (as in premature ejaculation in males), then legal psychoactive drugs become useful in that they will (as when it is a problem to sexual functioning) slow down the rate at which one becomes aroused and responds to sexual stimulation.

2. A psychological approach to biological sexual disorders can still be very helpful because (1) it is geared to improving communication between sexual partners, and (2) the behavioral aspects and techniques involved can help improve the physical sexual experience even if there are other physiological consequences resulting from the biological condition. Thus, though psychological sex therapy cannot offer a medical treatment for biological problems, it still can improve the communication, emotional understanding and sharing, and behavioral strategies involved in creating satisfying sexual relations.

MODULE 11.4 APPLICATION: COMBATING RAPE AND SEXUAL HARASSMENT

LEARNING OBJECTIVES

After you have mastered the information in this unit, you will be able to:

• Discuss steps we can take individually and as a society to combat rape and sexual harassment

OUTLINE

I.   How Common Is Rape and Sexual Harassment?
   A.   High incidence of rape, sexual assault among women
   B.   Estimate is that perhaps 25 percent of all American women raped at some point in their lives
   C.   Incidence of rape higher in the United States than in other industrialized countries
   D.   Males also can be raped; about 10 percent of rape survivors are male
   E.   Cases of sexual harassment usually not reported
   F.   Sexual harassment considered the most common form of sexual victimization (in U.S.)

II. Acquaintance Rape—The Most Common Type
   A.   Most rapes are experienced by women; committed by males whom they know
   B.   Occurs among 10 to 20 percent of all women
   C.   Often misperceptions, misattributions on the part of the male (or this is their claim)

III. What Motivates Rape and Sexual Harassment?
   A.   A crime of sexual violence, may be complex motives
   B.   Often a means of control or domination
   C.   May be an avenue to experience psychological revenge (especially if a history of prior abusive treatment from a woman, such as the mother)
   D.   May be an avenue to manifest social control or "superiority"

IV. What Are We Teaching Our Sons?
   A.   Some rapists have antisocial personalities (hatred towards society, no regard or empathy for victims)
   B.   Many other males exhibit normal behavior, except for commission of rape
   C.   May be a translation of the culturally approved practice of male domination (e.g., as occurs in sports)
   D.   Dating seen as an opportunity for the male to "score"
   E.   Use of alcohol may release inhibitions for aggressiveness (in males), cloud judgment

V.   Preventing Rape and Sexual Harassment
   A.   Approach socially and educationally
      1.   Teach respect for others (including respect towards women)
      2.   Clarify female perspective, and intent of female communication (e.g., "No" does not mean "Yes" or "Maybe")
   B.   Suggestions to help prevent rape
      1.   Have car keys handy when walking towards parking lot; drive with doors locked, windows up
      2.   Trust feelings, be firm, establish clear limits in dating
      3.   Keep home safe with locks, good lighting especially at entrances
      4.   Check credentials of service people
      5.   Avoid consuming alcohol on dates
      6.   Avoid walking alone at night, or in deserted areas
      7.   Meet first dates in a common, public area; do not get into the car of a new date
      8.   Be firm when establishing limits, refusing overtures

C. Suggestions to help counter sexual harassment
1. Maintain a professional attitude
2. Avoid meetings with harasser where others are not present
3. Keep a journal of events relating to harassment
4. Speak clearly to harasser that behavior is not welcome or acceptable
5. Speak to officials (at work, school, or wherever harassment occurs) responsible for handling sexual harassment complaints; review guidelines and grievance procedures
6. Consider legal actions

SUMMARY

In this module, you learn about acts of sexual coercion, which range from taunts and harassment to sexual assault and rape. Rape is using threats or force to compel an individual into sexual intercourse against that person's will. Harassment is unwelcome remarks, touching, overtures or pressure to engage in sexual relations, especially as a condition of employment or other aspect regarding how the individual being harassed will be treated.

Most acts of sexual coercion are committed by males against females, although some examples of the reverse do occur. Rape and sexual harassment are more common in the United States than in other industrialized countries, and reports suggest approximately one-quarter of all women will be raped at some point in their lives. Most rapes are committed against women under the age of eighteen. It is difficult to have exact figures because some rapes and many incidences of sexual harassment are not reported to officials. Most rapes occur when the parties are known to each other rather than occurring between strangers. This also makes reporting difficult since women may feel they are somewhat responsible if they are raped when on a date or elsewhere with someone they know. Also, reporting incidences of sexual coercion may be embarrassing, and may involve discussing personal, intimate experiences. Often alcohol has played a role in the occurrence of date rape.

Rape is more likely to involve issues of dominance, power, violence, revenge, anger, and perhaps cruelty than simply a desire for sexual gratification. As such, reasons behind the behavior of rapists may be complex. Because most cases of rape and sexual harassment are perpetrated by males, and often by males who appear otherwise normal with regard to their psychological characteristics, it is important to look at the cultural messages men still may be receiving as they grow up in our society.

Unfortunately, many family, community, and media experiences in which boys participate or to which they are exposed continue to communicate that masculinity is defined as the extent to which one shows physical aggression and dominance. There is an emphasis on overpowering others, and on "winning." Women may still be portrayed as the weaker sex and as a sexual tool or convenience for the male. These messages are not a reason to excuse sexual coercion by males, but they do suggest a place to start with regard to alleviating the problem.

It is hoped that social and educational messages will help change the perspective that leads to some incidences of rape. There are steps that individuals can take, too, which will help to prevent rape and successfully address incidences of sexual harassment. In order to help reduce the likelihood that you will be raped, be aware that rapes do occur, and be prepared. Avoid walking alone at night or in deserted areas. Have your car keys in your hand as you approach your car, and make sure no one is hiding around your car or in the back seat. Stay in areas that are well lit, and assure also that outside hallways and entrances to your home always have sufficient lighting. Keep windows locked; use deadbolts on doors. Avoid using alcohol when out on dates. Trust your feelings, know your standards, and be clear regarding limits and when refusing sexual overtures. Be careful regarding whom you let into your home. Check and verify the credentials of service people. Help resist sexual harassment by keeping a journal, stating your objections clearly, and avoiding the presence of the harasser especially if others are not around. Maintain a businesslike, professional attitude. Know the policies of your school, business, organization, or other institution, and communicate your concerns and experiences to the appropriate officials. Consider legal action, since harassment is a legal offense.

KEY TERMS

Rape

Statutory rape

Sexual harassment

SELF-TEST PRACTICE QUIZ

From the Key Terms select that which best matches the following:

1. _____ Sexual relations with an individual who is under the legal age of consent (whether or not that individual is a willing participant)

2. _____ Sexual intercourse with an individual against that person's will when threats, force, or other means are used to carry out the act

3. _____ Unwelcome and offensive gestures, jokes, taunts, touching, overtures, or demands for sexual activity especially as related to a condition of employment, advancement, or other standing within an institution or organization.

a. Rape

b. Statutory rape

c. Sexual harassment

ANSWER KEY

1. Statutory rape

2. Rape

3. Sexual harassment

CHAPTER 11 APPLICATION EXERCISE

Think of a movie you have seen recently or a television program that you enjoy and watch regularly. Are there both male and female leading roles? What are typical behaviors of each? What physical characteristics do the male stars have? What are the physical characteristics of the female lead roles? How is the "maleness" or "femaleness" of each cast member conveyed? Last, if included, what seems to be the attitude towards various sexual orientations? Towards sexual dysfunctions, coercion, or deviance?

CHAPTER 12

Personality

In Chapter 12 you learn about the many different explanations we have for personality. Personality is such a fascinating feature of ourselves. No wonder there are myriad ways to describe and explain it! There is debate as to what personality is, and, in fact, even if it exists. We tend to think of everyone as having a fairly consistent set of traits, which we can expect to encounter most every time we run into someone we know. But is that uniformity and consistency in personality really there? Or do we rely on classifications we have given friends and acquaintances (and even ourselves) because it makes our world more orderly and manageable? Most perspectives on personality presented in this chapter stem from the assumption that personality is fairly stable across time and situations. However, we want to remember that we may be underestimating situational factors and variation.

The earliest modern-day approach to personality was contributed by Sigmund Freud who felt that all real motivation behind our behaviors lay out of our awareness deep within the unconscious. He came to this view in part because he was influenced by Charles Darwin's theory that a species needs to ensure its survival and in part because he was fascinated with how hypnosis affected even our physical states. Hypnosis was a powerful force, Freud reasoned, yet we cannot see it nor remember being influenced by it. Perhaps other powerful, unseen forces influence us as well. Freud proposed a three-part personality structure, which he likened to an iceberg. He felt that the hidden motivation driving all behavior was a primitive desire for sexual gratification. Freud's developmental stages were characterized by a shift in the locus for that sexual gratification as a child grows older.

Trait theorists take a wholly different view regarding personality. We know innumerable words to describe personality and character. Do we need the thousands of different descriptors? Or can personality traits be distilled to fundamental or underlying factors? Trait theorists believe that this can be done. They believe human beings have a set of characteristics (traits) that by and large are stable over time and in a variety of situations. The 16PF, the five-factor model, and other tests have been derived to measure these underlying factors. What is still debated among trait theorists is how we acquire our personality traits. The two main explanations, which are well supported, are from genetic influence, and sociocultural experiences. How genetic input and environmental experience impact each other continues to be a major focus of study.

The social-cognitive perspective reminds us that much of our personality is probably the consequence of learned behavior. That is, each one of us has a long history of experience with the world, and our interactions often result in pleasant or unpleasant outcomes (to a behaviorist, these are reinforcers and punishments). Certainly, we keep characteristics that result in desirable outcomes, and we do not exhibit those that have led to unpleasant outcomes. Thus, learning is a major influence on personality. We can learn from experiences other than those where we are directly reinforced such as through observational learning and imitating behaviors of others. How we think about and interpret our behavior and its consequences also influences why we act as we do.

Last, the humanistic perspective turns inward again for an explanation of behavior. The humanistic perspective proposes that all of us are motivated from within to aspire towards self-actualization. Self-actualization involves discovering all of our unique abilities and putting them to best use. As we strive to do this, our efforts are revealed through our external behavior. Humanists emphasize the importance of the self in personality and that how one interprets a situation (this is a more subjective interpretation) is probably as important as objective features of the situation itself. An important tenet of humanism is the need to treat all people with unconditional positive regard. This means accepting, and valuing, others (and ourselves) simply for what we are, allowing everyone space for self-actualization.

How can we measure personality? Currently, both objective (e.g., the MMPI) and subjective (e.g., the inkblot test) measures are used. The MMPI is accepted as a reliable and valid measure. Always, though, it should be remembered that results of a personality test are just one source of information.

MODULE 12.1 THE PSYCHODYNAMIC PERSPECTIVE

LEARNING OBJECTIVES

After you have mastered the information in this unit, you will be able to:

- Define personality

- Describe the three levels of consciousness from Freud's theory

- Explain the structures of personality in Freud's theory

- Describe psychological defense mechanisms

- Explain the five stages of psychosexual development in Freud's theory

- Discuss some of the major contributions of other psychodynamic theorists

OUTLINE

I.   Sigmund Freud: Psychoanalytic Theory
     A.   Basics of psychoanalytic theory
         1.   Humans have sexual (and aggressive) instincts—for survival
         2.   These inborn forces must be balanced with needs of society
         3.   Psychoanalytic theory created to explain how this balance is achieved
     B.   Levels of consciousness
         1.   Mind is like an iceberg; most of mass lies out of range of visible detection
         2.   Contains three parts
             a)   Conscious—present awareness (tip of iceberg we can see)
             b)   Preconscious—stores past experiences and learning (easy to access)
             c)   Unconscious—primitive impulses, unacceptable desires, disturbing past experiences (the iceberg mass under the water that we cannot see); not easy to access
     C.   The structure of personality—consists of three (hypothetical) mental entities
         1.   Id ("it")
             a)   Operates only in unconscious
             b)   Only psychic structure present at birth
             c)   Contains animal drives, instinctive impulses
             d)   Basic energy that fuels our behavior
             e)   Functions according to pleasure principle—instant gratification, no regard for other considerations
         2.   Ego
             a)   Formed during first year of life
             b)   Realizes not all instinctual desires will be immediately satisfied
             c)   Learns how to cope with frustration, delay of gratification
             d)   Operates according to reality principle—satisfy demands in way that is acceptable to society

      3.   Superego
         a)   Internal moral guardian, conscience
         b)   Develops about ages three through five years
         c)   Internalizes norms, moral teachings to which we are exposed
         d)   Most of superego also unconscious
         e)   Judges, evaluates our actions and may impose shame
      4.   Ego negotiates (balances) between superego and id
      5.   Freud perceived these conflicts (among personality facets) as ongoing
         a)   Dynamic (constant challenges, interplay between the three)
         b)   Psyche—within the mind (so, "psychodynamic")
         c)   Always out of conscious awareness
  D. Defense mechanisms
      1.   Prevent anxiety that would occur if unconscious contents were in awareness
      2.   Repression—motivated forgetting (keeping troubling thoughts out of conscious awareness)
      3.   Other defense mechanisms: regression, displacement, denial, reaction formation, rationalization, projection, sublimation, regression, and displacement
      4.   Defense mechanisms can lead to, or be an attempt to hide, abnormal behavior
  E. Stages of personality development
      1.   Psychosexual stages—each characterized by focus on different body parts for sexual pleasure (erogenous zones)
      2.   All bodily processes sexual—because necessary for survival
      3.   Conflicts at each stage can lead to fixations (being "stuck" in a stage)
      4.   Freud's five psychosexual stages:
         a)   Oral stage—0 to 18 months; mouth, sucking
         b)   Anal stage—18 months to 3 years; fixation may make one either excessively fastidious or messy
         c)   Phallic stage—3 to 6 years; Oedipal, Electra complexes; much influence on personality
         d)   Latency stage—6 to 12 years; sexual impulses dormant (says Freud!)
         e)   Genital stage—puberty; incestuous desires forsaken

II.   Other Psychodynamic Approaches
  A. Common characteristic is emphasis on unconscious conflict
  B. Less sexual, aggressive emphasis, more focus on social relationships, tasks of the ego
  C. Leading neo-Freudians:
      1.   Carl Jung—analytical psychology
         a)   Broke close ties with Freud
         b)   More emphasis on current experiences (vs. early childhood)
         c)   Greater emphasis on conscious (vs. unconscious) processes
         d)   Have both a personal and a collective unconscious (collective unconscious contains accumulated knowledge of the species—explains cross-cultural similarities)
      2.   Alfred Adler—individual psychology
         a)   Also broke close ties with Freud
         b)   Emphasis on individual's unique potential
         c)   Important role for consciousness—creative self
         d)   Proposed concept of inferiority complex, since children start out small, with limited abilities; desire to overcome (drive for superiority)
      3.   Karen Horney—early feminine perspective
         a)   German physician and early psychoanalyst

> b)   Agreed that unconscious conflicts shape personality
> c)   Less emphasis on sex, aggression; more on social, cultural forces
> d)   Emphasized importance of parent-child relationships
> e)   Can move towards, away from, or against others
> f)   Opposed Freud's view of penis envy; females' inferiority more due to lower social status (and women admirable because of ability to reproduce)

III.   Evaluating the Psychodynamic Perspective
- A.   Most detailed and comprehensive theory on personality to date
- B.   Many terms have become part of everyday vocabulary
- C.   Possible greatest contribution—suggesting unconscious forces motivate behavior
- D.   Criticisms
  1.   Too much emphasis on sexual and aggressive drives
  2.   Lack of evidence to support many components (e.g., Oedipal complex, castration anxiety, penis envy)
  3.   Theory based largely on only a few case studies
  4.   Much of phenomena cannot be tested (or substantiated) scientifically
  5.   Is some support for repression, other defense mechanisms (functioning outside of conscious awareness)

SUMMARY

In this module you learn about the first modern view on personality. This and a large body of other work relating to human psychology were contributed by one of the most major figures in the field, Sigmund Freud. Freud did not begin in the field of psychology (psychology itself was just beginning to emerge), but rather in medicine, treating what were considered to be neurological disorders (such as hysteria). He was greatly influenced by a visit to Jean Martin Charcot, in France, where he saw individuals with no true physical cause for disorders be relieved of paralysis, or experience it, as a result of Charcot's hypnosis. Since these "mental" (from the hypnotic state) influences were so very powerful, it occurred to Freud that a major impact on our psyche and our behavior resulted from factors of which we are not even aware (they are unconscious). Freud was also much influenced by the views of Charles Darwin and thought that all behaviors necessary for survival were pleasurable in that an organism must desire to do them and enjoy the experience otherwise that organism would die. Since most crucial to human survival is that we reproduce ourselves, he came to see human sexuality as the primary motivator in all of existence. He felt that the human was born with this drive for sexual behavior, and that initially our sexual desires override any other consideration. This is the action of the id, the only personality structure Freud said was complete and functioning at birth. The id is driven to satisfy its desires regardless of the needs or condition of the rest of the social world (Freud pointed to the typical behaviors of a newborn baby). Freud's theory, known as psychoanalytic theory, was an explanation of how humans balance these inborn, powerful, and not always admirable inner drives with the need of the larger society for order and restraint. It was Freud's view that essentially all deeply impacting experiences relating to our personality occurred within the earliest years of our lives.

Freud's view of the personality was that there were three tiers, and the structure of personality resembled the features of an iceberg—most of what is truly powerful lies below the surface and out of our immediate sensory awareness. The innermost structure, the source of our energy, is the id, as mentioned above (the id is the massive part of the iceberg lying beneath the surface). The id operates by means of the pleasure principle—in other words, give me what I want, everything that I want, and right now. Obviously, this extremely selfish point of view will not make it far in the world, and Freud proposed that, after the first year of life, the child begins to develop an ego, which is more sensible (so to speak) and operates under the reality principle. The ego, according to Freud, is a negotiator, and compromiser. It is aware of the needs and boundaries established by society and attempts to find ways for the id to satisfy its desires yet stay within the confines of what is considered acceptable. This is an ongoing challenge. Because it is a lifelong task, and clearly involves conflicting demands among the parts of the personality, Freud's views are also referred to as psychodynamic theory. The "dynamic" part is that opposition and interplay among the personality forces. Freud did not see the aspects of personality as particularly harmonious. Eventually, for most people, according to Freud, we develop the superego. The superego parallels the notion of a conscience; we have internalized the moral values and beliefs espoused by the individuals and society surrounding us. The conscious part of the superego is our grasp of right and wrong. The powerful, unconscious part of our superego (according to Freud), notes all that we do and sits in judgment of our actions. Obviously, then, the superego can be the source of many feelings of guilt, shame, and self-condemnation. Part of our unconscious involves the use of defense mechanisms, another concept proposed by Freud. Defense mechanisms (such as denial, repression, sublimation, projection) help alleviate anxiety that arises when we fear that the aspects of our personality, in the id, may become visible or apparent to others. The "Freudian slip" (according to Freud) is when a hidden part of ourselves accidentally appears.

Freud believed that our personality developed in stages keeping in mind that the driving force in human existence, according to Freud, was the libido—sexual energy. Thus, Freud's stages of development were known as psychosexual stages. The emphasis is on sexuality (and, he added later, aggressive urges), and each stage represents a different body zone (an erogenous zone), which is the focus of that sexual pleasure for a given stage. Movement through the stages is due to shifts in the site of the reigning erogenous zone.

The earliest stage of psychosexual development is the oral stage. This involves the mouth region, and Freud believed sucking and other stimulation of the mouth was the greatest source of sexual gratification for the infant. One of the features of psychosexual development is the notion of fixation— one can be "stuck" in a stage and retain characteristics of that stage forever if the experience during that period involved too much or too little in the way of appropriate gratification. The anal stage is the second stage in psychosexual development, covering approximately the ages of 1 to 3 years. As the title suggests, the erogenous zone has now shifted to the anal region, and matters relating to urination, defecation, and control of these bodily processes become paramount. Again, aspects of personality are, according to Freud, heavily related to how a child is toilet-trained during this stage. The third stage of psychosexual development is the phallic stage, covering the ages in childhood of 3 to 6 years. This is the stage of development proposed by Freud that is perhaps most controversial of all. Freud said the locus of sexual pleasure is the phallus (the penis)—and, clearly, girls don't have one. Thus, according to Freud, female children experience penis envy and resent their mothers for allowing them to be created without a penis. Because girls don't have a penis like males do, they feel inferior. Women who seek out traditionally male occupations (at least, at the time that Freud practiced) were interpreted as trying to accomplish having a penis by imitating other aspects of being a male. Women who bore children bore them, in part, to have a male child and thus indirectly have the experience of having a penis. Also during this stage, boys go through the Oedipal phase, where, according to Freud, they sexually desire their mother and plot to destroy their father because he stands in the way of sexual gratification. Boys soon realize, though, that their father may detect this hatred and the boys experience castration anxiety—their fathers would castrate the sons to avoid a potential problem. This fear of castration is eventually resolved (according to Freud) by an identification with the same-sex parent; this is predominantly as a means of survival for the young boy. Ages 6 to 12 years in psychosexual development is known as a latency period, and in Freud's view sexual matters lay dormant while the child mastered many other skills and activities necessary to life. The final stage of psychosexual development was the genital stage, where the focus is on the genitalia of both sexes, and more appropriate (as opposed to desiring one's parents) sexual partners are chosen.

Many of Freud's views have been perceived as radical, then (during his lifetime) and now. His views were not accepted by the scientific community at the time he proposed them, but he did develop a group of followers (later known as neo-Freudians), many of whom themselves became prominent in psychology and made their own valuable contributions.

The greatest difficulty with the psychosexual perspective was that Freud was unwilling to consider any other substantially important influence on the human besides sexuality. His well-known protégés (Carl Jung, Alfred Adler, and Karen Horney, among others) all concurred regarding the existence and impact of the unconscious, but all suggested other influences (predominantly social and emotional) that were important as well. They emphasized that experiences after childhood were influential too. Many of these neo-Freudians eventually broke their formerly close ties with Freud because he grew increasingly obstinate regarding his own point of view. Carl Jung suggested the interesting notion of a collective unconscious (a common repository shared by all humans consisting of our common history, experiences, and understandings) in addition to the personal unconscious. Alfred Adler, who had experienced rather severe childhood illness, created the concept of the inferiority complex, suggesting that this develops naturally in children because they begin their lives smaller and weaker than others. Some of our motivation for behavior, according to Adler, is the drive to overcome these childhood feelings of inferiority. Karen Horney emphasized the powerful influence resulting from parent-child relationships. She was most critical of Freud regarding his views on women and his relegating of women to a second-class status (we recognize that in part Freud was reflecting the thinking and standards of his day). Horney argued that there was no more reason for women to be "jealous" regarding the male's penis than for men to regret that they were not born with a womb and the marvelous physical capacity to reproduce the human species. A key tenet in Horney's beliefs involved the emotional relationships, not only between parents and their children, but among all of us as we reach the adult years and beyond.

Without question Freud had substantial impact on the field of psychology. He certainly got us talking more about sex! He provided encompassing, detailed explanations for personality and how the structure of personality might be derived. However, it is difficult to scientifically prove much, if any, of Freud's theories. In part this is due to components of his theory not easily lending themselves to study—the unconscious or the preconscious, for example. In part, his views are based on limited case studies, and these do not at all necessarily represent the more general human experience. His views may also be a reflection of his own childhood and sociocultural experiences. We do not find evidence for the Oedipal complex, for example, one of the primary tenets in Freud's thinking. There is support for his notion of defense mechanisms, and the more general idea that influences, perhaps important influences, may be outside of our conscious awareness.

KEY TERMS

Personality

Psychoanalytic theory

Conscious

Preconscious

Unconscious

Id

Ego

Superego

Pleasure principle

Reality principle

Defense mechanisms

Repression

Denial

Reaction formation

Rationalization

Projection

Sublimation

Regression

Displacement

Erogenous zones

Fixations

Oral stage

Anal stage

Anal-retentive personality

Anal-expulsive personality

Phallic stage

Oedipus complex

Electra complex

Castration anxiety

Penis envy

Latency stage

Genital stage

Personal unconscious

Collective unconscious

Archetypes

Individual psychology

Creative self

Inferiority complex

Drive for superiority

Basic anxiety

Basic hostility

SELF-TEST PRACTICE QUIZ

From the Key Terms select that which best matches the following (Note: Not all Key Terms will be used.):

1. _____ The part of the human mind, according to Jung, that contains elements of the history of all humanity

2. _____ A defense mechanism where humans criticize others for faults that they themselves actually have

3. _____ According to Freud, the component of personality that is completely within the unconscious and is the seat of our sexual energy

4. _____ The behaviors and characteristics of the human that remain relatively consistent over time and across situations

5. _____ The standard by which the ego operates—finding socially acceptable ways to satisfy the id's primitive desires

6. _____ A tenet of psychoanalytic theory; it states that young children sexually desire their opposite-sex parent and wish to destroy the same-sex parent who is a rival

7. _____ The view of personality advocated by Freud

8. _____ A defense mechanism where plausible and acceptable (but inaccurate) explanations are provided to justify behavior

9. _____ The defense mechanism where painful or unacceptable thoughts and desires are kept out of conscious awareness

10. _____ A defense mechanism where the individual unconsciously refuses to recognize that a given phenomenon exists

11. _____ According to psychoanalytic theory, the problems and behaviors that result when an individual does not successfully move through a psychosexual developmental stage

a. Personality

b. Psychoanalytic theory

c. Conscious

d. Preconscious

e. Unconscious

f. Id

g. Ego

h. Superego

i. Pleasure principle

j. Reality principle

k. Defense mechanisms

l. Repression

m. Denial

n. Reaction formation

o. Rationalization

p. Projection

q. Sublimation

r. Regression

s. Displacement

t. Erogenous zones

u. Fixations

v. Oral stage

w. Anal stage

x. Anal-retentive personality

y. Anal-expulsive personality

z. Phallic stage

aa. Oedipus complex

bb. Electra complex

cc. Castration anxiety

dd. Penis envy

ee. Latency stage

12. _____ The fifth and last stage of psychosexual development, according to Freud

13. _____ The portion of the human mind that is completely out of conscious awareness

14. _____ The portion of the personality that, according to Freud, attempts to balance between the desires of the id and the demands and constraints of society

15. _____ The defense mechanism that involves redirecting unacceptable impulses and desires into more socially-acceptable avenues

16. _____ According to Freud, unconscious attempts to protect oneself from anxiety

17. _____ Personality characteristics that manifest a psychosexual fixation resulting from toilet training experiences that were too harsh and demanding

ff. Genital stage
gg. Personal unconscious
hh. Collective unconscious
ii. Archetypes
jj. Individual psychology
kk. Creative self
ll. Inferiority complex
mm. Drive for superiority
nn. Basic anxiety
oo. Basic hostility

18. Freud characterized personality structure as consisting of three basic components, which
   a. are the oral, anal, and phallic components.
   b. coexisted harmoniously, leading to the overall productivity of the organism.
   c. were predominantly in our conscious awareness.
   d. had conflicting and sometimes unacceptable objectives.

19. The level of consciousness that involves our awareness of our current state and of everyday events is the
   a. preconscious.
   b. conscious.
   c. unconscious.
   d. reality consciousness.

20. The id operates according to the _____ principle.
   a. pleasure
   b. reality
   c. unconscious
   d. moral

21. The superego usually develops during the _____ psychosexual stage.
   a. oral
   b. anal
   c. phallic
   d. genital

22. The task of the ego is

    a. balancing between desires of the id and moral boundaries prescribed by the superego.
    b. operating under the reality principle.
    c. finding acceptable avenues to satisfy the organism's desires for gratification.
    d. to accomplish all of the above.

23. Which of the following is a function of defense mechanisms?

    a. To prepare an organism to fend off threatening physical attacks
    b. To provide an excuse for what would otherwise be morally offensive behavior (such as sexual assault)
    c. To resolve underlying conflicts such as the experience of childhood sexual abuse
    d. To keep more unpleasant aspects of ourselves out of conscious awareness

24. Freud viewed basic bodily processes such as eating and elimination as sexual because

    a. they provide feelings of intense sexual pleasure.
    b. they are vital and necessary for an organism's survival.
    c. this perspective was part of the theory advocated by Jean Martin Charcot.
    d. his childhood experiences associated these activities with sexual behavior.

25. If an individual receives either too much or too little gratification at a psychosexual stage, that individual experiences

    a. repression.
    b. sublimation.
    c. fixation.
    d. reaction formation.

26. One may become excessively fussy, meticulous, and overly concerned with cleanliness and order if one receives too little gratification during the _____ stage.

    a. oral
    b. anal
    c. phallic
    d. latency

27. Cathy's id has an unconscious desire to kill people. This is unacceptable, so her ego manifests this desire as a conscious desire to engage in kickboxing instead. In transforming this desire into a more socially acceptable form, her ego is engaging in

    a. projection.
    b. displacement.
    c. sublimation.
    d. reaction formation.

28. According to psychoanalytic theory, boys imitate the behaviors of their fathers because

    a. society has taught them that this is proper male behavior.
    b. the behaviors are the result of castration anxiety.
    c. they have been operantly reinforced during childhood for doing so.
    d. most masculine behaviors are determined by genetics.

29. The term *archetype* refers to a

    a. primitive image that reflects humans' universal experiences.
    b. repressed memory.
    c. type of defense mechanism.
    d. stage during which young children have sexual desires for the opposite-sex parent.

30. Horney and Freud both believed that if children's parents are harsh or neglecting,
    a. children will repress their feelings of hostility.
    b. the pain of this experience remains in conscious awareness.
    c. children will commit aggressive acts that manifest their anger.
    d. long term consequences will usually be resolved in adulthood.

ESSAY QUESTION

1. What would you say are important contributions from Freud? What are some aspects of the theories he proposed that you do not see as helpful in promoting our understanding or healthy psychological adjustment?

ANSWER KEY

1. Collective unconscious
2. Projection
3. Id
4. Personality
5. Reality principle
6. Oedipus complex
7. Psychoanalytic theory
8. Rationalization
9. Repression
10. Denial
11. Fixations
12. Genital stage
13. Unconscious
14. Ego
15. Sublimation
16. Defense mechanisms
17. Anal-retentive personality
18. d
19. b
20. a
21. c
22. d
23. d
24. b
25. c
26. b

27. c

28. b

29. a

30. a

SAMPLE ANSWER TO ESSAY QUESTION

1. There is no doubt Sigmund Freud has been a tremendously influential figure in the history of psychology. Not all of that influence has, in fact, been good. Freud provided what remains the most comprehensive and detailed picture we have of personality. He proposed the useful and substantiated notion of the unconscious, or at least that not everything we do or that influences us is within the realm of our conscious awareness. Freud brought the topic of sexuality to the forefront as part of psychological development, and this aspect truly had been suppressed and ignored by the society of his time. Freud's theories, inadvertently, helped trigger the examination of women's roles in society and reflected the societal notion according females a lower status—a view that was then vigorously challenged. Although perhaps off base, psychosexual stages of development highlight the experiences of early childhood as crucial, and this is an understanding that is now widely advocated. Freud believed all stages of psychosexual development and movement through them were driven by desires for sexual gratification. He incorporated into his own practice what he learned from Charcot as far as treating non-organic "mental" disorders. Either because of him or in reaction to him (or both), Freud's psychodynamic theories spawned work by a number of neo-Freudians who themselves made substantial contributions to the field.

    The greatest drawback to Freud's views and theories is that, no matter how far-reaching and detailed they may be, they still may be wrong. It is next to impossible to test or to substantiate nearly all of the components that are fundamental to psychoanalytic thinking. How can we research the unconscious? How can we identify or verify the "negotiations" of the ego? Did you, or your adorable young son or daughter really hate the same-sex parent as a four-year-old and desire sexual relations and gratification involving the opposite-sex parent? Does sexuality truly motivate everything we do? Another, perhaps more subtle, drawback to Freud's theorizing is that he characterized the human as fundamentally selfish, dominated by sexual impulses and consumed (no matter how graciously the ego attempts to channel it) solely with obtaining one's own wants. Freud not only assumed that interpersonal conflict is unavoidable (competition for desired sexual targets, for example), but that the inner nature of the human, too, seethes with hostility and unrest no matter how well this seething conflict is masked by outward behavior. He does not propose that the human is inherently a creature of peace, regarding dealings both within and without the boundaries of the organism. Interestingly, the latency phase in psychosexual development covers the childhood ages of 6 to 12 years. During this time, according to Freud, the child's sexuality is dormant because psychological energies are directed elsewhere. It is a less comprehensive criticism of Freud's views, but the ages of 6 to 12 years (pre-puberty) are one time we can be sure sexual interest and activity are a focal point for the developing child.

MODULE 12.2 THE TRAIT PERSPECTIVE

LEARNING OBJECTIVES

After you have mastered the information in this unit, you will be able to:

- Describe the three types of traits in Allport's model

- Explain Cattell's view on the organization of traits

- Discuss the three traits represented in Eysenck's model of personality

- Describe the "Big Five" model of personality

- Explain the role of genes in personality

OUTLINE

I. The Approach of Trait Theorists
    A. Look at personality to explain behavior
    B. Relatively stable, enduring characteristics are traits
    C. Traits help explain behavior across situations
    D. Traits suggest why people differ with regard to personality
    E. Considerations: How do we measure traits? Are they learned, or inborn?

II. Gordon Allport: A Hierarchy of Traits
    A. Traits are physical entities buried in the brain
    B. Traits occur in a hicrarchy
        1. Cardinal traits—highest level; are pervasive throughout personality
        2. Central traits—basic building blocks; influence behavior in most situations
        3. Secondary traits—more superficial (e.g., preferences in clothing, music)

III. Raymond Cattell: Mapping the Personality
    A. Can we distill the traits that truly describe personality?
    B. Two basic levels of traits
        1. Surface traits
            a) We can infer from observations of behavior
            b) Examples are friendliness, helpfulness, emotionality
            c) Surface traits often occur together
            d) These linkages suggest more general, underlying traits
        2. Source traits
            a) Derived from factor analysis
            b) Developed 16 Personality Factor Questionnaire (16PF)

IV. Hans Eysenck: A Simpler Trait Model
    A. Constructed a simpler model with three major traits
    B. Eysenck's traits:
        1. Introversion-extraversion
        2. Neuroticism
        3. Psychoticism
    C. Eysenck Personality Inventory (EPI) measures these traits
    D. Variations in personality are due to biological (neurological) differences

V. The Five-Factor Model of Personality ("Big Five")
    A. The most widely adopted trait model of personality
    B. Five broad personality factors consistently found in personality research

1. Neuroticism
2. Extraversion
3. Openness
4. Agreeableness
5. Conscientiousness

C. A consolidation and integration of factors previously identified
D. Good support from cross-cultural studies
E. Consistency suggests underlying genetic component
F. Still not the final word regarding basic factors in personality
G. Can something so rich and varied as personality ever really be captured by broad categories?

VI. The Genetic Basis of Traits
A. Heredity has an important role in shaping personality
B. Genes are linked to neuroticism, shyness, aggressiveness
C. Trait of novelty-seeking linked to dopamine gene
D. Greatest focus is how environment, biology interact (mutually influential)

VII. Evaluating the Trait Perspective
A. Trait perspective has intuitive appeal
B. Trait terms are commonly used
C. Trait theories are basis of many personality tests
D. Criticisms:
1. Traits label but do not explain behavior
2. Behavior not at all necessarily stable over time or across situations
3. Do we need to consider situational factors?
4. Personality probably an interaction between traits, environment

SUMMARY

In this module you look at a second way of characterizing personality (Freud's psychodynamic model proposed inborn, unconscious motives). This way of looking at personality is the trait perspective. Personality theorists who adhere to the trait perspective believe that personality is relatively stable over time, but rather than emanating from the unconscious, as in Freud's model, trait theorists see personality as a function of where each human being falls relative to basic human characteristics. What these basic human characteristics are has remained something of a debate.

Gordon Allport (1897–1967) believed traits had a hereditary component, but were also influenced by environmental experience. In this sense, he was ahead of his time because that is the conclusion personality theorists have arrived at as of the current thinking. Allport divided traits into categories that fit a hierarchy. Cardinal traits were those overreaching characteristics that were consistent with an individual and present in most behavioral situations. Central traits were the middle ground, and he felt these were what typically characterized most people. The most transient, rather superficial traits were categorized as secondary traits. Raymond Cattell (1905–1998) also looked at traits as an explanation for behavior, and he began with many, which he then distilled down to a few (by means of the statistical procedure known as factor analysis—finding the central, underlying characteristic that was the common factor representing a cluster of related traits). He felt that there were surface traits (the obvious ones that we see in our daily interactions with others) and the deeper-level source traits; these source traits were the result of his factor analysis procedure. He could measure the degree of source traits by means of the personality test he invented, the 16 Personality Factor Questionnaire (16 PF). Each trait was not a single concept but a continuum, and the test taker could score anywhere along that continuum as to the degree of one pole or another that individual exhibited. Hans Eysenck (1916–1997) narrowed personality down to just three traits (or trait dimensions): introversion-extraversion, neuroticism, and psychoticism. He also created a personality scale to measure these traits—the Eysenck Personality Inventory (EPI). He concluded that there were four basic personality types, which were combinations of his personality dimensions. He felt that personality was biological in nature in that qualities of the human nervous system vary. These neurological differences, Eysenck believed, led to the different manifestations known as personality. The "Big Five" approach to personality is the modern-day distillation of previous personality theories and identified traits. This five-factor model (FFM) suggests the basic traits are: neuroticism, extraversion, openness, agreeableness, and conscientiousness. It is an interesting concept if everything about you reduces to these five trait dimensions! However, cross-cultural studies to date do provide solid support for this model.

Why would there be such universal findings of basic personality trait dimensions? Increasingly, especially as we gain a better ability to study genetic coding, we are turning to biology and the work of evolutionary psychologists to provide the answer. Indeed, already we know there are genes that are related to the manifestation of neuroticism, aggression, shyness, and novelty-seeking. Our focus in personality, in fact, has become a study of how "nature" and "nurture" influence each other. Much of the behavior exhibited by humans undoubtedly is a combination and interplay of genetic heritage and cultural-environmental experience.

The trait approach to personality is extremely useful, and fits the perspectives and assumptions of most individuals. It is helpful for classification purposes. However, one objection to the trait approach is that it, like "instinct" used elsewhere to explain human behavior, does not really explain behavior after all. Rather, it simply describes, or labels, certain personality features. A substantial argument against the trait theory approach is that perhaps we want personality in others, and ourselves, to be stable—but is it really? Have we, perhaps by choice, overlooked the influence of situations, and the unavoidable ensuing variability? We are surely more manageable and less threatening if we can think of humans as exhibiting fairly consistent personality and behavioral traits. However, with personality and other aspects of human behavior, we should not underestimate the power and influence of situational factors.

KEY TERMS

Traits

Cardinal traits

Central traits

Secondary traits

Surface traits

Source traits

Introversion-extraversion

Neuroticism

Psychoticism

Five-factor model (FFM)

SELT-TEST PRACTICE QUIZ

From the Key Terms select that which best matches the following (Note: Not all Key Terms will be used.):

1. _____ One of Eysenck's three personality dimensions, describing an individual who is characterized by volatility, anxiousness, and worry

2. _____ Allport's term for the most superficial and transient category of traits included in his personality trait hierarchy

3. _____ The most overriding and stable characteristics of personality, according to Allport

4. _____ One of Eysenck's three personality dimensions describing an individual who is characterized as being distant, unfeeling, antisocial, and hostile

5. _____ Underlying traits, according to Cattell, that represent a distillation of more apparent surface traits

6. _____ The general term for personality characteristics exhibited by an individual that are relatively consistent over time and across situations

7. _____ A term from Cattell's research on personality describing numerous characteristics that are obvious to an observer

8. _____ Fairly common personality characteristics that, according to Allport, are the basic building blocks influencing behavior in many situations (like generosity, independence)

9. _____ The current most widely advocated model of personality within the trait perspective where all of personality is revealed by means of five basic dimensions

10. _____ One of Eysenck's three personality dimensions, representing a continuum with regard to how sociable and outgoing, or how reserved, an individual is

a. Traits
b. Cardinal traits
c. Central traits
d. Secondary traits
e. Surface traits
f. Source traits
g. Introversion-extraversion
h. Neuroticism
i. Psychoticism
j. Five-factor model (FFM)

11. The trait perspective adheres to the approach that personality is

    a.   a set of characteristics describing an individual that are fairly stable across time and situations.

    b.   a function of unconscious conflicts and desires that are out of our awareness and often out of our control.

    c.   a consequence of one's thinking and the development of behavioral schemas.

    d.   dictated predominantly by whatever environment we happen to be in.

12. According to Allport, traits that are pervasively dominant and that few people truly have are known as _____ traits.

    a.   source

    b.   central

    c.   cardinal

    d.   holistic

13. Which of the following is NOT one of the "Big Five" personality traits?

    a.   extraversion

    b.   psychoticism

    c.   neuroticism

    d.   agreeableness

14. Which of the following is NOT a criticism of the trait approach to personality?

    a.   Traits function more to describe a personality feature than to explain it.

    b.   The trait approach does not help us make our interpersonal world more predictable.

    c.   Situational factors need to be considered as an influence on personality.

    d.   Whether genetics or environment create personality traits is not clear.

ESSAY QUESTIONS

1. How can biological differences in nervous system functioning explain the variation we see among human personalities? Explain Eysenck's view and also another way to look at nervous system reactivity relative to the introvert/extravert personality continuum.

2. Discuss how the "Big Five" (or five-factor model) approach to personality is in large part a combination and integration of previous trait theorists' work.

ANSWER KEY

1. Neuroticism

2. Secondary traits

3. Cardinal traits

4. Psychoticism

5. Source traits

6. Traits

7. Surface traits

8. Central traits

9. Five-factor model (FFM)

10. Introversion-extraversion

11. a

12. c

13. b

14. b

SAMPLE ANSWERS TO ESSAY QUESTIONS

1. Eysenck was onto something in thinking that biology was a factor in human personality variation. Eysenck's characterization was that nervous system qualities differed. In other words, an introvert (one who does not appear to seek a great deal of stimulation) had a nervous system that was already near optimal level, and little further arousal was required to keep the body functioning in an ideal neurological state. Extraverts, according to Eysenck, needed more stimulation because their basic nervous system functioning was further below that optimal level. Thus, extraverts had a greater need for activity and sensory stimulation (relative to that of an introverted person) to bring their nervous system activity up to that ideal level. Another way of looking at a role for neurology, which is somewhat different from Eysenck's suggestion, is that perhaps the nervous system of an introverted individual reacts more strongly to stimuli than would the nervous system of a more extraverted individual. So, for an introverted person, smaller doses (so to speak) of sensory stimuli would be sufficient. Thus, again (but for a different reason), the introvert needs less apparent stimulation than the extravert.

2. The work of all trait theorists has been to determine the set of true personality characteristics or dimensions, which then provide the means to represent all personality variations in the human. Although the trait approach seems intuitive, and inherently useful, this is a task that is easier said than done. Gordon Allport was the first contemporary personality theorist to adopt a trait perspective. There were many different personality traits in his model, and these traits were classified according to how extensive their influence on an individual was. Cardinal traits were the broadest, and according to Allport few people really had characteristics of this nature. Mother Teresa, for example, who devoted her life to serving and helping the poor in India or Joan of Arc might be viewed as having this cardinal trait of spiritual commitment. Allport's category of central traits again included many characteristics—these are the terms we use every day (helpful, friendly, competitive, a loner). Allport's central traits and Cattell's surface traits both covered the same kinds of concepts. Cattell took these many traditional trait labels and distilled them, he believed, into the truly accurate underlying dimensions of personality. Thus, the many different traits identified by Allport and later Cattell (as surface traits) were reduced to a smaller (and eventually much smaller) set of personality dimensions. The "Big Five" approach has built upon the many and extensive trait investigations carried out by earlier personality trait researchers.

MODULE 12.3 THE SOCIAL-COGNITIVE PERSPECTIVE

LEARNING OBJECTIVES

After you have mastered the information in this unit, you will be able to:

*   Explain expectancies and subjective values

*   Describe reciprocal determinism

*   Describe situation and personal variables

OUTLINE

I.   Personality as Resulting from Learned Behaviors
     A.   Another view besides Freud's and that of trait theorists
     B.   Personality is learned, like all of behavior
     C.   Total experience is history of reinforcements, punishments

  D. Exhibited personality characteristics are those strengthened by family, culture
II. Contemporary Version: Social-Cognitive Theory
  A. Broader view regarding learned behavior
  B. Consider cognitive, social aspects of behavior
  C. Includes expectancies, values, and role of imitation
  D. Humans think about and act on world, not just react to it
III. Julian Rotter: The Locus of Control
  A. To understand personality, know history of reinforcements—and some cognitive aspects
  B. Expectancies—beliefs regarding end result of behavior
  C. Subjective value—personal importance placed on various outcomes
  D. Locus of control—belief regarding source of forces that ultimately determine outcomes
   1. Internal locus of control
    a) Individual believes outcomes are primarily in his or her own hands
    b) "Internals" more likely to succeed in school, cope with pain, recover more quickly from minor surgery
   2. External locus of control—individual believes outcomes are due to forces out of one's control that one cannot influence
IV. Albert Bandura: Reciprocal Determinism and the Role of Expectancies
  A. Reciprocal determinism—cognitions, behaviors, and environmental factors influence each other
  B. Importance of observational learning
  C. Two types of expectancies
   1. Outcome expectations—what we predict about a given behavior
   2. Efficacy expectations—beliefs in one's ability to perform a behavior
  D. Self-efficacy—belief in personal effectiveness
   1. People high in self-efficacy more likely to choose challenging tasks and to succeed at them
V. Walter Mischel: Situation versus Person Variables
  A. Theoretical model has overlap with Rotter, Bandura
  B. Behavior influenced both by situation and internal personal factors
  C. Person variables
   1. Expectancies, subjective values (same as Rotter's model)
   2. Competencies—knowledge and skills we possess
   3. Encoding strategies—personal way of interpreting an event
   4. Self-regulatory systems and plans—self-directed strategy for obtaining goals
  D. Environment and personal factors interact to produce behavior
  E. Interactions of emotions with personal factors also important
   1. Emotional state influences how we encode experiences, form expectations
   2. Way that events are interpreted and processed (how we encode experiences) is related to subsequent emotional state
VI. Evaluating the Social-Cognitive Model
  A. Continues long history of impact from learning theorists
  B. Ongoing reminder of importance of environmental factors
  C. Learning approach enhanced by adding cognitive factors
  D. Behavioral and social-cognitive perspectives in therapeutic treatments
  E. Important to see humans as inquisitive, active, initiating agents (not just passive respondents)
  F. Criticisms from other personality perspectives (Freudian, trait, humanistic)

SUMMARY

In this module you learn about a third perspective regarding the source of personality—that proposed by the social-cognitive theorists. Social cognition is primarily an outgrowth of the behavioral perspective. Thus, its history is that of the behavioral school with influence from Pavlov, Watson, and Skinner. According to behaviorists, we exhibit certain personality characteristics now because we have been reinforced (received a pleasant or desirable outcome) when we exhibited the same behaviors in the past. We refrain from manifesting other behaviors because when we acted in that fashion in the past, the behaviors either were ignored or met with an undesirable outcome. Note that whether or not a behavior is reinforced is unrelated, actually, to how "good" or "bad" that behavior is. A "good" behavioral characteristic such as trust may not be supported by environmental experience. Counter-productive behaviors may be reinforced, perhaps inadvertently, or by a subgroup that holds a more aberrant set of values. The behavioral perspective in personality teaches us that personality traits that seem bizarre may be manifested because somewhere in a person's history that type of behavior was reinforced. "Good" personality characteristics may have gone without notice.

The more recent version of behaviorism (social cognition) recognizes that humans don't just react to their environment by being passively shaped by environmental experiences, but they also think about experiences, develop expectations, and initiate activity. This expansion to the traditional behavioral approach is considered by nearly all as an improvement and a better representation of how humans actually are influenced by and interact with the environment.

Central to the social-cognitive perspective on personality is the notion that humans develop expectations regarding the results of a behavior they may contemplate doing. We can predict with some accuracy what outcomes to our behavior will be, and that understanding impacts, of course, whether we will actually do that behavior we are contemplating. Another feature helping to determine whether or not we will exhibit a behavior is the value, or worth, we place on a potential outcome. If the outcome is something that we very much want, it is far more likely we will exhibit the actions necessary to achieve it. Expectancies and subjective value are personality concepts introduced by Julian Rotter. In addition, those of us who feel more helpless (an external locus of control) regarding what happens in our lives will likely exhibit less effortful personality characteristics than those of us who believe (an internal locus of control) that we are masters of our fate.

Albert Bandura proposed a personality model involving reciprocal determinism; that is, behavior, environment, and cognitions all influence each other. Bandura is well known for establishing the impact of observational learning on human behavior. Bandura pointed out that an individual does not have to experience direct reinforcement (the view held by the behaviorists) in order to learn a behavior. We can, and do, learn much vicariously—through watching what others do and the consequences they experience. Thus, certainly, part of personality attributes are the result of watching those to whom we are exposed. Bandura concurred with Rotter's view that our personality is affected by expectations; however, Bandura advocated that expectancies are of two different kinds. We have expectations about (1) what the outcome of a given behavior will be, and (2) whether our abilities are sufficient to carry out that behavior. Both of these expectations come into play with regard to whether we show certain personality characteristics or not. Predictions about whether or not we have the ability for a given behavior are known as efficacy expectations. It should be noted that the determination of self-efficacy is somewhat subjective. Whether or not we believe we have certain abilities, and our degree of confidence in those abilities, is closely related to prior successes that involved these abilities. Keep in mind that how successful we are has very much to do with whether we believe we will be successful.

Walter Mischel is best known for advocating the important role of situational factors in behavior and personality. His views also by and large parallel those of Rotter and Bandura. He endorses the position that both environment (situation variables) and characteristics of the individual (person variables) influence behavior and thus personality. Mischel notes a total of five relevant person variables:

expectancies, subjective values (both of these as in Rotter's model), competencies, encoding strategies, and self-regulatory systems and plans. Recently, Mischel has emphasized the impact of emotions on person variables. Our emotional state may influence how we think, how we evaluate ourselves, and how we perceive the environment. The social-cognitive approach to personality certainly advances our understanding in this field. Criticisms of the social-cognitive perspective arise from those who hold other theoretical positions regarding personality such as the perspectives discussed elsewhere in this chapter.

KEY TERMS

Social-cognitive theory

Expectancies

Subjective value

Locus of control

Reciprocal determinism

Outcome expectations

Efficacy expectations

Situation variables

Person variables

SELF-TEST PRACTICE QUIZ

From the Key Terms select that which best matches the following:

1. _____ According to Mischel, an influence on our behavior derived from our history of experience with the environment

2. _____ A factor in personality advocated both by Rotter and Mischel, relating to the consequence one anticipates as the result of a certain action or behavior

3. _____ The notion proposed by Bandura where behavior, cognitions, and environmental experience all interact and influence each other

4. _____ A concept proposed by Rotter, relating to where we think the major force determining the outcome of events in our lives emanates from

5. _____ A term proposed by Bandura that conceptualizes how likely we think it is that we can accomplish certain behaviors

a. Social-cognitive theory

b. Expectancies

c. Subjective value

d. Locus of control

e. Reciprocal determinism

f. Outcome expectations

g. Efficacy expectations

h. Situation variables

i. Person variables

6. _____ A personality perspective that is based on learning principles with the addition of cognitive processes and the notion that humans take a proactive role in their world

7. _____ A component in the personality approach advocated by Mischel, emphasizing the attributes and capabilities an individual brings to a behavioral setting

8. _____ A factor in personality advocated both by Rotter and Mischel, relating to how meaningful or what worth is placed on achieving a possible outcome

9. _____ A term proposed by Bandura that conceptualizes how likely we believe it to be that a certain end result will occur

10. Social-cognitive theory builds on our understanding that a powerful influence on behavior and personality
    a. is derived from our deep-seated fears and anxieties.
    b. involves actions and attributes we have manifested in the past and whether the end result of these was a positive or unpleasant experience.
    c. is derived from unconscious influences we are not really aware of.
    d. results from our striving to be the best person we can be.

11. Which of the following statements best represents the concept of an external locus of control?
    a. "If I study harder, I can improve my grades."
    b. "People can improve their health if they exercise more."
    c. "Getting the right job is simply a matter of being in the right time at the right place."
    d. "You can't just sit around waiting for the right person to come along—you have to go out and make it happen."

12. Recognizing the important influence that emotions have on how we evaluate ourselves and our environment was emphasized by the personality theorist
    a. Julian Rotter.
    b. Sigmund Freud.
    c. Albert Bandura.
    d. Walter Mischel.

13. How meaningful or important a certain outcome is to us is known as its
    a. efficacy expectation.
    b. outcome expectation.
    c. subjective value.
    d. personal value.

14. Which of the following is NOT a criticism of the social-cognitive perspective?
    a. It encourages us to view people as active problem-solvers.
    b. It has given rise to many widely-used therapeutic techniques.
    c. It has increased our understanding of how personality can be shaped by learning.
    d. It provides additional insight into the role of the unconscious in motivating behavior.

15. You decide you will greet whomever you encounter with a positive attitude. You smile and nod politely at the woman in line ahead of you at the grocery store. She smiles back and moves her cart in order to give you more room. This experience exemplifies Bandura's notion of

a. self-efficacy.
b. reciprocal determinism.
c. outcome expectations.
d. self-regulatory systems.

ESSAY QUESTION

1. What influence has social-cognitive theory had on psychological therapy approaches?

ANSWER KEY

1. Situation variables

2. Expectancies

3. Reciprocal determinism

4. Locus of control

5. Efficacy expectations

6. Social-cognitive theory

7. Person variables

8. Subjective value

9. Outcome expectations

10. b

11. c

12. d

13. c

14. d

15. b

SAMPLE ANSWER TO ESSAY QUESTION

1. The emphasis of social-cognitive theory and of behavioral theory upon which it is based is that everything about ourselves, our behavior, and our personality has been learned and is a consequence of our experience with the environment. This ideological perspective allows for two things within the field of psychology. One, it allows for a great deal of hope regarding therapy, for if poor behaviors and personality characteristics have been learned, they can be unlearned, and, better yet, more preferable behavioral and personality attributes can be learned instead. If the environment is fostering undesirable characteristics, we can change the environment and thus change the behavior. This is a very encouraging feature. Second, since influences on behavior and personality all exist in the real and tangible world, it is far easier to pin down what these influences are, describe them, and understand exactly how they have impact on what we do. Again, knowing precisely what we are dealing with, and being able to access it, helps us increase influences that are positive and minimize or eliminate the environmental sources producing undesirable results. Personality characteristics, then, are much more manageable.

Because of this understanding, social-cognitive and behavioral theories do play a substantial role in psychological treatment. Behavioral therapies examine the environment within which an individual is functioning. What seems to foster undesirable personality characteristics? Are there hidden reinforcers that, perhaps unbeknownst to us, keep it going? Where are incidences of desirable attributes formed? What leads to their formation? We can reproduce desirable characteristics elsewhere, and in others, when we know the experiential factors that lead to their manifestation. Cognitive-behavioral therapy adds the understanding that we need to include how people think about their behavior and about their experiences. Again, if we can change the thinking, there is a great likelihood we can change detrimental attributes and behaviors.

Certainly not everything about personality is a consequence of what we have learned or how we think about what we have experienced. There surely are other influences on personality as well. But, since any way that we can provide effective therapy is of value, we might as well use the sources we know of that are fairly easily identifiable and are close at hand.

MODULE 12.4 THE HUMANISTIC PERSPECTIVE

LEARNING OBJECTIVES

After you have mastered the information in this unit, you will be able to:

- Describe self-theory

- Explain the role of unconditional positive regard in the development of self-esteem

- Discuss the role of culture in self-identity

OUTLINE

I.   Humanistic Perspective
    A.   Conscious choice and personal freedom are crucial
    B.   Our ability to know ourselves, make choices, gives life meaning and direction
II. Carl Rogers: The Importance of Self
    A.   Self-theory—Rogers's theory of personality
        1.   The self is the source that directs how we experience the world
        2.   Inner drive leads us towards self-actualization (being all we can be)
    B.   Unconditional positive regard—acceptance of any person's basic worth
    C.   Conditional positive regard—valuing granted only when certain standards met
    D.   Self-ideals—sense of who we should be (sense of self-esteem is closely related)
III. Abraham Maslow: Self-Actualization
    A.   Humans capable of needs, achievements well beyond primitive instincts
    B.   We strive to develop our unique potentials
IV. Evaluating the Humanistic Perspective
    A.   Tremendous impact—focus on inner identity, self-direction, meaning in life
    B.   Emphasis on subjective, conscious experiences (e.g., our interpretation of them)
    C.   Criticisms
        1.   Difficult to study scientifically
        2.   Emphasis on self-fulfillment may lead people to become self-indulgent
V.   Exploring Psychology: Culture and Self-Identity
    A.   Culture influences sense of self
    B.   Collectivistic culture—self is defined as member of a group
    C.   Individualistic culture—self is defined in terms of unique, distinctive characteristics
    D.   Status and how it is attained are determined by culture

SUMMARY

This module discusses yet a fourth, and equally worthwhile, approach to personality that is based on our sense of who we are. Humanists believe individuals are striving towards self-actualization, which is the maximum fulfillment of our potential. Since, to a humanist, everyone is unique, only you yourself can truly know who you are and where you want to be headed. A core aspect of the humanistic view is unconditional positive regard. This means we treat all others, and ourselves, with respect and acceptance. This acceptance is appropriate whether or not we like or agree with characteristics exhibited by another. They are permitted their place in the world, as we are permitted and need ours. It is important to honor other people's views, even though they are not our own, because we know we need to be true to our own sense of self in order to progress. We need to discover who we are, like ourselves, and allow ourselves to follow the path that seems right for us. Respect and regard for ourselves, and respect and regard for others, should be approximately equally valued and practiced. We have a sense of ourselves (self-concept) and a sense of who we want to be (self-ideal). Self-esteem is a function of how closely these two match. We need to have regard for ourselves (self-esteem) in order to function well. The drive towards self-actualization is an inner need inasmuch as our striving toward self-actualization impacts our personality. Personality characteristics are determined from within. The humanistic view emphasizes the importance of having meaning and direction in our lives; thus the subjective experience of events and relationships is important. How the self interacts with the world and views the world determines how an individual will behave in the world.

Culture is a major influence on our sense of self; thus, culture is a strong determinant of personality. A basic difference between cultures is whether they are collectivistic (emphasis is on the group and community values) or individualistic (emphasis is on the individual and autonomy, self-worth).

KEY TERMS

Self-theory

Unconditional positive regard

Conditional positive regard

Self-ideals

Collectivistic culture

Individualistic culture

SELF-TEST PRACTICE QUIZ

From the Key Terms select that which best matches the following:

1. _____ A cultural view more typical of Asia and South America where the greater emphasis is placed on needs and roles within the communal group

2. _____ A theory of personality proposed by Carl Rogers emphasizing that the self is the force that interprets and acts upon the world

3. _____ Value and acceptance are accorded only when an individual meets our standards or does what we specifically direct

a. Self-theory

b. Unconditional positive regard

c. Conditional positive regard

d. Self-ideals

e. Collectivistic culture

f. Individualistic culture

4. _____   A cultural view more typical of the United States and other western countries where the greater emphasis is placed on the individual and his or her distinctive achievements

5. _____   A component in the theory proposed by Carl Rogers, which suggests the person we would like to be or think we ought to be

6. _____   Treating all individuals with respect and valuing whether or not they mirror the behaviors and principles we hold as our own standards

7. Knowing our true selves and trying to make full use of who we are is known as

   a. achievement orientation.
   b. unconditional positive regard.
   c. self-actualization.
   d. achievement motivation.

8. When we let children know that Mom or Dad will be unhappy if they don't try out for baseball or the school play, we are conveying a message of _____ to our children.

   a. unconditional positive regard
   b. action-oriented motivation
   c. energizing momentum
   d. conditional positive regard

9. According to Carl Rogers, our sense of self-esteem is based on

   a. how close we come to meeting our self-ideals.
   b. how much our parents and friends love us.
   c. our level of conditional positive regard.
   d. how much we are in touch with our unconscious.

10. If your status among your social group just rocketed up because you bought a Lamborghini, you probably live in a(n)

   a. collectivistic culture.
   b. individualistic culture.
   c. community located near a speedway.
   d. community located in an oil-producing state.

11. One drawback of the humanistic perspective is that it

   a. suggests that people look within for a sense of direction.
   b. advocates an attitude of respect towards all other living organisms, regardless of behavior.
   c. emphasizes the importance of meaningfulness and purpose in life, despite the demands of one's employment obligations.
   d. can lead to a focus on self that becomes excessive.

ESSAY QUESTION

1. Culture is certainly an influence on personality. How can extremes in cultural orientation cause problems for an individual or among family members?

ANSWER KEY

1. Collectivistic culture

2. Self-theory

3. Conditional positive regard

4. Individualistic culture

5. Self-ideals

6. Unconditional positive regard

7. c

8. d

9. a

10. b

11. d

SAMPLE ANSWER TO ESSAY QUESTION

1. Extreme collectivism or extreme individualism causes problems because the cultural attitude impacts personality. In an extremely collectivistic society, the individual and his or her identity become lost. There is no point in doing something individually remarkable because recognition for the unique achievement will not occur. Excessive individualism may lead a person to be concerned only with his or her accomplishments and personal gains. Regard for the well-being of others will be lost. Extreme views within a culture may also present problems when a family member has social contacts with other cultures. The end result may be a conflict involving cultural traditions and family values.

MODULE 12.5 PERSONALITY TESTS

LEARNING OBJECTIVES

After you have mastered the information in this unit, you will be able to:

- Describe self-report personality inventories

- Describe projective tests of personality

OUTLINE

I. History of Attempts to Measure Personality
   A. Character of Darwin and others judged on basis of physical features
   B. Phrenology—judging mental and personal attributes based on bumps on the head
II. Self-Report Personality Inventories
   A. Are objective tests; "yes/no" or "agree/disagree" format
   B. Minnesota Multiphasic Personality Inventory (MMPI)
      1. MMPI-2 has 567 true-false questions; yields scores on ten clinical scales
      2. Originally constructed to help diagnose psychological disorders
   C. Evaluation of self-report personality tests
      1. Reliability and validity supported by research
      2. Important to not base entire diagnosis on one test

III.   Projective Tests—use unstructured, ambiguous, open-ended stimuli
    A.   Rorschach test
        1.   As a child, Rorschach found inkblots interpreted differently
        2.   Scoring is complex; results must be interpreted by test administrator
    B.   Thematic Apperception Test (TAT)—stories about TAT's ambiguous scenes may reveal aspects of personality, psychological issues
    C.   Evaluation of projective tests—drawbacks include subjective nature of scoring, possible "pull" in features of ambiguous stimuli

SUMMARY

In this module, you learn about the avenues we have for measuring someone's personality. There are more objective approaches such as the MMPI (Minnesota Multiphasic Personality Inventory) and more subjective personality tests such as the Rorschach (inkblot) and TAT (Thematic Apperception Test). The MMPI consists of a great number of questions to each of which the respondent indicates *true* (it applies to the respondent) or *false* (it does not apply). The MMPI was originally designed to detect mental disorders, but it is now a very widely used personality test. The Rorschach test and TAT are useful too since they are more open-ended and reveal themes in a test-taker's responses. A problem with subjective tests, however, is that much rests on how they are scored. Interpretation is mostly in the hands of the test administrator. Self-report inventories (such as the MMPI) show consistent evidence of validity and reliability. In addition, these objective tests not only indicate scores on mental and clinical scales, but they reveal much about the test-taker's personality and interests.

KEY TERMS

Phrenology

Personality tests

Self-report personality inventories

Objective tests

Standard scores

Projective tests

SELF-TEST PRACTICE QUIZ

From the Key Terms select that which best matches the following:

1.   _____   A type of personality test where the test-taker is free to choose among test responses

2.   _____   Scores that have been converted to interpretable differences relative to the average score

3.   _____   Determining personality based on the pattern of bumps on the head

4.   _____   Tests that have a consistent and standardized method for scoring (such as the MMPI)

a.   Phrenology

b.   Personality tests

c.   Self-report personality inventories

d.   Objective tests

e.   Standard scores

f.   Projective tests

5. ＿＿＿＿＿ Tests such as the Rorschach and TAT, where scoring is more a matter of interpretation

6. ＿＿＿＿＿ Tests to evaluate fairly enduring behavioral features that characterize an individual

7. Scores on the MMPI are obtained by comparing the test-taker's responses to

   a. scores of other individuals taking the personality test at the same time.
   b. the mean and standard deviations of test-takers from the current year.
   c. patterns of responses reported by diagnostic groups and normal controls.
   d. subjective interpretations provided by the test administrator.

8. If you were asked to tell stories about some ambiguous scenes, you just took the

   a. MMPI.
   b. Rorschach test.
   c. Phrenology test.
   d. TAT.

ESSAY QUESTION

1. Why must we be careful about the results of any personality test?

ANSWER KEY

1. Self-report personality inventories

2. Standard scores

3. Phrenology

4. Objective tests

5. Projective tests

6. Personality tests

7. c

8. d

SAMPLE ANSWER TO ESSAY QUESTION

1. We always need to be careful about the results of any personality test because that is just one source of information about an individual. Self-report tests allow the respondent to reply however he or she wishes, and the responses may not always be forthright. A variety of indicators regarding personality and psychological dimensions should be used.

MODULE 12.6 APPLICATION: BUILDING SELF-ESTEEM

LEARNING OBJECTIVES

After you have mastered the information in this unit, you will be able to:

- Describe some ways of building self-esteem

OUTLINE

I.   Ways We Can Strengthen Our Self-Esteem
    A.   Acquire competencies—self-esteem is related to ability for accomplishments
    B.   Set reasonable goals
    C.   Have confidence in your abilities and likelihood of success
    D.   Create a sense of meaningfulness—think of what is really important to you
    E.   Be willing to accept level less than perfectionist
    F.   Moderate need for approval from others

SUMMARY

The humanistic school in particular emphasizes how important it is that we have a good sense of self-esteem. Self-esteem is our confidence in our selves and our belief that we are capable and effective individuals. Self-esteem is closely related to the successes we have achieved over the course of our lives. Of course, part of being successful is believing in our self-efficacy and choosing tasks that are at a level appropriate for us. The same holds true for developing a sense of self-esteem in children.

We can increase our sense of self-esteem by making sure we have skills and abilities that we want to have. It is important to be good at something, and everyone can be good at something. It may take a little effort to develop skills leading to proficiency. We want to set reasonable goals—our achievements should be geared to a level that we can realistically achieve. It is important to choose tasks at our level and believe that we will succeed. Meaningfulness in our lives and in our work is related to our sense of self-esteem. If we believe in ourselves, have developed some skills and proficiencies that we find useful, and find life meaningful, we will achieve enough of a sense of confidence that we will be less dependent upon the approval of others. We can set our own reasonable standards for achievement.

CHAPTER 12 APPLICATION EXERCISE

What do you think shapes our personality? Why are you the way you are? Take a few minutes to jot down a brief description of your characteristics. Ask a friend to add his or her list regarding your personality.

Now—analyze your personality. Review the different approaches to personality discussed in this chapter. Which has influenced you the most? Unconscious drives? A cluster of fairly stable traits you may have inherited? Habits and actions you imitate from seeing behavior in others? Situational factors? Characteristics that show themselves as you move towards self-actualization? Come up with your own explanation for personality and what best explains the characteristics you exhibit.

CHAPTER 13

Psychological Disorders

In Chapter 13 you learn about some of the many psychological disorders that are considered to constitute abnormal behavior. In the United States and many other countries, the *Diagnostic and Statistical Manual of Mental Disorders (DSM-IV-TR)* is used to help make the determination of psychological disorder. Diagnosing someone as mentally ill is not easy. We look for a set of characteristics to help decide possible psychological problems, but psychologically healthy people can show these characteristics at times also. To make a diagnosis, mental health professionals look for unusualness, degree of social deviance, evidence of emotional distress, maladaptive behavior, dangerousness, and, key to the severe psychotic disorders, distortions of reality.

Psychological disorders are grouped into categories, and disorders common to a classification share a pool of psychological symptoms. Abnormal behaviors presented in this chapter include anxiety disorders, dissociative disorders, somatoform disorders, mood disorders, schizophrenia, and personality disorders. When evaluating a person for psychological disturbance, we must always consider cultural factors. It is true that some behaviors may be accepted, or even expected, in some cultures and not in others. Also, the way in which symptoms are manifested may vary by culture.

Only recently have people with mental illnesses been treated somewhat benignly. For most of the history of humanity, people with psychological disorders were viewed as being possessed. They were thought to be controlled by supernatural forces or to be literally inhabited by demons. The standard treatment for "possession" was exorcism. More recently, including in the history of the United States, there was great concern about witches and witchcraft. People believed to be witches were persecuted and often burned at the stake. Finally, beginning about in the eighteenth century, we took a more accurate and compassionate look at psychological disorders as we began to learn more about the functioning of the human body in general. Due to medical advances, researchers began to regard psychological disorders as having similarities to physical disorders and illnesses. Although there were not many available options for actually treating psychological disorders at that time, at least the care provided to individuals suffering from mental illness became more humane than it had been.

Probably the most widespread disorders relating to Westernized societies are anxiety (in the classification of anxiety disorders) and depression (classified among the mood disorders). Most people will experience a psychological disorder at some time in their lives or certainly know someone who has. People suffering anxiety disorders tend to be agitated, cannot find peace, and often are consumed with perpetual worry. Phobias, panic attacks, and obsessive-compulsive disorder (OCD) are also included in the anxiety disorders classification. Dissociative disorders include dissociative amnesia, and dissociative identity disorder (which was formerly classified as multiple personality disorder). Somatoform disorders involve individuals who experience physical problems, but there is no obvious underlying physical cause (hypochondriasis is one example). The category of mood disorders (of which depression is one) also includes bipolar disorder, which in the past was referred to as manic-depression. Mood disorders affect our emotional state to the extent that we cannot function effectively. Schizophrenia is the most serious psychological disorder, in that it is classified as a psychotic disorder (the individual has truly lost touch with reality), it tends to affect individuals over the course of their entire lives, and its treatment consumes the bulk of our mental health expenditures. Personality disorders are the last classification of disorders presented, and the most-researched personality disorder is the antisocial personality (individuals with this disorder were previously known as psychopaths or sociopaths).

What are the causes of psychological disorders? The nature and manifestation of psychological disorders is complex, and as such we expect that a variety of factors contribute, probably in combination, to the emergence of the problem. Genetic, biological, cognitive, environmental, and unconscious influences all appear to be implicated in the experience of psychological disorder. With ongoing research we are continuing to learn more about these troubling, yet fascinating, disorders.

MODULE 13.1 WHAT IS ABNORMAL BEHAVIOR?

LEARNING OBJECTIVES

After you have mastered the information in this unit, you will be able to:

- Explain the criteria used to determine whether behavior is abnormal

- Discuss the major models of abnormal behavior

- Define psychological disorder

OUTLINE

I.   Charting the Boundaries Between Normal and Abnormal Behavior
    A.   Criteria for abnormal behavior—no behaviors exclusive to psychological disorder
        1.   Unusualness—experienced by only a few
        2.   Social deviance—not considered socially acceptable
        3.   Emotional distress—when prolonged, excessive, inappropriate
        4.   Maladaptive behavior—causes distress, self-defeating, self-destructive
        5.   Dangerousness—must consider within social context
        6.   Faulty perceptions or interpretations of reality—hallucinations, delusions, distortions of reality
        7.   Professionals use several criteria to make determination
    B.   Cultural bases of abnormal behavior
        1.   Always must consider social, cultural context when making evaluation
        2.   Disorders may take different forms in different cultures
        3.   Culture-bound syndromes—limited to occurring within just one culture
        4.   Behaviors may also be considered disordered or not, depending on era in history (e.g., evaluation of homosexuality)
    C.   Applying the criteria—apply several criteria in order to accurately evaluate
II.   Models of Abnormal Behavior
    A.   Early beliefs
        1.   Ancient times through Middle Ages—disturbed people thought possessed by demons or controlled by supernatural forces
        2.   Treatment was exorcism, or more severe
    B.   The medical model
        1.   Eighteenth and nineteenth centuries—medical advances
        2.   Shift to belief that mental disturbance is an illness
    C.   Psychological models
        1.   Psychodynamic (Freud)—disturbance due to unconscious conflict, stemming from childhood
        2.   Behavioral—disturbed, maladaptive behaviors learned the same way normal behaviors learned

3. Humanistic
   a) Disturbance due to encountering roadblocks on path to self-actualization
   b) Individuals have lost touch with inner self, over-concern with standards of others, distorted self-image

4. Cognitive
   a) Disturbances due to irrational, distorted thinking
   b) Interpreting negatively, exaggerating negative consequences

D. The sociocultural model
   1. Must evaluate in terms of social, cultural context
   2. Problem may lie with social ills, failures of society
   3. Labeling sufferers results in social prejudices; compounds problem

E. The biopsychosocial model
   1. Many useful models to explain abnormal behavior
   2. Disturbance is the result of combination, interaction of factors (including psychological, biological, sociocultural)
   3. Diathesis-stress model
      a) Diathesis is a predisposition, vulnerability (genetic or psychological)
      b) High stress triggers disorder, low stress does not

III. What Are Psychological Disorders?
   A. Basic characteristics of psychological disorders
      1. Also known as mental disorders, mental illnesses
      2. Disturbances of behavior, mood, thoughts, or perceptions, which impair functioning
   B. How many are affected?
      1. Fifty percent of Americans have a diagnosable disorder at some point
   C. How are psychological disorders classified?
      1. *Diagnostic and Statistical Manual of Mental Disorders (DSM-IV-TR)*
      2. Descriptions, diagnostic criteria for every recognized psychological disorder
      3. Multiaxial system—practitioner examines patient on many dimensions
      4. Widely used; some concern that reliability, validity not fully established; may rely too much on medical model

SUMMARY

In this module you are introduced to psychological disorder. Making the diagnosis of abnormal behavior is not easy because there are no human behaviors that are exclusive to the "disturbed" category. Psychologists look at a variety of criteria and use a combination of these criteria in their attempt to determine psychological status. Patterns of behavior for an individual are evaluated in terms of how unusual, how deviant, and how emotionally stressful they are. Psychologists also consider whether the behavior patterns are maladaptive (do they impede the individual's ability to function effectively?), dangerous to self or others, or involve distortions of reality. All of these factors are considered together, and a mental health professional almost always relies on the DSM-IV-TR *(Diagnostic and Statistical Manual of Mental Disorders)* as well, to help make a final diagnosis. The DSM-IV-TR lists every recognized psychological disorder, a description of that disorder, and standards for diagnosing whether or not that disorder is present in an individual. The DSM-IV-TR categorizes disorders by major groupings (e.g., whether the disorder affects mainly personality, or mood, or anxiousness, and the like). Increasingly we recognize that an awareness of the impact of culture is crucial in evaluating mental illness. Truthfully, some mental illnesses are acceptable in some societies (hearing voices, for example), and considered disordered in others. Some psychological problems take differing forms depending on the society. For example, among the Chinese, depression is manifested via headaches or other physical symptoms rather than by feelings of sadness as we would find in the United States.

The approach to and treatment of psychological disorders continues to improve, but disturbed behaviors were not always viewed as benignly even as they are today. The belief during most of human history was that mental illness was due to an individual being possessed—either controlled by unknown spirits or literally inhabited by demons. The accepted treatment was exorcism to rid the body of these forces. Even more severe means were utilized if exorcism seemed not to work. Beginning in the seventeenth century, substantial medical advances helped us understand much more about human functioning. For the first time, psychological disorder was approached in the same way as physical illnesses. This was the beginning of more humane treatment of the psychologically disturbed.

There are a variety of explanations regarding the cause of psychological disorder. These explanations parallel the various philosophical perspectives that comprise different approaches within psychology. The psychodynamic model, based on the views of Sigmund Freud, interprets psychological disorder as stemming from early childhood problems. These difficulties and conflicts are buried deep within the unconscious. The behavioral model, not surprisingly, points to maladaptive learning as the source of psychological problems. Poor behaviors are learned in the same way that more effective behaviors are learned. To humanists, psychological difficulties arise when we lose contact with our inner selves. Only our inner self knows the way to the self-actualization we seek, so when we lose clear contact with our inner self we have lost our sense of guidance and meaningfulness in the world. Cognitivists find psychological problems to be the result of distorted and self-destructive thinking. Change the thinking, and you change the maladaptive behavior. The most widespread contemporary approach to mental disorders is the biopsychosocial model. This model, as its name implies, looks at the combination of influences (genetic, biological, social, emotional, cultural, psychological) and how they interact to produce behavior.

KEY TERMS

Hallucinations

Delusions

Culture-bound syndromes

Dhat syndrome

Medical model

Biopsychosocial model

Diathesis-stress model

Diathesis

Psychological disorders

SELF-TEST PRACTICE QUIZ

From the Key Terms select that which best matches the following:

1. _____ An explanation for psychological disorder proposing that an individual may have a predisposition (usually genetic) to a disorder, but environmental experiences determine if the disorder becomes manifested

2. _____ An approach to psychological disturbance that interprets it as a physical disorder

3. _____ Distortions of reality that are manifested as false beliefs

4. _____ The general term for mental illnesses; distinctive patterns of abnormal behavior that impair functioning or cause distress

5. _____ A contemporary explanation for psychological disorder involving an integrated combination of known factors (emotional, genetic, environmental, and so forth)

6. _____ A predisposition or vulnerability

7. _____ Psychological disorders that only occur within a specific culture

8. _____ A psychological disorder found primarily in India involving excessive concern with losing semen during sleep

9. _____ Distortions of reality that involve perceiving stimuli that do not really exist

a. Hallucinations

b. Delusions

c. Culture-bound syndromes

d. Dhat syndrome

e. Medical model

f. Biopsychosocial model

g. Diathesis-stress model

h. Diathesis

i. Psychological disorders

10. Diagnosing psychological disorders is difficult because
    a. behaviors that are considered disturbed in one culture may not be viewed as abnormal in another.
    b. there are no human behaviors that are exhibited exclusively by psychologically disturbed individuals.
    c. some criteria used for diagnosis (for example, unusualness) may describe highly desirable behaviors as well.
    d. all of the above are factors when diagnosing psychological disorders.

11. Which of the following is NOT a criterion commonly used to distinguish normal from abnormal behavior?

    a. social deviance
    b. maladaptive behavior
    c. emotional distress
    d. legality

12. Whereas depression is manifested among Western cultures as the experience of sadness and lethargy, for Asian cultures, such as the Chinese, it is likely to appear in the form of

    a. stomach aches and ulcers.
    b. headaches and fatigue.
    c. muscle aches or tension.
    d. sleep difficulties.

13. Considering psychological disorder as an illness somewhat along the lines of physical sickness first appeared during the

    a. Middle Ages.
    b. sixteenth and seventeenth centuries.
    c. eighteenth and nineteenth centuries.
    d. twentieth and twenty-first centuries.

14. Attributing the cause of psychological disorder to poor or destructive behaviors learned as a consequence of reinforcements and punishments is a feature of the _____ model.

    a. cognitive
    b. psychodynamic
    c. humanistic
    d. behavioral

15. Attributing the cause of psychological disorder as resulting from a combination of genetic, environmental, and psychological factors is a feature of the _____ model.

    a. medical
    b. humanistic
    c. cognitive
    d. biopsychosocial

16. A vulnerability or predisposition to a disorder that increases the likelihood that this disorder will develop in an individual is known as a(n) _____.

    a. anxiety disorder
    b. diathesis
    c. immunological deficiency
    d. psychological propensity

17. The DSM is composed of five axes. What is the purpose of having this multiaxial system?

    a. It provides a way to distinguish different categories of disorders.
    b. It provides information on dealing with different insurance companies.
    c. It asks practitioners to conduct a comprehensive evaluation of the patient.
    d. It tells practitioners how to best treat their clients.

ESSAY QUESTION

1. We have a number of different models, or explanations, for abnormal behavior, such as the medical, psychological, and biopsychosocial models. What are the various psychological models, and how do they differ from each other?

ANSWER KEY

1.   Diathesis-stress model

2.   Medical model

3.   Delusions

4.   Psychological disorders

5.   Biopsychosocial model

6.   Diathesis

7.   Culture-bound syndromes

8.   Dhat syndrome

9.   Hallucinations

10.   d

11.   d

12.   b

13.   c

14.   d

15.   d

16.   b

17.   c

SAMPLE ANSWER TO ESSAY QUESTION

1.   We have a number of explanations regarding what mental illnesses are and why they occur. There are four different psychological explanations reflecting the major perspectives within the field of psychology. The historically earliest perspective was that advocated by Sigmund Freud (the psychodynamic model). His view was that the source of motivation and most of one's personality lay deep in the unconscious out of our awareness. Personality was comprised of often-conflicting components, according to Freud. Thus, the psychodynamic model explains psychological disorders as caused by deep-seated, unconscious conflicts often emanating from early childhood. Behaviorists, believing that everything about us is the result of learning through environmental experience, see disturbed behaviors as acquired the same way normal behaviors are acquired—through being reinforced, or not, for characteristics that we exhibit. Humanistic psychologists propose that disturbed behaviors arise from having lost one's way, so to speak, on the path towards self-actualization. Disorders can also result from a great disparity between what we think of ourselves and what we want to be. Cognitive psychologists trace psychological disturbances to errors in thinking and interpretation. Negative and irrational thoughts can lead us to misconstrue facts or a situation and then act inappropriately or ineffectively. Since all of these psychological models of abnormal behavior highlight important influences on human functioning, it is no wonder that a combined approach (the biopsychosocial model) is now taking center stage.

MODULE 13.2 ANXIETY DISORDERS

LEARNING OBJECTIVES

After you have mastered the information in this unit, you will be able to:

- Describe the various types of anxiety disorders

- Explain the causal factors implicated in anxiety disorders

OUTLINE

I.   Types of Anxiety Disorders
    A.   Basic characteristics of anxiety disorders
        1.   Most commonly experienced psychological disorders
        2.   Formerly classified as neuroses
        3.   Characterized by excessive, inappropriate agitation; impedes one's ability to function
    B.   Phobias
        1.   Affect seven to eleven percent of population
        2.   Irrational or excessive fear of object or situation
        3.   Types of phobic disorders
            a)   Social phobia—fear of being with others, speaking in public
            b)   Specific phobia—such as acrophobia (fear of heights), claustrophobia (fear of enclosed spaces)
            c)   Agoraphobia—fear of open spaces, going out in public
        4.   Individuals usually aware of problem; still cannot face source of fear
    C.   Panic disorder
        1.   Sudden episodes of sheer terror (panic attacks)
        2.   Many physiological symptoms; feeling as if one is dying or having a heart attack
        3.   Experience can be triggered by particular situations
    D.   Generalized anxiety disorder (GAD)
        1.   Pervasive, persistent fear, not related to specific object or location
        2.   Unrest, constant worry, feelings of dread and foreboding
    E.   Obsessive-compulsive disorder (OCD)
        1.   Behaviors or thoughts repeated over and over again
        2.   Obsessions are persistent thoughts; compulsions are rituals or repetitive behaviors
II. Causes of Anxiety Disorders
    A.   Biological factors
        1.   Anxiety disorders run in families—suggests a genetic link
        2.   Brain functioning may result in sense of alarm in some people
        3.   Overactivity in certain parts of the brain
    B.   Psychological factors
        1.   Classical conditioning—neutral stimulus paired with one that is frightening
        2.   Operant conditioning—negative reinforcement through relief of avoiding situation, engaging in compulsive behaviors
        3.   Cognitive models—possible misinterpretation of bodily cues; excessive, unrealistic concerns about others' social judgments

SUMMARY

In this module you learn about the largest class of psychological disorders, the anxiety disorders. Anxiety is a state of upset, unrest, worry, and the inability to relax. Anxiety may be chronic, as in generalized anxiety disorder, or short-term, such as the experience of a panic attack. Anxiety that is in response to a specific object or setting is known as a phobia. Phobias are unfounded, irrational, excessive fears. Obsessive-compulsive disorder is also classified as an anxiety disorder because the repetitive thoughts or behaviors are believed to be triggered by states of anxiety. Engaging in compulsive behaviors is thought to relieve anxiety, at least temporarily.

There are probably both biological and psychological causes leading to anxiety disorders. Biological causes include differences in activity level in parts of the brain as well as a genetic linkage (as indicated by twin and adoptee studies). Psychological factors including learning maladaptive (usually fear) responses to harmless situations because we have had an unpleasant experience in that kind of situation earlier. Avoiding anxiety-producing situations inadvertently reinforces the continuance of the avoidance behavior because the reduction in anxiety is a desirable outcome. Why go out in public when it is so stressful? Staying at home and watching television is much less anxiety-producing. A cognitive explanation for anxiety disorders is also a possibility. Some individuals may cognitively misinterpret signals from their bodies. A minor reaction or low level of arousal may be misinterpreted as signaling a serious threat or cause for alarm.

KEY TERMS

Anxiety disorders

Phobia

Social phobia

Specific phobia

Acrophobia

Claustrophobia

Agoraphobia

Panic disorder

Generalized anxiety disorder (GAD)

Obsessive-compulsive disorder (OCD)

Anxiety sensitivity

SELF-TEST PRACTICE QUIZ

From the Key Terms select that which best matches the following (Note: Not every Key Term will be used.):

1. _____ An anxiety disorder where the individual repeatedly engages in unproductive thoughts or ineffective behaviors

2. _____ An anxiety disorder involving excessive, irrational fear of enclosed spaces

3. _____ The experience of episodes of intense terror; overwhelming physical distress (but no underlying medical cause)

4. _____ A class of psychological disorders involving the episodic or chronic experience of agitation, worry, or unrest

5. _____ Feelings of unfounded, intense fear when faced with meeting or speaking with others

6. _____ An anxiety disorder where one is irrationally and excessively afraid of heights

7. _____ Intense, irrational fear in response to a particular object or situation

8. _____ Excessive, unfounded fear in response to objects or situations

9. _____ An anxiety disorder characterized by excessive fear of entering the public domain

10. _____ A persistent state of anxiousness and worry not connected to any single cause or situation

a. Anxiety disorders

b. Phobia

c. Social phobia

d. Specific phobia

e. Acrophobia

f. Claustrophobia

g. Agoraphobia

h. Panic disorder

i. Generalized anxiety disorder (GAD)

j. Obsessive-compulsive disorder (OCD)

k. Anxiety sensitivity

11. Someone who is afraid to enter open spaces where there are people and who eventually often becomes afraid simply to leave the home is suffering from
    a. social phobia.
    b. panic attack.
    c. agoraphobia.
    d. generalized anxiety disorder.

12. Someone who thinks or speaks the same phrase over and over again and who may engage in the same rituals precisely and repeatedly is suffering from _____, which is included in the broader psychological category of _____.
    a. phobic disorder; anxiety disorders
    b. obsessive-compulsive disorder; affective disorders
    c. generalized anxiety disorder; personality disorders
    d. obsessive-compulsive disorder; anxiety disorders
13. The individual who experiences an excessive, irrational fear of heights is suffering from
    a. agoraphobia.
    b. claustrophobia.
    c. acrophobia.
    d. arachnophobia.
14. Which of the following has been proposed as a biological cause for anxiety disorders?
    a. Heredity
    b. Overactivity in parts of the brain
    c. Biochemical changes in the brain which trigger internal alarms
    d. All of the above
15. Classical conditioning is proposed as a way phobias may be learned. If one has an irrational fear of stuffed teddy bears, it is possible that the presence of a stuffed teddy bear accompanied
    a. a pleasant or joyous experience, which has long been forgotten.
    b. an experience of pain or trauma, which may or may not have been forgotten.
    c. stuffed lions, zebras, and giraffes received as birthday gifts.
    d. the purchase of another, but smaller, stuffed teddy bear.
16. A cognitive explanation for panic attacks proposes that individuals with the disorder _____ neurological signals they receive about the state of their body.
    a. misinterpret
    b. ignore
    c. respond appropriately to
    d. think rationally about

ESSAY QUESTIONS

1. Phobias, panic attacks, generalized anxiety disorder, and obsessive-compulsive disorder all belong to the broader psychological category of disturbed behaviors known as anxiety disorders. What manifestations of symptoms do this class of disorders share?

2. One of the psychological explanations for avoidance behavior (staying away from objects or situations that frighten us) and perhaps for obsessive-compulsive disorder (OCD) is a reflection of the behavioral perspective. It is proposed that negative reinforcement serves to perpetuate the appearance of the undesirable behavior, even though the ineffectiveness or abnormality of the behavior may be obvious. How, exactly, does negative reinforcement work in this case?

ANSWER KEY

1. Obsessive-compulsive disorder (OCD)

2. Claustrophobia

3. Panic disorder

4. Anxiety disorders

5. Social phobia

6.   Acrophobia

7.   Specific phobia

8.   Phobia

9.   Agoraphobia

10. Generalized anxiety disorder (GAD)

11. c

12. d

13. d

14. b

15. b

16. a

SAMPLE ANSWERS TO ESSAY QUESTIONS

1.   Phobias, panic disorder, generalized anxiety disorder, and obsessive-compulsive disorder are all included in the anxiety disorders category because all are characterized by a state of excessive worry, agitation, or unrest. Phobias and panic attacks tend to be in response to a specific object or setting, and both are short-lived in that when one leaves the threatening situation or when the panic attack subsides, the psychological problem one was experiencing is no longer apparent. Phobias are irrational fears in response to objects or situations; panic attacks may be triggered by certain situations more than others but the precipitating factor is not so obvious as with phobias. Generalized anxiety disorder and obsessive-compulsive disorder tend to be more chronic. With generalized anxiety disorder there is no precipitating object or condition, and the individual is more or less always in a state of upset, worry, or concern. With obsessive-compulsive disorder, the worry or upset is not so obvious; in a sense, it is masked by the repetitive thoughts and repeated behaviors. These obsessions (repeated thoughts) and compulsions (repeated behaviors or rituals) may in fact be an attempt to relieve or deal with anxiety.

2.   Behavioral and social-cognitive psychologists point out that behaviors (whether good or bad) are learned and maintained when they are reinforced (a desirable outcome follows the behavior), and they tend to be suppressed when they are ignored or meet with an unpleasant consequence. These principles, whether we are aware of it or not, shape much of human behavior. Reinforcement (the desirable outcome) occurs in one of two ways. A positive reinforcer is a consequence following an action (a behavior) that involves obtaining something good—a paycheck, a good grade, a hug, or praise. Negative reinforcers are also good, but they probably are not quite as good as positive reinforcers. Negative reinforcers strengthen the occurrence of behaviors because they involve taking away something bad, or unpleasant, as a consequence of a manifested behavior. That, so to speak, is a desirable outcome also. Whether negative or positive, a reinforcer always increases the likelihood of the occurrence of the behavior it follows. Thus, reducing feelings of anxiety, either through avoidance or OCD symptoms, actually increases the occurrence of the disorder.

MODULE 13.3 DISSOCIATIVE AND SOMATOFORM DISORDERS

LEARNING OBJECTIVES

After you have mastered the information in the unit, you will be able to:

• Describe the dissociative and somatoform disorders

• Explain the causal factors implicated in dissociative and somatoform disorders

OUTLINE

I.   Dissociative Disorders—interfere with cohesive sense of self, unity of personality
    A.   Dissociative identity disorder (DID)
        1.   Also known as multiple personality or split personality
        2.   Two or more distinct personalities exist within same individual
    B.   Dissociative amnesia
        1.   Loss of memory about self or life experiences (no physical cause)
        2.   Usually a traumatic or stressful event involved
II. Causes of Dissociative Disorders
    A.   May be an attempt to distance self from psychological pain, conflict
    B.   DID—possible background of severe, repetitive physical abuse
    C.   DID diagnosis still in question
III. Somatoform Disorders—physical problem, no underlying physical cause
    A.   Conversion disorder
        1.   Called "hysteria" during time of Sigmund Freud
        2.   Loss of physical function, loss of feeling in a limb
    B.   Hypochondriasis—preoccupation with belief that one has a terrible illness
IV. Causes of Somatoform Disorders
    A.   Freud's explanation—manifestation of unconscious conflict
    B.   Secondary gain—"problem" may help individual avoid anxiety-producing situations
    C.   People may be reinforced for playing the "sick role"

SUMMARY

In this module you learn about two other classes of psychological disorders: The dissociative and the somatoform disorders. These categories are sometimes grouped together because they both may involve defenses against anxiety. Dissociative identity disorder (DID) was formerly called multiple personality disorder. Here the individual seems to have two or more complete personalities residing together (but apparently unknown to each other) within himself or herself. Dissociative amnesia is the forgetting of events or even one's own identity and life experiences. DID is a controversial diagnosis. There was severe and prolonged abuse in childhood in the backgrounds of well-known dissociative identity disorder cases. Dissociation seems to occur when people, knowingly or not, distance themselves from experiences or other aspects of their lives, probably because those aspects were painful or traumatic. Somatoform disorder occurs when there is something wrong with the body, or a part of the body, with no underlying physical cause. These disorders include conversion disorder (where a body part may appear paralyzed, lose feeling, or simply not function), and hypochondriasis, a well-known disorder where the individual continues to report symptoms of illnesses, but there is nothing medically wrong. Somatoform disorders may occur to help avoid difficult situations or even enable the sufferer to enjoy the concern and attempts at comfort from others.

KEY TERMS

Dissociative disorders

Somatoform disorders

Dissociative identity disorder (DID)

Conversion disorder

Hypochondriasis

Secondary gain

SELF-TEST PRACTICE QUIZ

From the Key Terms select that which best matches the following:

1. _____ One of the categories of psychological disorders where the individual experiences or reports physical problems but there is no evidence of a true medical condition

2. _____ A disorder in the classification of somatoform disorders where a person has lost the use of, or feeling in, a limb or other body part, but there is no underlying physical cause

3. _____ Formerly known as multiple personality disorder, a dissociative disorder where the individual exhibits two or more distinct personalities

4. _____ A class of psychological disorders involving disruptions in the unified sense of self such as loss of memory (for a traumatic event) or the creation of additional identities

5. _____ "Problem" actually helps sufferer avoid anxiety-producing situations

6. _____ Great concern that one has a serious illness (yet no apparent medical foundation)

a. Dissociative disorders

b. Somatoform disorders

c. Dissociative identity disorder (DID)

d. Conversion disorder

e. Hypochondriasis

f. Secondary gain

7. A controversial psychological disorder where an individual exhibits several personalities and that may involve a background of severe, prolonged physical abuse is
   a. hypochondriasis.
   b. dissociative identity disorder (DID).
   c. conversion disorder.
   d. dissociative amnesia.

8.   Which statement about people with hypochondriasis is NOT true?
    a.   They are preoccupied with thoughts of illness.
    b.   Their anxiety may make their physical symptoms even worse.
    c.   They are faking their symptoms.
    d.   They worry excessively about minor symptoms.

ANSWER KEY

1.   Somatoform disorders

2.   Conversion disorder

3.   Dissociative identity disorder (DID)

4.   Dissociative disorders

5.   Secondary gain

6.   Hypochondriasis

7.   b

8.   c

MODULE 13.4 MOOD DISORDERS

LEARNING OBJECTIVES

After you have mastered the information in this unit, you will be able to:

•   Describe the various types of mood disorders

•   Explain the causal factors implicated in mood disorders

•   Discuss the reasons for suicide and who is most at risk for committing suicide

OUTLINE

I.   Basic Characteristics of Mood Disorders
    A.   Severe, persistent disturbances of mood
    B.   Impair ability to function, will to live
II.   Types of Mood Disorders
    A.   Depressive disorders
        1.   Major depression
            a)   Extreme feelings of worthlessness, sadness, despondency
            b)   Experienced twice as often by women as men
            c)   Women may experience more stress, handle stress differently
        2.   Seasonal affective disorder (SAD)
            a)   Periods of depression during fall and winter
            b)   Treated successfully by exposure to bright light
        3.   Dysthymic disorder
            a)   More mild but chronic form of depression—may last for years
            b)   More common in women
    B.   Bipolar disorders—alternating, fairly extreme moods of elation, depression
        1.   Manic episodes—euphoria, boundless energy, possibly reckless
        2.   Cyclothymic disorder

    a) Milder mood swings than bipolar individual

    b) About as many men as women affected

III. Causes of Mood Disorders

  A. Psychological factors

   1. Psychodynamic explanation—anger against self

   2. Behavior model—too little reinforcement, especially social reinforcement

   3. Cognitive approach

    a) Aaron Beck (developed cognitive therapy)

    b) How people interpret events is related to depression

    c) Negative mind set, cognitive distortions are the problem

   4. Learned helplessness model (Martin Seligman)

    a) Stop making effort when people feel they have lost control over events

    b) Attributional style—how we explain outcomes

    c) Depressive attributional style—internal, global, stable interpretation for outcomes involving disappointments, experiences of failure

  B. Biological factors

   1. Chemical imbalances in the brain (involving neurotransmitters)

   2. Antidepressants (e.g., Prozac) increase levels of norepinephrine and serotonin

   3. Depression not just a lack of certain neurotransmitters

   4. Genetic link likely, especially with regard to bipolar disorder

IV. Exploring Psychology: The Personal Tragedy of Suicide

  A. Rate of occurrence

   1. 500,000 Americans each year make a serious attempt

   2. A leading cause of death among older teens, young adults

  B. Who is most at risk?

   1. Age—greatest among older adults

   2. Gender

    a) More women attempt suicide

    b) More males complete the act—use more lethal, violent methods

   3. Race/ethnicity—higher rate among white European Americans, Native Americans

  C. Factors in suicide

   1. Closely related to mood disorders, especially depression, bipolar disorder

   2. Suicide, like depression, may be linked to biochemical factors

   3. Disinhibition effect

    a) Possible result of low levels of serotonin

    b) Removes natural tendency to curb impulsive activity (including attempt to commit suicide)

   4. Alcohol dependence—again may lead to impulsivity

   5. Lack of coping responses among those who attempt, commit suicide

   6. Exit events—losing people who are sources of emotional support

   7. Copycat suicides among adolescents

SUMMARY

In this module you learn about the class of psychological disorders known as mood disorders. Mood disorders impact our emotional, or affective, state—how we feel. Individuals suffering from mood disorders usually are feeling sad and lethargic although some mood disorders involve a highly aroused or agitated state referred to as mania. One of the most common mood disorders is depression, and because of the misery one is experiencing when depressed, depression is closely linked to attempts at suicide.

The category of mood disorders includes depressive disorders and what are known as bipolar disorders. *Bipolar* is the term we now use for what was once called manic-depression. Major depression is the experience of extreme unhappiness, despondency, and feelings of unworthiness that lasts months or longer. About twice as many women as men suffer from depression. This may be linked to how women handle problems in their lives, but it may also be a result of the many kinds of stress women are prone to experience. Other depressive disorders are seasonal affective disorder, which is major depression as a result of lack of sunlight, and dysthymic disorder, which is milder but chronic depression. Individuals suffering from bipolar disorders exhibit alternating extremes of mood. Bipolar disorder is characterized by states of severe depression alternating with highly energized, perhaps abrasive, states known as manic episodes. There may be normal states of mood between the extreme periods, but the bipolar individual is characterized as mostly "highs" and "lows," with much less in the way of stable, moderate experience in comparison to individuals without the disorder. Cyclothymic disorder is like bipolar disorder, but the extremes of mood are not as pronounced.

It is thought that both psychological and biological factors cause mood disorders. Low levels of brain chemicals (especially norepinephrine and serotonin) are associated with an individual's experience of depression, and antidepressants that improve neurotransmitter functioning are used successfully to treat depression. Ongoing research suggests a genetic factor in mood disorders, especially for bipolar disorder. Psychological causes include cognitive factors, a lack of positive reinforcement, and learned helplessness. Freud's explanation of anger turned within is also a possible cause for mood disorders. Cognitive factors related to mood disorders involve how we think about our life experiences. If someone adopts a consistently negative pattern of interpreting events, misconstruing minor events as major catastrophes with consequences far-reaching and profound, life will be perceived as dismal and depression will result. These are called cognitive distortions. Learning theorists point out that reinforcement (a desirable consequence to our actions) is related to motivation, and if reinforcers diminish, motivation dwindles and one may feel depressed. Social reinforcers (emotional support, positive feedback from others) are particularly important. Martin Seligman introduced the notion of learned helplessness—that if we have experienced a lack of control in our lives, we may feel unable to influence our situation even if an opportunity does come along in the future. Seligman proposed that depression and learned helplessness are related to how one makes attributions about life events. This is somewhat related to the concept of cognitive distortions discussed above. If we make internal, global, and lasting attributions regarding an unsuccessful life event (known as a depressive attributional style), we are far more likely to experience depression.

There is a high risk for suicide among those who are clinically depressed or who are experiencing bipolar disorder. Though suicide is a leading cause of death among adolescents, young adults, and college students, still the highest rate of suicide occurs among the elderly. More women than men attempt suicide, but more men actually complete the act of suicide because men tend to use more violent, immediate means. There is a higher risk of suicide among white European Americans and Native Americans than among African Americans or Hispanic Americans. Alcohol use and low levels of neurotransmitters may have a disinhibiting effect—they lower the constraints we normally have on impulsive, destructive behavior. There is a higher incidence of suicide attempts among teenagers where a friend has just attempted suicide, and the use of drugs is related to the incidence of suicide. Last, individuals who attempt suicide may be less capable with regard to devising other, more effective ways of coping with problems. If such individuals also feel a lack of social and emotional support, the risk for attempting suicide is greater.

KEY TERMS

Mood disorders

Major depression

Seasonal affective disorder (SAD)

Dysthymic disorder

Bipolar disorder

Manic episodes

Cyclothymic disorder

Learned helplessness model

Attributional style

Depressive attributional style

Disinhibition effect

SELF-TEST PRACTICE QUIZ

From the Key Terms select that which best matches the following (Note: Not every Key Term will be used.):

1. _____ One kind of bipolar disorder, characterized by excessive, highly-charged levels of activity; may include extreme talkativeness and grandiose ideas or plans

2. _____ A type of mood disorder like major depression but the degree of depression is less severe

3. _____ One feature of alcohol use and low levels of some neurotransmitters; normal constraints on impulsive, perhaps harmful activities are diminished

4. _____ The pattern one tends to exhibit regarding explanations for life events

5. _____ A very common type of depressive disorder, where extreme feelings of sadness, lack of interest, unworthiness persist for an extended period of time

a. Mood disorders

b. Major depression

c. Seasonal affective disorder (SAD)

d. Dysthymic disorder

e. Bipolar disorder

f. Manic episodes

g. Cyclothymic disorder

h. Learned helplessness model

i. Attributional style

j. Depressive attributional style

k. Disinhibition effect

6. _____ A disorder included in the depressive disorders category where depression results from the lack of exposure to sufficient light (most likely to occur during fall and winter)

7. _____ A model, proposed by Martin Seligman, where prior experiences with events we could not control stifles future effort, even when opportunities we could impact occur

8. _____ A class of psychological disorders where one's feelings, or affective states, are impaired

9. _____ A mood disorder that is like bipolar disorder but the mood swings are less severe

10. _____ An attributional style that involves explaining events in a negative way; related to the incidence of depression

11. A person who feels very sad or low, has no energy, and has experienced sleeping problems for some months or more is probably suffering from

    a. major depression.
    b. bipolar disorder.
    c. manic-depression.
    d. cyclothymic disorder.

12. Why might women experience depression more frequently than men?

    a. Nervous system functioning in female organisms is less able to adapt to traumatic events.
    b. Women have fewer physical and psychological demands placed upon them, leaving more time for dwelling on problems and for worry and anxiety.
    c. Because women are more emotional, they experience more intense levels of all emotions.
    d. Women may differ from men in how much stress they experience and how they handle it.

13. The individual who has been feeling depressed and lethargic for some time then suddenly feels full of energy, is quite agitated, and rarely sleeps is probably experiencing

    a. a recovery from major depression.
    b. disthymic disorder.
    c. bipolar disorder.
    d. learned helplessness.

14. That one needs a balance between how much effort is expended and the rewards or gains as a result of that effort is an explanation for mood disorders proposed by

    a. Sigmund Freud.
    b. behaviorists and learning theorists.
    c. cognitive psychologists.
    d. Aaron Beck.

15. What is an exit event?
    a. a suicide attempt
    b. a depressive episode
    c. the loss of a supportive person in one's life
    d. none of the above

16. When one experiences a minor setback in life but interprets it as tragic with life-changing consequences one is
    a. creating cognitive distortions.
    b. later likely to engage in very positive interpretations and activities for balance.
    c. trying to find productive ways to manage life events.
    d. accepting the realities in life and taking steps to move on.

17. What is the most effective treatment for Seasonal Affective Disorder?
    a. electric shock therapy
    b. antidepressant medication
    c. exposure to bright lights
    d. cognitive-behavioral therapy

ESSAY QUESTION

1. How are individuals with mood disorders unlike people who do not suffer from this psychological problem? What does the usefulness of antidepressants tell us about the cause of mood disorders?

ANSWER KEY

1. Manic episodes

2. Dysthymic disorder

3. Disinhibition effect

4. Attributional style

5. Major depressive disorder

6. Seasonal affective disorder (SAD)

7. Learned helplessness model

8. Mood disorders

9. Cyclothymic disorder

10. Depressive attributional style

11. a

12. d

13. c

14. b

15. c

16. a

17. c

SAMPLE ANSWER TO ESSAY QUESTION

1.   Individuals with mood disorders are more likely to experience extremes of mood (or emotional state), with fewer and shorter periods of normal functioning between these extremes. The most common mood disorder is major depression; thus, many people with mood disorders exhibit chronic characteristics of sorrow, misery, lethargy, disruptions in sleeping and eating behaviors, and a loss of interest in life. Individuals with bipolar disorder show periods of abnormally elevated activity and agitation as well. These experiences of mood extremes are sufficient to substantially hamper one's psychological well-being and ability to function. Antidepressants are helpful in treating mood disorders. Because antidepressants influence the levels and functioning of neurotransmitters (messenger brain chemicals), especially norepinephrine and serotonin, this knowledge helps us understand that brain chemicals are important to regulating emotional states.

MODULE 13.5 SCHIZOPHRENIA

LEARNING OBJECTIVES

After you have mastered the information in this unit, you will be able to:

*   Define schizophrenia

*   Describe the three specific types of schizophrenia

*   Explain the causal factors implicated in schizophrenia

*   Discuss the diathesis-stress explanation for schizophrenia

OUTLINE

I.   Background Factors in Schizophrenia
    A.   Disorder most closely related to typical concept of madness
    B.   Involves bizarre, irrational behavior; roughly one percent of population is affected
    C.   Slightly more common, more severe, and with earlier onset in men
    D.   Tends to occur at uniform rates worldwide
    E.   Onset corresponds to transition from adolescence to adulthood
II. Symptoms of Schizophrenia
    A.   A psychotic disorder—inability to distinguish reality from fantasy
    B.   Experience things that in actuality do not exist
        1.   Hallucinations—perceptions not based on actual stimuli (e.g., hearing voices)
        2.   Delusions—adhering to beliefs that are clearly, completely false
    C.   Exhibit bizarre behavior, incoherent speech, illogical thinking (positive symptoms)
    D.   Thought disorder—ideas not really connected, organized, or meaningful
    E.   Includes extreme withdrawal, isolation, apathy, blunted emotions (negative symptoms)
    F.   Not all symptoms necessary for diagnosis of schizophrenia
III. Types of Schizophrenia
    A.   Disorganized
        1.   Confused behavior, hallucinations, disorganized delusions
        2.   May neglect personal hygiene, fail to control bodily functions
        3.   Inappropriate emotions, difficulty in relating to others
    B.   Catatonic
        1.   Bizarre movements, postures, grimaces
        2.   May adopt a motionless stupor, unresponsive for hours
        3.   Waxy flexibility—body can be molded without difficulty by others
        4.   A rare form of schizophrenia

      C.   Paranoid
          1.   Most common form of schizophrenia
          2.   Delusions of grandeur, persecution, or jealousy
          3.   May be accompanied by auditory hallucinations
IV.   Causes of Schizophrenia
      A.   Genetic factors
          1.   Heredity plays an important role
          2.   Higher rate of incidence among monozygotic than dizygotic twins
          3.   Higher incidence in adopted children whose biological parents afflicted
          4.   Expected that multiple genes are responsible for disorder
      B.   Biochemical imbalances
          1.   Dopamine pathways and dopamine receptors are implicated
          2.   Helpful antipsychotic drugs (e.g., Thorazine) reduce dopamine activity
      C.   Brain abnormalities
          1.   MRIs, CTs reveal abnormal brain development
          2.   Most affected areas are prefrontal cortex, limbic system
              a)   Prefrontal cortex helps organize thoughts, carry out plans
              b)   Limbic system involved in memories, emotional experiences
      D.   Psychosocial influences
          1.   Life stresses a factor, such as difficult family environment
          2.   Diathesis-stress model
              a)   Diathesis involves a genetic predisposition; creates vulnerability
              b)   Sufficient stressful experiences trigger onset of disorder

SUMMARY

In this module you learn about the leading serious psychological disorder, schizophrenia. Schizophrenia is a psychotic disorder, meaning the individual has truly experienced a break from reality. Hallucinations and delusions are common. The occurrence of schizophrenia coincides with our transition from adolescence to adulthood. Though about one-third of schizophrenics have severe enough symptoms that they require hospitalization, the experience of schizophrenia for nearly all who suffer it tends to extend throughout the course of life. A large portion of our national mental health expenditures (75 percent) is directed towards the treatment of individuals with schizophrenia.

Schizophrenics exhibit behavior that is irrational and bizarre. They show severe social impairments and, if they speak, their speech is usually incoherent. Thought patterns appear to be disorganized, and there is no logical connection in the arrangement and expression of ideas. Verbal utterances may become meaningless. Types of schizophrenia include disorganized, catatonic, and the most common, paranoid. Paranoid schizophrenics exhibit psychotic behavior and experience delusions, usually that they are being persecuted. Disorganized schizophrenics show confused behavior, blunted or inappropriate emotion, and do not attend to personal hygiene or bodily functions.

What causes schizophrenia? As with other abnormal behavioral disorders, we suspect a combination of biological, environmental, and psychological influences. There is clearly a genetic component to schizophrenia in that the incidence is higher among family members (including twins) sharing close or identical gene codes. It is expected that not just one gene, but multiple genes are a factor. However, even sharing an identical genetic heritage (as do monozygotic twins) results in a less than 50 percent concordance rate. The brain pathways and receptors for the neurotransmitter dopamine seem implicated, and drugs that reduce dopamine activity reduce the frequency and severity of psychotic symptoms. Brain imaging data provide evidence that the prefrontal and limbic portions of the schizophrenic brain have developed abnormally. The functions of these brain regions correspond to the decrements found in the behavior of schizophrenics. Life stressors are also considered to be a factor, and these may include an abusive family environment or other traumatic experiences. The diathesis-stress model proposes that a human may have a genetic predisposition (a diathesis) to a disorder, creating greater vulnerability. The disorder will not manifest in the individual, however, unless sufficient stresses and difficulties in life trigger its onset.

KEY TERMS

Schizophrenia

Psychotic disorder

Thought disorder

Positive symptoms

Negative symptoms

Disorganized type

Catatonic type

Waxy flexibility

Paranoid type

SELF-TEST PRACTICE QUIZ

From the Key Terms select that which best matches the following:

1. _____ Symptoms present in excess that suggest the diagnosis of schizophrenia, such as irrational behavior and utterances, hallucinations, and delusions

2. _____ A severe psychological disorder where an individual experiences a break with reality

3. _____ A psychotic disorder where an individual experiences hallucinations, delusions, disturbed thought patterns, extreme social impairment, and absent or inappropriate emotions

4. _____ One component in the behavior of catatonic schizophrenics where the body may be arranged to take any shape, even one that is probably very uncomfortable

5. _____ The most common type of schizophrenia where the disorder is accompanied by delusions (usually of grandeur or persecution)

a.   Schizophrenia

b.   Psychotic disorder

c.   Thought disorder

d.   Positive symptoms

e.   Negative symptoms

f.   Disorganized type

g.   Catatonic type

h.   Waxy flexibility

i.   Paranoid type

6. _____ One of the sub-types of schizophrenia where the individual exhibits confused behavior, inattention to bodily processes and personal hygiene, and inappropriate emotions

7. _____ One characteristic of schizophrenia where the organization and connection of expressed ideas is not apparent

8. _____ The lack of certain behaviors that suggests the diagnosis of schizophrenia such as the inability to establish and maintain social and emotional relationships

9. _____ A rare type of schizophrenia where the individual may assume and hold rigid body postures for many hours on end

10. The term *schizophrenia*, or "split brain," means
    a. the normal ties among thoughts, emotions, and perceptions are lacking.
    b. the corpus callosum joining the two hemispheres in the brain has been severed.
    c. an individual has experienced a severe brain injury.
    d. an individual will vacillate between rational and irrational behaviors.

11. The age at which the onset of schizophrenia is most likely to occur is
    a. early childhood (especially just prior to the start of school years).
    b. adolescence through young adulthood.
    c. the middle years of adult development.
    d. in late adulthood, when other mental faculties begin to fail.

12. The schizophrenic disorder that is accompanied by delusions and may be accompanied by auditory hallucinations is the _____ type of schizophrenia.
    a. disorganized
    b. catatonic
    c. paranoid
    d. psychotic-release

13. Which type of schizophrenia is characterized by unusual motor behaviors and postures?
    a. catatonic
    b. disorganized
    c. undifferentiated
    d. paranoid

14. A diathesis is a(n)
    a. experience of physical pain with no apparent underlying physical cause.
    b. treatment method for realigning dopamine activity receptors and pathways in the brain.
    c. medical device attached to the head to help reshape deformed regions of the cortex.
    d. state of vulnerability, possibly genetic in origin, increasing the likelihood that one will experience a disorder.

15. Ted believes that he is actually King Henry VIII of England. This type of bizarre belief is a
    a. hallucination.
    b. catatonia.
    c. delusion.
    d. negative symptom.

ESSAY QUESTION

1. Characterize the behavior of a typical individual who suffers from schizophrenia. What are the suspected causes of this psychotic disorder?

ANSWER KEY

1. Positive symptoms

2. Psychotic disorder

3. Schizophrenia

4. Waxy flexibility

5. Paranoid type

6. Disorganized type

7. Thought disorder

8. Negative symptoms

9. Catatonic type

10. a

11. b

12. c

13. a

14. d

15. c

SAMPLE ANSWER TO ESSAY QUESTION

1. An individual with schizophrenia seems to no longer have contact with, or at least a grasp of, reality. Schizophrenics experience perceptual disturbances (hallucinations) and false beliefs (delusions). Their behavior does not fit, or is unrelated to, the environment surrounding them. Often, a schizophrenic shows no emotional response to others and does not establish or maintain social contacts. Thought patterns appear to be disturbed, and this is most evident in the schizophrenic's speech. Ordinary words may be strung together, but their collective arrangement conveys no meaning. A schizophrenic is likely to neglect the most basic hygiene functions. Schizophrenia is a severe, pervasive disorder, and thus it probably is caused by a combination of factors. The diathesis-stress model is a good example of potential causal sources. Genetics alone is not a perfect predictor of schizophrenia. The diathesis-stress model suggests we may have a genetic predisposition, or vulnerability, for a disorder such as schizophrenia. Psychological and environmental factors then, if stressful, ultimately trigger the disorder's onset.

MODULE 13.6 PERSONALITY DISORDERS

LEARNING OBJECTIVES

After you have mastered the information in this unit, you will be able to:

- Describe the personality disorders

- Outline the characteristics associated with antisocial personality disorder

- Discuss the causal factors implicated in antisocial personality disorder

OUTLINE

I.   Background Characteristics of Personality Disorders
    A.   Excessively rigid patterns of behavior
    B.   Maladaptive because limits adjustment to environment, needs of others

II.   Types of Personality Disorders
    A.   Narcissistic personality disorder—inflated sense of self
    B.   Paranoid personality disorder—extreme suspiciousness, distrust of others
    C.   Schizoid personality disorder
        1.   Little or no interest in social relationships
        2.   Limited range of emotional expression
        3.   Appear distant and aloof
    D.   Borderline personality disorder
        1.   Stormy relationships with others
        2.   Unstable self-image, dramatic mood swings
    E.   Ten personality disorders identified by DSM
    F.   Antisocial personality disorder (APD)—the most widely studied

III.   Symptoms of Antisocial Personality Disorder
    A.   People with this disorder have also been labeled psychopaths, or sociopaths
    B.   Flagrant disregard for rules of society
    C.   Complete lack of regard for well-being of others
    D.   Not a psychotic disorder; antisocial personality is in touch with reality
    E.   Impulsive, irresponsible, take advantage of others
    F.   Lack remorse for misdeeds, mistreatment of others
    G.   Not concerned or threatened by punishment or possibility of punishment
    H.   May be unusually intelligent, exhibit superficial charm
    I.   Most often found in males

IV.   Causes of Antisocial Personality Disorder
    A.   Possible brain abnormalities in males
    B.   Lower levels of activity in frontal lobes of cerebral cortex
    C.   Possible structural damage to prefrontal cortex
    D.   Craving for stimulation may have genetic link
    E.   Environmental factors
        1.   Characteristics of homes, families where APD individuals raised
            a)   Lack of parental warmth
            b)   Parental neglect, rejection
            c)   Use of harsh punishment
            d)   Emotional, physical abuse
        2.   History of abuse may lead to lack of empathy, lack of genuine emotional ties
        3.   Failure to develop concern for others, moral compass, conscience
        4.   APD individuals treat others with callous disregard

SUMMARY

In this module you learn about the class of psychological disorders known as personality disorders, and most particularly about the widely studied disorder known as the antisocial personality. Individuals with antisocial personality disorder (APD) have also been referred to as psychopaths or sociopaths. Narcissistic personalities are self-focused; the paranoid personality is suspicious and mistrustful. Individuals with schizoid personalities have no real social interest in others, and they do not exhibit emotional warmth or empathy. Individuals who are diagnosed with borderline personality disorder have an unstable personality, show dramatic mood swings, and demonstrate an inability to form stable and peaceful relationships.

The antisocial personality is characterized by a lack of empathy and emotional response to others, combined with a disregard for others' well being and a tendency to take advantage. The individual with APD generally exhibits impulsive behavior and has no regard for rules of society. No regret for harm brought to others is apparent. Background characteristics of families where APD individuals are raised reveal a lack of warmth and caring, instances of harsh punishment, and emotional and physical abuse. There is some evidence that the APD individual may have brain functioning and structure that differs from that of normal individuals. Most individuals with APD are men. The threat of punishment or even actual punishment has little or no impact on individuals with APD.

KEY TERMS

Personality disorders

Narcissistic personality disorder

Paranoid personality disorder

Schizoid personality disorder

Borderline personality disorder

Antisocial personality disorder

SELF-TEST PRACTICE QUIZ

From the Key Terms select that which best matches the following:

1. _____ Emotional aloofness, lack of interest in social relationships

2. _____ Exaggerated image of and focus on oneself

3. _____ Impulsive, dispassionate behavior towards others, lack of regret for disregard, harm

4. _____ Erratic emotional behavior, unstable self-image, unstable personal relationships

5. _____ A category of psychological disorders involving rigid, maladaptive personality traits

6. _____ Exhibiting pervasive suspicion and mistrust of others

a. Personality disorders

b. Narcissistic personality disorder

c. Paranoid personality disorder

d. Schizoid personality disorder

e. Borderline personality disorder

f. Antisocial personality disorder

7.   Behaviors that include aloofness and emotional distancing, lack of interest in others, and a limited range of expressiveness are characteristic of the _____ personality disorder.

    a.   narcissistic
    b.   paranoid
    c.   schizoid
    d.   borderline

8.   Which statement about individuals with antisocial personality disorder is NOT true?

    a.   They are more likely to be male.
    b.   They may need higher-than-normal levels of stimulation.
    c.   They are psychotic.
    d.   They exhibit a lack of empathy toward others.

9.   Lower levels of activity in the brains of males with APD are found in the _____ lobes, the brain region responsible for inhibiting impulsive behavior.

    a.   frontal
    b.   parietal
    c.   occipital
    d.   temporal

ESSAY QUESTION

1.   Describe the characteristics of typical home life that we have found in the backgrounds of individuals diagnosed with antisocial personality disorder. How are these parental and familial characteristics related to the later behavior of an individual with APD?

ANSWER KEY

1.   Schizoid personality

2.   Narcissistic personality disorder

3.   Antisocial personality disorder

4.   Borderline personality disorder

5.   Personality disorders

6.   Paranoid personality disorder

7.   c

8.   c

9.   a

SAMPLE ANSWER TO ESSAY QUESTION

1.   People who show evidence of antisocial personality disorder tend to be raised in homes where there was not a great deal of parental warmth and caring. Family members probably were not involved in the activities of the child, and the child may have experienced outright neglect, emotional abuse, and physical abuse. There are reports of harsh punishments used in the homes of individuals who later develop APD. It appears that the early environmental experience of people who develop antisocial personality disorder involved being raised in a cold, unfeeling, and unresponsive emotional climate. Perhaps it is no wonder, then, that individuals with APD exhibit a cold and uncaring attitude towards others. People with antisocial personalities have no empathy or regard for the welfare of those around them, and exhibit no feelings of remorse or regret. They exhibit no respect for the rules of society and are unaffected by punishment or the threat of

punishment. It appears that individuals with APD exhibit the emotional behaviors with which they were raised.

MODULE 13.7 APPLICATION: SUICIDE PREVENTION

LEARNING OBJECTIVE

After you have mastered the information in this unit, you will be able to:

• Outline the steps you can take to help someone who is threatening suicide

OUTLINE

I.   Background Factors in the Occurrence of Suicide
    A.   Difficult to detect, even by professionals
    B.   A challenging situation, but there are steps one can take to help prevent
II. Facing the Threat—General Guidelines
    A.   Recognize that threatened suicide is serious
    B.   Also consider seriously indicators that are implied but not overt
    C.   Show warmth, compassion, understanding
    D.   Suggest alternatives
    E.   Evaluate immediacy of the event
    F.   Encourage the individual to agree regarding getting help
    G.   Take the individual to get help

SUMMARY

In this module you learn about steps you can take should someone you know indicate that he or she is considering suicide. Suicide is a life-threatening event and its mention, whether direct or indirect, should always be taken for the serious matter that it is. Detecting, understanding, and preventing suicidal behaviors are difficult even for professionals. Since you may well be in the company of someone who at some time may threaten suicide, keep the following steps in mind. Recognize that suicide is always serious. Try to determine how immediate the risk of a suicide attempt is. Even if your companion hints at considering suicide but does not say this outright, consider that a warning sign of a suicide attempt as well. Respond to the talk of suicide with warmth, compassion, and understanding. Gently suggest other ways that a problem might be solved. Take steps promptly to get the individual at risk to enlist the assistance of a professional, and accompany him or her if necessary.

CHAPTER 13 APPLICATION EXERCISE

Do you know someone with a psychological disorder? Reflect on that person's behavior. Do you think it is abnormal? If so, what makes you think so? List specific characteristics that lead you to believe the behavior is, or is not, disturbed. How serious does the disorder appear to be?

Can you think of causes that might contribute to the psychological difficulties? Do other members of the family show similar characteristics? Are there environmental factors that seem to keep the abnormal behavior going despite its maladaptiveness? How long has the individual had the disorder, and when did it begin? Does it fit any of the categories we have discussed in this chapter?

CHAPTER 14

Methods of Therapy

In Chapter 14 you learn about the various treatment methods that are available for individuals suffering from psychological disorders. These treatments include psychological intervention and biomedical therapies, which usually involve prescribing one or more of the available psychiatric drugs. In many cases the most effective approach to the treatment of abnormal behavior over the long run is a combination of biomedical and psychological interventions. Often, drug therapy is used to stabilize a patient and get symptoms of the psychological disorder under control. The development of drug therapies has been a tremendous breakthrough in the treatment of mental illness. However, drugs can only treat symptoms. Drugs alone do not provide a cure for psychological disorder, although they may contribute a great deal toward helping a patient manage debilitating symptoms and thus be able to live more effectively and productively. Once psychotropic drugs have helped moderate emotional extremes experienced by an individual or brought other maladaptive symptoms under control, then psychotherapy can proceed with a greater likelihood of success or long-term improvement.

The treatment of individuals exhibiting abnormal behavior was not always as compassionate and multi-faceted as it is today. Up until the late 1700s, people with psychologically aberrant behavior were thought to be possessed by demons or other spirits. The mentally ill were housed under dreadful conditions since they were regarded as strange and dangerous to society. In Paris, two Frenchmen took a different view and believed that if the psychologically disturbed were simply treated more humanely, they would be restored to normal functioning. This was known as the moral therapy approach. These Frenchmen, Jean-Baptiste Pussin and later Philippe Pinel, were both at various times in charge of a large mental hospital in Paris. They removed patients from chains, eliminated other harsh treatments, insisted that patients be treated with respect, and provided sunny, well-ventilated rooms. Dorothea Dix had a similar impact on the treatment of the mentally ill in the United States. This reform movement eventually dissipated, however, because moral therapy alone was not producing the desired normal behavior. Most patients were warehoused in large mental institutions with little hope or opportunity for recovery. In the mid-twentieth century there was again a reaction to the unpleasant conditions in which mental patients lived, and many individuals were removed from the mental institutions. This social movement was known as deinstitutionalization. The treatment of psychologically disturbed patients shifted to a community-based approach with the hope that more patients could be returned to their homes as long as support services were provided. While it is true that the more extensive and intensive the available psychological support systems are, the greater the likelihood that patients will recover to the point that they can be transitioned back into community life, still, the community-based mental health center approach also does not produce ideal results.

As mentioned above, a combination of psychotherapy and biomedical intervention provides the greatest promise for improvement among those suffering from psychological disorders. A variety of psychotherapy approaches are available, and research confirms that individuals who receive some kind of psychological treatment intervention fare better than those who do not. The major approaches to psychotherapy parallel the philosophical approaches found within the field of psychology. In other words, the psychodynamic perspective considers psychological problems to emanate from conflicts buried deep in the unconscious, and thus therapy is based on uncovering those conflicts and finding a better resolution. The humanistic perspective traces psychological disorder to losing touch with one's inner guidance and sense of self. Humanistic therapy is aimed at restoring that inner connectedness. Cognitive psychologists see disorder as resulting from erroneous thinking. Thus, cognitive therapy addresses reasoning and interpretation patterns with a view towards making thoughts more rational and realistic. The behavioral perspective proposes that maladaptive behaviors are learned and can be replaced when the client learns more effective living patterns. Psychiatric drugs can help manage aberrant psychological symptoms. Antianxiety drugs, antidepressants, and antipsychotics are among the drugs found useful in treating psychological disorders.

MODULE 14.1 PATHWAYS TO THE PRESENT: A BRIEF HISTORY OF THERAPY

LEARNING OBJECTIVES

After you have mastered the information in this unit, you will be able to:

- Describe how treatment of people with disturbed behavior has changed over time

- Discuss community-based mental health centers

- Explain whether the policy of deinstitutionalization has been successful

OUTLINE

I.   The Rise of Moral Therapy
    A.   Treatment emphasizing compassion and understanding toward mentally ill
    B.   Jean-Baptiste Pussin and Philippe Pinel (late eighteenth century France)
    C.   Pussin, then Pinel were medical directors at mental hospital
    D.   Treat patients humanely, release from chains
    E.   Dorothea Dix—United States—campaigned for kinder treatment
    F.   Dix's work led to establishment of 32 U.S. mental hospitals
    G.   By late nineteenth century, clear that moral therapy alone not successful

II. The Movement Towards Community-Based Care
    A.   Call for reform by 1950s
    B.   Transition to community mental health system (beginning in 1960s)
    C.   Social policy was deinstitutionalization
        1.   Mental hospitals vacated, closed
        2.   Community-based mental health centers created
            a)   Outpatient care; day treatment programs
            b)   Crisis intervention; supervised residential facilities
            c)   Criticism is that mental hospitals now are "revolving doors"
    D.   Success of deinstitutionalization is questionable
    E.   More intensive programs have better results

SUMMARY

In this module you learn about the beginnings of humane care for individuals suffering from mental disorders. The first attempt at compassion for the mentally ill occurred in France in the late 1700s. Jean-Baptiste Pussin was director of a large mental hospital in Paris and felt the mentally ill would recover if they were released from chains, freed from harsh treatments, and treated kindly. This approach was known as moral therapy. Pussin's successor, Philippe Pinel, continued the moral therapy approach. In the United States, not long afterwards (mid-nineteenth century), Dorothea Dix campaigned against the deplorable conditions under which the mentally ill were held and for improved treatment. Many mental hospitals were established as a result. However, moral therapy alone does not cure mental illness. The reform movement slowed, and again conditions deteriorated. Finally, beginning in the 1960s, there was a move away from mental hospitals and towards community-based mental health facilities. This movement is known as deinstitutionalization. Today's mental health centers provide an array of services for the psychologically disturbed. However, there is a tendency for patients to be admitted, treated, discharged—and then readmitted again a short time later. The success of deinstitutionalization thus far appears mixed.

KEY TERMS

Moral therapy

Deinstitutionalization

SELF-TEST PRACTICE QUIZ

From the Key Terms select that which best matches the following:

1. _____ A policy, begun in the United States in the latter half of the twentieth century, moving mentally ill individuals out of large hospitals and into community-based mental health programs

    a. Moral therapy

    b. Deinstitutionalization

2. _____ The approach, first begun by Pussin and Pinel, of attempting to bring about recovery for the mentally ill by eliminating harsh treatment and instituting compassionate care

3. Why did the treatment approach of moral therapy for mentally ill individuals begin to disappear in the late 1800s?

    a. Dorothea Dix campaigned effectively against moral therapy.
    b. The cost of this treatment method was prohibitively expensive.
    c. It was becoming apparent that moral therapy alone did not cure mental illness.
    d. Moral therapy was replaced by the establishment of individual mentors for each patient.

4. Which statement about deinstitutionalization is TRUE?

    a. It has met with mixed success.
    b. It was the primary method of treatment in the mid-nineteenth century.
    c. It was advocated by Jean-Baptiste Pussin.
    d. None of the above are true.

ESSAY QUESTION

1. Describe events leading up to the deinstitutionalization movement, and evaluate the success of deinstitutionalization to date.

ANSWER KEY

1. Deinstitutionalization

2. Moral therapy

3. c

4. a

SAMPLE ANSWER TO ESSAY QUESTION:

1. In the late 1700s and early 1800s, views shifted towards more humane treatment for the mentally ill. When it became apparent, however, that moral therapy alone did not cure mental illness, treatment of the mentally ill again deteriorated. In the latter part of the twentieth century, as a result of reform movements, community-based mental health programs were created, and most mentally ill were moved out of large institutions. Intensive treatment does help, but the problem of healing those with psychological difficulties has not been solved.

MODULE 14.2 TYPES OF PSYCHOTHERAPY

LEARNING OBJECTIVES:

- Define psychotherapy

- Describe the major types of mental health professionals

- Describe the major forms of psychotherapy

- Discuss whether psychotherapy is effective

- Discuss cultural factors that therapist need to consider when working with diverse groups

OUTLINE

I.   Background Factors in Psychotherapy
    A.   Psychologically based form of treatment to help with emotional, behavioral problems
    B.   Involves exchange of communication between client and therapist ("talk therapy")
II. Various Mental Health Professionals Provide Treatment (see Table 14.1 in text for review)
III. Psychodynamic Therapy
    A.   Traditional psychoanalysis
        1.   Root of problem is unconscious conflict, stemming from childhood
        2.   Free association—patient speaks whatever comes to mind
        3.   Dream analysis—examine latent content of dreams for real meaning
        4.   Interpretation
            a)   Insight—understanding regarding inner conflict, source
            b)   Resistance—client blocks when topic very sensitive
            c)   Transference relationship—client responds to therapist as if key individual in past unconscious conflict—helps with insight
            d)   Countertransference—therapist experiences carryover
    B.   Modern psychodynamic approaches
        1.   Focus is more on present, adaptive functioning
        2.   More direct approach by therapist, briefer therapy format
IV. Humanistic Therapy
    A.   Basic factors in humanistic therapy
        1.   Humans have free will, can make conscious, enriching choices
        2.   Focus is on the present, client's perception of issues and events
    B.   Client-centered therapy
        1.   Problems are a result of blocks on path to self-actualization
        2.   Therapy is to restore individual's ability to know own inner self
        3.   Emphasis is on empathy, genuineness, unconditional positive regard

    C.   Gestalt therapy
       1.   Important to blend conflicting parts of personality into a unified whole
       2.   Approach is direct, even confrontational; involves role playing

V. Behavior Therapy
    A.   Principles of learning are applied to make changes in behavior
    B.   Maladaptive behaviors have been learned, can be unlearned
    C.   Methods of fear reduction
       1.   Systematic desensitization—create fear hierarchy; maintain relaxed state
       2.   Gradual exposure—real-life objects or experiences used
       3.   Modeling—imitate others exhibiting adaptive behavior
    D.   Aversive conditioning—pair undesirable stimulus with unwanted learned response
    E.   Operant conditioning methods—may use token economy
    F.   Cognitive-behavioral therapy—combines behavioral methods with changing thinking

VI. Cognitive Therapies
    A.   Basic cognitive therapy approach
       1.   Root of problem is interpretation of events, rather than events themselves
       2.   Therapy is brief; focus is on present
    B.   Rational-emotive behavior therapy (REBT)
       1.   "ABC" approach developed by Albert Ellis—problem is irrational beliefs
       2.   Recognize irrationality of beliefs; adopt more effective strategies
    C.   Aaron Beck's cognitive therapy approach
       1.   Ineffective emotional reactions result from errors in thinking
       2.   Develop rational alternatives to cognitive distortions

VII. Eclectic Therapy—use combination of therapeutic approaches

VIII. Group, Family, and Couples Therapy
    A.   Group therapy
       1.   Therapy conducted among small number of participants
       2.   Less expensive; particularly helpful for social, interpersonal problems
       3.   May not provide sufficient confidentiality, individual attention
    B.   Family therapy—whole family as a unit may be problem, is focus of therapy
    C.   Couples therapy (marital therapy if applied to a married couple)
       1.   Both members of couple considered unit of treatment
       2.   Open communication channels, investigate power imbalances

IX. The Effectiveness of Psychotherapy
    A.   Measuring effectiveness
       1.   Meta-analyses: individuals who receive treatment vs. those who do not
       2.   Greatest gains shown in first few months of therapy
    B.   Which therapy is best?
       1.   Overall, all therapies better than receiving no treatment at all
       2.   Ongoing evaluation: type of therapy relative to particular problem
          a)   Behavioral and cognitive-behavioral—help anxiety, eating disorders
          b)   Token economies helpful for mental institution patients
          c)   Cognitive-behavioral appears helpful in treating schizophrenia
          d)   Psychodynamic therapy may help with depression, bulimia, borderline personality disorder
          e)   Humanistic best for connecting with inner self, finding direction
    C.   Accounting for benefits of therapy
       1.   Nonspecific factors
          a)   Common characteristics shared by different therapies
          b)   Include interpersonal relationship; expectation for improvement

      2.   Placebo effect—client does respond to positive expectancies
X.   Multicultural Issues in Treatment
    A.   Background considerations in multicultural treatment
        1.   Clients, therapists from a multitude of ethnic, racial backgrounds
        2.   Cultural bias destructive in therapeutic relationship
    B.   African Americans
        1.   Experienced a long history of oppression, discrimination
        2.   Hesitation and reserve to be expected; not a result of paranoid thinking
    C.   Asian Americans
        1.   Asian culture discourages open display of emotion, feelings
        2.   Matters relating to group valued over those relating to an individual
        3.   May approach therapist as authority figure, to direct behavior
    D.   Hispanic Americans
        1.   Strong emphasis on family interdependence
        2.   Therapist needs sensitivity regarding linguistic preferences
    E.   Native Americans
        1.   Remember customs, tribal culture (these may be source of comfort to client)
        2.   May be expectation that therapist will do most of talking
XI.   Exploring Psychology: Virtual Reality Therapy
    A.   Behavior therapy techniques—uses computer-generated simulated environments
    B.   Especially helpful for phobias
    C.   Advantages
        1.   Can arrange for environments that can be difficult to arrange in real life
        2.   Greater control over stimulus environments
        3.   Same people may be more willing to experience something virtually than in actuality

SUMMARY

In this module you learn about the many different types of therapy that are available for individuals with psychological problems. Problems both big and small can be helped by means of psychotherapy. Although there are many different approaches regarding how it is carried out, research does indicate that an individual getting any kind of therapy is more likely to show improvement than an individual getting no therapy whatsoever. The different therapeutic approaches parallel the underlying view on the nature of the human being and general explanations regarding human functioning that pertain to each perspective within the field of psychology. Cognitive psychologists take an approach that looks at thinking patterns, behavioral psychologists examine environmental influences, and so forth.

The traditional psychoanalytic perspective, founded on Sigmund Freud's ideas, portrays the inner nature of the human as full of conflict with primitive sexual desires motivating all of behavior. Traditional psychoanalytic therapy, then, is built around uncovering the repressed sources of conflict and bringing them to light. Once these deep-seated conflicts are in conscious awareness, the individual, with the aid of the therapist, can come up with better ways of working through and resolving these issues. Crucial to the process of psychoanalysis is free association. The patient is permitted and encouraged to free associate—to say whatever comes to mind, no matter how meaningless or relevant it may seem at the time. Freud also encouraged the recording and reporting of dreams, believing that dreams were "the royal road" to uncovering what was really going on in the unconscious. Psychoanalysts help the patient with dream interpretation. Psychological resistance means that the patient changes the subject or leaves the session whenever a certain topic emerges. This resistance is a signal that the topic is of great importance because of its obvious sensitivity. The process of transference in psychoanalysis means the patient starts to see the therapist in a role that was crucial in his or her past. Like resistance, interpreting transference too can be helpful since both of these phenomena reveal the traumatic childhood experiences that have led to the current psychological abnormality. Freud's psychoanalysis takes many years. Most current versions of psychoanalysis focus less on sexual drives and the unconscious and more on the here-and-now and finding adaptive solutions. Therapy tends to occur over a much shorter period of time.

Humanists believe that all of us are on the road towards self-actualization—discovering our unique inner potential and putting it to best use. Obviously, knowing our inner selves is crucial to living a psychologically healthy life. Problems arise, according to the humanistic perspective, when an individual has lost touch with that inner self and source of guidance or when our sense of ourselves is in conflict with what others have conveyed they think we should be or want us to be. The opinion of others may be conditional rather than unconditionally accepting as advocated by humanistic therapists. Thus, a humanistic therapist will try to help a client get back in touch with that inner self. Humanistic therapy is typically client-centered; that is, since every human is unique, only the client has the answer to his or her problems. The therapist acts mostly as a facilitator to help clients discover their own sense of self and their own aspirations. Since humanists think the source of psychological difficulty is others who were not supportive and accepting, humanistic therapists incorporate an approach of empathy, genuineness, and unconditional positive regard as they deal with their clients. The objective of humanistic therapy is to help clients reconnect with who they are and realize that they are completely acceptable as they are. Gestalt therapy is a form of humanistic therapy where again the objective is to aid the client in getting back in touch with that inner self and integrate all aspects of the personality. However, gestalt therapists may be more confrontational in the hope that this directness will help clients also be direct in confronting their true feelings at the moment.

Behavioral psychologists believe everything about the human has been learned directly through experience or indirectly through observation and imitation of others' behavior. Poor, offensive, ineffective, or maladaptive behaviors can be learned just as more desirable behaviors are learned. According to behaviorists, we adopt behaviors because in the past these behaviors have led to a pleasant outcome. We avoid exhibiting behaviors that have led to unpleasant outcomes. We may have, perhaps inadvertently, gotten "desirable" results from behavior that really is not productive. Our prior acceptable behavior may have gone unnoticed, leading to the decrease of its manifestation. Note that if a behavior has been learned, it can be changed by changing the consequences or by learning more effective behaviors. The treatment of fears (phobias and other anxiety disorders) may be approached behaviorally by means of systematic desensitization. With systematic desensitization, the client first reaches a state of relaxation, then slowly works her way up through a fear hierarchy. This is carried out over a period of therapy sessions. The objective is that the client will learn to replace a reaction of fear (such as to an object or situation) with a reaction of peace and calmness. This draws upon the behavioral phenomenon known as classical conditioning. The behavioral phenomenon of operant conditioning (behavior shaped by consequences) has therapeutic application in the form of behavior modification. This may be done in combination with the issuing of tokens (positive reinforcers) that can be exchanged for something the client wants. The objective of behavioral treatments is more preferable behaviors are reinforced and undesirable ones are not maintained.

Cognitive therapists, such as Aaron Beck and Albert Ellis, believe that the source of psychological problems is less the situations or events themselves, and more how we construe those situations or events. Cognitive psychologists believe that a key to good psychological health is keeping one's perspective. Was that event really the ruination of your life, or was it a setback that you are fully able and willing to overcome? Cognitive therapy involves encouraging clients to contemplate their thoughts, and how they interpret events in their lives. Albert Ellis, as part of rational-emotive behavior therapy, encourages clients to recognize that, for example, expecting everyone's approval all the time is irrational. Ellis also advocates a positive attitude. Thoughts such as "I can manage this" help create a more positive response and thus help prevent thinking that is self-defeating and that leads to self-defeating behaviors. Aaron Beck suggests that clients examine their negative emotional reactions. Beck points out that it is the negative emotional reaction that ultimately causes our problems. If we stay in touch with reality and truly examine our thoughts and emotional reactions for accuracy, we may well see that our negative interpretation is unfounded. Rational-emotive behavior therapy may be more direct and confrontational than Beck's cognitive therapy.

A popular approach to psychological problems is eclectic therapy. With eclectic therapy, the therapist calls upon all the available treatment methodologies. They may be used in combination, or one approach may help with one aspect of a problem while a different therapeutic approach is used for a different aspect of the problem. More clinical and counseling psychologists advocate an eclectic approach to psychotherapy than any other single methodology.

Therapy often is carried out in individual sessions with just client and therapist, but it also may take the form of group therapy, family therapy, or couples therapy. These basically constitute what their names imply. Group therapy can be advantageous in that it is less expensive, and participants may explore aspects of their problems that are shared by other group members. The experience of sharing with other group members particularly helps with relationship and social problems. In family therapy, there is no one individual with the problem. The source of the psychological difficulty is thought to lie within the entire family system, and thus the therapeutic approach addresses the family as a unit. Couples therapy (or marital therapy if the pair are married) addresses relationship issues, which very often involve the inability to communicate effectively, and/or power and control issues.

Though the effectiveness of psychotherapy is still undergoing detailed research, in general we know that any kind of psychotherapy results in more improvement for individuals than if they do not receive therapy at all. Statistical procedures known as meta-analyses compare the functioning of individuals who have received therapy with those who have not across hundreds of the individual studies that have been conducted. Still, some therapies may be more preferable for a given problem than others, and though we have initial findings, these matters are still being explored. It is thought that much of the reason why psychotherapy works lies with factors common to many approaches; these are known as nonspecific factors. Most likely these include the effectiveness and overall quality of the client-therapist relationship and the clients' hopes or expectations that the therapy will work and they will get better. Therapists need to remember that clients come from a wide range of ethnic and racial backgrounds. Therapy is most effective when practitioners are sensitive to the cultural factors pertaining to each of their clients.

One promising new avenue of therapy is virtual reality therapy, a type of behavior therapy involving simulated computer environments. This has the advantage of allowing people to have experiences that would be difficult to engage in actuality. It has proven particularly useful in the treatment of phobias.

KEY TERMS

Psychotherapy

Psychoanalysis

Psychoanalysts

Free association

Dream analysis

Interpretation

Insight

Resistance

Transference relationship

Countertransference

Behavior therapy

Systematic desensitization

Fear hierarchy

Gradual exposure

Modeling

Aversive conditioning

Cognitive-behavioral therapy (CBT)

Rational-emotive behavior therapy (REBT)

Cognitive therapy

Eclectic therapy

Group therapy

Family therapy

Couples therapy

Meta-analysis

Nonspecific factors

Placebo effects

Virtual reality therapy (VRT)

SELF-TEST PRACTICE QUIZ

From the Key Terms select that which best matches the following (Note: Not every Key Term will be used.):

1. _____ A helpful result of psychotherapy that occurs because the patient hopes and believes in the treatment and that the improvement will occur

2. _____ A type of therapy that involves utilizing aspects of any available therapeutic methodology in order to best treat the psychological disorder at hand

3. _____ One of the strategies involved in behavior therapy where the client observes the real-life adaptive behavior of others and attempts to imitate it

4. _____ The psychotherapy approach first begun by Sigmund Freud where the cause of psychological disorder is believed to be deep-seated, repressed, unresolved conflicts

a. Psychotherapy

b. Psychoanalysis

c. Psychoanalysts

d. Free association

e. Dream analysis

f. Interpretation

g. Insight

h. Resistance

i. Transference relationship

j. Countertransference

k. Behavior therapy

l. Systematic desensitization

m. Fear hierarchy

n. Gradual exposure

5. _____   The objective of psychoanalysis as devised by Freud; the patient comes to understand the connection between the psychological disorder and repressed childhood experiences.

6. _____   One component of psychoanalysis as developed by Sigmund Freud; the patient comes to regard the therapist as representing a key individual from an earlier difficult time and manifests this conceptualization during therapy sessions

7. _____   One approach to psychotherapy where the emphasis is on what the client has learned from experience either through classical or operant conditioning

8. _____   An approach to psychological treatment developed by Albert Ellis where the patient is challenged to evaluate the truth and rationality of beliefs underlying behaviors

9. _____   A type of psychotherapy developed by Aaron Beck where clients are encouraged to evaluate the truth of cognitive distortions underlying ineffective emotional reactions

10. _____   A behavioral approach to psychotherapy most specifically geared towards alleviating phobias and other fear-based disorders; involves gradually learning to replace response of fear with a response of calmness and relaxation

11. _____   A fundamental technique that is part of traditional psychoanalysis; the patient is completely free to say whatever comes to mind whether or not apparently meaningful

12. _____   A form of treatment for psychological disorders constructed around a supportive relationship between client and therapist and involving extensive verbal exchange

o.   Modeling

p.   Aversive conditioning

q.   Cognitive-behavioral therapy (CBT)

r.   Rational-emotive behavior therapy (REBT)

s.   Cognitive therapy

t.   Eclectic therapy

u.   Group therapy

v.   Family therapy

w.   Couples therapy

x.   Meta-analysis

y.   Nonspecific factors

z.   Placebo effects

aa.   Virtual reality therapy (VRT)

13. _____   A type of therapy built upon the basic behavioral approach but adding an awareness of one's thoughts and interpretations as important to behavior and psychological functioning

14. _____   Qualities that seem to contribute to a positive psychotherapeutic experience but do not appear to be exclusive to one approach to psychotherapy or another

15. _____   Treatment for psychological disorder involving approaching the entire family unit and its functioning as the presenting psychological problem

16. One difference between traditional psychoanalysis, as begun by Sigmund Freud, and modern psychodynamic approaches is that traditional psychoanalysis
    a.   discourages the use of free association.
    b.   is completed over a relatively brief span of time.
    c.   focuses primarily on the effects of primitive sexual instinct.
    d.   is conducted in a face-to-face manner.

17. In psychoanalysis, when the client begins to react to the therapist as if he or she were someone from the client's past with whom the client had troubling issues is known as
    a.   interpretation.
    b.   transference.
    c.   insight.
    d.   resistance.

18. Which of the following is NOT a technique commonly used in psychodynamic therapy?
    a.   systematic desensitization
    b.   interpretation of transference
    c.   dream analysis
    d.   free association

19. The source of psychological problems according to the humanistic view is
    a.   failing to adhere to behavioral standards established by close family members.
    b.   an excessive concern with one's own issues and inner feelings.
    c.   deep-seated sexual conflicts stemming from early childhood.
    d.   becoming out of touch with one's sense of direction towards self-actualization.

20. What do humanist therapists mean when they say that a therapist should be genuine?
    a.   Therapists should not lie about their feelings, even if they are bored by the client.
    b.   Therapists should be truthful when describing their qualifications.
    c.   Therapists should accept their clients for who they are and not judge them.
    d.   Therapists should attempt to see the world through their clients' eyes.

21. A novel behavioral therapeutic approach where a little boy became unafraid of white rabbits through repeatedly presenting a rabbit along with something pleasant was introduced by
    a.   John Watson.
    b.   Mary Cover Jones.
    c.   Albert Ellis.
    d.   Carl Rogers.

22. Behavior therapy is founded on the notion that a behavior (whether truly effective or not) is learned when an individual exhibits the behavior and it is then followed by a pleasant consequence (known as a reinforcer). To change that behavior, you would

    a. explain to the client that such behavior is not really effective.
    b. use dream analysis to detect the client's true underlying psychological issues.
    c. remove reinforcers for undesirable behaviors and apply reinforcers to strengthen other, more preferable or adaptive behaviors.
    d. gradually expose the client to low levels of electric shock.

23. The difference between systematic desensitization and gradual exposure is that systematic desensitization

    a. does not make use of a fear hierarchy.
    b. puts the client in real-life experiences.
    c. is more effective for personality disorders than for anxiety disorders.
    d. involves extensive use of the client's imagination.

24. The most widely endorsed therapeutic methodology presented in clinical psychology training programs in the United States is _____ therapy.

    a. cognitive-behavioral
    b. psychoanalytic
    c. rational-emotive behavior
    d. gestalt

25. In cognitive therapy, the source of psychological problems is believed to be not so much events or situations that occur but rather

    a. genetic influences that lead to consistent behavioral patterns across situations.
    b. a lack of unification among various aspects of one's personality.
    c. maladaptive behaviors resulting from emotional reactions that occur as a consequence of the interpretation of events and situations.
    d. genetic influences that lead to consistent thinking patterns across situations.

26. The cognitive therapy exercise where a client tries out his or her beliefs and perceptions in real life to see if they are actually true is known as

    a. virtual therapy.
    b. reality testing.
    c. modeling.
    d. the empty chair technique.

27. Which of the following is NOT a potential advantage of virtual reality therapy over other types of therapy?

    a. People may be more willing to take part in simulated experiences than real-life experiences.
    b. It provides greater control over the stimulus environment.
    c. Using virtual reality therapy may allow people to experience things that would otherwise be difficult for practical reasons.
    d. It is more effective than other therapies in helping patients deal with schizophrenia.

28. What is the goal of the statistical technique of meta-analysis?

    a. proving whether one type of therapy is more effective than another
    b. determining whether or not a study's results are statistically significant
    c. correcting for errors in data collection
    d. averaging the results of a large number of studies

29. It is likely that _____ best explain why there are psychological improvements in clients after therapeutic treatment.
    a. the principles involved in cognitive therapy
    b. the techniques involved in behavioral therapy
    c. nonspecific factors
    d. genetic factors
30. Sensitivity to the fact that some cultures discourage the open expression of emotions is particularly important when a therapist is treating _____ clients.
    a. African American
    b. Asian American
    c. Hispanic American
    d. Native American
31. Someone who draws from a variety of available psychological treatment methodologies, depending on the nature of the client's problem or problems, is a(n) _____ therapist.
    a. cognitive
    b. cognitive-behavioral
    c. rational-emotive behavior
    d. eclectic

ESSAY QUESTIONS

1. Briefly explain the traditional approach to psychoanalytic therapy.
2. What are empathy, genuineness, and unconditional positive regard? Why are they considered crucial to effective client-centered therapy?
3. Explain the relationship between events, beliefs, and consequences as presented in Albert Ellis's rational-emotive behavior model.

ANSWER KEY

1. Placebo effects
2. Eclectic therapy
3. Modeling
4. Psychoanalysis
5. Insight
6. Transference relationship
7. Behavior therapy
8. Rational-emotive behavioral therapy (REBT)
9. Cognitive therapy
10. Systematic desensitization
11. Free association
12. Psychotherapy
13. Cognitive-behavioral therapy (CBT)
14. Nonspecific factors
15. Family therapy

16. c

17. b

18. a

19. d

20. a

21. b

22. c

23. d

24. a

25. c

26. b

27. d

28. d

29. c

30. b

31. d

SAMPLE ANSWERS TO ESSAY QUESTIONS

1.   The traditional approach to psychoanalysis was begun by Sigmund Freud. Freud believed the cause of psychological abnormality lay out of an individual's conscious awareness and involved conflicting factors that were often related to early childhood experiences. Thus, to get to the cause of the psychological disorder, the therapist needed to gain access to and probe the client's unconscious. The objective is to bring these hidden conflicts to light (into conscious awareness), gain insight as to how they have impacted the client's life, and find a resolution that will cure problems (such as hysterical paralysis) and allow the client to invest energy in more worthwhile pursuits. Psychoanalysts believe that gaining access to the unconscious is difficult to do because the contents of the unconscious consist of selfish desires and unacceptable sexual and aggressive impulses. The patient does not want these unacceptable aspects to be seen by others, and it is concern about unintentional exposure of the unconscious that can lead to anxiety and other psychological disorders. Traditional psychoanalysts, then, instruct the patient to lie down on a couch and stay out of the patient's line of sight themselves in order to reduce reminders of the conscious world and make access to the unconscious easier. The patient is directed to free associate—to say whatever comes to mind—without regard to meaningfulness or apparent cohesiveness of the statements. Psychoanalysts believe these free associations and how they are reported by the patient (e.g., what thoughts seem to occur together), eventually suggest the conflicts within the unconscious. During psychoanalysis, the patient may exhibit transference; that is, he or she may begin to act as if the therapist were a key member in the patient's past, one with whom the patient had psychologically troubling experiences. The patient may also exhibit resistance. Here, the patient consistently avoids or fails to respond to a certain line of questioning presented by the therapist. Both transference and resistance are considered helpful by the psychoanalyst because both aid in bringing hidden difficulties to light. The analyst's role through all of the therapy sessions is to interpret what is happening and help the patient gain insight as to what underlying factors are and how they have influenced the patient's psychological state. Traditional psychodynamic therapy takes many months or, more often, years. Eventually the

patient comes to a conscious understanding of the underlying conflicting forces and, with this insight, is able to live more effectively.

2.   Empathy, genuineness, and unconditional positive regard are all key components in effective psychotherapy according to the humanistic viewpoint. Empathy means the therapist can perceive, and in fact can feel herself, the emotions and experiences of the client. Exhibiting empathy for the client's feelings and experiences helps confirm that the client's emotions and interpretations are valid, and are important to the therapist. Genuineness means the therapist is always his true self and conveys his own feelings, reactions, and characteristics honestly to the client. When the therapist is completely genuine and allows no falseness or facades in his own behavior, this sets the stage for the client to do the same. It suggests that the therapist values genuineness in others, thus encouraging clients to adopt an approach of genuinely detecting and reporting their own feelings. Unconditional positive regard means the therapist approaches the client as someone who is completely worthy and valuable exactly as he or she is at the moment. Everything about that client is completely acceptable and worthwhile, whether or not the client exhibits behaviors that parallel the therapist's behaviors and whether or not the client's behavior and personality characteristics are those that meet society's standards.

These approaches that are components of client-centered therapy are crucial because humanists believe psychological disorder stems from disliking oneself because one does not measure up to standards set by others. Or, psychological problems stem from losing touch with one's inner sense of guidance, again because others said the client "should" not feel or behave a certain way. The objective of client-centered therapy is to get the client back on track—back in touch with his or her feelings and that inner sense of guidance that leads the client to reaching self-actualization. Client-centered therapists let the client more or less direct what happens in therapy sessions; therapists act mostly as a facilitator, simply reflecting back what the client has conveyed. Thus, the client's connection with inner feelings and direction is restored, and the client develops confidence in and acceptance of his own sense of self-identity.

3.   The rational-emotive behavior model, upon which rational-emotive behavior therapy is based, is the view that thoughts and interpretations that are irrational lead to emotional distress, and maladaptive behaviors then result from this distress. The debilitating aspects of the process are not so much the events that happen to an individual but rather the individual's construal of events and the emotional reactions that spring from this interpretation. Albert Ellis's treatment method is to help clients face the irrationality of their thinking. Ellis suggests an "ABC" model to represent the relationship between events in a person's life and that person's resulting behavior. "A" stands for the events that occur in someone's life. We all have challenging experiences in addition to more pleasant ones. Thus, some life events, although presenting difficulties, are unavoidable. "B" stands for an individual's set of beliefs in light of which the individual makes an interpretation regarding the precipitating event. These interpretations are under our own control. Our beliefs impact how we construe a situation, and lead to "C" the emotional consequence of that interpretation. If one's beliefs are not logical (e.g., believing one must always be perfect or that one must always be completely acceptable to everyone else in every way possible), the emotional reaction will be maladaptive. No one can consistently reach unrealistically high standards, for example. Failure will inevitably result, and the sense of failure further diminishes one's ability to function effectively. Ellis challenged clients, sometimes in a confrontational manner, to recognize the irrationality of their beliefs. Rather than having events lead automatically to an emotional consequence, Ellis encouraged clients to be aware of the existing belief system through which the activating event is processed. With a more rational belief system, emotional reactions to events will not be so negative and debilitating. The client's response to an event will be more rational, and interpretations and resulting emotions will be kept in perspective. Rational-emotive behavior therapy also helps clients learn new, more adaptive behaviors and ways of dealing with others.

MODULE 14.3 BIOMEDICAL THERAPIES

LEARNING OBJECTIVES

After you have mastered the information in this unit, you will be able to:

- Discuss the major types of psychotropic or psychiatric drugs

- Compare and contrast the advantages and disadvantages of psychiatric drugs

- Define ECT, and explain how it is used

OUTLINE

I. Background Factors in Biomedical Therapies
   A. Many gains in biomedical treatments of individuals with psychological disorders
   B. Drugs have side effects; electroconvulsive shock, psychosurgery more controversial
II. Drug Therapy
   A. Basic approach in drug therapy
      1. Neurological transmission in the brain depends upon brain chemicals (neurotransmitters) to conduct messages from one neuron to another
      2. Some psychological problems (e.g., anxiety, mood, and eating disorders; schizophrenia) related to irregularities in brain chemical action
      3. Drugs have been developed that help alleviate abnormalities in functioning of these neurotransmitters
   B. Antianxiety drugs (minor tranquilizers)
      1. Category includes diazepam (Valium), chlordiazepoxide (Librium), and alprazolam (Xanax)
      2. Act on neurotransmitter gamma-aminobutyric acid (GABA)
      3. Enhance GABA's ability to keep neural flow calm, in check
   C. Antidepressants
      1. Increase availability of norepinephrine and serotonin (neurotransmitters) in the brain
      2. Tricyclics
         a) Examples are imipramine (Tofranil), amitriptyline (Elavil), and doxepin (Sinequan)
         b) Raise brain levels of norepinephrine and serotonin by interfering with reuptake process (reabsorption of these brain chemicals by transmitter cells)
      3. Monoamine oxidase (MAO) inhibitors
         a) Examples are phenelzine (Nardil) and tranylcypromine (Parnate)
         b) Inhibit action of MAO, which normally breaks down norepinephrine and serotonin in synapse
      4. Selective serotonin-reuptake inhibitors (SSRIs)
         a) Examples are fluoxetine (Prozac) and sertraline (Zoloft)
         b) Specifically raise levels of serotonin by limiting its reuptake
      5. Evaluation of use of antidepressant drugs
         a) Use of antidepressant medication has greatly increased in recent years
         b) Help relieve depression in 50 to 70 percent of cases
         c) Improvement usually modest
         d) SSRIs have less severe side effects, less dangerous regarding overdose
         e) Antidepressants may also help in treating anxiety disorders
         f) Serotonin implicated in regulation of mood, appetite
   D. Antipsychotics (major tranquilizers)
      1. Used to treat schizophrenia and other psychotic disorders

2.   First class of drugs (1950s): phenothiazines
   a)   Includes Thorazine, Mellaril, and Prolixin
   b)   Now possible to control most severe symptoms of schizophrenia
3.   Phenothiazines and newer antipsychotic drugs work by blocking action of dopamine at dopamine receptor sites
E.   Other psychiatric drugs
   1.   Mood-stabilizing drugs (such as lithium)—help with bipolar disorder
   2.   Anticonvulsant drugs help in treatment of epilepsy
   3.   Stimulant drugs
      a)   Methylphenidate (Ritalin) and others
      b)   Improve attention spans, reduce disruptive behavior
      c)   Work by increasing activity of dopamine in frontal lobes
F.   Evaluating psychotropic drugs
   1.   Do reduce or control symptoms of many psychological disorders
   2.   Psychotropic drugs do not provide a cure
   3.   Drugs alone do not teach more effective life skills
   4.   Each has risk of adverse side effects
      a)   Drowsiness from antianxiety drugs
      b)   Dry mouth and problems with sexual response (from antidepressants)
      c)   Muscular tremors, other motor problems from antipsychotic drugs
      d)   Most serious side effect of antipsychotic drugs—tardive dyskinesia (TD; permanent neurological damage to motor system)
      e)   Possible that clozapine (Clozaril, for treatment of schizophrenia) may have fewer neurological side effects
      f)   Some drugs lead to dependency, addiction, death from overdose
      g)   Concern (e.g., with widespread reliance on Ritalin) is overeagerness for "quick fix" regarding psychological problems
      h)   Antidepressants may lead to suicidal thoughts in children and adolescents
      i)   Psychotherapy may be more work, but appears crucial for long term drug-free improvement
      j)   Combination of psychotherapy and drugs together more effective than psychiatric drugs alone
III.   Electroconvulsive Therapy (ECT)
A.   Jolt of electricity is passed through brain of patient, resulting in convulsions
B.   May produce dramatic relief for individuals who are severely depressed
C.   Anesthesia, muscle relaxants used to prevent experience of pain or injuries
D.   Involves six to twelve treatments over period of several weeks
E.   Most likely to be used when patient does not respond to other therapies
F.   Perhaps regulates levels of neurotransmitters related to mood
G.   High rate of relapse; possible permanent memory loss—used as a last resort
IV.   Psychosurgery
A.   Brain is surgically altered to control deviant or violent behavior
B.   Prefrontal lobotomy
   1.   Previously most widely used psychosurgical technique
   2.   Nerve connections between frontal lobe and lower brain centers are severed
   3.   Eventually eliminated because of serious complications, death of patients
C.   More sophisticated psychosurgery techniques introduced in recent years
D.   Involve surgical alterations to smaller areas of the brain
E.   Again used only as a last resort; many concerns regarding later complications

SUMMARY

In this module you learn about another approach to treating psychological disorders. This approach involves the used of biomedical interventions. Biomedical therapies include the many currently available psychiatric drugs and other lesser-used biomedical interventions such as electroconvulsive shock therapy and psychosurgery. Far and away the most widely used biomedical treatments are the psychotropic drugs available to treat severe and less severe psychological disorders.

Psychotropic drugs are grouped into classes, the major classes being antianxiety drugs, antidepressants, and antipsychotics. All drug therapy is aimed at smoothing the workings of the brain's neurological pathways. Although neural messages are electrical in nature within the length of the neuron, they convert to chemical form when traveling from one neuron to the next. The neural messages are transmitted among many interconnecting neurons by means of chemical messengers called neurotransmitters. Note, then, that these neurotransmitters (such as norepinephrine, dopamine, and serotonin) are chemical in nature. It is here (at the junctures between neurons, which are called synapses) that the psychiatric drugs go to work. Because the drugs are chemicals, they are designed to affect the chemicals naturally present in the brain, the neurotransmitters. They also impact the neural sending and receiving sites (located on the ends of each neuron; not every neuron accommodates all brain chemicals) associated with these neurotransmitters. Although the underlying biological cause of abnormal behavior is not fully understood, irregularities in neural pathway functioning are associated with the presence of psychological disorder. Psychotropic drugs help to smooth the operations of these neural pathways by impacting the availability of relevant neurotransmitters and possibly by affecting the action at neural sending and receiving sites. The use of drugs helps, sometimes substantially, in the treatment of psychological disorder. When psychiatric drugs were first introduced in the 1950s, their use was a radical breakthrough in treating psychologically disturbed patients. It is important to recognize that the drugs do not provide a cure for the problem. However, in many cases, they control symptoms and make the psychological disorders more manageable.

Antianxiety drugs are minor tranquilizers, such as Valium and Xanax. All antianxiety drugs act upon the neurotransmitter gamma-aminobutyric acid (GABA), helping enhance its effects. Since GABA keeps neural impulses in check and flowing smoothly, individuals taking antianxiety drugs are expected to feel calmer and less prone to worry and agitation.

Antidepressants help keep the neurotransmitters norepinephrine and serotonin at sufficient levels within the brain. Both of these neurotransmitters are associated with mood or emotional states. The three major types of antidepressants are (1) tricyclics, (2) monoamine oxidase (MAO) inhibitors, and (3) selective serotonin-reuptake inhibitors (SSRIs). All of these antidepressants affect the levels of the neurotransmitters mentioned. Serotonin and norepinephrine levels are impacted because normally these brain chemicals are reabsorbed by transmitting neurons once the neural message has been passed to the next neuron. Antidepressants either limit the amount of the neurotransmitters that are reabsorbed from the synaptic gap, or stop the enzyme (MAO) that causes the neurotransmitters to be broken down once they have been released from the neural sending sites. Antidepressants have become very widely used. They are successful in the majority of cases in treating depression. They also help in the treatment of nearly all well-known anxiety disorders and in some eating disorders. Common antidepressants include Prozac and Zoloft (both SSRIs) and the tricyclic Elavil. It is important to remember that all drugs have side effects. Not all drugs work for all psychologically troubled clients, and many individuals stop taking medication because of unpleasant side effects.

Antipsychotics are major tranquilizers and are the ones used to treat schizophrenia (and other psychotic disorders). Antipsychotic drugs include Thorazine, Mellaril, and Prolixin. Again, while they control symptoms, antipsychotics do not provide a cure. However, being able to reduce and manage some of the most difficult aspects of schizophrenia (hallucinations, for example) is a tremendous step forward. Antipsychotics are effective because they appear to block receptor sites associated with the neurotransmitter dopamine. Though antipsychotics have been extremely helpful in treating serious psychological disorders, they also are the drugs with the most serious side effects. Long-term use of antipsychotic drugs damages the neurological systems of psychological patients most particularly the motor nervous system. Tardive dyskinesia (TD) is the most serious side effect of antipsychotic drugs, and the patient eventually will experience permanent impairment of motor functioning. Advanced tardive dyskinesia is characterized by various uncontrollable neurologically-directed movements.

Other psychiatric drugs such as lithium (for treatment of bipolar disorder) and stimulant drugs (such at Ritalin, for hyperactivity) help in the treatment of psychological disorder by managing maladaptive symptoms. Patients and therapists must resist the temptation to treat all psychological disorders with the apparent "quick fix" available through drug therapy. Biomedical therapies are not a substitute for psychological treatments, and psychotherapy is at least as effective as the available drug therapies. Often a combination of the two approaches is most effective. Biomedical therapies also include electroconvulsive shock therapy (to treat severe cases of depression especially when the sufferers have not responded to other forms of treatment) and psychosurgery. Both of these latter methods are quite controversial, rarely used and only in extreme cases as a last resort.

KEY TERMS

Psychotropic drugs

Antianxiety drugs

Antidepressants

Tricyclics

Monoamine oxidase (MAO) inhibitors

Selective serotonin-reuptake inhibitors (SSRIs)

Antipsychotics

Tardive dyskinesia (TD)

Electroconvulsive therapy (ECT)

Psychosurgery

Prefrontal lobotomy

SELF-TEST PRACTICE QUIZ

From the Key Terms select that which best matches the following:

1. _____ The most serious side effect from taking antipsychotic drugs; potentially disabling damage to the nervous system particularly that function directing motor activity

2. _____ A psychological surgical procedure (now no longer used) to control violent behavior; neural connections between the frontal lobes and other brain centers are severed.

a. Psychotropic drugs

b. Antianxiety drugs

c. Antidepressants

d. Tricyclics

e. Monoamine oxidase (MAO) inhibitors

f. Selective serotonin-reuptake inhibitors (SSRIs)

3. _____ A class of psychotropic drugs used to treat depression and other disorders by specifically increasing the availability of serotonin through limiting how much is reabsorbed

4. _____ Psychiatric drugs developed to treat psychological disorders by means of chemical and biological intervention

5. _____ One of the major classes of antidepressants, which are generally effective because they increase the availability of neurotransmitters by interfering with their reuptake

6. _____ A class of antipsychotic drugs developed to treat depression and other psychological disorders

7. _____ One of the major classes of antidepressants, which increases the availability of neurotransmitters related to emotional states by limiting the action of an enzyme that normally breaks down these neurotransmitters in the synapse

8. _____ Drugs used in the treatment of severe psychological disorders such as schizophrenia

9. _____ A controversial biomedical therapy for severe cases of depression where there is no real response to other forms of treatment; involves an electrical shock delivered to the head of a patient—the shock is of sufficient strength to induce convulsions

10. _____ A rarely used procedure involving surgical alterations to the brain in an effort to control dangerously psychologically disturbed behavior

11. _____ A class of psychotropic drugs developed to treat various anxiety disorders

g. Antipsychotics

h. Tardive dyskinesia (TD)

i. Electroconvulsive therapy (ECT)

j. Psychosurgery

k. Prefrontal lobotomy

12. The development of psychiatric drugs to treat psychological disorders has led to
    a. the complete relief of psychological disturbances.
    b. the ability to control the more debilitating aspects of abnormal behavior.
    c. an increased reliance on psychotherapy as a means for treating psychological problems.
    d. a minimization of side effects normally involved in psychological treatments.

13. Some antidepressant drugs are selective serotonin reuptake inhibitors (SSRIs). What is "reuptake"?

    a. release of neurotransmitters into the bloodstream
    b. reabsorption of neurotransmitters into neurons
    c. creation of new neurotransmitters
    d. the flow of nerve impulses

14. Antianxiety drugs act on the neurotransmitter

    a. norepinephrine.
    b. serotonin.
    c. GABA (gamma-aminobutyric acid).
    d. dopamine.

15. Prozac (fluoxetine) and Zoloft (sertraline) are in the drug classification

    a. antipsychotics.
    b. tricyclics.
    c. monoamine oxidase (MAO) inhibitors.
    d. selective serotonin-reuptake inhibitors (SSRIs).

16. Normally the brain chemical monoamine oxidase (MAO)

    a. smooths the flow of neural messages in the brain.
    b. interferes with the reabsorption of serotonin and dopamine.
    c. breaks down important mood-related neurotransmitters present in the synapses.
    d. blocks the action of dopamine at neural sending and receiving sites.

17. The most serious side effect to taking antipsychotic drugs is

    a. drowsiness.
    b. reduced sexual interest and sexual response.
    c. motor system functioning.
    d. permanent damage to intellectual functioning.

18. Messages are transmitted from one neuron to the next by

    a. interneurons.
    b. brain chemicals.
    c. connector neurons.
    d. nerve impulses.

19. A newer drug used in the treatment of schizophrenia that may have fewer side effects than traditional antipsychotics is

    a. clozapine.
    b. Thorazine.
    c. Elavil.
    d. chloropromazine.

20. Tricyclics fall into the category of _____ drugs.

    a. antidepressant
    b. antianxiety
    c. antipsychotic
    d. tardive dyskenisic

21. Which statement about electroconvulsive therapy (ECT) is NOT correct?

    a. It generally produces permanent improvements.
    b. It is usually a treatment of last resort.
    c. It may lead to memory losses.
    d. It usually requires a number of treatments to be effective.

22. Lithium is often used to treat

    a.   anxiety.
    b.   psychosis.
    c.   attention deficit disorder.
    d.   bipolar disorder.

23. In a prefrontal lobotomy,

    a.   the left brain hemisphere is severed from the right brain hemisphere.
    b.   the frontal lobe is severed from lower brain centers.
    c.   the thalamus is severed from the parietal and occipital lobes.
    d.   both the corpus callosum and the thalamus are removed.

24. Many people think it is odd that stimulant medications would be helpful for people with hyperactivity (ADHD). What is it that these medications are stimulating?

    a.   heart rate
    b.   GABA levels throughout the nervous system
    c.   dopamine activity in the frontal lobes
    d.   appetite

25. Tricyclics are likely to produce _____ severe side effects in comparison to selective serotonin-reuptake inhibitors (SSRIs).

    a.   less
    b.   about the same degree of
    c.   more
    d.   Cannot be determined; depends on the reaction of the individual patient

26. Psychotherapy has been shown to be _____ drug therapy with regard to treating psychological disorders.

    a.   more effective than
    b.   at least as effective as
    c.   slightly less effective than
    d.   much less effective than

27. Some drugs such as Valium raise concerns because

    a.   regular use can lead to physical and psychological dependency.
    b.   an overdose is often deadly.
    c.   they can become toxic if mixed with alcohol or other drugs.
    d.   they exhibit all of the above.

ESSAY QUESTIONS

1. How do the different classes of psychiatric drugs work? Briefly explain how each class of drugs works on the functioning of the neurological system.

2. Name the side effects or other concerns we have with at least four of five of the drugs or other biomedical therapies mentioned in this module.

3. Based on what you have read, what do you think is the best way to treat psychological disorders?

ANSWER KEY

1. Tardive dyskinesia (TD)

2. Prefrontal lobotomy

3. Selective serotonin-reuptake inhibitors (SSRIs)

4. Psychotropic drugs

5. Tricyclics

6. Antidepressants

7. Monoamine oxidase (MAO) inhibitors

8. Antipsychotics

9. Electroconvulsive therapy (ECT)

10. Psychosurgery

11. Antianxiety drugs

12. b

13. b

14. c

15. d

16. c

17. c

18. b

19. a

20. a

21. a

22. d

23. b

24. c

25. c

26. b

27. d

SAMPLE ANSWERS TO ESSAY QUESTIONS

1. Antianxiety drugs help keep patients calm and help reduce muscle tension. Antianxiety drugs bring these results about by enhancing one of the body's brain chemicals, a neurotransmitter called gamma-aminobutyric acid (GABA). The function of GABA is to keep neural impulses in check and keep a neural transmission from exciting activity in other nearby neurons. Specifically, the antianxiety drugs increase the sensitivity of GABA receptors.

   Antidepressants affect neurological functioning by increasing the available levels of neurotransmitters associated with emotional experience or mood states. Norepinephrine and serotonin seem to be the neurotransmitters most involved in neural communication regarding emotions. Antidepressants either interfere with, and thus limit or slow, the reuptake of these neurotransmitters (this is the function of tricyclics and SSRIs), or they reduce the action of an enzyme that breaks down these neurotransmitters once they have been released into the synapse (a synapse is the gap between one neuron and adjoining neurons, where the impulse transmission becomes chemical in nature). MAO inhibitors function in this latter fashion; monoamine oxidase (MAO) is the enzyme that normally degrades norepinephine and serotonin present in the synapse.

Antipsychotics work by blocking the action of dopamine at the dopamine receptor sites in brain neurons. Lithium is a major mood-stabilizing drug that is used in the treatment of bipolar disorder; other mood stabilizers are used in the treatment of epilepsy. Stimulant drugs help control hyperactivity and attention problems by increasing dopamine activity in the frontal lobes.

2.   Drug or other biomedical therapies are not a perfect solution to the problem of psychological disorders. Psychotropic drugs do not work for everyone and all drugs developed thus far produce side effects. A common side effect of taking antianxiety drugs is drowsiness. Antianxiety drugs such as Valium can be dangerous or fatal if mixed with other drugs or alcohol or taken in excessively high doses. A client taking antianxiety drugs runs the risk of developing physical or psychological drug addictions. Antidepressants can cause an uncomfortable condition called dry mouth and inhibit sexual responsiveness. Antipsychotic drugs lead to the most serious side effects; they impact motor neural system functioning and may cause permanent, irreversible damage. There is concern that there is excessive reliance on drugs to treat psychological disorders, and the side effects can be sufficiently unpleasant that many individuals stop taking medication for this reason. Both electroconvulsive therapy (ECT) and psychosurgery are very controversial procedures. They are used only as a last resort in the treatment of psychological problems that have failed to respond to other, less invasive interventions. In addition to the aversive nature of the physical procedure itself, both ECT and psychosurgery can produce complications. There is a high rate of relapse after ECT, and there may be permanent memory loss. Brain surgery can result in physical or other complications and may even result in death.

3.   It is clear that the best way to treat most incidences of abnormal behavior is through a combination of both psychological and drug treatment interventions. The great advantage of drug treatment is that drugs can reduce and control some of the most difficult characteristics associated with the experience of psychological disorders. Schizophrenic patients who are constantly experiencing delusions or hallucinations are a prime example. It is difficult to begin or proceed further with psychological intervention if a patient continues to hallucinate or seems unaware of his or her surroundings. A client who is severely depressed may simply be unable to concentrate during psychotherapy sessions. The point is that drug interventions can help manage the more debilitating symptoms of psychological disorder. In most cases, once these symptoms are under control, then psychological interventions such as verbal therapy sessions can begin or continue with some likelihood of success. Psychotherapy sessions will be much more effective if the emotional state of the client is under control. This stability can be facilitated through the use of mood-stabilizers (e.g., for bipolar disorder), antianxiety drugs, or antidepressants. Once a client is not experiencing severe mood swings or bouts of depression or severe anxiety, the client is much more able to attend to the benefits available in therapy sessions. Drug therapy is not effective for everyone, and results are usually acceptable but do not entirely eliminate the psychological disorder. Unlike drug treatments, psychotherapy has no unpleasant or harmful physiological side effects. There is a problem of relapse when drug treatments are used. It is best if both patient and therapist resist the notion that a drug is a panacea that will provide an instant solution to all psychological difficulties. Most likely, for long-term success, the client needs assistance with learning better life skills, better coping strategies, and better approaches to problem-solving. These gains can come about if a client also has access to quality psychotherapeutic intervention.

MODULE 14.4 APPLICATION: GETTING HELP

LEARNING OBJECTIVE

After you have mastered the information in this unit, you will be able to:

- Explain the steps people can take to find qualified mental health professionals

OUTLINE

I.   Steps for Finding Qualified Mental Health Professionals
- A.   Get recommendations from knowledgeable sources
- B.   Check with a local medical center or clinic
- C.   Consult with available services at college or university
- D.   Contact professional organizations (such as the American Psychological Association)
- E.   Look in yellow pages of telephone directory—but use these sources with caution
- F.   Check credentials, licensing, and affiliations of treatment providers
- G.   Investigate the type of therapy provided (behavioral, cognitive, or other)
- H.   Inquire regarding educational and professional background
- I.   Investigate the provider's experience in treating others with a similar problem
- J.   After initial consultation and evaluation, get a clear explanation of diagnosis and proposed treatment plan before making any commitments
- K.   Discuss costs and insurance coverage
- L.   Know policies for missed or canceled appointments
- M.   Learn details regarding any prescribed medications
- N.   Discuss any concerns, especially if the treatment recommendations do not seem appropriate to you
- O.   Consider a second opinion, especially if you are experiencing doubts
- P.   Be very cautious regarding online therapy services

SUMMARY

In this module, you learn about effective and reliable ways to find good mental health care providers. Almost anyone can call himself or herself a "therapist" or even a "psychotherapist." It is important to have a practitioner who is fully qualified and adheres to ethical standards when an individual is undergoing treatment for psychological disorders.

Suggestions for locating a qualified mental health professional include getting recommendations from people you know who have some knowledge and experience in the field of psychology and whose recommendations you can trust. These sources can include your physician, a local medical center, your college counseling or health center, or appropriate professional organizations. The yellow pages in your telephone directory are a possibility, but consider these sources with caution. Check the licensing of the mental health professional recommended to you, and verify educational background, professional affiliations, experience, and credentials. An ethical provider will have no hesitation in sharing all of this information and more with you. Investigate the type and history of experience the mental health professional has had with your particular disorder. Clarify the therapeutic approach that will be used (behavioral, psychoanalytic, or other) and how it is expected to help the type of problem you are experiencing. Be sure you know the diagnosis and proposed treatment plan before committing to anything. An understanding of costs, applicability of insurance coverage, and policies regarding missed or cancelled sessions should be part of your discussion with the therapist. If medication is to be prescribed, find out how it will work—how long it should take before you experience results, and what kind of side effects are possible. If you have concerns, mention them, and do not hesitate to seek a second opinion. Be particularly cautious of therapy services offered online.

CHAPTER 14 APPLICATION EXERCISE

Think of a movie or other program you have seen where individuals with psychological disorders are portrayed. What kind of treatment did they receive? How long was therapy continued? Were satisfactory results achieved? What was the site of the mental health services like? How does this media portrayal compare to what you know of psychotherapy in real life?

Have you yourself had a psychological disorder, or do you know someone who does? What kind of treatment therapy is involved, if any? If the individual is not getting psychological help of any kind—why is that so? What are the person's objections? Has the individual had a previous experience with medication causing unpleasant side effects? Did the person have difficulty with a therapist, the institution or mental health center, or the type of treatment involved?

If the individual (or you) is getting help from a mental health professional, how is the course of therapy going? Does therapy consist of psychotherapy talk sessions, biomedical interventions, or both? How long is treatment expected to last? Evaluate the psychological disorder as you see it, what type of treatment might be most effective, and note what you think of the results thus far.

CHAPTER 15

Psychology and Health

In Chapter 15 you learn about the field of health psychology and about the very close tie between psychological aspects of our lives and our physical health. We need to be aware of the many psychological factors in our lives and recognize that they impact our physical state. To a great extent our physical health is under our own control because the psychological factors that can affect it are under our own control.

Perhaps the most frequent psychological factor we deal with that impacts our physical health is stress. Stress is the pressure an organism experiences to adjust or adapt to its environment. Many people now consider life stresses and even high levels of stress unavoidable. True, to an extent stress is good for us, in that some stress keeps us alert and energized. With the many demands in our lives, however, it is easy for sources of stress to multiply in both number and intensity, leading to physical and psychological problems. When stress levels become too high, we experience distress.

Potential sources of stress (called stressors) are many and varied. They include the many hassles we encounter daily—getting through traffic or meeting the demands of school, work, family, and relationships. These are frequent or daily occurrences and usually are predictable. Life events, especially if they are unexpected, can cause intense stress. Stressful events often involve change. Certainly, changes in our life can be good! Going off to college, getting married, or starting a new job are events that we likely look forward to. Desirable events, however, can and do still cause stress. Other sources of stress are frustration (when our attempts at reaching a goal are blocked), conflict (when we must choose between opposing goals), and traumatic stressors. Experiencing traumatic stress can lead to the development of posttraumatic stress disorder (PTSD). Stress can be a function of one's personality type (such as the aggressive and hard-driving Type A personality) or result from the transition to a new culture and the necessity of fitting into that new culture.

Regardless of the type (or types) of stressors that are presented to us, our body tends to respond in the same kind of way. This underlying, fairly uniform pattern of reaction to stress is known as the general adaptation syndrome, which was proposed by Hans Selye. The general adaptation syndrome consists of three phases as a body attempts to respond to stress: the alarm stage, the resistance stage, and the exhaustion stage. If stressors are so intense and prolonged that the body's stored resources are fully depleted, death can actually result. Unfortunately, stress today is often unlike the experience of stress as our ancestors knew it. In earlier times, a stressor appeared, it was dealt with (in one way or another!), and then it was gone. Stressors today may be more subtle, but they also can be more prolonged. The body's way of meeting the demands of stressful situations is heightened arousal and the mustering of physical resources with which to meet a threat. Bodily functioning is kicked into overdrive, so to speak, due mostly to the secretion of stress hormones that cause bodily changes. Stress hormones (epinephrine and norepinephrine are important stress hormones) increase heart and breathing rate to move nutrients and oxygen to muscles more quickly. This reaction to stress is important for our survival, but the prolonged presence of stress hormones in our system and the continued elevation of our physical functioning have consequences. Interestingly, people vary in their thresholds for stress and in their ability to resist the negative effects of stress. A sense of optimism, confidence in our abilities and our ability to control what happens to us, and interpreting stressful situations as challenges all help us live effectively and moderate the negative impact of stress.

Psychological factors are also important in the experience of physical illness, and many physical disorders can be minimized or eliminated if healthy psychological and behavioral steps are taken. Smoking, diet, high blood pressure, amount of physical exercise, diabetes, and cholesterol levels are all implicated in our nation's leading killers, heart disease and cancer. Negative emotional states (e.g., anger and anxiety) are also implicated in physical illness along with excessive alcohol consumption. Some influences on our health we cannot currently control such as genetic factors. Since we are truly talking life and death, however, it seems like a good idea to improve the influences we can control.

MODULE 15.1 STRESS: WHAT IT IS AND WHAT IT DOES TO THE BODY

LEARNING OBJECTIVES

After you have mastered the information in this unit, you will be able to:

- Describe health psychology

- Define stress, and identify the major sources of stress

- Explain how the body responds to stress

- Explain how stress affects the immune system

- Discuss the psychological factors that buffer the effects of stress

OUTLINE

I. The Interrelationships Between Psychology and Physical Health
   A. Study of these relationships is called health psychology
   B. A particular concern of health psychologists is stress
      1. Stress involves pressure, demands placed on an organism to adjust to its environment
      2. Stress is inevitable, and moderate amounts keep us alert and energized
      3. Distress occurs when stress level too high to manage comfortably
      4. Excessive stress leads to physical and psychological problems
II. Sources of Stress (Stressors)
   A. Hassles
      1. Common, everyday annoyances
      2. Chronic stress—result of collective effect of daily hassles
         a) Chronic stress is a state of persistent tension or pressure
         b) Leads to feelings of exhaustion, irritability, depression
   B. Life events (major changes in life circumstances)
      1. Even good changes (marriage, promotion, birth of a baby) can result in stress
      2. Stress from life events occurs irregularly, sometimes unexpectedly
      3. Greater number of life events associated with higher incidence of physical health problems (note relationship is correlational, not causal)
      4. Stress threshold, coping abilities, optimism related to experience of stress
      5. Evaluation, interpretation of life event related to the level of stress it presents
      6. College Life Stress Inventory—evaluates degree of stress for college students
   C. Frustration
      1. Negative emotion when goals are blocked
      2. May result if goals set unrealistically high
   D. Conflict
      1. State of tension when two or more goals compete and demand resolution
      2. Approach-approach conflict

        a)   Simultaneously drawn towards two positive goals
        b)   Goals are mutually exclusive—choosing one eliminates possibility of choosing the other
        c)   Initially may vacillate between the two alternatives
        d)   Eventually choose one course of action or the other
        e)   Considered the least stressful type of conflict

3. Avoidance-avoidance conflict
        a)   Must choose between two opposing goals, both of which are unpleasant
        b)   Avoiding one unpleasant goal necessitates approaching the other
        c)   If no obvious resolution, decision may be put on hold
        d)   When conflict is very stressful, one may become immobilized

4. Approach-avoidance conflict
        a)   Goal has both positive and negative qualities
        b)   Resolution seems possible by adding up pluses and minuses
        c)   However, decision may flip-flop as various aspects considered

5. Multiple approach-avoidance conflict
        a)   Involves the most complex type of conflict
        b)   Two or more goals are involved
        c)   Each goal has compelling positive and negative attributes
        d)   Resolution sometimes possible by combining both goals
        e)   In other cases selection of one still results in concern over lost possibilities of the other

E. Traumatic stressors
1. Potentially life-threatening events
2. Natural or technological disasters, combat, accidents
3. Make maximum demands on coping abilities
4. Posttraumatic stress disorder (PTSD) may result
5. Characteristics of PTSD
        a)   Avoidance of cues associated with the trauma
        b)   Flashbacks, dreams, intrusive memories and images occur
        c)   Depression, anxiety impairs ability to function
        d)   May be chronically on guard, tense, on edge
        e)   Emotional experience may be numbed
        f)   Can develop months or years after traumatic experience
        g)   Vulnerability relating to coping skills, childhood history, severity of trauma, and available social support
6. PTSD found in many cultures; culture may influence ability to withstand stress

F. Type A behavior pattern (TABP)
1. Hard-driving, competitive, impatient, ambitious
2. In a rush, aggressive, intense
3. Unlike Type B behavior pattern, which is more relaxed and mellow
4. Type A individual at greater risk for heart disease (most likely it is the anger and negativity aspect of personality that contributes the risk)

III. The Body's Response to Stress
A. The general adaptation syndrome (stress response)—GAS
1. Much of what we know is due to research from Hans Selye ("Dr. Stress")
2. Body responds in similar ways to various kinds of stress
3. Alarm stage
        a)   Body's first response to a stressor (prewired for survival)
        b)   Body's defenses prepare for action
        c)   Fight-or-flight response (physical and emotional characteristics)

d)   May be physical or psychological source of stress
e)   Death will occur within hours if stressor extremely damaging
4.   Resistance stage
a)   Occurs if organism lives beyond alarm stage
b)   Stressor continues; body attempts to adapt
c)   Attempt is made to return to normal biological state
d)   Arousal remains high; may be negative emotional reactions
5.   Exhaustion stage
a)   Final stage if stressor continues
b)   Heart rate and respiration decrease to conserve bodily resources
c)   Continued exposure to stress still depletes body
d)   "Diseases of adaptation" may occur (kidney or heart disease, digestive disorders, allergies, depression)
6.   Original stress response meant to turn off rather promptly
7.   Stresses of today are more persistent, may be chronic
8.   Gender differences in response to stress
a)   Women engage in more nurturing behaviors during stress
b)   Males more likely to exhibit aggressive responses
B.   Stress and the endocrine system
1.   Endocrine system is a series of ductless glands throughout body
2.   Glands release secretions known as hormones
3.   Hypothalamus in brain controls responses of endocrine system
4.   Biological steps in stress response
a)   Hypothalamus secretes corticotrophin-releasing hormone (CRH)
b)   CRH stimulates pituitary gland to secrete adrenocorticotrophic hormone (ACTH)
c)   ACTH travels through bloodstream to adrenal glands (located just above kidneys)
d)   ACTH stimulates adrenal glands to secrete corticosteroids (stress hormones)
e)   Corticosteroids help body resist stress; make stored nutrients more available
f)   Adrenal medulla (inner layer in adrenal glands) secretes stress hormones epinephrine and norepinephrine
g)   Epinephrine and norepinephrine increase heart rate; blood sends more oxygen and nutrients more quickly to muscles
h)   Muscles then more capable of fight-or-flight response
IV.   Stress and the Immune System
A.   Immune system is body's primary defense against disease
B.   Diseases fought by means of lymphocytes (specialized white blood cells)
C.   Lymphocytes constantly circulate, alert for antigens
D.   Antigens activate immune system to produce antibodies
E.   Antigen is a recognizable foreign substance in the body
F.   Antibodies are specialized protein molecules that fit precisely into invading antigen (like key fitting into a lock)
G.   Antigen marked for destruction by "killer" lymphocytes
H.   "Memory" of an antigen possible due to prior exposure
I.   Immunity or resistance occurs due to this prior exposure (body is fully ready to respond, and quickly, to known antigen)
J.   Vaccination (immunization) also provides immunity
K.   Stress weakens immune system; individual more susceptible to disease
L.   Stress lowers production of immunoglobulin A and increases levels of interleukin-6
M.   Corticosteroids inhibit immune system's ability to respond to microbes
V.   Psychological Buffers to Stress
A.   Social support—friends, wide social network help buffer stress

    B.   Self-efficacy
       1.   Belief that we are capable of doing what we set out to do
       2.   High self-efficacy individuals view stressful situation as a challenge
       3.   Confidence in abilities strengthens will to persevere
    C.   Perceptions of control and predictability
       1.   Greater sense of control and predictability—less experience of stress
       2.   Locus of control
          a)   Internal locus of control—belief that one has considerable influence over events and outcomes (sense of ability to control may result in less experience of stress)
          b)   External locus of control—belief that fate is out of one's hands (likely to be more susceptible to experiencing stress)
    D.   Psychological hardiness (research by Kobasa, 1979)
       1.   Cluster of personality traits related to resilience to stress
       2.   Characteristics of individuals with psychological hardiness
          a)   Commitment—and belief that work is important
          b)   Openness to challenge
          c)   Internal locus of control
       3.   Stress is accepted as normal challenge of life, may be interesting
    E.   Optimism—key concept in positive psychology
       1.   Key concept in positive psychology
       2.   Associated with higher resiliency to stress
VI. Burnout
    A.   Physical and emotional exhaustion resulting from excessive stress
    B.   Associated with feelings of apathy, higher risk of health problems
    C.   Burnout due to imbalance between work and other facets of life
    D.   Vulnerability to burnout
       1.   Role conflict—competing demands for one's time
       2.   Role overload—inability to refuse additional responsibilities
       3.   Role ambiguity
          a)   Uncertain about others' expectations
          b)   Try to meet all demands on all fronts
VII. Exploring Psychology: Making it in America: The Challenge of Acculturative Stress
    A.   Acculturation is pressure to adopt characteristics of new culture
    B.   Economics, social support, and language proficiency related to adjustment
    C.   Adopting dominant language and customs may lead to financial success, but may also undermine family relationships
    D.   Bicultural theory—leading theory
       1.   Immigrants do best when they adopt to new culture but also maintain strong ethnic identity
    E.   Racism may also increase stress

SUMMARY

In this module you learn about the many aspects of stress and how the experience of stress can affect us. Life is impossible without some stress, and indeed a moderate level of stress helps keep us active, alert, and involved with life. Excessive stress, however, does take its toll in terms of both physical and psychological problems. Interestingly, stress cannot be precisely quantified. What is beyond the level of manageable stress to one person may be invigorating, engrossing, and challenging to another. Still, conflicts and demands can be so great that everyone may experience undesirable stress at some time. When levels of stress become too great, we experience distress. Distress means we have reached the point of physical and psychological suffering. The field of health psychology investigates the relationship between psychology and physical health.

Stress is the demand put on an organism to adapt to features of the environment. Sources of stress are termed stressors. Stressors often involve change whether for bad or for good. Certainly, marriage, job promotions or transfers, and the arrival of a new baby are positive experiences; yet, much stress accompanies each one of these events. Typical sources of stress include hassles (everyday annoying experiences), life events that are not expected or regularly occur, and frustration, which is most likely to occur when we are blocked in our attempt to reach a goal. Conflict also leads to much stress. There are four basic kinds of conflict. Approach-approach conflict is one, but it is not too stressful since both alternatives are desirable and resolution is simply a matter of choosing one over the other. Avoidance-avoidance conflict is more difficult (and therefore probably more stressful), because both possibilities are unpleasant outcomes. Avoidance-avoidance conflict means when we move away from choosing one alternative, we move towards selecting the other. Conflict tends to leave an individual vacillating between the choices. Avoidance-avoidance conflict can be so stressful than an individual literally cannot decide and becomes in essence immobilized. In approach-avoidance conflict, the same goal has both negative and positive aspects. This situation, too, can cause some difficulties. The positive features draw us to the goal, but then the negative features may well push us away again. Multiple approach-avoidance conflict is the most complex type of conflict. Two or more goals are involved, and each goal has both powerful positive and powerful negative aspects. Faced with choices where there is no one clear course of action can leave us feeling confused and stressed. Stress may come from traumatic experiences (which may result in posttraumatic stress disorder), from pressures to adjust to an unfamiliar culture, or as a function of personality (the Type A personality, for example).

How does our body respond to stress? Research by Hans Selye has revealed that, although there are specific variations, the body responds to many different types of stressors in the same general pattern. This pattern he termed the general adaptation syndrome (GAS). It should be noted that, historically, the experience of stress was probably a briefer event. A stressor would emerge, the organism would respond (and hopefully live through it), and then the threat passed. At that point the body's systems could return to normal. As most of us well know, this pattern is not always so with today's stress. Facing fairly intense stressors from a variety of sources on a daily basis can lead to chronic stress.

The first stage in the general adaptation syndrome is the alarm stage. This is the body's first reaction, and it prepares us to face the stress through means of the fight-or-flight response. Have you noticed that your heartbeat speeds up and your breathing rate quickens when you are faced with something frightening? Among other things these physiological changes get needed oxygen and nutrients to the body's tissues faster. The muscles may well be called upon to deal with the stress.

The second stage in the general adaptation syndrome is the resistance stage. Here, the body's energies have been elevated for some time and the body attempts to return to normal. However, if the stress is still present, arousal levels will still remain fairly high. If the stressor continues and the organism is still alive, the third stage, called the exhaustion stage, kicks in. Heart rate and respiration decrease in order to preserve what is possible among the body's energy stores. If the stressor continues beyond this point, the organism is at risk for developing stress-related diseases. Women are likely to show nurturing behaviors when intensely stressed; men are more likely to show aggressive behaviors.

When the body is faced with stress, the endocrine system becomes more active. The hypothalamus in the brain secretes a hormone that stimulates the pituitary gland to secrete ACTH (adrenocorticotrophic hormone). ACTH (transmitted by the bloodstream) stimulates the adrenal cortex of the adrenal glands (above the kidneys) to produce stress hormones known as corticosteroids. Corticosteroids aid in the body's reaction to stress by making stored nutrients more available. At the same time, the adrenal medulla (in the center of each adrenal gland) secretes norepinephrine and epinephrine, stress hormones that increase heart rate and thus move blood more quickly through the body bringing needed resources to the body tissues.

Stress, as you may have believed, does impair the functioning of our immune system and make us more susceptible to contracting illnesses. Normally, the immune system is primed to fight off disease by attacking antigens (substances in the body identified by the immune system as foreign) with specialized lymphocytes (white blood cells). During intensive stress, the ability to produce certain antibodies (which fight antigens) is lowered. Corticosteroids produced during the stress response do help the body meet an external threat, but their continuing presence within the body makes it more difficult to fight off invading microbes. If stress is prolonged and is the result of total concentration and investment in work without sufficient balance through other activities, burnout will result. Burnout involves a state of complete physical and psychological exhaustion.

Not everyone experiences debilitating stress on a regular basis, and some people are just more able to manage fairly high levels of stress compared to others. People with a high resistance to stress are characterized as exhibiting psychological hardiness. What psychological attributes contribute to an individual's ability to manage stress? Five major categories have been identified. The first attribute is having strong social and emotional support. Close relationships with others help us manage stress. The second attribute is a sense of self-efficacy. Self-efficacy means believing in oneself and that one has the ability to see an endeavor through successfully. Individuals high in self-efficacy see stress-producing situations more as a challenge than a problem. The third attribute is having a sense of control—over the stressful event and over our lives in general. Individuals with an internal locus of control (a sense that their actions are closely tied to the course of events and that they can influence those events) are less susceptible to feeling overwhelmed because of that sense of control. The fourth attribute is psychological hardiness—the psychological characteristics making one more resistant to stress. The last attribute is optimism (a positive outlook). Individuals who show more optimism experience less stress-related illness. The awareness of the great importance of optimism in our lives has lead to the development of a movement in psychology called positive psychology. Much of psychology to date has focused on what is wrong with people and how to fix it; those who advocate positive psychology emphasize that it is probably more effective and productive to focus on human strengths rather than on human weaknesses.

KEY TERMS

Health psychology

Stress

Distress

Stressors

Hassles

Chronic stress

Frustration

Conflict

Posttraumatic stress disorder (PTSD)

Type A behavior pattern (TABP)

Acculturative stress

General adaptation syndrome (GAS)

Alarm stage

Fight-or-flight response

Resistance stage

Exhaustion stage

Corticotrophin-releasing hormone (CRH)

Adrenocorticotrophic hormone (ACTH)

Adrenal glands

Adrenal cortex

Corticosteroids

Adrenal medulla

Immune system

Lymphocytes

Antigens

Antibodies

Vaccination

Psychological hardiness

Burnout

SELF-TEST PRACTICE QUIZ

From the Key Terms select that which best matches the following (Note: Not every Key Term will be used.):

1. _____ Specialized white blood cells that attack antigens

2. _____ The outer layer of the adrenal glands; secrete corticosteroids in response to stress

3. _____ The typical pattern of human response to stress, proposed by Hans Selye

4. _____ A state of tension where one must make a choice regarding goals that have positive and negative attributes

5. _____ A set of psychological characteristics that help an individual resist the impact of stress

6. _____ The field within psychology that investigates the relationship between psychological factors and physical health

a. Health psychology

b. Stress

c. Distress

d. Stressors

e. Hassles

f. Chronic stress

g. Life events

h. Frustration

i. Conflict

j. Posttraumatic stress disorder (PTSD)

k. Type A behavior pattern (TABP)

l. Acculturative stress

m. General adaptation syndrome (GAS)

7. _____   A particular behavior pattern involving impatience, competitiveness, and possibly aggression that may be associated with higher levels of experienced stress

8. _____   A feeling of pressure or tension due to the organism's need to adapt to certain environmental demands

9. _____   Our physical defense system, which, under normal conditions, fights off disease and helps keep us healthy

10. _____   Substances produced by the immune system that fit precisely into an antigen and mark it for destruction

11. _____   When stress has reached the level that it causes physical or emotional suffering and pain

12. _____   The second stage of response by the body to stress as characterized by the general adaptation syndrome (GAS) model

13. _____   The feeling typically experienced when one's path towards a goal is blocked

14. _____   When the experience of fairly intense stressful events is persistent

15. _____   The inner part of the adrenal glands; secretes stress hormones epinephrine and norpinephrine, which increase heart and breathing rates

n.   Alarm stage

o.   Fight-or-flight response

p.   Resistance stage

q.   Exhaustion stage

r.   Corticotrophin-releasing hormone (CRH)

s.   Adrenocorticotrophic hormone (ACTH)

t.   Adrenal glands

u.   Adrenal cortex

v.   Corticosteroids

w.   Adrenal medulla

x.   Immune system

y.   Lymphocytes

z.   Antigens

aa. Antibodies

bb. Vaccination

cc. Psychological hardiness

dd. Burnout

16. What is the difference between stress and distress?
   a. Stress may be a positive experience, while distress is always negative.
   b. Stress impacts physical health, but distress does not.
   c. Distress impacts psychological health, but stress does not.
   d. There is no difference between stress and distress.

17. When there seems to be no let up to the stress you experience and eventually you are beginning to feel tired, irritable, and depressed, you are suffering from
   a. physical illness.
   b. psychosomatic illness.
   c. chronic stress.
   d. final exam week.

18. Which statements about life events and physical health problems is TRUE?
   a. Life events are not related to physical health only to psychological health.
   b. Even positive events such as marriage may negatively impact health.
   c. The correlation between the two is very strong.
   d. None of the above statements are true.

19. Seth is facing a dilemma. He has accumulated a great deal of debt and is now forced with deciding whether to live a life of poverty or declare bankruptcy—both very unattractive options. Seth is experiencing a(n) _____ conflict.

    a. approach-avoidance
    b. approach-approach
    c. avoidance-avoidance
    d. multiple approach-avoidance

20. Which of the following is NOT a characteristic of posttraumatic stress disorder?

    a. Difficulty in feeling love or other strong emotions
    b. Flashbacks, intrusive memories, or dreams regarding the event
    c. Unwillingness to talk about the trauma that has been experienced
    d. Avoidance of situations that serve as reminders of the experience

21. The degree of acculturative stress experienced by an individual will be affected by that person's

    a. income.
    b. sense of ethnic identity.
    c. familiarity with the dominant culture's language.
    d. All of the above are correct.

22. Regarding stress and the body, which of the following is NOT correct?

    a. Some stress is good for us, in that it keeps us alert and energized.
    b. Stress is the result of a series of unpleasant life events.
    c. There is variation among individuals as to what level of stress becomes debilitating.
    d. Stress may be caused by desirable life events.

23. The fight-or-flight response is part of the _____ stage of the general adaptation syndrome.

    a. alarm
    b. resistance
    c. exhaustion
    d. resolution

24. Events including natural disasters, accidents, and physical or sexual assault are known as

    a. avoidance-avoidance conflicts.
    b. traumatic stressors.
    c. frustrations.
    d. debilitating factors.

25. In the general adaptation model, high levels of physiological arousal are first experienced during the _____ stage.

    a. alarm
    b. resistance
    c. exhaustion
    d. resolution

26. The research contributed by Hans Selye revealed that

    a. the body's response to extremes of temperature differs from the body's response to other stressors.
    b. the body's response to infectious agents differs from the body's response to other stressors.
    c. the body's response to psychological pressures differs from the body's response to other stressors.
    d. despite some stressor-specific reactions, in general the body responds to most kinds of stress in the same way.

27. Based on our body's response to stress, it appears that our physiology was designed to best accommodate
    a. lifestyles that really involve no stress.
    b. stressful experiences that are over rather quickly.
    c. stressful experiences no matter how long they may last.
    d. high stress or no stress—whatever life presents to us.

28. Heart rate and breathing rate decrease during the _____ stage of the general adaptation syndrome.
    a. alarm
    b. resistance
    c. exhaustion
    d. resolution

29. During stress, females are more likely to exhibit comforting and friendship behaviors and men are more likely to exhibit aggressive behaviors. These stress behaviors are most likely due to
    a. sexual and reproductive hormones.
    b. the general adaptation syndrome.
    c. cultural variation.
    d. observational learning.

30. Bodily reserves become seriously depleted during the _____ stage of the general adaptation syndrome.
    a. alarm
    b. resistance
    c. exhaustion
    d. resolution

31. The stress hormones epinephrine and norepinephrine are secreted by the
    a. hypothalamus.
    b. adrenal medulla.
    c. adrenal cortex.
    d. pituitary gland.

32. Making the nutrients stored in the body more easily available for use is a function of the
    a. hormone acetylcholine.
    b. lymphocytes.
    c. corticosteroids.
    d. pineal gland.

33. Specialized protein molecules that aid the body in fighting off harmful substances are called
    a. antibodies.
    b. lymphocytes.
    c. antigens.
    d. vaccinations.

34. Kayla is feeling pulled in all directions—her boss frequently insists that she stay late at work even though this means spending less time with her children. She feels forced to choose between being a good employee and a good mother. Kayla is experiencing
    a. role ambiguity.
    b. role conflict.
    c. acculturative stress.
    d. role overload.

35. Which of the following is NOT a characteristic of individuals who exhibit psychological hardiness?
   a. Commitment
   b. Recognition that what one is doing is not really going to change the world
   c. Viewing stressful situations as challenges, not problems
   d. Having an internal locus of control

ESSAY QUESTIONS

1. Describe and discuss some of the ways that stress can make us more vulnerable to physical illnesses or other health problems.

2. What is burnout? What seems to cause burnout, and what symptoms are exhibited by people experiencing burnout?

3. What are some of the factors that seem to moderate the extent to which people experience stress or suffer from its effects?

ANSWER KEY

1. Lymphocytes

2. Adrenal cortex

3. General adaptation syndrome (GAS)

4. Conflict

5. Psychological hardiness

6. Health psychology

7. Type A behavior pattern (TABP)

8. Stress

9. Immune system

10. Antibodies

11. Distress

12. Resistance stage

13. Frustration

14. Chronic stress

15. Adrenal medulla

16. a

17. c

18. b

19. c

20. c

21. d

22. b

23. a

24. b

25. a

26. d

27. b

28. c

29. a

30. c

31. b

32. c

33. a

34. b

35. b

SAMPLE ANSWERS TO ESSAY QUESTIONS

1. There is a distinct connection between the level of stress we experience and our ability to ward off disease. Stressors most likely to affect our physical health include loss of loved ones, exposure to traumatic events, divorce, prolonged unemployment, and chronic sleep problems. One clear way that stress impacts our physical health is that when an individual is under a great amount of stress, the individual's body produces less of the antibody immunoglobulin A. This antibody helps keep us from contracting cold viruses. Also, during stress, the human body is less able to fend off attacks by the Epstein-Barr virus.

    Another way that the physical state of the body is affected by stress is the damage done by corticosteroids when they linger within the physiological system. Corticosteroids are secreted by the adrenal glands during stress in order to help manage the stress better. Thus, of course, they are helpful in boosting the body's immediate ability to respond effectively to threats or trauma. However, continued stress leads to the continued secretion of these hormones. The continued presence of cortical steroids in the body reduces the immune system's ability to function optimally. Corticosteroids make the immune system less able to fight off invading microbes.

    Last, as pointed out in Hans Selye's research, when the physiological resources of the human body are severely depleted, as in the exhaustion stage of the general adaptation syndrome, the body becomes prone to "diseases of adaptation." These diseases include kidney and heart disease, psychological disorders such as depression, and digestive disorders. Thus, prolonged exposure or severe stressors leave the human body more vulnerable to health problems.

2. Burnout is a stress disorder that is related to chronic stress. However, burnout does not result from excessive levels of stress per se. Rather, it can be a consequence of devoting oneself exclusively to work-related demands and allotting no time or energy for other activities in life. Burnout is characterized by fairly high and persistent levels of physical and psychological exhaustion. An individual suffering from burnout may begin to feel apathetic towards occupational responsibilities and the people connected with those responsibilities. Motivation may be sapped. An individual experiencing burnout may be more prone to headaches, stomach disorders, and hypertension. There is a lack of energy, enthusiasm, and satisfaction as related to occupational tasks. The individual experiences chronic fatigue.

Burnout is most closely associated with a lack of balance regarding activities in one's life. This imbalance may be due to role conflict, role overload, or role ambiguity. In role conflict, competing demands for one's time where the matter cannot be rather promptly resolved may lead to burnout. Role overload is the inability to say "no" and to instead take on more and more responsibilities that really are beyond what is manageable. Role ambiguity is an uncertainty regarding meeting others' expectations. The response then is to try and do everything for everyone, which likely will lead to burnout. All of these difficulties in determining what an appropriate role is can lead to devoting all of one's time and energy to meeting demands. Burnout is likely to result when there is little or no relief from the focus on and time and energy invested in what one deems as one's work-related responsibilities.

3.   Not everyone experiences debilitating levels of stress, and not everyone interprets a stressful situation as an unpleasant experience. It appears that there are psychological factors that are related to how one perceives stress and how one deals with it. These psychological moderators of stress include our sources of social and emotional support, our confidence in our abilities and our ability to control what happens to us, the interpretation of stressful situations as opportunities or challenges and not problems, and an outlook of optimism.

Research indicates that having good friends and other sources of social support is associated with more resistance to physical disease. Self-efficacy means a person believes that he or she is competent and has the skills and abilities to meet and resolve a problem effectively. High self-efficacy is associated with the perception of stressful situations as challenges rather than as obstacles. How much we believe we can control what happens to us and how predictable events are in our lives are both related to how stressful these events are. Unpredictable and uncontrollable events are, of course, more stressful than those over which we have some influence or that we know may occur. The perception of the controllability of events is somewhat of a subjective matter. People vary in their locus of control; that is, people usually either take the perspective that they have a substantial impact on events and on outcomes of events that happen to them (an internal locus of control) or they believe that they are rather helpless and that whatever happens lies more or less in the hands of fate. Individuals with an internal locus of control manage stress more effectively and exhibit a greater resilience to its effects.

Another factor that buffers the impact of stress is what is called psychological hardiness. The concept of psychological hardiness is derived from the research of Suzanne Kobasa (1979), who studied business executives who were in high-stress positions but still remained physically healthy. The components of psychological hardiness are commitment to one's work, recognizing change as a normal part of life, and having an internal locus of control.

A last and important buffer regarding the impact of stress is one's outlook. Individuals who approach life with a basic attitude of optimism are generally more resilient to the effects of stress both physical and psychological. It should be noted, however, that these findings are correlational and not causal. Thus, we cannot assume that having a positive outlook causes us to be less affected by the experience of stress.

The importance of a positive outlook (e.g., optimism) has recently gained such recognition among individuals in the field of psychology that a movement has begun suggesting that the positive aspects of human functioning should be a major emphasis in psychological research—not just human weaknesses and how to fix them. Happily, negative emotions tend to decline over the lifespan, while positive emotions remain fairly steady. Expressing more positive emotions appears to be related to better psychological adjustment in one's later years.

MODULE 15.2 PSYCHOLOGICAL FACTORS IN PHYSICAL ILLNESS

LEARNING OBJECTIVES

After you have mastered the information in this unit, you will be able to:

- Explain how psychological factors are linked to the health of our heart and circulatory system

- Describe the roles played by psychological factors in the development of cancer

- Explain the roles of psychological factors in other health conditions such as asthma, headaches, and ulcers

OUTLINE

I.   Background Factors in Physical Health
    A.   Physical health is a function of many influences
    B.   Influences include heredity and exposure to infectious organisms
    C.   Physical health also related to behavior, lifestyle choices

II.   Coronary Heart Disease
    A.   Background factors related to coronary heart disease
        1.   The heart is muscle tissue, which needs oxygen and nutrients
        2.   Oxygen and nutrients are carried to heart by means of arteries (a type of blood vessel)
        3.   Coronary heart disease (CHD) results when flow of blood to heart is insufficient
        4.   Usual underlying cause for CHD is atherosclerosis
        5.   Atherosclerosis is the major form of arteriosclerosis (hardening of the arteries); it results from buildup of plaque along artery walls
        6.   Narrowed arteries (due to atherosclerosis) more likely to be location of blood clots
        7.   A blood clot in a coronary artery causes a heart attack (myocardial infarction, or MI), because flow of blood to heart is blocked
        8.   Severity of heart attack related to tissue damage from loss of oxygen
        9.   CHD is one of the leading causes of death in U.S.
    B.   Risk factors for CHD
        1.   Overall personal risk is related to individual risk factors
        2.   Prominent risk factors
            a)   Age—risk increases after age forty
            b)   Gender—men more likely to be affected
            c)   Family history
            d)   Hypertension (high blood pressure)
            e)   Factors related to lifestyle
        3.   CHD factors that can be controlled through behavior or medical treatment
            a)   Hypertension—can be controlled through medication
            b)   Smoking—doubles risk of heart attack
            c)   Obesity
            d)   Diabetes
            e)   Cholesterol levels
            f)   Lack of physical exercise
        4.   Adopting healthier lifestyle associated with reduced risks for individuals who have had heart disease in addition to those who have not
        5.   Currently non-Hispanic black Americans at greater risk
            a)   Higher rates of obesity, hypertension, and diabetes
            b)   Lower access to quality health care; may receive less aggressive treatment from physicians

    C.   Emotions and your heart
        1.   Emotions implicated in greater risk for heart disease
            a)   Hostility (one component in Type A personality)
            b)   Persistent anxiety
        2.   How emotions affect cardiovascular system
            a)   Persistent emotional arousal related to cardiovascular damage
            b)   Anger, anxiety result in release of epinephrine and norepinephrine (stress hormones)
            c)   Stress hormones increase heart rate, blood pressure, and strength of heart contractions—all add to burden on heart
            d)   Stress hormones (especially epinephrine) increase stickiness of blood clotting factors to protect against possible injury—may increase risk of dangerous blood clots within arteries
            e)   Individuals who anger easily may also develop higher levels of cholesterol, blood pressure
            f)   Other emotional distress also related to cardiovascular risk (such as depression, marital stress)

III.   Cancer
    A.   Cancer kills more Americans than heart disease
    B.   Disease occurs because body cells reproduce uncontrollably
    C.   Ability to regulate cell multiplication is lost
    D.   Malignant tumors are these masses of excess tissue
    E.   Tumors can originate in any body tissue or organ; can spread to other parts of body
    F.   Tumors damage vital body organs and systems, may result in death
    G.   Possible causes of cancer
        1.   Heredity
        2.   Exposure to cancer-causing chemicals
        3.   Exposure to some viruses
        4.   Two out of three cancer deaths in U.S. attributable to smoking and diet
        5.   Alcohol and excess sun exposure are also related
    H.   Risk factors in the development of cancer
        1.   Family history, age (older ages at greater risk)
        2.   Smoking
            a)   90 percent of lung cancer deaths directly attributable to smoking
            b)   Smoking related to other cancers, causes perhaps one-third of cancer deaths
            c)   Use of tobacco in other forms also harmful, can cause cancer
        3.   Diet and alcohol consumption
            a)   High levels of consumption of saturated fats—linked to prostate and colon cancers
            b)   Obesity is a significant risk factor
            c)   Heavy alcohol consumption raises risk of several cancers (including cancers of mouth, pharynx, and esophagus)
            d)   Alcohol also related to other health problems, especially diseases of the liver
        4.   Sun exposure
            a)   Prolonged sun exposure may lead to basal cell carcinoma (most common, least dangerous type of skin cancer)
            b)   Basal cell carcinoma accounts for 75 percent of skin cancers
            c)   Curable as long as detected early, surgically removed
            d)   Severe sunburn early in life related to occurrence of melanoma
            e)   Melanoma least common, most deadly skin cancer
            f)   Melanoma accounts for about 5 percent of skin cancers

5. Stress
   a) The role of stress with regard to cancer not yet fully established
   b) Persistent stress may affect immune system's ability to rid body of cancerous cells
   c) Health professionals provide counseling, other services to assist those with cancer; also promote cancer preventative behaviors

IV. Stress and Other Physical Disorders
   A. Asthma
      1. A chronic lung disease
      2. Bronchial tubes (airways) in lungs become obstructed
      3. Acute attacks—breathing is difficult; may become life-threatening situation
      4. Possible causes of asthma
         a) Allergies
         b) Respiratory infections
         c) Exposure to environmental pollutants such as cigarette smoke
         d) Genetic predisposition for asthma a possibility
         e) Stress may increase asthmatic's susceptibility for an attack
   B. Headaches
      1. Stress related to several kinds of headaches
      2. Muscle-tension headaches
         a) Stress may cause muscles in scalp, face, neck and shoulders to tense
         b) Experience is dull, throbbing pain and pressure on both sides of head
      3. Migraine headaches
         a) About one in ten Americans are affected
         b) A severe headache that can last for hours or days
         c) Piercing pain, usually on one side of the head
         d) Results from changes in blood flow to the brain
         e) Possibly caused by imbalances in serotonin (neurotransmitter)
         f) Serotonin involved in regulation of blood vessel size (in brain)
         g) Stress and other factors can trigger migraine attack
   C. Peptic ulcers
      1. About one in ten Americans suffer from peptic ulcers
      2. Sore that form on stomach or small intestine lining
      3. Usually caused by *H. pylori* bacterium
      4. Can have *H. pylori* in system but not develop ulcers
         a) Suggests that psychological factors play a role
      5. Stress in particular may increase release of stomach acid
      6. Stomach acid and *H. pylori* together may lead to ulcer formation

SUMMARY

In this module you learn about the psychological factors that may play a very large role in whether or not we contract a physical illness and how severe or prolonged our experience with that illness is. Some influences on our physical health we cannot completely control, especially those relating to our genetic heritage. Yet much regarding our overall health and longevity is affected by our behaviors and lifestyle choices. These behaviors and lifestyle patterns are entirely under our control.

The first major disease discussed in this module is heart disease. Coronary heart disease (CHD) occurs when blood vessels carrying nutrients and, even more importantly, oxygen to the heart become obstructed. Typically the blood vessels (arteries) have become narrowed (a condition known as atherosclerosis) because of the buildup of plaque (fatty deposits) along the inner artery walls. The obstructions, which are blood clots, are much more likely to become lodged in an artery and block it when the artery is narrow to begin with, because of the plaque buildup. If the artery is completely blocked, and oxygen is cut off to the heart, the heart tissue not supplied with sufficient oxygen is damaged or dies. The more heart tissue that is cut off from sources of oxygen and the longer this deprived condition lasts, the worse the heart attack. Though family history is a factor as to whether or not you are at risk for heart disease, many other psychological factors are implicated as well.

Smoking, obesity, cholesterol level, hypertension (high blood pressure), diabetes, and lack of physical activity are all implicated in the risk of heart attacks. All of these factors can be minimized through healthy diet, medications, and physical exercise. In one study of 84,000 nurses (Stampfer et al., 2000), those who followed a low-fat diet, did not smoke, and participated in regular exercise had a much lower risk of coronary heart disease compared to nurses in the study who did not adhere to these practices. Emotional equilibrium is also a factor in whether or not an individual develops heart disease. People who are chronically angry are at a higher risk for developing heart disease than people who are calmer and have a lower incidence of anger. Individuals who experience chronic anxiety, too, are at great risk for heart disease. How do our emotions affect us? Persistent anger or anxiety parallels the experience of stress and triggers the release of stress hormones. Stress hormones (such as epinephrine and norepinephrine) influence our body to prepare to react to a threat or stressor, and this preparedness includes an increase in heart rate, blood pressure, and strength of heart contractions. All of these physiological reactions to stress put greater demands on the heart. Factors in the blood that help it to clot are increased during stress (since the possibility of injury due to a threat is greater), and the increased ability to clot may be related to the formation of blood clots, which cause heart attacks. People who are frequently angry also are at greater risk for high blood pressure and high cholesterol levels. Both of these physical conditions are factors related to the incidence of heart disease.

Cancer kills even more Americans than heart disease. Cancer occurs when the normal reproduction of body cells becomes out of control, and body cells replicate in excessive numbers. This abnormal body tissue comprises malignant tumors, which can spread to any part of the body and that can result in death. Controllable factors in the occurrence of cancer are smoking, diet (especially a high fat diet), high levels of alcohol consumption, excessive exposure to the sun, and stress. Most of the cancer deaths in the United States can be traced to smoking or poor dietary habits. Although the relationship of stress to the incidence of cancer is not clearly established, it is proposed that stress impedes the immune system's ability to rid the body of cancerous cells, just as it fights off other harmful invaders such as antigens.

Stress does not cause asthma, as far as we know, but the experience of stress may make an asthma sufferer more prone to asthma attacks. Stress is definitely implicated in both kinds of headaches—muscle-tension headaches and migraine headaches. Stress may cause muscles of the head and neck region to tense and tighten up. Stress may trigger migraine headaches, which occur when blood flow in the brain is altered. The change in blood flow may occur because of imbalances in the levels of serotonin. Peptic ulcers seem to be caused by the *H. pylori* bacterium. However, most people with *H. pylori* in their systems do not develop ulcers. Thus, it is thought that a psychological factor, such as stress, may trigger the release of excess stomach acid, and stomach acid in combination with the bacterium leads to peptic ulcers.

KEY TERMS

Arteries

Coronary heart disease (CHD)

Atherosclerosis

Plaque

Arteriosclerosis

Heart attack

Malignant tumors

Basal cell carcinoma

Melanoma

Asthma

Migraine headache

Peptic ulcers

SELF-TEST PRACTICE QUIZ

From the Key Terms select that which best matches the following (Note: Not every Key Term will be used.):

1. _____ The most lethal form of skin cancer

2. _____ A lung disease characterized by temporary obstruction of the bronchial tubes

3. _____ A very intense headache, related to blood flow and possibly serotonin levels, in the brain

4. _____ The most common form of heart disease where coronary arteries become obstructed

5. _____ Blood vessels that carry oxygenated blood away from the heart and through the body

6. _____ Fatty deposits that can build up and narrow the inner walls of arteries

7. _____ The condition more commonly known as hardening of the arteries

8. _____ A common form of skin cancer that is treatable if discovered and removed promptly

9. _____ Also termed myocardial infarction; a life-threatening condition where the supply of oxygenated blood to the heart is cut off due to an arterial blood clot

10. _____ The formation of sores on the stomach lining or lining of the small intestine

a. Arteries

b. Coronary heart disease (CHD)

c. Atherosclerosis

d. Plaque

e. Arteriosclerosis

f. Heart attack

g. Malignant tumors

h. Basal cell carcinoma

i. Melanoma

j. Asthma

k. Migraine headache

l. Peptic ulcers

11. _____   What is formed in the body
when the orderly reproduction of cells is
disrupted and cell growth is out of
control; can cause destruction of other
body organs or systems

12. _____   The condition that occurs when
artery walls narrow due to buildup of
plaque

13. Psychological factors are related to the occurrence of a heart attack because _____
increase the risk of heart disease.

   a.   smoking and poor dietary habits
   b.   chronic anger or anxiety
   c.   a sedentary lifestyle and failure to control blood pressure
   d.   all of the above

14. The buildup of plaque, which causes arteries to become more narrow, is known as

   a.   arteriosclerosis.
   b.   atherosclerosis.
   c.   melanoma.
   d.   coronary heart disease (CHD).

15. Cancer occurs when

   a.   neurons lose the ability to communicate with one another.
   b.   heart muscle dies.
   c.   cells multiply uncontrollably.
   d.   plaque builds up in arteries.

16. The risks for cancer are _____ those for heart disease.

   a.   more pervasive than
   b.   less pervasive than
   c.   similar to
   d.   unrelated to

17. How many lung cancer deaths are directly attributable to smoking?

   a.   twenty percent
   b.   thirty percent
   c.   sixty percent
   d.   ninety percent

18. The dietary ingredient most related to the incidence of prostate and colorectal cancers is

   a.   dietary fiber.
   b.   saturated fat.
   c.   sugar and other sweeteners.
   d.   alcohol.

19. The leading cause of death in the United States for adults under age 85 is

   a.   homicide.
   b.   heart disease.
   c.   stroke.
   d.   cancer.

20. The most lethal but least common form of skin cancer is
   a. basal cell carcinoma.
   b. prostate cancer.
   c. melanoma.
   d. ulcerative cancer.
21. Which of the following is NOT considered a factor in the occurrence of migraine headaches?
   a. Stress
   b. Serotonin
   c. Hormonal fluctuations
   d. Number of pregnancies
22. The successful treatment of peptic ulcers involves
   a. surgery to remove bacterium-producing tissue.
   b. antibiotics to destroy any *H. pylori* present in the system.
   c. relaxing in milk baths at least once a day.
   d. all of the above treatments.

ESSAY QUESTIONS

1. What are the leading causes of death in the United States? Of factors relating to these deaths, which involve aspects of our lives that we cannot control? Which involve factors that we can control?

2. How are emotions related to the state of our physical health?

ANSWER KEY

1. Melanoma

2. Asthma

3. Migraine headache

4. Coronary heart disease (CHD)

5. Arteries

6. Plaque

7. Arteriosclerosis

8. Basal cell carcinoma

9. Heart attack

10. Peptic ulcers

11. Malignant tumors

12. Atherosclerosis

13. d

14. b

15. c

16. c

17. d

18. b

19. d

20. c

21. d

22. b

SAMPLE ANSWERS TO ESSAY QUESTIONS

1. The leading causes of death in the United States are cancer followed closely by heart disease. Currently, cancer is the leading cause of death for both men and women.

    Factors related to heart disease that we cannot control are our genetic heritage, age, and to an extent gender. Presently we cannot change our genetic heritage nor stop the process of aging. Men are somewhat more prone to heart disease than women, up until the age of 65. Black non-Hispanic Americans currently are at greater risk for heart disease than are other ethnic groups.

    Factors implicated in both heart disease and cancer that we can control include, most importantly, diet, exercise, and smoking. Smoking is implicated in very many illnesses, and nearly all deaths from lung cancer are attributable to smoking. It is possible to stop smoking, and there are programs available to help with this effort. Our risk for disease is lowered if we follow a healthy diet and particularly avoid foods high in saturated fats. A healthy diet will help keep weight under control; obesity is one of the factors related to heart disease. Even moderate exercise (such as a brisk walk) helps reduce the likelihood of heart disease. Other factors related to the leading causes of death are high blood pressure, diabetes, and cholesterol level. All of these can be controlled to an extent through diet and maintaining an appropriate weight; however, there are medications available that will provide further help in managing all of these physiological conditions. It is remarkable to think that so very many major factors relating to our longevity, physical health, and quality of life are simple things that we just need to practice every day.

2. We have already learned that a positive outlook (e.g., one of optimism) is an effective buffer for stress in our lives. This module presents the fact that negative emotions (most specifically anger and anxiety) put us at higher risk for physical health problems. For example, individuals who exhibit the Type A personality (hard-driving, competitive, aggressive) are at slightly greater risk for heart disease. This risk is most likely attributable to the fairly chronic anger state that many Type A personalities exhibit. Chronic anger and chronic anxiety trigger the stress response in the human body. Stress hormones such as epinephrine and norepinephrine are secreted, which is the normal reaction when the body is faced with stress. Chronic emotional arousal means these hormones are always present in the system. They tend to make the heart beat faster, increase blood pressure, and increase the number of heart contractions. Cholesterol levels may be affected. Persistently agitated emotional states, then, are clearly related to our physical health.

MODULE 15.3 APPLICATION: TAKING THE DISTRESS OUT OF STRESS

LEARNING OBJECTIVE

After you have mastered the information in this unit, you will be able to:

*   Explain some of the ways of removing distress from stress

OUTLINE

I.   Steps to Take the Distress Out of Stress
    A.   Maintain stress at a tolerable level
        1.   Reduce daily hassles
        2.   Know own limits
        3.   Adopt a reasonable schedule
        4.   Take frequent breaks
        5.   Develop more effective time-management skills
        6.   Learn to prioritize
    B.   Develop relaxation skills
        1.   Perhaps listen to music
        2.   Biofeedback, meditation, deep-breathing exercises may be helpful
        3.   Consider a stress-management course
    C.   Take care of your body
        1.   Get enough sleep
        2.   Follow a nutritious, balanced diet
        3.   Participate in regular exercise
        4.   Get regular medical check-ups
        5.   Avoid harmful substances
    D.   Gather information—whatever particular issue or illness you are facing, learn more about it
    E.   Expand your social network—social support is an important buffer against stress
    F.   Prevent burnout
        1.   Set reasonable limits and goals
        2.   Learn to say "no"
        3.   Delegate responsibilities
    G.   Replace stress-inducing thoughts with stress-busting thoughts
        1.   What is your reaction to disappointing or stressful events?
        2.   Are things blown out of proportion?
        3.   Review thought pattern in reaction to stress
        4.   Keep things in perspective
        5.   Remember advantage of self-efficacy (belief in one's capabilities)
        6.   Choose achievable goals
    H.   Don't keep upsetting feelings bottled up
        1.   Expressing feels helps minimize demands on autonomic nervous system
        2.   Share with a trusted friend, or consider writing in a journal
    I.   Control Type A behavior
        1.   Take things slower
        2.   Read books for enjoyment
        3.   Leave your computer at home
        4.   Avoid rushing through your meals
        5.   Engage in enjoyable activities
        6.   Develop relaxing interests
        7.   Set realistic daily goals
        8.   Hostility is not helpful

SUMMARY

In this Applications module you learn about ways to reduce unhealthy stress in your life. There are many things you can do you make the stress in your life manageable and make your life more satisfying and productive. First, review your typical daily pattern. How can you reduce the regular hassles you face? Try not to take on too much. Schedule tasks so you have a reasonable amount of time to get things completed. It is O.K. to take a break once in a while! Prioritize and delegate responsibility as needed.

Develop relaxation skills. Find what works for you as far as activities or surroundings that you find calming. Take good care of your body. This means that, in general, you get adequate sleep, eat reasonably healthy foods, and exercise regularly. Avoid harmful substances.

Whatever issue (an illness, or otherwise) you are facing—learn more about it. Being informed is usually less stressful than being mystified. There may be things you can do, too, to help with the adjustments necessary. Remember how important friends are. We can improve our own social skills, and strengthen emotional ties with our families and with other individuals emotionally important to us. There are clubs and organizations at schools and through the community where social activities are arranged, and guests or new members are welcome. Burnout can be prevented through keeping work-related responsibilities within reasonable limits. Allow time for other activities, and participate in these activities. If work demands exceed appropriate levels, learn to say "no," and to delegate responsibilities.

Remember the importance of positive thinking. Attend to your mind-set when you respond to life events. Avoid exaggerating the impact of something disappointing that happens to you. Believe in yourself and your ability to handle the events and situations that come your way. If you need to, sharpen your skills, and take advantage of opportunities where you can practice and improve your skills with a good likelihood of success. When you are emotionally upset, find a way to share it, either with a trusted friend or family member or through writing about your experiences and feelings in a journal. Reflect on whether you have the characteristics associated with the Type A personality. If so, recognize that this personality style can take a toll on your health. Find ways to relax and to reduce the sense of pressure and time constraints. Come up with a schedule that allows you sufficient time to get your work done and avoid taking on more obligations than what you can comfortably meet. Slow down, and take time to relax and enjoy your food and the company of others during meals. All of these steps will help make our lives both physically and psychologically healthier.

CHAPTER 15 APPLICATION EXERCISE

Think of the last time you were sick. What other things were going on in your life? Was it a period of extra stress or not? How did you become ill? How long did it take for the illness to run its course?

Do you think you are more prone to getting sick during periods of high stress? If so, what can you do to reduce the stress in your life?

CHAPTER 16

Social Psychology

In Chapter 16, you learn about the influences other people have on us and that we have on them. Human beings are very social creatures. As such, having the liking and acceptance of others is important to our own psychological well-being. Because acceptance from others is important, we are willing (to a greater or lesser extent) to mold and adapt our behavior in order to fit in with guidelines and standards established by the groups of which we are members.

Social perception involves how we come to know, understand, and think about our social environment. We form impressions of others from being exposed to them, and impressions can be formed quite quickly. If we rely too much on social schemas (a way of organizing our social perceptions), we fall into the trap of stereotyping. Stereotyping means making assumptions about others just because they are members of a particular group. In part, we do need to organize our social world so our lives run more smoothly and are manageable but not to the point that we and others are harmed by our prejudgments.

Because we are social creatures, we are always curious about others' behavior. We make attributions for behavior, which really are explanations we come up with as to why people do what they do. We also make attributions about our own behavior. Especially in Western cultures like the United States, there is a tendency to underestimate situational factors when interpreting the behavior of others. The fundamental attribution error is the tendency to make dispositional (e.g., it is due to an internal personality trait) attributions for the behavior of other people, disregarding what might be legitimate situational influences on that behavior. We develop attitudes about other persons, objects, or events; sometimes these attitudes can be changed. The correspondence between attitudes that we hold and behaviors we exhibit relative to those attitudes is not as high as one might think.

Social psychology also includes our liking for other individuals. Degree of liking tends to be influenced by four factors: similarity, physical attractiveness, proximity (nearness), and reciprocity. Although we tend to match up with partners who are about as physically attractive as we are, there seem to be standards for beauty (at least for the female face, thus far) that are fairly universal.

Why do people help others? Are there times when helping is truly purely altruistic—that is, we have no thought whatsoever as to what we might get out of it (including good feelings)? This is a debatable point in social psychology. Helping others also is not as obvious a matter as it might seem. Helping may, for example, put us or loved ones at risk. The situation may be confusing (is it really an emergency?) and if others are available to help, we are actually less likely to leap into the situation ourselves because surely someone else will.

Is the human by nature aggressive? That question we cannot fully answer. There are many factors related to aggression, and since it is such a complex behavior it is assumed that a variety of factors come into play when aggression is manifested. Aggressiveness may be instinctual behavior since at least in the past it was related to one's survival. Levels of testosterone are associated with levels of aggression, although again it is not a perfect correspondence. Aggression most clearly can be learned, particularly by means of behaviors modeled and reinforced at home. Prejudices are also passed on that way. Aggression may be the result of anger or frustration, but that is not always the case.

We are all members of groups, and our group membership (known as our group identity) is an important part of our self-concept or psychological identity. In other words, who we are is in part defined by our relationship with others. There is a pronounced tendency to conform (and this is not at all necessarily a bad thing!), and to obey directions from individuals in authority. Classic studies on conformity (by Asch, 1956), and on obedience (by Milgram in the 1960s) demonstrate these points well. Social facilitation describes the impact of the presence of others on our performance. As long as a task is familiar and not too difficult, our performance usually is enhanced when we have an audience. Performance usually is impaired if we are trying to carry out a difficult, unfamiliar task. Deindividuation is losing our sense of ourselves because we are caught up in a crowd.

MODULE 16.1 PERCEIVING OTHERS

LEARNING OBJECTIVES

After you have mastered the information in this unit, you will be able to:

- Define social perception

- Explain the major influences on first impressions and why first impressions often make lasting impressions

- Discuss the role of cognitive biases in judgments that we make about the causes of behavior

- Explain what attitudes are and how they are acquired

- Discuss how attitudes are related to behavior and how they change in response to persuasive appeals

OUTLINE

I.   Social Psychology and Social Perception
    A.   Social psychology—the study of how our thoughts, feelings, and behaviors are influenced by our social interactions with others and by the culture in which we live
    B.   Social perception—the process by which we come to form an understanding of our social environment, on the basis of three sources
        1.   Observations of others
        2.   Personal experiences
        3.   Information we receive
II. Impression Formation
    A.   Background information on impression formation
        1.   Impression formation—the process by which we form an opinion or impression of another person
        2.   First impressions usually formed quickly
        3.   Tend to be long-lasting and difficult to change
        4.   Affect how we relate to the person we have formed an impression of
    B.   Personal disclosure
        1.   More favorable impression formed of people willing to disclose personal information about themselves
        2.   Revealing too much too soon results in a negative impression
        3.   Cultural norms a factor in personal disclosure
    C.   Impressions as social schemas
        1.   Social schema
            a)   Impression is a type of social schema
            b)   Social schema is a mental image or representation we use to understand our social environment
            c)   Information about others is filtered through the social schema
            d)   Existing schema influences how we perceive new information

    D.   Stereotyping
1. Preconceived ideas about groups of people
2. Stereotypes can influence first impressions
3. Stereotyping a normal cognitive activity; helps us process social input more efficiently
4. May be some truth in commonly held stereotypes
5. Stereotyping on basis of race, ethnicity, gender, and the like is ineffective, unfounded

    E.   Self-fulfilling prophecies
1. Initial impression influences subsequent exhibited behavior towards that person
2. Behavioral message sent (perhaps unintentionally) then influences response of the other individual

III.   Attributions: Forming Personal Explanations of Events

    A.   Attribution—a personal explanation we form about the causes of behavior or events we observe
1. Dispositional causes—attributing behavior to internal traits
2. Situational causes—attributing behavior to external factors
3. Attributions are affected by cognitive biases

    B.   Fundamental attribution error
1. We tend to overlook situational factors when interpreting behavior of others
2. Tendency is to make internal attributions when interpreting behavior of others (our focus is on the actor, not surroundings)
3. Doesn't apply to displays of emotion—we tend to attribute those to the situation
4. Members of collectivist cultures less likely to make fundamental attribution error (less emphasis on the individual in these cultures)

    C.   Actor-observer effect
1. Tendency to attribute causes of our own behavior to external (situational) factors, make internal attributions regarding other people's behavior
2. Actor-observer effect probably due to differing perspectives (Heider, 1958)
3. Can alter actor-observer effect by changing presentation of the event
4. Personal contact, interaction with others increases our awareness of situational factors that impact their behavior

    D.   Self-serving bias
1. Tendency to attribute our personal successes to our own inner traits (internal attribution)
2. Tendency to make an external (situational) attribution with regard to things that did not work out well
3. Helps to keep our self-esteem intact
4. Much more widespread in Western than in Eastern cultures
      a)   Westerners value protection of self-esteem; Eastern cultures emphasize self-criticism, humility

IV.   Attitudes

    A.   An evaluation or judgment (either liking or disliking) regarding a person, object, or issue

    B.   Three components to attitudes
1. Cognitions—set of beliefs
2. Emotions—feelings of liking or disliking
3. Behaviors—what is manifested in actions

    C.   Sources of attitudes
1. Attitudes acquired from many sources in social environment
2. Sources include parents, teachers, peers, personal experiences, media
3. Individuals of similar backgrounds tend to hold similar attitudes
4. Possible genetic link to attitudes (resulting from commonality in intelligence, personality)

    D.   Attitudes and behavior
- 1.   We expect a strong correspondence between attitudes and actual behaviors
- 2.   Research reveals behavior only somewhat related to attitudes
- 3.   Possibly due to great variation in situational factors
- 4.   Correspondence related to stability and strength of attitude; also how directly it applies to a given situation

V.   Persuasion
- A.   We are constantly bombarded by messages designed to influence our attitudes
- B.   Frequently involve political figures or merchandise available for purchase
- C.   Relationship between appeals and possible attitude change
  - 1.   Elaboration likelihood model (ELM)
    - a)   Central route to attitude change—when motivation is high, have skills and knowledge needed for careful evaluation of message
    - b)   Peripheral route to attitude change—when motivation low; listeners more influenced by cues attending the message
  - 2.   Variables influencing persuasion
    - a)   Source—greatest influence when speaker credible, likable, similar
    - b)   Message—repetition, usually best to present both sides (with opposition side refuted), not appear to serve own interests
    - c)   Recipient—easier to persuade people of low intelligence, low self-confidence; also when people in a more positive mood (more likely to see message in a positive light)

SUMMARY

In this module you are introduced to the field of social psychology. Social psychology examines how the behavior of an individual is influenced by interactions with others. This module discusses factors related to the impressions we form of others and also describes attitudes and how attitudes may be changed. Social perception concerns how we come to perceive, or have an understanding of, others. As you might guess, social perception is something of a subjective process. Impressions of others tend to be formed rather quickly, yet they may be tenacious. That is, once an impression is formed, that impression may be somewhat resistant to change. An impression is one type of our social schemas—our way of categorizing the world so that we can function more effectively within it. Thus, once an impression is formed, all future information regarding the subject of that impression is filtered through the existing schema. We may no longer interpret new experiences with that person in a completely objective manner in part because of our expectations. Stereotypes can influence the formation of impressions because they constitute a preconceived set of beliefs about an individual simply because that individual is a member of a group. Stereotypes may bias our interpretations of another, and prejudicial behavior resulting from stereotyping is clearly wrong and unfounded.

Since humans are very social creatures, we are always trying to interpret and understand our social world. Why did that person you know glance down when you looked his way? Did your friends really enjoy your last party? To understand human behavior, we make attributions. Attributions are simply explanations as to why a behavior occurs. Attributions actually are somewhat difficult to make accurately since often we have access to only limited information. However, we usually go ahead and make attributions anyway! In part we need to so we can help make our complex social world more manageable. We tend to attribute behaviors to one of two sources—either internal (we believe the behavior occurred because of a fairly stable personality trait) or external (we believe the behavior occurred because of situational, or environmental, factors). Especially in Western, individualistic cultures, there is a tendency toward one kind of attribution error. This error is so pervasive in Western cultures, in fact, that it is known as the fundamental attribution error. That error is the tendency to underestimate situational factors when evaluating the actions of another. When we observe behavior, the actor performing that behavior is usually the focus of our attention. The actor is much more likely to attract our attention than are other features of the environment in which the actor appears. Probably that is the reason we tend to make internal attributions. We attribute the actor's behavior to personality characteristics. Interpreting our own behavior may be another story! The actor-observer effect is an expansion on the fundamental attribution error concept. The actor-observer effect includes the fact that we also tend to attribute our own actions (at least, when they do not come out well) to external, or situational, causes. The self-serving bias is the tendency to put what we do in the best light possible. In order to do that, we tend to make an internal attribution where we have succeeded and an external attribution where we have not.

Attitudes are how we feel about something—an object, a person, or an issue. Attitudes tend to have three components. These components include a cognitive aspect (what we believe), an emotional aspect (feelings of liking or disliking), and a behavioral aspect (what we convey through our actions). We get our attitudes from many sources. Interestingly, there may even be a genetic component linked (probably indirectly) to attitudes. Twins raised apart show more consistency in attitudes than can be explained by situational factors alone. Although we would expect the correspondence between what we believe and how we act regarding those beliefs to be quite high, in fact that is not the case. When attitudes and related behaviors are measured, there is only a modest correlation between the two.

Since we all have many attitudes, how likely is it that an attitude will change? This module also examines attitude change as a result of attempts at persuasion. The elaboration likelihood model (ELM) helps represent what occurs when persuasive attempts are made. For an intelligent audience motivated to attend to a persuasive message, the central route to persuasion is likely to be more effective. That is, features of the message itself will be attended to, and it is best if both sides of an argument (with the opposing side refuted) are presented. If an audience is not motivated to attend to a message, is fatigued, or is distracted, the peripheral route to persuasion is more likely to be effective. Here, the audience is probably not attending very closely to actual features of the message. Rather, they are likely to be influenced by peripheral characteristics—the attractiveness of the speaker, the tunefulness of the jingle, or how engaging the setting is. Variables influencing the effectiveness of persuasion messages include factors related to the source (the speaker), the message itself, and the recipient (the listener—if he or she is listening!). Communicators who are perceived as credible, likable, and similar to the listeners are more likely to change attitudes.

KEY TERMS

Social psychology

Social perception

Impression formation

Social schema

Stereotypes

Self-fulfilling prophecy

Attribution

Dispositional causes

Situational causes

Fundamental attribution error

Actor-observer effect

Self-serving bias

Attitude

Elaboration likelihood model (ELM)

SELF-TEST PRACTICE QUIZ

From the Key Terms select that which best matches the following (Note: Not every Key Term will be used.):

1. _____ Interpreting the behavior of an individual as a function of external (environmental) factors

2. _____ Putting ourselves in the best light by taking credit for our accomplishments and making situational explanations for what we have not done well

3. _____ How we feel about a person, object, or issue

4. _____ How we come to understand our social world

5. _____ The tendency to evaluate an individual and attribute characteristics simply because that individual is a member of a group

6. _____ When our behavior towards another inadvertently creates or encourages the behavior we are expecting

7. _____ Interpreting the behavior of an individual as a function of internal (e.g., personality, consistent traits) factors

8. _____ A field within psychology dealing with how our thoughts, feelings, and behavior are influenced by our interactions with others

9. _____ A mental representation (such as an impression) that helps us function more efficiently and effectively within our social environment

10. _____ The tendency to make internal attributions regarding others' behavior and external attributions regarding our own

11. _____ The process by which we develop an opinion or impression of another

a. Social psychology
b. Social perception
c. Impression formation
d. Social schema
e. Stereotypes
f. Self-fulfilling prophecy
g. Attribution
h. Dispositional causes
i. Situational causes
j. Fundamental attribution error
k. Actor-observer effect
l. Self-serving bias
m. Attitude
n. Elaboration likelihood model (ELM)

12. _____   The tendency to underestimate the impact of situational factors with regard to others' behavior

13. _____   An explanation we arrive at as to why an event or behavior occurred

14. _____   A representation of how attitude change due to persuasive messages may occur

15. The process of coming to understand our world through our experience with it is known as

    a.   social psychology.
    b.   social perception.
    c.   attribution theory.
    d.   the elaboration likelihood model (ELM).

16. An impression is a(n)

    a.   schema.
    b.   stereotype.
    c.   expectation.
    d.   attitude.

17. Once we have formed an impression, why is that impression rather resistant to change?

    a.   We tend to filter new information about a person based on the impression that already exists.
    b.   Our first impressions usually are quite accurate and there is no need to change.
    c.   Humans are by nature stubborn and resistant to change.
    d.   We have turned our focus to other, more pressing issues.

18. We have heard that Ms. Albright is very warm and caring. We greet her with an attitude of great warmth and make her welcome. Sure enough, she is just as warm and caring as others said that she was. What social psychological phenomenon is occurring here?

    a.   The central route to persuasion
    b.   The peripheral route to persuasion
    c.   The self-fulfilling prophecy
    d.   The fundamental attribution error

19. There is a very slow driver on the road in front of you. You think, "That guy must be ancient. He hasn't a brain in his head. Why do they let people like this guy on the road?" Just then there is a bend in the highway, and you see there is another, slow-moving vehicle right in front of the driver ahead of you. You have

    a.   made an external attribution.
    b.   inadvertently initiated a self-fulfilling prophecy.
    c.   committed the fundamental attribution error.
    d.   made good use of your driver education classes.

20. If you blame your friend's car accident on the weather rather than on his bad driving, you are making a(n) _____ attribution.

    a.   correlational
    b.   situational
    c.   dispositional
    d.   attitudinal

21. People in collectivist cultures where there is a greater emphasis on group needs and being a member of a group are _____ to make the fundamental attribution error relative to cultures like that of the United States.

    a. more likely
    b. less likely
    c. equally likely
    d. slightly more likely

22. According to Heider (1958), what is one reason that the actor-observer effect occurs?

    a. An audience tends to be fatigued and is not listening closely to the message.
    b. People with lower levels of intelligence and self-confidence are more likely to be persuaded.
    c. Attributions made about behavior may very well have to do with one's perspective.
    d. Our dispositional attributions are strengthened once we get to know the actor better.

23. Attitudes and behavior are likely to be consistent when the

    a. person feels free to choose whether or not to perform the behavior.
    b. person has difficulty remembering the attitude.
    c. attitude is not a very stable one.
    d. person is not very confident about the attitude.

24. The tendency to make dispositional attributions for personal successes and situational attributions for failure is known as the

    a. self-serving bias.
    b. actor-observer effect.
    c. self-fulfilling prophecy.
    d. fundamental attribution error.

25. If an audience is reasonably intelligent and motivated to listen to a message, persuasion is mostly likely to occur if

    a. the speaker relies on the peripheral route to persuasion.
    b. only one side of the argument is presented in detail.
    c. the message clearly presents why the alternative is beneficial to the speaker.
    d. the speaker creates the impression of being knowledgeable and trustworthy.

26. One characteristic of a message that is likely to result in attitude change, even if the information presented in the message in inaccurate, is

    a. repetition.
    b. an offer of money.
    c. clarification of the speaker's intent in presenting the message.
    d. the communication of threats or emotionally charged content.

ESSAY QUESTION

1. In general, with regard to impression formation, we form a more favorable impression when a person is willing to share personal information. However, too much information too soon has the opposite effect. Why might this be so?

ANSWER KEY

1. Situational causes

2. Self-serving bias

3. Attitude

4. Social perception

5. Stereotypes

6. Self-fulfilling prophecy

7. Dispositional causes

8. Social psychology

9. Social schema

10. Actor-observer effect

11. Impression formation

12. Fundamental attribution error

13. Attribution

14. Elaboration likelihood model (ELM)

15. b

16. a

17. a

18. c

19. c

20. b

21. b

22. c

23. a

24. a

25. d

26. a

SAMPLE ANSWER TO ESSAY QUESTION

1. It is true that we usually like people more if, when we first get to know them, they are willing to disclose somewhat more personal aspects and information about themselves. Perhaps this helps build a bridge between two people, and if the topic of conversation becomes a little more emotional, our emotional feelings about the entire exchange may become a bit more engaged. New social partners who disclose information that is too personal, in too great a quantity, and too soon, however, tend to elicit a more negative first impression. This occurs most probably because individuals who disclose a great deal of fairly personal information very early in social contact are perceived as being immature and less emotionally secure. They are also perceived as exhibiting poorer social and psychological adjustment than individuals who also share personal information but with more restraint.

    With regard to personal disclosure, it should be remembered that some standards for disclosure are a function of cultural norms. People who are members of East Asian cultures (such as China and Japan), for example, are likely to disclose less in the way of personal information and also to be uncomfortable with others who are highly personal, especially in the early phases of a social relationship. In such an instance, this reluctance to disclose and greater restraint regarding personal matters is more a reflection of cultural, than personal, characteristics.

MODULE 16.2 RELATING TO OTHERS

LEARNING OBJECTIVES

After you have mastered the information in this unit, you will be able to:

- Describe the major determinants of attraction

- Discuss the factors linked to helping behavior

- Define prejudice, and explain how it develops

- Discuss what can be done to reduce prejudice

- Explain the factors that contribute to human aggression

OUTLINE

I.   Attraction
    A.   Background factors in attraction
        1.   Includes feelings of liking, positive thoughts, positive actions
        2.   Liking and love both topics in social psychology
    B.   Similarity
        1.   Similarity serves as validation for each other
        2.   Common ground important but room in relationships for differences
    C.   Physical attractiveness
        1.   Physical attractiveness seems to be most important factor in initial attraction
        2.   Are gender and cultural differences regarding importance of attractiveness
        3.   Physical appearance affects how we are perceived (e.g., smiling, glasses)
        4.   Cross-cultural similarities in standards for facial beauty
        5.   Support for matching hypothesis—that we choose those similar in attractiveness
    D.   Proximity
        1.   Friends usually those who live (or sit in classroom) near us
        2.   Proximity increases opportunity to be exposed to, get to know, others
    E.   Reciprocity
        1.   Liking those who like us back
        2.   Reciprocal interactions build upon themselves, increase liking
II. Helping Behavior
    A.   Background factors in helping behavior
        1.   Story of Kitty Genovese
            a)   Stabbed to death in street in Queens, New York (1964)
            b)   Many neighbors watched, no one helped
            c)   In other situations, people risk careers and lives to help others, even strangers
            d)   What explains help in some cases, and not others?
        2.   Prosocial behavior—behavior that is beneficial to others
            a)   Altruism—pure helping, no thought of return (does this really exist?)
            b)   Helping to benefit helper
    B.   Bystander intervention
        1.   Result of a decision-making process
            a)   Is there a need for help?
            b)   Is it a true emergency?
            c)   Decision to assume personal responsibility
            d)   Choose form of help
            e)   Implement course of action

    2. Interpret situations in light of these factors

C. Influences on helping

  1. Situational ambiguity—less help likely when situation is confusing

  2. Perceived cost—less help likely if costs (including psychological) are high

  3. Diffusion of responsibility—less help likely when more people witness

  4. Similarity to those in need of help—also more help for kinship members

  5. Facial features—baby-faced people more likely to get helped

  6. Mood, gender, race

    a) More help likely when helper in a good mood

    b) More assistance still typically given to women

    c) Not helping may be a subtle way to express racism

  7. Attributions regarding the cause of need—more help to innocent victim

  8. Social norms—especially a factor when request is made in front of others

III. Prejudice

A. Background factors regarding prejudice

  1. A preconceived attitude, usually negative, without rational evaluation

  2. Has cognitive, emotional, and behavioral components

    a) Cognition—biased beliefs, stereotypes

    b) Emotion (usually negative)—feelings of prejudice

    c) Behavior—discrimination

  3. Often a disparity between voiced attitude and actual behavior

  4. Stereotypes and prejudices are resistant to change

  5. Prejudice and discrimination increase during social upheaval, scarcity

B. The development of prejudice

  1. An outgrowth of negative stereotypes

  2. Stereotypes are learned

  3. Everyone has some stereotypes—partly a cognitive, adaptive strategy

    a) In-group/out-group distinction

    b) Out-group homogeneity

C. Why some people are more prejudiced than others

  1. Learning and experience play key roles

  2. Parental influence, cognitive style, personality (e.g., authoritarian) are factors

D. Reducing prejudice

  1. Contact hypothesis (Gordon Allport, 1954)

    a) Social and institutional support

    b) Acquaintance potential

    c) Equal status—opportunity for contact on equal footing

    d) Intergroup cooperation—towards common goal

  2. Teaching empathy

  3. People can take steps to change beliefs and/or behavior

IV. Human Aggression

A. Background factors regarding aggression

  1. Stereotyping and prejudice can lead to more negative behaviors

  2. Much violence in the history of humanity, no less so in past century

B. Explanations for aggression

  1. Instinct

    a) A survival mechanism—protect family, species

    b) Aggressive, dominant males may produce stronger offspring

    c) Current view is aggression too complex to be explained just on basis of instinct (probably is a combination of causes)

  2. Biological influences

a) Possible abnormal brain circuitry (may involve serotonin)
b) Testosterone and aggression are related
3. Learning influences
a) Social-cognitive approach: children learn through observation, modeling
b) Aggressive behavior increases if reinforced
4. Sociocultural influences
a) Consider social stressors (social problems, child abuse)
b) Attempt to use aggression, violence for coercion
5. Alcohol use
a) Possibly implicated in half of homicides, one-fourth of rapes
b) Alcohol loosens inhibitions, restraints; affects judgment
6. Emotional influences
a) Frustration—when path to goal is blocked
b) Anger
c) Neither frustration nor anger necessarily lead to aggression
7. Environmental influences—outdoor temperature shown to be a factor
V. Exploring Psychology: How Does Racism and Stereotyping Affect Stereotyped Groups?
A. Racism
1. Negative perspective solely due to racial membership
2. May lead to lowered, internalized expectations
B. Stereotype threat
1. Awareness of others' negative outlook
2. May impair performance, lower motivation
C. Racism and stereotype threat may also affect physical health

SUMMARY

In this module you learn about the many social psychological factors involved in our relationships with others. Our interactions with others involve many pleasant circumstances such as social and emotional relationships and the opportunities we take to help each other. Our relationships can also have unpleasant aspects such as when prejudice or aggression materialize. All of these issues are studied by social psychologists, and it is hoped that as we learn more and gain more understanding about our relationships with others, the quality and harmony of interpersonal exchange may improve.

What attracts us to others? Social psychologists suggest that attraction tends to be based on four factors: similarity, physical attractiveness, proximity, and reciprocity. In general, we are most attracted to people who are like ourselves. Yes, individual differences can be interesting, but attractions are more likely to occur and be maintained when the social partners share common ground. Perhaps the reason for our attraction to others who are like us is because the characteristics in the other person validate who we are. When people spend time with each other, their attitudes can actually grow more similar. Physical attractiveness seems to be the predominant factor leading to initial attraction. There are gender and cultural differences, however. Men place more emphasis on the physical attractiveness of their partner, while women are more interested in attitude similarity or (in the Korean culture, for example) educational, occupational, or family background. The standards for what is beautiful in the human face are consistent across cultures, although there are of course some cultural variations. There also is a tendency for us to choose partners who more or less match us with regard to physical attractiveness (known as the matching hypothesis). Proximity (how close we are to others—in terms of where we live, where we sit in a classroom or office, and the like) is a distinct factor in attraction. In part, proximity gives you the opportunity to be exposed more often to another person (and vice versa!). Also, in part, we may be near others because of other similar background factors. Reciprocity means we like another person because that person has exhibited liking for us. The reaction to positive feedback from another is often, but not always, a feeling of liking in return.

Helping is a kind of prosocial behavior. Prosocial behavior means we engage in the behavior because it is beneficial to others. Do we ever help someone truly with no concern for what is in it for us? If so, this is known as altruism. We may also help because it feels good to do so or because we hope some time to be helped ourselves in the future. The intensive study of helping and of prosocial behavior in general was sparked in part by a brutal death nearly forty years ago. This involves the story of Kitty Genovese, who was repeatedly stabbed and left to die on a street near her home. What was shocking was that she was surrounded by neighbors who heard and saw the crime as it was being committed. No one went to help, and no one called the police until at least a half-hour had passed. By that point she could not be revived. With so many people aware of the murder and capable of helping why did no one go to her aid? The answer to this question has been proposed by Bibb Latane and John Darley (1970), based on research on the topic they call bystander intervention. According to this research, bystanders must make a number of decisions, which may involve their own welfare, before they act to provide help. These five steps are (1) recognizing the need for help, (2) determining that the situation is a true emergency, (3) feeling that one's own intervention is necessary, (4) deciding on how that help will be provided, and (5) taking action to intervene. What seems to lead people to help? If the situation is confusing, or if many others are around who could provide help also, intervention is less likely. It is harder to help when we put ourselves or our loved ones at risk. We are more inclined to help those who are like us and especially when we perceive that the person in need of help did nothing to bring on the problem. Social norms, the mood of the potential helper, and the gender of the person in need are also factors.

Prejudice and aggression are the more negative side of human behavior. Prejudice is an attitude, which may be related to stereotyping (a set of cognitions stemming from a person's membership in a particular group) and discrimination (the behavior of treating others in a biased or unfair manner simply because of their membership in a particular group). Prejudices emerge from negative stereotypes, and negative stereotypes are most likely learned. Children will imitate the behaviors and attitudes of their parents, and prejudices can be passed on in this way. There is a tendency also to see those like us as the in-group; others then form the out-group. Out-group homogeneity means we perceive "them" (the out-group) as all alike. Groups that experience prejudice and racism are hampered because they may internalize the attitudes conveyed towards them, and they are aware of the negative attitudes others hold. Prejudice among groups can be reduced by providing opportunities for all to get to know each other directly and on an equal footing. Organizations and institutions must support the effort to reduce prejudice, and a common goal for all involved groups is helpful.

There are many explanations for aggression, and aggression is a sufficiently complex behavior that there is probably a combination of causes. Proposed explanations for aggression include instinct (it may be helpful for survival), biological influences, learned behaviors, sociocultural influences, the consumption of alcohol (which lowers inhibitions and impairs reasoning), emotional influences, and environmental influences. Aggression and violence are more likely (but will not necessarily occur) when one is angry, feels frustrated, and if outdoor air temperature is high.

KEY TERMS

Attraction

Matching hypothesis

Proximity

Reciprocity

Prosocial behavior

Bystander intervention

Social norms

Prejudice

Discrimination

In-groups

Out-groups

Out-group negativism

In-group favoritism

Out-group homogeneity

Authoritarian personality

Contact hypothesis

Frustration

Racism

Stereotype threat

SELF-TEST PRACTICE QUIZ

From the Key Terms select that which best matches the following (Note: Not all Key Terms will be used.)

1. _____ A preconceived attitude towards an individual or group without direct experience

2. _____ Liking that occurs as a response to behavior indicating that another likes us

3. _____ A personality type that constitutes rigid, inflexible behaviors and attitudes

4. _____ Having positive thoughts, feelings, and behaviors with regard to another

5. _____ An approach for reducing prejudice involving the opportunity for members of different groups to get to know each other on an individual basis, with equal status, support from authority figures, and ideally working towards a superordinate goal

6. _____ Groups of which we are a member or with which we identify

7. _____ The idea that we are likely to choose as partners those who are similar to us with regard to physical attractiveness

a. Attraction

b. Matching hypothesis

c. Proximity

d. Reciprocity

e. Prosocial behavior

f. Bystander intervention

g. Social norms

h. Prejudice

i. Discrimination

j. In-groups

k. Out-groups

l. Out-group negativism

m. In-group favoritism

n. Out-group homogeneity

o. Authoritarian personality

p. Contact hypothesis

q. Frustration

r. Racism

s. Stereotype threat

8. _____ The action of offering help to a stranger who is in need

9. _____ The tendency to perceive individuals who are not in our in-group as being all the same

10. _____ The act of treating others with bias or unfairly because they are part of a particular group

11. _____ Simply being near another individual; a factor contributing to interpersonal attraction

12. _____ The awareness by members of a group who are accustomed to experiencing prejudice that there are negative attitudes held by others towards them

13. _____ A negative emotional state that typically occurs when one discovers that one's efforts at reaching or obtaining an objective are blocked

14. _____ Standards regarding what is acceptable that are held by a particular culture; there are subtle pressures on members of the culture to adhere to these standards

15. _____ Negative attitudes and behaviors directed towards individuals simply because they are members of a particular racial group

16. _____ Behavior on our part that fosters the well-being of others (it may or may not help our own outlook and well-being also)

17. Which seems to be the strongest predictor regarding whether or not you and someone you just met will date again?
   a. Similarity
   b. Physical attractiveness
   c. Proximity
   d. Reciprocity

18. When we help someone else with truly no thought or expectation as to what we might get out of it, we are said to have
   a. altruistic motives.
   b. a hidden agenda.
   c. a philanthropic personality.
   d. the reciprocity norm.

19. Ironically, a person in danger may be less likely to get help if there is a crowd nearby because everyone in the crowd may think, "Oh, I don't need to help because I'm sure somebody else will." This illustrates the concept of
    a. situational ambiguity.
    b. diffusion of responsibility.
    c. proximity.
    d. social norms.

20. People are generally more likely to help when
    a. the individual who needs help is an older male.
    b. the person needing help seems to have brought on the problem himself.
    c. it is uncertain as to whether there is a true need for help or not.
    d. they are in a good mood.

21. The behavioral component in the attitude of prejudice is
    a. experiencing negative feelings.
    b. stereotyping.
    c. discrimination.
    d. out-group homogeneity.

22. Which of the following increases the odds that a person will behave aggressively?
    a. the person is drunk
    b. the weather is hot
    c. the person has been previously reinforced for aggression.
    d. all of the above

23. Prejudice and discrimination are likely to increase
    a. during the winter months.
    b. when there is economic scarcity.
    c. when no obvious scapegoat is available.
    d. in inverse proportion to the success of welfare-to-work programs.

24. Based on research by Claude Steele and others, one way to alter the performance of individuals on a test (relative to what they might do under different circumstances) is to
    a. give the test to women first, and then to men participants.
    b. give the test to men first, and then to women participants.
    c. present equal numbers of verbal, practical, and analytical questions.
    d. change the name of the test.

ESSAY QUESTIONS

1. Based on research we have so far, are there cultural universals regarding what is considered beautiful in a face? Support your response with findings presented in the text.

2. Given the circumstances of the Kitty Genovese murder, we can conclude that making the decision to help is not a simple matter. Describe, referring to the research by Latane and Darley, steps we are likely to take when making the decision whether or not to intervene and provide help.

3. What are some of the reasons that may explain why humans exhibit aggressive behavior?

ANSWER KEY

1. Prejudice

2. Reciprocity

3. Authoritarian personality

4.   Attraction

5.   Contact hypothesis

6.   In-groups

7.   Matching hypothesis

8.   Bystander intervention

9.   Out-group homogeneity

10.   Discrimination

11.   Proximity

12.   Stereotype threat

13.   Frustration

14.   Social norms

15.   Racism

16.   Prosocial behavior

17.   b

18.   a

19.   b

20.   d

21.   c

22.   d

23.   b

24.   d

SAMPLE ANSWERS TO ESSAY QUESTIONS

1.   Research suggests that there is cross-cultural agreement on standards for beauty, at least with regard to the female face. Cunningham (1995) and others had raters from several races and cultures rate photographs of Asian, Hispanic, black, and white women. There was agreement among both male and female raters that features including high cheekbones, widely spaced eyes, a small nose and small chin are perceived as most attractive, regardless of racial origin. Both male and female faces were rated as more attractive if the features they exhibited were more in keeping with traditionally feminine characteristics. There are some individual cultural variations.

2.   Kitty Genovese was murdered while at least thirty-eight of her neighbors were aware of the assault and did nothing to intervene. Why did people around her not help? Latane and Darley (1970) proposed steps one may go through when considering whether to help another individual in need or not. The first step is to decide whether there really is a need for help. That seems clear in the Genovese case. The second step is to determine whether the situation really is an emergency. In the Genovese case, that also seems clear. Step three in Latane and Darley's model is perhaps the key. That step involves assuming personal responsibility. The fourth step is to decide what one is going to do to provide help, and the fifth step is to actually put that decision to help into action. This murder took place in an urban area. We can assume the neighbors were aware that many other people were at home and available to provide help also. It appears that the neighbors did not feel a need to get involved themselves—there were plenty of other people who

could do that. Another thing to consider in evaluating the response to the Genovese murder is the influence of the helping factor known as perceived cost. The murder was an assault with a knife. To provide any direct assistance was to put one's own life in danger. Still, a neighbor could have called the police. However, no one called until thirty minutes later.

3. Aggression is a very complex behavior, and there seems to be no single precipitating factor. Explanations that have been proposed for aggressive behavior include (1) that it is a survival instinct, (2) biological influences (may be related to levels of serotonin), (3) that it is a learned behavior, (4) sociocultural influences, (5) alcohol use (since alcohol tends to loosen inhibitions and impair reasoning), (6) emotional influences (particularly experiencing frustration or anger) and (7) environmental influences (incidences of aggression increase as the outdoor temperature rises). We can see some value in aggression for our ancestors in that it was literally necessary to fight off threats to home, family, and food sources. Aggression is most certainly learned. Children may learn both that aggression is an acceptable form of behavior (if it is modeled in the home) and to pick up pointers (so to speak) on how to aggress. If a youngster's aggressive acts meet with success and are not effectively discouraged, aggressive behavior is reinforced. All influences listed here are associated with the occurrence of aggression. No one influence or event always leads to aggressive behavior for all people. Yet, there is no shortage of aggression. Thus, psychologists adhere to the belief that aggressive behavior results from a combination of factors.

MODULE 16.3 GROUP INFLUENCES ON INDIVIDUAL BEHAVIOR

LEARNING OBJECTIVES

After you have mastered the information in this unit, you will be able to:

- Define social identity

- Discuss the significance of the Asch study on conformity

- Discuss factors that influence conformity

- Explain the principles that compliance techniques are based on

- Discuss why Milgram's findings were so disturbing and why his methods were controversial

- Explain how the presence of others affects individual performance

- Define deindividuation, group polarization, and groupthink

OUTLINE

I. Background Factors Regarding Group Influence
    A. Humans are very social creatures
    B. Since social connections vital, others wield powerful influence
II. Our Social Selves
    A. Two components of psychological identity (self-concept)
        1. Personal identity (individual identity)
        2. Social identity (group identity)
    B. Social identity more prominent in collectivist cultures
    C. Western cultures more likely to emphasize individuality, autonomy
III. Conformity
    A. Fitting our behavior to prevailing social standards
    B. Lack of conformity involves risk of social disapproval
    C. Asch study (a social psychology classic) on conformity

1. Judging length of lines (matching to a target line)
2. Three-fourths of participants gave wrong answer (to conform) at least once

D. Why do some people conform more than others?
  1. People assume the majority must be correct
  2. Greatest concern is being accepted by the group
  3. Simply easier to go along with group than disagree
  4. Other characteristics
     a) Women slightly more likely to conform than men
     b) More conformity among collectivist cultures than individualistic
     c) More conformity among individuals with low self-esteem, social shyness, especially strong need to be liked
     d) Conformity tends to decline with age (after childhood)

E. Situational factors
  1. More conformity when behavior public than in private
  2. Conformity increases as group size increases (up to three or four people)
  3. With dissent from anyone else in group—conformity drops sharply
  4. Note that some degree of conformity is helpful (groups run more smoothly)

IV. Compliance
  A. Acceding to requests or demands from others
  B. Factors related to compliance
    1. Authority figure
    2. Social validation
    3. Need for consistency in behavior
       a) Foot-in-the-door-technique (people who first comply with a small request are more likely to agree to a more demanding favor later)
       b) Bait-and-switch technique (people who have shown interest are more likely to comply with switch to more expensive product)
       c) Low-ball technique (people who have already made the decision to buy are more likely to accede to more expensive purchase offer)
    4. Door-in-the-face technique—based on reciprocity
       a) First request is large, unreasonable favor
       b) Greater compliance rates for smaller, follow-up task

V. Obedience to Authority
  A. Atrocities of Nazis during WWII raised questions
  B. Research program to test obedience created by Stanley Milgram (1960s)
    1. Cover story for experiment—the effects of punishment on learning
    2. Sixty-five percent of participants went to "severe shock" voltage
    3. Some variation related to proximity of "teachers" to "learners"
    4. Also raised questions regarding ethical treatment of subjects
  C. Why do people obey immoral commands?
    1. Socialization to obey authority
    2. Also some impact from social comparison, foot-in-the-door technique
  D. Evaluating Milgram's legacy
    1. Cannot duplicate study because of ethical considerations
    2. Hard to learn more about full nature of obedience (and authority)
    3. Perhaps more emphasis needed on personal responsibility

VI. Social Facilitation and Social Loafing
  A. Social facilitation
    1. Working harder when in presence of others
    2. Presence of others increases performance of dominant responses
    3. For complex tasks, presence of others impairs

B.   Social loafing
1.   Less effort expended when working as member of a group
2.   Thought is other group members will pick up slack
3.   Less likely to occur when individual performance is evaluated

VII. Mob Behavior
A.   Deindividuation—loss of personal sense of identity within a crowd
B.   May result in more destructive behaviors (than individual would exhibit when alone); inhibitions are loosened
C.   Results from sense of anonymity, shift of focus from self and inner standards to group and group actions

VIII. Group Decision Making
A.   Group polarization
1.   Tendency to adopt more extreme version of one's views when in a group
2.   Risky-shift phenomenon—extreme views may lead to more extreme actions
3.   Why does group polarization occur?
a)   Social validation—hearing others' similar views strengthens one's own views
b)   Normative influence—if group view is stronger than own personal view, personal view is adjusted to conform to intensity level of group
B.   Groupthink
1.   Concern to reach a consensus outweighs concern to critically evaluate issue
2.   Pressure is to conform to majority opinion
3.   Ways to minimize occurrence of groupthink (Janis, 1982, 1997)
a)   Encourage group members to consider all alternatives, weigh all evidence
b)   Group leader should avoid stating a preference at outset
c)   Call upon outsiders to voice opinions and analyses
d)   Encourage group members or outsiders to play "devil's advocate"
e)   Subdivide group; smaller groups review issues independently
f)   Hold several group meetings and evaluate all new information before final decision is made

SUMMARY

In this module you learn about how our membership in groups can influence us. Humans are very social creatures, and thus we value the opportunity to share social contact with others. Since we value social contact, the acceptance and opinions of others becomes important. We have a psychological identity (also known as a self-concept) that is derived in part from who we are as unique individuals but also in part of who we are due to the various groups to which we belong. Group acceptance and group membership matters. Thus, we may be inclined to conform to views or standards of a group even when they are not our own. Though there are, of course, no legal sanctions against social nonconformity, there certainly are social pressures to conform and repercussions if we do not. A classic study by Asch (1956) showed that, even among participants who did not know each other, and even when criteria for making judgments were completely clear, most participants disregarded their own evaluation and went along with inaccurate judgment of the group at least once. Greater levels of conformity are particularly likely to be found among individuals who lack self-esteem and who are especially in need of being liked and accepted by the group.

Others can sometimes get us to comply with what they want, or even feel that we should outright obey them because of their authority position. Compliance strategies include the foot-in-the-door technique (people are more likely to grant a larger request if they have first acceded to a lesser one), bait-and-switch, and low-balling based on our desire for consistency in our behavior. Beginning in the 1960s, Milgram researched the psychological factors regarding obedience to an authority. His work was undertaken in part because of the horrific acts carried out by the Nazis—many of whom were following

Instructions given by an individual in authority. Milgram's classic study on obedience involved participants who thought they were teaching another volunteer. For every wrong answer the "learner" in the study gave, the "teacher" (the only real participant in the study) was supposed to give the learner a shock. The shocks increased to a "severe shock" level. Though you might not expect it, approximately two-thirds of individuals participating in the study followed orders from an authority to administer shocks all the way up to and including the "severe shock" level. This study and ones like it cannot be repeated due to ethical considerations (i.e., the trauma experienced by the participants even though they found out later they were not really giving shocks). However, it does shed light on the fact that, under certain conditions, people will inflict severe harm on others because they are told to do so.

Other sources of group influence include social facilitation and social loafing. Social facilitation means the presence of others usually enhances our ability to perform well. A further clarification of social facilitation indicated that the facilitating effect occurred only when the task we were faced with was one that was not too difficult or was one that we knew very well. Social facilitation increases our ability at dominant responses; performance on a task that is difficult for us will usually be impeded. Social loafing conveys the finding that members of a group tend to expend less effort on a task than they would if they were doing it alone. Social loafing will usually will not occur, however, if it is made clear to group members that their individual contribution will be evaluated.

Deindividuation is the loss of awareness of ourselves and the loss of our sense of who we are. Deindividuation may occur when one is in a very large crowd or if one is dressed in a manner that hides one's own identity. This phenomenon, of course, can be dangerous if in the process of deindividuation you lose touch with your values and personal standards for behavior.

Desire to conform to the views of a group we value and the opinions of a forceful leader can lead to groupthink. Groupthink involves the process of minimizing and often withholding one's own opinions in deference to what appears to be the group's assessment. Obviously, groupthink can be a problem. Group decisions may be made that do not really reflect the best thinking of the individual group members. To help prevent groupthink, contrasting opinions should be encouraged, and members might meet in subgroups that would result in a greater variety of independent perspectives. New information should be welcomed.

KEY TERMS

Personal identity

Social identity

Conformity

Compliance

Social validation

Foot-in-the-door technique

Bait-and-switch technique

Low-ball technique

Door-in-the-face technique

Obedience

Legitimization of authority

Social facilitation

Social loafing

Deindividuation

Group polarization

Risky-shift phenomenon

Groupthink

SELF-TEST PRACTICE QUIZ

From the Key Terms select that which best matches the following:

1. _____ Following the directions of another because that person is an authority figure

2. _____ A term that describes the tendency to stifle one's own opinion when feeling pressure from desirable group to conform

3. _____ Gaining compliance to a smaller request in order to gain compliance to a larger one

4. _____ A sense of pressure to adjust one's behavior or views to standards set by a group

5. _____ Our sense of who we are which results from our membership in various groups

6. _____ When the presence of others improves our ability to perform tasks well

7. _____ The loss of awareness of ourselves and who we are when surrounded by many others

8. _____ The tendency in a group to adopt more extreme behaviors due to group polarization

9. _____ A compliance strategy where a tempting (though unrealistic) offer is extended first

10. _____ Our understanding of ourselves due to who we are as a unique individual

11. _____ Gaining compliance by requesting an impossibly demanding task first, then scaling back

12. _____ A strategy where compliance is gained first, then terms of agreement are subtly changed

a. Personal identity

b. Social identity

c. Conformity

d. Compliance

e. Social validation

f. Foot-in-the-door technique

g. Bait-and-switch technique

h. Low-ball technique

i. Door-in-the-face technique

j. Obedience

k. Legitimization of authority

l. Social facilitation

m. Social loafing

n. Deindividuation

o. Group polarization

p. Risky-shift phenomenon

q. Groupthink

13. _____ The tendency for group discussion to move members' individual opinions to more extreme levels

14. _____ Being inclined to go along with the request or demand of another

15. _____ Socialization leading us to accept and follow the demands of an authority figure

16. _____ Feeling more comfortable about our own characteristics because they are exhibited by others

17. _____ Doing less work because one's individual contribution to a group is not evaluated

18. The "me-orientation" is most prevalent among
    a. white European Americans.
    b. African Americans.
    c. Hispanic Americans.
    d. Asian Americans.

19. In Asch's (1956) study, when group members had to select one of three lines to match a target line, about _____ of the naïve study participants conformed to the group's incorrect answer at least once.
    a. one-quarter
    b. one-third
    c. one-half
    d. three-quarters

20. People soliciting donations for charities will often start by requesting a small amount of money; later, when the person is already in the habit of donating, the charity will start to ask for larger amounts. This is known as the _____ technique.
    a. door-in-the-face
    b. foot-in-the-door
    c. lowball
    d. bait-and-switch

21. In Milgram's research on obedience, the _____ was the only real naïve (e.g., not a collaborator with the researcher) participant in the study.
    a. "teacher"
    b. "learner"
    c. authority figure
    d. recipient of the shock

22. In which of the following settings for Milgram's research were obedience levels HIGHER than in the original study reported?
    a. When the research setting was moved from Yale to a commercial storefront
    b. When "teachers" and "learners" were placed in the same room
    c. When teachers could hear learners screaming through the walls
    d. When teachers were instructed to ask others to administer the shock for them

23. Being in the presence of others improves our ability at tasks
    a. on every occasion.
    b. when the task is particularly difficult.
    c. when the task is particularly easy.
    d. especially when the tasks involve academic skills.
24. People serving on trial juries may feel pressure from the group to reach a quick decision so that they can finish their jury duty. This emphasis on reaching a consensus rather than critically weighing the evidence is known as
    a. deindividuation.
    b. groupthink.
    c. group polarization.
    d. social facilitation.

ESSAY QUESTIONS

1. What are some reasons that people conform? Can you think of situations where conformity is good?
2. How is the "foot-in-the-door" technique related to findings in Milgram's study on obedience?

ANSWER KEY

1. Obedience
2. Groupthink
3. Foot-in-the-door technique
4. Conformity
5. Social identity
6. Social facilitation
7. Deindividuation
8. Risky-shift phenomenon
9. Bait-and-switch technique
10. Personal identity
11. Door-in-the-face technique
12. Low-ball technique
13. Group polarization
14. Compliance
15. Legitimization of authority
16. Social validation
17. Social loafing
18. a
19. d
20. b
21. a

22. d

23. c

24. b

SAMPLE ANSWERS TO ESSAY QUESTIONS

1.   People conform because social contact is important to us. We want acceptance from members of groups to which we belong, and we are willing to modify our behavior, at least to an extent, in order to help gain that acceptance. Part of our own understanding of ourselves, and our sense of who we are, is enmeshed in our relationships with others; this is known as our social identity. Thus, being connected to others is a fundamental part of us. We conform both to the general norms of our culture and to the more specific norms or standards established (formally or informally) by the groups in which we participate. Although often not clearly spelled out, there are social sanctions and repercussions for not conforming to either cultural or group standards.

     People may conform because they assume that the group must be correct, or they conform despite their own beliefs and attitudes because acceptance by the group is extremely important. Greater levels of conformity are found among individuals who have lower self-esteem, who exhibit social shyness, and who have a very high need to be liked and accepted by the group. Many times, of course, conformity is good, and perhaps we often conform without being aware of it. If we did not all stop on the red lights and go on the green, for example, we would indeed all be in trouble!

2.   In Milgram's study on obedience, participants played the role of someone teaching someone else (who was really a confederate of the researcher). Every time the learner gave a wrong answer, the teacher was instructed to administer an unavoidable shock to the learner. These shocks increased in standard increments of voltage for every wrong answer given. Milgram conducted this research in a variety of related formats, and in every case obedience to an authority, even when it meant administering severe shocks to an unknown fellow human being, was high. Milgram's study certainly emphasizes the importance of situational factors on behavior.

     The foot-in-the-door technique to gain compliance means beginning with a very low level of request. The obedience study began with a very low level of shock administered. Chances are results would have been different if participants were asked at the outset to administer the very highest level of "severe shock." Because the shock gradations were increased in fairly small steps, participants apparently were more likely to conform to the authority figure's demands.

MODULE 16.4 APPLICATION: PSYCHOLOGY GOES TO WORK

LEARNING OBJECTIVE

After you have mastered the information in this unit, you will be able to:

- Discuss some of the areas of interest to industrial/organizational psychologists today

OUTLINE

I.   Background Factors Regarding Industrial/Organizational Psychology
   A.   Workplace may be major site of interaction with others
   B.   Industrial/organizational psychology researches issues relating to optimizing occupational experience
II.   Job Satisfaction
   A.   The degree to which workers have positive feelings towards their occupation
      1.   Features of job
         a)   Job status

          b)   Pay, fringe benefits, childcare facilities
          c)   Interesting and personally fulfilling work
    2.   Features of worker
          a)   Happier with work when more satisfied with life in general
          b)   Those unhappy with one job tend to be unhappy at next
          c)   Personality traits predict job satisfaction (self-esteem, self-efficacy, emotional stability)
          d)   Job satisfaction similarities in identical twins, raised apart
    3.   Features of fit between attributional style and amount of control at work
          a)   For many people, more control leads to less job stress, more positive work experience
          b)   For some, prefer less control at work (people with negative attributional style—can avoid self-blame when things go wrong)
  B.   Important to not overgeneralize
  C.   Job satisfaction related to less absenteeism, less employee turnover
  D.   Job satisfaction moderately related to performance and worker productivity
III. Challenges of a Changing Workplace
  A.   Changes in the workplace
    1.   Less long-term job security
    2.   Jobs created, redesigned due to technology advances
    3.   Opportunity for home office, flexibility in hours and location
    4.   Becoming a more entrepreneurial workplace (more responsibility for one's own career development)
  B.   I/O psychologists help companies create effective, optimal work climate
  C.   Organizational culture—system of shared values, norms that exist within a company or other organization

SUMMARY

In this module, you learn about industrial/organizational psychology, a specialization within the field of psychology that is very closely related to social psychology. Industrial/organizational psychologists help businesses and other organizations with their workplace setting. Most of us spend a good deal of time in our employment settings, and it is often the location where many interpersonal exchanges occur as well.

Job satisfaction is extremely important for employee and administrator. Some features of job satisfaction are, of course, related to the job itself. These features include the prestige or status of the position, the financial compensation involved, how interesting and how personally fulfilling the position is. Some features of job satisfaction are related to the worker, in that people who are more satisfied with life overall tend to be happier with their jobs. Self-esteem, self-efficacy, and emotional stability are associated with higher levels of job satisfaction. Though not always true, having more control over the work one does is associated with a more positive work experience. Job satisfaction is related to less employee turnover and absenteeism and somewhat related to job performance.

The workplace is changing, sometimes rapidly. Advances in technology give us the opportunity to work at home or at least work from home more often. Long-term job security may be a thing of the past, and employees need to assume more responsibility for their own career and career development. It is important to stay current with technological advances because jobs and workplace settings are changing on an ongoing basis in response to these advances. Industrial/organizational psychologists help employers establish an organizational culture that maximizes the experience and effectiveness of the occupational setting.

KEY TERMS

Job satisfaction

Telecommuting

Organizational culture

SELF-TEST PRACTICE QUIZ

From the Key Terms select that which best matches the following (Note: Not every Key Term will be used.):

1. _____ A system resulting from the values held to be important by the organization and the guidelines established regarding acceptable behavior within the organization

2. _____ The degree to which an individual has positive feelings towards their occupation

   a. Job satisfaction

   b. Telecommuting

   c. Organizational culture

3. Which of the following would NOT be a task of an industrial/organizational psychologist?
   a. Design the work setting for optimal safety and efficiency
   b. Help all employees with job benefits and retirement planning
   c. Find the best fit between worker characteristics and job requirements
   d. Assure that the employment setting does not present barriers to individuals with disabilities

4. People who are happy with their current job tend to be people who
   a. are happier with life in general.
   b. were very unhappy at previous jobs.
   c. have jobs that are not particularly demanding or fulfilling.
   d. have jobs that allow them to work from home.

ESSAY QUESTION

1. What is the relationship between the self-serving bias and the amount of control people have over the work that they do?

ANSWER KEY

1. Organizational culture

2. Job satisfaction

3. b

4. a